ENCYCLOPEDIA OF
RELIGION
SECOND EDITION

ENCYCLOPEDIA OF RELIGION

SECOND EDITION

7

ICONOGRAPHY
•
JUSTIN MARTYR

LINDSAY JONES
EDITOR IN CHIEF

MACMILLAN REFERENCE USA
An imprint of Thomson Gale, a part of The Thomson Corporation

THOMSON
GALE

Detroit • New York • San Francisco • San Diego • New Haven, Conn. • Waterville, Maine • London • Munich

THOMSON
GALE

Encyclopedia of Religion, Second Edition

Lindsay Jones, Editor in Chief

For more information, contact
Macmillan Reference USA
An imprint of Thomson Gale
27500 Drake Rd.
Farmington, Hills, MI 48331-3535
Or you can visit our Internet site at
http://www.gale.com

LIBRARY OF CONGRESS CATALOGING-IN-PUBLICATION DATA

Encyclopedia of religion / Lindsay Jones, editor in chief.— 2nd ed.
p. cm.
Includes bibliographical references and index.
ISBN 0-02-865733-0 (SET HARDCOVER : ALK. PAPER) —
ISBN 0-02-865734-9 (V. 1) — ISBN 0-02-865735-7 (v. 2) —
ISBN 0-02-865736-5 (v. 3) — ISBN 0-02-865737-3 (v. 4) —
ISBN 0-02-865738-1 (v. 5) — ISBN 0-02-865739-X (v. 6) —
ISBN 0-02-865740-3 (v. 7) — ISBN 0-02-865741-1 (v. 8) —
ISBN 0-02-865742-X (v. 9) — ISBN 0-02-865743-8 (v. 10)
— ISBN 0-02-865980-5 (v. 11) — ISBN 0-02-865981-3 (v. 12) — ISBN 0-02-865982-1 (v. 13) — ISBN 0-02-865983-X (v. 14) — ISBN 0-02-865984-8 (v. 15)
1. RELIGION—ENCYCLOPEDIAS. I. JONES, LINDSAY, 1954-

BL31.E46 2005
200'.3—dc22 2004017052

This title is also available as an e-book.
ISBN 0-02-865997-X
Contact your Thomson Gale representative for ordering information.

Printed in the United States of America
10 9 8 7 6 5 4 3 2 1

EDITORS AND CONSULTANTS

Harvard Forum on Religion and Ecology
Ecology and Religion

JOSEPH HARRIS
Francis Lee Higginson Professor of English Literature and Professor of Folklore, Harvard University
Germanic Religions

URSULA KING
Professor Emerita, Senior Research Fellow and Associate Member of the Institute for Advanced Studies, University of Bristol, England, and Professorial Research Associate, Centre for Gender and Religions Research, School of Oriental and African Studies, University of London
Gender and Religion

DAVID MORGAN
Duesenberg Professor of Christianity and the Arts, and Professor of Humanities and Art History, Valparaiso University
Color Inserts and Essays

JOSEPH F. NAGY
Professor, Department of English, University of California, Los Angeles
Celtic Religion

MATTHEW OJO
Obafemi Awolowo University
African Religions

JUHA PENTIKÄINEN
Professor of Comparative Religion, The University of Helsinki, Member of Academia Scientiarum Fennica, Finland
Arctic Religions and Uralic Religions

TED PETERS
Professor of Systematic Theology, Pacific Lutheran Theological Seminary and the Center for Theology and the Natural Sciences at the Graduate Theological Union, Berkeley, California
Science and Religion

FRANK E. REYNOLDS
Professor of the History of Religions and Buddhist Studies in the Divinity School and the Department of South Asian Languages and Civilizations, Emeritus, University of Chicago
History of Religions

GONZALO RUBIO
Assistant Professor, Department of Classics and Ancient Mediterranean Studies and Department of History and Religious Studies, Pennsylvania State University
Ancient Near Eastern Religions

SUSAN SERED
Director of Research, Religion, Health and Healing Initiative, Center for the Study of World Religions, Harvard University, and Senior Research Associate, Center for Women's Health and Human Rights, Suffolk University
Healing, Medicine, and Religion

LAWRENCE E. SULLIVAN
Professor, Department of Theology, University of Notre Dame
History of Religions

WINNIFRED FALLERS SULLIVAN
Dean of Students and Senior Lecturer in the Anthropology and Sociology of Religion, University of Chicago
Law and Religion

TOD SWANSON
Associate Professor of Religious Studies, and Director, Center for Latin American Studies, Arizona State University
South American Religions

MARY EVELYN TUCKER
Professor of Religion, Bucknell University, Founder and Coordinator, Harvard Forum on Religion and Ecology, Research Fellow, Harvard Yenching Institute, Research Associate, Harvard Reischauer Institute of Japanese Studies
Ecology and Religion

HUGH URBAN
Associate Professor, Department of Comparative Studies, Ohio State University
Politics and Religion

CATHERINE WESSINGER
Professor of the History of Religions and Women's Studies, Loyola University New Orleans
New Religious Movements

ROBERT A. YELLE
Mellon Postdoctoral Fellow, University of Toronto
Law and Religion

ERIC ZIOLKOWSKI
Charles A. Dana Professor of Religious Studies, Lafayette College
Literature and Religion

ABBREVIATIONS AND SYMBOLS USED IN THIS WORK

abbr. abbreviated; abbreviation
abr. abridged; abridgment
AD *anno Domini,* in the year of the (our) Lord
Afrik. Afrikaans
AH *anno Hegirae,* in the year of the Hijrah
Akk. Akkadian
Ala. Alabama
Alb. Albanian
Am. *Amos*
AM *ante meridiem,* before noon
amend. amended; amendment
annot. annotated; annotation
Ap. *Apocalypse*
Apn. *Apocryphon*
app. appendix
Arab. Arabic
ʿArakh. *ʿArakhin*
Aram. Aramaic
Ariz. Arizona
Ark. Arkansas
Arm. Armenian
art. article (pl., arts.)
AS Anglo-Saxon
Asm. Mos. *Assumption of Moses*
Assyr. Assyrian
A.S.S.R. Autonomous Soviet Socialist Republic
Av. Avestan
ʿA.Z. *ʿAvodah zarah*
b. born
Bab. Babylonian
Ban. Bantu
1 Bar. *1 Baruch*
2 Bar. *2 Baruch*
3 Bar. *3 Baruch*
4 Bar. *4 Baruch*
B.B. *Bavaʾ batraʾ*
BBC British Broadcasting Corporation
BC before Christ
BCE before the common era
B.D. Bachelor of Divinity
Beits. *Beitsah*
Bekh. *Bekhorot*
Beng. Bengali
Ber. *Berakhot*
Berb. Berber
Bik. *Bikkurim*
bk. book (pl., bks.)
B.M. *Bavaʾ metsiʿaʾ*
BP before the present
B.Q. *Bavaʾ qammaʾ*
Brāh. *Brāhmaṇa*
Bret. Breton
B.T. Babylonian Talmud
Bulg. Bulgarian
Burm. Burmese
c. *circa,* about, approximately
Calif. California
Can. Canaanite
Catal. Catalan
CE of the common era
Celt. Celtic
cf. *confer,* compare
Chald. Chaldean
chap. chapter (pl., chaps.)
Chin. Chinese
C.H.M. Community of the Holy Myrrhbearers
1 Chr. *1 Chronicles*
2 Chr. *2 Chronicles*
Ch. Slav. Church Slavic
cm centimeters
col. column (pl., cols.)
Col. *Colossians*
Colo. Colorado
comp. compiler (pl., comps.)
Conn. Connecticut
cont. continued
Copt. Coptic
1 Cor. *1 Corinthians*
2 Cor. *2 Corinthians*
corr. corrected
C.S.P. Congregatio Sancti Pauli, Congregation of Saint Paul (Paulists)
d. died
D Deuteronomic (source of the Pentateuch)
Dan. Danish
D.B. Divinitatis Baccalaureus, Bachelor of Divinity
D.C. District of Columbia
D.D. Divinitatis Doctor, Doctor of Divinity
Del. Delaware
Dem. *Demaʾi*
dim. diminutive
diss. dissertation
Dn. *Daniel*
D.Phil. Doctor of Philosophy
Dt. *Deuteronomy*
Du. Dutch
E Elohist (source of the Pentateuch)
Eccl. *Ecclesiastes*
ed. editor (pl., eds.); edition; edited by

'Eduy. *'Eduyyot*
e.g. *exempli gratia,* for example
Egyp. Egyptian
1 En. *1 Enoch*
2 En. *2 Enoch*
3 En. *3 Enoch*
Eng. English
enl. enlarged
Eph. *Ephesians*
'Eruv. *'Eruvin*
1 Esd. *1 Esdras*
2 Esd. *2 Esdras*
3 Esd. *3 Esdras*
4 Esd. *4 Esdras*
esp. especially
Est. Estonian
Est. *Esther*
et al. *et alii,* and others
etc. *et cetera,* and so forth
Eth. Ethiopic
EV English version
Ex. *Exodus*
exp. expanded
Ez. *Ezekiel*
Ezr. *Ezra*
2 Ezr. *2 Ezra*
4 Ezr. *4 Ezra*
f. feminine; and following (pl., ff.)
fasc. fascicle (pl., fascs.)
fig. figure (pl., figs.)
Finn. Finnish
fl. *floruit,* flourished
Fla. Florida
Fr. French
frag. fragment
ft. feet
Ga. Georgia
Gal. *Galatians*
Gaul. Gaulish
Ger. German
Giṭ. *Giṭṭin*
Gn. *Genesis*
Gr. Greek
Ḥag. *Ḥagigah*
Ḥal. *Ḥallah*
Hau. Hausa
Hb. *Habakkuk*
Heb. Hebrew
Heb. *Hebrews*
Hg. *Haggai*
Hitt. Hittite
Hor. *Horayot*
Hos. *Hosea*
Ḥul. *Ḥullin*
Hung. Hungarian
ibid. *ibidem,* in the same place (as the one immediately preceding)
Icel. Icelandic
i.e. *id est,* that is
IE Indo-European
Ill. Illinois
Ind. Indiana
intro. introduction
Ir. Gael. Irish Gaelic
Iran. Iranian
Is. *Isaiah*
Ital. Italian
J Yahvist (source of the Pentateuch)
Jas. *James*
Jav. Javanese
Jb. *Job*
Jdt. *Judith*
Jer. *Jeremiah*
Jgs. *Judges*
Jl. *Joel*
Jn. *John*
1 Jn. *1 John*
2 Jn. *2 John*
3 Jn. *3 John*
Jon. *Jonah*
Jos. *Joshua*
Jpn. Japanese
JPS Jewish Publication Society translation (1985) of the Hebrew Bible
J.T. Jerusalem Talmud
Jub. *Jubilees*
Kans. Kansas
Kel. *Kelim*
Ker. *Keritot*
Ket. *Ketubbot*
1 Kgs. *1 Kings*
2 Kgs. *2 Kings*
Khois. Khoisan
Kil. *Kil'ayim*
km kilometers
Kor. Korean
Ky. Kentucky
l. line (pl., ll.)
La. Louisiana
Lam. *Lamentations*
Lat. Latin
Latv. Latvian
L. en Th. Licencié en Théologie, Licentiate in Theology
L. ès L. Licencié ès Lettres, Licentiate in Literature
Let. Jer. *Letter of Jeremiah*
lit. literally
Lith. Lithuanian
Lk. *Luke*
LL Late Latin
LL.D. Legum Doctor, Doctor of Laws
Lv. *Leviticus*
m meters
m. masculine
M.A. Master of Arts
Ma 'as. *Ma'aserot*
Ma 'as. Sh. *Ma' aser sheni*
Mak. *Makkot*
Makh. *Makhshirin*
Mal. *Malachi*
Mar. Marathi
Mass. Massachusetts
1 Mc. *1 Maccabees*
2 Mc. *2 Maccabees*
3 Mc. *3 Maccabees*
4 Mc. *4 Maccabees*
Md. Maryland
M.D. Medicinae Doctor, Doctor of Medicine
ME Middle English
Meg. *Megillah*
Me 'il. *Me'ilah*
Men. *Menaḥot*
MHG Middle High German
mi. miles
Mi. *Micah*
Mich. Michigan
Mid. *Middot*
Minn. Minnesota
Miq. *Miqva'ot*
MIran. Middle Iranian
Miss. Mississippi
Mk. *Mark*
Mo. Missouri
Mo'ed Q. *Mo'ed qaṭan*
Mont. Montana
MPers. Middle Persian
MS. *manuscriptum,* manuscript (pl., MSS)
Mt. *Matthew*
MT Masoretic text
n. note
Na. *Nahum*
Nah. Nahuatl
Naz. *Nazir*
N.B. *nota bene,* take careful note
N.C. North Carolina
n.d. no date
N.Dak. North Dakota
NEB New English Bible
Nebr. Nebraska

Ned. *Nedarim*
Neg. *Nega'im*
Neh. *Nehemiah*
Nev. Nevada
N.H. New Hampshire
Nid. *Niddah*
N.J. New Jersey
Nm. *Numbers*
N.Mex. New Mexico
no. number (pl., nos.)
Nor. Norwegian
n.p. no place
n.s. new series
N.Y. New York
Ob. *Obadiah*
O.Cist. Ordo Cisterciencium, Order of Cîteaux (Cistercians)
OCS Old Church Slavonic
OE Old English
O.F.M. Ordo Fratrum Minorum, Order of Friars Minor (Franciscans)
OFr. Old French
Ohal. *Ohalot*
OHG Old High German
OIr. Old Irish
OIran. Old Iranian
Okla. Oklahoma
ON Old Norse
O.P. Ordo Praedicatorum, Order of Preachers (Dominicans)
OPers. Old Persian
op. cit. *opere citato,* in the work cited
OPrus. Old Prussian
Oreg. Oregon
'Orl. *'Orlah*
O.S.B. Ordo Sancti Benedicti, Order of Saint Benedict (Benedictines)
p. page (pl., pp.)
P Priestly (source of the Pentateuch)
Pa. Pennsylvania
Pahl. Pahlavi
Par. *Parah*
para. paragraph (pl., paras.)
Pers. Persian
Pes. *Pesahim*
Ph.D. Philosophiae Doctor, Doctor of Philosophy
Phil. *Philippians*
Phlm. *Philemon*
Phoen. Phoenician
pl. plural; plate (pl., pls.)
PM *post meridiem,* after noon
Pol. Polish
pop. population
Port. Portuguese
Prv. *Proverbs*
Ps. *Psalms*
Ps. 151 *Psalm 151*
Ps. Sol. *Psalms of Solomon*
pt. part (pl., pts.)
1Pt. *1 Peter*
2 Pt. *2 Peter*
Pth. Parthian
Q hypothetical source of the synoptic Gospels
Qid. *Qiddushin*
Qin. *Qinnim*
r. reigned; ruled
Rab. *Rabbah*
rev. revised
R. ha-Sh. *Ro'sh ha-shanah*
R.I. Rhode Island
Rom. Romanian
Rom. *Romans*
R.S.C.J. Societas Sacratissimi Cordis Jesu, Religious of the Sacred Heart
RSV Revised Standard Version of the Bible
Ru. *Ruth*
Rus. Russian
Rv. *Revelation*
Rv. Ezr. *Revelation of Ezra*
San. *Sanhedrin*
S.C. South Carolina
Scot. Gael. Scottish Gaelic
S.Dak. South Dakota
sec. section (pl., secs.)
Sem. Semitic
ser. series
sg. singular
Sg. *Song of Songs*
Sg. of 3 *Prayer of Azariah and the Song of the Three Young Men*
Shab. *Shabbat*
Shav. *Shavu'ot*
Sheq. *Sheqalim*
Sib. Or. *Sibylline Oracles*
Sind. Sindhi
Sinh. Sinhala
Sir. *Ben Sira*
S.J. Societas Jesu, Society of Jesus (Jesuits)
Skt. Sanskrit
1 Sm. *1 Samuel*
2 Sm. *2 Samuel*
Sogd. Sogdian
Soṭ. *Soṭah*
sp. species (pl., spp.)
Span. Spanish
sq. square
S.S.R. Soviet Socialist Republic
st. stanza (pl., ss.)
S.T.M. Sacrae Theologiae Magister, Master of Sacred Theology
Suk. *Sukkah*
Sum. Sumerian
supp. supplement; supplementary
Sus. *Susanna*
s.v. *sub verbo,* under the word (pl., s.v.v.)
Swed. Swedish
Syr. Syriac
Syr. Men. *Syriac Menander*
Ta' an. *Ta'anit*
Tam. Tamil
Tam. *Tamid*
Tb. *Tobit*
T.D. *Taishō shinshū daizōkyō,* edited by Takakusu Junjirō et al. (Tokyo,1922–1934)
Tem. *Temurah*
Tenn. Tennessee
Ter. Terumot
Ṭev. Y. *Ṭevul yom*
Tex. Texas
Th.D. Theologicae Doctor, Doctor of Theology
1 Thes. *1 Thessalonians*
2 Thes. *2 Thessalonians*
Thrac. Thracian
Ti. *Titus*
Tib. Tibetan
1 Tm. *1 Timothy*
2 Tm. *2 Timothy*
T. of 12 *Testaments of the Twelve Patriarchs*
Ṭoh. *ṭohorot*
Tong. Tongan
trans. translator, translators; translated by; translation
Turk. Turkish
Ukr. Ukrainian
Upan. *Upaniṣad*
U.S. United States
U.S.S.R. Union of Soviet Socialist Republics
Uqts. *Uqtsin*
v. verse (pl., vv.)
Va. Virginia
var. variant; variation
Viet. Vietnamese

viz. *videlicet,* namely
vol. volume (pl., vols.)
Vt. Vermont
Wash. Washington
Wel. Welsh
Wis. Wisconsin
Wis. *Wisdom of Solomon*
W.Va. West Virginia
Wyo. Wyoming
Yad. *Yadayim*
Yev. *Yevamot*
Yi. Yiddish
Yor. Yoruba
Zav. *Zavim*
Zec. *Zechariah*
Zep. *Zephaniah*
Zev. *Zevaḥim*

* hypothetical
? uncertain; possibly; perhaps
° degrees
+ plus
– minus
= equals; is equivalent to
× by; multiplied by
→ yields

I
CONTINUED

ICONOGRAPHY

This entry consists of the following articles:

ICONOGRAPHY: ICONOGRAPHY AS VISIBLE RELIGION [FIRST EDITION]

Iconography literally means "description of images," but it also refers to a research program in art history that exposes the different meanings of images vis-à-vis the beholder.

WORDS AND IMAGES. Religious iconography defines a relationship between word and pictorial scheme, each of which follows its own logic. Visual forms are not discursive: they do not represent their message sequentially but simultaneously. While the meanings given through verbal language are understood successively, those given through visual forms are understood only by perceiving the whole at once. Susanne Langer, who argues for such a distinction in her *Philosophy in a New Key* (1951, pp. 79–102), calls this kind of semantics "presentational symbolism," indicating that we grasp it not by reasoning but by feeling. From this basic difference it follows that word and image sometimes compete against each other and sometimes supplement each other. There is no universal law for this rela-

CLOCKWISE FROM TOP LEFT CORNER. Relief of the ancient Egyptian deities Horus and Isis with Euergetes II at Kom Ombo in Aswan, Egypt. *[©Roger Wood/Corbis]*; Twelfth-century Byzantine mosaic of Christ with the Virgin Mary in Hagia Sophia, Istanbul, Turkey. *[©Charles & Josette Lenars/Corbis]*; Colossal stone Buddha (destroyed in 2001) in Bamiyan, Afghanistan. *[The Art Archive]*; Fifteenth-century Inca ruins at Machu Picchu in Peru. *[©Alison Wright/Corbis]*; The Dome of the Rock in Jerusalem. *[©Scala/Art Resource, N.Y.]* .

tionship; I shall illustrate some of the possibilities with examples from the history of ancient religions.

In ancient societies, the artist who shaped statues or carved stamps and seals was included among the artisans, a disparate group of producers who came to form a rank of their own. In Iran, as elsewhere, the three age-old social groups of priests, warriors, and peasants were joined in Parthian times (third century BCE–second century CE) by that of the artisans. But this new group was unable to elevate its status, as confirmed by the *Book of Ben Sira* (second century BCE). This text, which enumerates a list of craftsmen, acknowledges that without such skilled workers as the engravers of seals, the smith, or the potter, a city would have no inhabitants and no settlers or travelers would come to it. Yet, the writer points out, the artisans "are not in demand at public discussions or prominent in the assembly," since the assembly needs the wise men who are engaged in study rather than manual labor (*Ben Sira* 38:24–39:5).

The low reputation of the artisans is also reflected in the anonymity of their work. Artists working on behalf of a temple, a palace, or a private customer became alienated from their work. Although Greek vases were presumably signed by their painters for the first time about 700 BCE, the majority of artists were still unknown in later times and remained dependent on their patrons. The carvers of the Achaemenid rock reliefs (Iran, sixth–fifth century BCE), for example, relied completely on the political visions and models of the imperial court and were obliged to create a visual legitimation of Achaemenid kingship. (See Margaret Root's *The King and Kingship in Achaemenid Art*, Leiden, 1979).

Other trends of patronage can be observed with seals, stamps, amulets, and pottery. In Hellenistic Egypt, for example, the god Bes is represented in clay figures more often than the official and well-known Egyptian gods. The artisans in the provincial workshops obviously had to take into account the taste of private customers, who were looking for a deity able to avert evil powers and to protect men and women. The frightening appearance of Bes that the artisans shaped served as protection against such perils and met the demands of the laity (see Françoise Dunand in *Visible Religion* 3, 1985). The history of Greek vase paintings provides us with similar phenomena. While some paintings represent typically heroic attitudes toward dying, others display an unheroic, plebeian fear of death (see H. Hoffmann in *Visible Religion* 4, 1985–1986). Here the dependency on the court has been replaced by a dependency on citizens: the artisans were obviously serving civil demands and had to respond to changing social values. But in Egypt and Greece alike, the priests were scarcely able to control the artisans' relations with their customers. If there existed a market for religious objects and if there were influential lay employers, then priests could be expected to lose control of this part of religion. To make the point in positive terms: craft products sometimes reflect a popular comprehension of religion and thus can be used to trace the rulers' demands for political legitimation, on the one hand, and citizens' demands on the other. Yet, these materials have scarcely begun to be used for the study of political and civil conceptions of religion apart from the well-known priestly one.

Another factor should be noted: the scarcity of pictorial schemes. As there existed only a limited number of well-known stereotypes suitable for representing gods, we often find a certain break between image and inscription. A particularly dramatic example appears on a jar from Palestine (about 800 BCE), decorated with two figures similar to the Egyptian Bes (with feather crown, phallus, and crooked legs). An inscription declares: "I will bless you by Yahveh my [our] protector and his Ashera" (*Monotheismus im Alten Israel und seiner Umwelt*, edited by Othmar Keel, Fribourg, 1980, pp. 168–170). The pictorial representation of God of course violates the ban on images (*Ex.* 20:4), though this prohibition originally concerned cult statues *(pesel)* alone and was extended only later to a comprehensive ban on pictorial representation (Robert P. Carroll in *Studia theologica* 31, 1977, pp. 51–64). Nor does the chosen pictorial scheme fit the official literary conceptions of Yahveh. But this incongruency does not prove that inscription and image are disconnected. There were only a small number of pictorial schemes appropriate for the representation of sky gods. In the second and first millennia BCE, three main schemes were used: the figure of a seated old man with a beard, dressed in a long garment with a horn-crown on his head; the figure of a standing young man with a club in his right hand; and the figure of a wild bull (Peter Welten in *Biblisches Reallexikon*, 2d ed., Tübingen, 1977, pp. 99–111).

Here we obviously touch on a characteristic of all traditional imagery: it tends toward the most simple schemes, which will be evident to almost all beholders. We know that ancient Jewish literature was aware of these schemes. The psalms refer to Yahveh as a smiting god (*Ps.* 29, for example; see Othmar Keel's *Die Welt der altorientalischen Bildsymbolik und das Alte Testament*, 2d ed., Zurich, 1977, pp. 184–197), while *Daniel* 7:9 refers to Yahveh as the old god. These schemes were welcome as textual symbols, but for visual form they were rejected by the priests and prophets. Nonetheless, images such as Yahveh as Bes may well have been a pictorial representation not admitted by priests and prophets, and in fact, the ban on images so poorly argued in the Hebrew scriptures should be carefully reviewed in this context of pictorial schemes.

Further examples will suggest other aspects of the relationship between word and image. In India the concretization of gods in images reduced their geographical universality and emphasized their local function (Heinrich von Stietencron in *Central Asiatic Journal* 21, 1977, pp. 126–138). In Greco-Roman religions, gods that originally belonged to the same tradition could be split by different representations (Hendrik Simon Versnel in *Visible Religion* 4, 1985–1986). These are only two instances where images have had an impact on the conceptual tradition. But we can also observe the contrary: a ban on images in the literary tradition can deeply affect the pictorial representation. Medieval and modern Shīʿī Muslim artists usually paint their holy imams as men without faces; the incomplete and mutilated human figures testify to an image-critical tradition. In other cases, as in Munich in 1534–1535, a ban on images could result in full-fledged iconoclasm (*Bildersturm*, edited by Martin Warnke, Munich, 1973). Yet a thorough analysis of iconoclasm must pay close attention to the different functions these images have had: a political one in the case of state art, a civic one in the case of objects created by artisans for their fellow citizens, and finally, a sacerdotal one in the case of temple art. The destruction of rulers' emblems, the smashing of amulets, or the cleansing of the temple can all be justified by the same ban on images. But in fact each of these actions has its own rationale and must be described in separate terms.

APPROACHES TO ICONOGRAPHY AND ICONOLOGY. The study of iconography within the discipline of art history explores the symbolic references of pictorial representations. The first modern scholar to address such issues was Aby Warburg (1866–1929), who specialized in the art of the European Renaissance. Erwin Panofsky (1892–1968) proceeded to develop a comprehensive model for the description of pictorial arts based on three strata of meaning, each entailing particular analytical and terminological tools. According to Panofsky, the first level resides in the world of natural objects and events and is evident to every beholder. The second level, that of conventional meanings, can be detected in the motifs of works of art; it is the domain of iconography in the narrow sense of the word to identify these conventional meanings. Finally, there are underlying principles of *symbolic values*, in the sense defined by Ernst Cassirer, and he described the intuitive process of detecting them as *iconology* (see *Studies in Iconology*, pp. 3–31).

While Panofsky's design for reading images has been widely accepted, it has also been refined over time. Besides the Gestalt psychologists, the influence that Ludwig Wittgenstein (1889–1951) has exerted on the general theory of symbols has been felt in the field of iconology. In his *Philosophical Investigations* (1953), for example, Wittgenstein presents a figure that can be read as either a duck or a rabbit. What we see, he demonstrates, depends on our interpretation. In other words, there is no innocent eye; seeing is an active process, not a passive one. As recent research into pictorial representation emphasizes, the share of the beholder is decisive; the likeness between drawing and object is of minor importance. What might be called a critical rationalism of viewing dictates that when we read a drawing we are looking for stereotypes we have in mind already. This view, promoted most influentially by Ernst H. Gombrich (1977), implies that there is no clear-cut division between natural and conventional meanings as Panofsky maintained; reading images mainly involves the recognition of conventional schemes. Different cultures develop different schemes for identical objects; thus, we believe that we recognize likeness, but in fact we only recognize stereotypes well known in our own culture. Once the viewer's role is seen to be greater than Panofsky allowed, new problems are raised. How can we describe the way other people see their images? How do we distinguish between subjective association and objective perception? Where do we draw the line between true and false inference?

A second criticism of Panofsky's original scheme has been advanced by George Kubler, who reproaches the seeming preference for words over images in *The Shape of Time* (1962). Separating forms and meanings, he argues that artifacts have to be studied as forms of their own; their development must be traced regardless of the meanings connected with them. By including architecture and sculpture along with painting, Kubler has also conclusively extended the field. He reminds us that images and symbols are not free-floating but regularly connected with particular art forms and that, conversely, art forms have an affinal relationship with images and symbols. This phenomenon can be described in terms of iconological genres: images and symbols, like literary concepts, became institutionalized in genres (see Gombrich's introduction to *Symbolic Images*, 1972). The art form (a coin, for example, or a vase) is the place where an artisan combines a functional object with symbolic values. The study of continuity and variety in the designs of these art forms, therefore, yields insights into symbolic values. This analysis of iconological genres seems to offer a much more controlled approach to iconology than the intuition that Panofsky had in mind, since it allows us to discern between true and false implications.

It is evident that no verbal description can enter into details as much as a visual depiction. This means that each text leaves a certain free play to the imagination of the artist, and the manner in which artists have used this freedom is in no way accidental. To cite one example, the first Christian artists working in the Roman catacombs depicted Jesus as the Good Shepherd with a lamb on his shoulders, a motif obviously inspired by *Matthew* 18:12–14 and *Luke* 15:4–7. But there was a change in meaning: while the parables emphasize the concerns of the shepherd for the individual gone astray, the artists of the third century depicted Jesus with a lamb on his shoulders to emphasize the value of protection in the "age of anxiety." Later on, as social values changed, other motifs were demanded (see Moshe Barasch in *Visible Religion* 2, 1983). This episode neatly illustrates the subject of Panofsky's iconology: an image—in itself an illustration of a story—can be explained as a reflection of the symbolic value of an age, and therefore changes in the representation indicate changes in basic attitudes.

Panofsky himself perceived the risks connected with his approach. There is always the danger, he observed, that iconology, which should relate to iconography as ethnology relates to ethnography, will instead parallel the relationship between astrology and astrography (*Meaning in the Visual Arts*, p. 32). This danger of excessive interpretation is due to the very ambiguity of images and to the difficulty of comparing them. Every iconological statement must therefore be carefully argued and submitted to certain control. In the case of the history of Mediterranean religions and arts, two approaches appear to meet this fundamental demand, one focusing on styles, the other on the institutional function of images.

Changes of style. A comparison of art from early Egyptian and late Roman times immediately reveals certain changes in the means of depiction. The Egyptian mode, which Gerhard Krahmer has described as paratactical or preperspective (*Figur und Raum in der ägyptischen und griechisch-archaischen Kunst,* The Hague, 1931), can be seen on the famous Narmer Palette of about 2800 BCE. The details of the image are disconnected. Even the body is not a whole, for every part of it is depicted as an independent unit: head and legs are shown from the sides, eye and trunk from the front. The picture does not presuppose a spectator who perceives the depiction as a whole; rather, it tells a story by means of signs and symbols that are not interrelated. The visual and discursive systems of representation have not yet been separated: the visual does not evoke illusion, while the Egyptian system of writing represents discursive speech with pictorial symbols (see Herman te Velde in *Visible Religion* 4, 1985–1986). Only with classical Greek art does the depiction come to rely on an ideal beholder and deliberately evoke what we call illusion. These differences, of course, have nothing to do with skill or lack of it. More aptly, we should explain them in terms of a different *Kunstwollen*—a word used by Alois Riegl and only inadequately translated by "artistic intention" (Otto J. Brendel, *Prolegomena to the Study of Roman Art,* New Haven, 1979, p. 31). If one accepts the notion of *Kunstwollen,* however, the different artistic intentions remain to be explained.

At this point Panofsky again becomes useful because he looked for the symbolic values underlying artistic products. In this case, the change from paratactical to hypotactical (or perspectival) art can be analyzed as a change in worldview. By the fifth century BCE in Greece, an archaic conception of person and nature lacking the notion of organic coherence had been replaced by one stressing the organic interrelationship of different parts. Later on, in Hellenistic and Roman times, this organic conception of person and nature was replaced by yet another one stressing mechanical order. The individual object (a statue, for instance) then became part of a spatial scheme submitting different constructions and objects to a superior artificial order. The arrangements of space in late Roman art not only evoke military order but also reflect the values of a bureaucratic society that succeeded in crushing the civil structure of the *polis* (Hans Peter L'Orange, *Art Forms,* Princeton, 1965). There exist only a few of such large-scale comparisons of styles, but they are sufficient to prove the value of such an approach, and similar cases could be made for other cultures.

Genres. A second iconological approach describes and compares images as reflections of certain principles of decorum. Free-floating symbols can be assigned various meanings, but this variety will become more limited if symbols are regularly associated with specific art forms. The use of an object clearly influences the beholder's perceptions and associations: function guides the projection that the beholder makes. This phenomenon is also familiar from literature, where the reader's expectations are shaped by literary genre. The same holds true for visual representations: an image of a god on a coin evokes other associations than those summoned by the same image on an amulet: whereas the coin conveys political legitimacy, the amulet is associated with personal feelings of veneration. Thus, only by studying genres are we able to specify meanings, and only by studying institutional contexts can we discern between the true and false implications of images.

There are basically two theoretical models that can be invoked to explain the meaning of pictures: images can be read as elements of a structure, and they can be read as models of social reality. The two main theories of symbols, namely those of Claude Lévi-Strauss and Ernst Cassirer, are also used in the field of iconography. For Lévi-Strauss, the meanings of symbols are based on their own logical interrelationships, while for Cassirer, symbols provide a conceptual means to grasp reality.

These approaches can be illustrated with recent scholarship on Greek material. Herbert Hoffmann has studied the paintings on Greek vases as structural codes. The scenes on the vases illustrate myths, but these illustrations can be read as paradigms referring to social values. Death, for example, is sometimes represented as the monster Gorgon whom the hero courageously encounters, and sometimes it is represented as an ugly demon pursuing human beings. Behind the choice of different mythological themes hide two distinct conceptions of death, one heroic and the other plebeian (*Visible Religion* 4, 1985–1986).

An approach more in the line of Cassirer is used in Wiltrud Neumer-Pfau's study of possible links between Hellenistic Aphrodite statues and the social position of women. Such links are not unlikely, because ancient physiognomic literature postulated a connection between body posture and the moral qualities of the person depicted. In fact, the posture of the Aphrodite statues changed in the course of time. In the early Hellenistic period the nude Aphrodite is shown reacting to an unseen beholder who has disturbed her; thus the spectator looking at the beautiful nude woman is freed from feeling any guilt. Later statues portray the nude goddess as less shy and modest: she allows the invisible beholder to admire her. Finally there are statues showing the goddess frankly exposing her nude beauty to the spectator. The moral qualities ascribed to the subject have gradually changed, and this change cannot be isolated from the fundamental impact that ancient Near Eastern culture had on the social and legal position of women in the Greek world. While women were under male tutelage in ancient Greek society, they enjoyed a certain independence in Egypt and the Near East. Thus the change of visual representation reflects the change of social reality. (See Neumer-Pfau, *Studien zur Ikonographie und gesellschaftlichen Funktion hellenistischer Aphrodite-Statuen*, Bonn, 1982).

These two theoretical models are valuable tools for enlarging scientific knowledge about past and foreign cultures. Iconography as a description of how other cultures read their images enables us to reconstruct hitherto undiscovered aspects of ethos and worldview.

SEE ALSO Aesthetics, article on Visual Aesthetics; Archetypes; Architecture; Cassirer, Ernst; Colors; Human Body, article on Human Bodies, Religion, and Art; Images; Symbol and Symbolism.

BIBLIOGRAPHY

Gail, Adalbert J., ed. *Künstler und Werkstatt in den orientalischen Gesellschaften.* Graz, 1982. A collection of essays dealing with the social status of artists and artisans in different ancient and modern societies of the East; a valuable survey.

Gombrich, Ernst H. "Aims and Limits of Iconology." In *Symbolic Images: Studies in the Arts of the Renaissance.* London, 1972. An introductory essay expounding the idea of genres and the institutional function of images.

Gombrich, Ernst H. *Art and Illusion: A Study in the Psychology of Pictorial Representation.* 5th ed. Oxford, 1977. An excellently written book with many interesting examples; the main thesis is that reading images means recognizing mental stereotypes.

Hermerén, Göran. *Representation and Meaning in the Visual Arts: A Study in the Methodology of Iconography and Iconology.* Stockholm, 1969. A sagacious analysis of the conceptual framework of iconography and iconology; the main thesis is similar to that of Gombrich—seeing is an active process, not a passive one—but the author elaborates this idea more systematically than Gombrich along the lines of philosophical theories of symbols.

Kaemmerling, Ekkehard, ed. *Ikonographie und Ikonologie: Theorien, Entwicklung, Probleme.* Cologne, 1979. A collection of first-class essays, including the basic texts of Panofsky that discuss the program of Warburg and Panofsky.

Keel, Othmar. *Die Welt der altorientalischen Bildsymbolik und das Alte Testament.* 2d ed. Zurich, 1977. A book full of pictorial schemes; it analyzes the imagery of Old Testament texts with regard to these schemes.

Kubler, George. *The Shape of Time.* New Haven, 1962. A contribution to a theory of iconological genres; he criticizes Panofsky for emphasizing meaning derived from texts and argues in favor of art forms that can be studied independently of meanings.

Langer, Susanne K. *Philosophy in a New Key: A Study in the Symbolism of Reason, Rite, and Art.* 3d ed. Cambridge, Mass., 1951. Especially important for iconography is the distinction she makes between discursive and presentational forms.

Panofsky, Erwin. *Studies in Iconology: Humanistic Themes in the Art of the Renaissance* (1939). Reprint, Oxford, 1972. The introductory chapter expounds his basic program.

Panofsky, Erwin. *Meaning in the Visual Arts* (1955). Reprint, Chicago, 1982. Further studies based on his methodological approach.

Riegl, Alois. *Spätrömische Kunstindustrie.* 2d ed. (1927). Reprint, Darmstadt, 1973. The well-known book of Riegl describes the history of art from early Egyptian to late Roman times as stages of ancient worldview; many descriptive terms.

Visible Religion: Annual for Religious Iconography. Edited by H. G. Kippenberg. Leiden, 1982–. An annual reconstructing how visual representations have been read by other cultures. Published to date: vol. 1, *Commemorative Figures* (1982); vol. 2, *Representations of Gods* (1983); vol. 3, *Popular Religions* (1984); vol. 4, *Approaches to Iconology* (1985–1986).

H. G. KIPPENBERG (1987)

ICONOGRAPHY: ICONOGRAPHY AS VISIBLE RELIGION [FURTHER CONSIDERATIONS]

Since 1988, discussions related to the topic of iconography as a form of visible religion have expanded the boundaries previously established by Ernst Cassirer (1874–1945), Ernst Gombrich (1909–2001), Suzanne Langer (1895–1985), Erwin Panofsky (1892–1968), and Aby Warburg (1866–1929). The forms and directions of research questions have been re-shaped and re-formulated as the study of religion has been effected by the widening boundaries of gender studies, investigations of the body, and the study of economic, ethnic, engendered, and/or racial minorities. The study of art, ranging from art history through theories of appreciation, aesthetics, and art criticism has been expanded similarly to incorporate material culture, popular culture, and visual culture. The growing recognition among religious scholars of the significance and meaning of the iconographic elements in film, television, video, photography, and the mass media was prompted by the studies of Lynn Schofield Clark, Gregor Goethals, Stewart M. Hoover, Nissan N. Perez, and S. Brent Plate. New scholarship has extended the study of art and religion into geographic areas previously investigated to a lesser extent, such as Pre-Columbia, Latin America, Africa, and Oceania, as for example in the work of Carol Damian, Rosalind I. J. Hackett, and Albert C. Moore.

Interest in response theory (especially in relation to the arts) has affected the attitude toward and methodologies for the study of iconography. Attention in the last ten years has been placed on the religious valuing and influence of popular culture, and more recently, visual culture. These appear in the work of art historians such as Jeffrey F. Hamburger, Sally Promey, and Gary Vikan, and among religion scholars such as Erika Doss, Colleen McDannell, David Morgan, and Stephen Prothero. They have begun a transfer of interest from the traditional focus of iconographic analysis to new categories of engagement. Simultaneous to these renovations, reappraisals of the theories and methods developed by Cassirer, Gombrich, Langer, and most especially Panofsky, have reframed the fundamental starting points for analysis.

New Perspectives. As linguistic analyses and technology advance our understanding of the epistemological and aesthetic processes, future directions for the study of iconography as a form of visible religion will emerge in coordination with a growing recognition of global and multicultural discourses as pioneered in the comparative studies of traditional iconographic motifs by Helene E. Roberts. New modes of analyses will incorporate nonlinear patterns of thinking as initiated in the "visual thinking" of the philosopher Rudolf Arnheim and the creative linguistics of physician Leonard Shlain. Further, the studies of the significance of optics and vision as communicators of cultural values and ideas in the recent work of art historians James Elkins and Martin Kemp will impact the study of iconography as a form of visible religion.

The rapid transfer of information via visual global media raises new questions regarding the communication of information, knowledge, and ideas beyond the traditional boundaries of cultural and religious frames. The need for developing a methodology that incorporates globalism, multiculturalism, and modern technology will become more apparent, and hopefully filled in conjunction with the development of a language to discuss the visual. Similarly, the continuing study of the visual codes of traditional cultures, especially among indigenous peoples, provides the necessary foundation for current and future study significantly expanding the field of religious studies.

Bibliography

Almeida-Topor, H. d,' Michel Sève, and Anne-Elisabeth Spica, eds. *L'historien et l'image: de l'illustration?á la preuve: actes du Colloque tenu á l'Université de Metz, 11–12-mars 1994.* Metz, France, 1998.

Arnheim, Rudolf. *Visual Thinking.* Berkeley, Calif., 1997.

Berlo, Janet Catherine, ed. *Art, Ideology, and the City of Teotihuacan: A Symposium at Dumbarton Oaks, 8th and 9th October 1988.* Washington, D.C., 1992.

Bolvig, Axel, and Phillip Lindley. *History and Images: Towards a New Iconology.* Turnhout, Belgium, 2003.

Burke, Peter. *Eyewitnessing: The Uses of Images as Historical Evidence.* Ithaca, N.Y., 2001.

Bynum, Caroline Walker. *The Resurrection of the Body in Western Christianity, 200–1336.* New York, 1995.

Cassidy, Brendan, ed. *Iconography at the Crossroads: Papers from the Colloquium Sponsored by the Index of Christian Art, Princeton University, 23–24 March 1990.* Princeton, N.J., 1993.

Clark, Lynn Schofield. *From Angels to Aliens: Teenagers, the Media, and the Supernatural.* New York, 2003.

Dalle Vacche, Angela, ed. *The Visual Turn: Classical Film Theory and Art History.* New Brunswick, N.J., 2003.

Damian, Carol. *The Virgin of the Andes: Art and Ritual in Colonial Cuzco.* Miami Beach, Fla., 1995.

Doss, Erika. *Elvis Culture: Fans, Faith, and Image.* Lawrence, Kan., 2004.

Elkins, James. *Visual Studies: A Skeptical Introduction.* New York, 2003.

Ferretti, Silvia. *Il demone della memoria: simbolo e tempo storico in Warburg, Cassirer, Panofsky.* Cassale Monferrato, Italy, 1984.

Freedberg, David. *The Power of Images: A History of Response Theory.* Chicago, 1989.

Frese, Pamela R., and John M. Coggeshall, eds. *Transcending Boundaries: Multi-Disciplinary Approaches to the Study of Gender.* New York 1991.

Goethals, Gregor. *The Electronic Golden Calf: Images, Religion, and the Making of Meaning.* Cambridge, Mass., 1990.

Hackett, Rosalind I. J. *Art and Religion in Africa.* New York, 1996.

Hamburger, Jeffrey F. *Nuns as Artists: The Visual Culture of a Medieval Convent.* Berkeley, Calif., 1997.

Holly, Michael Ann. *Panofsky and the Foundation of Art History.* Ithaca, N.Y., 1984.

Hoover, Stewart M. *Mass Media Religion: The Social Sources of the Electronic Church.* Newbury Park, Calif., 1988.

Hourihane, Colum, ed. *Image and Belief: Studies in Celebration of the Eightieth Anniversary of the Index of Christian Art.* Princeton, N.J., 1999.

Kemp, Martin. *Visualizations: The Nature Book of Art and Science.* New York, 2001.

Kvaerne, Per. *The Bön Religion of Tibet: The Iconography of a Living Tradition.* Boston, 1995.

Lavin, Irvin, ed. *Meaning in the Visual Arts: Views from the Outside: A Centennial Commemoration of Erwin Panofsky (1892–1968).* Princeton, N.J., 1995.

McDannell, Colleen. *Material Christianity: Religion and Popular Culture in America.* New Haven, Conn., 1998.

Moore, Albert C. *Arts in the Religions of the Pacific: Symbols of Life.* London, 1997.

Morgan, David. *Visual Piety: A History and Theory of Popular Religious Images.* Berkeley, Calif., 1999.

Perez, Nissan N. *Revelation: Representations of Christ in Photography.* London, 2003.

Plate, S. Brent, ed. *Religion, Art, and Visual Culture: A Cross-Cultural Reader.* New York, 2002.

Promey, Sally. *Painting Religion in Public: John Singer Sargent's Triumph of Religion at the Boston Public Library.* Princeton, N.J., 2001.

Prothero, Stephen. *American Jesus: How the Son of God Became a National Icon.* New York, 2003.

Roberts, Helene E., ed. *Encyclopedia of Comparative Iconography.* 2 volumes. Chicago, 1998.

Shlain, Leonard. *The Alphabet Goddess: The Conflict between Word and Image.* New York, 1999.

Vikan, Gary S. *Sacred Images and Sacred Power in Byzantium.* Burlington, Vt., 2003.

Diane Apostolos-Cappadona (2005)

ICONOGRAPHY: TRADITIONAL AFRICAN ICONOGRAPHY

Africa is enormous, and the diversity of peoples and complexities of cultures in sub-Saharan black Africa warn against generalizations, especially when discussing visual images, the significance of which is inextricably linked to local religious and aesthetic sensibilities. Hence, in order to understand the iconography of traditional African religions, one must use a comparative approach. Only by examining the religious iconography of a variety of cultures can one fully understand how visual images represent distinctive ways of experiencing the world for the peoples of sub-Saharan Africa.

ANCESTORS AND KINGS: TWO CASE STUDIES. On the granary doors of the Dogon people of Mali, rows of paired ancestor figures called *nommo* stand watch over the precious millet stored within. Similar figures, at times androgynous, are placed next to the funeral pottery on ancestral shrines of families and on the shrine in the house of the *hogon,* the religious and temporal leader of a clan. Their elongated, ascetic bodies and proud, dispassionate faces image the Dogon's myths of origin, as well as their perception of themselves when life is filled with spiritual vitality, *nyama.*

Oral traditions recall a great drought in the fifteenth century that occasioned the migration of the Dogon in two successive waves from southwestern regions to the area of the Bandiagara cliffs and plateau. There they displaced the Tellem people, whose shrine sculpture they retained and used, and established themselves in small villages, often situated in pairs. In an environment largely devoid of permanent watercourses, the Dogon dug wells to great depths, cultivated subsistence crops of millet, and fashioned houses, shrines, and granaries of a mud-masonry architecture using the geometrical forms, such as cylinders, cones, and cubes, that can also be seen in Dogon wood sculpture.

The Dogon trace their descent to the "four families" who made the legendary migration, but this history of origins is inextricably intertwined with an elaborate creation mythology which profoundly informs their social and religious life. The variations in the myth, as in the sculptured forms expressing it, reflect the strong sense of individuality that each Dogon village possesses. It also permits the free play of the sculptor's imagination, whose work then generates new mythological interpretations.

Dogon myth, ritual, and iconography express a view of life in which, through a process of differentiation and pairing of related beings (*nommo*), an ordered, fruitful world is to be created. But the creative process of complementarity, or twinness, contains within it the potential of opposition and conflict. The primordial being, or *nommo,* who was a blacksmith, stole iron and embers from the sun and descended to earth within a well-stocked granary. It was he who led the descendants of the eighth *nommo* in civilizing the earth. Thus creation involves human participation through ritual actions that restore life and maintain an ordered world. Among the materials of the ritual process are village shrines representing a set of twins; shrine sculpture, as well as granary doors with their bas-relief of paired figures, snakes and lizards, zigzag patterns, and female breasts, all symbolically associated with the creation myth; geometric patterns or "signs" on shrine walls, which refer to the basic ontological properties of the world; funerary masquerades and dances through which the deceased is transformed into a venerated ancestor; and secret languages through which the incantations and texts describing the creation of the world and the appearance of death are conveyed from one generation to another. These are the means by which the Dogon can act effectively in their world, strengthen the creative process, and at the very least provide a momentary stay against confusion.

Among the Edo people along the coastal forest of southeast Nigeria, the iconography of the Benin kingdom reflects a culture with a very different spirituality, one shaped by a monarchical tradition. The present dynasty traces its origins to the fourteenth century, beginning with Oba Eweka I, who was fathered by Òraǹmíyaǹ, son of Odùduwà (Odua), the Yoruba creator-god and first king of Ife (although, according to oral tradition, even before Eweka, the Benin kingdom was said to have been ruled by the Ogosi kings). Thus, for centuries the political and religious life of the Edo people has focused upon the person and powers of the *oba,* or king.

The magnificently carved ivory tusks projecting from the top of the bronze memorial heads on the royal ancestral shrines (until the British punitive expedition of 1897) symbolized the powers of the king—his political authority and his supernatural gifts. While his authority depended upon statecraft and military conquest, it was by virtue of his descent from *obas* who had become gods and his possession of the coral beads, said to have been taken from the kingdom of Olokun, god of the sea, that the *oba* had *ase,* "the power to bring to pass," the power over life and death.

Over the centuries the royal guild of blacksmiths created more than 146 memorial bronze heads of deceased *obas*, queen mothers, and conquered kings and chiefs; and the royal guild of carvers portrayed on 133 ivory tusks the king, his wives, chiefs, and retainers, as well as leopards and mudfish, emblems of his power over forest and water and of his ability to move across boundaries distinguishing disparate realms. Although the memorial heads and the carved tusks were created in honor of particular *obas*, and the rites that are performed before them are always in the name of an individual *oba,* the bronze heads and carved figures do not portray the individuality of past *obas* in either form or expression. It is an aesthetic and a religious principle in Benin culture that the particular is subordinated to the general. The reigning *oba* depends upon the collective royal ancestors and yields to their commands, and the same is true of the iconography of the ancestral shrines and ritual artifacts of the Edo people generally. Thus, the ancestral shrines and their sculptures are not merely memorials but also serve as a means of communication with the living dead.

As in most other African religious traditions, the Edo distinguish between a high god, Osanobua, and a pantheon of deities that includes Olokun, god of the sea and bestower of wealth, Ogun, god of iron, and Osun, god of herbal leaves, whose shrines and rituals articulate the religious life for king and commoner as one of response to the powers upon which individuals are dependent but over which they have relatively little control. However, in a monarchical society, with its divisions of labor among craftsmen, hunters, farmers, warriors, and traders (with the Portuguese, Dutch, and British) and its high regard for individual enterprise and prowess, the Cult of the Hand, *ikegobo,* also known as *ikega,* provides a means for celebrating the ability of the individual to accomplish things and, within limits, to achieve new status. Containers for offerings to the Hand, crafted in bronze for kings and in wood for titled persons, bear images of power such as an *oba* sacrificing leopards, a warrior holding the severed head of an enemy, Portuguese soldiers with guns, or the tools and emblems of office for the blacksmith, carver, or trader. All shrines for the Hand bear the image of the clenched fist, showing the ventral side, with the thumb pointing upward and outward. The directness with which the ritual symbolism is expressed is unusual in African religious art but quite consistent with a ritual of self-esteem.

FORM AND MEANING. Notwithstanding the particularity of traditional African iconography, it is, in general, essentially conceptual and evocative. It is not representational and illustrative, and it is not abstract.

Although the principal subject of African art is the human figure, there is rarely any concern to portray individual likeness, even where a sculpture has been commissioned to commemorate a particular person, as in Akan funerary pottery, Yoruba twin figures, or, as noted above, the Benin bronze heads on royal ancestral shrines. And there is rarely any attempt to visualize in material form spiritual powers, although an elaborately constructed masquerade of cloth, wood, and raffia or a sculpted figure on a shrine may "locate" for ritual purposes the ancestral presence, the god, or the spirit. Rather, African iconography is primarily concerned with expressing the essential nature and status of those powers to which one must respond and with providing models of appropriate response to such powers.

Presence of power. Among the Ìgbómìnà Yoruba of southwestern Nigeria the costumes of the masquerades for the patrilineal ancestors, *eguńguń paaka,* combine materials of the forest with those of human manufacture, such as layers of richly colored cloths, bits of mirror, and beaded panels. The carved headdress portion often melds animal and human features. Packets of magical substances are secreted within the costume. It is the peculiar state of being of the living dead, who cross boundaries and move between two realms, who dwell in heaven yet profoundly affect the well-being of the living, that is materialized, for masquerades are created to reveal a reality not otherwise observable and to evoke an appropriate response, such as awe and dependency, on the part of the observer. Thus, among the Pende the concept of *mahamba* signifies an object, such as a mask, or a ritual given by the ancestors to the living for the common good and through which the ancestors periodically manifest themselves and communicate with their descendants.

A similar observation may be made about the reliquary figures of the Kota people of Gabon. Referred to as *mbulu-ngulu,* "image of the dead," the two-dimensional figures consist of large ovoid heads above simple, diamond-shaped wooden bases. On a shrine, the sculptured form is seated in a bark container holding the bones of several generations of ancestors. The ovoid face and coiffure are created by applying thin sheets or strips of brass and copper to a wooden form in a variety of interrelated geometric patterns. In every case, it is the power of the eyes that holds and penetrates the beholder, expressing the bond between the living and the deceased and the protective power of the ancestors in and for the life of the extended family.

It is not only the reality of the ancestral presence that Africa's religious art presents. Among the Ẹ̀gbá, Ẹ̀gbádò, and Kétu it is the power of "our mothers" that is celebrated in the spectacle of the Ẹ̀fẹ̀/Gẹlẹdẹ festival of masquerade, dance, and song at the time of the spring rains. "Our mothers," *àwọn ìyá wa,* is a collective term for female power, possessed by all women, but most fully by female ancestors and deities and by elderly women in the community who are thus able to sustain or inhibit the procreative process and all other human activities upon which the entire society depends. Balanced on the heads of the dancers—for they always appear in pairs—are sculptures depicting the composed face of a beautiful woman, above which there may be a dramatic scene of conflict between snakes and a quadruped, or scenes depicting domestic activities or social roles. The total sculpted image is perceived as a visual metaphor, often understood as having multiple levels of significance. Likewise, in the deliberate pairing of the delicate face masks and the massive forms and aggressive imagery of zoomorphic helmet masks of the Poro society among the Senufo people of the Ivory Coast one also observes images that refer to the complementary roles of female and male, both human and spiritual, by which life is sustained. In these masquerades, as in Kuba helmet masks worn by the king, African artists are not concerned with the representational illusion entailed in copying nature. Rather, they concentrate on that which they know and believe about their subjects, and they seek to construct images to which the distinctive spirituality of a people can react.

This is also true of emblems of office, such as the beautifully carved bow stands owned by Luba chiefs. The bow stands are considered sacred and are usually kept with ancestral relics, where only the chief and special caretakers are permitted to see them. The work images Luba political and spiritual power. It is through the maternal line that chiefs inherit their office. In the sculpted female figure at the top, woman as genetrix is conveyed in the lifting of the maternal breasts, the elaborately scarified abdomen, and the exposed genitals. The closed eyes of the serene face convey the inner, cerebral power that contrasts with the reproductive and nurturing power of her body. And the soaring three-pronged coiffure, expressing her status and beauty, repeats as an inverted pattern the sculptural treatment of the breasts and the legs, each of which frames a central vertical element. On ritual occasions, the chief's bow and arrows, signs of his political authority, would rest in her elaborate coiffure at the top of the staff. Below her, the metal tip of the staff is thrust into the earth, the realm of the ancestors. It is maternal power that provides the link with the ancestral power on which a Luba chief's power depends.

Models of response. Ritual sculpture provides not only images of the powers on which the living depend but also models for appropriate response to gods and spirits. The naked male or female with arms at their sides or touching their abdomens which appear on Lobi shrines in Burkina Faso, as well as the figure of a kneeling woman with a thunder-ax balanced upon her head and holding a dance-wand for the Yoruba god Sàngó, are images of man and woman as devotees, as inspirited and powerful. They are images through which persons see their spirituality and by which their spirituality is deepened.

The distinction between imaging the nature and status of spiritual powers and imaging the religious self in the posture of devotion and power cannot in most instances be clearly drawn: much African iconography combines the two processes, less so perhaps where there are ancestral associations and more often where the reference is to gods and spirits. On the shrines of the Baule people of the Ivory Coast, men and women place figures representing the spouse that they had in the other world before they were born. The figure is thus the locus for one's spirit-spouse and the place where one attends to the claims of that other. But at the same time the sculptures—many of them carved with great skill—present idealized images of male and female, often in the maturity of life, the hair or beard carefully groomed, the body decorated with scarification patterns and adorned with beads, the face composed, the stance well-balanced. Likewise, among the Igbo people of southeastern Nigeria, the tutelary gods of a town are imaged in wooden figures based upon an idealized human model, for the gods not only have life-giving powers but are also the guardians of morality. The sculptures—for they are often in groups—are looked upon as the "children" of the deity honored. Hence, in their presence the devotee is confronted with conceptions of the self that constrain him or her in thought and action to a deepened awareness of the self that that person is and is not.

Perhaps the most extraordinary images of self and of personal power are carvings that incorporate magical substances (in or on images) to the extent that they alter the human form of the image. They are found for the most part among the Songye and Congo peoples of the lower Congo basin. Some figures have an antelope horn filled with "medicines" projecting from the head, others have nails and small knives pounded into the body, or a magic-holding resin box embedded in the belly. They are visualizations in the extreme of ritual action as manipulative power. Using such carvings in conjunction with words of invocation, the priest or owner of the image engages with the evil in the world, either to project or deflect its aggressive power.

RITUAL ACTIVITY. It is evident that the iconography of African peoples must be understood in the context of ritual activity, where the world as lived and the world as imaged become fused together and transformed into one reality. There are essentially two types of rituals—those in which a person or group undergoes a change in status, usually referred to as rites of passage, and rituals of world maintenance, through which a person or group affirms and seeks to secure in the words and actions of sacrifice a worldview.

Rites of passage. Among many African peoples the masquerade is associated with rites of passage, as, for example, the seasonal rituals of sowing, tilling, and harvesting among the Bwa and Bamana, the funeral rites of the Dogon and the Yoruba, and the rituals of initiation of youth into the societies of the Dan and Mende peoples of West Africa.

Among the Mende people of Sierra Leone, Nowo, a female spirit, appears in dance and masquerade to girls being initiated into the Sande (also known as Bundu) ceremonial society. As far as is known, it is the only female mask danced by a woman in Africa. Although primarily associated with the Sande society and thought of as the Sande spirit, Nowo also appears in other ritual contexts. Her image is carved on the finals of the rhythm pounders used in the boys' initiation rites, on the staff carried by the leader of the men's Poro society, and on the carved mace of the Mende king, as well as on divination implements, women's ritual spoon handles, and on weaving-loom pulleys. But it is only to the female initiates into Sande that Nowo appears in the fullness of the masquerade and the movements of the dance.

In the rituals, Nowo is a spiritual presence and images the beauty and power, the nobility, of woman. Thick, dyed-black fiber strands, suspended from a wooden helmet mask, cover the dancer's body. The carved headdress depicts a composed face with faintly opened eyes that see but may not be seen. The head is crowned with an elaborate coiffure into which are woven cowrie shells and seed pods, symbols of wealth and fertility. Black is said to be woman's color, the color of civilized life. The glistening black surface suggests the lustrous, well-oiled skin with which the initiates will reenter the world. Nowo thus provides an image of the physical beauty and the spiritual power of woman to those about to take their place as adults in Mende society.

World maintenance rituals. The role of iconography in Africa's rituals of world maintenance is no less important than in rites of passage. Among the Yoruba, to cite only one example, paired bronze castings of male and female figures joined at the top by a chain, *ẹdan,* are presented to an initiate into the higher ranks of the secret society that worships Onílẹ̀, "the owner of the earth." The society is known as Ògbóni in Ọ̀yọ́ and the region once under the influence of the Ọ̀yọ́ Empire in the eighteenth century. In this instance Onílẹ̀ has feminine connotations and exists in a complementary relationship to Olódùmarè, the high god, who is usually thought of in masculine terms. Among the southern Yoruba, the same society is called Ọ̀ṣùgbó, who also worship Onílẹ̀.

However, the pronunciation of *Onílẹ̀* requires that the term be translated as "owner of the house." The house is the cult house, which is thought of as a microcosm of the universe. (Yoruba is a tonal language. The word *ilẹ̀* with a high tone on the concluding letter means "house," and with a low tone and shortened vowel refers to the "earth.") The secret, visualized in the linking of male and female, appears to refer to a vision of life in terms of its completion and transcendence of time.

The titled members of the Ògbóni/Ọ̀ṣùgbó society are the elders of the community. They are beyond the time of procreative concerns. For them, sexual differentiation is no longer as important as it once was. Furthermore, kinship distinctions are secondary to the worship of Onílẹ̀, because identification of person by patrilineage is replaced by the allegiance to the unity of all life in Onílẹ̀. Thus, the Ògbóni/Ọ̀ṣùgbó elders participate in the settling of conflicts that divide the body politic. The sacred emblems of the society, the *ẹdan,* are placed on those spots where the relationships among persons have been broken and blood spilled. Expressing the unity of male and female, they possess the power of reconciling and adjudicating differences and atoning through sacrifice for the violation of the essential wholeness of life, whether imaged in "earth" or "house."

The seated male and female figures present to the viewer the signs of their power and authority, *àṣẹ*. The female holds a pair of *ẹdan,* as she would twin children. The male figure, with clenched fists, makes the sign of greeting Onílẹ̀. Four chains with tiny bells are suspended from the sides of each figure's head. The number four, as well as multiples of four, are important in Ifa divination; Ọrúnmìlà (also called Ifá), the divination god, knows the secret of creation and the sacrifices that will make one's way propitious. Above the spare, ascetic bodies, the heads of the paired figures radiate with their *àṣẹ*. Twelve chains are suspended from the plate below each figure. Twelve is a multiple of three and four, also numbers associated with Ògbóni/Ọ̀ṣùgbó and Ifá ritual symbolism. In their combination, there is completion and wholeness born of the secret knowledge of Ògbóni/Ọ̀ṣùgbó and Ifá, a secret readily revealed to the informed eye.

See Also Dogon Religion; Edo Religion.

Bibliography

Biebuyck, Daniel. *The Arts of Zaire,* vol.1: *Southwestern Zaire.* Berkeley, Calif., 1985.

Ben-Amos, Paula. *The Art of Benin.* Revised edition. London, 1995.

Drewal, Henry John, and Margaret T. Drewal. *Gelede: Art and Female Power among the Yorùbá.* Bloomington, Ind., 1983.

Drewal, Henry John, John Pemberton III, and Rowland Abiodun. *Yorùbá: Nine Centuries of African Art and Thought.* New York, 1989.

Ezra, Kate. *Art of the Dogon.* New York, 1988.

Fagg, William B., and John Pemberton III. *Yorùbá Sculpture of West Africa,* edited by Bryce Holcombe. New York, 1982.

Fernandez, James. *Bwiti: An Ethnography of the Religious Imagination in Africa.* Princeton, N.J., 1982.

Fischer, Eberhard, and Hans Himmelheber. *Die Kunst der Dan.* Zurich, 1976.

Glaze, Anita J. *Art and Death in a Senufo Village.* Bloomington, Ind., 1981.

Horton, Robin. *Kalabari Sculpture.* Lagos, Nigeria, 1965.

Karp, Ivan, and C. Bird, eds. *African Systems of Thought.* Washington, D.C., 1979.

LaGamma, Alisa. *Art and Oracle: African Art and Rituals of Divination.* New York, 2000.

LaGamma, Alisa. *Genesis: Ideas of Origin in African Sculpture.* New York, 2002.

Lamp, Frederick. *African Art of the West Atlantic Coast: Transition in Form and Content.* New York, 1979.

Laude, Jean. *Les arts de l'Afrique noire.* Paris, 1966. Translated by Jean Decock as *The Arts of Black Africa.* Berkeley, Calif., 1971.

MacGaffey, Wyatt. "Complexity, Astonishment, and Power: The Visual Vocabulary of Kongo Minkisi." *Journal of Southern African Studies* 14, no. 2 (1988): 188–203.

Meyer, Piet. *Kunst und Religion der Lobi.* Zurich, 1981.

Pemberton, John, III, ed. *Insight and Artistry in African Divination.* Washington, D.C., 2000.

Rattray, R. S. *Religion and Art in Ashanti.* Oxford, 1927.

Roberts, Mary Nooter, and Allen F. Roberts, eds. *Luba Art and the Making of History.* New York, 1996.

Schildkrout, Enid, and Curtis Keim, eds. *African Reflections: Art from Northeastern Zaire.* New York, 1990.

Siroto, Leon. *African Spirit Images and Identities.* New York, 1976.

Strother, Z. S. *Inventing Masks: Agency and History in the Art of the Central Pende.* Chicago, 1998.

Thompson, Robert Farris. *African Art in Motion.* Los Angeles, 1974.

Thompson, Robert Farris. *The Four Movements of the Sun: Kongo Art in Two Worlds.* Washington, D.C., 1981.

Vogel, Susan M. *Baule: African Art, Western Eyes.* New Haven, Conn., 1997.

Vogel, Susan M., ed. *For Spirits and Kings: African Art from the Paul and Ruth Tishman Collection.* New York, 1981.

John Pemberton III (1987 and 2005)

ICONOGRAPHY: AUSTRALIAN ABORIGINAL ICONOGRAPHY

Art has a central place in Australian Aboriginal religion. The substance of Aboriginal ceremonies and rituals consists of enactments of events from the Dreaming, or ancestral past, events that are conserved in the form of the songs, dances, designs, and sacred objects that belong to a particular clan or totemic cult group. Such forms are referred to collectively by a word that can be translated as "sacred law," and it is as "sacred law" that art mediates between the ancestral past and the world of living human beings. Designs that were created in the Dreaming as part of the process of world creation are handed down from generation to generation as a means of maintaining the continuity of existence with the ancestral past.

Designs can be referred to then as "Dreamings," and they are manifestations of the ancestral past in a number of senses. Each originated as a motif painted on an ancestral being's body, as an impression left in the ground by that being, or as a form associated in some other way with ancestral creativity. In many regions myths relate how ancestral beings gave birth to or created out of their bodies the sacred objects associated with particular social groups and land areas. The meaning of the designs on the objects often refers to the acts of ancestral creativity that gave rise to the shape of the landscape; in this respect, the designs can be said to encode Dreaming events. Finally, designs can be a source of ancestral power. Paintings on the bodies of initiates are thought to bring the individuals closer to the spiritual domain; sacred objects rubbed against their bodies can have a similar effect. Upon a person's death in eastern Arnhem Land, designs painted on his or her chest or on the coffin or bone disposal receptacle help to transfer the soul back to the ancestral world for reincorporation within the reservoirs of spiritual power associated with a particular place. Art is linked with the concept of the cycling of spiritual power through the generations from the ancestral past to the present, a concept that characterizes Aboriginal religious thought. The same design may later be painted on an initiate's chest, signifying what Nancy Munn refers to in *Walbiri Iconography* (1973) as the intergenerational transfer of ancestral power, which conceptually integrates the Dreaming with present-day experience.

Aboriginal art varies widely across the continent. Any similarities that exist tend to reside in the properties of the representational systems that are employed—the kinds of meanings that are encoded in the designs and the way in which they are encoded—rather than in the use of particular motifs. One notable exception appears to be what Munn refers to as the circle-line or site-path motif (0 = 0 = 0), which forms a component of designs throughout Australia. In such designs, the circles usually refer to places where some significant event occurred on the journey of a Dreaming ancestral being, and the lines refer to the pathways that connect the places.

Likewise, designs in Aboriginal art exist independent of particular media. The same design in Arnhem Land may occur as a body painting, a sand sculpture, an emblem on a hollow log coffin, or an engraving on a sacred object *(rangga)*. In central Australia the same design may be incised on a stone disc *(tjurunga)*, painted on the body of a dancer in blood and down, or made into a sand sculpture. Further, it is the design that gives the object its particular ancestral connection: the designs are extensions of ancestral beings and are sometimes referred to as their "shadows." Thus, they can be used in different contexts for different purposes. The same basic design may be used as a sand sculpture in a curing ceremony, painted on the bodies of initiates to associate them with particular ancestral forces or signify membership in a social group, or painted on a coffin to guide a dead person's soul back to the clan lands for reincorporation within the ancestral domain.

SYSTEMS OF REPRESENTATION. Meaning in Aboriginal art is encoded in two distinct systems of representation, one iconic and figurative, the other aniconic and geometric. The iconography of Aboriginal religious art arises out of the interplay between these two complementary systems. This distinction extends outside the area of the visual arts to dance and ceremonial action, which involve some components and actions that are essentially mimetic and represent the behavior and characteristics of natural species, as well as other components that are abstract and have a conventional and nonrepresentational meaning. The balance between the figurative and the geometric varies from one region to another. The art of central Australia, of groups such as the Warlpiri, the Aranda, the Pintubi, and the Pitjantjatjara, is characterized by geometric motifs, whereas western Arnhem Land is associated with a highly developed figurative tradition. Nonetheless, there is a figurative component in central Australian art, and the *marayin* designs, clan-owned body painting designs used in certain western Arnhem Land initiation ceremonies, are largely geometric.

The forms of Aboriginal art are systematically linked to its various functions. The figurative art presents images of the Dreaming that at one level can be readily interpreted as representations of totemic species and the forms of ancestral beings. The X-ray art of western Arnhem Land, for example, is a figurative tradition that creates images of totemic ancestors associated with particular places, thus linking them directly to the natural world.

The title of Luke Taylor's book, *Seeing the Inside*, aptly expresses the capacity of X-ray art to look beyond the surface form of things. The figures are in part accurate representations of kangaroos, fish, snakes, and so on. However, they are more than that. The X-ray component, representing the heart, lungs, and other internal organs of the animal, adds an element of mystery to the figures and differentiates the representations from those of ordinary animals. Moreover, the art includes representations that combine features of a number of different animals in a single figure. For example, the figure of the Rainbow Snake, an important mythical being throughout Arnhem Land, may combine features of a snake, a kangaroo, a buffalo, an emu, and a crocodile. Such figures in X-ray art, together with songs and dances associated with them, are part of a system of symbolism that decomposes the natural world into its elements, breaks the boundaries between different species of animals, and alludes to the underlying transforming power of the Dreaming. The western Arnhem Land X-ray figures are public representations of the ancestral world and, painted on cave walls, are projections of the ancestral past into the present in a fairly literal form. Their presence on rock surfaces acts as a sign of the ancestral transformations that created the form of the landscape and a reminder of the creative forces inherent in the land.

Much of the ceremonial art and most of the secret art of Australia is, however, geometric in form. The geometric art encodes meaning in a more elusive way, well suited to a system of esoteric knowledge in which some of the meanings of art are restricted to the initiated. Without some assistance, its meaning will remain a mystery: in order to be understood it has to be interpreted and its meanings have to be revealed. Geometric art gives priority to no single interpretation, and as a person grows older he or she learns increasingly more about the meaning of particular designs. Thus, geometric art is potentially multivalent, and different meanings and interpretations can be condensed into the same symbol or design.

This property of geometric art enables it to encode the relationship between different phenomena or orders of reality. On one level, a circle in a design may represent a water hole, and the line joining it may represent a creek flowing into the water hole. On another level, the circle may be said to represent a hole dug in the ground and the line a digging stick. On yet another level, the circle may be interpreted as the vagina of a female ancestral being and the line as the penis of a male ancestor. All three interpretations are related, for digging in the sand is an analogue for sexual intercourse, and the water hole was created through sexual intercourse between two ancestral beings in the Dreaming. The design of which the circle is a part may belong to a particular clan and be identified as such. The design as a whole thus represents ancestral beings creating features of the landscape in territory associated with a particular social group. It is this set of associations that characterizes the iconography of Aboriginal art: the designs mediate between the present and the ancestral past by encoding the relationship between ancestral being, people, and place. Aboriginal religion firmly locates the identity of people in the spirituality of place, and designs infused with the power of ancestral beings provide an important transportable medium of connection.

The geometric art represents the ancestral world both semiotically and aesthetically, by expressing ancestral power in an artistic form. The Dreaming beings are often complex concepts, and their encoding in abstract representations provides one of the ways by which people develop shared understandings that help to order their collective experience of the ancestral past. For example, in the case of the Yolngu people of northeastern Arnhem Land, the Wild Honey ancestor consists of the whole set of things associated with the collection of wild honey: the hive, the bees, the honey; pollen and grubs; the paperbark tree where the hives are found and the swamps where the trees grow; the hunter, his baskets, and the smoke made by the fires he lights. All things associated with wild honey are attributes of the Wild Honey ancestor. In painting, the Wild Honey ancestor is represented by a complex diamond pattern representing the cells of the hive. The diamonds are cross-hatched in different colors to signify different components of the hive: grubs, honey, pollen, and bees. The bars across some of the segments represent sticks in the structure of the hive, and the dots within the circles represent bees at its entrance. On another level, elements of the design signify smoke, flames, and ash from the hunter's fire, and on still another level, the diamond pattern represents the rippling of floodwater as it passes beneath the paperbark trees. The Wild Honey ancestor is all of those things and more.

Systems of Interpretation. As people go through life they learn the meanings of designs such as the Wild Honey pattern; they associate it with places created by the ancestral being and with ceremonies that celebrate that being's creative power. For the individual, the design is no longer an abstract sign but a manifestation of the ancestral being concerned. Aesthetic aspects of the design reinforce this understanding, as Howard Morphy has shown in *Ancestral Connections*, his book on the aesthetics and iconography of Yolngu ritual art. In northeastern Arnhem Land, Yolngu body paintings convey a sense of light and movement through the layering of finely cross-hatched lines across the skin surface. Similar effects are created in central Australian painting through the use of white down and the glistening effect of blood, fat, and red ocher. These attributes of paintings are interpreted by Aboriginal people as attributes of the ancestral being: the light from the ancestral being shines from the painting as symbol or evidence of the power of the design.

Throughout much of Australia, rights to designs and other components of "sacred law" are vested in social groups that exercise some control over their use and have the responsibility to ensure that they continue to be passed down through the generations. Such rights are of considerable importance, as "sacred law" provides the charter for ownership and control of land. Hence, designs not only represent sources of ancestral power but are politically significant in demonstrating rights over land and providing a focal point for group solidarity and identity. This dimension is reflected in the iconography insofar as designs often vary on the basis of group ownership, each group holding rights to a unique set of designs.

There is enormous regional variation in Australian Aboriginal art, and the specific symbolism of the designs can only be understood in their regional context. However, the underlying principles of the art have much in common everywhere. Moreover, belief in the spiritual power and mediating functions of the designs is to an extent independent of knowledge of their meaning. For both these reasons, designs and other components of ritual can be passed on to other groups—from neighboring or even quite distant places—and become part of those groups' ancestral inheritance. In this respect, religious iconography is integral to the process of religious change, enabling religious ideas to be exchanged with other groups and diffused across the continent. Changes also can occur internally through the Dreaming of new designs. This allows the iconographic system to adjust to sociopolitical reality or to the creation of new groups and the demise of existing ones. However, from the Aboriginal viewpoint, such changes are always revelatory: they ultimately have a Dreaming reference and will always be credited to the past. The designs not only encode meanings that help endow everyday events and features of the landscape with cosmic significance, but are themselves extensions of those Dreaming ancestors into the present.

Since the 1970s, through the popularity of Aboriginal bark and acrylic paintings, art has become an increasingly important means by which Aboriginal people communicate religious ideas to a wider audience. While non-Aboriginal audiences have been attracted by the aesthetic dimension of the works, they also have been exposed to the religious ideas and values that are integral to them. Exhibitions of Aboriginal art emphasize the religious values that the works embody: the idea of the Dreaming, the immanence of the sacred in the form of the landscape, and the emergent nature of spirituality.

Aboriginal people also have responded to and accommodated religious ideas through their art. Yolngu artists from Arnhem Land carried on a dialogue with Christianity from the arrival of the first missionaries in 1935. This dialogue resulted in the placing of painted panels of Yolngu religious art on either side of the altar of the new church built in 1962. Subsequently, as Fred Myers has shown, the Pintubi artist Linda Syddick's paintings combine Christian themes concerning crucifixion with reflections on separation and identity stimulated by the science fiction character E.T., all represented through central Australian iconography. This dynamic aspect of Australian Aboriginal art and its capacity to reach diverse audiences within and outside the society is one of the factors that has enabled Aboriginal religion to continue to make a contribution to global religious discourse.

SEE ALSO Dreaming, The; Tjurungas; Wandjina.

BIBLIOGRAPHY

Berndt, Ronald M., ed. *Australian Aboriginal Art.* New York, 1964. A pioneering volume, with essays by Ted Strehlow, Charles Mountford, and Adolphus Peter Elkin, that provides a broad coverage of Aboriginal art and its religious significance.

Elkin, A. P., Ronald M. Berndt, and Catherine H. Berndt. *Art in Arnhem Land.* Melbourne, Australia, 1950. The pioneering work on Australian Aboriginal art, placing the art of Arnhem Land in its social and mythological context.

Groger-Wurm, Helen M. *Australian Aboriginal Bark Paintings and Their Mythological Interpretation.* Canberra, Australia, 1973. A good account of northeastern Arnhem bark paintings, with detailed interpretations of their meanings.

Kleinert, Sylvia, and Margo Neale, ed. *The Oxford Companion to Aboriginal Art and Culture.* Melbourne, Australia, 2000. A comprehensive reference work on Aboriginal art and religion.

Morphy, Howard. *Ancestral Connections: Art and an Aboriginal System of Knowledge.* Chicago, 1991. A detailed account of the iconography of the paintings of the Yolngu people of northeast Arnhem Land, including their meanings and ritual context.

Morphy, Howard. *Aboriginal Art.* London, 1998. A comprehensive and richly illustrated introduction to Aboriginal art with broad regional and historic coverage.

Mountford, Charles Pearcy. *Records of the American-Australian Scientific Expedition to Arnhem Land.* Vol. 1: *Art, Myth and Symbolism.* Melbourne, Australia, 1956. A comprehensive collection of paintings from western and eastern Arnhem Land and Groote Eylandt. The collection is extensively documented with accounts of Aboriginal myths. The documentation is somewhat general and not always accurate, but its coverage is excellent.

Munn, Nancy D. *Walbiri Iconography.* Ithaca, N.Y., 1973. A detailed account of the representational systems of the Warlpiri of central Australia and the religious symbolism of the designs. This is a classic work on the geometric art of central Australia.

Myers, Fred R. *Painting Culture: The Making of an Aboriginal High Art.* Durham, N.C., 2002. A detailed account of the central Australian acrylic art movement that provides insights into its cultural context and religious significance in addition to its developing global market.

Taylor, Luke. *Seeing the Inside: Bark Painting in Western Arnhem Land.* Oxford, 1996. A rich account of western Arnhem Land X-ray and ceremonial art covering equally the social and conceptual dimensions of artistic practice.

Watson, Christine. *Piercing the Ground: Balgo Women's Image Making and Relationship to Country.* Freemantle, Australia, 2003. A rich account of the iconography of desert paintings from Balgo with a particular emphasis on the tactile dimension of their cultural aesthetics.

HOWARD MORPHY (1987 AND 2005)

ICONOGRAPHY: NATIVE NORTH AMERICAN ICONOGRAPHY

Iconography is a living force in North American Indian religious life, past and present. Rooted in mythical imagery, it informs the content of individual dreams and nourishes the themes of contemporary Indian art. A study of the iconography of a people provides a unique opportunity to gain insight into what Werner Müller calls the "pictorial world of the soul" (*Die Religionen der Waldlandindianer Nordamerikas,* Berlin, 1956, p. 57).

The following exposition of the major themes of religious iconography in North America is restricted to the evidence of the late-nineteenth and twentieth centuries of ethnographic research. As a result, the beautiful pottery and stone remains of the prehistoric peoples of the Southwest and Southeast are not represented here, nor are the remains of the Mound Builder cultures of the river regions.

The iconographical themes follow the general lines of myth and religious beliefs. As such, they can be cataloged in the following manner: the cosmos, supreme beings, tricksters/culture heroes, guardian beings, other mythic beings, astronomical beings, weather beings, animal beings, vegetation beings, human beings, geological beings, and abstract symbols. But it is not always the case that the verbal images of the myths are equivalent to iconographical images: one notorious example of divergence is the Ojibwa trickster, Rabbit, who, when pictured, is actually human in form.

Concerning the wide variety of media used, the following general distribution can be observed: in the Far North—ivory, bone, and stone; the Northeast and Southeast Woodlands—wood, bark, skin, quillwork, and beadwork; the Plains—skin, beadwork, pipestone, quillwork, and painting of bodies and horses; the Northwest Coast—cedar, ivory, argillite, blankets, and copper; California—baskets and some stone; the Southwest—sand painting, wood, stone, baskets, pottery, jewelry, and dolls.

THE COSMOS. Cosmologies vary from tribe to tribe in both content and imagery. But whereas the mythical image of the universe (its cosmography) may be highly detailed, the iconographical rendering is necessarily restricted. The cosmos is most often graphically limited to those elements that characterize its basic nature and structure, including its nonvisual aspects.

The most widespread symbol of the whole cosmos is the ceremonial lodge, house, or tent. The fundamental idea of the ceremonial lodge, such as the Delaware *xingwikáon* ("big house"), is that all of its parts symbolize, and in ritual contexts actually are, the cosmos. Usually the realms of this cosmos are interconnected with a central post, which is conceived of as extending itself like a world tree up to the heavens. Renewing such a house constitutes the actual renewal of the cosmos.

Similar ideas are found among the Plains Indians, for whom the sacred camp circle constitutes an image of the world, and the central pole of the Sun Dance tipi, the whole cosmos. In fact the Crow call this tent the "imitation" or "miniature" lodge, a replica of the Sun's lodge.

Representations of the cosmos can refer to the more subtle manifestations of the world, as in the sand paintings of the Luiseño of California, but they can also approach the reality of topographical maps, as in the sand paintings of the neighboring Diegueño. In a completely different approach to the visualization of the cosmos, the well-known Navajo sand painting of Father Sky and Mother Earth illustrates the anthropomorphic representation of the cosmos.

Concerning nonvisual aspects of the cosmos, it is not uncommon that ethical ideals or holistic images of proper human life, which are extensions of the theological bases of many cosmologies, are also visualized iconographically. The most common image of this type is that of the right, or the beautiful, path. The Delaware big house has a circular path on its floor, which the visionary singers and other participants in the big house ceremony walk and dance upon. This path is called the Good White Path, the symbol of the human life. It corresponds to the Milky Way, which is the path of the souls of the dead. The Ojibwa bark charts of the Midewiwin ceremony consist of illustrations of the degrees of initiation into the Mide secret society. All of the degrees are represented as connected by the path of the initiate's life, starting in the image of the primordial world and ending upon the island of direct communication with the supreme being. This path is pictured with many detours and dramatic occurrences.

SUPREME BEINGS. Among the myriad images found in North American Indian iconography are certain divine beings whose representations cut across taxonomic groups; these include supreme beings, tricksters/culture heroes, guardian beings, and other mythical beings. Since the majestic, all-encompassing supreme being is difficult to visualize, its morphology is relatively simple. When not visualized as some object or animal intimately associated with the supreme being, its form tends to be anthropomorphic. For example, the Ojibwa song charts visualize the supreme being, Kitsi Manitu, with a pictograph of a human head, belonging to an initiate in the Mide secret society.

On the other hand, the all-pervasiveness of the supreme being among the Plains Indians can result in the use of symbols of lesser deities to represent it. Thus Wakantanka, of the Oglala Lakota, has various manifestations such as the Sun, the Moon, Buffalo, and so on, all of which are pictured on hides or, as with Buffalo, represented by a buffalo skull.

TRICKSTERS/CULTURE HEROES. The most widespread iconographic trickster type is theriomorphic: Raven, Coyote, or Rabbit. The most well-known image is that of Raven among the Northwest Coast tribes, a character who encompasses all of the classical features of the trickster. He is pictured in raven-form on virtually every object throughout the Northwest, usually in the context of a mythical event that somehow affected the ancestor of the house in which the object is found, be it house pole, settee, or some other form. As part of shamanic paraphernalia, his image imparts one of his main characteristics: that of transformation. Even though the trickster is an animal, in mythical thought he can change to human form, and this process is often reflected iconographically, as with the Navajo Coyote and the Delaware and Ojibwa Rabbit.

The culture hero is a divine or semidivine mythic figure who, through a series of heroic deeds—especially the theft of such an important item as fire or light—starts humanity upon its cultural road. When he is not the theriomorphic trickster, he is often simply visualized as a human being.

GUARDIAN BEINGS. Guardian beings associate themselves most often on a personal level with single individuals, and they function as guardians who bring blessings to their human partners. In the Plains and Northern Woodlands cultures, to seek and receive a personal vision of just such a guardian is necessary in order to secure an individual's station in life. These guardians can appear in just about any form taken from the natural or the mythological world. Among the Oglala it may be necessary to paint a version of one's vision on the tipi in order to secure its validity, although generally images of the guardian are painted on shields.

In the cultures of the Far North and Arctic areas, the shaman and his guardians are a constant iconographic theme. His guardians are portrayed in several general ways: as diminutive human beings clustered near the shaman or as human faces clustered together, as a human visage under an animal visage such as seen in Alaskan masks, as an animal form reduced in size and resting on the head or shoulders of the shaman, as birdlike shamans or shamans in transformation, as flying spirits being ridden by shamans, as an animal or human being with skeletal markings, or as flying bears or other usually flightless beasts. These images are portrayed in contemporary drawings, ivory sculpture, masks, stone sculpture, bone sculpture, drumsticks, shaman staff, and so on. Throughout North America the shaman also uses organic parts of his guardians in his ritual paraphernalia, or else he can use the entire skin of his guardian animal to transform himself.

Guardians appear in nonvisionary and nonshamanistic cultures as well. The Pueblo deities of the six world regions are considered to be guardians of humanity. Another type of guardian is Rainbow Serpent, pictured on almost all Navajo sand paintings. This figure encircles the entire painting but remains open toward the east. Its function is to keep the evil spirits out of the reinstated cosmic region.

Other Mythical Beings. Among the mythological figures who are pictured iconographically, one important group is that of monsters. The most common monster motif is an image of the primordial horned, flying serpent, the cause of floods and earthquakes. He is known all over the Americas and is generally pictured in exactly the form described. Another monster known all over North America is Thunderbird, usually pictured on shields, shirts, and beadwork as an eaglelike creature.

There is also a whole group of evil beings who, in one form or another, are believed to exercise a malignant and dangerous influence on humanity. Such creatures are usually theriomorphic but not necessarily so.

Astronomical Beings. The sun, the moon, and the stars are pictured as beings throughout North America. The sun is portrayed most intensely where it is strongest, in southeastern and southwestern North America. The Hopi portray the Sun, Taawa, anthropomorphically but, in keeping with Hopi iconography, he wears a mask that consists of a circular disk fringed with radiating feathers and horsehair. This radial representation of the sun is the most common image known. The Ojibwa, on the other hand, have a completely different image, which is horned, winged, and legged.

The moon is usually represented in its quarter phase, although images of the full moon are sometimes found. The stars most often pictured are the Morning Star (Venus), the Pleiades, Orion, Altair, the constellation Ursa Major (which is invariably pictured as a heavenly bear), and the Milky Way. Stars are shown with four, five, and six points and are often associated with human figures.

Meteorological Beings. This group consists of Thunder, Wind, Rain, and Lightning. Thunder is often pictured as the Thunderbird, but other birds can also be used. Wind, on the other hand, is generally associated with the cardinal regions and therefore not visualized directly. Cultures with anthropocentric morphology, however, such as the Navajo and the Ojibwa, picture even this being in human shape.

Rain is usually illustrated as lines falling from cloud symbols or as a being from which rain is falling. Lightning is always shown as zigzag lines regardless of the tribe in question. The lines usually end in arrowheads, for there is a conceptual link between lightning and arrows. Lightning and thunder are usually considered to be the weapons of the widely known Warrior Twins.

Animal Beings. There are a number of animals which are known and visualized throughout North America, such as the bear, the deer, and the buffalo. However, other animals peculiar to a particular region are the more common iconographical subjects, such as the whales and seals of the northern coasts, or the lizards and snakes of the desert regions. The general rule is that the animal is depicted in its natural form.

Representations of animals may signify the spirit or master of their species or the form of some deity, guardian being, or primordial creature, or they may indicate the totem animal. All animal images used in ritual contexts have religious significance. But the most common use of animal images occurs in heraldry, which casts some doubt on the exclusively religious significance of its use and meaning.

The Northwest Coast Indians are the most conspicuous users of totem symbols. These symbols are represented in literally every conceivable medium: poles, house fronts, hats, aprons, spoons, bowls, settees, boat prows, spearheads, fishhooks, dagger handles, facial painting, masks, speaker staffs, paddles, drums, rattles, floats, bracelets, leggings, pipes, and gambling sticks. The question of religious significance may be resolved by the fact that the totem animal is considered either a direct ancestor of the clan or somehow associated with an ancient human ancestor. Thus the symbol at least, if not its use, has religious meaning.

Vegetation Beings. Corn is the plant most commonly visualized. The representation can simply refer to the plant itself, but frequently a maize deity is being invoked. The latter is the case throughout the Southwest, whether among the Pueblo or the Athapascan peoples. The maize deity is usually clearly anthropomorphized. Hallucinogenic plants such as peyote, jimsonweed, or the strong wild tobaccos are more or less realistically pictured; such images refer to the deities of these potent plants. Others beings who somehow influence plant growth are also visualized iconographically; these include the Yuki impersonations of the dead, who have a decided influence on the abundance of acorns, or the Hopi impersonations of cultic heros and heroines whose rituals influence crop growth.

Human Beings. This category concerns not only human ancestors but also a miscellaneous collection of beings that have human form. The first type are effigies of once-living human beings. These are most commonly figured on Northwest Coast mortuary poles, but they are also found elsewhere: the Californian Maidu, Yokuts, Luiseño, and Tubatulabal, for example, all burn effigies of prominent people two years after their deaths.

Human images can also be material expressions of the ineffable. During the Sun Dance the Shoshoni and the Crow each bring out a stone image in diminutive human shape, which is then attached to a staff or the center pole of the tent. It is said to represent the spirit of the Sun Dance. Human images, such as dolls, can symbolize or are actually considered to be small spritelike creatures who can have an array of functions and duties and who play a part in ceremonial contexts as well. Human representations can also signify the heroes or founders of cults; such is the case with many images on Pueblo altars and other representations on Northwest Coast poles.

Geological Beings. This category of images is based on a type of religious geomorphology. It is not a numerically dominant theme, but it is nonetheless of singular importance. The most prominent geological being envisioned is Mother Earth, although it is seldom that direct representations of it occur. In such anthropocentric iconographies as that of the Navajo, it is no problem to illustrate Mother Earth as a somewhat enlarged female human being. Usually, however, Mother Earth is symbolized by some fertility image, such as an ear of corn, or by a circle. Among the Delaware, the earth is symbolized by the giant tortoise who saved humankind from the flood and upon whose back the new earth was created by Nanabush. Sods of earth can also be used to represent Mother Earth, as in the Cheyenne buffalo-skull altar in the medicine lodge.

Another group of geological beings consists of images of mountains. Except for isolated pockets of flatlands and desert basins, most of North America is covered with mountains, and these are usually believed to be alive or at least filled with life, that is, they are the abodes of the gods. This feature of mountains is highly important and is also recognized iconographically.

Finally, some mention should be made of stones and prehistoric implements. Animacy or power is attributed to implements such as ancient pipe bowls, mortars, and blades, any odd-shaped stones, and stones resembling animal, vegetable, or human outlines. Such stones symbolize whatever they resemble.

Abstract Symbols. The dynamic and highly stylized geometric patterns on Southwest Indian pottery, which represent categories already discussed (such as clouds, rain, lightning, the sun, and so on), also belong to the category of abstract symbols. Cultures with highly developed artistic iconographies, such as those of the Northwest Coast, the Southwest, and the Woodlands peoples with their birchbark illustrations, also develop series of signs referring to abstractions inherent to their systems. On the Ojibwa Midewiwin scrolls, for example, the symbol of bear tracks in a particular context represents a priest's four false attempts to enter the Mide lodge. These four false attempts can also be symbolized by four bars.

See Also North American Indians; Shamanism, article on North American Shamanism; Tricksters, article on North American Tricksters.

Bibliography

There is unfortunately no comprehensive work on the religious iconography of the North American Indians. Information about iconography is found in the original ethnographic data on various peoples published in the annual reports and the bulletins of the Bureau of American Ethnology. An ethnographic approach to art in North America, with emphasis on prehistoric art, can be found in Wolfgang Haberland's *The Art of North America*, translated by Wayne Dynes (New York, 1964). General works on the art of American Indians are numerous; the most comprehensive is Norman Feder's *American Indian Art* (New York, 1971). Another useful study is Frederick J. Dockstader's *Indian Art of the Americas* (New York, 1973).

For the Indians of the Far North, see Jean Blodgett's *The Coming and Going of the Shaman: Eskimo Shamanism and Art* (Winnipeg, 1979) and Inge Kleivan and Birgitte Sonne's *Eskimos: Greenland and Canada*, "Iconography of Religions," sec. 8, fasc. 1 (Leiden, 1984). Concerning the Northeast and Southeast Woodlands tribes, see Frank G. Speck's *Montagnais Art in Birch-bark, a Circumpolar Trait*, "Museum of the American Indian, Heye Foundation, Indian Notes and Monographs," vol. 11, no. 2 (New York, 1937), and *Concerning Iconology and the Masking Complex in Eastern North America*, "University Museum Bulletin," vol. 15, no. 1 (Philadelphia, 1950). For the Plains Indians, see Åke Hultkrantz's *Prairie and Plains Indians*, "Iconography of Religions," sec. 10, fasc. 2 (Leiden, 1973), and Peter J. Powell's *Sweet Medicine: The Continuing Role of the Sacred Arrows, the Sun Dance, and the Sacred Buffalo Hat in Northern Cheyenne History*, 2 vols. (Norman, Okla., 1969). For Indians of the Northwest Coast, see Charles Marius Barbeau's *Totem Poles*, 2 vols. (Ottawa, 1950–1951), and Franz Boas's *Primitive Art* (1927; new ed., New York, 1955). Concerning the Pueblo Indians of the Southwest, see my *Hopi Indian Altar Iconography*, "Iconography of Religions," sec. 10, fasc. 4a (Leiden, 1986), and Barton Wright's *Pueblo Cultures*, "Iconography of Religions," sec. 10, fasc. 4 (Leiden, 1985). For the Navajo Indians of the Southwest, see Sam D. Gill's *Songs of Life: An Introduction to Navajo Religious Culture*, "Iconography of Religions," sec. 10, fasc. 3 (Leiden, 1979), and Gladys A. Reichard's *Navajo Medicine Man: Sandpaintings and Legends of Miguelito* (New York, 1939).

Armin W. Geertz (1987)

ICONOGRAPHY: MESOAMERICAN ICONOGRAPHY

Each major Mesoamerican culture developed its religious imagery in a distinctive fashion, although all were historically interlinked and drew from the common pool of Mesoamerican stylistic-iconographic tradition. This type of pictorialization was especially important in an area cotradition that lacked fully evolved phonetic scripts. It constituted an effective technique of visually communicating in a standardized, codified manner the basic concepts of the religious-ritual systems that played such a crucial sociocultural role in pre-Hispanic Mesoamerica.

ISSUES OF INTERPRETATION. The Mesoamerican iconographic systems that were functioning at the time of the Spanish conquest in the early sixteenth century can be interpreted with the aid of a broad range of data, including written sources compiled in Spanish and in the native languages. The iconographies of the earlier cultures must be studied without the assistance of texts of this type and pose much greater interpretative difficulties. The technique most often employed has been to invoke similarities between the Conquest period images, whose connotations are reasonably well understood from ethnohistorical information, and those of the earlier traditions, assigning to the latter generally similar meanings. This procedure, employing the elementary logic of working from the known to the unknown, is often referred to as the "direct historical approach" or "upstreaming."

This technique has been criticized, particularly when long temporal spans are involved. Disjunctions between form and meaning in religious imagery, it has been pointed out, have been common in iconographic history (above all in the Western tradition with the sharp ideological breaks that accompanied the rise of Christianity and Islam). However, those who sustain the validity of the direct historical approach argue that no major disjunctions of the type that occurred in the West took place in pre-Hispanic Mesoamerica. They cite various examples of imagic continuity from Olmec to Aztec and suggest that Mesoamerica can be more fitly compared to pre-Christian Egypt or to India and China, areas well known for their long-term iconographic continuities of form and meaning. These disagreements among leading scholars indicate that considerable caution is advisable when appraising the accuracy of interpretations of religious images and symbols of the more ancient Mesoamerican cultures.

OLMEC. Most archaeologists agree that the earliest sophisticated religious iconographic system in Mesoamerica was that of the Olmec, which flourished between about 1200 and 400 BCE (Middle Preclassic), and was centered in the Gulf Coast region of eastern Veracruz and western Tabasco. Olmec style, which conveyed religious concepts imaginatively and effectively, was one of the most striking and original esthetic expressions ever achieved in pre-Hispanic Mesoamerica. Unfortunately, accurately ascertaining the connotations of the intricate Olmec symbol system presents formidable difficulties, and interpretations of prominent students often differ radically.

A major characteristic of Olmec iconography is the blending of anthropomorphic and zoomorphic features. Much of the controversy surrounding the interpretation of Olmec iconography has focused on these fused images, which often exhibit additional overtones of infantilism and dwarfism. The most popular interpretation has been that they merge feline with human characteristics, and the term *were-jaguar* has become fashionable to refer to them. Frequently cited in support of this interpretation are two well-known Olmec monumental sculptures from two small sites near the great Olmec center of San Lorenzo, Veracruz, that supposedly represent a jaguar copulating with a human female, thus producing a hybrid feline-human race, the "jaguar's children." In this view, the composite creature, connoting rain and terrestrial fertility, constituted the fundamental Olmec deity, the archetypical ancestor of all later Mesoamerican rain-and-fertility gods. However, another interpretation would give preeminence to crocodilian rather than feline imagery; the rattlesnake and the toad also have their vigorous proponents.

Other Olmec composite beings are recognized, but opinions differ concerning the precise zoological identification of their constituent elements. A considerable case has been presented for the importance of a polymorphic, essentially saurian creature with various aspects. Called the Olmec Dragon, it has been postulated as the ancestor of a variegated family of celestial and terrestrial monsters prominent in later Mesoamerican iconography.

To what extent Olmec religious imagery indicates the existence of discrete, individualized deities has also elicited considerable debate. Some scholars argue for a fairly sizable Olmec pantheon, often linking its members with prominent contact-period gods. Others view Olmec symbolism as connoting various generalized supernaturalistic concepts but not recognizable deities—which, in their opinion, did not emerge in Mesoamerica until much later. However, it seems likely that at least prototypical versions of various later deities were already being propitiated in "America's first civilization."

IZAPA. A series of closely interrelated stylistic and iconographic traditions known as "Izapan," after the major site of Izapa, Chiapas, Mexico, flourished between about 500 BCE and 250 CE (Late Preclassic-Protoclassic) in the area flanking the Isthmus of Tehuantepec, concentrated in the Pacific slope region of Chiapas, Guatemala, and El Salvador. Izapan iconography bears a close relationship to Olmec, from which it partly derives, but its formats are generally somewhat more complex. The style is most typically expressed by low-relief carving, commonly on the perpendicular stone monuments known as stelae, which are sometimes fronted by plain or effigy "altars."

Izapan iconography frequently displays a narrative quality in its compositions, depicting a variety of ritual-mythic scenes, some of considerable complexity. These scenes are often framed by highly stylized celestial and terrestrial registers, interpreted as monster masks. As in Olmec, polymorphic creatures, ostensibly merging feline, saurian, and avian elements, are common. Even more than in the case of Olmec, identifying recognizable deities is difficult, but prominently featured in Izapan iconography is the profile mask of the "long-lipped dragon," depicted in numerous variants including the "scroll-eyed demon." Another significant Izapan composite creature was the "bi- and tricephalous monster," apparently with both celestial and terrestrial connotations. Also prominent on Izapan monuments are downward-flying, winged, anthropomorphic beings, downward-peering celestial faces, combat scenes (humanoid figures versus double-headed serpentine creatures), polymorphic bird monsters, cosmic trees with "dragon-head roots," and diminutive human ritual celebrants accompanied by various ritual paraphernalia. This region during the Late Preclassic and Protoclassic periods produced some of the most iconographically intriguing sculptures of Mesoamerica.

Classic Lowland Maya. The Izapan tradition led directly into the most sophisticated of all Mesoamerican iconographic and stylistic traditions, that of the Classic Lowland Maya (c. 25–900 CE) As in the case of Izapan, which lies in its background, Maya art in general is essentially two-dimensional and painterly but is also more structured and mature in its expressive power than the earlier tradition. Nearly all of the most common Izapan iconographic themes were retained and often further elaborated. These included the bi- and tricephalous polymorphic celestial-terrestrial creature now frequently conceived as the "ceremonial bar" held by the rulers, the long-lipped dragon in numerous manifestations that eventually evolved into the long-nosed god of rain (Chac), celestial and terrestrial enclosing frames, cosmic trees, and avian composite creatures (serpent birds). Some deities that were clearly prototypical to those represented in the iconography of Postclassic Yucatán can be discerned in Maya religious art of the Classic period. Classic Maya stelae—accurately dated, erected at fixed intervals, and containing long hieroglyphic texts—display profile and frontal portraits of the great Maya dynasts. Their elaborate costumes are replete with religious symbols that invested them with the aura of divinity.

A particularly complex Lowland Maya iconography is portrayed on Late Classic painted ceramic vessels usually encountered in burials. An extensive pantheon of underworld supernaturals is featured in these scenes. It has been suggested that they frequently display connections with the Hero Twins of the *Popol Vuh*, the cosmogonical epic of the Quiché Maya of Highland Guatemala. The representations on these vessels were probably derived at least in part from painted screenfold paper books. Although no Classic period examples have been found, the surviving Postclassic specimens (known as Codex Dresden, Codex Paris, and Codex Madrid) provide some notion of the magnitude and importance of this lost Classic Maya "iconographic archive." The recent progress that has been made in the decipherment of Lowland Maya hieroglyphic writing has resulted in a considerably improved understanding of the meaning of the religious imagery so richly developed in this most spectacular of ancient New World cultures.

Monte Albán. Another major Mesoamerican cultural tradition, connected in its origins with Olmec and having some Izapan ties, was that of Monte Albán, so named from the huge site near the modern city of Oaxaca. Already well developed in Late Preclassic times (Monte Albán I-II, c. 600 BCE–100 CE), its full flowering occurred during the Classic period (Monte Albán IIIa–b, c. 100–700 CE). Monte Albán iconography is one of the richest and most structured in pre-Hispanic Mesoamerica. There is general agreement that a numerous pantheon of individualized deities was portrayed, especially in the famous funerary urns, theomorphic ceramic vessels placed in tombs. Many deities are identified by their "calendric names," the day in the 260-day divinatory cycle on which they were believed to have been born. Some can be tentatively connected with deities known to have been propitiated by the Zapotec-speakers who occupied most of the area around Monte Albán at the time of the Conquest, including the basic rain-and-fertility god, Cocijo. The walls of a few tombs at Monte Albán display painted images of deities or deity impersonators, some of them identical to those depicted on the ceramic urns. The hieroglyphic writing of Monte Albán is still poorly understood, but it has been of some aid in interpreting the iconography of one of the greatest of the Mesoamerican Classic civilizations.

Teotihuacan. Dominating the Classic period (c. 100–750 CE) in central Mexico—and spreading its influence throughout Mesoamerica—was the dynamic civilization of Teotihuacan, centered in the urban metropolis known by that name at the time of the Conquest and located about twenty-five miles northeast of Mexico City. Teotihuacan iconography, evidenced by a plethora of ceramic and stone pieces and numerous mural paintings, was one of the most intricate and variegated of ancient Mesoamerica. Symmetry and repetitiveness were hallmarks of Teotihuacan formats, which, particularly in the murals, include processions of ritual celebrants, frontal anthropomorphic and zoomorphic images flanked by profile figures, and complex scenes involving numerous personages engaged in a variety of activities. The dominant theme was clearly the promotion of fertility, featuring what appear to have been at least two major aspects of the preeminent rain-and-fertility deity that was prototypical to the Aztec Tlaloc. Aquatic and vegetational motifs are ubiquitous.

To what extent clear-cut deity representations are present in Teotihuacan iconography, as in the case of the earlier Mesoamerican traditions already discussed, has generated considerable differences of opinion. Various motif clusters have been defined, which some have suggested might have connoted distinct cults. Certain images have also been identified as discrete deities of the Aztec type, and they have often been labeled with Nahuatl names. They include Tlaloc, the rain-and-earth god; a female fertility deity who may be the prototype of various Aztec goddesses (Chalchiuhtlicue, Xochiquetzal, Teteoinnan, and others); an old fire god (Aztec Huehueteotl or Xiuhtecuhtli); the flayed god (Xipe Totec); a butterfly deity, the Fat God (possibly prototypical to Xochipilli/Macuilxochitl, the Aztec god of sensuality); and, perhaps, prototypes of Quetzalcoatl, the feathered serpent creator-and-fertility god; Xolotl, god of monsters and twins; and Tecciztecatl, the male lunar deity. As in earlier and contemporary Mesoamerican traditions, composite zoomorphic images are another hallmark of Teotihuacán iconography. Some, such as the feathered serpent, may have served as the "disguises" or avatars of various deities, as in the Aztec system.

Classic Veracruz. During the Early Classic period (c. 100–600 CE), after the fade-out of the Olmec tradition in the Gulf Coast region, a distinct regional stylistic and iconographic tradition emerged, climaxing during the Late Classic and Epiclassic periods (c. 600–900 CE). It was best expressed at the major site of El Tajín, in northwest Veracruz, where a sophisticated style of relief carving, featuring double-outlined, interlocking scroll motifs, decorates a number of structures; these include the famous Pyramid of the Niches, two ball courts with friezes portraying complex sacrificial rituals connected with the ball game, and even more complicated ceremonial scenes on a series of column drums in the Building of the Columns.

The most famous exemplars of Classic Veracruz iconography are the handsomely carved stone objects worn by the ball players or replicas thereof: yokes (ballgame belts); *hachas*, thin stone heads; and *palmas*, paddle-shaped stones, the latter two objects attached to the yokes worn by the players. Sculptured on these pieces are various anthropomorphic and zoomorphic beings, especially a monstrous creature probably symbolizing the earth. A major tradition of ceramic sculpture also flouished in this region during the Classic period. Some examples appear to represent deities that were prototypical to those of Postclassic times. They include the Old Fire God; versions of Tlaloc and long-lipped beings probably related to the iconographically similar Izapan and Maya rain-and-fertility deities; male and female figures wearing human skins, evidencing rituals similar to those of the Aztec fertility deities Xipe Totec and Tlazolteotl/Teteoinnan; the Fat God; perhaps a proto-Ehécatl (wind god); and a whole complex of smiling figures seemingly expressing aspects of a cult of sensuality—possibly involving the ritual ingestion of hallucinogens—similar to that of Xochipilli/Macuilxochitl of later times. Complex ceremonial scenes are also represented on mold-pressed, relief-decorated ceramic bowls.

Xochicalco. With its apparent *floruit* during the Epiclassic period (c. 750–900 CE), the extensive hilltop site of Xochicalco flourished in what is now the state of Morelos, Mexico, and gave rise to another distinctive stylistic and iconographic tradition, mainly expressed in relief sculpture. The greatest amount of sculpture decorated one remarkable structure, the Pyramid of the Feathered Serpent. Aside from huge, undulating representations of the feathered serpent, various cross-legged seated personages, reflecting Lowland Maya stylistic influence, are depicted, many identified with their name signs and in some cases, seemingly, place signs as well. Calendric inscriptions are also present, and some scholars have suggested that the carvings may commemorate a major gathering of priests to discuss calendric reform and other ritual-religious matters. Another possibility is that this conclave involved some important dynastic event, perhaps a royal coronation. Other Xochicalco monuments, such as three elaborate stelae now in the Museo Nacional de Antropología, feature hieroglyphic inscriptions and different deities, including a version of the rain god, Tlaloc, and a fertility goddess.

Toltec. At the outset of the Postclassic period a new political and cultural power arose north of the Basin of Mexico, at Tollan, modern Tula, in the state of Hidalgo. Flourishing between about 900 and 1200, Tollan was a major metropolis, capital of an extensive empire. Its stylistic and iconographic tradition was quite eclectic and represented an amalgam of various earlier traditions (Teotihuacan, Xochicalco, El Tajín, and others).

Toltec iconography is known primarily from relief sculpture, decorated ceramics, figurines, and some remarkable cliff paintings at Ixtapantongo, southwest of Tula in the Toluca Basin. The relief carvings frequently depict armed, elaborately attired personages on quadrangular pillars and, in processional files, on bench friezes. Some of these figures are identified with their name (or title) signs and seem to depict actual individuals. The militaristic flavor of Toltec imagery was also expressed by alternating representations of predatory animals and birds: jaguars, pumas, coyotes, eagles, and vultures. Recognizable deity depictions are rare in the reliefs but can be more readily identified in the ceramic figures and especially in the Ixtapantongo cliff paintings. Many appear to be prototypical forms of Aztec deities: Tlaloc, Quetzalcoatl, Xipe Totec, various fertility goddesses, *pulque* deities, solar and Venus gods, and others. Toltec iconography was particularly haunted by the feathered-serpent icon symbolizing Quetzalcoatl; the related "man-bird-jaguar-serpent" motif was also important.

Mixteca-Puebla and Aztec. During the Toltec period a new stylistic and iconographic tradition was apparently emerging to the southeast, centered in southern Puebla, Veracruz, and western Oaxaca (the Mixteca), which has been labeled "Mixteca-Puebla." During the Postclassic period its pervasive influence was felt throughout Mesoamerica, as a kind of final iconographic synthesis of the earlier traditions already described. In contrast to its predecessors, it was characterized by a greater depictive literalness, plus a particular emphasis on symbolic polychromy. An extensive pantheon of anthropomorphic and zoomorphic supernaturals was represented with relatively standardized identificatory insignia.

The Aztec sytlistic and iconographic tradition, which flourished in central Mexico during the last century or so before the Conquest, can be considered, from one aspect, a regional variant of Mixteca-Puebla. It differs principally in displaying an even greater naturalism in human and animal imagery. It also was expressed much more frequently in monumental three-dimensional stone sculpture, particularly deity images. Because of the wealth of available ethnohistorical documentation, the Aztec iconographic tradition can be interpreted with considerably more success than any other Mesoamerican system. Virtually all of its principal symbols have been correctly identified as well as the great majority of the numerous deity depictions, which include almost every member of the crowded pantheon mentioned in the primary sources. Those who advocate maximum utilization of the direct historical approach in the analysis of pre-Hispanic Mesoamerican iconography stress the importance of this extensive corpus of information concerning the Aztec system as a key point of departure for interpreting the much less well-documented pre-Aztec traditions.

SEE ALSO Aztec Religion; Maya Religion; Mesoamerican Religions, article on Mythic Themes; Olmec Religion; Temple, article on Mesoamerican Temples; Toltec Religion.

BIBLIOGRAPHY

Acosta, Jorge R. "Interpretación de algunos de los datos obtenidos en Tula relativos a la epoca Tolteca." *Revista mexicana de estudios antropológicos* 14, pt. 2 (1956–1957): 75–110. A useful, well-illustrated summary of the archaeological aspect of Toltec culture by the principal excavator of Tula. Includes some discussion of the iconography.

Caso, Alfonso. "Calendario y escritura en Xochicalco." *Revista mexicana de estudios antropológicos* 18 (1962): 49–79. An important study of Xochicalco iconography, focusing on the hieroglyphic writing system and calendric inscriptions.

Caso, Alfonso. "Sculpture and Mural Painting of Oaxaca." In *Handbook of Middle American Indians*, edited by Robert Wauchope and Gordon R. Willey, vol. 3, pp. 849–870. Austin, Tex., 1965. Well-illustrated discussion of Monte Albán iconography through sculpture and wall paintings.

Caso, Alfonso. "Dioses y signos teotihuacanos." In *Teotihuacan: Onceava Mesa Redonda, Sociedad Mexicana de Antropología*, pp. 249–279. Mexico City, 1966. A broad survey of Teotihuacan iconography, extensively illustrated.

Caso, Alfonso, and Ignacio Bernal. *Urnas de Oaxaca*. Memorias del Instituto Nacional de Antropología e Historia, no. 2. Mexico City, 1952. The classic study of the effigy funerary urns of the Monte Albán tradition, illustrated with hundreds of photographs and drawings.

Coe, Michael D. *The Maya Scribe and His World*. New York, 1973. A beautifully illustrated catalog featuring principally Late Classic Lowland Maya painted ceramic vessels, with perceptive analyses of their complex iconographic formats and accompanying hieroglyphic texts.

Joralemon, Peter David. *A Study of Olmec Iconography*. Dumbarton Oaks Studies in Pre-Columbian Art and Archaeology, no. 7. Washington, D.C., 1971. The most comprehensive study of Olmec iconography, profusely illustrated by line drawings. Includes "A Dictionary of Olmec Motifs and Symbols."

Kampen, Michael Edwin. *The Sculptures of El Tajín, Veracruz, Mexico*. Gainesville, Fla., 1972. An important monograph describing and analyzing the sculptural art of the greatest of the Classic Veracruz sites. Includes a catalog of all known Tajín carvings, illustrated with excellent line drawings.

Kubler, George. *The Iconography of the Art of Teotihaucan*. Dumbarton Oaks Studies in Pre-Columbian Art and Archaeology, no. 4. Washington, D.C., 1967. Significant pioneer discussion and analysis of Teotihuacan iconography, utilizing a linguistic model requiring that "each form be examined for its grammatical function, whether noun, adjective, or verb." Includes a table of approximately one hundred Teotihuacan motifs and themes.

Kubler, George. *Studies in Classic Maya Iconography*. Memoirs of the Connecticut Academy of Arts and Sciences, vol. 18. New Haven, 1969. Preliminary but broad-ranging consideration of Classic Lowland Maya iconography, with special attention to dynastic ceremonies, ritual images, and the "triadic sign."

Nicholson, H. B. "The Mixteca-Puebla Concept in Mesoamerican Archaeology: A Re-Examination." In *Men and Cultures*, edited by Anthony F. C. Wallace, pp. 612–617. Philadelphia, 1960. Discusses and defines the Postclassic Mesoamerican Mixteca-Puebla stylistic and iconographic tradition conceptualized as a "horizon style," with some consideration of its origins and the mechanism of its diffusion.

Nicholson, H. B. "The Iconography of Classic Central Veracruz Ceramic Sculptures." In *Ancient Art of Veracruz: An Exhibit Sponsored by the Ethnic Arts Council of Los Angeles*, pp. 13–17. Los Angeles, 1971. A concise discussion of the iconography of Classic Veracruz ceramic figures, with suggestions that some of them probably represent specific deities.

Nicholson, H. B. "The Late Pre-Hispanic Central Mexican (Aztec) Iconographic System." In *The Iconography of Middle American Sculpture*, pp. 72–97. New York, 1973. Summary discussion of the iconographic system of Late Postclassic central Mexico, with specification of its leading diagnostics.

Parsons, Lee A. "Post-Olmec Stone Sculpture: The Olmec-Izapan Transition of the Southern Pacific Coast and Highlands." In *The Olmec and Their Neighbors*, edited by Elizabeth P. Benson, pp. 257–288. Washington, D.C., 1981. Perceptive, well-illustrated discussion of the Izapan and related stylistic and iconographic traditions as manifested in the Pacific Slope region of Chiapas-Guatemala and adjacent highlands.

Quirarte, Jacinto. *Izapan-Style Art: A Study of Its Form and Meaning*. Dumbarton Oaks Studies in Pre-Columbian Art and Archaeology, no. 10. Washington, D.C., 1973. A significant pioneering attempt to define the leading formal and iconographic features of the Izapan stylistic and iconographic tradition; well illustrated with numerous line drawings.

Robicsek, Francis, and Donald M. Hales. *The Maya Book of the Dead: The Ceramic Codex; The Corpus of Codex Style Ceramics of the Late Classic Period*. Charlottesville, Va., 1981. Extensive album of photographs (including full-surface rollouts and color) of Late Classic Lowland Maya ceramic vessels with scenes and hieroglyphic texts related to the surviving ritual-divinatory paper screenfolds. Includes iconographic analysis and preliminary decipherment of the texts.

H. B. NICHOLSON (1987)

ICONOGRAPHY: MESOPOTAMIAN ICONOGRAPHY

Any discussion of the religious iconography of ancient Mesopotamia is hampered by the fact that we have, on the one hand, religious texts for which we possess no visual counterparts and, on the other, representations—sometimes extremely elaborate ones—for which we lack all written documentation. Mesopotamia lacked raw materials such as stone, metal, and wood, and these had to be imported. As a result stone was often recut and metal was melted down; nor has wood survived. In time of war, temple treasures were carried off as booty, and divine statues were mutilated or taken into captivity, so that virtually none remains. Indeed we should know very little of Mesopotamian sculpture of the third and second millennia BCE were it not for the objects looted by the Elamites in the late second millennium BCE and found by the French in their excavations at Susa in southwestern Iran from 1897 onward. In time of peace the temples themselves frequently melted down metal votive objects in order to produce others. Occasionally a hoard of consecrated objects was buried near the temple, however, presumably to make room for others. The Tell Asmar and Al-ʿUbaid hoards dating to the second quarter of the third millennium BCE are two examples of this practice. In only a few cases has fragmentary evidence survived to indicate how temples were decorated (the leopard paintings at Tell ʿUqair, for instance), but their elevations are often depicted on monuments and seals, and facades decorated with date-palm pilasters or water deities have been found. The decoration of secular buildings, among them the painted murals from the palace at Mari and the limestone reliefs that ornamented the palaces of the Assyrian kings, provide some evidence for religious iconography.

Our best sources for religious iconography are therefore the small objects that are more likely to have survived. Plaques and figurines made of local clay often illustrate a more popular type of religion. At certain periods painted pottery is the vehicle for representations that have religious significance. Decorated votive metal vessels, stone maces, and small bronze figures also occasionally survive. Without seals, however, our knowledge would be extremely scant. Prehistoric stamp seals were replaced during the second half of the fourth millennium by small stone cylinders that were used as marks of administrative or personal identification until the end of the first millennium BCE. These cylinder seals were carved with designs in intaglio and could be rolled across clay jar-sealings, door-sealings, bullae, tablets, or their clay envelopes so as to leave a design in relief. Such miniature reliefs are the vehicle for the most complex and tantalizing iconographic representations.

EARLY IMAGERY. Nude female figurines are among the earliest artifacts to which a religious significance can be attached. Among the prehistoric figurines of Mesopotamia are the tall, thin, clay "lizard" figures with elongated heads, coffee-bean eyes, slit mouths, and clay pellets decorating the shoulders. "Lizard" figurines have been found at southern sites in both male and female versions though the latter is dominant. Farther north, at Tell al-Sawwan, female figurines and male sexual organs were carved from alabaster. These figurines also have elongated heads and prominent eyes but are more rounded in shape. In the north, clay figurines often have abbreviated heads, and the emphasis is on a well-rounded, full-breasted body. An opposite trend is attested, however, at Tell Brak, where "spectacle" or "eye idols" were found in a late fourth-millennium temple. Here the eyes are emphasized to the exclusion of everything else, and there has even been debate as to whether they might not, in fact, represent huts. Although there is always a risk in attributing a religious significance to a figurine when there is no written evidence to corroborate this, it does seem likely that these figures had fertility connotations.

Animal combats. One motif that seems to have had a special significance throughout Mesopotamian prehistory and history shows a heroic male figure in conflict with wild animals. A pot of the Halaf period (c. 4500 BCE) shows an archer aiming at a bull and a feline. A figure traditionally known as the priest-king appears on a relief and a seal of the Uruk period (late fourth millennium) shooting or spearing lions and bulls, and the same theme reappears in the Assyrian reliefs of the ninth and seventh centuries BCE and forms the subject of the Assyrian royal seal. After the hunt the king is shown pouring a libation over the corpses, thus fulfilling his age-old function as representative of the god and protector of the country against wild cattle and lions. This function must have been particularly important when animal husbandry and agriculture were in their infancy but would have lost some of that immediacy in Assyrian times, when animals had become scarce and were specially trapped and released from cages for the hunt.

At certain periods the theme of animal combat became dominant in the iconographic repertoire. For several centuries during the third millennium, and at various times later on, heroes are shown protecting sheep, goats, and cattle from the attack of lions and other predators. Generally the heroes are either naked except for a belt, with their shoulder-length hair falling in six curls, or they are kilted and wear a decorated headdress. They are often assisted by a mythic creature who has the legs and horns of a bull and a human head and torso. Attempts have been made to equate the figures with the legendary king Gilgamesh and his wild companion Enkidu, but the evidence is lacking. We probably have here an extension of the theme already discussed, with the emphasis on the protection of domesticated animals from their aggressors. Prehistoric stamp seals showing figures who often wear animal masks and who are involved with snakes, ibex, and other animals probably reflect a more primitive animistic religious tradition.

Early urban imagery. The advent of an organized urban society in the second half of the fourth millennium led to the development of more varied vehicles for the transmission of iconographic concepts. Some examples of monumental sculpture have survived, among them an almost lifesize female head which was probably part of a cult statue. The wig and the inlay that once filled the eye sockets and eyebrows have vanished and make this sculpture particularly attractive to modern Western aesthetic taste. Uruk, where the head was found, was the center of worship of the fertility goddess Inanna, and a tall vase is decorated with a scene where the robed goddess in anthropomorphic form, accompanied by her symbol, the reed bundle, receives offerings from a naked priest and a (damaged) figure who wears a crosshatched skirt; this latter is probably the priest-king mentioned above. In his role as *en* ("lord") he is depicted feeding flocks and cattle, engaging in ritual hunts, or taking part in religious ceremonies; in his role as *lugal* ("owner") he triumphs over prisoners. He too has survived in sculpture in the round, on reliefs, and on cylinder seals.

Other significant motifs are known only from their impression on clay sealings. It seems that certain types of seals were used by particular branches of temple administration: boating scenes used by those connected with fishing and waterways, animal file seals for those dealing with herds. Certain designs, for instance those showing variations on a pattern of entwined snakes and birds, are more difficult to fit into this scheme of things. Other seals are squat, often concave-sided, and cut with excessive use of the drill to form patterns. These might have been used by an administration dealing in manufactured goods since potters and weavers are depicted. Some show a spider pattern, and it is tempting to associate these with the temple weavers, whose patron deity was the spider-goddess Uttu. Some more abstract patterns are difficult to interpret.

If we have dealt at some length with this early period it is because many of the iconographic concepts found later have their roots in the late fourth-millennium repertoire, including depictions of both the physiomorphic and the anthropomorphic form of deities, cult scenes with naked priests, the attitude of worship with hands clasped and large, inlaid eyes to attract the deity's attention, as well as the royal hunt, the sacred marriage, and banquet scenes. Even such quasi-abstract concepts as the rain cloud received its iconographic shape during this period, as testified by seal impressions showing the lion-headed eagle. Later he is shown on seals, vessels, reliefs, and particularly on a huge copper relief that adorned the temple at Al-ʿUbaid.

LATER DEVELOPMENTS. Banquet scenes were especially popular in Early Dynastic times (mid-third millennium) and are often associated with scenes of war: seals, plaques, and mosaic panels depict these ritual banquets, which are probably to be interpreted as victory feasts in some contexts and as marriage feasts in others. They are to be distinguished from later neo-Hittite funerary meals, but the preparation of food for the gods is a favorite iconographic motif in the second half of the second and early first millennia BCE.

Deities and their attributes. The representation of deities developed slowly, though by the middle of the third millennium they were wearing horned headdresses as a means of identification. In Akkadian times (2340–2180 BCE) distinct iconographies were established for the more prominent deities, and their position facing left became fixed, though the detailed representations of myths on seals of this period are generally incomprehensible to us. The role of some deities can be identified by the attributes they hold, others by the sprigs of vegetation, streams of water, rays, or weapons which issue from their shoulders. Often these serve only to establish that the deity is, for instance, a vegetation or a warrior god without being more specific.

In fact, it is only a very few representations which can actually be identified with any degree of certainty. Plows are frequently depicted, especially on Akkadian seals, but this is not always a shorthand for Ninurta (who is, however, depicted in a chariot on the famous Stela of the Vultures). Warrior gods on Old Babylonian seals are probably also to be equated with him in many cases, and he appears on Assyrian reliefs. The temple of Ninhursaga at Al-ʿUbaid was decorated with friezes showing dairy scenes. There are clear representations of the water god Enki/Ea in his watery house or with water flowing from his shoulders on Akkadian seals. His Janus-faced attendant, Usmu, is also shown, as is the Zu bird who stole the tablets of destiny. Later the water god fades from the iconography and comes to be represented by a turtle. A neo-Assyrian seal showing a divine figure running along the back of a dragon is often taken to represent the Babylonian god Marduk with the primeval monster Tiamat, but there is no proof that this is so.

The moon god Nanna/Sin was a major deity, but there are surprisingly few representations of him. A stele from Ur and one of the wall paintings from the palace of Mari are perhaps the most convincing representations of this god, but where gods in boats can be identified with any certainty, they seem to be the sun god. The moon's crescent below the sun disk is also extremely common. The iconography of the sun god Utu/Shamash is, however, well attested. He is frequently shown with rays rising from his shoulders, placing his foot on a mountain and holding the saw-toothed knife with which he has just cut his way through the mountains of the east. Often he is accompanied by his animal attribute, the human-headed bull (probably a bison), or by attendants who hold open the gates of dawn. Scorpions likewise can be associated with the sun god, but they are also symbols of fertility and attributes of the goddess of oaths, Ishara. A famous plaque shows the sun god seated in his temple in Sippar; he also appears as the god of justice, holding a symbolic rod and ring, on the law code of Hammurabi of Babylon.

From Old Babylonian times onward the storm god Adad occurs frequently, often standing on a bull and holding a lightning fork. His consort Shala may appear briefly, on seals and in the form of mass-produced clay figurines of the Old Babylonian period, as a nude goddess, shown frontally. Ishtar (Inanna), the Uruk fertility goddess, appears on Akkadian seals holding a date cluster, calling down rain, and often winged with weapons rising from her shoulders as goddess of war. It is this last aspect that becomes predominant, and the Old Babylonian representations are so standardized that it is tempting to see in them the depiction of a well-known cult statue. It may be her aspect as "mistress owl" which is shown on the famous Burney relief (on loan to the British Museum). Her earlier symbol, the reed bundle, is later replaced by a star. One early seal may show her consort Dumuzi (Tammuz) as a prisoner in the dock, but otherwise he is difficult to identify. Ningirsu is often identified as a lion-headed eagle or thunderbird. There are several representations of what is probably Nergal as a warrior god. The god in the winged disk on Assyrian reliefs has generally been identified as Ashur but is more likely the sun god Shamash. Amurru, the god of the Amorites, appears on Old Babylonian seals accompanied by a gazelle and holding a crook.

Unidentifiable figures. From the wealth of symbols which represent deities, many can only be tentatively identified. The Babylonian boundary stones show these symbols on podia and list names of deities, but there is often no correlation between image and text. This is also the case on Old Babylonian seals of the earlier part of the second millennium BCE where we have frequent representations of unidentifiable figures and a large number of inscribed seals mentioning divine protectors: the names do not generally have any bearing on the representation. It seems that the owners of the seals were "hedging their bets" and invoking some deities in pictorial form, others in written form, and still others by their symbols.

It has also been suggested that the deities invoked most frequently were those most likely to be depicted; again this cannot be so since Ishtar, for instance, is frequently depicted and is almost never mentioned in the inscriptions. It is likely that certain deities had a well-established iconography (like the popular saints of medieval Christianity), probably based on a commonly known cult statue or wall painting, while others were invoked by name because their iconography was not as immediately recognizable. The picture becomes even more complex in neo-Assyrian times when demons played an ever-increasing part in religion: we have descriptions of the demons, but these are difficult to reconcile with the representations.

The rich and tantalizing iconography of Mesopotamia is also responsible for key images in the Judeo-Christian tradition. To cite only one example, the huge, winged, human-headed lions and bulls which decorated and protected the Assyrian palace entrances are the basis for Ezekiel's vision (*Ez.* 1:4–13) and by extension for the symbols of the four evangelists as we know them, combining human intelligence with the wings of the eagle and the strength of the bull or lion, the most powerful creatures in heaven and on earth.

SEE ALSO Mesopotamian Religions, overview articles.

BIBLIOGRAPHY

There is no recent study of Mesopotamian religious iconography. An early attempt at bringing order out of chaos is Elizabeth Douglas Van Buren's *Symbols of the Gods in Mesopotamian Art* (Rome, 1945). This is still a useful book but has been superseded to a large extent by Ursula Seidl's detailed study of the Babylonian boundary stones, *Die babylonischen Kudurru-Reliefs* (Berlin, 1968). The symbols which appear on these stones are analyzed, the various possible interpretations and identifications are discussed, and examples from all periods are listed.

Most studies on religious iconography have appeared in catalogs of cylinder seals, beginning with Henri Frankfort's pioneering attempt to relate the seal designs to the texts in his *Cylinder Seals* (London, 1939). Edith Porada's *Corpus of Ancient Near Eastern Seals in North American Collections,* vol. 1, *The Pierpont Morgan Library Collection* (Washington, D.C., 1948), is also a mine of information. The same author has more recently edited *Ancient Art in Seals* (Princeton, 1980), which includes an essay by Pierre Amiet relating the iconography of Akkadian seals to a seasonal cycle. In her introduction Porada summarizes the advances in glyptic studies which have taken place since Frankfort wrote. Many of the objects referred to here are illustrated in André Parrot's *Sumer* (London, 1960) and *Nineveh and Babylon* (New York, 1961) or in J. B. Pritchard's *The Ancient Near East in Pictures relating to the Old Testament* (Princeton, 1969).

DOMINIQUE COLLON (1987)

ICONOGRAPHY: EGYPTIAN ICONOGRAPHY

The principal iconographic sources for ancient Egyptian religion are the representations of scenes, both ritual and mythological, carved in relief or painted on the walls of Egyptian temples and tombs, as well as the numerous images and statues of gods and pharaohs. Additionally, there are many objects of ritual or practical function decorated with carved or painted religious motifs, and finally, numerous hieroglyphic signs belonging to the Egyptian writing system are representations of gods, religious symbols, and ritual objects. These types of sources remain constant throughout the more than three thousand years of ancient Egyptian history from the Old Kingdom to the Roman period (c. 3000 BCE–395 CE).

Egyptian gods were depicted both as human beings and as animals; a composite form combining a zoomorphic head with a human body enjoyed special popularity in relief and statuary alike. Anthropomorphic representations of Egyptian gods relate to their mythological functions and reveal narrative aspects of their relationships, whereas other forms may be defined as their "metamorphoses" or symbols, emphasizing one particular feature or event. In this symbolic realm one divinity could be represented by various animals or objects—for example, the cow, the lioness, the snake, and the sistrum (a musical instrument) are all manifestations of the goddess Hathor. Conversely, one animal could embody various gods; thus, the protective cobra that appears on the forehead of each pharaoh could be identified with almost all goddesses. The divine identity of an animal may differ in various local pantheons. Particularly numerous were iconographic variations of the sun god, which illustrate various phases of the sun's *perpetuum mobile.* Some male gods associated with generative powers (Min, Amun-Re, Kamutef) are depicted ithyphallically. A particular shape, that of a mummified human body, was attributed to Osiris, the god of the dead. This form also occurs in some representations of other gods, especially when they appear in the realm of the dead. Diads and triads of gods, frequent in Egyptian statuary, as well as larger groups of divine beings represented in reliefs and paintings, are visual expressions of various relationships among numerous divinities. Syncretistic tendencies in Egyptian religion, popular after the Amarna period, take concrete form in the composite features that combine the iconographic features of different gods.

Scenes carved on the walls of tombs and temples as well as on furniture and ritual objects most frequently show the gods in the company of a king making offerings or performing other ritual acts (such as censing, purifying with water, or embracing the god). All representations of the king facing a divinity illustrate the ongoing relationship of reciprocity between them. In return for the precious object that he presents to the god, the pharaoh receives symbols of life, strength, stability, many years of kingship, and the like.

STATUARY. Numerous Egyptian statues made of all possible materials, such as stone, wood, gold, bronze, and faience, represent one, two, or three gods often accompanied by a king. Both gods and king wear crowns and hold characteristic insignia, among which the most frequent are the sign of life (*ankh*) and various types of scepters. Many elements of the king's dress are identical with those of the gods, thus visualizing the divine aspects of the monarch's nature. The shape of their artificial beards is distinctive, however: the beard of the god is bent forward at the end, while that of the king is cut straight in its lower part.

The size of the statues varies according to their function. Small bronze statuettes of votive character were common, especially in the first millennium BCE. Many represent animals sacred to Egyptian gods; sometimes these figures are set on boxes containing mummies of the animals represented. The mummified bodies of larger animals, such as bulls, ibis, crocodiles, and cats, have been found buried within special necropolises near places connected with the cults of various gods.

Large stone statues served as cult objects in Egyptian temples. Pairs of colossal effigies of the seated king usually stood in front of the temple pylons. The sphinx, with its body of a lion and head of the king, was often placed in the front of the temple to symbolize the monarch's identity as solar god. Rows of sphinxes lined both sides of processional ways leading to the principal temple entrances.

FUNERARY ART. Another important part of our knowledge about ancient Egyptian iconography comes from the decoration of Egyptian tombs and coffins that comprises the great Egyptian religious "books"—literary compositions that combine spells of magical, mythological, and ritual character with pictures illustrating Egyptian visions of the netherworld. The most ancient of these "books" are the Pyramid Texts carved on the walls of some of the rooms inside the royal pyramids (Old Kingdom, c. 3000–2200 BCE). The illustrations accompanying this sort of text appear for the first time in the Book of Two Ways, which is part of the Coffin Texts (Middle Kingdom, 2134–1600 BCE) painted on the sides of wooden coffins.

Subsequent literary compositions of religious character are generally accompanied by elaborate tableaux, often in the form of vignettes drawn above a column of text written on papyrus. From the New Kingdom (1569–1085 BCE) on, the most popular of these "books" was the *Book of Going Forth by Day* (the so-called *Book of the Dead),* a copy of which was a necessary element of the funerary offerings of every noble. The visual aspects of royal eschatology are best known from a composition called *Amduat* (That Which Is in the Netherworld), which was painted or carved on the walls of royal tombs. Illustrations show the nightly wandering of the sun god through the netherworld. Beginning with the New Kingdom and continuing into the Roman period, fragments of these "books" also decorate many tombs, coffins, and ritual objects belonging to the nobles.

TEMPLES. As the abode of the gods, Egyptian temples were accessible only to the kings and priests. The king, considered the mediator between the gods and the people, is usually shown in front of the gods in the ritual scenes that decorate the temple walls, although in reality it must have been the priests who performed the rituals in the king's name.

The sanctuary, usually situated at the far end of the temple along its axis, contained the sacred image of the god to whom the temple was dedicated. The statue of Amun-Re, the chief divinity of Thebes and the state divinity since the time of the New Kingdom, stood inside a shrine on a portable bark placed upon a sled. In Theban temples this effigy is often represented in connection with the Opet Feast or the Beautiful Feast of the Valley, during which it was transported along or across the Nile on a huge ceremonial boat adorned with reliefs and statues.

Narrative cycles. Many temple scenes form standardized sequences of pictures showing summarily, sometimes almost symbolically, successive episodes of mythicized rituals that often refer to important historical events, such as the miraculous birth of the king, his coronation, his victories over enemies, his jubilee, and the founding of the temple. These representations appear in the inner parts of the temple, together with tableaux depicting the daily ritual performed before the statue of the temple's principal deity and scenes showing various offerings being made. Often the iconographic repertory of the decoration of the pillared hall—the central part of many temples—constitutes something of a "showcase," reviewing in abbreviated form all the important elements of the temple's relief decoration.

The interior of the walls enclosing the courts are often decorated with episodes of the most important feasts, while the grandiose tableaux found on the exterior of the walls and on the gates (frequently in the form of pylons) commonly illustrate the king's military achievements. Standard scenes on the pylon faces show the king smiting foreign captives, presenting them to a god, and images of the king offering a figure of the goddess Maat—the personification of truth, justice, and order—to the main divinity of the temple. Another iconographic pattern frequently occurring on the pylons and on the socle of royal thrones is the symbolic representation of subjugated peoples, the so-called ring-names, showing legless human figures, with hands bound, behind an oval ring containing the name of the foreign province. The facial features of these figures were meant to characterize the physiognomy of each particular people.

Symbolic motifs. In addition to these scenes referring to particular events, the temple walls are also decorated with numerous motifs of a more symbolic nature, which give visual form to religious, political, or geographical ideas. The so-called geographical processions, for instance, symbolize the provinces of Egypt in the form of hefty divinities personifying the Nile, each bearing offerings in their hands.

Various iconographic patterns invented by the Egyptians give shape to the idea of the unification of Lower and Upper Egypt. The central motif of a great number of them is the heraldic symbol called *sma-tawy*, which is composed of two plants, papyrus (for Lower Egypt) and a kind of bulrush (for Upper Egypt), bound together around the spinal cord and the lungs of an animal. Two divine personifications of the Nile—the motive power of this unification—are often shown holding and binding together the two plants

Geographical and religious at the same time, the concepts of the country's division into two parts—either north and south or east and west—belong to the most important principles prevailing in Egyptian iconography. They find expression in symmetrical or antithetical compositions of scenes placed in the axial rooms of temples and tombs, as in the disposition of the various gods representing north and south or east and west, especially on the decoration of lintels, doorposts, and rear walls.

The netherworld. The Egyptian realm of the dead lay in the west. The best illustration of ancient Egyptian visual concepts of the netherworld appears in the decoration of New Kingdom royal and noble tombs situated in west Thebes; these iconographic patterns remained a favorite and repeated subject right up to the Roman period. Of the two principal groups of scenes depicted there, the first, usually found in the first room of the tomb, refers to various episodes in the earthly life of the deceased, including such religious ceremonies or feasts as the Beautiful Feast of the Valley, the royal jubilee, the New Year festival, or the harvest feast. Included in all these scenes are processions, offerings (including burnt offerings), incense burning, and performances with playing, singing, and dancing. Of special importance among Egyptian musicians was the harpist, who came to be represented by the squatting figure of a blind man shown in profile.

The other group of scenes, found in the inner room, illustrates various episodes of the funeral rites, such as the embalming ritual, the symbolic "pilgrimage to Abydos" by boat, and various processions with the mummy being dragged on sledges. The ritual of "opening the mouth" was one of the most important ceremonies of the long funeral cycle. Performed on the statue of the deceased or on his mummy, it was composed of episodes including censing, pouring libations, purifying, and "opening the mouth" with special instruments, all of which were intended to revive the spirit of the deceased.

Cult of the dead. Of particular importance in every tomb were the places intended for the cult of the deceased. These featured niches with statues of the dead person (and sometimes of members of his family), stelae often depicting the deceased adoring and making offerings to various gods or royal personages, and lastly, false-door stelae constituting a symbolic passage between the realm of the dead and the world of the living.

Enabling the deceased to enjoy the sight of the shining sun is another idea that predominates in the eschatological visions depicted and described on the walls of royal tombs. Such great religious compositions as the *Amduat*, the *Book of Gates*, and the *Book of Caverns* depict, among other things, the nightly journey of the sun god, who is often identified with the king. The monarch is thus endowed with the ability to reappear in the morning as a form of the solar divinity.

Most important in each tomb, however, was the burial chamber, commonly situated underneath the accessible rooms at the bottom of a deep vertical shaft. Here were contained the sarcophagus with the mummy of the deceased and all the funerary offerings, including the four Canopic jars for the viscera of the deceased, the mummiform figures known as *shawabtis* (*ushabtis*), a copy of the *Book of Going Forth by Day* written on papyrus, and various ritual objects. The sarcophagi and coffins, made of wood or stone, took the form of cubical or body-shaped cases decorated with painted or carved religious motifs. The four Canopic jars were associated with the four sons of the royal deity Horus, with the four cardinal directions, and with the four protective goddesses; they each had distinctive stoppers, often representing the heads of the four sons of Horus or simply anthropomorphic heads. Numerous *shawabtis* holding various objects, such as hoes, baskets, or religious symbols, and most frequently made of faience or stone, accompanied the deceased in his tomb in order to help him in the netherworld. In some tombs the number of these figures were considerable: more than one thousand were recovered in the tomb of King Taharqa (r. 689–664 BCE). Particularly rich were the grave goods of the royal tombs; the most complete version of such a funeral outfit has been found in the tomb of Tutankhamen (r. 1361–1352 BCE) located in the Valley of the Kings, the New Kingdom necropolis in west Thebes.

The evolution of iconographic patterns in the three-thousand-year course of ancient Egyptian history parallels general changes in religious concepts, which are themselves a function of political and social changes. A "democratization" of religious beliefs during the Middle Kingdom and the Second Intermediate period resulted, on the one hand, in the depiction of direct relations between gods and human beings and, on the other hand, in identifying the dead with the god Osiris. Religious conflicts during the eighteenth dynasty, probably reflecting political struggles and culminating in the "heresy" of Amenhotep IV-Akhenaton, led first to a disproportionate emphasis on solar cults and then to a development of religious concepts concerning the realm of the dead, with a dual focus on Osiris and the solar god. The union of these two once-competing deities occurs frequently after the Amarna period and contributes to a development of theological concepts as well as their iconographic renderings. This syncretism increases during the Third Intermediate period and generates an unparalleled variety of forms during the Ptolemaic period.

SEE ALSO Pyramids, article on Egyptian Pyramids; Temple, article on Ancient Near Eastern and Mediterranean Temples.

BIBLIOGRAPHY

The most complete and up-to-date compendium of information concerning the iconography of ancient Egyptian religion is *Egypt*, volume 16 in the series "Iconography of Religions," edited by the Institute of Religious Iconography, Groningen. Each of the thirteen fascicles of this volume, arranged in chronological sequence, contains rich photographic materials and a detailed bibliography. Encyclopedic information on particular subjects can be found in Hans Bonnet's *Reallexikon der ägyptischen Religionsgeschichte*, 2d ed. (Munich, 1971), and in *Lexikon der Ägyptologie*, 6 vols., edited by Hans Wolfgang Helck, Eberhard Otto, and Wolfhart Westendorf (Wiesbaden, 1972–). Bonnet's *Ägyptische Religion* (Leipzig, 1924) may be consulted as a valuable complement to these publications. There is an amazing scarcity of scientific literature in English, but see Manfred Lurker's *The Gods and Symbols of Ancient Egypt*, revised by Peter A. Clayton (London, 1980).

KAROL MYSLIWIEC (1987)

ICONOGRAPHY: GRECO-ROMAN ICONOGRAPHY

The religious structures of both Greeks and Romans conform to the typical patterns of divinity and belief found among the Indo-European peoples. Most notable of these is an organized pantheon of deities related by birth or marriage and presided over by a god of the sky who is both ruler and father (e.g., Zeus Pater and Jupiter). Nevertheless, although it is clear that such gods accompanied the movement of the Indo-Europeans into Greece and Italy, it is impossible to state with certainty what iconographic representation, if any, was used to worship them during this earliest period. The attempt to discern early iconographic patterns is further hampered by the fact that both peoples were invaders whose later religious outlook was influenced by older, settled cultures. When the Greeks arrived at the beginning of the second millennium BCE, they found not only an indigenous population on the mainland (whom they called the Pelasgians) but also the flourishing civilization of nearby Crete, whose art and architecture show evidence of Egyptian and Near Eastern influences. Thus, not only all the gods who constituted the classical Greek pantheon but also their iconography must be considered the products of a long process of syncretism and synthesis of Indo-European, pre-Hellenic, Cretan, and Near Eastern concepts of divinity. Similarly, the Indo-European settlers in Italy mixed with a variety of peoples already well established on the peninsula. Therefore, any attempt to understand the development of the form and content of Greco-Roman iconography must necessarily entail a consideration of the often disparate parts of the traditions.

MINOAN-MYCENAEAN ICONOGRAPHY (2000–1200 BCE). The study of Cretan (Minoan) religion may be compared to a picture book without a text. The two symbols of Minoan civilization, the double ax and the horns of consecration, clearly had religious significance, perhaps as tools of worship, but their function is not understood. From the archaeological evidence, however, which includes frescoes, seals, and figurines, one may conclude that the representation of the divine was both anthropomorphic and theriomorphic. Found are depictions of female deities encoiled by snakes or with birds perched upon their heads; these figures may explain the prominence of snakes in later Greek religion as well as the association of Greek deities with specific birds. In addition, animal-headed figures reminiscent of contemporaneous Egyptian material have been uncovered. One such type, a bull-headed male, may be the source for the Greek myth of the Minotaur. Also found are representations of demonlike creatures who appear to be performing various ritual acts; these have been cited as evidence of Mesopotamian influence. A number of seals portray the figures both of a huntress, who is called "mistress of the beasts" and whom the Greeks associated with Artemis, and of a male deity, who stands grasping an animal by the throat in each hand. Finally, the seals present strong evidence for the existence of tree cults and pillar cults, the survival of which perhaps may be seen in the Greek myths about dryads, the woodland spirits of nature who inhabit trees. To what extent the traditions of Minoan iconography immediately influenced the Greeks can be explored through a consideration of Mycenaean remains. Indeed, although the Linear B tablets from Pylos have provided valuable linguistic evidence about the names of the earliest Greek deities, most of our information, as in the case of Crete, comes from archaeological sources. From the excavations at Mycenae have come a number of clay snakes, and at Tiryns a fresco depicts a crocodile-headed creature reminiscent of those seen on Crete. Persistence of the Minoan traditions may also be found in the Lion Gate of Mycenae, over which two lions, carved in relief and leaning on a central pillar, stand guard. Providing further evidence for the continuing influence of Minoan iconography are a number of Mycenaean seals, rings, and ornaments that display representations of sacred trees, bird-decorated shrines, and demons carrying libations. To what extent, however, the continuity of form indicates a continuity of content is difficult to determine. In 1969, further excavations at Mycenae uncovered the Room of the Idols, which contained a quantity of clay statues with arms either raised or outstretched. Although possessing only an approximation of human form, each has a distinctive individuality; it has been suggested they may be the earliest representations of those Olympian gods later described by Homer. However, perhaps most characteristic of Mycenaean religious iconography are the thousands of clay statuettes called *phi* and *psi* figurines (after their distinctive shapes). Although most are rendered recognizably female by the accentuation of the breasts, they do not necessarily portend future anthropomorphic representation. They are often found in graves, but there is no general agreement as to their function. It is possible that they once served as votive offerings but that, like much of later Greek art originally sacred in nature and function, they became separated from their original purpose.

Archaic and Classical Iconography. The difficulty of establishing the continuity of the iconographical tradition from the Mycenaean into the later periods of Greek history is illustrated by a comment of the historian Herodotus (fifth century BCE), who credits Homer and Hesiod with describing the gods and "assigning to them their appropriate titles, offices, and powers," but who concedes that the two poets had lived not more than four hundred years before him. Homer and Hesiod are in fact our earliest sources for the iconography of the Greek gods after the Mycenaean age. But another four hundred years separate the destruction of Mycenae and the life of Homer, and the poet's descriptions of the Olympian gods bear little resemblance to the representations of the divine found at Mycenaean sites. Hesiod's account of the birth of the gods in his *Theogony* indicates that, while earlier generations of deities were often monstrous in appearance as well as behavior, the victorious Olympian gods, with Zeus as their ruler, were clearly anthropomorphic. Homer elaborates upon this concept, describing not only their very obviously human physical appearance but also their often all-too-human behavior. It has been suggested that the source for the relentlessly anthropomorphic quality of the Greek gods in both literature and art is a general rejection of the concept of an abstract deity. Despite criticism by philosophers such as the pre-Socratic Xenophanes, who commented rather cynically that "mortals consider that the gods are born and that they have clothes and speech and bodies like their own," or Plato, who banned poets from his ideal state because they told lies about the gods, the Greeks persisted in depicting their gods as human in form and action. Nevertheless, there is a great deal of evidence to indicate that, in the conservative ritual of Greek religion, the older forms of representation of the divine persisted. Aniconic images of the divine, such as the *omphalos* at Delphi, provide proof of its survival. This stone, which in Greek myth was described as the one that Rhea gave to Kronos to swallow when he wished to devour his infant son Zeus, and that the ruler of the Olympians then placed at the center of the world, is clearly a baetyl, a sacred stone that contains the power of the divine. Similarly, the widespread appearance of the herm, a pillar on which was carved an erect phallus and that acted as an agent of fertility and apotropaic magic, points to the survival of earlier conceptions of the divine. Myth also provides a clear illumination of the remnants of a theriomorphic iconography: Zeus changes himself into a bull in order to rape Europa and into a swan in order to seduce Leda; Athena and Apollo metamorphose themselves into vultures to watch the battle between Hector and Ajax. The amalgamation of a number of functional deities during the Archaic and Classical periods can be seen in the great variety of epithets by which each god was addressed. In the use of such epithets, we see once again the particularism of Greek religion. The disparate types, which link seemingly unconnected functions from both the world of nature and the world of humans in a single deity, are probably a result of the continuing processes of synthesis and syncretism described above. Owing to the conservative nature of Greek religion, no epithet was ever discarded. Thus, the most primitive expression of the power of nature embodied in the god as well as the most sophisticated conceptions of divine political power can be found in the iconography, but it is clear that not all aspects of a deity can be equally well expressed through the various cultic epithets. Nevertheless, many of the epithets of the Olympians can be considered as proof of older iconographic substrata that reveal functions closely linked to the world of nature: horselike Poseidon, owl-eyed Athena, cow-eyed Hera, cloud-gathering Zeus. Although deities were often portrayed with their attributes of nature—the thunderbolt of Zeus, the trident of Poseidon—the connection between iconography and function may at times be difficult to establish because it is clear that many of the earlier "nature" functions of individual deities could not be expressed with clarity in the monuments. The frequent dichotomy between mythic meaning and ritual function also presents one with difficulties in understanding the iconography of a particular god. In Greek myth, Poseidon is clearly the god of the sea, who appears in sculpture and vase painting brandishing his trident or rising from the sea in his chariot. Yet, Poseidon was also worshiped as a god of horses, and he is depicted on coins in the form of a horse. Likewise, the Artemis of myth is the eternal virgin, yet it is clear from both cult and iconography that she was worshiped as a goddess of fertility. It would seem that myth often serves to create a coherent portrait while religious ritual and practice see no such need. The medium, too, often shapes iconographic conceptualization: the narrative of myth can be more readily portrayed in vase painting and reliefs than through freestanding sculpture. The evolution of the form and content of Greek iconography as a means of expressing spiritual ideals generally parallels that of Greek art, especially in sculpture. The earliest religious sculpture and architecture were executed in wood and have vanished; but in the seventh century BCE we see the development of monumental stone architecture and sculpture. The most representative forms of sculpture are the *kouros* and the *kourē* (female) figures that stand rigidly with stylized features and dress. Perhaps votive offerings, they have been variously identified as divine or human but may represent something in between: an idealized existence shared by gods and mortals alike. One cannot divorce iconography from the history of Greek art and architecture, for there is no such concept as purely hieratic art: the Classical Apollo, for example, is not only presented as the youthful god, naked and beardless, but comes to embody the idealization of youth. Similarly, a bronze statue of a muscular, bearded god with his left arm stretched out in front of him and his right arm extended behind as if to hurl something is identified as either Zeus or Poseidon; without lightning bolt or trident, it is impossible to distinguish between the spheres of sky and sea. Increasing emphasis on the beauty of the human form in repose and in action informs both Greek sculpture and the understanding of the divine. Furthermore, iconography is linked not only with the development of the artistic ideal but with that of the political as well. As the institutions of the state evolved, the original gods of nature were made citizens of the polis and given civic functions as protectors and benefactors of the city. Thus, the gold and ivory statue of Athena in the Parthenon portrayed the armed goddess in full regalia as the protector and patron of Athenian civilization, the goddess who had led her people to victory against the Persians. The Parthenon itself is a symbol of the bond between Athena and her city, for the temple frieze depicts the procession of the Panathenaea, a festival held in honor of both the goddess and the powerful city that worshiped her, the pediment portrays scenes from the life of Athena, and the metopes record various victories of Greeks over barbarians. Similarly at Olympia, which served as the religious and political center of Greece during the Classical period, the Phidian Zeus sat enthroned in the inner sanctuary of the great temple, the concrete expression of the god's power and majesty. Crafted of gold and ivory, nearly twelve meters high, the Lord of the Universe held in one hand a statue of Victory and in the other a golden scepter on which sat an eagle. Behind the throne were the Graces and Hours, goddesses of the seasons and regulators of nature. The worlds of nature and culture become one. Phidias himself reportedly said that he had meant to portray the king in his supremacy as well as in his magnanimity and nobility. The god may be seen as the source out of which all reality—sacred and profane—flows. The temple itself was also an expression of the all-encompassing might of Zeus: twenty-eight meters wide, sixty-nine meters long, and twenty meters high, its colossal size emphasized those attributes of power and universality that Phidias had sought to convey in his sculpture.

HELLENISTIC AND ROMAN ICONOGRAPHY. The declining political fortunes of the Greek states after the Peloponnesian War paved the way for the rise of Macedon and the magnificent career of Alexander the Great. His military conquests produced a new cultural synthesis of East and West that radically altered the perception and portrayal of the divine; for although the Classical understanding of the nature of deity survived, it was now informed by new religious, social, and political ideals. Absolute monarchy, an altered concept of the divine as embodied in Eastern mystery cults, and the rise of a middle class eager to display its wealth all contributed to the development of different iconographic sensibilities. Religious iconography in the Hellenistic period presents a curious admixture of Eastern and Western values, of monumentalism and individualism, of divine rationality and pathos, amalgams that expressed themselves in the formal magnificence of the tomb of Mausolus at Halicarnassus as well as in the representations of Aphrodite that emphasize her naked human beauty, in sleeping satyrs and playful cupids as well as in the struggling Laocoön doomed by the gods. The Great Altar of Zeus at Pergamum, with its wide monumental stairway, was encompassed by a frieze that, in depicting the ancient Greek myth of the war between the Olympians and the Giants, displays a remarkable range and intensity of human emotions. In a world where kings were hailed as living gods and apotheosis was a constant possibility, and where gods suffered and died, the division between sacred and profane iconography became even less distinct. With the conquest of the Hellenistic kingdoms the Romans acquired the values that had informed later Greek religious art and architecture. Although the earlier Etruscan culture of Italy had been strongly influenced by Greek and Oriental ideologies, it shows evidence of a religious outlook distinct from both. Tomb paintings from the Archaic period, for example, portray lively Dionysian revels and rowdy funeral games that, while drawing on Greek sources, perhaps indicate a more optimistic view of the afterlife than that of the Greeks. Roman iconography, on the other hand, reflects the conscious choice of the Greek ideal. Roman religion seems to have remained rooted in nature to a much greater extent than civic Greek religion had; the early anthropomorphic representations of Mars and Jupiter are exceptions, perhaps occasioned by their clear identification with the political rather than the agricultural life of the Roman people. Mars was the father of Romulus and Remus and thus the ancestor of the Roman people; but even so it was the she-wolf, nurse of the twin boys, who became the emblem of Rome's auspicious origins. Only when old Italic spirits of nature became identified with their anthropomorphic Greek counterparts did the Romans build temples as houses for their gods and represent them in human form. The conservative values of Roman religion not only inhibited the development of a distinctive iconography but at the same time led to the adoption of those elements in Hellenistic art that seemed best to reflect those values. Although Augustus's attempt to recreate the old Roman religious values through the resurrection of archaic rituals and priesthoods and the rebuilding of ancient temples and shrines was ultimately unsuccessful, his Altar of Augustan Peace (Ara Pacis) illustrates the Roman understanding of the connection between traditional expressions of piety and political success. One of its panels depicts Augustus offering solemn sacrifice; another reveals Mother Earth holding on her lap her fruitful gifts. The peace and prosperity of mortals and gods are attributed to Augustus's piety and devotion. More than three hundred years later, the Arch of Constantine was to reflect the same themes: celebrating the victory of the emperor over his enemies, its inscription attributes his triumph to the intervention of an unnamed divine power and his own greatness of spirit. Over three millennia, the iconography of Greek and Roman religion became increasingly concrete, locating the divine first in nature, then in objects, and finally within the human realm.

See Also Temple, article on Ancient Near Eastern and Mediterranean Temples.

Bibliography

Boardman, John. *Greek Art.* Rev. ed. New York, 1973. A useful and thorough survey of the development of Greek art forms from the Mycenaean age through the Hellenistic period.Dumézil, Georges. *Archaic Roman Religion.* 2 vols. Translated by Philip Krapp. Chicago, 1970. An analysis of early Roman religion that depends primarily on a structural analysis of Indo-European religious institutions and mythologies.Farnell, Lewis R. *The Cults of the Greek States* (1896–1909). 5 vols. New Rochelle, N. Y., 1977. Although lacking recent archaeological and linguistic evidence, this work remains the standard reference for ancient sources on Greek religion in all its forms.Guthrie, W. K. C. *The Greeks and Their Gods.* London, 1950. A well-balanced view of the origins of each of the Greek gods, with detailed discussion of the multidimensional roles of the divine in Greek society.Hauser, Arnold. *The Social History of Art,* vol. 1. New York, 1951. A combination of art criticism and social analysis, Hauser's work attempts to define the cultural forces that determine artistic sensibilities.Nilsson, Martin P. *A History of Greek Religion* (1925). Translated by F. J. Fielden. 2d ed. Oxford, 1949. Emphasizes the continuity of tradition between Minoan and Mycenaean ritual and practice.Nilsson, Martin P. *Greek Piety.* Translated by Herbert Jennings Rose. Oxford, 1948. This short work presents a thoughtful study of the various social, historical, and political forces that shaped Greek attitudes about the nature of the divine.Peters, F. E. *The Harvest of Hellenism.* New York, 1970. A historical, cultural, and religious survey of the Greek and Roman world after Alexander.

Tamara M. Green (1987)

ICONOGRAPHY: HINDU ICONOGRAPHY

Viṣṇu, Śiva, and Devī are the basic visual images of Hinduism. Each of these deities is worshiped in a concrete image *(mūrti)* that can be seen and touched. The image is conceived in anthropomorphic terms but at the same time transcends human appearance. With certain exceptions, Hindu images have more than two arms. Their hands, posed in definite gestures, hold the attributes that connote the deity's power and establish its identity. While the images are concrete in their substantiality, they are but a means of conjuring up the presence of deity: this is their essential function. The image serves as a *yantra,* an "instrument" that allows the beholder to catch a reflection of the deity whose effulgence transcends what the physical eye can see. The divine effulgence is beheld in inner vision. As a reflection of this transcendental vision, the image is called *bimba.* This reflection is caught and given shape also by the *yantra,* a polygon in which the presence of deity during worship is laid out diagrammatically. The *yantra* is constructed with such precision that the "image" emerges in its unmistakable identity.

Deity, beheld by the inner eye, by an act of "imagination," is translated in terms of the image. In this respect the image is called *pratimā*—"measured against" the original vision of the deity as it arose before the inner eye of the seer. Iconometry in the case of the anthropomorphic three-dimensional image corresponds to the geometry of a linear *yantra.* Thus the anthropomorphic image is at the same time a reflection of a transcendental vision and a precise instrument for invoking the divine presence during worship in the manmade and manlike figure of the image. It has its place in the temple, where it is worshiped not only as a stone stela in high relief in the innermost sanctuary but also on the outside of the walls. There, a special niche or facet of the wall is allotted to each of the images embodying aspects of the image in the innermost sanctuary.

Viṣṇu, Śiva, and Devī (the Goddess) are represented in many types of images, for each of these main deities has multiple forms or aspects. These are carved in relief in niches on the outer side of the temple walls, each niche suggesting a sanctuary correlated in the main directions of space to the central image—or symbol—in the innermost sanctuary. While the images of Viṣṇu and Devī are anthropomorphic and partly also theriomorphic, the essential form in which Śiva is worshiped is in principle without any such likeness.

Śiva. The main object of Śiva worship is the *liṅga.* The word *liṅga* means "sign," here a sign in the shape of a cylinder with a rounded top. The word *liṅga* also means "phallus" however; some of the earliest Śiva *liṅgas* are explicitly phallus shaped. However, this sign is not worshiped in its mere anthropomorphic reference. It stands for creativity on every level—biological, psychological, and cosmic—as a symbol of the creative seed that will flow into creation or be restrained, transmuted, and absorbed within the body of the yogin and of Śiva, the lord of yogins. In its polyvalence the *liṅga* is Śiva's most essential symbol, while the images of Śiva, each in its own niche on the outside of the temple wall, are a manifestation of Śiva in a particular role offering an aspect of his totality.

The images of Śiva visualize the god's two complementary natures: his grace and his terror. Like all Hindu divine images, that of Śiva has multiple arms; their basic number, four, implies the four cosmic directions over which extends the power of deity in manifestation. Śiva's image of peace and serenity in one of its forms, Dakṣiṇāūmurti, is that of the teacher. Seated at ease under the cosmic tree, he teaches the sages yoga, gnosis, music, and all the sciences. In another image, standing as Paśupati, "lord of animals," Śiva protects all the "animals," including the human soul.

He is also the celestial bridegroom, Sundaramūrti, embracing his consort (Āliṅganamūrti) or enthroned with her (Umāmaheśvara), while as Somāskanda the seated image of the god includes his consort, also seated, and their dancing child. These images assure happiness within the human condition, whereas Ardhanarisvara, the "lord whose half is woman," the androgyne god, his right half male and left half female, is an image of superhuman wholeness.

Myths and legends in which Śiva annihilates or pardons demons of world-threatening ambition are condensed in images of him as victor over destructive forces and death (Tripurāntaka, Kālāri). Another class of images visualizes the god as a young, seductively naked beggar (Bhikṣātaṇa) and, in a later phase of the selfsame myth, as an image of terror, an emaciated, skeletal—or, as Bhairava, bloated—god who is sinner and penitent on his way to salvation. Bhairava is an image of the lord's passion on his way to release. There he dances as he danced on the battlefield in his triumph over fiends. Śiva's dance is the preeminent mode of the god's operation in the cosmos and within the microcosm, in the heart of man. The image of Śiva Nāṭarāja dancing his fierce dance of bliss subsumes ongoing movement and stasis in the rhythmic disposition of limbs and body as if the dance were everlasting: in his upper hands are the drum and flame, the drum symbolizing sound and the beginning of creation, the flame symbolizing the end of creation; one arm crosses over the body and points to the opposite, while his raised foot signals release from gravity and every other contingency in the world. The whole cycle of the eternal return is laid out in the *yantra* of Śiva's dancing image. In another image, that of the cosmic pillar, Śiva reveals himself to the gods Brahmā and Viṣṇu; an endless flaming pillar of light arises from the netherworld. The image of Lingodbhava shows the anthropomorphic figure of Śiva within the *liṅga* pillar bursting open.

The *liṅga* as both abstract symbol and partly anthropomorphic shape is the main Saiva cult object. In some of the sculptures, a human head adheres to the cylinder of the *liṅga*, or four heads are positioned in the cardinal directions, implying a fifth head (rarely represented) on top. Five is Śiva's sacred number, and the entire Saiva ontology—the five senses, five elements, five directions of space, and further hierarchic pentads—is visualized in the iconic-aniconic, five-faced *liṅga*. This concept underlies the image in the innermost sanctuary of the Caturmukha Mahādeva Temple in Nachna Kuthara, near Allahabad (sixth century), and that of Sadāśiva in the cave temple of Elephanta, near Bombay (mid-sixth century). These are ultimate realizations and constructs embodied in sculptural perfection.

The facial physiognomy of the image reflects the nature of the particular aspect or manifestation of the god. His calm, inscrutable mien as well as Bhairava's distorted countenance are shown with many nuances of expression that convey the significance of each particular manifestation, defined as it is by specific attributes and cognizances. The ornaments, however, the necklaces, belts, earrings, and so on, are not essentially affected by the specific manifestation. Likewise some of Śiva's attributes, particularly the trident, serpent, crescent moon, rosary, and antelope, are part of the god's image in more than one manifestation. Invariably, however, Śiva's crown is his own hair. He is the ascetic god, and his crown shows the long strands of the ascetic's uncut hair piled high on his head in an infinite variety of patterns, adorned by serpents, the crescent moon, and the miniature figure of the celestial river Gaṅgā (Ganges) personified. Lavish presentation here nonetheless constitutes iconographic economy, for each of the various symbols implies an entire myth, such as that of the descent from heaven of the river goddess Gaṅgā, whose impact would have wrought havoc on earth had not Śiva offered his hair as a temporary station for her.

An essential cognizance particular to Śiva among gods—though not present in every Śiva image—is the god's third eye (which also graces deities derived from the Śiva concept, such as Devī and Gaṇeśa). Vertically set in the middle of Śiva's forehead above sun and moon, his two other eyes, the third eye connotes the fire of the ascetic god. It broke out when Pārvatī, his consort, playfully covered the god's other eyes with her hands: darkness spread all over the cosmos. This fire also blazed forth to destroy the god Kāma, "desire," in his attempt to wound Śiva with his arrow.

Whether distinguished by one symbol only or by a combination of symbols, the identity of Śiva is unmistakable in his images. There is also no inconsistency if, for example, the crown of Śiva, lovingly enthroned with Pārvatī, is wreathed with skulls (Umā-Maheśvara from Belgavi, Karnataka, twelfth century). The total being of Śiva is present in the particular aspect.

Facing the *liṅga*, the image of Nandin, the zebu bull carved in the round and stationed in front of the entrance of the temple or in its hall, is at the same time the animal form of Śiva, his attendant, and conveyance (*vāhana*). In more than one respect, Nandin, the "gladdener," conveys Śiva.

VIṢṆU. The pervader and maintainer of the universe is represented by his anthropomorphic image in the innermost sanctuary. Invariably the image stands straight like a pillar, and its four arms symmetrically hold the god's main attributes: conch, wheel, mace, and lotus. The conch—born from the primordial ocean—with its structure spiraling from a single point, is a symbol of the origin of existence. The wheel represents the cycle of the seasons, of time. The mace stands for the power of knowledge, while the lotus flower symbolizes the unfolded universe risen from the ocean of creation. According to their respective placement in the four hands of the Viṣṇu image, these four attributes define the particular aspect under which the god is worshiped according to the needs of the worshiper. Each of the twenty-four images—the total permutations of the four symbols in the four hands—has a name. The supreme god, Viṣṇu has a thousand names in which those of the twenty-four images are included.

In addition to the standing image in the innermost sanctuary—an anthropomorphic version of the concept of the cosmic pillar—Viṣṇu may assume two other positions, seated and recumbent. Indeed, no other Hindu god—except a Viṣṇu-derived allegory, Yoganidrā—is shown recumbent, and together, these three positions render the mode of the god's pervasive presence in the cosmos and during its dissolution, when in yoga slumber Viṣṇu reclines on Śeṣa, the serpent whose name means "remainder," floating on the waters of the cosmic ocean. In South India each of the three types of images occupies its own innermost sanctuary, on three levels in three-storied temples. According to the needs of the worshiper, each of these three types of images fulfills four goals: total identification with the god, desire for wish fulfillment in worldly matters, desire for power, and desire for success by magic. According to their desired efficacy on these four levels, the images are more or less elaborate in the number of attendant divinities, with the images granting wish fulfillment on the worldly plane the most elaborate.

The twenty-four varieties of the four-armed, standing Viṣṇu image are emanations (*vyūhas*) of the supreme Viṣṇu. Four of the emanations, Saṃkarṣaṇa, Vāsudeva, Pradyuma, and Aniruddha, are considered primary, though their names occur as the thirteenth, fourteenth, fifteenth, and sixteenth in the list of twenty-four.

Theological doctrine and its supporting imagery each follow an inherent logic. The *vyūha* or emanation doctrine is as relevant to the twenty-four types of the Viṣṇu image as the *avatāra* or incarnation doctrine, according to which the supreme Viṣṇu was fully embodied in a specific shape, be it that of fish or boar or man or god. One or the other of these incarnate forms, however, including that of the dwarf (Vāmana) or of Kṛṣṇa, also figures among the twenty-four varieties of the main cult image of Viṣṇu.

Viṣṇu is also conceived in his fivefold aspect: as ultimate, transcendental reality (*para*); in his emanation (*vyūha*); in his incarnation (*vibhava*); as innermost within man (*antaryāmin*), the inner controller; and as *arcā* or consecrated image, this fifth instance being an *avatāra*, a "descent" into matter.

Each *avatāra* is assumed by the supreme Viṣṇu for a particular end, as the situation demands. Yet each *avatāra* or divine descent, though known to have come about at a definite time, remains valid for all times. The number of *avatāras* or incarnations (*vibhavas*) is generally accepted as ten, but twelve further *vibhavs* are also described. The ten shapes are those of the (1) fish (Matsya); (2) tortoise (Kūrma); (3) boar (Varāha); (4) man-lion (Narasiṃha); (5) dwarf and "[god who took] three strides" (Vāmana and Trivikrama); (6) Rāma with the ax (Paraśurāma), who reestablished the leading position of the brahmans; (7) Rāma, the ideal king; (8) Kṛṣṇa; (9) Buddha; and (10) Kalkin, the redeemer yet to come. In niches of the temple wall, the *avatāras* are imaged in anthropomorphic, theriomorphic, or combined anthropo-theriomorphic shapes.

The Matsya *avatāra* incorporates a deluge myth, telling how a grateful small fish saved by Manu in turn saved Manu, who became the founder of present-day mankind. The tortoise myth tells of the cosmic tortoise that lent its body as the firm support for the world mountain, which served as a churning stick at the churning of the primeval ocean. The third of Viṣṇu's descents similarly illustrates a creation myth out of the cosmic waters. While the Matsya *avatāra* establishes the existence of mankind on earth and the Kūrma *avatāra* guarantees the firmness of its support, the boar incarnation shows Viṣṇu as the savior who lifted the earth from the depth of the ocean waters to the light of the sun. In the man-lion incarnation, Viṣṇu assumes this combined shape, bursting out of a pillar in the demon king's palace in order to disembowel this fiend who had questioned Viṣṇu's omnipresence. The fifth incarnation, the dwarf, gained from the demon king Bali a foothold on which to stand and took the threefold stride by which he traversed the cosmos. The four following *avatāras* appeared in the shape of man as hero or god. The images of Kṛṣṇa as the child of superhuman powers (Balakṛṣṇa) and as flute-playing young god have their own visual iconography, particularly in metalwork. Two forms of Kṛṣṇa are unlike other images of Hindu gods. The one is Jagannātha, "lord of the world," whose center of worship is in Purī, Orissa; the other is Śrī Nāthjī, whose center of worship is Nāthadvāra in Mewar, Rajasthan. Both these images are roughly hewn and painted wooden chunks only remotely anthropomorphic. From the sixteenth century on, Kṛṣṇa appears in miniature paintings incomparably more frequently than any other Hindu god. In front of Viṣṇu temples, the image in the round of Viṣṇu's partly anthropomorphic vehicle, the bird Garuḍa, is supported by a high pillar.

DEVĪ. The Great Goddess, Devī, represents the creative principle worshiped as female. She is Śakti, the all-pervading energy, the power to be, the power of causation, cognition, will, and experience. She is the power of all the gods; she wields all their weapons in her main manifestations or images. She is the origin of the world, the conscious plan of creation, the mother; she is the goddess Knowledge. Her main image is that of Durgā in the act of beheading the buffalo demon, the mightiest of the demons whom she defeats. This huge, dark, demonic animal, an embodiment of stupidity, is her archenemy. In her image as killer of the buffalo demon, the young and lovely goddess is accompanied by her mount, the lion.

In certain traditions the buffalo demon while still in human shape adored the goddess. In some of the sculptures of the goddess as slayer of the demon—his body that of a man, his head that of a buffalo—he ecstatically surrenders to her as she slays him. When not depicted in action but standing straight in hieratic stance, the goddess is supported by a lotus or a buffalo head.

The Great Goddess has many forms. Like Śiva she has three eyes; like Viṣṇu, in her form as Yoganidrā, "yoga slumber," she is represented lying, an embodiment of Viṣṇu's slumber. Yoganidrā is most beautiful and has only two arms, whereas the Goddess displays from four to sixteen arms in her other images. Although the lion is the *vāhana* or vehicle of the Great Goddess, as Rambhā she rides an elephant; as Gaurī, the White Goddess—the aspect under which the gods contemplate her—she stands on an alligator. In her horrific, emaciated aspects, the owl is her vehicle. Like Śiva, the Goddess is seen in divine beauty or in a shape of horror as Kālī or Cāmuṇḍā.

When worshiped in her own image, the Goddess is the center of the composition, but as the *śakti* or creative power of a god she is figured by his side, smaller in stature, and with only two arms, for she is the god's consort. Pārvatī is Śiva's consort, whereas Bhūdevī and Śrīdevī—the goddess Earth (Bhū) whom Viṣṇu rescued in his boar incarnation, and the goddess Splendor (Śrī)—are shown by Viṣṇu's side.

If the images of these gods are cast in bronze, they are modeled in the round. These are processional images, meant to be visible from all sides, in contrast to the stone images in the innermost sanctuary or on the temple walls, where they confront the devotee as he or she approaches them. However, where the image of Devī is represented as the supreme goddess, she may be flanked or surrounded by smaller figures of gods and demons who play a role in the particular myth represented. Attendant divinities may further enrich the scene.

Devī is not only represented in her own right as supreme goddess or as the consort of one of the main gods, she is also embodied as a group, particularly that of the "Seven Mothers" (*saptamātṛkās*) where, as Mother Goddess, she is shown as the *śakti* of seven gods, including Brahmā, Viṣṇu, and Śiva. Brahmā, although the creator in ancient times, is rarely figured in the present-day Hindu pantheon and has but few temples of his own. In South India his image figures on the south wall of a Viṣṇu temple opposite that of Śiva Dakṣiṇāmūrti on the north wall.

Brahmā's consort Sarasvatī, the goddess of knowledge and speech, is worshiped in her own image to this day. The image of the "Seven Mothers" arrayed in one row are worshiped in their own sanctuary. Another assemblage of "group goddesses," though of lower hierarchical standing, is worshiped in hypaethral temples, which allow their total of sixty-four images to be worshiped separately. The iconography of the Goddess has its counterpoint in the (originally imageless) diagrams. Both these instruments of contemplation of the goddess—her image and the geometrical diagram—are man-made. The Goddess is also worshiped as a stone in its natural shape.

Stones in themselves are sacred. A *śālagrāma* stone, a fossilized ammonite embedded in dark stone, represents Viṣṇu, with the spiral of the fossil structure evoking Viṣṇu's wheel. The *śālagrāma* is worshiped in domestic rituals. Similarly another stone, the *bāṇaliṅga*, washed by the water of the river where it is found into *liṅga* shape, is sacred to Śiva. Among *liṅgas*, which can be made of any material, whether clay or precious stone, the *svayambhū liṅga*, a natural outcrop of rock like a menhir, has special sanctity.

Today most of the preserved images are made of stone or metal. The few paintings that have survived over the last four centuries are in watercolor on paper, as a rule small in size, and narrative rather than iconic. To this day the gods are painted in their iconographic identity on walls of houses and on portable paper scrolls. Color, according to ancient texts, was essential to the image: its use was primarily symbolic and expressive of the nature of the respective deities. However, different colors in different texts are prescribed for the same deity.

GAṆEŚA. Gaṇapati or Gaṇeśa, the lord of hosts and god of wisdom, who is also called Vighneśvara ("the lord presiding over obstacles"), has an obese human body topped by the head of an elephant. Worshiped throughout Hinduism, he is invoked at the beginning of any enterprise, for his is the power to remove obstacles but also to place them in the way of success. His shape is a symbol charged with meaning on many levels. His huge belly, containing the world, is surmounted by his elephant head, signifying the world beyond, the metaphysical reality. The head is maimed; it has only one tusk, thus signifying the power of the number one, whence all numbers have their beginning. Every part of Gaṇeśa's shape is a conglomerate symbol, and each is accounted for by more than one myth. According to one tradition, the dichotomy of Gaṇeśa's body resulted from Śiva's beheading of Vighneśvara, Pārvatī's son, in a fit of anger. Śiva then ordered the gods to replace Vighneśvara's head with that of the first living being they met. This was an elephant; they cut off its head and put it on Vighneśvara's body. According to another source, Gaṇeśa was the child Kṛṣṇa whose head was severed by Śani (Saturn) and replaced by that of the son of Airāvata, elephant of the god Indra.

In the *Ṛgveda* (2.23.1) Gaṇapati is a name of Bṛhaspati, the lord of prayer, the lord of hosts. From the fifth century CE, images of Gaṇeśa are numerous. An elephant-headed deity is shown on an Indo-Greek coin of the mid-first century CE. Today, Gaṇeśa is invoked at the beginning of all literary compositions and all undertakings. Every village, every house has an image of Gaṇeśa, seated, standing, or dancing—like Śiva. Some of his images have a third eye. In one of his (generally) four hands he holds the broken-off tusk. His vehicle is the mouse or the lion. In his form as Heramba, Gaṇapati has five heads; as Ucchiṣṭa Gaṇeśa, he is accompanied by a young goddess. He is red, yellow, or white in different varieties of his image.

SEE ALSO Avatāra; Durgā Hinduism; Gaṇeśa; Goddess Worship, article on The Hindu Goddess; Maṇḍalas, article on Hindu Maṇḍalas; Mūrti; Śiva; Temple, article on Hindu Temples; Viṣṇu; Yantra; Yoni.

BIBLIOGRAPHY

Banerjea, Jitendra. *The Development of Hindu Iconography.* 2d ed. Calcutta, 1956. A handbook particularly dealing with the beginnings and historical typology of Hindu images.

Coomaraswamy, Ananda K. *The Dance of Shiva* (1918). Rev. ed. New York, 1957. Interpretation of an iconographic theme based on original sources.

Courtright, Paul B. *Gaṇeśa.* New York, 1985. The first comprehensive and insightful presentation of Gaṇeśa.

Eck, Diana L. *Banaras, City of Light.* New York, 1982. A topical study in depth, relating the icon to its setting.

Gopinatha Rao, T. A. *Elements of Hindu Iconography* (1914–1916). 2 vols. in 4. 2d ed. New York, 1968. The standard survey of Hindu iconography.

Kosambi, D. D. *Myth and Reality.* Bombay, 1962. An exposition of the roots of iconic and aniconic traditions.

Kramrisch, Stella. *The Hindu Temple* (1946). Reprint, Delhi, 1976. An exposition of architectural form in relation to the iconography of its images.

O'Flaherty, Wendy Doniger. *The Origins of Evil in Hindu Mythology.* Berkeley, 1976. A study in depth of the interrelation of gods and demons in Hindu mythology.

Shah, Priyabala, ed. *Viṣṇudharmottara Purāṇa.* 2 vols. Gaekwad's Oriental Studies, vols. 130 and 137. Baroda, 1958 and 1961. The most complete and ancient treatise (c. eighth century CE) of Hindu iconography.

Shulman, David D. *Tamil Temple Myths.* Princeton, 1980. An indispensable background study for South Indian iconography.

Śivaramamurti, Calambur. *The Art of India.* New York, 1977. The best-illustrated and best-documented presentation of Indian sculpture.

Zimmer, Heinrich. *Artistic Form and Yoga in the Sacred Images of India.* Translated and edited by Gerald Chapple and James B. Lawson. Princeton, 1984. A clarification of the function and relation of iconic, sculptural form and abstract, linear diagram.

STELLA KRAMRISCH (1987)

ICONOGRAPHY: BUDDHIST ICONOGRAPHY

In Buddhism, the very nature of a sculptural image is complex. Not only have the conception and function of images varied over the course of Buddhist history, but also according to the particular ritual, devotional, and decorative context in which they are situated. Although there has been considerable scholarly debate about the matter, it seems clear that Buddhists began to depict the Buddha very early on, perhaps even before he died, although no such images survive. The Buddha himself is recorded in some commentaries on the Pali *suttas* to have said that images of him would be permissible only if they were not worshiped; rather, such images should provide an opportunity for reflection and meditation. However, in other commentarial texts images also are discussed as viable substitutes for the absent Buddha. In any case, virtually all Buddhist temples and monasteries throughout the world contain sculptural images—of the Buddha, *bodhisattvas,* minor divinities, *yakṣas,* and significant monks and saints. These images range from very simple early Indian stone sculptures of the Buddha, standing alone delivering a *dharma* talk, to incredibly intricate medieval Japanese depictions of a *bodhisattva* like Kannon with a thousand heads, elaborate hand gestures, and iconographic details.

IMAGES OF ŚĀKYAMUNI (THE "HISTORICAL BUDDHA"). The earliest surviving Buddhist sculpture dates to roughly the third century BCE, and the images that were produced contextually functioned as decorations and visual "texts" in monasteries. Significantly, however, the Buddha himself is absent from these very early images. Instead of his physical form, early Buddhist artisans employed a range of visual symbols to communicate aspects of the Buddha's teachings and life story:

1. The wheel of *dharma,* denoting the preaching or "turning" of his first sermon, and also, with its eight spokes, the eight-fold Buddhist path.
2. The bodhi tree, which represents the place of his enlightenment (under the tree) and comes to symbolize the enlightenment experience itself.
3. The throne, symbolizing his status as "ruler" of the religious realm, and through its emptiness, his passage into final *nirvāṇa.*
4. The deer, evoking both the place of his first sermon, the Deer Park at Sārnāth, and also the protective qualities of the *dharma.*
5. The footprint, which denotes both his former physical presence on earth and his temporal absence.
6. The lotus, symbolic of the individual's journey up through the "mud" of existence to bloom, with the aid of the *dharma,* into pure enlightenment.
7. The stupa, the reliquary in which the Buddha's physical remains are contained—a powerful symbol of both his physical death and continued presence in the world.

Later Buddhism added countless other symbols to this iconographic repertoire. In the Mahāyāna, for instance, the sword becomes a common symbol of the incisive nature of the Buddha's teachings. In the Vajrayāna, the *vajra,* or diamond (or thunderbolt), is a ubiquitous symbol of the pure and unchanging nature of the *dharma.*

Much of the very early art produced in India is narrative in both form and function, presenting episodes from the Buddha's life and, particularly, scenes from his prior lives. At sites such as Bhārhut and Sāñcī in modern Madhya Pradesh, Bodh Gayā in modern Bihar, and Amarāvatī in modern Andhra Pradesh, huge stupas were erected as part of the large monastic complexes that were built in these locations beginning in the third century BCE. In addition, elaborate carvings were made on and around these stupas, particularly on the railings that encircled the monuments themselves. Many of these were scenes from the Buddha's prior lives, which also were verbally recorded in the *Jātaka* and *Avadāna* literature. These included representations of prior Buddhas, as well as depictions of key events in the Buddha's life such as miraculous conception, his birth, and his departure from the palace in search of enlightenment.

Typically, it has been assumed that because the earliest Buddhist artistic images did not depict the Buddha, there must have been a doctrinally-based prohibition against such depictions. First articulated by the French art historian Alfred Foucher in 1917, this idea—generally referred to as the "aniconic thesis"—has deeply influenced our understanding of early Buddhist art. The basic assumption has been that there must have been a prohibition against representing the Buddha in the early centuries after his death. Perhaps this was because the Buddha had, at the time of his *parinirvāṇa,* passed forever out of existence, and therefore could only be represented by his absence.

In the late twentieth century scholars began to rethink this basic assumption, arguing that perhaps these early sculptures are not reflective of a theological position, but instead frequently represent scenes after the Buddha's death, scenes of worship at prominent places of pilgrimage linked to key events in his life—such as Bodh Gayā, Lumbinī, and Rājagaha—and are thus intended to serve as ritual records and blueprints, and visual prompters for correct veneration. In any case, what seems clear is that early Buddhists had a complex understanding of both the form and function of the Buddha's representations, and that any attempt to articulate a univocal theory of early Buddhist art is probably misguided, precisely because of the complex interactions of original intent, ritual and aesthetic context, and individual disposition. Fundamentally, then, Buddhist images project an open potential.

Actual images of the historical Buddha began to appear sometime around the turn of the first millennium, prominently in two regions: in Mathura, near modern Agra, and in Gandhara, in what is now modern Afghanistan. In Mathura, large standing images of the Buddha were made in red sandstone. The Buddha in these images is depicted as broad shouldered, wearing a robe, and marked by various *lakṣaṇas,* the thirty-two auspicious marks with which he was born. Described in several early texts, these included the *uṣṇīṣa,* or protuberance atop the head, elongated earlobes, webbed fingers, and *dharmacakra* on the palms. In the Gandhara region, the Buddha typically was depicted in what appears to be a Greek style of representation, wearing a robe that resembles a toga, and with distinctly Western facial features. These details may be evidence that an iconographic exchange took place with the Greeks who inhabited the region at the time of Alexander the Great. Many of the Gandharan Buddha images depict him seated, forming the *dharmacakra mudrā*—literally the "turning of the wheel of *dharma* gesture"—with his hands. In other images he is presented in a meditative posture, his body withered by the years of extreme asceticism that preceded his enlightenment. These different iconic forms were employed by Buddhist artisans (and their royal, monastic, and lay patrons) to emphasize different moments in the Buddha's life story, and to convey visually different aspects of the *dharma.*

By the fifth century CE, the Buddha was represented in a large array of forms and sizes. Some of these representations were truly colossal, cut from cliffs and reaching upward of 100 feet—a practice that would continue throughout the Buddhist world for the next millennium. The sheer size of these images seems to have been intended to convey an understanding of the superhuman qualities of the Buddha, many of which were also expressed in contemporary biographical stories contained in various Nikāyas, the *Lalitavistara, Buddhacarita,* and several other well-known texts. Furthermore, such massive images would have served as a potent means of attracting new followers.

Stone and metal sculptures of the Buddha were produced in abundance throughout India. These were in addition to painted images, many of which were in caves, such as those that form the massive monastic complexes at Ajantā and Ellora. Many of these images presented the Buddha in a single pose, representing a particularly significant moment in his life. Among these, the giving of his first sermon was especially common. The Buddha typically is seated in such images, forming the *dharmacakra mudrā.* Oftentimes, he is flanked by several smaller figures: the five monks who first heard the sermon, the laywoman Sujatā who offered him the modest gift of food that gave him strength to attain enlightenment, two deer, and an image of the wheel.

Another common form is the Buddha at the moment of defeating the evil Māra—the embodiment of temptation, illusion, and death in Buddhism. In these images, the Buddha is seated in what is sometimes called the *bhūmisparśa mudrā,* or "earth-touching gesture," visually evoking the moment when the Buddha calls the earth goddess as witness to his enlightenment, and marking the final defeat of Māra. This iconographic form, sometimes presenting the Buddha as a crowned figure and including the seven jewels (*saptaratna*) of the ideal king, became extremely popular in medieval north India, where it seems to have been complexly involved in royal support of Buddhism by the Pālas, the last line of Buddhist kings in India, evoking as it does the image of the *Dharmarāja,* the righteous ruler.

By the eighth century, a fairly common means of representing the Buddha—especially in the monastic stronghold of northeastern India—was a standardized set of eight scenes known as the *aṣṭamahapratiharya.* This presented a kind of condensed version of the Buddha's life—birth, enlightenment, first sermon, various miraculous events in his biography, and death—that enabled the viewer of the image to participate ritually and imaginatively in the entire life of the Buddha by looking at and venerating a single image. In this sense, then, such images were more than visual texts or narratives; they served as means to embark upon visual pilgrimages. As such, they not only recorded past events in the Buddha's life and ongoing ritual activity, but also allowed the viewer to participate in the Buddha's life. In short, they evoke a sense of the Buddha's continued presence in the world despite his physical absence.

Bodhisattvas. As the various Mahāyāna schools emerged and developed in India, Tibet, and later in East Asia, the Buddhist pantheon expanded tremendously and was reflected in both art and iconography. In India, particularly in the northeast, there was a virtual iconographic explosion after the eighth century. Although images of various *bodhisattvas* had been produced in the early art of Gandhara and Mathura, they became particularly prominent in the Mahāyāna. Images of Mañjuśrī were quite common in India after about the fifth century, and he is sculpturally depicted in dozens of forms. Typically, he is depicted as a handsome young man holding aloft a sword—the incisive sword of wisdom, with which he cuts through delusion and ignorance—in one hand and a lotus in the other. A consistent element in his iconography is the representation of the book—sometimes he holds the text aloft, sometimes it rises out of a lotus to one of his sides. In contemporary iconographic manuals, this is described as the *Perfection of Wisdom* text, of which he is the manifestation. In the Vajrayāna context, Mañjuśrī frequently is depicted in a wrathful form, as Yāmantaka, a buffalo-headed demon who does battle with Yāma, the god of death. Avalokiteśvara, the embodiment of compassion and the bodhisattva who sees all suffering and comes to the aid of his devotees, is perhaps the single most popular figure in the Buddhist world after the Buddha himself. He is depicted in a vast range of forms. Avalokiteśvara frequently is shown with several eyes, denoting his compassionate omniscience, and sometimes with multiple heads, as in the *das'amukha* (ten-faced) iconographic form prevalent particularly in Nepal.

In addition, Avalokiteśvara almost always has multiple hands, in which he holds various implements that aid him in his salvific endeavors. In the *Saddharmapuṇḍarīka Sūtra* and several other Mahāyāna texts, he is described as a great protector whom one invokes against a standardized set of perils (snakes, beasts, robbers, poisons, storms, and so forth), which are sometimes iconographically depicted with him. Avalokiteśvara becomes extremely popular in East Asia, where he is known as Kannon (in Japan) and Kuan-yin (in China); as Kannon, he sometimes is depicted with 1,000 heads, and as Kuan-yin he is manifested as a female figure. Maitreya, the Buddha of the future, is often depicted as a crowned, royal figure (often with a Buddha image or stupa in his forehead). He typically displays the *dharmacakra mudrā,* the gesture of religious discourse, since it is he who will deliver the final version of the *dharma* that will release all beings from *saṃsāra.* In medieval China, after the Tang period, Maitreya is sometimes iconographically transformed into Budai, a jovial, pot-bellied figure who spreads good cheer and is the special friend of children.

Transcendent Buddhas. The various Mahāyāna schools articulated complex understandings of the continued presence and power of the Buddha in the world, understood broadly as *buddhatā,* or "buddhaness." One particularly common manifestation of *buddhatā* was the five celestial Buddhas, sometimes called Jina or Dhyāni Buddhas. More properly deemed the *pancatathāgātas,* this set represents the manifestation of different aspects of the Buddha's teaching and salvific power, and is depicted in both sculpture and painting (particularly *maṇḍala* paintings in the Vajrayāna). The five celestial Buddhas are Vairocana, Akṣobhya, Ratnasambhava, Amitābha, and Amoghasiddhi.

Iconographically, each of five Buddhas bears specific symbols and a specific color (when painted in a *maṇḍala,* for example), as well as specific *mudrās.* For instance, Akṣobhya (the "unshakable one") occupies the eastern quadrant of the *maṇḍala* and displays the *bhūmisparśa mudrā,* since he is the manifestation of the Buddha's steadfastness and unshakable calm, even in the face of Māra, or the embodiment of death. Vairocana, the "radiant one," is the manifestation of the Buddha's supreme *dharma,* and thus his standard iconographic form displays the *dharmacakra mudrā.* In the Pure Land schools that developed in China and later took root in Korea and Japan, Amitābha, the Buddha of the West, became particularly important. In a wide variety of images—stone and metal sculptures, bas-reliefs, cave temples, and paintings—Amitābha frequently is depicted at the center of a large entourage of *bodhisattvas* and buddhas, or more commonly is presented in a standard triad, flanked by Avalokiteśvara and Maitreya. As Amida, Amitābha continues to be very popular in contemporary Japan, and is depicted in a variety of modern images including metal and plastic sculptural forms, paintings, and even animated comic books.

Wrathful Figures. With the rise of the Vajrayāna in northeastern India around the ninth century, and its later development in Tibet, the divine pantheon expanded to a seemingly limitless degree, with a vast range of Buddha families, *bodhisattvas,* goddesses, *yoginīs,* and all manner of fierce divinities. There are numerous categories of wrathful beings in the Vajrayāna pantheon, including *vajradhāras, herukas, lokapālas,* and *dharmapālas.* These beings are projections of the base aspects of human nature: lust, anger, delusion, greed, and so on. However, when propitiated these figures are transformed into saviors who destroy the passions of the mind and protect the faithful. Their faces are depicted with strikingly wrathful expressions, their mouths contorted into angry smiles, from which protrude long fangs, sometimes dripping with blood.

Particularly in Tibet, *maṇḍalas* frequently depict vastly complex Buddha families and their associated divinities. Meditation and rituals focused on such divinities typically are intended to bring the divinity to life. For instance, in the practice of deity yoga the meditator can bring the divinity to life in him or herself by realizing the inseparability of the self and the divinity. In the esoteric schools that developed in Japan, the *lokapālas* often flank a central *bodhisattva* and are depicted as sometimes fierce and menacing dark-skinned foreigners. Consistent with the early literature that lays out Buddhism's basic cosmological view, in a relative sense, such beings are very real and very active in the world. However, in an absolute sense they ultimately are creations of our minds, and therefore, like everything else, are empty. Therefore, the iconographic presentation of these divinities is intended to provide an opportunity for meditation on the very nature of reality.

WISDOM GODDESSES. A range of divine and semidivine female figures also is depicted in Buddhist iconography, many of which are elaborately described in medieval texts such as the *Sādhanamālā* and *Niṣpannayogāvalī.* The female divinity Tārā emerges in the Mahāyāna as a divine savior who protects and nurtures her devotees. Her name literally means "star," and she was perhaps originally associated, in particular, with guiding sailors. Tārā is sometimes referred to as *jagat tarinī,* the "deliverer of the world." She is depicted in numerous forms—sometimes seated with a book, sometimes standing displaying variations of the *abhāya mudrā* (the gesture of no fear) or making a hand gesture of giving—and is intimately associated with the lotus, denoting her characteristic purity. In addition to her very common benevolent forms, in the Vajrayāna Tārā is sometimes depicted as wrathful figure who transforms into the benign savior for her devotees when properly worshiped. Tārā was and continues to be extremely popular throughout the Mahāyāna and Vajrayāna worlds, particularly in Nepal and Tibet, and she is frequently associated with Avalokiteśvara. Sometime around the seventh century, the *Perfection of Wisdom* texts (Prajñāpāramitā sūtras) became personified in the figure of *prajñāpāramitā,* wisdom incarnate, the divine "mother" of all enlightened beings. She typically is seated, legs crossed, and has either two or four arms. *Prajñāpāramitā* almost always forms the *dharmacakra mudrā,* holding both a lotus (emblematic of the purity of her teachings) and the text of which she is the embodiment.

SAINTS, ARHATS, AND MONKS. As Buddhism spread beyond India, an elaborate iconographic lexicon related to arhats, monks, and saints emerged. In China, the veneration and representation of important patriarchs became prominent; arhats were frequently represented, occasionally individually but more commonly in groups. In the Chan schools in particular, where monastic lineage was central, portraits of important patriarchs were common. Most prominent was Bodhidharma, who typically is depicted as an aged monk deep in mediation. Sometimes, he is depicted floating in the ocean atop a reed, representing his voyage from India to China. Bodhidharma also is represented in a kind of aniconic form, as an abstract face painted on papier-mâché or wooden balls, and occasionally as a lascivious old man, often in the company of courtesans. This conveys Chan's understanding that enlightenment can be found in the most mundane, and even the most conventionally polluting, of activities. In Tibet, images of Padmasambhava, who is said to have introduced Buddhism and tamed the demons who inhabited the region, are common. He frequently is depicted as a robed monk with a crown, often holding an alms bowl and *vajra.* Prominent monks such as Atīśa and Xuanzang are common in both the sculpture and painting of China and Japan. Particularly in Japan, individual monks, often specific to a particular monastery, are presented in remarkably realistic images, sometimes life-size, three-dimensional sculptures. As with images of Śākyamuni, such sculptures function as meditational aids to be emulated, pedagogical prompters, and outright objects of devotion.

IMAGES AND RITUAL. The *Sādhanamālā* and *Niṣpannayogāvalī* are two medieval Indian iconographic manuals, written in Sanskrit and still used in the early twenty-first century. These texts—and the countless other lesser-known manuals that deal with three-dimensional icons, paintings, and *maṇḍalas*—describe in sometimes minute detail the proper way to construct an image. They cover the purifying rituals to be performed prior to the start of work, the materials to be used, the iconographic details, the specific proportion, as well as detailed instructions for the ritual practices that are associated with the image.

From the moment they appeared in the Buddhist world, visual images were intended to narrate aspects of the Buddha's life and teachings, and therefore function on the ground as visual texts to be read. In addition, they were very much intended to be objects of ritual worship. A wide range of texts are available for making and consecrating Buddhist images, from locally-produced manuals in the vernacular to pan-Buddhist iconographic manuals. Perhaps the most common form of worship in the Buddhist world is *buddha pūjā,* literally "honoring the Buddha." This is a ritual that typically involves making some sort of offering to a Buddha image (or to a relic or a stupa), such as a flower, a small lamp, food, or even money. Many images, particularly the stelae that were abundantly produced in the medieval Indian milieu—although this also is an iconographic theme on some of the very earliest Buddhist images—actually depict such worship as part of the sculpture. These depictions usually are found along the base of the image, at what would in a ritual context be eye-level for the worshiper. The iconography in such cases, then, serves as a kind of visual guide to proper ritual action.

Across the Buddhist world, image construction and consecration are embedded in elaborate ritual structures. Images are made by specially trained and sanctified artisans, who follow extremely precise iconographic guidelines that dictate the proportions and specific details of a particular image. In northern Thailand, for instance, images are constructed using local ritual texts that include iconographic proportions, recitation of special protective chants (*paritta*), and elaborate consecration rituals, which "enliven" the image. Of particular interest in this regard is a clearly articulated correlation between the various parts of the image—which in the ritual becomes the "form body" (*rupakāya*) of the Buddha—and the *dhammakāya*, or "teaching body" of the Buddha. According to these Thai texts—and there are similar manuals in other ritual contexts in Tibet, China, Japan, Sri Lanka, and other Asian countries—a properly constructed and consecrated Buddha image is one that makes the ritual participant feel as though he or she is in the presence of the Buddha himself.

For the laypeople and monks who participate in such rituals, the Buddha image has a special apotropaic power, often heightened by the accompanying recitation of *paritta* texts and various *mantras*. In some instances, part of the consecration ritual involves the "instructing" of the image in the life story and teachings of the Buddha, which provides, also, the opportunity for the laity to receive this same instruction. Finally, the construction, consecration, and ritual veneration of images in virtually all Buddhist contexts provide an opportunity for laypersons to generate merit by way of donations made to the image—food, money, material objects—and by sponsoring such rituals.

Frequently, Buddhist iconography is intended to focus the mind of the worshiper on the Buddha and his teachings, serving as a visual aid and helping the practitioner to engage in *buddha anusmṛti*, or "recollection of the Buddha." This important form of meditation involves contemplating the Buddha's magnificent qualities and internalizing them, very often with the use of a sculpture or painting. The iconography of such images, then, serves a mimetic function in that the meditator is to emulate the iconographically presented Buddha. In the process, the practitioner creates a mental image by internalizing the external iconographic form, thereby becoming like the image, and like the Buddha himself.

SEE ALSO Bodhidharma; Buddha; Buddhism, overview article; Buddhist Meditation, articles on East Asian Buddhist Meditation, Theravāda Buddhist Meditation, and Tibetan Buddhist Meditation; Buddhist Philosophy; Lotus; Mudrā; Stupa Worship; Temple, articles on Buddhist Temple Compounds.

BIBLIOGRAPHY

For a broad-ranging orientation to Buddhist iconography, see Fredrick W. Bunce's *Encyclopedia of Buddhist Demigods, Godlings, Saints and Demons*, two volumes (New Delhi, 1994). *The Image of the Buddha* (Paris, 1978), edited by David L. Snellgrove, focuses on the development and function of Buddha images across the tradition. A good initiation into the Tantric pantheon and its complex iconography is found in Marie-Thérèse Mallmann's *Introduction à l'iconographie du tântrisme bouddhique* (Paris, 1975). Two of the most comprehensive studies of Buddhist iconography are Lokesh Chandra's *Buddhist Iconography* (New Delhi, 1991), which focuses particularly on the Tibetan pantheon, and his *Dictionary of Buddhist Iconography* (New Delhi, 2004). For an excellent study of the particular iconography of Eastern India, and especially the later esoteric schools that were prevalent, Thomas Donaldson's *Iconography of the Buddhist Sculpture of Orissa*, two volumes (New Delhi, 2001), is a treasure trove of information. In *Imaging Wisdom: Seeing and Knowing in the Art of Indian Buddhism* (London, 1999), Jacob Kinnard examines medieval Indian Buddhist sculpture specifically related to the important faculty of *prajna*. For a useful foray into the medieval iconographic manuals, see Benoytosh Bhattacharyya's *Indian Buddhist Iconography: Mainly Based on the Sadhanamala and Other Cognate Tantric Texts of Rituals* (Calcutta, 1958). Tucci's *Theory and Practice of the Mandala* (London, 1961) remains a useful study. For the recent debate about the aniconic thesis, see Susan Huntington's "Early Buddhist Art and the Theory of Aniconism" (*Art Journal*, 1990); Vidya Dehejia's "Aniconism and the Multivalence of Emblems" (*Ars Orientalis*, 1992); and Susan Huntington's response, "Aniconism and the Multivalence of Emblems: Another Look," (*Ars Orientalis*, 1993). Donald Swearer's *Becoming the Buddha: The Ritual of Image Consecration in Thailand* (Princeton, 2004) presents a richly detailed examination of the ritual construction and use of buddha images in northern Thailand as well as a useful comparative survey of ritual praxis associated with images. For an important postmodern-oriented essay, see Bernard Faure's "The Buddhist Icon and the Modern Gaze" (*Critical Inquiry*, 1998). Finally, for a fascinating collection of essays, see *Living Images Japanese Buddhist Icons in Context* (Stanford, 2002), edited by Robert H. Sharf and Elizabeth Horton Sharf.

JACOB N. KINNARD (2005)

ICONOGRAPHY: DAOIST ICONOGRAPHY

Like Daoism, Daoist iconography is not easily described as a unity. The focus in this entry will be on the visual expressions of the organized religion whose origins can be traced to the second century CE, but this religion and its iconography cannot be understood without reference to the intellectual and religious developments that formed its background.

BACKGROUND. Many of the tenets that the Daoist religion came to embrace evolved during the last four centuries BCE, the period that forged the worldview of imperial China. A chief concern for the competing rulers of the late Warring States period (403–221 BCE) and the founders of the succeeding Qin (221–206 BCE) and Han (206 BCE–220 CE) dynasties was the sanction of political power, based on the previous conception of a mandate (*ming*, also meaning "destiny" and "life") bestowed by heaven (*tian*) on one who possessed perfect virtue or "inner power" (*De*). From the fourth century BCE on, Chinese thinkers speculated about the relationships between this inner power, the concept of an ineffable way (Dao) underlying the functions of the cosmos as a whole, and the notion of *ming* in its double sense as heaven's mandate to rule and as the mandate of life granted by heaven to each individual. To many of these philosophers, *de* or inner power, believed to derive from the ability of aligning oneself with the Dao, was the prerequisite quality of both the sage ruler and the saint capable of preserving his life. In the *Dao de jing* (Scripture on the way and inner power), attributed to the paradigmatic figure of the "Old Master," Laozi, the saint and sage ruler are equivalent. This also holds for the texts *Guanzi* (compiled between the fourth and the second centuries BCE) and *Huainanzi* (submitted to the Han emperor Wu in 139 BCE). The book *Zhuangzi* (the earliest parts are attributed to the fourth-century BCE philosopher Zhuang Zhou), however, envisages the ideal, "fully realized person" (*zhenren*)—whether female or male—gaining boundless freedom by forsaking all political aspirations.

While some Warring States rulers quickly caught on to the idea of a direct connection between heaven-endowed power and longevity or immortality, a dialogue between various court professionals (astrologers, calendarologists, and health specialists) and philosophers led to the systematization of a theoretical framework by which the cosmic functions of the great Dao could at least approximately be understood and controlled. Modern Western scholars have termed the resulting system—based on the theories of yin and yang, of *qi* (the vital pneuma and material basis of the universe), and of the five cosmic driving forces (*wuxing*; also rendered five elements, phases, or agents)—*Chinese correlative cosmology*. Its symbolic expressions included animal figures (e.g., the tiger and the dragon standing for yin and yang), color schemes, and trigrams derived from the ancient *Yi jing* (Book of changes). The system, which united the divine, natural, social, and moral orders into one interconnected whole, henceforth became the mainstay not only of traditional Chinese cosmo-political thought, but also of the gamut of Chinese sciences, including medicine and the immortality arts, and of Chinese religion in general.

Just as, according to correlative cosmology, the order of the cosmos was manifest in the human realm in the form of administrative structures, the universe as a whole came to be viewed as administered by a bureaucracy of divine forces. The figure of the Yellow Emperor took the central position, analogous to the elemental force of "yellow" earth, among a group of five celestial thearchs correlated with the *wuxing*. By the early Han dynasty, the Yellow Emperor was the paradigm for the sage ruler. Believed to have not only civilized the world, but also succeeded in the cultivation of life, he became the model for Emperor Wu's (r. 140–87 BCE) quest for universal rule and immortality. But some two hundred years later, the emperors of the declining Han dynasty pleaded their hopes for longevity, male posterity, and the dynasty's survival before a far more powerful divinity: Laozi, who by then was seen as the very embodiment of the eternal Dao itself.

Demonstrative of the experience that for ordinary humans immortality is attainable only in an afterlife, most artifacts testifying to ancient Chinese beliefs about the cultivation of life have been discovered in tombs. A second-century BCE Han tomb in Mawangdui contained the almost perfectly preserved body of a woman belonging to the high aristocracy. A painted silk banner presenting the lady's ascent from the tomb to the immortal realms covered the innermost of four coffins encasing her. Other finds in tombs of Han dynasty elites include Boshan (Universal Mountain) censers, incense burners with perforated, mountain-shaped lids depicting the marvelous world of the immortals; bronze mirrors, whose backsides show the Queen Mother of the West, often along with her male counterpart, the King Father of the East; and so-called money-trees, stylized tree-sculptures in bronze with coin-shaped leaves, their branches carrying divinities such as the Queen Mother of the West, immortals, and fabulous beasts.

The Queen Mother, a deity of ancient origin, became one of the foremost idols of the Han immortality cult. By the second century CE, she was believed to rule over a paradise of immortals on the mythic Kunlun Mountain located at the far western rim of the Han empire. Her picture—identified by her phoenix-patterned headdress, her throne flanked by a tiger and dragon, and animals such as a bird, hare, toad, and fox—frequently adorns Han dynasty stone sarcophagi and mortuary architecture. As Wu Hung has demonstrated, her increasingly iconic representation—showing her frontally, seated, and centered—derives from images of the Buddha, which became known in China around the same time. Indeed, in the second century CE, the Buddha (recognizable by the *uṣṇīṣa* protuberance on his head, his halo, Ghandaran-style gown, and hand gestures or *mudrās*) began to appear in Chinese funerary art as an equivalent of the Queen Mother of the West, promising, like her, immortality beyond the tomb.

Evidently, the hope for postmortem immortality in some paradisiacal region was counterpoised by fears of an afterlife in the drab realms of death. Texts excavated from graves of commoners reveal that the netherworld was already in the late fourth century BCE imagined as a bureaucratic institution. By the second century CE, this administration was believed to be headquartered in China's Five Sacred Mountains and ruled by the Celestial Emperor or Yellow God. The texts usually express people's trepidation at the possibility of untimely death, either on account of an error in the netherworld bookkeeping, or because the deceased might have suffered or committed severe wrongs during life. Surviving family members buried human figurines of ginseng and lead with the bodies of the deceased to redeem their guilt and serve as surrogates for the living, lest they might fall ill and die by implication.

EARLY DAOIST RELIGION. Early Daoists shared and refined this broader worldview as they constructed their tradition between the second and fifth centuries CE. Among several politico-religious movements in the second century, the Way of the Celestial Master alone survived and established the fundamental liturgical and organizational structures of the Daoist religion. Celestial Master followers worshiped Laozi as the supreme embodiment of the Dao, whose limitless pneumata (*qi*) could, however, take the shape of innumerable other divinities. Originally more concerned about death and its harbinger, disease, than the pursuit of immortality, Celestial Master priests sent petitions to the Three Bureaus, the other world's legal institution, to relieve parishioners from the consequences of the crimes of deceased family members. Subordinated to the Three Bureaus were twelve hundred officials, including their civil and military staffs, whose divine intervention could be invited depending on the specific circumstances of each case.

These were fairly concrete notions about a bureaucratically functioning spirit world, wholly inscribed in Laozi's divine body of the Dao, but, in accord with the *Dao de jing*'s assertion that the Dao ultimately has no concrete forms, early Daoists hesitated to give outside visual form to any of these ideas. A second-century commentary to that scripture, whose author stood at least close to the Celestial Master religion, even warns against picturing the Dao in the form of innercorporeal divinities. This evidently marked an extreme, since anthropomorphic visualizations of the numinous forces indwelling the body—a microcosm of Laozi's cosmic body—quickly became central to the Daoist work of regulating universal flows through meditation. The fourth-century Shangqing (Higher Purity) scriptures contain the most detailed instructions for such visualizations, although there are prior guidelines for actualizing microcosmic deities—even Laozi himself—through mentally created images of their appearances, including their size, garb, headgear, coloring, and accoutrements.

Apart from this eidetic technique of imaging, however, Daoists presented the forces of the divine preferably in abstract, symbolic ways. Diagrams, sacred maps, and various forms of secret script early on played important roles. The yin-yang symbol (*taiji tu*) with its two comma-shaped fields inscribed in a circle, which became so prominent from the Song dynasty (960–1279) on, may not just be traced to a Tang dynasty (618–907) Buddhist antecedent, as Isabelle Robinet has shown, but to even earlier Daoist, albeit nontransmitted, diagrams. Maps of the interior of the Five Sacred Mountains existed already in early medieval times, even though the extant diagrams only replace the long-lost originals. But the chief key to access divine forces was writing. This accounts for the centrality of Daoist *fu*, secret tallies (or talismans), which Daoists drew in order to tap particular numinous sources. Moreover, from the fourth and fifth centuries on, Daoist scriptures were held to incorporate the blueprint of the cosmos itself in their original celestial-script versions. That is why so much weight was put even on the calligraphic quality of the transcripts of such scriptures in human hands.

Daoist Sculpture. Concrete material images, however, constituted in Daoist eyes only crude attempts to give fixed shape to the ever-changing modalities of the Dao and its hypostases. Fully sculpted icons of durable materials presented the bottom rank on that scale, and were considered dangerous, because their coarse materiality might easily invite impure and potentially malevolent spirits instead of the deities whose likeness they purportedly produced. Even in late imperial times, Daoist texts frequently mention demons possessing such icons as causes of disease, but already a fifth-century source, attributed to the famous southern Chinese Daoist Lu Xiujing (406–477), complains that lay believers installed sculpted images in their ritual chambers like the followers of vulgar cults. Curiously, despite all Daoist claims of the formlessness of the Dao, a seventh-century Buddhist author accuses precisely Lu Xiujing of plagiarizing Buddhist icons in sculptures of Daoist Heavenly Worthies (an epithet of the Dao's embodiment as supreme deity in three different aeons).

Archaeologically, the earliest examples of Daoist sculpture date indeed to the fifth and sixth centuries CE; but they come from north China, where the Daoist Kou Qianzhi (d. 488) supposedly first promoted such icons. These images, carved on stelae and dedicated by private donors to the weal of the government and the happiness of their ancestors, ostensibly relate to a well-known Buddhist practice of merit-transfer. Indeed, there are indications that religious differences barely mattered to followers of the custom. Several of the stone monuments combine images of both Buddhist and Daoist divinities, which are distinguished only by minor features. While the figures of buddhas and *bodhisattvas* feature *uṣṇīṣas* or crowns and monastic garb, Daoist deities, often bearded and holding fans, wear hats and belted Chinese garments. Otherwise, the posture and grouping of the Daoist gods, with the chief divinity flanked by two attendants, conform entirely to Buddhist iconography. Nor are there differences in the appearance of Daoist deities identified by distinct titles; whether a figure is referred to as Lord Lao (specifically Laozi as the body of the Dao) or Heavenly Worthy (a general appellation for hypostases of the Dao), their images are the same. Only late in Daoist history, the Three Purities, or main hypostases of the Dao, developed their individualized iconographies with Yuanshi tianzun (Heavenly Worthy of Prime Origin) holding a pearl, Lingbao tianzun (Heavenly Worthy of the Numinous Treasure) carrying a scepter, and Daode tianzun (Heavenly Worthy of Dao and De) retaining the features of the white-haired, bearded Lord Lao (Laozi).

While Six Dynasties (220–589) Daoist sculpture was predominantly a matter of private devotion, the situation changed dramatically under the Tang dynasty, which traced its ancestral line to Laozi and therefore strongly supported Daoism in its official cult. Tang emperors established a nationwide network of Daoist temples in which large freestanding statues of the holy ancestor were set up. Empress Wu (r.

684–705), before she founded her own interim dynasty and turned to Buddhism for legitimization, decreed that sculptures of Laozi's mother should accompany those of Laozi; and Xuanzong (r. 712–756), the most powerful of the emperors of the re-established Tang, even had his own likeness installed in temples along with images of Laozi.

If statuary began to play a role in state-endorsed Daoist temples in connection with the imperial cult, the rules for the production and worship of these images followed Buddhist models. A relatively early Daoist source (ascribed a pre-Tang date by many scholars, but more probably compiled in the early Tang) determines a code of "auspicious marks" (Skt., *lakṣaṇa*) for different types of icons and, prescribing monthly vegetarian offerings and ritual cleansings for them, ascertains their sacrality. In the early tenth-century, a prominent court Daoist welcomed all ideological efforts at demonstrating the miraculous powers of Daoist over Buddhist icons.

Still, Daoists remained reluctant about attributing statuary a central place in their innermost ritual practice. Even today, effigies are generally eschewed in the inner sanctum of the enclosed temporary altar constructions, where the essential rites of Daoist services take place. As a rule, only painted images of the Daoist high divinities are allowed here, while sculpted icons from community temples and household altars are relegated to the outer areas of the sacred space as onlookers. If statues have any immediate ritual functions, such as the figures of altar guardians, messengers, or the newly deceased in funeral services, they are made of paper. These images are animated at the beginning of the ritual through the so-called eye-opening rite (*kaiguang*), and burned as soon as the spirits legitimately possessing them during the ritual have fulfilled their tasks.

DAOIST PAINTING. Court support was also a chief factor in the development of Daoist painting. Wu Daozi (fl. 710–760), reportedly a Daoist priest, created his famous murals and scroll paintings on both Buddhist and Daoist themes under Emperor Xuanzong's sponsorship. None of his originals has survived, but textual references and transmitted works of later artists, most of whom placed themselves in Wu Daozi's tradition, bespeak the main features of his style: movement, dramatic facial expressions, individualized figures, and narrative composition.

Beautiful examples of the illustrative art that the Daoist pictorial tradition eventually produced survive in the fourteenth-century murals of the Eternal Joy Temple (Yongle gong in Shanxi province) depicting the lives of the Immortals (*xian*) Lü Dongbin and Wang Chongyang. But more expressive of what inspired Daoist painting at its core is the brilliant rendition of the theme known as the "Audience with the Origin" in the temple's main hall. The frescoes show the various monarchs of the Daoist universe, including the Jade Emperor; the Purple Tenuity Emperor of the North Pole; the Queen Mother of the West; her spouse, Lord of the Dao in the East; Houtu, the royal matriarch of earth; and their retinues, all turning towards the Dao, which in its threefold aspect was represented by statues of the Three Purities (now lost).

Depictions of the Daoist pantheon at audience with the Dao's higher hypostases may go back to the tenth century. Other examples of narrative religious painting in China, such as the tableaus related to the "Water and Land" ritual of universal salvation (*shuilu zhai*) and the earlier "transformation pictures" (*bianxiang*) of hell (which existed already by the seventh century and of which Wu Daozi reportedly also was a master) are associated with Buddhism; and Buddhism is considered to have inspired Daoist painting in general. But such paintings on Buddhist themes were early on connected with popular performances and rituals in China and likely received indigenous Chinese and Daoist influence from the beginning. Surviving "Water and Land" frescoes, hell frescoes, and scrolls of the thirteenth and fourteenth centuries and beyond, at least, clearly manifest the impact of Daoism (which then had incorporated them in its liturgy) in their hierarchic-bureaucratic vision of the numinous realms and the inclusion of Daoist gods.

Nonetheless, Buddhist iconography unquestionably shaped the appearance of Daoist deities. One example is the Great Monad Heavenly Worthy Saving from Suffering (Taiyi jiuku tianzun), who, already by the tenth century, had assumed features of the *bodhisattvas* Avalokiteśvara (Guanyin), Kṣitigarbha (Dizang), and Mañjuśri (Wenzhu). Central to Daoist funerary rituals, Taiyi jiuku tianzun is still represented on painted scrolls next to the Three Purities in mortuary altar settings. Particularly influential was the submerged Tantric Buddhist tradition in China. As Daoist liturgical texts of the twelfth through fourteenth centuries show, esoteric Buddhist rituals and popular spirit possession practices greatly enriched the Daoist exorcistic tradition and its pantheon of star deities, thunder gods, and divine marshals or generals. As a result, some Daoist deities, such as the multi-handed Mother of the Seven Dipper Stars (Doumu), became directly modeled on Tantric divinities. In others, the multiple eyes, heads, and arms of Tantric spirits were combined with traditional Daoist symbols and the names and features of popular gods; in the chief thunder gods, iconographic synthesis produced new chimerical shapes. Daoist sources nonetheless understand these composite divinities in quintessentially Daoist terms as manifestations of pure cosmic forces, re-created through the cycling and blending of corporeal *qi* in visual meditations. As in earlier Daoist texts, these visualizations follow exact descriptions of the deities' semblance and attributes and their cosmological significance; only the iconographic vocabulary has become far more diverse. Even the *fu* tallies, originally abstract graphs designed to contract divine powers, take in these late ritual manuals, often the form of calligraphic pictures of the deities and their symbols.

The general agreement between such liturgical sources and depictions of Daoist divinities in late imperial and modern religious paintings suggests a connection between ritual performance and pictorial representation. Indeed, just as the Audience with the Origin was not merely an iconographic theme, but originally denoted the culmination of Daoist meditation (when the divinities of an adept's or priest's bodily microcosm are brought face to face and merged with the original oneness of the Dao), authentic artworks, and particularly paintings, were to reflect the internal visions of Daoist priests and the iconographic codes thereby established. That this continuity between liturgy and the visual arts always remained an ideal and never led to the iconographic standardization achieved in the Buddhist tradition is partly due to Daoism's internal diversity and comparatively loose organization, partly to difficulties in institutionalizing links between clerical and art traditions, and, of course, also to the disruptions of modern times.

While already in the twelfth and thirteenth centuries, scrolls portraying the Three Purities, the Jade Emperor, the Purple Tenuity Emperor, the Heavenly Worthy Saving from Suffering, and other Daoist high divinities surrounded the inner, most sacred area of Daoist altars, these paintings, surprisingly, were not accorded full sacred status. Even today, the actual seat of Daoist divinities during rituals is in the *shenwei*, small tablets inscribed with their names, not in the paintings. An exception here is the Daoist tradition of the Yao minority, which clearly emphasizes the sacrality of altar paintings through special rites of consecration and deconsecration (once they have outlived their ritual life spans).

Daoist Iconography in Popular Chinese Art and Religion. Daoist visions of gods and immortals, as well as demonic beings and their realms, have had a tremendous influence on popular religious iconography. Temple murals and altar hangings evidently played important roles, but Daoists also propagated their views through narrative and performance arts. The most eloquent proof of this exists perhaps in some of the great vernacular novels of the sixteenth through eighteenth centuries that feature the eminently hybrid pantheon of popular Chinese religion, including immortals, Daoist and Buddhist divinities, and entirely composite and often even renegade gods, all under the Jade Emperor's rule. Even contemporary Chinese cite these novels as sources of information about the backgrounds, functions, symbolism, and iconography of the deities worshiped by them, whether in statues and murals in community temples, or in wood-block book illustrations and New Year's pictures at home. As these explanations again are frequently traced to Daoist liturgical literature, they point—in line with the motto favored by late imperial Daoists, that all religious paths eventually run into the Great Way—to Daoism as the most important factor in the formation of popular Chinese religion and iconography.

See Also Afterlife, article on Chinese Concepts; Calligraphy, article on Chinese and Japanese Calligraphy; Dao and De; Daoism; Temple, article on Daoist Temple Compounds; Xian; Yinyang Wuxing.

Bibliography

Bokenkamp, Stephen R., with Peter Nickerson. *Early Daoist Scriptures*. Berkeley, 1997. Contains several important early Daoist texts in English translation, including individual introductions and thorough annotations. Peter Nickerson's contribution is of special interest in context with early Celestial Master liturgy and its connection with previous mortuary rituals.

Davis, Edward L. *Society and the Supernatural in Song China*. Honolulu, 2001. The most comprehensive analytical study of Daoist ritual in the Song dynasty and later.

Harper, Donald. "Resurrection in Warring States Popular Religion." *Taoist Resources* 5, no. 2 (1994): 13–29. An important article on popular afterlife beliefs in the Warring States period.

Kamitsuka Yoshiko. "Lao-tzu in Six Dynasties Taoist Sculpture." In *Lao-tzu and the Tao-te-ching*, edited by Livia Kohn and Michael LaFargue, pp. 63–87. Albany, N.Y., 1998. A concise and highly informative essay on early Daoist sculpture.

Katz, Paul R. *Images of the Immortal: The Cult of Lü Dongbin at the Palace of Eternal Joy*. Honolulu, 1999.

Lemoine, Jaques. *Yao Ceremonial Paintings*. Bangkok, 1982. A richly illustrated, exceedingly interesting introduction to the ritual paintings of the Yao minority people living in the mountainous regions in south and southwestern China, who, by the thirteenth century at the latest, were collectively converted to Daoism.

Little, Stephen, and Shawn Eichman. *Taoism and the Arts of China*. Chicago and Berkeley, 2000. This catalog of an unprecedented exhibition in Chicago and San Francisco is a treasure trove of stunning illustrations, including both distinctly Daoist works and others that are more widely related to Daoist concepts and themes. The authors have made efforts at contextualizing their examples with Daoist history, thought, and liturgy. With five essays on particular topics by different experts, this is the most up-to-date book-length publication on Daoist arts and iconography.

Loewe, Michael. *Ways to Paradise: The Chinese Quest for Immortality*. London, 1979. A classic on immortality and afterlife beliefs in early China.

Reiter, Florian C. "The Visible Divinity: The Sacred Image in Religious Taoism." *Nachrichten der deutschen Gesellschaft für Natur-und Völkerkunde Ostasiens* 144 (1988): 51–70. The article studies the guidelines concerning Daoist temple imagery in an early (pre-Tang/beginning of Tang) Daoists liturgical code.

Robinet, Isabelle. *Taoism: Growth of a Religion*. Translated by Phyllis Brooks. Stanford, Calif., 1997. A lucid introduction to the history of Daoist thought up to the mid-fourteenth century by one of the foremost scholars in the field. Includes an illuminating discussion of the importance of script and scripture in Daoism, and provides information on the evolution of the yin-yang symbol.

Seidel, Anna. "Traces of Han Religion in Funeral Texts Found in Tombs." In *Dokyo to shukyo bunka*, edited by Akizuki Kan'ei, pp. 21–57. Tokyo, 1987. One of the famous late author's pioneering studies of the mortuary cult of the Han dynasty in connection with the early Daoist religion of the Celestial Master movement.

Stevens, Keith. *Chinese Gods: The Unseen Worlds of Spirits and Demons.* London, 1997. An introduction to the icons of popular Chinese religion, richly illustrated and with copious ethnographic commentaries that help readers see the interconnections between Chinese everyday religion and Daoist and Buddhist imagery.

Teiser, Stephen. "'Having Once Died and Returned to Life': Representations of Hell in Medieval China." *Harvard Journal of Asiatic Studies* 48, no. 2 (1988): 433–464. An outstanding iconological study on Chinese Buddhist representations of hell in medieval times.

Verellen, Franciscus. "'Evidential Miracles in Support of Taoism': The Inversion of a Buddhist Apologetic Tradition in Late T'ang Dynasty China." *T'oung Pao* 77/78 (1991–1992): 217–263. An exceedingly interesting account of how a late medieval court Daoist turned the tables on Buddhist polemics against Daoist liturgical and iconographic plagiarism.

Wu Hung. *The Wu Liang Shrine: The Ideology of Early Chinese Pictorial Art.* Berkeley, 1989. An authoritative in-depth study of Han dynasty tomb art and iconography with focus on an offering shrine of 151 CE.

URSULA-ANGELIKA CEDZICH (2005)

ICONOGRAPHY: CONFUCIAN ICONOGRAPHY

Over the centuries, the terms "Confucian" and "Confucianism" have been constructed in different ways, both in China and in the West. The adjective "Confucian" here is used loosely, referring not only to the writings of Confucius (551–479 BCE) but also to that larger body of learning and praxis transmitted in other (often older) ancient classical texts and their later commentaries (which are being compiled to this day). This collection of works is very diverse and its boundaries are difficult to determine. The more important titles, which date to Warring States times (403–221 BCE) or earlier, are the *Book of Odes* (*Shijing*), *Book of Documents* (*Shangshu*), *Book of Rites* (*Liji*), *Master Zuo's Commentary on the Spring and Autumn Annals* (*Chunqiu Zuozhuan*), and the *Analects* of Confucius. Somewhat later is the Han dynasty (206 BCE–220 CE) *Book of Filial Piety* (*Xiaojing*). The term "iconography" is used here in a very general sense to refer to visual depictions of the phenomena recorded in such classical texts, and it also refers to later products of the visual culture that was based in some fashion upon that written legacy.

CONFUCIAN DIVINITIES AND MYTHIC BEINGS. Early texts describe an expansive pantheon of divinities, numinous powers, ideal beings, and culture heroes. These include the Lord on High; heaven and earth; spirits of mountains and rivers; powers of cold, heat, and celestial bodies; mythic suprahuman beings; sage rulers; and ancestral spirits, to name a few.

Historiographic issues. The ways in which these beings were visually understood in pre-Han times, however, is unclear. The pre-Han archaeological record preserves depictions of a wide range of mythic beings. However, they are neither readily identifiable nor easily associated with figures from "Confucian" written works.

More specifically, using painted or sculpted figural images as objects of reverence to depict these beings is not clearly attested in early texts. Later Confucian historiography, beginning at least as early as the Song dynasty (960–1279), insisted that anthropomorphic images of deceased human beings, or of nonhuman divinities, were not used in ritual contexts in Warring States times or earlier. Both written records and the archaeological record as it was then known support this notion.

For example, according to the *Book of Rites,* ancestors were instead "imaged" (*xiang,* a term used as both noun and verb) or represented by a personator (or impersonator) of the dead. The personator (*shi*) was a living descendant of the deceased who temporarily took upon the identity of the departed ancestor, whose laid-out body was simultaneously called a *shi,* during commemorative rites that feted the personator/deceased with food and liquor. The consanguineous relationship between the dead and the personator (the bodies of descendants were moreover considered consubstantial with those of their forebears) often ensured a close physical resemblance between the personator and his or her ancestral "prototype."

Personators were not widely used after the Warring States era, but the notion that an image should resemble its prototype became crucial in later times, when validity of an image was determined by its perceived similitude to its prototype. Some Chinese scholars of the Song and Ming (1368–1644 CE) dynasties believed that the custom of using personators to image the deceased was in fact the origin of the later use of anthropomorphic images in sacrificial offerings. According to this historiographic interpretation, after Warring States times the living descendant was replaced with painted or sculpted images of the deceased, which were held to high standards of semblance.

Such ancestral portraits were widely used by the Song dynasty, and were called *ying,* or "shades." Conceptually, the term *ying* incorporates the meanings of both "shadow" and "reflection," and can be understood as an emanated projection from the human body that is visible in sunlight and reflected in mirrors and other clear or flat surfaces, such as the surface of an ancestral painting used in rites to commemorate the deceased. In folk tales such as the Ming dynasty *Peony Pavilion,* shades sometimes become doppelgängers of the original body and take on lives of their own—even after the prototype body is deceased. Ancestral portraits are still widely used in modern times, although they have been largely replaced by photographs, which ensure greater verisimilitude than paintings. In fact, the modern expression "to photograph" is literally *she ying,* "absorb the shade."

Images in early China. Confucian images often emerge from or appear in mortuary, visionary, or other liminal contexts. One of the earliest known textual descriptions of an image in a Confucian text is of an image (*xiang*) created to depict a man seen in a vision. The *Book of History* records how a bereft ruler went into mourning and underwent the usual austerities of isolation, fasting, silence, and occlusion of the senses. This typically led to visionary experiences, and not unexpectedly the ruler saw in a dream a man whom he understood was to be his helpmate or body-substitute. This helpmate would replace the ruler while he remained secluded in mourning. The ruler ordered an image created of the man he saw and sent it about the kingdom until someone was located who resembled it. This person was then established as the ruler's prime minister. Visions of the deceased, as well as the living, were commonplace in the pre-sacrificial vigils of commemorative offerings presented by pious descendants to their ancestors. It was here that one could see them again, even though they were now in the realm of spirits, which were otherwise formless, invisible, and ineffable.

PHYSICAL APPEARANCE OF CONFUCIAN FIGURES. Virtually nothing is known of the actual physical appearance of particular figures from Confucian lore, or even of Confucius himself.

Han dynasty iconography. By Han times, thinkers and artists began to create their own visual interpretations of important figures. Extant sculpted stone bas-reliefs on shrines, tombs, and steles from the Han and early medieval periods (to 618 CE) depict narrative representations of daily life, historic figures, mythic beings, and prognosticatory omens. These reliefs were didactic in nature and, when located in tombs or shrines, were the backdrop for the mortuary rites convened there.

Confucius appears frequently in these early depictions, never alone and sometimes accompanied by a retinue of disciples and even by half-human, half-animal hybrid creatures. He is yet far from being depicted as the premier sage of the *Analects*—or even as the "uncrowned king" that contemporary philosophical texts claim him to be—but is more commonly shown to be a pedant instructed by recluses, farmers, or even children. He frequently appears in conversation with the legendary Laozi and the child prodigy Xiang Tuo. The assemblage of these three figures constitutes an admixture of mythic accounts from several textual sources, some of which are not "Confucian." In this grouping, Confucius is understood to be a middle-aged man who is the pupil of both the older master ("Lao" means simply "old" or "elderly") and the precocious child. Tales of Confucius's apocryphal conversations with Xiang Tuo appear in Dunhuang literature (a trove of documents dating to Tang times discovered in the Dunhuang caves of Central Asia), and both texts and illustrations of the encounter are still commonly included in yearly almanacs distributed among Chinese populations worldwide.

Other bas-reliefs from Han and early medieval times depict culture heroes and heroines from antiquity: the model rulers Yao, Shun, and Yu; exemplars of filial piety; paragons of female courage; and men of remarkable character. The medium does not allow for "realistic" renderings, and the figures are highly stylized and sometimes only identifiable by virtue of their insignia or textual cartouches. Didactic representations, such as those of the Wu clan shrines in Shandong, depict their subjects in the very act of performing virtuous deeds: a wife allows herself to be murdered in order to save her husband and father; the culture hero Yu digs the waterways that preserved the world from floods; a mother rescues a nephew at the expense of her own child.

Early medieval images. These Han images are murals in shrines, but during the Tang dynasty (618–907), spirits of all kinds also were represented at their "spirit places" (*shenwei*) on temple altars by spirit tablets (*zhu*), which were vertical planks that recorded the name and title of the divinities they represented. Written records indicate that by this time period, Confucius and other famous literati also were represented by two- or three-dimensional anthropomorphic images on altars where they were given state-sponsored food offerings. Debates ensued over how certain figures should be represented; being depicted sitting rather than standing was considered a mark of honor. These arguments paralleled debates over which textual or spiritual traditions should be granted greater authority: personal disciples of Confucius, or later scholars who transmitted the learning of a particular classic. Because few Tang images exist, their actual appearance is unknown.

One of the most widely known depictions of Confucius is traditionally attributed to the famous Tang painter Wu Daozi (fl. 710–760), although the image's authenticity is questionable. This rendering depicts Confucius as a solitary standing figure, hands held at his chest. A long beard attests to his age and seniority; he is no longer a pupil who bows politely to seek wisdom from others, but is an autonomous, iconic figure presented visually as a model of authoritative gravitas. It is this Confucius who is the subject of modern sculptures in Chinatowns throughout the world.

In other Tang and Song renderings, Confucius is no longer accompanied by his "teacher," Xiang Tuo, who has instead been replaced by Confucius's favorite disciple, Yan Hui. In contrast to the child prodigy, Yan Hui was noted for his humility. Elsewhere, Confucius is found in poses similar to those of the Buddhist layman Vimalakīrti: he sits on a raised platform and holds a fan. However, instead of an entourage of monks and *bodhisattvas,* he is accompanied by his disciples. These images exist as narrative scrolls on paper and silk, and also as stone carvings displayed in temples.

POLITICAL AND SOCIETAL ACCEPTANCE. Some Song scholars began to express discomfort with anthropomorphic renderings of both historic figures and spirits of natural phenomena, particularly when they were used in ritual contexts.

Images in the Song dynasty. The brothers Cheng Hao (1032–1085) and Cheng Yi (1033–1107) questioned the use of ancestral portraits, especially those wanting in verisimilitude. In addition, Chen Chun (1159–1223) ridiculed the practice of depicting the spirit of sacred Mount Tai as a human king. Taking anthropomorphizing to its logical conclusion, Chen wondered where such a geographically isolated mountain range was likely to find a queen. Distaste for perceived Buddhist influences on Chinese practices, and for the charlatanry that passed for Buddhism, was not far below the surface. Zhu Xi (1130–1200) was troubled that images of Confucius were depicted in ahistorical Buddhist poses, and Cheng Hao ordered the decapitation of a Buddhist statue that gained notoriety by purportedly emitting rays of light.

Elsewhere, artists of the Song dynasty found their subjects in classical texts. Such famous artists as Li Gonglin (c. 1041–1106) created illustrations for the *Book of Filial Piety*, and others illustrated the *Women's Book of Filial Piety*. These works were created in the hand scroll format: a long scroll of paper or silk about one foot in height and several yards in length was illustrated alternately with text passages and accompanying illustrations. Intended for the moral edification and aesthetic appreciation of the viewer, the scroll would be unfurled slowly and the images viewed one at a time, perhaps with the help of an instructor. The twelfth-century painter Ma Hezhi and his calligraphic collaborator, Song emperor Gaozong (1107–1187; r. 1127–1162) chose as their subject the verses of the ancient *Book of Odes*. The cryptic verses and liturgical hymns of the *Odes* were believed to embody the epitome of human sensibility, and were thus a fitting subject for the ruler himself.

For millennia, vessels of bronze and objects of jade have been the vehicles for presenting food offerings and displaying pious sentiments to spiritual beings, and even illustrations of those objects bear iconic status. Several compilations of woodblock illustrations, depicting ritual objects, were created during the Song dynasty. Thereafter, this genre remained popular for centuries. Some of these texts were created for an audience of connoisseurs and antiquarians. However, others were intended as handbooks for those who officiated at rites or were used as visual inventories of sacred objects appreciated for their own sake. The display, arrangement, directionality, and number of particular objects used in ritual performances was of great concern, and Ming (1368–1644 CE) and Qing (1644–1911 CE) dynastic records provide line illustrations that document the placement of each goblet and saucer for spiritual beings of all ranks.

Images in later imperial times. In the Ming, scholars began to question more fundamentally the use of anthropomorphic images in sacrificial offerings. To some thinkers, human-shaped images of clay or paint created by mere artisans blasphemed the subtle formlessness of spirits. Images that did not look like their prototypes were considered invalid. Images of Confucius, for example, could not possibly look like Confucius, for none of them even looked like one another. Others presented xenophobic arguments against Buddhist customs imported from India and against Mongolian Buddhist tendencies (China had been ruled by Mongol people in the thirteenth and early fourteenth centuries) toward iconophilia. By the 1530s, sentiment against anthropomorphic images in temples to Confucius and other literati was so strong that they were ordered eliminated by imperial decree. Sculpted images of clay were replaced by wooden tablets that bore only the names and titles of the deceased. In officially sponsored temples, images remain largely absent from temple altars to this day, although during the late Ming dynasty the ban was occasionally circumvented by hiding images inside temple walls.

Paradoxically, even as sculpted images were being cleansed from the altars of officially sponsored temples, other kinds of images flourished. The expansion of the publishing industry resulted in an unprecedented variety of woodblock illustrations. Many illustrated collections that depicted important events (largely apocryphal) in the life of Confucius were printed, as were illustrated books of filial piety and ritual paraphernalia. Another popular genre was collected volumes of portraits of famous people: historical figures, rulers and ministers, sages and worthies, local heroes, filial children, and exemplars of women's virtues.

In late imperial times Confucius also was popularly depicted in "Three Teachings" images that illustrated how the Confucian, Daoist, and Buddhist traditions (represented by Confucius, Laozi, and Śākyamuni Buddha, respectively) were deeply interrelated. Not everyone believed that Buddhism was a heterodox religion that profaned the teachings of the sages of ancient China. To make the philosophical point that the three traditions were different manifestations of a common substratum, the three figures are sometimes shown schematically as intertwining shapes that form one body, or *ti* (a term that can be applied to a human body as well as a canonical corpus). Other depictions recall the Han representation of Confucius, Laozi, and the child Xiang Tuo. However, in the late imperial images Xiang Tuo is replaced by an infant named Śākyamuni, who is held in Laozi's arms.

During the Qing dynasty, images of Confucius were largely proscribed from official temples and shrines to Confucian sages and worthies, but they were not eliminated at the Kong (the Chinese family name of Confucius) ancestral temples in Qufu in Shandong province, which also maintained a collection of family portraits of "the Sage's" descendants. During the early twentieth century, there was a revival of interest in visual depictions of Confucius. At this time, Confucian associations from around the world returned to Qufu to locate "real" images of Confucius that could be duplicated and distributed in large quantities to promote the values of the *Analects*. The search for verisimilitude was partially fueled by the development of photography.

Twentieth-century trends. During the first half of the twentieth century, political regimes employed images of Confucius or of the Kong family temples to promote their own agendas. In China, the facade of a temple also is understood as a *mian*, or face. Several governments featured Confucius's visage, or that of his temple at Qufu, on their currency. By doing so, they attempted to fortify their own cultural legitimacy and establish a cultural symbol that was palatable to the hundreds of diverse cultural and ethnic groups within China. Even the Japanese puppet government of Manchuria adopted Confucius on its currency, thus claiming sovereignty over the cultural homeland of Shandong.

With the establishment of the avowedly iconoclastic People's Republic of China in 1949, however, religious and cultural symbols of all kinds (other than those promoted by the Communist Party) were erased in the name of revolution. Even though thinkers such as Kuang Yaming tried to depict Confucius as a "man of the people," "Confucianism" became synonymous with cultural stagnation and economic backwardness. In the civil strife of the Cultural Revolution, the Confucian images at Qufu were disemboweled and paraded around the town in dunce caps, much as if they were living entities. Communist propaganda distributed to adults and children depicted Confucius as a hideous, deceitful, and decrepit old man who was deservedly punished for his reactionary ways by muscular young peasants and laborers.

CONTEMPORARY DEVELOPMENTS. By the end of the twentieth century, revolutionary zeal was supplanted by financial ambition as China became a larger force in the world economy. As China reshaped its image of itself as a nation among equals, it rehabilitated its own culture heroes. Municipal governments and schools refashioned their own civic monuments and replaced statues of Mao with public sculptures of famous world figures from the sciences, the arts, and philosophy. In addition to Newton, Copernicus, Einstein, and Beethoven, these included representations of Confucius. In cinema, the mythic life of Confucius has been featured in several lengthy television series and feature films, where he is often depicted as a virtuous man who successfully withstands adversity.

Confucian temples in Taiwan continue to preserve the Ming tradition of using tablets instead of images, and their walls are dominated by textual and calligraphic icons, when decorated by anything at all. Blood-red tablets mark the names of hundreds of famous literati and invoke their bodies of written work. Inside shrines, altars stand before oversized calligraphed renditions of the *Great Learning,* clearly marking the text as an object of reverence.

In Beijing, which has been an imperial capital since the fifteenth century, the presence of numinous powers also is marked by simple tablets, as well as extensive architectural structures and sacred spaces. The late-imperial Temple of Heaven complex at the southern end of the north-south axis of the city marks the sacrality of the earth with a large open-air circular altar; of heaven, with a smaller, closed structure roofed in blue tiles. The larger Hall of Yearly Harvests architecturally represents the intersection of time and space: the numerical arrangement of columns and shrines marks the four seasons, twelve months, and calendrical days of the year. This complex is oriented with additional temples to the sun and moon in other quadrants of the city's cosmography, making all of Beijing a sacred space shared by humans and spiritual powers.

SEE ALSO Chinese Religion, overview article; Confucianism in Japan; Confucianism in Korea; Confucianism, overview article; Confucius; Temple, article on Confucian Temple Compounds.

BIBLIOGRAPHY

For early depictions of the human body in Chinese art, see Helmut Brinker's "The Concept of the Human Body in Chinese Art," in *Symbolik des menschlichen Leibes,* edited by Paul Michel (Bern, Switzerland, 1995), pp. 49–81. Bas-reliefs of the Wu clan shrine are explored in Wu Hung's *The Wu Liang Shrine: The Ideology of Early Chinese Pictorial Art* (Stanford, Calif., 1989). For ancestral portraits, see *Worshipping the Ancestors: Chinese Commemorative Portraits* by Jan Stuart and Evelyn S. Rawski (Washington, D.C., 2001) and Patricia Ebrey's "Portrait Sculptures in Imperial Ancestral Rites in Song China," in *T'oung Pao* 83 (1997), pp. 42–92. Song depictions of Confucian sages and texts are discussed in Julia K. Murray's "The Hangzhou *Portraits of Confucius and Seventy-two Disciples* (*Sheng xian tu*): Art in the Service of Politics" (*Art Bulletin* 74, 1992, pp. 7–18), as well as her *Ma Hezhi and the Illustration of the* Book of Odes (Cambridge, U.K., 1993). For the *Classic of Filial Piety,* see Richard M. Barnhart's *Li Kung-lin's* Classic of Filial Piety (New York, 1993). For late-imperial narrative scenes in the life of Confucius, see Julia K. Murray's "Varied Views of the Sage: Illustrated Narratives of the Life of Confucius" in Thomas A. Wilson, ed., *On Sacred Grounds: Culture, Society, Politics, and the Formation of the Cult of Confucius* (Cambridge, Mass., 2002), pp. 222–264. For Chinese pictorial collections of sculptures, paintings, and architectural monuments related to the Confucian tradition see the *Rujia tuzhi* (A collection of Confucian images) compiled by Xu Lingyun et al. (Shandong province, China, 1994) and *Dazai Kongzi* (O Great Confucius), edited by Zhang Zuoyao (Hong Kong, 1991). The art and architecture of the temple of Confucius in Qufu is documented in *Qufu Kongmiao Jianzhu* (Architecture of the Confucian temple in Qufu), edited by the Qufu Cultural Administration (Beijing, 1987). For the religious and philosophical significance of images of Confucius, see Deborah Sommer, "Destroying Confucius: Iconoclasm in the Confucian Temple," in Thomas A. Wilson, ed., *On Sacred Grounds: Culture, Society, Politics, and the Formation of the Cult of Confucius* (Cambridge, Mass., 2002), pp. 95–133. Revivals of Confucius as a subject matter for artists is documented in the *Jinian Kongzi danchen 2550 zhounian quanguo meishu zuopin Zhongguohua zuopin ji* (Collection of Chinese paintings from the national art exhibition to commemorate the 2,550th birthday anniversary of Confucius), edited by the editorial committee of the national art exhibition to commemorate the 2,550th birthday anniversary of Confucius (Beijing, 1999). For a European exhibition featuring works related to Confucius and time, see *Confucius: a l'aube de humanisme chinois,* edited by Jean-Paul Desroches (Paris, 2003). For more theoretical studies of visuality in China, see Craig Clunas's *Pictures and Visuality in Early Modern China* (Princeton, N.J., 1997).

DEBORAH SOMMER (2005)

ICONOGRAPHY: JEWISH ICONOGRAPHY [FIRST EDITION]

Jewish iconography, whether actually represented in works of art or existing only as traditional imagery (and occasionally referred to in literature), was determined from the first by the biblical "prohibition of images." This prohibition, transmitted in the Bible in several versions, could be understood (1) as forbidding, in a religious context, all images, regardless of their subject matter (*Ex.* 20:4, *Dt.* 4:15–18), or (2) specifically forbidding the depiction of God and the ritual use of such a depiction as an idol (*Dt.* 27:15). While the first interpretation of the prohibition did not prevail (the Bible itself provides evidence of this in *1 Kgs.* 6:23–29, *Ez.* 8:5–12), the other was consistently implemented. Possibly the most striking feature of Jewish iconography throughout the ages is the systematic avoidance of any depiction of the figure of God. To a large extent this is also true for saintly personages: though hagiographical literature emerged in Judaism, it was not accompanied by any visual imagery of saints. From the beginning, then, Jewish religious iconography developed in marked contrast to the traditions predominant in the Christian West. Since the loss of political independence in 71 CE, Jewish imagery could not be formed within the framework of a state art and did not enjoy any official support for its symbols. As the art and imagery of a religious minority, however, it flourished in the Diaspora throughout the ages. The iconography that emerged within these limitations developed mainly in a few periods and thematic cycles.

HELLENISM. The meeting between Judaism and the Greek world—a process that lasted from early Hellenism to late antiquity (roughly, second century BCE to fifth century CE)—resulted in a body of religious images. While the Mishnah and Talmud were being compiled (roughly second to sixth centuries CE) Jewish communities produced a large number of representations, which have been uncovered in Jewish remains (mainly synagogues and burial places) from Tunisia to Italy and eastward to the Euphrates; sites in Israel are particularly rich. Occasionally this imagery includes human figures, either in biblical scenes or in pagan myths (frequently the image of Helios, the Greek sun god).

More often, however, these survivals show objects with definite ritual connotations. Most prominent are the seven-branched *menorah* (candelabrum), Aron ha-Qodesh (the Ark of the Covenant), *lulav* and *etrog* (palm branch and citron), and shofar (ceremonial animal horn). These objects (which reflect the crystallization of Jewish ritual) have no strict hierarchy, but the *menorah*, and the Ark of the Covenant, representing the law itself, are more important than the others. When both are shown together, they always occupy the central place. Besides such explicitly ritual objects, Jewish remains abound in artistic motifs, taken over from Hellenistic art, whose symbolic character is obscure. A good example is the vine, most likely derived from contemporary Dionysian imagery and often found in Jewish cemeteries. But whether in Jewish communities it carried the meaning of salvation that it had in the pagan world is a matter of dispute. Some modern scholars tend to see these motifs as "decoration" devoid of articulate symbolic meanings; others, especially Goodenough, attribute established symbolic meanings to them.

MIDDLE AGES. In the European Middle Ages, especially between the thirteenth and fifteenth centuries, Jewish religious imagery developed further. The illumination of manuscripts is the central aesthetic medium of the period; of particular significance are the manuscripts produced in Spain, Italy, and Germany. All these manuscripts are of a ritual nature, the most important groups being the Haggadah for Passover and prayer books for the holidays, the *maḥzor.* The illuminations (and later, printed illustrations) represent many ritual utensils, but they also include, more often than in Jewish art of other periods and media, human figures, especially in biblical scenes. The iconographic repertoire is enlarged by mythical motifs, attesting to messianic beliefs. Among these motifs are the legendary beasts (such as the *shor ha-bar,* a kind of wild ox), on which the just will feast on the day of redemption; these are particularly prominent in manuscripts produced in Germany. The future Temple that, according to common belief, is to be built after the redemption, is another frequent mythical motif, especially in Spanish and German manuscripts; it is sometimes patterned after contemporary Christian models. Both the temple building and the ritual utensils (the latter sometimes rendered on the opening folios of Bible manuscripts produced in Spain) may be taken as expressions of "the ardent hope and belief" to see the "restored Temple in the messianic future." In countries under Islamic rule, Jewish art readily adapted the aniconic attitude and the repertoire of decorative motifs common among the Muslims, although in literature, visual imagery continued to thrive in the form of metaphors and descriptions.

QABBALISTIC SYMBOLISM. The qabbalistic tradition is a special field of iconographic creation. Qabbalistic literature abounds in visual metaphors, since the authors often tend to express (or to hide) their thoughts and mysteries in visual images and descriptions of supposed optical experiences. Since the beginnings of Jewish mysticism in late antiquity, a continuous tradition of visual symbols has persisted. Considerably enriched in the Middle Ages, and in the seventeenth century, this tradition remained unbroken up to, and including, Hasidic literature. The central image of qabbalistic symbolism is the Tree of Sefirot. The godhead is imagined as structured in ten spheres, each of them representing a "divine quality" (Heb., *sefirah*). The shape and place of the spheres, and the spatial relationships between them, are firmly established in the qabbalistic imagination. The overall pattern vaguely resembles a tree (hence the name), but the basic character of the image is abstract rather than figurative. Though the Tree of Sefirot has frequently been depicted (mainly in simple form, primarily in popular printed editions) and has exerted some influence on contemporary Jewish painters, the image is not primarily an artistic one; rather, it is still widely known from the literary sources.

Qabbalistic literature produced other visual symbols, among them the images of broken vessels, scattered sparks, Adam Qadmon (primordial man) as a figure of God, and so forth. Scholem has also shown that an elaborate color symbolism emerged in the qabbalistic literature. In modern civil societies, Jewish iconography is still in the process of formation and has not yet been properly studied.

See Also Biblical Temple; Qabbalah; Synagogue.

Bibliography

For the imagery of the Hebrew Bible (though not necessarily in art only) still useful is Maurice H. Farbridge's *Studies in Biblical and Semitic Symbolism* (1923; reprint, New York, 1970). Erwin R. Goodenough's *Jewish Symbols in the Greco-Roman Period*, 13 vols. (New York, 1953–1968), has a rich collection of photographs; the text is stimulating, albeit sometimes arguable. Mainly for the Middle Ages, see Jacob Leveen's *The Hebrew Bible in Art* (1944; reprint, New York, 1974). For early modern times, see *Beauty in Holiness: Studies in Jewish Customs and Ceremonial Art*, edited by Joseph Gutmann (New York, 1970), a catalog of Jewish artifacts from the Prague Museum shown at the Jewish Museum in New York.

Much can be learned from the discussion of single problems. See, for example, *The Temple of Solomon*, edited by Joseph Gutmann (Missoula, Mont., 1976). Another individual problem is discussed by Zofia Ameisenowa in "The Tree of Life in Jewish Iconography," *Journal of the Warburg and Courtauld Institutes* 2 (1938–1939): 326–345. Qabbalistic imagery is best discussed in Gershom Scholem's *Major Trends in Jewish Mysticism*, 3d rev. ed. (New York, 1954), esp. pp. 205–243. A highly interesting study of a particular subject in qabbalistic symbolism is Scholem's "Farben und ihre Symbolik in der jüdischen Überlieferung und Mystik," *Eranos Yearbook* 41 (1974): 1–49, *The Realms of Colour* (with English and French summaries).

Moshe Barasch (1987)

ICONOGRAPHY: JEWISH ICONOGRAPHY [FURTHER CONSIDERATIONS]

In his 1987 *Encyclopedia of Religion* article, Israeli art historian Moshe Barasch surveyed some of the important issues and artistic genres in the history of Jewish art as they were understood by historians of Jewish art of his generation. Within that community, scholars were often reacting against a deep prejudice against Jewish art—and even the possibility of Jewish art—that was deeply ingrained in the Western discourses on art and on the relation of art and Judaism. This reaction against prevalent notions that Judaism was aniconic (without symbols or icons), iconophobic, or otherwise antithetical to art resulted in the discovery, publication, and exhibition of artifacts of Jewish art and archaeology.

Apologetics and Early Research. With few exceptions, late nineteenth- and twentieth-century scholarship did not face the prevailing prejudice against Jewish artistic production head on. Rather, it was refuted indirectly through discovery, scholarly publication, and the public exhibition of Jewish art (often in museums established by Jewish communities for the purpose). Early scholarship was carried out mainly by non-Jewish scholars, generally with Jewish financial backing. This was thought to afford this research with greater veracity. Notable among scholarly writings of this early period was art historian J. von Schlosser's pathbreaking work on Hebrew manuscripts, *Die Haggadah von Sarajevo: Eine spanisch-judische Bilderhandschrift des Mittelalters* (1898), with Jewish scholar D. H. Müller and a contribution by David Kaufmann; classicists Heinrich Kohl and Carl Watzinger's *Antike Synagogen in Galilaea* (1916); and Heinrich Frauberger's revolutionary work on Jewish ceremonial art, *Üeber Alte Kuntusgegenstände in Synagoge und Haus* (1903).

Since World War I the majority of scholarship has been carried out by Jews, usually within the contexts of Judaic studies. The prominent exceptions all focused on the Greco-Roman period: Carl Kraeling's exceptional final report of the Dura Europos synagogue, Kurt Weitzmann's interest in this material for the study of early Christian art, and Erwin R. Goodenough's provocative *Jewish Symbols in the Greco-Roman Period* (1953–1967). Zionist and Israeli scholarship has been particularly prominent as Jewish art scholarship was formulated in nationalist terms. E. L. Sukenik's studies of Jewish archaeology—particularly his discovery of ancient synagogues and Second Temple (536 BCE–70 CE) period tombs—and Mordecai Narkiss's studies of ceremonial art and his project of building the Bezalel National Museum (now part of the Israel Museum in Jerusalem) are notable, particularly Narkiss's *The Hanukkah Lamp* (1939, in Hebrew). His son Bezalel Narkiss's work during the second half of the century focused on medieval manuscripts and the assembly of an *Index of Jewish Art* to serve as an adjunct to the Princeton Index of Christian Art, which is the main project of his Center for Jewish Art at the Hebrew University of Jerusalem. Narkiss founded *The Journal of Jewish Art* (now *Jewish Art*) in 1974 as an annual, although for the last decade it has appeared less frequently. At midcentury important contributions were made, particularly by expatriate Germanophones in America and Israel—most prominently by Rachel Wischnitzer, Franz Landsberger, Michael Avi-Yonah, and Stephen S. Kayser. More recently, Isaiah Shachar, Joseph Gutmann, Rachel Hachlili, Abraham Kampf, Carole Krinsky, Shalom Sabar, Vivian Mann and others have made Jewish art from antiquity to the modern period widely available and known. Much of this scholarship has focused on primary publication of artifacts (and in Mann's case, also primary texts) and building the corpus of Jewish art. The varied audiences for whom scholars wrote are significant. Some focused on academic Jewish studies contexts (e.g., M. Narkiss, Wischnitzer, Kayser, Kraeling, Shachar, Gutmann, Sabar, and Mann), others located their work within general art history and archaeology (e.g., Avi-Yonah, Kraeling, Weitzmann, B. Narkiss, Gutmann, Krinsky, and Hachlili), and still others sought to integrate it within the history of religions approach (e.g., Goodenough).

More recently social historians with less of an object-focus have developed interests in Jewish art. Most prominent among these are Richard I. Cohen and Ezra Mendelsohn. Explicit reflection on the study of Jewish art has been rare. Perhaps the most interesting conceptualization developed during the first half of the twentieth century was presented by German/Israeli art historian Heinrich Strauss, who, against the tide, referred to Jewish art as a "minority art." Most reflection tended to be apologetic, as in Cecil Roth's introduction to his seminal widely influential edited volume, *Jewish Art,* first published in 1956 and still in print in Hebrew. Roth's anthology, which begins with the Biblical period and concludes with then-contemporary art and architecture, was intended to serve as an introduction to Jewish art through the ages. He begins this monumental project with the apology that "the conception of Jewish art may appear to some to be a contradiction in terms: for there is a widespread impression that in the past visual art was made impossible among the Jews by the uncompromising prohibition in the Ten Commandments. . ." (Roth, 1961, p. 11).

As late as 1988 archaeologist Rachel Hachlili introduced her important study, *Ancient Jewish Art and Archaeology in the Land of Israel* with the confession: "For some time now I have felt the need for a comprehensive study, which would support my thesis for the existence of an ancient Jewish art." (Hachlili, 1988, p. xxi). For most of the twentieth century the backdrop for Jewish study of this material was often the need to prove and legitimize its very existence. This project has been intertwined with the opening and expansion of Jewish museums (of which there are now around fifty in the United States alone), the Center for Jewish Art, excavation of archaeological sites, the publication of popular books, and the use of Jewish art as a source of symbols by the State of Israel. Ideology has generally not impinged on the quality of scholarship. During the closing decades of the century the apologetic impulse was in steep decline both in the public sphere and in scholarship.

Beginning during the mid-1990s and continuing into the twenty-first century, a major reevaluation of the place of Jewish art in Western culture has been undertaken by Annabelle Wharton, Catherine Soussloff, Kalman Bland, Margaret Olin, Yaakov Shavit, Avner Holtzman and other scholars. This reassessment is very much in motion, although it has already begun to receive some critical response. Writing in the postmodern mode, each of these scholars has focused on the historiography of Jewish art, setting scholarship of the late nineteenth and twentieth centuries within the general discourses on art and Judaism during this period. This scholarship follows a general trend in history writing during this period, in which reevaluation of humanities scholarship across the spectrum has been a major preoccupation.

The contemporary art world's ambivalent attitude toward Judaism was addressed in Norman Kleebatt's *Too Jewish: Challenging Traditional Identities,* a major traveling exhibition of contemporary art with Jewish themes organized by the Jewish Museum in New York in 1996. Annabelle Wharton (1994) was the first to address these issues in an American academic context, focusing on the colonialist ways that the Dura Europos synagogue has been studied since its discovery in 1932 and the ways that these approaches have colored interpretation. The academic watershed, however, was Catherine Soussloff's edited volume, *Jewish Identity in Modern Art History,* published in 1999. The assembled studies, composed by historians and art historians (although significantly, no specialists in Jewish art) suggest the absolute ambivalence (if not contempt) that art historical scholarship, often carried out by Jews, has shown toward Judaism and Jewish art. The importance of this volume is in the fact that it brought together scholars working in diverse areas of art history to shine a focusing lens on the issue of art historical constructs of Jewish visual culture. This early statement of the problem was the harbinger of the first monographs to approach Western conceptions of Jewish art.

Kalman Bland, a contributor to Soussloff's volume and a colleague of Wharton's at Duke University produced the first monograph on Jews and art. Bland discussed the nineteenth century philosophical roots of this phenomenon in his *The Artless Jew: Medieval and Modern Affirmations and Denials of the Visual* (2000). Still schematic in its approach, Bland succeeds in tracing the denial of Jewish visuality to the thought of Immanuel Kant (1724–1804), who praised Jews for being aniconic like German Protestants, and G. W. F. Hegel (1770–1831), who damned them for the same supposed aniconicism. Bland also began to show ways that Jews of different allegiances responded to these approaches. In general, classical Reform Jews, who denied Jewish peoplehood also denied the existence of Jewish art, a national art being impossible for a nonpeople. This conception brought Judaism close to Protestant ideals. The stakes in Jewish aniconism were large for Protestants, who believed that the earliest Christians were aniconic—like the ancient Jews, their religion corrupted by pagan influences, resulted in Christian art, and the "idolatry" of the Catholic church. Jews committed to Jewish peoplehood (both Zionist and non-Zionists), however, reacted strongly to the notion that Judaism was artless and set out to prove this paradigm wrong. These Jews found support in Catholic praise of ancient Jewish art, which Catholic scholars saw as the predecessor to their own artistic tradition. It is not surprising that the earliest Jewish art scholarship was centered in Catholic Budapest, where Kaufmann and his students worked within a generally supportive intellectual environment—and not in Protestant lands.

Margaret Olin, a contributor to both Kleebatt's and Souseloff's volumes, published *The Nation Without Art: Examining Modern Discourses on Jewish Art* in 2002. This monograph presents case studies in the historiography of art history regarding Jews. Olin's discussions of nineteenth and twentieth century conceptions in the German academy and

Jewish responses to this artlessness are particularly relevant. Olin's main focus is the notion that each nation has a unique and distinctive national art (with its own style and iconography), and the problems created by such classifications. For Judaism in particular, notions of Jewish peoplehood and nationality were basic to the construction of Jewish identity during the nineteenth and twentieth centuries and hence the existence or nonexistence of Jewish art was an important statement of Jewish self-understanding and the ways that Jews were viewed by the majority Western cultures. Olin focuses on Zionist responses to Jewish artlessness, David Kaufmann's early scholarship on Jewish art, and art historical approaches to the Dura Europos synagogue, as well as attitudes toward more contemporary art by Jews. Her study of Dura is particularly insightful, exposing a deeply anti-Semitic strain in European scholarship (associated with proto-Nazi scholar Josef Strzygowski, who placed the origins of Christian art firmly in the East, in a Jewish context) and ways that it influenced scholarship on Jewish art at midcentury (particularly by the philo-Semitic German expatriate art historian, Kurt Weitzmann). Her discussions of more contemporary manifestations, as expressed in studies of Clement Greenberg, George Segal, and others point to the continuation of this phenomenon through the second half of the century.

Parallel to the development of this corpus, Yaakov Shavit (1992; 1997) followed by Avner Holtzman (1999) has focused on ways that Zionists conceptualized art against the background of Eastern European Jewish ambivalence toward non-Jewish art forms and the place of art in Jewish-Palestinian culture of the pre-State era before 1948.

SECOND WAVE. The second wave of studies dealing with these issues is being written by historians who are applying the insights of previous studies directly to the study of ancient art and religion. In a series of articles influenced by Olin and others, British classicist and art historian Jaś Elsner has moved from a rather negative position vis-à-vis Jewish art and its relation with Christian art during late antiquity to a position that subsumes Jewish, Christian, and pagan art together under a broader category of Late Antique art. According to Elsner's new approach, Jewish art is not merely a backdrop to Christian art but an equal. Steven Fine's *Art and Judaism During the Greco-Roman Period* (2005) discusses ways that the "artless Jew" trope affected historiography of ancient Judaism, particularly the work of E. R. Goodenough, M. Smith, and Smith's students (among them Jacob Neusner, S. J. D. Cohen, and Lee Levine). The assumption that Jews are artless was transformed by Goodenough into the notion that whereas Jews created art, the Talmudic rabbis were anti-art. Extant Jewish art was therefore often conceived as nonrabbinic. Reevaluating ancient Jewish attitudes toward art as reflected in both literary and archeological sources, Fine demonstrates coalescence between Jewish and general Greco-Roman art except in areas in which Jewish values (which were scripture-based, but open to varying interpretations and circumstances) were at variance with general attitudes.

Recent developments in the historiography of Jewish art have changed the conceptual frame within which this discipline functions. By exposing the often anti-Semitic (and sometimes anti-rabbinic) roots of many of these conceptions, scholars of the late twentieth and early twenty-first century have created a level playing field in which the study of Jewish material culture may be pursued without engaging in the types of implicit and overt apologetics that were so often necessitated during the nineteenth and twentieth centuries.

BIBLIOGRAPHY

Bland, Kalman P. *The Artless Jew: Medieval and Modern Affirmations and Denials of the Visual.* Princeton, N.J., 2000. The first monograph on Western discourse on Jewish art, Bland also briefly surveys Jewish attitudes toward the visual, as well as selected issues of aesthetics in Jewish thought.

Cohen, Richard I. *Jewish Icons: Art and Society in Modern Europe.* Berkeley, Calif., 1998. Cohen presents historical case studies of the reception of Jewish art during the nineteenth century.

Elsner, Jaś. *Imperial Rome and Christian Triumph: The Art of the Roman Empire AD 100–450.* Oxford, 1998.

Elsner, Jaś. "Cultural Resistance and the Visual Image: The Case of Dura Europos." *Classical Philology* 96, no. 3 (2001): 269–304.

Elsner, Jaś. "The Birth of Late Antiquity: Riegl and Strzygowski in 1901." *Art History* 25, no. *3* (2002): 358–379.

Elsner, Jaś. "Archaelogies and Agendas: Reflections on Late Ancient Jewish Art and Early Christian Art." *Journal of Roman Studies* 93 (2003): 114–128. Influenced by Olin and others, Elsner's discussion of ancient Jewish art reflects a marked shift from the traditional anti-Jewish bias of art history to a far more reflective stance.

Fine, Steven. *Art and Judaism During the Greco-Roman Period: Toward a New "Jewish Archaeology."* Cambridge, U.K., 2005. Fine provides a thorough analysis of the ways that Jewish art and Jewish archaeology relation has been constructed in America, Palestine/Israel, and Europe against the backdrop of Western thought. The work of Sukenik and Goodenough are contextualized.

Frauberger, Heinrich. *Üeber Alte Kuntusgegenstände in Synagoge und Haus.* Frankfürt, Germany, 1903.

Goodenough, Erwin R. *Jewish Symbols in the Greco-Roman Period.* New York, 1953–1968. Goodenough's assemblage of Jewish archaeological remains from antiquity was important for the development of interest in this material beyond Jewish studies circles. His theory, that this material bespeaks an ancient nonrabbinic "mystical Judaism" that created this art, while widely refuted, occasioned a profound reevaluation of previous paradigms for the interpretation of ancient Judaism.

Hachlili, Rachel. *Ancient Jewish Art and Archaeology in the Land of Israel.* Leiden, 1988.

Holtzman, Avner. *Aesthetics and National Revival—Hebrew Literature Against the Visual Arts* [in Hebrew]. Tel Aviv, 1999. Holtzman, focusing mainly on literary sources, nuances and expands on Yaakov Shavit's discussion of art within early Zionism.

Kohl, Heinrich, and Carl Watzinger. *Antike Synagogen in Galilaea.* Leipzig, 1916.

Mann, Vivian, ed. *Jewish Texts on the Visual Arts.* Cambridge, U.K., 2000. Mann translates and comments on important Jewish texts that exemplify academic reflection on the place of art in Judaism.

Mendelsohn, Ezra. *Painting a People: Maurycy Gottlieb and Jewish Art.* Hanover, N.H., 2002. A historical study of an important late-nineteenth-century Jewish painter.

Narkiss, Mordecai. *The Hanukkah Lamp* [in Hebrew]. Jerusalem, 1939.

Olin, Margaret. *The Nation Without Art: Examining Modern Discourses on Jewish Art.* Omaha, Neb., 2001. Olin focuses on the art historical discourse on art and Judaism, showing how this discipline encouraged and developed the notion that the Jews are "the nation without art. "

Roth, Cecil, and Z. Ephron. *Jewish Art* [in Hebrew]. Tel Aviv, 1956/57.

Roth, Cecil, ed. *Jewish Art.* Revised by B. Narkiss. 2d ed. London, 1971. A compendium of eighteen articles on Jewish art from Biblical times to the mid-twentieth century, this volume is still the standard reference work for the study of Jewish art.

Sabar, Shalom. "The Study of Jewish Art and Its Development" [in Hebrew]. *Mahanayim* 11 (1995): 264–275. Sabar surveys the history of scholarship on Jewish art from the nineteenth century to the 1990s, and is particularly strong in his description of Germanophone scholars.

Shavit, Yaakov. *Athens in Jerusalem: Classical Antiquity and Hellenism in the Making of the Modern Secular Jew.* Tel Aviv, 1992; reprint, Portland, Ore., 1997. Shavit's work was the first monograph to approach the place of art in Zionist culture.

Sousloff, Catherine, ed. *Jewish Identity in Modern Art History.* Berkeley, Calif., 1999. A watershed in the study of attitudes toward art and Judaism in art history, Sousloff's volume presents a broad discussion of the place of Jews and of Judaism in the historiography of art.

Von Schlosser, J., and D. H. Müller. *Die Haggadah von Sarajevo: Eine spanisch-judische Bilderhandschrift des Mittelalters.* With a contribution by David Kauffmann. Vienna, 1898.

Weitzmann, Kurt, and Herbert L. Kessler. *The Frescoes of the Dura Synagogue and Christian Art.* Washington, D.C., 1990. Weitzmann, and his student, Kessler, treat the Dura synagogue within the context of Christian art, postulating that this building is a missing link between a hypothesized Jewish tradition of manuscript illumination and early Christian art.

Wharton, Annabel Jane. "Good and Bad Images from the Synagogue of Dura Europos: Contexts, Subtexts, Intertexts." *Art History* 17, no. 1 (1994): 1–25.

Wharton, Annabel Jane. *Refiguring the Post Classical City: Dura Europos, Jerash, Jerusalem, and Ravenna.* Cambridge, U.K., 1995. Wharton was the first American scholar to discuss problematic Western views of Jewish art, focusing on the Dura Europos synagogue.

STEVEN FINE (2005)

ICONOGRAPHY: CHRISTIAN ICONOGRAPHY

For the greater part of Christian history, the church's images have been drawn from its liturgical texts, scriptures, and pedagogy, and they have been rendered in the styles of the particular age and place the images served. In modern times, the sources for Christian iconography have expanded to include psychological, sociopolitical, and nontraditional elements.

The most distinctive characteristic of Christian iconography is its preoccupation with the person and role of Jesus Christ (and his followers). The image of Christ as earthly founder and heavenly savior is central to the religion, especially insofar as the church defines itself as the body of Christ on earth. Thus the changing repertoire of images of Jesus and his followers reveals the nature of the religion in its many cultural and historical manifestations.

EARLY CHRISTIANITY. Early Christian art surviving from the first half of the third century reflects the diversity of the Greco-Roman context from which it emerged. The earliest iconographic figures, borrowed directly from late antique conventions, were placed in new compositional and environmental settings on jewelry and other minor arts. For example, the common pose of the shepherd Endymion, a reclining male nude resting on one elbow with ankles crossed, was the type borrowed by artists to depict the Old Testament figure of Jonah resting under an arbor. For Christians, Jonah represented an image of resurrection and, as such, was used in funerary paintings and low-relief carvings on sarcophagi. Old Testament figures used in early Christian iconography appeared almost exclusively as typologies of Christ and his followers.

The earliest images of Christ were concerned with his person and role on earth and were borrowed from classical types of teaching figures, miracle workers, and heroes. Conventions for depicting divine attributes were missing, and there was no attempt at historical accuracy. Jesus did not look like an early-first-century Jewish man from Palestine, but like a Roman teacher-philosopher or like an Apollo-type mythic hero such as the Christos-Helios mosaic figure in the necropolis of Saint Peter's Basilica in Rome. Frustration with the limitations of these typologies seems to have led to symbolic representations, such as the ubiquitous Christ as Good Shepherd and the emblematic cross and wreath symbolizing the Trophy of Victory on sarcophagi. The Good Shepherd image was adapted from pagan culture, while the Trophy was the earliest representation of the Christian cross.

IMPERIAL CHRISTIANITY. Following the adoption of Christianity as a state religion by the Roman emperor Constantine in the early fourth century, the figure of Christ as the imperial reigning Lord emerged. Jesus enthroned as the leader of the church, or in the heavens as an imperial judge, reflected the power the church had gained in that era. Within a hierarchically structured society, Jesus was depicted as a reigning philosopher-emperor who dispensed grace and judgment above all earthly power (see, for instance, the enthroned Christ in the apse mosaic of Santa Pudenziana in Rome).

Theological teachings and conciliar rulings are reflected in the Christian iconography that followed. From the fourth through the sixth century the figure of Jesus, elevated to a ruler over all, came to represent the power of the church over state and society. Christ seated in majesty above the heavens in the apse mosaic of the mausoleum of Santa Constanza in Rome (c. 350) or in the apse mosaic of the Church of San Vitale in Ravenna, Italy (c. 550), reflects Christological formulations. Mary appears as an enthroned queen in the mosaics of Santa Maria Maggiore, Rome, after the Council of Ephesus in 431, which declared her *theotokos,* Mother of God. Two types of Christ figures occupy the twenty-six mosaic panels of the Christ cycle in San Apollinare Nuovo in Ravenna (c. 520). The figure in the scenes of Christ's ministry and miracles is an Apollo type—young, beardless, and dressed in royal purple—while the figure in the scenes of Christ's last days on earth is a philosopher type—older, bearded, also dressed in purple. These two figure types reflect Pope Leo the Great's late-fifth-century theological treatise on the two natures of Christ.

Explicit representation of the crucifixion of Jesus is conspicuously absent from early Christian iconography prior to the fifth century. The visual representation of Jesus' crucifixion and resurrection was reserved to be seen only for those who have been baptized. By the early fifth century, on rare occasions, crucifixion scenes appeared on liturgical objects and other church furnishings, such as the wooden doors of the Church of Santa Sabina in Rome. Nonetheless, the crucifixion is missing as an episode in the Christ cycle of the nave mosaics in the early-sixth-century Church of San Apollinare Nuovo in Ravenna. Once the crucifixion came to be widely depicted, the preferred type in both East and West through the ninth century was a robed, open-eyed, victorious Christ hanging on the cross, such as the ones in the illuminations of the Rabula Gospels from Mesopotamia (dated 586) or on the wall decorations of the Church of Santa Maria Antiqua in Rome.

From early Christian times to the ninth century, themes of rescue, delivery, and victory were dominant. Figures introduced as graced believers eventually became regal symbols of transcending powers. Mary, for instance, in third-century Roman fresco painting, was a Roman citizen; in the fourth century she acquired the dress of an aristocratic lady, and in the fifth, she was the queen of heaven. By the ninth century she was a reigning personification of the church.

BYZANTINE ART. Within the art of the Eastern Orthodox Church, the image (as icon) relates to the liturgy in a manner distinguished from that of its Western counterparts. An icon can appear in a variety of media: painting, mosaic, sculpture, or illuminated manuscript. Its subject matter includes biblical figures, lives of the saints, and scenes and narrative cycles that relate specifically to the liturgical calendar. To the present day, Byzantine tradition relies heavily on iconography in its worship. On the iconostasis—the screen extending across the front of the worship space in the Byzantine tradition—icons of Christ, Mary, and the saints appear as physical representations of the real spiritual presence of these figures for the worshipers, thereby creating the most integral and dynamic use of iconography in worship among all Christian traditions.

Over the centuries, rules for iconographers in the East were formalized, and copy books determined the style and subject matter of iconography. Paintings of the crucifixion in the Byzantine tradition, for example, often include the figures of Mary and Saint John at the foot of the cross in attitudes of grief, and the corpus traditionally hangs in a limp curve against the rigidity of the cross. This form then became popular in the West, especially in medieval Italy, and influenced painters such as Cimabue (d. 1302?).

Icons of the Madonna as the Blessed Virgin, Mother of God, emphasizing her role as mediator and eternal spirit of consolation and blessing, are numerous in Eastern iconography, but the single most imposing and austere composition in Byzantine iconography is the Pantocrator icon of Christ. The frontal presentation of this image emphasizes the presence of Christ as coeternal and coexistent with God the Father. Theologically, the Pantocrator gave visible form to the church's teachings on the consubstantiation of Father and Son, just as the Transfiguration icon visualized its teachings on the incarnation of God in Christ. The religious and social power of icons in society is reflected in the Iconoclastic Controversy of the eighth and ninth centuries, which produced a body of writings on the theology of iconography never again matched in Christian history.

MIDDLE AGES. While saints, heroes, and narrative episodes from scripture dominated medieval iconography, rich patterns of decoration and reference to everyday contemporary life worked their way into the art of the church in the West. Sculptural programs on church buildings and marginalia in illuminated manuscripts introduced genre scenes such as the symbols for the labors of the months and images for the seven liberal arts.

Christian iconography produced in the eighth and ninth centuries became regionally acculturated as its Roman origins disappeared in the face of indigenous expression. Elaborate decorated surfaces enclosed Christian symbols and figures, where, in the service of beautiful patterns, iconography became abstract and emblematic, especially on painted vellum in books.

During the ninth and tenth centuries a shift in emphasis from Christ the victor to Christ the victim took place in the thinking of the church; accordingly, images of the crucifixion with the victorious reigning Lord on the cross were replaced by those of the suffering human victim. The Gero Crucifix in the Cathedral of Cologne, Germany (c. 960), is one of the earliest representations of Christ as a suffering, dying figure. Under the influence of Anselm (d. 1109) the emphasis on the purpose of Christ's sacrifice shifted from the act necessary to defeat the devil to the act necessary to satisfy God on behalf of the world. Christian iconography of the crucifixion reflected that shift. Simultaneously, the role of Christ as a stern and eternal judge was emphasized in sculptural programs on the exterior of monastic churches such as those at Moissac and Autun in France. Images of Mary as mediator, together with the lives of the saints as models of virtue and fidelity, presented an array of images for instruction and contemplation.

By the twelfth century the decorative, narrative, and didactic role of the arts gave way to an explicitly sacramental function, one in which the imagery appeared in a context believed to be a model of the kingdom of heaven, the church building. Iconography in the church was believed capable of building a bridge that reached from the mundane world to the threshold of the divine spirit. Described in twelfth-century Christian literature as anagogical art, iconography served as an extension of the meaning of the Mass. Visual images led believers from the material to the immaterial (see Suger, 1979). In a Gothic cathedral the sculptural programs (statue columns, tympana, archivolts, capitals, screens) and painted glass included figural compositions that narrated scripture, historical events, literature, and daily life, and all were considered to have an anagogical function.

In the Gothic era a proliferation of Old Testament imagery reflected renewed theological and political interests in manifestations of God working within and through royal hierarchies. During this period the suffering Christ of the Romanesque style became a more benign savior. More types of Christ figures appear in the sculptural program and stained glass of Chartres Cathedral from the twelfth and thirteenth centuries than in the most elaborate Romanesque iconographic schemes. The quantity of figures was more important to the Gothic planners than to any of their predecessors, owing to the twelfth-century belief in the anagogical function of art.

In the late Gothic period (approximately the fourteenth and fifteenth centuries) across northern Europe, the iconography of Christianity was populated with aesthetically appealing, elegant figures and decorative surfaces known in modern scholarship as the International Style. Attitudes, dress, and colors emphasized soft, flowing lines, gentle expressions, and rich textures.

Renaissance and Reformation. Christian iconography of the Renaissance in Italy acquired classically human characteristics as interest in Greco-Roman literature and art was revived. Jesus and his followers appeared in a human guise heretofore unknown. Scenes of biblical episodes and historically religious significance were given the illusion of three-dimensional settings that emphasized their reality in the natural world. Fifteenth-century Renaissance art reflected renewed interest in pagan mythology and Christian subject matter alike; therefore, pagan iconography competed with traditional Christian iconography. Proportion, perspective, and human experience were new ingredients in the iconography of the Renaissance. For example, between 1495 and 1498 Leonardo da Vinci completed the *Last Supper* on the wall of the refectory of Santa Maria della Grazie in Milan, Italy. Leonardo's painting of the figures within a perspectival view of a room centered on Christ renders the moment as one of self-conscious and anxious questioning among the twelve apostles. This painting has become the most popular and most often reproduced object of Christian iconography.

In an age in which "man was the measure of all things," the types of human figures ranged between idealized and ethereal images, such as Raphael's *Madonna del Granduca* (1505) and the anxious and suffering figures in Michelangelo's Sistine Chapel *Last Judgment* (1536–1541). In the latter, terror lurks in the consciousness of the sinful, and the blessed rise passively to a severe and enigmatic Lord.

In northern Europe in the fifteenth and sixteenth centuries, exaggerated realism in the treatment of subject matter and pre-Reformation currents of thought shaped Christian iconography. Matthias Grünewald's famous crucifixion panel in the Isenheim Altarpiece (1510–1512) presents Christ as a victim whose physical appearance betrays mutilation and disease; the panel emphasizes divine participation on behalf of human suffering.

Specifically Reformation iconography illustrated biblical teaching and liturgical practices by the reformers. Lucas Cranach the Elder, a painter and a friend of Martin Luther, presented the subject matter of one of Luther's sermons in the figure of the crucified Christ in the Wittenberg Altarpiece of 1545. Here, Christ appears classically proportioned, alive, and without signs of maltreatment. Albrecht Dürer's engravings and woodcuts, known to a wide-ranging public, in some instances reflected contemporary religious thought as well. Whereas the old *Andachtsbild* (image for contemplation) tradition in medieval Christian iconography served prayer and meditation, many of Dürer's engravings engaged the intellect and gave focus to religious thought and theological propositions.

Reacting against "papist" imagery, Reformation iconoclasts destroyed vast amounts of iconographic imagery and liturgical furnishings. For its part, the Roman Catholic Church consciously appropriated iconographic programs in their churches in order to counteract the reforming movements. The Council of Trent, held in the middle of the sixteenth century, formulated instructions on the uses of iconography on behalf of the church. If the Reformation in some areas limited or forbade the use of images in the church, the Counter-Reformation encouraged a proliferation of them, thereby stimulating the introduction and expansion of the Baroque style of art. Eventually the church's use of Baroque forms extended beyond traditional sculptural programs and painted panels to wall-surface decor, ceiling plaster, frescoes, elaboration of vestments and liturgical vessels, and extensive programmatic designs for altars and chapels. Dramatic highlighting, theatrical effects, and atmospheric illusions were used with iconographic programs to convince believers that the authentic home of spirituality and the true seat of the church's authority was in the Roman Church.

Seventeenth and Eighteenth Centuries. Protestant iconography in the seventeenth century emphasized individual experience, and images of Jesus stressed his humanity and participation in the human condition. Rembrandt's portraits of Jesus, for example, show a thirty-year-old Jewish man; his *Deposition from the Cross* (1634) emphasizes a Christ broken and dead. Roman Catholic iconography, by contrast, stressed the sacramental presence of a heroic Christ in programmatic sequences, such as Peter Paul Rubens's early altarpieces and Nicolas Poussin's two series of paintings entitled *The Seven Sacraments* from the 1640s.

Eventually, architects created iconographic environments in church interiors that approximated a heavenly realm, decorated with ethereal figures of saints. As the German Rococo churches attest (see, for example, the Bavarian pilgrimage churches of Balthazar Neumann at Vierzehnheiligen and Dominikus Zimmermann at Wies), the setting for the sacrament was an integration of iconography and architecture that established a place separate from the natural world.

The New World. While the excesses of Rococo iconographic decoration engulfed worship spaces in eighteenth-century Europe, the New World seemed austere by contrast. Late-seventeenth-century Christian iconography in North America consisted primarily of small, colorful panel paintings for the Spanish-American communities of the Southwest and of a conservative form of monochromatic portraiture on the East Coast. The art of the Southwest reflected a Spanish Roman Catholic culture with its indigenously adapted Baroque forms. By contrast, the arts introduced by the Puritans in New England were understated to the point of asceticism and iconoclasm. The elimination of imagery and decoration left a Christian iconography of simple abstract elements created by natural materials and excellent craftsmanship. Early American meetinghouse architecture symbolized a community's place of contact with itself and with God, specifically the word of God. Shaker communities, for instance, made a virtue of functional beauty and created a repertoire of objects that were revered for their clarity of form and usefulness. Cemetery art in eighteenth-century New England relied on simple abstract symbols reduced to line drawings in stone, representing angels' heads or skulls with wings.

The earliest Christian imagery in North America, as found in Western Hispanic communities and the Puritan centers in the East, drew on separate European traditions and enjoyed no cross-fertilization. In the Southwest, images of Christ's crucifixion served Roman Catholic liturgical traditions, public and private. In New England any iconography that suggested a Roman Catholic influence was considered "papist" and inappropriate. Not only were images of the crucifixion rare, but many churches refused to display the symbol of the cross in order to avoid appearing idolatrous.

By the late eighteenth century, the major trends in Christian iconography were competing with the secularization of Western culture and the impact of the Enlightenment. The American and French revolutions witnessed the destruction of institutional hierarchies and the great Christian monuments associated with them. In France, for instance, the dismantling of the medieval monastery at Cluny and the destruction of royal imagery on Gothic churches at Notre-Dame and St.-Denis in Paris demonstrated the negative power of Christian iconography that appeared to be royalist.

Nonetheless, during this period the private vision of artists dealing with Christian themes added an enigmatic dimension to religious iconography. For instance, William Blake's figures from the late eighteenth century combined traditional Christian subject matter with his own imaginative intuition. Whereas the human condition had always impinged upon and shaped the priorities of traditional Christian iconography, personal insight shaped primary subject matter in the latter half of the eighteenth century.

Nineteenth Century. Prior to the Enlightenment, the life of the Christian church, theologically and liturgically, influenced the images and forms of art directly: Christian iconography reflected the "mind" of the church. In the nineteenth century, Christian iconography served more private and artistically formal purposes. The recovery of historical styles in nineteenth-century art and architecture carried with it renewed interest in Christian iconographic themes. The English Pre-Raphaelites, for example, sought to recover the artistic values and qualities of the high Middle Ages. (See, for example, the Edward Burne-Jones mosaic decoration for Saint Paul's Within-the-Walls in Rome, begun in 1881.) Generally speaking, nineteenth-century Christian iconography was created to celebrate a popular style—whereas in the past, style had been shaped by its ecclesiastical settings and patrons.

Claims about the sublime as perceived in nature or in the depths of human consciousness created new aspects of religious iconography in the eighteenth and nineteenth centuries. After the Enlightenment, the canon of iconographic subject matter became open-ended. As the formal aspects of artistic production became foremost for artists who in previous centuries would have been concerned with narrative force and meaning, iconographic expression became more independent and individual. For instance, Vincent van Gogh (d. 1890), who in his early life had been a Christian missionary, created a personal iconography that eschewed, for the most part, any specifically Christian subject. Paul Gauguin's (d. 1903) paintings of Old Testament subjects, the crucifixion, or religious imagery from life in Tahiti created a recognizable but private iconography that reflected individual interests and goals. The institutional church, for the most part, disengaged itself from major artists and movements. Under these circumstances, by the late nineteenth century a great part of Christian iconography had become copy work, sentimental and remote from the society at large.

Twentieth Century. A highly individualized Christian iconography was shaped in the twentieth century by the religious consciousness of individual artists. The German expressionists, for example, insisted upon interpreting and revealing their individuality. When Wassily Kandinsky (d. 1944) wrote *Concerning the Spiritual in Art,* what was revealed in the art included the feelings of the artist and the expressive properties of color. Emil Nolde's nine-part *Life of Christ* altarpiece (1911–1912) combines Nolde's interest in the impact of color with a traditional Christian format. George Rouault, more than any other recognized twentieth-century artist, sought to create compelling Christian imagery. His 1926 *Miserere* series compares Christ's suffering with twentieth-century experiences of human sufferings in war. The work of Max Beckmann (d. 1950) equates the fall of Adam and Eve with the grotesque dimensions of the human condition under fascism. In contrast, the most popular and most often reproduced image of Jesus in the United States in the first half of the twentieth century was W. H. Sallmon's *Head of Christ* (1940), a sentimental, idealized figure with widespread influence.

Fantasy painters such as Salvador Dali and Marc Chagall used Christian subject matter in a unique manner in order to suggest visions of the mind or vistas of a dreamworld fashioned out of the subconscious. Paintings such as Dali's *Sacrament of the Last Supper* (1955) and Chagall's *White Crucifixion* (1938) identify a private vision in which traditional Christian iconography is reinterpreted. Pablo Picasso's *Guernica* (1937) has been interpreted as Christian iconography because some traditional imagery appears to enhance its reference to human terror and death, and because it suggests religious meanings. Abstract art in the twentieth century created the possibility for a broadly Christian iconography without recognizable subject matter. For instance, the purely abstract compositions of Piet Mondrian (d. 1944) were intended to provide an image of universal truths, religious in nature, that reflected theosophical beliefs.

Radical individuality and sociopolitical realities influenced the content of Christian iconography in the twentieth century. Revolutionary movements produced Christian iconography that placed traditional religious figures in advocacy relationships with human beings suffering social and political injustice. In predominantly Communist countries, socialist realism that emphasized the heroic stature of the worker or the revolutionary fighter replaced Christian iconography. In other cultures, indigenous forms were integrated into Christian imagery. African sculpture, South American painting, and Asian graphics, for example, often provided indigenous twentieth-century iconography. One aspect of the Christian ecumenical movement around the world was to encourage the diverse international community to reclaim and clarify their cultural heritages. Liturgical arts and iconography in non-Western cultures emphasized their individual locales and traditions.

Following the lead of religious leaders such as the Dominican artist-priest M. A. Couturier (1905–1957) from France, who encouraged abstract and modern artistic treatment of Christian themes, various modern artists entered the arena of religious art. In France, Henri Matisse's windows and wall drawings at Vence, from the late 1940s; Le Corbusier's chapel at Ronchamp (1950–1955); and the stained glass, tapestries, and altar cloth of Fernand Léger at Audincourt (1951) all present Christian iconography in specifically twentieth-century forms.

In the United States, the work of the abstract expressionists from the early 1950s to the 1970s summarized much of the religious consciousness that had been expressed in modern art during the first half of the century by various abstract and expressionist movements. In works such as Robert Motherwell's *Reconciliation Elegy* (1962), Mark Rothko's chapel in Houston, Texas (1970), or Barnett Newman's *Stations of the Cross* (1958–1962), religious subject matter seems identical with expressions of radical individuality.

The twentieth century also saw the emergence of Christian iconography in new media, notably film and electronic communications. Biblical stories presented in films with such titles as *The Bible, The Ten Commandments, The King of Kings,* and *The Gospel according to St. Matthew* engaged a public separate from the church. The mass media, which now included home video, offered traditional Christian subject matter in extended narrative form as dramatic entertainment. In 2004 the film entitled *The Passion of the Christ* drew worldwide attention. Such presentations of Christian stories are a form of Christian iconography, but in their cultural context they appear to be no more than stories from one literary source among many, iconography for entertainment rather than worship.

CONCLUSION. The function of Christian iconography has varied in each generation. It has always been a living language of images invented by the religious consciousness of communities and individuals. Until the modern era, the figures of Jesus and his followers were always central to iconographic programs, but during the twentieth century the focus shifted to the individual iconographer on the one hand and to major cultural presentations of the stories on the other. At the end of the twentieth century and the beginning of the twenty-first century, individual parishes, independent religious communities, and various national responses have introduced their own Christian themes to the iconographic vocabulary. For instance, the so-called African experience or Asian experience have been given renewed attention through their arts.

Religious art continues to be affected to some extent by political and social forces. Censorship efforts on the part of religious communities have attracted headlines, but these efforts have not been effective in the general public. Pornography has been attacked for religious reasons but remains a major media industry. Antireligious attitudes have caused small episodes of outrage, but in the end the art world has not been seriously affected.

Within the large variety of Christian communities around the world, expanded interest in iconographic imagery has produced a wealth of artistic activity. Nevertheless, the proliferation of art in the Christian church has not become a major factor in the art markets of the world. Leading collectors of Christian art, for instance, have not been identified, and museums do not offer major collections of Christian art unless it has some other value than just being religious.

However, interest in religions, generally, has risen in the twenty-first century for political reasons, and interest in religious art and architecture has increased accordingly. It may be that the academy and the general public will become more interested in the arts of world religions in the near future because religion has become a central theme. Other factors leading toward a larger role for religious art are the expanding place of museums in society and the relaxation of the traditional split, in the United States at least, between church and state.

Another tendency that is emerging in the twenty-first century has to do with the way various distinctive cultures in the world have artists who are reinterpreting the Christian biblical stories in their own cultural vernacular. Earlier efforts that translated the biblical story into the major languages of the world have led artists to apply traditional Christian iconographic themes to a variety of modern cultural settings. Such works of art also remind observers that the same was true when Christian iconography was first invented and emerged within the context of the Roman Empire. Cultural settings have always shaped Christian iconography and will continue to do so.

See Also Aesthetics, article on Visual Aesthetics; Basilica, Cathedral, and Church; Iconoclasm; Icons; Images, article on Veneration of Images; Monastery.

Bibliography

Bottari, Stefano. *Tesori d'arte cristiana.* 5 vols. Bologna, Italy, 1956–1968. Excellent photo-essays on major architectural monuments and their contents from early Christian times to the twentieth century. The principles of selection, however, are not clear, and the views printed are sometimes eccentric. Many color illustrations and ground plans.

Cabrol, Fernand, et al., eds. *Dictionnaire d'archéologie chrétienne et de liturgie.* 15 vols. Paris, 1909–1953. Essential material for the history of Christian iconography, architecture, and worship. Illustrations, although small in size and few in number, include good ground plans. A classic research and reference source.

Didron, Adolphe Napoléon. *Christian Iconography, or, The History of Christian Art in the Middle Ages* (1851–1886). 2 vols. Translated by Ellen J. Millington. New York, 1965. Organized thematically, with each essay treating historical sources in depth. Limited illustrations but valuable for theories concerning iconography.

Ferguson, George. *Signs and Symbols in Christian Art* (1954). New York, 1961. Remains the most reliable single-volume handbook on the subject.

Hall, James. *Dictionary of Subjects and Symbols in Art* (1974). Rev. ed. New York, 1979. Includes Christian subject matter.

Kirschbaum, Englebert, and Wolfgang Braunfels, eds. *Lexikon der christlichen Ikonographie.* 8 vols. Rome, 1968–1976. Vols. 1–4, *Allgemeine Ikonographie,* edited by Kirschbaum, present general articles on Christian iconography, alphabetically arranged; vols. 5–8, *Ikonographie der Heiligen,* edited by Braunfels, present the legends of the saints and their imagery in a separate alphabetical sequence. Both series of volumes include excellent bibliographies and summaries. Illustrations are relatively few in number and small in size.

Réau, Louis. *Iconographie de l'art crétien.* 3 vols. in 6. Paris, 1955–1959. Includes a historical overview (vol. 1), Old and New Testament iconography (vol. 2), and an iconography of the saints with legends and cult status (vol. 3). Very few illustrations.

Schiller, Gertrud. *Ikonographie der christlichen Kunst.* 4 vols. in 5. Gütersloh, Germany, 1966–1976. Offers excellent essay introductions to Christian themes in art and their sources, covering presentations of Christ (vols. 1–3), the church (vol. 4, pt. 1), and Mary (vol. 4, pt. 2). An exemplary study with many well-selected and clearly printed illustrations. The first two volumes have been translated by Janet Seligman as *The Iconography of Christian Art,* vol. 1, *The Incarnation and Life of Christ* (Boston, 1971); and vol. 2, *The Passion of Christ* (Boston, 1972).

Suger, Abbot. *On the Abbey Church of St. Denis and Its Art Treasures.* Edited and translated by Erwin Panofsky. 2d ed. Princeton, N.J., 1979.

John W. Cook (1987 and 2005)

ICONOGRAPHY: ISLAMIC ICONOGRAPHY

Islam is generally considered an iconoclastic religion in which the representation of living things has been prohibited from its very beginning. However, the Qurʾān nowhere deals with this problem or explicitly speaks against representation. Rather, the prohibition of pictorial activities was derived from certain *ḥadīth,* the traditions attributed to the prophet Muḥammad and his followers. It has often been argued that the development of figural painting in Iran was due to Iran's Shīʿī persuasion, which would have taken these *ḥadīth* less seriously, but this idea likewise is not in keeping with historical fact, because the Shīʿīs follow the tradition as strictly as the Sunnīs, and furthermore, Shiism was declared Iran's state religion only in 1501.

Islam's attitude toward representation is basically in tune with the stark monotheistic doctrine that there is no creator but God: To produce a likeness of anything might be interpreted as an illicit arrogation of the divine creative power by humans. Such an attitude may have hardened at the time of the Byzantine Iconoclastic Controversy; thus, in Persian poetical parlance, "pictures" are often connected with (Christian) "convents." Furthermore, the Islamic prohibition may have first been concerned primarily with sculpture, for sculptures—as they existed in the Kaʿbah in Mecca in pre-Islamic times—could lead humankind again into idolatry, and, indeed, hardly any sculptural art developed in Islam until recently.

EMERGING IMAGERY. The feeling that representation was alien to the original spirit of Islam resulted in the development of abstract ornamental design, both geometric and vegetal, notably the arabesque as the endless continuation of leaves, palmettes, and sometimes animal-like motifs growing out of each other; it also gave calligraphy its central place in Islamic art. However, it would be wrong to claim that early Islam was without any pictures. In secular buildings such as palaces, there was no lack of representations of kings, musicians, dancers, and the like, and expressions in Persian poetry such as "like a lion painted in the bathhouse" point to the existence of wall painting (albeit with the additional, negative meaning of "something lifeless"). Decorative painting on ceramics includes not only more or less stylized animal or human figures as individual motifs but also scenes from (often unidentified) tales and romances. Although the Arabic and Persian texts scribbled around the rims of the vessels sometimes give a clue to the scene, little is known about such pictorial programs, which are found on metalwork as well. Theories about pre-Islamic (Sassanid or Turkic) or astronomical symbolism have been proposed. In the early Middle Ages, certain Arabic books were illustrated either for practical purposes, namely medical and scientific manuscripts, or for entertainment, as in the *Maqāmāt* (Assemblies) of al-Ḥarīrī or the animal fables known as *Kalīlah wa-Dimnah.*

New stylistic features came with the growing Chinese influence during the Mongol occupation of Iran in the late thirteenth century. (Persian literature speaks of China as the "picture house," where Mani, the founder of Manichaeism, acts as the master painter.) Henceforward, illustrative painting developed predominantly in Iran, where the great epic poems (an art form unknown to the Arabs) inspired miniaturists through the centuries to the extent that the iconography of Firdawsī's *Shāh-nāmah* (Book of kings) and Niẓāmī's *Khamsah* (Quintet) became almost standardized. Early historical works, such as the world history of Rashīd al-Dīn (d. 1317), were rather realistically illustrated. Human faces are clearly shown (and later sometimes mutilated by orthodox critics), and even the prophet Muḥammad appears with his face uncovered.

The same originally held true for a branch of painting that has continued from the fourteenth century to the present day, namely, pictures of the Prophet's night journey (*isrā*ʾ, *miʿrāj*) through the heavens on the mysterious steed Burāq. In the course of time, Muḥammad's face was covered partly, then completely; at present, no representation of the Prophet is permitted at all: In the numerous popular pictures of the Miʿrāj, he is represented by a white rose or a cloud. Burāq, meanwhile, has become a centerpiece of popular iconography: Pictures of this winged, donkey-shaped creature with a woman's head and a peacock's tail not only appear today on cheap prints but are also painted on trucks and buses, especially in Afghanistan and Pakistan, as a kind of protective charm.

Truck painting in these areas has developed into a new art form, and the religious and political ideals of the owners become visible in the pictorial and calligraphic decorations of their vehicles. Similarly telling are wall paintings in Turkish or Afghan coffee- or teahouses, where one may find realistic scenes from the *Qiṣaṣ al-anbiyā*ʾ (Stories of the prophets) or allusions to folk romances.

There was and is apparently no aversion to representing angels in Miʿrāj scenes, romances, or works on cosmology, or else as single figures, even in relief on walls. Their faces are always uncovered. Gabriel with his many enormous wings and Isrāfīl with the trumpet of resurrection are most prominent.

Islamic painting reached its zenith in Iran and India in the sixteenth and seventeenth centuries, when, partly under the influence of European prints, naturalistic portraiture was developed to perfection. The Mughal emperor Jahāmgīr (r. 1605–1627) inspired the court painters to express his dreams of spiritual world-rule in his portraits by using the motif of the lion and the lamb lying together, or by showing him in the company of Ṣūfīs.

THE SHAPE OF SPIRITUALITY. Portraits of Ṣūfīs and dervishes are frequent in the later Middle Ages: Many drawings capture the spiritual power or the refinement of a solitary Muslim holy man or illustrate the "sessions of the mystical lovers" (*majālis al-ʿushshāq*). Ṣūfīs are also shown as teachers or in their whirling dance. However, little has been done to identify them, although the color of their garments (or the shape of their headgear) sometimes betrays their affiliation with a certain Ṣūfī order (thus, a cinnamon- or rose-colored frock is typical of the Ṣābirī branch of the Chishtīyah). Colors are also used to indicate the spiritual state the mystic has reached.

Manuscripts of the Qurʾān and *ḥadīth*s were never illustrated but were written in beautiful calligraphy that sometimes assumes an almost "iconic" quality, as Martin Lings has pointed out. Qurʾanic themes, however, as retold in the stories of the prophets or in poetry such as the *Yūsuf and Zulaykhā* by Jāmī (d. 1492), have developed a pictorial tradition of their own. Some mystical epics, especially ʿAṭṭār's *Manṭiq al-ṭayr* (The conversation of the birds), have inspired painters, but the few examples of Rūmī's *Mathnavī* with pictures, which date from fourteenth-century India to nineteenth-century Iran, lack any trace of Ṣūfī spirituality.

Sometimes seemingly simple motifs are interpreted mystically; this author's Turkish Ṣūfī friends explain the frequent use of tulips on the tiles in Turkish mosques with the fact that the word *lālah* ("tulip") has the same letters and thus the same numerical value as the word *Allāh*, that is, sixty-six. This is also true for the word *hilāl*, "crescent," and the *hilāl* has come to be regarded as the typical sign of Islam although its first appearance on early Islamic coins, metalwork, and ceramics had no religious connotations. It seems that in the eleventh century, when some churches (such as Ani in Armenia) were converted into mosques, their cross-shaped finials were replaced with crescent-shaped ones. A *ḥājj* ("pilgrimage") certificate of 1432 shows drawings of the sacred buildings in Mecca with such crescent finials. The Ottoman sultan Selim I (r. 1512–1520) used the *hilāl* on his flag, but only in the early nineteenth century was it made the official Turkish emblem, which appeared on postage stamps in 1863. Other Muslim countries followed the Turkish example, and now it is generally seen as the Islamic equivalent of the Christian cross (thus, the Red Crescent parallels the Red Cross).

There was no inhibition in representing pilgrimage sites in medieval guidebooks for pilgrims. In the late nineteenth century, photographs of the holy cities of Mecca and Medina became prized possessions of pilgrims and of those who were unable to perform the *ḥājj,* just as many Muslim homes now contain prints, posters, or wall hangings with representations of the Kaʿbah and/or the Prophet's mausoleum.

While naturalistic representation of the Prophet and his family was increasingly objected to, other ways of presenting him developed. One might put a *ḥadīth* in superb calligraphy on a single page or write his *ḥilyah,* an elaboration of the classical Arabic description of his outward and inward beauty, in a special calligraphic style, as was done in Turkey from about 1600. The Prophet's footprints on stone, or representations of them, along with more or less elaborate drawings of his sandals, still belong to the generally accepted items in the religious tradition. One could also produce "pictures" of saintly persons such as ʿAlī ibn Abī Ṭālib from pious sentences written in minute script (although in Iran quite realistic battle scenes showing the bravery and suffering of Ḥusayn and other members of the Prophet's family are also found in more recent times).

Calligraphic images have become more and more popular: The letters of the word *bismillāh* ("in the name of God") can be shaped into birds and beasts; Qurʾanic passages of particular protective importance, such as the "throne verse" (*sūrah* 2:256), appear in animal shape; and whenever a calligraphic lion is found, it usually consists of a formula connected with ʿAlī, who is called the "Lion of God" (Asad Allāh, Ḥaydar, Shir, and so forth). Most frequently used is the invocation "Nādi ʿAlīyan . . ." ("Call ʿAlī, who manifests wondrous things . . ."), which appears on many objects from Safavid Iran and Shīʿī India, as do the names of the twelve Shīʿī *imāms.* The names of the Panjtan (Muḥammad, ʿAlī, Fāṭimah, Ḥasan, and Ḥusayn) combined with the word *Allāh* are used to form human faces, as in the Bektāshī tradition in Turkey. The names of protective saints such as the Seven Sleepers (*sūrah* 18) are also used as a calligraphic design (but their figures appear as well in Persian and Turkish painting, with their faithful dog Qiṭmīr or his name always in the center). Invocations of Ṣūfī saints may be written in the shape of a dervish cap (typical is that of Mawlānā Rūmī); other pious exclamations appear as flowers or are arranged in circular form.

Indeed, the most typical and certainly the most widely used means of conveying the Islamic message was and still is calligraphy. The walls of Persian mosques are covered with radiant tiles on which the names of God, Muḥammad, and ʿAlī in the square Kufic script give witness to the Shīʿī form of faith; Turkish mosques are decorated with Qurʾanic quotations or with an enormous *Allāh.* In Turkey, various calligrams are based on the letter *w,* and the central statements of the faith are written in mirrored form.

Lately, under European influence, a very colorful popular iconography has developed in some parts of the Muslim world. On posters, religious motifs from various traditions are strung together in highly surprising form: Raphael's little angels appear along with the Lourdes Madonna around a deceased Muslim leader in a lush Paradise, or an apotheosis of Ayatollah Khomeini is coupled with the earthbound figure from Andrew Wyeth's *Christina's World.* (Here one is reminded of some pictures in the Indian Ismāʿīlī tradition that show ʿAlī as the tenth *avatāra* in the blue color of Kṛṣṇa, with Hanuman the "monkey-chief" carrying the royal umbrella over ʿAlī's white mule, Duldul.) Such syncretistic pictures are certainly not acceptable to the large majority of pious Muslims. On the other hand, the calligraphic traditions are gaining new importance from Morocco to Indonesia, and some attempts at producing a kind of Qurʾanic scriptorial picture (thus Sadiqain and Aslam Kamal in Pakistan) are remarkably successful and deserve the attention of the historian of religion and the art lover.

See Also Calligraphy, article on Islamic Calligraphy; Mosque.

Bibliography

Most histories of Islamic art deal with the topic of so-called iconoclasm in Islam. One of the latest publications is Mazhar Şevket Ipşiroğlu's *Das Bild im Islam: Ein Verbot und seine Folgen* (Vienna, 1971), which stresses the Ṣūfī influence on Islamic painting but is not completely convincing. The only scholar who has devoted a good number of studies to Islamic iconography is Richard Ettinghausen; out of his many valuable works I shall mention especially "Hilāl in Islamic Art," in *The Encyclopaedia of Islam,* new ed. (Leiden, 1960–), with a thorough historical survey; "Persian Ascension Miniatures of the Fourteenth Century," in *Oriente ed occidente nel medio evo* (Rome, 1957), which treats the early pictorial development of the ascension theme; and his religious interpretation of a Mughal painting of Jahāmgīr preferring a Ṣūfī to worldly rulers, "The Emperor's Choice," in *De Artibus Opuscula XL: Essays in Honor of Erwin Panofsky,* edited by Millard Meiss (New York, 1961), vol. 1. See also Ettinghausen's *Islamic Art and Archaeology: Collected Papers,* prepared and edited by Myriam Rosen-Ayalon (Berlin, 1984). The volume dedicated to Ettinghausen, *Studies in Art and Literature of the Near East,* edited by Peter Chelkowski (Salt Lake City, 1974), lists more of his relevant works and contains some articles pertinent to the problem of iconography.

The best pictorial introduction to the *miʿrāj* miniatures is *The Miraculous Journey of Mahomet,* edited by Marie-Rose Séguy (London, 1977), based on a Uighur manuscript from the Timurid court at Herat. Popular painting has been dealt with in Malik Aksel's *Türklerde dinï resimler* (Istanbul, 1967), a delightful book with many examples of folk painting and calligraphic pictures from the Bektāshī tradition. A very useful introduction into Islamic iconography in Africa (a much neglected topic) is René A. Bravmann's *African Islam* (London, 1983). The calligraphic and iconographic aspects of the Qur'ān are lucidly explained in Martin Ling's The *Quranic Art of Calligraphy and Illumination* (London, 1976). A general survey of the calligraphic tradition in connection with the mystical and poetical expressions can be found in my *Calligraphy and Islamic Culture* (New York, 1984).

ANNEMARIE SCHIMMEL (1987)

ICONS. The term *icon* (from the Greek *eikōn,* "image") is applied in a broad sense to all sacred images worshiped by Christians in eastern Europe and the Middle East regardless of the image's media; thus icons may be mosaics, frescoes, engravings on marble or metal, or prints on paper. In its current use the term describes portable sacred images painted on wood, canvas, or glass.

BEGINNING AND GROWTH OF THE VENERATION OF ICONS. Portable icons first appeared in Egypt in the third century. The oldest works that have been preserved to this day bear a striking resemblance to the funeral portraits that replaced the masks on the anthropoid coffins of the Hellenistic period. The Judaic tradition, which relied on the biblical prohibition of the use of images in religious worship, was confronted in the eastern Mediterranean area with the Greek tradition, theoretically substantiated by Neoplatonism, according to which the material symbol is an expression of spiritual reality and the image has a didactic function. This latter tradition gained ground even in some Jewish communities; for example, frescoes based on biblical subjects were painted on the walls of the synagogue at Dura-Europos (present-day Salahiyeh, Syria) in the third century. It was the Greek tradition that caused the emergence as early as the second and third centuries of sacred imagery in the Christian church, which had originally used only symbols (e.g., the cross, lamb, fish, and dove). The didactic function of images was generally accepted throughout the Christian world, but the veneration of images did not spread to all areas: It remained a specific cult of Christianity in the Greco-Byzantine tradition.

The earliest icons, like the Hellenistic funeral portraits, originally had a commemorative value: They were representations of martyrs, apostles, the Virgin, and Jesus Christ. As early as the fourth century a typology of characters took shape, and their sacred nature was marked by a nimbus. The authenticity of portraits was an essential concern: The images of Christ and the Virgin were believed to be of miraculous origin, "made without hands" (Gr., *acheiropoiētos*); those of the saints were rendered according to descriptions preserved by traditional—oral or written—sources. The oldest icon representing the Virgin originated in Palestine and, with the exception of the visage, was attributed to the apostle Luke; the visage was said to have been painted miraculously, without the touch of the human hand. According to tradition, the representation of Christ relied on a portrait Jesus had sent to the king of Edessa, Abgar Ukkama, "the black" (d. 50 CE), and on the veil of Veronica, said to bear the imprint of the Savior's face (recent research suggests that the name Veronica derives from the Latin *vera icona,* "true face").

As Christian icon painting developed after the fourth century, themes relating to the historical cycles of Christ's mission (miracles, scenes from his life) and then events from the lives of saints and from the history of the Christian church were introduced. In the sixth century icon worship spread throughout the Byzantine Empire. Icons were displayed to the faithful in churches or during processions, and they were also to be found in private homes. They were either in one piece or were combined from two or three pieces, forming, respectively, diptychs and triptychs. The strength of the development of icon worship, the miraculous powers attributed to certain icons, and the fact that in the minds of the faithful icons were identified with the character they represented, aroused, even from the beginning, opposition and hostility from some of the fathers of the church. This led in the eighth century to the iconoclastic crisis, which resulted in the destruction of a large number of icons, especially in areas under the direct authority of the Byzantine emperors. Nevertheless iconoclasm was unable to prevent the further development of icon worship at the periphery of the empire; hence the oldest icons, dating from the fifth and sixth centuries, were preserved in Georgia (Transcaucasia), on Mount Sinai, and in Cyprus. With the official restoration of the veneration of icons in 843, the practice of veneration became generalized not only in the Byzantine Empire but also in other regions where the Eastern Orthodox church had become predominant, such as the Balkan Peninsula and Russia.

Following the triumph of the doctrine claiming the legitimacy of icon worship many more wall icons were displayed in sanctuaries, and the iconostasis (Gr., *eikonostasis,* "support for icons") was introduced, a screen of icons that separated the altar from the nave of the church. The iconostasis apparently developed from the *templon,* a barrier made of stone, marble, or ivory that enclosed the main apse or chancel, where the sacred table was contained.

THEOLOGY OF ICONS. The final elaboration of the theology of icons resulted from the disputes caused by iconoclasm and the rules formulated by the Second Council of Nicaea (787). The earliest elements of the doctrine had already been enunciated in the second to the fourth centuries. Arguing against the Christian apologists who condemned idols as "devilish," such Neoplatonic thinkers as Celsus (latter half of the second century), Porphyry (c. 234–c. 305), and Emperor Julian the Apostate (d. 363) attempted to give a metaphysical justification of sacred images and statues as material symbols expressing external and spiritual realities and fulfilling at the same time a significant didactic function. According to Neoplatonists the relationship between image and prototype is not one of sameness: Images serve only as vehicles by which to approach the divine prototype, which is hidden from humans because of the limitations of their corporeality. The arguments adduced by the Neoplatonists are to be found in subsequent developments of Christian theology. Thus, the concept according to which "sensible images are vehicles whereby we accede, as far as possible, to divine contemplation" was clearly stated by Dionysius the Areopagite (c. 500) in his treatise *Ecclesiastical Hierarchy* (1.2). The relationship between image and its divine prototype would be later clarified in the same vein in the writings of John of Damascus (c. 679–749) and other authors of the Eastern church.

The Christian authors of the eighth and ninth centuries who formulated the theology of icons relied on a belief that icon worship was a consequence of the incarnation of the Son of God. According to Germanus I, patriarch of Constantinople (r. 715–730), the Son could be portrayed because he "consented to become a man." An icon representing Christ is not an image of the "incomprehensible and immortal Deity" but rather that of the "human character" of the Logos (the Word) and serves as proof that "indeed he became a man in all respects, except for sin." Christ could be represented only "in his human form, in his visible theophany." John of Damascus, who wrote three treatises in defense of "sacred icons," gave the following definition of the painted image of the Deity: "I represent God the Invisible not as invisible but to the extent he became visible to us by partaking of flesh and blood."

John of Damascus and, especially, Theodore of Studios (759–826) and Nikephoros, patriarch of Constantinople (r. 806–815), further clarified the relationship between the sacred image, or icon, and its divine prototype. To them image is essentially distinct from the original: It is an object of relative veneration (Gr., *proskunēsis skhetikē)*. Through the mediation of the icon the faithful actually address the prototype it represents, and so the relative veneration of the image becomes adoration (Gr., *latreia*) that is exclusively offered to the Deity. This distinction between adoration of the model and relative veneration of its image removed the danger of turning icons into fetishes, a danger that was inherent in their worship. Theodore of Studios emphasized that "veneration was not due to the essence of the image but rather to the form of the Prototype represented by the image . . . since matter cannot be subject to veneration."

These clarifications stressed the intimate connection between the theology of icons and the Christological question posed by the heresy of docetism, which questioned the real humanity of Christ and claimed that Christ's body was only apparent. In contradistinction, the icon was claimed to represent the image of an incarnation of the Son of God, thus, according to Germanus, "proving that he invested our nature by means other than imagination." Indescribable by his divine nature, Christ is describable by the complete reality of his historical humanity.

According to Theodore of Studios, "the fact that God made man after his likeness showed that icon painting was an act of God." The theology of icons confers upon icons an almost sacramental role. As the early painters saw it, their art did not belong to aesthetics but rather to liturgy. The perfection of form was no more than an adequate expression of the doctrine. The painter was not an artist in the modern sense of the word but a priest: His talent was a necessary, but not sufficient, condition. He was chosen and guided by a master; the beginning of his apprenticeship was marked by a ritual (e.g., prayer and benediction) quite similar to that of an initiation.

The earliest painters of icons never signed their works because their individuality was believed to be of no consequence. (The first icons to be signed, in the fifteenth and sixteenth centuries, signaled the beginning of decadence in the art of icon making.) Seen as mere interpreters of the truth, the painters of old had to follow strict rules: The subjects of their paintings could only be previously established models, scenes from the holy books, or, more rarely, acknowledged visions; they did their work after having fasted and received the Eucharist; and some even mixed holy water with their colors.

Diffusion of the Cult of Icons. After the conclusion of the iconoclastic crisis, icon painting in Byzantium, under the Palaeologus dynasty (1261–1453), witnessed a remarkable period in which artistic perfection was reached; that style further influenced the art of icon making down to the present time. In the Greek territories the main icon-producing centers were Mount Athos and the imperial workshops in Constantinople, Thessalonica, and, after the fall of Byzantium, Crete. Cretan painters, having remained outside the area of Ottoman domination between 1453 and 1669, produced a great many works that were disseminated throughout the Orthodox world. Their icons displayed a certain lavishness, to be explained by the comfortable conditions in which they were produced; they were increasingly influenced by the contemporary Italian painting not only in the rendering of human visages and bodies, and of space, but even in iconography.

In eastern and southeastern Europe the cult of icons was disseminated by the early missionaries and through contacts with Byzantium. At first icons were brought from the Byzantine territories, but later they began to be produced in local workshops: at Preslav and Veliko Tŭrnovo in Bulgaria; at the courts of Serbian kings and Romanian princes; in Walachia and Moldavia; and in major monasteries in all these countries. They were characterized by their faithfulness to the Byzantine prototypes, but starting in the eighteenth century, popular local tastes made an impact on the choice of colors, the design of costumes, and the decoration of space. The union of a part of the Eastern Orthodox Romanians in Transylvania with the church of Rome gave rise to a unique phenomenon in Eastern Christian art: Icons were painted on glass by peasant artists, producing works that strongly resembled naive folk painting.

Of the oldest icons imported to Russia after the baptizing of the Russians in 988, only works of Byzantine origin dating from the eleventh century have been preserved. In the same century the earliest local icon-making centers began to emerge, first in Kiev and then in Novgorod and Vladimir-Suzdal. The earliest masters were from Byzantium, but soon a specific Russian style took shape; it developed from a spiritualized and ascetic attitude to a search for artistic and didactic effects, a taste for minute detail, and naturalism. The Council of the Hundred Chapters held in Moscow in 1551 reacted against the penetration of Western elements into the art of icon painting and put down rigid, mandatory rules to be followed by painters. This led to a proliferation of handbooks that provided authorized versions (Ch. Slav., *podliniki,* "outlines") of the holy images; these guides were equivalent to the ones used in the Byzantine Empire beginning in the eleventh century. The reforms enacted by Peter the Great (r. 1682–1725) inhibited the further development of icon painting, and the art subsequently lapsed into conservatism.

In the East after the Council of Chalcedon (451), the church (under the patriarchates of Antioch and Jerusalem) followed the orthodox doctrine upheld against Monophysitism. In the seventeenth century the style of icon painting known as Melchite developed under new influences—Arabic, in terms of decoration; western European, in terms of subject matter.

See Also Docetism; Iconoclasm; Images, article on Veneration of Images.

Bibliography

The scientific study of icons began in the latter half of the nineteenth century as part of the new discipline of Byzantology and enlisted especially Russian contributions; an essential bibliography is to be found in Oskar Wulff and Michael Alpatoff's *Denkmäler der Ikonenmalerei* (Leipzig, 1925), pp. 298–299. Earlier research included icons, described as "panel paintings" or "portable images," in studies on Eastern Christian iconography, among which the fundamental work remains Gabriel Millet's *Recherches sur l'iconographie de l'Évangile aux quator-zième, quinzième, et seizième siècles* (Paris, 1916). In western Europe and America icons were "discovered" as works of art and spiritual creations only after World War I, when the Christian Orthodox tradition was reassessed by Catholic and Protestant scholars; see David Talbot Rice's *Byzantine Art,* 2d ed., rev. & enl. (Baltimore, 1968). Most experts approach icons as works of art within the general framework of Byzantine or, particularly, Russian art—for example, André Grabar's *Byzantine Painting,* translated by Stuart Gilbert (New York, 1953), and Tamara Talbot Rice's *Icons,* rev. ed. (London, 1960). The theology of icons has been systematically studied and clarified mainly by Western Orthodox authors since the 1950s; the most profound works are Leonid Ouspensky and Vladimir Lossky's *The Meaning of Icons,* translated by G. E. H. Palmer and Eugénie Kadloubovsky, rev. ed. (Crestwood, N.Y., 1982); and Leonid Ouspensky's *Essai sur la théologie de l'icone dans l'église orthodoxe* (Paris, 1960). Most writings about Eastern Orthodox Christianity contain pertinent chapters on icons: Timothy Ware's *The Orthodox Church,* rev. ed. (Baltimore, 1964); Paul Evdokimoff's *L'orthodoxie* (Paris, 1959); and John Meyendorff's *Byzantine Theology: Historical Trends and Doctrinal Themes* (New York, 1979). Photographs of the oldest, fifth- to sixth-century, icons have been published in Georgios A. Sotiriou and Maria Sotiriou's *Icones du Mont Sinai/Eikonec the Monha Cina* (in Greek and French), vols. 1 and 2 (Athens, 1956–1958). New information about the role of icons during the posticonoclastic period is to be found in Manoles Chatzedakes's "L'évolution de l'icone aux onzième à treizième siècles et la transformation du templon," and Tania Velmans's "Rayonnement de l'icone à l'onzième siècle," in *Actes du quinzième Congrès international d'études byzantines,* vol. 1 (Athens, 1979), pp. 333–366, 375–419. For icons of the Middle East, see Sylvia Agémian's important study in my collection titled *Les icones melkites* (Beirut, 1969).

New Sources

Barasch, Moshe, Jan Assmann, and Albert Baumgarten. *Representation in Religion: Studies in Honor of Moshe Barasch.* Leiden, 2001.

Belting, Hans. *Likeness and Presence: A History of the Image before the Era of Art.* Chicago, 1994.

Comack, Robin. *Painting the Soul: Icons, Death Masks, and Shrouds.* London, 1997.

Damian, Theodor. *Theological and Spiritual Dimensions of Icons According to St. Theodore of Studion.* Lewiston, N.Y., 2002.

Eastmond, Antony, Liz James, and Robin Cormack. *Icon and Word: The Power of Images in Byzantium.* Aldershot, U.K., 2003.

Jeffreys, Elizabeth, and Robin Cormack. *Through the Looking Glass: Byzantium through British Eyes.* Aldershot, U.K., 2000.

Nelson, Robert S. *Visuality Before and Beyond the Renaissance: Seeing as Others Saw.* Cambridge, U.K., 2000.

Temple, Richard. *Icons and the Mystical Origins of Christianity.* Rockport, Mass., 1992.

Velmans, Tania, and Elka Bakalova. *Le grand livre des icônes des origines à la chute de Byzance.* Paris, 2002.

Virgil Cândea (1987)
Translated from Romanian by Sergiu Celac
Revised Bibliography

IDEALISM

IDEALISM. Idealism is the metaphysical view that reality is of the nature of mind. It stands in contrast with scientific philosophies, such as naturalism, realism, and pragmatism that assume that natural life in the natural world is philosophy's appropriate point of departure. Idealism is not grounded in an empirical evaluation of fact. It is grounded in an intuitive evaluation of meaning. Because all philosophy presupposes that things have a meaning and that something, at least, of that meaning can be known, all philosophy has an idealistic element.

Idealism does not deny the reality of the physical world. It insists only that the apparent self-sufficiency of the natural world is deceptive. Nature seems to go its own way, to be self-sufficient, eternal, and operating on the basis of its own laws without need of a creator or outside force to initiate and sustain its motions, but idealism maintains that it relies on mind or spirit or idea for its forcefulness, purposiveness, and inherent meaning. Idealism therefore always distinguishes between appearance and reality, but its emphasis can either be objective or subjective. Subjective idealism sees the physical world as metaphysically insubstantial. Objective idealism regards physical substance as a necessary counterpart of mind.

SUBJECTIVE IDEALISM. The doctrine of the world as *māyā* or illusion in Śaṅkāra's Advaita Vedānta philosophy in India is the most systematic statement of subjective idealism, although George Berkeley's philosophy is the best-known statement of subjective idealism in the West. Berkeley observed that one's visual perception of the physical world is that of shapes and colors, not of any substantial "thing." People project "physical substance" into the picture because they assume that there must be some "thing" that "has" these perceived qualities.

All one ever knows, however, are the perceived qualities. Reality, therefore, is a perception on the part of a perceiver. Hence Berkeley's principle *esse est percipi* ("to be is to be perceived"). He pointed out that one seems to see distance; in fact, however, three-dimensional depth perception is a learned projection of the mind, not a physical reality that impinges directly on one's senses. He added that the physical sciences are not concerned with some "substantial" reality of a physical object, but rather with those perceptions known to mind. To test a yellow metal to see if it is gold, for example, the chemist does not test "substance," but properties—solubility in different acids, combining proportions, and weight. The "substance" of gold is only a fact of experience that these properties bring together. Berkeley concluded that the distinction between what Locke had called primary qualities and secondary qualities—real "substance" as opposed to "appearances" (of color, shape, etc.)—was mistaken. Nature is, he insisted, whole. If space is mental, then all the other qualities of the natural object must also be mental. Reality is entirely an observer's perception.

But what of objects that are alone and unobserved by any human knower, like the tree in the deserted forest or the living-room furniture in the dead of night? Berkeley argued that natural laws hold for events past as well as future because there is an eternal mind to think them. The living-room sofa exists as an object in the eternal perception of the mind of God. God alone guarantees the eternal endurance and order of nature.

The most consistent subjective idealist in modern Western philosophy was G. W. Leibniz, who held that each self is a "monad" of self-enclosed experience. He accepted a plurality of worlds—my world must be different from yours—and solipsism, the view that each person is *solus ipse,* a "windowless monad."

Here subjective idealism runs afoul of the "ego-centric predicament." Confined to his or her own ideas, the self-confessed solipsist nevertheless assumes that he or she knows what it might be like *not* to be so confined; otherwise the assertion has no significance. Each self is conscious, necessarily, of what it is not, in order to know itself as a distinct and separate entity. Solipsism, therefore, is self-refuting.

OBJECTIVE IDEALISM. Objective idealism, mindful of this pitfall, grants to naturalism that the physical world is given from "outside" one's self, and must be received passively, but agrees with subjective idealism that one's experience of this given world is, in large part, an interpretation shaped by one's own mind. Both subjective and objective idealism are rooted in the intuition that reality is essentially mind. Objective idealism is distinguished by a nondual view in which the physical world shares metaphysical reality.

The historic relation between idealistic philosophy and religious reflection stems from this common concern for showing how an immaterial power gives the material world its reality and true being. The idealistic commitment to mind as ultimately real expresses, in the language of experience, a view that overlaps the religious commitment to spirit as the enabling power of being. This tradition in Western philosophy was first explored systematically by Plato, for whom reality lay in the eternal forms, or ideas, that were the meaning of any particular thing. These particulars, however, were always imperfect because they were necessarily material. Matter, for Plato, is an admittedly indispensable context for existence. More significantly, however, it is a hindrance to realization of the true meaning of things, which is their ideal form. Plato is unclear as to why nature should exist, and matter remains a dark and unresolved dilemma in his philosophy. Aristotle gave matter greater status by making it the counterpart of form or idea in any particular. Matter is therefore the possibility of a new form. Mind or spirit or form shapes matter, as the idea of a pot in the mind of a potter transforms a lump of clay into a utensil for human use.

Plato and Aristotle incline toward idealism but remain dualists. It was only after Immanuel Kant that idealism offered an integrated view of reality that did justice to natural fact. Beginning with the radical distinction between mind and matter with which René Descartes had first fashioned the modern mind, idealists argued that mind and matter are different but interdependent. J. G. Fichte argued that will is the essence of mind, and will requires the recalcitrant opposition of material stuff in order for work to teach the moral lessons of industry, perseverance, and devotion to factual truth. For Fichte, nature is "the material for our duty, made sensible." For Friedrich Schelling and G. W. F. Hegel, nature is necessary in order that mind attain full self-awareness. Hegel argued that useful knowledge is always acquired through a double movement: first one gains an intimate knowledge of the particular thing, and then one learns something of what it is not. To know one's own language for what it truly is, for example, one must know something of a different language. So, to generalize from that experience, mind must know something that is not mind. It must wander in an alien world before it can return home to know itself truly for the first time. Nature, therefore, is the "otherness of spirit," the alien land in which the mind wanders in order to gain full possession of itself. Or, to put it less metaphorically, natural objects are the necessary content of mind. There is no thought without an object; one must think something. Whereas subjective idealism, in both the monadology of Leibniz and the Advaita Vedānta of Śaṅkara, argues that mind alone is the really real, objective idealism argues that objective nature is a necessary condition for the reality of mind. Reality is therefore not a univocal state; it is a dialectical process.

IDEALIST ETHICS. Idealism also proposes an ethics, developed from its metaphysical view that mind or spirit constitutes an eternal and purposive transcendent order. As the metaphysical reality of any particular is derived from the idea that is its ultimate meaning, so the norms and values of human behavior are derived from the transcendent idea of love, power, justice, or so forth.

Unlike modern naturalisms, which regard ethical values as entirely relative to the social and psychological needs of natural groups, idealism holds that there are what Kant called categorical imperatives, or moral absolutes. Kant stated the foundational principle of all idealistic ethics, people always should be treated as ends in themselves and never as a means to some end; but his dogmatic categorical imperative lacks metaphysical justification. It was his successors who developed an independent metaphysics that could flesh out Kant's intuitive insight with a rational argument. Hegel supplemented the Kantian view with a dialectical interpretation of concrete freedom that seeks to ally itself with whatever is objectively rational and universal in the laws and institutions of one's community. This view turned idealism toward social realism. Josiah Royce later argued that the objective reason that Hegel sought in institutions could not be found there if, as Hegel himself noted, institutions rise and fall. Rejecting Hegel's conservatism, Royce argued that one's loyalty is not just to the institutionalized rationality of the past but to the hoped-for rationality of the future. For Royce, therefore, one's primary loyalty is not to institutions but to those creative causes that some institutions sometimes serve. There will be different interpretations as to what these causes should be, but the authentic common spirit of cause-servers everywhere will always be one of loyalty. Royce's categorical imperative is therefore that one should be loyal to loyalty wherever it is found.

Various forms of idealism were influential during the nineteenth and early twentieth centuries when there was confidence in reason and hope for the future. The prevailing spirit since the late twentieth century has become skeptical of rationalization and pessimistic about the future, so idealistic philosophy is less influential. However, when religious thinkers look for a rational and universal language of experience in which to articulate the dramatic, poetic, and mythological convictions of the great religions with their message of a divine *Logos* that assures the ultimate fulfillment of a divine purpose, that language is inescapably some form of idealism.

SEE ALSO Metaphysics; Naturalism; Nature, article on Religious and Philosophical Speculations.

BIBLIOGRAPHY

Plato's dialogues all focus on the idealist issue, and Plotinus's third-century *Enneads* bears resemblance to the Advaita Vedānta philosophy in India, which Śaṅkara articulates in his ninth-century *Commentary on the Brahma Sutra.* Kant's *Religion within the Limits of Reason Alone* (1793), translated by Theodore M. Greene et al. (New York, 1960), identifies mind and spirit in idealistic fashion, and Hegel's *Lectures on the Philosophy of Religion* (1832), 3 vols., translated by E. B. Speirs and J. B. Sanderson (London, 1895), is the first systematic statement of idealistic philosophy of religion in the West. Josiah Royce's *The Problem of Christianity,* 2 vols. (New York, 1913), and William Ernest Hocking's *The Meaning of God in Human Experience* (New Haven, Conn., 1912) are the best-known systematic statements in the American philosophical tradition.

The best secondary sources on idealism are in the major histories of Western philosophy. For a technical discussion of philosophical ideas and their development, Wilhelm Windelband's *History of Philosophy,* translated by James H. Tufts (New York, 1893), is still unsurpassed. For idealism as an influential strand of modern intellectual culture, see John Herman Randall, Jr.'s *The Making of the Modern Mind* (New York, 1976) and Randall's two-volume *The Career of Philosophy* (New York, 1962–1965), especially volume 2, *From the German Enlightenment to the Age of Darwin.* The most recent significant interpretation of a major religious tradition in the light of an idealistic philosophy is Paul Tillich's three-volume *Systematic Theology* (Chicago, 1951–1963).

New Sources

Beiser, Frederick. *German Idealism: The Struggle against Subjectivism, 1781–1801.* Cambridge, Mass., 2002.

Henrich, Dieter, *Between Kant and Hegel: Lectures on German Idealism.* Edited by David Pacini. Cambridge, Mass., 2003.

McCumber, John. "The Temporal Turn in German Idealism: Hegel and After." *Research in Phenomenology* 32 (2002): 44–60.

Pinkard, Terry. *German Philosophy 1760–1860: The Legacy of Idealism.* New York, 2002.

Pippin, Robert. *Idealism as Modernism: Hegelian Variations.* New York, 1997.

LEROY S. ROUNER (1987)
Revised Bibliography

IDOLATRY. The word *idolatry* is formed from two Greek words, *eidōlon,* "image," and *latreia,* "adoration." Etymologically, *idolatry* means "adoration of images." Authors have given *idolatry* and *idol* widely differing definitions thereby revealing the complexity of the problem. Eugène Goblet d'Alviella uses the term *idol* to mean images or statues "that are considered to be conscious and animate" and sees idolatry in the act of "regarding an image as a superhuman personality" (Goblet d'Alviella, 1911, p. 126). In a relatively recent article, J. Goetz (1962), trying to get a better grip on the problem, establishes, first, that in the wake of etymology idolatry "designates the adoration of images by emphasizing the specific nature of the cult surrounding the objects, a cult of adoration, which strictly speaking expresses a feeling of absolute dependence, especially through sacrifice." He then states that the terms *idolatry* and *idol* remain inaccurate, and that "the authors who have tackled the problem of idolatry most often defined the idol as an object in anthromorphic form, intended to represent a spirit, the object of worship." Finally, venturing onto the terrain of religious phenomenology, he risks a definition of *idol:* "any material object that receives a form of worship more or less structured," idolatry being this form of worship.

The concept of idolatry originated in a very specific historico-religious context: the monotheism of Israel. Consequently, an authentic approach to the concept must refer to the Hebrew scriptures. In his research on the prophetic reaction to pagan religious concepts, Christopher R. North presents two ideas taken directly from the prophets. First, "Idolatry is the worship of the creature instead of the Creator and, to make matters worse, the creature is made by man, who is himself a creature" (North, 1958, p. 158). He then states: "Idolatry is the worship of what in modern terms we should call process, the 'life-force,' the *élan vital,* or what we will, instead of the Creator who transcends and is in some sort external to creation" (ibid., p. 159). Finally, here is another, more recently formulated definition: "Idolatry may be defined as the worship of an idol (*eidōlon,* image, portrait) considered as a substitute for the divine" (M. Delahoutre, "Idolâtrie," *Dictionnaire des religions,* Paris, 1984).

This brief survey should help situate this article's discussion. The concept of idolatry originated in the application of the second commandment. It acquired definitive formulation in censure by the prophets of Israel of the pagan cults and their influence on the chosen people. This biblical heritage passed into the New Testament and early Christianity, blazing its way through the forest of pagan cults. The monotheism of Islam adopted this Judeo-Christian concept and made it one of the foundations of its beliefs and its faith.

Beginning with these notions formed with the help of the dogmatic thought as well as the polemic stance of the three great monotheisms, the historian of religions enlarges his vision of idolatry by studying this religious phenomenon through the behavior of *homo religiosus* in relation to the representation of divinity. However, this study becomes vast and includes other very important aspects: images for worship, symbolism in religions and cults, religious art, veneration of images, iconoclasm. The present study is limited to idolatry, which it will approach on two levels: On the one hand, the historico-religious fact that the three great monotheisms censured the worship of idols; and, on the other hand, the phenomenon of humankind's attitude of worship in the presence of a visible representation of divinity. The study of these two aspects is made with reference to the historical documentation left by the *homo religiosus* concerned.

HISTORICAL SEMANTICS. In ancient Greek texts since Homer one rarely finds the word *eidōlon.* Formed from *eidos* (n.), "aspect, shape," the word *eidōlon* has diverse meanings: "phantom, undetermined form, image reflected in a mirror or in water." It also means an image formed in the human mind. Thus in the ancient Greek world, *eidōlon* did not have a religious meaning.

One must therefore turn to the biblical Greek world, where *eidōlon* is found in the Septuagint. Used 70 times in the protocanonical texts, it translates 16 different Hebrew words, as for example *aven,* vanity; *elil,* nothing; *gillulim,* excrement; *pesel,* carved statue; *tselim,* image. For these protocanonical texts the Vulgate uses *idolum* 112 times and *simulacrum* 32 times in order to translate 15 Hebrew words. *Eidōlon* also appears many times in the apocryphal writings. The Hebrew Bible uses 30 different nouns in order to talk about idols and mentions 44 pagan divinities. Thus *eidōlon* designates the false gods and does so with a scornful nuance, for they are vanity, lies, nothingness, vain images, molded metal, carved wood. It is therefore through choices made by Greek translators of the Bible that *eidōlon* acquired the religious sense of representing a pagan divinity considered to be a false god. Thus the Septuagint gave *eidōlon* a new pejorative and polemical meaning. (By extension, *eidoleiōn* means a temple in which idols are found.)

Eidōlon passed into the Greek New Testament. The word does not occur in the Gospels, but it appears elsewhere (*Acts* 7:41, 15:20; *Rom.* 2:22; *1 Cor.* 8:4, 8:7, 10:9, 12:2; *2 Cor.* 6:16; *1 Thes.* 1:9; *1 Jn.* 5:21; *Rev.* 9:20). The Vulgate sometimes translates it as *idolum* and sometimes as *simulacrum.* One passage (*1 Cor.* 7:10) has the word *eidoleion,* "temple of idols," which the Vulgate preserves, Latinizing it as *idolium.* The New Testament passages show that in the eyes of the compilers, the pagan gods have no substance (*Gal.* 4:8). Behind their worship hides the work of demons (*1 Cor.* 10:19).

The word *eidōlon* passed into patristic terminology. Its usage is common from the second century on. In the *Epistle of Barnabas,* the *eidōla* are the pagan gods to which the Hebrews turned in the desert. Justin Martyr (*1 Apology* 64.1) designates as an *eidōlon* a statue of Kore, who was considered to be the daughter of Zeus. In speaking of pagan gods, Clement of Alexandria made use of all the richness of Greek vocabulary of his time. Evidence of this can be found in chapter 4 of the *Exhortation to the Heathen,* devoted to statues of gods, *agalmata.* He calls them idols (4.53.1) and includes them among the demons (4.55.1), which are impure and base spirits. He invites his readers to approach these statues (*agalmata*) in order to uncover the error that they conceal: "Their exterior clearly shows the mark of your demons' inner dispositions" (4.57.1). Later he reproaches the Greeks for having given themselves models of sensuality in these idols (4.61.1). Justin proclaims that Christ came to liberate people from the domination of idols (*Dialogue with Trypho* 113.6). These pagan gods are only phantoms that take possession of the human spirit and give the pagans the illusion of divine worship (Athenagoras, *Libellus* 23). These few samples, taken from the arsenal of the polemic of the apologists and the Greek fathers, show how the meaning of *eidōlon* expanded in the Greek world during the first centuries of the common era.

The Latin fathers adopt the same vocabulary and an identical stance. Tertullian shows that the pagan gods have no substance (*Apologetics* 10.2); then he attacks the statues as inert matter, *simulacra* made of material related to that of vases and ordinary utensils (12.2). In a similar fashion, Firmicus Maternus speaks of the *imagines consecratas* of public pagan worship (*Octavius* 24.5). Augustine gives a definitive structure to this criticism of idolatry made by the Latin apologists. Speaking of the pagan gods, he shows the semantic relationship between *simulacrum* and *idolum*: "*simulacra*, which in Greek are called idols" (*Expositions on the Psalms* 135.3). In his eyes, the idol worshipers are *daemonicolae*. The idol lets the demon make his own revelation (Mandouze, 1958).

The words *eidōlolatria* and *eidōlolatrēs* are found neither in secular Greek texts nor in the Septuagint nor in the writings of Philo Judaeus. They are a specific contribution of the New Testament and Christian literature of the first Christian centuries. Paul considers idolatry a grave sin and puts it on the list of sins that Christians must avoid (*1 Cor.* 5:10–11, 6:9, 10:7, 10:14; *Gal.* 5:20; *Col.* 3:5; *Eph.* 5:5). The writer of *1 Peter* 4:3 speaks in analogous fashion of the worship of idols that ought to be rejected by Christians. The same idea appears in *Revelation* 21:8 and 22:15.

The use of the two words becomes constant in Greek patristic literature. Clement of Alexandria even leaves a definition of idolatry: "the extension to numerous divinities of what is reserved for the one true God" (*Miscellanies* 3.12). The Christian church opposed idols and condemned their manufacture. The second-century apologists left a veritable arsenal of arguments on which Christian polemicists would draw until the age of Augustine.

IDOLATRY AND THE HEBREW SCRIPTURES. The formal condemnation of idolatry is found in *Exodus* 20:3–5. The biblical God (whose unvocalized name is YHVH) simultaneously forbids the worship of foreign gods and the making of images that claim to represent him, because it is impossible to represent the God of Israel. A confirmation and amplification of this commandment are found in *Deuteronomy* 4:12–19. The interdiction pertains to both theriomorphic and anthropomorphic images. It pertains also to symbolic animal representations of the divinity. Thus idolatry is vested with a double aspect: the idolatrous worship of Yahveh as well as the worship of false gods.

The Mosaic prohibition. The second commandment forbids the making of representations of the divinity (*Ex.* 20:4–6; *Dt.* 4:15–19 and 5:6–9; *Lv.* 26:1). A rigorous tendency took this Mosaic prohibition literally by banishing all ornamentation of religious buildings. This tendency, which became widespread among the Pharisees, insisted on the spiritualization of God and radically opposed the danger of idolatry. A more liberal tendency has always existed, however, as attested by the animal and human decoration of certain synagogues discovered by archaeologists.

Idolatrous worship of YHVH. Biblical texts refer to this worship on various occasions. The Hebrew tribes underwent the influence of Canaanite culture (*Jgs.* 3:5–6, *Dt.* 7:1–5). Micah of the tribe of Ephraim made a *pesel* and a *massekhah*, a carved image and idol of cast metal (*Jgs.* 17:1–13), perhaps an image of God. After his victory over Midian, Gideon made use of the gold taken from the enemy to make and set up an *efod* (*Jgs.* 8:22–27). Moreover, there is evidence of the tauriform cult of YHVH in the northern kingdom of Israel after the schism of 935 (*1 Kgs.* 12:26–32, *2 Kgs.* 15:24). In *1 Kings* 12:28, Jeroboam presents God, symbolized by the bull (Hadad and Teshub, fertility gods), as the liberator of Israel at the time of the flight from Egypt. The writer of *2 Kings* 15:24 speaks of the erection of statues of divine bulls. This is the religious tradition of the golden calf.

The prophets fought the use of images because they represented the danger of superstition. *Hosea* 3:4 assails the stelae (*matstsebot*) erected next to the altars, the *efod*, which are either images or instruments for interrogating Yahveh, and the *terafim*, which closely resemble the *efod*. Thus, the prophet aims at the elimination of even the accessories to worship. Jeremiah went even further, proclaiming around 587 BCE that he would no longer speak of the Ark of the Covenant of Yahveh, which would be neither remembered nor missed, and which would never be built again (*Jer.* 3:16).

The prophetic argument is simple. It rejects all tangible representation of God as dangerous because the image is distinct from God. Hosea, moreover, refers to the past, to the youth of Israel, and to the flight from Egypt (*Hos.* 2:17). Thus, prophetic polemics find support in the Mosaic tradition. It is in this context that the incident of the golden calf (*Ex.* 32) must be understood and seen in terms of a protest against the worship of the tauriform Yahveh. Clearly, one is confronted here with a total rejection of the symbolism of the idol.

Idolatry as worship of false gods. The second aspect of idolatry holds a much larger place in the Bible; to understand it is necessary to review the history of idolatry in Israel. The ancestors of the chosen people practiced polytheism. Joshua recalled this in his address to the assembly at Shechem: The father of Abraham and Nahor served other gods (*Jos.* 24:2, 24:14), and even in Egypt some Hebrews worshiped pagan divinities. Upon their return from Egypt, the seminomadic Hebrew tribes who settled in Canaan came under the influence of the surrounding pagan culture and were always tempted to adopt their gods (*Jgs.* 10:6; *1 Sm.* 7:4, 12:10). Furthermore, kings often advanced polytheism by the introduction of foreign wives who kept their gods (*1 Kgs.* 11:7, 11:33). Amos accuses his contemporaries of worshiping Sakkuth and Kaiwan (*Am.* 5:26), two astral divinities. The prestige of the Assyrian pantheon exercised a profound influence on the populations of Israel. During the reign of Manasseh (688–642 BCE) a serious religious crisis broke out. Shaken by the triumphs of the Assyrians and the Chaldeans, the faithful turned to the gods of the conquerors (*2 Kgs.* 21:1–9, 23:4–14). They worshiped the sun, the moon, the *baals*, and the Astartes (*Jer.* 2:8, 7:9). Nergal and other divinities reigned in the sanctuaries (*2 Kgs.* 17:30–31). After 587 came the trial of exile, followed by a spiritual reform. The prophets' orations were beneficial for the piety of Israel, which regained consciousness of its monotheistic faith. Upon returning from exile, they were vigilant about keeping their distance from idolatry, which continued to threaten the people because of the populations that remained in Palestine, especially in Samaria. The reaction against idolatrous cults was especially characteristic of the syncretic attempts under Antiochus IV Epiphanes (*2 Mc.* 6:2). The entire Jewish nation drew tightly together around the faith in Yahveh.

The most formidable opponents of idolatry were the prophets and their prophecies. At the solemn unveiling of the golden calf at Bethel, a prophet appeared before Jeroboam and announced Yahveh's threat (*1 Kgs.* 13:1–32). Elijah and Elisha fought against the worship of Baal and his priests (*1 Kgs.* 18:22–40). Amos reproached his Judean compatriots for letting themselves be seduced by idols (*Am.* 2:4). Hosea spoke harshly also, because in his eyes the worship of Israel had become idolatry (*Hos.* 4:12–13). Isaiah attacked the idols and announced their fall (*Is.* 2:20, 17:7–8, 30:22).

One of the important themes of the prophetic polemic is the emptiness of false gods. Idols are nothing but stone and wood (*Jer.* 16:20). Hosea does not hesitate to liken idolatry to fetishism, for in his eyes the image is set up in place of God (*Hos.* 8:4–6). Isaiah writes veritable satires of the Babylonian gods, whom he compares to nothingness (*Is.* 44:14–17). These mindless gods are carried about by beasts of burden (*Is.* 46:1–2). The theme of the idol as vacuous will continue its march, to be exploited by subsequent prophets (*Bar.* 6, *Dn.* 13:65–14:42). Moreover, it will crystallize into an imposing number of ironic and scornful terms: *nothingness, insubstantial puff of wind, lie, corpse.* Ezekiel's favorite word is *gillutim* ("dunghill"). Derision of false gods is a biblical tradition antedating the prophets and continuing after the exile (Preuss, 1971).

The *Wisdom of Solomon,* written in Greek on the eve of the common era, holds a veritable trial of idolatry, especially in chapters 13–15. The author rejects the worship of nature, idolatry, and zoolatry (worship of animals). However, while remaining completely faithful to the biblical tradition, he reflects his time by paying homage to the beauty of nature and works of art. He attacks the Stoic conception of gods according to which Zeus was the ether, Poseidon the ocean, and Demeter the earth (*Wis.* 13:1–19). He attacks the dynastic cult of the Ptolemies (14:17–20) and the mystery religions (14:23). In his view, the adherents of zoolatry have completely lost their reason (15:18–19). It is in terms of an authentic Yahvism that he judges pagan religions. He considers idolatry a fundamental disorder because it gives the name of God to that which is not God (13:2, 14:15, 14:20). Furthermore, the faithful adore dead idols that are incompetent and powerless. This disorder, which comes from seduction, leads to a mental aberration that in the end produces a moral deficiency among the faithful, who fall into error if not into lechery. Yet even while condemning these mistaken ideas from which Abraham and the chosen people escaped, the author speaks of his admiration for art. The *Wisdom of Solomon* has left a veritable synthesis of biblical polemics against idols, a synthesis into which certain ideas from the contemporary Greek world have already entered.

IDOLATRY AND CHRISTIANITY. The study of idolatry from the point of view of early Christianity is linked to problems of the birth of Christian art and the question of images, their worship, and the refusal to worship them. The attitude to adopt toward idols had been prescribed to the Christians from the first decades of the church. The Christians coming from Judaism had very strong traditions. Christians who converted from paganism radically separated themselves from idols and their worship. They all lived in the midst of pagan populations who had proliferated temples, altars, statues, sacrifices, processions, and festivals in Egypt, Greece, Rome, and the Middle East. The rapid expansion of Christianity into the provinces of the empire obliged the church to take very clear positions in regard to pagan cults.

The biblical heritage. Traces of the Old Testament opposition to idols are found in the New Testament, where *eidōlon* appears several times in the Pauline epistles. *Galatians* 4:8 takes up the common theme of pagan gods who have no substance. In *1 Corinthians* 10:19, Paul states that when one venerates idols, one is appealing to demons. This idea had already appeared in *Deuteronomy* 32:17 and was developed after the exile as a result of the success of demonology. The Pauline polemic revives the notion that the pagans offer sacrifices to demons. Demonolatry is also denounced in *Revelation* 9:20. The double biblical theme of the emptiness of idols and the demonic character of idolatry will be taken up later by the apologists and the church fathers.

The biblical heritage concerning idols also reached Christians by a second route, namely that of Philo Judaeus. In *Allegory of the Law* Philo tries to differentiate the divinity from any human likeness, because "anthropomorphism is an impiety greater than the ocean" (*On the Confusion of Tongues* 27). In *On the Decalogue* (52–80) and *Of the Contemplative Life* (3–9), he writes two accounts of the pagan gods. Both follow the same five-point outline: (1) a critique of the deification of the elements (earth, water, air, fire); (2) a critique of the deification of the sun, the moon, and the cosmos; (3) a critique of the gods considered as actors in mythology; (4) an attack against idolatry; and finally (5) a critique of zoolatry. J. Schwartz (1971) has called this "the Philonian schema." It influenced the critique of idolatry by Greek and Latin apologists, who drew on it for part of their own polemical material. On the subject of the worship of statues and divine images, Philo writes, "Their substance is of rock and wood, which was completely formless just a little while before. . . . Fragments which were their brothers or their family have become vessels for bath water or foot-washing basins" (*On the Contemplative Life* 7).

The Greek apologists and fathers. In his first *Apology* (9.1–5), Justin Martyr collects the principal themes of second-century polemics against idols: The human form is not suitable to divinity; idols have no soul and are made from a base substance; they are works of depraved artisans and bait for thieves; they bear the names of maleficent demons in whose appearance they are clothed. In his *Apology* Aristides of Athens has no sympathy for the idols of the Greeks. He severely condemns the sin of worshiping created things but is even harsher toward the barbarians, who revere earth, water, the sun, and the moon, and create idols they present as divinities. In his *Libellus,* another Athenian, Athenagoras, attempts to show that making statues of divinities is recent. All such statues are the works of people whose names are known. The artists have therefore made gods who are younger than their creators. In short, all these idols are no more than fragments of creation that the faithful adore in place of the creator. After this interpretation of idolatry in the sense of fetishism, Athenagoras explains the manipulation of idols by demons. The demons urge the faithful to block around the idols, then during the sacrifices they lick the blood of the victims. But all these gods had once been humans. A heritage of the secularized Greek age of the centuries just prior to the Christian era, this theme of euhemerism was to be a weighty argument, one the Fathers would use continuously.

Clement of Alexandria wrote his *Protrepticus* in order to convince the worshipers of the gods of what he held to be the stupidity and baseness of pagan myths. He first tries to determine the origin and nature of idols. Blocks of wood and pillars of rock in ancient times, they became human representations thanks to the progress of art, of which the author gives a well-documented survey. Then Clement poses the fundamental question: Where did the gods represented by idols come from? The historical response to this question, inspired by euhemerism, is the deification of human beings, of kings who have declared themselves divine, and of kings by their successors. Clement then gives a theological answer, partly inspired by Plato: The pagan gods are demons, shadows, infamous and impure spirits. Consequently,the error and moral corruption of idolatry becomes clear. The error is serious, for it leads the faithful to worship matter and demons as divine. The corruption of morals is a consequence of error: Idols excite lust and sensuality, which were invented by demons. To idolatry, Clement opposes the adoration of the true God, who shows humanity its proper dignity. Clement indicates this path of happiness by invoking *Deuteronomy* (5:8), *Exodus* (20:4), the *Sybilline Oracles* (4:4–7, 24:27–30), and Christian doctrine (*1 Pt.* 2:9; *Rom.* 6:4; *Jn.* 8:23). Chapter 4 of the *Protrepticus* is a veritable synthesis of the Christian concept of idolatry at the end of the second century.

The Latin apologists. The position taken by the Latin apologists in regard to the pagan gods constitutes a final stage. Here one again finds the Philonian schema of the *De vita contemplativa* (3–9). Yet, this schema is not a dead weight that condemns the argumentation of the Fathers to die-hard conservatism. Two facts emerge from the study of these documents: On the one hand, the researcher is witnessing a permanent renewal of the antipolytheistic argument; on the other hand, the authors take into account changes in the pagan cults, especially the rise of the mystery cults with their new religiosity. The documents appear at intervals from the late second to the fourth century: *To the Nations, Apology,* and *On Idolatry* by Tertullian; *Octavius* by Minucius Felix; *To Donatus, To Quirinius, To Demetrianus, Quod idola di non sint* by Cyprian; *Divinae institutiones* and *Epitome* by Lactantius Firmianus; and *De errore profanorum religionum* by Firmicus Maternus.

The pagan gods are not idols, states Tertullian: "We stopped worshiping your gods once we realized they do not exist" (*Apology* 10.2). He first substantiates his statement through history, for it is known where these gods were born and where their tombs are. He reproaches the pagans for claiming that their gods became gods after death because of their merits in the service of humans. After these considerations inspired by euhemerism, Tertullian tackles the question of *simulacra.* The statues are only inert matter, just like vases, dishes, and furniture. Insensitive to outrage or homage, these statues are given over to commerce if not to destruction. Tertullian treats these questions at greater length in *On Idolatry,* which undertakes to show that idolatry is the gravest sin, encompassing all others. He condemns painting, modeling, sculpture, and participation in public festivals, because idolatry hides beneath seemingly innocent actions. Furthermore, he forbids Christians to teach or to conduct business, for both pursuits require contact with idols. In short, all the powers and dignities of this world are alien to God; for this reason, Christians must likewise be forbidden the military life.

The Latin apologists also developed the idea that pagan gods are demons. Demonology held a place of honor at the beginning of the common era. Both Greek and Latin apologists transformed the false gods into demons. The fathers seized the opportunity to turn these demons, intermediary beings between humanity and divinity, into characters lurking in the shadows of idols. Minucius Felix explains that "the demons hide behind statues and sacred images and, by exhaling their breath," exercise their mysterious effects—spells, dreams, prodigies (*Octavius* 27.1–3). In *To the Nations* Tertullian speaks of the pagan gods represented by idols that the demons use as masks to deceive men, and in *On Idolatry,* he curses artists and workers who fashion these bodies for the demons. Minucius Felix does not hesitate to make the demons the beneficiaries of sacrifice. Taking up Tertullian's notion that the devil, in the mysteries of Mithra, mimics the Christian faith, Minucius Felix accuses the devil of having plagiarized Christian ritual in the religions of Mithra and Isis. Firmicus Maternus develops this theory further and discovers the devil everywhere in paganism—in idolatry, zoolatry, the deification of sovereigns, and astrology. Thus a shaken paganism faces a decisive condemnation of idolatry and idols.

Augustine. In his *Against the Pagans,* completed in 311, the convert Arnobius attacked paganism, denounced the anthropomorphism of the pagan cult, ridiculed the pagans' conception of the gods, censured their myths, and attacked the mystery cults. His disciple Lactantius, converted, like him, under the persecution of Diocletian, and began his *Divinae institutiones* in 304. Lactantius demonstrates that monotheism is the only form of belief in God consistent with truth and reason. Speaking of the general evil of polytheism, he explains it by euhemerism and by the ruse of demons who get themselves adored under divine names first in families and then in cities.

On August 24, 410, the hordes of Alaric entered Rome and subjected the city to pillage. The pagans accused the Christians of having destroyed the worship of the gods and thus chased away the city's protectors. Augustine's answer was the *City of God,* written between 413 and 426, whose twenty-two books constitute the last great apologetic work against ancient paganism.

The pagan gods were a prime target, but Augustine found himself confronting a paganism with multiple and contradictory aspects. Besides the divine populace of country rituals, there were the gods of the classical pantheon, deified men, and a Stoic pantheism that turned Jupiter into a world soul. Throughout the first ten books of *City of God,* Augustine launches a critique, in turn acerbic and ironic, of the Roman gods, polytheism, and mythology. To strike a fatal blow at the idols, he brings in Varro, Cicero, Seneca, Euhemerus, Apuleius, and Plato. He tries to fight Varro's theology with its false gnosis of etymologies of divine names and its tripartition of gods introduced by poets, philosophers, and heads of state. But Augustine knows that idols are not mere beings without substance, invented during the course of history. These idols are also in the hearts of worshipers, for idolatry consists of worshiping creation or a part of it as God. This theme is developed in *On Christian Doctrine* and *On True Religion,* in which Augustine, not content with a critique of the idol, launches a critique of the idol's worshiper, whom he considers a devil worshiper.

Thus, an essential aspect of Augustine's criticism of idolatry is his study of demonology. After having reviewed some of the major themes of his predecessors, he virtually psychoanalyzes the work of demons in the life of idol worshipers. Evoked by humans, demons take possession of idols. The *simulacra* become animate, and the work of demons can be achieved because the idol is no longer inert: An invisible *numen* is present. The idol serves as body for the demon. It receives life from the demon, to whom it lends itself. By this means, the demon accomplishes his revelation. For this reason, Augustine repeats incessantly, "The gods are demons, and worshipers of idols are worshipers of demons." Yet in book 8 of *City of God,* he diminishes the power of demons somewhat, because they are not gods. For Augustine, these false gods are lying angels who continue their struggle against the true God. The malice of the sin of idolatry is thus exposed.

Christianity since Augustine. Ever since the conversion of the empire to Catholicism, paganism had been in retreat. After one last revival under the emperor Julian, it found a tough opponent in Theodosius the Great (r. 379–395), who forbade idolatry as a crime of lèse-majesté. The fifth century witnessed the demolition of temples and idols; Augustine gave the final blow to pagan theology. But the church remained vigilant in order to uproot the last implantations of paganism and squelch its influence among the people. This preoccupation would be translated in three ways: penitential discipline enacted against the sin of idolatry; the teaching of morality, beginning with the writings of Tertullian; and the constant purification of Christian worship and vigilance regarding the veneration of saints. Several great controversies, especially iconoclasm and the Reformation, show that idolatry remained a preoccupation. In the sixteenth and seventeenth centuries, Protestants often accused the Catholic church of maintaining ceremonies and traditions tainted by idolatry. Recent discussions about the cult of the saints, the worship of images, and the origin of Christian worship show the historical and theological importance of the problem.

Idolatry and Islam. An Arab proverb recorded by al-Maydānī says, "When you enter a village, swear by its god." On the eve of the Hijrah, Arab tribes venerated many gods. In his work *Kitāb al-aṣnām* (Cairo, 1914), Ibn al-Kalbī described the prosperity of the cult of idols in the pre-Islamic age (Jāhilīyah). These idols were *anṣāb,* or raised stones; *garis,* or stones upon which the blood of sacrifice was poured; sacred trees; and statuettes that were bought and sold at fairs and markets. Another word used by al-Kalbī, which is also found in the commentators of the Qurʾān, is *ṣanam* (pl., *aṣnām*), "an object venerated next to God." The word has a Semitic origin and seems close to the Hebrew *semel,* "representation." The word is found five times in the Qurʾān (6:74, 7:134, 14:38, 21:58, 26:1), designating the "idol" rejected by Muslims. In the pre-Islamic age *ṣanam* designated diverse objects: statues sculpted like the god Hubal, statues around the Kaʿbah in Mecca, and sacred trees and stones. These stones, which received libations and became objects of worship, were *anṣāb* (sg., *nuṣub*); the Arabs carried them in their migrations. Therefore *ṣanam* does not mean "divinity."

Al-Azraqī says that in Mecca there was an idol in every house. Through this proliferation of idols, the Arab invoked divinity. The gods of this vast pantheon brought the divine into the everyday realities of existence. The distinctions between various epiphanies resided in the names given them and the numerous sanctuaries. Onomastic documentation takes one back to a distant age where these idols existed, epiphanies of the divine. In addition, Hellenism introduced into Arab paganism heroes, ancestors, and genies from Petra, Palmyra, and other Hellenistic cities.

Another word is *shirk* (*mushrikūn*), which designates the act of associating a person with divinity; it is the word for polytheism. In the Qurʾān the word appears in the Medina *sūrahs*, where its use is frequent in Muḥammad's attacks on the associators, the *mushrikūn* (*sūrah* 6:94, 10:19, 30:12, 39:4). Such persons are to be avoided by believers. One must not pray for them, even if they are relatives (9:114). Their sin will not be pardoned. The word *kāfir*, "unbeliever," is more general and includes both the associators and the possessors of scripture (Jews and Christians). In the Qurʾān *shirk*, "associator," is the opposite of *muslim*, "worshiper of God." *Shirk* retains this meaning in the *ḥadīth*.

Muḥammad's opposition to idolatry is a Judeo-Christian inheritance. Abraham becomes the prototype of the monotheistic faith that Muḥammad espouses. Abraham is to the prophets what the Arabs are to other Muslim peoples. Beginning with Abraham's revelation, Muḥammad goes on to see in Islam not only the true monotheism but primordial hanifism (from *ḥanīf*, one who follows the original and true monotheistic religion; a Muslim), which was transmitted by Abraham's son Ishmael, following in his father's footsteps. It is in this original path that one discovers the Qurʾān's opposition to idolatry.

Idols are the enemies of God and his worshipers. Referring again to Abraham, the Qurʾān condemns them along with the whole Semitic ancestral tradition, which is the origin of their worship, a worship radically opposed to the worship of the one true God (26:69–83). The same idea is found in the text of *sūrah* 21:53/52 to 70, which tells how Abraham smashed the idols worshiped by his countrymen. These idols had no substance and were incapable of creating anything (25:3–5/4). Moses had to intervene against the sons of Israel who, after their flight from Egypt, began to worship the idols that they made for themselves (7:134/138). Thus Muḥammad orders his followers to avoid the stain of idolatry and to serve God in complete fidelity (22:31/30).

Throughout the whole Qurʾān is found opposition to idols and idolatry. One must turn away from them (15:94) for they bring unhappiness to their worshipers (41:5/6), who are nothing but liars upon whom God will inflict torment after torment (16:88/86–90/88). The idolators' error is a grave one because they have no faith in God (12:106), to whom they compare mere creatures (30:30). A terrible punishment awaits them: They will be treated like their idols (10:29/28), who will abandon them to their sad fate when they stand before the fire (6:23–29). Because of the seriousness of this error, the law of the Qurʾān demands that Muslims neither marry a woman idolator nor give their daughters to idolators in marriage (2:220–221). The Qurʾān makes a distinction between idolators (associators) on the one hand, and possessors of scripture on the other, that is to say, Jews and Christians. However, the two categories of non-Muslims are guilty of infidelity in respect to God, as emphasized in surah 98. In *sūrah* 22:17 (evidently a later text), is found the opposition between Muslims on the one hand, and Jews, Christians, Sabaeans, and Zoroastrians on the other. The Qurʾān demands that Muslims fight idolators (9:36).

Idolatry consists of associating a god or gods with God (51:51, 50:25–26). This idea keeps recurring; it is the Qurʾān's definition of idolatry, whence the word for associators. Idolatry is an insult to God, because honors reserved for him alone are bestowed on false gods. *Sūrah* 17:111 shows that there are three degrees of association: children, associates in kingship, and protectors (sg., *walī*). The idea of the protector is found several times in the Qurʾān. In *sūrah* 39:4/3, saints are divinities that the faithful worship because they consider them intermediaries who will bring them closer to God. From the beginning, in Islam, fear of idolatry led to the suppression of all mediation between the faithful and God. Association in kingship consists of putting false gods on an equal footing with the one and only God (14:35/30, 26:92, 26:98). It involves an actual insult to God, for the power of the Creator is given to beings who have no substance (32:3/4, 40:69/67, 29:41/42). These idols are only names (12:40); God is the sole master of the world and people. A third means of association consists of attributing children to God (43:81), an idea that appears repeatedly in diverse forms. The Qurʾān is undoubtedly alluding to polytheistic myths and statues of divinities in temples. *Sūrah* 23:93/91 tells of the quarrels of the gods who claim to be superior to each other. There is also mention of goddesses, daughters of God (43.15, 52:39). The most famous passage is *sūrah* 53:19–21, satanic verses about the three goddesses of the Kaʿbah. These goddesses were highly honored in the pre-Islamic Arab world, with great financial returns for the tribe of Quraysh. At the beginning of his preaching, the Prophet did not dare touch them. After the seizure of Mecca in 630, however, he had all the idols of the Kaʿbah destroyed in his presence.

The essence of idolatry resides in the insult to God by the associators, who confer on mere creatures the honors and worship reserved for the Unique, the Creator, the Master of the World. Like the apologists and the Fathers of the church, the Qurʾān insists on the work of the demon who impels men toward idols. Abraham asks his father not to worship Satan (19:45/44), who turns men away from the worship of

God (27:24). The demon is the patron of idolators (16:65/63) and as such is opposed to God (4:118/119). Consequently, idolatry becomes the demon's auxiliary (25:57/55). In *sūrah* 4:117, the Qur'ān says that idolators pray only to females, or to a rebellious demon.

Allāh is the creator God, judge, dealer of retribution, unique and one in himself, all-powerful, and merciful. He reveals himself through his prophets. He does not show himself, but is recognized in the signs of the universe, in the signs of God, *āyāt Allāh*. He can be known only by his word, his names, his attributes, and his deeds. In any case, he cannot be represented by an image or a representation. Islam is a religion without icons.

IDOLATRY AND HOMO RELIGIOSUS. Idolatry is a historical-religious concept that finds expression in the response and behavior of the three great monotheisms when confronted with the beliefs and the practices of the polytheistic religions they encountered along their way. This concept was developed in the course of discussions and confrontations with these monotheisms: three religions of the Book, depositories of a revelation, animated by prophecy and doctrines of salvation—religions that join humanity to a personal God who appears in history. Idolatry means divine worship of beings who are not God in the eyes of those who have defined worship as idolatrous. The word has a negative and pejorative connotation because to the faithful of a monotheistic religion, attitudes, behaviors, and rites that should be strictly reserved for the true God are turned by the idolator toward false gods. Thus, idolatry is a fundamental religious disequilibrium due to two paradoxical facts: on the one hand a divine cultus, on the other a substitute for the divine that is not God.

Fetishism is a historical-religious concept developed in the modern age by ethnologists and historians of religions, with a view to explaining the creeds of primal black peoples of western Africa. In *Du culte des dieux fétiches* (1760), Charles de Brosses tried to apprehend humankind in its archaic state of raw nature. He observed that ancient peoples worshiped animals, trees, plants, fountains, lakes, seas, stars, and rivers as contemporary primitives still do. To this worship, de Brosses gave the name *fetishism,* a term formed from the Portuguese *feitiço* ("witchcraft, bewitched subject"). Humanity sees an active presence in the fetish, which provokes fear and the need for protection. Humankind obtains protection through the observance of rites. Thus, the fetishist worships the object directly, unlike in polytheism, which de Brosses viewed as a more structured religion in which symbols are characterized above all by the image and the statue.

Research has made the notion of fetishism more precise. Fetishism is the belief in the existence of a power, concentrated in beings or objects, that humanity must harness for its own well-being. This power is obtained by means of individual or collective rites. The beneficial result will be a function of the force obtained; therefore humankind uses a whole web of rituals in order to increase the force and then capture it. The context here remains one of worship, but one in which ritual receives the greatest emphasis.

This parallel between two phenomena of worship, idolatry and fetishism, will allow one to better situate idolatry as a religious phenomenon perceived by the historian of religions. In this view, idolatry is the worship of a divinity represented by a substitute for the divine, called an idol. To grasp the different dimensions of this worship, the historians of religions center their research on *homo religiosus* at work in the exercise of this worship. They seek to understand human behavior through human rites and in the implementation of the human symbolic system.

In the Greco-Roman world, voices were raised against the adoration of divinity in human form by Heraclitus, Xenophanes, Pythagoras, Euripides, Diogenes and the Cynics, and Stoics such as Zeno and Seneca. Reflecting on the divinity, these thinkers tried to establish themselves as intermediaries between the philosophers' religion and that of the people. In this area, Plutarch's thought becomes apparent. Seeking to avoid the two extremes of superstition and atheism, he emphasizes that divine life and intelligence are not subordinate to humans. Likewise, he refuses the application of gods' names to insensate natures or inanimate objects (*De Iside* 66–67). In Egypt, he confronts zoolatry, which may lead to repugnant aberrations because of the worship of sacred animals. However, observing that the Egyptians were extraordinary inventors of symbols and emblems, Plutarch accepts the symbolism of the divine manifested in the life of beings. Consequently, he approves of those for whom these beings are an occasion to worship the divine.

During the first century of the common era, Dio Cocceianus (Chrysostomos) of Prusa, writing an apology for Greek art, affirmed: "We invest God with the human body since it is the vessel of thought and reason. In the complete absence of a primitive model we seek to reveal the incomparable and the invisible by means of the visible and the comparable, in a higher manner than certain barbarians who, in their ignorance and absurdity, liken the divinity to animal shapes." For Dio, plastic beauty expresses the divine. A century later the eclectic Platonist Maxim of Tyre treated the question of the legitimacy of portraying the gods. He notes that the Persians adored the divinity in the ephemeral image of fire; that the Egyptians contemplated their gods in objects and beings worthy of scorn; and that though the images may vary, the essential thing is to worship divinity: "God, the father of all things and their creator, existed before the sun and is older than the sky. . . . Since we cannot grasp his essence, we seek help in words, names, animal shapes, figures of gold, ivory, and silver" (*Philosophumena* 2.10).

Augustine leaves numerous allusions to the allegorical interpretation of idolatry by pagan authors. In *Expositions on the Psalms* 113 he speaks of certain people who claim that their worship does not really address itself to the elements themselves but to the divinities who are their masters. The same idea is found elsewhere in the same work (96), where the idolator declares that he worships the statue he sees, but submits to the god he does not see; the statue is only a substitute for the divinity. The pagan authors targeted by Augustine are perhaps the emperor Julian, Porphyry, and Varro.

The history of religions approaches idolatry in terms of those four fundamental aspects of religious belief and practice that *homo religiosus* has been evolving from prehistoric times down to the present: the sacred, myth, rite, and symbol. The idol represents a hierophany in which humans perceive a manifestation of the sacred that clothes the object in a new dimension. This dimension is obtained by means of rites consecrating the objects of worship, altars, divine statues, and temples: Sacral presence and sacred space are indispensable. Through consecration, the image or object now belongs to the divinity and can no longer serve a secular use. The Egyptian rituals for opening the mouth, eyes, nose, and ears of a statue made to represent a divinity attest to a theology of the sacred in which the idol is an incarnation of power and life, a personification; it evokes the greatness of the god. Greek art tried to render this sacral dimension through the whiteness of marble or through protective coatings applied to the idols. Worship reactualizes myths that put the worshiper in contact with primordial time and furnish him models for his life. Thanks to this celebration, humanity again becomes contemporary with the primordial event, which awakens and maintains its awareness of a world distinct from the secular world.

This mythical behavior of *homo religiosus* is likewise found in Christian worship, but with an essential difference: The return to a primordial event is not a return to mythical time, but to the historical time of the life of Christ. The Incarnation is effected in a historical time: The Christians who celebrate the mysteries of Christ know that they are simultaneously attaining the historical time of Jesus and the transhistoric time of the Word of God.

Idolatry is the area in which rites and symbols are multiplied. For humankind, it is a matter of transcending the human condition through contact with the sacred. The human reference point remains the archetype. This is the role of ritual. Religions have left extraordinary documentation on the rites of celebration, as for instance the sacrificial rites of ancient Greece and Rome, as well as sacred meals with mystical participation of the gods through statues led in procession; rituals of sacrifice with three fires in the Indo-European world; rites of *soma* in India and of *haoma* in Iran; the symbolism of the cults of Cybele and Mithra; the rites of daily worship in Egyptian temples; the power of the rite and of the word in the imitation of the primordial gesture of the god Thoth, creator of the cosmos; funeral rituals of embalming in ancient Egypt, linked to the Osiris myth; and the symbolism of the altar and of gestures in Hindu temples. Incorporated in the life and existence of *homo religiosus*, the symbolism of worship has the function of revelation, for it is the language of hierophany. It reveals a dimension that transcends the natural dimension of life. Consequently, it introduces a new significance into the life of individuals and society. In the celebration of worship, such sacred symbolism, myths, and rites help humankind to penetrate the mystery of salvation, a mystery that is represented by the holy history of human religion and culture.

See Also Anthropomorphism; Demons; Devils; Fetishism; Hierophany; Iconoclasm; Iconography, article on Jewish Iconography; Images; Synagogue.

Bibliography

Barthélémy, Dominique. *God and His Image.* New York, 1966.

Baumer, Iso, Hildegard Christoffels, and Gonsalv Mainberger. *Das Heilige im Licht und Zwielicht.* Einsiedeln, Switzerland, 1966.

Baynes, Norman H. "Idolatry and the Early Church." In *Byzantine Studies and Other Essays,* pp. 116–143. London, 1955.

Bevan, Edwyn Robert. *Holy Images: An Inquiry in Idolatry and Image-Worship in Ancient Paganism and in Christianity.* London, 1940.

Campenhausen, Hans von. "Die Bilderfrage als theologisches Problem der alten Kirche." In *Tradition und Leben,* edited by Campenhausen, pp. 216–252. Tübingen, 1960.

Clerc, Charly. *Les théories relatives au culte des images chez les auteurs grecs du deuxième siècle après J.-C.* Paris, 1915.

Dubarle, A. M. *La manifestation naturelle de Dieu d'après l'écriture.* Paris, 1976.

Duesberg, Hilaire. "Le procès de l'idolâtrie." In *Les scribes inspirés,* vol. 2. Paris, 1939. Second edition (1966) written in collaboration with Irénée Fransen.

Gelin, Albert. "Idoles, idolâtrie." In *Dictionnaire de la Bible, supplément,* vol. 4. Paris, 1949.

Gilbert, Maurice. *La critique des dieux dans le Livre de la Sagesse.* Rome, 1973.

Goblet d'Alviella, Eugène. "Les origines de l'idolâtrie." In *Croyances, rites, institutions,* vol. 2, pp. 125–147. Paris, 1911.

Goetz, J. "Idolâtrie." In *Catholicisme hier, aujourd'hui, demain,* vol. 5. Paris, 1962.

Mandouze, André. "Saint Augustin et la religion romaine." In *Recherches augustiniennes,* vol. 1, pp. 187–223. Paris, 1958.

Marion, Jean-Luc. *L'idole et la distance: Cinq études.* Paris, 1977.

Michel, A. "Idolâtrie, idole." In *Dictionnaire de théologie catholique,* vol. 7. Paris, 1921.

North, Christopher P. "The Essence of Idolatry." In *Von Ugarit nach Qumran,* edited by Johannes Hempel and Leonhard Rost, pp. 151–160. Berlin, 1958.

Prat, Ferdinand. "Idolâtrie, idole." In *Dictionnaire de la Bible,* vol. 3. Paris, 1912.

Preuss, Horst Dietrich. *Verspottung fremder Religionen im Alten Testament.* Stuttgart, 1971.

Sauser, Ekkart. "Das Gottesbild: Eine Geschichte der Spannung von Vergegenwärtigung und Erinnerung." *Trierer Theologische Zeitschrift* 84 (1975): 164–173.

Schwartz, J. "Philon et l'apologétique chrétienne du second siècle." In *Hommages à André Dupont-Sommer,* edited by André Caquot and M. Philonenko, pp. 497–507. Paris, 1971.

Vermander, Jean-Marie. "La polémique des Apologistes latins contre les Dieux du paganisme." *Recherches augustiniennes* 17 (1982): 3–128.

Will, Robert. *Le culte: Étude d'histoire et de philosophie religieuses.* 3 vols. Paris, 1925–1935.

New Sources

Bernand, Carmen, and Serge Gruzinski. *De l'idolâtrie: une archéologie des sciences religieuses.* Paris, 1988.

Deacon, Richard. *Image and Idol: Medieval Sculpture.* London, 2001. Exhibition catalog.

Flynn, Tom. *The Body in Three Dimensions.* New York, 1998.

Gombrich, E. H., and John Onians. *Sight and Insight: Essays on Art and Culture in Honour of E. H. Gombrich at 85.* London, 1994.

Guillou, André, and Janice Durand. *Byzance et les images: cycle de conférence organisé au musée du Louvre par le Service culturel du 5 octobre au 7 décembre 1992.* Paris, 1994.

Hawting, G. R. *The Idea of Idolatry and the Emergence of Islam: From Polemic to History.* Cambridge, U.K., 1999.

Julius, Anthony. *Idolizing Pictures: Idolatry, Iconoclasm, and Jewish Art.* New York, 2001.

Kamerick, Kathleen. *Popular Piety and Art in the Late Middle Ages: Image Worship and Idolatry in England, 1350–1500.* New York, 2002.

Mazur, Eric Michael. *Art and the Religious Impulse.* Lewisburg, Pa., 2002.

Mills, Kenneth. *Idolatry and Its Enemies: Colonial Andean Religion and Extirpation, 1640–1750.* Princeton, 1997.

JULIEN RIES (1987)
Translated from French by Kristine Anderson
Revised Bibliography

IGBO RELIGION. The Igbo are the largest ethnic group of southeastern Nigeria, numbering about fifteen million people in 2000. Until the mid-twentieth century the overwhelming majority of Igbo were farmers, raising yams as their staple crop. Traditionally, the Igbo lived in villages or village-groups surrounded by their farms. The village-group was the primary unit of political authority; there was no sustained tradition of centralized states within Igbo society. Rather, there were strong ties of the village community, the extended family system, age-group associations, and the various religious organizations that were important to community life. The Igbo have been exposed to Christian missionary activity since 1841; in 1857 an Anglican mission was opened at the important town of Onitsha along the Niger River. The Roman Catholics came in 1885. By the mid-twentieth century most Igbo had adopted Christianity, though the tensile strength of Igbo traditional religion sustained millions of devotees.

Igbo religion distinguishes between three types of supernatural beings: God, the spirits, and the ancestors. Ndigbo believe that there is only one supreme being, who is variously known in different parts of Igboland as Chukwu, Chineke, Ezechitoke, Osebuluwa or Obasi di n'elu. Each name privileges certain attributes. He created the world and sustains it from above, and one of his praise names is "the one who is known but never fully known." Igbo parents honor Chukwu by naming their children in praise of his power: Chukwudi ("God lives"), Chukwu nyelu ("God gave"), Chukwuneke ("God creates"), Chukwuma ("God knows"), Chukwuka ("God is greater"), Ifeanyichukwu ("nothing impossible with God"), Chukwuemeka ("God has been very kind"), Kenechukwu ("thank God"), Ngozichukwu ("blessing of God"), Chukwumailo ("God knows my enemies"), and Chukwujioke ("God is the sharer").

Chukwu is seen as a powerful, munificent God, the one who holds the knife and the yam and provides people with wealth, rain, and children, and who is merciful toward rich and poor, male and female, child and aged. Every morning the father of the family offers prayers to the supreme being. Chukwu does not intervene in the minor details of human existence, however; such matters he leaves to the spirits and ancestors, who are often described as his messengers.

The spirits *(alusi)* are powerful beings who inhabit the three dimensions of space—sky, earth (land and water), and ancestral world. There are several categories of spirits. Powerful sky deities manifest through thunder, lightning, sun, and moon; nature spirits inhabit rocks, hills, caves, trees, and land or farms. The guardian spirit of the earth is Ani/Ala, the earth mother. There is also a spirit associated with each day of the Igbo four-day week: Eke, Orie, Afor, and Nkwo. Patron spirits serve as guardians of hunters, farmers, fishermen, medicine men, and other professional guilds; the matron spirit is called Nne Miri or Mami Wata. Marine spirits inhabit rivers and streams. Human spirits, called *chi,* determine each individual's destiny. Spirit forces energize medicine that individuals can conjure and deploy for strength, protection, or to harm enemies. Ancestral spirits are the living dead who inhabit the spirit world but are involved in the lives of progenies in the human world. During festivals, they visit the human world as guests in form of masquerades. Evil spirits live in both human and spirit worlds. Only those who lived honest lives, did not die from inexplicable diseases, and had full burial rites can be ancestors or reincarnate. The spirits of evil people wander as *akalogolu* who appear on lonely farm roads to frighten people. Among the most dreaded evil spirits are *ogbanje*—spirits who manifest as children, covenanted to return to the marine world after a brief sojourn among human families. Their mission is to participate exuberantly in life events, tantalizing parents with their excessive beauty, friendliness, joy of living, and precocious habits. Near the appointed time of return, they develop unusual illnesses and die very suddenly. *Ogbanje* spirits tend to possess females. Parents consult *dibia afa* (divining healers, as opposed to *dibia ogwu,* who are adept with herbs), make sacrifices to marine spirits, and use facial scarifications on the children to discourage their return to the human world. Body marks at birth may betray an *ogbanje* child (modern medicine suspects sickle cell anemia).

Benevolent spirits have shrines, priests, and religious festivals as part of their worship. The wicked spirits receive no regular cultic activity except the occasional offering made with the left hand as the supplicant asks to be left alone. Major ancestors have statues, which recall their spiritual power, located at a family shrine. Before drinking palm wine, the Igbo pour out a few drops in honor of the ancestors. The ancestors are believed to help the living reap a good harvest, have many children, and protect the family from misfortunes. Ancestors may also be reincarnated among the children of their descendants.

Acts of religious worship permeate daily life and are often conducted on behalf of family or village groups. A father's morning prayer to Chukwu is offered on behalf of his entire family. Individuals invoke the name of a spirit or even that of Chukwu when they sense danger, have cause to rejoice, when they sneeze, or when they approach a spirit's shrine. Prayers also accompany ritual sacrifice. They are offered to God, the spirits, and the ancestors, and can be prayers of petition, praise, or thanksgiving. The Igbo perceive time as cyclical, from birth to death and reincarnation. Rites of passage are celebrated: naming ceremonies, puberty rites, marriage rites, membership in secret and open societies, adult roles in communal governance, and funerary rites. Both the poor, *ogbenye,* and the rich, *ogalanya,* are judged after this life by their honest commitment to communal values.

Sacrifice is central in Igbo religious life. Sacrifices are offered for the expiation of sins, for protection from misfortune, to petition for assistance, and to offer thanks. Most are offered to spirits and ancestors, but in certain cases sacrifices of white chickens are offered directly to Chukwu. Sacrifices at family shrines are performed by the senior man of the family. Each spirit has its own priests who perform sacrifices at the shrine. Offerings include eggs, chickens, fruits, goats, cows, and (in a few rare cases of community sacrifices) human beings. Sometimes the victim—animal or human—is offered to a spirit and a little of its blood is shed as a sign of an offering, but the victim is allowed to live as a devotee who is consecrated to the spirit. Human sacrifices are sometimes connected with adjudication of disputes at oracular shrines. Oracles are graded according to purview. The three with the widest geographical patronage that extended beyond Igboland were Ogbunorie, Igwe-ka-Ala, and Ibin Ukpabi. The last acquired notoriety because the Arochukwu, who served as middlemen in the transatlantic slave trade manipulated the oracle by soaking the stream near the ravine that housed the oracle with red ochre wood and declaring that Ibin Ukpabi had eaten the guilty party in the arbitration. Meanwhile, they sneaked the hapless victim through the forest to a waiting slave boat. The colonial government conducted a raid on the Arochukwu community between 1901 and 1902, but could not wipe out the oracle. They followed this with four other four raids between 1912 and 1925 against the oracle, still to no avail.

Healing is central to Igbo religion. *Ndi dibia ogwu* (herbalists) employ a variety of techniques to discern the spiritual cause of a particular malady or misfortune: a violation of taboos/prohibitions, moral failure, an offense against a spirit, or a bad personal fate *(chi).* A spirit, *agwu,* possesses the herbalist after he recites incantations, and it identifies the herb and the location in the forest for the cure.

Social control models include socialization into acceptable values *(omenali),* restriction through satires and peer joking relationships, punishment for those who flout the salient values, and reward for those who uphold them. Each control is legitimized with religion. For instance, theft from a farm threatens the food security of the community, so the elders invoke the spirits of Ahiajioku (the god of the yam who also guards farms), Ani/Ala (the earth mother), or ancestors to detect and punish the thief. The earth spirit and ancestors serve as guardians of morality. The most serious crimes are abominations committed against the earth spirit, such as patricide, suicide, incest, theft of crops or livestock, giving birth to twins, and killing sacred animals. Itinerant priests from Nri conduct the expiation of such abominations. Ndigbo employ covenants with the gods of their fathers to preserve social order, enhance the well-being of individuals and communities, and preserve the highest values, *nka na nzere*—long life and prosperity. They sacralize the whole of life.

See Also God, article on African Supreme Beings.

Bibliography

Afigbo, A. E. *The Image of the Igbo.* Lagos, Nigeria, 1992.

Agbasiere, Joseph Thésèse. *Women in Igbo Life and Thought.* London and New York, 2000.

Aguwa, Jude C. U. *The Agwu Deity in Igbo Religion: A Study of the Patron Spirit of Divination and Medicine in an African Society.* Enugu, Nigeria, 1995.

Amu, Boniface-Peter. *Religion and Religious Experience in Igbo Culture and Christian Faith Experience.* Bonn, Germany, 1998.

Arinze, Francis A. *Sacrifice in Igbo Religion.* Ibadan, Nigeria, 1970.

Egwu, Raphael Amobi. *Igbo Idea of the Supreme Being and the Triune God.* Würzburg, Germany, 1998.

Henderson, Richard N. *The King in Every Man: Evolutionary Trends in Onitsha Ibo Society and Culture.* New Haven, Conn., 1972.

Ikenga-Metuh, Emefie. *God and Man in African Religion: A Case Study of the Igbo of Nigeria.* 2d ed. Enugu, Nigeria, 1999.

Ilogu, Edmund. *Christianity and Igbo Culture.* New York, 1974.

Ilogu, Edmund. *Igbo Life and Thought.* Onitsha, Nigeria. 1985.

Kalu, Ogbu U., ed. *Embattled Gods: Christianization of Igboland, 1841–1991.* London and Lagos, Nigeria, 1996; Trenton, N.J., 2003. See especially chapter 2, "Enduring Covenants: The Igbo and Their Gods."

Ogbuene, Chigekwu. *The Concept of Man in Igbo Myths.* Frankfurt am Main, Germany, and New York, 1999.

FRANCIS A. ARINZE (1987)
OGBU KALU (2005)

IGNATIUS LOYOLA (c. 1491–1556) was the author of *Spiritual Exercises,* founder and first superior general of the Jesuits, and a Christian saint. Iñigo López de Loyola was born to noble, wealthy Basque parents in the castle at Loyola, near Azpeitia, Guipúzcoa province, in northernmost Spain. Beginning in the mid-1530s he more and more frequently called himself Ignatius, although he also used his baptismal name Iñigo (Enecus in Latin). Up to 1521 his career gave no premonition of his subsequent development into one of the most influential religious figures of the sixteenth and later centuries.

EARLY LIFE AND EDUCATION. In the patriarchal family in which Iñigo spent his boyhood, loyalty to Roman Catholic doctrines was unquestioning, and observance of religious practices and moral standards was about average for its social class. At about the age of twelve Iñigo received the tonsure; but his father may well have intended this not to mark the start of a clerical vocation, but merely to be the means of procuring the income from a local benefice at his disposal.

A momentous change in the youngster's life occurred when he was between twelve and sixteen years of age. His father (who died in 1507, long after his wife) accepted the invitation of Juan Velázquez de Cuéllar to receive the boy into his home at Arévalo in Castile, and there raise him as if he were his own son, while preparing him for a career in politics, public administration, and arms. The wealthy and famous Velázquez would act as the boy's patron at the royal court, while utilizing his services as a page. Velázquez was the master of the royal treasury and a confidant of King Ferdinand the Catholic; his wife was an intimate friend of the queen. Baldassare Castiglione's famous *Book of the Courtier* (1528), a manual for the training of the polished gentleman and model courtier, details the type of education furnished to the young page, with emphasis on courtly manners and conversation, proficiency in music and dancing, fastidiousness about dress and personal appearance, devotion to the ruler, and skill in arms. Iñigo's literary schooling proved superficial, consisting mainly of avid reading of tales of chivalry, then very popular. As he later admitted, his mind was filled with the military and amorous adventures of Amadis of Gaul and other fictional heroes. These novels proved an important formative influence, however, for they fired an ambition to gain fame by great feats of arms.

As Iñigo developed into manhood—short (about five feet, two inches tall) but robust, well-formed, fair-haired with long locks—his activities included gaming, dueling, and amorous affairs. In 1515 he and his brother Pero, a priest, were hailed before a secular court for some unspecified deeds of premeditated violence perpetrated at night during the carnival at Azpeitia. They escaped sentence by appealing to an ecclesiastical court, whose judgment remains unknown. Another revealing incident took place a few years later in Pamplona. While Iñigo was walking along a street, a group of men headed in the opposite direction shoved him against a wall. Drawing his sword, he chased them and would have run them through had he not been restrained.

When Velázquez died in 1517, his page promptly entered the service of the duke of Nájera, viceroy of Navarre, as a courtier, with obligations to military duty if needed. During the revolt of the Comuneros, Iñigo fought in the forefront of the duke's forces in the victorious storming of Nájera (September 1520), but he refused to participate in the customary sack of the town as an act unworthy of a Christian or a gentleman. When the French invaded Navarre in 1521 and attacked Pamplona, its capital, the townsfolk surrendered without a struggle. Almost alone at a council of war, Iñigo advocated resistance to death in the fortress above the city. In the absence of a priest, he prepared for the end by following a medieval custom of confessing his sins nonsacramentally to a comrade-in-arms. During the six-hour bombardment of the citadel on May 21, a cannonball struck Iñigo, injuring his left leg and breaking his right one below the knee. This calamity moved the small garrison to surrender; it also effected a metamorphosis in the wounded man's life.

Chivalrously but inexpertly, the French tended Iñigo's injuries and then permitted their vanquished enemy to be carried back to his family home on a litter. In resetting the limb there, the surgeon shortened the broken leg and left a large, unsightly protrusion on the kneecap. Impelled by vanity, by a determination to return to his former lifestyle, and by romantic notions about impressing a lady of very high, perhaps royal, lineage, whose name is still the subject of conjectures and who may have been an imaginary figure, Iñigo insisted on further surgery. The lump was sawed off and the leg was stretched almost to normal length. During all these excruciatingly painful operations, performed without anesthesia, the iron-willed patient voiced no complaint.

To while away the tedium of convalescence, the sick man turned to reading. Because the meager family library lacked his preferred tales of chivalry, he accepted Spanish versions of Ludolph of Saxony's life of Christ and Jacobus de Voragine's *Golden Legend,* a collection of saints' lives. As he kept rereading and reflecting on these two famous works of edification, Iñigo developed an aversion for his worldly ideals and ways. He resolved to serve and imitate Christ alone and to emulate the deeds of the saints, although in a manner as yet undetermined.

SPIRITUAL LIFE AND LEADERSHIP. Early in 1522 Iñigo left home and started on a pilgrimage to the Holy Land. Soon he took a vow of perpetual chastity, dismissed his two servants, and disposed of all his money. At the Benedictine monastery of Montserrat on March 22–25, he gave away his mule and his fine clothes, donning a coarse pilgrim's garb of sackcloth. Then he made a knightly vigil of arms, praying all night before the altar of Our Lady, where he discarded his sword and dagger. From Montserrat he proceeded to the nearby town of Manresa, where his stay, originally intended to last only a few days, extended to eleven fateful months. At Manresa, the pilgrim, as he now termed himself, refused to divulge his true identity. He led a life of great austerity and underwent bodily penances so severe that they permanently impaired his rugged constitution. Unkempt in appearance, he obtained food and lodging by begging, a practice he was to follow for years. At times he dwelt in a cave. Besides devoting seven hours daily to prayer on his knees, he read pious books, especially the *Imitation of Christ,* and performed works of charity.

At Manresa Iñigo also composed the substance of *Spiritual Exercises,* although he continued revising and expanding the text until 1541. In its opening paragraph the slender book describes spiritual exercises as "every method of examination of conscience, of vocal and mental prayer, and of other spiritual activities that will be mentioned later . . . to prepare and dispose the soul to rid itself of all inordinate attachments; and after their removal, to seek and find God's will concerning the disposition of one's life for the salvation of the soul." Along with a number of annotations, rules, and notes, the text proposes points for methodical meditations and contemplations on various Christian doctrines and on some key topics original to the author, but mostly on incidents in the life of Christ.

Divided into four stages, called weeks, the exercises in their fullness are meant to occupy the memory, imagination, understanding, and will of a retreatant, under a director and secluded from temporal affairs, for thirty days, although considerable elasticity in length is permitted. Primarily the book is a manual of practical directives for a retreat director. Highly compressed and lacking in literary embellishments, the text is not designed for continued pious reading in the usual sense. The book was mainly the product of the author's own experiences within himself and with others. It soon won acclaim as a spiritual masterpiece, original, unified, outstanding for its sound religious psychology and pedagogy, and remarkably well organized. Its contents manifest the essence of Ignatian and Jesuit spirituality, and it has exerted an enormous influence throughout the Catholic world down to the present day. As early as 1548, Paul III's *Pastoralis officii* gave what has been termed the most explicit and honorable papal approval ever accorded a book. A long list of popes have added their own commendations, culminating with Pius XI, who in 1922 officially designated Ignatius as the patron saint of spiritual exercises.

From Manresa the pilgrim traveled by foot and by ship to Jerusalem, arriving on September 4, 1523, by way of Barcelona, Gaeta, and Rome and Venice. Only because he was denied permission to reside permanently in the Holy City, where he had hoped to spend his days visiting the sacred places and evangelizing, did he decide to return to Spain. He set sail for Venice on October 3, 1523, and arrived in Barcelona in February 1524.

Study, motivated by a desire to help souls, preoccupied the next eleven years. After applying himself to Latin in Barcelona (1524–1526), Iñigo undertook university courses in philosophy at Alcalá (March 1525–June 1527) and Salamanca (July–September 1527). Extracurricular apostolic activities won the student a number of followers, mostly women, and aroused official suspicions regarding his apparent adherence to the heretical Alumbrados. During their investigations, diocesan officials at Alcalá imprisoned the uncomplaining suspect for forty-two days and those at Salamanca for an additional twenty-two, but in both cases Iñigo was exonerated. To escape the restrictions attached to his freedom, he migrated to the University of Paris (1528–1535), where he gained a master of arts degree in philosophy in 1534 and then studied philosophy for a year and a half.

In Paris, new followers were attracted by Iñigo's spiritual exercises. On August 15, 1534, in a chapel on Montmartre, he and six companions vowed to dedicate their lives to the good of their neighbors, while observing strict poverty, and to journey to Jerusalem on pilgrimage or, if this proved impossible (as it did because of war), to place themselves at the disposal of the pope. Three others joined in the renewal of this vow a year later, bringing to ten the original membership of the as yet unforeseen Society of Jesus.

Heading for Jerusalem, Ignatius traveled in December 1535 to Venice, where his nine companions joined him in January 1537. He and six of the nine were ordained priests there the following June. After long deliberations with the whole group, Ignatius resolved to make their association a permanent, structured one, to be called the Society of Jesus. His First Formula of the Institute, a brief draft of a constitution, received solemn confirmation from Paul III on September 27, 1540, canonically establishing it as a religious order. The new order aimed at the salvation and perfection of its members, popularly known as Jesuits, and of all humankind. To this end it incorporated a number of innovations in its organization, manner of life, and scope of ministries.

In 1541 the other nine cofounders of the Society of Jesus unanimously elected Ignatius superior general for life. Under his leadership, membership increased rapidly, reaching about 940 at the time of his death, on July 31, 1556. Members dispersed throughout Europe and penetrated Africa, Asia, and the Western Hemisphere. They engaged in numerous pastoral, educational, and missionary labors, while moving to the forefront of the work of the Catholic revival and Counter-Reformation. As head of the highly centralized society, Ignatius played the key role in all this activity, as well as in the internal development of the order. He it was who devised, organized, supervised, or at least approved all these ministries, keeping in close contact with them through an enormous correspondence; some seven thousand of his letters have since been published. Besides admitting new members, choosing superiors, and regulating the spiritual life of his fellow religious, he composed the Jesuit Constitutions, along with other religious instructions and rules. In Rome he founded the tuition-free Roman College (now the Gregorian University) and the German College to train priests for Germany. In addition he founded and won support for several charitable institutions.

Because of his rare combination of talents, Ignatius influenced modern religious life as few have done. He was at once a man of prayer, a contemplative, a mystic who reported many visions, a man of action, and a born leader not only in individual spiritual direction but also in practical projects of great magnitude. He was zealous in promoting the greater glory of God, and he was a sharp judge of persons and events: reflective, imperturbable, prudent, decisive, and wise in adjusting means to ends. His mode of government, while stressing obedience, was paternal, not at all military, as is sometimes argued. In personal contacts he was inevitably courteous, tactful, grave but pleasant and genial. He was beatified in 1609 and canonized in 1622.

See Also Jesuits.

Bibliography

For editions of the writings by Ignatius in their original languages and in translations, as well as for the enormous secondary literature about him, see *Bibliographie ignatienne* (1894–1957), edited by Jean-François Gilmont, S.J., and Paul Daman, S.J. (Paris, 1958), containing 2,872 entries; *Orientaciones bibliográficas sobre San Ignacio de Loyola,* edited by Ignacio Iparraguirre, S.J., vol. 1, 2d ed. (Rome, 1965), with 651 items; and *Orientaciones bibliográficas sobre San Ignacio de Loyola,* edited by Manuel Ruiz Jurado, S.J., vol. 2 (Rome, 1977), adding another 580 items (both volumes contain evaluative comments and references to important book reviews). Complete annual bibliographies appear in *Archivum Historicum Societatis Iesu,* published since 1932 in Rome. An important source, although incomplete, brief, and ending in 1538, is *The Autobiography of St. Ignatius Loyola, with Related Documents,* translated by Joseph F. O'Callaghan and edited with an introduction and notes by John C. Olin (New York, 1974). Ignatius's best-known work is available in several English translations; a particularly good version is *The Spiritual Exercises of St. Ignatius* by Louis J. Puhl, S.J. (Westminster, Md., 1952), reprinted many times. *The Constitutions of the Society of Jesus* has been translated, with an introduction and commentary by George E. Ganss, S.J. (Saint Louis, Mo., 1970). The best biography available in English is by Paul Dudon, S.J.: *St. Ignatius of Loyola* (Milwaukee, 1949). *Saint Ignatius Loyola: The Pilgrim Years* (London, 1956), by James Brodrick, S.J., covers the years 1491–1538 only and is written by a superior stylist. *The Jesuits, Their Spiritual Doctrine and Practice: A Historical Study* (Chicago, 1964), by Joseph de Guibert, S.J., is an authoritative study.

John F. Broderick (1987)

IGNATIUS OF ANTIOCH (c. 35–c. 107) was a bishop and Christian saint, martyred in Rome. His name may be derived from the Latin *ignis,* which means "fire," but nothing is known of his origins. Origen relates that Ignatius was the second bishop of Antioch after Peter, but Eusebius of Caesarea writes that he was the third bishop of Antioch after succeeding Peter and Euodius (d. around 69) and thus the predecessor of Heron of Antioch (70–107). He may have met the apostles and most probably John and Paul, but there is no confirmation of this. In his letter to the Ephesians (9.2), he calls himself *theophoros,* that is, "God-bearer," a man who bears in himself God and Christ. Indeed, his letters show him to be an exceptional man with an exceptional faith in Christ.

Although Ignatius lacked formal education, his rule as bishop was an illustrious one. During the persecutions of Emperor Trajan he was arrested, condemned, and ordered to be executed at Rome. Because of his high reputation, his execution in Rome would provide an example to the growing numbers of Christians in the East and at the same time an entertainment for the Romans, who delighted in witnessing the execution of prominent Christians. On his way to Rome, Ignatius was taken under the guard of ten soldiers to Smyrna, whence he wrote letters to the Christians of Ephesus, Magnesia Tralles, and Rome. From Troas he wrote letters to the churches in Philadelphia and Smyrna and to Polycarp, bishop of Smyrna. Apparently, throughout the long and exhausting journey, he was received by the Christian communities with great respect and reverence. Finally he was executed in the Colosseum of Rome. Another tradition, originating in Antioch and recorded in the sixth century by John Malalas, holds that Ignatius suffered martyrdom in Antioch, but such information is without any historical foundation. The Eastern church commemorates Ignatius's name on December 20 and the Western church on February 1.

Most patrologists today accept the authenticity of seven letters of Ignatius. Because of Ignatius's emphasis on the importance of the office of bishop, a dispute arose among patristic scholars during the fifteenth and then during the sixteenth centuries concerning the authenticity of the letters. Although there are four versions of these letters, the dispute has settled on the authenticity of the so-called long recension and short recension. The first contains thirteen letters and the second only three (those to the Ephesians, Romans, and Polycarp). Through vigorous discussion and debate by John Pearson (1672), Joseph B. Lightfoot (1885), and others, the authenticity of the seven letters has been accepted. Most recently, J. Rius-Camps (1980) advanced the theory that a forger, availing himself of the genuine ending of the letter to the Ephesians, and through a process of interpolation and plagiarism, composed three spurious letters to the churches of Philadelphia and Smyrna, and to Polycarp. The chief motive of the alleged forger, according to Rius-Camps, was to emphasize church unity and absolute obedience to the bishop. Such an elaborate hoax cannot be proved beyond dispute. The seven letters of Ignatius can still claim credibility and acceptance.

Although not a man of secular erudition, Ignatius, with his simplicity of style, his biblical language and idioms, and his emotional and passionate devotion to Jesus Christ, is one of the most attractive of the early church fathers. His great faith, humility, and willingness to suffer martyrdom for Christ are reflected movingly in his letters, which emphasize three central themes: Christ, the unity of the church under the bishop, and the Eucharist. He is probably the first father of the church to emphasize in clear terms both the divinity and the humanity of Christ: "There is only one physician—of flesh yet spiritual, born yet unbegotten, God incarnate, genuine life in the midst of death, sprung from Mary as well as God, first subject to suffering then beyond it—Jesus Christ our Lord" (*Letter to the Ephesians* 7.2). He is ready to die for Christ and only for him. "Of no use to me will be the farthest reaches of the universe or the kingdoms of this world. I would rather die and come to Jesus Christ than be king over the entire earth" (*Letter to the Romans* 6.1).

Ignatius is the first Christian writer to use the term *catholic* for the church, and he insists on the unity of the church under the auspices of the bishop. In his letter to the church at Smyrna he says

> You should all follow the bishop as Jesus Christ did the Father. Follow, too, the presbytery as you would the apostles; and respect the deacons as you would God's law. Nobody must do anything that has to do with the Church without the bishop's approval. You should regard that Eucharist as valid which is celebrated either by the bishop or by someone he authorizes. Where the bishop is present, there let the congregation gather, just as where Jesus Christ is, there is the Catholic Church. (8.1–8.2)

Other letters declare the bishop to be *tupos,* or likeness, of God the Father and charge that nothing should be done "without the bishop." This unity under the bishop must have practical applications. To the Magnesians he writes, "Hence you must have one prayer, one petition, one mind, one hope, dominated by love and unsullied joy—that means you must have Jesus Christ. . . . Run off—all of you—to one temple of God, as it were, to one altar, to one Jesus Christ, who came forth from one Father, while still remaining one with him, and returning to him" (7.1–2).

Ecclesiastical unity should be expressed most especially during the Eucharist. Ignatius admonishes the Ephesians to

> assemble yourselves together in common, every one of you severally, man by man, in grace, in one faith and one Jesus Christ, who after the flesh was of David's race, who is Son of Man and Son of God, to the end that you may obey the bishop and the presbytery without distraction of mind; *breaking one bread, which is the medicine of immortality and the antidote that we should not die but live for ever in Jesus Christ.* (20.2)

To the Philadelphians, he writes: "Be careful, then, to observe a single eucharist. For there is one flesh of our Lord, Jesus Christ, and one cup of his blood that makes *us* one, and one altar just as there is one bishop along with the presbytery and the deacons, my fellow slaves" (4.1). The message is clear: one God the Father, one Jesus Christ, one Holy Spirit, one church, one Eucharist, one altar, one bishop. Only through this kind of unity will the Christians prove themselves real disciples of Christ and will Christ dwell in them.

The impact of Ignatius's letters was great. He dispelled the notion that the new religion offered a magical way of salvation and propagated the teaching that only through real unity in the life of the church and in the sharing of the corporate eucharistic life will Christians taste the joy of salvation and become members of the kingdom of God.

BIBLIOGRAPHY

A complete bibliography is available in Johannes Quasten's *Patrology,* vol. 1 (Utrecht, 1950), pp. 63ff. Texts of the letters can be found in *The Apostolic Fathers,* edited and translated by Joseph B. Lightfoot (1956; reprint, Grand Rapids, Mich., 1973); *The Epistles of Saint Clement of Rome and Saint Ignatius of Antioch,* edited and translated by James A. Kleist, S.J., "Ancient Christian Writers," no. 1 (Westminster, Md., 1946); and *Early Christian Fathers,* edited by Cyril C. Richardson, "The Library of Christian Classics," vol. 1 (Philadelphia, 1953). Especially valuable discussions of the letters are found in John Romanides's "The Ecclesiology of Saint Ignatius of Antioch," *Greek Orthodox Theological Review* 7 (Summer 1961–Winter 1962): 53–77; and in J. Rius-Camps's *The Four Authentic Letters of Ignatius, the Martyr,* "Orientalia Christiana Analecta," no. 213 (Rome, 1980).

GEORGE S. BEBIS (1987)

IGNORANCE SEE KNOWLEDGE AND IGNORANCE

IʿJĀZ is the concept of the "miraculousness of the Qurʾān." That the Qurʾān is the miracle of Muḥammad is an Islamic doctrine of the utmost importance because it is held to prove the divine source of the holy Book, and hence its authority, as well as the authenticity of the Prophet to whom it was revealed. But what constitutes this miracle is a subject that has engaged Muslim thinkers for many generations. By the early part of the third century AH (ninth century CE), the word *iʿjāz* had come to mean that quality of the Qurʾān that rendered people incapable of imitating the Book or any part thereof in content and form. By the latter part of that century, the word had become a technical term, and the numerous definitions applied to it after the tenth century have shown little divergence from the key concepts of the inimitability of the Qurʾān and the inability of human beings to match it even when challenged.

The idea of the challenge is based on several verses of the Qurʾān: in *sūrah* 52:33–34 there is a challenge to produce a discourse resembling it; in *sūrah* 17:88, to bring forth a like of it; in *sūrah* 11:13, to contrive ten *sūrahs* similar to it; in *sūrahs* 10:38 and 2:23–24, to compose only one *sūrah* matching it, the latter *sūrah* adding, "and you will not." The Qurʾān declares also that even if men and jinn were to combine their efforts, they would be incapable of producing anything like it (17:88) or even like one surah of it (10:38).

The argument, as in *Ḥujaj al-nubūwah* (Proofs of prophethood) of al-Jāḥiẓ (d. AH 255/869 CE), that Muḥammad's pagan Arab contemporaries failed to take up the challenge to discredit him, although they were masters of rhetoric and strongly motivated by opposition to Islam and by tribal pride, led some Muslim thinkers to associate the miracle with the Qurʾān's sublime style. Others supported this argument by reference to the contents of the Qurʾān, highlighting its information about the distant past, its prophecies of future and eschatological events, its statements about God, the universe, and society—all of which were beyond an unlettered man like Muḥammad.

Early in the theological discussion, al-Naẓẓām (d. 846) introduced the concept of the *ṣarfah* ("turning away") and argued that the miracle consisted in God's turning the competent away from taking up the challenge of imitating the Qurʾān, the implication being that otherwise the Qurʾān could be imitated. This notion was acceptable only to a few, such as Hishām al-Fuwaṭī (d. 833?), ʿAbbād ibn Sulaymān (ninth century), and al-Rummānī (d. 996). On the whole, the Muslim consensus continued to hold to the stylistic supremacy of the Qurʾān. In his systematic and comprehensive study entitled *Iʿjāz al-Qurʾān*, al-Bāqillānī (d. 1013) upheld the rhetorically unsurpassable style of the Qurʾān, but he did not consider this to be a necessary argument in favor of the Qurʾān's uniqueness and emphasized instead the content of revelation. On the other hand, al-Qāḍī ʿAbd al-Jabbār (d. 1025) insisted on the unmatchable quality of the Qurʾān's extraordinary eloquence and unique stylistic perfection. In volume 16 of his extensive *Al-mughnī* (The sufficient book), he argued that eloquence (*faṣāḥah*) resulted from the excellence of both meaning and wording, and he explained that there were degrees of excellence depending on the manner in which words were chosen and arranged in any literary text, the Qurʾān being the highest type.

The choice and arrangement of words, referred to as *naẓm*, have been treated in several books entitled *Naẓm al-Qurʾān*, such as those by al-Jāḥiẓ, now lost, al-Sijistānī (d. 928), al-Balkhī (d. 933), and Ibn al-Ikhshīd (d. 937). Al-Rummānī offered a detailed analysis of Qurʾānic style in his *Al-nukat fī iʿjāz al-Qurʾān* (Subtleties of the Qurʾān's inimitability) and emphasized the psychological effect of the particular *naẓm* of the Qurʾān without, however, disregarding other elements of content that render the Qurʾān inimitable. His contemporary al-Khaṭṭābī (d. 998) argued in his *Bayān iʿjāz al-Qurʾān* (Clarification of the Qurʾān's inimitability) that the source of *iʿjāz* the insuperable manner in which Qurʾanic discourse binds meaning and wording, using various styles that combine literary qualities characteristic of the Qurʾān alone and that are conducive to a special psychological effect.

The author who best elaborated and systematized the theory of *naẓm* in his analysis of the *iʿjāz* is ʿAbd al-Qāhir al-Jurjānī (d. 1078) in his *Dalāʾil al-iʿjāz* (Indicators of inimitability). His material was further organized by Fakhr al-Dīn al-Rāzī (d. 1209) in his *Nihāyat al-ījās fī dirāyat al-iʿjāz* (Extreme concision in the comprehension of inimitability) and put to practical purposes by al-Zamakhsharī (d. 1144) in his exegesis of the Qurʾān entitled *Al-kashshāf* (The elucidator), rich in rhetorical analysis of the Qurʾanic style.

Hardly anything new has been added by later writers on *iʿjāz*. In modern times, Muṣṭafā Ṣādiq al-Rāfiʿī (d. 1937) emphasized two points in explaining the sources of *iʿjāz* in his *Iʿjāz al-Qurʾān wa-al-balāghah al-nabawī-yah* (Cairo, 1926), namely, the insufficiency of human capabilities to attempt an imitation and the persistence of this inability throughout the ages. A more recent writer, ʿAbd al-Karīm al-Khaṭīb, offers four points in the same vein in his two-volume study *Iʿjāz al-Qurʾān: Dirāsah kāshifah li-khaṣāʾiṣ al-balāghah al-ʿarabīyah wa-maʿāyīrihā* (An elucidating study of the characteristics of Arabic rhetoric and its criteria; 2d ed., Beirut, 1975), namely, the absolute truth of the Qurʾān; its authoritative, all-knowing tone of speech; its beautiful *naẓm*; and its spirituality, which derives from the spirit of God.

SEE ALSO Qurʾān; Tafsīr.

BIBLIOGRAPHY

Abdul Aleem's article "ʿIjazu'l-Qurʾān *[sic]*," *Islamic Culture* 7 (1933): 64–82, 215–233, surveys the development of the *iʿjāz* doctrine and the major works on the subject. A shorter survey can be found in the introduction to *A Tenth-Century Document of Arabic Literary Theory and Criticism*, edited by G. E. Von Grunebaum (Chicago, 1950), which also contains a well-annotated English translation of the sections on poetry of Muḥammad ibn al-Tayyib al-Bāqillānī's *Iʿjāz al-Qurʾān*. J. Bouman's *Le conflit autour du Coran et la solution d'al-Bāqillānī* (Amsterdam, 1959) analyzes the theological discussions on *iʿjāz* in their historical background and presents al-Bāqillānī's in detail. John Wansbrough argues in his *Quranic Studies: Sources and Methods of Scriptural Interpretation* (Oxford, 1977), pp. 77–83 and 231–232, that the dogma of *iʿjāz* developed more as an assertion of the Qurʾān's canonical status within the Muslim community than as evidence of Muḥammad's prophethood.

ISSA J. BOULLATA (1987)

ĪJĪ, ʿAḌUD AL-DĪN AL-

ĪJĪ, ʿAḌUD AL-DĪN AL- (AH 680?–756/1281?–1356 CE) was a Muslim theologian and jurist of the Il-khanid period. He originated from a well-to-do family of notables and judges living in the town of Īg in the province of Shābankārah, near the strait of Hormuz in the Persian Gulf. As a young man, he tried to make a career at the court of the Mongol dynasty reigning in Iran, the Il-khanids in Tabriz, and succeeded in winning the favor of the powerful vizier Rashīd al-Dīn Faḍl Allāh, a Jew who had converted to Islam when the Mongols themselves finally gave up their inherited shamanist or Buddhist convictions. Rashīd al-Dīn gave him a teaching post at a mobile "university" that accompanied the Il-khanid ruler Öljeitu during his campaigns, but because al-Ījī was a Sunnī, his position may have become precarious when Öljeitu turned to Shiism in 1310. In the long run, he seems to have returned to Shābankārah, where, after the death of his father in 1317, he had to administer large estates that secured the wealth of his family in the form of a charitable trust *(waqf)*. When Rashīd al-Dīn was executed in 1318, al-Ījī severed his relations with the court and returned only when Rashīd al-Dīn's son Ghiyāth al-Dīn managed to take over the vizierate in 1327; he then became chief judge of the empire. However, with the end of the Il-khanid dynasty in 1335, he moved to Shiraz where he found the protection of the provincial ruler Abū Isḥāq Injü and became chief judge of the town. His salary was much lower than before, but he enjoyed the atmosphere of an art-loving court and the company of poets such as Ḥāfiẓ Shirazi (d. 1390?). This phase of quiet life lasted for almost twenty years until, in 1354, al-Ījī's patron was driven out of Shiraz by Mubāriz al-Dīn, a rival ruler whose sphere of influence also included Shābankārah. Al-Ījī therefore prudently knotted secret connections with the new man and escaped to his native town shortly before Shiraz was captured. His treason did not, however, go unnoticed. Apparently at the initiative of a former adherent of Abū Isḥāq Injü, he was imprisoned in a fortress near Īg and died there in 1356.

Al-Ījī was a prolific writer. Many of his works are dedicated to Ghiyāth al-Dīn or Abū Isḥāq. Intended as systematic handbooks for teaching in high schools, they have no claims to originality, but they are well structured and reflect the long scholarly tradition of the Muslim East, which had never been completely interrupted by the Mongol invasion. They cover the disciplines of scholastic theology, jurisprudence (according to the Shāfiʿī school), Qurʾanic exegesis, rhetoric and dialectics, ethics, and, to a certain extent, historiography. Their popularity is attested by the great number of commentaries on them. Some of them are still used in religious universities such as al-Azhar in Cairo. They have, however, been almost completely neglected in Western scholarship. The most important work among them is the *Kitāb al-mawāqif* (Book of stations), a concise *summa theologica* that, after the example of Fakhr al-Dīn al-Rāzī, explains traditional Ashʿarī doctrine in philosophical terms borrowed from Ibn Sīnā (Avicenna). It consists of six books, of which only the last two deal strictly with theological problems, which are subdivided into matters depending on reason (the essence of God and his attributes) and on revelation (eschatology, belief and sin, and so forth). The first four books are concerned with the general conceptual framework of theological discourse: epistemology, philosophical principles (such as necessity, possibility, eternity, and contingence), accidents, and substances.

BIBLIOGRAPHY

Further biographical information can be found in my article "Neue Materialien zur Biographie des ʿAḍudaddīn al-Īgī," *Die Welt des Orients* 9 (1978): 270–283. The *Kitāb al-mawāqif* was first analyzed in Louis Gardet and Georges C. Anawati's *Introduction à la théologie musulmane* (Paris, 1948). I have translated and commented upon the first chapter of the *Kitāb al-mawāqif*, on epistemology, in my *Die Erkenntnislehre des ʿAḍudaddīn al-Īcī* (Wiesbaden, 1966).

JOSEF VAN ESS (1987)

IJMĀʿ. The Arabic term *ijmaʿ*, which means "agreement" or "consensus," becomes in Islamic jurisprudence the designation for one of the four sources of law posited by classical Sunnī theory, namely the consensus of the Muslim community. This consensus ranks as the third of the four sources, the first, second, and fourth of which are the Qurʾān, the *sunnah* (custom) of the prophet Muḥammad, and analogical reasoning (*qiyās*). For the majority of Sunnī legal theorists, the work of constructing legal rules is carried on by qualified scholars, called *mujtahids*, on behalf of the community as a whole. Whatever these scholars agree upon is therefore constitutive of the consensus of the community, and it is not necessary for them to take into account the views of an unqualified laity. The majority of theorists further hold that an authoritative consensus is fully constituted at the very moment when the community's living scholars agree unanimously on a rule of law; it is not necessary to allow additional time for individual scholars to reconsider their decisions or to wait until the entire body of scholars involved in the consensus has passed away, thus eliminating any possibility of reconsideration. Once constituted, a consensus is irrevocable. It represents, in the view of all Sunnīs, an infallible and immutable statement of the divine law, or *sharīʿah*. As such, it is worthy to be made the basis of further legal constructions by individual scholars through either interpretation or analogical deduction. It is for this reason that *ijmāʿ* is included among the sources of law.

Sunnī theorists agree that the authority of consensus must rest upon revealed declaration and that all attempts to base that authority upon purely rational considerations are futile. The only self-constituted authority is that of the Creator-Lord; the authority of consensus can be nothing more than its derivative. However, the search for a clear-cut divine endorsement for the authority of consensus has been one of the most arduous tasks undertaken by classical Islamic jurisprudence. The various loci classici employed in this search have all proved to be in some degree problematic: The relevant Qurʾanic passages allow diverse interpretations, and the relevant dicta of the Prophet (as recorded in *ḥadīth*, the literary embodiment of the *sunnah*) are not only open to differing interpretation (despite their being in some cases more precise than the Qurʾān in their support of the authority of consensus, as in the case of the well-known dictum, "My community will never agree upon an error") but are also fraught with text-critical uncertainties. Scholarly opinion has therefore been divided as to whether or not the textual evidence for the authority of consensus is entirely conclusive. Among those who acknowledge that it is not, compensation for the resulting element of uncertainty is found in the principle that on issues relating to human conduct, an authority need not be conclusively grounded in the texts in order to acquire validity, so long as there is sufficient textual evidence to make the legitimacy of that authority more likely than its nonlegitimacy. In this view, the case for the authority of consensus thus rests upon the principle of the sufficiency of probable textual evidence.

While a few Sunnī theorists have conceded to the consensus the privilege of engendering rules that have no demonstrable textual basis, the great majority have restricted its role to granting finality to rules constructed on the basis of the texts. Accordingly, the consensus must emerge from the exegetical deliberations of individual scholars. Individuals qua individuals can at best, according to the general view, produce only probable constructions of the law; their exegesis can never be more than tentative. This exegesis is in fact called *ijtihād* ("exertion," whence the term *mujtahid*) precisely because of its tentative character. The exegetes, as fallible mediators of the divine law, exert themselves in the effort to achieve, through philological procedures and analogical reasoning, the most accurate construction of that law possible *for them.* When the results of their efforts are confirmed by the consensus of their contemporaries, then, and only then, do these results acquire the stature of an infallible and immutable pronouncement. This confirmation may take the form of either explicit espousal or silent consent. The theorists differ, however, as to the value of the latter. The confirmation must, furthermore, be unanimous; a consensus cannot be constituted by a mere majority.

Because the Islamic tradition does not provide for the public certification or official convening of legal scholars and because unanimity on a scale vast enough to embrace the entire Muslim world would be difficult to achieve in the best of circumstances, the consensus, as conceived in the classical theory, has been virtually unrealizable throughout the greater part of Islamic history. While few theorists have accepted the view of Dā'ūd al-Ẓāhirī (d. AH 270/884 CE) and his followers, which restricted the prerogative of consensus making to the first generation of Muslims who were still alive after the Prophet's death, it is not surprising that the classical theorists have generally drawn their examples of consensus from that generation. In so doing, they have implied that only in the earliest period of Islam, when those Muslims who had been in sufficient contact with the Prophet to be deemed authorities ("Companions of the Prophet") were still concentrated in one locality, did the circumstances required for the constitution of a true consensus exist and that thereafter the consensus has remained more a theoretical possibility than a historical actuality. The notion that the consensus is identifiable with Muslim public opinion is distinctly modern.

In Shīʿī theory, consensus is reckoned among the sources of law, but it cannot, according to that theory, be regarded as properly constituted unless the divinely appointed leader, the imam, is present within the community. Because the word of the imam is considered infallible apart from the consensus, the consensus is deprived of the role it occupies in Sunnī theory as the infallible finalizer of rules of law and becomes, in effect, the community's affirmation of solidarity with the imam, such that its teaching and his are one and the same. Thus, from the Shīʿī point of view, the consensus may be deemed a source of law only by special license, and this status is granted only insofar as the consensus is presumed identical with the doctrine of the imam.

BIBLIOGRAPHY

There is as yet no monograph in a Western language devoted specifically to *ijmaʿ*. For a more extensive survey of the subject than the above, see the article "Idjmāʿ" by Marie Bernand in *The Encyclopaedia of Islam,* new ed. (Leiden, 1960–). On the controversies over the authority of consensus, see George F. Hourani's "The Basis of Authority of Consensus in Sunnite Islam," *Studia Islamica* 21 (1964): 13–60. The standard Islamicist view of *ijmaʿ* and its historical development can be found within the pages of Joseph Schacht's *An Introduction to Islamic Law* (Oxford, 1964). For a French translation of the writing of an important classical author, Abu'l Ḥusayn al-Baṣrī, on *ijmaʿ*, see Marie Bernand's *L'accord unanime de la communauté comme fondement des statuts légaux de l'Islam* (Paris, 1970).

BERNARD G. WEISS (1987)

IJTIHĀD.

The Arabic word *ijtihād,* which in ordinary usage means "strenuous endeavor," has become in the Muslim scholarly tradition a technical term for the endeavor of an individual scholar to derive a rule of divine law (*sharīʿah*) directly from the recognized sources of that law without any reliance upon the views of other scholars. Since these sources consist preeminently of texts, namely the Qur'ān, the *ḥadīth* (narratives recording the divinely sanctioned custom of the Prophet), and dicta expressing the consensus of Muslim scholars, *ijtihād* is a fundamentally text-related activity embracing two principal tasks: the authentication of texts and the interpretation of texts. These entail not only deliberation upon actual texts but also the working out of appropriate methodological principles. In carrying on *ijtihād,* a scholar, while not relying for final answers upon other scholars, does interact with scholars holding contrary opinions in a setting of a highly formalized process of disputation. The rules of law that the great scholars of the past have arrived at through *ijtihād* are recorded in the literature of *fiqh,* whereas the methodological principles of *ijtihād* are set forth in the literature of *uṣūl al-fiqh.*

THE TASKS OF IJTIHĀD. The text-critical tasks entailed in *ijtihād* relate mainly to *ḥadīth* and, to some extent, to historical material used to determine the existence of a consensus in an earlier generation. The Qurʾān itself is considered by Muslim scholars to be of incontestable authenticity and therefore not in need of attestation through formal text-critical procedures. The focus of attention in all Muslim text criticism is upon the "chain of transmitters" *(isnād),* rather than upon the contents of the texts themselves. The examination of these chains itself entails a complex methodology, which is explored at length in the *uṣūl al-fiqh* literature. Considered as a purely individual scholarly activity, this transmission-criticism claims to be able to establish, at the very most, the *probable* authenticity of a text, although the degree of probability may—as in the case of "sound" (*ṣaḥīḥ*) *ḥadīth*—be very high. Once the degree of probability of a text's authenticity has been determined, the scholar faces yet another task before he may proceed to interpret the text: He must determine whether or not, during the course of the Prophet's lifetime, the text was abrogated by some other text, for only if it was not may he endeavor to derive a rule from it.

The process of deriving rules from the texts entails two distinct activities: (1) the determination of rules that lie within the meaning of the text, and (2) the determination of any additional rules that may be deemed analogous to these rules. The first of these activities constitutes a derivation of rules from the texts in the sense that it brings to light rules that are not immediately obvious from any particular text taken in isolation. One seldom encounters in the texts legally precise statements of rules, that is to say, statements having a form such as "*x* is obligatory upon all Muslims without exception" (*x* representing an unambiguous reference to a human act considered as a class or category). Such statements, which are necessary to the development of law in Islam, must therefore be extrapolated from the texts by scholars. In carrying on this task, scholars must deal with a host of problems relating to the language of the texts. A good example of these problems is the imperative form of the verb, which appears frequently in the sorts of texts that Muslim legal scholars tend to focus upon. One may not assume from the presence of an imperative in a text such as *aqīmū al-ṣalāt* ("Perform the prayer," *sūrah* 2:43 and elsewhere) that an obligation is intended, for imperatives are used not only to impose obligations but also to invite, exhort, warn, permit, and so on. If, therefore, an obligation is intended, this can be known, according to the majority of Muslim scholars, only from the context. This context need not consist of the larger passage immediately surrounding the text in question, since *any* text within the corpus of recognized texts may shed light on any other text. This being the case, each text must be interpreted in the light of the entire corpus of texts, since virtually no text is free of some degree of ambiguity, vagueness, or generality. As the corpus of texts is vast and the greater part of it—namely, the *ḥadīth*—is subject, in greater or lesser degree, to text-critical problems, the work of Muslim legal scholars is perceived by the scholars themselves to be extremely demanding, and one can thus readily appreciate why they chose to call it *ijtihād.*

The use of analogical reasoning (*qiyās*) to deduce further rules from rules established through exegesis of the texts has been a matter of considerable controversy among Muslims. The main living adversaries of this method are the Twelver Shīʿī scholars. Among Sunnīs of all four surviving schools of law, the method is universally accepted, although an earlier school, namely that of Dāʾūd al-Ẓāhirī (d. 884), rejected it, and there is some evidence of its having been rejected by some scholars within earlier "traditionist" circles out of which the Ḥanbalī school arose. In any case, *ijtihād* is clearly not to be identified solely with *qiyās*, as some Western writers have been wont to do, since *ijtihād* has been as vigorously undertaken by opponents of analogical reasoning as by its partisans. In place of analogical reasoning, some Twelver Shīʿī scholars have espoused certain more strictly rational operations as valid methods of legal inquiry, which they have subsumed under the heading of *ʿaql* ("reason").

In consideration of the enormity of the text-critical, interpretive, and deductive tasks just described, the Sunnī scholarly tradition acknowledges that certainty about rules of divine law is rarely possible and that the formulations of rules that emerge out of *ijtihād* represent the opinions (*ẓann*) of scholars, not hard knowledge *(ʿilm).* That this is so is especially evident in the face of differences of opinion that arise among scholars. On the other hand, the exegetical tentativeness of the rules constructed by scholars is deemed among Sunnīs to be no barrier to the validity and binding character of these rules. If the *ijtihād* of a scholar is truly representative of his very best efforts, then the opinions emerging from it are binding upon the scholar himself and upon all less qualified persons (*muqallids*, lit., "imitators") who choose to follow his teaching.

The practice of following the opinion of a scholar in preference to engaging in *ijtihād* on one's own is called, in Arabic, *taqlīd* ("imitation"). Through the *taqlīd* of the majority of Muslims, the *ijtihād* of scholars, whose number must necessarily be relatively small, is able to acquire authority within society at large and thus to engender law as a social force. The Shīʿī tradition recognizes both *ijtihād* and *taqlīd* but allows less scope for variation of opinion, emphasizing its preference for knowledge over opinion.

MUJTAHIDS. Since the law of God comprehends, in principle, the whole of life, it must be continually expounded as novel life situations present themselves. Consequently, the exercise of *ijtihād* is not a right but a responsibility, one that rests in every age upon the community as a whole. As with all communal responsibilities, it is discharged by the few (that is, the appropriately qualified scholars) on behalf of the many and could in principle be discharged by a single scholar. Those who engage in *ijtihād* bear the title of *mujtahid,* which, though in form a participle, becomes thus denotative of a status. While the claim to this status is theoretically a matter of individual conscience, any such claim becomes effective only after it has been validated by a substantial number of scholars. The validity of such a claim is considered to be contingent upon the satisfaction of certain requirements, which are discussed at length in the *uṣūl al-fiqh* literature. These fall into two general categories: (1) mastery of the belief system of Islam and of its rational basis and (2) mastery of the rules of legal interpretation, text criticism, and (among Sunnīs) analogical deduction.

Eventually Muslim scholarship drew distinctions between different ranks within the general status of *mujtahid*, the highest being that of the "unrestricted *mujtahid*" (*mujtahid muṭlaq*), whose holders are free to engage in *ijtihād* within any field of law and to disregard the established doctrine of any school. *Mujtahids* in the various subordinate ranks, on the other hand, were bound to the general doctrine of a particular school and permitted to explore only those questions that had not been fully resolved within that school or were restricted to certain fields of law. The rigor of the scholarly qualifications varied from rank to rank.

Muslim jurisprudents debated the issue of whether it was possible for the Muslim community to exist in any age without the presence of at least one *mujtahid* (a situation commonly referred to in later Muslim literature as "the closing of the door of *ijtihād*"), but a consensus seems never to have been reached on this matter. The general presumption of Muslim scholarship down to the modern age seems, in any case, to have been that *ijtihād* is, at least in its restricted forms, an ongoing process, even if it be on occasion temporarily interrupted. The requirements for the rank of *mujtahid muṭlaq*, however, were regarded as so demanding as to render the claim to this high rank extremely rare. Muslim jurisprudence has generally shown great deference for the great *mujtahids* of the early centuries of Islam, especially the founders of the schools of law. In Shīʿī Islam, this deference is intensified by the fact that the founders of Shīʿī law were none other than the infallible imams.

In the modern age, the concept of *ijtihād* has sometimes been applied, in an entirely unprecedented manner, to reformist legislation introduced by, or at least subject to the ratification of, elected parliamentary bodies. It has also been adopted by a variety of reform-minded Muslim thinkers, both "modernist" and "fundamentalist," as a rationale for programs calling for fundamental social change or intellectual reorientation.

See Also Qiyās; Uṣūl al-Fiqh.

Bibliography

While virtually every general work on Islam or Islamic law—for example, Joseph Schacht's *An Introduction to Islamic Law* (Oxford, 1964)—deals to some extent with the subject of *ijtihād*, there is as yet no major scholarly monograph in a Western language on the scholarly activities that constitute *ijtihād*. For a cursory discussion, see my "Interpretation in Islamic Law: The Theory of *Ijtihad*," *American Journal of Comparative Law* 26 (1978): 199–212, and Abdur Rahim's *The Principles of Muhammadan Jurisprudence according to the Hanafi, Maliki, Shafii and Ḥanbalī Schools* (1911; reprint, Westport, Conn., 1981), pp. 69–115, 137–192.

Bernard G. Weiss (1987)

IKHWĀN AL-MUSLIMŪN, AL- See MUSLIM BROTHERHOOD

IKHWĀN AL-ṢAFĀʾ

IKHWĀN AL-ṢAFĀʾ (Brethren of Purity) is a pseudonym assumed by the authors of a well-known encyclopedia of the philosophical sciences who described themselves as a group of fellow-seekers after truth. Members of a religio-political movement, they deliberately concealed their identity so that their treatises, entitled *Rasāʾil Ikhwān al-Ṣafāʾ* (Epistles of the Brethren of Purity), would gain wider circulation and would appeal to a broad cross-section of society.

Authorship and Dating. Over the centuries, the authorship of the *Epistles* has been ascribed to the Muʿtazilah, to the Ṣūfīs, to Imam Jaʿfar al-Ṣādiq, and to the great astronomer and mathematician al-Majrīṭī. The assertion of Abū Ḥayyān al-Tawḥīdī (d. 1023) that the treatises were composed by a group of learned men in Basra during the middle of the tenth century was widely accepted. Al-Qifṭī (d. 1248), the famous biographer of physicians and philosophers, expressed his skepticism of al-Tawḥīdī's attribution by acknowledging the prevalence of the belief that the treatises were composed by an ʿAlid imam. In 1932 Husayn Hamdani stated that the Ismāʿīlī Mustaʿlī-Ṭayyibī tradition attributes the *Epistles* to the hidden imam Aḥmad. He also pointed out marked features of the treatises that are manifestly Ismāʿīlī in character.

The Ismāʿīlī character of the *Epistles* is therefore no longer in dispute. What is yet to be determined is the precise identity of their authors within the Ismāʿīlī movement. Zāhid ʿAlī and Wilferd Madelung consider the authors to have been Qarāmiṭah from Basra. On the basis of al-Tawḥīdī's comments and certain information provided by another contemporary Muʿtazilī author, al-Qāḍī ʿAbd al-Jabbār (d. 1025), S. M. Stern also implies that the authors were Qarāmiṭah from Basra. Yves Marquet affirms the Ismāʿīlī authorship of the *Epistles* and suggests that the composition might have begun under the hidden imams and that the authors mentioned by al-Tawḥīdī might have been later editors.

Abbas Hamdani has pointed out the weaknesses in al-Tawḥīdī's assertion and the untrustworthiness of his report and has published the earliest reference to the *Epistles* found in the Ismāʿīlī literature. He therefore rejects the Qarmati authorship of the *Epistles* and argues that they were compiled by the Ismāʿīlīyah as an ideological spearhead before the establishment of the Fatimid state in North Africa in 909.

Contents of the Epistles. *Rasāʾil Ikhwān al-Ṣafāʾ* consists of fifty-two philosophical treatises arranged in four groups, a compendium (*Al-risālah al-jāmiʿah,* ed. Jamīl Ṣalībā, Damascus, 1949), and a compendium of the compendium (*Risālat jāmiʿat al-jāmiʿah,* ed. ʿĀrif Tāmir, Beirut, 1959). The four sections are (1) "The Mathematical Sciences," fourteen treatises on numbers, geometry, astronomy, music, geography, theoretical and practical arts, morals, and logic; (2) "The Physical and Natural Sciences," seventeen treatises on physics, generation and corruption, mineralogy, botany, the nature of life and death, the nature of pleasure and pain, and the limits of human beings' cognitive ability; (3) "The Psychological-Intellectual Sciences," ten treatises on the metaphysics of the Pythagoreans and of the Brethren themselves, the intellect, the cycles and epochs, the nature of love, and the nature of resurrection; and (4) "The Divine Religious Sciences," eleven treatises on beliefs and creeds, the nature of communion with God, the creed of the Brethren, prophecy and its conditions, actions of the spiritual entities, types of political constitutions, providence, magic, and talismans.

The Brethren attempted to popularize learning and philosophy among the masses. Appealing to a multiplicity of races and religions, they developed a strong strain of interconfessionalism. Their attitude toward other religions is therefore strikingly liberal. They argued that religious differences stem from accidental factors such as race, habitat, and time and do not affect the unity and universality of truth.

The complete text of the *Epistles* was first published in 1305–1306/1887–1889 in Bombay, then in 1928 in Cairo (ed. Ziriklī), and most recently in 1957 in Beirut. However, a critical, reliable edition based on the widely scattered original manuscripts of the treatises has yet to be compiled.

SOURCES OF THE EPISTLES. The *Epistles* draw on a variety of sources. The Greek element has been dominant throughout; for example, Ptolemy in astronomy, Euclid in geometry, Hermes Trismegistos in magic and astrology, Aristotle in logic and physics, Plato and Neoplatonists in metaphysics. Another pervading influence is that of the Pythagoreans, especially in arithmetic and music. Of the Neoplatonists, Plotinus and Porphyry exercised the strongest influence. In astrology there are traces of Babylonian and Indian elements. There are also stories of Indian (Buddhist) and Persian (Zoroastrian and Manichaean) origin, and quotations from the Bible. Despite these diverse sources the authors have achieved a remarkable overall synthesis.

PARABLES AND THE ANIMAL STORY. The Brethren employ fables, parables, and allegories to illustrate and prove their doctrine while concealing their own identities; as a result, much of their doctrine remains hidden from the careless reader. The reason they give for hiding their secrets from the people is not their fear of earthly rulers, but a desire to protect their God-given gifts. To support their contention they invoke Christ's dictum not to squander the wisdom by giving it to those unworthy of it.

The dispute between humans and animals (part of the twenty-second epistle, entitled "On How the Animals and Their Kinds Are Formed") is an allegorical story in which the animals complain to the just king of the jinn about the cruel treatment meted out to them by human beings. In the course of the debate, the animals refute humanity's claim of superiority over them by denouncing the rampant injustice and immorality of human society. This fable is a good example of the Brethren's sociopolitical criticism of Islamic society couched in animal characters. The most severe criticism is leveled against the wealthy (who go on amassing fortunes without caring for the needy), the privileged, and the ruling classes. The point is rendered more explicitly in the compendium *(Al-risālah al-jāmiʿah),* wherein it is stated that the animals in the story symbolize the masses who blindly follow their rulers, and the humans represent "the advocates of reasoning by analogy" (those who deduce legal prescriptions from the Qurʾān and the *sunnah* by reasoning and by analogy), the disciples of Satan, the adversaries of the prophets, and the enemies of the imams.

The story enjoyed wide popularity among the masses. It was translated into Hebrew during the fourteenth century and was rendered into Urdu-Hindustani by Mawlavī Ikrām ʿAlī (Calcutta, 1811). In modern times it was translated into English by L. E. Goodman as *The Case of the Animals versus Man before the King of the Jinn* (Boston, 1978).

PHILOSOPHICAL SYSTEM. The philosophical system of the *Epistles* is a synthesis of reason and revelation wherein the cosmos is viewed as a unified, organic whole. The philosophical structure and the cosmology are derived from Neoplatonism and Neo-Pythagoreanism. Eclectic in nature, the system draws on various faiths and philosophies, with a strong undercurrent of rationalism. The Brethren offered a new political program under the aegis of an ʿAlid imam, and their utopia, referred to as *al-madīnah al-fāḍilah al-rūḥānīyah* ("the spiritual, virtuous city") or *dawlat ahl al-khayr* ("the government of virtuous people"), was to be governed by a lawgiving philosopher-prophet. The organization and arrangement of the *Epistles* and their classification of the sciences reflect this ultimate objective.

God is described as absolutely transcendent, beyond all thought and all being. He is the One, the originator and the cause of all being. He is unique in every respect, and nothing can be predicated of him. The universe, which is quite distinct from the divine unity, is related to God by its existence *(wujūd),* permanence (*baqāʾ*), wholeness (*tamām*), and perfection *(kamāl).* The universe is derived by emanation *(fayḍ),* whereas creation, when it is spoken of, is understood as a form of adaptation to theological language.

The superstructure of the hierarchy of beings originates with the intellect emanating from God. The intellect, therefore, is described as the first existent being that emanates from God's munificence *(jūd).* It is a simple spiritual substance with the qualities of permanence, wholeness, and perfection. It contains the forms of all things and is in fact the cause of all causes. Second in the hierarchy is the soul, which emanates from the intellect. It is a simple spiritual substance with the qualities of permanence and wholeness but lacking the quality of perfection. Third in the hierarchy is prime matter, which emanates from the soul. It is a simple spiritual substance that has permanence but lacks wholeness and perfection. It is also susceptible to form.

The cause of the intellect's existence is God's munificence, which emanates from him. The intellect accepts God's munificence and virtues (permanence, wholeness, and perfection) instantaneously, without motion, time, or exertion, on account of its proximity to God and its utmost spirituality. Because of its perfection it overflows with munificence and virtues into the soul. But as its existence is through the intermediacy of the intellect, the soul is deficient in receiving the virtues, and thus its status is below that of intellect. To procure goodness and virtue, it turns sometimes to intellect and at other times to matter. Consequently, when it turns to intellect for goodness, it is distracted from doing good to matter, and vice versa. Being imperfect, the soul becomes attached to matter, which lacks not only the virtues but also the desire to receive them. The soul, therefore, turning to matter, takes special care in its advancement by acting on the matter and by making manifest the virtues inherent in it. Hence the soul is afflicted with exertion, hardship, and misery in reforming and perfecting matter. When matter accepts the virtues, it attains wholeness, while the soul achieves its own perfection. When the soul turns to the intellect, is attached to it and united with it, it attains tranquillity.

The process of emanation terminates with matter. As the soul acts on matter, the matter receives its first form—the three dimensions (length, breadth, and depth)—and thereby becomes absolute body (*al-jism al-muṭlaq*) or universal matter (*hayūlā al-kull*). Thenceforth begins the realm of the composite (*ʿālam al-murakkabāt*). Next, absolute body takes its first form, which is circular because that is the best form. Thus, the spheres and the stars are formed from absolute body. Subsequently come the nine spheres beginning with the outermost sphere, which encompasses all spheres. Next to it is the sphere of fixed stars, followed by the spheres of Saturn, Jupiter, Mars, the sun, Venus, Mercury, and the moon. The higher the position of the sphere, the purer and finer its matter. The spiritual force that directs and manages each sphere is called the particular soul of that sphere.

Under the sublunar world comes the physical matter (*hayūlā al-ṭabīʿah*) of the four elements, fire, air, water, and earth. The earth, being farthest from the One, is the coarsest and darkest kind of physical matter. The active force of the soul that operates on the four elements through heat, cold, dryness, and wetness is known as "the nature of generation and corruption." It moreover produces the generated beings that form the three kingdoms of minerals, plants, and animals. The active force operating on each of these generated beings is called the particular soul. Thus, the process wherein the soul mixes the elements to various degrees and thereby produces the generated beings terminates with man, who is the culmination of that process. Humanity is therefore the noblest of all creation, and the rest of the three kingdoms have been made subservient to it. The unity and complexity of the human being's soul and body make him or her a microcosm. Humans, by virtue of their position, are the central link in the long chain of beings; below them is the animal kingdom and above them is the world of angels, and they are connected to both. In the Perfect Human Being, who has realized his divine origin, the process of generation in descending order comes to an end and the reverse journey in ascending order starts. The human being, therefore, fulfills the purpose of creation.

The *Epistles* occupy a unique position in the history of Islamic thought and exercised a great influence on the Muslim elite. The existence of a large number of manuscript copies of the text scattered throughout the Muslim countries is an eloquent witness to their popularity and influence.

BIBLIOGRAPHY

To the extensive bibliography provided by Yves Marquet in his article "Ikhwān al-Ṣafāʾ," in *The Encyclopaedia of Islam,* new ed. (Leiden, 1960–), the following studies should be added: Abbas Hamdani's "Abū Ḥayyān al-Tawḥīdī and the Brethren of Purity," *International Journal of Middle East Studies* 9 (1978): 345–353, and "An Early Fatimid Source on the Time and Authorship of the *Rasaʾil Ikhwān al-Ṣafāʾ*," *Arabica* 26 (February 1979): 62–75; Hamid Enayat's "The Political Philosophy of the *Rasāʾil Ikhwān al-Ṣafāʾ*," in *Ismaili Contributions to Islamic Culture,* edited by Seyyed Hossein Nasr (Tehran, 1977); and Ian R. Netton's *Muslim Neoplatonists* (London, 1982).

ISMAIL K. POONAWALA (1987)

IKKYŪ SŌJUN (1394–1481) was a poet, calligrapher, Zen eccentric, and revitalizer of the Daitokuji line of Rinzai Zen. Ikkyū was likely, as legend suggests, the unrecognized son of the hundredth emperor of Japan, Gokomatsu (1377–1433; r. 1392–1412), by a rather low-ranking court lady. At an early age, perhaps for lack of any other option, his mother placed him in the Gozan temple of Ankokuji, in Kyoto. He spent the rest of his childhood in Ankokuji and in Tenryūji, yet another Gozan establishment. A quick student, Ikkyū was precocious in both scriptural studies and in the literary arts that had become a focus of the aesthetically oriented Gozan movement.

In 1410 Ikkyū left Tenryūji to live in the streetside hermitage of the eremetic monk Kenʾō Sōi (d. 1414). Kenʾō belonged to the Daitokuji-Myōshinji lineage of Rinzai. Because these two temples had long been out of the Gozan orbit patronized by the shoguns, and because Kenʾō lacked formal certification of enlightenment from his own master, Ikkyū's decision to take him as spiritual master left the young monk doubly removed from the orthodox Zen establishment and clearly illustrates his desire to reach the substance of the Zen tradition rather than grasping for the formal honors offered by the power brokers of his day.

Ikkyū's devotion to the rigors of meditative life in preference to the aesthetic glory and institutional pomp of establishment Zen led him, after Ken'ō's death in 1414, to leave Kyoto to join the circle of the demanding master Kasō Sōdon (1352–1428), twenty-second abbot of Daitokuji, at his small hermitage at Katada on the shores of Lake Biwa. There, in 1420, Ikkyū attained *satori* but following the example of his early master, Ken'ō, refused to accept Kasō's certification.

Shortly thereafter, apparently following an extended squabble with Kasō, Ikkyū left Katada to spend several years in Sakai, a booming port town on the Inland Sea. There he gained a reputation for wild eccentricity, in part due to his repeated bouts of tavern and brothel hopping. These establishments, he claimed, were far better sources of enlightenment than the corrupt temples of Kyoto and Kamakura. Even Daitokuji came under his criticism, and although he was briefly appointed abbot of Daitokuji's Nyoi-an subtemple in 1440, he soon stormed out in disgust at the temple's general pretentiousness and in particular at the role taken there by Kasō's chief disciple, Yōsō Sōi (1376–1458).

By the 1440s Ikkyū had once again taken up practice of the arts. He was eventually to become known for his unconventional poetry and his powerful, at times even unsettling, calligraphy. He was, as well, the confidant and friend of a number of key figures in the development of the new urban middle-class arts—the *nō* playwright Komparu Zenchiku (1405–1468); the early tea master Murata Shukō (1427–1502); the painters Bokkei Saiyo (dates unknown) and Motsurin Shōtō, also known as Bokusai (d. 1492), who wrote the earliest biography of Ikkyū; and the *renga* poet Sōchō (1448–1532)—and was thus an important conduit for Zen ideas and attitudes geographically outward from Kyoto and socially downward to the largely nouveau riche audience for these emerging arts.

In his later years, Ikkyū made peace with the hierarchy of Daitokuji and was appointed abbot of the temple in 1474, at a time when the temple was but a shell, its buildings having been almost entirely destroyed in the early battles of the Ōnin War (1467–1477). It was, indeed, in no small part Ikkyū's connections with the upwardly mobile merchant class of Sakai that provided the funds for the rebuilding and revitalization of Daitokuji and laid the foundation for it and its sister temple, Myōshinji, to fill the spiritual vacuum left by the intertwined collapse of the Ashikaga shogunate and the Gozan establishment. Ikkyū's final years were also marked by his famous autumnal affair with a blind woman singer called Mori. He died in 1481 at the age of eighty-seven. Popular fiction of the Tokugawa period made much of Ikkyū's eccentricities and transformed him from a serious historical figure into an amusing, but stereotypical, folk image, an image whose most recent manifestation was as the hero of a cartoon show on Japanese television.

Several literary works are attributed to Ikkyū. The most important of these are his collection of more than a thousand poems, the *Kyōunshū* (Crazy-cloud anthology), and the related collection the *Jikaishū* (Self-admonitions). He was also the author of six prose works on Buddhist themes: the prose poem *Gaikotsu* (Skeletons); *Amida hadaka* (Amida laid bare); *Bukkigun* (The war of the buddhas and demons); *Mizukagami me-nashi gusa* (Mirror for the sightless), which includes the sometimes separated *Futari bikuni* (Two nuns); *Kana hōgo* (A vernacular sermon); and *Maka hannya haramitta shingyō kai* (Explication of the Heart Sūtra). Two *nō* librettos, *Yamamba* (Old woman of the mountains) and *Eguchi,* are also ascribed to Ikkyū, but these attributions are doubtful. A fair number of examples of his extraordinary calligraphy survive, as do a number of forgeries.

SEE ALSO Calligraphy; Gozan Zen.

BIBLIOGRAPHY

The fullest, though by no means either complete or perfect, treatment of Ikkyū in English is my own *Zen-Man Ikkyū* (Chico, Calif., 1981). Also useful are Donald Keene's biographical sketch, "The Portrait of Ikkyū," most easily available in his *Landscapes and Portraits* (Tokyo and Palo Alto, Calif., 1971), Sonja Arntzen's annotated translations of several dozen poems from the *Kyōunshū, Ikkyū Sōjun: A Zen Monk and His Poetry* (Bellingham, Wash., 1973), and her *Ikkyū and the Crazy Cloud Anthology* (New York, 1986). The best study of Bokusai's critical biography of Ikkyū is Hirano Sōjō's *"Ikkyū oshō nempu" no kenkyu* (Kyoto, 1977), which includes the whole of Bokusai's original text. The best, though still incomplete, study of Ikkyū's poetry is Hirano's *Kyōunshū zenshaku,* 2 vols. (Tokyo, 1976–). Ikkyū's prose pieces can be found in *Ikkyū oshō zenshū,* edited by Mori Taikyo (Tokyo, 1913). The fullest representation of his calligraphy is Tayama Hōnan's *Zenrin bokuseki kaisetsu* (Kamakura, 1965) and *Zoku Zenrin bokuseki kaisetsu* (Kamakura, 1965). Serviceable modern biographies on Ikkyū in Japanese include Furuta Shōkin's *Ikkyū* (Tokyo, 1946), Ichikawa Hakugen's *Ikkyū: Ransei ni ikita zenja* (Tokyo, 1971), and Murata Taihei's *Ningen Ikkyū* (Tokyo, 1963). For general background on the age in which Ikkyū lived, *Japan in the Muromachi Age,* edited by John Whitney Hall and Toyoda Takeshi (Berkeley, Calif.,1977), and Martin Collcutt's fine *Five Mountains: The Rinzai Zen Monastic Institution in Medieval Japan* (Cambridge, Mass., 1981) are especially valuable.

New Sources

Ikkyu. *Wild Ways: Zen Poems of Ikkyu.* Translated by John Stevens. Boston, 1995.

Stevens, John. *Three Zen Masters: Ikkyu, Hakuin, Ryokan.* Tokyo, 1993.

JAMES HUGH SANFORD (1987)
Revised Bibliography

ILLUMINATIONISM SEE ISHRĀQĪYAH

ILMARINEN. According to the list of pagan Finnic gods compiled in 1551 by Michael Agricola, who introduced the Reformation to Finland and established the Finnish literary language, Ilmarinen was the creator of both wind and calm weather and controlled travel on water. There is no evidence that Ilmarinen was ever worshiped, but what is probably the oldest stratum of *Kalevala*-type poetry concerning the exploits of Ilmarinen connects him with various cosmogonic acts. Elias Lönnrot's redaction of the *Kalevala* includes material from this ancient folk tradition but increases the number of his appearances, featuring him in twenty-seven out of the fifty divisions of the epic. Lönnrot also enhances Ilmarinen's personality with a human dimension.

The name *Ilmarinen* is probably derived from the Finno-Ugric word *ilma,* meaning "air," and, by extension, "weather" and "world." The Udmurts (Votiaks), distant relatives of the Finns and inhabitants of the region northeast of Moscow between the Kama and Vyatka Rivers, called their sky god Ilmar or Inmar. A famous Saami (Lapp) witch drum, presented in 1692 as an exhibit in court, depicts a god named Ilmaris as having the power to raise and calm storms at sea.

Among the epithets applied to Ilmarinen in the epic tradition is "shaper of the mysterious, luck-bringing *sampo.*" *Sampo* is a difficult term, and scholarly research has produced more than sixty definitions for it, but according to the most widely held view, the *sampo* is a support of the world. A close derivative of the term is *sammas,* meaning "statue." A frequent substitute or parallel for the term is *kirjokansi,* meaning "brightly worked cover," which in other contexts stands for the sky. Certain Saami cult images in stone and wood are believed to be late representations of the *sampo.*

One folk poem places the forging of the *sampo* shortly after the genesis of the sky, earth, sun, moon, and stars, all of which, the poem claims, were formed by the breaking of an eagle's (in some versions, a waterfowl's) egg. The poem, which goes on to relate how Ilmarinen and his brother Väinämöinen steal the *sampo,* resembles the ancient Nordic sagas. But the epithet "shaper of the mysterious, luck-bringing *sampo*" refers to the tradition in which Ilmarinen creates the *sampo* himself, as in the episode in which, as a result of this act, he wins a competition against his brother for the beautiful maid of Pohjola. Together, Väinämöinen and Ilmarinen strike the primeval spark in the upper aerial regions.

Ilmarinen is also credited with forging a golden maid, who eventually proves no match for a real women. Ilmarinen as smith-god later developed into a culture hero who makes useful objects for people and takes part in various adventures, including love-quests.

See Also Finnish Religions; Lemminkäinen; Väinämöinen.

Bibliography

Fromm, Hans. *Kalevala.* Munich, 1967. See the index, s.v. *Ilmarinen.*

Honko, Lauri. "Ilmarinen." In *Wörterbuch der Mythologie,* edited by H. W. Haussig, vol. 1, *Gotter und Mythen im Vorderen Orient,* pp. 309–311. Stuttgart, 1965.

Krohn, Kaarle. *Kalevalastudien,* vol. 3, *Ilmarinen,* and vol. 4, *Sampo.* Folklore Fellows Communications, nos. 71–72. Helsinki, 1927. Krohn's six-volume work, although partially outdated, still gives the most thorough summary of the sources of the *Kalevala.*

New Sources

DuBois, Thomas A. *Finnish Folk Poetry and the Kalevala.* New York, 1995.

Matti Kuusi (1987)
Revised Bibliography

IMAGES

This entry consists of the following articles:

VENERATION OF IMAGES
IMAGES, ICONS, AND IDOLS

IMAGES: VENERATION OF IMAGES

The veneration of images involves humans or other subjects showing respect and homage to objects that visually represent, point to, or embody sacred beings or realities held to be especially worthy of honor. While such practices have been disputed in many religious traditions and decisively rejected by a few, the veneration of images has been a remarkably widespread form of ritual practice throughout history in many parts of the world.

The English terms used here, *veneration* and *image,* both derive from Latin, but they may be adequately used to translate such indigenous terms as the Indic *mūrtipūjā.* Deriving from the same etymological root as Venus, goddess of beauty and love, veneration refers both to feelings of deep respect and reverence toward some person or thing and to practices by which that respect and reverence are demonstrated or enacted. These practices may be bodily gestures, physical offerings, verbal expressions, emotional dispositions, or mental presentations. The subjects making these acts of veneration are most often humans but may also include animals, semidivine beings, divinities, other images, or even nature itself. Recipients may be venerable living persons like kings or religious teachers, remains or relics of venerable persons, images of divine or human beings, other objects considered particularly sacred such as holy books, or invisible presences. The range of religious practices of veneration then is very broad, and the veneration of images is only one part of this larger category.

The term *image* comes from Latin *imago,* which denotes an imitation, a copy, a likeness, among several other meanings. In its earliest English usage, image referred to a fabricated imitation or representation of the external form of an object and applied particularly to sculpted figures of saints and divinities that were treated as objects of religious devotion. As an ideal type, the veneration of images may be taken as venerative acts directed toward physical icons that represent divinities or other sacred beings anthropomorphically. However, divine beings are notoriously multiform, and they are promiscuous in making themselves present in a great variety of objects. Not just sculpted images but paintings and drawings, abstract forms, diagrams, stones, trees, and other physical objects as well as mentally projected visualizations may serve as objects of veneration. More than simply signifying those beings, icons are often considered and honored as living beings, animated by the actual presence of the beings they represent.

In every ritual culture that engages with images, venerative practices take on a distinctive pattern in accord with the broader practices and premises of that tradition. Some ritual cultures may specify, for example, who is eligible to perform image worship according to criteria of birth, gender, age, initiatory status, or special training, whereas others leave the practice open to all devotees. Some may require that the worshiper undertake special preparations, such as physical purifications or mental concentration, before entering into worship, or that one wear special clothing. So too ritual cultures may prescribe how the image is to be prepared: its conception, fabrication, consecration, and regular maintenance as a venerated object. Ritual cultures may differ from one another as to the specific vocabulary of actions one should employ in venerating images and in the degree to which they formalize a prescribed etiquette of veneration. Religious traditions may develop distinctive theological understandings of the relationship of the image to the deity it represents, instantiates, or embodies. They may ascribe agency—moving, talking, miracle working—to the image or to the deity acting through it. Finally, different ritual cultures understand the efficacy of venerative practices in varied ways.

Widespread and varied as it is, the veneration of images has been a fiercely disputed practice. Even within ritual cultures strongly attached to the worship of images, adherents debate not only proper methods and understandings of such practices but also their ultimate value. Greek philosophers like Xenophanes and Heraclitus and Hindu ones like Śaṅkara sought to deprecate or delegitimate the venerative practices of their own societies. In some cases religious traditions have defined themselves through a shared opposition to the worship of images. Around the sixth century BCE Israelite prophets began to articulate a critique of the image-related practices of their Near Eastern neighbors, and this decisive break with image veneration subsequently became a defining feature of Judaism. Similar critiques were later deployed by the other Abrahamic monotheisms, Christianity and Islam, in their own moments of self-definition. Among all religions, Christians have shown perhaps the most complex historical ambivalence toward images, and this has led to several episodes of intense internal controversy and iconoclastic destruction.

Critiques of image worship originating with the Greeks and the Israelites have also had a decisive impact on the scholarly study of religion, as many scholars have observed. Earlier generations of comparative religionists constructed teleological schemes in which the veneration of images figured lower on an evolutionary scale than aniconic forms of religiosity. Others developed what Peter Brown calls "two-tiered" models, where intellectual elites allegedly detach themselves from such popular practices as the worship of images. More subtly, as Leo Oppenheim noted in 1964, a scholarly ambivalence toward "idols" has often led scholars away from the serious investigation of image veneration in other religious traditions and toward the study of religious practices considered more comprehensible and acceptable in Western terms.

Only in the last two decades of the twentieth century, with calls to "rematerialize" the study of religion, did the exploration of the veneration of images, in its great historical and ethnographic variety as well as its history of dispute, become a more central topic in the history of religions and related disciplines. In his wide-ranging study *The Power of Images* (1989), the art historian David Freedberg seeks to identify and substantiate an innate human responsiveness to the image. At the other pole, the intellectual historian Alain Besançon, in *The Forbidden Image* (2000), traces a common philosophical disposition toward the absolute underlying the history of Western opposition to images from the Greeks up to twentieth-century Russian painters. In between the iconophilic and the iconoclastic, many scholars working in particular religious traditions have begun to explore more deeply the multiplicity of image-venerating ritual cultures. Drawing on this scholarship, this article outlines several examples of historical traditions that have practiced the veneration of images. It is not intended as comprehensive, but it does aim to illustrate some of the variety this practice takes in different settings and some of the ways it has been disputed.

MESOPOTAMIANS. Among the earliest known religious images are numerous female figurines, commonly called *Venuses,* found in European, Asian, and Middle Eastern archaeological sites and dating to the late Paleolithic and Neolithic periods. Some scholars have seen these as icons in a widespread cult of the "Great Goddess" linked to fertility and the emergence of agriculture. While they are intriguing as possible evidence for the ancient veneration of images, indications of how or even if these objects were employed ritually remains sketchy.

The earliest full evidence for image veneration comes from the early urban civilizations of Mesopotamia. Archaeological evidence, inscriptional records, and later texts all point to a ritual culture centered around images starting as early as the Sumerian period of circa 2500 BCE and continuing for nearly two thousand years. Within the Mesopotamian ritual culture, images that represented the gods were consecrated through a rite of "mouth opening," then were maintained inside temples with regular offerings, and were processed outside their temples for annual festival celebrations. The best documented of these involve deities closely associated with city-states, such as Marduk in Babylonia and Anu in Uruk. Cults of these palladial deities were highly institutionalized and closely related to the political order.

In Mesopotamia the key ritual by which a human-made wooden statue was transformed into an animate divine icon was known as "opening the mouth" *(mīs pī)*. As cited by Christopher Walker and Michael B. Dick in "The Mesopotamian *mīs pī* Ritual," "The statue cannot smell incense, drink water, or eat food without Opening the Mouth." Motifs of gestation and birth appear throughout the mouth-opening rites, for the ritual sought to give birth to the living presence of the deity. Moreover the ritual distances the image itself from any suggestion of human fabrication. Artisans would have their hands symbolically cut off with a wooden sword, and they were required to swear that they had not created the image. Rather, they averred, the patron deities of their guild had done so.

Once consecrated, the image took its place on a pedestal in the temple, often located in an elevated part of the city. The wooden image would be plated with gold, dressed in sumptuous clothing, and adorned with jewelry. It would be surrounded by other images that composed the god's family and court, much as a king would sit in state surrounded by attendants. The daily services for such divine rulers were carried out by ritual specialists and consisted chiefly of elaborate feasts. At Uruk the god Anu ate twice a day. His meals, specified in detailed texts, included milk, beer, and other drinks; meat; bread; cake; fruit; and sweets. Musicians played during the repast, and priests burned incense to perfume the sanctum. After the god had eaten his fill of the offerings, the remainders were taken to the king as particularly potent nourishment. Receiving god's leftovers was a definite marker of royal status.

Kings were also present in the temples in the form of royal images. Starting around 2100 to 2000 BCE, consecrated images of ruling kings were introduced as both venerators of the gods and recipients of veneration. A standing figure of the king might offer worship to the seated image of the god, while a seated image of the king could receive worship from his human acolytes.

In addition to the regular patterns of daily worship, the divine images celebrated special festivals. Central to many of these were public processions. If cultic practices within the temple were restricted to the religious and political elite, processions were occasions for much broader participation. The image-deities would leave their private temple-palaces and journey through the streets of the city to a festival temple in the countryside. On such occasions the more general public veneration reasserted the special relationship between deity and city-state.

GREEKS. In the *Iliad*, Homer describes Hekabe's veneration of an image. The Trojan warrior Hector, Hekabe's son, leaves the battle to ask the women and elders of the city to solicit the aid of the gods. Hekabe calls together the women and then selects her most beautiful brocaded robe as a presentation. The women process to the temple of the goddess Athena, on the Troy acropolis. The temple priestess Theano allows them to enter, and while the women cry out aloud, Theano takes Hekabe's robe and places it on the seated image's knees. The priestess petitions Athena. If the goddess favors the Trojans by "breaking the spear" of their fierce opponent Diomedes, she prays, they will sacrifice twelve young heifers on her altar. Athena evidently does not agree to the terms, for as Homer relates, she turns away her head. Deities may be swayed by offerings but remain ultimately autonomous in their powers.

From Homer's time through the classical period (roughly 800–300 BCE), the Greek gods and goddesses were present in anthropomorphic forms in myriad temples throughout the Greek world. Some ancient icons, like the famous olive wood Athena Polias in Athens, were said to have "fallen from the sky," whereas others were explicitly associated with their human sculptors, such as the Athena Parthenos, also on the Acropolis in Athens, made by the celebrated Pheidias (between 447 and 438 BCE). The purpose of images was to make the gods visible to humans and to facilitate interactions between them. As Pythagoras is supposed to have said, "People who enter a temple and see the images of the god close up get a different mind" (Burkert, 1988). Greeks interacted with their gods in three ritual ways: sacrifice, votive offerings, and prayer.

Of these, animal sacrifice was preeminent in Greek ritual culture. Sacrificial altars were placed before the images in their temples. However, sacrifice does not require image or temple. A sacrifice offered on an altar in the open air could just as easily reach the gods dwelling on Mount Olympus. Greeks also made offerings of more permanent objects in association with vows. As Hekabe presented her brocaded gown to Athena, petitioners offered all sorts of valuable items to the gods in their temples: garments, vessels, weapons acquired as war booty, bronze tripods, gold bricks, statuettes, and votive tablets. Votive offerings (*anathema*) were showpieces meant to delight the recipient deity as well as to impress other human visitors to the temple. The gods and goddesses evidently enjoyed seeing themselves, for many of the tablets featured their representations along with the donor in the act of prayer or sacrifice. Greek temples often filled up with these showpieces, so much so that it might become difficult to see the deity. The sumptuous wealth deposited in the temples also made it necessary to protect them from thieves and looters. A common depiction of the temple priestess shows her holding a large key.

Beyond these special acts of worship, scholars know something about the ordinary etiquette of the Greek cult of images. Water basins near the temple entry indicate that physical purification was a prerequisite to entering. Once inside, worshipers greeted the divine image by falling to their knees and sought physical contact by touching or kissing it. Bodily acts of bathing and dressing the image were common venerative practices. Ritual specialists mediated these acts of worship between humans and the gods, as the priestess Theano did with Hekabe's exchange with Athena. Unfortunately, however, Greek ritual specialists did not leave behind records of their priest craft. Scholars do not know exactly how they performed the ritual of installation for new images or the daily liturgical routines for maintaining deities in their livelihood. And while Greek authors copiously recorded the mythological deeds of their gods and goddesses, they wrote little about the theological conception of the divine image. Much of what is written moreover is the work of critics.

To subvert the image worship of their fellow Greeks, the pre-Socratic philosophers Xenophanes (c. 560–478 BCE) and Heraclitus (c. 540–480 BCE) presented two primary arguments. According to Xenophanes, humans project their own attributes, with all their human flaws, onto the gods. If horses had hands and could create images of the gods, he argued, gods would appear as horses. Images are projections of humanity, not true representations of the divine. Heraclitus focuses on the materiality of images. To pray to a sculpted image is like trying to hold a conversation with a house; the image does not hear and does not give. Later Greek satirists picked up on the theme of an image's inanimate helplessness. So in parodies like "The Battle of the Frogs and Mice," Athena complains that mice are nibbling away at her garments and fouling up her garlands. It is not possible to say how broadly these critical views were shared among Greeks of the classical period, though it is certain that many continued to address prayers to images and to present new robes to Athena.

JAINS. The earliest Indic inscription to refer to a venerative icon, dating to the first century BCE, concerns an image of Mahāvīra called the "Kalinga Jina." The inscription reports how this icon, evidently of political import, had previously been taken away by the Mauryan ruler and was now recovered and ritually installed by Kharavela, ruler of the Kalinga territory. In addition to inscriptional evidence, archeological finds and early Jain texts indicate that the Jains developed and maintained a flourishing culture centering around the worship of Jina images in the early centuries CE.

Early Jain texts prescribe worship practices similar to those later classified as the eightfold *pūjā*, which is still the central form of worship among the majority Śvetāmbara Jain community. The eightfold *pūjā* is an individual form of image veneration. After first purifying himself or herself, a Jain worshiper enters the temple, approaches the image of worship, honors it with mantras, and circumambulates it in a clockwise direction. Worshipers mark their foreheads with sandalwood paste and then offer the eight components of worship. The first three offerings are applied directly to the body of the image: worshipers pour bathing water over it, smear marks of sandalwood paste on its limbs, and adorn it with flowers. The following five offerings are made in front of the image, not onto it. Worshipers offer incense, lamps, broken rice grains, food, and fruit before the image. After these physical offerings (*dravya-pūjā*) have been given, worshipers should perform mental veneration (*bhāva-pūjā*), an inward contemplation of the exemplary qualities of the Jina.

Among Jains, the dominant understanding of these venerative practices is reflexive. Because the Jain *Tīrthaṃkaras* are fully liberated beings who do not engage in the world after liberation, Jain worshipers do not expect them to inhabit their icons, and they do not expect them actually to consume food or fruit. Nor do they seek direct aid from the *Tīrthaṃkaras* in their lives. Jains view the veneration of images as an act of renunciation that is valuable for a worshiper in the shedding of karmic bondage. During each offering, worshipers recite verses that interpret the actions in terms of key Jain values and the worshipers' own states. While offering food, worshipers identify the Jina as the "noneating one" and express a wish that through renunciation they might also reach this state.

This austere conception of image veneration did not prevent Jains from developing an opulent temple culture, which reached its apogee in the image-filled hilltop temple cities of Shatrunjay and Mount Abu. Nor did it preclude lively devotional practices, such as the Jain laywomen who sing hymns of praise to accompany rituals of worship.

However, the issue of image worship was central to the primary sectarian split among the Śvetāmbara Jains. Starting from the critique of the fifteenth-century monk Lonka, the faction that came to be called the Sthānakvāsins argued that image worship is a feature of a corrupt world age and advocated instead mental worship and the veneration of living ascetics. The majority group remaining loyal to their image practices came to be called Murtipujakas, the image worshipers.

BUDDHISTS. Buddhist traditions often ascribe the first images of the Śākyamuni Buddha to the founder's own lifetime. When the Buddha left Kausambi to teach elsewhere, the story goes, King Udayana requested that the monk Maudgalyāyana supervise the fabrication of a stand-in image so that the king might continue to pay respects to the teacher during his absence. Thus was made the "Udayana Buddha." When Śākyamuni returned to Kausambi, the animated image rose to honor its prototype. But the Buddha understood the pedagogic value of the image, for he honored it in return and predicted that it would play a great role in disseminating his teachings.

Modern historians of Buddhism have usually discounted such claims. While the question of the "origin of the Buddha image" has long been a topic of vigorous scholarly debate, a general consensus ascribes the earliest three-dimensional images of the Buddha to the period of the Kushans, who ruled during the first through the third centuries CE. The innovative step of fabricating physical icons of the Buddha was taken, more or less simultaneously, in two centers of the Kushan dominion, the Gandhara region of northern Pakistan and the city of Mathura.

Whenever the Buddha image did appear historically, the etiquette of veneration was already well established within Buddhist ritual culture. The earliest recipient of such honor was the Śākyamuni Buddha himself. Early Buddhist texts are replete with accounts of humans, animals, semidivine Nāgas and *Yakṣas,* divinities like Indra and Brāhmaṇ, and even nature itself demonstrating veneration to the body (*śarīra*) of the Buddha through acts of prostration, circumambulation, flower garlanding, gift giving, and reciting of verbal praises. With the Buddha's *parinirvāṇa* and cremation, Buddhist venerative practices shifted to the Buddha's physical remains (also called *śarīra*) and other objects or places associated with this life. His relics were interred in moundlike stupas. These became flourishing cult centers of Buddhist veneration at least by the time of the Mauryan emperor Aśoka (r. 260–230 BCE). Worshipers honored the stupas, enlivened by the presence of Buddha's remains, much the same way they had once honored the teacher: with prostrations and circumambulations, flowers and incense, banners and parasols, and food offerings. More ambitious donors might arrange to have the entire stupa decorated with lamps or to have musicians serenade it. These appear to have remained relatively spontaneous and unstructured practices, because there are few liturgical prescriptions within the early Buddhist literature.

The introduction of the Buddha image offered another way of making the Buddha present. But there were debates over the degree of this presence. Worshipers might address the image as if it were the living Buddha, but as with the Jains, they generally understood the efficacy of veneration to reside not in the recipient but in the karmic benefits of the pious act itself. The image of the Buddha was a particularly fertile "field of merit" in which to sow the seeds of generous acts, but the Buddha did not directly reward such acts.

On the other hand, by the Gupta period in the fourth and fifth centuries CE, inscriptions point to a greatly enhanced sense of the Buddha's presence. During this period Indian monastic layouts regularly set aside a special cell, facing the entrance, where the Buddha image resided. Monks were assigned to tend to the needs of the Buddha, and endowments provided for the regular supply of flowers, incense, oil lamps, and other requisites to the Buddha. Moreover the inscriptions speak of the Buddha as the owner of the monastic property. Clearly the Buddha image became more fully established as a real living presence in the institutional life of the monastery. This significant change in Buddhist ritual culture may correspond to the introduction of new, more expansive philosophical ideas about the nature of Buddha's personhood.

Buddhist image practices figured prominently in the spread of Buddhism from India to other parts of Asia. According to tradition, Emperor Ming (r. 58–75 CE) of the Han dynasty had a dream of a radiant golden Buddha flying through the air and promptly sent emissaries to India to bring back Buddhist Scriptures and the famous Udayana Buddha. Images were so central to the early implantation of Buddhism that the Chinese referred to Buddhism as the "religion of images." The wealth of Buddhist imagery and venerative practices appear to have stimulated other competing ritual cultures of China, including Daoists and Confucians, to integrate some aspects of image veneration.

HINDUS. Modern Hinduism may well feature more venerated images per capita that any other religious tradition. This was not always the case, though. In early India the primary forms of public religion receiving elite patronage were aniconic. The Vedas (composed roughly 1500–300 BCE) prescribed an elaborate program of fire sacrifices to deities who remained invisible. The earliest images of recognizable Hindu deities date from the Kushan period, contemporary with the early Jain and Buddhist images, and the earliest texts describing protocols for image worship appeared still later, around the fifth and sixth centuries CE. By the early medieval period (700–1200 CE), however, Hindu elites and ritual specialists had positively embraced the icon as an instrument of religious practice, and the veneration of images became the normative ritual culture of the public sphere.

In the early medieval period Hindu priests articulated new theologies and elaborate ritual programs for their divine images, and their formulations have continued to be influential over many centuries. For these Hindus, images are understood as one of the means by which a deity who is both transcendent and immanent makes himself or herself present and accessible to human votaries. Vaiṣṇava theologians speak of Viṣṇu's "incarnation as an image," parallel to his other incarnations (*avatāra*). Just as Viṣṇu manifests himself in human and animal bodies, so he can also enter into fabricated physical representations of himself.

Hindu image veneration places much emphasis on the act of seeing, known as *darśana.* A physical representation enables worshipers to see their god, who might otherwise remain beyond their ken, and the beauty of the divine body attracts their gaze and awakens their devotion. But the gaze is reciprocal; the god looks back. The key moment in consecrating a new Hindu image is not opening the mouth, as the Mesopotamians would have it, but opening the eyes. So Hindus often refer to the act of worship as "taking *darśana,*" seeing and being seen by the deity present in the icon.

Hindu image veneration is offered daily, both by devout worshipers in private home shrines on their own behalf and by priests in public temples on behalf of the entire community. Prescriptions in medieval Śaiva priestly guides, for example, call for elaborate preparatory purifications. The worshiper, the place of worship, the icon, the substances to be offered, and even the *mantras* to be used in worship must all be purified. The priest approaches the primary icon, the abstract Śiva linga. Though Śiva is considered to be already present in the linga, the priest performs a detailed invocation, such that Śiva becomes "specially present" there for the duration of worship. At this point the offerings or services (*upacāras*) that are the core of Hindu image veneration may begin.

Through these services, the worshiper treats the divine person present in the icon as an especially esteemed guest or as the sovereign lord of the cosmos. Priestly guides suggest that one may offer five, eight, sixteen, or as many as twenty-five services, depending on one's resources and ambitions. Among these services are many of the same offerings employed in Jain and Buddhist worship, such as flowers, incense, lights, prostrations, hymns, and food. If they share some of the venerative vocabulary, though, Indic ritual cultures have different ideas about many details, such as food offerings. According to Viṣṇu worshipers, that god partakes of the subtle portion of the food, and the substantive remains of Viṣṇu's meal, transfigured by contact with the divine, are then distributed to the community of worshipers as a physical manifestation of Viṣṇu's grace, called *prasāda.* Śaiva Siddhāntins also believe Śiva eats the subtle portion of food offerings, but they consider food that has come into contact with Śiva too powerful for human consumption. In Śaiva temples leftovers are passed on to another image, one of Śiva's semidivine followers, who is better able to handle them.

In medieval India, with its great temples, image veneration became the most visible manifestation of Hindu religiosity but not without opposition from other Hindus. Those loyal to the earlier Vedic practices of aniconic sacrifice fought a long discursive battle against the veneration of images. Others, like the devotional Vīraśaivas, satirized the cult of images in favor of more spontaneous and unmediated expressions of devotion (*bhakti*). Still others, like the nondualist philosopher Śaṅkara (c. 700–750 CE), advocated more "subtle" forms of practice as superior, such as "mental *pūjā*" offered through meditation to a nonsubstantive and imperceptible Supreme.

Hindus have selectively adapted new technologies to their practices of image veneration. New print technologies were adopted in the late nineteenth century and the twentieth century to enable the mass reproduction of inexpensive lithographic "God pictures," which pilgrims can purchase and incorporate into their home shrines. Large temples employ monitors to televise the venerated image so that a larger audience may partake of *darśana.* And with the development of the Internet, prominent Hindu temples in India have developed websites so that far-flung worshipers can offer cyber veneration.

Over the centuries, despite internal and external critiques, Hindus have maintained their practices of image veneration, modifying and transforming them along the way. When Hindus emigrated from India in the nineteenth and twentieth centuries, images traveled with them. The multitude of new temples that Hindus constructed throughout the United States and the United Kingdom in the late twentieth century demonstrate the flexibility and vitality of Hindu venerative practices.

INCAS AND ANDEANS. In the fifteenth century and the early sixteenth century the Incas of Cuzco (Peru) built a large empire, subordinating more than one hundred different ethnic groups over an area along the Pacific Coast and through the Andean Highlands. Within this newly established empire the Incas promoted a central state religion. They recognized a hierarchy of gods, in which the highest were Viracocha, the creator, and the Sun, first descendent of Viracocha. This imperial cult, however, coexisted uneasily with the ritual traditions of the conquered cultures, who had their own divine figures and practices. Both the Incas and their subjects venerated images.

In the center of Cuzco the Incas constructed a massive temple for the Sun, whom the Incas took as their own ancestor. Within the temple the Sun appeared in the form of a young boy made of pure gold. The image was put to bed at night and awakened in the morning. At noon women brought him his meal: a dish of maize, a serving of meat, and a cup of maize beer. After the Sun had consumed what he would of his meal, the remainders were burned in a silver cauldron, and the beer was poured into a drain through which it nourished the earth. Officiants then raised their hands to the Sun and proclaimed their gratitude. Normally access to the inner sanctum was highly restricted, and ritual officiants observed high degrees of personal purification before entering. On special occasions, however, the Sun image was brought out into the central square of the city and received his meal in a more public setting.

The Incas constructed new Sun temples in areas they brought under control, and they required their subjects to show veneration to the Sun. Often these Sun temples competed directly with the shrines of local deities, called *huacas.* In Cajamarca on the coast, for instance, one of the most powerful of the *huacas,* named Pachacámac, occupied a massive pyramid temple. The Incas built a still taller temple to the Sun next to it. Local stories reflected the tension that subsisted between these two cult deities in which Pachacámac reluctantly ceded his preeminent status.

Huacas had once been superhuman beings walking the earth, and they were responsible for creating the landscape. But after completing their creative deeds or through conflict with another deity, the *huacas* turned into stone, sometimes in icon form and other times simply as prominent parts of the natural landscape. In such physical forms they lived on and continued to play a role in human affairs. *Huacas* were unpredictable. They were benevolently responsible for the health and prosperity of the community, but they might also bring disease, earthquakes, and crop failure. Therefore it was wise to attend to their needs assiduously.

Pachacámac resided in his pyramid in the form of a wooden pole whose top was carved in the figure of a man. Here too access was strictly limited. Priests fasted for a year before they could enter the inner sanctum. Properly attended and solicited, this deity, like many other *huacas,* could speak. Pilgrims from throughout the area brought him gifts of gold and textiles, conveyed their messages to Pachacámac through the priests, and hoped to receive an answer. In addition to the local *huacas,* Andeans also venerated special lineage gods in icon form and household deities who appeared as small animal-shaped stones.

The Inca Sun, the more localized *huacas* and other deities, and their icons were all part of the complex ritual culture of the Andean region that the Spanish conquistadores encountered in 1532. As Catholics, the Spaniards brought with them a different attitude toward images.

CRITICS OF THE IMAGE: JEWS, CHRISTIANS, AND MUSLIMS. Most image-venerating ritual cultures coexist with their critics, as shown, for the public worship of images seldom appears as an uncontested practice. It is possible also to trace a more sustained critique of images and their veneration in the West, deriving from both Greek and Israelite sources. Early Christian critics of the image drew on Greek writings as well as the Hebrew Bible in formulating their positions, and later the Islamic founders adapted them to their own theological vision.

Scholarship suggests that the strong monotheism and vigorous prohibition of image veneration in the Hebrew Bible may reflect the triumph of one group of "Yahweh-alone" partisans among the Israelites in the wake of the disastrous events of the sixth century BCE. After the destruction of Jerusalem in 586 BCE and the debilitating exile, this group advanced its own vision of the Israelite past and its notion of a proper Israelite ritual culture by exercising a dominant role in editing the Bible.

The Hebrew Bible opposes the veneration of images in two main ways. One is through direct prohibition. The Israelites were surrounded by ritual cultures, such as those of Mesopotamia and Egypt, that represented their gods in image form. In the second commandment Yahweh distinguishes himself as the God who refuses to be so represented. An insistence on Yahweh's exclusive divinity in the first commandment coupled with the prohibition of images defines a distinctive identity for the Israelites and helps insure that they will not assimilate the cults of their neighbors. The second method of articulating opposition was through prophetic parody, such as those of Jeremiah and Isaiah. Jeremiah carefully describes all the steps in fabricating an icon: the cutting of the tree in the forest, carving the wood into an image, decorating it with silver and gold, and nailing it into place. However, he asserts, these practices are false. With its material roots, the image is "only wood." There is no breath of life in it. Like Heraclitus, the Hebrew prophets argued that an image of wood or stone, fashioned by human hands, necessarily remained inanimate and could not serve as a vehicle for a god like Yahweh.

Early Christians, true to their Jewish legacy, maintained a critical attitude toward the use of images. Paul's encounter with the Greek images of Athens, recorded in the *Acts of the Apostles*, serves as a paradigm. In Athens, Paul was revolted by the sight of "a city given over to idolatry." However, in his speech to the Areopagus council, he did find one monument to praise: an empty altar inscribed "To an Unknown God." In Paul's view this unrepresented divinity is the one the Christians worship. God does not reside in human-made shrines or images, because God is not dependent in any way on human hands. Following Paul, the early Christian writers of the second and third centuries CE attacked image veneration from several different angles. Justin Martyr (c. 100–165 CE) argued that images are without souls and cannot represent God. As essentially demonic forms, they constitute an insult to God. Tertullian (c. 155–220 CE) focused on the social dangers of idolatry and held that image veneration could unleash unwelcome emotional outbursts. Moreover in Tertullian's view idolatry was an index of pagan culture, and it was crucial for Christians to distinguish themselves from the dominant Roman culture.

A more complex attitude began to develop in the fourth century CE, as Christianity itself became the dominant culture. With Emperor Constantine's conversion around 313 CE, the Christian movement became an imperial religion. Whereas early Christians had been criticized for their impoverished ritual culture, with no altars and no temples, now Christians began to develop their own architecture and art. They also destroyed competing pagan images, such as those of Zeus. The introduction of a Christian representational art was also criticized from within. Augustine (354–430 CE) disapproved of those who would look for Christ on painted walls rather than in his written word. Other Christians looked for ways to accommodate the didactic value of Christian institutional imagery with the negative attitude toward images. Most influential was the distinction articulated by Pope Gregory I (r. 590–604 CE). Images are placed in churches, he ruled, not for worship, but solely for instructing the minds of the ignorant. Christian images would be officially educational and not venerative in purpose.

Gregory's distinction provided one important legitimation but did not finally resolve the issue for Christians. The greatest debate, usually known as the Iconoclastic Controversy, began in the next century. By the eighth century the veneration of icons—painted images of holy persons regarded as particularly powerful and efficacious—had become widespread throughout churches and monasteries. Worshipers prostrated before the images, kissed them, and solicited their aid. During the same period the Byzantine Empire suffered political reversals at the hands of an expanding Ummayad Islamic polity, and this sense of threat from a more iconophobic religious community contributed to the vigor of the debate. Some argued that God was using Islam to punish Christians for having fallen into idolatry.

Similar to the Israelites, early Muslims insisted first on the principle of *tauhid*, the exclusive divinity of Allāh. Images pose a threat to that divine hegemony, for there is always a danger that humans may come to venerate those images rather than Allāh. Moreover Muslims identified Allah as sole creator. The *ḥadīth* traditions therefore especially condemn those who make images, because they seem to be laying claim to the creative prerogative of Allah. Later Muslims in some settings adopted more relaxed attitudes toward representational art, but the Islamic prohibition on the veneration of images remained firm.

Against this political background, Emperor Leo III initiated the controversy in 726 CE with an effort to purge from the church "the idolatry of image worship." The iconodules, notably John of Damascus (675-749), responded by defending the "relative worship" of images without idolatry. As representations of the material appearances of Jesus, Mary, and saints in the flesh, their images could suggest or evoke for viewers spiritual realities that lay beyond. Leo's next move was more forceful. In 730 CE he ordered all holy images removed from churches and all recalcitrant bishops removed from their positions. This put Christians in a new position altogether, for it required that they destroy not only pagan images but also statues and paintings of Jesus Christ and revered saints. The battle was joined for several decades, with repeated episodes of iconoclasm and persecution. Finally, in 787 CE the iconodule Irene (acting as regent for her son Constantine and later as empress) convened a council at Nice with monks sympathetic to her cause and issued a new decree. Holy images of Christ, Mary, and the saints may be set up in churches and honored with relative worship, though the highest form of veneration would be reserved for the imageless divine nature alone.

The unstable position of "relative worship" did not prevent further debates among the Christians. However, it did provide a reasonable legitimation for the icon-veneration practices as they developed in the Eastern Church, and it also laid the groundwork for the main institutional position of Western Christianity during the medieval period. With the Protestant Reformation of the sixteenth and seventeenth centuries, the battle of images surfaced once again. Starting in the 1520s Christians in many parts of Europe acted to reform their ritual culture by entering churches and cleansing them of images and other sacerdotal objects.

CONQUEST, CENTRALIZATION, AND ACCOMMODATION. Images and the ritual practices of veneration do not exist in isolation. They enter into larger religious debates about divinity and the world and into political struggles as well. In *Kings and Councillors* (1936), the anthropologist A. M. Hocart observed that religious iconoclasm and political centralization have gone hand in hand throughout history. In Hocart's genealogy of iconoclasm, the Egyptian king Akhenaton (fourteenth century BCE) is the earliest recorded opponent of image veneration and the first to seek a single unified divine cult. This went with Akhenaton's attempts to unite Egypt politically. Hocart followed his observation into the twentieth century and British-ruled Fiji, where the centralizing agenda of the Colonial Office sought to suppress the dispersed icons of the local spirit cults. Powers committed to colonial control have often—though by no means always—opposed the image venerating ritual cultures of the colonized.

In the Andes region, when the Incas conquered their neighbors, they extended their state cult into the region, but this did not entail the suppression of local *huaca* cults. Both groups of icons could live side by side, albeit in a hierarchical relationship. When the Spanish arrived in 1532, however, they proceeded along different lines. The public extinction of all prominent sites of indigenous idolatry was a key element in the policy of conquest. In Cuzco they systematically looted the Temple of the Sun, desecrated it, and converted it into a monastery. In Cajamarca, they broke down the door that kept Pachacámac sequestered and erected a tall cross on his shrine.

The Spanish victory in the Andes was rapid, and the Inca Sun images in their highly visible temples quickly succumbed. Many of the more deeply rooted local *huacas* were not so easy to conquer. By the seventeenth century the veneration of *huacas* was still widely practiced, though now their rites were performed in secret. Believing the process of Christianization incomplete, church authorities initiated a series of inquisitions to extirpate idolatry. Their task had become complex, however, for the boundaries of what were initially distinct ritual cultures had become permeable. Many Andean peoples viewed Christianity not as an exclusive salvific message but as one new source of spiritual powers among many. They incorporated Catholic practices with older local ones, even as the old ways were adapted to fit new circumstances. Ritual healing specialists might maintain icons of Jesus Christ and Mary along with those of *huacas* and lineage gods to employ their powers in curing the sick. Christian celebrants might venerate the local *huacas* with offerings of guinea pig and llama blood at the start of the feast of Saint Peter.

To the inquisitors all this appeared as idolatry. They collected the idols and publicly destroyed them. But even as they did so, other churchmen recognized that the links their parishioners made between Catholic statuary and their longstanding deities enhanced religious devotion. Statues of the Virgin Mary might take on characteristics of Pachacámac, Andean goddess of the earth, and the Inca Sun might lend its rays to Jesus' halo. Devotees believed that notable images like the Virgin of Copacabana performed miracles and made pilgrimages to solicit their help. The new venerative practices might not meet Pope Gregory's principle concerning pedagogic imagery only nor qualify with John of Damascus as relative worship. Yet out of these mutual accommodations Catholic churchmen and local Andean converts constructed a new ritual culture in which the veneration of significant Christian images played an important role.

VENERATION IN THE SECULAR WORLD. At first glance modern secular cultures might not seem hospitable to the religious veneration of images. Yet scholars have persuasively argued that venerative practices of a ritual character may be found in many secular locations.

In the context of national struggle, a religious image like the Virgin of Copacabana in Bolivia may come to be revered as a popular icon of nationhood without leaving her cathedral. Political elites in many secular polities generate their own iconographies of the nation in the form of flags, statues, and monuments intended to symbolize or embody founders, leaders, and national ideals. Examples range from the ubiquitous personal imagery and the extraordinary Victory Arch erected by Ṣaddām Ḥusayn in Iraq to public monuments like the Statue of Liberty and Mount Rushmore in the United States. Such national icons have their own venerative rites: ceremonial dedications, pilgrimage itineraries, and on-site guides who enforce proper decorum and instruct viewers on their meaning. Likewise acts of iconoclasm directed at these instantiations of the nation, from flag burning to the toppling of Ḥusayn's statue during the U.S. invasion of 2003, take on an iconic significance of resistance or conquest.

Visitors to modern art museums may also recognize that they are entering settings for secular ritual. In these temples viewers are asked to observe respectful conduct and to pay close, contemplative visual attention to the images they encounter there. Indeed many of the objects—particularly those in the Mesopotamian, classical, medieval, and non-Western sections—formerly resided in religious institutions, where some of them received their proper ritual offerings. Now relocated to the comprehensive institutions of the West, these same images are understood by new audiences to embody the collective artistic accomplishment of their cultures and of humanity as a whole. Museum viewers may hope for a transformative experience not through the intervention of Athena or Śiva but through a kind of communion with the artists and cultures of the collective human past.

See Also Icons; Idolatry.

Bibliography

General comprehensive studies of image veneration are rare. David Freedberg, *The Power of Images: Studies in the History and Theory of Response* (Chicago, 1989), is an ambitious attempt to explore a broad panorama of image-related practices. Alain Besançon, *The Forbidden Image: An Intellectual History of Iconoclasm* (Chicago, 2000), represents an erudite attempt to trace a Western genealogy for the critique of images. Among calls for the rematerializing of religious studies, Joanne Punzo Waghorne, *The Raja's Magic Clothes: Re-Visioning Kingship and Divinity in England's India* (University Park, Pa., 1994), is broad and persuasive. Peter Brown, *The Cult of the Saints: Its Rise and Function in Latin Christianity* (Chicago, 1982) presents the notion of "two-tiered" models in the study of religion. The term *ritual culture* as used in this article is drawn from Lawrence Alan Babb, *Absent Lord: Ascetics and Kings in a Jain Ritual Culture* (Berkeley, Calif., 1996).

A fine overview of image-veneration practices in Mesopotamia is A. Leo Oppenheim, *Ancient Mesopotamia: Portrait of a Dead Civilization* (Chicago, 1964), pp. 183–198. The volume edited by Michael B. Dick, *Born in Heaven, Made on Earth: The Making of the Cult Image in the Ancient Near East* (Winona Lake, Ind., 1999), contains valuable articles, including a detailed study of the mouth-opening consecration, by Christopher Walker and Michael B. Dick, "The Mesopotamian *mīs pī* Ritual," pp. 55–121. Also important are two essays by Irene J. Winter, "'Idols of the King': Royal Images as Recipients of Ritual Action in Ancient Mesopotamia," *Journal of Ritual Studies* 6 (1992): 13–42, and "Opening the Eyes and Opening the Mouth: The Utility of Comparing Images in Worship in India and the Ancient Near East," in *Ethnography and Personhood*, edited by Michael W. Meister (Jaipur, India, 2000), pp. 129–162.

An excellent brief introduction to Greek temple culture is Walter Burkert, "The Meaning and Function of the Temple in Classical Greece," in *Temple in Society*, edited by Michael V. Fox (Winona Lake, Ind., 1988), pp. 27–47. Burkert's *Greek Religion, Archaic and Classical* (Oxford, 1985), remains the standard overview; whereas Jan N. Bremmer, *Greek Religion* (Oxford, 1994), provides a valuable supplement to Burkert based on continuing research. For a detailed treatment of votive offerings, see F. T. van Straten, "Gifts for the Gods," in H. S. Versnal, *Faith, Hope, and Worship* (Leiden, Netherlands, 1981), pp. 65–151.

Earlier scholarship on the Jains most often viewed the worship of Jina images as a borrowed and nonessential practice within the Jain tradition. John E. Cort's article, "Bhakti in Early Jain Tradition," *History of Religions* 42 (2002): 59–86, provides an important revision, demonstrating that venerative practices were an integral part of the Jain tradition from an early period. Valuable studies of Jain ritual culture utilizing both ethnographic and textual materials are those of Babb, cited above, and John E. Cort, *Jains in the World: Religious Values and Ideology in India* (Oxford, 2001). Also noteworthy for its treatment of devotional practices among Jain women is M. Whitney Kelting, *Singing to the Jinas: Jain Laywomen, Mandal Singing, and the Negotiations of Jain Devotion* (Oxford, 2001). For an overview of Jain disputes over image worship, see Paul Dundas, *The Jains* (London, 1992).

For Buddhist traditions concerning the earliest Buddha image, see Martha L. Carter, *The Mystery of the Udayana Buddha* (Naples, Italy, 1990). The scholarly literature on the origins of the Buddha image is vast. Works of John S. Strong are particularly valuable for their description of the ritual culture of early Indian Buddhism. See especially Strong's "*Gandakuti*: The Perfumed Chamber of the Buddha," *History of Religions* 16 (1977): 390–406. On the Buddhist cult of relics, a useful starting point is Kevin Trainor, *Relics, Ritual, and Representation in Buddhism: Rematerializing the Sri Lankan Theravāda Tradition* (Cambridge, U.K., 1997). Donald K. Swearer, *Becoming the Buddha: The Ritual of Image Consecration in Thailand* (Princeton, N.J., 2004), considers many issues surrounding the veneration of the Buddha image in the Theravāda school and provides a detailed ethnographic account of an image consecration. The essays of Gregory Schopen have significantly altered the study of Indian Buddhism and its material practices. Many of these essays are in Schopen's collection *Bones, Stones, and Buddhist Monks: Collected Papers on the Archaeology, Epigraphy, and Texts of Monastic Buddhism in India* (Honolulu, 1997). On the role of images in East Asian Buddhism, see the volume edited by Robert H. Sharf and Elizabeth Horton Sharf, *Living Images: Japanese Buddhist Icons in Context* (Stanford, Calif., 2001).

A good point of entry into the ritual cultures of Hindu image venerators is the collection edited by Joanne Punzo Waghorne and Norman Cutler, *Gods of Flesh/Gods of Stone: The Embodiment of Divinity in India* (Chambersburg, Pa., 1985). Diana L. Eck, *Darśan: Seeing the Divine Image in India* (Chambersburg, Pa., 1985), explicates this important underlying concept in Hinduism. For a more detailed explication of Hindu worship as practiced by the Śaiva Siddhānta school, see Richard H. Davis, *Ritual in an Oscillating Universe: Worshiping Śiva in Medieval India* (Princeton, N.J., 1991). Among many valuable ethnographic accounts of image worship in Hindu temples, one of the most comprehensive is Françoise L'Hernault and Marie-Louise Reiniche, *Tiruvannamalai: Un lieu saint śivaïte du Sud de l'Inde*, vol. 3, *Rites et fêtes* (Paris, 1999). On Hindu disputes over the veneration of images, see Richard H. Davis, "Indian Image-Worship and Its Discontents," in *Representation in Religion: Studies in Honor of Moshe Barasch*, edited by Jan Assmann and Albert I. Baumgarten (Leiden, Netherlands, 2001), pp. 107–132.

For the Andes, Kenneth J. Andrien, *Andean Worlds: Indigenous History, Culture, and Consciousness under Spanish Rule, 1532–1825* (Albuquerque, N.Mex., 2001), offers a good starting point. Sabine MacCormack, *Religion in the Andes: Vision and Imagination in Early Colonial Peru* (Princeton, N.J., 1991), reconstructs Andean religion at the time of Spanish conquest and offers a nuanced portrait of Spanish perceptions of indigenous ritual culture. Verónica Salles-Reese, *From Viracocha to the Virgin of Copacabana: Representation of the Sacred at Lake Titicaca* (Austin, Tex., 1997), stresses continuity in the complex interactions of the *huacas* and the inquisitors in the seventeenth and eighteenth centuries. See also Kenneth Mills, *Idolatry and Its Enemies: Colonial Andean Religion and Extirpation, 1640–1750* (Princeton, N.J., 1997).

Moshe Barasch, *Icon: Studies in the History of an Idea* (New York, 1992), provides an excellent brief account of Western critiques of the image, ranging from Greeks and Israelites through the iconoclastic controversy. For a more detailed exploration of the biblical view, see Michael B. Dick, "Prophetic Parodies of Making the Cult Image," in *Born in Heaven, Made on Earth*, edited by Michael B. Dick (Winona Lake, Ind., 1999), pp. 1–53. Two works reconsider early Christian art in light of disputes over the image, Thomas F. Mathews, *The Clash of Gods: A Reinterpretation of Early Christian Art* (Princeton, N.J., 1993); and Paul Corby Finney, *The Invisible God: The Earliest Christians on Art* (New York, 1997). Works on the iconoclastic controversy are too numerous to mention. Among several works that explore iconoclastic practices of the Protestant Reformation, a noteworthy study is Lee Palmer Wandel, *Voracious Idols and Violent Hands: Iconoclasm in Reformation Zurich, Strasbourg, and Basel* (New York, 1995). David Morgan addresses the Christian ambivalence toward images in *Visual Piety: A History and Theory of Popular Religious Images* (Berkeley, Calif., 1998). A. M. Hocart, *Kings and Councillors: An Essay in the Comparative Anatomy of Human Society* (Cairo, 1936, Chicago, 1970) discusses iconoclasm and political centralization.

Among studies of secular iconography of the nation, Samir al-Khalil, *The Monument: Art, Vulgarity, and Responsibility in Iraq* (Berkeley, Calif., 1991), explores the significance of Ṣaddām Ḥusayn's Victory Arch; whereas Albert Boime, *The Unveiling of National Icons: A Plea for Patriotic Iconoclasm in a Nationalistic Era* (Cambridge, U.K., 1998), traces the history and interpretations of five key American icons: the flag, the Statue of Liberty, Mount Rushmore, the Marine Corps Monument, and the Lincoln Memorial. In *Civilizing Rituals: Inside Public Art Museums* (London, 1995), Carol Duncan analyzes art museums as ritual settings for the visual contemplation of art objects. Richard H. Davis, *Lives of Indian Images* (Princeton, N.J., 1997), follows Hindu religious objects as they are relocated and reinterpreted in Western museums and other settings.

RICHARD H. DAVIS (2005)

IMAGES: IMAGES, ICONS, AND IDOLS

One way to categorize religious traditions is whether or not they accept or advocate the use of two- and/or three-dimensional objects to symbolize or embody the divine. Some traditions, such as temple Hinduism, Buddhism, and Orthodox and Catholic Christianity, see the use of such images as central to their theologies and rituals. In these traditions images can serve three functions. They can be understood to be representations or likenesses of deities, symbols of deities, or the deities themselves. Other traditions, such as some schools of Islam, Judaism, and Reformed Protestant Christianity, are iconoclastic or otherwise oppose the use of images. Still others, such as Lutheran Christianity and the Advaita Vedānta school of Hinduism, are ambivalent or indifferent to the use of images.

Scholars of art and religion generally prefer the use of the terms *image* and *icon* to *idol*, as they argue that the former terms are more objective and less judgmental. For most English speakers the word *idol* is inevitably associated with *idolatry* or *heathen idolatry*, and so brings with it theological implications of the biblical and Protestant critiques of images. *Idolatry* in this theological usage is just one of a number of forms of false religion, so one finds actions, beliefs, and ideologies as varied as market capitalism, warfare, violence, the contemporary U.S. military and its budget, nuclear weapons, undue reliance on technology, an individualistic focus on self rather than community, slavery, racism, apartheid, patriarchy, adulation of cultural heroes, contemporary mass media, National Socialism, Communism, nationalism, and even scientific objectivity decried by their critics as forms of idolatry.

Anthropologists, on the other hand, tend to be comfortable using the word *idol* and argue that it more accurately reflects the theological and ritual understanding of Hindus, Buddhists, and Jains who themselves use *idol* in English. Furthermore, they say not to use the term is to disrespect those who in good faith do use it, by implying that their use of the term betrays an ignorance of the negative connotations of *idolatry* in Abrahamic theologies. Still other scholars of religion prefer to use *idol* on the grounds that *image* is too neutral a term. These scholars argue that *image* does not convey adequately the depth of feelings aroused by idols in both devotees and critics. Notwithstanding the good arguments in favor of using *idol*, this essay will use *image*.

TYPES OF IMAGES. The difference between an *image* and an *icon* is in many cases an arbitrary one. In Christian usage, *icon* refers only to two-dimensional representations of Jesus Christ, the Virgin Mary, or a saint, and so for many English-speakers *icon* calls to mind a two-dimensional object. Many scholars follow this theological distinction and use the term *icon* to refer only to two-dimensional objects. Most historians of art and religion use *image* to refer to any of many material objects, both of two and three dimensions, and restrict the use of *icon* to an image that is ritually consecrated and/or in some way participates in the divine substance of that which it represents.

Three-dimensional images can be of stone, metal, wood, lacquer, or clay. An image can be a figurative likeness (iconic) or abstract (aniconic). In India, the original image at a shrine is oftentimes an aniconic natural feature, understood to be a manifestation of divine power. As its popularity grows, patrons build increasingly elaborate shrines around the image and replace the original natural image with a humanly crafted iconic one.

Two-dimensional images generally are iconic. They can be on paper, wood, or cloth, and the figure can be painted, woven, or embroidered.

Some traditions, such as Buddhism and Catholic Christianity, employ both two- and three-dimensional images. Others, such as Hinduism and Jainism, exhibit a preference for three-dimensional images over two-dimensional ones. In Eastern Orthodox Christianity only two-dimensional images function as formal liturgical icons. Some objects, such as Hindu, Buddhist, and Jain *maṇḍalas* and *yantras*, are low-relief carvings and castings that at the same time share visual features with two-dimensional icons.

Iconic images can be anthropomorphic and so represent a human form. Other iconic images depict animals, divine beings that combine human and nonhuman traits, or inanimate symbols such as a cross, a book, or a throne. The multiplication of images leads to issues of identity, as different forms are used to depict the same deity. Traditions with iconic images therefore develop an iconography, a detailed formal canon of distinguishing features of anatomy, color, clothing, ornamentation, and attributes held in the hands that allow the viewer to identify which deity or saint is depicted. The multiplication of images can also contribute to understandings of divinity as plural and diverse. Complex iconographies contribute to explicit polytheisms, with many deities, such as we find in the Hindu, Buddhist, Jain, Shintō, Daoist, Egyptian, and Greco-Roman traditions. They also contribute to implicit polytheisms of minor deities and/or saints, such as we find in Catholic and Orthodox Christianity. In contrast, explicit monotheisms tend to employ a simplified iconography or be iconoclastic.

The physical nature of images connects them to many other objects in the material culture of religions, such as relics, shrines, altars, clothing, staffs, scepters, ritual implements, and books. Only some of these objects, such as images, relics, books, and in some cases clothing, engender long-standing and heated ideological disagreements. Images and relics in particular have been the focus of extended critiques and defenses, since they are most clearly tied to theological understandings of the relationships among divinity and humanity, and spirit and matter.

Images serve different functions in religious life. Some of them are visual symbols. They can be visual tools in the meditation of specially trained religious practitioners, who use two- or three-dimensional forms as props for visualization of deities. Images, especially two-dimensional ones with narrative themes, serve to educate people concerning essential religious truths or the history of a religious community. The Catholic pope Gregory the Great in the sixth century thus termed images "books of the illiterate." This equation of images with books is often found in elite criticisms of images as being suitable only for commoners or other more childlike and less-educated members of a religious community.

Images often appear on the outside of temples and shrines. Here they can serve as markers of sectarian identity. On the outside and inside of temples images can also serve an ornamental function, as they add to the grandeur of a building.

CONSECRATION. When images function as visual markers, there is usually no need to prepare the image through special consecratory rituals. But many other functions do require such rituals. In particular, the Mesopotamian, Egyptian, Hindu, Buddhist, and Jain traditions developed complex rituals whereby images are infused with divine presence or otherwise consecrated for ritual use.

Mesopotamian texts from the first half of the first millennium BCE describe in detail a two-day ritual sequence for consecration that involved multiple mouth-washings (Babylonian *mīs pî),* each of which involved mouth-opening rites (Babylonian *pīt pî).* References to these rituals are found in texts from as early as the twenty-second century BCE. Egyptian texts from the first half of the first millennium BCE describe a consecration ritual also known as the opening of the mouth; some texts also describe these rituals as involving the opening of the eyes, nose, and ears of the image. Hindu images are consecrated in multiday-festivals that both install vital breath in the image (Sanskrit *prāṇa pratiṣṭhā*) and anoint the image with pure water and many other liquids (*abhiṣeka*). Jain consecration rituals distinguish between the enlivening of the image through opening its eyes in a rite called literally the "eye-needle" (Sanskrit *añjana-śalākā*), and the establishment (Sanskrit *pratiṣṭhā*) of the image on an altar for worship. Buddhist rituals throughout Asia employ the two ritual paradigms of opening the eye of the image (Sanskrit *netra-pratiṣṭhāpana*) and anointing it (*Buddha-abhiṣeka*). In Tibetan Buddhist consecrations the focus is on the establishment (Tibetan *rab gnas*) of the Buddha-nature (Tibetan *ye shes sems dpa'*, Sanskrit *jñānasattva*) in the image. Tantric Buddhist consecrations involve placing consecrated objects such as scriptures and relics inside the image. In East Asia, some images are consecrated by placing the cremated ashes and other relics of a deceased Buddhist master in a cavity in the image. The periodic reconsecration of the wooden image of the Hindu deity Jagannātha in Orissa also involves transferring a sacred object from the old image into a cavity in the back of the new one. These rituals show the overlap between icons and relics.

IMAGES AS DIVINE PRESENCE. All these rituals effect the transformation of the image from a humanly manufactured object into a receptacle or real presence of divinity. In the Mesopotamian case the image is understood to have been produced by the cooperation of humans and gods. In many traditions there are stories of images that either were created by divine beings, or else were spontaneously material incarnations of the deity him- or herself.

This dual character of the image, as at once humanly created and a body for the divine, is reflected in various ways in the rituals. In the Mesopotamian ritual priests use a wooden sword symbolically to cut off the hands of the artisans, whereas the artisans themselves swear an oath that the image was made not by them but by their craft deities. In the Buddhist ritual in Sri Lanka the act of painting in the eye of the image to open it is considered so dangerous that no one can look at the image during this process, and even the craftsman who performs the act must do it with a mirror. This would appear to indicate a powerful presence in the image, greater than anything within normal human experience.

It is often not clear whether the image is a representation of a particular deity, or is the deity itself. The language of hymns and rituals, as well as stories concerning images, allow for both interpretations. Some paintings of images clearly depict an image in a temple. In others it is unclear if the painter has depicted the deity or an image of the deity.

A further ambiguity seen in consecration rituals is whether the image is the sole abode of a particular deity, or the abode of a deity who equally resides in other images. While the language and actions of the consecration ritual usually indicate that the image has now become a permanent abode of the divine, the language and actions of some daily rituals simultaneously indicate an understanding that the ritual practitioner invokes the deity into the image and then dismisses the deity at the conclusion of the ritual. Most images are the subject of annual or periodic rituals of purification and renewal. In some cases these rituals consist of a set of purifications; in others the image itself is repaired, reornamented, or even, as in the case of the Jagannātha, entirely refabricated.

In some traditions, such as the Mesopotamian, Egyptian, Hindu, and Mahāyāna Buddhist, there is little or no theological problem caused by positing the presence of the deity, either in whole or as a partial incarnation, in the image. But other traditions deny this possibility. In Theravāda Buddhism and Jainism the Buddha and the Jina, respectively, are understood no longer to be present in this world in a tangible sense. These traditions engage in more complicated explanations of what, if anything, is present in the image, and tie the presence to the intentions and actions of the Buddha or Jina several thousand years ago. Christian theology also denies the possibility of *real presence* in an icon or image, reserving this (according to the Eastern Orthodox, Catholic, and some Protestant traditions) to the sanctified bread and wine in the Eucharist. A careful analysis of rituals and stories in traditions that theoretically deny presence, however, shows that many people act *as if* there were a divine presence in the image, so scholars must beware placing too much emphasis on theological arguments of absence.

Images and miracles. Stories of images frequently recount miracles. Some miracle stories account for the existence of the image itself, as the image or deity arranges for a person, animal, or deity to find or receive the image and install it for worship in a shrine. For example, in the early sixteenth century the image of Śrīnāthjī that had earlier appeared from within the sacred Mount Govardhan summoned the Vaiṣṇava saint Vallabhācārya (Vallabha, 1479–1531) and revealed its true identity, and in 1672 the image, which had been removed from the danger of spoilage by the Mughal rulers, indicated its eventual home in Nathdwara by preventing the bullock cart carrying it from leaving that site. In 1531 in Guadalupe the Virgin Mary appeared to the Mayan Indian peasant Juan Diego and left an image of herself on a cloth. In circumstances where there is extensive iconoclastic opposition to and destruction of images, many miracle stories relate how images saved themselves from destruction and thereby verified the theological correctness of the cult of images. Miracle stories also recount ways that images have saved cities and towns from hostile armies. The *Hodegetria* icon of the Virgin Mary was displayed by the emperors of Constantinople to help protect the city from invaders. Politically and socially important images also become the source of attention for the state's enemies. The *Hodegetria* was sought by the Venetian conquerors of Constantinople in 1204, and later cut into four pieces by the Turkish conquerors of the city in 1453. While the Venetians were unable to locate and seize the *Hodegetria* icon, they did seize another icon of Mary, the *Nicopeia*, which had been on the chariot of the defeated commander of the Greek army, and transported it and many other images back to Venice for installation in the cathedral of San Marco.

Most miracle images come to have a distinct personality that is indicated by its name. Examples of these are the Emerald Buddha in Thailand, the Zenkōji icon of Amida, Japan, the Jain Śaṅkheśvara Pārśvanātha in Gujarat, India, the Infant Jesus of Prague, the *Hodegetria* icon of the Virgin Mary, and the Vladimir Mother of God icon now in Saint Petersburg, Russia. These images are readily identifiable to members of the religious community. Replicas of these images are known by the same name, and the spread of such images creates a *replication cult.* Replication cults appear to be most prominent in Buddhism, Jainism, and Christianity. As Hinduism has spread outside of India in recent decades, many temples built in Europe and the United States represent a replication cult, such as the temple outside of Pittsburgh, Pennsylvania, that replicates the temple of Veṅkateśvara in Tirupati in southern India. Related to replication cults is the widespread practice of pilgrims obtaining inexpensive replicas of icons to take home and place in a household shrine. These reproductions tend to be two dimensional more often than three dimensional, and rarely undergo formal consecration rites. Just as consecrated images exhibit an ambiguity concerning whether they are the sole and unique abodes of particular deities, so also replication images at once share in the presence of the original and point away from themselves to that unique and easily identifiable original.

Images and religious conversions. Images often play an important role in the spread of religions and in conversions. Chinese texts call Buddhism "the teaching of the [Buddha] images" (*xiangjiao*). The introduction of Buddhism into the Korean kingdom of Silla in the early sixth century was effected by a miracle, as the severed head of a pro-image martyr spouted a fountain of pure white blood. The introduction of Buddhism into Japan later in the same century was also effected by a miracle, as an image that opponents had thrown into a canal arranged for a commoner to rescue it and in return revived his dead son. Images have also proved to be bridges between different religious communities, such as the Virgin Mary of Guadalupe in Mexico, of whom there were different but overlapping understandings by the indigenous Mayans and the conquering Spaniards.

RITUAL USES OF IMAGES. Consecrated images are the foci of many rituals. Viewing an image is itself an efficacious ritual in many traditions, which leads to the elaborate ornamentation of images. In many cases, such as Hindu, Jain, and Christian images, the ornamentation is so extensive that it almost totally covers the image, so the image's identity is established more by the ornamentation than by the underlying "original" image. In Hinduism, Buddhism, and Jainism images are offered flowers, incense, lamps, edibles, and other physical substances. In Hindu Vaiṣṇava traditions the deity is understood to consume the subtle essence of the offerings that are then returned to the person as *prasāda*, literally "divine grace." In contrast, Jain and Hindu *Śaiva* traditions explicitly restrict such transactions. Hindu, Buddhist, and Jain rituals also involve the anointing of images with water, milk, and other liquids in a ritual idiom that shares much with the consecration of kings. In Christianity devotion to an image is usually expressed through kissing it and praying in front of it.

Rituals can differ according to the deity symbolized or embodied by the image. In Jainism, the eight-part ritual offering (Sanskrit *aṣṭaprakārī pūjā*) is done only to images of the enlightened and liberated Jinas, whereas images of unliberated deities receive a different number of offerings. The Eastern Orthodox theologian Saint John of Damascus distinguished between veneration (Greek *proskinesis*, Latin *dulia*) directed toward a saint, and worship (Greek *latreia*, Latin *latria*), which is appropriate only toward Jesus as God. This distinction was adopted by Catholic theologians, who added an intermediate rite of special veneration (*hyperdulia*) in which the Virgin Mary was named the Mother of God.

Image cults often involve processions, in which an important image is periodically taken out of the shrine and processed around the village or neighborhood. In some cases it is the central image of a shrine that is processed. In other cases the main image remains permanently in the shrine, and a portable image stands in for it in the procession. Processions spread the power and blessings of the image throughout the geographical area encompassed by the procession. In traditions such as Hinduism before Indian independence, in which entry to many temples was prohibited to some lower castes, the procession also allows access to the image on the part of the total population.

Vows taken before an image may have the same binding significance as those taken before the deity or a religious leader. In the Jain tradition, for example, a person should be initiated into monkhood by another monk, but several twentieth-century Digambara monks initiated themselves in front of Jina images. Shingon Buddhist monks in medieval Japan also performed self-ordinations in front of Buddha images to start new monastic lineages. Buddhist monks in many traditions perform rites of confession in front of Buddha images.

COMMISSIONING AND MAKING OF IMAGES. The most obvious reason people commission images for installation in shrines is devotion to and faith in the deity represented by the image, although in the case of replication cults this devotion may be directed to the particular icon as much as to the deity. This devotion may be a generalized response to the deity on the part of the donor, or it may be motivated by a request from the deity or other miraculous event. In many traditions the donation of images earns religious merit for the donor. Images are donated as the result of vows, in which a person pledges to donate an image in response to the fulfillment of a particular desire for health, success, or other form of well-being. Images can be donated to enhance the social prestige of the donor. This intention is often underscored by an inscription or other testimonial, such as inclusion of a portrait of the donor in the painting or sculpture, that publicly links the image to the donor's name.

In many cultures images are made by hereditary craftsmen. In India there is no requirement that the craftsmen be of the same religious tradition, so the Vaiṣṇava stone carvers of Jaipur also make images for *Śaivas*, goddess worshipers, and Jains, and in some places in India nonconsecrated images are even made by Muslims. In other traditions there is an expectation that the craftsman be within the same tradition, for the making of a religious image, especially one to be consecrated, requires a higher degree of moral purity or spiritual insight than making a nonreligious image. In some Tibetan Tantric esoteric traditions the painters of *thangkas* are expected to have taken formal initiation in the cult of the deity. Old Believers of the Russian Orthodox Church said that the only way to be sure that an icon was not actually an icon of the antichrist was to insist that icon painters live in a state of near-monastic spirituality and simplicity. Painters of Greek Orthodox icons are also expected to be in a condition of heightened reverence, for icon painting is understood not as a form of artistic self-expression, but as an act in imitation of the first image of Christ, the icon "made without hands" (Greek *acheiropoietos*) or cloth true portrait (Greek *mandylion*) made when Christ imprinted the features of his face on a cloth.

ICONOCLASM AND JUSTIFICATIONS OF IMAGES. Traditions that devote extensive theological and ritual attention to images almost always generate countermovements in criticism or opposition to images. The destruction of images (iconoclasm) is oftentimes accompanied by criticisms of other aspects of the material culture of the religion, of priestly hierarchies with special prerogatives and extensive powers, and of theological decentralizing through either polytheism or the development of cults of multiple subsidiary deities or saints. In some cases, as in the critiques of the Ārya Samāj in Hinduism, the Sthānakavāsīs and Terāpanthīs in Jainism, and Lutherans in Christianity, iconoclasm is nonviolent and aims at convincing people to ignore and eventually reject images. In other cases, such as the Christian Iconoclastic Controversy of the eighth and ninth centuries and the Calvinist Reformation, the iconoclasm was more violent, with extensive destruction of images. Iconoclastic movements also lead to the development of self-conscious defenses of images and the cult of images. Saint John of Damascus and Saint Theodore of Studion articulated the Orthodox Christian theology of the image during the Iconoclastic Controversy, the Council of Trent confirmed the Catholic theology of images in response to the Protestant Reformation, and Mūrtipūjaka Jain thinkers developed their philosophy of images in response to the Sthānakavāsī critiques. Iconoclastic opposition to images can also come from outside a tradition. It can be physically nonviolent, as in the case of the Christian polemics against Hindu idols in nineteenth- and twentieth-century India, or it can result in the violent overthrow of images as witnessed most recently in 2001 by the destruction of the Buddha images at Bamiyan in Afghanistan by the Taliban.

SEE ALSO Iconography; Icons; Idolatry.

BIBLIOGRAPHY

The literature on images and icons is extensive, with significant contributions from historians of religion, art historians, and anthropologists. The following bibliography includes the most recent and authoritative sources, each of which contains further extensive bibliographies.

Barasch, Moshe. *Icon: Studies in the History of an Idea.* New York, 1992.

Belting, Hans. *Likeness and Presence: A History of the Image before the Era of Art.* Translated by Edmund Jephcott. Chicago, 1994.

Bentor, Yael. *Consecration of Images and Stūpas in Indo-Tibetan Tantric Buddhism.* Leiden, 1996.

Besançon, Alain. *The Forbidden Image: An Intellectual History of Iconoclasm.* Translated by Jane Marie Todd. Chicago, 2000.

Camille, Michael. *The Gothic Idol: Ideology and Image-Making in Medieval Art.* Cambridge, U.K., 1989.

Cormack, Robin. *Painting the Soul: Icons, Death Masks, and Shrouds.* London, 1997.

Cort, John E. *Jains in the World: Religious Values and Ideology in India.* New York, 2001.

Davis, Richard H. *Lives of Indian Images.* Princeton, N.J., 1997.

Davis, Richard H., ed. *Images, Miracles, and Authority in Asian Traditions.* Boulder, Colo., 1998.

Dick, Michael B., ed. *Born in Heaven, Made on Earth: The Making of the Cult Image in the Ancient Near East.* Winona Lake, Ind., 1999.

Eck, Diana L. *Darśan: Seeing the Divine Image in India.* 3d ed. New York, 1998.

Eckel, Malcolm David. *To See the Buddha: A Philosopher's Quest for the Meaning of Emptiness.* Princeton, N.J., 1992.

Eire, Carlos M. N. *War against the Idols: The Reformation of Worship from Erasmus to Calvin.* Cambridge, U.K., 1986.

Faure, Bernard. *Visions of Power: Imagining Medieval Japanese Buddhism.* Translated by Phyllis Brooks. Princeton, N.J., 1996.

Freedberg, D. *The Power of Images: Studies in the History and Theory of Response.* Chicago, 1989.

Gombrich, Richard. "The Consecration of the Buddhist Image." *Journal of Asian Studies* 26 (1966): 23–36.

Halbertal, Moshe, and Avishai Margalit. *Idolatry.* Translated by Naomi Goldblum. Cambridge, Mass., 1992.

Hiromitsu, Washizuka, and Roger Goepper. *Enlightenment Embodied: The Art of the Japanese Buddhist Sculptor (7th–14th Centuries).* Translated and edited by Reiko Tomii and Kathleen M. Friello. New York, 1997.

Humphrey, Caroline, and James Laidlaw. *The Archetypal Actions of Ritual: A Theory of Ritual Illustrated by the Jain Rite of Worship.* Oxford, 1994.

Image and Ritual in Buddhism. Thematic issue of *History of Religions* 34, no. 3 (February 1995).

Kailasam, Bala, dir. *Vaastu Marabu.* Watertown, Mass., 1992.

Kieschnick, John. *The Impact of Buddhism on Chinese Material Culture.* Princeton, N.J., 2003.

Kinnard, Jacob N. *Imaging Wisdom: Seeing and Knowing in the Art of Indian Buddhism.* Richmond, U.K., 1999.

McCallum, Donald F. *Zenkōji and Its Icon: A Study in Medieval Japanese Religious Art.* Princeton, N.J., 1994.

Miles, Margaret. *Image as Insight: Visual Understanding in Western Christianity and Secular Culture.* Boston, 1985.

Morse, Anne Nishimura, and Samuel Crowell Morse, eds. *Object as Insight: Japanese Buddhist Art and Ritual.* Katonah, N.Y. 1995.

Ouspensky, Léonid, and Vladimir Lossky. *The Meaning of Icons.* Translated by G. E. H. Palmer and E. Kadloubovsky. 2d ed. Crestwood, N.Y., 1982.

Padoux, André, ed. *L'Image Divine: Culte et Méditation dans l'Hindouisme.* Paris, 1990.

Pelikan, Jaroslav. *Imago Dei: The Byzantine Apologia for Icons.* Princeton, N.J., 1990.

Schopen, Gregory. *Bones, Stones, and Buddhist Monks: Collected Papers on the Archaeology, Epigraphy, and Texts of Monastic Buddhism.* Honolulu, 1997.

Sharf, Robert H., and Elizabeth Horton Sharf, eds. *Living Images: Japanese Buddhist Icons in Context.* Stanford, Calif., 2001.

Shepherd, Rupert, and Robert Maniura, eds. *Depicted Bodies and Present Souls.* London, 2004.

Strickmann, Michel. *Mantras et Mandarins: Le Bouddhisme Tantrique en Chine.* Paris, 1996.

Swearer, Donald K. *Becoming the Buddha: The Ritual of Image Consecration in Thailand.* Princeton, N.J., 2004.

Tambiah, Stanley Jeyaraja. *The Buddhist Saints of the Forest and the Cult of Amulets.* Cambridge, U.K., 1984.

Tarasov, Oleg. *Icon and Devotion: Sacred Spaces in Imperial Russia.* Translated and edited by Robin Milner-Gulland. London, 2002.

Tripathi, G. C. "Navakalevara: The Unique Ceremony of the 'Birth' and the 'Death' of the 'Lord of the World.'" In *The Cult of Jagannātha and the Regional Traditions of Orissa,* edited by Anncharlott Eschmann, Hermann Kulke, and Gaya Charan Tripathi, pp. 223–264. New Delhi, 1978.

Waghorne, Joanne Punzo, and Norman Cutler, eds. *Gods of Flesh/Gods of Stone: The Embodiment of Divinity in India.* Chambersburg, Pa., 1985.

JOHN E. CORT (2005)

IMAGINATION SEE AESTHETICS; ART AND RELIGION

IMAMATE.

IMAMATE. The Arabic term *imam* means in general "leader" or "master." In nontechnical usage it is often applied to a leading authority in a field of scholarship or to the leader of a community. As a technical term in Islamic law and theology, it refers to the legitimate supreme leader of the Muslim community and also to the leader of the ritual prayer (*ṣalāt*). The imamate, as the office of imam, will be dealt with here in these two technical senses.

SUPREME LEADERSHIP OF THE MUSLIM COMMUNITY. The question of leadership, in theory and practice, has historically evoked different responses within the different branches of Islam.

The Sunnīs. Representing the great majority of Muslims, the Sunnīs have generally viewed the historical caliphate as the legitimate leadership of Islam after the prophet Muḥammad. For them, the imam is thus identical with the ruling caliph. Actual rule, even if reduced to a minimum, is indispensable for the legitimacy of the imam. Throughout history, however, the Sunnīs were primarily concerned with preserving the unity and solidarity of the Muslim community under a single imam and were prepared to compromise on the ideal of his legitimacy and justice. Sunnī theory generally held that the true and exemplary caliphate, meaning the vicegerency of prophecy (*khilāfat al-nubūwah*) was restricted to the first four, or "Rightly Guided" (Rāshidūn) caliphs, Abū Bakr, ʿUmar, ʿUthmān, and ʿAlī. This view was embodied in a well-known *ḥadīth* attributed to Muḥammad, according to which the caliphate was to last for only thirty years after his death and to be followed by mere autocratic kingship (*mulk*). Sunnīs considered the first four caliphs to be the most excellent of humankind after Muḥammad and thus entitled to his succession as leaders of the community.

This judgment did not apply, however, to the later caliphs, many of whom were seen as unjust and impious. While the later caliphate was thus recognized to be imperfect, Sunnī doctrine viewed it still as a divinely sanctioned and indispensable institution and stressed the obligation of every Muslim to obey and actively support the established imam, be he just or oppressive, pious or immoral, except in violation of the religious law. Conservative traditionalist opinion, especially that of Ḥanbalī jurists, virtually equated power and legitimacy, affirming the validity of the imamate gained by usurpation. In their view, the imamate could become binding without any act of recognition by the Muslim community. The only prerequisite for the rightful imam was that he be a Muslim of the Quraysh, the tribe of Muḥammad.

A less radical view of the caliphate was taken by another current of Sunnī thought, represented in particular in the legal school of al-Shāfiʿī. The Shāfiʿī jurists did not confine the legitimate imamate to the most excellent of the community and allowed that a less excellent candidate might be chosen, especially in order to avoid discord. They considered the late caliphate essentially as a legitimate continuation of the ideal rule of the four Rightly Guided caliphs, to be judged by the standards they had set. On this basis they elaborated a comprehensive legal doctrine concerning the qualifications, election, rights, and duties of the imam. Their activity reached its peak with al-Māwardī (d. 1058), whose book *Al-aḥkām al-sulṭānīyah* (The statutes of government) came to be widely regarded as an authoritative statement of classical Sunnī teaching on the imamate.

Classical theory. Classical Sunnī theory considered the imamate as an institution necessary for the legitimacy of all acts of government. Thus it held that the Muslim community was under the obligation to set up an imam as its supreme head at all times. It allowed for only a single imam at any time and considered rival caliphs, even if they were in clear control of part of the Islamic world, to be illegitimate. The imam was to be of Qurayshī descent, male, major, free, physically fit, and capable to execute the political and military duties of the office. He was to have the knowledge of the religious law required for the judgeship and probity as required for legal testimony. The imam could be either appointed by his predecessor or elected. These alternative modes of investment were based on the fact that the second caliph, ʿUmar, was appointed by his predecessor, Abū Bakr, but, before his death, set up an electoral council (*shūrā*) of six prominent companions of the Prophet to choose his successor. The later caliphs in most instances appointed their successors, commonly their sons.

In the case of election, the law considered any Muslim of probity, discernment, and with knowledge about the nature of the office qualified to act as an elector. The number of electors required to make the election binding on the whole Muslim community was generally held to be small, and a common view considered a single elector sufficient. The legal doctrine here reflected the fact that in the absence of an appointed successor a handful of powerful men were usually able to impose a successor of their choice. The election was not intended to be a free choice between candidates, but a selection of the "most excellent" in religious terms. The election of the "less excellent" was viewed as permissible only for proper cause.

The imamate became legally invalid through loss of liberty and of mental or physical fitness. Many Shāfiʿī authorities also held it to be forfeited by loss of probity through immoral conduct, injustice, or heterodoxy; this view was denied, however, by others and by Ḥanbalī and Ḥanafī opinion in general. In practice there was no way to apply this rule. Sunnī law defined the duties of the imam as: guarding the faith against heresy, protecting the peace in the territory of Islam, defending it against external enemies, conducting *jihād* against those outside the territory of Islam resisting its supremacy, enforcing law and justice between disputants, administering punishments *(ḥudūd)* under the religious law, collecting legal alms and other taxes and the fifth of war booty due to the imam, spending revenue according to the provisions of the law, and appointing trustworthy and qualified officials in delegating his authority.

Subsequent developments. The overthrow of the Abbasid caliphate in Baghdad by the Mongols in 1258 confronted Sunnī legal theory with a new situation. The Abbasid shadow caliphate set up by the Mamluk sultans in Cairo was generally ignored. After the Ottoman conquest of Egypt in 1516, the claims of the Ottoman sultans to the caliphate gained some popular support. Sunnī jurists, however, mostly considered the imamate to be in abeyance. Relying on the legal principle of necessity (*ḍarūrah*), they maintained that because the actual exercise of power was essential to the imamate, its functions had devolved upon the rulers of the Muslim world, whoever they were. The formal abolition of the Ottoman sultanate (1922) and caliphate (1924) by the Turkish National Assembly has led to a renewed interest in the question of a supreme and universal leader of Islam. Although some modernists have denied the need for the imamate, others among them, as well as fundamentalists, have advocated its restoration. Here the ideal model is the caliphate of the four Rightly Guided caliphs rather than the later dynastic caliphate. Modernists have stressed in particular the principle of rule by consultation (*shūrā*), often seen to imply the need for an elected parliamentary council to advise the supreme ruler, and the principle of election rather than appointment by the imam's predecessor.

The Shīʿah. While Sunnī Muslims were essentially motivated to back the actual holder of supreme power as the guarantor of the unity of the Muslim community, the Shīʿah have primarily emphasized the principle of legitimacy of the imam, which they see vested in the family of the prophet Muḥammad. The majority of Shīʿī imams, except among the Zaydīyah, never held political power, though the Shīʿah considered them solely entitled to the supreme leadership of the Muslim community and viewed the historical caliphs, with the exception of ʿAlī, as illegitimate usurpers. Partly as a result of their lack of political power, the Shīʿah have tended to endow their imams with great religious authority and to place the imamate at the center of religion.

Twelvers. Twelver Shīʿī doctrine bases the imamate on the permanent need for a divinely guided, infallible ruler and teacher of religion. This need was recognized through human reason rather than revelation. After the age of the prophets had come to a close with Muḥammad, these divinely guided leaders were the imams, beginning with Muḥammad's cousin and son-in-law, ʿAlī. They were, like the prophets, fully immune from sin and error and shared the same function and authority, though they would not bring a new divine scripture because the Qurʾān was final. The imamate thus assumed the same religious significance as prophecy. Ignorance or disobedience of any of the imams constituted infidelity equal to ignorance or disobedience of the Prophet. For the Twelvers, the imamate is handed down by divinely directed designation (*naṣṣ*) of the successor. Thus the great majority of the companions of Muḥammad and the Muslim community at large had become apostates when they recognized Abū Bakr as the imam in place of ʿAlī, who had been publicly designated by Muḥammad as his successor. After Ḥasan and Ḥusayn, the grandsons of Muḥammad, the imamate was to be transferred only from father to son among the descendants of Ḥusayn.

In 874 the death of the eleventh imam without apparent son caused a crisis that was eventually resolved by the affirmation that a son had been born to him and continued to live on earth, though in concealment (*ghaybah*) from humankind. The twelfth imam was identified with the eschatological Mahdi or Qāʾim who is expected to appear before the end of the world and to rule it in glory. Because the twelfth imam is present on earth and may show himself to some of the faithful in person or in a dream, he is held to be essentially still able to fulfill his supreme function of conveying infallible divine guidance. His more practical legal duties and rights have either been assumed gradually by the Shīʿī *ʿulamāʾ* (religious scholars), who claim a general deputyship of the imam during his concealment, or remain in abeyance.

Twelver Shīʿī tradition ascribes to the imams numerous miracles and supernatural powers. They are described as having complete command of all crafts and languages, including those of animals. Though they are not endowed with a natural knowledge of the hidden, God gives them knowledge of anything they wish to know: "what has been and what will be." Because they inherit the knowledge of the prophet Muḥammad, they are perfectly informed of both the outer (exoteric) and the inner (esoteric) meaning of the Qurʾān. They are in possession of all revealed scriptures as well as books containing secret knowledge, including the *Saḥīfah, Jafr, Jāmiʿah,* and the *Muṣḥaf* of Fāṭimah. They receive divine guidance from an angel who speaks to them and informs them, though unlike the messenger prophets, they do not see him.

The imams are endowed with the Holy Spirit. In numerous passages of the Qurʾān they are evoked by terms such as "the light of God," his "witnesses," his "signs," those "firm in knowledge." They are the "vicegerents" of God on earth and the "gates" through which he may be approached. In popular piety the privilege of the imams to intercede with God for the sinners of their community has always loomed large and has inspired the frequent pilgrimages of the faithful to their tombs. Later esoteric Twelver Shīʿī teaching, influenced by Ṣūfī and Ismāʿīlī thought, defined the permanent essence of the imamate as *walāyah,* the quality of a *walī,* "friend of God," and as the esoteric aspect of prophecy. The imam was viewed as the initiator to the mystical truths.

Ismāʿīlīyah. When, after the sixth imam, Jaʿfar al-Ṣādiq, the Ismāʿīlīyah separated from the group developing into the Twelver Shīʿah, they retained the idea of a permanent need for a divinely guided, infallible leader and teacher but developed from it a cyclical view of the history of the true religion. For the Ismāʿīlīyah, prophetic revelation progresses through seven eras. Each of the first six is inaugurated by a "speaker prophet," who brings a scripture with a law and is followed by a "silent fundament." The fundament reveals the esoteric truth concealed in the scripture and is followed by seven imams in sequence, the seventh of whom rises in rank to become the speaker of the following era. The imam takes the place of the speaker prophet in guarding and applying the literal aspect of the revealed law, while his *ḥujjah* ("proof"), representing the rank below the imam in the hierarchy, succeeds the fundament in revealing the esoteric truths to the initiate.

In the sixth era, that of Muḥammad and Islam, ʿAlī was the fundament and Jaʿfar al-Ṣādiqʿs grandson Muḥammad ibn Ismāʿīl the seventh imam from Ḥasan. As such he was expected, after his imminent advent from concealment, to rise in rank to become the seventh speaker prophet, who was identified with the Mahdi and Qāʾim. This early Ismāʿīlī expectation was modified in the tenth century by the rise of the Fatimid caliphs, who claimed to be imams. Some Ismāʿīlī backers of the Fatimid caliphate recognized the first Fatimid caliph as the Mahdi, while others continued to expect the early return of Muḥammad ibn Ismāʿīl and considered the Fatimids his lieutenants. As Fatimid rule continued, however, these eschatological expectations receded, and the Fatimid caliphs were viewed as a continuous line of imams within the era of Islam.

After the fall of the Fatimid dynasty, the Ismāʿīlīyah survived mainly in two branches. The Ṭayyibīyah recognized al-Ṭayyib, an infant son of the Fatimid caliph al-Āmir about whose fate nothing is known, as their imam and denied his death. They hold that al-Ṭayyib, though in concealment, remains in touch with his community and will return. He is not identified, however, with the eschatological Qāʾim. In later Ṭayyibi gnostic thought, the imam is described as having both a human nature (*nāsūt*) and a divine nature (*lāhūt*). His human, physical nature, also called the "camphoric figure," is composed of the vapors that arise from the souls of the faithful three days after their death. The divine nature is described as a light temple formed by the assembly of light points of the souls of the faithful and the teaching hierarchy. This light temple will, after the death of the imam, rise to the horizon of the Tenth Intellect, the demiurge, where it will assemble with the temples of the other imams to form the immense light temple of the Qāʾim.

The Nizārī branch recognized Nizār, a son of the Fatimid caliph al-Mustanṣir, as their imam and has continued to adhere to a line of present imams leading, for the great majority, to the Aga Khans. The proclamation of the resurrection (*qiyāmah*) in 1164 and the subsequent return to an age of concealment brought major reforms of the esoteric doctrine of the imamate. The imams were now raised in rank above the prophets. As a potential Qāʾim, each imam was held to have the authority to suspend or apply the religious law as the circumstances required. The imam was in his spiritual essence defined as a manifestation of the divine word or command, the cause of the spiritual world. The faithful attain spiritual birth, or resurrection, through recognition of the essence of the imam. In the era of concealment, spiritual union with the imam was restricted to his *ḥujjah,* who was his gate for the faithful and the sole dispenser of spiritual truth.

Zaydīyah. Unlike other Shīʿī Muslims, the Zaydīyah do not consider their imams divinely protected from error and sin and do not recognize a hereditary line of imams. They hold that after the first Shīʿī imams, ʿAlī, Ḥasan, and Ḥusayn, who were appointed by the prophet Muḥammad through a descriptive designation, the imamate belongs to any qualified descendant of Ḥasan or Ḥusayn who rises against the illegitimate rulers. Apart from his descent, the legal qualifications of the imam are substantially the same as in Sunnī law. Special emphasis is placed, however, on religious learning, competence to render legal judgment, moral integrity, and courage. Zaydī imams have generally been scholars of rank and authors of the most authoritative Zaydī religious works. The imamate becomes legally binding upon the issuance of a formal call to allegiance (*daʿwah*) and rising against illegitimate rule, not through election or appointment by a previous imam. After his call to allegiance, recognition and active backing of the imam is incumbent upon every believer. The imamate is forfeited by loss of any of the qualifications, in particular by moral offenses. According to the prevalent doctrine, only the most excellent claimant is entitled to the imamate, and if a more excellent candidate arises to claim it, the excelled imam must surrender it to him. This has been disputed, however, by some later authorities. In practice rival claims to the imamate have often divided the allegiance of the Zaydī communities, both in Yemen and in the coastal regions south of the Caspian Sea.

Although in Zaydī legal theory there must always be a qualified candidate for the imamate, the Zaydī imamate has often been in abeyance for prolonged periods. The list of recognized imams has never been definitely fixed, though there is consensus on many of them. Many Zaydī ʿAlīd rulers did not claim the imamate or were not recognized as imams by later Zaydī opinion because they did not fulfill the requirements, especially that of religious learning. These were often considered as "restricted" imams, or "summoners" (*duʿāt*), with limited authority.

Khārijīs. Whereas the Shīʿah historically based their repudiation of the Sunnī caliphate on the principle of legitimacy, the Khārijīs founded their opposition on an uncompromising concept of the justice and moral integrity of the imam. In Khārijī doctrine the imam loses his legitimacy by any violation of religious law and must be removed, by force if necessary. The unjust or immoral imam and his supporters are to be treated as infidels unless they repent. ʿUthmān and ʿAlī are viewed as initially legitimate imams who became infidels by their illicit acts and thus were rightfully murdered. Any Muslim who does not dissociate himself or herself from them and their supporters shares their state of infidelity. Likewise any Muslim who does not affirm solidarity with just imams such as Abū Bakr and ʿUmar is an infidel. The Khārijīs also unanimously rejected the elitist Sunnī doctrine restricting the imamate to the Quraysh. They held that any qualified Muslim, even of non-Arab and slave origin, was eligible. An exceptional view extended this egalitarian principle to women as well. The other qualifications and functions of the imam were similar to Sunnī doctrine, with special emphasis on the Qurʾanic duty of "commanding what is proper and prohibiting what is reprehensible" and on the imam's leadership of the *jihād* against non-Khārijī Muslims.

Only the most moderate sect of the Khārijīs, the Ibāḍīyah, survived the first centuries of Islam. The Ibāḍīyah took a more accommodating view toward non-Khārijī Islam at large, and their doctrine came to recognize different types of imams corresponding to the four states in which the community of the faithful could face its enemies. These include the state of manifestation, when the community was strong enough to overcome the opponent; the state of defense, when it could merely hope to ward off the enemy; the state of self-sacrifice, when a small group of the faithful seeking martyrdom would choose to attack a powerful enemy; and the state of concealment, when the faithful were forced to live under the rule of the opponent and to practice dissimulation. Only the imam of the state of manifestation was entitled to exercise all the functions of the imamate.

Leadership of the Ritual Prayer. The ritual prayer, which is obligatory for every Muslim five times daily, may be performed individually or in group with a leader who is called the imam. The same applies to several special prayers, which are merely recommended, on the occasion of festivals and solar or lunar eclipses, prayers for rain, and supererogatory and funeral prayers. In most of these cases group prayer, preferably in a mosque, is the recommended form whenever possible. The congregational Friday prayer, which is generally obligatory for those in easy reach of a congregational mosque (*jāmiʿ*), can only be performed in group with an imam.

The imam must face the *qiblah,* the direction toward Mecca. In the mosque he stands in front of the *miḥrāb,* or prayer niche, which indicates this direction. In the early time of Islam a staff or lance was placed in the ground before him. The congregation stands in rows behind the imam; no one is permitted to be in front of him. If there is only a single worshiper following the prayer, he may stand at the imam's right, and a second one may stand at his left. The members of the congregation must strictly follow the imam in every movement and recitation. While the imam recites in a loud voice, however, they should generally not be heard. If the congregation is too large for everyone to see and hear the imam, special "conveyors" (sg., *muballigh*) may be employed to repeat his *takbīrs*, marking the transition to the next phase of the prayer, for the worshipers in the back rows or outside the mosque.

The obligation to imitate strictly the movements of the imam applies even if a worshiper belongs to another legal school prescribing different prayer rituals. While this rule has been generally accepted among the four Sunnī schools, there have at times been problems. Some Ḥanafī authorities held that raising the hands during the bowing (*rukūʿ*) and lifting the head, as practiced by the Shāfiʿīyah and others, invalidates the prayer and ruled that a Ḥanafī must not pray behind a Shāfiʿī imam. This matter provoked friction between the two schools for centuries.

A group praying outside a mosque may generally choose its own imam. Preferably he should be the most worthy among them, with particular consideration given to probity, knowledge of Qurʾanic texts for recitation during prayer, knowledge of the ritual, and freedom from speech defects. While a woman may act as prayer leader only for other women, the imam may be a minor boy, a slave, or a moral offender among men and women alike. Prayer led by an imam with a speech defect is invalid. In a private home, the owner is most entitled to lead the prayer even if otherwise more worthy men are present.

Mosques have generally appointed official imams. Whenever the official imam or a substitute appointed by him is present, he is entitled to lead the prayer. In the congregational mosques or others maintained by the caliph, his governors, or, in modern times, the government, the imam is appointed by them. In private mosques maintained by individuals or local communities, the imam is chosen by the neighborhood. Once chosen he cannot be removed except for cause. The imam has usually the right to choose and direct the muezzin, who makes the call to prayer.

The imam of the Friday congregational worship may be appointed separately from the imam of the daily prayers. He is normally also the preacher (*khaṭīb*), who delivers the official sermon (*khuṭbah*) with the prayer for the ruler before the Friday prayer. In early Islam the Friday congregational prayer in particular was led by the caliph himself in the capital and by his governors in the provincial capitals. Later they generally deputed imams. The Friday prayer remained closely associated with government authority, however, and some of the legal schools held it to be invalid without the presence of the supreme imam (caliph) or his appointed representative. In Twelver Shiism, for instance, the Friday worship has been generally held to be in abeyance in the absence of the rightful supreme imam. Only when the Safavids established a Shīʿī regime in sixteenth-century Iran did the matter become controversial, and some Shīʿī jurists maintained that Friday worship was obligatory in the presence of a qualified legal scholar. Today the Friday prayer is performed among the Twelver Shīʿah, though not as widely as among Sunnīs. Sunnī concern for maintaining the unity of Islam by backing the established rulers, whatever their moral failings, found expression in the affirmation contained in many Sunnī creeds that every Muslim must "pray behind every imam, be he righteous or immoral." The Shīʿah and Khārijīs generally reject this attitude and prohibit prayer behind an imam who is known to be either immoral or heterodox.

SEE ALSO Aga Khan; Caliphate; Ghaybah; ʿIsmah; Nubūwah; Walāyah.

BIBLIOGRAPHY

There is no comprehensive study of the imamate. The institutional development of the caliphate is analyzed by Thomas W. Arnold in his *The Caliphate* (Oxford, 1924); the second edition contains a chapter on the abolition of the caliphate and its aftermath by Sylvia G. Haim (New York, 1965). See also Emile Tyan's *Institutions du droit public musulman* (Paris, 1954–1957), volume 1, *Le califat,* and volume 2, *Califat et sultanat.* The most authoritative medieval treatise on the Sunnī (Shāfiʿī) legal doctrine of the imamate, al-Māwardī's *Kitāb al-aḥkām al-sulṭānīyah,* has been translated into French by Edmond Fagnan, as *Les statuts gouvernementaux* (Algiers, 1915). Modernist views are discussed by Malcolm H. Kerr in his *Islamic Reform: The Political and Legal Theories of Muḥammad ʿAbduh and Rashīd Riḍā* (Berkeley, Calif., 1966) and by Henri Laoust in the introduction to his *Le califat dans la doctrine de Rašīd Riḍā* (Beirut, 1938), which contains the translation of a major work on the subject by a conservative modernist.

Twelver Shīʿī doctrine is described by Dwight M. Donaldson in *The Shiʿite Religion* (London, 1933), and later esoteric teaching by Henry Corbin in *Histoire de la philosophie islamique,* vol. 1 (Paris, 1964), pp. 53–109. For Ṭayyibi esoteric doctrine, see the analysis and annotated translation of a typical Ṭayyibi treatise on the subject in chapter 4 of Henry Corbin's *Trilogie ismaelienne* (Tehran, 1961). Nizārī doctrine after the *qiyāmah* is described by Marshall G. S. Hodgson in *The Order of Assassins* (1955; reprint, New York, 1980), pp. 160–175. Rudolf Strothmann's *Das Staatsrecht der Zaiditen* (Strasbourg, 1912) discusses Zaydī legal doctrine and practice. Khārijī doctrine is analyzed by Elie Adib Salem in *Political Theory and Institutions of the Khawārij* (Baltimore, 1956), especially in chapter 4. For details of the legal rules concerning the imamate of the ritual prayer, see chapter 9 of al-Māwardī's work cited above and *Nawawī, Minhaj et Talibin: A Manual of Muḥammadan Law according to the School of Shafī,* translated by E. C. Howard (1914; reprint, Lahore, 1977), pp. 42–69.

WILFERD MADELUNG (1987)

ĪMĀN AND ISLĀM.

Islām, a noun derived from the verb *aslama* ("to submit or surrender [to God]"), designates the act by which an individual recognizes his or her relationship to the divine and, at the same time, the community of all of those who respond in submission. It describes, therefore, both the singular, vertical relationship between the human being and God and the collective, horizontal relationship of all who join together in common faith and practice.

In its communal aspect *islām* has come to be the commonly accepted term for the religion of the followers of the prophet Muḥammad and today claims many millions of adherents. As the personal act of response to the oneness of God and his commands *islām* often has been viewed as coordinate with another term basic to Muslim theology. This is *īmān,* most commonly understood as faith, from the verb *amana* ("to be secure, to place one's trust [in God]"). While *islām* as a verbal noun appears only eight times in the Qurʾān, *īmān* is found over five times as often in the sacred scripture.

QURʾANIC CONTEXT. The Qurʾān as understood by Muslims is not a theological document per se, although it does reveal something of the being and will of God. It is rather a record of the revelations to the prophet Muḥammad that details the ways in which men and women of faith are to respond to the fact of divine oneness. It also sets forth the specific ways in which they are to conduct their daily lives in preparation for the reality of the final day of judgment and recompense. Terms such as *islām* and *īmān* therefore are not defined and analyzed in the Qurʾān. In some instances they are apparently interchangeable in meaning, and in others Qurʾanic usage seems to suggest that the two have different emphases, particularly as they relate to works. In one place only (sura 49:14) is a clear discrimination between *islām* and *īmān* implied.

Here a distinction is drawn between the verbal acknowledgment of *islām* by the tongue and the *īmān* that has entered the heart. The suggestion that *islām* is the outward sign and *īmān* the inward, however, runs counter to the general understanding of the Qurʾān that they are essentially synonymous and that they both designate the religious response by which one heeds the message of God's oneness and thereby escapes the eternal retribution of the Day of Resurrection.

Ḥadīth. Many kinds of references to *islām* and *īmān* are to be found in the collections of *ḥadīth,* the narratives or "traditions" that record the community's memory of the sayings and actions of the prophet Muḥammad and his companions. Individual traditions often fail to suggest a distinction between *islām* and *īmān.* The Prophet is sometimes quoted as having indicated that the essentials of *islām* are the Shahādah, the twin testimonies to the oneness of God and the prophethood of Muḥammad, as well as the other duties constitutive of formal *islām,* with no specification of the components of faith. More often, however, the reports seem to imply that the terms connote at least different aspects of the same response, if not two separate kinds of responses.

One particularly interesting narrative found in a range of renditions presents the Prophet defining *islām* as clearly distinct from *īmān.* In the best-known version the story is told about a stranger with a beautiful face, black hair, and a white robe (usually understood to be the angel Gabriel) who joins the Prophet and a group of his companions and asks "What is *islām?*" (or, in other versions, "Tell me about *islām*"). The Prophet answers that *islām* is the performance of certain duties. The specifics of these duties differ in the various renditions of this *ḥadīth,* but the most commonly cited are witnessing that there is no god but God and that Muḥammad is his Messenger (*shahādah*), submitting to God with no association of anything else, performing the prayer ritual (*ṣalāt*), paying the alms tax (*zakāt*), observing the Ramaḍān fast (*ṣawm*), and making the pilgrimage *(ḥājj).* If the first two of these are combined, the list then reflects the elements that commonly have been accepted in Islām as the five duties that constitute the "pillars" (*arkān*) of the individual Muslim's religious responsibilities.

After this enumeration the stranger assures the Prophet that the definition is correct. He then goes on to ask about *īmān* and is told that it consists of faith in the following (again differing somewhat according to the several versions): God, his angels, his books (or book), his messengers (or messenger), the resurrection, the garden and the fire, and other eschatological realities. Though less commonly classified than the *arkān,* the elements in this list generally are identified as the key components of the creeds that have been developed by members of the Muslim community. Several versions indicate that after thus defining *islām* and *īmān* the stranger asks the Prophet, "If I do that am I a *muslim* and a *muʾmin?*" to which the Prophet responds "Yes."

The continuation of the story includes commentary on *iḥṣān,* a third element beyond *islām* and *īmān,* which the Prophet says is the state of being perfected and serving God as if he were always before your eyes. From the structure of the narrative it is clear that the discussion was intended to suggest degrees of religious response, with *islām* as the first and most basic and *iḥṣān* as the last and highest. This kind of ranking is supported by another commonly cited narrative in which the Messenger of God says that *islām* is external while *īmān* belongs to the heart. For reasons that are not entirely clear, scholastic theology (*kalām*) did not generally develop the concept of *iḥṣān* but centered its subsequent discussions primarily on the first two terms.

Other *ḥadīths* seem to suggest that faith is a component element of *islām.* When asked about *islām* on one occasion the Prophet is said to have replied, "Witness that there is no god but God and that I am the Messenger of God, and have faith in all foreordinations, their good and evil, their sweetness and bitterness." On another occasion, the Prophet says that the more virtuous *islām* is *īmān,* which consists of faith in God, his angels, his books, his messengers, and the resurrection. Here *īmān* becomes a kind of subdivision of *islām,* with the most virtuous *īmān* said to be the emigration (Hijrah) and so on through a series of subcategories. In several traditions *islām* seems to consist of *īmān* plus works, as when the Prophet says that one should say "I have faith" and walk the straight path.

Theology. The respective definitions of *islām* and *īmān* became increasingly important in the early Muslim community as the nation of Islām grew through great numbers of conversions, and its members early on began to struggle with the question of who was or was not a Muslim. In a variety of ways, and for political as well as theological reasons, sects, schismatic groups, individual thinkers, and schools of theology adopted positions by which they tried to determine membership in the Islamic community. To this end clearer and firmer distinctions came to be drawn between *islām* and *īmān,* and the various groups in the young Muslim community often defined their positions according to those distinctions.

Khārijīs. Theological speculation is often said to have begun with the political movement of the Khārijīs, the earliest of the Muslim sects. It was, however, a movement not of passive reflection but of active involvement in the effort to purify Islam. As decades passed after the death of the Prophet, some began to feel that those in power were betraying the basic understanding of the faith. All the members of the community were being called *muʾminūn* ("persons of faith") regardless of the degree of their piety and their adherence to the essentials of Islam. The Khārijīs, in their zeal to ensure that the Muslim community was led by those most qualified in matters of faith and obedience, focused attention on the question of who is a true *muslim/muʾmin* and who is a *kāfir* (best defined not as unbeliever or infidel but as one who actively rejects the will of God). *Īmān* and *islām* were seen by the Khārijīs as essentially synonymous: Both include verbal and intellectual assent as well as works and are in absolute opposition to *kufr* ("rejection"). Rather than trying to define the *muslim/mu'min* the Khārijīs concentrated on the *kāfir* and adopted often ruthless means of condemning and in fact excommunicating such a person from the community.

Murji'ah. The sect known as the Murji'ah (lit., "those who postpone") was politically and, on this issue, theologically opposed to the Khārijīs. This group felt that it is wrong to condemn a member of the community as a *kāfir,* no matter what his or her actions. Judgment of human conduct and final determination of one's state of punishment or felicity must be left in the hands of God, they said, postponed until the Day of Resurrection.

Gradually, however, this doctrine came to mean for them not simply the postponement of judgment. In addition, they gave works a place of secondary importance behind faith by saying that good works are not a necessary indication of faith. This was in distinction to the Khārijīs, who stressed the importance of outward acts of piety in conformity with God's laws. The Murji'ah thus became the first in the Muslim community specifically to address the question of the internal structure of *īmān.* While there clearly were different schools of Murji'ah (al-Khaṭīb al-Baghdādī breaks them into three main groups, and al-Ash'arī identifies twelve different strands), their overall contribution to Islamic theology was in their identification of the nature of faith as separate from works and in their assurance for the *mu'min* of a place in paradise despite his or her failure to observe the laws of God.

Virtually all of the succeeding theoretical discussions about the nature of faith took as their starting point the issues and problems raised by the various schools of the Murji'ah. There was general acceptance of the Murji'ī thesis that the main elements to be considered in the understanding of *īmān* are affirmation (*taṣdīq*) and verbal acknowledgment (*iqrār*) of that affirmation. (While most later thinkers stressed the primary significance of *taṣdīq* as heartfelt affirmation, however, the Murji'ah rather understood affirmation as intellectual assent or knowledge.) While they assented to the importance of *taṣdīq* and *iqrār* as necessary constituents of *īmān,* the Murji'ah clearly rejected works.

As a consequence of this doctrine the Murji'ah, in clear opposition to the Khārijīs, did not believe that the quality of one's faith could be determined by the commission of sins, even major or grave sins. One school of the Murji'ah, the Karrāmīyah, went so far as to maintain that *īmān* consists strictly of the saying of the two *shahādahs,* the testimony of the oneness of God and the prophethood of Muḥammad, and involves neither affirmation nor works.

Later discussion. The debates between sects such as the Khārijīs and the Murji'ah were based on crucial questions of membership in the Muslim community and were therefore far from strictly intellectual issues. They were, in fact, quite often matters of life and death. As time passed, however, and the community began to stabilize after its initial growth, a stage was reached in which these kinds of questions were seen less as issues requiring decisive action and more as matters of intellectual engagement and decision. Thus the nature of *islām* and *īmān* continued to be discussed by the leading thinkers of the community.

One way of treating the relationship of, or distinction between, submission and faith is to consider which is the broader category under which the other is subsumed. Not surprisingly, different Muslim interpreters and schools of theology have reached different conclusions, often based on traditions from the Prophet such as those cited above.

If one understands *islām* as consisting of the five pillars or duties (the testimony, prayer, fast, alms tax, and pilgrimage) it is possible to argue that the first of these, witnessing to God's oneness and the prophethood of Muḥammad, can be considered an act of faith. In that way *īmān* is part of the larger category of *islām.* Thus Ash'arī theologians such as al-Bāqillānī (d. 1013), for example, concluded that all *īmān* is part of *islām,* but not all *islām* is part of *īmān.* Al-Ash'arī (d. 935) himself said that *islām* is wider than *īmān* and that therefore not all the former is part of the latter.

The later Ḥanbalī thinker Ibn Taymīyah (d. 1328) carefully developed another way of seeing this relationship in his analysis of the *ḥadīth* in which the Prophet seems to rank *islām, īmān,* and *iḥsān.* Because of the very ranking, he said, *iḥsān,* while characteristic of the most select number of the faithful, in fact connotes the most inclusive definition. That is, the person of faith (*mu'min*) must by definition be a submitter (*muslim*), and the person of perfection (*muḥsin*) must therefore be both of the former. *Īmān,* therefore, contains *islām.* Ibn Taymīyah's conclusion was more than academic. It is clear, he felt, that *islām* is an external act while *īmān* is a matter of the heart. For Ibn Taymīyah the Ash'arī conclusion that *islām* is wider than *īmān* implies that while all those who submit are persons of faith, not all who profess faith are *muslims,* a conclusion with which he totally disagreed. And in fact the majority Ash'arī view was that although faith can exist without *islām,* failure to do the works characteristic of *islām* is a grave sin. For Ibn Taymīyah, to have faith but not to do works of obedience is an impossible contradiction.

While some in the Muslim community continued to debate these and other theological issues, others turned to the task of systematizing the conclusions reached by thinkers within the various schools into creedal formulations. One of the most popular of the creeds over the centuries has been the *Sharḥ al-'aqā'id* of the Ḥanafī jurist al-Nasafī (d. 1143). The creed was later commented on by the Ash'arī scholar al-Taftāzānī (d. 1389). *Īmān,* said al-Nasafī, is affirmation (*taṣdīq*) of that which the Prophet brought from God and confession (*iqrār*) of it. While acts of obedience may increase, faith neither increases nor decreases. Then, in a very interesting conclusion, he declares that *īmān* and *islām* are one; they are so, al-Taftāzānī explains, because obedience (*idh'ān*) is the essence of both *islām* and *taṣdīq,* which, in al-Nasafī's definition, is *īmān.*

Despite the common element of obedience, al-Taftāzānī did not completely identify the terms but rather said that one cannot exist without the other. In the Ḥanafī creed *Fiqh akbar II* (Greater understanding II), attributed to Abū Ḥanīfah (d. 767) but probably written in the tenth century, *īmān* and *islām* share the common ingredient of submission and overlap so much that they are essentially interchangeable.

Qur'ān commentators analyzing the eight verses in which *islām* is mentioned all have stressed the essential component of submission, usually in relation to God's initiative. To the extent to which they have dealt with faith in relation to submission they have made it clear that *īmān* (most commonly defined as *taṣdīq* and *iqrār*) is identified in some clear ways with *islām.* The degree to which they have equated the terms, however, has varied considerably. In his monumental commentary on the Qur'ān, *Jāmi' al-bayān 'an ta'wīl āy al-Qur'ān,* al-Ṭabarī (d. 923) suggests a kind of bipartite *islām.* On one level is the verbal acknowledgment of submission by which one becomes part of the community of Islam, and on a deeper level is that *islām* that is in fact coordinate with the act of faith (*īmān*) and that involves the complete surrender of the body, the mind, and the heart. Fakhr al-Dīn al-Rāzī (d. 1209), in the *Mafātīḥ al-ghayb* (Keys to the mystery), insists that while the two are different in generality they are one in existence. If *islām* is not of the heart, he said, it cannot be called *islām.* Muḥammad Rashīd Riḍā, the twentieth-century Egyptian author of the *Manār* commentary, suggested a similar interpretation when he said that the true meaning of both *islām* and *īmān* is what he calls *īmān khāṣṣ,* interiorized faith, which is the only means of salvation. In this understanding *islām* and īmān converge in a single reality (*ḥaqīqah*).

Most Qur'ān commentators through the centuries, however, have seen *islām* and *īmān* as more distinct than al-Ṭabarī, al-Rāzī, or Rashīd Riḍā have. They admit that *islām* can have a purely external meaning, while *īmān* always involves confirmation of the heart. Although they differ in their attempts to interpret the distinctions between the terms, in no instance have they seen them as irreconcilable. And despite the variety of responses reflected in the works of theology, general usage of the terms *islām* and *īmān* has revealed some common understanding both of their respective definitions and of the ways in which these terms together express the totality of the Muslim's response to the being and will of God.

SEE ALSO Ummah.

BIBLIOGRAPHY

Works in Arabic

For a full collection of traditions from the prophet Muḥammad in which the terms *islām* and *īmān* are used, see Ibn Ḥanbal's *Musnad,* 6 vols. (1895; reprint, Beirut, 1969). The earliest extensive Qur'ān commentary that analyzes the relation of the terms in their scriptural usage is Abū Ja'far Muḥammad al-Ṭabarī's *Jāmi' a-bayān 'an ta'wīl āy al-Qur'ān,* 30 vols. in 12 (Cairo, 1954–1968). Of the several creedal formulations dealing the juxtaposition of faith and submission in the thinking of the early Muslim community, one of the most popular is 'Umar ibn Muḥammad al-Nasafīyah's *Sharḥ al-'aqā'id,* with commentary by Sa'd al-Dīn al-Taftāzānī (Cairo, 1974). A rich treatment of the meaning of faith and its relation to submission is found in the *Kitāb al-īmān* of the fourteenth-century theologian Ibn Taymīyah (Damascus, 1961).

Works in Western Languages

Such basic works as A. J. Wensinck's *The Muslim Creed* (1932; reprint, New York, 1965) and Louis Gardet and M. M. Anawati's *Introduction à la théologie musulmane,* 2d ed. (Paris, 1970), are helpful for a general understanding of the significance of the *īmān/islām* discussions in the development of Islāmic theology. More specific treatments such as Helmer Ringgren's *Islām, 'aslama, and muslim,* "Horae Soederblomianae," vol. 2 (Uppsala, 1949), and "The Conception of Faith in the Koran," *Oriens* 4 (1951): 1–20, analyze Qur'anic usage of the terms. Toshihiko Izutsu provides an extensive study of the interpretation of *īmān* in the history of Islamic thought, with a chapter on its relation to *islām,* in *The Concept of Belief in Islamic Theology* (Tokyo, 1965).

JANE I. SMITH (1987)

IMMANENCE SEE TRANSCENDENCE AND IMMANENCE

IMMERSION SEE BAPTISM

IMMOLATION SEE SACRIFICE

IMPLICIT RELIGION. In the age of secularization and debate within the social sciences on how to approach the religious factor, two trends have intersected. One proclaims a progressive disenchantment with a decline of the religious factor's role and plausibility; within a wide range of social attitudes, religion seems destined to social irrelevance or to occupying a purely personal dimension. The second trend of thought sees a recovery and renewal of the role of religion in contemporary society, after a period of neglect, with particular reference to ancient religions.

The concept and problem of implicit religion is situated within a different perspective. Beyond the oppositions that locate the religious factor amongst those "religious" institutions balanced between death and resurrection, this concept initiates the observation that there is a widespread separation between believing and belonging, and in particular between the numerous paths of existentialism within a culture and the dimensions of daily life with specific intentionality and therefore specific dimensions of ultimate meaning.

The concept of implicit religion is recent, and arose as a result of semantic difficulties related to reflection on the meaning and value of religiousness itself. Dietrich Bonhoeffer, during his imprisonment, proposed that a supernatural deviation of the spiritualistic tendencies of Catholicism and Protestantism usually results in a tendency to make sacred the world. Both Catholicism and Protestantism achieve the same result, that is, conceiving Christian life as based on the idea of a separation from the world. Bonhoeffer's proposal becomes dramatic when he reaches the conviction that there exists an insurmountable incompatibility between faith and religion.

The evocation of implicit religion is therefore not merely an academic expedient or a pleonastic concept. It is rather an analytical occasion, an instrument of the less visible and differentiated layers of the radical demand for meaning that exists in human life. Nor can it be interpreted as an indirect proof within the line of the resurgence of the religious factor.

The term *implicit religion* is one among a number of terms that have become familiar in the literature of sociology of religion, including *invisible religion* (Luckmann, 1967) *common religion* (Towler, 1974, pp. 145–162), *surrogate religion* (Robertson, 1970), *quasi-religion*, and *para-religion* (Greil, 1993). These terms have been introduced to help scholars deal with that which appears to be like religion, but is not actually religion, as well as that which does not appear to be religion, but actually is religion. Another such concept is *civil religion*, which refers primarily to a more integrated set of values and symbols that is, to some degree, actually held in common by a group of people (Bellah, 1970).

The concept of implicit religion, according to Edward Bailey, refers to people's commitments, whether or not they take a religious form. The study of implicit religion began in earnest in 1968, in the context of debate about secularization, and concentrated upon the spirituality and ethos of secular expression. This focus was determined because religious studies already generally concentrated on organized forms of religious belief, ritual, and community. In his conclusion to three studies on implicit religion in contemporary society, Bailey wrote:

> Implicit religion which largely includes the empirical Christianity as well as the secular face of contemporary society, unlike archaic religion, is neither ecstatic nor corporate; and unlike historical religion, it is neither segmented nor visionary. So for most men, religion in general, and implicit in particular, is, and is likely to remain, dimensional in character, with extensive influence, rather than relational, with specific power. Yet moderation, or even inertia, can be held to as doggedly as apocalyptic or eschatology is preached or conversions are pursued. Belief may be fanatical, although still implicit (Bailey, 1983, p. 81).

Through the discussion of these relationships a number of questions relating to the meaning and application of the term *implicit religion* are raised. Wilhelm Dupré discusses various areas in which the critical potential of implicit religion becomes obvious (Dupré, 1991). These areas appear in situations in which developments in implicit religion account for considerable modifications in both the explicit religion and the cultural environment, and they extend as far as the many instances in which the concept of implicit religion has a critical impact on the perception of reality. Through a consideration of the main criteria used to define such concepts, a systematic but tentative typology is suggested.

In attempting to locate implicit religion within this typology, it has been found that it might be equivalent to: (1) a nonreligious meaning system; or (2) Thomas Luckmann's invisible religion; or it may include (3) generically both a nonreligious meaning system and invisible religion; or (4) even more generically nonreligious meaning systems, invisible religion, para-religion, and quasi-religion. Some scholars have appealed for a more appropriate conceptual tool kit and terminology to deal with this range of phenomena (Hamilton, 2001, pp. 5–13). To this end, the 1980s saw the appearance of sociologist Arnaldo Nesti's *Il religioso implicito* (1985) and the first issue of the journal *Religioni e Società*, both focusing on issues of implicit religion in society.

Although the notion of implicit religion is recent, one can find traces of it within the traditional social sciences. Even though the term itself and its exact references are not used in the socioreligious sphere, the problem and the dynamics from which its meaning and form derive are perceivable (Weber, 1920–1921; Schutz, 1932).

Max Weber's contributions, particularly regarding the polytheism of values, include the topic of intentionality in Edmund Husserl, the social character of *Lebenswelt* in Alfred Schutz (1932), and lessons connected to the dark side of personality in C. G. Jung. As an example, it is advisable to remember that the "polytheism of values" implies that the antagonism between different divinities has become "an everyday reality," depriving itself from any residual fascination coming from the myth. "To know how to face such an everyday life" is the difficult duty of modern humans, in opposition between the ethics of conviction and the ethics of responsibility. For Weber, the meaning of the polytheistic experience marks the descending course of Jewish-Christian monotheism and implies a viewpoint including the subject's act, whose meaning cannot be traced back to an exclusive theodicy (Weber, 1920–1921, pp. 264–265).

According to Nesti, implicit religion is a phenomenon, an analytical cipher of the difficulties of existential independence and of the symbolic-prescriptive transignification in progress in contemporary society, particularly in Western Christianity. The extent of such religiousness involves three factors. The first factor is connected to symbols and beliefs and rules and practices characteristic of the explicit "religious factor." Between the explicit morphology and the meaning dimension correlated to it, a level that is in itself ambivalent is wedged in: consider silence and voice phenomenology, as well as the symbolicity of ritual dynamics.

The second factor must be traced among the "topoi" critical to the Christian "religious system" as a source of plausibility. Thus, an implicit religiousness can be traced in: (1) Christianity without faith; (2) Christianity without church; and (3) Christianity from an esoteric approach. A third factor must be reconstructed outside and in contrast to the "religious system" itself. There is, thus, an implicit hidden religiousness outside the "sacred fence." In particular, such an implicitness is acquired in: (1) agnosticism; (2) skepticism characterized by the art of living in the uncertainty of the present; and (3) atheism as metaphor provided with a radical meaning.

The specific nature of implicit religion lies in the attempt to override prejudices and stereotypes with the mechanism of forced repetition, so as to understand life and the world as experienced by people in the process of living. It is necessary to go beyond such common schemes as the identification of the religious with churches, sects, and institutions, or the dichotomy of secular and sacred, as well the antonyms visible and invisible, sacred and profane.

The outlined survey, in all its diversity, refers to a presence, to a unifying principle. Even if the word and the exact reference is missing within the socioreligious tradition, the perception of its issues and of the dynamic from which its meaning derives, is not absent. By applying the concept of implicit religion, we are induced to pass beyond conventional representations of religion to a concept of religion that begins with the experience of the subject, and thus to a new reading of the religious within the objective religious pluriverse.

See Also Invisible Religion; Popular Religion; Secularization; Society and Religion.

Bibliography

Bailey, Edward. "The Implicit Religion of Contemporary Society: An Orientation and Plea for Its Study." *Religion* 13 (1983): 69–83.

Bailey, Edward. "The Implicit Religion of Contemporary Society: Some Studies and Reflections." *Social Compass* 37, no. 4 (1990): 483–498.

Bailey, Edward. *Implicit Religion in Contemporary Society.* Kampen, Netherlands, 1997.

Bellah, Robert N. *Beyond Belief: Essays on Religion in a Post-Traditional World.* New York, 1970.

Cipriani, Roberto, and Arnaldo Nesti. "Due interventi sul religioso implicito." *Religioni e Società* 14 (1992): 77–92.

Dupré, Wilhelm. "Implicit Religion and the Meaning of the Religious Dialogue." *Studies in Interreligious Dialogue* I, no. 2 (1991): 129–145.

Greil, Arthur L. "Exploration along the Sacred Frontier: Notes on Para-Religions, Quasi-Religions, and Other Boundary Phenomena." In *The Handbook on Cults and Sects in America,* edited by David G. Bromley and Jeffrey K. Hadden. Greenwich, Conn., 1993.

Hamilton, Malcolm. "Implicit Religion and Related Concepts: Seeing Precisions." *Implicit Religion* 4 (2001): 5–13.

Luckmann, Thomas. *The Invisible Religion: The Problem of Religion in Modern Society.* New York, 1967.

Nesti, Arnaldo. *Il religioso implicito.* Rome, 1985.

Nesti, Arnaldo. "Lo religioso hoy: Arquitectura de un Labirinto. Primeros Apuntes." *Universidad de Mexico* no. 610 (2002): 11–22.

Nesti, Arnaldo, ed. *La religione implicita: Sociologi e teologi a confronto.* Bologna, Italy, 1994.

Robertson, Roland. *The Sociological Interpretation of Religion.* Oxford, 1970.

Schutz, Alfred. *Der Sinnhafte Aufbau der sozialen Welt: Eine Einleitung in die Verstehende Sociologie.* Vienna, 1932.

Towler, Robert. *Homo Religiosus: Sociological Problems in the Study of Religion.* London, 1974.

Weber, Max. *Gesammelte Aufsätze zur Religions-soziologie.* Tübingen, Germany, 1920–1921.

Arnaldo Nesti (2005)

IMPURITY See PURIFICATION

INANNA.

Inanna, the Sumerian astral deity representing the planet Venus, was known throughout the Mesopotamian world. The Akkadians (and later the Assyro-Babylonians) called her Ishtar. For both the Sumerians and the Akkadians she was the principal goddess in their respective pantheons. Inanna-Ishtar's closest counterparts to the west are the Canaanite Astarte and the later goddesses of Greece and Rome, Aphrodite and Venus.

When the Semitic Akkadians settled in the lower Tigris-Euphrates Basin, they assimilated the preexisting, predominantly Sumerian culture. Comparative Semitic evidence suggests that the Akkadian Venus deity was originally masculine but became completely feminized when identified with the female Sumerian deity Inanna. Because of the eventual syncretism of the Sumerian and Akkadian pantheons, the traditions concerning Inanna-Ishtar are extremely complicated. By one such tradition she is the daughter of the sky god An, by another the daughter of the moon god Nanna-Sin (and thereby the sister of the sun god Utu-Shamash), and by still another the daughter of Enlil or Ashur. Similarly, Inanna-Ishtar was associated with more than one consort, alternately Zababa of Kish, Ashur, An, and Dumuzi (called Tammuz by the Akkadians). Although her main cult center was Uruk, she was worshiped in many other localities, each of which gave her rather diverse epithets and characteristics.

Inanna in Sumerian and Akkadian Mythology. The myth entitled "Inanna Takes Command of Heaven" tells the story of how Inanna managed to bring down the Eanna, "the house of An," from heaven and thus become "mistress of heaven." Unfortunately the text has many lacunae, missing many passages of this remarkable adventure. The narrative begins with the decision of Inanna to take control of the Eanna and her appeal to her brother Utu for help in this task. The inner motives of the goddess, if her words are accurate, are the result of her wounded pride at being raped and a vague promise by An. However, no one knows where on earth the house of An is. Consequently, Inanna asks the assistance of a fisherman who has experience in sailing in the marsh. He willingly agrees, and after repeated attempts Inanna finally finds the Eanna in the marsh. It is impossible to know what defenses An had set up so the house would not be robbed, but certainly the scorpion with which Inanna fights must have been one. The text resumes with An's hurt and regret for the theft that has occurred, but at the same time he makes the prudent decision to leave things as they are. The Eanna will from now on be the "most splendid temple in Sumeria." A summary of the myth is given in lines 159–163, where the theft that has taken place and the new reality are once more emphasized. The Eanna will be the abode of the rule of Inanna, who is praised as "the greatest of all the heavenly gods."

Completely different in tone is the narrative better known as the "The Descent of Inanna to the Underworld." It could be renamed "The Ascent of Inanna to the Land of No Return" because, on the basis of continuing scholarship and the recovery of less ambiguous epigraphic evidence, the country to which the goddess goes is once again the Kur, "the mythical mountain" located east of Sumer, in modern Iran. As Silvia Chiodi (1994) has shown, there is no mention in the Sumerian texts that the mythical Kur—from which life arose, including the gods and plants, and to which the spirits of the dead return, as it were to return to the life-giving element from which they originated—is located beneath the earth. Besides, the ambiguous verb *e11* (to go up and to go down) used in this myth has been greatly clarified in the myth of Inanna and Shukalletuda by the variant verb *íla*, which can mean nothing except "to go up." The myth, which is written in an expansive, grandiose style and in highly poetic language, describes the attempt, on this occasion unsuccessful, made by Inanna to expand her sphere of influence by taking control of the Kur, the undisputed realm of Queen Ereshkigal.

After Inanna has decided upon this action, she leaves earth and the sanctuaries dedicated to her, dresses in an appropriate fashion with clothes and jewels that symbolize her divine power, and sets off on her journey. Before she leaves she tells her faithful ambassador Ninshubur that if things go wrong she must go to Nippur, Ur, and Eridu to plead for the assistance of the gods on her behalf. Inanna presents herself at the gates of the great palace, which is defended by seven walls, and asks Neti to allow her to come in. Neti asks her to wait so he can obtain permission from the queen. Ereshkigal apparently agrees but orders that Inanna should observe all the rituals customary in the Kur. No one may enter her realm dressed in finery, as the mistress of heaven had intended to do. So Inanna is allowed to enter, but at every gate she has to take off part of her clothing. When she comes before Ereshkigal, she is completely naked. Ereshkigal has a fit of uncontrolled rage when she sees her sister and turns her into a "corpse."

"Three days and three nights have passed," and Ninshubur carries out the orders Inanna gave her. Ninshubur goes to Nippur first and then to Ur, where she begs the gods of the two towns to save Inanna, who is being held in the Kur. But the two gods are unyielding. Ninshubur must go to Eridu. There the god Enki feels sorry for Inanna, although he criticizes the way she has behaved. Enki creates two sprites and gives them the job of saving Inanna by bringing her "the food of life and the water of life." Galatur and Kurgarra, the two sprites, go down to the underworld, and after a detailed discussion with Ereshkigal, they are allowed to take away the corpse of Inanna, which they bring back to life. But no one may break the unbending rules of the underworld, so Inanna must provide a substitute in her place. When she leaves the Kur, she is accompanied by demons ready to seize and take back the one who is to replace her. On her return Inanna meets Ninshubur first, then Shara her son, then Lulal, but she refuses to allow the demons to take any of them because they had mourned the disappearance of the goddess. Continuing the journey, the group arrives in Uruk, where Inanna's husband Dumuzi, instead of weeping, is amusing himself. The goddess becomes angry and lets the demons take Dumuzi. However, Dumuzi asks the god Utu to transform him into a serpent to escape from the demons trying to capture him.

In the variant from Ur, the demons are tired of the goddess's outbursts and ask her to return to the Kur, so Inanna hurries to have her husband seized. At this point the appeal to Utu and the request to be transformed into a serpent are repeated, and Dumuzi takes refuge in the house of his sister Geshtinanna. The demons arrive at Geshtinanna's house and ask for her brother, but she does not reveal that he has taken refuge with her. The demons nevertheless find Dumuzi in the sheepfold, where they capture him. When the main text resumes, the fate of the fly is decided, for reasons that elude the reader, and Inanna decides that Dumuzi's sister should share his fate: "six months for him, six months for her." The concluding doxology sweetly praises the queen of the underworld. Similar descriptions of the land of the dead are in the myth of Nergal and Ereshkigal and the classic *Epic of Gilgamesh.*

Of the two Akkadian recensions of the myth, the Middle Assyrian version, because of its shortness (a mere eleven lines), does not provide new information of any importance. The New Assyrian recension is 138 lines long and is complete, but a comparison with the Sumerian version of the so-called "descent" of Inanna to the underworld, over 400 lines long, is required despite their clearly different cultural milieus. The main events and divine characters are certainly similar if not identical. The queen of the underworld in both myths is the same, Ereshkigal, the Sumerian goddess who rules the realm of the dead. The heavenly goddess who goes to the other world is Inanna in the Sumerian myth, whereas in the New Assyrian myth it is Ishtar. The two goddesses had been amalgamated by Mesopotamian religious tradition. The other gods who become involved are mostly the same, starting with Dumuzi and ending with Sin and Ea (Nanna and Enki, respectively). The herald is different, Ninshubur in the Sumerian recension, Papsukkal in the New Assyrian version.

The New Assyrian account, though more condensed and concise than the Sumerian version, still provides substantial new elements. For example, the scribe stresses the disastrous consequences for humanity and livestock caused by Ishtar's departure from the earth, described by Papsukkal when he tries to get first Sin and then Ea to secure the release of the goddess from the underworld. He also describes the far from pleasant nature of life in the underworld, not only for the dead but also for the queen of the underworld. In place of the two sprites, Galatur and Kurgarra, created by Enki to save Inanna, here Ea creates "Asushunammir, the court jester," who is assigned the task of moving Ereshkigal. The ending of the story is also different. In the New Assyrian version the return of Dumuzi from the underworld altogether with the dead is mentioned, albeit optatively, something which is quite incomprehensible, as Wolfram von Soden (1967) points out in his commentary on the passage.

Once again the Kur is the main focus of Inanna's attention in the following myth, which illustrates the fundamental point that the Sumerians considered the "mythical mountain" the source of life and all good things. Inanna turns to her brother Utu, the sun god, and asks if she can sail with him in his daily journey across the vault of heaven toward the Kur to enjoy the wonderful plants there. She is particularly interested in discovering the secret of female charms and the techniques of love with man. Only after she has experienced what love may mean is she prepared to go back to the city of her birth and resume her family role as mother, mother-in-law, and sister-in-law. The text concludes with a new hymn to the sun god that emphasizes his assistance to all those in trouble, from travelers to widows and orphans. The final sentence expresses the joy and relief of all those who can travel in his light.

Another interesting Sumerian text begins with a description and a hymn to the goddess with clear warlike qualities. An auto-eulogy describes the activities of Inanna and observes that only the Kur has refused to submit. The goddess dresses suitably and appears before her father An, seeking justice. She virtually asks him to agree to her interfering in the Kur, but An strongly advises his daughter against such action because he is convinced that this is another of Inanna's tantrums. Inanna remains implacable and engages in deadly combat with the Kur. She sends a torrent of water and a burning fire to subdue the lively spirits of the Kur, and she reduces the mountain, previously an earthly paradise, to a silent desert. At this point the goddess describes the outcome of the war and sets out the fate of the vanquished. She follows with a new, haughty auto-eulogy, in which she praises her memorable victory over the Kur. The concluding doxology is addressed to Nisaba, the goddess of academia, from where this text definitely originated.

In Sumerian literature the following myth is often called "Theft of the Divine Powers by Inanna from Enki." In fact, nothing could be more inaccurate and inconsistent. On this occasion Inanna has done nothing wrong to anyone, and what has been considered "theft" is in fact a completely voluntary gift from the god of wisdom. As the myth begins the goddess of Uruk is standing in front of a mirror admiring her beauty, including her private parts. Inanna is not content, however; she needs something further to complete her portrait. So she decides to go to Enki and ask him for something related to sex. The god of wisdom foresees her visit and gives orders for Inanna to be received with full honors. When Inanna arrives, Enki's herald Isimud extends full hospitality and lays on a banquet for the guest, which Enki attends. But Enki drinks too much and becomes drunk. At this point Enki volunteers to give Inanna divine powers or the essence of all things, and she accepts them happily. She makes a list of all the good things she has received, loads the gifts on her ship and sets off back to Uruk.

When Inanna has left port, Enki becomes himself again and, aware that he has been thoughtless, wants to recover the divine powers now heading to Uruk. After an interlude about a frog, whose fate is determined by Enki, the god sends Isimud on a mission to ask Inanna to return the gifts she has been given. Six times Inanna, with the aid of Ninshubur's magic, manages to prevent the monsters sent by Enki from taking control of her ship, which is sailing the arc of heaven. The ship finally reaches Uruk, where it is welcomed joyfully. Enki still cannot take in what has happened and sends his herald to Uruk with a list of the goods taken by Inanna. Meanwhile, the joyous atmosphere at Uruk affects everyone. Inanna renames all the city districts and assures her people of all the benefits that will result from the arrival of the divine powers. At this point Enki has no choice but to accept the loss and forecast the undoubted future greatness of Uruk.

LOVE STORIES. Among the accounts of the lovers and love stories of the goddess is the myth of "Inanna and Shukalletuda." The main theme is the misfortune of Inanna when she is raped by a mortal man, who must be punished with death. The story begins with a description of the goddess Inanna and her journey to the Kur, where she aims to enhance her divine powers. After the first break comes the story of the creation of the palm tree by Enki and the raven. Now the second main character Shukalletuda is introduced, seen trying desperately to water a flowerbed. Then follows the key moment in the myth, the rape of the virgin Inanna while she is resting under the shade of the only poplar in the garden. When Inanna realizes what has happened to her, she intends to punish the perpetrator. She sends plagues to the earth, first putting blood in the wells of the country, then she sends a hurricane and a sandstorm, in the end completely sealing off every road in the land.

Shukalletuda has been able to escape the anger of the goddess by hiding among his own people, so the goddess turns to Enki for help. Enki allows her to find Shukalletuda, who is condemned to death. The wrongdoer tries to excuse himself, explaining to the goddess that he was not really to blame, but this only angers her even more. Her only promise is that the name of Shukalletuda will be remembered in song after his death. After Shukalletuda's fate has been settled there is a hymn of praise for the holy Inanna.

The myth concerning the death of Dumuzi, the beloved husband of Inanna, on the other hand, is part of a series of stories about the strained relationship between Inanna, the mistress of heaven and of Uruk, and Dumuzi, the shepherd whom she loves, at least according to the love poems that have survived. A completely negative view of the lovers of Inanna is presented in the three redactions of the *Epic of Gilgamesh* that recount the episode when Ishtar falls in love with the hero. The passage in which Gilgamesh rejects Ishtar's offer that he become her husband, completely enraging the goddess, who at once sets about punishing him for this insult by sending down to earth the Bull of Heaven, has no equivalent in the Sumerian story of the same episode, where the reason for the quarrel seems to be political rather than emotional. To find anything like what is described here, it is necessary to resort to Sumerian literary texts on love concerning the goddess Inanna.

The detailed list of the jilted lovers of Ishtar spans the human and divine worlds and even includes the beasts of the earth, who have all received scant reward for their love of the goddess. Following is a list of the lovers and their rewards:

Dumuzi year after year of mourning

the bird Alallu broken wings

lion ditches dug

horse bridle, whip, and reins

shepherd changed into a wolf

Ishullanu the gardener turned into a mole

It can be understood why Gilgamesh refuses her enticing offer, especially when it becomes clear that the goddess is offering the king of Uruk a kingdom in the underworld.

The myth of "Ishtar and Saltu" was intended to be sung and includes notes on how it should be sung, as well as evidence of a refrain. It is reasonable to conclude that it was divided into more than ten songs that tell of the occasion when the gods were forced to take strong measures to curb the high spirits of the goddess. Its composition can be dated with certainty to the Old Babylonian period, more accurately during the reign of Hammurabi, who is mentioned by name. At the beginning the goddess and all her qualities are described, especially the strength that makes her so cut out for war. But the goddess certainly overdoes matters, because all the gods, particularly the god of wisdom Ea, find her behavior completely unacceptable. Ea decides to check the goddess's reckless behavior by creating a match for her. The new creature is formed from the dirt underneath the nails of the god of wisdom, and she is aggressive as well as beautiful. The god Ea gives her the task of defeating Ishtar, along with useful advice. Ishtar has learned of the changed situation, however, and sends her herald Ninshubur to find out what Saltu (meaning "strife") is like and how powerful she is. The contest between the two goddesses is fierce, but because they are evenly matched, neither wins or loses. Ishtar, at this point in the story, has a new name, Agushaya. She is unable to bear the shame of defeat, so she turns to Ea, asking him for an explanation of the changed situation and to eliminate her opponent. Ea willingly agrees to what Ishtar asks, reconfirming the function of the goddess on earth and inviting humanity to celebrate a feast to mark the creation of Saltu and the ultimate victory of Ishtar. In the doxology Ishtar and her patron Ea are praised for the defeat of Saltu.

SEE ALSO Dumuzi; Gilgamesh; Goddess Worship, overview article; Hierodouleia; Hieros Gamos; Mesopotamian Religions, overview article.

BIBLIOGRAPHY

Abusch, Tzvi. "Ishtar's Proposal and Gilgamesh's Refusal: An Interpretation of the Gilgamesh Epic, Tablet 6, Lines 1–79." *History of Religions* 26 (1986): 143–178.

Abusch, Tzvi. "Ishtar." In *Dictionary of Deities and Demons in the Bible*, edited by Karel van der Toom, Bob Becking, and Pieter W. van der Horst, pp. 847–855. Leiden, 1995.

Attinger, Pascal. "Inana et Ebiæ." *Zeitschrift für Assyriologie* 88 (1998): 164–195.

Chiodi, Silvia Maria. *Le concezioni dell'Oltretomba presso i Sumeri.* Memorie dell'Accademia Nazionale dei Lincei, Classe di Scienze Morali, Storiche e Filologiche, ser. 9, vol. 4, fasc. 5. Rome, 1994.

Farber-Flügge, Gertrud. *Der Mythos Inanna und Enki unter besonderer Berücksichtigung der Liste der me.* Studia Pohl 10. Rome, 1973.

Frymer-Kensky, Tikva. *In the Wake of the Goddesses.* New York, 1992.

Groneberg, Brigitte. "Philologische Bearbeitung des Agushaya-hymnus." *Revue d'Assyriologie* 75 (1981): 107–134.

Harris, R. "Inanna-Ishtar as Paradox and a Coincidence of Opposites." *History of Religions* 31 (1991): 261–278.

Heimpel, Wolfgang. "A Catalog of Near Eastern Venus Deities." *Syro-Mesopotamian Studies* 4 (1982): 9–22.

Lambert, W. G. "The Cult of Ishtar of Babylon." In *Le temple et le culte*, pp. 104–106. Istanbul, 1975.

Pettinato, Giovanni. *Mitologia Sumerica.* Turin, Italy, 2001.

Sefati, Yitschak. *Love-Songs in Sumerian Literature: Critical Edition of the Dumuzi-Inanna Songs.* Bar-Ilan Studies in Near Eastern Languages and Culture. Ramat Gan, Israel, 1998.

Soden, Wolfram von. "Kleine Beiträge zu Text und Erklärung babylonischer Epen." *Zeitschrift für Assyriologie* 58 (1967): 189–193.

Van Dijk, J. J. A. "Inanna raubt den 'grossen Himmel': Ein Mythos." In *Festschrift für Rykle Borger zu seinem 65. Geburtstag am 24. Mai 1994. Tikip santakki mala bašmu,* edited by Stefan M. Maul, pp. 9–38. Groningen, Netherlands, 1998.

Volk, Konrad. *Inanna und* Šukalletuda*: Zur historisch-politischen Deutung eines sumerischen Literaturwerkes.* Wiesbaden, Germany, 1995.

GIOVANNI PETTINATO (2005)
Translated from Italian by Paul Ellis

INCANTATION. The practice of incantation (Lat., *incantatio,* from *incantare,* "to chant a religious formula") differs considerably from culture to culture. For the purposes of this cross-cultural overview, however, incantation can be understood as the authorized use of rhythmically organized words of power that are chanted, spoken, or written to accomplish a desired goal by binding spiritual powers to act in a favorable way.

Since incantation uses words to move spiritual powers and accomplish a desired result, this practice is related to other uses of sacred language such as prayer, invocation, blessing, and cursing. Verbal formulas associated with prayer beseech the spiritual powers for certain actions or maintain communication by praise and submission. However, verbal formulas associated with incantation are designed to perform the desired result by "obliging" (Lat., *obligare,* "to bind") spiritual powers. Invocation, blessing, and cursing are used with both prayer and incantation.

THE POWER OF INCANTATION. Even though practices of incantation differ widely from culture to culture, its validity or efficacy appears to depend on cultural consensus about a number of primary factors, namely, the power of the chanted verbal formula, the authority of the incantor, the receptivity of spiritual forces both good and evil, the connection with the religious or mythological tradition, and the power of the accompanying ritual.

The power of the formula. Societies that use incantations understand them to be performative, that is, they accomplish what they say. The act of chanting the verbal formula itself has power. Scholars have put forth a variety of explanations concerning the effect incantations have for people. Older theories considered incantation to be a form of magic, an attempt to control and manipulate the forces of nature. More recent theories have suggested that incantations are expressive of needs and wishes or symbolize a desired result, or that they have the psychological effect of restructuring reality in the minds of people. Although these explanations may provide certain insights into the meaning of incantation, it must be remembered that, to the people involved, the proper chanting of the formula itself has performative power. To them it does not express or symbolize some other action—it *does* it. When, for example, the incantation experts of the Trobriand Islanders chant over the newly planted yam vines, "Raise thy stalk, O taytu. Make it flare up, make it lie across!" (Malinowski, 1935, vol. 1, p. 146), the people know that the "hearing" of these commands by the tubers is what makes them sprout and grow.

It is not, however, just any words that have such power. Incantations are special verbal formulas that in a variety of ways, depending upon the particular cultural tradition, tap into sacred power. They may, for example, contain powerful scriptural expressions, mantras, or sacred names. They are usually rhythmically organized and chanted repeatedly. They may use special devices such as foreign or unintelligible words, "abracadabra" nonsense phrases. The Anglo-Saxon medical-incantation treatise *Lacnunga* provides an example, using powerful names and impressive nonsense words:

> Sing this prayer over the black blains nine times: first, Paternoster. "Tigath tigath tigath calicet aclu cluel sedes adclocles acre earcre arnem nonabiuth aer aernem nidren arcum cunath arcum arctua fligara uflen binchi cutern nicuparam raf afth egal uflen arta arta arta trauncula trauncula. [In Latin:] Seek and you shall find. I adjure you by the Father, Son, and Holy Spirit that you grow no larger but that you dry up. . . . Cross Matthew, cross Mark, cross Luke, cross John." (Grattan and Singer, 1952, p. 107; my trans.)

It should be noted that, although the primary power of an incantation resides in its oral presentation, once these formulas could be written down, the chirographic (handwritten) text itself contributed to the potency of the incantation. From before 600 CE come Jewish-related Aramaic incantation texts written by experts on bowls and designed to ward off various sorts of evil. Such power could now be extended even into the realm of the dead, as in the case of Middle Kingdom Egyptian incantations inscribed on the inside wall of coffins, by which the various gods and demons encountered by the soul would be bound to act beneficially.

The chanter's authority. Closely connected to the power of the verbal formula is the authority of the incantors. These may be experts in terms of learning or ecclesiastical authority, like Daoist priests or Christian monks; they may be people who have been specially initiated into the use of such power, like various kinds of shamans; they may be charismatic holy ones who keep certain special observances or practices that sanction their authority. In the incantation itself, the chanter often clothes himself in the aura of divine authority and power. A Malay shaman, drawing authority from both Hinduism and Islam, outroars a thunderstorm:

> Om! Virgin goddess, Mahadewi! Om!
> Cub am I of mighty tiger!
> 'Ali's line through me descends!
> My voice is the rumble of thunder, . . .
> By virtue of my charm got from 'Ali

And of Islam's confession of faith. (Winstedt, 1925, p. 59)

Receptivity of the spiritual forces. The power of the incantation further derives from the people's shared understanding of the nature and receptivity of the spiritual powers to be moved and bound by the powerful words. That spiritual entity may be simply an object or person that is to perform in a certain way. At other times, the incantation invokes, with careful mention of names, spirits, or gods who control aspects of nature and life, empowering or binding them to act beneficially. Ritual specialists of Java, when burying the umbilical cord of a newborn baby, intone the following words: "In the name of God, the Merciful, the Compassionate! Father Earth, Mother Earth, I am about to leave in your care the birthcord of the baby. . . . Don't bother the baby. This is necessary because of Allah. If you do bother him, you will by punished by God" (Geertz, 1960, p. 46).

A great many incantations are addressed to evil spirits or demons, conjuring them to leave or stay away. It is extremely important that the incantor name and identify the origin and characteristics of the evil power in order to bind it. Pre-Spanish Maya incantations, for example, list detailed knowledge about the evil spirit of the disease, recounting its parentage, its lustful impulses that inspired its shameful birth, and all its characteristics; they then proceed to consign the spirit to the foul-smelling underworld or to cast it into the wind to fall behind the sky. An Aramaic incantation becomes very specific in naming one of the many demons: "I adjure you, Lilith Ḥablas, granddaughter of Lilith Zarnai, . . . the one who fills deep places, strikes, smites, casts down, strangles, kills, and casts down boys and girls, male and female foetuses," while another text conjures by name nearly eighty demons and spirits of evils or sicknesses (Isbell, 1975, pp. 61, 121–122), showing that, occasionally, an incantation will name a whole series of evil spirits and demons—just to be sure that the right one is included.

Connection of the chant with tradition. The successful operation of the incantation depends on its connection with the religious or mythological tradition of the people. In one way or another, the incantation fits the specific human circumstance into the larger pattern of sacred existence and power as known in the religion of the people. Incantations in which such patterns are made explicit can be called narrative incantations. For example, Scottish incantations are regularly grounded in stories or legends about Christ and his disciples, as in this example: "Christ went on an ass, / She sprained her foot, / He came down / And healed her foot; / As He healed that / May He heal this, / And greater than this, / If it be His will to do" (Carmichael, 1928, vol. 2, p. 17). An ancient Egyptian narrative incantation, relating at great length how Isis rescued her son Horus from a scorpion's bite, concludes with the main point: "It means that Horus lives for his mother—and that the sufferer lives for his mother likewise; the poison is powerless!" (Borghouts, 1978, pp. 62–69).

The accompanying ritual actions. While incantations can be used alone without any accompanying actions, in most cultures the chanting of incantations is usually associated with the power of other ritual actions. The incantation may be related to a ritual object that it empowers with sacred force. For treating a child with worms, the Javanese doctor chants over a special herb: "In the name of God, the Merciful, the Compassionate! Grandmother spirit, Grandfather spirit. . . . The harmful worms—may they all die. The good worms—may they stay for the whole length of the child's life" (Geertz, 1960, p. 93). Cherokee specialists almost always chant their incantations over tobacco, "remaking" or empowering the tobacco to perform the desired benefit. A Daoist priest chants this incantation over a small puppet as he rubs it over a patient: "Substitute, be thou in place of the fore part of the body, . . . be thou in place of the back parts, . . . be thou in place of the left side, that health may be ensured to him for year upon year" (de Groot, 1967, vol. 6, p. 1260). Incantation texts are often accompanied by directions for ritual actions. For example, an ancient Mesopotamian incantation for potency commands: "Let the ass swell up! Let him mount the jenny! Let the buck get an erection! Let him again and again mount the young she-goat!"; then the ritual directions follow: "Pulverized magnetic iron ore you put [into] puru oil; you recite the incantation over it seven times; the man rubs his penis, the woman her vagina with the oil, then he can have intercourse" (Biggs, 1967, p. 33). Incantation and ritual together accomplish the desired result.

FORMS OF ADDRESS. Within the great diversity of forms taken by the incantation formulas in different cultures and even within the same culture, a number of standard types can be discerned in the way spiritual powers are addressed. Many operate with the command form, using imperatives or statements of obligation to bind the spiritual powers to the desired action. Other incantations use the declaratory mode to establish the hoped-for result. And there are other incantations that approach the prayer mode, beseeching or charming the spiritual powers to take the beneficial action. Many times, of course, incantations use a combination of these three forms.

The command form, at its simplest, consists in naming the spiritual power and binding it to the desired action with an imperative. The High German "Pro Nessia" incantation from the ninth century CE, driving out the worm spirit that causes disease, is pure command:

> Go out, nesso,
> with the nine little ones,
> out from the marrow into the veins,
> from the veins into the flesh,
> from the flesh into the hide,
> from the hide into this arrow.
> Three paternosters. (Hampp, 1961, p. 118; my trans.)

In Burma, an exorcist addresses many powers of the supernatural world in a general incantation in order to focus his powerful command on the *ouktazaun* (minor spirit) that is possessing his client: "To all the *samma* and *brahma devas* of the sky heavens; to all the ghosts, monsters, and other evil creatures; to the ogres of the earth; to the master witches and the wizards; to the evil nats and the *ouktazauns:* I command you to leave. I command you by the glory of the Triple Gems [Buddha, Dhamma, and Sangha]" (Spiro, 1967, p. 177).

Very often incantations use a declaratory mode to perform the intended result of binding evil forces or compelling the good, declaring the desired state to be a reality in the present or the future. A Cherokee incantation designed to break up a happily married couple, for the benefit of a forgotten lover, simply declares the result to be so:

> Now! Very quickly pillow your head upon the Soul of the Dog, outside, where there is loneliness!
>
> Your name is ______.
>
> In the very middle of your two bodies loneliness has just come to think.
>
> You are to be broken in the Pathway.
>
> Now! Where the joining is has just come to be divided.
>
> Your two souls have just come to be divided somewhere in the Valley.
>
> Without breaking your soul, I have just come to stupefy you with the Smoke of the Blue Tobacco. (Kilpatrick and Kilpatrick, 1965, pp. 139–140)

When the Trobriand sorcerer tours the gardens with their budding leaves, he intones, "The yam rises and swells like a bush-hen's nest. The yam rises and swells like a baking-mound. . . . For these are my yams, and my kinsmen will eat them up. My mother will die of surfeit, I myself will die of repletion" (Malinowski, 1935, vol. 1, p. 146). It is in this declaratory mode that blessings and curses are often formulated, focusing on the person or thing to be involved and declaring the favorable or unfavorable state to be a reality.

A third mode of expression in many incantations is that of beseeching or charming the sacred powers to act benevolently. This form approaches that of prayer and, at times, is indistinguishable from it. Yet the typical expressions, "May you," "Let God," "I ask you," and the like, can also be understood as compelling or binding the spiritual powers, not just beseeching them. A Burmese doctor chants a prayer-spell over a sick girl, repeating it three times as he empowers many spiritual beings for action: "May the five Buddhas, the nats, and the Brahmas rest on the forehead [of the patient]; may Sakka rest on the eyes and ears, Thurasandi Devi on the mouth, and Matali on the hands, feet, and body, . . . and may they guard and protect me" (Spiro, 1967, p. 152). And the Malay incantor turns even to Iblis (Satan) and the other spirits and devils and firmly requests direct action on behalf of his lovesick client:

> In the name of God, the Merciful, the Compassionate!
> Friend of mine, Iblis!
> And all ye spirits and devils that love to trouble man!
> I ask you to go and enter the body of this girl,
> Burning her heart as this sand burns,
> Fired with love for me. (Winstedt, 1925, p. 165)

PURPOSES OF INCANTATION. Purposes for the use of incantation differ widely and cover the whole gamut of life needs of individuals and societies. It is possible, however, to classify incantations, according to their purpose, into three broad categories: defensive, productive, and malevolent.

Defensive incantations. Among defensive incantations, a major purpose is prophylactic or apotropaic, that is, warding off evil spirits and their troubles, especially in the critical passages of life. Classic among apotropaic incantations are those widespread in the ancient Near East, directed against demonic powers called liliths—ghostly paramours of men, who attack women during their periods and at childbirth and who devour children. An incantation bowl binds these demons:

> I adjure you, every species of lilith, in the name of your offspring which demons and liliths bore. . . . Woe, tramplers, scourgers, mutilaters, breakers, disturbers, squeezers, muzzlers, and dissolvers like water. . . . You are fearful, terrified, and bound to my exorcism, you who appear to the sons of men—to men in the likeness of women and to women in the likeness of men—you who lie with people during the night and during the day. (Isbell, 1975, pp. 17–18)

Vedic incantation from ancient India is directed against the fiends who cause pregnant women to abort: "The blood-sucking demon, and him that tries to rob health, Kanva, the devourer of our offspring, destroy, O Prisniparni [medicinal plant], and overcome!" (*Atharvaveda* 2.25.4, as cited in Bloomfield, 1964, p. 22). The Egyptian Coffin Texts testify to the need for incantations to ward off the evil powers who feast on the soul in the passage of death.

The other major use of defensive incantations is for the expulsion of evil powers that have taken up abode. A Malay Muslim shaman exorcises the demon of disease, reciting first the creation story and then chanting,

> Where is this genie lodging and taking shelter?. . .
> Genie! if thou art in the feet of this patient,
> Know that these feet are moved by Allah and His prophet;
> If thou are in the belly of this patient,
> His belly is God's sea, the sea, too, of Muhammad. . . .
> (Winstedt, 1925, pp. 62–63)

Sickness can also be seen as the result of attack by rival humans, and then the appropriate measure is a counterincantation. The Atharva priest of ancient India chants over a special ritual plant: "The spell which they skillfully prepare . . . we drive it away! . . . With this herb have I destroyed all spells. . . . Evil be to him that prepares evil, the curse shall recoil upon him that utters curses: back do we hurl it against him, that it may slay him that fashions the spell" (*Atharvaveda* 10.1.1, 4–5, as cited in Bloomfield, 1964, p. 72).

Productive incantations. A second purpose of incantation is beneficial, that is, it promotes growth, health, and happiness either by urging on the responsible inherent powers or by causing beneficial interference by divine powers. A curer in Java uses a massage and a spitting ritual with this incantation:

In the name of God, the Merciful, the Compassionate!
May the Prophet Adam repair [the person],
May Eve order [the person].
Untangle the tangled veins,
Right the dislocated bones,
Make the fluids of the body feel pleasant, . . .
Health falls with my white spittle,
Well, well, well, by the will of God. (Geertz, 1960, p. 94)

A great many incantations of the productive type have to do with love and sexual attraction, marriage, home and family, potency, successful birth, and the like. The Cherokee, for example, have a large variety of love incantations, for creating loneliness in the desired person, for retaining affection of a wandering mate, for acclimatizing a newlywed wife, or compelling a runaway spouse to return. Cherokee men and women can use incantations to "rebeautify" themselves and thus become attractive to a potential mate:

Now! I am as beautiful as the very blossoms themselves!

I am a man, you lovely ones, you women of the Seven Clans! . . .

All of you have just come to gaze upon me alone, the most beautiful.

Now! You lovely women, already I just took your souls! I am a man!

You women will live in the very middle of my soul.

Forever I will be as beautiful as the bright red blossoms! (Kilpatrick and Kilpatrick, 1965, pp. 86–87)

At times, productive incantations are needed to bring about pregnancy, as this one from ancient India: "Into thy womb shall enter a male germ, as an arrow into a quiver! May a man be born there, a son ten months old!" (*Atharvaveda* 3.23.2, as cited in Bloomfield, 1964, p. 97).

Malevolent incantations. A third purpose of incantation is related to the need to harm, punish, or take revenge on enemies or rivals. A jilted woman can target her erstwhile lover with this fierce imprecation:

As the best of the plants thou art reputed, O herb; turn this man for me today into a eunuch that wears his hair dressed! . . . Then Indra with a pair of stones shall break his testicles both! O eunuch, into a eunuch thee I have turned; O castrate, into a castrate thee I have turned! (*Atharvaveda* 6.138.1–3, as cited in Bloomfield, 1964, p. 108)

The Cherokee bent on revenge learns from the shaman to recite the name of his adversary, repeating the following incantation four times and blowing his breath toward him after each rendition: "Your Pathways are Black: it was wood, not a human being! Dog excrement will cling nastily to you. You will be living intermittently. . . . Your Black Viscera will be lying all about. . . . Your Pathway lies toward the Nightland!" (Kilpatrick and Kilpatrick, 1967, p. 127).

CONCLUSION. Incantations, as rhythmic or formulaic words of power used to accomplish a desired goal by binding spiritual powers, have sometimes been considered as magic rather than religion, or as a form of religious practice lower than prayer. It is true that incantations oblige the powers to perform the action rather than prayerfully request them for it. And it is also true that incantations have to do with self-interest, sometimes at the expense of others. Yet they do represent a religious mode of being in the world, albeit a mode of aggression rather than simple submission to spiritual powers. The power of chanted words fits the events of human life into the pattern of the sacred realities that underlie and support human existence. Far from being trivial, incantations provide help for whatever deeply troubles or concerns humans: health, birth, love, marriage, family, prosperity, death. Human existence is understood as a drama involving the interaction of many spiritual powers, and, through the power of the chanted formula, a restructuring of these powers is performed so that life can become more healthy, secure, prosperous, and happy.

SEE ALSO Magic; Mantra; Names and Naming; Spells.

BIBLIOGRAPHY

Among the many works that include incantations from all over the world, the following provide a representative survey from ancient, medieval, and modern cultures.

Biggs, Robert D. *Šà. zi. ga: Ancient Mesopotamian Potency Incantations.* Locust Valley, N.Y., 1967. Translations and textual studies of incantations used in Mesopotamian society for this universal sexual problem.

Bloomfield, Maurice, trans. and ed. *Hymns of the Atharva-Veda.* Delhi, 1964. Reprint of "Sacred Books of the East," vol. 42 (Oxford, 1897). Translations and interpretations of the most important incantations and hymns of the fourth Veda from ancient India by one of the outstanding American Sanskritists of the nineteenth century.

Borghouts, J. F., trans. *Ancient Egyptian Magical Texts.* Leiden, 1978. Translations of a representative range of incantations from ancient Egypt, dealing with concerns of everyday life, mostly from the Middle Kingdom and later.

Carmichael, Alexander. *Carmina Gadelica: Hymns and Incantations,* vol. 2. Edinburgh, 1928. Various incantations collected orally in the highlands and islands of Scotland and translated into English.

Geertz, Clifford. *The Religion of Java.* Glencoe, Ill., 1960. Extensive information about incantations in this important study of the Javanese religious system, which combines Islam and native spirit beliefs.

Grattan, J. H. G., and Charles Singer. *Anglo-Saxon Magic and Medicine.* Oxford, 1952. Some incantations and healing rituals especially from the semipagan text *Lacnunga,* translated into modern English.

Groot, J. J. M. de. *The Religious System of China* (1892–1910). 6 vols. Reprint, Taipei, 1967. Especially volume 6 of this multivolumed work contains traditional Chinese rituals and incantations against specters.

Hampp, Irmgard. *Beschwörung, Segen, Gebet: Untersuchung zum Zauberspruch aus dem Bereich der Volksheilkunde.* Stuttgart,

1961. A rich sourcebook for incantations from German cultures, providing also a study of types and purposes.

Isbell, Charles D. *Corpus of the Aramaic Incantation Bowls.* Missoula, Mont., 1975. Texts and translations of all the published Aramaic texts inscribed on incantation bowls, from Jewish-related societies in Babylon.

Kilpatrick, Jack Frederick, and Anna Gritts Kilpatrick. *Walk in Your Soul: Love Incantations of the Oklahoma Cherokees.* Dallas, 1965. Incantations used in situations of love and marriage among the Cherokee.

Kilpatrick, Jack Frederick, and Anna Gritts Kilpatrick. *Run toward the Nightland: Magic of the Oklahoma Cherokees.* Dallas, 1967. Incantations of the Cherokee for use in various situations.

Malinowski, Bronislaw. *Coral Gardens and Their Magic.* 2 vols. London, 1935. Texts of many incantations interspersed with descriptions of the Trobriand Islanders to the east of New Guinea, with important interpretations by this famous anthropologist.

Roys, Ralph L., trans. and ed. *Ritual of the Bacabs.* Norman, Okla., 1965. Translations of healing incantations from the pre-Spanish Maya culture.

Spiro, Melford E. *Burmese Supernaturalism: A Study in the Explanation and Reduction of Suffering.* Englewood Cliffs, N.J., 1967. A careful study of the Burmese spiritual world, including translations of incantations used in this Buddhist culture.

Winstedt, R. O. *Shaman, Saiva and Sufi: A Study of the Evolution of Malay Magic.* London, 1925. Includes translations of many incantations in a study of religious practices in Malay culture, which mixes Islamic, Hindu, and indigenous religious influences.

THEODORE M. LUDWIG (1987)

INCA RELIGION.

The pre-Columbian Andean cultures, of which the Inca empire was the final heir, extended over a geographical area that the Inca believed corresponded to the four quarters (*tahuantinsuyu*) of the world. At the time of the Inca empire's fall to Spanish forces under Francisco Pizarro in 1532, the Inca occupied large portions of present-day Ecuador, Peru, Bolivia, and Chile. The great Andean civilizations flourished in this setting of contrasting ecosystems (coastal desert ribbed with fertile valleys, arable highlands at altitudes of more than four kilometers, Amazonian and montane rain forests) that offered resources for pursuing a variety of means of subsistence, including fishing, hunting and gathering, agriculture, and the herding of llamas, guanacos, and alpacas.

HISTORICAL BACKGROUND. The great pre-Inca civilizations that flourished in what is now Peru were the Chavín (after about 800 BCE), the Nazca and Moche (c. 100–800 CE), the Tiahuanaco (c. 200–1000), the Huari (c. 800–1200), and the Chimu (c. 1200–1400). None of these cultures, the Inca included, appears to have possessed a written language, though this function was filled, to some extent, by the use of *quipus*, or knotted strings. (The geometric plastic arts of the ancient Andean peoples may one day be shown to comprise a system of ideograms.) Aside from scattered archaeological evidence—including figurative and abstract images on stone and wood, funerary pieces, and some fresco fragments—we possess documents (written in Spanish and, less frequently, in Quechua) that were composed during the years following the Conquest and that detail the religious practices of indigenous Andean peoples. (The Inca were reported to have painted mythological scenes on canvas and wood, but these are now lost.)

Despite their separation in time and the contrasts between their ecological milieus, the Andes high cultures and their religious systems manifested a common spirit. Religious practices permeated all aspects of public and private life. These religions for the most part included cults of the dead, of ancestors, of a founding culture hero, and of a divine king. Offerings and sacrifices (often human) were performed, and reflected beliefs in the needs of the "living corpse" and in the exigencies of the cosmic powers on which the cycles of nature depended. These deified powers were portrayed as monstrous beings that combined human, animal, and vegetable traits. The images of the principal deity throughout these cultures were basically variations on constant themes. This deity, which in images is variously characterized as an anthropomorphized feline (a puma or jaguar), a one- or two-headed serpent, a condor, or an ear of maize, is often portrayed brandishing weapons or other instruments.

The temples of the urban centers of these civilizations were built either in the form of truncated, stepped pyramids or as series of enclosures. Some possessed underground vaults, with or without labyrinths. In some locations, temple architecture is suggestive of the structure of the cosmos, comprising three vertical levels. Elsewhere, rows or circles of stones testify to astral observations and to cults connected to the organization of sacred time and space, in which the movements of the sun, moon, and stars, the alternations of day and night and dry and rainy seasons, the cycles of the earth and sea, and human, animal, and vegetable fecundity all seem to play a role. Calendars were based on the cycles—individually or in combinations—of the sun, the moon, the planet Venus, and the Pleiades. The Sun and Moon pair of deities and the pair composed of this couple's sons (often seen as enemy twins) were important pan-Andean deities. Among coastal groups, the Moon, represented in bird form and associated with the sea and the dead, was the preeminent deity. Divine symbols and religious rites were not, however, always directly related to the ecosystem within which the particular culture flourished, as is evident when one compares pre-Inca iconography with Inca mythology and with the myths of present-day Amazonian peoples.

INCA COSMOLOGY. The Inca religious system is usually attributed to either the Inca Tupac Yupanqui or his predecessor, the Inca Pachacuti, and dates to at most one hundred years before the European conquest. The expansion of Cuzco, the Inca capital, was carried out in the name of the superiority of its gods over those of other peoples who, once they were assimilated into the empire, left their principal idol (or its replica) in the Inca capital. The colonization, or federation, was founded on a system of reciprocity overseen by Cuzco. Certain cults and temples were richly endowed by the Inca (the title given the head of the empire); others were suppressed. The great social and religious leaders of the empire went regularly to the capital city, and the Inca brought colonies of collaborators (*mitima*) to the temples of the empire and sometimes had himself named priest of honor. The sanctuaries of the provinces paid tribute in kind to Cuzco, contributing, for example, young children to be sacrificed during the Capacocha ceremony, which was held to ensure the Inca's health and prosperity. Rites of communion were held periodically to ensure the political and religious cohesion of the empire. Generally, these rites took place at the Temple of the Sun, in the center of the *tahuantinsuyu,* which center was located at the junction of the two rivers of Cuzco. Slow processions or rapid messengers departed from and returned to this center, traveling along the roads that divided the empire into four regions (*chinchaysuyu* to the northwest, *antisuyu* to the northeast, *contisuyu* to the southwest, and *collasuyu* to the southeast) or along the forty-one *ceque* (theoretical lines radiating from the center, on which 428 shrines were placed), and returned. Although the Inca authorized the conservation of certain regional religious structures in the cities of the empire, they also reproduced Cuzco's geometrical organization of sacred space and built replicas of the capital's principal temples in all the ceremonial centers. The bipartition of villages and adjacent territories—the distribution in halves—was common throughout the Andes. In Cuzco these halves were called *hanan* (which roughly means "high, superior, right, masculine") and *hurin* ("low, inferior, left, feminine"). Other categories of opposition and complementarity could intersect or be superimposed over this base, determining various socioreligious complexes. Such halves (or moieties) were linked respectively with the cosmic powers of the lower and upper worlds, and with two cardinal points.

The inhabitants of the Andean region worshiped a great number of gods, idols, and spirits, which were designated by the generic name *huaca,* a term that was also applied to the shrines. The oral traditions frequently related the adventures of the great *huacas* (gods or parents of gods), their births and metamorphoses; the magical creation of wells, lakes, and irrigation canals; hunts, rivalries, wars, and conquests of lands, waters, and women who were captured by force or trickery; and the powers of the *huacas* over men and men's duties toward them. All this took place "in the time when the *huacas* were men . . . afterward they were turned into stone." Each family—and, at the higher level, each village and province—claimed to descend from a given *huaca* (a particular man-god, conquering ancestor, founder, or civilizer), who represented a cosmic power and whom they venerated in the form of a mummy, a stone, an animal, or a constellation of stars. The codification of these beliefs was founded on the oppositions and complementaries of nature—binary or ternary (e.g., man-woman, the head and the two arms), biological and parental, or cultural (conqueror-conquered, interior-exterior, etc.)—expressed in the representation of cosmic forces. Similarly, certain numbers, probably the results of astronomical calculations, gave order to the sacred.

INCA GODS. The kings of Cuzco, reputed to be sons of the Sun, formed a religious, cosmic, and territorial imperial structure in which the Sun reigned over the Andean highlands and the heavens and the god Pachacámac ruled over the lowlands and the underworld.

The Coricancha, the great Temple of the Sun in Cuzco, was flanked by two golden pumas and its walls were covered with gold and silver plaques. The halls contained statues and cosmic representations, and the mummies—or their replicas—of earlier kings and queens. There were three sculptural triads of the Sun; each included a father and two sons, each triad symbolizing, respectively, the heavenly body, its light, and its vital warmth. One of these statues, Punchao, depicts two pumas between whom is seated a man with serpents at his waist and rays emanating from his shoulders. It contained a reliquary filled with a powder made from the entrails of dead kings. The temple sheltered a large number of priests (the first priest was a close relative of the Inca) and the "virgins of the Sun" (*aclla*), who dedicated themselves to making cloth and corn beer for the cult of the Sun, and who also served as concubines to the Inca (who was himself the manifestation of the Sun) or to dignitaries.

From the dark bowels of the cosmos, Pachacámac caused earthquakes and sent pestilence. With his wife Pachamama ("mother of the earth"), he ruled the waters of the underworld, and, with his daughters, he controlled the depths of the sea. His temple was located at the seacoast. Although represented by a golden fox, he was also worshiped in the form of a wooden pillar, which was sculpted in a dark chamber atop a truncated adobe pyramid.

Illapa, who represented thunderbolts, lightning, rain, hail, snow, and frost, was venerated by a large cult in the highlands. He was conceived of as a triad (father, brother, and son). One of the three was represented by a man holding a club in one hand and a sling in the other. It was said that the *huacas*, sons of Illapa from whom various tribes were descended, had been thrown off a mountaintop and were raised by humans. They were identified with the mountain and became masters of its animals and plants. The mountains were personified and arranged hierarchically and were the object of a cult.

The serpent Amaru represented the striking thunderbolt and also the animal or monster who, according to the myths, rose from the lake and moved toward the upper world. With one head at each of his extremities, Amaru symbolized communication between the upper and lower parts of the cosmos.

Women were the principal participants in the cult of Quilla, the Moon, who was the sister and wife of the Sun.

The Coya ("queen") was believed to be the daughter of the Moon, just as the Inca was believed to be the son of the Sun. The anthropomorphic statues of Quilla were silver, while those of the Sun were gold. A lunar calendar was used along with a solar calendar. Quilla was associated with the earth and the dead. Traditionally, she pursued dead thieves into the underworld at night. One month of the year was especially sacred to her. Men also worshiped her, in Cuzco and elsewhere, particularly in the temple of Nusta, which was located on an island in Lake Titicaca.

When they were not visible, the stars, like the sun and the moon, were believed to go under the earth. The Milky Way—thought of as two rivers—may have inspired the construction of the Coricancha at the junction of the two rivers of Cuzco. Among the constellations, that of the llama, visible during the dry season, was of special importance to cattle raisers. The Pleiades were associated with the rainy season. If they appeared clearly at the end of May, a good harvest was augured.

After death, one of the two souls that were attributed to a man returned to its place of origin, either before or after a journey strewn with obstacles, and dwelt in the land of the souls, which was not unlike the world of the living. The kind of afterlife enjoyed by this soul was conditional on the type of death, social rank, and virtues of the dead. The other soul remained in the body, which had to be preserved intact, and which had the same needs as the living person. The bodies of nobles, kings, and queens were mummified, kept by their families, and often moved about. The mummies of ancient kings—or their replicas—were set out hierarchically in parallel series (*hanan* and *hurin*) of four. At the head was the common founding ancestor, theoretically androgynous, of whom the first was Manco Capac. The ancestors, associated with the netherworld and germination, were considered oracles of the past, the future, and distant events, and they were consulted by expert priests.

Viracocha was the supreme god of the Inca. The Spanish missionaries—monotheists and monogenists—would have liked to make him or perhaps Pachacámac into a creator god who was unique, abstract, and infinite. But in Andean thought, each tribe had been transformed (rather than created) from water, earth, animals, and so forth, by a particular god at the beginning of a cosmic cycle, and the role of all deities was to have given, and to continue to give, the breath of life and strength *(cama)* to humankind and to nature.

Viracocha was one of these personified gods. He was also a complex deity and was thought of as both one and many, the principle of transformation. Two others of his names were Con-Ticsi-Viracocha and Pachayachachic ("he who gives order to the world") and he had a large family with several sanctuaries. Viracocha was associated with water and the foam of Lake Titicaca, whence he had come, and with the foam of rivers and the surface of the ocean, where, according to some myths, he (in human form) disappeared to the northwest, walking on the waves. These attributes associated him with the rainy season, and others made him the representative of the fire of the heavens and of the triumphant Sun. Under the name of Huari Viracocha (an androgynous being) he was able to draw to himself all the cosmic functions of the upper and lower worlds. He had created the sun, the moon, the stars, and the prototypes of the Andean tribes—including the Inca—thus separating night from day and ushering in the solar cosmic cycle, which he entrusted to the Inca Manco Capac. The latter, accompanied by his brothers and sisters (the Ayars), was plunged into the earth by Viracocha and reemerged from the central window of Pacaritambo, to the south of Cuzco, at dawn, in order to reflect the first appearance of the sun. Viracocha's sons, Imaymana and Tocapu, taught the Andeans the names and virtues of the flora and fauna. Their travels, like Viracocha's, may have corresponded to astronomical observations.

Some prayers to Viracocha have been preserved. Around 1575, a number of prayers were recorded by Fray Cristóbal de Molina (collected in *Las crónicas de los Molinas,* Lima, 1943). The first of these may be rendered in English as follows:

> O Creator, you who are at the ends of the earth, peerless, who has given being and force to men, who has said, "Let this one be man and that one be woman." You made them, you gave them shape, you gave them being. Let them live in health, free from danger, in peace. Wherever you may be, whether up in the heavens, below with Thunder, or with the clouds of the storm, listen to me, answer me, grant me my prayer, give us eternal life. Keep us forever in your hand. This offering, receive it, wherever you are, O Creator.

Inca Rites. The Inca was considered to be the son of the Sun and the Earth, Viracocha's chosen one and equal. In this world, between the two vertical halves of the cosmos, he was the synthesis of their opposition, acting as center and mediator. A *huaca* himself, he had ambiguous powers over the *huacas*, with whom he either negotiated or made war. He contributed to the upkeep and vigor of the cosmic cycle in which he lived by seeing that the order of Pachayachachic was respected. Specialized priests (for such matters as divination, interpreting oracles, making sacrifices, hearing confessions, etc.) conducted the rites that measured the cycles of agriculture and husbandry, which were spread throughout the year, and which corresponded to the solstices and equinoxes, the alternation of rainy (October to March) and dry seasons, and the alternation of day and night. Each month a particular segment of Cuzco society dedicated itself to the prevailing cult. One of the most important festivals was Hanan Raymi (held at seedtime in December), during which the initiation rites of the young nobility took place, and after which the Citua was celebrated to expel the illnesses brought on by the rains. Another important ceremony was Inti Raymi, which took place at harvest time in June.

The great religious ceremonies were publicly celebrated in Cuzco. The sacrifices were designed to nourish and placate the gods, and offerings were selected from the great complementary ecosystems of nature (plants, birds, shells, the blood of animals—particularly llamas—and humans) and culture (maize, coca, pepper, corn beer, cloth, statuettes). At the center of the ceremonial place was the *usnu,* a small edifice on which the Inca sat enthroned and that was pierced at its base by underground canals leading to the temples of Viracocha, the Sun, and Illapa. Here the Sun was given "drink," which acted to placate and balance the powers of the lower and upper worlds. The *usnu* may also have served as an astronomical observatory. The golden statues of Viracocha, the Sun, and Illapa, the silver statue of the Moon, and the mummies of dead sovereigns—or their replicas—were set out on ceremonial occasions.

The performance of these ritual duties was also intended to ward off cataclysms *(pachacuti),* especially those caused by excessive heat ("suns of fire") or water (floods). Such cataclysms were believed to result from the dissatisfaction of the cosmic powers of the upper and lower worlds. They were believed to have occurred before, ushering in new cycles, and it was thought that they could happen again. These ideas, which were based on the observation of the movements of the sun and moon and the oppositions of day and night, dry and rainy seasons, and fire and water, were projected through time to construct an explanation of the history of the world. In any case, the important Quechua word *pacha* means both "time" and "space."

CONCLUSION. It is impossible to show in this short essay the wealth and the complexity of the official Inca religion, which was itself superimposed over the no less rich religions of the conquered provinces. Religion imbued and governed all private and public activities of the Andean people. Daily tasks and major undertakings alike were performed with equal passion and competitive spirit, for the dualism of the religion imparted its dynamism to society. The great ritual festivals of participation and communion involved the population from the capital as well as that from the countryside, thus assuring the cohesion of the social and ethnic groups of the empire. The deification of power guaranteed its intangibility and the stability of the social order. Finally, it is known that piety was general, and that members of the elite did not hesitate to offer their children for sacrifice.

To be sure, no Andean religious books exist. But there is much to discover in the colonial documents. Recent years have seen considerable progress, especially in scholarly knowledge of Andean astronomy. Religion, culture, and philosophy were built around several fundamental ideas: the opposition of contraries, the search for their conciliation in a harmonious equilibrium, and concern for the natural and human laws, which religion had as its object to predict and to regulate.

But this religion also had its failings in regard to the social order, owing especially to the importance attributed to the oracles and to the divinization of the Inca, factors that certainly facilitated the conquest of the empire by the Spaniards. Given the present state of Andean studies, it is difficult to talk about theology in connection with Inca religion. One can, however, speak of a complex metaphysic in connection with the major god Viracocha, the conception of whom was forced to enrich and complexify itself during the final days of the empire.

The religious spirit of the Andeans revealed its full intensity after the Spanish conquest, especially in the cruel but vain attempts to make the indigenous priests confess the locations of hidden treasures. After the official religion had been forbidden and destroyed by the invaders, after it had disappeared with the empire, the rural religions, which in general antedated the Inca conquest, continued to be practiced secretly despite the fierce assaults of the itinerant Inquisition upon the Indians. During the colonial centuries, the indigenous religions formed the core around that crystallized the spirit of resistance and the preservation of the cultural identity of the Andeans.

SEE ALSO Calendars, article on South American Calendars; Knots.

BIBLIOGRAPHY

Duviols, Pierre. *La lutte contre les religions autochtones dans le Pérou colonial: "L'extirpation de l'idolâtrie" entre 1532 et 1660.* Lima, 1971. A history of the itinerant Inquisition (called "the extirpation of idolatry") against the Indians, its methods and the reactions of the indigenous peoples.

Duviols, Pierre. "Punchao, ídolo mayor del Coricancha: Historia y tipología." *Antropología andina* 1 (1976): 156–182. Shows the continuity in one of the representations of the Andean solar god.

Duviols, Pierre. *La destrucción de las religiones andinas: Conquista y colonia.* Mexico City, 1977. Studies the means used to suppress the Andean religions and the efforts to replace them with Christianity.

Lumbreras, Luis G. *The Peoples and Cultures of Ancient Peru.* Washington, D.C., 1974.

Mariscotti de Görlitz, Ana María. *Pachamama Santa Tierra.* Berlin, 1978. Monograph on this topic.

Murra, John V. *The Economic Organization of the Inca State.* Greenwich, Conn., 1980. Numerous references to the economics of religion.

Pease, Franklin. *El pensamiento mítico.* Lima, 1982. Anthology of ancient Andean myth, preceded by a study.

Platt, Tristan. "Symétries en miroir: Le concept de *yanantin* chez les Macha de Bolivia." *Annales, economies, sociétés, civilisations* 33 (1978): 1081–1107. Analysis of the concepts of reflection and the double among the Macha of Bolivia.

Rostworowski de Diez Canseco, María. *Estructuras andinas del poder: Ideología religiosa y política.* Lima, 1983. Study of a large number of current works, focusing on the theme of dualism.

Rowe, John Howland. "The Origins of Creator Worship among the Incas." In *Culture in History: Essays in Honor of Paul Radin,* edited by Stanley Diamond, pp. 408–429. New York, 1960.

Taylor, Gerald. "*Camay, Camac,* et *camasca* dans le manuscrit Quechua de Huarochiri." *Journal de la Société des American-*

istes 63 (1974–1976): 231–244. Analyzes an important concept in Andean thought.

Urbano, Henrique. *Wiracocha y Ayar: Héroes y funciones en las sociedades andinas.* Cuzco, Peru, 1981. Anthology of ancient Andean myths, preceded by an attempt at interpretation using the trifunctional model of Georges Dumézil.

Urton, Gary. *At the Crossroads of the Earth and Sky: An Andean Cosmology.* Austin, 1981. Analysis of contemporary Andean astrological beliefs in terms of pre-Columbian Andean astronomy.

Zuidema, R. Tom. *The Ceque System of Cuzco: The Social Organization of the Capital of the Inca.* Leiden, 1962. Analyzes the geometrical and arithmetical organization of the sacred space of Cuzco.

Zuidema, R. Tom. "Mito e historia en el antiguo Perú." *Allpanchis* (Cuzco) 10 (1977): 15–52.

Zuidema, R. Tom. "Hierarchy and Space in Incaic Social Organization." *Ethnohistory* 30 (1983): 49–75.

New Sources

Bauer, Brian S. *The Sacred Language of the Inca: The Cusco Ceque System.* Austin, Tex., 1998.

Dean, Carolyn. *Inka Bodies and the Body of Christ: Corpus Christi in Colonial Cuzco, Peru.* Durham, N.C., 1999.

Drasat, Penny. *Elemental Meanings: Symbolic Expression in Inka Miniature Figurines.* London, 1995.

MacCormack, Sabine. *Religion of the Andes: Vision and Imagination in Early Colonial Peru.* Princeton, N.J., 1991.

Salles-Reese, Veronica. *From Viracocha to the Virgin of Copacabana: Representation of the Sacred at Lake Titicaca.* Austin, Tex., 1997.

Sullivan, William. *Secret of the Incas: Myth, Astronomy and the War against Time.* New York, 1996.

Urton, Gary. *The History of a Myth: Pacariqtamba and the Origin of the Inkas.* Austin, Tex., 1990.

Villoldo, Alberto, and Erik Jenresen. *Journey to the Island of the Sun: The Return to the Lost City of Gold.* San Francisco, 1992.

PIERRE DUVIOLS (1987)
Translated from French by Erica Meltzer
Revised Bibliography

INCARNATION. The concept of incarnation (Lat., *incarnatio,* "being in flesh") has been applied in the Christian community to the mystery of union between divinity and humanity in the person of Jesus Christ. More generally, the concept has been extended to take into account a variety of forms of incarnation that the history of religions has described in various lands and among different peoples. The term *incarnation* is broadly defined here as the act or state of assuming a physical body (as a person, an animal, a plant, or even an entire cosmos) by a nonphysical entity such as the soul, the spirit, the self, or the divine being.

Typologically speaking, there are two sharply contrasting evaluations of incarnation. One of them is a tragic view, according to which the union of the soul, the spirit, or the self with the world of matter, hence with the physical body, is interpreted as a fall from its proper place into an alien abode, an imprisonment, or an enslavement. Salvation consists, according to this view, in the soul's escape from the world into which it has fallen by dissociating and liberating itself through purifications, rites of initiation, or meditation, from the chains of its captivity. There is, on the other hand, a positive interpretation of incarnation, which sees the assumption of a bodily form by the soul, the spirit, or the divine being as occurring for the purpose of saving or sanctifying the phenomenal world. This type of bodily manifestation is seen, for example, in the leaders of small tribal communities, the founders of religions, and the heads of theocratic states. In a certain sense, the history of religions has been the history of persistent battles fought between these two distinctive visions of the incarnation.

THE "PRIMITIVE" TRADITION. The belief in the divine incarnate can be attested as early as the late Paleolithic period, in a considerable number of pictures of human beings in animal forms, often in dancing posture. Among the best known is a figure of the "great sorcerer" in a Trois Frères cave, sporting a deer's head crowned with huge antlers. The same cave has also preserved the portrayal of a dancer disguised as a bison, playing a bow-shaped instrument, possibly a kind of flute. It is certain that the early hunters wore masks and skins of animals for the celebration of their magico-religious ceremonies. These masked figures and many parallel examples were probably believed to be the incarnations of spirits or divine beings akin to the Lord of the Animals.

Wearing masks has been one technique for incarnating souls or spirits in premodern societies. In Inner Asia, for example, a shaman's mask symbolizes the incarnation of a mythical personage (ancestor, mythical animal, or god). For its part, the costume transforms the shaman into a spiritual being. In Polynesia and Melanesia, the souls or spirits of dead ancestors are believed to come from the land of the dead at certain fixed times, especially when the old year passes into the new year. They appear in disguise, wearing terrifying masks and strange costumes; the "dead" call on villagers, praising them for their good conduct and rebuking them severely for any wrongdoing they have committed. The "dead" also perform the rites of initiation for young novices. Finally, they give blessings for a good crop in the coming months and, after receiving hospitality from the villagers, return to their homeland far across the sea. In fact, the spirits of the dead are impersonated by members of secret societies (e.g., the Dukduk of the Bismarck Archipelago, the Arioi of the Marquesas Islands), but these awe-inspiring "sacred visitors" wield such terror over the noninitiated that they are truly believed to be the incarnations of the ancestral spirits. Significantly, the arrival of the spirits from the world beyond announces the renewal of time, the advent of the new year, and the renovation of the entire universe. A similar belief in the sacred visitors (*marebito*) is also attested in Japan.

The belief in the preexistence and incarnation of souls is abundantly documented in the "primitive" world. According to the Caribou Inuit (Eskimo), for example, the immortal soul of a dead person leaves his body, ascending to the supreme being Pinga in heaven who receives it. If the person lived properly according to the rules of life, Pinga lets the soul assume a bodily form, human or animal. Such a belief is also widespread among the North American Indians. Especially noteworthy is the belief found among the Aranda in central Australia, according to which every human being has two souls: the mortal soul, which comes into being with the fetus as a result of intercourse between the parents, and the immortal soul, which predates and really creates the entire human personality. More concretely, the immoral soul is a particle of life of the totemic ancestor who unfolded his sacred history in the beginning of mythical time; every individual is what he is today because of the incarnation in him of the immortal soul, a spark of his primeval ancestor's life. The Aranda becomes aware of this mystery of life as he undergoes the rites of initiation, in which he learns the sacred history of his ancestors. It is a sort of anamnesis, a remembering of the preexistence of his immortal soul in the mythical sacred history—a recollection accompanied by the acute realization of the immortal soul's involvement in temporary, phenomenal existence.

Greece, India, Iran. The ancient Greek doctrine of metempsychosis presupposes the incarnation of preexistent and immortal souls in successive bodies, human and animal, and even in inanimate substances. Pythagoras certainly believed in the transmigration of souls (Xenophanes, frag. 7); according to him, the human soul, despite its immortality, has been imprisoned in the body and condemned to a cycle of reincarnation due to the fall from its original state of bliss. A similar idea was held by Empedocles: The immortal human soul has fallen from its proper abode into the world, into the physical body, due to its primal sin. Condemned to the physical world, the fallen soul is destined to wander through a series of incarnations until it is restored to the primeval state of bliss from which it has fallen. Plato contrasts the immortal part of the soul, which the Demiurge has created, with the mortal part, including perception, which is added by the created deities at the moment of union with the body (e.g., *Timaeus* 69c–d). Immediately before incarnation, the immortal soul drinks from the waters of Lethe ("forgetfulness"); "burdened with a load of forgetfulness and wrongdoing," the soul "sheds her wings and falls to the earth" (*Phaedrus* 248c), that is, it falls into the physical world, into the body that is a "tomb" (*Gorgias* 493c), imprisoned by the cycle of becoming and incarnation. But, it is still possible for the immortal soul to learn, to recall its extraterrestrial experience of the perfect condition that existed prior to the fall (cf. especially *Meno* 81c–d). For Plato, to live fully and meaningfully is, after all, to remember a discarnate, purely spiritual existence; it is an anamnesis of the soul's true identity, that is, a recognition of its heavenly origin.

This Greek mythology of the soul, more or less hostile to the world of matter and the physical body, was incorporated into Gnosticism, a set of doctrines characterized by anticosmic dualism. Humankind, as viewed by the Gnostics, is constituted by three components: the self, the soul, and the body. The physical body belongs to the deficient world of nature (*phusis*), but the soul is also part of this evil world. Psychic human activities arise from and are limited by the continual flux of natural events. It is only the self that transcends the evil world. It is divine in nature, hence not subject to time and change; it is indestructible. Where is the original home of the divine self, the spiritual part of humanity? The Gnostic myth narrates, with manifold variations, the fate of the self, its origin in the world of light, its tragic fall into the alien world, and its imprisonment in the physical body. Salvation consists, in the last analysis, in the emancipation of the self from the dark world of matter and the physical body and its return to its genuine home, the world of light.

India presents a doctrine similar to gnosticism, namely, Sāṃkhya-Yoga, whose central message may be summed up as follows: (1) humanity's destiny in the world is conditioned by the mysterious interplay between the self (*puruṣa*), which is indestructible, eternal, and not subject to change, and matter (*prakṛti*), which is subject to time and transformation and which constitutes humankind's psychophysiological complex; (2) the self is essentially a stranger to the world of matter, into which for unknown reasons it has fallen and been enslaved, resulting in the oblivion of its original, true identity; and (3) deliverance (*mokṣa*) begins when the self remembers its eternal freedom and tries to dissociate itself through the practice of yoga from the world of matter.

However, in India the tragic view of the incarnation coexists peacefully with another, more positive view. The Hindu god Viṣṇu, out of his profound concern for the welfare of the universe, has frequently embodied himself wholly or partially in the phenomenal world. According to one of the earliest versions of the doctrine contained in the *Bhagavadgītā*, he incarnates himself in the person of Kṛṣṇa, but he is also able to manifest himself in other bodily forms, human and animal. "Whenever the law of righteousness withers away," Viṣṇu declares, "I come into being age after age for the protection of the good, for the destruction of evildoers, and for the setting up of the law of righteousness" (*Bhagavadgītā* 4.7–8). While Hindu myths and rituals have concentrated attention on Viṣṇu's ten primary incarnations, in some formulations four saviors appear as his *avatāras*, or incarnations, each ushering in one of the four cosmic ages constituting a *mahāyuga,* a complete cosmic cycle. In the *kṛtayuga,* which lasts 4,800 divine years (with one divine year corresponding to 360 human years), Viṣṇu makes his appearance as the sage Kapila, while in the *tretāyuga,* lasting 3,600 divine years, he appears as the universal monarch Cakravartin. In the third cosmic age, *dvāparayuga,* of 2,400 divine years, the supreme being incarnates himself as the sage Vyāsa, and in the final cosmic age, *kaliyuga,* lasting 1,200 divine years, he will manifest himself as Kalki, a sort of messianic figure who will come in glory to establish the golden age, judging the wicked, rewarding the virtuous, and ruling over the entire universe in peace and prosperity.

The ancient Iranians of the Parthian period had an ardent hope or expectation for Mithra incarnate, who would come at the end of the world as the great universal monarch and savior. This king and savior will descend on the Mount of Victories in the form of a column of light or a shining star to be born in a cave. He will be given birth by a human mother, but in truth he is of heavenly origin; he descends from above with the light, that is, he is the child of light. There were, in fact, magi who lived near the Mount of Victories; every year, at a certain fixed date, they climbed the mountain in which there was a cave, and quietly prayed to the heavenly god for three days, waiting for the appearance of the star.

KINGS, EMPERORS, IMAMS. The status of kings was often defined in terms of God incarnate. In ancient Egypt, for example, the king was believed to be divine in essence. His coronation, usually celebrated at the beginning of the new year, signified not an apotheosis but an epiphany, a self-manifestation of the god. As long as he ruled, the king was identified with the god Horus; in fact, he was Horus incarnate in his early existence, but upon his death he was mystically assimilated to Osiris, the god of rebirth and immortality.

The Greco-Roman world generally dissociated itself from the notion that the king was the incarnation of a certain god, despite the fact that royal titles such as *The Young Dionysos* and *Epiphanes* were often used by kings in the Hellenistic period. According to Arthur Darby Nock, the only exception was Ptolemy XIII of the mid-first century BCE, who demonstrably considered himself to be Dionysos incarnate, probably under the influence of the pharaonic conception of the king as Horus incarnate.

While the Chinese emperor was generally called Son of Heaven (*tianzi*) and as such was considered the earthly representative of Heaven or heavenly will, some emperors were regarded as incarnations of the Buddha. For example, the founder of the Northern Wei dynasty (386–534), Taizi, was regarded by the eminent monk Faguo as the Tathāgata in person, an incarnation of the Buddha. This idea was iconographically represented in the caves of Yungang to the west of Datong, the capital of the empire until 494. Moreover, toward the end of the seventh century the Empress Wu Zhao, who was a strong supporter of Buddhism, was considered to be the incarnation of Maitreya, the future Buddha. Among the Tibetans, the Dalai Lama has been accepted as an incarnation of the bodhisattva Avalokiteśvara.

In ancient Japan, the emperor was explicitly called the *akitsumi kami* ("manifest *kami*"), that is, the god who manifested himself in human form in the phenomenal world. The essential part of the Japanese conception of sovereignty was the belief in the emperor's heavenly origin, and this belief was clearly expressed in the myths of Ninigi, the grandson of the sun goddess Amaterasu. Ninigi is born in the heavenly world and then descends onto the summit of Mount Takachiho, carrying the three items of the sacred regalia as well as the heavenly mandate guaranteeing his eternal sovereignty on earth. The emperor was identified with this mythic figure at the annual harvest festival as well as on the occasion of his enthronement festival.

In Islam, more particularly among the Shīʿah, the imam enjoyed a truly exalted and significant status; while among the Sunnīs an imam is no more than a leader of congregational prayer at a local mosque, among the Shīʿah the imam was endowed with a power at once political and religious. Like the caliph, he was one who ruled the community in mercy and justice, but unlike the caliph, who had no legal authority, the imam was empowered to interpret the *ḥaqīqah,* or esoteric meanings of the Qurʾān and Islamic law. This power was based on the Shīʿah conviction that Muḥammad's charisma, or spiritual gift, which he received from God, would be transmitted genealogically only within his household. It was natural that the imam became the central focus of Shīʿah faith to such an extent that he was believed to be the embodiment of the divine light. Some extreme sects of the Ismaʿīlī movement went even further in believing that the imam was the incarnation of the godhead itself. The Druze of the Lebanon Mountains hold the Caliph Ḥākim (r. 996–1021) of the Fatimid dynasty in Egypt to be the incarnation of the godhead, now in concealment but with the promise of a return.

BUDDHISM. Buddhism was founded by Siddhārtha Gautama of the Śākya clan in India, who left his home in quest of truth, devoted himself to the practice of meditation, and finally attained enlightenment. Hence he is also called the Buddha, the Enlightened One. During the early centuries of the history of Buddhism, this historical Buddha commanded the primary attention of Buddhists.

However, as a new trend of the Buddhist movement called the Mahāyāna developed in the course of the second century BCE, a shift occurred in Buddhology; emphasis was now placed less on the historical Buddha than on the Eternal Buddha. This Eternal Buddha is transcendent, absolute, and infinite, embodying the universal and cosmic truth. Hence he is called the *dharmakāya* ("body of the law"), the essential Buddha who is the ultimate reality as viewed by Mahāyāna Buddhism. The Eternal Buddha does not wish, however, to hold himself aloof from the phenomenal world; out of his deep compassion for humanity in pain and suffering he has incarnated himself in the person of Siddhārtha Gautama, as the *nirmāṇakaya* ("body of transformation").

This doctrine is elaborated, for example, in the *Saddharmapuṇḍarīka Sūtra,* also known as the *Lotus Sūtra.* The scripture presents the Buddha in two aspects: his absolute aspect in the form of the Eternal Buddha, which is dealt with in the section following chapter 15, while the section preceding this chapter is concerned with his relative aspect in the person of the historical Śākyamuni Buddha, who assumed human form for the sake of benefiting all sentient beings. According to the doctrine of the "Tendai school" in medieval Japan, the absolute and the relative are in essence qualitatively equal; they represent the two different aspects of the Buddha but, in reality, are one and the same.

Japanese Buddhism, more particularly, the Shingon school of Buddhism, has also unfolded what may be called a cosmotheism, a fascinating conception of the cosmos as the embodiment of the Buddha Mahāvairocana. The place of central importance in Shingon Buddhism is occupied no longer by the historical Buddha but rather by the Cosmic Buddha Mahāvairocana (Jpn., Dainichi, "great sun"); just as the sun is the source of light, illuminating the whole universe and giving life to all forms of existence, so Mahāvairocana is the Great Illuminator of all existence, both animate and inanimate. He is transcendent, absolute, and eternal because he is identified with the *dharmakāya.* However, Mahāvairocana is not only transcendent but also immanent in the universe. This Buddha is cosmic in nature because, according to Shingon Buddhism, he embodies himself in the six great elements constituting every form of existence in the universe: earth, water, fire, wind, space, and mind. These six elements are interfused and in a state of eternal harmony. In fact, the whole universe is viewed as the "*samaya* (symbolic) body" of the Buddha Mahāvairocana. When the universe is referred to as the Buddha's *samaya* body, it means two things at the same time: First, the cosmos symbolizes and points to the ultimate reality, Mahāvairocana identified with the *dharmakāya;* and second, while the ultimate reality embodies itself in the cosmos, for its part the cosmos participates substantially in the ultimate reality itself. Accordingly, the cosmos is a sanctified world endowed with the quality of the sacred, assuming profound soteriological value.

CHRISTIANITY. That God was incarnated in the person of Jesus of Nazareth in order to save humankind is a basic tenet of Christianity. One of the earliest confessions of faith pronounced by the primitive church (*Phil.* 2:6–2:11) speaks of the preexistent divine figure Christ Jesus, who condescended to take on human form, won victory in his death over the cosmic forces of evil, and reigns now with God in heaven. In the *Gospel of John,* dating from the end of the first century, Christ Jesus is presented as the incarnate Word (Logos) of God (*Jn.* 1:1–1:14). In sharp contrast to the portrait of the life of Jesus in the synoptic Gospels, John identifies him as the preexistent divine being who, descending from heaven, moves mysteriously through human life, proclaiming heavenly messages and working miracles, and who even foretells his ascension to heaven following his impending suffering and death. John's language may sound preeminently Gnostic, but the content of his central message, namely, that the divine Logos had become human flesh, was certainly anti-Gnostic.

Christian Gnostics accepted the belief that Christ was the divine Logos, the chief intermediary between God and humans. However, they rejected the idea that the Logos took on human flesh, because to them the flesh was both evil and insubstantial. Characteristically, they denied the reality or historicity of the incarnation: The human life of Christ was spiritual but not material; Christ hovered over mortal life, never really participating in the birth, suffering, and death of the historical Jesus. The Christian church set itself against this docetic view in such affirmation of the Apostles' Creed as "God the Father Almighty, creator of heaven and earth." By implication this was an affirmation of the goodness of all God's creation, material as well as spiritual. Similar affirmations concerning Jesus' birth, suffering, and death were directed against the Gnostic denial of the incarnation of Jesus Christ. Moreover, the assertion in the Apostles' Creed of the resurrection of the dead affirmed the salvation of the whole person and not merely the discarnate soul, spirit, or self. It is thus significant that Christian orthodoxy affirmed the humanity of Christ and the goodness and reality of the cosmos against Gnosticism and any form of the Gnostic view of man and the universe. "After the Incarnation," Mircea Eliade states in his *Myth and Reality* (p. 172), "the World has been reestablished in its original glory." The phenomenal world, humanity's world, the world as it is, is a *sanctified* cosmos because Jesus Christ the Savior has dwelt in it.

The Christian church attempted to articulate the nature of the person of Jesus Christ as God incarnate at the First Council of Nicaea (325). It adopted a creed that included such phrases to define Christ as "begotten not made," "begotten before all ages," and "of one essence with the Father." Thus Christ was declared to be *homo-ousios,* "consubstantial," with God the Father, a doctrine that was to be formulated later by Augustine as *una substantia tres personae* ("one substance in three persons"); Christ was essentially divine without being a kind of "second God." Once this result was generally accepted, a further question arose: How are the divine and human elements related to each other in the person of the historical Jesus? After apparently endless debates and anathemas, the orthodox view was formulated at the Council of Chalcedon (451): Two natures of Christ, divine and human, are perfectly blended in one person; Jesus Christ is *vere Deus vere homo* ("truly God and truly man").

TWENTIETH-CENTURY VIEWS. While the affirmative view of incarnation has apparently won the victory, the tragic view of the destiny of the soul, as it was classically expressed by Plato, Gnosticism, and Sāṃkhya-Yoga, is far from dead; on the contrary, it has often asserted itself ever since. In fact, as Martin Buber has aptly stated, human self-understanding has gained "depth" in those crisis periods in history when humankind has felt homeless in the physical world in which it lives, becoming aware of its acute alienation from the world. The twentieth century, one such crisis period, demonstrated a keen interest in the Gnostic outlook on life and the universe, as it is reflected in the writings of C. G. Jung, Hermann Hesse, and Martin Heidegger. For Heidegger, for example, the world is no longer a home for modern humankind but an alien realm; humanity is homeless in the world. Moreover, humankind lives in a period of cosmic night, and the darkness of this cosmic night is to continue for some time. According to him, the soul is not in its proper place in this evil world; here, it is a stranger, imprisoned in the physical body. The soul is destined to leave this world behind and, becoming "a blue soul," to set out for the dark wandering, journeying toward the land of the evening.

SEE ALSO Avatāra; Docetism; Kingship; Masks; Reincarnation; Soul.

BIBLIOGRAPHY

There is no single book dealing with the problem of incarnation in the general history of religions. On masks and their religious meaning in prehistory, see Johannes Maringer's *Vorgeschichtliche Religion: Religionen im steinzeitlichen Europa* (Einsiedeln, Switzerland, 1956), pp. 184ff., edited and translated by Mary Ilford as *The God of Prehistoric Man* (New York, 1960), pp. 146ff.

Hutton Webster offers basic information on the periodic return of the ancestral spirits in Polynesia and Melanesia in his *Primitive Secret Societies* (New York, 1980). On the Aranda conception of the immortal soul, there is a fascinating account in Mircea Eliade's *Australian Religions: An Introduction* (Ithaca, N.Y., 1973), pp. 44–59.

The incarnation of the soul in the Greek philosophical tradition has been competently discussed by W. K. C. Guthrie in *The Earlier Presocratics and Pythagoreans* (pp. 306ff.) and *The Presocratic Tradition from Parmenides to Democritus* (pp. 249ff.), volumes 1 and 2 of his *A History of Greek Philosophy* (Cambridge, U.K., 1962 and 1965). The best single book on the Gnostic view of the destiny of humankind and its immortal soul in the world remains Hans Jonas's *The Gnostic Religion,* 2d ed., rev. (Boston, 1963). On Sāṃkhya-Yoga, there is a concise account in Robert C. Zaehner's *Hinduism* (London, 1962), pp. 67ff. Focusing his attention on the fate of the immortal self in the world, Mircea Eliade has compared Gnosticism with Sāṃkhya-Yoga in his essay "Mythologies of Memory and Forgetting," now included in his *Myth and Reality* (New York, 1963), pp. 114–138. There is a fine comparative study of the avatar beliefs of India and the Christian doctrine of the incarnation in Geoffrey Parrinder's *Avatar and Incarnation* (New York, 1970).

The eschatological expectation of the birth of the savior Mithra in ancient Iran has been elucidated by Geo Widengren in his *Iranisch-semitische Kulturbegegnung in parthischer Zeit* (Cologne, 1960), pp. 62–86. See also Mircea Eliade's *Méphistophélès et l'androgyne* (Paris, 1962), pp. 60ff., translated by J. M. Cohen as *The Two and the One* (Chicago, 1965), pp. 51–55.

Major problems of Greco-Roman kingship have been discussed authoritatively by Arthur Darby Nock in volume 1 (pp. 134ff.) and volume 2 (pp. 928ff.) of his *Essays on Religion and the Ancient World* (Cambridge, Mass., 1972), with an introduction by Zeph Stewart. On the conception of kingship in ancient Japan, see my article "Sacred Kingship in Early Japan: A Historical Introduction," *History of Religions* 15 (1976): 319–342.

Mahāyāna Buddhism has attempted to explain the historical Buddha Śākyamuni as an incarnation of the Eternal Buddha. See, in this connection, a brief but illuminating account of the doctrine of the "three bodies" (*trikāya*) of the Buddha by T. R. V. Murti, *The Central Philosophy of Buddhism,* 2d ed. (London, 1970), pp. 284–287. On the conception of the cosmos as the embodiment of the Buddha Mahāvairocana, see *Kūkai: Major Works,* translated, with an account of Kūkai's life and a study of his thought, by Yoshito S. Hakeda (New York, 1972), pp. 76ff.

On the history of the Christian doctrines of the incarnation, there is an admirable account by Jaroslav Pelikan in *The Emergence of the Catholic Tradition, 100–600,* volume 1 of his *The Christian Tradition* (Chicago, 1971).

New Sources

Bassuk, Daniel. *Incarnation in Hinduism and Christianity: The Myth of the God-Man.* Basingstoke, U.K., 1987.

Cross, Richard. *The Metaphysics of the Incarnation: Thomas Aquinas to Duns Scotus.* New York, 2002.

Davies, Oliver, and Denys Turner, eds. *Silence and the Word: Negative Theology and Incarnation.* New York, 2002.

Kingston, Richard. *God and One Person: The Case for Non-Incarnational Christianity.* Basingstoke, U.K., 1993.

Luoma, Tapio. *Incarnation and Physics: Natural Science in the Theology of Thomas F. Torrance.* New York, 2002.

Sheth, Noel. "Hindu Avatara and Christian Incarnation: A Comparison." *Philosophy East and West* 52 (January 2002): 98–126.

Smith, James K. A. *Speech and Theology: Language and the Logic of Incarnation.* New York, 2002.

MANABU WAIDA (1987)
Revised Bibliography

INCENSE. The term *incense* (from Latin *incendere,* to burn or kindle) has the same meaning as the word *perfume,* i.e., the aroma given off with the smoke (*per fumar*) of an odoriferous substance when burned. Incense may then be associated with the perfume arising from the burning of substances that produce a pleasant odor. Aloe, camphor, cloves, sandalwood, myrrh, frankincense, cedar, juniper, balsam, galbanum, and turpentine have been used as incense. Since ancient times incense has been an important part of religious rites and practices in various regions of the world. Incense has been used to appease the gods, sanctify a place or an object, display reverence and respect, honor commitments, tie bonds, and seal promises and friendships. Valued as a precious commodity, it was offered as a gift to honored personages: Frankincense and myrrh were two of the gifts the wise men of the East brought to the infant Jesus.

In association with concepts of purity and pollution, incense plays a major role in purification rites and customs. Incense smoke is used for these purposes because of the transforming powers of fire, as well as the seemingly purificatory powers of sweet smells. Because its fragrance is thought to be pleasing to the gods, incense has played an important role in worship and is used in ceremonies of offering, prayer, intercession, or purification. It is used to attract the attention of, or establish a connection with, a deity and is also used to exorcise evil or harmful forces.

The Far East and India. In Chinese, the word *xiang* can mean both "aromatic" and "incense." In China incense was sometimes burned in conjunction with aesthetic enjoyments like reading, writing compositions, or performing music; in Japan it was an important part of the tea ceremony. In Chinese Daoism, incense was used to disperse evil and to appease the gods; it was also employed in rituals for the cure of disease. Considered a punishment for evil deeds committed by the sufferer himself or by an ancestor, illness was regarded as a punishment by the San Guan (Three Officials), the judges and officials of the dead. During the rituals for curing sickness, a formal appeal was made to mitigate and revoke the officials' judicial severity. Using the rising flame and smoke from the incense burner in the center of the oratory to transmit a message borne by spirits exteriorized from within his own body, the Daoist libationer submitted petitions (*zhang*) to the appropriate bureau of the Three Heavens (San Tian), where officials pronounced judgment on the appeal and marshaled celestial forces against the offending demons responsible for the illness. Incense played a major role in another Daoist ritual for fending off disease, the Mud and Soot Retreat or Retreat of Misery. The ritual was usually performed outdoors at a specially delimited sacred area, or altar (*tan*). It was a ceremony of collective contrition where the combined effects of clouds of incense, the light of many lamps, and the sound of the chanted liturgy produced a cathartic experience in the participants.

Incense is also central to the Daoist Jiao liturgy, which renews the community through communication with the gods. Jiao rites may be held for the ordination of priests or the birthdays of gods or may be held to ward off calamities. For the Jiao ritual, a village feast is held outside the temple, and an esoteric liturgy is performed inside the closed temple. In the temple ritual the main incense burner, the central object in the temple, is the focus of the rite. A symbolic incense burner is "lighted" inside the body of the main priest, whose meditation transforms him into a mediator with the divine and makes possible the efficacy of the rite. Incense is employed for the ecstatic symbolic journey to heaven performed inside a sacred area demarcated by five buckets of rice. Together with the burning incense, a document is burned ("sent off to heaven") as a "memorial to the throne" (*zhang*), which announces to Heaven the performance of the liturgy.

Incense also forms an important part of the Buddhist ritual ceremonies in Korea. When taking the vows of Buddhist priesthood, young initiates undergo a rite called Pultatta, or "receiving the fire." In this ceremony a moxa, or cone of burning incense, is laid upon the arm of the novice after the hair has been shaved off; the ignited cone is then allowed to burn slowly and painfully into the flesh. The remaining scar is considered a mark of dedication and holiness and commemorates the ceremony of initiation. Incense is used in ancestor worship as well; tablets containing the names of the departed written in gilt and black characters are placed on every household altar, where sacrifices are offered and incense burned.

At least until the late nineteenth century, incense timekeepers were used in Japanese Buddhist temples to mark the intervals at which the priest struck the great bell to call the people to prayer. The use of incense to measure time was an idea borrowed from China, and so in Japan these sticks were called "Chinese matches." In China the first literary mention of incense being used as a time indicator appears in the sixth century, although it may have been used much earlier. It was widely used from the tenth century on. To make the timekeepers, hardened-paste incense was prepared in sticks or spiral coils and marked into hourly intervals. Depending on the season, the burning time of the sticks was usually between seven to eleven *ke,* one *ke* being equivalent to about a half an hour of modern time. Sometimes a continuous trail of powdered incense was marked off into equal lengths and burned to indicate how much time had passed. The legacy of using incense sticks as timekeepers has been transferred to Hawai'i, where many Japanese and Chinese have migrated.

In India, incense is used in both Hindu and Buddhist rituals. In Hindu rites it is offered in temples as an act of homage before the statue of the devity; in the *āratī* ceremony, for instance, the increase censer or stick is rotated before the image of the deity in order to make an offering and evoke blessings. Fragrant incense was also used to waft prayers to the gods and to drive off foul-smelling demons.

The Ancient Near East. In ancient Egypt, incense was frequently used in cultic rituals. According to Plutarch, the Egyptians burned incense to the sun three times a day; Herodotos recounts that incense was daily burned before an image of a cow. Sacrifices were offered to the pharaoh, and incense was burned before him in the coronation procession. The importance of offering incense is evident from the title of a courtly official, the "Chief of the House of Incense." It was also an important element of funerary practices, because the soul of the dead was considered to ascend to heaven by the smoke of the burning incense.

Incense also figures in Mesopotamian mythology. In the Mesopotamian *Epic of Gilgamesh,* Gilgamesh's mother Ninsuna supplicated the gods, asking them to protect and befriend her son. She burned incense and offered it to the god of creation, Shamash, to show her reverence and receive his blessings. As Gilgamesh embarked on his mission to kill the Evil One, Huwawa, he heard the words of his mother and remembered the fragrant aroma of the incense.

Judaism, Christianity, Islam. According to the Hebrew scriptures, in ancient Israel incense was considered a holy substance and was reserved for Yahveh; it was included with the bread offered to him on the Sabbath (*Lv.* 24:7). Incense was placed in the Tent of Meeting (*Ex.* 30:34) and was used in the offerings of the first fruits (*Lv.* 2:15–16); it was offered in censers on the Day of Atonement when the high priest appeared before the mercy seat (*Lv.* 16:12ff.). Its use as a perfume is indicated in *Song of Songs* 3:6, which states that it was used to scent Solomon's couch. In Psalm 141 incense is likened to prayer.

Until the time of Constantine, incense was not used in public worship ceremonies of the Christian church. Its use as an offering was severely condemned by the early Fathers (e.g., Cyril of Alexandria and John Chrysostom) because of its association with pagan practices. Christians were identified by their refusal to burn incense before a statue of the emperor; Saturninus and Sisinnius were martyred for their refusal to do so. Those Christians who capitulated in order to escape death were known as *turificati,* or burners of incense. However, by the ninth century incense was used in some churches for the dedication and consecration of the altar. Incense was later incorporated into the liturgical services of both the Eastern Orthodox and Western churches.

In the Islamic tradition, incense is burned to create a pleasant aroma in places of worship, although it does not have any specific religious significance. The Muslims of India burn incense sticks on auspicious occasions such as weddings, births, or religious festivals. Incense is frequently offered at the tombs of saints, which people visit in order to obtain blessings. In the Ṣūfī *samā*ʿ incense is often burned as the *dhikr* is chanted.

BIBLIOGRAPHY

Atchley, E. G. C. F. *A History of the Use of Incense in Divine Worship.* London, 1909.

Lucas, A. "Cosmetics, Perfumes and Incense in Ancient Egypt." *Journal of Egyptian Archaeology* 16 (May 1930): 41–53.

Schoff, Wilfred H. "Aloes." *Journal of the American Oriental Society* 42 (1922): 171–185.

Smith, G. Elliot. "Incense and Libations." *Bulletin of John Rylands Library* 4 (September 1917–January 1918): 191–262.

Van Beek, Gus W. "Frankincense and Myrrh." *Biblical Archaeologist* 23 (September 1960): 70–95.

HABIBEH RAHIM (1987)

INCUBATION SEE ASKLEPIOS; DREAMS

INDIAN PHILOSOPHIES.

Over the past four hundred years India has witnessed a break in its sociocultural and intellectual life with which it is still in the process of coming to terms. It is not, contrary to general belief, the legacy of colonialism that Indian philosophy and culture has had to contend with, but rather the compelling influence of the structure, rationality, and method of the European Enlightenment and its modernity. Since the eighteenth century, academic attempts at recovery of the classical tradition, efforts at translation, and philosophical analyses have all been mainly in the shadow of this modernity which separates as well as differentiates the study of science, politics and religion/metaphysics or *jñā a, karma* and *bhakti.*

Thus, contemporary scholarship in Indian philosophy is divided between, on the one hand, Indological enquiry engaged in the clarification and preservation of an "authentic" classical Indian philosophy, in all its details, and, on the other hand, an orientalist interest in appropriating the tradition to compare and compete with Western philosophy accepting the latter's standards and parameters of philosophical discussion. For a thorough and comprehensive history of Indian philosophy S. N. Dasgupta's five volumes titled *History of Indian Philosophy* (1922–1955) still represent the most systematic attempt. J. N. Mohanty's *Classical Indian Philosophy* (2000) is a lucid and independent exposition based on a classification according to issues in epistemology, ethics, or politics and religion. In *Presuppositions of India's Philosophies* (1991) by Karl Potter, the reader will find a serious attempt to consider and articulate the technical aspects of Indian philosophy in a manner in which they can address fundamental issues in philosophy and not be restricted to discussions within the tradition itself. Nevertheless, since a discussion of method and structure is lacking in these studies, even Potter's analysis does not ultimately succeed in bringing to bear the implications of what he himself characterizes as the speculative orientation of Indian philosophy towards the realization of freedom.

According to the *Sangarva Sūtra,* the Buddha classified his discussants into four categories—traditionalists, rationalists, metaphysicians, and experimentalists—and regarded himself as an example of the class of experimentalists (see Mohanty, 2000). It is this epistemological space for experiment within the framework of tradition that this article will attempt to trace.

THE STRUCTURE OF ORTHODOX AND HETERODOX SYSTEMS. Indian philosophy is generally thought to be comprised of six orthodox systems of thought—Nyāya, Vaiśeṣika, Sāṃkhya, Yoga, Mīmāṃsā, and Vedānta—and three so-called heterodox systems: Cārvāka, Jainism, and Buddhism. The orthodox schools are so described because they accept the authority of the Vedas, whereas the heterodox do not. However, the development of the schools is not linear and is characterized by a dialectical relationship entailing contradiction, correspondence, and complementarity, for which reason they are better approached as mutual elucidations rather than as a series of attempted improvements or revisions. Perhaps this is why they are called *darśanas.* Showing and seeing are both a part of the meaning of the term *darśana*; therefore, the term *revelation* appropriately defines it, implying the possibility of a plurality of revelations of the One.

Thus one may argue that the unity in plurality and plurality in unity of all religious tradtions—Hindu, Muslim, Sikh, and Christian, vernacular and classical, and not merely of the six orthodox and three heterodox schools—defines the limit of Indian philosophy. The basis for this unity lies in the fact that they represent experiments with the method of non-dualism of knowledge, praxis, and faith. Gandhi was not the first nor the last of the martyrs to testify to this in his writing and in his life. Dara Shikoh, the eldest son of Shahajahan, the Mogul emperor of India, held guilty of apostasy and martyred in 1609, wrote in the preface to his *Sirri-i-Akbar* (1067; a translation of the Upaniṣads) that it was his conviction that "the utterances of God elucidate and explain one another."

The different systems represent attempts to understand the epistemological, cosmological, and metaphysical presuppositions that underlie the relation between the Origin and the universe, the Unmanifest and the manifest, and the Unity and the plurality. It may be argued that there is a division of focus between the schools: Nyāya and Vaiśeṣika address epistemological questions, the first from the point of view of the subject or knower and the other from the point of view of the object of knowledge. Sāṃkhya and Yoga are cosmological schools, the first addressing the question of the macrocosm and plurality, and the second, unity, the microcosm, and humankind as witness. Mīmāṃsā and Vedānta are primarily metaphysical systems, the former focusing on praxis or means and the latter on the nature of the end. The three sets can be seen as different modes of understanding the relation between God, man, and nature through *jñāna* (knowledge), *karma* (praxis), and *bhakti* (faith).

The Cārvāka school (founded prior to first millennium BCE), Jainism (founded in the sixth century BCE), and Buddhism (dating to the sixth century BCE) present vernacular critiques of the Vedic tradition. They consider the epistemological, cosmological, and metaphysical presuppositions of civil society and material culture, and do so with an emphasis on the vernacular,which is seen as capable of expressing not merely the lay but also the sacred, on custom, and on the crafts, as opposed to orthodox Hinduism's focus on Sanskrit, tradition, and the sciences. Thus they lay the foundations for the tradition of the saints and the modern religions of Vīraśaivism (also known as Liṅgāyatism; founded in the twelfth century CE; in using the term *Liṅgāyatism* we are avoiding the usual orientalist opposition of Saivism versus Vaisnavism and drawing attention to the self description of the follower of this religion as the *the wearer of the* liṅga—which is the sign of the union of Śiva and Śakti), Sikhism (originating in the sixteenth century CE); and Gandhism (developed in the twentieth century CE). It may then perhaps be more apt to classify Indian philosophies according to their relationship to either the Śravaṇa tradition (of the hearers of the Word) or the Śramaṇa tradition (of the "laboring" devotee), rather than on the basis of orthodoxy or heterodoxy.

The focal point of Jainism's critique is the recognition that the Truth is always relative to a point of view, even if it seems absolute from a particular perspective. The hegemony of a single tradition as custodian of the Truth is thus broken. Buddhism characterizes reality as suffering, and thus finds it essential to demonstrate the impermanence or momentariness *(kṣaṇabhaṅgavāda)* of this reality, as the condition for the possibility of liberation *(nirvāṇa)* from it.

The Cārvākas are materialists representing the lay point of view. Knowledge of their perspective is mainly derived from representations made by philosophers who opposed them. They are characterized as infidels or sophists, or as proponents of a form of nature lore. This last description suggests that Cārvāka could be seen as representing a kind of metaphysical materialism that bridges the classical and vernacular traditions. Though Cārvāka rejects *mokṣa* (liberation) as a goal to be achieved outside and beyond this world, it asserts its possibility in this world, without the usual associations of pain and penance, associating it with pleasure instead. It is significant that the four elements—earth, water, air, and fire—are held to be eternal. The soul or consciousness does not exist independently of the body. It springs from a mixing of the elements that is characterized by their individual potencies, and that forms a fifth element, as it were. Formulated this way, Cārvāka philosophy can be seen as presenting a counter-Advaitic point of view. If Advaita argues the ultimate identity of the individual soul with *brahman,* the Unmanifest and transcendent principle of the universe, the Cārvākas argue the ultimate identity of the soul and the body, in this world, thus presenting the other limit of the spectrum. If the Mīmāṃsākas defend the potency of the Word, the Cārvākas defend the potency of matter. They together define the limits of the relationship between spirit and matter, the Word and the flesh, *mantra* (invocation) and *prasāda* (consecrated offering/partaking).

Thus Jainism, Buddhism, and the Cārvākas represent principles of civil society in their respective engagements with continence, the love of all creation being its positive force, suffering and its overcoming, and pleasure and its possibility in this world. All three schools are strongly critical of the ritualism of Hindu society and its making a travesty of the *varnāśrama* classification of society, resulting in a rigid social hierarchy between *brahmans, kṣatriyas, vaiśyas* and *śūdras*. The *āśramas* refer to the different roles or stages that members of each of the *varṇas* pass through in life. Classical Hinduism talks of four *āśramas*: *brahmachārya* (of the novice), *gṛhastha* (of the householder), *vanaprastha* (of the recluse), and *sannyāsa* (of the renouncer of society). *Saṃnyāsāśrama* frees man from the laws that govern *varṇa:*

> For the social system of caste was always surrounded in India by a penumbral region, as it were, of non-caste, where flourished the renunciatory religious orders whose principles abrogated those of caste, lineage, and birth: and the fourth *āśrama (saṃnyāsa)* constituted a door through which the individual was recommended to pass from the world of caste to that of its denial. The mutual relation of the two worlds, and I have no doubt that it was mutual, is of the greatest significance to a full understanding of either of them. (Uberoi, 1996, p. 14)

It may be argued that with the rejection of *varṇa,* Jainism and Buddhism followed a classification of society into only two classes, the monastic *(bhikṣu)* and the householder *(gṛhastha),* mediated by the congregation or *saṃgha.* Significantly, the tantric tradition also holds that only these two *āśramas* characterize society in *kaliyuga* (Kālī age).

Unity, Plurality, and the Trinity. The term referring to the Unity or the One is Brahman. The conceptualization of its nature and role and the theological issues that surround it make Brahman in many ways analogous to Yahveh in the Judaic tradition, God in the Christian tradition, and Allāh in the Islamic tradition. Just as with these three traditions, a central concern of Indian philosophies has been to relate the one to the plurality that characterizes the manifest world. As with Christianity, Trinity mediates between Unity and plurality. In place of the trinity of the Father, the Son, and the Holy Ghost, the Vedic tradition posits the trinity of Brahmā, the Creator; Viṣṇu, the All Pervading (Spirit); and Maheśvara/Śiva, the Destroyer. Brahmā is the eternal conceiver of name and form that constitute the very essence of plurality in the universe. Viṣṇu is the breath of God, as it were, the Holy Spirit that pervades the universe and enables nature to reflect the attributes of its maker. Finally, Śiva is the destroyer not of the plurality of the universe as is generally believed, but of the duality of unity and plurality. Thus he is the beginning and the end, the first and the last, marking at once the destruction of plurality and the realization of Unity—as well as the destruction of Unity and its manifestation in the plurality. This is the theological role envisaged for Christ and Muḥammad who are in their respective religions mediator and intercessor, between God, humans, and nature.

Three possible relations between the Unity and the plurality emerge from this understanding of the Trinity, and these three positions are reflected in the points of view of the three major thinkers of the metaphysical schools of Vedānta, namely: (1) of the plurality emerging or being carved out of the Unity (the position held by Śaṅkara, of the Advaita school); (2) of the Unity and the plurality being independent realities, as it were, though bound by the Holy Spirit/*prāṇa* (the position held by Madhva, of the Dvaita school); and (3) of the Unity in the plurality (the position held by Rāmānuja, of the Viśiṣṭādvaita school).

The common reading of the Advaitic school is that it regards the universe constituted by name and form as a mere illusion *(māyā).* This leads to the misconception by contemporary scholars that the reality of this world must be forsaken to achieve identity of the individual soul *(ātman)* with Brahman. In fact Śaṅkara's position is that Brahman projects himself in the universe only in name and form. This of course implies that in reality He does not change or project himself but the statement has the added significance that Brahman, if he may be known in this universe, can be known only through name and form. To consider the universe of name and form as independent of Brahman is the illusion. Name and form are then neither real nor unreal, neither self nor not-self. Thus Śaṅkara effectively demonstrates the contradiction and complementarity, the difference and correspondence, that exist in the relation between Brahman and the universe. In Swami Gambhirananda's translation of Śaṅkara's *Brahma-Sūtra Bhāṣya,* Śaṅkara writes:

> Nothing but Brahman can be different from name and form, since the whole of creation consists of a manifestation of name and form. And the manifestation of name and form in an absolute sense is not possible for anything but Brahman; for the Upanishad mentions that Brahman is the agent of their revelation: "Let me manifest name and form by Myself entering as the individual soul." (1972, p. 239)

And Śaṅkara goes on to explain this further:

> the intention here is to declare the identity of the individual soul and Brahman (and not agentship). From this very declaration of the manifestation of name and form, creatorship etc., as the indicatory signs of Brahman become stated ipso facto. (1972, p. 239)

It may be argued then that to know name and form is to know them in their relation to the Unity/Brahman, which is to say to know them as a sign, symptom, or symbol *(liṅga)* of the relation between Unity and plurality. The name is a sign of the covenant between God, humans, and nature.

Depending on which type of relationship between the Unity and the plurality is assumed, names may refer either to substance, attribute, or relation. When plurality is seen to emerge from the Unity, names primarily refer to substance and there can be no real separation of substance and attribute. Śaṅkara thus posits that the essential nature of Brahman is such that a distinction cannot be made between substance and attribute, and for him the ultimate goal is the identity of the individual soul with Brahman. For those for whom Unity and duality are conceived of as separate realities, name and form may refer either to substance, to attributes of substance, or to relations between substance and attributes. Thus Madhva sees the possibility of attaining to three types of goals—of gods, seers, and humans, according to the merit of one's actions. These correspond respectively to the names of substance, of relations, and of attributes. For those for whom Unity exists in the plurality, all names and forms refer to a relation of the two. According to Rāmānuja, Brahman therefore has only auspicious attributes while the name and form of other objects in the universe may refer both to good or evil attributes.

Sāṃkhya, which means "number," characterizes the plurality of the universe as being constituted of *liṅgas* (specific combinations of the constituents of matter—*sattva, rajas,* and *tamas*) that in their turn individually associate with *puruṣa,* the spirit that is witness, enjoyer, and seeker of liberation, thus giving rise to a plurality of *puruṣas*/persons. The Sāṃkhyakārikā characterizes their relation thus: "From their association, the non-intelligent *liṅga* becomes intelligent as it were; and so too, though agency is of the constituents, the indifferent One (Puruṣa) becomes agent as it were"(Īśvara Kṛṣṇa [Īśvarakṛṣṇa], 1948, ch. 20, pp. 43–44). *Prakṛti and puruṣa* come together so that *prakṛti* ("nature") may be contemplated on through *liṅga* by *puruṣa* and so that *puruṣa* in turn may be released from the three-fold misery that constitutes the universe; this is the necessary condition for the possibility of creation. Here the use of the term *liṅga,* indicating a particular form of the specific person evolving from this association, is significant since it points to the fact that it is only through *puruṣa* seeing himself in name and form that liberation is possible. According to Yoga, then, it is *liṅga* that is the object of meditation. Unlike knowledge by inference or testimony, *liṅga* refers to the determinate object and the individual soul, and not to something general. Such knowledge arising from the meditation upon the *liṅga* is "truth/reality-bearing."

From this, one can argue that though it is a topic not given much attention in the secondary literature, the mediation between Brahman and the universe—or between transcendence and empirical existence—is the crux of the issue, and not the nature and reality or unreality of one or the other. Such mediation is achieved through the specific example (of *liṅga*) and its contemplation. Thus, knowledge of name and form as signs of this mediation is the basis of knowledge *(jñāna),* vocation (*karma),* and invocation *(bhakti).* It is not by accident then that the saints of the Bhakti and tantric traditions, the new religions of Liṅgāyatism (Virasairism) and Sikhism, and Mohandas Gandhi's experiments with Truth, share a recognition of the potency of the name. Bhakti does not, as is generally believed, have its basis merely in experience, or simple faith, but in an understanding of the theory of names as the quintessence of the classical tradition and as crucial to the mediation between God, humankind, and nature—in other words, to the mediation of religion, politics, and science. This mode of prayer is considered to be available to men and women of all *varṇas.*

Jñāna, Karma,* and *Bhakti. Philosophers like Karl H. Potter and Jitendra Nath Mohanty have attempted to find unity in the variety of systems that comprise Indian philosophy by claiming that they are all, with the possible exception of Cārvāka, metaphysical schools with the goal of achieving liberation or *mokṣa.* However, not all schools articulate such an engagement with *mokṣa* explicitly, nor are they all necessarily theistic. Other scholars attempt to make a distinction between the schools on the basis of whether a particular system follows the path *(mārga)* of *jñāna, karma,* or *bhakti.* Here the specific meaning these terms take on in a particular system is of importance. For instance, it is often said that Śaṇkara Vedānta accepts *jñāna mārga* and is of the view that all *karma* ceases when the identity of Brahman and *ātman* is achieved. It is only a sense of agency that assumes the distinction of subject and object that is denied here and not action. So, there may be action but it is as if there is none. Thus the dichotomization of the question of *jñāna, karma,* and *bhakti* in contemporary readings is a forced one. Failure to understand their unity and method arises from an incomplete realization of the implications of the fact that Indian philosophies do not separate the scientific or cognitive from the spiritual, nor do they separate theory from practice or means from ends. Furthermore, it may be argued that there exists a unity of method amongst the different systems. They all attempt, with varying emphasis, a non-dualism which presupposes a necessary and systematic relation between *jñāna, karma,* and *bhakti.* It is significant that etymologically *bhakti* means "partaking," referring to humanity's share in Creation, through labor in production and reproduction. Thus humanity's participation in this universe, in *jñāna, karma,* and *bhakti,* involves the principle of compassion for all creatures. One may note therefore that according to the *Nyāyasūtra,* compassion is a necessary requirement for the person who may bear witness—that is, for the speaker of truth *(āpta).* By inference, then, truth must itself be such that it embodies this principle of compassion. If the trinity of Brahmā, Viṣṇu, and Śiva represents the conditions for the possibility of the Unity translating itself into the plurality, *jñāna, karma,* and *bhakti* represent the means or conditions for the possibility of the realization of the Unity in the plurality by humankind.

Texts: *Śruti, Smṛti,* and *Itihāsa.* Texts of the Vedic tradition are classified into three categories: (1) *śruti,* or revelation, comprising a compendium of hymns found in the four Vedas (*Ṛk, Sāma, Yajur,* and *Atharva*), rituals in the Brāhmaṇas, and interpretations of vedic sacrifice in the Āraṇyakas, which include the Upaniṣads; (2) *smṛti,* meaning remembrance; and (3) *itihāsa,* meaning history or proof.

Etymologically, *śruti* refers to "that which is heard." As has been said already, the orthodox systems of philosophy accept the authority of the Vedas, which are *śruti* texts. *Śruti* is eternal and impersonal *(apauruṣeya).* Some interpret *apauruṣeya* to mean nonhuman and infer a transcendental author of *śruti.* As the etymology of the term *śruti* suggests however, what is indicated is a "hearer" and not a transcendent speaker. Thus it is an eternal and universal revelation that may be heard by one who is chosen (or, that is, has the capacity to "hear"), and the ones who hear may speak in different tongues *(vāṇi).* Thus *śruti* and *vāṇi* make a pair, the one ineffective without the other. This is demonstrated by the fact that the Mīmāṃsaka, who believe in the eternalness of the Word, deny the possible contradiction to this assumption posed by the fact that a variety of sounds may associated with a single letter, by explaining that the modification of letter sounds is only in the hearing.

The philosophical systems and treatises in science, politics, medicine, art, architecture, and so on are classified as *smṛti. Smṛti* etymologically means remembrance (of *śruti*), and refers to the invocation of the name, which, as has been said, is the sign of the covenant between God, humankind, and nature. Thus *smṛti* in conjunction with *śruti* refers to the law that governs religion, politics, and science and identifies the law of God as the law of nature. Each discipline works out the laws in their specific determination in that specific science in such a way that the application of the law is at once the invocation of God/Unity by that specific name and the means to the realization of Unity through that calling and discipline. This presumes therefore the love of the All (creation) and makes necessary the principle of nonviolence in the constitution and application of all laws whether in science, religion, or politics.

Itihāsa, or "history," includes the Purāṇas and the two great Indian epics, the *Rāmāyaṇa* and the *Mahābhārata.* They embody the dialogic and dramatic defense of and attack on the truth of the *śruti* and *smṛti* in the history and living experience of man in his relation to God, society, and nature.

EXPERIMENTS WITH TRUTH: RELIGION, PHILOSOPHY, AND CIVIL SOCIETY. This section will deal with Liṅgāyatism (Virasaivism), Sikhism, and Gandhism as examples of religio-philosophical schools that experiment with truth, and thus herald the modern period of Indian philosophy and history. Like Jainism, Buddhism, and Cārvāka philosophy, they also represent the vernacular tradition and the strength of civil society with regard to religion and the state. They critique Hindu dogma and ritualism, and its rigid and alienating social stratification. Without denying the essential truth of the Vedas, they emphasize the importance of experiment and of a living faith. Their example serves as proof of the existence of a principle of motion within Indian philosophy, society, and history.

It is not often noticed that the critique of *varṇāśramadharma,* in whatever form, is accompanied by a realization of the necessary relation between the theory of the name and *bhakti.* This is significant because the social stratification along lines of *varṇa* was based on a division of labor and office. The theory of the name and *bhakti* together bring into focus the relation between vocation and invocation, labor and sacrifice, and service and office in the "partaking" of the creative and reproductive aspect of the universe. It may be said, then, that they announce for the modern age a theory and method of following one's calling and conscience, which, while breaking away from medieval class hierarchy and rigidity, does not lapse into dichotomies of opportunism and idealism, or of individualism and communism.

Lingayatism was founded by Basava (also known as Basavaṇṇa or Basaveśwara) in South India in the twelfth century CE. It proposed a system of thought called Śakti-viśiṣṭādvaita, which argues that the principles of Unity (Śiva) and the potency (Śakti) to become plurality are inalienably and necessarily united in the *liṅga* (sign). The trinity that forms the conditions for the possibility of the transfiguration of the plurality through the realization of the Unity consists of *sthala* (substance/substratum), *liṅga* (sign/relation), and *aṅga* (part/attribute of the body of Śiva). *Liṅga* and *aṅga* are in a relation of complementarity and correspondence, as the object of service or worship is to the one who offers service or worship, as the macrocosm is to the microcosm, and as the whole is to the part. One may read Lingayatism as referring to a theory of signs and the trinity above as referring to the names of substance, relation, and attribute. Since the sign itself mediates between Unity and plurality, it refers to the category of relation.

The Vīraśaiva initiate wears a *liṅga* around his neck as a sign of being in a constant state of worship; the *aṅga* being incomplete without the *liṅga,* they are witness, each to the other. *Kāyaka,* the orderly conduct of life in this world, is itself "heaven" *(kailāśa).* The Liṅgāyat is at once householder and renouncer, as Śiva himself is. Thus the division of society into the monastic and householder's way of life established by Jainism and Buddhism is overcome. The potency (Śakti) of the One (Śiva) has two modes—Śakti and *bhakti.* Though *bhakti* is a modification of Śakti, paradoxically it is the former that is considered superior since the latter is the impulse towards separation and plurality, veiling herself and her Lord, while *bhakti* is the impulse towards unity with the Lord. Men and women, high and low, all without exception have equal access to salvation in and through their respective vocation and station in society.

Sikhism carries further the experiment to bridge the dichotomy between religion and civil society and between the householder and the renouncer by taking into account their relation with a third category, the political, represented by the state. As J. P. S. Uberoi comments:

> The new departure of Sikhism, in my structural interpretation, was that it set out to annihilate the categorical partitions, intellectual and social, of the medieval world. It rejected the opposition of the common citizen or householder versus the renouncer, and of the ruler versus these two, refusing to acknowledge them as separate and distinct modes of existence. It acknowledged the powers of the three spheres of *rājya, sannyās [saṃnyāsa],* and *gṛihasta [gṛhastha],* but sought to invest their virtues conjointly in a single body of faith and conduct, religion-in-society-and-history, inserted by grace and effort as mediation between heaven and the world, or the *ātma* and *Paramātma,* the individual and the All, as the modern Indian form of non-dualism of self, the world and the other. (1996, p.16)

Uberoi argues that the five, along with an unstated sixth, symbols of Sikhism—the *kēś* (unshorn hair) and *kaṅga* (comb) of Saṃnyāsa yoga, the uncircumcised state which is not stated but structurally indicated and the *kachh* (tailored loin garment) of *gṛhastha* yoga, and the *kirpan* (sword) and *kaṛa* (band of ritual constraint) of *rājya* yoga—signify the assumption of the offices of these three spheres, by an "ordered renunciation of renunciation," and not as opposed to one another

The five symbols of Sikhism may be fruitfully compared with the eight *āvarṇas* ("sheaths") of the Vīraśaiva, which form four pairs of symbols—*gurū* (example) and *liṅga* (sign of the unity of Śiva and Śakti), *jaṅgama* (the *jīvanamukta* "moving"/living in this world) and *vibhūti* ("ashes," symbolizing renunciation), *rudrākṣa* (Śiva's eye, indicating the status of being witness) and *pādodaka* (the water that has cleansed the feet of *gurū, liṅga,* and *jangama,* indicating service), and *prasāda* ("grace"; the potency of that which we partake of through one's vocation in the presence of the congregation) and *mantra* (invocation/potency of the name). These pairs reflect the juxtaposition of form and name, being in the world and renunciation, through self-restraint and self-denial with respect to the world and the other, the inner and outer aspects of worship, and grace and potency in the world and the word respectively. Though it is perhaps right to argue that Vīraśaivism, unlike Sikhism, does not oppose religion and society to the state, the two traditions are nonetheless united in assigning primacy to the worship of the name, the life of renunciation in (and not "of") this world, and worship through sacrifice and service.

With Sikhism is introduced the notion of the *saṃgha* (or congregation) as a society of the saved, membership of which is the condition for the reception of service and worship. This may be compared with Liṅgāyatism, which emphasizes the service and worship of the Ishtalinga (a personal deity) and the union of Śiva and Śakti symbolizing the possibility of creation, production, and reproduction of the species as the condition for the possibility of its reception The notion of the congregation also plays a significant role in Gandhi's philosophy.

The trinity that forms the foundation of Gandhian philosophy is comprised of truth, nonviolence, and experiment. Gandhi demonstrates through example and experiment that the study of the self cannot be separated from the study of the other and the world, in religion, politics, and science, and therefore that the truth of the one can not be independent of that of the other. According to him the adherence in spirit and practice to the principle of nonviolence, based on a love that embraces the meanest of God's creatures, alone can be the method of investigation by which one may arrive at the truth. Thus he was as much against vivisection as a means of scientific study and progress as he was against the evil of untouchability as a social institution:

> I abhor vivisection with my whole soul. I detest the unpardonable slaughter of innocent life in the name of science and society so-called, and all the scientists' discoveries stained with innocent blood I count as of no consequence. If the circulation of blood theory could not have been discovered without vivisection then humankind could well have done without it. And I see the day clearly dawning when the honest scientist of the West will put limitations upon the present methods of pursuing knowledge. Future measurements will take note not only of the human family but of all that lives and even as we are slowly but surely discovering that it is an error to suppose that Hindus can thrive upon the degradation of a fifth of themselves or that people of the West can rise or live upon the exploitation and degradation of the Eastern and African nations, so shall we realize in the fullness of time, that our dominion over the lower order of creation is not for their slaughter, but for their benefit equally with ours. For I am as certain that they are endowed with a soul as that I am. (*Collected Works*, vol. 29, pp. 325–326)

Thus Gandhi presents a new theory of experiment as the discovery of nonviolent means of realizing truth in every aspect of life with the self as the subject and the object of study in its relation of service to God, humankind and nature; it is new as much to the idea of the Indian tradition as it is to the modernity of the Enlightenment. Without deferring to either, it establishes the conditions for the possibility of true *swaraj (svarāj)* or self-rule of individual, society, and nation through labor, service, self-denial, and self-sacrifice in religion, politics, and science. The *satyāgrahi,* the nonviolent seeker after truth, equipped with fearlessness and a spirit of self-sacrifice, and invoking the name of God *(Rāmanāma),* is at once devotee, community/political worker, and scientist, combining service and experiment in faith, experiment and faith in service, and faith and service in experiment.

Denying that *varṇa* and *āśrama* had anything to do with caste, Gandhi drew attention to the fact that *varṇāśrama* asserts the law governing one's being in in society, refers to the calling by which we earn our bread, defines one's duty not right, and emphasizes that all callings must necessarily be conducive to the welfare of all humanity. From this he concludes: "It follows that there is no calling too low and none too high. All are good, lawful and absolutely equal in status. The callings of a Brahmana—spiritual teacher—and a scavenger are equal, and their due performance carries equal merit before God and at one time seems to have carried identical reward before man" (1987, pp. 12–13).

According to Gandhi individual prayer is only a prelude to collective prayer and is ineffective without the latter. It is a necessary means to the realization of the brotherhood of man and the fatherhood of God, and to the realization of membership in society, and is necessary training for the use of the "weapon" of *satyāgraha* ("soul force"). Congregational prayer lays the foundation for the unity in plurality and the plurality in unity of religions, which is achieved through equality and difference, and complementarity and competition between them:

> It becomes man to remember his Maker all the twenty-four hours. If that cannot be done we should at least congregate at prayer time to renew our covenant with God. Whether we are Hindus or Musalmans, Parsis, Christians or Sikhs, we all worship the same God. Congregational worship is a means for establishing the essential human unity through common worship. (1987, pp. 194–195)

CONCLUSION. The method of the non-dualism of *jñāna, karma,* and *bhakti,* in Indian philosophy, is based on a presupposition of the necessary relation between theory and practice, fact and value, means and ends, and the individual and the collective. This method therefore defines the nature and scope of both the dialectic within the scriptural traditions and between them and the vernacular traditions. The specific examples of issues and of religions discussed above demonstrate, albeit not exhaustively, the existence of a principle of motion within Indian philosophy that inspires the direction and development of its problematic in history and society.

In method, spirit, and project Indian philosophies present a species of modernity diametrically opposed to the modernity that derives from the European Enlightenment. The former presents a systematic working out of experiments to consider the necessary relation between religion, politics, and science in philosophy, history, and society, whereas, the project of the latter is to separate, systematically, their study in theory and practice.

SEE ALSO Buddhist Philosophy; Cārvāka; Jainism; Mīmāṃsā; Nyāya; Sāṃkhya; Vaiśeṣika; Vedānta; Yoga.

BIBLIOGRAPHY

Dasgupta, Surendranath. *A History of Indian Philosophy.* 5 vols. Cambridge, U.K., 1922–1955.

Gandhi, Mohandas Karamchand. *The Essence of Hinduism.* Ahmadabad, India, 1987.

Gandhi, Mahatma [Mohandas Karamchand Gandhi]. *Collected Works.* 100 vols. New Delhi, 1956–1994. A CD-ROM version has also been released in 98 volumes (New Delhi, 1999).

Īśvara Kṛṣṇa [Īśvarakṛṣṇa]. *The Sāṃkhyakārikā.* Edited and translated by S. S. Suryanarayana Sastri. Madras, India, 1948.

Mohanty, Jitendra Nath. *Classical Indian Philosophy.* Lanham, Md., 2000.

Potter, Karl H. *Presuppositions of India's Philosophies.* Delhi, 1991.

Sakhare, M. R. *History and Philosophy of Liṅgāyat Religion.* Belgaum, 1942. Includes an introduction to and translation of *Liṅgadhāranachandrikā* by Nandikesvara.

Śaṅkarācārya [Śaṅkara]. *Brahmā-Sūtra Bhāṣya.* Translated by Swami Gambhirananda. Calcutta, 1972.

Uberoi, Jitendra Pal Singh. *Religion, Civil Society, and the State: A Study of Sikhism.* Delhi and New York, 1996. A comparative study of the traditions of Hinduism, Sikhism and Islam from the point of view of what he identifies as Sikhism's as well as Gandhi's problematic—that of forging an Indian modernity out of medievalism based on pluralism and principles of contradiction, correspondence and complimentarity.

ANURADHA VEERAVALLI (2005)

INDIAN RELIGIONS

This entry consists of the following articles:

AN OVERVIEW
RURAL TRADITIONS
MYTHIC THEMES
HISTORY OF STUDY

INDIAN RELIGIONS: AN OVERVIEW

The Indians, anthropologically a mixture of immigrant Aryans and partly autochthonous peoples, gradually elaborated a many-sided, highly developed culture rooted in the archaic structure of the human mind. This culture is characterized by an often almost complete integration of heterogeneous elements, by unity in diversity, by homogeneity despite the utmost variety and complexity of its ethnic and social composition, by a multitude of languages and different cultural patterns, and by a great diversity in mental character and socioreligious customs, cults, beliefs, practices, and ways of life varying widely both regionally and, within the same region, from class to class. Indian culture gives free scope to the emotional and imaginative sides of human nature, to speculative, more or less visionary thinking and modes of apprehension, and it has long preserved the cohesion of its provinces: religion, art, literature, and social organization.

VEDISM. The religious life reflected in the oldest Indian literature in preclassic Sanskrit, the Veda (from about the thirteenth century BCE), is that of a predominantly ritual and sacrificial system (Vedism) developing, almost in seclusion, at first in the Punjab, later in the Ganges Plain, among the immigrant Aryans (Indo-Europeans), whose ideas and representations of the divine constitute an almost unified synthesis embodied in an elaborate mythology partly paralleled by ritual equivalences. Vedic thought was based on the belief in an inextricable coordination of nature, human society, ritual, and the sphere of myth and the divine; it was also founded on the belief that these spheres influence one another continuously and that men have, by means of ritual, an obligatory part to play in the maintenance of universal order and the furtherance of their common interests. In later times also, Indians have constantly sought correspondences between objects and phenomena belonging to distinct spheres of nature and conceptual systems. Many hymns and individual stanzas of the oldest literary corpus (the *Ṛgveda Saṃhitā*, an anthology drawn from family traditions) were intended for the cult and used in the liturgy of spectacular solemn (*śrauta*) ceremonies, which gradually increased in number, length, and complexity. These ceremonies were to ensure the orderly functioning of the world for the benefit of noble or wealthy patrons. The rites were performed in the open on a specially prepared plot—there were no temples or idols—by specialized officiants. Part of this literature was employed, along with texts from the *Atharvaveda Saṃhitā,* in the domestic or magic ritual performed by a householder or single priest to ensure an individual's health, safety, success, prosperity, and longevity. These texts and the ritual formulas of the *Yajurveda,* which invariably fulfill some ritual function, are collectively called *mantras*. They are believed to be revelations of aspects of the divine, the product of the exalted experiences of sages (*ṛṣis*) and hence constitute sacred and inherently powerful verbal formulas for producing a desired result. Some Vedic *mantras* remained in Hinduist rites, which, however, generally require other ones.

No definite chronology can be established for Vedic literature or the development of religious ideas and ritual practices. It is known that the collections of hymns were succeeded by the Brāhmaṇas, texts that discuss rites and rituals and explain their origin, meaning, and validity. These sacral acts, being the counterpart of the cosmic drama, are in fact also the symbolic expression of speculations about the origin and functioning of the universe and the significance, activity, and operation of the powers, personal and impersonal, presiding over its provinces and manifesting their presence and influence. Thus the ceremonious construction of a special place for the ritual fire is believed to reintegrate the creator god, enabling him to continue his creative activity and to bring about a transformation and higher existence of the patron of the sacrifice, who in and through this ritual is identified with the creator and delivered from death. Mainly based on the Brāhmaṇas are the Śrauta-sūtras, manuals in which the rites are for practical purposes systematically and authoritatively described. No information is given on the earlier, prehistoric cult, which cannot be reconstructed. These works arrange the solemn rites in three classes: the partly inherited bloodless sacrifices, the more elaborate animal sacrifices, and the typically Indian soma ceremonies. In the course of time these elite *śrauta* rituals fell largely into disuse and were superseded by Hinduist rites performed at the expense of and for the benefit of much larger parts of the population.

HINDUISM. Some prehistoric forms of Hinduism—the civilization of the Hindus, consisting of their beliefs, practices, and socioreligious institutions—must have existed at the Vedic period, especially in the unrecorded religion of the lower classes, and probably earlier. Domestic ritual, which is entirely different from the solemn rites, consists of many rites that, though described and systematized by *brahman* authorities in the Vedic Gṛhyasūtras, are in essence not typically Vedic, or rather constitute Vedic varieties of widespread rites of passage, rites of appeasement, cult of the dead, and so on. Later chapters of this literature show markedly non-Vedic and post-Vedic influences, such as strong leanings toward Vaiṣṇava ritualism, which attest to the gradual incorporation of non-Vedic rites and substitution of extra-Vedic elements for those recognized by the original compilers of Hindu rites and practices. Gradually these elements became more prominent.

Non-Aryan influences. How much influence was exerted by the religions of the non-Aryan inhabitants of India on the formation and development of Hinduism is a matter of dispute. Although aborigines may have contributed some elements, their religion is generally different in many respects (e.g., they do not venerate the cow, and they allow their widows to remarry). The Vedic religion had no demonstrable relation with the great civilizations of Harappa, Mohenjo-Daro, and vast regions to the east of the Indus Valley (c. 2500–1500 BCE). As long as the graphic symbols on seals from these sites are not convincingly deciphered and the language is not identified (that it was Dravidian—the name of non-Aryan languages of southern India—is still unproved conjecture), most of the conclusions drawn from archaeological material and argumentation regarding links with elements or characteristics of older and even contemporary Hinduism remain as speculative as the hypothesis of a predominantly influential Dravidian substratum. Do the clay figurines of women really attest to some form of worship of a mother goddess that continued in the historical period, or to the existence of a prehistoric Śaiva *śakti* cult? Is the figure of a male dancer identical with the dancing Śiva? The wide distribution in various countries of, for instance, objects that may have been amulets or votive offerings should prevent one from hastily regarding their occurrence in Hinduist religions as an uninterrupted continuance of a function supposedly attributed to certain Indus objects.

General characteristics. The main current of Hinduism, the so-called great tradition, is a remarkably continuous whole. The tendency to maintain continuity has always been deep-rooted but did not exclude the constant accretion and integration of further elements derived from non-Aryan peoples, extraneous sources (invaders on the northwestern frontier may have contributed to the custom of *satī*, the self-immolation practiced by widows, for example), and the activities of individual religious leaders. While continuity and change have been the prevailing patterns, incorporation and synthesis between the new and the traditional usually were more obvious than the often almost imperceptible elimination of those elements that no longer had a useful and recognizable function. Nevertheless, it is more common to draw upon the past than to invent anew, and apparently original ideas may be foreshadowed by concepts apparent centuries earlier. Thus many features of Hinduism have their roots in the Vedic past, and some characteristic ideas inherited from that past and developed in a few main currents—primarily doctrines of salvation—have up to the present largely determined the Indian view of life and the world.

The older Upaniṣads are the first recorded attempts at systematizing Indian philosophical thought. They are esoteric supplements to the Brāhmaṇas, intended for advanced pupils with a bent for reflection, abstract speculation, and philosophical discussion rather than ritual theory, and therefore answering the needs of ascetics and anchorites. Few Indians are inclined to reject the contents of these Upaniṣads, with which every subsequent philosophy had to show itself in accord. While emphasizing the philosophical value of the Vedic tradition, they are essentially concerned with describing the nature of what is alternately called *brahman* (the Absolute) or *ātman* (universal soul), and its relation with the individual soul (often called *jīva*). The realization of the identity of the latter with the former came to be substituted for the ritual method of conquering death and attaining integral life, the ultimate goal of all speculation. Being compilations, the Upaniṣads do not present a homogeneous philosophical theory, but there was a move to reconcile the references to the dualistic and evolutionistic doctrines of what was to become the influential Sāṃkhya school of philosophy with the prevailing monistic doctrines. Hinduism, directed by these works toward monism, has largely sought its inspiration in them.

There are a number of more or less constant elements of Hinduism. The central focus of India's spiritual life is the belief in and search for an uncreated eternal, fundamental principle (*brahman*), the ultimate source and goal of all existence. *Brahman* is the One that is the All and the sole reality, which transforms itself into the universe, or causes all existence and all beings to emanate from itself, and which is the self (*ātman*) of all living beings. *Brahman* may also be conceived of as a personal "high god" (usually as Viṣṇu or Śiva), characterized by sublime and adorable qualities. Further elements are the confidence that one's own existence and the culture of one's community are founded on an eternal and infallible basis, and the craving for building one's life and ideals on this firm foundation; the recognition of a pristine body of religious literature (the Veda) as an eternal and absolute authority considered to be *brahman* appearing as words, however unknown its contents; and acknowledgment of the spiritual supremacy by birth of the *brahmans*, another manifestation of *brahman,* who are regarded as representing the norm of ritual purity and who enjoy social prestige. The keystone of Hinduist ethics is the belief in the unity of all life and its corollary respect for life and fellow feeling with all living beings *(ahiṃsā);* the doctrine of transmigration and rebirth (*saṃsāra,* a post-Vedic term), first adumbrated in one of the oldest Upaniṣads (c. 600 BCE), and its complement, the belief in *karman* (previous acts) as the factor determining the condition into which a being is reborn, a consequence of a cyclic view of all worldly processes and existence. These doctrines encourage the opinion that mundane life is not true existence (the so-called Indian pessimism) and hence relate to the conviction that human endeavor should be directed toward final emancipation (*mokṣa*) from the mechanism of *karman* and transmigration, the only goal of this effort being the One (*brahman*) that is beyond all phenomenal existence. In view of the above, Hinduism exhibits a natural tendency to speculation hand in hand with religion as well as to a monistic philosophy and mysticism that has left intact traditional mythology and common beliefs. Finally, it is characterized by a complex polytheism subsumed in a fundamental monotheism and by a propensity to ascribe the attributes of other gods to the deity one is worshiping.

Early history. The history proper of Hinduism begins with the emergence of the great works on *dharma,* the totality of traditional custom and behavior that, agreeing with standards considered to derive their authority from the Vedas, manifests and maintains order and stability. This is also the age of the epics, especially the *Mahābhārata* (c. 300 BCE–300 CE), that "encyclopedia of Hinduism" that shows, even then, what appears to be a varied and confused conglomerate of beliefs and practices. However, there are two main currents, soteriologies when viewed from their doctrinal aspect and religions from the viewpoint of their adherents: Vaiṣṇavism and Śaivism. Neither current is in itself a unity. Yet all Vaiṣṇavas are essentially monotheistic, believing in Viṣṇu as their immanent high god (Īśvara), although in many contexts he appears as one of the divine polytheistic figures (*devas*). In the Vedas, Viṣṇu represents universal pervasiveness; his beneficent energy, in which all beings abide, reaches the world through the *axis mundi,* the central pillar of the universe. Vaiṣṇavas often worship him through his manifestations or incarnations (*avatāras*), such as Rāma or Kṛṣṇa. These and other originally independent figures had fused with Viṣṇu mainly as a result of the tendency to identify the various representatives of the Highest Person with the Primeval Person (Puruṣa), whose self-limitation, according to a Ṛgvedic hymn, inaugurated the era of creation. Preference for an *avatāra* is mainly traditional; in the North, Kṛṣṇa is more often worshiped; in the South, it is Rāma, Viṣṇu himself, or Viṣṇu's consort, Śrī. In many myths the versatile Viṣṇu performs, often in well-known Indian places, great and miraculous deeds to confirm the *dharma,* protect humanity, and preserve the world. The *Bhagavadgītā,* an episode of the *Mahābhārata* and the most seminal of all Vaiṣṇava works, founded Vaiṣṇava ethics: Fulfilling their duties disinterestedly, humans should realize God's presence in themselves, love him and their fellow beings devotedly, and dedicate all their actions to him so as to earn the prospect of final emancipation.

The Hinduist worship, in many different groups and currents, of Śiva in his various manifestations results from a complex development to which the often malevolent outsider god Rudra of the Vedas has contributed much. (There may also have been Dravidian influences.) Rudra, primarily representing the untamed aspects of uncultivated nature, was called Śiva ("the mild one") when the benevolent and auspicious aspects of his nature were emphasized. Śaivism is an unsystematic amalgam of pan-Indian Śaiva philosophy, local or folk religion, mythological thought, and popular imagery. Śiva's many-sided character, to which accreted features of great gods as well as demoniac powers, is split up into many partial manifestations representing aspects of his ambivalent nature. As Īśvara he is the unique and almighty Supreme Person, representing an abstract, sole principle above change and variation, less human than Viṣṇu, and much less active, although elsewhere, in his role as Nāṭarāja the dancer, he originates the eternal rhythm of the universe. He is both mild and terrible, a creator and destroyer, an ascetic and a sexualist. Thus Śiva represents a composite god who is a unity to his devotees, and he plays many apparently contradictory roles in myths, which, on various levels, resolve logically irreconcilable contradictions.

BUDDHISM AND JAINISM. The same period saw the spread of two heterodox soteriologies, heterodox because they reject the authority of the Veda and the social prejudices of the *brahmans*, although they scarcely attack the fundamentals of Hindu belief and practices. The way in which the early Buddhists presented their doctrines has much in common with the oldest Upaniṣads, which must antedate the spread of the Aryan culture to the south and the activity of Gautama (c. 560–480 BCE). Gautama, the Buddha, first gave an exposition of his basic doctrine in Banaras. He taught that those who wish to be delivered from *saṃsāra* and the automatism of *karman,* which does not rely upon a permanent transmigrating soul (whose existence the Buddha denied), should realize four basic truths: (1) earthly existence is pain; (2) the cause of pain is craving for existence, leading to rebirth; (3) cessation of that craving is cessation of pain; (4) an eightfold path leads to that cessation. Final deliverance is realized only in an ascetic and monastic life by those who, after having successfully observed definite rules of life and reached complete meditation (*samādhi*), experience the undefinable state of *nirvāṇa,* the cessation of all becoming. The daily activities of Buddhist monks were recitation, meditation, instruction, and collecting alms from the laity (who largely continued adhering to Hindu belief and observing Hindu practices). As the number of adherents increased, the Buddhist order received large gifts that led to the establishment of monasteries. The multiplying order spread to different parts of India, including the south and Sri Lanka (third century BCE). In the beginning of the fourth century BCE the community began to be split by successive schisms, each of which made its own collection of canonical texts. After about 500 CE, Indian Buddhism began to decline.

The Buddha was not the only illuminated teacher who, after renouncing the world, organized his initiates into a community. In Bihar one of his contemporaries, Vardhamāna Mahāvīra, reformed an existing community and founded the predominantly monastic Jainism, which spread to northern and central India, Gujarat, and the Deccan, and in the last few centuries BCE split into two groups, not on philosophic disagreement but on points of rules for the monks. Jainism is systematic and has never changed in its basic ideology. Its philosophy is dualistic: It posits nonliving entities (including space and time) pervaded by (partly transmigrating, partly emancipated) immaterial and eternal souls; the world, eternal and changeless, is not governed by a supreme being; the system is characterized by the absence of gods (*devas*); *karman* is the central power that determines the destiny of unemancipated souls. Humans have to perfect their souls and those of their fellow creatures; *ahiṃsā* and universal tolerance are the main duties and cardinal virtues. Whereas the adherents of Buddhism were from a variety of social classes, Jainism attracted the wealthy and influential. The Jains erected beautiful temples with statues of their perfect souls (*siddhas*) and produced an enormous body of moral and narrative literature. Nowadays they often tend to return to Hinduism, against whose social order they have never revolted.

HINDUISM AFTER ABOUT 300 BCE. When Buddhism and Jainism enjoyed royal protection, they could extend their influence. However, the masses doubtless always remained Hinduist, even under the Maurya dynasty (c. 326–c. 187 BCE), from which time the epigraphical records left by kings create the impression of a Buddhist supremacy, and in the first and second centuries of the common era, when foreign rulers accorded Buddhists protection. Until the fourth century, inscriptional and numismatic evidence of Vaiṣṇavism and Śaivism is scanty, but the period of the Gupta dynasty (320–c. 500 CE), which patronized the *brahmans* and the Hinduist communities, saw the full development of classical Sanskrit and the rise of a non-Buddhist architectural style. The construction of a temple, a rite based on mythical reality, a sacrifice leading to a higher level of self-realization for the builder, is, like the construction of the great Vedic sacrificial fire-place (usually, though inaccurately, called "fire altar"), always the material expression of the doctrine of reintegration. At the temple the god is worshiped through his image (*mūrti*), whose beauty contributes to its force as a sacred instrument. In elaborate ceremonies the god, as an exalted personage and royal guest, is offered food, flowers, and incense. His iconography, consecration (introduction of the god's spirit), and installation, as well as the *mantras* used, the significance of the material and requisites, and the spirit animating the execution of temple and images, are all meticulously described. This daily worship (*pūjā*) probably continues many non-Aryan elements that were gradually received by the higher classes and incorporated into the Brahmanical literature. *Pūjā* is also performed at home by the householder. As far as the uncomplicated older private cult survived, it was supplemented by the traditional (*smārta*) cults of Viṣṇu, Śiva, and other gods, morning and evening rites, oblations in the consecrated fire, recitation, and mental adoration.

During many centuries after about 300 CE there arose an enormous body of mainly Vaiṣṇava and Śaiva literature. The Puraṇas, stemming from various circles and regions, but significantly all attributed to the redactor of the Vedas and the *Mahābhārata* and claiming to be inspired, deal with cosmogony, cosmology (the universe exists cyclically, its eternal return implying the eternal return of souls to bondage and suffering), mythology and legends, principles and philosophy, religious practices and ceremonies, local cults and sanctuaries, sacred rivers and places of pilgrimage. The many, still-influential Āgamas, also in Sanskrit, mainly teach the practical realization of religious truths, while largely governing temple and household ritual and the traditional religious life and behavior of Hindus. Their subject matter is theoretically divisible into four categories: higher knowledge, which gives access to final emancipation; physical, mental, and psychic concentration, that is, complete control of all corporeal and mental functions, leading to the same goal (yoga); meritorious works; and rites, including the many socially and religiously important festivals that are believed to stimulate and resuscitate the vital powers of nature. The Āgamas favor various philosophical doctrines. A feature of the Vaiṣṇavāgamas, usually called Saṃhitās, is *bhakti,* "participation (of the soul in the divine)," devout and emotional worship and adoration of a personal deity in a spirit of deep affection, amounting to surrender to God. Because these works also teach non-Vedic tenets, they are often considered heterodox, in that they deviate from the Hindu *dharma.* Some religions, such as the northern Śaiva Pāśupatas, have propagated consciously divergent rites and practices. Most Vaiṣṇavas, among them the Pāñcarātras, however, deny that they deviate from the generally accepted tradition; many southern Śaivas regard their Āgamas (although with no certain proof) as the sanskritization of an originally Dravidian tradition; some assume the influence of oral esoteric doctrines. In fact, numerous elements are, notwithstanding argumentation to the contrary, non-Brahmanical in origin.

Śaiva Religions and Tantrism. Some religions of India do deviate from common Hinduist traditions and institutions. In contrast to the Śaiva Siddhāntins of the Tamil-speaking South—who, basing themselves also on the mysticism of the Śaiva Tamil saint-poets (Nāyaṉārs), teach that God in the shape of a spiritual guide, or *guru,* graciously permits himself to be realized by the purified soul—the Vīraśaivas, or Liṅgāyats, in southwestern India (not mentioned before the twelfth century) abandon many traditional elements (e.g., caste, image worship). Doctrinal dissent is always possible. The religio-philosophic idealist and monist Kashmir school of Śaivism disagrees in certain important respects with the teaching of Śaṇkara (eighth century), the founder of Advaita monism, derived from the Upaniṣadic Vedānta as a system of absolute idealism that is mainly followed by the intellectual elite. Śaṇkara, a native of Malabar who resided in Banaras and traveled throughout India, was a superb organizer; he established a monastic order and monasteries (*maṭhas*), which, like the many hermitages (*āśramas*) and the great shrines, became centers of religious activity and contributed to the realization of his ideal of Hindu unity.

From about 500 CE, Tantric ritual and doctrines manifest themselves more or less frequently in Buddhism, Śaiva Siddhānta, and Pāñcarātra. Tantrism, primarily meant for esoteric circles, yet still an important aspect of Hinduism, is a systematic quest for spiritual excellence or emancipation through realization of the highest principle, the bipolar, bisexual deity, in one's own body. The possibilities of this microcosmos should be activated, sublimated, and made to exert influence on the macrocosmos, with which it is closely connected (physiological processes are thus described with cosmological terminology). Means to this end, partly magical, partly orgiastic, include recitation of *mantras*, contemplation of geometrical cosmic symbols (*maṇḍalas*), leading the performer of the rites to the reintegration of consciousness; appropriate gestures (*mudrās*), and meditation. Tantric *pūjā* is complicated and in many respects differs from conventional ceremonies. Especially in Bengal, Tantrism has tended to merge with the Śākta cult. The term *Tantra* commonly applies to Śaiva or Śākta works of the Tantric tradition. Śāktism, not always clearly distinguishable from Śaivism, is the worship of the Supreme as divine creative energy (*śakti*), a female force that creates, regulates, and destroys the cosmos; when regarded as a person, she usually is Śiva's spouse, often the dreadful goddess Durgā or Kālī. In contrast to the so-called right-hand Tantrists, who emphasize yoga and *bhakti,* the left-hand Tantrists seek to realize the union of the male and female principles in the One by combining control of the senses with the sexual act; in addition, they make sacramental use of what is forbidden (e.g., meat) to the *brahmans*.

Vaiṣṇava Religions and Bhakti. Although Vaiṣṇavism, less coherent than Śaivism, had, in the sixth century, spread all over India, it reached predominance in Tamil Nadu, which became the cradle of important schools and movements that still have many adherents. The tradition known as the Śrī Vaiṣṇavas was inaugurated between about 900 and 1130 by Yāmuna, the first apologist of Vaiṣṇava theology, and consolidated by the great philosopher Rāmānuja (c. 1017–1137). The Śrī Vaiṣṇavas introduced into their temple ceremonies the recitation of Tamil hymns of the Āḻvārs, which evince a passionate belief in and love of God. Considering these poets and their great teachers (*ācāryas*) integral parts (*aṃśas*) of God's nature, they often worship images of them in their temples. According to Rāmānuja, *brahman* is as a "person" (*puruṣa*) the sole cause of his own modifications (emanation, existence, and absorption of the universe), immaterial, perfect, omnipotent, the soul of all being, the ultimate goal of all religious effort, to which God induces the devotee who wishes to please him. The purificatory significance of the ritual, meritorious works, disinterested discharge of duties, and *bhakti* are emphasized.

The influential *Bhāgavata Purāṇa* (c. 900?), also composed in Tamil Nadu, teaches that God through his incomprehensible creative ability (*māyā*) expands himself into the universe, which is his outward appearance. On the basis of this teaching, Bengal Vaiṣṇavism developed the theory of a relation of inconceivable difference in identity and identity in difference between God and the world, as well as the belief that God's creative activity is his sport (*līlā*). The emotional and erotic description of young Kṛṣṇa's sport with the milkmaids (*gopīs*), who represent souls pervaded by *bhakti* who yearn for God, enjoys lasting popularity. In this Purāṇa, *bhakti* religiosity was expanded, deepened, and stimulated by singing, meditation, and looking at Kṛṣṇa's image. As the safest way to God, *bhakti,* a mystical attitude of mind involving an intuitive, immediate apprehension and loving contemplation of God, often overshadows the devotee's aspirations to final emancipation and assumes a character of uncontrollable enthusiasm and ecstasy, marked by tears, hysteria, and fainting.

In northern and central India the *bhakti* movement flourished from the thirteenth to the eighteenth century, producing a vast and varied literature in vernacular languages. Even today these areas feel the influence of a long succession of saint-poets, passionate itinerant preachers (among them Caitanya, in Bengal, 1485–1533), and *gurus*. These mystics and religious (rather than social) reformers propagated public singing of their devotional songs and *kīrtana* (the praise of God's name and glory), and preached a nonextremist way of life. While so addressing the masses, *bhakti* influenced almost all religious communities and contributed as a unifying force considerably to a revival of Hinduism.

Reaction to Foreign Religions. The revival of Hinduism in the south and the spread of the *bhakti* movement also prepared the Indians to withstand the proselytizing of external religions, particularly Islam. From 1000 CE onward, the Muslims conquered the Northwest, made Delhi their capital, and extended their influence to Bengal, the Deccan, and the

South, destroying temples and idols and making many converts, particularly among the untouchables. But Islam scarcely affected the Hindu way of life; rather, it provoked a counterreaction in the form of increased adherence to the Hindu *dharma* and the Hindu religions and stricter observance of rites and ceremonies. Nevertheless, the presence of Islam in India involved an age-long conflict between strict monotheism and the various manifestations of Hinduism. In one field, however, Islam and Hinduism could draw near to each other: Muslim and Hindu mystics have in common the idea of an all-embracing unity. To be sure, the Ṣūfīs made this idea a channel of Islamization, but some Indian spiritual leaders tried to bridge the gulf between Islam and Hinduism. Kabīr (c. 1450–1525), an itinerant ascetic, mystic, and strictly monotheist poet and eclectic teacher and preacher, rejected traditional ritual and Brahmanical speculation but retained the belief in basic concepts such as *karman* and *saṃsāra.* In the course of time his syncretistic religion became largely Hinduized. Nānak (1469–1539) was likewise a strict monotheist who stated that any pluralistic and anthropomorphous idea of the Supreme should dissolve in God's only form, the really existent. An opponent of caste and idolatry, he organized his followers, the Sikhs, in an exclusive community, an amalgam of Islam and Hinduism, which gradually was transformed into an armed brotherhood hostile to Islam but separated from the Hindus. Supreme authority resides in their holy scripture (*Granth*), the reading of which is their main form of worship.

India's contact with the West, Christianity, and modern life since the early nineteenth century has led to the emergence of many new religious movements and spiritual groups, as diverse in their principles, ideals, and reactions to foreign influences as the personalities of their founders; most distinguish themselves from traditional devotional movements by a more pronounced interest in ethical, social, and national issues. The extent of their influence in India has, however, often been exaggerated in the West, for the beliefs and customs of the Indian masses are still largely traditional.

The first product of this cultural encounter, the Brāhmo Samāj, a partly social, partly religious organization, was founded by the Bengali *brahman* Ram Mohan Roy (1772–1833), who, using modern vehicles of propaganda such as the press, advocated social reform and a reformation of Hinduism, which, if purged of abuses and with its monotheistic features underscored, might become the foundation of a universal religion. Schisms resulting mainly from the activities of the *bhakti* mystic Keshab Chandra Sen (1838–1884) led to the coexistence of various small groups of differing aims and ideals. In the second half of the nineteenth century, anti-Muslim and anti-Western ideas as well as religious nationalism led to movements of reformation and modernization or to the propagation of what was considered the essence of traditional Hinduism. One such reformation movement representing the former tendency is the Ārya Samāj, founded in 1875 by Dayananda Sarasvati (1824–1883). Sarasvati advocated absolute adherence to the religion of the Vedic hymns, which he regarded as a continually misinterpreted source of pure monotheism, moral and social reform, and guidance toward the right way to salvation; however, most of the doctrines Sarasvati accepted (e.g., *karman*) were post-Vedic. Opposed to foreign religions, the Ārya Samāj propagates a refined nationalist and democratic Hinduism without symbols and local cults but including the worship of God with praise, prayer, meditation, and daily ceremonies. The main object of Ramakrishna (1836–1886), perhaps the best-known modern Hindu saint, was the propagation of the Vedānta as a superior and comprehensive view of life that synthesizes all faiths on a higher level of spiritual consciousness. A devotee of Rāma and later of Kṛṣṇa, he practiced the Vaiṣṇava form of love; convinced that Hinduism, Islam, and Christianity all lead to the same God, he also adopted Christian methods. Under his disciple Vivekananda (1862–1902), who turned the trend of Vedānta philosophy toward new values, the Ramakrishna Mission (founded 1897) became, in India, an important force for spiritual regeneration and unification.

SEE ALSO Ājīvikas; Bengali Religions; Brāhmaṇas and Āraṇyakas; Buddhism; Cārvāka; Durga Hinduism; Gāṇapatyas; Hindi Religious Traditions; Hinduism; Indo-European Religions, overview article; Indus Valley Religion; Jainism; Kṛṣṇaism; Marathi Religions; Parsis; Śaivism; Saura Hinduism; Sikhism; Sinhala Religion; Tamil Religions; Vaisnavism; Vedas; Vedism and Brahmanism.

BIBLIOGRAPHY

Carman, John Braisted. *The Theology of Rāmānuja: An Essay in Interreligious Understanding.* New Haven, Conn., and London, 1974.

Eliot, Charles. *Hinduism and Buddhism: A Historical Sketch* (1921). 3d ed. 3 vols. London, 1957.

Embree, Ainslie T., ed. *The Hindu Tradition: Readings in Oriental Thought.* New York, 1966.

Gonda, Jan. *Aspects of Early Viṣṇuism* (1954). 2d ed. Delhi, 1969.

Gonda, Jan. *Change and Continuity in Indian Religion.* The Hague, 1965. A series of essays and monographs aiming at a fuller appreciation of the many difficulties with which the historian of the Indian religions is confronted.

Gonda, Jan. *Viṣṇuism and Śivaism: A Comparison.* London, 1970. The Jordan Lectures for 1969.

Gonda, Jan. *Medieval Religious Literature in Sanskrit.* Wiesbaden, 1977.

Gonda, Jan. *Die Religionen Indiens.* 2 vols. Vol. 1, *Veda und älterer Hinduismus,* 2d rev. ed. Vol. 2, *Der jüngere Hinduismus.* Stuttgart, 1963, 1978. Comprehensive, detailed, and well-documented histories of all aspects of Vedism and Hinduism. Translated into French as *Les religions de l'Inde,* 2 vols. (Paris, 1962–1965) and into Italian as *Le religioni dell'India,* 2 vols. (Milan, 1981).

Gonda, Jan. *Vedic Ritual: The Non-Solemn Rites.* Leiden and Cologne, 1980.

Gupta, Sanjukta, Dirk Jan Hoens, and Teun Goudriaan. *Hindu Tantrism.* Leiden, 1979.

Keith, Arthur Berriedale. *The Religion and Philosophy of the Veda and Upanishads* (1925). 2 vols. Reprint, Westport, Conn., 1971.

Moore, Charles A., ed. *The Indian Mind: Essentials of Indian Philosophy and Culture.* Honolulu, 1967.

O'Flaherty, Wendy Doniger. *Śiva: The Erotic Ascetic.* London, 1981. Reprint of *Asceticism and Eroticism in the Mythology of Śiva* (1973). An original discussion of various aspects of Śaivism and Indian mythology in general.

Renou, Louis. *Religions of Ancient India.* London, 1953. The Jordan Lectures for 1951.

Renou, Louis, and Jean Filliozat. *L'Inde classique: Manuel des études indiennes.* 2 vols. Paris, 1947–1953.

Zaehner, R. C. *Hinduism.* London, 1962.

New Sources

Aleaz, K. P. *Dimensions of Indian Religion: Study, Experience, and Interaction.* Calcutta, 1995.

Baird, Robert D., ed. *Religion in Modern India.* New Delhi, 1998.

Heehs, Peter, ed. *Indian Religions: A Historical Reader of Spiritual Expression and Experience.* New York, 2002.

Larson, Gerald James. *India's Agony over Religion.* Albany, N.Y., 1995.

Lopez, Donald S., Jr., ed. *Religions of India in Practice.* Princeton, N.J., 1995.

Madan, T. N., ed. *Religion in India.* Delhi and New York, 1992.

Perrett, Roy, ed. *Indian Philosophy of Religion.* Dordrecht and Boston, 1989.

Sharma, Arvind, ed. *Women in Indian Religions.* New Delhi and New York, 2002.

Young, Katherine K., ed. *Hermeneutical Paths to the Sacred Worlds of India: Essays in Honour of Robert W. Stevenson.* Atlanta, 1994.

JAN GONDA (1987)
Revised Bibliography

INDIAN RELIGIONS: RURAL TRADITIONS

The religious beliefs and practices of rural India reflect the influence of three general cultural traditions that throughout history have mingled and mixed in varying degrees. Grouped generally, these traditions are those of agricultural cultures, food-gathering communities, and nomadic societies.

Since the third millennium BCE the most stable groups within these three traditions have been those of the agricultural cultures, which are typified by their development of written script and by their emergent sophistication in the production of artifacts reflecting a pervasive consciousness of the earth and its vegetation. The myth-bound lives of people in these cultures have long been linked to the cycles of time experienced in the circular movement of the seasons and in the resulting change in the earth's character. The fundamental energy that gave life to sprouting seeds was commonly understood to be feminine and was represented in female images—although a variety of icons, figurines, and magical geometric drawings painted on home floors and walls also reveal a pervasive worship of the sun, water, grain, and other natural phenomena. Possessed of an archaic knowledge of tools and agricultural methods, these people were India's first inventors and creators and have given as their cultural inheritance to India agrarian technologies that until recently remained unchanged for five thousand years.

A second general cultural stream arose from the archaic food-gatherers living in India's forests and mountain regions and whose myths reflect the notion that they are the firstborn of the earth. Made up mostly of tribal societies with a remote past and no recorded history, these groups established kingdoms and ruled large areas of the vast interior of India, but then disappeared again into the wilderness, where they lived in caves, hunted animals, and collected wild foodstuffs from the dark and pathless forests. These peoples, too, experienced life as power and developed magical and sacerdotal means by which they could please or combat the intensely felt but unseen and terrible potencies of the natural world. Like the ancient agriculturalists, they also felt kinship with the earth but in their case revered the animals and wild plants of the forest rather than of the domestic arena. They, too, knew the earth intimately and understood her to whisper her secrets to them as long as they did not wound her breasts with the plough.

The third cultural stream was comprised of nomadic peoples, wanderers across the lands who have bequeathed to their descendants a racial memory of ancient migrations across wild deserts, over rugged mountains, and through lush valleys. These were cattle herders and horse riders who first entered India, the land of rivers, seeking water for their stock. They had a penetrating visual vocabulary based on an astute appreciation of color and light. Their rituals and art forms share in this vibrant experience of the world. Their bards and dancers were vigorous drinkers who lived a free and spontaneous life full of the passion of war and love.

India's rural religious traditions arose from the confluence of these three cultural streams. These ancient societies are the predecessors of the rural people today whose farming techniques, arts, and rituals give form to primordial tribal myths. When women today paint ceremonial drawings, when artisans create fecundative images, when singers and performers tell of epic conquests, they concretize the legends and mysteries of these ancient groups. From this archaic unconscious come rural myths of cosmic power, of cyclical destruction and creation, of natural processes in which human beings live their lives.

Women of today's higher castes in northern Mithila recount a myth that is identical both in form and meaning to a legend sung by autochthonous women of the deep south who worship the goddess Pedammā. The long history of the myth indicates a substratum of powerful and energetic female memories, the unconscious source of which is transmitted through feminine culture and given form in the act of communication between mother and daughter. In this myth are to be found remnants of ancient wisdom regarding creative power that carries the germ of its own destruction. Out of this tradition arises values that are deeply understood by the women of Mithila, who say with great simplicity that "these insights come from a time without beginning; we carry this wisdom in our wombs."

Candrakālā Devī, a traditional artist of Mithila, narrates the following myth:

> First there was Ādi Śakti ("primordial power"), another name for whom was Mahāmāyā ("great creator"). She was the one, alone. She desired [a partner] and, displaying her *māyā,* created the manifest world out of the void. A cosmic egg appeared and the new male gods Brahmā, Viṣṇu, and Śiva emerged when it hatched. As these gods grew to young manhood, Ādi Śakti turned with fiery passion to Brahmā and sought to marry him. Brahmā recoiled, saying, "You are our mother!" The goddess laughed at him and reduced him to ashes. The same thing happened to Viṣṇu: He, too, retreated, filled with horror and he, too, was consumed by fire. The luminous goddess then approached Śiva, the young, beautiful, long-limbed youth who, hearing her demands, smiled and accepted her as his bride.

The story's versions as told in the South and the North are the same to this point. But now they diverge. In the legend as told in Mithila (in the North), Śiva responds to the goddess Ādi Śakti by asking her to accept him as her disciple. She agrees to his request, and Śiva learns from her the secrets of life and various incantations for raising the dead. Having mastered these mysteries and ancient secrets of power, Śiva then destroys the primordial Ādi Śakti by engulfing her with flame and reducing her to ashes, promising to her as he does so that he will marry her again after many aeons when she is reborn as Satī, the daughter of Daksa. The story acknowledges that this second marriage did, indeed, eventually take place.

The Dravidian variant—one in which passionate youth is said to lead irrevocably to old age and decrepitude—is darker and more archaic. As in the northern version, Śiva agrees to marry Ādi Śakti after the goddess has reduced Brahmā and Viṣṇu to ashes for refusing to do so. In the southern account Śiva is then said to ask Ādi Śakti if he may have as a gift from her the brilliant jewel that shines as brightly as ten thousand suns and that rests on her forehead. Infatuated, she agrees to the request and hands the jewel to her young lover. As he takes it from her hand the goddess ages frightfully, as if centuries had just elapsed in the moment's duration. Formerly a beautiful goddess who lived unhindered by time, she is now suddenly a bent and undesirable old woman. Time, the devourer of all things, has entered the world. Śiva merely smiles; for he is Kālā, the lord of time. With this action, the new gods have taken over. The primordial primacy of female power is reduced to ashes, its brilliance usurped. The female takes second place in the Puranic pantheon to the male.

Candrakālā Devī molds images of Ādi Śakti out of clay and paper pulp to which has been added *methi* (cumin seed), ground to a paste. The image of the goddess has many arms, an elongated body, and hollow eyes. She is reminiscent of the ancient and universal Mātalas, the earth mothers. Their gaunt, passionless, masklike faces have crater-deep eyes, stark with the secrets of death and life.

Images of Ādi Śakti, the primeval mother, are made at harvest time. Also known as Aṣṭabhuja ("eight armed"), she holds in her hands the cosmic egg as well as a cup that holds the seed or blood to fertilize the fields; she also holds the sun and moon, the earth (depicted as a flat plate and covered with grass and sprouts of other plants), two bullocks pulling a plow, a plowshare, a flower, and a sword.

By the beginning of the second millennium (no one knows exactly how early), groups of peoples migrated into India from the Northwest. They were not of one tribe, nor had they all reached the same levels of cultural development or of artistic abilities. The best-known of these migrating groups were the Vedic Aryans. Strong, heroic, and proud of their identity, these people had wandered the steppes for generations, never settling long enough to establish any cities.

The Vedic Aryans were warriors who brought with them into the river valleys of northern India the songs and poems that came to be included in the *mantras* (hymns) of the Vedic religious textual tradition. Their songs were robust, loud, and full of life: hymns to the awesome processes of nature; invocations to Aditya, the sun god; praises to Vāyu, the wind, and to Uṣas, the maiden of the dawn. Moving into the decaying or destroyed Harappan urban areas, the Vedic Aryans introduced to those agricultural peoples the instruments of war, new dimensions of language, new volumes of sound, new relationships with nature, and pulsing vitality.

In successive waves through the centuries the Vedic Aryans moved on their horse-driven chariots along the densely forested banks of the Indus, Ganges, and Yamunā rivers. It took a thousand years for them to reach the Narmada River in central India (in modern Madhya Pradesh), by which time they had merged into the cultures of the vast hinterland through intermarriage and by adopting local customs, skills, and tools.

It is likely that the Vedic Aryans found the original inhabitants of India living at various levels of technological culture, those groups living within the walled cities of Mohenjo-Daro and Harappa contrasting vividly with the Paleolithic societies living in the dense forests along the banks of the Ganges or in the caves of the Vindhya Mountains. Five-thousand-year-old ruins scattered throughout the Harappan sites indicate that the people of the Indus Valley had established a highly developed society: They had discovered the wheel, with which they transformed their methods of transportation and increased the sophistication with which they molded their clay pots; they had developed simple tools with which they could measure angles and with which they could build structures with precision and accuracy; they had learned to grow and spin cotton, to weave and dye cloth, to mold clay, and to cast bronze into figurines.

Intense intellectual and psychological activity accompanied the tremendous revolution in technology and the production of tools brought about by these early city dwellers. They had developed a script to illumine their pictographs, and they practiced yoga and other meditative techniques to expand their minds.

With the fall of the cities to natural and martial forces, large numbers of people took refuge in the wilds of central India, traveling all the way to the banks of the Narmada and Tapti rivers and even farther south. They carried with them into the inner lands of the subcontinent their knowledge of agriculture, technology, ritual, and magic. The influence of these urban skills and perceptions appear in their symbols, worship, and magical practices.

The migrations of nomadic peoples onto the fertile plains of India were to continue through the centuries. One of the most important of these tribes to the development of Indian culture and its rural traditions were the Ahirs, who came to be known in the epic *Mahābhārata* as the "snake-loving" Abhiras.

The figure of Kṛṣṇa also was known as Māyōṉ or Māyavan in ancient Tamil *saṃgam* literature; the dark-skinned, non-Aryan god emerged in the culture of Mathurā and reflects a mixture of elements from Ahir and tribal backgrounds. The name itself, *Kṛṣṇa* ("dark one"), is pregnant with early Aryan scorn; but it was Kṛṣṇa who was to supply the generative vitality that transformed Indian arts and culture.

Stories about the personalities and affairs of Kṛṣṇa, of the Goddess, and of other local heroes were collected by the compilers of the epic poems the *Mahābhārata* and the *Rāmāyaṇa.* These tales, as well as myths and legends recounted in the various Purāṇas, traveled by word of mouth through the vast lands of India. Transmission of these stories was enhanced by their widespread multifaceted use of song, dance, mime, drama, and iconography. These various media allowed all kinds of people, particularly members of those tribal groups living outside the mainstream of society, to experience the sensory nature of the divine presence and to express the immediacy of that presence through an active, personal, and contemporaneous participation.

Rural painters and balladeers drew their inspiration and source material from Ahir love songs, accounts of brave and victorious heroes, and tales of the Puranic gods and their erotic adventures. The most famous of these ballads was the *Lorikagan,* which was composed in Avadhi (a dialect of Hindi) and which recounts the love held by Lorik, an Ahir from the Mithila country, for Chaṇḍa, the wife of Śrīdhara. According to the tale, Śrīdhara had become impotent as a result of a curse placed on him by the goddess Pārvatī. Chaṇḍa then fell in love and eloped with Lorik. Śrīdhara searched for the couple, only to be killed by Lorik when he found them. The young couple then approached the master gambler Mahāpatra Dusadh and engaged him in a game of dice. Lorik lost Chaṇḍa and all his wealth to Mahāpatra Dusadh. But Chaṇḍa argued with Dusadh that the stakes involved in the game did not include her clothing and demanded that the gambling continue. On resumption of the game she sat down in front of Dusadh and exposed her beautiful body. Intoxicated by the sight of Chaṇḍa's nakedness, Dusadh lost control of the game and was defeated by Lorik, who later killed him. This legend finds expression in paintings, theater, and song.

The tribal kings of central India also had an ancient bardic tradition. The Gond *rāja*s included in their courts official tribal genealogists and musicians known as Pardhans, who recounted to the royal household the ancient stories of the Gond hero-kings and warriors. Serving also as priests and diviners, in time the Pardhans absorbed Hindu legends, gods, and even ethics into their tribal epics, ballads, and other expressions of folklore.

A Pardhan today worships his musical instrument, the *bana,* as the god Bara Pen. "As his sacred books [are] to a Brahmin, as his scales [are] to a Bania, as his plough [is] to a Gond, so is the bana to the Pardhan" (Hivale, 1946, p. 66).

It is said that the original Pardhan was timid when he first played his wonderful new music in the house of the Gond brothers. But he played so divinely that all those residing in the heavenly as well as earthly worlds were enchanted. Even the supreme god, Nāyāyaṇ Deo, stood watching in amazement. Then the Pardhan forgot his shyness and completely lost himself in his music. He danced ecstatically with his *bana,* with which he produced sounds the world had never heard before. On that day, it is said, three new *par*s (sounds or combination of sounds) known as Sarsetī Par, Nāyāyaṇ Par, and Pujan Par were first created.

Pābujī is a folk hero who is especially popular among the Bhils, a tribal group living in Rajasthan. According to legend, Pābujī was suckled as an infant by a lioness and grew to be a brave warrior. He was given a powerful black mare named Kāḷmī by Devaḷ, a *cāraṇ* woman of a pastoral community. In return for this gift Pābujī promised to protect Devaḷ's life and cattle, and he eventually died in the attempt to keep his promise. Among the Bhils are a group of bardic musicians (*bhopā*s) who travel through the countryside with a fifteen-foot long painted scroll known as the Pābujī-ka-Pad (Pābujī's scroll). In its center lies the main figure, a portrait of Pābujī himself, painted in vibrant red, black, olive, and yellow ocher. Surrounding this main figure are depictions of warriors engaged in battle, images of horses, lions, and tigers, and scenes of heroic incidents that serve to illustrate the legend of Pābujī. Performers reenact stories based on that legend at night. The scroll is stretched out, oil lamps are lit, and the *bhopā* sings his story. As he sings, a woman lifts the lamp to the cloth in order to illumine for the crowd the figures of warriors on horseback, animals, birds, and other elements of the tales. She joins with the *bhopā* in singing the refrain and, at times, dances.

The bards of the Santāls in Bengal and Bihar are known as *jādu paṭuā* ("magic-painters"), who carry from village to village their painted *paṭs* depicting scenes from the Purāṇas as well as their own tribal cosmogonic and anthropogonic myths.

The fundamental assumptions of male supremacy in Brahmanic culture were established by the time of the classical law books such as the *Manusmṛti* (c. 200 BCE–100 CE) and the various Dharmaśāstras. According to these and other texts, a girl was dependent on her father and then, as a woman, was inferior to her husbands and sons. Such ideals of Indian womanhood as obedience and faithfulness to the male were embodied in the images of the goddesses Sītā and Savitrī.

Vedic learning was closed to women by the time of the *smṛti* ("remembered") literatures. However, in the vast and flat countryside that encircled the cities and in the rural life of the village and fields surged a powerful, flexible, ancient, and secret undercurrent among women, wandering yogins, Tantric adepts, and magician-priests, who focused their religious sensibilities on the primeval female, Śakti, and on Śiva, the mysterious god of the autochthonous tribes.

The earliest, almost primordial, images of the earth mother glorified a feminine creative principle made manifest by the image itself, which often celebrated the secrets of birth and death. The dark earth-bound goddess was a mother, yet a virgin, for "no father seemed necessary to the society in which she originated" (Kosambi, 1962, p. 90). Originally represented aniconically through hieroglyphs and vegetation symbols, through the centuries the primeval mother came to be represented in animal and finally in anthropomorphic images of Śakti, who had a thousand names and forms. Potent with the energy of life itself, and holding within herself the essence of her earlier incarnations, she had the capacity to heal and transform. Such earlier forms find expression in the hieroglyphic triangle resting on her heart or generative organs. Her vegetal nature appeared in the plants she held in her hands. Her animal incarnations were transformed into the various beasts on which she rode. As the primary physical and spiritual essence of the universe, Śakti was alive in the experience of color, form, taste, and fragrance. In her final form she was Durgā—the holder of all life, brighter than a thousand suns.

Tantric texts describe Durgā's symbols: "The Goddess of renowned form assumes in times of protection the form of a straight line. In times of dissolution, she takes the form of a circle. Similarly for creation she takes the brilliant appearance of a triangle" (Sastry, 1906, p. 280).

A new priesthood and new relationships with the gods became inevitable with the rise of the male godhead into the Puranic pantheon. The emergent potent male deity was known as the *kṣetrapal* (guardian of the field and womb), Thakur Dev. The *kṣetrapal* protected and fecundated the earth and field, the body of the goddess. In the religious rites the people expressed their search for cosmic transformation, embodied in the act of sexual union between the God and Goddess. Agricultural magic fused with alchemical and Tantric practices.

Either the aboriginal magician-priest known as the *baiga* or a priest from the potter, the barber, or the *camār* community presided at ceremonies worshiping trees and river-washed stones held at the village or forest shrines honoring the primeval mother, the Goddess, various deities, or the tribal hero. The potency of his magic was recognized and accepted by the villagers and householders living in the sheltered rural societies. The Tantric doctrines outlined in the Āgama and Nigama textual traditions, the frenzied ecstatic worship of Śakti through ritual performance and *mantra*-recitation, had pervaded the Indian psyche to the depths of the cultural subconscious. In prosperous villages the Puranic gods were worshiped; but along with this praise, and at a deeper level, a worship of the pre-Vedic deities continued and the practice of Tantric rituals remained.

One of the attributes of the Goddess was *jāgaritṛ* (wakefulness). Through practicing such *vrata* ("vow") rites as fasting, meditative concentration, and other observances, the woman votary directly invoked the power of the goddess by awakening her power (*śakti*) inherent in various symbols, stones, trees, and water pots. She drew geometric shapes (*maṇḍalas*) on the ground and on the wall of houses, worshiped the interlocking triangle known as the *yantra* dedicated to the Goddess, and performed in the darkness various rituals accompanying the sprouting of corn. Songs, dance, and image-making flourished as part of the ceremonies. The worshiper hoped through creative expression, *vrata,* and ritual song and dance to awaken Śakti and to ensure that, once awakened, that primal energy was not dissipated or dispersed.

Unlike the temporary clay images of the *grāma mātṛkās* ("village mothers"), which have mysterious links with the earth and its cyclical patterns of creation and destruction, the images of the *vīras* (deified "heroes") and the *kṣetrapals* are shafts embodying virility and power carved in stone and wood. Rising as pillars to the sky and toward the sun and yet rooted in the earth, the harsh simplicity of the flat visual planes thus gives to the images a heroic dimension representing the sanctity of the immovable and the eternal divine presence.

The term *vīra* ("hero") is often used to refer to the valiant ancestors killed in battle while protecting women, fields, and cattle. It also is used to describe the alchemists, yogins, magicians, and enlightened ones who gained control over and conquered the ways of their bodies and minds. Both types of *vīras* were deified and worshiped in the form of the *vīrakāḻ* and *pāḻiā* stones. The *vīra* cult itself is an ancient one that centers on an admixture of ancestor worship, veneration of the heroic protectors and guardians as well as of magicians and seers, and praise of such figures as the Hurā Purā (deified heroes) or the Āyi Vaḍil (deified ancestors) of the Bhil tribes. The cult also includes the worship of a wonderfully rich symbolic complex associated with the *yakṣas*, spirits of the forests and rivers known by the compilers of the *Atharvaveda* and the Purāṇas. Depicted as having tall male bodies (which they are mysteriously able to transform), the *yakṣas* were regarded at first as malevolent beings, but underwent a significant change at some point when they became associated and identified with the *kṣetrapals* and the *vīrās*, with whom they protected and watched over the welfare of the earth and the Goddess.

India's most powerful symbol of the hero is a rider on a horse. Carved in memorial stones or cast in metal icons and amulets, the image displays the vitality and energy of the heroic male.

Elements of the *vīra* cult evolved through time into the worship of Śiva, the supreme god of rural India. Śiva is described as late as the third century CE as a *yakṣa* who is to be propitiated in the wild regions beyond the village walls. Rural customs still exist in India that reflect Śiva's autochthonous origins. In the Punjab and in Himachal Pradesh, for example, women are not permitted the worship of Śiva. Women in Uttar Pradesh can worship Śiva in the form of the *liṅga,* but they must carry their offerings to the god in the corner of their *sārīs* and must never allow their hand to touch the phallic form as they circumambulate it.

The tribal Bhils worship Śiva as their first ancestor. The Gonds of Bastar sing an epic, Lingo pen, in which they describe the appearance of Śiva in human form:

> There the God Mahādev was ruling from the upper sea to the lower sea. What was Mahādev doing? He was swimming like a rolling stone, he had no hands, no feet. He remained like the trunk [of a tree]. Then Mahādev performed austerities for twelve months. And Bhagavān [i.e., Śiva] came and stood close to Mahādev and called to him. "Thy devotion is finished, emerge out of the water." He said, "How shall I emerge? I have no hands, no feet, no eyes." Then Mahādev received man's form. Thus man's form complete was made in the luminous world. (Hislop, 1866, pp. 2–3)

Next to their drawings of the corn goddess the Warlis of Maharashtra often display an image known as Pāñc Siryā Dev, a headless male figure with five sheaves of sprouting corn emerging from his body. Among the Bhils of Gujarat a five-headed figure with an erect penis is cast in metal and is called Pāñc Mukhi Dev. Both images are linked to Śiva and to cultic fertility rites.

In some regions of West Bengal the roles and personalities of Śiva and the sun god fuse into the worship of Dharma Thākur. The *maṇḍala* (village headman) performs rituals centered on the marriage of Śiva and Gaurī at which Kalighat painters used to congregate in order to sell their paintings to pilgrims.

At the Nilā Gajan or Gambhira festivals Śiva is worshiped as Nilākaṇṭha (*nilā* is an indigo cloth worn by low-caste devotees of Śiva who worship the planets and for whom the Gambhira is a key harvest ritual). Singing abounds in these rites. One song describes Śiva as a cultivator of cotton and as one who loves Koch tribal girls:

> The month of Baisakh came,
> The farmer ploughed the field;
> The month of Āṣāḍh came,
> God Śiva planted cotton seeds,
> As the planting was over,
> Śiva went to the quarter of the Koch women.
> He stayed and stayed on there,
> Until he knew that cotton had grown.
> Śiva returned to gather cotton,
> He placed the stuff in the hands of Gaṅgā,
> She spun yarn out of it.
> Śiva wove a piece of cloth,
> The washerwoman Netā washed it clean,
> She washed it by water from the ocean of milk.
> (Bhattacharya, 1977, pp. 60–61)

Having become the central deity in rural areas, Śiva then became the figure from which all of the minor rural gods emerged. The elephant-headed Gaṇeśa ("lord of the folk"), for example, is regarded as the son of Śiva, though no legend specifically relates the nature of his birth. Originally worshiped as a malevolent spirit and the creator of obstacles, Gaṇeśa underwent a transformation during the time of the composition of the Purāṇas and assumed the role of protector of the people and the remover of obstacles. Hanumān (or Māruti), the devotee of Rāma, is also known to be an incarnation of Mahābhairav, who, in turn, is one of Śiva's many manifestations. No forest or village masculine deity is free of an intimate association with Śiva, the central personality of the cosmos and locus of the processes of creation and destruction.

Deep within the religious practices and ideologies of rural India lie the recognition of cosmic transformation marked by the flexive flow of creation and destruction, the appreciation of the vital forces of life, and the longing to be protected from the powers of the physical and spiritual worlds. The gods fuse and merge, or they are transformed, or they vanish with the receding forests and disappearing tribes. New gods come into being and new rituals emerge, bringing with them changes in the form and content of religious expressions. But the sacredness and the mystical power of rural religious sensibilities survive the many changes in deities and rituals throughout history.

SEE ALSO Alchemy, article on Indian Alchemy; Bengali Religions; Goddess Worship, article on the Hindu Goddess; Hindi Religious Traditions; Horses; Indus Valley Religion; Kṛṣṇa; Mahābhārata; Maṇḍalas, article on Hindu Maṇḍalas; Marathi Religions; Purāṇas; Rāmāyaṇa; Śāstra Literature; Śiva; Tamil Religions; Tantrism; Yantra.

BIBLIOGRAPHY

Archer, William G. *The Vertical Man: A Study in Primitive Indian Sculpture.* London, 1947.

Bhattacharya, Asutosh. *The Sun and the Serpent Lore of Bengal.* Calcutta, 1977.

Dasgupta, Sashibhushan. *Obscure Religious Cults.* Calcutta, 1962.

Elmore. W. T. *Dravidian Gods in Modern Hinduism.* Lincoln, Neb., 1915.

Elwin, Verrier. *The Baiga.* London, 1939.

Hislop, Stephen. *Papers relating to the Aboriginal Tribes of the Central Provinces.* Nagpur, 1866.

Hivale, Shamrao. *The Pardhans of the Upper Narbada Valley.* Oxford, 1946.

Jayakar, Pupul. *The Earthen Drum: An Introduction to the Ritual Arts of Rural India.* New Delhi, 1980.

Kane, P. V. *History of Dharmaśāstra.* 2d ed., rev. & enl. 5 vols. in 7. Poona, 1968–1975.

Kosambi, D. D. *Myth and Reality.* Bombay, 1962.

Kramrisch, Stella. *Unknown India: Ritual Art in Tribe and Village.* Philadelphia, 1968.

Oppert, Gustav. *On the Original Inhabitants of Bharatavarṣa or India* (1893). Reprint, Delhi, 1972.

Reeves, Ruth. *Cire Perdue Casting in India.* New Delhi, 1962.

Shamasastry, R. *The Origin of the Devanagari Alphabets.* Varanasi, 1973.

New Sources

Durrans, Brian, and T. Richard Blurton, eds. *The Cultural Heritage of the Indian Village.* London, 1991.

Epstein, T. Scarlett, A. P. Suryanrayana, and T. Thimmegowda, eds. *Village Voices: Forty Years of Rural Transformation in South India.* Thousand Oaks, Calif., 1998.

Kapur, Tribhuwan. *Religion and Ritual in Rural India: A Case Study in Kumaoon.* New Delhi, 1989.

McMullen, Clarence O. *Religious Beliefs and Practices of the Sikhs in Rural Punjab.* New Delhi, 1989.

Sharma, Kanhaiyalal. *Rural Society in India.* Jaipur, 1997.

Vishnu, Asha. *Material Life of Northern India: Based on an Archaeological Study: (3rd Century B.C. to 1st Century B.C.)* New Delhi, 1993.

Wiser, William H., and Charlotte Viall Wiser. *Behind Mud Walls: Seventy-Five Years in a North Indian Village.* Berkeley, 2000.

PUPUL JAYAKAR (1987)
Revised Bibliography

INDIAN RELIGIONS: MYTHIC THEMES

India, like other civilizations, has myths that deal with themes shared by all human beings—the great themes of life and death, of this world and the world beyond—which she inflects with her own personal colorations and thus makes different from the myths of other civilizations. Moreover, Indians have been inspired to create myths on themes that have not appealed to other civilizations with the same intensity, or on themes that simply do not exist outside of India. One can go further in laying out this spectrum of the general and the particular, beginning with the universals and moving through large shared cultures (such as the Indo-European) down through India as a whole until one reaches the many particular, local traditions within India. This approach views myths on the analogy of languages (as F. Max Müller taught), which can be broken down into language families (again, the Indo-European), languages, dialects, and regional dialects. Indeed, if one wishes, one can go still further, until one reaches, in India, at least a single language (or dialect) that is said to be spoken by a single person. So, too, at the end of the line (and perhaps at the beginning of the line too, *in illo tempore*), each myth exists in a unique version in the mind of the individual who knows it.

In attempting to present an overview of Indian mythic themes, the author of this article has chosen to begin with the great universal themes as they appear in their Indian incarnations (primarily Hindu forms, though with some passing references to the Buddhist variants of the pan-Indian themes) and to move through the narrower Indo-European functions of the myths in India to variants that are uniquely Indian. There the article shall perforce stop; it would be impossible to trace the regional subvariations in an essay of limited size and wide range, and of course the subsubvariations in the minds of all the individual myth-knowers are infinite. But it must never be forgotten that these subvariations do exist (and have been recorded in some of the books listed in the bibliography attached to this article) and that, moreover, they flow not only downstream (from the pan-Indian to the local) but upstream, from the local to the pan-Indian, in a cybernetic process that lends the great myths much of their particular flavor, texture, and vivid detail.

ANIMALS. Although it is no longer believed, as it once was, that all mythology is somehow connected with totemism, it is certainly still true that you cannot have a mythology without animals. Animals and gods are the two communities poised on the frontiers of the human community, the two "others" by which humans define themselves. And though all animals can be mythical, certain animals tend to be more mythical than others, more archetypal, if the reader will. Birds and snakes recur throughout the mythologies of the world, both individually and as a matched pair. Individually, birds (and eggs) are symbols of creation; their wings make them part of the kingdom of heaven, where they come to function as symbols of God (in Christianity) or of the magic woman from the other world (the swan-maiden of European folklore). Snakes slough their skin to become symbols of rebirth, or bite their tails to become symbols of infinity (the Uroboros); they bring about the loss of innocence (as in the *Book of Genesis*) or the loss of immortality (as in the *Epic of Gilgamesh*). Together, birds and snakes symbolize the elements of air and subterranean water, spirit and matter, good and evil, or simply the principle of opposition, through the observed natural enmity of the two species.

All of this symbolism is found in Indian mythology, together with more narrowly Indo-European themes: the killing of the dragon-serpent (Indra killing Vṛtra, Kṛṣṇa subduing Kāliya); the battle between birds and snakes (the quarrel between Vinatā, the mother of snakes, and Suparṇā, the mother of birds, in the opening books of the *Mahābhārata*). Also found in the *Mahābhārata* are traces of the more subtle Indo-European theme of the battle between the snake and the horse (of which is found echoes in paintings of Saint George, always mounted on his white horse, killing the dragon): In the course of the quarrel between Vinatā and Suparṇā, the black snakes form the hairs of the tail of the sacred horse, a trick that leads eventually to a great sacrifice in which snakes are killed in place of the usual stallion. But as might be expected in a country as snaky as India, snake symbolism is more luxuriant than it is elsewhere. The *nāgas,* half serpent, half deity, who inhabit the waters of the lower world, participate in many myths and adorn most temples; Viṣṇu sleeps on Ananta, the serpent of eternity, and Śiva wears snakes for his bracelets, his necklaces, his sacred thread, and (with occasionally embarrassing results) his belt. Birds of a rich mythological plumage are equally pervasive; Viṣṇu rides on the *garuḍa* bird (a descendant of the Vedic sunbird), Skanda on a peacock (an appropriate emblem for the general of the army of the gods), and Brahmā on a royal goose or swan (the *haṃsa* that is also a symbol of the transmigrating soul).

Another important Indo-European pair of animals, the horse and the cow, remain essential to the mythology of the Vedas and to that of later Hinduism. The stallion loses in India some of his ancient power as a symbol of royal, martial, and fertile functions (the Indo-European triad), although he remains an important figure on the local, village level, where one still encounters many minor horse deities and equine heroes, as well as charming terra-cotta horses, some of enormous size. The mare became in India a symbol of the voracious female who must be tamed (like the submarine fire in the form of a mare held in check by the waters of the ocean, until the moment when she will emerge at doomsday to destroy the universe). But the animal who truly usurped the stallion's place of honor is the cow, which became symbolic of all the values of the society of the newly settled Ganges Valley (in contrast with the nomadic, warring Indo-European society that was so well symbolized by the stallion); the cow represented motherhood, nourishment, chastity, and noninjury (the cow being an animal able to furnish food without having to be slaughtered). The bull plays a relatively minor role, primarily as Nandi, the vehicle of Śiva.

A more purely Indian symbol is the elephant, representing royalty, power, wisdom, fertility, longevity, and much else. The mother of the future Buddha dreamed, upon conceiving him, that a white elephant had entered her womb; Lakṣmī, the goddess of good fortune, is lustrated by two elephants; elephants support the earth and the quarters of the sky; the god Gaṇeśa, patron of scribes and of all enterprises, has the head of an elephant, the source of his cunning and of his ability to remove obstacles. At the other end of the Indian animal spectrum is the dog, already maligned in Indo-European mythology (Kerberos, the dog of Hades, appears in the *Ṛgveda* as the two Sārameyas, the four-eyed brindled dogs of Yama, the king of the dead). In India, the dog became a vehicle for all the negative values of the caste system; he was regarded as unclean, promiscuous both in his eating habits and in his (or, more often, her) sexual habits; dogs are said to be the food of untouchables (who are called "dog-cookers," *śvapakas,* in Sanskrit). Yet Yudhiṣṭhira, the righteous king in the *Mahābhārata,* refused to enter heaven until the gods allowed to enter with him the dog that had followed him faithfully through all his trials, a dog who turned out to be none other than the god Dharma himself, incarnate.

In addition to these individual animals, Indian mythology teems with animals of a more miscellaneous sort. Every Indian god has an animal for its vehicle (*vāhana*). This association means not only that the god is literally carried about on such an animal (for the elephant-headed Gaṇeśa is awkwardly mounted on a bandicoot, or large rat) but also (and more importantly) that the animal "carries" the god in the way that a breeze "carries" perfume, that the god is always present in that animal, in all of its manifestations (the bandicoot, for example, shares Gaṇeśa's nimbleness of wit and ability to get past anything, and so is indeed an appropriate vehicle for the god). This is the only sense in which animals (including cows) are sacred in India; the tendency not to kill them (which does not, unfortunately, generally extend to a tendency not to ill-treat them) arises from something else, from the concept of noninjury (*ahiṃsā*) that discourages the taking of any life in any form. In addition to these official vehicles, many gods appear in theriomorphic or semitheriomorphic forms; Viṣṇu becomes incarnate as the man-lion Narasiṃha, but he also is often represented with the head of a boar and the body of a man in his *avatāra* as the boar. When Śiva makes war on Viṣṇu the boar, he takes the form of a *śarabha,* a beast with eight legs, eight tusks, a mane, and a long tail.

More generally, whether or not people get the gods they deserve, they tend to get the gods that their animals deserve; the natural fauna of any country has a lot to do with the ways in which the people of that country perceive their gods. For example, two animals that play an important role in Indian mythology are the monkey and the tiger. Although neither of these animals is the vehicle of a god, the monkey is a cousin of Hanuman, the monkey ally of Rāma, the divine hero of the *Rāmāyaṇa,* and the tiger sometimes replaces the lion as the vehicle of the goddess Devī (especially in places where lions have long been extinct). But the influence of monkeys and tigers extends far beyond their recorded roles in the mythology. The ingenious mischievousness of the monkey and the uncanny cruelty and beauty of the tiger are qualities that have found their way into the images of many Hindu gods and goddesses. If Judaism has a mythology of lions, and

Christianity a mythology of sheep, India has a mythology of monkeys and tigers.

The Tree and the Mountain at the Center of the Earth. Many, if not all, of the mythologies of the world have located a tree or a mountain, or both, at the center of the world. In India, the sacred mountain is Mount Meru, the golden mountain, wider at its peak than at its base. The sacred tree, too, is inverted, the banyan with its roots in the air. The particularly Indian variants of this myth begin in the *Ṛgveda,* where the sacred *soma* plant, which bestows immortality on the gods, functions as the *axis mundi,* or cosmic pillar, in propping apart heaven and earth. The same *soma* plant is said to have been stolen from heaven by Indra, mounted on an eagle, who carried the plant down to the mountains of earth. This is the Indian variant of the Indo-European myth of the theft of fire; Prometheus carried fire down to earth in a hollow fennel stalk, while Indra (who also embodies the lightning bolt) carries the fiery liquid of *soma* in its own hollow stalk. The association of the mountain, the sacred plant, and the theft continued to produce offshoots in later Hindu mythology. In the *Rāmāyaṇa,* Hanuman is sent to fetch a magic plant that will revive the fallen hero; he flies to the magic mountain and, unable to decide which plant it is that he wants, uproots the entire mountain and brings it to the battlefield. Elsewhere in the *Rāmāyaṇa,* and in the *Mahābhārata,* the gods and demons join forces to use the sacred mountain Mandara as a churn with which they churn the waters of the ocean to obtain the *soma.* As soon as they get it, the demons steal the *soma* from the gods, and the gods steal it back again.

Snakes are also associated with the mountain and the magic plant (as is the serpent in Eden) and with the cosmic waters: When the serpent Vṛtra has wrapped himself around a mountain, holding back the waters (which are homologous both with the *soma* juice that Indra loves and with the rains that he controls), Indra pierces him so that the waters flow again; it is a snake, Vasuki, who is used as the rope for the churn when the gods and demons churn the ocean for *soma*; and when Viṣṇu sleeps on the serpent of eternity in the midst of the cosmic ocean, a lotus plant grows up out of his navel—the navel of the universe. This web of associations forms the framework for the many local myths about particular trees (banyan trees, coconut palms, the sacred mango tree in the temples of South India) and particular plants sacred to particular gods (the *tulsi* of Viṣṇu, the *rudrākṣas* of Śiva).

Cosmogony, Theogony, and Anthropogony. Most Indian mythologies seem to agree about the way in which the universe is arranged: It has a sacred mountain in the center, and concentric oceans and continents around the center; the sacred mountain connects the earth with heaven above and the underworld below. This is the basic Indian cosmology. But there are many different explanations of how the universe came to be the way that it is; these are the Indian cosmogonies. The earliest source, the *Ṛgveda,* refers glancingly to many different theories of creation. Sometimes the world is seen as the result (often apparently a mere by-product) of a cosmic battle, such as the victory of Indra over Vṛtra, or as the consequence of the seemingly unmotivated act of separating heaven and earth, an act that is attributed to several different gods. These aspects of creation are woven in and out of the hymns in the older parts of the *Ṛgveda* (books 2–9). But in the later, tenth book one encounters for the first time hymns that are entirely devoted to speculations on the origins of the cosmos. Some of these hymns seek the origins of the existence of existence itself, or of the creator himself, the golden womb or golden embryo (later to become the golden egg or the golden seed of fire in the cosmic waters). Other hymns speculate upon the sacrifice as the origin of the earth and the people in it, or upon the origins of the sacrifice itself. Sacrifice is central to many concepts of creation, particularly to those explicitly linked to the sacrificial gods or even sacred speech itself, but it also appears as a supplement to other forms of creation, such as sculpture or the spreading out of dirt upon the surface of the waters.

In more anthropomorphic conceptions, creation takes place through a primeval act of incest. In the Brāhmaṇas, the incestuous father is identified as Prajāpati, the lord of creatures; his seed, cast into the fire in place of the usual oblation of clarified butter or *soma* juice, was distributed into various life-forms, ritually creating the living world. Later Indian cosmogonies in the epics and Purāṇas continue to combine the abstract with the anthropomorphic. Sometimes the universe is said to arise out of the waters of chaos, from a flame of desire or loneliness that expresses itself in the creation of living forms as well as such abstract entities as the year, logic, grammar, and the thirty-six musical scales. Sometimes a single god (Brahmā, the creator, or Śiva or Viṣṇu, according to the sectarian bias of the text, or even an undifferentiated sort of Vedantic godhead) arises out of the primeval waters and begins to create, more precisely to emit, the world from within himself; this emission (*prasarga*) is the act of projecting his mind onto formless chaos to give it the form that is its substance. In this latter case, the god usually continues to create by taking the form of an androgyne or by producing a woman out of his own body. From there creation proceeds through anthropomorphic methods, often by a combination of sexual intercourse and the generating of ascetic heat, or *tapas.*

The link between abstract cosmogony and highly inflected anthropogony is made explicit in the Purāṇas, which are traditionally expected to deal with five basic topics: the primary creation (of the universe) and the secondary creation (of gods and humans and all the other living creatures); the dynasties of the sun and of the moon (that trace their lineage back to those divine celestial bodies and forward to the rulers at the time of the recension of the text that contains the list); and the ages of the Manus or ancestors of humans, generally said to be fourteen (the present time is the seventh Manus age). A different sort of cosmogony-cum-anthropogony begins back in the *Ṛgveda.* This is the Indo-European theme of the dismemberment of a cosmic giant or primeval man (Puruṣa), a theme that also appears, outside of India, as the dismemberment of the primeval androgyne. In the *Ṛgveda,* this man is the victim in a sacrifice that he himself performs; the moon is born from his mind, the sun from his eye, the gods from his mouth, and so forth. Moreover, from this dismemberment there arise the four classes, or *varṇas,* of ancient Indian society: the *brahmans* from his head, the rulers and warriors from his chest, the workers from his arms, and the servants from his feet. The Indian text thus extends the three original Indo-European functions that Georges Dumézil taught researchers to recognize (priest-kings, warriors, and producers of fertility) by adding a fourth class that is "outside" the original three, for these three alone receive the epithet "twice-born" (that is, reborn at the time of initiation) throughout Indian social history.

But the myth of the dismembered man says little about theogony, and the *Ṛgveda* contains no systematic narration of the birth of the gods as a whole, although the births of various gods are described in some detail: Indra, kept against his will inside his mother's womb for many years, bursts forth out of her side and kills his own father; Agni, the god of fire, is born of the waters; and so forth. One important late hymn does speak of the birth of the gods in general, from a female called Aditi (Infinity), who is more particularly the mother of the sun and who remains the mother of the solar gods or *adityas* (who are contrasted with the *daityas,* or demons, the sons of Diti) throughout later Indian mythology.

In the epics and Purāṇas, the creation of the gods (and, in turn, of humankind and the animals) is usually attributed to whichever god is regarded by the text in question as the supreme god; thus the Vedic tendency to worship several different gods, but to regard the god one is addressing at the moment as God (a kind of theological serial monogamy that F. Max Müller dubbed henotheism or kathenotheism, "one god at a time") continues into post-Vedic theogonies and anthropogonies.

ESCHATOLOGY AND DEATH. At the end of each aeon comes doomsday, or *pralaya,* when the universe is destroyed by a combination of fire and flood until at last the primeval waters of chaos close back over the ashes of the triple world. In anthropomorphic terms, this is regarded as the moment when God, whose waking moments or whose dream has been the source of the "emission" of the universe from his mind, falls into a deep, dreamless sleep inside the cosmic waters. And at the end of that sleep, at the end of the period of quiescence, the universe, and the consciousness of the god, is reborn once more out of the waters of chaos.

Thus, eschatology is necessarily the flip side of cosmogony; the wave set in motion by the act of creation is already destined to end in a certain kind of dissolution. The particular Indian twist on the Indo-European model, which added a fourth class to the original three in the anthropogony, places its stamp on the Indo-European eschatology, with its twilight of the gods. First of all, India developed, like Greece, a theory of four ages of declining goodness; where the Greeks named these ages after metals, the Indians called them after throws of the dice, the first and best being the *kṛta-yuga,* which is followed by the *tratā,* the *dvāpara,* and finally the present age, or *kaliyuga* (the equivalent of snake-eyes in dice). The choice of the metaphor of dice, with its implication of a fortuitous, impersonal controlling mechanism (which is, moreover, a negative one—the house always wins), is not itself fortuitous; it expresses a basic Indian belief in the inevitable loss of goodness and happiness through the fault of no conscious agent, but just "through the effects of time." The Indian version of the loss of Eden (which appears in Buddhist and Jain as well as Hindu texts) further emphasizes a change in quality between the first three ages and the fourth: The first three are the mythic ages, while the last is real, happening now. And the "end" that comes after the fourth age is not the end at all; the linear decline is combined with the circular pattern of cosmogony and eschatology that has already been seen, and the end becomes the beginning. Time spirals back in on itself like a Möbius strip.

This eternal circularity of time is further developed in India within the context of the unique Indian mythology of *karman,* according to which there is a substance that is intrinsic to all action (*karman,* from the Sanskrit verb *kṛ,* cognate with the Latin *creo,* "to do, to make") and that adheres to the transmigrating soul throughout its life and across the barrier of death, determining the nature of the next rebirth. There are many assumptions embedded in this theory: that there is a transmigrating soul; that one's positive and negative actions are tallied up and carried across the bottom of the ledger page at the end of each life. But the mythology of *karman* reveals a hidden ambivalence in the values expressed by the theory of *karman.* That is, in many myths of *karman,* people want to go on being reborn, in better and better conditions of life, and ultimately in the heaven of the gods. These are the myths within the Vedic and Puranic corpus that exalt *pravṛtti,* or active involvement in worldly life (*saṃsāra*). But there are many other myths in which people want to escape from the wheel of rebirth, to cease from all activity (*nivṛtti*), to find release (*mokṣa*); these are myths influenced by Vedānta and by Buddhism and Jainism. In this latter view, the universal eschatology is replaced by the individual eschatology (or soteriology), the ultimate dissolution of the individual soul (*ātman*) in its final release from the universe itself.

A parallel development took place in the mythology of death. In the *Ṛgveda,* death is vaguely and uneasily alluded to as the transition to a place of light where the ancestors live, a place ruled by Yama, the primeval twin and the first mortal to die. Much of the subsequent mythology of the Brāhmaṇas is an attempt first to explain the origin of death and then to devise means by which death may be overcome, so that the sacrificer will be guaranteed immortality. The Upaniṣads then begin to speak of the terrors of re-death, and to begin to devise ways of obtaining not immortality but release from life altogether, *mokṣa.* And in medieval Hinduism, *bhakti,* or the passionate and reciprocated devotion to a sectarian deity (Śiva, Viṣṇu, or the Goddess), was thought to procure for the worshiper a kind of combination of the Vedic heaven and the Vedantic release: release from this universe into an infinite heaven of bliss in the presence of the loving god. In this way, the mythology of *bhakti* resolved the conflict between the Vedic desire for eternal life and the Vedantic desire to be free of life forever.

Householder and Renouncer, *Dharma* and *Mokṣa*. A similarly irreconcilable conflict of values is addressed in the Hindu mythology of the householder and the ascetic. Again, one can, if one wishes, see this simply as the Indian version of the widespread theme of the conflict between involvement in the world and a commitment to otherworldly, spiritual values, the conflict between God and mammon. But one can still view the development of this theme within the particular context of Indian intellectual history, more particularly as another instance of the pattern that adds a (transcendental) Indian fourth to an older, Indo-European societal triad. Originally, there were three stages of life, or *āśrama*s, in ancient India: student, householder, and forest dweller. That this was in fact the original triad is substantiated by the three "debts" that all Hindus owe: study (the first stage), the debt owed to the Vedic seers, or *ṛṣi*s; the oblation (performed by all married householders) to the ancestors; and sacrifice (offered by the semirenunciatory forest dweller) to the gods. And there were three goals of life: (*puruṣārtha*s): success (*artha*), social righteousness (*dharma*), and pleasure (*kāma*). At the time of the Upaniṣads and the rise of Buddhism, Jainism, and other cults of meditation and renunciation, a fourth stage of life was added, that of the renouncer (*saṃnyāsin*), and a fourth goal, *mokṣa.* Although these fourth elements were basically and essentially incompatible with the preceding triads, revolutionary negations of all that they stood for, the dauntless eclecticism of Hinduism cheerfully embraced them as supplements or complementary alternatives to the other three. (Similarly, the *Atharvaveda,* a text wholly incommensurate to the other three Vedas in style and purport, was tacked on as the fourth Veda during roughly the same period.) This conjunction of opposites inspired many ingenious responses in the mythology. In some myths, the covert, ancient, antiascetic bias of worldly Hinduism was expressed through tales of hypocritical, lecherous, and generally carnal renouncers; in others, the self-deceptive aspirations of otherworldly householders were dashed or ridiculed. In yet others, the uneasy compromise of the forest dweller—half householder, half renouncer, and the worst half of both—was exposed as a double failure; the myths in which Śiva mocks the sanctimonious sages of the Pine Forest and their sex-starved wives, or the myths in which the impotent and jealous sage Jamadagni curses his lubricious wife, Reṇukā, are important examples of this genre.

The mythology of renunciation, particularly as it interacted with the mythology of the ancient, nonrenunciatory orthodox caste system, gave rise to an important cycle of myths about kings and untouchables. Even in the Vedic period, the ritual of royal consecration included a phase in which the king had to experience symbolically a kind of reversal, renunciation, or exile before he could take full command of his kingdom. In the later mythology of the epics, this theme is crucial: Both the heroes of the *Mahābhārata* and Rāma in the *Rāmāyaṇa* are forced to dwell in exile for many years before returning to rule their kingdoms. In several of the early forms of this myth, the period of exile is spent in association with untouchables; thus Hariścandra, Viśvāmitra, and other great kings are "cursed" to live as untouchables among untouchables before being restored to their rightful kingship. In terms of world (or at least Indo-European) mythology, one can see this theme as the Indian variant of the motif of the true king who is kidnapped or concealed for his own protection at the time of his birth (the slaughter of the innocents) and raised among peasants before returning to claim his throne. This theme is well known through such figures as Moses, Jesus, Oedipus, Romulus, or even Odysseus, and, in India, Kṛṣṇa. But the particularly Indian aspect of this theme emerges from two special applications of the phenomenon of renunciation or exile.

First, this experience happens not only to kings but also to *brahman*s, many of whom are cursed or otherwise condemned to live as untouchables for a period before they are ultimately restored to their brahmanhood. This adventure is neither politically necessary nor psychosexually expedient (in the Freudian mode); it is simply an aspect of the initiation into suffering and otherness that is essential for the fully realized human being in Indian myths. For the king, at the top of the political scale, the experience among the untouchables is a descent from power to impotence; for the *brahman,* at the top of the religious scale, it is a descent from purity to defilement. The experience of impotence is regarded as just as essential for the wise execution of power as the experience of defilement is essential for the dispassionate achievement of purity.

Second, the Indian development of the myth of renunciation and exile does not always end with the resumption of political power. The most famous example of this alternative denouement is the myth of Gautama, the Buddha Śākyamuni, who dwelt among the Others not by actually leaving his palace to live as an untouchable but by seeing and empathizing with the quintessential "other" from the standpoint of a young king who had been sheltered from every form of weakness or sadness: the vision of an old man, a sick man, a dead man, and a renouncer. As a result of this vision, the Buddha left his palace, never to return again. This myth served as a paradigm not only for many Buddhist (and Buddhist-influenced) myths of renunciant kings but also for many local, sectarian myths about saints and the founders of heterodox traditions, who left the comfort of orthodoxy to dwell among the Others—not necessarily true untouchables, but non-*brahman*s, even women, people who did not know Sanskrit and had no right to sacrifice—and who never returned.

A final cycle within the corpus of myths of renunciation is the series of myths in which "good" demons "renounce" the canons of demonality in order to become ascetics or devotees of the sectarian gods. The myth of the demon Prāhlada, who loved Viṣṇu and was saved from the attacks of his truly demonic father by Viṣṇu in the form of the man-lion, is the most famous example of this genre. One could view these myths as covert attacks on the threat posed by the ideal of asceticism to the worldly basis of conventional Hinduism: Anyone who strove for renunciation, instead of remaining within the bourgeois, sacrificial Hindu fold, was "demonic." To this extent, the myths of good demons can with profit be related to other, non-Indian myths about conscientious devils and saintly witches, myths in which religious innovators or inspired misfits are consigned by the religious establishment to the ranks of the ungodly. But, as always, the Indian variant is peculiarly Indian; here, these myths become myths about caste, and although there are many systems that may resemble caste, there is nothing outside India that duplicates the caste system.

The myths of the good demon are myths in which the overarching, absolute, pan-Indian values of universal *dharma* (*sanātana dharma,* which includes truthfulness, generosity, and noninjury) are pitted against the specific, relative, mutually contradictory, and localized values of "one's own *dharma*" (*svadharma*), which is peculiar to each caste. Thus, some castes may be enjoined to kill animals, to kill people in battle, to execute criminals, to carry night soil, or even to rob. As the *Bhagavadgītā* relates, it is better to do one's own duty well (even if it violates absolute *dharma*) than to do someone else's duty (even if it does not violate absolute *dharma*). The good demon—good in relativistic, demonic terms—would be good at killing and raping, not good at telling the truth. Thus, in the mythology of orthodox Hinduism, the gods send Viṣṇu in the form of the Buddha to corrupt the "good" demons, to persuade them (wrongly) to give up Vedic sacrifices in favor of noninjury and Buddhist meditation. Stripped of their armor of absolute goodness, the demons are destroyed by the gods, while the demons who remain safely within the fold of their relative goodness survive to contribute their necessary leaven of evil to the balance of the universe. In the later mythology of *bhakti,* however, which successfully challenged caste relativism, the "good" demons are not destroyed; on the contrary, they are translated out of the world entirely, forever absolved of the necessity of performing their despicable duties (despicable in absolute terms), to dwell forever with the God for whom caste has no meaning.

These myths may also express the conflict between life-affirming Vedic values (which, traditionally, have included killing one's enemies in battle as well as killing sacrificial animals) and life-renouncing Vedantic values (of which *ahiṃsā,* the ideal of noninjury, is the most famous if not the most important). They may also be viewed as conflicts between contradictory cosmogonies. The traditional Hindu universe, or "world egg," was closed; those who died must be reborn in order to allow life to recirculate; those who were virtuous had to be balanced by others who were evil in a world of limited good. This reciprocity was further facilitated by the *karman* theory, which held that one's accrued good and bad *karman* could be transferred, particularly through exchanges of food or sexual contact, from one person to another; if one gained, the other lost. Thus, if there are to be saints, there must be sinners. Nor may the sinners refuse to sin, or the demon to rape and pillage, if the saint is to be able to bless and meditate. (Or, in another part of the forest, the householder must not refuse to sacrifice and produce food if the renouncer is to be able to remain aloof from sacrifice and yet to go on eating.) Yet the renouncer wished, ideally, to leave this universe altogether; the good demon wished to abandon demondom forever. The *bhakti* mythology of good demons was thus inspired to create a series of liminal heavens in which the devotee, or *bhakta,* demonic or human, could satisfy the absolute demands of universal *dharma* while disqualifying himself from, rather than defying or explicitly renouncing, the demonic demands of his own *svadharma.*

GODS VERSUS DEMONS. But it is a mistake to view demons as merely the symbolic expression of certain human social paradoxes. Demons *exist,* and are the enemies of the gods. Indeed, in India that is what demons primarily are: non-gods. In the earliest layer of the *Ṛgveda,* which still shares certain important links with Avestan mythology and looser ties with the Olympian gods and Titans, gods and demons were not different in nature or kind; they were brothers, the children of Prajāpati, the lord of creatures. The demons were the older brothers, and therefore had the primary claim on the kingdom of heaven; the gods were the usurpers. The gods triumphed, however, and post-Vedic mythology (beginning with the Brāhmaṇas) began to associate the divine victors with a cluster of moral virtues (truthfulness, piety, and all the other qualities of universal *dharma*) and the demonic losers with the corresponding moral flaws. The "good" demons of the medieval pantheon, therefore, were not so much upstarts as archconservatives, reclaiming their ancient right to be as virtuous as the gods of the arriviste establishment.

These palace intrigues in heaven had interesting repercussions on earth, in the relationship between humans and gods. In the *Ṛgveda,* humans and gods were pitted against demons. Humans and gods were bound to one another by the mutually beneficial contract of sacrifice: The gods kept humans prosperous and healthy in return for the offerings that kept the gods themselves alive and well and living in heaven. The demons were the enemies of both gods and humans; the major demons or *asuras* (the ex-Titans) threatened the gods in heaven, while the minor demons, or *rākṣasas* (more like ghouls or goblins), tormented people, both in their secular lives (killing newborn children, causing diseases) and in their sacred offices (interfering with the sacrifices that maintained the all-important bond between heaven and earth).

But with the rise of the ideal of renunciation as a challenge to the sacrificial order, these simple lines were broken.

For demons might offer sacrifice, but if they sacrificed to the gods they strengthened their enemies, which went against their own interests, while if they offered the libations into their own mouths (as they were said to do in the Brāhmaṇas) they exposed their innate selfishness, and the powers of truth and generosity abandoned them, taking with them their power to overcome the gods in battle. But if demons amassed ascetic power they could not be faulted on traditional moral grounds—for they had, in effect, renounced traditional moral grounds—and their power could not be neutralized by the powers of the gods. In this situation, demons were like human ascetics, who could bypass the entire Brahmanic sacrificial structure and strike out as religious loners, outside the system, with powers that, although gained by nonsacrificial methods, could nevertheless challenge the sacrificial powers of the gods on equal grounds, because the heat (*tapas*) generated by the ascetic was of the same intrinsically sacred nature as the heat generated by the sacrificial priest. In the myths, this challenge is expressed by the simple transfer of heat: The *tapas* generated by the demonic or human ascetic rises, as heat is wont to do, and heats the throne of Indra, the king of the gods; Indra immediately recognizes the source of his discomfort (for it recurs with annoying frequency) and dispatches from heaven a voluptuous nymph (an *apsaras*) to seduce the would-be ascetic by siphoning off his erotic heat in the form of his seed. In this middle period, therefore, the epic period in which Indra ruled in heaven, humans and demons could be pitted against the gods.

A further realignment took place with the rise of the great sectarian gods, Viṣṇu and Śiva. The mythology of the "good" demon brought into play a mythology of the "good" untouchable or the good non-*brahman* in local and vernacular traditions; one aspect of this development has been seen in the myths of the king among the untouchables. For in *bhakti* mythology the devotional gods are on the side of good humans and good demons alike; they are against only evil humans and evil demons. The straightforward lines of Vedic allegiance are thus sicklied o'er with the pale cast of morality. While in classical orthodox Hinduism, it was one's action that mattered (ortho*praxy*), now it was one's thought that mattered (ortho*doxy*). Thus, devotional Hinduism can be generous to untouchables, and even to Buddhists and Muslims, whose ritual activities made them literally anathema to orthodox Hinduism, but it can be bitterly intransigent toward wrong-thinking Hindus (and, of course, to wrong-thinking Muslims, Buddhists, and untouchables), no matter how observant they might be of caste strictures governing behavior. In this view, what one is (demon or untouchable) or what one does (kill, tan leather) is not so important as what one thinks, or, even more, feels (love for the true God).

ILLUSION. This emphasis on what is thought or felt in contrast with what is done or brought into existence is basic to all of Indian mythology. Its roots go back to the Vedas, where the gods use their powers of illusion (*maya*) not merely to delude the demons (themselves masters of illusion) but to create the entire universe. The Upanisadic doctrine that the state of unity with the godhead is closer to dreaming sleep than it is to waking life (and closest of all to dreamless sleep) paved the way for the concept, already encountered in the myths of cosmogony, that the universe is merely a projection or emanation from the mind of a (sleeping) god, that humankind is all merely a dream of God. The belief that the gods are seen most closely in one's dreams is encountered widely outside of India and accounts, in part, for the universal value set on premonitory dreams. But just as Indian philosophy, particularly Mahāyāna Buddhist philosophy, developed the doctrine of illusion to a pitch unknown in other forms of idealism, so too Indian mythology played countless imaginative variants on the theme of dreams and illusion.

In its simplest form, the theme could transform any myth at all into a myth of illusion: At the end of any number of complex adventures, the god appears *ex machina* to say that it was all nothing but a dream. All is as it was at the beginning of the story—all, that is, but one's understanding of what the situation *was* at the beginning of the story. This is a motif that is known from other cultures (although not, one suspects, from any culture that could not have borrowed it from India). But in its more complex form, the theme of illusion is combined with the folk motif of the tale within a tale, the mechanism of Chinese boxes, with the peculiar Indian Möbius twist: The dreamers or tellers of tales are dreaming of one another, or the dreamer of the first in a series of nested dreams, one within the other, turns out to be a character inside the innermost dream in the series. Ultimately, the worshiper is dreaming into existence the god who is dreaming him into existence.

THE PANTHEON. This article has left until last the theme that is usually regarded as the meat and potatoes of mythology: the pantheon of gods and goddesses. These will all be treated separately elsewhere in this encyclopedia, so for this author it remains only to remark upon their interrelationships and the patterns of their interactions. The basic structure of the Indian pantheon might be viewed, appropriately enough in the home of *homo hierarchicus,* in terms of a decentralized hierarchy. At the center of the pantheon is a single god, or a godhead, recognized by most Hindus. They may refer to it (him/her) as the Lord (Īśvara), the One, the godhead (*brahman*), or by a number of other names of a generally absolute character. This godhead is then often identified with one of the great pan-Indian gods: Śiva, Viṣṇu, or the Goddess (Devī). The concept of a trinity consisting of Brahmā the creator, Viṣṇu the preserver, and Śiva the destroyer is entirely artificial, although it is often encountered in the writings of Hindus as well as Western scholars. If there is any functional trinity, it is the triangle of Śiva, who is married to Devī, who is the sister of Viṣṇu.

On the third level of differentiation, Viṣṇu may be worshiped in the form of one of his *avatāras* (of which Rāma and Kṛṣṇa are by far the most popular), and Śiva may be worshiped in one of his "manifestations" or "playful appearances" on earth. Devī is often identified with a local goddess who brings as her dowry her own complex mythology. In general, local gods are assimilated to the pan-Indian pantheon through marriage, natural birth or adoption, or blatant identification: Durgā marries Śiva; Skanda is the natural son of Śiva; the demon Andhaka becomes Bhṛngin, the adopted son of Śiva; and Aiyanar *is* Skanda, a god by another name. These assimilations work in the upstream direction as well; the pan-Indian concept of the dancing Śiva probably originated in South India, and the erotic liaison of Kṛṣṇa and Rādhā in Bengal. Such cross-fertilizations result in gods and goddesses who are truly and literally multifaceted; their many heads and arms reflect not merely the many things that they are and can do, but the many places they have come from—and are heading toward.

At this point, the pantheon splinters into a kaleidoscope of images and tales that demonstrate how the one God became manifest right here, in Banaras or Gujurat or Madurai, how this particular temple or shrine became the center of the earth. For, like a hologram, the entire Indian mythological panorama is always present in its entirety in every single spot in the Indian world.

SEE ALSO Avatāra; Bhakti; Birds; Cosmology, articles on Hindu Cosmology, Jain Cosmology; Dharma, article on Hindu Dharma; Elephants; Horses; Karman; Mahābhārata; Māyā; Monkeys; Nāgas and Yakṣas; Purāṇas; Rāmāyaṇa; Saṃnyāsa; Snakes; Tapas; Varṇa and Jāti.

BIBLIOGRAPHY

There are several good introductory collections of Indian myths. Both my own *Hindu Myths* (Harmondsworth, U.K., 1975) and Cornelia Dimmitt and J. A. B. van Buitenen's *Classical Hindu Mythology* (Philadelphia, 1978) give translations of selected central texts. The latter inclines more to folkloric and localized Sanskrit traditions; the former leans more toward the classical themes and includes a detailed bibliography of primary and secondary sources. The available surveys are useful as reference works: Sukumari Bhattacharji's *The Indian Theogony* (Cambridge, U.K., 1970), Alain Daniélou's *Hindu Polytheism* (London, 1964), V. R. Ramachandra Dikshitar's *The Purāṇa Index* (Madras, 1955), E. Washburn Hopkins's *Epic Mythology* (1915; reprint, New York, 1969), A. A. Macdonell's *Vedic Mythology* (1897; reprint, New York, 1974), Vettam Mani's *Puranic Encyclopaedia* (Delhi, 1975), and Sören Sörensen's *An Index to the Names in the Mahābhārata,* 13 pts. (London, 1904–1925).

Most of the primary sources for Indian mythology in Sanskrit are now available in English translations of varying reliability. For the *Ṛgveda,* see my *The Rig Veda* (Harmondsworth, U.K., 1982); for the Brāhmaṇas, see Arthur Berriedale Keith's *Aitareya and Kauṣītaki Brāhmaṇas* (Cambridge, Mass., 1920); Julius Eggeling's *The Śatapatha Brāhmaṇa,* 5 vols., "Sacred Books of the East," vols. 12, 26, 41, 43, and 44 (Oxford, 1882–1900; reprint Delhi, 1966); Willem Caland's *The Pañcaviṃśa Brāhmaṇa* (Calcutta, 1931); and A. A. Macdonell's *The Bṛhaddevatā Attributed to Śaunaka* (Cambridge, Mass., 1904). The *Mahābhārata* has been completely if awkwardly translated by Pratap Chandra Roy and K. M. Ganguli, 12 vols. (1884–1896; 2d ed., Calcutta, 1970); a fine new translation by J. A. B. van Buitenen, terminated by his death when he had completed only five of the eighteen books (Chicago, 1973–1978), is in process of completion by the University of Chicago Press at the hands of a team of translators. The *Rāmāyaṇa* has been completely if clumsily translated by Hari Prasad Shastri, 3 vols. (London, 1962), and is now being properly translated by Robert P. Goldman and others and published by Princeton University Press.

The Purāṇas, which are the main sources for the study of Hindu mythology, are now becoming available in English translations in several different series: "Ancient Indian Tradition and Mythology" (AITM), published by Motilal Banarsidass in Delhi; the "All-India Kashiraj Trust" (AIKT), in Varanasi; and two older series that have recently been resurrected, the "Chowkhamba Sanskrit Series" (CSS), in Varanasi, and the "Sacred Books of the Hindus" (SBH), originally published in Allahabad and now republished in New York by AMS Press. These are the Purāṇas that have emerged so far:

Agnipurāṇam. 2 vols. Translated by M. N. Dutt. CSS, no. 54. Calcutta, 1901; reprint, Varanasi, 1967.

Bhāgavata. 4 vols. Translated by Ganesh Vasudeo Tagare. AITM, nos. 7–10. Delhi, 1976.

Brahmāṇḍa. 5 vols. Translated by Ganesh Vasudeo Tagare. AITM, nos. 22–26. Delhi, 1983.

Brahma-vaivarta Purāṇam. 2 vols. Translated by Rajendra Nath Sen. SBH, no. 24. Allahabad, 1920–1922; reprint, New York, 1974.

Śrimad Devī Bhāgavatam. Translated by Swami Vijnanananda. SBH, no. 26. Allahabad, 1922–1923, issued in parts; reprint, New York, 1973.

Garuḍapurāṇam. Translated by M. N. Dutt. CSS, no. 67. Calcutta, 1908; reprint, Varanasi, 1968.

Kūrma Purāṇa. Translated by Ahibhushan Bhattacharya and edited by Anand Swarup Gupta. Varanasi, 1972.

Liṅga Purāṇa. 2 vols. Edited by Jagdish Lal Shastri and translated by a board of scholars. AITM, nos. 5–6. Delhi, 1973.

Markandeya Purāṇa. Translated by F. Eden Pargiter. Bibliotheca Indica. Calcutta, 1888–1904, issued in parts; reprint, Delhi, 1969.

Matsya Purāṇam. 2 vols. Translated by a *taluqdar* of Oudh. SBH, no. 17. Allahabad, 1916–1919.

Śiva Purāṇa. 4 vols. Edited by Jagdish Lal Shastri and translated by a board of scholars. AITM, nos. 1–4. Delhi, 1970.

Vāmana Purāṇa. Translated by Satyamsu M. Mukhopadhyaya and edited by Anand Swarup Gupta. Varanasi, 1968.

Viṣṇu Purāṇa. Translated by H. H. Wilson. London, 1940; 2d ed., Calcutta, 1961.

For a complete list of Sanskrit editions of the Purāṇas, see my *Hindu Myths,* cited above.

There are also several useful studies of selected Indian mythic themes. Still the best introduction is Heinrich Zimmer's *Myths and Symbols in Indian Art and Civilization,* edited by Joseph Campbell (1946; reprint, Princeton, 1972). Also helpful is Arthur Berriedale Keith's *Indian Mythology,* vol. 6, pt. 1, of *The Mythology of All Races,* edited by Louis H. Gray

(1917; reprint, New York, 1964). There are also a number of books devoted to particular gods or mythic themes: for Tamil mythology, David Dean Shulman's *Tamil Temple Myths* (Princeton, N.J., 1980); for gods and demons, my *The Origins of Evil in Hindu Mythology* (Berkeley, Calif., 1976); for cosmology, Richard F. Gombrich's "Ancient Indian Cosmology," in *Ancient Cosmologies,* edited by Carmen Blacker and Michael Loewe (London, 1975); for Kṛṣṇa, John Stratton Hawley's *Krishna, the Butter Thief* (Princeton, N.J., 1983) and *At Play with Krishna* (Princeton, N. J., 1981); for Śiva, my *Śiva, the Erotic Ascetic* (Oxford, 1981); for Devī, *The Divine Consort: Rādhā and the Goddesses of India,* edited by John Stratton Hawley and Donna M. Wulff (Berkeley, Calif., 1982) and my *Women, Androgynes, and Other Mythical Beasts* (Chicago, 1980); for the myths of illusion, my *Dreams, Illusion, and Other Realities* (Chicago, 1984). Finally, no study of Indian mythology can fail to take into account the writings of Madeleine Biardeau, particularly her *Clefs pour la pensée hindoue* (Paris, 1972); *Études de mythologie hindoue,* 4 vols. (Paris, 1968–1976); and her essays in the *Dictionnaire des mythologies,* edited by Yves Bonnefoy (Paris, 1981).

New Sources

Coomaraswamy, Ananda Kentish. *Yaksas: Essays in the Water Cosmology.* New York, 1993.

Doniger, Wendy. *Splitting the Difference: Gender and Myth in Ancient Greece and India.* Chicago, 1999.

Flueckiger, Joyce Burkhalter. *Gender and Genre in the Folklore of Middle India.* Ithaca, N.Y., 1996.

Jamison, Stephanie. *The Ravenous Hyenas and the Wounded Son: Myth and Ritual in Ancient India.* Ithaca, N.Y., 1991.

Kinnard, Jacob N. *Seeing and Knowing in the Art of Indian Buddhism.* Richmond, U.K., 1999.

Leslie, Julia. *Myth and Mythmaking.* Collected Papers on South Asia, 12. Richmond, U.K., 1996.

Sherer, Alistair. *The Hindu Vision: Forms of the Formless.* London, 1993.

Vaudeville, Charlotte. *Myths, Sins, and Legends in Medieval India.* New York, 1996.

WENDY DONIGER (1987)
Revised Bibliography

INDIAN RELIGIONS: HISTORY OF STUDY

As is the case with other great traditions, the study of and interest in Indian religions cannot be described in terms of academic research alone; nor is it confined to the accumulation of factual information. It also involves questions of motivation, hermeneutic conditions, religious commitment, philosophical reflection, and interaction and dialogue between India and the West. It reflects the work and attitudes of missionaries and philologists, travelers and philosophers, anthropologists and theologians. It has roots and repercussions in the general trends and developments of Western science, religion, and philosophy. Its impact upon Indian as well as Western self-understanding is undeniable and still growing. More than other religions, Indian religions and specifically Hinduism are integrated into the totality of forms of culture and life, and to that extent, Indian studies in general have a direct or indirect bearing upon the religion of Hinduism. In such broad and comprehensive application, the term *religion* itself has become subject to questioning and reinterpretation.

BEGINNINGS OF INDOLOGICAL RESEARCH. Although institutionalized Indological research and systematic and organized study of Indian religions are not older than two centuries (initiated in part by the foundation in 1784 of the Asiatic Society of Bengal and by the establishment in 1814 of the first chair for Indian studies at the University of Paris), the Western encounter with the Indian religious tradition was by no means an unexpected and unprepared event. Since the days of classical Greece, and in particular since the Indian campaign of Alexander the Great (327–325 BCE), there has been interest in and speculation about Indian wisdom and religion. On the one hand, such interest was nurtured by the idea that the origins of the Greek religious and philosophical tradition were to be found in the East; on the other hand, it may also have reflected a search for alternatives and correctives to the Greek tradition. In spite of this interest, however, verifiable contacts between West and East were rare; the linguistic and cultural barriers were usually insurmountable. Even Megasthenes, the Greek ambassador at the Maurya court in Pataliputra (today Patna, Bihar) from 302 to 291 BCE, was unable to explore Indian religion in its original textual sources. The rise of the Sassanid empire and then of Islam virtually precluded direct contacts between India and Europe for many centuries, and there was little more than a repetition and rearrangement of the materials inherited from Greek and Roman antiquity. However, a highly original and thorough study of India, based upon textual sources as well as travel experiences and accompanied by an unprecedented hermeneutic awareness, was produced in Arabic by the great Islamic scholar al-Bīrūnī (973–1051). But his work remained unknown in contemporary Europe, and even in medieval Islam it was a unique and somewhat isolated phenomenon.

The Portuguese explorers who reopened direct Western access to India (a development marked by Vasco da Gama's arrival in 1498 in the South Indian port city of Calicut) were motivated not by any interest in Indian religion or philosophy but by trade and missionary interests. Yet, the urge to teach and to proselytize turned out to be a powerful incentive to explore the contexts and conditions for spreading the Christian message. For several centuries, missionaries were the leading pioneers in the study of Indian languages and of Indian religious thought. Their greatest representative, Roberto de Nobili (1577–1656; active in Madurai, South India), learned Tamil and Sanskrit and acquired and unequaled knowledge of the Indian tradition. But his writings remained unpublished during his lifetime and were only recently rediscovered. The work of another missionary, Abraham Roger's Dutch-language *De opendeure tot het verborgen heydendom* (The open door to the hidden heathendom), published in 1651, was translated into other European languages and widely used as a sourcebook on Indian religion. The works of travelers like François Bernier and Jean-Baptiste Tavernier provided additional information.

The ideological movements of Deism and the Enlightenment opened new perspectives on India and on non-Christian religions in general. One characteristic argument (used, for example, by Voltaire) was that the basic ideas concerning God and religion are older, more original, and less deformed in the ancient cultures of Asia than in the Christian West. Similarly, a certain deistic openness toward a universal religion can be found in the works of two eighteenth-century British pioneers of the study of Hinduism, Alexander Dow and John Z. Holwell. Like them, the French scholar A.-H. Anquetil-Duperron (1731–1805) did not have direct access to Sanskrit; instead, his Latin version of fifty Upaniṣads, published in two volumes in 1801–1802 under the title *Oupnek'hat* and of seminal importance for the appreciation of Indian religious thought in continental Europe, was based upon a Persian translation (*Sirr-i Akbar,* 1657). Even William Jones (1746–1794), founder of the Asiatic Society of Bengal and one of the most influential pioneers of modern Indology, initially studied Persian before gaining access to the Sanskrit language. Charles Wilkins (1749–1836), the first English translator of the *Bhagavadgītā* (1785), and Henry Thomas Colebrooke (1765–1837), whose wide-ranging studies set new standards for Indian studies, continued the work of Jones. The general British attitude toward India was, however, under the impact of more practical interests, and, accordingly, it viewed Indian religion most often in its association with social, administrative, and political issues.

The situation was significantly different in continental Europe, and specifically in Germany, where the Romantic movement produced an unparalleled enthusiasm for ancient India, celebrated as the homeland of the European languages and of true religion and philosophy. German scholars contrasted the original spiritual purity and greatness of India with a progressive degeneration and obscuration in more recent times. In several cases, this enthusiasm led to a serious study of the original sources and to a more sober assessment; a certain disenchantment, for example, is documented in Friedrich Schlegel's classic *Über die Sprache und Weisheit der Indier* (On the language and wisdom of the Indians, 1808). August Wilhelm Schlegel, who shared his brother's early enthusiasm, became the first professor of Indology in Germany (at the University of Bonn in 1818) and a pioneer in the philological treatment of Indian texts. The Romantic influence persisted to the time of F. Max Müller (1823–1900), a German-born leader of nineteenth-century Indology and at Oxford University an influential advocate of comparative religion and mythology. In general, the discovery of the Indian materials had a special, often decisive impact upon the development of comparative studies in the humanities.

CLASSICAL INDOLOGY. Textual and historical scholarship of the nineteenth century has laid the foundations for the current access to ancient and classical Indian sources. Dictionaries prepared during this period as well as catalogs of manuscripts and editions and translations of religious texts are still considered indispensable. Throughout the nineteenth century there was a particular fascination with the Vedas, the oldest religious literature of Hinduism, and especially with the *Ṛgveda.* The first complete editions of the *Ṛgveda* were prepared by F. Max Müller (1849–1874) and Theodor Aufrecht (1861–1863). Müller saw in it the origins and early developments of religion as such; his contemporary Rudolf Roth took a more philological approach. Interest in the vast ritualistic literature of the Brāhmaṇas remained more limited, and pioneering work was done by Albrecht Weber (1825–1901) and Willem Caland (1859–1932). For earlier scholars the Vedas had been primarily a record of Indo-European antiquity, and at the core of its religious impulse they had seen a mythology of natural forces. Subsequently, other dimensions of the Vedas were emphasized, and they were interpreted more specifically in their Indian context and with reference to later developments. Moreover, Western interest in the Vedic and Upaniṣadic texts further enhanced their reputation in India. Between 1816 and 1819 the Bengali reformer Ram Mohan Roy published Bengali and English translations of some of the Upaniṣads, which in Anquetil-Duperron's Latin version had already impressed European thinkers, most conspicuously Arthur Schopenhauer; Roy is an early example of an Indian author who contributed to the modern exploration and dissemination of ancient Indian religious documents. Toward the end of the nineteenth century, Schopenhauer's admirer Paul Deussen (1845–1919) made further significant contributions to the study of the Upaniṣads and to the Vedānta system, which is built upon the interpretation of the Upaniṣads.

The great epics the *Mahābhārata* and the *Rāmāyaṇa* were studied as both religious and literary documents. In particular, the most famous episode of the *Mahābhārata,* the *Bhagavadgītā,* which was first translated into English by Charles Wilkins (1785) and has since appeared in numerous new translations and editions, has become in the present time the most popular piece of Indian religious poetry in the West. The Purāṇas, by contrast, attracted much less interest in spite of the outstanding efforts of H. H. Wilson (whose English translation of the *Viṣṇu Purāṇa* was published in 1840) and Eugène Burnouf (whose edition and French translation of the *Bhāgavata Purāṇa* was published 1840–1847; a French version based upon a Tamil version had been published in 1788). A full exploration of this vast literature has begun only in the twentieth century. Serious scholarly work on the Tantras has lagged behind still further and is still in its infancy. The collection and description of Tantric manuscripts begun by Rajendralal Mitra and others, and the editions and studies done in this area by John George Woodroffe (pseudonym, Arthur Avalon), the chief justice of Bengal, broke new ground. R. G. Bhandarkar's *Vaiṣṇavism, Śaivism and Minor Religious Systems* (1913) gave an authoritative summary of the information on sectarian Hinduism available at the time it was written.

Apart from his extensive Vedic studies and his contributions to other fields such as Brahmanic literature, Albrecht Weber laid the foundations for modern Jain studies, an area in which he was followed by scholars like Georg Bühler and Hermann Jacobi, who established the distinctive and extra-Vedic character of the Jain tradition. Another representative Indologist of the nineteenth century, Monier Monier-Williams (1819–1899), tried to combine textual learning with an understanding of living Hinduism and of practical missionary and administrative problems; this effort was visible, for example, in his work *Modern India and the Indians* (1878). By and large, popular Hinduism and the practical, institutional, or social dimensions of Indian religions were not among the topics of classical Indological research. Up to the beginning of the twentieth century, these phenomena were recorded principally by missionaries in accounts such as the controversial yet very influential report of Jean-Antoine Dubois entitled *Hindu Manners, Customs and Ceremonies* (1816, a translation of a French manuscript completed in 1805–1806). Further valuable information on social and religious life was provided by various gazetteers of India. Missionaries or scholars with missionary background also contributed richly to the study of religious literature in vernaculars, especially in South India, where they compiled most of the early dictionaries of Dravidian languages; and they produced as well the first accounts of the tribal religions of India, which are more or less outside the great scriptural traditions. The missionary J. N. Farquhar covered the whole range of Hindu religious literature in his still useful *Outline of the Religious Literature of India* (1920); his *Modern Religious Movements in India* (1915) is one of the first surveys of neo-Hinduism and related phenomena.

PHILOSOPHICAL APPROACHES TO INDIAN RELIGIONS. The results of Indological research have affected the thought of various Western theologians and philosophers. In turn, Western systems of thought have provided motivations and interpretive frameworks for the study of Indian religions or have even influenced Indological research directly. These influences are exemplified by three important nineteenth-century philosophers, namely, G. W. F. Hegel (1770–1831), Arthur Schopenhauer (1788–1860), and Auguste Comte (1798–1857).

Hegel rejects the Romantic glorification of India. Nonetheless, he is a careful witness of the beginnings of Indological research and deals with Indian religious thought and life in considerable detail. In Hegel's view, the way of the *Weltgeist* ("world spirit") leads from East to West. Eastern and in particular Indian thought represents an introductory and subordinate stage of development that has been transcended (*aufgehoben,* i.e., canceled, conserved, and exalted all at once) by the Christian European stage. The inherent and distinctive principle of Indian religion and philosophy (systems that Hegel sees as inseparable) is the orientation toward the unity of one underlying "substance." God is conceived of as pure substance or abstract being (*brahman*), in which finite beings are contained as irrelevant modifications. The individual human person has to subdue and extinguish individuality and return into the one primeval substance. In this light, Hegel tries to give a comprehensive and coherent interpretation of all phenomena of Indian life and culture and to establish the basically static, ahistorical character of the Indian tradition. Whatever the deficiencies of this interpretation may be, it has had a significant impact upon the treatment of India in the general histories of religion, and it has largely contributed to the long-lasting neglect of Indian culture in the historiography of philosophy.

Schopenhauer's association with Indian thought is much more familiar to Western readers than that of Hegel, and his attitude is conspicuously different. He does not accept any directedness or progression in history, and he can recognize insights and experiences of foreign and ancient traditions without having to subordinate them to the European standpoint. In the religious metaphysics of Vedānta and Buddhism he rediscovers his own views concerning the "world as will and representation" and the undesirability of existence, and he claims these traditions as allies against what he considers to be the errors and evils of the Judeo-Christian tradition, such as the belief in historical progress and in the uniqueness of the human person. He sees the Old Testament as a worldly book without the genuine sense of transcendence and of final liberation that he discovers in the Indian religious documents. In the New Testament he finds more to appreciate; his speculations that its teachings were influenced by Indian sources are not uncommon in the nineteenth century. He hopes that the Indological discoveries will initiate a "New Renaissance." While in fact this may not have happened, Schopenhauer's ideas nevertheless have stimulated much interest in Indian and comparative studies, though largely outside the academic world. Among the followers of Schopenhauer who contributed to the textual exploration of Indian religion and philosophy Paul Deussen remains the most outstanding example.

Comte does not show any noticeable interest in Indian thought, but his conception of "positive philosophy" and his programmatic ideas about transforming philosophy into sociology and anthropology (i.e., the systematic study of the human phenomenon) have set the stage for important developments in European, specifically French intellectual and scholarly life, such as the work of Lucien Lévy-Bruhl, Émile Durkheim, and Marcel Mauss in ethnology, sociology, and religious studies. In general, these writings have provided a broad ideological background for the anthropological and sociological study of religion. Paul Masson-Oursel's *La philosophie comparée* (1923; translated as *Comparative Philosophy,* 1926) reflects this tradition in its own way. By juxtaposing and comparing the "facts" of philosophical and religious thought in India, China, and Europe, Masson-Oursel tries to explore the full range of human potential and to discover the basic regularities of its development. Indeed, he presents himself as a disinterested cartographer of the human mind, an observer no longer attached to one particular cultural tradition or metaphysical viewpoint.

The three approaches just outlined remain exemplary and influential. There are, of course, numerous variants, as well as other, genuinely different approaches. Among the latter is a wide spectrum of attempts to find a common core or horizon of religiosity or a "transcendent unity of religions" (as proposed by Frithjof Schuon) or to approach the Indian tradition in the name of "religious experience" or "comparative mysticism" (as proposed by Rudolf Otto); another approach, with a psychological and agnostic emphasis, was taken by William James. Again, instead of Hegel's European self-confidence or the rigid Christian absolutism of such theologians as Karl Barth, there is now found a variety of more or less far-reaching ideas about encounter and dialogue, adaptation, and even synthesis. Among Catholic theologians, Karl Rahner has set new standards of openness toward other religions. Psychological or psychoanalytic methods and viewpoints have repeatedly been applied to the study of Indian religions, most conspicuously and influentially in the works of C. G. Jung and some of his followers. Other methodologies or ideologies, too, have had an explicit or implicit bearing upon the study of Indian religions; in particular, structuralist orientations have gained momentum. A Marxist interpretation of the Indian tradition exists as well, represented by Walter Ruben and others.

Scientific Contributions. The study of Indian religions by anthropologists and other social scientists is largely a phenomenon of the period after 1945. These studies rely principally on field investigations of living communities to generate their descriptions and models of Indian religions, and only indirectly on historical works or classical textual sources.

From their predecessors in the study of Indian religions, social scientists have inherited the following major questions about Indian religions. What is the nature and structure of the dominant religious traditions of India? What is the relationship between the legacy of norms, concepts, and beliefs contained in the great textual traditions of India and the day-to-day religious lives of its people? In what way does religion in India affect social structure (and, in particular, the caste system)? To what degree do the religions of India inhibit its economic development and vigor? Social scientists have inherited also a tendency to focus on Hinduism, the majority religion of the subcontinent, so that minority religions, including Islam, have till recently not been the focus of sustained research except insofar as they support or refute ideas about Hindu social forms.

In the period since 1945, social scientists trained principally in India, England, France, and the United States have translated these overarching questions into a series of more manageable ones about the functioning of religion at the village level of Indian society, addressing the following subjects: the ritual aspects of hierarchy in village life; the structure of the village pantheon; the links between social mobility and changed religious practices; the Hindu grammar of purity and pollution; indigenous ideas about power and authority; Indian explanations of fate, misfortune, and determinacy; and Hindu conceptions of space and time, death and liberation. Although much of this investigation has been conducted and communicated within the village framework, there has been throughout this period a concomitant countertradition of synthetic works that aim to capitalize on and generalize from these many local studies. The four decades after 1945 can, for expository convenience, be divided into three phases, which are sequentially discussed below. The following discussion focuses on major or representative works, approaches, and authors, rather than on more specialized, peripheral, or transient trends.

The first phase, which began in 1945, was dominated by the publication of *Religion and Society among the Coorgs of South India* by M. N. Srinivas (1952). In this study, Srinivas used the term *Sanskritization* to characterize a general mobility strategy that enabled Coorgs, and many other groups, either to enter the social fold of Hinduism or to rise within its hierarchy. This concept, which has been much invoked, debated, and refined since then, rested on the assumption of a critical historical, linguistic, and conceptual gap between local religious beliefs and customs and those of what Srinivas called "Sanskritic Hinduism," that is, the Hinduism of esoteric texts, literate priests, and cosmopolitan centers. This approach dovetailed very fortuitously with the ideas of the American anthropologist Robert Redfield regarding the difference between "great" and "little" traditions in peasant civilizations. Subsequently, an influential group of anthropologists centered at the University of Chicago set themselves to refining, synthesizing, and operationalizing the ideas of Redfield and of Milton Singer as they applied to Indian religions and society. A collection of essays edited by McKim Marriott and titled *Village India* (1955) signals the beginning of this trend, and Singer's *When a Great Tradition Modernizes* (1972) marks its zenith. This latter work also contains the most thorough anthropological critique available of Max Weber's influential thesis about the antagonism between caste ideology (with its Hindu assumptions) and modern capitalistic enterprise. This first phase, rooted in the empirical study of village religion, was dominated by the problem of reconciling village-level diversities with what were perceived as pan-Indian uniformities in religious belief and practice.

In the second phase, inaugurated by the publication of *Homo Hierarchicus: The Caste System and Its Implications* by Louis Dumont (1966; first English translation, 1970), this problem was largely replaced by a concern to analyze the conceptual core of Hinduism. Dumont, whose intellectual starting point was the opposition of pure and impure in Hindu thought (an opposition first remarked by Celestin Bougle, 1908), denied the conceptual gap between "great" and "little" traditions on the grounds of a shared conceptual scheme that animated Indian religious systems at all levels. He argued that the Hindu religious understanding of hierarchy was the philosophical basis of the caste system, and suggested that there was a radical incompatibility between approaches appropriate to the analysis of Western societies, which assume the axiomatic importance of equality and the individual, and those appropriate to the study of Indian society, with its cultural axiom of hierarchy—based on religiously defined purity—and its assumption of the priority of the social group. Dumont's work, in spite of its controversial qualities, has generated two decades of anthropological and sociological writing on India characterized by a concern with hierarchy, an almost exclusive focus on Hinduism, and a tilt toward the conceptual rather than the behavioral aspects of religious life in India.

Starting approximately in 1975, there has been a turning away from some of these larger debates and a return to more focused ethnographic and thematic investigations. Recent approaches have included anthropological analysis of both specific Hindu texts and textual traditions in an effort to learn of their cosmological assumptions; more systematic effort to investigate the local incarnations and involutions of dominant civilizational concepts; and a rediscovery of oral traditions, which, together with local performance genres, reveal important variations on civilizational themes and motifs. This most recent phase continues to explore traditional problems in the study of Indian religions, but makes more explicit and self-conscious use of methods and theories developed recently in folklore, linguistics, and philosophy. But perhaps the most promising recent trend has been the turn toward historical analyses of religious institutions, processes, and symbolic forms, a shift that has involved renewed dialogue between historians and anthropologists. This trend has produced a number of studies reminding researchers that Indian religions are not unchanging ways of expressing timeless truths.

Recent Trends and Developments. There is no single spectacular work separating modern from traditional Indology; instead, there is continuation and expansion, combined with gradual changes in orientation. The tradition of classical Vedic scholarship has been continued by Heinrich Lüders, Louis Renou, Jan Gonda, and others; these scholars have also reexamined the problems of continuity and change between Vedic and Hindu India. The quantity of available source materials has increased rapidly, and more scholars of different geographical, cultural, and religious origins and disciplinary backgrounds participate now in the process of research, which is no longer a primarily European affair. In the United States, the tradition of classical Indology (first represented by scholars such as William Dwight Whitney and Maurice Bloomfield) continues to some extent; but the study of Indian religion is pursued more vigorously in the context of other disciplines and of so-called area studies in the university curriculum. In Japan, which adopted Western academic institutions and methods of research in the late nineteenth century, research interests have focused on Buddhism, but much significant work has been done also on the other religious traditions of India, primarily in the field of textual studies (by Ui Hakuju, Nakamura Hajime, and others). From the beginning of modern Indology, the participation of Indians as collaborators in the process of research and as interpreters of their own tradition has been indispensable. In the twentieth century, particularly since India's independence (1947), their role has become more active, and their growing presence at Western universities, specifically in North America, has had a significant impact upon the exploration and teaching of Indian religions. Indian scholars have not traditionally been attracted by historical and philological methods; yet certain massive projects necessitating such methods could be executed properly only in India. Such a project was the critical edition of the *Mahābhārata,* which was inspired by Western philologists but actually produced in India (by V. S. Sukthankar and others). More recently, Indians have begun a systematic textual exploration of the Purāṇas, Āgamas, and Tantras, and of the vast devotional and philosophical literature of the sectarian movements. Still, there is on their part some reluctance to devote serious scholarly attention to religious literature considered to have lesser theoretical status (such as the *māhātmya* literature) or written in a vernacular language. The wide field of connections between religious texts on the one side and art, architecture, and iconography on the other also remains an important area for further studies; scholars like Ananda K. Coomaraswamy and Stella Kramrisch have made stimulating, though to some extent controversial, contributions in this area.

Much work remains to be done in the study of Indian religions. A new area of research (and speculation) was opened during the 1920s by the archaeological discovery of the pre-Vedic Harappan civilization; the religious practices of this civilization and its connection with Vedic India are still open to question. The Vedas themselves are being approached in new and unorthodox ways, for example, in the *soma* studies of R. Gordon Wasson. The vastness of classical and later Sanskrit materials available for study is made evident by the New Catalogus Catalogorum (edited since 1949 by V. Raghavan, continued by K. Kunjunni Raja), a comprehensive listing of extant Sanskrit texts. In addition, the materials in Prakrit (specifically in Jainism) and numerous South and North Indian vernaculars still await comprehensive cataloging and exploration. These are particularly relevant for the study of sectarian and theistic movements, such as the South Indian Śaiva Siddhānta or Śrī Vaiṣṇava traditions; moreover, the increasing awareness of the details and inner differentiations of the Hindu tradition leads to new questions concerning its identity and coherence and its manifold and ambiguous relations to Buddhism and Jainism, but also to Islam, which has been present in India for more than a thousand years, and finally to Christianity. This emergent complexity has been an occasion for discussions concerning the meaning and applicability of the idea of tolerance in the Indian context. Furthermore, because of the pervasive role of religion in India, its study has to be based upon a wide variety of sources, including, for example, the Dharmaśāstras (law books); the work of such Dharmaśāstra scholars as P. V. Kane is immediately relevant for the study of Indian religion. More specifically, philosophical literature supplements religious literature because it is, with few exceptions, built upon religious foundations or motivated by religious goals; it also provides religious practices and ideas with a theoretical framework that at times challenges conventional Western understanding of such theological concepts as revelation, grace, or creation. Such interdependence gives the work of historians of Indian philosophy—for example, Surendranath Dasgupta—obvious importance for the study of Indian religion.

In the past few decades, the relationship of textual norms and theories to actual religious life has become an increasingly significant issue. A variety of nontextual approaches have been suggested to correct or supplement the understanding that can be gained from the texts alone. Combinations of textual and nontextual methods have been applied to such topics as the caste system, world renunciation, religious devotion (*bhakti*), and the doctrine of *karman* and rebirth in order to clarify not only their theoretical meaning but also their practical functions in the life of the Indian people. By means of such combined methods, local cults are correlated and contrasted with the standards of the great traditions; precept and practice, text and social context are investigated in their mutual relations. The pioneering works of Max Weber (1864–1920) continue to have an impact upon the sociological study of Indian religion. Anthropologists and other specialists have tried to construe theoretical frameworks to be applied to the textual-contextual continuum and to provide heuristic models for further research in this direction.

In a general and inevitably simplifying sense, it may be said that three basic attitudes dominate the current study of Indian religion:

(1) the historical and philological approach, which derives its data and its direction from the Indian texts themselves and is primarily interested in historical reconstruction;

(2) the sociological and anthropological approach, which tries to understand religious life in a functional manner, with reference to—or even directly in terms of—social, economic, ethnographic, political, and behavioral phenomena; and

(3) the more existentially or ideologically involved approaches, which find in the Indian religious tradition a genuine religious, philosophical, or theological challenge and which respond to it in the name of specific worldviews or religious convictions.

These three approaches are not mutually exclusive; they can be and have been combined with one another. Still, they represent clearly distinguishable types of scholarly interest and orientation.

Finally, the development of Indological studies in the West has had a remarkable influence on India's interpretation of its own traditions. Not only do Indians now participate in the Western study of their religious past, but they also respond to it and to the challenge of Western thought in general, thus opening a religious dialogue with potentially far-reaching implications. Traditional Indian thought had not previously sought such dialogue or shown interest in non-Indian traditions, and yet it has produced a rich heritage of debate and refutation, as well as of coordination and harmonization of different standpoints. But foreign religions, including Islam and Christianity, did not become part of this process until the beginning of the nineteenth century, when Hinduism opened itself to the impact of Western ideas and entered into a fundamentally new relationship with the non-Indian world. At that time, Ram Mohan Roy (1772–1833) and others initiated a movement of reform and modernization of Hinduism that combines apologetics and self-affirmation with reinterpretation, adaptation, and universalization.

Thus, Western ideas and terms have been used not only to interpret the Indian religious tradition to foreigners but also to articulate a new Indian self-understanding. Modern reinterpretations of such key concepts as *dharma* exemplify the ambiguity of India's reaction to the Western challenge and specifically to the Christian notion of religion. In response to missionary activities, Christianity and other religions have been readily incorporated into traditional Hindu schemes of concordance, where they appear as different approaches to the same goal or as preliminary stages on a path often seen as culminating in the philosophical religion of Advaita Vedānta. In this context, "comparative religion" has found many advocates in India; similarly, against the Hegelian subordination of Asian thought to that of the West, Brajendranath Seal (1864–1938) formulated his program of "comparative philosophy." In general, there has been a tendency to respond to science and technology and to Western political domination by invoking religion and spirituality, which have been presented as genuinely Indian phenomena by such successful advocates of neo-Hinduism as Vivekananda (1863–1902; represented Hinduism at the World Parliament of Religions, Chicago, 1893). The concept of religious experience plays a crucial role in the modern self-presentation of Hinduism in the West. In increasing numbers, Indian scholars, teachers, gurus, and founders of syncretistic movements have come to the West and contributed to a growing awareness of the Indian religious tradition. At the same time, these developments are themselves continuations and transformations of the tradition, and they are a legitimate topic of study and research. Among those who have contributed to the scholarly and critical evaluation of Neo-Hinduism, Paul Hacker (1913–1979) ought to be mentioned especially.

The hermeneutic and religious position of neo-Hinduism is still problematic and tentative and has had difficulties in finding an adequate language for presenting the Indian religious tradition to the modern world. Accordingly, the situation of the religious dialogue between India and the West is still precarious. Nonetheless, the fact that the Indian religious tradition is no longer just an object of Western study but now speaks back to the West, questioning some of the very basic presuppositions of Western historical research, is in itself a highly significant event. It affects not only the modern Western perception of India but also the religious and philosophical situation of the modern world.

BIBLIOGRAPHY

Dandekar, R. N., and V. Raghavan, eds. *Oriental Studies in India.* New Delhi, 1964. A survey of Asian, primarily Indian, studies with sections on Vedic, Dravidian, and Islamic studies, philosophy and religion, archaeology, and so on, including a list of centers of teaching and research in India.

Dell, David, et al. *Guide to Hindu Religion.* Boston, 1981. A generously annotated bibliography of studies of Hinduism, covering such areas as history of Hinduism, religious thought, sacred texts, rituals, sacred locations, soteriology; emphasis on more recent contributions; not always fully reliable.

Gonda, Jan, et al. *Die Religionen Indiens.* 3 vols. Stuttgart, 1960–1963. One of the most comprehensive surveys of research on the religions of India, primarily from the standpoint of textual and historical studies. This survey is further extended in Gonda's *Viṣṇuism and Śivaism: A Comparison* (London, 1970).

Hacker, Paul. *Kleine Schriften.* Wiesbaden, 1978. A comprehensive collection of articles in German and English by a scholar whose studies of Indian religion combine a thoroughly philological orientation with theological and philosophical commitment; important methodological discussions and references to neo-Hinduism.

Halbfass, Wilhelm. *Indien und Europa: Perspektiven ihrer geistigen Begegnung.* Basel, 1981. A study of the intellectual and spiritual encounters between India and Europe, of the patterns of mutual understanding in the areas of religion and philosophy, and of the beginnings of Indological research.

Holland, Barron. *Popular Hinduism and Hindu Mythology: An Annotated Bibliography.* Westport, Conn., 1979. A useful bibliographical guide (including sections on "sacred literature," etc.), although the annotations are extremely short and often not very helpful.

Mandelbaum, David G. *Society in India.* 2 vols. Berkeley, Calif., 1970. This general introduction to the anthropological study of Indian civilization also contains (in chapters 28–31 of volume 2) the best introduction, for the nonspecialist, to the social and historical dynamics of Indian religions.

O'Flaherty, Wendy Doniger, ed. *Karma and Rebirth in Classical Indian Traditions.* Berkeley, 1980. A collection of essays, by authors with varied backgrounds, on one of the most fundamental ideas in Indian religious thought.

Otto, Rudolf. *Mysticism East and West: A Comparative Analysis of the Nature of Mysticism* (1932). New York, 1960. Although somewhat obsolete, still an exemplary approach to the Indian religious tradition by a liberal Christian theologian.

Radhakrishnan, Sarvepalli. *The Hindu View of Life* (1927). London, 1968. Not a contribution to the academic study of Hinduism, but one of the most eloquent and successful statements of neo-Hinduism, exemplifying its basic patterns of reinterpretation and modernization.

Renou, Louis. *Bibliographie védique.* Paris, 1931. An exemplary bibliography of scholarly literature on the Vedas. A sequel to this work is R. N. Dandekar's *Vedic Bibliography,* 3 vols. (Bombay and Poona, 1946–1973).

Schwab, Raymond. *La renaissance orientale.* Paris, 1950. Translated by Gene Patterson-Black and Victor Reinking as *The Oriental Renaissance* (New York, 1984). A comprehensive and richly documented account of the seminal period between 1770 and 1850, when the foundations were laid for modern Indology and for a new appreciation of Indian religion and philosophy; equally detailed on academic and nonacademic developments; analyzes thoroughly the intellectual background of Indian and Oriental studies. The translation is not always reliable.

Smith, Bardwell L., ed. *Hinduism: New Essays in the History of Religions.* Leiden, 1976. A collection of eight contributions, exemplifying recent approaches to the study of Hinduism, including structuralism.

Windisch, Ernst. *Geschichte der Sanskrit-Philologie und indischen Altertumskunde.* 2 vols. Strasbourg, 1917–1920. Though incomplete, somewhat obsolete, and not extending beyond 1900, this remains the most thorough and comprehensive survey of the history of Indology and of the textual exploration of Indian religion.

Zimmer, Heinrich. *Myths and Symbols in Indian Art and Civilization* (1946). Edited by Joseph Campbell. Princeton, 1972. A somewhat idiosyncratic, yet stimulating and influential study of Hindu religion and mythology, with particular reference to its visual illustrations.

New Sources

Baird, Robert D. *Essays in the History of Religions.* New York, 1991.

Bhargava, Rajeev. *Secularism and Its Critics.* New York, 1998.

Bosch, Lourens van den. *Friedrich Max Müller: A Life Devoted to Humanities.* Boston, 2002.

Gilmartin, David, and Bruce B. Lawrence, eds. *Beyond Turk and Hindu: Rethinking Religious Identities in Islamicate South Asia.* Gainesville, Fla., 2000.

Jones, Kenneth W., ed. *Religious Controversy in British India.* Albany, 1992.

Lopez, Donald S., ed. *Religions of India in Practice.* Princeton, N.J., 1992.

Madan, T. N., ed. *Religion in India.* New York, 1991.

Young, Katherine K. *Hermeneutical Paths to the Sacred Worlds of India: Essays in Honor of Robert W. Stevenson.* Atlanta, 1994.

WILHELM HALBFASS (1987)
ARJUN APPADURAI (1987)
Revised Bibliography

INDO-EUROPEAN RELIGIONS

This entry consists of the following articles:

INDO-EUROPEAN RELIGIONS: AN OVERVIEW

The study of Indo-European religion has a relatively recent origin, for the very existence of the Indo-European language grouping was not recognized until a celebrated lecture given by Sir William ("Oriental") Jones in 1786. Speaking to the Royal Asiatic Society of Bengal, Jones first observed that there were striking philological similarities between Greek, Latin, Sanskrit (the ancient language of India), and Persian, too numerous and precise to be explained by simple borrowing or chance. Going further, he suggested that the Celtic and Germanic languages exhibited many of the same features and argued that all of these geographically and historically far-flung languages were best understood as separate derivates of a common parent language, a language nowhere preserved in written form, but which might be reconstructed through systematic comparison of the derivate stocks.

Later research has confirmed the relations among these languages, adding not only Germanic and Celtic firmly to the family now known as Indo-European but also Baltic, Slavic, Armenian, Albanian, Anatolian (chiefly Hittite), and Tokharian (an obscure language found in western China and Turkestan). Rigorous and systematic comparison of words in these various languages has permitted scholars to posit numerous prototypes as a means to explain the systematic resemblances that have been adduced. As a simple example of how this is done one might consider certain words for "god," assembling a set of correspondences (to which other reflexes might be added) as shown in table 1.

From these correspondences, along with the knowledge of Indo-European phonetics gained from hundreds of other such comparisons, linguists can reconstruct a prototype **deywo-s* (the asterisk denotes a reconstructed form unattested in any written source), which means "god, deity." Phonetic rules explain the various sound shifts in each language, but one must also note semantic changes in certain stocks, each of which is instructive for the history of the corresponding religion. Thus, for instance, the old word for "god" has become the most important word for demonic beings in Avestan (the Iranian language in which the most ancient Zoroastrian scriptures were composed), a transformation that seems to originate in the prophet Zarathushtra's renunciation of the old Indo-Iranian pantheon.

The Greek reflex of **deywo-s* has also lost its sense as "deity," being replaced in this usage by *theos*. The older term survives as an adjective, however, which reveals one of the fundamental attributes of deity in Indo-European thought: gods are celestial beings, characterized by light, for the word **deywo-s* (whence the Greek *dios,* "celestial") is derived from a verb that means "to shine." In contrast, one of the most important words for "human" identifies people as "terrestrial" beings (note the relation of the Latin *homo,* "man," and *humus,* "soil"), while humans and deities are further contrasted in other terminology that identifies them as "mortals" and "immortals" respectively.

This relatively simple example reveals some of the possibilities and some of the pitfalls of research into Indo-European religion. Careful examination of lexical items provides insight into the nature of thought on religious topics. But each of the separate Indo-European families differs from the other families in important regards, and just as Latin phonology differs from Iranian phonology for all that they are related (to cite but one example), so Roman religion is not identical to Iranian: a *deus* is not the same thing as a *daēva.*

Reconstruction that proceeds along linguistic lines is relatively safe, however, compared to research that seeks out correspondences in the myths, rituals, laws, cosmologies, and eschatologies of the various Indo-European peoples and that attempts to recover their hypothetical antecedents. Such research is possible, to be sure, but in all instances it is extremely risky and difficult, involving the adducement of parallel phenomena (usually called "correspondences" or "reflexes") attested in the religions of several different Indo-European families; the study of each reflex in its cultural specificity; the isolation of those features that the scattered reflexes hold in common; the explanation of those features that diverge (often called "transformation"); and the positing of a hypothetical prototype that is capable of accounting for evident similarities, along with a train of historical development that explains the forces producing each transformation. Finally, the reconstructed prototype ought to be set within a plausible set of assumptions regarding the nature of Indo-European culture in general.

Based on linguistic and archaeological research, the ancient Indo-European peoples are generally considered to have been semisettled pastoralists, whose wealth consisted of relatively large herds, including domesticated sheep, pigs, goats, and, most important, cattle. Horses were also highly significant, especially when yoked to chariots and used in warfare, but cattle remained the normal draft animals for peaceful purposes, the source of most foods, and the fundamental measure of wealth. Some agriculture seems to have been practiced, although this was much less important and prestigious an activity than herding or war. The pursuit of warfare, especially the raiding of livestock from neighboring peoples, was facilitated not only by use of chariots but also by an elaborate weaponry built on a single metal, probably copper or bronze.

Linguistic data are insufficient to posit the existence of either a homeland or a proto-Indo-European community, and it is possible to view the similarity of the various Indo-European languages as the cumulative result of complex borrowings, influences, and cultural interrelations between multiple social and ethnic groups over many centuries. Some scholars have sought to employ archaeological evidence to demonstrate a specific point of origin for proto-Indo-European society. Of such theories, the most widely accepted is that of Marija Gimbutas, who has delineated what she calls the Kurgan culture, dating to the middle of the fifth millennium BCE and located in the southern Russian steppes, in the area that stretches from the Urals to the land north of the Black Sea, and including such groups as the Jamna culture of the Ural-Volga region north of the Caspian and the Srednii Stog II culture north of the Black Sea.

MYTHIC LEGITIMATIONS OF SOCIETY, ECONOMY, AND POLITY. Comparison of texts in which are described the patterns of social organization among the Indian, Iranian, and Celtic peoples reveals a common structure, which is also preserved in the ideal republic envisioned by Plato. This system is characterized by the distinction of three hierarchically differentiated classes—or "functions," as they are called by Georges Dumézil (1958), who was first to recognize their importance. Moreover, it is possible to reconstruct a number of myths that describe the origin of these classes, their nature, and their sometimes problematic interrelationships.

Most important of these is the creation myth, a complex, polyphonic story that told how the world was created when the first priest (often bearing the name Man, *Manu) offered his twin brother, the first king (often named Twin, *Yemo), in sacrifice, along with the first ox. From Twin's body, the world was made, in both its material and social components. Portions of two reflexes of this myth may conveniently be cited: the first, from the Indic "Song of Purusa" (*Ṛgveda* 10.90.11–14) dates to about 900 BCE; the second, the Old Russian *Poem on the Dove King,* is mentioned in sources dating to the thirteenth century CE and was still circulating orally in the nineteenth century:

When they divided Purusa, how many pieces did they prepare?
What was his mouth? What are his arms, thighs, and feet called?
The priest was his mouth, the warrior was made from his arms;
His thighs were the commoner, and the servant was born from his feet.
The moon was born of his mind; of his eye, the sun was born;
From his mouth, Indra and fire; from his breath, wind was born;
From his navel there was the atmosphere; from his head, heaven was rolled together;
From his feet, the earth; from his ears, the directions.

Our bright light comes from the Lord,
The red sun from the face of God,
The young shining moon from his breast,
The bright dawn from the eyes of God,
The sparkling stars from his vestments,
The wild winds from the Holy Spirit.
From this our little Tsars are on earth—
From the holy head of Adam;
From this princes and heroes come into being—
From the holy bones of Adam;
From this are the orthodox peasants—
From the holy knee of Adam.

Language	Phonetic Form	Semantic Sense
Latin	*deus*	"deity"
Lithuanian	*diēvas*	"deity"
Greek	*dios*	"celestial"
Hittite	*^{d}Šiuš*	"deity"
Sanskrit	*deváḥ*	"deity"
Avestan	*daēva*	"damon"

TABLE 1. Indo-European words for "God"

Although this article shall return to the cosmic dimensions of this myth, it is its social contents that are of concern now. Among these, the following four should be noted:

(1) Society consists of vertically stratified classes, with priests or sovereigns in the first position, warriors in the second, and commoners—those entrusted with the bulk of productive labor—in the third. To these, a fourth class of relative outsiders—servants, or the like—was sometimes added, as in the Indian example cited above.

(2) The characteristic activity of each of these classes is explained and chartered by the part of Twin's body from which they originated. Thus, the intellectuals who direct society by exercise of thought and speech come from his head; those who defend society by their physical prowess come from his chest (heart) and arms; those who produce food, reproduce, and provide material support for the other classes come from the lower body, including belly, loins, legs, and feet.

(3) The priest, following the model of Man, has as his prime responsibility the performance of sacrifice, sacrifice being the creative act *par excellence.*

(4) The king, following the model of Twin, combines within himself the essence of all social classes and is expected to sacrifice himself for the good of the whole.

Another myth, which has as its central character the first warrior, whose name was Third (*Trito), provided an analysis of the warrior class. Within this story, it was related that cattle originally belonged to Indo-Europeans but were stolen by a monster, a three-headed serpent who was, moreover, specifically identified as a non-Indo-European. Following this theft, it fell to Third to recover the stolen cattle, and he began his quest by invoking the aid of a warrior deity to whom he offered libations of intoxicating drinks. Having won the god's assistance, and himself fortified by the same intoxicant, Third set forth, found the serpent, slew him, and recovered the cattle, which had been imprisoned by the monster.

This myth, which is attested in more reflexes than any other (its traces are still apparent in countless fairy tales), speaks to the eternal themes of wealth and power. It asserts, first, that cattle—the means of production and of exchange in the most ancient Indo-European societies—rightly belong exclusively to Indo-Europeans, falling into other hands only as the result of theft. Theft is condemned here because of its reliance on stealth and treachery, and it is set in contrast to raiding, which—far from being condemned—is heartily endorsed. Raiding emerges as a heroic action sanctioned by the gods, hedged with ritual, and devoted to regaining what rightfully belongs to the Indo-European warrior or his people. Throughout Indo-European history, Third in his various reflexes has remained the model for warriors, who repeatedly cast themselves in his image—raiding, plundering, and killing their non-Indo-European neighbors, convinced all the while that they were engaged in a sacred and rightful activity.

Yet another myth emphasized the importance of the commoner class to the social totality, although no individual heroic figure was provided as a model for commoners. Rather, the myth begins with separation and even hostility existing between the generalized representatives of the upper classes and those of the commoners. After an inconclusive struggle, however, members of all classes recognize their need for one another, and they merge into a larger, all-encompassing society. Thereafter the classes are expected to cooperate and live harmoniously, although the commoners continue to occupy a subordinate position, a considerable portion of their labor being diverted for the support of the noble classes of priests, warriors, and kings. At the level of mythic ideology, however, if not of actual social process, commoners were assured of their superiority to even the most privileged members of society, for an important set of myths, recently studied by Cristiano Grottanelli, focused on the conflict of a humble woman who was the mother of twins (thus signifying abundant reproductive power) with a king's horses (the emblem of martial and royal power), in which the lowly woman emerged victorious.

COSMOLOGY AND THE GODS. While Georges Dumézil and his followers have consistently argued that the Indo-European pantheon mirrored the organization of social classes, other scholars have at times been skeptical of this view. Chief among its difficulties is the fact that Dumézil's proposals include none of the gods for whom names can be linguistically reconstructed, all of whom are personified natural phenomena—Shining Sky (*Dyeus), Sun (*Swel), Dawn (*Ausos), and so forth—while reconstructible names exist for none of the deities he proposes.

In general, as noted above, deities were characterized as radiant celestial beings. In addition to the **deywo-s*, however, there was another class of divinities associated with the waters beneath the earth's surface and with darkness. These deities—whose names were regularly formed with the preposition signifying downward motion (**ne-*, as in Latin *Neptunus*, Greek *Nēreus*, Germanic *Nerthus*, Sanskrit *Nirṛti*)—figure in myths that are nothing so much as meditations on the interconnections between "above" and "below," involving immergence into and emersion out of the world ocean, as has recently been demonstrated by Françoise Bader.

Speculation on the nature of the cosmos also forms an important part of the creation myth, the social contents of which was touched on above. It must be noted, however, that beyond this social discourse, the myth established a series of homologic relations between parts of the human body and parts of the physical universe—that is to say, an extended parallelism and consubstantiality was posited between the microcosm and the macrocosm. Many texts thus tell of the origin of the sun from the eyes of the first sacrificial victim, stones from his bones, earth from his flesh, wind from his breath, and so forth, while others invert the account—as for instance, in the following medieval accounts, the first Germanic and the second Slavic:

> God made the first man, that was Adam, from eight transformations: the bone from the stone, the flesh from the earth, the blood from the water, the heart from the wind, the thoughts from the clouds, the sweat from the dew, the locks of hair from the grass, the eyes from the sun, and he blew in the holy breath. (from the Old Frisian *Code of Emsig*)

> And thus God made man's body out of eight parts. The first part is of the earth, which is the lowliest of all parts. The second is of the sea, which is blood and wisdom. The third is of the sun, which is beauty and eyes for him. The fourth is of the celestial clouds, which are thought and weakness. The fifth is of the wind—that is, air—which is breath and envy. The sixth is of stones, that is, firmness. The seventh is of the light of this world which is made into flesh, that is humility and sweetness. The eighth part is of the Holy Spirit, placed in men for all that is good, full of zeal—that is the foremost part. (from the Old Russian *Discourse of the Three Saints*)

In these and other texts the elements of the physical universe are converted into the constituent parts of a human body, as cosmogony (a story of the creation of the cosmos) becomes anthropogony (a story of the creation of humankind). In truth, cosmogony and anthropogony were regarded as separate moments in one continuous process of creation, in which physical matter eternally alternates between microcosmic and macrocosmic modes of existence. Bones thus become stones and stones become bones over and over again, matter and change both being eternal, while the body and the universe are only transient forms, alternate shapes of one another.

RITUAL ACTION. The myths that have been under consideration were closely correlated with and regularly represented in numerous ritual forms. Thus, the creation myth was inextricably connected to sacrifice, the most important of all Indo-European rites. Insofar as the first priest created the world through the performance of a sacrifice in which a man and an ox were the victims, so each subsequent priest recreated the cosmos by sacrificing humans or cattle. This was accomplished through manipulation of the homologies of macrocosm and microcosm, such that when the victim was dismembered, its material substance was transformed into the corresponding parts of the universe. Thus, for example, an Indic manual of ritual practice, the *Aitareya Brāhmaṇa* (2.6), provides instructions for the sacrificial dismemberment of an animal victim in terms drawn directly from the creation myth:

> Lay his feet down to the north. Cause his eye to go to the sun. Send forth his breath to the wind, his life-force to the atmosphere, his ears to the cardinal points, his flesh to the earth. Thus, the priest places the victim in these worlds.

Without this matter drawn from the bodies of sacrificial victims all the items of the material world—earth, stones, sun, wind, water, and the like—would become depleted; it is only because they are replenished in sacrifice that the cosmos continues to exist.

If sacrifice is thus a sort of "healing" of the cosmos based on principles articulated in the creation myth, medical practice was also based on the same principles and bears a curious relation to sacrifice. For if in sacrifice the priest shifted matter from the body to the universe, then in the healing of a broken limb—as attested in the famous Second Merseberg Charm and corresponding materials throughout the Indo-European world—the healer took matter from the universe and restored it to a broken body, creating new flesh, bones, blood, and the like out of earth, stones, and water.

Royal investiture was based on yet another elaboration of ideas contained within the creation myth, as is suggested by the researches of Daniel Dubuisson. Investigating accounts of ancient "coronation" rituals in Ireland and India, he has shown that a king was ritually constructed by having the essential properties of the three Indo-European social classes placed within his body, symbolic gifts, clothing, unctions, and the like being employed toward this end.

Other rituals were closely related to the myth of Third. Embarking on cattle raids—which were raised to the status of a sacred act as a result of this mythic charter—Indo-European warriors invoked the assistance of martial deities, poured libations, partook of intoxicating drinks, and aspired to states of ecstatic frenzy. Moreover, each young warrior had to pass through certain initiatory rituals before he attained full status as a member of the warrior class. Regularly his first cattle raid was something of a rite of passage for the young warrior, and other initiations were consciously structured on the myth of Third and the serpent. It appears that in some of these, a monstrous tricephalous dummy was constructed, and the initiand was forced to attack it. If able to summon up the necessary courage to do so, he discovered that his seemingly awesome opponent was only a joke, with the implicit lesson that all of his future enemies, however fearsome they might seem, would be no more formidable than this dummy. Those enemies, of course, were to be cast in the role of the serpent—a monster, a thief, and, what is most important, an alien (i.e., a non-Indo-European)—the plunder and murder of whom was established by myth as not only a rightful but also a sacred act.

While the use of intoxicants was an important part of warrior ritual, these had other applications as well. The oldest Indo-European intoxicating beverage was mead, later followed by beer, wine, and a pressed drink known as *soma* to the Indians and *haoma* to the Iranians; the symbolism and ideology surrounding all of these remained relatively constant. In all instances, the drink appears as a heightener of abilities and activities. When consumed by a priest, it increases his powers of vision and insight. Similarly, it makes a poet more eloquent, a warrior more powerful, a king more generous and just.

A large group of rituals served to forge bonds of community and to cement important social relations. Extremely important in this regard were certain formalized reciprocal obligations, including hospitality and gift exchange, whereby individuals, lineages, and even larger units were brought into repeated contact and friendly interchange. Marriage also must be considered as a prolonged exchange relationship between social groups, given the predominant preference for exogamy. An individual marriage was thus as much a part of an ongoing exchange between lineages or clans as it was a permanent bond between two individuals.

Verbal rituals—including those of vow, oath, and treaty—played a highly important part in the establishment and preservation of social bonds; accordingly, truth and fidelity were cardinal virtues. Initially, this must be related to the lack of literacy among the most ancient Indo-European peoples, a state of affairs that also contributed to the high development of verbal art (epic poetry, for instance) and mnemonic techniques. But even after the introduction of writing among the scattered Indo-European peoples, a marked preference for the oral transmission of religious lore remained, for the spoken word was perceived as a live vehicle, in contrast to the dead written letter, and was preferred accordingly.

If verbal rituals could serve to establish social connectedness, they could also be used to sunder unwanted connections, as is attested in a formula of outlawry that survives in Hittite and Germanic reflexes, the former dating to 1600 BCE. Here, particularly disreputable individuals (an abductor and murderer in the first instance, a grave robber in the second) are told "You have become a wolf" and "May he be a wolf" respectively, the wolf being the most feared predator of pastoral societies, a dangerous outsider ever to be kept at bay. Ironically, however, it was not only outlaws who were regarded as wolves, for Indo-European warriors also styled themselves wolflike beings, as is attested by the many ethnic names derived from the word for "wolf" (thus the Luvians, Lykians, Hirpini, Luceres, Dacii, Hyrcanii, and Saka Haumavarka), personal names so formed (Wolfram, Wolfhart, Wolfgang), and the Greek term *lussa* ("rabies, wolfish rage"), which denotes the highest pitch of fury attained by heroes such as Achilles and Hector in the *Iliad*. Apparently what legitimated the wolfish violence of these heroes is that it was directed outside the community of Indo-Europeans, in contrast to that of outlaws, which was directed internally, an inference that is supported by the fascinating name of a heroic warrior attested in the *Ṛgveda:* Dasyave Vṛka, "wolf to the Dasyu," that is, to the non-Indo-European.

DEATH, RESURRECTION, AND ESCHATOLOGY. A central issue in Indo-European religions, as in most religions, was what becomes of an individual after death. Although several scholars have devoted attention to certain details of funerary ideology, the full nature of Indo-European thought on this topic remains to be worked out. Among the major contributions thus far are the studies of Hermann Güntert (1919), who showed that there was a goddess *Kolyo ("the coverer") whose physical form incarnated the mixture of fascination and horror evoked by death, for she was seductively beautiful when seen from the front, while hiding a back that was repulsive—moldy and worm-eaten—in the extreme. Paul Thieme (1952) has also contributed an important study of the view of death as a reunion with departed ancestors, and Kuno Meyer (1919) has shown that in Ireland as in India it was the first mortal (*Yemo, the twin) who founded the otherworld.

If ideas regarding the fate of the soul are unclear—no reconstructible word approximates the semantic range of the English *soul,* the nearest equivalent being a term for "life-breath"—those on the fate of the body are extremely precise and reveal a remarkable religious content. For death is seen as the last sacrifice that an individual can offer, in which his or her own body is itself the offering. Moreover, that body is transformed into the elements of the physical universe, just as were those of Twin at the time of creation, each death being not only a sacrifice but a representation of the cosmogonic sacrifice. Such a view is preserved, for instance, in Euripides' *The Suppliant Women:*

> Let the corpses now be covered with the earth,
> From which each of them came forth to the light
> Only to go back thither: breath to the air
> And body to earth. (531–534)

Or in the funeral hymn of the *Ṛgveda:*

> Your eye must go to the sun. Your soul must go to the wind. You must go to the sky and the earth, according to what is right.
> Go to the waters, if you are placed there. You must establish the plants with your flesh. (10.16.3)

This is not a final fate, however, for it would seem that nothing within the cosmos was perceived as final. Just as cosmogony was seen to alternate with anthropogony, so also death and resurrection. That matter that assumes its cosmic form when one specific human body dies will once again assume bodily form when that specific cosmos itself dies, as must inevitably happen. Greek, Germanic, and Indo-Iranian evidence permits reconstruction of a temporal scheme involving four world ages, the first of which is most pure and stable, followed by ages in which human virtue and the very order of the cosmos gradually break down. At the end of the fourth world age, there is an apocalyptic collapse, followed by the creation of a new, pure, and regenerated world. One of the cardinal features of the eschatological destruction of the cosmos, however, is the resurrection of the dead, their bodies being formed out of the material substance freed when the cosmos falls apart. The new creation that follows is then in most versions accomplished with an initial act of sacrifice. Descriptions of the resurrection are preserved, *inter alia,* in the *Pahlavi Rivāyat Accompanying the Dādistān i dīnīg,* a Zoroastrian text of the ninth century CE, and in Plato's *Politicus:*

> [In order to accomplish the resurrection] Ohrmazd summons the bone from the earth, the blood from the water, the hair from the plants, and the life from the wind. He mixes one with the other, and in this manner, he keeps on creating. (*Pahlavi Rivayat* 48.98–107)

> When the transition of the old people to the nature of a child is completed, it follows that those lying [dead] in the earth are put back together there and brought back to life, the process of birth being reversed with the reversal of the world's rotation. (*Politicus* 271b)

Behind these formulations stand several very simple, yet very profound, principles: (1) matter is indestructible; (2) matter is infinitely transmutable; (3) living organisms and the physical universe are composed of one and the same material substance; (4) time is eternal. While change is thus constant, it is also meaningless, for nothing that is essentially real is ever created or destroyed. Worlds come and go, as do individuals of whatever species, but being—material being—is always there.

The gods are also subject to the same rhythms of dissolution and reemergence, but in truth the gods seem to have been of much less concern than mythic ancestors such as Man, Twin, and Third. Certain statements made above, however, must be corrected in light of what has just been said about the nature of time and the cycles of creation and destruction. For whereas this article initially called these figures the "first" king, priest, and warrior respectively, it must now be concluded that they were merely the first of the current world age, time and the world receding infinitely into the past as well as stretching eternally into the future.

BIBLIOGRAPHY

Among the most interesting and important general studies of Indo-European religion are (in chronological order): Joseph Vendryes's "Les correspondances de vocabulaire entre l'indo-iranien et l'italo-celtique," *Mémoires de la Société de Linguistique de Paris* 20 (1918): 265–285; Hermann Güntert's *Der arische Weltkönig und Heiland* (Halle, 1923); Paul Thieme's *Mitra and Aryaman* (New Haven, 1957); Georges Dumézil's *L'idéologie tripartie des Indo-Européens* (Brussels, 1958); Émile Benveniste's *Indo-European Language and Society,* translated by Elizabeth Palmer (Coral Gables, Fla., 1975); Franco Crevatin's *Ricerche d'antichità indeuropee* (Trieste, 1979); and my own *Priests, Warriors, and Cattle: A Study in the Ecology of Religions* (Berkeley, Calif., 1981).

Specialized studies of particular merit are Marija Gimbutas's numerous articles on the archaeological record of the Indo-

Europeans, most complete of which to date is "An Archaeologist's View of PIE in 1975," *Journal of Indo-European Studies* 2 (Fall 1974): 289–308; Georges Dumézil's three-volume *Mythe et épopée* (Paris, 1968–1973), in which he demonstrates the ways in which many myths were transformed into epic, pseudohistory, and other genres; Stig Wikander's *Der arische Männerbund* (Lund, 1938) and Lily Weiser's *Altgermanische Jünglingsweihen und Männerbunde* (Baden, 1927) on warriors; Wilhelm Koppers's "Pferdeopfer und Pferdekult der Indogermanen," *Wiener Beiträge zur Kulturgeschichte und Linguistik* 4 (1936): 279–411, and Kasten Rönnow's "Zagreus och Dionysos," *Religion och Bibel* 2 (1943): 14–48, on sacrifice (both to be used with caution, however); Daniel Dubuisson's "Le roi indo-européen et la synthèse des trois fonctions," *Annales économies sociétés civilisations* 33 (January–February 1978): 21–34, on kingship; Hermann Güntert's *Kalypso* (Halle, 1919); Kuno Meyer, "Der irische Totengott und die Toteninsel," *Sitzungberichte der preussischen Akademie der Wissenschaften* (1919): 537–546; and Paul Thieme's *Studien zur indogermanischen Wortkunde und Religionsgeschichte* (Berlin, 1952) on death and the otherworld; and my own *Myth, Cosmos, and Society: Indo-European Themes of Creation and Destruction* (Cambridge, Mass., 1986) on the creation myth.

Two papers presented at a panel on Indo-European religion held during the Ninth International Congress of Anthropological and Ethnographic Sciences (Vancouver, 1983) were of considerable importance: Françoise Bader's "Une mythe indo-européene de l'immersion-émergence" and Cristiano Grottanelli's "Yoked Horses, Twins, and the Powerful Lady: India, Greece, Ireland and Elsewhere."

On the problems and insecurities of research in this area in general, see Ulf Drabin, "Indogermanische Religion und Kultur? Eine Analyse des Begriffes Indogermanisch," *Temenos* 16 (1980): 26–38; Jean-Paul Demoule, "Les Indo-Européens ont-ils existé?" *L'histoire* 28 (1980): 108–120; and Bernfried Schlerath, "Ist ein Raum/Zeit Modell für eine rekonstruierte Sprach möglich?" *Zeitschrift für vergleichende Sprachwissenschaft* 95 (1981): 175–202.

New Sources

Ballantyne, Tony. *Orientalism and Race: Aryanism in the British Empire.* New York, 2002.

Berry, Ellen E., and Anesa Miller Pogacar. *Re-Entering the Sign: Articulating New Russian Culture.* Ann Arbor, 1995.

Davidson, H. R. *Myths and Symbols in Pagan Europe: Early Scandinavian and Celtic Religions.* Syracuse, N.Y., 1989.

Davidson, H. R. *The Lost Beliefs of Northern Europe.* New York, 1993.

Green, Miranda. *Symbol and Image in Celtic Religious Art.* New York, 1989.

Mallory, J. P. *In Search of the Indo-Europeans: Language, Archaeology and Myth.* London, 1991.

Siebers, Tobin. *Religion and the Authority of the Past.* Ann Arbor, 1993.

Winn, Shan M. M. *Heaven, Heroes, and Happiness: The Indo-European Roots of Western Ideology.* Lanham, Md., 1995.

Bruce Lincoln (1987)
Revised Bibliography

INDO-EUROPEAN RELIGIONS: HISTORY OF STUDY

Strictly speaking, the history of comparative Indo-European studies begins in the late eighteenth century as a direct result of the momentous discovery that the ancient languages now classified as "Indo-European" (e.g., Latin, classical Greek, Sanskrit, Old English, Old Persian, Old Icelandic, Old Church Slavonic, Old Irish, Hittite, etc.) all stemmed ultimately from a common source, that is, Proto-Indo-European. As shall be seen, it soon became apparent that the speakers of these languages, which can be considered along with their progeny as members of a grand "family" of languages, shared more than simply a common linguistic heritage, and that among the most important features of this extralinguistic, Indo-European heritage was a common body of religious beliefs and practices.

To be sure, the taproots of the discipline can be traced back to classical antiquity, to the theories of Euhemerus (fl. 300 BCE) and other Greek and Roman scholars who attempted to come to grips with the origin and meaning of myth. It is also possible to trace the immediate source of the ideas that flowered in the nineteenth century to the ideas of such eighteenth-century precursors as Bernard de Fontenelle (1657–1757), Giovanni Battista Vico (1668–1744), and Charles de Brosses (1709–1777), who first suggested that a search for natural metaphors might be preferable to the traditional euhemeristic and allegorical approaches that had heretofore been the rule. These ideas may also be traced as well to that curious (albeit all-pervasive) philosophical, literary, and artistic movement called Romanticism, adumbrated in the works of J. G. Herder (1744–1803), which profoundly influenced most of the scholars who first began to conceive of a distinctly Indo-European religious tradition in the early nineteenth century. But these ideas belong properly to the general history of comparative mythology and religion; for the purposes of this article, the survey begins with the discovery of the Indo-European language family.

Discovery of the Indo-European Language Family. Until the last quarter of the eighteenth century, most theories about the nature and origin of language were grounded in philosophical speculation, much of it centering on the idea of degeneration. Thus, the primordial language was often held to be Hebrew, since it must have been spoken in the Garden of Eden. Following the ancient notion of degeneration from an assumed "Golden Age," many writers on the subject maintained that Greek was a degenerate form of Hebrew, Latin a degenerate form of Greek, and that the modern languages of Europe were all degenerate offspring of Latin.

However, thanks to the voyages of discovery and the rapid expansion in European awareness of the range and diversity of human languages, and impelled by the romantic emphasis on national origins, which effectively precluded the notion that all languages were necessarily descended from Hebrew, scholars had begun to suspect that the degeneration hypothesis, whether secular or religious, was inadequate to explain the historical relationships among languages. Nowhere was this more obvious than in India, which, by the latter part of the eighteenth century, had become in effect the private preserve of the British East India Company. As European awareness of this vastly complex region deepened, it became clear that Sanskrit, the ancient language of the Hindu sacred texts, occupied a position in religious and literary affairs similar to that occupied by Latin in Europe during the Middle Ages. Indeed, several scholars, beginning with Filippo Sassetti in 1600, had remarked on the curious similarities between Latin and Sanskrit, but these similarities defied explanation in terms of the "degeneration hypothesis," as Sanskrit was patently as ancient as either Latin or classical Greek. Furthermore, the modern languages of North India—Hindi, Bengali, and the rest—seemed to bear the same immediate relationship to Sanskrit as French, Spanish, Italian and other members of what later came to be called the Romance languages did to Latin.

The problem was finally solved in 1786 by William Jones (1746–1794), who is generally considered the founder of scientific linguistics. An amateur philologist (he was reputed to have been fluent in some twenty-two languages), Jones had recently been appointed chief justice of the East India Company's establishment at Calcutta, and in his off-hours he immediately set about learning Sanskrit. In September 1786, at a meeting of the Royal Asiatic Society of Bengal, he gave an after-dinner speech in which, for the first time, the idea of the language family was first clearly articulated. As Jones saw it, the relationship among Sanskrit and the ancient languages of Greece and Rome, as well as those spoken by the ancient Germans and Iranians, was that of a set of orphaned siblings: all were descended from a common parent language that had long since disappeared. That parent language, however, might be reconstructed by rigorously comparing the grammars and lexicons of these attested languages. The whole ensemble could be described as a family tree, one to which Hebrew, Arabic, and other Semitic languages did not belong, for they were members of another, wholly distinct language family.

Thus was born both comparative philology and the idea of the Indo-European language family. Although Jones himself never followed up his monumental discovery, others soon did, and by the beginning of the third decade of the next century the science of comparative philology, together with the discipline now referred to as comparative Indo-European religious studies, was well under way.

Almost from the outset, the practitioners of this new science, almost all of them steeped in romantic idealism, found themselves confronted by more than simply a set of linguistic similarities. The primary source materials—the *Ṛgveda,* the *Mahābhārata,* the *Iliad,* the Iranian Avesta, the Icelandic Eddas, and so forth—were religious and/or mythological texts, and it soon became apparent that the gods, heroes, rituals, and events described in these texts could be compared using the same basic methodology that Jones and others had developed, that is, the *comparative method,* which is predicated on the assumption that anterior stages and/or prototypes can be systematically reconstructed from attested evidence, linguistic or otherwise. Thus, comparative mythology, and especially comparative Indo-European mythology, rapidly took its place as a sister discipline of comparative philology.

EARLY NINETEENTH CENTURY. As might be expected, many early nineteenth-century scholars, even those who were not directly concerned with Indo-European linguistic studies, had something to say about various aspects of the newly discovered parallels among the several Indo-European pantheons. This was especially true in Germany, where romantic concern with the origins of the *Volk* (German and otherwise) had become almost a national passion. Thus, Karl O. Müller (1797–1840) and G. F. Creuzer (1771–1858) drew heavily, albeit selectively, upon the linguistic evidence in their attempts to reconstruct the prototypes of Greek and other Indo-European gods and heroes. Even the philosopher G. W. F. Hegel (1770–1831), in whose works Romantic idealism reached the apex of its development, seems to have been strongly influenced by the new comparativism, and, as Richard Chase puts it, "longed for a 'polytheism in art' and imagination, a plastic and mythological philosophy" (*Quest for Myth,* 1949, p. 39).

Most of the pioneer philologists, among them Franz Bopp (1791–1867), Friedrich Schlegel (1772–1829), and Rasmus Rask (1787–1832), also made important contributions to comparative Indo-European mythological and religious studies. In many respects, the most distinguished member of this group was Jacob Grimm (1785–1863), who, with his brother Wilhelm (1786–1859), was responsible for amassing the great collection of tales that bears their name. However, Jacob Grimm was more than a mere collector of folk tales; he was also a preeminent philologist, and in 1823 he articulated the principle that later came to be known as "Grimm's law," which firmly established the phonological connections among Latin, Greek, and the ancient Germanic languages. His most important single contribution to Indo-European religious studies was a two-volume work entitled *Deutsche Mythologie* (1835). In it he developed the thesis that the *Märchen* he and his brother had collected were the detritus of pre-Christian Germanic mythology. This argument is bolstered by a host of etymologies, as well as comparisons to other Indo-European traditions. A good example of the latter is Grimm's suggestion that the ancient Scandinavian account of a war between the gods (Óðinn, Vili, and Vé) and an earlier generation of giants (Ymir et al.) is cognate to the Greek Titanomachy, or the war between the Olympians and the Titans (that is, between Zeus and his siblings and the supernatural beings of the previous generation, led by Kronos).

Elsewhere in Europe and in America interest in mythology, if not exclusively Indo-European mythology, also ran high. In Britain, for example, most of the Romantic poets—Wordsworth, Coleridge, Blake, Shelley, Keats, Byron, and others—drew extensively upon mythological themes; and

Thomas Bulfinch's *The Age of Fable* (1855) popularized the study of mythology like no other work before it. Thus, by the middle of the nineteenth century, the science of comparative philology had reached maturity, interest in mythology and the history of religions had become widespread, and the stage was set for the appearance of the first grand paradigm in the history of Indo-European religious studies.

The First Grand Paradigm: F. Max Müller and the Naturists. In his seminal book, *The Structure of Scientific Revolutions* (1970), the eminent philosopher of science Thomas S. Kuhn makes a persuasive case for the proposition that all scientific knowledge expands in what amounts to an ascending and ever-widening spiral. In its earliest stages a new discipline necessarily finds itself groping for a central focus, for an overarching model in terms of which theories can be generated. Eventually, however, thanks to the efforts of a few scholars, a breakthrough is made, and there emerges a grand paradigm, which not only organizes the knowledge heretofore gained, but by its very nature generates a host of new discoveries and/or interpretations. The emergence of such a paradigm is revolutionary in its impact, and constitutes a quantum leap forward in the history of a discipline.

Kuhn, of course, focuses his attention upon the growth of the physical sciences, which so far have known at least two grand paradigms—Newtonian mechanics and quantum mechanics/relativity—and which may well be on the verge of a third. But the model applies generally. For example, in the history of linguistics, William Jones's discovery led to that discipline's first grand paradigm, which indeed precipitated the study of Indo-European religions. However, it was not until the 1850s, almost sixty years after Jones's death, that Indo-European religious studies finally achieved its own grand paradigm.

The person most responsible for this "revolution" was F. Max Müller (1823–1900), a German-born Sanskrit scholar, philologist, and student of Indian religions who had studied with Bopp and the eminent French Sanskritist Eugène Burnouf. Shortly after completing his formal studies, Müller accepted a position at Oxford University as a lecturer in Sanskrit and Indian religions; as it turned out, he spent the rest of his career there, eventually becoming one of the Victorian era's most distinguished men of letters.

In 1856, seven years after arriving at Oxford, Müller published a long essay entitled simply "Comparative Mythology" (published in *Oxford Essays,* 1856), and the revolution was launched. Although he went on to publish a veritable library of books, as well as innumerable collections of essays, articles, introductions, and so forth, most of his basic ideas were laid out in "Comparative Mythology."

Solar mythology and the "disease of language." First and foremost among Müller's ideas was the notion that the gods and heroes of the "Aryan" (i.e., Indo-European) peoples were basically metaphors for the sun, in all its aspects. To be sure, this was not a brand-new idea. In 1795, Charles-François Dupuis (1742–1809) had suggested that Jesus Christ was a solar metaphor and that the twelve apostles could be interpreted as the signs of the zodiac. But it was Müller who escalated the notion into a full-blown paradigm, one that had special relevance to the ancient Indo-European-speaking domain. Moreover, as a philologist, Müller insisted that the key to understanding these solar metaphors lay in the etymologies of divine names.

Müller asserted that language, including Proto-Indo-European, which he identified in effect with the earliest form of Sanskrit, was in its pristine state eminently rational. Objects such as the sun, the moon, stars, and other natural phenomena were labeled without reference to any divine beings or concepts, as the earliest dialects were incapable of expressing abstractions. But as time went on, Müller concluded, a curious malady set in, a "disease of language," the prime symptom of which was metaphor. What had begun as simple, descriptive terms gradually evolved into increasingly complex and abstract metaphors, and these in turn came to take on a life of their own. In short, by the time the earliest religious texts (e.g., the *Ṛgveda* and Hesiod's *Theogony*) were composed, the disease of language had become terminal; myth and religion had replaced reason and rationality. By judicious use of the comparative method, however, one could cut through the layers of metaphoric accretion and arrive at the root meanings underlying divine and heroic names. Thus, for example, the equation between Zeus and the Indian figure Dyauh, which clearly stemmed from a Proto-Indo-European conception of the sky god, could be traced back to a series of abstract conceptions relating to light, brightness, dawn, and so on, which, in turn, ultimately derived from metaphors for various solar attributes. Although he admitted that other natural phenomena play a part in generating mythical metaphors, Müller constantly emphasized the sun as the prime source of Indo-European religious inspiration: "I am bound to say that my own researches have led me again and again to the dawn and the sun as the chief burden of the myths of the Aryan race" (*Lectures on the Science of Language,* 1864, p. 520).

Müller's solar mythology rapidly began to gain adherents, both in Great Britain and abroad. Perhaps the most important of these was the English classicist George W. Cox (1827–1902), author of *The Mythology of the Aryan Nations* (1887). Despite his obsession with "pan-Aryanism" and with solar and other natural metaphors, Cox added a new and important dimension to comparative Indo-European mythology through his emphasis upon structural as well as etymological equations. As shall be seen, this prefigured more recent theories about the nature of the Indo-European religious tradition. Another major disciple was the Semitist Robert Brown (b. 1844), who extended the paradigm far beyond the Indo-European domain and used it to explain the ancient Near Eastern divinities as well as those of the *Ṛgveda.* Two American scholars, John Fiske (1842–1901) and Daniel G. Brinton (1837–1899), also made significant contributions to the literature of solar mythology. In *Myths and Mythmakers* (1888) Fiske attempted to reconcile the meteorological and solar varieties of naturism, and Brinton, in *The Myths of the New World* (3d ed., 1896), sought to demonstrate the parallels between North American Indian and Indo-European mythological figures.

It should be pointed out that Müller's was by no means the only naturistic school of comparative Indo-European mythology to flourish in the late nineteenth century. Indeed, the "first paradigm," as it has been termed here, actually included several rather distinct subparadigms, all of which shared essentially the same methodology and basic assumptions. For example, in 1859 Adalbert Kuhn (1812–1881) published his famous *Die Herabkunft des Feuers und des Göttertranks,* in which thunderstorms and their attendant bolts of lightning, rather than the sun, were conceived to be the prime source of Indo-European (and other) mythological and religious metaphors. Kuhn's most famous onomastic equation, later shown to be totally incorrect, was the assumed etymological connection between Prometheus and the Indian figure Pramantha. Both were seen as archetypal "fire bringers," and Kuhn and his followers were as assiduous in discovering other Indo-European fire gods as Müller and others were in discovering their solar divinities. Another prominent naturist was the Italian philologist Angelo de Gubernatis (1840–1913), who emphasized animal metaphors; thus, where Müller and Kuhn saw the sun and the lightning bolt, Gubernatis saw wild beasts, especially beasts of prey. Still others sought to find lunar and/or stellar metaphors in the Indo-European and other ancient mythological traditions.

Collapse of the first paradigm. While Müller, Kuhn, Cox, and the rest were developing their naturistic models, another scholarly approach to myth and religion per se was quietly taking a shape that would ultimately prove to be the undoing of these models. This approach was fostered by the pioneer anthropologists, such as E. B. Tylor (1832–1917), John Lubbock (1834–1913), and John McLennan (1827–1881), who, as might be expected, came to focus their attention not on the Indo-European tradition, but rather on the vast corpus of data that had come to light relative to the beliefs and practices of contemporary "primitive" peoples. In his *Primitive Culture* (1871), for example, Tylor laid the foundations for the theory of animism, that is, the notion that all religious beliefs are rooted in the concept of the human soul. The anthropologists were for the most part not trained philologists—although they did, of course, make use of the comparative method in its broadest sense—and therefore were not as attuned to etymologies and the metaphoric significance of names. The result was a profoundly different conception of the origin and evolution of human religious beliefs.

By the late 1880s the naturists and the anthropologists found themselves on a collision course. The anthropological attack was led by a brilliant and iconoclastic Scotsman, Andrew Lang (1844–1912). A sometime disciple of Tylor, Lang set about to destroy naturism in general and the theories of Max Müller in particular. In a series of books, essays, and popular articles he hammered at Müller's assumptions and etymologies, and by the end of the century had effectively demonstrated the weaknesses in the naturistic paradigm so effectively that it did not long survive the death of its chief proponent in 1900.

It would be impossible here to trace all of the thrusts and counterthrusts that marked this famous scholarly debate, but Lang's principal objections can be summed up as follows: (1) Müller's theory—and, by extension, the theories of Kuhn, Cox, Fiske, and the rest—was implicitly based on the fallacious linkage of "degradation" to Original Sin, which, although the chosen people in this instance were the so-called Aryans (i.e., Indo-Europeans) rather than the Jews, was modeled on traditional Judeo-Christian historiography and did not take into account the comparative data from contemporary non-Western cultures; (2) too much emphasis was placed upon language and linguistic processes, especially metaphor and etymology, and too little on the differential effects of the social, cultural, and physical setting wherein myths and religious concepts originated; and (3) there was too much concern with origins and not enough with the historical development of myths and mythmaking, nor was enough attention paid to the universal, evolutionary stages evident in the Indo-European tradition. Needless to say, Müller attempted to answer these charges as best he could, and indeed his criticisms of unilineal evolutionism are remarkably similar to those of later critics. But in the end Lang was triumphant, and solar mythology, together with the other varieties of naturism that had flourished since the middle of the century, went into a permanent eclipse.

EMPIRICAL REACTION AND EMERGENCE OF NEW MODELS: 1900–1920. Thus passed the first grand paradigm in comparative Indo-European religious studies. As the new century dawned, the majority of scholars working in the field—classicists, Indologists, Germanists, Celticists, and so forth—rapidly abandoned the naturistic/etymological approach in favor of more intense efforts to explain the various Indo-European religious traditions on their own terms. As in other disciplines at this time, including anthropology, a new spirit of empiricism came to the fore, marked by a growing distrust of comparativism. Most of these specialists, as they may be termed (e.g., the Celticist Joseph Vendryes), relied heavily on the methods of textual criticism, phrasing their analyses in terms of new translations, new specific etymologies, and the like. Indeed, save for the purposes of linguistic reconstruction, the idea of a common Indo-European religious and/or mythological heritage was rarely mentioned in the first two decades of the twentieth century.

At the same time, unrelated, for the most part, to Indo-European studies, several new theoretical models for the study of religion emerged, two of which were to have an important impact on the future development of this discipline.

In his massive survey of primitive religion, *The Golden Bough* (3d ed., 12 vols., 1911–1915), James G. Frazer (1854–1941) came to the conclusion that religion everywhere was rooted in magic, and that all belief systems, including those of the ancient Indo-European-speaking communities, were predicated on a sacrificial ritual wherein a god was killed and replaced so as to renew the world. Among Frazer's prime examples was the death of Baldr, the Apollo-like son of the chief Norse god, Óðinn, who, thanks to the machinations of Loki, was unintentionally killed at the peak of his youthful vigor by his sibling, the blind god Hǫðr. Thus, through a form of "sympathetic magic" the gods, and the forces they incarnated, were periodically manipulated so as to keep them perpetually vigorous and fertile. Although largely rejected by subsequent generations of anthropologists, Frazer's influence lingered on in the so-called ritualist school of mythology associated with Jane E. Harrison, Francis M. Cornford, Jessie L. Weston, Gilbert Murray, F. R. S. Raglan, and H. J. Rose, all of whom drew heavily on Greco-Roman beliefs and practices in the formulation of their theories (indeed, most were classicists by academic training).

A second theoretical development occurred in France under the aegis of Émile Durkheim (1858–1917), one of the founding fathers of contemporary social science. In 1903, in collaboration with his principal student and disciple, Marcel Mauss (1872–1950), Durkheim published a short monograph entitled "De quelques formes primitives de classification: Contribution à l'étude des représentations collectives" (*Année sociologique* 6, 1903, pp. 1–72), which argued that social classification systems are necessarily "collectively represented" in a society's belief systems. This was followed in 1912 by his *magnum opus, Les formes élémentaires de la vie religieuse* (translated as *The Elementary Forms of the Religious Life*, 1917), in which he persuasively demonstrated that society itself is the stuff of the divine and that humans necessarily fashion their gods as collective representations of fundamental "social facts." To be sure, Durkheim's prime examples were drawn from the belief systems of the Australian Aborigines, but the implications for the study of religion per se were clear: a new primary source of religious metaphors had been identified, and the immediate implications for the study of Indo-European belief systems were also clearly present from the outset, as Durkheim's ideas themselves were in some measure influenced by the demonstration (1907) of Antoine Meillet (1866–1936) that the Iranian god Mithra (equivalent to the Vedic god Mitra) was the personification of the idea of "contract." Indeed, as shall shortly be demonstrated, Meillet, perhaps the most eminent Indo-European philologist of his time, had more than a little to do with the development of the second grand paradigm in Indo-European studies.

Neo-Comparativists and the Search for a New Paradigm: 1920–1938. Although comparative Indo-European religious studies suffered a marked decline in the generation following Müller's death, the basic questions he and his colleagues had addressed regarding the fundamental similarities among the several ancient Indo-European pantheons remained, and in the early 1920s the pendulum began to swing once again in the direction of what can best be labeled neo-comparativism. For example, Albert Carnoy began to speak in no uncertain terms about a "religion indo-européenne," and shortly thereafter, although they differed widely in inspirations and orientation, a number of German scholars, among them Walter F. Otto, Hermann Güntert, Friedrich Cornelius, and F. R. Schröder, came to the same general conclusion: that it is impossible to understand any single ancient Indo-European religious system without reference to a common set of deities, rituals, and myths, and that it is indeed possible to conceive of such a common Indo-European tradition without reference to the discarded theories of Müller and Kuhn. Another driving force in this new effort was provided by Meillet, who, although he himself never attempted with Indo-European mythological materials the kind of broad synthesis that characterizes his *Introduction à l'étude des langues indo-européennes* (1922), encouraged his students to undertake such studies. One of these students was Georges Dumézil (1898–1986), a young philologist and historian of religions who took his doctorate under Meillet in 1924.

Like the other neo-comparativists, Dumézil sought to find a viable theoretical basis upon which to build a new paradigm for comparative Indo-European mythology. In his early studies, for example, *Le festin d'immortalité* (1924), *Le crime des Lemniennes* (1924), and *Le problème des Centaures* (1929), which focused on what he came to call the "ambrosia cycle," that is, the common Indo-European traditions surrounding the preparation and consumption of a deified beverage (*soma,* mead, ambrosia, and so forth), he drew heavily on Frazer's theory of death and rebirth and of the ritual sacrifice of the king. But as he himself later observed, the Frazerian model ultimately proved to be insufficient for his purposes; it simply could not explain the multitude of common motifs that pervaded the several Indo-European traditions.

After a decade of grappling with the problem, Dumézil took an extended leave from his academic duties in the early 1930s and undertook the study of ancient Chinese religion under the guidance of Marcel Granet (1884–1940), an eminent Sinologist who had also been one of Durkheim's most devoted disciples. Yet although the project began as an attempt to gain a perspective on the Indo-European tradition by coming to grips with a wholly different ancient belief system, it ended by providing Dumézil with the framework he had been searching for and that he came to call *la méthode sociologique.* Thus, in 1938, not long after he had completed his studies with Granet, Dumézil achieved the breakthrough he had been seeking, and the second grand paradigm in Indo-European studies was born.

The Second Grand Paradigm: Dumézil and the New Comparative Mythology. Although the breakthrough itself came in 1938, the first hint of what Dumézil now refers to as the tripartite ideology actually surfaced shortly before he began his Chinese studies. In 1930 he published an article comparing the three divisons of ancient Scythian society—the "Royal Scyths," the "Warrior Scyths," and the "Agricultural Scyths," each of which was believed to have descended from one of the sons of the primeval figure Targitaus (Herodotos, 4.5–4.6)—with the three *varṇas*, or classes (later to become full-fledged castes) of Vedic India: the Brāhmas (priests), the Kṣhatriyas (warriors), and the Vaiśhiyas (herders and cultivators, that is, the food producers). He also recognized that the sovereignty of the Royal Scyths was based on the myth that their ancestor, Targitaus's youngest son, had managed to recover three fiery golden objects, a cup, an ax, and a yoked plow, each symbolic of one of the social divisions, that had fallen from the sky, although the full import of this symbolism did not become apparent until the new paradigm had fully crystallized. Two years later, in 1932, the linguist Émile Benveniste arrived independently at a similar conclusion relative to the parallels not only between the Scythian and Indian situations, but also among these two and the social classes of ancient Iran. However, all of the societies concerned belonged to the Indo-Iranian substock, and at the time there seemed to be no reason to conclude that this tripartite hierarchy of priests (or priest-kings), warriors, and cultivators was necessarily pan-Indo-European.

Nevertheless, in the years that followed, Dumézil began to pick up hints of an analogous structure in the Roman tradition (see, for example, *Flamen-Brahman,* 1935), especially in the makeup of the most ancient of the Roman priestly colleges, the *flamines maiores.* Could the distinctions between the *flamen Dialis,* or chief priest of Jupiter, the *flamen Martialis,* who presided over the cult of the war god Mars, and the *flamen Quirinalis,* who served the popular divinity Quirinus, an incarnation of the mass of Roman society, reflect the same structure he and Benveniste had discovered in the Indo-Iranian tradition, especially in light of the probable etymological connections between the two terms *flamen* and *brahman*? It was not until he had focused his attention upon the ancient Germanic pantheons in the course of giving a series of lectures at the University of Uppsala in Sweden in the fall of 1938 that he finally came to the realization that this threefold hierarchy was in fact pan-Indo-European, and that it was reflected in both the structure of the pantheons and the structure of society itself, especially in the system of social stratification. And here, of course, his recent exposure to Durkheimian theory in the course of his studies with Granet served him well. The Old Norse gods Óðinn, Thórr, and Freyr reflected the same basic type of social organization, even though the priestly, or Brahmanic, level had long since disappeared as a viable social entity by the time the myths were transcribed by Snorri Sturluson and Saxo Grammaticus. Óðinn (Odin), like Jupiter and the Vedic god Varuṇa, was a collective representation of ultimate sovereignty; Thórr was the incarnation of the warrior stratum and thus was cognate to Mars and Indra; while Freyr (together with his father Njorðr), like Quirinus and the Vedic Asvins ("divine horsemen"), represented the producing classes, that is, the herders and cultivators upon whom the other two classes depended for nourishment.

Dumézil's discovery was in large measure confirmed by his Swedish colleague Stig Wikander's conclusive demonstration that among the most prominent features of ancient Indo-European social organization was the *comitatus* ("war band"), which typically formed itself around the person of a chief. According to Wikander, the *comitatus* was mythologically reflected by such otherwise diverse phenomena as Indra and his Marut (i.e., the Rudriyas) and the war bands that followed Irish heroes like Cú Chulainn and Finn (see *Der arische Männerbund,* 1938). Thus, thanks to Wikander, who became one of Dumézil's earliest and most productive supporters (see below), a major piece of the puzzle had fallen into place.

A preliminary statement of the new model appeared in *Les dieux des Germains* (1939), which was based on the lectures Dumézil had given in Sweden, and for the next decade the discoveries came thick and fast. Dumézil rapidly came to the conclusion that the sovereign level, shortly to be labeled the "first function," was in fact represented by two complementary divinities: Varuṇa, Jupiter, and Óðinn were primarily concerned with the maintenance of cosmic order (e.g., the Vedic concept of *ṛta*), while Mitra, Týr, and the otherwise obscure Roman divinity Dius Fidius were concerned with social and juridical sovereignty. This idea of the "joint sovereignty" formed the major focus of *Mitra-Varuna: Essai sur deux représentations indo-européennes de la souveraineté* (1940). The first comprehensive statement of the new paradigm appeared a year later in a book entitled *Jupiter, Mars, Quirinus* (1941). Although Dumézil here focuses on Rome and its mythological origins, this book spelled out in detail for the first time the concept that came to be known as the "three functions" of social organization, that is, the "first function" (cosmic and juridical sovereignty in all its manifestations), the "second function" (the exercise of military prowess), and the "third function" (the provision of nourishment, health, physical well-being, wealth, the welfare of the masses, etc.).

In short, by the end of the 1940s, in a remarkable series of books, monographs, and shorter works, Dumézil had fully articulated the basic elements of the second grand paradigm in comparative Indo-European religious studies. The Iranian and Celtic traditions had been brought into the picture, and a great many secondary themes had been discovered; for example, the recognition that the juridical sovereign (e.g., Mitra and Týr) typically had two ancillary manifestations, each of whom was concerned with an aspect of this function. In the Vedic texts, these were the figures Aryaman and Bhaga, who represented, respectively, the Aryan community itself, along with its most basic social relationship, marriage; and the equitable distribution of goods and rewards. This idea was first enunciated in *Le troisième souverain* (1949).

In his first articulations of the new paradigm Dumézil had relied heavily on the previously mentioned Durkheimian proposition that "social facts" give rise to "supernatural facts," or "collective representations." However, as he himself observed, around 1950 his orientation began to shift, and he took what amounted to a long step beyond strict Durkheimianism and "la méthode sociologique." Adopting what in retrospect may be called a more structuralist perspective, he began to conceive of the three functions as expressions of a deep-seated, tripartite ideology that was manifest in both social and supernatural contexts, but which ultimately lay outside either sphere. Thus, the functions were gradually redefined as "un moyen d'analyser," a method of analysis, and this revised orientation is, in some respects, not dissimilar to the structuralist vision espoused by Claude Lévi-Strauss (b. 1908). There is, however, a major difference between the two French scholars: Lévi-Strauss (in such works as *Le cru et le cuit,* 1964) is concerned primarily with the "deep structure" of the human mind per se, while Dumézil remains committed to the proposition that the tripartite ideology is uniquely Indo-European, and that other major language families, such as the Sino-Tibetan, the Hamito-Semitic, and the Uto-Aztecan, are probably characterized by their own unique ideologies. Perhaps the best way to describe this approach is to label it "structural relativism."

In the course of the next three decades more important discoveries were made, not only by Dumézil himself, but also by the scholars who have come to adopt the paradigm. One of the earliest of these was Stig Wikander, who in 1947 demonstrated the extent to which the heroes of the *Mahābhārata* (Yudhiṣṭhira, Arjuna, Bhīma, Nakula, and Sahadeva) were at bottom transpositions of the major Vedic divinities (Mitra, Varuṇa, Indra, and the Nāsatya) and showed that the tripartite ideology could be detected at the epic as well as the mythological level. Other early followers of Dumézil were Lucien Gerschel, Jan de Vries, Edgar Polomé, Robert Schilling, Jacques Duchesne-Guillemin, François Vian, and Marie-Louise Sjoestedt.

In the late 1950s and early 1960s a new generation of scholars was attracted to the Dumézilian model, including Jaan Puhvel, Donald J. Ward, Françoise Le Roux, and myself, and the paradigm was extended even more broadly. Among the major subthemes discovered by Dumézil and his colleagues over the years, in addition to Wikander's 1947 breakthrough, were (1) the "three sins of the warrior," that is, the recognition that Indo-European warrior figures (e.g., Indra, Herakles, and the Norse figure Starkaðr) typically commit three canonical "sins," one against each of the functions, and (2) the "war between the functions," manifested principally in the Roman and Germanic traditions, wherein representatives of the first two functions defeat representatives of the third and incorporate them into the system, rendering it complete (e.g., the Sabine war and the conflict between the Æsir and Vanir).

In the early 1970s Dumézil pushed the paradigm in yet another important direction (see *Mythe et épopée,* vol. 2, 1971, especially "L'enjeu du jeu des dieux: Un héros") through his discovery that Indo-European warrior figures such as the Vedic character Śiśupāla are in the final analysis but counters in a game played by the gods, and that the gods themselves can be sorted into "dark" and "light" categories—that is, those who represent the chaotic forces of nature and those who seek to control these forces. In the Indian tradition this dichotomy is reflected in the difference between the "dark" divinity Rudra and the "light" divinity Viṣṇu; in ancient Scandinavia it appears in that between Óðinn and Thórr. The full implications of this discovery are being probed by several of Dumézil's disciples, among them Udo Strutynski and the author of this article.

In the course of what may be termed his *phase de bilan,* Dumézil's remarkable scholarly output continued unabated. Among his subsequent books were a reexamination of the Indo-European concept of sovereignty (*Les dieux souverains des Indo-Européens,* 1977) and a disquisition on Indo-European attitudes toward marriage (*Mariages indo-européens,* 1979). He also published several collections of earlier writings, all of which bear on one or another aspect of the tripartite ideology. Dumézil's career was capped in 1979 when he was elected to the Académie Française.

This is not to imply that the "new comparative mythology" has become universally accepted by Indo-Europeanists. Indeed, almost from the outset it has been the subject of intense and persistent criticism from a variety of scholars, many of whom have suggested that Dumézil imposed the tripartite model on the data, and that it has no existence save in the minds of the researchers concerned. Among the most persistent of these critics was Paul Thieme, an Indologist, who asserted on numerous occasions that Dumézil's interpretation of the Indic pantheon, especially the role played by the god Aryaman, was wholly incorrect. Thieme interpreted the Sanskrit root *ari-* to mean "stranger" rather than "the people" (or "the shining ones"), the common meaning of most ethnic self-identification terms, modern as well as ancient—for example, Hopi, Diné (Navajo), and so forth. Other prominent critics have included H. J. Rose (who took Dumézil to task for ignoring the "manaistic" basis of Roman religion), Jan Gonda, Angelo Brelich, the Germanist E. A. Philippson, and John Brough, a Sanskrit scholar who claimed to have discovered the tripartite ideology in the Bible and therefore asserted that it was not uniquely Indo-European.

Dumézil vigorously responded to these and other criticisms, and to date no single critic has emerged as a potential "Andrew Lang" as far as this paradigm is concerned. Indeed, it is fair to say that the majority of contemporary scholars in the field of comparative Indo-European mythology and religion continue to make effective use of the general theoretical and methodological framework developed by Dumézil and his colleagues in the course of the last five decades. A good example is Joël Grisward, whose brilliant analysis of the medieval French legends of Aymeri de Narbonne and the extent to which they have Indo-Iranian counterparts (see his *Archéologie de l'épopée médiévale,* 1981) is, as Dumézil himself noted, perhaps the most important contribution to the new comparative mythology since Wikander's discovery of epical transposition in 1947. Another excellent example can be seen in Udo Strutynski's convincing demonstration that the English weekday names, at least from Tuesday through Friday, and their cognates in other modern Germanic languages, represent a persistence of a tripartite ideological formula—that is, "Týr's day," "Óðinn's day," "Thórr's day," and "Frigg's day" (see his "Germanic Divinities in Weekday Names," *Journal of Indo-European Studies* 3, 1975, pp. 363–384).

It would be impossible in the space of this brief article even to mention, let alone discuss in any detail, all of the significant research that has been pursued since the late 1960s by specialists in comparative Indo-European religion and mythology who have oriented their work around the Dumézilian paradigm. For example, Atsuhiko Yoshida, a Japanese Hellenist who studied with Dumézil for the better part of a decade, has demonstrated the strong probability that the development of Japanese mythology was profoundly influenced, either directly or indirectly, by Indo-European themes in the late prehistoric period (that is, the fourth and fifth centuries CE), and that the most likely source of this influence was one or another tribe of North Iranian-speaking steppe nomads (Scythians, Alans, etc.) that managed to reach East Asia during this period (Yoshida, 1977). The late Ōbayashi Taryō, an anthropologist at the University of Tokyo, and the author of this article subsequently joined Yoshida in this effort. Bruce Lincoln has published a book comparing Indo-Iranian and contemporary East African religious attitudes toward cattle (*Priests, Warriors, and Cattle,* 1981). David Cohen has expanded the understanding of the "three sins" typically committed by the Indo-European warrior (see above) in a penetrating analysis of the Irish hero Suibhne ("Suibhne Geilt," *Celtica* 12, 1977, pp. 113–124).

In France, Daniel Dubuisson, who took his doctorate under Dumézil in 1983, has attempted to develop a quasi-mathematical approach to Indo-European myth, based in large part on his Indological research. More recently, in 1994, he published a major overview of the current status of comparative Indo-European mythology. Bernard Sergent has illuminated the dual kingship at Sparta by judicious application of the Dumézilian paradigm ("La représentation spariate de la royauté," *Revue de l'histoire des religions* 189, 1976, pp. 3–52). And in 1984 Dean A. Miller investigated the trifunctional implications of the "three kings" in Sophocles' *Oedipus at Colonus* from what can best be termed a neo-Dumézilian standpoint. Other scholars who have extended the paradigm in a variety of new and potentially important directions include Steven O'Brien, Miriam Robbins, Alf Hiltebeitel, David B. Evans, and Jean-Claude Rivière.

SOME RECENT DEVELOPMENTS. Like all grand paradigms that have been pushed to their effective limits, the Dumézilian paradigm is fraying a bit at the edges, and several of the most important recent advances in Indo-European religious studies have involved matters that transcend the tripartite ideology. One of these is the matter of "dark" and "light" divinities mentioned earlier. Indeed, Dumézil himself suggested that this dichotomy cuts across the three functions, and perhaps reflects a more fundamental binary structure that underlies social and supernatural tripartition. If this proves to be the case, it may well be that the ideological model Dumézil first detected some fifty-odd years ago is but a special case of a broader and more deep-seated mental template, as it were, that is shared by *homo religiosus* as a whole. Such a template, if it exists, would closely parallel the presumably universal "deep structure" of the human psyche posited by Lévi-Strauss.

Another extremely significant development involves the nature of the common Indo-European cosmology, something Dumézil never really came to grips with and which, heretofore, had defied all attempts at elucidation via the tripartite ideology. In 1975, Puhvel and Lincoln, working independently, reached compatible conclusions; they agreed that the elusive cosmology was in fact embedded in a theme, present in the Roman, Indo-Iranian, and Norse traditions, wherein a primeval being kills his twin and makes the world from the latter's remains. This theme closely approximates the nearly universal concept of what Adolf E. Jensen calls the "*dema* deity," that is, a sacrificial victim whose body parts provide the *materia prima* of either the world itself or some important part thereof (as in the Ceramese myth of Hainuwele; see Jensen, *Myth and Cult among Primitive Peoples,* 1963).

For Puhvel, the point of departure was the pseudo-historical account of Romulus and Remus, in which the latter is killed shortly after the founding of Rome. Underlying the names *Romulus* and *Remus,* Puhvel suggests, are **Wironos* ("man") and **Yemo(no)s* ("twin"), to which may be compared *Yama* (Skt.), *Yima* (Av.), and *Ymir* (ON), as well as *Mannus* and *Tuisto,* mentioned in Tacitus's *Germania.* Although Romulus/*Wironos did not explicitly "make the world" from Remus/*Yemos's remains, Remus's death seems clearly to have been somehow essential to the building of the city, like a sacrificial offering, and the fact that Remus's "crime" consists of jumping over the newly dug foundation for the city wall implies that the victim's essence was in one way or another mixed with the mortar that eventually filled the ditch. Lincoln's point of departure was the Indic manifestation of the theme and its implications as they relate to the *dema*-deity concept, that is, the account in *Ṛgveda* 10.90 wherein Manu (i.e., "man") sacrifices Yama (or Puruṣa, as he is called in the Vedic text) and creates the world from his corpse. (Unlike Remus/*Yemos, Puruṣa was a willing victim, and Manu is credited with originating the institution of religious sacrifice; however, the basic context of the two accounts is remarkably similar.) As luck would have it, Lincoln sent a draft of his manuscript to Puhvel for comment and criticism, and the result was a pair of seminal articles that in 1975 appeared back-to-back in *History of Religions.*

The paradigmatic implications of this discovery are still under investigation, and various questions have been raised by scholars. Does the ideology itself spring from this primordial sacrifice? Is it possible that the account of Romulus and Remus, who began life as the foster children of a shepherd, became warriors, and finally went off to found a city, is a euhemeristic survival of an ontological myth wherein the three functions emerge successively after a primeval fratricide? And is there a connection between the *dramatis personae* of this primeval drama and the dark/light dichotomy (see above)? Or does the theme in question lie totally outside the parameters of the paradigm? As yet no clear answers have been provided to these questions.

Yet another extremely significant discovery relating to Indo-European religion was N. J. Allen's 1987 compelling case for the existence of a "fourth" ideological function (or "F4," as he labels it) that lies outside the tripartite paradigm per se and can thus be described as "other." A good exmaple of a "fourth function" phenomenon in the Indic tradfition the Shurdra caste, that is, the non-Aryan outisders, who are "other" to the three twice-born Aryan *varna* (that is, the Brāhmaṇs, Kṣhatriyas and Vaiśhiyas, who reflect "F1," "F2" and "F3," respectively). This concept adds a new and extremely important dimesion to the Dumézilian paradigm, the implications of which are only just beginning to be appreciated.

The common denominators among the the several Indo-European epic traditions have also been the subject of some important recent research. For example, Dean A. Miller's book *The Epic Hero* (2000) has materially advanced the understanding of this most important aspect of the Indo-European worldview, while Julian Baldick's (1994) convincing demonstration that the *Iliad* is fundamentally cognate not to the *Mahābhārata,* as has long been held, but rather to the *Rāmāyana,* has led some scholars, including the author of this article, to the conclusion that the two epics in question are, at bottom, reflexes of a common Indo-European concern with abducted brides and their rescurers. Other reflexes of this concern may include the medieval European tale of Tristan and Isolde and the Middle High German Kudrun epic, both of which involve figures broadly similar to Helen, Sītā, Rāma, Menelaus, Agamamnon, and the rest. Moreover, Baldick has gone on to suggest that the *Mahābhārata* is cognate to the *Odyssey,* in that they both involve accounts of exiled kings who eventually return to reclaim their thrones after a climactic battle (e.g., the Battle of Kurukshetra in the *Mahābhārata,* in which the Pāndava defeat their enemies and restore Yudhisthira to his rightful throne, and Homer's account of the slaying of Penelope's suitors by Odysseus and Telemachus).

Finally, the importance of binarism in the Indo-European tradition, that is, the all-pervasive difference between "light" and "dark," which, as has been noted, Dumézil came to recognize late in his career, is something that may link it to far older Nostratic and even, perhaps, Eurasiatic traditions dating as far back as the Upper Paleolithic (that is, prior to 10,000 BCE), has begun to be recognized (see Littleton 2002). Indo-European religion is thus beginning to be grounded in the broader context of the Eurasian tradition, which took shape in Central Asia millennia before anything identificable as Proto-Indo-European appeared on the scene.

In sum, as the field of Indo-European religious studies enters its third century it remains a vigorous and intellectually viable discipline. In the course of the last two hundred-plus years it has managed to develop and then transcend one grand paradigm (naturism) and is currently dominated by a second (the new comparative mythology). How long this second paradigm will continue to reign is uncertain; as has been indicated, there are already signs that it may have begun to outlive its usefulness. But whatever may be the ultimate fate of the Dumézilian model—and one suspects that it will eventually become a "special case" of a much broader paradigm, the outlines of which cannot yet be clearly perceived, although Allen's aforementioned seminal discovery of a fouth function does provide a glimpse of what may lie ahead—the discipline itself will almost certainly persevere, and will continue to contribute important insights not only into a fundamental aspect of the heritage shared by all Indo-European speakers, but also into the nature of religion per se.

SEE ALSO Comparative Mythology.

BIBLIOGRAPHY

Allen, N. J. "The Ideology of the Indo-Europeans: Dumézil's Theory and the Idea of a Fourth Function." *International Journal of Moral and Social Studies* 2 (1987): 23–39. A significant discovery that adds an important new dimension to the study of Indo-European religion.

Baldick, Julian. *Homer and the Indo-Europeans: Comparing Mythologies.* London, 1994. The author contends that the *Iliad* is cognate to the *Rāmāyana* in that both reflect an "abducted bride" mythologem, while the *Mahābhārata* is cognate to the *Odyssey.* An important reassessment.

Dorson, Richard. "The Eclipse of Solar Mythology." In *Myth: A Symposium,* edited by Thomas A. Sebeok, pp. 25–63. Bloomington, Ind., 1965. The definitive study of the Müller-Lang controversy.

Dubuisson, Daniel. *Mythologie du xxeme siecle (Dumézil, Lévi-Strauss, Eliade).* Lille, 1993. An important overview of contemporary comparative Indo-European mythology and religion by one of Dumézil's chief students.

Dumézil, Georges. *L'idéologie tripartie des Indo-Européens.* Brussels, 1958. Remains the most succinct overview of Dumézil's thesis.

Dumézil, Georges. *Camillus.* Berkeley, Calif., 1980. A translation by Annette Aronowicz and Josette Bryson of the "Camillus" sections from *Mythe et épopée,* vol. 3 (Paris, 1973) and related passages from *Fêtes romaines d'été et d'automne* (Paris, 1975). Includes a definitive introduction by Udo Strutynski.

Dumézil, Georges. *The Stakes of the Warrior.* Berkeley, 1983. A translation by David Weeks of the "L'enjeu du jeu des dieux:

Un héros" section of *Mythe et épopée,* vol. 2 (Paris, 1971). Includes a masterful introduction by Jaan Puhvel, which puts the "dark/light" dichotomy into its proper perspective.

Feldman, Burton, and Robert D. Richardson, eds. *The Rise of Modern Mythology, 1680–1860.* Bloomington, Ind., 1972. A comprehensive anthology of the major eighteenth- and early nineteenth-century contributions to comparative mythology, from Vico and Fontenelle to F. Max Müller.

Grisward, Joël H. *Archéologie de l'épopée médiévale.* Paris, 1981. A brilliant application of the tripartite model to a medieval French epic, the saga of Aymeri de Narbonne.

Larson, Gerald James, C. Scott Littleton, and Jaan Puhvel, eds. *Myth in Indo-European Antiquity.* Berkeley, 1974. A symposium on various aspects of the Dumézilian model and related subjects. Includes papers by Littleton, Puhvel, Strutynski, David Evans, Mary R. Gerstein, Steven E. Greenebaum, Edgar Polomé, Marija Gimbutas, Jeannine Talley, Matthias Vereno, and an essay by Dumézil entitled "'Le Borgne' and 'Le Manchot': The State of the Problem." This essay concerns yet another Indo-European subtheme: the loss of an eye and a hand, respectively, by the cosmic and juridical representatives of the first function, for example, Óðinn, who gives up an eye in exchange for wisdom, and Týr, who loses a hand while swearing what amounts to a false oath, as well as the Roman figures Horatius Cocles, who is one-eyed, and Mucius Scaevola, who also loses a hand while swearing falsely.

Lincoln, Bruce. "The Indo-European Myth of Creation." *History of Religions* 15 (1975): 121–145. A seminal contribution to the understanding of the Indo-European cosmogonic myth; see the article by Puhvel listed below.

Littleton, C. Scott. *The New Comparative Mythology: An Anthropological Assessment of the Theories of Georges Dumézil.* 3d ed. Berkeley, 1980. A comprehensive review of the origins and current state of the "second paradigm," that is, the Dumézilian model. Includes a discussion of the major criticisms that have been directed against the model, as well as an essay comparing Dumézil and Lévi-Strauss, and an extensive bibliography of works by Dumézil and other contributors to the new comparative mythology.

Littleton, C. Scott. "Gods, Myths and Structures: Dumézil." *Encyclopedia of Continental Philosophy,* edited by Simon Glendinning, pp. 558–568. Edinburgh, 1999. A recent overview.

Littleton, C. Scott. "The Binary 'Spine' of Dumézil's Tripartite Indo-European Ideology: A Pan-Nostratic/Eurasiatic Feature?" *Cosmos* 14 (2001): 69–84. Discusses the extent to which Indo-European binarism has deep Eurasian roots.

Meillet, Antoine, "Le dieu indo-iranien Mitra." *Journal asiatique* 9 (1907): 143–159. A seminal article on the Vedic god Mithra and the extent to which he is a "collective representation" of the idea of "contract"; had an impact on Durkheim and later on the development of Dumézil's theory.

Miller, Dean A. *The Epic Hero.* Baltimore, 2000. An important contribution to the understanding of the Indo-European warrior figure as manifested in epics.

Puhvel, Jaan. "Remus et frater." *History of Religions* 15 (1975): 146–157. Reprinted in Puhvel's *Analecta Indoeuropaea* (Innsbruck, 1981), pp. 300–311. Together with the article by Lincoln listed above, this paper probes the Indo-European cosmogonic myth and concludes that it is based on a primeval sacrifice of "Twin" by "Man." An extremely significant contribution to the new comparative mythology.

Puhvel, Jaan, ed. *Myth and Law among the Indo-Europeans.* Berkeley, 1970. A symposium on the new comparative mythology. Includes papers by Puhvel, Littleton, Strutynski, Donald Ward, Jacques Duchesne-Guillemin, Edgar Polomé, Calvert Watkins, James L. Sauvé, Robert L. Fisher, and Stephen P. Schwartz.

Rivière, Jean-Claude, ed. *Georges Dumézil à la découverte des Indo-Européens.* Paris, 1979. A symposium marking Dumézil's election to the Académie Française in 1979. Includes essays by several of his colleagues and former students, including Rivière, Robert Schilling, François-Xavier Dillmann, Jean Varenne, Joël Grisward, Georges Charachidzé, and Alain de Benoist, editor of *Nouvelle école.* Original versions of some of these essays were published, together with other materials, in a 1973 issue of *Nouvelle école* devoted to Dumézil.

Vries, Jan de. *Perspectives in the History of Religions.* Translated by Kees W. Bolle. Berkeley, 1977. A succinct survey of the history of religious and mythological thought from classical antiquity to modern times. De Vries was an early disciple of Dumézil, and he includes an interesting section on his theories (pp. 182–186).

Ward, Donald. *The Divine Twins: An Indo-European Myth in Germanic Tradition.* Berkeley, 1968. An important contribution to the study of the "third function" and the role played in dioscurism in the Indo-European ideology.

Wikander, Stig. "Pandava-sagan och Mahabharata's mytiska förutsättningar." *Religion och Bibel* (Lund) 6 (1947): 27–39. Demonstrates that the heroes of the *Mahābhārata* reflect the tripartite ideology and were derived from the Vedic divinities. Wikander's essay was a major step forward in the development of the new comparative mythology.

Yoshida, Atsuhiko. "Japanese Mythology and the Indo-European Trifunctional System." *Diogenes* 98 (1977): 93–116. Summarizes the evidence suggesting that Japanese mythology, as expressed in the *Kojiki* (712 CE) and the *Nihonshoki* (720 CE), was influenced by the tripartite Indo-European ideology at some point in the late prehistoric period.

C. Scott Littleton (1987 and 2005)

INDRA. In India the worship of the god Indra, king of the gods, warrior of the gods, god of rain, begins properly in the *Ṛgveda,* circa 1200 BCE, but his broader nature can be traced farther back into the proto-Indo-European world through his connections with Zeus and Wotan. For although the *Ṛgveda* knows a sky father called Dyaus-pitṛ, who is literally cognate with Zeus-patēr and Jupiter, it is Indra who truly fills the shoes of the Indo-European celestial sovereign: He wields the thunderbolt, drinks the ambrosial *soma* to excess, bestows fertility upon human women (often by sleeping with them himself), and leads his band of Maruts, martial storm gods, to win victory for the conquering Indo-Aryans.

In the *Ṛgveda,* Indra's family life is troubled in ways that remain unclear. His birth, like that of many great warriors and heroes, is unnatural: Kept against his will inside his mother's womb for many years, he bursts forth out of her side and kills his own father (*Ṛgveda* 4.18). He too is in turn challenged by his own son, whom he apparently overcomes (*Ṛgveda* 10.28). But the hymns to Indra, who is after all the chief god of the *Ṛgveda* (more than a quarter of the hymns in the collection are addressed to him), emphasize his heroic deeds. He is said to have created the universe by propping apart heaven and earth (as other gods, notably Viṣṇu and Varuṇa, are also said to have done) and finding the sun, and to have freed the cows that had been penned up in a cave (*Ṛgveda* 3.31). This last myth, which is perhaps the central myth of the *Ṛgveda,* has meaning on several levels: It means what it says (that Indra helps the worshiper to obtain cattle, as he is so often implored to do), and also that Indra found the sun and the world of life and light and fertility in general, for all of which cows often serve as a Vedic metaphor.

It was Indra who, in the shape of a falcon or riding on a falcon, brought down the *soma* plant from heaven, where it had been guarded by demons, to earth, where it became accessible to humans (*Ṛgveda* 4.26-27). Indra himself is the *soma* drinker *par excellence;* when he gets drunk, as he is wont to do, he brags (*Ṛgveda* 10.119), and the worshiper who invites Indra to share his *soma* also shares in the euphoria that *soma* induces in both the human and the divine drinker (*Ṛgveda* 9.113). But Indra is a jealous god—jealous, that is, of the *soma,* both for lofty reasons (like other great gods, he does not wish to allow mortals to taste the fruit that will make them like unto gods) and for petty reasons (he wants to keep all the *soma* for himself). His attempts to exclude the Aśvins from drinking the *soma* fail when they enlist the aid of the priest Dadhyañc, who disguises himself with a horse's head and teaches them the secret of the *soma* (*Ṛgveda* 1.117.22).

But Indra's principal function is to kill enemies—non-Aryan humans and demons, who are often conflated. As the supreme god of the *kṣatriyas* or class of royal warriors, Indra is invoked as a destroyer of cities and destroyer of armies, as the staunch ally of his generous worshipers, to whom Indra is in turn equally generous (Maghavan, "the generous," is one of his most popular epithets). These enemies (of whom the most famous is Vṛtra) are often called Dāsas or Dasyus, "slaves," and probably represent the indigenous populations of the subcontinent that the Indo-Aryans subjugated (and whose twin cities, Mohenjo Daro and Harappa, in the Indus Valley, may have been the citadels that Indra claims to have devastated). But the Dāsas are also frequently identified with the *asuras,* or demonic enemies of the gods themselves. The battles thus take place simultaneously on the human and the divine levels, and are both political and cosmogonic.

Indra's reputation begins to decline in the Brāhmaṇas, about 900 BCE, where his supremacy is preempted by Prajāpati, the primordial creator. Indra still drinks the *soma,* but now he becomes badly hungover and has to be restored to health by the worshiper. Similarly, the killing of Vṛtra leaves Indra weakened and in need of purification. In the epics, Indra is mocked for weaknesses associated with the phallic powers that are his great glory in the *Ṛgveda.* His notorious womanizing leads, on one occasion (when the sage Gautama catches Indra in bed with Ahalyā, the sage's wife), to Indra's castration, though his testicles are later replaced by those of a ram (*Rāmāyaṇa* 1.47–48); in another version of this story, Indra is cursed to be covered with a thousand *yonis* or vaginas, a curse which he turns to a boon by having the *yonis* changed into a thousand eyes. When Indra's excesses weaken him, he becomes vulnerable in battle; often he is overcome by demons and must enlist the aid of the now supreme sectarian gods, Śiva and Viṣṇu, to restore his throne. Sometimes he sends one of his voluptuous nymphs, the *apsaras,* to seduce ascetic demons who have amassed sufficient power, through *tapas* ("meditative austerities"), to heat Indra's throne in heaven. And when the demon Nahuṣa usurps Indra's throne and demands Indra's wife, Śacī, the gods have to perform a horse sacrifice to purify and strengthen Indra so that he can win back his throne. Even then Indra must use a combination of seduction and deceit, rather than pure strength, to gain his ends: Śacī goads Nahuṣa into committing an act of hubris that brings him down to a level on which he becomes vulnerable to Indra.

Old Vedic gods never die; they just fade into new Hindu gods. Indra remains a kind of figurehead in Hindu mythology, and the butt of many veiled anti-Hindu jokes in Buddhist mythology. The positive aspects of his person are largely transformed to Śiva. Both Indra and Śiva are associated with the Maruts or Rudras, storm gods; both are said to have extra eyes (three, or a thousand) that they sprouted in order to get a better look at a beautiful dancing *apsaras;* both are associated with the bull and with the erect phallus; both are castrated; and both come into conflict with their fathers-in-law. In addition to these themes, which are generally characteristic of fertility gods, Indra and Śiva share more specific mythological episodes: Both of them seduce the wives of *brahman* sages; both are faced with the problem of distributing (where it will do the least harm) certain excessive and destructive forces that they amass; both are associated with anti-Brahmanic, heterodox acts; and both lose their right to a share in the sacrifice. And just as Indra beheads a *brahman* demon (Vṛtra) whose head pursues him until he is purified of this sin, so Śiva, having beheaded Brahmā, is plagued by Brahmā's skull until he is absolved in Banaras. Thus, although Indra comes into conflict with the ascetic aspect of Śiva, the erotic aspect of Śiva found new uses for the discarded myths of Indra.

SEE ALSO Jupiter; Prajāpati; Śiva; Vedism and Brahmanism.

BIBLIOGRAPHY

For a detailed summary of the mythology of Indra, see pages 249–283 of Sukumari Bhattacharji's rather undigested *The Indian*

Theogony (Cambridge, U.K., 1970). For a translation of a series of myths about Indra, and a detailed bibliography of secondary literature, see pages 56–96 and 317–321 of my *Hindu Myths* (Harmondsworth, U.K., 1975). For the sins of Indra, see Georges Dumézil's *The Destiny of the Warrior* (Chicago, 1970) and *The Destiny of the King* (Chicago, 1973), and my *The Origins of Evil in Hindu Mythology* (Berkeley, Calif., 1976). For the relationship between Indra and Śiva, see my *Śiva: The Erotic Ascetic* (Oxford, 1981), originally published as *Asceticism and Eroticism in the Mythology of Śiva* (1973).

New Sources

Jamison, Stephanie W. *The Ravenous Hyenas and the Wounded Sun: Myth and Ritual in Ancient India.* Ithaca, N.Y., 1991.

WENDY DONIGER (1987)
Revised Bibliography

INDUS VALLEY RELIGION is the goddess-centered religious system of the urban civilization that emerged in the Indus Valley of western India around 2500 BCE and declined into a series of successor posturban village cultures after 1750 BCE. The antecedents of this religion lie in the village cultures of Baluchistan and Afghanistan, which were part of a larger regional cultural system in western Asia that also included the village cultures of southern Turkmenistan and the Elamite culture of southwestern Iran. Common religious patterns within this larger region continued into the early stages of urbanization in Elam, Turkmenistan, and the Indus Valley, after which the unification of the local regions and subsequent historical changes led to separation: Elam was drawn into the orbit of Sumerian and Akkadian culture; Turkmenistan was settled by new groups from the northern steppes; and Indus settlement shifted eastward into the Ganges-Yamuna Valley in the North and Gujarat and the Deccan Plateau in the South as the original cities in the Indus Valley were abandoned. After the entry of Aryan tribes into northern India around 1500 BCE, the continuity of Indus Valley religion is found mainly in the Dravidian cultures of South India, although various elements were also preserved in the village cultures of North India and in the synthesis of Aryan and non-Aryan cultures that marked late Vedic and post-Vedic developments in the Ganges-Yamuna Valley.

THE WESTERN ASIAN SETTING. The evolution of the Neolithic cultures of western Asia that preceded the Indus civilization cannot yet be reconstructed in detail, but a pattern is emerging from current evidence that sheds new light on the basic features of the Indus Valley religious system. Archaeological research in southern Turkmenistan has revealed a continued sequence of village cultures north of the Kopet Dagh Mountains from at least 6000 BCE onward, culminating in a regional urban culture at Namazga and Altin around 2500 BCE. Research on the proto-Elamite and proto-Dravidian languages points to a common proto-Elamo-Dravidian ancestry among a pastoral people moving southward from Central Asia into Iran sometime between 8000 and 6000 BCE, combining the herding of goats, sheep, and cattle with the cultivation of wheat and barley, and gradually separating into two branches: a proto-Dravidian branch that settled eastward in Afghanistan and Baluchistan, and a proto-Elamite branch that continued westward across southern Iran to the Zagros Mountains. The broadly based set of common cultural features established throughout western Asia in this early period and reinforced by later interregional contacts is reflected in similar patterns of proto-urban development and urbanization between 3500 and 2500 BCE in the various localized regions.

Because the Indus civilization's script has not been deciphered, the proto-Dravidian identification of the Indus language remains uncertain. There is broad scholarly consensus, however, that a form of proto-Dravidian was the dominant language of the Indus urban culture, and this is substantiated by parallels between cultural and religious features of the Indus civilization and later Dravidian village culture. These parallels, in conjunction with the pre-urban cultural affinities with Elam and Turkmenistan, provide a framework for interpreting the evidence from village and urban sites in the Indus Valley region and constructing a hypothetical picture of Indus Valley religion.

The single most significant religious feature in all of the western Asian village cultures is the importance of female powers or goddesses, as evidenced by stylized clay and terracotta female figurines in a variety of types that appear—often in conjunction with figurines of bulls or rams—from the early levels of village culture on into the urban periods in Turkmenistan, Elam, and the Indus Valley. Whether they represent specific goddesses or powers is impossible to determine without more information, and the villages are mute. Evidence of coherent mythologies only appears in the richer range of artifacts at the urban level, and by then, in all of the urban regions, clearly defined goddesses had become part of complex urban cultic systems that reflect at least in part differences in regional urbanization. Enough affinities remain, however, to provide clues to the Indus Valley system.

Turkmenistan, where extensive excavation has been carried out, provides a valuable point of reference for parallel developments in Afghanistan, Baluchistan, and the Indus Valley. Turkmenistan village sites show four millennia of clay and terracotta goddess figurines and figures of male animals, most often rams and bulls. The goddesses appear in a variety of styles and are often marked with painted stripes, dot-centered circles, or clusters of pocked depressions; most have concentrated attention on the breasts, thighs, and buttocks, and they often have either no arms or vestigial stumps. One distinctive type, the so-called foot profile style, shows the truncated legs and torso of a female in a semireclining posture.

Evidence from early sites indicates that special areas were set aside as shrine rooms for a likely domestic cult. Enclosed village shrines appear by the fifth or fourth millennium along with a new type of Namazga III "foot profile" figurines with elaborate hairdos. The Bronze Age Namazga IV culture, concurrent with developments in early Elam and the pre-Indus village cultures of Baluchistan and Afghanistan, has evidence of more elaborate shrines and a range of figurine types. Finally, around 2500 BCE, a full urban culture appeared in the Namazga V period that was contemporary for several centuries with the early phases of the Indus cities.

Urbanization in Turkmenistan brought not only greater complexity but also dramatic new religious forms. A massive brick platform, with three stepped tiers reaching forty feet in its final height, was built on the edge of the Namazga V site of Altin. This was certainly a center for public rituals, and implies a class of professional priests or priestesses. A richly endowed burial of a woman holding two female figurines in her hands has been tentatively named a "priestess's grave." Namazga V figurines are in a new and highly abstract style: flat fiddle-shaped cutouts with no legs, stylized triangular arm extentions, pinched maskedlike faces usually without a mouth, conical breasts, and a stippled pubic triangle with a vaginal line. There is evidence of a more standardized iconography and a clearer identification of individual figurines, including the use of different hair styles and engraved markings that resemble signs found in the Elamite and Indus writing systems.

Goddess worship in Turkmenistan clearly survived the transition from Neolithic to Bronze Age culture and subsequent urbanization. The styles of representation changed, the identities and meanings of individual goddesses may have varied, and the form of cultic practice certainly differed dramatically at the urban level from that in early villages, but the goddesses and their powers remained the central focus of religious life throughout the millennia. Much the same pattern can be seen also in the Elamite culture of southwestern Iran.

The foundation of Elamite culture was laid by proto-Elamite-speaking settlers who brought wheat and barley cultivation and the herding of sheep, goats, and cattle into the southern Zagros Mountain region of Iran sometime after 7000 BCE. By 4000 BCE, cultivation had been carried into the lowlands of Khuzistan at the western base of the Zagros, providing an agricultural base for urbanization. Sumer, across the Tigris in southern Mesopotamia, achieved urbanization around 3500 BCE. By 3200 BCE, Khuzistan and the Zagros highlands had been united in the rival urban civilization of Elam, with a highland capital at Anshan near later Persepolis and a lowland capital at Susa. Within the next two centuries, a proto-Elamite script had been developed and Elam had extended its influence eastward along a trade network that passed through Tepe Yahya in southern Iran as far as the Nal village culture of southern Baluchistan.

The expansion of Elamite urban culture was limited to the early third millennium, and its eastern trading centers had been abandoned several centuries before the first Indus cities emerged. The similarity between the later Indus script and the proto-Elamite script provides circumstantial evidence for the transfer of writing during this period, because the proto-Elamite script had been replaced by cuneiform by the middle of the third millennium; there is, however, no evidence of direct Elamite influence on Indus urbanization. Yet if Elam cannot be assigned a significant causal role in the creation of Indus civilization, it nonetheless provides an important model for understanding Indus Valley religion because of the many evident parallels between the two traditions.

Pre-urban cultural levels at Persepolis and Susa reveal a familiar pattern of female figurines and goddess worship, and painted pottery at these sites reveals a related concern for serpents as objects of religious veneration—a combination found also in the Dravidian villages of South India, and further evidence for an earlier common culture. Terracotta female figurines from Susa and other sites in the early third millennium show that goddess worship survived the transition from agricultural villages to urbanization in Elam as in Turkmenistan. The religious data from urban proto-Elamite sites such as Susa, however, are much richer than that of Turkmenistan and reveal not only the importance of goddesses in urban religious life but also an elaborate system of myths, symbols, and cultic practices.

Cylinder seals in a distinctive proto-Elamite style provide the most valuable evidence for the symbolism of this period. Many of the motifs in the proto-Elamite seals can be traced back to painted designs on earlier village pottery, but the more elaborate seal designs reflect a new urban sophistication: complex mythic or ritual scenes; symbolic designs involving mountains, trees, and animals (bulls and rams most often, but also lions and other felines); and an androgynous bovine in a variety of humanlike poses characteristically found in the figurines of goddesses. This latter figure is most likely the animal form or surrogate of the main Elamite fertility goddess, a moon goddess who was born from the Primeval Bull and was both the protector and soul of cattle—roles certainly consistent with the symbolism of the seals. None of the other figures can be identified with any certainty, and the meaning of individual symbols and scenes remains obscure in the absence of explanatory myths. In general, however, the symbolism reflects a developed fertility religion with its roots in the village past—probably a mountain past—but with new dimensions and new meanings in the urban culture: a religion in which the village goddesses have become patron deities of the city as well.

Cylinder seals, supplemented by other data, allow at least a partial reconstruction of proto-Elamite cultic practices. One seal shows a goddess or priestess being drawn in procession in a chariot flanked by moon symbols and horned cattle; another shows a tree in procession in a similar chariot, also with horned cattle and moon symbols; another shows an image or shrine on a palanquin flanked by attendants carrying moon symbols and what are either snakes or snake symbols in their hands. The goddess being honored in all of these scenes is almost certainly the moon goddess, whose connection with trees, serpents, and horned animals is indicated on a seal from the late third millennium that shows priests wearing belts or girdles of snakes around their waists and a device on their heads that combines the symbolism of crescent-shaped horns and trees.

Ritual processions and pilgrimages to sacred sites were apparently important features of Elamite religion. Elamite reliefs from around 2000 BCE depict long lines of worshipers in procession, confirming the evidence from earlier proto-Elamite seals. Sumerian texts from the same period describe similar practices associated with the moon goddess Inanna, whose characteristics closely match those of the main Elamite goddess with whom she was later assimilated. A hymn to Inanna vividly describes a parade of priestesses, musicians with harps, drums, and tambourines, and a priest who sprinkles blood on the goddess's throne, and notes that men in the procession "adorn their left side with women's clothing" while women "adorn their right side with men's clothing" (Wolkstein and Kramer, 1983, p. 99).

The centers of Elamite worship were the shrines and temples erected for the goddess, usually in high places and with an associated sacred grove. In Susa, temples to the major deities were located on an elevated sacred area on the western edge of the city between the river and the royal establishment. The main ritual activity in the temples was animal sacrifice, and raised altars with drains attest to the emphasis on blood in these sacrificial rites. The major sacrificial festival to the goddess at Susa was descriptively called a "day of the flowing sacrifice" in tribute to the quantity of blood offered on this occasion.

THE ELAMO-DRAVIDIAN PATTERN. The significance of these features of Elamite religion for comparative purposes is the light they shed on those aspects of Indus Valley religion for which there is no available Indus evidence. Indus seals and votive figurines, for example, suggest that Indus religion was based on some form of animal sacrifice centered around goddesses, but there is no direct evidence of ritual practice. Indus stamp seals, however, depict goddesses, trees, tigers, and horned animals such as rams, bulls, and water buffaloes in various combinations in mythic or cultic scenes. In other symbolic settings snakes appear as sacred animals. One scene portrays a line of androgynously appareled worshipers parading before a buffalo-horned goddess in a tree. This is the same basic set of symbols—goddesses, trees, lions/tigers, horned animals, snakes, and androgynous figures—found on Elamite cylinder seals, and indicates a significant body of shared religious concepts that reflect the common proto-Elamo-Dravidian ancestry and presuppose a common ritual practice. The relevant ritual in Elamite religion was blood sacrifice to the goddess, as it was also, along with many of the same symbols, in later Dravidian village religion. It is thus highly likely that Indus Valley religion followed the same Elamo-Dravidian pattern.

This is not a case of wholesale borrowing of Elamite religion or of basing Indus urban culture on external models. There are well-documented influences from Turkmenistan for at least a millennium prior to urbanization in the Indus Valley, and there must have been some degree of contact with Elam during the late stages of Indus urbanization to account for the similar scripts. Indus urbanization may have been stimulated by these contacts, just as trade and interregional contacts stimulated urbanization throughout western Asia. The similarities between Indus urban culture and other western Asian cultures, however, were general family resemblances, like those between the Elamite and Dravidian language systems. Indus urban culture was both unique and uniquely Indian, as much a product of the regional setting as of the common western Asian heritage, with characteristic features that were deeply rooted in the pre-urban cultures of Afghanistan and Baluchistan.

The groundwork for Indus urbanization was laid by a series of village cultures in the highlands west of the Indus Valley, the earliest of which dates from around 6000 BCE. Archaeological research since the 1950s has revealed several early aceramic settlement sites with subsequent pottery development and domestication of local plants and animals, proving that the Indus region contributed to the Neolithic revolution and was not just a recipient of imported culture. By the early fourth millennium local village cultures had been established in northern and central Baluchistan, and by the mid- to late fourth millennium these cultures had been linked by trade with the Namazga III culture of southern Turkmenistan.

By around 3000 BCE, when Elam was extending its influence eastward, the Nal culture had emerged in southern Baluchistan and the Nal-related Amri culture had expanded into the southern Indus Valley. By early in the third millennium another related culture known as Kot Dijian had expanded northward along the Indus from the region of later Mohenjo-Daro as far as the later sites of Harappa and Kalibangan. These new developments laid the foundation for urbanization.

Goddess worship was an integral part of Indus village culture, as can be seen from the example of Mehrgarh, the oldest known continuous settlement site within India proper. Discovered in the 1970s at the eastern end of the Bolan Pass, Mehrgarh spans the range from aceramic settlement around 6000 BCE to the brink of urbanization around 2600 BCE. Goddesses in the form of female figurines appear at every cultural level, and their evolution is intertwined with the development of the Indus region.

The earliest figurines from Mehrgarh date from the sixth and fifth millennia, a period when pottery was being developed, cultivation was expanding, and local animals—especially humpbacked cattle (zebus)—were being domesticated to replace the earlier reliance on hunting. The style of these first Indian village goddess figurines was the "foot profile" style found also in Turkmenistan, and this style continued essentially unchanged down to around 3000 BCE. At that point, reflecting Mehrgarh's greater involvement in regional trade, there was a convergence toward the pinched-faced, goggle-eyed "Zhob mother goddesses" from the Zhob culture in northern Baluchistan. During the village's final century, from 2700 to 2600 BCE, nude goggle-eyed female figurines were being produced commercially by the thousands at Mehrgarh and are for the first time in a standing position like Zhob figurines. Nude male figures, also standing, with shoulder-length hair and Zhob-like goggle eyes, suggest for the first time the possibility of a divine couple.

The end of Mehrgarh's final century marks the beginning of urbanization. As in Turkmenistan, the new iconography of female figurines and the appearance of male figurines coincided with the building of monumental ritual platforms. At Mehrgarh, the platform was a massive structure of brick faced with plaster with a colonnade of square mud-brick columns in front. This was contemporary with others in the larger contiguous area, one of which, near Quetta, had drains in the center and a stone-built hollow containing a jawless human skull, perhaps evidence of a "building sacrifice" in the platform's construction. Near this platform were found figurines of females and cattle with painted stripes.

Other platform structures of note belonged to the Kulli culture, which gradually replaced the Nal culture in southern Baluchistan after about 3000 BCE and was still flourishing when the Indus civilization emerged on its eastern boundaries about five centuries later. Near the fertile stretches of the Porali River elaborate ceremonial centers were built on a new vast scale: At one typical site are two stone-built platforms about thirty feet high with ramps to the top and, nearby, a complex of over forty buildings. The Kulli ceremonial centers are set apart from the nearby agricultural villages with which they share common artifacts such as pottery and figurines. As the latter include both goddess figurines and striped cattle, it is likely that the cattle were votive offerings to the goddess. The whole combination, with platforms, wells, and drains, clearly suggests a ritual pattern involving sacrifice and ablution. The goddess figurines show a combination of originally Elamite postures with other styles (Zhob, Mehrgarh) developed regionally in western India. Although the Indus Valley civilization synthesizes elements from all these cultural styles, Kulli figurines and ceremonial centers provide its most direct prototypes.

Harappa and Mohenjo-Daro. The Indus civilization has been widely noted for its rapid development and continued stability over a seven-hundred-year period from around 2500 to 1750 BCE. Over an estimated 500,000 square miles, the same basic cultural features recur from the cities to the several hundred towns and villages so far discovered. Such uniformity is striking, because unlike the concentrated settlement patterns in Mesopotamia, Indus sites were often well over fifty miles apart. It was the long-established base of village agriculture—wheat and barley cultivation along with cattle herding—that by the mid-third millennium provided the base for urbanization. The new cities, however, also broke with traditional village cultural patterns, and imposed new developments upon them. The two largest, Harappa and Mohenjo-Daro, both seem to go back to the civilization's beginnings. Their founding was no doubt decisive in setting the new political, economic, and religious styles. To the north, Harappa was built over an earlier Kot Dijian farming village, while to the south, Mohenjo-Daro's new urban culture dominated and soon replaced the neighboring village of Kot Diji and the local culture of Amri farther south. Similarly, at the smaller Indus city of Kalibangan farther east, the imposition of the new urban culture included construction of an Indus style ritual platform on the mound of an earlier fortified Kot Dijian agricultural settlement.

Mohenjo-Daro and Harappa were both built on a similar plan, one that smaller sites replicate. The cities were divided into two basic components: a lower city, about three miles in circumference with rectangular grid streets, and an upper area on each city's western edge formed by a brick-walled platform on an artificial mound that leveled some twenty feet above the surrounding plain. The massive exterior walls of the two major cities, over forty feet thick at the base, served to protect against flooding: Mohenjo-Daro from the Indus River, Harappa from the Ravi. Mohenjo-Daro was the larger of the two, and in most matters preserves the best evidence, as most of the Harappa mound was destroyed either by erosion or by its dismantling in 1856 by British engineers to provide ballast for a railroad. It was not until the early 1920s that the antiquity of Indus sites was recognized.

The lower city's residential and commercial character is evident at Mohenjo-Daro. The exterior baked-brick walls lining the main street were for the most part without adornment or direct street access. Residences range from barrack-like dwellings to multistoried complexes, two of which have been dubbed a palace or hostel, but the typical residence was of a still-common South Asian type: small rooms around a central courtyard. Interspersed among residences were various shops and ateliers, and a large area with threshing floors has been found at Harappa. The lower city shows no clear evidence of dominant religious structures. In continuation of village patterns, there probably was a domestic cult centered in the home, perhaps connected with the terracotta female figurines and the elaborate drainage system that suggests a concern for hygiene and purity. But for the culture's larger religious patterns one must turn elsewhere, and first of all to the raised platform mound on the western edge of the urban complex.

The standardization of the urban plan suggests that dominant political and religious sanctions lay behind the civilization's conservatism. It is noteworthy that the two major cities show none of the gradual growth that occurred in Mesopotamian cities, but were built from the very beginning with their dominant platform mounds. One may assume from this that the civilization's basic values were set and preserved by those who established these structures, and that their functions were connected with the architectural eminences they created.

These platform structures—often misleadingly called citadels—did not have a primarily defensive purpose. Though the heavily walled mounds at some of the more decentralized locations like Harappa and Kalibangan may have been used defensively, and the Mohenjo-Daro platform had watchtowers fortified with pellets, it is noteworthy that at a time when Mesopotamian rulers had for several centuries raised large armies to extend their power, the Indus cities leave no traces of arrows, spears, or swords.

Rather than citadels, the monumental platforms are thus no doubt continuations of the structures found at pre-urban village sites, but on a far grander scale, with a surface area large enough for several big buildings. With such structures, they differ from unoccupied platforms elsewhere (most notably Altin in Turkmenistan). But they bear a resemblance to the "acropolis" at Elamite Susa, also on the west of the city, and the purpose is clearly similar: to give prominence to the institutions and activities set apart and above. It is even possible, with the Kulli culture as an intermediary, that Elam provided the model for the Indus platforms, as for its script. But in specific features the Indus platform reflects an independently emergent tradition with its own cultural dynamics.

Most of the structures on the Mohenjo-Daro mound have been variously identified. A large columned building was probably an assembly hall; another has been dubbed a college. Definite is a granary; with grain as the primary measure of wealth and medium of exchange, the control of grain distribution was tied to civic authority. Yet most distinctive was a structure called the Great Bath.

The Great Bath itself was both literally and no doubt also symbolically the center of this complex. A large rectangular bitumen-lined tank in a colonnaded courtyard, it had steps leading down into its water from both ends. Clearly the steps were for bathing, and possibly for crossing from one end to the other. Moreover, the trouble taken to build such an *elevated* bath probably reflects an intensified concern for purification already evident in the lower city. In later Indian notions, higher waters are purer. Quite likely the whole complex—with wells, bathing rooms, and bath—served for the performance of purification rites supervised or enacted by priests. And because it was situated adjacent to the granary, such concerns probably also tied in conceptually with an interest in agricultural fertility.

In all this one is faced with a combination of concerns similar to those that underlay the practices connected with the platform mounds of pre-Indus villages. There is a new assertion of political, economic, and religious authority in the building of such massive structures in the heart of the riverine plain. The platforms themselves, however, must have been more than *assertions* of power by a new urban elite; they must also have been intended as *sources* of power: not because they were dominant physically, but because they provided a stage for rituals that would bring the ascendant cultural forces into harmony with the divinely empowered order of nature so evident in the nearby rivers, herds, and fields of grain.

One representation of divinity in Indus sites has been met: the terracotta female figurine, a surviving type from pre-urban village cultures, with the closest analogues being from Kulli and Zhob. Similar figurines also reappear in classical periods of Hinduism and serve as models for the *yakṣīs* on early Buddhist stupas. The basic Indus type has bare breasts, tapered or full-length legs, a girdle, heavy pendant necklaces, and an elaborate hairdo. Whether one or more goddesses is represented is uncertain, but parallel evidence from Elam suggests an iconographic differentiation. A few male figurines have also been found. While human figurines are predominantly female, animal figurines are invariably male. Most common are various bovines: zebu, short-horned bulls, and water buffalo. Most likely different kinds of potency were represented: that of the female in the form of the anthropomorphic goddess, that of the male in animal form, perhaps linked with symbols of civic power.

INDUS VALLEY SEALS. For further insights into the religious conceptions of the Indus Valley civilization, however, one must turn to a new iconography that has no precedent in the pre-urban village cultures. This comes from the controversial evidence of the Indus Valley seals. Here again, however, one must reckon with prior developments in Sumer and Elam, which produced cylinder seals earlier than the flat steatite (soapstone) stamp seals—measuring about ¾–1¼ inches per side—of Indus sites. Although Elamite seals are linked typologically to Sumer, their subjects are distinctively Elamite, and in certain cases present images with Indus counterparts, indicating the likelihood of iconic cross-fertilization. Thus, two cylinder seals from Susa seem to draw on familiar Indus motifs: one a series of bulls eating from a manger, and the other a composite bull-antelope with long wavy horns facing a stylized pipal tree.

It is not, however, only the older urban civilizations that shed light on the Indus seal iconography, but also the likely continuities from Indus urban culture to the Dravidian village culture of South India. For not only is there the likelihood of linguistic continuities, but there is also archaeological evidence of cultural continuities from the Indus civilization, through Gujarat, to the Dravidian culture of the Deccan Plateau. Moreover, the urban models that the Indus cities provided during the Indus period not only reshaped village life in Indus times, but transmitted patterns that long outlived the Indus cities.

The Indus Valley stamp seals, found by the hundreds, confirm impressions gained from the terracotta figurines, most notably the tendency to accentuate female power in human form and male power through animal forms. But the situation with the seals is also more complex, as there are also humanized males and human-animal and even human-animal-plant composites of apparently both genders. Of single animals, many are drawn from nature: short-horned bulls, zebu, buffaloes, rhinoceroses, tigers, elephants, antelopes, crocodiles. Composite human-animal forms reach such complexity as one with tiger hind quarters, ram forepart, bull horns, elephant trunk, and human face. Others show animal heads radiating from a central trunk.

The most frequently depicted seal animal is a "unicorn" bull or ox of generalized bovine traits with a single erect horn that faces an apparently sacred object, perhaps a brazier or incense burner. The unicorn's horn is sometimes shown as a thin curved shaft crossed by lines that taper toward the tip, suggesting an affinity between animal and plant forms. Some of the naturally drawn animals also sometimes face simpler brazier or manger type objects. It is thus likely that "real" animals were linked with ritual symbols as well, and mythologically marked no less than the more clearly "mythic" figures like the composites, multicephalics, and unicorns.

It is the seals with humanoid figures, however, that take one beyond the general sense of mythic and ritual markers to evidence for a cult with a complex of sacrificial symbols. Females appear in various such scenes, but the most important are a series of scenes that portray a recurring ensemble involving goddesses, trees, tigers, and water buffaloes. Three seals show these interrelationships most dramatically. In one, a slender goddess with a crescent-shaped headdress kneels on a branch of a neem (margosa) tree, her arm outstretched toward a tiger below that turns its neck around to face her. The goddess's position replicates a worshiping pose in other seals and suggests that she beckons the tiger with her outstretched arm. In the second seal, the goddess, now descended from the neem tree, stands behind the tiger about to seize it from the back. Yet both goddess and tiger are strikingly transformed. The goddess has assumed multiple traits of the water buffalo: Along with filling out the stylized crescent horns, her legs and feet have become flanks and hoofs and her ears pointed and flapped. Meanwhile, the tiger has sprouted horns that replicate the serrated V branch and leaf pattern of the neem, which now stands behind the goddess.

These two seals seem to suggest that the goddess has her primary affinity with the buffalo, and an opposition to the tiger. But a third seal shows a fusion of the goddess and the tiger, joined together so that the goddess retains a standing human form as the forepart of a tiger's body that extends back from her hips and rear. Here, where the goddess's affinity is with the tiger, she has wavy ram's horns rather than buffalo-like horns. There is thus the suggestion that while the goddess has affinities with both the tiger and the buffalo, the two animals themselves remain in an oppositional and unfused tension.

This sense of a tiger-buffalo opposition is further reinforced in the so-called proto-Śiva seal from Mohenjo-Daro. But before discussing this seal, one should observe the primary seal evidence for a connection between the transformational themes that link the goddess to these and other animals and to a sacrificial cult. Clearest in this regard is the so-called ritual seal from Harappa depicting a goddess in the U-shaped twin branches of a stylized pipal tree, which rises from a circular platform base or altar. The goddess has crescent buffalo-like horns and a pony tail like the goddess who descends toward the tiger from the neem. But her horns have a third central peak, and she does not have the hind legs or hoofs of the buffalo. Standing at rest, her bangled arms loose at her sides, she observes a horned and pony-tailed figure much like herself kneeling at the base of the pipal in the same "suppliant" posture that the goddess in the neem adopts toward the tiger. The kneeling suppliant has led before the goddess in the pipal a composite animal with buffalo hind quarters, ram horns and forepart, and a large masklike human face. Seven figures in thigh-length tunics, single backward-curving horns, pigtails, and bangled arms stand or possibly file before this scene, which clearly depicts the essentials of a sacrifice. The horned goddess is the recipient of an offering, its composite nature no doubt representing something of the range of victims she receives: the ram, buffalo, and the human face. Whether all are real offerings, or the human face solely symbolic, cannot be ascertained.

The kneeling figure making the offering in the "ritual seal" has an intermediate status between the horned goddess whose dress he affects and the composite human-animal he offers. The precise nature of his sacrificial role eludes researchers. But it is striking that the combination of elements that the seals configure remain coherent in the setting of still-current South Indian village rituals. In that Dravidian context, the neem, a female tree, is itself a form of the goddess. It is linked to her fierce side, and more specifically to the forms she takes to "cool" and thus overcome violent forces like smallpox, fevers, and various demons. The pipal, on the other hand, is the male tree the goddess marries, so the two trees will be planted to actually intertwine. It is highly suggestive that while the seal goddess on the neem branch descends to overcome the fierce and *wild* tiger, the goddess in the pipal stands tranquilly in a position to receive as a sacrifice the composite of human and *domesticated* animals that would seem to reflect the range of her regular cult.

Since the discovery of the Indus civilization, the one seal most central to a succession of different interpretations of the religion has been the so-called proto-Śiva seal from Mohenjo-Daro. This designation, however, now appears to have been based on a combination of misattributions: most notably the "three heads" that actually outline the dewlap of a buffalo face, and the "trident" headdress that actually consists of buffalo horns enclosing a central fan-shaped and stylized tree or sheaf of grain reminiscent of the tree-and-horns headpiece worn by Elamite and Sumerian priests. Moreover, above this "mitre" is what looks like a stylized pipal tree. The main figure is thus a humanlike water buffalo with a buffalo head and horns, axially centered on representations of a plant and/or tree. He sits with his knees out to the side and his feet drawn in below an erect phallus. The posture has usually been identified as yogic, though it is also reminiscent of the posture of the androgynous bovine seated in the pose of the goddess on an Elamite seal. Possibly the series of V-shaped stripes that end at his waist—sometimes regarded as necklaces—represent tiger stripes, making him a figure in whom the tiger-buffalo tension finds a resolution in a yogic or more likely regally dominant self-discipline.

The central buffalo figure in the "proto-Śiva" seal seems to be the male counterpart to the goddess, who herself combines both tiger and buffalo attributes in various transformational modes. But in this male figure, what remains tense and dynamic in the goddess seems to find poise, dominance, and resolution. This is especially suggestive in view of the four animals that surround him, for the tiger and buffalo appear among these along with the elephant and rhinoceros. By analogy with later Indian iconographies, the four together are likely to have had a directional symbolism: the elephant linked with the east, the rhino with the west, the tiger with the north, and the buffalo with the south. Most strikingly, while the elephant and rhinoceros appear indifferent to each other, both facing east, the tiger and buffalo, which most directly flank the buffalo-man's horns, face each other in a state that has the look of combative arousal. Furthermore, a stick figure appears over the back of the charging tiger: possibly a form of the goddess herself.

Of the four "wild" animals on the seal, two—the elephant and water buffalo—are susceptible to some degree of domestication even though they retain their "wild" traits. There is some evidence that elephants were captured and trained for heavy forest work during the Indus period, and it is likely that domestication of the water buffalo for agricultural use in the river valley was one of the major achievements of the Indus civilization, complementing the village cultures' earlier domestication of the zebu in the highlands. It is significant that the water buffalo played the main symbolic role in Indus urban culture instead of the zebu, despite the latter's longstanding economic importance. This suggests that the buffalo had a critical role in the riverine agriculture on which the Indus system was based, and that it symbolized the control of both nature and culture that made urban civilization possible.

The central water buffalo figure on the proto-Śiva seal seems to have the same general symbolic meaning of power-under-control as does the bull in Mesopotamian symbolism, and like the latter it probably also represents the king or ruling authority. Because the figure is male, it may be assumed that the Indus rulers also were male, as the few examples of protrait sculpture at Mohenjo-Daro suggest. There is little doubt, however, that the Indus people considered the goddess to be the real power and the ruler only her surrogate, empowered by her and thus responsible to her and for her. This is certainly consistent with the symbolism of the seal, where the central figure seems to bring into a regulated and authoritative image the various forces that the goddess oversees: agriculture, animal sacrifice, and the dangerous forces associated with the truly wild regions beyond the domain of civilization.

What kind of authority—priestly, political, economic—this figure represented still remains uncertain. The urban background of the ritual complex on the platform mound leaves all these possibilities open, and the distinctively Indian features of Indus symbolism make it risky to explain the Indus civilization on the basis of other urban cultures, even the closely related proto-Elamite culture. There is little doubt, however, that Indus Valley religion played a major role in establishing and maintaining that authority, and there is even less doubt that sacrifices to the goddess were the primary form of cultic practice. All of the external evidence—earlier village cultures, contemporary and related western Asian urban cultures, and later Dravidian culture—points to this conclusion, and the Indus evidence seems to confirm it.

CONCLUDING OBSERVATIONS. Taking the evidence as a whole, it is possible to construct a model of Indus Valley religion that explains its major known features and its place in the Indus civilization. The central element was certainly worship of the goddess at both the domestic and public levels, with corresponding levels of cultic practice. At the domestic level, votive sacrifices involving figurines were the likely form of worship, with a related emphasis on bathing and ritual purity. At the public level, represented by the raised platform mounds, worship must have involved more powerful blood sacrifices.

Mohenjo-Daro seems to have been the major cultic center for the system as a whole and the site for the most important sacrifices. Indus symbolism and later Dravidian practice point toward water buffalo sacrifices as the most important cultic rituals. The buffalo is the husband of the goddess in Dravidian cult sacrifices, and on Indus seals he appears as both the goddess's surrogate and the symbol of centralized rule; it is likely that Indus cultic practice involved these elements, at least on major ceremonial occasions, but there is no direct evidence for how this might have been conceptualized.

The interpretation of Indus Valley religion cannot proceed beyond such speculation at the present time. Much has been learned about the Indus civilization since its discovery in the 1920s, and the pattern of Indus Valley religion is beginning to emerge from the growing body of data, but there are still many gaps to fill. The major task, moreover, has hardly begun: to trace the contributions of the Indus system to later Indian religious developments and to understand the place of the Indus system in the larger pattern of religious history.

SEE ALSO Goddess Worship; Hinduism; Indian Religions, articles on Mythic Themes, Rural Traditions; Iranian Religions; Nāgas and Yakṣas; Prehistoric Religions, article on The Eurasian Steppes and Inner Asia; Tamil Religions; Vedism and Brahmanism.

BIBLIOGRAPHY

The most useful single source on village cultures and urbanization in Turkmenistan and western India is S. P. Gupta's *Archaeol-*

ogy of Soviet Central Asia and the Indian Borderlands, vol. 2 (Delhi, 1979), which presents a judicious overview of the archaeological evidence and current interpretive theories. An assessment of the archaeological data from Turkmenistan sites is provided by the Soviet prehistorians V. M. Masson and V. I. Sarianidi in *Central Asia: Turkmenia before the Achaemenids* (London, 1972), edited and translated by Ruth Tringham and published initially in English as volume 79 of the "Ancient Peoples and Places" series. The best and most comprehensive survey of cultural development in India from earliest times through the establishment of Indus urban culture is Walter A. Fairservis, Jr's. *The Roots of Ancient India,* 2d rev. ed. (Chicago, 1975), which examines the relevant evidence from all of the regional village cultures, discusses the factors that led to urbanization, and describes the basic features of the Indus civilization. The most accessible summary of the evidence from Mehrgarh is Jean-François Jarrige and Richard H. Meadow's "The Antecedents of Civilization in the Indus Valley," *Scientific American* 243 (August 1980): 122–133.

A variety of data on proto-Elamite religion is available in *A Survey of Persian Art,* edited by Arthur U. Pope and Phyllis Ackerman (1938–1939; reprint, London, 1964–1965), especially in the sections by Phyllis Ackerman on cult figurines and early seals (vol. 1, chaps. 11 and 14, and accompanying plates in vol. 7). A summary of Elamite history, culture, and religion is provided in Walther Hinz's *The Lost World of Elam: Recreation of a Vanished Civilization* (New York, 1973). Diane Wolkstein and Samuel Noah Kramer's *Inanna: Queen of Heaven and Earth* (New York, 1983) supplements what is known of Elamite goddesses with a comprehensive portrait of the closely related Sumerian goddess Inanna. The argument for a common origin of the proto-Elamite and proto-Dravidian languages is presented in David W. McAlpin's *Proto-Elamo-Dravidian: The Evidence and Its Implications* (Philadelphia, 1981). The significance of the Elamite trading center at Tepe Yahya for understanding interregional contacts in West Asia is discussed in Carl C. Lamberg-Karlovsky and Martha Lamberg-Karlovsky's "An Early City in Iran," *Scientific American* 224 (June 1971), and in Carl C. Lamberg-Karlovsky's "Trade Mechanisms in Indus-Mesopotamian Interrelationships," *Journal of the American Oriental Society* 92 (1972).

Data from the early excavations at Mohenjo-Daro are contained in John Marshall's *Mohenjo-Daro and the Indus Civilization,* 3 vols. (London, 1931), and E. J. Mackay's *Further Excavations at Mohenjo-daro,* 2 vols. (New Delhi, 1938). A valuable synthesis and interpretation of Indus evidence is presented in Mortimer Wheeler's *The Indus Civilization,* 3d ed. (Cambridge, U.K., 1968), and in his *Civilizations of the Indus Valley and Beyond* (London, 1966). A survey of Indus data up to the mid-1970s is provided in Walter A. Fairservis, Jr's. *The Roots of Ancient India* (Chicago, 1975), supplemented by his *Allahdino I: Seals and Inscribed Material* (New York, 1976). Many of the most important contributions to the ongoing study of the Indus civilization are found in two volumes edited by Gregory L. Possehl: *Ancient Cities of the Indus* (New Delhi, 1979) and *Harappan Civilization: A Contemporary Perspective* (New Delhi, 1982). Possehl's own initial work on Indus culture in Gujarat is presented in his *Indus Civilization in Saurashtra* (Delhi, 1980).

Understanding Indus Valley religion has been a concern of investigators since Marshall and Mackay offered their first tentative interpretations, and the issue receives significant attention in the cited works by Wheeler and Fairservis. Indus seals in particular have been studied for clues to Indus religious concepts, with the so-called proto-Śiva seal receiving the greatest interest. A major new interpretation of the symbolism on this seal is found in Alf Hiltebeitel's "The Indus Valley 'Proto-Śiva,' Reexamined through Reflections on the Goddess, the Buffalo, and the Symbolism of *vahanas,*" *Anthropos* 73 (1978): 767–797. Earlier interpretations of this seal and of other supposedly related Indus data are challenged in Doris Srinivasan's "Unhinging Śiva from the Indus Civilization," *Journal of the Royal Asiatic Society* (1984 pt. 1): 77–99. New insights into the meaning of Indus seals, especially those dealing with goddess-and-tiger motifs, are presented in Pupul Jayakar's *The Earthen Drum: An Introduction to the Ritual Arts of Rural India* (New Delhi, 1980), a beautifully illustrated book that interprets Indus religious data by drawing comparisons with the art and religious practices of later Indian folk traditions.

New Sources

Allchin, Bridget. *Origins of a Civilization: The Prehistory and Early Archaeology of South Asia.* New Delhi, 1997.

Bryant, Edwin. *The Quest for the Origins of Vedic Culture: The Indo-Aryan Migration Debate.* New York, 2001.

Kennedy, Kenneth A. R. *God-Apes and Fossil Men: Paleoanthropology of South Asia.* Ann Arbor, Mich. 2000.

McIntosh, Jane. *A Peaceful Realm: The Rise and Fall of the Indus Civilization.* Boulder, Colo., 2002.

Possehl, Gregory L. *The Indus Age: The Writing System.* Philadelphia, 1996.

Possehl, Gregory L. *The Indus Civilization: A Contemporary Perspective.* Walnut Creek, Calif., 2002.

Ratnagar, Shereen. *Understanding Harappa: Civilization in the Greater Indus Valley.* New Delhi, 2001.

Sharma, A. K. *The Departed Harappans of Kalibangan.* New Delhi, 1999.

Thapar, Romila. *Early India: From the Origins to* AD *1300.* Berkeley, Calif., 2003.

Thomas J. Hopkins (1987)
Alf Hiltebeitel (1987)
Revised Bibliography

INITIATION

This entry consists of the following articles:

AN OVERVIEW
MEN'S INITIATION
WOMEN'S INITIATION

INITIATION: AN OVERVIEW

The term *initiation* in the most general sense denotes a body of rites and oral teachings whose purpose is to produce a radical modification of the religious and social status of the person to be initiated. In philosophical terms, initiation is equivalent to an ontological mutation of the existential condition. The novice emerges from his ordeal a totally different being: he has become "another." Generally speaking, there are three categories, or types, of initiation.

The first category comprises the collective rituals whose function is to effect the transition from childhood or adolescence to adulthood, and which are obligatory for all members of a particular society. Ethnological literature terms these rituals "puberty rites," "tribal initiation," or "initiation into an age group."

The other two categories of initiation differ from puberty initiations in that they are not obligatory for all members of the community; indeed, most of them are performed individually or for comparatively small groups. The second category includes all types of rites of entering a secret society, a *Bund*, or a confraternity. These closed societies are limited to one sex and are extremely jealous of their secrets. Most of them are male, constituting secret fraternities (*Männerbünde*), but there are also some female societies. However, in the ancient Mediterranean and Near Eastern world, such sites, or "mysteries," were open to both sexes. Although they differ somewhat in type, we can still classify the Greco-Oriental mysteries as secret confraternities.

Finally, there is a third category of initiation, the type that occurs in connection with a mystical vocation. On the level of archaic religions, the vocation would be that of the medicine man or shaman. A specific characteristic of this third category is the importance of personal experience. Initiation in secret societies and those of the shamanic type have a good deal in common. What distinguishes them in principle is the ecstatic element, which is of greatest importance in shamanic initiation. Despite their specialized uses, there is a sort of common denominator among all these categories of initiation, with the result that, from a certain point of view, all initations are much alike.

PUBERTY RITES. The tribal initiation introduces the novice into the world of spiritual and cultural values and makes him a responsible member of society. The young man learns not only the behavior patterns, techniques, and institutions of adults but also the myths and the sacred traditions of the tribe, the names of the gods, and the history of their works; above all, he learns the mystical relations between the tribe and supernatural beings as those relations were established at the beginning of time. In a great many cases, puberty rites, in one way or another, imply the revelation of sexuality. In short, through initiation, the candidate passes beyond the "natural" mode of being—that of the child—and gains access to the cultural mode; that is, he is introduced to spiritual values. Often, on the occasion of the puberty rites the entire community is religiously regenerated, for the rites are the repetitions of operations and actions performed by supernatural beings in mythical time.

Any age-grading initiation requires a certain number of more or less dramatic tests and trials: separation from the mother, isolation in the bush under the supervision of an instructor, interdiction against eating certain vegetable or animal foods, knocking out of an incisor, circumcision (followed in some cases by subincision), scarification, and so forth. The sudden revelation of sacred objects (bull-roarers, images of supernatural beings, etc.) also constitutes an initiatory test. In many cases, the puberty initiation implies a ritual "death," followed by a "resurrection" or a "rebirth." Among certain Australian tribes the extraction of the incisor is interpreted as the neophyte's "death," and the same significance is even more evident in the case of circumcision. The novices isolated in the bush are likened to ghosts: they cannot use their fingers and must take food directly with their mouths, as the dead are supposed to do. Sometimes they are painted white, a sign that they have become ghosts. The huts in which they are isolated represent the body of a monster or a water animal: the neophytes are considered to have been swallowed by the monster, and they remain in its belly until they are "reborn" or "resuscitated." The initiatory death is interpreted either as a *descensus ad inferos* or as a *regressus ad uterum*, and the "resurrection" is sometimes understood as a "rebirth." In a number of cases, the novices are symbolically buried, or they pretend to have forgotten their past lives, their family relations, their names, and their language, and must learn everything again. Sometimes the intiatory trials reach a high degree of cruelty.

SECRET CULTS. Even on the archaic levels of culture (for example, in Aboriginal Australia), a puberty initiation may entail a series of stages. In such cases sacred history can be revealed only gradually. The deepening of the religious experience and knowledge demands a special vocation or an outstanding intelligence and willpower. This fact explains the emergence both of the secret cults and of the confraternities of shamans and medicine men. The rites of entrance into a secret society correspond in every respect to those of tribal initiations: seclusion, initiatory tests and tortures, "death" and "resurrection," bestowal or imposition of a new name, revelation of a secret doctrine, learning of a new language. A few innovations are, however, characteristic of the secret societies: among these are the great importance attached to secrecy, the particular cruelty of initiatory trials, the predominance of the ancestors' cult (the ancestors being personified by masks), and the absence of a supreme being in the ceremonial life of the group. In the *Weiberbünde*, or women's societies, the initiation consists of a series of specific tests, followed by revelations concerning fertility, conception, and birth.

Initiatory "death" signifies both the end of the "natural," acultural man and the passage to a new mode of existence, that of a being "born to the spirit," that is, one who does not live exclusively in an immediate reality. Thus the initiatory "death" and "resurrection" represent a religious process through which the initiate becomes "another," patterned on the model revealed by gods or mythical ancestors. In other words, one becomes a real man to the extent that one resembles a superhuman being. The importance of initiation for the understanding of the archaic mind centers essentially in the fact that it shows that the real man—the spiritual one—is not automatic, is not the result of a natural process. He is "made" by the old masters, in accordance with the models revealed by divine beings in mythical times. These old masters form the spiritual elite of archaic societies. Their main role is to transmit to the new generations the deep meaning of existence and to help them assume the responsibility of real men, and hence to participate actively in the cultural life of the community. But because culture means, for archaic and traditional societies, the sum of the values received from supernatural beings, the function of initiation may thus be summarized: it reveals to every new generation a world open to the transhuman; a world, one may say, that is transcendental.

Shamans and Medicine Men. As for shamanic initiations, they consist in ecstatic experiences (e.g., dreams, visions, trances) and in an instruction imparted by the spirits or the old master shamans (e.g., shamanic techniques, names and functions of the spirits, mythology and genealogy of the clan, secret language). Sometimes initiation is public and includes a rich and varied ritual; this is the case, for example, among the Buriats of Siberia. But the lack of a ritual of this sort in no way implies the absence of an initiation; it is perfectly possible for the initiation to be performed in the candidate's dreams or ecstatic experiences. In Siberia and Central Asia the youth who is called to be a shaman goes through a psychopathic crisis during which he is considered to be tortured by demons and ghosts who play the role of the masters of intiation. These "initiatory sicknesses" generally contain the following symbolic elements: (1) torture and dismemberment of the body, (2) scraping of the flesh and reduction to a skeleton, (3) replacement of organs and renewal of blood, (4) a sojourn in the underworld and instruction by demons and the souls of dead shamans, (5) an ascent to heaven, and (6) "resurrection," that is, access to a new mode of being, that of a consecrated individual capable of communicating personally and directly with gods, demons, and souls of the dead. A somewhat analagous pattern is to be found in the initiations of Australian medicine men.

The little we know about Eleusis and the initiations in the Hellenistic mysteries there indicates that the central experience of the initiand (*mustēs*) depended on a revelation concerning the death and resurrection of the divine founder of the cult. Thanks to this revelation, the *mustēs* acceded to another, superior mode of being, and concurrently secured for himself a better fate after death.

The Meaning of Initiatory Ordeals. In many puberty intiations, the novices must not go to bed until late in the night (see some examples in Eliade, 1958, pp. 14–15). This initiatory ordeal is documented not only among nonliterate cultures (e.g., Australia, coastal California, Tierra del Fuego) but even in highly developed religions. Thus, the Mesopotamian hero Gilgamesh crosses the waters of death to find out from Utanapishtim how he can gain immortality. "Try not to sleep for six days and seven nights!" is the answer. But Gilgamesh at once falls asleep, and Utnapishtim wakes him on the seventh day. Indeed, not to sleep is not only a victory over physical fatigue but is above all a demonstration of will and spiritual strength; to remain awake is equivalent to being conscious, present in the world, responsible.

Another puberty initiation ordeal is the interdiction against eating for a few days, or against drinking water except by "sucking it through a reed" (Australia, Tierra del Fuego). Among some Australian tribes, the dietary prohibitions are successively removed as myths, dances, and pantomimes teach the novices the religious origin of each kind of food. But most puberty ordeals are cruel and terrifying. In Africa, as in Australia, circumcision is equivalent to death; the operators, dressed in lion and leopard skins, attack the novices' genital organs, indicating that the intention is to kill them. In the Kongo or the Loango coast, boys between ten and twelve years old drink a potion that makes them unconscious. They are then carried into the jungle and circumcised. Among the Pangwe, the novices are taken to a house full of ants' nests and are badly bitten; meanwhile, their guardians cry, "You will be killed; now you must die!" (See examples in Eliade, 1958, pp. 23ff., 30ff.) Excesses of this kind sometimes result in the death of the boy. In such cases the mother is not informed until after the period of segregation in the bush; she is then told that her son was killed by the spirit, or that, swallowed by a monster with the other novices, he did not succeed in escaping from its belly.

The assimilation of initiatory tortures to the sufferings of the novices in being swallowed and digested by the monster is confirmed by the symbolism of the cabin in which the boys are isolated. Often the cabin represents the body or the open maw of a water monster, a crocodile, for example, or of a snake. In some regions of Ceram the opening through which the novices pass is called the snake's mouth. Being shut up in the cabin is equivalent to being imprisoned in the monster's body. On Rooke Island (Umboi), when the novices are isolated in a cabin in the jungle, a number of masked men tell the women that their sons are being devoured by a terrifying, demonic being. In New Guinea, the house built for the circumcision of the boys has the form of the monster Barlun, who is believed to swallow the novices; that is, the building has a "belly" and a "tail." The novice's entrance into the cabin is equivalent to entering the monster's belly. Among the Nor-Papua the novices are swallowed and later disgorged by a spirit whose voice sounds like a flute. The initiatory cabin represents not only the belly of the devouring monster but also the womb. The novice's "death" signifies a return to the embryonic state.

It is in the interval between initiatory "death" and "resurrection" that the Australian novice is gradually introduced to the sacred history of the tribe and is permitted to witness, at least in part, its pantomimes and ceremonial dances. Learning the myths of origins, that is, learning how things came into existence, the novice discovers that he is the creation of supernatural beings, the result of a specific primordial event, the consequence of a series of mythological occurrences, in short, of a sacred history. Such revelations, received through the ordeals of a ritual "death," characterize most of the age-grading initiations. The "resurrection," or "rebirth," proclaims the coming into being of a new person: an adult aware of his religious condition and of his responsibilities in the world.

From Tribal Initiation to Secret Cult. Female puberty initiations are less widespread than boys' initiations, although they are documented in the ancient stages of culture (Australia, Tierra del Fuego, and elsewhere). The rites are less developed than those for boys' initiations. Furthermore, girls' initiations are individual; that is, they begin with the first menstruation. This physical symptom, the sign of sexual maturity, compels a break—the young girl's separation from the community. The length of the girl's segregation varies from culture to culture: from three days (in Australia and India) to twenty months (New Zealand), or even several years (Cambodia). Consequently, in many parts of the world, the girls do in the end form a group, and then their initiations are performed collectively, under the direction of their older female relatives (as in India) or of other old women (Africa). These tutors instruct them in the secrets of sexuality and fertility and teach them the customs of the tribe and at least some of its religious traditions—those accessible to women. The instruction is general, but its essence is religious: it consists in a revelation of the sacrality of women. The girl is ritually prepared to assume her specific mode of being, that is, to become a "creator of life," and at the same time is taught her responsibilities in society and in the world—responsibilities that are always religious in nature.

Among some peoples, there are several degrees of female initiation. Thus, among the Yao of Thailand initiation begins with the first menstruation, is repeated and elaborated during the first pregnancy, and is only concluded with the birth of the first child. There are also a number of women's cult associations, most probably created under the influence of the male secret societies. Some African female secret associations include masculine elements (for instance, the directress, symbolizing a leopard, attacks and "kills" the novices; finally they "kill" the leopard, and free the novices from its belly). Among the Mordvins of Russia there existed a secret women's society whose emblem was a hobbyhorse and whose members were called "horses." But such masculine influences have been exercised chiefly on the external organization of female societies. (On female intiations, see Eliade, 1958, pp. 44ff., 78ff., and especially Lincoln, 1981.)

The morphology of men's secret societies is extremely complex, and their origin and history are still obscure. But there is a continuity between puberty rites and rites of initiation into men's secret societies. Throughout Oceania, for example, both initiations of boys and those requisite for membership in the men's secret societies involve the same ritual of symbolic death through being swallowed by a sea monster, followed by resurrection—which indicates that all the ceremonies derive historically from a single center. In West Africa, we find a similar phenomenon: the secret societies derive from the puberty initiations. (For other examples, see Eliade, 1958, pp. 73ff., 153.)

The socioreligious phenomenon of secret male cults and masked confraternities is especially widespread in Melanesia and Africa. As in the tribal initiations, the rites for entrance into men's secret cult societies present the well-known pattern: seclusion, initiatory ordeals and tortures, revelation of a secret doctrine, bestowal of a new name, instruction in a special language.

In the two American continents, the climbing of a tree or a sacred pole plays an important role not only in puberty initiations (as, for example, in the north of the Gran Chaco, and among the Mandan, the Kwakiutl, and the Pomo) but also in public festivals (the Festival of the Sun held by the Ge; various festivals among the Tupi, the Plains Indians, the Salish, the Delaware, the Maidu), or in the ceremonies and healing séances of shamans (Yaruro, Araucanian, Maidu). The climbing of the tree or of the sacred pole has the same goal: to meet with the gods or heavenly powers in order to obtain a blessing, whether a personal consecration, a favor for the community, or the cure of a sick person.

Martial and Heroic Initiations. In ancient Greece, some heroic scenarios can be identified in the saga of Theseus; for example, his ritual descent into the sea (an ordeal equivalent to a journey into the beyond) or his entering the labyrinth and fighting the monster. Other initiatory ordeals survived in the famous Spartan discipline of Lykurgos, under which an adolescent was sent away to the mountains, naked, to live for a full year on what he could steal, being careful to let no one see him. In other words, Lacedaemonian youths led the life of a wolf for a whole year.

Among the ancient Germans, a young man had to confront certain ordeals typical of the initiations of warriors. Tacitus tells us that among the Chatti the candidate cut neither his hair nor his beard until he had killed an enemy. A Taifali youth had to bring down a boar or a wolf; among the Heruli, he had to fight unarmed. Through these ordeals, the young man took to himself a wild animal's mode of being; he became a dreaded warrior in the measure in which he behaved like a beast of prey. Such warriors were known as berserkers, literally, "in shirts (*serkr*) of bear," or as *úlfheðnar*, "men with the skin of a wolf." They thought that they could metamorphose themselves into wolves by the ritual donning of a wolfskin. By putting on the skin, the initiand assimilated the behavior of a wolf; in other words, he became a wild-beast warrior, irresistible and invulnerable. "Wolf" was the appellation of the members of the Indo-European military societies.

The martial initiatory ordeal *par excellence* was the single combat, conducted in such a way that it finally roused the candidate to the "fury of the berserkers." The ancient Germans called this sacred force *wut*, a term that Adam of Bremen translated as *furor*; it was a sort of demonic frenzy, which filled the adversary with terror and finally paralyzed him. The Irish *ferg* (lit., "anger") is an almost exact equivalent of this same terrifying sacred experience, specific to heroic combat.

The initiation of the youthful hero Cú Chulainn admirably illustrates such tumultuous and burning "fury." While still a little boy, Cú Chulainn asked his uncle, the king of Ulster, for arms and a chariot, and set off for the castle of his uncle's three famous adversaries. Although those heroes were supposed to be invincible, the little boy conquered them and cut off their heads. But the exploit heated him to such a degree that a witch warned the king that if precautions were not taken, the boy would kill all the warriors in Ulster. The king sent a troop of naked women to meet Cú Chulainn, and the lad hid his face, that he might not see their nakedness. Thus they were able to lift him from the chariot and place him in successive vats of cold water to extinguish his wrath (*ferg*). The first vat burst its staves and its hoops; the next boiled with big bubbles; "the third vat into which he went, some men might endure it and others not. Then the boy's *ferg* went down, and his garments were put on him" (*Táin Bó Cuailnge*, trans. Joseph Dunn, London, 1914, pp. 60–78).

INITIATION IN THE CHRISTIAN AND WESTERN WORLD. Initiatory scenarios can be recognized in many medieval and postmedieval religious, mystical, and esoteric groups, some, but not all of them, considered heretical by the ecclesiastical authorities. The matter is too complex, and as yet insufficiently researched, to permit a brief summary. Still, throughout almost all of rural Europe, and down to the end of the nineteenth century, the ceremonies marking the passage from one age class to the next still reproduced certain themes characteristic of traditional puberty initiations. Furthermore, the symbols and rituals of a secret society can be recognized in the military organizations of youth: the ordeals of their entrance, their peculiar dances (for example, the Scottish sword dance), and even their costumes. Also, the ceremonial of the artisans' guilds has an initiatory pattern, especially among the blacksmiths and masons. Finally, the closed milieus of the alchemists contained many recognizable elements; indeed, the *opus alchymicum* implies the well-known pattern of initiation: tortures, "death," and "resurrection" (Eliade, 1978, pp. 142ff.).

It is significant that in medieval and postmedieval times, some initiatory patterns were conserved in the oral as well as written literatures, for instance, in folk tales, in the Arthurian cycle, in the neo-Greek epic *Digenis Akritas*, in the ecstatic poems of *Fedeli d'amore*, and even in certain children's games (see some examples in Eliade, 1958, pp. 124ff.; Eliade, 1969, pp. 120ff.). No less significant is the survival of initiatory scenarios in many pre-Romantic and Romantic novels, from Goethe's *Wilhelm Meister* to Balzac's *Séraphita*. With regard to the initiatory rituals practiced by the various secret associations of the same period, only that of Freemasonry seems to prolong an authentic tradition. Most other secret groups are recent creations, and their initiation rites were either constructed by their founders or inspired by certain esoteric literature. The same phenomenon of improvising secret associations with more or less complicated initiatory ordeals continued into the twentieth century (see Eliade, 1976, pp. 58ff.).

But such pseudo-initiatory improvisations have a religious significance. In recent times, literary critics have recognized initiation themes in much modern European and American literature; Nerval (*Aurélia*), Jules Verne (*Voyage au centre de la terre, L'île mystérieuse*), T. S. Eliot (*The Waste Land),* and many other contemporary writers, such as Sherwood Anderson, F. Scott Fitzgerald, Thomas Wolfe, and William Faulkner, have made use of this notation (see Eliade, 1969, pp. 123ff.). Other authors have deciphered initiatory scenarios in contemporary plastic arts and especially in cinema. Thus, in the modern Western world, initiatory symbols have survived on the unconscious level (i.e., in dreams and imaginary universes). It is significant that these survivals are studied today with an interest difficult to imagine sixty or seventy years ago. In the desacralized Western world, the sacred is present and active chiefly in the realms of the imaginary. But imaginary experiences are part of the total human being, no less important than his diurnal experiences. This means that the nostalgia for initiatory scenarios, a nostalgia deciphered in so many literary and artistic creations, reveals modern man's longing for a total and definitive renewal, for a *renovatio* capable of radically changing his existence.

SEE ALSO Berserkers; Frenzy; Mystery Religions; Ordeal; Shamanism.

BIBLIOGRAPHY

The important critical literature published through the late 1950s is noted in my *Birth and Rebirth: The Religious Meanings of Initiation in Human Culture* (London, 1958), pp. 137ff., reprinted under the title *Rites and Symbols of Initiation* (New York, 1965). See also the more recent critical bibliographies cited in "Initiation and the Modern World" in my *The Quest: History and Meaning in Religion* (Chicago, 1969), pp. 112–126.

Angelo Brelich's *Paides e parthenoi* (Rome, 1969) is invaluable for its rich documentation and insightful analyses. Frank W. Young presents a sociological interpretation in his *Initiation Ceremonies: A Cross-Cultural Study of Status Dramatization* (Indianapolis, 1965). The best monograph on female initiation is Bruce Lincoln's *Emerging from the Chrysalis: Studies in Rituals of Women's Initiation* (Cambridge, Mass., 1981).

On secret cults, see M. R. Allen's *Male Cults and Secret Initiations in Melanesia* (London, 1967), an exemplary analysis of initiation ceremonies in New Guinea; *Secret Societies,* edited by Norman MacKenzie (New York, 1967); *Classes et associations d'âge en Afrique de l'Ouest,* edited by Denise Paulme (Paris, 1971); and Robert S. Ellwood Jr.'s *Religious and Spiritual Groups in Modern America* (Englewood Cliffs, N.J., 1973). On the initiation pattern among alchemists, see my *The*

Forge and the Crucible, 2d ed. (Chicago, 1978). For a discussion of initiatiory ordeals among secret societies improvised in this century, see my *Occultism, Witchcraft, and Cultural Fashions: Essays in Comparative Religions* (Chicago, 1976).

MIRCEA ELIADE (1987)

INITIATION: MEN'S INITIATION

The word *initiation* implies a new beginning, as the Latin *initium* suggests. By means of a rite of passage or transition, a person is separated from one social or religious status and incorporated into another. From a religious perspective, initiation may be seen as an encounter with the sacred. The transition is therefore a profound one, with the initiand emerging from the passage changed not only socially but existentially and spiritually as well. This radical transformation is almost universally symbolized by images of death and rebirth. One is not simply changed; one is made new.

The study of initiation in general, particularly in primitive society, has been almost synonymous with the study of men's initiation in particular. This situation exists, in part, because the vast majority of ethnologists, anthropologists, and even untrained observers were male and, therefore, had greater access to the secret rituals of their own sex. More germane, however, is the fact that male initiations are frequently given more importance, both social and religious, than female initiations. They are, in any event, usually more elaborate and therefore more conspicuous than their female counterparts. Men's initiation may be divided into three categories: puberty rites; specialized initiations into secret societies or confraternities; and specialized initiations into religious vocations or mystical careers.

PRIMITIVE PUBERTY RITES: METHODOLOGICAL APPROACHES. These invariably obligatory rituals effect the transition from childhood or adolescence to manhood. The boy is separated, often quite literally, from the world of women and children, emerging from his seclusion a man in the company of men. For the male, the arrival of biological puberty is not as punctuated an event as it is for the female. Male initiations are therefore largely cultural rather than biological transitions. Relatedly, boys are usually initiated in groups.

The nature and purpose of male puberty rites have been interpreted from three primary perspectives: history of religions, anthropology, and psychoanalytically oriented schools of psychology. Although they emphasize different aspects of the ritual, these approaches often complement rather than conflict with one another.

Historians of religion, most notably Mircea Eliade, are essentially concerned with interpreting the meaning of the ritual, particularly its symbols of transformation, such as death and rebirth. Historians of religion seek to make intelligible the existential moment experienced by the initiand himself. Their inquiry ranges well beyond primitive society in general and puberty rites in particular in an effort to discern universal patterns in initiation per se. As a consequence this approach is more concerned with cross-cultural symbols than it is with either the varying social frameworks in which those symbols appear or the structure of the rite as such.

By comparison, structure is a primary concern for the anthropologist. Beginning with Arnold van Gennep's *Rites of Passage* (1909), the "career" of the initiand has been analyzed from the perspective of its three basic stages: "separation" from one social status, "transition," and "incorporation" into another social status. Like Eliade, van Gennep clearly recognized the religious dimension of initiation in primitive society. Developing the views of van Gennep and Bronislaw Malinowski, contemporary anthropology concerns itself primarily with how the rite "functions" in primitive society. Its emphasis is, therefore, on how rites reinforce social values, maintain social stability, promote group solidarity, and provide needed instruction and psychological support for the individual.

Unlike Eliade and van Gennep, however, the contemporary social sciences regard initiation as an essentially secular activity. Concerning themselves almost exclusively with male initiation, they suggest that adolescent boys, because of their increasing prowess, strength, and sexual capacities, threaten the order of society and its social equilibrium. Puberty rites help socialize these individuals, thereby allaying their socially disruptive potential. Although theories that stress group solidarity are applicable in a primitive context, they often shed little light on individual initiations in post-primitive society.

Psychoanalytically oriented schools of psychology have shown great interest in men's puberty rites. In fact, it is only this particular aspect of primitive society that has attracted their attention. Using Freudian theory, particularly oedipal conflict and castration anxiety, as a starting point, most exponents of these schools concern themselves not with puberty rites in general but rather with ritual details such as circumcision.

PUBERTY RITES: PATTERNS AND ISSUES. From a cross-cultural standpoint, three comprehensive traits characterize male puberty rites in primitive society. First, as noted, is the structure of separation, transition, and incorporation. This scenario is frequently correlated with images of death and rebirth. Second is the disclosure of sacred knowledge, particularly mythical paradigms. Third is the performance of ritual operations on the body and the often related presence of ordeals.

Separation and incorporation/death and rebirth. As illustrated by Eliade, separation from childhood and the female realm is often dramatic and symbolized by death. In Australia, for example, mythical beings in the form of masked men snatch the boys from their mothers and "devour" them. The mothers mourn for the novices just as one mourns for the dead.

The transitional period between separation and incorporation is often prolonged, particularly in the elaborate rituals afforded the male. This period, referred to as one of "liminality," has attracted increasing attention. The social anthropologist Victor Turner draws particular attention to the "liminal persona" as one that is neither this nor that, neither here nor there, but rather betwixt and between. The period of liminality is one of ambiguity and paradox. The initiand may be seen as neither living nor dead, but as both at the same time. Much of the symbolism accompanying this rite is accordingly bivalent. The hut in which the secluded initiand dwells, for example, symbolizes both devouring monster and generative womb, that is, both death and rebirth. During this period, the initiand is seen as pure possibility or primal totality. Males are often dressed as females, thus representing androgyne. Again, they are neither male nor female, but both. The liminal persona is in many ways "invisible," living beyond the norms and categories of society. Traditional taboos and moral injunctions do not apply to him. Liminal personas are sacred, even dangerous. It is therefore often necessary that they be purified before reentering society.

Disclosure of knowledge and mythical paradigms. Some scholars, particularly the psychoanalytically oriented, have suggested that little, if any, significant knowledge is imparted during initiation. Most other scholars, however, suggest that instruction is, in fact, central to the primitive rite. A more significant issue concerns the type of knowledge imparted. Sociologists emphasize instruction in behavior that will be appropriate to the new social status of the person. Historians of religion tend to emphasize the revelation of sacred myths and the true meaning of ritual objects. To a certain degree these two forms of knowledge are interrelated; it is through the myth that the initiand learns who he is and what he is to be. It is, however, the revelation of sacred myth and, relatedly, divine-human relations that require the ritual to be kept secret from women and the uninitiated. Almost always, it is the men only who receive instruction in these matters. Male initiation frequently takes place on a secluded and sacred ground to which women have no access. According to the myths in many cultures, it is on this very ground that the first initiation took place. Among the Kamilaroi of Australia, the sacred ground is the first camp of the All-Father, Baiame. The novices not only learn of mythical events, they reexperience them, returning to the primordial time when the first initiation took place.

Ritual operations and ordeal. Ritual operations on the body are widely performed during primitive puberty rites. The body may be cut, scarred, pierced, branded, or tattooed in innumerable ways, often with great ingenuity and artistic skill. The operation symbolizes differentiation from uninitiated individuals as well as permanent incorporation in a new group. Particularly painful operations, along with harsh treatment, tests of endurance, and other imposed hardships are common in all but the most archaic of male initiations. Invariably, such an ordeal symbolizes ritual death and has a mythological model.

Although van Gennep regarded genital operations as simply another form of bodily modification with no unique significance, circumcision in particular has attracted uncommon interest and generated great controversy. Circumcision of males at puberty is a widespread, if not universal, practice among archaic tribes. Many societies see it as equivalent to initiation itself and regard uncircumcised men as children. Mythologies and rituals of circumcision are generally dramatic; death symbolism is often conspicuous. The masters of initiation frequently portray mythical animals that seize and symbolically destroy the genitals of the novice. Like Freud himself, many psychoanalytically oriented scholars see in male puberty rites a ritual confirmation of Freudian theory. They regard circumcision as a symbolic form of castration and a primary means of generating castration anxiety within the adolescent male. The ritual act is seen as an ongoing repetition of a primal punishment imposed by a primal father on his rebellious sons. The ritual produces submission to the father's will and reinforces the taboo against incest. Adherents of this school regard ordeal as the essential aspect of the ritual and see instruction as insignificant or peripheral.

Far less prevalent than circumcision is the practice of subincision, whereby the undersurface of the penis is slit open. The initial cut is made some time after circumcision, but may be subsequently lengthened until the incision extends along the entire penile urethra. The wound is periodically opened and blood is drawn. Various explanations and interpretations have been offered. In certain cases, particularly where the incision is explicitly equated with a vulva, the intent of the rite is apparently to provide the male, in symbolic fashion, with both sex organs. The initiand takes on a bisexual or androgynous character, thereby emulating a divine totality. Relatedly, the blood periodically drawn from the reopened wound may symbolize menstrual blood. In Australia and elsewhere, blood is sacred, and males are often anointed with it during the initiation ritual.

The psychologist Bruno Bettelheim offers interpretations of both circumcision and subincision in primitive society. He observes that adolescent boys experience anxiety because they lack a clear biological confirmation of sexual maturity such as the female's first menstruation. Departing from mainstream Freudian theory, Bettelheim sees circumcision as a means of allaying rather than increasing anxiety. Circumcision, in effect, demonstrates to the boys their sexual maturity. Subconsciously at least, they desire it. Their anxiety alleviated, they can more easily adjust to their new social roles. Subincision, for Bettelheim, is rooted in the male's subconscious envy of the female, her sexual organs, and her reproductive ability. Such envy may be seen as the male counterpart of "penis envy" experienced by females, according to Freudian theory. The ritual of subincision creates a vagina; its periodic opening recreates menstruation; and the ritual, according to Bettelheim, helps the male master his envy of the opposite sex.

Despite evident differences, ritual homologues of the primitive puberty rite are found in every major religion: confirmation in Christianity, Upanayana in Hinduism, and bar mitzvah in Judaism, to name a few. This last-named rite will serve as a representative illustration. Properly speaking, the term *bar mitzvah* refers not to the ritual but rather to the initiand. On the day following his thirteenth birthday, the Jewish male becomes a "son of the commandments," as the term suggests. Separated from religious and moral childhood, he is incorporated into a life of ethical responsibility and ritual obligation. He is incorporated, too, into the *minyan*, the ten persons necessary for the recital of public prayer. Of great importance is the first public reading of the Torah (the Pentateuch) by the initiand. This simultaneously demonstrates his religious knowledge and his place in the adult world. In many communities an examination was given prior to the ceremony. In certain traditional communities the boy is expected to present a *derashah*, or scholarly discourse on the Talmud (the collection of Jewish law and tradition), at the celebration that follows. The initiand's investiture with sacred objects is also central to the rite, as it was for the primitive youth. Having become a bar mitzvah, the male is obligated and permitted to wear the *tefillin*, two cubical leather boxes containing four biblical passages, expressing four basic precepts. The two containers, connected to leather thongs, are ritually bound to the arm and the forehead during recitation of the morning prayers. These boxes contain passages from the Pentateuch (*Dt.* 6:4–9; 11:13–21) requiring the Jew to "bind" the Law as a sign between the eyes and on the hand (arm). This the bar mitzvah now does literally and for the first time.

SPECIALIZED INITIATIONS. Religious man (*homo religiosus*) seeks an ever-increasing participation in the sacred. Initiations of a specialized nature are therefore appropriate. These rites are invariably voluntary. Particularly in primitive society, puberty rites enable the novice to fully enter the human condition. Specialized initiations, by comparison, enable the individual to transcend that condition. In primitive, classical, and modern society, specialized initiations for men may be divided into two categories: (1) initiation into secret societies or male confraternities and (2) initiations into religious vocations or mystical careers. These specialized initiations are morphologically similar to puberty rites. Patterns and motifs characteristic of primitive puberty rites reappear in specialized initiations, even those in classical and modern society.

Initiation into secret societies. Initiations into primitive secret societies or male confraternities tend to be more selective, more severe, more dramatic, and more secretive than puberty rites. Again, however, we find the ubiquitous symbols of death and rebirth or resurrection. The "mystery" cults of the ancient Greco-Roman world may clearly be regarded as secret societies. The Greek word *mustērion* indicates a rite performed only for initiates. Unlike the formalized state religions of the time, the "mysteries" afforded the worshiper a highly personal experience. Invariably the mysteries promised a resurrection or rebirth beyond the grave. This posthumous resurrection found its temporal equivalent and precondition in ritual rebirth. It was, in fact, at a highly secret initiation during which sacred objects were revealed that this rebirth took place. Invariably, too, the triumph or rebirth of the initiand found its model in the paradigmatic victory of a god or celestial hero.

Although most Hellenistic "mysteries" were open to both sexes, there was one major exception. Mithraism, the secret cult surrounding the celestial Mithra, was open only to men. This confraternity, with its evidently masculine and austere emphasis, had a particular appeal for the soldiers of Rome. The paradigmatic myth relates how the lord Mithra sacrificed the primal bull. From its dying body and shed blood issued the bread and wine of a fecund earth. Plants and animals, too, sprang forth as new life issued from death. Relatedly, at the initiation rite, the new member was baptized in the blood of the dying bull, after which he shared a sacred meal of bread and wine. This ritual feast found its model in the original banquet celebrated by Mithra after the ritual slaying.

Just as Mithra ascended to heaven, passing through the seven planetary spheres, so too does the initiand pass through seven stages or grades of initiation. The seven ritual grades correspond also to the planetary journey of the initiand's own soul after death, winning for him immortality beyond the grave.

The initiatory process was characterized by test and ordeal, befitting the military and austere constituency of the confraternity. Although information here is obscure, it appears that the initiand was branded, subjected to extremes of heat and cold, and, with hands bound, possibly hurled across a pit. The use of crypts and tombs as sites of initiation clearly reinforced the death imagery. Initiation at the mysteries, including the Mithraic rite, was essentially concerned with effecting a personal transformation of the initiand rather than simply imparting information.

In the modern world, initiations into secret societies have become semireligious vestiges of their archaic counterparts. Although the actual experience of transcendence, sacrality, and renewal has become rare, the desire for it often remains. This is clear in modern Freemasonry. Initiation to the level of master mason will serve as a representative example. Although Freemasonry began as an institution in the seventeenth century, it has generated a mythology, or legendary history, according to which its origins are to be found in the biblical reign of Solomon and the building of his temple. According to this mythology, the master architect, Hiram Abiff, was slain by assailants just before the completion of the temple, because he refused to divulge the secrets of a master mason. His actions at that time constitute the paradigmatic gestures now reiterated and explained during the ritual of initiation. As he died, so now dies the initiand. A coffin, an open grave, or the depiction of a grave on the floor make this symbolically clear, as do the skull and crossbones surrounding it. The initiand is "lowered" into the grave from which he is, however, "resurrected," symbolizing his rebirth and incorporation into the circle of master masons who assist in the resurrection. The ordeal accompanying the ritual is essentially symbolic rather than real. Just as Hiram Abiff refused to divulge the secrets of a master mason to the uninitiated, so does the initiand now swear himself to secrecy under penalty of death. Not only are his knowledge of myth and symbol tested at this level, but higher levels of knowledge and interpretation are disclosed. The tools of the stonemason assume a sacred significance as ritual objects. Their symbolic significance, which invariably contains a moral message, is now disclosed.

Initiation into a religious vocation. A representative illustration is afforded by the Buddhist monk. Prior to the ordination proper, initiation into a probationary period takes place. This step, the *pravrajyā*, or "going out," literally implies a "departure" or separation from the normal world. This initiation often takes place at the age of eight and, like the Upanayana in Hinduism, is a homologue of primitive puberty rites. In some Buddhist countries of Southeast Asia, the novice is sometimes so cut off from the world that no woman, not even his mother or sister, may approach him. Having attained the age of twenty and completed the probationary period, the novice undergoes ordination proper, or *upasaṃpadā*. Here again, separation from the world and symbolic death are evident. In Laos, the women of the house ritually weep on the eve of the ordination, reminiscent of primitive practice. It is frequently the Buddha himself, leaving behind his world of pleasure, who provides the mythical and paradigmatic model for the ritual activity. In Cambodia, for example, the future monk, dressed in princely robes to represent the Buddha's preascetic life, rides toward the monastery amid the joyous cries of friends and relatives who represent the gods in their praise of the future Buddha. Others attempt to hinder the initiand's progress, just as Māra, the Buddhist devil, attempted to impede the future Buddha.

Ordination, or *upasaṃpadā* is, however, literally an "arrival." The initiand is very clearly "incorporated" into the body of monks, the Buddhist order, as is evident at the completion of the rite when the monks surround the newly ordained member, symbolizing refuge in the Buddha, his teachings, and the order itself. The exact moment at which the monks close in around the novice is carefully recorded, as his rebirth takes place and his new life begins at this time. The assumption of a new name is commonplace.

Many of the ordination activities find their model in the events that transpired at the council of Rājagṛha shortly after the Buddha's death. The participants at this council and their activities demonstrate a mythical quality. Just as Ānanda, the Buddha's favorite disciple, was tested by the early *arhats* or "enlightened ones," so now is the novice tested and subjected to ordeal. Just as Ānanda did then, so must the initiand now confess his sins, be banished from the gathering, and then be permitted to return. In Tibet and elsewhere the initiand is presented with certain sacred objects such as robes and books.

The Roman Catholic rite (sacrament) of ordination to the priesthood also illustrates many traditional initiatory motifs. The rite is, however, public, as are its ritual equivalents (e.g., Buddhist ordination) in most modern religions. After a period of candidacy, the ordinand is examined, declared worthy, and presented to the bishop for election. Just as Jesus selected priests for his ministry, so is the ordinand now selected. The paradigmatic Jesus serves as model throughout the rite. He is referred to not only as teacher and shepherd, but also as priest. His paradigmatic death and rebirth-resurrection are continually evident. The bishop states in the revised rite: "In the memorial of the Lord's death and resurrection, make every effort to die to sin and to walk in the new life of Christ."

Central to the rite is the "laying on" or "imposition of hands" by the bishop. Already in the Old Testament (*Nm.* 8:5–11), the tribe of Levi is "set apart" for service to God by this gesture. As the Latin *ordo* (a social body separate from the people at large) originally made clear, the priest is set apart or separated from the people by this rite. Yet, following the laying on of hands by the bishop, all the priests present lay their hands upon the ordinand. This ancient ceremonial is a symbol of incorporation, homologous to the Buddhist monks surrounding their new member. Like the Buddhist initiand, the Roman Catholic ordinand is "received into" an order.

After being anointed on the palms, the new priest is empowered to offer Holy Communion (the Eucharist) for the first time. The sacred objects are given him: a chalice of wine and a paten (silver plate) with the host (bread). Just as Jesus offered bread and wine, so now does the ordinand. In the Mass they become the body and blood of Christ; thus the last supper becomes a contemporary event and the Lord's death and resurrection are shared by the congregation.

SEE ALSO Blood; Circumcision; Mithraism; Ordeal; Rites of Passage.

BIBLIOGRAPHY

A pioneering work, now dated but still useful and interesting as an introduction, is Arnold van Gennep's *Les rites de passage* (Paris, 1909), translated by Monika B. Vizedom and Gabrielle L. Caffee as *The Rites of Passage* (Chicago, 1960). Hutton Webster's *Primitive Secret Societies*, 2d ed., rev. (1932; reprint, New York, 1968), is also a pioneering work, first published in 1908. It views secret societies from the perspective of their political power. Written by the noted historian of religions, Mircea Eliade, *Rites and Symbols of Initiation: The Mysteries of Birth and Rebirth* (New York, 1958) is the best overview of initiation in general and male initiation in particular. It confines itself largely but not exclusively to primitive society. *Initiation*, edited by C. Jouco Bleeker (Leiden, 1965), is a collection of essays in several European languages, including English. It represents various methodological approaches and deals with ritual in numerous religious traditions. The article by Eliade contains an excellent, even if now slightly dated, bibliography. John W. M. Whiting,

Richard Kluckhohn, and Albert Anthony's "The Function of Male Initiation Ceremonies at Puberty," in *Readings in Social Psychology*, edited by Eleanor E. Maccoby et al. (New York, 1958), is a frequently cited and stimulating article combining sociological and psychological theory. Frank W. Young's *Initiation Ceremonies: A Cross-Cultural Study of Status Dramatization* (Indianapolis, 1965) views the primitive rite from the perspective of its social function. Michael Allen's *Male Cults and Secret Initiations in Melanesia* (Melbourne, 1967) combines sociological and psychological perspectives and sees the rite as a means of reinforcing sexual identity. Bruno Bettelheim's *Symbolic Wounds: Puberty Rites and the Envious Male* (Glencoe, Ill., 1954) is a little classic. It is readable, controversial, even provocative, and in many ways superior to the sociological and psychological works that have followed it. For further information on Buddhist initiation, see Paul Lévy, *Buddhism: A "Mystery Religion"?* (New York, 1968).

WALTER O. KAELBER (1987)

INITIATION: WOMEN'S INITIATION

Although rituals of women's initiation resemble in numerous ways those celebrated for men, there are also highly significant differences that reflect the biological and—more importantly—the social distinctions between men and women. For instance, it has often been noted that whereas males are usually initiated as a group, women's initiation is quite frequently performed separately for each individual. In part, this may result from the fact that a dramatic individual physiological event—the onset of menstruation—marks the moment at which women's initiation is to take place in many cultures. But one should also note that whereas strong sociopolitical solidarity is established among those males who are initiated together as a corporate group or age-set, the isolation of women in initiation reflects and helps perpetuate a situation in which females are not integrated into any broadbased, powerful, or effective sociopolitical unit.

The task of initiatory rituals is the making of an adult: the transformation of a child into a productive, responsible member of society, prepared to assume the rights and obligations of the particular status marked out for him or her by tradition. Within any ritual of women's initiation, one may thus expect to find encoded the expected norms of female existence as defined by a given society, for it is in that ritual that girls are led to adopt those norms, or—to put it differently—that those norms are imposed on each girl by society as a whole. Here, the observations of Simone de Beauvoir in *The Second Sex* (New York, 1961) are particularly appropriate: "One is not born, but rather becomes, a woman. No biological, psychological, or economic fate determines the figure that the human female presents in society; it is civilization as a whole that produces this creature, intermediate between male and eunuch, which is described as feminine" (p. 249).

Although women's initiation is widely practiced—statistical studies show it to be current among more of the world's peoples than its male counterpart—it has rarely received the degree of attention directed toward men's corresponding rituals. In part, this unfortunate state of affairs may exist because male fieldworkers have been unable to gain admission to these ceremonies, or they may simply have been uninterested in making the attempt. Thus, only a few examples have been reported in any real detail, and still fewer subjected to thorough analysis. Some attempts have been made to draw conclusions from statistical surveys based on the Human Relations Area Files (New Haven), but the findings proposed—correlating performance of women's initiation with matrilocal residence patterns, for instance—have been called into serious question. The field remains largely unexplored, and more work is urgently needed.

Among the examples that have been most thoroughly reported and studied is the Nkang'a ritual of the Ndembu, witnessed by Victor and Edith Turner. This ceremony, which is performed for each Ndembu girl at the time when her breasts begin to develop, but before her menarche, consists of three stages that lead up to the initiand's marriage. The first of these phases, Kwing'ija ("causing to enter"), begins when the prospective bridegroom of the initiand exchanges arrows with the mother of his bride-to-be and also gives an arrow to a specially selected woman who will serve as the girl's instructress and who presides over her initiation. On the next day, dances are held for the girl by the women of her village (men being for the most part excluded) at a consecrated *mudyi* tree just outside the village. The *mudyi* tree, which is the focus of this day's rituals, has strong symbolic associations to numerous referents; among these are the central Ndembu principle of matrilineal descent, the relation of mother and child, female breasts and their milk, and, more broadly, life, learning, the tribe as a whole, and tribal custom in general. Throughout the day's dancing, the initiand lies motionless and naked in a clear *regressus ad uterum,* tightly wrapped within a blanket. Meanwhile, another important symbolic item is introduced to the ceremonial apparatus: After the bridegroom's (phallic) arrow has been inserted into the roots of the *mudyi* tree, a string of white beads, representing the emergent fertility of the initiand, the children she will bear to her husband, and the continuity of her matrilineage, is draped over the arrow. Shortly before this, the women sing:

> They are giving you Nkang'a.
> You have grown up, my child,
> When you have passed puberty you will be pregnant.

Late in the day, a seclusion hut is prepared for the initiand on the side of the village opposite the *mudyi* tree; at sunset she is taken there, carried through the village on the back of the instructress. Here she will spend some weeks or even months, in the second stage of the rite, Kunkunka ("seclusion in the hut"). During this time, she is subjected to numerous ritual interdictions and is given detailed instruction, primarily in dance and in sexual technique. Men may not enter the seclusion hut, with one significant exception: When the girl is first placed within, her future bridegroom enters to light a new fire for her, representative of their impending marriage. The white beads with which the initiand was earlier presented are now wrapped around a miniature bow (the female counterpart to the male arrow) and placed at the apex of the seclusion hut, where an arch is formed of two poles from the *mudyi* tree, symbolic of the female thighs spread in the position of intercourse. The apex thus represents the genitals, and the beads, once again, the children the initiand will bear. Throughout her period of seclusion, however, the initiand is forbidden to look up and see this mystery that rests over her.

The final phase of the ritual, Kwidisha ("bringing out"), begins with a number of mock confrontations between the kinship group of the initiand and that of her bridegroom, in which the latter group is expected to prevail. At dawn, after a night of dancing, the initiand, once again wrapped in a blanket, is carried from her seclusion hut to a place outside the village. There she is washed, shaved, rubbed with oil and red earth, adorned with rattles, and dressed in a skirt, although her now more fully developed breasts remain exposed. Most importantly, her hair is carefully coiffed, leaving a central part into which the string of white beads is placed. The entire coiffure is then covered with densely packed oil and earth. Many of the women present also remove their beads and place them on the head and shoulders of the novice, so that she bears upon her the fertility of all womankind while hiding her own personal fertility as a secret within.

Once adorned, the initiand is led to the village dance place, where she dramatically exhibits the dance skills she has acquired while in seclusion, receiving compliments and gifts from all assembled. In these dances, she is at the height of her power, as is evident from the fact that at a certain moment she is given the eland-tail switch, emblem of the village headman's authority, to carry. Shortly thereafter, however, she must kneel before the drums of the men of the village, dance kneeling, and then spit before the drums "in blessing and thanksgiving." When the dance is concluded, the initiand is led to her bridegroom's hut, where the marriage is consummated. If all goes well, on the following morning the newly married woman, her initiation complete, washes and takes the white beads from her hair in the presence of her husband, shaking the red earth—perhaps signifying the blood of parturition or menstrual blood—from her hair. The beads are then carried to her mother, who will keep them until the rituals for her daughter's first pregnancy are performed, at which time the beads are returned to her.

In assessing this complex and fascinating ritual, Victor Turner (1968) has called attention above all to the way in which it serves to adjust the Ndembu social field when it has been temporarily disrupted by the emergence of a female member from childhood to adult status. This transition calls into focus the deep-seated contradiction in Ndembu social organization between matrilineal descent and virilocal residence: When a girl reaches maturity and marries, she is lost to her lineage, the very lineage that she is expected to perpetuate through the birth of her children. Thus, in the ritual she is first systematically separated from her mother and then gradually handed over to her husband through the intermediary of the instructress; at the same time, the mother is reassured that her daughter's children—represented by the string of white beads—will be returned to her and will ensure the continuity of her matrilineage, as well as the continuity of the Ndembu people as a whole.

Beyond this, one must also consider the effects of the Nkang'a ritual on the initiand herself, for her fertility—what makes her a woman and no longer a girl—is symbolically and ceremonially created within the course of the ritual through her association with the *mudyi* tree, with the apex of the seclusion hut, and, above all, with her string of white beads. But for all that a woman's creative power in fertility is celebrated, her position of sociopolitical subordination is also unambiguously asserted: After a brief flirtation with power as she carries the eland-tail badge of authority, she is quickly forced to kneel before the men's drums.

The ways in which traditional social definitions of ideal female nature are effectively impressed upon successive generations of women through initiation rituals are given striking expression in the Kinaaldá ("first menstruation," or perhaps "house sitting") ceremony of the Navajo, as reported by Charlotte Johnson Frisbie (1967) and others. A major part of this four-night, five-day ceremony is the repeated massaging of the initiand by older women of known good character. Known as "molding," this practice has as its explicit goal the definitive reshaping of an individual woman, both in terms of bodily form and moral character: for it is stated that at the time of her initiation, a girl's body becomes soft again, as it was at birth, so that she is susceptible to the pressures exerted on her by the hands, minds, and speech of those around her.

The events of the Kinaaldá are all patterned upon the first Kinaaldá, performed for the goddess Changing Woman (also known as White Shell Woman), recounted at length in the blessingway, one of the longest and most important of Navajo sacred chants. The initiand is dressed as Changing Woman, and she is systematically identified with her through sacred songs, just as the girl's family dwelling, where the ritual is celebrated, is identified with that occupied by the goddess at the dawn of time.

Changing Woman, in the opinion of many the most important of Navajo deities, is an enormously complex figure who defies easy categorization. In part the paramount representative of the abstract principle *hózhǫ́* (lit., "beauty," but also "harmony," "balance," "goodwill," etc.), the Navajo *summum bonum,* she is also identified with the earth, vegetation, fertility, growth, abundance, and ideal womanhood. Moreover, as recounted in the blessingway, having become pregnant by the Sun, she gave birth to the twin culture heroes of Navajo mythology, who rid the world of monsters and established civilization as humans know it.

For the first four days of the Kinaaldá, the initiand's actions are quite restricted. Most of her time must be spent in the family hogan grinding corn, and through her vigorous labor at this time it is expected she will come to be industrious—industry being a highly prized female virtue for the Navajo—for the rest of her life. Repeatedly she is "molded," and three times each day she must run eastward from the hogan in pursuit of the Sun. Ultimately, this pursuit seems to be successful, and it is implied that the initiand will conceive by the Sun, as did Changing Woman. But this will not happen until the initiand is thoroughly assimilated to the goddess in the course of an all-night sing held for her on the fourth night of the ritual. In the songs chanted at that time, the family hogan is identified with that of Changing Woman, located at Gobernador Knob, the sacred mountain where she was born out of the union of Sky and Earth. Further, all those who attend the sing take on the identity of the gods who participated in the initiation of Changing Woman; most important, the initiand is herself thoroughly identified with the goddess, as in the following song:

> I am here; I am White Shell Woman, I am here.
> Now on the top of Gobernador Knob, I am here.
> In the center of my white shell hogan I am here.
> Right on the white shell spread I am here.
> Right at the end of the rainbow I am here.

At dawn on the fifth day, as an all-night sing comes to a close, the initiand runs to the east for the last time, toward the rising sun that has just cast its light on her through the hogan's eastern door. Shortly thereafter, the participants in the sing move outside to eat a sweet circular corn cake that has been baking in an earth oven overnight. Compressed within this cake are symbols of the sun and earth, male and female, vegetation, pregnancy, birth, the four cardinal points, and the zenith and nadir. All partake of this cake except the initiand, who offers it to the others as if she herself has given birth to it and to all it represents. The Kinaaldá is expected to ensure universal rebirth consequent upon a woman's initiation, for as Changing Woman was told at the first such ritual, as a result of its proper performance, "there will be birth. Vegetation, as well as all without exception who travel the surface of the earth, will give birth; that you will have gained."

Emergent sexuality is celebrated as the means for the renewal of life, society, and the cosmos in both the Kinaaldá and the Nkang'a rituals, although ceremonies of female initiation celebrated within cultures that hold a more ambivalent attitude toward sex can be expected to treat things quite differently. Thus, for example, as Audrey I. Richards reported in her 1956 study of the Bemba of Northern Rhodesia, among the Bemba sexual intercourse is considered a "hot" activity that can pollute domestic and ritual fires by which approach ought be made to the ancestral spirits central to all cultic activity. Only if a man and wife purify themselves after sex, using a small secret pot conferred upon the wife at the time of her initiation (Chisungu), may these dangers be avoided. The Chisungu—which is somewhat unusual in that it is a corporate ritual in which a group of girls are secluded together for a month or more—thus involves considerable instruction in the mysteries of sexuality, pollution, and purification. By the application of those principles that are learned during initiation, and through the pot that is conferred only upon those who have been initiated, women are able to bring the dangers of sexuality under control. But the tensions, anxiety, and aggression implicit in male-female relations are emphatically dramatized in the culminating acts performed on the final night of the ceremony, when mock bridegrooms appear at the Chisungu hut, singing loudly, "I have tracked my game, / Now I have speared my meat," after which they symbolically carry off their "brides."

Such ambivalence toward emergent female sexuality is not particularly common among agricultural populations, who regularly associate a woman's fertility with the desired fertility of the land. But among peoples whose means of subsistence is hunting and/or fishing, the situation is different, for there it is often perceived that an excess of human fertility results in overpopulation that threatens a fragile ecosystem. Such considerations clearly affect the cultural norms of ideal womanhood as they are transmitted—or better, continually recreated—in initiatory rituals. Thus, for instance, the initiand in the Tucuna Festa das Moças Novas (Festival of the New Maiden) is menaced by a variety of demons (the *noo*) who, according to the myths of this fishing people of the northwest Amazon, avenge themselves mercilessly on those who disrupt the delicate balance of humans and game. Isolated within the large familial residence (*maloca*) in a chamber that bears the name of the underworld of the *noo,* the initiand is told these spirits will kill her, suck the viscera from her body, and carry off her empty corpse, should she violate any of her ritual prescriptions; each night she hears the "voices" of the *noo* in the form of sacred trumpets hidden from women's view by men. Upon emerging from her seclusion chamber—like a butterfly from a cocoon, according to Tucuna metaphor—the initiand is again assaulted by the *noo,* now represented by a host of masked dancers, who only in the course of a wild night of drink and dancing shed their costumes and resume human identity. Should the girl survive this ordeal, she is taken on a symbolic tour of heaven, earth, and multiple underworlds, and is finally bathed in a contraceptive solution passed upward from her feet to her head, "to prevent her becoming prematurely pregnant." Only when these magico-ritual checks upon her potentially excessive fertility have been established is the Tucuna woman accorded adult, marriageable status.

In general, specialized initiatory rites for women tend to disappear in urban and later in industrial societies; often they blend into marriage ceremonies or into those lacking gender specificity, such as graduation from school. Still, it is sometimes possible to recognize the traces of older women's initiation rituals within a new context and dramatic program. Thus, for example, such scholars as Angelo Brelich and Walter Burkert have been able to show how, within the Greek *polis,* broader rituals of women's initiation came to be narrowed so that only a few individuals, drawn always from wealthy, prominent families, passed through a series of initiatory schemata, serving perhaps as representatives of all women in general. In his *Lysistrata* (lines 641ff.), Aristophanes preserves a list of the age-grades through which these women passed: *arrēphoros, aletris, arktos,* and *kanēphoros,* each status conferred by ritual means. While the details of each grade are complex, it may be noted briefly that the last two of these were celebrations and consecrations of a young girl's virginity prior to marriage: As an *arktos* (lit., "bear") she took up residence with Artemis in the wilds; as a *kanēphoros* she carried a basket holding sacred objects for the Panathenaia festival celebrated in honor of Athena. (Artemis and Athena were the goddesses most protective of virgins and virginity.) Having played the role of *kanēphoros,* however, a girl was considered eligible for marriage; in myths such as that of Oreithyia women are abducted and raped while or shortly after appearing as *kanēphoros.*

Although they may appear in combination in any specific ritual complex, four general "ideal types" of women's initiation have been recognized. These are (1) rituals of bodily mutilation, involving such operations upon the initiand's physical self as tattooing, scarification, clitoridectomy, or other genital surgery as well as such processes as the Navajo "molding"; (2) rituals involving identification with a mythic heroine, whether goddess, culture heroine, primordial ancestress, or some other prototypical figure; (3) rituals involving a cosmic journey, in which the initiand is symbolically conveyed to heavens, underworlds, the four quarters, and other places of cosmologic significance, as a means of lifting her beyond her normal locus and identity; (4) rituals focused upon the play of opposites, wherein such normally exclusive categories as male/female, human/divine, above/below, right/left, black/white, and wild/tame are somehow united within the initiand, establishing her as a being who transcends the dualities of fragmented mundane existence.

In all of these types, three interrelated levels of transformative action are regularly claimed to be accomplished. First, it is claimed that rituals of women's initiation transform a girl into a woman, conferring upon her marriageable status. Second, it is claimed that they renew society, providing it with new members ritually empowered to play productive and reproductive roles for the good of the social totality, whether lineage, tribe, or other corporate entity. Third, it is claimed that they renew the cosmos, by virtue of the homology between the initiand's fertility and that of nature at large. This last claim is the most audacious and fascinating of all.

It must be emphasized, however, that in contrast to male initiations, women's rites do not usually advance those who have completed them toward political offices of power and prestige. For while the status of a woman may be ritually changed from that of child to adult (from unmarriageable to marriageable or even married), the woman's sphere of influence and activity has been restricted in virtually all human societies to the home. In light of this, it appears a reasonable hypothesis that the exorbitant claims of cosmic transformations wrought by women's initiation and of the cosmic significance of an adult female life offer a form of false consciousness that deflects women's attention and lives from the sociopolitical arena, offering a religio-cosmic ground of meaning and action in place of the sociopolitical one reserved—and preserved—for men.

See Also Feminine Sacrality.

Bibliography

The chief attempts to draw theoretical generalizations regarding rituals of women's initiation are D. Visca's "Le iniziazioni feminili: Un problema da riconsiderare," *Religioni e Civiltà* 2 (1976): 241–274; my *Emerging from the Chrysalis: Studies in Rituals of Women's Initiation* (Cambridge, Mass., 1981); and Judith K. Brown's "A Cross-Cultural Study of Female Initiation Rites," *American Anthropologist* 65 (1963): 837–853. The last of these, however, has been subjected to severe criticism by Harold E. Driver in his "Girls' Puberty Rites and Matrilocal Residence," *American Anthropologist* 71 (1969): 905–908.

Among the finest anthropological case studies of specific data are Victor Turner's *The Drums of Affliction: A Study of Religious Processes among the Ndembu of Zambia* (London, 1968), pp. 198–268; Charlotte J. Frisbie's *Kinaaldá: A Study of the Navaho Girl's Puberty Ceremony* (Middletown, Conn., 1967); Audrey I. Richards's Chisungu: *A Girls' Initiation Ceremony among the Bemba of Northern Rhodesia* (London, 1956); Kathleen E. Gough's "Female Initiation Rites on the Malabar Coast," *Journal of the Royal Anthropological Institute* 85 (1955): 45–80; and Judith Modell's "Female Sexuality, Mockery, and A Challenge to Fate: A Reinterpretation of South Nayar talikettukalyanam," *Semiotica* 50 (1984): 249–268. Classicists have also made considerable progress in the reconstruction of women's initiations as practiced in the ancient world. Among the best of these studies are Angelo Brelich's *Paides e Parthenoi* (Rome, 1969) and Walter Burkert's "Kekropidensage und Arrephoria: Vom Initiationsritus zum Panathenäenfest," *Hermes* 94 (1966): 1–25.

New Sources

Beidelman, T. O. *The Cool Knife: Imagery of Gender, Sexuality, and Moral Education in Kaguru Initiation Ritual.* Washington, D.C., 1997.

Dodd, David B., and Christopher A. Faraone, eds. *Initiation in Ancient Greek Rituals and Narratives: New Perspectives.* New York, 2003.

Dowden, Ken. *Death and the Maiden: Girls' Initiation Rites in Greek Mythology.* New York, 1999.

Gruenbaum, Ellen. *The Female Circumcision Controversy: An Anthropological Perspective.* Philadelphia, 2001.

Kratz, Corinne Ann. *Affecting Performance; Meaning, Movement, and Experience in Okiek Women's Initiation.* Washington, D.C., 1994.

Lutkehaus, Nancy C., and Paul B. Roscoe, eds. *Gender Rituals: Female Initiation in Melanesia.* New York, 1995.

Vida, Vendela. *Girls on the Verge: Debutante Dips, Gang Drive-bys, and Other Initiations.* New York, 1999.

BRUCE LINCOLN (1987)
Revised Bibliography

INNER ASIAN RELIGIONS. Inner Asia, essentially a historical concept, was that great land mass surrounded by the civilized worlds of Rome, Greece, Arabia, Persia, India, and China. Central Eurasia, the more scholarly term for the region, should not be confused with Central Asia, which, in the strict sense, comprises the modern-day Uzbek, Turkmen, Kirghiz, Kazakh, and Tajik republics; or, in a broader sense, adds Chinese Turkistan (Sinkiang). Until modern times, the boundaries that separated Inner Asia from the rest of the Eurasian land mass were in constant flux, expanding or contracting according to the relations of the peoples within Inner Asia toward the surrounding sedentary states.

Inner Asia is a vast area with a multitude of peoples, speaking a variety of languages, possessing distinct religious practices, yet culturally united in a unique civilization. The languages spoken in Inner Asia belong to a number of linguistic families, the largest of which is Altaic (comprising the Turkic, Mongol, and Tunguz languages), followed by Uralic (the Finno-Ugric and Samoyed languages), Paleosiberian or Paleo-Asiatic, Indo-Iranian, and the isolated languages of the Caucasus. The noninstitutionalized forms of religion in Inner Asia, as reported by early travelers and recorded by historians, were most evident in their myths of origin, in the ceremonial activities present in daily life, such as rituals performed before hunting or connected with funerals, and in art. Tolerance of outside religions was the norm, rather than the exception, and Buddhism, Islam, and Christianity all exerted great influence on the region.

Ecologically, Inner Asia is divided into four great longitudinal belts: the tundra in the far north, the forest (taiga), the steppe, and finally the desert in the south. The existence of these four separate zones has led to the inaccurate stereotyping of the economic activity practiced in the north by the Finno-Ugric, Samoyed, and Tunguz peoples as hunting, fishing, and gathering, and that practiced in the south by the Turkic and Mongol peoples as exclusively nomadic herding. However, just as hunting and limited agriculture were a part of Turkic and Mongol economies, so was animal husbandry a part of the economy of the more northern peoples. The prevailing climatic conditions severely limited agricultural potential without manmade changes in the environment, giving rise to one of the most important unifying features of Inner Asia: the relationship between horse and pasture. As the mainstay of Inner Asian economy, the horse, dependent only on pasture, was either traded for basic necessities, particularly armaments that could only be manufactured by the surrounding sedentary civilizations, or used for military conquest. It thus became the key to the rise of the great nomadic civilizations.

Major problems arise in dealing with the history of Inner Asia. Indigenous written material is extremely scant, existing only from the eighth century CE. Much of the Inner Asian tradition was preserved only orally, transmitted by storytellers, singers, shamans, and priests. Most often the early history of Inner Asia was recorded by the surrounding civilizations, eager to protect their own ways of life and highly critical of different customs and manners. Because the written records are in a variety of nonindigenous languages, the correct identification of names in Inner Asia presents problems. Ethnonyms and toponyms, not to mention personal names and titles, that appear, for example, in Chinese sources are extremely difficult to equate with names or terms given in Greek or Arabic sources. When a name such as *Scythian* or *Hun* or *Turk* first appeared, it meant a specific people; later, the name would often become a generic term applied to any barbarian people. Imprecise geographical knowledge only added to the problems; distances were exaggerated, and few people from the surrounding sedentary civilizations had actually visited Inner Asia. The history of the region therefore must be filtered from ideas and ways hostile to its peculiar civilization and drawn from the precious scraps of indigenous material—written fragments, archaeological data, art—often literally scraped out of the desert sands or the frozen soil of the tundra.

To most peoples from other parts of the world, Inner Asia was seen as one vast zone. The world, from the time of Homer (c. tenth century BCE) until the beginning of the Russian expansion into Asia in the late sixteenth century, saw Inner Asia as a land shrouded in mystery and myth, defined only by its barbarousness. It was the inhospitable land of the north, unfit for man or beast.

ANCIENT VIEWS OF INNER ASIA. Early Chinese and Classical Greek sources spoke of Inner Asia, but many of the peoples mentioned were imaginary and showed the civilized world's lack of real knowledge about the region. To the Greeks these were the peoples who inhabited such places as the City of Perpetual Mist or the Rhipaean Mountains. These regions and the peoples who lived there were removed, beyond the pale of Greek civilization, their barbarous nature, according to Hippocrates (460?–377? or 359? BCE), directly determined by the environment in which they lived. The Greek geographer and historian Strabo (c. 63 BCE–24 CE) reminded his readers that before the Black Sea was navigable the barbarous tribes surrounding it as well as the fierce storms on it caused it to be called Axine ("inhospitable"); not until the Ionians established cities on its shores did it become known as Euxine ("hospitable"). This case is an example of one of the myths perpetuated about Inner Asia by external historians: the lack of cities was equated with a lack of civilization. On the other side of Inner Asia, the Chinese held similar views. The Inner Asian lived in the "submissive wastes," the "great wilderness," the region of the "floating sands," in the barren lands "where frost came early." The "five grains" would not grow there. Chinese emperors were often challenged by their ministers on the wisdom of trying to expand

Chinese territory into these wastelands. This attitude perpetuated another myth: the lack of agriculture meant the people were uncivilized.

Early Medieval Judaic, Christian, and Islamic Views. In the Judeo-Christian and Islamic traditions, the peoples of Inner Asia had been driven into the barren, desolate lands of the north, to the hidden, dark regions of the world—to the land of Gog and Magog. When Jeremiah was asked by the Lord what he saw, he answered, "I see a seething pot; and the face thereof is toward the north" (*Jer.* 1:13). Within this "seething pot" were the unknown kingdoms of the north, which, at the end of time, would rise and the contents spill upon the land, bringing death and destruction. Classical Arab and Persian geographers (ninth to eleventh century) located Gog and Magog in the fifth and sixth climes and warned of their cold, bestial nature, but others recognized their brave, warriorlike qualities. To al-Kāshgharī (fl. eleventh century) they were an army, the army of the prophet Muḥammad, to be sent out when he was angry with a people. This army, called Turk, would come at the end of time. The fear that medieval man had regarding the peoples of the north was also manifest in the *Roman d'Alexandre*, in which the hordes of Gog and Magog are sealed off behind an iron gate.

The armies of Inner Asia did not exist in myth alone; the fears of medieval man had been justified by repeated invasions from the steppe lands. Walls—such as the Roman *limes* or the Great Wall of China—were monuments of the civilized world's futile attempt to contain the encroaching and often unknown peoples from Inner Asia. When the hordes of Inner Asia broke through, they did bring death and destruction with a terrible swiftness. It was because of such invasions that the peoples of Inner Asia first entered recorded history in some detail and accuracy.

The History of Inner Asia. The peoples of Inner Asia who lived in the tundra and taiga were widely dispersed in small communities and posed no threat to their neighbors. It was the peoples of the steppes, formed in large tribes with vast herds of sheep, goats, camels, cattle, and horses, who were highly mobile and had the organizational ability to lead military excursions against their sedentary neighbors. When these peoples first appear in historical sources, they come from two great steppe regions: the south Russian (or Pontic) steppe and the Mongolian steppe.

Scythians. The first important Inner Asian people, the Indo-Iranian Scythians, appeared on the south Russian steppe in the eighth century BCE and began to fade out of the historical scene around 175 BCE, although some remnants survived until the third century CE. While little is known about their origin, a detailed description of their mode of life and some remarks on their history are given by Herodotos (c. 480–420 BCE) in book 4 of his *Histories.* The Scythians were the first historically known people to use iron, and having defeated the Cimmerians, they assumed full command of the south Russian steppe. Their greatness as steppe warriors was recognized when Darius I (r. 521–486 BCE), king of Persia, led a campaign against the Scythians north of the Black Sea from 516 to 513. These Scythian mounted archers soon frustrated Darius by seemingly fleeing before him, attacking when and where he least expected, all the while drawing him farther and farther into their land. In the end, Darius was forced to retreat to Persia. This type of warfare and the ability of the skilled horseman to turn and shoot behind him—the Parthian shot—became a trademark of the Inner Asian warrior.

In Persian sources these people were called Saka, and three kinds were enumerated: the Saka beyond the sea, the pointed-hat Saka, and the Saka who revered Hauma. The Scythians of Herodotos lived north of the Black Sea, while the Saka of Persian sources lived beyond the Oxus River (the modern Amu Dar'ya) and south of this area in Iran. The social structure of the Scythians was tripartite: agriculturists, warriors, and priests. They had cities, centers of metallurgy, and a highly developed, stylized animal art.

Animals, particularly horses and cattle, as well as humans were sacrificed as offerings to the gods. Herodotos listed the Scythian gods with what he thought were their Greek equivalents, the supreme deity being Tabiti (Vesta). Images, altars, and temples were used. Scythian soothsayers were called into service when the king was ill; Enarees, womenlike men among the Scythians, practiced divination; elaborate funeral and burial rites, a strong will to protect the tombs of their ancestors, and prescribed ceremonies for oath taking existed. By the late second century BCE, the ethnically and linguistically related nomadic tribes of the Sarmatians began to replace the Scythians, who had reached a degree of civilization perhaps unparalleled by any other Inner Asian empire.

Xiong-nu. On the eastern edge of Inner Asia, the Xiong-nu were the first clearly identifiable and important steppe people to appear on the borders of China, constantly menacing the frontier with raids that sometimes penetrated deep into Chinese territory. Their center of power was the Mongolian steppe. Appearing in Chinese sources around 230 BCE, an account of the Xiong-nu was provided by the grand historian of China, Ssu-ma Qian (c. 145–86 BCE). By about 56 BCE internal revolts had begun to rack the Xiong-nu empire and some tribes moved to the west; in 48 CE the Xiong-nu finally split into two major groups: the Southern Xiong-nu and the Northern Xiong-nu. The former continued to be a serious threat to China and finally faded from the historical scene around 400 CE, while the Northern Xiong-nu remained on the original homeland of the Mongolian steppe. The Northern Xiong-nu never regained their former power, however, and about 155 CE they were destroyed by another steppe people, the Xianbei.

The language of the Xiong-nu is unknown. Long thought to be Mongol or Turkic, more recent studies seem to indicate that it comprised some elements of the Yenisei branch of the Paleosiberian languages. Since the eighteenth century, it has been popular to equate the Xiong-nu of the east with the Huns of the west: at best the theory is controversial.

The military power of the Xiong-nu, like that of the Scythians, lay in their remarkable skill as highly disciplined mounted archers. In fact, Ssu-ma Qian considered warfare their main occupation. Made up of numerous tribes, the Xiong-nu confederation was most highly organized in its relations with foreign states, depending upon the horse for both military superiority and for economic gain. The Chinese set up border markets in an attempt to weaken the Xiong-nu by supplying them with luxuries and fostering a dependence on Chinese goods. Even though there was a hereditary aristocracy within the Xiong-nu confederation, internal organization was loose, each tribe having its own pastures. A son would marry his stepmother when his father died; a brother would marry a deceased brother's widow—both practices aimed at preventing the extinction of the clan.

At set times of the year, sacrifices were offered to ancestors, gods, heaven and earth, while auspicious days were chosen for major events, and the stars and moon were consulted for military maneuvers. Burials were elaborate, particularly for the ruler, with many of his concubines and loyal ministers following him in death. Although condemned by the Chinese for lacking in morals, not understanding court ritual, and not showing respect for the aged, the Xiong-nu had laws, customs, and manners of their own that contradicted the ethnocentric views of the Chinese.

Yuezhi, Wusun, and Kushans. The Xiong-nu greatly affected the history of Inner Asia to the west and south of their domains where, in 160 BCE, they inflicted a terrible defeat on the Yuezhi, an Indo-European people located on the Chinese border of modern Gansu province. This caused the Yuezhi to divide; the Lesser Yuezhi moved to the south while the Greater Yuezhi began moving west. As the latter migrated through the Ili River valley, they abandoned the Mongolian steppe to the complete control of the Xiong-nu, while they themselves displaced the Sai (or Saka) tribes. The majority of the Yuezhi continued to move west into the Greek state of Bactria. At about the same time, the Chinese emperor Wudi (r. 140–87 BCE) sent Chang Qian to the Greater Yuezhi to form an alliance against the Xiong-nu. Leaving in 139, Chang Qian had to pass through Xiong-nu territory, where he was detained and held prisoner for more than ten years. Chang Qian's account, made to the Chinese emperor on his return, brought the first real knowledge of the western regions to China, information that would allow China to expand westward and become actively involved in Central Asia. Although his mission to the Yuezhi failed, he was sent again in 115 to try to form a different alliance against the Xiong-nu, this time with the Wusun, another people probably of Iranian origin, who accepted the gifts that Chang Qian brought as well as an imperial princess to become the wife of their ruler, but who also refused to cooperate. It was not until the Xiong-nu empire was disintegrating that the Wusun inflicted serious defeats on them.

The Yuezhi tribes that settled in Bactria were later united under one tribe, the Kushans, probably in the first century BCE. Besides Bactria, their kingdom included extensive domains in Central Asia and large portions of Northwest India, where centers of Greco-Buddhist art were established at Gandhāra and Mathurā. The Kushan period is extremely controversial, and the dates and order of kings are widely disputed. But it was during the reign of Kaniṣka, a patron of Buddhism, that this Indian religion began to spread into Central Asia and China, heralding a new era for the region. Chinese monks began to travel to India and Sri Lanka to obtain the Buddhist sūtras, passing through Dunhuang, Khotan, and Turfan on the edge of the Tarim Basin, as well as Ferghana and Sogdiana. Most notable are the accounts left by the monks Faxian (traveling from 399 to 413 CE) and Xuanzang (traveling from 629 to 645). Buddhist texts had to be translated into Turkic languages; the routes used by pilgrims were destined to become active trade routes, linking east and west.

Huns. With the appearance of the Huns toward the end of the fourth century CE, a new movement began on the south Russian steppe. Rumors of invasions spreading fear and panic reached Jerome (c. 347–420) in Palestine, where he wrote that these "wolves of the north"—the Huns—spared neither religion nor rank nor age." It was with this turmoil on the steppe north of the Sea of Azov that the *Völkerwanderung,* or migration of the peoples, began. The name *Hun* first appears in the writings of Ptolemy (fl. second century CE), but later historians of the Huns such as Ammianus Marcellinus (c. 322–400), Priscus (fl. fifth century), and the less reliable Jordanes (fl. sixth century) portray a culture typical of Inner Asian society and very different from Roman civilization. Aided by civil wars in Italy that occupied the Roman army, some Hun tribes had established themselves by 409 on the Roman *limes* and in the Roman province of Pannonia (on the right bank of the Danube). When, in 434, a Hun king named Rua died, he was succeeded by his nephews, Bleda and Attila.

Hun penetration into Europe and the displacing of existing tribes were instrumental in the formation of modern Europe. Aetius, the great fifth-century general and power broker of the Western Roman Empire, provoked some Hun tribes to attack the Burgundians in 437 in order to shatter Germanic power and to strengthen Roman rule in Gaul. The Visigoths, who had been pushed from the east into the Toulouse area, forced the Vandals into Spain and North Africa, an event that caused great consternation to the entire Roman Empire. However, Aetius's attempt to use the Huns to defeat the Visigoths failed in 439. Turmoil continued, this time in the Eastern Roman Empire with the Persian decision to attack Byzantium; at the same time, Attila attacked the Byzantines from the north, gaining new treaty concessions. Then in 445 Attila murdered Bleda, thus becoming the sole ruler of the Hun tribes of Pannonia. In the end, a nervous Aetius allied himself with the Visigoths to meet Attila in the Battle of the Catalaunian Plain (451) near Troyes, France, where the Visigoth king Theodoric II lost his life and the Romans withdrew in a battle that left neither Hun nor Roman the victor. With Attila's death in 453, Hun influence on Europe rapidly crumbled.

Where the Huns had originated is unknown, but written sources leave no doubt on their physical appearance, which was clearly mongoloid. No text in the Hun language has been found; archaeological finds from Hun areas remain controversial. What is certain is that despite their impact on the formation of Europe, the Huns never attained the power of the great Inner Asian states such as those of the Türks or the Mongols.

Xianbei and Ruanruan. As already mentioned, the Northern Xiong-nu state was replaced around 155 CE by that of the Xianbei, who probably spoke a Mongol language. Through this victory, the Xianbei became the dominant tribal confederacy on the Mongolian steppe. With other nomadic peoples, including the Southern Xiong-nu and the Wuhuan, they continued attacks on China but were repulsed, particularly by the famous Chinese general Cao Cao. When the Xianbei first appeared, during the Wang Mang interregnum (9–23 CE), they had no supreme ruler; unified leadership is not ascribed to them until just before their defeat of the Xiong-nu. Oral tradition embellished this first leader, Tanshihuai (d. between 178 and 183), with a "miraculous birth," heroic qualities, and the wisdom to be a chief, yet the Xianbei failed to create a lasting empire in this fragmented period of steppe history.

From approximately 400 to 550 a new power emerged on the Mongolian steppe: the Ruanruan (or Jou-jan). Their origins are uncertain but future research may clarify their relation to the Hua and to the Avars who appeared in Europe in the fifth century. According to a widely accepted but yet unproven theory, the Ruanruan in the east are identified with the Avars in the west. Personal names, as given in Chinese, do not appear to be either Turkic or Mongol, but it is with the Ruanruan that the title *kaghan* is first used for the ruler. In 546 the last ruler, A-na-kui, was approached by a man named Bumin (Tumen), whom he called a blacksmith slave, and who had the audacity to request the hand of one of A-na-kui's daughters. He was rudely refused—so the story goes—whereupon Bumin and his followers revolted, overthrew the Ruanruan, and established their own Türk empire.

Türk. The appearance of the Türk—the first Inner Asian people whose language is known and the first also to use with certainty a Turkic idiom—marks a turning point in the history of the steppe. According to Chinese sources they were metallurgists employed by the Ruanruan, but it is not clear whether the revolt led by Bumin (d. 552) was social in character or a minority uprising. After Bumin's death the empire split, one group, led by his son, establishing itself on the Mongolian steppe, while the other group, under the leadership of his brother Ishtemi, ruled over the more western part of the empire. They encountered the Ephthalites (or White Huns) on the borders of Persia. The Türk made an alliance with Sasanid Persia (226–655), encircled and destroyed the Ephthalites, establishing thereby a common border with Persia, but also obtaining control of the lucrative silk trade. Because of its commercial interests—represented mainly by Sogdian merchants—the Western Türk empire then found itself embroiled in the conflict between Persia and Byzantium. Persian attempts to stop silk from reaching Byzantium forced the Türk to go directly to Byzantium by a northern route. It was for this reason that embassies were first exchanged between Türk and Byzantium, opening up entire new horizons for Romans as well as for the Chinese. The first Türk embassy, headed by a Sogdian named Maniakh, reached the court of Justin II (r. 565–578) in 567. The Türk embassy remained in Constantinople, then part returned to the Türk with the Byzantine ambassador Zemarkhos. A later Greek ambassador arrived at a Türk camp at the death of the ruler and witnessed the funeral rites, which included laceration of the faces of the mourners and the sacrifice of horses and servants. The Western Türk empire disintegrated around 659.

The Eastern Türk empire, in a semipermanent state of war with China and plagued by internal dissension, was finally defeated in 630. Chinese rule then lasted until 682 when the Türk revolted and again seized power, forming a second Türk empire that was overthrown in 743 by the revolt of three Turkic tribes: the Basmil, the Karluk, and the Uighur. It was from the period of the second Türk empire that the first indigenous texts from Inner Asia—as stated above, written in a Turkic language—have been found. The most famous of these are funeral-stela inscriptions written in a runiclike alphabet found in the area of the Orkhon River and dedicated to the Türk ruler, Bilge Kaghan (r. 716–734), his brother Kül Tegin, and the prime minister Tonyuquq. These texts give not only a history of the Türk people but also provide valuable insight into Türk society and customs, including their belief in *tengri* ("heaven, sky"), in the sacred mountain of Ötükän, and in the erection of *balbal* (stone pillars) on the tomb of a warrior inscribed with the name of an enemy he had killed. Chinese sources recorded three Türk legends of origin quite different from one another: the child raised by a wolf, the child born of the spirit of wind and rain, the child born of the spirit of the lake. Such a multiplicity of ancestral traditions would suggest that the Türk empire was most likely a confederation of tribes of diverse origin.

Avars, Khazars, and Bulgars. The Greek historian Priscus wrote of a migration of peoples taking place from 461 to 465 on the south Russian steppe. An embassy from the Oghur, Onoghur, and Saroghur had arrived in Byzantium, reporting that they had been pushed by the Sabir, who in turn were being displaced by a people in Central Asia called Avar. For almost a century there was no news of them, but in 558 the Avars, now in the Caucasus, sent an embassy to the Byzantine emperor Justinian I (r. 527–565) requesting land in exchange for military protection. Fleeing from the

Western Türk, the Avars were given asylum in the Byzantine Empire by Justin II, an act that infuriated the Türk, who considered the Avars their own, fugitive subjects. It is a well-documented Inner Asian concept that ruling tribes owned the peoples whom they had conquered. Settled in the Carpathian Basin, the Avars remained there for some two and a half centuries, becoming an effective wedge between the northern and southern Slavs. When they had arrived in the Carpathian Basin, the Avars found two Germanic tribes, the Gepids, whom they destroyed, and the Lombards, who fled and settled in northern Italy. The Avars also menaced the Byzantines and the Franks. In 626 the Avars and the Persians jointly attacked Constantinople and were defeated only when the Byzantine forces destroyed the Persian fleet as it attempted to cross the Bosphorus.

Meanwhile, the south Russian steppe continued to be a place of turmoil. The Turkic-speaking Khazars became increasingly powerful with the weakening of the western Türk, and by the mid-seventh century achieved independence. Christian and Islamic missionaries had already had some influence among the Khazars, but in 740 the Khazar ruler and his entourage adopted Judaism. Not an empire bent on conquest, but practicing a settled, mixed economy based on cattle breeding, agriculture, and trade, the Khazars nevertheless caused some movement on the steppe and prevented Arab and Islamic penetration into eastern Europe. Pushed by the Khazars, the Bulgars (a Turkic-speaking people who had lived on the Pontic steppe from the late fifth century) split around 680. One group, moving north to the Volga-Kama region, was, in 921, visited by an Arab embassy described by one of its members, Ibn Faḍlān, who left an invaluable account of both the Khazars and the Volga Bulgars. A Christian Bulgar prince, Kovrat, and his son Asparukh led other Bulgar tribes, mostly Turkic, to the lower Danube region where Asparukh created a Bulgar state between 679 and 681. Some of the Bulgars settled with the Avars in the Carpathian Basin, but the formation of this Bulgar buffer state between the Avars and Byzantium effectively ended Avar-Byzantine relations by 678. As a result, the Avars led a reasonably quiet life for over a century until they were attacked and greatly weakened (although not defeated) in 791, 795–796, and 803 by Charlemagne. The Avars slowly disappeared over the next eighty years until Hungarian (Magyar) tribes filled the vacuum and maintained the non-Slavic wedge in central Europe.

Uighurs. The final blow to the Türk empire was delivered by the Uighurs who, as we have seen, had been a part of the Türk confederacy. Their language was basically the same as that of the Türk, with some of their texts written in runic script and some in a script borrowed from the Sogdians, one that would become a major script used in Inner Asia. Unlike the Türk, whom they overthrew in 743, the Uighurs often allied themselves with China; thus, during the reign of Mouyu the Uighurs helped China to quell the An Lushan rebellion (755–757). When Mouyu visited Luoyang in 762–763, he was converted to Manichaeism, which had been propagated in China by the Sogdians. A description of his conversion appears on the trilingual inscription (in Uighur, Sogdian, and Chinese) of Karabalghasun, the Uighur capital city. When Mouyu returned home he took Manichaean priests with him and made Manichaeism the state religion. Thus, the Uighurs became the first Inner Asian people to adopt an institutionalized, major religion. Many Uighurs disliked the influence gained by Sogdians in Uighur affairs and an anti-Sogdian faction, led by the uncle of Mouyu, revolted and killed the *kaghan* and his family. There followed a succession of rulers embroiled in family intrigues, plagued by assassinations and suicide. Even so, Sogdian and Manichaean influence remained in a kingdom dominated by Buddhism. An Arab traveler, Tamīm ibn Baḥr, visited Karabalghasun in 821 and left an account of what he saw. Of particular interest are his remarks about the flourishing town of Karabalghasun and other small settlements, located in richly cultivated areas. The picture he draws contradicts the stereotyped image of the incompatibility of Inner Asian civilization and urban development. In 840 the Uighurs were attacked by a new Turkic power, the Kirghiz, who lived north and west of the great Mongolian steppe.

Not absorbed into the new ruling Kirghiz confederacy, the Uighurs moved. Some went to China, settling in today's Gansu province, where some of their descendants can still be found; the majority moved to the Tarim Basin and created a new state centered on the city of Kocho (850–1250), where a sophisticated, multilingual, and multiethnic civilization developed. A cultured leisure class in the refined society supported Buddhism, Manichaeism, the arts and letters, and lavish entertainments. Here, the Uighurs adopted a completely sedentarized life based on agriculture supported by extensive irrigation works. As Kocho was a main stop on the east-west trade route, economic prosperity played a major role in the growth of Uighur civilization. When the Kitans, a Mongol people who overthrew the Kirghiz in 924, offered to let the Uighurs return to their former steppe lands, the Uighurs declined to move, preferring their life in Kocho. In 1250, the kingdom of Kocho voluntarily submitted to the Mongols. Uighur script was adopted by the Mongols and many Uighur scribes became skilled administrators for the Mongols. The famous German Turfan expeditions of 1902–1903, 1904–1905, and 1905–1907, led by A. Grünwedel and Albert von Le Coq, unearthed from the dry sands of the Tarim Basin the glories of the kingdom of Kocho: unparalleled art treasures including Manichaean and Buddhist frescoes and manuscripts in many languages, illuminating the splendor of Uighur civilization.

Mongols. The rise of Mongol power and the domination of the Chinggisid states brought unification to Inner Asia in a way that had not existed since prehistoric times.

Central Asia before the Mongol conquest. Arab penetration into Central Asia began in 652 and culminated in the Battle of Talas (751), thus permitting the spread of Islam into Central Asia. Wars with the Uighurs had forced the Karluk west and in 999 they seized Bukhara, an act that brought strong Turkic influence to the region. Farther to the west on the steppe north of the Black and Caspian seas lived the Turkic tribes of the Kipchaks (known also as Cumans or Polovtsy), whose move to these regions is shrouded in mystery. To the south of them, the Oghuz tribes—mentioned in the Orkhon inscriptions—were steadily moving westward, into Anatolia, where they were to form the basis of the Ottoman state.

The rise of Inner Asian powers in Manchuria. A mixture of forests rich in game, agricultural land made fertile by abundant rainfall, and pastures suitable for horse and cattle breeding determined the basic economy of Manchuria. The settled way of life also made pig raising an important feature of all Manchurian civilizations. In the fourth century, the Mongol-speaking Kitan began to gain dominance in the region, entering into relations with China in 468, but by the sixth century, they came under Türk domination. A new Kitan rise to power was signaled by their attack and defeat of the Kirghiz ruling over the Mongolian steppe in 924; they then expanded their rule over North China, adopting the Chinese dynastic title of Liao (927–1125). In 1125 Kitan domination was replaced by that of the Jurchen, a Tunguz-speaking Manchurian people who had been Kitan subjects. The Jurchen assumed the Chinese dynastic title of Chin (1125–1234) and maintained their rule over northern China until the Mongol conquest. When the Jurchen moved into North China, some Kitan tribes, with the permission of the Uighurs, moved west across the Tarim Basin through the kingdom of Kocho to Central Asia, where a third Kitan state was founded (after those of Manchuria and China), that of the Karakitai (Black Kitan or Kitai) centered at Bala-sagun in the Chu River valley.

Chinggis Khan and the Mongol conquest. Between Central Asia and Manchuria, two major mongolized Turkic tribes, the Naiman and the Kereit, were vying for power in the eleventh century. Both tribes had been strongly influenced by Nestorianism; the conversion of the Kereit around 1000 was related by the Syriac chronicler Bar Hebraeus (fl. thirteenth century). The first united Mongol kingdom ended in the late eleventh century, followed by a period of internecine warfare between Mongol tribes and against the neighboring Tatar tribes. It was not until Chinggis (known as Temüjin before he was elected khan) had defeated all of his rivals that a new and powerful Mongol state emerged. These events, chronicled in *The Secret History of the Mongols* (mid-thirteenth century), were only the first shadows of what was to come as the Mongol empire spread over the Eurasian continent.

Chinggis, angered by the Naiman leader Küchlüg, who had defeated the Karakitai in Central Asia, began the great push west, defeating the Naiman in 1218, and then led a punitive campaign against Khorezm aimed at avenging the murder of Mongol envoys. Before Chinggis's death in 1227, Central Asia had been devastated, and the campaigns of the famous Mongol generals Jebe and Sübetei had spilled into Georgia, across the Caucasus, and into Russian territory, where the Russian forces and their Cuman allies were defeated in the Battle of Kalka in the late spring of 1223. The Mongols advanced as far as the city of Bulgar where they were turned back at the very end of the year 1223. With the death of Chinggis, the Mongol empire was to be divided among his four sons. But the eldest son, Jochi, predeceased Chinggis and his appanage of the westernmost Mongols, the so-called Golden Horde, went to his son, Chinggis's grandson, Batu. Of the remaining sons, Čagadai's domains were in Central Asia, Tolui remained on the homeland, and Ögedei was elected great khan in 1229.

The Mongols in Europe. Defeating Bulgar in the winter of 1237–1238, the Mongols then swept into eastern and central Europe with a great offensive begun in the winter of 1239–1240: Kiev fell on December 6, 1240, German forces were defeated at the Battle of Liegnitz on April 9, 1241, and the Hungarian army fell two days later. Suddenly, in 1242, the Mongols withdrew from Europe and returned to the rich pastures of the south Russian steppe. All of Europe now accepted the Mongol threat as real, however, an attitude that opened a period of rapprochement in Mongol-Western relations, begun by Pope Innocent IV (r. 1234–1254) at the Council of Lyons (June 1245). Three groups of papal emissaries were sent to the Mongols: the Dominican Ascelinus, the Dominican Andrew of Longjumeau, and the Franciscan Giovanni da Pian del Carpini, who brought back the first extensive accounts of the Mongols, as did the later Franciscan missionary William of Rubrouck, who journeyed to the Mongols from 1253 to 1255.

The Golden Horde and the Il-khanids. With Batu's death in 1256, his brother Berke (r. 1257–1267) became ruler of the Golden Horde. He converted to Islam, thus placing the Golden Horde at odds with the Il-khanids of Persia. The Il-khanids came to power under Hülegü, who sacked Baghdad in 1258 and ended the Abbasid caliphate. The Mamluk sultan Baybars (r. 1259–1277), powerful foe of the Crusaders but also of the Mongols, defeated the Il-khanid forces in the Battle of Ain Jalut (1259), thereby stopping the Mongol conquest of the Arab world. During the reign of the Il-khan Arghun (r. 1284–1291), Buddhism was declared the state religion and close contact was maintained with Europe, particularly with the Vatican and the kings of France and England. Under severe economic pressure, Il-khanid Persia declined and religious tension forced Gazan (r. 1295–1304) to proclaim Islam the official religion. With the death of Abu Saʿīd in 1335, Il-khanid Persia fragmented. Meanwhile, the power of the Golden Horde reached its apogee under Özbeg (r. 1313–1341), but attempts to expand its territory brought it into military conflict with ambitious Muscovite princes and the great military leader Timur (Tamarlane; 1336–1405) in Central Asia. Finally, the Golden Horde split into three successor states: the khanates of Kazan, Astrakhan, and the Crimea.

The Mongols in China. It was Khubilai (r. 1260–1294), the last great Mongol khan, who brought China under Mongol rule (the Yuan dynasty, 1264–1368). With the extended visit of Marco Polo to Khubilai's court (1271–1292) the first reliable information about China came to the West. After the death of Khubilai, Mongol rule in China began to weaken until they were overthrown in 1368 by the Chinese. What remained of Mongol power returned to the steppe where the western Mongols (Oirats, Dzungars, Kalmuks) became a factor in Central Asia, with two successive Oirat states menacing the territory between the western Mongolian steppe and the Caspian Sea from the mid-fifteenth century until their final defeat in 1758 at the hands of the Chinese.

With the decline of the Mongol empire, the patterns of Inner Asian civilization were well established. The development of firearms eliminated the advantages of the Inner Asian warrior: the economic structure of Inner Asia could not technologically advance. The change from land routes to sea routes considerably diminished Inner Asia's role as an intermediary between east and west. Even though the last Chinese dynasty, the Qing (1644–1911) was Manchu, founded by Tunguz-speaking peoples from Manchuria, it rapidly became sinicized, losing much of its Inner Asian character at a very early date. The simultaneous penetration by Russia and China had profoundly changed the structure of Inner Asian civilization. The history of these later periods, not typically Inner Asian, does not shed light on what made the civilization of Central Eurasia unique.

SEE ALSO Buddhism, article on Buddhism in Central Asia; Chinggis Khan; Hun Religion; Hungarian Religion; Islam, article on Islam in Central Asia; Manichaeism, overview article; Missions, article on Buddhist Missions; Mongol Religions; Nestorian Church; Prehistoric Religions, article on The Eurasian Steppes and Inner Asia; Sarmatian Religion; Scythian Religion; Tengri; Turkic Religions.

BIBLIOGRAPHY

The classic definition of Inner Asia can be found in Denis Sinor's "Central Eurasia," in *Orientalism and History,* 2d rev. ed., edited by Denis Sinor (Bloomington, Ind., 1970), pp. 93–119, and expanded in textbook form in his *Inner Asia: History, Civilization, Languages; A Syllabus* (Bloomington, Ind., 1969). Sinor's *Introduction à l'étude de l'Eurasie Centrale* (Wiesbaden, 1963) is the basic bibliographic work for the study of Inner Asia and is invaluable for the author's opinion on research in a field dominated by French, German, Russian, and Hungarian scholarship. Other histories of Inner Asia that can be consulted with profit include René Grousset's *The Empire of the Steppes: A History of Central Asia,* translated by Naomi Walford (New Brunswick, N.J., 1970); Wilhelm Barthold's *Turkestan down to the Mongol Invasion,* 3d ed. (London, 1968); and the collection of essays in the *Handbuch der Orientalistik,* vol. 5.5, *Geschichte Mittelasiens,* under the general editorship of Bertold Spuler (Leiden, 1966).

For the art of Inner Asia, Karl Jettmar's *The Art of the Steppes,* translated by Ann E. Keep (New York, 1967), provides an excellent introduction plus ample illustrations both in black and white and in color. The best book on the epic in Inner Asia is Nora K. Chadwick and Victor Zhirmunsky's *Oral Epics of Central Asia* (Cambridge, U.K. 1969), but it concerns only the Turkic-speaking peoples.

For a discussion of the early Arab penetration into Inner Asia, which opened the region to Islam, H. A. R. Gibb's *The Arab Conquests in Central Asia* (London, 1923) remains a useful account. In a similar vein, Owen Lattimore's *The Inner Asian Frontiers of China* (New York, 1940) and *Studies in Frontier History: Collected Papers 1928–1958* (Oxford, 1962) are unique in that much of Lattimore's life has been spent in the region.

The most extensive portrayal of the life of the Scythians can be found in Ellis H. Minn's *Scythians and Greeks: A Survey of Ancient History and Archeology on the North Coast of the Euxine from the Danube to the Caucasus* (Cambridge, U.K. 1913). The most detailed account of the Huns is J. Otto Maenchen-Helfen's *The World of the Huns: Studies in Their History and Culture,* edited by Max Knight (Berkeley, 1973). Annemarie von Gabain's work on the Uighur kingdom of Kocho, *Das Leben im uigurischen Königreich von Qočo: 850–1250,* in "Veröffentlichungen der Societas Uralo-Altaica," vol. 6 (Wiesbaden, 1973), is unparalleled.

For the Mongols there is an abundance of material. René Grousset's *Conqueror of the World,* translated by Denis Sinor in collaboration with Marian MacKellar (Edinburgh, 1967), is the best book on the life of Chinggis. For the Mongol Il-khans and the Golden Horde, Bertold Spuler's *The Muslim World: A Historical Survey,* vol. 2, *The Mongol Period* (Leiden, 1960); *Die Goldene Horde: Die Mongolen in Russland, 1223–1502,* 2d ed. (Wiesbaden, 1965); and *Die Mongolen in Iran* (Leipzig, 1939) are by far the most useful in this complex period of Mongol history.

New Sources

Dani, Ahmad Hasan, V. M. Masson, J. Harmatta, B. A. Litvinovskii, and Clifford Bosworth. *History of Civilizations of Central Asia.* 4 vols. Paris, 1992–2000.

Elverskog, Johan. *Uygur Buddhist Literature.* Turnhout, Belgium, 1997.

Foltz, Richard. *Religions of the Silk Road: Overland Trade and Cultural Exchange from Antiquity to the Fifteenth Century.* New York, 1990.

Frank, Andre. *The Centrality of Central Asia.* Amsterdam, 1992.

Heissig, Walther. *The Religions of Mongolia.* Translated by Geoffrey Samuel. London, 1980.

Klimkeit, Hans-Joachim. *Gnosis on the Silk Road: Gnostic Parables, Hymns & Prayers from Central Asia.* San Francisco, 1999.

Lieu, Samuel. *Manichaeism in Central Asia and China.* Leiden, 1998.

Sinor, Denis, ed. *The Cambridge History of Early Inner Asia.* New York, 1990.

RUTH I. MESERVE (1987)
Revised Bibliography

INNOCENT I (r. 401–417) was a bishop of Rome. Nothing is known about Innocent's early life save the fact that, according to Jerome, he was the son of his predecessor, Anastasius I (r. 399–401). His episcopacy took place during the period of Rome's decline and witnessed some important events, namely, the displacement of Milan by Ravenna as the seat of imperial administration in the West (c. 404) and the sack of Rome in 410 by Alaric the Goth. Only thirty-five of Innocent's letters survive, in a variety of sources. A few are short administrative documents, but others are more personal and reveal a vigorous personality with decided views. The severe proscriptions against heretics issued at Rome in 407 by the emperor Flavius Honorius and later incorporated into book 16 of the Theodosian Code were probably inspired by Innocent.

In ecclesiastical matters Innocent took a strong stand with regard to the prerogatives of his see, which he viewed as the ultimate court of appeal in all important ecclesiastical cases, claiming Roman supremacy over church councils and church courts. Through his letter to Decentius, bishop of Gubbio, Innocent was the first pope to voice such a claim of dominion in the realm of liturgy as well. The church at Gubbio was considering using some liturgical rites (probably deriving from Gaul) that deviated from Roman practice. Innocent asserted that Decentius should not depart from the Roman norm—an understandable attitude, because Gubbio was a suffragan see—but went on to censure all other churches in the West (Spain, Gaul, Sicily, and Africa) for not following Roman usage. This stand of Innocent's was without precedent. The letter to Decentius remains a precious historical source on the Roman liturgy of this period.

Innocent's letters to Victricius and Exsuperius, bishops of Rouen and Toulouse, deal with numerous points of ecclesiastical discipline. His statement (to Exsuperius) that marital relations are forbidden to married men from the time of their ordination may indicate that his own birth occurred early in the career of his father, Anastasius I. Other groups of letters show Innocent's involvement with events in Africa and the East. His correspondence with the bishops of Africa deals with the Pelagian controversy; five bishops, including Augustine, had appealed to Innocent for a condemnation. He denounced the error but did not contest the decision of the Palestinian bishops, who had pardoned Pelagius. In the East, Innocent intervened as a supporter of John Chrysostom, the persecuted and exiled bishop of Constantinople, and of Jerome in his struggle with John, bishop of Jerusalem. Innocent also brought the churches of eastern Illyria, which had been part of the Eastern Empire since 388, back into Western jurisdiction.

The principles and precedents established by Innocent became the foundation for many of the claims later made by the medieval papacy. Innocent's policies reflect both his own strong personality and the ecclesio-political situation of the time, when the ascendancy of a new Rome at Constantinople, and the decline of the old Rome, helpless before Alaric, invited the consolidation and assertion of power by the incumbents of the see of Peter, the only apostolic see in the West.

BIBLIOGRAPHY

Innocent I's letters can be found in J.-P. Migne's *Patrologia Latina*, vol. 20, *Epistolae et decreta* (Paris, 1845), cols. 457–637. Not all are genuine; see Eligius Dekkers's *Clavis Patrum Latinorum* (Bruges, 1961), vol. 1, no. 1641. Only the letter to Decentius exists in a good critical edition, with commentary: *La lettre du pape Innocent Premier à Décentius de Gubbio, 19 mars 416,* edited and translated by Robert Cabié (Louvain, 1973). On the emergence of new papal claims and Innocent's role in that development, see Myron Wojtowytsch's *Papsttum und Konzile von den Anfängen bis zu Leo I, 440–461: Studien zur Entstehung der Überordnung des Papstes über Konzile* (Stuttgart, 1981), especially pages 205–264. Wojtowytsch (p. 205, n. 1) stresses that a new study of Innocent I is needed, although Erich Caspar's chapter on Innocent in his *Geschichte des Papsttums,* vol. 1, *Römische Kirche und Imperium Romanum* (Tübingen, 1930), pp. 296–343, still remains important. Gerald Bonner's review of Wojtowytsch's *Papsttum und Konzile* in the *Journal of Ecclesiastical History* 34 (July 1983): 451–453 suggests some added reasons for the fourth-century shifts in papal attitudes.

For Jerome's letter identifying Anastasius I as Innocent's father, see Epistle 130, sec. 16, of Isidor Hilberg's edition in *Corpus Scriptorum Ecclesiasticorum Latinorum,* vol. 56 (Vienna, 1918), p. 196.

PAUL MEYVAERT (1987)

INNOCENT III

INNOCENT III (Lothar of Segni, 1160?–1216) was a pope of the Roman Catholic church (1198–1216). Innocent was the son of Trasimund of Segni, a count of Campagna, and Clarissa Scotti, daughter of a distinguished Roman family. He was educated first in Rome, possibly at the Schola Cantorum; then in Paris, where he studied theology; and finally in Bologna, where he probably studied law for a short time. Clement III elevated him to the cardinal diaconate of Saints Sergius and Bacchus in 1190. Before becoming pope, Innocent was active in the Curia Romana and took part in a number of legal cases as an auditor. As cardinal, he wrote three theological tracts, *De miseria humane conditionis* (Misery of the human condition), *De missarum misteriis* (Mysteries of the Mass), and *De quadripartita specie nuptiarum* (Four typologies of marriage), in addition to sermons. *De missarum misteriis* and *De miseria humane conditionis* enjoyed enormous popularity until the sixteenth century. Innocent was not a profound theological thinker. His thought was derivative and conventional, even a little old-fashioned.

When Innocent became pope in January 1198, the political situation in Italy and the German empire was very unstable. Emperor Henry VI had died in 1197 after subjecting most of the Italian peninsula to imperial authority. He left a young son, the future Frederick II, and two rival claimants for the imperial throne, his brother, Philip of Hohenstaufen, and Otto of Brunswick. Innocent skillfully extracted promises from both candidates that they would respect the integrity of the papal states. He regained control over the city of Rome and gradually reasserted papal hegemony over the Patrimony of Saint Peter. Although he eventually turned to Henry VI's young son Frederick in 1212, Innocent used the rivalry of Philip and Otto to establish the pope's right to judge a disputed imperial election in an important decretal, *Venerabilem.* He also indicated the importance of imperial affairs for the church by entering many letters, papal and secular, in a special register, the *Regestum super negotio imperii.*

Lack of imperial leadership during his pontificate permitted Innocent to strengthen papal prerogatives outside the papal states and inside the church. He received the kingdom of Sicily as a fief and was regent to young Frederick. In the Roman church he reorganized the Curia and managed the complex administrative and judicial affairs with consummate skill. He developed a new vision of papal monarchy, using earlier traditions, but with a powerful change of emphasis. An ingenious biblical exegete who cleverly used the Bible to support his vision of papal monarchy, he exalted the pope and his authority within the church as no earlier pope had done, and also attempted to mediate the affairs of secular rulers. He extolled the pope's status as Vicar of Christ, placing him above man but below God. The pope exercised divine authority granted by Christ only to him and held fullness of power (*plenitudo potestatis*) within the church.

Innocent formulated most of his ideas about ecclesiastical government early in his pontificate. His theories had practical consequences of strengthening the judicial hierarchy of the church, underlining the pope's position of supreme judge, and, at the same time, fundamentally destroying the last vestiges of the decentralized church of the early Middle Ages. He demanded the subordination of the bishops to the pope and insisted that all episcopal translations, resignations, and depositions fall entirely under papal jurisdiction. His anonymous biographer and other chroniclers drew a picture of a pope with enormous capacity and skill in judicial affairs, who frequently participated in the cases before the papal court and enjoyed the exercise of authority.

During Innocent's pontificate, law became a central concern of ecclesiastical government. He authenticated a collection of his decisions and sent them to the law school in Bologna in 1209–1210. This collection, the first officially promulgated code of canon law, signaled Innocent's awareness that the papacy was an institution with many of the same concerns as secular states. He heard appeals from all parts of Christendom, issued rulings on disputed points of law, and established a professional cadre of trained men in Rome to carry out his policies.

CRUSADES. Innocent called for a new, papally led crusade in August 1198 and imposed a special tax on the clergy to support it. Although the Fourth Crusade (1202–1204) lacked strong leadership and sufficient money, Constantinople, capital of the Byzantine Empire, was successfully assaulted in 1204. Innocent hoped that the conquest of Constantinople would result in the reunification of the Latin and Greek churches, but his hopes were in vain.

In 1218 he summoned another crusade, for which he made final arrangements at the Fourth Lateran Council (1215). Although he died before the Fifth Crusade (1217–1221) departed, it bore his imprint. Financed by the church and directed by the papacy, this crusade was a more sophisticated attempt to elaborate the policies Innocent had conceived in 1198. It was the last attempt of the papacy to organize a crusade without strong secular leadership.

Innocent also turned his attention to the proliferation of heretics, especially in the papal states. In 1199 he issued *Vergentis,* which decreed that condemned heretics should be dispossessed of their lands because heresy is treason. In effect, he defined the church as a state that the heretics had betrayed. This new conception of heresy led to his calling a crusade against the heretics of southern France, the Albigensian crusade (1208–1229). An army was gathered together under the leadership of a papal legate, Arnold Amalric, and at a heavy cost in lives the crusade was successful in extirpating heresy in Languedoc.

PASTORAL CARE AND REFORM. Innocent exalted the authority of the pope but also had a profound understanding of his pastoral duties. His ability to balance power and solicitude marks him as the greatest pope of the Middle Ages. In November 1215, some 412 bishops convened in Rome to take part in the Fourth Lateran Council. The council's seventy-one canons reflect Innocent's concerns. Heresy and the crusade were important items on the agenda—canon 8 established the foundations for the Inquisition—but the canons covered a wide range of other topics. Canon 18 forbade the participation of clerics in ordeals, which necessitated changes of judicial procedure in secular courts; canon 21 dictated that all Christians should confess their sins and receive Communion once a year; canon 50 changed the limits of consanguinity and affinity for marriage from seven to four degrees. Innocent also promulgated a number of canons regulating the lives of the clergy and the administration of churches.

The Fourth Lateran Council was the most important general council of the Middle Ages and provided a fitting end to Innocent's pontificate. Its canons are a measure of Innocent's strengths and serve as a guidepost for his policies. Innocent may have, in the words of the thirteenth-century Franciscan Salimbene, involved the church too much in worldly affairs, but he was a militant pastor and a great monarch.

BIBLIOGRAPHY

Ernest F. Jacob's chapter on Innocent in the *Cambridge Medieval History,* vol. 6, edited by J. R. Tanner et al. (1929; reprint, Cambridge, U.K., 1957), pp. 1–43, though dated, is still readable and full of insights. For a longer treatment, Helene Tillmann's *Pope Innocent III* (1954), translated by Walter Sax from the German (New York, 1980), is sympathetic but not uncritical, and sprinkled with keen observations. Christopher R. Cheney's *Pope Innocent III and England,* "Päpste und Papsttum," vol. 9 (Stuttgart, 1976), is a brilliant study, the sum of a lifetime's work, and broader than its title might indicate. Three German scholars have recently discussed Innocent's thought and policies: Helmut Roscher's *Papst Innocenz III. und die Kreuzzüge* (Göttingen, 1969) examines all aspects of Innocent's crusades; Manfred Laufs's *Politik und Recht bei Innocenz III.* (Cologne, 1980) describes the dispute between Philip of Hohenstaufen and Otto of Brunswick, and Innocent's handling of this complex problem; Wilhelm Imkamp's *Das Kirchenbild Innocenz' III., 1198–1216,* "Päpste und Papsttum," vol. 22 (Stuttgart, 1983), explores the theological basis of Innocent's ecclesiology. Brian Tierney gives a masterful analysis of Innocent's ideas on the relationship of church and state in "'Tria quippe distinquit iudicia. . . .': A Note on Innocent III's Decretal *Per venerabilem,*" *Speculum* 37 (1962): 48–59. Innocent's vision of papal monarchy is studied in my book *Pope and Bishops: The Papal Monarchy in the Twelfth and Thirteenth Centuries* (Philadelphia, 1984). Editions of Innocent's works cited at the beginning of the article can be found in Cheney and Imkamp.

KENNETH PENNINGTON (1987)

INNOKENTII VENIAMINOV (John Popov Veniaminov, 1797–1879), known in English as Innocent, was a Russian Orthodox missionary to Alaska, bishop of Siberia and Alaska, and metropolitan of Moscow. Born into a poor clerical family in the village of Anga, near Irkutsk (south-central Siberia), John Popov received his early education from his father, the church sacristan. From 1806 to 1818 he attended the seminary in Irkutsk, where he was an outstanding student. During this period, his surname was changed to Veniaminov.

After his marriage, Veniaminov served as a priest in Irkutsk. When the Russian-American Company called for volunteers to serve as missionary priests, he at first refused, but changed his mind after hearing of the zeal of the Aleuts for the Christian message. In 1823 he set out with his wife, son, brother, and mother for the fourteen-month journey to Unalaska in the Aleutian chain. His first task there was to build his own house and a church.

Veniaminov studied the Aleutian language, creating an alphabet and teaching the Aleuts to read and write. One of the books he wrote in Aleut, *A Guide to the Way to the Heavenly Kingdom,* was translated into Russian and went through forty-six editions. Veniaminov was also an outstanding scientist and anthropologist. A series of his articles, published in Russia, aroused so much interest that they also were published in French and German journals. His three-volume *Notes on the Islands of the Unalaska District* remains a basic reference work. Veniaminov's main interest, however, was in the conversion of the Aleuts. His careful work in evangelism and teaching left an established church.

After ten years in the Aleutians, Veniaminov was transferred to Sitka in southeast Alaska and commenced work among the Tlingit, a tribe previously hostile to both Russian culture and religion. Upon completing fourteen years of missionary service, he returned to Russia to oversee the printing of his Aleutian translations. When his wife died, he entered the monastic ranks, taking the name Innokentii. He was then made bishop of the newly created Diocese of North America and Kamchatka (1840).

Innokentii returned to Sitka in 1841, but was not content to direct affairs from his episcopal residence. He traveled widely over his scattered diocese, visiting areas that had rarely seen a priest. He changed his episcopal residence three times to be on the front line of the missionary expansion of his diocese. As the result of his efforts, the synod enlarged his diocese and elevated him to archbishop in 1850.

In 1868, at the age when he normally would have retired to a monastery, Innokentii was elected primate of the Russian church. This honor was truly a crown to his life's work, as it enabled him to submit new plans and to press for reforms in the Orthodox church. The most far-reaching project was the establishment of the Orthodox Missionary Society (1870), which put Russian missionary activity on a sound financial footing for the first time. The society was an attempt to mobilize the whole church by the formation of local diocesan committees, and its work continued into the twentieth century.

Innokentii's influence extended beyond his own dioceses. He encouraged Nikolai Kasatkin, Orthodox chaplain to the Russian consulate in Hakodate, Japan, to learn Japanese. Kasatkin credited Innokentii's advice and example as part of the impetus that resulted in the establishment of the Japanese Orthodox church. Innokentii worked toward the establishment of an independent Diocese of North America with the episcopal see to be located in either San Francisco or New York. He was canonized on October 6, 1977, by the Holy Synod of the Church of Russia and honored with the title Evangelizer of the Aleuts and Apostle to America.

BIBLIOGRAPHY

Innokentii's writings and a biography are available in seven volumes in *Innokentii Mitropolit Moskovskii i Kolomenskii, Tvoreniia* (Writings) and *Pis'ma* (Letters), edited by I. P. Barsukov (Moscow, 1883–1888; Saint Petersburg, 1897–1901). The only full-length biography in English is Paul D. Garrett's *Saint Innocent, Apostle to America* (Crestwood, N.Y., 1979). Valuable information is found in Josef Glazik's *Die russisch-orthodoxe Heidenmission seit Peter dem Grossen* (Münster, 1954), Hector Chevigny's *Russian America: The Great Alaskan Venture, 1741–1867* (New York, 1965), and Gregory Afonsky's *A History of the Orthodox Church in Alaska, 1794–1917* (Kodiak, Alaska, 1977). Two articles in *Saint Vladimir's Theological Quarterly* refer to materials in the U.S. Library of Congress: Vsevolod Rocheau's "Innocent Veniaminov and the Russian Mission to Alaska, 1820–1840," 15 (1971): 105–120; and Dmitry Grigorieff's "Metropolitan Innocent: The Prophetic Missionary," 21 (1977): 18–36; they are excellently researched introductions.

JAMES J. STAMOOLIS (1987)

INQUISITION, THE

This entry consists of the following articles:

THE INQUISITION IN THE OLD WORLD
THE INQUISITION IN THE NEW WORLD

INQUISITION, THE: THE INQUISITION IN THE OLD WORLD

The long history of the Inquisition divides easily into two major parts: its creation by the medieval papacy in the early thirteenth century, and its transformation between 1478 and 1542 into permanent governmental bureaucracies—the Spanish, Portuguese, and Roman Inquisitions, all of which endured into the nineteenth century. What unites both phases is the struggle of the Roman church to suppress various forms of heresy, which ecclesiastical authorities believed posed serious threats to proper worship in Christian communities. It is worth stressing that, for more than five centuries, the average European Christian approved of the activities of the Inquisitions. Inquisitions had no coercive powers and depended upon the cooperation of local people to denounce heretics and upon local secular authorities to punish them. Interestingly, the inquisitors never composed written justifications for their activities because their basic purpose seemed self-evidently beneficial to good Christians. Until the mid-eighteenth century, inquisitors almost never encountered serious opposition, except in rare situations where heretics either formed a majority or were deeply embedded among the local ruling class. For example, in the sixteenth century the Spanish Inquisition was perceived as an instrument of foreign tyranny by both Catholic Neapolitans and heretical Netherlanders; in both cases an ultimately successful "popular" opposition was manipulated by local magnates.

Originally directed primarily against the Cathars of southern France, inquisitors spread to many other regions of continental Europe; only places that rarely used canon law, such as the British Isles or Scandinavia, never had them. After eliminating the Cathars, papally appointed inquisitors targeted primarily Waldensians, but they also investigated a variety of other heretics, including the Spiritual Franciscans and the antinomian "Brethren of the Free Spirit" (who never existed as an organized sect) as their activities spread into northern Italy, Germany, the Low Countries, Switzerland, Bohemia, and northeastern Spain. After 1430, inquisitors in Switzerland and Germany further broadened their range of activity by helping define and punish the newly defined offence of diabolical witchcraft (it was a "mixed" crime, punishable by either inquisitors or secular courts). Meanwhile, in a different kind of extension, King Ferdinand and Queen Isabella created the Spanish Inquisition to punish Jewish behavior among Spain's large and influential communities of converted Jews; a generation later, another state-run Inquisition was created in Portugal for the same purpose. After 1520 the spread of Protestantism gave fresh business to inquisitors wherever the institution survived or was rebuilt, as in Italy. After 1540 the largest group of heretics arrested in Spain were baptized Muslims, who outnumbered converted Jews and Protestants combined.

MEDIEVAL INQUISITIONS: ORIGINS AND PROCEDURES. Unlike Byzantium, the Latin church felt no need to develop any special proceedings against heretics until the twelfth century. Two separate but almost simultaneous developments created the preconditions for a revived and intensified investigation of religious dissenters. The first development was the great increase in heresy in several parts of western Europe. By the twelfth century, the Cathars appeared to form the most dangerous group. However, their political strength was broken after 1209 by a new type of crusade, directed against internal rather than external enemies of the church. As Catharism was gradually eliminated during the thirteenth century, it was replaced by other, more widespread, forms of organized heresy, not imported from the East but indigenous. Consequently, defining and condemning heretical beliefs and practices occupied much of the papacy's attention at the time of the third and fourth Lateran councils in 1179 and 1215.

Ever since the conversion of Constantine and the Christianization of the Roman Empire, heresy had been a punishable crime. The primary responsibility for disciplining heretics rested with the hundreds of bishops scattered across Christian Europe, who had the authority to use the ancient Roman procedure of *inquisitio,* involving *ex officio* investigations. Throughout the Middle Ages and beyond, each bishop had the right to name an inquisitor for his diocese or even perform the duty himself. The most famous medieval inquisitorial register, describing the elimination of the last Cathar heretics in the Pyrenean village of Montaillou, was kept by an early fourteenth-century French bishop who later became pope. Subsequently, the trial of a famous German mystic, Meister Eckhardt (1328), was begun by the archbishop of Cologne, but it was later transferred to the papal court. Moreover, although much inquisitorial history has been written as though papally appointed inquisitors were the only zealous pursuers of heretics in medieval Europe, the inquisitors were always less violent, and often less zealous, than secular judges in dealing with heretics. The Albigensian Crusade, with its powerful (if apocryphal) slogan "Kill them all! God will know his own!" offers vivid testimony of just how bloodthirsty ordinary Christians could be.

However, the spread of heresy led the medieval papacy, whose power had increased steadily since the Investiture controversy, to substitute its own central authority for local episcopal inquisitions, especially during the pontificate of Innocent III (1198–1216). Like most major medieval popes, Innocent had been trained in the relatively new discipline of canon law; it was a fateful coincidence that church law, based largely on Roman precedents, developed simultaneously with heresy in twelfth-century western Europe. With his decretal of 1199, *Vergentis in senium,* Innocent III took the crucial step of combining heresy with the Roman-law doctrine of *lèse-majesté,* thereby accusing heretics of treason against God and enabling both ecclesiastical and secular authorities to apply the full force and procedure of Roman law against them. In 1207, Innocent III also ordered that the houses of convicted heretics be torn down and their property (like that of convicted traitors) confiscated: one part of the proceeds went to the accuser, one part to the court, and the remainder was invested in building prisons. After the murder of a papal legate in 1208, Innocent III proclaimed the Albigensian crusade, a twenty-year campaign that decisively tilted the long-term trend of the Western Christian clergy away from persuasion of unbelievers in favor of coercion.

Besides the growth of heresy and canon law, one must also consider the role of the new Dominican order, founded in 1220, before one can understand the thirteenth-century papal Inquisition. Saint Dominic did not intend to punish heretics but to convert them—his order, founded in the old Cathar capital of Toulouse, was (and is) named the Order of Preachers. But the founder's stress on proper theological training, together with the fact that the new order was directed by a minister-general responsible only to the pope, made the Dominicans uniquely valuable in Rome's ongoing struggles against heresy, and they quickly became inquisitors as well as preachers. In 1231, Gregory IX commissioned a German Dominican monk as a judge-delegate under papal authority with orders to go anywhere he wished to preach and also to "seek out diligently those who are heretics or reputed as heretics." Although medieval inquisitors included Franciscans and other clerics, Dominicans dominate medieval inquisitorial history, from the diary-like notices of the early Dominican Pelisso describing the activities of inquisitors at Toulouse in the 1230s to the careers of Tomás de Torquemada and the German authors of the *Malleus maleficarum* in the 1480s. It is certainly no accident that both major fourteenth-century codifiers of inquisitorial procedure, a Frenchman and a Catalan, were Dominicans.

Between 1230 and 1260, such legally trained popes as Gregory IX and Innocent IV completed the process of transforming their delegated judges into papal inquisitors of heretical pravity. The process was piecemeal; no single papal bull or other document provides an exact official date of birth for the medieval papal Inquisition, but some benchmarks do emerge. Besides his commission to the German Dominican prior, in 1231, Gregory IX also issued the decretal *Excommunicamus,* clarifying that death was the appropriate punishment for unrepentant heretics. A short manual for papally delegated inquisitors, produced at Toulouse around 1248 or 1249, outlined the correct procedures they should follow, from their original appointment through the pronunciation and implementation of final sentences against convicted heretics. In 1252, Innocent IV's bull *Ad extirpandum* legalized the use of torture to detect heretics and compel confessions, although inquisitors could not apply it themselves.

The basic procedures of medieval inquisitors changed relatively little between the short guide of 1248–1949 and the far more elaborate manual of Nicolas Eymeric a century and a quarter later, and they changed even less between Eymeric and the nineteenth century. Nearly always, inquisitorial procedure followed normal rules of canon law. The newly appointed inquisitor, normally assigned to a particular region for a specified number of years, began with a sermon that urged his listeners to denounce suspected heretics and announced a grace period, during which voluntary confessions that implicated fellow heretics would be accepted without legal consequences. Officially, repentance rather than punishment of heretics remained the primary purpose of the inquisitors: they wanted heretics to abjure their errors, accept whatever penance was imposed upon them, and assist the Inquisition. Hearings were held in private, but the penances were always pronounced in public, with all physical punishments carried out by local secular officials.

Inquisitorial punishments emphasized shaming and humiliating heretics rather than killing them. No first offender who confessed at any stage of the trial was executed; only obdurate heretics and repeat offenders were "relaxed to the secular arm." Most offenders were therefore punished with some mixture of monetary fines, whippings, and imprisonment (a sentence of "perpetual" imprisonment generally meant seven years and could be reduced for good behavior). Many penitents were also forced to wear special garments in public. Like secular courts under Roman law, inquisitors could also condemn heretics who were already dead or absent, after which they might burn a skeleton or an effigy and confiscate property from their heirs.

Much ink has been shed, especially in Protestant countries, about the legal iniquities of the Inquisition. However, in many ways it provided a fairer form of justice than most secular courts or jury trials. Because inquisitors, unlike secular courts, were ultimately concerned with saving the soul of the accused, their prisons were better run than secular jails (clever prisoners tried to be transferred from secular to inquisitorial jurisdiction, but never the reverse). Inquisitors discounted the truthfulness of confessions wrung out under torture, and generally employed torture only against heretics who had already been convicted in order to discover their associates and leaders. Although defendants had no right to choose their own lawyers, inquisitors provided prisoners ample opportunity to name and discredit all of their personal enemies and provided a free "public defender" to avoid formal miscarriages of justice. In terms of procedure, inquisitors were unusual in only one significant respect: as their earliest guide of 1248–1949 insisted, "we do not deviate from established legal procedure except that we do not make public the names of witnesses." They did this in order to protect the well-being of their informers, employing a simpler and cheaper method than the current witness-protection program used in the contemporary United States. This famous provision served the Inquisition well: for six hundred years, there was no serious effort to change it.

Another common misconception about both the medieval and modern Inquisitions is their role in the ugly record of European witchcraft. It is undeniable that fifteenth-century inquisitors in the Swiss and northern-Italian Alps contributed heavily to transferring the notion of a satanic conspiracy from secret nocturnal meetings of heretics to gatherings of old women who cast harmful spells on their neighbors. Moreover, a German inquisitor produced the *Malleus maleficarum,* Europe's first and most famous practical guide to conducting a witch trial. However, theory is one thing and practice is another. Even in the fifteenth century, most "witches" were executed by secular rather than inquisitorial courts. After 1530, fewer than fifty were executed by all Inquisitions combined, a tiny number compared with the nearly forty thousand burned by Europe's secular courts. Around 1615 the Spanish Inquisition, not usually considered an example of "enlightened" justice, pioneered the skeptical investigation of material evidence and confessions of witchcraft.

THE "MODERN" INQUISITIONS: SPAIN, PORTUGAL, ROME. Two major limitations of the thirteenth-century inquisitorial system should be stressed. One was institutional: papally appointed inquisitors lacked any permanent organization or central direction. The other limitation was geographical: in several parts of medieval Europe, including places with numerous heretics, such as England or northern France, heresy cases were tried by secular rather than inquisitorial courts. In its long history, the papally appointed Inquisition eventually managed to partially overcome the first difficulty, but it never overcame the second. In fact, after the Protestant Reformation, the Inquisition's sphere of activity shrank considerably: a generation after a German Dominican inquisitor gave Europe its first detailed guide for trying witches in 1486, the Inquisition disappeared from the Holy Roman Empire and Bohemia after Martin Luther's successful defiance of papal inquisitors. In 1539 a former inquisitor was himself burned for heresy by a secular court at Toulouse, the Inquisition's original birthplace in southern France. After the mid-sixteenth century, the Inquisition's history was essentially reduced to Mediterranean Catholic Europe, south of the Alps and Pyrenees, where it had been reshaped into three government-controlled permanent institutions—the Spanish, Portuguese, and Roman Inquisitions.

The oldest and most famous of the "big three" was the Spanish Inquisition. Chartered by the papacy in 1478 at the request of Spain's "Catholic kings," Ferdinand and Isabella, in order to discipline and punish crypto-Jewish behavior among their uniquely large and prominent population of *conversos,* or baptized Jews, the Spanish Inquisition held its first *auto-de-fe* at Seville in 1480 and lasted until its third and final abolition in 1836. The most important departure separating Spain's Holy Office from its medieval predecessors is that its inquisitor-general (Torquemada was the first) was named and paid by the king and merely approved by the pope. Since the inquisitor-general appointed all of his local subordinates, the Spanish Inquisition became effectively a branch of the royal government (in Spanish court protocol, the Supreme Council of the Inquisition occupied fifth place in the hierarchy). The Inquisition was also the only royal institution that functioned identically in both Isabella's Castile and Ferdinand's Aragon. With few and insignificant exceptions, the papacy exercised no supervision or control over its operations.

The overall pattern of its activities falls into four stages. A bloodthirsty first half-century was directed almost exclusively against Spain's numerous and influential communities of baptized Sephardic Jews (*conversos*). Incomplete records suggest at least two thousand of them were burned, along with an approximately equal number of cadavers and effigies (one of Torquemada's earliest rules insisted that "trials of the living must never take precedence over trials of the dead"). Although the scale of its public slaughter of "Judaizers" was unprecedented in the annals of the medieval Inquisition, such numbers appear small by modern standards; the number of Jews killed at Nazi gas chambers in one August day of 1944 probably surpassed the number of officially Christian *conversos* executed by Spain's Holy Office across three and a half centuries.

Afterwards, between 1530 and 1630, the Spanish Inquisition greatly extended the range of its investigations while reducing its relative severity: about ten people were executed each year throughout the entire system. Spanish *conversos* now accounted for barely 10 percent of those arrested or executed, while Protestants (mostly foreigners) and especially *Moriscos* (baptized Muslims) comprised its principal heretical prisoners. The following century (1630–1730) saw a greatly reduced rate of activity—annual executions dropped from ten to two—and Judaizers, now principally immigrants from Portugal, again became its primary victims, especially during a final and little-explored surge of cruelty in the 1720s. In the final century of its activities, the Spanish Inquisition did relatively little damage to anyone before Napoleon abolished it in 1808; it was restored twice, once after Spanish liberals abolished it in 1821.

The range of the activities of the Spanish Inquisition from 1530 to 1630 is indeed remarkable. During this century every tribunal held regular *autos de fe* with a variety of prisoners, and submitted annual reports to the Supreme Council (enabling historians to follow their activities with remarkable precision). Most of its forty thousand prisoners were ordinary Spaniards, often charged with blasphemy or infringing the requirements of the Council of Trent; the Holy Office became the coercive arm of Spanish confessionalization. Many were charged with "mixed" crimes, like bigamy or witchcraft, which could be tried in either royal or inquisitorial courts. Men accused of homosexual or bestial "sodomy," another "mixed" crime, which inquisitors judged in only three northeastern tribunals, accounted for 170 burnings, almost as many as Protestantism or Islam. However, the Spanish Inquisition executed only two dozen witches—a smaller number than those killed for "opposition to the correct and proper functioning of the Holy Office" (e.g., by murdering its witnesses, reminding us again why their names were concealed). In a truly bizarre extension of inquisitorial logic, several dozen prisoners were charged with heresy for smuggling horses to French Protestants.

The Spanish Inquisition developed extremely long arms, both geographically and socially. During the reign of Philip II, it expanded to the Americas, establishing tribunals in Mexico City, Lima, and later Cartagena (Colombia). Although most subjects of the Aztec and Inca empires were converted to Catholicism before the Inquisition was introduced, the Holy Office cannot be considered a form of "colonial" exploitation; Philip II had ruled that native Americans were not "reasonable people" (*gente de razón*) and thus not subject to the Inquisition, although mestizos and baptized African slaves were subject to it. Meanwhile, its reach in Spain was boundless; almost nobody was exempt from the Spanish Inquisition, one of the few European institutions that—then or now—overrode all social privileges. The Inquisition imprisoned and punished numerous powerful *conversos* holding important offices; it also punished some high-ranking "pure-blooded" Spaniards, including an archbishop of Toledo, Philip II's most trusted private secretary, and the grandee who headed the crusading order of Montesa. In such cases, the Spanish Inquisition did not take lives, but it most certainly ruined careers.

When Ferdinand and Isabella expelled Spain's remaining practicing Jews in 1492, many of them took the short and easy route across the Portuguese border. Five years later, when Portugal's king wanted to marry a Spanish heiress, Spanish diplomatic pressure provoked forcible Christian baptisms of thousands of these Jewish religious refugees. It was only a matter of time before Portugal's extremely unconverted "New Christians" encountered a virtual carbon copy of the Spanish Inquisition, which the papacy chartered in 1536 and reinforced in 1547.

The Portuguese Inquisition was even more closely connected to the crown than the Spanish model. Portugal's first inquisitor-general was the son of a king and eventually became king himself. During the Spanish occupation of Portugal (1580–1640), his second successor combined the offices of viceroy and inquisitor-general. Because Portugal was much smaller than Spain, the Portuguese Inquisition had only three European tribunals, but it expanded overseas even sooner, establishing a tribunal in India by 1560. Although relatively harmless after 1774, Portugal's Holy Office lasted until 1821. Its remarkably well-preserved records show a tenacious obsession with Judaizing by descendants of the New Christians of 1497: they accounted for almost 80 percent of all trials in mainland Portugal and for almost all of its thousand-plus public executions between 1540 and 1761. In India, Asian Christians formed the majority of the Portuguese Inquisition's thirteen thousand prisoners, but even here most of those burned were Sephardic New Christians.

In 1542, frightened by the Protestant movement in Italy, Pope Paul III created the Roman Inquisition with the bull *Licet ab initio*. Like its Iberian counterparts, it was restricted by some "enlightened" princes after the mid-eighteenth century and suffered greatly from Napoleon; but unlike them, it revived quickly and held jurisdictional power until the unification of Italy in 1861. The Roman Inquisition continues to exist in toothless form, being renamed the Congregation for the Doctrine of the Faith in 1965. Because Italy remained politically divided until 1861, the Roman Inquisition was far more complicated than either Iberian model. The Congregation of the Holy Office, a standing committee of cardinals, often presided by the pope in person, regulated a network that eventually included forty-six tribunals; a few of them (e.g., Malta) lay outside Italy, while large parts of modern Italy (e.g., the entire south plus Sicily and Sardinia) avoided it. Within Italy, the Inquisition resembled a governmental agency only in the ten tribunals of the papal states. The Roman Inquisition's largest single cluster (fifteen tribunals) belonged to the Venetian Republic, which imposed various restrictions on its standard operations; minor restrictions affected the Inquisition elsewhere. Whereas almost all inquisitors in Spain or Portugal after 1550 were secular clerics trained in canon law, the Roman Inquisition followed medieval precedents by appointing only Dominican (or sometimes Franciscan) monks.

Unlike the Spanish and Portuguese tribunals, the origins of the Roman Inquisition had nothing to do with baptized Jews; perhaps not coincidentally, there is enough evidence to affirm that the Roman Inquisition seems far less bloodthirsty than either Iberian tribunal. The likeliest guess is that the Roman Inquisition put only about 125 people to death, the vast majority being Italian Protestants; about half of its victims were burned in Rome and two dozen others were drowned secretly in Venice. The Roman Inquisition succeeded in its original purpose of controlling Protestantism on the Italian peninsula, but it did so through suffocation rather than burning it out. The most convincing explanation for the Roman Inquisition's success is the co-optation of confessors, who were required to denounce to the Holy Office any penitent admitting any unorthodox behavior.

Public knowledge of the operations of the Roman Inquisition was hampered until 1997 by the closing of its central archive and the disappearance of the records of its trials, which were mostly destroyed in Napoleon's time. To some extent, the lack of quantitative information about the Inquisition's operations has been offset by the exceptional richness of a few famous trials that have been studied in exemplary depth. The Roman trial of the Florentine mathematician and astronomer Galileo Galilei in 1634, which ended with the condemnation of Copernican astronomy and the perpetual house arrest for this aged prisoner, surely constitutes the single most famous case in the history of any Inquisition. Its execution in 1600 of another Copernican and renegade Dominican monk, Giordano Bruno, is known to all Italians. The Inquisition's two trials of Domenico Scandella, better known as "Menocchio," an obstinate and argumentative miller in a remote village of northeastern Italy who was finally executed in 1599, have made him almost as famous.

DID THE INQUISITIONS SUCCEED? Both the medieval and modern forms of the Inquisition compiled a mixed record with respect to their principal purposes. Dominic saw Cathars as the most dangerous heretics of his day, and a century after his death they had been eliminated. However, the Waldensians, who constituted the principal targets of the fourteenth- and fifteenth-century inquisitors, outlasted their persecutors and still exist today. The record of the early modern state-run Inquisitions is comparably mixed. It is difficult to deny that the Roman and Iberian Inquisitions played a major role in eliminating all serious traces of native Protestantism in Mediterranean Europe. But the baptized Muslims of Spain could not be coerced into behaving like Tridentine Catholics, and their expulsion in 1609 constituted a major defeat for the Spanish Holy Office.

The Spanish Inquisition's record with Sephardic *conversos* remains controversial. One could assert, however, that the relative scarcity of prosecutions after 1530 implies that most of them, like the ancestors of Saint Teresa of Avila or the Jesuit general Diego Laynez, became proper Catholics. Although Portuguese New Christians resisted Tridentine Catholicism far more stubbornly, part of the explanation is surely the circumstances of their 1497 "conversion," and Portuguese historians claim that their persecution across eight or nine generations has social rather than religious roots.

SEE ALSO Heresy, article on Christian Concepts; Marranos; Persecution, article on Christian Experience; Torquemada, Tomás de.

BIBLIOGRAPHY

Much useful material can still be found in Henry Charles Lea's three-volume *History of the Inquisition of the Middle Ages,* first published in 1887, and his four volumes on the Spanish Inquisition, but they must be supplemented by more recent scholarship. Edward Peters's *Inquisition* (Berkeley, 1988) provides an excellent introduction to the long-term history and mythology of this institution, while the best survey of the modern state-run Inquisitions is Francisco Bethencourt, *L'Inquisition à l'époque moderne: Espagne, Italie, Portugal, XVe-XIXe siècle* (Paris, 1995). Both have extensive bibliographies. The standard English-language history is Henry Kamen, *The Spanish Inquisition: A Historical Revision* (New Haven, Conn., 1997). By far the most interesting case study of the medieval Inquisition is Emmanuel Le Roy Ladurie, *Montaillou: The Promised Land of Error,* translated by Barbara Bray (New York, 1978), and for the modern Inquisitions, Carlo Ginzburg, *The Cheese and the Worms: The Cosmos of a Sixteenth-Century Miller,* translated by John Tedeschi and Anne Tedeschi (Baltimore, 1980).

WILLIAM MONTER (2005)

INQUISITION, THE: THE INQUISITION IN THE NEW WORLD

The institution developed by the Roman Church to combat heresy in the Old World operated in several forms in the New World. Initially organized under papal authority in Italy, France, and Germany during the thirteenth century, inquisitions emerged under royal auspices in the Iberian kingdoms of Castile, Aragon, and Portugal in the late fifteenth and mid-sixteenth centuries. They became part of the colonial apparatus in Spanish and Portuguese America from the sixteenth to the early nineteenth century. Although its procedures and goals were essentially the same in both hemispheres, the institution confronted several unique and changing circumstances in the New World and adapted its organization, jurisdictions, and operations accordingly. Beginning with the delegation of authority to a series of bishops and missionaries, the Holy Office of the Inquisition (as the institution was known in both Spain and Portugal and their dominions) expanded its presence with periodic visitations, networks of operatives, and, in Spanish America, autonomous tribunals, alongside related episcopal activity that addressed heterodoxy among the indigenous inhabitants. Over the course of three centuries, the institution went from being a modest instrument for rooting out heresy to facilitate evangelization, to an elaborate bureaucratic organization attempting to control moral, spiritual, and intellectual life in the colonies. But it experienced a long period of decline before its final dissolution in the face of Enlightenment ideas and independence movements.

OLD WORLD ORIGINS. Although the Spanish and Portuguese Inquisitions functioned as separate entities in the New World, they shared similar and somewhat related origins. The Catholic Monarchs, Ferdinand of Aragon and Isabella of Castile, initially brought the institution to the Iberian peninsula to help effect the political and religious consolidation of what would become Spain, an area in which three faiths—Christianity, Judaism, and Islam—had co-existed for several centuries. Responding to growing public anti-Semitism and allegations that certain "New Christians" or *conversos* (recent converts to Roman Christianity from Judaism or Islam) were still practicing their old religion, the monarchs secured a series of papal bulls, between 1478 and 1483, authorizing the appointment of inquisitors and the establishment of tribunals and a Supreme Council (known as the Suprema) under royal control. By the summer of 1492, the Inquisition had executed many wealthy *conversos* and confiscated their assets, while Isabella and Ferdinand had given Jews the ultimatum of conversion or expulsion. Tens of thousands went to Portugal, only to face a similar order to convert in 1497 from King Manuel. After a series of negotiations and papal concessions between 1531 and 1547, the Portuguese Holy Office came into being, along the lines of the neighboring Spanish model, with regional tribunals and a General Council under the monarchy's control. Both countries would integrate the institution into the ecclesiastical and political machinery of their colonial empires.

The inquisitorial procedures employed in the New World had already taken their general form in the peninsula before crossing the Atlantic. When an inquisitor first came to an area or embarked upon a new campaign, the populace was assembled in the main church for a solemn ceremony. In a display of unity between the temporal and spiritual realms, the civil and ecclesiastical authorities offered their deference and support to the inquisitor, who issued an "edict of faith" or monitory, warning of the iniquities of heresy and outlining the various offenses that the Holy Office then considered to be heretical or otherwise unorthodox or immoral. Confessions and denunciations were solicited and duly recorded during a prescribed grace period, after which the inquisitor summoned additional testimony about those implicated in the information gathered.

Three credible denunciations judged sufficiently culpable by examiners (theologians and canonists) could lead to an individual's arrest and the initiation of proceedings. The identity of accusers and witnesses was kept secret, although a list of enemies provided by a suspect could bring about the nullification of denunciations thought to stem from enmity. Defendants had the benefit of legal counsel and the opportunity to address the charges and testimony against them. Those who confessed to offenses were assigned penance, while those who denied the charges were incarcerated and often had their assets sequestered to cover their maintenance while in custody. Inquisition officials sometimes employed prison informants and torture to obtain additional information or confessions before or after conviction or sentencing. Penalties for minor offenses included fines, flogging, and various lighter forms of penance aimed at publicly humiliating the offender. Those convicted of major heresies usually had their assets confiscated and could receive exile, imprisonment, galley service, or even death in the case of an obstinate or repeat offender. The Inquisition's goal was to get convicts to admit their guilt, receive absolution, and then be reconciled with the Church. Unreconciled heretics were turned over or "relaxed" to the secular authorities for civil execution, usually by fire at the stake, although last-minute confessions normally entitled the condemned to strangulation before burning.

The procedural process culminated with another solemn ceremony, in this case an auto-da-fé (act of faith), in which the authorities announced and implemented the sentences of all the recent offenders, who appeared in penitential garb before the entire community. The public humiliation of penitents in these elaborate and dramatic affairs served as a deterrent against heterodoxy and an effective form of social control. Although these general procedures stayed remarkably constant throughout the colonial period, several changes in terms of organization, jurisdiction, and the delegation of authority occurred during the early decades of colonization, as the Holy Office experimented with ways to extend its reach across the Atlantic.

Early Development in the Americas. Inquisitorial activity initially arrived in the Americas to assist in Spain's evangelical mission. From the Church's perspective, Spanish dominion in the New World derived from a papal donation that required the monarchs of Castile to oversee the conversion of the indigenous population to Christianity. When Columbus returned to the Caribbean in 1493 on his second voyage, he brought a missionary contingent led by Bernardo Buyl, an apostolic delegate who, some have speculated, may have possessed and exercised inquisitorial authority during his brief stay in the hemisphere. In 1510, Columbus's son Diego Colón, as governor of Hispaniola, asked the king for the authority to name an inquisitor on the island. Bartolomé de las Casas, in turn, called for the introduction of the Inquisition to help protect Indian neophytes and mentioned that two heretics already had been burned in a report he addressed to Cardinal Francisco Ximénez de Cisneros in 1516. Ximénez, who was then inquisitor general as well as regent of Castile, responded the following year with an order granting bishops "in the Indies" apostolic powers to deal with heretics and apostates observing the "sects of Moses and Muḥammad." Many years later, Henrique, the king and inquisitor general of Portugal, would likewise extend apostolic authority to the bishop of Salvador da Bahia in Brazil.

These delegations of apostolic inquisitorial authority to bishops in the Americas were expressly granted in addition to the episcopal authority they already held, as ecclesiastical judges or ordinaries, to conduct inquisitions within their own dioceses. Along with bishops, the Holy Office also selected monastic superiors to be inquisitors, thus the first two appointed in the New World in 1519 were Alonso Manso, the bishop of San Juan (Puerto Rico), and Pedro de Córdoba, the Dominican vice-provincial in Hispaniola. In 1522, as the activity of Spanish conquistadores and missionaries moved farther away from the established dioceses and sees in the Caribbean, Charles V obtained the *Omnímoda,* a papal concession extending episcopal powers to monastic prelates more than two days' travel from a bishop, which allowed them to try inquisitorial cases as ordinaries. These apostolic, episcopal, and monastic forms of inquisitorial authority and jurisdiction would be variously combined at different times and places, as the Holy Office and church officials tried to adapt to rapidly changing developments in the New World.

Regarding the first two inquisitors, Córdoba died in 1521, but Manso continued to execute his charge in the Caribbean until 1539. In 1524 the Holy Office attempted to erect a Tribunal of the Indies under the San Juan bishop. It was expected to support itself, as the peninsular tribunals did, from penitential fines and the assets confiscated from heretics, which in the Americas then, and for some time to come, were meager at best. Manso nevertheless managed to appoint auxiliaries in the islands and conduct various cases against the colonists, although contemporaries complained to the Crown that the activities of the bishop and his delegates were often arbitrary, despotic, and in excess of their authority.

As the Spanish colonial project advanced onto the continent, inquisitorial activities expanded alongside the conquest and conversion effort. After the 1521 fall of Tenochtitlan, the great Mesoamerican urban center in the Basin of Mexico, priests accompanying the conquistador Fernando Cortés tried various cases, the earliest known involving an Indian accused of concubinage. A short time later, Franciscan missionaries began arriving to convert the millions of native inhabitants in what would become the viceroyalty of New Spain. Their superior Martín de Valencia served as inquisitor and apparently was the first to condemn Indians to the stake for practicing idolatry. Beginning in 1526, a series of Dominican prelates exercised the charge, including Domingo de Betanzos, who tried several cases of blasphemy among the conquistadores and settlers, and Vicente de Santa María, who held the first auto-da-fé in Mexico and relaxed two New Christians for "Judaizing."

The next apostolic inquisitor was Juan de Zumárraga, a Franciscan who became the first bishop of Mexico and whom the Holy Office authorized to organize an episcopal tribunal. Between 1536 and 1543 he conducted at least 152 cases involving European, Indian, black, and *mestizo* (mixed European and Indian) men and women, whose range of offenses included blasphemy, bigamy, heretical propositions, Judaism, Protestantism, idolatry, sorcery, and superstition. He initiated several proceedings against Indian practitioners and elites he considered impediments to the evangelization campaign. The most notable of these cases culminated in the 1539 execution of Carlos Ometochtzin, a prominent native leader accused of being a "dogmatizing heretic," and earned Zumárraga a reprimand from the Suprema and the removal of his inquisitorial authority.

VISITATIONS AND AUTONOMOUS TRIBUNALS. The activities of both Zumárraga and Manso prompted a reexamination of inquisitorial organization in Spanish America at a time when the Crown was attempting to implement the reforms lobbied for by Las Casas in the "New Laws" of 1542. Faced with these excesses and economic realities in the New World, the Holy Office abandoned the idea of tribunals in favor of the inquisitorial *visita,* an official visitation or inspection conducted for a given amount of time. In 1544, the Spanish crown sent Alonso López de Cerrato to the Caribbean and Francisco Tello de Sandoval to New Spain to inspect all colonial institutions and enact various reforms. The Holy Office made them both apostolic inquisitors and assigned Tello, who had served as an inquisitor in Toledo, to review the finances and cases of Zumárraga's tribunal (especially the trial of Carlos Ometochtzin), and Cerrato to do the same with Manso's record. In 1546, Pedro de la Gasca, of the Suprema, was sent to the new viceroyalty of Peru to put an end to the civil unrest among the colonists and to reassert royal authority. While the institution clearly had become an important tool in the monarchy's strategy to consolidate colonial rule, it would be nearly another quarter-century before the Inquisition would achieve its definitive form and presence in Spanish America.

Within a few years, the *visitadores* had left and inquisitorial authority reverted back to the bishops and monastic prelates acting as ordinaries. In New Spain, at least, it seems that the Crown made a conscious effort to avoid further abuses when appointing the Dominican theologian Alonso de Montúfar, who had been an examiner for the Holy Office in Spain, as the new archbishop of Mexico. For the next two decades episcopal activity increased throughout Spanish America, but during these years of the Counter-Reformation and the Council of Trent (1545–1563), it focused primarily on the growing presence of Protestants and on maintaining orthodoxy among the clergy, leaving the Indians relatively unmolested.

This was not the case, however, in the wave of monastic activity in New Spain during the 1560s that climaxed with a brutal inquisition directed by Diego de Landa in Yucatan. Claiming authority from the *Omnímoda,* the Franciscan provincial unleashed a reign of terror upon thousands of Maya Indians after finding some "idols" in a cave. Many were tortured, harshly disciplined, or committed suicide to avoid interrogation, before the first bishop of Yucatán, Francisco de Torral, intervened and sent Landa back to Spain to answer for his actions. Although Landa eventually was exonerated, this episode was influential in Philip II's decision to establish permanent tribunals of the Holy Office in Spanish America and to remove the Indians from its jurisdiction.

In 1569, after an accumulation of petitions complaining of abuses against both Spaniards and Indians, increased penetration of foreign Protestants and Protestant literature, and a general concern about unorthodox and immoral behavior in the colonies, the Crown authorized the creation of two autonomous tribunals, directly subordinate to the Suprema, in the capitals of the American viceroyalties. The Mexico City tribunal had jurisdiction over all of New Spain, from New Mexico to Panama to the Philippines, while the Lima tribunal in the viceroyalty of Peru covered all of Spanish South America until 1610, when a third tribunal was established in Cartagena to monitor New Granada (roughly Colombia and Venezuela) and the Caribbean islands.

Although numbers varied over time and by location, the bureaucracy of these tribunals consisted of inquisitors, prosecutors, secretaries, notaries, examiners and consultants, defense advocates, constables, jailers, and guards, as well as treasurers and accountants to manage the revenue and property acquired in fines and confiscations. The vast territorial jurisdictions of the American tribunals also required establishing provincial branches, each run by a commissary, who initiated investigations and proceedings, transferred serious cases to the main tribunal, and was assisted by a notary, a constable, and a jailer. Inquisitors and commissaries additionally relied on a network of lay officials known as familiars, dispersed throughout the empire, who supplied intelligence and assisted in investigations and arrests. The Holy Office also maintained inspectors in the ports to prevent prohibited books and suspected heretics from entering the colonies and fugitives from leaving.

In contrast to the experience in Spanish America, the Portuguese never created an autonomous tribunal in the New World. Although the Crown in 1560 established an overseas tribunal at Goa (India) whose jurisdiction extended from the Cape of Good Hope to the Far East, Portugal's Atlantic holdings, including Brazil, remained under the authority of the Lisbon tribunal. In 1579, Cardinal-King Henrique invested apostolic inquisitorial authority in the bishop of Salvador da Bahia, António Barreiros, to act in consultation with a group of Jesuit theologians, just one year before Philip II consummated his claim to the Portuguese throne and ushered in sixty years of Spanish rule. Although the Holy Office of both countries maintained their autonomy in the "Iberian Union," the Spanish Crown nevertheless pressured the Portuguese institution to proceed against *conversos* suspected of "Judaizing" in the colonies. Until that time inquisitorial activity in Brazil had been minimal and many New Christians and Jews emigrated there to avoid persecution in Portugal, or paradoxically were exiled there by the Holy Office. From the very beginning of colonization, they had been instrumental in providing capital and developing enterprises, first in brazilwood, then sugar production, and finally gold mining in the eighteenth century. In 1591, the General Council of the Inquisition appointed Heitor Furtado de Mendonça to conduct the first Holy Office visitation (*visitação*) and he spent five years dispatching cases in the northeast provinces. In 1622, Philip IV ordered the creation of an autonomous tribunal in Brazil that never materialized, most likely because of opposition from Flemish interests in Pernambuco and Bahia, the Jesuits, and even the Holy Office itself, which preferred to maintain peninsular control over inquisitorial activity in the colony. Thus the Lisbon tribunal continued its vigilance through a combination of periodic Holy Office visitations, diocesan visitations conducted by bishops and ordinaries, and a network of commissaries and familiars, who identified and forwarded suspects to Portugal. Although inquisitors investigated a wide variety of offenses, most of the cases originating in Brazil involved New Christians, many of whom were denounced by "Old Christians" for purely economic or political reasons.

Inquisitional Activities and Offenses. Pursuing "Judaizing" *conversos* was also a priority for the new tribunals in Spanish America, as many Portuguese New Christians had entered Peru, New Spain, and New Granada during the period of the Iberian Union (1580–1640). In Mexico, there were two periods of heightened activity against *conversos.* The first came between 1585 and 1601, and was dominated by the prosecutions of members and associates of the Carvajal family. The second occurred from 1642 to the great autos-da-fé of 1647 and 1649, when the Holy Office arrested and tried hundreds of New Christians, fearing their subversion after Portugal's extrication from Spanish hegemony in 1640. In Peru, such activity steadily increased until peaking with the "Great Conspiracy" and the extraordinary 1639 auto-da-fé in Lima.

Protestantism, since the beginning of the Counter-Reformation, was considered especially dangerous and had been one of the primary reasons for establishing the American tribunals. Generically referring to it as the "heresy of Luther," the inquisitors made little distinction between Lutherans, Anglicans, Calvinists, and other sectarians and usually dealt with them all quite harshly. The condemned offenders included pirates, smugglers, and shipwreck victims captured on Iberian-American shores, French Huguenot interlopers (notably in Florida and Brazil), and English and German merchants who ventured, legally or illegally, into Spanish and Portuguese ports and cities in the New World. By the mid-seventeenth century, however, prosecutions of foreign Protestants had declined because of treaty obligations and pragmatic commercial concerns.

Inquisition officials also worried about blasphemy and the spread of various "heretical propositions" associated with Protestantism or other Old World movements. Common examples were denying the virginity of Mary, criticizing the veneration of saints and images, questioning the existence of Purgatory or the notion of original sin, claiming that the Mass had no significance or that excommunication offended God, or rejecting the sacrament of confession or the Eucharist. Blasphemy cases, ubiquitous throughout the colonial period, also included slaves who renounced their faith in the heat of being punished or mistreated by their masters. In terms of Old World movements, in addition to Erasmians, the Inquisitors were especially concerned with adherents of Spanish Illuminism and Quietism, who aspired to spiritual perfection through mystical reflection and direct union with God, because they often counseled others to forsake the Church's intercessory role. Moreover, believing they were incapable of sin in that direct union sometimes led to sexual transgressions. These *alumbrados,* many of them pious women (*beatas* and nuns), included mystics and visionaries, who issued prophecies and claimed to receive divine revelations. They were steadily prosecuted well into the eighteenth century, along with their followers and supporters, many of whom were members of the regular clergy. Inquisitors also tried clerics for other theological errors and a variety of offenses related to church discipline and the sacraments, such as improperly celebrating the Eucharist, marrying while in the consecrated state, or soliciting sex in the confessional.

The Holy Office also began to monitor familial and sexual morality, especially after the Council of Trent's pronouncements upholding the dissolubility of monogamous marriage and the prohibition of deviant moral behavior that was quite common in the New World. Bigamy, for example, was one of the most frequently tried offenses, surely reflecting the long distances, poor communications, and personal mobility in the Americas. Concubinage also thrived in the colonial environment, between conquistadores and Indian women, masters and slaves, native elites and subjects, and others preferring cohabitation to marriage. Although jurisdiction over adultery, fornication, and sodomy (at this time meaning any sexual activity not destined for procreation) traditionally resided with the civil authorities, the Holy Office increasingly intervened in cases it deemed to have heretical implications because they contradicted Tridentine decrees.

Thus inquisitors were often more interested in disciplining offenders for certain commonly held beliefs—such as fornication was not a sin, or living together was better than being in a bad marriage—than for the acts themselves.

Other inquisitorial activity related to the indigenous inhabitants and their Christian conversion. The evangelization of the Indians in the New World was uneven at best and often involved "guided syncretism," indigenization, and transculturation, which incorporated many native beliefs and practices, and "relapses" were common. When establishing the American tribunals, the Spanish Crown decided that the transgressions of these neophytes should not elicit the Holy Office's harsh sentences for heresy or apostasy, but rather more lenient responses from episcopal authorities acting as ordinaries. The Holy Office, nevertheless, continued to investigate Indian heterodoxy to gather evidence against the rest of the population who *were* under its jurisdiction. It turned its findings over to the episcopal courts, which had established their own special tribunals under various names (Provisorato de Indios, Tribunal de Naturales, Inquisición Ordinaria). Headed by the *provisor* or vicar general of the diocese, these Indian tribunals also employed inquisitorial methods, issued edicts of faith, held autos-da-fé, and meted out penitential sentences that included haircutting, flogging, incarceration, forced labor, and exile for offenses such as bigamy, concubinage, idolatry, superstition, and sorcery. In Peru, successive Lima archbishops, especially Pedro de Villagómez (1641–1671), augmented these tribunals with systematic extirpation campaigns in indigenous communities conducted by a *visitador* of idolatries. Throughout their existence, these episcopal tribunals often clashed with the Holy Office over jurisdictional matters, which became even more complicated when cases of Indian bigamy and polygamy were returned to its authority in 1766. In Brazil, baptized Indians had always remained under the Portuguese institution's jurisdiction. During the first visitation in Bahia, the *visitador* Furtado investigated a Tupi millenarian sect called Santidade that integrated elements of Catholicism, prophesied the end of slavery and the Portuguese, attacked colonial interests, and astonishingly enjoyed the protection of a powerful planter and sugar mill owner. In both Spanish and Portuguese America, however, the vast majority of inquisitorial cases concerned whites, blacks, *mestizos,* and other racial mixtures rather than the Indians.

By the seventeenth century, the population was becoming more diverse with increasing European immigration, continued importation of African slaves, and a rising number of American-born whites, *mestizos,* and other miscegenational combinations. In this dynamic biological and social environment a vibrant and fluid popular culture emerged in which African, American Indian, and European beliefs and practices were creatively combined in ways that deviated from the orthodoxy that the Holy Office was entrusted to maintain. This was especially apparent in the genre of cases the inquisitors variably classified as superstition, sorcery (*hechicería/feitiçaria*), or witchcraft (*brujería/bruxaria*), which involved male and female practitioners of all racial backgrounds. This activity included astrology, fortunetelling, necromancy, and other forms of divination, the healing practices of *curanderismo,* the use of magic, spells, curses, charms, bundles, talismans, and potions for protection or to elicit desired effects, and the use of peyote, mushrooms, coca, and other psychoactive substances to induce visions, revelations, and prophecies. Early on, the inquisitors vigorously pursued such offenses as true heresies thinking they were dealing with supernatural powers linked to the devil, but years later when this activity had grown beyond all control, their interest waned as they increasingly attributed these cases to chicanery and ignorance among the lower classes.

By the late seventeenth century, inquisitional activity had already peaked and was in a state of decline. In Spanish America, a shift occurred around mid-century as cases of major heresies such as "Judaizing" and Protestantism gave way to lesser offenses among the clergy and the masses, resulting in diminishing revenue in fines and confiscations for the Holy Office and fewer and less elaborate autos-da-fé. During the eighteenth century, although bigamy and solicitation still dominated the docket, the institution started to take on a more political character as Spain's Bourbon monarchs sought to defend royal absolutism from liberal republicanism. The Index of Prohibited Books, begun in 1559, was now burgeoning with works from the Enlightenment, which inquisitors tried to suppress by monitoring imports, presses, booksellers, and private collectors. In the latter half of the century, cases citing "disloyalty to the Crown," sedition, Freemasonry, materialism, or republicanism as heretical offenses began to appear and during the turbulent years of popular uprisings and independence wars the Holy Office sided with the royalists. Nevertheless, after years of bitter financial and jurisdictional disputes, even the local royal authorities showed little sympathy when the Spanish Inquisition was suppressed in 1813 and definitively abolished in 1820. In Brazil, after some late activity involving *conversos* in Minas Gerais, the last Holy Office visitation occurred in 1763, several decades before the liberal Portuguese Constituent Assembly dissolved the institution in 1821.

BIBLIOGRAPHY

There is no comprehensive, combined treatment of Spanish and Portuguese inquisitorial activity in the New World. Most scholarship, with the notable exception of *The Inquisitors and Jews in the New World* (Coral Gables, Fl., 1974) and other works by Seymour B. Liebman, focuses on one or the other empire.

For Spanish activity, the pioneering works of Chilean historian José Toribio Medina should still be consulted. His *Historia del Tribunal del Santo Oficio de la Inquisición de Lima* (Santiago, 1887), . . . *en Chile* (Santiago, 1890), . . . *de Cartagena de las Indias* (Santiago, 1899), . . . *en las provincias del Plata* (Santiago, 1899), and . . . *en México* (Santiago, 1905) represent the first systematic treatments of the Inquisition in these areas and have reappeared in subsequent editions with useful retrospective introductions by leading scholars. Another important early synthesis is found in Henry Charles Lea's *The Inquisition in the Spanish Dependencies* (New York, 1908), which emphasizes the institution's jurisdictional conflicts, financial corruption, and inhibiting effect on intellectual development. The apostolic, episcopal, and monastic activities before the arrival of the first permanent tribunals are covered in Medina's *La primitiva inquisición americana, 1493–1569* (Santiago, Chile, 1914), a topic that Álvaro Huerga has reexamined in "La pre-inquisición hispanoamericana, 1516–1568," in *Historia de la Inquisición en España y América,* edited by J. Pérez Villanueva and B. Escandell Bonet (Madrid, 1984–2000), vol. 1, pp. 662–700. This three-volume set contains other useful essays concerning general historiography, documentary sources, administrative and economic structures, and regional activities of the Holy Office in the Spanish colonies. Additional scholarship along these and other lines is found in *Cultural Encounters: The Impact of the Inquisition in Spain and the New World,* edited by Mary Elizabeth Perry and Anne J. Cruz (Berkeley, Calif., 1991), and *Women in the Inquisition: Spain and the New World,* edited by Mary E. Giles (Baltimore, Md., 1998).

Within Spanish America, New Spain has received the most attention owing to the survival of nearly all the records generated by the Mexico City tribunal. Richard E. Greenleaf's "Historiography of the Mexican Inquisition: Evolution of Interpretations and Methodologies," in *Cultural Encounters,* pp. 248–276, provides a good overview of this scholarship, and his *Zumárraga and the Mexican Inquisition, 1536–1543* (Washington, D.C., 1961) and *The Mexican Inquisition in the Sixteenth Century* (Albuquerque, 1969) cover early activity. Inga Clendinnen examines Landa's monastic inquisition in *Ambivalent Conquests: Maya and Spaniard in Yucatan, 1517–1570* (Cambridge, U.K., 1987). On Mesoamericans, the Holy Office, and the Provisorato, see Greenleaf's "The Inquisition and the Indians of New Spain: A Study in Jurisdictional Confusion," *The Americas* 22, no. 2 (1965): 138–166. Solange Alberro offers a broad synthesis and statistical analysis of the most active phase of the Mexican tribunal in *Inquisition et société au Mexique, 1571–1700* (Mexico City, 1988), also available in a Spanish translation of the same year. For the later period, see "The Inquisition in Eighteenth-Century Mexico," *The Americas* 22, no. 2 (1965): 167–181, by Lewis A. Tambs, and Ruth Behar's "Sex and Sin, Witchcraft and the Devil in Late-Colonial Mexico," *American Ethnologist* 14, no. 1 (1987): 34–54. The two-volume *Inquisición novohispana,* edited by Noemí Quezada, Martha Eugenia Rodríguez, and Marcela Suárez (Mexico City, 2000), presents a diverse sampling of research at the close of the millennium.

Concerning other Spanish-American areas, Carlos Esteban Deive studies Caribbean activity in *Heterodoxia e inquisición en Santo Domingo, 1492–1822* (Santo Domingo, Dominican Republic, 1983). For the Cartagena tribunal, see Fermina Álvarez Alonso's *La Inquisición en Cartagena de Indias durante el siglo XVII* (Madrid, 1999) and Anna María Splendiani's four-volume *Cincuenta años de Inquisición en el Tribunal de Cartagena de Indias, 1610–1660* (Bogotá, Colombia, 1997). On the Lima tribunal, see the three-volume *La Inquisición de Lima, 1569–1820* (Madrid, 1989–1998) by Paulino Castañeda Delgado, Pilar Hernández Aparicio, and René Millar Carvacho. The extirpation campaigns in Peru are examined by Kenneth Mills in *Idolatry and Its Enemies: Colonial Andean Religion and Extirpation, 1640–1750* (Princeton, N.J., 1997).

For Brazil, Sonia A. Siqueira's *A inquisição portuguesa e a sociedade colonial* (São Paulo, Brazil, 1978) provides a good institutional overview. Denunciations and confessions from the first visitation have appeared in several editions, the most recent being *Denunciações e Confissões de Pernambuco, 1593–1595,* edited by José António Gonsalves de Mello (Recife, Brazil, 1984), and *Confissões da Bahia,* edited by Ronaldo Vainfas (São Paulo, Brazil, 1997). Vainfas reconstructs a native millenarian movement from inquisition documents in *A heresia dos índios: catolicismo e rebeldia no Brasil colonial* (São Paulo, Brazil, 1995) and looks at sexual morality and the institution in *Trópico dos pecados: moral, sexualidade e Inquisição no Brasil* (Rio de Janeiro, Brazil, 1997). Regional studies of New Christians and the Inquisition include José Gonçalves Salvador's *Cristãos-novos, Jesuítas e Inquisição: aspectos de sua atuação nas capitanias do Sul, 1530–1680* (São Paulo, Brazil, 1969), Anita Novinsky's *Cristãos novos na Bahia* (São Paulo, Brazil, 1972), and Neusa Fernandes's *A Inquisição em Minas Gerais no século XVIII* (Rio de Janeiro, Brazil, 2000). Geraldo Pieroni provides an interesting study of Portuguese penitents exiled to Brazil in *Os excluídos do reino: a Inquisição portuguesa e o degredo para o Brasil colônia* (São Paulo, Brazil, 2000).

Scott Sessions (2005)

INSECTS appear in mythology not only as the gods, often as the creators of the world, but also as messengers to the gods. They serve sometimes as the agents of creation and frequently function as symbols of the human soul. Moreover, some insects, such as cicadas, beetles, and scarabs, often symbolize rebirth, resurrection, or eternal life.

According to the Lengua, a South American tribe of the Gran Chaco, a god in the shape of a huge beetle created the world and peopled it with mighty spirits. He holds aloof, however, from his creation and is not invoked in prayer. The butterfly is often worshiped as a god, sometimes as the creator. In Madagascar and among the Naga of Manipur, some trace their ancestry to a butterfly. According to the Pima of North America, at the time of beginning the creator, Chiowotmahki, assumed the form of a butterfly and flew over the world until he found a suitable place for humankind.

It is, however, the spider that plays a prominent part in the myths of North American Indians; it appears as the creator (e.g., among the Sia Pueblo Indians) or culture hero, or at least as the trickster (among the Dakota Indians). The Jicarilla Apache believe that at the time of beginning, when creatures lived in the underworld, the spider spun a web in the hole leading up to the earth and, together with the fly, came up on it before the people emerged. The spider and the fly were told by the Holy Ones to make a web and extend it to the sky in order to bring down the sun. According to the Navajo, Spider Man and Spider Woman are supernatural beings who instructed their mythical ancestors in the art of weaving and established the four warnings of death. The spider is also conspicuous in West African myths. In some myths, he is creator of the world; in others, he plays the role of culture hero, as in the stories in which he steals the sun. However, his usual role is that of a crafty and cunning trickster who prospers by his wits.

In Hindu mythology, ants are compared to a series of Indras. One day Indra in his palace receives a visit from a boy dressed in rags, who is Viṣṇu in disguise. While the boy speaks of the innumerable Indras who people the innumerable universes, a procession of ants appears in the great hall of the palace. Noticing them, the boy suddenly stops and bursts into laughter. "What are you laughing at?" asks Indra. The boy replies, "I saw the ants, O Indra, filing in long parade. Each was once an Indra. Like you, by virtue of pious deeds each one ascended to the rank of a king of the gods. But now, through many rebirths, each has become again an ant. This army is an army of former Indras."

In West Africa, ants are often viewed as the high god's messengers. In the Romanian creation myth, the bee serves as God's messenger. It also helps God to complete his creation with advice that it overhears from the hedgehog. Although the angry hedgehog puts a curse on it, condemning it to eat only ordure, God blesses the bee so that the filth it eats may become honey.

The bee is still an important symbol in Islam. The Qurʾān explicitly mentions it as a model of an "inspired" animal, and both Muḥammad and, even more, ʿAlī are connected in folklore with the pious and useful bee. Honey becomes sweet, it is said, because the bees hum blessings for the Prophet as they go about their work.

In some earth-diver myths, which speak of the origin of the earth from the primordial waters, insects serve as agents of creation. According to the Garo of Assam, the goddess Nosta-Nōpantu was to carry out the work of creation on behalf of the god Tattaro-Robuga. To get a particle of soil from the bottom of the primeval ocean, she sent in turn a large crab, a small crab, and a dung beetle. Only the dung beetle succeeded in bringing up a little clay, and from this Nosta-Nōpantu formed the earth. The Semang Negritos of the Malay Peninsula (such as the Menik Kaien, Kintak Bong, and Kenta tribes) similarly believe that the earth was brought up from the primeval ocean by a dung beetle, although in this version the insect seems to have dived on its own initiative. Among the Shan of Burma, the divers are ants. In North America, too, insects are known as earth divers among the Cherokee. In contrast to earth-diver myths are stories that speak of the celestial origin of the earth—as in the Indonesian and Micronesian cosmogonies—and in these myths, too, insects play an important role. The Toba and the Batak of Sumatra, for example, have preserved the tradition that a swallow and a large dung beetle brought down a handful of earth from the sky.

While bees, ants, and dragonflies often symbolize the souls of the dead, the image of the butterfly as the human soul is widely diffused in Europe, Asia, and the Pacific islands. The early Greeks sometimes depicted the soul as a diminutive person with butterfly wings, and later as a butterfly. A similar belief was shared by the Romans. The Maori of New Zealand believe that the soul returns to earth after death as a butterfly, and in the Solomon Islands a dying person, who has a choice as to what he will become at death, often chooses to become a butterfly. In Japan, the motif has been incorporated into *nō* dramas, and in the world of Islam, it is one of the favorite images of Sufism: The moth that immolates itself in the candle flame is the soul losing itself in the divine fire.

The cicada, on account of its metamorphosis, was well known in ancient China as a symbol of rebirth or renewal of life. According to the Arawak of Guyana, at the time of beginning the creator came down to earth to see how humankind was getting along. But humans were so wicked that they tried to kill him; so he deprived them of eternal life and bestowed it instead on animals that renew their skin, such as serpents, lizards, and beetles. In ancient Egypt the scarab, a beetle of the Mediterranean region, was identified with the sun god Khepri and thus became a symbol both of the force that rolled the sun across the heavens and of the rising sun, self-generated. Scarab amulets made of green stone set in gold were placed over the heart of the dead during the funeral ceremony as a sign that just as the sun was reborn, so would the soul of the deceased be born again.

Insects are not always viewed as beneficent creatures. According to Northwest Coast Indians such as the Tlingit, the Haida, and the Tsimshian, mosquitoes are pests that originated from the ashes of an ogre's burned body. The same motif is found among the Ainu and in southern China. In Japanese mythology, spiders appear as a symbol of the evil forces that were subjugated by the heavenly gods before the imperial dynasty—and with it, Japan—was established.

See Also Tricksters.

Bibliography

On insects playing a role in cosmogonic myths, see Mircea Eliade's *Zalmoxis, the Vanishing God: Comparative Studies in the Religions and Folklore of Dacia and Eastern Europe* (Chicago, 1972), pp. 76–130. See also Charles H. Long's *Alpha: The Myths of Creation* (New York, 1963), pp. 44ff. There is a fine study of scarab symbolism in the Greco-Roman world in *Fish, Bread, and Wine,* volume 5 of Erwin R. Goodenough's *Jewish Symbols in the Greco-Roman Period* (New York, 1956), pp. 172ff. Schuyler Cammann discusses the symbolism of the cicada in his very useful essay "Types of Symbols in Chinese Art," in *Studies in Chinese Thought,* edited by Arthur F. Wright (Chicago, 1953). On the origin of mosquitoes, see Gudmund Hatt's *Asiatic Influences in American Folklore* (Copenhagen, 1949), pp. 89–90. On the Islamic symbolism of insects, there is an admirable study in Annemarie Schimmel's *The Triumphal Sun: A Study of the Works of Jalaloddin Rumi,* rev. ed. (London, 1980), pp. 108ff.

New Sources

Cherry, R. H. "Insects in the Mythology of Native Americans." *Entomology* 39 (1993): 16–21.

Gosling, David L. *Religion and Ecology in India and Southeast Asia.* New York, 2003.

Hoyt, Erich. *The Earth Dwellers: Adventures in the Land of Ants.* New York, 1996.

Hoyt, Erich, and Ted Schulz. *Insect Lives: Stories of Mystery and Romance from a Hidden World.* New York, 1999.

Lauck, Joanne Elizabeth. *The Voice of the Infinite in the Small: Re-Visioning the Insect-Human Connection.* Boston, 2002.

MANABU WAIDA (1987)
Revised Bibliography

INSPIRATION. As it appears in the general history of religions, *inspiration* may be defined very broadly as a spiritual influence that occurs spontaneously and renders a person capable of thinking, speaking, or acting in ways that transcend ordinary human capacities. Taken in this general sense, the term refers to a form of religious experience that is widely distributed and found in a great variety of forms. Taken more narrowly, the actual term (which derives from the Latin *inspirare,* "to blow or breath upon") implies the existence of a *spiritus,* or "breath," that is breathed into the soul and enlivens it. Although inspiration may often be conceived in this way, its specificity as a religious phenomenon should not be located in an explicit notion of spiritual breath or divine spirit, because such a notion may be absent in cases where one would still wish to speak of inspiration. In such cases, inspiration may be attributed to the direct action of a god, or even to the effects of a particular kind of food or drink. What is common to most forms of inspiration is its efficacy as an influence that motivates or facilitates action, very often in the form of inspired speech or song. An understanding of inspiration is thus closely related to questions of human agency and its transcendence.

The use of the term *inspiration* should probably be restricted to those cases where human agency is transformed but not totally displaced. This would make it possible to contrast inspiration with trance, because in the latter, human agency is simply canceled out, to be replaced in most cases by the action of a possessing god, spirit, or ancestor. The notion of possession itself, however, which need not always imply a state of trance, can sometimes be used to account for particularly intense experiences of inspiration. The essential point is that inspiration never leads to a state of complete dissociation of the personality and subsequent amnesia, as is the case with trance.

One of the earliest historical forms of inspiration is that experienced by the *ṛṣis,* or poet-seers, of the *Ṛgveda.* In composing their liturgical hymns, the *ṛṣis* often invoked their gods to inspire their songs. The gods Mitra and Varuṇa, the Aśvins, and in particular the god Agni were asked to stimulate the visions of the seers, to animate or impel their speech, and to set their songs in motion. The verbs used in these contexts convey a sense of power: *cud-* ("to impel, animate"); *tuj-* ("to strike, instigate"); *hi-* ("to set in motion, urge on"). One of the most famous verses in the *Ṛgveda* (3.62.10), the so-called Gāyatrī, is in fact a prayer addressed to the god Savitṛ, asking for such inspiration, a verse that is recited daily by traditional Hindus. This example of the inspiration of the Vedic seers may be taken as representative of the phenomenon of inspiration among the ancient Indo-European peoples generally. This is illustrated most clearly by the Indo-European root **vat-* ("to blow," or more figuratively, "to inspire"). This root not only appears in the *Ṛgveda* and *Avesta* but also underlies the Latin word *vates* ("seer, prophet, poet") and the Old Irish term *fáith* ("prophet, seer").

The Vedic seers also sought inspiration by drinking a special beverage called soma, which was used in the Vedic sacrifice. Here again one finds Indo-European parallels, both in the *haoma* found in ancient Iran, and in the legendary mead of the ancient Scandinavians, a drink that was believed to make anyone who drank it a poet or a visionary.

Whatever its exact source, inspiration is experienced as an impulse that either comes from without, or, if it arises within, does so spontaneously, in independence of the individual's will. In principle this trait distinguishes it from the ecstatic experience that is the defining characteristic of shamanism, because once initiated the shaman is capable of acting on his own and controlling the inhabitants of the spirit world for his own ends. This autonomy is what gives shamans their importance as "technicians of the sacred." The inspired person is by contrast much more dependent upon a continuing source of inspiration.

In classical India an experience of spontaneous inspiration was sometimes referred to as *pratibhā,* a "flash" of insight that arose in an inexplicable way, free of any intentional cognitive act on the part of the subject. In Indian poetics, *pratibhā* became a common term for poetic inspiration. In early Mahāyāna Buddhism, it took on a distinctly religious value, referring to the inspired speech uttered spontaneously by a disciple in praise of the Buddha. It is, however, in later Hindu devotionalism (*bhakti*) that are found the most striking Indian examples of inspiration. In inspired states that are often hard to distinguish from states of possession, the devotees of Viṣṇu and Śiva (the Āḻvārs and Nayanars) composed thousands of hymns in honor of their god. One of the greatest of these, the Vaiṣṇava poet-saint Nammāḻvār (9th–10th century CE), spoke of being taken over by Viṣṇu, such that Viṣṇu himself sang through his mouth (*Tiruvāymoḻi* 7.9.1).

The connection of inspiration with poetry and song was also recognized in ancient Greece, where poets sought the inspiration of the Muses, much as their Indian counterparts might pray to Sarasvatī, the goddess of eloquence. Plato describes the inspiration of the Muses as a form of mania ("madness or frenzy") and makes the poet's art wholly dependent upon it. It is because the poet's mind is "taken away" by the gods that the reader knows that it is the gods who speak and not the poet himself. Poets are "simply inspired to utter that to which the Muse impels them" (*Ion* 534).

Poetic inspiration was not the only type of mania that Plato recognized, however. In the *Phaedrus* (265a–b) he distinguishes four different types: Besides the poetic mania of the Muses there are also prophetic, telestic (ritual), and erotic forms of mania. All save the telestic are described as forms of inspiration (*epipnoia*). In many respects the most important of these was prophetic or mantic inspiration, the type given by Apollo for purposes of divination, and most important in connection with the Delphic oracle. Although the famed "frenzy" of the Pythia at Delphi has been shown to be largely a product of the literary imagination (Lucian's in particular), there is no doubt that she was at all periods believed to be genuinely inspired by the god Apollo. Mention should also be made of those enigmatic, quasi-legendary figures of antiquity, the sibyls. Their inspired oracles were collected and consulted at Rome, while many later Christians looked upon some of them as pre-Christian prophecies of Christ.

The fact that Plato classified both poetic and prophetic inspiration as forms of madness is indicative of the Greek tendency to view inspiration in terms of possession, a tendency already noted in South India, and which is very widespread among tribal cultures the world over. Inspiration as a form of mania is conceived of as a manifestation of *enthousiasmos,* literally the presence of a god within the inspired person, that is, possession. It shall be seen that this theory exerted an important influence on some early Jewish and Christian theories of inspiration, only later to be rejected.

In the ancient Near East inspiration was closely associated with the phenomenon of prophecy. In its earliest form, the Near Eastern prophet served primarily as a counselor of the chief or king, giving advice in the form of inspired oracles. His role was distinguished from that of the cultic priest by the fact that the latter employed technical means of divination while the prophet relied primarily on inspiration. The more familiar figure of the prophet as the inspired critic of both king and cult derives from the later history of prophecy in Israel, where the prophet became the divinely elected spokesman of Yahveh. The ecstatic behavior and utterances of prophets such as Saul, Elijah, and Elisha were the effect of the powerful spirit (*ruaḥ*) of God. In the later, so-called classical prophets the experience of inspiration is less violent and takes on the character of a close personal encounter.

In general the role of the prophet in this more familiar noncultic sense and the nature of inspiration as a religious phenomenon seem to be very intimately connected. The spontaneity and dynamism that characterizes inspiration achieve an almost paradigmatic realization in the figure of the itinerant prophet, who feels free to confront the established centers of power in the name of his god. It is surely not by chance that some of the clearest instances of inspiration among the peoples of Africa are found among the African tribal prophets who have appeared since the end of the nineteenth century in struggles against foreign domination. Prophetic inspiration, in one form or another, has historically been an important factor in a large number of nationalistic, nativistic, and resistance movements.

The experience of inspiration in the early Christian communities was interpreted as the outpouring of the Spirit predicted by the prophet Joel, and was dramatically symbolized by the descent of the Holy Spirit in a rush of wind and in tongues of fire at Pentecost (*Acts* 2). The inspiration of the Spirit brought with it a variety of ecstatic experiences, which included speaking in tongues and a revival of prophecy. In the light of such experiences, and given the Christian belief in the divinity of the Holy Spirit, it is not surprising that some early Christians found theories of inspiration congenial that were hardly distinguishable from theories of possession. Thus the apologist Athenagoras could say that the Spirit made use of the prophet as a flute player makes use of a flute. Justin Martyr also seems to have had a "mantic" view of inspiration. Such theories may well have derived from Philo Judaeus, who explicitly ascribed scriptural prophecy to divine possession, in this undoubtedly being influenced by Plato. As a whole, however, the Christian tradition resisted such notions, and from the time of Origen on affirmed the importance of the active involvement of the inspired subject.

The Christian theological concept of the Holy Spirit as a divine person gave the concept of inspiration a theological importance that it could not have in either Judaism or Islam, where the strong sense of divine immanence implied in such a notion was viewed with suspicion. This is made clear by the role ascribed to inspiration in the constitution of the scriptures of these three religions. While affirming the supreme authority of the Torah, the rabbis denied that it was inspired. Rather it was given directly to Moses by God verbatim. The intervention of an inspired author would have served only to weaken its authority. Only the Prophets and the Writings could properly be described as inspired. Similarly in Islam, a clear distinction is drawn between revelation (*waḥy*), which is applied to the *verbatim* transmission of the Qurʾān to Muḥammad through the angel Gabriel, and inspiration (*ilhām*), which is restricted to the inspiration of individuals on matters that are of primarily personal concern. In Christianity, by contrast, it is precisely the concept of inspiration that is traditionally invoked to account for the authoritativeness of scripture.

This should not be taken to mean, however, that the concept of inspiration is unimportant in either Judaism or Islam. The rabbinical notion of the *ruaḥ ha-qodesh* (lit., "holy spirit"), while not to be confused with the Christian notion, nevertheless fulfills some of the same functions. It was used by the rabbis to explain prophetic inspiration, and was also believed to be present to holy souls, and in particular to those who taught the Torah in public. According to a Midrash, "All that the righteous do, they do with the power of *ruaḥ ha-qodesh*" (*Tanḥumaʾ Va-yeḥi* 13).

In Islam the fact that the revelation made to Muḥammad is distinguished from the inspiration received by the individual believer should not prevent anyone from recognizing in Muḥammad an inspired prophet. Nor can one fail to note the similarity between the oracular structure of some of the earliest *sūrahs* of the Qurʾān and the inspired oracles encountered elsewhere in the history of religions, in particular among the *kāhin,* or soothsayers, of pre-Islamic Arabia.

The later Ṣūfīs recognized the validity of another type of ecstatic utterance, called *shaṭḥ,* which they believed to be divinely inspired. The saying of al-Hallāj, "Anā al-ḥaqq" ("I am the Truth"), is probably the most famous of such utterances, but one that unfortunately encouraged misunderstandings that eventually led to his death. Inspiration did not always take such a dramatic form, however. The experience of *ilhām* remained an essentially inner experience that was believed to be authoritative only for the saintly soul who received it as a gift from God.

These few examples must suffice to illustrate the variety of ways in which inspiration has been experienced from the earliest times down to the present day. Throughout human history are found such examples of men and women who are open to a form of experience that ultimately defies any attempts to explain, or even understand. Friedrich Nietzsche put it beautifully, in describing his own personal experience of inspiration: "One hears—one does not seek; one takes—one does not ask who gives: a thought suddenly flashes up like lightning, it comes with necessity, unhesitatingly—I have never had any choice in the matter" (Nietzsche, 1954).

SEE ALSO Beverages; Enthusiasm; Glossolalia; Oracles; Prophecy; Shamanism; Sibylline Oracles; Spirit Possession.

BIBLIOGRAPHY

A broad view of inspiration in its variety of forms in the history of religions is provided by N. Kershaw Chadwick's *Poetry and Prophecy* (Cambridge, U.K., 1942) and Edwyn Robert Bevan's *Sibyls and Seers: A Survey of Some Ancient Theories of Revelation and Inspiration* (London, 1928). A more recent work by Gilbert Rouget, *Music and Trance: A Theory of the Relations between Music and Possession* (Chicago, 1985), while dealing primarily with possession trance, does have some interesting things to say about inspiration and is to be recommended.

Much information on inspired poets among Indo-European peoples can be found in *Indogermanische Dichtersprache,* edited by Rüdiger Schmitt (Darmstadt, 1968), although this book is aimed at the trained philologist. For a more accessible sampling of the hymns of the Vedic *ṛṣis,* see Wendy Doniger O'Flaherty's *The Rig Veda* (Harmondsworth, U.K., 1981). The inspired speech of the Mahāyāna Buddhists is discussed by Graeme MacQueen in "Inspired Speech in Early Mahāyāna Buddhism," *Religion* 11 (1981): 303–319 and 12 (1982): 49–65. On Nammāḻvār, see A. K. Ramanujan's *Hymns for the Drowning: Poems for Viṣṇu by Nammāḻvār* (Princeton, N.J., 1981), especially the very helpful afterword.

For a general view of inspiration among the Greeks, see E. R. Dodds's *The Greeks and the Irrational* (Berkeley, Calif., 1951). A more recent work by Joseph Fontenrose, *The Delphic Oracle* (Berkeley, Calif., 1978), proposes a fundamental revision of traditional views of the inspiration of the Pythia at Delphi. On the inspiration of the Muses, one may consult Eike Barmeyer's *Die Musen: Ein Beitrag zur Inspirationstheorie* (Munich, 1968).

A wealth of information on inspiration among the Greeks, Hebrews, and early Christians can be found in the article on *pneuma* in the *Theological Dictionary of the New Testament,* edited by Gerhard Kittel (Grand Rapids, Mich., 1968). Johannes Lindblom's *Prophecy in Ancient Israel* (Philadelphia, 1962) is also a rich resource. Johannes Pedersen's short study, "The Role Played by Inspired Persons among the Israelites and the Arabs," in *Studies in Old Testament Prophecy* (Edinburgh, 1950), is helpful for the attention it gives to early Arabic sources. For rabbinical theories of inspiration, see Paul Billerbeck's "Der Kanon des Alten Testaments und seine Inspiration," excursus 16 of the *Kommentar zum Neuen Testament aus Talmud und Midrasch,* by Hermann L. Strack and Paul Billerbeck (Munich, 1928). For inspiration in Islam, see Fazlur Rahman's *Prophecy in Islam: Philosophy and Orthodoxy* (London, 1958), Annemarie Schimmel's *Mystical Dimensions of Islam* (Chapel Hill, N.C., 1975), and the articles on *waḥy, ilhām,* and *shaṭḥ* in the *Shorter Encyclopaedia of Islam,* edited by H. A. R. Gibb and J. H. Kramers (Leiden, 1974).

Friedrich Nietzsche's account of his own experience of inspiration while engaged in writing his *Thus Spake Zarathustra* was included by his sister in her introduction to that work and is reproduced in the Modern Library edition of Nietzsche's major works, *The Philosophy of Nietzsche* (New York, 1954), pp. xix–xxxiii.

New Sources

Alexander, Anna, and Mark Roberts. *High Culture: Reflections on Addiction and Modernity.* Albany, N.Y., 2003.

Anthony, Brian Patrick. "Nature's Cathedral; The Union of Theology and Ecology in the Writings of John Muir." *Ecotheology* 7 (July 2002): 74–81.

Berger, Michael S. *Rabbinic Authority.* New York, 1998.

Pearce, Joseph. *Literary Converts: Spiritual Inspiration in an Age of Unbelief.* San Francisco, 1999.

Schniedewind, William Michael. *The Word of God in Transition: From Prophet to Exegete in the Second Temple Period.* Sheffield, U.K., 1995.

DAVID CARPENTER (1987)
Revised Bibliography

INTELLECTUALS are persons who produce or intensively study intellectual works. Intellectual works are coherent complexes of symbolic configurations that deal with the serious or ultimately significant features of the cosmos, the earth, and human beings. An intellectual work is unified by logical connectedness and the substantive identity of its subject matter, and it is set forth in a conventional form.

Religious intellectual works are those that deal with transcendent powers and their verbal, physical, and inspirational manifestations. They deal with the relations of transcendent powers to texts that are regarded as sacred, and with the influence of transcendent powers in the genesis and working of the cosmos, in human life and destiny, and in the norms that guide human action.

Religious activities, both intellectual and practical (i.e., religious practices), have as their objective the engendering or maintaining of a state of belief that comprises a relationship to transcendent powers. Religious intellectual activities, embodying this particular state of mind or belief, aim at attaining and transmitting knowledge or understanding of transcendent powers and their manifestations. The attainment of a religious state of mind encompasses practices such as the performance of prescribed rituals, the incantation of sacred songs, the reiteration of sacred words, and the ingestion, handling, and bearing of sacred objects. Such practical religious activities are infused with symbolic components and are hence intimately related to the intellectual religious activities that have constructed their underlying symbolic configurations. The intellectual elucidation of the meaning of practical religious activities and objects creates an intimate bond between the intellectual and practical spheres of religious activity.

Bodies of religious beliefs and practices differ, however, in the degree to which beliefs and practices have been elaborated and rationalized. Religions that are built around sacred texts are more susceptible to an elaborate variety of interpretations than are those that have no sacred texts. These elaborate interpretations are possible only on the basis of prolonged and intensive study by religious intellectuals who study the religious intellectual works that are central to the complex of beliefs espoused by the religious community and who produce works of their own.

"Primordial" and "World" Religions. Not all religious communities, that is, communities with common religious beliefs and practices, cultivate or depend upon intellectuals. The majority of these religions without intellectuals are primordial religions, that is, the religions of societies that define themselves by locality and lineage and in which no written texts contain their fundamental ideas. Such religions have beliefs and ritual practices, but they do not have doctrines. Their religious beliefs remain centered on local, occasional, and functional deities. Their rituals often have been codified, as was the case with Roman religion, and they sometimes have developed priesthoods as distinct professional strata; but, having no sacred books, they generally have no religious intellectuals to construct doctrines that could become integrally connected with their ritual observances. The larger, differentiated, and literate societies that continue to adhere to their primordial religions have produced intellectuals, including religious intellectuals, but the latter have had no ecclesiastical role. In these societies, such as those of ancient Greece and Rome, the construction of theological-philosophical theories has been left to laymen whose theories remained outside the realm of religious practice and influence.

Both in theory and in fact, however, the line dividing primordial religions from "world" or "universal" religions, that is, doctrinal religions that have acquired their doctrines through the work of religious intellectuals, cannot be precisely delineated. A primordial religion could in principle acquire an intellectual constituent. Its mythological pantheon could be rationalized and its rituals given a more pronouncedly transcendent reference; its magical procedures could be given a more explicit symbolic interpretation. World religions contain much that has been taken from the primordial religions that were indigenous to the territories from which they emerged or into which they entered. Yet no primordial religions that were indigenous to the territories from which they emerged or into which they entered can be turned into world religions without sacred or canonical texts and without intellectuals to construct doctrine from these texts.

Doctrine. The world religions have been primarily doctrinal religions in which articles are defined and ritual observances prescribed; belief and observance are required of members. Buddhism, Christianity, and Islam are unqualifiedly such religions. Confucianism has no primordial qualifications: It is open to all who can study the classical texts. In Hinduism, one is in principle a Hindu by being born into a Hindu caste, but it is also a religion centered around sacred writings and the rituals prescribed in the sacred writings. In this respect, Judaism is also in a marginal position. It is certainly a religion of doctrines insofar as it has a tradition contained in a sacred text and elaborated by commentary, but it is also a primordial religion: A Jew is one who is born of Jewish parents. Nevertheless, both of these world religions, despite this primordial element, have allowed prominent places to religious intellectuals.

Although the world religions, once established, recruit their members from among the offspring of their existing members, in order for transmission and expansion to occur, there must be a doctrine that is susceptible to simplification and exposition. Even if the founder of the religion is, in Max Weber's terms, an "exemplary" rather than an "ethical" prophet, this exemplification has to be transformed into expoundable and teachable doctrine as a condition of its expansion. The doctrine is precipitated into intellectual works; the construction of this doctrine is the accomplishment of religious intellectuals.

Primordial religions have expanded territorially with the movement of their adherents, but they have not expanded to become the religions of entire societies to which they were not indigenous. Having no doctrines, they could not become world religions.

The combination of the written works, commentary, and systematic speculations of religious intellectuals has given to the world religions an influence in world history that the fragmentary, unwritten, and inchoate beliefs of the devotees of primordial religions could not achieve. The self-confidence of the propagators of the world religions within and outside the societies of their origin has rested, in part, on the collective consciousness of participation in a system of beliefs that answers urgent ultimate questions. It was difficult for the devotees of doctrineless religions to stand up against the forceful proclamations and denunciations of a world religion that possessed an elaborated and rationalized doctrine. To the charismatic force of the prophetic founder and his sacred text was added the derivative charismatic force of an elaborated doctrine that expanded the concentrated and intense charisma of the founder. Local primordial religions fell before the expansion of the world religions pushing outward from their centers of origin.

In contrast, world religions have been resistant to one another's expansion. The Chinese, for example, were fortified by the intellectually elaborated outlooks of Confucianism and Buddhism against the intellectual argument of Christian missionaries. The expansion of world religions has been made primarily at the expense of primordial religions that have had no significant intellectual rationalization to resist attacks from an intellectually elaborated world religion. As world religions have expanded, the primordial religions, as visible collective entities, have been all but obliterated. They have survived within this expansion only through their unacknowledged assimilation. Their traditions were powerful enough to survive in fragmentary form, but they were not sufficiently rationalized to be able to survive as recognizable wholes.

Tradition and Originality. An affirmative attitude toward a particular tradition is inherent in the activities of religious intellectuals, because they claim to carry forward sets of beliefs that rest on the revelations of a founder, or a divinely engendered sacred text, or both. Religious intellectuals are committed to a tradition that continues, with some attenuation, the sacrality of the founding moment or period in the past. All subsequent truths must be demonstrably continuous with that sacred past event or sequence of events.

Originality in the world religions is admitted only for the founder of the religion or for the sacred scriptures in which the founder serves as the voice of a transcendent power. This conception of the originating sacredness of a body of scriptures does not acknowledge any subsequent originality by the religious intellectuals who take upon themselves the responsibility for expounding and interpreting them.

Prophetic—charismatic, founding, and renewing—originality is acknowledged in most world religions. Interpretative rationalizing originality is not acknowledged as originality. Yet originality does occur within the traditions of Buddhism and in the work of Jewish rabbis, Roman Catholic and Protestant theologians, Islamic theologians and Hindu philosophers. It is not, however, regarded as originality. It is treated either as clarification of unchanging doctrine or it is rejected as heretical. In addition to rationalizing interpretative originality, there is in the world religions the originality of the mystic who, while affirming his acceptance of the most fundamental objects of the religion, breaks out of the constraints of rationalized theological doctrine and routine ritual.

Religious intellectuals are not less creative or less original than secular intellectuals who produce works of science, literature, and art that are appreciated for their creativity or originality. Because the meaning of a sacred text is not self-evident, interpretation is necessary. Interpretation is intended to discern the "true," or preexistent, meaning of a sacred text. The successful discovery of this "true" meaning is perceived to be not an addition to existing knowledge but a reassertion and confirmation of an already existent truth. Nevertheless, a considerable degree of originality within the tradition might in fact be attained.

When intellectuals elaborate doctrines that are based on inherently problematic sacred texts, divergent and hence conflicting doctrinal currents of belief appear. Such conflicts have occurred in every world religion and have led to intense disputes until one current has become prevalent over the others and has been established as the orthodox position. There is, however, an important difference between a prevailing doctrine that is orthodox solely through a substantial intellectual consensus and a prevailing doctrine that is promulgated as orthodox by an authoritative institution. An authoritatively promulgated doctrine is a dogma. Where there is dogma, heterodoxies are proscribed, and their intellectual proponents are suppressed.

The authorities that the religious intellectuals must confront are the authority of the sacred writings and the doctrines formed from them, the authority of the religious intellectual community, and that of ecclesiastical institutions. In principle, the authority of the sacred writings is inviolable. In fact, however, the authority of these writings is the authority of the prevailing doctrinal tradition and of those who espouse it within the institution. Critical interpretation of sacred texts is thus perpetually a potential threat to the effective "official" authority of the religious institution.

Within more complex societies, even those of very restricted literacy, there have been some self-taught laypersons different in their occupation and status from the majority of religious intellectuals in their society. They may be called lay or amateur religious intellectuals. Sometimes they have been merchants or craftsmen, sometimes scribes, officials, or soldiers. These laymen have studied the texts zealously and sometimes arrived at conclusions different from the prevailing doctrines. They have also resented the pretensions of the officially acknowledged and self-assertive priestly, academic, or monastic religious intellectuals. Their dissenting interpretations of sacred writings have occasionally broken into passionate public dissent from the prevailing doctrines and from the priestly and academic representation of those doctrines. These autodidactic intellectuals, sometimes reinforced by renegades from the more established stratum of religious intellectuals, have often furiously denounced the main body of the priesthood as departing fundamentally from the "true" meaning of the sacred texts. The priests, and especially the higher level of the priestly hierarchy, have been accused of excessive subservience to the ruling house and to the powerful landowning families.

Heterodox or dissenting doctrines have occasionally been the work of intellectuals within the priesthood itself. Such interpretations at first lived an "underground" life. Some of them were cultivated in seclusion by dissenting, autodidactic religious intellectuals. The latter have often been subtle, learned, and ingenious.

Among the greatest of these intellectuals who were critical of the priestly or orthodox interpretation have been those prophets who were founders of new religions, that is, religions that declared themselves to be distinct from the hitherto prevailing body of religious belief and its proponents. The Buddha, Jesus, and Muḥammad were such prophets. They were the beneficiaries of new revelations or illuminations.

Jesus said he was divinely chosen to fulfill the mission of earlier prophets. The Buddha was a profoundly original prophet, but he too was a continuator of Hinduism. Muḥammad claimed to be not only the recipient of a new revelation but to have realized more truly the religion of Abraham and Jesus. In contrast, Confucian scholars in China claimed no authority from revelation, and they did not bring forth prophets from their ranks.

There have also been prophets who have claimed to realize the true intentions of long-accepted doctrines against those who had falsified them. The Hebrew prophetic intellectuals did not claim at any time to found a new religion. They demanded the restoration of the religion of the Jews to its prior condition of purity. Martin Luther, John Wyclif, and the monastic reformers of Christian religious orders must be placed in the same category as the prophetic intellectuals who thought that their religious community had departed from its original meaning and had succumbed to the ways of the earthly world.

Religious intellectual traditions alter as they pass from region to region and from generation to generation. The world religions—Hinduism, Buddhism, Confucianism, Judaism, Christianity, and Islam—have experienced numerous doctrinal vicissitudes and variations. They have survived largely because their doctrines have been received and retransmitted with modifications and increments by religious intellectuals. Without the constant reaffirmation and modifications of doctrinal traditions by religious intellectuals, there could be no religious communities with more or less uniform practices and beliefs over extended periods and large geographical areas.

Secular and Religious Intellectual Activities. In no large societies have religious intellectual activities been the only intellectual activities. Yet except in ancient Greece and Rome, most intellectual activities in the societies of the ancient world were carried on by religious intellectuals. In the modern age, the increased volume of intellectual works, the increased differentiation of objects of intellectual activity, and the increased specialization of intellectuals in dealing with aspects of the world (which is now thought to be relatively independent of transcendent powers) have been associated with a great increase in the proportion of secular intellectuals and a recession of the jurisdiction of religious intellectuals.

In territories where autonomous intellectual traditions—both religious and secular—were well developed, religious intellectuals often assimilated intellectual traditions that lay outside their own religious tradition. This occurred, for example, in Christianity and later in Islam when they became established in the territory of Hellenistic civilizations. Christian intellectuals found affinities between their own Christian beliefs and Platonic, and later Aristotelian, philosophy. Islamic intellectuals quickly absorbed the Hellenistic philosophical and scientific knowledge that had been cultivated in Syria and other parts of the Middle East under the Seleucids and the Romans. By the end of the European Middle Ages, Christian religious intellectuals drew knowledge directly from ancient secular Western sources. By the seventeenth century, both the quantity and the intellectual authoritativeness of secular intellectual works gained the ascendancy. Religious intellectuals absorbed some of this secular knowledge and attempted to render it compatible with Christian belief.

The humanistic intellectuals of the Renaissance, taking up the traditions of the secular cultures of Greece and Rome, continued to be Christians, but their attention moved toward the study of earthly things. After the Reformation this differentiation and multiplication of secular intellectuals continued. Religious intellectuals also declined more and more in status in comparison with secular intellectuals.

Religious intellectuals now constitute a small minority of the intellectuals of European and American societies. Many of them have made very far-reaching concessions to the substantive and technical standards of secular intellectuals. They have accepted the findings of the research of physical and biological scientists and the approaches and analyses of secular historians and social scientists.

In modern times, religious intellectuals have confined their intellectual activities to religious objects in a restricted sense: theological studies, textual and historical analysis of sacred writings and their commentaries, the archaeology of sacred sites, church history and the history of religious doctrines, and closely related topics. But even within some of these restricted spheres of religious study, a secular criterion of validity has prevailed. Secular modes of study in the analysis of religious phenomena have become predominant, and in certain fields, such as church history, the history of doctrines, and the sociological and anthropological study of religion, the techniques of research and the interpretations of secular intellectuals have come to predominate.

For centuries, religious intellectuals were an integral part of the political life of their respective societies. The earthly centers of power could not claim the legitimacy of their ascendancy without its attestation by religious intellectuals. It was thought that social order could be assured only if the earthly center was properly aligned with the transcendent center. The earthly centers called upon religious intellectuals for administrative services. The education of young persons and children was entrusted to religious intellectuals. There was, by and large, a relationship of mutual support between religious intellectuals, princes, and great landowners. In the bourgeois age, religious intellectuals became more critical of the new plutocratic elite and of the bourgeois order of society. In Western European countries and North America religious intellectuals increasingly joined with secular intellectuals in oppositional political activities.

In the once-colonial territories, now sovereign states, "traditionalistic," revivalistic religious intellectuals have become more active. In these countries, during the period of foreign rule, traditional religious intellectuals had been mainly passive toward the foreign rulers. Indigenous rulers enjoyed the same submission of intellectuals in Asian societies that remained independent. Such passivity among traditional religious intellectuals is no longer so common. In Iran, for example, they have succeeded in establishing a theocracy. In a few other Islamic countries, they have been influential enough to compel secular military and civilian rulers to designate their states as "Islamic" and to install "Islamic constitutions." Christian religious intellectuals in the formerly colonial societies have not been so active politically; in their religious intellectual activities, they have sought to overcome their "alien" situation by reinterpreting Christianity to render it compatible with indigenous cultural traditions.

In Western countries in the twentieth century religious intellectuals narrowed their intellectual activities in accordance with the prevailing tendencies toward specialization and professionalization. At the same time, they acquired many of the scientific, cultural, moral, and political traditions of the secular intellectuals. In many respects, religious intellectuals in Western countries have become very much like secular intellectuals.

BIBLIOGRAPHY

Arnold, Thomas W. *The Caliphate.* 2d ed. Oxford, 1965.

Baron, Salo W. *The Jewish Community: Its History and Structure to the American Revolution.* 3 vols. Philadelphia, 1942.

Burkert, Walter. *Greek Religion.* Cambridge, Mass., 1985.

Eliot, Charles. *Hinduism and Buddhism.* 3 vols. 3d ed. London, 1957.

Gibb, H. A. R., with Harold Bowen. *Islamic Society and the West,* vol. 1, *Islamic Society in the Eighteenth Century.* Oxford, 1950.

Goldziher, Ignácz. *Die Richtungen der islamischen Koranauslegung* (1920). Leiden, 1952.

Harnack, Adolf von. *The Constitution and Law of the Church in the First Two Centuries.* London, 1910.

Hooke, S. H. *Prophets and Priests.* London, 1938.

James, E. O. *The Nature and Function of Priesthood.* London, 1955.

Le Bras, Gabriel. *Institutions ecclésiastiques de la chrétienté médiévale.* Paris, 1959.

Marrou, Henri Irénée. *A History of Education in Antiquity.* New York, 1956.

Moore, George Foot. *Judaism in the First Centuries of the Christian Era, the Age of the Tannaim.* 3 vols. Cambridge, Mass., 1927–1930.

Nilsson, Martin P. *Geschichte der griechischen Religion.* 2 vols. 3d ed. Munich, 1967–1974.

Ryan, John. *Irish Monasticism: Origins and Early Development.* Dublin, 1931.

Schacht, Joseph. *The Origins of Muhammadan Jurisprudence.* Oxford, 1950.

New Sources

Belief in God and Intellectual Honesty. Ruurd Vuldhuis, Andy F. Sanders and Heine J. Siebrand, editors. Assen, Netherlands, 1990.

Christian Faith and Greek Philosophy in Late Antiquity: Essays in Tribute to George Christopher Stead, 9th April 1993. Lionel R. Wickham and Caroline P. Bammel, editors. Leiden, Netherlands, 1993.

Enlightenment and Religion: Rational Dissent in Eighteenth-Century Britain. Knud Haakonssen, editor. New York, 1996.

Exchange of Ideas: Religion, Scholarship and Art in Anglo-Dutch Relations in the Seventeenth Century. Simon Groenveld and Michael Wintle, editors. Zutphen, Netherlands, 1994.

Meeting of Minds: Intellectual and Religious Interaction in East Asian Traditions of Thought: Essays in Honor of Wing-tsit Chan and William Theodore de Bary. Irene Bloom and Joshua A. Fogel, editors. New York, 1996.

Religion and Twentieth-century American Intellectual Life. Michael J. Lacey, editor. New York, 1996.

Religion, Learning, and Science in the Abbasid Period. M.J.L. Young, J.D. Latham, and R.B. Serjeant, editors. Cambridge, 1989.

Taylor, Clarence. *Black Religious Intellectuals: The Fight for Equality from Jim Crow to the Twenty-First Century.* New York, 2002.

EDWARD SHILS (1987)
Revised Bibliography

INTELLIGENT DESIGN

INTELLIGENT DESIGN studies features of objects that signal the action of an intelligent cause. Designed objects, like Mount Rushmore, exhibit characteristic features that point to an intelligence. Such features or patterns constitute *signs of intelligence.* Proponents of intelligent design, known as design theorists, purport to study such signs formally, rigorously, and scientifically. Intelligent design may therefore be defined as the science that studies signs of intelligence.

Intelligent design is controversial because it purports to find signs of intelligence in nature and specifically in biological systems. According to the evolutionary biologist Francisco Ayala (2004), Charles Darwin's greatest achievement was to show how the organized complexity of organisms could be attained apart from a designing intelligence. Intelligent design therefore directly challenges Darwinism and other naturalistic approaches to the origin and evolution of life. Leading proponents of intelligent design include Michael Behe, Phillip Johnson, and William Dembski. Leading critics include Kenneth Miller, John Haught, and Michael Ruse.

Although intelligent design is incompatible with a naturalized, nonteleological understanding of evolution, it has no complaint against evolution per se. Intelligent design is compatible with common descent, the claim that all organisms trace their lineage to some last universal common ancestor. At the same time intelligent design is also compatible with special creation, the claim that organisms, except for small-scale evolutionary changes, were all separately created.

Given this flexibility, intelligent design is not readily shoehorned into the usual spectrum of explanations for evolutionary change, which places naturalistic evolution at one end, scientific creationism at the other, and theistic evolution somewhere in the middle. Intelligent design argues that intelligence played a discernible role in the history of life. Whether that intelligence acted through an evolutionary process or by special creations is a separate question, and proponents of intelligent design come down on both sides of this question. (Behe, for instance, accepts common descent.)

Defining Signs of Intelligence. The idea that an intrinsic intelligence or teleology inheres in and is expressed through nature has a long history and is embraced by many religious traditions. The main difficulty with this idea since Darwin's day, however, has been to discover a conceptually powerful formulation of design that can fruitfully advance science. What has kept design outside the scientific mainstream since the rise of Darwinism has been the lack of precise methods for distinguishing intelligently caused objects from unintelligently caused ones.

For design to be a fruitful scientific concept, scientists have to be sure they can reliably determine whether something is designed. Johannes Kepler, for instance, thought the craters on the moon were intelligently designed by moon dwellers. It is now known that the craters were formed by purely material factors (like meteor impacts). This fear of falsely attributing something to design only to have it overturned later has hindered design from entering the scientific mainstream. But design theorists argue that they now have formulated precise methods for discriminating designed from undesigned objects. These methods, they contend, enable them to avoid Kepler's mistake and reliably locate design in biological systems.

As a theory of biological origins and development, intelligent design's central claim is that only intelligent causes adequately explain the complex, information-rich structures of biology and that these causes are empirically detectable. To say intelligent causes are empirically detectable is to say there exist well-defined methods that, based on observable features of the world, can reliably distinguish intelligent causes from undirected natural causes. Many special sciences have already developed such methods for drawing this distinction—notably forensic science, cryptography, archaeology, and the search for extraterrestrial intelligence (SETI). Essential to all these methods is the ability to eliminate chance and necessity.

The astronomer Carl Sagan wrote a novel about SETI called *Contact* (1985) that was later made into a movie. Sagan based the SETI astronomers' methods of design detection squarely on scientific practice. Why do the radio astronomers in *Contact* draw such a design inference from the signals they monitored from distant space? SETI researchers run signals collected from space through computers programmed to recognize preset patterns. These patterns serve as a sieve. Signals that do not match any of the patterns pass through the sieve and are classified as random.

After years of receiving apparently meaningless, random signals, the *Contact* researchers discover a pattern of beats and pauses that corresponds to the sequence of all the prime numbers between 2 and 101. (Prime numbers are divisible only by themselves and by one.) That startles the astronomers, and they immediately infer an intelligent cause. When a sequence begins with 2 beats and then a pause, 3 beats and then a pause, and continues through each prime number all the way to 101 beats, researchers must infer the presence of an extraterrestrial intelligence.

The rationale for this inference is that nothing in the laws of physics requires radio signals to take one form or another. The prime sequence is therefore contingent rather than necessary. Also the prime sequence is long and hence complex. Note that if the sequence were extremely short and therefore lacked complexity, it could easily have happened by chance. Finally, the sequence is not merely complex but also exhibits an independently given pattern or *specification* (it is not just any sequence of numbers but a mathematically significant one—the prime numbers).

Intelligence leaves behind a characteristic trademark or signature—what within the intelligent design community is now called *specified complexity.* An event exhibits specified complexity if it is contingent and therefore not necessary, if it is complex and therefore not readily reproducible by chance, and if it is specified in the sense of exhibiting an independently given pattern. Note that a merely improbable event is not sufficient to eliminate chance—by flipping a coin long enough, one will witness a highly complex or improbable event. Even so, one will have no reason to attribute it to anything other than chance.

The important thing about specifications is that they be objectively given and not arbitrarily imposed on events after the fact. For instance, if an archer fires arrows at a wall and then paints bull's-eyes around them, the archer imposes a pattern after the fact. On the other hand, if the targets are set up in advance (specified) and then the archer hits them accurately, one legitimately concludes that it was by design.

The combination of complexity and specification convincingly points the radio astronomers in the movie *Contact* to an extraterrestrial intelligence. Note that the evidence is purely circumstantial—the radio astronomers know nothing about the aliens responsible for the signal or how they transmit it. Design theorists contend that specified complexity provides compelling circumstantial evidence for intelligence. Accordingly specified complexity is a reliable empirical marker of intelligence in the same way that fingerprints are a reliable empirical marker of an individual's presence. Moreover design theorists argue that purely material factors cannot adequately account for specified complexity.

BIOLOGICAL DESIGN. In determining whether biological organisms exhibit specified complexity, design theorists focus on identifiable systems (e.g., individual enzymes, metabolic pathways, and molecular machines). These systems are not only specified by their independent functional requirements but also exhibit a high degree of complexity.

In *Darwin's Black Box* (1996) the biochemist Michael Behe connects specified complexity to biological design through his concept of *irreducible complexity.* Behe defines a system as irreducibly complex if it consists of several interrelated parts for which removing even one part renders the system's basic function unrecoverable. For Behe, irreducible complexity is a sure indicator of design. One irreducibly complex biochemical system that Behe considers is the bacterial flagellum. The flagellum is an acid-powered rotary motor with a whiplike tail that spins at twenty thousand revolutions per minute and whose rotating motion enables a bacterium to navigate through its watery environment.

Behe shows that the intricate machinery in this molecular motor—including a rotor, a stator, O-rings, bushings, and a drive shaft—requires the coordinated interaction of approximately forty complex proteins and that the absence of any one of these proteins would result in the complete loss of motor function. Behe argues that the Darwinian mechanism faces grave obstacles in trying to account for such irreducibly complex systems. In *No Free Lunch* (2002) William Dembski shows how Behe's notion of irreducible complexity constitutes a particular instance of specified complexity.

Once an essential constituent of an organism exhibits specified complexity, any design attributable to that constituent carries over to the organism as a whole. To attribute design to an organism one need not demonstrate that every aspect of the organism was designed. Organisms, like all material objects, are products of history and thus subject to the buffeting of purely material factors. Automobiles, for instance, get old and exhibit the effects of corrosion, hail, and frictional forces. But that does not make them any less designed. Likewise design theorists argue that organisms, though exhibiting the effects of history (and that includes Darwinian factors such as genetic mutations and natural selection), also include an ineliminable core that is designed.

INTELLIGENT DESIGN AND RELIGION. Intelligent design's main tie to religion is through the design argument, and perhaps the best-known design argument is William Paley's. Paley published his argument in 1802 in a book titled *Natural Theology.* The subtitle of that book is revealing: *Evidences of the Existence and Attributes of the Deity, Collected from the Appearances of Nature.* Paley's project was to examine features of the natural world (what he called "appearances of nature") and from there draw conclusions about the existence and attributes of a designing intelligence responsible for those features (whom Paley identified with the God of Christianity).

According to Paley, if one finds a watch in a field (and thus lacks all knowledge of how the watch arose), the adaptation of the watch's parts to telling time ensures that it is the product of an intelligence. So too, according to Paley, the marvelous adaptations of means to ends in organisms (like the intricacy of the human eye with its capacity for vision) ensure that organisms are the product of an intelligence. The theory of intelligent design updates Paley's watchmaker argument in light of contemporary information theory and molecular biology, purporting to bring this argument squarely within science.

In arguing for the design of natural systems, intelligent design is more modest than the design arguments of natural theology. For natural theologians like Paley, the validity of the design argument did not depend on the fruitfulness of design-theoretic ideas for science but on the metaphysical and theological mileage one could get out of design. A natural theologian might point to nature and say, "Clearly the designer of this ecosystem prized variety over neatness." A design theorist attempting to do actual design-theoretic research on that ecosystem might reply, "Although that is an intriguing theological possibility, as a design theorist I need to keep focused on the informational pathways capable of producing that variety."

In his *Critique of Pure Reason* (1781) Immanuel Kant claimed that the most the design argument can establish is "an architect of the world who is constrained by the adaptability of the material in which he works, not a *creator* of the world to whose idea everything is subject" (Kant, 1929, p. 522). Far from rejecting the design argument, Kant objected to overextending it. For Kant, the design argument legitimately establishes an architect (that is, an intelligent cause whose contrivances are constrained by the materials that make up the world), but it can never establish a creator who originates the very materials that the architect then fashions.

Intelligent design is entirely consonant with this observation by Kant. Creation is always about the source of being of the world. Intelligent design, as the science that studies signs of intelligence, is about arrangements of preexisting materials that point to a designing intelligence. Creation and intelligent design are therefore quite different. One can have creation without intelligent design and intelligent design without creation. For instance, one can have a doctrine of creation in which God creates the world in such a way that nothing about the world points to design. The evolutionary biologist Richard Dawkins wrote a book titled *The Blind Watchmaker: Why the Evidence of Evolution Reveals a Universe without Design* (1996). Even if Dawkins is right about the universe revealing no evidence of design, it would not logically follow that it was not created. It is logically possible that God created a world that provides no evidence of design. On the other hand, it is logically possible that the world is full of signs of intelligence but was not created. This was the ancient Stoic view, in which the world was eternal and uncreated and yet a rational principle pervaded the world and produced marks of intelligence in it.

The implications of intelligent design for religious belief are profound. The rise of modern science led to a vigorous attack on all religions that treat purpose, intelligence, and wisdom as fundamental and irreducible features of reality. The high point of this attack came with Darwin's theory of evolution. The central claim of Darwin's theory is that an unguided material process (random variation and natural selection) could account for the emergence of all biological complexity and order. In other words, Darwin appeared to show that the design in biology (and by implication in nature generally) was dispensable. By showing that design is indispensable to the scientific understanding of the natural world, intelligent design is reinvigorating the design argument and at the same time overturning the widespread misconception that the only tenable form of religious belief is one that treats purpose, intelligence, and wisdom as by-products of unintelligent material processes.

Bibliography

Ayala, Francisco. "Design without Designer: Darwin's Greatest Discovery." In *Debating Design: From Darwin to DNA,* edited by William A. Dembski and Michael Ruse, pp. 55–80. Cambridge, U.K., 2004.

Beckwith, Francis J. *Law, Darwinism, and Public Education: The Establishment Clause and the Challenge of Intelligent Design.* Lanham, Md., 2003. Examines whether intelligent design is inherently religious and thus, on account of church-state separation, must be barred from public school science curricula.

Behe, Michael J. *Darwin's Black Box: The Biochemical Challenge to Evolution.* New York, 1996. An overview of intelligent design's scientific research program.

Dawkins, Richard. *The Blind Watchmaker: Why the Evidence of Evolution Reveals a Universe without Design.* New York, 1996. An impassioned defense of Darwinism against any form of teleology or design.

Dembski, William A. *No Free Lunch: Why Specified Complexity Cannot Be Purchased without Intelligence.* Lanham, Md., 2002.

Dembski, William A. *The Design Revolution: Answering the Toughest Questions about Intelligent Design.* Downers Grove, Ill., 2004. These two Dembski works include overviews of intelligent design's scientific research program.

Dembski, William A., and Michael Ruse, eds. *Debating Design: From Darwin to DNA.* New York, 2004. This anthology places intelligent design in conversation with Darwinian, self-organizational, theistic approaches to evolution.

Forrest, Barbara. "The Wedge at Work: How Intelligent Design Creationism Is Wedging Its Way into the Cultural and Academic Mainstream." In *Intelligent Design Creationism and Its Critics: Philosophical, Theological, and Scientific Perspectives,* edited by Robert T. Pennock, pp. 5–53, Cambridge, Mass., 2001. A history of the intelligent design movement by a critic of that movement.

Giberson, Karl W., and Donald A. Yerxa. *Species of Origins: America's Search for a Creation Story.* Lanham, Md., 2002. Discusses intelligent design's place in the science and religion dialogue.

Haught, John F. *God after Darwin: A Theology of Evolution.* Boulder, Colo., 2000. A theological critique of intelligent design.

Hunter, Cornelius G. *Darwin's God: Evolution and the Problem of Evil.* Grand Rapids, Mich., 2001. Provides an interesting analysis of how intelligent design and Darwinism play off the problem of evil.

Kant, Immanuel. *Critique of Pure Reason.* Translated by N. K. Smith. New York, 1929.

Manson, Neil A., ed. *God and Design: The Teleological Argument and Modern Science.* London, 2003. This anthology situates intelligent design within broader discussions about teleology.

Miller, Kenneth R. *Finding Darwin's God: A Scientist's Search for Common Ground between God and Evolution.* New York, 1999. A critique of intelligent design's scientific research program.

Paley, William. *Natural Theology; or, Evidences of the Existence and Attributes of the Deity, Collected from the Appearances of Nature.* London, 1809.

Peters, Ted, and Martinez Hewlett. *Evolution from Creation to New Creation.* Nashville, Tenn., 2003. Discusses intelligent design's place in the science and religion dialogue.

Rea, Michael C. *World without Design: The Ontological Consequences of Naturalism.* Oxford, 2002. Probes intelligent design's metaphysical underpinnings.

Sagan, Carl. *Contact.* New York, 1985.

Witham, Larry. *By Design: Science and the Search for God.* San Francisco, 2003. A good overview of intelligent design that evenhandedly treats its scientific, cultural, and religious dimensions by a journalist who has personally interviewed the main players in the debate over intelligent design and who allows them to tell their story.

Woodward, Thomas. *Doubts about Darwin: A History of Intelligent Design.* Grand Rapids, Mich., 2003. A history of the intelligent design movement by a supporter.

William A. Dembski (2005)

INTERLACUSTRINE BANTU RELIGIONS.

The term *interlacustrine Bantu,* as used here, encompasses a variety of peoples who live between the Great Lakes of east-central Africa and speak closely related Bantu languages.

Their territory includes some of the most densely populated regions of Africa, consisting of all of Uganda south of the Victoria Nile, the states of Rwanda and Burundi, and a substantial portion of northwest Tanzania. Before independence, most of the area was divided into a number of traditional kingdoms, the largest of these being Rwanda and Burundi in the south and the four Uganda monarchies of Buganda, Bunyoro, Toro, and Ankole in the north. There were also about a dozen smaller but structurally similar units in the Tanzanian sector. The mass of the people are agriculturalists, but in many areas a cattle-owning minority, called Huma, or Hima, in the north and Tutsi in the south, formed a dominant and hereditary upper class.

Today most of the people of the region are at least nominally Christians; there is also a substantial minority of Muslims. But the indigenous cults are still widespread and are remarkably similar throughout the area.

The Spirit Powers. All the peoples of the area have the idea of a supreme being, known as Imana in the south, Ruhanga in the Nyoro-speaking north, and Katonda in Uganda; the last two names mean "creator." In some myths the hierarchical class structure mentioned above is ascribed to him, which to a certain degree may have sanctioned its acceptance by the less privileged. But, in a familiar pattern, the creator god, having made the world, was disappointed by it and withdrew from active participation in human affairs. Shrines are not made for him, nor are sacrifices offered as they are to the other gods (though here Buganda seems to have been an exception). In contrast to the lesser spirit powers, no mediumship cult is dedicated to the supreme being. He is, however, thought to be generally well disposed toward humans, and brief prayers and thanks may be offered up to him on a casual basis.

Far more significant in everyday life are the powerful spirits known as *embandwa* or *emandwa.* The most important of these form a group of hero-gods, whose names are well known throughout the area. They are linked in the south with a quasi-mythical ruler called Ryangombe and in the north with a shadowy ruling dynasty whose members are called *cwezi.* These heroic figures are the subject of a rich mythology; sometimes they are represented as the earliest descendants of the creator, sometimes as having come from a distant country. In either case they were great warriors, larger than life, and the doers of marvelous deeds. They were accompanied by retinues of kin and servants, and their women are included among their number. Like the Greek gods, some are identified with particular features of the environment; thus Wamara is associated with rain and rivers, Kagoro with thunder and lightning, Mulisa with cattle and cattle herding, Mugasa with the Great Lakes, and so on.

Eventually this heroic race vanished from the world: some say that the *cwezi* disappeared into one of the lakes in the area; Ryangombe is said to have been killed by a wild buffalo while hunting. But whatever their fate, it is believed that they left the institution of spirit mediumship behind for the benefit of their successors. This institution involved both possession and mediumship; it is believed that the possessing spirit, while "in the head" of its medium, may enter into communication with the living within an accepted framework of values and beliefs. Traditionally, these cults focused especially on the hero-gods who were, and still are, regarded as primarily beneficial, concerned especially with human fecundity. In Bunyoro and some neighboring areas the *cwezi* are known as the "white" *embandwa;* the color white signifying purity and blessing. These traditional cults, centered on the *cwezi* in the north and on Ryangombe and his associates in the south, may be said to form the core of interlacustrine Bantu religions.

There are many other spirits of nonhuman and sometimes of foreign origin that can be approached through mediumship ritual. These are sometimes known in the northern areas as the "black" *embandwa,* and they include spirits associated with the bush, with certain illnesses, and with some neighboring countries. In the interlacustrine area (as elsewhere in Africa) more recent spirits have come to represent new and formidable forces of all kinds, such as hitherto unknown illnesses, manifestations of Western power such as motorcars, airplanes, and even army tanks, as well as such abstract qualities as "Europeanness." All these elements and a great many more have been readily incorporated into the mediumship cults.

In addition to the high god and the wide and growing variety of *embandwa* spirits, there are the ghosts of the dead. Ghost cults are not necessarily ancestor cults. An ancestor cult is concerned with the deceased forebears of a lineage, who are usually conceived as a collectivity and are believed to be directly interested in the well-being of their descendants. Though traces of such a cult are still found in parts of the interlacustrine area, it has none of the importance of such fully developed cults as have been described among, for example, some West African peoples.

But the cult of ghosts is important throughout the region. It is believed that ghosts are left by people after they die; diffused like the wind, such ghosts are sometimes associated with a shadowy underworld, and it is thought that they may bring death, illness, or other calamity on those who have injured or offended them while they were alive. Ghosts are not necessarily kin or affines of their victims, though very often they are. Disputes are especially likely to arise within a person's circle of relatives, and it is believed that these may readily take the form, postmortem, of ghostly vengeance. Anyone, relative or not, who dies with a grudge against another may "leave a ghost" to obtain revenge.

Throughout the interlacustrine area, ghosts are seen as malevolent rather than benevolent, more concerned to punish than to reward. They are feared rather than revered, though if they cannot be exorcised it is desirable to remain on good terms with them. In either case, recourse must be had to the possession cults.

CULTS. Generally people have recourse to the cults as a response to some misfortune, and when things go wrong, the first step is to consult a diviner. He, or possibly she, using one of a wide variety of techniques, is likely to ascribe the client's trouble to an *embandwa* spirit, an offended ghost, or sorcery. If the responsible agent is found to be an *embandwa* spirit or a ghost there are two possibilities. If the ghost is that of a stranger (or of a very distant relative) or if the affliction is attributed to a minor spirit such as might be sent by a sorcerer, then there are special ritual techniques for exorcising it and either destroying it or turning it away from its intended victim forever.

But the more important *embandwa,* and the ghosts of closely related kin or affines, cannot be dealt with so summarily. The afflicted person must become initiated into the mediumship cult as the spirit's human medium. This establishes an enduring relationship between person and spirit, a relationship that should be sustained from time to time by further possession ritual. In the course of these séances the possessing power is believed to be able to communicate with the living through its medium, who is supposed to be in a state of trance while this is happening. The spirit may begin by announcing its identity, and then greet and be greeted by all present. It may go on to explain what offended it and ask for food and drink—an offering that should be given to it there and then while it is "in the medium's head." Or it may demand the sacrifice or dedication to it of a cow or a goat, or the building for it of a spirit hut. And it may, if it is the ghost of a close kinsman, ask for the reconciliation of quarreling family members. Before it "leaves the head" of its medium, a spirit, if it is mollified, is likely to bless all present and to promise them good fortune, and especially more children, in the future. Séances are dramatic occasions, involving drumming, dancing, and the singing of special songs, and mediums may assume the language and gestures appropriate to their possessing spirits.

While possessed, mediums appear to be in a state of trance and may claim afterward that they have no recollection of what happens to them when they are possessed. But evidence from several parts of the area indicates that complete dissociation is seldom, if ever, achieved; generally, the medium is "putting on an act." But this does not mean that they are fraudulent; the play they are performing is a religious one, a "liturgical drama" in Luc de Heusch's phrase. And, in addition to providing a ritual means of influencing powers over which there are no other means of control, the mediumship cults are also a source of dramatic entertainment in their own right.

Admission to the cults requires a complex (and expensive) cycle of initiation ritual, often lasting for several days and culminating in the possession of the novice by the spirit concerned. The pattern of cult initiation is broadly similar throughout the area. First, the initiate's change of status is stressed. He, or more probably she, is reborn into a new family, that of her fellow mediums, and this rebirth may be symbolically enacted. Second, the secrets of cult membership have to be learned; in particular, the novice may be told how to simulate possession and mediumship even though she does not actually achieve these states. Threats of the fearful consequences of disclosure confirm the candidate's commitment to secrecy. And third, the process of initiation puts the aspirant in a condition of ritual impurity, needing special ritual to remedy it.

SOCIAL CONTEXT. Important throughout much of the area was the role of the household medium, in the Nyoro-speaking region called *omucwezi w'eka* or, if female, *nyakatagara.* One member of the family, usually female and preferably initiated while still a child, links the domestic group with one of the traditional *embandwa* spirits as its medium: this spirit is supposed to have a special concern for the well-being of the family members. Here especially the purity and auspiciousness of the traditional cults are stressed; for only a gentle and well-mannered child is acceptable to the spirits as a household medium. In some areas there is, in addition, a broader association between particular traditional spirits and particular clans, but generally this does not involve any special ritual over and above the "domestic" cults just mentioned.

The relationship between the *embandwa* cults and the traditional kingships was commonly one of implicit or explicit opposition. In several kingdoms, most notably those of Bunyoro and Rwanda, members of the royal clan (including the king himself) were debarred from participation in the mediumship cults. Kings in the interlacustrine region were not priests. Instead, they maintained priests at court—professional mediums who, like everyone else, were subject to the royal authority. Among the larger kingdoms it was only in Buganda, by far the most politically centralized of the interlacustrine states, that the royal line was closely identified with the mediumship cult. The official Ganda cult centered on the ghosts of former kings, whose tombs, carefully maintained, provided the locus for state ritual. But even here it was the *lubale* (i.e., *embandwa*) "priests," and not the king, who were the mediums for the royal ancestors.

In the twentieth century the opposition between religion and state was exemplified in the rise and decline of the Nyabingi cult. This cult focused on a powerful female *embandwa* called Nyabingi and her associates, whose cult has been ascribed to various sources but may have originated in northern Rwanda, whence it spread rapidly into southwest Uganda. It appears to have begun as a reaction both against the traditional Ryangombe cults and against Rwanda's ruling class, the pastoral Tutsi. But with the coming of European colonial power, the cult became a protest movement against all governmental authority. In the 1920s a revolt by Nyabingi adherents against the local administration was crushed by military force, though the cult survived in attenuated form for many years.

It is not surprising that the *embandwa* cults found themselves in opposition to the Christian mission churches, which, with only very limited justification, regarded them as being involved with witchcraft. Because the traditional cults were generally seen as beneficent and as being especially concerned with childbearing, attempts by government officials and missionaries to eradicate them were readily interpreted by the traditionally minded as aimed, in the long term, at the elimination of the indigenous peoples themselves. Mention should also be made here of the revivalist and fundamentalist Balokole ("the Saved Ones") movement within the Anglican church. Although this movement affected only a small minority of Christians, its uncompromising evangelism brought it into conflict not only with the *embandwa* cults—with which it had certain things in common, for example, the notion of being "born again"—but also with the secular authorities.

How, finally, is one to explain the continued survival of the cults, old as well as new, throughout much of the area? Some of the reasons are implicit in what has been said above. But among the most important of them is the cults' eclecticism. Inimical aspects of the environment, and in particular the disruptive effects of social change, are not denied or rejected; rather they are assimilated and dealt with through dramatic ritual. To give concrete expression to the forces that shape human lives (even if this is done in symbolic form) provides the interlacustrine Bantu with one basis for coping with these forces.

SEE ALSO East African Religions, article on Northeast Bantu Religions.

BIBLIOGRAPHY

Three works adopt a comparative approach. In his *Entre le Victoria l'Albert et l'Édouard: Ethnographie de la partie anglaise du Vicariat de l'Uganda* (Rennes, 1920), the missionary P. Julien Gorju gives a good account of the cults and of initiation into them in the Uganda kingdoms. Luc de Heusch's *Le Rwanda et la civilisation interlacustre: Études d'anthropologie historique et structurale* (Brussels, 1966) contains a comprehensive analysis of the Ryangombe cult in Rwanda, taking account also of comparable data from neighboring areas. And Iris Berger's *Religion and Resistance: East African Kingdoms in the Precolonial Period* (Tervuren, Belgium, 1981), although largely concerned with historical reconstruction, includes an up-to-date review and assessment of current information on the cults over the whole area as well as a useful bibliography. Berger notes in particular the important role played in the cults by women.

There are several brief accounts of the religious beliefs and rituals of particular peoples in the area; see, for example, Lucy P. Mair's "Religion and Magic," chapter 9 of her book on the Ganda, *An African People in the Twentieth Century* (1934; New York, 1965); J. J. Maquet's "The Kingdom of Ruanda," in *African Worlds,* edited by Daryll Forde (London, 1954); and John Beattie's "Spirit Mediumship in Bunyoro," in *Spirit Mediumship and Society in Africa,* edited by John Beattie and John Middleton (New York, 1969). A monograph by a Norwegian anthropologist, Svein Bjerke, *Religion and Misfortune: The Bacwezi Complex and the Other Spirit Cults of the Zinza of Northwestern Tanzania* (Oslo, 1981), provides a detailed account, based on field research, of the cults among one of the less well known peoples of the region. Relevant to the study of religion in its political context is Elizabeth Hopkins's "The Nyabingi Cult of Southwestern Uganda," in *Protest and Power in Black Africa,* edited by Robert I. Rotberg and Ali A. Mazrui (Oxford, 1970), a history of the rise and influence of an anticolonial spirit cult. Finally, for an African academic's view of his own traditional religion, see Abel G. M. Ishumi's "Religion and the Cults," chapter 6 of his *Kiziba: The Cultural Heritage of an Old African Kingdom* (Syracuse, N.Y., 1980)

JOHN BEATTIE (1987)

INTERMEDIATE BEINGS SEE ANGELS; DEMONS; DEVILS; FAIRIES; GHOSTS; MONSTERS

INTERNATIONAL SOCIETY FOR KRISHNA CONSCIOUSNESS

INTERNATIONAL SOCIETY FOR KRISHNA CONSCIOUSNESS (ISKCON) is the missionary form of devotional Hinduism brought to the United States in 1965 by a pious devotee of Kṛṣṇa who wanted to convert the English-speaking world to "God-consciousness." By 2003, ISKCON had become an international movement with more than 350 temples and centers worldwide (approximately fifty in the United States).

ESTABLISHED AS CHARISMATIC MOVEMENT. The founding guru of ISKCON, A. C. Bhaktivedanta Swami Prabhupada, was born Abhay Charan De in 1896 in Calcutta. Educated in a Vaiṣṇava school and later in Scottish Church College, he was a sporadically successful businessman in the pharmaceutical industry. However, after he was initiated in 1922 by Bhaktisiddhanta Sarasvati, a Gauḍiya (Bengali) Vaiṣṇava, in the line of the sixteenth-century saint and reformer Caitanya, he began increasingly to invest time and money in his religious interests. In 1944 Prabhupada established the magazine *Back to Godhead,* and in 1952 he formed the Jhansi League of Devotees. He gave up his life as a householder (*gṛihastha*) in 1954 and took the formal vows of an ascetic (*saṃnyāsin*) in 1959.

In September 1965, at the age of sixty-nine, Prabhupada arrived in New York City with less than ten dollars in his pocket and a suitcase full of his translations of the Kṛṣṇa scripture, called the *Śrīmad Bhāgavatam.* He lived with various Indian and American supporters in Manhattan, where he daily chanted and sang the praises of Kṛṣṇa. Prabhupada's lectures and devotional services initially attracted many counterculture youths, and preaching centers were established in Los Angeles, Berkeley, Boston, and Montreal. By the early 1970s, Los Angeles had become the headquarters of ISKCON and its publishing office, the Bhaktivedanta Book Trust, which has printed more than fifty different translations and original works by Prabhupada and hundreds of other ISKCON treatises since his death.

From the earliest years of the movement, Prabhupada's disciples have been known for their public chanting (*saṅkīrtan*) of the Hare Kṛṣṇa mantra and their distribution of *Back to Godhead* magazine and Prabhupada's books. Like his Indian godbrothers, Prabhupada believed that the recitation of God's name was necessary for salvation. Further, his guru had instructed him to bring "Krishna consciousness" to the English-speaking world. Consequently, the "Hare Krishnas" have been both very visible and evangelical in India, America, and globally.

In July 1970, Prabhupada formed a Governing Body Commission (GBC) of twelve advanced devotees to administer an increasingly widespread and complex ISKCON and to allow him to spend his time preaching and translating. At this same time, he instituted a series of standardized religious practices that made ISKCON devotees more like their Indian counterparts. Male devotees who entered the temple had to wear the traditional saffron dress of the monastic novice and shave their heads, while women wore traditional Indian saris. All temples were to follow a daily regimen of rising at 4:00 AM for morning devotional services *(pūjā),* chanting sixteen rounds of the Kṛṣṇa mantra on 108 prayer beads *(jāpā),* and attending a lecture on a scriptural passage. A clear distinction was made between *brahmācarin,* or "student," devotees who intended to take the four monastic regulative principles (no meat eating, no intoxicants of any kind, no sexual activity of any kind, and no gambling) and *gṛihasta,* or "householder," devotees who intended to live in marriage (often outside the temple) and who might also take a modified version of the four vows.

EXPANSION AND EXTERNAL OPPOSITION. Throughout the 1970s and early 1980s, ISKCON became more conscious of its Indian roots at the same time that it was expanding to every continent on the globe. Prabhupada frequently returned to India from 1970 until his death in Vṛndāvana, India, in November 1977. He received a hearty welcome from most Indians, who jokingly called his devotees "dancing white elephants." He established temples and preaching centers near Bombay, in Vṛndāvana (the birthplace of Kṛṣṇa), and in Māyāpur (the birthplace of Caitanya). By the early 1980s, the Bombay temple had more than six thousand Indian "lifetime" congregational members, and the Vṛndāvana temple was included on most Kṛṣṇa pilgrims' circuits. Back in America, Indian immigrants became members of ISKCON temples and were often strong supporters of this transplanted devotional Hindu movement.

Prabhupada circled the globe eleven times in his twelve years of missionary activity and established temples in England and continental Europe as well as in India, Australia, and South Africa. Just before his death, he appointed eleven disciples as initiating gurus to keep his Caitanya chain of discipleship unbroken and to missionize the rest of the world. By the mid-1980s his disciples had established forty-five temples or farms in Europe, ten in Africa, thirty-five in Asia, and forty in South America. Whereas the full-time membership of the American temples remained constant or declined in the decade after Prabhupada's death, ISKCON branches grew rapidly overseas, where they often found more welcoming environments.

During the 1990s, ISKCON's primary growth came in the former Soviet states with twenty temples formed in Russia alone. In April 1998, ISKCON's status as an accepted Hindu tradition was confirmed as the prime minister helped inaugurate a new temple and museum complex in New Delhi, India.

Throughout its history in America, ISKCON has encountered opposition from anticult groups such as the Citizens' Freedom Foundation, the Cult Awareness Network, and the American Family Foundation. The movement's methods of book distribution and fund-raising have most often been at the heart of both external and internal criticism. These questionable practices were often the result of the unbounded enthusiasm of devotees and organizational inconsistencies during the first two decades of ISKCON's development. The early decades of this charismatic movement also spawned several internal crises that fully emerged after the founder's death.

INTERNAL CRISES. Existing leadership problems were heightened after the founder's death. ISKCON began as a charasmatic movement founded on the strength of Prabhupada's pious faith and practices. While the administrative and religious authority of the founder could be transferred to his eleven appointed successors, his piety and depth of faith could not. The initial practice was for the eleven guru successors to provide spiritual and administrative leadership for a geographical "zone" and to act as though they were Prabhupada (i.e., they initiated disciples, accepted guru worship, and so on). Some of the new ISKCON gurus even claimed that their individual authority was superior to that of the GBC. But one by one, many of these young gurus succumbed to the temptations of sex or the abuse of their power. By the late 1980s, six of the original eleven had either voluntarily stepped down or had been removed by the GBC. By the mid-1980s the GBC authorized the inauguration of nearly two dozen new initiating gurus and assigned more than one guru to each geographical zone where devotees lived. Throughout the 1990s the guru and leadership debates continued with many Kṛṣṇa devotees (including some gurus) defecting to start their own movement or to become the disciple of one of the Indian godbrothers of Prabhupada. Several waves of reform during the 1980s and 1990s altered the power and scope of individual gurus. In 2003 the supreme court in India was asked to adjudicate leadership squabbles among temple leaders who quarreled over the powers of current ISKCON gurus in India. In the absence of the founding guru, the GBC and the appointed gurus together have tried to provide leadership for the worldwide movement in the face of economic and legal crises that have threatened the movement's very survival.

A second serious internal crisis for ISKCON has been the abuse of children. In the early 1970s the number of married devotees was rising, and some of the initial devotees accepted the life of the "renounced" *saṃnyāsin.* This shift of authority in the Kṛṣṇa temples to the celibate devotees created a lower social status for families (and especially women and children) than had been true in the 1960s. Schools for children called *gurukulas* (guru schools) were established in Dallas and Los Angeles in America and in Vrindaban, India. The schools were often run by *saṃnyāsins* who had no experience in child rearing, and initially parents were strongly discouraged from maintaining contact with their children. In 1974, stories of child abuse (e.g., harsh punishments and psychological depravations) arose surrounding the Dallas *gurukula.* Less than a year later the school was closed, and school reforms were put in place. Yet throughout the 1970s into the early 1980s, abuses ranging from overzealous corporeal punishment and food deprivation to sexual abuse occurred in some *gurukulas* with some children.

In 1990 the GBC established policies requiring abuse-prevention training and mandatory reporting of abuse allegations in Kṛṣṇa schools. In 1996, ten former *gurukula* students spoke at an annual North American GBC meeting about their abuse. As a result, the Children of Krishna organization was formed to provide counseling and educational resources for Kṛṣṇa youth. In 1997 a professionally staffed Child Protection Office was formed to investigate and adjudicate child abuse allegations. However, in June 2000, a $400 million lawsuit was filed on behalf of former *gurukula* students against two dozen Kṛṣṇa temples. The case was dismissed from federal court in 2002 but refiled on behalf of ninety-one former students in the Texas State Court. In 2003 the ISKCON temples named in the suit sought Chapter 11 bankruptcy protection. All of the boarding *gurukulas* in the United States had closed their doors by the mid-1990s, but Kṛṣṇa day schools continue to educate many devotee children.

The third persistent internal issue of considerable magnitude concerns the role and status of women in ISKCON. Since the Middle Ages in India, Vaiṣṇava and other devotional traditions have afforded women greater spiritual status than traditional Vedic beliefs and practices had. However, it is still often assumed in India that a woman's material body requires her to be "protected" by her father in her youth, her husband in her middle years, and her sons in her old age. When Prabhupada first came to America, he treated women and men devotees with considerable equality. Women were permitted to lead worship services, to give lectures on the Kṛṣṇa scriptures, and even to hold offices in temples. He argued that spiritually there was no difference between men and women, which was a more liberal view than most of his Indian godbrothers. But with the ascendency of the *saṃnyāsin,* or "renounced," movement in the early 1970s, women found themselves to be second-class devotees in ISKCON. From the mid-1970s through the mid-1990s, women devotees in most temples were forbidden to lead chanting, to give *Bhāgavatam* class, or to hold high offices in a temple or the GBC.

In the late 1980s and early 1990s, some women and men came forward to insist on the equal spiritual, social, political status that women had enjoyed earlier under Prabhupada. In the mid-1990s some temple leaders in Europe and the United States said that discrimination against women must cease and permitted women to engage in religious and leadership roles equal to men. In 1996 an American woman devotee was appointed to the GBC, which had previously been open only to men (i.e., gurus and laymen). This act signaled that women could be equal to men as "advanced devotees" and policymakers for ISKCON—even though men alone can be gurus. In 1997 ISKCON held its first conference for Women's Ministry and explored the pent-up issues that previously had been taboo. In 1998 a second woman was added to the international GBC, and in 2000, at the International GBC meeting in Mayapur, India, a resolution was passed that provided for the "equal facility, full encouragement, and genuine care and protection of women members of ISKCON." By 2000, several temples in Europe and the United States were led by women presidents. However, the role of women in ISKCON still depends to a considerable degree on whether they live in or outside India, and on whether the local temple practices derive from the notions of the equality of spirit or they insist on the differentness of gender. The role of women in ISKCON will always be lodged in the context of a Hindu and Indian view of women that will make full equality difficult to achieve. And yet ISKCON is constantly molded by global processes of institutionalization and accommodation that include pressure to give women a greater voice.

Institutionalization and Maturation. ISKCON is truly an international religious movement and, as such, is very diverse, depending on whether the locus is the Los Angeles temple, the Bhaktivedanta Manor in London, or the pilgrimage center in Māyāpur, India. Yet there are certain common trends toward the "Hinduization" of ISKCON that bring it into the sphere of other Vaiṣṇava traditions in India and have attracted many Indian members to its temples throughout the world. Likewise, there are trends toward institutional maturation in ISKCON that are revealed in an acadmic seriousness that has led more than a dozen leading devotees to earn Ph.D.s in the 1990s and the creation of several academic journals. ISKCON has created leadership classes for temple officials that range from economic and managerial lessons to instructions on the proper place and treatment of children and women in the movement. ISKCON has initiated interfaith conversations such as the "Vaishava-Christian Dialogue" and has established a European ministerial college in England. To be sure, its "Indianness" (e.g., circular concept of time, or *saṃsāra*) and "Hinduness" (e.g., its focus on Kṛṣṇa rituals and scriptures) will always make ISKCON a minority religious tradition outside of India. Still, its capacity to accommodate its beliefs and practices globally according to the medieval Vaiṣṇava dictum of "time, place and circumstance" should serve it well into the future as it seeks an enduring place in the religious landscape of a twenty-first-century multicultural world.

SEE ALSO Caitanya; Kṛṣṇaism; New Religions, overview article; New Religious Movements, articles on New Religious Movements in Europe, New Religious Movements in the United States; Vaiṣṇavism, overview article.

BIBLIOGRAPHY

J. Stillson Judah's study of California devotees, *Hare Krishna and the Counterculture* (New York, 1974), is now dated, but its emphasis on ISKCON's origin as a religious alternative to and embodiment of countercultural values and attitudes is still instructive. An anthropological study that focuses on the Boston, New York, London, and Amsterdam temples is Francine Jeanne Daner's *The American Children of Krishna* (New York, 1976). Daner also places the rise of ISKCON in the context of "counterculture religions" as well as in the framework of Erik Erikson's identity theory of personality development. Larry D. Shinn's *The Dark Lord: Cult Images and the Hare Krishnas in America* (Philadelphia, 1987) is based on more than one hundred interviews of Krishna devotees conducted over two years in fourteen temples throughout America and India and presents the various aspects of the American Krishna faith in the framework of anticult criticisms and a history of religions perspective on this devotional Indian faith. For a good summary of the child abuse issue, see E. Burke Rochford. "Child Abuse in the Hare Krishna Movement: 1971–1986," *ISKCON Communications Journal* 6 (1998): 43–69. For a reflective essay concerning the role and status of women in ISKCON see Kim Knott, "Healing the Heart of ISKCON: The Place of Women," in *The Hare Krishna Movement: The Post-Charismatic Fate of a Religious Transplant,* edited by Edwin F. Bryant and Maria L. Ekstrand (New York, 2004). The Bryant and Ekstrand book is remarkable in the scope and coherence of its essays and for its inclusion of insiders' and outsiders' perspectives. For an insider's report on the way that ISKCON has responded to many of its growth pains and crises in the 1970s and 1980s, see Nori J. Muster, *Betrayal of the Spirit* (Chicago, 2001). For a good example of the institutionalization and "Hinduization" of ISKCON, see Malory Nye, *Multiculturalism and Minority Religions in Britain: Krishna Consciousness, Religious Freedom, and the Politics of Location* (Richmond, U.K., 2001).

LARRY D. SHINN (1987 AND 2005)

INTI was the Inca sun god, worshiped in the Andes at the time of the Spanish conquest in the first half of the sixteenth century. The Sun was the Inca's dynastic ancestor and imperial god. The Inca ruler was believed to be the son of the Sun; his commands were divine oracles. According to one variant of the Inca creation myth, the Sun, having been created by the god Viracocha on a sacred island in Lake Titicaca (on the Bolivian-Peruvian Altiplano), rose over the lake and spoke to the first Inca ruler, Manco Capac, to whom he gave instruction in Sun worship. The Sun was the most important sky god, with Thunder (or Weather), Moon, and the star deities trailing in rank. There may have been a tripartite division of the Sun, but this is not clear. As was often true in New World religions, the Sun had various aspects or names. Inti was the royal deity; he was also identified with Punchao, the Sun of the day—that is, daylight. There may also have been specifically identified Suns of solstices or other astronomical events.

Inca sun worship was intimately integrated with the growing of maize. The sun was of vital importance in an expanding agricultural society mostly situated in hail-ridden altitudes with frequent frosts. The sun also regulated planting times. In the Inti Raymi ("sun festival"), held at the winter solstice (June), priests made a pilgrimage toward the east, and a ceremony took place in which the Inca ruler lifted a cup of *chicha* (a fermented maize drink) to the Sun, then sprinkled the liquid on the ground. There were sacrifices to the Sun on neighboring hills.

The legend of the founding of Cuzco, the capital city, indicates the agricultural basis of Inca religion. The wandering Inca, led by Manco Capac, were told to establish the city in a place where a gold rod given to them by the Sun would sink into the earth with one blow, indicating good planting ground. The Coricancha ("golden enclosure"), begun by Manco Capac as a humble shrine on the spot where the rod sank, was later expanded into the Temple of the Sun, an impressive structure of finely worked stone buildings around a courtyard; the facade was decorated with sheets of gold that reflected sunlight. (Manco Capac had originally presented himself to the Cuzco Valley people dressed in sun-catching gold ornaments.)

The Coricancha was the primary religious center, a place of pilgrimage, and a model for other Sun temples throughout the vast Inca empire. The priests of the Sun were of the highest rank (the chief priest was a relative of the Inca ruler), and there were many of them. At the Coricancha lived the "chosen women," wives of the Sun, who performed ritual duties including the preparation of ceremonial maize and *chicha* and the weaving of fine cloth to be offered to the Sun. At Inti Raymi, maize was specially prepared by them because it was thought to be a gift from the Sun. During several festivals only maize could be eaten. It was grown in the garden of the Coricancha, and three times a year, during festivals, maize plants fashioned of gold were displayed there. The best lands and largest herds of llamas belonged to the Sun, who also received the finest offerings, including pure-white llamas and objects of gold.

SEE ALSO Manco Capac and Mama Ocllo; Viracocha.

BIBLIOGRAPHY

Bernabé Cobo's *History of the Inca Empire* (Austin, 1979) is a valuable early source on myth and rite. Burr C. Brundage's *Lords of Cuzco* (Norman, Okla., 1967) includes a description of Inti Raymi, and J. H. Rowe's *An Introduction to the Archaeol-*

ogy of Cuzco (Cambridge, Mass., 1944) includes a detailed section on the Coricancha.

Elizabeth P. Benson (1987)

INTOXICANTS
See BEVERAGES; PSYCHEDELIC DRUGS

INTUITION.

The term comes from the Latin *intuitio,* which is derived from *intueri,* meaning to look at attentively (with astonishment or admiration), gaze at, contemplate, or pay attention to. At first confined to direct visual experience, the term came to denote the process of insight as well as its object. Intuition in this first sense is a direct "look" at a particular thing that shows itself immediately in its concrete fullness without the mediation of any other knowledge, procedure, or content. The roots of this meaning lie in the visual character of the Greek, Arabic, and Hebrew mentalities as reflected in the Platonic-Augustinian tradition. In the later and wider sense, the word designates the direct apprehension of an object in its present, concrete reality through either sense perception (including memory and imagination) or the intellect. *Intuition* is today almost exclusively understood in a metaphorical sense; the word designates the human capacity for instant and immediate understanding of an object, a person, a situation, and so forth. The immediacy of intuition sets it in opposition to the discursive function of the intellect, which is mediated by concepts and propositions. In this sense, intuition entails the direct, nonmediated presence of the object to the knowing faculty; it sometimes extends to a partial or total fusion of subject and object. Knowledge of this kind excludes all rational, gnoseological, or even psychological analysis or justification.

The many, sometimes divergent, uses of the word can be classified into several distinct types: (1) sensory (aesthetic) or empirical intuition is a nonconceptual, nonrational grasp of reality; (2) intellectual, logical, or mathematical intuition is the self-evident grasp of fundamental ideas, axioms, principles, or truths; (3) essential intuition is a grasp of the inner essence of a thing, a being, a cause, a situation; and (4) spiritual intuition is the immediate contemplation of the highest order of things, an insight gained neither through the senses nor through intellectual reflection, but stemming from the "inner man" and akin to the receiving of a revelation.

The Philosophical Tradition. In Plato's works, especially the dialogue *Phaedrus,* with its myth of the soul that contemplates the heavenly ideas before its embodiment, intuition is of these eternal essences, which are visible only to the intellect. In Plotinus, for whom the *nous* is able to apprehend the true world in itself, and the Neoplatonic mystics, the role of intuition in the spiritual sense looms large. Aristotle recognized the existence of intuitive knowledge (*Posterior Analytics* 1.9.76a21) in relation to the first principles, which are not in need of any demonstration. Augustine of Hippo, who believed that "the truth lies in the inner man," considered intuition a form of mental contemplation. Thomas Aquinas attributed to God the veritable creative intuition; he defined human intuitive cognition as "the presence, in some way, of the intelligible to the intellect" (*Commentaries on the Sentences* 1d3.94a5). The medieval scholastics used "intuitive cognition," as opposed to "abstractive cognition," to designate knowledge in which the object is delivered directly to the senses. For Descartes, intuition constitutes each successive link in a chain of deductions that are noninferential concepts of the "pure and attentive mind." For Spinoza, it is the third and highest degree of cognition. Kant recognized only sensible intuition. The German Idealists (Schelling, Fichte, Schopenhauer) and Husserlian phenomenologists viewed intellectual intuition as a deep and instantaneous understanding of things, essences, and situations given in perception. For Henri Bergson, intuition signifies an immediate awareness akin to instinct and sympathy, capable of penetrating its object while unfolding in the unique, qualitative time ("duration") of each living being. Bergson opposed intuition to intelligence, the proper dimensions of which are geometrical space and mechanical clock-time; for him, intuition alone is capable of grasping the dynamic nature of things in its original simplicity.

Religious Intuition. In religion, the term *intuition* functions on several levels; the specific meanings are mostly variants of the spiritual intuition defined previously. The following aspects of religious intuition may be distinguished: (1) the understanding of divine commands; (2) the perception of the divine in religious or numinous experience, in the sense of a peering into the mysterious elusive presence of the transcendent in ways simultaneously sensory (seeing, hearing, or "smelling" divinity), intellectual, and suprasensory; (3) the illuminating understanding of the meanings hidden in metaphors and other literary tropes of sacred writings; and (4) the means of communicating and communion among believers.

All forms of mysticism and Gnosticism rely on intuition in the formulation of cognitive claims regarding the ineffable understanding of religious mysteries. The highest states of mystical contemplation may be conceived as uninterrupted chains of intuitive acts. The experience of nonduality in Advaita Vedānta, for example, is based on the insight of oneness and the disappearance of the distance between subject and object. "Suchness" (*tathatā*) in Mādhyamika Buddhism may be called an intuition of the ultimate as the invisible reality underlying all things. The Buddha's enlightenment constitutes an intuitive peak—the highest form of mystical contemplation. Zen Buddhism, with its abhorrence for the discursive intellect, emphasizes *satori* as the immediate grasp of the Buddha nature. The crux of Zen meditational disciplines, whether of gradual enlightenment (in the "*zazen* only" Sōtō school) or of sudden enlightenment (the *kōan*-solving Rinzai school), lies in the all-pervading illumination of the mind, an insight that reaches into that which is beyond any subjectivity or objectivity.

In Jewish mysticism, the secret contents of the Qabbalah are considered highly intuitive, obtained by a form of supernatural illumination. The poverty of ordinary human faculties does not allow proper cognition; intuition alone, tantamount in its "fine points" to divine inspiration, can create a felicitous "science of God" that reasoning is incapable of encompassing. Hence the claim, characteristic of Jewish mysticism, that true tradition and true intuition coincide, a tenet that plays an important part in the history of Qabbalah, that of maintaining the balance between tradition and innovation.

In Islam, intuition plays a role in connection with *al-ʿaql,* a cognitive faculty often mentioned in the Qurʾān that binds humankind to God (the root *ʿql* means literally "to bind"). Religious knowledge is participatory knowledge, higher than rational yet not opposed to the intellect. Direct vision by a "third eye," as opposed to the indirect knowledge yielded by intellectual ratiocination, is emphasized. In Islamic theology and philosophy, but especially in Ṣūfī mysticism, where the heart is traditionally considered the locus of intelligence and spirituality, the actually intuitive "knowledge of the heart" is connected with the creative imagination of the perfected universal man; such knowledge alone counts before the divine and is essential for salvation. In the esoteric tradition, some commentators of the Qurʾān considered the intuitive faculty a gift of revelation by the Holy Spirit (the archangel Gabriel), an illumination received by the intellect.

In Daoism, the doctrine of "no knowledge" or "ignorance" is aimed at obtaining true wisdom or intuition. Creativity is unconscious of accumulated technical knowledge, but it relies on the certainty and precision of intuitive knowledge.

SEE ALSO Knowledge and Ignorance.

BIBLIOGRAPHY

Bahm, A. J. *Types of Intuition.* Albuquerque, 1960.

Bergson, Henri. *Introduction à la métaphysique.* Paris, 1903.

Hadamard, Jacques. *Subconscient, intuition, logique dans la recherche scientifique.* Paris, 1947.

Husserl, Edmund. *Ideas: General Introduction to Pure Phenomenology* (1913). Translated by W. R. Boyce Gibson. London, 1931.

Lévinas, Emmanuel. *Théorie de l'intuition dans la phénoménologie de Husserl.* New ed. Paris, 1963.

Lonergan, Bernard J. F. *Insight: A Study of Human Understanding.* London, 1957.

Nasr, Seyyed Hossein. "Intellect and Intuition: Their Relationship from the Islamic Perspective." *Studies in Comparative Religion* 13 (Winter–Spring 1979): 65–74.

Palliard, Jacques. *Intuition et réflexion.* Paris, 1925.

Penzo, Giorgio. "Riflessioni sulla intuitio tomista e sulla intuitio heideggeriana." *Aquinas* 9 (1966): 87–102.

Pritchard, Harold Arthur. *Moral Obligation.* Oxford, 1949.

Schuon, Frithjof. *L'œil du cœur.* Paris, 1950.

Stace, W. T. *Mysticism and Philosophy.* Philadelphia, 1960.

Thompson, D. G. "Intuition" and "Inference." *Mind* 3 (1878): 339–349, 468–479.

Verdú, Alfonso. *Abstraktion und Intuition als Wege zur Wahrheit in Yoga und Zen.* Munich, 1965.

New Sources

Curnow, Trevor. *Wisdom, Intuition and Ethics.* Amherst, N.Y., 1999.

Davis-Floyd, Robbie, and P. Sven Arvidson, eds. *Intuition, the Inside Story: Interdisciplinary Perspectives.* New York, 1997.

Holt, Lynn. *Apprehension: Reason in the Absence of Rules.* Burlington, Vt., 2002.

Sternberg, Robert, and Janet Davidson, ed. *The Nature of Insight.* Cambridge, Mass., 1995.

Stratton-Lake, Philip, ed. *Ethical Intuitionism: Re-evaluations.* New York, 2002.

ILEANA MARCOULESCO (1987)
Revised Bibliography

INUIT RELIGIOUS TRADITIONS. The Inuit (Eskimo) live in the vast Arctic and sub-Arctic area that stretches from the eastern point of Siberia to eastern Greenland. Of the approximately 105,000 Inuit, 43,000 live in Greenland, 25,000 in Arctic Canada, 35,000 (plus 2,000 Aleut) in Alaska, and 1,500 (plus a small number of Aleut) in Russia. Language has been used as the basic criterion for defining the Inuit as an ethnic group. The "Eskimo languages" (as they are invariably referred to) are divided into two main branches, Inuit and Yupik. Inuit is spoken from northern Alaska to eastern Greenland, forming a continuum of dialects with mutual comprehension between adjacent dialects. Varieties of Yupik are spoken in Siberia and in southern Alaska as far north as Norton Sound.

The word *Eskimo* seems to be of Montagnais origin and has been erroneously believed to mean "eater of raw meat." The word *Inuit* means "people." *Inuit* as a self-designation is used primarily in Canada and, to some extent, in Greenland (where the more common self-designation is *Kalaallit*). *Yupik* means "a real person," just as *Inupiat,* which is the self-designation in northern Alaska, means "real people." *Inuit,* however, is the common term used to designate themselves collectively by the members of the Inuit Circumpolar Conference, an organization established in 1977 by representatives from Greenland, Canada, and Alaska.

Traditionally the Inuit are divided into many geographic groups. The members of each group, or band, were connected through kinship ties, but the band was without formal leadership. The nuclear family was the most important social unit, but the extended family often cohabited and worked cooperatively. Dyadic relationships, such as wife-exchange partners and joking partners, were also common.

Today, most Inuit live in the so-called Arctic area, north of the treeline and the 10° celsius July isotherm. The Inuit were hunters who adapted to the seasonal availability of various mammals, birds, and fish. Hunting sea mammals with harpoons was characteristic, but hunting inland during the summer was also part of the subsistence pattern of many Inuit. A few groups in northern Alaska and in Canada have spent the entire year inland, hunting caribou and fishing for arctic char. In southern Alaska, the wooded valleys along the long rivers were inhabited by Inuit who relied upon the great run of the fish as well as the migrations of sea mammals and birds.

Most Inuit in Canada lived in snow houses during the winter; others settled in winter houses built of stone and sod or wood. Stone lamps that burned blubber were used for heating, lighting, and cooking. Skin boats and, except in southern Greenland and Alaska, dog sledges were used for transportation; kayaks were used for seal hunting and large, open umiaks for whale hunting. Although some Inuit are still hunters and fishermen, today's Inuit societies are modernized. Money economy has replaced subsistence economy; modern technology and education have been introduced; television plays an important role; and so on. Except for the small population in Siberia, the Inuit have become Christians, and even the Inuit in Siberia no longer observe their religious traditions.

Historically, the Inuit held many observances to insure good hunting, and in the small and scattered hunting and fishing communities many local religious practices were observed. Generally, ritual life was more elaborate in Alaska than in Canada and Greenland. In Alaskan settlements there were usually one or more big men's houses, called *qarigi* among the Point Barrow Inuit and *qasiq* among those of the Bering Sea, where people gathered for social and religious feasts. In Canada, the Inuit built temporary festival snow houses, but no eyewitness accounts exist of festival houses in Greenland.

RELATIONS BETWEEN MEN AND ANIMALS. According to eastern Inuit religious tradition, each animal had its own *inua* (its "man," "owner," or "spirit") and also its own "soul." Within the western Inuit religious tradition, the *inua* seems to have been identical to the soul. The idea of *inua* was applied to animals and implements as well as to concepts and conditions (such as sleep). Lakes, currents, mountains, and stars all had their own *inua,* but only the *inua* of the moon, air, and sea were integral to the religious life of the Inuit.

Since the Inuit believed that the animals they hunted possessed souls, they treated their game with respect. Seals and whales were commonly offered a drink of fresh water after they had been dragged ashore. Having received such a pleasant welcome as guests in the human world, their souls, according to Inuit belief, would return to the sea and soon become ready to be caught again, and they would also let their fellow animals know that they should not object to being caught. When the season's first kill of an important species of seal was made, the meat was distributed to all of the inhabitants of a settlement. This practice divided the responsibility for the kill among the entire community and increased the possibility of good hunting.

Inuit rituals in connection with the polar bear are part of an ancient bear ceremonialism of the circumpolar regions of Eurasia and North America. In southern Greenland, for example, the head of a slain polar bear was placed in a house facing the direction from which the bears usually came so that the bear's soul could easily find its way home. During the five days that the soul was believed to require to reach its destination the bear was honored: its eyes and nostrils were closed so that it would not be disturbed by the sight and smell of human beings; its mouth was smeared with blubber; and it was given presents.

Whaling was of great social, economic, and ritual importance, especially among the North Alaska Inuit. In the spring, all hunting gear was carefully cleaned, and the women made new clothes for the men. The whales would not be approached until everything was cleaned. During the days before the whaling party set out, the men slept in the festival house and observed sexual and food taboos. The whaling season terminated with a great feast to entertain the whales.

TABOOS, AMULETS, AND SONGS. Unlike cultic practices in connection with the deities, which had relatively minor significance, taboos, amulets, and songs were fundamentally important to the Inuit. Most taboos were imposed to separate the game from a person who was tabooed because of birth, menstruation, or death. A separation between land and sea animals was also important in many localities, reflecting the seasonal changes in hunting adaptation. An infringement of a taboo might result in individual hardship (for example, the loss of good fortune in hunting, sickness, or even death), but often, it was feared, the whole community would suffer. Usually a public confession under the guidance of the shaman was believed sufficient to reduce the effect of the transgression of a taboo.

Amulets, which dispensed their powers only to the first owner, were used primarily to secure success in hunting and good health and, to a lesser degree, to ward off negative influences. Parents and grandparents would usually buy amulets for children from a shaman. Amulets were usually made up of parts of animals and birds, but a wide variety of objects could be used. They were sewn on clothing or placed in boats and houses.

One way to increase the effect of the amulets was through the use of food totems and secret songs. Used primarily to increase success in hunting, secret songs and formulas were also used to control other activities and were often associated with food taboos. Songs were either inherited or bought. If a song was passed on from one generation to the next, all members of the family were free to use it, but once it was sold it became useless to its former owners.

RITES OF PASSAGE. In many localities in Canada and Alaska, women had to give birth alone, isolated in a small hut or tent. For a specified period after the birth, the woman was subjected to food and work taboos. Children were usually named after a person who had recently died. The name was regarded as a vital part of the individual, and, in a way, the deceased lived on in the child. The relationship resulted in a close social bond between the relatives of the deceased and the child.

The family celebrated particular stages in a child's development, especially in connection with subsistence activities. For example, when a boy killed his first seal, the meat was distributed to all the inhabitants of the settlement, and for each new important species a hunter killed, there was a celebration and ritual distribution.

Death was considered to be a passage to a new existence. There were two lands of the dead: one in the sky and one in the sea (or underground). The Inuit in Greenland considered the land in the sea more attractive because people living there enjoyed perpetual success in whale hunting; those in the sky, on the other hand, led dull existences. It was not the moral behavior of the deceased that determined the location of his afterlife, but rather the way in which he died. For example, men who died while whaling or women who died in childbirth were assured of an afterlife in the sea. Conceptions of the afterlife, however, differed among the Inuit. The Canadian and Alaskan Inuit believed the most attractive afterlife was found in the sky. Some Inuit had either poorly conceptualized beliefs in an afterlife or no beliefs at all.

While death rituals usually included only the nearest family members and neighbors, the Great Feast of the Dead, celebrated in the Alaskan mainland from the Kuskokwim River to the Kotzebue Sound, attracted participants even from neighboring villages. The feast was given jointly, and the hosts' social status was demonstrated by the quantity of food, furs, clothing, and implements that were given away.

The Bladder Feast, an important calendar feast celebrated in Alaska from Kodiak Island to Point Hope, was held in midwinter. At this feast, the bladders of all the seals that had been caught during the previous year were returned to the sea in order that their souls might come back in new bodies and let themselves be caught again. The skins of all the small birds and animals that the boys had caught were displayed in the festival house, and gifts were given to human souls, to the souls of the seals, and to those who were present.

SHAMANS. In Greenland and Canada, the shaman (*angakkoq*) played a central role in religion. In Alaska, however, where it was common for an individual to become a shaman as the result of a calling, many rites did not demand the expertise of the shaman. Prospective shamans often learned from skilled shamans how to acquire spirits and to use techniques such as ecstatic trances. In Greenland and Labrador, the apprentice was initiated by being "devoured" by a polar bear or a big dog while being in trance alone in the wilderness. After having revived, he was ready to become master of various spirits.

Shamans in Greenland always used a drum to enter a trance. Masks were also instrumental, especially in Alaska, both in secular and religious connections. The shaman might summon his familiar spirits to the house where a séance was taking place, or he might go on a spiritual flight himself. The Canadian shaman might, for example, go down to the *inua* of the sea, that is, the Sea Woman, to get seals. In Alaska, a shaman on Nunivak Island would go to the villages of the various species of animals in the sea. In the Norton Sound area he would go to the moon to obtain animals for the settlement.

Although shamans were the principal revealers of unknown things, some other people could also acquire information from the spirits by using a simple technique called *qilaneq*. It required that an individual lift an object and then pose questions, which were answered affirmatively or negatively according to whether the object felt heavy or not.

Shamans also functioned as doctors. For example, they would suck the sick spot where a foreign object had been introduced or try to retrieve a stolen soul. Sorcerers—often believed to be old, revengeful women—were also common, and shamans were sometimes called to reveal them. There were instances, however, in which the shaman himself was accused of having used his power to harm someone; in such cases the shaman could be killed.

THE DEITIES. The Inuit of Canada and Greenland believed that the *inua* of the sea, the Sea Woman, controlled the sea animals and would withhold them to punish people when they had broken a taboo. Franz Boas (1888) transcribed the name given to her by the Inuit on Baffin Island as *Sedna*, which probably means "the one down there."

The Inuit of eastern Baffin Island ritually killed Sedna during a feast that was held when the autumn storms came and whose purpose was to make sealing possible again. The Sedna ceremony included, *inter alia*, a ritual spouse exchange and a tug-of-war, the result of which predicted the weather for the coming winter.

While Sedna represented the female principle of the world, the *inua* of the moon, Aningaaq, represented the male principle. An origin myth tells how he was once a man who committed incest with his sister. She became the sun, he the moon. Otherwise the sun played no part in the religion of the Inuit, but the moon was associated with the fertility of women. He was recognized as a great hunter, and some Alaskan Inuit believed that the moon controlled the game.

The air was called Sila, which also means "universe" and "intellect." The *inua* of the air was a rather abstract but feared figure; if it was offended when taboos were broken, it would take revenge by bringing storms and blizzards.

The Raven appeared, primarily in Alaska, as a creator, culture hero, and trickster in a cycle of myths that included those of the earth diver and the origin of the light. The Raven, however, played a negligible role in religious practices.

The differences between and sometimes vagueness in Inuit religious ideas may be related not only to their wide and scattered distribution but also to the fact that their societies had a loose social organization and were without a written language before contact with the Europeans. For all Inuit, however, a close and good relationship with the animals on which they depended for their survival was believed to be of vital importance.

SEE ALSO Bears; Sedna; Tricksters, article on North American Tricksters.

BIBLIOGRAPHY

An excellent survey of Inuit culture from prehistoric to modern times is given in the *Handbook of North American Indians*, vol. 5, edited by David Damas (Washington, D.C., 1984). The best survey of Inuit religion is Margaret Lantis's article "The Religion of the Eskimos," in *Forgotten Religions*, edited by Vergilius Ferm (New York, 1950), pp. 311–339. Lantis is also the author of *Alaskan Eskimo Ceremonialism* (New York, 1947). This well-documented book is based primarily on literary sources, but it also contains Lantis's field notes from Nunivak. A review of the religion of the Inuit in Canada and Greenland has been written by Birgitte Sonne and myself as an introduction to a collection of plates that illustrate the religious life of these people in *Eskimos: Greenland and Canada* (Leiden, 1985), vol. 8, pt. 2, of the series "Iconography of Religions." A strong visual impression of the Bering Sea Inuit culture in the nineteenth century is found in William W. Fitzhugh and Susan A. Kaplan's *Inua: Spirit World of the Bering Sea Eskimo* (Washington, D.C., 1982). This is a fascinating book that examines how the spirit world manifests itself in all areas of the life of these Inuit. A study of the religion of two Inuit groups in Canada is given in J. G. Oosten's *The Theoretical Structure of the Religion of the Netsilik and Iglulik* (Mappel, Netherlands, 1976). Information that has been gathered on rituals in connection with animals is presented in Regitze Soby's article "The Eskimo Animal Cult," *Folk* (Copenhagen) 11/12 (1969–1970): 43–78. The position of the Inuit shaman has been analyzed by Birgitte Sonne in "The Professional Ecstatic in His Social and Ritual Position," in *Religious Ecstasy*, edited by Nils G. Holm (Stockholm, 1982), pp. 128–150, and by Daniel Merkur in his *Becoming Half Hidden: Shamanism and Initiation among the Inuit* (Stockholm, 1985).

Among the many valuable and often quoted books by Knud Rasmussen is *The Netsilik Eskimos: Social Life and Spiritual Culture* (Copenhagen, 1931). This book presents material that Rasmussen collected from various groups of Inuit who had had limited contact with the Euro-American world. Among the many valuable studies on the Alaskan Inuit, two should be mentioned: Robert F. Spencer's *The North Alaskan Eskimo: A Study in Ecology and Society* (Washington, D.C., 1959) and Ann Fienup-Riordan's *The Nelson Island Eskimo: Social Structure and Ritual Distribution* (Anchorage, Alaska, 1983).

An extensive bibliography for Inuit religion is given by John Fisher in his article "Bibliography for the Study of Eskimo Religion," *Anthropologica* n.s. 15 (1973): 231–271.

New Sources

Albanse, Catherine L. *Nature Religion in America: From the Algonquin Indians to the New Age.* Chicago, 1990.

The Cambridge History of the Native Peoples of the Americas. 3 vols. New York, 1996–2000.

Dorais, Louis-Jacques. *Quagtag: Modernity and Identity in an Inuit Community.* Toronto, 1997.

Eber, Dorothy Harley. *When the Whalers Were Up North: Inuit Memories from the Eastern Arctic.* Kingston, 1989.

Mills, Antonia, and Richard Slobodin. *Amerindian Rebirth: Reincarnation Belief among North American Indians and Inuit.* Toronto, 1994.

Seidelman, James Turner, and Harold Seidelman. *The Inuit Imagination: Arctic Myth and Sculpture.* London, 1994.

Tester, Frank James and Peter Kulchysi. *Tammarit (Mistakes): Inuit Relocation in the Eastern Arctic.* Vancouver, 1994.

INGE KLEIVAN (1987)
Revised Bibliography

INVISIBLE RELIGION. The term *invisible religion* was introduced by the German sociologist Thomas Luckmann and became widespread following the publication in 1963 of *Das Problem der Religion in der modernen Gesellschaft*, published in English as *The Invisible Religion: The Transformation of Symbols in Industrial Society.* The concept of invisible religion emerged from the difficulty of maintaining a traditional religious life in societies to which the industrial revolution brought radical differentiation processes, both in social structures and ways of living, as people were forced, in mounting progression, to change residences, workplaces, habits, and worldviews. Luckmann agrees with sociologists who consider the secularization trend, which they view as a crisis of ecclesiastic-oriented religion, as irreversible. On the other hand, and more importantly, Luckmann extends the significance of religion by arguing that one's worldview, as an objective social and historical reality, fulfills an essentially religious function. This "elementary social form of religion," according to Luckmann, is universal in human society.

In his book, Luckmann considers the notion—diffused in nineteenth-century philosophy and among the secularization theorists of the following century—that modern life is without religion, if not essentially areligious; that is, that the "irrationality" of religion should yield precedence to the "rationality" of modern life. Luckmann argues that this idea is partially wrong. It is true that, unlike Australian aboriginal societies and those of ancient Egypt and medieval Europe, postindustrial societies seem secular and rationalistic. Their political and economic institutions no longer need traditional legitimizations, especially religious ones. Most people living in modern industrial societies do not consider themselves to be tied to each other by officially institutionalized religious communities, dogmas, and religious rituals. Taking all these circumstances into account, Luckmann agrees that modern social structures are "secular." Nevertheless—and this is his central thesis—human beings in modern societies, no matter how much their lives differ from that in other cultures and societies, have not lost the "religiousness" that has characterized human life (as opposed to the lives of other species) since ancient times. Therefore, even the deep social and cultural changes that produced "modernity" have not changed the fundamentally religious nature of human existence.

In his analysis of the "religious nature of human existence," Luckmann refers to the writings of his mentor Alfred Schutz (1899–1959), particularly those dealing with the concepts of "appresentation" and "symbol/transcendence." Schutz claimed that when human beings perceive an object, they perceive directly only certain aspects of it, but other aspects that do not appear to them directly are immediately grasped as well. The directly perceived part of the object "appresents" the unseen part. Schutz also introduced a concept of transcendence that became important to Luckmann's concept of religion. In his essay "The Transcendence of Nature and Society: Symbols" (1932). Schutz argues that everything that surrounds human beings (e.g., the world, the cosmos) goes "beyond" their direct experience of time and space. The social environment in which people live refers to a horizon of potential social environments, just as in space there exists an infinity of objects that cannot be reduced to the human capacity for manipulation and control—they are "beyond." Humans can only apply to them appresentative references of a higher order, the "transcendent." From this point Schulz tackles the issue of symbol, which he defines in the following way: "A symbol can be defined in first approximation as an appresentational object, fact, or event within the reality of our everyday life, whereas the other appresented member of the pair refers to an idea which transcends our experience of everyday life" (1962–1966, vol. 1, p. 331). Thus, the issue of transcendence is located, according to Schutz, in the appresentative relationship between two realities: fact, which is a part of everyday life; and idea, which transcends and refers to something other than everyday life.

The religious problem in Luckmann is based on this relationship, to which he confers a social dimension. Luckmann distinguishes the *transcendent,* which is such only in relation to what is referred as "immanent," from *religion,* which is normally seen as the whole of human experience made visible and localized in symbols, holy places, and holy temples, and the people and activities concerned with them. All this is evident, according to Luckmann, in the case of tribal religions, ancestral cults, universal religions (especially when institutionalized under the form of churches and sects), and so on. Furthermore, the historical institutionalization of the symbolic and sacred nucleus of a worldview is included in the specifics of a universally human social process. The fundamental function of religion is therefore to transform the members of the species *Homo sapiens* into actors belonging to a specific historical-social order. Any component of social reality that is essential to this function can be legitimately called *religious,* whether or not it refers to the supernatural explicitly or implicitly.

Luckmann insists that the fundamental function of religion—that is, the transformation of the members of a species into morally responsible actors within a social order—is motivated by historical deposits of social interaction: "The objectivation of a symbolic universe as a system of meaning presupposes that the subjective experiences entering into its construction be meaningful. The meaningful quality of subjective experience, however, is a product of social processes" (1967, pp. 44–45). This meaningfulness is a "quality," so "it is inkeeping with an elementary sense of the concept of religion to call the transcendence of biological nature by the human organism a religious phenomenon. . . .We may, therefore, regard the social processes that lead to the formation of Self as fundamentally religious" (p. 49).

Here Luckmann's approach diverges from that of Schutz. The concept of transcendence in Schutz is born from the experience of going beyond the contingent that every person experiences everyday. Thus, the present natural and social environment refers to a horizon of potential natural and social environments, and an opening is made manifest to a double transcendent infinity of the natural world and the social world. Transcendence, according to Schultz, marks the expressive limits and the limits of movement of human beings, while it also enables people to construct a complex net of socially approved terminals between significants and meanings. This "net" constitutes the symbolic activity of humans. The symbol, being a typically human construction, is a link between the two poles: (1) a fact or an event within the reality of everyday life, and (2) an idea that transcends everyday experience.

In accordance with the research of anthropologists, ethnologists, and historians of religion, Schutz considered hierogenetic and mythopoetic activities to be typical activities of the human mind. The framework in which Luckmann locates the notion of transcendence is more radical. He strongly emphasizes its social construction as the giver of meaning to the symbolic process because "it is true that a genuinely isolated subjective process is inconceivable" (1967, p. 45). He also recovers the terms *religion* and *religious,* qualifying them as intrinsic modalities to the self's transcendent process and to the world belonging to the symbolic-cognitive aspects of the human species. Such a process presents a twofold modality: (1) an organism becomes a self when devoting itself with others to the construction of a universe of objective and moral significance; and (2) transcendence of biologic nature is a universal phenomenon of humankind. Luckmann identifies in the formation of consciousness and conscience "the universal yet specific anthropological condition of religion" (1967, p. 49).

According to Luckmann, the worldview as an "objective and historical social reality performs an essentially religious function and can be defined as an *elementary form of religion*" (1967, p. 53). In turn, religion as traditionally intended can be defined as a worldview with "social, objective, and historical reality." Religion manifests itself in particular social institutions that are the product of the articulation of a sacred cosmos within the worldview, which is in turn constituted by a set of representations that refer "to a domain of reality that is set apart from the world of everyday life" (1967, p. 61). According to this perspective, religious representations constitute a sacred universe definable as a specific and historical form of religion.

Throughout history there have existed societies characterized by a diffusion of religious ceremonies that were expressed through experience and the acknowledgment of the extraordinary. But the boundary between everyday life and the extraordinary is far from clear-cut; therefore, theoretical elaboration of the sacred did not occur. Societies belonging to this type (especially the simpler and more primitive forms of social organization, such as societies of hunters and gatherers) show a remarkable variety of cultural content, in spite of their basic similarities in social structure and in their social, "diffused" form of religion. According to Luckmann, a transformation of great importance in the social form of religion is an element of the framework of socio-structural "adaptations" of the so-called agricultural revolution. Sedentary life, high population density, urbanization, and the institutionalization of power are associated with a marked growth in the institutionalization of religious ceremonies, which, in relation to centralized power and the canonization of sacred life, could lead to a high level of stability in the theocratic variants of ancient hydraulic civilizations. In the West, the next great transformation consisted in the complete specialization of religious ceremony, and eventually in the appearance of the problems associated with pluralism and secularization.

In *The Invisible Religion,* Luckmann examines some of the most important conditions characterizing the institutionalization of religion in the post-Constantine church. Such a process constitutes the background of what was his main interest: the raising of a new, "privatized" social form of religion in the industrial societies of the West. As for the relationship between individual religiosity and social forms of religion, Luckmann maintains that in tribal societies an individual religiosity is modeled exclusively by the social form of religion relatively diffused, whereas in societies characterized by the presence of a "theocratic" institutionalization of religious and political forms, the modeling of individual religiosity by the social form of the prevailing religion remains similar, despite a more complex stratification of society. Churches present the individual with "official" models. But other models begin to enter into competition—and when conditions of pluralism are established for economic and political reasons, the circumstances under which full institutional specialization can succeed cease to exist.

According to Luckmann, if at least one religion is accessible in the condition of "diffused" politico-religious and specialized institutionalization, the individual can deviate from such forms of religion for merely contingent reasons. But if other models are in competition, various systematic types of individual religious development are possible: fundamentalism, syncretism, new religious movements, a return to traditional devotion, or detachment from any form of religion. In the case of institutional specialization, orthodox and heterodox models are in competition. The privatized social form of religion is characterized by the fact that—from a sociological point of view—talking of orthodox and heterodox models makes little sense. In fact, in an interview granted to the Italian journal *Religioni e Società* in 1986, Luckmann stated that:

> A wide range of different actors are involved on the social scene in the social constructions of several kinds of transcendence. The fundamental structure of the process is the one of a "market." There are mass media and there are Christian churches that, in addition to being monuments to a former period characterized by institutional specialization of religion and despite some restoring and fundamentalist tendencies, are trying to reinsert in the processes of modern social constructions of transcendence. Moreover sub-institutional communities have emerged, more or less recent and religious (in the traditional sense), which are trying to play an important part in this process. (Prandi, 1986, p. 37)

Luckmann's complex theory thus comes to the idea that, in modern life, social structure has ceased to mediate coherently between subjective conscience and its experiences of transcendence, and between the communicative reconstruction of such experiences and the competing social constructions of the "sacred universes." At any rate, the present co-location of religion in society—that is, its privatization—is not characterized by something that *is,* but rather by something that *is not.* It is characterized by the absence of compulsory social models, generally plausible with regard to persistent universal human experiences of transcendence.

See Also Implicit Religion; Secularization; Society and Religion; Sociology, article on Sociology of Religion; Study of Religion.

Bibliography

Beyer, Peter. "Secularization from the Perspective of Globalization: A Response to Dobbelaere." *Sociology of Religion* 60, no. 3 (1999): 289–301.

Dobbelaere, Karel. "Towards an Integrated Perspective of the Processes Related to the Descriptive Concept of Secularization." *Sociology of Religion* 60, no. 3 (1999): 229–247.

Grassi, Piergiorgio. "Sulla religione invisibile." In *La religione nella costruzione sociale,* pp. 111–124. Urbino, Italy, 1980; 2d ed., 1989.

Luckmann, Thomas. *Das Problem der Religion in der modernen Gesellschaft.* Freiburg, Germany, 1963. Translated by Luckman as *The Invisible Religion: The Transformation of Symbols in Industrial Society* (New York, 1967).

Prandi, Carlo. "La religione invisibile: Un riesame del contributo di Thomas Luckmann." *Religioni e Società* 1 (1986): 40–48.

Schutz, Alfred. *Collected Paper,* 3 vols. Vol. 1: *The Problem of Social Reality,* edited by Maurice Natanson; Vol. 2: *Studies in Social Theory,* edited by Arvid Brodersen; Vol. 3: *Studies in Phenomenological Philosophy,* edited by I. Schutz. The Hague, 1962–1966.

Swatos, William H., Jr., and Kevin J. Christiano. "Secularization Theory: The Course of a Concept." *Sociology of Religion* 60, no. 3 (1999): 209–228.

CARLO PRANDI (2005)

IOANN OF KRONSTADT (Ivan Il'ich Sergeev, 1829–1908), also known as John of Kronstadt, was a Russian Orthodox priest. Ioann was born in the village of Suro in the Arkhangelsk province of Russia and at the age of ten was sent to the parochial school in Arkhangelsk. He later entered the seminary there, finishing at the top of his class in 1851. He then enrolled in the Theological Academy of Saint Petersburg, one of the four graduate faculties of theology in the empire. High-strung, physically weak, overworked, and radically committed to his life of study, prayer, ascetic discipline, and spiritual struggle, Ioann suffered greatly during these academic years. An added burden was the constant necessity to support himself by outside work. He finished the academy near the bottom of his class in 1855, was ordained deacon on November 11 of that year, and priest on the very next day.

Before accepting priestly ordination, Ioann dreamed of becoming pastor of Saint Andrew's Cathedral in the port city of Kronstadt, a naval base and penal colony on the island of Kotlin in the Gulf of Finland near Saint Petersburg. Kronstadt, teeming with outcasts and criminals, was notorious as a place of dirt, darkness, and sin. Because parish priests as a rule could not be celibate, Ioann married Elizaveta Nesvitskii, the daughter of Saint Andrew's retiring pastor, but he never consummated the marriage, a fact that has caused much debate because it remains unclear whether the bride had consented to such an arrangement.

Ioann served as pastor of the Kronstadt church until his death on December 20, 1908. His priestly career was distinguished by numerous acts of social, charitable, and educational work, both personal and institutional. Ioann established philanthropic agencies such as the Home for Constructive Labor, which provided free schools, workshops, training centers, libraries, counseling services, medical care, and food, for people of all ages. He also taught religious classes in the parish school for thirty-two years, not freeing himself from this obligation until 1889.

Ioann's greatest fame, however, was not as a philanthropist or a pedagogue but as a man of prayer. He was sought by people of all classes and religions from all parts of the Russian empire and beyond as an intercessor before God. From early in his priestly career he began the unprecedented practice, even for monastics, of celebrating all of the Orthodox church services every day, including the eucharistic liturgy. He did so with great fervor and devotion, spending long hours at the altar praying for those who begged his intercession. He often added his own words to the official church prayers and always insisted that the thousands of people who thronged to his church each day participate fully in the worship by receiving Holy Communion. To make this radically innovative practice possible, Ioann further instituted public confession whereby the crowds of penitents openly acknowledged their sins before all while the praying priest walked about the church bestowing absolution and offering counsel.

Ioann, who had come to be known as the "all-Russian pastor," was violently attacked by his detractors for his radical practices, and only the protection of the tsar kept him from becoming the object of punitive action. His spiritual diary, *My Life in Christ,* is a classic of contemporary Russian Orthodox spirituality.

BIBLIOGRAPHY

Ioann of Kronstadt's spiritual diary, *Moia zhizn' vo khriste (My Life in Christ),* is available in the original Russian (Moscow, 1892), and in English translation by Ernest E. Goulaeff (1897; reprint, Jordanville, N. Y., 1971). English excerpts from this work can be found in *The Spiritual Counsels of Father John of Kronstadt,* edited by W. Jardine Grisbrooke (London, 1967; Greenwood, S.C., 1983), and G. P. Fedotov's *A Treasury of Russian Spirituality* (1950; reprint, Belmont, Mass., 1975). A two-volume work in Russian analyzing Ioann of Kronstadt's life and work, containing letters, photographs, and a church service in his honor, is I. K. Surskii's *Otets Ioann Kronshtadtskii* (Father John of Kronstadt), 2 vols. (Forestville, Calif., 1979–1980). The best work in English is *Father John of Kronstadt: A Life,* by (Bishop) Alexander Semenoff-Tian-Chansky (Crestwood, N.Y., 1979).

THOMAS HOPKO (1987)

IPPEN (1239–1289), also known as Chishin; a Japanese holy man, founder of the Jishū, an order of Pure Land Buddhist itinerants. Ippen was born in the province of Iyo (modern Ehime Prefecture) to a long-powerful military clan, the Konō, which had recently suffered a serious defeat in the Jōkyū War of 1221. Ippen's grandfather died in exile, and Ippen, three of his brothers, and his father all became monks. At the age of twelve, Ippen was sent to Kyushu to study the doctrines of the Seizan branch of the Jōdo (Pure Land) sect. Upon the death of his father in 1263, he returned to household life in Iyo. Perhaps because of intraclan strife, he left home again eight years later, and spent the rest of his life on the road as a holy man (*hijiri*).

Ippen initially went on pilgrimages to the great Buddhist temples and Shintō shrines and underwent austerities in the mountains of Shikoku. While on a pilgrimage to Kumano in 1274, he had the climactic experience of his life. The Shintō deity (*kami*) of the main shrine, believed to be a manifestation of Amida Buddha, appeared before him and commanded him to distribute to all people, regardless of their belief or unbelief, purity or impurity, paper talismans (*fuda*) on which were printed the words "Namu Amida Butsu" ("Homage to Amida Buddha"). This Ippen did for the rest of his life, traveling throughout the Japanese archipelago.

By 1278, Ippen had attracted a small group of followers that he called the Jishū, or "time group," referring to its chanting of Amida's name at all times. Before his death, this group numbered perhaps more than two hundred men and women, and Ippen had established rules for group poverty and incessant wayfaring. In addition, he had enrolled 251,724 names in a register of lay supporters.

In 1279, this Jishū began its distinctive dance (*odori nembutsu*) celebrating the instantaneous salvation available in Amida's name. Originally spontaneous and ecstatic, the dance became a regularized performance by members of the Jishū on the grounds of shrines and temples, and in other public areas such as beaches and markets. After being brutally driven out of Kamakura, the shogunal capital, in 1282, Ippen led his Jishū to the provinces around the imperial capital (modern Kyoto). Here he met with great success and was even invited to many notable temples and shrines. In 1288, Ippen led his group to his home in Iyo and then back across the Inland Sea, where he died in 1289. He is buried near the modern city of Kobe.

Ippen interpreted the Pure Land sutras to mean that Amida's enlightenment and the rebirth (*ōjō*) of all beings into Amida's Pure Land were precisely the same event. Since Amida's enlightenment had occurred ten *kalpa*s ago, so too must have the rebirth of all beings. Both, furthermore, had their origin in "Namu Amida Butsu," the "six-character name" established through the vows Amida had made while still a bodhisattva. For this reason, the name alone was sufficient to effect the rebirth attained ten *kalpa*s ago and to obliterate the distinctions between then and now, between this world and the Pure Land, and indeed between all beings and buddhahood. Ippen's paper talismans, therefore, immediately saved all who received them, regardless of their faith, practice, or morality. The dance served as a celebration of this absolutely universal salvation.

Ippen's thought was largely derived from that of the Seizan branch of the Jōdo sect, itself strongly influenced by Esoteric *(mikkyō)* Buddhism. His originality lay in using these ideas to employ for Buddhist salvation existing popular traditions of shamanistic holy men and magic. The Jishū became the largest itinerant order of medieval Japan, absorbing earlier, similar groups, and several of its members were important in the literature and arts of the Muromachi period (1338–1573). Many samurai supported the Jishū, attracted by its endorsement of Shintō, and used its members both as a cultural entourage and as participants in funeral and memorial services. The fortunes of the order declined dramatically, however, with the turmoil that swept the country at the end of that period, and the Jishū continues in the early twenty-first century as only a minor Buddhist sect with headquarters in the city of Fujisawa.

Nevertheless, the practices and beliefs of the Jishū were widely diffused among the Japanese during the medieval period. Ippen's dance, for example, continues as a feature of folk Buddhism in several regions and is tied to the legendary founding of the Kabuki theater. The *Ippen hijiri e* (Illustrated life of the holy man Ippen), a work of twelve scrolls completed in 1299, is one of the masterpieces of Japanese painting and the single most important source for studying popular life in thirteenth-century Japan.

See Also Nianfo.

Bibliography

A collection from the 1750s of Ippen's sayings, letters, and verse has been translated and annotated by Dennis Hirota as *No Abode: The Record of Ippen,* rev. ed. (Honolulu, 1997). For the Jishū, see S. A. Thornton, *Charisma and Community Formation in Medieval Japan: The Case of the Yugyō-ha (1300–1700)* (Ithaca, N.Y., 1999). In Japanese, the best works are Ōhashi Toshio's *Ippen: Sono kōdō to shisō* (Tokyo, 1971), Kanai Kiyomitsu's *Ippen to Jishū kyōdan* (Tokyo, 1975), and Imai Masaharu's *Jishū seiritsu no kenkyū* (Tokyo, 1981).

James H. Foard (1987 and 2005)

IQBĀL, MUḤAMMAD (1877–1938), influential Muslim poet-philosopher of the Indian subcontinent. Born at Sialkot (presently a Pakistani town on the border of India), Iqbāl received his early schooling in his native town and his college education at Lahore (where he studied philosophy with the British Islamicist T. W. Arnold). In 1905 he went to Europe, where he followed M'Taggart's lectures in philosophy, took his doctorate from Munich with a thesis on the development of metaphysics in Persia, and was called to the bar from Lincoln's Inn in London in 1908. In the same year he returned to Lahore where he taught for a while at the Government College and pursued a hectic but unsuccessful law practice. He was knighted in 1922 for his contributions to poetry (about 60 percent of which is in Persian and 40 percent in Urdu). In 1927 he was elected to the Punjab Legislative Assembly, and in 1930 he gave the historic presidential address to the annual session of the Muslim League at Allahabad, wherein he suggested that the solidly Muslim areas of northwest India might be given autonomy so that Muslims could run their affairs according to Islamic norms, the idea that later took the shape of Pakistan. During his last years he was often ill and did not appear in public after April 1936. He died on April 21, 1938, and was buried in the complex of the Imperial Mosque of Lahore. Iqbāl's commitment to the creation of Pakistan was a direct result of his philosophic thought, which was so powerfully expressed in his poetry.

Iqbāl had displayed his unusual talent as a moving and eloquent poet with a "grand style" even in his college days. Before going to Europe he had been a Platonic idealist, an Indian nationalist, and a romanticist of the past who sang hymns to the Himalayas, to intercommunal understanding, and to universal love. In Europe, he discovered Islam with a vengeance, having been shocked by his experience of the European double standards that combined liberal morality and democracy at home with colonial exploitation abroad and, even at home, with the capitalistic exploitation of the working classes. Coupled with this disillusionment he saw the increasing dilapidation of human values in the machine age and the decline of the family institution. But looking at the Eastern and particularly the Muslim societies, he found them in deep somnolence. At this point, he discovered the "true Islam" of the Qurʾān and of Muḥammad, an Islam that was dynamic and not static; in its dynamism he discovered a creative impulse that directed the raw materials of history into a positive moral channel. The modern West, unlike the world of Islam, was industrious enough, but it lacked a positive moral direction for the uplift of humanity; it was inventive but not creative and was, in fact, destructive to the human moral fiber. Henceforth, he invited the whole world, both Muslim and non-Muslim, to join this energizing and ethically positive Islam.

In the development of this dynamic philosophy, which is expressed in Bergsonian vitalistic terms (although unlike Bergson, Iqbāl regards God as being outside the process of history), the key role is played by the twin terms *khudī* ("self") and *ʿishq* ("absorbing love," or *élan vital).* The goal of this ethical dynamism is to expand and fortify the self (which is the only way to individual survival after death), since only when an enlarged and fortified self is realized can a meaningful community of the faithful be launched on earth as the prophet Muḥammad was able to do. Although in the early years of his intellectual development after his discovery of Islam Iqbāl was not optimistic about a similar reawakening on the part of the Muslim community at large, he did eventually come to place his faith in such a development. Through both his poetry and his major prose work, *The Reconstruction of Religious Thought in Islam* (chapter 5), he tried to urge Muslims to create a new future through *ijtihād,* literally "exerting oneself," a Muslim legal term for independent reasoning, which Iqbāl used to describe the exercise of new creative thought within the framework of Islam.

Iqbāl, who had been known as a good poet in Urdu early on, first indicated his concern with the Muslim cause in the two great poems *Shikwah* (Complaint) and *Jawāb* (Answer, that is, God's response to the complaint), but he subsequently turned to Persian in order to reach a larger group of educated Muslims. His *As-rār-i khudī* (Secrets of the self), first published in 1915, speaks of that individual human core that should be strengthened until it reaches its highest fulfillment. The duties of this "self" in the community were discussed two years later in the *Rumūz-i bīkhudī* (Mysteries of selflessness). The Persian collection *Payām-i mashriq* (Message of the East) acknowledges Iqbāl's spiritual debt to Goethe, who was his Western guide as much as Mawlānā Rūmī was his Eastern master. His major Persian work is the *Jāvīd-nāmah* (Jāvīd's book), written for his son in 1932. In this spiritual journey through the spheres in Rūmī's company, he discusses religious, political, and social problems with Muslim and non-Muslim poets and thinkers alike. Among his Urdu poetry, *Bāl-i Jibrīl* (Gabriel's wing) is outstanding.

The titles of Iqbāl's works point to his understanding of himself: he wanted to use "the rod of Moses" (*ẕarb-i kalīm*) and assumed the role of "the sound of the camelbell" (*bāng-i darā*) that had led the Muslims in the caravan of the Prophet back to Mecca. The general impression among Westerners that Iqbāl indulged in romanticization of the past glory of Islam is not correct. While he did show romanticizing tendencies before his "conversion," after his discovery of the dynamic nature of Islam, he was anything but a romanticist of the past. He continually called for the creation of a new future, although he singled out, for the sake of inspiration, certain past achievements of the Muslims, as, for example, in his poem *The Mosque of Cordoba,* which appears in *Bāl-i Jibrīl.*

Bibliography

Iqbāl's collected Persian poetic works have been published in Tehran (1964) and in Pakistan (1973), while his collected Urdu poetic works were published in Pakistan in 1975 and reproduced in India in 1980. *The Reconstruction of Religious Thought in Islam* has had (like his poetic works) a number of printings, including a recent one from Lahore in 1960. A major part of his Urdu poetry has been translated into English by V. G. Kiernan under the title *Poems from Iqbal* (London, 1955); some of his Persian poetic works have been translated by Reynold A. Nicholson and A. J. Arberry, although several still await translation.

Translations into German by Annemarie Schimmel include *Payām-i Mashriq as Botschaft des Ostens* (Wiesbaden, 1963); *Jāvīd-nāmah* as *Das Buch der Ewigkeit* (Munich, 1967); and *Muhammad Iqbal, Persischer Psalter* (Cologne, 1968), with selected poetry and prose. Iqbāl's Urdu poetry has also been translated into German by Johann Christoph Bürgel as *Steppe im Staubkorn* (Bern, 1983). Italian translations by Alessandro Bausani include "Il ʿGulšan-i raz-i ğadid' di Muhammad Iqbāl," *Annali Istituto Universitario Orientale di Napoli,* n. s. 8 (1958): 125–172; *Il poema celeste* (Rome, 1952); and *Poesie di Muhammad Iqbal* (Parma, 1956). There are also French, Czech, Dutch, Arabic, and Russian translations available, and much of his work has been translated into the regional languages of Pakistan.

There has been a plethora of works on Iqbal, not all of good quality. The following three should give a comprehensive introduction to Iqbāl's thought as well as his biography and bibliographies: Syed Abdul Vahid's *Iqbal: His Art and Thought* (Lahore, 1944); Annemarie Schimmel's *Gabriel's Wing: A Study into the Religious Ideas of Sir Muhammad Iqbal* (Leiden, 1963); and *Iqbal: The Poet-Philosopher of Pakistan,* edited by Hafeez Malik (New York, 1971).

New Sources

Biswas, Lakshmi. *Tagore and Iqbal: A Study in Philosophical Perspective.* Delhi, 1991.

Hyder, Syed Akbar. "Iqbal and Karbala: Re-Reading the Episteme of Martyrdom for a Poetics of Appreciation." *Culture Dynamics,* 13 (November 2001): 339–363.

Maruf, Mohammed. *Iqbal's Philospһy of Religion.* Lahore, 1988.

Masud, Muhammad Khalid. *Iqbal's Reconstruction of Ijitihad.* Lahore, 1995.

Siddiqi, Nazir. *Iqbal and Radhakrishnan: A Comparative Study.* New Delhi, 1989.

FAZLUR RAHMAN (1987)
Revised Bibliography

IRANIAN RELIGIONS. Because of the scarce and fragmented data in our possession, we do not know the religions of ancient Iran, other than Zoroastrianism, as organic systems endowed with a specific pantheon, a mythology, particular creeds, cosmogonic and cosmological ideas, and precise eschatological notions. We can postulate the existence of other religions only through a careful analysis of those elements contained within Zoroastrianism that can be linked to a pre-Zoroastrian paganism and through an Indo-Iranian comparison. That is to say, we have no sources, other than the Zoroastrian, for any Iranian religion. Some scholars have viewed as testimony of a non-Zoroastrian cult those few religious references found in the royal Achaemenid inscriptions (sixth to fourth century BCE), as well as Herodotus's mention of "the Persian religion" (1.131–132), although, as is well known, Herodotus never refers to Zarathushtra (Zoroaster). Given these meager materials, we cannot be sure that the cults referred to were not affected in some way or at some time by the Zoroastrian "reform." In fact, it is probably most prudent to consider the religion of the Achaemenids—whose inscriptions also never mention Zarathushtra—as belonging to the Zoroastrian tradition and as a stage in its troubled and complex historical development.

Having said this, it is nonetheless possible to reconstruct a few essential elements of ancient Iranian religions through traces of ideas and beliefs that appear to be independent of the Zoroastrian tradition. Some of these are completely original, but most are held in common with ancient, especially Vedic, India. Such elements pertain mainly to rituals, the pantheon, concepts of death and the afterlife, and cosmology.

Rituals included libations *(zaothra),* offered both to Āpas ("water") and to Ātar ("fire"). The latter was called Agni by the Indians. The libations offered to water were a blend of three ingredients: milk and the juice or leaves of two plants. Those offered to fire were also a blend of three ingredients: dry fuel, incense, and animal fat. In both the libations to water and fire, called *āb-zōhr* and *ātakhsh-zōhr* in late Zoroastrian literature, we find the symbolism of the number three, which also occurs in a number of Brahmanic practices, as well as the blending of ingredients from the animal and vegetable worlds.

These offerings to water and fire, typical of a daily and familiar ritual, were also at the heart of the priestly ritual called the Yasna by the Iranians and Yajña by the Indians, from the root *yaz* ("sacrifice, worship"). Animal sacrifice was certainly practiced in the oldest Yasna and was accompanied by prayers that made it sacred and justified it as a religious act through which the spirits of the household animals being sacrificed became absorbed into a divine entity called Gēush Urvan, the "soul of the bull." Herbs also played an important role in the Yasna, and the priest who carried out the sacrifice held a bundle of herbs in his left hand, called a *baresman* by the Iranians. In time the bundle of herbs was discarded in favor of a bundle of consecrated twigs.

Undoubtedly, *haoma* (*soma* in India) constituted a central element in the cult. The offering made to the waters at the conclusion of the Yasna was prepared by blending milk, the leaves of a plant, and the juice squeezed from the stems of a different plant. The substance's name, *haoma,* applied to both the sacrificial matter and its *yazata,* that is, the "being worthy of worship," or deity, whom it represented. *Haoma,* which was endowed with hallucinogenic and stimulating properties and was seen as a source of strength for warriors, inspiration for poets, and wisdom for priests, was extracted in a stone mortar during a preparatory ritual, after which the consecrated substance was consumed by the priests and by those taking part in the ceremony.

The premises, the instruments, and the ingredients for the ceremony were purified with water in a meticulous and careful way. Purifying and disinfectant properties were also attributed to cattle urine *(gōmez),* a substance that played an important role in the Zoroastrian ritual of the Great Purification, Bareshnūm, as well as in the initiation of priests and corpse bearers, in accordance with practices and notions that were certainly Indo-Iranian in origin.

Libations offered to water and fire, essential components in the ceremonial aspects of the cult, cannot be understood without an awareness of the complex symbolism linked to those two elements, both in Zoroastrian and pre-Zoroastrian Iran, as well as in ancient India. The Indo-Iranian background is particularly evident in the symbolism of fire: in the three ritual fires and in the five natural fires found in Iranian and Indian thought. We can trace the concept of the three fires, those of priests, warriors, and farmers, as well as the concept of five fires burning before Ahura Mazdā, in the bodies of men, animals, plants, clouds, and the earth, respectively, to the Indo-Iranian background. Two *yazatas,* Apam Napāt ("grandson [or son] of waters") and Nairyōsanha ("of manly utterance"), are linked to fire and have Indian counterparts in Apāṃ Napāt and Narāśaṃsā, an epithet for Agni, whose name also belongs to a different god in the Vedas.

Concerning the pantheon, an Indo-Iranian comparison provides considerable help in reconstructing the pre-Zoroastrian religious environment in Iran. There are many divine entities that derive from a common cultural heritage, although they do, at times, present significant differences. Particularly important in such comparisons is the section of the Avesta known as the *Yashts,* or hymns to the various *yazatas*, which mostly perpetuate the worship of gods from an ancient, pre-Zoroastrian cult through a veil of Zoroastrianization after the fact. Worthy of mention, in addition to the cult gods Āpas, Ātar, Gēush Urvan, and Haoma, are the nature gods, such as Asman ("heaven"), Zam ("earth"), Hvar ("sun"), Māh ("moon"), and the two winds, Vāta and Vāyu. A juxtaposition with the Vedic religion clarifies many aspects of an ancient theology dating back to a period that we can definitely call proto-Indo-Iranian. According to some scholars, a few of these divine beings, as well as others well known to the Zoroastrian tradition, such as Zrvan (Zurwān) and Mithra, were originally high gods of Iranian religions other than the Zoroastrian and were thus in competition with Ahura Mazdā, the creator god of Zoroastrianism. Apart from a few specific details in the theories propounded by various scholars (H. S. Nyberg, Stig Wikander, Geo Widengren), and apart from the complex question of the so-called Zurvanist heresy, it is hard not to recognize a certain degree of verisimilitude in their reconstructions, as we find embedded in the Zoroastrian tradition, and not only in the *Yashts,* clear traces of a plurality of heterogeneous elements gradually absorbed and modified.

The Iranian pantheon, like the Indian, was subdivided into two main groups of divine beings, *ahuras* and *daivas*, although there exists sufficient evidence to hold that in Iran the latter word at one time indicated the gods in general. This can be inferred from the Avestan expression *daēva/mashya,* analogous to the Vedic *deva/martya,* to which correspond the Greek *theoi/andres (anthrōpoi)* and the Latin *dii/hominesque,* all of which mean "gods and men." *Daivas*, as gods of an ancient polytheism condemned by Zarathushtra, acquired negative connotations only with the Zoroastrian reform. This happened also with some of the Indo-Iranian gods, such as Indra, Saurva (Śarva in India), and Nāṅhaithya (Nāsatya in India). The term *ahura* ("lord"; *asura* in India), on the other hand, maintained its positive connotations and became part of the name of the supreme god of Zoroastrianism, Ahura Mazdā, as well as being attached to the name of some of the ancient gods from the Indo-Iranian pantheon, such as Mithra (Mitra in India) and Apąm Napāt.

We are not able to establish whether, behind the image of Ahura Mazdā, which was probably created by Zarathushtra himself, there lies the Vedic Indian god Varuṇa or an Indo-Iranian god named Ahura or Asura. This problem, however, is not critical, for even if Zarathushtra's god were a sublimation of the ancient Varuṇa by the Iranian prophet's great religious reform, Varuṇa would certainly have already attained a higher status than that of other gods, such as Mitra or the other sovereign gods of the Indo-Iranian pantheon (Dumézil, 1968–1973).

If the Iranian Mithra corresponds to the weaker Indian Mitra, then Anāhitā, the other great divine being of the triad mentioned in the Achaemenid inscriptions, corresponds to the Indian Sarasvatī, through the Avestan Aredvī Sūrā Anāhitā. The latter, however, presents some very complex problems. Most likely, this ancient Indo-Iranian goddess was subject at an early date to the influence of religious concepts belonging to the Anarian substratum of the Iranian world. Even Herodotus (1.131), speaks of an "Assyrian" and an "Arabian" origin of the great goddess, who certainly shows traits typical of the Great Goddess of the most ancient settled civilizations of the Near and Middle East. In fact, in attempting to reconstruct Iranian religions other than Zoroastrianism, one must rely heavily on elements obtained through an investigation of the Indo-Iranian background. One must, however, try to ascertain, with the help of archaeological findings, what part was played by the Anarian substratum, from the Elam civilization to the so-called Helmand civilization, which came to light in the 1960s during excavations at Shahr-i Sokhta, in Iranian Seistan. A thorough investigation into more recent times is also necessary in order to see whether there are to be found, among the religions of the Hindu Kush, between Nuristan and Dardistan, any fossilized remains of ancient proto-Indo-Aryan religions (Jettmar, 1975; Tucci, 1977).

An Indo-Iranian comparison also provides many other elements pertaining to the pantheon, as well as mythical figures and epos. The latter has been the object of particularly detailed study in recent decades (Dumézil, 1968-1973; Wikander, 1949-1950; Molé, 1953). In this context, we find cast in a leading role the Iranian god Verethraghna, whose Indian name, Vṛtrahan ("slayer of the dragon Vṛtra"), is an epithet of the god Indra. Behind the sacred figure of Verethraghna, who represented victory in the Zoroastrian tradition, was, most likely, the idea of overcoming an obstacle to the activity of the cosmos, which is manifest through the flow of waters.

In the cosmogony of pre-Zoroastrian Iran, we find signs of a myth of separation of heaven and earth, in which the figure of Vāyu, the god of wind and of the atmosphere, the intermediate zone, must have played an important role. It is likely also that the doctrine of seven consecutive creations, of the sky, of water, earth, vegetation, animal life, man, and fire, which we find in late sources, in fact dates from very ancient times.

Essential elements are also provided by an Indo-Iranian comparison in matters pertaining to cosmology. Both Iranians and Indians believed that the world was divided into seven regions, whose Avestan name was *karshvar* (Pahl., *kēshwar;* Skt., *dvīpa*), and that it was surrounded by a mountain range. The central region was called Khvaniratha in Iran and Jambūdvīpa in India, and at its center was a high mountain, called Mount Harā in Iran and Meru or Sumeru in India. South of the mountain was the Tree of All Seeds, just as, in Indian cosmography, we find the Jambū Tree south of Mount Meru. The Tree of All Seeds was thought to be at the center of the great sea Vourukasha, to the south of the mountain standing at the center of the world, also called, in Avestan, Hukairya ("of good activity") or, in Pahlavi, Hukar and Cagād i Dāidīg ("the lawful summit").

The views of death and of the afterlife in the most ancient Iranian religions, before the Zoroastrian reform, seem to have included the survival of the soul *(urvan)*. After wandering around the earth for three days, the soul was thought to enter a gray existence in a subterranean world of shadows, ruled by Yima, the first king, or king of the Golden Age, and the first man ever to have died. (The figure of Yima seems to correspond, although not without some question, to the Indian Yama.) There also appears to have been a notion of survival of a sort of "double" of the soul, the *fravashi,* linked to a concept of immortality typical of an aristocratic and warrior society, in which were present the values of the Indo-Iranian *Männerbund* (Wikander, 1983). There was, as well, the idea of a terrible trial to be overcome by the dead man's spirit: the crossing of Chinvat Bridge, a bridge that could become wider or narrower, to the width of a razor's edge, depending on whether the dead man had been just *(ashavan)* or evil *(dregvant)*. There was probably a test, analogous to this trial after death, used in initiation rites (Nyberg, 1966).

Traces of a common concept of initiation can be found in both Iran and India. It is related to the basic Indo-Iranian religious idea of *asha* (in the Avesta) or *ṛta* (in the Vedas), which remained central even in Zarathushtra's reform, although modified by partly new and different aspects. If we compare the Indian and the Iranian ideas, we can see clearly that a vision of *asha* (or of the sun, which, in turn, is the visible manifestation of the Vedic *ṛta*), was considered by both as a step in the spiritual fulfillment of the believer, who thus became *ashavan* (Av.; OPers., *artāvan*), that is, a participant in the supreme state of possessing *asha/ṛta*. In fact, the Indo-Iranian concept, which the Zoroastrian tradition transformed into one of the Amesha Spentas, contained various positive meanings, from that of truth (its exact translation) to that of a cosmic, ritual, and moral order. The Iranian *ashavan* (Pahl., *ahlaw/ardā[y]*) and the Indian *ṛtāvan* stood, although with different shades of meaning, for "the initiate" and, more generally, for those who, alive or dead, would succeed in penetrating a dimension of being or existence different from the norm.

The idea of the need for an initiation in order to achieve the supreme state of *asha/ṛta,* held in common by the ancient Indo-Iranian world and by what we may call "Aryan mysticism" (Kuiper, 1964), was also linked to the experience of illumination and of the mystic light. The blessed state of *asha* manifests itself through light (*Yasna* 30.1), and *asha* is to be found in "solar dwellings" (*Yasna* 53.4, 32.2, 43.16). The initiate is, then, first of all a "seer," one who has access to the mysteries of the otherworld and who can contemplate a luminous epiphany.

The experience of a mystical light and a complex symbolism connecting spirit, light, and seed form part of a common Indo-Iranian heritage and constitute, therefore, specific elements of an ancient Iranian religion that precedes Zarathushtra's reform. It may not be pure coincidence that we find in the *Gāthās* no mention by Zarathushtra himself of the concept of *khvarenah* ("splendor"), which was a notable aspect of Iranian religious thinking; yet we see it becoming part of the Zoroastrian tradition, as, for example, in *Yashts* 19. *Khvarenah* is a luminous and irradiating force, a sort of igneous and solar fluid (Duchesne-Guillemin, 1962), that is found, mythologically, in water, in *haoma,* and (according to an anthropological concept found in the Pahlavi tradition) in semen.

Khvarenah is an attribute of Mithra, of royalty, of divine and heroic figures belonging to a national and religious tradition, of Yima, of Zarathushtra, and of the Saoshyant; it does not have an exact Indian counterpart but is found in a context that, both literally and in terms of mythological structure, is strictly analogous to the Indian. In the Indian tradition, we find concepts concerning light—its splendor, its activity, its energy, and its effects—such as *ojas* (Av., *aojah*), *varcas* (Av., *varecah*), and *tejas,* meaning, respectively, "strength," "energy," and "splendor," concepts that closely resemble some in Iranian anthropology. The same adjective is used to describe "splendor" in both Iran and India: *ughra* (Av.) and *ugra* (Skt.), meaning "strong."

The Iranian religions other than Zoroastrianism, can, as we have seen, be partially reconstructed, not as organic systems, but rather in some of their particular and characteristic elements: cult and pantheon, cosmogony and cosmology, individual eschatology, anthropology, and psychology, as well as a concept of the experience of initiation substantially common to the entire ancient Indo-Iranian world. Such a common heritage was handed down in ancient Iran by schools of sacred poetry, which left their mark both on Zarathushtra's *Gāthās* and on the *Yashts* of the Younger Avesta.

SEE ALSO Ahura Mazdā and Angra Mainyu; Ahuras; Anahita; Chinvat Bridge; Cosmology, articles on Hindu Cosmology, Jain Cosmology; Daivas; Fravashis; Haoma; Indo-European Religions; Khvarenah; Magi; Mani; Manichaeism; Mazdakism; Mithraism; Saoshyant; Yazatas.

BIBLIOGRAPHY

Preeminent among general reference works on Iranian religions is H. S. Nyberg's important *Irans forntida religioner* (Stockholm, 1937), translated by Hans H. Schaeder as *Die Religionen des alten Iran* (1938); 2d ed., Osnabrück, 1966. Among other invaluable references are Geo Widengren's *Stand und Aufgaben der iranischen Religionsgeschichte* (Leiden, 1955); Jacques Duchesne-Guillemin's *La religion de l'Iran ancien* (Paris, 1962), translated as *Religion of Ancient Iran* (Bombay, 1973); Geo Widengren's *Die Religionen Irans* (Stuttgart, 1965), translated as *Les religions de l'Iran* (Paris, 1968); and Mary Boyce's *A History of Zoroastrianism,* vol. 1 (Leiden, 1975).

On particular aspects of Iranian religions, the following works are recommended. On ceremonials, see Mary Boyce's "*Ātaš-Zōhr* and *Āb-Zōhr,*" *Journal of the Royal Asiatic Society* (1966): 100–118. For a discussion of the Iranian pantheon and an Indo-Iranian comparison, see Émile Benveniste and

Louis Renou's *Vṛtra et Vṛthragna* (Paris, 1934) and Stig Wikander's *Vayu* (Uppsala, 1941). On epos, see Stig Wikander's "Sur le fonds commun indo-iranien des épopées de la Perse et de l'Inde," *La nouvelle Clio* 1–2 (1949–1950): 310–329; Marijan Molé's "L'épopée iranienne après Firdōsī," *La nouvelle Clio* (1953): 377–393; Georges Dumézil's *Mythe et épopée,* 3 vols. (Paris, 1968–1973); and Prods Oktor Skjærvø, "Eastern Iranian Epic Traditions II: Rostam and Bhīsma," *Acta Orientatia Academiae Scientiarum Hungaricae* 51 (1988): 159–170. On the religions of the Hindu Kush, see Karl Jettmar's *Die Religionen des Hindukush* (Stuttgart, 1975) and Giuseppe Tucci's "On Swāt: The Dards and Connected Problems," *East and West,* n. s. 27 (1977): 9–103.

For discussion of the common Indo-European background of some concepts of the most ancient cosmography, see G. M. Bongard-Levin and E. A. Grantovskij's *De la Scythie à l'Inde: Énigmes de l'histoire des anciens Aryens,* translated by Philippe Gignoux (Paris, 1981). On the concept of the Iranian *Männerbund,* see Stig Wikander's *Der arische Männerbund* (Lund, 1983) and my "Antico-persiano *anušya-* e gli immortali di Erodoto," in *Monumentum Georg Morgenstierne,* vol. 1, "Acta Iranica," no. 21 (Leiden, 1981), pp. 266–280. For discussion of the concept of *asha* and Aryan mysticism, see F. B. J. Kuiper's "The Bliss of Aša," *Indo-Iranian Journal* 8 (1964): 96–129.

On initiation, see Jacques Duchesne-Guillemin's "L'initiation mazdéenne," in *Initiation: Contributions to the Theme . . .* edited by C. Jouco Bleeker (Leiden, 1965), pp. 112–118, and on the common Indo-Iranian background of initiation through possessing *asha* and the experience of light, see, in particular, my "Ašavan: Contributo allo studio del libro di Ardā Wirāz," in *Iranica,* edited by me and Adriano V. Rossi (Naples, 1979), pp. 387–452. See also Andrea Piras, "Visio Avestica, I: Prolegomena à l'étude des processus visuels dans l'Iran ancien," *Studia Iranica* 27 (1988): 163–185.

For comparison of the Indo-Iranian notions of *ojas/aojah, varcas/varecah,* and so on, see Jan Gonda's *Ancient-Indian 'ojas', Latin '*augos', and the Indo-Iranian Nouns in -es/-os* (Utrecht, 1952), pp. 57–67, and my "Licht-Symbolik in Alt-Iran," *Antaios* 8 (1967): 528–549. On the ancient Iranian tradition of sacred poetry, which was Indo-Iranian (and, more generally, Indo-European) in origin, see the various contributions by J. Wackernagel, Hans H. Schaeder, and Paul Thieme to *Indogermanische Dichtersprache,* "Wege der Forschung," vol. 165, edited by R. Schmitt (Darmstadt, 1968).

GHERARDO GNOLI (1987)
Translated from Italian by Ughetta Fitzgerald Lubin

IRENAEUS (c. 130–c. 200) was a bishop of Lyons (177/78–c. 200), theologian, and antiheretical writer. Claimed by both Roman Catholics and Protestants as their progenitor, Irenaeus framed the catholic concept of authority that helped to pull diverse churches together in a period of identity crisis created by gnosticism, Marcionism, and other movements. Opposing the radical accommodation of Christian thought to Hellenistic culture, he pointed to canon and creed as interpreted by bishops in churches of apostolic foundation. Until the discovery of a gnostic library at Nag Hammadi (modern-day Chenoboskion, Egypt) in 1945, Irenaeus's treatise *Against Heresies* also supplied the main and most reliable information on gnostic thought.

LIFE. Nothing is known of Irenaeus's ancestry or of the date or place of his birth. He grew up, however, in Smyrna, where he sat at the feet of Polycarp, the distinguished bishop martyred about 155, who, according to Irenaeus, had known the apostles, specifically John, in Asia. From Polycarp perhaps he drew his penchant for biblical theology, for, he observed, Polycarp "related all things in harmony with the scriptures," which he then noted "not on paper, but in my heart." Irenaeus witnessed Polycarp's debate with Anicetus in Rome about 155 and studied in Justin's school, gaining much from Justin's apologetic methods but diverging sharply from him in his partiality for a biblical theology rather than for Platonism. After 164 he went to Lyons, where he was ordained a presbyter. He narrowly missed the pogrom that took place in Lyons and Vienne in 177, when Pothinus, the nonagenarian bishop of Lyons martyred in the persecution, sent him to Rome with a letter for Eleutherius (pope, r. 175–189) in which Pothinus characterized his protégé as "zealous for the covenant of Christ" and "among the first as a presbyter of the church."

On returning to Lyons, Irenaeus succeeded Pothinus as bishop. When Victor, bishop of Rome (189–199), rashly excommunicated the Christians of Asia because they observed Easter according to the Jewish Passover, whatever day of the week that might fall on, and not always on a Sunday, as in Rome, Irenaeus intervened with a stern rebuke. Writing in the name of "the brethren in Gaul," he pointed out that although variety of practice was customary among Christians from ancient times, they had always lived in peace with one another. Victor's predecessors in Rome, he added, all adhered to the Roman custom but did not excommunicate the Asians on account of a different practice. Anicetus and Polycarp once had a direct confrontation; although neither could persuade the other to change, they remained in communion with each other. Apart from his writing activities, little more is known about Irenaeus's career as bishop of Lyons. About 576 Gregory of Tours reported that Irenaeus was martyred in the persecution under Septimius Severus, but the lateness of the account makes this unlikely.

WRITINGS. Two major works of Irenaeus—*Refutation and Overthrow of Knowledge Falsely So-Called* (usually referred to as *Against Heresies*) and *Proof of the Apostolic Preaching*—have survived. In addition, three letters—one to Blastus, *On Schism;* a second to Florinus, *On Monarchy* or *That God Is Not the Author of Evil;* and a third to Victor on the Easter controversy—are quoted partially or wholly in the *Church History* of Eusebius. Other works have survived only in fragments or not at all, including a treatise against Valentinian gnosticism titled *On the Ogdoad;* an apology, *On Knowledge, against the Greeks;* and comments on scriptures under the title *Dissertations.* Irenaeus's works, especially the treatise

Against Heresies, circulated widely and exerted a widespread influence on Christian theology in subsequent centuries, particularly in the West.

Composed at the request of a friend and usually dated 185–189, *Against Heresies* is somewhat repetitious and disjointed. In book 1 Irenaeus outlines the gnostic system of Valentinus and his pupil Ptolemaeus and refutes it briefly on the grounds of inconsistency and diversity, especially in handling scriptures (in contrast to the unity of the catholic church's teaching); in a similar way he sketches and refutes the practices and thought of the Marcosians; and he gives thumbnail sketches of the variegated teachings of other heretical teachers or sects: Simon Magus (the archheretic, according to Irenaeus), Menander, Saturninus, Basilides, Carpocrates, Cerinthus, the Ebionites, the Nicolaitans, Cerdo, Marcion, Tatian, and the Encratites, Barbeliotes, Ophites, Sethians, and Cainites. In book 2 Irenaeus undertakes a more detailed rational refutation of the Valentinian system with its elaborate cosmology. In book 3 he constructs his famous argument for catholic teaching based on scriptures and tradition. In book 4 he pursues the refutation of Marcion (d. 160?) that he begins at the end of book 3. Following in the train of his teacher Justin, whose treatise *Against Marcion* is no longer extant, Irenaeus argues from scriptures the oneness of the God of the Old Testament and the God who had disclosed himself in Jesus of Nazareth. Christ bore witness to the God of the Old Testament; the scriptures of the Old Testament bore witness to the Christ of the New. In book 5 Irenaeus sustains chiefly the Christian doctrines of resurrection of the flesh, incarnation, and last things against gnostic "spiritualizing." Like his teacher Justin, Irenaeus adopts the eschatology of the *Revelation to John* with its expectation of the millennial reign of Christ.

The *Proof of the Apostolic Preaching,* long lost but rediscovered in an Armenian translation in 1904, is a catechetical treatise, addressed to a certain Marcianus, that Irenaeus describes as "a manual of essentials." Basically a summary of salvation history, the first part focuses on theological matters (divine monarchy, Trinity, baptism) and the second on christological matters (Jesus as Lord, Son of David, Christ, Son of God; the glory of the Cross; the kingdom of God). "Proofs" for various doctrines come principally from the Old Testament.

THOUGHT. Irenaeus, responding to gnostics and Marcionites rather than presenting an apology to Gentiles, rejected Justin's concept of the Seminal Logos who illuminated the minds of both Jews and Greeks. Although he could praise Plato faintly, he had few compliments for nonbiblical writers and writings. He placed his confidence, rather, in the Old Testament and in writings beginning to be collected into a New Testament. Against Marcion and some of the gnostics, he asserted vigorously that one and the same God inspired both. In his understanding of inspiration he came closer to the rabbinic concept of the spirit indwelling an individual who faithfully adheres to the established tradition of truth than to the Greek mantic theory, but he never denied the latter. He regarded the Old Testament in the Greek Septuagint as canonical in its entirety. Although the limits of his New Testament canon are not clear, he left no doubt that it included at its core the four Gospels and thirteen letters of Paul.

In his polemic against the gnostics Irenaeus criticized especially their use of allegorical exegesis, but he himself resorted freely to this method even in interpretation of the New Testament, the first orthodox writer to do so. He struggled to solve problems posed by the Old Testament by way of a theory of progressive education of the human race; but, although biblical, he lacked historical sensitivity in treating of the Old Testament. In the final analysis, Irenaeus saw the basis of religious authority as the tradition committed to the churches by the apostles, as a collective and not as an individual witness. The "living voice," a continually renewed understanding of the church's heritage, was his actual authority.

Irenaeus's theology reflected throughout a strong biblical and especially Pauline slant. Against gnostic and Marcionite dualism he affirmed Jewish monotheism. One God, the creator, created ex nihilo and not through emanations (as in Valentinian gnosis). To prove at once the immanence and the transcendence of God, Irenaeus developed the distinctive doctrine of "the two hands of God." Through the Son and the Holy Spirit (or the Word and Wisdom), God acted directly in creation, not through intermediaries, and God continues to act in inspiration or revelation. Scholars have often tried to decide whether Irenaeus held to an "economic," or "modalist," concept of the Trinity (that God appeared at one time as Father, at another time as Son, at a third time as Holy Spirit), but the "two hands" doctrine is scarcely compatible with such a concept. For Irenaeus, God is the living God of the Old Testament. Although he counterbalanced this understanding with ideas drawn from the philosophical leanings of earlier apologists, he always leaned heavily toward the biblical side. Whereas Justin thought of the Logos as the hypostatized Divine Reason, for example, Irenaeus conceptualized the Logos as the Word of God depicted in *John* 1:1–14. Also, whereas Justin could call the Logos a "second God" (*deuteros theos*), a part of God, for Irenaeus the Logos is God—God self-disclosed.

Unlike his precursor Justin, Irenaeus was also profoundly biblical and Pauline in his doctrine of redemption. According to his famous recapitulation theory, Jesus traversed the same ground as Adam but in reverse. Through his obedience he overcame the powers that hold humankind in thrall—sin, death, and the devil. To establish his theory, Irenaeus contended that Jesus experienced every phase of human development—infancy, childhood, youth, mature adulthood—sanctifying each by obedience. On the basis of a comment in the *Gospel of John* ("You are not yet fifty," *Jn.* 8:57), he argued that Jesus lived to age fifty. To be sure, alongside the motif of Christus Victor in his recapitulation theory, Irenaeus also gave attention to the Greek concept of divinization by way of the vision of God in the incarnate Son. "He became man," said Irenaeus, "in order that we might become divine." This idea, however, did not dominate his theology as did that of recapitulation. As Irenaeus used it, moreover, it had both Pauline and Johannine roots. Thus, although nodding to Hellenism, Irenaeus did not depart from a strong biblicism.

There has been much debate among Protestant scholars about Irenaeus's emphasis on free will. In opposition to the gnostic division of humankind into three groups—material, psychic, and spiritual—he insisted on the survival of freedom even after the fall. Distinguishing "image" (*eikon*) and "likeness" (*homoiosis*) in the *Genesis* account of creation, as did Valentinus, he held that the fall affected only the "likeness." The "image," the whole bodily and spiritual nature with no added supernatural gift, was unaffected. Loss of the divine "likeness," however, resulted in a disordered human nature, death, and enslavement to Satan. Thus every person is born in sin, but this does not mean, as it did to Augustine, inheritance of guilt. Realizing that moral responsibility necessitates freedom of choice, Irenaeus viewed sin as wrong moral choice by a responsible agent. Although this meant that he sometimes minimized the need for grace, he was far from being a forerunner of Pelagius (fl. 410–418), who emphasized "natural grace" almost to the exclusion of supernatural. The fall, Irenaeus would say, attenuated free will, although it did not obliterate it.

In his understanding of the church Irenaeus again reproduced much of Paul's thought. The church is Israel under a new covenant, the true Israel, the priestly people of God. Although he believed in a universal priesthood, Irenaeus nevertheless lacked Paul's concept of the church as the body of Christ. He understood the church rather as a corporation composed of individuals and seldom spoke of being "in Christ" or "in the Spirit."

Irenaeus did not comment at length on the sacraments. Baptism, according to him, is a sign of faith and marks the beginning of the Christian life. He presupposed adult baptism, although one allusion connected with his recapitulation theory has often been pressed in support of infant baptism. The Eucharist, or Lord's Supper, played a minor role in his thinking. With Ignatius he could designate it "the antidote of life," or with Justin he could say the elements were "no longer common bread." Yet he preferred the phrase "the new oblation of the new covenant." Rich as his writings were in the formation of catholic theology, however, he did not approach the medieval idea of transubstantiation. The Eucharist is a "sacrifice" of praise symbolic of the recapitulating death of Christ; it proclaims and sets forth Christ's saving truth, the raison d'être of the church.

Irenaeus's understanding of ecclesiastical authority has evoked fierce debate between Protestants and Roman Catholics, for the meaning of a crucial statement is uncertain. Citing Rome as an example of an "apostolic" church, "founded and organized by Peter and Paul," and possessed of a reliable succession of bishops, Irenaeus added, "Ad hanc enim ecclesiam propter potiorem principalitatem necesse est omnem convenire ecclesiam." Roman Catholics have preferred to translate this sentence as "For it is necessary that every church agree with this church on account of its more powerful authority"; Protestants as "For it is necessary that every church come together with this church on account of its greater antiquity." Lack of a Greek original makes certainty impossible.

In eschatology, Irenaeus followed in the footsteps of his mentor Justin. Indeed, he was more rigorous than Justin in demanding adherence to millenarian beliefs. Countering the gnostics' dualism, he attached great importance to the idea of general resurrection, and he insisted on a resurrection of the flesh. Curiously, unlike Justin, he expected the general resurrection and the Last Judgment of both human beings and fallen angels to precede the millennium. Citing Papias (c. 60–130), bishop of Hierapolis, he believed the devil and his angels (demons) would be consigned to an everlasting fire while the saints would reign with Christ during the millennium. This millennial vision capped Irenaeus's theory of the evolution of religion.

INFLUENCE. Irenaeus's integration of biblical and Hellenistic thought, more cautious than that of his predecessor Justin or his contemporary Clement of Alexandria, was to have a significant impact in subsequent centuries. Eastern theology adopted his Christus Victor motif and his idea of the perfectibility of human nature consummated in immortality. A strong emphasis on free will in Eastern thinking probably also has its roots in Irenaeus. In the West both Roman Catholics and Protestants have claimed Irenaeus and Augustine as their leading mentors. Roman Catholics have cited Irenaeus on authority, Protestants on the Bible. Neither, however, has felt entirely at ease with the bishop of Lyons. Although Irenaeus came up with a "catholic formula" for truth, he left much uncertainty about Rome's place in safeguarding it. Similarly, although he was basically a biblical theologian, the Protestant reformers felt uncomfortable with both his idea of authority and his "Pelagian" tendencies. In the present ecumenical climate, fresh studies of Irenaeus are aiding in the reexamination of theology that must inevitably accompany progress toward Christian unity.

BIBLIOGRAPHY

The standard text of Irenaeus's treatise *Against Heresies* is *Sancti Irenaei libros quinque adversus haereses,* 2 vols., edited by W. W. Harvey (Cambridge, U.K., 1857). A complete English translation can be found in volume 1 of *The Ante-Nicene Fathers,* edited and translated by Alexander Roberts and James Donaldson (1867; reprint, Grand Rapids, Mich., 1975). Irenaeus's catechetical work appears in two English translations: *The Demonstration of the Apostolic Preaching,* translated by J. Armitage Robinson (London, 1920), and *Proof of the Apostolic Preaching,* translated and annotated by Joseph P. Smith, S.J. (Westminster, Md., 1952) for the series "Ancient Christian Writers." The standard English biography of Irenaeus is F. R. M. Hitchcock's *Irenaeus of Lugdunum*

(Cambridge, U.K., 1914). Valuable comprehensive studies of Irenaeus's theology include John Lawson's *The Biblical Theology of Saint Irenaeus* (London, 1948) and Gustaf Wingren's *Man and the Incarnation: A Study in the Biblical Theology of Irenaeus,* translated by Ross Mackenzie (Edinburgh and Philadelphia, 1959).

E. GLENN HINSON (1987)

IROQUOIS RELIGIOUS TRADITIONS.

The League of the Iroquois consisted, at the time of contact with Europeans, of five "nations" (the Mohawk, Oneida, Onondaga, Cayuga, and Seneca). In 1724, these groups were joined by the Tuscarora to form the Six Nations of the Iroquois. These tribes form part of a larger complex of Iroquoian-speaking peoples. The northern language group of which the members of the league are a part also includes the Saint Lawrence Iroquois, Huron, Wyandot, Susquehanna, Nottoway, Erie, Wenro, and Neutrals. The Cherokee form the southern language group. The separation between the northern and southern groups probably occurred between three and four thousand years ago, with further dialects developing over time.

Geographically, the early-seventeenth-century Iroquois inhabited the area from 42° to 44° north latitude and from 74° to 78° west longitude. In the late seventeenth century, the League of the Iroquois controlled territory from the Mohawk Valley in the east to Lake Erie in the west, and from Lake Ontario in the north to the mountains of western and south-central New York State and northwestern Pennsylvania in the south.

At contact the Iroquois were a matrilineal and matrilocal people living in clusters of longhouses situated on hilltops. The villages were usually palisaded and semipermanent. The men involved themselves in hunting, fishing, and making war; the women took care of the fields and gathered berries, nuts, and roots. The clan mothers elected the fifty sachems, or chiefs, who guided the external policies of the league from Onondaga.

COSMOLOGY. The cosmological structuring of space into three tiers provides the Iroquois with the basic categories with which to interpret human experience. The sky world and the underworld represent extremes of both a spatial and an existential nature. The sky world is order, goodness, warmth, light, and life. The underworld is chaos, evil, coldness, darkness, and death. In the in-between world—the world of ordinary human experience—the qualities of both worlds are intertwined in a myriad of ways. One of the ways is cyclical, as when night follows day; another is antagonistic, as when good struggles with evil.

Mythically, this world was the creation of two twins, one good and the other evil. The former, the Master of Life, was the creator of flora and fauna. He held the sky world in mind at all times while creating living things, and he gave customs to humans modeled after those of the sky world. His brother tried to imitate his creative acts, but what issued instead were all of the nasty, noxious, and monstrous forms of life. The evil twin is described as cold and hard, like ice and flint, and his influence is believed to infect all areas of existence. Each of the twins left behind spirit-forces and other manifestations of his orientation and power. The general thrust of Iroquois religion is toward increasing and renewing the power of those forces that sustain life and reducing or eliminating those forces that diminish life, such as disease and pain.

COMMUNITY RITUALS. To live in harmony with the spirit-forces is the essential requirement of Iroquois religion. These fundamental relationships that sustain community life are renewed, intensified, and celebrated in the calendrical cycles of the Longhouse religion. This final form of the Iroquois ceremonial cycle crystallized in the nineteenth century under the influence of the Seneca prophet Handsome Lake (1735–1815). The Longhouse religion, as it is practiced today, is a synthesis of elements from the hunter-gatherer traditions of the Middle Woodland and early Late Woodland periods (300–1000 CE) and the agricultural complex that gradually took hold during the Late Woodland period (1000–1500 CE).

The fundamental attitude of the Iroquois community toward the benevolent spirit-forces of the universe is thanksgiving. Thus all Iroquois ceremonies begin and end with a thanksgiving address, a paean to all the forces of earth, sky, and the sky world that create, support, and renew life. The address is divided into three main parts. The first part includes prayers of thanksgiving for the earth, waters, plants and trees, animals, birds, and the "three sisters" (the staple Iroquois foodstuffs—maize, beans, and squash). The second section gives thanks to those spirit forces that have greater power: wind, thunder, sun, moon, and stars. The final section gives thanks to the spiritual guides of the Iroquois: Handsome Lake, the creator, and the Four Beings (protectors of humans and messengers from the creator to Handsome Lake).

The epitome of the synthesis represented by the Longhouse religion is the Midwinter festival. Concentrated into its eight days are all of the major themes and components of Iroquois ceremonialism. The first half of the Midwinter rite is the older and contains many elements from the hunting-forest complex that centered on shamanic practices. It is given over to the symbolic expulsion of the old year through rites of confession, ashes-stirring, and dream fulfillment, as well as medicine-society curing ceremonies, False Face society rituals, and the White Dog sacrifice (no longer practiced). These expiatory and cathartic rituals clear the path for the new year and for the second half of the festival, whose structure largely reflects the farming-village complex. The "four sacred rituals"—a feather dance, a skin (or drum) dance, a personal chant, and a bowl game—are considered the gifts of the creator, modeled after ceremonies in the sky world. A tobacco invocation, a kind of thanksgiving address, beseeches all of the spirit-forces to bless the people during the coming year. Both the Our Sustenance Dances and the performance by the Husk Faces anticipate a fruitful agricultural season. The yearly ceremonial cycle unfolds from the Midwinter festival and returns to it.

While the ceremonial cycle may vary slightly from longhouse to longhouse, a representative list would include the Midwinter festival, the Bush Dance, and the Thanks-to-the-Maple, Seed Planting, Strawberry, Raspberry, Green Bean, Thunder, Little Corn, Green Corn, and Harvest ceremonies.

MEDICINE SOCIETIES. Not only has Iroquois religion been concerned with affirming and intensifying life, it has also been concerned with countering those things that diminish life. The spirit-forces that assist humans in this battle revealed themselves long ago and entered into covenants with individuals, families, and societies. Through fasting, dream-visions, and ecstatic states, the ancient shamans sought to divine the causes of illness, pain, famine, and sudden or widespread death. Other shamanic specialists had their own ceremonies and skills that brought healing power. At times groups of shamans who possessed similar secrets joined together into sodalities. With the demise of individual shamanism, these "medicine societies" grew in importance in Iroquois life and became the preserver of the ancient shamanic traditions.

The significance of medicine society rituals in Iroquois life differs from that of the communal ceremonies. The latter are thanksgiving-celebrative, follow the agricultural cycle, are directed toward the major spirit-forces, and are held in the longhouse. The former are power-evocative and occasional, invoke the tutelary spirit of the particular medicine society, and are usually conducted in private homes. Membership in a society is generally limited to those who have been cured by one of that society's rituals. The medicine societies have their own myths, songs, dances, prayers, costumes, and ritual paraphernalia. A listing of Iroquois medicine societies and their major characteristics follows.

1. *The Society of Medicine Men* (also known as Shake the Pumpkin) is the largest medicine society. Most members of the other societies also belong to it. The society began with a covenant relationship between the medicine animals and its founders. In return for feasts offered in their honor, the animals promised to cure diseases, ease pain, and get rid of bad luck. Practices of this society, such as juggling red-hot coals and wearing masks without eye holes, are quite ancient.

2. *The Company of Mystic Animals* includes the Buffalo, Otter, Bear, and Eagle societies. In varying degrees the members imitate their tutelary animals in their dances, songs, and practices. They continue the shamanic tradition in which humans and animals communicate with, and can be transformed into, one another.

3. *The Little Water Medicine society,* like its ally in the Eagle society, was originally associated with war and the healing of wounds received in war. The Iroquois say that its medicine, concocted from parts of animals, birds, and plants, is the most potent made by any society. Ceremonies are held at night, several times a year, to renew the medicine.

4. *The Little People society* (also known as Dark Dance) also holds its ceremonies at night. This society fosters a good rapport with the *jo-ga-oh* ("little people"), elflike spirits who help humans in a variety of ways and who adopt many different forms for mischievous purposes.

5. *The False Face society* is the favorite of the Iroquois. The wooden masks worn by its members are filled with power. Reverence and ritual surround both their carving and their care. The most common practices of the Faces today were noted among the Huron by seventeenth-century observers: blowing ashes, handling hot coals, imitating hunchbacks, and carrying sticks. It is quite possible that the Faces came to the Iroquois from the Huron. The False Face society holds rites for cleansing the community of disease in the spring and fall. It sponsers rites at Midwinter both for its own members and for the broader community in the longhouse and performs individual curing rites when needed.

6. *The Husk Faces* are dedicated to the agricultural spirits. They also cure by blowing ashes and handling hot coals. During Midwinter they burst into the longhouse and announce that they are going to the other side of the world to till the crops.

7. *The Towii'sas society* is a woman's society honoring corn, beans, and squash. It participates in the Green Corn ceremony and also has its own curing ceremonies.

8. *The Ohgiwe society* conducts ceremonies for people who have been dreaming of ghosts. A feast is held to feed the ghost and to dissuade it from bothering the living. Just as the sharing of food brings harmony into human relationships, so does it harmonize relations between living and dead. The Iroquois both respect and fear the dead and therefore conduct a number of feasts for them. In addition to the feasts conducted by the Ohgiwe society, there is a community Feast of the Dead (also called Ohgiwe) that is held annually or semiannually. All souls, but especially those of the recently deceased, are invited. Songs and dances are performed, and a post-midnight feast is held. There are also frequent family feasts for the dead during the winter months. These celebrations both fulfill the family's obligations to the dead and serve as a means of bringing together relatives of the deceased.

THE INDIVIDUAL. In traditional (i.e., pre-nineteenth-century) Iroquois lore, access to the power and guidance of the spirit-forces was not limited to the community (through its collective ceremonial life) nor to the curing societies. The individual Iroquois had an array of spiritually vital allies, including charms, medicine bundles, guardian spirits, and his or her own soul.

The most common medium for communication with these forces was the dream-vision. During puberty rites of shamanic training a guardian spirit would reveal itself to the individual through the dream-vision. The spirit could take the form of a human being, or animal, or a bird such as a raven or crow. An intimate and powerful relationship was established between the person and the guardian spirit. A person who had such a friendship had greater inner power and confidence than one who did not. The guardian spirit revealed its desires in dreams. To ignore this ally or to fail to understand its desires could result in illness. Such an illness signified a dangerous disruption of the relationship between spirit-forces and humans. Should someone become ill, his dreams would be consulted to ascertain what the guardian spirit desired. Sometimes the efforts of everyone in the community would be needed to fulfill the dream. They willingly undertook this.

Similarly, an alienation could occur between a person's ego and soul. The Iroquois believed that the soul was the source of biological as well as mental well-being. Dreams were its language. To lose touch with or deny the desires of the soul could cause it to revolt against the body. Dreams were carefully investigated in order to avoid such a possibility or to remedy it when illness occurred. The dream-guessing rite that even today forms a part of the Onondaga Midwinter festival was performed quite frequently by the seventeenth-century Huron. The ill person's soul's desire would be given in riddle form; whoever guessed it correctly had to fulfill the desire. This might involve an object, a feast, the performance of a particular ritual, or any of a number of other actions.

Dreams were also thought to contain warnings about future events—events whose actual occurrence might be prevented by acting out the dream and thereby fulfilling it. Thus, a warrior who dreamed that he had been captured, bound, and tortured by an enemy might, upon waking, ask his fellow tribesmen to tie him up and make cuts or burns in his flesh in order that the greater pain and shame predicted by the dream might be avoided. Dreams also affected hunting, fishing, military, and political plans.

There was no aspect of life among the ancient Iroquois and Huron that was not touched by the dream. Religiously it played both a conservative and an innovative role. That is, it confirmed within an individual's experience the culturally transmitted religious system while also initiating changes in the beliefs and rituals that constituted this system. It would not be going too far to say that most of Iroquois religion was constructed of dream material. Through this building process, the individual hierophany became symbolized and available to all. The last series of significant changes introduced into Iroquois life by the dream resulted from the revelations given to Handsome Lake, which were eventually institutionalized into the present-day Longhouse religion.

Today the majority of Iroquois live on reservations in Canada and New York State. Perhaps one-fourth of the approximately twenty thousand Iroquois adhere to the traditionalist Longhouse religion. In addition to the ceremonies described above, they perform partial recitations of the *Gaiwiio* ("good word") of Handsome Lake on the first mornings of both the Midwinter festival and the Green Corn ceremony. This formalization of the dream-vision revelations received by the prophet from 1799 until his death in 1815 provides the moral, ceremonial, social, and theological context in which followers of the Longhouse religion live. A complete recitation by an authorized preacher may occur every other fall at a meeting of the Six Nations, depending upon which longhouse is sponsoring the meeting.

SEE ALSO Handsome Lake.

BIBLIOGRAPHY

The main source for information on seventeenth-century Huron religion, which also provides some insight into Iroquois life, is *The Jesuit Relations and Allied Documents,* 39 vols. (1896–1901), edited by Reuben Gold Thwaites (New York, 1959). The nineteenth century marked the beginning of modern studies on Iroquois religion. Midcentury produced Lewis H. Morgan's classic *The League of the Ho-de-no-sau-nee, or Iroquois* (1851; reprint, New York, 1966). The most complete collection of Iroquois cosmological stories is found in J. N. B. Hewitt's "Iroquois Cosmology," which was published in two parts in the *Annual Report of the Bureau of American Ethnology* 21 (1899–1900) and 43 (1925–1926). An excellent, thorough study of the Midwinter festival is found in Elisabeth Tooker's *The Iroquois Ceremonial of Midwinter* (Syracuse, N.Y., 1970). For an introduction to and translation of a thanksgiving address, see Wallace L. Chafe's "Seneca Thanksgiving Rituals," *Bureau of American Ethnology Bulletin* 183 (1961). A much more thorough, if complex, comparison of several thanksgiving addresses along with a study of other events in the ritual cycle is M. K. Foster's *From the Earth to Beyond the Sky: An Ethnographic Approach to Four Longhouse Speech Events* (Ottawa, 1974). Valuable information on the medicine societies, along with the only full translation at present of "The Code of Handsome Lake" (i.e., the *Gaiwiio*), is found in a collection of Arthur C. Parker's writings, entitled *Parker on the Iroquois,* edited by William N. Fenton (Syracuse, N.Y., 1968). Fenton has done this century's most important work among the Iroquois. Among his numerous articles, special mention should be made of "An Outline of Seneca Ceremonies at Coldspring Longhouse," *Yale University Publications in Anthropology* 9 (1936): 3–22; and "Masked Medicine Societies of the Iroquois," in the *Annual Report of the Smithsonian Institution* (Washington, D.C., 1940), pp. 397–430. An indispensable collection of articles on the Iroquois and their neighbors can be found in the *Handbook of North American Indians,* vol. 15, *Northeast* (Washington, D.C., 1978).

DONALD P. ST. JOHN (1987)

IRVING, EDWARD (1792–1834), was a controversial Scottish minister associated with the founding of the Catholic Apostolic church. Born in Annan, Dumfriesshire, Irving was educated at the University of Edinburgh. After serving as a schoolmaster at Haddington in 1810 and Kirkcaldy in 1812, he was licensed to preach in the Church of Scotland in 1815. He became Thomas Chalmers's assistant at Saint John's, Glasgow, in 1819 but left Scotland in 1822 to become pastor of Caledonian Chapel, a small, struggling congregation in Hatton Garden, London. His dynamic preaching drew such large crowds that a new church had to be built at Regent Square in 1827.

Avowal of controversial doctrines soon undercut Irving's popularity. In the mid-1820s, Irving became a millenarian through the influence of James Hatley Frere, Henry Drummond, and Drummond's Albury Circle. He published *Babylon and Infidelity Foredoomed of God* (1826), in which he predicted the second coming of Christ in 1864; translated *The Coming of Messiah in Glory and Majesty* (1827), a millenarian work by the Spanish Jesuit Manuel Lacunza; lectured on the *Book of Revelation* at the University of Edinburgh (1828); and was a regular contributor to Drummond's prophetic journal *The Morning Watch* (1829–1833).

Citing his *The Doctrine of the Incarnation Opened* (1828) and *The Orthodox and Catholic Doctrine of Our Lord's Human Nature* (1830), the London Presbytery in 1830 charged Irving with teaching the sinfulness of Christ's human nature. He vigorously denied the charge, arguing that though Christ shared humanity's weak and infirm nature, his reliance on the Holy Spirit kept him without sin. Further, Irving refused to recognize the presbytery's authority.

Irving also believed in the continuation of the charismata of apostolic times and urged his congregation to pray for their outpouring. In the fall of 1831, glossolalia, faith healing, and prophetic visions broke out at Regent Square. As a result, Irving was deposed from the church in 1832 and excommunicated by his Scottish presbytery in 1833. He then became a wandering preacher, while several hundred of his London parishioners established the sacramental, millenarian, and charismatic Catholic Apostolic church. Eventually Irving was ordained a deacon in the new church, but he never assumed any significant leadership role. He died at Glasgow and was buried in the cathedral there.

Always the controversialist, Irving attacked the cold and somewhat complacent spirit of orthodoxy in the Church of Scotland. Through his adoption of millenarian and charismatic views, he became an early shaper of those movements in British and American evangelicalism.

Bibliography

Irving's works are found in *The Collected Writings of Edward Irving,* 5 vols. (London, 1864–1865), edited by Gavin Carlyle. For studies of Irving's life, one may consult H. C. Whitley's *Blinded Eagle* (London, 1955), the work of an unabashed admirer, and Margaret Oliphant's *The Life of Edward Irving,* 2 vols. (London, 1862), a fine example of Victorian biography. A helpful examination of Irving's associations is Andrew L. Drummond's *Edward Irving and His Circle* (London, 1938). Irving's theology is analyzed in C. Gordon Strachan's *The Pentecostal Theology of Edward Irving* (London, 1973).

Timothy P. Weber (1987)

ISAAC, or, in Hebrew, Yitsḥaq; the second of the biblical patriarchs and the only son of Abraham and Sarah. Although not known from elsewhere, the name *Yitsḥaq* conforms to a well-known Northwest Semitic type and means "may God smile"; Ugaritic texts from the thirteenth century BCE refer to the benevolent smile of the Canaanite god El. The Bible, however, ascribes the laughter to Isaac's mother, who was amazed to learn that she would have a child despite her advanced age.

Isaac is the only patriarch whose name was not changed. The Bible treats him primarily as Abraham's son or the father of Jacob and Esau. He was the first ancestor of the Israelites to be circumcised on his eighth day in accordance with God's command (*Gn.* 17:12). At an unspecified age he was taken to be sacrificed in order to test Abraham's faithfulness; however, Isaac himself did little except ask why his father had not brought an animal for the offering. His later marriage to Rebecca, a cousin, was arranged by Abraham and provided comfort to Isaac after his mother's death. In his old age, Isaac was deceived into giving Jacob the blessing intended for the older Esau.

Isaac's only independent actions are found in *Genesis* 26, in which he tells King Abimelech that Rebecca is his sister, a story reminiscent of one told twice about Sarah and Abraham. The same chapter mentions his involvement in agricultural activities and his resolution of a dispute over water rights between his shepherds and those of Abimelech. Isaac died at the age of 180 and was buried alongside Rebecca at Machpelah.

Postbiblical Jewish interpretations focus largely on the story of Abraham's intended sacrifice of Isaac, called the *ʿaqedah* ("binding"), and often elaborate his role beyond the biblical description. According to one version he actually died and was then revived. Christian tradition, perhaps attested as early as the writings of Paul (*Rom.* 8:32), views this incident as prefiguring the Crucifixion. Paul contrasted Isaac, representing Christianity, with Ishmael, the rejected older son who symbolizes Judaism (*Gal.* 4:21–30).

Bibliography

An excellent survey of modern scholarly insights into the patriarchal narratives is Nahum M. Sarna's *Understanding Genesis* (New York, 1966). Rabbinic legends are collected in Louis Ginzberg's *The Legends of the Jews,* 2d ed., 2 vols., translated by Henrietta Szold and Paul Radin (Philadelphia, 2003). Shalom Spiegel's *The Last Trial,* translated by Judah Goldin (New York, 1967), summarizes a vast array of postbiblical legends pertaining to the binding of Isaac (*Gn.* 22).

Frederick E. Greenspahn (1987 and 2005)

ISAAC THE SYRIAN (d. 700 CE?), also known as Isaac of Nineveh, was a bishop in the ancient Nestorian church of Syria; a monk, recluse mystic, and creative writer whose discourses have had widespread influence on Christian and, some think, Ṣūfī spirituality. The English world at first greeted his work, originally written in Syriac, with culture-bound coolness, but has eventually come to recognize him as one of the most sublime and original mystic writers of the Christian East.

Little is known about Isaac's life. Born in a region around the Persian Gulf, he became a monk and for a time the bishop of Nineveh (modern Mosul), an office he resigned after only five months. He then withdrew to one of the monasteries in the mountains of Huzistan (southwestern Iran), where he practiced strict solitude (hesychasm) as a way of pursuing unceasing communion with God. In order not to break the rule of solitude, as Isaac himself relates in a stirring personal account, he refused to go to the deathbed of his brother, a monk in another monastery. Toward the end of his life a burning love led Isaac to write a profusion of illuminating discourses on Christian perfection—the fruit of his assiduous study of scripture, his reading of Christian authors, and his own experiences, about which he is discreetly modest.

Isaac's writings were translated into Greek, Coptic, and Arabic, and became influential from Byzantium to Ethiopia. Later Latin and Spanish translations made him known to the West. The Greek translation (ninth century) was printed in a partly critical edition by Nikēphoros Theotokēs (1770), and this edition was in turn the basis of a Russian translation by Feofan the Recluse (nineteenth century), excerpts of which were rendered into English by Eugénie Kadloubovsky and G. E. H. Palmer in *Early Fathers from the Philokalia* (1954). Earlier, A. J. Wensinck, working on Paul Bedjan's critical edition of the original Syriac discourses (1909), had published his English translation of *Mystic Treatises by Isaac of Nineveh* (1923), valuable but unfortunately inadequate in correctly rendering key patristic terminology derived from the Greek fathers. A new translation, *The Ascetical Homilies of St. Isaac the Syrian,* based on the Greek and Syriac, is in preparation by the Holy Transfiguration Monastery, Brookline, Massachusetts.

Only the earnest student will be rewarded by reading Isaac's work in English; wide cultural differences, the sublimity of Isaac's thought, and the fact that it is addressed principally to other solitaries, not ordinary Christians, add to other problems of translation. Although he cites Evagrios of Pontus, Theodore of Mopsuestia, and others who are in some respects suspect to orthodox theology, there is nothing specifically Nestorian about Isaac's Christology. Isaac strictly avoided dogmatic disputations and was completely grounded in the traditions of Eastern Christianity's piety and spirituality. He frequently quoted not only the Old and New Testaments but also the ascetics of Egypt and eminent church fathers such as Ephraem of Syria, Athanasius, Basil of Caesarea, Gregory the Theologian, and Chrysostom. Isaac was interested primarily not in mysticism but in God; his originality lies in his luminous descriptions of the deep stirrings of the Holy Spirit in the heart, the new birth, the gift of tears, and profound stages of prayer leading to ecstasy. For him the goal of Christian perfection is the love of God, of "the food of angels . . . which is Jesus."

BIBLIOGRAPHY

Bejan, Paul, ed. *Mar Isaacus Ninivita de perfectione religiosa.* Paris, 1909.

Kadloubovsky, Eugénie, and G. E. H. Palmer, trans. *Early Fathers from the Philokalia.* London, 1954.

Theotokēs, Nikēphoros. *Isaak tou Syrou Eurethenta Asketika* (1770). Reprint, Athens, n.d. (1960s).

Wensinck, A. J., trans. and ed. *Mystic Treatises by Isaac of Nineveh.* Amsterdam, 1923.

THEODORE STYLIANOPOULOS (1987)

ISAIAH

ISAIAH (fl. 740–701 BCE), or, in Hebrew, Yeshaʿyahu or Yeshaʿyah, was a Hebrew prophet. Isaiah, son of Amoz, prophesied during the reigns of Uzziah, Jotham, Ahaz, and Hezekiah, kings of Judah (see *Is.* 1:1). He was a contemporary of the prophets Micah and Hosea and lived soon after Amos. (Amos and Hosea were active in Israel, or Ephraim, while Micah prophesied in Judah.) This was the period of the Syro-Ephraimite war (734/3–733/2 BCE), in which these kingdoms to the north of Judah surrounded Jerusalem, threatening to replace the house of David (*Is.* 7:1–6 [verse citations are according to the English version]). It was also the time of the Assyrian invasions, a chain of military campaigns that caused the fall of the northern kingdom of Israel in 722 and made Judah a vassal of the Assyrian Empire. During this stormy political period, Isaiah addressed the political elite and the people of Jerusalem, delivering God's word, which often did not correspond with the rulers' political views. He repeatedly criticized the rulers for the prevailing social injustices.

COMPOSITE NATURE OF THE *BOOK OF ISAIAH.* *Isaiah* contains sixty-six chapters and is the largest prophetic book in the Hebrew Bible. The existing structure had appeared by the beginning of the second century BCE. *Ben Sira* apparently knows *Isaiah* as a whole (*Sir.* 48:17–25), and the Dead Sea Scrolls, as well as the New Testament, regard the entire sixty-six chapters as a single composition. There are, indeed, certain stylistic usages that are common to the entire book, such as the combination "Holy of Israel" (*Is.* 1:4, 5:16, 5:19, 5:24, 6:3, 10:20, 12:6, 30:11, 30:12, 30:15, 31:1, 41:14, 41:16, 41:20, 43:3, 43:14, 45:11, 47:4, 48:17, 49:7, 54:5, 55:5, 60:9, 60:14) and the expression "Thus says God," in the imperfect tense instead of the usual perfect, "said" (*Is.* 1:11, 1:18, 33:10, 41:21, 66:9; cf. 40:1, 40:25).

Contrary to these early sources, however, modern scholarship on *Isaiah* generally differentiates between chapters 1–39 of the book and chapters 40–66, treating them as distinct major works by different authors. The first 39 chapters of *Isaiah* bear the title "The Vision of Isaiah the Son of Amoz" (1:1); chapters 40–66 are ascribed to an anonymous prophet to whom scholars refer as "Second Isaiah," or "Deutero-Isaiah." Some scholars also recognize the existence of a "Third Isaiah," or "Trito-Isaiah," the author of chapters 56–66, because the tone and approach of these chapters is more critical and condemning than that of chapters 40–55.

The division of the *Book of Isaiah* into two sections follows from the fact that the two parts are concerned with two distinct historical periods, the Assyrian and the Persian, and different political situations during these periods, which are reflected in the different topics and particular prophetic themes of the book. The author of the first part is concerned with social problems and concentrates on the moral and ethical misconduct of the rulers of Jerusalem, while the author of the second part responds to the national religious crisis of the exiled Jewish community in Babylonia. Accordingly, speeches of judgment distinguish the first part, while words of encouragement and oracles of salvation characterize the second. The prophet of the second part anticipates the collapse of Babylon in 539 BCE and the triumph of Cyrus II (558–529), the founder of the great Persian Empire. He knows about the destruction of the Temple in Jerusalem (587/6 BCE), and assigns Cyrus the task of building the new temple (*Is.* 44:28, 45:1; cf. 52:5, 52:11). Historical evidence thus dates the second part of *Isaiah* to the second half of the sixth century BCE, approximately two centuries later than the first part. The division in *Isaiah* was already recognized in the twelfth century CE by the Hebrew commentator Avraham ibn ʿEzra (in his commentary on *Is.* 40:1), and the literary-thematic distinction has recently been confirmed by a computer analysis (Y. T. Radday, *The Unity of Isaiah in Light of Statistical Linguistics,* Hildesheim, 1973).

But how were these distinct compositions tied together? One can only speculate. Perhaps it was just a technical matter in which a shorter scroll was attached to a longer one for preservation, and the origin of the work as two separate manuscripts was later forgotten. Or perhaps the combination was intentional, the product of a school of religious thought that sought to create a continuous ideological composition in which the period of judgment had been fulfilled, thus confirming the old Isaian prophecies and pointing out the validity of the new ones concerning the new era of salvation. Or perhaps the composer of the second book considered himself Isaiah's faithful disciple. This hypothesis may explain the lack of superscription in the second part as well as the similarity of idioms and phrases in the two parts. For example, in a rare passage in which Second Isaiah refers to himself, he describes God's word as *limmudim,* "teaching" (*Is.* 50:4), language that resembles that of Isaiah (*Is.* 8:16). Isaiah's spiritual disciple responds to his teacher's feeling of "distress and darkness" (*Is.* 8:22), which caused the master to seal his testimony (*Is.* 8:16–17). The disciple feels that times have changed. He notices that God again reveals himself (*Is.* 40:5), and he considers himself the one who bears the leader's testimony.

The First Isaiah. It appears that Isaiah, the son of Amoz, was from Jerusalem (unlike his contemporary Micah, who grew up outside the city). He was familiar with city life (see, e.g., *Is.* 3:16–23), and Jerusalem was the center of his activity. He married a woman whom he called "the prophetess" (*Is.* 8:3). They had at least two sons, whose names are associated with their father's prophetic message (cf. *Hos.* 1:3–9): Shearjashub (lit., *She'ar yashuv,* "a remnant shall return"; *Is.* 7:3) and Maher-shalal-hash-baz (lit., "pillage hastens, looting speeds"; 8:3). Isaiah may have had a third son, ʿImmanuʾel ("God is with us"; 7:14; cf. 8:18), whose name refers to trust in God even in moments of political despair. Isaiah is rarely mentioned outside of his book, but is referred to in *2 Kings* 19–20 and *2 Chronicles* 26:22, 32:20, and 32:32, where he appears not just as a prophet but as the king's healer and the court chronicler. All the sources indicate that Isaiah was closely associated with King Hezekiah, especially during the Assyrian siege of Jerusalem. He had access to the king (*Is.* 7:1ff.) and was the king's political counselor (37:1ff.). He makes frequent reference to the forms and vocabulary of the wisdom literature and is clearly familiar with the scribal profession (30:8; cf. *2 Chr.* 26:22).

There are a number of traditions about Isaiah's role and activities that make it difficult to reconstruct the "real" Isaiah. His close ties with Hezekiah as portrayed in the narrative (*Is.* 36–39, *2 Kgs.* 19–20) may create the impression that he functioned as a court prophet, but his confrontation with King Ahaz (*Is.* 7) depicts him as an independent prophetic figure. The portrayal of Isaiah as a healer in *Kings* 20:1–7 is significant—"And Isaiah said: bring a cake of figs. And let them take and lay it on the boil, that he may recover" (*2 Kgs.* 20:7)—and is repeated in the appendix of the *Book of Isaiah* (*Is.* 38:1–8). That *Isaiah* inserts this deed of healing at the end of Hezekiah's poem as an excursus may reflect a tendency to minimize Isaiah's role as a healer and portray him instead in the role of God's messenger, who does not perform miracles in the tradition of the earlier prophets (such as that of Elisha, described in *2 Kgs.* 2–5). Note, however, that even in chapters 1–35, which deal directly with Isaiah's prophecy, the prophet does not appear only as God's messenger but performs symbolic acts in the tradition of the earlier prophets, such as Elijah. For example, he walks barefoot and naked in Jerusalem for three years as a symbol of the fate that would overtake Egypt and its ally Ethiopia at the hands of Assyria (*Is.* 20:1–6). One must keep in mind, however, that this is but a single episode.

Speeches and additional material. The major critical issue surrounding the book of Isaiah is the determination of his original speeches. It has been noted that even chapters 1–39 do not constitute a single composition. The poetic, oratorical language is replaced in chapters 36–39 with a historical narrative (as well as Hezekiah's prayer in 38:10–20). The *Book of Isaiah* seems to have a long literary history. Rabbinic sources hint at an editorial process in which it was not Isaiah himself who wrote the book but later scribes (Hezekiah and his school). Modern criticism attempts to establish clear criteria for the distinction between the authentic and the added material. Some scholars distinguish between oracles of judgment and prophecies of salvation, with the latter, reflecting the days to come, considered a later theological addition. Style is another criterion for analyzing the editorial process. Isaiah is regarded as a poet. Thus some hold that only the material in verse is authentic. Accordingly, passages such as 1:18–20, which breaks the poetic structure, and 4:2–6, a prosaic text differing from the poetic material surrounding it, are considered late. Similarly, this view does not regard texts such as 2:2–4/5 and 11:1ff., which are prophecies of salvation, as Isaiah's compositions. It has also been suggested that verses referring to the fall of Assyria (e.g., 8:9–10, 10:16–19, 10:20–23, 10:24–27, 10:33–34) are the product of an "Assyrian redaction" added in the period of Josiah's territorial expansions and Assyrian decline, toward the end of the seventh century BCE. The goal of the redactor, in this view, was to update Isaiah's original prophecy and show how it was fulfilled through God's determination of political events. Thus there is a complete theological paradigm: First God appears as the accuser and punisher of Israel, and later he reveals himself as Israel's savior. Scholars of the redactional school such as Barth, Clements, and Kaiser assume that Isaiah was not a prophet with a complete political vision, but merely a deliverer of judgmental oracles.

It is the opinion of this author, on the other hand, that Isaiah had a politico-religious worldview that was not limited to contemporary conditions. As a man of vision, he had a total religious concept which looked beyond the day of judgment which was imminent. Isaiah was not just a social critic and man of protest; his proclamation of judgment led to his prophetic outlook for the future as well. There is neither stylistic nor philological evidence that the oracles designed for the days to come (included in chapters 1–35) are products of later hands, unless one imposes on the text specific external critical theories (for certain exceptions, see below). Rather than regarding style (verse versus prose) as the criterion for distinguishing between the original and added text, one should consider that stylistic variations and mixing of styles may be the function of the subject matter and may have been intentional in a particular prophetic message. Subject and function determine Isaiah's style; the question of how it has been said is related to the issue of what has been said. Isaiah employs a significant variety of stylistic forms: *mashal* ("parable"; 5:1ff.), comparison (1:2–3), vivid description (1:4–9), polemic discourse (1:10–17), lament (1:21), satire (3:4ff.), vision (6:1ff.), prediction (7:7–9), and narrative (7:11ff., 8:1ff.), among many others.

The rich language and varied stylistic modes reveal that the prophet was not a narrator who merely reported events. Isaiah sought to appeal to his audience by the force of his language, a goal that, in light of the prophetic office, requires the use of religious language. This language uses metaphor and an imaginative style to create an array of sensory impressions. For example, the description of the foreign influence in Judah is hyperbolic: "Their land is filled with silver and gold, and there is no end to their treasures; their land is filled with horses, and there is no end to their chariots" (2:7). The prophet's stylistic technique creates a vivid and dynamic word picture. The poem of the vineyard in 5:1ff. aims to illustrate a specific aspect of the people's misconduct. The use of a parable, that is, the rhetorical description of the situation in a different context, enables Isaiah to focus his audience's attention and get their sympathy. If he had presented his criticism directly, it might have been rejected by the hostile audience. Another illustration of this technique is the vision of the future in 4:2–6, written in a prose style and following the description, in vivid imagery, of the corrupted daughters of Zion (3:16ff.). The present reality is described in verse in order to stir the emotions and move the audience. However, in this context if a description of the future were delivered in verse, it might have been received as an imaginative discourse having nothing to do with the present reality. Isaiah therefore employs a prosaic style, the language of historical fact, and the address, though it refers to the days to come, seems to have an air of reality.

Chronological order of the speeches. The speeches of chapters 2–5 (as well as those of 1:21–31) differ thematically from the material of 7:1ff., and it has been suggested that each topic mirrors a different political era. The sharp social criticism is replaced by political addresses. The first cycle of speeches (chaps. 2–5) is assigned to the days of Uzziah (c. 787–c. 736), a time of political stability, security, and economic prosperity (see *2 Kgs.* 15:1–7, *2 Chr.* 26:1–23). The social and political elite of Jerusalem regained their strength, creating severe social tension in Judah that affected the poor. Isaiah criticizes the rulers for oppressing their citizens. The speech of 7:1ff. refers to the days of Ahaz (who became king probably in 741 and was coregent until 725), during the Syro-Ephraimite war. Here Isaiah is responding to political developments rather than to the domestic situation. This historical reconstruction of Isaiah's activity assumes, however, that 1:4–9, which describes a major war that has endangered Jerusalem, is either not in order or that the whole of the chapter is an introduction to Isaiah's prophecy and does not belong to his early activity in the days of Uzziah. However, if one does not ignore 1:4–9 and read chapters 1–5 chronologically in their existing order, they reflect a period of war that had gravely threatened Jerusalem. Isaiah is concerned here with the cause of the military disaster. He indicates that corrupt domestic conditions are the reason for the political and military defeat and the people's suffering, which are God's punishment. In chapters 7–8 however, he focuses on King Ahaz's foreign policy. Isaiah's major thrust is directed not toward Uzziah's time but Ahaz's.

Isaiah's prophecy is thus a series of responses to specific political and domestic situations that, in his view, are mutually related. He reveals his deep involvement with and specific viewpoint regarding these political events and offers his unique prophetic interpretation of the political situation through a series of speeches that attempt to persuade. Isaiah does not speak as a political analyst or as a political philosopher; he uses rhetoric or any other means of appeal to reach his audience (see, e.g., 7:10ff.). Accordingly, the various speeches must be analyzed as a whole, and each speech or vision studied in light of Isaiah's thematic prophetic ideology and not as a separate entity. Prophecies of salvation follow from oracles of judgment, and both are integrated into Isaiah's prophetic worldview.

Political context and arrangement of the speeches. The book deals with two major political events that shocked Judah: the Syro-Ephraimite war and the Assyrian threats (734–701). Isaiah's prophecy is presented in light of his overall prophetic conception, which does not see the actual events as mere politico-military developments, although they shaped the prophet's political views. In the Syro-Ephraimite war the kings of Aram (Syria) and Ephraim (Israel) sought to fight against Assyria and needed Judah's active support. Ahaz, the Judahite king, refused, and as a result the northern coalition launched a military attack meant to replace Ahaz with their favorite, who was not a descendant of the house of David (see *Is.* 7:1–6). God's sacred promise to David and his house of an eternal throne in Jerusalem (see *2 Sm.* 7:1–17) was thus endangered. The sacred status of the house of David is the starting point of Isaiah's prophetic responses. It forces him to deal with the cause of the problem, which was, in his view, the social and ethical misconduct of the rulers (see 1:4–5, 1:10–17, 1:21–23, 3:14–15, 3:16ff., 5:1ff.). The war is God's punishment (see 1:4–9). At the last moment (1:9) the city will be purified, and justice will be restored (1:25–27, 2:2–4/5, 4:2–6; hence the above-mentioned connotation of the name of Isaiah's son Shear-jashub, "a remnant shall return." This teleology, the faith that God will interfere on behalf of the people and for the sake of Jerusalem, leads Isaiah to oppose Ahaz's political attempts at saving himself by means of the foreign powers of Assyria or Egypt (7:18–25), and to assure the king that the enemies of the north will collapse (7:5–9). Furthermore, a series of speeches delivered by Isaiah emphasize the continuity of the Davidic dynasty (9:1–6, 11:1ff.). Chapters 10–11 should be read with the implications of the Assyrian threat in mind. Aram and Ephraim, Judah's enemies, had collapsed, and Judah itself was powerless against Assyria. The new political development invited the prophet's interpretation, and Isaiah delivers a series of speeches that interpret the meaning of the situation. Again, he points to moral and ethical misconduct as the cause of the military threat (10:1–4). God's response is direct: Assyria is his means of punishment (10:5–6), but that empire overestimates its power and will be punished (10:7ff.).

It has been suggested that the collection of oracles against the nations in chapters 13–23 may include material that is not Isaian (particularly chapters 13–14 and perhaps also chap. 23). The collection, which includes a prophecy against Judah concluding with a personal attack on two officers (22:1ff.), is an integral part of Isaiah's prophetic ideology. The structure of this collection resembles the work of Amos, who starts with a series of oracles against the nations and climaxes with a prophecy against Israel (1:2–2:16), his major point. The common theme in Isaiah's prophecies against the nations is that they will suffer military defeat. Isaiah repeatedly reveals his basic religious and political belief that the international political situation does not exist in a vacuum but is determined by God, who does not exclude Judah. Consequently, Judah's efforts to protect itself through military and political means will fail (22:1ff.).

The visions of chapters 24–35 abstractly summarize once again Isaiah's prophetic ideology: God's absolute universal domination and his punishment for misbehavior in the form of military defeat (24:1–5, 24:21–23, 28:14–22, 29:13–14, 30:1–3, 34:1ff.). Isaiah, a master of language, moves from visionary to more concrete speech and characteristically, concludes with an optimistic vision of the future (35:1ff.). It is unnecessary, therefore, to regard chapters 34–35, with their enthusiastic tone, as part of Second Isaiah's prophecy, as a number of scholars suggest.

Such a thematic reading of Isaiah's speeches raises the question of the place and function of chapter 6, which is regarded by many as Isaiah's call, his "inaugural vision." Was it originally placed at the beginning of the book? If so, why would the message of the vision be to harden the hearts of the people (6:9, 6:10)? Perhaps this is, in fact, a response to the people's stubbornness and their denial of Isaiah's earlier comments on their political and military troubles. In this light the vision of chapter 6 would seem to be in its correct chronological setting, reflecting Isaiah's despair over the people's unresponsiveness.

Alternatively, those who read *Isaiah* as a series of discrete speeches of judgment have suggested that the book's editors intended its literary structure to reflect a specific theological view that incorporated the late prophecies of salvation. For example, the literary passage 5:25–30 may be read together with a group of invective threats in 9:8–21, and the *hoy* ("woe") oracle of 10:1–4 may be associated with a series of *hoy* oracles in 5:8–24. It has been suggested as well that these two series of threats and *hoy* oracles were broken apart and rearranged in a chiastic order. The intent was to frame Isaiah's actual encounter with Ahaz in a way that would recall the fall of Israel and would also warn seventh-century Judah (the time of Josiah) by recalling the realization of Isaiah's words. Thus, in this view, the prophecies were rearranged, and the book was edited in light of the political climate of Josiah's times.

"Second Isaiah." The Babylonians exiled the social and political elite of Judah (see *2 Kgs.* 24:12–26, *Jer.* 52:16–30) to Babylonia. Evidence suggests that many of the Jews in exile preserved their national and religious identity. The Sabbath emerged as the expression of the covenant between God and the Jewish people, a view that has distinguished the Jews since the exilic period (see *Is.* 56, 58:13–14). The exilic period is also noted for its nationalistic-religious literary activity.

The masterpiece of biblical historiography, the Deuteronomist work, was developed and shaped in this period. Nevertheless, there was a feeling of despair in the exiled Jewish community. The prophet Ezekiel asked hopelessly, "How are we to go on living?" (*Ez.* 33:10; see also 37:11). *Lamentations* repeatedly conveys a feeling of pessimism: "There is no one to comfort me" (*Lam.* 1:2, 1:16, 1:17, 1:21). Psalm 137 also reflects a hopeless situation, and Second Isaiah himself struggles with an attitude of religious and national despair: "A voice says: 'cry'! And I said: 'What shall I cry?' All flesh is grass and all its beauty is like the flower of the field" (*Is.* 40:6; RSV). The people felt the fall of Jerusalem, the destruction of the Temple in 587/6 BCE, and then the exile to be a hopeless situation that resulted from God's disappearance from the political stage. The exiles were indifferent to the momentous developments that were occurring on the international scene. The sensational victories of Cyrus I, king of Persia, did not affect the pessimistic religious attitude of the Jewish community in Babylonia. In 539 BCE, however, Babylonia surrendered to Cyrus II, and in 538 Cyrus announced his famous declaration allowing the Jewish community in exile to return to Jerusalem and restore the Temple (*Ezr.* 1:3–5 [*2 Chr.* 36:23], 6:3–5).

An important issue in the interpretation of Second Isaiah's prophecy is thus whether he addressed the exiles before or after the fall of Babylonia. Cyrus's edict is not quoted in Second Isaiah's speeches, and in light of his struggle with his audience's skepticism about God's control of contemporary political events, the speeches would sound inappropriate if Cyrus had already publicly granted permission to rebuild the Temple in Jerusalem. One should also take into account that Second Isaiah's description of the fall of Babylonia is not realistic. In contrast to inscriptions that report that the city fell peacefully, Second Isaiah describes Marduk, Babylon's god, being carried into captivity (46:1–2), which suggests that the prophet prophesied prior to 539 BCE.

The unknown prophet, the so-called Second Isaiah, was aroused by these significant political developments and considered that his prophetic goal was to persuade the exilic community that the immediate future held great promise and new hope. He considered the great king, Cyrus II, to be an agent of God, "who says of Cyrus: 'He is my shepherd. And he shall fulfill all my purpose,' saying of Jerusalem; 'she shall be built,' and of the Temple, 'your foundation shall be laid'" (44:28; see also 45:12–13). He rejected the spiritual crisis of the exiles and proclaimed two major themes: that God is not hidden from the Jewish people and that God is directing the new political events on their behalf. But first, Second Isaiah had to struggle with and reject the basis of the religious crisis. The cry "there is no one to comfort me" (*Lam.* 1:21) was replaced with "Comfort, comfort my people, says your God" (*Is.* 40:1). Furthermore, there was no reason for the people's feeling of guilt that they suffered because of their forefathers' sins; a new spiritual and religious era has begun: Jerusalem's warfare has ended and she has been pardoned (40:12). This explains the absence of threat, so characteristic of the biblical prophets, in Second Isaiah's speeches and sheds light on his style. His aim was to persuade, to appeal to his audience through words of comfort and encouragement, not by means of threat and judgment.

The major issue in research on Second Isaiah is the demarcation of the prophetic speech. There are almost no formal indications of the beginning or end of the address. In general, two opposite approaches have been taken. The first considers the book to be a product of planned literary activity and regards Second Isaiah's work as composed of large units. The second approach argues that Second Isaiah delivered his speeches orally, and that the book is a collection of a number of short, distinct oracles. This approach raises the issue of the arrangement of the material and the editorial principles behind it. It has been suggested that the short, independent oracles were arranged mechanically according to a principle of keywords or similarity of theme, with each speech placed on the basis of its association with the preceding unit. One should note, however, that the question of defining the individual speech depends on the function of Second Isaiah's prophecy, which was to change his audience's religious attitude. He thus appealed to his audience by employing numerous means of persuasion; he thus relies on argument and style. Second Isaiah paid close attention to the organization of his addresses; each emerged from and is a response to a particular situation. An analysis of the text in light of the prophet's rhetorical goal and his efforts to affect his listeners reveals that his speeches are not short thematic oracles but are relatively long, thus enabling him to develop his argument at some length.

Second Isaiah was a master of language and employed his skill to stress his point and attract the attention of his audience. He often repeats himself to emphasize a certain point. On the other hand, he often varies his style by using a colorful and rich vocabulary to create an aesthetic effect. He is very flexible in his use of language and often employs unusual words or phrases with the intention of providing variety and avoiding clichés.

The beginning of Second Isaiah's prophecy, 40:1–2ff., is a good illustration of his style. His first announcement, "Comfort, comfort my people" is brief and clear. The entire section, verses 1–2, is explicit in structure, with no coloration or figures of speech, and is designed to express clearly and straightforwardly his primary announcement. But the audience may miss a message delivered in such an unadorned style. Therefore, Second Isaiah uses the stylistic device of repetition and repeats the key word of his message, *comfort.* The reiteration of the word is intended to make a deep impression on the audience. The verb *comfort* in the form used here was coined by Second Isaiah based upon the lament "no one comforts her" (*Lam.* 1:2). Yet Second Isaiah uses it in a positive sense, to stress the motif of rejoicing, while in *Lamentations* the expression connotes religious despair. Thus at the beginning of his address, Second Isaiah employs a familiar expression in a way that changes its meaning. By using a familiar expression in an unexpected manner, he attracts attention and also cancels its earlier, negative meaning. In addition, verse 1 reverses the normal order and places the opening formula, "says your God," at the end. Because Second Isaiah wants to convey his message's immediacy, he has adjusted the formula accordingly. In addition, as is well known, rhyme is not highly developed in biblical prosody. In order to unify the various elements in a verse, the biblical poets developed the literary device of the sound effect. Sound plays an important role in this verse. *Alliteration* holds the verse together and focuses attention on the consonant *ḥeit*(*ḥ*) in the opening words *"nahamu, nahamu."* The sound is then repeated at the end of verse 2 (*ḥaṭṭo'teikhah*) thus binding the entire statement into a whole.

The songs of the "servant of the Lord ['eved YHVH]" have received special attention from scholars. There are four poems that speak about the servant (42:1–4, 42:5–7, 49:1–6, 50:4–9) and an additional two poems that may be related to them (50:10–11, and 52:13–53:12). These poems share a common theme: Their subject, the servant, suffers when he is ignored by the people who surround him. In the future, however, the servant will be recognized as God's servant, who has a mission to restore justice, which will be fulfilled. The poems occupy a distinct place in the history of sacred interpretations and have theological significance in the histories of Jewish and Christian religious interpretation. The major critical issue for Second Isaiah is whether to isolate the poems from their context or to consider them as an integral part of his prophecy. There is the further question of the identity of the servant, with scholars divided between an individual and a collective identity. Thus there have been various attempts to identify the servant as a specific public or historical figure, such as Jeremiah, Josiah, Zerrubbabel, or even the prophet himself. Second Isaiah makes other allusions to the servant of God, however (41:8ff., 41:13, 42:19, 44:1–2); and in light of the frequent references to Israel as God's servant (see, e.g., 49:3), it has been suggested that the servant be seen as the people of Israel, sympathetically portrayed by Second Isaiah to arouse hope and a feeling of mission and fulfillment as well as to convey the message that the current suffering has not gone unnoticed. Another view holds that the servant is neither a particular figure nor a group, but the combination of a mythological cultic and royal figure.

"THIRD ISAIAH." Concerning chapters 56–66, it has already been mentioned that these may constitute a separate collection by another anonymous prophet, called Third Isaiah, or Trito-Isaiah, who was active after Second Isaiah, during the time of Ezra and Nehemiah, in the fifth century BCE. Third Isaiah is no longer located in Babylonia but is based in Judah. His prophecies presuppose the existence of the Temple in Jerusalem (which was dedicated in 515). There is no clear thematic line in this work as is found in the speeches of Second Isaiah. The collection of Third Isaiah emphasizes ritual requirements. It starts with words of encouragement to those who observe the Sabbath, including the eunuchs, and stresses the importance of Sabbath worship (56:1–8). It continues with a critique of the leaders (56:9–12), a short lament on the death of the righteous (57:1–2), a stormy attack on foreign cults (57:3–13), a prophecy of comfort (57:14–19), and a criticism of those who fast ritually without thought (58:1–7). Chapters 60–61 contain another prophecy of salvation in the style of Second Isaiah. In 63:7–64:11 there is a communal lament, and 66:1–4 rejects both the building of the Temple and the sacrificial cult. This attitude reflects a view opposite that held by the prophets Haggai and Zechariah, who encouraged and supported the rebuilding of the Temple. It has been suggested that Third Isaiah was a disciple of Second Isaiah and his redactor as well. Another view holds that Second Isaiah returned to Jerusalem following Cyrus's edict and continued his prophetic activity there. His prophecies in Judah would then constitute chapters 49–66, in which Zion is the background for the speeches (see 49:14ff., 51:17–23, 54:1ff., 60:1ff., 62:1–9).

TEXTS OF ISAIAH FOUND AT QUMRAN. The scrolls found in 1947 on the northwestern shore of the Dead Sea reveal two almost complete manuscripts of the entire *Book of Isaiah,* dated to the second or first century BCE. As a rule, the scrolls of *Isaiah* reflect the Masoretic text. Of the two scrolls, one (found in Cave I) shows certain corrections and interlineations from a more popular edition, but these are mainly matters of spelling and stylistic characteristics rather than important editing. This scroll shows indications that it may actually have been composed of two manuscripts: There is evidence that the existing chapter 34 was started on a new sheet of leather, which may mean that it was a new manuscript. This may have influenced the modern critical division of the book into Isaiah of Jerusalem and Second Isaiah (and the remainder of the book).

BIBLIOGRAPHY

Isaiah 1–39

Barth, Hermann. *Die Jesaja-Worte in der Josiazeit.* Neukirchen, 1977.

Clements, R. E. *Isaiah 1–39.* Grand Rapids, Mich., 1980.

Kaiser, Otto. *Isaiah 13–39.* Translated by R. A. Wilson. Philadelphia, 1974.

Kaiser, Otto. *Isaiah 1–12.* 2d ed. Translated by R. A. Wilson. Philadelphia, 1983.

Wildberger, Hans. *Jesaja.* 3 vols. Neukirchen, 1972–1983.

Isaiah 40–66

Elliger, Karl. *Jesaja II.* Neukirchen, 1970–.

Gitay, Yehoshua. *Prophecy and Persuasion: A Study of Isaiah 40–48.* Bonn, 1981.

Kaufmann, Yeḥezkel. *History of the Religion of Israel,* vol. 4, *From the Babylonian Captivity to the End of Prophecy.* Translated by Clarence W. Efroymsen. New York, 1977.

Muilenburg, James. "Isaiah 40–66 (Introduction and Exegesis)." In *The Interpreter's Bible,* vol. 5, pp. 381–419, 422–773. New York, 1956.

Westermann, Claus. *Isaiah 40–66: A Commentary.* Translated by David M. G. Stalker. Philadelphia, 1969.

New Sources

Berrigan, Daniel. *Isaiah: Spirit of Courage, Gift of Tears.* Minneapolis, 1996.

Clements, Ronald Ernest. *Isaiah and the Deliverance of Jerusalem: A Study of the Interpretation of Prophecy in the Old Testament.* Sheffield, 1984.

Davies, Andrew. *Double Standards in Isaiah: Re-evaluating Prophetic Ethics and Divine Justice.* Leiden and Boston, 2000.

Hayes, John Haralson, and Stuart A. Irvine. *Isaiah, the Eighth Century Prophet: His Times and His Preaching.* Nashville, 1987.

Irvine, Stuart A. *Isaiah, Ahaz, and the Syro-Ephraimitic Crisis.* Atlanta, 1990.

Leclerc, Thomas L. *Yahweh Is Exalted in Justice: Solidarity and Conflict in Isaiah.* Minneapolis, 2001.

Quinn-Miscall, Peter D. *Reading Isaiah: Poetry and Vision.* Louisville, 2001.

Schmitt, John J. *Isaiah and His Interpreters.* New York, 1986.

YEHOSHUA GITAY (1987)
Revised Bibliography

ISHIDA BAIGAN (1685–1744) was a Japanese philosopher of the Tokugawa period (1603–1868) who developed the concept of a moral or ethical philosophy known as Shingaku. Ishida was born on September 15, 1685, in the village of Tōge in Tamba province (modern Kameoka City, Kyoto prefecture), the second son of a farmer. At the age of ten (eleven by Japanese count) he was sent to Kyoto as a merchant's apprentice. There he spent his leisure time studying Shintō doctrine and attending lectures by local Confucian scholars, Buddhist monks, and experts on the Japanese classics.

When Ishida reached the age of about thirty-five he began to feel an inner restlessness; he felt that he did not know the nature of human beings. In his search for a guide or a direction, he met a Buddhist monk, Ryōun, who led him to an awakening of the spirit such as that described by the Chinese founder of Daoism, Laozi. It was then that Ishida realized that humanity's true nature was egoless. In his writings, he pointed out that once one understood this aspect of human nature, one's life would automatically coincide with what he called the "universal principle" and one's *kokoro* ("soul" or "spirit") would be content and at peace. Ishida believed it would be possible to reach an egoless, natural state and to acquire instinctive knowledge by meditative restraint of the senses. In accordance with his convictions, he lived as a celibate ascetic, although he acknowledged that social responsibilities were also inherent in his view of human nature.

In 1727 Ishida left the service of the Kyoto merchant; two years later, he began to conduct lectures at his home in Kyoto. At these lectures, which were free and open to all, Ishida encouraged his listeners to seek individual awakening through meditation. To make learning accessible to all, Ishida distributed simplified manuscripts of his interpretations of Chinese and Japanese classical literature. He repudiated the critiques of scholars, whom he believed were interested only in the meanings of words. Ishida strove instead to capture the essence of the classics as he understood them, although his views did not always agree with the original intent of the authors.

In his search for a fundamental principle, Ishida believed that the first and last step in the learning process was to understand the human heart and thereby gain insight into human nature. He adopted the term *jinsei,* which refers to the total capacity of the mind, from the Chinese Confucian thinker Mengzi. According to Ishida, one must utilize all one's spiritual and mental capacity to overcome desires. Only when one's *kokoro* is empty and free of human desires is it possible to unite with the universal spirit. Overcoming the ego and its desires will enable one to carry out one's duty in life. One can then develop a spirit of self-sacrifice toward one's ruler, be properly filial toward one's parents, and discover one's proper vocation in life.

BIBLIOGRAPHY

A number of works have been published on Ishida Baigan and his philosophy of Shingaku, or practical ethics. Robert Bellah's *Tokugawa Religion: The Values of Pre-Industrial Japan* (Glencoe, Ill., 1957) clarifies the religious morals of the Tokugawa period, morals that had their origin in Ishida's concept of ethics and that played a part in the modernization of Japan. Readers of Japanese will want to consult a translation of this seminal work, *Nihon kindaika to shūkyō rinri* (Tokyo, 1981), translated by Hōri Ichirō and Ikeda Akira. Ishikawa Ken's *Shingaku, Edo no shomin tetsugaku* (Tokyo, 1964) discusses Ishida's philosophy and its applicability to the common people. Sakasai Takahito focuses on Ishida's conversion to popular morality in "Sekimon shingaku no igi to genkai, sono tsūzoku dōtoku e no tenraku ni tsuite," *Rikkyō keizaigaku kenkyū* 18 (February 1965). Another work that deals with Ishida's ethics is *Sekimon shingaku,* edited by Shibata Minoru (Tokyo, 1971), in volume 42 of "Nihon shisō taikei." Finally, Takenaka Yasukazu's *Sekimon shingaku no keizai shisō* (Tokyo, 1962) emphasizes the economic aspects of Ishida's ethical philosophy.

New Sources

Takemura, Eiji. *The Perception of Work in Tokugawa Japan: A Study of Ishida Baigan.* Lanham, Md., 1997.

HAGA NOBORU (1987)
Translated from Japanese by Irene M. Kunii
Revised Bibliography

ISHMAEL, or, in Hebrew, Yishma'e'l; eldest son of Abraham. Ishmael's mother was Hagar, an Egyptian slave girl whom Sarah gave to Abraham because of her own infertility; in accordance with Mesopotamian law, the offspring of such a union would be credited to Sarah (*Gn.* 16:2). The name *Yishma'e'l* is known from various ancient Semitic cultures and means "God has hearkened," suggesting that a child so named was regarded as the fulfillment of a divine promise.

Ishmael was circumcised at the age of thirteen by Abraham and expelled with his mother at the instigation of Sarah, who wanted to ensure that Isaac would be Abraham's heir (*Gn.* 21). In the New Testament, Paul uses this incident to symbolize the relationship between Judaism, the older but now rejected tradition, and Christianity (*Gal.* 4:21–31).

In the *Genesis* account, God blessed Ishmael, promising that he would be the founder of a great nation and a "wild ass of a man" always at odds with others (*Gn.* 16:12). He is credited with twelve sons, described as "princes according to their tribes" (*Gn.* 25:16), representing perhaps an ancient confederacy. The Ishmaelites, vagrant traders closely related to the Midianites, were apparently regarded as his descendants. The fact that Ishmael's wife and mother are both said to have been Egyptian suggests close ties between the Ishmaelites and Egypt. According to *Genesis* 25:17, Ishmael lived to the age of 137.

Islamic tradition tends to ascribe a larger role to Ishmael than does the Bible. He is considered a prophet and, according to certain theologians, the offspring whom Abraham was commanded to sacrifice (although *sūrah* 37:99–111 of the Qur'ān never names that son). Like his father Abraham, Ishmael too played an important role in making Mecca a religious center (2:127–129). Judaism has generally regarded him as wicked, although repentance is also ascribed to him. According to some rabbinic traditions, his two wives were Aisha and Fatima, whose names are the same as those of Muḥammad's wife and daughter. Both Judaism and Islam see him as the ancestor of Arab peoples.

BIBLIOGRAPHY

A survey of the Bible's patriarchal narratives can be found in Nahum M. Sarna's *Understanding Genesis* (New York, 1966). Postbiblical traditions, with reference to Christian and Islamic views, are collected in Louis Ginzberg's exhaustive *Legends of the Jews*, 2d ed., 2 vols., translated by Henrietta Szold and Paul Radin (Philadelphia, 2003).

FREDERICK E. GREENSPAHN (1987 AND 2005)

ISHMAEL BEN ELISHA SEE YISHMA'E'L BEN ELISHA'

ISHRĀQĪYAH,

ISHRĀQĪYAH, from *ishrāq* ("illumination"), is the name of a school of esoteric philosophy in Islam. The two major currents of thought in the development of Islamic philosophy, one exoteric and the other esoteric, are known respectively as *falsafah* ("scholastic philosophy," derived from Aristotle and Plato) and *'irfān* (a special type of philosophy derived from a metaphysical experience of Being through spiritual realization). Introduced into the West from the twelfth century onward through numerous translations from Arabic to Latin, it was *falsafah* that almost exclusively came to constitute "Islamic philosophy" in the West, while the other important tradition, that of *'irfān*, was left in complete obscurity. But *'irfān* has always been a creative force in Islamic spirituality, and as such it has produced a type of philosophy that is quite different from, and in many respects sharply opposed to, *falsafah*.

IMAGINAL THINKING. The word *philosophy* tends to suggest the inner act of thinking as a logical outcome of reason. One has to be reminded, however, that philosophic thought is not necessarily activated only on the level of pure reason. Because human consciousness is extremely complicated and multilayered, various forms of thinking can be realized at different levels of the mind. "Imaginal" thinking is one of them.

"Imaginal" thinking, also known as "mythopoeic thinking" or "mythopoesis," is a peculiar pattern of thinking that evolves through interconnections and interactions among a number of archetypal images in a particular depth-dimension of consciousness. In the technical terminology of Islamic *'irfān*, this depth-dimension is called the *'ālam al-mithāl*, meaning literally the "world of symbolic images." The type of philosophy produced by this kind of thinking naturally manifests remarkable differences from philosophy as a product of pure reason.

Imaginal thinking is not confined to Islamic *'irfān*. Quite the contrary; many different systems of philosophy that have come into being in various Asian regions reflect self-expressions of "imaginal" consciousness. The "illuminationism" (*ishrāqīyah*) of Suhrawardī represents one case, the "unity of being" (*waḥdat al-wujūd*) of Ibn 'Arabī another. Complicating the matter with regard to the Islamic variety of "imaginal" or esoteric philosophy, however, is the fact that the majority of the first-rate thinkers in this domain were also great masters of Scholastic, exoteric philosophy, so that both the "imaginal" and the rational modes of thinking appear in subtle entanglements on the textual surface of their works. This is notably the case with men like Suhrawardī and Ibn al-'Arabī.

Suhrawardī, in particular, is known to have written three voluminous books on scholasticism, *Kitāb al-talwīḥāt*, *Kitāb al-muqāwamāt*, and *Kitāb al-muṭāraḥāt*, the famous trilogy attesting to his rarely surpassed accomplishment as an exoteric philosopher, prior to embarking upon the production of his major work on Illuminationism, *Ḥikmat al-ishrāq* (Theosophy of Illumination). As indicated by the title, this is essentially a product of imaginal thinking, representing a peculiar kind of esoteric philosophy based on a metaphysical experience of light. Yet it begins with a sober exposition of the principles of Aristotelian logic before gradually becoming an "imaginal" presentation of the hierarchic structure of the angels of light. It is important to note that this seemingly odd combination of the exoteric and esoteric modes of thinking, together with the very conception of *ishrāq*, can be traced back to Ibn Sīnā (Avicenna).

IBN SĪNĀ AND "ORIENTAL PHILOSOPHY." In a number of respects, and particularly with regard to the idea of *ishrāq*, Ibn Sīnā may be considered an important precursor of

Suhrawardī. Quite characteristically, however, in Ibn Sīnā's work the rational and "imaginal" modes of thinking are still consciously and methodically separated from one another, so that *falsafah* and *ʿirfān* are conceived as two independent and essentially different types of philosophy (although in the process of the structuralization of Ibn Sīnā's symbolic narratives, we sometimes notice technical concepts of Aristotelianism creeping into the "imaginal" space of *ʿirfān*).

It is important to note that of the two types of philosophy Ibn Sīnā himself laid greater weight on the imaginal (i.e., esoteric) than on the rational (i.e., exoteric). At the outset of his *magnum opus*, the famous *Kitāb al-shifaʾ* (Book of Remedy, known in the West in Latin translation as *Sufficientia*), which is a huge systematic exposition of Peripatetic philosophy, Ibn Sīnā declares that what he is going to write does not represent his personal thought but is intended to acquaint the students of philosophy with the thought-world of the ancient Greeks, Aristotle in particular.

As for his own "true thought," he seems to have long cherished the idea of giving a direct expression to it in a completely different book, *Al-ḥikmat al-mashriqīyah* (Oriental Philosophy), of which the now extant *Manṭiq al-mashriqīyīn* (The Logic of the Orientals) is only the introductory part. Whether completed or not, the book itself has not come down to us. Besides this work we have a few short treatises of esotericism and some symbolic tales from his own pen.

Ibn Sīnā's use of words meaning "Orient" and "Oriental" is significant here, for the word *mashriq* ("Orient"), from the root *shrq*, literally means the "place (*ma-*) where what is designated by the root *shrq* becomes activated," that is, the original point of "illumination" (*ishrāq*). The "Orient," in other words, is not a geographical notion, but a term designating the East in a mythopoeic or spiritual geography.

The "Orient" in this particular context is the sacred locus from which the divine light makes its appearance, illuminating the whole world of being, "the place where the sun rises," the ultimate origin of all existence. In the Persian commentary on Ibn Sīnā's mythic-symbolic tale, *Ḥayy ibn Yaqẓan* (a proper name, literally "Living, son of Wakeful"), one of his disciples (Abū ʿUbayd al-Juzjānī?) explicates the symbolism of "Orient" and "Occident" in the following manner. Utilizing in his own way the Aristotelian theory of the distinction between "form" and "matter," he begins by stating that matter in and by itself has no existence, whereas form is the source of existence. Matter, in other words, is pure nonexistence. But his Iranian frame of reference naturally and immediately translates this proposition into another, namely, that matter in itself is sheer darkness. And he assigns matter (as darkness) to the Western region of the cosmos in the "imaginal" map of his symbolic geography.

The implication of this position is clear. Ibn Sīnā defines the Orient as the original abode of form (light), and thus symbolically as the world of "forms," or existential light, while the Occident is the world of "matter," that is, of darkness and nonexistence.

Matter turns into existence only by the influx of the all-existentiating luminous energy of form, coming from the divine Orient through the intermediary of ten angels—the number limited to ten in conformity with the ten celestial spheres of Hellenistic astronomy. Directly reflecting the divine light, the angels embody the highest degree of existential luminosity, while all other beings and things that become luminous (i.e., existent) through the illuminating activity of the angels are less bright (i.e., less densely existent). The existential luminosity naturally grows less and less intense as the rays of the divine light go down the scale of being (i.e., become further and further removed from its original source), until they merge almost totally into the darkness of matter when they reach the lowest stage of being.

As long as they do exist factually, the "things" in the empirical world are not sheer darkness. They are shadowy existents, faint reflections of the divine light. But since it is matter that is overwhelmingly dominant in this domain, the empirical world is "imaginally" represented as a world of darkness. In some privileged cases (notably the prophets), however, the human consciousness may suddenly flare up in glorious light under the influence of the Active Intellect (Gabriel, the angel of revelation), illuminating the world of darkness in which the souls of ordinary human beings are imprisoned—a typical theme of Gnosticism.

Such, in brief outline, is the general plan of the "Oriental philosophy" of Ibn Sīnā. Underlying it is clearly a vision of the cosmos as the interplay of light and shadow, a vast "imaginal" field in which the divine light appears in infinitely various and variegated forms, determining itself in accordance with various degrees of interfusion with material darkness through the light-transmitting activity of the angels. It is a Gnostic vision of the world permeated with the "imaginal" presence of the angels of light.

SUHRAWARDĪ, FOUNDER OF THE ISHRĀQĪ SCHOOL. The esoteric worldview manifested in Ibn Sīnā's philosophy, with its strong Gnostic influences, was inherited in turn by Shihāb al-Dīn Yaḥyā ibn Ḥabash ibn Amīrak al-Suhrawardī (1153–1191), the real founder of the Illuminationist school in Iran. Significantly enough, Suhrawardī, who has come to be known by the honorary title Shaykh al-Ishrāq, "master of illumination," traces the "tradition" of his Illuminationist philosophy back to Hermes Agathodaemon (who appears in Islam under the figure of the prophet Idrīs). It must be remembered that long before the rise of Islam, the Mediterranean school of Hermetism had established itself in Alexandria, and from this center it had infiltrated into the wide domain of the Middle East. There, in the city of Harran, the "followers of the prophet Idris," the Sabaeans who venerated the *Corpus Hermeticum* as their scripture, cultivated the esoteric learning of Hermetism and propagated it in various directions. Through one of these it must have reached Suhrawardī.

In the "imaginal" dimension of Suhrawardī's consciousness, however, the history of Illuminationism (which he straightforwardly identifies with the history of philosophy in general) takes on a remarkably original and peculiar form. Ishrāqī wisdom as the only authentic actualization of the "perennial philosophy" (*ḥikmah ʿatīqah*) of mankind has its ultimate origin in the divine revelations received by the prophet Idris, that is, Hermes, who thereby became the forefather of philosophy. This Hermetic wisdom was transmitted to posterity through two separate channels: Egyptian-Greek and ancient Iranian. The first branch of Hermetic wisdom, after flourishing in ancient Egypt, went to Greece, where it produced such Gnostic sages as Pythagoras, Empedocles, Plato, and Plotinus. The tradition was maintained in Islam by some of the eminent early Ṣūfīs, including Dhū al-Nūn (d. 859) and Sahl al-Tustarī (d. 896).

The second branch of Hermetism, represented in ancient Iran by the mythical priest-kings Kayūmarth, Farīdūn, and Kay Khusraw, developed into the Sufism of Bāyazīd al-Basṭāmī, generally known in the West as al-Bisṭāmi (d. 874), and Manṣūr al-Ḥallāj (d. 922).

Suhrawardī considered himself the historical point of convergence between the two traditions, unifying and integrating into an existential, organic whole all the important elements of the Hermetic wisdom elaborated in the long course of its historical development. And to the integral whole of Gnostic ideas thus formed Suhrawardī gave a peculiar philosophical reformulation, structured in terms of the Zoroastrian symbolism of light and darkness—the term *Zoroastrianism* here understood in the sense of the spiritual, "esoteric" teaching of Zoroaster as distinguished from the "exoteric."

East-West symbolism. In approaching Suhrawardī's Illuminationist philosophy, the first thing we must pay attention to is the symbolism of East and West. *Qiṣṣat al-ghurbah al-gharbīyah* (The Narrative of the Occidental Exile), which he composed in Arabic—most of his symbolic tales or narratives are in Persian—makes it clear that he attaches the same "imaginal" meanings to "Orient" and "Occident" as did Ibn Sīnā. Thus, the Orient for him too means the Orient of lights, the sacred place in which divine light originates, the source of spiritual as well as cosmic illumination, whereas the Occident is the abyss of material darkness, in which the human soul is imprisoned and from which it must set itself free so that it may go back to its real home, the Orient.

Hierarchy of lights. Rejecting (or radically modifying) the Aristotelian doctrine of hylomorphism, which explains every existent in terms of a conjunction of matter and specific form, Suhrawardī employs a completely different ontology, of Gnostic origin, explaining all things as degrees of light (or as various mixtures of light and darkness); the Aristotelian "form" thereby appears metamorphosed into an angel as a luminous being. Suhrawardian philosophy thus turns out to be an ontology of light, with varying degrees of intensity, in a hierarchical order.

Light, says Suhrawardī, is that which illuminates itself, and by so doing illuminates all other things. Light, otherwise expressed, is that which exists by and in itself (i.e., light *is* existence) and by its own existence brings into existence all things. Light thus defies definition, while all other things can and must be defined in reference to it. Light, in short, is nothing other than the ontological "presence" (*ḥuḍūr*) of the things; it is the ultimate source of all existence. It follows, therefore, that the whole world of being must be realized as a grandiose hierarchy of lights, beginning with the absolute light in the highest degree of luminosity and ending with the weakest lights just about to sink into the reign of utter darkness (*ghasaq*), that is, absolute nonexistence.

What stands at the top of this cosmic hierarchy of light is the "light of lights" (*nūr al-anwār*), which, in the terminology of Islamic theology, is God. Beneath it, spreading down to the domain of the densely dark bodies in the physical world, are various degrees of light (existence), which, in Suhrawardī's system, characteristically appear in the guise of angels who govern the world of being.

Unlike Ibn Sīnā's angelology, which is Neoplatonic, Suhrawardī's is fundamentally Zoroastrian. Rather than being limited to ten (corresponding to the ten heavens of Ptolemy), the number of angels is innumerable. Their function, moreover, is not limited to the Neoplatonic angels' triple intellection of their origin, of themselves, and of those that come out of them. As a result, the hierarchy of Suhrawardī's angelology is far more complicated than that of Ibn Sīnā. There are, to begin with, two different basic orders of angels, "longitudinal" (*ṭūlī*) and "latitudinal" (*ʿarḍīi*), with regard to their successive generations, their spatial disposition, and their functions.

Longitudinal and latitudinal order. The longitudinal order of angels lays the primary foundation of the world of being in its entirety as a "temple of light," or rather, a dazzling complex of "temples of light" (*hayākil al-nūr*, sg., *haykal al-nūr*), radiant with angels reflecting the "light of lights" and mutually reflecting each other. Their procession is described by Suhrawardī in the following manner.

From the "light of lights," representing the highest and ultimate point of cosmic-metaphysical luminosity, proceeds the archangel Bahmān, who is the "nearest light" (*nūr aqrab*). Directly contemplating his own origin, the "light of lights," the archangel Bahmān reflects it without any intermediary. And this immediately brings into being another light-entity, or archangel, which is doubly illuminated, receiving as it does illumination directly from the "light of lights" and from the first light from which it has arisen. The double illumination of the second light immediately generates the third light, which is now illuminated four times, once by the "light of lights," once by the first light, and twice by the second light (the second light being, as we have just seen, itself doubly illuminated). And so continues the downward procession of the archangels, resulting in the constitution of the "longitudinal" order of lights. Each one of these angelic lights is called in Suhrawardī's technical terminology a "dominating light" (*nūr qāhir*), with "forceful domination" (*qahr*) one of the basic principles determining the activity of these angels.

This longitudinal order of archangels of light has in itself two mutually opposed aspects, the masculine and the feminine, from the former of which issues an essentially different order of angels, the latitudinal. Unlike the archangels of the longitudinal order, the latitudinal angels do not generate one another, but simply coexist horizontally, positioned side by side, thus constituting the world of eternal "archetypes" that are "imaginal" equivalents of the Platonic ideas. Suhrawardī calls them in this capacity the "lords of the species" (*arbāb al-anwāʿ*; sg., *rabb al-nawʿ*). Every thing in the empirical world specifically stands under the domination of a lord of the species; in other words, every individual existent in our world has its corresponding metaphysical archetype in the angelic dimension of being, somewhat like the ontological relationship between the individual and universal realms in Platonic idealism. Each existent in the empirical world is technically called the "talisman" (*ṭilasm*) of a particular angel governing and guarding it from above. And the angel in this capacity is called the "lord of the talisman" (*rabb al-ṭilasm*).

As for the feminine aspect of the longitudinal order of angels, it primarily has to do with such negative attributes as being dominated, being dependent, being receptive to illumination, being remote from the "light of lights," nonbeing, and so on. The fixed stars and the visible heavens come into being from it as so many hypostatizations of the luminous energies of the archangels. And this marks the ending point of the Orient and the beginning point of the Occident.

The latitudinal order of angels gives rise to still another order of angels, whose basic function is to govern the species in the capacity of vicegerents of the "lords of the species." These deputy angels are called by Suhrawardī the "directive lights" (*anwār mudabbirah*; sg., *nūr mudabbir*). Using the characteristic Persian word *ispahbad*, meaning "commander-in-chief," Suhrawardī calls them also "light-generalissimos" (*anwār isfahbadīyah*). These are the angels who are charged with maintaining the movement of the heavens, and who, as the agents of the "lords of the species," govern all the species of the creatures in the physical world, including human beings, whose shared "lord of the species" is the archangel Gabriel (Jibrīl). The "deputy governor" (*ispahbad*, the "light-generalissimo") of Gabriel resides in the inmost part of the soul of each human being, issuing directions concerning his or her internal and external acts.

As will be clearly observable even from this very brief, and necessarily incomplete, exposition, Suhrawardī's Illuminationist worldview is fundamentally mandalic in nature. The world of being in its entirety is conceived or imaged as a vast cosmic mandala composed of innumerable angels of light spreading out in geometric designs along longitudinal and latitudinal axes. Here we have a typical product of mandalic consciousness completely self-realized in the form of a vision of the whole world of being appearing as an "imaginal" space saturated with light.

POST-SUHRAWARDIAN DEVELOPMENTS. Suhrawardī's life was extremely short; in the citadel of Aleppo where he was imprisoned as a propagator of anti-Islamic "new ideas" he was murdered at the age of thirty-eight in the year 1191. But after his death the influence of his Ishrāqī teaching grew stronger in the Islamic world, particularly in Iran, where it exercised the greatest influence on the historical formation of the philosophy of Shiism.

The long chain of followers of the Master of Illumination begins with Shams al-Dīn Shahrazūrī (thirteenth century), who studied personally under Suhrawardī or under one of his direct disciples. He wrote the first systematic and most extensive commentary on the *Ḥikmat al-ishrāq*, thereby preparing the ground for subsequent interpretations of this fundamental work of Illuminationism. It was, as a matter of fact, in complete reliance on this commentary that Quṭb al-Dīn Shīrāzī (d. 1311) composed his famous commentary on the *Ḥikmat al-ishrāq*.

Shahrazūrī was in reality a far more original thinker than Quṭb al-Dīn Shīrāzī, and his commentary was far more important and interesting than Quṭb al-Dīn's, which is now known to be an abbreviated version. Quṭb al-Dīn's fame, however, soon overshadowed that of his great predecessor, so that his commentary came to be regarded as virtually *the* commentary on the *Ḥikmat al-ishrāq*; thus from the early fourteenth century until today almost all those who have been interested in Suhrawardian Illuminationism have read or studied the book mainly through the interpretation given by Quṭb al-Dīn.

The historical importance of Quṭb al-Dīn lies in the fact that besides being an ardent propagator of Illuminationism, he was also a disciple of Ṣadr al-Dīn Qūnawī (or Qunyawī), a personal disciple of Ibn al-ʿArabī and his son-in-law, and that through this channel he was well versed in the *waḥdat al-wujūd* type of philosophy. In fact, Quṭb al-Dīn is counted among the greatest expositors of Ibn al-ʿArabī's ideas. Combining thus in his own person these two important currents of the post-Avicennian Islamic philosophy, Quṭb al-Dīn fundamentally determined the subsequent course of the development of the Ishrāqī school. Indeed, after Quṭb al-Dīn, Suhrawardian Illuminationism quickly assimilated into its structure the major ideas of the "unity of existence" that had been independently developed by the school of Ibn al-ʿArabī.

The work of integration reached its first stage of completion in the Safavid period in Iran. The two centuries of the Safavid dynasty (1499–1720), during which the city of Isfahan was the political and cultural center and Twelver Shiism was the recognized form of Islam, realized what is often called the "renaissance of Islamic [Shīʿī] culture." It was in the flourishing city of Isfahan that the intellectual heritages of Ibn al-ʿArabī and Suhrawardī were harmoniously integrated into an organic whole through the works of generations of outstanding thinkers. These thinkers are now referred to among historians of Islamic philosophy as the "school of Isfahan," the greatest figure in which is uncontestedly Ṣadr al-Dīn Shīrāzī (popularly known as Mullā Ṣadrā, 1571–1640).

Mullā Ṣadrā's philosophy is a colossal and complicated system, synthesizing ideas derived from various sources in conjunction with his own quite original thoughts. As regards Illuminationism, Mullā Ṣadrā made thoroughly explicit what had from the beginning been implicit (and occasionally explicit), namely, the complete identification of "light" with "existence." In this way, "existence" became totally synonymous with "luminosity." The existence of each thing is in the metaphysical-"imaginal" vision of Mullā Ṣadrā nothing other than a degree of light, a luminous issue or illumination from the "light of lights." The "light of lights" itself is completely identified with what is referred to in Ibn al-ʿArabī's *waḥdat al-wujūd* system as the "one," that is, existence in its primordial state of absolute undetermination, but ready to start determining itself in an infinity of different ontological self-manifestations.

See Also Falsafah; Hermetism; Ibn al-ʿArabī; Ibn Sīnā; Images; Mullā Ṣadrā; Nūr Muḥammad.

Bibliography

Works by Suhrawardī in Translation

Shihaboddin Yaḥyā Sohravardi's "L'archange Empourpré," translated by Henry Corbin, in *Documents spirituels,* vol. 14 (Paris, 1976), is a collection of symbolic narratives and short essays of Suhrawardī, translated into French from Persian and Arabic, with copious notes. It is indispensable for all those seeking initiation into the mystical world of the Master of Illumination.

Works on Suhrawardī and Illuminationism

Seyyed Hossein Nasr's "Shihāb al-Dīn Suhrawardī Maqtūl," in *A History of Muslim Philosophy,* edited by M. M. Sharif (Wiesbaden, 1963), vol. 1, pp. 372–398, is by far the best introductory exposition of the Illuminationism of Suhrawardī. See also his "The School of Iṣpahān," in the same source, vol. 2, pp. 904–932, and "The Spread of the Illuminationist School of Suhrawardī," *Islamic Quarterly* 14 (July–September 1970): 111–121, a short but important paper that traces the historical development of Illuminationism in Iran, India, and Turkey down to modern times. See also Henry Corbin's *Sohrawardī et les platoniciens de Perse,* vol. 2 of *En Islam iranien* (Paris, 1971), one of the most important works on Suhrawardī.

New Sources

Walbridge, John. *The Wisdom of the Ancient East: Suhrawardi and Platonic Orientalism.* Albany, 2001.

Ziai, Hossein. *Knowledge and Initiation: A Study of Suhrawardi's Hikmat al-ishraq.* Atlanta, 1990.

Toshihiko Izutsu (1987)
Revised Bibliography

ISHTAR See INANNA

ISIDORE OF SEVILLE

ISIDORE OF SEVILLE (560–636), bishop of Seville (603–636), proclaimed "eminent teacher and an honor to the church" by the Council of Toledo of 653. Member of an eminent Andalusian family, Isidore was prepared to inherit the see of Seville by his older brother Leandro, also bishop of Seville. In his youth the king, Leovigild (r. 569–586), was able to stabilize the Visigothic kingdom, in which a minority of Visigoths (Germanic peoples who entered the Iberian Peninsula in the fifth century) and a vast majority of ancient inhabitants (the Hispano-Romans) coexisted. Under Reccared (d. 601) the Goths abjured the Arian doctrine and embraced the Catholic faith (c. 589). In 614 the Jews were forced by Sisebut to convert to Christianity.

Through his pastoral leadership, Isidore imbued the Visigothic church with the same concerns that dominate his writings: respect for the political authority of the Goths, incitation for increasing participation of the Hispano-Romans in the life of the church, and an overriding intellectual and moral commitment. A famous orator, he presided at the Council of Seville of 619 and at the Council of Toledo of 633. Mild and conciliatory, Isidore was a man of great human and Christian optimism; he struggled with his own strict education and with the intransigent atmosphere of the church after the triumph of catholic orthodoxy against the Arians, and over tensions with Jews after 614.

Isidore's writings, cataloged by his friend Braulio (d. 651), bishop of Zaragoza, may be grouped as follows:

1. biblical studies;
2. handbooks for clergy and monks: *Concerning the Ecclesiastical Offices, A Monastic Rule, Vademecum of the Catholic Faith for Use in Discussion with the Jews,* and *Catalog of Heresies;*
3. guides for personal and public spiritual development: *Synonyms* and *Sentences;*
4. works on civic education: *About the Universe,* an explanation of the system of the world and of natural phenomena for the purpose of preventing fear and superstition;
5. works extolling the national glory: *History of the Goths, Vandals, and Suevi; Praise of Spain; Chronicle of the World;* and *Catalog of Illustrious Men,* an innovation in this genre insofar as it introduces persons distinguished by their pastoral activity; and
6. works on general education, based largely upon linguistic or grammatical explanations: *Differences between Words,* his first writing, and *Etymologies,* on which he labored until his death and which was completed by Braulio.

He also wrote poems and letters, and he probably took part in preparing the *Collectio canonica Hispana* (Collection of church councils), covering both ecumenical and Spanish councils. Both Christian and non-Christian authors are cited in Isidore's writings with admiration and appreciation.

Isidore is best known through his *Synonyms* (known in manuscripts as "Soliloquies," a dialogue between humanity and its reason), which employed a new technique of parallel phrases with progressive variation of words. This work was simultaneously a source of practical vocabulary and a mechanism of catharsis that promoted in the reader a unified spirituality. It includes simple moral teaching and formulas for spiritual enlightenment. In three books, *Sentences* (*On the Greatest Good* in manuscripts) summarizes the spiritual organization of the human community by duties and obligations. It is in the form of easily memorized proverbs based upon Christian authors, and it combines moral knowledge with living experience. *Etymologies* (also named *Origines*), in twenty books, classifies and defines, according to a personal system of etymological interpretation, all the knowledge of Isidore's time as drawn from ancient sources through commentaries, glosses, and scholastic handbooks. In the Middle Ages it was considered the basic reference work for understanding texts and for coherently interpreting the world.

BIBLIOGRAPHY

An extensive critical introduction and systematic bibliography can be found in my introduction to *San Isidoro de Sevilla, Etimologías,* vol. 1, edited by José Oroz Reta, "Biblioteca de autores cristianos" (Madrid, 1982). See also J. N. Hillgarth's "The Position of Isidorian Studies," *Studi medievali* 24 (1983): 817–905. In French, see Jacques Fontaine's *Isidore de Séville et la culture classique dans l'Espagne wisigothique,* 2 vols. and suppl. (Paris, 1983); "Isidore de Séville," in the *Dictionnaire de spiritualité,* vol. 7 (Paris, 1971); and *Isidore de Séville. Genèse et originallé de la culture hispanique au temps des visigoths* (Turnhout, Belgium, 2000).

MANUEL C. DÍAZ Y DÍAZ (1987 AND 2005)
Translated from Spanish by Maria Elisa Guirola

ISIS is one of the most important deities in the Egyptian pantheon. The hieroglyph for her name was the throne, and she was portrayed with a headdress in the shape of a throne. Scholars postulate that Isis was the personification of the throne or that her name means "the one who has ruling power." Jan Bergman concludes in "Isis" (1980, col. 188) that the explanation of her name points to a later priestly interpretation. The name Isis appears securely for the first time in the fifth dynasty (2465–2325 BCE) and in the *Pyramid Texts* at the end of the Old Kingdom (2650–2152 BCE). The first depiction of the goddess occurred almost a thousand years after the first textual mention in the eighteenth dynasty (1539–1295 BCE).

In the Heliopolitan rendering of the nine premier Egyptian gods, Isis was the daughter of Geb and Nut (Earth and Sky). Osiris was her brother and husband, Horus their son. Seth and Nephthys, also offsprings of Geb and Nut, were Isis and Osiris's opponents. Seth killed his brother Osiris and dismembered him, and Isis searched for the scattered body parts across Egypt. She found all the parts except for the phallus. Isis then fashioned a replacement for the missing part and reassembled her brother-husband's body. With the help of Thoth, she revived Osiris for a short time. In this period of revival Isis conceived Horus, who became his father's avenger.

Being a mother herself, Isis helped women in childbirth. In the New Kingdom (1539–1069 BCE), Isis was depicted as midwife. Greco-Roman renderings of Isis show her with a knot on the front of her dress. This knot indicated life and protected pregnant women as well as their babies. The goddess was also a healer. When a scorpion stung and killed her son Horus, Isis revived him. In another myth Isis fashioned a snake that bit the supreme god Re. As Re lay dying, Isis promised to heal him if he gave up his secret name and thus world dominion. Re refused at first, but in the end he gave Isis what she sought. In another succession myth, Horus raped and decapitated his mother, the latter as punishment for Isis's disloyalty when she did not allow the destruction of her brother Seth. The Greek writers Diodorus Siculus (1.13–27) and Plutarch (*De Iside et Osiride,* 12–19) provide the most continuous myths surrounding Isis. Various aretologies emphasize her henotheistic, singular divine force of creation; she was the goddess with a thousand names (*myrionyma*).

Isis was linked to the goddess Hathor. She wore Hathor's headdress, the cow horns. In his "Isis," Bergman points to another connection with Hathor (Bergman, 1980, col. 189f.). After Horus decapitated his mother, she received a cow head as replacement. Like the cow horns and cow head, Isis acquired the uraeus snake from Hathor. In addition, Isis was equated with Selket and appropriated that goddess's animal form, the scorpion. Isis was also linked to the female hippopotamus, a white sow, and a lion. Bergman notes that the goddess appears as a water- and food-providing tree goddess. In the celestial sphere Isis was connected with Sothis or Sirius, the Dog Star (Canis Major). She was the bringer of the Nile's annual flooding (Bergman, 1980, col. 192), which was essential for Egypt's agriculture. Isis's manifestations are manifold due to syncretism, an inbuilt fluidity that allowed gods to merge with each other. Depictions of Isis from Egyptian to Greco-Roman times show this confluence of representative elements most succinctly. Isis was not only *myrionyma* in name but also in terms of her iconographic signifiers.

DISSEMINATION OF THE CULT. Greeks, who had economic links with Egypt since the seventh century BCE, knew of Egyptian deities. They explained these deities by way of analogies. In this way Isis was equated with Demeter (Herodotos, *Histories,* 2.42ff.). The Ptolemaic period, however, ushered in a more intensive propagation of the cult of Isis outside Egypt. In this era, as in Roman times, the most important temple structure of Isis was on the island of Philae in southern (Upper) Egypt. Alexander's successor, Ptolemy I Soter, chose Sarapis as his dynasty's guardian deity. This god then became Isis's Hellenized consort.

An inscription from Pireus (Vidman, 1969, inscription no. 1), the port city of Athens, dated to 333 BCE suggests that cult adherents were first Egyptians who had economic ties with Athens. By the end of the third century BCE Athenian citizens held the various priesthoods. On Delos, the most important location for the westward dissemination of the cult, Egyptians held the priesthoods initially, followed by Delians and then Athenians. Françoise Dunand demonstrates in *Le culte d'Isis dans le bassin oriental de la Méditerranée* (1973) that, in all of Greece, Isis had the lowest impact on the Peloponnese. Michel Malaise shows in "La diffusion des cultes égyptiens dans les provinces européennes de l'Empire romain" (1984) that merchants were the most important propagators of the cult. When Archelaos, a general of Mithridates VI, the king of Pontos, captured the island of Delos in 88 BCE, Italian merchants returning to Italy brought with them the goddess Isis and intensified the goddess's presence where she was already known before this time.

Isis, for example, was established before 88 BCE in the port cities of Pompeii, Puteoli, and Ostia. The temple of Isis in Pompeii was built toward the end of the second century BCE, the temple of the Alexandrian gods in Puteoli dates to approximately 105 BCE. However, it seems that, in the wake of the forceful return of Italian merchants from Delos, Isis made her way to Rome. The second century CE author Apuleius states in his *Metamorphoses*, also known as *The Golden Ass* (11.30), that the first association of Isiac priests (*collegium pastophorum*, college of carriers of sacred objects) in Rome was founded at the time of the dictator Sulla (82–79 BCE). An inscription, unfortunately now lost, established a strong connection between Delos and Rome (Vidman, 1969, inscription no. 377). In "Iside Capitolina, Clodio e i mercanti di schiavi" (1984) Filippo Coarelli convincingly dates the inscription to 90–60 BCE and points to families of slave traders as a decisive link between the Aegean island and the capital. Ladislav Vidman suggests in *Isis und Sarapis bei den Griechen und Römern* (1970) that the Late Republican period was favorable to the Egyptian cult. Subsequent research showed that it was not unbridled passions of the simple and disfranchised that brought about this acceptance. Egyptian scenes and representations of Isis's headdress, rattles (*sistra*), Egyptian snakes (uraei), obelisks, and lotus flowers were components of an artistic repertoire. Control marks on coins were not expressions of a social revolution but an artistic realization of a Late Republican cultural reality.

The reactions against the cult in 58, 53, and 48 BCE were of a political nature (Tertullian, *Ad Nationes*, 1.10; Dio Cassius, 40.47 and 42.26). The Roman Senate found itself stripped of its political power and, as a consequence, dictated these expulsions of the cult of Isis. Expulsion as well as acceptance and subsequent introduction of a foreign cult into Rome's religious system were privileges of the Senate. These actions demonstrated, confirmed, and secured the Senate's political authority. Isis, however, did not disappear from Rome. Far from it, the triumvirate in charge of restoring the Republic voted in favor of a temple of Isis in 43 BCE (Cassius Dio, 47.15.4). Two later regulations (28 and 21 BCE; Cassius Dio, 53.2.4 and 54.6.6) curtailing the cult within the city of Rome were intended by Augustus to demonstrate his resolve vis-à-vis the traditional code of behavior (the *mos maiorum*) and the traditional, Greco-Roman gods.

In 19 CE Tiberius ordered the removal of Jews and Isis worshipers from Rome (Tacitus, *Annals*, 2.85.5; Josephus, *Antiquities*, 18.72; Suetonius, *Life of Tiberius*, 36.1). It has been suggested that the emperor intended to cleanse the capital of foreign cults, especially those perceived as undermining Roman morality, but is seems more likely that the reason was political. Germanicus, Tiberius's designated successor, had traveled to Egypt and, in a public relations stunt, opened the granaries. Unfortunately, this gesture of generosity led subsequently to famine in Rome (Tacitus, *Annals*, 2.67). Germanicus also visited Memphis without imperial permission. The priests of Memphis, the guardians of the living and dead Apis bulls, made and unmade pharaohs, even if only symbolically at this time (Maystre, 1992).

In the Roman construct of reality, politics and religion were intertwined; hence Rome's success was thought dependent on the gods and the gods favored a people who worshiped them properly and in a timely fashion. Whenever a political crisis occurred that undermined Rome's social order, the problem was thought to lie in the religious sphere; that is, it was believed that the gods had turned away from the Romans, who had failed in their ritual performance. Isis was Alexandria's most powerful god, and the city had the largest number of Jewish inhabitants in the Roman Empire. The expulsion of Jews and Isis worshipers from Rome demonstrated the emperor's political power and symbolized the reestablishment of traditional order.

With the consolidation of the new political order (the principate, which began with the emperor Augustus [r. 27 BCE–14 CE]) and the integration of Egypt as a province of the Roman Empire, Isis and her cult could no longer be thought illegal. The cult was officially recognized at the end of Caligula's reign or at the beginning of Claudius's. The first to establish this time period was Georg Wissowa in *Religion and Kultus der Römer* (1971), and Anthony Barrett in *Caligula* (1989, pp. 220f.) further developed the argument. The connection with the imperial house (the *domus Augusta*) occurred during the reign of Vespasian (69–79 CE). Vespasian had been proclaimed emperor by his troops while he was in Alexandria. Upon his return to Rome, he and his son Titus stayed in the temple of Isis in the Field of Mars, the *Iseum Campense*, the night before their triumphal procession into Rome (Josephus, *Jewish Wars*, 7.123f.). Domitian, Vespasian's youngest son, renovated many temples of Isis during his reign (81–96 CE). After Vespasian's acclamation in Alexandria, the family had a connection to Isis, and their subsequent actions are demonstrations of piety toward the goddess.

There was an increasing interest in Egyptian and Egyptianizing objects at the time of the emperor Hadrian (114–141 CE), which had to do with the emperor's interest in Egypt. The city of Alexandria possessed the most important libraries of antiquity. Hadrian was a philhellene (a lover of Greek culture), and the Alexandrian libraries were the guardians of Greek literature and culture. It also happened that Hadrian's beloved Antinous had drowned in the Nile while visiting Egypt with the emperor. The death of a friend and accessibility to a cherished cultural heritage made Egypt so prominent in Hadrian's life that it brought about a new artistic movement. Even Hadrian's villa outside Rome featured an Egypt-inspired area.

Inscriptions asking for the well-being (*salus*) of the imperial household (*domus Augusta*) in the name of Isis's Hellenistic consort Sarapis appear predominantly in the period after Emperor Marcus Aurelius's victory over the Quadi, a Germanic people. István Tóth established in "Marcus Aurelius' Miracle of the Rain and the Egyptian Cults in the Danube Region" (1976) that the dedicators of these inscriptions were the emperor's generals. As the Quadi were close to victory on a blazing hot day, Arnouphis, a *hierogrammateus* (cultic scribe) and member of Marcus Aurelius's entourage, induced rain and alleviated the Roman legions' debilitating thirst. The Romans thus gained the advantage over their adversaries (Cassius Dio, 71.8). Isis and her consort Sarapis were now fully accepted guarantors of the Empire's well-being. Ultimately, at the time of the Severi (193–235 CE), the Roman dynastic ideology corresponded to the pharaonic-Ptolemaic one. Like Vespasian more than a century earlier, the legions of the East had made Septimius Severus, the founder of the dynasty, emperor.

RELIGION PRACTICES. Two major festivals in honor of Isis are known: the public launching of the ship of Isis—the *navigium Isidis,* or *ploiaphesia*—which was celebrated on March 5 (Apuleius, *Metamorphoses,* 11.8–17), and the finding of Osiris—the *inventio* or *heuresis Osiridis*—from October 28 to November 3. A cult association had five *antistites* (priests or carriers of sacred objects), *pastophori* or *hierophoroi,* who in the cult hierarchy were below a *sacerdos,* priest. These five carried various insignia during a procession (Apuleius, *Metamorphoses,* 11.10). A *sacerdos* (man or woman) held his or her position for a year, sometimes for life. The lower priesthoods and cult positions were most often held for life. Inscriptions name guardians of temples (*neokoroi* or *zakoroi),* who may have helped during sacrifices. In the West the *pastophori* were equated with *hierophoroi* (both carriers of sacred objects) or *hagiophoroi* (carriers of the sacred) during imperial times. Greeks living in Egypt translated the title of the highest priest in the cult as *prophetes* (prophet). Outside Egypt, however, a *prophetes* is best thought of as *pastophorus.* In the Egyptian system the dresser (*stolistes*) held the second highest position after the prophets. Documentation, however, records dressers of statues only in Athens in the second and third century CE.

In the West there is only one inscription of a dresser, an *ornatrix fani* (Vidman, 1969, inscription no. 731). Scribes (*scriba, grammateus,* or *hierogrammateus*) (Apuleius, *Metamorphoses,* 11.17), follow the dressers in the Egyptian priestly hierarchy. They are, however, like astrologers *(horoskopoi* or *horologoi)* and singers *(hymnodoi),* not documented outside Egypt. *Therapeutai* or *cultores* were cult adherents without rank and function. The official heading the *ploiaphesia* in March, the *nauarchus, trierarchos, hieronautes,* or *naubates,* is only known through inscriptions from Rome's imperial period. He or she was not a priest but a lay member of the cult association. In general, one notes that priests and lay cult functionaries could have the same designation. In addition, not every dedicator of an inscription was a cult initiate. Most of the personal inscriptions were put up in fulfillment of a vow (ex-voto), and most of the official ones (*pro salute imperatoris,* for the well-being of the emperor) were political in nature.

In Roman times, temples of Isis (*Isea*) were most often found outside the religious border of a city (the *pomerium)* and in an aqueous area in the vicinity of a river, an important water source, a marsh, or a port. Unlike Greco-Roman temples, *Isea* were not oriented toward public spaces. Even the innermost part of a temple of Isis, the *cella* (*naos*), opened only inward. The doors of the temple were opened and closed in connection with a morning and an afternoon ceremony. Sacrifice was given during these ceremonies. Although Plutarch mentions sacrifice of a white and a saffron-colored rooster to Osiris (Plutarch, *De Iside et Osiride,* 61; see Griffiths, 1970, p. 518) and red cattle to Seth (Plutarch, *De Iside et Osiride,* 31; Griffiths, 1970, pp. 414–415), his treatise does not reveal what kind of sacrifice Isis received. Apuleius, in his *Metamorphoses* (11.21ff.), indicates that there were three initiation rituals. Whether this was indeed true is not known with certainty. As was the case with other mystery cults, the preparations of an initiate included abstinence and purification. The initiate (*mystes*) experienced death and through it achieved new life. In contrast to public cults, social standing did not translate to a comparable position in the hierarchy of this mystery cult. The origins of the Isiac mysteries are not easily discerned, but it seems that there was an Egyptian element (Bianchi, 1980; Griffiths, 1970, pp. 390–392; Plutarch, *De Iside et Osiride,* 27; Junge, 1979; and Kákosy, 1999). The premier temple of Isis, the *Iseum* on Philae, closed its doors forever during the reign of Justinian I (527–561 CE).

SEE ALSO Goddess Worship, article on Goddess Worship in the Hellenistic World; Mystery Religions.

BIBLIOGRAPHY

Barrett, Anthony A. *Caligula.* London, 1989.

Bergman, Jan. *Ich bin Isis: Studien zum memphitischen Hintergrund der griechischen Isisaretologien.* Acta Universitatis Upsaliensis, Historia Religionum, 3. Uppsala, 1968.

Bergman, Jan. "Isis." In *Lexikon der Ägyptologie*, edited by Wolfgang Helck and Eberhard Otto, vol. 3, pp. 186–203. Wiesbaden, Germany, 1980.

Bianchi, Ugo. "Iside dea misterica: Quando?" In *Perennitas: Studi in onore di Angelo Brelich*, pp. 9–36. Rome, 1980.

Coarelli, Filippo. "Iside Capitolina, Clodio e i mercanti di schiavi." In *Alessandria e il mondo ellenistico-romano: Studi in onore di Achille Adriani*, edited by Nicola Bonacasa and Antonino Di Vita, vol. 3, pp. 461–475. Studi e materiali, Istituto di Archeologia Università di Palermo, 6. Rome, 1984.

Dio Cassius. *Roman History*. Translated by Earnest Cary. Cambridge, Mass., 1961–1969.

Diodorus Siculus. *Works*. Translated by C. H. Oldfather. Cambridge, Mass., 1946.

Dunand, Françoise. *Le culte d'Isis dans le bassin oriental de la Méditerranée*. Études préliminaires aux religions orientales dans l'Empire romain, 26. Leiden, Netherlands, 1973.

Floriani Squarciapino, Maria. *I culti orientali ad Ostia*. Études préliminaires aux religions orientales dans l'Empire romain, 3. Leiden, Netherlands, 1962.

Griffiths, J. Gwyn, ed. and trans. *Plutarch's "De Iside et Osiride."* Cardiff, Wales 1970. Includes commentary.

Griffiths, J. Gwyn, ed. and trans. *The Isis-Book (Metamorphoses, Book XI) Apuleius of Madauros*. Études préliminaires aux religions orientales dans l'Empire romain, 39. Leiden, Netherlands, 1975.

Herodotos. *Histories*. Translated by Robin Waterfield. New York, 1998.

Josephus, Flavius. *The Jewish War*. Translated by H. St. J. Thackeray. Cambridge, Mass., 1997.

Junge, Friedrich. "Isis und die ägyptischen Mysterien." In *Aspekte der spätägyptischen Religion*, pp. 93–115. Göttinger Orientforschungen, Reihe 4, Ägypten, vol. 9. Wiesbaden, Germany, 1979.

Kákosy, László. "Mysteries in the Isiac Religion." *Acta Antiqua Academiae Scientiarum Hungaricae* 39 (1999): 159–163.

Lembke, Katja. *Das Iseum Campense in Rom: Studie über den Isiskult unter Domitian*. Heidelberg, Germany, 1994.

Malaise, Michel. "La diffusion des cultes égyptiens dans les provinces européennes de l'Empire romain." In *Aufstieg und Niedergang der römischen Welt*, vol. 2, 17.3, pp. 1615–1691. Berlin and New York, 1984.

Maystre, Charles. *Les grands prêtres de Ptah de Memphis*. Freiburg and Göttingen, Germany, 1992.

Merkelbach, Reinhold. *Isis regina, Zeus Sarapis*. Stuttgart, 1995.

Roullet, Anne. *The Egyptian and Egyptianizing Monuments of Imperial Rome*. Études préliminaires aux religions orientales dans l'Empire romain, 20. Leiden, Netherlands, 1972.

Suetonius. *Lives of the Twelve Caesars*. Translated by Robert Graves. New York, 2001.

Takács, Sarolta A. *Isis and Sarapis in the Roman World*. Religions in the Graeco-Roman World, 124. Leiden, Netherlands, 1995.

Taylor, Lily Ross. *The Cults of Ostia*. Bryn Mawr, Pa., 1912. Reprint, Chicago, 1976.

Tertullian. *Ad Nationes*. In *The Ante-Nicene Fathers*, vol. 4., edited by Alexander Roberts and James Donaldson. Grand Rapids, Mich., 1969.

Tóth, István. "Marcus Aurelius' Miracle of the Rain and the Egyptian Cults in the Danube Region." *Studia Aegyptiaca* 2 (1976): 101–113.

Totti, Maria. *Ausgewählte Texte der Isis- und Sarapis-Religion*. Hildesheim, Germany.

Tran, Vincent Tam Tinh. *Essai sur le culte d'Isis à Pompéi*. Paris, 1964.

Tran, Vincent Tam Tinh. *Le culte des divinités orientales en Campanie en dehors de Pompéi, de Stabies et d'Herculanum*. Études préliminaires aux religions orientales dans l'Empire romain, 27. Leiden, Netherlands, 1972.

Turcan, Robert. "Isis of the Many Names; or, Our Lady of the Waves." In *The Cults of the Roman Empire*, edited by Robert Turcan, translated by Antonia Nevill, pp. 75–129. Oxford and Cambridge, Mass., 1996. French edition, *Cultes orientaux dans le monde romain*, Paris, 1989.

Vidman, Ladislav. *Isis und Sarapis bei den Griechen und Römern*. Religionsgeschichtliche Versuche und Vorarbeiten, 29. Berlin, 1970.

Vidman, Ladislav, comp. *Sylloge inscriptionum religionis Isiacae et Sarapiacae* (SIRIS). Religionsgeschichtliche Versuche und Vorarbeiten, 28. Berlin, 1969.

Wild, Robert A. *Water in the Cultic Worship of Isis and Sarapis*. Études préliminaires aux religions orientales dans l'Empire romain, 87. Leiden, Netherlands, 1981.

Wissowa, Georg. *Religion and Kultus der Römer*. Munich, 1971.

SAROLTA A. TAKÁCS (2005)

ISLAM

This entry consists of the following articles:

ISLAM: AN OVERVIEW [FIRST EDITION]

The root *slm* in Arabic means "to be in peace, to be an integral whole." From this root comes *islām*, meaning "to surrender to God's law and thus to be an integral whole," and *muslim*, a person who so surrenders. It is important to note that two other key terms used in the Qurʾān with high frequency have similar root meanings: *īmān* (from *amn*), "to be safe and at peace with oneself," and *taqwā* (from *wqy*), "to protect or save." These definitions give us an insight into the most fundamental religious attitude of Islam: to maintain wholeness and proper order, as the opposite of disintegration, by accepting God's law. It is in this sense that the entire universe and its content are declared by the Qurʾān to be *muslim*, that is, endowed with order through obedience to God's law; but whereas nature obeys God's law automatically, humanity ought to obey it by choice. In keeping with this distinction, God's function is to integrate human personality, both individual and corporate: "Be not like those who forgot God, and [eventually] God caused them to forget themselves" (*sūrah* 59:19).

ORIGIN AND HISTORY. Muslims believe that Islam is God's eternal religion, described in the Qur'ān as "the primordial nature upon which God created mankind" (30:30). Further, the Qur'ān claims that the proper name *Muslim* was given by Abraham (22:78). As a historical phenomenon, however, Islam originated in Arabia in the early seventh century CE. Two broad elements should be distinguished in that immediate religious backdrop: the purely Arab background and the penetration of Judeo-Christian elements. The Qur'ān makes a disapproving reference to star worship (41:37), which is said to have come from the Babylonian star cult. For the most part, however, the bedouin were a secular people with little idea of an afterlife. At the sanctuaries (*ḥarams*) that had been established in some parts, fetishism seems to have developed into idol worship; the most important of these sites was the Kaʿbah at Mecca.

The bedouin Arabs believed in a blind fate that inescapably determined birth, sustenance (because of the precarious life conditions in the desert), and death. These Arabs also had a code of honor (called *murūwah*, or "manliness") that may be regarded as their real religious ethics; its main constituent was tribal honor—the crown of all their values—encompassing the honor of women, bravery, hospitality, honoring one's promises and pacts, and last but not least, vengeance (*tha'r*). They believed that the ghost of a slain person would cry out from the grave until his thirst for the blood of vengeance was quenched. According to the code, it was not necessarily the killer who was slain in retaliation, but a person from among his kin equal in value to the person killed. For reasons of economics or honor, infant girls were often slain, and this practice, terminated by the Qur'ān, was regarded as having had religious sanction (6:137).

In southwestern Arabia, a rather highly sophisticated civilization had existed since the Sabian period, with a prosperous economy and agriculture. The Sabian religion was, at the beginning, a trinitarian star cult, which was replaced, in the fourth century CE, by the monotheistic cult of al-Rahman (a term that appears to have traveled north and found a prominent place in the Qur'ān, where it means "the merciful"). In the sixth century CE, Jewish and Christian ideas and formulas were adopted, with the term *al-Raḥmān* applied to the first person of the Trinity.

As for the Judeo-Christian tradition, it was not only present where Jewish and Christian populations existed (Jews in Medina—pre-Islamic Yathrib—in the south and in Khaybar in the north; Christians in the south, in Iraq, in Syria, and in certain tribes), but it had percolated in the air, generally speaking. Indeed, there had been Jewish and Christian attempts at proselytizing the Meccans, but these were unsuccessful because the Meccans wanted a new religion and scripture of their own, "whereby they would be better guided than those earlier communities" (35:42, 6:157). In the process, the Meccans had nevertheless come to know a good deal about Judeo-Christian ideas (6:92), and several people in Mecca and elsewhere had arrived at the idea of monotheism. Even so, they could not get rid of the "intermediary gods" for whom they had special cults, and there was still no cult for God, whom they called "Allāh," or "the God." In addition to these limitations, there was also a great disparity between the rich and the poor and disenfranchised in the thriving commercial community of Mecca. Both of these issues are strongly emphasized from the beginning of the Qur'anic revelation, making it clear that the primary background of Islam is Arab rather than Judeo-Christian, although the latter tradition has strongly influenced Islam. In its genesis, Islam grew out of the problems existing in an Arab Meccan society.

Early development of the community. During a twelve-year struggle in Mecca (610–622 CE), the prophet Muḥammad had gathered a devoted group of followers, largely among the poor but also among the well-to-do merchants. Yet his movement seemed to reach an impasse because of the unflinching opposition of the mercantile aristocracy, which saw in it a threat to both of their vested interests—their Kaʿbah-centered religion, from which they benefited as custodians of the sanctuary and recipients of income from the pilgrimage, and their privileged control of trade. After Muḥammad and his followers emigrated from Mecca to Medina in 622 (the beginning of the lunar Islamic calendar, called the *hijrī*, or "emigration," calendar), at the invitation of the majority of the Arab inhabitants there, he became the head of both the nascent community and the existing polity. However, while he gave laws, waged peace and war, and created social institutions, he never claimed to be a ruler, a lawgiver, a judge, or a general; he referred to himself always as a messenger of God. As a result, not only were Islamic "religious" doctrine and ritual in the narrower sense regarded as Islamic but so were the state, the law, and social institutions. Islam is thus the name of a total way of life and does not merely regulate the individual's private relationship with God.

In Medina, then, the Prophet was able to institute his social reforms through the exercise of the religious and political power that he had been denied in Mecca. After three battles in which Muslims gained the upper hand over the Meccans and their allies, Islam, now in rapid ascendancy, was able to take Mecca peacefully in AH 8/630 CE along with a large part, if not the whole, of the Arabian Peninsula. In Medina, too, the Muslim community (*ummah muslimah*) was formally launched in 2/624 as the "median community," the only community consciously established by the founder of a religion for a specific purpose, as the Qur'ān speaks of those "who, when we give them power on the earth, shall establish prayers and welfare of the poor and shall command good and forbid evil" (22:41). At the same time, the Qurʾān (22:40) provided this community with the instrument of *jihād* (utmost exertion in God's cause, including peaceful means but also cold and hot war). Finally, Mecca was declared to be the goal of annual pilgrimage for the faithful and also the direction (*qiblah*) for prayer instead of Jerusalem. Both the constitution and the anchoring of the community were complete.

After a brief lapse into tribal sovereignty following the Prophet's death, Arab resistance to the acknowledgment of Medina's central authority was broken by force. The tribesmen's energies were turned outward in conquests of neighboring lands under the banner of Islam, which provided the necessary zeal for rapid military and political expansion. Within a century after the Prophet's death, Muslim Arabs were administering an empire stretching from the southern borders of France through North Africa and the Middle East, across Central Asia and into Sind. Muslim rule in the conquered territories was generally tolerant and humane; there was no policy of converting non-Muslims to Islam. The purpose of *jihād* was not conversion but the establishment of Islamic rule. Nonetheless, partly because of certain disabilities imposed by Islamic law on non-Muslim subjects (mainly the *jizyah*, or poll tax—although they were exempt from the *zakāt*, or alms tax levied on Muslims, the *jizyah* was the heavier of the two, particularly for the lower strata of the population) and partly because of Islamic egalitarianism, Islam spread quickly after an initial period during which conversions were sometimes even discouraged. This was the first phase of the spread of Islam; later on, as we shall see, Muslim mystics, or the Ṣūfīs, were the main vehicles of Islamic expansion in India, Central Asia, and sub-Saharan Africa, although the role of traders in the Indian and Indonesian coastal areas and China must not be minimized. Even in the twentieth century, Turkish soldiers brought Islam to South Korea during the Korean War.

Several major developments in this early period affected the religious texture of the Muslim community as a continuing phenomenon. Less than half a century after the Prophet's death, political dissensions over succession led to civil war. A number of groups called the Khārijīs ("those who went out") declared war on the community at large because it tolerated rule by "unrighteous" men; they claimed that a Muslim ceased to be a Muslim by committing a reprehensible act without sincerely repenting, and that other Muslims who did not regard such a person as non-Muslim also became non-Muslim. In reaction to the Khārijīs and the ensuing civil strife, the community (both the Sunnī mainstream and the Shīʿah, or party of ʿAlī) generally adopted a religious stand that not only was tolerant of religious and political deviations from strict Islamic norms but was even positively accommodating toward them. The members of the community who took this stand were known as the Murjiʾah (from *irjāʿ*, meaning "postponement," in the sense of not judging a person's religious worth, but leaving it to God's judgment on the Last Day). The net result of this basic development was that excommunication was ruled out so long as a person recognized the community as Muslim and professed that "there is no god but God and Muḥammad is his prophet."

This formula created or rationalized accommodation for an amazing range of different religious opinions and practices under one God and Muḥammad's prophethood. Oddly enough, the only systematically rigid and illiberal school of doctrine that persecuted its opponents, after it became state creed under the Abbasid caliph al-Maʾmūn in the first half of the ninth century, was the liberal rationalist school of the Muʿtazilah. The emergence of this school was largely the result of the impact on the Islamic religion of the wholesale translations of Greek works of science, philosophy, and medicine into Arabic on the orders of al-Maʾmūn. The Muʿtazilah tried to create necessary free space by insisting on freedom of human will and God's rational justice, but the Muslim orthodoxy, countering with doctrines of the inefficacy of human will and the absolutism of God's will and divine predeterminism, actually provided more accommodation for varying opinions and human actions and thereby halted the growth of the rationalist school.

With the advent of the Abbasids, there were other political, social, and religious changes as well, among them the improvement of the status of the Iranians, who, under Umayyad rule, were denied an identity of their own as "clients" (*mawālī*) of the Arab tribes; and the espousal and implementation of legal measures created by the religious leadership, which had been largely alienated from the Umayyads. All of these developments combined to facilitate the rapid spread of Islam.

Medieval and later developments. With the weakening of the central caliphal authority in Baghdad, the tenth century saw not only the virtual fragmentation of the Abbasid Empire and the rise of *de facto* independent rulers (sultans and emirs) in the provinces but the almost ubiquitous rise of the Shīʿah. While Baghdad came under the political and fiscal "management" of the orthodox Twelver Shīʿah through the Persian Buyid family, Egypt and North Africa came under the rule of the Ismāʿīlī Fatimids. But if the Buyids were able to influence Islamic practices in some ways—such as the observance of ʿĀshūrāʾ, the tenth of Muḥarram (the first month of the Islamic calendar) as the commemoration of the martyrdom of the Prophet's grandson Ḥusayn at the hands of the Umayyad troops—Fatimid rule, by and large, did not leave much of a trace on later Muslim thought and institutions, despite the fact that the Ismāʿīlīyah had offered a revolutionary ideology claiming to usher in a new world order through the establishment of a universal religion.

In purely religious terms, indeed, it was not so much Shiism as the rise and spread of Sufism that constituted the new and greatest challenge to Islamic orthodoxy, in terms of ideas and spiritual orientation, and indeed, it was Shiism that suffered most, in terms of following, as a result of the new movement. From modest beginnings as an expression of refined piety on the part of a spiritual elite in the eighth and ninth centuries, Sufism became a mass religion from the eleventh century onward. In its origins as a deepening of the inner "life of the heart," Sufism was largely complementary to the outer "life of the law," which was the domain of the *ʿulamāʾ*, the religious scholars who functioned as custodians of the *sharīʿah* (sacred law) and never claimed to be pastors or custodians of the soul.

In its later development, however, through networks of brotherhoods that spread from the shores of the Atlantic to Southeast Asia, it practically took the place of "official" Islam, particularly in the countryside. Feeding on certain pantheistic ideas of eminent Ṣūfīs and generating latitudinarian, indeed protean, tendencies, it served to convert to Islam large populations in the Indian subcontinent, Central Asia, Africa, and Indonesia. A long line of orthodox Ṣūfīs, beginning in the eighth and ninth centuries and culminating in the monumental work of al-Ghazālī (d. 1111), struggled hard, with a good measure of success, to bring about a synthesis that would ensure a respectable place for Ṣūfīs spirituality in the orthodox fold. After the advent of Sufism, and particularly after al-Ghazālī's success, the number of converts to Islam expanded dramatically, and the number of Shīʿah shrank equally dramatically, apparently because the demands for an inner life that Shiism had satisfied through its esoteric claims were now satisfied by Sufism.

During the thirteenth and fourteenth centuries, Islam penetrated into the Malay archipelago largely through Arab traders, who went first to the coastal areas of Java and Sumatra and afterward to Malaysia. Shortly after the advent of Islam, however, these lands fell under western European domination. Because the structure of British power in Malaysia differed from Dutch colonialism in Indonesia, in that British overlordship was exercised through regional sultans whereas the Dutch ruled directly, Islam was inhibited in Indonesia: a large percentage of the population of the interior remained *abangans*, or "nominal Muslims," whose life is still based on ancient custom (*ʿādat*) under a thin Islamic veneer. Recently, however, a large-scale thrust of islamization has changed this picture considerably. In Djakarta, for example, a little more than a dozen years ago, there were only a few cathedral mosques for Friday services, but now the number has multiplied spectacularly; indeed, there is a mosque attached to every government department. This process of "consolidation in orthodox Islam," necessitated by the initial compromises made by Ṣūfīs with local cultures, has been going on for some decades in the Indian subcontinent as well.

In Africa south of the Sahara, Islam appears to have penetrated through both traders and pilgrims. Although, as noted above, Islam spread there through the influence of Ṣūfī orders, one unique feature of African Islam seems to be the combination of Sufism with militancy, the latter acclaimed as the result of the Islamic teaching on *jihād*, although it is also congruent with the spirit of local tribalism.

Africa is the only continent where Muslims are in the majority, while in Europe, Islam now constitutes the second largest religion, mainly comprising emigrants from Muslim lands but a few Western converts as well. In North America, Muslims are said to number around two million, most of whom are emigrants from Muslim countries. But there is also in the United States a significant phenomenon of conversion among local blacks, originating in the social protest movement against white ascendancy. The earliest group, known as the Black Muslims, called itself the Nation of Islam during the lifetime of its founder, Elijah Muhammad, and was a heterodox movement. After his death in 1973 it moved closer to the rest of the Muslim community, taking the new name of American Islamic Mission and receiving financial help from oil-rich Arab countries such as Saudi Arabia, Libya, and Kuwait. (The organization was dissolved in 1985.) There are also other numerous, though small, Afro-American Muslim groups scattered throughout the United States.

Arriving at a precise estimate of the Muslim population in China presents a serious problem. According to data collected unofficially by Chinese Muslims in 1939–1940 and extrapolations from these data in terms of population growth, Chinese Muslims might number close to one hundred million in the 1980s. The official Chinese figure given in the early sixties, however, was ten million, a figure revised to between fifteen and twenty million two decades later (religion is a factor not counted in the Chinese census). According to the 1979 United Nations statistics, the world Muslim population is just under one billion.

The Systematic Content of Islam With the rise of Islamic legal and theological thought in the eighth century CE, a framework had to be articulated within which religious developments were to be set. The most basic sources in this framework were the Qurʾān and the *sunnah* of the Prophet.

The Qurʾān. The God of the Qurʾān is a transcendent, powerful, and merciful being. His transcendence ensures his uniqueness and infinitude over and against all other creatures, who are necessarily characterized by finitude of being and potentialities. Hence God is all-powerful, and no creature may share in his divinity (belief in such sharing is called *shirk* and is condemned in the Qurʾān as the most heinous and unforgivable sin). This infinite power is expressed, however, through God's equally infinite mercy. The creation of the universe, the fact that there is plenitude of being, rather than emptiness of nothing, is due solely to his mercy. Particularly with reference to humanity, God's creation, sustenance, guidance (in the form of revelations given to the prophets, his messengers), and, finally, judgment, are all manifestations of his power in mercy.

God created nature by his command "Be!" In fact, for whatever God wishes to create, "He says, Be! and there it is" (36:82). But whatever God creates has an orderly nature, and that is why there is a universe rather than chaos. God puts into everything the proper "guidance" or "nature" or laws of behavior to make each part fit into the entire pattern of the universe. "All things are measured" (e.g., 54:49), and only God is the measurer; hence he alone is the commander, and everything else is under his command. This command, which is a fact of automatic obedience in the case of nature (3:83), becomes an "ought" in the case of humans, for whom moral law replaces natural law. Nature is, therefore, a firm, well-knit machine without rupture or dislocations.

Here it is interesting and important to note that while the Qurʾān patently accepts miracles of earlier prophets (67:2–3), in response to pressure from Muḥammad's opponents for new miracles (e.g., 2:23, 10:38, 11:13), the Qurʾān insists that it is itself the Prophet's miracle, and one that cannot be equaled. As for supernatural miracles, they are out of date because they have been ineffective in the past (17:59, 6:33–35). Nature is, therefore, autonomous but not autocratic, since it did not bring itself into being. God, who brought nature into being, can destroy it as well; even so, although the Qurʾān, when speaking of the Day of Judgment, often invokes a cataclysm that strongly suggests destruction (see, for example, *sūrah* 81), in many verses it speaks instead of a radical transformation and a realignment of the factors of life (e.g., 56:60–63). Finally, the universe has been created for the benefit of human beings, and all its forces have been "subjugated" to them; of all creatures, only they have been created to serve God alone (e.g., 31:20, 22:65).

In its account of the human race, while the Qurʾān holds that humans are among the noblest of God's creatures and that Adam had indeed outstripped the angels in a competition for creative knowledge, a fact testifying to his unique intellectual qualities, it nevertheless criticizes them for their persistent moral failures, which are due to their narrow-mindedness, lack of vision, weakness, and smallness of self. All their ills are reducible to this basic deficiency, and the remedy is for them to enlarge the self and to transcend pettiness. This pettiness is often represented by the Qurʾān in economic terms, such as greed, fraud, and holding back from spending on the poor (as was the case with the Meccan traders): "If you were to possess [all] the treasures of the mercy of my lord, you would still sit on them out of fear of spending [on the needy]" (17:100). It is Satan who whispers into people's ears that they would be impoverished by spending, while God promises prosperity for such investment (2:268). Instead of establishing usurious accounts to exploit the poor, believers should establish "credit with God" (2:245, 57:11, 57:18 et al.).

In its social doctrine and legislation, the Qurʾān makes a general effort to ameliorate the condition of the weak and often abused segments of society, such as the poor, orphans, women, and slaves. People are asked to free slaves on freedom-purchasing contracts, "and if they are poor, you give them from the wealth God has bestowed upon you" (24:33). An egalitarian statement concerning males and females is made, but the husband is recognized as "one degree higher" (2:228) because he earns by his strength and expends on his wife. Polygamy is limited to four wives with the provision that "if you fear you cannot do justice [among them], marry only one" (4:3), and the further admonition that such justice is impossible "no matter how much you desire" (4:129). Kind and generous treatment of wives is repeatedly emphasized; celibacy is strongly discouraged, although not banned outright. The basic equality of all people is proclaimed and ethnic differences discounted: "O you people, we have created [all of] you from a male and a female, and we have made you into different nations and tribes [only] for the purpose of identification—otherwise, the noblest of you in the sight of God is the one who is the most righteous" (49:13).

In the economic field, the widespread practice of usury is prohibited. The *zakāt* tax is levied on the well-to-do members of the community; it was meant as a welfare tax to be spent on the poor and the needy in general, but *sūrah* 9:60, which details the distribution of *zakāt,* is so comprehensive in its scope that it covers practically all fields of social and state life. In general, fair play and justice are repeatedly advised. Detailed inheritance laws are given (4:7ff.), the main feature of which is the introduction of shares to daughters, although these shares are set at half of what sons receive. Communal affairs are to be decided through mutual consultation (*shūrā baynahum,* 42:38), a principle that has never been institutionalized in Islamic history, however.

One noteworthy feature of the moral teaching of the Qurʾān is that it describes all wrong done against anyone as "wrong done against oneself" (*ẓulm al-nafs,* as in 2:231, 11:101, 11:118). In its teaching on the Last Judgment, the Qurʾān constantly talks of "weighing the deeds" of all adult and responsible humans (101:6–11, 7:8 et al.). This doctrine of the "weight" of deeds arises out of the consideration that people normally act for the here and now; in this respect, they are like cattle: they do not take a long-range or "ultimate" (*ākhirah*) view of things: "Shall we tell you of those who are the greatest losers in terms of their deeds? Those whose whole effort has been lost [in the pursuit of] this life [i.e., the lower values of life], but they think they have performed prodigies" (18:104). The rationale of the Last Judgment is to bring out the real moral meaning, "the weight" of deeds. But whereas the Last Judgment will turn upon individual performance, the Qurʾān also speaks about a "judgment in history," which descends upon peoples, nations, and communities on the basis of their total performance and whether that performance is in accord with the teaching of the divine messages brought by their prophets: many nations have perished because of their persistence in all sorts of disobedience and moral wrong, for "God gives inheritance of the earth [only] to good people" (21:105).

The Qurʾān, therefore, declares unequivocally that God has sent his messages to *all* peoples throughout history and has left none without guidance (35:24, 13:7). These messages have been essentially the same: to reject *shirk* (associating anyone with God) and to behave according to the law of God. All messages have emanated from a single source, the "Mother of All Books" (13:39) or the "Hidden Book" (56:78) or the "Preserved Tablet" (85:22), and although every prophet has initially come to his people and addressed them "in their tongue" (14:4), the import of all messages is universal; hence it is incumbent on all people to believe in all prophets, without "separating some from the others." For this reason the Qurʾān is severely critical of what it sees as proprietary claims upon God's guidance by Jews and Christians and rejects Jewish claims to special status in strong terms (62:6, 2:94–95, 5:18, et al.). Despite the identity of divine messages, moreover, the Qurʾān also posits some sort of development in religious consciousness and asserts that on the Last Day every community will be judged by the standards of its own book and under the witness of its own prophet(s) (4:41, 16:84, et al.). The Qurʾān protects, consummates, and transcends earlier revelations, and Muḥammad is declared to be the "seal of the prophets" (33:40).

Finally, the Qurʾān states five basic constituents of faith (*īmān*): belief in God, in angels, in revealed books, in God's messengers, and in the Last Day. Corresponding to these five items of belief, a fivefold practical doctrine was formulated very early on. These "Five Pillars" include (1) bearing witness in public at least once in one's lifetime that "There is no god but God and Muḥammad is his prophet"; (2) praying five times a day (before sunrise, early afternoon, late afternoon, immediately after sunset, and before retiring), while facing the Kaʿbah at Mecca; (3) paying *zakāt*; (4) fasting during Ramaḍān (the ninth month of the Islamic lunar year), with no eating, drinking, smoking, or sexual intercourse from dawn until sunset, when the daily fast is broken; and (5) performing the annual pilgrimage to the Kaʿbah at least once in one's adult lifetime, provided one can afford the journey and leave enough provisions for one's family.

The pilgrimage is performed during the first ten days of the last month of the Islamic year. One may perform the lesser pilgrimage (*ʿumrah*) at other times of the year, but it is not a substitute for the great pilgrimage (*al-ḥajj al-akbar*). The pilgrimage has, through the centuries, played an important role, not only in strengthening general unity in the global Muslim community but also in disseminating religious ideas both orthodox and Ṣūfī, for it provides the occasion for an annual meeting among religious leaders and scholars from different parts of the Muslim world. For the past few decades, it has also served to bring together political leaders and heads of Muslim states. In recent years, too, because of new travel facilities, the number of pilgrims has vastly increased, sometimes exceeding two million each year.

Sunnah. The word *sunnah* literally means "a well-trodden path," but it was used before Islam in reference to usage or laws of a tribe and certain norms of intertribal conduct accepted by various tribes as binding. After the rise of Islam, it was used to denote the normative behavior of the Muslim community, putatively derived from the Prophet's teaching and conduct, and from the exemplary teaching of his immediate followers, since the latter was seen as an index of the former. In the Qurʾān, there is no mention of the term *sunnah* with reference to the Prophet's extra-Qurʾanic precepts or example, but the term *uswah ḥasanah*, meaning a "good model" or "example" to be followed, is used with reference to Muḥammad's conduct as well as the conduct of Abraham and his followers (33:31, 60:4, 60:6). The term *uswah* is certainly much less rigid than *sunnah* and does not mean so much a law to be literally implemented as an example to be matched.

Even so, there is clear evidence that the concept of *sunnah* was flexible in the early decades of Islam because, with hardly any written codifications of the *sunnah* (which was used in the sense of an ongoing practice rather than fixed formulas), there was no question of literal imitation. As political, legal, and theological dissensions and disputes multiplied and all kinds of positions sought self-validation, however, the opinions of the first three generations or so were projected back onto the Prophet to obtain the necessary authority, and the phrase *sunnat al-nabī* (the *sunnah* of the Prophet) gradually took the place of the term *sunnah*.

During the second and third centuries AH, the narration and codification of the *sunnah* into *ḥadīth* was in full swing. A report that claims to convey a *sunnah* (or *sunnahs*) is called a *ḥadīth*. It is reported that while earlier people used to accept a *ḥadīth* as genuine on trust alone, after the civil wars of the late first to early second centuries AH, a *ḥadīth* was accepted only on the basis of some reliable authority. From this situation emerged the convention of the *isnād*, or the chain of guarantors of *ḥadīth*, extending from the present narrator backward to the Prophet. The *isnād* took the following form: "I, So-and-so, heard it from B, who heard it from C, who said that he heard the Prophet say so-and-so or do such-and-such." Then followed the text (*matn*) of the *ḥadīth*. A whole science called "principles of *ḥadīth*" developed in order to lay down meticulous criteria for judging the reliability of the transmitters of *ḥadīth*, and the discipline stimulated in turn a vast literature of comprehensive biographical dictionaries recording thousands of transmitters' names, their lives, character, and whether a transmitter actually met or could have met the person he claims to transmit from. The canons for criticizing transmitters were applied rigorously, and there is hardly a transmitter who has escaped criticism.

The experts on *ḥadīth* also developed canons of "rational critique" alongside the critique of the chains of transmission, but they applied the former with far less rigor than they did the latter. Although the specialists divided *ḥadīth* into several categories according to their "genuineness" and "reliability," to this day it remains the real desideratum of the science to work out and apply what is called historical criticism to the materials of *ḥadīth*. The six authoritative Sunnī collections of *ḥadīth* date from the third century AH, while the famous Shīʿī collection of al-Kulīnī, *Al-kāfī* (The Sufficient), dates from the early fourth century. In modern times, the authenticity of *ḥadīth* and hence of the recorded *sunnah* of the Prophet (although not so much the biographies of the

Prophet and historical works) has come under general attack at the hands of certain Western scholars and also of some Muslim intellectuals—and this is happening increasingly—but the *ʿulamāʾ* have strenuously resisted these attacks because a large majority of Islamic social and political institutions and laws are either based on *ḥadīth* or rationalized through it.

Law. The well-known dictum among Western Islamicists that, just as theology occupies the central place in Christianity, in Islam the central place belongs to law is essentially correct. Law was the earliest discipline to develop in Islam because the Muslims needed it to administer the huge empire they had built with such astonishing rapidity. Recent research has held that the early materials for Islamic law were largely created by administrators on the basis of *ad hoc* decisions and that, in the second stage, systematic efforts were made by jurists to "islamize" these materials and bring them under the aegis of the Qurʾān and the *sunnah.* (The content of the latter, in the form of *ḥadīth,* developed alongside this activity of islamization.) This picture is probably too simplistic, however, and it would be more correct to say that the process of subsuming administrative materials and local custom under the Qurʾān and the *sunnah* went hand in hand with the reverse process of deriving law from the Qurʾān and whatever existed by way of the *sunnah* in the light of new administrative experiences and local custom.

Although clarification of this issue requires further research, it is certain that up to the early third century AH the schools of law were averse to the large-scale use of *ḥadīth* in the formulation of law and that, in fact, some scholars explicitly warned against the rise of "peripheral *ḥadīth*" and advised the acceptance of only that *ḥadīth* that conformed to the Qurʾān. However, the need for the anchoring authority of the Prophet had become so great that in the latter half of the second century AH al-Shāfiʿī (d. 204/819) made a strong and subsequently successful bid for the wholesale acceptance of "reliable" *ḥadīth*—even if narrated by only one person. As a result, *ḥadīth* multiplied at a far greater rate after al-Shāfiʿī than before him. Nevertheless, the followers of Abū Ḥanīfah (d. 767) continued to reject a single-chain *ḥadīth* in favor of a "sure, rational proof derived from the *sharīʿah* principles," just as the followers of Mālik (d. 795) continued to give preference to the early "practice of Medina" over *ḥadīth.*

The final framework of Islamic jurisprudence came to recognize four sources of law, two material and two formal. The first source is the text of the Qurʾān, which constitutes an absolute "decisive proof"; the second is *ḥadīth* texts, although these can vary from school to school, particularly between the Sunnī and the Twelver Shīʿī schools. In new cases, for which a "clear text" (*naṣṣ*) is not available, a jurist must make the effort *(ijtihād)* to find a correct answer himself. The instrument of *ijtihād* is analogical reasoning (*qiyās*), which consists in (1) finding a text relevant to the new case in the Qurʾān or the *ḥadīth,* (2) discerning the essential similarity or *ratio legis* (called *ʿillat al-ḥukm*) between the two cases, (3) allowing for differences (*furūq*) and determining that they can be discounted, and (4) extending or interpreting the *ratio legis* to cover the new case. This methodology, although neatly formulated in theory, became very difficult to wield in practice primarily because of the differences of opinion with regard to "relevant texts," particularly in the case of *ḥadīth.*

The fourth source or principle is called *ijmāʿ*, or consensus. Although the concept of consensus in the sense of the informal agreement of the community (for Islam has no churches and no councils to produce formal decisions) has in practice an overriding authority, since even the fact and the authenticity of a Qurʾanic revelation are finally guaranteed by it, there is no consensus on the definition of consensus: it varies from the consensus of the *ʿulamāʾ*, through that of the *ʿulamāʾ* of a certain age, to that of the entire community. There is also a difference of opinion as to whether a certain consensus can be repealed by a subsequent one or not; the reply of the traditionalists is usually, though not always, in the negative, while that of modern reformers is in the positive.

A special category of punishments called *ḥudūd* (sg., *ḥadd*) was established by jurists and includes penalties specified in the Qurʾān for certain crimes: murder, theft, adultery, and false accusation of adultery, to which was later added drunkenness. The theory is that since God himself has laid down these penalties, they cannot be varied. But in view of the severity of the punishments, the jurists defined these crimes very narrowly (adultery, for example, is defined as the penetration of the male organ into the female) and put such stringent conditions on the requisite evidence that it became practically unattainable (for example, in order to prove adultery, four eyewitnesses to the sexual act itself were required). The legal maxim "Ward off *ḥadd* punishments by any doubt" was also propounded, and the term *doubt* in classical Islamic law had a far wider range than in any other known system of law. In addition, Muslim jurists enunciated two principles to create flexibility in *sharīʿah* law and its application: necessity and public interest. The political authority, thanks to these two principles, could promulgate new measures and even suspend the operations of the *sharīʿah* law. In later medieval centuries, the Ottoman rulers and others systematically promulgated new laws by invoking these particular principles of the *sharīʿah.*

After the concrete and systematic establishment of the schools of law during the fourth and fifth centuries AH, original legal thought in Islam lost vitality; this development is known as "the closure of the door of *ijtihād.*" It was not that new thinking was theoretically prohibited but rather that social, intellectual, and political conditions were unfavorable to it. However, a procedure known as *talfīq* (lit., "patchwork") was introduced whereby, if a certain provision in one legal school caused particular hardship, a more liberal provision from another could be borrowed, without necessarily taking over its reasoning. Thus, given the impracticality of the Ḥanafī school's regulation that a wife whose husband has disappeared must wait more than ninety years before remarrying (according to the reasoning that the wife must wait until her husband can be presumed dead through natural causes), the Mālikī school's provision that such a wife may marry after four years of waiting (Mālik reasoned that the maximum period of gestation, which he had himself witnessed, was four years) was taken over in practice.

Of the four extant Sunnī schools of law, the Ḥanafī is prevalent in the Indian subcontinent, Central Asia, Turkey, Egypt, Syria, Jordan, and Iraq; the Mālikī school in North Africa extends from Libya through Morocco; the Shāfiʿī, in Southeast Asia, with a considerable following in Egypt; and the Ḥanbalī school, in Saudi Arabia. Within Shīʿī jurisprudence, the Jaʿfarī (Twelver Shīʿī) school prevails in Iran. At one time, the "literalist" (Ẓāhirī) school was represented by some highly prominent jurists, but it has practically no following now, while the Khārijī school is represented in Oman, and to a limited extent in East and North Africa.

It must finally be pointed out that when we speak of Islamic law, we mean all of human behavior, including, for example, intentions. This law is therefore very different from other systems of law in the strict sense of the term. Islamic law does not draw any line between law and morality, and hence much of it is not enforceable in a court, but only at the bar of conscience. This has had its advantages in that Islamic law is shot through with moral considerations, which in turn have given a moral temper to Muslim society. But it has also suffered from the disadvantage that general moral propositions have very often not been given due weight and have been selectively construed by jurists as mere "recommendations" rather than commands that must be expressed in terms of concrete legislation: the result has been an overemphasis on the specific dos and don'ts of the Qurʾān at the expense of general propositions. For example, the Qurʾanic verse 4:3, permitting polygamy up to four wives, was given legal force by classical Muslim jurists, but the rider contained in the same verse, that if a person cannot do justice among co-wives, then he must marry only one, was regarded by them as a recommendation to the husband's conscience that he should do justice.

Theology. At an elementary level, theological speculation in Islam also began very early and was occasioned by the assassination of ʿUthmān, the third caliph (d. 665), but its rise and development was totally independent of the law, and the first great theological systems were constructed only in the third and fourth centuries AH. The first question to become the focal point of dispute was the definition of a true Muslim. The earliest political and theological schism was represented by the Khārijīs (from *khurūj*, meaning "secession"), who contended that a Muslim ceases to be a Muslim by the commission of a single serious sin such as theft or adultery, no matter how many times that person may recite the profession of faith, "There is no god but God and Muḥammad is his prophet," unless he or she repents sincerely. They held that ʿUthmān and ʿAlī (the fourth caliph) had both become *kāfirs* (non-Muslims), since the former was guilty of serious maladministration, including nepotism, and the latter had submitted his claim to rule to human arbitration, even though he had been duly elected caliph. The Khārijīs, who were exemplars of piety and utterly egalitarian, and who believed that the only qualification for rule is a person's goodness and piety, without consideration of race, color, or sex, were mostly bedouin, which largely explains both their egalitarianism and their fanaticism. They were "professional rebels" who never united but always fought successive governments in divided groups and were almost entirely crushed out of existence by the middle of the second century AH.

While the Khārijīs were not a systematic theological school, a full-fledged school, that of the Muʿtazilah, soon developed from their milieu. These thinkers, who emerged during the second and third centuries AH, held that while grave sinners do not become *kāfirs*, neither do they remain Muslims. Their central thesis concerned what they called "God's justice and unity," which they defended to its logical conclusion. God's justice demands that human beings have a free and efficacious will; only then can they be the locus of moral responsibility and deserve praise and blame here and reward and punishment in the hereafter. They carried this belief to the point of holding that just as God, in his justice, cannot punish one who does good, neither can he forgive one who does evil, for otherwise the difference between good and evil would disappear. This position certainly offended religious sensitivities, since the Qurʾān repeatedly mentions that God will forgive "whom he will" (2:284, 3:129 et al.).

For the Muʿtazilah, God plays no role in the sphere of human moral acts, except that he gives man moral support provided man does good by himself; God's activity is limited to nature. All anthropomorphic statements in the Qurʾān were interpreted by the Muʿtazilah either as metaphors or as Arabic idioms. They rejected *ḥadīth* outright because much of it was anthropomorphic and refused to base law upon it on the ground that *ḥadīth* transmission was unreliable. They further held that good and evil in terms of general principles (but not the positive religious duties) were knowable by human reason without the aid of revelation but that revelation supplied the necessary motivation for the pursuit of goodness. In conformity with this view, they believed that one must rationally ponder the purposes of the Qurʾanic ordinances, for in laying these down, God had a positive interest in furthering human well-being (*maṣlaḥah*). This presumably means that law should be rationally grounded; there is, however, no evidence that the Muʿtazilah ever attempted to work out a legal system.

On the issue of God's unity, the Muʿtazilah rejected the separation of God's attributes from his essence, for this would entail belief in a multiplicity of eternal beings, amounting to polytheism. They did not deny that God is "living," "knowing," and "willing," as divine activities, but they denied that God is "life," "knowledge," and "will," as substantives. The development of this particular doctrine was possibly influenced by Christian discussions on the nature of the Trinity, and how and whether three hypostases could be one person, because the terms in which it is formulated are all too foreign to the milieu of pristine Islam. As a consequence of this doctrine, the Muʿtazilah also denied the eternity of the Qurʾān, the very speech of God, since they denied the substantiality of all divine attributes. When their credo was made state creed under Caliph al-Maʾmūn, they persecuted opposition religious leaders such as Ibn Ḥanbal (d. 855), but because of these very doctrines—denial of God's forgiveness and of the eternity of the Qurʾān—they became unpopular, and Caliph al-Mutawakkil (d. 861) brought Sunnism back to ascendancy.

What is in fact called Sunnism means nothing more than the majority of the community; it had its content defined in large measure as a reaction to the Khārijīs and the Muʿtazilah, for Sunnī orthodoxy is but a refined and sophisticated form of that popular reaction that crystallized against these groups. There, no small role was played by popular preachers and popular piety, which had already found its way into *ḥadīth*. In doctrinal form, this reaction can be described as Murjiʾism (from *irjāʿ*, "postponement"), the belief that once adults have openly professed that there is no God but Allāh and Muḥammad is his prophet, if there is no reason to suspect that they are lying, mad, or under constraint, then such people are Muslims, irrespective of whether their deeds are good or whether their beliefs quite conform to orthodoxy, and that final judgment on their status must be "postponed" until the Last Day and left to God.

In conscious opposition to the Khārijīs and the Muʿtazilah, the Murjiʾah were content with minimal knowledge of Islam and Islamic conduct on the part of a believer. On the question of free will, they leaned heavily toward predestinarianism, and some were outright predestinarians. There is evidence that the Umayyad rulers supported the Murjiʾah, apparently for their own political ends, since they were interested in discouraging questions about how they had come to power and set up a dynastic rule that abandoned the first four caliphs' model and high moral and political standards. However, it would have been impossible for these rulers to succeed if popular opinion had not swung toward the Murjiʾah, particularly in reaction against the Khārijīs.

The chief formulator of the Sunnī creed was Abū al-Ḥasan al-Ashʿarī (d. 935), a Muʿtazilī who later came under the influence of the traditionists (*ahl al-ḥadīth*) and turned the tables on his erstwhile preceptor and fellows among the Muʿtazilah. For al-Ashʿarī, people cannot produce their own actions; rather, God does, and neither man nor nature has any powers or potencies before the actual act. At the time of the act, for example, when fire actually burns, God creates a power for that particular act. Thus God creates an action, while human beings "appropriate" or "acquire" (*kasaba*) it and thereby become responsible for "their" acts. The Ashʿarī theologians are, therefore, atomists in terms of both time and space, and they reject causation and the entire idea of movement or process. God is under no obligation to do what human beings call justice; on the contrary, whatever God does is just. Justice involves reference to certain norms under which the agent works; since God has no norms to obey, there is no question of doing justice on his part. He also promised in the Qurʾān that he will reward those who do good and punish those who do evil, and this is the proper and only assurance we have of the fate of human beings; if he had chosen to do the reverse, no one could question him. It also follows that good and bad are not natural characteristics of human acts, but that acts become good or bad by God's declaration through the revelation that he has been sending since Adam, the first prophet. It is, therefore, futile to probe rationally into the purposes of divine injunctions, for these are the result of God's will.

On the question of divine attributes, al-Ashʿarī taught that these are real, although they are "neither God, nor other than God." God has an eternal attribute of "speech," which al-Ashʿarī called "psychic speech," manifested in all divinely revealed books. Although the Qurʾān as God's "psychic speech" is eternal, as something recited, written, and heard it is also created: one cannot point to a written copy of the Qurʾān or its recital and say "This is eternal."

A contemporary of al-Ashʿarī, the Central Asian theologian al-Māturīdī (d. 944), also formulated an "official" Sunnī creed and theology that in some fundamental ways was nearer to the Muʿtazilī stance. He recognized "power-before-the-act" in man and also declared good and bad to be natural and knowable by human reason. Whereas al-Ashʿarī belonged to the Shāfiʿī school of law, which was based principally on *ḥadīth*, al-Māturīdī was a member of the Ḥanafī school, which gave greater scope to reason. Yet, in subsequent centuries, the former's views almost completely eclipsed the latter's, although in the Indian subcontinent such prominent thinkers as Aḥmad Sirhindī (d. 1624) and Shāh Walī Allāh of Delhi (d. 1762) criticized Ashʿarī theology. The reason behind this sweeping and enduring success of Ashʿarī theology seems to be the overwhelming spread of Sufism (particularly in its pantheistic form), which, in theological terms, was much more akin to Ashʿarī thought than to that of Muʿtazilah or even the Māturīdīyah, in that it sought to obliterate the human self in the all-embracing and all-effacing self of God, the most important nodal point of this conjunction being al-Ghazālī.

In the intellectual field, as we shall see, Sufism grew at the expense of theology and utilized the worldview of the Muslim philosophers. On the moral and spiritual planes, however, the powerful corroboration of theology and Sufism stimulated the vehement reaction of the jurist and theologian Ibn Taymīyah (d. 1328). Struggling all his life against popular Ṣūfī superstitions, against worship of saints and their shrines, and against Ashʿarī theology, he tried to resurrect the moral activism of the Qurʾān and the *sunnah*. He regarded the Muʿtazilī denial of God's role in human actions as an error but considered the Ashʿarī denial of human free and effective will as extremely dangerous and, in fact, stated that pantheistic Ṣūfīs and the Ashʿarī theologians were considerably worse than not only the Muʿtazilah but even the Zoroastrians. He held that the Zoroastrians' postulation of two gods was undoubtedly an error but argued that they had been forced into this belief by the undeniable distinction between good and evil that both Ashʿarī theology and pantheistic Sufism virtually obliterated, leaving no basis for any worthwhile religion. (As we shall see, a similar argument was conducted within Sufism by a later Indian Ṣūfī, Aḥmad Sirhindī.) Ibn Taymīyah sought to solve the perennial problem of free will versus divine omnipotence by saying that the actual application of the principle of divine omnipotence occurs only in the past, while the *sharīʿah* imperatives are relevant only to the future. His teaching remained more or less dormant until the eighteenth century, when it inspired the Wahhābī religious revolution in the Arabian Peninsula.

Sufism. The mainspring of Sufism lay in the desire to cultivate the inner life and to attain a deeper, personal understanding of Islam. Among the many proposed etymologies of the word *ṣūfī*, the most credible is the one that derives it from *ṣūf*, meaning "coarse wool," a reference to the kind of garb that many Ṣūfīs wore. The first phase of this spiritual movement was definitely moral, and the works of most early Ṣūfīs, those of the second and third centuries AH, show a preoccupation with constant self-examination and close scrutiny of one's motivation.

Ṣūfī doctrine. The dialectic of the trappings and self-deception of the soul developed by Ḥakīm al-Tirmidhī (d. 898) in his *Khatm al-awliyāʿ* (The seal of the saints) provides one extraordinary example of spiritual insight, but this strongly moral trend continues from Ḥasan al-Baṣrī (d. 728) through al-Muḥāsibī (d. 857) to his pupil al-Junayd (d. 910). The essence of their doctrine is moral contrition and detachment of the mind from the "good things" of the world *(zuhd)*. But from its very early times, Sufism also had a strong devotional element, as exemplified by the woman saint Rābiʿah al-ʿAdawīyah (d. 801). The goal of love of God led to the doctrine of *fanāʾ* or "annihilation" (that is, of the human self in God). There were definitely Hellenistic Christian influences at work here. But the annihilation ideal was soon amended into "survival (*baqāʾ*) after annihilation," or (re)gaining of a new self, and this formula was given different interpretations.

Most Ṣūfīs taught that, after the destruction of the human attributes (not the self), mortals acquire divine attributes (not the divine self) and "live in" them. The firm view of the orthodox and influential Ṣūfīs al-Junayd was that when a person sheds human attributes and these attributes undergo annihilation, that person comes to think that he or she has become God. But God soon gives that person the consciousness of otherness (not alienation) from God, which is extremely painful and is only somewhat relieved by God's also giving the consolation that this is the highest state attainable by human beings. Yet there were also Ṣūfīs who, most probably under the influence of Hellenistic Christianity, believed in human transubstantiation into God. In 922, al-Ḥallāj, a representative of this school, was charged with having uttered the blasphemous statement "I am God" and was crucified in Baghdad. Yet, a somewhat earlier mystic, al-Bisṭāmī (d. 874), who is said to have committed even graver blasphemies, was never touched by the law. It may be, as some contend, that the real reasons behind al-Ḥallāj's execution were political, or it may be related to the fact that al-Ḥallāj was in the capital, Baghdad, whereas al-Bisṭāmī lived in an outlying province.

This example of such divergent interpretations of a fundamental doctrine should warn us that with Sufism we are dealing with a truly protean phenomenon: not only do interpretations differ, but experiences themselves must differ as well. However, under pressure from the *ʿulamāʾ*, who refused to acknowledge any objective validity for the Ṣūfī experience, the Ṣūfīs formulated a doctrine of "spiritual stations" (*maqāmāt*) that adepts successively attained through their progressive spiritual itinerary (*sulūk*). These stations are as objectifiable as any experience can be. Although the various schools have differed in the lists of these stations, they usually enumerate them as follows: detachment from the world *(zuhd)*, patience (*ṣabr*), gratitude (*shukr*) for whatever God gives, love (*ḥubb*), and pleasure *(riḍā)* with whatever God desires.

After the violent death of al-Ḥallāj, another important doctrine of the dialectic of Ṣūfī experience was developed by orthodox Ṣūfīs. According to this doctrine, the Ṣūfī alternates between two different types of spiritual states. One type is the experience of unity (where all multiplicity disappears) and of the inner reality. In this state the Ṣūfī is "absent" from the world and is "with God"; this is the state of "intoxication" (*sukr*). The other state, that of "sobriety" (*ṣaḥw*), occurs when the Ṣūfī "returns" to multiplicity and is "with the world." Whereas many Ṣūfīs had earlier contended that "intoxication" is superior to "sobriety" and that, therefore, the saints (*awliyāʾ*) are superior to the prophets (who are "with the world" and legislate for society), the orthodox Ṣūfīs now asserted the opposite, for the goodness of saints is limited to themselves, whereas the goodness of prophets is transitive, since they save the society as well as themselves.

On the basis of this doctrine, al-Ḥallāj's famous statement was rationalized as "one uttered in a state of intoxication" and as such not to be taken at face value. But it was al-Ghazālī who effected a meaningful and enduring synthesis of Ṣūfī "innerism" and the orthodox belief system. A follower of al-Ashʿarī in theology and of al-Shāfiʿī in law, al-Ghazālī also studied thoroughly the philosophic tradition of Ibn Sīnā (known in the West as Avicenna, d. 1037), and although he refuted its important theses bearing on religion in the famous work *Tahāfut al-falāsifah* (The Incoherence of the Philosophers), he was influenced by it in important ways as well. He then adopted Sufism as his "way to God" and composed his *magnum opus, Iḥyā' ʿulūm al-dīn* (The Revivification of the Sciences of the Faith). His net accomplishment lies in the fact that he tried to infuse a new spiritual life into law and theology on the one hand and to instill sobriety and responsibility into Sufism on the other, for he repudiated the Ṣūfī *shaṭaḥāt* (intoxicated utterances) as meaningless.

Within a century after al-Ghazālī's death, however, a Ṣūfī doctrine based on out-and-out monism was being preached by Ibn al-ʿArabī (d. 1240). Born in Spain and educated there and in North Africa, Ibn al-ʿArabī eventually traveled to the Muslim East; he lived for many years in Mecca, where he wrote his major work, *Al-futūḥāt al-makkīyah* (The Meccan Discoveries), and finally settled in Damascus, where he died. Ibn al-ʿArabī's writings are the high-water mark of theosophic Sufism, which goes beyond the ascetic or ecstatic Sufism of the earlier period, by laying cognitive claims to a unique, intuitive experience (known as *kashf,* "direct discovery," or *dhawq,* "taste") that was immune from error and radically different from and superior to the rational knowledge of the philosophers and the theologians.

Ibn al-ʿArabī's doctrine, known as Unity of Being *(waḥdat al-wujūd),* teaches that everything is in one sense God and in another sense not-God. He holds that, given God, the transcendent, another factor that in itself is not describable "either as existent or as nonexistent" comes to play a crucial role in the unfolding of reality. This factor is neither God nor the world; it is a "third thing," but it is God with God and world with the world. It is the stuff of which both the attributes of God (for God as transcendent has no names and no attributes) and the content of the world are made. It is eternal with the eternal and temporal with the temporal; it does not exist partially and divided in things: the whole of it is God, and the whole of it is the world, and the whole of it is everything in the world. This "third thing" turns out finally to be the Perfect or Primordial Human Being (who is identified with the eternal, not the temporal, Muḥammad), in whose mirror God sees himself and who sees himself in God's mirror. This immanent God and Human Being are not only interdependent but are the obverse and converse of the same coin. There is little doubt that Ibn al-ʿArabī represents a radical humanism, a veritable apotheosis of humanity.

This monistic Sufism found certain devoted and distinguished exponents in Ibn al-ʿArabī's school, in both prose and poetry, the most illustrious and influential representative of the latter being Jalāl al-Dīn Rūmī (d. 1273), whose *Mathnavī* in Persian has been hailed as the "Qurʾān in the Persian language." Through poetry, moreover, it has had a profound and literally incalculable influence on the general intellectual culture of Islam, in terms of a liberal humanism, indeed, latitudinarianism, and among the lower strata of Islamic society even antinomianism. A striking feature of this antinomianism, where orthodoxy was unashamedly scoffed at and ridiculed for its rigidity and narrow confines, is that it was tolerated by the orthodox only when it was expressed in poetry, not in prose. Also, because of the latitude and broad range of Ṣūfī spirituality, from roughly the twelfth century to the impact of modernization in the nineteenth century, the more creative Muslim minds drifted from orthodoxy into the Ṣūfī fold, and philosophy itself, although it remained rational in its methods, became mystical in its goals.

I have already noted the severe reaction against Ṣūfī excesses on the part of Ibn Taymīyah in the fourteenth century. It may be mentioned here that for Ibn Taymīyah the ultimate distinction between good and evil is absolutely necessary for any worthwhile religion that seeks to inculcate moral responsibility, and further, that this distinction is totally dependent upon belief in pure monotheism and the equally absolute distinction between man and God. He sets little value on the formal fact that a person belongs to the Muslim community; he evaluates all human beings on the scale of monotheism. Thus, as seen above, he regards pantheistic Ṣūfīs (and, to a large extent, because of their predestinarianism, the Ashʿarīyah as well), as being equivalent to polytheists; then come the Shīʿah and Christians because both consider a human being to be a divine incarnation; and last come Zoroastrians and the Muʿtazilah, since both posit two ultimate powers.

Later, the Indian shaykh of the Naqshbandī order, Aḥmad Sirhindī (d. 1624), undertook a similar reform of Sufism from within. His massive *Maktūbāt-i Aḥmad Sirhindī* (Letters), the main vehicle of his reform, besides the training of disciples, was twice translated into Ottoman Turkish and was influential in Turkey; in the Arab Middle East, his reformist thought was carried and spread in the nineteenth century. Sirhindī, who accepts Ibn al-ʿArabī's philosophical scheme at the metaphysical level, introduces a radical moral dualism at the level of God's attributes and, instead of identifying the temporal world with the stuff of divine attributes, as Ibn al-ʿArabī does, regards that world as being essentially evil, but evil that has to be transformed into good through the activity of the divine attributes. The basic error of the common Ṣūfīs, for him, is that instead of helping to transform this evil into good, as God wants to do through his attributes, they flee from it. The spiritual heights to which they think they are ascending are, therefore, a pure delusion, for the real good is this evil, "this earth," once it has been transformed. But this realization requires a constant struggle with evil, not a flight from it. It is a prophet, then, not a saint, who undertakes the real divine task, and the true test of a person's ascent to real spiritual heights is whether he or she reenters the earth in order to improve and redeem it. Despite the efforts of Ibn Taymīyah, Sirhindī, and other figures, however, Ibn al-ʿArabī's influence has been, until today, very strong in the Muslim world, not just on Sufism but on Islamic poetry as well.

Ṣūfī orders. Up to the twelfth century, Sufism was a matter of limited circles of a spiritual elite that might be aptly described as "schools" with different spiritual techniques and even different spiritual ideologies. From the twelfth century on, however, they developed into networks of orders, involving the masses on a large scale. Systems of Ṣūfī hospices—called variously *zāwiyahs* (in Arabic), *tekkes* (in Turkish), and *khānagāhs* (in Iran and the Indian subcontinent)—where the Ṣūfī shaykh lived (usually with his family in the interior of the building) and guided his clientele, grew up from Morocco to Southeast Asia. Although in some of the hospices orthodox religious disciplines such as theology and law were taught along with Ṣūfī works, orthodox education was generally carried on in the *madrasahs*, or colleges, while only Ṣūfī works were taught in the Ṣūfī centers.

Ṣūfī orders can be divided into those that are global and those that are regional. The most global is the Qādirī order, named after ʿAbd al-Qādir al-Jīlānī (d. 1166), with branches all over the world that are tied only loosely to the center at Baghdad. Somewhat more regional are the Suhrawardī and the Naqshbandī orders. The latter, which originated in Central Asia in the thirteenth century, formulated an explicit ideology early in its career to try to influence the rulers and their courts, with the result that they have often been politically active. One of its branches, the Khalwatīyah, played a prominent role in modernizing reform in Turkey during the eighteenth and nineteenth centuries. Several of the Ṣūfī orders have been associated with guilds and sometimes, particularly in Ottoman Turkey, have been directly involved in social protests and political rebellions against official oppression and injustice.

Another broad and important division is that between urban and "rustic" orders. The former, particularly the Naqshbandī order and its offshoots, were refined and close to the orthodoxy of the *ʿulamāʾ*, with the result that an increasingly large number of the *ʿulamāʾ* gradually enrolled themselves in these urban Ṣūfī orders, particularly the orthodox ones. By contrast, many of the rustic orders were without discipline and law (*bī-sharʿ*), especially in the Indian subcontinent, where they were often indistinguishable from the Hindu *sādhūs* (monks). With the spread of modernization, Sufism and Ṣūfī orders have suffered greatly; in Turkey, they were suppressed by Mustafa Kemal Atatürk in the 1920s, and their endowments were confiscated by the government. It is interesting to note, however, that since the mid-twentieth century some orders have experienced a revival in the industrial urban centers of Muslim lands, probably in reaction to the excessively materialistic outlook generated by modernization, while in Central Asia their underground networks are waging anti-Soviet activities in an organized manner. Correspondingly, in the West, several intellectuals, such as Frithjof Schuon and Martin Lings, have actively turned to Ṣūfī devotion to escape the spiritual vacuity created by their own overly materialistic culture.

Sects. There are two broad divisions within the Muslim community, the Sunnīs and the Shīʿah. The theological views and the legal schools of the Sunnīs—the majority of the community—have been dealt with above. The Shīʿī schism grew out of the claim of the Shīʿah (a word meaning "partisans," in this context "the partisans of ʿAlī") that following the Prophet, rule over Muslims belongs rightfully only to ʿAlī, Muḥammad's cousin and son-in-law, and to his descendants. This doctrine, known as "legitimism," was opposed to the Khārijī view that rule is open to any good Muslim on a universal basis and to the Sunnī view, which was no more than a rationalization of actual facts, that "rulers must come from the Quraysh," the Prophet's tribe, but not necessarily from his clan or house.

The Shīʿah, in early Islam, were primarily sociopolitical dissidents, sheltering under the umbrella of "the house of the Prophet" but actually representing various elements of social protest against Umayyad Arab heavy-handedness and injustices. But it was not long before they began establishing an ideological and theological base for themselves. Until well into the third century AH, Shīʿī theology was crude and materialistic: it asserted that God was a corporeal being who sat on an actual throne and created space by physical motion. Hishām ibn al-Ḥakam (d. 814?), among the best known of the early Shīʿī theologians, is reported to have said that God was "a little smaller than Mount Abū Qabīs." There were several other early Shīʿī theologians who attributed some kind of body, including a physical body, to God, but beginning in the latter half of the ninth century, Shīʿī theology was radically transformed, inheriting and asserting with increasing force the Muʿtazilī doctrine of human free will against the Sunnīs.

In the thirteenth century CE, through the work of the philosopher, theologian, and scientist Naṣīr al-Dīn Ṭūsī (d. 1273), philosophy entered Shīʿī theology, a process that was further facilitated by Ṭūsī's student, the influential theologian al-Ḥillī (d. 1325). In his work on the creed, *Tajrīd al-ʿaqāʾid* (Concise Statement of the Creeds), which was subsequently commented upon by both Shīʿī and Sunnī theologians, Ṭūsī describes man as "creator of his own actions." Ṭūsī, however, rejects the philosophical thesis of the eternity of the world. Here it is interesting to compare this Shīʿī development with the Sunnī position that was articulated about three-quarters of a century earlier at the hands of Fakhr al-Dīn al-Rāzī (d. 1209), who expanded the official Sunnī theology by incorporating into it a discussion of major philosophical themes. But whereas the Shīʿah accepted many philosophical theses into their theology, al-Rāzī and other Sunnīs after him refuted all the philosophical theses point by point, thus erecting a theology that was an exclusive alternative to philosophy. Against this background is probably to be understood the fact that while philosophy was exorcised from the curricula in the Arab world from the thirteenth century on and declined sharply in the rest of the Sunnī world, it reached its zenith in Shīʿī Iran in the seventeenth century and continues unabated until today, although many of the orthodox Shīʿah continue to oppose it.

In law, the Twelver Shīʿī school has long been recognized as valid by the Sunnīs, despite differences, the most conspicuous being that Shīʿī law recognizes a temporary marriage that may be contracted for a fixed period—a year, a month, a week, or even a day. Among the Shīʿah, the nearest school to Sunnism, particularly in law, is that of the Zaydīyah in Yemen, whose founder Zayd ibn ʿAlī (d. 738), a brother of the fifth imam of the Shīʿah, was a theology student of the first Muʿtazilī teacher, Wāṣil ibn ʿAṭāʾ (d. 748).

But the most characteristic doctrine of the Shīʿah is their esotericism. This has a practical aspect called *taqīyah*, which means dissimulation of one's real beliefs in a generally hostile atmosphere. This doctrine, apparently adopted in early Islamic times, when the Shīʿah became a subterranean movement, as it were, in the wake of political failure, subsequently became a part of Shīʿī dogma. But in its theoretical aspect esotericism is defined by the doctrine that religion, and particularly the Qurʾān, has, besides the apparent, "external" meaning, hidden esoteric meanings that can be known only through spiritual contact with the Hidden Imam. In the early centuries of Islam, this principle of esotericism was probably unbridled and fanciful in its application, as is apparent from the ninth- to tenth-century Qurʾān commentary of al-Qummī. But as Shiism was progressively permeated by rational thought, esotericism became more systematic, even if it may often seem farfetched (as in certain philosophical interpretations of the Qurʾān). As pointed out earlier, the Ṣūfīs also patently practiced esotericism in understanding the materials of religion, particularly the Qurʾān; the ultimate common source of both Shiism and Sufism lies in Gnosticism and other comparable currents of thought, and, indeed, Ibn al-ʿArabī's interpretations are often purely the work of his uncontrolled imagination.

Beginning from about the middle of the tenth century, when the Sunnī caliph in Baghdad came under the control of the Shīʿī Buyid dynasty, there were public commemorations of the martyrdom of Ḥusayn at Karbala on the tenth of Muḥarram (ʿĀshūrāʾ). These ceremonies caused riots in Baghdad and still do so in some countries such as Pakistan and India today. The commemoration is traditionally marked by public processions in which participants lamenting the death of the Prophet's grandson beat their breasts and backs with heavy iron chains. Scenes of Ḥusayn's death are re-created in passion plays known as *taʿziyahs*, and he is eulogized in moving sermons and poetry recitals. Fed from childhood with such representational enactments of this event, a Shīʿī Muslim is likely to develop a deep sense of tragedy and injustice resulting in an ideal of martyrdom that is capable of being manipulated into outbursts of frenzied emotionalism, like the spectacular events of the Iranian Revolution.

Shīʿī subsects. In the first and second centuries of the Islamic era, Shiism served as an umbrella for all kinds of ideologies, with a general social protest orientation, and the earliest heresiographers enumerate dozens of Shīʿī sects, several with extremely heretical and antinomian views. The main surviving body, the Ithnā ʿAsharīyah, or Twelvers, number probably between fifty and sixty million people. All other sects (except the Zaydīyah of Yemen) are regarded even by the Twelvers themselves as heretical extremists (*ghulāt*). The main one among these, the Ismāʿīlīyah, or Seveners, broke with the Twelvers in a dispute over which son of the sixth imam was to be recognized as the latter's successor: the Twelvers refused to recognize the elder son, Ismaʿil, because he drank wine, while the Seveners did recognize him (thus the name Ismāʿīlī) and continue to await his return.

The Ismāʿīlīyah established a powerful and prosperous empire in North Africa and Egypt from the tenth to the twelfth centuries. Prior to this, the Ismāʿīlīyah had been an underground revolutionary movement, but once they attained political power, they settled down as part of the status quo. Since the late eleventh century, they have been divided into two branches: the Nizārīyah, commonly known by the name Assassins, who were active in Syria and Iran, and in recent years have been followers of a hereditary Aga Khan, and the Mustaʿliyah, who are mainly centered in Bombay. Ismāʿīlī philosophy, which is reflected in the *Rasāʾil Ikhwān al-Ṣafāʾ* (Epistles of the Brethren of Purity), produced by a secret society in the late ninth century, is essentially based on Neoplatonic thought with influences from Gnosticism and occult sects.

The Ismāʿīlī sect, which was organized and propagated through a well-knit network of missionaries (*duʿāh*), adheres to a belief in cyclic universes: each cycle comprises seven Speakers, or Messengers, with a revelation and a law; each Speaker is followed in turn by one of the seven Silent Ones, or Imams. The last imam, when he appears, will abrogate all organized religions and their laws and will institute a new era of a universal religion. During the leadership of the third Aga Khan (d. 1957), the Ismāʿīlī community started drawing closer to the mainstream of Islam, a trend that seems to be gaining further strength at present under Karim Aga Khan's leadership: Ismāʿīlī intellectuals now describe their faith as the " Ismāʿīlī *ṭarīqah* [spiritual order] of Islam." There are other "extremist" subsects within the Shīʿah, including the Druze, Nusayriyah, and ʿAlawīyūn. Of these, the Druze are the most prominent. This sect arose in the eleventh century as a cult of the eccentric Fatimid ruler al-Ḥakīm, who mysteriously disappeared in 1021.

Later sects. In more recent times, there have been two noteworthy sectarian developments, one within Shīʿī Islam in mid-nineteenth-century Iran and the other within Sunnī Islam in late nineteenth-century India. During an anticlerical movement in Iran, a certain Muḥammad ʿAlī of Shiraz claimed to be the Bāb, or "Gate," to God. He was executed by the government under pressure from the *ʿulamāʾ* in 1850. After him, his two disciples, Subḥ-i Azal and Bahāʾ Allāh, went different ways, and the latter subsequently declared his faith to be an independent religion outside Islam. While the origin of the Bahāʾī religion was marked by strong eschatological overtones, it later developed an ideology of pacifism and internationalism and won a considerable number of converts in North America early in the twentieth century. In

Iran itself, Bābīs and Bahā'īs are frequent targets of clerical persecution, and many of them have been executed under the Khomeini regime.

The Sunnī sect called the Aḥmadīyah arose in the 1880s when Ghulām Aḥmad of Qadiyān (a village in East Punjab) laid claim to prophethood. He claimed to be at once a "manifestation" of the prophet Muḥammad, the Second Advent of Jesus, and an avatar of Kṛṣṇa for the Hindus. It is possible that he wanted to unite various religions under his leadership. After his death, his followers constituted themselves as an independent community with an elected *khalīfah* (successor; i.e., caliph). When the first caliph died in 1911, the Aḥmadīyah split in two: the main body carried on the founder's claim to prophethood under Aḥmad's son, Bashīr al-Dīn, while the other, the Lahore group, claimed that Ghulām Aḥmad was not a prophet, nor had he claimed to be one, but rather that he was a reformer or "renovator" (*mujaddid)* of Islam. Both groups have been active with missionary zeal, particularly in Europe and America. In 1974, the National Assembly of Pakistan, where the main body had established its headquarters after the creation of the state, declared both groups to be "non-Muslim minorities."

Modernism. In the eighteenth century, against a background of general stagnation, a puritanical fundamentalist movement erupted in Arabia under Muḥammad ibn ʿAbd al-Wahhāb (1703–1792). The movement called for a return to the purist Islam of the Qur'ān and the *sunnah* and its unadulterated monotheism, uncompromised by the popular cults of saints and their shrines. Ibn ʿAbd al-Wahhāb married into the family of Saʿūd, a chieftain of Najd, who accepted his teaching and brought all Arabia under his ruling ideology. At the same time, in the Indian subcontinent, Shāh Walī Allāh of Delhi, a highly sophisticated intellectual (said to have been a fellow student of Ibn ʿAbd al-Wahhāb during his stay in Medina), also advocated a return to pristine Islam although, unlike his Arabian contemporary, he was a Ṣūfī at a high spiritual level.

In the nineteenth century a reformist militant group called the Jihād movement arose out of Walī Allāh's school, and three more movements followed in Africa—the Sanūsī in Libya, the Fulbe in West Africa, and the Mahdists in the Sudan. Although these three movements emerged from different environments, common to all of them was a reformist thrust in terms of the recovery of the "true pristine Islam" of the Qur'ān and the Prophet, particularly emphasizing monotheism; an insistence upon *ijtihād*, that is, rejection of the blind following tradition in both theology and law in favor of an attempt to discover and formulate new solutions to Islamic problems; and finally, resort to militant methods, including the imposition of their reformist ideologies by force. In addition, these movements generally brought to the center of consciousness the necessity of social and moral reforms as such, without recourse to the rewards and punishments of the hereafter. In other words, all three were characterized by a certain positivistic orientation.

While these premodernist reform movements laid great emphasis on *ijtihād*, in practice their *ijtihād* meant that Muslims should be enabled to disengage themselves from their present "degenerate" condition and to recover pristine Islam. Also, it is a general characteristic of all fundamentalist movements that in order to "simplify" religion and make it practical, they debunk the intellectualism of the past and discourage the growth of future intellectualism. In such cases education becomes so simplified that it is virtually sterile, thus leaving little possibility for *ijtihād*. Of the fundamentalist groups I have described above, the progenitors of the Indian and Libyan movements were sophisticated and accomplished scholars, but the leaders of the other three had only a modicum of learning and were primarily activists.

Nonetheless, these movements signaled real stirrings in the soul of Islam and paved the way for the intellectual activity of the Muslim modernists—Muslims who had been exposed to Western ideas and who, by integrating certain key ones among them with the teaching of the Qur'ān, produced brilliant solutions to the crucial problems then faced by Islamic society. The influence of premodernist reformism upon the modernists is apparent from the fact that they keep the Qur'ān and the tradition of the Prophet as ultimate referents for reform while criticizing or rejecting the medieval heritage. Thus, although their individual views regarding, for example, the relationship between faith and reason differ, all of them insist on the cultivation of positive sciences, appealing to numerous verses of the Qur'ān that state that the entire universe has been made subservient to good ends of humankind and that we must study and use it.

In the political sphere, citing Qur'ān 42:38, which says that Muslims should decide all their affairs through mutual consultation (*shūrā*, actually a pre-Islamic Arab institution confirmed by the Qur'ān), the modernists contended that whereas the Qur'ān teaches democracy, the Muslims had deviated from this norm and acquiesced to autocratic rule. Similarly, on the subject of women, the modernists argued that the Qur'ān had granted equal rights to men and women (except in certain areas of economic life where the burden of earning and supporting the family is squarely laid on men), but the medieval practice of the Muslims had clearly departed from the Qur'ān and ended by depriving women of their rights. Regarding polygamy, the modernists stated that permission for polygamy (up to four wives) had been given under special conditions, with the proviso that if the husband could not do justice among his co-wives then he must marry only one wife, and that finally the Qur'ān itself had declared such justice to be impossible to attain (4:129).

Of the half-dozen most prominent names in Islamic modernism, two were *ʿulamā'*-trained along traditional lines: Jamāl al-Dīn al-Afghānī (1839–1897), a fiery activist with a magnetic personality, and his disciple, the Egyptian shaykh Muḥammad ʿAbduh (1845–1905). Three were lay intellectuals with modern education: the Turk Namik Kemal (1840–1888) and the two Indians Ameer Ali (d. 1928) and

Muḥammad Iqbāl (1877–1938), while the Indian Sayyid Ahmad Khan (1817–1898), the most radical of them all in theological views, was a premodern lay-educated scholar. Yet, despite their differences and the fact that none of them, except for al-Afghānī and ʿAbduh, ever met any of the others, they shared the basic tenet—*à la* premodernist reform movements—that medieval Islam had deviated on certain crucial points from the normative Islam of the Qurʾān; this argument runs through all the issues that they discuss.

However, while these modernists sought reform within their own societies, they also waged controversies with the West on the latter's understanding of Islam, and some of them, particularly Iqbāl, argued about the West's own performance on the stage of history. Iqbāl bitterly and relentlessly accused the West of cheating humanity of its basic values with the glittering mirage of its technology, of exploiting the territories it colonized in the name of spreading humanitarian values, which it itself flouted by waging internecine wars born of sheer economic savagery, and of dewomanizing the women and dilapidating the family institution in the name of progress. Iqbal was an equally strong critic of the world Muslim society, which for him represented nothing more than a vast graveyard of Islam. He called the whole world to the "true Islam" of the Qurʾān and the Prophet, a living, dynamic Islam that believed in the harnessing of the forces of history for the ethical development of mankind.

Iqbāl and others, such as the Egyptian Rashīd Riḍā (d. 1935), proved to belong to a transitional stage from modernism to a new attitude, perhaps best described as neofundamentalism, for unlike the fundamentalism of the premodernist reform movements, the current neofundamentalism is, in large measure, a reaction to modernism, but it has also been importantly influenced by modernism. This influence can best be seen on two major issues: first, the contention that Islam is a total way of life, including all fields of human private and public life, and is not restricted to certain religious rites such as the Five Pillars (to which the Islam of the traditionalist *ʿulamāʾ* had become practically confined); and, second, that cultivation of scientific knowledge and technology is desirable within Islam.

Besides emphasis on technology (although Iran appears to pay only lip service to science and technology), neofundamentalists have, on the one hand, oversimplified the traditionalist curriculum of Islamic studies, and, on the other, embarked upon a program of "islamization" of Western knowledge. Besides these points, the most basic factor common to the neofundamentalist phenomena is a strong assertion of Islamic identity over and against the West, an assertion that hits equally strongly at most modernist reforms, particularly on the issue of the status and role of women in society. This powerful desire to repudiate the West, therefore, leads the neofundamentalist to emphasize certain points (as a *riposte* to the modernist, who is often seen as a pure and simple westernizer) that would most distinguish Islam from the West. Besides the role of women, which is seen to lie at home, the heaviest emphasis falls on the islamization of economy through the reinstitution of *zakāt* and the abolition of bank interest (which is identified with *ribā*, or usury, prohibited by the Qurʾān). No neofundamentalist government in the Muslim world—including Iran and Pakistan—however, has been successful in implementing either of the two policies, while the Libyan leader Muʿammar al-Qadhdhāfī has declared that the modern banking institution is not covered by the Qurʾanic prohibition of *ribā*.

Neofundamentalism is by no means a uniform phenomenon. Apart from the fact that there exist, particularly in the Arab Middle East, extremist splinter groups of neofundamentalists that are strikingly reminiscent of the Khārijīs of early Islamic times, on most crucial issues, such as democracy or the nature of Islamic legislation, even the mainstream elements are sharply divided. While in Libya, for example, Muʿammar al-Qadhdhāfī has taken a most radical stand on legislation, repudiating the precepts of *ḥadīth* as its source and replacing them with the will of the people, the current rulers of Pakistan and Iran show little confidence in the will of the people. The most interesting attitude in this connection is that of the religious leaders of Iran: while almost all reformers since the mid-nineteenth century—including Shīʿī thinkers such as Ameer Ali—have insisted that there can be no theocracy in Islam since Islam has no priesthood, the Iranian religious leaders are asserting precisely the opposite, namely, that Islam does have a priesthood and that this priestly class must rule, a position expounded even prior to the Islamic Revolution by Ayatollah Khomeini, the chief ruler of Iran, in his work *Vilāyat-i faqīh* (Rule of the jurist, 1971).

Finally, the phenomenon of international Islamic conferences in modern Islam is also to be noted since, in the absence of political unity in the Muslim world, these help the cause of unity of sentiment, if not uniformity of mind. The beginnings of this phenomenon go back to the 1920s, when conferences were held in Cairo and Mecca to deliberate on the possibility of reinstituting the caliphate after Atatürk abolished it with the secularization of the Turkish state. But from the mid-1940s on, as Muslim countries gained independence from European colonial rule, the sentiment for international Muslim gatherings became progressively stronger. In the mid-1960s all the national and international private Islamic organizations became affiliated with the semiofficial Saudi-sponsored Muslim World League (Rābiṭat al-ʿĀlam al-Islāmī), headquartered in Mecca; the league finances Islamic causes both in the Muslim world and in Western countries, where large numbers of Muslim settlers are building mosques and Islamic centers and developing Islamic community life, including programs for education.

At the same time, since the 1969 Muslim Summit Conference held in Rabat, Morocco, an Islamic Secretariat has been set up in Jiddah, Saudi Arabia, as the administrative center for the Organization of Islamic Conferences (OIC) on the state level. Besides holding summit meetings, this organization maintains a developmental economic agenda through which interest-free development banks have been set up, financed principally by oil-rich Arab countries to help poorer Muslim countries (this is in addition to the aid given to non-Muslim countries). All these conferences, whether organized by the OIC or the World Muslim League, discuss political problems affecting the Muslim world and try to formulate a common response to them, through the United Nations and its agencies or through other channels.

Islam's attitude to other religions. According to Qur'anic teaching divine guidance is universal, and God regards all peoples as equal. Every prophet's message, although immediately addressed to a given people, is nevertheless of universal import and must be believed by all humanity. Muḥammad himself is made to declare, "I believe in any book God may have revealed" (Qur'ān 42:15), and all Muslims are required to do likewise. This is so because God is one; the source of revelation is one, and humankind is also one. The office of prophethood is, in fact, indivisible.

Muslims, however, have, from earliest times, considered Muḥammad to be the bearer of the last and consummate revelation. Nevertheless, there is a tension within the Qur'ān itself on this issue. In keeping with its fundamental teaching that prophethood is indivisible, the Qur'ān, of course, invites Jews and Christians to Islam; it insists on the unity of religion, deplores the diversity of religions and religious communities, which it insists is based on willful neglect of truth, and denounces both Jews and Christians as "partisans, sectarians," with "each sect rejoicing in what itself has" (30:32).

On the other hand, it states that although religion is essentially one, God himself has given different "institutions and approaches" to different communities so that he might "test them in what he has given them," and that they might compete with each other in goodness (5:48), which implies that these different institutional arrangements have positive value and are somehow meant to be permanent. In fact, the Qur'ān categorically states that whether a person is a Muslim or a Jew or a Christian or a Sabian, "whosoever believes in God and the Last Day and does good deeds, they shall have their reward with their Lord, shall have nothing to fear, nor shall they come to grief" (2:62; see also 5:69). This tension is probably to be resolved by saying that it is better, indeed incumbent upon humankind to accept Muḥammad's message, but that if they do not, then living up to their own prophetic messages will be regarded as adequate even if it does not fulfill the entire divine command.

The organization of Muslims as a community—which was inherent in the message of the Prophet—set in motion its own political and religious dynamics. The Qur'ān itself, while strongly repudiating the claims of Jewish and Christian communities to be proprietors of divine truth and guidance, frankly tells Muslims also (for example, in 47:38) that unless they fulfill the message they cannot take God for granted. Soon after the time of the Prophet, however, the community came to be regarded as infallible, and a *ḥadīth* was put into currency that the Prophet had said "My community shall never agree on an error." This development was necessitated partly by intercommunal rivalry, but largely by the internal development of law, since the doctrine of legal consensus had to be made infallible.

In his last years, the Prophet decided on the policy of forcible conversion of Arab pagans to Islam and gave religious and cultural autonomy to Jews and Christians as "people of the Book" (although Jews were driven out of Medina by Muḥammad and later from the rest of the Arabian Peninsula by ʿUmar I). Muslims had to determine for themselves the status of Zoroastrians, Hindus, and Buddhists when they conquered Iran and parts of Northwest India. It was decided that these populations were also "people of the Book" since they believed in certain scriptures, and consequently they were allowed to keep their religion and culture, like the Jews and Christians, on payment of the poll tax (*jizyah*). In contrast with their stance toward Jews and Christians however, Muslims were prohibited from having social intercourse or intermarrying with these other groups.

Indeed, when the community became an imperium, further developments took place that had little to do with the Qur'ān or the *sunnah* of the Prophet but rather were dictated by the logic of the empire itself. The law of apostasy, for example, which states that a Muslim apostate should be given three chances to repent and in the case of nonrepentance must be executed, has nothing to do with the Qur'ān, which speaks of "those who believed and then disbelieved, then once again believed and disbelieved—and then became entrenched in disbelief" (4:137; see also 3:90), thus clearly envisaging repeated conversions and apostasies without invoking any penalty in this world. It is, therefore, important to make these distinctions and to treat historic Islam not as one seamless garment but rather as a mosaic made up of different pieces.

There are numerous other laws that are the product neither of the Qur'ān nor of the Prophet's *sunnah*, but of the Islamic imperium, such as the inadmissibility of evidence of a non-Muslim against a Muslim in a criminal case. In this legal genre also falls the juristic doctrine that the world consists of three zones: the Abode of Islam (*dār al-Islām*), where Muslims rule; the Abode of Peace (*dār al-ṣulḥ*), those countries or powers with whom Muslims have peace pacts; and the Abode of War (*dār al-ḥarb*), the rest of the world. This doctrine was definitely the result of the early Islamic conquests and the initial Islamic law of war and peace resulting from them. But during the later Abbasid period, the concept of *jihād* was formulated in defensive terms, because the task then was the consolidation of the empire rather than the gaining of further territory through conquest. To this general problem also belongs the consideration advanced by several Western scholars that Islam cannot authentically be a minority religion because the presumption of political power is built into its very texture as a religion. What is true is that Islam requires a state to work out its sociopolitical ideals and programs, but this does not mean that Muslims cannot live as a minority; indeed they have done so throughout history. The Qurʾān, in fact, envisages some sort of close cooperation between Judaism, Christianity, and Islam, and it invites Jews and Christians to join Muslims in such a goal: "O People of the Book! Let us come together on a platform that is common between us, that we shall serve naught save God" (3:64).

SEE ALSO African American Religions, article on Muslim Movements; Aḥmadīyah; ʿAlawīyūn; Arabian Religions; Ashʿarīyah; ʿĀshūrāʾ; Assassins; Attributes of God, article on Islamic Concepts; Bābīs; Bahāʾīs; Caliphate; Creeds, article on Islamic Creeds; Darwīsh; Domestic Observances, article on Muslim Practices; Druze; Elijah Muhammad; Eschatology, article on Islamic Eschatology; Falsafah; Folk Religion, article on Folk Islam; Free Will and Predestination, article on Islamic Concepts; God, article on God in Islam; Ḥadīth; Ḥaram and Ḥawṭah; Ibn ʿAbd al-Wahhāb, Muḥammad; Iʿjāz; Ijmāʿ; Ijtihād; Ikhwān al-Ṣafāʾ; Imamate; Īmān and Islām; Islamic Law, articles on Personal Law and Sharīʿah; Islamic Religious Year; Islamic Studies; Jamāʿat-i Islāmī; Jihād; Kaʿbah; Kalām; Khānagāh; Khārijīs; Madhhab; Madrasah; Malcolm X; Maṣlaḥah; Modernism, article on Islamic Modernism; Mosque; Muḥammad; Muslim Brotherhood; Muʿtazilah; Nubūwah; Pilgrimage, article on Muslim Pilgrimage; Qarāmiṭah; Qiyās; Qurʾān, article on Its Role in Muslim Practice and Life; Ṣalāt; Ṣawm; Shahādah; Shiism, articles on Ismāʿīlīyah and Ithnā ʿAsharīyah; Sufism; Sunnah; Tafsīr; Taqīyah; Ṭarīqah; Taʿziyah; Ummah; Uṣūl al-Fiqh; Wahhābīyah; Worship and Devotional Life, article on Muslim Worship; Zakāt.

BIBLIOGRAPHY

General Works

For a general survey of Islam, see *The Cambridge History of Islam*, vol. 2, *The Further Islamic Lands, Islamic Society and Civilization*, edited by P. M. Holt, Ann K. S. Lambton, and Bernard Lewis (Cambridge, 1970), and my own book entitled *Islam*, 2d ed. (Chicago, 1979). Richard C. Martin's *Islam: A Cultural Perspective* (Englewood Cliffs, N.J., 1982) gives a good description of Islamic religious practice. For a developmental view of Islam in a global setting, see Marshall G. S. Hodgson's *The Venture of Islam*, 3 vols. (Chicago, 1974). A collection of essays rarely matched for perspective interpretation of Islamic civilization is H. A. R. Gibb's *Studies on the Civilization of Islam* (Boston, 1962). Two other works of general interest are *The Legacy of Islam*, edited by Thomas W. Arnold and Alfred Guillaume (London, 1931), and *The Legacy of Islam*, 2d ed., rev., edited by C. E. Bosworth and Joseph Schacht (Oxford, 1974).

Topical Studies

For the general reader and the scholar alike, an excellent guide to the Qurʾān is *Bell's Introduction to the Qurʾān* (Edinburgh, 1970), W. Montgomery Watt's revised and enlarged edition of a work published in 1953 by Richard Bell. My own study, *Major Themes of the Qurʾān* (Chicago, 1980), is a systematic presentation of the views of the Qurʾān on God, man, society, revelation, and so on. Among translations of the Qurʾān, three can be recommended: *The Meaning of the Glorious Koran*, translated and edited by M. M. Pickthall (New York, 1930); *The Koran Interpreted*, translated by A. J. Arberry (New York, 1955); and *The Message of the Qurʾān*, translated by Muḥammad Asad (Gibraltar, 1980). Both Pickthall's and Arberry's translations have been frequently reprinted and are readily available, but Asad's painstaking and thoughtful translation is well worth seeking out.

Two works on *ḥadīth* that may profitably be consulted are Ignácz Goldziher's *Muslim Studies*, 2 vols., edited by S. M. Stern and C. R. Barber (Chicago, 1966–1973), and Alfred Guillaume's *The Traditions of Islam* (1924; reprint, Beirut, 1966).

Among the many works devoted to the Prophet's biography, none is entirely satisfactory. Alfred Guillaume's *The Life of Muḥammad: A Translation of [Ibn] Isḥāq's "Sīrat Rasūl Allāh"* (1955; reprint, Lahore, 1967), an English translation of the first extant Arabic biography (second century AH), is the best guide one has at the present. W. Montgomery Watt's *Muhammad at Mecca* (London, 1953) and *Muhammad at Medina* (London, 1956) may be usefully read as secondary sources.

On Islamic theology the following works are recommended: *A Shiʿite Creed: A Translation of "Risālatu'l-Iʿtiqādāt" of Muhammad b. ʿAlī Ibn Bābawayhi al-Qummī*, edited and translated by A. A. Fyzee (London, 1942); D. B. Macdonald's *Development of Muslim Theology, Jurisprudence and Constitutional Theory* (1903; reprint, New York, 1965); W. Montgomery Watt's *The Formative Period of Islamic Thought* (Edinburgh, 1973); and A. J. Wensinck's *The Muslim Creed: Its Genesis and Historical Development* (1932; reprint, New York, 1965).

For information on Islamic law the following works are useful: *Law in the Middle East*, edited by Majid Khadduri and Herbert J. Liebesny (Washington, D. C., 1955); J. N. D. Anderson's *Islamic Law in the Modern World* (New York, 1959); Noel J. Coulson's *A History of Islamic Law* (Edinburgh, 1971); and Joseph Schacht's *An Introduction to Islamic Law* (Oxford, 1974).

Numerous works on Sufism are readily available. Among them are Reynold A. Nicholson's *The Mystics of Islam* (1914; reprint, Beirut, 1966) and *Studies in Islamic Mysticism* (1921; reprint, Cambridge, 1977); A. J. Arberry's *Sufism: An Account of the Mystics of Islam* (London, 1950); J. Spencer Trimingham's *The Sufi Orders in Islam* (New York, 1971); and Anne-marie Schimmel's *Mystical Dimensions of Islam* (Chapel Hill, N. C., 1975).

For Islamic political thought and education, the following works are useful: A. S. Tritton's *Materials on Muslim Education in the Middle Ages* (London, 1957); E. I. J. Rosenthal's *Political Thought in Medieval Islam* (Cambridge, 1958); Bayard Dodge's *Muslim Education in Medieval Times* (Washington, D. C., 1962); Ann K. S. Lambton's *State and Government in Medieval Islam*, vol. 1, *The Jurists* (London, 1981); Hamid Enayat's *Modern Islamic Political Thought* (Austin, 1982); and my own *Islam and Modernity: Transformation of an Intellectual Tradition* (Chicago, 1982).

The most important statements on Islamic modernism by Muslim modernists themselves are Syed Ameer Ali's *The Spirit of Islam: A History of the Evolution and Ideals of Islam*, rev. ed.

(London, 1974), and Muḥammad Iqbāl's *Reconstruction of Religious Thought in Islam* (1934; reprint, Lahore, 1960). General writings on and critiques of Islamic modernism by modern Western scholars include H. A. R. Gibb's *Modern Trends in Islam* (Chicago, 1947); G. E. von Grunebaum's *Modern Islam: The Search for Cultural Identity* (Los Angeles, 1962); and Wilfred Cantwell Smith's *Islam in Modern History* (Princeton, 1957).

The following are important regional treatments: Charles C. Adams's *Islam and Modernism in Egypt* (1933; reprint, New York, 1968); Wilfred Cantwell Smith's *Modern Islam in India* (London, 1946); Albert Hourani's *Arabic Thought in the Liberal Age, 1798–1939,* 2d ed. (Cambridge, 1983); Bernard Lewis's *The Emergence of Modern Turkey* (London, 1963); Niyazi Berkes's *The Development of Secularism in Turkey* (Montreal, 1964), a mine of information despite its secularist bias; and J. Boland's *The Struggle of Islam in Modern Indonesia* (The Hague, 1971).

New Sources

Black, Antony. *The History of Islamic Political Thought: From the Prophet to the Present.* New York, 2001.

Bloom, Jonathan, and Sheila Blair. *Islam: A Thousand Years of Faith and Power.* New Haven, Conn., 2002.

Esposito, John L., and John Obert Voll. *Makers of Contemporary Islam.* New York, 2001.

Fischer, Michael M. J. *Debating Muslims: Cultural Dialogues in Postmodernity and Tradition.* Madison, Wisc., 1990.

Nasr, Seyyed Hossein. *Islam: Religion, History, and Civilization.* San Francisco, 2002.

Powers, Paul R. "Interiors, Intentions, and the 'Spirituality' of Islamic Ritual Practice." *Journal of the American Academy of Religion,* 72 (June 2004): 425–460.

Renard, John. *Seven Doors to Islam: Spirituality and the Religious Life of Muslims.* Berkeley, 1996.

Schimmel, Annemarie. *Deciphering the Signs of God: A Phenomenal Approach to Islam.* Albany, 1994.

Rippon, Andrew. *Muslims: Their Religious Beliefs and Practices.* New York, 2001.

Wilson, Peter Lamborn. *Sacred Drift: Essays on the Margin of Islam.* San Francisco, 1993.

FAZLUR RAHMAN (1987)
Revised Bibliography

ISLAM: AN OVERVIEW [FURTHER CONSIDERATIONS]

The "Preface" to the first edition of *The Encyclopedia of Religion* (1987), edited by Mircea Eliade, highlighted the "radical change of perspective" and the "impressive advances in information and understanding" that had affected religious studies and that underlined the impetus behind a new *Encyclopedia.* In his entry, "Islam: An Overview," Fazlur Rahman sought to capture and synthesize some of these changes and advances in rewriting an understanding of the Muslim strand in the religious history of humankind. His continuing influence on scholarship in the field is a testimony to his contribution to *The Encyclopedia of Religion* and to wider scholarship on Islam.

Fazlur Rahman belonged to a small group of Muslim academics who received training in two different contexts: a traditional Muslim one (primarily from his parents and also from private tutors) and a modern, Western academic experience. He became over time one of the most prominent representatives of bringing to the study of Islam a scholarly approach and to an interested world a reflection of an "enlightened" Islam. In the course of his academic life he faced open hostility from those who rejected and undermined his approach and a level of indifference or even suspicion from modern Muslim intellectuals, who having adopted a more secularized view, regarded his emphasis on the relevance of faith as misplaced.

These footnotes to the article, as it were, engage some of the issues he raised in the light of further advances, changes, and challenges in current scholarship, and also suggest additional perspectives that take into account developments in the ongoing history of Muslims and scholarly discourse in the wider academic world.

The first set of questions arises with regard to the uses and meanings of the term *Islam.* This remains a major concern of contemporary scholars and a significant topic of debate. This has highlighted the need for a clearer distinction between *Islam* understood as a defined faith tradition, that is to say as a theologically organized system of beliefs and rituals, on one hand, and the historical contexts and developments that have engaged Muslims in articulating their faith on the other. The historian Marshall G. S. Hodgson proposed a set of concepts such as *Islamdom, Islamicate,* and the like to differentiate various historical representations of Islam. Although Fazlur Rahman was aware of the necessity of such distinctions (he mentions the need to "treat historic Islam not as one seamless garment but rather as a mosaic made up of different pieces") the logic of his stance awaits a fuller development, precisely to avoid the kind of reductionist stance that the editors of the first edition clearly wished to avoid.

In the same article, Fazlur Rahman stated that, "Islam is . . . the name of a total way of life and does not merely regulate the individual's private relationship with God." Such a view builds on the concept of the precedent set by the Prophet to create institutions and manage the community's growth and development as a Prophet, not merely as a ruler, a lawgiver, a judge, or a military head. This interpretation, which has been supported by many modern Muslim interpreters, had been challenged by several of his contemporaries including, Ali Abderraziq, Ma'ruf Rusafi, and more recently Mohamed Arkoun, among others. According to their perspectives, the kind of leadership exercised by the Prophet in his life was to be understood as an "exceptional" and historically contingent moment in history. It was much later, and very gradually, that the fusion of religion and temporal matters (including politics) was constructed, first by the invention of the title "caliph" ("successor" of the Prophet), and during the Abbasid dynasty later, with the definition of a caliphate modeled in theory, if not always in practice, as a theocracy.

The historical reality of the lived experience of Muslims was that they drew the conceptual framework of their collective life, in ethics and politics, from diverse sources, including Persian and Indian traditions, Greek philosophy, and local customs. In reality, as Fazlur Rahman shows, political power had become de facto separate from religio-legal power. From that perspective one can only study Islam as it has been appropriated, interpreted, and invoked in human contexts, by Muslims and non-Muslims, in contrast to Islam as an essentialist notion or as a purely metaphysical idea "out there." The focus on the histories, cultures, and material contexts of people for whom Islam has been and continues to be a powerful force can thus benefit from all of the critical scholarly apparatus and questions that arise across the full spectrum of the study of religion. Given such an approach, it might be inappropriate to speak of a mainstream construction of "orthodoxy" because all Muslim traditions did not invoke or appropriate the sources in the same way. This would suggest a more comparative approach in the study of Muslim societies, when, like other religions, developments within were affected by interactions—theological, cultural, legal, and political—that had profound effects on how certain patterns came to monopolize Muslim discourse. This is not to suggest that religious traditions themselves do not invoke normativeness; rather that the goal of religious studies is to show how such notions are developed, constructed, and institutionalized, and that Islam like other religions is plural and pluralistic.

This has interesting implications for understanding historical appropriation in contemporary Muslim history and societies where Muslims, like others, are increasingly seeking inspiration and markers of identity from the past. This constituted an important part of Fazlur Rahman's scholarly work. Mohamed Arkoun, Abuzayd and Abdul Karim Soroush have more recently addressed the relationship of new methodologies and approaches to the study of Islam and of the Qur'ān and identified the limitations of both traditional scholarship and modern Muslim apologetics. The idea of religious reform that Fazlur Rahman sought to analyze as it emerged from the nineteenth century onwards has in contemporary contexts taken on an urgent relevance in global affairs and scholarly and public debates, within and outside Muslim societies.

The first "reformists" of the nineteenth century were Muslim intellectuals, including religious scholars, officials, and senior functionaries in administration, originating from similar social strata and having received more or less identical training in legal and religious matters. They were individuals who belonged to the tiny minority who had access to the written heritage of Muslims, and who could compare the current status of affairs with norms, models, and rules set by earlier generations. Their judgment was that Muslims had fallen short of the real expectations of their faith and the achievements of their predecessors. Such a view, however, took no account of the variety of formations within the larger Muslim *ummah*. The focus on the views of certain reformers distorted both how Muslims had experienced their respective histories but also the different way in which they memorialized their past. The need for redress or rectification (this is the original meaning of their main slogan, *iṣlāḥ*) was therefore identified with a kind of return to normality, that is, a movement back to fundamentals as they were enacted by earlier generations. The early Muslim community was considered de facto as more pious (thus the expression *salaf salih*). This "normativeness" was retrospectively imagined to mirror values similar to those exemplified in European contexts of the time, including rationality, toleration, and ethically determined behavior.

The increasing availability of primary sources for groups such as the Shīʿah, Khwarij, Muʾtazilah, and others suggests that we can no longer accept a monolithic view of how Muslims enacted responses to change. The pluralization of discourses within the early community, as indeed within different communities of interpretation, needs now to become an integral part of the study of Islam. This becomes particularly relevant in addressing significant shifts or "turns" in the history of Muslim thought. Contemporary scholarship highlights, for instance, the mode and process by which al-Shāfiʿī's synthesis of jurisprudence assumed a normative dimension. A similar pattern would occur later in the dynamics of legal formulation in Twelver Shiism. However these "turns" occurred after long periods of debate, challenge, and even competition, which, when allied to particular political contexts, created conditions for the empowerment of certain traditions over others. This offers a more nuanced view of the flow of Muslim intellectual history and its consequences for representing the primacy of law over philosophical thought and for the widespread influence of Sufism to offer alternative patterns for expressions of piety and personal direction.

Early reformers did not ignite the mass mobilization they had hoped for, and were therefore not able to give impetus to a sustainable process for redressing the conditions through a reform of ideas and practices grounded in Islam. However, their thought contributed, on the one hand, to creating support for nationalist movements and, on the other hand, to reviving conservative trends that considered the return to the purity of the norms and the pristine models of the past as the panacea. A few Muslim thinkers did recognize major shifts in history with the advent of the industrial revolution in Europe and its links to dramatic social change as well as unprecedented developments in science, technology, and the arts. Those among them who called for a reexamination of the self based on proper acknowledgement of this turn were rejected as unfaithful to the sacred heritage and to the cause of Muslim self identification and emancipation. The most lasting effect of the first reformist wave was therefore the establishment of a *salafī* (traditionalist) trend and the laying of seeds for more radical perspectives to emerge in time. There was however a shared belief that the modern state was a key mode through which to liberate Muslims from foreign domination and to re-Islamize society through reenactment of the original norms. The older dynamic between faith, power, and governance thus found new spaces in which to be played out.

The more globalized environment of the last few decades has, in spite of dramatic failures to create stable civil societies in many parts of the Muslim world, opened worlds of meanings, concepts, and methods that have prompted alternative views and attitudes for a new generation of Muslims. In the last two decades, the cumulative efforts of scholars across the globe have resulted in the accumulation of new data and categories of interpretations. The interplay of the two has shed new light and raised more questions for an emerging generation of scholars, who, while investigating the historicity of forms and expressions of Islam, are also questioning the stability of assumptions about what were regarded as core religious beliefs, institutions, and ethical principles. The analysis and intelligent adaptation of values inherited by Muslims to modern conditions was an important goal for the generation led by Fazlur Rahman. It seems appropriate that the next phases will build on that legacy to develop a space for discussion of Islam within a more universal framework within the history of religions.

BIBLIOGRAPHY

The various entries on Islam in the encyclopedia indicate the significant growth in scholarship on Islam that has taken place in the last two decades. Ebrahim Moosa has edited Fazlur Rahman's selected articles in a volume entitled *Revival and Reform in Islam* (Oxford, 1999). See Abdullah Saeed's article in Taji-Farouki text cited below.

An example of recent works that illustrate the increasing complexity of developments in early Islamic thought based on a vast array of primary sources are:

Cook, M. A. *Commanding Right and Forbidding Wrong in Islamic Thought.* Cambridge, 2003.

Crone, Patricia. *Medieval Islamic Political Thought.* New York, 2004.

Van Ess, Josef. *Theologie und Gesellschaft im 2. und 3. Jahrhundert Hidschra.* Berlin, 1991–1997.

On some of the issues related to reform and reformulation, see:

Abderraziq, A. *Islam and the Foundations of Political Power.* Cairo, 1925.

Arkoun, M. *The Unthought in Contemporary Islamic Thought.* London, 2002.

Nafi, Basheer M., and Taji-Farouki, Suha. *Islamic Thought in the Twentieth Century.* London, 2004.

Rusafi, M. *The Personality of Muhammad.* Cologne, 2002.

Safi, O. *Progressive Muslims.* Oxford, 2003.

Schulze, R. *A Modern History of the Islamic World.* New York and London, 2002.

Soroush, A. K. Please consult his personal web page, http://www.drsoroush.com.

Taji-Farouki, Suha, ed. *Modern Muslim Intellectuals and the Qur'an.* Oxford, 2004.

There are a number of encyclopedia and institutional initiatives that are worth noting:

Aga Khan University Institute for the Study of Muslim Civilisations (ISMC), London. See http://www.aku.edu/ismc.

Center for Maghrib Studies (CEMAT) in Tunis: The Qur'anic Studies Project. See http://www.la.utexas.edu/research/mena/cemat.

Center for Islamic Studies (ISAM) has published the Turkish version of the *Encyclopaedia of Islam.* See http://www.isam.org.tr.

Institute of Ismaili Studies (IIS), London. See http://www.iis.ac.uk.

International Institute for the Study of Islam in the Modern World (ISIM), Leiden. See http://www.isim.nl.

International Institute of Islamic Thought & Civilisation (ISTAC), Kuala Lumpur, Malaysia. See http://www.iiu.edu.my/istac.

McAuliffe, Jane Dammen. *Encyclopaedia of the Qur'an.* Leiden, 2001 and ongoing.

AZIM NANJI (2005)
ABDOU FILALI-ANSARY (2005)

ISLAM: ISLAM IN NORTH AFRICA

The term *North Africa* usually denotes the region that includes the countries of Libya, Tunisia, Algeria, Morocco, and Mauritania. Because this region corresponds to what Arab writers call the Maghreb (the "west"), this article shall use both terms here with no distinction of meaning. The unity of this region originates in its continuous settlement: From the dawn of history it has been inhabited by Berbers who came mostly from the banks of the Red Sea and who were later joined by Europeans, Semites, and blacks. North Africa was in contact with all the great civilizations of antiquity and became an integral part of the Islamic world at the end of the seventh century CE. Although it has never become wholly Arabized like Greater Syria and Egypt, it was totally Islamized, with the exception of a Jewish minority that has always been in existence there. Moreover, from the twelfth century CE, the vast majority of the population has followed the Mālikī legal tradition (*madhhab*).

In North Africa as elsewhere, Islam may be considered either as a religion or as a form of culture, and according to the point of view adopted, the same facts may be interpreted in quite different ways. In the following pages Islam is referred to not as a culture that has been more or less influenced by the Qur'anic message but as a religion. Discussion will center on the movements, the works, and the people who have formed the feelings and the religious behavior of the inhabitants of the Maghreb.

PRE-ISLAMIC RELIGION. The message of the prophet Muḥammad itself bore the marks of Arab polytheisms, and the Islamization of North Africa was likewise influenced by the religious situation already present there.

The prehistoric substrate. The prehistory of the Berbers remains obscure. The Libyan inscriptions guard their secrets, and funerary monuments and rock drawings can be interpreted in diverse ways according to whether Egyptian, Mediterranean, or Saharan influences are discerned in them. Scholars do agree, however, on two points: The ancient Berbers did not differentiate between magic—a technique used to harness the powers of nature—and religion—the worship of a divinity with a more or less distinct identity. Later their divinities were exclusively local ones.

Thus, say the specialists, it is better to refer not to a Berber religion as such, but to a specific attitude toward the sacred, which the inhabitants of North Africa associate even today with caves, springs, certain trees, certain stones, and so on. This strategy of the sacred was aimed at satisfying basic needs, such as causing rain, curing an infertile woman, or guaranteeing victory. Its presence has been noted by writers as far apart in time and space as the Greek historian Herodotus (sixth century BCE), the Moroccan traveler Ibn Battutah (fourteenth century CE), and the Finnish anthropologist Edward Westermarck (twentieth century). The notion of *barakah* (a polymorphous power linked to holiness), the institution of the *zāwiyah* (a brotherhood centered on a sanctuary), the *ziyārah* (cult of saints), the *shaṭḥ* (a ritual dance), and the *sama*ʿ (ritual music) have all played an important role in the religious feeling of the Maghreb people until quite recently, despite the fact that official Islam has opposed them for centuries; many anthropologists maintain that such features can only be explained in terms of this fundamental attitude toward the sacred that had already colored the Phoenician religion, Roman polytheism, and Christianity well before the arrival of Islam.

The Phoenico-Punic influence. The Phoenicians reached the shores of North Africa at the beginning of the first millennium BCE, founded Carthage, and set up a large number of trading posts along the coast. A seafaring nation of traders, they did not venture far into the interior until well into the fifth century BCE. What was their influence on local culture? Historians differ in their assessments, but they all maintain that it was crucial, for the Berbers were also from the East. The punicization of Maghrebi culture did not coincide, however, with the period when Carthage was at the height of its power: It was only after the city was overcome and destroyed (146 BCE) that the *aquellids* ("kings") of Numidia and Mauritania adopted the most characteristic features of Carthaginian civilization. Both epigraphic and archaeological discoveries have shown that the cult was colored by the Phoenico-Punic religion, that the goddess Tanit was accorded an important position, and that child sacrifice, so loathsome to the Romans, was commonplace. This speeding up of the process of punicization seems to have been a deliberate challenge to imperial Rome. According to Stéphane Gsell, the French specialist on ancient African history, it also prepared the population for Islamization later on.

Romanization and christianization. Roman polytheism as it spread to the peoples of North Africa was inseparable from Romanization, which had been, in many respects, quite remarkable. But, challenged by the Carthaginian divinities and soon undermined by Christian propaganda, the Roman religion never had time to gain a permanent foothold. Many studies have shown that it was profoundly africanized. Latin names only superficially mask pre-Roman divinities: Jupiter has been identified with Amun, Saturn—that most African of gods—with Baal-Hammon, Juno-Caelestia with Tanit, Asklepios with Eshmun, and so forth.

The problem of specific local characteristics also arises with reference to African Christianity. The new religion rapidly made converts, especially in the towns, as can be seen from the number of followers affected by the persecutions of the third century CE. Nor can one forget the appearance of such great thinkers as the apologist Tertullian (d. after 220 CE), Cyprian, bishop of Carthage (d. 258), and Augustine the church father (d. 430). However, the most significant phenomenon during this period was undoubtedly the Donatist schism, which deeply divided Roman Africa throughout the fourth century. Whether this was an attempt to found a national church or a movement of social protest, the basic point is that it reveals a permanent aspect of the psychology of the Maghrebians. They seem to accept foreign cultures easily enough but select from them one element that they then transform into a symbol of their own identity. In this sense it may be said that the Donatists foreshadowed the Muslim Khārijīs of three centuries later.

Berber religiosity. North Africa was thus subjected in turn to Egyptian, Phoenician, Greco-Roman, and Christian influences, without any real alteration of its fundamental religious attitude. Foreign religions, which gave the appearance of being accepted without any difficulties, were in fact profoundly transformed on the day-to-day level. Professions of faith, institutions, and cults changed, but what remained intact was a type of religiosity: Characterized by its vehemence, its extremism, and its tendency to intellectual simplification, it is to be found at each stage of the development of Maghrebi Islam.

Excessive intellectualism was linked with a strong attachment to the humblest of popular cults, as though the North Africans refused to see religion as a means of individual salvation: The social always took precedence over the individual, the concrete and useful over the purely spiritual. For them, religion was above all a communal ethic. The simpler and clearer the creed, the better it fulfilled its role. Both local cults and elaborate dogma, however far apart they might seem to be from a purely formal point of view, nevertheless tended toward the same end: holding the social body together.

A single religious consciousness expressed in diverse religious forms—this is a hypothesis of continuity that many specialists would be reluctant to accept. However, a number of historians have adopted it, at least as a starting point for their work, even if it has proved necessary to alter it later for a clearer explanation of how the Maghreb became Muslim.

Islamization, in North Africa as elsewhere, was a dual process. Islam originated as a set of beliefs and behaviors indigenous to the Arabs of the Middle East, but the long and rich experience of the Maghrebi population that received it was also to determine its final form. Three centuries before the appearance of the first Muslim missionaries, the region, with the exception of Carthage, was totally free from foreign influence. Independent principalities, whose internal histories are relatively obscure, had come into being. Epigraphic evidence proves that the Punic religion and Christianity persisted, that Judaism was spreading, and that Donatism and Manichaeism were flourishing again. It was within this extremely complex situation, with its strange syncretisms, that Islam was to develop. The belief that North Africa went directly from Christian orthodoxy to Sunnī Islam is nothing but an illusion.

The Arab Period. This term, inadequate as it might seem, refers to the period from the second to the fifth Muslim centuries (seventh to eleventh centuries CE). With its own distinctive features, the period was Arab only in a very restricted sense. But under this rubric shall be considered first of all the conquest, or the taking of political power by the warriors from the Middle East; second, Islamization, or the adoption of rites and beliefs defined by the Qur'ān; and finally, Arabization, in its dual ethnic and cultural senses as a change in the actual makeup of the population and as the adoption of Arab language and customs. These three developments were far from identical.

The conquest. The first Arab armies arrived in Ifrīqiyā (formerly known as Byzacene) in AH 26/647, but the conquest began only nine years later, when ʿUqbah ibn Nāfiʿ founded the city of Kairouan as a permanent base for his soldiers. ʿUqbah decided to skirt the northern towns that had been fortified by the Byzantines and to follow the inland route of the high plateaus, where the independent principalities had been set up. At first these tactics paid off, for the Arab general, after defeating the Berber chief Kusaylah, was able to cross the whole country as far as the Atlantic Ocean without meeting any further resistance. However, on his way back he found that the Berbers and the Byzantines had united to cut off his lines of communication, and his army, which he had misguidedly divided into small groups, was wiped out. Another leader of the conquest, Ḥassān ibn al-Nuʿmān, drew the logical conclusions from this defeat and decided to attack Carthage, which was the center of Byzantine power. He took it by storm in 691, lost it, then recaptured it definitively in 695. It was at that moment that the mountain people of the Aures, who had fought fiercely for their independence against the Vandals and the Byzantines during the past two centuries, rose up in revolt under the leadership of a woman the Arabs called al-Kāhinah ("the sorceress"). Because the conquerors are interested only in our wealth, al-Kāhinah reasoned, let us turn our land into a desert and they will leave. She then gave the order to cut down all the trees, thus causing a terrible deforestation with consequences that are still felt today. Is this truth or legend? In either case, this last-ditch effort did not have the anticipated results. The Arabs did not leave the devastated land, and al-Kāhinah, seeing how things were turning out and herself unable to surrender, advised her sons to go over to the enemy. Military operations continued for another ten years or so in the west of the country. The new general, Mūsā ibn Nuṣayr, returning to the policy of one of his predecessors, Abū al-Muḥājir, widely applied the system of *walā'* ("adoption") and took into the Arab aristocracy the sons of the vanquished leaders. This ethnic interpenetration was so rapid that the conquest of Spain, which began in 711, was led by a *mawlā* ("client") of Mūsā, the Berber Ṭāriq ibn Ziyād.

Unlike the centralized monarchies of Egypt, Persia, and Spain, whose destinies were sealed by the outcome of a single battle with the Muslims, the Maghreb was conquered definitively only after a half-century of fighting. There were several reasons for this. Mountainous, compartmentalized, and politically fragmented, the country was always difficult to conquer. The Arabs were faced with several different groups: Rūm (Byzantines), Afranj (Romans), Afāriq (punicized Berbers), nomad and sedentary peoples. Each of these groups had its own defense tactics and had to be countered by an appropriate attack. Berber resistance varied between the policy of Kusaylah and that of al-Kāhinah, and the Arab strategy also wavered between the rigor of ʿUqbah and the liberalism of Abū al-Muḥājir. Moreover, the conquering armies felt the repercussions of the crises that shook the Muslim caliphate from 660 to 694.

Some historians who are not specialists on Islam believe that the first Arab conquerors were nomads such as the Banū Hilāl, who invaded the country more than three centuries later. This belief is wholly erroneous; they were in fact highly skilled horsemen, trained in the latest cavalry tactics. Most of them came from Syria and were the descendants of people who had been in contact with the Romans and the Byzantines for generations. Thus they came to the Maghreb as heirs of ancient civilizations. As time went on, the neo-Byzantine character of the Arab administration became more and more obvious.

Arabization. From an ethnic point of view, the process of Arabization seems to have been very limited in scope. According to the most reliable historians, the number of Arabs settled in the country during the first Muslim century did not exceed fifty thousand. The local population, especially in Ifrīqiyā, was already fairly mixed; this characteristic was accentuated by the conquest, for the "Arab" armies in fact included Byzantines, Persians, and, very early on, Berbers, probably nomads, who were later known as Zanātah.

The adoption of Arab customs, habits, costume, and language was doubtless very rapid; the early Arab chroniclers all emphasize the Himyarite (Yemenite) origin of the Berbers, which suggests that a feeling of distant ethnic solidarity existed. The system of *walā'* meant that many Berber clans were linked with the Qahtanites (southern Arabs). The word *berber* rapidly lost its original etymological meaning and came to designate the inhabitants of isolated mountain regions. Since Islamization, the fundamental distinction in North Africa has been sociocultural rather than ethnicolinguistic.

Cultural arabization was naturally enhanced when political authority was in Arab hands. During the period under consideration the power of the Arabs was solidly established in what is now Tunisia and in that part of Spain bordering on the Mediterranean. These were populated, prosperous regions, easy to defend, where the Punic influence had been deep and lasting. Kairouan and Cordova, the capitals of the two provinces, maintained uninterrupted relations with the other Muslim metropoles and were the starting points for the spread of Arab culture and orthodox Islam.

After the conquest the Maghreb was governed by emirs appointed by the Umayyad caliphs in Damascus. With the Abbasid Revolution of 750, which saw the capital transferred to Baghdad, the empire became more Persian than Arab, more Asian than Mediterranean. The western provinces, which from then on would be more difficult to watch over, began to break away one after the other. In 755 an Umayyad prince who had fled to Spain founded an independent emirate there. In 787 Idrīs I, a descendant of ʿAlī ibn Abī Ṭālib, did the same in Morocco. Finally, in 800, Ifrīqiyā achieved autonomy under the Aghlabid dynasty, with the consent of the caliph.

In the ninth century, the Umayyad and Aghlabid emirates exercised military and commercial control over the whole of the western Mediterranean. Muslim Spain, which became a caliphate in 929, retained its preeminence right up to the great crisis of 1009; its capital, Cordova, was the equivalent of Baghdad or Cairo. The western half of the Maghreb lived in the sphere of Spain's cultural and political influence; the princes of Ceuta, Fez, Tlemcen, and elsewhere, whether Arabs or Berbers, were clients of the caliph of Cordova, and as such they spread Andalusian culture and Umayyad orthodoxy.

As for the Aghlabid emirate, it fell victim to the propaganda of the Shīʿī Fatimids, who maintained that only the descendants of ʿAlī and Fāṭimah, the cousin and daughter respectively of the prophet Muḥammad, could legitimately lay claim to the caliphate. One of their *dāʿīs* ("missionaries") who had come from the Yemen settled among the Kutāmah Berbers in the mountainous region of Little Kabylia. There, surrounded by a population favorable to the ʿAlids and out of the reach of Aghlabid power, he patiently bided his time. The Aghlabid army, weakened by the quarrels that split the reigning family, was crushed at al-Urbus (ancient Laribus) in 909, and the residence of the emirs, Raqqādah, was taken by storm. A year later the real pretender arrived and officially adopted the title of ʿUbayd Allāh al-Mahdi. But for the victorious Fatimids Ifrīqiyā was no more than a base for the conquest of the Abbasid empire. Once they had taken command of Egypt in 969, they abandoned Ifrīqiyā to their Kutāmah allies. Thus two dynasties were born: the Zirids in what is now Tunisia, and the Hammadids in the east of present-day Algeria; both were descendants of Zīrī ibn Manād, the army general who became regent after the departure of the Fatimid caliph, and both were to prosper until the mid-eleventh century.

Applied to this period, then, the term *Arab* is clearly inadequate. It was indeed princes from the East who founded states and created cities where the army, the administration, and the religious institutions spread Arab culture, but very early on political power was shared; without the Awribah, Idrīs I would never have reigned, and without the Kutāmah, ʿUbayd Allāh could never have laid claim to the caliphate.

There is no doubt that the process of Arabization was very slow. Epigraphic finds have shown that Punic and Roman-Christian influences subsisted for a long time after the conquest, but the importance of such relics must not be exaggerated. The narratives that tell the story of the beginning of the Fatimid dynasty show clearly that the Kutāmah homeland, although it was far from the capital and isolated by its mountainous surroundings, was nevertheless open to the influence of the cities, which were themselves wholly given over to the distinctive values of Arab culture. Arabization was set in motion by Arab governors, but it did not cease when the power passed into Berber hands, as can be seen from the behavior of the Zirid and Hammadid princes, who were direct descendants of the Ṣanhājah Berbers.

Islamization. In 660 a serious crisis split the eastern Muslim community. Two opposing clans were struggling for the caliphate: the supporters of Muʿāwiyah and the Umayyad family in general, and the followers of ʿAlī ibn Abī Ṭālib and, by extension, the Hashimites, the Prophet's clan. Later there appeared a more neutral faction who maintained that authority should be conferred by election and that the caliph could be non-Qurayshī and even non-Arab. The last mentioned were known as Khārijīs; the second were called Shīʿah; and the first, *ahl al-jamāʿah,* that is to say, the supporters of the majority, who were later to become the Sunnīs (orthodox ones). At first all three factions were similarly Arab; but when the conquering Umayyads set up a predominantly Qurayshī administration in Damascus, the Shīʿah and the Khārijīs turned toward the newly converted, and, confronted by Sunnism—an official, conservative, moderate Islam that was also an Arab Islam—they took up a non-Arab and sometimes even a frankly anti-Arab stance.

Islam spread more rapidly in North Africa than did the Arab language. This was a paradoxical result of the schismatic propaganda, for the autonomy movement, which was directed against the political power of the Arabs and their clients, endowed Islam with a profoundly national character.

After the death of al-Kāhinah in 701, the conquest was almost completed. The new rulers, seeking to reorganize the country, imposed a regular tax system. But since the decline of the Roman Empire the population had become used to living in small, independent communities. As early as 720 the Berbers of Ifrīqiyā rose up and killed the emir, Ibn al-Ḥabḥāb. In 740 a more serious revolt broke out in northern Morocco and soon spread throughout the whole of North Africa. One of the main rebel chiefs, Maysarah, had lived in Kairouan, where he had come under the influence of the Ṣufrīyah, who were Khārijī extremists. Thus the Berbers rose up in the name of those values of justice, equality, and austerity that had been taught by Islam itself but that, in the Berber view, had been betrayed by the Umayyads. In 740, on the banks of the Chelif River, in the center of what is now Algeria, the flower of the Arab aristocracy fell in the Battle of the Nobles *(ghazwat al-ashrāf)*. Thenceforth, the western half of the Maghreb was independent. The struggle continued to the east, but no decisive battle was won against the rebels. The new rulers of the empire, the Abbasids, despairing of a rapid victory over this distant province, delegated their authority to Ibrāhim ibn al-Aghlab, a brilliant general who had defended Zāb, in the south of present-day Tunisia, against the insurgents; this event led to the birth of the Aghlabid dynasty within the frontiers of what had been Roman Africa.

The Khārijīs were now in command of the central and western Maghreb, but they soon proved to be incapable of establishing a great state. As proponents of absolute equality, they refused any form of hierarchy or discipline; they accepted without discrimination all those who shared their beliefs. They had a taste for theological controversies and, in case of disagreement over a point of dogma, they would depose their imams and, in some cases, kill them. The principalities that they founded after 754 had shifting frontiers and rudimentary structures. Entrepôt towns such as Tāhart in western Algeria and Sijilmāsah in southwestern Morocco were situated at the junction of the important communication routes between east and west, between the Sahara and the Mediterranean, and as such were busy and prosperous despite their political instability. The state of Barghwāṭah, founded at the same period on the rich Atlantic plains, was just as prosperous, according to travelers in the tenth century; the fruit of the Khārijī revolt, it tended more and more toward a very broad syncretism.

After Khārijīsm, it was Shiism that dominated the political and religious history of the Maghreb. Indeed, the founding of the Idrisid kingdom was probably not fortuitous. There is some evidence for the existence of a real network of Shīʿī missionaries who took to the western routes from Medina or Iraq to spread their good word. They began by questioning students and pilgrims from the Maghreb about the state of mind of their countrymen. If the latter seemed to nurture some sympathy for the ʿAlīds and if they were unhappy with their rulers, then a missionary was sent over to find out firsthand what the situation was and perhaps prepare the ground for the arrival of the ʿAlīd pretender. The success of Idrīs I encouraged several of the descendants of Ḥasan ibn ʿAlī to follow his example. In the middle of the eleventh century, nearly a dozen Ḥasanid princes were established in the west of Algeria. Some confined themselves to the role of honored guests, while others were regarded as local chiefs, although their ambitions were limited by the fact that they had no armies. Owing to the presence of so many ʿAlid "guests," Shīʿī ideology was able to permeate Maghrebi society, sometimes replacing Khārijī thought, sometimes combining it with older beliefs to produce strange syncretisms. One example may be found in the region of Ghumārah, south of Tetuan, where a pseudo-prophet called Hāʾ Mīm founded a separate cult in conjunction with his aunt, Tangīt. The victory of the Fatimids would be incomprehensible without the preliminary activity of the Shīʿī missionaries. The notion of Mahdi (messiah), the dispenser of justice who brings to a close an era of injustice, may or may not have sounded the echo of ancient beliefs, but henceforth it was to become a permanent aspect of the mentality of the Maghreb, before taking on official status with the Almohads.

The Islam that was spread among the Berbers by the schisms now seems to be very unorthodox, but can one really speak of orthodoxy in relation to that far-off time when no remotely hierarchical institution existed? As long as there was no strong state capable of imposing an official ideology throughout North Africa, there was room enough for different interpretations of dogma, and these ultimately deepened the impact of the Qurʾanic message. The Fatimids were the first to attempt the political and ideological unification of the Maghreb; the Khārijīs were almost completely eradicated, with the exception of the Mzab region in southern Algeria and Jabal Nafūsah to the west of what is now Libya, where communities persist down to the present day. It was with the Almoravids that Mālikī Sunnīsm was to triumph, mainly because islamization had already been achieved through the activity of the schismatics.

Literary works. Berber literature has always been basically oral. Berber prophets such as Ṣāliḥ of the Barghwāṭah or Hāʾ Mīm of the Ghumārah probably employed oral means of communication. Although the eleventh-century Andalusian geographer al-Bakrī asserts that the Barghwāṭah had a Qurʾān in Berber, no trace of this has been found so far.

If no written document exists to shed light on the syncretisms, this is not so for the Khārijīs. After the fall of Tā-hart, the survivors fled to Mzab with their sacred books, and in this way two important works were saved. The first, *Kitāb akhbār al-Rustumīyīn* (Memorable Events in the History of the Rustimid Imams), was written by Ibn al-Ṣaghīr (d. 894), who was alive at the time of the events he recorded; the second, *Kitāb al-sīrah wa-akhbār al-aʾimmah* (Lives and Works of the Imams), is a later work—its author, Abū Zakarīyāʾ, lived in the eleventh century—although it remains with in the limits of the period under consideration. Both texts are concerned above all with enlightening the faithful; nevertheless they provide some historical information and clues to the psychology of the Khārijīs in the Maghreb.

The early Shīʿī movement did not leave behind comparable works; it is known only through the prehistory of the Fatimid dynasty as it was recorded by Qāḍī al-Nuʿmān ibn Ḥayyūn (d. 974). This writer was the main ideologue of the Fatimids. In his major work, *Iftitāḥ al-daʿwah* (Our First Missions), he describes, with remarkable objectivity and accuracy, the region that escaped the political control of the Aghlabids while remaining open to their cultural influence.

The most important works of this period, however, were conceived in Kairouan. Until the eleventh century, profane literature was dominated by émigrés from the East, but local writers won renown in the field of religious culture. At first Ifrīqiyā followed the example of Baghdad and adopted the legal tradition of Abū Ḥanīfah (d. 768), but it soon came to favor that of Mālik ibn Anas (d. 796). What was the reason for this preference? It seems that there were several. Students and pilgrims from the Maghreb went more readily to the Hejaz, Malik's home, than to Iraq, where Abū Ḥanīfah was born. Because he had lived all his life in Medina, Mālik seemed to guarantee greater fidelity to the tradition of the Prophet. Many of the inhabitants of the Maghreb wished, perhaps unconsciously, to dissociate themselves from the East but without falling into the schisms. Finally, the Mālikī school, which was simpler than the Ḥanafī, was better suited to the society of Ifrīqiyā, which was still predominantly rural and thus relatively homogeneous.

But whatever the causes, the results were of major importance. The Mālikī school in Kairouan took decisive steps toward the ideological unification of the Maghreb. ʿAbd al-Salām ibn Saʿīd, known as Saḥnūn (d. 854), set down in his *Mudawwanah* (a handbook of Mālikī law) the code of the civil society of the Islamic Maghreb. Doubtless many ancestral or even prehistoric customs persisted, but they were judged by reference to the model laid down in the *Mudawwanah.* From now on the Mālikī *faqīh* (jurisprudent) was one of the two most important figures in society. The other was the *ʿābid* (man of God) who disdained any honors offered him, was always ready to criticize the powers that be, and thus was able to channel popular discontent. The master among these was Buhlūl ibn Rāshid (d. 799), who, along with others like him, was said to have prepared the blossoming of those brotherhoods (*zawāyā*) that were so characteristic of Berber religiosity. If Sunnism prevailed in the end, it was thanks to men like him, whose example suggested how to influence the government by means other—and better—than bloody rebellion. As the society became more urbanized and more stable, such an example found even greater echoes. These ascetics have not left any written works, but their attitude has been described in detail and their sayings recorded in the *manāqib* (hagiography) literature, beginning with the *Ṭabaqāt ʿulamāʾ Ifrīqiyā wa-Tūnus* (Biographies of the religious scholars of Ifrīqiyā and Tunis) by Abū al-ʿArab Muḥammad ibn Tamīm (d. 944).

When, in the middle of the tenth century, the Kutāmah Berbers inherited a stable, prosperous state that soon gained its autonomy, they encouraged the growth of a genuinely local literature. The second Zirid emir, al-Manṣūr ibn Buluggīn (984–996), left Raqqādah, the former Aghlabid residence, and went to live in great luxury in Ṣabrā-Manṣūrīyah, where the court life, so typical of Islamic civilization, favored the development of *ādāb* (profane literature). Here may be mentioned the names of three men whose fame extended far beyond the frontiers of Ifrīqiyā. Ibrāhīm ibn al-Raqīq (d. 1027) was chancellery secretary and a committed Shīʿī; his vast historical work, *Taʾrīkh Ifrīqiyā wa-al-Maghrib,* served as a reference for all subsequent chroniclers, although very little of it has come down to the present. Muḥammad ibn Saʿīd ibn Sharaf (d. 1067) was known as both a poet and a historiographer; his treatise of literary criticism, *Masāʾil al-intiqād,* has been translated into several European languages. Ḥasan ibn Rashīq (d. 1064), a poet and anthologist, has left to posterity a book of rhetoric (*Kitāb al-ʿumdah*) that is remarkable for the depth of its analysis and the elegance of its style.

The mosques of Kairouan and Sousse, the remains of the palace in Raqqādah, the fortresses of Belezma and Baghāʾī, the citadels of Sousse and Monastir, all bear witness to the wealth of the reigning dynasties and the adaptation of Islamic art to North Africa. The architecture of this period resulted from a harmonious symbiosis of the Byzantine heritage, the influence of Abbasid Iraq, and a spirit of sobriety that was expressed in the asceticism of a man such as Buhlūl.

THE BERBER PERIOD. The culture of Ifrīqiyā reached its peak in the eleventh century and then spread throughout the Maghreb as a result of the unifying policies of the Almoravid, Almohad, and Marinid dynasties. For want of a better name, the three hundred years from the mid-eleventh to the mid-fourteenth century, when supreme power was in the hands of the Berber dynasties, is known as the Berber period, but the term is as unsatisfactory as the adjective *Arab* that this article applied to the previous three centuries. Indeed, neither arabization nor islamization had been halted, and on the contrary, it was in this period that they reached the point of no return.

The three Berber dynasties practiced an imperial policy aimed at the unification of the Maghreb; although this attempt failed in the end, it left indelible traces. In the eleventh century there was an obvious difference between the eastern and western halves of the Maghreb. The former was Arab in culture and politically unified, while the latter was fragmented into numerous principalities that were fought over by the rulers of Cordova and Kairouan. Maghrāwah and Miknāsah, alternately serving the interests of one and the other, wore themselves out in a series of fruitless conflicts. Quite suddenly and for various reasons, the caliphate of Cordova disappeared in 1031, and the Zirid and Hammadid emirates in 1052; with this vacuum on the North African political scene, the time of the western Maghreb had come. The Almoravid Lamtunah, starting from the Atlantic region of the Sahara, built an empire around Marrakesh (founded in 1062); this empire, which lasted until 1146, stretched from Andalusia to the Sahara and from Algiers to the Atlantic. The Almoravids were replaced by the Almohads, whose main strength came from the Maṣmūdah of the High Atlas; extending the empire they had inherited as far as Tripoli, they reigned in Marrakesh until 1276 and, under the name of the Hafsids, in Tunis until 1573. Then came the turn of the Zanātah shepherds from the borders of Algeria and Morocco, who, as the Marinids and then the Wattasids, reigned in Fez until 1550 and, as the Zayyanid-ʿAbd al-Wadids, in Tlemcen until 1554.

Unlike the Kutāmah, the Berber groups from the western Maghreb had not set out at the call of an Arab refugee. In both cases, however, the seizure of power by a Berber dynasty was accompanied by cultural Arabization that owed its fast pace to the luxurious life of the court. Ethnic Arabization was intensified too, because the Banū Hilāl Bedouins, who were responsible for the fall of the Zirid and Hammadid emirates, continued to emigrate to the Maghreb right up to the fifteenth century; the last to arrive, the Banū Maʿqil, Arabized the province of Shangīṭ, which lies to the north of what is now Mauritania.

The Almoravid movement. One of the leaders of the Lamtūnah, on his way back from a pilgrimage to Mecca, attended the lessons given by Abū ʿImrān al-Fāsī, a famous man of law from Morocco. "My countrymen," he told the teacher, "know nothing of true Islam and have need of a guide. Who would you recommend?" Abū ʿImrān replied, "Go on my behalf to see Wajjāj, who knows your region well." Wajjāj in turn directed the Lamtūnah chief to a *faqīh* from Sijilmāsah called ʿAbd Allāh ibn Yāsīn. When they got back to the Sahara, the warrior chief and the missionary founded a *ribāṭ* (monastery) where the future leaders of the movement gathered together; for this reason they were given the name *al-murābiṭūn,* transformed by the Spanish into Almoravids. Later, under the leadership of Yūsuf ibn Tāshfīn, the disciples of Ibn Yāsīn set out to conquer a vast empire.

This story closely resembles that of Abū ʿAbd Allāh, the Fatimid *dāʿī,* apart from the fact that this time the missionary was Sunnī. The Almoravid movement in the West, like the Seljuk movement in the East, belonged to the vast counteroffensive launched by the Abbasids in the eleventh century to destroy Shiism and repel the Christian crusade. One of the spiritual fathers of the movement, the Mālikī *qāḍī* al-Bāqillānī (d. 1013), was Abū ʿImrān's teacher, and it was with the blessing of the grest jurisprudents of the East that Yūsuf ibn Tāshfīn overthrew the Andalusian princes and took the title of Amīr al-Muslimīn ("commander of the Muslims"), which symbolized his supreme authority in the Muslim West under the suzerainty of the Abbasid caliphs.

In the new Almoravid state the *faqīhs* held pride of place. Chosen from among the early adherents of the movement, they set out to defend and spread the official ideology. They gave advice to local emirs, kept a close watch on the verdicts of the courts, preached asceticism to the governed and austerity to the governing. Qāḍī ʿIyād of Ceuta (d. 1149) was the embodiment of this clerical caste. He left many works, two of which were of considerable importance. His *Shifāʾ* (Book of Healing), which draws a complete portrait of the Prophet, simultaneously gives readers an example to follow at every moment of their lives, thus proving that, contrary to Shīʿī thought, they had no need of an imam to guide them to the truth. In the *Kitāb al-madārik* (Book of Exploits), he drew up a long list of the celebrities of the Mālikī school. This book completed the work that Abū al-ʿArab had begun by putting together what can be considered a veritable patrology of Maghrebi Islam.

However, in spite of the wholehearted support of the state, Mālikī preeminence was short-lived, and with the coming of the Almohad dynasty the Maghreb was once more to experience a schism. Official Almoravid ideology seems to have lagged behind the sociointellectual evolution of the rest of the Islamic world. Whereas in the East, thanks to al-Ghāzalī (d. 1111), Sunnism had succeeded in integrating dialectical theology (*kalām*), logic (*manṭiq*), and mysticism (*taṣawwuf*); and while in Andalusia, Ibn Ḥazm (d. 1064) was pioneering new directions in juridical thought, the Mālikīyah of the Maghreb remained blindly attached to the school of Kairouan and refused any kind of reform. When in power they applied a reactionary policy in the true sense of the term, refusing to systematize the *fiqh* in the manner of al-Shafiʿī (d. 820), condemning and burning all the works of al-Ghāzalī, and declaring war on popular piety. They formed an isolated, activist minority that refused the spirit of the *sunnah,* that is, to choose the middle way and always seek the consensus of the majority. It was not until they had suffered bitterly from the persecution of the Almohads that they discovered the virtues of moderation.

The Almohads. From a political point of view, the Almohad century represented the apogee of North African history, but from a religious point of view it was simply an interlude. The official ideology, which from the very beginning had been opposed by the *ʿulamāʾ* and later was to be seen as schismatic by a majority of the population, was eventually repudiated by the descendants of those who had established it in the first place. How can its appearance be expalined? Was it a belated offshoot of earlier schisms? An original creation stemming from the Berber mentality? A national religion comparable with what was to become Twelver Shiism in Persia? All of these remain questions without answers.

Muḥammad ibn Tūmart, the Almohad ideologue, unlike Ibn Yāsīn, was not the propagandist of a movement that was external to his native region. Toward 1107 he left southern Morocco for Cordova, where he immersed himself in the teachings of Ibn Ḥazm, then traveled on to Iraq where, according to some biographers, he may have met al-Ghazālī. About 1116 he began to return homeward, stopping off for a long time in Alexandria, Tunis, Bougie, Tlemcen, Fez, and Meknes. In each of these cities he set himself up as the arbiter of morals, antagonizing the local authorities but gaining disciples who, like ʿAbd al-Muʾmin al-Gūmī, became fanatical followers. When he arrived in the Almoravid capital of Marrakesh, he challenged the *faqīh*s and led them into theological controversies for which they were ill prepared. An advocate of strict monotheism *(tawḥīd)* who made no concessions to popular imagination, he accused his adversaries of anthropomorphism (*tajsīm*). In fact, *Almohad* is a Spanish distortion of the Arabic *al-muwaḥḥid* ("unitarian").

Expelled from the capital in 1121, Ibn Tūmart took refuge in Tinmal in the High Atlas; there, surrounded by his followers, and with the support of the Hintātah Berbers, a clan of the Maṣmūdah, he put himself forward as a candidate for the imamate. He spent seven years organizing a veritable revolutionary army, then set out in 1128 to attack Marrakesh. The Almoravid empire was still in the prime of youth, and the attacking army was repelled with serious losses, although Ibn Tūmart's forces were able to regain a place of refuge without being pursued. Ibn Tūmart died soon after this defeat, but he left behind him a perfectly tuned instrument of warfare. His successor, ʿAbd al-Muʾmin, had only to choose tactics of attrition to overcome the power of the Almoravids.

Ibn Tūmart was closely involved in the ideological training of his disciples and for their benefit wrote a series of theological texts that have come down to the present. Like the Khārijīs, he held that faith (*imān*) should not be passive, and he believed that he had to actively follow good and fight against evil. Like the Muʿtazilah, he defined the divine attributes in strictly rational terms, with recourse if need be to *taʾwīl* (allegorical interpretation). As the leader of an independent school, he applied *ijtihād,* following his own opinions without reference to a particular legal school. As a pretender to political power, he claimed ʿAlid ancestry and presented himself as the infallible imam (*maʿṣūm*), the Mahdi whose coming had been so long awaited by the weak and the oppressed. Here one is far from the Mālikī school, but the only point that was really unacceptable to a Sunnī Muslim was the doctrine of infallibility, and this was to be abandoned in Marrakesh in 1229 and later in Tunis by the Hafsids. If Ibn Tūmart had contented himself with claiming the right to *ijtihād,* the *faqīh*s would have have been able to do no more than question his abilities, without ever going so far as to condemn him for heresy.

The arrival of a man such as Ibn Tūmart in a region that was so far from the great cultural centers shows to what extent the Maghreb had been Islamized; however, it would be a serious error to consider the Almohads a purely local phenomenon; their ideology expressed a general desire to go beyond the narrow legalism of the Mālikī school, to apply logic to both law and theology. This was in fact achieved in the following century. To the extent that there is today a homogeneous Maghrebi people, in spite of their internal diversity, this is the result of the policy of the Almohad caliphs. Ibn Tūmart owed his victory to the support of the Maṣmūdah in the Moroccan High Atlas, who were then to play a leading role in the empire. However, his successor, Caliph ʿAbd al-Muʾmin, came from western Algeria, and, according to the chroniclers, he brought forty thousand of his countrymen with him to Morocco in order to reinforce his personal power. During his later campaigns, when he came up against the Zanātah, Arabized Berbers migrating along the Algerian-Moroccan borders, he moved them to the regions of Meknes and Taza; he likewise sent the Banū Hilāl, Arab Bedouins from Ifrīqiyā, to the Atlantic plains. He imposed military service on both groups and in return granted them *iqṭāʿ*s, tax farms for vast tracts of land. Thus there came into being a caste of soldiers who were superimposed on the local population and who brought with them their Arab culture and language. In this way the Arabization of the plains and plateaus of the Maghreb was completed. Both toponymy and anthroponymy bear witness to the fact that the same groups were to be found everywhere.

This period also saw the development of a pietistic religious movement that had its origins in Almoravid times. Encouraged by the victory of the Almohads, it was nonetheless distinguished from them from the beginning by its aims and methods. Ibn Tūmart's intellectualism was permeated with great fervor, and yet its austerity left no room for the religious sentimentality that the people doubtless needed. Numerous ascetics left for the countryside to spread the word of God to the people in a colorful language that was simple enough to be understood by the least educated. Only a very few of them were real *faqīh*s, and some were even quite uneducated, but they were all men of God. They settled in lodges (*zāwiyah*s) far from any town, where they spent their days in prayer and meditation. For the scattered populations that still had no fixed homes, these lodges became centers where they could gather, and in fact they were the forerunners of what are today the *mawasim* (annual fairs; sg., *mawsim*). The biographies of these men, the greatest of whom was ʿAbd al-Salām ibn Mashīsh (d. 1128), can be found in the *Tashawwuf* of Ibn al-Zayyāt. It was with this movement that Islam truly became the culture of the people of the Maghreb.

Two centuries later than Ifrīqiyā but on a larger scale, the western Maghreb in its turn witnessed a court life that was to familiarize it with Arab-Islamic civilization. By emulating the Andalusian émigrés, Moroccans such as Abū Jaʿfar ibn ʿAṭīyah (d. 1158), Ibn Ḥabbūs (d. 1174), and Aḥmad al-Jarāwī (d. 1212) distinguished themselves in the field of profane literature. A school of historiography also came into being, and through it are obtained the first glimpses of the interior of the western Maghreb. The most important authors in this field were Ibn al-Qattān, who lived during the reign of Caliph al-Murtaḍā (1248–1266), ʿAbd al-Wāḥid al-Marrākushī (d. 1230), and Ibn ʿIdhārī (d. after 1213). For the first time, too, a Maghrebi capital, Marrakesh, could be compared with Cordova or Cairo. The celebrated Andalusian philosophers and jurists Ibn Ṭufayl (d. 1185) and Ibn Rushd and Ibn Zuhr (who both died in 1198) lived there for many years and wrote some of their most important works there. During the Almohad period the art of the Maghreb reached the height of its greatness and harmony. Rigor, sobriety, and modesty were the characteristics ascribed to the ideology of Ibn Tūmart and to the collective psychology of the Maghrebi people.

The post-Almohad period. The Almohad empire, exhausted by its wars in Andalusia against the combined forces of Christendom, finally gave way to three dynasties that divided the North African territory among themselves. Under the descendants of Abū Ḥafṣ ʿUmar, one of the first disciples of Ibn Tūmart, Ifrīqiyā once more became autonomous within its former frontiers. The Hafsids remained loyal to Almohad ideas for a certain time, then dissociated themselves and were reconciled with the Mālikī *ʿulamāʾ*. The rest of the Maghreb was shared between two Zanātah groups: the Marinids in Fez and the Zayyanids in Tlemcen. The Marinids, who considered themselves the sole rightful heirs of the Almohads, attempted to rebuild the empire but failed, and after 1350 the three dynasties coexisted more or less peacefully.

The Maghreb of the fourteenth century was homogeneous. Various names were used for what was in fact the same political organization, the Almohad *makhzan* (state government) that had been directly inherited by some and copied by others. The army was dominated everywhere by the Banū Hilāl, the bureaucracy by the Andalusian émigrés who brought with them their refined system of etiquette. The retreat of the Andalusians from Spain marked the third step in the cultural arabization of the country. Fashions in dress or cooking, language, music, architecture, decoration, all the framework of a certain kind of middle-class existence, still bear witness to this cultural influence today. The same names, the same customs, the same way of speaking are to be found in Fez, Tlemcen, and Tunis.

The failure of Ibn Tūmart's extremism left the field clear for a renewed Sunnism that was both faithful to the heritage of the past and open to the new questions that the Almohad crisis had brought to light. The Marinids, who had no ideological pretensions, took the advice of the *ʿulamāʾ* and, following the example of the Seljuks in the East, set up *madrasah*s, colleges where the Islamic disciplines were taught from an orthodox viewpoint. These were immediately copied by the Zayyanids and Hafsids. The teaching was organized by the authorities, but its content was defined by the consensus of the *ʿulamāʾ*, based on a tradition that was nurtured by the vast body of biographical literature of the *ṭabaqāt*. The growing number of pupils led to a need for manuals; thus began the era of dry, hermetic summaries that soon required long commentaries (*shurūḥ*). This was perhaps an inevitable development, but one that turned out to be negative in the long run.

Official Islam. As the reigning dynasties grew weaker, the *ʿulamāʾ*, without ever becoming truly independent, gained more power and put the finishing touches on an official ideology that was characterized by moderation, simplicity, and positivity. For a long time Sunnī Islam had been faced with a precise problem: the rationalization of law, theology, and mysticism. The Ẓāhirī and Shāfiʿī jurists claimed that it was possible to reduce the various Qurʾanic dictates to a few laws. The Muʿtazilī and Ashʿarī theologians wanted to derive all the attributes of God from a single principle. The mystics of the school of Ibn ʿArabī (d. 1240) justified their metaphysical monism with the desire to be identified with God. The Mālikī *faqīh*s, taking a completely different viewpoint, considered this attempt at systematization useless methodological extremism. For them, Islam is above all a divine order (*amr*) that is self-evident. The duty of the Muslim is to obey this order; hence the cardinal importance of the notion of *bidʿah,* innovation in regard to ritual. The Prophet is by definition the perfect believer; why go beyond what he taught his followers? Does this not imply either that he was not perfect or that he did not transmit faithfully the message of God?

Because Islam is above all a *sharīʿah* (law; lit., "path"), *fiqh* is the central discipline in Islamic science. The community can always do without theologians and mystics, as in Medina at the epoch of the Prophet, but it cannot live without *faqīh*s, who form an integral part of the governing elite. And because *fiqh* fills a social need, it must be founded on a simple *ʿaqīdah* (profession of faith), that of the *salaf* ("ancestors"); any attempt to complete it or to clarify it would lead inevitably to endless dissension. *Fiqh,* the constitution of the Muslim community, is a positive element and must be accepted as such; it is justified by the will of God, which is itself inseparable from the final good of humanity.

Such an attitude is easy to understand in the light of the disastrous consequences that partisan rifts have had throughout the history of Islam, but it is impossible to ignore the fact that as this attitude became more widespread, it tended to discourage any form of intellectual curiosity. Indeed, the last achievements in the exact and natural sciences date from no later than the fifteenth century in the Maghreb.

The history of the Maghreb seems to come to a standstill at the moment when Islam assumed its definitive characteristics. Contemporary scholars were aware of this and attempted to record, in encyclopedic form, the knowledge handed down from past centuries. One such example in the field of law is the *Miʿyār* (Norm) of al-Wansharīsī (d. 1508). Ibn Khaldūn (d. 1406), the greatest thinker ever produced by the Islamic Maghreb, also endowed his famous *Muqaddimah* (Prolegomena) with an encyclopedic content. This work was the conclusion of a deep reflection on the history of the Maghreb, widened to include the entire Arab-Islamic past. The author, who had been a serious student of Greco-Arab philosophy and who was personally inclined toward mysticism, nevertheless remained absolutely faithful to Mālikī methodology. In two brilliant chapters of his main work, he contrasts the positivism of *fiqh* with the rationalism of *kalām* on the one hand, and the monism of mysticism on the other. More important, he reveals the sociological basis for such a contrast: Universal history, according to him, had evolved from *ʿumrān badawī* (rural civilization) to *ʿumrān madanī* (urban civilization). In the Maghreb the two kinds of culture exist side by side, resulting in a structural dichotomy. In the city, society tends naturally toward a religion of reason, whereas rural society upholds a naturalist religion: The sultan (the political authority) plays the role of mediator between the two forms of social life; his official ideology, Mālikī *fiqh,* must necessarily remain at an equal distance from rationalism and naturalism, hence its qualities of positivism and moderation.

THE ISLAM OF THE ZĀWIYAHS. During the fourteenth and fifteenth centuries the Maghreb underwent a general crisis. Nomadic life spread at the expense of a ruined agriculture; commerce languished and plunged the cities into profound inactivity. The Spanish and the Portuguese, masters of the seas, conquered many ports on the North African coasts. Faced with such unfavorable developments and already weakened by incessant wars, the three reigning dynasties collapsed.

The Ottoman Turks. This period began with the Portuguese seizure of Ceuta in 1415 and ended with the defeat of the Spanish in Tunis in 1574, and of the Portuguese in Wādi al-Makhāzin near Larache in 1578. Morocco was saved by an outburst of nationalism, the rest of North Africa by the Ottoman Turks.

Ottoman sovereignty theoretically persisted in Algeria until 1830, in Tunisia until 1881, and in Libya until 1911. However, from 1710 on, each of these provinces gained its autonomy. The official language was Turkish, but Arabic remained the language of culture. The Ottomans reintroduced Ḥanafī law into the Maghreb; the resulting competition with Mālikī law rekindled interest in long-neglected disciplines such as *uṣūl al-fiqh* (fundamental principles of law) and *kalām.* In Morocco, under the new Saʿdid dynasty, the social and political scene was dominated by the Ṣūfī brotherhoods.

The marabout movement. Popular pietism, which had been launched under the Almoravids and the Almohads, covered the country with a network of *zāwiyahs* where ascetics lived—in theory at least—cut off from the world. In reality they taught children and even adults the rudiments of religion; they used the offerings they received from the population to help the poor and give shelter to travelers; in cases of conflict they served as mediators. The person who was called *ṣāliḥ* (man of good works), *walī* (man of God), *sayyid* (lord), and *shaykh* (leader) had become an indispensable figure. The last two terms indicate that he was endowed with a spiritual authority that the *qāʾid* (representative of the central powers) could not easily ignore.

Up to this time the *zāwiyahs* fulfilled a social need and completed the work of the *makhzan.* When the latter turned out to be incapable of getting rid of the Portuguese who had settled on the coasts, the *zāwiyahs* were transformed into *ribāṭs,* rallying centers for warriors. (Here the word *murābiṭūn*—as with Almoravids earlier—yields *marabout* in French and English.) The man who symbolized this transformation was Muḥammad ibn Sulaymān al-Jazūlī, the author of a celebrated book of prayers concerning the Prophet called *Dalāʾil al-khayrāt* (The Signs of Blessings); his *zāwiyah* was located in Afūghvl, near present-day Safi. He died in 1465, before the Portuguese occupation of the city, but his disciples, who later led the struggle for freedom, considered that he had prepared them spiritually for their task. All the *zāwiyahs* founded later were linked to al- Jazūlī and, through him, to ʿAbd al-Salām ibn Mashīsh.

The marabout movement was based on the legacy of several centuries. To the tasks of education and moral reform it added a political program—the struggle against foreign domination—and this was its originality. The majority of its leaders prided themselves on being *sharīfs* (descendants of the Prophet through his daughter Fāṭimah); victory over the invaders gave them a social importance that was based on an assumption of holiness (*barakah*). From this time on, being a marabout and being a *sharīf* were closely linked in the eyes of the people if not in reality.

FROM BROTHERHOOD TO PRINCIPALITY. The parent *zāwiyah,* which was a center for teaching and meditation, trained missionaries whose task was to spread the good word far and wide. The followers gathered in a special chapel, also known as a *zāwiyah,* to recite their *wird* ("litany"). Thus the *ṭarīqah* (brotherhood) came into being. With the weakening of the central power and the gradual splitting up of the country, the people turned more and more to the shaykhs of *zāwiyahs* who thus became, sometimes much against their will, the new political leaders. Similar circumstances surrounded the birth of the great North African brotherhoods: the Nāṣirīyah and Wazzānīyah in the mid-seventeenth century, and the Darqāwīyah, Tijānīyah, and Sanūsīyah during the nineteenth century. The *zāwiyah* thus took on diverse forms: it could be a monastery, brotherhood, or principality. On the one hand, it united the faithful over and above their traditional splits; on the other hand, it created new splits with its activism. In fact the *zāwiyah* competed with the political authority and the clerical institution on their respective grounds. In the eyes of his disciples, the shaykh was in possession of a beneficial power that enabled him to work wonders (*karāmāt*). When he died he became the object of a cult (*ziyārah*) because of his power of intercession (*shafāʿah*). From the point of view of its organization, the brotherhood had something of a secret society or, at the very least, a private club about it. The principle of the brotherhood posed a problem for orthodoxy. However, until the beginning of the nineteenth century, every inhabitant of the Maghreb, literate or illiterate, was a member of one or several of them. Because it was a family affair, women and children were included in the brotherhood even if they did not usually participate in the ceremonies. The authorities and the clerics were unable to rise up openly against such a widespread practice.

The zāwiyah and the naturalist substratum. Each brotherhood produced a vast body of hagiographic literature listing the qualities that placed its successive leaders among the chosen and omitting any details of their behavior that were not quite orthodox. Nevertheless the official religious hierarchy remained suspicious. What was the true practice of the *zāwiyah*? Those who knew it from the inside were sworn to secrecy, while those who remained outside could say nothing with authority. Were the old pre-Islamic cults lingering on in the *zāwiyahs*? The Sunnīs insinuated that this was so but were unable to produce solid proof. And in any case, even if the naturalist cults were kept up in secret, they were reinterpreted in an Islamic language. The notions of *barakah, karāmah, shafāʿah,* and *sirr* ("secret") were directly linked to the teachings of the Prophet.

For three centuries the Islam of the brotherhoods, characterized by faith in hereditary grace, a supererogatory cult, and a hierarchical organization (which related it to the Shīʿī *daʿwah*), dominated the scene in the Maghreb so overwhelmingly that any outside observer took it for the true Islam, with the doctrine of the jurists being mere rationalization. Later history showed that this was not the case. From the mid-nineteenth century on, scriptural Islam returned in force; then began the long struggle against the *zāwiyahs* that finally brought them into disrepute. And yet one question remains: If the brotherhoods were so popular, was it not because they fulfilled an affective need that official Islam was unable to satisfy? Whatever the case, they gave rise to a renewal of literary expression. Whereas classical Arabic poetry (the *qaṣidah,* "ode") was becoming bogged down in a welter of archaisms and stylistic artifices, the new emotionalism that emerged from the brotherhoods gave rise to *malḥūn,* poetry in the spoken language that was meant to be sung. Created by artists versed in the subtleties of classical prosody, *malḥūn* produced genuine masterpieces.

THE ISLAM OF THE SALAFĪYAH. Throughout the Maghreb, the second half of the eighteenth century was a period of recovery. The power of the central authority was reinforced, trade revived, and the cities prospered again. At the same time as did the Wahhābīyah of Arabia, the *faqīhs* of the Maghreb began to criticize the most absurd aspects of popular religiosity. Their movement claimed to continue the inspiration of the first Muslims *(salaf),* hence the name Salafīyah conferred on it by historians.

Pre-Salafīyah and Salafīyah. The Salafīyah were not the first reformers to appear in the modern history of Islam, so how can they be distinguished, apart from chronology? The ʿAlawid sultans of Morocco, Muḥammad III (d. 1790) and Sulaymān (d. 1822), seeking to return to a simpler form of religion, criticized the subtleties of the jurists and the supererogatory practices of the brotherhoods. Muḥammad ibn al-Madanī Gannūn (d. 1885) spoke out vehemently against music and ritual dances. The book written by Ibn al-Ḥājj (d. 1336) against all kinds of innovation, *Al-madkhal* (The Introduction), was reprinted, and numerous clerics published summaries of it. Thus, from the mid-eighteenth century on normative Islam began to regain control, but it was in the minority and it attacked only the most aberrant aspects of the marabout movement, never its basic tenets. This phase is what this article shall call the pre-Salafīyah.

The Salafīyah in the proper sense of the term appeared at the end of the nineteenth century, when several Arab countries, including Algeria (in 1830) and Tunisia (in 1881), came under the yoke of European imperialism. The movement expressed an awareness of the failure of traditional Islamic society in the face of foreign domination, as well as a desire for radical reform in the intellectual and social domains. From this standpoint the Islam of the *zāwiyahs* appeared as a distortion of true Islam, an alteration that lay at the origin of the decadence of the Muslims. The Salafīyah declared total war on maraboutic Islam.

The North African Salafīyah formed part of the movement that had been launched by the pan-Islamic leader Jamāl al-Dīn al-Afghānī (d. 1897) and his Egyptian disciple Muḥammad ʿAbduh (d. 1905). The review *Al-ʿurwah al-wuthqā* (The Strongest Bond), which they published for a short time in Paris, was widely read by enlightened Tunisians. ʿAbduh himself stayed briefly in Tunisia and Algiers in 1901/2. The Cairo review *Al-manār* (The Lighthouse), launched at ʿAbduh's instigation in 1898 by his disciple Rashīd Riḍā, had an immediate influence on the pupils of the *madrasahs*. It shaped the minds of such future leaders of Islamic reformism as the Tunisian Bashīr Ṣfar (d. 1937), the Algerians Ṭayyib al-ʿUqbī (d. 1962) and ʿAbd al-Hamīd ibn Bādīs (d. 1940), and, to a lesser extent, the Moroccans Abū Shuʿayb al-Dukkālī (d. 1940) and al-ʿArbī al-ʿAlawī (d. 1962).

The critique of the zāwiyahs. In 1937 the Algerian Mubārak al-Mīlī (d. 1962) published a pamphlet called *Risālat al-shirk wa-maẓāhirih* (Aspects of Polytheism), in which he summarized the main criticisms leveled by the Salafīyah against the brotherhoods. From the point of view of faith, he argued, the practices of the brotherhoods are tainted with *shirk* ("associationism"). Those who give offerings believe that this is the price to be paid for the intercession of the patron saint of the *zāwiyah.* However much the shaykh maintains that it is God alone who really intervenes, the donors still believe that it is the saint; they associate another being with God and thus commit the worst of sins.

From a legal point of view, the brotherhood is an innovation. Its members frequent a chapel, not a mosque, and this in order to recite prayers rather than the Qurʾān; they fast during periods other than the month of Ramaḍān and go on pilgrimages to places other than Mecca. According to the Salafīyah, this is a cult that has elements in common with Islam and yet is distinct from it. New *zāwiyahs* are created every day, and the Muslim community, instead of being united around the Qurʾān, is splitting up into sects that rise up against one another. Finally, from a social point of view, the *zāwiyah* is a school of *taqlīd* (the act of following blindly) and *tawakkul* (fatalism). The disciple follows the shaykh in the belief that he can work wonders. Thus parasitism is encouraged. The *zāwiyah* is indeed active, but only in that it recruits people and takes them away from a productive life. In short, for the Salafīyah the *zāwiyahs* divide the Muslims, disarm them morally, impoverish them economically, and enslave them spiritually. They mark a reappearance of the paganism (*jāhilīyah*) that the Prophet had fought against. A return to the religion of the one God is a return to freedom, to a sense of action and solidarity, in other words, to the qualities responsible for the greatness of the ancestors.

From Salafīyah to nationalism. The Salafīyah were at work in a Maghreb that was dominated by European colonialism; they were not members of the *ʿulamāʾ*, even if they had been taught in such traditional institutions as the Zaytūnah in Tunis or the Qarawīyīn in Fez. They were fighting above all against the leaders of the *zāwiyahs*, but they also criticized the *faqīhs* who, prudently favoring middle-of-the-road solutions, had little liking for their vehemence. The Salafīyah drew their strength from the anticolonialist feelings harbored by the majority of the North African people. In response to the question "Why have we been colonized?" the Salafīyah gave a forceful answer: "Because we have been morally disarmed by the brotherhoods." The reply to this criticism came from Aḥmad ibn ʿAliwah (d. 1934) in Algeria and from Aḥmad Skīraj (d. 1944) in Morocco, but because it was purely religious in form it caused little stir.

The triumph of Salafīyah can be explained by the social and political environment of the time. As the cities became poorer, the Islam of the brotherhoods predominated. Then, during colonization, the cities recovered their prosperity and gave rise to a new merchant class whose lifestyle owed nothing to the practices of the *zāwiyahs*. It was from this class that Salafīyah drew the strength that enabled it to confront the colonial administration, the shaykhs of the brotherhoods, and the prudent *ʿulamāʾ*. However, because it was at once a religious and a sociopolitical movement, the Salafīyah had to follow the same evolution as the society, which, becoming ever more urbanized and politicized, obliged it to merge first with liberalism, then with nationalism, and finally with socialism. In this way the movement lost its specificity, as illustrated by the careers of ʿAbd al-ʿAzīz al-Thaʿālibī (d. 1937) in Tunisia and ʿAllāl al-Fāsī (d. 1974) in Morocco, who began as Salafī thinkers and wound up nationalist leaders.

POLITICAL ISLAM. In the present-day Maghreb, the state completely dominates both the society and the individual. Traditional institutions—*madrasahs*, *zāwiyahs*, *ḥabūs* (religious foundations)—are under the close supervision of their respective ministries. In Morocco the *ʿulamāʾ*, organized on a national level in a *jamʿīyat ʿulamāʾ al-Maghrib* (Moroccan ʿUlamāʾ Association) and in each province in a *majlis ʿilmi* (ʿUlamāʾ Council), are consulted on questions concerning dogma or the life of society in general, but they are allowed no say whatsoever in political affairs. In Algeria, the FLN (National Liberation Front), the sole political party, monopolizes public activity by law; in Tunisia, it is the dominant PSD (Destourian Socialist Party); in Libya, the people's committees, while the *ʿulamāʾ*. are no more than civil servants.

The new dichotomy. After their liberation from the colonial yoke, the states of the Maghreb adopted the Salafi position as their official ideology. What has become of the Islam of the *zāwiyahs*? Scholars do not agree on this subject. The religious evolution of the Maghreb seems to have followed two quite separate paths. On the one hand, there are the Khārijī and Shīʿī schisms, which, containing elements of prehistoric polytheism, influenced the Almohads and the practices of the brotherhoods; on the other hand, there is strict monotheism, expressed at first through the Kairouan Mālikīyah, later redefined by the Sunnism of the thirteenth and fourteenth centuries and revived by the modern Salafīyah. This dichotomy could explain Ibn Khaldūn's opposition between rural and urban civilization. If so, the growing urbanization and industrialization of the independent Maghreb, which requires an increasingly rationalist religiosity, constantly reinforces the Salafīyah to the detriment of residual naturalist practices.

However, urbanization itself creates new needs. The city is never wholly middle class; it also contains a subproletariat that remains close to its peasant roots and an intelligentsia that is socially mixed and vulnerable to unemployment. The former group (the women in particular) indulges in magical practices, while the latter zealously seeks out mystical emotion or political activism. Under these circumstances, there could well be a revival of the *zāwiyahs*, but they would be used to fulfill a role that is defined more by present needs than by the legacy of the past. This fact is common to all the great cities in the world.

Political temptation. The Salafī ideology, which is spread among the masses by the machinery of the state, retains its original activist character. As the state is not always faithful, in practice, to Qurʾanic prescription, individuals who adopt this ideology find themselves on the horns of a dilemma: Either they envisage it as a purely spiritual exercise or they derive a program of political reform from it. Now this dilemma is not confined to the Maghreb; it takes on a particular form only to the extent that religious experience in the Maghreb has distinct features.

North Africa has never produced intellectual mystics like the Andalusian Ibn ʿArabī, the Egyptian Ibn al-Fāriḍ (d. 1235), or the Persian Jalāl al-Dīn Rūmī (d. 1273); rather, it is a land of ascetics, educators, missionaries, and *mujāhids* (warriors of the faith), all of whom were close to the ordinary people and sensitive to the problems of the community. In the same way the great Mālikī *ʿulamāʾ* were inclined to practicality and moderation, with little concern for methodological subtleties. It is most significant that the greatest author born in the Maghreb, Ibn Khaldūn, chose as his field of investigation the history and evolution of societies. In the Maghreb more than anywhere else, Islam seems to have been less individualist and intellectual, much more pragmatic and concerned with the community. One can also assume that it will retain these characteristics in the future, particularly in the absence of any opposing tendency thus far. The practice of the *zāwiyah,* wherever it remains in evidence, is increasingly purified by the *ʿulamāʾ*. In people's minds Islam is above all a law (*sharīʿah*) that expresses the solidarity of the faithful, as can be seen in the way the majority is still attached to the fasting at Ramaḍān and the pilgrimage to Mecca. Islam as it is envisaged by the Society of Muslim Brothers (al-Ikhwān al-Muslimūn) does have a certain influence on official Salafī thought, but until now it has remained peripheral.

SEE ALSO Berber Religion; Christianity, article on Christianity in North Africa; Judaism, articles on Judaism in the Middle East and North Africa to 1492 and Judaism in the Middle East and North Africa since 1492; Khārijīs; Modernism, article on Islamic Modernism; Rites of Passage, article on Muslim Rites; Shiism; Ṭarīqah.

BIBLIOGRAPHY

For a general historical introduction, see Jamil M. Abun-Nasr's *A History of the Maghrib* (Cambridge, 1971) and my *L'histoire du Maghreb: Un essai de synthèse* (Paris, 1970), translated by Ralph Manheim as *The History of the Maghrib: An Interpretive Essay* (Princeton, 1977). The problem of the pre-Islamic substrate is dealt with in François Decret and Muhammed Fantar's *L'Afrique du Nord dans l'antiquité: Histoire et civilisation des origines au cinquième siècle* (Paris, 1981). See also Marcel Bénabou's *La résistance africaine à la romanisation* (Paris, 1976) and W. H. C. Frend's *The Donatist Church: A Movement of Protest in Roman North Africa* (1952; reprint, Oxford, 1971). These are to be compared with ethnographical studies such as Edward Westermarck's *Ritual and Belief in Morocco,* 2 vols. (1926; reprint, New Hyde Park, N. Y., 1968), and Émile Dermenghem's *Le culte des saints dans l'Islam maghrébin,* 4th ed. (Paris, 1954).

Mohamed Talbi's *L'émirat aghlabide 184–296/800–909: Histoire politique* (Paris, 1966) summarizes and criticizes the literature concerning the beginnings of Islam. Roger Le Tourneau's *The Almohad Movement in North Africa in the Twelfth and Thirteenth Centuries* (Princeton, N. J., 1969) gives a brief survey of the work of Ibn Tūmart and his successors. The Almohad organization is described in J. F. P. Hopkins's *Medieval Muslim Government in Barbary until the Sixth Century of the Hijra* (London, 1958). For the *zāwiyahs* see T. H. Weir's *The Shaikhs of Morocco in the Sixteenth Century* (Edinburgh, 1904) and Jacques Berque's *Al-Yousi: Problèmes de la culture marocaine au dix-huitième siècle* (Paris, 1958).

The Salafī movement is studied in depth by Ali Merad in his *Le réformisme muṣūlman en Algérie de 1925 à 1940: Essai d'histoire religieuse et sociale* (The Hague, 1967) and by Arnold H. Green in his *The Tunisian Ulama, 1873–1915: Social Structure and Response to Ideological Currents* (Leiden, 1978). The account given by ʿAllāl al-Fāsi in *The Independence Movements in Arab North Africa,* translated by Hazem Zaki Nuseibeh (Washington, D. C., 1954), is an important one. A defense of maraboutism is presented in Martin Lings's *A Moslem Saint of the Twentieth Century: Shaikh Aḥmad al-Alawi,* 2d ed. (Berkeley, Calif., 1973).

The anthropological point of view can be found in Clifford Geertz's *Islam Observed: Religious Development in Morocco and Indonesia* (New Haven, Conn., 1968), which uses Weberian concepts, and Ernest Gellner's *Muslim Society* (Cambridge, 1981), which is more structuralist. Dale F. Eickelman's *Moroccan Islam, Tradition and Society in a Pilgrimage Center* (Austin, 1976) is descriptive. Vincent Crapanzano's *The Hamadsha: A Study in Moroccan Ethnopsychiatry* (Princeton, 1973) is more limited in scope. To the list can be added the self-criticism of Paul Rabinow in *Reflections on Fieldwork in Morocco* (Berkeley, Calif., 1977). The present-day situation is analyzed acutely and competently by Elbaki Hermassi in *Leadership and National Development in North Africa* (Berkeley, Calif., 1972) and by Mohammed Arkoun in *La pensée arabe* (Paris, 1975).

ABDALLĀH LAROUI (1987)
Translated from French by Glyn Thoiron

ISLAM: ISLAM IN ANDALUSIA

Al-Andalus was the name used by the Muslim population of the Iberian Peninsula for the territory that was under Muslim rule from the times of the conquest in 711 CE until the fall of the Nasrid kingdom of Granada in 1492. That territory varied through the centuries. During the Umayyad period (eighth–tenth centuries), Muslims ruled most of the regions of the Iberian Peninsula, with the exception of part of the lands situated north of the river Duero and south of the Pyrenees, where Christians managed to establish small independent kingdoms. A major shift in the balance of power between Muslims and Christians occurred in 1085, when Toledo, the former Visigothic capital, was lost forever to the Muslims when it fell into the hands of the king of Castile, Alfonso VI.

The Muslim conquest of al-Andalus had taken place during the Umayyad caliphate, with its seat in Damascus, and some of the settlers in the Iberian Peninsula were clients of the Umayyads. When the latter's rule was put to an end by the new dynasty of the Abbasids (who moved their capital to Baghdad), a member of the fallen dynasty, ʿAbd al-Raḥmān I (r. 756–788), escaped from the massacre of his family and with the help of the Umayyad clients managed to establish himself as ruler of al-Andalus. The new Umayyad emirate had Cordova as its capital. During the ninth century, the Umayyads fought hard to maintain their power in the Iberian Peninsula, shaken by the attempts of Arabs, Berbers, and local converts to establish autonomous political governments. The eighth Umayyad ruler, ʿAbd al-Raḥmān III (r. 912–961), succeeded in regaining control of al-Andalus and proclaimed himself caliph in order to give a firmer basis to his rule and to counteract the danger represented by the establishment of a Fāṭimid (Shīʿī) caliphate in North Africa, while taking advantage at the same time of the decline of the Abbasid caliphate in the East. Political unity, general stability, economic flourishing, and cultural achievements were some of the traits of the tenth century, although the minority of the third Umayyad caliph and the military reforms carried out by his powerful chamberlain, al-Manṣūr ibn Abi ʿAmir, eventually opened the door to civil war.

The conquest of Toledo in 1085 was partly the result of the political fragmentation of al-Andalus that took place during the eleventh century. The administrative centralization achieved during the tenth century disappeared with the collapse of the (second) Umayyad caliphate. It was abolished in 1031, but before that date independent Muslim kingdoms had already arisen, the most important being those of Seville, Toledo, and Zaragoza. With different ethnic backgrounds, the rulers of the so-called Party or Taifa kingdoms were engaged in a complex internal political game of war and peace, in which the intervention of the Christian kingdoms played a major role. Muslim military weakness led to the payment of tribute to those Christian kingdoms. This situation was novel in al-Andalus and almost exceptional in the Muslim world, as the predominant historical experience of Muslims had been until then one of conquest and rule, not of submission to non-Muslims. But money was not a deterrent to Christian military expansion, as became clear when Barbastro and Coimbra fell into Christian hands in the years 1063–1064, followed by Coria in 1079 and Toledo in 1085.

By this time, the need to seek military help outside al-Andalus had become acute and an appeal was made to the Almoravids by some of the Taifa rulers. Of Berber origin, the Almoravid dynasty had succeeded in establishing a unitary kingdom in the Maghreb (nowadays Morocco), having as its capital Marrakech. The powerful Almoravid army crossed the Straits of Gibraltar and defeated the Christians in the battle of Zallaqa (1086), although they were unable to regain most of the territory already lost to the Christians or to retain some major towns (Valencia was in Christian hands from 1094 to 1102, Zaragoza was taken in 1118, Lisbon in 1147, Tortosa in 1148). Almoravid political legitimization revolved around the abolition of illegal taxes and the pursuit of holy war *(jihād)*. As this program failed, the support the Almoravids had attracted both among the elites and the masses of al-Andalus declined and by the third decade of the twelfth century, political and religious movements aiming at autonomous government had begun in several towns, shaking Almoravid rule in al-Andalus. The Almoravids were facing, at the same time, a new religious movement in their Maghrebi territory, that of the Almohads, who threatened Almoravid power both politically and ideologically.

The Almohad movement was founded by the Berber Messianic reformer Ibn Tumart; his successor as political leader was also a Berber who adopted an Arabic genealogy in order to proclaim himself caliph. The movement started in the south of Morocco in the first decades of the twelfth century, expanding from there to dominate the whole of the Maghreb (Morocco, Algeria, Tunisia) and al-Andalus. Aiming at a radical political and religious revival, the Almohads found support among disparate groups in Andalusi society who shared some of their puritanical reformist policies, although it was mostly the use of violence that helped them suppress, at least for some time, the opposition of those groups and individuals that either disagreed with their program or were against its more extremist aspects. Although the Almohads were able for some time to check Christian military advance, their armies suffered a major defeat in the battle of Las Navas de Tolosa in the year 1212. This defeat had been preceded and was followed by the loss of major towns in what was left of al-Andalus: Silves was conquered in 1190, Cordova in 1236, Valencia in 1238, Murcia in 1243, and Seville in 1248.

While Almohad rule collapsed both in the Maghreb and in al-Andalus, there were attempts at replacing it with local forms of government. This happened in al-Andalus according to a pattern that had been followed before during the collapse of Umayyad and Almoravid rules. Military men, urban elites, and charismatic leaders aimed at creating viable political and military entities in order to ensure the maintenance of the remaining territory under Andalusi rule. Only one such attempt succeeded, that founded by Ibn al-Ahmar in Granada and the surrounding area. From the middle of the thirteenth century until 1492, the Nasrid kingdom of Granada managed to survive by taking advantage of the internal dissensions both among the Christian kingdoms and those Muslim states that had been created in North Africa after the demise of the Almohad empire. The political unity achieved by Isabel of Castille and Fernando de Aragón signaled the end of the small Muslim kingdom of Granada. In the same year that Christopher Columbus disembarked in America and Jews were expelled from Spain, Granada was conquered and al-Andalus as a political entity ceased to exist. But the term survived in the form of Andalucía, the name given to the southern regions of Spain, this being the area where Muslim rule had lasted longest.

ARABIZATION, ISLAMICIZATION, AND THE RELIGIOUS MINORITIES OF AL-ANDALUS. The Muslim armies that conquered the Iberian Peninsula were formed mostly of Berbers, with small groups of Arabs. The number of the Arabs increased when a Syrian army sent by the Umayyad caliph in Damascus to suppress a Berber revolt in North Africa sought refuge in al-Andalus. The first Umayyad ruler, ʿAbd al-Raḥmān I, attracted other members of his family to his capital. The number of Arabs also increased by intermarriage with the local population, as their descendants became Arabs due to their strict patrilineal genealogical system, and also through the establishment of patronage ties with other ethnic groups. Arabic tribal affiliations (*nisbas*) became a distinguishing feature of the Andalusi population, in contrast to that of the Maghreb (Morocco), where Arab settlement was scarce. Arabic ethnicity and language were cultivated and praised by men of letters and poets, and also by historians, both under Umayyad rule and during the eleventh century, when the legitimization of some of the Taifa kings, such as the Abbasids of Seville, was grounded on their Arab ancestry.

It is difficult to establish for how long the Berber conquerors and first settlers of al-Andalus managed to preserve their own language, which has left very few traces. When ʿAbd al-Raḥmān III proclaimed himself caliph in 929, one of his policies was the consolidation of an Andalusi identity which, while not suppressing the Arab component, stressed the Islamic unifying factor. This Andalusi identity was felt to be under threat when new groups of Berbers, maintaining their language and tribal organization, settled in al-Andalus and seized political power in the eleventh century. The possibility (that many saw as a danger) of a Berberization of al-Andalus increased when the Iberian Peninsula became part of the Berber Maghrebi empires of the Almoravids and the Almohads. The complex dynamics at play between Arab and Berber ethnicities through the history of al-Andalus still await a monographic study.

Muslim Arabs substituted the Visigoths as rulers over the local Hispano-Roman population, who were (even if only nominally) Christians and whose languages were Latin and Romance. They, together with the Jews, became "protected peoples" (*dhimmis*), being allowed to preserve their religion and their community life, although always in a position of subordination to the Muslims. The Christians of al-Andalus are commonly referred to as Mozarabs, although this term (not found in the Arabic sources) should be limited to the Arabized Christians in order not to obscure the complex linguistic and cultural situation of the Christian communities living under Muslim rule.

The language, culture, and religion, often inextricably linked, of the new rulers had a deep attraction for those Christians who were more directly in contact with the Muslims. Latin culture was still predominant in the ninth century, but in the tenth century the Christians of al-Andalus started to translate their religious literature (the Psalms, the canons of the Visigothic church) into Arabic. The bishop Recemundo (also known as Rabiʿ ibn Zayd) took part in the translation into Arabic of Latin and Greek works (such as Orosius's historical work, Dioscorides's treatise, and the famous Cordovan Calendar) that was carried out during the Umayyad caliphate. This trend towards acculturation had been harshly fought in the previous century by two Cordovan Christians, Eulogius and Alvarus, who promoted the movement of the so-called voluntary martyrs. These were Christian men and women, some of them born from religiously mixed marriages, who voluntarily sought martyrdom by publicly insulting Islam in reaction to what was perceived as the increasing loss of their identity. The church hierarchy did not favor their movement, which eventually faded away.

The linguistic and cultural Arabization of the Christian population took place with different rhythms and characteristics according to location and social and economic status. The issue of Romance-Arabic bilingualism of the indigenous population of the Iberian Peninsula has been hotly debated in spite of, or more precisely, because of the scarcity of available sources and the contradictory interpretations to which those sources have been subject. Even if demography was in principle favorable to the Romance language spoken by the local population, Romance monolingualism survived only among those sectors who were rural, poor, illiterate, and Christian. Bilingualism was characteristic of the urban settings, while Arabic was the dominant language among the literate groups of society. In the tenth century, Arabic became the predominant written language and in the eleventh and twelfth centuries, the predominant spoken language. Arabic monolingualism (with diglossia between written Arabic and the spoken dialects) became the norm from the thirteenth century onward. The experience of al-Andalus thus differed from that of Iran, where the local language survived the process of Islamicization. Also in contrast to Iran, there was no cultural *shuʿubiyya* in al-Andalus, that is, the glorification and preservation of the pre-Islamic culture as part of the struggle of the convert local populations to achieve equality with the new rulers.

In opposition to what happened with Latin and Romance language and culture, the Jews of al-Andalus were able to maintain Hebrew as their religious and literary language and it became pivotal in the defence of their cultural identity, while at the same time they carried out a deep absorption of Arabic language and culture. In this context, a golden age was made possible. As David Wasserstein (1997) has put it, almost all the greatest poets writing in Hebrew in the Middle Ages were Iberian (Judah ha-Levi, Ibn Gabirol, Samuel Ha-Nagid, Moses Ibn Ezra), and some of the most important works of Jewish thought are also the product of Iberian Jewry (the *Kuzari*, the *Guide for the Perplexed)*.

With the general exception of the Jews, Arabization was closely linked to the process of conversion to Islam. An early majority of Muslims in the population of al-Andalus was achieved in the first half of the tenth century and from that time onward, Christians lost the demographic battle.

The Hegemony of Malikism and Its Alternatives. The main distinguishing feature of Andalusi Islam is its lack of the religious pluralism expressed by the co-existence of the four legal schools (Malikism, Ḥanafism, Shafiʿism, and Hanbalism) recognized within the Muslim Sunnī world from the tenth century onwards. While Malikism reigned supreme in al-Andalus, Ḥanafism seems to have been banned, while the attempts at introducing Shafiʿism and Traditionalist trends akin to Hanbalism failed. The main alternatives to Malikism were locally produced: the Cordovan Ibn Hazm's Zahirism, a legal school generally considered too radical for Sunnīsm, and the Almohad program of religious revival and reform.

The early Muslim settlers of al-Andalus were soldiers. Their religious and legal needs were catered for by their leaders, acting as judges and directors of prayer. The legal doctrine associated with a Syrian jurist, al-Awzaʿi (d. 773), is generally considered to have been followed by those judges, until it was replaced by Medinan (from Medina, the town in the Arabia Peninsula where the Prophet ruled and died) jurisprudence at the time when a new scholarly class was being formed. The emergence and consolidation of a scholarly milieu can be documented from the late eighth and early ninth century onwards. The first scholars (*ʿulamāʾ*) came mostly from the army milieu, which they left in what seems to have been a process of professional diversification on the part of the ruling elites. Soon, local converts devoted themselves to learning as a means to social advancement. By traveling to the central lands of Islamdom for commerce, in search of knowledge, and to carry out the pilgrimage, Andalusis became aware of and integrated themselves into the Muslim world of scholarship.

Umayyad rule had lasting consequences in how this world was shaped in the Iberian Peninsula. As the tenth-century geographer al-Muqaddasi noted, among the early schools of law, the one associated with Abū Ḥanīfah (d. 767) and later known as Ḥanafism was rejected. The Abbasids, the dynasty that had put an end to Umayyad rule, had generally favored this legal trend that was also supported by the Aghlabids, their representatives in Ifrīqiyah, so that the Umayyads of al-Andalus could only view it with suspicion. Furthermore, Ḥanafism was associated with ʿAlī and the town of Kufa and some of its doctrines were considered to be pro-Shīʿah. This again could only favor its rejection on the part of the Umayyads, whose rise to power had taken place by fighting against ʿAlī's party. The other major legal trend in the eighth century was that associated with Medina and more specifically with Mālik ibn Anas (d. 796). It has been said that Andalusi scholars adopted the latter's legal doctrine because their travels took them to Egypt and the Ḥijāz, where they studied with Mālik's pupils. But if geography certainly had a role, it was associated with politics, as the first Andalusi scholars did not travel to Iraq, the center of Abbasid power. Also, some aspects of Medinan-Mālikī doctrine were seen as being congenial with Umayyad history and legitimacy.

An Andalusi scholar of Berber origin, Yahya ibn Yahya al-Laythi, had a crucial role in bringing together Mālik's and his pupils' doctrines and the Umayyads of al-Andalus. A revolt against al-Hakam I (r. 796–822) that took place in Cordova during the year 817 and in which Yahya ibn Yahya took part made it clear to the Umayyad emir that the emerging group of scholars could channel either popular opposition or support to the ruler and that without them Umayyad power could be put in jeopardy. For his part, Yahya ibn Yahya realized how advantageous the ruler's support was in getting the upper hand for his own followers in the struggle among the emerging factions of scholars. A pattern of collaboration between the ruler and the scholars was established and Māliki ʿulamaʾ started serving the Umayyads as judges, legal experts and advisers, and in other legal charges. A rapidly growing body of legal literature began to be transmitted in al-Andalus and soon also to be authored by Andalusi scholars, such as ʿAbd al-Mālik ibn Habib (d. 852–853), al-ʿUtbi (d. 868–869) and others.

By the tenth century, Andalusi jurists belonged, with few exceptions, to the Mālikī legal school. Andalusi Mālikīs were well integrated in chains of teachers and pupils, whose relationships, achievements, and social practices started to be recorded in biographical dictionaries. A number of legal treatises were used for the training of pupils. The proclamation of the Umayyad caliphate in 929 consolidated Malikism as an "official" legal school, making it a crucial element of the Andalusi identity promoted by both rulers and scholars, and thus separating al-Andalus from heterodox Fāṭimid North Africa and also marking it within the Sunnī world. The Umayyad caliphs of Cordova stressed the association of Malikism with Medina, the town where the Prophet had acted as ruler, thus implying that by following this legal school, Medina had been relocated in the Iberian Peninsula and that it was as if the Prophet himself was ruling again over the Muslims.

But even if al-Andalus was Mālikī and only Mālikī, this does not mean that it was monolithic. There were always discrepancies within the school, most of them deriving (or said to derive) from the various interpretations of Mālik's teachings by his pupils and also from the latter's own contributions to the body of legal doctrines and practices. The existence of such legal differences *(ikhtilaf)* was accepted, as it was the inevitable result of the human effort at understanding (*fiqh*) the revealed law (*sharīʿah*), but it also led to polemics and sometimes to harsh attacks against those jurists with whom one disagreed, attacks which could even become accusations of religious deviation. One of the main areas of disagreement was how to carry out the process of traditionalizing the early body of Mālikī literature, which contained very little reference to Prophetic tradition (*ḥadīth*).

During the ninth century, "the conviction became absolute that law is justified only if it can be related hermeneutically to Prophetic exempla, and not if it is presented discursively as emanating from an ongoing juristic tradition" (Calder, pp. 18–19). The Eastern jurist al-Shāfiʿī (d. 820) devoted himself to the science of the fundaments of law *(usul)* and forcefully argued that law had to be derived from both Qurʾān and *ḥadīth,* and that the methodology for such derivation had to be strictly regulated. At the same time, great effort was made in the central lands of Islamdom to make available compilations of *ḥadīth* to the jurists.

These tendencies would soon echo in al-Andalus. Andalusis started traveling to Iraq by the second half of the ninth century and brought back the doctrines of the Traditionalists. Some of those Andalusis won to Traditionalism were radicals, who rejected Malikism and tried to introduce Shafiʿism. The Cordovan Baqi ibn Makhlad (d. 889), who wrote a voluminous compilation of *ḥadīth* (now lost), excelled among them. But his extremism provoked the legal establishment and he was accused of heterodoxy. The ruler, who saw the advantage of scholarly infighting, saved his life. Eventually, those Mālikīs who were receptive to the new trends managed to Traditionalize their legal doctrines without becoming Shāfiʿī. This was a long process and its complete story still needs more study. The most prominent jurists along this road were Ibn Waddah (d. 900), al-Asili (d. 1002), Abū ʿUmar ibn ʿAbd al-Barr (d. 1071), Abu-l-Walid al-Baji (d. 1081), Ibn Rushd al-Jadd (d. 1126), Abū Bakr ibn al-ʿArabi (d. 1148), and al-Shatibi (d. 1399). In their writings dealing with *ḥadīth* literature, Qurʾān commentary, and legal methodology, they carried out the adaptation of Malikism to the new legal trends. Of crucial importance were the commentaries written by Ibn Rushd al-Jadd of the two founding texts of Western Malikism, Sahnun's *Mudawwana* and al-ʿUtbi's *Mustakhraja,* as his effort was directed at connecting the legal doctrine found in those two early texts with the Qurʾān, the Prophetic Tradition, the consensus and analogical reasoning (*qiyas*), the four legal sources established by al-Shāfiʿī. In other words, Ibn Rushd al-Jadd was able to insert early Mālikī legal opinion (*ra'y*) within the context of *usul* methodology, without much substantial change being introduced in traditional Andalusi Maliki practice.

The endeavor of these reforming Mālikī jurists from the time of Abū ʿUmar ibn ʿAbd al-Barr onwards was greatly influenced by the challenge posed by Ibn Hazm's doctrines to Andalusi Malikism. Ibn Hazm (d. 1064) left Malikism to become a Ẓāhirī, thus adhering to a very literal interpretation of the religious sources (Qurʾān and *ḥadīth*), limiting consensus to that of the companions of the Prophet and rejecting analogical reasoning. After abandoning an unsuccessful career in the dangerous waters of Taifa politics, Ibn Hazm dedicated his life to producing a complete alternative to the Mālikī legal system. According to Ibn Hazm, Mālikīs considered it wrong to act according to the contents of a *ḥadīth* if the practice of the community was contrary to it. He put all his considerable intellectual gifts to work to reverse that trend, making *ḥadīth* the basis for practice. Had he succeeded, it would have meant the disruption of the Andalusi scholarly milieu and a complete renovation of the urban elites, closely associated, as in any other Islamic region, to the world of scholarship. Ibn Hazm's aims probably included this social, and eventually political, disruption, in which he might have seen a solution for the problems he denounced in Andalusi society under the Taifa kings. But Ibn Hazm did not succeed in making al-Andalus adhere to his legal vision. Nevertheless, he left an enduring legacy. Mālikīs were forced to react to the formidable challenge represented by his writings and his doctrines, so that the most able of Mālikī scholars devoted their energies to refuting Ibn Hazm. And by doing so, Malikism was inevitably changed.

Part of Ibn Hazm's vision can be found in the religious and legal policies of the Almohads. Their struggle for radical reform was formulated as a return to the times of the prophet Muḥammad, whose teachings had been revived by their Messianic founder, the Mahdi Ibn Tumart. The latter's successor, the Almohad caliph, was to ensure correct interpretation of the religious sources and the disappearance of diversity of opinion through his acting as the vicar of God or caliph, and through the training of a body of scholars, the *talaba,* charged with the diffusion and control of Almohad theological and legal doctrines. In many ways, this version of Almohadism was closer to Shiism than to Sunnīsm, so that the proposal has been made to name this experiment of radical reform the "Sunnīticization of Shiism" (Fierro, 1999, p. 232, note 23). It eventually failed, not only because of the political and military collapse of the Almohads, but also because Malikis soon reacted against those aspects of Almohadism that represented a departure from the Sunnī understanding that, as important as revelation is, the historical experience of the Muslim community has always to be taken into account. Those with totalitarian leanings who try to dismiss that historical experience put themselves in the margins of Sunnism.

Religious Doctrines and Practices. Legal and law-related writings constitute the main body of the Muslim literature written and transmitted in al-Andalus. Islamic jurisprudence (*fiqh*) regulated the relations among men and also between man and God, and Andalusi scholars, like their colleagues in the rest of the Islamic world, devoutly engaged in the search of God's norms to humankind, an effort that at the same time allowed them gaining a livelihood as *qadis,* jurists, notaries, and teachers.

A special feature of this endeavor is the rich tradition of *fatawa* literature, where the legal opinions on a variety of issues formulated by Andalusi jurists were collected. As Hallaq has pointed out, whether in his capacity as a private legal expert or as an advisor to the court, the jurisconsult determined the law. The *fatawa* literature thus represents a privileged vantage point from which to analyze the interplay between law, society, and religion. Studies devoted to it in the past decades have opened new and promising venues of research on many aspects of Andalusi social and religious practices. This literature gives information mostly on urban areas. The possibility of learning about what was going on in rural areas is limited, although archaeology (which has greatly developed in the last decades) has made them better known, while the incorporation of anthropological knowledge has also opened new perspectives, as in the case of the function of holy men and charismatic leaders among the Berbers.

Qurʾanic and *ḥadīth* literature, as well as theology, have not been paid as much attention as law. Recent interest on the Almohad period might give more impulse to the study of theology, as correct belief became one of the fundaments of Almohad religious policies (the population ruled by the Almohads was supposed to learn by heart the Almohad profession of faith). This trend was related to developments taking place in the rest of the Islamic world and in it the impact of the famous thinker and reformer al-Ghazālī (d. 1111) can be detected. The reception of al-Ghazālī's works and ideas in the Islamic West has been subject to many studies, mostly related to the issue of the spread of Sufism that took place in the twelfth century with figures such as Ibn al-ʿArif, Ibn

Barrajan (both died in 1141) and Ibn Qasi (d. 1151), who did not limit himself to the study and teaching of Ṣūfī doctrines, but also engaged in a political career as a charismatic ruler in the troubled times that preceded the Almohad caliphate. The most famous Andalusi Ṣūfīs are Ibn Masarra (d. 931), better understood now thanks to the publication of his works that were thought to be lost by Asín Palacios in his often quoted monograph; Ibn Sabʿin (d. 1269); and especially Muhyi al-din Ibn al-ʿArabi (d. 1240). The latter, like many other Andalusi Ṣūfīs, spent much of his life outside al-Andalus. In fact, Ṣūfīs did not find in the Iberian Peninsula an atmosphere as congenial to their presence as that existing elsewhere, especially in the Maghreb, where Ṣūfīs and more generally holy men accomplished a variety of functions for which there were competing figures or arenas in al-Andalus. The twelfth century, especially in the Almohad period, witnessed not only the flourishing of Sufism, but also that of philosophy. The career and written production of Ibn Rushd (Averroës) is closely linked to the Almohads's religious and intellectual program. Although Averroës's philosophical work transcended that program, Averroës's most lasting influence is to be found not in Islamdom but in Christian Europe.

Andalusis were keen in portraying their religious history as an unbroken tradition of orthodoxy, without heretical sects, and on the few occasions in which they appeared they were soon annihilated. This image evokes historical developments that supported religious uniformity in al-Andalus, but it also reflects the powerful capacity of Andalusi scholars of assimilating the changes taking place in their milieu and therefore making them almost invisible.

Muslims under Christian Rule. The religious experience of Muslims in the Iberian Peninsula also had a specific trait: that of the Mudéjares, the Muslims who had neither migrated nor converted when their lands were conquered by the Christians but who continued to live as Muslims under Christian rule. They were able to temporarily maintain the use of Arabic, while progressively acquiring the language of the conquerors. This bilingualism was short-lived in some areas, such as Castile, where Arabic was lost, while in the Kingdom of Valencia it lasted longer. A curious form of linguistic survival was to use Arabic letters to write Romance (the so-called *aljamiado* or *aljamía*), not because those who used *aljamiado* wanted to ignore the Romanic script but because they sought to keep themselves linked to the sacred language of the Qurʾān. The use of *aljamía* was a profession of faith, a sign that indicated the users' belonging to the Muslim community.

The status of the Mudéjares came progressively under threat after the conquest of the last Muslim kingdom. The Mudéjares of Granada and Castile were forced to convert to Christianity in 1501 and 1502, those of Valencia in 1521 and 1522, those of Aragon in 1524, in a process that by 1526 signaled the end of Islam as a permitted religion in the Iberian Peninsula. These forced converts are known as Moriscos. Efforts for the Christianization of the Moriscos were carried out according to policies closely intertwined with contemporary debates about the conversion of the Indians of America. In spite of the inevitable, but slow, process of religious and cultural assimilation, the new Christians were suspect in their religion and often denounced as a potential fifth column for the Muslim enemies of the Spanish crown. Also, there was rejection on the part of some sectors of Christian society of their cultural difference. After their rebellion in Granada in 1568, the persecution of the Moriscos at the hands of the Inquisition increased and the remaining communities grew weaker. Their expulsion was discussed in 1582, the first decree was promulgated in 1609, and between 1610 and 1614 the Moriscos were forced to leave the Iberian Peninsula. With them, the small amount of Arabic that still survived disappeared as a spoken language. The dispersion of the Moriscos in Muslim lands and their eventual acculturation to the new context also meant the disappearance of the Andalusi dialectal bundle. For a while, they preserved the Romance language in the new lands where they settled, even producing works in Castilian in Tunis.

Surviving legal opinions dealing with the issue of whether Muslims were allowed to live under Christian rule, mostly formulated by jurists who did not live in the Iberian Peninsula, show a powerful tendency to reject this possibility, arguing that residence in a non-Muslim territory precluded following fundamental tenets of the Islamic religion and was thus equated with religious and cultural corruptions such as eating carrion, blood, or pork. This attitude must have been demoralizing for the religious elites of Mudéjares and crypto-Muslim Moriscos who did not emigrate (emigration to Muslim lands was economically difficult, if not impossible, for the more humble members of the community). Even so, they managed to develop varied and fruitful strategies for religious and cultural survival, the study of which has offered and is still offering new perspectives on the general issue of the interplay between normative and local Islam. *Aljamiado* literature preserved the fundamentals of religion and law, as well as Muslim sacred history, and made them available to the community at large. Sophisticated forgeries such as the Gospel of Saint Barnabas and the Lead Tablets of the Sacromonte of Granada tried to demolish the distinction between "old Christian" and "new Christian" as a rationale for the elimination of the Moriscos, in an attempt to ensure the physical permanence in the Iberian Peninsula of the descendants of its former Muslim inhabitants.

The Legacy of al-Andalus. As in other Islamic societies, in al-Andalus Muslim rulers allowed the existence of Christian and Jewish communities as *dhimmis,* although there were episodes of persecution under certain political and religious circumstances, such as the pogrom of Granada in 1066, the expulsion of the Christians to North Africa in 1126, and the forced conversion of the Jews under the Almohads. Eventually, both non-Muslim communities either disappeared from al-Andalus or saw their numbers greatly diminished, although their Arabo-Islamic acculturation had lasting consequences.

But before exploring them, what was their contribution to Andalusi cultural and intellectual achievements? Echoes of the Latin tradition in astrology, medicine, geography, history, and perhaps agronomy have been identified in early Andalusi culture. The most famous example is the Cordovan Calendar. But there was nothing comparable to the impact of Hellenistic culture in the Eastern Islamic civilization and thus Saʿid of Toledo, writing in the eleventh century, stated that the scientific development of al-Andalus was not indebted to any indigenous tradition. The related issues of the possible influence of Romance lyrics in the appearance of new poetical forms *(muwashashat* and *azjal)* in al-Andalus and of the possible influence of such forms in Western poetry have been (and still are) widely and ardently debated. The *muwashashat* encapsulate verses in Romance called *kharjas.* They have attracted a passionate interest from Arabists, Hebraists, and Romanists, giving rise to hugely divergent interpretations and becoming one of the cornerstones of the presentation of al-Andalus as the land of the three cultures or the land of religious *convivencia* (living together). This largely mythical presentation has had a recent flourishing, owing once again more to contemporary needs than to historical accuracy.

Less open to debate is the impact that Andalusi Christians and Jews had in Latin Christendom and in Jewish culture. In the case of the Christians, those who emigrated to Christian lands brought with them artistic skills that modern scholarship has analyzed as representing a specific Mozarabic art, unique to the Iberian Peninsula. The Christians who lived in Muslim lands conquered by the northern Christians kept for some time the use of Arabic, as shown by the rich collection of Arabic documents from Christian Toledo (eleventh to thirteenth centuries), and they also preserved the old Visigothic church ritual.

But it was mostly the highly Arabicized Jews who played a crucial role in the transmission of Arabic culture and science to Christian Spain and Europe. They are closely associated with the so-called school of translators of Toledo, a label which is merely a way to express in a simple manner the complex linguistic and intellectual process through which Arabic works were translated into other peninsular languages (Latin, Romance languages, Hebrew). The need to translate arose mainly for two reasons.

On the one hand, knowledge of the "other" was necessary in order better to confront the Muslims or to convert them, especially when Christian expansion led to the presence of Muslim communities inside Christian territory. In the twelfth century, Latin Christendom started the serious study of Islam, thanks mainly to the encouragement given by Peter the Venerable of Cluny to the translation of Muslim religious texts. Raymond Lull (1232–1316), who called himself Christianus Arabicus, developed a philosophical-apologetical system with the aim of convincing the infidel Muslims of the truth of the Catholic faith, arguing not against, but rather from their own faith, which he had deeply studied. On the other hand, translation was needed to take possession of the knowledge achieved by the Muslims in philosophy, science, and other fields. For example, Christian historical works written in the thirteenth century, like those produced under the patronage of Alfonso X the Wise, were highly indebted to Arabic chronicles, in the same way that the Arab geographers had learned about the Iberian Peninsula from Latin sources. But the translation effort concentrated mostly on the field of the "sciences of the ancients."

The Greek and Latin legacy was sought where it was known to have been preserved, in those Arabic works containing translations from that legacy, but also the original contributions made by Muslims themselves. In fact, in searching for the scientific and technical knowledge of antiquity, the Christians had to acknowledge the importance of the additions made in the Arabo-Islamic civilization. That search started early, as shown by the manuscripts of Ripoll monastery (in Catalonia). The main impulse took place in the twelfth century, when Hermann of Carinthia and Robert of Ketton worked in the Ebro valley, while Dominicus Gundisalvus and Gerard of Cremona centered their activities in Toledo. The exact sciences, linked to astrology and magic, attracted the first translating efforts, but philosophical and medical treatises were soon incorporated. Andalusi Aristotelianism had a lasting influence in Latin and Hebrew philosophy.

Averroës's works were already translated in the first half of the thirteenth century, shortly after having been written, provoking the well-known reaction of both attraction and rejection in Christian Europe. Alfonso X the Wise promoted the translation from Arabic into the vernacular, employing mostly Jews, of a wide range of works dealing with magic, astrology, astronomy, games, and literature. Arabic vocabulary penetrated into these vernacular languages, mainly in the fields of agricultural products and techniques, building crafts, clothing, and food. Mudéjar art, like its counterpart Mozarabic art, singles out Spain from the rest of western Europe with the exception of Sicily. Spanish medieval literature is indebted in both contents and form to Arabic literature. The Muslim religious influence on peninsular Judaism has acknowledged manifestations in the fields of mysticism and theology, while its influence on Christianity is less widely accepted. This reflects the tensions that have existed (and continue to exist) in the construction of a Spanish Catholic national identity, while similar debates (such as that on the debt of Dante's *Divine Comedy* to Muslim eschatology) show that the study of religious interaction has been, and still is, a contested field.

The al-Andalus cultural and intellectual legacy should not be sought only in what is now known as the West. Andalusi Islam produced works and developed doctrines and practices that had a lasting influence in the Muslim world at large. Following Christian expansion in Muslim lands,

Andalusi intellectual elites started a process of emigration to other regions of Islamdom. Its rhythm and peculiarities are not yet well known, but it helped disseminate Andalusi cultural achievements among Muslims. Any look at the contents of extant Muslim libraries reveals that the list of Andalusi "best-sellers" in Muslim religious literature is substantial and that in certain areas, such as North and Central Africa, Islam cannot be understood without reference to the thought and works of Andalusi scholars.

Bibliography

Acién Almansa, Manuel. *Entre el feudalismo y el Islam: ʿUmar ibn Hafsun en los historiadores, en las fuentes y en la historia.* Jaén, Spain, 1994; reprinted with a new introduction, 1997. Monograph on the issue of pre-Islamic feudalism in al-Andalus and the formation of an Islamic society.

Adang, Camilla. *Islam frente a judaísmo: La polémica de Ibn Hazm de Cordova.* Madrid, 1994.

Addas, Claude. *Ibn ʿArabi ou la quête du Soufre Rouge.* Paris, 1989. Analysis of the Ṣūfī Muhyi al-din Ibn ʿArabi's Andalusi background.

Arié, Rachel. *L'Espagne musulmane au temps des Nasrides (1232–1492).* Paris, 1973; new ed., 1990.

Arnaldez, Roger. *Grammaire et théologie chez Ibn Hazm de Cordoue: Essai sur la structure et les conditions de la pensée musulmane.* Paris, 1956; reprint, 1981.

Ashtor, Eliyahu. *The Jews of Moslem Spain.* 3 vols. Philadelphia, 1973–1984; reprint, 1992, with a new introduction by D. J. Wasserstein. This general history of Jewish presence in al-Andalus needs to be updated, as Wasserstein shows in his introduction.

Asín Palacios, Miguel. *Abenmasarra y su escuela. Orígenes de la filosofía hispano-musulmana.* Madrid, 1914. Reprinted in Miguel Asín Palacios, *Tres estudios sobre pensamiento y mística hispanomusulmanes,* Madrid, 1992. English translation, *The Mystical Philosophy of Ibn Masarra and His Followers,* by Elmer H. Douglas and Howard W. Yoder, Leiden, 1978. Still influential, although outdated. J. van Ess's work is a good guide to more recent bibliography.

Asín Palacios, Miguel. *Abenházam de Córdoba y su Historia Crítica de las ideas religiosas.* 5 vols. Madrid, 1929.

Baer, Yitzhak F. *A History of the Jews in Christian Spain.* Translated by L. Schoffman. Philadelphia, 1961–1966. Spanish translation by José Luis Lacave, 2 vols., Madrid, 1981. Still useful on the presence and influence of Andalusi Jews in Christian Spain.

Bosch Vilà, Jacinto. *Los almorávides.* Tétouan, Morocco, 1956. 2d ed., with a preliminary study by Emilio Molina, Granada, 1990.

Bulliet, Richard. *Conversion to Islam in the Medieval Period: An Essay in Quantitative History.* London, 1979. It contains a chapter on al-Andalus.

Burman, Thomas E. *Religious Polemic and the Intellectual History of the Mozarabs, c. 1050–1200.* Leiden, 1994. A discussion of religious polemic between Christians and Muslims.

Burnett, Charles. "The Translating Activity in Muslim Spain." In *The Legacy of Muslim Spain,* edited by Salma Khadra Jayyusi. Leiden, 1992.

Burns, Robert I. *Muslims, Christians, and Jews in the Crusader Kingdom of Valencia.* Cambridge, U.K., 1984.

Calder, Norman. *Studies in Early Muslim Jurisprudence.* Oxford, 1993. The discussion of the traditionalizing of the ancient schools of law includes references to al-Andalus.

Christys, Anne. *Christians in al-Andalus (711–1000).* Richmond, U.K., 2002. A critical presentation of some of the main issues, with bibliography.

Coope, Jessica. *The Martyrs of Córdoba: Community and Family Conflict in an Age of Mass Conversion.* Lincoln, Neb., 1995.

Cornell, Vincent. *Realm of the Saint: Power and Authority in Moroccan Sufism.* Austin, Tex., 1998. With references to Andalusi Sufism, which still lacks a monograph.

Corriente, Federico. *Arabe andalusí y lenguas romances.* Madrid, 1992. Study of the Arabic language spoken in al-Andalus.

Cruz Hernández, Miguel. *Historia del pensamiento en al-Andalus.* Seville, Spain, 1985. An overview of philosophy in al-Andalus.

Cruz Hernández, Miguel. *Abu al-Walid Ibn Rushd (Averroes): Vida, Obra, Pensamiento, Influencia.* Cordova, Spain, 1997. An overview of Averroës's biography and philosophy.

De las Cagigas, Isidro. *Los mozárabes.* Madrid, 1947–1948. Useful though dated monograph on the Mozarabs.

Dodds, Jerrilyn, ed. *Al-Andalus: The Art of Islamic Spain.* New York, 1992.

Epalza, Míkel de. *Los moriscos antes y después de la expulsión.* Madrid, 1992. A useful and updated presentation on the Moriscos.

Estudios onomático-biográficos de al-Andalus. Volumes 1–14. Madrid and Granada, 1988–2004. Studies on the world of Andalusi scholarship.

Ferhat, Halima. *Le Maghreb aux XIIème et XIIIème siècles: les siècles de la foi.* Casablanca, 1993. With references to Andalusi Sufism, which still lacks a monograph.

Fernández Félix, Ana. *Cuestiones legales del islam temprano: la ʿUtbiyya y el proceso de formación de la sociedad islámica andalusí.* Madrid, 2004. A study of one of the earliest legal texts written in al-Andalus and its contribution to the formation of an Islamic society.

Fierro, Maribel. *La heterodoxia en al-Andalus durante el periodo omeya.* Madrid, 1987.

Fierro, Maribel. "Opposition to Sufism in al-Andalus." In *Islamic Mysticism Contested: Thirteen Centuries of Controversies and Polemics,* edited by Frederick de Jong and Bernd Radtke. Leiden, 1999.

Fierro, Maribel. "The Legal Policies of the Almohad Caliphs and Ibn Rushd's Bidayat al-mujtahid." *Journal of Islamic Studies* 10, no. 3 (1999): 226–248.

Fierro, Maribel. *Al-Ándalus: saberes e intercambios culturales.* Barcelona, 2001. A concise presentation on the intellectual history of al-Andalus.

Fierro, Maribel, ed. *Judíos y musulmanes en al-Andalus y el Magreb: Contactos intelectuales.* Madrid, 2002. Collection of studies on intellectual contacts between Jews and Muslims.

Fierro, Maribel, and Julio Samsó, eds. *The Formation of al-Andalus.* Part II: *Language, Religion, Culture and the Sciences.* Aldershot, U.K., 1998. Collection of studies on the process of Arabization and Islamicization of al-Andalus, with a useful bibliography.

García-Arenal, Mercedes. *La diáspora de los andalusíes.* Barcelona, 2003. A concise presentation on religious minorities in al-Andalus and the Muslim minority in Christian Spain.

García-Arenal, Mercedes, ed. "En torno a los Plomos del Sacromonte." *Al-Qantara* 23 (2002): 295.

Glick, Thomas. *Islamic and Christian Spain in the Early Middle Ages.* Princeton, N.J., 1979. A good overview on intercultural influences.

Glick, Thomas F. *From Muslim Fortress to Christian Castle: Social and Cultural Change in Medieval Spain.* New York, 1995. An overview of the contribution made by French and Spanish archaeological research to a better understanding and sometimes radical revisions of Andalusi history.

Guichard, Pierre. *Al-Andalus: Estructura antropológica de una sociedad islámica en Occidente.* Barcelona, 1978; reprint, Granada, 1998. Highly influential monograph on the issue of tribalism in al-Andalus and the formation of an Islamic society.

Guichard, Pierre. *Valence et la Reconquête (XIe–XIIIe siècles).* 2 vols. Damascus, 1990–1991. Spanish translation, *Al-Andalus frente a la conquista cristiana: los musulmanes de Valencia (siglos XI–XIII),* by Josep Torró Abad, Madrid, 2001. A monograph on the transition from a Muslim to a Christian polity in the Valencian area.

Guichard, Pierre. *Al-Andalus: 711–1492.* Paris, 2000. Good, short, and manageable introduction to the history of al-Andalus.

Guichard, Pierre, and Vincent Lagardère. "La vie sociale et économique de l'Espagne musulmane aux XIe-XIIe siècles à travers les *fatwas* du *Mi'yar* d'al-Wansarisi." *Mélanges de la Casa de Velázquez* 26, no. 1 (1990): 197–236. It highlights the importance of *fatawa* literature for the history of al-Andalus.

Hallaq, Wael H. *A History of Islamic Legal Theories: An Introduction to Sunni usul al-fiqh.* Cambridge, U.K., 1997.

Harvey, L. P. *Islamic Spain: 1250–1500.* Chicago, 1992.

Historia de España Ramón Menéndez Pidal. Madrid, 1957–2003. Spanish translation by Emilio García Gómez of the *Histoire de l'Espagne musulmane* by Evariste Lévi-Provençal. Volumes 5 and 6 are devoted to the Umayyad period under the title *España musulmana hasta la caída del Califato de Córdoba (711–1031 d.C.).* María Jesús Viguera has coordinated volume 8, no. 1 (The Taifa Kingdoms), volume 8, no. 2 (Almoravid and Almohad periods), volume 8, nos. 3 and 4 (The Nasrid Kingdom). A major work of reference for Andalusi political, social, and cultural history, where the interested reader can find an extensive and updated bibliography.

Huici Miranda, Ambrosio. *Historia política del imperio almohade.* Facsimile edition with a preliminary study by Emilio Molina López and Vicente Oltra. 2 vols. Tétouan, Morocco, 1956–1957; reprint, Granada, 2000.

Jayyusi, Salma Khadra, ed. *The Legacy of Muslim Spain.* Leiden, 1992.

Kennedy, Hugh. *Muslim Spain and Portugal:. A Political History of al-Andalus.* London, 1996.

Lagardère, Vincent. *Les Almoravides jusqu'au regne de Yusuf b. Tashfin (1039–1106).* Paris, 1989.

Lagardère, Vincent. *Les almoravides. Le djihad andalou (1106–1143).* Paris, 1998.

Lirola Delgado, Jorge, and José Miguel Puerta Vílchez, eds. *Enciclopedia de al-Andalus: Diccionario de Autores y Obras Andalusíes.* Tomo I. Granada, 2002. A biographical dictionary of Andalusi scholars.

Maíllo, Felipe. *¿Por qué desapareció al-Andalus?* Buenos Aires, 1997. An exploration of the reasons for the political and military fall of al-Andalus.

Makki, Mahmud ʿAli. *Ensayo sobre las aportaciones orientales en la España musulmana y su influencia en la formación de la cultura hispano-árabe.* Madrid, 1968. Study of the reception of Arabic and Islamic literature in al-Andalus.

Marín, Manuela. *Individuo y sociedad en al-Andalus.* Madrid, 1992. Study of the social and intellectual trends in al-Andalus during the Umayyad period.

Marín, Manuela. "Learning at mosques in al-Andalus," In *Islamic Legal Interpretation. Muftis and Their Fatwas,* edited by Muhammad Khalid Masud, Brinkley Messick, and David Powers. Cambridge, Mass., 1996.

Marín, Manuela. *Al-Ándalus y los andalusíes.* Barcelona, 2000. A concise presentation on the political and social history of al-Andalus.

Marín, Manuela. *Mujeres en al-Ándalus.* Madrid, 2000. Includes a study of women's religious practices.

Marín, Manuela, ed. *The Formation of al-Andalus,* Part 1: *History and Society.* Aldershot, U.K., 1998. Collection of studies on the early history of al-Andalus with a useful bibliography.

Martinez-Gros, Gabriel. *Identité andalouse.* Paris, 1997. Study on the formation of an Andalusi identity.

Menocal, Rosa María. *The Arabic Role in Medieval Literary History: A Forgotten Heritage.* Philadelphia, 1989.

Menocal, María Rosa, Raymond P. Scheindlin, and Michael Sells, eds. *The Cambridge History of Arabic Literature: The Literature of al-Andalus.* Cambridge, U.K., 2000.

Meyerson, M. D. *The Muslims of Valencia in the Age of Fernando and Isabel: Between Coexistence and Crusade.* Berkeley, Calif., 1991.

Molénat, Jean-Pierre. *Campagnes et monts de Tolède du XII au XVème siècle.* Madrid, 1997. An important contribution to the history of the Mozarabs in Christian Spain.

Monroe, James T. *The Shuʿubiyya in al-Andalus.* Berkeley, Calif., 1970. Analysis of the rarity of *shuʿubi* trends.

Nirenberg, David. "Muslims in Christian Iberia, 1000–1526: Varieties of Mudejar Experience." In *The Medieval World,* edited by Peter Linehan and Janet L. Nelson, London, 2001. An evaluation of the different perspectives on Mudéjar Islam.

Rubiera, María Jesús. *Literatura hispanoárabe.* Madrid, 1992. A short introduction to Andalusi literature and poetry.

Rubio, Luciano. *El "ocasionalismo" de los teólogos especulativos del Islam: su posible influencia en Guillermo de Ockam y los "ocasionalistas" de la Edad Moderna.* El Escorial, Spain, 1987. An important contribution to the history of theology and philosophy in al-Andalus.

Sáenz-Badillos, Angel, and Judith Targarona Borrás. *Diccionario de autores judíos (Sefarad. siglos X–XV).* Cordova, Spain, 1988. A useful guide to the literary production of Andalusi Jews.

Samsó, Julio. *Las ciencias de los antiguos en al-Andalus.* Madrid, 1992. A good introduction to the Andalusi contribution in the "rational" sciences.

Scales, Peter C. *The Fall of the Caliphate of Córdoba: Berbers and Andalusis in Conflict.* Leiden, 1994.

Simonet, Francisco Javier. *Historia de los mozárabes de España* (1897–1903). Amsterdam, 1967. In spite of its shortcomings, still offers a complete overview to date on the Christians living under Muslim rule.

Urvoy, Dominique. *Pensers d'al-Andalus. La vie intellectuelle à Cordoue et Sevilla au temps des Empires Berberes (fin XIe siècle – début XIIIe siècle).* Toulouse, France, 1990. An overview of intellectual trends during the Almoravid and Almohad periods.

Urvoy, Dominique. *Averroès: Les ambitions d'un intellectuel musulman.* Paris, 1998. A useful presentation of Averroës's life and work.

Van Ess, Joseph. *Theologie und Gesellschaft im 2. und 3. Jahrhundert Hidschra. Eine Geschichte des religiösen Denkens im frühen Islam.* 6 vols. Berlin, 1991–1997. It contains valuable analyses of developments in al-Andalus.

Vernet, Juan. *La cultura hispanoárabe en Oriente y Occidente.* Barcelona, 1978. New ed., *Lo que Europa debe al Islam de España,* Barcelona, 1999. French translation by Gabriel Martinez Gros, *Ce que la culture doit aux arabes d'Espagne,* Paris, 1985. Overview of Christian and Jewish contributions to Andalusi scientific culture and Andalusi contributions to Europe.

Viguera, María Jesús. *Los Reinos de Taifas y las invasiones magrebíes.* Madrid, 1992.

Wasserstein, David. *The Rise and Fall of the Party-Kings: Politics and Society in Islamic Spain, 1002–1086.* Princeton, N.J., 1986.

Wasserstein, David. "The Muslims and the Golden Age of the Jews in al-Andalus." *Israel Oriental Studies* 17 (1997): 179–196. A discussion of the issue of the Jewish golden age in the Iberian Peninsula.

Wiegers, Gerard. *Islamic Literature in Spanish and Aljamiado: Yça of Segovia (d. 1450), His Antecedents and Successors.* Leiden, 1994. A good presentation on Aljamiado literature.

Zwartjes, Otto. *Love Songs from Al-Andalus: History, Structure and Meaning of the Kharja.* Leiden, 1997. Balanced presentation of the issue of poetical borrowings between Arabic and European vernacular languages.

MARIBEL FIERRO (2005)

ISLAM: ISLAM IN SUB-SAHARAN AFRICA

Islam entered Africa within decades of its inception in the seventh century CE. In North Africa its spread was related to the empire-building process which took Islam to Morocco and Spain in the far west and to India in the east whereas in the rest of Africa its diffusion followed a different path. The African dimension goes back to 615 CE when the first Islamic migration to Abyssinia, now called Ethiopia, took place, though its impact there at this early stage is not clear. A few years later, the epoch-making *hijrah*, or migration, by Muḥammad and his persecuted band of followers to Medina created the political center of the nascent Islamic state built in Arabia. The task of spreading Islam beyond the Arabian peninsula to other regions, including North Africa to the fringes of the Sahara, was left to Muḥammad's successors or caliphs.

Scholars, until recently, have not paid sufficient attention to the Islamic intellectual tradition and culture in sub-Saharan Africa which is generally treated as a periphery of the Islamic heartland in the Middle East. Moreover, studies about Islam in Africa are often marred by the view that gained currency during the colonial era, namely that African Islam represented a syncretic or diluted version of the faith, stripped of elements of its higher tradition. This view is difficult to understand given that Islam is indeed a religion of great synthesis which (in the areas where it has spread) has interacted with local cultures, enriching them and being enriched by them. The study of Islam in sub-Saharan Africa is now entering into a new and very interesting phase (for instance, witness local and international efforts to help save old manuscripts relating to Tombouctou's intellectual heritage) as scholars begin to look at Africa's literary tradition and contributions to aspects of Islamic law, mysticism, devotional matters, theology, and history in Arabic or local languages. The number of Qurʾanic translations in African languages, using the Arabic or Latin alphabet, moreover, has also been growing steadily and testifies to this increased urgency to produce written material for African Muslims.

Knowledge of the history of Islam in sub-Saharan Africa before the sixteenth century comes mainly from the works of Arab geographers and historians such as al-Bakr, al-Zuhri, Ibn Batuta, and others. Archaeological excavations of important centers of trade, such as Kumbi Saleh, Awdaghust, Jenne, Kilwa, and others, have added further to the knowledge of these cities by allowing for historical reconstruction. Finally, oral traditions have become an increasingly important source for the study of this history as they present information (in legendary form) of kings such as Sundiata, the founder of Mali, which can be critically assessed to provide insights into what is remembered and emphasized about the past. The sources of information become more varied after the sixteenth century and include written material in Arabic by local Muslims, oral traditions and ethnographic data, and European records in the era of European expansion and domination of the Atlantic system.

ISLAM IN THE SAHARA AND THE SAHEL. Islam made its presence felt in much of Africa (the east coast and Horn of Africa as well as West Africa) mainly through trade and migration. In the Sahara region and beyond it, for instance, Islam was introduced from North Africa by the Berbers, mostly members of Khārijī sects, through the trans-Saharan trade as early as the eighth or ninth century. They had their centers in the oases at the northern side of the Sahara in Sijilmasah, Tahart, Wargla, and Ghadames. With the expansion of this mainly salt-for-gold trade, important trading towns such as Awdaghust, Tadmeka, and Kawwar also sprang up at the southern end of the Sahara. Beyond them lay the important African states of Ghana (with Kumbi Saleh as its capital), Gao, and Kanem in the region that was known as the Sahel (which means in Arabic the "shore" of the desert). This was the region where the desert and the savanna meet and where Sahelian cities served as terminus points for a very vibrant international trade.

The Khārijī influence in North Africa had declined by the tenth and eleventh centuries due to a number of factors, including the Shīʿī Fāṭimid conquest of North Africa, the destabilizing migration of the Arab Hilalian nomads, and the rise of the Almoravid movement among the Sanhaja Berbers of southwestern Sahara and the Mauritanian coast. The latter factor was especially important in entrenching the Sunnī Mālikī school of law in the region against both the Ḥanafī (supported by the Aghlabids) and the Shīʿī Fāṭimids. Mālikī scholars had arrived in North Africa as early as the ninth century and had successfully won the support of both the pastoralists and traders among the Berbers who became the vehicle for dissemination of Islam into the Sahara and beyond it in West Africa.

The increasing interest in the wider Arab/Muslim world in the source of gold for the trans-Saharan trade led to Ghana receiving mention in Arabic writings as early as the eighth century. Nevertheless, it was only after Muslim traders from North Africa began to settle in the largest Sahelian states by the eleventh century that more detailed descriptions of these states appear. For instance, the Arab geographer in Islamic Spain, al-Bakr, described Ghana's capital, Kumbi Saleh, as constituting two separate towns situated at a short distance from each other. One was a distinctly Muslim town, set aside for Muslim merchants who had their own mosques, and the other, the royal town, consisted of a palace and conical huts where the imperial indigenous form of religion was practiced. The king, who was known to be a man of justice and extended his friendship to the Muslims, appointed many of them, as the literati in society, to ministerial positions. Similarly, Gao, on the Niger, east of the river bend, was also divided into Muslim and royal towns although the king in this case was a Muslim. It was only in Takrur, on the lower Senegal River, that the Muslim king was reported as carrying out a vigorous campaign of conversion among his subjects and neighbors.

By about 1050 CE the kingdom of Ghana had expanded to include the Berber town of Awdaghust. A few decades later the king and the people of Ghana, according to al-Zuhuri who wrote in the twelfth century, had converted to Islam under the influence of the Almoravids (al-Murabitun). Some scholars have read the early sources as suggesting that this conversion was not attained by peaceful means. Recent careful study, however, has raised doubts about this conquest hypothesis which is considered to be more fiction than fact. In any case, Ghana continued to thrive as a state until the thirteenth century when its decline began due to a combination of factors, including Bure gold fields opening up farther south in the savanna country, new trans-Saharan routes developing farther east of Awdaghust, over-exhaustion of resources in this marginal Sahelian zone for food and iron production, and the continuous pressure from Berber pastoralists in search of new pastures for their stocks. Mali by then had emerged as the dominant power in the region.

MALI: THE WEST-AFRICAN PATTERN OF ISLAMIZATION. From an early period, political developments in West Africa were continually shaped by the trading network which depended on the trans-Saharan routes being extended to new sources of gold to the south. These trading networks developed among local African groups, mostly of Soninke origin (related to the rulers of Ghana), such as the Mande (Wangara/Dyula) whose area of operation was over a wide area, extending from as far west as Senegal to northern Nigeria in the east. This trade network, which led to exposure to Islam as a result of trading transactions with North Africans, was closely associated with the diffusion of Islamic studies, including mysticism in the later centuries, and enabled Islam to penetrate peacefully beyond the Sahel into the savanna area. Initially Islam was the religion of the African traders, then the rulers (who sought Muslim prayers if those of local priests failed), and finally (due to the efforts of Muslim scholars in later centuries) commoners among various African communities.

The cross-cultural trade in many parts of Africa, apart from reinforcing cultural self-identity and nurturing religious commitment, fostered a pluralist structure in which commerce, Islam, and the indigenous system supported the urban network. In this way a balance was established between local ritual prescriptions and those of universal Islam.

Islam in Africa was (as in many parts of the world where it reached) primarily an urban religion (with an urban ethos) which fostered commitment to its religious system, ranging from ethnic self-identity to Islamic self-identity, universal and trans-ethnic in scope. Islamic penetration in the rural areas, on the other hand, made slow infiltration over a long period of time with significant gains awaiting a much later period. The religion therefore entered much of Africa peacefully through the agency of trade and later gained status after the migrant community (purveyors of the written word and the visual symbols of Islam) became integrated into the political structure. Finally the ruling elite embraced the faith and appropriated its symbols for political purposes.

The level of commitment to Islam varied from one region of Africa to another and was influenced by a number of factors, including the length of interaction between Islam and the traditional religion, societal organization between centralized and non-centralized or "stateless" ones (in West Africa evidence suggests that Islam was not often adopted by segmentary societies), the compatibility or incompatibility of the world views of the two religious systems, and the level of resilience of the indigenous integrative symbols to sustain traditional structures of the local religion. Islam is based on a written scripture, prescribed ritual, a historical and historicizing tradition, and a supra-ethnic religious identity. Its interaction with traditional African religions is therefore governed by the tension between the supra-ethnic universality of its *ummah* and the ethnocentrism of traditional African religion. As one scholar has put it, for the African, the ethnic group is the matrix in which his or her religion takes shape, the meaning of myth communicated, and a person's sacramental relation to nature experienced. This means that when the traditional symbols of an ethnic group are challenged by a new system, recombination of old and new forms may appear to reorganize the group and to compensate for any loss. More specifically, becoming a Muslim and joining this universal *ummah* involves offering prayers in a mosque frequented by members of other ethnic groups, adoption of Muslim behavior patterns and dress code in some cases, and using a certain language (e.g., in the case of East Africa, Kiswahili). The Kano Chronicle, a written version of the oral traditions not committed to writing until the nineteenth century, brings out clearly the struggle between the two religious systems, the Islamic and the traditional one, after the symbolic tree is cut down and a mosque built in its place.

In the case of Mali, despite the influence of Islam among the Malinke chiefs prior to the founding of the empire by Sundiata, the latter is presented in the Arabic sources and oral traditions as a great hunter and a magician who mobilized the resources of his people against the Sosso in the name of the ancestral tradition, not Islam. Yet, when Mali expanded and was transformed from a small chiefdom to a sprawling multi-ethnic empire extending into the Sahel region, its Muslim rulers (including the famous Mansa Musa with his lavish pilgrimage to Mecca) shifted their attachment over time from traditional religious references to a more universal Islamic outlook.

Mali reached the height of its power in the fourteenth century during the reign of Mansa Musa (1312–1337) and Mansa Sulayman (1341–1360) when the specifically Muslim character came to be reflected by the many mosques and centers of Islamic learning, such as Tombouctou. Ibn Batuta visited Niani, the capital of Mali in 1352/3 and reported attending an official Islamic festival which attracted the presence of the king as well non-Muslims. He spoke highly of the people's efforts to study the Qurʾān from memory, their hospitality, and their love of justice, though he deprecated their pre-Islamic customs which he still found to be in vogue.

By the end of the fourteenth century and certainly the beginning of the fifteenth century, the Mali empire was in decline with a series of weak rulers, dynastic struggles, and loss of control to the Tuareg and later to Songhai over the Sahel (the region where Islam had been more firmly established). The outer provinces (such as the Mossi areas to the south of the Niger bend) broke away and went their separate way, with the Mali state contracting to its original borders on the upper Niger.

SCHOLARS AND RULERS: TOMBOUCTOU IN SONGHAI. While traders played a major role in the dissemination of Islam across the various trading networks in the region, the work of entrenching and deepening peoples understanding and commitment to the faith was left to the religious scholars (*ʿulamāʾ*). The term *ʿulamāʾ* covers a range of Muslim religious personalities, from the learned elite of the Muslim world who is steeped in one or more of the Islamic sciences—including Qurʾanic exegesis, Islamic jurisprudence, and so on—to the teacher/preacher/healer/holy man who provides services of a magical-religious nature to both Muslims and non-Muslims. The latter played similar religious, social, and political roles as did the African priest/healer/diviner whose traditional shrines served the same type of function as did the mosque, God's house, or sanctuary. These Muslim healers maintained a level of neutrality in the political affairs of the places where they resided. This served to enhance their powers as they were not perceived to be a threat to the local political elite.

Muslim scholars provided their services at the centers of political power, in chiefly and kingly courts as well as at major trading and learning centers, such as Tombouctou which provided an important link between the Sudanic savanna and the Berber Sahara. The city produced its own indigenous scholars, some of whom, under the rule of Mansa, were sent to Fez in Morocco to further their studies. In the fifteenth century, the Sanhaja scholars (under the patronage of another Berber group, the Tuareg, who were their kin) became prominent in Tombouctou. They gained the title of the people of Sankore, owing to their residence in the quarter of the Sankore mosque.

Unlike their counterparts in West Africa, the Sanhaja scholars of Tombouctou did not shy away from the political message of Islam. They articulated the concerns of the merchants of Tombouctou about guarding the autonomy of the city which was conquered by Sonni Ali in 1469 thus setting off a bitter conflict. By then the kingdom of Gao had blossomed to become the empire of Songhai under the ruthless leadership of Sonni Ali, who persecuted scholars who opposed him, a fact noted in Arabic sources, while respecting those who collaborated with him. This is an early example of confrontation between religious scholars and a ruler of a West African kingdom.

After Sonni Ali's death in 1492, his son was soon ousted by Askiya Muḥammad Ture (1493–1528), one of the generals who had formed an alliance with discontented elements in the western provinces of Songhai. Ture, founder of the Askiya dynasty, strengthened the administration of the empire and consolidated the earlier conquests of Sonni Ali. He used Islam effectively to reinforce his authority, by involving the Tombouctou scholars in his pro-Islam policy, and to unite the various regions of his kingdom. His pilgrimage to Mecca a few years later brought him to the attention of the Muslim world as one concerned about the affairs of Islam. He returned with the title of *amir al-muʾminin* (commander of the faithful), conferred upon him in Cairo, which made him the politico-religious head of the Muslim community (*ummah*) in western Sudan.

Askiya Muḥammad's politics of appeasing potential opponents helped integrate even the Tuareg of the Sahara into the empire, a development that safeguarded the commercial interests of Tombouctou. For their part, the scholars of Tombouctou favored piecemeal changes in the Songhai empire and did not call for radical transformations of the type advocated by al-Maghili, a visiting scholar from the oasis of Tuat in the northern Sahara. Al-Maghili's responses to Askiya Muḥammad's questions represent the most sustained criticism of the religious and political situation in West Africa prior to the Islamic revolutions of the eighteenth and nineteenth centuries.

Among Askiya Muḥammad's great achievements was his revival of Tombouctou as a great center of Islamic learning. During this period the Mālikī scholars from Tombouctou visited Cairo, a major source of Islamic intellectual influence in the region, on their way to and from Mecca. In Cairo they studied mainly under eminent Shāfiʿī scholars from whom they assimilated the science of *ḥadīth* (the prophetic traditions), *taṣawwuf* ("mysticism"), and *balāghah* (rhetoric). In this way, scholarship in Tombouctou was broadened beyond the narrow parochialism of the Mālikī school that seems to have stifled intellectual life in the Maghreb at that time. One representative of this scholarly tradition was the famous Tombouctou scholar Ahmad Baba, who, along with the other leading scholars in the city, were exiled to Morocco following the invasion of Tombouctou in 1591. His excellence in Islamic erudition was acknowledged when scholars from the major towns of Morocco came to hear his lectures in Marrakech.

The Moroccan conquest transformed the autonomous town governed by its own patriciate of scholar families into the seat of an authoritarian military government. The outcome was that once again, as during the time of Sonni Ali, scholars led the resistance. The continued intellectual prominence of Tombouctou was confirmed by the two most important Arabic chronicles of West Africa, *Taʿrikh al-Sudan* (History of Sudan) and *Taʿrikh al-Fattash* (The researcher's history [of Takrur]), both of which were written there in the middle of the seventeenth century. They form part of the local Arabic historiography which documents, among other things, the rise and gradual decline of Tombouctou.

Tombouctou, which once had the status of a major center of learning and commerce, declined slowly, under the contested rule of the descendants of the Moroccan conquerors. Feuding factions struggled for power within Tombouctou and Tuareg nomads pressed the town from the outside. Arma (Moroccan) rule finally collapsed in 1737 when the Tuareg seized the town and became the dominant power on the Niger bend. Once commerce was affected, it did not take long for the decline in Islamic scholarship to set in. With military and political ascendancy passing into the hands of the Tuareg, learning and also spiritual leadership migrated to the nomads' camp. By the middle of the eighteenth century, the Kunta, a nomadic clan of Arab and Berber descent, exercised influence over the whole of Muslim West Africa.

The mediating and integrating functions of Islamic learning in the segmentary societies of the Saharan nomads was expressed through the influence of the marabouts who attempted to establish harmony between warring groups. These maraboutic lineages were also involved in trade, employing a network of disciples and followers. The transformation or conversion of religious prestige to economic resources and political assets accounts for the rise of the Kunta as a dominant scholarly and commercial network. Their leader, Sidi al-Mukhtar al-Kabir (1728–1811), a reputable scholar and a great mystic, reinvigorated the Qādirīyah Ṣūfī order, which until then had not played a particularly distinctive role in the religious life of the Sahara for more than two centuries. He was highly revered by the Tuareg and through his influence over them extended his patronage over Tombouctou. Through his disciples he facilitated the diffusion of his Qadiri teachings among many Muslim groups in the savanna.

Islam in the Savanna. The collapse of the imperial system in western Sudan, which had been sustained by the successive powerful states of Mali and Songhai, weakened the position of Islam in the savanna. There were now no longer patrons of learning like the great kings Mansa Musa and Askiya Muḥammad, with their strong commitment to Islam and its promotion in their respective states. Moreover, by the seventeenth century, Muslims were living under the auspices or authority of lesser chiefs who were strongly influenced by their traditional heritage. Yet, all was not lost, as Muslim traders were venturing farther afield, to the fringes of the forest, opening new areas to the influence of Islam. This allowed Islam (the religion of urban centers, generally followed by merchants, scholars, and the like in the age of the great empires) to filter into the countryside by the seventeenth and eighteenth centuries.

The Bambara of middle Niger, who had previously resisted Islamization during the period of the Mali empire, became more open to Islam when they entered a process of state formation of their own. The Scottish explorer Mungo Park reported in 1796 seeing many mosques in the Bambara capital. Bambara chiefs began to practice Islam while retaining traditional rituals. The Islam practiced by their chiefs accommodated local ritual practices, a pattern that recurs throughout the regions where Islam spread in Africa and Asia.

The role of Muslims as advisers to rulers and as specialists with access to supernatural power was transmitted from the middle Niger (central parts of modern Mali) to the Volta basin, where several patterns of Islamization and integration had developed. In Gonja, Dagomba, Mamprusi, and Wa (present-day northern Ghana), Muslims of Dyula and Hausa origin had assimilated many aspects of the local cultures in addition to adopting local languages. Moreover, Muslims had become integrated into the sociopolitical system of these states. In the area west of the Black Volta River (modern Ivory Coast), the Dyula managed to maintain their cultural and linguistic identity either as residents of states, such as Buna and Gyaman, or as independent communities among stateless peoples. The exception was in Kong and Bobo-Dioulasso (formerly Upper Volta, now Burkina Faso) where the Dyula forged their own states.

Farther west, in the shared border area of Ivory Coast, Guinea, and Mali, the Dyula lived among Mande warriors and peasants, from whom they differed only in their commercial activities and Islamic faith. They were two contrasting groups, one of warriors (Mande) and the other of Muslims (Dyula). This dichotomy between warriors and Muslims held true over a large area of western Sudan and the Sahara. Thus warriors who exercised political authority, shed blood, and indulged in imbibing alcohol (which played the symbolic role of differentiating the two communities) often professed Islam but were not committed Muslims.

THE EARLY *JIHĀD* MOVEMENTS. The *jihād* movements of West Africa represented a phase in the diffusion (often through the agency of Ṣūfī orders) and further entrenchment of Islam in the region. Part of the process of conveying Islam from the urban areas to the countryside and from the elite to the common people, *jihād* movements had the literary consequences of stimulating, in some cases, the production of Islamic material in Arabic or in the indigenous languages. It was partly a response to mounting levels of violence, abuse of political power, and the enslavement of people (including Muslims) in the age of the transatlantic slave trade.

With the rise of militancy in the 1670s, a crisis came about which pitted activist scholars against the traditional political elite. Nāṣir al-Dīn, a Berber scholar from the southwestern part of present day Mauritania where the Almoravid movement had originated, challenged the political supremacy of the nomadic Arab Hassani warriors. He was an ascetic scholar known for his religious charisma (*barakah*). He called for repentance and mobilized his devoted disciples for a jihad in 1675.

In West Africa, the *jihāds* succeeded in bringing about the political ascendancy of Islam not through conquest or expansion from the outside, but through the uprising of Muslim militants who lived within pluralistic societies including non-believers as well as men and women of varying degrees of commitment to Islam. West African *jihāds* can therefore be considered religious uprisings that accomplished a long evolutionary process.

While the military efforts of Nāṣir al-Dīn failed, his example most likely inspired the revolutionary movements which seized power in the following areas: Bundu, in present-day Senegal (c. 1700); Futa Jalon, in present-day Guinea (c. 1725); and Futa Toro (c. 1776). The scholars who led these movements, like Nāṣir al-Dīn before them, adopted the title of *al-imām* which implied political and religious leadership. They were Torodbe, members of scholarly lineages in Futa Toro.

Of the post-*jihād* states, the one in Futa Jalon was the least stable as it was plagued by internal conflicts and the lack of political integration of non-Fulani groups in the state. The one in Futa Toro did not fare any better as the leader, the *almamy imām* ʿAbd al-Qadir, and his successors were unable to establish effective central authority.

KANEM-BORNU AND HAUSALAND TO 1800. Kanem, in present-day Chad, northeast of Lake Chad, was one of the earliest states mentioned in Arabic sources, with references to the area in Arabic texts dating to the middle of the ninth century. But Islam was introduced into Kanem by Muslim traders from Tripoli and Fezzan (in present-day Libya) only at the beginning the twelfth century, at least a century after it had gained a foothold in Takrur and Gao.

Unlike the situation in western Sudan where the spread of Islam was facilitated by the trans-Saharan trade which linked the network of trading routes to the gold fields, in central Sudan the trade in captives with North Africa in exchange for goods, such as horses, dominated the economy and inhibited the spread of Islam. There was no comparable trading and scholarly diaspora across an expanding network of routes; instead, there was a Sahelian state which, even at the height of its military power, expanded, not southward into the savanna, but northward into the Sahara, eventually reaching the Fezzan. These contacts across the desert though led to the growth of Islam among the Kanuri-speakers. Islam, however, did not enter Baghirmi, the first Islamized state south of Lake Chad, until as late as the sixteenth century.

The above notwithstanding, the fact remains that the influence of Islam in Kanem was far more sustained than in western Sudan as judged by developments such as the state's expansion of its northern borders to as far as the southern part of modern Libya in the thirteenth century, Kanem kings underscoring the importance of Islam by performing pilgrimage, and the establishment of an Islamic school in Cairo for Kanem students and scholars. Sometime in the fourteenth century, the Saifawa dynasty, in order to stave off a complete disintegration of the state, located in a very precarious and fragile environment, moved its capital to the grassland region of Bornu in the southwestern corner of Lake Chad (present-day Nigeria). Bornu, formerly a tributary state of Kanem, had access to a wider trading network. This led the Saifawa dynasty in the fifteenth century to establish trading links with the Hausa which enabled them to exchange salt and horses for Akan gold, ushering in a period of prosperity.

The Kanem-Bornu state reached its peak under the rule of mai Idris Alawma (1570–1603), when government officials were Muslim and the capital, N'Gazargamu, emerged as an important center of Islamic learning. Muslim scholars were highly respected, exempt from taxes, and looked to for advice. Other scholars who wished to maintain their independence and keep their distance from political authorities created their own Muslim communities in the countryside. It was in this state, which became the most Islamized of all African states prior to the Islamic revolution in Hausaland, that Islam filtered more widely to the common people. Yet, even here, African ancestral elements remained at the symbolic and organizational levels.

Islam reached Hausaland during the fourteenth century when the Mali empire flourished and when the Saifawa dynasty relocated its capital to Bornu. This was the period when the Wangara trading diaspora was established on the eastern fringes of the Mali empire in Hausaland at the same time that a direct trade route from Hausaland to Tripoli was developed. These Wangara traders and the scholars who accompanied them provided services to Hausa rulers as they had done elsewhere in West Africa. Despite the employment of Wangara scholars at the courts, however, pre-Islamic beliefs continued to exist. Clearly, a struggle between the two religious systems existed as indicated by the Kano Chronicle.

By the end of the fifteenth century, King Rumfa of Kano attempted to make some reforms by ordering the symbolic tree to be cut down and a mosque built in its place. It is believed that the king, under the influence of al-Maghili, who visited Kano in 1493, installed Muslim judges and encouraged the construction of mosques. Moreover, Tombouctou scholars on their way to the pilgrimage visited Kano and neighboring Katsina to the north where they taught briefly. The outcome was the development or nurturing of a body of Hausa scholars in the region.

Some of the Muslim scholars who served at the courts of the Hausa rulers were later to become the object of criticism by later reformers. The former were seen as worldly scholars who had compromised Islamic teachings by their association with political authorities.

Revolution and Reform in Hausaland. The practice of living in separate communities (*jamaʿat*) with their followers in the countryside had already began to develop among some pious-minded scholars who avoided both the kingly courts and the trading centers. Instead, they lived and preached among the peasants in the rural areas and contributed to the radicalization of attitudes. Some scholars became champions of the peasants and couched their grievances in Islamic idiom or language. The increasing production of devotional literature in Hausa by the eighteenth century contributed further to an Islamic awareness among the people.

Revivalist or reformist ideas gained momentum in different parts of the Muslim world in the eighteenth century and fed into *mahdī* expectations and millenarian excitement which, widespread in the Muslim world, dated back to the fifteenth century. Since the thirteenth century, Ṣūfī orders had developed ecstatic practices and antinomian tendencies, but in the eighteenth century, they shifted their orientation toward greater adherence to the *sharīʿah*. Mysticism of the speculative kind, with its focus on otherworldliness, was increasingly being supplanted by the strands which emphasized involvement in societal affairs and even political activism. While Muḥammad Abdul Wahhab's struggles against syncretism in Saudi Arabia went as far as rejecting the whole mystical tradition, the reform movements of West Africa sought reform within the Ṣūfī traditions of the area.

Several reasons have been suggested for this militancy. First, there was the religious excitement, particularly at al-Azhar, which influenced various parts of the Muslim world. In western Sudan this was expressed either through a radical Qadiriyah, or as was the case later, through a radical Tijaniyya. Second, Islamic messianism or millenarian expectations, which were quite widespread in West Africa, explains this tendency to radicalism. In particular the ideas of the eighteenth-century Egyptian scholar al-Suyuti had gained currency. Suyuti predicted that a *mahdī* would appear at the end of the eighteenth century. Even earlier than this was al-Maghili who presented in a radical way the doctrine of a rejuvenator or renewer of Islam *(mujaddid)*. These seminal ideas took root and may partly explain the religious-political eruptions of the later centuries. Membership in Ṣūfī orders by these leaders, with special powers being attributed to them, increased the prestige and influence on their followers. Third, the institution of pilgrimage played an important role in preparing the careers of certain leaders for an active political life. Apart from legitimizing their role, the institution of pilgrimage was important in launching the career of certain leaders on a reformist course. The Tijani order became the moving force behind several later revolutions of the nineteenth century. Fourth, there was a growing Islamic consciousness on the part of the more learned Muslim scholars; this awareness went hand in hand with a call for radical reform. These were the *sharīʿah*-minded scholars who aimed at forging Islamic states. They articulated some of the local political and socioeconomic grievances but in the language or idiom of Islamic reform. They championed what has been called the "radical tradition" which Thomas Hodgkin defined as follows:

> A tradition which emphasizes the rights of common people against their rulers, takes an egalitarian attitude to social differences, is concerned with changing institutions as a precondition of changing human beings, demands the widest possible diffusion of knowledge and education, stresses the idea of an international community, the need for puritanism in personal life and the urgency of social change—justifying in some circumstances the use of revolutionary methods to achieve it. ("The Radical Tradition in Muslim West Africa," in *Essays on Islamic Civilization,* edited by D. P. Little, 1976, p. 103)

Shehu Usuman dan Fodio (Uthman Dan Fodio), a Fulani religious leader, belonged to the autonomous scholarly communities of Torodbe/Toronkawa who kept their distance and avoided making any accommodations with the Hausa elite of Gobir. They were neither traders nor pastoralists although they shared cultural values with the Fulani pastoralists who, like them, carried arms and also excelled in horse riding.

Usuman, the charismatic and missionizing teacher, along with his followers engaged in preaching around the villages. His scrupulousness as a scholar won him many sympathizers among the oppressed and exploited peasants. He called for responsible leadership committed to a moral vision of society, not a corrupt one which ruled arbitrarily. As the tensions mounted between Usuman and the king of Gobir, Usuman, whose life was in danger, was forced to disengage from society by moving from Degel to an alternative place (Gudu) to establish a new just society based on his Islamic reformist program. In effect, he and his followers performed a *hijrah*, or migration, following the example of the prophet, a preparatory stage for the *jihād*.

Once open conflict erupted between the king of Gobir and his Muslim protagonists, Usuman declared a *jihād* which, after its initial success, attracted other disaffected groups, including Fulani pastoralists who resented arbitrary seizure of their stocks. These military campaigns, which lasted from 1804 to 1810, engulfed not just the Hausa states, but also western Bornu, Adamawa, Nupe, and the Yoruba state of Ilorin (the basis of Islam's later impressive inroads among the Yoruba in the forest region of Nigeria). The outcome was a sprawling empire or Sokoto caliphate, with a number of separate emirates, which was ruled by a caliph (*Amir al-Muslimin*). Usuman retired into a religious life and left the administration of the new state to his brother and son.

Thus the Muslim scholars were able to realize their vision of creating an Islamic state. The ideals and values of the reformers were never realized although they remained normative and guided Usuman's successors. More importantly, Hausa society became transformed with the state and its institutions became Islamized. Another major outcome was that the Hausa ruling elite were replaced by a new Fulani one that adopted Hausa language and culture. Nevertheless, not all pre-*jihād* structures and practices were eliminated, as evidenced by the continued existence of some communities of non-Muslim Hausa speakers known as Maguzawa.

THE ṢŪFĪ ORDERS AND THE NINETEENTH-CENTURY *JIHĀDS* IN WESTERN SUDAN. Following Shehu Usuman's example, Ahmadu Lobbo conducted a *jihād* in 1818 against Fulani syncretists in Massina on the middle Niger south of Tombouctou. The state that he established, which lasted until 1864, was criticized by the Kunta and even Sokoto leaders for not being free of narrow-minded concerns and bigotry.

The first wave of *jihāds* or religiously inspired revolutions in West Africa were for the most part led by members of the Qadiri order (for instance, Usuman) while the later ones were mainly headed by Tijanis. The most important of these was the one led by al-Hajj ʿUmar (1794/97–1864), the Tijani leader in West Africa. His pilgrimage to Mecca and his appointment while there to Tijani leadership in West Africa confirmed him in his reformist mission to challenge syncretic Islam as well as other Ṣūfī orders, including Qādirīyah. He used Islam to forge a large Islamic state incorporating the regions of Segu, Kaarta, and Massina, which make up large parts of the present republic of Mali. His influence spread rapidly, perhaps too rapidly, explaining why he clashed with the French as well as the established groups in Massina. Despite his death in 1864, his state survived for the next several decades amidst French imperialistic and colonial advances in the region. Further south, on the fringes of the forest zone, during the decade of the 1860s, Samoury Toure (1835/40–1900), a long distance trader, attempted to unite various southern Mande peoples and states into a vast political system.

THE PROGRESS OF ISLAM IN ETHIOPIA AND THE HORN OF AFRICA. The economic, cultural, and political relations between Ethiopia and Arabia, separated only by the Red Sea, predate the coming of Islam by many centuries. In fact, this much earlier contact is evidenced by the presence of the locally evolved Geez, an Afro-Asiatic language, which bears the imprint of the interaction between south Arabians and the local Ethiopian groups. While in the seventh century Muslim refugees had migrated to the Aksum court to escape Meccan persecution, by the eighth century Muslims had settled on the Dahlak Islands off the Ethiopian coast, and by the ninth century there were Muslim communities along the long-distance trade routes into the interior. Islam expanded southwards, from the Harar area, in the direction of the Sidama principalities but not in the north where the Christian power was well established and well entrenched.

The growing power of Ifat and other Muslim states threatened the interests of an expanding Christian kingdom under the Zagwe kings who controlled the Ethiopian highland region. By the early fourteenth century, however, Ifat had been defeated. Yet, another Muslim state, Adal, asserted itself and began to recruit support from the Somali pastoralists who were increasingly being proselytized. More importantly, Adal controlled Harar, the most important center of trade and Islam in the interior, and also Zeila, on the Somali coast, south of modern Djibouti, which by the end of the ninth century had become a significant alternative Muslim trading settlement. Somali coastal settlements developed into thriving towns, the most significant of which was the sultanate of Mogadishu.

At the end of the fifteenth century or early sixteenth century, a Muslim general, Ahmad Gran, became the ruler of Adal and took on the title of *imām*. He saw Christian Ethiopia, then ruled by the Solomonid dynasty, as a threat to Muslim security. He articulated his policy toward Christian Ethiopia, which showed signs of breaking up, in religious terms and went on to overrun major sections of it with Ottoman-supplied firearms. The timely intervention by a Portuguese force, which came to the aid of Ethiopia, led to the two forces together defeating and killing Ahmad Gran in 1543 and thus saving the kingdom.

In the sixteenth century the pastoral Oromo, from northeast of Lake Turkana, moved into the southern highlands of Ethiopia, a region destabilized by the warfare, and pushed as far east as the plateau of Harar. Those that came into contact with Adal Muslims converted to Islam while others elsewhere became Christians. The Oromo became a major factor in the expansion of Islam from the eighteenth century onwards. Today they form the largest ethnic group in Ethiopia with probably more than half being Muslim.

Islam in East Africa and the Interlacustrine/Central Region. For centuries, even before the advent of Islam, there had always been contact between the East African coast and western Asia. Traders from south Arabia, the Persian Gulf, and western India took advantage of the monsoon winds to visit East Africa in pursuit of commercial opportunities.

The advent of Islam in Arabia in the seventh century marked the turning point in the trading relations between the two regions. The eastern Bantu speakers had already expanded to this coastal area probably by the midpoint of the first millennium CE, if not earlier. However, the growing commerce between Arabia and East Africa led to an increased migration to the area. The migrants appear to have come from a number of areas, but mainly from southern and, to a lesser extent, eastern Arabia. They first settled on the Benadir (Somali) coast in the ninth and tenth centuries, setting up settlements in Merca, Mogadishu, and Barawa. In later centuries, most notably the twelfth, traders from this region—Africans and proto-Swahili speakers, including probably some African-Arabs—also moved southward along the coast as far as Kilwa and established their settlements there. This is the period of the Shirazi myths as found in a number of chronicles. More immigrants from Hadhramawt and Yemen followed later, although their numbers were much smaller in relation to the local African coastal urban population. The cumulative result of the gradual changes brought about by the interaction between the immigrants and the dominant African Bantu-speaking groups was the creation of a new urban ethos in which Islam blended with the indigenous local culture to produce Swahili Islam. Although the coastal area had not become fully Islamized by this time, by early 1330s when Ibn Batuta visited East Africa, he indicated that there were many Muslims to be found in the thriving coastal towns such as Kilwa, whose inhabitants he makes clear were of dark skin. Swahili culture and language were by then fully evolved that he could speak of the coast as Sawahil country. It took another century or two, however, before Islam became part of the Swahili identity.

There was a period when the founding of Swahili coastal towns was attributed to Asian and Middle Eastern colonizers. This is the Asian perspective or hypothesis popularized by colonial scholarship which denied Africans with a contribution in the evolution of historical towns in their own region. The overwhelming evidence from records of earlier travelers and geographers, recent archaeological findings, and linguistic studies are all, however, in favor of the African perspective, crediting Africans with establishing their own towns. This does not deny the fact that Middle Eastern Muslim immigrants, whether as refugees from the Middle East or attracted by commercial opportunities in the region, were absorbed into Swahili population over a long period of history as evidenced by the culture of the Swahili which is both Muslim and African.

Although Islam reached East and West Africa around the same time, the methods and timing of its diffusion in the two regions presents some interesting contrasts. To begin with, Islam in West Africa had penetrated inland from Sahel into the savanna and as far as the fringes of the forest by the end of the fifteenth century. In East Africa, on the other hand, Islam remained confined to the coastal area for a long time before it was introduced into the interior, for instance, in Buganda in 1840. The spread of Islam in West Africa, moreover, was not associated with one particular ethnic or linguistic grouping the way it was in East Africa. For the most part, Islamization in East Africa went hand in hand with Swahilization, a process by which members of different ethnic groups became integrated into the Muslim Swahili community. In fact, the introduction of Islam in the hinterland of East Africa is closely connected to the extension of Muslim trading communities along the coast as far as northern Mozambique to the Interlacustrine region (which includes present Buganda/southern Uganda, Rwanda, Burundi, eastern Congo, and Malawi). Another significant difference is that religious upheavals in East Africa did not play a role as an instrument of conversion the way they did in some areas of West Africa. This means that there was no territorial expansion of Islam from the coast to the interior. There was a marked absence of empires like those of Ghana, Mali, and Songhai; instead, East Africa produced several dozen trading city states at the height of its commercial prosperity by the fifteenth century. Also, whereas East Africa was incorporated into the world of the west Indian Ocean, West Africa, through the trans-Saharan trade, was more connected to North Africa with which it traded for a long time.

The coming of the Portuguese to coastal East Africa at the end of the fifteenth century, as crusaders with commercial interests in the East, disrupted the Indian Ocean trade and also put to an end the first Muslim period of the East African coast. The brutal rule of the Portuguese provoked rebellions from time to time, and by the end of the seventeenth century, the Portuguese had been expelled from the coastal area north of Mozambique through a combination of local resistance and the rising power of Oman. Omani influence did not take hold until the 1830s when the sultan of Oman moved his capital to Zanzibar. This was a period of a commercial revival, including an expansion in slave trade, as well as growth in higher Islamic education along the coastal region and the development of the Ibadi school of thought in East Africa. Additionally, during the colonial period, Muslim communities from the subcontinent, Sunnī and Shīʿah, migrated to East Africa, adding a cosmopolitan dimension to the presence of Islam there.

Islam in South Africa. The highly urbanized Muslim minority communities of South Africa, with people of mainly Malay and Indian descent, have their origins in the developments starting from the mid-seventeenth century. As the Dutch began colonizing the Indonesian archipelago, the Cape of Good Hope functioned as a convenient place of exile for Indonesian political leaders. These exiles included Muslim learned men such as the scholar saint Shaykh Yusuf. A revered figure and a leader of an alternative culture, Shaykh Yusuf led foreign, non-white members of excluded or isolated groups who maintained their Islamic faith and perpetuated it among the slaves, convicts, and freed convicts from India and the Indonesian archipelago. Given the racial attitudes of nineteenth-century white South African society, many African slaves (liberated "Prize Negroes" or Africans freed by the British from intercepted slave ships) who could not be assimilated into white Christian culture found themselves turning to Islam. The final phase of Islam's entrenchment in South Africa through immigration came with the introduction of indentured labor service from India for the sugarcane fields in Natal. A significant number of these foreign workers were Muslim and succeeded in establishing a base for the faith in the region. Over a century later, Islam had survived in South Africa and even entered into a radical phase among some of its followers during the period of apartheid. The location of the South African Muslim communities on the periphery of the Muslim world in a secular Westernized world has allowed for some of its scholars to offer interesting modernist interpretations of Islam that are in keeping with progressive trends.

Islamic Art and Architecture. Treatment of the diffusion of Islam in Africa from both the east and the north would be remiss if the cultural dynamics of the interaction between the Islamic system and values and those of traditional African ways of thinking, especially in the area of visual representation, were not present or discussed at least briefly. The question that first needs to be asked is whether the old forms and symbols of the indigenous African system were discarded as a result of the encounters between Islam and traditional African religions? Did Islam, with its supra-ethnic universality, and the local African culture, with its ethnically centered identity, blend sufficiently during the process of Islamization on the continent to produce an Islamic art in Africa?

In the artistic and architectural domains there was a unique blending of Islamic structure and African representation. Once a balance had been reached between the local religious practices and the universal ritual prescriptions of Islam, the next step was to cast the imagery and iconography of African ancestral pillars, shrines, and so on into Islamized form. Where Islam was introduced, such items as charms, amulets, certain types of clothing, and prestige goods were incorporated into local societies. More importantly, the local altar-shrine was transformed into the mosque in such a way that the physical configuration represented a leap into verticality. Thus, the single, towering pyramidal earthen cone became the *miḥrāb*, while also serving as a minaret, with its system of projecting wooden pickets extending out of this massive structure. The ends of these wooden pickets served as a scaffold for workers to climb and repair the walls. The ancestral conical structure or pillar (in the Voltaic tradition) was now redirected to a new focal center, that of Mecca. In certain cases, as Prussin and Bravmann have observed, some of the mosques that were built in Mali had *miḥrābs* that evoked the image of an African mask, which traditionally represent powerful forces. This is how the mosques were constructed by the Mande of West Africa with Islam clearly inspiring the use of certain architectural features in the spatial configuration. The Islamic architectural tradition, mediated through the Maghrebian heritage, in turn inspired the architectural imagery or style represented by the thatched domes of the Senegal-Guinea mosques and maraboutic shrines, following the example of the domed cities of Tripoli and Cairo.

Islamic-type designs were also emulated and led to the adoption of arabesque wall patterning instead of the attached African charms. This calligraphy allowed for a new system of spatial organization. More than this, Islamic script was used in decorative ways even in non-Muslim areas such as modern-day Ghana, where in the nineteenth century, the Asantehene, head of the Ashanti confederacy, wore clothes with Arabic writing in various colors. Islam had clearly filtered through Ashanti politico-religious structure such that, as one scholar has noted, both in terms of ideas and in the realm of the arts, it provided a medium through which the ideology of the Ashanti was communicated.

Cultural Dynamics. Islam, which for many centuries coexisted well with traditional African religion, gradually over time attempted to replace it as the dominant faith of some regions. What made this possible was that the Islamic faith was much more adaptable in Africa, with minimum requirements for new members, including at the very least a change of name after reciting the testimony of faith. The observance of Islamic duties along with the understanding of the faith were supposed to follow later. For the first generation of Muslims, introduction to Islamic cultural values was what came first whereas Islamization itself could take generations to realize. At this level, there was accommodation to social and political structures of authority. This was the period when the learned Muslims, as in West African kingdoms, played a key role in administration and diplomacy. Eventually, however, a number of these African rulers adopted Islam and in doing so may partly have undermined the basis of their legitimacy as guardians of African ancestral religious traditions. Nevertheless, they did not completely renounce ties with the African traditional religion, which continued to be the religion of many of their subjects. This arrangement assisted in maintaining order although it did not please some West African Ṣūfī leaders of the eighteenth and nineteenth centuries who launched their *jihāds* and reform movements of Islamic revivalism, some of which had *mahdī* and messianic overtones, to establish Islamic states.

Islam during the Colonial Period. While there were some Muslim leaders who resisted colonialism—such as Muḥammad ibn ʿAbd Allāh (1864–1920) of the Salihiyah order in Somalia, al-Hajj ʿmar, and Samori (Guinea and Mali)—many others chose accommodation and collaboration. Colonialism facilitated the growth of Islam in areas of Africa as far apart as Tanzania (Tanganyika) in East Africa and Senegal in West Africa through the activities of Muslim brotherhoods (Ṣūfī orders), traders, and others. For some African groups, the loss of power with the onset of colonial rule made them gravitate towards Islam which was seen as an alternative to the prevailing colonial order. The difficulties of a new life under the colonial system, which uprooted the African from his or her traditional universe, presented Islam with an opportunity to provide a new framework as meaningful and all-embracing as the old African one. This, for instance, happened with Amadou Bamba's Murid brotherhood in Senegal, which converted thousands of people whose earthly kingdoms had been destroyed by colonialism. In 1888 Bamba established Touba/Tubaa as a great holy city, some claim it to rival Mecca, where he was buried in 1927. Every year hundreds of thousands of his followers visit his tomb on the anniversary of his death. Generally speaking, for the uprooted African who joined the faith, the Muslim supra-ethnic *ummah* provided solidarity and a sense of belonging not very different from that of the African village or ethnic one. Moreover, while the Islamic prescriptions replaced the indigenous ones, in matters of worship, however, the Muslim ritual prayer did not completely dislodge the traditional rituals of seeking to appease one's ancestors. In fact, Muslim religious leaders and teachers performed, in some cases, the same kind of role as the African healers and medicine men in carving out the domain of popular religion.

Islam therefore spread rapidly during the colonial period and became the majority faith in Senegal, Gambia, Guinea, Mali, Niger, and northern Nigeria where Shehu Usuman's descendants continued to exercise influence. Islam also made progress in areas such as Burkina Faso, the northern parts of the Ivory Coast, Ghana, Togo, Benin, and the "middle belt" of Nigeria where twenty to forty percent of the population is Muslim. Were it not for the resilience of traditional religions and the activities of Christian missions, Islam would most likely have been a majority religion here too.

POPULAR ISLAM IN AFRICA. Despite Muslim efforts to purge African elements from their faith, Islam continued to display a level of indigenization or Africanization in West Africa. In spite of producing such well-known major religious Fulani reformers of the nineteenth century, including Shehu Usuman dan Fodio, in northern Nigeria, women still tend to follow the traditional cults, including the bori spirit cult, even with the sustained impact of Islam in Hausaland for centuries. According to some scholars, there must be a level of affinity between the two religious systems which allows this to happen. For instance, the belief in mystical powers (*jinn* or invisible supernatural creatures) allows Islam to be accommodated to the African spirit world, which is important to understanding the African religious universe. In fact, the ancestral beliefs have been recombined with Muslim practice to form a new "folk" religion with emphasis on saint veneration, which popular Islam and Sufism reinforce and which approximates local ancestor veneration.

The diagnosis and treatment of illnesses attributed to occult forces in Africa have provided an opportunity for Muslim healing traditions to flourish and allowed for the services of Muslim healers and holy men, who provided additional healing choices to local practitioners, to be in high demand. The appearance of new epidemic diseases such as smallpox and cholera, which arose in the nineteenth and twentieth centuries in hinterland East Africa and which the local people could not adequately deal with, led people to turn to the Muslim healing system. Muslim prayers and amulets were more popular than Muslim secular remedies in this atmosphere of suspicion, which took the form of sorcery and witchcraft accusations. As has been noted, apart from the fact that Muslim amulets were believed to embody the words of the Supreme Being and not that of the intermediary powers, making them therefore more portent as the Ashanti believed, Muslim literacy played a role as a potential source of healing. Furthermore, Ṣūfī masters who had attained a closeness to God through following the path of spiritual enlightenment were believed to have special powers which made their prayers efficacious. This *barakah*, or blessing power which heals, was passed on in families and explains why the scholarly Ṣūfī lineages of the Sahara have played a pivotal role in mediating Islam between North and West Africa.

Modern developments in the Muslim world have undermined, to some extent, the influence of the *ṭarīqah* (Ṣūfī orders) in some parts of Africa such as Tanzania. Yet, the commitment to a mystical engagement with faith continues to be strong in West Africa and especially in Senegal, although even there it is facing the challenge of the Salafī reformers, also known as Wahhābīs, a term that is not used approvingly. Sufism, far from being a predominantly rural phenomenon which would fade away as Muslim societies became increasingly modernized, has continued to thrive and to engage African Muslims of the urban centers as well. It is true to say though that for some educated young African Muslims who are discomfited by magical practices, saint veneration, hierarchy, and authoritarianism of some Ṣūfī orders, the Salafī message has proved attractive.

The Salafī religious revivalism, despite its attractiveness to younger Africans, is generally conservative and traditional; to the extent that this is true, Salafī reform and Ṣūfī traditionalism are constantly engaged in an overlapping movement of interaction. Will they creatively synthesize from the values of their common Islamic heritage while acknowledging the entanglements and creative encounters between and within cultures? It remains to be seen what the outcome of this clash will be. It is clear though that underlying the conflict between them are struggles for power and control of the Muslim community in places as far apart as Uganda, Nigeria, and Mali.

WOMEN AND ISLAM. With respect to gender issues, Islam did not introduce patriarchy to Africa. In fact, many African societies were patriarchal and polygamous even before their encounter with Islam. Nevertheless, where Islam was introduced and its values incorporated in the socioeconomic and political structures of these societies (especially those with a propensity for state or empire building), a hierarchical social organization resulted in which there were clear demarcations of male and female spheres of activity. This, of course, did vary from society to society. For instance, the Yoruba women of southwestern Nigeria continued to be market women even after the coming of Islam whereas their Hausa counterparts in northern Nigeria tended to lead more secluded lives. It is significant to note that the Mahdiyya movement, which was established in 1941 in southern Nigeria by the scholar Muḥammad Jumat Imam, emphasized the education of women, their attendance of mosques together with men, and their inclusion in public affairs. By way of comparison, among the Tuareg-Berbers of the Sahara, who tend to be matriarchal, their unveiled women continued to enjoy far more freedom of movement than their Arab counterparts in North Africa.

Mysticism, and its chant practices and the spirit possession cults, provided an opening or opportunity for the acceptance of female authority, for instance, Sokna Magat Diop of the Murids, or religious leadership located within the female realm. Moreover, the Qādirīyah order did not challenge the female leadership of Shaykh Binti Mtumwa, a former slave or person of low status, who founded a branch of the order in Malawi and was successful in attracting many women. Therefore, both possession cults and Ṣūfī brotherhoods have allowed women to establish a sphere of action in hierarchical societies where control of the state is a male domain. These orders have incorporated women in both East and West Africa, especially in the area of education and fund raising, although women have a much larger scope in Senegal than Nigeria in brotherhood leadership.

There are Muslim women who, during the period of economic hardship at the end of the twentieth and beginning of the twenty-first centuries, have began to articulate issues of cultural authenticity rooted in Islamic identity in opposition to what has been perceived as Western cultural domination. They reject Western feminism, which they see as an extension of Western cultural domination and which sets Western values and ideas as the normative values. The role of these women has expanded as liberalization of the political process and the emergence of multi-party politics have led them to establish organizations and to embrace a particular agenda, including the Muslim dress code, and become involved in cultural politics. The Islamists and radical reformist activists are engaged in contesting existing gender relations and social justice. Islamists use the text (scripture) as their framework, whereas the secular activists' frame of reference is based on certain abstract concepts such as egalitarianism, humanism, human rights, and pluralism, concepts which have emerged from Western discourses on the subject.

The above examples indicate that the roles of men and women are constantly changing, especially due to urbanization, education, and cross-cultural contacts. For some women these changes have generated new freedom and opportunities for self-improvement.

ISLAMIC LAW IN AFRICA. In the political domain, Islam united much of Africa in the past and was willing to accommodate local, including legal, practices. Nevertheless, as the level of Islamization deepened, learned Muslim scholars began to call for a strict interpretation of the *sharīʿah* or Islamic law which they saw as different from the African legal and customary practices. Some obvious areas of difference included, for instance, the emphasis on individual ownership of land (and property inheritance through the male side of the family), whereas in various African societies land belonged to the community. Also, some have suggested, the way Islamic law was interpreted tended to give men more power over property matters than perhaps was the case in some African societies. Yet, comparative data across a number of African societies is needed to make this a meaningful comparison.

Unlike its African counterpart which is customary and unwritten, Islamic law, which covers both public and private life, is written, providing an extensive institutional framework within which Muslim *qāḍī* analyze legal issues and deduce new laws to handle new situations in the *ummah*. Its emphasis is on the rights or obligations of individuals, whereas African customary law (in which economic and social relations, especially in "stateless" societies, were regulated by customs maintained by social pressure and the authority of elders) is based on kinship ties in matters of marriage and property. It extends to commercial and criminal law and also has rules regarding the conduct of political leaders or those entrusted with authority. In their encounter with other legal systems, European colonial powers left these systems functioning in some societies (for instance, in Sudan and Nigeria as part of the British self-serving policy of indirect rule) while in others they allowed Muslim judges to apply Islamic civil and family law, except in criminal matters, which were tried by European courts. In the post-colonial period, the scope of Islamic law, where it is applied, is limited to religious issues and civil cases as the modern trend, with its emphasis on equal rights of citizens, is to have laws that apply across the board without recognizing any distinctions based on religion or gender.

The decision to recognize or not recognize Islamic laws in many African states after independence has created tensions and political controversy, especially when the secular elites have sought to forge a uniform system of law or at least have attempted to modify Muslim personal law, in aspects such as marriage for girls, to bring it in line with the inherited Western law and African customary practices. There has been a wide variety of responses to this dilemma regarding how much scope to give to religious laws. Mozambique, for instance, has made attempts to recognize traditional and religious marriages (thus doing the basic minimum) whereas Sudan has made *sharīʿah* the law of the state. The call by Muslim groups in northern Nigeria for nationalization of Islamic law has unleashed the *sharīʿah* debate, a source of tension in national politics in a country where at the very least only half or slightly more than half the population is Muslim. In African Muslim societies in general, however, it has been noted that there is often an anti-state discourse underlying the call for Islamic law by Muslim groups. These groups seek to foster their religious and cultural autonomy in societies where the state and secular institutions have neglected to respond to their needs.

ISLAMIZATION OF AFRICAN LANGUAGES. Arabic as the language of Islam has provided abstract concepts, particularly religious ones, which reveal Islamic modes of thought and expression. Islamic influence is, in fact, revealed both at the explicit and suggestive levels in languages as different as the Berber dialects, Hausa, Fulani, Mandingo, Swahili, and Somali, to name just a few. These languages have absorbed the Islamic worldview, though at some level languages such as Swahili have been progressively secularized over time, during and after the colonial period, making them more neutral. Since the eighteenth century, religious poems, sermons, devotional prayers, and litanies have been committed to writing in some of these Muslim languages of Africa, and legal manuals have been translated from Arabic to these languages.

The written word has been held in such high esteem in Islamic culture that wherever Islam has reached in Africa versions of its script have been adopted in those regions of sustained contact. Moreover, Islamic penetration of Africa introduced Arabic as the language of religious discourse among scholars, official correspondence between Islamized states, and historical writing during the period of the Muslim kingdoms. The priceless Tombouctou Arabic manuscripts, which still survive though precariously, once fully studied and analyzed by scholars will likely demolish the conventional historical view of Africa as a purely "oral continent." Both East and West Africa have also produced Afro-Islamic literature, from the panegyrics of the Prophet to poetry, based on local languages that have absorbed many Arabic words in the spheres of religion, politics, and commerce. In some of these areas, the written word though has competed with the oral literature, especially among such clan-based people as the Somali.

FUTURE OF ISLAM IN AFRICA. In the twenty-first century's era of globalization, Islam in Africa will continue to oscillate between accommodation and reform (both internally and externally generated), particularism and universalism, quietism and political activism, although increasingly the latter is the case in a significant number of countries in this era of Islamic resurgence worldwide. Islam has sought to penetrate Western secular cultures whose institutions and ideologies have not functioned well in Africa. In Muslim northern Nigeria, for instance, the *sharī'ah* debate is seen by some as masking concerns with Nigeria's federal system and is taking the form of cultural self-determination, cultural insecurity (in the wake of Western-driven globalization), and as a political-bargaining strategy for a region that thinks it is losing influence. Similarly, in Uganda in the 1990s, the increasing radicalization of Muslim Salafī and reformist groups, revealing social-economic forces at play and issues of inclusion or "full-citizenship," was partly a response to what was perceived as the failure of national institutions to provide social services.

SEE ALSO Aḥmadiyah.

BIBLIOGRAPHY

By far the single most important volume to date on the history of the development of Islam in Africa is *The History of Islam in Africa*, edited by Randall Pouwels and Nehemia Levtzion, (Athens, 2000). This will no doubt remain the definitive study on the subject for some time. Earlier works, though dated, that laid the foundations of serious study of Islam in sub-Saharan Africa include those by J. Spencer Trimingham, *Islam in the Sudan* (Oxford, 1959), *Islam in Ethiopia* (Oxford, 1952), *Islam in West Africa* (Oxford, 1959), *A History of Islam in West Africa* (Oxford, 1962), and *Islam in East Africa* (Oxford, 1964). For broad historical outlines of the regions where Islam spread, consult the relevant sections in *The Cambridge History of Africa*, eight volumes, (London, 1975). Other useful texts include Peter Clark's *West Africa and Islam* (London, 1982) and *Islam in Tropical Africa*, second edition, edited by I. M. Lewis (Oxford, 1980).

The Institute for the Study of Islamic Thought in Africa (ISITA) at Northwestern University has produced a series of important publications, such as "Arabic Literature of Africa," in a projected six volume series, of which the first four have already appeared. They include Volume 1: *The Writings of Eastern Sudanic Africa to c. 1900*, edited by R. S. O'Fahey, (Leiden, 1994) and Volume 2: *The Writings of Central Sudanic Africa to c. 1900*, edited by John Hunwick, (Leiden, 1996). The proceedings of the yearly ISITA colloquia have also produced *The Transmission of Knowledge in Islamic Africa*, edited by Scott Reese, (Leiden, 2004).

The most significant Arabic sources are now available in English or French translations. Among them are those that appear in the series "Fontes Historiae Africanae." Many external Arabic sources before the sixteenth century are collected in the *Corpus of Early Arabic Sources for West African History*, edited by Nehemia Levtzion and J. F. P. Hopkins (Cambridge, U.K., 1981). Four chronicles from Tombouctou are now available in French: *Ta'rikh al-Fattash*, translated by O. Houdas and M. Delafosse (Paris, 1913); *Ta'rikh al-Sudan*, translated by O. Houdas (Paris, 1899); *Tadhkirat al-Nisyan*, translated by O. Houdas (Paris, 1913–1914); *Tombouctou au Milieu du dix-huitieme siecle d'apres la Chronique de Mawlay al-Qasim*, translated by M. Abithol (Paris, 1982). Al-Maghili's text has been translated by John O. Hunwick as *Shari'ah in Sunghay: The Replies of al-Maghili to the Questions of Askiya al-Hajj Muḥammad* (London, 1985). On the *jihād* in Sokoto, see 'Abd Allah ibn Fudi's *Tazyin al-Waraqat*, translated by M. Hiskett Ibadan, 1963, and Usuman dan Fodio's *Bayan wujub al-hijrah*, translated by F. H. al-Masri. See also al-Hajj Umar's *Bayan ma Waqa'a*, translated by M. Mahibou and J. L. Triaud, (Paris, 1983).

On Islam in the early states of western Sudan, see Levtzion's *Ancient Ghana and Mali* (London, 1973). This may be followed by John Hunwick's *Timbuctu and the Songhay Empire: Al-Sadi's Tarikh Al-Sudan down to 1613 and Other Contemporary Documents* (Leiden, 1999) and Elias Saad's *Social History of Timbuctu: The Role of Muslim Scholars and Notables,*

1400–1900 (New York, 1983). A new approach to the study of Muslim religious figures was opened by Lamin O. Sanneh's *The Jakhanke: The History of an Islamic Clerical People of the Senegambia* (London, 1979) and *Piety and Power* (New York, 1996). In *Muslim Chiefs and Chiefs in West Africa* (Oxford, 1968), Levtzion has analyzed patterns of integration of Muslims into the sociopolitical system of West African states. See also *Rural and Urban Islam in West Africa* (Boulder, Colo., 1987), edited by Levtzion and J. Humphrey.

For more information about two south Saharan societies that influenced West African Islam, see H. T. Norris's *The Tuaregs: Their Islamic Legacy and Its Diffusion in the Sahel* (Warminster, U.K., 1975) and C. C. Stewart's *Islam and Social Order in Mauritania* (Oxford, 1973).

On the important role of Sufism in Africa, see H. T. Norris's *Sufi Mystics of the Niger Desert: Sidi Mahmut and the Hermits of Air* (Oxford, 1990), *Charisma and Brotherhood in African Islam*, edited by D. C. O'Brien and C. Coulson (Oxford, 1988) and Bradford G. Martin's *Muslim Brotherhoods in Nineteenth Century Africa* (New York, 1976). Essays on the precursors and leaders of the *jihāds* are presented in *Studies in West African Islamic History: The Cultivators of Islam*, edited by John R. Willis, (London, 1979). For the major *jihād* movements and products of the *jihād*, see Mervin Hiskett's *The Sword of Truth: The Life and Times of Shehu Usuman dan Fodio*, second edition, (Evanston, Ill., 1994); B. B. Mack and J. Boyd's *One Woman's Jihad: Nana Asma'u, Scholar and Scribe* (Bloomington, Ind., 2000); Michael Gomez's *Pragmatism in the Age of Jihad* (Cambridge, U.K., and New York, 1993); Yves Person's *Samori: Une revolution dyula*, three volumes, (Nimes, France, 1968–1975); and Thomas Hodgkin's "The Radical Tradition in Muslim West Africa," in *Essays on Islamic Civilization*, edited by D. P. Little, (Leiden, 1976).

On Islam during the period of French colonialism in Africa, see Christopher Harrison's *France and Islam in West Africa, 1860–1960* (Cambridge, U.K., and New York, 2003). For Islam in the modern politics of Africa, consult *Religion and National Integration in Africa: Islam, Christianity, and Politics in the Sudan and Nigeria*, edited by John Hunwick, (Evanston, Ill., 1992), A. El-Affendi's *Turabi's Revolution: Islam and Power in Sudan* (London, 1991), *African Islam and Islam in Africa*, edited by D. Westerlund and E. E. Rosander, (London, 1997), and Lansine Kaba's *The Wahhabiyya: Islamic Reform and Politics in French West Africa* (Evanston, Ill., 1974).

Specialized studies on Islam in East Africa have also began to appear, including Anne Bang's *Sufis and Scholars of the Sea: Family Networks in East Africa, 1860–1925* (London, 2003); Randall Pouwels' *Horn and Crescent* (Cambridge, U.K. and New York, 1989); Abdin Chande's *Islam, Ulamaa, and Community Development in Tanzania* (San Francisco, Calif.,1998); *Islam in Kenya*, edited by Mohamed Bakari and Saad Yahya, (Nairobi, Kenya, 1995); and August Nimtz Jr.'s *Islam and Politics in East Africa: The Sufi Order in Tanzania* (Minneapolis, 1980). Interpretive studies, with numerous illustrations that represent the best of Muslim artistry and design in Africa, are offered in Rene Bravmann's *African Islam* (London, 1983); Labelle Prussin's *Hatumere: Islamic Design in West Africa* (Berkeley, Calif., 1986); and *Islamic Art and Culture in Sub-Saharan Africa*, edited by K. Dahl and B. Sahlstrom, (Uppsala, Sweden, 1995).

On popular Islam, as well as encounters between African ancestral religions and Islam, see Dean Gilland's *African Religion Meets Islam: Religious Change in Northern Nigeria* (Lanham, Md., 1986), and David Owusu-Ansah's *Islamic Talismanic Tradition in Nineteenth Century Asante* (Lewiston, N.Y., 1991). On Islam in the periphery, see A. Tayob's *Islam in South Africa: Mosques, Imams, and Sermons* (Gainesville, Fla., 1999).

NEHEMIA LEVTZION (1987)
ABDIN CHANDE (2005)

ISLAM: ISLAM IN THE CAUCASUS AND THE MIDDLE VOLGA

When the first Arab invaders appeared in eastern Transcaucasia in the seventh century, the Caucasus was a borderland between the nomadic world to the north and the old sedentary world to the south, and between the Greek civilization in the West and the Iranian world in the East. It had a highly sophisticated urban civilization where several world religions, including Judaism, Manichaeism, Zoroastrianism, and Christianity, were already well entrenched. Among the Christians, the Georgians and Alans were Orthodox, and the Armenians and Albanians were monophysites. Unlike Central Asia, which has been characterized by religious tolerance, the Caucasus for centuries has been the fighting ground for three great monotheistic religions—Christianity, Judaism, and Islam.

ISLAM IN THE CAUCASUS. The spread of Islam was inhibited by powerful political rivals who reinforced religious rivalries. The Turkic Khazar empire in the north formed an effective barrier against the progress of the conquering Arabs north of Derbent; the Christian Georgian and Armenian principalities, backed by the Byzantine Empire, presented an insuperable obstacle to Muslim progress westward.

The slow Islamization of Dagestan. The Arabs penetrated into Azerbaijan in 639; local rulers agreed to become subordinate to the caliph but retained their Christian faith. In 643, the Arabs reached Derbent (which they called Bāb al-Abwāb) and in 652 attempted to move north of the city but were heavily defeated by the Khazars. For almost a century the territory of present-day Dagestan was disputed between the Khazars and the Arabs, as expeditions and counterexpeditions succeeded each other almost without interruption and without any decisive victory. Not until the governorship of Marwān ibn Muḥammad (734–744) were the Khazars decisively defeated in Arrān. Derbent, solidly held by an Arab garrison, became the northernmost bastion of Islam facing the world of the Turkic nomads. Several thousand Arab settlers from Syria and northern Iraq were established in northern Azerbaijan by the governor Maslamah ibn ʿAbd al-Malik.

First inroads. Notwithstanding several Khazar expeditions between 762 and 799, by the end of the eighth century Islam was already the dominant religion of Arrān and of the coastal plain south of Derbent. Even so, Christian and Jewish communities survived in the area. Indeed, in 1979 there were in northern Azerbaijan and southern Dagestan some 5,919 monophysite Christian Udins, the last survivors of the Albanian church. There were also about 30,000 "Mountain Jews," or Dagh Chufut, the descendants of the Jewish military colonists established in the Caucasus by the Sassanid kings. In recent years, most of them have migrated to Israel.

The progress of Islam into the mountains was, by contrast, slow and difficult. According to Dagestani legends, Maslamah ibn ʿAbd al-Malik (r. 723–731), having conquered all Dagestan, imposed Islam on the local rulers. In reality, the submission of the indigenous chieftains was purely formal. As soon as the Arab control weakened, the local population reverted to their ancient religion. In some instances, after Dagestani rulers embraced the new religion, their subjects remained Christian, Jewish, or animist. The northern Caucasian mountain area remained virtually untouched by Islam into the tenth century. In southern Dagestan, the ruler of Tabasaran professed Islam, Christianity, and Judaism simultaneously. All three religions were represented among the Zirīhgarāns of central Dagestan. The Lezghians of southern Dagestan were "infidels." Sarīr, in the Avar country of western Dagestan, had a Christian prince (Orthodox of Georgian rite), but his subjects were in the majority animist, with traces of Zoroastrianism. Samandar in northern Dagestan was governed by a Jewish prince related to the Khazar khagan, but all three religions were represented among his subjects. The majority of the Iranian Alans of the central Caucasus were Christian Orthodox of Byzantine rite, while the Kabardins and the Cherkess were animist, with a Christian minority. On the Black Sea coast the Abkhaz paid tribute to the Arabs but remained Christian. At the end of the tenth century, the borderline of the *dār al-Islām* ("abode of Islam") was still situated three miles north of Derbent. Islam was solidly rooted only in Derbent, which was an important fortress, a prosperous economic center, and one of the wealthiest cities of the Arab caliphate, and also in the Lakh country of central Dagestan. According to a local legend, a mosque was built in the Lakh capital, Kazi-Kumukh, in 777.

This first period of Islamization of the Caucasus (through the tenth century CE) was marked by exceptional religious tolerance. Not only did the three monotheistic religions coexist peacefully, but there was toleration of those not originally included among the "people of the Book" (*ahl al-kitāb*)—Zoroastrians and animists. In short, Islam was only superficially superimposed on a deeply rooted set of pre-Islamic beliefs, customs, and rites.

Further expansion. In the eleventh century, a new phase of Islamization began. The Khazar empire had been destroyed in 965 by the Russes, thus removing the main obstacle to relations between the Muslim Bulgar kingdom in the far north and the lands of the caliphate on the one hand, and to the Islamization of the Turkic nomads beyond Derbent on the other. Meanwhile, in the south, the foundation of the Seljuk empire improved security along the trade routes and favored the peaceful penetration of Islam into the mountains. This movement was facilitated by two additional phenomena. First, in the tenth century, the old clanic formations were replaced by stronger feudal principalities in Dagestan: the Nutzal of Avar, the Ūsmīyat of Kaytāk in the Darghin country, the Shāmkhālat of Kazi-Kumukh (central Dagestan), and the Maʿṣūmat of Tabasaran in southern Dagestan (Lezghian country). By the end of the eleventh century the rulers of these principalities were already Muslim, and their vassals and subjects tended to follow the example of the suzerain. Second, there was a total disappearance of the old alphabets (Aramaic, Pahlavi, Albanian) formerly used to transcribe the local languages. These were replaced by Arabic, which became and remained henceforward the only literary language of the area.

In the eleventh and twelfth centuries, the majority of the Darghins and the Lakh of central Dagestan became Muslims, and Islam penetrated into western and northern Dagestan. By contrast, the more remote territories, bypassed by the main trade routes—in particular, the Chechen and Ingush countries—preserved a purely prefeudal (clanic) society and were resistant to Islam.

In the middle of the twelfth century, a visitor to Dagestan, Abū Ḥāmid al-Andalusī of Granada, discovered traces of Christianity and Zoroastrianism among the Zirīhgarāns; he also found many Christians and animists among the Avars.

Mongol era. The Mongol invasion did not modify the complicated religious situation of the northern Caucasus. As elsewhere, in Central Asia, in the Bulgar country, or in Iran, the first wave of Mongol invaders were animists, Nestorian Christians, or Buddhists, and generally hostile to Islam. But the destruction wrought by the expeditions of Sübetey and Djebe (1220) and of Batu (1239) were not followed by religious persecution. During the Mongol rule, Caucasian Islam ceased to be exclusively the religion of rulers and of elites and became more deeply rooted in the popular elements. The Caucasus was divided between two rival Mongol khanates, the Golden Horde in the north and the khanate of the Il-khanids in Iran. The third khan of the Golden Horde, Berke (r. 1257–1266), embraced Islam, and although his successors reverted to their ancestral religion, they remained tolerant and even favorable toward Islam.

In 1313, Uzbek Khan, a Muslim, became the ruler of the Golden Horde. His reign marked the final victory of Islam among the Turkic nomads roaming the immense steppe area between the Crimea and the Volga. One of the Turkic tribes, the Nogai Horde, played an important role in the Islamization of the northern Caucasus during the fourteenth century. It was through the Nogais that Islam made inroads for the first time among the Cherkess, the Kabardins, and the Chechen. Also, in the first half of the fourteenth century, the Ṣūfī brotherhoods began to appear in the northern Caucasus as well. Shaykh Muḥammad al-Baṭāʾiḥī of the

Rifāʿī *ṭarīqah* (order) founded a *khānqāh* ("lodge") in Machar in the steppeland of the northern Caucasus. This *ṭarīqah* disappeared a century later, however.

Timurid rule. The final phase of Islamization in Dagestan took place in the late fourteenth and early fifteenth centuries, during the reign of Timur (Tamerlane). The great conqueror led several expeditions into Azerbaijan and Dagestan between 1385 and 1395. He took a personal interest in the destruction of the last survivals of pre-Islamic religions, and Islam became henceforward the only religion of the Lakh of central Dagestan. In turn, the Lakh became the champions of Islam against those neighbors remaining animist or Christian. The city of Kazi-Kumukh, the capital of the principality of the Shāmkhālat Lakh, was the new center for the Islamization of Dagestan and the lands beyond its western frontiers, and it was the Lakh missionaries who brought Islam to the Chechen and the Kumiks. Timur also dealt a deadly blow to the power of the Christian Alans of the north-central Caucasus (the ancestors of the Ossets). The Christian Alans had been the mightiest nation of the Caucasus, and their decline was followed by a new expansion of Islam in the northern Caucasus.

During Timur's period, the majority of the Kāytāks became good Muslims. Earlier, the Kāytāks were considered as "people without faith" (*bī-dīn*) or as a "people of bad faith." Subsequently, the Lezghians of southern Dagestan and the Avars turned Muslim as well.

It was in this high, mountainous territory that Christianity held out longest, and its survival was important to the Georgian kings' efforts to protect their coreligionists. The village of Karakh in the high Avar country did not adopt Islam until 1435. The Dido and the Andi tribes remained Christian until 1469, and Gidatl became Muslim in 1475 or 1476.

At the end of the fifteenth century, two new Muslim powers appeared on the Caucasian scene, and their influence on the process of Islamization became decisive. The Ottoman Empire brought the spirit of *jihād* (religious war) to the Caucasus. The rulers of the Crimean khanate dominated the lowlands of the western and central Caucasus. The Ottoman advance was marked by the gradual conversion of the Laz of the southwestern Caucasus (they were formerly Christian) and of the Abkhaz of the Black Sea coast. At the same time the Crimean Tatars introduced Islam among the western and eastern Cherkess tribes. Derbent and Shirvan in eastern Transcaucasia were conquered by the Safavids in 1538. As a consequence, the Twelver Shīʿī rite of the Safavid rulers became the dominant form of Islam in Azerbaijan.

In the middle of the sixteenth century, Sunnī Islam of the Shāfiʿī rite was solidly established in Dagestan, while the Ḥanafī rite was making steady progress in the western Caucasus. The tribes of the central Caucasus, however—the eastern Cherkess, the Kabardins, the Ossets, the Balkars, the Karachays, the Chechen, and the Ingush—were for the most part Christian or pagan, and only the upper level of their feudal aristocracy had adopted Islam.

Battle with Muscovy. After 1556, the power of Muscovy appeared in the Caucasus. As a consequence, relations between Islam and Christianity were dramatically modified. Specifically, the era of religious tolerance came to an end, and the Caucasus entered a new period of religious confrontation. Both Moscow and Istanbul favored their coreligionists. Temrük, the great Kabardian prince (a Muslim), accepted Russian sovereignty and married his daughter, Maria (converted to Christianity), to Ivan the Terrible. The central Caucasus was thus opened to Russian influence. Christian missionaries were sent in great numbers, and churches were built in Kabardia, among the eastern Cherkess, and in Ossetia. In 1584, Muscovy began its military advance southward, and three years later, the Russians reached the Terek Valley. In 1590, their vanguards appeared on the Sunzha River, threatening Dagestan, but already the Crimean Tatars and the Ottomans were reacting vigorously. In the same year, the Ottomans, advancing from the south, occupied Derbent; in 1587 the Crimean khan had already invaded and ruined Kabardia, Moscow's principal ally in the northern Caucasus. In 1594, there was a major confrontation: on the banks of the Sulaq River in northern Dagestan, a Russian army was opposed by a joint force of Ottomans, Tatars, and Dagestanis. In a furious battle, with all the characteristics of a "holy war," the Russians were pushed back. They returned in 1604 and were once again heavily defeated. Thus, the first *jihād* in Dagestan and the religious competition in Kabardia between Christianity and Islam ended with a complete Muslim victory. Russian influence was pushed back as far as Astrakhan and the Lower Volga. Kabardia, strategically the most important area of the northern Caucasus, became a solid Muslim bastion.

In the seventeenth and eighteenth centuries, the Ottoman Turks and the Crimean Tatars continued their steady efforts to introduce Islam among the remaining Christian or pagan tribes of the northwestern Caucasus. These tribes included the Karachay, the Balkars, the western Cherkess, the Abazins, and the Abkhaz. In 1627, southwestern Georgia was conquered by the Turks, and a part of its population embraced Islam. The descendants of these Georgian Muslims, the Adzhars, totaled from 100,000 to 150,000 people late in the twentieth century.

The period of the "Holy Wars." The Russian advance toward the Caucasus, suspended in 1604, was resumed in 1783 after the conquest of the Crimea and the occupation of the steppe areas north of the Kuban River.

Naqshbandīyah. The arrival of the Russians, this time with overwhelming force, coincided with the appearance of the Naqshbandīyah Ṣūfī brotherhood in the northern Caucasus. This was a Turkistani order founded in Bukhara by Muḥammad Bahāʾ al-Dīn Naqshband (1317–1389). For more than a century, the adepts of the Naqshbandīyah were the organizers of the "holy war" against the advancing conqueror. It was during the struggle against the "infidels" and the "bad Muslims" who served them that Islam became the dominant religion of the northern Caucasus and that its character was fundamentally modified. At the end of the eighteenth century, the superficially Islamized communities were tolerant toward their neighbors who remained Christian. They also tolerated those who remained attached to numerous pre-Islamic beliefs and rites and followed various non-Muslim customary laws (*ʿādāt*). But a century later, Caucasian Islam, deeply rooted in the rural masses, was characterized by its rigorous conservatism, by its intolerance toward non-Muslims, and by its strict adherence to *sharīʿah* law.

The first Naqshbandī *jihād* against the Russians was led by Imām Manṣūr Ushurma, a Chechen who was probably the disciple of a *shaykh* from Bukhara. The movement began in 1785 in Chechnya and spread to northern Dagestan and the western Caucasus. But Manṣūr was captured in 1791 in Anapa and died two years later in the fortress of Schlüsselburg. It was a short-lived attempt to stop the advance of the invaders. Even so, during Manṣūr's rule Islam became deeply rooted in Chechnya, formerly only about one-half Muslim.

After Manṣūr's defeat, the Naqshbandīyah disappeared from the northern Caucasus for nearly thirty years, and during this period the Russians, almost unopposed, made substantial advances. The *ṭarīqah* reappeared in the 1820s in the province of Shirvan, however, with the Naqshbandī missionaries coming this time from the Ottoman Empire. The second Naqshbandī *murshid* ("guide") to preach "holy war" was Shaykh Muḥammad of Yaraglar. He was the master of Ghāzī Muḥammad and Shāmil, the first and the third *imāms* of Dagestan. The long and fierce resistance of the mountaineers lasted from 1824 to 1859, when Shāmil was finally defeated and captured. Despite its failure, this second Naqshbandī *jihād* left an indelible impact on northern Caucasian Islam. Shāmil liquidated forever the traditional customary legal system and replaced it with the *sharīʿah*. Moreover, in the nineteenth century, classical Arabic became the official written language of the imamate and also the spoken intertribal language of Dagestan and Chechnya. Thus, for the first time in history, the northern Caucasian population was united by a strong religious, linguistic, and cultural bond. Finally, the intense work of the Naqshbandī missionaries in the central and western Caucasus achieved the Islamization of all Cherkess and Abazin tribes. During Shāmil's rule, Dagestan became an important center of Arabic culture. Its scholars, the so-called Arabists, were exported to the entire Muslim world.

Qādirīyah. After 1859 and the subsequent Russian occupation of the Caucasus, the Naqshbandīyah went underground. Its leaders migrated to Turkey or were deported to Siberia. Some became *abrek,* "bandits of honor," forming guerrilla groups in the mountains. Another Ṣūfī order, the Qādirīyah (or Kunta Haji *ṭarīqah*), replaced the Naqshbandīyah on the front line of religious resistance. This order appeared in the Chechen country in the 1860s, when "infidel" domination had become a fact of life. It was different, at least at the outset, from the militant Naqshbandīyah in that its ideology was inspired by the mystic search for God rather than by "holy war." Even so, it was rapidly outlawed by the authorities and was obliged to go underground. At that point, the Qādirīyah became another center of military resistance to the Russian presence. Both the Naqshbandī and the Qādirī *ṭarīqahs* played an active part in the anti-Russian revolt of 1877–1878 in Dagestan and Chechnia.

The Qādirīyah were vigorous missionaries. Because of their activities, the Ingush, who had remained animist until the fall of Shāmil, finally became Muslim. The last animist Ingush village was converted to Islam in 1864.

The Russian Revolution provided the Ṣūfī adepts with the opportunity to shake off Russian rule. During this period, the Naqshbandīyah surfaced and made one last attempt to expel the "infidels." They fought for four years—from 1917 to 1921—first against the White armies of Denikin, then against the Red Army. Their resistance was finally crushed in 1921, and after their defeat, both Ṣūfī brotherhoods were subjected to a long and bloody persecution. But they survived. In 1928, the Qādirīyah and the Naqshbandīyah joined together in a revolt in Dagestan and the Checheno-Ingush republic. This armed uprising was followed by similar revolts in 1934 and 1940–1942. The revolt during World War II was led by nationalists, but the Qādirīyah were numerous among the guerrilla fighters.

The level of religious feeling among the Muslim population of the Caucasus is quite high, especially in Dagestan and in the Checheno-Ingush republic, where more than 80 percent of the population are considered "believers." The strength of Islam in the northern Caucasus is due, in part, to the intense activity of the Ṣūfī brotherhoods. The *ṭarīqahs* still control a network of houses of prayer and Qurʾanic schools, where children are taught Arabic and receive the rudiments of the Muslim faith. The schools and mosques are often organized around the holy places of pilgrimage, generally tombs of Ṣūfī *shaykhs*.

Ṣūfī *ṭarīqahs* are especially active in the Checheno-Ingush republic and in northern Dagestan, while they are not represented in the central and western Caucasus. The Naqshbandīyah dominates Dagestan, northern Azerbaijan, and the western districts of Chechnya. In the northern Caucasus, the Qādirīyah, more popular and more dynamic, is divided into four sub-*ṭarīqahs*, called *wirds*. These are the Batal Haji, Bammat Giray Haji, Chim Mirza, and Vis (Uways) Haji. The Qādirīyah *ṭarīqah* is predominant in the Checheno-Ingush republic and is spreading into western Dagestan.

ISLAM IN THE MIDDLE VOLGA. As early as the fifth or sixth century a few Turkic tribes, the ancestors of the Volga Bulgars, began settling in the territory of the Middle Volga. These tribes were the first Turks to settle down and to abandon the nomadic way of life.

Islamization: trade, conquest, Sufism. The area—the Kama River and the Urals—was situated at the crossroads of two main trade routes during the Middle Ages. The fur route ran from northern Russia-Siberia (Arḍ al-Ẓulm, the "Land of Darkness" of the Arab geographers) to the Muslim Middle East, and the Silk Road linked northern and central Europe to China. The Turkic Bulgars were traders in furs, slaves, amber, and ivory. Accordingly, they traveled widely, some as far as Baghdad and Gurganj on the Amu Darya, coming into contact with Arab merchants as early as the ninth century. It is through such trade relations that Islam penetrated into the Middle Volga, initially from Khorezm, then from Baghdad farther west.

The Bulgar kingdom. In 921, the Bulgar king, Almas, received an embassy sent by Caliph al-Muqtadir and converted to Islam on May 12, 922. His example was followed rapidly by the ruling elite of the kingdom. At the end of the tenth century, most of the Bulgars were already Muslim, and there were mosques and schools in virtually every village. For three hundred years, the Middle Volga area remained a Muslim island—the northernmost vanguard of the *dār al-Islām*—completely surrounded by Christian or animist neighbors. Its ties with the faraway Muslim world were maintained through the Volga trade route.

In spite of, or perhaps because of, their isolation, the Bulgars were zealous Muslims from the beginning. They played a role in the conversion of some nomadic Turkic tribes, the Pechenegs and Cumans, to Islam. They also nursed hopes of spreading Islam to the Russians, who were at that time still animists. In 986 a Bulgar embassy was sent to Kiev with the aim of converting the grand prince, Vladimir. The Russian Primary Chronicle recounts that some time later, Vladimir, in search of a suitable religion, also received representatives of Western and Eastern Christianity and of Judaism and heard each speak in turn of the merits and tenets of his faith.

Little more is known about the cultural history of the Bulgar kingdom prior to the thirteenth century. One may assume that Islam remained the religion of the Turkic city-dwellers, the feudal elite, and the merchant class, while the rural population, of whom the majority was ethnically Finnic, remained animist.

The Golden Horde. The Bulgar kingdom was destroyed by the Mongols around 1236. This was a major disaster that left the country devastated and ruined. But its Islamic character survived. The economic and political center was transferred from the valley of the Kama River to the Volga, near what is now the city of Kazan. Subsequently, Kazan became one of the most prosperous trading centers of the Golden Horde. In this area there was a biological and cultural merging of the indigenous Muslim Turks and the invading Mongols, with the less numerous Mongols assimilated by the Muslim Turks. Even so, the new nation was called "Tatar," the name of a Mongol tribe.

During the period of the Golden Horde, Uzbek Khan (r. 1313–1341) adopted Islam as the official religion of the Mongol rulers. This example was followed by all the Turkic and Mongol tribes roaming in the steppes between the former Bulgar kingdom and the Black and Caspian seas. Islam gained a firm footing in the Crimea as well.

Sufism. It was also during the period of the Golden Horde—between the thirteenth and fourteenth centuries—that Sufism was brought to the Volga region. It was introduced by adepts of a mystical Turkistani brotherhood, the Yasawīyah *ṭarīqah,* founded by the Turkic poet and mystic Aḥmad Yasawī (d. 1166?). Thanks to the efforts of the Ṣūfī preachers, Islam was no longer limited to being the religion of rulers and scholars: it became deeply rooted in the countryside among the rural populations and even among the nomadic tribes.

In 1445, with the weakening of the Golden Horde, Kazan became the capital of an independent Tatar khanate that lasted until 1552. It was a wealthy city, a world capital of the fur trade, and a brilliant cultural center famous for numerous mosques and *madrasahs*. In the late fifteenth and the early sixteenth centuries, a new Ṣūfī brotherhood became active in Kazan—the Naqshbandīyah *ṭarīqah,* which, as mentioned above, later opposed Russian advances in the northern Caucasus. An intellectual order representing the city elites, the Naqshbandīyah practiced the silent *dhikr,* or Ṣūfī prayer litany. In contrast, the Yasawīyah practiced the "loud" *dhikr* with songs and ecstatic dances reminiscent of old Turkic shamanistic rituals. The influence of the Naqshbandīyah on Tatar literature became predominant, and nearly all the Tatar poets from the sixteenth to the nineteenth century were adepts of the order, including Muḥammadiyar, the sixteenth-century author of *Tukhfat-i mardān* (The gift for the courageous) and *Nūr-u ṣudūr* (The light of the soul), Mawlā Qulī in the seventeenth century, Utyz Imānī al-Bukhārī (1754–1815), ʿAbd al-Manih Kargaly (1782–1826), ʿUbayd Allāh Ṣāḥib (1794–1867), and Shams al-Dīn Zakī Ṣūfī (1825–1865).

Russian rule. In 1552, the khanate was destroyed by the Russians and its territory was incorporated into the Muscovite state. In 1556 and 1598, two other Muslim remnants of the Golden Horde, the khanates of Astrakhan on the Lower Volga and of Sibir (or Tumen) in western Siberia, were conquered and annexed by Muscovy. Their inhabitants, whether Muslim or animist, were incorporated into the fabric of Russian Orthodox society. They were treated as Russian subjects, but were denied those rights reserved to Christians. Only by religious assimilation, that is, by their conversion to the Orthodox faith, could the Tatars become the equals of the Russians. Russia, except for Spain, was the only European power to attempt systematically to convert its Muslim subjects to Christianity. Missionary activity was begun in 1555 by Arkhiepiskop Gurii, the first archbishop of Kazan. This initial attempt at conversion was relatively liberal. Tsar Ivan the Terrible, who was tolerant in religious matters, advised the Kazan missionaries to work "through persuasion and not through compulsion." The effort was partly successful and resulted in the conversion of a large community of Christian Tatars—the Old Converts (Starokriasheny; Tatar, Taze Kryash). However, the majority of the converts were former animists, not Muslims.

The anti-Muslim campaigns. The campaign of conversions, interrupted during the seventeenth century, was resumed with a new vigor under Peter the Great and continued violently until the reign of Catherine II. Mosques were destroyed, Qur'anic schools were closed, and special schools were opened for the children of the converts. At the same time, Muslim counterproselytism was punishable by death. The climax was reached under the reign of Empress Anna (1730–1740), when some forty to fifty thousand New Converts (Novokriasheny; Tatar, Yeni Kryash or Aq Kryash) were added to those who had been converted during the sixteenth century.

To strengthen the religious pressure, civil and economic coercion was added. The feudal landed nobility, considered by the Russian rulers as their most dangerous adversary, was either physically liquidated or deprived of its feudal rights (Muslim landlords were forbidden to have non-Muslim serfs), dispossessed of its property, and ruined. Muslim urban dwellers, merchants, clerics, and artisans were expelled from Kazan. Tatar farmers were forced to leave the best agricultural lands along the river valleys and were replaced by Russians.

After more than a century of sustained pressure, the very existence of the Islamic civilization in the Middle Volga was in danger. But the pressure produced conflicting results. The landed nobility disappeared as a class; although some of its representatives became Christian, its most dynamic elements remained Muslim and became merchants, traders, and small industrialists. Expelled from the cities, the Tatars took refuge in the countryside. By the seventeenth century, Tatar Islam presented a curious and unique feature in the Muslim world: it had become a rural religion with its most famous mosques and *madrasahs* situated in small villages. In the same way, Tatar merchants expelled from the cities of the Volga-Kama area migrated eastward, where they formed trading colonies in Siberia, the Kazakh steppes, along the Lower Volga, in the Caucasus, in Turkistan, and as far as China. Already in the seventeenth century, the Tatar nation, reduced to a minority in its Volga homeland, had become a diaspora community led by a dynamic merchant class. Religious persecutions against Islam created a lasting hatred among all the Tatars—Muslim and Christian alike—against Russia and the Russians.

During the reign of Catherine II, the anti-Muslim campaign was halted and even reversed. The empress, who personally deemed Islam to be "a reasonable religion," succeeded in gaining the sympathies of the Tatars. She closed the schools for Christian converts and allowed the Tatars to return to Kazan and to build mosques and Qur'anic schools in the cities of the Middle Volga and the Urals. Religious persecution was stopped, and a *modus vivendi* was achieved between the Russian state and its Muslim subjects. The Russian authorities even helped Tatar "clerics" to build mosques in the Urals and in the Kazakh steppes. By a 1773 decree they were granted religious freedom, and in 1782, a Muslim spiritual board (*muftiat*) was established in Orenburg and invested with authority over all religious matters. The chairman of the board was appointed by the Ministry of the Interior in Saint Petersburg. Those Tatars who had been converted to Christianity began to return to Islam. Finally, the last decade of the eighteenth century was marked by a new phenomenon: the massive conversion to Islam of the indigenous Finnic tribes of the Middle Volga region. These tribes—Cheremiss, Mordvins, Udmurts—were formerly animist or superficially Christianized; after conversion, there was rapid "tatarization."

The pressure against Islam was renewed under Nicholas I and Alexander II, however. By new methods, including education and propaganda, efforts were made to attract Tatars to Christianity. In 1854, a special anti-Muslim missionary department was organized by the Kazan Theological Academy. In 1863, a new educational policy was elaborated by Nikolai Il'minskii, a missionary and orientalist professor at the Religious Academy of Kazan. His aim was to create a new native Christian elite of Tatar intellectuals, educated along European lines but retaining the use of its native language. This Christian elite, which had not broken its links with the national past, was charged with missionary work among its Muslim brethren. As a result of this effort, assisted by an intense and brilliant propaganda campaign, more than 100,000 Muslims and almost all the remaining animists from the Volga area were converted.

The economic threat from Russia. Yet another danger threatened the Tatar nation: Its economic prosperity was in jeopardy. During the late eighteenth century and the first half of the nineteenth, the Tatar merchant class had been allied with the young Russian capitalists and had acted as an intermediary between Russian industrial towns and the markets of Turkestan. But that fruitful cooperation was not to last: During the second half of the nineteenth century, after Russian armies had opened the gates of Turkestan to Russian enterprise, Russian capitalists were able to dispense with the Tatar middlemen. The two bourgeoisies had become rivals, and the Tatar bourgeoisie, as the weaker, appeared to be doomed. The economic threat, coupled with the resumption of the policy of religious and educational assimilation, produced a lively reaction among the Tatar bourgeoisie during the reign of Alexander III. The *jadid* reformist movement, which has been properly called "the Tatar renaissance" of the nineteenth century, was the direct consequence of this threat, as well as of the desire to unify all the Muslim and Turkic peoples on the basis of a religious, ethnic, and cultural ideology. The Tatar merchants, supported by the young intelligentsia and the modernist *'ulamā'*, or religious scholars, were aware that a successful resistance would involve confronting

Russian imperialism with another imperialism. They knew that it would be necessary to extend their economic and cultural scope to all Muslim peoples of the empire, and that they would have to constitute themselves as the leaders of Russian Islam and, taking advantage of the linguistic similarity and of their common religion, propagate the notions of pan-Islam and pan-Turkism.

The *jadid* renaissance. In the middle of the nineteenth century, the Tatar community was a curious element in the Muslim world. It had survived centuries of political and religious pressure, and, led by its merchant bourgeoisie, it had reached a high economic and cultural level. In the Middle Volga area, the proportion of literate Tatars was greater than among the Russians, especially among women. The Tatar bourgeoisie was aggressive and dynamic, able to compete successfully against its Russian counterpart. But at the same time, the Tatar elite lived intellectually in a conservative medieval world. Indeed, their strict conservatism had protected their community from contamination by a technically more advanced Russian establishment and preserved its Islamic character. But by the end of the nineteenth century, it had become obvious that "the Tatar oxcart" could no longer compete effectively with the Russian "steam engine." In order to survive in a modern world, it was necessary for the Tatars to modernize their intellectual *Weltanschauung* rapidly and thoroughly. Without questioning the religious foundation of Muslim society, Tatar reformers applied themselves to modernizing Islam by imitating the spirit of Western liberalism.

The reformist movement manifested itself in almost all the Muslim countries, from the Ottoman Empire to Indonesia, but nowhere was it so dramatic and so deep as in the Tatar country. There, the problem facing the native elite was not merely how to regain its lost power; rather, it was concerned with survival itself.

Theological reform. The movement began in the early nineteenth century with an attempt by Tatar *'ulamā'*, educated in Bukhara, to break with the conservative Central Asian traditionalists who had dominated the spiritual life of Russian Muslims. The first to challenge their scholasticism was Abu Nasr Kursavi (1783–1814), a young Tatar teacher in a Bukhara *madrasah.* Accused of impiety by the emir of Bukhara and by the *muftī* of Orenburg, he was obliged to flee to Turkey. Later challengers included Shihabeddin Mayani (1818–1889), the greatest and the most respected among Tatar scholars, and a generation of modernist theologians including Ibrahim Khalfin, Husein Faizkhanov (1825–1902), Rizaeddin Fahreddin Öglu (1859–1936), and Musa Jarullah Bibi (1875–1945). Their action restored life and vigor to the Muslim religion in Russia and exercised an undeniable influence on the neighboring countries. Especially affected was the Ottoman Empire, where the prestige of Tatar *jadid* thinkers was invoked by all those who sought to undermine the authority of medieval scholasticism.

By the beginning of the twentieth century, Tatar Islam was endowed with a powerful religious establishment consisting of thousands of mosques and schools (*maktabs* and *madrasahs*) using the *jadid* system of teaching. It also included a brilliant new literature inspired by the challenge of the modern world and committed to religious and political reforms, along with a rich, diverse, and sophisticated periodical press in the Tatar language.

Language and literature. One figure dominated the literary scene of the Tatar world. The Crimean Tatar Ismail Gaspraly (Gasprinskii) (1851–1914) was a historian, philologist, novelist, and politician. Over a period of twenty-five years, he developed in his magazine, the celebrated *Terjümān,* published from 1883 in Bakhchisarai, the doctrine of a liberal modernist pan-Turkism summed up in its watchword, "unity of language, of thought, and of action" (*dilde, fikirde, işte birlik*). Gaspraly called for the union of all the Turkic peoples of Russia and for a new Muslim culture, which would be in contact with the West through the medium of Russian and Ottoman models. To achieve this unity he elaborated and used in his *Terjümān* a common pan-Turkic language based on a simplified Ottoman Turkish that would be understood by all the Turks from the Balkans to China.

Gaspraly also reorganized the teaching system, and his model *madrasah* in Bakhchisarai was imitated throughout Russia, especially in the Volga Tatar country. Some of the reformed *madrasahs*—such as the Huseiniyeh of Orenburg, Aliyeh of Ufa, Rasuliyeh of Troitsk, and Muhammadiyah of Kazan—were among the best educational establishments of the Muslim world.

At the turn of the century, in response to the great effort made by the people as a whole, the cultural level of the Volga Tatars had been raised to a remarkable degree. The cities, particularly Kazan, Orenburg, Ufa, Troitsk, and Astrakhan, had acquired the character of genuine intellectual centers.

Politics. After 1905, the reform renaissance passed beyond the confines of education, language, and theology and became a political movement, an attempt to shake the pressure of the West without abandoning the Islamic basis of the Tatar society. The defeat of Russia by Japan in 1905, revealing Russia's weakness and stirring the hope of revenge among the subject peoples of the empire, was the psychological shock that transformed cultural reformism into a political movement. For the Muslims, and particularly for the Tatars who at that time were playing the role of the unquestioned intellectual leaders of Russian Islam, this defeat demonstrated that the tsarist empire was not invulnerable and that a political struggle was possible.

Between 1905 and 1917, the Tatar political scene became highly diversified and sophisticated, with all political trends involved. At the extreme right were the ultraconservatives, represented by a puritanical Ṣūfī brotherhood, God's Regiment of Vaysī, a dissident offshoot of the Naqshbandīyah. Founded a half-century earlier, in 1862, the brotherhood rejected the authority of the Russian state and refused to pay taxes or perform military service. Moreover, it condemned all the other Muslims as "infidels" for their submission to Russian rule. The Vaysī brotherhood was persecuted by the Russian authorities and brought to trial several times. In 1917, its adepts sided with the Bolsheviks; their leader, Shaykh Inan Vaysov, was killed by the Tatar counterrevolutionaries while fighting alongside the Red Army. Less radical was the traditionalist (*qadim*) wing of the Tatar community, which dominated the official Islamic administration until the revolution. Its representatives were conservative in religion and politics. They were law-abiding citizens, hostile to the reformist movement, loyal to the tsarist regime, and personally loyal to the Romanov monarchy.

The majority of Tatars belonged to the liberal and radical trends. The liberals, followers of Ismail Gaspraly, believed that open struggle against Russia would be impossible and ill-fated. They advocated peaceful cooperation between Russia and the Muslim world, arguing that this would be of great and lasting advantage to Islam. The liberals dominated the Tatar national movement until the revolution, but even though they were culturally united, they were politically divided. A few liberals sought to satisfy their demands within the framework of the tsarist autocracy; the majority envisaged a more or less lasting cooperation with the Russian liberal bourgeoisie. After 1908, Tatar leaders convinced of the impossibility of achieving reforms and equality of rights with the Russians by legal methods within the framework of the tsarist regime began to migrate to Turkey. Alternatively, they moved nearer to various socialist-Marxist or non-Marxist parties, giving birth to an original cultural and political movement, Muslim socialism. After the revolution, Muslim socialism became Muslim communism. From Russian (or European) socialism, Muslim communism borrowed its phraseology, certain features of its agrarian program, its methods of propaganda, and organization; even so, it remained deeply rooted in the Islamic tradition.

Until the Revolution, even the most radical left-wing Tatar group, the Uralchylar (officially controlled by the Russian Marxists), refused to break away from Islam and to follow the antireligious line of the Bolsheviks.

Tatar Islam under the Soviet regime. For the majority of the Tatar *jadids*, the Russian Revolution provided an occasion to fulfill their century-long struggle for the modernization and the secularization of their society. They took advantage of the downfall of the Romanov monarchy in February 1917 to create an independent religious establishment. The first All-Russian Muslim Congress, held in May 1917 in Moscow, abolished the tsarist practice whereby the *muftī* of Orenburg was appointed by the Russian minister of the interior. At this congress they elected their own *muftī*, Galimjan Barudi, a *jadid* scholar. The first ten years of the new regime were relatively quiet for the Muslims of the Middle Volga. Local power belonged to the Tatar communists, former *jadids* who had joined the Bolshevik Party without breaking completely with their Islamic background.

The leader of the Muslim communists was a Volga Tatar, Mīr Said Sultan Galiev (1880–1936?), a companion of Stalin and, in the 1920s, the highest-ranking Muslim in the Communist Party hierarchy. Although Mīr Said Sultan Galiev was a dedicated Marxist and an atheist, he believed that "no antireligious propaganda may succeed in the East as long as it remains in the hands of the Russians"; he also believed that "the main evil threatening the Tatars [is] not Islam, but their political backwardness" ("Metody antireligioznoi propagandy sredi Musul'man," *Zhizn' natsional'nostei,* Dec. 14, 1921; Dec. 23, 1921). Sultan Galiev was denounced by Stalin as a bourgeois nationalist and was arrested in 1923; he reemerged briefly in 1925 but was arrested again in 1928. He and all his companions disappeared in the decade-long purge that followed.

The liquidation of Galiev and his followers marked the beginning of a full-scale government offensive against Islam. It began with the foundation of the Tatar branch of Sughushchan Allahsyzlar (the "union of godless militants") and the appearance in 1924 of an antireligious periodical press in Tatar, Fen ve Din ("science and religion"), replaced in 1928 by Sughushchan Allahsyzlar. By 1929 all religious institutions, such as religious schools, religious courts, and *waqfs*, had disappeared. During the 1930s most of the mosques were closed or destroyed. In 1931, 980 parishes with 625 "clerics" remained in the Tatar A.S.S.R. By comparison, in 1889 the *muftī* of Orenburg had 4,645 parishes (sg., *mahalle*), served by 7,497 "clerics," under his jurisdiction. In the mid-1930s the anti-Islamic campaign culminated with the massive arrest of Muslim clerics accused of counterrevolutionary activity and espionage for Japan. The *muftī* of Orenburg, Kashaf Tarjemani, was arrested and executed.

During World War II, in 1942, one of the few surviving *jadid* clerics, Abdurrahman Rasuli (Rasulaev), approached Stalin with a view toward normalizing relations between the Soviet government and Islam. Stalin accepted the proposal, and a concordate was established. Persecutions were suspended, anti-Islamic propaganda lessened, and the *muftiat* reestablished (in Ufa instead of Orenburg). Abdurrahman Rasuli was appointed *muftī* and occupied this post until his death in 1962.

SEE ALSO Jihād; Modernism, article on Islamic Modernism; Ṭarīqah.

BIBLIOGRAPHY

Abdullaev, M. A., and M. V. Vagabov. *Aktual'nye problemy kritiki i preodoleniia Islama.* Makhachkala, 1975. A biased but well-documented Soviet work on Islam in Dagestan.

Abdullin, Yahya. *Tatarskaia prosvetitel'naia mysl'.* Kazan, 1976.

Avksentiev, Anatolii. *Islam na Severnom Kavkaze.* Stavropol, 1973. Well-documented propaganda.

Bennigsen, Alexandre, and Chantal Lemercier-Quelquejay. *Les mouvements nationaux chez les Musulmans de Russie: Le Sultangalievisme au Tatarstan.* Paris, 1960.

Davletshin, Timurbek. *Cultural Life in the Tatar Autonomous Republic.* New York, 1953. In Russian.

Fisher, Alan. *The Crimean Tatars.* Stanford, 1978.

Ibragimov, Galimjan. *Tatary v Revoliutsii 1905 goda.* Kazan, 1926.

Ishmuhametov, Zinnat. *Sotsial'naia rol' i evoliutsiia Islama v Tatarii (Istoricheskie ocherki).* Kazan, 1979. One of the few Soviet works on Islam in the Tatar country.

Marjani, Shihabeddin. *Mustafadh ul-akhbar fi ahvali Qazan ve Bolghar.* 2 vols. Kazan, 1897–1900.

Minorsky, Vladimir. *The Turks, Iran and the Caucasus in the Middle Ages.* London, 1978.

Sattarov, Magsad. *Islam dini galyglary haggynda.* Baku, 1967. A biased but serious Soviet work on Islam in Azerbaijan.

ALEXANDRE BENNIGSEN (1987)
FANNY E. BRYAN (1987)

ISLAM: ISLAM IN CENTRAL ASIA

Geographically, Central Asia (comprising modern Kazakhstan, Kyrgyzstan, Tajikistan, Turkmenistan, and Uzbekistan) may be divided into three zones: the oasis belt (sometimes called Transoxiana), which stretches from Iran to China along the main river valleys of the southern tier, mainly through Uzbekistan, but also encompassing contiguous areas of the other states; the steppe-desert zone in the northern and central tiers (Kazakhstan) and in the far south (Turkmenistan); and the high mountain zone in the southeast (Badakhshan, part of Tajikistan).

ISLAMICIZATION OF CENTRAL ASIA. Islam penetrated these regions in different forms and at different times. The cultural and ethnic heritage of local populations was very diverse. This influenced the way in which they responded to Islam. The chief distinction was between the sedentary, largely urbanized population of the oasis belt and the nomads of the steppes and deserts. The scattered communities that inhabited the high mountain zone had their own, quite distinct, traditions; they had little direct contact with the peoples of the plains, so they played little part in the cultural, social, and religious developments in the region.

Oasis belt. In 622 CE, the year of the *hijrah* (Muḥammad's flight from Mecca to Medina and the accepted commencement of the Muslim era), the population of the oasis belt of Central Asia was mainly of Iranian origin, but there was also a substantial Turkic element. There was a flourishing urban tradition in the region, particularly in cities such as Merv, Samarqand, and Bukhara. Moreover, the so-called Silk Road—a transcontinental network of trade routes—linked Central Asia to China, India, and Iran, and also to the Black Sea and Europe.

Prior to the introduction of Islam, the main religions of the oasis belt were Zoroastrianism, Buddhism, and Manichaeism. There were Nestorian Christian communities in several of the cities (a bishopric was established at Merv in the fourth century and at Samarkand in the sixth century) and a significant Jewish presence in the Samarkand-Bukhara area. In the southwest (modern Turkmenistan), there were traces of Hellenistic cults.

Islam was brought to the region by the Arab armies that invaded Khorasan and Transoxiana in the mid-seventh century. In 705 CE Qutaybah ibn Muslim, who became governor of Khorasan, established his principal seat at Merv. Until his death in 714 he repeatedly undertook campaigns eastwards into the Ferghana Valley and beyond. By the beginning of the ninth century the oasis belt had been so thoroughly integrated into the Muslim world that Caliph Maʿmūn made Merv, instead of Baghdad, his capital from 813 to 817.

At first the Arabs imposed Islam by force. Later, however, a more moderate approach to the Islamicization of the region was adopted. The form of the faith that came to be practiced in this part of Central Asia was initially Sunnī Islam of the Ḥanafī school of law. Central Asian scholars traveled throughout the Muslim world. Several made major contributions to the development of applied and theoretical sciences, as well as to Islamic philosophy and jurisprudence. Known to history by the Arabicized forms of their names, they include al-Bukhārī (compiler of one of the fundamental collections of the *Traditions of the Prophet*, still revered and consulted today), at-Tirmidhī, al-Farghānī, and al-Khwārazmī in the ninth century; al-Fārābī, al-Bīrūnī, and Ibn Sīnā (Avicenna) in the tenth century; and Nāṣir-i Khusraw in the eleventh century.

In the early thirteenth century, Mongol hordes conquered Central Asia. Initially, they inflicted huge damage, destroying cities, wrecking the irrigation systems that supported agriculture, and disrupting long-haul trade. In time, however, peace returned and the cultural and intellectual life of the oasis belt revived. The Mongol rulers were eventually Turkicized and Islamicized. Under Tamerlane (1336–1405) and his successors (the Timurid period), there was a new flowering of Muslim scholarship. Eminent thinkers of the day included the astronomer-ruler Ulugh Beg (who reigned in Samarkand from 1409 to 1449) and the poet Alisher Navoi (1441–1501).

From the sixteenth century onward, however, Transoxiana became increasingly isolated from the rest of the Islamic world. There were several reasons for this. One was that routes from Central Asia to the Arab lands were blocked by hostile neighbors and long-running wars. To the south, Shāh Ismāʿīl (1485/1486–1524), founder of the Safavid dynasty, established Twelver Shiism as the state religion of Iran, thus adding an ideological element to the power struggle that was then in progress with the Sunnī Sheibanid dynasty of Transoxiana. To the northwest, the nascent Russian state was advancing into the Volga region, defeating the Tartar khans of Kazan in 1552 and of Astrakhan in 1556. Across the Caspian Sea, the Ottomans and the Safavids were fighting for possession of the Caucasus. Transoxiana itself, wracked by internecine strife, was fragmenting into small, semi-independent principalities. Meanwhile, a change was taking place in patterns of global trade as sea routes began to replace the arduous transcontinental land routes across Central Asia. Factors such as these led to economic decline and intellectual stagnation. Increasingly, a highly conservative form of Muslim education took hold in the *madrasahs* (Muslim colleges).

The steppes and deserts. At the time of the Arab invasion of the oasis belt, the steppes and deserts were inhabited by Turkic-speaking nomadic pastoralists. By religion they were shamanists. Islam took far longer to influence these peoples than it did the sedentary population of the oasis belt. Their way of life precluded the establishment of fixed, centrally located institutions. Thus, it was itinerant Ṣūfī missionaries who played the decisive role in spreading the new faith in this region. The Islamicization of the nomads in the areas that bordered the oasis belt was probably completed by the mid-tenth century, albeit superficially. The remoter regions, however, were scarcely affected by Islam until the eighteenth century or later.

The high mountains. The high mountains and valleys of Badakhshan, today part of Tajikistan, have been inhabited from time immemorial by small Pamiri tribes of Eastern Iranian origin. Most of these people were eventually converted to the Ismāʿīlī sect of Shīʿī Islam, which spread northwards from centers in Afghanistan and India from the late eleventh century onwards. A few groups, however, adopted Sunnī Islam. Until the twentieth century, the Pamiris were almost entirely isolated from the Muslim communities, both sedentary and nomadic, of the Central Asian lowlands.

Sufism and Ishanism. Sufism, the mystical tradition of Islam, began to penetrate Central Asia in the immediate aftermath of the Arab invasion. The first centers appeared in Balkh and Nishapur in the eighth and ninth centuries. Later, Merv, Bukhara, Khwarezm, and other cities in Transoxiana became bastions of Sufism. The early adepts were disciples of the Baghdad school of mystics. Indigenous Central Asian orders began to appear towards the end of the twelfth century.

The first major figure in the development of Central Asian Sufism was Yūsuf Ḥamadānī (1048–1141). After a period of study in the major centers of the Middle East, he moved to Central Asia and spent most of his adult life there; he established a *khānqāh* (Ṣūfī monastery) in Merv that came to be known as the "Kaʿbah of Khorasan." Two parallel chains of authority were derived from him. One led to Aḥmad Yasavī (d. mid-twelfth century), who crystallized the spiritual legacy that had been bequeathed to him into the *ṭarīqah* (path) of the Yasavī order. The other led to Bahāʾ ad-Dīn an-Naqshbandī (1318–1389), who formulated the *ṭarīqah* of the Naqshbandī order. Both these orders were to expand far beyond the confines of Central Asia. The former attracted adherents throughout the Turkic-speaking world, while the latter spread to India and China, as well as to the Ottoman Empire and, in more recent times, to Western Europe.

The chief distinction between the Naqshbandīyah and the Yasavīyah was that the former practiced a silent or hidden (*khafiyah*) *dhikr* (set of devotions), the latter a vocal or loud (*jahrīya*) *dhikr*. The Yasavī *ṭarīqah*, which contained elements of ritual that were reminiscent of shamanistic practices, was particularly successful among the Turkic-speaking nomads of the steppes and deserts; the Naqshbandī *ṭarīqah* tended to appeal more to the sedentary, Iranian-speaking population. However, there was no rigid boundary between their different spheres of influence; the Naqshbandī order, for example, had many adherents among the nomads. Two other great orders that attracted a substantial following in Central Asia were the Kubrawīyah, whose *ṭarīqah* was crystallized by Najm al-Dīn al-Kubrá (1145–1221), and the Qādirīyah, who traced their *ṭarīqah* to ʿAbd al- Qādir Gīlānī (twelfth century).

The most influential *ṭarīqah* in Central Asia, in terms of political weight, was the Naqshbandī. The foundations of their control over state affairs were laid during the Mongol period, when they played a pivotal role in the conversion of the conquerors to Islam. Since the Mongol khans not only became rulers of Transoxiana, but also assumed leadership of the tribal confederations of the steppes, the Naqshbandī order acquired a privileged position among both the sedentary population and the nomads. They consolidated their position under Tamerlane, who was himself possibly a *murīd* (disciple) of one of the teachers of Bahā al-Dīn an-Naqshbandī. Tamerlane did, however, also show the Yasavīyah signs of favor, notably by the construction of a superb (and materially well-endowed) mausoleum over the tomb of Aḥmad Yasavī at Turkestan. This city was later captured by the Kazakhs; thereafter, the Yasavī *shaykhs* (spiritual leaders) came to exert a strong influence over the nomad khans and sultans. Several Kazakh nobles were buried near the tomb of Yasavī, thus emphasizing the nexus between the spiritual and civil sources of authority.

During the fourteenth to eighteenth centuries, the leading Ṣūfī *shaykhs* occupied a dominant position in the political life of the Central Asian khanates. Some, such as Hoja Aḥrār (1404–1490), became great magnates, possessing vast tracts of agricultural land, as well as urban settlements, together with the attendant income arising from the dwellings, crafts, and trade that were located on such land. The position of particular Ṣūfī dynastic lines was further underpinned by intermarriage with the ruling families. Throughout most of the sixteenth century, Naqshbandī *shaykhs* acted as kingmakers, playing off one pretender to the throne against another. However, their influence waned in the next century, especially under the Manghit dynasty, which came to the throne in 1753, and they never regained their former political power. Their spiritual power was also gradually eroded.

There is another mystical tradition in Central Asia that is related to Sufism but has characteristics of its own. It is frequently termed *Ishanism* to distinguish between the major orders described above and the largely autonomous, local networks of mystics whose activities were mainly associated with popular (i.e., folk, lay) religion. In the early Islamic period the distinction is perhaps an irrelevance: it is difficult now to determine whether or not semi-legendary figures such as Ḥakīm-ata or Chopan-ata were fully fledged initiates of a Ṣūfī order. Later, however, there does appear to have been a divergence. By the early nineteenth century this resulted in the proliferation of local *ishans*, each of whom established his own *ṭarīqah*, with a personal circle of devotees.

The phenomenon was most widespread in rural areas, where every village or nomad community sought to secure the presence of an *ishan* of their own; allocations of free land and water were set aside for this purpose. Often, *ishans* would have charge of a particular shrine or holy place, which gave them added legitimacy and authority. The fact that they generally had a modicum of education also helped to enhance their standing amongst their neighbors, most of whom were illiterate. The duties of an *ishan* included a variety of social, as well as quasi-religious, quasi-magical functions: they dispensed protective amulets and healing potions, gave counsel and comfort, and conducted prayers, rituals, and ceremonial invocations for divine assistance and protection. There was a strong dynastic element in Ishanism. In several areas there existed whole clans of "holy" families; strictly endogamous, they traced their lineage (not necessarily reliably) back to Arab forebears.

INDIGENIZATION OF ISLAM. Islam, in the form that it was first brought to Central Asia by the Arabs, retained its formal, doctrinally regulated character in the learned institutions in the cities, but elsewhere it was modified by local traditions and beliefs. In some areas, for example, Zoroastrian practices were absorbed, while in others, traces of Buddhism, Manichaeism, or Hellenistic cults became embedded in local Muslim beliefs and observances; shamanism and pantheism provided an even broader substratum of pre-Islamic references.

Among the most tenacious of the ancient customs was the cult of "saints"—the veneration of figures who were regarded as protectors and intercessors. They may or may not have had identifiable historical antecedents, but in any case they were the focus of cults that usually had ancient, non-Islamic origins. Such figures were often associated with a number of widely scattered sites, and specific biographical details varied accordingly. The best known included Burkut-baba, who was regarded by the Turkmen as having the power to ensure rain; Chopan-ata, widely regarded as a protector of sheep; and Kanbar-ata, regarded as a protector of horses. Individual saints (usually inherited from pre-Islamic traditions) were associated with particular crafts and occupations. Fertility cults, especially those connected with the annual farming cycle, were also preserved in one form or another.

Shrines to such individuals were to be found in many parts of the region; these were often associated with much older forms of faith, now reinterpreted within the framework of Islam, as elsewhere in the Muslim world. Such places were often located by springs, caves, trees, or cliffs. It was common practice (and has remained so up to the present) to visit these holy places to pray for assistance and good fortune. Generally this act of supplication was sealed with the ritual sacrifice of an animal (usually a sheep) and by lighting candles or leaving scraps of material tied to twigs. Another common feature, reminiscent of pre-Islamic ancestor cults, was the emphasis on showing respect for the dead; this was especially common in rural areas. The healing and soothsaying arts of the shamans also continued to be practiced.

TSARIST RULE. The northern rim of Central Asia (northern Kazakhstan) was brought under Russian control towards the end of the eighteenth century. By the middle of the century, Russian troops were poised to take the oasis belt. The subjugation of the khanates of this region was completed within less than a decade. Bukhara and Khiva retained some degree of autonomy as protectorates, albeit after ceding a portion of their lands to the Russian crown.

Tsarist policies towards Islam fell into two categories: those employed among the nomads of the steppe region and those employed among the sedentary population of Transoxiana. In the steppe region, the new administration deemed it politic to show good will and even support for Islam in order to win the loyalty of the nomad Kazakh aristocracy, who were strongly Muslim in their convictions, if not always observant in their practices. Tartars from the Volga region (under Russian rule since the mid-sixteenth century), who, like the Kazakhs, were Sunnī Muslims of the Ḥanafī school, were encouraged to inculcate a perceived Islamic orthodoxy in the steppes. The Tsarist authorities allocated funds for the printing of Muslim literature and for the construction of mosques in the steppes (prior to this the Kazakhs had possessed very few mosques, and those only in their winter grazing grounds). The Tartar missionaries were at first much resented by the nomads, who were accustomed to a much freer, more heterodox interpretation of Islam. Educated, urbanized Kazakhs, such as Shokan Valikhanov (1835–1865) and Ibrai Altynsaryn (1841–1889), were also deeply disturbed by the Tartars' attempts to spread a form of Islam that they perceived to be narrowly dogmatic and, moreover, alien to Kazakh tradition. Nevertheless, the zealous proselytizers from the Volga gradually succeeded in introducing a more orthodox element into local worship.

In the mid-nineteenth century, Russian policy towards Islam in the steppe region began to change. Belatedly, a campaign was launched to convert the Kazakhs to Christianity. However, it met with little success. At the same time, measures were introduced to curb Muslim activities. The interface between Islam and the Russian administration was brought under the jurisdiction of the Tsarist Ministry of Internal Affairs. New measures included restrictions on the number of mullahs in a given district. In addition, mosques and other Muslim educational establishments could only be opened with official sanction, and the collection of obligatory Islamic taxes (*zakāt, ṣadaqah*) was prohibited. Yet even under these conditions the network of formal Islamic institutions continued to expand. In 1895, for example, there were only thirty-one *mekteb* (primary schools) in the Steppe Territory, but by 1913 this number had increased to 267. There were also *madrasahs* in most of the bigger cities.

In Transoxiana the situation was somewhat different. The main urban centers fell to the Tsarist troops comparatively quickly. Thereafter, relations between the Russians and the local population were remarkably amicable. Eugene Schuyler (an American official who made an extensive visit to the region in 1873) commented, "what was strange for Mussulmans, [was that they] spoke in the highest terms of the Russian Emperor. The conduct of General Tchernaief made a most favourable impression upon the natives and from that time on there was not the slightest trouble of any kind on the part of the native population."

The institutional framework of Islam in Transoxiana largely was retained, although some of the highest offices of the *ʿulamāʾ* (trained Muslim scholars; e.g., Shaykh-al Islām and Kazi Kalan) were later abolished. Muslim courts continued to function, albeit under the nominal control of colonial officials and with some restriction of their powers. Islamic education at *mekteb* and *madrasah* levels was provided as previously, although gradually, and to a limited extent, alternative forms of schooling became available (principally, the Russo-Native schools and the reformist "new method" Muslim schools). Christian institutions began to appear, but they were few in number and served the needs of the immigrant population; missionary work was virtually nonexistent (and initially specifically prohibited). One Islamic obligation that became easier to observe under Russian rule was the *ḥajj*. The Tsarist authorities organized special travel facilities for the pilgrims and made provision for consular support, quarantine, and other such needs; by the end of the century, some twenty thousand "Russian" Muslims, mostly Central Asians, were making the pilgrimage annually.

Muslim reformist *(jadīd)* trends in the tsarist period. The Muslim reformists in Central Asia (known as *jadīds* or *jadīdists*, from the Arabic word for "new") constituted not so much a group as a broad trend. Relatively few in number, they were united by common convictions and aspirations rather than by set programs (although distinct clusters did eventually emerge, including some with specific sociopolitical agendas). The aim of the reformists was to modernize Central Asian society, without abandoning the Islamic framework. The first to propound these ideas were Kazakhs such as Ibrai Altynsaryn (1841–1889) and Abai Kunanbayev (1845–1904) in the mid-nineteenth century. Later, in Transoxiana, Bukharans such as Donish (c. 1828–1897) and Fitrat (1886–1938) began to follow a similar line of thought.

The reformists, especially in the early period, were drawn mostly from wealthy merchant families or the local aristocracy. They were familiar with traditional Muslim scholarship and also, either through further study in Russian institutions or through travel and personal contacts, had some knowledge of European culture. This dual experience on the one hand gave them a great admiration for Western science and technology, but on the other hand it strengthened their faith in Islamic values. They were particularly concerned with modernizing the system of education in Central Asia by introducing Western-style methods of teaching (*uṣūl-i jadīd*, "new method": hence the term *jadīdist*). However, they were interested in a wide range of social and political issues; some were remarkably radical in their views, advocating the overthrow of the emir, on the grounds that he was not fulfilling his obligations as a Muslim ruler, long before the Bolsheviks put forward this idea.

The reformist movement in Central Asia was greatly strengthened by the influx of Muslim activists from other parts of the Russian empire in the late nineteenth and early twentieth centuries, since the concept of modernization within Islam was already far better established in intellectual circles in the Volga region, Crimea, and Transcaucasia. The incomers, especially the Tartars, played an important role in establishing a local, independently owned press and in implementing educational innovation. They also gave a certain impetus to the politicization of the Central Asian reformists. Some of these joined Tartar-dominated Muslim political groupings, some moved closer to the liberal Russian Constitutional Democrats (Kadets), and some were drawn to the Socialists and later to the Communist Party.

The significance of the reformist movement in Central Asia lies more, perhaps, in the fact that it appeared at all than in any specific achievements. Similar trends were emerging at the same period in other parts of the Muslim world, notably in Turkey, India, and Egypt. In Central Asia the process was more difficult and fraught with greater obstacles. First, there was the physical remoteness of the region, which hampered the development of links with like-minded thinkers elsewhere; some contacts were established, but for the most part they were sporadic. Second, the reformists were frequently under pressure from the *ʿulamāʾ*. A few members of the *ʿulamāʾ* were sympathetic to reformist ideas, but most were bitterly opposed to any form of innovation. The conservative faction was particularly powerful in Bukhara, where it had the support of the emir. In the Governorate-General of Turkestan, which was under Russian rule, the situation was somewhat easier, though even here the colonial administration was careful not to offend the *ʿulamāʾ*. The reformists also faced many practical problems. These included poor communication networks, a low level of literacy, and few printing facilities. Not surprisingly, they made little impact outside a relatively narrow circle of urban intellectuals. This might have changed had they had time to build up a broader base, but this did not happen: the reformist movement was abruptly terminated once Soviet rule was established.

SOVIET PERIOD. Soviet rule was first established in Tashkent in September 1917, and shortly thereafter it was extended to the industrial centers of the northern tier. The Turkestan Autonomous Soviet Socialist Republic, encompassing the Tsarist Governorate-General of Turkestan, was created in April 1918 as an administrative unit within the Russian Soviet Federative Socialist Republic. In 1920 the emir of Bukhara and the khan of Khiva were deposed and their states transformed into the nominally independent People's Soviet Republics of Bukhara and Khorezm, respectively. In 1924 the People's Republics of Bukhara and Khorezm were formally annexed and the whole of Central Asia was repartitioned into five administrative units, the precursors of the independent states of today, namely, Uzbekistan, Turkmenistan, Tajikistan, Kazakhstan, and Kyrgyzstan.

Soviet policies towards Islam went through a number of different phases. Moreover, they were often not implemented uniformly; much depended on local conditions at any given time. This apparent lack of consistency may be ascribed to the fact that such policies were motivated not solely by the desire to eradicate the religion, but more broadly, to secure the triumph of socialism and victory in the class war. This was most clearly reflected in the first years of Soviet rule (1917–c.1925), when pragmatism, more often than not, prevailed over ideology. Had the Bolsheviks taken precipitate action against the Muslim clerics they would have risked alienating the very people whose support they were aiming to attract. Moreover, Soviet power was as yet far from securely established in the region, and counterrevolutionary forces in various parts of Central Asia (*basmachi*) were using religion as a means of rallying support, calling themselves the "Army of Islam" and claiming that they were defending the faith against the infidel.

In late 1917, V. I. Lenin and Joseph Stalin made a famous appeal, "To all the Toiling Muslims of Russia and the East," assuring them that from that day forth their "beliefs and customs, national and cultural institutions would be free and inviolable." In March 1919, at the Second Conference of the Communist Party of Turkestan, a Muslim Bureau was created for the express task of carrying out agitational work among the indigenous population. Material was prepared in the local languages and services at mosques, which brought together large numbers of people, were used for spreading Communist ideas. Believers were admitted to the Party and for some years thereafter constituted a significant proportion of the membership. Muslim trade unions were set up for local craftsmen (e.g., tanners, cobblers); so, too, were soviets of Muslim deputies and soviets of Muslim workers.

Meanwhile, the social, legal, and economic basis of Islam was being systematically dismantled, to be replaced by Soviet institutions. From 1918 to 1924 a number of laws and decrees were put in place that established the legal framework for the secularization of society. These included the right of freedom of conscience, the separation of church and school, and the marriage and family laws. In 1921, at the Tenth Party Congress, a resolution was passed calling for the launch of a comprehensive antireligious campaign. However, in the Turkestan and Kirghiz/Kazakh Autonomous Soviet Socialist Republics, conditions were still too unstable for decisive steps to be taken in this direction. In 1919 attempts had been made to close down Muslim schools and courts and to confiscate *waqf* property (i.e., endowed trusts), but this aroused such anger amongst the local population (not to mention giving a tactical advantage to the *basmachis*) that in 1922 these measures were relaxed. Nevertheless, it became increasingly difficult for the schools and the courts to continue to function and their numbers fell rapidly.

By 1925 the Soviet government was in a strong enough position to take a much firmer line towards Islam. The *waqf* lands were nationalized as part of Union-wide land and water reforms. Muslim schools and courts were phased out by 1927 to 1928. The Arabic script, which had been used in Central Asia for over a thousand years and was, moreover, the script in which the Qurʾān was written and therefore of great religious significance, was abolished in favor of the Latin script (in turn to be replaced by the Cyrillic alphabet in 1940); the whole world of Muslim scholarship was thus effectively rendered inaccessible to future generations of Central Asians. The campaign for the emancipation of women, which was intensified during these years, was likewise used to undermine Islam by portraying the religion as a source of ignorance, oppression, and social injustice.

Atheistic propaganda was intensified in the late 1920s. Republican branches of the Union of Atheists, later renamed Militant Atheists, were set up at this time and large quantities of antireligious materials (books, journals, brochures, posters, etc.) were produced in the local languages. Outreach activities (e.g., lectures and discussion groups) were used to underline and amplify this message in schools and the workplace, and in social and professional organizations. Women, who were generally more devout than men, were singled out as special targets for anti-Islamic propaganda; wherever possible they were drawn into atheistic work. From 1925 onward, discriminatory legislation was introduced to limit the rights of religious functionaries of all faiths. Initially, clerics were deprived of the right to elect, or be elected, to soviets. The Law of Religious Associations (which remained in force from 1929 to 1990) made such activities as the provision of religious education for minors, proselytizing, and fundraising for religious purposes illegal. Beginning in about 1930, arbitrary arrests and executions were used to eliminate Muslim leaders who refused to cooperate with the authorities; Muslim literature, or any material at all in the Arabic script, even if nonreligious, was liable to be confiscated and the owner severely punished. All but a few mosques were closed. Some were destroyed, and some were used for other purposes, often of an emphatically antireligious nature (e.g., bars or atheistic museums). All the *madrasahs* were abolished. No religious literature was published. The annual *ḥajj* was suspended, and contacts with foreign Muslims virtually ceased.

After the outbreak of World War II there was an abrupt change of policy: the repression of the 1930s was suddenly replaced by a spirit of cooperation. In Central Asia an official Muslim administration, known as the Muslim Board for Central Asia and Kazakhstan, was established in Tashkent. Its responsibilities included the upkeep of mosques and the appointment of clerics. In 1944 the *ḥajj* was officially reinstated, though only a very small and select group of clerics were able to benefit from this. The following year the Mir-i Arab *madrasah* in Bukhara was reopened, becoming the only Muslim educational institution in the whole of the Soviet Union. The number of functioning mosques was slightly increased, and the public celebration of religious ceremonies became a little easier. The loyalty of the Muslim community and their contribution to the Soviet war effort was acknowledged in the central press, a clear indication that Islam was no longer regarded with the categorical disapproval of the 1930s.

This trend towards greater accommodation continued in the postwar period, despite renewed bouts of religious persecution in the mid-1950s and early 1960s. In 1971 another *madrasah* was opened in Tashkent, the second in the Soviet Union. In 1974 it was officially named the Ismāʿīl al-Bukhārī Institute, to commemorate the AH 1,200th anniversary of al-Bukhārī's birth. The motivation for this policy was not born of a greater degree of tolerance towards Islam, but rather of a desire to present the Soviet Union in a favorable light to the developing world, particularly the oil-rich Arab countries of the Middle East. This entailed creating at least a facade of acceptance toward Soviet Islam. To further this aim, selected students from the *madrasah* were allowed to go to Islamic universities in Egypt and other Arab countries to complete their Qurʾanic studies and to perfect their Arabic. A small number of religious publications were permitted, including several editions of the Qurʾān and a journal, *Muslims of the Soviet East,* originally printed in Uzbek and Arabic, later in several other languages. These publications were intended for the *ʿulamāʾ,* Muslim scholars, and for foreign Muslims, not for local distribution. During this period the restoration of major Islamic monuments in Central Asia was undertaken, and Muslims from abroad were encouraged to visit the region, though in official delegations with set programs, rather than for private, individual purposes. Soviet Muslims became regular participants in international Islamic conferences and hosted some such events in their own republics. They also played a prominent part in the international peace movement, acting as mouthpieces for the Soviet government's views on such issues as nuclear disarmament and the Palestinian-Israeli conflict in the Middle East.

Parallel Islam. The Soviet policies of the 1920s and 1930s were aimed at bringing about the radical transformation of Central Asian society. They included positive measures, such as the introduction of mass literacy and compulsory education, the provision of social welfare services, and the emancipation of women, as well as measures specifically aimed at destroying the legacy of the past, such as the purges and the antireligious campaigns. They were implemented with such force and speed that they could not but have an impact. Consequently, a significant level of modernization was achieved in a very short space of time. One aspect of this was a marked degree of external secularization. Some of the older generation certainly continued to perform the prescribed ritual prayers and other obligations in private throughout the Soviet period. Younger members of the family (it was not uncommon for three or even four generations to live together) learnt by example, and out of respect for their elders they tried to keep these practices alive. However, the meaning underlying the words and the gestures was gradually forgotten, and by the 1960s even those who considered themselves to be devout were often reduced to the mechanical repetition of incomprehensible formulae.

Western writers, especially in the 1980s, often made a distinction between so-called official (*ʿulamāʾ*-led) and unofficial or parallel (Ṣūfī- or *ishan*-led) Islam. The latter was supposed in some way to be more "genuine." The majority of Central Asians do not appear to have subscribed to this categorization. On the contrary, those who attended the mosque might also be in contact with an *ishan,* and vice versa. Moreover, some members of the *ʿulamāʾ* were from Ṣūfī/*ishan* lines; they, too, kept alive some beliefs and practices, even if largely in a private, personal capacity.

The observances that were most persistently maintained were those connected with rites of passage: male circumcision, marriage ceremonies (though these came to be somewhat influenced by European and Christian practices), and above all, burial services. The obligation to honor the deceased took precedence over almost all other considerations, to the point even of jeopardizing career prospects, since it was seen not only as a mark of respect to the dead, but also as an affirmation of membership in the community. Social customs such as the payment of *kalym* (in Islamic legal terminology, *mahr*—the dower or bride price paid by the groom) and, to a lesser extent, polygamy and the underage marriage of girls, although forbidden by law, continued to be practiced surreptitiously. Dietary prohibitions regarding the consumption of pork and alcohol were observed unevenly. The pressure on men to conform to standard Soviet norms was far greater than on women, since the latter tended to live and work in environments that were more culturally homogeneous, thus less vulnerable to external influences.

Group outings to holy places, especially *mazars* where saints were buried, remained popular, but in general were regarded as social occasions, without any specific religious significance. Several other traces of religious practices, reinterpreted as folk tradition, persisted throughout much of the Soviet period. These included the blessing given in traditional crafts (e.g., pottery, carpet-weaving) by the "master" to the "freed" apprentice as a sign that the latter's training was complete.

Islamic resurgence. The resurgence of Islam in Central Asia began in the early 1970s with the emergence of a small-scale revivalist movement in the Ferghana Valley. The Soviet press referred to its adherents as Wahhābīs, implying that they were backed by foreign sponsorship (presumably from Saudi Arabia), but there is no evidence to indicate that they received either external influence or support during this period. It is possible that the movement drew its inspiration from an ascetic sect that was active in the area at the beginning of the century. It is more likely, however, that it was a spontaneous, grass-roots reaction against the relentless materialism of Marxism-Leninism and its sterile doctrine of "scientific atheism" (similar revivals in other religions were to be observed in many parts of the Soviet Union at that time).

Another and stronger impetus for the reintroduction of Islamic values was the shift in government policy. From 1989 on, the Soviet authorities adopted a conciliatory approach toward Islam. This was to some extent the result of greater tolerance towards religion throughout the Soviet Union, but more specifically, it was an attempt to combat the perceived threat of Iranian-style Islamic revolution by bolstering a sense of pride in indigenous Islamic traditions. A new *muftī* was elected at this time, Muḥammad Ṣadyk Muḥammad Yūsuf Hoja-ogli (b. 1952). He had previously been the rector of the Tashkent *madrasah.* A young and highly educated cleric (graduate of the two Soviet *madrasahs,* followed by postgraduate studies in Libya), Muḥammad Ṣadyk was a persuasive proponent of government policies, but he also worked hard to improve conditions for the practice of Islam. His efforts met with official approval and he received substantial support from the authorities, who not only gave him a prominent role in public affairs, but also made several concessions to the Muslim community, such as permission to open more mosques, the relaxing of restrictions concerning the pilgrimage to Mecca, and the increased provision of religious literature.

These measures generated a surge of gratitude to the Soviet state and specifically to Soviet President Mikhail Gorbachev, the architect of this new liberalism. There was a genuine sense of satisfaction that the validity of Central Asian culture had been recognized and was finally being accorded proper respect. For the great majority of the population this was sufficient: at this stage there were few who were in favor of religion assuming a more dominant role in society.

Only in Tajikistan was the picture somewhat different. Here, the Islamic revival soon acquired a political aspect. The first Islamic political party in Central Asia was the Islamic Rebirth Party (IRP) of Tajikistan. It began as an offshoot of the all-Union Islamic Rebirth Party, founded in Astrakhan (on the Volga) in June 1990. However, the Tajik party soon began to follow an independent course; it was formally registered by the Tajik authorities in October 1991. Thus, on the eve of the collapse of the Soviet Union, in this one republic, Islam was not only beginning to play a significant role in public life but was also operating with a degree of autonomy that was not to be found elsewhere in the region.

Post-Soviet Islam. The Soviet Union was formally abolished in December 1991. Few had expected its sudden collapse. When the Central Asian states gained independence at the end of 1991 there was much speculation, within the region and abroad, as to the possible impact of the "Islamic factor" on politics and society. In Tajikistan the IRP joined other independent political parties to form an antigovernment alliance. Confrontation between the two factions soon escalated into violence, triggering the outbreak of civil war in mid-1992. The IRP and other opposition parties were banned by the government. They moved to Afghanistan and continued to fight the government from there. The IRP formed the core of this resistance movement. Thus, the conflict came to be seen as a struggle between Islamists and secularists. However, the situation was more complex. Although Islam was undoubtedly a major factor in the conflict, it was not the sole cause. Rather, it was an aggravating feature in the struggle for national supremacy that broke out between different socio-regional groupings in the aftermath of independence. The conflict continued sporadically for five years. It was formally brought to a close in June 1997, when a peace treaty was signed by the warring factions. Despite the shortcomings of this agreement, and the imperfect manner in which it was implemented, it remained in force as of 2004. This has permitted a certain amount of political and economic restructuring to take place. In 1999 several independent political parties were granted registration (or re-registration), including the Islamic Rebirth Party.

Elsewhere in Central Asia, post-Soviet Islam exhibits three tendencies. These can be described as traditional Islam, government-sponsored Islam, and radical Islam.

Traditional Islam. Traditional Islam is characterized by a conservative, overall passive attitude to religion. Moreover, there is great attachment to popular practices which, though understood as being Islamic, are contrary to orthodox teachings. This is the form of Islam that is still espoused by the great majority of Central Asian Muslims. However, the situation is beginning to change. In the immediate aftermath of independence there was great enthusiasm for mosque construction. In Kyrgyzstan, for example, there were only thirty-four mosques open for worship in 1987, but by 1994 there were almost a thousand; in Uzbekistan in the same period the number rose from eighty-seven to some three thousand. The same phenomenon was to be observed in the other Central Asian states. Moreover, many Muslim schools and *madrasahs* were opened and courses were provided for children and adults in the study of Arabic, the Qurʾān, and related religious topics. By the second half of the 1990s this upsurge of interest in Islam had somewhat abated. Nevertheless, among the younger generation there has been a distinct change of outlook. Mosque attendance has increased again, particularly in the south (notably the Ferghana Valley and southern Kazakhstan). Thus, a more orthodox form of Islam is gradually replacing the indigenous syncretic beliefs and practices of the past.

Government-sponsored Islam. This form is a continuation of the late Soviet-era policy of co-opting religion to serve the needs of the state. Today, the constitutions of all the Central Asian countries enshrine the principle of the division of religion and state. Yet throughout the region, Islam has been elevated to a status akin to that of a state ideology. This seems to have been prompted by the conviction that unless urgent action was taken to fill the ideological vacuum left by the discrediting of Marxism-Leninism (which possibly had more support in Central Asia than elsewhere in the Soviet Union), anarchy would follow. Consequently, in all the Central Asian states an immediate campaign was set in motion to emphasize the role of Islam as an integral component of the national heritage, and likewise of the ethical foundation of the state. This message was conveyed through the teachings of Muslim clerics, as well as through the pronouncements of senior political figures and editorial and documentary features in the mass media. In Uzbekistan and Kyrgyzstan this dual ethical-national significance was made explicit when the presidents swore their respective oaths of office on both the constitution and the Qur'ān. On a personal level, the heads of state (all former Communist Party members who came to power under Soviet rule) have been at pains to establish Muslim credentials. This has included fulfilling the lesser (*ʿumrah*) pilgrimage to Mecca.

Since independence, new laws on religion and on religious associations have been passed in the Central Asian states. The law adopted in Uzbekistan in 1998 is regarded as the most restrictive. However, the draft amendments that are currently under consideration in Kazakhstan and Kyrgyzstan propose measures that are almost equally severe. Political parties of a religious orientation are proscribed everywhere except in Tajikistan, where in mid-1999, in the run-up to parliamentary elections, the Islamic Rebirth Party, outlawed in 1993, was again legalized. In all five states, religious communities must be officially registered by the authorities. If not, they are likely to be prosecuted and to suffer personal harassment, as well as the confiscation or destruction of community property. Most of the so-called nontraditional faiths (i.e., those that have only recently been introduced into the region) have experienced great difficulties in securing registration; insofar as they operate at all, their activities are regarded as illegal, and therefore criminal.

The form of Islam favored by the Central Asian governments of today is based on the teachings of orthodox Sunnī Islam of the Ḥanafī school of jurisprudence. However, the sphere of application is strictly limited. There is little question, for example, of introducing elements of *sharīʿah* law (Muslim canon law) into the legal framework of these states. The main concern at the governmental level is to promote "good" Islam, which, it is implied, is beneficial to the development of the state; and to banish "bad" Islam, which represents a threat to stability. To underline this last point, frequent reference is made to Tajikistan and Afghanistan, where, it is alleged, the spread of "bad" Islam has brought misery and suffering. Yet there is no public debate in any of the Central Asian countries as to where, and on what basis, the dividing line should be drawn between the acceptable and the unacceptable. Thus, men who grow beards (a traditional Muslim sign of piety) are regarded with suspicion, particularly in Uzbekistan, where they run the risk of summary arrest. Why these manifestations, which are in keeping with orthodox Muslim practice, should be labeled extremist, while other aspects of Islamic behavior should be encouraged, is not discussed.

The institutional control of Islamic activities in Central Asia today largely follows the Soviet model. However, whereas under Soviet rule there had been a unified, overarching administration for all the Muslims of the region (i.e., the Muslim Spiritual Directorate of Central Asia and Kazakhstan), separate national administrations, each headed by a *muftī*, were established in the early 1990s. In Tajikistan, the office of *muftī* was abolished in 1996, and the work of the *muftīyāt* was reorganized; the chief Muslim authority is now the chairman of the council of *ʿulamāʾ*. In the other states, the *muftīyāt* remains responsible for administering Muslim affairs within the state and maintaining formal contacts with Muslims abroad. The work of the *muftīyāt* is closely monitored by a Committee (or Council) for Religious Affairs, a body that serves as the interface between the government and the religious communities (yet another Soviet-era survival). The interests of Muslims, as well as adherents of the other established faiths (chiefly Orthodox Christianity and Judaism), are officially represented in this body. Such "nontraditional" faiths as Bahāʾī, Pentecostal Christianity, and Jehovah's Witnesses are regarded with suspicion and given little opportunity for official representation. In Turkmenistan the *muftīyāt* and the Committee for Religious Affairs have virtually merged into a single entity, as the chairman of the latter body is the deputy *muftī*, while the *muftī* is deputy chairman of the Committee.

The *muftīyāt* is responsible, among a number of other functions, for the formal examination and registration of Muslim clerics. Unregistered preachers are liable to criminal prosecution. The ostensible aim of registration is to disbar unqualified individuals from holding religious posts. At the same time, however, registration enables the state authorities to keep a close check on the ideological orientation of the religious establishment. Clerics who hold views that do not conform to the official line, or who are felt to be lacking in loyalty to the government, can be excluded from the system.

The most marked example of government control over the Muslim establishment is in Uzbekistan. The last *muftī* of the Soviet era, Muḥammad Ṣadyk, was forced from office in the wake of accusations of Wahhābī sympathies and financial improprieties. In 1993 he went into voluntary exile, though he later returned to live as a private individual in Tashkent. Since the mid-1990s the official Muslim hierarchy has been relegated to a subordinate role, remarkable chiefly for its unquestioning support of government policies. Elsewhere in the region, state control of the religious establishment is also increasing, though it is still well below the Uzbek level. Kyrgyzstan has, as of 2004, shown a fairly consistent commitment to maintaining the independence of the religious establishment. This appeared to falter in December 1996, when covert government pressure resulted in the ousting of Muftī Kimsanbai-aji Abduraḥmān uulu (elected in 1993), a cleric who had a large following within the Muslim community but was suspected by some of Wahhābī leanings. However, he was reinstated as *muftī* in 2000.

Radical Islam. The radical trend embraces a loose grouping of activists who want to purge Islam of the distortions that have been introduced over time. They are collectively referred to as Wahhābīs, a term that today, as during the Soviet era, is a generic expression of abuse rather than a literal description of religious affiliation.

From the early 1990s onward, the radical trend has been gaining ground. In Tajikistan, it was one of the factors that led to the outbreak of the civil war. Elsewhere in the region the main expression of radical Islam has been the emergence of clandestine groups, based in Uzbekistan and adjacent areas of Kazakhstan and Kyrgyzstan. There are no reports of Islamist movements in Turkmenistan, which could mean either that they do not exist or that they are suppressed more effectively than elsewhere.

It is impossible to set a figure either to the number of individuals who are involved, or to the number of separate groups. Names of some of these groups have appeared in various sources from time to time, though with almost no background information. These include Adolat (Justice); Akromiya (named after their founder, Akrom Yuldashev), they are also known as the Iimonchilar (Believers) or Khalifatchilar (Caliphate Supporters); the Tawba (Repentance) movement; and Islom lashkarlari (Soldiers of Islam). The first such group to acquire wide notoriety was the Islamic Movement of Uzbekistan. It was formed around 1996 under the leadership of Ṭāhir Yoldashev and Jumabai Khojiev and may have attracted members from some of the earlier groups. Based predominantly in the Ferghana Valley, the great majority of its members were Uzbeks. The movement was also active in southern Kyrgyzstan and southern Kazakhstan, where it was said to find support among local Uzbek minorities. In 2001 there was a move to rename the party the Islamic Movement of Turkestan, but this does not appear to have been implemented.

Likewise in the mid-1990s, a very different, and potentially far more powerful, radical element appeared. This was Ḥizb ut-Taḥrīr (transliterated in various forms, including Ḥizb al-Taḥrīr, and usually translated as the "Liberation Party"). A transnational Islamist organization, it was created in 1953 in Jerusalem; it soon attracted a substantial following in Jordan and spread to other countries in the Muslim world. In several countries it was banned as a dangerously subversive organization and its members were imprisoned. The headquarters of the movement are not known, though it is credibly suggested that they are based in the United Kingdom. It is not known how the Ḥizb ut-Taḥrīr is funded, but it produces numerous publications and has an impressive Internet presence.

The first Ḥizb ut-Taḥrīr leaflets reportedly appeared in Tashkent in 1992 or 1993, but the movement does not seem to have established a definite presence in the city until 1995. There were an estimated eighty thousand Ḥizb ut-Taḥrīr members in Uzbekistan in 2004. Since 2001, Ḥizb ut-Taḥrīr documents have referred to Uzbekistan as a *wilāyah* (province) of an imagined worldwide Islamic state. The party has launched excoriating attacks on the Uzbek government and, in particular, on President Islom Karimov, who is depicted as an archenemy of Islam. It is not known whether Ḥizb ut-Taḥrīr and the Islamic Movement of Uzbekistan are in any way linked. Initially, they were separate organizations, but in the late 1990s there were rumors to suggest that some degree of rapprochement had taken place.

On February 16, 1999, there was an attempt on the life of President Karimov in Tashkent, the capital of Uzbekistan. Within hours of the incident, "Islamic fundamentalists" were being blamed for the outrage. This triggered a renewed onslaught on devout Muslims. The incident was used as an excuse to conduct a campaign against all shades of dissident opinion. According to reports from numerous sources, tens of thousands of people were arrested. It is difficult to verify such estimates, but certainly the fear of reprisals caused many Uzbeks to flee across the border into neighboring states, from where some of them launched attacks on Uzbekistan. A serious clash occurred when armed fighters crossed into Kyrgyzstan in August 1999 with the aim, according to official sources, of invading Uzbekistan "in order to establish an Islamic state." Estimates of the size of this force vary greatly, but it seems likely to have numbered some five hundred men. When the guerrillas reached the border they found Uzbek troops blocking their route; they thereupon retreated into the Kyrgyz mountains, taking with them a number of hostages, including four Japanese geologists. The hostages were released in October 1999, reputedly after the Japanese government paid a large ransom. There were similar armed clashes in the same area in mid-2000, though on a smaller scale.

There is no information as to why such attacks were mounted at precisely this juncture. It may have been retaliation for the repression that followed the February assassination attempt on Karimov. It is also possible that it was part of a struggle between local mafia barons to gain control of lucrative narcotic-trafficking routes. In September 2000 the U.S. State Department placed the Islamic Movement of Uzbekistan on its list of international terrorist organizations to which U.S. citizens are forbidden to give assistance, and whose members are denied entry into the United States.

Foreign influences. The Islamic revival in the Central Asian states is to some extent inspired and supported by Muslims in other countries. Some of the financing for the building of mosques and *madrasahs*, as well as the restoration of Islamic monuments, has come from abroad, from both private sources and government funds. Students from Central Asia have gone in large numbers (a few hundred a year) to study in countries such as Turkey, Egypt, and Pakistan. Since independence, many thousands of Central Asians have performed the pilgrimage to Mecca, some already two or three times. In the early 1990s, and again in 1999, the travel expenses of several thousand pilgrims were covered by the Saudi monarch. All the Central Asian states have now joined the Organization for Islamic Conference, hence there are also institutional links with the Muslim world.

The main foreign influence, however, has come from missionaries. Following the collapse of the Soviet Union they flocked to Central Asia from many parts of the Muslim world to preach and to open schools. At first they were warmly welcomed. Gradually, though, the mood in the region began to change. On the one hand, the traditionalists—the mass of ordinary believers—objected to being told that some of their most respected customs (for example, those connected with burials) were not authentic and should be replaced by more orthodox procedures. On the other hand, the state authorities also became uneasy that the missionaries were encouraging independent Islamic thought. Uzbekistan was the first to impose restrictions on Muslim missionaries from abroad; in 1992 to 1993 some fifty Saudi preachers were expelled. Other expulsions followed, and since then the activities of foreign Muslims have been very carefully monitored. A similar tendency can be observed in the other states.

Foreign commentators initially expected Iran to play the lead role in the re-Islamicization of Central Asia. In fact, Iranian clerics have been conspicuous largely by their absence. After the collapse of the Soviet Union, delegations from Iran began to visit the Central Asian states and to acquire first-hand familiarity with the region. They soon realized that an Islamic revolution along the lines of the Iranian model was not a realistic prospect; this was partly because of the low level of knowledge of Islam among the population at large, but also, and very importantly, because of the lack of a trained, independent-minded *ʿulamāʾ*. The fact that the Iranians represent the Shīʿī tradition also placed them at a disadvantage. By contrast, Sunnī Muslim missionaries were active from the first years of independence. Turkish Muslims have played the most prominent role. Proportionately, they are more numerous than any other ethnic group.

The great majority of the Turkish missionaries are Nurcus, followers of Bediüzzaman Said Nursī (1876–1960), and of his disciple Fethulla Gülen (b. 1938). The Nurcus opened hundreds of schools and commercial enterprises in all the Central Asian states. They appeared to be propagating a moderate, modernized version of Islam, and their teaching programs concentrated on scientific subjects and technical skills. However, on a more informal level, through extracurricular contacts and through the distribution of translations into the local languages of the *Risale-i Nur* (The Epistle of Light), the corpus of teachings of Said Nursī, they seem to have been disseminating a more radical message. There are increasing concerns that their ultimate political project is the creation of an Islamic state. They are also accused by some of having a pan-Turkic agenda. Because of such suspicions, their newspaper *Zaman* (Time) was banned in Uzbekistan in 1994; several teachers were expelled at about the same time. In other Central Asian states a similar sense of unease is emerging regarding the activities of this group, and consequently their work is now being more closely monitored.

Turkish influence has also played a part in the revival of Sufism. Great Ṣūfī orders such as the Naqshbandīyah and Qādirīyah had been influential in Central Asia in the past, but even before the Soviet era they had lost much of their power. Under Soviet rule, insofar as anything of this tradition of mysticism survived, it was in the form of popular syncretic practices. In the early 1990s, adepts from Turkey began to reintroduce Sufism to the region, focusing their efforts mainly on Uzbekistan and southern Kazakhstan. Initially, this was welcomed by the secular authorities in Uzbekistan, who professed admiration for Ṣūfī philosophy. An indication of official approval occurred when President Karimov made his first post-independence visit to Turkey, and Mukhtarkhan Abdullayev, a self-avowed Ṣūfī, was included in his entourage; Abdullayev, who was subsequently appointed *muftī* (1993–1997), was formally inducted into the Naqshbandī order on this occasion. Later, however, the Uzbek government's attitude towards Sufism changed. It continued to be revered as a historical and cultural phenomenon, but attempts to revive Ṣūfī brotherhoods were firmly repressed; the movement was eventually driven underground.

Fears that foreign Muslims were fomenting religious extremism and militancy in Central Asia continued to grow. The enthusiasm for sending students to Islamic institutions in Turkey, Egypt, and other Muslim countries was tempered with concerns that, once abroad, they would be exposed to radical ideas. The Uzbek authorities were the first to react to this perceived threat, going so far as to accuse Turkish Islamists of using these students as a fifth column. It was alleged that while in Turkey several of these students underwent terrorist training. On their return home, so it was claimed, they set up cells of activists in villages and towns. Thereafter, other governments in the region also became suspicious of the education offered by foreign Muslims and cut back on the number of religious students who were allowed to go abroad to study.

Islamic literature. In Central Asia there has not as yet emerged a homegrown Muslim intellectual tradition expounding a coherent vision of Islam in the modern world. Equally, awareness of the existence of contemporary thought in other parts of the Islamic world is not well developed. Almost the only literature that is available (though how widely is a moot point) is that which is produced clandestinely by Ḥizb ut-Taḥrīr. The state authorities in Kyrgyzstan and Uzbekistan report that large consignments of the party's journal *al-Waʿī* (Consciousness), as well as leaflets and books, have been circulated. Titles of confiscated material include *Islom nizomi* (The Islamic Order), *Hizbut-Tahrir tushunchalari* (Concepts of Ḥizb ut-Taḥrīr), and *Siyosat va khalqaro siyosat* (Politics and International Politics); these texts are sometimes in Arabic, sometimes in competent Kyrgyz or Uzbek translations. Several underground printing presses have been discovered. Local editions of such works are said to have been produced in print runs of one thousand or so. Distribution of these tracts is mostly covert: typically, copies are scattered in public places under cover of night, or handed out by casual hired labor. The Central Asian governments, especially the Uzbek, are deeply concerned about the effect that this literature might have. Anyone who is found in possession of such material runs the risk of arrest, and consequently most people are afraid to handle it. Thus, it is very difficult to judge how much of it is actually read by the population at large. Elsewhere there are examples of efforts to produce materials in local languages, such as Tajik, for example, to provide a wider readership with the benefits of the Muslim scholarship that originated in their own region.

POST-SEPTEMBER 2001. Following the terrorist attacks on the United States in September 2001, a U.S.-led coalition commenced military operations against the Taliban and al-Qāʿidah bases in Afghanistan. In the following months, coalition bases were established in Uzbekistan and Kyrgyzstan. In the course of this campaign, many of the Central Asian guerrillas who were fighting alongside the Taliban and al-Qāʿidah were killed. It was claimed (though not conclusively confirmed) that Juma Namangani, leader of the Islamic Movement of Uzbekistan, had also been killed. Certainly the movement was badly damaged, and despite rumors that it was regrouping, it had not undertaken any significant actions as of early 2004. Meanwhile, in the Central Asian states the authorities began pursuing their own "war on terror" by arresting hundreds of so-called religious extremists. The main targets are members of Ḥizb ut-Taḥrīr, although little credible evidence of criminal activity has been produced against them. Human rights organizations are particularly concerned about the situation in Uzbekistan, where prisoners are reportedly subjected to physical and psychological torture.

The persecution of radical Islam is accompanied by ongoing attempts to promote government-sponsored Islam. Official Islamic institutions continue to function, and in Uzbekistan have even been enhanced (e.g., by the opening of the Islamic University in Tashkent). The aim is to inculcate a "positive" interpretation of Islam in society. Ultimately, however, better knowledge of the faith might make it more difficult to control the responses of believers. The struggle between radical Islam and "official" Islam seems likely to continue.

SEE ALSO Buddhism, article on Buddhism in Central Asia; Inner Asian Religions.

BIBLIOGRAPHY

Akiner, Shirin. "Islam, the State, and Ethnicity in Central Asia in Historical Perspective." *Religion, State, and Society: The Keston Journal* 24, nos. 2/3 (1996): 91–132.

Akiner, Shirin. *Tajikistan: Disintegration or Reconciliation?* London, 2001.

Akiner, Shirin. "The Politicisation of Islam in Post-Soviet Central Asia." *Religion, State, and Society: The Keston Journal* 31, no. 2 (2003): 97–122.

Amnesty International. "Central Asia: No Excuse for Escalating Human Rights Violations." Available from http://www.web.amnesty.org/ai.nsf/Recent/EUR040022001.

Babadjanov, Bakhtiyar, and Muzaffar Kamilov. "Muḥammadjan Hindustani (1892–1989) and the Beginning of the 'Great Schism' among the Muslims of Uzbekistan." In *Islam in Politics in Russia and Central Asia*, edited by Stéphane Dudoignon and Komatsu Hisao, pp. 195–219. London and New York, 2001.

Ḥizb ut-Taḥrīr. Official website. Available from http://www.hizb-ut-tahrir.org.

Human Rights Watch. "Memorandum to the US Government Regarding Religious Persecution in Uzbekistan." *HRW World Report 2001: Europe and Central Asia.* August 10, 2001. Available from http://www.hrw.org/backgrounder/eca/uzbek-aug/persecution.htm.

Keston Institute: Resources for the Studies of Communist Countries and Religious Affairs. Available from http://www.starlightsite.co.uk/keston/.

Mardin, Şerif. *Religion and Social Change in Modern Turkey: The Case of Bediüzzaman Said Nursī.* Albany, N.Y., 1989.

Ro'i, Yaacov. *Islam in the Soviet Union: From World War II to Perestroika.* London, 2000.

Trofimov, Dmitri. "Friday Mosques and Their Imams in the Former Soviet Union." *Religion, State, and Society: The Keston Journal* 24, nos. 2–3 (1996): 193–219.

SHIRIN AKINER (2005)

ISLAM: ISLAM IN CHINA

Muslims within the present-day borders of the People's Republic of China, and indeed within the borders of late imperial China and its republican successor, can be divided broadly into two categories. First, there are the Chinese-speaking Muslims, known today as the Hui, who are distributed throughout the whole of the country. There are Hui mosques and communities in all provinces of China and in most towns and cities, including Beijing, but there are significant Hui concentrations in the northwest provinces of Gansu and Qinghai, the Ningxia Autonomous Region, and the southwest province of Yunnan. In both the northwest and the southwest it is possible to speak of clear and well-defined Muslim societies rather than minority communities in a wider non-Muslim society. In appearance and language there is very little to distinguish the Hui from the majority population of China, the Han, although they do retain some elements of Arabic and Persian vocabulary in their speech when communicating with fellow Muslims. In addition, many Hui, especially in rural areas, wear distinctive head covering—caps for men and variations on the veil or scarf for women—as a symbol of their Islamic identity. Although these emblems of cultural and religious identity were suppressed during the Cultural Revolution of the 1960s and 1970s, they have been readopted since the 1980s with considerable pride.

There are also Muslims in Xinjiang in the far northwest of China, bordering the former Soviet Central Asian states of Kazakhstan and Kyrgyzstan. Xinjiang is also known as Eastern Turkestan to the indigenous Turkic peoples, but this name is not popular with the Chinese authorities. Although Chinese is an important administrative and business language in this region, the bulk of the population are speakers of Turkic languages, of which by far the most important is Uighur, a language closely related to the Uzbek tongue. The Islam of Xinjiang is practiced separately from the Islam of the Chinese-speaking regions, and the Xinjiang Muslims have their own mosques and other religious organizations. This separation is made more complex by a tradition of anti-Chinese nationalism and political separatism that is intimately connected with Islam as practiced in Xinjiang, but this tradition is not shared by China's Hui Muslims.

This two-part division of Islam in China is not as precise as this brief account suggests. For example, there have been a number of Hui Muslim communities in Xinjiang for well over a century and a half as a result of the rebellions and political upheavals of the late nineteenth century.

Although the term *Yisilanjiao* (a Chinese transliteration for *Islam*) is now in common use in China, in earlier times Islam was more commonly referred to as *Huihu jiao* or *Huijiao*, terms that did not restrict it to Chinese-speaking Muslims, or as *Qingzhenjiao* (the religion of purity and truth). This latter term persists in the names of mosques in China, which are almost all known as *qingzhensi* (temples of purity and truth).

The First Muslims in China. It is impossible to be precise about the year in which Islam first reached China. Contacts between China and the Middle East probably predate the beginning of the prophecy of Muḥammad in 610 CE by many centuries. As early as the Han dynasty (206 BCE–220 CE) Chinese imperial envoys had reached the Arab world, and the official chronicles of that time contain accounts of diplomatic and trade missions to Western Asia and particularly Persia. The Indian Ocean trade routes in use between the fourth and sixth centuries were dominated by Arabic- or Persian-speaking merchants, mainly from the Arabian or Persian Gulf, who made landfall in the ports of China's southern and southeastern coast.

The origin of these maritime traders is usually said to be *Dashi* in the Chinese histories; this term has been translated as "Arabia," although there is reason to think that it is in fact a much less precise term, which included the Persian-speaking world and probably the whole of the region that was eventually conquered by Arab armies in the name of Islam. The name *Dashi* may be connected with the word *Tajik.* In any case, there is clear documentary evidence of visiting groups of traders from the Middle East as early as the sixth century, and some Chinese scholars of Islam have dated the origin of Islam in China to that period.

The Tang dynasty (618–907 CE) was the golden age of medieval China and the period during which China was without doubt the greatest empire in Asia. It was renowned for the efficiency of its civil service; for its sophisticated and multiethnic urban culture, especially in the capital Chang'an (present-day Xi'an); and for its poetry and the beginnings of a great tradition in both landscape painting and ceramics. The greatness of the Tang is often attributed to China's openness to foreign cultures, particularly to the developing Muslim cultures beyond its inner Asian frontiers, some of which were treated as military protectorates of the Chinese empire. The imperial family of the Tang dynasty was of mixed Chinese and Central Asian ancestry, and this link with what would eventually become part of the Islamic world had a profound influence on Tang culture.

Although Chang'an was a magnet for Muslim, as well as Buddhist and Manichaean, officials, traders, and spiritual leaders from Central Asia, the clearest evidence for a Muslim presence in China in this period comes from the southeastern coastal city of Quanzhou in what is now the province of Fujian. Traders from the Middle East had settled in the port city, and during the twentieth century historians and archaeologists uncovered a profusion of gravestones and stelae inscribed in Arabic and Persian. This important collection of inscriptions provides evidence of a thriving Muslim community that was already well established in the early part of the eighth century and that became highly developed by the end of the Southern Song dynasty in the thirteenth century, the last Chinese dynasty before the Mongol invasion.

The Arab Mosque in Quanzhou, which is the only one remaining from that period, was built in the eleventh century. It was constructed in the style favored in the Arab world of that time. On its walls are inscriptions in Arabic, including quotations from the Qur'ān and an account of the history of the mosque, its construction in 1009 to 1010, and its reconstruction in 1310 to 1311 by Aḥmad bin Muḥammad Quds, who came originally from Shiraz in Persia. Stelae in other parts of Quanzhou record the construction of mosques that are no longer extant by Muslims from Yemen and Central Asia. The inscriptions on gravestones and tombs excavated in the city indicate clearly that the majority of Muslims in Quanzhou were of Persian origin, although most inscriptions are in Arabic rather than Persian. The descendants of some of these sojourners from the Middle East remained in Fujian, married local Han Chinese women, and are now classified as part of the Hui ethnic group. The province of Fujian remains one of the most outward looking in China, and the people of Fujian have a tradition of emigration to Taiwan, Southeast Asia, and more recently Europe.

Muslims and the Mongol Conquests. It is clear that there was already a significant Muslim presence in China by the time of the Mongol conquests of the thirteenth century. These conquests, which changed the political and social map of the whole of East, Central, and South Asia, also had the effect of increasing the Muslim population of China. Chinggis Khan (c. 1162–1227), who unified the Mongols and led them to their early military victories, ordered that when his armies captured such cities as Samarkand and Bukhara the craftsmen should be spared the otherwise wholesale slaughter. The craftsmen were conscripted into the service of the Mongols and at first were assigned to the building of defense works for sieges. They were later taken back to China, effectively as slaves, where they were required to build the new Mongol capital cities of Karakorum and Dadu (Beijing). Other Central Asians were pressed into service as soldiers, and over a period of many years, women and children were transported to China, as were some scholars and aristocrats.

It is not possible to say how many of these conscripts were Muslims because this was the period of the gradual Islamization of Central Asia, but the later growth of strong Muslim communities in northwestern China suggests that these forced migrants were the conduit for the transmission of the faith into China. The vast majority of migrants were men, and their intermarriage with Han Chinese, Tibetan, and other local women created the Chinese-speaking Hui ethnic group.

Consolidation During the Ming Dynasty. During the Ming dynasty (1368–1644), which is considered to be a period of high Chinese culture sandwiched between two "barbarian" dynasties, the Mongols and the Manchus, the Chinese-speaking Muslim population of China grew numerically and established itself as a permanent part of Chinese society, notably in the provinces of Gansu and Shaanxi, but also in Yunnan. Whereas before the Mongol conquest these Chinese Muslims could be seen as sojourner communities with an attachment to their original homelands in Central Asia, Persia, or the Arabian Peninsula, during the Ming they evolved into settled communities, living side by side with Han Chinese, although not always harmoniously. They gradually lost their knowledge of the Arabic and Persian languages as Chinese became their normal method of everyday communication. The Hui Muslims spoke the regional Chinese language of whichever part of the country they settled in, but to this day they retain elements of Arabic and Persian in their vocabulary, which is a testimony to the origins of their forebears.

Although it was in the rural areas of the northwest of China that the greatest concentration of Hui Muslims could be found during the Ming period, the spiritual and intellectual center of Chinese Islam was the city of Nanjing in the valley of the Yangtze River. Nanjing was chosen as the first capital of the Ming by Zhu Yuanzhang when he became the Hongwu emperor in 1368. Although the capital was moved to Beijing in 1403, Nanjing remained a city of considerable influence for centuries and served as the capital of the Guomindang Nationalist government from 1928 to 1937.

The Hongwu emperor (Ming Taizu, to accord him his correct posthumous title) was favorably disposed towards Muslims, many of whom were brought to the capital as tax collectors and interpreters or to serve in other official posts. Among the Muslim thinkers who flourished in Nanjing was Wang Daiyu (1585–1657), who was born into an ancient and distinguished family of court astronomers and educated in the tradition of the pioneering Islamic teacher Hu Dengzhou (1522–1597). Hu Dengzhou played a key role in the establishment of Muslim education in Shaanxi, and his methods were conveyed to Nanjing by Wang Daiyu's teacher, Ma Junshi (c.1628–1690). Wang Daiyu's teachings were greatly influenced by Confucian ideas and by the language of Confucianism. He was writing for a Muslim constituency that had virtually lost its ability to read Arabic or Persian, and also for a Han Chinese audience that he wished to inform about Islam. His major work, the *Zhengjiao zhenquan* (A true commentary on the orthodox faith), which quotes frequently from the Qurʾān, was an attempt to express the central tenets of Islamic thought in an understandable Chinese style. Purists disapproved of his efforts, objecting to the use of any languages other than Arabic or Persian, but Wang Daiyu's writings were welcomed by the majority of educated Hui who could rarely read anything other than Chinese.

Liu Zhi (c. 1664–c. 1739), perhaps the best-known Muslim scholar of the Qing dynasty, was also born in Nanjing in the late seventeenth century. He developed Wang Daiyu's use of the terminology of Confucianism to translate Islamic concepts into Chinese. Liu Zhi was also the first translator of the Qurʾān into Chinese, although he translated only part of the text. Liu Zhi's major works are *Tianfang xingli* (Islamic philosophy), *Tianfang dianli* (Islamic ritual), and *Tianfang zhishen shilu* (The last prophet of Islam).

Conflict and Rebellion During the Manchu Qing Dynasty. In 1644 China was in the grip of a major rebellion. Peasant armies led by Li Zicheng attacked Beijing in April, and the Chongzhen emperor, the last of the Ming line, hanged himself on Jingshan, a hill that overlooks the Forbidden City. Into this confusion marched the armies of the Manchus, a seminomadic, partly Sinicized people from northeastern China, who over the next thirty years proceeded to capture the capital, conquer the whole of China, and establish themselves as the ruling elite for almost three hundred years. Manchu policy was to expand their Qing dynasty (1644–1911) into Inner Asia, and they successfully consolidated their control over Mongolia, Xinjiang, and Tibet, redrawing the map of China. The present boundaries of the People's Republic of China are effectively those of the Qing.

There was resistance to the Qing expansion, and in the northwest Muslims fought the Manchus, as did the Han. Widespread insurrections against the new dynasty took place in Gansu in 1648 and 1649. Although these were ruthlessly crushed, the distinctiveness and separateness of Muslims was maintained, and the Muslim population grew throughout the eighteenth century. The Islamic educational system was reinforced and reformed, and Sufism began to make its appearance in northwestern China, brought there by traveling Ṣūfī mystics, as well as pilgrims returning from the *ḥājj* to Mecca who had come into contact with Ṣūfīs in Central Asia or the Arab world. Sufism took deep root in the poor and isolated northwestern regions, and it remains an important part of the religio-political structure to this day.

Expanding populations and the competition for scarce resources, particularly land and water, led to religious and ethnic conflict. Muslim Hui villages were reinforced for defensive purposes, and there were frequent clashes with neighboring communities of other ethnic groups, often with Han but also with Tibetans and the Qiang, who lived in the Tibetan borderlands. There was also conflict between Muslim villages and between adherents of different Ṣūfī orders and other sects.

In the second half of the nineteenth century these conflicts escalated and became so explicitly anti-Qing in their nature that the imperial government designated them as rebellions and deployed its substantial armies to crush them. China as a whole was going through a crisis during this period. Westerners had been pushing for an extension of trade with China, which led to the Opium War (1839–1842) and the defeat of China at the hands of the British Navy. In southern China the quasi-Christian Taiping rebellion (1851–1864) presented a serious challenge to Qing authority, which it aimed to replace. Nian bandit militia controlled much of north-central China at the same time.

In 1855 in Yunnan, Han and Hui miners came into conflict over mineral rights, and the local government and landowners indiscriminately slaughtered Muslims. In August 1856 the Muslim Du Wenxiu rose in rebellion and took the city of Dali as the base for an independent Islamic state (a caliphate), which he ruled until he was defeated and beheaded in 1873.

However it was in the northwest that rebellion was most savage and its repression most devastating. As in Yunnan, the roots of the conflict lay in disputes over land and other issues between Hui and Han villages, and the Muslim Hui took up arms against the landlords' militia. Their forces eventually attacked major towns and the capital of Shanxi province, Xi'an. Qing forces were dispatched to put down the rebellion, and the Muslim armies withdrew westward to Gansu, the Hui heartland. The Hui forces in Gansu were centered at four locations, all of which were associated with one or more of the Ṣūfī orders. All of these orders had sacred sites that were built around the tombs of their revered ancestral *shaykhs*, and the mosques and *madrasahs* in these tomb complexes served as headquarters for the Hui resistance. The Hui uprising was eventually suppressed in 1873 with great brutality and loss of life by the armies of the Qing regime. The whole of northwestern China had been devastated by the conflict, and the practice of Islam was dealt a near mortal blow. Hui communities were forcibly resettled away from their traditional lands and the graves of their founding *shaykhs*. Ṣūfī organizations were outlawed, and many mosques were closed, destroyed, or converted to Buddhist temples.

There were further serious episodes of communal violence in Gansu and neighboring areas in 1894 to 1895. The origins of the conflict were complex and included factional disputes between Ṣūfī orders and clashes between Hui and Han landlords and officials. The insurrection was eventually suppressed by Qing forces under the command of Muslim officers. By the twentieth century, because of this history of rebellion, Chinese-speaking Muslims had acquired a reputation for rebellion, fierceness, and conflict with the Chinese state. In defeat, many of the public practices of Islam were concealed or reduced in scale, and the Muslim communities strove to portray themselves as loyal citizens of the empire.

ISLAM IN CONTEMPORARY CHINA. Islam in contemporary China is mainly of the Sunnī tradition and adheres to the Ḥanafī school of law. Muslims of this tradition are known as Gedimu, a Chinese transliteration of the Arabic *al-qadīm* (the ancient), in deference to the longevity of this form of mainstream Islam in China. Gedimu Islam is characterized by adherence to *sharīʿah* law and the five major precepts of Islam; the attestation that there is only one Allāh; prescribed prayer and purification; the giving of alms; the fast at Ramaḍān; and the *ḥājj* pilgrimage to Mecca. This is no different from the rest of the Islamic world, although Chinese Muslims have interpreted the precise requirements in their own way. In particular the *ḥājj* has at times been impossible for the majority of Chinese Muslims, partly because of poverty and the impossibility of travel over such long distances, and partly because of restrictions imposed on travel by different regimes.

The practice of Gedimu Islam is centered on the *imām* (*ahong* in Chinese, from the Persian *akhond*), who presides over the town or village mosques. While some of the *imāms* inherit their role, others are elected by their community. There was a tradition of *imāms* circulating from community to community and of some being brought into China from Central Asia. The Gedimu celebrate the major Islamic festivals of Qurban (ʿĪd al-Aḍḥā), the festival of sacrifice that is celebrated during the month of pilgrimage; Bayram (ʿĪd al-Fiṭr), celebrated at the end of Ramaḍān; and Mawlid, the birthday of the prophet Muḥammad.

Islamic education. Islamic education has been as important to Muslims in China as in other parts of the Muslim world. Muslim education among the Gedimu includes primary school level *maktab*, which concentrate on instruction in Arabic and the basic requirements of *sharīʿah*, and the *madrasahs*, which are for more advanced students who are planning to train as *imāms* or as theologians. Education for younger students usually occurs in the mosques. Areas where there are larger concentrations of Hui usually have separate primary and middle schools for Muslim children, although the curriculum is the same as in the mainstream schools. The issue of education for girls and women is as controversial in Chinese Islam, as elsewhere. Single sex schools for girls were closed during the Cultural Revolution, but reopened in 1987 to conform to Hui disapproval of coeducation. The closure of these schools for ten years substantially affected schooling and literacy rates among Hui women because many Hui parents would not allow their daughters to attend coeducational schools.

Among the reopened girls' schools is the Tongxin Girls' Hui Middle School, a boarding school in Tongxin in central Ningxia. The school is spacious, modern, and well equipped by the standards of northwest China. All the girls board at the school because their families live in Hui villages around Tongxin. Other rural Hui children attend the Tongxin Number 2 Hui Middle School. Pupils here also board, go home on Saturday afternoons, and return to the school on Sunday evening. Children who live in the town attend the Tongxin Number 1 Hui Middle School. The effect of mixed schools on Hui girls is illustrated by the school attendance and literacy figures for Guyuan prefecture in southern Ningxia. It is an overwhelmingly Hui region, but only 4.7 percent of school pupils were Hui girls in 1986. Half the Hui women in the region were illiterate, whereas the illiteracy rate for women as a whole in the region was 34.4 percent.

As part of the resurgence of Islam in China, eight Islamic academies for the training of clergy were opened during the 1980s, the most important being in Beijing, Yinchuan, and Urumqi. By 1988, four hundred students had been enrolled in four- to five-year courses that included the study of the Qurʾān, Islamic culture, and management. The aim of the academies was to train researchers, teachers, and high-ranking personnel engaged in international Islamic academic exchanges. Many of the students were *ahongs* who had been serving as clergy for some time but had been unable to obtain formal theological training because of restrictions on religion during the Cultural Revolution.

The Ningxia Islamic Academy (Ningxia Yisilanjiao jingxueyuan) in the Western suburbs of Yinchuan, the capital of the Ningxia Autonomous Region, was built with funds provided by the Islamic Development Bank. The government of the Ningxia Autonomous Region also authorized a loan of 2,300,000 *renminbi* to enable construction to take place. Further technical support was provided by a visiting Saudi engineer in February 1986 and October 1988. By October 2001, the academy was fully functional, with well-attended classes taking place in Arabic, Islamic law, and computing.

The Tongxin Arabic Language School was founded in 1985, also with aid from the Islamic Development Bank, to promote economic and cultural exchange between China and Islamic countries of the Middle East. The design of the building is similar to the Islamic Academy in Yinchuan, but unlike the academies its role is almost entirely secular. It is designated a "secondary vocational school," specializing in training translators and interpreters at the elementary and intermediate level, although the students are of university age. As of 2004, Tongxin Arabic Language School was the only state-run Arabic school in China, although there were privately run Arabic schools in Shaanxi province and elsewhere. The three-year program includes Arabic language and history, general Islamic studies, and nationality theory and policies. By 1988 Tongxin Arabic Language School had ninety-eight students, mostly Hui, and twenty-nine staff members. By 1992 the school's 260 students were all Hui, with three of its graduates working in the Ministry of Foreign Affairs as Arabic translators. Although many of the students were from Ningxia, there were also some from Xi'an and elsewhere. Teachers at the school have studied in Kuwait, Egypt, Syria, and Saudi Arabia. Teaching materials were provided by the Foreign Languages College in Beijing, and supplemented by newspapers and other materials from the Arab world.

Mosques. The most obvious physical expression of the presence of Islam in China is the mosque. *Zhongguo Qingzhen zonglan* (Survey of mosques in China) estimated in 1995 that there were approximately twenty thousand mosques of different types and sizes throughout China. While they are concentrated in traditional Muslim regions in the northwest and southwest, mosques are found throughout China, even in the smallest towns. Beijing alone has at least forty mosques, the most famous being the Ox Street (Niu Jie) Mosque, which has become a showpiece for the country's tolerance of Islam.

Although mosques in China have the same basic characteristics of mosques throughout Islam, with a prayer hall, a *minbar* or pulpit from which the *imām* delivers sermons, a *mihrāb* that points in the direction of Mecca, and rooms for ritual *wuḍūʾ* ablutions, there is great variation in style and size. Some Chinese mosques are built in a style that is similar to Chinese or Mongolian Buddhist temples, and indeed some mosques are converted temples. Others, particularly those built since the 1970s, have deliberately rejected Chinese architectural models and favor a Middle Eastern style. The minaret is no longer universal and was discontinued in some mosques after the suppression of the rebellions of the 1860s when many Muslim communities tried to maintain a low profile. Some, such as the Id Gah Mosque in the center of Kashgar, are grand in scale, but there are smaller mosques. One mosque in the Helan Mountains outside Yinchuan consists of one room backing onto a Buddhist temple.

Shiism and China. Chinese Muslims assert that there is no Shīʿī Islam in either the Hui or Turkic Muslim communities in China, apart from the Ismāʿīlī Shiism of the small community known as the Pamir Tajiks (more accurately, the Wakh), who live in the mountains in the far west of Xinjiang. However, Hui scholars have detected the broad influence of Shīʿī culture and practices on Chinese Islam, notably in the popularity of personal names associated with the family and followers of ʿAlī, the cousin of the prophet Muḥammad and the first Shīʿī *imām* in the schism that followed the death of the Prophet. This influence is not surprising in view of the close connections between Islam in China and the Persian-speaking world, and it has been suggested that the existence of women's mosques in Chinese Islam is due in large part to this hidden Shīʿī influence.

Chinese Sufism. The influence and persistence of Sufism in China is far clearer. Ṣūfī orders (*menhuan*) or brotherhoods (they are mainly a male preserve) have proliferated, especially in northwestern China; they are typically based around the tomb of the founding *shaykh* of the order. This applies to both the Chinese-speaking Hui areas and to Xinjiang, although the Xinjiang Ṣūfī orders operate independently of the others. Historically there have been conflicts between orthodox Gedimu Islam and the Ṣūfī orders, but individuals and families frequently have ties to both traditions. The leadership of the Chinese Ṣūfī orders is usually hereditary, although it is common for a childless *shaykh* to nominate a successor, or for a son-in-law to be brought in to the family to take on that role. The authority of the *shaykh*, as in Ṣūfī orders throughout the Islamic world, relies heavily on the tradition of succession, the *silsilah*, traced back as far as the prophet Muḥammad.

The history and structure of the Ṣūfī orders in China is complex: they are fissiparous in the extreme and often reflect family divisions among the Ṣūfīs. Nevertheless, these orders play an important political and social role in China's Muslim areas, and local government officials are conscious of the need to conciliate them and allow them representation, in proportion to their importance, in local united front bodies. The oldest Ṣūfī orders in China made their appearance in the second half of the seventeenth century. They are the Qādarīyah, which had its origins in twelfth-century Baghdad, and the Kubrawīyah, which emerged in Central Asia during the thirteenth century.

Of all the different Ṣūfī orders, the Naqshbandīyah, which is also important in Central Asia, is the most influential in China. It is rarely referred to by that name among Chinese-speaking Muslims, but the Khufīya and Jahrīyah orders, which exert a powerful influence among the Hui in northwestern China, are subdivisions of the Naqshbandīyah. The Khufīya have traditionally been more inclined to take the side of the government and have produced a number of distinguished military leaders. They are also known as the *laojiao* (literally, the "old teaching"). The Jahrīyah, although also part of the Naqshbandīyah movement, were for many years the main rivals of the Khufīya and became known as the *xinjiao* (the "new teaching") to distinguish them from their competitors. These two terms are generally avoided because there has been considerable confusion by both Western and Chinese writers, who have taken the *laojiao* to be equivalent to the mosque-based Islam of the Gedimu.

The Jahrīyah trace their origins to the arrival in the eighteenth century of Ma Mingxin in Gansu after a long period of study in Bukhara and Yemen. He established his spiritual headquarters in Hezhou, now known as Linxia. The main feature of Jahrīyah religious practice, which distinguishes this group from the Khufīya, is their use of the vocal *dhikr*. The *dhikr* is the Ṣūfī remembrance of Allāh; it is performed in silence by the Khufīya. The Jahrīyah vocalized the *dhikr* and added ritualized movements of the head and body, as well as breathing techniques. The Jahrīyah were more radical and aimed at a purer form of Islam: many adherents adopted a simple and ascetic style of life, rejecting material goods and refusing to pay taxes to the government. This brought them into conflict with the Khufīya, who sought accommodation with the authorities. Ma Mingxin was executed in 1781, as were many of his relatives and thousands of his followers, many of them Turkic Salars. In spite of this and further repression after the rebellions in the late nineteenth century, the Jahrīyah flourished underground, maintaining their faith by the secret practice of the vocal *dhikr*. Despite the original asceticism of the order, the leaders of the Jahrīyah in the early twentieth century are reputed to have made a fortune from agriculture and commerce.

One of the strongest outposts of Jahrīyah Islam in China in the twenty-first century is in Jingyuan county, a poor mountainous area in the far south of the Ningxia Hui Autonomous Region. Almost the entire population of Jingyuan is classified as Hui Muslim (97.8 percent of a total population of 81,432 in 2000). The county government is proud of this heritage and of the way that it has integrated the different Ṣūfī orders into the local power structure, with representation on the Jingyuan Islamic Association in proportion to the numbers of the different sects. The Gedimu are in the majority, followed by the Jahrīyah and the Yihewani. There are also two Khufīya mosques. Most of the Jahrīyah live in mountain villages, where they maintain the tombs of their founding *shaykhs*. Some of the men wear the distinctive six-sided white hat of their order, rather than the white skull cap that is worn by most rural Hui men. In economic and social terms the entire region is underdeveloped, even by the standards of northwest China. The Yihewani (Ikhwānī) sect has also been influential in the northwest; the Yihewani has a role similar to that of the Ṣūfī orders, but often in opposition to them.

Members of these Islamic orders may also be involved in secular social and political organizations. For example, the *shaykh* of a Ṣūfī *menhuan* might also be the chairman of the local Chinese People's Consultative Committee, the united front body established by the Chinese Communist Party to ensure the cooperation of ethnic, religious, and other minorities.

Ṣūfī tombs. After the mosques, the most visible manifestations of Islam in China are the tombs of the Ṣūfī *shaykhs* (*gongbei*). Some of these are simple constructions; in others the tomb is the focus for a substantial collection of buildings that may include a mosque, school, residential accommodation for students, and guest accommodation for visiting worshipers. In Ningxia and Gansu, where the tomb cults are the most highly developed, the tombs are frequently located in remote villages and on isolated hills, but distance is no object to devotees of the orders based there. Thousands of members of the Ṣūfī orders to which the tomb complexes belong make pilgrimages on feast days such as the anniversary of the death of the founding *shaykh*.

Muslims and the Chinese Communist Party. The extent to which religious observance has been possible among China's Muslims has varied considerably according to the current policies of the central government in Beijing and the way in which these policies were interpreted in the Muslim areas. When the Chinese Communist Party came to power in 1949 it had built up a degree of credibility among the Hui Muslims after the creation of autonomous local governments in Muslim areas during the Long March. The early 1950s was a period of conflict as mosques and Ṣūfī orders attempted to retain their landholdings in the face of a countrywide land reform campaign that was designed to redistribute land to the poor. Some *waqfīyah* land owned by mosques and Ṣūfī orders was confiscated, but the authorities were at that stage still relatively tolerant of religious belief and did not seek to suppress Islam in general, although they did move against some of the more radical Ṣūfī *menhuan*, which were treated in a similar way to Daoist and Buddhist secret societies and were outlawed if they were deemed to pose a threat to the security of the new state.

Conflict between Muslims and the Chinese Communist Party increased significantly with the Great Leap Forward of 1958 and the program of collectivization that led to the creation of communes. Conflict between the government and Muslims was further intensified during the Cultural Revolution, which began in 1966 and lasted for approximately a decade. Collectivization, the anti-rightist campaign of 1957, and the Great Leap Forward marked a turn towards a more radical policy associated with Mao Zedong's wish to speed China's transformation into a socialist society. The component of this transformation that most affected religious organizations was religious system reform (*zongjiao zhidu gaige*), which was implemented in 1958. Muslim communities, including the Hui, lost more of their land and buildings; many mosques were closed, and religious activities were restricted. Some Hui businesses, including *ḥalāl* restaurants, restaurants that provided meals produced according to the dietary laws of Islam, were also brought under state or collective ownership under parallel programs to "socialize" industry and commerce.

The aim of the Chinese government was to create a pan-Chinese identity that would subsume minority ethnic and religious identities. As a result, Muslims kept a low profile. During the Cultural Revolution, mosques and tomb complexes were attacked in the Red Guards' campaign against *sijiu* or the "four olds" (old customs, old habits, old culture, and old thinking). In fact, during the Cultural Revolution, the ultra-leftist leadership around Mao maintained that China's nationality problem had been solved, and thus there was no longer any need for different policies for ethnic minorities. As a result, policies specific to minority cultures were dropped, and China's minority peoples were expected to adopt the majority Han culture. The concept of regional autonomy came to be seen as outdated, minority schools and colleges were closed, the use of minority languages was restricted or even banned, and many cadres of minority nationality were replaced by Hans.

Most of China's mosques were closed and many were badly damaged or even completely destroyed in the Red Guard crusade to destroy all remnants of what they regarded as an archaic and obsolete feudal culture. It is not clear to what extent this was an interethnic conflict. There is some suggestion that Red Guards from a Hui background wanted to be in the forefront of the attacks on mosques so as to demonstrate their ardent support of Mao Zedong. Although many mosques were destroyed, some communities managed to protect their places of worship and are deeply proud of their achievements to this day. The study of Islam, along with study in most other fields, was paralyzed during the Cultural Revolution. It was only in the 1970s that articles relating to Islam began to appear again in publications concerning archaeology and international relations.

Like other religions, Islam has been regulated by the Chinese state through the Religious Affairs Bureau, created in 1954 by the State Council. The Religious Affairs Bureau established the Chinese Islamic Association, to which all officially organized mosques belong. The Chinese Islamic Association has been the main instrument of the Communist Party's control over Muslims in China. Because of this, a number of independent or radical groups, notably the Ṣūfī orders, have declined to register with it. This has created a conflict between Muslim groups acceptable to the state and those regarded as unpatriotic and dissident. The Chinese Islamic Association was in abeyance during the Cultural Revolution, like most state organizations, but was resurrected during the "reform and opening" period when Deng Xiaoping came to power in 1978 to 1979.

The Shadian incident. One of the most serious incidents involving Hui Muslims during the Cultural Revolution occurred in the Yunnan village of Shadian near the border with Burma. In 1967, Shadian, like much of China, was divided between rival Cultural Revolution groups. The Red Guards insisted on the mosques being closed and burned copies of the Qur'ān and other religious texts. Others attempted to preserve the constitutional rights of ethnic minorities. The Red Guards claimed the support of the central Cultural Revolution group and were supplied with arms by the Peoples Liberation Army (PLA). In July 1968, the Red Guards surrounded Shadian and fired on the mosque and houses. Several people were killed, but the Red Guards were kept out of the village. Shadian became a haven for the more conservative elements in the region. In November 1968, the Revolutionary Committee of Yunnan ordered a propaganda team into Shadian. The team chose to billet themselves in the main mosque of the village, ate pork while they were there, and threw the bones into the well that the faithful used to wash before prayer. The propaganda team humiliated the Hui to prove their revolutionary fervor, and their activities provoked a violent response from the Muslims of Shadian.

In October 1973, Ma Bohua, a secondary school teacher, led a movement to retake the mosque and open it for prayer. Ma Shaomei, a Muslim and the secretary of the local Communist Youth League, was arrested in May 1974. His fellow Muslims surrounded the office of the propaganda team and demanded that he be set free, but negotiations and appeals to the provincial government on freedom of religion grounds were not successful. In December 1974, the Hui community in Shadian established a Hui militia with Ma Bohua as commander and Ma Shaomei named formally as political commissar. In May 1975, units of the PLA, which had stationed outside Shadian, attempted to enter the village, but they were barred by the villagers. On December 23, leaflets produced by the Provincial Party Committee were dropped by helicopter on Shadian, denouncing counterrevolutionaries and reactionary *imāms.* The Hui responded by burning the leaflets in front of the building where the propaganda team was staying. Negotiations for the Hui to surrender their weapons failed, and the Chinese authorities accused them of cooperating with the Soviet Union and of wanting to establish an independent Islamic republic. These accusations were later blamed on the Gang of Four: Mao Zedong's wife, Jiang Qing, and three of her political associates from Shanghai. This group spearheaded the Cultural Revolution during the 1970s and attempted to take control of the Chinese Communist Party while Mao was ill and dying.

PLA troops entered Shadian during the early morning hours of July 29, 1975, with artillery, flame-throwers, and incendiary bombs. At least nine hundred Hui were killed and six hundred injured during fighting that lasted eight days. Hundreds more were killed in military action in the surrounding villages. Between four hundred and seven hundred PLA soldiers probably died. Shadian was effectively razed, and after the massacre the remaining population had to be relocated, in an echo of the Qing government's policies for dealing with uprisings. After the death of Mao and the arrest of the Gang of Four, there was a "reversal of verdicts" on the Shadian massacre. Those who had resisted the troops were no longer to be regarded as counterrevolutionaries, given the special circumstances of the time, and their organization, Ḥizb Allāh (Party of God), was not to be considered an illegal secret society but a legitimate religious organization.

Chinese Islam after Mao. For Muslims throughout China, the situation changed radically after the end of the Cultural Revolution and the death of Mao Zedong in 1976. Since 1979 there has been a remarkable resurgence of Muslim communities and Islamic religious activity. This is attributed by the government press to the influence of *gaige kaifang,* the reform policies of Deng Xiaoping. China's Muslims have been allowed something of a renaissance, with the rebuilding of mosques demolished during the Cultural Revolution; the publication of Muslim books, journals, and newspapers; and the realization that China had to convince the Muslim world, with which it wished to trade and establish political alliances, that Islam could be practiced freely in China. Since 1979, the five provinces and regions of northwest China with significant Muslim populations—Gansu, Qinghai, Shaanxi, Ningxia, and Xinjiang—have organized five colloquia on Islamic issues, and others have been held in Beijing and in the southeastern coastal areas. Studies on Islamic culture in China and in the rest of the Islamic world have experienced a resurgence, and hundreds of books have been published in the field.

According to statistics published in official news and academic publications, since 1979 more than 20,000 mosques have opened (or, more accurately, reopened, since they were forced to close during the Cultural Revolution). Hundreds of thousands of copies of the Qurʾān and other Islamic classics have been printed and distributed. In addition, the magazine of the government-controlled Islamic Association of China, *Zhongguo Musilin* (Muslims in China), which was inaugurated in 1953, has renewed publishing in both Chinese and the Uighur language. It is estimated that some two thousand Chinese Muslims visit Mecca annually on state-supervised *ḥājj.* The official New China News Agency reported the departure in 1988 of a group of forty-four "Chinese Muslims from Xinjiang," who left on pilgrimage on June 10, with five hundred more who were due to leave for Mecca via Pakistan "in the next few days." According to statistics released by religious authorities in Xinjiang, 6,500 people of different Muslim ethnic groups made the pilgrimage to Mecca from 1980 to 1987.

With the collapse of the Soviet Union and the reemergence on the borders of China of independent Central Asian republics with Islamic histories and traditions, the role of China's Muslims, many of whom share common ethnic and linguistic ties with their Muslim neighbors, is likely to become more significant. However, at the beginning of the twenty-first century, the role of Islam in former Soviet Central Asia hangs in the balance, with tensions between secular nationalist and Islamic movements, as well as competition between Iran and Turkey for influence.

It is very difficult to arrive at a precise figure for the number of people who can properly be called *Muslim* in modern China. The term *Muslim* is used rather loosely to include both those who are active believers and those who belong to communities that by tradition have been Muslim for centuries, irrespective of whether the majority of the members are believers or visit mosques regularly. The government of the People's Republic of China has never collected statistics on religious adherence; the only figures available cover ethnic minority groups that are nominally and traditionally Muslim. Still, many Chinese who formerly considered themselves to be loyal Communists and possibly even atheists identify closely with the Islamic culture of their communities. Some Communist Party members are also believers, and some have become *ahongs*.

The Chinese authorities recognize ten ethnic groups as Muslim: Hui, Uighur, Kazakh, Uzbek, Tajik, Tartar, Khalkhas, Dongxiang, Salar, and Baoan. The total number of Muslims within the borders of China at the beginning of the twenty-first century has been officially estimated at about fourteen million, but many scholars consider this to be an underestimate. There are villages and other communities petitioning to be recognized as Hui or as another ethnic group. Estimates of China's Muslim population before World War II often gave a round figure of fifty million, giving rise to suspicions of genocide. The problem with this figure is that there was no reliable census in China before 1953, and the statistical source of the fifty million figure is far from clear. China's 1990 census suggests a Muslim population of over seventeen million, and a round figure for the 1990s of twenty million Muslims in China would be a reasonable working estimate.

The Hui of Ningxia. The Ningxia Hui Autonomous Region is the province with the highest Hui population and the largest concentrated Hui residential area. At the end of 1985, the Hui population in the autonomous region was 1,337,561, which was 32.3 percent of the total population of the province and 18 percent of the total Hui population of China. Although the Hui are distributed throughout the region, there are two areas of concentration: one in the southern mountainous area, which includes Tongxin, Haiyuan, and Xiji counties, as well as the Hui county of Jingyuan, where the Hui constitute 96.9 percent of the total population; the other in Wuzhong and Lingfu counties in the Yinchuan area in the north of the region, where the Hui populations are respectively 55.2 and 48 percent of the total population.

Ningxia is on the upper and middle reaches of the Yellow River and is approximately 66,000 square kilometers in area. It has water and mineral resources, including gypsum and coal. Irrigation and canals on the Yinchuan plain date back to the Qin dynasty (221–206 BCE) and were further developed during Han, Tang, and Xixia rule. The Ningxia plain is known locally as "the Jiangnan on the Wall." Jiangnan means "south of the Yangzi" and is the highly productive region south of the Yangzi River. Agriculture in the region includes wheat, paddy rice, hemp, oil-bearing crops, and melons and other fruit. People living in the Ningxia grasslands produce fur and skins, including Tibetan lambskins. Sheep are particularly important in the foothills of the Helan mountain range, and tree planting has been both an end in itself and a barrier to the drift of the desert.

To the Han officials who control the region, Ningxia is relatively unproductive and backward in commerce, education, culture, science, and technology. They complain of fast population growth and ignorance of the concept of a commodity economy. The cities on the bend of the Yellow River and surrounding rural areas have developed much more quickly than the mountainous areas of southern Ningxia. Southern Ningxia holds 59 percent of the area and 43 percent of the population of the autonomous region, but the gross value of industrial and agricultural output was only 9.6 percent of the regional total in 1987.

The importance attached to the promotion of a Muslim region can be seen in Ningxia's thirtieth-anniversary celebrations on October 25, 1988. The People's Bank of China announced the issue of a commemorative one *yuan* coin that depicts the Great Mosque in Yinchuan on one side and two young Hui women on the other. Celebratory speeches inevitably praised "nationality solidarity" and unity, claimed that disputes between the Hui and Han nationalities had "all but vanished," and maintained that Hui officials occupied most of the senior posts in the autonomous region and its cities. However, at a meeting with cadres in Yinchuan on September 27, 1988, senior Communist Party figure Wang Zhen, former commander of Chinese military units in Xinjiang, called for measures to increase the number of cadres from minority nationalities. It was revealed that although Hui people accounted for 32.5 percent of the total population of the region, they constituted only 14.5 percent of the cadres, even though most of the leading posts at all levels were occupied by cadres of Hui origin.

Religious observance. Religious observance in Ningxia was stifled during the Cultural Revolution. Many mosques were completely destroyed and others lost much of their land. For Muslims in China, the most important feature of the reform program associated with Deng Xiaoping has been the possibility of rebuilding or reopening mosques. There are no accurate figures for these losses, but some examples will illustrate the point.

The Nanguan (South Bar) Mosque is the largest in Yinchuan. In the courtyard is a shop where the Qurʾān and other devotional materials are on sale, with a display of photographs depicting the destruction of the mosque in the mid-1960s, the makeshift prayer hall made up of mats and tables that the congregation used thereafter, and the reconstruction of the mosque in a Middle Eastern style in the mid 1980s. By 1991 the mosque was fully active with a *madrasah* enrolling about a dozen boys. Also in Yinchuan, the Xiguan (West Bar) Mosque, which is said to date to the 1880s, was rebuilt in 1981 in a Middle Eastern style. The Wuzhong Mosque in Wuzhong, a busy market town south of Yinchuan, was built in 1778 and extended twice during the late nineteenth century. After severe damage during the Cultural Revolution, it was reconstructed in 1979, with further repairs carried out in 1987, although the present mosque occupies far less land than the original. The Najiahu Mosque in Najiahu village near Wuzhong was also badly damaged during the Cultural Revolution, but the prayer hall, with its mixture of Chinese and Islamic architecture, remained untouched.

The Great Mosque in Tongxin, a predominantly Hui town in central Ningxia, functioned as a Buddhist temple during the Mongol conquest and it has the appearance of a temple. It was rededicated as a mosque when it was taken over by local Muslims after the expulsion of the Mongols in the late fourteenth century and the congregation now follows the Yihewani sect. The Great Mosque in Tongxin escaped damage during the Cultural Revolution, and the congregation is proud of its role in defending the mosque. As of 2001, the congregation was flourishing; according to the *ahong*, several dozen Muslims came to the mosque daily, with hundreds on Fridays.

Islamic literature is available in Muslim centers in China, but with certain serious restrictions. The magazine *Zhongguo Musilin* is published nationally and the Qurʾān is available in both Chinese and Arabic. Commentaries and other classic devotional literature, such as the writings of the Ming dynasty Muslim scholar Wang Daiyu, are published openly and are sold in state bookshops in Ningxia and Gansu, as well as in Beijing. Religious publications are also available in Urumqi bookshops. Few Islamic publications are available in bookshops in Kashgar, but religious works in Arabic and Chinese can be bought from street stalls in the Kashgar bazaar. In Linxia, the main Hui area of southwestern Gansu and Guanghe, new and secondhand books on religious topics and Arabic-language courses are on sale from barrows or stalls on the main streets. There is also a widespread network of underground or unofficial Islamic publishing, with *ahongs* publishing and distributing their own books, but these are difficult for outsiders to obtain.

Chinese officials treat the Muslim sects as if they were political factions. There are considered to be six Muslim factions in Ningxia: the Gedimu, Yihewani, Hufuye, Zhehelinye, Gadelinye, and Sailaifeiye. In the view of Chinese Communist Party officials, the Ningxia Hui belong to six factions, all Sunnī, the largest faction having 33,000 members and the smallest 1,000. Government policy is to treat factions equally, with each faction having its own representatives in people's congresses and the local committees of the Chinese People's Political Consultative Conference, an organization designed to integrate non-Communists into the Chinese polity.

In a report on Islam in Ningxia, published in 1989, the New China News Agency claimed that fights between the factions had become rare, but disclosed that there had been a clash between two groups in 1984 over the building of a mosque in Xiji county. More than one thousand people participated in the conflict; two people were killed and over a hundred injured. Other sources suggest that the conflict may have been more serious, and not an exceptional occurrence. According to an article in the latest issue of *Liaowang* (Outlook), conflicts between Muslims in Ningxia are common, and some have led to violence. Since 1978, two factions of the Zheherenye group (the name is derived from the Arabic word *Jahrīyah*) in Xiji county have clashed on numerous occasions, with several hundred and sometimes thousands of people participating. These clashes have led to at least three deaths and five serious injuries. Generally the local government does not intervene in religious disputes, which are resolved through the mediation of religious organizations, although major cases that undermine production and cause casualties are dealt with according to the law.

Local experts maintain that there are no essential differences among the factions, except in the conduct of religious rituals. For example, one faction performs elaborate religious ceremonies, while another may simplify them. Although the differences are minor, conflicts among the factions can be fierce, sometimes culminating in armed fights, mostly for economic benefits or to win people over from other factions. In fact, these "minor" differences have been the most important source of conflict between Chinese Ṣūfī orders for centuries.

Muslim communities and the economic reform program. Mosques in Ningxia benefited from China's move towards a market orientated economy by developing business interests that helped to finance their religious activities. For example, in August 1986, the Nanguan Mosque in Yinchuan, which is the longest established and largest mosque in the region, set up a Muslim services company. It manages an Islamic hotel with sixty to seventy beds, a canteen, grocery, shop, and clinic. By 1988, the mosque had made a profit of over 100,000 yuan. The regional government gives preferential treatment to mosques involved in business, including tax exemption for the first three to five years. The Nanguan Mosque employed thirty-six local people in the mid-1980s, and the poor, the young, and the elderly received free medical treatment in the clinic. Plans for developing the business interests of the mosque included the creation of an Islamic bazaar in Yinchuan, supported by foreign investment.

In 1989, Hui Muslims in Qinghai opened their own Islamic bank, the Muslim savings deposit center run by the Xining City Bank of Industry and Commerce. The bank took 150,000 *renminbi* in deposits in its first month. Some Muslims were wary of the new bank, but the provincial party secretary, Yin Kesheng, attempted to reassure them by saying "We must run the Muslim savings center as a place with genuine minority nationality and Muslim characteristics. Muslim money should be used for Muslim affairs. . . More bonus savings schemes should be organized in view of the needs of religious believers." The Hui people have a tradition of involvement in trade and finance and are likely to prosper in the more open financial environment created by the reform program.

ISLAM IN XINJIANG. Although Xinjiang (or Eastern Turkestan, to use the name preferred by many of its inhabitants) has been under formal direct Chinese control as a province of the empire since 1884, and since 1955 as an autonomous region of the People's Republic of China, the culture, society, and politics of the region and the role of Islam differ so much from that of the rest of China that it is necessary to consider it separately.

The main population of Xinjiang is not Chinese but Uighur. The Uighurs are Central Asian Muslims whose Turkic language is closely related (some say almost identical) to Uzbek; it is also related, but less closely, to the other Central Asian languages of Kazakh and Kyrgyz. Although the Uighurs have had close contact with the Han for centuries, they have struggled to maintain their distinctive Islamic society and social structure, especially in the south of Xinjiang. In addition to the Uighurs, Xinjiang is home to communities of Kazakhs, Kyrgyz, and Mongols, as well as some Russian families whose ancestors have been in the region for centuries. There are also Chinese-speaking Hui Muslims living in Xinjiang. However, by far the largest non-Uighur group are the Han Chinese. While a minority of the Han have roots in Xinjiang as far back as the nineteenth or even eighteenth centuries, the vast majority are more recent immigrants. Xinjiang's Han population includes demobilized soldiers from the Communist forces that took control of Xinjiang in 1949, and members of the quasi-military Xinjiang Production and Construction Corps, a powerful body that combines border defense functions, farming, and land reclamation, and employs many former PLA soldiers, prisoners released from the network of labor camps that stretches throughout Xinjiang, young people from the towns and cities sent down to the countryside (*xiafang*) in the aftermath of the Cultural Revolution, and traders from eastern China hoping to make their fortunes on the new frontier in the far west.

This Han population almost outnumbers the Uighurs, making them feel that they are a colonized nation and that their culture is under serious threat. Resistance to control from Beijing dates back to an insurrection led by Yakub Beg (1820–1877), the independent governments that controlled Kashgaria in the 1930s, and the East Turkistan Islamic Republic, which was established in Yining (also known as Ghulja) in the 1940s. Since the Chinese Communist Party came to power in 1949, resistance has been clandestine and was hardly acknowledged officially until the 1990s, when separatist demonstrations and terrorist acts could no longer be ignored. Even so this resistance was presented as essentially motivated by pan-Turkism and Uighur nationalism against the Han. In fact, there was and is a major religious component to the resistance, and there is strong evidence to suggest that Ṣūfī organizations, often operating through unlicensed *madrasahs* and unofficial mosques, are the organizational backbone to the resistance. The Chinese government and its Xinjiang arm enacted legislation to control such unregistered organs, and also issued instructions to police and customs officials to seize what were said to be large quantities of religious material being imported into Xinjiang. This included copies of the Qurʾān, exegetical literature, and sermons by radical clerics both in text form and on tape. Much of this was imported from Pakistan, and Pakistani traders were openly selling this material in small shops in Kashgar in the 1990s.

Although Islam has been more thoroughly repressed in Xinjiang than in other parts of China, it remains an important part of the fabric of the regional society. Although mosques often maintain a low profile, they remain the center of the community, especially in the more remote rural areas. In addition to their obvious role in worship, funerals, and so on, the mosques are the natural focus for community activities, welfare organizations, and, at times, popular protest against what are seen as government policies inimical to Islam.

The resistance to Beijing that has manifested itself in popular insurrections—notably in 1997 in Yining and in bomb attacks in Urumqi, Kashgar, and Beijing—has become more overtly Islamist in nature. Slogans at demonstrations are frequently Islamic, as well as nationalist, and the existence of clandestine Islamist organizations with names such as *Zhenzhudong* (Party of Allāh) has been reported.

BIBLIOGRAPHY

Bai Shouyi. *Zhongguo Yisilanjiao shi cungao* (Collected papers on Chinese Islam). Yinchuan, China, 1982.

Broomhall, Marshall. *Islam in China: A Neglected Problem.* London, 1910; reprint, 1987.

Chen Dasheng, ed. *Quanzhou Yisilanjiao shike* (Islamic inscriptions of Quanzhou). Fuzhou, China, 1984.

Chu, Wen-djang. *The Moslem Rebellion in North-West China 1862–1878: A Study of Government Minority Policy.* Paris, 1966.

Dillon, Michael. *China's Muslims.* Hong Kong, 1996.

Dillon, Michael. *China's Muslim Hui Community: Migration, Settlement, and Sects.* Richmond, UK, 1999.

Dillon, Michael. *Religious Minorities in China.* London, 2001.

Dillon, Michael. *Xinjiang: China's Muslim Far Northwest.* London, 2004.

Feng Jinyuan. *Zhongguo de Yisilanjiao* (China's Islam). Yinchuan, China, 1991.

Gao Zhanfu. *Xibei Musilin shehui wenti yanjiu* (Research on social issues in northwestern Muslim society). Lanzhou, China, 1991.

Gladney, Dru C. "Muslim Tombs and Ethnic Folklore: Charters for Hui Identity." *Journal of Asian Studies* 46, no. 3 (1987).

Gladney, Dru C. *Muslim Chinese: Ethnic Nationalism in the People's Republic.* Cambridge, Mass., 1991; 2d ed., 1996.

Leslie, Donald Daniel. *Islam in Traditional China: A Short History to 1800.* Canberra, Australia, 1986.

Lipman, Jonathan N. *Familiar Strangers: A History of Muslims in Northwest China.* Seattle, 1997.

Ma Tong. *Zhonguo yisilan jiaopai yu menhuan zhidu shilue* (Brief history of sects and the Ṣūfī pathway system in China's Islam). Yinchuan, China, 1983/1999.

Ma Tong. *Zhongguo xibei yisilanjiao jiben tezheng* (Basic characteristic of Islam in northwest China). Yinchuan, China, 2000.

Mian Weilin. *Ningxia Yisilan jiaopai gaiyao* (Muslim sects in Ningxia). Yinchuan, China, 1991.

Wang, Jianping. *Glossary of Chinese Islamic Terms.* Richmond, U.K., 2001.

Wu Jianwei, ed. *Zhongguo Qingzhen zonglan* (Survey of mosques in China). Yinchuan, China, 1995.

MICHAEL DILLON (2005)

ISLAM: ISLAM IN SOUTH ASIA

One in three Muslims today is of South Asian origin. With a Muslim population of over 300 million, South Asia (India, Pakistan, Bangladesh) is home to the largest concentration of Muslims in the world. The significance of the region's vast and diverse Muslim communities extends far beyond the present-day political boundaries of South Asia. Over the centuries, Muslims from the region have also emigrated, mostly for economic reasons, to other parts of the world such as Southeast Asia, East and South Africa, the Gulf states, Fiji, and the Caribbean. In more recent decades, Muslims of South Asian origin have come to constitute a substantial proportion of immigrant populations in Europe, the United Kingdom, Canada, and the United States.

Notwithstanding their impressive numerical strength, South Asia's Muslims are a minority when considered within the context of the subcontinent's total population. Awareness of this minority status has been an influential factor affecting their history, particularly in contemporary times. In the early decades of the twentieth century, the rise of nationalist movements to free India from British colonial rule was marked by a growing anxiety among some Muslim intellectuals and leaders about the status of Muslim minorities in an independent postcolonial India ruled by a Hindu majority. Many feared that Muslims would not be able to practice their faith and nurture their cultural traditions freely in a nation governed by a non-Muslim majority. As prominent Hindu and Muslim leaders began to conceptualize their respective communities as constituting two separate nations, demands increased for the partition of the subcontinent and the creation of two states, India and Pakistan. The birth of Pakistan in 1947, an independent nation-state in which Muslims would form a majority, marked the first time in modern history that a nation-state was founded to protect a religious community.

Indo-Muslim civilization, contrary to the discourse of some contemporary politicians and religious leaders, has not been exclusively Muslim; adherents of other faiths as well have played an important role in its formation and have been deeply affected by it. In premodern India, for instance, Hindus were well represented in the imperial bureaucracy of Muslim rulers, holding coveted positions at courts such as chief secretary, chief minister, treasurer, and commander of the royal armies. Muslim royal patronage of Hindu poets, writers, musicians, and artists was also quite common. At present, Hindus and Sikhs in some parts of India still visit the shrines of Muslim holy men in the hope of receiving spiritual blessing. During worship, they may sing devotional songs composed by Muslim mystics. In a more secular context, they attend poetry recitals where audiences enjoy listening to the *ghazal,* a form of Arabo-Persian mystical poetry that enjoys widespread popularity all over the subcontinent. The participation of non-Muslims in many aspects of Muslim culture demonstrates that in South Asia peoples of different religious affiliations could and did come together in profound ways.

The Emergence of Muslim Communities in South Asia and the Problem of "Conversion." The earliest Muslim presence in the subcontinent can be traced to immigrants who came to earn a living, to conquer, to teach religion, and to seek refuge. According to tradition, the first Muslim immigrants were Arab traders who, as early as the eighth century, settled in many of the seaports along the western and southern coasts of India. Later, the descendants of these merchant communities moved to major cities inland as well as farther south to Sri Lanka. In 711 a small Arab expedition, under the command of the seventeen-year-old general Muḥammad ibn Qāsim, was sent to the Arabian Sea to subjugate pirates who had been pillaging Arab trading ships. The expedition conquered parts of Sind (southern Pakistan) and, with the assistance of local allies, founded a state that survived for nearly three centuries. These early Arab mercantile and political connections laid the basis for the strong affinity of later Muslim communities in southern and southwestern India with the Arab world and Arabian culture. In contrast, in other regions of the subcontinent, especially the north and northwest, the first contacts with Muslims were through various Central Asian tribes and clans, mostly consisting of Turks who had been culturally "Persianized." As a result of political turmoil in Central Asia and Afghanistan in the tenth century, groups of Turks and Afghans crossed the Himalayas and entered India from the northwest. Initially, these groups seem to have been interested in acquiring booty rather than settling in the region. Over the next several centuries, however, they established kingdoms in North India, Bengal, the Deccan, and western India. The most famous of these Central Asian dynasties were the Mughals, founded in 1526 by the Emperor Bābur. With the strong support of local Hindu allies such as the Rajputs, the Mughals were eventually able to consolidate control over a vast portion of India, creating an empire under whose auspices there was a veritable renaissance in Indo-Muslim literature, art, and architecture.

The establishment of sultanates and empires led to an influx of a variety of classes of individuals. Some sought administrative positions in the newly established states, while others looked for appointments to legal positions such that of *qāḍī* ("judge"). Poets and artists also flocked to the subcontinent from Central Asia and Iran in search of royal patronage, especially after they experienced difficulties in securing patronage in their homelands. Religious scholars (*'ulamā'*) and preachers, both Sunnī and Shī'ī, as well as Ṣūfī *shaykhs* and their disciples, were also attracted to the new land.

While immigrant Muslims and their descendants played a significant role in the development of the Islamic tradition in the region, historically they constituted only a small fraction of the entire Muslim population. The vast majority of Muslims in South Asia are clearly of indigenous origin, although some, for reasons of social prestige, may still claim Arab or Persian descent. Unfortunately, the processes by which they became Muslim are not well understood. Colonial, religious, nationalist, and communitarian agendas have so influenced perspectives on this subject that, as British historian Peter Hardy comments, "to attempt to penetrate the field of the study of the growth of Muslim populations in South Asia is to attempt to penetrate a political minefield" (Hardy, 1979, p. 70). Traditionally, various theories have been advanced: that people converted under duress at the point of the sword, or to acquire political and economic patronage, or to escape the evils of the Indian caste system. Various Ṣūfīs have also been regarded as "missionaries" who were responsible for the peaceful spread of Islam through their charismatic personalities, the miracles they performed, and the religious folk songs and poems they composed.

Recent scholarship has raised important questions on the issue of conversion to Islam. All the theories mentioned above have been criticized for either being flawed or being inadequately supported by convincing historical or sociological evidence. In addition, scholars have disagreed about the processes involved. For instance, Carl Ernst in *Eternal Garden: Mysticism, History, and Politics at a South Asian Sufi Center* (1992) questions the idea that Ṣūfī folk poetry was explicitly composed to convert people to Islam, observing that some of these compositions are so heavily laden with Islamic material that "it is difficult to imagine them as devices to impart knowledge of Islam to non-Muslims" (pp. 166–168). He argues that the verses could only have been directed at an audience already familiar with the Islamic tradition. On the other hand, Richard Eaton, in *Sufis of Bijapur, 1300–1700* (1978), contends that the authors of Dakkani folk songs, whose lyrics contained Islamic teachings, primarily desired to secure for themselves the role of mediators or intermediaries between God and the people (Muslim and non-Muslim) who recited these songs. If, he writes, in the process of singing these songs local populations became familiar with or acculturated to popular forms of Islamic practice, the phenomenon should not be construed as "conversion" in the sense of a "self-conscious turning around in religious conviction and belief." Nor should the authors be considered missionaries or "self-conscious propagators," even though this is the general context in which Ṣūfīs tend to be viewed (pp. 172–173).

Complicating the discussion of why and how so many South Asians became Muslim is the inadequacy of the term *conversion* itself. In his book *The Rise of Islam and the Bengal Frontier, 1204–1760* (1993), Richard Eaton correctly points out that the notion of conversion, with its presumption of conscious intentionality and individual choice regarding religious belief, is derived from a Protestant missionary model, and has been projected unconsciously on the historical context of premodern South Asia. As he convincingly demonstrates, the diffusion of Islamic ideas in premodern Bengal took place at a mass level and was as much associated with the clearing of forests and the spread of agrarian civilization as with changes in doctrine and practice. The inadequacy of the term "conversion" is further apparent when we observe that, in many regions of South Asia, Islamic beliefs were often expressed in ways that did not totally reject the conceptual and social framework of indigenous cultures. Intrinsic to this approach was the acceptance of both indigenous beliefs and newer Islamic ones in an integrated manner. If an individual retained previous beliefs and practices and saw continuities between the old and the new, could this process be called "conversion," a term that usually implies complete abandonment of the old in favor of the new? Given that the religious identity of a community is fluid, is it more appropriate to view the process as one of acculturation, rather than conversion, involving not a sudden act but rather a slow and gradual process, perhaps over several generations, during which adherents respond to changing contexts? Obviously, these and many other unanswered questions concerning the evolution of Muslim communities in South Asia will require a great deal more research before we have satisfactory explanations. In view of the historical, social, and cultural complexities involved, what is clear is that a mono-dimensional approach that limits explanations to a single factor is far too simplistic to explain why so many South Asians today identify themselves as Muslim.

DIVERSITY OF TRADITIONS. Much contemporary political, religious, and academic discourse on the Islamic tradition in South Asia is dominated by the conception that Muslims of South Asia form a single homogeneous Muslim community. Typically in such discourses, the political fortunes of the great Turko-Persian Muslim dynasties, such as the Mughals, and the experiences of North Indian Persian- and Urdu-speaking Muslim elite communities, have come to be the only lenses through which Muslim experiences throughout the subcontinent are perceived. Historically, the concept of a single undifferentiated Muslim community is a relatively recent development and its emergence is clearly a result of the religiously based idiom of British colonial rule, the growth of religious nationalism, and the politics of electoral representation. Thus, the demand for the creation of Pakistan and its underlying premise of Muslims comprising a single unified nation should not mislead us into thinking that common religion (Islam) has always been a strong unifying bond among diverse Muslim groups in South Asia.

Historically, socioeconomic status, class, caste, ethnicity, and sectarian affiliation have been far more significant identity-markers among South Asian communities, Muslim and non-Muslim alike, than religious affiliation. Indeed Muslims in South Asia are characterized by a rich diversity that mirrors the diversity of the subcontinent itself. This diversity stems, on the one hand, from the different ethnic and linguistic groups to which they belong. It is a cultural diversity that is reflected, for example, in the many Indic languages and literary genres used in Muslim devotional literatures, in musical genres such as the *qawwālī* that are rooted in North Indian musical traditions, and in the mosques that incorporate local traditions of design. Diversity may also be theological, stemming from the many ways Muslims understand and interpret their faith. Even within overarching categories, such as Sunnī, Shīʿah, or Ṣūfī, there exist several subgroups and divisions with significant differences. A Sunnī may be Deobandi or a Brelvi; a Shīʿah may be Ithnāʿasharī (Twelver) or Ismāʿīlī, either Nizārī or Mustaʿlī (Bohra); a Ṣūfī may belong to one of the major orders such as the Chishtīyah or Naqshbandīyah, or not belong to an order at all. In this way, the Islamic tradition in South Asia is comprised of multiple communities of interpretation. Each community has its particular way of conceiving Islam. Each is shaped by its specific sociopolitical and cultural context in the way it understands universally held Islamic beliefs, such as the belief that the Qurʾān is the embodiment of divine revelation or that the Prophet Muḥammad is God's final messenger.

The plurality of traditions that characterizes Islam in South Asia can best be explored within a framework that takes into account the role of both cultural and doctrinal/theological elements in creating competing definitions of what is considered "Islamic" and "non-Islamic." Historically, the relationship between culture and religious doctrine among Muslim communities has been such that in many cases, as we shall see below, cultural and religious identities are conflated. Frequently, socioeconomic factors such as class and caste have played a significant role in this interaction.

Defining Islam: The Role of Culture. Several studies of the Islamic tradition in South Asia have remarked on a dichotomy within the tradition between two contradictory facets. Frequently at odds which each other, the two facets or strands represent radically different perspectives on what it means to be a Muslim in the South Asian environment. One facet looks to what are perceived to be universal norms observed in the worldwide Muslim community, particularly those represented by Arabo-Persian culture, for guidance and inspiration. The other facet seeks to acculturate and root the practice of Islam within the many local cultures of the subcontinent. The dynamic interaction between these two facets, manifest in the thoughts and attitudes of Muslim thinkers, statesmen, poets, and artists through the centuries, provides a useful lens through which to view the complex interaction between culture and religion in the determining of identity.

The first facet, under the influence of a strictly legalistic interpretation of Islam based on the classic traditions of *sharīʿah* and religious jurisprudence, appealed to Arabian and Persian traditions to determine the religious and cultural norms and mores for Muslim communities in South Asia. On account of its extraterritorial ethos and legalistic outlook, Annemarie Schimmel, the renowned scholar of South Asian Islam, has characterized this facet as being "Mecca-oriented" or "prophetic." Historically, this facet was associated mostly with the ruling and intellectual elite, often referred to as the *ashrāf* ("nobility"). In northern India, the *ashrāf* were Persianized Turks and Iranians who had come to South Asia from Central Asia, Afghanistan, and Iran as soldiers, rulers, traders, religious scholars, artists, poets, and refugees. Favoring Persian as the official language of administration, as well as of literary culture, they lived mostly in or near an axis stretching from Lahore to Delhi to the Deccan, an axis that Richard Eaton has aptly termed South Asia's "central Perso-Islamic axis." They also participated in an extensive transnational and cosmopolitan nexus of Turko-Persianate culture that, at least until the eighteenth century, connected them with the elites of Central Asia, Iran, Afghanistan, and even the Ottoman Empire. Beyond the Perso-Islamic axis, we find, along the western and southwestern coasts of India, a more Arab-centered tradition with closer historical and cultural links to Arabia. Among Muslims communities, such as the Māppiḷḷas of Kerala, the category of *ashrāf* included *sayyids,* those who claimed descent from the Prophet Muḥammad, as well as populations of Arab origin whose ancestors had come to the regions as traders and merchants at least as early as the eighth century, making them some of the first Muslim immigrants to South Asia.

Conscious of their privileged status, as well as their ethnic and cultural difference from the subcontinent's indigenous populations, the *ashrāf* were anxious to prevent their religious and cultural identity from being absorbed and overwhelmed by an environment they considered to be alien and antithetical to their values. In their desire to maintain the purity of their identity, they disparaged and rejected all Indian cultural manifestations—from Indian languages, which they considered unworthy of recording any Islamic literature, to indigenous Indian Muslims, whom they contemptuously called the *ajlāf* ("mean, ignoble wretches"). Al-Baranī (d. c. 1360), a medieval historian, refers, in his chronicle *Fatāwā Jahāndārī,* to local converts as "pigs, boars, and dogs" who ought not to be given too much education lest "it bring honor to their mean souls." Even today, it is hardly surprising that many South Asian families continue to assert their superior social status by proudly claiming a Central Asian, Iranian, or Arab ancestry and refusing to marry Muslims with indigenous family roots, even though the *ashrāf* have lost effective political power.

To preserve and protect their religio-cultural identity from encroachment by "idolatrous" Indian customs and beliefs, the *ashrāf* cultivated a strong extraterritorial ethos, one that appealed to the Islamic heartlands as a source of cultural and religious norms and mores. We can discern this extraterritorial ethos in the works of many of the subcontinent's influential Muslim thinkers, scholars, and theologians. Thus, the fourteenth-century Suhrawardi Ṣūfī Makhdūm-i Jahāniyān Jahāngasht (d. 1385) insisted that his followers use Arabic terms such as Allāh to refer to God, rather than Indic vernacular terms (such as *nirañjan,* "the one without attributes"). Similar sentiments were echoed several centuries later by Shāh Walī Allāh (1703–1762), one of the great reformers of South Asian Islam, who writes in his treatise *Tafhimat al-ilāhiyya:* "We are an Arab people whose fathers have fallen into exile in the country of Hindustan; Arab genealogy and the Arabic language are our pride" (vol. 2, p. 246). He further demanded that the Muslims of India substitute the customs of the Arabs for the foreign customs they had adopted. These foreign customs, he felt, were not compatible with their Islamic identity. The twentieth-century poet-philosopher Muḥammad Iqbāl (1877–1938) also reflects this ethos in his Urdu work, *Bang-i dara,* in which he sees himself as a bell around the neck of the lead camel in the caravan of the Prophet Muḥammad, calling the Muslim community of India to return to its true homeland in Mecca. The conflation of an Islamic identity with Arabo-Persian culture is also apparent in the emergence of such linguistic forms as Arwi, a form of Tamil that is heavily influenced by Arabic.

Intensely at odds with this extraterritorial Arabo-Persian facet is an assimilative and adaptationist aspect that may be described as being local, or South Asia–focused, as well as more mystically oriented. Representatives of this strand generally espoused an esoteric or mystical vision of Islam in which external manifestations of culture, such as language, were not seen as fundamental to being Muslim. Consequently, they not only were more open to, and tolerant of, the South Asian cultural milieu, they also actively fostered interpretations of Islam that could be more readily understood within the contexts of indigenous religion and culture.

The *shaykhs* of the Chishtī Ṣūfī order, for instance, actively promoted the creation of devotional poetry on Islamic mystical themes in local languages. In its ethos, expressions, and similes, this poetry is strikingly similar to Hindu *bhakti* (devotional) poetry. Beyond developing a common poetical language, some Ṣūfīs also adapted the Indian disciplines of Yoga and meditation to practices inherited from the classical Arabo-Persian Ṣūfī tradition. In an identical spirit, the authors of the extensive *pūthī* religious literature from medieval Bengal attempted to incorporate various figures of Hindu mythology, particularly Kṛṣṇa (Krishna), an *avatāra* of the Hindu deity Viṣṇu (Vishnu), into the historical line of prophets that ends with the Prophet Muḥammad. In Tamil Nadu, Muslim authors such as Umaru Pulavar (d. 1703), used the genre of the *purāna,* conventionally employed to recount the deeds of various Hindu deities, to narrate in poetic form the biography of the Prophet Muḥammad, using traditional Tamil literary conventions and customs to create a distinctively Tamil flavor. In Sind and Punjab, Ṣūfī poets appropriated to an Islamic context the theme of *viraha* (love-in-separation) and the symbol of the *virahinī* (the woman longing for her beloved), both associated in the Hindu devotional traditions with the longing of the *gopīs* (cow-maids), particularly Radha, for the deity Kṛṣṇa. Following the conventions of Indic devotional poetry, these Ṣūfī poets represented the human soul as a longing wife, or bride, pining for her beloved husband or bridegroom, who may be God, the Prophet Muḥammad, or the Ṣūfī *shaykh.*

Although such localized or acculturated understandings of Islam have frequently been characterized as syncretistic, mixed, or heterodox, they are perhaps better understood as attempts to "translate" universal Islamic teachings within "local" contexts. The validity of approaching vernacular Muslim poetry through the lens of "translation theory," as articulated by Tony Stewart (2001), is confirmed by the fact that communities who recite and sing vernacular religious poems frequently regard them as texts that encapsulate the teachings of the Arabic Qurʾān. For instance, Sindhi-speaking Muslims in southern Pakistan consider Shāh ʿAbdul Laṭīf's poetic masterpiece in the Sindhi language, the *Risālo,* to be a revered book that contains within it the essence of the spiritual teachings of the Qurʾān. Through his exegetical remarks on dramatic moments and events in popular Sindhi folk romances, Shāh ʿAbdul Laṭīf is perceived to be conveying in the Sindhi vernacular Qurʾānic ideas on the spiritual significance of the human situation. In the Punjab, poems attributed to Punjabi Ṣūfī poets such as Bullhe Shāh (d. 1754) and Vāriṣ Shāh are also commonly regarded as spiritual commentaries on Qurʾānic verses, particularly those associated with Sufism or Islamic mysticism. Similarly, the *ginān*s of the Khoja Ismāʿīlī communities of western India and Pakistan, composed in various vernacular languages such as Gujarati, Hindi, Punjabi, and Sindhi and embodying the teaching of Ismāʿīlī preacher-saints, have also been regarded as secondary texts embodying the inner signification of the Qurʾān.

Of the two facets, "the prophetic and Mecca-oriented" and "the mystical and South Asia–centered," it is the latter, by advocating that there was no contradiction between being a Muslim and fully embracing indigenous cultures, that has always stressed the common cultural links that South Asian Muslims share with their non-Muslim compatriots. With their contradictory attitudes toward the South Asian milieu and differing definitions of what constitutes an Islamic identity in a predominantly non-Muslim environment, it was inevitable that representatives of the two strands would come into conflict with one another. Indeed, one approach to interpreting the history of Islam in South Asia is through an analysis of the constant interplay and interaction of these two facets.

SUNNĪ ISLAM. The vast majority of Muslims in South Asia are Sunnī, relying on Sunnī *ʿulamāʾ,* or religious scholars, for guidance on matters of faith. Generally speaking, the Shāfiʿī school of jurisprudence prevails among Sunnī communities in southern and southwestern India and Sri Lanka, whereas the Hanafī school is widespread elsewhere in the subcontinent. Little is known of the coming of Sunnī *ʿulamāʾ* to the early Muslim settlements established by Arab traders on the southwest coast of India. Although the sixteenth-century Malayali author Zayn al-Dīn al-Maʿbarī suggests in his *Tuḥfat al-mujāhidīn* (Gift of the holy warriors) that preachers from Arabia founded the first mosques in Kerala, he does not indicate specific dates. In 1342 the Moroccan Arab traveler Ibn Baṭṭūṭah found in the region mosques and *qāḍīs* of the Shāfiʿī school of law being supported by Muslim seamen and merchants. There are several indications that Sunnī *ʿulamāʾ* were already established in northern India in the eleventh and twelfth centuries: the presence of the scholar-Ṣūfī Shaykh ʿAlī al-Hujwīrī in Lahore, where he died between 1072 and 1077; the travels of Fakhr al-Dīn al-Rāzī (1149–1209), the theologian and exegete, in the Punjab; and the praise heaped by Muslim historians on various rulers for establishing mosques and encouraging scholars to move to India. The Mongol devastation of cities in the Middle East and Central Asia in the mid-thirteenth century triggered a further migration of Sunnī scholars to India, making easier the task of appointing *qāḍīs* for the growing number of Muslim-ruled states in northern India. This new influx may partially explain why the Hanafī school of law supplanted the Shāfiʿī school as the dominant Sunnī rite in northern India.

During the earlier periods of Muslim history in North India, the teaching centers of Sunnī *ʿulamāʾ* appear to have been informal schools attached to mosques rather than separate *madrasahs,* or religious colleges. The same can be said of Bengal, where inscriptions from the thirteenth to the fifteenth centuries also refer to *madrasahs* being attached to mosques. Although the first independent *madrasah* was established in 1472 at the city of Bidar in the Bahmanid state in the Deccan by the Persian minister Maḥmūd Gāwān, it is only in the eighteenth century that institutions such as the Farangī Mahal in Lucknow and the Madrasa-i Raḥīmiyya in Delhi began to enjoy widespread fame as centers of Sunnī scholarship. The Farangī Mahal developed into a leading religious college after it received substantial financial support in 1691 from the Mughal Emperor Aurangzeb (d. 1707). Its curriculum, the *dars-i Niẓāmī,* heavily emphasized theology and philosophy as opposed to colleges in Delhi, such the Madrasa-i Raḥīmiyya, founded by Shāh Walī Allāh's father Shāh ʿAbd ar-Raḥīm, which were repositories of *ḥadīth* studies. The nineteenth century was the age of the *madrasah* in South Asia, because Sunnī *ʿulamāʾ* responded to British colonialism and the spread of Western-style education by setting up a network of colleges to provide an alternative Islamic education to Muslim youth. Most significant among these was the Dār ul-ʿUlūm at Deoband, created to train *ʿulamāʾ* who could promote and uphold "correct" Islamic belief and practice within Muslim communities. A bastion of Sunnī learning to this day, Deoband continues to attract students from all over the world. Historically, it had a network of affiliate branches established at places such as Muradabad, Saharanpur, and Darbhanga. Later, colleges founded in such widely separated centers as Madras, Peshawar, and Chittagong regarded themselves at Deobandi. An alternative curriculum to that of Deoband was offered at Nadwat al-ʿulamāʾ, founded in Lucknow by Shiblī Nuʿmānī (d. 1914), allowing its students to combine traditional Islamic subjects with secular "Western" subjects, including English. However, this institution was not successful in meeting its educational goals, for its curriculum soon reverted to the traditional *dars-i Niẓāmī* model.

Sunnī Islam in South Asia has evolved into several strands so that Sunnī Muslims are often categorized according to the particular *ʿulamāʾ* group they follow: the Deobandis uphold the interpretation of the four classical schools of Sunnī jurisprudence, developed in the late ninth and tenth centuries, as constituting orthodox Islam; the Barelwīs are more accepting of popular practices, such as visiting tomb shrines, and other Ṣūfī rituals that the Deobandis would disapprove of; the Ahl-i Ḥadīth, particularly strong in certain regions of Pakistan, are more right wing and puritanical in their interpretation, which is strongly influenced by the Wahhābīs.

The Sunnī *ʿulamāʾ* obtained material support from a variety of sources. All Muslim rulers in South Asia appointed *qāḍīs,* royal tutors, *khaṭībs* (mosque preachers), and *imāms* (mosque prayer leaders) and paid them in cash or by income from tax exempt land. Others received income from *waqfs,* or endowments. *ʿUlamāʾ* who did not enter service (for which they were often more respected) relied on gifts from the faithful, fees in money or kind for private tuition, or income from cultivation or trade, though this latter case was uncommon. Sometimes a noted scholar would accept a royal pension or subvention from a government official, without the obligation to perform a public function. The *ʿulamāʾ* of the Dār ul-ʿUlūm at Deoband broke new ground under British rule: they opened subscription lists and drew voluntary contributions from Muslims at all social levels, though chiefly from the well-to-do.

The social status of the *ʿulamāʾ* was high. Indeed, at all times, though not at all places, a good proportion of them belonged to families with a history of being appointed to prominent political and religious positions. As *sayyids* and *shaykhs,* many took pride in claiming an ancestry outside South Asia, reaching back to seventh- or eighth-century Arabia. Some openly despised Muslims with indigenous roots. To maintain their social status, *ʿulamāʾ* married within extended families, or at least within the elite circles of the *ashrāf.* Sometimes the pursuit of a recognized course of study according to recognized methods could enable a Muslim from a lower social class or even a convert to gain acceptance among the general body of the *ʿulamāʾ*. Such social mobility is more fully documented in modern than in medieval times: for example, the family of Sayyid Ḥusayn Aḥmad Madanī of Deoband was thought to have been weavers; Mawlānā ʿUbayd Allāh Sindhī, also a prominent Deobandi *ʿalīm,* was born a Sikh. Of course, the high status of an *ʿalīm* might have very local recognition: the rural *mullā* and *maulawī* in many parts of South Asia is often not learned in Arabic and would not be recognized outside his neighborhood as an equal of scholars fluent in Arabic, Persian, and Urdu.

Shīʿī Islam. Shīʿī communities, of both Ismāʿīlī and Ithnāʿasharī (Twelver) varieties, are a minority comprising approximately ten percent of the total Muslim population in South Asia. It is not, however, unusual to find them concentrated within certain urban neighborhoods and cities, thus forming local majorities. Although reverence for the family of the Prophet Muḥammad has been strong in South

Asia, the public articulation of a Shīʿī identity waited on favorable political and social developments, both in the larger Muslim world as well as in parts of South Asia.

Ismāʿīlī communities. The earliest Shīʿī communities in South Asia were Ismāʿīlī. Regarded as subversive by the Abbasids of Baghdad and by Sunnī warlords who took effective control of the eastern Muslim world by the middle of the ninth century CE, Ismāʿīlīs nevertheless managed in the tenth century to establish strongholds in Sind, the area around Multan, as well as Gujarat. There is evidence that the Ismāʿīlī dynasty that ruled Sind during this period had connections with the Fatimids in Egypt, a dynasty that claimed the Shīʿī imamate and caliphate on the basis of its direct descent from the Prophet. Judging by information from historical chronicles, these early Ismāʿīlī communities were persecuted by Turko-Persian Sunnī warlords who began to invade South Asia from the tenth century onwards. In 1094 the Ismāʿīlīs split into two branches, the Mustaʿlīs and the Nizārīs, over the issue of succession to the Fatimid imamate. In South Asia, the Mustaʿlīs are popularly known as the Bohras, a term probably derived from the Gujarati *vohora* ("trader"), while the Nizārīs are often called Khojas, from the Persian *khwaja* ("lord, master"), or Aga Khanis, based on the fact that they follow the guidance of the Aga Khan, a honorific title used by their living *imāms*. Both Ismāʿīlī communities, concentrated mostly in Gujarat and Sind as well as in some of the major urban centers of South Asia, have been heavily involved in trade, commerce, and the professions.

Bohra communities were probably in existence in Gujarat by the middle of the twelfth century and certainly before the conquest of Gujarat by the Delhi sultan that began in 1299. Their origins can be traced to a series of preachers who came to the region from Yemen, an important center of Mustaʿlī history. Because Bohras believe that their *imām* is in occlusion, the affairs of the community are run by his representative, the *dāʿī muṭlaq*, who controls all activities of the community. He is assisted by *shaykhs*, *mullās*, and *ʿāmils* ("agents") who are, however, only executive functionaries and do not participate in the formulation of doctrine and principles of right conduct. For several centuries, the headquarters of the *dāʿī muṭlaq* was in Yemen. In the sixteenth century, however, as a result of a major dispute over the issue of succession to the office of *dāʿī muṭlaq*, the Bohras split into two factions: the Sulaimanī and the Dāʾūdī. The former owe allegiance to a *dāʿī* still based in Yemen, whereas the latter pledge loyalty to a *dāʿī*, often called *syednā* ("our master"), whose headquarter is in Mumbai.

The history of Khoja communities can be traced at least to the eleventh and twelfth centuries when, according to tradition, Nizārī Ismāʿīlī *imāms*, then resident in Iran, sent *dāʿīs* to Punjab, Sind, Gujarat, and possibly Rajasthan, to preach the Ismāʿīlī faith. Also known as *pīrs*, these preacher-saints composed *ginān*s, hymn-like songs in various vernacular languages through which they elaborated a highly devotional and mystical understanding of the Shīʿī concept of *imām*. Particularly interesting was the attempt to explain the concept of the *imām* within the framework of Vaisnavite Hindu thought. The *ginān*s continue to be the mainstay of Khoja devotional life today. In the 1840s the living *imām* of the Nizārīs, Ḥasan ʿAlī Shāh, Aga Khan I, moved from Iran to India and asserted his leadership over the Khoja community. This resulted in some schisms among the Khojas, but the majority continued to pledge their allegiance to the Aga Khan and, after him, his descendants who, as living Shīʿī *imāms*, have absolute power of decision over belief and practice. Sultan Muḥammad Shāh, Aga Khan III (d. 1957), utilized this authority to institute a wide range of religious and social reforms, some of which, such as abolishing the veil and promoting female education, were aimed at improving the status of Ismāʿīlī women. His successor, Karīm Al-Ḥusaini, Aga Khan IV, has continued the transformation of the community in South Asia by making it part of a transnational network of social, economic, and educational institutions that links it with Nizārī Ismāʿīlī communities in other parts of the world. Known as the Aga Khan Development Network, it seeks to improve the standard of living of Ismāʿīlī and non-Ismāʿīlī communities in the countries in which it operates.

Twelver or Ithnāʿasharī communities. Unlike Ismāʿīlī Shiism, Twelver Shiism in South Asia has often enjoyed official patronage by certain rulers and states. In the fifteenth century, following a substantial migration of Twelver Shīʿahs from Iran to the court of the Bahmanid Sultanate in the Deccan, the Bahmani sultan Aḥmad I (1422–1436) declared himself to be Shīʿī, though the dynasty's public position continued to be ambiguous. Of the successor states to the Bahmanis, Bijapur supported the Twelver Shīʿī position from 1510 to 1534 and again between 1558 and 1580; Golkonda's Quṭb Shāhi dynasty was Shīʿī from its foundation under Qulī Quṭb al-Mulk (1496–1543); and the kingdom of Ahmadnagar supported Twelver Shiism from the reign of Burhān I (1509–1553). The establishment of Mughal rule made northern India a safer place for Shīʿī scholars. The Shīʿī Safavid Shāh of Iran, Ṭahmāsp I (1524–1576), assisted the emperor, Humāyūn (d. 1556), in reestablishing the Mughal position in eastern Afghanistan by 1550, and Shīʿī Persians formed an important element of the Muslim elite of the Mughal Empire. They became particularly prominent during the reign of the Mughal emperor Jahāngīr (d. 1627) when many Twelver Shīʿī poets and scholars emigrated from Iran seeking positions at the Mughal courts. In 1611 Jahāngīr married Mihrunnisā, also called Nūr Jahān, the daughter of an Iranian nobleman. Because the emperor was not too interested in matters of state, Nūr Jahān became the de facto ruler of the empire. Her father and brother were appointed to positions of great influence while her niece, Mumtāz Mahal, was married to the emperor's son Shāhjahān. The most famous monument of Indo-Muslim architecture, the Taj Mahal, was erected in Mumtāz Mahal's memory. After the collapse of the Mughal empire, Twelver Shiism continued to be favored by certain regional dynasties.

In the eighteenth century, under the *nawābs* of Awadh, Lucknow became the Twelver Shīʿī cultural and educational capital in South Asia.

While the official acceptance of Shīʿī Islam in court circles attracted prominent Shīʿī scholars and theologians to India, there was always the danger that they could be persecuted when there were shifts in the political climate at courts. Shāh Faṭhullāh Shirāzī (d. 1589) and Qāḍī Nūrullāh Shustarī (d. 1610) rank among two prominent Twelver Shīʿī scholars who experienced mixed fortunes in India. Shāh Faṭhullāh Shirāzī, an important Iranian scholar who was invited to Bijapur by the Shīʿī ruler ʿAlī ʿĀdil Shāh I (d. 1580), initially enjoyed great respect at the court. ʿAlī ʿĀdil Shāh's successor, however, was not favorably disposed to Shiism. Consequently, Shāh Faṭhullāh found himself imprisoned. Shortly thereafter he was invited to join the more tolerant court of the Mughal emperor Akbar where he became one of the leading intellectuals. He played an influential role within the emperor's inner circle, being appointed to several significant administrative and political posts. Qāḍī Nūrullāh Shustarī, one of the greatest scholars of Twelver Shiism in his time, came to India in 1584 seeking a position at the court of Akbar. Two years later, on the basis of his excellent knowledge of Arabic and command over both Shīʿī and Sunnī jurisprudence, he was appointed *qāḍī* of Lahore, earning for himself the reputation of being an impartial and honest judge even in cases involving Sunnī law. His fame apparently incited the jealousy and anger of some of his Sunnī rivals who instigated the Mughal emperor, Jahāngīr, to have him flogged to death. He is thus sometimes called the "third martyr" of Twelver Shīʿī Islam.

THE ṢŪFĪ ORDERS. Religious authority in post-Prophetic Islam is legitimized by appealing to different sources. The authority of the *ʿulamāʾ*, of whatever persuasion, as interpreters of Islam flows from recognition of their learning. The authority of the Shīʿī *imāms* is based on esoteric knowledge acquired on the basis of physical descent from the Prophet Muḥammad. The authority of the Ṣūfī masters flows from the recognition that they have had (or are preparing themselves and others to have) direct, intuitive experience of divine realities and that divine grace might endow them with special spiritual powers. These powers, often believed to continue after physical death, are seen as evidence of them having attained the status of *awliyāʾ* ("friends [of God]"). By the twelfth century CE, seekers on the mystical path had developed distinct spiritual disciplines and methods and formed themselves into fraternities organized around *khānqāhs* ("hospices"). Each fraternity was headed by a *shaykh,* or *pīr,* responsible for guiding disciples on the path, appointing deputies, admitting novices to full discipleship, training and investing a successor, and possibly controlling a network of centers.

The arrival of Ṣūfī orders. Although Shaykh ʿAlī al-Hujwīrī, the author of the famous Ṣūfī manual *Kashf al-maḥjūb* (The disclosure of the veiled) settled and died in Lahore in 1071, the arrival of members of Ṣūfī orders in South Asia was broadly contemporary with the Ghurid invasions at the end of the twelfth century. One of the earliest was the Chishtī order from Afghanistan, introduced by Khwājah Muʿīn ad-Dīn who settled in Ajmer (Rajasthan) in the 1290s. His successor, Quṭb ad-Dīn Bakhtiyār Kākī (d. 1235), spread Chishtī influence to Delhi. Bakhtiyār Kākī's chief disciple, Farīd ad-Dīn, called *Ganj-i Shakar* ("the treasury of sugar"; d. 1265), settled in Pakpattan by the Sutlej, thus consolidating a Chishtī position in the Punjab. During the lifetimes of the two great *shaykhs* of fourteenth-century Delhi, Niẓām al-Dīn Awliyāʾ (1238–1325) and Nāṣir ad-Dīn Maḥmūd, *Chirāgh-i Dihlī* ("the lamp of Delhi," 1276–1356), branches of the Chishtī order were established in other regions: in Bengal by Shaykh Sirāj ad-Dīn (d. 1357), in Daulatabad by Burhān ad-Dīn (d. 1340), and in Gulbarga by Sayyid Muḥammad Gisū Darāz ("of long locks," 1321–1422). Other Chishtī mystics settled in Malwa and Gujarat. The Suhrawardīyah were the other principal group of Ṣūfīs active in sultanate South Asia, antithetical in their rituals and practices to the Chishtīyah. Their spiritual headquarters were in the southwest Punjab: at Multan where Shaykh Bahāʾ ad-Dīn Zakarīyāʾ (1182–1262) resided, and at Uchch where Sayyid Jalāl ad-Dīn Surkhpush ("red-dressed") Bukhārī (d. 1292) and his grandson Jalāl ad-Dīn Makhdūm-i Jahāniyān ("lord of the mortals," 1308–1384) lived. In Bengal, a leading Suhrawardi master was Shaykh Jalāl ad-Dīn Tabrīzī (thirteenth century). In Kashmir, the intellectually influential Kubrawīyah order gained a foothold through a visit by Sayyid ʿAlī Hamadānī between 1381 and 1384. An offshoot of this order, the Firdawsīyah, attained fame in Bihar through Sharaf ad-Dīn ibn Yaḥyā Manerī (1263–1381).

From about the middle of the fifteenth century onwards, other Ṣūfī orders made their appearance in South Asia, notably the Qādirīyah, the Shaṭṭārīyah, and the Naqshbandīyah. Muḥammad Ghawth (d. 1517), claiming to be tenth in succession to the founder of the Qādirīyah, ʿAbd al-Qādir al-Jīlānī (1077–1176), settled at Uchch, but before that Qadiri Ṣūfīs had settled at Bidar about the time it became the capital of the Bahmani sultanate in 1422. The Bijapur sultanate also became a major center for the Qādirīyah. The Shaṭṭārīyah was another order that became influential in the Deccan as well as North India. Introduced from Iran by Shaykh ʿAbd Allāh al-Shaṭṭār (d. 1485), the order spread to Gujarat under the guidance of Muḥammad Ghawth of Gwalior (1485–1562/3), attracting the attention of the Mughal emperors Humāyūn and Akbar. The Naqshbandīyah, a conservative Central Asian Ṣūfī order, became prominent from the seventeenth century onwards when its members began to challenge the established forms and practice of Sufism in South Asia. It was introduced by Khwājah Muḥammad al-Bāqī Billāh (1563/4–1603), who initiated, in his last years, the most influential member of the order in South Asia, Shaykh Aḥmad Sirhindī (1564–1624).

Qalandārs. Another important category of Muslim holy men consisted of a variety of wandering mendicants, who were distinguished from "respectable" Ṣūfīs by scantiness of dress and the wearing of bizarre iron insignia, and who oftentimes exhibited aggressive attitudes toward Ṣūfīs belonging to the mainstream orders. They went by a variety of names—*qalandārs*, Ḥaydarīs, Madārīs. Because they seemed to be indifferent or antagonistic to the observance of prescribed religious and social norms, they have been termed *be-shar'*, that is, those who are outside religious law. Some of them, like the Madārīs (so called after a Jewish convert, Shāh Madār, who migrated to South Asia from Syria), smearing their naked bodies with ashes, using hashish, and ignoring Muslim religious duties, seemed to be indistinguishable from Hindu ascetics and yogis. Yet certain great *shaykhs* of the orders, notably the Chishtī, recognized some of them as men of genuine intuitive experience. Although so evidently outside the Muslim "religious establishment," it is possible to regard them as being important in communicating some identifiable Islamic religious beliefs and practices among Muslims and non-Muslim populations in rural and urban areas. The most famous of these *qalandārs* was La'l Shahbāz ("Red Falcon," d. 1325), the subject of one of the most popular Ṣūfī praise songs in South Asia. His tomb shrine at Sehwan in Sind still attracts thousands of pilgrims, including many *be-shar'* dervishes, although many of the immoral and illegal activities that historically gave this shrine notoriety have now been purged.

Religious and social roles of Ṣūfīs. As a mystical philosophy, Sufism has deeply impacted the lives of Muslims as well as non-Muslims in the Subcontinent. Beyond the realm of religious thought and practice, Sufism has influenced social, economic, cultural, and even political dimensions of everyday life. The development of literary and musical traditions in many South Asian languages bears the deep impress of Sufism. Not surprisingly, members of Ṣūfī orders have been regarded, by some scholars, to be "bridge-people," interpreting and adjusting Islamic concepts and practices to the psychology of different populations. They have also been responsible for introducing new emphases and rites into the Islamic tradition. By the time that Ṣūfī orders came to the Subcontinent, Sufism had become more of a devotional than a mystical movement, embracing a collection of cult associations that centered on the *shaykh,* or *pīr,* who was more approachable to the masses than the *'ālim,* or religious scholar. To be sure, discussions of more speculative and philosophical formulations of Sufism were taken up toward the end of the fourteenth century, yet these were limited to elite inner circles of disciples. At a popular level, a *shaykh/pīr* was seen as playing an intercessory role between humans and the divine. This role was often understood to be a physical manifestation of their special charisma, inherited through a *silsilah* ("spiritual chain") going back to the Prophet Muḥammad. Rather than adhering to the classical conception of his role as that of as a teacher and guide along the path to personal experience of divine truths, the *shaykh* had became a charismatic figure with special spiritual powers and energies. The *dargāh,* or tomb-shrine, began to supplant the *khānqāh* ("hospice," "retreat") in the popular imagination. Exclusive membership in, or allegiance to, particular orders became less important—indeed some adepts now belonged to more than one order. Some orders gained appeal; others fell from favor. Perhaps these responses were related to the way in which members of particular orders responded to the local cultural environment. Traditionally, Mu'īn ad-Dīn Chishtī is represented as having gained many followers after promoting the use of music in his *khānqāh.* No doubt, too, willingness to use the local vernacular for devotional poetry would enhance a *shaykh*'s appeal. Ṣūfīs belonging to larger Ṣūfī orders appear to have been more willing than the *'ulamā'* to found *khānqāhs* away from the principal centers of political power and thus seem to have drawn more of the allegiance of the rural and small-town populations to themselves. Certain orders, notably the Qādirīyah and the Shaṭṭārīyah in Bijapur, were more urban-based.

Rulers of the day quickly recognized the popular appeal of *shaykhs/pīrs* among Muslim populations and wished to turn that appeal to their own advantage. *Shaykhs* were offered pensions and tax-free lands. Most Ṣūfī orders were willing to accept royal largesse. For example, the Suhrawardīyah in the Punjab have always enjoyed state patronage, while the Qādirīyah and Shaṭṭārīyah accepted land grants in seventeenth-century Bijapur. The Chishtī order, in particular, attracted a great deal of royal patronage. Ironically, the early Chishtīs were vehemently against any close association with those in political power, for they considered such contact to be detrimental to a person's moral and spiritual well-being. By the early fourteenth century, however, the order began to rise in prominence precisely on account of the enormous royal patronage it was attracting. As Muslim rulers of Turko-Persian ancestry began to establish kingdoms in the subcontinent, they associated their own personal fortunes and those of their dynasty with that of the Chishtī order. A ruling dynasty's patronage of Chishtī *dargāhs* could strengthen its claims of legitimacy in the eyes of the local population and also bestow upon it spiritual blessings for continued prosperity and success. As a consequence, a pattern of growing political patronage of Chishtī shrines emerged in many parts of northern India, from Gujarat to Bengal. Naturally, the "mother" *dargāh* at Ajmer where Mu'īn ad-Dīn Chishtī, the founder of the order, is buried, received a great deal of royal attention, all the more so due to its frontier location.

The most generous and loyal patrons of the Chishtīyah were members of the Mughal dynasty who were firmly convinced their worldly success was due to the blessings of the Chishtī shaykhs. As a result, not only did Mughal emperors bestow lavish endowments for the support of the Ajmer *dargāh* and sponsor several construction projects, they also actively involved themselves in its management by appointing its administrators and titular heads. The emperor Akbar (d. 1605) was a particularly ardent devotee, undertaking fourteen pilgrimages to the shrine, several of them on foot. Two of these pilgrimages, those of 1568 and 1574, were made immediately after conquering Chittor and Bengal, respectively, victories he attributed to the blessings of Muʿīn ad-Dīn Chishtī. Akbar's reverence for and devotion to the Chishtīs increased significantly when Shaykh Salīm Chishtī, a descendant of Muʿīn ad-Dīn, correctly predicted the birth of the emperor's son. In gratitude, he performed a pilgrimage to Ajmer, walking on foot all the way from Agra. He also had his new capital city, Fatehpur Sikri, built near Salīm Chishtī's *khānqāh* as a tangible way of symbolizing the close Mughal-Chishtī alliance that continued for the next two generations. In the seventeenth century the Naqshbandīyah, a Central Asian Ṣūfī order, vied against the Chishtīyah for the attention of the Mughals, for they had great political ambitions to influence aspects of state policy. Clearly, it is difficult to accept fully the contention that Ṣūfī orders represented an organized religious establishment in medieval India independent of different political establishments.

MUSLIM RELIGIOUS LIFE IN SOUTH ASIA: THE CULTS OF PERSONALITY. The character of Muslim piety in South Asia has been predominantly "person"-centered. As in other parts of the Muslim world, a central focus of "person"-centered piety has been the figure of the Prophet Muḥammad. Not only is the *Milād an-nabī,* his birthday, widely celebrated, but shrines housing relics, such as his footprint or his hair (e.g., Hazratbāl in Kashmir), attract many pilgrims. The Prophet has commonly been venerated through an extensive corpus of poems and songs in major South Asian languages, some even composed by Hindu poets. Although love for him and appeals for his intercession are common themes, many of these poems accord him a superhuman, or mystical status that at times appears to compromise strict notions of monotheism. The poems often reveal a Prophet who has been acculturated to specific regional contexts and perceived through lenses that have been influenced by a variety of literary conventions. Thus, epics in medieval Bengali *pūthī* literature see him as an *avatāra,* and poems in Tamil address him as a baby, while Sindhi poems beseech him as a bridegroom for whom the bride lovingly longs. Devotion to him has become the hallmark of a Muslim identity, defining the boundary between Muslim and non-Muslim, so that attacks on his character and personality have frequently sparked riots. It is hardly surprising that revivalists who sought to strengthen Muslim identity in the eighteenth and nineteenth century identified themselves as members of the Ṭarīqah-i-Muḥammadīyah ("the Muḥammadan Path") and appealed for a renewed commitment among Muslims to the Prophetic paradigm.

Several religious figures and personalities have been heirs to the Prophet's authority and/or charisma, giving rise to different types of "person"-centered devotionalism. For example, the Prophet's immediate family members, particularly his grandson Ḥusayn, tragically martyred at Karbala in 680 CE, have come to be widely venerated in South Asia, especially during the month of Muharram, not only by Shīʿī communities but by Sunnī Muslims as well. In many localities, Hindus, too, have participated in the commemorative Muharram processions. Ḥusayn and some of the martyred Shīʿī *imāms* and the family of the Prophet have been the subject of many elegies composed in several languages, including Urdu, Sindhi, and Gujarati.

Most ubiquitous in South Asia is the devotion to the Ṣūfī *shaykh/pīr.* Belief in the supernatural powers of Ṣūfī *shaykhs/pīrs,* deceased or living, has led to the proliferation of *dargāhs* and *mazārs* ("tomb-shrines") all over South Asia, frequented by devotees seeking to cure illnesses, ward off evil, fulfill desires, or gain admission to paradise. In some cases, these tomb shrines are associated with mythical figures (such as Khwājah Khiẓr or the Nau Gaz ["Nine Yard"] *pīr*). So strong is the shrine tradition in South Asia that even a legendary Ṣūfī such as ʿAbd al-Qādir al-Jīlānī (d. 1166), who is actually buried in Baghdad, has many shrines dedicated to him all over southern India. Interestingly, the *dargāh* in South Asia has not remained an exclusively Muslim institution; Muslim and non-Muslim alike participate in common rituals and ceremonies—such as kissing or touching the tomb, offering flowers, and lighting incense—in the hope of receiving spiritual blessing. It has also provided the only space where Muslim women can participate in public worship because as a rule in South Asia they do not attend mosques.

Of a different character and nature are a variety of movements centered around persons who have acquired religious authority on the basis of claims to a prophet-like status. Because these movements pose a challenge to the central authority of the Prophet Muḥammad, they have often been controversial. Many of these movements have been millenarian in nature. For instance, in the late fifteenth century, Sayyid Muḥammad of Jaunpur (1443–1505) declared himself to be the *Mahdī* ("guided one") of the Sunnī tradition who would lead the world to order and justice before the day of resurrection. His followers, who eventually formed the Mahdawī community, claimed for him a rank equal to that of the Prophet and clustered around him as though around a *pīr.* Needless to say, the group was intensely persecuted by Sunnī *ʿulamāʾ*, who saw the *Mahdī* as a threat to their authority. Bāyazīd Anṣārī (1525–1572/3), born at Jallandar in the Punjab, was a Pathan who claimed to be a *pīr-i raushan* ("a luminous master") in direct communication with God, who shone his divine light upon him. Bāyazīd's followers regarded him as combining perfections of the paths of law, mysticism, and wisdom attained through gnosis. In the last stage of their spiritual ascent, these disciples were allowed to exempt themselves from some of the obligations of the *sharīʿah.* Gathering support from among his fellow Pathans, Bāyazīd Anṣārī became the head of a religio-political movement that seriously challenged Mughal authority in northwest India. In 1581 the Mughal court itself was the setting of a personality cult around the figure of the Emperor Akbar, the so-called *din-i ilāhī* ("divine religion"), which some have declared to be an apostasy from Islam. More of a mystical order with limited membership in which the emperor was viewed as *insān-i kāmil* ("the perfect man"), the *din-i ilāhī* eclectically combined lofty ideas from various religious traditions as well as Sunnī ideas of the caliph and the just ruler to present Akbar as the earthly homologue and symbol of God's truth and justice. Interestingly, Akbar himself seems never to have directly made any claims to prophecy or divinity.

Even a figure such as Shaykh Aḥmad Sirhindī (d. 1624)—considered the bastion of religious conservatism during the reign of Akbar's son, Jahāngīr—gave himself prophetic airs. Because he arrived in India as the expected renovator of Islam at the beginning of the second Islamic millennium, Sirhindī was popularly referred to as the *mujaddid-i alif-i thānī.* He claimed that the "perfections of Prophethood," which had disappeared after the death of the Prophet Muḥammad, would reappear in deserving persons, such as himself, because they were the Prophet's heirs. He also regarded himself as the *qayyūm,* an intermediary between man and God through whom flowed all spiritual and material benefits. On account of his elevated status, he considered it his duty to point out in his many letters to the Emperor Jahāngīr and the Mughal nobility various "un-Islamic" practices that were being tolerated in the realm. These letters, described by Jahāngīr in his memoirs, *Tuzuk-i Jahāngīrī,* as a "bunch of absurdities," earned Sirhindī a short spell in prison so that, as the emperor puts it, "his disturbed disposition and confused mind would calm down a little."

The reaction to the emergence of these personality cults has often been in the form of a call for the reassertion of the paradigmatic role of the Prophet Muḥammad and his companions. Yet these types of movements have continued to emerge in South Asia to our day, the most recent being the Aḥmadīyah, founded by Mīrzā Ghulām Aḥmad (1835–1908). Influenced by the *mujaddid* and *mahdī* traditions, Ghulām Aḥmad claimed that he was a "non-legislative" prophet whose responsibility it was to ensure the correct implementation of the message revealed by the "legislative" prophet, that is, Muḥammad. Viewed within the historical context of other movements, his ideas were not so strange or idiosyncratic. However, when his followers expressed them within the context of a Pakistani nation that was increasingly moving to an Islamist political ideology, they stirred a violent backlash from religious conservatives. In 1974 the Pakistani legislature passed a bill that declared the followers of Ghulām Aḥmad to be non-Muslim. It believed that a line had been crossed and that the state had to take on the role of defining legitimate religious identity.

MOVEMENTS OF ISLAMIC RENEWAL AND REFORM. The eighteenth and nineteenth centuries witnessed a mushrooming of movements for reform and change among Muslim communities in several regions of South Asia. While the nature and character of these movements varied according to regional contexts, they were, broadly speaking, in response to factors that were internal and external to the communities concerned. Internally, there seems to have been a widespread need to cure a spiritual and religious malaise that some felt had affected the way in which Islam was being practiced. Externally, the establishment of European, particularly British, colonialism and the emergence of nationalism presented a whole new set of challenges: new lifestyles, new educational systems, and new economic, social, and political structures. The arrival of Christian missionaries intent on converting Muslims (and Hindus) posed another kind of threat. For Muslim elites in North India, the collapse of Mughal rule in the face of onslaughts from the Marathas, Sikhs, and the British was also traumatic for it meant a loss of political and economic power. Many among the elite interpreted disempowerment as a sign of God's displeasure and a sign that Muslims needed to reinvigorate their relationship with Islam in the face of rapid change.

Early revivalist movements. The first attempts to advocate sociopolitical reform using Islam as a basis can be traced to Shāh Walī Allāh (d.1762), the great theologian of Delhi, who believed himself to be a renovator *(mujaddid)* of Islam. As *mujaddid,* he was the Prophet's vice-regent with the special duty of purifying religion from infidel practices such as visiting tomb-shrines. Through his numerous writings, the most important being *Ḥujjat Allāh al-Bālighah* (The perfect proof of God), Shāh Walī Allāh's ideas had a deep impact on later generations of reformists, ranging from conservatives to modernists. He believed himself to be called upon by God to demonstrate that a harmony of apparently different views existed or could be achieved among a whole range of religious sciences. A strong advocate of Muslim unity in the face of loss of political power, he attempted intellectually to reconcile differences between Sunnī schools of jurisprudence and competing philosophies of mysticism (*waḥdat al-wujūd* ["unity of existence"] and *waḥdat ash-shuhūd* ["unity of vision"]), although his ecumenism did not extend to Shīʿī communities. Shāh Walī Allāh felt strongly that Muslims would be better able to resolve their sociopolitical problems if they lived in accord with the precepts of their faith. In this regard, they needed to understand the Qurʾān for themselves without relying on the secondary interpretations of commentaries. To make the scripture more accessible, he translated it into Persian, paving the way for a later translation into Urdu by his sons. To deal with the loss of political power, he wrote a number of letters inviting neighboring Muslim rulers, such as Aḥmad Shāh Abdalī, to reestablish Muslim rule in North India. Unfortunately, Shāh Walī Allāh's Afghan friends and religious brethren plundered and looted Delhi after they conquered it!

No doubt inspired by Shāh Walī Allāh's activism, his grandson, Ismāʿīl Shahīd (d. 1831), became the theoretician for the energetic *mujāhidīn* reformist movement of the early nineteenth century initiated by Aḥmad Barēlī (Aḥmad of Rai Bareilly; d. 1831), a charismatic preacher who wanted to purge Islam of its accretions and corruptions. Ismāʿīl

Shahīd's work *Taqwiyat al-imān* (Strengthening of faith) calls Muslims to righteous action in accord with God's command in order to improve their situation in this world and the next. Preaching a type of reformed Sufism, purged of "polytheistic" practices, the *mujāhidīn* movement, in keeping with the ideology of the Ṭarīqah-i-Muḥammadīyah, emphasized the importance of the Prophet Muḥammad as a paradigm. Following the example of the Prophet's *hijrah* ("emigration") from Mecca to Medina, in 1826 Aḥmad Barēlī led a group of *mujāhidīn* from British India to Pathan borderlands, from where they waged *jihād* against the Sikhs in a futile attempt to create an Islamic state in the Punjab modeled after the Prophet's Medina. Both reformers were killed by Sikh forces at the battle of Balakot in 1831. (The hold of the Prophet Muḥammad's *hijrah* over Muslim sentiment was to be further demonstrated in 1920 when, on the urging of mosque *imāms* and *pīrs,* about thirty thousand Muslims from the province of Sind and the Frontier Province migrated to Afghanistan as their *dār al-Islām,* or "abode of Islam.")

Regional revivalist movements. Reform and revivalist movements were not simply confined to areas traditionally associated with Muslim political power in North India. There were significant ones in regional contexts as well. By way of illustration, we will cite three cases.

In Bengal, Hajjī Sharīʿat Allāh (1781–1840) initiated the Farāʾiḍī movement. Having lived in the Hejaz in Arabia for about eighteen years, he sought to teach Bengali Muslims the correct way to observe the obligatory duties *(farāʾiḍ)* of Islam, to abandon reverence for *pīrs,* and to forsake "Hinduized" life ceremonies. On the grounds that there were no properly constituted Muslim rulers and *qāḍīs* in nineteenth-century India, the Farāʾiḍīs abandoned Friday and *ʿīd* ("festival") prayers. Under Hajjī Sharīʿat Allāh's son Dudū Miyān (1819–1862) violence broke out between the movement's largely peasant following and their landlords. Throughout the nineteenth century, a variety of Sunnī scholars and teachers, including Karāmat ʿAlī Jawnpurī (d. 1873), a follower of Aḥmad Barēlī willing to accept British rule, devoted themselves to trying to get rid of polytheistic attitudes and practices among Muslims in Bengal, while disagreeing among themselves about the acceptability of Sufism or about which school of Sunnī jurisprudence should be followed.

In the far south, among the Māppiḷḷas, as the Muslims of Kerala are called, *ʿulamāʾ* such as Sayyid ʿAlawī (d. 1843/4) and his son Sayyid Faḍl (d. 1900), though creating no formal organization, perpetuated among Māppiḷḷa peasant farmers a tradition of resistance to Hindu landlords. Among Māppiḷḷa urban classes who had lost employment and suffered a decline in trading because of European colonial rule, the movement became anti-British. Throughout the nineteenth century, Māppiḷḷa grievances were expressed through riots, culminating in the Māppiḷḷa rebellion of 1921, which was brutally squashed by the British. In demanding the formation of Moplastan, a separate state for Māppiḷḷa Muslims in south Kerala, these leaders, like the *mujāhidīn* in the north, employed an idiom that invoked the first Muslim community created in Medina by the Prophet Muḥammad in 622 CE.

In the west, in Sind, the nature of the revival movement took on a less overtly political and more spiritual and literary hue. Under the influence of a reformist movement initiated by members belonging to the conservative Naqshbandī Ṣūfī order, various poets undertook to instruct people about the basic duties of Islam using simple verse forms. In doing so, they sought to avoid the emotional expressions of piety found among more "intoxicated" Ṣūfī groups. Miyān Abūʾl Ḥasan (d. 1711) composed the *Muqaddimat as-Ṣalāt,* a long didactic poem on Islamic ritual prayer. Another Naqshbandī, Makhdūm Muḥammad Hāshim (d. 1761) was a prolific author of several works that explained the essentials of Islam in didactic Sindhi verse. His principal works included: the *Farāʾiḍ al-Islām* (The obligations of Islam), dealing with Islamic law and correct behavior; *Tāfsir Hāshimī,* a rhymed commentary on the last part of the Qurʾān; and *Qūt al-ʿĀshiqīn* (The nourishment of the lovers), which describes the virtues and miracles of the Prophet Muḥammad.

RESPONSES TO BRITISH COLONIAL RULE. In the aftermath of the 1857 rebellion and the failed attempt to overthrow British control, Muslim elites in North India were forced to come to terms not only with British political supremacy, but also with the growing presence of Western cultural institutions, particularly churches, schools, and colleges. Their reactions took various forms, the principle division being between modernists and conservatives.

Modernists: The Aligarh movement. The first major figure to argue that the changes Muslims were experiencing in the nineteenth century were compatible with Islam was Sir Sayyid Aḥmad Khān (d. 1898). As a young man, Sir Sayyid was well trained in theology in the tradition of Shāh Walī Allāh as well as in Muʿtazilah rationalism. In keeping with the spirit of the Ṭarīqah-i-Muḥammadīyah, with which he was affiliated, the book he wrote to help Muslims examine the life and exemplary of the Prophet Muḥammad lacked the customary hagiographic elements. He was convinced that in order to progress under colonial rule, Muslims must accept a future shaped by absolute loyalty to British power. Furthermore, he felt that Muslims should participate fully in the Western-style educational system being established by the British in India so that they would not become a social and economic underclass. As a Muslim, he wished to demonstrate that God was not being mocked when young Muslims, attending British-influenced schools and colleges in hope of advancement, were being taught a natural science that appeared to contradict divine revelation. He argued that the word of God and the work of God, revelation and nature as understood by nineteenth-century Western science, are wholly in harmony. Apparent discrepancies between the Qurʾānic account of the natural world and that of Western scientists are, in fact, attributable to misunderstandings of the language of the Qurʾān. He also advocated a rational approach to the Qurʾān based on fresh *ijtihād,* since Islam, in his interpretation, is a religion that accommodates historical change. The mandates of the *sharīʿah,* as interpreted by generations of religious scholars, needed to be reexamined to determine whether they were, in fact, the essential mandates of faith. To promote his ideas and provide young Muslims with Western-style higher education, he fought for and eventually founded the Anglo-Muhammadan College, which later became Aligarh Muslim University.

Sayyid Aḥmad Khān's approach enjoyed the support of several important personalities who formed the basis of the so-called Aligarh movement. Among its members were several prominent literati who wrote Urdu poetry and prose to disseminate its ideas. Most prominent among these was Alṭāf Ḥusayn Ḥālī (d. 1914), the author of *Madd wa gazr-i Islām* (The ebb and flow of Islam), a epic poem considered to the Aligarh movement's most enduring literary monument. Popularly known as the *Musaddas,* after its six-line stanzas, it contrasts the past glories and achievements of Islamic civilization with the miserable status of Muslims of Ḥālī's time. Among the other notable members of the Aligarh circle were: Naẓīr Aḥmad (d. 1912), a pioneer in the development of the Urdu novel, who highlighted the need to educate Muslim women in his fiction; Mumtāz ʿAlī, the publisher of *Tahzīb al-niswān,* a journal dedicated to women's issues; Ameer ʿAlī (d. 1928), the author of *The Spirit of Islam,* a book intended primarily for British readers, emphasizing the essential compatibility between Islam and Western liberalism; and Chirāgh ʿAlī (d. 1895), a modernist interpreter of the Qurʾān, who, among other things, demonstrated that the Islamic scripture was actually intended to ameliorate the position of women and implicitly prohibited polygamy. Chirāgh ʿAlī's most controversial stand was in regards to the *ḥadīth* literature, which he considered entirely fabricated and therefore unworthy as a basis of Islamic jurisprudence.

Sir Muḥammad Iqbāl. The poet-philosopher Sir Muḥammad Iqbāl ranks among the most significant thinkers of modern Islam. Because he was the first to advocate the idea of a separate Muslim homeland, he is also widely perceived as the spiritual founder of Pakistan. He has became such a towering figure that every religious, political, and social movement in contemporary Indo-Muslim thought has turned to his writings in order to find justification for its position. In addition to receiving training in Islamic studies (he was influenced by Sir Sayyid Aḥmad Khān and Shiblī, two significant figures in the Aligarh movement), he studied philosophy at the Universities of Cambridge and Munich. Through his prose and poetic works, he reveals a unique way of interpreting and expressing Islamic concepts and ideas through a skillful combination of Western and Eastern intellectual and literary tools. He offered a conception of the God-human relationship through which he intended to inspire Muslims to action. The life goal of the individual ego, he believed, should be that of actualizing in thought and deed the infinite possibilities of the divine imagination. Humans, he believed, as vicegerents of God on earth, have an active duty to develop themselves to the highest potential. Some of his ideas, such as the call to free the interpretation of Islam from the fetters of tradition and the scholarship of *ʿulamāʾ,* and the demand for *ijtihād,* were typical of Islamic reformers. His claim that human beings can actively participate within a dynamic creation, his call for individual action and responsibility, and his conception of the Qurʾān as revelation that unfolds in time and eternity were unusual and for some controversial. Yet his thought had a tremendous appeal for those Muslims who were searching for leaders with an intellectual and political vision.

Conservatives: The Deobandi *ʿulamāʾ*. The theological school of Deoband, founded in 1867 by Rashīd Aḥmad Gangohī (d. 1905) and Muḥammad Qāsim Nanawtawī (d. 1880), represented a conservative response among Sunnī *ʿulamāʾ* to the establishment of British rule and the spread of Western culture. Although the theologians of Deoband accepted the British as rulers, they found Western culture to be wanting and inappropriate for the faithful to emulate. The objective of the school was thus to establish and maintain a correct standard of Islamic practice for (Sunnī) Muslims to follow at a time when they were exposed to many non-Islamic influences. The theologians of Deoband prided themselves in upholding the authority of the four traditional schools of Sunnī jurisprudence, and in time, their school acquired an outstanding reputation, enrolling students from many parts of the Islamic world. Deobandi leaders assumed the status of Ṣūfī *shaykhs* and initiated disciples, but the special miracles that were attributed to them were depicted as being exercised to influence people to follow the *sunnah,* the custom of the Prophet. In this regard, they were strongly opposed to anything that was not in keeping with Prophetic tradition, such as worship at Ṣūfī shrines, belief in the intercession of *pīrs,* or elaborate birth, marriage, and death rituals. Deobandi theologians vigorously defended the need to accept the interpretations and consensus of earlier Sunnī scholars and jurists and attacked all dissenting voices. Rashīd Aḥmad Gangohī, for example, dismissed Sir Sayyid's pro-Western and neorationalist approach as "deadly poison." Muḥammad Qāsim acquired a stellar reputation for his polemical disputations with Hindu and Christian missionaries. A later Deobandi scholar, Ashrāf ʿAlī Thanwī (d. 1943) achieved fame for his work *Bihisti zevar* (Heavenly jewelry), a conservative guidebook for the education of Muslim women. The prestige of Deoband as the guardian of Sunnī Islam was enhanced in the late nineteenth and early twentieth centuries when its scholars played a leading role in refuting the claims of Ghulām Aḥmad, the founder of the Aḥmadīyah movement, particularly his challenge to the finality of Muḥammad's prophethood.

Other groups. The emphasis on the Prophetic paradigm as a source of guidance for Muslims facing change formed the focal point of another reformist group, Ahl-i Ḥadīth, led by Siddiq Ḥasan Khān (d. 1890), a religious scholar who had married, in the midst of much controversy, the widowed princess of Bhopal. Though the Ahl-i Ḥadīth stressed the exclusive primacy of the Qurʾān and the *ḥadīth* as fundamental guides in life, they rejected the interpretive authority of the founders of the four Sunnī schools. Their treatment of the *ḥadīth* as a form of implicit revelation that elaborated authoritatively the explicit revelation of the Qurʾān led them into conflicts with two groups. On the one hand they opposed members of the Aligarh movement who exhibited skepticism toward the authenticity of the *ḥadīth;* not surprisingly, they dubbed Sayyid Aḥmad Khān "the modern prophet of nature-worshippers," and the latest instigator of evils in Muslim society. On the other hand, they engaged in a vitriolic polemical war with a counter-group led by ʿAbdullāh Chakralavī and called the Ahl-i Qurʾān. As its name suggests, this movement advocated total reliance on the Qurʾān as the most perfect source of guidance; the Qurʾān according to them contained all the basic injunctions for Muslims and left them free to decide on other matters. For example, they regarded the call to prayer and the performance of *ʿīd* and funerary prayers as not essential Islamic obligations because they are not mentioned in the Qurʾān. A third important group was comprised of those *ʿulamāʾ* who did not see the need to change or modify the various customs and practices that had developed among Sunnī Muslim communities in South Asia. Led by Aḥmad Riḍā Khān (d. 1921), with their major centers at Bareilly and Badaʾun, they accepted a variety of intercessory figures in Islam, from the Prophet Muḥammad to the *shaykhs* and *pīrs* of the *dargāhs.* The Barelwīs, as they came to be called, observed the birthdays of the Prophet and of the Ṣūfī *pīrs*—a practice that the Deobandis and others found objectionable on the grounds that such celebrations implied that the dead were present. An important offshoot of the Deobandi movement is the Tablighi-jamāʿat, founded in the 1920s by Mawlānā Muḥammad Ilyās (d. 1944). Its principal objective is to reach out to ordinary Muslims individually and provide guidance on matters of faith through a network of self-taught teachers traveling from house to house. Initially conceived as a response to the efforts of Hindu movements such as the Shuddhi and Sangathan to forcibly convert Muslims, it has become one of the most influential grassroots religious movements in South Asia, with considerable influence at the international level as well.

Defining Muslim Identity in Colonial India. It is in the nineteenth century, during the establishment of British colonial rule over South Asia, that we witness a gradual evolution of cultural distancing and alienation between Muslim and non-Muslim. The very "idiom" of British rule was communalist, systematically institutionalizing South Asia into a nation of communities defined along religious lines. The census and ethnographic surveys conducted under British auspices highlighted religious markers of identity to the detriment of others, forcing people to identify themselves primarily in religious terms. Through such colonial instruments, South Asian Muslims from diverse socioeconomic, ethnic, and sectarian backgrounds, began, for the first time, to perceive themselves as belonging to a distinct community and, eventually, to a nation distinct from the subcontinent's non-Muslim population.

As the variety of revivalist and reform movements discussed above began to clarify their respective positions as to what it meant to be a Muslim under the circumstances of colonial rule, they offered a wide spectrum of definition concerning Islamic identity. These definitions sought to differentiate more sharply the Muslim from the non-Muslim by turning for guidance to scriptural sources such as the Qurʾān, the *sunnah* of the Prophet Muḥammad, and the tradition of the historical past. In the process, any practices considered to be syncretistic and accommodating to local custom were suspect. Significantly, none of the definitions allowed for Muslims to observe customs or rituals that were part of the South Asian cultural environment. Practices, customs, and ideas that were prevalent among Muslims and recognized as local or indigenous were deemed to be "un-Islamic." This was contrasted to the "Islamic" values represented by Perso-Arabic culture.

A suspicion of the local as "un-Islamic," or "Hindu," and a privileging of the "Arabo-Persian" as "Islamic," combined with a conception of Islam and Hinduism as closed systems of thought, couched in communalist and nationalist terms, radically changed perceptions of different elements of South Asian culture. As literature, music, dance, and language came to be viewed through religious lenses they became politicized within the realms of colonial and nationalist discourse. For instance, Muslims with personal names derived from local Indian systems of nomenclature began changing them in favor of Arabic or Persian ones to reflect their Muslim identity. Dramatic changes occurred in how languages were perceived: there were attempts to "Islamicize" Indic vernacular languages and literatures, such as Bengali, by injecting into them more words of Arabic and Persian origin and using the Perso-Arabic script to write them. Urdu, written in the Perso-Arabic script and with a highly Persianized vocabulary, was increasingly perceived as a symbol of Islamic identity, while Hindi, written in the Devanagari script and with a highly Sanskritic vocabulary, became a symbol of Hinduism. In this emotionally charged atmosphere, it became politically and culturally difficult, if not impossible, for many Hindu writers to continue writing in Urdu, or for Muslim writers to cultivate Hindi.

The twin processes of Islamicization—defined in this case as the adoption of Perso-Arabic cultural elements and mores—among Muslims and Sanskritization among Hindus resulted in a cultural distancing between Muslim and Hindu in many regions of the subcontinent. Muslim groups realized that their status as Muslims depended on their cultural distinctiveness from Hindu groups and vice versa. As sociologist Imtiaz Aḥmad correctly observes in "Exclusion and Assimilation in Indian Islam" (1976) the ultimate result of this variety of Islamicization was disjunction; it had profound significance in shaping interaction among Muslims and Hindus by sharpening cultural differences between them. Ultimately, cultural distancing facilitated the rise of the two-nation theory—the idea that Muslims and Hindus constitute two separate cultures and nations—and the demand for partition. It also partially explains why the lack of a shared common culture has intensified the Muslim-Hindu violence that has marked the history of contemporary South Asia.

Post-Partition South Asia. The emergence of the two-nation theory as the political platform on which Muḥammad ʿAlī Jinnāḥ (d. 1948) and the Muslim League were able to garner support for the idea of Pakistan was not unexpected, for it had historical roots. The seeds for its germination had already been sown decades earlier. Sir Sayyid Aḥmad Khān's advocacy for separate political rights for Muslims; Sayyid Aḥmad Shahīd's *mujāhidīn* movement and the quest for a *dār al-Islām;* the Khilāfat movement of the 1920s and its futile attempt to preserve the Sunnī caliphate and the ideal of Muslim political sovereignty; Sir Muḥammad Iqbāl's call for a consolidated Muslim state within a federal India—all can be seen, retrospectively, as paving the way for the creation of Pakistan. Nevertheless, many *ʿulamāʾ*, including a significant number of Deobandis, were opposed to the idea of Pakistan on two grounds: firstly, they did not trust the westernized elite who led the Pakistan movement and secondly, they considered nationalism to be a Western ideology that was detrimental to transnational Muslim unity. Not surprisingly, Ḥusayn Aḥmad Madanī, a leader of the Deoband *ʿulamāʾ*, issued a *fatwā* forbidding Muslims to support the idea of Pakistan and declared Jinnāḥ, who was popularly called *Quaid-i Aʿẓam* ("The Great Leader"), to be *Kāfir-i Aʿẓam* ("The Great Infidel"). Among other opponents were Abūʾl Kalām Azād (d. 1958), a scholar and commentator on the Qurʾān and an ardent proponent of a composite Hindu-Muslim nationalism; and Maulānā Mawdūdī (d. 1979), who founded the Jamāʿat-i Islāmī to counter the Muslim League and the drive for a Muslim homeland. Ironically, the Jamāʿat-i Islāmī was able to fully express its political program only after it became actively involved in Pakistan, the very state whose creation Mawdūdī had opposed.

Ostensibly founded to allow Muslims a safe haven in which to practice their religion and nourish their cultures without fearing the tyranny of a non-Muslim majority, Pakistan has, since its foundation, grappled with the problem of defining the role of Islam in the organization of the state. Muḥammad ʿAlī Jinnāḥ, the founding father, had a vision of a "Muslim" state that was secular and liberal. It was "Islamic" in that it was to be devoted to nurturing and protecting the cultural, social, and political interests of Muslims. In this vision, the state did not interfere with the religious beliefs and practices of its Muslim (and non-Muslim) population. In contrast, groups such as Mawdūdī's Jamāʿat-i Islāmī envisioned an "Islamic" state whose underlying political ideology was religious and whose function it was to ensure that Islam (meaning, of course, their interpretation of it) was being correctly followed and implemented. Over its fifty odd years of existence, the Pakistani polity has become the battleground for struggles between secularists, modernists, and Islamists, and has oscillated between different visions of the role of Islam in public life. To promote national unity, the state had at its foundation appealed to religion as a binding ideology to hold together different ethnic groups. Yet, as the secession of Bangladesh from Pakistan in the bloody civil war of 1971 demonstrates, religious ideology alone is not sufficient to hold Muslim communities together. Ethnic and language loyalties are much stronger forces than faith in fostering community. Today, ethno-nationalist tensions between Sindhis, Muhajirs, and Punjabis continue to plague Pakistan.

In the 1980s General Ẓiā ul-Ḥaqq, with the support of the Jamāʿat-i Islāmī, was able to implement programs of Islamicization, in which the government enforced religious practices that it determined as being "Islamically" correct and proscribed those that it considered incorrect. Although instituted to promote national unity through uniformity, these programs have proven to be divisive as there is no consensus in Pakistani society on basic questions such as what is "true" Islam, who is a Muslim, or even who is, in fact, responsible for the enforcement of religious codes. As a result of Islamicization policies, tensions between Shīʿah and Sunnī have intensified, frequently leading to violence. Discord between different groups, even within the majority Sunnī community, has heightened because it has been impossible to reach agreement over which interpretation of Islam should be the basis for state policy. Many changes in personal and family law, introduced as part of the Islamicization program, have been detrimental to the status of Muslim women, leading to opposition from women's rights organizations. Groups such as the Aḥmadīyah, who claim to be Muslim, have been proclaimed a non-Muslim minority by the state and subjected to persecution. Although constitutionally protected, Christian and Hindu minority communities in Pakistan live apprehensively in a nation that has yet to come to terms with ethnic and religious pluralism.

The situation in Bangladesh has been different from that of Pakistan, mainly because the state emerged as an expression of Bengali ethnonationalism—the majority of Bangladeshis being speakers of Bengali—not common religion. Nevertheless, since its foundation, the role of Islam in this Muslim-majority state has become a topic of debate and contention. The first constitution in 1972 affirmed the secular character of the state and prohibited political parties founded on the basis of religious affiliation. Three years later, after a military coup, the government of Ziaur Rahman (1975–1981) began to replace secularist ideals with more religious ones, eventually resulting in the declaration of Islam as a state religion in 1988. Religious political parties, principally the Jamāʿat-i Islāmī, following the pattern in Pakistan, have campaigned for Islam to become the ideology of the state. So far they have been unable to win widespread electoral support for their cause.

As for India, in the aftermath of the partition Muslim communities there have been consistently perceived as the "other," especially as the nation-state of India was itself formed in opposition to the Islamic "other"—Pakistan. Consequently, many Muslims have experienced a steady marginalization economically, socially, and politically, especially as the nation's politics have come to be increasingly influenced by right-wing Hindu ideologies. At various times, the situation of Muslim minorities has been precarious as they have been victimized by bloody pogroms provoked by Hindu extremist groups. The demolition of the Babri mosque in December 1992 and the riots that followed, as well as the massacres of Muslims in Gujarat in 2003, have severely shaken the self-confidence of many of India's Muslims in the supposedly secular nature of the state.

Surveying the history of Muslim communities in South Asia, it is clear that religiously based nationalisms and the politics of communalism in the contemporary period have been detrimental to the composite culture that Muslims have shared for many centuries with other religious groups. As previously shared cultural elements have become increasingly politicized along religious lines, the divide between Muslims and Hindus has widened. In the politically charged atmosphere created by the rise of religious right-wing political parties in India and Pakistan, and to a limited extent in Bangladesh, traditions of inter-religious and intra-religious pluralism have been jeopardized. Religious intolerance and stereotyping are on the rise. As a result, the history of Islam in South Asia has been grossly misrepresented. Perpetuated by Muslim and non-Muslim groups alike, these stereotypes and distorted interpretations of history and doctrine have had the unfortunate consequence of creating a marked increase in the dehumanization of the "other"—whether Muslim or Hindu, Shīʿī or Sunnī.

See Also Aḥmadiyah; Jamāʿat-i Islāmī; Ṭarīqah.

Bibliography

The most comprehensive and scholarly handbook is Annemarie Schimmel's *Islam in the Indian Subcontinent* (Leiden, Netherlands, 1980), which has full bibliographies. Muḥammad Mujeeb's *The Indian Muslims* (London, 1967) is a sensitive interpretation of Muslim responses to the South Asian setting. *India's Islamic Tradition, 711–1750,* edited by Richard Eaton (New Delhi, 2003), and *Beyond Turk and Hindu: Rethinking Religious Identities in Islamicate South Asia,* edited by David Gilmartin and Bruce Lawrence (Gainesville, Fla., 2000), contain important essays on Muslim and Hindu interactions in premodern South Asia in regional contexts, the dynamic overlapping of religious cultures, and the fluid nature of constructions of religious identity. These essays are a marvelous antidote to the strictly communalist and nationalist readings of history favored in some circles. Finally, Tony Stewart's "In Search of Equivalence: Conceiving the Muslim-Hindu Encounter through Translation Theory," *History of Religions* 40, no. 3 (2001): 260–287, represents a significant contribution to the study of vernacular Muslim literature.

Sufism in South Asia has attracted a great deal of attention from scholars, some of whom have axes to grind. Important studies include the various works by Khaliq Ahmad Nizami; Yohanan Friedmann's *Shaykh Ahmad Sirhindī: An Outline of His Thought and a Study of His Image in the Eyes of Posterity* (Montreal, 1971); Richard Eaton's *Sufis of Bijapur, 1300–1700: Social Roles of Sufis in Medieval India* (Princeton, N.J., 1978); *Muslim Shrines in India: Their Character, History, and Significance,* edited by Christian Troll (Delhi,1989); and Carl Ernst's *Eternal Garden: Mysticism, History, and Politics at a South Asian Sufi Center* (Albany, N.Y., 1992).

Important studies on minority Muslim communities include S. A. A. Rizvi's *A Socio-Intellectual History of the Isna ʿAshari Shiʿis in India,* 2 vols. (Delhi, 1986); Azim Nanji's *The Nīzarī Ismāʿīlī Tradition in the Indo-Pakistan Subcontinent* (Delmar, N.Y., 1978); Juan Cole's *Roots of North Indian Shiʿism in Iran and Iraq: Religion and State in Awadh, 1722–1859* (Berkeley, Calif., 1988); Yohanan Friedmann's *Prophecy Continuous: Aspects of Ahmadi Religious Thought and Its Medieval Background* (Berkeley, Calif., 1989); Vernon Schubel's *Religious Performance in Contemporary Islam: Shiʿi Devotional Rituals in South Asia* (Columbia, S.C., 1993); and Jonah Blank's *Mullahs on the Mainframe: Islam and Modernity among the Daudi Bohras* (Chicago, 2001).

Among the growing number of studies that focus on the regional development of Islamic traditions, the most significant are Stephen Dale's *Islamic Society on the South Asian Frontier* (New York, 1980); Asim Roy's *The Islamic Syncretistic Tradition in Bengal* (Princeton, N.J., 1983); David Gilmartin's *Empire and Islam: Punjab and the Making of Pakistan* (Berkeley, Calif., 1988); Rafiuddin Ahmed's *The Bengal Muslims 1871–1906: A Quest for Identity* (Delhi, 1991); and Richard Eaton's *The Rise of Islam and the Bengal Frontier, 1204–1760* (Berkeley, Calif., 1993).

For modern developments, the standard survey is Azīz Aḥmad's *Islamic Modernism in India and Pakistan, 1857–1964* (London, 1967); dated but still a classic is Wilfred Cantwell Smith's *Modern Islam in India: A Social Analysis,* rev. ed. (New York, 1972). Imtiaz Aḥmad discusses in detail the impact of Islamicization on Muslim-Hindu relations in his "Exclusion and Assimilation in Indian Islam," in *Sociocultural Impact of Islam on India,* edited by Attar Singh (Chandigarh, India, 1976), pp. 85–105. More specialized studies on individual figures or movements include Christian Troll's *Sayyid Ahmad Khan: A Reinterpretation of Muslim Theology* (New Delhi, 1978); Annemarie Schimmel's *Gabriel's Wing: A Study into the Religious Ideas of Sir Muḥammad Iqbāl* (Leiden, Netherlands, 1963); Barbara Metcalf's *Islamic Revival in British India: Deoband, 1860–1900* (Princeton, N.J., 1982); Gail Minault's *The Khilafat Movement: Religious Symbolism and Political Mobilization in India* (New York, 1982); and S. Vali Reza Nasr's *Mawdudi and the Making of Islamic Revivalism* (New York, 1996).

The experiences of Muslim women in South Asia are long overdue for scholarly attention. Among a few pioneering works are Patricia Jeffery's *Frogs in a Well: Indian Women in Purdah* (London, 1979); *Separate Worlds: Studies of Purdah in South Asia,* edited by Hannah Papanek and Gail Minault (Columbia, Mo., 1983); Gail Minault's *Secluded Scholars: Women's Education and Muslim Social Reform in Colonial India* (Delhi,

1998); and Shemeem Abbas's *The Female Voice in Sufi Ritual: Devotional Practices of Pakistan and India* (Austin, Tex., 2002).

Ali S. Asani (2005)

ISLAM: ISLAM IN SOUTHEAST ASIA

Southeast Asia is in some respects a forgotten world of Islam, for much the same reasons as its counterparts in West and East Africa. Neither its arrival nor its development there was spectacular, and the languages of the local Muslim communities did not become vehicles for works of universal and commanding stature as had Arabic, Persian, Turkish, and some of the vernaculars of the Indian subcontinent. Yet, Islam in Southeast Asia has its own styles and its own temper and intellectual traditions. It merits full recognition as a major cultural zone of the domain of Islam in its own right. Its sacral practices and folk beliefs that color and live alongside the profession of Islam no more invalidate that basic allegiance than do the sacral practices and folk beliefs of Muslims elsewhere, including those in the Middle East. Indeed, Southeast Asia is the home of at least one-fifth of the world's Muslims. Indonesia alone, with over 130 million Muslims, is the largest such community in the world.

Historical Geography. Southeast Asia is best described as a great archipelago, a huge land mass that juts southward between the Indian subcontinent and China and then fragments at its extremity into a complex of thousands of islands, the largest of which are Sumatra, Borneo (Kalimantan), Java, and Mindanao, while the smallest hardly registers on the map. Today this region is identified with the modern nation-states of Myanmar, Vietnam, Laos, Kampuchea, Thailand, Malaysia, Singapore, Brunei, Indonesia, and the Philippines. All of these nation-states have Muslim communities. In Myanmar, Kampuchea, and Vietnam they are insignificant minorities. In Thailand, the Muslim community, though still a minority, has a distinct profile. In Malaysia, Indonesia, and Brunei, on the other hand, Islam has an imposing position. Farther to the east, in the Philippines, it constitutes a significant cultural minority that is in some respects a part of the Philippine nation, but in others, the nucleus of a national entity attempting in various ways to establish its autonomy, if not independence.

Structures in transition. In seeking to understand the historical evolution and contemporary significance of these communities, it is necessary to distinguish between the modern nation-states of the contemporary world, and the traditional distribution of centers of power in Southeast Asia. These new nation-states, emerging in the wake of decolonization, were largely set within the borders established by the colonial powers that had created them. The capital cities of such states, Kuala Lumpur and Jakarta for example, are a focus of the national personality of the political entities in which they are set. They are the gateway, the immediate point of identification, the seat of government, to which their inhabitants turn. They have a status that defines the other parts of the nation as provinces.

Nevertheless, and although it might seem, from a contemporary perspective, that these nations have always existed in some form or another and that their present role derives simply from the expulsion of colonial powers and the recovery of a national sovereignty that has been lost, the reality is far more complex and the results of decolonization more radical. In fact, the creation of such states has turned the traditional world of Southeast Asia on its head. The role of such capital cities with a strong central authority dominating the political, economic, and religious life of the region is very recent.

Traditionally, centers of political power in Southeast Asia were distributed among a wide range of focal points that served as harbors for the exchange and transshipment of goods; these points became the sites of port cities, which from time to time grew strong enough to wield an extensive political authority. Such sites were diverse, discrete, numerous, scattered, and largely unstable centers of activity; they had relations with each other on the basis of rivalry and self-interest, without the direct hegemony of a central authority or any stable and continuing point of reference. Unlike the great cities of the Middle East and South Asia, which enjoyed stability over centuries, if not millennia (one need only mention Cairo, Alexandria, Damascus, Baghdad, or Delhi), centers of power in traditional Southeast Asia rarely maintained their position for more than a century, and the authority they enjoyed was very different from that of the modern capital cities in the region. The historiography of the region, in its many languages, reflects this character in the emphasis that it lays on genealogy of founders and traditional rulers in its accounts of the origins of settlements.

These circumstances have important implications for an understanding of Islam and the processes of Islamization in the region. On the one hand, its origins need to be seen in the planting of numerous local traditions of Islam at focal points in the archipelago. In the course of time, these traditions coalesced and emerged for a while as Islamic city-states or fissiparated and disappeared as significant entities, to be succeeded by new ones. On the other hand, the establishment of modern nation-states with single centers of authority has laid the foundation for a new kind of Islamic tradition with a national character, and these centers in turn have exercised a normative influence on the development of such traditions.

The diversity of Southeast Asia. From earliest times, Southeast Asia has been a region with a variety of peoples, social structures, means of livelihood, cultures, and religions. Denys Lombard, admittedly writing of the modern period, puts it this way:

> We are in fact dealing with several levels of mentality. . . . The thought processes of fringe societies in which "potlatch" is a prevailing custom (the Toraja); those of concentric agrarian societies (the Javanese

> states and their off-shoots at Jogja and Surakarta); those of trading societies (Malay towns, *pasisir* [Javanese coastal centers]); those of the societies living in large modern towns, and above all, the interplay of these various processes on each other, and their interrelationships.

If the first broad distinction to be made is temporal and political, between the constellation of modern nation-states and that of the traditional period, another is geographical: between continental (excluding the Malay Peninsula) and insular Southeast Asia. The former includes the states of Vietnam, Kampuchea, and Thailand; the latter, the Malay Peninsula and the islands of what are now Indonesia and the southern Philippines.

To be sure, each has economic and social elements in common—settled rice cultivation, slash-and-burn shifting cultivation, fishing and seafaring, trading and piracy, gold mining, along with elements of megalithic culture, ancestor worship, and the numerous rituals and beliefs associated with rice cultivation. Yet they are separated by a division into two great language families—the Austronesian, of which the most important representatives are Malay and Javanese, and the Mon Khmer, of which the most important are Thai and Burmese—and the communications barrier between these language families is much greater than that between related members within one family or the other. Equally important, both parts of the great archipelago responded vigorously to religious traditions stemming from the Indian subcontinent long before the birth of Islam. In continental Southeast Asia, Theravāda Buddhism became dominant, whereas Mahāyāna Buddhism in one form or another flourished in Sumatra and Java, in particular, in the empire of Srivijaya (seventh to fourteenth centuries) based on South Sumatra, and in Mataram (Central) and Majapahit (East) East Java (seventh to sixteenth centuries). These great divisions correspond to those regions in which Islam secured a dominant position and those in which it did not.

Languages. Southeast Asia is an area of great linguistic diversity: There are over three hundred languages in the Indonesian area alone. Of these languages, Malay was known throughout the region as a lingua franca as early as the sixteenth century. During the period already discussed, it had also been established as a vernacular of Islam and as a language of the court for areas as far afield and diverse as Malacca, Aceh, and Makassar. It is this very early diffusion of the language, with its religious, economic, cultural, and chancellery roles, that led to its adoption in the twentieth century, in slightly different forms, as the national language of both Malaysia and Indonesia, where it became known as Bahasa Malaysia and Bahasa Indonesia, respectively. Of course, other languages of the same family were to become vehicles of Muslim learning and culture, in particular Javanese, Sundanese, Madurese, and some of the languages of southern Sulawesi (the Celebes). Although Javanese had a far richer literary tradition than did Malay, none had the latter's widespread social and geographical diffusion, and none could challenge its authority as the ideal medium for the vernacularization of Islam.

Its role as a language of Islam is also made evident by the well-nigh universal use of a form of the Arabic script for its written transmission up to modern times, supplanting a script of Indic derivation that had been used for inscriptions before the coming of Islam. Other languages that accepted the Arabic script include Taosug and Maranouw from the southern Philippines, and it was also used alongside (but never supplanted) scripts derived from Indian syllabaries for writing Javanese and Sundanese.

There is only one example of the use of an Indic script for an already Islamized Malay. This is found on a tombstone from Minye Tujuh in Aceh marking the grave of a Queen Alalah, daughter of a Sultan Malik al-Zahir, who was a khan and a son of a khan (the title suggests a foreign origin). Dated in the equivalent of 1389 CE, it is written in an Indian script, and possibly in an Indian meter; if this is so, it shows a remarkable skill, even at this early period, in using Arabic loanwords within the requirements of Indic meters. The Malay inscription on the Trengganu stone, it will be recalled, was written in the Arabic script. The fact that there is a gap of almost two centuries between this tombstone and the earliest surviving manuscripts simply emphasizes how arbitrary are the constellations of chance that provide material for knowledge of the progress and forms of Islam in the region.

By the seventeenth century Malay had absorbed a rich stratum of Arabic loanwords and the acceptance of Arabic structures, along with some elements of Arabic morphology, provides striking evidence of the permeation of the region by an Islamic ethos and its modulation to the expression of Islamic ideas. Many of these ideas relate to religious matters, for example, those relating to the ritual prayer, marriage, divorce, and inheritance. Some Arabic words have undergone a narrowing: that is to say, they have lost a general meaning and kept only a religious one. Others range from technical terms, relating to religious matters and the administration of religious law, or terms of medicine, architecture, and the sciences, to the most common everyday expressions. Sometimes the words are so thoroughly assimilated that they would pass unrecognized unless one were able to identify them as Arabic by following through the patterns of sound change that Malay imposes on the loanwords it absorbs. Most remarkable is the adoption of an Arabic word to refer to local systems of culture, law, and traditional usage: *adat* (Arab., *ʿadah*). In fact, the concept identified by the word is so characteristically Malay that it would not be recognized as an Arabic word unless its origin were pointed out. The number of common Arabic words in Malay—whether borrowed directly from Arabic or indirectly from other languages such as Persian—is well over a thousand. With the growing intensity of Islamic awareness since the 1980s, the number continues to increase as individuals respond to an increasing need to demonstrate their Muslim identity.

It is not only Malay that has received a large corpus of Arabic loanwords; the same is true of many of the Malay-related languages in Sumatra, Java, and Borneo, notably Javanese, Sundanese, Madurese, Acehnese, and Minangkabau. The establishment of Muslim communities in the Philippines likewise brought numbers of loanwords to various Philippine languages. In Tagalog the number is relatively small, but in the southern Philippines, where Muslim communities are concentrated, they are more numerous.

Southeast Asia in world trade. The great archipelago of Southeast Asia lies across the sea routes between the Indian Ocean and the China Sea. In both divisions of the region there were some points open to a range of contacts with the outside world, and others where access was more difficult and where a lifestyle conditioned by such remoteness was preserved.

For centuries before the Christian era, the trading system of the Indian Ocean had been dominated by the Yemenis, who traded in gold, gums, spices, rhinoceros horn, and ivory from the east coast of Africa. For this early period, it is not possible to identify place names accurately, but it is known that the Yemenis brought their goods to the land of gold, *suvarna bhumi,* the term by which Southeast Asia was referred to in some Sanskrit texts.

In the beginning of the Christian era, both continental and insular Southeast Asia reacted to, and in a remarkable way were fecundated by, contact with Indian cultural influences carried to the focal trading centers referred to earlier, which were to be creative for over a millennium. A constant succession of Hindu and Buddhist influences was established in particular regions, with various phases carrying the different traditions, schools, and artistic styles of these great religions and modifying each other as they were adapted to the new environment.

The Coming of Islam. Up to the tenth century CE there is very little evidence of the presence of Islam in Southeast Asia. Indeed, although the Portuguese conquerors of Malacca in 1511 give us some important information about the progress of Islam in the region, apart from a few archaeological remains, reports by Chinese merchants, and the records of individual travelers such as Marco Polo and Ibn Baṭṭuṭah, both of whom give descriptions of North Sumatra, there is little concrete documentation until the sixteenth century. By that time, however, with the appearance of the Dutch and British trading companies in the region, the evidence of widespread Islamization is considerable. The territories of the Islamic commonwealth in Southeast Asia were so vast that the process of their creation has been called "the second expansion of Islam," alluding to the original expansion from Arabia into North Africa and the Fertile Crescent. Unlike that first period of extraordinary growth in the seventh century, however, the spread of Islam in Southeast Asia was hesitant, modest, and discreet: what was achieved in one century in the Middle East took at least half a millennium in Southeast Asia.

There is too little evidence to document in detail the beginnings of this process, yet a reasonable working hypothesis may be formulated as follows: as soon as there were Muslim sailors aboard ships sailing under whatever flag in the Indian Ocean trading system and disembarking goods or individuals at points in Southeast Asia, there was the possibility of a Muslim presence at those points with a concern for the implementation of the norms of Islamic community life. This could have been as early as the end of the eighth century. Hardly anything is known of the history of trading settlements along the littoral of Southeast Asia during this period; however, reliable evidence for the presence of Muslims in China from the beginning of the eighth century, suggests that Muslim seamen and merchants were already breaking their long voyages at one or another of the numerous natural harbors along the coasts of Sumatra, the Malay Peninsula, Borneo, and northern Java, the Celebes and the southern Philippines. The unloading of goods to await transshipment with the change of the monsoon, the establishment of warehouses and semipermanent settlements, and trading and intermarriage—and other relationships—with the local peoples were all factors that could combine to establish small, viable and possibly stable Muslim communities.

Given the diversity and discontinuities of the region, the provenance of Southeast Asian Islam is not a practical topic for discussion, although hypotheses have located it anywhere from Egypt to Bengal. Some Indonesian writers have sought to discover for it an Arabian origin that can be dated as early as the eighth century. One thing is certain: all movement of ideas and peoples from West and South Asia to Southeast Asia is related to the maritime history of the Indian Ocean (although it is possible that some communities included those who had made part of the journey by land across the Indian subcontinent, or even the "great circle" route via the Silk Road through Central Asia, and then by sea from Canton to the islands). The greater the number of Muslims involved in the trading system, the greater the diversity of the Muslim tradition that became diffused, and the greater the probability of Muslims coming together in sufficient numbers to generate a critical mass—a Muslim community that could become stable, put down roots through intermarriage with local women who embraced Islam, and play a distinctive role on equal terms with other local communities. Such Muslim communities may have included Arabs from what may be called an Arab diaspora in the early years of the Islamic commonwealth; but from that era, very little direct information has survived. The process of consolidation was however slow. It is not until the thirteenth century that Islamic communities appear with a political profile, as port city-states ruled by sultans. The earliest of these sultanates was that of Pasai, on the east coast of North Sumatra; it was succeeded by others. The appearance of such city-states must be seen as the culmination of a long period of Muslim presence with a low profile, a circumstance that has made the ethnic mix of the communities—whether local, Indian, Persian, Arab or even Chinese—difficult to determine.

Once Islam achieved a political presence in the region, further growth and the exercise of political power became possible. By this time the trading system of the Indian Ocean was largely in Muslim hands; this assured economic power to Muslims, and Muslim mercantile law served to generate business confidence. The power and self-confidence of the Muslim states gave them a position as power brokers and allies. Marriage alliances that required a profession of Islam doubtless had a role as well.

First traces. The earliest archaeological evidence is slight: a lone pillar in the region of Phanrang on the mid-east coast of Vietnam, inscribed in Arabic and dating from the tenth century. The French scholar Ravaisse (quoted by S. Q. Fatimi in *Islam Comes to Asia*) believes it to indicate that

> there existed there in the eleventh century an urban population of whom we know little. They were very different from the indigenous people in race, belief and habits. Their ancestors must have come about a century earlier, and must have married native women. They were merchants and craftsmen living in a perfectly well-organized society mixing more and more with the natives. They asked one of themselves to act as their representative and defender with respect to the authorities of the place. He was called Shaikh al-Suq ["master of the market"], and was assisted by the Naqib (a merchant or craftsman in charge of the management of the community to which he belonged). Along with him were "notables who, enriched by their commerce, occupied an important place."

Another piece of evidence from roughly the same period suggests that there was a Muslim presence at Leren on the north coast of Java. This is a tombstone with a date corresponding to 1082 CE, marking the grave of a merchant's daughter. It provides no certain evidence of a Muslim community; even the date cannot be taken for granted since tombstones were frequently imported long after a burial. Near Jolo (southern Philippines) is the venerated grave of a foreign Muslim with a date corresponding to 1310 CE, the site of which has been used for the coronation of a number of the sultans of Sulu. In Trengganu, an east-coast state on the Malay Peninsula, a fragment of a stone pillar inscribed in Malay in Arabic script which may be dated between 1321 and 1380—a fragment of the inscription is missing—marks the presence of a Muslim community. By the fifteenth century there is sporadic but more substantial evidence of Muslims in the East Javanese empire of Majapahit, again from gravestones. Probably they belonged to communities of merchants, but this too is hardly more than surmise. Just as there were Muslims in Java, there is evidence that there were Muslims in the great Buddhist empire of Srivijaya (seventh to thirteenth centuries) based on South Sumatra, an empire that thrived on trade and maintained close relations with China and India.

The earliest evidence that substantiates not simply the presence of Muslims in the region but the existence of an Islamic maritime sultanate dates from the thirteenth century. This is a tombstone of Malik al-Saleh, the first Muslim ruler of Pasai, in North Sumatra, the date given for his death corresponding to 1297. Reports of foreign travelers confirm that many of his subjects were Muslims. What circumstances enabled the Muslim community to achieve a critical mass and generate a state in which the ruler could style himself sultan, and what processes led to this event, we cannot tell. Likewise there is little evidence as to the ethnic composition of this state: to what extent was it local, to what extent foreign? (And even the term *foreign* at this time begs a number of questions.) Many of the titles and names attributed to the personalities of this sultanate in a local chronicle have a South Indian ring to them.

Nonetheless, from this point on, the documentation of Islam at the political level is relatively straightforward, and it is possible to chronicle the emergence of states with Islamic rulers. Even though internal records are sparse and their human and cultural dynamics remain in the shadows, at the very least their names are recorded by foreign visitors.

The sultanates. It has been posited that Pasai is the earliest Muslim state in the Malay world and its ruler as the first sultan there. The only evidence of his life comes from his tombstone. It is however striking that his name is eponymous with that of the Ayyubid ruler al-Malik al-Saleh (r. 1240–1249) who restored Jerusalem to Islamic rule in 1244. But Pasai was at least referred to by Marco Polo and Ibn Baṭṭuṭah in the thirteenth and fourteenth centuries. Although the extent of its political authority is not known, it occupied a strategic position at the entrance to the straits of Malacca and was a convenient point for exchanging goods and taking on board supplies of water and firewood. Moreover, by making alliances with either pirates or nascent states on the other side of the straits, it was able to ensure that shipping did not go elsewhere, and that port taxes were paid.

Malacca. Malacca, on the west coast of the Malay Peninsula, inherited the mantle of Pasai. Far more is known of its history than that of Pasai, from both local and foreign sources. It became Muslim shortly after its foundation around 1400, and via its dependencies, both on the Malay Peninsula, where it established the dynasties of the Malay sultanates, and on the east coast of Sumatra, it served as a conduit for Muslim influence to other parts of the archipelago. Various factors were involved here: local traders from Thailand to the north and the neighboring islands were attracted to its emporium, Muslim traders from Bengal, India, and further afield found scope for business activities opened up in its trading partners and dependencies, and it attracted foreign *ʿulamāʾ* (religious scholars; sg., *ʿālim*), principally from the Indian subcontinent, although many of them may have had Arab blood and used this Arab descent to their advantage. Although Malacca held an important position, however, it was not unique. There were many smaller states that played an analogous role along the littoral of East Sumatra, the north coast of Java, Borneo, Sulawesi (Celebes), and later the Spice Islands (Moluccas) and the southern Philippines. In every case the same kind of processes that were illustrated at Malacca were taking place, perhaps on a smaller scale, perhaps on a larger scale, and they had been happening even before the birth of Malacca. It must be stressed that there is no "big bang" explanation for the coming of Islam to Southeast Asia; such claims as the Portuguese statement that Java was converted from Malacca must be regarded as hyperbole.

Successor states. After Malacca fell to the Portuguese in 1511, it was such smaller states that were to grow in stature: Aceh, Palembang, Banten, Ceribon, Demak, Surabaya, and Makassar, as well as smaller centers in the Spice Islands and Mindanao. Each of them became integrated into the Muslim trading system, each became a center of Islamic learning, and each, by a continuing process of osmosis, attracted people from the interior into contact with these cities. In every case, networks of family, Ṣūfī order *(ṭarīqah),* guild, and trade association relationships gradually served to diffuse Islam back into the interior, although it was transmitted at different levels of intensity and perceived in rather different ways according to the cultural backgrounds of the various communities.

Special attention should be drawn to Aceh, which first came to prominence in the 1520s and reached its apogee during the reign of Sultan Iskandar Muda (1607–1636). During the first half of the seventeenth century it was the dominant economic and political power of the region. It conquered the northern half of the Malay Peninsula and northern and parts of central Sumatra, gaining control of the pepper areas and enforcing a trading monopoly. Aceh was the first Muslim state in the region to have extended intercourse with Europe, and European dignitaries, including James I of Britain, as well as the Ottoman Empire. It is also noteworthy for a surviving legacy of Islamic learning: for the first time we have historical information about a state in the region generating works of Islamic scholarship that remain accessible to us, some of which are used in schools throughout the Malay world even today. In addition, experts are able to identify individual Acehnese scholars, both in Aceh and in the holy cities of Mecca and Medina, and the teachers with whom they studied. Indeed, one of the great ministers of state between 1600 and 1630, Shams al-Dīn was a noted *ʿālim* and bore the title Shaikh al-Islam. There are eyewitness reports from British, Dutch, and French sailors on the celebration of the conclusion of the fast of Ramaḍān (ʿĪd al-Fiṭr) and the festival of the sacrifice marking the climax of the pilgrimage rites in Mecca. It is also possible to establish and describe some of the relations between Aceh, the Mughal court, and the Ottoman Empire.

The Islamic history of Aceh during this period is better known than that of any of its neighbors, but analogous centers of lesser political power played a major role elsewhere in the region as Islam moved inland during the seventeenth century. In Sumatra, for example, the inland highlands of the Minangkabau region, territories rich in gold and pepper and which for centuries had established this part of the island in a network of trading systems, became Muslim. This area was to put a distinctive stamp on its interpretation and realization of Islam by maintaining a matrilineal social structure alongside a commitment to Islam that was among the staunchest in the archipelago.

Another inland region where Islam became established was the state of Mataram in Central Java, which was, until its defeat by the United Dutch East India Company in 1629, the largest single state on the island. Even after the defeat, it maintained this status, a status that added special significance to the fact that its ruler, Susuhunan Agung (1613–1645), assumed the title of sultan and in 1633 established the Islamic calendrical system in Java.

Beginnings of the colonial era. From the early sixteenth century, European powers, or trading companies representing them began an increasing encroachment on the region, establishing themselves as participants in its economic and political life. Early in the sixteenth century (1511), the Portuguese captured Malacca; in the second half of the sixteenth century, the Spanish established their rule in the Philippines; at the beginning of the seventeenth century, the Dutch East India Company took the first steps toward acquiring an empire in the East Indies, fighting a war of attrition against the Portuguese as it did so. In the eighteenth century, British East India Company began to establish trading posts in Sumatra, and on the Malay Peninsula. Islamization nevertheless continued. Throughout the region more people were gradually drawn into the new religion, to the basic recognition of transcendence implicit in the confession "There is no god but God." To be sure, numerous cults survived alongside this confession, together with practices and rituals and the use of spells and magical formulas that derived from the Indic and even megalithic traditions. Nevertheless there was a continuing momentum toward the subordination and finally the subsuming of the spiritual concepts of such traditions into the terminology of Islam: thus numerous Javanese spirits were largely included within the Islamic category of spiritual beings, the *jinn.* Doubtless the intensity of response to the more exclusive demands of Islam waxed and waned, yet amid all these communities where Islam had been planted, some degree of formal recognition was given to positive Islamic law, particularly in relation to diet, to burial of the dead, to marriage, to circumcision, and to the fast, even though the performance of the daily prayer might be lax. Indeed it is striking how the pre-Islamic cult of the dead reflected in the building of great mausolea for the Javanese god-kings, and the extravagant sacrifices of buffalo still carried on today in non-Muslim areas such as the Torajas (Central Sulawesi), faded away with the acceptance of Islam.

The ḥājj played an important role; some individuals who made it stayed to study for years in the holy cities of Mecca and Madina, or elsewhere in the Middle East; the Ṣūfī orders also played a role, and religious teachers, traversing the Muslim world, gave fresh life to communities and religious schools and often held the ear of local rulers. The constant retelling of stories of the prophets and the heroes of Islam and the cultural adaptation of these stories to local conditions gradually created a unitary and universalistic frame of reference for local and world history and established Islamic concepts—of the creation, of the sending of God's messengers culminating in Muḥammad, of the community, and eventually of the resurrection of the body—as the norm and benchmark by which all competing systems of ideas were to be measured and into which they were largely to be assimilated.

SPIRITUAL AND CULTURAL DIMENSIONS. The modalities by which islamization progressed throughout the region and the cultural achievements it set in train are far richer in character than a political survey can communicate, although it can establish a framework within which these dimensions can be situated. Discussion of these achievements is inevitably centered on the territories that now constitute Malaysia and Indonesia, due to the weight of population. By comparison, within the framework of this article, despite their intrinsic interest and importance, Thailand, the other mainland states, Singapore, Brunei, and the Philippines can only receive passing mention.

Let us consider in a little more detail some of the cases we have mentioned. The community at Phanrang lived and governed itself apart from its neighbors. Typologically this situation is difficult to account for. Thus the hypothesis that it was founded by descendants of a community of Shīʿī refugees who fled from a persecution by the Umayyad governor al-Ḥajjāj (d. 714) is plausible. It will be noted later that although today the region is Sunnī, there are some remnants of Shīʿī influence from the past, such as the commemoration of the martyrdom of Ḥasan and Ḥusayn in a coastal region of western Sumatra—albeit only as popular entertainment, not grief and self-flagellation.

Processes of Islamization. The descriptions of the sultanate of Pasai referred to earlier make a clear distinction between the Muslim community of the city itself and those people of the hinterland who were still unbelievers. This distinction suggests that an originally foreign community became settled over a number of years, and that an individual with sufficient charisma at one point proclaimed himself sultan. The coastal port of Malacca on the other hand presents an example of a mercantile state whose ruler professed Islam soon after its foundation. The case of Aceh is different again, in that it appears to have arisen after the amalgamation of two small Muslim states in the north of Sumatra into a single state that was to dominate the straits of Malacca for the greater part of the seventeenth century.

The importance of Aceh cannot be exaggerated. It was known in popular parlance as the Veranda of the Holy Land (Arabia). Aspiring pilgrims and scholars from all parts of the archipelago would make the journey in stages over a period of years. Aceh was the last port of work and residence and study that they would encounter before leaving their own region of the world and heading out across the Bay of Bengal. It was also the first place of call on their return journey. And the intensity of religious education, debate, and teaching in Aceh, as well as the constant movement of peoples of diverse ethnic groups, ensured a wide dissemination of religious ideas and, to some extent, a normalization of religious life through the distribution of networks of religious affiliations. (*Ṭarīqahs* can be identified in north Sumatra since at least the second half of the sixteenth century).

The acceptance of Islam by Sultan Agung of Mataram (r. 1613–1646) is a special case. His kingdom was not a port-state but was located in the interior and was based more on wet rice cultivation than commerce. It was the prestigious heir to the great Śiva Buddha tradition of East Java and included in its territories the sites of the great Buddhist stupa, the Borobudur, and other Hindu and Buddhist shrines built during the seventh, eighth, and ninth centuries. Yet for Agung, this history was not enough, nor was his title of *susuhunan.* To all this he added the title of sultan, purchased from Mecca; thus he assumed a dignity which, although largely symbolic, had a major role in elevating the status of Islam in Java (although not necessarily the conversion of Java to Islam).

As C. C. Berg points out in a seminal article (1955), kings and princes operated as factors of acceleration and deceleration of the Islamization process in Java. In this instance, Agung played a role of acceleration, paradoxically in the wake of his defeat by the Dutch East India Company in 1629. This event turned him toward whatever enemies of the Dutch could be found in the seas and islands of the archipelago: the Portuguese and communities of Muslim merchants. As a Muslim by profession, if not by passion until 1629, he soon became a Muslim in search of authority and power. Whatever his psychological motivations, he changed the face of his kingdom and its cultural character by introducing the Muslim calendar with the announcement that from 1 Muḥarram 1043 AH, a date corresponding to July 8, 1633 CE, this calendrical system should operate in Java alongside the traditional Javanese system of Saka years. Symbolically this was an act of great importance, because it meant that the Islamic calendar based on the date of the *hijra,* became the global, universalistic event in relation to which events in Javanese society and history were to be recorded.

In the last analysis, however, the creative achievement of a religion is to be seen in the lives of the individuals it inspires, the intellectual activity it generates, and the dimensions it adds to spiritual, cultural, and social life. But one of the difficulties in coping with the early story of Islam in Southeast Asia is the absence of historical figures to whom one can attribute the early spread of the religion.

It is striking that, in the Malay texts at least, there are no historical figures to whom the primal conversion of a state to Islam can be attributed. The same holds true for the preaching of Islam in Java as presented by Javanese court chronicles. This is not to say that such figures are always nameless, or that they may not be based on individuals who did once exist, but certainly in the way they are presented, there is little that could be described as a personality base. In his contribution to Nehemia Levtzion's *Conversion to Islam* (1980), Jones gives an account of ten conversion myths from different parts of the archipelago. The account from the *Sejarah Malayu* (Malay Annals) is typical: the ruler of Malacca had a dream in which he saw Muḥammad, who ordered him to recite the Muslim Shahādah ("witnessing"): "There is no god but God, and Muhammad is his Messenger." The prophet then told him that the following day, at the time of the afternoon prayer, a ship would arrive from Jidda with a religious teacher on board whom he was to obey. When the king awoke, he found he had been circumcised. At the time foretold on the following day the ship arrived, and the religious teacher came down from it. There and then he performed the afternoon prayer on the beach, and the bystanders gathered round asking: what is this bobbing up and down. The king, on hearing what was happening went down to the beach to welcome him, and together with all his courtiers and subjects embraced Islam.

An intriguing feature of this work is that many of the religious teachers described in its pages are presented as figures of fun. There is the eccentric who takes sling shots at kites flown over his house, and there is the religious teacher who is teased by a tipsy court officer because he cannot pronounce Malay words correctly. There is also the mystically inclined teacher who refused to accept the sultan as a religious disciple unless he left his elephant behind at the palace and came to him humbly on foot.

Of these figures, one may possibly be identified: Sadar Jahan, the religious adviser to Sultan Ahmad Shah of Malacca. When Ahmad Shah came out on his elephant to face the Portuguese attack that destroyed the city in 1511, Sadar Jahan accompanied the sultan. Under a hail of musket shots he begged his master to retreat to a safer position with the words: "This is no place to discuss *tawḥīd* (mystical union)." He has been identified with a scholar-jurist-diplomat Fayd Allah Bambari, known as Sadr-i Jahan, who was sent by King Ayaz from Gujarat via Jidda to negotiate a defensive wall from Hormuz to Malacca against the Portuguese incursion into the Indian Ocean. He arrived in Malacca by ship in 1509 to stiffen Malaccan resistance to the Portuguese and is presumed to have been killed during the sack of the city. The identification is not wholly certain. Nevertheless, the evidence is sufficient to show that as early as the fifteenth century, religious teachers from various parts of the Muslim world took part in the religious life of the Southeast Asian sultanates.

The propagation of Islam in Java is traditionally attributed to *wali songo* (nine saints) who made their debut between thirteenth and fourteenth centuries. The number nine probably has more to do with cosmology than arithmetic, since this figure subsumes the eight points of the compass and the center. Each is associated with a different region of Java. They are associated with the origin of elements of Javanese culture such as the Javanese shadow theater and gamelan orchestra, which existed long before Islam. All are presented as figures with a mystical insight into the reality of things; they have a role in the founding of dynasties and are not subject to the laws of nature. One of them, Siti Jenar, was executed for uttering words that claimed identity between himself and God. It has been conjectured, in my view with little foundation, that this event—if indeed it occurred—is a doublet of the al-Ḥallāj story.

It is only from the late sixteenth century that it becomes possible to identify individuals among religious teachers, gain access to the works they wrote, and so lay the foundations for an intellectual and spiritual history of Islam in this region, a task pioneered by Peter G. Riddell (2001). However, since the information available about such figures is very sparse—there is little evidence available in the form of biographical or autobiographical writing—it is not possible to do much more than situate them within a general framework of the intellectual and spiritual life of the region to the degree that this can be established.

Local scholarship. This absorption of Arabic words in large measure derived from the study of Arabic works on the fundamental Islamic disciplines of Qurʾanic exegesis, traditions, and jurisprudence, as well as Ṣūfī practice and spirituality (i.e., *tafsīr, ḥadīth, fiqh,* and *taṣawwuf*). There is no documentation of the early stages of the development of these studies, although there is no reason to doubt that the seeds from which they grew were planted at least as early as the thirteenth century. Indeed, it should be stressed again that there were Islamic communities in the region long before the earliest evidence for Islamic states.

It is only from the late sixteenth century that manuscripts from these traditions survive, whether in Arabic (mostly representing key works from the Islamic tradition) or in Malay or other regional languages such as Javanese. The Arabic manuscripts, some doubtless copied on the instructions of, or at least the permission of, a teacher in the Muslim Holy Land are of various levels of difficulty. Of works of *tafsīr,* that known as *Al-Jalālayn* is the most popular. Van Ronkel (1913) lists a significant number of manuscripts from various parts of the archipelago, some with interlinear translations, or at least annotations, in Malay or Javanese, sometimes with a dedication to a local ruler. There may be a temptation to look down on *Al-Jalalayn.* In fact it contains *multum in parvo* and is an excellent work for early levels of study, ideally suited for students who, though trained in an Islamic school, are not native speakers of Arabic. After *Al-Jalālayn,* al-Bayḍāwī's *Anwār al-tanzīl* takes pride of place, followed by al-Khāzin's *Lubāb al-taʾwīl fī maʿānī al-tanzīl.* There are in addition fragments of Ṣūfī commentaries, including al-Bayhaqī's *Kitāb al-tahdhīb fī al-tafsīr* copied in 1652, which for a manuscript with a Southeast Asian provenance is very early indeed. There is even a work by al-Dānī on the seven recitations (*qirāʾat*) of the Qurʾān. It should be stressed that these manuscripts represent the tip of the ice-berg in relation to the number of those unknown from that period, or simply lost.

Collections of *ḥadīth,* especially those of al-Bukhārī, are numerous, and with them commentaries; the same collections of forty *ḥadīth (Al-arbāʿīn),* especially that of al-Nawawī, were also popular. To these may be added a selection of works on history and biography, jurisprudence, astronomy, and *taṣawwuf.* A Ṣūfī text that appears to have been popular, on the basis of the number of surviving manuscripts, is *Al-ḥikam al-ʿAṭāʾīyah* of Ibn ʿAṭāʾ Allāh; this work too is often accompanied by commentaries. There are treatises on the Shādhilī, Naqshbandī, and ʿAlawī orders and a sprinkling of works in the Ibn al-ʿArabī tradition, both by Ibn al-ʿArabī himself and by his great commentator, al-Kāshānī. Of such manuscripts, one of the most striking contains the introduction to the commentary on Ibn al-Fāriḍ's poem *Al-tāʾīyah al-kubrā* by Saʿīd ibn ʿAlī al-Farghānī (d. 1299).

Given how heterogenous and arbitrary such a listing is, it is clear that these manuscripts have only survived by chance. What has been lost begs the imagination. Nevertheless, the evidence is enough to show that many basic Arabic works were accessible to scholars in this region, and that a variety of traditions was represented.

Pioneers of vernacularization. We have already mentioned interlinear translations, glosses, and annotations on Arabic manuscripts. These represent in embryonic form beginnings of the vernacularization of Islam and the Islamic disciplines into Malay and the other regional languages. How early this began it is not possible to determine. The manuscripts that are extant, surviving as they do largely by chance, are not a sure guide as to the kind of works that were first achieved in local languages.

Ḥamzah Fanṣūrī. The earliest Malay author known is Ḥamzah Fanṣūrī (d. c. 1593). Few details of his life are known, but a significant number of his writings have survived. Apart from the ravages of a tropical climate, many were destroyed by a later *ʿālim* who accused him of heresy. Those that do remain however show him to have been a great religious poet. From them it is clear that he made the pilgrimage to Mecca, and that he embraced a particular formulation of Ṣūfī theosophy, apparently an Arabo-Iranian one based on the Ibn al-ʿArabī tradition as it was reformulated and extended by al-Jīlī, and may have included Shīʿī elements. If it had, this would at least be consistent with the stories of Shīʿī heroes in Malay discovered in Aceh early in the seventeenth century.

A verse from one of his *syaʾir* (poems made up of end rhyming quatrains) gives a good example of the ascetic theology of the Ibn al-ʿArabī school of mysticism:

> Regard heat and cold as one and the same; Abandon greed and avarice; Let your self will melt like wax, Then your elusive goal you will gain.

It should not be supposed that this is the earliest instance of original Islamic writing in Malay. The technical skill in which religious ideas are handled in his quotations suggests that he represents a culminating point in a long tradition.

Shams al-Dīn. Another major figure is Shams al-Dīn, the guide and teacher of Iskandar Muda, sultan of Aceh from 1607 to 1636. Shams al-Dīn reflects a tradition from North India, in which the manifold self-manifestations of the Divinity, the supreme Reality (al-Haqq) characteristic of the Ibn al-ʿArabī tradition was reduced to a convenient seven, and this framework, which was rapidly adopted by the Naqshbandī, Shādhilī and Shaṭṭārī orders, soon became part of the stock-in-trade of the mystical tradition in all parts of the archipelago. An important figure of state, Shams al-Dīn was the author of a significant corpus of writings in both Arabic and Malay. He is in fact the first local author known to have written original works in Arabic, a tradition which was long to continue. The single most important work that he used as the basis for his teaching was a summary of the key ideas of Ibn al-ʿArabī's system set out in a framework of seven grades of being proceeding from the undifferentiated Absolute through six manifestations to the Perfect Man first formulated by the Indian *ʿālim* Muḥammad ibn Fadl Allah (d. 1590) and effectively displaced that of al-Jīlī, which had been used by Ḥamzah Fanṣūrī.

ʿAbd al-Raʾūf. By the second half of the seventeenth century, ʿAbd al-Raʾūf (1615–1690) had prepared a full rendering of the Jalālayn *tafsīr* in Malay. It was extended by one of his students, Dāwūd al-Rūmī, by selections from the *qirāʾāt* literature and citations from the *tafsīrs* of al-Khāzin and al-Bayḍāwī. It is still reprinted with the misattribution on the cover title *Tafsīr al-Bayḍāwī.* This rendering into Malay of the Jalālayn means in effect that there was a full vernacularization of the Qurʾān in Malay, albeit embedded in an authoritative commentary before the end of the seventeenth century.

In addition to these works, others written in Malay include, for example, simple summaries of the Muslim creed, such as al-Sanūsī's *Umm al-barāhīn* (Mother of proofs), and hundreds of works on topics such as the mystical practice of various *ṭarīqahs* (the Naqshbandīyah, Shaṭṭārīyah, and Shādhilīyah in particular), the twenty attributes of God, *tawḥīd* (the unity of God), the application of Islamic law on various topics, and eschatology. One example is a four-volume abridgement of al-Ghazālī's *Iḥyāʾ ʿulūm al-dīn* (The revivification of the religious sciences) by an expatriate scholar, ʿAbd al-Ṣamad of Palembang, who compiled it around 1780 in Ṭāʾif, Arabia. It is still reprinted in various parts of Malaysia and Indonesia, and although there are now more academically prepared translations of the full work in Indonesian published in the Roman script, they have not totally supplanted the earlier version.

Progress from the study of the foundation texts of Islam together with the religious disciplines deriving from them, and vernacularizing their content, to the generation of original works reflecting the needs of the new environment was at first slow. In the premodern period, there is little in Malay that can stand beside the literary and intellectual achievements of Islam in Arabic, Persian or Turkish. In part this is due to an extended dominance of the oral tradition in the transmission of knowledge. But in any case the cultural achievements of Islam in Southeast Asia are different in character to those of the Middle East. This is only to be expected given the tremendous differences in the human ecology of monsoon Southeast Asia and the wide range of traditions and forms of social organization that had their home there from conditions prevailing in the Arab world.

Literary activities fecundated by Islamization. These are of various kinds. Important among them is a historiography. Certainly there is an influence of both Arabic and Persian historiography on the writing of Malay court chronicles. Such works were given an Islamic flavor by the use of Arabic words such as *sejarah* (Arab., *shajara* [t al-nasab]), meaning family line, chronicle, or history, and *silsilah,* or lineage, in the titles to indicate a genealogy or succession of rulers. The Malay chronicle of the kingdom of Malacca that purports to give an account of the antecedents and genealogy of the Malaccan sultanate (1400–1511), for example, is known as the *Sejarah Melayu.* Although popularly known in English as *The Malay Annals,* the title really means a genealogy of the Malays, by which is meant the Malay rulers of Malacca. The work, it may be noted, although it spans a century, and presents vivid vignettes of court life, has no dates.

There are a number of similar court and dynasty based histories of the states of the Malay peninsula. Despite Arabic words in their titles, however, many of them have more in common with the Malay folk tradition than of Arabo-Persian historiography. In fact, up to the late nineteenth century only in a few cases did works of this kind develop with the concern for date and fact that characterizes Muslim historiography as a whole. One is the historical writing of Nūr al-Dīn al-Rānīrī, an itinerant scholar of Gujarati origin (an illustration of the significant role expatriate *ʿulamāʾ* played in the religious life of the region). Although only in Aceh between 1637 and 1642, he wrote in Malay the *Bustan al-Salatin* (The garden of kings), a universal history, including a book on the history of Aceh, which is one of the most important and reliable sources for the history of the sultanate. (Aside from his importance as a historian, he was a vicious polemicist, who while he enjoyed the patronage of the Acehnese court, had many of the writing of Ḥamzah Fanṣūrī and Shams al-Dīn burnt, and their followers executed.) Another example of historical writing in the Islamic tradition is the *Tuhfat al-nafis* (Dedication to the noble endeavour), a history of the Riau archipelago, by Raja Haji Ali of Riau, written in the wake of an Islamic revival in the late nineteenth century.

In addition there are works literary in character, some of them based on the prophets of the pre-Muslim era, on events in the life of the prophet Muḥammad and his companions, and on the heroes of Islam. Some of these are extant in manuscripts from the beginning of the seventeenth century. Early stories that have been discovered include Malay renderings of the story of Joseph and Potiphar's wife, possibly from a Persian source, was copied in 1604, and alongside it versions of the story of Iskandar Dhu al-Qarnayn (Alexander the Great) and other stories of the prophets of Islam. The 1612 rescension of *The Malay Annals* opens with a version of the story of Alexander's invasion of India and presents him as the ultimate ancestor of the Malacca dynasty. This story then was well known, and the name Alexander popular. Iskandar it may also be remarked, was the name of the greatest ruler of Aceh (Iskandar Muda, r. 1607–1636).

Other stories that became popular from this period centered on the Prophet's uncle Amīr Ḥamzah and the Shīʿī hero Muḥammad ibn al-Ḥanafīyah. *The Malay Annals* suggests that versions of these stories were preserved in the Malacca library and as of 1511 were held in great esteem. The reference to them may be apocryphal: it indicates that they were to be recited to the Malaccan soldiers to give them courage for battle against the Portuguese on the following day, a battle that was to end in the Portuguese occupation of Malacca. Nevertheless, their symbolic role was well known at the time that the 1612 rescension of *The Malay Annals* was compiled. Equally important, the popularity of such works suggests at least the presence of a Shīʿī flavor to Islam in Aceh during this period. Shīʿī or not, there is certainly a strong Persian flavor in the literary works that were rendered into Malay, the most outstanding of which at this early period is a version of the *Ṭūṭīnāmah* (Book of the parrot) known in Malay as *Hikayat bayan budiman* (Story of the wise parrot).

There is in addition a wholesale collection of stories of Islamic provenance that has found its way into Malay and Javanese and other related languages. Such stories derive more from the popular than the belletristic traditions, and more of them have come via the Indian subcontinent than directly from the Arab Middle East, although even here the distinction is not absolute. Stories and fables in Arabic have been rendered into a variety of local vernaculars, and thence passed on to reappear in the languages of the Malay-Indonesian archipelago.

It must be remembered that stories about the heroes of Islam, while having a role as religious instruction, were equally important as entertainment and became widely popular. As a result, these heroes became part of community education for all levels of society and all ages, and thus, by allowing popular audiences to share in the experience of other communities of these heroes, they served to create a general pan-Islamic consciousness. Manuscript catalogues include numerous copies of stories of Muḥammad ibn al-Ḥanafīyah and Amīr Ḥamzah; there are collections of stories of the prophets and tales of the individual prophets including Adam, Abraham, Noah, and Moses. In Java, the story of Joseph was especially popular.

To these, however, should be added stories quite divorced from these religious figures, but which derive from Islamic sources and which have an Islamic ethos. These include many tales that appear in collections such as *The 1,001 Nights,* and classics such as the *Ṭūṭīnāmah* referred to earlier. Among other collections of stories are the *Kalīlah and Dimnah,* which was known as early as 1736, and the *Bakhtiyār-nāmah* (Book of Bakhtiyār), a kind of reversal of the *1,001 Nights* that is a grand story of a young prince who is accused by ten viziers of having an affair with a chambermaid, but who postpones his execution by telling stories until the truth is discovered. This theme, it may be noted, was famous in Persian and Turkish popular literature, as well as in medieval Latin.

How these tales were first rendered into Malay is not known: They may have been carried by the oral tradition and set down in writing by court scribes, according to established literary conventions, to be recited on royal occasions, or there may have been some kind of committee composed of reader, oral translator, and scribe. It is certain, however, that such stories were preserved in court libraries, that access to them was restricted to senior court officials, and that the sultan had the authority to declare which might be read.

This composite Islamic tradition, whether formed directly from Arabic sources or mediated through Indian vernaculars, remains popular throughout Muslim Southeast Asia in numerous retellings, adaptations, and even dramatizations. In West Java, a cycle of Amīr Ḥamzah stories has become part of the repertory of the puppet theater. Evidence of this past and present popularity, apart from observation, can be gleaned from the catalogues of Malay, Javanese, and Sundanese manuscripts, to mention only a few.

Revival and reform movements. Islamicized Southeast Asia was an integral part of the Muslim world. In consequence there was a sensitivity to and identification with an Islamic ethos, which although at times not totally unequivocal, rendered such Muslim communities responsive to movements that caught the imagination and fired the enthusiasm of their coreligionists in other parts of the Muslim world. One such movement was the Wahhābī uprising in Arabia during the last quarter of the eighteenth century. Inspired by the ideal of cleansing Islam from accretions and practices that were held to be incompatible with *tawḥīd,* the unity of God, it resorted to force to put Islamic law and ritual observances into effect. A group of Sumatran scholars in Arabia when the Wahhābīs conquered Mecca in 1803, returning home filled with enthusiasm for the ideals of the movement led to the rise of the Padri movement in the Minangkabau area of Central Sumatra. This movement set itself against the traditional elite, which it regarded as compromising with non-Islamic practices and values, whether reflected in the lifestyle of the traditional rulers or in the matrilineal descent system of the region. Their reaction was to lead to a civil war that gave the Dutch government an opportunity to intervene on the part of the traditionalists and to defeat the leader of the revolt, Imām Bondjol, in 1842.

It may well have been also that the Java War (1826–1830) between rival members of the royal court likewise took part of its energy from this ferment in Islam. It should not be imagined that the expansion of Islam was always peaceful, or that even the relationships among different traditions of Islam were without conflict. One need only recall the persecution and book burning in Aceh between 1637 and 1642, sometimes referred to as an attempt by the so-called Shuhūdīyah ("unity of witness") school of mysticism to suppress the Wujūdīyah ("unity of being") tradition; the wars waged by Sultan Agung's successor, Amangkurat I, in the 1660s against the more *shariʿa* minded Muslim communities of the north coast of Java; and the scatological and even obscene diatribes written in Javanese to make fun of the professional *ʿulamāʾ* in the nineteenth century.

It must be emphasized however that the modes of participation of Southeast *ʿulamāʾ* in the wider world of Islam were complex and diverse. They were certainly not limited to the transmissions of varying forms of Islamic radicalism. Much of their work and thinking was conveyed in treatises they wrote in Arabic. The Indonesian scholar Azyumardi Azra has made a detailed study of the networks of religious teachers binding together the geographically separate zone of the Muslim world in the seventeenth and eighteenth centuries. They continued and continue. Some of the works they produced are minor tracts devoted to issues that became shibboleths, for example, whether the commencement of the fasting month was to be decided by the sighting of the moon or by calculation, or whether the formulation of intention before beginning a ritual prayer should be made aloud or mentally. Such material has only a local and historical importance. Occasionally, however, a substantial work appears and wins an established position. One such text was *Marah labid* (Rich pasture), a two-volume Qurʾān commentary of about one thousand pages by a Muḥammad Nawawi al-Jawi, scholar from Banten, on the north coast of West Java. He was born in 1815, went to study in the Muslim Holy Land in 1830, and died in Mecca in 1893. Published in Cairo by the well-known firm of Halabi in 1887, *Marah labid* is still available in the Middle East and remains popular as an intermediate-level work in religious schools in many regions of Malaysia and Indonesia. His Arabic style is fluent and lucid, and the great scholar, Fakhr al-Dīn al-Rāzī's (d.1210) *Mafatih al-ghayb* is among his primary authorities. The work is accordingly rich in its spirituality and the sheer humanistic values that it expresses. It is also worth drawing attention to a large (thousand-page) commentary on al-Ghazali's *Minhaj al-ʿabidin ila jannat rabb al-ʿalamin* by an East Javanese scholar from the region of Kediri, recently republished in Surabaya. In addition to such major works, there are hundreds of minor ones issuing from Arabic printing presses scattered over Sumatra, Java, the Malay Peninsula, and Borneo, where both private and state supported *madrasah* abound.

Al-Afghānī ʿAbduh and the reformist movement. It was these same networks that were to bring the reformist movement inspired by Jamāl al-Dīn al-Afghānī and Muḥammad ʿAbduh from the Middle East to Sumatra, Java, and the

Malay Peninsula, to be diffused from there to southern Thailand, and paradoxically, from Hadrami communities in Java back to southern Arabia.

It soon fecundated a vigorous counterpart in Southeast Asia. In particular, students from the Malay world in the Middle East, especially those studying at al-Azhar University in Cairo, were inspired by ʿAbduh, Rashīd Riḍā, and their followers, and as they returned to Malaya and the Indies, they carried the new ideas with them. It coincided with a growing sense of national identity and resentment to Dutch and British rule. ʿAbduh's reformist program was based on four main points: the purification of Islam from corrupting influences and practices; the reformation of Muslim education; the reformation of Islamic doctrine in the light of modern thought; and the defence of Islam. The establishment of the reformist journal *Al-manār* (The lighthouse), published between 1898 and 1936 under the editorship of ʿAbduh and later that of Rashīd Riḍā, directly inspired two counterparts in the Malay world. *Al-imām* (The imām), published in Singapore between 1906 and 1908, transmitted the views of *Al-manār* and ʿAbduh's earlier journal, *Al-ʿurwah al-wuthqā* (The indissoluble bond), and published translations of their articles into Malay. Its layout followed that of *Al-manār*. *Al-munīr* (Illumination), established in the major West Sumatran port town of Padang, was published between 1911 and 1916; it too referred regularly to *Al-manār* and published translations from the Egyptian journal.

Al-manār in turn reflected the interest that it generated in Southeast Asia: from the very year of its founding, it included articles, in Arabic, either written by Southeast Asian Muslims studying in Cairo or contributed by *ʿulamāʾ* from a wide range of places in the Indies, including Singapore, Batavia, Malang, Palembang, Surabaya, and Sambas (Borneo), some on a range of Southeast Asia–related topic. An 1898 article, for example, reports on a request by some Javanese Muslims to the Dutch colonial government for them to be allowed to acquire Ottoman citizenship; other articles address complaints of Dutch harassment of Muslims, problems of marriages between *sayyids* (the Muslim elite) and Muslim commoners, and the humiliations of quarantine regulations imposed on Muslims making the pilgrimage. A 1909 article from Palembang tells how *Al-manār* had inspired the Muslims of the region to form associations and financial unions to support Islamic schools to teach Arabic, the religious disciplines, and secular subjects. Two years later, another interesting entry praises the periodical for creating an intellectual movement among Muslims and describes how a school director had been inspired by *Al-manār* to introduce the Berlitz method of teaching foreign languages in his school. A 1930 communication from Sambas was particularly important, for it requested Rashīd Riḍā to put to the famous writer Shakīb Arslān certain questions relating to reasons for the backwardness of Muslims and the progress of other peoples. The response to this request, first published in three parts in *Al-manār,* was to become Arslān's well-known book *Limādhā taʾakhkhara al-Muslimūn wa-taqaddama al-ākharūn* (Why do the Muslims lag behind and the others progress?), which was in due course to be translated into Malay. The episode is important because it indicates the seriousness and care of the response of Egyptian scholars to the queries and difficulties of their Southeast Asian coreligionists.

The educational dimension of the reform program quickly made itself felt. Here a few examples will suffice. The work of To'Kenali (1866–1933), a scholar from Kelantan, an east-coast state of the Malay Peninsula, is representative of many, including some who became famous in Patani and Cambodia (Kampuchea) at the turn of the century. He went to Mecca at the age of twenty and stayed in the Middle East for twenty-two years before returning to Kelantan in 1908. In 1903 he traveled to Egypt to visit al-Azhar and other educational institutions. It is possible that he met ʿAbduh on this occasion. There is no doubt, however, that he had absorbed the educational ideals of the movement. He quickly became famous as a teacher was appointed assistant to the *muftī* in Kelantan with responsibility for Islamic education in the state, and set up a network of schools. He introduced Malay textbooks in religious knowledge and devised a system of graded instruction in Arabic grammar. Indeed, one of his students (born in Mecca of Malay parents in 1895), on returning to Kelantan in 1910, was inspired by him to compile an Arabic-Malay dictionary with entries and definitions in part based on the famous and widely respected Lebanese Arabic-Arabic dictionary *Al-munjid.* His work was first published in 1927, and is still available.

The reform, however, was reflected not only in textbooks, but also in classroom organization. The traditional method of teaching was known as the *ḥalaqah* ("study circle"), where students, irrespective of age, would sit in a circle around the teacher, who would present material to be learned by rote. The introduction of the classroom method, where the students sat in rows and used graded texts, together with the encouragement of active class participation, was a remarkable change of style. No less remarkable was the inclusion of secular subjects in the curriculum. Schools inspired by the reform movement multiplied in various parts of the archipelago, sometimes identified with individuals, sometimes initiated within the framework of an organization. Many sprang up and disappeared like mushrooms.

Of those founded by individuals, one that became important was the Sumatra Thawalib school founded in 1918. Another was the Sekolah Diniyah Putri in Padang Panjang, a religious school for girls founded in 1921 by a woman named Rahmah al-Yunusiyah. Designed to train students in the basic rules and practices of Islam and in the understanding of the principles and applications of Islamic law, particularly in matters of special concern to women, the school also set out to give girls an education in those matters that would enable them to run their homes efficiently and care for the health and education of their children. While from one

COMMERCE OF IMAGES

Although certain definitions of religion would like to portray worship and the contemplative life as devoid of anything so profane or secular as commerce, in fact, work, trade, and religion are often inseparable, and can even be indistinguishable. And no religion is without fundamental economic aspects. If commerce is broadly understood as any system of exchange in which goods, services, or capital act as a medium of human relations, it is not difficult to see how commerce also characterizes much religious behavior. Human traffic with the divine may be described as a commerce of sorts, and often precisely as a system of exchange in which human beings barter for goods and services that will enhance their lives. Images are often the coin by which the metaphysical economy of exchange is conducted with the gods or divine forces whose benefits may be acquired by the expenditure of moral or spiritual capital betokened by the image. In other cases, images promote or facilitate consumption that is infused with religious meaning.

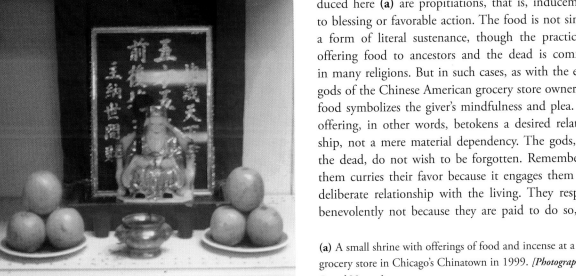

(a) A small shrine with offerings of food and incense at a grocery store in Chicago's Chinatown in 1999. *[Photograph by David Morgan]*

The food and incense offered to earth gods by a Chicago Chinatown grocer in the small shrine reproduced here **(a)** are propitiations, that is, inducements to blessing or favorable action. The food is not simply a form of literal sustenance, though the practice of offering food to ancestors and the dead is common in many religions. But in such cases, as with the earth gods of the Chinese American grocery store owner, the food symbolizes the giver's mindfulness and plea. The offering, in other words, betokens a desired relationship, not a mere material dependency. The gods, like the dead, do not wish to be forgotten. Remembering them curries their favor because it engages them in a deliberate relationship with the living. They respond benevolently not because they are paid to do so, but

(b) **Above.** Nineteenth-century ex-votos for the Virgin Mary on a church wall in Vilsbiburg, Germany. *[©José F. Poblete/Corbis]* (c) **Right.** Wooden prayer tablets with requests for favors from the gods for sale at a Shintō shrine in Kyoto, Japan. *[©Catherine Karnow/Corbis]*

out of their sense of gratitude to the human recognition of their needs or because of the respect they are due. Such an economy humanizes the otherwise unpredictable power of the divine. A world in which the devout can engage the divine in acts of civility is a world less hostile and inhumane. The earth gods invoked by the grocer's shrine respond by promoting the sale of food in a way that parallels their propitiation in rural China, where they could assist good harvests.

The practice of displaying thanks for healings and deliverance or posting petitions for such blessings is familiar in Roman Catholicism and Shintō. Small paintings **(b)** are commissioned and displayed in cathedrals by those who wish to thank the Mother of God for her intervention in difficult circumstances. Public displays of this visual form of thanks are an essential part of the ritual since they are a kind of reciprocation that recognizes the Virgin's benevolence. Catholic women often post their petitions and thanks to Saint Jude at his shrines or in shrine publications as part of seeking his assistance in overcoming obstacles. Shintō pilgrims who visit shrines and holy places, such as mountains in Japan, display their petitions on pieces of wood purchased and then deposited at the shrines **(c)**.

In the later Middle Ages in Europe, Christians were able to procure time off from extended stays in purgatory for themselves or dead loved ones by purchasing indulgences, which were delivered as tokens on paper **(d)**. Letters of indulgence were drawn up by ecclesiastical authorities and awarded to particular churches or religious orders, authorizing the sale of indulgences to those who visited shrines or churches where they might venerate relics or images and offer prayers. Indulgences were often associated with pilgrimage churches and offered lucrative benefits to the towns, orders, bishoprics, and the Vatican. Images and medallions were sold at pilgrimage sites as tokens of pilgrimage and as devotional items that were used in prayer and even enshrined for devotion afterward. Sales at religious festivals helped ensure local artisans of income and boosted local economies, as well as church coffers **(e)**.

(d) Right. A sixteenth-century woodcut flyer advertises indulgences to be purchased from John Tetzel, an indulgence seller. *[©Bettmann/Corbis]* **(e) Below.** Jörg Breu the Elder, *Sale of Indulgences*, c. 1530, woodcut. *[©Art Resource, N.Y.]*

Festivals such as Ramaḍān, Ro'sh ha-Shanah, Christmas, and Easter are commonly celebrated the world over by the sale of all manner of decorations **(f)**. Muslims, like their Christian and Jewish counterparts, purchase inexpensive, brightly decorated items for domestic display **(g)**. These objects are often mass-produced, but typically recall premodern forms of craft and handmade production. Highly decorative, they incorporate explicitly religious symbols and motifs that will encourage ritual mindfulness during the festival and support rituals of gifting that

(f) **Top.** Ramaḍān decorations for sale in 2003 in Beirut, Lebanon. *[AP/Wide World Photos]* **(g)** **Left.** A decoupage calligram by an unknown artist of a figure at prayer. This popular image can be found in the homes of many pious Muslims. *[UCLA Fowler Museum of Cultural History; photograph by Don Cole]*

are common on the occasions of such holy days. Even daily devotional life finds a hearty place for artistic goods, as seen in two different African religious marketplaces, which show an Ethiopian Orthodox priest and lay persons patronizing image peddlers outside of a temple in Addis Ababa **(h)** and two Muslim men in front of a vendor's glass painting display in Dakar, Senegal **(i)**. Consumption, therefore, is a familiar form of religious observance. Religious practices such as Vodou, which are perhaps most commonly experienced as forms of problem-solving by practitioners, rely on proprietors who create the material

(h) Top. Religious images for sale near an Ethiopian Orthodox Church compound in Addis Ababa in 1999. *[Photograph by David Morgan]* **(i)** Right. Senegalese men view images of Ṣūfī leaders and tourist themes for sale in 2001 in Dakar. *[UCLA Fowler Museum of Cultural History; photograph by Lynne K. Brodhead]*

(j) **Top.** Two Haitian merchants display Vodou items for sale in the Iron Market in Port-au-Prince in 1994. *[Photograph by Doran Ross]* **(k) Above.** The *Colporteur on his Rounds*, an illustration from *The Sunday at Home* (vol. 8, no. 345, December 6, 1860, page 776). *[Courtesy of the Billy Graham Center Museum, Wheaton, Ill.]*

culture of liturgy, ritual action, and petition that priests and laity purchase in commercial shops for later use **(j)**.

Religion is market-friendly even among those traditions that criticize and seek to reform certain economic practices. By challenging and ultimately subverting the metaphysical economy of indulgences used among Roman Catholics, the renegade monk Martin Luther and the Reformation he led and inspired replaced it with an alternative economic system of belief. Arguing that God himself provided the means of redemption in a theology of substitutionary atonement, in which the debt of sin was paid for by the sacrificial blood of Christ's death, Luther rejected the believer's dependence on an economic relationship with the divine that was mediated by the ecclesiastical hierarchy.

Inspired by the success of Luther's use of print and the commercial viability of print production, Protestants formed tract and bible societies that published and distributed materials domestically and internationally, often as the cornerstone of their mission outreach **(k)**. In effect, Protestantism tended to transform faith into the affirmation of a message that was inexpensively circulated on a vast scale as mass-produced information or "news." These printed items were often illustrated, since images both attracted consumers and effectively condensed information into economically viable forms of advertisement.

Advertisement was understood as a form of evangelism, as the mural painted by an evangelical sign painter in Los Angeles **(l)** clearly shows. The pithy, attention-grabbing image was accompanied by the richly visual language of the Bible to deliver its urgent message in a direct way.

The very efficacy of Protestantism's use of imagery in mass-produced media during the nineteenth and twentieth centuries encouraged the exploitation of biblical narrative as a form of mass entertainment. Cecil B. De Mille's sensational portrayal of the life of Moses in *The Ten Commandments* (1956) was not only a box office hit in the United States, but in several countries. The promotional poster reproduced here **(m)** advertised the film to Japanese viewers in a way that capitalized on the star power and charisma of the Hollywood commodities of celebrity and extravaganza.

Making work and religion indistinguishable is not a peculiarly Protestant habit. Islam anticipated the integration of work and belief by centuries. This is perhaps most assiduously practiced by the Mourides, a Senegalese Ṣūfī ethnic group that regards work as a spiritual practice par excellence. This attitude is strongly conveyed by the

(l) ABOVE. *Mire of Sin*, a mural by John B. D. at the Emmanuel Baptist Rescue Mission in Los Angeles. *[©Camilo José Vergara, reproduced by permission.]* **(m)** LEFT. A Japanese poster advertising Cecil B. De Mille's 1956 film *The Ten Commandments. [Courtesy of the Billy Graham Center Museum, Wheaton, Ill.]*

(n) An image of Amadou Bamba, a Mouride saint, on the wall of a hubcap shop in Dakar, Senegal, in 1994. *[Photograph by Mary N. Roberts and Allen F. Roberts]*

intermingling of the portrait of the Mouride saint, Amadou Bamba, on a wall of a hubcap shop in Dakar **(n)**. Buying hubcaps at this store promises a special blessing to devout consumers. For Muslims and Christians, business is an ideal medium for religious practice because it carries belief into the heart of the daily world, infusing the most mundane acts with a transcendent significance.

Bibliography

Andersson, Christiane, and Charles Talbot, eds. *From a Mighty Fortress: Prints, Drawings, and Books in the Age of Luther, 1483–1546.* Detroit, 1983.

Cosentino, Donald J. *Vodou Things: The Art of Pierrot Barra and Marie Cassaise.* Jackson, Miss., 1998.

Morgan, David. *Protestants and Pictures: Religion, Visual Culture, and the Age of American Mass Production.* New York, 1999.

Orsi, Robert A. *Thank You, St. Jude: Women's Devotion to the Patron Saint of Hopeless Causes.* New Haven, 1996.

Roberts, Allen F., and Mary Nooter Roberts. *A Saint in the City: Ṣūfī Arts of Urban Senegal.* Los Angeles, 2003.

Zarur, Elizabeth Netto Calil, and Charles Muir Lovell, eds. *Art and Faith in Mexico: The Nineteenth-Century Retablo Tradition.* Albuquerque, N. Mex., 2001.

David Morgan (2005)

standpoint the discipline of the institution was strict and the scope for individual development narrow, it won the confidence of isolated village communities, and in fact, its students gained wider horizons than those girls who remained in the interior. In fact it played an important role in advancing the status and self-respect of women in the community.

This school was, in fact, a strikingly original institution (and was to inspire the founding of the Kullīyat al-Banāt within al-Azhar in 1957). Yet it was based on simple premises: a universalistic presentation of Islamic teaching in combination with secular subjects—history, geography, bookkeeping, domestic science and the like—and the founder's determination to establish an institution that would present itself in every respect as an alternative to the Dutch system, from curriculum to the yearly cycle of festivals and the Islamic calendar (Friday was the day off) to student dress. It guarded its independence and refused offers of subsidy from the Dutch government. It still flourishes today and during the 1930s had branches in Java and the Malay Peninsula.

The Muhammadiyah. The most famous and long-lived of all socioreligious reformist movements in the Indies was the Muhammadiyah, founded in 1912 in Yogyakarta (Central Java) by Kiai H. A. Dahlan. At first it was an exclusively male organization, but before long it had as an affiliate a parallel women's organization called ʿAʾisyiyah, through which women could play an independent role in furthering its ideals. These included improving the basic observance of the norms of Islamic life, and a vigorous dedication to *tabligh* (religious instruction). But its goals went further than this. The organization was determined to propagate the ideas of the reformists concerning the purification of Islam from traditional accretions, in particular from the animistic beliefs that were so much part of the world view of the Javanese peasantry, and from the religious attitudes and values of the upper classes, for whom the Hindu-Buddhist traditions of the pre-Islamic period—traditions embodied in the Javanese shadow theater—were still very much alive. A special target for attack was the cult of saints' tombs.

The organization consciously adopted the institutional structures of the Dutch, and its members made a careful study of the techniques of Christian missionary organizations. Carrying on vigorous missionary activities, it expanded into journalism and publishing and established mosques, religious endowments, orphanages, and clinics. But its central role was in education, where it set up an entire system from primary school to teacher training colleges. Like Toʾ Kenali in Kelantan on the Malay Peninsula, the Muhammadiyah together with ʿAʾisyiyah carried on the impulse generated by Muḥammad ʿAbduh to reform the traditional Islamic educational system—by grading teaching materials and classes, by sitting students at desks faced by teachers with blackboards, and by assessing their progress with formal examinations and the award of individual marks that determined when they could move from one grade to the next.

The Muhammadiyah's strict and responsible methods of organization and financial management ensured its stability, and by the 1930s it had established branches as far afield as North, Central, and South Sumatra, Borneo, and Sulawesi, thus taking on a protonational character.

Another aspect of the reformist movement was its campaign against the Ṣūfī *ṭarīqah.* For the reformers the *ṭarīqah* represented the one element in traditional Islam that most contributed to the backwardness of Muslims and the lack of respect they had in the world. They held that the *ṭarīqah* promoted a passive otherworldliness, that it discouraged initiative, and that the dedication to the *shaykh,* the head of the branch, overshadowed devotion to the Prophet and God himself. In addition, the ascetic exercises of members and their fondness for reciting sacred formulas were considered intellectually harmful, often paving the way for the absorption of non-Islamic practices. In short, the reformists took over and applied all the arguments marshaled against the *ṭarīqah* by the *Al-manār* tradition. There is a reasonable documentation of debates between the two sides on the issue. Conventional wisdom is that the Ṣūfī orders in the Dutch East Indies, were almost a spent force by the 1930s, with their followers to be found only in the remoter rural areas. Rumors of their demise have long been exaggerated, often by the Reformists. Certainly on the Malay Peninsula they continued to fare well, and maintained a social role there, as they still do. Indeed, one of the leading figures of religious reform and revival in Kelantan was Wan Musa, who, when he studied in Mecca with his father, was introduced to the theosophy of Muḥyī al-Dīn ibn al-ʿArabī and inducted into the Shādhilīyah *ṭarīqah.* He introduced the reforms of ʿAbduh and Rashīd Riḍā into Kelantan and rejected *taqlīd,* or unquestioning acceptance of precedent, yet defended the institutional role of the *ṭarīqah* and preserved the content of Ṣūfī doctrine, stressing in his instruction the role of intellect, intuition, and emotion.

Some idea of the continuing role of the Indonesian *ṭarīqah* at a public level by 1955 can be gained from the fact that an attempt to obtain representation for these movements in the national parliament at the first general election resulted in the election of one member, a Naqshbandī. This, of course, is not necessarily an index of the relative strength of *ṭarīqah,* only that many *ṭarīqah* members did not see the national parliament as an appropriate forum for *ṭarīqah* activity.

The Nahdlatul Ulama. The Reformist movement as represented by Muhammadiyah (today an estimated membership of 20,000) and other organizations did not go unchallenged, and there has been a tendency to exaggerate its successes. The traditionalists had their own support base and intellectual resources. They too developed their own organizations in response to the challenge presented by the reformists. Of them, the most important was the Nahdlatul Ulama (lit., "revival of the *ʿulamāʾ*"), founded in 1926, which is today (2003) the largest religious organization in Indonesia with an estimated membership of thirty million, It stood for the traditional role of the *'ulamā'*. It accepted the realities of development and history, and was tolerant of many of the religious practices in religious life that the Reformists condemned. Thus it opposed the puritanical neo-Hanbalism implicit in the Reformists' reliance on the Qur'ān and *sunnah* alone. One of its basic principles was the requirement to adhere to one or another of the four schools of law as the basis for the application of *fiqh*, and in Indonesia this meant, in practice, the Shāfi'i school. Although defense of the *ṭarīqah* was not a formal part of its program, in practice, as a result of its cultural tolerance, it did so, and provided a wide space for the mystical tradition.

The Japanese interregnum and beyond. By the end of the 1930s there was a rich and diverse tapestry of Islamic thought, activity and aspiration in the region, although under colonial rule, these did not have a high profile, nor any direct or decisive role in government. The Japanese occupation hastened the development of national self-awareness and laid the groundwork for the organization and development of movements that would undermine attempts to restore colonial authority after the war. This was to have implications for the role of Islamic movements in the newly independent states of Indonesia (proclaimed August 17, 1945) and Malaya (established 1957, becoming the Federation of Malaysia in 1963). In each of these nations there have been differences in the articulation of Islamic movements, and hence a different story that continues in progress.

Malaysia. The current dominant political party at the national level, is the United Malay National Organisation, generally identified by its acronym UMNO. It was founded in 1946 in the wake of British constitutional proposals for the territory after the Japanese surrender.

In Malaya (after 1963 Malaysia), up to the time of independence in 1957 religious parties did not have a high political profile: to be a Malay is, by definition, to be a Muslim, to live by Malay custom, and to speak the Malay language. At this time the Malays comprised little more than half the total population of the territory they shared with Chinese and Indians. Their urban presence and participation in economic was limited. They could only manifest their identity in the persons and ceremonial role of the sultans of the nine states on the peninsula and in the profession of Islam. The situation was one in which in which the Malay language and even survival of the Malay race was at stake. At first there was little scope for a competing religious party. In any case, to be a Malay was to be a Muslim, and the sultans were the ultimate authorities over religion and Malay custom in their states. Nevertheless, a dedicated religious party was founded in 1951, the Pan-Malayan Islamic Party (PMIP). Its concern was that the constitution of an independent Malaya be built on Islamic structures and institutions. At this stage it had little direct influence on the outcome of policy, and in 1957, Malay became essentially a secular state, with Islam as the national religion, and thus part of the state structure, but with guarantees of freedom for other religions. Race riots in 1969 resulted in the declaration of a state of emergency. Constitutional rule was restored in 1971 with the swearing in of a National Front coalition government, in which the PMIP took part. In 1973 it changed its name to Partai Islam Se-Malaysia (PAS), and in 1977 was forced to withdraw from the National Front government. PAS was from then on an opposition party, its program based on a radical Islamization of the nation. Its influence has since waxed and waned. In the wake of the economic crisis of the 1990s and the dismissal and imprisonment of the deputy prime minister Anwar Ibrahim in 1998, it drew a significant measure of the support of Malay voters away from UMNO. It is however more important than its parliamentary representation at the national level suggests. On the one hand it functions as a kind of Islamic ginger group. By claiming to be more Islamic than UMNO, it can impel UMNO towards more Islamic policies at the national level. But more seriously, it has a significant influence at state level, and the lines between federal and state authority are not clearly drawn. PAS currently holds power in the two northern states of Kelantan and Trengganu, and has influence in a number of others. It urges a full implementation of Islamic law, and is concerned with the active promotion of what is deemed good, and the prohibition of evil. The result is that at state level aspects of what is deemed to be Islamic law is imposed on Muslims: the sale of alcohol banned, social relations between the sexes restricted, and offences such as taking food during the daylight hours of the month of Ramaḍān, or failing to attend the Friday prayer are punishable by religious courts. Malay translations of the Bible are not allowed to include words such as *Allāh, imān* and *rasūl* that are deemed to be Islamically specific. A high profile is accorded to Islam in the way the nation presents itself to the world, although not much more than 50 percent of the population is Muslim. Considerable funds from the public purse are devoted to *da'wa*, which can be understood as presenting Islam to the non-Muslim population, or making those who are Muslims better Muslims, or both. By these means, the government is trying to cut the ground from under the feet of radicals. At the same time it is supporting programs that inculcate a broader understanding of religion. There are sophisticated programs in Islamic studies at university level, and in 1983 was founded the International Islamic University it Kuala Lumpur. It has established itself as a high quality institution with faculties across the disciplines alongside Islamic revealed knowledge and human sciences, Arabic, *fiqh* and *uṣūl al-fiqh*. It has a highly trained and internationally qualified staff, and over ten thousand students. Languages of instruction are Arabic and English.

Indonesia. The role of Islam and Islamic movements in postcolonial Indonesia has been far more directly involved in the political process, on a far greater scale, and at times to much greater dramatic effect. With the Japanese occupation, all Muslim associations were dissolved and then reconstituted into an umbrella organization encompassing both reformists and traditionalists, the Majlis Shura Muslimin Indonesia, or Consultative Assembly of Indonesian Muslims, known widely by its acronym Masyumi. After the war, the organization broke up into two main wings: the one that kept the name Masyumi became the political wing of the reformist movement and drew most of its strength from Sumatra and the large towns in Java, while the other, Nahdlatul Ulama, now took a public role as a political party and derived most of its strength from the rural areas of East Java. An index to the standing of the parties, and therefore the distribution of attitudes, is furnished by the results of the 1955 elections, in which the Masyumi won 57 seats and the Nahdlatul Ulama won 45 out of a total of more than 250. Even taking into account the seats held by minor religious parties, this meant that more than half of the Muslim electorate had cast its vote for nonreligious parties.

With the proclamation of Indonesian independence on August 17, 1945, two days after the Japanese surrender, and with the transfer of sovereignty by the Dutch in 1950, Muslim groups exerted considerable pressure to have Indonesia declared an Islamic state, with the provisions of Muslim law binding on Muslims.

It was only after long and bitter debates between religious factions and the secular nationalists in the few months prior to the Japanese surrender that a compromise was reached, and the Pancasila ("five pillars"), a set of five principles formulated by Sukarno, first president of the republic, were with certain qualifications accepted as the basis of the new state. Since the first of these principles was belief in one God, this formula made Indonesia a nonconfessional state without making it a secular one. A corollary of this charter was the establishment of a ministry of religion early in the republic's history. This ministry was to take care of the needs and interests of every religious community in the country (although later there were to be difficulties as to the terms under which the Hindu Balinese and the Javanese mystical groups might be included within its terms of reference).

Religious revolts. The compromise, however, did not last long. After the proclamation of independence, the secular nationalists dropped the references to the position of Islam in the state agreed to in it. For the hard-line Muslims, this was a confirmation of their worst fears. The disillusion and bitterness generated on the Muslim side led to three major risings against the republican government. The first and most dangerous broke out before independence from the Dutch had been secured. After several months of guerrilla activity, Kartosuwirjo (1923–1962), a former medical student, proclaimed the establishment of the Islamic state of Indonesia on August 7, 1949, in the mountainous regions of West Java and was inaugurated as *imām* of the state. He and his movement conducted a guerrilla war, the Darul Islam revolt, against the government until 1962, when Kartosuwirjo was captured, and he and five of his associates were executed. The movement, while at first idealistic and attracting at least tacit support among some members of the Muslim political parties, gradually degenerated into a terrorist group that caused great human and material damage over West Java for more than ten years. It plundered and destroyed farms and peasant holdings to get financial resources and was behind several attempts to assassinate President Sukarno.

Two other major religious revolts inspired by the ideal of making Indonesia an Islamic state and realizing in it a *dār al-Islām* (Arab., "abode of Islam"; Indon., *darul Islam*) were to break out. One was on the island of Sulawesi in 1952, with the leader of the movement, Kahar Muzakkar, accepting a commission from Kartosuwirjo in West Java as commander of the fourth division of the Islamic army of Indonesia. With varying levels of success he managed to maintain his movement until early 1965, when he was encircled and shot by republican forces. The other revolt, in late 1953, was led by Daud Beureu'eh in Aceh, a region already referred to on several occasions for the strength of its Islamic traditions. This rising too was associated with the West Javanese movement. Daud Beureu'eh proclaimed an Islamic state of Aceh and styled himself "Commander of the Faithful" (Amīr al-Mu'minīn, the historic title of the Muslim caliphs), but after nine years of struggle he made his peace with the central government in 1962. The details of these struggles belong more to political history than to that of Islam. It is important to observe, however, that these three very serious uprisings, costly in human lives and property, were put down by Muslim soldiers under a Muslim president of a national state based on an ideology, the Pancasila, that did not recognize exclusive claims on the part of any one religious tradition. Also that radical Islam on such a scale made its debut in Southeast Asia many years before the Iranian revolution.

Islamic policies in opposition. On a predominantly political level, the years between 1950 and 1965 saw continued but decreasingly successful efforts by the Muslim parties to gain by political means the power required to make Indonesia an Islamic state. They were never sufficiently strong to outnumber or wily enough to outmaneuver the alliance between the "secular" nationalists and the radical left-wing parties. In the last resort they could claim loyalty to the Indonesian state by recognizing the Pancasila as the state ideology. And this they did by claiming that only Islamic theology could supply an adequate content to the first of these five principles: belief in one God.

The elimination of Sukarno as a political force in 1965 in the wake of an attempted communist coup, and the destruction of the Communist Party, led to a revival of Muslim expectations of a positive Islamic stance in government. These expectations were again disappointed, although Muslim mass action had one spectacular success in blocking a proposed marriage law which would have undercut the authority of religious courts, and allowed civil marriage in 1973. The position of the Suharto government was that Islam had no place in politics. Its role was spiritual and cultural, and in the political arena it represented as much a danger to the integrity of the state as had the Communist Party. In 1973 the number of parties eligible to contest parliamentary elections was reduced to four, and none was permitted to campaign in the name of a religion, or to use religious symbols, such as the Crescent Moon, or the Kaʿbah. Toward the end of the decade, the government began to insist that every organization within the state accepted the Pancasila as its sole ideological foundation, and in 1984 the Nahdlatul Ulama—now a social religious and not a political body, accepted this stipulation.

During the 1980s, the former Muslim parties though in secular garb were able to provide a significant measure of dissent to the increasingly authoritarian and corrupt Suharto government. If, during the 1950s their goal had been Indonesia as an Islamic state, their role now was to raise a voice of protest against corruption, secularism, consumerism, and the excesses of an open economy. At the same time the Islamic resurgence and ferment that began with the Arab-Israel war in 1973 and shifted in high gear with the Iranian revolution, did not bypass Southeast Asia.

In Malaysia there have been waves of Islamic enthusiasm since the early 1970s, and there is considerable pressure to Islamize life in the country. This has taken the form of moves to introduce Islamic banking; promulgation of rules for social behavior, especially in the form of *khalwat* laws, which prohibit situations of "suspicious proximity" between the sexes. There was a heightened concern that all products handled should be *ḥalāl*, not just those concerned with food. Often Malays were reluctant to eat in non-Muslim households in case non-*ḥalāl* material had touched the crockery. Such concerns resulted in conditions being imposed on the handling and selling of pork that virtually excluded it from the menus of international hotels.

People thus were becoming aware of their Muslim heritage and identity. Increasingly women wore the Islamic head-covering. There was a growing preoccupation with the observance of the prayer times and the Ramaḍān fast. Islamic schools saw a surge in enrollments, and Islamic symbols and motifs were used even in the commercial advertising of everyday products.

During this period observers have noted a marked increase in religious fervor. This is particularly evident in the university campuses and among civil servants: it is reflected in the observance of daily prayers and the fast, in the numbers of Muslims making the pilgrimage to Mecca, and in women's dress. In addition, various religious associations have sprung up, all dedicated to spreading Islamic teachings, but with different emphases.

In response to this developing situation, President Suharto, in Riddell's phrase, became a born-again Muslim. He made the pilgrimage with a fanfare of publicity in 1991. He presided over the establishment of a state Islamic Bank, and the launch of a government sponsored Islamic newspaper, *Republika*. The vice-president, B. J. Habibie played a major role in founding the Indonesian Association of Muslim Intellectuals (ICMI), designed to develop a sophisticated and modern understanding and practice of Islam among professionally qualified people.

These attempts to harness a growing commitment to Islam were not sufficient to save Suharto from a groundswell of discontent. In 1998 he was forced to resign. The then vice-president (Habibie) succeeded him, and one of his first decisions was to permit the formation of new political parties. Ninety were formed, of which twenty-nine were Islamic based (although not all qualified to stand for election). When general elections were held the following year, secular parties gained 58.3 percent of the vote, and the five principal Islamic based parties, 38.5 percent. And of the Islamic parties contesting the election, only three, representing no more than 14.5 percent of the electorate, had Indonesia as an Islamic state as part of their program. In the wake of these elections, Abdurrahman Wahid, a former leader of the Nahdlatul Ulama was appointed president, and Megawati Sukarno Putri of a secular party became vice president. In 2001, Abdurrahman Wahid was impeached. Sukarno Putri thereupon became president, and Hamzah Haz, leader of the other major Islamic party became vice president.

At a macro-level, the most striking result of this election is the drop in support for the idea of an Islamic state. In 1955, the two principal parties campaigning on the program of an Islamic state gained around 42 percent of the vote. In 1999, those in favor of an Islamic state gained around 14.5 percent. In light of the high profile of Islamic radicals in the region, these figures are significant. Relatively few Indonesian Muslims support Islamic political movements. The majority is content to live and work within the status quo, Javanese dominated though it is, and with Islamic styles of behavior and forms of worship tacitly accepted as religious norm of social life.

CONCLUSION. In a sense, no conclusion is possible, for the story is open-ended. An account of such events at what one might call the macro-level gives very little sense of Islam as it is lived, its dynamics, values, aspirations, frustrations, and the challenges it faces in a rapidly changing world among the Muslims of the region. Among them is great variety, and a wide range of emphases.

To the superficial observer, there is at first sight little outward evidence of Southeast Asia's widespread Islamic allegiance. There is little of the exuberant architecture that so characterizes Muslim civilization in South and West Asia. Traditional forms of music and the dance, styles of dress, social structures, systems of inheritance, and personal and family law all suggest a complex of cultures that owes little to Islam. Observers coming from the Middle East, taking as a norm outward manifestations of Islam in the Arab world, where so much that was local custom at the time of the Prophet is now inseparable from the Islamic tradition, may be perplexed at the variety and distinctiveness of Southeast Asian Islam. They may even regard much of what they see there as non-Islamic, forgetting that in the early years of Islam, much in Middle Eastern culture was non-Islamic, but with the passage of time was transmuted and given an Islamic meaning and identity.

In each of the nation-states of the region, Islam has a different profile. In Thailand, it is represented by a minority, ethnically Thai, but in general geographically limited to the southeast of the country. In Malaysia Muslims are today up to 60 percent of the population. Islam is to a high degree an emblem of Malay ethnicity and Malay kingship. To be a Malay is to be a Muslim, and it is through their profession of Islam that the Malays define their identity in relation to other races in their multiracial nation, notably the Chinese. In Singapore, Muslims are a small minority in what is essentially a Chinese state, and almost all are ethnically Malay. In Indonesia, Muslims are an overwhelming majority, almost 90 percent of the population, but are distributed among a variety of (related) ethnicities which while having an individual ethnic region as a point of origin, are widely dispersed, and share in taking part in national civic life on equal terms in the professions and the instrumentalities of government. In the Philippines, Muslims are a minority, largely defined by ethnicity, and geographically concentrated in the south.

For the great majority of Muslims in all these regions, being a Muslim is as natural, as unreflective as breathing, whether a particular community places a high or low value on external observances such as the fast and the ritual prayer and whatever the regional observances it chooses to decorate and enhance its Islamic practice at rites of passage. Religion then has to do primarily with personal devotion, morality, and events in the life cycle. To the superficial observer, many of the Javanese peasantry, for example, might not appear to be Muslims at all. Yet relatively few claim exclusive allegiance either to Buddhism, which is enjoying a revival, or to the mystical sects. For the great majority, what perception they have of transcendence is of Islamic transcendence. Even if this is the limit of their commitment, it is sufficient for them to be identified as Muslims.

The governments of both Malaysia and Indonesia have invested a great deal of effort and funding in Islamization projects, projects designed to raise the level of Islamic consciousness, and strengthen belief and practice within the framework of constitutional government and civil administration. In so doing, they are attempting to cut the ground from under the feet of the Muslim radicals for whom any formal recognition of religious pluralism is anathema. The inevitable result is that despite good intentions, non-Muslim religious communities, though tolerated and even respected, do not have the same right to present themselves in public life as have Muslims.

Islamic education at tertiary level has an important contribution to make. Reference has already been made to the International Islamic University in Kuala Lumpur. Indonesia has established IAIN (State Universities of Islamic Studies) in virtually every province which combine training in the religious disciplines with secular subjects. They are designed to produce graduates in Islamic law, education, and preaching, and to produce graduates with a well-rounded education qualified to serve in the various departments of religious administration in the public service.

Alongside the government system there is a large number of smaller institutions that teach in Arabic and graduate hundreds of students who travel overseas for higher learning; sometimes these students attend secular institutes in Australia, Britain, and Canada, for example, but of course they go more often to religious ones in India, Pakistan, Saudi Arabia, and Egypt. Indeed, students from Indonesia and Malaysia have a very high profile at al-Azhar in Cairo, and at the celebration of the millennium of al-Azhar in April 1983, Southeast Asian students were the most prominent community of foreigners studying at the institution, as indeed they are on the pilgrimage to Mecca. Nevertheless, the diffusion of graduates of these institutions is uneven, and there is a significant number of Muslim thinkers who have developed an intellectual interest in the role of religion in the modern world, outside of the traditional Islamic disciplines of *fiqh* and *kalām,* some under the influence of the minority Lahore Aḥmadiyah, who have a small presence in Indonesia.

Thus there is a deep reservoir of concern for and expertise in religious matters that study clubs, workshops and associations can draw on vigorously to debate religious issues. Such issues include the validity of traditional procedures of Qurʾān interpretation, the status of many of the positive prescriptions of *fiqh*, and the authority religious institutions should exercise in society. Riddell gives an account of these debates in *Islam and the Malay-Indonesian World.* Striking are the words of Abdurrahman Wahid, former president of Indonesia, speaking of why he declined to join ICMI, "As long as they think Islam is an ideology, then I will not participate. Islam is a way of life. Its adherents should follow it voluntarily, not needing any legislation from the state." There is however in the region as much as in the wider world of Islam a simmering cauldron of ideas on the realization and rethinking of Islam in the contemporary world, that has generated a baffling range of terms to designate various tendencies—traditionalists, modernists, neo-modernists, reformists without even coming to the usual catalogue of terms of abuse and mutual recrimination among such groups.

Events such as the September 11, 2001, outrages in the United States, the consequent American-led invasion of Afghanistan, the increasing bitterness between Israelis and Palestinians, the Bali bombing in October 2002, and finally the invasion of Iraq in 2003, have heightened the sensitivities of many exposed nerves among numbers of Muslims. In our region, as elsewhere, there are groups of radicals inspired by the ideas of Ḥasan al-Banna, founder of the Muslim Brotherhood, Mawdudi, and the writings of Sayyid Qutb—readily available in Indonesian/Malay translation.

The mentality exemplified by the Egyptian Takfir wa al-Hijra (Denounce and Abandon) groups, and in turn al-Qāʿidah, has its representatives in Southeast Asia. It is represented in the Jamaʾa Islamiyya (al-Jamaʿatuʾl-Islamiyya) associated with the Bali bombings in October 2002, itself an heir of the Darul Islam movement that terrorized large areas of Indonesia in the 1950s. It is expressed in the activities of the Abu Sayyaf movement in the Philippines, and likewise in the violence of the virtual civil war with Christians in the Moluccas, and the bombing of churches in different parts of the country in Christmas 2000.

The leaders of such fringe groups, with international backing, can draw on latent resentment at past wrongs, and the frustrations and despairs attending much of daily life in Indonesia, to create a turmoil, totally disproportionate to their numbers.

It is clear that virtually every movement in the Islamic world and every emphasis and school has found a counterpart in Southeast Asia alongside local responses to them. Even in the architecture of the mosque, there is a distinctive regional style alongside the domes and minarets and arched masonry imported from the Middle East: splendid timber structures with rising tiers of tapering hipped roofs supported on multiple columns. I have referred to the long tradition of local *ʿulamāʾ* settling as expatriates in the Middle East, either permanently or on a long-term basis. Indonesian and Malaysian Muslims have not gone to the Middle East only to study. Numbers of them have gone west as volunteers to fight for what they perceived as the defense of Islam, whether in Bosnia, Afghanistan, or Iraq. There is likewise the continuing tradition of *ʿulamāʾ* from the Middle East and South Asia becoming domiciled in Southeast Asia. There is a strength and vitality in Islamic life expressed in a wide range of religious perceptions and enthusiasms both at individual and community levels. The region is not simply a passive, partial and selective recipient of Islam. It has its traditionalists, it has its *jihadi* warriors, but also among its scholars are pioneers of new ways of acculturating Islam in the modern world and facing its challenges. Every issue is faced, not least those to do with the position of women in society. They are faced with an outspokenness and courage that would not be tolerated in many other areas of the Islamic world. How the balance of the various elements will shift for good or for ill in the years ahead is an unanswerable question. Whatever the future holds, Southeast Asia is a distinctive and vibrant cultural zone of the Islamic world, which in some areas gives leadership to it. Further consideration of it merely as a periphery of that world (sadly still fashionable in some quarters) should be put to rest.

SEE ALSO Acehnese Religion; Javanese Religion; Modernism, article on Islamic Modernism; Southeast Asian Religions, article on Insular Cultures; Ṭarīqah.

BIBLIOGRAPHY

Unfortunately no single basic work on Islam in Southeast Asia yet exists. What follows should serve as a guide to the general reader and not as an exhaustive list. For the historical context within which Islam plays its various roles in Southeast Asia, John Sturgus Bastin and Harry J. Benda's exquisitely written and lucid *A History of Modern Southeast Asia: Colonialism, Nationalism, and Decolonization* (Englewood Cliffs, N.J., 1968) makes sense of the region as a whole, from Burma to the Philippines. D. G. E. Hall's *A History of South-East Asia,* 4th ed. (London, 1981), is still the basic work for a historical survey of Southeast Asia as a whole from the earliest times up to 1950. A very useful source book is *Readings on Islam in Southeast Asia,* edited by Ahmad Ibrahim (Singapore, 1985). See also Barbara Andaya and Leonard Andaya's *A History of Malaysia* (London, 1982) and M. C. Ricklefs's *A History of Modern Indonesia, c. 1300 to the Present* (Bloomington, Ind., 1981).

The Modern Period

C. van Dijk's *Rebellion under the Banner of Islam: The Darul Islam in Indonesia* (The Hague, 1981) is an admirably lucid analysis of revolts against the republican government in Indonesia between 1950 and 1965 directed toward the transformation of the nation into an Islamic state. Clifford Geertz's *The Religion of Java* (Chicago, 1976) is a masterpiece of sensitive ethnographic description, despite its somewhat mechanistic division of Javanese society into Santri (Muslim), *abangan* (peasant), and Prijayi (aristocratic bureaucrat), and its lack of depth in understanding the historical context of Javanese religion. Peter G. Gowing's *Muslim Filipinos: Heritage and Horizon* (Quezon City, Philippines, 1979), an excellent survey of the Muslim communities in the Philippines from the earliest days up to the 1970s, has a particularly useful bibliography. *The Crescent in the East: Islam in Asia Major,* edited by Raphael Israeli (London, 1982), includes chapters on Islam in Burma, Malaysia, Thailand, Indonesia, and the Philippines. *Islam in Public Life,* edited by John L. Esposito (New York, 1986), includes chapters on Islam in public life in Malaysia and Indonesia that give a reasonable account of the state of play in each nation. See also B. J. Boland's *The Struggle of Islam in Modern Indonesia* (The Hague, 1982); G. W. J. Drewes's "Indonesia: Mysticism and Activism," in *Unity and Variety in Muslim Civilization,* edited by Gustave E. von Grunebaum (Chicago, 1955), pp. 284–310; my "An Islamic System or Islamic Values?: Nucleus of a Debate in Contemporary Indonesia," in *Islam and the Political Economy of Meaning: Comparative Studies in Muslim Discourse,* edited by W. R. Roff (Berkeley, 1986); and Astri Suhrke's "The Thai Muslims: Some Aspects of Minority Integration," *Pacific Affairs* 43 (Winter 1970–1971): 531–547.

Specialized Studies

S. Q. Fatimi's *Islam Comes to Malaysia* (Singapore, 1963) is a short, provocative, but delightfully written book that elaborates a role attributed to Ṣūfīs in the preaching of Islam in Southeast Asia, with a particularly interesting analysis of the inscribed pillar discovered at Phanrang. *Islam in South-East Asia,* edited by M. B. Hooker (Leiden, 1983), a collection of seven essays that add up to a fresh and vigorous approach to Islam in Southeast Asia, brings together perspectives derived from studies in ethnography, Islamic philosophy and law, and literature. Christiaan Snouck Hurgronje's *The Achehnese,* 2 vols., translated by A. W. S. O'Sullivan (Leiden, 1906), is a classic work of description of what from many aspects is the single most important Muslim community in Southeast Asia. *Islam in Asia,* vol. 2, *Southeast and East Asia,* edited by Raphael Israeli and myself (Boulder, Colo., 1984), includes such topics as a sociological analysis of Islamization in Java, Qur'anic exegesis in Malaysia and Indonesia, and the reciprocal relationships between Islamic Southeast Asia and the heartlands of Islam. Clive S. Kessler's *Islam and Politics in a Malay State: Kelantan 1838–1969* (Ithaca, N.Y., 1978) is an excellent microstudy of a small town in a Malay state that has wide implications for all Malaysia. *Conversion to Islam,* edited by Nehemia Levtzion (New York, 1979), is a very useful collection of essays providing a foundation for a comparative study of conversion to Islam. *Kelantan: Religion, Society, and Politics in a Malay State,* edited by W. R. Roff (Kuala Lumpur, 1974), is a most useful collection of material on Islamic life and movements in Kelantan that also presents a convincing paradigm for other regions. See also Muhammed Abdul Jabbar Beg's *Arabic Loan-Words in Malay: A Comparative Study* (Kuala Lumpur, 1982); C. C. Berg's "The Islamisation of Java," *Studia Islamica* 4 (1955): 11–142; Christine E. Dobbin's *Islamic Revivalism in a Changing Peasant Economy: Central Sumatra, 1784–1847* (London, 1983); my "Islam in Southeast Asia: Reflections on New Directions," *Indonesia,* no. 19 (April 1975): 33–55; and Deliar Noer's *The Modernist Muslim Movement in Indonesia, 1900–1942* (Singapore, 1973).

Esposito, John L., ed. *Islam in Asia: Religion Politics and Society.* Oxford, 1987. This includes chapters on Malaysia and Indonesia giving a competent and lucid account of developments in both countries up to the date of publication.

Hefner, Robert W. *Civil Islam: Muslims and Democratization in Indonesia.* Princeton, N.J., 2000. A general and sympathetic account of the adaptation of Islamic movements in Indonesia in coming to terms with civil society.

Hooker, Virginia, and Norani Othman, eds. *Malaysia: Islam, Society and Politics.* Singapore, 2003. A collection of essays taking as a point of departure the work of Clive S. Kessler, a sociologist who has specialized in the role of PAS in the northern states of the Malay Peninsula.

Laffan, Michael Francis. *Islamic Nationhood and Colonial Indonesia: The Umma below the Winds.* London, 2003. A study of the contribution of study in the Middle East (Egypt, Mecca, and Madina) by southeast Asian students towards the end of the nineteenth century to the evolution of Indonesian (and Malaysian) nationalism.

Riddell, Peter G. *Islam and the Malay-Indonesian World Transmission and Responses,* London, 2001. A recent, important, pioneering work with an emphasis on intellectual development from primary sources, up to the year of publication.

Riddell, Peter G. "The Diverse Voices of Political Islam in Post-Suharto Indonesia." *Islam and Christian-Muslim Relations* 13, no. 1 (2002): 65–84. A lucid and succinct account of rapid changes taking place in the Muslim political scene after the resignation of President Suharto.

Salim, Arskal, and Azumardi Azra, eds. *Shariʿa and Politics in Modern Indonesia.* Singapore, 2003. An account of debates concerning the feasibility of implementing Shariʿa law in Indonesia.

Literature

For an introduction to Islamic writing in the regional vernaculars, C. C. Brown's *Sĕjarah Mĕlayu; or, Malay Annals* (Kuala Lumpur, 1970) is a somewhat mannered but readable translation of the 1612 rescension of the *Sejarah Melayu.* G. W. J. Drewes's *The Admonitions of Seh Bari* (The Hague, 1969) is an edition and translation of a manuscript of a Javanese Primbon (student notebook) brought back to Europe around 1598; his *Directions for Travellers on the Mystic Path* (The Hague, 1977) includes a very valuable index and bibliography. Richard Winstedt's *A History of Classical Malay Literature* (Kuala Lumpur, 1969) is a difficult book to read, in a number of ways insensitive and obtuse, but nevertheless deserving sympathetic, careful study. See especially those chapters dealing with Muslim legends, cycles of tales from Muslim sources, and Islamic theology, jurisprudence, and history. See also L. F. Brakel's *The Hikayat Muhammad Hanafiyyah* (The Hague, 1975).

A. H. Johns (1987 and 2005)

ISLAM: ISLAM IN MODERN EUROPE

Muslims have been present in Europe almost as long as Islam has existed, most commonly as merchants traveling across the Mediterranean and the Black Sea, but also as captives in war and, less commonly, as slaves. Before modern times there were three main periods that left significant traces of a Muslim presence in Europe. In 711 CE a mainly Berber army crossed from North Africa into Spain at Gibraltar, quickly expanding northwards until they were stopped by Charles Martel (c. 688–741) at the Battle of Poitiers in 732. Muslim rule was thus established in most of Spain. Centered in Seville and Córdoba, its hold over the northern provinces was never firm, and it was from that direction that the Christian *reconquista* gradually pushed back Muslim rule beginning around the late tenth century. The kingdom of Granada held out for more than two centuries until its defeat in 1492 marked the end of Muslim rule in the region. It was to be another century before the remaining Muslim populations, in the meantime forcibly relocated to the northeast, were finally expelled. During these centuries, Muslim Spain was a major center of culture and learning and, together with a much shorter period of Muslim domination in Sicily and southern Italy (approximately two centuries until the late eleventh century), the region served as a rich route for the diffusion of Arabic and Islamic culture into Europe.

The second and third periods are interrelated, and they commence with the spread of a series of Mongol empires across Central Asia into the Middle East and eastern Europe in the thirteenth century. Originally holding various shamanist beliefs, the Mongol rulers controlling the kingdoms after the rapid breakup of the empire became Muslim. Of these kingdoms, the most significant for the purposes of this entry was that of the Khanate of the Golden Horde, whose territories covered southern Russia and western Siberia. During the fifteenth and sixteenth centuries, the khans were gradually pushed back by the growth of the Ottoman and Russian states, until the final fall of the Khanate of Kazan to Russia in 1552. The population, known in Europe as Tartars, were then able to move around within the growing Russian Empire, leaving major Muslim communities in present-day western Ukraine and the regions of the Crimea and the Volga River valley. During the period of Joseph Stalin (1879–1953) and World War II, large portions of this population were forcibly removed to Soviet Central Asia with great loss of life. Only since the 1980s have their descendants been able to return to their homes.

The growth of the Ottoman Empire constitutes the third period. Starting less than a century after the first Mongol conquests, the Ottoman family established a small state in Anatolia and soon became a major competitor to what was left of the Byzantine Empire. Over a period of two hundred years, the Ottomans were able to expand both in Anatolia and into the Balkans, until they finally conquered Constantinople in 1453 and made it their new capital, Istanbul. Over the following centuries, Muslim merchants, craftsmen, soldiers, and administrators settled in all the towns and cities of Ottoman southeast Europe. At the same time, parts of the indigenous population converted to Islam, especially in such communities as the Bogomils, which had developed forms of Christianity that found them persecuted by both the Orthodox and the Roman Catholic churches. On the whole, these converted communities lived in the countryside and only started moving into towns in the nineteenth and twentieth centuries. Significant communities of Turkish descent remain in present-day southeast Europe only in Serbia, Bulgaria, and Greece, while the descendants of the indigenous Slavic and Albanian communities are spread across the southern half of the Balkans: Albanians in Albania itself, as well as in southern Serbia and Kosovo, Macedonia, and northwestern Greece; and Slavs in Bosnia-Herzegovina, with small numbers, usually called Pomaks, in Bulgaria and Greece.

Western Europe—Islam before 1945. The contemporary presence of Muslim communities in western Europe constitutes a fourth period in this historical context. Before 1945, three countries led the way, namely Germany, Britain, and France. There are records of early Muslim immigration and settlement in German-speaking lands following the earliest contacts in southeastern Europe with the expanding Ottoman Empire. The two failed sieges of Vienna in 1529 and, especially, in 1683 left behind stragglers, deserters, and prisoners of war. More Muslims arrived and settled during the eighteenth century as Prussia expanded its interests eastward. Thus a group of Tartar cavalry ended up in the hands of Frederick I the Great (1712–1786), who made arrangements for them to observe weekly prayer in the barracks at Potsdam. By the mid-nineteenth century a Muslim cemetery had been established in Berlin, and in 1866 a mosque was opened. The Muslim presence in Germany, which had been united by Otto von Bismarck (1815–1898), grew substantially as the country developed its diplomatic and economic relationships with the Ottomans in the last few decades before the outbreak of World War I. By this time provisions were being made jointly by the German and the Ottoman-Turkish governments to address the spiritual needs of Muslim prisoners from Russia, Britain, and France. After the defeat in 1918, the fortunes of the Muslim communities declined, only to resume growth during World War II when the Third Reich recruited extensively among the Muslim nationalities of the Soviet Union.

The Austro-Hungarian Empire of the Habsburgs shared much of this history, with the major difference that, as the Ottoman Empire retreated in southeastern Europe during the nineteenth century, Austria-Hungary actually acquired direct rule over territories inhabited by substantial Muslim populations. This happened in 1878 when the Austro-Hungarian Empire occupied Ottoman Bosnia-Herzegovina. Smaller Muslim communities had existed on the margins of Habsburg territory, and even before 1878 laws had been passed governing Muslim family affairs. Soon after 1878 there was a resident *muftī* in Vienna. In 1909, Austria incorporated Bosnia-Herzegovina formally, and three years later passed a law recognizing the "followers of Islam of the Hanafite rite as a religious community," a facility available within the 1867 constitution.

In the United Kingdom and France, the history of Muslim settlement is even more directly linked to the history of empire than is the case with Germany, whose relationship to Istanbul before 1914 might be termed "proto-imperial." Already in the seventeenth and eighteenth centuries, the East India Company was crewing many of its ships from the territories of its factories in India. When these ships returned to ports in Britain, these men were laid off and left to fend for themselves, until public outrage forced the company to establish boarding houses for them in the 1820s. The Muslim component in Britain grew significantly after the opening of the Suez Canal in 1869. Companies shipping to and from India now recruited cheap labor at the new coaling station in Aden, which led directly to the establishment of Yemeni and Somali settlements in British ports. By the end of the century, these communities were finding religious structure and identity with the arrival of a *shaykh* of the ʿAlawī Ṣūfī order, an order of Algerian origin that had developed an offshoot in Yemen.

In the major ports of Liverpool and London, Muslim settlers came not only from India and Aden but also from West Africa. British merchants and aristocrats started to forge links with their counterparts in various parts of the empire and occasionally supported the education in Britain of the sons of the native colonial elites. Others Muslims, especially from Indian princely families, found their own way to Britain. The first formal mosques were established in London and Liverpool around 1890. The circle around the mosque in London, at Woking, obtained support both from the British establishment and certain Indian princes, as well as from the Saudi ambassador, so that it was possible in 1944 to acquire land in Regent's Park and start the planning for what was to become London's Central Mosque and Islamic Centre, which opened in 1977.

The foundations of Muslim settlement in France are linked closely to the French imperial project in North Africa, where Algeria was invaded in 1830. Businessmen, students, and exiles were most noticeable among the early French Muslim community, including such figures as Jamāl al-Dīn al-Afghānī (1838/9–1897) and Muḥammad ʿAbduh (1849–1905), who were exiled for a time from Egypt towards the end of the century by the British. But labor migration was an early dimension, especially with thousands of Algerians working in the olive oil industry around Marseille shortly before World War I. During the war, the need for both agricultural and industrial labor grew massively, especially when the French government started forcible requisition of Algerians, possibly as many as two thirds of the 200,000 or so who arrived during the war. In recognition of the Algerians, Moroccans, and Tunisians who had served as civilians and soldiers during the war, the French government provided funding for the building of the Paris Mosque and Islamic Centre, which opened in 1929. Labor migration continued erratically after the war, and after the French defeat in 1940 the Vichy Republic requisitioned Algerian laborers to help build the German Atlantic defenses. North Africans in France, and particularly Algerians in Paris and Marseilles, became involved in the campaigns for independence as early as the 1920s. Some observers have suggested that the rebellion, which started in the mid-1950s and led to independence in 1962, was essentially financed by Algerian émigrés in France.

WESTERN EUROPE—IMMIGRATION AFTER 1945. After the end of World War II, the devastated economies of western Europe initially met their growing labor needs from the pool of returning soldiers. But by the early 1950s it became clear that the sources had to be widened. In mainland Europe, the first regions that provided workers for the industrial heartlands of northern Europe were the countries of southern Europe: Spain, Portugal, Italy, Greece, and Yugoslavia. But there were early signs that this was not sufficient. The first immigrants to Britain from the Caribbean arrived in 1948, and through the 1950s large numbers of people started arriving from India. In 1957 an agreement between Turkey and the German state of Schleswig-Holstein assured the first official arrival in Europe of Turkish workers, while in France the numbers of Muslims coming from the traditional North African sources continued to increase gradually.

During the 1960s immigration of Muslims into Europe expanded almost explosively. Nearly half a million Moroccans arrived in France in the decade beginning in 1962, while the Algerian number doubled to 750,000, and the first 140,000 Tunisians arrived. Labor migration into Germany, the Netherlands, Belgium, and the Scandinavian countries tended to take place under the auspices of bilateral treaties between governments, particularly with Turkey, Morocco, and Tunisia. In just three years (1960–1962), the number of Turkish workers in Germany increased tenfold, and it continued growing until it reached over 600,000 in 1973. In addition there were many thousands of other nationalities of Muslim background. Similar developments took place in Scandinavia, the Netherlands, Belgium, Austria, and Switzerland, although in these areas the figures were, by 1973, still in the tens of thousands. The economic crisis caused by the rise of oil prices in the two years after 1972 put the brakes on the influx of Muslims into Europe, as most mainland European countries closed their doors to labor immigration.

In the United Kingdom this halt to immigration had taken place already in 1962. Following a period dominated by immigration from the Caribbean and India, social tensions were beginning to appear. In response to riots in London in 1958, a national debate initiated limits on immigration from colonies and former colonies, which until that point had been unrestricted. The debate alerted other groups to the danger that access might be cut off, and during the next several years, until the Commonwealth Immigration Act of 1962 came into effect, large numbers of Muslim immigrants arrived, including nearly 100,000 from Pakistan alone. Smaller groups had also arrived during this period, including Greek and Turkish Cypriots who were fleeing crises in their home country. In the late 1960s and early 1970s, significant numbers of Asian Muslims, mostly of Gujarati origin, arrived in Britain from Kenya and Uganda, where Africanization policies had made their positions untenable.

The closing of the gates in 1962, and again from 1973 to 1974, did not lead to an overall decline in immigration, however. To the contrary, instead of young men coming with the intention of returning home after a few years, they now decided to stay and bring in wives and children. In Britain the result was that the number of people of Pakistani and Bangladeshi origin in the 1981 census was about 360,000, and ten years later 636,000. In France, while the number of Algerians stabilized in the two decades after 1973, the number of Moroccans more than doubled to over 570,000 in 1990 and the Tunisians by about 50 percent to over 200,000. In Germany over the same period, the number of Turks also more than doubled to 1.5 million.

By this time, Germany was also beginning to show signs of a new phase in immigration, in which the emphasis was increasingly on refugees and asylum seekers. This change was caused by two basic factors. The relentless and progressive restrictions on immigration for work and immigration of dependents made the refugee route gradually more attractive, despite its costs both in cash and in terms of involvement with criminal networks. In addition, the Muslim world witnessed a number of destabilizing political crises that uprooted populations and devastated economies. As a result, Lebanon, Iran, Somalia, Afghanistan, Iraq, and Palestine joined the list of sources for Muslim migrants to western Europe.

Common to the large majority of Muslim immigrants during these phases was their origins in certain rural regions or, in the case of Turkey in particular, in the rural immigration areas of major cities of the countries of origin. The Muslim immigrants to Europe therefore came from the more culturally conservative sections of society, in which religion had continued to play an important role. Most of the labor migrants found semiskilled or unskilled labor, and a high proportion of them had only a primary school background—the first generation of women immigrants were often illiterate. It is to this background that some social scientists attribute the low rates of educational success and high rates of unemployment among young people, which often characterize Muslim communities in Europe at the beginning of the twenty-first century. The causes are not unequivocally clear, but the experience of, for example, East African Asians in Britain, would seem to support the analysis, as there seems to be little correlation between religion and educational and economic success among this mixed Muslim, Hindu, and Sikh group whose urban roots are to be found in commerce and the professions.

A further factor is the encounter with racism and xenophobia, widespread in European cities, both west and east. This has encouraged minority communities to construct and preserve internal solidarity and has supported tendencies towards residential concentrations in specific parts of the cities and towns where they live. This is also a factor in contributing to widespread educational failure and partial or complete exclusion from a number of occupations.

Settlement and Organization of Muslim Communities. The closing of the gates of labor immigration in 1962 in the United Kingdom and in 1973 and 1974 on mainland western Europe was a turning point. Leading as it did to the settlement of families, it also, in effect, contributed to making Islam visible and to the forming of consciously Muslim communities. Until that point, with a few notable exceptions, migrant workers had related to their host societies in almost exclusively economic terms. They lodged cheaply, often in boarding houses run by people from their own background. In industry, Muslim workers tended to be concentrated in specific sectors and often worked in their own gangs or shifts, with employment mediated, again, by people of their own background. With the arrival of Muslim families, however, interaction with the institutions of the host society necessarily expanded, especially in terms of access to housing, health and social services, and education.

It is significant that the countries into which these immigrants arrived had extensive state welfare systems, in which the price of gaining benefits was a broad and deep contact with complicated official bureaucracies. Women were especially affected in the areas of health and education, often in ways that men in their cultural tradition were unused to dealing with, but which at the same time frequently touched on aspects of individual and family honor, personal hygiene, and religious ritual. By such routes, Islam suddenly became a matter of conscious significance, and ways of dealing with these issues were sought.

It is thus no coincidence that an immediate consequence of the beginnings of family reunion was the growth of the number of mosques and prayer houses in Europe. British official statistics show that from the mid-1960s, starting from a base of only thirteen, an average of seven new mosques were registered annually. From 1975, when hopes grew of financial support from the Middle East (hopes that often turned out to be in vain), the annual number of new mosques jumped to between twenty and thirty. A similar development can be observed in other western European countries after the 1973 to 1974 period.

Mosques and prayer houses were usually founded by local communities to meet specific needs, primarily the performance of regular prayer, especially the congregational Friday noon prayer, *jumʿah*, and the Islamic instruction of children. Most communities initially employed people from their home villages or regions to perform these tasks. In Britain this tended to mean men who met the accustomed criteria of a village or small-town *imām*, usually someone with minimum training and without any serious Islamic scholarship or experience of the country of settlement.

Not long after this first stage of local organization, organizations with regional or national significance in the countries of origin began to establish themselves, either by invitation of the communities or individuals settled in Europe or by their own initiative. Given the official sponsorship of much Turkish settlement in Germany, it was natural that Turkish religious institutions should have immigrated with the settlers. This development included Turkey's official Department of Religious Affairs, the *Diyanet*, as well as several of the unofficial Islamic movements prevalent in Turkey. These groups had the added advantage that they could function much more freely in Germany than in Turkey, although there were joint German-Turkish efforts to limit their activities after the September 1980 military coup d'état in Turkey. The same Turkish institutions quickly came to pay a role in other countries with Turkish settlement, especially the Netherlands, Belgium, and Switzerland. They found their activities to be more difficult in Sweden, where the government actively discouraged external interference; in Britain, where the Turkish communities mostly came from Cyprus and had little interest in control from Ankara; and in France, where the rigid divide between state and religion was a major obstacle.

North African governments, especially those of Algeria and Morocco, similarly attempted to retain a degree of control over their émigrés, and they established a number of organizations in such countries as France, the Netherlands, and Belgium. Some of these organizations have had a degree of independence, while others, especially Moroccan ones, were long controlled directly by the respective embassies. Pakistani and Bangladeshi state structures have not intervened in the affairs of their communities in Europe. In the United Kingdom, it has often been a matter of political parties in the country of origin seeking support, especially financial support. In addition, various mainstream Islamic movements that were independent of their governments were often quick to establish roots among the new Muslim communities in Europe, sometimes at their own initiative and sometimes at the initiative of followers who had joined the migration.

Eastern Europe. The presence of Muslim communities in eastern Europe can be traced back many centuries to the existence of Mongol/Tartar states and the Ottoman Empire. The region referred to here does not fully coincide with the eastern Europe of the pre-1990 Soviet system; rather it includes Albania, the former Yugoslavia, and Greece, but not eastern Germany, the former Czechoslovakia, or the Baltic states. In those countries, which were members of the Warsaw Pact, the official ideology of the network of Communist parties initially regarded nationalities as being of secondary importance compared with the solidarity of the proletariat. But by the time most of these countries came under Soviet domination after World War II, Soviet ideology had moved towards an acknowledgement of a role for nationalities within the overall system. This is of significance in a region where traditional religious adherence was a major factor in determining national identities during the nineteenth and early twentieth centuries.

The Warsaw Pact countries followed the Soviet lead by exercising very tight control over all religions within a generally antireligious ideology and public policy. All public manifestations of traditional religion, in the form of religious buildings, organizations, and education, were often brutally suppressed. In the case of Islam, official institutions were sponsored and controlled by the government, usually with an officially recognized head who was given the title of *muftī* or chief *muftī*. The few mosques that were allowed to function were placed under the direction of the official institution, and the content of the Friday sermon was often dictated centrally.

In Albania, especially under the rule of Enver Hoxha (1908–1985), atheist policy went further and all forms of religion, organized or otherwise, were banned and persecuted. Data from the 1930s suggest that over 70 percent of the Albanian population was Muslim at that time. In Yugoslavia, the government of Josip Broz Tito (1892–1980) decided in the 1960s to recognize the Slavic population of Bosnia-Herzegovina of Muslim heritage as a nationality distinct from the Croats and the Serbs, although all of them shared essentially the same language. For reasons having to do with both domestic and international politics, the term used to refer to them was "Muslims in the national sense." Most religious communities in the region had experienced a very strong process of secularization, which Communist rule hastened. This was the case very markedly with the Muslims of Bosnia and Albania, so the Yugoslav concept of Muslim by nationality carried strong contradictions.

Muslims in Greece were for decades after World War I synonymous with Turks. The postwar settlement had included massive exchanges of population between Greece and Turkey, with thousands of ethnic Greeks leaving their homes in western Anatolia, especially in and around Smyrna/Izmir, and, similarly, with large numbers of ethnic Turks leaving Western Thrace. The position and rights of remaining communities on both sides were governed by peace treaties, especially the 1923 Treaty of Lausanne. On both sides, the mutual mistrust that has been sustained into the present has meant that these minorities have been under close observation and control by their respective governments. As a result, both governments have repeatedly been found remiss in their application of article 9 of the European Convention on Human Rights, which deals with religious freedom, to which both countries are signatories.

During the 1980s, as the old order was beginning to display its weaknesses, some Communist politicians sought to maintain their position by appealing to national chauvinism. In Yugoslavia, the targets of this increasingly violent trend were, during the 1990s, the "Muslims in the national sense," namely the Bosnian Muslims and the Albanians of Kosovo and Macedonia. In Bulgaria, the regime also adopted this tendency and in the mid-1980s implemented a "national" policy that involved forcing people with Muslim names, Turks or Pomaks, to adopt Bulgarian names. The ensuing mass exodus to Turkey was a major factor leading to the fall of the Communist regime in that country.

Since the collapse of the Soviet system, all of the countries of this region have had to review their policies towards their religious minorities, including their Muslim communities, especially after signing the European Convention on Human Rights. On the whole, while there remain Muslim institutions that have inherited the mantle of the official bodies of the Communist period, they have become more distanced from the state. At the same time, it has become possible for other Muslim organizations and movements to establish themselves, and there has been a major growth in the number of mosques sponsored by local communities. In many of the countries concerned, a growth in immigration from the Muslim world has also been recorded. Some of the roots of this development can be found in students from the Arab world who were sponsored by the Communist governments. But other Muslim immigrants are businesspeople and people looking for work. In Bulgaria a large proportion of those who fled the Communist name-changing policy returned to their properties after the regime changed, but many subsequently returned to Turkey to escape the economic collapse. Like most of the other countries under consideration here, Bulgaria has, since the late 1990s, begun attracting immigrants from various parts of the Muslim, especially Arab, world.

Austria. A small, generally well-educated Bosnian Muslim community was established in Vienna during the late Habsburg period until the empire fell apart during World War I. Most of the contemporary Muslim population in Austria immigrated as workers during the 1970s, particularly from Turkey. During the 1980s, when labor migration slowed down, more Muslim immigrants arrived as businesspeople, students, and diplomats attached to the international institutions in Vienna, to be followed during the 1990s by a new wave of workers brought in by demand from employers, as well as thousands of refugees from the wars in the former Yugoslavia. Turks constituted about half of the estimated 300,000 Muslims in Austria in 1997, some 4 percent of the total population of the country. Only a minority of Austrian Muslims have acquired citizenship, and about half of the Muslim population lives in and around Vienna, with the rest living in the northern and western industrial regions of the country.

Belgium. The Muslims of Belgium originate from Morocco (125,000 in 1999) and Turkey (71,000), followed by other Arab nations (Algeria, Tunisia, Lebanon, and Syria), as well as Bosnians and Pakistanis, making up altogether about 370,000, or 3.7 percent of the Belgian population. Most Muslim immigrants arrived in Belgium in the 1960s and early 1970s, followed by smaller numbers of refugees in the 1980s and 1990s. Changes in the laws of citizenship in 1984 and 1991 have led to almost half of these immigrants acquiring Belgian citizenship. Turks are concentrated in the industrial areas of north Belgium, while most Moroccans live in Brussels and in the south.

Bulgaria. The 2001 Census recorded 967,000 Sunni Muslims and some 53,000 Shīʿahs, making up some 12.9 percent of the total population. In terms of ethnicity, there were 747,000 Turks (a decline of over 50,000 since the 1992 census, mainly due to emigration to Turkey), 150,000 Bulgarians ("Pomaks"), 140,000 Roma ("Gypsies"), and about 5,000 Tartars and Circassians.The more than 5,000 Arab settlers, concentrated in 1992 in the major cities, especially Sofia, have increased significantly in number since then. Ethnic Turks are concentrated in the south, southeast, and northeast, with Pomaks in the Rhodope Mountains of the south, and Roma dispersed all over the country.

Denmark. Denmark's estimated total of 150,000 Muslims in 2000, making up about 2.8 percent of the population, is among the most ethnically mixed in Europe. Major groups include Turks, former Yugoslavs (especially Bosnians), Somalis, Iraqis, Pakistanis, Palestinians, and Moroccans, as well as smaller groups of other Arab and South and Central Asia nationalities. This reflects the accumulated effect of labor migration occurring during the 1967 to 1973 period, as well as refugee flows in the 1980s. Acquisition of Danish citizenship has been slow. Denmark's main concentrations of Muslims are found in Copenhagen, Aarhus, and Odense, with significant smaller groups in the industrial towns of eastern Denmark.

Finland. Official statistics for 1999 allow an estimate of some twenty-thousand Muslims in Finland, or about 0.4 percent of the population. A small group, less than one thousand, are Tartars whose presence, mostly in Helsinki and Turku, dates back to the nineteenth century when Finland was part of Russia and their forebears arrived as traders. The majority of Muslims living in Finland today have come from the eastern Arab world and Somalia, mostly as refugees during the 1980s and 1990s. Most of them live in and around Helsinki, with smaller numbers in the main cities of the south and southwest.

France. Estimates of the number of Muslims in France are based on statistics concerning nationality, which suggest that between four and five million Muslims, up to 7 percent of the population, lived in France at the end of the twentieth century. By far the largest proportion come from North Africa, of which over 1.5 million are Algerians, with approximately one million Moroccans and about 350,000 Tunisians, as well as some 450,000 so-called Harkis, the descendants of Algerians who sided with the French during the war of independence. There are a further 350,000 Turks, some 250,000 Muslims from sub-Saharan Africa, and over 100,000 Muslims from the Middle East. The major period of immigration occurred in the three decades before 1974, after which Algerian figures stabilized due to a subsidized policy of return, while the numbers of Muslim immigrants from other regions continued to increase. The largest concentrations of Muslims are to be found in the industrial areas of Paris, Lyon, and Marseilles, as well as in smaller towns in eastern France. Turks are also prevalent in forestry and light industry in the Alsace-Moselle region. Most Muslims of North African origin have French citizenship, and the rate of naturalization among Turks grew during the 1990s.

Germany. In 2000, just over three million Muslims were estimated to be resident in Germany, making up 3.2 percent of the population. Three-quarters of these are of Turkish origin, followed by Bosnians, Iranians, Moroccans, and Afghans. Germany long maintained that it was a country of temporary migration, not immigration and settlement. The majority of Turks arrived in Germany during the 1960s and early 1970s, while the other nationalities arrived mainly as students or refugees. Only in 1998 did Germany ease access to citizenship, so about 90 percent of Germany's Muslims remain legal foreigners. Most Muslims live in the former West Germany in the limited inner city districts of Berlin, Cologne, Hamburg, Munich, and Frankfurt am Main, and in the Ruhr district cities of Düsseldorf and Duisburg.

Greece. The main Muslim populations in Greece are those of Western Thrace, whose rights as a religious and ethnic minority are protected by the 1923 Treaty of Lausanne, and the Albanians, mostly immigrants from Albania and Macedonia since the early 1990s, making up altogether about 370,000 people (3.7 percent of the total population) at the beginning of the twenty-first century. While the Turks remain concentrated in the towns and villages of Western Thrace, Albanians have spread to wherever there is dynamic economic activity, including both the major cities and the countryside and, more recently, also the islands. Significant numbers of immigrants from the Muslim world, in particular the Middle East, have settled in Athens and other major cities since the 1980s, but figures are unreliable.

Hungary. The majority of the twenty to thirty thousand Muslims in Hungary came as students from Arab, South Asian, and Central Asian countries. They make up less that 0.3 percent of the Hungarian population.

Ireland. A small community of Muslims of different origins, mostly students and businesspeople, are concentrated in Dublin. They total approximately 15,000, or 0.3 percent of the Irish population.

Italy. Due to the high proportion of unregistered immigrants in Italy, figures are unreliable, but best estimates suggest a Muslim population of as many as 700,000, or about 1.2 percent of Italy's total population. The largest groups are Moroccans and Albanians, followed by smaller but still significant numbers of Tunisians, Senegalese, Egyptians, Pakistanis, Algerians, and Bosnians. Less than 5 percent of the Muslims in Italy have Italian citizenship. With few exceptions, most arrived during the 1980s and 1990s, among them a high proportion of refugees, especially from Albania and Bosnia. Most live in Italy's northern industrial regions and around Rome.

Luxembourg. According to Muslim estimates there were upwards of seven thousand Muslims in Luxembourg (1.6 percent of the population) in 2000, two-thirds being from Bosnia-Herzegovina. The principality signed a labor agreement with Yugoslavia in 1970, which led to the first wave of immigrants, who were followed by refugees during the 1990s.

Netherlands. Official statistics record almost 700,000 Muslims in 1999 in the Netherlands, equivalent to 4.6 percent of the population. The two largest groups are the almost 300,000 Turks and 250,000 Moroccans, with smaller numbers of Surinamese, Iraqis, Somalis, Iranians, Pakistanis, and Afghans. Over half have become Dutch citizens. The major immigration of Turks and Moroccans took place during the 1960s and 1970s to meet the demand for labor. Later arrivals came primarily as refugees. The population is overwhelmingly urban, concentrated particularly in Amsterdam, Rotterdam, The Hague, and Utrecht.

Norway. During the 1970s and 1980s, people from Pakistan, Morocco, and Turkey started arriving in Norway in search of work. Since then more have arrived as refugees. Estimates at the end of the twentieth century suggest a Muslim population of between 100,000 and 150,000, or about 3 percent of Norway's population. Most of Norway's Muslims live in and around Oslo, with smaller numbers in other major cities.

Poland. With a total of about fifteen thousand people concentrated in the major cities, Muslims make up only 0.038 percent of Poland's population. About one-third of the country's Muslims are Polish citizens of Tartar origin, mostly from areas near the Ukrainian border. The rest came as students during the 1980s, or as traders and refugees in the following decade.

Portugal. Between half and three-quarters of Portugal's Muslims are citizens; most came from colonial Mozambique and are of Indian origin. The remainder of Portugal's thirty to forty thousand Muslims (0.3 to 0.4 percent of the population) came from former Portuguese colonies, particularly Guinea-Bissau, and from Arab countries. The latter arrived mostly during the 1990s, while the earliest major immigration was caused by the decolonization processes of the 1970s and 1980s.

Romania. A total of about sixty thousand Muslims make up less that one quarter of 1 percent of Romania's total population. The majority are citizens of the centuries-old Turkish, Tartar, and Albanian communities, concentrated in the Dobruja region of southeast Romania. In recent decades small numbers of students and traders, especially from the Arab world and Central and South Asia, have settled in Romania.

Spain. According to Spain's 1996 census, there were between 300,000 and 400,000 Muslims in the country, comprising about 1 percent of Spain's population. Nationality statistics for 2000 indicate that about 250,000 originate from North Africa, mostly Morocco, and about 22,000 from sub-Saharan Africa, with smaller numbers from the Middle East and South Asia. Only a minority of Spain's Muslims have Spanish citizenship. The main period of immigration started in the 1980s, with immigrant workers settling around Catalonia and Madrid, and subsequently as workers in the tourist industry of the Mediterranean coast.

Sweden. Estimates for 2000 indicate between 250,000 and 300,000 Muslims live in Sweden, about 4 percent of the population. Although some arrived during the 1960s and 1970s looking for work, most came as refugees during the 1980s and the 1990s from a number of countries, with Iraqis, Iranians, Turks (especially of Kurdish descent), Bosnians, and Palestinians from Lebanon, Syria, and Jordan being the largest groups. By far the largest numbers of Sweden's Muslims live in and around Stockholm, with sizable communities also in Gothenburg and Malmö.

Switzerland. The federal census of 2000 recorded approximately 310,000 Muslims, or 4 percent of Switzerland's total population. Over half have their origins in the former Yugoslavia, especially Macedonia and Bosnia-Herzegovina. Many immigrated for work before the collapse of Yugoslavia, while many of the later arrivals came as refugees. About 20 percent of Switzerland's Muslims are of Turkish origin, mostly arriving during the 1970s and early 1980s. They are settled in all the major cities, particularly Zurich, Bern, Basel, Lausanne, and Geneva. Few of the Muslims living in Switzerland have succeeded in meeting the country's strict citizenship requirements.

United Kingdom. The United Kingdom's 2001 census recorded some 1.6 million Muslims, constituting 2.7 percent of the population. The main period of immigration was during the 1960s and 1970s, with continued family reunion occurring thereafter, along with a rise in the number of refugees during the 1990s. People of South Asian origin make up more than half of the country's Muslims, about half of whom were of Pakistani origin. Other significant groups come from the Arab world, Turkish Cyprus, and the commonwealth countries of western and eastern Africa. Outside of London, which has the most mixed population, including the most

Arabs, the largest Muslim communities, with South Asians dominant, are to be found in the West Midlands, West Yorkshire, Manchester, and Glasgow.

Public Participation. At the official level, one of the major challenges to European states with Muslim populations has been how to incorporate Islam, as well as other religions that have appeared in Europe since 1945, into the patterns of church-state relations that have been built up through centuries of sometimes conflicted history. Although society and politics during the late twentieth century became increasingly secular in nature, most European states are not formally secular in the sense of a clear separation between church and state. Patterns range from the clear church-state separation introduced in France in 1905 and integral to the constitutions of Ireland and most nations of eastern Europe, to countries such as Denmark and Greece that retain a state church or one church in a highly privileged position. In between are states such as Belgium, Austria, Spain, and Germany that offer official forms of recognition for religions, and others, such as Italy, that retain concordats with Rome. But the official status often does not reflect the influence of traditionally dominant churches. In some cases they have an impact far above their official status, as in the case of the Catholic Church in Ireland and Poland, or, conversely, far below their official status, as with the Evangelical Lutheran Church in Denmark.

Muslims have had to find their way through this confusion, and they have achieved legal recognition in several countries where it is available, including Austria (1979), Belgium (1974), and Spain (1992). In other such countries, including Germany, some of the Swiss cantons, and the Alsace-Moselle region of France, such legal recognition was still to be obtained as of 2004. Recognition brings with it different privileges in different countries. In Austria, legal recognition gives Muslims access to the state broadcast media and provides for religious instruction in schools, the latter a privilege that also comes with recognition in Belgium. For a long time it was the view in Germany that recognition was required before access to religious instruction in state schools was possible. More recently, German politicians and educators have begun supporting the view that religious education can go ahead without recognition.

Whatever the legal situation, for most European Muslim communities, acknowledgment of them as an inherent part of public life is more than a mere formality. During the 1990s the French government became involved in the sponsorship of a Muslim representative body. To achieve this, French authorities have had to enter into ever greater compromises with the country's Muslim communities. A broadly based *Conseil Français du Culte Musulman,* sponsored by the Ministry of the Interior, was elected in April 2003. The establishment of the Muslim Council of Britain in 1997 served a similar purpose for a number of years, but it never succeeded in broadening its initial base of support among Britain's Muslim communities, and its role as interlocutor with the government remained circumscribed.

That such national Muslim representation developed in France and Britain is due in part to the citizenship status of most people of Muslim background in these countries. In Great Britain, commonwealth citizens have the right to vote and to stand for election, and access to citizenship for the children of residents is accorded by birth or a relatively unrestricted process of naturalization after five years of residence. French rules are slightly different, but the principle of citizenship by birth is also the legal foundation there. So in both countries there has been a long tradition of political participation, which is only gradually spreading to the rest of Europe as laws are changed. This was the case in Germany at the end of the 1990s, when limited access to dual citizenship and citizenship by birth were introduced. In some countries, such as the Netherlands and in the Scandinavian countries, political participation at the local level was encouraged by the introduction during the 1980s of the right to vote and to stand for election in local government for foreigners of longer than three years of residence.

Education. Education has been a priority for Europe's Muslim communities. For most Muslim parents, education has been seen as the key to a better future for their children and their families, and European governments have regarded their educational systems as one of the main tools for building national identity and, therefore, for the integration or assimilation of people of foreign origin. At the same time, modern child-centered educational thinking, linked with a liberal and pluralist view of Europe, has required a recognition and validation of children's cultural identities.

The United Kingdom was among the first countries to restructure syllabuses of religious education to take into account the presence of faiths other than Christianity, when local authorities introduced "multi-faith" religious education during the 1970s. The Education Reform Act of 1988 specified for the first time that Christianity was the be the main faith taught, but the law also guaranteed the teaching of other religions, most prominent among which have been Islam and Judaism. In other European countries where religion is taught in state schools, the curriculum was traditionally linked to a specific Christian tradition. In some cases, as in Germany, the churches have cooperated in expanding the curriculum to include knowledge of other world religions, especially Islam and Judaism, while some countries, including Norway and Sweden, have restructured their official programs on British lines. In Eastern Europe since the collapse of Communist regimes, changes are only slowly taking place, since in most cases the priority has been the reintroduction of religious instruction in the parents' faith after decades of atheistic indoctrination.

As the teaching of Islam has spread in schools, so Muslim organizations have become increasingly involved in designing syllabuses and teaching materials, as well as contributing to the training of teachers. Since the national, linguistic, and cultural origins of Muslims in many countries are mixed, Muslims have had to become accustomed to an internal pluralism that was often absent from the regions of origin. This involvement in education has thus often required Muslim participants to reach a consensus on what should be taught as Islamic faith and practice, and also how to deal pedagogically with the variety of cultural forms through which Islam finds expression in society. It remains a fact, however, that the main cultures of origin continue to influence the image of Islam that is variously presented in schools across Europe.

ISLAMIC MOVEMENTS AND TRENDS. The countries of origin have also played a major role in determining the Islamic trends that became established in various places. The vast majority of Muslims in western Europe are Sunnīs who tend to identify with the legal and ritual schools (*madhhab*) of their parents. There are a number of Shīʿī communities in the United Kingdom, notably Ithnāʿasharīs and Ismāʿīlīs; they are primarily of Iranian, Arab, and South Asian origin. The Iranian government has long played a role that, in the Hamburg Mosque on the Alster Lake, predates the Islamic revolution of 1979. But other groups are also to be found, such as the Khoei Foundation in London with its link to the eponymous family of Iraqi Shīʿī scholars. The Ismāʿīlī community has a major center in London, and promotes philanthropic and developmental activities through the Aga Khan Development Network.

However, it is often the Muslim movements that arose in the Muslim world during the nineteenth and twentieth centuries that have been most visible. So among Muslims of Indian subcontinent origin, the Deobandi and Brelwi movements remain strong and continue to reproduce their mutual controversies after settling in Europe. To them must be added the network of organizations emanating from the Jamāʿat-i-Islāmī, founded by Abū'l A'la Mawdūdī (1903–1979). Among North African Arabs, branches of the National Liberation Front continued to exercise influence for many years, but during the 1990s younger Arabs increasingly found themselves attracted to organizations linked to the Muslim Brotherhood, a trend also to be noted among Muslim students elsewhere in western Europe, and in some cases institutions supported and funded by individuals or organizations from the Persian Gulf and Saudi Arabia.

From the beginning, Turks were split between an educated minority that tended to support the official secularism of the tradition of Kemal Atatürk (1881–1938) and a majority that through the 1970s became increasingly organized through federations of mosques. These federations were run by either the local representatives of the *Diyanet*, a network that was expanded significantly after the September 1980 coup in Ankara; the Milli Görüş movement; or the more Ṣūfī-oriented Süleymanli movement.

While most movements remain ethnically identified, some have established high levels of cooperation across borders based on a sympathy of ideas. This has most clearly been the case in cooperation between organizations based in the Muslim Brotherhood, the Jamāʿat-i-Islāmī, and the Milli Görüş. But a few movements have crossed ethnic and national borders, above all the Tablighi-jamāʿat. This movement originated in the context of the Indian Deobandi movement but spread around the world during the 1950s and 1960s. During the 1980s it particularly found followers in France among North Africans, where it was know as *Foi et pratique*, and very soon after the regime changes in eastern Europe itinerant Tabligh preachers were seen in Bulgarian villages.

Ṣūfī networks, although generally less visible than other, more formal organizations, have developed a strong presence in Europe. In the Balkans the Bektāshī network, traditionally strong among Albanians, is also to be found among ethnic Turks in Bulgaria. Related to the Bektāshīs, and currently going through major revival and change, are the so-called Alevis. Originating in Anatolia (and not to be confused with the Syrian group of the same name), many Turks and Kurds of Turkish nationality are now publicly professing to be Alevis. In some instances, especially among the Balkan village communities, it is difficult to distinguish between these movements and isolated traditional popular religious practices, but it is also clear that, with the growth of communications and freedom of movement, the two forms of expression are being linked.

Other more traditional Ṣūfī orders are also widespread, especially various branches of the Naqshbandī order, prevalent among both Turks and South Asians. Among communities from sub-Saharan West Africa, especially among the Senegalese, the *marabout* networks retain significant influence, including economic influence. New European cross-border networks have arisen as offshoots from the more traditional orders, the most well-known of these probably being that of the Cypriot Shaykh Nazim al-Haqqani (b. 1922), whose followers, although limited in number, range from Central Asia through Europe to North America.

Smaller, more extreme groups have made themselves noticed since the early 1990s, usually when the media have temporarily linked them to political events. This was the case at the time of the Bosnian crisis early in the decade, the period of the Algerian civil war from the middle of the decade, and in the aftermath of the September 11, 2001, attacks on the Pentagon and the World Trade Center. Most well-known among these groups is the Ḥizb al-Taḥrīr network, which has appeared in most European countries and in former Soviet Central Asia.

As a younger, educated generation appears in the Muslim communities in both eastern and western Europe, many European Muslims are beginning to develop European forms of Islam. On the one hand, they are loosening their adherence to the culturally specific forms of Islam identified with their parents and countries of origin; on the other hand, they are working out those dimensions of Islam that they regard as essential to being a Muslim, while also exploring how to be Muslim in ways that harmonize with being European. This has, among other things, given rise to a debate within

Muslim circles concerning an Islamic "minority law": *fiqh al-aqalliyāt.* It is this field above all that will determine during the first quarter of the twenty-first century the extent to which European Islam can integrate and to which the central Islamic lands will continue to influence Muslim identity in Europe.

BIBLIOGRAPHY

There has been an explosion in literature on this subject since the early 1990s. Detailed bibliographies can be found in Wasif Shadid and P. Sjoerd van Koningsveld, eds., *Religious Freedom and the Position of Islam in Western Europe: Opportunities and Obstacles in the Acquisition of Equal Rights* (Kampen, Netherlands, 1995); Felice Dassetto and Yves Conrad, eds., *Musulmans en Europe occidentale: Bibliographie commentée* (Paris, 1996); and Jochen Blaschke et al., eds., *Muslims in Europe: A Bibliography* (Berlin, 2002). Much of the present entry is based on Jorgen S. Nielsen, *Muslims in Western Europe*, 2d ed. (Edinburgh, 1995), together with the substantial thematic discussion and updating, including Eastern European material, to be found in Brigitte Maréchal, Stefano Allievi, Felice Dassetto, and Jorgen Nielsen, eds., *Muslims in the Enlarged Europe* (Leiden, 2003), which includes an extensive bibliography. The country statistics are from Brigitte Maréchal, ed., *L'Islam et les musulmans dans l'Europe élargie: Radioscopie* (Louvain-la-Neuve, Belgium, 2002).

JORGEN S. NIELSEN (2005)

ISLAM: ISLAM IN THE AMERICAS

Muslims have been arriving in the New World from the sixteenth century to the present. The horrors of the lives of Muslim slaves mark the first accounts, while the horrors of the lives of Muslim immigrants in the aftermath of the tragedies of September 11, 2001, mark the latest accounts. Muslims have settled in almost every part of the Americas. Their relationships with other immigrants and with indigenous peoples have been as varied as their success in planting Islam in the religious landscape.

There have been problems with accurately documenting the earliest arrivals. Various accounts of Muslims arriving in North America prior to Columbus have yet to be proven. Recent research on Muslim slaves from West Africa, however, has been much more definitive. It is now documented that Muslims were among the first African slaves to arrive in the New Worlds, as early as 1501. These Muslims were from regions ranging form Senegal to Chad and from the southern border of the Sahara to the northern fringes of the tropical forest. The African Muslim diaspora was spread from North America to the Caribbean and on to South America. The size of the African diaspora is still in dispute; estimates range from 9.5 million to 20 million, with Muslims comprising anywhere from 10 to 30 percent of slaves over a period of three hundred and fifty years. While data now exists on the numbers and percentages of various ethnic groups, in only a few countries is religious affiliation noted in censuses. What is uncontested is the fact that Muslim African slaves were scattered across every region of the Americas.

SLAVES AND PLANTATION COMMUNITIES. Significant numbers of African Muslim slaves were literate in Arabic, making them unique in the slave community. There exist short biographies of at least seventy-five of these slaves who were brought to North America between 1730 and 1860. The earliest known biography is a fifty-four-page volume, *Some Memories of the Life of Job Ben Solomon,* written in 1734 by an Englishman. From these and other accounts, what emerges is a clear history of the struggle to retain Muslim faith and Arabic literacy. Most researchers agree that the slaves who proved most difficult to convert to Christianity were the Muslims. Muslims were also the most difficult to keep in slavery: the first slave revolt in the New World was led by Muslims in 1522. Catholics sought to convert Muslims because conversion provided a moral justification for the institution of slavery, while Protestants generally oppressed slaves on the grounds that they would be morally bound to free slaves that had been converted to Christianity. Forced and mass conversions were persistently resisted by many Muslims, as shown by rebellions in the French West Indies and in North America.

There are a variety of reports on the religious life of Muslim slaves in historical documents, ranging from the reports of slave masters to Works Progress Administration accounts from descendants of slaves in the early twentieth century. The Muslim practices of *ṣalāt* (prayer) and *ṣawm* (fasting), along with the retention of Arabic words and phrases, stand out in these accounts. Though prayer was one religious practice often hidden by slaves, accounts of public prayers were recorded. The story of Yarrow Mamont praying in public is reported by Charles Peale, who painted his portrait in 1819. Other non-Muslim slaves, such as Charles Ball, writing in the early nineteenth century, tell of hearing prayers spoken in Arabic. Muslims slaves in Brazil used prayer rugs—pieces of cloth or animal skins—and are reported to have actively fasted during the month of Ramaḍān, and to have celebrated the feast that marks the end of Ramaḍān. Though impoverished, slaves are even said to have made gifts of whatever they possessed.

Through faith, practice, and dreams, Islam did survive in the Americas despite the brutalities and dislocations of slavery. The willpower of African Muslim slaves was remarkable. The distinctive lifestyle of the Muslim was imprinted on the consciousness of descendents. Muslims had much difficulty maintaining modesty in the face of degradation. As much as slave owners tried to keep slaves humiliated by keeping them nude, Muslim slaves put on as many clothes as they could find, including head wraps and caps. The use of Arabic names along with slave names assisted in identity preservation, and Muslim names can presently be found among people all over the Americas and the Caribbean. For example, the Sea Islands off the coasts of South Carolina and Georgia provide a significant slave-made reservoir of African Muslim names. Muslim slaves also maintained Islamic dietary regulations against pork despite the meager, limited offerings of plantation living.

Muslims are forbidden to eat dead meat, blood, and the flesh of swine and to drink wine or other forms of alcohol. In the Caribbean, slaves were forced to drink alcohol as part of a diet designed to increase productivity and were given it as a bonus for hard work. Muslim slaves rejected both alcohol and pork with such consistency that at least one Caribbean governor complained in writing that continued punishment was not working. There are additional documented accounts of Muslim slaves' refusal to eat non-halal meats (meats not slaughtered according to Islamic law). Other Islamic traditions, such as circumcision and polygamy, were also retained. There are accounts from Brazil of Muslim slaves practicing circumcision on boys at ten years of age. The practice of polygamy, though not wide-spread in the Americas, was understood in the West as an expression of the natural immorality of slaves.

In several historical accounts, Muslim slaves are described as "uppity" or "arrogant" because of their persistence in pursuing their religious practices and literacy. One account from Cuba claimed that Muslims stayed to themselves. The deliberate separation of slaves from the same ethnic groups had much the same effect on Muslims as it had on other slaves—it created loneliness and depression. The only difference was that the practices of Islam and knowledge of Arabic acted as cultural bridge-builders between Muslims of different ethnic groups. Though some Muslim slaves were literate and others semi-literate, slavery remained the circumstance of almost all African Muslims for generations in North America. In 1837, however, decades before the Emancipation Proclamation, Sir Andrew Halliday reported that Trinidad boasted a free Muslim community. In Brazil, as early as 1850, many Muslim indentured servants were able to pool their resources to buy their freedom and then either remain in the country or go back to Africa.

The resourcefulness of Muslim slaves in the Americas extended to obtaining Qurʾāns and to communication across the Americas, especially to and from Brazil. One documented report speaks of the importation of Qurʾāns from Europe for sale to Muslim slaves. Slaves went into debt, buying about one hundred Qurʾāns every year. It is also documented that Arabic Qurʾāns were in use on the Sea Islands. The sale and transport of slaves between the Caribbean and North America also facilitated the transmission of Qurʾāns. Slaves also wrote their own Qurʾāns from memory. Benjamin Larten, a Jamaican slave, apparently displayed his Qurʾān in 1835 to author Richard Madden.

Some of those Muslim slaves who previously had been teachers continued to teach, especially in Brazil. As a result of various revolts, some of the names of these slaves and freedmen are known. Newspapers published accounts of the revolts and the names of the participants to aid in their recapture. In addition, the names of slaves who were tried in court for holding classes appear in legal documents; two such names are Dandea Aprigio and Sanem. Evidence of structured Qurʾanic schools among slaves is mostly found in Brazil, though it is known that there were some schools established on the North American continent. The most renowned religious slave manuscript is the Ben-Ali diary, which is a thirteen-page document in Arabic. Arabic was not only used in the context of attempts to practice and preserve Islam, however. It was also used to transmit the plans for uprisings. One letter confiscated in 1835 during a revolt in Bahia, Brazil, was a call to "take the country and kill the whites." The separation of people in each tribe was a tried-and-true method of keeping control of communication and possible revolt. This generally worked on captives, but not for Muslims who, though separated from members of their tribes, could still communicate using Qurʾanic Arabic.

Islam endured in the Americas primarily due to the persistence of the Atlantic slave trade, which resulted in a continuous arrival of slaves. It was only in the last decades of the nineteenth century that the steady flow of new arrivals began to wane. By then, many descendants of African Muslim slaves were so removed in time (up to more than fifteen generations) from their homelands that much of the Islamic tradition was lost. Some descendants turned to Christianity, some turned to a blend of Christianity and Islam, while others gave up on religion. Many researchers currently assert that Islamic influences can be readily observed in black syncretic religion. There is overwhelming scholarly agreement, however, that Muslim communities comprised of Americans of African descent were not seen again until the twentieth century.

Islam in the Americas: Nineteenth and Twentieth Centuries. After the horrendous period of chattel slavery, Islam was spread through most of the Americas by immigrants, exiles, and refugees from the Muslim world—primarily from the Arab world and South Asia. In some regions Muslims formed exclusivist communities that only engaged the majority community when necessary. Other Muslims actively engaged themselves in the social and political life of their adopted country. In the Caribbean, where descendants of African Muslims remained after slavery, immigrant (primarily South Asian) Muslims made no efforts to blend into and strengthen the existing Muslim community. On the other hand, in those places where the majority of immigrants were Arab Muslims, there were significant efforts to merge with any existing Muslim community.

Islam in the Caribbean and South America. The terms *Caribbean* and *South American* refer to aggregations of countries, not to specific areas within legally defined boundaries. Thirty-one countries form the Caribbean, which is divided into English, French, Spanish, and Dutch linguistic regions. The majority of the countries are English-speaking. The total Muslim population by country varies from 4 to 15 percent. The largest Muslim populations are in English-speaking countries such as Guyana and Trinidad and Tobago. There are small communities made up of Muslims of African descent, but the greatest number of Muslims are descendents of immigrants from India and Indonesia who came as indentured servants. In French-speaking countries, such as Guadeloupe, Guyana Françoise, Haiti, and Martinique, the Muslim community is mainly composed of African Muslim immigrants from West Africa. Martinique is also home to a very wealthy immigrant Palestinian Muslim community supported by Saudi Arabia.

Muslims on the Spanish-speaking islands—Cuba, the Dominican Republic, and Puerto Rico—claim an Islamic heritage in the Americas dating back to the days of slavery and trace their history prior to slavery back to Islamic Spain during the eighth to fifteenth centuries. Thus, many trace their ultimate cultural ancestry to northern Africa and the Moriscos—Moors who were forcibly converted to Christianity. These Muslims are aware that Moriscos were enslaved with other Africans during the Atlantic slave trade. There are also much Islamic and Moorish retention in this sector of Caribbean society, especially in language and names.

In the Caribbean, Muslims continue to experience life as minorities. Christian missionaries continue to try to convert Muslims—though there is also increasing evidence that Muslims are trying to convert Christians. In 2002, reports in local newspapers asserted that of the few conversions that take place, most are from Christianity to Islam.

The history of Muslims in Mexico is difficult to trace. Spanish conquistadors from both Cuba and Spain came to pillage Mexico's resources in the early 1500s. The indigenous population was subdued and forcibly converted to Catholicism during this time. Many in the native population died as a result of the importation of European diseases and from starvation, as Europeans devastated the farming land and depleted water resources. Mexicans themselves regained control only in the 1900s.

Historians are divided over when Islam came to Mexico and who brought it. Some claim it was introduced by Syrian immigrants, whereas others point to Turkish immigrants. One recent (2002) study estimated that 10 percent of the Syrian-Lebanese immigrant community were Muslim. Today this community is one of the richest and contains more than 250,000 people. The history of Islam in Mexico is largely undocumented, with the exception of a sixteenth-century book called *Un Herehe y un Musulman.* Written by Pascual Almazan, this recounts the exploits of Yusuf bin Alabaz, who came to Mexico after expulsion during the *Reconquista* in Spain. Today, Islam is a recognized entity following the establishment of the Muslim Center de Mexico in 1994 in Mexico City. There are also centers in Monterrey, Torrion, Guadalajara, and San Cristobal de las Casa.

Islam in Cuba has not been documented before the twentieth century. At the start of the twenty-first century, Muslims in Cuba continue to pray at home because there is no mosque where they can freely congregate. There is an Arab House built by a wealthy Arab in the 1940s, which houses an Arabic museum, a restaurant, and a prayer space for diplomats. Monies are currently being solicited for the building of a mosque. In the late twentieth century, a representative of the Muslim World League making his own solicitations on behalf of Cuban Muslims referred to the example of a small town, Pilaya de Rosacio, which has a Muslim population of 40 percent.

If the number of Muslim organizations and centers is any indication, there are Muslims all over other areas of South America. The origins of Islam in Chile have not been researched, but census reports show that in 1854 two Muslims from the Ottoman Empire came to Chile. Given that the Ottoman Empire (the last Muslim empire), which fell in 1929, covered a great deal of the Arab world, it is difficult to state ethnic origins of these immigrants. It is also only presumed that they were Muslim, for religion was not noted in the Chilean census of 1865. However, by 1895 the census did note the presence of 58 Muslims who lived in Tarapaca, Atacama, Valparaiso, and Santiago—all in the north of the country. By 1907 there were approximately 1,500 Muslims, all of them immigrants. The first Islamic institution in Chile was the Society of Muslim Union of Chile, founded in 1926. Interestingly, the numbers of Chilean Muslims rises and falls throughout the twentieth century for reasons that are unaccounted for in any reports. Through the 1970s and 1980s there were no religious leaders or mosques in Chile. In the 1990s the construction of Al-Salam Mosque was begun, following which other mosques were built in Temuco and Iquique. At the beginning of the twenty-first century, it is estimated that there are 3,000 Muslims in Chile, many of whom are Chilean by birth. The majority are Sunnī, but there are both Shīʿī and Ṣūfī communities present as well. Muslims, still a small minority group, generally face great pressure to convert to Christianity.

In times past, Rio de Janeiro was one of the disembarkation points for those millions abducted or sold from Muslim Africa. The native population learned about Islam primarily through Muslim behavior—prayer and abstention from pork and alcohol. Islamic revivals are reported to have occurred frequently enough over the centuries to leave a permanent mark. In 1899 the Cairo-based magazine *Al-Manar* published in its August issue an article entitled "Islam in Brazil." Here it was noted that the Muslim communities in Rio were made up of direct descendants of Muslim slaves. During the 1920s, Arab immigrants and traders added to Brazil's Islamic presence. Now, university students lead the way in teaching about Islam. There are currently five large Islamic organizations in Brazil: in São Paulo, Recife, Rio de Janeiro, Boa Vista, and Florianopolis.

Venezuela currently has fifteen Islamic civic associations in ten states. Arab immigrants, Venezuelans, and Creoles have come together to make Islam a known tradition. The closest estimate of when Islam came to Venezuela is "centuries ago." Estimates of the number of Muslims range from 700,000 to almost a million. Venezuelan Muslims have many of the same problems as Muslims in other countries where Muslims are a minority and Islam is a potentially competing faith—issues revolving around dress, political participation, civic concerns, and Christian missionizing.

Muslims in Peru trace their ancestry to the Spaniards and the Moros. As Moros fled persecution in Spain, they settled in many South and Latin American countries. In Peru they have had a lasting influence on dress, food, architecture, and both the social and political systems. Women who covered their hair were called *las tapadas Limenas* (The covered ones from Lima). There are also the famous *balcones lumenas,* which are protruding balconies done in a style known as *Arabescos*—a term clearly referring to an Islamic heritage. Twentieth-century Islam in Peru is dominated by Palestinian Arabs who arrived in the 1940s, fleeing Jewish persecution. Today, after several aborted construction projects, Peruvian Muslims (there are no estimates of their numbers) still have no mosques, but they do have the Asociacion Islamica del Peru in Lima and a school.

Argentinean Muslims currently number between 900,000 and one million. If Arabs and other ethnic groups are included this number increases to three million. It is reported that Muslims first arrived in Argentina around 1870 from Syria, Lebanon, and Palestine. Today, there are mosques all over the country, as well as nine Islamic centers. Bolivia traces its Islamic heritage to immigrants from the Ottoman Empire, but as with Chile the ethnicities of the Muslims who came is unknown. The first mosque however, was not commissioned until 1992, in Santa Cruz. There are already three civic organizations, known as Centro Islamico Bolivanos.

What is significant about the Islamic presence in the Caribbean and South America is that it has survived for so long. The patterns that lie behind the introduction of Islam into various countries appear to be multifold: in some countries the Islamic presence can be traced to the Atlantic slave trade; in others it is due to the influx of refugees caused by the Spanish persecution of non-Christians in Spain; in yet others it is the result of Muslims fleeing a ravaged Ottoman Empire in search of opportunities or of Arab refugees fleeing persecution by Jews in Palestine; and in others still it is attributable to the arrival of Muslim Indians, both indentured servants and immigrants seeking better opportunities. Regardless of the origin of the Islamic presence, it has endured and is currently growing.

ISLAM IN CANADA. The Canadian Census of 2001 lists 579,640 people, or 2 percent of Canada's population, as Muslim, an increase of 128.9 percent from the 1991 census. Ontario Muslims have more than doubled to 352,500, while the number of Muslims in Quebec increased by 141.8 percent. The median age is 28.1 years. As of 2004, there were more than eighty mosques, with additional locations rented or leased for prayers, such as Masjids and Islamic Centers. There are, in addition, various other centers where Muslims congregate for prayers and community activities.

The earliest authenticated account of Muslims in Canada is provided by the census of 1871, which lists thirteen Muslim residents. The first mosque, Al-Rashid, was built in Edmonton, Alberta, in 1938. Canadian Muslims hail from at least forty different countries from all over the Muslim world and all over the Americas. Until the census of 2001, the largest non-Christian minority were Jews, but Muslims now hold this distinction. A significant Muslim presence first began to develop in the 1970s, after the "White Canada" policy of 1891 was abandoned, with immigration coming predominately from the Arab world and South Asia. Mosques, which are mostly in major cities, are found in nine of the ten Canadian provinces, the exception being Prince Edward Island. A few dozen of these mosques have Islamic schools associated with them.

Canadian Muslims initially put their energies into building or acquiring facilities for prayers. This quickly extended to procuring additional spaces for religious education on the weekends. By the 1980s, full-time schools were established, and by the 1990s, specialized social services organizations were in place. The focus of these social services organizations was on pre- and post-marital counseling, teaching parenting skills, spiritual counseling, domestic and substance abuse issues, and *imām* training. Though the Qurʾān encourages Muslims to extend their social projects to the non-Muslim communities in which they live, this has only happened in a few instances.

On the other hand, Canadian Muslims have been much more successful than their U.S. counterparts regarding the media. Canada has a multifaith television channel, Vision TV, on which one host, a Muslim woman, uses two thirty-minute weekly programs to facilitate discussion of issues involving Muslims and Islam.

One study completed in the 1990s in Ottawa concluded that Muslims found "their comfort level fairly high" in Canada. Because many Muslim immigrants to Canada are professionals who earn enough to live quite comfortably, this experience is almost a foregone conclusion. With regard to less tangible issues, however, there are many concerns. Many Muslims find that the general media are hostile to Islam and Muslims. They discern "unfair or inaccurate stereotyping of their cultures" in movies, documentaries, and television series. On the other hand, many Muslims are hostile to media that exalt alcohol, causal sex, and lifestyles that are at best immodest. Even though Canadian society places a high premium on tolerance and pluralism, there is ongoing debate over the rising numbers of "nonwhite" citizens. Despite the official abandonment of the White Canada policy in the late 1960s, the desire to maintain the "whiteness" of Canada persists.

There are also substantial problems with racism inside the Muslim community. Many of the ethnic communities are extremely ethnocentric. There is little brotherhood or sisterhood when it comes to interracial marriages among Muslims. Assertions of a "color-blind" Islam fall by the wayside when it comes to marriage and private spaces. Other contentious issues arise out of the impact of influences from the larger Canadian community. Gender issues have become increasingly significant, as Muslim women from all ethnic groups learn of the efforts of the women's movement to enhance the quality of women's lives. This has led to disagreements over pervasive male-only leadership in most community functions and organizations.

Observers of and participants in the Canadian Muslim community note that Muslim communities in Canada are not doing a good job of dealing with interethnic tensions, parent-youth tensions, and the frustrations of women. Some say that Muslims, despite being drawn to the relatively comfortable lifestyle of the West, are still conditioned by the oppressive and repressive cultures of the Muslim world. For many Canadian observers, and for many young Muslims as well, the Muslim community seems terrified of social freedoms and of working cooperatively with other faith-based communities.

Whereas many Christian communities actively pursue interreligious dialogue, Muslims, with the exception of a few individuals and communities, generally do not. Even where multifaith awareness is critical—in prisons, hospitals, and hospices—Muslim involvement in dialogue and outreach is limited. Though Muslims are everywhere in the work force, intercultural exchange is infrequent. Some prominent Canadian Muslims lament a focus on the "homeland" that has been slow to change, even in the wake of repression of the community since the tragic events of September 11, 2001.

Since September 11, 2001, some Canadian Muslims have found themselves targeted. Provincial governments have reactivated their use of "security certificates," which give them the power to vote extrajudicially on "whether an immigrant should be shipped back to his or her country (if an immigrant) or stripped of citizenship (if he or she is already a citizen)." With one exception, the security certificate has only been used against Muslims. Project Shock provides subjects for the security certificate. This sixty-million-dollar Mountie-led effort, shadows, documents, and interrogates Muslims in Canada as part of the fight against terrorism. Under this effort, Canadian governments formed Integrated National Security Enforcement Teams (INSETs) that secretly investigate potential suspects. Civic commitment and community renown have not protected Muslims from co-workers who call police or INSETs to report suspicious behavior. The increase in racial profiling and human rights violations is currently becoming increasingly alarming.

In a recent poll by Tandem News, 43 percent of Canadians said they supported the idea of requiring immigrants to carry photo identification. At the same time, many Canadians (64 percent) opposed declaring war on Iraq with the United States, and after September 11, 2001, many non-Muslim Canadians have sought out information on Islam and Muslims. Muslim groups in Canada have begun the planning for a class-action suit in Ottawa against the security certificates and unlawful detentions.

The potential for detention and deportation in the United States, meanwhile, has caused some U.S. Muslims to flee to Canada. These new immigrants, largely Pakistani in origin, have come in the hundreds. In January 2003 in Ontario alone, over four hundred Pakistanis sought asylum, though only about 55 percent will have their applications accepted. Those who are denied must return to the United States, where they will be detained and possibly deported. As the United States continues to surveil and arrest its Muslim citizens and residents, Canadian Muslims fear that their lives will become even more difficult.

ISLAM IN THE UNITED STATES: NINETEENTH AND TWENTIETH CENTURIES. In 2000, Cornell University and Zogby International published two separate surveys of Muslims in the United States. Working from a figure of seven million Muslims, they estimated that almost half of U.S. Muslims are African American and almost half are immigrants. Though the United States census does not track religious affiliation and surveys have margins of error, some useful information can be gleaned from their findings. Over half of the U.S. Muslim population is under forty years of age and more than half have a college degree. More than half of the Muslim population earns more than $50,000 per year in occupations that range from entrepreneurial ventures to medicine. However, Muslims are virtually absent in professions that make public policy and consciously assert influence over public opinion, and these numbers are not changing. Muslim families are at least 25 percent larger than the average American family. The story of how Muslims are faring in the United States is really two separate stories: one of indigenous Americans and one of immigrant Americans.

During the nineteenth century the Muslim presence in the United States was negligible. Muhammad Alexander Webb, a multi-talented convert who worked as a diplomat, founded the American Islamic Propaganda Movement in 1893. He lectured on Islam, wrote books, and published a periodical entitled *The Moslem World.* Few traces of his movement remained after his death in 1916, however. In the early decades of the twentieth century a few hundred Arab Muslims from Syria represented the primary presence of Islam in the United States, along with a few fledgling communities of African Americans. For many of these largely uneducated but entrepreneurial immigrant Muslims, life was severe in Jim Crow America. The Immigration Act of 1897 had limited immigration from the Ottoman Empire under the overarching category of restrictions on Orientals, mimicking Canada's White Canada policy. Arab immigrants (mostly male) settled in the Midwestern states and along the East Coast. While many changed their given names to English nicknames to facilitate assimilation, others viewed their tenure in the United States as temporary. A shortage of Muslim women led to marriage to Christian women for some and a bachelor life for others.

Even with restrictive immigration policies, the United States also admitted about forty thousand Turks, Kurds, Albanians, and Bosnians between 1900 and 1925. Almost simultaneously, Islam was developing a presence in some of the segregated black communities of the East Coast and Midwest. Sometime during the second decade of the twentieth century, the Moorish Science Temple, led by Noble Drew Ali, emerged. The 1920s witnessed the creation of the Aḥmadiyah movement in Islam (1921), the Universal Islamic Society (1926), the First Muslim Mosque of Pittsburgh (1928), and the Islamic Brotherhood (1929). This collage of philosophies and ideological positions marked the beginning of an expansion of Islam among African Americans that would eventually make them the biggest single ethnic group among U.S. Muslims. While immigrant Muslims sought the American Dream, Americans of African descent sought refuge from their American nightmare.

The first sixty-five years of the twentieth century was an especially horrible and violent time for black Americans. Inequality was enforced through Jim Crow laws (extensions of the slave codes) in southern states, and through convention in many of the northern states. Complete or nearly complete segregation in all public places was basic to the U.S. social order. Blacks had no rights that whites had to respect. In reaction to strict segregation, a wave of lynchings, and suffering caused by the Great Depression, blacks began increasingly to turn to Islam. The rise of ideologies that use Islam as their basis, at least in part, owes everything to the state of the nation.

The Moorish Science Temple of America, founded in Newark, New Jersey, in 1913 by Timothy Drew (later Noble Drew Ali), was the first of these ventures into Islam. Noble Drew Ali believed that Morocco was the original land of African Americans, whom he called Asiatics and Moors. Drew Ali claimed that after traveling to Morocco he converted to Islam and received permission to spread Islam in America. This account has been spread for almost a century by community members, but the evidence for this voyage and for meetings between Drew Ali and various Islamic dignitaries has never been documented. Some researchers assert that Drew Ali may have met Muslims from various parts of the world who had immigrated to the East Coast. However it was that he came into contact with Islam, Drew Ali took elements of Islam and combined them with other religious teachings to formulate the *Holy Koran of the Moorish Science Temple of America.* The book's cover asserts that the book had been "divinely prepared by the Prophet Noble drew Ali, by the guiding of his father, God, Allah."

Members of the Moorish Science Temple constructed a new way of life for themselves. They abstained from alcohol, gambling, and pork consumption and embraced clean living, fasting, and prayer. Women covered their heads with turbans made from seven yards of cloth, while men donned fezzes. Modesty of dress was evidenced through the wearing of loose clothing. The *Holy Koran of the Moorish Science Temple* provided a template for personal relationships and etiquette for the public sphere. Moors, as members were called, gained a reputation for clean living, honesty, and frugality—a reputation reflected in some of the works of the Harlem Renaissance. Moors were also entrepreneurial. They manufactured and sold oils and herbal remedies throughout the black community. The popularity of Moorish Science enabled Noble Drew Ali to open ten chapters within ten years in cities in both the Northeast and Midwest. By 1928 he had established seventeen temples in fifteen states.

In the face of competition from numerous other ideologies seeking the allegiance of the black community, the Moorish Science temple taught a very simple definition of Islam: "The cardinal doctrine of Islam is the unity of the Father, Allah, we believe in One God." Perhaps because his community did not follow all of the tenets of Islam and because of his heretical designation of himself as prophet, Drew Ali did not refer to his movement's religion as Islam, but as *Islamism.*

Another Islamic movement embraced by some in the black community was Aḥmadīyah, which has its origins in South Asia. Aḥmadī publishing houses in India were prolific in the production of English-language Islamic materials. During the early years of the twentieth century, most of the English Qurʾāns, English study materials, biographies of the prophet Muḥammad, and Islamic history texts distributed in the United States were produced by them. Most African American Muslims had little knowledge of the debates and conflicts associated with this particular Islamic reform movement in its country of origin, and they eagerly embraced the limited brand of Islamic harmony it advocated. In a social environment in which prophets were many and varied and the safety of every descendant of slaves was at risk, the Aḥmadī version of Islam became popular. As these South Asians embraced African Americans and publicly decried the violence against them, Islam gained a further foothold in the black community. One difference with this community however, was the absence of black nationalism.

Druse Mohammed, son of a Mamlūk military commander, also reported to be a mentor of Marcus Garvey, was a pan-African founder of the Universal Islamic Society in Detroit in 1926. An apparently tireless advocate for human rights, he challenged Europeans to accept an Islam-based universalism as an extension of Enlightenment ideals. He saw Islam as an alternative to Western imperialism. His ideas were readily embraced by African Americans, for whom the Islamic ideal of universal brotherhood was a welcome alternative to the racist practices of Protestant Christianity. Unfortunately, the only accounts of the Universal Islamic Society that exist are a few small pamphlets.

Shaykh Daoud Ahmed Faisal's Islamic Brotherhood (1924; also incorporated as the State Street Mosque and the Islamic Mission) was the first African American Sunnī Muslim group in the United States. Here, as with the Aḥmadīyah movement, the Qurʾān, biographies of Prophet Muḥammad, and accounts of Islamic history formed the central texts. Unlike Aḥmadīyah and the Garvey movement, Shaykh Faisal focused his community efforts directly on the social problems of the black community. Just as Noble Drew Ali sought publicly to distinguish his movement from philosophies of Ethiopianism, black Christian sects, and Garvey's movement, Faisal distinguished Sunnī Islam from both the previously mentioned movements and the Moorish Science Temple. There are nevertheless some curious similarities between Drew Ali and Faisal. Shaykh Faisal also asserted that he received a letter—in his case from Jordan, in 1925—authorizing him to spread Islam. Whatever the genesis of the Islamic Brotherhood, it has been estimated that the group inspired over sixty thousand conversions to Islam during Shaykh Daoud Faisal's lifetime. This community initially used the Qur'āns and other Islamic literature published by the Aḥmadiyah, but then began producing their own translations.

By 1930, Islam was firmly planted in the black religious landscape. The Great Depression had taken more of a toll on blacks than on whites, and the resultant stress led to the emergence of more prophets and more Muslim communities. The First Mosque of Pittsburgh (1928), a Sunnī congregation, was originally affiliated with the Aḥmadiyah movement, but, armed with knowledge of the Qur'ān and Arabic, they began to challenge the core tenets of the Aḥmadī Mission and its focus on its founder as a prophet. After ten years of fund-raising, this black community bought out the Aḥmadī and moved fully into Sunnī Islam. The 1930s also witnessed the beginnings of the Nation of Islam, a black community that spoke to the hearts of many black Americans and raised the reactionary hatred of white and black Christian communities.

The Nation of Islam had its origins in a collaboration between Wali Fard Mohammed (his ethnicity is still being debated) and Elijah Poole (later known as Elijah Mohammed). It did not become known for its form of Islam, but for its rhetoric attacking Protestant Christian America's treatment of blacks. By publicly labeling whites "the Devil" and detailing the many ways whites sought black genocide, the Nation of Islam insured its popularity among blacks and the hatred and fear of whites. Unlike the Moorish Science Temple, the Nation used the Holy Qur'ān as its focus, augmented by Elijah Mohammed's *How to Eat to Live* and *Message to The Black Man*, and a compilation of Fard Mohammed's lectures called the *Supreme Wisdom.* Like the Moorish Science Temple, the Nation claimed an Asiatic heritage and declared Islam to be original religion of the black man. Also like the Moorish Science Temple, the Nation deviated from Islamic orthodoxy by declaring the holy status of its founders: according to their teachings, Fard Mohammed was God in person and Elijah Mohammed was the messenger of God. The Nation practiced most of the central tenets of Islam, though it adapted them to the social needs of blacks in America. One example was their adaptation of the practice of Ramaḍān (the month of self-restraint), which they moved to December. This shift was seen as necessary both to avoid the temptation to overspend during the Christmas season, and to counteract the focus on Christian celebrations, which imaged the Creator, God, as a white man.

As the Nation of Islam matured, it established temples across the United States in every major city. It is estimated that at its peak there were more than 500,000 registered members. Many researchers assert that much of the growth of the Nation during the 1950s can be attributed to media focus on the charismatic leadership of Malcolm X (formerly Malcolm Little; also known much later as El Hajj Malik Shabazz). The Nation organized itself around Islamic notions of abstention from consumption of pork, gambling, alcohol, narcotics, and lewd behavior. Women were required to attend Muslim Girls Training class in order to learn home economics, and Civilization classes to learn about world and black history. Men were required to become members of the Fruit of Islam, from which they learned about the proper nature of marital relationships, how to conduct themselves privately and publicly, crafts, and the martial arts. While the men donned suits with white shirts and bow ties, the women wore a uniform consisting of a long tunic over a long skirt, with a matching veil.

Building a "righteous nation" that would be independent of whites was the goal. The Nation quickly developed the best drug and narcotics detoxification programs around, and simultaneously developed a wide range of businesses, both to keep members away from the temptations of drug use and to provide a road to self-esteem. Their efforts resulted in the first black parochial school system, a nationwide chain of food stores, cleaners, clothing-manufacturing factories, and restaurants. They acquired farms and, in order to import various goods, entered into contracts with Muslims overseas. They published a national newspaper, books, and pamphlets. The black community took pride in these accomplishments and identified, though distantly, with the Nation's efforts. Perhaps because of the Nation's success, but more likely because of its rhetoric, the U.S. media decided, in the 1950s, that the Nation was the only important manifestation of Islam in the African American community. Naturally, this paved the way for confrontations with other expressions of Islam, especially Sunnī Islam. This antagonistic relationship between different strains of African American Islam characterized the greater portion of the twentieth century.

The Nation of Islam, with a great deal of media assistance, became strongly associated with opposition to the methodologies used by the civil rights movement. Media cast the conflict as one between black separatism and integrationism, totally ignoring the root cause of all black protest—white oppression. Most African American Muslims opposed Martin Luther King's tactics of putting women and children at the front of protest lines to face armed white men with attack dogs. While black Christians hoped that white Christians would eventually find their faith incompatible with the continued persecution of blacks, most African American

Muslims believed that if white society's understanding of Christianity had permitted the violence thus far, change was unlikely. These opposing views became associated with their most ardent voices—Malcolm X and Martin Luther King.

During this period, African American Muslim inmates began to sue the federal government for the right to use Arabic/Muslim names and for the freedom to practice Islam—including the right to have halal meat, Qur'āns, prayer rugs, and so on. After a series of successful litigations, these prisoners firmly established Islam as a part of America's religious landscape. Despite the fact that the actual number of African American Muslims was not that large, Islam began to exert a great deal of influence in the black community. In fact, one of the reasons that African Americans of all religious persuasions supported the Civil Rights Act of 1964 was that it revoked the Oriental Exclusion Act of the 1920s, which prevented immigration from the Muslim world.

By the 1970s, African American Muslim communities had grown in size and religious sophistication. The original communities—the Moorish Science Temple, the Aḥmadīyah, and the Nation of Islam—all widened their membership within the black community. Shaykh Daoud Faisal's community developed into separate entities under the general umbrella of Darul Islam (The Abode/House of Islam). There were at least fourteen philosophically different expressions of Islam in the African American community. The original communities maintained their organizational structures, practices, and beliefs, while the newer communities sought out contact with the Muslim world. Members of the Darul Islam communities traveled to the Sudan, Jordan, Saudi Arabia, Egypt, and Morocco to learn Arabic and pursue Islamic studies. Controversy over the definitions of Islam in the United States increased at an accelerated rate. Despite the debates, African American Muslims introduced Islam into the worlds of music, sports, education, health care, and social services, all fields in which they were represented in significant numbers.

The Ansarullah Nubian Islamic Hebrews, led by As-Sayyid Isa Al-Haadi, developed communities across the United States. Starting in 1971 they published over 200 books, almost three hundred cassette tapes, and dozens of videotapes and newspapers. The community in New York City owned a recording studio that provided a base for rhythm-and-blues, rap, and pop musicians. Members of this community lived communally, practicing collective ownership and control of property and goods. Children were raised with Arabic as their only language and were schooled inside the community. Leveling charges of racism and "sectism" at Saudi Arabia, this community found its origins in the Sudan.

Yusuf Muzaffaruddin Hamid led the Islamic Party of North America, which was based primarily in Washington, D.C., but had extensions later on in Georgia and the Caribbean. Hamid journeyed throughout the Muslim world to study the various popular Islamic movements of the 1960s. When he returned, he built an organization dedicated to sharing knowledge of Islam with the general black population of Washington, D.C. While there are only a few publications from this community, they had a very positive and influential impact on black Washington, as they worked to reform drug users and prostitutes and provide tutorial and mentoring services.

One community that became especially renowned among young musicians is the Five Percent Nation, an offshoot of the Nation of Islam. Formally known as the Nation of Gods and Earths, this group was founded in New York City in 1964 by Clarence 13X, a former member of the Nation of Islam. The name of the group came from the Nation of Islam's "Lost Found Nation Lessons." The Five Percent were those who taught righteousness, freedom, justice, and equality to the entire human family. They were destined to be poor, righteous teachers and to struggle especially against the elite. Their connection to Islam, though tenuous at best, remains, and they have been a conduit for young African Americans seeking to explore Islam as a worldview.

With the death of the Honorable Elijah Muhammad in 1975, the Nation of Islam fell into philosophical debates that reached their zenith in a split. Wallace Muhammad declared that his father, Elijah, had always been leading the community toward Sunnī Islam, though he was in error in taking so long. Louis Farrakhan and other ministers disagreed. Wallace (now known as Warithudeen) led those Nation members who followed him through a series of doctrinal and organizational changes. His group first called themselves Bilalians after Bilal ibn Ribah, an Abyssinian slave who converted to Islam and was the first muezzin (person who calls the community to prayer). Several years later (1982), they emerged as the American Muslim Mission. Since the 1990s the community has been called the Muslim American Society, though it is involved in a dispute with an immigrant group over the rights to the name. The original Nation has also gone through changes and further divisions.

Many in the Nation who did not follow Warithudeen Muhammad gave their allegiance to Louis Farrakhan. Some of the philosophical changes that occurred under Louis Farrakhan's leadership mimicked the changes initiated by Warithudeen Muhammad, but they developed over a much longer period of time. In the 1980s Minister Farrakhan solicited aid from African Muslim *imāms* in slowly moving his group into the fold of a more traditional Islam, while maintaining the focus on the concerns in the black community. Others in the original Nation chose neither Farrakhan nor Muhammad as their leader. Rather they selected another very outspoken minister, Silas Muhammad. Minister Silas Muhammad has primarily made his presence felt in the international arena of human rights debates in the Hague. Still others chose Elijah Muhammad's brother, John Muhammad, while some decided to continue with the original platform of the Nation, acknowledging only the Honorable Elijah Muhammad as leader.

Most communities of African American Muslims are still in the process of maturation. Members of most communities have continued to study overseas in the Muslim world, but there has not been much in the way of literary production. Represented most heavily in the worlds of music and sports, African American Muslims rarely enter the political fray. Their apolitical stance is attributable both to the fatigue and despair that followed the civil rights movement and to the discouragement of "learned" members of the immigrant communities. Recently, however, there has been some increase in political activism and a number of Muslims have run for and now hold political and judicial offices.

European-American Muslims have been present in Islam in the United States at least since the conversion of Alexander Webb in the late nineteenth century. Though few in number, their diligence regarding outreach across ethnic barriers and to the larger white society, along with their novelty, has kept them in the forefront of the communities to which they belong. The number of European-American Muslims is growing, and is currently estimated to be in the tens of thousands.

Latino Americans have been converting to Islam for the last thirty years, largely from Catholicism but also from Pentecostal Christianity. Since many do not change their names upon conversion, there numbers are hard to track. One recent survey of mosques found Latino mosques in New York, Los Angeles, Newark, and Chicago. This survey also concluded that 6 percent of American converts are Latino. Most Latino-American Muslims consider Islam a natural heritage and point to the many Arabic words and names in Spanish. Many converts to Islam have spoken at conferences and seminars on their conversions, citing differences with the Catholic Church over the concept of the Trinity and also the notion of "mysteries of the Church" behind such concepts.

Alianza Islamica, founded in 1975 by a group of Puerto Rican converts, was the first Latino Muslim association in the United States. Working closely with African American Muslims, they are at the forefront of battles against urban gang activity, drug dealing, and prostitution. They sponsor mentoring and cultural programs, along with forums on HIV and AIDS. Like African American Muslims, they have had myriad problems with immigrant Muslims. Since the founding of Alianza Islamica, quite a few Latino Muslim organizations have emerged, such as the Latino American Dawah Organization, which works to educate Latinos about Islam.

Students and professionals from the Muslim world began immigrating to the United States in the late 1960s. At first, many immigrants prayed with African Americans, but as their numbers grew they formed communities based on common language, common ethinicitcty, and, when possible, common regional origin. Arab Muslim students formed the first Muslim Student's Association (MSA) in 1963. The MSAs firmly established Islam as an available worldview among the educated elite. Muslims, recruited as healthcare professionals, scientists, and technology experts, brought an Islamic presence to places where it had not previously been. It is estimated that Muslims currently comprise a significant percent of the physicians, architects, and scientists in large corporations and hospitals. The architect of the Sears Tower in Chicago was a Muslim.

Immigrant Muslims in the United States come from eighty-four countries. Predominately, they are Sunnī Muslim, but there are also Shīʿī, Ṣūfī, and Ismāʿīlī communities. Researchers report that Shīʿī and Ismāʿīlī Muslims make up 15 to 20 percent of the immigrant Muslim population, and that the majority of Muslim university professors belong to one of these two groups. In the various Sunnī Muslim communities, the competition for leadership is fierce. Arabs have the greatest say in defining Islam, while South Asians vie with them and with each other for authority. Some differences between groups are becoming sharper, while at the same time recognition of common ground is also increasing. Most of the immigrant communities still tend to be ethnocentric, staying away from each other and from the larger American community.

Both Arab and South Asian Muslims have formed a number of professional and social organizations, many of which are national. These organizations have assisted them in settling in the United States and provide venues for discussions of intracommunity issues and general social gatherings. They also facilitate marriages between young adults. Whether Sunnī or Shīʿī, most immigrants marry endogamously, maintain traditional customs at home, and predominately speak Arabic, Urdu, or their mother tongue.

Ṣūfī orders have increased their numbers in the last two decades. Some are Sunnī, others Shīʿī. Most of the members are white, middle- and upper-middle-class American converts, but there are also a small number of immigrant and African American converts. African Muslim immigrants come from a variety of countries, but they are small in number, with Somali refugees forming what is perhaps the largest single ethnic group. All immigrant communities have established an informal economy through networks connecting them with their former homelands.

Few Muslims live in rural America. The suburbs of major cities continue to be where residential communities are established and mosques are built. Yet immigrant Muslims have not yet become an integral part of these suburban communities. The Islamic presence, however, is visible. This visibility and lack of community participation has led to vandalism of mosques and attacks on individual Muslim families, especially in the period since September 11, 2001.

Since that date, 13,740 Muslims have been detained and ordered into deportation proceedings (as of 2004). Many Muslims from countries targeted by the U.S. government for support of terrorist activities have fled to Canada or simply gone "home." The immigrant Muslim community lives in perpetual fear of night raids, of their coworkers calling the FBI or CIA, and of mosque invasions and deportations. The actions of the U.S. government have encouraged various media personalities to attack Islam and Muslims, leading in turn to several Constitutional debates about the First Amendment. As a result, immigrant Muslims are debating to what extent they can or should become "Americans."

SEE ALSO African American Religions, article on Muslim Movements; Malcolm X; Nation of Islam.

BIBLIOGRAPHY

Balderston, Daniel, Mike Gonzalez, and Ana M. López, eds. *Encyclopedia of Contemporary Latin American and Caribbean Cultures.* New York, 2000. This volume contains sections on topics such as: General History, Religion and Politics, Globalization and Latin American Religion, and the Transnational Character of Latin American Religion.

Brah, Avtar. *Cartographies of Diaspora: Contesting Identities.* New York, 1996. Explores the interrelationships of race, gender, class, sexuality, ethnicity, generation, and nationalism in different discourses, practices, and political contexts. Maps theoretical and political shifts in approaches to questions of difference and diversity.

Diouf, Sylviane A. *Servants of Allah: African Muslims Enslaved in the Americas.* New York, 1998. An impressive book drawing on Diouf's Senegalese heritage, her familiarity with Islam and Arabic, and her translations of relevant French, Spanish, and Portuguese documents from both sides of the Atlantic.

Forte, Maximilian Christian. *Against the Trinity: An Insurgent Imam Tells His Story: Religion, Politics, and Rebellion in Trinidad and Tobago.* Binghamton, N.Y., 1996. A personal narrative.

Gomez, Michael A. "Muslims in Early America." *Journal of Southern History* 60, no. 4 (November 1994): 671–718. Gomez examines the diverse African regions and cultures from which Muslim slaves came, and establishes links between these cultures and the present-day African American community. This article was later expanded in Gomez's *Exchanging Our Country Marks: The Transformation of African Identities in the Colonial and Antebellum South* (Chapel Hill, N.C., 1998).

Korom, Frank J. *Hosay Trinidad: Muharram Performances in an Indo-Caribbean Diaspora.* Philadelphia, 2002. Beyond basic historical and ethnographic data, *Hosay Trinidad* offers a thoughtful and rigorous exploration of the Trinidadian *Muharram:* its contradictions and controversies and the complex interaction of the local and global influences that shape it.

Mallon, Elias. *Neighbors: Muslims in North America.* New York, 1989. In an effort to facilitate interfaith relations, this book provides interviews with Muslims who talk about their families, their work, and their spiritual journeys.

Nimer, Mohamed. *The North American Muslim Resource Guide: Muslim Community Life in the United States and Canada.* New York, 2002. This useful resource offers an overview of mainstream Muslim life in North America and provides basic information about Muslim Americans and Muslim Canadians. It includes population statistics, as well as immigration information that tracks the settlement of Muslim people in the Americas. American Muslim participation in the political process is given special attention. The book also reviews various recent events with special significance for Islamic-Americans, especially in relation to the September 11 terrorist attacks.

Pulis, John W. *Religion, Diaspora, and Cultural Identity: A Reader in the Anglophone Caribbean.* Library of Anthropology, no. 14. Amsterdam, 1999. This volume is a much-needed and long overdue addition to the literature of Caribbean studies. Drawing upon ethnographic and historical research in a variety of contexts and settings, its contributors explore the relationship between religious and social life.

Quick, Abdullah Hakim. *Deeper Roots: Muslims in the Americas and the Caribbean before Columbus to the Present.* London, 1996. A brief look at the history of Islam in the Caribbean that provides some amazing material concerning early Muslim settlements—long before the arrival of Columbus.

Richardson, E. Allen. *Islamic Cultures in North America: Patterns of Belief and Devotion of Muslims from Asian Countries in the United States and Canada.* New York, 1981. A very descriptive book.

Waines, David. *An Introduction to Islam.* Cambridge, U.K., 1995. A fairly comprehensive look at Islam and its spread, from the perspective of a believer.

Waugh, E. H., Baha Abu-Laban, and Regula B. Qureshi, eds. The *Muslim Community in North America.* Edmonton, Alberta, 1983. One of the first comprehensive treatments of immigrant Muslims in North America, especially Canada. Community concerns and issues are explored in detail.

Yousif, Ahmad. *Muslims in Canada: A Question of Identity.* Ottawa, Ontario, 1993. An excellent review of old and new Canadian immigrant communities. Family life and mosque- and school-building projects are explored along with attendant issues and concerns.

AMINAH BEVERLY MCCLOUD (2005)

ISLAMIC LAW

This entry consists of the following articles:

ISLAMIC LAW: SHARĪʿAH

Sharīʿah is an Arabic term used to designate Islamic law. It originally referred to a path trodden by camels to a water source, and the commonly used Arabic phrase *al-sharīʿah al-islāmīyah* may be translated as "the Islamic way." In the case of Islamic law, the way is one that leads the righteous believer to Paradise in the afterlife. The *sharīʿah* is not deemed a religious law by virtue of the subject matters it covers, for these range far beyond the sphere of religious concerns strictly speaking and extend to the mundane affairs of everyday life. Rather, its religious character is due to the Muslim belief that it derives from divinely inspired sources and represents God's plan for the proper ordering of all human activities. Although Muslims agree that they are bound by the *sharīʿah,* the interpretations of its requirements have differed historically according to sectarian and school divisions and, in modern times, also according to differing views of how the *sharīʿah* applies in the changed circumstances of present-day societies.

The interpretations of the requirements of the *sharīʿah* are contained in the *fiqh*. In a general sense, *fiqh* means "knowledge" or "understanding," but it is also used in the more specific sense of Islamic jurisprudence. *Sharīʿah* and *fiqh* are often treated as synonymous terms designating the body of rules constituting Islamic law. However, *fiqh* can also refer to the science of interpreting the *sharīʿah*.

ORIGINS AND NATURE. The historical origin of the *sharīʿah* lies in the revelation that Muslims believe was given to the prophet Muḥammad by God through the vehicle of the archangel Gabriel in the last decades before the Prophet's death in 632 CE. This divine revelation was later recorded in a text known as the Qurʾān. Although only a small portion of the Qurʾān concerns strictly legal questions, it sets forth a number of general principles regarding how Muslims are to conduct themselves. The Qurʾān is replete with commands to believers to abide by God's limits, to obey God and his Prophet, and to judge according to what God has laid down. It contains many references to God's laws and commands. The prevailing view among Muslims is that the Qurʾān laid the underpinnings for a distinctively Islamic legal order and one that all Muslims are bound to follow as a token of their submission (*islām* in Arabic) to the will of God.

From this kernel the *sharīʿah* grew into a vast corpus of law. One of the great, challenging issues of Islamic intellectual history has been that of defining the relationship between the text of divine revelation and subsequent legal development, an effort that has entailed the working out of a theory of resources to provide an Islamic theoretical basis for resolving legal problems not explicitly addressed in the Qurʾān.

Sharīʿah rules were part of the positive law applied by the government of the early Muslim community, which was originally conceived as an entity where political and religious loyalties would be coterminous. At the same time, the *sharīʿah* was also understood as a system of moral guidance for the individual believer.

In the Islamic view, governments exist only to ensure that the *sharīʿah* is properly administered and enforced. Governments are subordinate to the *sharīʿah* and must execute its commands and prohibitions. In other words, what Islam envisages is a scheme of divine nomocracy, in which the law is the medium of social control—truly, a government of laws, not of men.

Should the government of a Muslim society fail in its obligation to uphold the *sharīʿah* as the positive law, or the judges of this world fail in their obligation to administer justice in accordance with the *sharīʿah,* the individual believer would still be held to the responsibility incumbent upon all Muslims to conform their behavior to the *sharīʿah*. On the Day of Judgment each Muslim will be held to account for any personal failures to comply with the commands and prohibitions of the *sharīʿah*.

Classification of acts. The dual nature of the *sharīʿah* as positive law and deontology, serving the combined functions of law and of what in some other religious systems might be moral philosophy, is reflected in the fact that Muslim jurists distinguish between two fundamentally different ways of classifying human acts. One way is to assess the moral character of acts, an assessment that corresponds to the deontological quality of the *sharīʿah*. For this task there exists a fivefold scheme of classification, according to which an act may be mandatory, recommended, neutral (that is, entailing no moral consequences), blameworthy, or prohibited. Knowledge of this classification scheme enables pious Muslims to follow a meritorious course of conduct that will ensure their salvation on the Day of Judgment.

The second way of classifying acts reflects the fact that the *sharīʿah* is meant to be used as the positive law of Muslim societies. The fundamental distinction made by Muslim jurists in this connection is between acts that are legally binding and valid and those that are of no legal effect or invalid. They also distinguish between licit acts and illicit acts warranting the imposition of penalties or exposing the actor (and potentially persons in privity with the actor) to legal liability. The classifications in the two schemes are not correlated; from knowledge of how an act is to be evaluated from the ethical standpoint, one cannot draw any automatic conclusions about the legal validity or invalidity of an act or whether it is punishable or goes unpunished by worldly authorities. Likewise, one cannot safely make assumptions about how acts will be classified from an ethical standpoint based on whether they are legally valid or not or whether they entail penalties or legal liability.

The precise nature of the relationship between the *sharīʿah* and Islamic theology is not easy to delineate and has been the subject of disagreement among Muslim scholars of Islamic philosophy, theology, and law over the centuries. However, throughout the history of Islam there has been a tendency to emphasize the elaboration of exact standards for conduct rather than setting detailed standards for what Muslims should believe, and, by extension, to require adherence to the standards of orthopraxis rather than demanding orthodoxy of creed.

Principal divisions. The two principal divisions of the *sharīʿah* are based on the subject categories of legal rules. The first category is that of the *ʿibadāt,* or strictly religious obligations. These comprise the believer's duties vis-à-vis the deity. In this category one finds very extensive rules regarding precisely how to carry out the acts of worship and religious observances incumbent on the individual Muslim. The performance of daily prayers (*ṣalāt*), the pilgrimage to Mecca (*ḥājj*), the practice of fasting during the month of Ramaḍān (*ṣawm*), and the payment of the alms tax (*zakāt*) are all regulated by the rules of *ʿibadāt.* These, along with the profession of faith (*shahādah*), constitute the so-called pillars of the faith in Islam. Ancillary rules such as those for identifying sources of ritual pollution and setting forth the requirements for the ablutions necessary to achieve a state of ritual purity, the techniques for correct preparation of a corpse for burial, and the selection of a prayer leader in a given congregation are likewise included in the *ʿibadāt* category.

The Islamic concern for orthopraxis in religious matters clearly emerges from any examination of the very exacting scheme of *ʿibadāt* rules. While some specific provisions of *ʿibadāt* rules vary according to sectarian and school divisions, one finds considerable agreement on the fundamental features of the *sharīʿah* in this area. Within a given sect, the rules of *ʿibadāt* have tended to remain relatively stable and uncontroversial over the centuries.

The other main category of *sharīʿah* rules is that of the *muʿamalāt,* which regulate the conduct of interpersonal relations rather than the relationship of the believer to the deity. There is considerable diversity among the sects and schools regarding the *sharīʿah* rules in this category. In the early twenty-first century there is also significant controversy about the degree to which these rules, originally formulated by medieval jurists, need to be updated and reformed in the light of modern circumstances.

HISTORICAL DEVELOPMENT. The question of the historical development of the *sharīʿah* cannot be fairly discussed without acknowledging the deep and persistent cleavage between the views set forth in modern Western scholarship and the views of the majority of Muslim scholars. The positions that have been taken by Western scholars regarding the historical development of Islamic law challenge deeply held convictions of most Muslim scholars and are strongly reprehended by the latter. The nature of the differing views and their implications will be explained in what follows.

The relation of the Qurʾān to previous law. As already noted, the Qurʾān provided the original kernel of *sharīʿah* law. Most of the Qurʾānic verses dealing with legal questions were transmitted to the Prophet in the decade after the Hijrah, or flight from Mecca to Medina (622 CE).

An unresolved dispute in Islamic jurisprudence stems from the question of whether the rules set forth in the Qurʾān should be regarded as a break with the preexisting system of western Arabian customary law or whether the revelations came to modify and reform some aspects of that law while otherwise retaining it. Some Muslim scholars have concluded that the great unevenness in depth of coverage of different topics in Qurʾanic legislation should be taken to imply that the resulting gaps were intended to be filled by reference to those pre-Islamic customary laws that were not changed by the Qurʾān, while others see in it a fresh starting point for legal development.

The Sunnī-Shīʿī division. The death of the prophet Muḥammad in 632 CE marked the end of the period of Qurʾanic revelation to the Muslim community. Until the Umayyad dynasty (661–750) came to power, the community was ruled by four leaders known as the Rāshidūn, or the "Rightly Guided [Caliphs]." The assumption of leadership by the Umayyads had great consequences for both sectarian and legal developments. Repudiating the Umayyads, the Shīʿī and Khārijī factions both broke away from the main body of Muslims, who came to be called Sunnīs, and their respective legal orientations thenceforth diverged. The Khārijīs (also known as the Ibadiyah) believed that the leadership of the Muslim community should be determined by elections and that Muslims had the right to rebel against an unqualified ruler. This Khārijī position has generally been regarded as heretical by other Muslims, and although small Khārijī communities have survived in remote areas of the Muslim world, Khārijī thought has been marginalized by the majority. The Shīʿī faction believed that the first three caliphs had usurped the rule of the community, which in their view should have passed to the fourth of the Rāshidūn, ʿAlī ibn Abī Ṭālib (d. 661), a cousin and son-in-law of the Prophet. While Sunnī Muslims subsequently looked to the pronouncements and examples of all of the Rāshidūn for authority on how the community should be governed and for guidance on questions of Islamic law, the Shīʿah repudiated the authority of all but the caliph ʿAlī.

Not only did the Shīʿah believe that the caliph ʿAlī had been the rightful successor of the Prophet, but they also believed that leadership of the community rightfully still belonged to ʿAlī's blood descendants after the civil war that resulted in his death and the establishment of a hereditary monarchy by the victorious Umayyads. Those of the caliph ʿAlī's descendants who inherited his authority were known as *imāms*, and like him they were believed by the Shīʿah to share the same divine inspiration that had enabled the Prophet, while himself not divine, to make authoritative pronouncements on *sharīʿah* law. That is, their *imāms* were qualified to interpret the divine will for humankind and could thus serve as an ongoing link between God the Lawgiver and the community after the death of the Prophet. The Shīʿī community subsequently split into subsects over questions of who was entitled to succeed to the position of *imām.* The largest of the subsects, the Twelvers, believes that the last imam, who disappeared in 874, went into a state of occultation from which he is expected eventually to return, while the other subsects follow lines of *imāms* whose descent has continued into the modern era.

The earliest stage of *sharīʿah* law. For Sunnīs the possibility of divine revelation and the making of new Islamic law ceased with the death of the Prophet. Subsequent generations of Muslims who were concerned with how to establish a legal system on an Islamic basis were thus faced with a problem of scarce source material. Although there is little information on the development of legal thought in the generations immediately following the death of the Prophet, it does not appear that this problem was initially of great concern to the leaders of the community, who were preoccupied with the challenges of meeting the military threats to the growing Islamic polity and administering its rapidly expanding territory. *Ad hoc* measures and a spirit of pragmatism appear to have characterized much of the decision making of the early political leaders, who also served as judges.

A view common in Western scholarship is that as the new empire absorbed its early conquests of Syria, Iraq, Egypt, and Iran, it was also exposed to influences from the local civilizations, which included the very highly developed legal cultures of Romano-Byzantine law, Jewish law, Sasanid law, and the law of the Eastern Christian churches. An assumption commonly made by Western scholars is that educated converts to Islam from these cultures perpetuated the legal traditions of the conquered civilizations, which, in a syncretic process, were assimilated into the nascent Islamic legal culture. According to this perspective, the ostensibly Islamic derivation of much of *sharīʿah* law is the product of later attempts to create Islamic pedigrees for legal principles actually borrowed from other legal traditions by linking them to Islamic sources. Most Muslim scholars absolutely reject this view and take the position that *sharīʿah* law owes no debt whatsoever to any non-Islamic tradition. In any event, it must be said that the historical and comparative legal research that would be needed to prove or disprove scientifically either of these two theses has never been undertaken, and the dispute about the relation of the *sharīʿah* to other legal traditions in the areas first conquered by the Islamic empire cannot be resolved at present.

Ancient law schools. The jurisprudence of the Sunnī branch of *sharīʿah* law had its beginnings in what are called the ancient schools of law. Within a century of the Prophet's death there were prominent law schools in various cities in Iraq, Syria, and the Ḥijāz. It appears that the scholars in these ancient schools felt free to resort to ratiocination to develop legal rules for new situations and that they may also have been influenced in their approach to legal questions by the judicial practice of the tribunals set up by the Umayyad rulers. While individual scholars did attain renown in this period, what was viewed as the normative legal standard was the consensus of the scholars in a given locality, or the *sunnah*—roughly, "custom"—of the school. Some attempts were made to establish Islamic derivations for such local custom, which might be ascribed to early authorities in the first generation of the Muslim community, including the Prophet himself.

The traditionist movement. Meanwhile, a second movement was under way, that of the traditionists, who began to make their influence felt in the course of the second century after the Prophet's death. The traditionists did not accept the authority of the *sunnah* of the ancient schools, nor did they accept the practice of the scholars of those ancient schools who relied on juristic opinion to resolve legal questions. Instead, the traditionists proposed that accounts relating the sayings and doings of the Prophet should be treated as legally binding statements of law. The traditionists collected traditions, known as *ḥadīth* (pl., *aḥadīth*), which purported to record the Prophet's sayings and his reactions to the different situations he had confronted.

Unlike the Qurʾān, the final version of which was written down in 653 and which most Muslims believe accurately represents God's speech, the authenticity of the *ḥadīth* literature was immediately challenged by Muslim scholars unsympathetic to the traditionists' thesis. The early traditionists tried to meet their opponents' criticisms by developing criteria for distinguishing sound *ḥadīth* from those that were not genuine, an effort that resulted in the development of an elaborate science of *ḥadīth* criticism. The dispute regarding the authenticity of the *ḥadīth* has persisted to the present and has meant that a substantial part of Islamic jurisprudence is and always has been a source of controversy among Muslims.

The genuineness of the *ḥadīth* literature is yet another point on which modern Western scholars tend to find themselves in disagreement with many of their Muslim counterparts. The prevailing view among Western scholars has been that most, if not all, of the *ḥadīth* are pious forgeries put into circulation by traditionists of the first and second Muslim centuries with a view to creating Islamic pedigrees for rules of law that had originally been the products of juristic reasoning or judicial practice, that were inherited from Arabian customary law, or that were borrowed from other legal cultures. Western scholarship has generally evaluated the traditional science of *ḥadīth* criticism as inadequate for differentiating historically accurate accounts from later fabrications. In the view of most Muslims, including those who have reservations about the genuineness of some of the *ḥadīth* and the adequacy of *ḥadīth* scholarship, these Western criticisms are excessively harsh. Wholesale dismissals of the *ḥadīth* literature as a product of later forgeries and of the traditional science of *ḥadīth* criticism as defective are rarely encountered in Muslim scholarship.

The beginnings of the classical law schools. Despite the initial resistance that it encountered, the traditionists' position steadily gained ground at the expense of the influence of the ancient schools of law in the second century after the death of the Prophet. The ancient schools did not disappear but adapted in differing degrees to the new trends in legal thought. It is in the second century AH (ninth century CE) that the foundations were laid for the development of what were subsequently to become the classical *sharīʿah* schools. Each school came to be referred to by the name of an eponymous founder, but it should be noted that the views of the scholars who gave their names to schools did not always prevail among their immediate disciples, much less among their later followers.

The oldest of the classical Sunnī schools is the Mālikī, which originated in Medina and was named after the prominent legal scholar and traditionist Mālik ibn Anas (d. 796). Respect for the *sunnah* of Medina as the place most closely associated with the mission of the Prophet and the first Muslim community persisted in the legal thought of the Mālikī school.

The Ḥanafī school was meanwhile developing in the context of the legal community in Kufa in southern Iraq. Although the school was named after a prominent local jurist, Abū Ḥanīfah (d. 767), its followers actually often showed greater deference to the views of two of his disciples, Abū Yūsuf (d. 798) and al-Shaybānī (d. 805). The Ḥanafī school bore many traces of influences from the Iraqi environment in which it developed. Ḥanafī jurists attached great importance to systematic consistency in legal thought and the refinement of legal principles. They used juristic speculation to develop rules and characteristically resolved legal questions through formalistic approaches.

Muḥammad ibn Idrīs al-Shāfiʿī (d. 820), the founder of the school that bears his name, was associated with the city of Medina. He ranks prominently in the history of Islamic legal thought and promoted the eventual triumph of the traditionist thesis in classical Islamic legal thought. According to al-Shāfiʿī, the *sunnah* of the Prophet as embodied in the *ḥadīth* totally superseded the *sunnah* of the ancient schools as a normative legal standard. Al-Shāfiʿī thus elevated the *sunnah* of the Prophet to the status of a source of law coequal with the Qurʾān. He articulated the view, which subsequently found widespread acceptance, that the *sunnah* of the Prophet explained the meaning of the Qurʾān.

Having established the Qurʾān and the much more extensive corpus of *ḥadīth* literature as the material sources of the *sharīʿah,* al-Shāfiʿī rejected the use of juristic opinion or speculative reasoning in formulating legal principles and insisted that jurists be restricted to the use of analogical reasoning (*Qiyās*), to extend principles in the sources to cover problems not explicitly addressed in the texts of the Qurʾān and *ḥadīth.* In his view, only by insisting that jurists limit themselves to such careful, piecemeal extensions of principles in the texts could one be sure that the jurists were not injecting undue subjective elements into their interpretations of *sharīʿah* requirements or distorting the rules set forth in the sources. Al-Shāfiʿī also refused to accord any weight to juristic consensus and held that the only binding consensus would be one among all members of the Muslim community. Despite his prestige, al-Shāfiʿī was unable to prevail on this last point even among members of his own school, who, like most Sunnī Muslims, came to believe that *ijmāʿ*, or the consensus of all the jurists in a given generation, could conclusively validate the correctness of a legal proposition and foreclose further debate. In general outlines, the jurisprudence developed by later members of the Shāfiʿī school has much in common with that of the Ḥanafī school.

The last of the classical Sunnī schools crystallized around Aḥmad ibn Ḥanbal (d. 855), a traditionist from Baghdad who traveled widely among different centers of learning. Subsequent members of the Ḥanbalī school have shared Ibn Ḥanbal's traditionist orientation and his concern for the consensus of the companions of the Prophet, but individual Ḥanbalī scholars have taken diverging opinions on questions of jurisprudence. The doctrines of the Ḥanbalī school, and particularly those of its more idiosyncratic members, are difficult to characterize, so that it is necessary to be wary of generalizations purporting to describe broad features of Ḥanbalī doctrine.

Other schools of law founded in the first centuries of Islam have not survived into the modern era. Perhaps the most influential of these was the Ẓāhirī school founded by Dāwūd ibn Khalaf (d. 884). It takes its name from the Arabic *ẓāhir,* meaning "that which is apparent" and referring to the insistence of this school that the *sharīʿah* required literal adherence to the words of the Qurʾān and the *sunnah.* In the Ẓāhirī school, human interpretations of their meanings were not binding.

The development of the legal doctrines of the early Shīʿī schools, aside from their shared doctrine regarding the *imāms*' title to succeed to the leadership of the community, seems to have begun somewhat later. It is important to note that while sectarian disputes in Islam often led to the development of bitter intellectual antagonisms and sometimes took on political dimensions, within the Sunnī sect legal scholars generally demonstrated great tolerance of and even respect for divergent opinions on the part of members of the four classical schools, all four of which were regarded as equally orthodox.

The Islamizing impetus in Islamic legal development that had been encouraged by the traditionist movement was also promoted by the official policies of the Abbasid dynasty, which justified its overthrow of the Umayyads in 750 on the basis of its greater claims to Islamic legitimacy and piety. The Abbasids manifested a desire that all persons in their domains, including the rulers, should follow the commands and prohibitions of the *sharīʿah.* They elevated the *sharīʿah* to the status of the official law to be applied in the courts by *qāḍīs,* or judges, who were required to be well versed in it. However, before many decades passed, it became abundantly clear that for the Abbasids, promoting the cause of the *sharīʿah* was entirely subordinate to the achievement of their dynastic political objectives. As a result, many jurists who were unwilling to readjust their idealistic views of the role that Islamic law should play in the governance of the Muslim community to the dictates of political expediency retreated from all contact with government and the administration of justice. It became common for great jurists to shun positions in courts and to retire to lives of scholarship and academic disputations. With this abjuring of political involvement, the basic elements in Sunnī law on the subject of how the Muslim community should be governed tended to remain fixed at the stage of elaborating models derived from the era of the Rāshidūn caliphs, despite the fact that the practical relevance of these models had been superseded by changed historical realities.

Uṣūl al-fiqh. With the development of the classical schools of Islamic law came the articulation of the principles of *uṣūl al-fiqh,* the roots or sources of jurisprudence. Although the *uṣūl* are often called sources of the *sharīʿah,* only the Qurʾān and the *sunnah* are material sources. Ultimately, the study of *uṣūl al-fiqh* is concerned with establishing a science of proofs of the Islamic derivation of substantive legal principles, thus enabling the jurist to discern which legal rules are correct statements of *sharīʿah* principles. The rules shown by this science to be authentically Islamic are known as the *furūʿ al-fiqh,* the branches of jurisprudence. The study of *uṣūl* has been one of the major preoccupations of Muslim jurists over the centuries and continues to be so in the early twenty-first century. As the subsequent history of the development of the *sharīʿah* demonstrates, the influence of al-Shāfiʿī on the fomulation of the classical Sunnī theory of *uṣūl al-fiqh*—a formulation that was basically complete by the ninth century—was considerable.

The first root of the *fiqh* is the Qurʾān. In the prevailing view, it is to be treated as the eternal and uncreated word of God, part of his essence. Although the Qurʾanic revelation constitutes the starting point for the development of the *sharīʿah,* a relatively small portion of *sharīʿah* rules can be traced directly to the text of the Qurʾān. Aside from setting forth rules regarding acts of worship and the rituals that they entail, the Qurʾān includes extensive provisions on intestate succession, many on domestic relations and the status of women, a few criminal laws, and some rules of evidence and contracts.

Muslim jurists developed an elaborate methodology to interpret the Qurʾān, and, in fact, the legal significance of the Qurʾān cannot be properly understood without an appreciation of this methodology. Muslim jurists themselves have differed over the legal significance of many specific lines of the Qurʾān. Some differences in the legal principles derived from the Qurʾān relate to the sectarian divisions of Islam; perhaps the most striking example lies in the laws of intestate succession among the Sunnīs and the Twelver branch of the Shīʿah. From the same Qurʾanic verses, which are more extensive on this subject than on any other legal topic, the two groups have derived markedly contrasting legal rules. In the Sunnī view, the Qurʾān meant to retain, with only limited modifications, the pre-Islamic Arabian scheme of agnatic succession, in which males inheriting through the male line got a major part of the estate. By contrast, the Twelver Shīʿī jurists held that, in designating inheritance shares for females and the children and parents of the deceased, the Qurʾān was implicitly repudiating the customary law of pre-Islamic Arabia and setting forth a completely different scheme of succession. As a result, Sunnī law favors inheritance by agnatic kinsmen, while that of the Twelvers favors the inheritance by the children and parents of the deceased, including females.

Al-Shāfiʿī succeeded in persuading subsequent jurists that the *sunnah* of the Prophet should be treated as the second root of Islamic jurisprudence and a source co-equal with the Qurʾān. It is generally accepted among Muslims not only that the Prophet was a perfect human being and thus worthy of emulation, but also that he enjoyed divine inspiration and thus could make no error in matters of religion or *sharīʿah* law. As noted, challenges to the authenticity of the *ḥadīth* literature on which the understanding of the Prophet's *sunnah* rested generated a science of *ḥadīth* criticism to weed out unsound or dubious accounts. In addition, methodologies were worked out to reconcile seeming contradictions and inconsistencies in different *ḥadīth* and between *ḥadīth* and verses of the Qurʾān. As in the case of the Qurʾān, reading the *ḥadīth* literature without a grasp of how orthodox Islamic scholarship interprets the legal implications of the *ḥadīth* and the relevant jurisprudence can lead to erroneous conclusions.

Most Sunnī Muslims have taken the view that the *ḥadīth* assembled in certain classic collections, such as those of al-Bukhari and Muslim, which date from the latter part of the third century AH, should be regarded as genuine, while members of the other sects rely on their own *ḥadīth* collections, which include many *ḥadīth* accounts that conflict with those in other collections and support their respective sectarian legal positions. Challenges to the authenticity of the *ḥadīth,* which have repeatedly arisen in various forms over the history of Islam, have important implications for the *sharīʿah.* Since the *ḥadīth* literature is very extensive (classical collections contain more than four thousand reports) and covers a much wider range of topics than the legal verses in the Qurʾān, it has supplied the Islamic rationale for a major part of *sharīʿah* law, which would forfeit its Islamic legitimacy if the *ḥadīth* literature were discredited.

Qiyās, reasoning by analogy, is a method for expanding the rules in the Qurʾān and *sunnah* to cover problems not expressly addressed in the sources. Most Sunnīs accept *qiyās* as the third root of *fiqh. Qiyās* involves the application of a legal ruling from a case mentioned in the Qurʾān or *sunnah* to a subcase not mentioned in the text but sufficiently related to permit coverage by analogical extension. Even though many jurists insisted on the use of *qiyās* on the theory that extending the scope of principles in the Qurʾān and *sunnah* by analogical reasoning minimized the risk of distorting those principles, a number of Sunnī jurists remained critical of its limitations on the grounds of the subjective element it involved. The extension of rules through *qiyās* ultimately involves human judgment, since it is first necessary to identify the reason underlying the original rule set forth in the text. In practice, jurists have been far from unanimous in their identification of these underlying reasons, with the result that they have extended the rules of the Qurʾān and *sunnah* in different ways. The reliance on analogical reasoning meant that Sunnī jurists analyzed series of concrete instances of application of specific rules rather than trying to abstract general rules from the sources. As new issues arose and generated Islamic rules coined by the use of analogy, these rules were added to the earlier compilations without attempts to synthesize and codify the underlying legal principles.

Twelver Shīʿī jurists do not accept the Sunnī model of *qiyās.* Many of them use forms of juristic reasoning that are not limited to drawing analogies in order to construe the meaning of the Qurʾān and *sunnah.* Known as the Uṣūlīyah, Twelver Shīʿī jurists who believe that *sharīʿah* rules can be extended by human reason have historically been opposed by another faction of jurists, the Akhbariyah, who insist that rules generated by human reason cannot be binding statements of *sharīʿah* law and argue that the Qurʾān and the *sunnah* of the Prophet and the Shīʿī *imāms* alone provide trustworthy guidance.

Ijmāʿ refers to the retroactive ratification of the correctness of an interpretation of *sharīʿah* requirements. Most Sunnīs treat *ijmāʿ*, which is constituted by the consensus of all the jurists of one generation, as the fourth root of *fiqh.* According to the majority Sunnī position, once a legal principle has won such unanimous endorsement, it becomes definitively established and cannot be challenged by subsequent generations. Al-Shāfiʿī's different view of *ijmāʿ* has already been noted. Prominent Ḥanbalī scholars have been among those who have rejected the binding force of *ijmāʿ* as defined by the majority; they claim that only the consensus of the companions of the Prophet could bind later Muslims. Also among the critics of the Sunnī view of *ijmāʿ* are the Twelver Shīʿah, who have historically taken a variety of positions on the significance of *ijmāʿ* and how it is constituted.

This bare summary of the basic principles of *uṣūl al-fiqh* does not begin to do justice to the tremendously complex and subtle analysis that Islamic legal scholarship is capable of bringing to bear on questions of the Islamic derivation of legal rules. Problems of *uṣūl al-fiqh* have attracted the attention of many of the finest Muslim scholars over the centuries and are still capable of generating controversy and provoking important intellectual developments.

In addition to the fundamental rules of *uṣūl al-fiqh,* there are subsidiary law-finding principles that are used to interpret the requirements of *sharīʿah* law. These principles provide the jurist with guidelines for resolving questions of *sharīʿah* law where the usual sources offer no unequivocal answer or where the facts of the case mean that the application of an otherwise dispositive principle will produce an unsatisfactory result. Predictably, these subsidiary principles vary considerably according to school and sectarian affiliations, and even within one school individual jurists may display different views on their use. An example of such a subsidiary principle is *maṣlaḥah* (considerations of public welfare), which was particularly emphasized in Mālikī jurisprudence. By reference to the criterion of *maṣlaḥah,* Muslim jurists can adjust their interpretations of *sharīʿah* requirements to promote the well-being of society.

Jurists and the development of the *sharīʿah.* With the foundation of the classical schools of Islamic law and the formulation of the fundamental principles of *uṣūl al-fiqh,* the *sharīʿah* became a jurists' law, and exhaustive training in law and ancillary disciplines was essential for interpreting how the *sharīʿah* applied to a given problem. The jurist, or *faqīh* (pl., *fuqahāʾ*), came to enjoy great prestige as a result of his monopoly of expertise regarding the sacred law. The prominence and power of the *fuqahāʾ* as a class in Muslim societies has in some instances led to the misperception that Islam envisages a theocratic system of government. In fact, it is the *sharīʿah* itself that is supposed to be the instrument of social control, and the *fuqahāʾ*, in theory powerless to alter the law, are no more than its faithful interpreters. For the most part, the *fuqahāʾ* have eschewed direct participation in the affairs of government and an overt role in political life.

The task of interpreting the requirements of the *sharīʿah* is termed *ijtihād,* and the person performing the interpretation is termed a *mujtahid.* The exercise of *ijtihād* by the early jurists defined the basic contours of the *sharīʿah* by the start of the tenth century CE. It has been widely believed that in Sunnī jurisprudence, the *fuqahāʾ* were deemed to be bound by the solutions to legal problems that had been reached by jurists of earlier generations on the grounds that the latter, being closer in time to the prophet Muḥammad, were less likely to fall into error than scholars of later generations. This bar to reexamination of previously decided questions of *sharīʿah* law has been termed "the closing of the door of *ijtihād.*" Never recognized by Twelver Shīʿī law, deference to established tradition may have inhibited innovative thought and retarded legal reform in Sunnī circles, although not in the Ḥanbalī school, where many jurists denied that they could be bound by the *ijtihād* of their predecessors. However, the proposition that the doctrine of *taqlīd,* or obedience to established legal authority, immutably fixed *sharīʿah* doctrines at an early stage and had a stultifying impact on the evolution of *sharīʿah* law has been challenged. Whether and to what degree *taqlīd* actually inhibited jurists from adjusting legal doctrines to respond to the exigencies of their changing environment needs to be reevaluated.

Of course, even if Sunnī jurists did consider themselves bound in areas where there had been *ijtihād* by the jurists of the first centuries, they were left free to resolve questions that had not been definitively settled by their predecessors. In Muslim societies, important new problems of *sharīʿah* law were traditionally referred for resolution to a qualified *mujtahid.* In Sunnī environments this function was exercised by scholars who had attained the status of *muftī,* meaning that they were able to issue *fatwās*, or binding legal rulings, on such problems. A *muftī* might act in a private capacity, advising individuals who came to him with inquiries about how the *sharīʿah* applied to a problem, but jurists were appointed as official or governmental *muftīs* by rulers. *Fatwās* that were widely respected and collected for further use and study could be incorporated in *fiqh* works and could acquire considerable currency and authority.

In contrast to the important role played by *fatwās* in the development of *sharīʿah* rules, only rarely were decisions rendered by *qāḍīs* in actual cases treated as authoritative in the *fiqh* literature. Most of the *fuqahāʾ* did not recognize judicial precedent as binding, perhaps because in the wake of the disenchantment with government after the first Abbasids many of the more eminent *fuqahāʾ* preferred to disassociate themselves from the court system and often declined to serve when offered judgeships. The one important exception in this regard occurred in Morocco, where *ʿamal,* or judicial practice, was considered authoritative.

The Mature Classical Law Schools. From the tenth century until the disruptive impact of European imperialism made itself felt in India in the eighteenth century, and in the other parts of the Muslim world in the nineteenth century, there was no major discontinuity in the development of doctrines of the classical law schools. Instead, one could say that this period was devoted to refining and amplifying the early treatments of Islamic jurisprudence.

As the schools matured, their doctrines became more elaborate—often, as already noted, deviating from the views of their eponymous founders. Although the schools did not require that all members adhere to precisely the same doctrines, within each school there tended to be a core of doctrines that enjoyed widespread acceptance and that embodied a distinctive approach to the resolution of legal problems. The jurists of the different schools wrote treatises on *fiqh* that were evaluated and reevaluated by their peers and successors. Some works gained particular renown and respect and were widely circulated and studied. The same work would often be recopied with added commentaries and supercommentaries in the margins by subsequent scholars. As the *fiqh* literature expanded, it was typical for the jurists in a given locality to select one of the more highly regarded treatises from what was the dominant legal school as the authoritative statement of legal doctrine in their jurisdiction. They also prepared summaries of the classical statements of a school's doctrine, which were meant to be easier to use and understand than the scholarly originals. Even so, works of *fiqh* were intelligible only to learned specialists. Institutions of higher learning were set up to train students in *fiqh* and related fields, the first and most enduringly influential of which was al-Azhar in Cairo, founded in 972.

One of the ancillary subjects essential for aspiring *fuqahāʾ* to master was classical Arabic, the language of God's speech in the Qurʾān and the language of the *ḥadīth.* Arabic has continued to be the essential language for the study of the *sharīʿah.* No translated versions of the Qurʾān or the *ḥadīth* are adequate for use in scholarly investigations. All of the classical *fiqh* works are also in Arabic. Although some have become available in translations, these are of very uneven quality and must be used with great caution.

The schools spread far from their original settings. Adherence to one school or another, as well as sectarian allegiances, changed in accordance with the many political upheavals and vicissitudes suffered by the different parts of the Muslim world over the centuries, and the patterns of school and sect distribution varied significantly at different eras of Islamic history. One of the prerogatives of the Muslim ruler was to select the law of a sect or, more commonly, of a Sunnī school that would become the official norm in his domains and would be applied by the courts. In some large cities, court staffs would include judges from different schools and sects, so that the law applicable in a given case could be selected to correspond to the affiliations of the parties.

It should be recalled that all of the four classical Sunnī schools are considered equally orthodox. Although concerns for doctrinal consistency and coherence mandated that a jurist follow the established doctrine of his school, it was not unusual for jurists to study the *fiqh* of other Sunnī schools or even to refer extensively to the opinions of other schools in treatises. This approach was less common, however, when *fiqh* principles of other sects were involved. The protracted polemics between the Sunnī and Twelver Shīʿī camps on the question of temporary marriage, which the former claim is prohibited and akin to prostitution and which the latter argue is clearly established in the Qurʾān and the *ḥadīth,* is an example of the hostile attitudes that were engendered by sectarian disputes about interpretations of the requirements of *sharīʿah* law. However, Sunnī jurists have been prepared to accord some deference to the *fiqh* of the Zaydī Shīʿah, since the Zaydīyah are considered to be more moderate and closer to Sunnīs in their views than the other Shīʿī sects.

Geographical distribution of the schools. The long sponsorship of Ḥanafī law by the Ottoman sultans meant that the Ḥanafī school came to predominate in most of their former territories in the eastern Mediterranean. As the major Sunnī school of the Indian subcontinent as well, the Ḥanafī school is by far the largest school of law.

The adherents of the Mālikī school tend to be concentrated in the western portions of the Muslim world, particularly in North and West Africa, although one does find them in other parts of the Arab world, including the Hejaz and Kuwait. The distribution of members of the Shāfiʿī school tends to correspond to patterns of major trade routes, with Shāfiʿī communities mostly concentrated in coastal areas. One finds large numbers in East Africa, Ceylon, Malaysia, and Indonesia. The Ḥanbalī school has dwindled in size to such a point that its adherents are scarcely found outside central Saudi Arabia. The widely appreciated originality and intellectual distinction of some of its medieval *fuqahāʾ* has, however, allowed it to retain an influence entirely out of proportion to its numbers.

The Twelvers, by far the most numerous branch of the Shīʿah, claim the adherence of a majority of the people of Iran and, probably, Iraq, as well as sizable minorities in Pakistan, eastern Arabia, and Lebanon. Since 1501 Twelver Shiism has been the official religion of Iran, and it has come to be particularly identified with that country. As noted, a deep and important cleavage in Iranian Twelver Shīʿī legal thought has divided the Akhbārī and Uṣūlī subschools.

The followers of the Aga Khan belong to the Ismāʿīlī branch of Shīʿī Islam. His ancestors once ruled an Ismāʿīlī state, the powerful and intellectually influential Fatimid empire (909–1171), from their capital in Cairo, but in the early twenty-first century the Ismāʿīlīyah are everywhere in the minority and are widely scattered around the globe. Sizable communities remain in the Indian subcontinent and East Africa. The Zaydīyah are concentrated in the Yemen Arab Republic (North Yemen), which was ruled until the 1960s by a Zaydī *imām.*

A very small but intellectually significant group whose law cannot receive its due here is that of the Khārijīs or Ibāḍīyah, many of whom have managed to survive in the more remote parts of the Muslim world, such as the Berber areas of North Africa and in Oman.

Although a ruler is free to select the school of law that will apply on his territory, this selection binds only the formal legal system. In the absence of unusual external pressures mandating a change in allegiance, individual Muslims remain free to follow the school of their choice. Typically, Muslims consider themselves followers of the same school as their fathers, and even within the Sunnī sect, where all four schools are deemed equally orthodox, it is unusual for a Muslim to change school affiliation.

Comparisons of the rules of the classical *fiqh*. In detail the rules of the various Sunnī schools are often different enough to affect the outcome of a legal dispute. On the average legal question, the degree of doctrinal difference between a given Sunnī school and a Shīʿī school is often not much greater. Notwithstanding the different approaches that Sunnī and Shīʿī *fiqh* purport to have to the sources of law, aside from their differences regarding who should rule the Muslim community, one finds few major divergencies except on some points of religious ritual and worship, certain rules of marriage and divorce, and the laws of inheritance.

A comparison of the *muʿamalāt* rules of the medieval *fiqh* literature with rules in other medieval legal systems of the Middle East and Europe, whether secular or religious, reveals many broad similarities. The single most distinctive accomplishment of the medieval *fuqahāʾ* from the standpoint of comparative legal history lies in their very sophisticated and complex schemes of intestate succession.

Principal figures. The founders of the schools of Sunnī law and the imams of the Shīʿī sects, who enjoyed the same capacity as the prophet Muḥammad to make authoritative pronouncements regarding the requirements of the *sharīʿah,* would have to be ranked in the forefront of the principal figures in the history of Islamic law. Given the vast corpus of writings on the *sharīʿah,* it is impossible to present any summary treatment without risking unfair omissions of outstanding figures. The following list must therefore be understood to be only a selection of persons who are representative of some of the important aspects of the Islamic legal heritage and suggestive of its variety and richness.

An early jurist who is notable for a conception of the role of the *sharīʿah* different from that of his more orthodox contemporaries was Ibn al-Muqaffaʿ (d. 756). He unsuccessfully urged the Abbasid caliph al-Manṣūr to end the confusion and disparities in the *sharīʿah* resulting from conflicting interpretations by the jurists of the early law schools by systematizing and codifying the *sharīʿah.* He argued that the *sharīʿah* should be enacted into uniform legislation that would apply throughout the caliph's domain; his failure to convince others of the correctness of his ideas meant that the *sharīʿah* continued to be viewed as a jurist's law independent from and untouchable by political authorities.

Before its extinction, the once-influential Ẓāhirī school enjoyed a flowering in Muslim Spain. The most famous and distinguished Ẓāhirī thinker was Ibn Ḥazm (d. 1065), a vigorous polemicist who made many enemies in the course of his harsh attacks on the doctrines of other law schools. He challenged the authenticity of much of the *ḥadīth* literature, rejected *qiyās* and the rules it produced, limited *ijmāʿ* to that of the companions of the Prophet, and insisted that, in the absence of explicit commands in the Qurʾān and *sunnah,* all conduct should be regarded as outside the concern of religious law.

One of the most eminent figures in Islamic intellectual history, al-Ghāzalī (d. 1111) examined the teachings of the *sharīʿah* in relation to his own theological and philosophical views. Although he is best known for his searching inquiry into the theological fundamentals of Islam, al-Ghāzalī also wrote a number of important books of Shafiʿi *fiqh.* In his greatest work, *Iḥyāʾ ʿulūm al-dīn* (The revivification of religious sciences), al-Ghāzalī sought to achieve a synthesis of the teachings of Islam and to define the role of the *sharīʿah* in relation to other aspects of religion. His work may constitute the most accomplished statement of what passed for Sunnī orthodoxy in medieval Islam.

One of the most original medieval jurists was the Ḥanbalī Ibn Taymīyah (d. 1328), who had an influential disciple in Ibn Qayyim al-Jawziyah (d. 1350). Ibn Taymīyah strongly attacked the doctrine of *taqlid* that bound Muslims to the interpretations of the early jurists. He argued that qualified Muslim thinkers should be free to return to the Qurʾān, *sunnah,* and consensus of the companions of the Prophet and interpret them afresh. Muḥammad ibn ʿAbd al-Wahhāb (d. 1792), the leader of the puritanical Wahhābī reform movement that won many followers in Arabia and elsewhere, invoked Ibn Taymīyah's ideas in his rejection of the authority of the classical law schools and his insistence on fresh *ijtihād.*

Theories about the need to identify and follow the fundamental policies underlying *sharīʿah* provisions and to interpret these provisions in a manner responsive to social needs were developed by the Mālikī jurist al-Shāṭibī (d. 1388). Ibn Nujaym (d. 1562) was a Ḥanafī jurist who extracted what he saw as the fundamental *sharīʿah* principles from the specific instances of applications of rules set forth in the *fiqh.* While not himself a jurist, the Mughal emperor Awrangzib ʿĀlamgīr (d. 1707) made his mark on Islamic legal history by ordering the composition of the famous

Fatāwā ʿĀlamgīrīyah, a thorough compilation of Ḥanafī *fiqh.*

Muḥammad ʿAbduh (d. 1905) served as Grand Muftī of Egypt and in that capacity and in his writings on Islamic law proposed rationalist and liberal reformist interpretations of the *sharīʿah.* The influential Salafīyah movement inspired by ʿAbduh and led by his disciple Rashīd Riḍā advocated a return to a purified version of the *sharīʿah* meant to be more authentic than the versions developed in the course of the centuries devoted to the study of medieval *fiqh.* An example of ʿAbduh's approach may be seen in his famous argument that the *sharīʿah* prohibits polygamy. Dismissing traditional support for polygamy among the *fuqahāʾ,* ʿAbduh returned to the Qurʾān and offered a novel reading of two critical verses, which he claimed were to be taken together, although they had previously been held to apply to different issues. *Surāh* 4:3 of the Qurʾān was traditionally interpreted to allow a man to wed up to four women at a time, with a moral injunction to marry only one if he could not treat additional wives justly. *Surāh* 4:129, which says it is not possible for a man to deal equally with his wives, was traditionally interpreted as offering reassurance to the polygamous husband that he was not sinning if he felt stronger attraction to and affection for one of his wives. Treating the injunction to deal equally with wives in the earlier verse as a legally binding precondition for a valid marriage, ʿAbduh used the later verse as evidence that this precondition could not in practice be met, so that in the *sharīʿah,* no polygamous marriage could be valid. ʿAbduh's practice of interpreting *sharīʿah* rules to serve the ends of enlightened social policies had far-reaching intellectual repercussions. His ideas encouraged many Middle Eastern Muslims in the first half of the twentieth century to accommodate liberal political, economic, and social reforms in their interpretations of Islamic law.

Among the principal figures of Twelver Shīʿī jurisprudence, Muḥammad ibn al-Ḥasan al-Ṭūsī (d. 1067) wrote a number of works that became treated as classic statements of principles of Shīʿī *fiqh,* as were the writings of Muhaqqiq al-Ḥillī (d. 1277). An important representative of the Akhbari faction of Twelver Shiism was Muḥammad Bāqir al-Majlisī (d. 1699), who, in addition to producing an encyclopedic statement of *fiqh,* also served as a judge and became the most powerful judicial figure under the Safavids. After the Safavids made Twelver Shiism the state religion of Iran, he, like many major Shīʿī jurists, attempted to define the proper political relationship between the Shīʿī clergy and the state. Al-Majlisī conceived of a powerful, independent political role for the clergy. A jurist of similar eminence, but representing very different tendencies in Twelver thought, was Murtaḍā Anṣārī (d. 1864). A member of the Uṣūlī school, which predominated in Iran in the nineteenth century, he wrote a major treatise on the Uṣūlī theory of sources. His writings promoted the view that each layperson was bound to follow the legal interpretations of the most learned of living jurists, the *marjaʿ-i taqlīd,* whose *ijtihād* became absolutely binding on his followers. He took the view that public law was not a true concern of the *sharīʿah* and stressed instead its ethical dimensions. The single most important Ismāʿīlī jurist is Qāḍī al-Nuʿmān (d. 974), who served as the highest judge in the Fatimid empire and also wrote a great treatise of Ismāʿīlī law.

Principal subjects. Classical *fiqh* works have similar, although not always identical, subject divisions. They begin with a section on the very extensive *ʿibadāt,* the obligations of the individual to God discussed above. The remaining subjects belong to the *muʿamalāt* category, including (in a representative, though not exhaustive, list) marriage, divorce, manumission of slaves, oaths, criminal penalties, relations between the Muslim community and non-Muslims, treasure troves, missing persons, partnership, religious trusts, sales, guarantee contracts, transfers of debts, rules for judges, evidence, legal claims, acknowledgments of legal obligations, gifts, hire, the purchase of freedom by slaves, the defense of compulsion, incapacity, usurpation and damage of property, preemptive purchases, partition, agency, contracts for cultivation of agricultural land, slaughter of animals (for food), animal sacrifice, hateful practices, cultivation of waste lands, prohibited drinks, hunting and racing competitions, pledge, personal injuries, blood money and fines, intestate succession, and wills.

Historically, the areas of *sharīʿah* law that were most developed in the classical *fiqh* corresponded to the areas where *qāḍʿis* in the *sharīʿah* courts were best able to retain jurisdiction over disputes, while legal issues in other areas tended to be dealt with by secular tribunals with more flexible procedures and greater enforcement powers, such as the police tribunals. The *sharīʿah* rules of intestate succession and family law are the two most developed portions of the *sharīʿah,* and recourse to *sharīʿah* courts was very common for resolution of disputes on these subjects. The *sharīʿah* courts also had jurisdiction over pious endowments *(awqāf;* sg., *waqf),* which were very important legal institutions in traditional Islamic societies, allowing for the consolidation and protection of private property and often providing the financial basis for schools, hospitals, mosques, and other public institutions. *Waqfs* continued to serve such functions until the twentieth century, when they were generally abolished or significantly reformed. The *shariʿah* law of contracts, and particularly of sales contracts, is also quite extensive. The difficulties of complying with some of the *sharīʿah* contract rules—such as the prohibition of interest—spawned an ancillary legal literature by some Ḥanafī and Shāfiʿi jurists on how to circumvent inconvenient rules by means of ingenious exploitation of legal technicalities (the so-called *ḥiyal,* or "legal tricks").

The Situation in Recent Times. The situation of the *sharīʿah* in recent times has two significant dimensions, corresponding to its dual nature as a positive law and a deontology.

Beginning in the nineteenth century, the *sharīʿah* was increasingly supplanted as a positive law in the legal systems of Muslim countries by borrowed European law. Historically, substantive *sharīʿah* rules survived in the legal systems of modern Muslim countries in rough proportion to the importance traditionally accorded to the subject area involved, but even in those areas where the *sharīʿah* was able to maintain itself, it was nonetheless subjected to some reforms. In the twentieth century, *sharīʿah* reform became one of the major legal problems faced by Muslim societies and provoked protracted political and intellectual controversies. Despite popular and clerical support for retention of the *sharīʿah,* governments have generally moved as quickly as political constraints permit in the direction of westernization. In the 1970s the political influence of forces favoring the retention and/or renewal of the *sharīʿah* began to make itself felt, and a process of abrogating westernizing reforms and reinstating *sharīʿah* law began in Libya, Iran, Pakistan, Egypt, Sudan, and Kuwait. How far the process of Islamization will proceed and what the future role of the *sharīʿah* as a positive law will be are at present uncertain.

Also in the twentieth century, Muslim intellectuals concerned with questions of *fiqh* subjected the medieval versions of the *sharīʿah* to critical reexamination and brought new interpretive approaches to the *sharīʿah* sources. The variety in modern approaches to the *sharīʿah* is reminiscent of the situation prevailing in the first centuries after the death of the Prophet, before the doctrines of the classical schools coalesced. There are still many conservative thinkers who defend the validity of the medieval *fiqh.* Arrayed against them are many who support new interpretations of what the *sharīʿah* means. Adding to the fragmentation of legal doctrines is the fact that with the spread of educational opportunities and the increase in literacy, many Muslims who are educated but have not pursued a traditional course of study at a religious institution are contributing interpretations of the *sharīʿah.* In other words, laypersons who belong to the modern educated elite do not necessarily feel that they must defer to the specialized knowledge of the *fuqahāʾ* and are prepared to challenge the monopoly formerly enjoyed by the *fuqahāʾ* to make authoritative statements on *sharīʿah* law. As a result, it has become very difficult to make generalizations about contemporary *sharīʿah* doctrines.

The westernization of legal systems in the Muslim world. The westernization of the legal systems of Muslim countries began with the impact of European imperialism on Muslim societies in the eighteenth and nineteenth centuries. The legal systems of Muslim societies subjected to direct colonial rule underwent distinctive transformations in relation to the legal culture of the colonizing power. Thus, there developed in Muslim parts of India under British rule a peculiar blend of common law and elements of the *sharīʿah* that became known as Anglo-Muhammadan law. This unique, hybrid law was progressively reformed to eliminate what were regarded as the more archaic features of the *sharīʿah* elements, and it remained influential in the legal systems of India and Pakistan after they achieved independence in 1947. Algeria was part of France from 1830 until independence in 1962, and as a French colony, it also developed a hybrid legal system, known as *le droit musulman algérien,* which incorporated many French features.

Eager to strengthen their relatively backward and weak societies in the face of threatened European domination, most elites in the independent countries of the Muslim world tended to see the *sharīʿah* as an obstacle to the achievement of essential modernization. Governments first replaced those parts of the *sharīʿah* that were viewed as impeding economic transformation, such as *sharīʿah* commercial law, or those possessing features that seemed particularly archaic by modern standards, as in the cases of *sharīʿah* procedural and criminal law.

It was not always the substance of *sharīʿah* rules that troubled modernizers. Their arcane formulation and their diffuse mode of presentation in medieval *fiqh* treatises meant that only specialists with a mastery of medieval legal Arabic and an extensive traditional training could find answers to legal questions in a reasonably efficient manner. The cumbersome form of the *fiqh* works could be compared with the streamlined, systematized legal compendia to be found in nineteenth-century continental European codes. Growing impatience with the *fiqh* works encouraged a definite preference for codified law.

At the early stages of this legal reform process, one possibility for saving the *sharīʿah* from eclipse by Western law seemed to be that of vastly simplifying and systematizing its presentation. Attempts were made to codify the *sharīʿah* in the late nineteenth century, the most notable accomplishment being the promulgation of the Ottoman Majalla in 1877. Starting with some general principles of *sharīʿah* law taken from Ibn Nujaym, the Majalla presents a codification of the law of obligations derived from the views of various Ḥanafī jurists. The Majalla proved its utility, surviving for decades in former Ottoman territories well after they had obtained their independence from the empire. A later code, the Ottoman Family Rights Law of 1917, constituted an original attempt to codify *sharīʿah* law on that subject by reference to the doctrines of more than one Sunnī law school. This was the first important instance of the application of the technique of *takhayyur,* or picking and choosing the most apt principles from the doctrines of different schools and combining them in an arrangement that had no precedent in the classical *fiqh.* However, the preference for wholesale importation of Western law codes was ultimately so strong that there was soon little incentive to pursue projects for devising further codes on a *sharīʿah* basis.

Another factor mandating change from the old *sharīʿah*-based system of law was the international political setting. The rulers of Muslim states in the nineteenth and twentieth centuries were obliged to deal with a historical reality that was vastly different from what had been contemplated in early *sharīʿah* theory. The *sharīʿah* was originally conceived as a law whose application would be coextensive with religious affiliation. The world was to be converted to Islam, and there would result one community of believers with a common political allegiance and a common obligation to follow the *sharīʿah.* This conception did not envisage the appearance of obstacles in the way of the realization of this ideal, such as the fragmentation of the Muslim community into separate and mutually hostile political units, the development of national identities and the rise of modern nationalism, the failure of large non-Muslim communities within the Muslim world to convert, and the need to deal with non-Muslim countries possessed of greater economic and military resources.

The continued existence of non-Muslim communities had necessitated one legal adaptation at an early stage of Islamic history, namely, the allowance of separate religious laws and courts for minority communities. Members of the minority religious communities on Muslim territory were permitted to follow their own religious laws in matters of personal status and in transactions between themselves while remaining subject to the *sharīʿah* in their interactions with outsiders or in their public activities. This practice was highly developed under the Ottoman Empire, where it was known as the *millet* system.

Under outside pressures, this system was further modified by a practice of according a special legal status to non-Muslims from the powerful European states: from the medieval period onward, certain states exacted from Muslim governments agreements, or "capitulations," according extraterritorial status to their nationals. Originally granted only by way of exception, capitulatory privileges were expanded apace with growing European influence. An example of the resulting system of extraterritoriality can be seen in the powerful Mixed Courts of Egypt, set up in 1875, expanded after the British occupation in 1882, and continuing until 1949. Originally established as alternatives to the "native courts" for cases involving foreigners, the Mixed Courts were able to extend their jurisdiction to a wide variety of cases, including those involving Egyptians, in instances where the courts detected some "foreign interest" in the outcome. One reason for the exaction of these concessions, the demands for which became increasingly onerous as Muslim power and wealth declined and that of the West grew, was the Western perception that the substantive provisions of the *sharīʿah* were "primitive" and "barbaric" by modern European legal standards, and that the justice meted out by the traditional courts was arbitrary. European powers also objected to the inferior legal status accorded to non-Muslims under the *sharīʿah* and exploited this as a pretext for political intervention. In attempts to forestall such intervention, the Ottoman sultan promulgated the Haṭṭ-i Şerïf of Gülhane in 1839 and the Haṭṭ-i Humâyûn of 1856, officially establishing the principle that Ottoman citizens regardless of their religion should be equal in terms of their legal rights and obligations.

Retention of *sharīʿah* law as the law of the land in these political circumstances thus presented obstacles to setting up a unified national legal system and entailed exposure to risks of compromising the sovereignty and national dignity of the Muslim states. The reluctance of governments to continue to make such sacrifices provided an impetus for law reform that would place legal systems in Muslim countries on a par with the emerging modern international standard.

The formation of modern nation-states in the Muslim world starting in the nineteenth century and the subsequent collapse of the Ottoman Empire in World War I prompted Muslims to reassess the relationship between the *sharīʿah* law and the new political entities into which the Muslim world had been divided. Although the claims of the Ottoman sultans to be the legitimate successors of the Prophet had been based on tenuous legal and historical arguments, some Sunnīs saw in the sultan-caliphs an embodiment of the original *sharīʿah* notion that religious allegiance—not nationality—should determine political loyalties. With the ouster of the last of the Ottoman sultan-caliphs in 1924, there ended any real chance in the Sunnī world of preserving an Islamic caliphate, a government under which all Muslims would share a common political and religious allegiance.

Iran's *ʿulamāʾ* faced a momentous question at the turn of the twentieth century, when a growing movement favored the establishment of a democratic government, and the Constitutional Revolution of 1905–1909, led to the overthrow of the Qajar dynasty. To the *ʿulamāʾ*, accepting this revolution meant acknowledging the legitimacy of a government based on the principle of popular sovereignty and the law-making authority of the people's representatives. Such changes were seen by some as a challenge to the theoretical primacy of the imamate and the exclusive prerogative of the *ʿulamāʾ* to determine and declare the law. Other important jurists, such as Muḥammad Naʾīnī (d. 1936), however, took the position that, pending the return of the Hidden Imām from the state of occultation, it was impossible to have a government that truly accorded with *sharīʿah* ideals and that it was therefore permissible for Iran to adopt a constitutional form of government in the interim.

The acceptance of the idea in the Sunnī and Shīʿī camps that laws should be enacted on a national basis by representatives of the people did not by itself entail a reduction of the role of the *sharīʿah.* However, the attendant pressures for systematic uniformity meant that statutes enacted by the state inevitably replaced the old, decentralized system of jurists' law. Thus, the realization that laws would henceforth be made by national governments encouraged the acceptance of the idea that there should be neutral, secular laws that could apply to all persons on the national soil. The typical pattern in Muslim countries in the nineteenth century, and more particularly in the twentieth century, was to abandon the *sharīʿah* in favor of imported European law save in matters of personal status and religious trusts, and occasional token provisions in other fields such as the law of contracts.

The timing of the adoptions of Western law was related to the chronology and extent of various countries' exposure to European imperialism. The Ottoman Empire was therefore the first Muslim state to adopt Western laws, followed shortly by the semiautonomous province of Egypt. The first French-based codes to be introduced in the Ottoman Empire were in the areas of commercial law (1850), penal law (1858), and commercial procedure (1861). The countries that remained most insulated from such influences—Afghanistan, the Yemen, and Saudi Arabia—were the last to undertake westernization of their legal systems. In most countries, legal westernization was largely completed by the 1950s. Alone among Muslim countries, Turkey, under the leadership of Kemal Atatürk after the collapse of the Ottoman Empire, abandoned the *sharīʿah* in favor of a completely secular legal system. At the opposite extreme, Saudi Arabia has retained the *sharīʿah,* or more specifically, Ḥanbalī *fiqh,* as the official norm, which has prevented the government from openly undertaking legislative activity, including the enactment of a constitution.

In contemporary Muslim countries the desire on the part of the governments for legal modernization combined with the need to show respect for the *sharīʿah* has resulted in various compromises. In the area of personal status, a number of reforms, by and large modest ones, have been enacted in Muslim countries with a view to improving the status of women in matters of marriage, divorce, support, and child custody. The boldest reforms in this area were enacted in the Tunisian Code of Personal Status of 1956, the Iranian Family Protection Law of 1967 (since abrogated by the revolutionary government), and the South Yemen Family Law of 1974. Only a few very cautious reforms of aspects of the *sharīʿah* law of intestate succession have been undertaken.

Even Muslim states with westernized legal systems generally enshrine Islam in the national constitution as the state religion and stipulate that the *sharīʿah* is a source of law or even the source of all laws. In some constitutions there are provisions stating that laws must accord with the *sharīʿah* or that they may be reviewed and nullified if they are found to violate the *sharīʿah.* In the past such provisions often had little more than symbolic significance, but as supporters of the *sharīʿah* gained political strength in the 1970s throughout the Islamic world, there was increasing pressure for reinstatement of *sharīʿah* rules and the abrogation of imported laws that conflict with *sharīʿah* principles. Thus, the *sharīʿah* is tending to be treated more and more as a fundamental law in the legal systems of Muslim countries.

Islamization campaigns. The circumstances in which the replacement and reform of the *sharīʿah* took place resulted in political tensions between the westernized elites and other, more traditional segments of Muslim societies. The masses remained attached to the idea of the supremacy of *sharīʿah* law, anticipating that its reinstatement would cure endemic political, economic, and social ills. The *fuqahāʾ* continued to study and defend the *sharīʿah* and were offended by their displacement by the new class of lawyers and judges trained in Western law; as traditional guardians of the *sharīʿah* heritage, the *fuqahāʾ* also retained prestige and a popular following among the masses. Meanwhile the forces of what has come to be known as political Islam, in which Islam was converted to a populist political ideology, won support from disaffected urban dwellers for their proposals for Islamization.

The political potency of this combination was illustrated in the 1978–1979 Islamic Revolution, which was spearheaded by prominent Twelver Shīʿī *faqih,* Ayatollah Khomeini, who had as one of his goals the reinstatement of *sharīʿah* law. Khomeini had written prior to the revolution about the requirements for Islamic government and posited that the state should be ruled by the foremost *faqih* of the era. Although other Iranian *fuqahāʾ* disputed the correctness of Khomeini's views, his accession to power and the ability of allied *fuqahāʾ* to ensconce themselves in leading positions in the government meant that Iran was transformed into a theocracy. Western law was replaced by *sharīʿah* principles in many areas, sometimes with variations on the traditional *sharīʿah* rules that reflected the politics of the revolutionary situation. The unpopularity of theocratic rule jeopardizes the survival of this attempt to establish a new version of Islamic government.

Regimes in the Muslim world have responded to the demonstrated popularity of Islamization programs by enacting selected principles of *sharīʿah* law in statute form. Libya was the first country to undertake such initiatives in the 1970s, and its example was subsequently imitated in Pakistan and Sudan and to a lesser degree in some other countries. These measures did not mean that the governments were relinquishing control over the legal systems, which remained basically Western in character and structure. The major emphasis in such Islamizing legislation tended to be on reenactment of Qurʾanic criminal laws and imposing restraints on women in the name of protecting morality. During the brief rule of the Taliban in Afghanistan (1996–2001), an Islamic emirate was established committed to implementing a particularly harsh version of Islamic law. It is premature to predict the long-term consequences of the turnabout in the fortunes of the *sharīʿah,* but it is clear that the position of imported Western laws in the legal systems of the Muslim world is not secure and that the *sharīʿah* retains considerable potency as a countermodel.

Contemporary reformulations of the *sharīʿah.* At the same time that there is mounting pressure for the reinstatement of the *sharīʿah,* there is growing diversity of opinion on what the requirements of the *sharīʿah* are and how they should be applied in modern circumstances. Previously settled issues of Islamic law are being reopened and reexamined.

While some contemporary Muslims, particularly those educated in traditional Islamic institutions of higher learning, consider medieval *fiqh* treaties authoritative, there is a marked and growing tendency to treat such works as secondary legal sources that are useful but not conclusive guides on questions of *sharīʿah* science and substantive rules. The old hierarchies of sources and the established methodologies for interpreting them are also questioned by contemporary thinkers. Although the traditional techniques of legal reasoning from the sources are also rejected by many modern students of the *sharīʿah,* no consensus about what new methodology should replace the ones used by the traditional scholars is discernible.

Increasingly, Muslims turn directly to the Qurʾān and *sunnah* for guidance. The tendency has also mounted to give precedence to the Qurʾān over the *sunnah*—because of either a more critical appraisal of the reliability of the *ḥadīth* literature or a conviction that the Qurʾān was intended to serve as the primary source of *sharīʿah* principles. While it is rare for Muslims to reject the authenticity of the entire *ḥadīth* literature, it has become more common for them to evaluate negatively the traditional science of *ḥadīth* criticism. As a result, there has been a greater willingness to discard or discount the legal value of *ḥadīth* that are not demonstrably genuine.

A noteworthy development in contemporary Sunnī legal thought is that on questions of methodology and substance alike there is a tendency to disregard the former school divisions. When seeking enlightenment from past scholarship, modern Sunnīs commonly treat the views of all the classical Sunnī schools and also the extinct schools as deserving of consideration. Thus, the process of *takhayyur* exemplified in the Ottoman Family Rights Law of 1917 is now routinely utilized.

Many contemporary interpretations of the *sharīʿah* tend to reflect ideological visions of the social order that should result from the application of the *sharīʿah.* In these interpretations the *sharīʿah* does not function only as a criterion for the legal validity or permissibility and ethical character of human acts but as a blueprint for the perfect ordering of all social relations and the solution to the problems of achieving social harmony and justice. The latest ideologized versions of the *sharīʿah* reflect all the different ideological currents that are contending for the loyalties of peoples in the Muslim world from the most conservative to the most radical, so that this ideologization of Islamic legal thought has led to a polarization of opinions. Topics that have given rise to particularly important disagreements include remedies for maldistribution of wealth, the sanctity of private property, the nature of Islamic government, human rights, and the role of women. At the same time that new feminist interpretations of the sources are winning popularity, other theories calling for drastic curbs on women's rights are being put forward.

Because the latest ideological perspectives characteristic of contemporary Islamic thought have few counterparts in the traditional *fiqh* and do not correspond to any of the traditional school or sectarian divisions of the *sharīʿah,* they have created new divisions and alliances along ideological lines. The willingness on the part of Sunnī and Shīʿī Muslims to utilize the economic and political theories presented by members of the other sect is growing. Thus, on the theoretical level, all the old doctrinal certainties are now challenged by modern attempts to understand the *sharīʿah* in relation to the great political, economic, and social questions confronting Muslim societies. It is premature to predict which of the many presently competing versions of the *sharīʿah* will ultimately find favor with the majority of Muslims, but it is clear that many Muslims believe that the answers to these questions must be sought by reference to the *sharīʿah.*

SEE ALSO Abū Ḥanīfah; Abū Yūsuf; Ḥadīth; Ḥanābilah; Ijmāʿ; Ijtihād; Madhhab; Mālik ibn Anas; Maṣlaḥah; Pilgrimage, article on Muslim Pilgrimage; Qāḍī; Qiyās; Qurʾān; Ṣalāt; Ṣawm; Shāfiʿī, al-; Shahādah; Sunnah; ʿUlamāʾ; Uṣūl al-Fiqh; Worship and Devotional Life, article on Muslim Worship; Zakāt.

BIBLIOGRAPHY

An older study offering a general reference with extensive indexes and bibliography is Joseph Schacht's *An Introduction to Islamic Law* (Oxford, 1964). An excellent reference work is *The Encyclopaedia of Islam,* 4 vols. and supplement (Leiden, 1913–1938), and its condensed version, the *Shorter Encyclopaedia of Islam* (1953; reprint, Leiden, 1974). A new edition of the larger version has been issued alphabetically in fascicles since 1960. To use these works it is necessary to know the Arabic terms for different aspects of Islamic law.

A bibliography of works in many languages is Erich Pritsch and Otto Spies's "Klassisches Islamisches Recht," in *Orientalisches Recht* (Leiden, 1964), pp. 220–343, suppl. vol. 3 of *Der Nahe und der Mittlere Osten,* first part of *Handbuch der Orientalistik.* An old but still usable general book is Nicolas P. Aghnides's *Muḥammadan Theories of Finance* (New York, 1916), with a much broader scope than the title suggests. Materials on recent scholarship on Islamic law are included in *A Bibliography of Islamic Law, 1980–1993,* edited by Laila Al-Zwaini and Rudolph Peters (Leiden, 1994).

Unparalleled in its depth of analysis and a uniquely valuable contribution to the comparative study of Islamic jurisprudence is Yvon Linant de Bellefonds's *Traité de droit musulman comparé,* 3 vols. (Paris, 1965–1973), covering aspects of contract and family law. A readable short historical survey of the development of the *sharīʿah* from the beginnings to the modern period is Noel J. Coulson's *A History of Islamic Law* (1964; reprint, Edinburgh, 1971). A general survey by an important Muslim scholar is S. R. Mahmassani's *Falsafat al-Tashrīʿ fi al-Islam: The Philosophy of Jurisprudence in Islam,* translated by Farhat J. Ziadeh (Leiden, 1961). A. A. Fyzee's *Outlines of Muhammadan Law,* 4th ed. (Bombay, 1974), combines a general introduction to the *sharīʿah* with a discussion of features of Anglo-Muhammadan law.

A thorough and critical examination of the doctrines of the Mālikī school in comparison with the Shāfiʿī school can be found in David Santillana's *Istituzioni del diritto musulmano malichita,* 2 vols. (Rome, 1925–1938). One of the great medieval encyclopedias of *fiqh* is that of the Ḥanbalī scholar Muwaffaq al-Dīn ibn Qudāmah, *Al-mughnī,* 12 vols., edited by Tāhā Muḥammad al-Zaynī (1923–1930; reprint, Cairo, 1968–), notable for its balanced treatment of the doctrines of the different Sunnī schools and still a standard reference work. An erudite exposition on the early development of the *sharīʿah* is Joseph Schacht's *The Origins of Muhammadan Jurisprudence* (Oxford, 1950), now contested by Wael Hallaq in *A History of Islamic Legal Theories: An Introduction to Sunnī uṣūl al-fiqh* (New York, 1997). A collection of essays of high scholarly merit is Robert Brunschvig's *Études d'islamologie,* 2 vols. (Paris, 1976). Useful chapters on the interrelationship of theology and law in Islam can be found in the short volume edited by G. E. von Grunebaum, *Theology and Law in Islam* (Wiesbaden, 1971). An older work on this topic by one of the major European scholars of Islam is Ignácz Goldziher's *Introduction to Islamic Theology and Law,* published in German in 1910 and translated by Andras and Ruth Hamori (Princeton, N. J., 1981). A thorough treatment of the legal position of non-Muslims in Muslim society is Antoine Fattal's *Le statut légal des non-musulmans en pays d'Islam* (Beirut, 1958). The doctrines of the different law schools regarding intestate succession are clearly set forth in Noel J. Coulson's *Succession in the Muslim Family* (Cambridge, U.K., 1971). The administration of justice in the setting of traditional Islamic civilization is Émile Tyan's *Histoire de l'organisation judiciaire en pays d'Islam,* 2d ed. (Leiden, 1960). An informative collection of studies of *fatwās* is *Islamic Legal Interpretation: Muftīs and Their Fatwās,* edited by Muḥammad Khalid Masud et al. (Cambridge, Mass., 1996). A probing examination of medieval jurisprudence on political resistance and rebellion can be found in Khaled Abou El Fadl, *Rebellion and Violence in Islamic Law* (Cambridge, U.K., 2001).

Valuable assessments of Twelver Shīʿī law are in *Le Shīʿisme imāmite: Colloque de Strasbourg, 6–9 mai 1968,* edited by Toufic Fahd et al. (Paris, 1970). A useful examination of Twelver Shīʿī legal doctrines is Harold Löschner's *Die dogmatischen Grundlagen des Shīʿitischen Rechts* (Cologne, 1971). Islamic institutions and the role of the clergy in Iran are examined in detail in Shahrough Akhavi's *Religion and Politics in Contemporary Iran* (Albany, N.Y., 1980). An insightful comparative study of Islamic family law is Ziba Mir-Hosseini, *Marriage on Trial: A Study of Islamic Family Law* (London, 1993).

A distinguished assessment of early liberal reformist thought is Malcolm H. Kerr's *Islamic Reform: The Political and Legal Theories of Muhammad Abduh and Rashid Rida* (Berkeley, Calif., 1966). A survey of reform of the *sharīʿah* in legal systems in the Muslim world is presented in J. N. D. Anderson's *Law Reform in the Muslim World* (London, 1976). A proposal for an enlightened approach to interpreting the requirements of Islamic law can be found in Fazlur Rahman's *Islam and Modernity* (Chicago, 1982). Feminist perspectives on Islamic law from many different sources and countries are published by the nongovernmental organization Women Living under Muslim Laws.

ANN ELIZABETH MAYER (1987 AND 2005)

ISLAMIC LAW: PERSONAL LAW

The area of personal law is often considered to be the main bastion of Islamic law. One reason for this is that the Qurʾān devotes greater attention to subjects such as marriage, divorce, and inheritance than it does to any other legal topic. In this sense the law of personal status represents an entrenched part of the religion, and Muslims have by and large regarded adherence to its principles as a criterion of the religious propriety of individuals and governments. It is, therefore, not surprising to find that the *sharīʿah* law of personal status has remained largely applicable in Muslim countries today in spite of recent reforms that have adapted many aspects of the classical law to suit the requirements of modern life. Reform of the *sharīʿah* law is a phenomenon of the twentieth century and, because of the continuing relevance of the law of personal status to the Muslim community, has been concentrated mainly in that area. Other portions of the *sharīʿah,* such as criminal law, taxation, and constitutional law, have either fallen into abeyance or remained relatively untouched by modern reformist legislation. Under the renewed influence of Islamic movements in the 1970s and 1980s, however, these other areas of the law have also begun to attract the attention of reformers as the effort is made to revive their significance.

In modern-day Islam, the Ḥanafī school commands a greater following than any other school of law. This survey is, therefore, based on *sharīʿah* law as developed within the framework of the Ḥanafī school. Wherever Ḥanafī law diverges from the law of the other three Sunnī schools (Shāfiʿī, Mālikī, and Ḥanbalī), their differences are outlined. References to Shīʿī law generally relate to the Twelver Shīʿī school, which is mainly adhered to in Iran and has the largest following of all the branches of Shīʿī Islam.

MARRIAGE. Like any other private contract, marriage under *sharīʿah* law is concluded by the mutual agreement, oral or written, of the parties or their representatives. The only formality required is the presence of two witnesses at the conclusion of the contract, and even this is not necessary under Shīʿī law. Formalities usually observed, such as ceremonies performed in the presence of a religious leader, are matters of customary practice and not a legal requirement.

The requirements of a marriage contract are basically the same in all *sharīʿah* schools. First, the parties or their representatives must be legally competent persons, and second, there must be no legal impediment to marriage. Sanity and majority are the basic requirements of the legal capacity to contract. Legal majority is established with physical puberty, which is attained upon proof of sexual maturity rather than at a specific age. Unless proven otherwise, a boy below the age of twelve and a girl below the age of nine are legally presumed to be minors. Similarly, both sexes are presumed to have attained majority with the completion of the fifteenth year. A boy or girl who has reached the minimum age of majority but is still below fifteen is permitted to marry provided he or she shows signs of puberty. A person who has attained majority (*bāligh*) and is of sound mind (*ʿāqil*) has rights and obligations, must fulfill religious duties, and incurs criminal responsibility. The minor (*saghīr*) and the insane (*majnūn*) are wholly capable of contracting marriage. The idiot (*ma'tūh*) and the imbecile, who are incapable of managing their own affairs, have the capacity only to conclude purely advantageous transactions, such as the acceptance of a gift, but they are not permitted to contract marriage. A major who is incompetent (*safīh*) may be subjected to interdiction (*ḥajr*) and placed under the supervision of the authorities, and this procedure could lead to restrictions on his capacity to contract. An adult woman has the capacity to contract her own marriage only in Ḥanafī and Shī'ī law. According to the other three Sunnī schools, her marriage guardian (*walīy*) must conclude the contract on her behalf. All schools recognize, in principle, the compulsory power of the marriage guardian, which is known as *ijbār.* The guardian is accordingly authorized to contract his ward, whether the ward is male or female, in marriage at his discretion regardless of the ward's wishes. But the precise extent of this power varies among the schools. In Ḥanafī law, only minor wards are subject to *ijbār,* and the power is absolute only when exercised by the father or paternal grandfather. In all other cases, the ward has the right to repudiate the marriage on attaining puberty. This option of puberty (*khiyār al-bulūgh*) is, however, lost by the affirmative act of consummating the marriage. Guardianship in marriage is vested in the nearest male relatives in accordance with the order of priorities that is applied in inheritance, that is, the father, grandfather, brother, nephews, uncles, and cousins, and failing them, the female relatives.

Under the Ḥanafī doctrine of *kafā'ah* (equality), the guardian of an adult female may oppose the marriage of his ward on the ground that the prospective spouse is not her equal. This doctrine is, however, mainly applicable to the man, who is required to be the equal of his prospective wife in respect of lineage, religion, freedom (as opposed to slavery), piety, means, and profession. If, however, both the guardian and bride fail to raise the question of equality before the contract, neither can have the marriage annulled upon discovery that the husband is not the equal of his wife. In both the Shāfi'ī and Mālikī schools, the adult virgin is denied the right to conclude her own marriage; because the guardian himself is concluding the marriage, the doctrine of *kafā'ah* is not applicable under these schools.

Marriage is prohibited between close relatives. Relationships that constitute permanent impediments to marriage fall into three categories: (1) blood relationship (*garābah*), which implies that a man may not marry any of his lineal descendants, lineal ascendants, the offspring of his parents, or the immediate child of any grandparent; (2) affinity (*muṣāharah*), which creates a bar to marriage between a man and the ascendants or descendants of his wife, or the wife of any of his ascendants or descendants; (3) fosterage (*raḍā'*), which arises when a woman breast-feeds the child of someone else. Fosterage creates a bar to marriage not only between foster brothers and sisters, but also between the foster mother and all her relatives on the one side, and her foster children, their spouses, and descendants on the other.

In addition, difference of religion is a bar to marriage: A Muslim woman may not marry a non-Muslim man unless he professes Islam. A Muslim man is, on the other hand, allowed to marry a *kitābīyah,* that is, a woman who follows a religion that has a revealed scripture, such as Judaism or Christianity. The Qur'ān further prohibits both Muslim men and women from marrying polytheists or fire worshipers. Finally, a man may not marry a woman who is already married or who is observing *'iddah,* that is, the waiting period that a woman must observe following a divorce, with the exception of a divorce ending an unconsummated marriage. *'Iddah* usually lasts for three menstrual cycles or, where the wife proves to be pregnant, until the delivery of the child. The main purpose of *'iddah* is to determine a possible pregnancy prior to marriage. A widow must observe a waiting period of four months and ten days following the death of her husband.

The marriage contract is classified into three types, namely valid *(ṣaḥīḥ),* irregular *(fāsid),* and void *(bāṭīl).* A marriage contract is valid when it fulfills all the legal requirements. This contract brings about a fully effective union that renders intercourse lawful between the spouses, entitles the wife to dower and maintenance, obligates the wife to be faithful and obedient to the husband, and creates prohibited degrees of relations and mutual rights of inheritance between the spouses.

A void *(bāṭīl)* marriage is one that is unlawful from the outset and that does not create any rights or obligations between the parties. In such a marriage no illicit sexual intercourse (*zinā'*) is considered to have been committed if the parties were unaware that the marriage was void. Marriage with a woman within the prohibited degrees and marriage that is brought about without the consent of the adult parties are void. The offspring of a *bāṭīl* marriage is illegitimate.

An irregular *(fāsid)* marriage, on the other hand, is not unlawful in itself, but involves some irregularity of a temporary nature that could be rectified by means of a new contract. Marriage without witnesses, marriage with a fifth wife (the maximum limit being four), marriage with a non-*kitābīyah* (a woman who is neither Jewish nor Christian), and marriage with a woman undergoing *'iddah* are examples of *fāsid* marriages. Such a marriage may be terminated by either party or by a judge, should it come to his notice. A *fāsid* marriage has no legal effect before consummation, but when consummated, the wife is entitled to dower and maintenance, and the issue of the marriage is legitimate. A *fāsid* marriage does not create any right of inheritance between the parties.

Islamic law requires the husband to pay his wife a dower (*mahr*). The amount of dower and the terms of its payment are matters of agreement between the parties. Anything that can be considered as goods *(māl)* may be given as a dower, but objects that are prohibited in Islam, such as wine and pork, are excluded from the definition of *māl.* If no dower is specified in the contract, the wife is entitled to a "proper" dower *(mahr al-mithl)*, that is, a dower that is equivalent to the dower usually received by women of similar status. A dower may be paid at the time of the contract, or it may be deferred, in whole or in part, subject to the agreement of the parties. A deferred dower remains a debt on the part of the husband and is payable upon the dissolution of the marriage by death or divorce. In the event of a divorce prior to consummation, the wife is entitled to half the specified dower; if no dower is specified in the contract, the wife is entitled to a gift (*mutʿah*), which consists of a set of clothing.

The husband is bound to maintain his wife as soon as she cohabits with him. Should she refuse to cohabit or refuse herself to him, the husband is relieved of his duty, unless her refusal is for a lawful cause such as the husband's failure to pay the dower or unsuitability of the lodging for a person of her status. In such cases, the wife's refusal to cohabit does not relieve the husband of his duty of maintenance, which includes food, clothing, and accommodation. According to the majority of jurists, the wife is entitled to maintenance in a style that conforms to the husband's status, regardless of her own premarital position. Should the husband desert his wife without providing for her maintenance, a judge may authorize the wife to make the necessary arrangements at her husband's expense. The wife is not, however, entitled to a decree for past maintenance unless the claim is based on a specific agreement. Shāfiʿī and Shīʿī law, on the other hand, entitle the wife to claim her past maintenance. The general rule in maintenance is that no individual who is capable of maintaining himself is entitled to receive maintenance from others; the only exception is the wife, who is entitled to maintenance regardless of her own financial status. The father is bound to maintain his sons until they attain puberty, and his daughters until they are married; he is also responsible for the maintenance of a widowed or divorced daughter. The law entitles every blood relative to maintenance provided that, if male, he is a child and destitute, and if a female, she is destitute whether a child or an adult. A widow is not entitled to maintenance during the period of *ʿiddah* following her husband's death, because in this case she would be entitled to a share of the inheritance. The liability of a person to support these relatives is generally proportionate to his or her share of their inheritance.

The *sharīʿah* entitles the husband to discipline his wife lightly when she transgresses. The law is not precise as to how and when the husband is entitled to do so, nor indeed as to what amounts to a transgression (*maʿṣiyah*). She must not dishonor him, refuse herself to him without lawful excuse, or cause him loss of property that is deemed unacceptable according to normal social usage. The wife is entitled to visit her parents once a week and other relatives once a year, even without the permission of her husband. She may also leave the husband if he refuses to pay her a dower. Similarly, unreasonable requests by the husband—that she should accompany him on long journeys, for example—may be refused by her. The wife retains her full capacity to enter contracts and transactions with regard to her own property as if she were not married. Indeed, the law recognizes no merger of either the personality or the property of the wife into that of her husband's. Separation of property is the norm in *sharīʿah* law and is presumed to apply unless the parties make a specific agreement to the contrary. If a man beats his wife without reason (even lightly), or beats her for cause but exceeds moderation, he is liable to punishment following her complaint to the court.

Islam allows a man to marry up to four wives simultaneously provided that he does not combine, as co-wives, two women so closely related that if either of them were a male, they would themselves be within the prohibited degrees of marriage. Each of the co-wives is entitled to a separate dwelling and to an equal portion of the husband's time and companionship.

Modern legislation in Muslim countries has either sought to restrict the practice of polygamy or to abolish it altogether. At the one extreme is the Tunisian law of 1957, which prohibits polygamy outright. At the other is the Moroccan law of 1958, which entitles the wife to seek judicial divorce if she has suffered injury as a result of polygamy. Syria, Iraq, and Pakistan have adopted a middle course by requiring official permission before a polygamous marriage is contracted. The modernists have generally justified their reforms by direct resort to the Qurʾān and a reinterpretation of the Qurʾanic verse on polygamy (5:4), which permits polygamy but at the same time expresses the fear of injustice in polygamous relationships. Modern reformers have reasoned that the fear of injustice in a polygamous marriage is bound to be present in every case of polygamy and therefore have concluded that abolishing polygamy is consistent with the Qurʾanic dispensations.

Marriage under Sunnī law is a lifelong union, and any stipulation that sets a time limit to it nullifies the contract. Shīʿī law, however, recognizes temporary marriage, known as *mutʿah*. This is a contractual arrangement whereby a woman agrees to cohabit with a man for a specified period of time in return for a fixed remuneration. *Mutʿah* does not give rise to any right of inheritance between the parties, but the issue of *mutʿah* is legitimate and entitled to inheritance. As the reader will note, *mutʿah* also signifies a gift of consolation to a divorced woman; the word appears in the Qurʾān in both senses (2:236, 4:24), hence the origin of its double legal meaning.

Modern legislation in most Muslim countries compels marriage registration, and failure to comply is usually liable to legal sanctions. The law similarly requires the express consent of the parties to a marriage in order for it to be valid. To facilitate meeting the consent requirement, parties to a marriage contract must be of marriageable age. This age is almost everywhere enacted at sixteen for females and eighteen for males. Modern reforms concerning the age of marriage have thus departed from the classical *sharīʿah*, which stipulated no specific age for marriage and only presumed the minimum and maximum ages of legal majority; the age of marriage established under the new codes also signifies the age of majority for all legal purposes. A marriage in which the parties have not reached the specified age is denied registration and may render the parties liable to statutory penalties. As a result of the enactment of a statutory age for marriage, child marriage has been effectively abolished in most Muslim countries. Similarly, the powers that the marriage guardian enjoys under classical *sharīʿah* law have, as a result of the age provisions, been either abolished or substantially restricted.

DIVORCE. Marriage under *sharīʿah* law may be dissolved either by the husband at his will, by mutual agreement of the spouses, or by a judicial decree. All the *sharīʿah* schools recognize the husband's right of unilateral repudiation, known as *ṭalāq*. Sunnī law requires no formalities as to the manner in which a *ṭalāq* may be pronounced. A husband of sound mind who has attained puberty may effect *ṭalāq* orally or in writing without assigning any cause. Any words indicative of repudiation may be used, and no witnesses are necessary for the pronouncement. In Shīʿī law, *ṭalāq* must be pronounced in the presence of two witnesses, and the exact term *ṭalāq* must be used. Whereas in Ḥanafī law *ṭalāq* pronounced by way of jest or in a state of intoxication is nonetheless valid, in both Shāfiʿī and Shīʿī law, *ṭalāq* is valid only when accompanied by a definite intention.

The husband can delegate his power of *ṭalāq* to his wife or to a third person who may then pronounce it according to the terms of the authorization (*tafwīḍ*). Thus there can be a valid agreement between the spouses authorizing the wife to repudiate herself if the husband marries a second wife, and the wife can exercise the power when the occasion arises.

In Sunnī law, *ṭalāq* is classified as "approved" (*ṭalāq al-sunnah*) or "disapproved" (*ṭalāq al-bidʿah*), according to the circumstances in which it is pronounced. The former is generally revocable, whereas the latter is irrevocable and terminates the marriage tie immediately upon pronouncement. The "approved" *ṭalāq* may consist of either a single repudiation pronounced during a clean period, that is, a period between menstruations, known as *ṭuhr*, followed by abstinence from sexual intercourse for the whole of the waiting period (*ʿiddah*), or it may consist of three repudiations pronounced during three successive *ṭuhr*s. In the former case, *ṭalāq* becomes final after the expiration of the *ʿiddah*, whereas in the latter, it becomes final upon the third pronouncement. Until the *ṭalāq* becomes final, the husband has the option to revoke it, and this may be done either expressly or by implication, through the resumption of normal marital relations. The "disapproved" *ṭalāq* may consist of a single repudiation which is expressly declared to be final, or it may consist of three repudiations pronounced at once. Shīʿī law does not recognize the "disapproved" form of *ṭalāq*.

Divorce by mutual agreement may take one of two forms: *khulʿ*, in which the wife secures her release from the marital tie by offering the husband financial consideration, commonly the return of the dower, which is accepted by the husband; or *mubāraʾah*, which is a dissolution of marriage on the basis of mutual release of the spouses from any outstanding financial commitments arising from the marriage. In both cases, the divorce is final and extrajudicial, effected simply by the mutual agreement of the parties.

With respect to judicial dissolution, Ḥanafī law is the most restrictive of all the *sharīʿah* schools. This law allows a woman to seek a dissolution (*faskh*) of her marriage from a *qāḍī* (Islamic judge) under four specific conditions: If she was married at a young age by a guardian other than her father or grandfather, she can ask the *qāḍī* to dissolve the marriage upon attaining puberty; if insane, upon regaining her sanity; if the husband is sexually impotent; or if he is a missing person and ninety years have elapsed since the date of his birth. All the other schools, including the Shīʿī, authorize the *qāḍī* to grant a judicial divorce in cases where the husband is suffering a physical or mental disease. Whenever it is proved that the disease is incurable, the court is to order dissolution immediately, but if it is a disease that requires time to cure, the court must order a stay of judgment for one year. The Shāfiʿī and Ḥanbalī schools also consider a husband's willful refusal to support his wife and a husband's desertion as valid grounds for a judicial divorce. Even more liberal is the Mālikī school, which recognizes the husband's illness, his failure to maintain, desertion for more than one year for whatever reason, and injurious treatment (*ḍarar*) as valid grounds for judicial divorce. According to the last ground, the wife can demand a judicial dissolution by claiming that cohabitation with her husband is injurious to her in a way that makes the continuation of marital life impossible for a person of her status. A decree of divorce granted on any of these grounds is final, except in the case of failure to maintain, where the court's degree effects only a revocable divorce, and the husband can resume normal marital relations during the period of *ʿiddah* if he proves that he can support his wife.

And finally, apostasy from Islam by either of the spouses operates as an immediate and final dissolution of the marriage without any judicial intervention. If both spouses renounce Islam simultaneously, their marriage is permitted to endure. Conversion to Islam by the husband alone where both spouses were Jewish or Christian does not impair the marriage, and the wife may retain her religion. However, if a Christian or Jewish woman, married to a man of the same faith, becomes a Muslim, the marriage is dissolved unless the husband also adopts Islam.

A final divorce, whatever its mode may be, renders sexual intercourse unlawful and entitles the wife to remarry after completing the waiting period of *ʿiddah*. If the marriage is not consummated, she is free to marry immediately. A triple *ṭalāq* renders remarriage between the divorced couple unlawful until the woman marries another person; only after the dissolution of this latter marriage may she remarry her former husband. Upon a final divorce, mutual rights of inheritance cease between the parties, and any outstanding dower becomes immediately payable to the wife. She is entitled to maintenance only during her *ʿiddah.*

Modern reforms of divorce law in Muslim countries have been primarily directed at restricting the husband's power of unilateral divorce on the one hand, and at increasing the remedies available to the wife in cases of injurious circumstances on the other. The main restriction on the husband's power of unilateral *ṭalāq* comes from the abolition of the irrevocable forms of *ṭalāq.* The husband is thus no longer able to terminate his marriage immediately by pronouncing a final and irrevocable *ṭalāq.* Legislation in some Muslim countries also entitles the wife to financial compensation for any injury she may have sustained as a result of the husband's abuse of his power. In the traditionally Ḥanafī countries, the wife's position has been enhanced by legislative measures, which entitle her to a judicial divorce on grounds substantially the same as those recognized under Mālikī law. Modern legislation has also departed from the Ḥanafī position that ignores intention in *ṭalāq* by adopting provisions under which *ṭalāq* is only valid if accompanied by a definite intention. The Tunisian law of 1957 is the most far-reaching of the modern reforms in that it abolishes all forms of extrajudicial divorce, whether by *ṭalāq* or by mutual consent. By abolishing the husband's power of unilateral *ṭalāq,* the Tunisian law effects complete equality between the spouses in divorce.

INHERITANCE. In pre-Islamic Arabia, succession was purely tribal and agnatic, that is, the heirs were normally the closest male relatives, and women and minors were excluded. A fundamental reform that the Qurʾān brought about was to assign definite shares to female relatives. According to the Islamic scheme of inheritance, a female generally receives half the share of a male. The deceased fictitiously remains the owner of the estate until his obligations are fully discharged. The creditors can, therefore, only assert their claims against the estate and not against the individual heirs. All funeral expenses, debts, and bequests have to be paid in full before the estate can be distributed among the heirs.

An essential condition of inheritance is that the heir must survive the deceased. In doubtful cases, arising, for example, when persons who would inherit from one another have died without proof of who died first, neither can inherit from the other according to the majority, but Shīʿī and Ḥanbalī law entitle both to inherit from one another. Similarly, inheritance can only pass to an heir who exists at the time of the death of the deceased, except when a man leaves a pregnant widow, in which case the share of an unborn male child is reserved for the offspring. If the child is female, she will receive her normal share of inheritance, and the remainder of the reserved portion reverts back to the estate to be redistributed among the heirs proportionate to their normal shares.

The birth of a child, whether male or female, may affect the position of an heir in a variety of ways. He or she may be excluded from succession, have their share reduced, or in some circumstances, become entitled to a larger share. In all cases, the present heirs are, according to the majority view, entitled to take their minimal shares and reserve the largest share for the unborn child. This is the share of a male child under Ḥanafī law, whereas the Shāfiʿī, Ḥanbalī, and Shīʿī law assume that twin boys or twin girls will be born, and the other heirs are entitled to the share they would receive in one case or the other, whichever is less. In Mālikī law the distribution is completely suspended until the birth of the child. All schools are unanimous, however, in suspending the distribution of the estate in the event that all the other heirs would be totally excluded by the birth of the child. Excluded from succession are the following: one who has caused the death of the deceased; a non-Muslim as the heir of a Muslim and vice versa (a bequest, however, can be made to a non-Muslim), and a slave who, under classical law, is not capable of owning property.

The heirs are mainly divided into three groups: those who are entitled to a prescribed share, known as Qurʾanic heirs (*dhawū furūḍ*); those who receive the remainder, known as agnatic heirs (*ʿaṣabah*); and distant kindred (*dhawū al-arḥām*), persons who are related to the deceased in the female line and fall into neither of the first two categories. In the absence of all three, the estate goes to the public treasury *(bayt al-māl).*

The Qurʾān allots shares to eight relatives, namely the daughter, mother, father, husband, wife, brothers, and sisters. But the rules regarding the daughter have been extended, by analogy, to the daughter of a son, and those regarding the parents, to the grandparents. In addition, a distinction has been made between a full sister, a half sister on the father's side, and a half sister on the mother's side. The total number of Qurʾanic heirs has thus been raised to twelve.

A daughter who has no brothers is entitled to half the estate, and two or more daughters share equally in a portion of two-thirds. But if daughters inherit along with sons, they become *ʿaṣabah* and receive half the portion of the sons. A son's daughter without brothers inherits half the estate; if there are two or more son's daughters, their share is two-thirds. A son's daughter is excluded if that son has two or more sisters inheriting along with him. The father inherits one-sixth in the presence of a son, and in the presence of a daughter or a son's daughter, one-sixth plus any residue. In the absence of descendants, the father inherits as the nearest *ʿaṣabah.* The father's father inherits one-sixth, but he is excluded if the father is alive. The mother's portion is one-sixth if there are children and one-third if there are none. The mother's mother inherits one-sixth, but she is excluded if the mother is alive. One full sister in the absence of brothers inherits one-half, and two or more, two-thirds. A half sister on the father's side receives the same share as a full sister, but both are excluded in the presence of a son, or a son's son, or the father. Both a half brother and a half sister on the mother's side receive one-sixth, and two or more share a third among them, but they are excluded by descendants and male ascendants. The husband receives a quarter if there is a descendant, and in the absence thereof, a half. The wife inherits one-half of what the husband would receive under the same circumstances.

Sometimes the number of qualified Qurʾanic heirs or the sum of their shares may be larger than the whole of the estate. In this case, their shares are reduced under the principle of proportionate reduction, known as *ʿawl.* For example, if the deceased is survived by a husband and two full sisters, their shares will be one-half and two-thirds respectively, which exceed unity. Hence, the share will be reduced to three-sevenths and four-sevenths respectively.

The agnatic heirs (*ʿaṣabah*) inherit the remainder of the estate after the Qurʾanic heirs have received their shares. The *ʿaṣabah* are divided into the following classes, in order of priority: (1) the son and his descendants in the male line; (2) the father and his ascendants in the male line; (3) the male descendants of the father; (4) descendants of the paternal grandfather; and (5) descendants of the paternal great-grandfather. Any member of a higher class totally excludes any member of a lower class, except that the brothers of the deceased are not excluded by the grandfather. Among the relatives of the same class, the nearer in degree to the deceased excludes the more remote: In class three, for example, a nephew will be excluded by the deceased's brother. Among agnatic relatives of the same class and the same degree, germanes have priority over consanguines. Thus, for example, the germane brother of the deceased totally excludes the consanguine brother.

If there is no *ʿaṣabah* and the Qurʾanic heirs do not exhaust the estate, the remainder is proportionately distributed among the Qurʾanic heirs under the principle of reversion, known as *radd.* For example, if the deceased is survived by his mother and a daughter, their shares will be one-sixth and one-half; because these are less than unity, they will be increased to one-quarter and three-quarters respectively.

BEQUESTS. All the *sharīʿah* jurists agree that a person who is adult and sane has the capacity to make a bequest, while bequests made by a minor or a mentally defective person, a person acting under compulsion, or under temporary loss of reason (through, for example, intoxication) are void. A bequest may be oral or written, and any words, or even signs, may be used provided they clearly indicate the testator's intention. All free individuals, juristic persons, and fetuses in the womb, whether Muslim or non-Muslim, and irrespective of domicile, are capable of receiving a bequest. Any object of value that is considered as goods *(māl)*, including income and usufruct arising out of the property owned by the testator, may be given in bequest. A bequest is invalid if made in pursuit of unlawful purposes, such as promoting a brothel. Further, no Muslim may bequeath more than one-third of the residue of his estate after the payment of debts and other charges. In Sunnī law, a bequest made in favor of a legal heir is void unless the other heirs consent to it. Similarly, a bequest that exceeds the bequeathable third does not take effect without the consent of the surviving heirs. In Sunnī law, such consent must be obtained after the death of the testator, whereas in Shīʿī law it may be obtained either before or after the testator's death. Shīʿī law also permits the testator to bequeath to any person, including a legal heir, within the limit of one-third. Without the consent of the surviving heirs, bequests amounting to more than one-third of the estate must be reduced to the maximum of one-third.

A testator may specify the order in which several of his bequests are to be executed, and this order will be observed until the bequeathable third is exhausted. If no order is specified and the limit of one-third is exceeded, the abatement will be proportionate in Sunnī law, whereas under Shīʿī law the first in chronological order prevails. A bequest is null and void if made in favor of a person who has caused the death of the testator. And finally, if the legatee predeceases the testator, the bequest lapses in Ḥanafī law, but passes on to the heir of the deceased legatee in Shīʿī law.

PATERNITY. Paternity is the legal relation between father and child that is created by a legitimate birth. The paternity of a child is normally established by marriage between its parents. Maternity on the other hand is not dependent upon marriage. In Sunnī law, the maternity of a child, whether the offspring of marriage or of adultery, is established in the woman who actually gives birth to the child. Thus if a man commits adultery and a child is born, it is considered to be the child of its mother and inherits from her and her relations. But the man is not considered to be the father of the child, for paternity is established only through marriage. In Shīʿī law, however, an illegitimate child has no legal relationship with either its father or its mother.

The law normally presumes that a child born to a married woman is the legitimate child of her husband. This presumption, however, operates within the limits of what the law recognizes as the minimum and maximum duration of the gestation period. According to all the *sharīʿah* schools, the minimum period of gestation is six months. The maximum period varies between nine months (Shīʿī), two years (Ḥanafī), four years (Shāfiʿī), and five to seven years (Mālikī). In Ḥanafī law, therefore, the paternity of the child is ascribed to the husband if it is born after not less than six months of marriage, and within not more than two years after the dissolution of marriage. The only method by which the husband can challenge the presumption of legitimacy and disown his child is to resort to the imprecation procedure, known as *liʿān.* According to this procedure, the husband must swear four oaths that the child is not his and then invoke the curse of God upon himself if he is lying. This effects an immediate and final divorce according to the majority view, whereas in Ḥanafī and Shīʿī law, the marriage subsists until the court orders the parties to separate. If the wife confesses to the adultery, the penalty is imprisonment according to Ḥanafī law, and death by stoning according to the other schools (Ḥanafī law forbids the enforcement of capital punishment for *zinā'* unless it is proven by the testimony of four witnesses). Alternately, she may deny the charge by swearing four solemn oaths to plead her innocence and finally calling upon herself the wrath of God if she was in fact guilty. Regardless of whether the wife confesses or denies the charge, as a consequence of *li'ān* the child is disowned by the husband.

Either of the spouses, or failing this, the judge, may initiate the *li'ān* proceedings. The traditional law of *li'ān* does not, however, provide for the eventuality where the wife might initiate a charge of adultery against the husband. In the event that the wife accuses the husband of *zinā'*, she would normally be required to prove the accusation by the testimony of four witnesses, in which case the husband would be liable to the capital punishment for *zinā'*. But if she fails to provide the required proof, she would herself be liable to punishment for slanderous accusation *(qadhf)*, which is eighty lashes. In neither case, however, would recourse be made to *li'ān*, for the latter is invoked only when the husband accuses his wife of *zinā'*, and not vice versa. If the husband accuses his wife of *zinā'* but fails to resort to *li'ān*, he too would be liable to the punishment of *qadhf*. Some jurists have held the view that the wife's unproven accusation of *zinā'* would provide sufficient grounds for judicial separation on the basis of injury (*ḍarar*).

Where the paternity of a child cannot be proved by establishing a marriage between the parents at the time of conception, the law recognizes acknowledgment (*iqrār*) as a method whereby such a marriage and legitimate descent can be established. This method can be used only if real paternity is possible; thus the acknowledged child must be at least twelve and one-half years younger than the acknowledging parent, because this interval represents the minimum period of gestation added to the minimum age of puberty. In addition, one person may acknowledge the paternity of another on the following three conditions: the child is of unknown paternity; there is no definite proof that the child is the offspring of adultery; and the acknowledgment does not contradict another person's presumption of paternity. An acknowledgment need not be expressed in words, but may be implied by the deliberate conduct of one person who treats another as his legitimate offspring. Subject to repudiation by an acknowledgee who is adult and sane, an acknowledgment of paternity is binding for all purposes, and once effected, it is irrevocable.

The *sharī'ah* law of paternity has been criticized mainly for accepting gestation periods of two years (Ḥanafī law) or more, which has encouraged people to claim the paternity of illegitimate children for purposes of inheritance. In a 1929 law, the Egyptian legislature reduced the maximum period of gestation to one year. Consequently, no claim of paternity on behalf of a child born more than one year after the termination of the marriage can be heard in Egyptian courts. Furthermore, the Egyptian law provides that proof of nonaccess between the spouses because their marriage or for one year preceding the birth of a child would debar a claim of the legitimacy of such a child. Syria, Tunisia, and Morocco have also adopted these measures with minor variations, and one year represents the maximum period of gestation in these countries. It may be added that the modern law provision enabling a husband to prove that he had no physical access to his wife during the possible time of conception supersedes the procedure of *li'ān*. In appropriate circumstances, therefore, the new rules of evidence will determine the disputed paternity of a child. Proof of nonaccess, under modern law, would also seem to defeat the claim to inheritance of a child in embryo, at least where the basis of such a claim is the legitimacy of the child, and would, in turn, overrule the provision of the traditional law concerning the reservation of a portion of the estate for such a child. The fundamental rules governing the custody of children (*ḥaḍānah*) are common to all the *sharī'ah* schools. Following the dissolution of a marriage, the custody of the young children belongs to the mother, but she loses this right if she remarries, in which case custody reverts to the father. The mother's right to custody terminates with the completion of seven years in the case of male children, and in case of female children, with the onset of puberty.

BIBLIOGRAPHY

An accurate exposition of the *sharī'ah* law of marriage and divorce can be found in al-Marghinānīs *Al-hidāyah,* a twelfth-century source book of Ḥanafī law, translated by Charles Hamilton as *The Hedaya, or Guide,* 4 vols., 2d ed. (Lahore, 1957). A source book on the law of inheritance is Sirāj al-Dīn al-Sajāwandi's *Al-sirājīyah,* the text and translation of which will be found in a modern work by al-haj Mahomet Ullah ibn S. Jung, *The Muslim Law of Inheritance* (Allahabad, 1934). The whole range of personal law is treated by D. F. Mulla's *Principles of Mahomedan Law,* 16th ed. (Bombay, 1968), a well-known Ḥanafī law text that is also informative on the application of this law in India and Pakistan. F. B. Tyabji's *Muslim Law: The Personal Law of Muslims in India and Pakistan,* 4th ed. (Bombay, 1968) is skillfully classified and comprehensive on all the major schools of *sharī'ah* law. A. A. Fyzee's *Outlines of Muhammadan Law,* 4th ed. (Bombay, 1974) is more informative on Shī'ī personal law, and its introductory chapter gives background information on the sources and history of the *sharī'ah.* The best single book on the law of inheritance and its modern reforms remains Noel J. Coulson's *Succession in the Muslim Family* (Cambridge, U.K., 1971). A useful collection of the statutory laws of various Muslim countries, with special reference to modern reforms, can be found in Tahir Mahmood's *Family Law Reform in the Muslim World* (Bombay, 1972). Herbert J. Liebesny's *Law of the Near and Middle East* (Albany, N.Y., 1975) is also very useful on the application of *sharī'ah* law in various Muslim countries. For the status of women, see John L. Esposito, *Women in Muslim Family Law* (Syracuse, N.Y., 1982).

There are many good books in Arabic on the subject. Muḥammad abū Zahrah's *Al-aḥwāl al-shakhṣīyah* (Cairo, 1957) is written in readable style and deals with the whole range of the *sharī'ah* personal law. 'Abd al-Raḥmān al-Sabūni's *Madā ḥurriyat al-zawjayn fī al-ṭalāq,* 2 vols., 2d ed. (Beirut, 1968) is most comprehensive on the *sharīʿah* law of divorce in its various schools. And finally, Muhammad Zayd al-Ibyānī's *Sharh al-aḥkām al-sharīʿah fī al-aḥwāl al-shakhṣīyah,* 3 vols. (Beirut, 1976), is a useful modern work on the whole range of the *sharīʿah* personal law.

M. Hashim Kamali (1987)

ISLAMIC PHILOSOPHY See FALSAFAH

ISLAMIC RELIGIOUS YEAR. The Islamic religious year is highlighted by two major events that are enjoined by the Qurʾān and that are celebrated all over the Muslim world. These are the pilgrimage, or *ḥājj,* which culminates in the ʿĪd al-Aḍḥā (Feast of Sacrifice), in the last lunar month, and Ramaḍān, the month of fasting, which ends with the celebration of the ʿĪd al-Fiṭr (Feast of Fast Breaking) on the first day of the next month, Shawwāl. Because the twelve-month calendar of Islam is based on a purely lunar year of 354 days, these events have no fixed relation to the seasons of the 365-day solar year. Over the course of years, they may occur in spring, summer, autumn, and winter. Thus, no connection with pre-Islamic solar feasts can be made, nor can any tradition of agricultural cults be traced. (Celebrations of the solar seasons do occur in various parts of the Muslim world, but they are not based on the Qurʾān or on *ḥadīth.*)

The beginning of each month of the Muslim calendar is reckoned from the appearance of the new moon, which must, according to tradition, be reported by at least two trustworthy witnesses. Because religious leaders in some Muslim countries do, in fact, rely on astronomical calculation of the first appearance of the crescent while others continue to follow the Qurʾanic prescription of actually seeing the moon, differences of one day in reckoning the beginning or end of a month are common. The date may also vary according to local weather conditions.

Certain days of the week are considered to be endowed with good or bad qualities, as can be understood from relevant collections of *ḥadīth.* Friday, the day of communal prayer at noon, is always regarded as auspicious, and Monday and Thursday carry positive aspects, as do the "white nights" before and after a full moon.

The year begins with the month of Muḥarram. Its tenth day, ʿĀshūrāʾ, was suggested as a fast day by the Prophet but subsequently became associated with the death of Muḥammad's grandson, Ḥusayn ibn ʿAlī, who was killed in the Battle of Karbala on 10 Muḥarram 81 / October 10, 680. Although this day is a time of mourning for all Muslims, it is the Shīʿah, the "party" of ʿAlī, who have attached very special significance to Ḥusayn's martyrdom and to the entire month of Muḥarram. Thus, Sunnī Muslims do not subscribe to the elaborate celebrations developed in later centuries, particularly in Iran and India, where commemorations extend through the first ten days of the month. During this period women wear subdued colors, preferably black, with no jewelry. Men and women hold separate gatherings (*majālis*) during which a male or female preacher reminds the audience of the suffering of Ḥusayn and the other imams. The preacher recounts legends of the events at Karbala; singers recite threnodies; and those present beat their breasts, call blessings upon the Prophet, and profusely shed tears. "Weeping for Ḥusayn opens the door to Paradise," it is said, and the tears themselves are collected for future use as a panacea.

During the first ten days of Muḥarram, special craftsmen prepare *taʿziyahs*, or *tābūts*, tall, domed, wooden structures (up to thirty feet high) that represent the tombs of the imams. Beautifully carved and gilded or painted, they are carried in the ʿĀshūrāʾ processions along with colorful standards lofted in memory of Ḥusayn's standard-bearer, Jaʿfar. A lavishly caparisoned white horse is led as a symbol of Ḥusayn's mount, Dhū al-Janāḥ, and of the white horse on which the Hidden Imam is expected to ride when he finally reappears. During these processions many people flagellate themselves with chains from which hang small knives (wounds thus inflicted never become septic), and fire walking is sometimes performed. In some areas, such as the Deccan, ʿĀshūrāʾ processions at times assumed almost carnivalistic aspects, as eighteenth-century miniatures show. Late in the day the small *taʿziyahs* are buried in a place designated as "Karbala," while the more precious ones are stored, along with other implements, in *ʿāshūrā-khānahs* or *imām-bārahs*, large buildings for the meetings of the Shīʿī community. A special dish with numerous ingredients is cooked in remembrance of the mixed food in Karbala, prepared from whatever happened to be in the heroes' bags. In Turkey, sharing this *aṣure* with neighbors is a custom among both Sunnī and Shīʿī families.

In nineteenth-century Lucknow, *taʿziyah* rites were continued until the tenth day of the following month of Ṣafar, thus marking forty days of mourning from the start of Muḥarram. Among the Shīʿah, no weddings are celebrated in Muḥarram, and the month has always been a time when communal or sectarian feelings run high. Not infrequently, rioting results. The Ismāʿīlī community, at least since the time of Aga Khan III (r. 1885–1957), does not participate in Muḥarram because it has a *ḥāẕir imām* ("present imam") in the Aga Khan and need not look back to Ḥusayn's death.

Various literary and dramatic genres have also developed around the events at Karbala. The genre of *maqtal Ḥusayn,* poetry or prose telling of Ḥusayn's suffering, has been known since the early Middle Ages, and the *marthiyah,* or threnody, began to be developed by Indian poets about the beginning of the seventeenth century. This latter genre, which originated in the Deccan and spread to northern India, found its finest expression at the Shīʿī court of Lucknow in the nineteenth century. In Iran, and to a lesser degree in Iraq and Lebanon, the martyrdom of Ḥusayn came to be re-created in *ta'ziyah* plays interweaving numerous mythical elements to establish the martyrdom as the central event in the history of the universe.

In the month of Ṣafar, which follows Muḥarram, a sad mood used to prevail among Muslims because the Prophet once fell ill during this period. The last Wednesday of the month, when the Prophet felt better, was a day of rejoicing.

Rabīʿ al-Awwal ("first Rabīʿ"), the third lunar month, is marked by the Mawlid al-Nabī ("birthday of the Prophet") on the twelfth. The day is celebrated as the date of the Prophet's birth *(mīlād)* although it was actually the date of his death and is also widely commemorated in that connection. Nonetheless, the joyful celebration of Muḥammad's birthday began comparatively early; it was introduced on a larger scale in Fatimid Egypt, where the rulers, descendants of Muḥammad's daughter Fāṭimah, remembered the birthday of their ancestor by inviting scholars and by distributing sweets and money, a feature that has remained common. Ever since, the pious have felt that celebrations of the Mawlid have a special blessing power (*barakah*).

The first major celebration of the Mawlīd al-Nabī is described for the year AH 604/1207 CE in Arbalāʾ (modern Irbil, in northern Iraq), where the Ṣūfīs participated actively. The Mawlid became increasingly popular first in the western and then in the central Islamic lands. A special genre of poetry known as *mawlūd* developed in almost all Islamic languages. In Turkey the *mevlûd* by Süleyman Çelebi (d. 1409), telling in simple verse the miracles connected with the birth of the Prophet and describing his life, is still sung. In many countries, candles are lit—in Turkey the day is still called Mevlûd Kandili (Lamp Feast of the Birth)—and the Mawlid provides an occasion for donning festive clothes, burning incense, and distributing sweets. Orthodox circles have traditionally taken issue with the use of candles because of the similarity to Christmas celebrations; likewise they have disallowed musical performances and deemed that only the recitation of the Qurʾān seems permissible on a day that also marks the Prophet's death. The stories that have been traditionally recited reflect the people's love and veneration of the Prophet, whose birth, according to some eighteenth-century writers, was "more important than the Laylat al-Qadr," the night when the Qurʾān was first revealed, for it meant the arrival of "mercy for the worlds" (*sūrah* 21:107). Lately, however, there is a growing tendency to demythologize the contents of Mawlid literature; the speeches and poems offered on that day, and throughout the month in many countries, are meant to remind people of the ethical and social role of the Prophet, the "beautiful model" (*sūrah* 33:21) of his community. Newspapers and television publicize this attitude.

The following month, Rabīʿ al-Thānī ("second Rabīʿ"), has no ritual justified by the Qurʾān or *ḥadīth*. However, in many areas, especially in India and Pakistan, the eleventh marks the anniversary of ʿAbd al-Qādir al-Jīlānī, whose Ṣūfī order, the Qadiriyah, is the most widespread fraternity. The month is therefore called simply Yārhīñ, meaning "eleven" in Sindhi. As on other saints' days, flags are flown, meetings are convened to recite eulogies for the saint, and food is cooked and distributed in his name.

No religious events, other than local saints' days, are noted for the following two months, Jumādā al-Ūlā ("first Jumādā") and Jumādā al-Ākhirah ("last Jumādā"), but the seventh lunar month, Rajab, is blessed by celebration of the Prophet's *Miʿrāj*, his heavenly journey, which took place on the night of the twenty-seventh. In Turkey, this is again a *kandil,* or "lamp feast," on which people fast during daytime. In other areas, such as Kashmir, it used to be celebrated for a whole week. Although the celebration of the *Miʿrāj* cannot vie in popularity with the Prophet's birthday, the mystery of the Prophet's heavenly journey has deeply impressed Muslim piety and poetry. Other events commemorated in Rajab include the first nights of the month, *raghāʾib,* celebrated in some areas (notably Turkey) as the time when Āminah conceived the Prophet, as well as ʿAlī's birthday, celebrated by all Shīʿī communities on 13 Rajab.

In the following month, Shaʿbān, a non-Qurʾanic but very popular feast is the Laylat al-Barāʾah (Pers., Shab-i Barāt), celebrated on the night of the full moon. Historically this is the night when the Prophet entered Mecca triumphantly, but in Muslim folklore it is considered to be the night when the "writing conferring immunity is written in heaven" or, more generally, the night during which the fates for the coming year are fixed. Therefore pious Muslims fast, pray, and keep vigils. On the whole, however, and especially in Indo-Pakistan, the night is celebrated with illuminations and fireworks. Orthodox critics object to such displays as symptoms of Hindu influence, even though the Shab-i Barāt is mentioned in a non-Indian environment as early as the twelfth century, in a poem by Sanāʾī of Ghaznah (d. 1131). The Shīʿī community celebrates the birthday of Imam Mahdi, the last of the twelve imams, on this day.

The month of Ramaḍān is the most demanding of the Islamic year, especially when it falls in the hot season. Each day, Muslims must fast from the moment there is enough light to distinguish white from black threads until the sun has completely set. The order to abstain from food, drink, smoking, sex, and even from injections or intake of fragrance requires a strong intention (*nīyah*) of the fasting person. He or she will then break fast with an odd number of dates and some water before proceeding to the evening prayer. The problem of how to keep the fast in northern countries during the long summer days has aroused much controversy; one solution is to break fast at the time when the sun sets in the next Muslim country or on the forty-fifth degree of latitude. For every day that the fast is neglected, or cannot be performed because of illness, pregnancy, or menstruation, the observant Muslim is obliged to compensate either by fasting some other day or by feeding a number of the ever present poor.

The Laylat al-Qadr ("night of power"; *sūrah* 97), during which the first revelation of the Qur'ān took place, is one of the last odd-numbered nights in Ramaḍān, generally considered the twenty-seventh. In its honor people may spend the last ten days of Ramaḍān in seclusion, and those who do not fast otherwise will try to do it during that period. The pious hope for the vision of the light that fills the world during this blessed night. The Ismāʿīlīs pray all night in their Jamāʿāt-khānah. Many people perform the *tarāwiḥ* prayers (a long sequence, including twenty to thirty-three *rakʿahs* of prayers and prostrations) after breaking the fast. Then they may enjoy the lighter side of life: The illumination of mosques and the activities of all kinds of entertainers that used to be a regular part of every Ramaḍān night. A second meal is taken before the first sign of dawn.

The ʿĪd al-Fiṭr (Feast of Fast Breaking), which brings release from the month-long abstinence at daylight, is called the "lesser feast," but it is most eagerly awaited as a celebration of the return to normal life. Its Turkish name, *Şeker Bayrami* ("sugar feast"), points to the custom of distributing sweets. After the morning prayer of 1 Shawwāl in the spacious *ʿīdgāh,* it is customary to put on new clothes and to visit friends. The sigh that one has no new clothes for the feast is a touching topic in Islamic love poetry.

After the ʿĪd al-Fiṭr there is no major feast in Shawwāl or in Dhū al-Qaʿdah. The later month is used for preparations for the pilgrimage (*ḥājj*), which takes place in Dhū al-Ḥijjah.

On 10 Dhū al-Ḥijjah, the ʿĪd al-Aḍḥā, or ʿĪd al-Qurbān (Feast of Sacrifice), called the "major feast," is celebrated in the valley of Minā, near Mecca, with thousands, and now millions, of Muslims ritually slaughtering sheep or larger animals and thus reenacting the substitution of a ram for Ismāʿīl, whom Abraham was willing to sacrifice (*sūrah* 37:102). Because this is the only feast in which the community celebrates the memory of a mythical event, every Muslim is called upon to repeat the slaughter at home; theologians do not accept the substitution of money for the sacrificial animal, as some liberal Muslims have suggested. According to popular belief, the slaughtered animal will carry its owner across the Ṣirāṭ Bridge to paradise. The meat of the animal sacrificed at home is distributed to the poor, and the hide is given to a charitable foundation. The Indo-Muslim designation of the feast as Baqar ʿĪd (Cow Feast) and the slaughtering of cows have often caused Hindu riots during these days. The return of the pilgrims is duly celebrated, as one can witness every year at the airports of Muslim countries. Later in the month, on 18 Dhū al-Ḥijjah, the Shīʿī community celebrates the ʿĪd al-Ghadīr (Feast of the Pond), the day on which Muḥammad invested ʿAlī as his successor near the pond Khumm.

Every place in the Islamic world has special celebrations for commemorating local saints. Some of these festivities, called *ʿurs* (spiritual "wedding"), attract tens of thousands of people. Almost all of them follow the rhythm of the lunar year. The *ʿurs* of Aḥmad al-Badawī in Tanta, Egypt, is celebrated, however, according to the solar year in early June, when the Nile is rising, and may be connected with pre-Islamic fertility rites. In Turkey, the anniversary of the birth of Mawlānā Rūmī is now celebrated on December 17. Likewise, Ismāʿīlīs celebrate the Aga Khan's birthday according to the common era.

Some Muslim festivals are connected with the solar year. The most important is Nawrūz, the Persian New Year, which occurs at the vernal equinox. It is celebrated in a joyous way wherever Persian culture spread, even in Egypt. It is customary that seven items have to be on the table (in Iran, the names of these seven must begin with the letter *s*). Orthodox Muslims have often objected to the celebration of Nawrūz, but for most people the beginning of spring has always been too delightful to be neglected. The Bektashī order of Ṣūfīs in Turkey have explained Nawrūz as ʿAlī's birthday and have thus Islamized it. Another Turkish celebration, Hidrellez, combines the feasts of the saint-prophet Khiḍr and of Ilyās, associated with the biblical Elijah. The day falls on May 6 and is connected with a change of winds and weather.

An interesting way of depicting the sequence of the ritual year is found in a poetic genre of Indo-Pakistan called *bārahmāsa* ("twelve months"). It is derived from Hindu tradition and in its Islamized forms describes the twelve months through the words of a lovesick young woman who experiences in Muḥarram the pain of seeing her beloved slain, celebrates his birthday in Rabīʿ al-Awwal, and finally meets him in Dhū al-Ḥijjah, when visiting either the Kaʿbah in Mecca or the Prophet's tomb in Medina.

Muslim mystics, as strictly as they might have adhered to ritual, have spiritualized the liturgical year. The Feast of Sacrifice—whether it be named ʿĪd al-Aḍḥā, ʿĪd al-Qurbān, or ʿĪd al-Naḥr—has meant, for them, to sacrifice themselves before the divine Beloved, and the true *ʿīd* has been to see the face of the Beloved whose very presence makes every day a feast for the lover.

SEE ALSO ʿĀshūrāʾ; Mawlid; Nowrūz; Pilgrimage, article on Muslim Pilgrimage; Ṣawm; Worship and Devotional Life, article on Muslim Worship.

BIBLIOGRAPHY

Gustave E. von Grunebaum's *Muhammedan Festivals* (New York, 1951) gives a general survey of the Islamic festivals, mainly based on classical sources. See also the article "Muslim Festivals" in Hava Lazarus-Yafeh's *Some Religious Aspects of Islam* (Leiden, 1981), pp. 38–47. E. W. Lane's *An Account of the Manners and Customs of the Modern Egyptians,* 3 vols., 3d ed. (1846; reprint, New York, 1973) deals with the seasons as they were celebrated in early nineteenth-century Cairo, while Jaʿfar Sharif's *Islam in India, or the Qanun-i-Islam,* translated by G. A. Herklots and edited by William Crooke (1921; reprint, London, 1972), describes the Muslim year as celebrated in India, particularly in the Deccan. For the Muḥarram ceremonies, the best introduction is *Taʿziyeh: Ritual and Drama in Iran,* edited by Peter J. Chelkowski (New York,

1979), and the classic study of the *ḥājj* is still Christiaan Snouck Hurgronje's *Het Mekkansche feest* (Leiden, 1880).

ANNEMARIE SCHIMMEL (1987)

ISLAMIC STUDIES [FIRST EDITION]. Islamic studies encompass the study of the religion of Islam and of Islamic aspects of Muslim cultures and societies. At the outset we must recognize that the word *Islam* itself is used in very different senses by faithful Muslims, for whom it is a norm and an ideal, and by scholars (Muslim and non-Muslim Islamicists), who refer to it as a subject of study or a kind of symbol for the focus of their inquiry, as well as by the larger public in the West who are outsiders and give different appreciations of what is felt by them to be "foreign." By extension, a sharp distinction must be made between normative Islam (the prescriptions, norms, and values that are recognized by the community as embodiments of divine guidance) and actual Islam (all those forms and movements, practices and ideas that have in fact existed in the many Muslim communities in different times and places). In other words, Islamic data sought for the sake of scholarly understanding are not the same as the ideals that Muslims as adherents of Islam attach to them, the meaning they attribute to them, or the truth they recognize in them.

This familiar distinction between practice and ideal, fact and (subjective) meaning of religious data must be maintained not only for the purpose of analysis and understanding but also for the making of valid comparisons. Practices may be compared with practices, ideals with ideals, but the practice of something in one religion should not be compared with the ideal of the same thing in another religion. From a scholarly point of view, moreover, we have no reason to say that any particular Muslim society represents Islam as a norm and an ideal better than another. We must proceed by reporting the various ideas and practices that prevail in one or another group and by trying to explain differences and discover their implications. Whatever the eternal truth of Islam at all times and places, its ideas and practices at different times and places are to be studied as they present themselves.

THE SCOPE OF ISLAMIC STUDIES. On the basis of these distinctions, it is possible to identify three different enterprises that come under the general rubric of Islamic studies:

1. *The normative study of Islamic religion* is generally carried out by Muslims in order to acquire knowledge of religious truth. It implies the study of the Islamic religious sciences: Qur'anic exegesis (*tafsīr*), the science of traditions (*ʿilm al-ḥadīth*), jurisprudence (*fiqh*), and metaphysical theology (*kalām*). Traditionally pursued in mosques and special religious colleges (*madrasahs*), it is now usually carried out in faculties of religious law (*sharīʿah*) and of religious sciences (*ʿulūm al-dīn*) at universities or special Islamic institutes in Muslim countries. It should be noted, however, that normative studies of Islam can also be undertaken by non-Muslims, such as Christians seeking to proselytize among Muslims or to develop a theology of religions in which a particular place is assigned to Islam.
2. *The nonnormative study of Islamic religion* is usually done in universities and covers both what is considered by Muslims to be true Islam (the Islamic religious sciences in particular) and what is considered to be living Islam (the factual religious expressions of Muslims). This nonnormative study of Islamic religion can be pursued by Muslims and non-Muslims alike, wherever they observe the general rules of scholarly inquiry. This is the research that is generally called "Islamic studies."
3. *The nonnormative study of Islamic aspects of Muslim cultures and societies* in a broader sense is not directed toward Islam as such. It takes a wider context into consideration, approaching things Islamic from the point of view of history and literature or cultural anthropology and sociology, and not specifically from the perspective of the study of religion.

My focus in this essay is on the two nonnormative forms of study, which we may call Islamic studies in the narrower (2) and the wider (3) sense. In the narrower sense of Islamic studies, the focus is on Islamic religion as an entity in itself; the wider sense of Islamic studies deals with data that are part of given Muslim communities and are culled from the Islamic experience but that may or may not possess a religious (i.e., Islamic) significance for particular Muslim groups.

In the case of studies of particular Muslim communities, a further distinction can be made. On the one hand, some general concept of Islam may be held implicitly or explicitly by the researcher, even if the research is limited to one or to a few concrete situations. In research of this kind, notwithstanding its specialized character, Islam as a whole remains within the horizon of the researcher. On the other hand, there are studies dealing with Muslim communities of a specific area and period that do not take into consideration any general concept if Islam. Yet this research still belongs implicitly to Islamic studies in the wider sense to the extent that Islamicists may find it useful.

HISTORY OF ISLAMIC STUDIES IN THE NARROWER SENSE. The rise of scholarly interest in Islam as a religion represents in part a critical response to numerous images of Muḥammad and Islamic religion in general that were widespread in medieval Europe. Although Arab science and philosophy were appreciated and admired, Islam was projected as the great adversary of Christianity. The first effort to acquire a more scholarly knowledge of the Islamic religion on the basis of the sources was made by Peter the Venerable, abbot of Cluny (c. 1094–1156), who financed a team of translators working in Spain. One of the results was the first Latin translation of the Qur'ān, which was completed in 1143 by Robert Ketton.

Since the beginning of the sixteenth century, Arabic and other so-called Islamic languages (notably Persian and Turkish) have been studied in European universities; language competency was the first prerequisite for the investigation of Islam. Another prerequisite was a serious study of Islamic history, carried out first (from the sixteenth century) as a history of Muslim peoples, especially the Turks, and later (from the eighteenth century on) as a history of Islamic religion, which, thanks to the Enlightenment, could be appreciated more adequately. Noteworthy indeed is the objective description of Islamic religion, based on Muslim sources, presented by Adrian Reland in his *De religione mohammedica libri duo* (1705; 2d ed., 1717). Such approaches were to lead to the rise of Islamic studies as a discipline based on textual criticism and historical analysis with a view to the writing of a history of Islamic religion and culture. As a modern field of scholarship, Islamic studies emerged around the middle of the nineteenth century, with the publication of biographies of Muḥammad by Gustav Weil (1843), William Muir (1861; rev. ed., 1912), and Aloys Sprenger (3 vols., 1861–1865). Early studies of the Qurʾān were Weil's *Historisch-kritische Einleitung in den Koran* (1844; 2d ed., 1878) and Theodor Nöldeke's *Geschichte des Qorans* (2 vols., 1860; 2d rev. ed., 1909–1938). Alfred von Kremer's *Geschichte der herrschenden ideen des Islams* (1868) and *Culturgeschichtliche Streifzüge auf dem Gebiete des Islams* (1873) were the first attempts to present the history of Islam as an integrated whole.

Islamic studies as part of Oriental studies. The development of Islamic studies in the nineteenth century was part of the general development of Oriental studies, commonly called "Orientalism." This effort was the first serious intellectual encounter between Europe and another civilization, albeit a unilateral encounter and one in which current cultural images of the "Orient" unavoidably played a role. Oriental studies were largely patterned after the classical studies that had arisen in the sixteenth century; they were based on philology in the broad sense of the term, that is, the study of a particular culture through its texts. Islamic studies in this sense lead to nonnormative accounts of Islamic religion as described under (2), above. The field has always been a demanding one, presupposing an intensive study of Arabic and other "Islamic" languages, on the basis of which text editions can be prepared and textual studies, including textual criticism and literary history, can be carried out. Familiarity with the texts, in its turn, is a prerequisite for the further study of history. Supplemented by the study of other Islamic expressions in art and architecture and in present-day religious life, textual, historical, and anthropological research together prepare the way for the study of Islamic culture and religion.

Within the Orientalist tradition, Islamic studies were conceived of as a cultural discipline and exhibited certain assumptions of European civilization of the time, notably the superiority of Western civilization and the excellence of its scholarship. Stress has generally been laid on the differences between Islamic civilization and European culture, with an ethnocentric bias toward the latter. Beyond the interest in its origins, a certain predilection can be discerned for the "classical" period of Islamic civilization, a preference that can also be observed in other branches of Oriental studies. Specialization increasingly led to detailed studies, and the ideal of a comprehensive view of Islam often came down simply to mastering an extraordinary mass of facts. Just as the preponderance of facts in Oriental studies has given Islamic studies a rather "positivist" orientation, the approach to Islamic religion too has been essentially based on establishing historical facts with little attention being paid to the problem of the meaning of these facts, which is a problem of interpretation.

The nonnormative study of Islamic religion. The history of Islamic religion has been approached in three basic ways. A great number of historians, following the example set by Julius Wellhausen (1844–1918) in his various studies on the early Islamic period, have focused on the external history of Islam. Later historians such as Claude Cahen and Bernard Lewis have shown how much light can be thrown on particular Muslim institutions and movements by viewing them against the background of economic, social, and political history.

Another kind of historical research concentrates rather on what may be called the inner developments in Islamic religion and culture. This approach was introduced by one of the major figures in the field, Ignácz Goldziher (1850–1921), who tried to establish the basic framework of an intellectual history of Islam. Another scholar working along these lines was Helmut Ritter (1892–1971), who revealed the inner connections among a great number of religious concepts, mainly theological and mystical, as they developed in history.

Somewhere between the general historians and the historians of religion are cultural historians of the medieval period such as Carl Heinrich Becker (1876–1933), Jörg Kraemer (1917–1961), and Gustav Edmund von Grunebaum (1909–1972), all of whom set religious developments within wider cultural frameworks, which were related in turn to political and military history. The name of Marshall G. S. Hodgson (1921–1968) should also be mentioned here because of his efforts to situate the total history of Islam within a culturally oriented world history.

These three types of historical study are also reflected in the vast number of specialized historical researches on particular Muslim communities of the past, as well as in studies dealing with the contemporary history of Muslim societies. Here I must limit myself to indicating the major points of the history of research into broad topics, mentioning some names but omitting many others of no less significance. (The categories that follow are those set out by Charles J. Adams in his 1976 survey, "Islamic Religious Tradition.")

Muḥammad. Various approaches have developed since the mid-nineteenth-century biographies mentioned earlier.

In a two-volume biography, *Mohammed* (1892–1895), Hubert Grimme gave an account of the social factors in Muḥammad's life and stressed the Prophet's aspect as social reformer; Frants Buhl assembled all historical materials available at the time for a substantial biography of Muḥammad in *Das Leben Muhammed* (1930; 2d ed., 1955). Tor Andrae studied later Muslim views of Muḥammad as a prophet and paradigmatic figure in his *Die person Muhammeds in lehre und glauben seiner gemeinde* (1918). A breakthrough in establishing the context of Muḥammad's life and work is W. Montgomery Watt's two-volume study, *Muhammad at Mecca* (1953) and *Muhammad at Medina* (1956), which focuses attention on the social and economic changes in Arabia (Mecca) that Muḥammad tried to address in his prophetic activity. Maxime Rodinson's thought-provoking biography, *Mohammed* (1961; Eng. trans., 1971), interprets historical data from a similar perspective but adds a psychological dimension. An era in which Western scholarship recognizes the originality of Muḥammad's achievements seems to have dawned, following a period during which stress was placed by Jewish scholars on the Jewish influences on Muḥammad and by Christian scholars on Christian influences. Biographies of Muḥammad written by Muslims are too numerous to be treated here in full. The classic one is that by Ibn Isḥāq (d. 767?), translated by A. Guillaume as *The Life of Muhammad* (1955). E. S. Sabanegh studied some modern Egyptian biographies of Muḥammad in his *Muhammad b. Abdallah "le Prophete": Portraits contemporains, Egypte 1930–1950* (1982).

The Qurʾān. After the important translation into English by George Sale (1697?–1736), published in 1734 with a famous "preliminary discourse," a great number of translations of the Qurʾān have seen the light. I may mention those by Richard Bell (1937), A. J. Arberry (1955), and Marmaduke Pickthall (1930), this last being recognized by Muslims. The classic study of the Qurʾanic text remains that of Theodor Nöldeke in its three-volume second edition (1909–1938), enlarged and revised with the help of colleagues. Arthur Jeffery published two important studies, *The Textual History of the Qurʾān* (1937) and *The Foreign Vocabulary of the Qurʾān* (1938). Rudi Paret's conscientious German translation (1962) was subsequently accompanied by his important commentary (1971). Important is Angelika Neuwirth's *Studien zur Komposition der mekkanischen Suren* (1981). John Wansbrough's *Quranic Studies* (1977) has brought the accepted theory on the early collation of the Qurʾanic text into question.

It is noteworthy that while great progress has been made with regard to the textual-critical, linguistic, and literary aspects of the Qurʾān, the study of its contents, concepts, and worldview—that is, its meaning—has only started to take off. In this connection Toshihiko Izutsu's semantic analyses of the Qurʾān, *The Structure of the Ethical Terms in the Qurʾān* (1959; rev. ed., 1966) and *God and Man in the Koran* (1964), have played a pioneering role. Needless to say, critical studies of the Qurʾān and of Muḥammad have offended some Muslim sensibilities in much the same way that source criticism of the Bible has offended some biblicist Christians.

The study of the Qurʾān implies that of Muslim commentaries (*tafsīrs*) of the Qurʾān. See Helmut Gätje's *Koran und Koranexegese* (1971) and compare Mohammed Arkoun's *Lectures du Coran* (1982).

Ḥadīth. Goldziher's critical stand in *Muhammedanische Studien*, vol. 2 (1890; Eng. trans., 1971), with regard to the historical dating of *ḥadīths* ("traditions") that were ascribed to Muḥammad or his companions but were in fact later creations, was carried further by Joseph Schacht (1902–1969) in *The Origins of Muhammadan Jurisprudence* (1950) and led to a debate on their authenticity not only among Muslims but also in Western scholarship. Later work by Fuat Sezgin in the first volume of his *Geschichte des arabischen Schrifttums* (1967) has led to a reconsideration of the extreme criticism by Goldziher and Schacht, although the falseness of many of the attributions to Muḥammad remains acknowledged. Since the *sunnah* (consisting of *ḥadīths*) is the second source, after the Qurʾān, of religious knowledge and law in Islam, here too Muslims are particularly sensitive to scholarly criticism from outside. See G. H. A. Juynboll's *The Authenticity of the Tradition Literature: Discussions in Modern Egypt* (1969).

Law. The structure of religious law (*sharīʿah*) in Islam, its ideal character, and the rules of juridical reasoning by Muslim jurists were first elucidated by Goldziher and by Christiaan Snouck Hurgronje (1857–1936), who also studied its application, side by side with customary law, in Indonesia. Further studies in depth were carried out by Éduard Sachau (1845–1930), Gotthelf Bergsträsser (1886–1933), and especially Joseph Schacht, who summarized his findings in *An Introduction to Islamic Law* (1964). Current trends toward Islamicization in Muslim countries are again arousing interest in its juridical aspects. Among the scholars who have worked on changes in the application of the *sharīʿah* in modern Muslim states, the names of J. N. D. Anderson and Noel J. A. Coulson deserve particular mention.

Metaphysical theology. It has been only in the course of the twentieth century that Islamic theological speculation (*kalām*) has been revealed in its originality. An important study on early Muslim creeds is A. J. Wensinck's *The Muslim Creed* (1933). Georges Anawati and Louis Gardet's *Introduction à la théologie musulmane* (1948) demonstrates the structural similarity of medieval Islamic and Christian theological treatises. Here and in other works these authors stress the apologetic character of Islamic theology. On the other hand, Harry A. Wolfson, in *The Philosophy of the Kalām* (1976) is attentive to parallels between Islamic, Christian, and Jewish theological thought. Important are recent studies by Richard M. D. Frank and J. R. T. M. Peters on Muʿtazilī theology.

Islamic philosophy. In the wake of T. J. de Boer's handbook on the subject, *The History of Philosophy in Islam* (1901;

Eng. trans., 1903; reprint, 1961), philosophy in Islam was taken to be the continuation of Aristotelian philosophy with Neoplatonic overtones. Important work on this philosophical line appears in Richard Walzer's *Greek into Arabic* (1962). Subsequently, however, it has become clear that there are other old philosophical traditions of a more gnostic nature in Islam. They can be found in Shīʿī intellectual circles, both Iranian Twelvers and Ismaʿīlī Seveners. We owe this discovery mainly to the investigations of Henry Corbin (1903–1978), whose works, such as *En islam iranien* (4 vols., 1971–1972), revealed hidden but still living spiritual worlds. See also Heinz Halm's *Die islamische Gnosis: Die extreme Schia und die ʿAlawiten* (1982).

Mysticism. Muslim mystical thought and experience have attracted serious scholarly attention in the West only in the course of the twentieth century, especially through the work of Reynold A. Nicholson (1868–1945) and Louis Massignon (1883–1962). The former concentrated on certain major works and their authors, such as *The Mathnawīi* of Jalāl al-Dīn Rūmī; the latter focused on the development of mystical terminology and produced a four-volume biography of the tenth-century mystic al-Ḥallāj (1922; Eng. trans., 1982). This line of study has been pursued for mystical poetry by A. J. Arberry (1905–1969) and later by scholars such as Annemarie Schimmel in *Mystical Dimensions of Islam* (1976). Muslim mystical orders have also received considerable attention, for instance by J. Spencer Trimingham and F. de Yong.

Islamic art and architecture. This field deserves a separate status among the disciplines making up Islamic studies, since it deals with materials other than texts and is linked with art history in general. Among scholars who deserve mention are K. A. C. Creswell (1879–1974), and Richard Ettinghausen (1906–1979), and at present Oleg Grabar and Robert Hillenbrand. The study of this field is now becoming more integrated into the broader cultural history of Islam.

Religious institutions. In recent decades important breakthroughs have been made in the understanding of the relationships between Islamic religious institutions and the societies in which they function. In *La cité musulmane* (1954), Louis Gardet attempted to sketch the outline of the ideal society in terms of orthodox Islam, while H. A. R. Gibb and Harold Bowen addressed the eighteenth-century Muslim "religious structure," especially with regard to processes of modernization in parts 1 and 2 of *Islamic Society and the West* (1950–1957). Considerable attention has been paid to religious authorities (*ʿulamāʾ*, Ṣūfī shaykhs) with their different roles in society. *Scholars, Saints and Sufis*, edited by Nikki R. Keddie (1972), reflects much of this research through the early 1970s. Important in this respect is A. C. Eccel's study *Egypt, Islam and Social Change: Al-Azhar in Conflict and Accommodation* (1984). See also Michael Gilsenan's *Recognizing Islam: An Anthropologist's Introduction* (1982) and *Islamic Dilemmas: Reformers, Nationalists and Industrialization*, edited by Ernest Gellner (1985).

Living Islam. Travelers, civil servants such as Christiaan Snouck Hurgronje, and anthropologists such as Edvard A. Westermarck (1862–1939) had already in the nineteenth century given descriptions of actual Muslim life, and this kind of research has increased considerably in the twentieth century, mainly through the efforts of anthropologists. Rudolf Kriss and Hubert Kriss-Heinrich, for example, wrote a handbook of popular Islam, *Volksglaube im Bereich des Islams* (2 vols., 1960–1962); Klaus E. Müller dealt with current beliefs and practices among sectarian groups in Islam in his *Kulturhistorische Studien zur Genese pseudoislamischer Sektengebilde in Vorderasien* (1967); and Constance Padwick has studied prayer manuals in actual use in Egypt in *Muslim Devotions* (1961).

Since the 1960s several important studies of living Islam in the broader context of society and its structure have been published by social scientists, among them Clifford Geertz, who, in *Islam Observed* (1968), compares Moroccan and Javanese Islamic structures. Other books in this vein, focusing on Ṣūfī structures, are Michael Gilsenan's *Saint and Sufi in Modern Egypt* (1973) and Ernest Gellner's two works on Morocco, *Saints of the Atlas* (1969) and *Muslim Society* (1981). To this same category belong the numerous writings by Jacques Berque that deal with Arab society and the role of Islam within it. The literature on the status of women in Muslim societies is growing rapidly. See for instance *Women in the Muslim World*, edited by Lois Beck and Nikki R. Keddie (1978).

Modern developments in Islam. Scholarly surveys of modern developments in Muslim countries commenced with a 1932 volume edited by H. A. R. Gibb, *Whither Islam? A Survey of Modern Movements in the Moslem World*, which was followed by the same scholar's *Modern Trends in Islam* (1947) and by Wilfred Cantwell Smith's *Islam in Modern History* (1957). It has since become clear that recent developments should be described according to the country within which they occur and that although certain patterns can be established as valid for nearly all Muslim countries, in each country various groups, including the government, have their own articulation of Islam. A major contribution to this formulation is *Der Islam in der Gegenwart*, edited by Werner Ende and Udo Steinbach (1984). Events in revolutionary Iran have shown, moreover, that Islamicists in the Orientalist tradition simply have not been adequately equipped to interpret what happens in Muslim countries. On the other hand, *Religion in the Middle East: Three Religions in Concord and Conflict*, edited by A. J. Arberry (2 vols., 1969), may be mentioned here as an example of objective and impartial information about the three major religions that coexist in the Middle East, in an environment ridden with political tensions, where religions can be abused for all kinds of purposes, and where good relations among the three traditions have been hampered by claims of exclusivity.

PRESENT-DAY ISLAMIC STUDIES IN THE WIDER SENSE. As in other scholarly fields and disciplines, new issues have come under discussion in Islamic studies, whether through the internal development of scholarly research or through current developments in Muslim countries, which developments demand interpretation.

Methodological issues. Intense epistemological debates seem to have been absent from Islamic studies until the 1960s, chiefly because of the inherited pattern established by the scholarly tradition. Yet there have been other currents in Islamic studies too, and with the incorporation of textual research within a larger cultural and even religious perspective, scholars such as Louis Massignon, Gustav E. von Grunebaum, Wilfred Cantwell Smith, and Clifford Geertz have been able to see the Islamic universe in new ways. We shall point here to three matters of paramount importance: (1) the questioning of Islamic identities, (2) the increased assertion of Islamic identities, and (3) Islam as a living religion and faith.

Questioning Islamic identities. Among Western scholars who have reevaluated accepted readings of the Islamic tradition, John Wansbrough has opened up critical research with regard to the text of the Qurʾān in the aforementioned *Quranic Studies* and has extended this inquiry to early Islamic history in *The Sectarian Milieu* (1978). In an even more controversial work, *Hagarism: The Making of the Islamic World* (1977), Patricia Crone and Michael Cook have argued that the historical formation of Islamic religion and civilization can be explained in terms of a complex network of Jewish-Arab relations. While their argument has found little favor, it may well lead other scholars to reconsider the role of historically falsified material in their research.

Asserting Islamic identities. The growing participation of Muslim scholars in the field of Islamic studies has had the opposite effect to that mentioned above. An intention to assert Islamic identities becomes evident in books such as *Islamic Perspectives: Studies in Honor of Sayyid Abul Ala Mawdudi,* edited by Khurshid Ahmad and Zafar Isḥāq Ansari (1979), and *Islam and Contemporary Society,* edited by Salem Azzam (1982). One important contribution of Muslim scholars is that of making Muslim forms of understanding available to other Islamicists; their work should lead, moreover, to discussions within the Muslim community. Noteworthy, for instance, is Mohammed Arkoun's semiotic approach in *Lectures du Coran* (1983) and Fazlur Rahman's studies on the history of Islamic thought, for instance in his *Prophecy in Islam: Philosophy and Orthodoxy* (1979).

Islam as a living religion. Recent methodological and epistemological concerns have been stimulated in large part by a growing interest in Islam as a living religion and faith, which is connected with certain political solidarities and social and economic issues. As a result, the meaning of events and processes in Muslim countries is studied more and more in their contemporary cultural and Islamic framework. Three questions are paramount in these Islamic studies in the wider sense:

1. Which kinds of groups support and transmit various particular interpretations of Islam, and who are the leaders of these groups?
2. How do particular changes occurring in the religious institutions (or in institutions legitimized by religion) relate to changes in society at large, and what are the consequences of such social changes for the institutions concerned (and vice versa)?
3. What general social functions do various Islamic ideas and practices perform within particular Muslim societies, apart from the specifically religious meaning they are meant to have?

Such questions can also be asked about Muslim societies of the past, provided that historical data are available to answer them. Indeed, it is a mark of epistemological progress that subjects excluded from investigation fifty years ago for lack of methodological tools can now come under the purview of Islamic studies. We can think of the distinctions that can be made now between religious and other (e.g., political) meanings of Islamic data, and of our better insight in the appeal that particular Islamic ideas and practices can have for specific groups.

Tradition in a wider sense. The notion of tradition, too, has attracted new attention in Islamic studies among both historians and anthropologists, who recognize that successive generations of Muslims have interpreted their lives, their world, and history through the religious and cultural framework, or "tradition," of the society into which they have been born. On the one hand, we have the normative "great" tradition with elements ranging from the Qurʾān and parts of the *sharīʿah* to particular creeds, practices of worship, and paradigmatic figures and episodes in Islamic history. On the other hand, for each region we must add numerous elements of the local "little" tradition, including legendary events in the history of the region, miracles and blessings of particular saints, the meritorious effect of particular practices, and so on, all of which constitute local, popular religion.

New topics of research. As a result of these and other methodological issues, new topics of research have come within our horizon, of which the following may be mentioned as examples.

Revitalization of Islam. Different forms of Islamic revitalization have been signaled by both Muslim and non-Muslim observers in a number of countries. While the media have addressed the political and "exotic," even abhorrent dimensions of this revitalization, scholarly investigation is needed to distinguish various sectors of life and society in which such revitalization takes place (as well as its religious from its nonreligious aspects) according to both Islamic criteria and criteria developed by the scientific study of religion. Preceding movements of reform and renewal should be taken into account.

Ideologization of Islam. During the last hundred years a great number of Islamic ideologies have developed; what for centuries was considered a religion based on revelation seems to have evolved in certain quarters into an Islamic system or ideology of a cognitive nature, in which the dimension of faith and religious knowledge seems to have given place to a definite set of convictions and values. This ideologization responds to a need for rationalization and may serve apologetic purposes, against criticism from the West, for instance, or against secularizing trends within society. Often the predicate "Islamic" suggests that a correspondence is sought between the older cultural and religious tradition and the solutions proposed for the problems of the present.

Islam, political action, and social and economic behavior. After a period of Western domination in which a political articulation of Islam was mostly impossible, Islam has again come to play various political roles, in both more conservative and more progressive quarters, usually bypassing the authority of those schooled in religious law (the *ʿulamāʾ*). So the question arises: what are the possibilities and the limits of the political, social, and economic use and abuse of Islam? Islam has permitted very different economic systems (including a form of capitalism) as Maxime Rodinson (1966) has demonstrated. We may go on to ask in what ways Islam can be related positively or negatively to economic development, and to determine what basic values economic development is subordinated to within the Islamic framework. That Islam is articulated basically as a way of life and as social behavior has become evident again, for instance, by the recurrence of the veil and by expressions of solidarity with Muslims in other parts of the world.

Muslim self-interpretations. In the course of the history of Islamic studies, serious hermeneutical mistakes, that is, errors of interpretation, have been made. Western scholars for instance tended to reify Islam, forgetting that "Islam" in itself does not exist, that "Islam" is always Islam *interpreted*, and that Muslims keep this interpretive process going. Much more attention should be paid to what Muslim authors, speakers, groups, and movements actually mean when they express themselves in particular situations, free from interpretations or explanations imposed from outside. Carrying out study in collaboration with Muslim researchers is appropriate here as in many fields.

Interaction and image formation. It is perhaps a sign of renewal of Islamic studies that Islam is no longer studied only as an isolated culture, tradition, and religion that may have assimilated outside influences, but that more attention is given to the spread of Islam, processes of interaction with other communities, and Muslim images of other religions and of the non-Muslim world generally. This direction of inquiry is evidenced first by works of Arab scholars like Albert Hourani, Abdallah Laroui, and others, as well as by publications like Bernard Lewis's *The Muslim Discovery of Europe* (1982) and *Euro-Arab Dialogue: Relations between the Two Cultures*, edited by Derek Hopwood (1985). This area of study has been opened up as a consequence of the recognition of Islamic religion and culture as an autonomous partner in international religious and cultural relations, which are linked, in turn, to political and other relationships. The recent establishment of considerable Muslim communities living side by side with a non-Muslim majority in a number of Western societies may also have made both North America and Western Europe more sensitive to the plurality of religions and cultures in daily life.

Study of religion in Islamic societies. The study of religion as a focus of Islamic studies has received considerable attention in the work of Wilfred Cantwell Smith, especially in his *On Understanding Islam* (1980). The major epistemological problem in Islamic studies is still apparently the difficulty involved in correlating scholarly categories of description, analysis, and interpretation with the adequate "reading," conceptualization, and translation of the raw data of Islamic realities. Since "Islam" is not an empirical datum in the same way as is an actual text, a practice, or even an ideal, the way in which Islam is "thematized" and what is held to be the "reality" of Islam largely depend on the concepts and categories with which a particular scholar is working. It is only logical that certain sets of concepts will lead to Islam being denied any "reality," or at least to the denial of the possibility of scholarly knowledge of any such reality. This does not mean that such a position precludes important work in Islamic studies but rather that, in this case, the concept of "Islam" makes little scholarly sense.

How should we then approach and study religion in the context of Islamic studies? Our starting point must be the recognition that Islam is always linked to persons, to societies, and to the Muslim community at large. Whereas texts, monuments, social practices, and so on, be they sacred or profane, somehow exist in themselves, this is not the case for "Islam," which exists first of all as a meaning for people, both Muslims and outsiders (including non-Muslim Islamicists). The subjective meaning of a particular datum, however, may be different for each person; in abstract terms, religious meanings are not inherent in particular facts. If we are interested in such meanings, accurate scholarly study of the religious aspects of Islam should avoid using general terms derived from Western parlance, such as *religion*, *worldview*, *ideology*, *faith*, and so on, and should instead start by looking at those data that possess significance for groups of Muslims—data that can be said to have a semiotic or symbolic value for Muslims.

Islam as a *religion*, in the strict sense of the word, can probably best be called a network of signs, or a semiotic system; when such signs are internalized, they become symbols. Interestingly enough, the Qurʾān hints at this process. Indeed, Islam constitutes the right human response to the *āyāt* ("signs," sometimes translated as "symbols") that have been provided mankind in the Qurʾān, in nature, and in history. The *āyāt* are nexus points of divine revelation and human reflection. Making full use of reason, Muslims are enjoined to draw right conclusions from these *āyāt* for their lives on earth, for the life and order of society, and for eternal bliss. Muslims are called upon to abandon themselves to the God who sent the *āyāt* and to obey his will as communicated through them. They should appeal to others to follow and understand the signs as well. They should, before all else, understand the Qurʾān itself as a "sign" revealed to humankind. Religion in the Islamic sense is faith (in God), knowledge (of the God-given signs), and a way of life accordingly.

Insofar as this interpretation corresponds with the Islamic notion of what religion is, it avoids stamping Islamic data with Western-coined concepts that are part of ideals, views, ideologies, and faiths fundamentally alien to Islam as Muslims see it. Paralleling the Muslim's focus of interest, this approach discovers the sense of the universe, humanity, and society, and the rules of right behavior and correct thinking, by means of the study of the *āyāt* that are recognized as providing meaning, orientation, and guidance. A study of Islam as a network of signs will reveal certain permanent vehicles of religious meaning, which permit communication between Muslims despite varying circumstances of place and time. By approaching Islam as a communicative, religious sign system, we avoid the one extreme of reifying Islam (and the concomitant search for an eternal essence), as well as the other extreme of denying any reality to Islam as measured against the material world.

BIBLIOGRAPHY

Full bibliographic data for the literature referred to in the section on the history of Islamic studies, above, can be found in Charles J. Adams's "Islamic Religious Tradition," in *The Study of the Middle East*, edited by Leonard Binder (New York, 1976), pp. 29–96. For further bibliographic data, see *A Reader's Guide to the Great Religions*, 2d ed., edited by Charles J. Adams (New York, 1977), pp. 407–466.

Islamic Studies: A Tradition and Its Problems, edited by Malcolm H. Kerr (Malibu, Calif., 1983), deals admirably with the full scope of Islamic studies. On the history of Islamic studies, see Maxime Rodinson's "The Western Image and Western Studies of Islam," in *The Legacy of Islam*, 2d ed., edited by Joseph Schacht with C. E. Bosworth (Oxford, 1974), pp. 9–62. Rodinson has elaborated his views in his *La fascination d'Islam* (Paris, 1980).

My own study, *L'Islam dans le miroir de l'Occident*, 3d ed. (Paris, 1970), focuses on five prominent Islamicists: Goldziher, Snouck Hurgronje, Becker, Macdonald, and Massignon. This work may be supplemented with my essay "Changes in Perspective in Islamic Studies over the Last Decades," *Humaniora Islamica* 1 (1973): 247–260.

The following works treat the development of Islamic studies in particular European countries. England: A. J. Arberry's *Oriental Essays: Portraits of Seven Scholars* (New York, 1960). France: Claude Cahen and Charles Pellat's "Les études arabes et islamiques," in *Cinquante ans d'orientalisme en France, 1922–1972*, a special issue of *Journal asiatique* 261 (1973): 89–107. Germany: Rudi Paret's *The Study of Arabic and Islam at German Universities: German Orientalists since Theodor Nöldeke* (Wiesbaden, 1968) and Johann Frick's *Die arabischen Studien in Europa* (Leipzig, 1956). Netherlands: J. Brugman and F. Schrödder's *Arabic Studies in the Netherlands* (Leiden, 1979). Spain: James T. Monroe's *Islam and the Arabs in Spanish Scholarship, Sixteenth Century to the Present* (Leiden, 1970).

Islamic studies in the West have not escaped criticism by Muslim Islamicists. See, for instance, A. L. Tibawi's *English-Speaking Orientalists: A Critique of Their Approach to Islam and Arab Nationalism* (Geneva, 1965) and *Second Critique of English-Speaking Orientalists and Their Approach to Islam and the Arabs* (London, 1979). The following works also deserve mention in this connection: Anouar Abdel Malik's "Orientalism in Crisis," *Diogenes* 44 (1963): 103–140; Abdallah Laroui's *The Crisis of the Arab Intellectual* (Berkeley, 1976); Edward Said's *Orientalism* (New York, 1978); and Sadiq al-Azm's "Orientalism and Orientalism in Reverse," *Hamsin* 8 (1981): 5–26.

Finally, I have discussed methodological issues at greater length in "Islam Studied as a Sign and Signification System," *Humaniora Islamica* 2 (1974): 267–285; "Islamforschung aus religionswissenschaftlicher Sicht," in *XXI. Deutscher Orientalistentag, 24–29. März 1980 in Berlin: Ausgewählte Vorträge*, edited by Fritz Steppat (Wiesbaden, 1982), pp. 197–211; and "Assumptions and Presuppositions in Islamic Studies," *Rocznik Orientalistyczny* 43 (1984): 161–170. For an application, see *Islam: Norm, ideaal en werkelykheid*, edited by me (Weesp, Netherlands, and Antwerp, 1984).

JACQUES WAARDENBURG (1987)

ISLAMIC STUDIES [FURTHER CONSIDERATIONS]. The study of Islam is both an ancient and a modern endeavor. It has its roots among Muslims in a long-established and continuing tradition of scholarship and interpretation of their own faith. Among others, particularly medieval Christians, the study was motivated by polemical ends aimed at establishing self-authenticity and preeminence by attributing to Islam, often pejoratively, error or willful misappropriation. This tendency has lingered on, though the medieval constructions and assaults on Islam have assumed different forms and emphases. The academic study of modem Islam, on the other hand, grew primarily out of the Enlightenment tradition of European scholarship and interest in Asian and African cultures and peoples, and by the nineteenth and twentieth centuries it had assumed some of the normative contours and institutional patterns that are associated with the general discipline of thought and expertise known as *Oriental studies* or *Orientalism.*

Orientalism, Edward Said's (1935–2003) critique of the discipline, its assumptions, and practitioners, first published in 1978, elicited a steady stream of responses, some of which were denunciatory and hastened to defend the discipline and its authority; others, more self-reflective, began submitting the discipline to greater introspection and even rethinking in the light of developments in other disciplines. What is noteworthy is that such a turn towards self-reflection, though stimulated in this case by someone outside the discipline, was by no means the first of its kind. Such a process has had its own history within Islamic studies and Orientalism and was part of a general trend in academic culture after World War II.

In 1953, a conference of leading European Islamicists was organized by Gustav von Grunebaum (1909–1972) as part of a larger effort to examine the relationship among Muslims, as well as between Islam and the various cultures and civilizations to which it had spread over time. This marked probably the first organized and self-conscious endeavor in recent times to undertake a historical and critical self-understanding of the discipline in the light of developing methods and theories in the social sciences, particularly Robert Redfield's notion of "great" and "little" traditions. It was noted at the time that the methods and assumptions used to study the history of Islam lagged a century behind those used for European history.

A year later, at another conference, Claude Cahen (1909–1991) reemphasized the point, quoting Bernard Lewis (b. 1916) to the effect that the history of the Arabs had been written in Europe chiefly by historians who knew no Arabic and Arabists who knew no history. Cahen argued that a new direction was necessary, one that would go beyond the hitherto philological orientation and study Muslim society as a total integrated organism. The sponsors and participants of such conferences, which took place against the backdrop of events and changes in the Muslim world, noted and emphasized the need to better understand Muslim civilization and history, and thereby the social and political problems of the Near East. They were conscious that the assumptions and methods of past generations of scholars, though meritorious in their own right, had become increasingly outmoded and detached from developments in other disciplines, as well as the changing realities in the relationship between Europe, the Americas, and the Muslim world.

The next two decades of the 1960s and 1970s represented for Asia and Africa the era of decolonization, nationalism, and revolution, whose impact was no longer local or regional but was becoming increasingly global. These were turbulent times in the academic community as well. A newer, more assertive tone emerged to which many scholars from the now so-called Third World allied themselves. It argued for the dismantling and deconstruction of established metaphysical and epistemological systems and the "Eurocentric" institutional apparatus that accompanied them. This would not be the only straw in that wind of change, but, among other things, it caused a questioning and revising of many of the assumptions of humanistic and social-scientific inquiry into other cultures. This debate, whose contemporary games are played out within interdeterminate frameworks called postmodernism and post-structuralism, but also across disciplines in programs of "cultural studies," affected Islamic studies only marginally. In part, this insulation explains both the defensiveness of the established community of Islamicists against criticisms and the need felt by an emerging group of dissatisfied younger scholars to escape from the narrower confines of philologically oriented scholarship to a more open-ended discourse, from which, in certain cases, they embraced uncritically the many new theories that had emerged.

The community of scholars in Islamic studies had indeed grown larger and more diverse, and the subject matter too complex, to be contained any longer within one interpretive community. The debate about "Orientalism" reflected and heightened the ambivalence within the field. Its significance, in retrospect, seems to lie more in the way it highlighted this predicament through wider public discourse and by placing it within ongoing academic debates than in its particular claims and critique against European scholarship.

Said's claims and insights regarding the historical and ideological conditions necessary to produce a discipline such as Islamic studies intertwined issues of representation and construction of the discipline to reveal a Eurocentric pattern of domination and authority. At a time of cultural and political collision and preoccupation with assertions of identity and difference in some parts of the Muslim world, his linking of power and knowledge and his arguments against a hegemonic misrepresentation of Muslims by the West played into the hands of rhetoricians emboldened by its anti-imperialist and anti-Western stance. This narrow focus and the controversy the book aroused diverted attention from the scholarly task and the opportunity to engage in a wider intellectual dialogue and exchange. The theorizing and extension of the boundaries of knowledge was by no means limited to Islamic studies. Broadly speaking, the process reflected the larger debate (some might say disarray) among various communities of interpretation in the humanities and the social sciences on the questions of the role of intellectuals and scholarly settings in representing and misrepresenting various human groups and cultures and upon the stability of authors and texts as repositories of meaning.

There also developed, in due course, as each European power established trade and colonies, a need to undertake studies of structures and peoples in their immediate settings, in particular the study of existing legal and social practices. While much of the collection of such information was an official task, it did involve individuals with scholarly interests, who subsequently helped encourage greater interest in the study of Muslim society, contemporary to them. However, the primary source of Islamic studies remained textual (based on available and selected texts) and the mode of analysis remained philological (with Arabic, Persian, and Turkish having priority). The history of European scholarship was by no means monolithic. At times, it appears as competing and is certainly diverse. It also reflected the economic and religious involvement of these various countries and their own power relations within Europe.

However, the pattern of historical-linguistic scholarship on Islam remained general for a long time and was often insulated from developments in other areas of humanistic scholarship that affected academic trends in fields such as history and literature. The 1953 conference referred to earlier marked something of a departure, particularly for the study of economic and social history and institutions. The focus of traditional Islamic studies, the Middle and Near East, was shifted to include interactions between Muslims, Africans, and other Asian peoples, and current sociological and anthropological perspectives came to be employed in the analysis of the spread and development of Islam.

Two new global factors would affect the study of Islam in the 1960s: the institutionalization of the Cold War and the decolonization and creation of new nation-states in much of Africa and Asia, including the Muslim regions of these two continents. There was a corresponding development in the growth of higher education and research in Europe and North America (accompanied by the migration of scholars and ideas from the former to the latter), and a transplanting of emerging intellectual trends in the theory and practice of scholarship. These factors highlighted attempts to study what were presumed to be the disorienting effects of colonial rule and the need to develop institutional strategies necessary to address the challenges, as well as the asymmetries, created by independence.

A colloquium held in 1961, the *Colloque sur la Sociologie Musulmane*, affirmed the need to refine methods and develop new concerns informed by social science. Baber Johansen, in discussing the development of Islamic studies in Germany, reflected on the loss of the dominant paradigm of historicism since the 1960s. The changes in German society after World War II, and the subsequent breakdown of the colonial system, led to university reform and a restructuring of Oriental studies. Scholarly authority shifted to the disciplines of social sciences, with their promise of better understanding of the transformation of economic, political, and social life at home and abroad. The same patterns can be said to have affected Britain, France, the Netherlands, and other Western European countries during the same period. The Russian example (and that of some other Eastern European countries) presents a special case. It suggests the strong constraint of ideologically grounded scholarship of a different kind—molded as it was by assumptions that governed intellectual and cultural life in the Soviet Union. In its engagement with some countries of the Muslims world an effort was also made to infiltrate intellectual life in these countries with a competing agenda meant to foster the Soviet Union's hegemonic aspirations. The collapse of the Soviet Union has opened up the space both in Russia and various Central Asian Republics to a revision and a restatement. The contours of this new trend are still uncertain, though considerably new archival and manuscript material has become available.

It is also during this period that the study of Islam expanded in Canada and the United States, in particular with the establishment of area-studies centers funded by government sources and foundations. It has been argued that such centers, particularly in the United States, while advancing the study of regional languages and cultures, tended to have their intellectual rationale subverted by the matrix of Cold War concerns, strategies, and ambiguities. This led to a fragmentary approach that very often separated and pitted those who were in the humanities against their counterparts in the social sciences who were studying the same region. The various uses to which the conclusions of Thomas Kuhn's *Structure of Scientific Revolutions* (first published in 1962) could be applied suggested how even the most objective pursuits of scientific knowledge could be analyzed to understand how these conclusions operated within contingent and historicized contexts. The presumed failure of "bias-free" assumptions and methods came to be evoked in those social-science disciplines that studied other cultures and societies. This undermining of confidence in the inherited paradigms was also exacerbated by the availability of many works by those who lived or wrote from the perspective of the Third World. In time, as these ideas took hold, the construction of knowledge became linked to issues of power and representation. Existing textual authority came to be questioned, and many pretentious and arbitrary claims came to be made for and against established "canons." Said's work was a reflection and a development of this trend. The history of Islamic studies reveals that there never was at any time in the past a fixed paradigm that operated universally; the boundaries were constantly being revised, not always by design but invariably because the dynamics of Muslim engagement with their history and heritage was changing as dramatically as the relationship of Europe and North America with the Muslim world.

The abundance of current scholarship portrays the intellectual, spiritual, and institutional pluralism of Islam, showing the development of a wide variety of Muslim societies within local and global contexts and illustrating the diversity that exists among individual Muslims, traditions, and periods of history. This scholarship also suggests Western scholars need to rethink the ways in which they have geographically and intellectually mapped the Muslim world. Past legal constructs such as "Dar al-Islam" and "Dar al-Harb" have become irrelevant, which is not to say that they cannot be invoked for ideological reasons. The manner in which European scholarship in the past perceived the Muslim world, with a presumed center—the "Near East" or "Middle East"—led to the marginalization of large groups of Muslims who did not inhabit that geopolitical space, and this marginalization affected the focus and practice of scholarship.

In addition to resisting the imposition of old boundaries, there is the caveat against present-mindedness and the undue focus on what has been termed *Islamist* or *radical* expressions, and the violent behavior associated with it on a global scale. While their relevance to contemporary politics and current affairs cannot be dismissed, it would be erroneous and limiting to make it the primary expression of Muslim identity in the modern world. There is among contemporary Muslims, as in all religious traditions, an inherent tension. One pattern expresses the growing differentiation in and separation of spheres and activity of life in which the inherited tradition occupies a place of differing degrees of personal and collective commitment. Another seeks to reintegrate all spheres within a totalizing conception of "Islam," which some wish to impose on other Muslims. Still others seek broader intellectual, ethical, and practical directions without assuming a parochial or doctrinaire approach. The tools of intellectual modernity that are employed in all cases cannot be homogeneous. The task of scholarship is to further develop and refine mediating categories and tools of comprehension that allow one to negotiate the space between concept and practice, embeddedness and expression, past and present.

An encouraging trend in Islamic studies is the cosmopolitan profile of the scholars and their methods in the field. A number of modern universities in the Muslim world have established specific centers or institutes for the study of Islam to complement more traditional and normative places of advanced study. A new generation of Muslim scholars is being created in countries such as Indonesia, Turkey, and Malaysia whose interests are less parochial and whose methods are linked to those practiced in academic institutions in the rest of the world. The migration of European scholars to the Americas has been followed by the migration of scholars from the Muslim world to both Europe and the United States. As Muhsin Mahdi (b. 1926) points out, one cannot easily separate contemporary scholarship in terms of "Western" and "Muslim." When combined with the rapid changes in communication made possible by advances in technology, such as the internet, collaboration between scholars within a continent and across continents has become much easier. This cross-fertilization is reflected in the fact that Islamic studies now radiates from within many departments and disciplines and finds expression in collaborative projects, institutes, journals, and associations. This new constellation of interests and constituencies has generated a profusion of scholarship and augurs well for a transnational scholarly landscape.

The field of Islamic studies will continue to be more diverse and encompassing in its scope than in the past. There are many possibilities open for adding to its subject matter and methods, including the role of Islam as a cultural force of great diversity; the increasing public participation in society by women (whose contributions and role still await detailed study within Islamic studies); the history of rural, agricultural, and mountainous peoples of the Muslim world; and new interactions among Muslims now living in the West. In this way, a vibrant humanistic scholarship can contribute to knowledge, linking the fifth of humanity that is Muslim to others, among whom Muslims live and with whom they increasingly share the task of building mutual understanding.

BIBLIOGRAPHY

This essay is meant to supplement the article by Jacques Waardenburg in the first edition of *The Encyclopedia of Religion* and to introduce some broader perspectives and developments in the field. It is based primarily on the "Introduction" in Azim Nanji's *Mapping Islamic Studies* (1997).

Abou El Fadl, Khaled. *And God Knows the Soldiers: The Authoritative and Authoritarian in Islamic Discourse.* London, 2001.

Abu Lughod, Lila, ed. *Remaking Women: Feminism and Identity in the Middle East.* Princeton, 1998.

Akbar, Ahmed. *Postmodernism and Islam: Predicament and Promise.* London, 1992.

Bunt, Gary. *Islam in the Digital Age: E-jihad, Online Fatwas, and Cyber Islamic Environments.* London, 2003.

Cooke, Miriam. *Women Claim Islam: Creating Islamic Feminism through Literature.* London, 2000.

Erturk, Korkut A., ed. *Rethinking Central Asia: Non-Eurocentric Studies in History, Social Structure, and Identity.* Reading, Pa., 1998.

Geertz, Claude. *Local Knowledge: Further Essays in Interpretive Anthropology.* New York, 1983.

Gole, Nilufer. *The Forbidden Modern: Civilization and Veiling.* Ann Arbor, Mich., 1998.

Hodgson, Marshall G. *Rethinking World History: Essays on Europe, Islam, and World History.* Introduction by Edmund Burke III. Cambridge, U.K., and New York, 1993.

Hourani, Albert. *Islam in European Thought.* Cambridge, U.K., 1991.

Huntington, Samuel P. *The Clash of Civilizations and the Remaking of World Order.* New York, 1996.

Kerr, Malcolm, ed. *Islamic Studies: A Tradition and Its Problems.* Malibu, Calif., 1980.

Macfie, A. L., ed. *Orientalism: A Reader.* Edinburgh, 2000.

Nanji, Azim, ed. *Mapping Islamic Studies.* Berlin and New York, 1997.

Rahman, Fazlur. "Approaches to Islam in Religious Studies: Review Essay." In *Approaches to Islam in Religious Studies,* edited by Richard C. Martin. Tucson, Ariz., 1985.

Ramadan, Tariq. *Western Muslims and the Future of Islam.* New York, 2004.

Said, Edward. "Orientalism Reconsidered." In *Literature, Politics, and Theory: Papers from the Essex Conference,* edited by Francis Baker et al. London, 1986.

Sells, Michael A., and Emran Qureshi, eds. *The New Crusades: Constructing the Muslim Enemy.* New York, 2003.

Waardenburg, Jacques. *Islam: Historical, Social, and Political Perspectives.* Berlin, 2002.

World Policy Institute Dialogue. "Clash of Civilizations or Clash of Perceptions: In Search of Common Ground for Understanding." Granada, Spain, 2002.

AZIM NANJI (2005)

ʿIṢMAH. The Arabic term *ʿiṣmah* means "immunity" from sin or error. *ʿIṣmah* is discussed by the Sunnīs in relation to the Prophet Muḥammad and other prophets, and by the Shīʿah in relation to not only the prophets but, most importantly, the *imāms,* the charismatic descendants of ʿAlī ibn Abī Ṭālib who stand at the center of Shīʿī piety. The paths taken by Sunnīs and Shīʿah with regard to *ʿiṣmah* throw much light on the different development and character of the two traditions.

The idea of immunity is latent in the tendency of *Homo religiosus* to attribute outstanding qualities to special persons. This tendency was already evident in the first centuries of Islam in efforts to dissociate Muḥammad from polytheism in his early life and Ṣūfī and Shīʿī exaltation of the saints and *imāms*. It was, however, only in the eighth century (AH second century), under the influence of theology and in answer to problems raised by possible error on the part of religious authorities, that immunity was made explicit and expounded systematically. This development may be contrasted with the case of Judaism, in which theology did not gain as much importance and the question of inerrancy was consequently not raised, so that the prophets and other revered figures were largely left with their errors and sins.

The word *ʿiṣmah* itself is not found in the Qurʾān, but other forms of the base root *ʿ-s-m* do appear, for example, "God will protect [*ʿ-s-m*] you from the people" (5:67), "those who take refuge [*ʿ-t-s-m*] in God" (4:146). It thus seems likely that the choice of the term for *immunity*, in which God "protects" certain persons from error, was indirectly suggested by the Qurʾān; related words are used in similar senses before *ʿiṣmah* ever acquires a technical sense—for example, a community can be *maʿṣūm*, specially taken care of or "protected" by God.

The Qurʾān itself, however, is unconcerned with problems raised by the capacity for error or sin on the part of the prophets whose stories it relates. One passage (80:1–10) even tells how the Prophet of Islam was reproached by God for turning away from a blind man who wanted to hear his preaching. Apart from tendencies toward semi-deification seen in some Shīʿī and Ṣūfī circles, early Muslim non-theological tradition also accepted prophets and other revered persons as merely human, albeit outstanding humans who may work miracles. The canonical books of Sunnī *ḥadīth*, collected in the mid- to late ninth century, contain traditions that freely admit lapses on the part of the prophets (e.g., Adam's sin, the Prophet's warning to his followers that he might judge in error). Early Shīʿī *ḥadīth* texts—including the mid-tenth-century canonical *al-Kāfī* —do not refer to *ʿiṣmah* or construct any theory of immunity, even as they virtually imply it by referring to the pure essence and perfect knowledge of Muḥammad and the *imāms*. Later Shīʿī works that wish to uphold *ʿiṣmah* are compelled to rely mostly on statements attributed to the *imāms* that do not address the subject directly, or on clearly late material such as long disquisitions attached to the eighth *imām*, ʿAlī al-Riḍā. Nevertheless, by the mid-eighth century the belief that the *imāms*, or at least ʿAlī, did not commit any fault was already attributed to an unnamed group of Shīʿah. The belief must have been an extremist one, for these persons did allow that the Prophet committed faults. The pioneering Shīʿī theologian Hishām ibn al-Ḥakam (d. 179/795–796) then begins to systematize this belief, explaining that the Prophet may sin because he can be corrected by revelation (which the *imāms* cannot); Shīʿī sources also credit Hishām with describing the quality that prevents sin as freedom from all covetousness, envy, anger, and appetite, and calling it "*ʿiṣmah*."

By at least the late eighth century, immunity was also taken up by the great rationalist theologians of Islam, the Muʿtazilah, perhaps initially because of contacts with Shīʿah but finally because of a certain fit with the Muʿtazilī worldview. The Muʿtazilah insisted that a just God was bound to do the best for his creatures, and thus, they concluded, he would not allow revelation to be compromised through faults on the part of its bearers. Because the aim of the Muʿtazilah was not to idealize any personality but to secure a principle of their system; they spoke of the prophets altogether, not even necessarily privileging Muḥammad. Rigorous logic caused them to extend *ʿiṣmah* to any circumstance that might damage that principle, to the time not only after but also before a prophet's mission and to "any trait," as the Qāḍī ʿAbd al-Jabbār puts it in the eleventh century, "liable to cause aversion."

The Shīʿī theological argument for *ʿiṣmah* was finally assembled as they themselves adopted the Muʿtazilī rationalist worldview. The argument was that God could not grant supreme authority, whether in religion or temporal rule, to any person liable to error or sin, because such persons would then lead others into the same error, which would mean that God had failed to do the best possible for his creation and was thus not perfectly just. Therefore, so the reasoning goes, there must necessarily exist persons who are immune to whom such authority may be given; and these are none other than the prophets and their successors, the *imāms*, to whom complete allegiance is consequently owed. This is the basic argument of the Shīʿī doctrine of immunity to this day.

The theological notion of *ʿiṣmah* was entirely in harmony with veneration of the *imāms* and soon spread over the rest of the tradition. Early-tenth-century exegetical works such as the *tafsīrs* of ʿAyyāshī and Qummī are unconcerned with the errors and sins of prophets related in the Qurʾān; modern editors add long notes to "correct" them on this point. Not long after, however, the traditionist Ibn Bābawayh (d. 991) presents textual instead of rational proofs to establish the necessity (*wujūb*) of immunity, also pointing out that because immunity is an inner quality, it is only through the designation of the text (*naṣṣ*) that the *maʿṣūm* can be known. The scholars move on to treat the many problematic passages of the Qurʾān and tradition; Shaykh Ṭūsī (died c. 1067), for instance, argues that it is not possible that Muḥammad would have turned away from the blind man, since that would be contrary to his demonstrated character and prophetic mission, the one who turned away being rather one of the Quraysh nobles hostile to him. Proof texts for *ʿiṣmah* are also adduced, for example, Qurʾān 33:33: "God wills, O People of the Household, that all impurity be removed from you and that you be cleansed most thoroughly."

ʿIṣmah entered Sunnism also from the direction of theology. It is first mentioned in the tenth-century Ḥanafī creed *Fiqh Akbar II* (in which some scholars have also detected

Muʿtazilī influence). Sunnī theologians continued to affirm immunity, but they were more reticent than their Muʿtazilī and Shīʿī counterparts, for they were not as willing to undertake the extensive interpretation of the scriptures required to make them accord with *ʿiṣmah,* and they were also wary of blurring the boundary between human and divine. Thus, many Sunnīs allowed sin and error (excluding unbelief) before the prophets' missions, and even minor sins after, though with some added proviso, such as that they would be unintentional or not of the kind that would affect their preaching.

Sunnī scholars had originally been drawn into giving qualified assent to the doctrine of *ʿiṣmah* by the problem laid before them of establishing a guaranteed starting point for religion. Already by the eighth century, however, they found a partial escape by locating immunity in the consensus (*ijmāʿ*) of the scholars, as expressed in the *ḥadīth,* "My community shall never commit an error." This solution had the added virtue of securing the ongoing process of the tradition, and the Shīʿah were later to adopt a version of it by asserting that the unanimous consensus of their own scholars was certainly correct, since the infallible Twelfth Imām was also a scholar hidden among them.

Though the groups most attached to the literal meaning of the Qurʾān and *ḥadīth,* the Ḥanbalīs and extremist "Ḥashawīyah," were drawn by their fideism toward some acceptance of the prophets' sins, the grandfather of modern Ḥanbalī-Wahhābism, Ibn Taymīyah (d. 1328), does affirm *ʿiṣmah.* The Wahhābīs are fiercely opposed to any veneration of humans, including the Prophet; but they too have been compelled to admit *ʿiṣmah* in order to secure the Qurʾān and especially, *ḥadīth* on which they rely so heavily. Thus, Shaykh Bin Bāz, Grand Mufti of Saudi Arabia until his death in 1999, explains that all the prophets were *maʿṣūm* in that which they communicated from God, and that Muḥammad was immune from major sins, though not from minor sins or error in worldly affairs concerning which he did not express certainty or issue any command—in which case God made him aware of the sin or error so that he then desisted from it.

The Shīʿah have tended to maximize immunity. This tendency is driven partly by the theological impulse toward systematization; the logic of *ʿiṣmah* in order for it to hold must be applied to all bearers of revelation and all circumstances in the life of a *maʿṣūm.* Thus, the Sharīf al-Murtaḍá (d. 1044 or 1045) composed a book entitled *Complete Exoneration of [All] the Prophets and Imāms;* and the immunity of the *maʿṣūms* is finally extended not only to the time before their missions but even unintentional commission of minor sins and (against all other Muslim opinion) inadvertent error (*sahw*). Immunity for the Shīʿah also embraces nonreligious affairs. Modern Shīʿī scholars continue to produce a considerable literature explaining and defending *ʿiṣmah.*

The Shīʿī focus on *ʿiṣmah* is driven primarily, however, by veneration of the *imāms,* and here it becomes absolutely central to Shīʿī piety, in which the twelve imāms, the Prophet, and Faṭimah are referred to collectively as the fourteen *maʿsums.* Any questioning of immunity would be for Twelver Shīʿah a very great heresy, partly because of the deep sectarian emotions attached to it. Thus, opponents of the controversial Lebanese cleric Sayyid Muḥammad Faḍlallāh have accused him of undermining the prophets' *ʿiṣmah,* a charge he has strongly denied.

Contemporary popular Sunnism has been pulled in the opposite direction. Partly under the growing influence of the spirit of Wahhabism, Sunnīs are likely, while still venerating the prophets, to insist on their humanity, one of the Qurʾanic proof texts commonly cited being "I [Muḥammad] am only a mortal like you. . ." (18:110).

BIBLIOGRAPHY

For the positions of additional sects and thinkers, including Shīʿī groups who have held views different than those of the majority Twelvers, refer to W. Madelung and E. Tyan's "ʿIṣmah" in *The Encyclopaedia of Islam,* 2nd ed., edited by H. A. R. Gibb, vol. 4, p. 182 (Leiden, Netherlands, 1977).

al-Asadābādī, ʿAbd al-Jabbār ibn Aḥmad. *Sharḥ al-uṣūl al-khamsah.* Edited by ʿAbd al-Karīm ʿUthmān. Cairo, 1965.

Ashʿarī, Abū al-Ḥasan. *Maqālāt al-islāmīyīn,* 2d ed. Edited by Muḥammad Muḥyi al-Dīn ʿAbd al-Ḥamīd. Cairo, 1969–1970.

Bar-Asher, Meir M. *Scripture and Exegesis in Early Imāmī Shiism.* Leiden and Jerusalem, 1999.

Bin Bāz ʿAbd al-ʿAzīz. *Majmū fatāwá wa-maqālāt mutanawwiʿah.* 17 vols., see vol. 6, pp. 290–291. Riyad, Saudi Arabia, 1421 (2001–2002).

Calverley, Edwin E., and James W. Pollock, eds. and trans. *Nature, Man and God in Medieval Islam.* 2 vols. Leiden, Netherlands, 2002.

Donaldson, Dwight M. *The Shiite Religion.* London, 1933.

Ibn Bābawayh. *Maʿānī al-akhbār.* Mashhad, Iran, 1408 (1987–1988).

Ibn Baṭṭah, ʿUbayd Allāh ibn Muḥammad. *al-Sharḥ wa-al-ibānah ʿalá uṣūl al-sunnah wa-al-diyānah (Profession de foi d'Ibn Batta).* Translated by Henri Laoust. Damascus, Syria, 1958.

Laoust, Henri. *Essai sur les doctrines sociales et politiques de Taki-d-Din Ahmad b. Taymiyya.* Cairo, 1939.

McDermott, Martin J. *The Theology of al-Shaikh al-Mufid.* Beirut, Lebanon, 1978.

Majlisī, Muḥammad Bāqir. *Biḥār al-anwār.* 2d revised edition, 110 vols; see vol. 11, pp. 72–126, vol. 17, pp. 108–110, vol. 25, pp. 191–211. Beirut, Lebanon,: 1403 (1983).

Schmidtke, Sabine. *Theologie, Philosophie und Mystik im Zwölferschiitischen Islam des 9./15. Jahrhunderts.* Leiden, 2000.

Schmidtke, Sabine. *The Theology of al-Allamah al-Hilli.* Berlin, 1991.

Sharīf al-Murtaḍá. *Tanzīh al-anbiyāʾ wa-al-aʾimmah.* Beirut, 1989.

Ṭūsī, Muḥammad ibn al-Ḥasan. *al-Tibyān fī tafsīr al-Qurʾān.* Beirut, 1990.

Zayn al-ʿĀbidīn, ʿAbd al-Salām. *Murājaʿāt fī ʿiṣmat al-anbiyāʾ min manẓūr Qurʾānī.* 1421 (2000).

L. CLARKE (2005)

ISMAILIS See SHIISM, *ARTICLE ON* ISMĀʿĪLĪYAH

ISRAEL See JACOB; JEWISH PEOPLE; ZIONISM

ISRAELITE LAW

This entry consists of the following articles:

AN OVERVIEW
PERSONAL STATUS AND FAMILY LAW
PROPERTY LAW
CRIMINAL LAW
STATE AND JUDICIARY LAW

ISRAELITE LAW: AN OVERVIEW

In all societies, law is an absolutely necessary bracket that, through a common compulsory way of acting, guarantees the ties between individuals, groups, and communities usually drifting apart due to their different material and ideal interests. Law assumes this task of promoting the cohesion of society through two basic functions. First, it minimizes violence by regulating social conflicts; second, it secures norms by means of sanctions and thus stabilizes expectations of behavior into socially acceptable actions.

The Codification of Law in the Ancient Near East and in Israel. Norms of behavior enforced through the penalty of sanctions and the rules for minimizing violent conflicts were primary forms of law originally transmitted orally. In state-run societies, legal functions tended to be taken over by the state or were put under public supervision. In monarchies, if and for what function laws were written down and codified depended upon the scope of the incarnation of legal functions in the king who embodied public power.

In Egypt, the king's competence for legal decisions could not be restricted by written laws or laws arranged in collections of legal rules. This was because the pharaoh, the son of the sun-god, was looked upon as the incarnation of justice and law (*ma'at*). Thus there were not any Egyptian law collections from the pre-Persian period but only several legal decrees of the king. In Mesopotamia, the gods empowered the king to enforce the law. The king could delegate his task to subordinate authorities. Contrary to Egyptian law and justice (Akkadian: *kittu*[*m*] *u mīšaru*[*m*]), the law and justice incarnated in the king were of meta-divine origin, because the gods themselves—like the sun-god Shamash, who is the god of justice—have obtained law and justice. Thus they were only viewed as non-derivable powers who even transcended the gods' universe as well as the king's functions, including the instruction of the gods to the king to enforce the law. Due to this difference between Egypt and Mesopotamia concerning the legitimation of the legal functions of the king, it was possible to codify and collect laws in Mesopotamia without restricting his legal functions.

At first, the Mesopotamians began to write down and to arrange law collections—like that of old Babylonian Eshnunna—which are considered to be descriptions of legal practice, in order to teach and exercise legal decision-making. The law codes were arranged for two purposes: on the one hand, for the education of scribes, on the other hand, for the sophisticated propagation of legal reforms—like the Middle-Assyrian laws—or for the documentation of such a reform—like the Hittite laws. On a secondary stage of literary development, such law collections—like that of Hammurabi—may have been framed by a prologue or an epilogue, according to the royal ideology that serves for the public presentation of the king's function to enforce laws. Likewise in this function, the laws remained descriptive and did not bind the judgments of the court to which the gods—particularly Shamash—were entitled through their cultic decision-making. In Persian jurisprudence of the Achaemenids, the decrees of the king functioned as unchangeable laws for the courts. However, in Persia, as in Egypt, law collections were not codified. In Persia, they also restrained the function of the king for dispensation to jurisdiction by enacting laws together with the state god Ahura Mazdā. But in addition to the decrees of their king, the Persians allowed the enforcement of codified local laws in provinces of defeated nations for order's sake.

In the ancient Near East, laws never gained a critical distance from the king and thus from the state as well. Only in Israel and Greece, where the legal sphere kept its distance from the king, laws—in Israel given by God or in Greece by the will of the people—confronted the state in written form through a prescriptive character bestowed on them. The written legal texts took over functions which were usually filled by the king in the ancient Near East. With the words "the law is the king of all" (*nómos ho pántōn basileús*), Pindar (born about 520 BCE) furnished a conception for a breakthrough which was true of the Hellenic form of justice and also applied to Israel. But in contrast to Greece, Jewish law was not legitimated by the will of the people in the polis, but it expressed God's will, the source of law and justice (*mišpatusdaqā*). In Greece, *nómos* was the commonly valid norm which an individual was not allowed to violate; nevertheless, it could be altered by the polis. The act of writing down the laws allowed them to be revised, making legal reform possible. However, the consistent deduction of the law from God's will in Israel confined Old Testament law in a way that prohibited legislation or judicial revision initiated by the people. Furthermore, this raised problems concerning the adaptation of laws revealed by God as a legal source to new sociohistorical circumstances because God cannot be contradictory to himself. Within the Bible, legal revisions can only be mediated by scribal techniques in order to prove the identity of revised and revising law and of God's will. This form of inner-biblical judicial revision became the origin of the methods of Rabbinic interpretation of the Bible.

A History of Biblical Law. The Israelite laws had their origins in three functions: first, to secure expectations of socially acceptable behavior by criminal law, second, to regulate conflicts by compensation law (thereby decreasing violence), and third, to regulate intercourse with the divine sphere by sacral law. The form-historical differentiation of Israelite law, which analyzes the typical forms and structures of biblical texts into a casuistic and an apodictic type covered these different functions. The casuistic laws (*mišpatim*), consisting of a protasis (i.e., the definition of the case) and an apodosis (i.e., the legal consequence, as in *Ex.* 21:18–19) served the regulation of conflicts. They stemmed from the judicial practice at local courts where conflicts between families were settled. The apodictic laws as criminal law (*hoq/huqqāh/mis wāh/Torah*) comprised the legal rules of capital law (e.g., *Ex.* 21:12.15–17), the prohibitives of the Decalogue, the bans on incest (*Lv.* 18), and the law of curse (*Dt.* 27). The apodictic laws originated in the family but in the preexilic period were transferred to the local courts which begin to settle cases of family law, as well. In pre-Deuteronomic sacral law, the intercourse with the divine sphere was defined by the order of festivals (*Ex.* 23:14–19; 34:18–26), by the law on first fruits or firstlings (*Ex.* 22:28–30), on the fallow year and the rest day (*Ex.* 23:10–12), as well as by the sacral commands of taboos (*Ex.* 22:17–19).

At local courts, initiatives were taken to collect legal rules of casuistic law on similar themes. *Exodus* 22:6–14 contains a small collection of three laws dealing with depositing, herding, and renting of animals. In this manner, cases of human negligence can be delimitated from those of force majeure. Such collections served the purpose of contributing to the continuance of juridical decisions by transmitting them in written form and by inferring abstract laws from the decisions. Moreover, rule authority was enhanced by mutual explanation of the legal rules. That entailed a larger diversification concerning the delimitation of cases. More complex collections were those of the law of property (*Ex.* 21:33–22:14), law of bodily injuries (*Ex.* 21:18–32), and family law (*Dt.* 21:15–21a; 22:13–29; 24:1–5; 25:5–10). These collections had ingeniously been arranged through editorial networking by the scribe-scholars of wisdom literature and served to educate, as did the cuneiform law codes originally in Mesopotamia. Most of the legal rules of the above-mentioned biblical collections, however, had an indigene Israelite origin and were not received from Mesopotamian law. This is also true of the law on the "goring ox" (*Ex.* 21:35–36) which had an Israelite origin although a parallel law exists in the codex of Eshnunna from the first half of the second millennium; the similarity does not have to be explained through legal reception. The notion of "common law" can only be applied in Mesopotamia and Israel in so far as in both countries compilations of legal rules serve for education and the legal rules are descriptive in character.

In the pre-Deuteronomic period, the direct influence of cuneiform law on Israelite law was confined to editorial compilation techniques of legal rules for the purpose of education. Neither the individual laws applied in daily legal practice nor their compilations in the framework of the scribes' curriculum required an explicit legitimation of law, because the function of the laws in settling conflicts and securing norms was self-evident due to general prevention. But when in the eighth and seventh centuries BCE social stratification of Israelite society increased, implying poor and rich classes, the natural obviousness of the establishments of laws became lost. A vertical law concerned with providing protection for the benefit of underprivileged people had to be established in addition to a horizontal law relating to the regulation of conflicts (*Ex.* 21:2–11; 22:20–26; 23:10–12). In order to enforce the vertical law against the interests of the political and economic elite, it needed a religious legitimation. Judean priests took over the small law collection that was compiled for educational reasons, and treated them like the sacral laws by attributing their legal source to YHWH. The ruptures of social conflicts enforced the religious legitimation of law and can be learned from the covenant code in *Exodus* 21–23, which got its name from the covenant ceremony in *Exodus* 24:3–8, where Moses read it out. In that way, Zadokite priests at the temple of Jerusalem transferred their comprehension of law, which had its source in the sacral law, to the law-collections which were formed in the course of legal education. Intellectuals from priestly circles, not looking to promote their own interests, worked for the benefit of underprivileged people in society. Already in the covenant code, they charted the program of a society that was based on the solidarity with poor people and thus expressed God's will.

After the laws of the covenant code had been supplied with a theological legitimation, the priests of Judea could use them as a tool for defying cultural and political claims to hegemony in the seventh century BCE that were laid by the supreme power of Late Assyria. They inserted a revision of the covenant code (*Dt.* 12;14–26) into a loyalty oath (*Dt.* 13; 28) that was adopted in a subversive way from a loyalty oath to the neo-Assyrian king Esarhaddon by referring the royal demand for loyalty to YHWH, thus divesting the Assyrian king of it. The revision of the covenant code in the Deuteronomic law responded to the centralization of the cult combined with the reorganization of the judicial system by King Josiah (622/21 BCE) and elaborated on the social program of the covenant code through release of debts (*Dt.* 15:1–11) and prohibition of usury (*Dt.* 23:20–21). The cult of the Assyrian imperial god Assur, which had its center at the temple of Assur in the city of Assur, made up the counterpart to the cult of YHWH centralized in Jerusalem (*Dt.* 12). If evidence is found implying that the Judean legal tradition was superior to the Assyrian one, it must be shown that there are not any inconsistencies, despite the contradictions to the covenant code which are due to the revision. Law legitimated by its divine origin must be free of tensions; God cannot contradict himself. The scribe-authors accomplished this task by turning the text of *Deuteronomy,* which interprets the covenant code, into the hermeneutical key of the interpreted text in the covenant code. The legislation of asylum illustrates this process in a paradigmatic way. While in *Exodus* 21:13–14 the respective local sanctuaries were declared to be an asylum, the verses in *Deuteronomy* 19:2–13 provided cities of asylum all over the country after abolishing local sanctuaries and centralizing the cult. Henceforth *Exodus* 21:13–14 is considered to be a reference to the asylum function of the central sanctuary in Jerusalem. Therefore the revised laws of the covenant code were not "recycled," as Bernard M. Levinson suggests, but continued to be valid together with the revised law. This explains why the covenant code could be located in the Pentateuch pericope in terms of being a part of the Sinai revelation, whereas the Deuteronomic link with Moab renders this emphasis impossible.

In the late preexilic period, *Deuteronomy* was held as a direct expression of God's will which was linked to the central sanctuary in Jerusalem and did not yet refer to Moses as an intermediary. But after the loss of the Temple, *Deuteronomy* had to be adapted to the new situation of the exilic period. This was done by setting Deuteronomic law in a frame (*Dt.* 5:9–10; 28:1–14, 45–68) that combined the law with Moses and God's mount and incorporated the Decalogue into *Deuteronomy* 5. Moreover, *Deuteronomy* was now read as an interpretation, thus imposing the covenant obligations on God's people at God's mount (*Dt.* 26:16–19). In the covenant code and preexilic *Deuteronomy*, the king was not mentioned at all, because the legal functions of the king were replaced by the written text of the laws as expression of God's legal will. In the exilic period, when there was no longer an acting king, the Deuteronomists integrated the theme of kingship into the Deuteronomic law (*Dt.* 17:14–20) but divested it programmatically of all political functions and stylized the king to be the first pious man of Torah among his people. The king was now no longer the source of law as in the ancient Near East but subdued under the divine Torah.

After the fall of kingship even the understanding of time, which in the ancient Near East was embodied in the king and therefore was only conceivable as royal time, became separated from the king by transferring the origin of the law to Mount Horeb, also known as Mount Sinai. Now the law was embedded in a time structure of an ideal "history" as a story of Israel's origin which was remote from the king. In this way the Torah created a link between law and historical narrative. At the same time free prophecy was domesticated by restricting it to Mosaic prophecy as the only legitimate one according to prophetic law (*Dt.* 18:9–22). Previously, prophecy was blamed for the fractionation of the society in Israel and in Judah, thereby entailing its fall, as the contradiction between true and false prophecy could not be solved. At this point the triumphant advance of law over prophecy began, an event which would be finished in the postexilic period (*Zec.* 13:2–6). In an additional framework of *Deuteronomy* (*Dt.* 1–3; 29–30), the revelation at Mt. Horeb appeared to be a prelude for the proclamation of the law by Moses and for the covenant making in the land of Moab. Thus *Deuteronomy* not only encouraged the second generation (*Dt.* 1:19–46) to hope for their return from exile by scheduling the promulgation of *Deuteronomy* on the day before their entrance into the Promised Land beyond the river Jordan (*Dt.* 29–30), but it also fostered the expectation that the faults would be expiated after the death of the sinful older generation and that a new history would start on taking possession of the land.

Furnishing the idea of the covenant in Moab, the exilic *Deuteronomy* stood out against the rival conception of the priestly code which also stemmed from the period of exile and which declared that God's indwelling in the tabernacle of the congregation as well as the establishment of the expiatory cult ministered by the Aaronite priests was the goal and summit of creation and universal history (*Gn.* 1–11). The covenant with Israel was transferred to the time of the Patriarchs and linked to Abraham (*Gn.* 17). Furthermore, it was held to be a covenant made by mere grace, independent from the law.

In consequence for the priestly code, all of Israel could not fail the covenant once again. Only individuals who refused circumcision should be expelled from the ethnic community. According to the priestly code, the liability to the law was not particularly imposed on Israel but on all mankind as follows from the Noachite commands (*Gn.* 9:1–7). Mankind also can neither fail the Noachite commands nor the covenant made with them on the basis of those commands as God promises to refrain from another flood and thus from the extinction of mankind.

The postexilic scribes faced the task to jointly mediate the two different exilic drafts of the narrative foundation of Israel's revelation of the law of the Torah, as expressed in *Deuteronomy* and the priestly code. If YHWH, the God of Israel, was One according to the First Commandment in the Decalogue, hence his history with Israel and his revealed will of the Torah respectively can be only one. In this respect the postexilic literary history of the Torah theologically was a function of the First Commandment in the Decalogue. The postexilic scribes accomplished the task to adapt the priestly code and the law of *Deuteronomy* which was combined with the *Book of Joshua*. They succeeded in doing so by means of their scribal erudition. In the fifth century BCE they formed a Hexateuch (*Gn.* 1 through *Jos.* 24) in which possession of the land of Israel (*Jos.* 13–21) was the goal of creation and universal history (*Gn.* 1–11). In that way they rejected the claim of the Persian imperial ideology that the god Ahura-Mazdā had assigned an appropriate place to all nations in the world, the center of which was Persepolis. While the authors of the Hexateuch considered the possession of the land to be the central *Heilsgut* (fruit of salvation), the Zadokite priests in the Diaspora challenged this view because they identified the Torah as this good of salvation. They held that Israel was present wherever Jews observe the Torah of YHWH. *Ezra* 7 preserved the remembrance that the Diaspora theology was adopted in Jerusalem, beginning with *Ezra*. This process was also reflected in the Pentateuch. The *Book of Joshua* became separated from it and the Sinai pericope was expanded instead by interpolating the Decalogue, the covenant code, and the holiness code (*Lv.* 17–26). Thus this pericope became the typical location for the revelation of the Torah *kat exochen.*

Prophetic circles of the postexilic period examined the Torah-theology of the Pentateuch in a critical way. Circles that felt bound to the tradition of the prophet Ezekiel required a "new spirit" as precondition for fulfilling the Torah which was fixed in a written form by Moses (*Ez.* 11:19; 36:26–27). Other circles that stood by the tradition of the prophet Jeremiah depreciated the written Torah of Moses and expected a Torah which was written by God on the human heart (*Jer.* 31:31–34). Consequently they declared the scribes' erudition of the Torah to be useless (*Jer.* 8:8–9). The draft of a constitution of the post-exilic Israel in *Ezekiel* 40–48 did not combine the Torah with Moses and Sinai but with the Temple in Jerusalem instead. It could not prevail as a part of the Torah and only entered into the canon under the protecting authority of the priest-prophet Ezekiel. The subsequent Temple Scroll that bound the Temple to the Torah looked for a connection with the Sinai tradition of the Pentateuch (*Ex.* 34), but the Temple Scroll was ruled out and did not get accepted into the canon of the Hebrew Bible.

See Also Law and Religion.

Bibliography

Alt, Albrecht. *Die Ursprünge des israelitischen Rechts.* Leipzig, Germany, 1934. Translated by Robert A. Wilson as *Essays on Old Testament History and Religion.* Garden City, N.Y., 1967, pp. 101–171. Basic study and critical analysis of apodictic and casuistic law in the Old Testament.

Greengus, Samuel, and Rifat Sonsino. "Law." In *The Anchor Bible Dictionary,* edited by David Noel Freedmann, vol. 4, pp. 242–254. New York, 1992. A short summary of the development of biblical law with a good bibliography.

Houtman, Cornelis. *Das Bundesbuch. Ein Kommentar.* Leiden, Netherlands, 1997. Basic commentary on the covenant code.

Jackson, Bernard S. *Studies in the Semiotics of Biblical Law.* Sheffield, U.K., 2000. Theories of cognitive development are used to explain the development of biblical law.

Lafont, Sophie. *Femmes, Droit et Justice dans l'Antiquité orientale.* Fribourg, Switzerland, and Göttingen, Germany, 1999. Basic study of gender aspects in ancient Near East criminal law.

Levinson, Bernard M., ed. *Theory and Method in Biblical and Cuneiform Law: Revision, Interpolation, and Development.* Sheffield, U.K., 1994. Critical discussion of R. Westbrook's hypothesis of an ancient Near East "common law."

Levinson, Bernard M. *Deuteronomy and the Hermeneutics of Legal Innovation.* New York, 1997. Application of proto-rabbinical exegetical methods, described by Michael Fishbane (*Biblical Interpretation in Ancient Israel.* Oxford, 1985) to the revision of the covenant code in *Deuteronomy.*

Lévy, Edmond, ed. *La codification des lois dans l'Antiquité.* Paris, 2000. Important contributions to the motives for codification of law in antiquity.

Matthews, Victor H., Bernard M. Levinson, and Tikva Frymer-Kensky, eds. *Gender and Law in the Hebrew Bible and the Ancient Near East.* Sheffield, U.K., 1998. Collection of papers related to aspects of gender-studies in ancient Near East and biblical law.

Otto, Eckart. *Theologische Ethik des Alten Testaments.* Stuttgart, Germany, 1994. Basic ethics of the Hebrew Bible in a wide range of ancient Near East legal history.

Otto, Eckart. *Das Deuteronomium. Politische Theologie und Rechtsreform in Juda und Assyrien.* Berlin, 1999. Study of the literary and legal history of Deuteronomic law.

Otto, Eckart. *Das Deuteronomium im Pentateuch und Hexateuch.* Tübingen, Germany, 2000. Study of the *Book of Deuteronomy* as part of the Pentateuch.

Roth, Martha T. *Law Collections from Mesopotamia and Asia Minor.* Atlanta, Ga., 1995. Best collection of texts and translations of cuneiform law.

Watts, James W. *Reading Law: The Rhetorical Shaping of the Pentateuch.* Sheffield, U.K., 1999. Rhetorical criticism that explains the literary formation of the Pentateuch.

Weinfeld, Moshe. *Deuteronomy and the Deuteronomic School.* Oxford, 1972; reprint, Winona Lake, Ind., 1992. Important study of intellectual impacts on *Deuteronomy.*

Weinfeld, Moshe. *Justice in Ancient Israel and the Ancient Near East.* Jerusalem and Minneapolis, 1995. Important study of ancient Near East patterns to realize social justice.

Westbrook, Raymond. "Biblical and Cuneiform Law Codes." *Revue Biblique* 92 (1985): 247–264. Study that proves the descriptive character of ancient Near East and biblical law.

Westbrook, Raymond. *Studies in Biblical und Cuneiform Law.* Paris, 1988. Collection of studies that promote the hypothesis of an ancient Near East and biblical "common law."

Westbrook, Raymond, ed. *A History of Ancient Near Eastern Law,* 2 vols. Leiden, Netherlands, 2003. Basic collection of studies of all fields of ancient Near East legal history, with good bibliographies.

Eckart Otto (2005)

ISRAELITE LAW: PERSONAL STATUS AND FAMILY LAW

Biblical laws concerning personal status may relate to individuals as members of larger segments of society (slaves, poor, aliens, women), or they may govern relations between persons in a household, as in laws governing the treatment of slaves, and those stipulating the relations between members of the family. These categories are followed in the discussion below.

Personal Status. One of the essential characteristics of Israelite law is that there are no legally defined social classes among free Israelites. This contrasts with the laws of Hammurabi, which assume two classes of free men, the *awilum* ("man," the higher class) and the *mushkenum* (a poorer class, perhaps only partially free, partially in royal service), with notable differences in the treatment of each, as, for example, in the prescription of penalties for assault by a member of one group against a member of the other. In Israelite society the economic differences between rich and poor never resulted in differences in their treatment before the law. Nevertheless, there are clear distinctions between free Israelites and slaves, between men and women, between adults and minors, and, to a lesser extent, between Israelites and foreigners, and between king and subjects.

Slaves. Israelite law distinguishes between foreign and Israelite slaves and, to a lesser extent, between male and female slaves. Foreign slaves could be bought or, theoretically, acquired as prisoners of war. Once acquired, they were expected to be slaves permanently (*Lv.* 25:46). Israelites, however, could not be slaves permanently. The law allowed a free man to sell his children into slavery or to sell himself in order to escape poverty or debt (*Lv.* 25:39); he is required to sell himself if he cannot otherwise pay the penalty for having committed a robbery (*Ex.* 22:2). An Israelite would also be a slave if he or she were born to slaves (*Ex.* 21:4). But the male Israelite "slave" (almost certainly the meaning of *ʿeved ʿivri*) was to be set free in the Sabbatical (seventh) year unless he chose to make his status permanent, which decision was formalized in a ceremony in which his ear was pierced. According to *Exodus* 21:7–8, female slaves were not freed according to the laws that freed male slaves; this may be because a woman was sold as an *amah,* a term which may imply concubinage, for she was to be set free if her master's sons denied her matrimonial rights (*Ex.* 21:11). In *Deuteronomy* 15:12–17 female slaves were treated like male slaves, possibly an indication that by this time it was written (no later than the seventh century BCE) Hebrew women were not sold into concubinage. Foreign women could be taken as concubines in war; they could subsequently be divorced but not sold (*Dt.* 21:10–14). *Deuteronomy* 15:12–17 requires that freed slaves be given substantial provisions. According to *Leviticus* 25:40, debt-slaves were to be released in the Jubilee (fiftieth) year. Yet there is some indication in *Jeremiah* 34:8–16 that people in ancient Israel were not punctilious about obeying the laws regarding manumission.

Although a fully recognized institution, slavery was considered an undesirable state of existence. There was a death penalty for kidnapping free Israelites to use or sell as slaves (*Ex.* 22:15, *Dt.* 24:7). Israelites discovered to be slaves of non-Israelites were to be redeemed (*Lv.* 25:47–54), and fugitive slaves (Israelite or foreign) were not to be given up to their masters (*Dt.* 23:16–17). Israel was to ameliorate the condition by treating slaves well and treating Israelite slaves as if they were hired laborers (*Lv.* 25:40, 25:53). The law adjured these efforts on the slaves' behalf in the remembrance that the Israelites had been slaves in Egypt (*Dt.* 15:15) and that they continued to be the slaves of God, who had redeemed them (*Lv.* 25:55). Slaves were to be considered members of the household: They were to be circumcised (*Gn.* 17:23) and could thereupon eat the Passover sacrifice (*Ex.* 12:44); priest's slaves could eat of the holy offerings (*Lv.* 22:11). Slaves shared in sacrificial meals (*Dt.* 12:11–12, 12:18) and in feasts (*Dt.* 16:11, 16:14) and observed the Sabbath (*Ex.* 20:10, 23:12; *Dt.* 5:14–15). Slaves could be beaten; but if they died of a beating, their death would be avenged (*Ex.* 21:20), and if they were permanently injured, they were to be set free (*Ex.* 21:26–27). Slaves could acquire their own property and might ultimately be able to redeem themselves (*Lv.* 25:29).

The poor. Although there were no formal classes in Israelite society, there were distinctions between wealthy and poor. The "book of the covenant" stipulates that one should not impose usury on loans to the poor (*Ex.* 22:25), that cloaks taken as pledges be returned by sundown (*Ex.* 22:26–27; cf. *Dt.* 24:12–3), and that poverty not result in mistreatment before the law (*Ex.* 23:6). *Deuteronomy* further stipulates that a hired worker be paid immediately (*Dt.* 24:14–15) and prescribes the giving of charity to the poor even when the Sabbatical is near (*Dt.* 15:7–11), at which time the produce was to be left for the poor (*Ex.* 23:11). The seventh year was to some extent a time for the redistribution of wealth, in that debts were to be canceled (*Dt.* 15:1). The difference between rich and poor may have increased after the development of the monarchy, and the unequal distribution of wealth is an important theme of the prophets, who condemned the accumulation of capital by the rich.

Resident aliens. Immigrants to Israel and the original inhabitants of the land were considered *gerim* (sg. *ger,* "resident alien"). This designation also extended to the Levites, who had no tribal territory of their own, and, in the early days, to an Israelite outside the territory of his own tribe. *Gerim* are often grouped with the poor, widows, and orphans, who were to be allowed to collect fallen fruit and olives and glean at harvest time (*Lv.* 19:10, 23:22; *Dt.* 24:19–21) and to share in the tithe of the third year (*Dt.* 14:29) and the produce of the Jubilee (*Lv.* 25:6). The Israelites were to treat them well, remembering that they too had been *gerim,* in Egypt (e.g., *Ex.* 22:20); the laws that apply to them, thus, are generally found within law addressed to the free Israelites. *Gerim* had equal status with Israelites in civil and criminal law; in religious law the one recorded difference is the statement in *Deuteronomy* 14:21 that a *ger* may eat a dead carcass; *Leviticus* 17:15, however, forbids this. *Gerim* observed the Sabbath (*Ex.* 20:10, *Dt.* 5:14) and the Day of Atonement (*Lv.* 16:29); they offered sacrifices (*Lv.* 17:8, e.g.) and participated in religious festivals (*Dt.* 16:11, 16:14); and they observed the laws of purity (*Lv.* 17:8–13) and, if circumcised, could partake of the Passover sacrifice (*Ex.* 12:48–49).

Minors. A person was considered a fully adult member of Israel, counted as such in the census, at age 20 (*Ex.* 30:14); this was also the age above which the Israelites who had come out of Egypt were condemned to die in the desert without reaching the promised land (*Nm.* 14:29). At least in theory, children below that age were under the jurisdiction of their father, who could contract marriages for them and even sell them into slavery to pay his debts and to whom they owed allegiance. A rebellious son could be accused by his parents and thereupon stoned (*Dt.* 21:18–21). There are no specific regulations relating to minors. They were, however, treated as individual persons before the law in matters of punishment, for, unlike the ancient Near Eastern codes, biblical law did not allow the punishment of children for the crimes of their parents. For example, the death of a victim who was a minor son did not entail the execution of the minor son of the offender in biblical law as it did in Babylonian law (*Ex.* 21:31; cf. laws of Hammurabi 229f.).

The king. The king in Israel occupied a special intimate relationship with God: As God's appointed and anointed, his person was inviolable (*2 Sm.* 1:14), and cursing the king was tantamount to cursing God and was punishable by death (*2 Sm.* 19:21–22; *1 Kgs.* 21:10, 21:13). The Israelite king was not regarded as divine, and his close relationship with God, expressed as sonship (*2 Sm.* 7:14), was understood to arise from adoption (cf. *Ps.* 2:7) rather than divine paternity. The king was not a lawgiver but his role in the legal system was twofold: to uphold the laws in his capacity as judge and to obey fully the laws of God, who is Israel's only legitimate lawgiver. A king who disobeyed God's laws might lose all of his kingdom, as did Saul (*1 Sm.* 13:13) and Jeroboam (*1 Kgs.* 14:7–11), or part of his domain, as did David. The divine promise of a dynasty to the House of David made the rulers of the southern kingdom of Judah less concerned with the possibility of losing the throne. However, the deeds or misdeeds of a king could influence the fortunes of the land, for God could bring pestilence, military defeat (as under David, *2 Sm.* 24:13), or drought as a consequence or royal apostasy (as under Ahab, *1 Kgs.* 17:1).

Two passages deal with royal prerogative. In one, in his effort to discourage the people from establishing a monarchy, Samuel warns them that a king will take their sons as soldiers and their daughters as domestics, that he will tithe their property, and that he will appropriate their fields to give to his servants (*1 Sm.* 8:11–18). The other passage, *Deuteronomy* 17:14–20, sets limits to the grandiosity of the monarch, declaring that the king should not acquire many horses or wives or much wealth and that he should copy a book of the Law, keep it with him, and read it so that he learns to keep the law and not act arrogantly toward his people. Despite Samuel's warning that a king would appropriate fields, the kings did not simply commandeer property. David bought a threshing floor (*2 Sm.* 24:24); Omri bought the hill of Samaria (*1 Kgs.* 16:24); and even Ahab did not feel free to simply commandeer the vineyard of Naboth (*1 Kgs.* 21). Kings did, however, confiscate the land of those who had committed treason: David took Mephibosheth's land to give to Ziva after Ziva reported that Mephibosheth was planning to take the throne (*2 Sm.* 16:1–4) and Ahab set out to take Naboth's vineyard after Naboth was falsely convicted and executed for having cursed the king (*1 Kgs.* 21:13–16). Nor did the kings of Israel exercise unrestrained power over their subjects' lives: Jezebel made sure that Ahab was convicted and executed by the courts, and David maneuvered Uriah so that he would be killed in battle (*2 Sm.* 11)—neither king killed the inconvenient subjects outright.

Women. The laws present a picture of women as socially inferior to men. In terms of family life, a woman was expected to be subordinate first to her father and then, when married, to her husband. This subordination also found expression in economic matters. Women did not normally hold property, though they could inherit if there were no male heirs. This right of inheritance is presented in the Bible as a special divine decree to answer the needs of the daughters of Zelophehad (*Nm.* 27:1–11), which was soon modified to require daughters who inherited their father's property to marry within the "family of the tribe of their father" in order to keep the ancestral holdings in the paternal estate (*Nm.* 36:1–9). A comparison with near Eastern law shows that the laws of Lipit-Ishtar, written in Sumerian about 1900 BCE, contain a proviso whereby if a man had no sons, his unmarried daughters could inherit his property.

The inferior economic position of women is also indicated by the fact that when a person took a vow to dedicate members of his family (to temple service?) or to donate their monetary worth, an adult male was valued at fifty shekels and a woman at thirty (*Lv.* 27:3–4). It is also clear that women did not have equal right of disposition of the family property, for the male head of the household could annul the vows of women under his authority if he did so the day that he heard them (*Nm.* 30:5–8). Nevertheless, there is no hint that women could be considered thieves if they took or sold family property (as is the case in the Middle Assyrian laws, according to which the wife who took something and gave it to another is labeled a thief, and the receiver, a fence); on the contrary, the "woman of valor" of *Proverbs* 31 is particularly praised for her commercial ability and independent enterprise.

Some of the laws of sexual purity were applicable to both men and women. After sexual intercourse, both partners had to bathe in water and were considered impure until the evening (*Lv.* 15:16–18). In case of genital discharges (as in gonorrhea), both men and women were isolated until seven days after the discharge stopped and were then to bring an offering of two birds (*Lv.* 15:1–15, 15:25–29). In addition, women were instructed to remain isolated during menstruation (*Lv.* 15:19–24) and childbirth (*Lv.* 12:1–8). The impurity of menstruation was contagious: A man would become impure by having sexual relations with a menstruating woman (for which he could also expect divine punishment). Furthermore, he would become impure by touching her, sitting on a seat on which she sat, or eating food that she had cooked. This resulted in total isolation, although it is not known whether women were isolated in their own homes or spent the week in women's hostels (to which there is no textual reference). The "impurity" of the menstruating woman was not believed to bring danger to others (as is the case in many other cultures). Nevertheless, it became a metaphor for contamination (*Jer.* 13.20, *Lam.* 1.9, *Ez.* 36.17) and clearly was used to the denigration of women.

Despite the image portrayed by the legal documents, the biblical narratives indicate that women did not have a particularly weak position with respect to their husbands. The Shunammite woman entertained Elijah without prior consent from her husband (*2 Kgs.* 4:8–17), and Abigail commandeered large amounts of her husband's supplies to bring them to David (*1 Sm.* 25). The legal documents may, therefore, be affirming ideals rather than prescribing reality.

Women were generally expected to fit into a domestic niche, as wife and/or mother. However, there were also non-domestic roles. The queen had a powerful position, and might, as Jezebel and Athaliah did, exercise the power of the throne (*1 Kgs.* 18–19; *2 Kgs.* 9:30–37, 11:1–16); the position of queen-mother also seems to have had some importance, as may be inferred from the fact that Asa removed his mother Maacah from that position (*1 Kgs.* 15:13). "Wise women," who are mentioned in the time of David (*2 Sm.* 14, 20:16–22), may have been some sort of village elders. Deborah was a political and judicial leader (*Jgs.* 4–5); Deborah, Miriam (*Nm.* 12:2), Huldah (*2 Kgs.* 22:14–20), and Noadiah (*Neh.* 6:14) are recorded as prophetesses.

FAMILY LAW. This picture of family law is incomplete: The law corpora were not intended to be comprehensive, and frequently they omit matters that were well known in that culture or were not of concern to the writers. The picture can be filled in to some extent with details from the few narrative accounts of family life contained in the historical books. Important information also comes from the law collections of the ancient Near East, because it is clear that there was a common jurisprudential tradition in the area.

The Bible reveals two social systems. The first, the older system, is the extended family of the patriarchal period. The male head of the family had great power over his children, both male and female, in that he could contract marriages for them. Girls would leave their father's house in order to enter the dominion of the head of the family into which they were marrying. In the event of the husband's death, the woman stayed in her new family, either as the mother of children or, if there had been no children, by being given in marriage to her deceased husband's brother through the institution of the levirate. In such a system women were completely dependent on the kindness and attentiveness of the males in their lives and could affect events only by influencing them, as through persuasion or trickery. If a man were abusive, a woman had no recourse, and the principle of male disposition of women lent itself to such abuses as Lot's offer of his daughters to the men of Sodom (*Gn.* 19:8), the Levite's offer of his concubine to the men of Gibeah (*Jgs.* 19:24), and Jephthah's sacrifice of his daughter (*Jgs.* 11).

The other major social pattern is the monogamous family depicted in *Genesis* 3:6. This was the dominant pattern during the history of the biblical state (apart from the royal family, which continued the patriarchal pattern). At marriage, the girl moved from her father's house to that of her husband, and was thereafter under her husband's (rather than her father's or father-in-law's) domination. Polygyny was possible, but certainly not the norm. The ancient Near Eastern law collections also envision polygyny, or rather *bigyny* (having two wives), but severely limit the circumstances under which a man could take a second wife.

Marriage. The stages by which a marriage was contracted are not detailed in the biblical laws, but information is available, from both biblical narrative and the Near Eastern legal compilations, and the close agreement between these sources indicates that they reflect a biblical and Near Eastern reality. A preliminary agreement was reached between the fathers (or between the groom and the bride's parents), and then the groom or, frequently, the groom's father, paid a sum, the "bride-price," to the girl's father. There was also a dowry, though this does not seem to have been essential, and there was another custom, not universally observed, in which the father of the bride returned the bride-price to the couple at the completion of the marriage (unlike Lagan, who did not; *Gn.* 31:15). The bride-price was not a purchase, for the girl was not considered property, but it did guarantee the groom certain rights over the girl. At this point, once the bride-price was paid, the girl was "betrothed," which was an inchoate form of marriage. The marriage could still be canceled by either party (with appropriate financial penalties). Nevertheless, the bridegroom at that point owned the girl's sexual and reproductive capacity, and any sexual relations with a betrothed girl was considered adultery. The betrothed girl would stay in her father's house until the groom came to call for her (which could be a duration of years if she had been betrothed very young). At that point he would bring her to his house, and the marriage was complete.

Divorce. The details of divorce are also not clearly defined in the Bible. The laws in *Exodus* do not mention divorce; *Deuteronomy* does not describe the procedure but does mention the requirement of a bill of divorce (*Dt.* 24:1) and the stipulation of the two occasions on which the husband cannot divorce his wife: when he has acquired his wife after rape (*Dt.* 22:28–29) or when he has falsely accused his wife of not having been a virgin as a bride (*Dt.* 22:13–21). These laws prevented men, to some extent, from divorcing unloved brides who would have been at a great disadvantage in the Israelite socioeconomic system. Because the details are not provided, it is not known whether divorce was always at the prerogative of the husband; the laws of Hammurabi indicate that a woman could apply to the court for divorce (with the risk that her case would be investigated; and if she were found to have been a bad wife, she would be executed). There is evidence that early Jews on Elephantine (in Egypt) and in Palestine believed that the Bible allowed female-initiated divorce. In the postbiblical period it has been taken for granted that only husbands could initiate divorce proceedings.

Extramarital relations. A woman's sexual capacities were under the control of the head of the household. Girls were expected to be virgins at marriage. If a bridegroom accused his bride of not being virginal, their bedsheets were to be examined: if there was no blood on the sheets, she would be stoned; if she was proved innocent, her husband could never divorce her (*Dt.* 22:13–21). If a nonbetrothed girl was seduced, the seducer had to pay the full virgin's bride-price to her father, who decided whether to give her in marriage (*Ex.* 22:16–17). *Deuteronomy* provides that the seducer must pay the bride-price, take the girl as his wife, and never divorce her (*Dt.* 22:28–29); it is possible that the Deuteronomic rule concerned rape, but it may also have applied to any illicit sex with a virgin. The penalty for adultery was death for the married woman and her lover (*Lv.* 20:10); the extramarital relations of a married man were not considered adultery. If a man suspected his wife of adultery, he had the right to accuse her, and she would then undergo a solemn oath procedure (drinking the "bitter waters"). If, innocent, she suffered no ill effects, she could return to her husband. If she were guilty, she would ultimately be punished by God, who could cause her belly to swell and her thigh to fall; that is, some disaster to her fertility could occur, possibly a prolapsed uterus (*Nm.* 5:11–31). Even if she did not suffer these dire consequences and, moreover, demonstrated her fertility by later bearing a child, her husband could not be penalized for making a false accusation.

See Also Kingship, article on Kingship in the Ancient Mediterranean World; Menstruation.

Bibliography

Boecker, Hans Jochen. *Law and the Administration of Justice in the Old Testament and Ancient East.* Translated by Jeremy Moiser. Minneapolis, 1980.

Driver, G. R., and John C. Miles, eds. and trans. *The Babylonian Laws.* 2 vols. Oxford, 1952–1955.

Falk, Ze᾿ev. *Hebrew Law in Biblical Times: An Introduction.* Jerusalem, 1964.

Frymer-Kensky, Tikva. "The Strange Case of the Suspected Sotah." *Vetus Testamentum* 34 (January 1984): 11–26.

Vaux, Roland de. *Ancient Israel,* vol. 1, *Social Institutions.* 2d ed. Translated by John McHugh. London, 1965.

Whitelam, Keith W. *The Just King: Monarchical Judicial Authority in Ancient Israel.* Journal for the Study of the Old Testament Supplements, no. 12. Sheffield, 1979.

New Sources

Glass, Zipporah G. "Land, Slave Labor and Law: Engaging Ancient Israel's Economy." *JSOT* 91 (2000): 27–39.

Matthews, Victor H., Bernard Levinson, and Tivka Frymer-Kensky, eds. *Gender and Law in the Hebrew Bible and the Ancient Near East.* Sheffield, U.K., 1998.

Pressler, Carolyn. *The View of Women Found in the Deuteronomic Family Laws.* Beihefte zur Zeitschrift für die alttestamentliche Wissenschaft, no. 216. Berlin and New York, 1993.

Rattray, Susan. "Marriage Rules, Kinship Terms and Family Structure in the Bible." *SBLSP* 26 (1987): 537–544.

Rofé, Alexander. "Family and Sex Laws in Deuteronomy and the Book of Covenant." *Henoch* 9 (1987): 131–159.

Tappy, Ron E. "Lineage and Law in Pre-exilic Israel." *Revue Biblique* 107 (2000): 175–204.

Turnham, Timothy John. "Male and Female Slaves in the Sabbath Year Laws of *Exodus* 21:1–11." *SBLSP* 26 (1987): 545–549.

Westbrook, Raymond. *Property and the Family in Biblical Law.* Journal for the Study of the Old Testament Supplement Series, no. 113. Sheffield, U.K., 1991.

Tikva Frymer-Kensky (1987)
Revised Bibliography

ISRAELITE LAW: PROPERTY LAW

Like Israelite law in general, Israelite property law is marked by a concern for the rights of the individual. In particular an attempt is made, at least in theory, to safeguard the rights of the less fortunate (the poor, widows, orphans, etc.). As will be seen in this article, Israelite property law shares many points of contact, both in actual detail and in terminology, with property laws found elsewhere in the ancient Near East.

Conveyance of Property. As expressed ideally in the laws of the Hebrew Bible, the only transference of property in ancient Israel should be through inheritance. Every Israelite family was allocated a plot of land at the original apportionment, traditionally held to have been in the time of Moses and Joshua (*Nm.* 26:52–54, 33:54; *Jos.* 13–22), and it was believed that this ancestral plot should remain, if not in the family's possession, then at least in the possession of the clan. Thus there really should be no sale of land. Theological justification for this point of view is given in *Leviticus*: "But the land must not be sold beyond reclaim, for the land is Mine; you are but strangers resident with Me" (*Lv.* 25:23). This view regards God as owner of all property and the Israelites as only temporary tenants who may not buy or sell land. The duty of redemption and the institution of the Jubilee year (for both, see below) tend to corroborate this point of view, as does the complete absence in the Bible of laws concerning the renting of property.

Sale of land. While there is some evidence that this view of the inalienability of property was current in monarchical times (as can be gathered from Naboth's response to Ahab in *1 Kings* 21:3), there can be little doubt that the very emergence of the monarchy and the growth of the cities led to sweeping sociological changes as far as land ownership was concerned. Because of debt, many small farmers were forced to sell their farms to a new landed aristocracy. The situation became so serious that by the time of the eighth century the old Israelite society based on the small farmer had been destroyed. This was the situation that attracted the opposition of the prophets who denounced the land-grabbing practices of the new aristocracy. For example, Isaiah complains, "Ah, those who add house to house and join field to field, till there is room for none but you to dwell in the land!" (*Is.* 5:8). Similarly, Micah condemns those who "covet fields, and seize them; houses and they take them away. They defraud men of their homes, and people of their land" (*Mi.* 2:2).

Contracts of sale. The Bible records a number of property transactions, including Jacob's purchase of land at Shechem (*Gn.* 33:18–20), David's purchase of the threshing floor from Araunah (*2 Sm.* 24:24), Omri's purchase of the hill of Samaria, site of his future capital, from Shemer (*1 Kgs.* 16:24), and Boaz's purchase of a field from Naomi (*Ru.* 4:9). Two transactions are recorded in detail: when Abraham purchases the Cave of Machpelah (*Gn.* 23:3–20) and when Jeremiah, fulfilling his duty as near kinsman, redeems (purchases) the land in Anathoth from his impoverished cousin Hanamel (*Jer.* 32:6–15). In these two transactions there are elements that conform to standard ancient Near Eastern real estate documents.

In Abraham's purchase, one can discern the strict attention that is paid to ensure that the transaction conforms to all the details of ancient Near Eastern law. Thus, as required by early Mesopotamian law, two stages in the transfer of the property can be seen: payment of the price by the transferee to the transferor and taking possession of the property by the transferee. Hence it is twice said that the field was transferred to Abraham, once after Abraham weighed the silver for Ephron, that is, after payment of the price (*Gn.* 23:17), and then again after he buried Sarah (*Gn.* 23:20), that is, after he took possession of the field.

Another reflection of Mesopotamian law may be seen in the passage about Jeremiah's redemption of land that describes in detail the writing of a real estate contract (*Jer.* 32:6–15). Two copies of the deed of sale are made and witnessed, all "according to rule and law" (*Jer.* 36:11). Both are kept in the archives, but one is sealed as the official permanent record, and the other is unsealed for consultation when necessary. This reflects the Mesopotamian practice of enclosing a contract in a clay envelope that shows a copy of the same contract on the outside.

REDEMPTION OF HEREDITARY LAND AND THE JUBILEE YEAR. In accordance with the principle, expressed above, of the inalienability of land, a person's patrimony should ideally never be sold. However, should a man, due to economic straits, have to sell his land, then the law provides relief for its retrieval in two ways. First, the debtor's nearest family member is given the option of first refusal to the property (redemption). Second, in the absence of a family redeemer, the property ultimately reverts back to the debtor in the Jubilee year.

Redemption. Among the Israelites, the redemption of property from indigent family members was regarded not only as a moral obligation but also as a noble form of social action (*Lv.* 25:25–34). Two examples in the Bible of family members redeeming property (already mentioned) are Jeremiah redeeming his cousin's field at Anathoth (*Jer.* 32:6–9) and Boaz redeeming the field belonging to Naomi (*Ru.* 4:1–10). Note that in these cases the land is not restored to the impoverished kinsman but becomes the property of the redeemers. (For a contrary opinion, see Levine, 1983). Under the laws of the Jubilee, however, the land reverts back to the original owner. In both cases, the clan is protected from the alienation (loss) of the property.

The Jubilee year. The law of the Jubilee year (*shenat ha-yovel*) is set out in *Leviticus* 25. Three regulations concerning property ought to be mentioned here:

(1) Anybody who is forced to sell ancestral lands may reclaim them every fiftieth year, pointing to the principle that land cannot be irrevocably sold (*Lv.* 25:10, 25:13, 25:28).

(2) Because land cannot be irrevocably sold, what can be sold is only so many harvests (*Lv.* 25:15–16). Consequently every sale of land becomes a kind of lease for a number of years before the next Jubilee.

(3) Town houses, other than those belonging to Levites, are not subject to the Jubilee law. If they are not redeemed within one year of purchase, then the seller can never reclaim them (*Lv.* 25:29–30).

The terminology used to describe property that cannot be reclaimed is *tsemitut* ("beyond reclaim"), a term that has both semantic (*tsamit,* "beyond reclaim") and functional parallels in real estate documents from Ugarit in the thirteenth century BCE.

The original intention of the Jubilee law is much debated. There are two major schools of thought. One holds that in the Jubilee law the old tribal principle of inalienability of the land was affirmed, but because of the new social realities, the land laws were relaxed. Hence when the new economic order, which was not tied to the land or to patrimony, came into being, irrevocable sales in the cities were permitted (Weinfeld, 1980). The other school believes that the law is a later (postexilic) reworking of the Sabbatical year (on which all agree it is patterned) by the Priestly school. The principle here is that of *restitutio in integrum,* "a restoration to an original state": The land has to be returned to its original owner and thereby effect a restoration of the structure of Israelite society as it had been divinely ordained in ancient days (Noth, 1977).

Scholars also differ on the question of whether the Jubilee law was ever actually put into effect. The problem is aggravated because of the paucity of references in the rest of the Bible. The Jubilee is not referred to in any historical text, not even in postexilic ones. Outside of *Leviticus* 25, it is mentioned only in *Leviticus* 27:17–25 and briefly in *Numbers* 36:4 and *Ezekiel* 46:17. The protests of the prophets concerning land monopoly may indicate that the Jubilee law was not observed in preexilic times, and, because Nehemiah makes the people promise to observe the Sabbatical year but says nothing about the Jubilee year (*Neh.* 10:32), the same may probably be said for postexilic times as well.

RIGHTS OF INHERITANCE. The norm in ancient Israel was that a man's property was inherited by his sons, the firstborn receiving a double share (*Dt.* 21:15–17). In the event that a man had no sons, the line of inheritance was transferred through a scale of family members: from daughters to brothers to uncles and, ultimately, to the nearest kinsman of the deceased (*Nm.* 27:8–11). It is noteworthy that there is no provision in this list for a man's widow (see below). While the principle of primogeniture was the rule, there are numerous cases recorded in which the firstborn did not get the preferential share. Indeed, a significant motif in the narrative sections of the Bible is that the younger son eventually supplants the older both in cases where property is concerned (e.g., Ishmael and Isaac, Esau and Jacob, Reuben and Joseph, and Manasseh and Ephraim) and in cases of succession to the throne (e.g., Eliab and David and Adonijah and Solomon).

Rights of daughters. According to *Numbers* 27:1–11, daughters originally were not eligible to inherit any part of the family estate. Only after the case of the daughters of Zelophehad was provision made for daughters to inherit on a limited basis: They could inherit providing the deceased had no sons (*Nm.* 27:8) and they married within the clan, so that the patrimony would not be transferred to another tribe (*Nm.* 36:6–9). There is a reference in the *Book of Job* to Job's daughters inheriting alongside their brothers (42:15). However, because of the fact that *Job* is set in a non-Israelite locale, scholars generally do not regard this as standard Israelite practice.

Rights of widows. As already indicated, the line of inheritance in *Numbers* makes no provision for the widow, not even for the usufruct of her husband's property. This is unusual because in most ancient Near Eastern law collections (e.g., the Code of Hammurabi and Hittite and Assyrian laws) the widow is appropriately provided for. This omission is usually explained by the supposition that it was incumbent on the eldest son, who receives a preferential share of the estate, to provide for his mother and the unmarried female members of the family. It is also pointed out that widows, although not specifically mentioned in the line of inheritance, were provided with some degree of protection in the laws concerning the levirate.

The laws of the levirate state that should a man die without leaving a son, the brother of the deceased must marry the widow. The first child of this marriage is to be considered the heir of the deceased (*Dt.* 25:6). By this device, the estate of the deceased would be preserved, because his inheritance would pass to the child. However, there are indications that these laws were not widely observed (e.g., in the story of Judah and Tamar; see *Gn.* 38), and the penalties for nonobservance were insignificant (*Dt.* 25:7–10, *Ru.* 4:7–8). There was no incentive other than moral duty for the brother to perform what may well have been regarded as a most onerous and unwelcome task (Davies, 1981). For by assuming the duty, the brother not only lost his claim to his own brother's estate—because if there were no heir, he and his brothers would be next in line (*Nm.* 27:9)—but in certain cases performance of the levirate could actually be damaging to his own estate (by having to take responsibility for the widow as well as managing his dead brother's land). Performance of the levirate must therefore have been considered a magnanimous act by the brother: He was assuming obligations without necessarily deriving any corresponding benefits.

Childless couples. In the ancient Near East, having an heir was of paramount importance. Should a wife remain childless, her husband could marry another woman. To forestall this, the woman might give her own personal slave to her husband to bear the children for her. Children born of such unions were thought of symbolically as the wife's. Examples of barren women giving maids to their husband include Sarah, who gives Hagar to Abraham (*Gn.* 16:3), Rachel, who gives Bilhah to Jacob (*Gn.* 30:3), and even Leah, who, not barren but no longer bearing children, gives Zilpah to Jacob (*Gn.* 30:9–13). Children of such marriages had the same rights of inheritance as natural children (e.g., Ishmael in *Gn.* 17:18, 21:10).

Another method that was very common in the ancient Near East, and to which childless couples often resorted, was adoption. Although there are no laws of adoption in the Bible, the institution may underlie some of the patriarchal narratives, for example, in Abraham's complaint that because he was childless, Dammesek Eliezer would inherit from him. (*Gn.* 15:2–4).

Bibliography

There is as yet no work exclusively dealing with Israelite property laws of ownership and inheritance. Material on this subject can be garnered from general works on Israelite law and institutions. Still the classic among these is the chapter "Economic Life" by Roland de Vaux in his *Ancient Israel,* vol. 1, *Social Institutions,* 2d ed. (London, 1965), pp. 164–177. Particularly useful is the survey of Israelite law by S. E. Loewenstamm in his article "Law" in *The World History of the Jewish People,* edited by Benjamin Mazar, vol. 3, *Judges* (Tel Aviv, 1971), pp. 231–267.

On specific topics, Edward Neufeld's article "The Emergence of a Royal-Urban Society in Ancient Israel," *Hebrew Union College Annual* 31 (1960): 31–53, is helpful for understanding the changing economic conditions in Israel at the time of the monarchy. Baruch A. Levine's study "Late Language in the Priestly Source: Some Literary and Historical Observations," in *Proceedings of the Eighth World Congress of Jewish Studies . . . , Bible Studies and Hebrew Language* (Jerusalem, 1983), pp. 69–82, deals with the terminology of land tenure. Robert North's *Sociology of the Biblical Jubilee* (Rome, 1954) is a full-length treatment of most aspects of the Jubilee, which may be supplemented by the relevant sections in Martin Noth's *Leviticus* (Philadelphia, 1977), pp. 181–193, and in Moshe Weinfeld's *Mishpaṭ u-tsedaqah be-Yisra'el uva-'amim* (Jerusalem, 1985), pp. 104–106. Articles dealing with different aspects of rights of inheritance are Zafrira Ben-Barak's "Inheritance by Daughters in the Ancient Near East," *Journal of Semitic Studies* 25 (Spring 1980): 22–33; Eryl W. Davies's "Inheritance Rights and the Hebrew Levirate Marriage," *Vetus Testamentum* 31 (1981): 138–144, 257–268; and Tikva Frymer-Kensky's "Patriarchal Family Relationships and Near Eastern Law," *Biblical Archeologist* 44 (Fall 1981): 209–214.

New Sources

Heltzer, Michael. "About the Property Rights of Women in Ancient Israel." In *Shlomo: Studies in Epigraphy, Iconography,*

History and Archaeology in Honor of Shlomo Moussaieff, edited by Robert Deutsch, pp. 133–138. Tel Aviv-Jaffa, Israel, 2003.

Mbuwayesango, Dora Rudo. "Can Daughters Be Sons? The Daughters of Zelophehad in Patriarchal and Imperial Society." In *Relating to the Text: Interdisciplinary and Form-Critical Insights on the Bible*, edited by Timothy J. Sandoval and Carleen Mandolfo, pp. 251–262. London, 2003.

Ollenburger, Ben Charles. "Jubilee: 'The Land Is Mine; You Are Aliens and Tenants with Me.'" In *Reclaiming the Old Testament: Essays in Honour of Waldemar Janzen*, edited by Gordon Zerbe, pp. 208–234. Winnipeg, Man., 2001.

Sicherman, Harvey. "'Foremost in Rank and Foremost in Power:' Conflict over the First-born in Israel." *Jewish Bible Quarterly* 31 (2003): 17–25.

Westbrook, Raymond. *Property and the Family in Biblical Law.* Journal for the Study of the Old Testament Supplement Series, no. 113. Sheffield, 1991.

DAVID MARCUS (1987)
Revised Bibliography

ISRAELITE LAW: CRIMINAL LAW

Criminal law is a modern legal concept that relates to punitive actions taken by society when confronted by conduct that is considered socially harmful, morally offensive, or a threat to fundamental values or norms. Crimes are public offenses because the community, often acting through its authoritative representation, punishes the offender. The claims of any injured individual are submerged into the public actions of the community; society as a whole reacts as if it were the injured party. The punishment imposed on the criminal offender is often corporal: death, mutilation, or beating. Punishment might also be exile, imprisonment, or public humiliation. Sometimes monetary fines are imposed as well, but these go to the state, not to an injured individual.

In modern times, crimes are to be distinguished from torts, which belong to the category of civil law. Torts are offenses that society is satisfied to leave private. To redress a tort, the injured individual either acts alone or seeks the aid of kinfolk or powerful allies (self-help). In more developed societies, the king or government might help the individual enforce his claims. But the injured individual acting privately in civil law can exact only indemnity or monetary compensation from the offending party.

BIBLICAL CONCEPTS. The literary books that constitute the Hebrew Bible only partially reveal the legal practices of ancient Israelite society. One can, however, discern elements of criminal law among the stated commandments or prohibitions and casuistic legal formulations as well as in the details of narrative elements. All of this ancient evidence must be considered, although, to be sure, one does not know the extent to which it reflects the ancient realities or actual practices.

One cannot tell whether the ancient Israelites articulated a conscious distinction between criminal and civil law. Clearly, the lines between private and public offenses were drawn differently from those of modern, Western societies. Some offenses like battery (*Ex.* 21:18–19 [verse citations unless otherwise specified are to the Eng. version]) and theft (Masoretic text *Ex.* 21:37, 22:3), which today are criminal or public, were still considered to be private torts in the Bible. Conversely, offenses such as witchcraft (*Ex.* 22:18, *Lv.* 20:27, *1 Sm.* 28:3), adultery (*Lv.* 20:10; *Dt.* 22:20–24; *Ez.* 16:38–41, 23:45–49), and violation of the Sabbath (*Ex.* 31:14–15, 35:2; *Nm.* 15:32–36), which in modern secular societies are either private torts or nonactionable, were in the Bible considered serious public offenses or crimes.

There are no special Hebrew terms for *crime* and *criminal;* the same words, *sin, transgress,* and so forth, are used to describe both human offenses against other people and those against God. Religious and secular concerns are commingled, and most of the extant criminal laws are presented as God's own pronouncements. In this sense, all crimes are offenses against God. But one cannot assert that all sins are crimes. God may punish all sins, but the term *crime* is here reserved to describe only those public offenses that were punished by Israelite (i.e., human) society.

CRIMES AGAINST KING, PARENTS, AND CIVIL AUTHORITIES. The biblical narratives relate that the death penalty was meted out by the king for treason (*1 Sm.* 22:13–19; *1 Kgs.* 1:50–53, 2:23–24), regicide (*2 Sm.* 1:14–16, 4:9–12; *2 Kgs.* 14:5–6), cursing God or king (*2 Sm.* 19:21–23; *1 Kgs.* 2:46, 21:9–16; cf. *Ex.* 22:28, *Lv.* 24:10–16), "treasonous" prophecy against the state (*Jer.* 26:8–24, *2 Chr.* 24:19–21), and witchcraft (*1 Sm.* 28:9–10). These executions were carried out by the king's men; at other times, by mass actions such as stoning, preceded by a public trial. "Treasonous" prophecy was sometimes treated as a minor crime, punished by imprisonment, beating, or exile (*1 Kgs.* 22:13–27; *Jer.* 20:2, 32:2–3; *Am.* 7:9–13).

There was a stated duty to obey both parental and civil authority. The death penalty was prescribed for those who rebelled against the courts (*Dt.* 17:8–13) as well as against the ruler (*Jos.* 1:18). There are similar provisions for striking a parent (*Ex.* 21:15), cursing a parent (*Ex.* 21:17, *Lv.* 20:9), or rebelling against parental commands (*Dt.* 21:18–21).

SEXUAL OFFENSES. The death penalty was also prescribed for a variety of sexual offenses: adultery (in addition to the references cited above, see *Gn.* 20:3, 38:24; *Dt.* 22:22–24), sexual relations of a man with his father's or son's wife (*Lv.* 20:11–12) or with his mother or daughter (*Lv.* 20:14), rape of a married or even a betrothed woman (*Dt.* 22:25–27), bestiality (*Ex.* 22:19, *Lv.* 20:15–16), male homosexuality (*Lv.* 20:13), and prostitution engaged in by the daughter of a priest (*Lv.* 21:9).

IDOLATRY. The biblical laws reflect the long conflict with idolatry and polytheism that came to a climax at the end of the monarchy. The death penalty is prescribed for a variety of idolatrous acts (*Lv.* 20:2–5, *Dt.* 17:2–7) as well as for promoting idolatry to others (*Dt.* 13:1–5, 13:6–11, 18:20–22;

cf. the general slaughter of idolaters in *Exodus* 32:27). *Deuteronomy* 13:12–18 assigns the death penalty to an entire city and its livestock; all other possessions and goods were considered *ḥerem,* that is, to be dedicated to God and burned by fire (cf. *Ex.* 22:20).

Homicide and Manslaughter. The biblical response to homicide hovers between the spheres of private and public law. The relatives and allies of the victim retained the right to take action; society allowed them to slay the offender or to accept monetary compensation for the death of kin. Their choice of action, however, depended upon whether death was due to negligent homicide, involuntary manslaughter, or murder; the free or unfree status of the victim was also a factor to be considered. The negligent owner of the ox that fatally gored a person (*Ex.* 21:28–32) only owed compensation for a dead slave but was subject to the death penalty if the victim was a free man. The owner, however, was allowed to negotiate compensation in that case, too; but the ox was put to death in either case. A man who committed involuntary manslaughter could rightfully be slain by the relatives of the victim; but the civil authorities could intervene to grant the manslayer asylum (a form of exile) in a "city of refuge" (*Ex.* 21:12–13, *Nm.* 35:1–34, *Dt.* 19:1–13). The normal penalty for murder was death (*Gn.* 9:6, *Ex.* 21:14). In most cases, vengeance was taken by kin or allies of the victim (*Gn.* 4:11–15, *2 Sm.* 14:4–11; cf. the case of wrongful vengeance, *2 Sm.* 3:26–30, *1 Kgs.* 2:5–6). Public outrage could sometimes boil over into community action against the slayer (*Ex.* 21:14; *Dt.* 19:11–12; Jgs. 20:12–13; *Ez.* 16:38–41, 23:45–49).

The giving of compensation in cases of murder is strongly condemned in *Leviticus* 24:21 and *Numbers* 35:31–34 (cf. *Lv.* 24:18), because biblical law generally considers murder a public, not private, offense. Glimpses of that practice, however, may be seen in *2 Samuel* 21:1–4 and *1 Kings* 20:39. There is evidence that compensation was given for a number of other offenses where the death penalty was prescribed. Compensation for adultery is suggested in *Proverbs* 6:30–35 (in *Leviticus* 19:20–22 the slave status of the female obviates punishment). Compensation replaces the death penalty for breaking a solemn oath in *1 Samuel* 14:24–46 but not in *Judges* 11:30–40. One may also note the institution of *ʿerekh* ("monetary equivalents"), which could be offered in place of a dedicated object, including persons (*Lv.* 27:1–33), except in the case of *ḥerem* (*Lv.* 27:29). *ʿErekh* is offered in order to redeem potential victims of exile or death in *2 Kings* 23:35.

Theft. Even more than the response to homicide, the responses to theft hover between public and private law. Kidnapping and sale of a person was punished by death (*Ex.* 21:16, *Dt.* 24:7), but the theft of animals was settled by compensation (MT *Ex.* 21:37, 22:3). There are, nevertheless, hints of capital punishment in the outbursts of King David in *2 Samuel* 12:5–6 (cf. *1 Sm.* 26:16) and of Jacob in *Genesis* 31:32. A thief caught stealing during the day was not to be killed, but a thief caught in the night could be slain without penalty (*Ex.* 22:2). This same distinction, between daytime and nocturnal theft, also appears in the Babylonian laws from Eshnunna (modern-day Tell Asmar, Iraq; sections 12–13). The taking of property belonging to God (*ḥerem*) was punished by death (*Jos.* 7:1, 7:18–26).

Multiple Penalties. One encounters the actual commingling of private and public concerns in cases where a criminal penalty was imposed in addition to the payment of compensation. The man who brought a false charge of adultery against his betrothed wife was punished on two levels: The father of the woman received monetary compensation, and the man was beaten (*Dt.* 22:13–19). Beating could apparently also be added, as a criminal penalty, to the settlements reached in civil or private disputes (*Dt.* 25:1–3).

Talion. Battery, as noted above, was normally a private offense. But battery became a criminal or public matter if it caused serious, permanent injury or death (*Ex.* 21:20–23). The criminal penalties varied according to the injuries sustained; one finds repeated expression of this principle of *lex talionis* (*Ex.* 21:23–25, *Lv.* 24:19–20; for false accusation, see *Dt.* 19:15–21). The harshness of the talionic rules has led some interpreters, both ancient and modern, to question their literal application, especially in noncapital cases. One could compare the offering of compensation in place of the death penalty for homicide, discussed above. Yet there are instances where talion was literally imposed: the cutting off of thumbs and toes in *Judges* 1:6 and mutilation for battery leading to serious injury in *Deuteronomy* 25:11 (there is no exact talionic parity between male and female in this case).

There is some textual evidence that the harsher practices of earlier times were gradually modified or eased in later times. This is reflected, for example, in the discontinuation of the practice of assigning collective guilt for crimes committed by one individual (*Dt.* 24:16, *2 Kgs.* 14:5–6; cf. *2 Sm.* 21:1–9, *2 Kgs.* 9:24–26). Similarly, for the change in the treatment of the corpses of the executed, one may contrast *2 Samuel* 21:9–14 with *Deuteronomy* 21:22–23.

Criminal Law and Sacred Law. Divine as well as human punishment was expected for some criminal offenses, such as cursing a parent (*Dt.* 27:16), bestiality (*Dt.* 27:21), sexual relations of a man with his son's or father's wife (*Dt.* 27:20, 27:23), Sabbath violation (*Ex.* 31:14). These mark points of overlap between criminal and sacred law. Sacred law involved God and human, and it transcended the human agencies of court, judge, and so forth. It has been noted that the Decalogue (*Ex.* 20:2–17, *Dt.* 5:6–21) addresses areas of concern that are also treated in the criminal laws; similarly, *Leviticus* 18:8–23 promises divine punishment for offenses that are given societal penalties in *Leviticus* 20:10–21. (Jewish commentators of late antiquity came to consider offenses lacking societal penalty to be a category of lesser crime, punishable by beating; see Mishnah *Makkot* 3.1–10 and Maimonides' *Mishneh Torah,* Sanhedrin 18–19.)

BIBLIOGRAPHY

Diamond, A. S. *Primitive Law, Past and Present.* London, 1971. A good general historical introduction to ancient law.

Greenberg, Moshe. "Some Postulates of Biblical Criminal Law." In *Yehezkel Kaufmann Jubilee Volume,* edited by Menahem Haran, pp. 5–28. Jerusalem, 1960.

Haase, Richard. "Körperliche Strafen in den altorientalischen Rechtssammlungen." *Revue internationale des droits de l'antiquité* 10 (1963): 55–75. A comparative study of corporal punishments in ancient Near Eastern law collections. This work adds useful perspective to the consideration of biblical materials.

Jackson, Bernard S. "Reflections on Biblical Criminal Law." In his *Essays in Jewish and Comparative Legal History,* pp. 25–63. Leiden, 1975. Contains a thoughtful critique of earlier studies.

Phillips, Anthony. *Ancient Israel's Criminal Law.* Oxford, 1970. Useful for its bibliography and scope; Phillips approaches the subject from a viewpoint different from Diamond's.

New Sources

Chinitz, Jacob. "Eye for an Eye—An Old Canard." *Jewish Bible Quarterly* 23 (1995): 79–85.

Dyk, Peet J. van. "Violence and the Old Testament." *Old Testament Essays* 16 (2003): 96–112.

Falk, Ze'ev Wilhelm. *Hebrew Law in Biblical Times: An Introduction.* 2d ed. Provo, Utah, and Winona Lake, Ind., 2001.

Greenberg, Moshe. "More Reflections on Biblical Criminal Law." *Scripta Hierosolymitana* 31 (1986): 1–17.

Phillips, Anthony. "The Decalogue—Ancient Israel's Criminal Law." *Journal of Jewish Studies* 34 (1983): 1–20.

SAMUEL GREENGUS (1987)
Revised Bibliography

ISRAELITE LAW: STATE AND JUDICIARY LAW

In ancient Israel, laws were regarded as divinely ordained. The upholding of the laws, therefore, devolved upon the state, the religious establishment, and the people. Although the state could, presumably, impose sanctions for breaches of law, most cases were decided on the local level, and punishment was executed by the people as a whole (as in stoning), by the family of the victim (as in cases of murder), and by God.

JURISDICTION. There were several different strands of jurisdiction and authority in ancient Israelite law. Priests were in charge of religious matters, which included the important determination of secular and profane, pure and defiled (*Lv.* 10:10, *Ez.* 44:23; cf. *Dt.* 33:10). They oversaw the expiation of those misdeeds that could be expiated (*Lv.* 5:1–13; see below); they were involved in the trial of false witnesses; and they were members of the superior court envisioned in *Deuteronomy* (*Dt.* 17:8–13) and in the judicial reform under Jehoshaphat (*2 Chr.* 19:11). Alongside this priestly jurisdiction was a secular legal system that included the elders of the towns, the king, and judges and their officers.

Trials were usually held in the villages before the local elders. The typical procedure for such trials has been reconstructed by Donald A. McKenzie (1964). The adversaries would come before the elders (normally at the town gate) to lay out their case. The elders would take their seats; the defendant would be given a prominent place (*1 Kgs.* 21:9) with the plaintiff on his right (*Zec.* 3:1). The witnesses would be sitting and later would rise to bear testimony; if the case were very important, citizens would be summoned to attend (*1 Kgs.* 21:9). The plaintiff would state his case; then the defendant would state his, after which the witnesses would rise to bear witness (*Dt.* 19:16. *Ps.* 35:11). The elders would discuss the matter and rise to give their verdict (*Ps.* 3:8, 35:2), declaring the defendant innocent or guilty. In the case of a guilty verdict, they would then oversee an immediate punishment. The informality of such procedures is indicated in chapter 4 of *Ruth,* in which Boaz waits at the gate for his kinsman and then convenes a court with what seems to be a random ten of the elders of the town.

Alongside this local system was the jurisdiction of the kings. There is a strong tradition, shared by Israel and Mesopotamia, that the kings were responsible for upholding justice. The kings of Israel, however, were not lawgivers, for Israel's laws were held to come directly from God. They were, however, responsible for judging fairly, for seeing that justice was done, and for upholding the cause of the powerless. From the revelation of the Law, biblical narrative depicts Israel's leaders as arbiters of justice: Moses is seen as a judge (*Ex.* 18:13); the charismatic leaders of the premonarchical period (the "Judges") are said to have judged Israel; Samuel rode a justice circuit (*1 Sm.* 7:15–16); and both David and Solomon are shown making judicial decisions (*2 Sm.* 15:2, *1 Kgs.* 3:16–28). However, there is no instance in which a case was referred from the elders to the king, nor is there any case in which a king overrode the decision of a local court. The royal system seems to have operated separately and may have been open to any citizen.

The stories of the decisions of the king, moreover, do not show formal trials. In the two phony disputes that David "decided," the parables of Nathan (*2 Sm.* 12:1–6) and of the wise woman of Tekoa (*2 Sm.* 14:4–7), only one party is heard—an outsider (Nathan) or a pleader. Similarly, when the woman whose son Elisha had restored to life comes before the king to reclaim her lands, nothing is heard of or from whoever is presently working those lands (*2 Kgs.* 8:1–6). The impression one gets from these stories is that individuals would come to plead their case before the king in order to convince him—without formal process—and thus have the king become their advocate. It is in this sense that Absalom tells the Israelites coming to David for justice that they will find no "hearer" from the king (*2 Sm.* 15:2–6), that is, that the king will not grant them a sympathetic audience and act on their requests. Similarly, Josiah is said to have judged the case of the poor (*Jer.* 22:15–16). The only known case in which the king heard from both litigants is that of the two prostitutes before Solomon (*1 Kgs.* 3:16–28). The kings do not appear to have instituted trials at which they would preside. Even in the case of Naboth, where the charge was treason (cursing the king), Jezebel and Ahab did not preside: Jezebel went through the regular channels of the elders and nobles of the city in order to have Naboth convicted (by perjured testimony) (*1 Kgs.* 21:8–14).

At some time during the monarchy, most probably under Jehoshaphat, the system of trial by elders or by king was either augmented or superseded by the appointment of judges and their executives throughout the land and by the establishment of a superior court in Jerusalem to which the local elders and judges could bring cases that they could not decide. In the organization of the judiciary under Jehoshaphat (*2 Chr.* 19:5–11), the superior court had a dual composition: Matters relating to God were referred to the priest in charge, Amariah; the "king's matters," to Zebadiah. This system of installing royally appointed judges throughout the land, as well as a superior court to which they could refer, is also envisioned in *Deuteronomy* (*Dt.* 16:18–9, 17:8–13).

Decision Making. Israelite trials were based on an accusatorial system in which the plaintiff bore testimony against the defendant. In effect, there was no difference between an accuser and a witness. This system is inherently vulnerable to the subverting of justice by false witnesses. Two mechanisms act to minimize this danger: the requirement of two (male, free, Israelite) witnesses for conviction and the institution of retributive punishment for bearing false witness or making a false accusation. *Deuteronomy* 19:15–21, as the laws of Hammurabi in Mesopotamia, requires the false witness or accuser to receive the punishment that the accused would receive if convicted: payment of equivalent damages if the case was pecuniary, and forfeiture of life if the case was capital. This provision is a change from the Sumerian system, which prescribed a fine for false witnesses, but is similar to the laws of Hammurabi. These precautions were not entirely sufficient; they did not prevent Jezebel from finding two witnesses willing to commit perjury (*1 Kgs.* 21:10), nor the two elders in Susanna from perjuring themselves; the Pharisaic insistence on intense cross-examination of witnesses in capital cases was meant to increase the safeguards against false conviction by means of witnesses.

In the absence of two witnesses, the courts did not have the authority to decide a case. This is the reason for the indictment of someone who hears the *alah* (here a judicial curse meant to call out witnesses) but does not speak up (*Lv.* 5:1). Certain cases could not be left undecided, and recourse would be had to divine intervention, either through divination, an oracle, or an oath procedure. Two types of divination used in Israel were lots and the Urim and Tummim. Lots could be used to determine whether an accused person was guilty, as in the case of finding the culprit who took booty from Jericho (*Jos.* 7:14–15). They would not be sufficient to convict; for after Achan was selected by the lots, his tent was searched, and even after the goods were found, he was asked to confess (*Jos.* 7:22–25). The Urim and Tummim were in the hands of the priests and also functioned to determine whether an accused were guilty (*1 Sm.* 14:38–42). Neither method of divination is heard of after the full establishment of the monarchy. Solomon's willingness to decide the case of the two prostitutes (in which there were no witnesses) may be an indication that the monarchy now considered itself strong enough not to need divine legitimation for its decisions; the recorded feeling of the people was that "the wisdom of God was in him to do judgment" (*1 Kgs.* 3:28).

Decision by oracle is heard of in such cases as blasphemy (*Lv.* 24:12) and Sabbath offenses (*Nm.* 15:34); the accused would be put under guard until a divine decision was heard. Such matters may have continued to be decided by divine oracle even under the monarchy, for *2 Chronicles* records that people might come to the superior court for the argument of a case or for God's judgment (*2 Chr.* 19:8).

God could also be involved in the judicial process by means of an exculpatory oath by the accused, in which the accused placed himself under God's jurisdiction in affirming his innocence (*Ex.* 22:7–10, *Lv.* 5:20); the court would believe him under the supposition that he would not risk divine retribution for commiting a falsehood. A particularly solemn form of exculpatory oath is the procedure for the suspected adulteress (*Soṭah*): The woman accused by her husband stood "before the Lord" and drank a potion that contained dust from the sanctuary and the dissolved words of the oath in which she affirmed her innocence and her belief that the waters would not harm her if she was innocent but would cause infertility if she was guilty (*Nm.* 5:11–31). After drinking the potion, the woman was free to go and would "bear her penalty" (that is, she would await divine retribution). If she was guilty, "her belly shall distend and her thigh shall fall," which may indicate a prolapsed uterus and certainly indicates future infertility. If she was innocent, she would ultimately be totally vindicated by becoming pregnant, and her husband would not be penalized for making a false accusation. Although this procedure is sometimes called an ordeal, it differs from true ordeals in two ways: (1) no divine decision is immediately apparent and (2) God himself rather than the human court is expected to punish the woman.

Execution of the Decision. There are several different kinds of penalties. Fines might be exemplary, multiple payments such as the repayment of double, fourfold, or fivefold damages for theft (*Ex.* 22:1–4). Or, specific penalties could be prescribed, such as the guilt offering (*asham*) of a ram imposed for violating a slave woman designated to marry (*Lv.* 19:20–21) or the payment of the standard bride-price to the father of a deflowered virgin (*Ex.* 22:16–17). In certain cases the amount of the penalty is determined by the family of the injured party. Thus, after an ox had gored someone to death, its owner was to pay whatever was demanded of him in order to ransom his own life (*Ex.* 21:30), and after having caused a woman to miscarry, one was to pay whatever the woman's husband and the judge decided (*Ex.* 21:22).

There is little corporal punishment in the Bible. The most common instance of it is scourging, or flogging, limited by law to forty lashes (*Dt.* 25:1–3). A woman who touched a man's genitals while protecting her husband in a fight could have her hand cut off (*Dt.* 25:11–12). This was the only specific mutilation prescribed in the Bible, in contrast to Babylonian and Assyrian law (e.g., Laws of Hammurabi 192, 193, 194, 205, 218, 282; Middle Assyrian Laws 4, 5, 8, 9, 15, 18, 20, 44, 52).

A question is raised by the law of talion (*lex talionis*) that requires equal retaliation in cases of assault and battery (*Lv.* 24:19–21). Given the lack of mutilation practiced in Israel, it has been suggested that talion is a statement of judicial principle rather than a concrete description of practice and that the actual penalty was the payment of compensation money computed by talionic principles. This is almost certainly the case with the other two statements of the talionic principle in the Bible, the accidental injury to a pregnant woman (*Ex.* 21:23–25) and the penalty for false witnesses (*Dt.* 19:19–21): If there were no judicial penalties of mutilation, then the mention of talionic mutilations must have been a judicial maxim to express the principles of equivalent retaliation. Equivalent retaliation stopped with the accused. In Mesopotamia the child or wife of a perpetrator could be punished for a misdeed against the child or wife of the injured party. In Israel this was not allowed (*Ex.* 21:31, *Dt.* 24:16), although a belief that God would punish and reward the children (*Ex.* 20:5) was held until the days of Jeremiah and Ezekiel (*Jer.* 31:30, *Ez.* 18).

Capital Punishment. Death by burning is prescribed for two sexual offenses (*Lv.* 20:14, 21:9, cf. *Gen.* 38:24). Death by the sword is prescribed for an idolatrous city (*Dt.* 13:15; cf. *1 Kgs.* 18:40, *2 Kgs.* 23:30). The most common penalty mentioned in capital cases is stoning. The stoning was to be held before the judges; the witnesses cast the first stone, followed by the rest of the people (*Dt.* 17:7), who were thus collectively acting to rid themselves of the guilt of the misdeed. There is a difference of opinion as to whether stoning was in fact the common mode of execution (Phillips, 1970), or whether it is specifically mentioned only for those cases in which it was used, cases in which there had been a major offense against the hierarchical order of the universe (J. J. Finkelstein, 1981; Tikva Frymer-Kensky, 1983).

In cases of murder, the agent of execution was the "blood redeemer" (*go'el ha-dam*), who was obligated to avenge the murdered party. He was to chase the culprit, who could escape to one of the cities of refuge, set up to be places where a person who had accidentally killed someone could go for a trial. If the person was found to be an intentional murderer, he was handed over to the blood redeemer; if found to be an accidental murderer, he stayed in the city of refuge (a kind of quarantine) until the death of the priest. If he left before that, the blood redeemer was charged with executing him. The reason for this law is explicit: The blood of the slain pollutes the Land of Israel; thus accepting money as restitution for murder or even allowing an accidental murderer to leave the city of refuge would pollute the Land of Israel (*Nm.* 35:9–34, *Dt.* 19:1–12). The blood redeemer is normally taken to mean the closest male relative of the slain, whose job it would be to protect the family. Anthony Phillips (1970), however, has argued that the blood redeemer was, on the contrary, the appointed representative of the local court, whose job it was to carry out the court's instructions.

Expiation. Despite the fact that Israel's law had a fundamentally religious base, there was little expiation in the legal system. Someone who ignored the charge for witnesses and did not come forth, who swore a false oath, or who touched impurity might bring a conscience sacrifice, the *asham* (*Lv.* 5:1–13, traditionally translated as "guilt offering"). In the case of the discovery of a murdered corpse when the murderer cannot be found, the elders of the city were to perform the ritual of the heifer whose neck is broken, attesting to their lack of culpability, averting the blood pollution of their land, and expiating the failure of the legal system (*Dt.* 21:1–9).

Bibliography

Falk, Ze'ev. *Hebrew Law in Biblical Times: An Introduction.* Jerusalem, 1964.

Finkelstein, J. J. *The Ox That Gored.* Transactions of the American Philosophical Society, vol. 71, pt. 2. Philadelphia, 1981.

Frymer-Kensky, Tikva. "Tit for Tat: The Principle of Equal Retribution in Near Eastern and Biblical Law." *Biblical Archeologist* 43 (Fall 1980): 230–234.

Frymer-Kensky, Tikva. "Pollution, Purification and Purgation in Biblical Israel." In *The Word of the Lord Shall Go Forth,* edited by Carol L. Meyers and M. O'Connor. Winona Lake, Ind., 1983.

Frymer-Kensky, Tikva. "The Strange Case of the Suspected *Soṭah.*" *Vetus Testamentum* 34 (January 1984): 11–26.

Greenberg, Moshe. "Crimes and Punishments." In *The Interpreter's Dictionary of the Bible,* edited by George A. Buttrick, vol. 1, pp. 733–744. Nashville, 1972.

McKenzie, Donald A. "Judicial Procedure at the Town Gate." *Vetus Testamentum* 14 (1964): 100–104.

Milgrom, Jacob. *Cult and Conscience: The Asham and the Priestly Doctrine of Repentance.* Leiden, 1976.

Phillips, Anthony. *Ancient Israel's Criminal Law: A New Approach to the Decalogue.* Oxford, 1970.

Ploeg, J. P. M. van der. "Les anciens dans l'Ancien Testament." In *Lex Tua Veritas: Festschrift für Hubert Junker,* edited by Heinrich Gross and Franz Mussner, pp. 175–191. Trier, 1961.

Ploeg, J. P. M. van der. "Les juges en Israel." *Populus dei: Studi in honore del card. Alfredo Ottaviani per il cinquantesimo di sacerdozio,* vol. 1, pp. 463–507. Rome, 1969.

New Sources

Ball, Milner S. *Called by Stories: Biblical Sagas and Their Challenge for Law.* Durham, N.C., 2000.

Carmichael, Calum M. "Biblical Laws of Talion." *Hebrew Annual Review* 9 (1985): 107–126.

Fitzpatrick-McKinley, Anne. *The Transformation of Torah from Scribal Advice to Law.* Journal for the Study of the Old Testament Supplement Series, no. 287. Sheffield, U.K., 1999.

Friedmann, Daniel. *To Kill and Take Possession: Law, Morality, and Society in Biblical Stories.* Peabody, Mass., 2002.

Hanks, Gardner C. *Capital Punishment and the Bible.* Scottdale, Pa., 2002.

Knoppers, Gary N. "The Deuteronomist and the Deuteronomic Law of the King: A Reexamination of a Relationship." *ZAW* 108 (1996): 329–346.

Rofé, Alexander. "The Laws of Warfare in the Book of Deuteronomy: Their Origins, Intent and Positivity." *JSOT* 32 (1985): 23–44.

TIKVA FRYMER-KENSKY (1987)
Revised Bibliography

ISRAELITE RELIGION. In 1979 two silver amulets dating to the late seventh to sixth centuries BCE were discovered in a burial cave in Ketef Hinnom, outside of Jerusalem. The smaller of these amulets reads: "Blessed be [he or she] by Yahweh, the helper and dispeller of evil. May Yahweh bless you (and) protect you, and may he cause his face to shine upon you and grant you peace." The larger amulet mentions "the covenant" and Yahweh's "graciousness to those who love him," refers to Yahweh as "our restorer," and concludes with the benediction: "May Yahweh bless you and protect you, may he cause his face to shine. . . ." This blessing is a slight variant of the priestly benediction in *Numbers* 6:22.

These two amulets, worn by the deceased, provide an entry into a number of aspects of ancient Israelite religion. They show the interplay between family religion and state religion, linking domestic burial practice with the religion of the Jerusalem Temple, where priests recited the priestly benediction during the sacrificial rites; they show how domestic religion placed Yahweh in the protective role of helper and dispeller of evil; they show the importance of the covenant to individual Israelites; and they suggest that the dead too belong to Yahweh's covenant and require Yahweh's protection. Some of these ideas were rejected by various biblical writers, particularly the aspects linked to magic and the cult of the dead. Nonetheless, the amulets provide a countervoice, testifying to authentic Israelite belief and practice in the late preexilic era. They provide a perspective onto the complex weave of Israelite religion, involving the nature of God, the relationship between God and humans, the functions of the covenant, the Temple, and sacrifice, the varieties of religious practice and belief, and the status of sacred texts. Each of these topics was subject to controversy, negotiation, and reinterpretation during the course of Israelite history.

GOD AND THE GODS. Yahweh (יהוה) is the proper name of the God of ancient Israel. He is also called El, literally "God," and Elohim, also meaning "God," although the latter was originally a plural noun meaning "gods, pantheon." By a remarkable act of theological reduction, the complex divine hierarchy of prior polytheistic religion was transformed into the authority of a sole high god. However, Yahweh was not the only god in Israelite religion. Like a king in his court, Yahweh was served by lesser deities, variously called "the Sons of God," "the Host of Heaven," and similar titles. This host (the word also means "army") sometimes fought battles of holy war (cf. the battle of Jericho, where Joshua meets the divine "captain of Yahweh's army"; *Jo.* 5:13–15) and were also represented as stars (*Jgs.* 5:20: "the stars fought from heaven;" also *Jb.* 38:7). These lesser deities attend Yahweh in heaven, as in the prophet Micaiah's vision: "I saw Yahweh seated on his throne with all the Host of Heaven standing beside him, to his right and left" (*1 Kgs.* 22:19). At times they are also equated with the gods of other nations: "He established the boundaries of the nations according to the number of the Sons of God" (*Dt.* 32:8 with Qumran and the Septuagint; similarly, *Dt.* 4:19). A third category of divine beings (after Yahweh and the Sons of God) consisted of messenger gods, called angels. The angels carry Yahweh's messages to earth, as illustrated by Jacob's dream vision of the angels ascending and descending the celestial staircase that links heaven and earth (*Gn.* 28:12). In late biblical books, the Sons of God and the angels merge into a single category and proliferate: In Daniel's vision of the heavenly court, "thousands upon thousands serve him" (*Dn.* 7:10).

The tripartite hierarchy of the divine world—Yahweh, the Sons of God or Heavenly Host, and the angels—derives from the earlier structure of Canaanite religion. According to the texts from Ugarit (c. 1200 BCE) and other Canaanite sources, the high god of the Canaanite pantheon was El, whose wife, the mother of the gods, was Asherah. The other gods of the pantheon are collectively called the Children of El and are subservient to El's authority, although some—particularly Baal, Anat, Astarte, and Resheph—are prominent deities. A third category consists of servants and messenger gods. This hierarchy is structurally equivalent to that of Israelite religion, with some striking differences. On the level of high god, El seems to have merged with Yahweh, who absorbs El's name and has many of his attributes. Asherah in Israelite religion becomes the name of a sacred pole or tree in local Yahwistic shrines, although there are hints in some texts that she was worshiped as a goddess in some times and places. The second tier of deities, the Children of El *(bn ʾil),* have the same title in Israelite religion (Sons of God; *bene ʾel* or *bene haʾelohim),* but in Israelite religion have been demoted into relatively powerless beings. Resheph, for example, rather than an independent god of war and disease, seems to become a personification of disease, accompanying Yahweh's awesome march into battle (*Hb.* 3:5). Yahweh replaces or absorbs the functions of all of the active gods of the pantheon, hence like El, he is the beneficent patriarch and judge; like Baal, he is the divine warrior; and like Asherah and her daughters, he dispenses "blessings of breast and womb" (*Gn.* 49:25). Israelite religion, like Israel's language and culture, is a child of the Canaanite or West Semitic world.

One of the distinctive features of Israelite religion is the absence of a wife or consort for Yahweh. Yahweh is a male god, but he is not depicted as a sexual being. It is possible, although far from certain, that some local traditions may have rectified this situation. Several inscriptions from the eighth century invoke blessings "by Yahweh and his asherah." The grammar of these invocations most likely indicates that "his asherah" refers to a sacred pole or tree rather than a goddess, because a proper name cannot have a possessive suffix, and sacred poles or trees called asherahs are mentioned in the Bible as features of local shrines. However, Asherah is El's wife in Canaanite religion, and she might be Yahweh's wife in these local cults, perhaps represented by the sacred pole or tree. In several instances in the Bible, the name Asherah clearly refers to a goddess: According to the *Book of Kings,* King Asa's mother made a statue of Asherah, which King Asa destroyed (*1 Kgs.* 15:13); 400 prophets of Asherah were supported by Queen Jezebel (*1 Kgs.* 18:19; lacking in the Septuagint, the Greek translation of the Hebrew scriptures); and a statue of Asherah was placed in the Jerusalem Temple by King Manasseh and later destroyed by King Josiah (*2 Kgs.* 21:7; 23:6). Whether these statements are historically accurate or whether in some cases they are false accusations against "wicked" royalty (like Jezebel and Manasseh), they nonetheless clearly attest that Asherah could be understood as the name of a goddess. The symbolism of the sacred pole or tree called the asherah or asherim (the plural form is masculine in gender) remains suggestive but obscure. It may be a depersonalization of Asherah into a religious symbol of Yahweh worship, perhaps representing an attribute of Yahweh's divinity such as fertility or abundance (in the metonymy of the tree); it may signify that the goddess Asherah was worshiped alongside Yahweh; or perhaps more likely, the sacred pole or tree was subject to differing interpretations, with a floating symbolic register.

Early biblical texts seem to acknowledge that gods of other nations exist (*Dt.* 32:8). The nations each have their own god, but Yahweh is Israel's god. This seems to be the earliest sense of the first commandment, "You shall have no other gods beside me" (*Ex.* 20:3). Yahweh is Israel's high god, who delivered his people from slavery and oppression, and therefore he is entitled to Israel's worship and loyalty. Moreover, Yahweh is superior to the other gods, as proclaimed in the early hymn, the Song of the Sea: "Who is like you among the gods, O Yahweh? Who is like you, glorious in holiness, awesome in praise, working wonders?" (*Ex.* 15:11). Other national gods exist, but Yahweh is Israel's god and he is the greatest god. The worship of Yahweh functions as a unifying agent of Israelite culture and religion. This type of worship is sometimes called monolotry (the worship of one god without denying the existence of others) or henotheism (belief in one god without denying the existence of others). A more thoroughgoing monotheism, which denies the existence of other gods, is a product of the prophetic and Deuteronomistic critique during the eighth through the sixth centuries BCE.

In addition to the major categories of divine beings, the human dead are also referred to as gods. When King Saul has a sorceress summon the ghost of the prophet Samuel, she calls the ghost an Elohim (*1 Sm.* 28:13). Elsewhere the shades of the dead are called gods (*Is.* 8:19) and "holy ones" (*Ps.* 16:3). Although divination by consulting the shades of the dead is prohibited in *Deuteronomy* 18:11, it may have been a fairly common local practice. Statues called teraphim were also used for divination (*Ez.* 21:26; *Zec.* 10:2) and are once referred to as gods (*Gn.* 31:30). These were probably statues of dead ancestors who bestowed blessings on their descendants and could be invoked for divination. These practices indicate that the dead were not connected to the world of the gods as full-fledged deities, but as shadowy intermediaries between the world of the living and the divine realm. The world of the dead was the subterranean Sheol, not in heaven where Yahweh and his divine entourage dwelled, but somehow their shadowy existence was in some respects divine and included godlike foresight into the future.

On a different level the human king functioned as a quasidivine intermediary between the divine and human realms. The king is at times referred to as the son of God (*Ps.* 2:7; 2 *Sm.* 7:14) and the firstborn of God (*Ps.* 89:28), and in one text the king seems to be addressed as Elohim (*Ps.* 45:7). The language of divine kinship in these texts indicates that God adopts the reigning king as his earthly son, which corresponds to the king's role as God's chosen representative or intermediary on earth. As portrayed in the royal psalms, the king is the earthly guarantor of cosmic order, defeating the enemies—both human and cosmic—and establishing harmony and peace. The king partakes of the divine through the sacral office of kingship, which ideally ensures "abundant authority and peace without end" (*Is.* 9:6). In the Second Temple period (536 BCE–70 CE), in the absence of a reigning king, the concept of the king as a quasidivine intermediary stimulated the expectation of a royal messiah, the future Davidic king, hedged with divinity, who will defeat chaos once and for all.

HUMANS AND GOD. Aside from the special status of the king, humans have varying kinds of relationship with God. In the priestly creation account of *Genesis* 1, God creates humans "in the image of God," a phrase that suggests a democratization of the king's status. As God's earthly image, humans are collectively to rule the earth and all of its creatures (*Gn.* 1:26–28). Humans—including male and female—are god-like mediators between God and the world. To be created in "the image of God" also implies a spiritual, moral, or intellectual component that transcends ordinary creaturely existence. Humans are more than animals but less than gods, and they are the pinnacle of creation (see also *Ps.* 8:4–9). A less exalted status is given to humans in the Yahwistic (denoted as J) creation myth in the Garden of Eden (*Gn.* 2:4–3:24). There the first human is created as a laborer, "to work and protect" the garden (*Gn.* 2:15). This status is similar to that in older Mesopotamian creation myths, in which humans are created to be the laborers of the gods. In the course of the Garden of Eden story, the humans become "like gods, knowing good and evil" (*Gn.* 3:5, 22), gaining a god-like aspect comparable to the lofty status of humans in *Genesis* 1. In this story the desire to be god-like leads to higher knowledge and self-awareness, but also leads to pain, suffering, hard agricultural subsistence, and consciousness of death, that is, the ordinary fare of human existence. Unlike the original situation in paradise, the human world is limited by pain and mortality, but it is also enriched by a god-like knowledge of good and evil. This divine quality includes moral discernment of good and evil and, through the semantic range of the verb "to know," sexual maturity ("they knew that they were naked," *Gn.* 3:7; "the man knew his wife, Eve," *Gn.* 4:1). Human existence contrasts with the perfection of paradise or divine existence, yet humans have some degree of divinity, or likeness to divinity.

Humans, however, also have a propensity toward evil. This flaw gives rise to various problems and solutions. In *Genesis* 6, God responds to the collective problem of human evil by sending the flood. In both versions of the flood story (the Yahwistic and priestly versions, edited together in *Gn.* 6–9), God saves the sole righteous man and begins a new era of human existence. This new era, according to the Priestly version, is distinguished by the first laws and covenant (*Gn.* 9:1–17), establishing clear limits to human violence, particularly the slaughter of animals and murder. The Noachic covenant and its laws, which apply to all earthly creatures, are a first step toward the great promulgation of laws and covenant to Israel at Mount Sinai. In the Yahwistic version of the flood, human evil is not decisively controlled, rather Yahweh resigns himself to the persistence of human evil, promising that despite their corrupt nature he will never again destroy humans (*Gn.* 8:21). In the Yahwistic narrative the problem of evil is relieved by Yahweh's compassion for humans, and later by his election of Abraham, who will teach justice and righteousness to his children, and through whom all the earth's peoples will be blessed (*Gn.* 12:1–4; 18:19).

The human propensity for evil creates the need for religion, which, through its stories, rites, and laws, teaches morality, regulates behavior, and restores a beneficial relationship with God and the cosmos. People—including Israelites and foreigners—can choose to disobey the religious norms, in which case God will send destruction (e.g., Sodom and Gomorrah). But there remains a mutuality of interest in the continuance of human existence: God desires justice and morality, and from Israel he also desires worship, and in return he grants his blessing. God and humans are linked in a relationship of mutual benefit, regulated by a divinely sanctioned cosmic order. In situations in which this cosmic order has been disrupted or destroyed, God's relationship with Israel, or with humans generally, becomes a critical problem.

FAMILY RELIGION AND STATE RELIGION. The worship of God took different forms in various social contexts in ancient Israel. The most notable distinction is between family religion and state religion. In the domestic domain of family religion, portrayed most directly in the patriarchal narratives, Yahweh is the "god of the father" who provides blessings of offspring, abundance, healing, and protection for members of a household or lineage. The worship of the "god of the father" and the reverence for the lineage ancestors were complementary features of family religion. Problems of infertility (e.g., Sarah, Rebekah, Rachel), marriage (e.g., Isaac, Jacob), inheritance (e.g., Ishmael and Isaac, Jacob and Esau), family strife (e.g., Jacob and Laban, Joseph and his brothers), and famine (e.g., Abraham, Isaac, Jacob) are occasions when family religion becomes prominent in these stories and in Israelite domestic life.

Archaeological excavations shed additional light on family religion. Many Israelite houses had domestic shrines featuring incense altars and cultic stands, where incense and food offerings were made, probably accompanied by prayers and vows. Also common in these domestic shrines were bowls of sheep or goat knuckles, which were used for divination, and clay figurines (including females with prominent breasts, horses with male riders, birds, and rattles), whose function is unknown. These clay objects presumably figured in family religion, although it is unclear whether they were deities, ancestors, the worshiper, or had other functions or uses. Ethnographic parallels indicate that such inexpensive figurines could be used in a variety of ways: as religious icons, decorations, or even toys. It is possible that the female figurines represented major or minor goddesses in Israelite religion. A variety of other religious practices were at home in family religion, including memorial offerings to the dead (*Ps.* 16:3–4; *Dt.* 26:14), divination by means of statues of the ancestors, and protective magic (cf. the mortuary amulets from Ketef Hinnom and the biblical references to male and female sorcerers).

The worship of gods other than Yahweh is occasionally attested in domestic contexts in the biblical text, such as the family worship of the Queen of Heaven (probably a local form of Ishtar or Astarte; *Jer.* 7:17–18; 44:15–25); women planting ritual gardens and mourning for Adonis, Tammuz, or Baal (*Is.* 17:10–11; *Ez.* 8:14; *Zec.* 12:11); and the offering of incense to the Host of Heaven on rooftops (*Jer.* 19:13; *Zep.* 1:5). The latter, at least, is the worship of Yahweh's heavenly entourage. It is possible that family religion also included a ritual of passing children through fire as a rite of initiation or redemption, perhaps called a *molech* offering (or *mulk*) or an offering to the god Molech (e.g., *Dt.* 18:10; 2 *Kgs.* 23:10). This may have been a symbolic attenuation of an older rite of child sacrifice. Many of the practices of family religion were deplored by various biblical writers (e.g., *Dt.* 18:9–11), and they were officially anathematized by King Josiah (2 *Kgs.* 23).

State religion was rooted in the public structures of political authority and descends from the prestate tribal religion. In the early period, tribal and pan-tribal identity was activated most directly during pilgrimage festivals and military crises. For example, the Song of Deborah (*Jgs.* 5) describes the call of the tribes to war (not all of them come) and depicts Yahweh as the mighty divine warrior and savior of the tribal confederation. The Song of the Sea (*Ex.* 15), perhaps recited at tribal festivals, describes Yahweh as the mighty warrior and national savior in his triumph over Pharaoh's army at the Exodus and his delivery of his people to the Promised Land. Jerusalem became the royal capital and the center of the state religion for the southern kingdom of Judah, whereas Dan and Bethel were the official state shrines for the northern kingdom of Israel. State religion regulated the system of sacrifices offered at the central shrines, which supported the guild of official priests. The king was the patron of the state religion, which in turn provided the charter for his sacral authority; the king maintained the Temple (or, in the northern kingdom, the official shrines), appointed the chief priests, and at times presided over the sacrificial ceremonies (e.g., *1 Kgs.* 8:62–66). The Jerusalem Temple and the dynasty of Davidic kings were symbolically linked, as illustrated by the proximity and names of the two institutions: the Temple was the House of Yahweh (*bet yhwh*), which stood next to the somewhat larger palace of the royal dynasty, the House of David *(bet david).* The centralization of worship at the Temple, promulgated by Kings Hezekiah and Josiah, concentrated the sacrificial tribute in Jerusalem and exalted and extended the authority of the royal house.

It is useful to distinguish a third type or level of religious worship, local religion, which mediates between family and state religion. Regional shrines served local families and lineages, functioning as a unifying feature in Israelite society. There is evidence that Yahweh was worshiped in various local manifestations: He was invoked in blessings as "Yahweh of Samaria" and "Yahweh of Teman" in eighth-century inscriptions from Kuntillet ʿAjrud, and Absalom speaks of his vow to "Yahweh in Hebron" (*2 Sm.* 15:7). These local manifestations of Yahweh were no doubt conceived as the same god, but worshiped with local variations and accents. The local shrines—and the local priests who gained their living by the sacrifices offered there—were anathematized by the prophets and *Deuteronomy.* The exhortation "Hear O Israel, Yahweh our God, Yahweh is one" (*Dt.* 6:4) may be a criticism of the multiplicity of Yahwehs worshiped at the local shrines and an affirmation of Yahweh as worshiped in the Jerusalem Temple. In some respects state religion was a version of local religion, because Yahweh in Zion is a local manifestation of Yahweh who becomes the authorized state god, a jealous god inimical to the local cults.

COVENANT AND LAW. Ancient Israel called itself *ʿam yhwh* (the people of Yahweh; *Jgs.* 5:11; *1 Sm.* 2:24; *2 Sm.* 1:12). This term implies a relationship of kinship or fealty between the people and their god. In many biblical texts, particularly from the eighth century BCE and later, this relationship is called a *berit* (covenant, pact; e.g., *Hos.* 6:7; 8:1; *Ex.* 24:7–8). The Priestly source structures its portrayal of history as a sequence of three covenants: the Noachic covenant (*Gn.* 9:8–17), the Abrahamic covenant (*Gn.* 17), and the Mosaic covenant (beginning with *Ex.* 6:1–8). According to this scheme all creatures have a covenant with God (the Noachic covenant), but Israel has a special covenant with God. Only to Israel at the time of Moses does God reveal his true name, Yahweh, which signals his most complete self-revelation (*Ex.* 6:3). The Mosaic covenant consists of rules or stipulations that Israel must abide by, and in return Yahweh will make his sacred presence dwell in the midst of the people in his Tabernacle. Hence the construction of the Tabernacle—a desert image of the Temple—has a prominent place in the account of the covenant at Sinai (*Ex.* 25–40). The covenant is a divine–human bond between Yahweh and Israel and is also an interhuman bond—a system of law, ethics, and ritual practice—that regulates Israelite life.

Preeminent among these laws are the Ten Commandments (*Ex.* 20:1–14; *Dt.* 5:6–18), which crystallize the basic tenets of the covenant. In their present form, the first five commandments are explicitly religious, each referring to Yahweh, and the second five are more explicitly secular and do not refer to Yahweh. In the earlier form of the Ten Commandments, which apparently consisted of ten brief sentences, this twofold division may have more naturally fallen between the fourth commandment ("remember the Sabbath day, to make it holy") and the fifth commandment ("honor your father and mother"). In any case, the sacred and the secular commands are complementary aspects of the covenant, together forming a coherent religio-ethical order. Notably, the Ten Commandments are addressed to the people Israel as a series of exhortations ("You [plural] shall. . . .") and has no explicit penalties. The Commandments are community rules anchored not by penalties but by the authority of Yahweh. This authority is rooted in the memory of his salvific deeds on Israel's behalf: "I am Yahweh your God, who brought you out of the land of Egypt, out of the house of slavery" (*Ex.* 20:1). The legal and ethical order of the covenant is guaranteed by the past deeds of Yahweh that created the conditions for Israel's existence. Israel's willing assent to the laws ("all that Yahweh has spoken we will do and obey"; *Ex.* 24:7) is an expression of covenant loyalty to her divine patron.

The effective consequences of the covenant are made explicit in the blessings and curses in *Leviticus* 26 and *Deuteronomy* 27 and 28 (which show some borrowings from the curses in contemporary Assyrian treaties). If Israel obeys the covenantal stipulations, Yahweh will grant Israel his blessings; if Israel disobeys, Yahweh will send curses and destruction. This collective responsibility for Israel's destiny becomes the historiographical key for the Deuteronomist's account of Israelite history in the books of *Deuteronomy* through *Kings.* The destruction of the northern kingdom by Assyria and the southern kingdom by Babylon are due to both kingdoms' disobedience to the covenant, particularly to the first and second commandments (*2 Kgs.* 17:7–23; 23:26–27). The classical prophets' oracles of doom also rest on this covenantal foundation: Because the people have disobeyed the covenant, Yahweh will deliver them to destruction. The preexilic prophets occasionally provide a glimpse of Yahweh's blessings should Israel repent, and this prospect of future blessing becomes a prominent theme in the exilic and postexilic prophets (and in the postexilic expansions of previous books). The conceptual fabric of the covenant is implicit in much prophetic discourse, including in its pointed social criticism, prophecies of doom, and evocations of an ideal order.

TEMPLE AND PSALMS. The local shrines in Israel served as sacred centers where earth and heaven meet and where the worshiper could draw near to Yahweh's presence. The foundation legend of the shrine at Bethel in *Genesis* 28 illustrates the cosmic function of Israelite shrines: Jacob sees "a staircase standing on the earth with its top reaching to heaven" (*Gn.* 28:12) and encounters God. At Bethel Yahweh grants the patriarchal blessing to Jacob and promises to protect him, and Jacob makes a vow: "If I return in peace to my father's house, Yahweh will be my God, and this rock that I set up as a standing stone will be a house of God (*bet ʾelohim*), and of all that you give me, I will give a tenth to you" (*Gn.* 28:21–22). The sacred site of Bethel (lit., "house of God") is a cosmic axis where the human and the divine realms meet, where the ancestor enters into a bond with God, and where his descendants renew this bond. At this holy site the worshipers offer vows, libations, tithes, and sacrifices. As seen in its name, this "house of God" is a place where God dwells on earth, where the worshiper can enter into God's holy presence.

The Temple in Jerusalem partakes of all these aspects of the local shrines and eventually displaced them. As the central shrine of state religion, it had the patronage of the king and was graced (according to *1 Kgs.* 6) with the finest Phoenician workmanship. It was built with Lebanon cedars, elsewhere called "cedars of God" (*Ps.* 80:11; cf. "cedars . . . in the garden of God," *Ez.* 31:8). A divine quality seems to inhere in this wood (the Cedar Forest of Lebanon is described as a divine preserve in the ancient Babylonian epic of Gilgamesh and is considered "the secret abode of the gods"). The Temple is an image of divine paradise, as evoked by the engravings of trees, flowers, and protective cherubim on the cedar panels and gold overlay. Similar to the Garden of Eden, the Temple is a sacred place where God dwells and where ordinary humans cannot enter. (Only priests could enter the Temple's interior, and only the high priest could enter its most holy inner sanctum, and then only once a year on the Day of Atonement.) Unlike the Garden of Eden, the Temple's location was known, and worshipers could approach God's holy presence in the Temple courtyard, and indeed were required to do so. There they would bring sacrifices and hear (or chant) sacred songs.

Many of the poems in the book of *Psalms* are sacred songs about the Temple, some sung in the Temple courts and some by pilgrims on their way to Jerusalem. In the language of these songs, the Temple is on Yahweh's "holy mountain," where worshipers who are pure of hands and heart (i.e., deeds and spirit) can enter into his salvific presence and receive his blessing (*Ps.* 24:3–6). The humble worshiper has only one wish: "to dwell in the House of Yahweh all the days of my life, to see the beauty of Yahweh, and to contemplate [him] in his Temple" (*Ps.* 27:4). This experience of divine presence is available in the sacred space and sacred time of the Temple, where Yahweh once celebrated his victory over chaos (*Ps.* 24:1–2, 7–10). At the Temple, the worshiper joyfully feasts in God's presence, drinks from the "fountain of life," and sees the light of God (*Ps.* 36:9–10). It is an earthly experience of a divine paradise, a place where, for a time, one can return to the perfect existence that humans once had in the Garden of Eden.

Because the Temple was the divinely sanctioned cosmic center, its destruction by the Babylonian army in 586 BCE was a major religious crisis. In the psalms this event is depicted as a reversion to primeval chaos, when evil forces ran riot. Thus *Psalm* 74 invokes "God, my king from of old" to restore the order of creation as he did in primeval times when he defeated the dragons of chaos. In this mythic construal of historical events, the enemy's destruction of the Temple is a temporary victory, because the divine king will once more arise to vanquish the enemy. The tragedy of the present is an interlude between God's victories of the primeval past and the imminent future. This cyclical or periodizing view of history is a key ingredient in the rise of apocalypticism: the expectation that God and his holy allies (angels and one or more messiahs) will soon appear to vanquish evil and suffering. In the new era to come, God will build a new Temple, more glorious than the first (see Ezekiel's angelic tour of the new Temple in *Ezekiel* 40–48), and the rivers of paradise will once more flow from the Temple (*Ez.* 47:1–12).

SACRIFICE. The major ritual action at the Israelite sacred shrines was sacrifice. Usually this involved the killing and offering of an animal from the domestic flocks (sheep, goat, or cattle), although grain offerings could serve as a substitute. Sacrifices in general are referred to as a gift (*minḥa*), a slaughter (*zebaḥ*), or an offering or bringing-near (*qorban*). These terms point to some of the basic dimensions of sacrifice. The sacrifice is a ritualized meal or feast in which meat is slaughtered (the consumption of meat was a special occasion in ordinary life, as in *Gn.* 18:1–8), transferred from the domestic setting to sacred space, where it takes on the character of gift or tribute to the deity and celebrates the bond between worshiper and deity. The sacrificial system has various components, each of which has distinctive shades of meaning.

The types of sacrifice most commonly referred to are the voluntary sacrifices called burnt offering (*ʿola*) and well-being offering (*shelamim*). The burnt offering is the type offered by Noah after the flood (*Gn.* 8:20) and by Abraham at Mount Moriah (*Gn.* 22:13), and both types are offered by Moses at Mount Sinai (*Ex.* 24:5) and Solomon at the dedication of the Jerusalem Temple (*1 Kgs.* 8:64). Both types are commanded by Yahweh at Mount Sinai in one of the few passages that comment on their significance: "You shall make for me an earthen altar, and sacrifice on it your burnt offerings and your well-being offerings from your flocks and herds. In every place where I cause my name to be remembered, I will come to you and bless you" (*Ex.* 20:21). Performing these sacrifices at the sacred sites is a way of worshiping or remembering Yahweh, and with each ritual of remembrance, Yahweh grants his blessing. Memory and the circulation of blessings are the focus of the ritual. The worshiper remembers Yahweh and pays homage to him, and also remembers the great sacrificial events of the past that founded the people (e.g., the Sinai covenant, the dedication of the Temple). Yahweh remembers his bond with his people and responds to their tribute with his blessing, which recapitulates the pattern of his relationship with the ancestors. In this ritual event, which takes place in family, local, and state religion, the social roles of the Israelites in their families, clans, and tribes are reaffirmed and sacralized, as is the worshiper's metaphysical role in the larger structures of reality.

The burnt offering and well-being offering form a complementary pair and were usually offered in sequence. The burnt offering, performed first, is entirely burnt into smoke, serving as a greeting-gift to Yahweh. The smoke is the pleasing odor that rises to Yahweh, summoning him to the sacrifice. The well-being offering, performed next, is shared by Yahweh and the worshiper, but with different portions and by different culinary means. The fat or suet is burnt into smoke (like the technique of the burnt offering), which rises to Yahweh as his pleasing odor. The meat is boiled in a pot for the worshipers, with a portion going to the officiating priests. The well-being offering is sometimes aptly rendered as a "communion offering," because in it the worshiper and Yahweh share a ritual meal in each other's presence. Yet even as they share a common meal, the difference of their respective portions signifies the metaphysical difference between Yahweh and humans. Yahweh's portion is smoke—a nonmaterial substance, rising from the earth to heaven, pointing to his divine nature. This is a substance that humans, as earthly beings, cannot eat. The humans' portion is meat stew, which is solid and cooked in a pot, corresponding to human physicality and material culture. Yahweh transcends human existence, just as his sacrificial cuisine differs from theirs. The ritual meal effects communion between the worshipers and Yahweh but also expresses metaphysical difference and hierarchy.

In the priestly system of sacrifice (presented in *Lv.* 1–16), several additional types of sacrifices are mandated for purification of sins. Each is a specialization of the well-being sacrifice, with the suet burnt into smoke for Yahweh and the meat boiled for the officiating priest. The most important purificatory sacrifice is the "sin offering" (*ḥatta't*), sometimes called the "purification offering." This offering purifies the worshiper and the Temple from the worshiper's inadvertent sins and impurities. Situations that require such purifying sacrifices include physical contact with an unclean person or object, menstrual impurity, unintentional failure to testify in a legal matter, and transitions of ritual status such as the initiation of priests. These are all situations in which a person is temporarily "out of place," whether physically, legally, or socially. A special purification offering is performed by the high priest on the Day of Atonement to cleanse the Temple of the Israelites' deliberate transgressions (*Lv.* 16:16). The system of purification offerings ensures the continued availability of Yahweh's presence in the Temple by keeping it cleansed from the "dirt" of Israel's impurities and sins. It also provides a solution to the problem of human evil by regulating and cleansing its effects, thereby warding off another divine punishment like the great flood. The priestly system of sacrifice is, in this respect, a ritual theodicy, in which Yahweh forswears punishment as long as Israel atones for its sins.

Several of the classical prophets criticize the legitimacy of sacrifice, stating that Yahweh does not want or accept the people's sacrifices (*Am.* 5:21–25; *Hos.* 6:6; *Is.* 1:10–17; *Mi.* 6:6–8; *Jer.* 7:21–23). These prophetic texts set up a contrast between ritual and ethics; Yahweh denounces the former and requires only the latter. It is not clear whether this contrast in prophetic rhetoric is absolute or relative; that is, whether ritual is empty under any circumstance, or whether it is empty only under the current circumstance of unethical behavior. In either case, the traditional practice becomes the object of critique and its meaning problematized. These questions about the relation between ritual practice and ethical disposition provide the ground for later transformations in Judaism and Christianity, when sacrifice becomes obsolete after the destruction of the Second Temple (70 CE). Some of the meanings and functions of sacrifice were preserved in other significant rites, most prominently the Passover Seder (a ritual meal which recalls the Passover sacrifice) and the Eucharist (a ritual meal which recalls both the Passover Seder and Jesus' sacrifice).

The Prophetic Critique. The religious critiques of the classical prophets (eighth through the sixth centuries BCE) effected, over several centuries, significant shifts in the structures of belief and practice in Israelite religion. Many aspects of traditional religious practice such as sacrifice, worship at local sacred sites, and the use of various types of religious iconography came under scathing attack. Veneration of other divine beings, including Yahweh's entourage, the Heavenly Host, was defined as sacrilege. Political institutions, such as kingship and the ruling elite, came under attack. The classical prophets regarded Israelite society—particularly the ruling classes—as ethically corrupt, and the major religious institutions and traditions were part of the problem. Hence they were defined as empty and abhorred by Yahweh. Hosea's writings against Samaria are the beginnings of the critique:

> Israel rejects what is good. . . . They made kings, but not by me; They made officers, but not by my knowledge; With their silver and gold, they made images. . . . (I) reject your calf, O Samaria, I am furious with (it). . . . A craftsman made it, but it is not a god; Yahweh will shatter the calf of Samaria. (*Hs.* 8:3–6)

In this speech, kingship, the political administration, the sacred sites, and the religious iconography are all denounced.

The "calf of Samaria" was the bull pedestal or throne of Yahweh at the royal shrines of Bethel and Dan. Analogous to the sphinx-like cherubs above the Ark in the Jerusalem Temple, the calf is a divine creature, but not a high god. But the physical representation of any divine being or aspect of divinity is castigated by the classical prophets, including the old standing stones at the local shrines. This is a critique of religious symbolism as such. Sacrifice too is an empty rite, as in Isaiah's oracle:

> What do I need of all your sacrifices, says Yahweh, I am sated with burnt offerings of rams, And the suet of fatlings; The blood of bulls, lambs, and goats, I do not desire. When you come to appear before me, Who asked these of you, trampling my courts? (*Is.* 1:11–12)

The critique of traditional religious symbols and practices comes to a climax in Jeremiah's Temple Sermon: "Thus says Yahweh of Hosts, God of Israel, Make good your ways and actions, and I will let you dwell in this place. Do not place your trust in empty words, saying 'The Temple of Yahweh, the Temple of Yahweh, the Temple of Yahweh.' . . . You are placing your trust in empty words which are of no avail" (*Jer.* 7:3–8). In a situation in which the people are morally corrupt, even the Temple—the religious institution par excellence—is devoid of value. In the absence of ethical behavior, all religious symbols and rituals are vacant.

As part of the prophets' religious critique, the divine realm is reconceived such that Yahweh becomes the sole high god of all the nations. Rather than being the best of gods, as in older texts, Yahweh is the only god: "Yahweh is the true God, He is the living God and eternal King" (*Jer.* 10:10). The gods of other nations are mere illusions. Second Isaiah (i.e., the "second author" who wrote segments of the book of *Isaiah*) makes this point in his exilic oracles: "I am God, there is no other; I am god, there is none like me" (*Is.* 46:9). In this new conception of God, the former anthropomorphic traits are purged: God is beyond human imagination, omniscient and omnipresent. The prophetic critique produced the classical monotheism of Judaism, Christianity, and Islam.

The new conceptual forms of the prophetic critique are closely related to the classical prophets' social positions as liminal or status-inconsistent figures. Unlike kings and priests, the authority of these prophets derived from their verbal power and personal qualities, outside of inherited or appointed hierarchies. (There were other prophets who were royal retainers; e.g., Nathan in David's court.) The prophets whose social backgrounds are cited had inconsistent status: Amos was a southern rancher prophesying in the northern kingdom, Jeremiah was from a disenfranchised priestly lineage, and Ezekiel was a priest in exile. As prophets they were religious mediators, hearing Yahweh's words in heaven and relating them to humans on earth. From their betwixt-and-between positions, they drew new distinctions between symbol and reality, signs and things, in a manner unthinkable within the traditional structures of religious thought. This practice of social and religious critique is characteristic of a variety of intellectual elites in what Karl Jaspers called the Axial Age (Eisenstadt, 1986). The classical prophets are ancient Israel's Axial critics.

The prophetic critique was appropriated by the royal administration of Josiah (and perhaps earlier, Hezekiah) to justify the centralization of religious authority in the Jerusalem Temple, the central shrine of state religion. Both kings, according to the biblical texts, destroyed the local shrines (*2 Kgs.* 18:4–6, 22; 22:8–20). Sacrifice could henceforth only be offered at the Temple. This aggregation of power to the capital city enhanced the prestige of the king and the Jerusalem priesthood. It may have been facilitated, in part, by the Assyrian destruction and depopulation of the Judean countryside during the reign of Hezekiah and the concomitant expansion of Jerusalem's population. Josiah's renewed efforts to consolidate religious centralization in Jerusalem was accompanied by the discovery of "the scroll of the law" (*2 Kgs.* 22; an early form of *Deuteronomy*), which mandated that Israel only worship at one site, "the place that Yahweh your God will choose, among all your tribes, to place his name there" (*Dt.* 12:5). *Deuteronomy*, a sublimely spiritual book, integrated the prophetic critique with the triumph of the state religion.

Other Theodicies. The classical biblical view of the relation between God's justice and human suffering can be seen most clearly in the psalms of lament and thanksgiving. Worshipers, who are suffering or have recently been delivered from suffering, attribute their painful state either to their own sins or to the malefic influence of their enemies. The worshipers trust that God will deliver them from suffering and evil or offers thanks for already having been delivered. At the end, the worshipers rejoice and offer sacrifices of thanksgiving to Yahweh. The sequence of importuning, trust, deliverance, and thanks is typically dramatized with motifs from the old myth of God's primeval victory over his cosmic enemies. As in the Canaanite myth of Baal, the cosmic enemies par excellence are Sea and Death. For example, the suffering that afflicts the worshipers are "the ropes of Death . . . the flood-torrents of Belial . . . the ropes of Sheol . . . the snares of Death" (*Ps.* 18:5; similarly, *Ps.* 69:2–3, 15–16; 88:4–8; 116:3; *Jon.* 2:3–4). God rescues the worshiper from these chaotic regions with his mighty hand: "He reached down from on high, he took me, he drew me from the mighty waters, he saved me from my fierce enemy" (*Ps.* 18:17); and "he lifted me out of the desolate Pit, the miry clay" (*Ps.* 40:3; similarly, *Ps.* 30:4; *Jon.* 2:7). In these psalms, the victory of God over evil and suffering are portrayed as a recapitulation of his primeval victories over chaos. The myth of the Divine Warrior forms the master plot for his victory over evil and suffering in the present.

The classical prophets transformed this constellation of ideas in their concept of the Day of Yahweh, which will be directed against Israel for its evil deeds (*Am.* 5:18–20; *Is.* 2:12–17; *Zep.* 1:2–18). The leaders and people of Israel are now the "enemies," and Yahweh will punish and destroy them for the injustices they have committed. The military destruction of the northern kingdom by the Assyrians and the southern kingdom by the Babylonians vindicated these utterances of the classical prophets, thereby investing their writings with increased authority, leading to their eventual canonization.

During and after the Babylonian exile (586–538 BCE), new shifts occurred in the old patterns of theodicy. In the proto-apocalyptic writings of *Second Isaiah, Ezekiel,* and other prophetic texts, God's future victory over the enemy (the Babylonians, other foreign nations; e.g., Gog of Magog and his allies in *Ez.* 38–39 and Death and the sea dragon Leviathan in *Is.* 25:8, 27:1) will lead to a golden age of peace and joy. The divine destruction of evil and suffering will be a cosmic transformation in which this era will be no more and a golden age will dawn. These apocalyptic ideas grew in force in the late Second Temple period, particularly after the Antiochene persecutions, stimulating the formation of apocalyptic communities at Qumran (an Essene order) and among the early Christians. In these apocalyptic groups, the cosmic enemies are both earthly and heavenly. The earthly enemies include Rome and other foreign nations, and also Jews who are not in the inner group of the righteous elect. The heavenly enemies are Satan and his armies of wicked angels and demons, who will be vanquished in cosmic battle with God, his angelic army, and one or more messianic figures.

An alternate transformation of the old pattern of theodicy occurs in the poetic dialogues of the book of *Job.* Job laments his suffering in language rooted in the psalms of lament, but maintains that he is innocent of any sin or wrongdoing. His comforters, who maintain the traditional claim that suffering is merited by past sinful acts, are repudiated by Job and later by God (*Jb.* 42:7). Job insists that God is treating the innocent man as his enemy ("Am I the Sea or the Dragon?"; *Jb.* 7:12), which impugns the idea of divine justice. When God appears to Job in the storm cloud, he uses the language of divine mastery over chaos to intimidate Job into silence. God's ways are beyond Job's understanding, and he recants: "I spoke without understanding, of things too wondrous for me, which I did not know" (*Jb.* 42:3). After recanting, Job is delivered from suffering, but the reasons are not the traditional ones. God's relationship to human evil and suffering is no longer comprehensible, if any such relationship even exists. Humans seem to be more or less insignificant in God's sight, and his victory over cosmic chaos—represented by Leviathan and Behemoth—no longer has any metaphoric relation to the defeat of human suffering.

A similar view is articulated in the book of *Ecclesiastes,* in which the language of the divine victory over chaos is entirely lacking. A general absence of meaning (*hevel*; emptiness, vanity, logical absurdity) pervades the world that we inhabit, and human suffering is only alleviated by death. Humans should cultivate simple pleasures and a tempered pursuit of wisdom, but not worry overmuch about the apparent absence of divine justice. *Ecclesiastes* holds that God is just, but what happens in the world is often unjust. Life and wisdom are God's gifts, and to ask for more is to invite anguish. "God made humans straightforward, but they have sought great reasons for things" (*Eccl.* 7:29). *Ecclesiastes,* like *Job,* stresses the limits of human understanding, offering a skeptical and pragmatic alternative to the traditional biblical views of theodicy.

THE SCRIPTURALIZATION OF RELIGION. During the preexilic period, religious knowledge circulated orally, particularly in the rites and festivals of family, local, and state religion. Elders, priests, and prophets were the primary religious authorities. Toward the end of the monarchic period a shift begins to occur in the locus of religious knowledge, from oral tradition to the written word. *Second Kings* 22 describes the discovery in the Jerusalem Temple of a "scroll of the teaching" (*sefer hatorah;* probably an early version of the book of *Deuteronomy*) that authorizes King Josiah's religious reforms. *Deuteronomy* 17:18–20 instructs the king to read a scroll that is "a copy of this teaching" throughout his days to ensure his just rule. In these scenes the authority of the written word begins to take the place of the prophets and priests—the latter are limited to copying the scroll or pronouncing on its authenticity. The image of God's word as a textual product is vividly portrayed in the initiatory vision of the prophet Ezekiel, who becomes a prophet when God commands him to swallow a scroll: "I ate it, and it became as sweet as honey in my mouth" (*Ez.* 3:3). God's word has become a text, which the prophet recites to the people.

Henceforth the history of Israelite religion is inseparable from the history of the text and its interpretation. The canonical moment for this history, according to the biblical portrayal, is Ezra's reading of "the scroll of the teaching of Moses" (*sefer torah moshe*; an early version of the Pentateuch; i.e., the first five books of the Bible) accompanied by learned men who "explain the teaching to the people" (*Neh.* 8:7). The function of religious specialists was now to read and interpret the authoritative text to discern the true meaning of God's already textualized word. A striking example of the new concept of divine revelation during the Second Temple period is Daniel's vision in *Daniel* 9, in which the pious Daniel reads the book of *Jeremiah* to learn when the redemption of Jerusalem will occur, then he prays, mourns, and fasts. The angel Gabriel arrives from heaven to reveal the scriptural secrets: "Daniel, I have now come to impart knowledge to you" (*Dn.* 9:22). God's word is contained in a text, but it takes further divine revelation to understand its true meaning.

Once religion becomes textualized, each community needs a divinely inspired or authorized interpreter, or class of interpreters, to discern the scriptural secrets. The Teacher of Righteousness at Qumran and Jesus of Nazareth are prominent examples of inspired teachers of scriptural secrets during the latter part of the Second Temple period. New institutions arose, such as the Pharisees and rabbis, whose authority was rooted in their ability to interpret scripture. Hillel, according to rabbinic tradition, "renewed the Torah" by the wealth of his interpretations, touching many aspects of Jewish life and law (Sukkah 20a). As Gershom Scholem observed, commentary became the major vehicle for religious discourse in Judaism. In Christianity "the word become flesh," but its gospel was also a text, and Christianity preserved its Jewish origins as a scriptural religion. By the end of the Second Temple period, Israelite religion had been transformed into a plurality (including Essenes, Pharisees, Samaritans, Christians, Gnostics, and Platonists) of cultures of interpretation.

SEE ALSO Biblical Exegesis, article on Jewish views; Biblical Literature, article on Hebrew Scriptures.

BIBLIOGRAPHY

Albertz, Rainer. *A History of Israelite Religion in the Old Testament Period.* 2 vols. Louisville, Ky., 1994. The most comprehensive recent history of Israelite religion, marked by attentiveness to differences of social context and corresponding distinctions of religious perspective and practices.

Barkay, Gabriel, Marilyn J. Lundberg, Andrew Vaughn, and Bruce Zuckerman. "The Amulets from Ketef Hinnom: A New Edition and Evaluation." *Bulletin of the American Schools of Oriental Research* 334 (2004): 41–71. The fullest decipherment of two important inscriptions.

Cross, Frank M. *Canaanite Myth and Hebrew Epic: Essays in the History of the Religion of Israel.* Cambridge, Mass., 1973. The major synthesis of the relationship between Canaanite and Israelite religion. A rich source of insights into many aspects of Israelite religion.

Dearman, John A. *Religion and Culture in Ancient Israel.* Peabody, Mass., 1992. A fine introduction to the subject, with careful attention to sociopolitical contexts and analyses.

Eisenstadt, S. N., ed. *The Origins and Diversity of Axial Age Civilizations.* Albany, N.Y., 1986.

Levenson, Jon D. *Sinai and Zion: An Entry into the Jewish Bible.* Minneapolis, 1985. A thoughtful presentation of key topics such as monotheism, covenant, and the symbolism of sacred space in Israelite religion.

Miller, Patrick D. *The Religion of Ancient Israel.* Louisville, Ky., 2000. A comprehensive study of some major topics, including the origins and diversity of Israelite religion, sacrifice, holiness and purity, and religious specialists.

Niditch, Susan. *Ancient Israelite Religion.* New York, 1997. An engaging introduction to aspects of Israelite religion, with attention to folkloric perspectives.

Ringgren, Helmer. *Israelite Religion.* Translated by David E. Green. Philadelphia, 1966; reprint, Lanham, Md., 1988. A classic study marked by wide learning and sound judgment and the best general introduction to the subject.

Scholem, Gershom. "Revelation and Tradition as Religious Categories in Judaism," *The Messianic Idea in Judaism.* New York, 1971. A seminal essay on the centrality of biblical interpretation in the history of Judaism.

Smith, Mark S. *The Early History of God: Yahweh and the Other Deities in Ancient Israel.* 2d ed. Grand Rapids, Mich., 2002. A thorough and judicious treatment of the relationship between Yahweh and the Canaanite deities, including the difficult issues of Asherah and the emergence of monotheism.

Toorn, Karel van der. *Family Religion in Babylonia, Syria and Israel: Continuity and Change in the Forms of Religious Life.* Leiden, 1996. A penetrating study of family religion in the ancient Near East, shedding important light on neglected aspects of Israelite religion.

Zevit, Ziony. *The Religions of Ancient Israel: A Synthesis of Parallactic Approaches.* London, 2001. A thorough survey of archaeological and textual data on the plurality of practices and beliefs in Israelite religion in the preexilic period.

RONALD S. HENDEL (2005)

ISSERLES, MOSHEH

ISSERLES, MOSHEH (c. 1520–c. 1572), known by the acronym RaMa (Rabbi Mosheh), was a Polish rabbi, halakhist, and scholar. Isserles was born in Kraków to one of the most powerful families of the Jewish community of sixteenth-century Poland and rose very rapidly to a position of prominence in the rabbinical world of Ashkenazic Jewry. Isserles's wealth and social status, as well as his ties by marriage to other prominent intellectual and communal figures in Polish Jewry, allowed him to wield substantial authority at a young age, primarily through the important *yeshivah* that he established in Kraków. His contributions to Jewish law and learning were vastly influential, and he was one of the few eastern European rabbis of his age to be venerated as a saintly leader for centuries after his death.

Isserles was trained in the Talmudic academy of Shalom Shakhna of Lublin, where he imbibed a fundamental commitment to the Ashkenazic traditions brought to Poland from Germany in the fifteenth century. He returned to his native Kraków to take up the position of its chief rabbi and remained in this post in the Polish capital until his death. The Rama synagogue in Kraków, which he built with his own wealth in 1553 as a memorial to his first wife, stands to this day as one of the most significant emblems of Jewish religiosity and learning in eastern Europe.

Isserles's prowess in Jewish law was revealed in his *responsa,* first published in Kraków in 1640, that displayed a distinctive synthesis of rigor and flexibility. While adhering to the Ashkenazic tradition of conservative interpretation, the Rama's rulings argued for a considerable degree of leniency in situations of severe economic or social stress and emphasized his belief in the importance of local customs in determining law. One *responsum* also detailed Isserles's controversial dedication to the study of philosophy: Taken to task by his senior colleague Shelomoh Luria for citing Aristotle as an authority of note, Isserles proclaimed his commitment to the Maimonidean view of the relation between philosophy and theology while explaining that he had only read Aristotle through the medium of medieval Hebrew texts. Isserles opposed the contemporary practice of teaching mysticism to the young and untried. However, in a number of quasi-philosophical works, the most important of which was *Torat ha-ʿolah* (The doctrine of the offering; 1570), a symbolic analysis of the commandments concerning the ancient Temple in Jerusalem, he attempted to demonstrate the confluence of Jewish philosophy and Qabbalah.

Isserles also published a large number of commentaries and glosses on various parts of the Bible, the Talmud, and other rabbinic literature. But his major scholarly accomplishment and claim to fame was his participation in one of the crucial legal enterprises in Jewish history, the creation of the *Shulḥan ʿarukh.* As a leading but relatively inexperienced jurist, Isserles recognized the need for a guide to Jewish law that would collate the rulings of recent scholars with classic interpretations and traditions. He had only begun to prepare such a compendium when he learned that the great Sefardic sage Yosef Karo of Safad had just published his *Beit Yosef,* an exhaustive code of Jewish law. Isserles revised his plan and produced his *Darkhei Mosheh,* which abridged Karo's work yet differed from it by insisting on the authority of local custom and recent precedents in determining correct rulings. Ten years later, Karo himself issued an abridgement of his original work, now entitled the *Shulḥan ʿarukh*—the "set table." Isserles responded by writing his *Mappah*—the "tablecloth"—which was an extensive commentary on Karo's work that argued for the pertinence of Ashkenazic customs and recent rulings. Immediately accepted as a critical amplification of Karo's work, Isserles's glosses were incorporated into the now collaborative *Shulḥan ʿarukh,* which became the authoritative codification of Jewish law and the object of continuous scholarly interest and debate.

BIBLIOGRAPHY

There exists no critical scholarly study of Mosheh Isserles or his works. The most successful reverential treatment is Asher Siev's *Rabbi Mosheh Isserles* (New York, 1972), in Hebrew. A useful summary of Isserles's legal works can be found in the standard, if dated, history of Jewish law, Haim Chernowitz's *Toldot ha-posqim,* vol. 3 (New York, 1947), pp. 36–73. An excellent description of Isserles's role in composing the *Shulḥan ʿarukh* is available in Isadore Twersky's elegant essay "The *Shulhan ʿAruk:* Enduring Code of Jewish Law," reprinted in *The Jewish Expression* (New Haven, Conn., 1976), edited by Judah Goldin. Chapters 4–6 of Moses A. Shulvass's *Jewish Culture in Eastern Europe: The Classical Period* (New York, 1975) may also be consulted.

New Sources

Ben Sason, Yonah. *Mishnato ha-iyunit shel ha-Rema.* Jerusalem, 1984.

Fishman, David Eliahu. "Rabbi Moshe Isserles and the Study of Science among Polish Rabbis." *Science in Context* 10 (1997): 571–588.

Shulman, Yaacov Dovid. *The Rema: The Story of Rabbi Moshe Isserles.* New York, 1991.

MICHAEL STANISLAWSKI (1987)
Revised Bibliography

IŠTAR SEE INANNA

ĪŚVARA,

ĪŚVARA, meaning "the lord," is the chief term used in Indian religion and philosophy to designate a supreme personal god. Goddess worshipers employ the feminine form, *īśvarī.* The noun comes from the Sanskrit root *vīś,* which means to own, rule, be master of, or be powerful. The meaning of the term developed over the history of South Asian literature.

In the earliest strata, the hymns of the *Ṛgveda* (c. 2000 BCE) prefer the epithets *īśaṇa* or *īśa* (from the same root) to designate the power of such deities as the universal sovereign Varuṇa, guardian of the cosmic order; Agni, the god of fire; Indra, lightning-hurling leader of the gods; and Puruṣa, the Cosmic Person, who was dismembered to create the universe. Though powerful, these early "lords" are not supreme personal deities. The term *īśvara* itself first occurs in the latest collection of Vedic hymns, the *Atharvaveda,* where it is extended from the god Agni (fire) to Vayu (wind), Prāṇa (life energy), and Kāla (time)—all later associated with the supreme god, Rudra-Śiva, also called Great Lord (Maheśvara). Later the Brāhmaṇas, priestly books elaborating sacrifice, elevate the god Prajāpati (Lord of Progeny), as the embodiment of Vedic sacrifice, creator, preserver, and ruler of the world. This lord is equated with *brahman,* the underlying Absolute.

In the last portion of the Veda, the Upaniṣads (800 BCE–200 CE), where the mystical link between *brahman* and the innermost soul (*ātman*) are explored, the concept of *īśvara* emerges fully. Although early Upaniṣads focus more on the mystical equation of *brahman* and *ātman,* later Upaniṣads, such as the *Śvetāśvatara* coalesce personal and impersonal conceptions of divinity into *īśvara* as a single, supreme, gracious, personal god. Here Rudra ("the howler"), a Vedic storm god also known as Śiva ("the beneficent one"), creates the world, pervades it, and dwells in humans as their soul, ruling all. Though he is lord of the external world, it is knowledge of the lord in meditation (yoga) as the inner soul that brings ultimate liberation.

The roughly contemporaneous *Bhagavadgītā* (c. 200 BCE), the most popular portion of the epic *Mahābhārata,* develops the concept even further with respect to Viṣṇu-Kṛṣṇa, the other principle deity to whom the term *īśvara* is applied. Like Śiva, Viṣṇu is an early Vedic god who grows in stature as he is identified over time with popular divinities, here with Vāsudeva, Nārāyaṇa, and Kṛṣṇa. With Kṛṣṇa as *avatāra,* or the incarnate "descent" of the transcendental lord as an earthly prince, *īśvara* becomes vividly personal. The *Bhagavadgītā* establishes devotion (*bhakti*) as a new path to salvation, alongside the earlier paths of ritual action (karma) and inner knowledge (*jñāna*). Kṛṣṇa is seen as Supreme Lord (*parameśvara*), the very foundation of *brahman,* beyond the universe, its creator and ruler. Kṛṣṇa is also revealed as the ultimate person (*puruṣottama*), immanent within the human heart. While clearly preferring devotion, the spiritual disciplines (yogas) of the *Bhagavadgītā* poetically synthesize the sacrificial, introspective, and devotional paths to liberation. This tendency to prefer and elevate the path of devotion (whether to Viṣṇu, Śiva, or in later times the goddess) to a supreme personal deity continues in the sectarian literature of the epics and Purāṇas, becoming from the medieval period to modern times the mainstream of Hindu spirituality.

In philosophical literature, other conceptions of *īśvara* hold sway. Sāṃkhya explains the world and its operation impersonally, in terms of the dual principles of matter and pure consciousness—without recourse to *īśvara*. The Yoga philosophy of Patañjali maintains a similar dualism, yet includes *īśvara* as the ultimate exemplar of pure consciousness. Here devotion to *īśvara* through repetition of his holy sound *Oṃ* is only seen as an optional means to achieving the meditative insight and absorption that alone grants liberation. In Yoga, *īśvara* is neither the efficient nor the material cause of the universe. The philosophy of Karma Mīmāṃsā, like heterodox schools of Buddhism and Jainism, emphasizes the law of cause and effect—the doctrine of karma—such that the need for an *īśvara* figure to create and maintain the universe is unnecessary. The Nyāya-Vaiśeṣika schools, though probably opposed to *īśvara* originally, in later commentarial literature support *īśvara*, the author and teacher of Vedic revelation, as an eternal being who combines eternally existing atoms according to karma to create, maintain, and dissolve the universe.

Śaṁkara's nondual Vedānta philosophy has famously subrated *īśvara* as "lower *brahman*," For Śaṁkara, "higher *brahman*" is an absolute beyond all qualities (*nirguṇa*) and description. To ordinary worldly perception this higher *brahman* is ignorantly seen as *īśvara*, the personal god replete with qualities (*saguṇa*). Alternatively, Rāmānuja's qualified nondual Vedānta understands *īśvara* as ultimately real, a personal deity eternally possessing all good qualities, distinct from the material world and souls, though dwelling in it and ruling them—a view more consistent with the growth of devotional theism in the last millennium.

BIBLIOGRAPHY

Chemparathy, George. *An Indian Rational Theology: Introduction to Udayana's Nyayakusumajali.* Vienna, 1972. Overview of theism in Nyāya-Vaiśeṣika philosophy.

Gonda, Jan. *Change and Continuity in Indian Religion.* The Hague, 1965.

Gonda, Jan. *Visnuism and Sivaism: A Comparison.* London, 1970; New Delhi, 1976.

Goyal, S. R. *A Religious History of Ancient India, Up to c. 1200 A.D.* Meerut, India, 1984–1986. A comprehensive treatment of Indian theism by an eminent historian.

Keith, Arthur Berriedale. *The Religion and Philosophy of the Veda and Upanishads* (1925). 2d ed. 2 vols. Westport, Conn., 1971. A classic source.

Klostermaier, Klaus K. *Mythologies and Philosophies of Salvation in the Theistic Traditions of India.* Waterloo, Ontario, 1984.

Pande, Susmita. *The Birth of Bhakti in Indian Religion and Art.* New Delhi, 1982.

LLOYD W. PFLUEGER (2005)

ITHNĀ ʿASHARĪYAH SEE SHIISM, *ARTICLE ON* ITHNĀ ʿASHARĪYAH

ITŌ JINSAI (1627–1705) was a Japanese *kangakusha* (Sinologist), educator, and Confucian philosopher. In 1681 Jinsai opened a private school, the Kogidō, in Kyoto and thus founded the Kogakuha, the school of Ancient Learning, a school of thought opposed to the Shushigakuha and the Yōmeigakuha, based on the thought of the Chinese thinkers Zhu Xi and Wang Yangming, respectively. The Kogidō, where Jinsai educated hundreds of students from the upper classes, continued uninterruptedly under Ito family management until 1871, when it gave way to the modern curriculum adopted from the West.

Jinsai, known for his personal modesty, forgiving nature, and broadmindedness toward other convictions, such as Buddhism, deserves credit not only as an outstanding moral teacher of the Tokugawa period but also as a scholar whose interests lay beyond his country's boundaries. Unlike the *kokugakusha,* the scholars of National Learning (Kokugaku), he prepared Japan for the assimilation of Western ideas in the mid-nineteenth century. He was highly appreciated by the Imperial House, and his main works were presented to the throne. His achievements were publicly recognized by the Meiji emperor in 1907, and those of his gifted son Tōgai (1670–1736), by the Taishō emperor in 1915. Jinsai's grave can still be seen at the Nison'in, a Buddhist temple in the Saga district, northwest of Kyoto.

Based on two books, the *Analects* of Confucius and the *Mencius,* Jinsai's thought has several features that are rare, if not unique, for a Japanese Confucianist. Jinsai resolutely discards all Buddhist and Daoist accretions to authentic, pre-Han Confucian doctrines. His cosmogony ascribes the origin of all things to a single cosmic yet anthropomorphous force. He honors the classic *yinyang* theory, which explains change and motion, but sees the origin of both *yin* and *yang* in one supreme ultimate, in turn equivalent to the moral concept of a supreme law governing all things. This law is benevolent and free from defects. Jinsai takes his monism one step further in his definition of Heaven, whom he calls ruler, conserver, supreme judge, and benefactor of humanity. Heaven is personified, although it is not always clear whether it is distinct from nature. In daily life, Jinsai showed the utmost respect for spiritual beings. With great forbearance he trusted in Heaven as a witness to his sincerity.

Jinsai's moral system flows from his anthropomorphic cosmology: Humankind is originally good and bent toward perfection. There is no need for Daoist or Zenlike abstention and meditation. There is balance between intellect and will, although freedom remains undefined beyond the pregnant phrase "Will means directedness toward good." Practically, virtue is manifest in the four cardinal virtues: humaneness or love, justice, propriety, and wisdom. These are reducible to two, humaneness and justice, whose apex unites in the supreme virtue, humaneness.

Jinsai's life was a paean to that virtue, even though he stood, with the dignity befitting a scholar, somewhat aloof from his surroundings. His educational principles paralleled his character, holding the middle between an exaggerated intellectualism and an unenlightened voluntarism. He was confident that a pupil, launched on his own way, runs no risk of being swept off his feet as long as he stands on the bedrock of classical learning and takes to heart the great lessons of history.

Among Jinsai's works, the following are best known and have gone through several editions: *Dōjimon* (1707), a question-and-answer presentation condensing his philosophical doctrines for classroom use; *Go-Mō jigi* (1683), a commentary on the *Analects* and *Mencius;* and the *Kogakusensei bunshu* (1717), an anthology prepared by Tōgai from his father's unpublished papers. Jinsai's originality has been challenged, but without success. Whether he came in contact with Ricci's *Tianzhu shi yi,* written to prove the existence of a unique God, remains a moot point.

The measure of Jinsai's influence must be found not only in his life and writings; even more, it lies in the lives and work of his many pupils. He imparted to them a critical spirit, for he doubted where others blindly believed, and he formed his own conclusions when it was still fashionable to follow the Song masters. His philosophy has a peculiar human appeal. The moral order is not a mere haphazard rule, but a providential guide, based upon the inherent nature of things.

Jinsai's legacy is still highly regarded in Japan, because he penetrated to the very core of the national spirit. To no mean extent, Jinsai could claim to be an educator of his people. Not only did he stir in his followers something that they felt was deeply embedded in their national way of life, but he impressed on them that Confucianism is inherently associated with the good that lies between two extremes. Jinsai's lasting success is explained by the fact that, in his efforts to accomplish the ideal that he contemplated, he found a way to blend two seemingly paradoxical qualities: equanimity of mind and passionate devotion to a cause. In this, he found a way that is Japan.

BIBLIOGRAPHY

The only monograph available in English is my own, *Itō Jinsai: A Philosopher, Educator and Sinologist of the Tokugawa Period* (1948; reprint, New York, 1967).

JOSEPH J. SPAE (1987)

IUPITER DOLICHENUS.

The god known in the Latin-speaking part of the Roman Empire as Iupiter Dolichenus was a local god of Syrian origin. His cult as a major cosmic god became widespread in the Empire in the second century CE, and he was given the majestic epithets of the Roman Jupiter (Optimus and Maximus). Although honored with Roman religious formulae, certain specific dedications have nonetheless retained evidence of his exotic origin.

Doliche (modern Dülük, in Turkey, near Gaziantep) was a town of Commagene beside the Euphrates—and thus at the crossroads of Anatolian, Syrian, and Iranian influences—and had come under Roman sway at the time of Pompey (106–48 BCE). Its local god (whose sanctuary has not yet been excavated) was derived from the Hittite-Hurrian Teshub, a weather god who had absorbed some of the characteristics of the Aramaic Hadad, a Syrian storm god. In the absence of literary sources giving details of his myth, the way he is portrayed sheds light on his character. Typical iconography shows him upright on a bull, holding a double-bladed axe and thunderbolt and wearing a Persian crown or Phrygian cap. From the Hellenistic period on, he also wears military armor. The fixed religious formula describing the god—*ubi ferrum nascitur* (where iron is born)—recalls both his theogony and a powerful nature. The theology of the great god providing prosperity, the universal lord, "eternal guardian of the entire cosmos" (Hörig and Schwertheim, 1987, no. 376), is displayed via complex symbolic ornamentation, in which he is surrounded by attendants making clear his cosmic sovereignty (the Dioscuri, the Sun, the Moon). Like the Anatolian and Syrian master gods he is accompanied by a female consort, whose character was borrowed from the goddess Hebat/Hepet of the Hurrian/Hittite substrate. In the Roman Empire she was known widely as Iuno Dolichena, or sometimes Regina, like the Roman goddess.

The cosmic power of the god explains his support among the military (around half the devotees in about 650 dedications). The geographical extent of his spread is along the lines of the militarized areas as far as Hadrian's Wall in Brittany, and sometimes the trade routes with the East. Even in places where easteners were numerous, such as the *Vrbs* (the City of Rome), the face of the cult was still romanized. The oriental image of the god merged into the Roman melting pot during stages of integration: under Hadrian in Africa and Rome (two sanctuaries on the Equiline and the Aventine), then from the middle of the second century in the Danube provinces (Pannonia and Noricum, with the outstanding collection of Mauer-an-der-Url). The significant number of soldiers highlights the fact that the majority of the faithful were male. However, the cult was not barred to women, who took part in family dedications (Hörig and Schwertheim, 1987, no. 381) or offered silver plaques on their own (Hörig and Schwertheim, 1987, nos. 303 and 304).

The military factor enlightens the period of time over which the evidence is spread as well, from Hadrian (117–138) to Gallienus (253–268 [The last dedication is dated in

260]). The growing interest for the god under the Severan emperors betrays mainly the military situation rather than an official support from a dynasty originating from Emesa. The reasons for the cult's disappearance have caused scholarly debate. In the absence of clear proof of an "Illyrian backlash" by Maximinus the Thracian (235-238), the military crisis, which arose in 235, saw fighting and destruction in the frontier regions, which are sufficient explanation of the disaffection with a cult that persisted elsewhere (in Rome, for example). Under Gallienus, who redrew the *limes* (frontier) along the Rhine and the Danube, Shapur I captured Doliche and destroyed the temple. The disappearance around this time of devotions in the Empire might mean that the Doliche as a religious metropolis played a significant part in the organization of the cult, perhaps by sending out priests (a number have Syrian names); most likely the existence of the city served as a symbolic point of reference.

The cult was well organized. Even if it was not actually sent out by the main temple, the priesthood, which was linked to Doliche, ensured a proper framework, which could explain why the conception of the god was more or less consistent. As far as we know, the structure of groups of the faithful was established on a basis of *collegia*, at least in Rome. Cult sites (more than fifteen have been excavated) were long-standing and well maintained (Hörig and Schwertheim, 1987, no. 547). The *Dolichena* (temples of the god) that have been preserved are varied in size with no "canonical" plan. We have only a partial idea of the rituals that took place, probably sacrifices with ritual meals (attested at Zugmantel [Germania] and at the Aventine temple). Raised votive hands and bronze triangles with complex symbolism might have served as religious emblems for display or procession, and mounted silver plaques served as an ornate display.

The two great heavenly lords of Doliche and Heliopolis in Syria, which had similar theologies, are jointly invoked on several documents (Hörig and Schwertheim, 1987, nos. 183 and 221). Another Syrian Baal "from the mountain," Jupiter Turmasgades, was also *sunnaos* (housed in the same temple) of Dolichenus (at Doura Europos and in Dacia). However, the god who was closest to Iupiter Dolichenus was Mithras, due to the similar beliefs and social composition of their followers. Apart from these usual associations within polytheistic systems, the god of Doliche borrowed little from other great gods, except the testimony of two bronze plaques, which show an influence of Isis' religion (Hörig and Schwertheim, 1987, nos. 512 and 511). In contrast, the god is often figured with the characteristics of a Latin Jupiter, with scepter and thunderbolt, along with an eagle (Hörig and Schwertheim, 1987, no. 515, for example).

Since the god of Doliche, like the Roman god Jupiter, was a god of power and victory, his followers, some of them high-ranking military officers, included the emperors and their families in their prayers. The link between the god of Doliche and the Empire started as early as his "meeting" with Rome at the beginning of the common era. It was figured on a civic stamp that shows a *dexiosis* (shaking hands) between the god and an Imperator. Even so, the cult of Dolichenus was not, as one might think, an official army cult, a religion of the military camps. Of course, this god with a military aspect, and possibly in Roman guise, was well able to act as divine patron in the eyes of military units. More generally, this god of victory, and thus of salvation, may be seen as a "great" benevolent god, in keeping with the trend of religious developments in the second and third centuries.

SEE ALSO Aramean Religion; Blessing; Hittite Religion; Hurrian Religion; Roman Religion, article on the Imperial Period; Teshub.

BIBLIOGRAPHY

Epigraphical and archaeological data are published by Monika Hörig and Elmar Schwertheim, *Corpus Cultus Iovis Dolicheni* (Leiden, 1987); for Rome, see Gloria M. Belleli and Ugo Bianchi, eds., *Orientalia Sacra Urbis Romae Dolichena et Heliopolitana. Recueil d'études archéologiques et historico-religieuses sur les cultes cosmopolites d'origine commagénienne et syrienne* (Rome, 1997). Rainer Vollkommer discusses iconographical typology in "Iuppiter Dolichenus," *Lexicon Iconographicum Mythologiae Classicae* 8, no. 1 (1997): 471–478. The standard study is Pierre Merlat, *Jupiter Dolichenus. Essai d'interprétation et de synthèse* (Paris, 1960). It has been updated by Monika Hörig in "*Iupiter Dolichenus,*" *Aufstieg und Niedergang der Römischen Welt II* 17, no. 4 (1984): 2136–2179, and by Elmar Schwertheim in "*Iupiter Dolichenus.* Seine Denkmäler und seine Verehrung," in *Die orientalischen Religionen in Römerreich*, edited by Marteen J. Vermaseren, pp. 193–212 (Leiden, 1981). German readers should see Michael P. Speidel, *Juppiter Dolichenus. Der Himmelsgott auf dem Stier* (Stuttgart, 1980). For a focus on the army issue, see Michael P. Speidel, *The Religion of Jupiter Dolichenus in the Roman Army* (Leiden, 1978).

NICOLE BELAYCHE (2005)
Translated from French by Paul Ellis

IZANAGI AND IZANAMI, in Japanese mythology, are the universal parents and creators who produced the land, mountains, rivers, waves, trees, fields, wind, fog, and the deities ruling these things. According to the early written chronicle of Japan called the *Kojiki,* they appeared on the Takama no Hara, or High Plain of Heaven, as brother and sister. Standing on the Bridge of Heaven, they churned the ocean's water with a jeweled spear, then drew the spear up. The brine that dripped from the tip of the spear became the first Japanese island, Onogoro. Izanagi and Izanami descended onto the island, erected there a high pillar and a hall, then circled the pillar in opposite directions. When they met, they were united, and thus the islands of Japan were born.

After the birth of the islands, various other deities were born of the two creator-parents. But when the fire god Kagutsuchi was born, the mother goddess Izanami was burned to death by the heat. Like the Greek Orpheus,

Izanagi descended to the land of Yomi (the underworld) to bring back his wife. His attempt ended in failure when he peered into a dark room with his torch against Izanami's wishes, only to find there her decaying corpse. Pursued by the enraged Izanami and her subordinate demons, Izanagi fled. Finally, the two deities stood face to face at the entrance of the underworld and agreed upon a divorce. It was decided that Izanagi should rule the living and Izanami the dead (a motif paralleling that of Tane and Hina in Polynesia). Izanagi then returned to the earth, where he purified himself in a stream. From his purified eyes and nose appeared three great deities: Amaterasu (the sun goddess), Tsukiyomi (the moon god), and Susano-o (the violent god). These deities were appointed rulers of heaven, night, and the ocean. Izanagi thereupon returned to the celestial abode, where he remained.

Somewhat different versions of the creation myth are recorded in the other ancient Japanese chronicle, the *Nihonshoki.* In it, the three great deities are born of both Izanagi and Izanami, not of Izanagi alone. There is no descent to the underworld by Izanagi, who retires permanently to a hidden palace on the island of Awaji in the Inland Sea. Since ancient times, there has been an Izanagi shrine on Awaji, and the divine couple have been worshiped by the fishermen and divers of this and neighboring islands. The myth of *kuni-umi* ("birth of the islands from the sea") seems to have originated with the Awaji fishermen. In the most primitive form of the story the divine couple created only Awaji and its tiny neighboring islands, but the myth must eventually have grown in scale to include the creation of all the islands of Japan.

The *Kojiki* as well as the *Nihonshoki* record that the two deities gave birth first to Awaji. According to another account in the *Nihonshoki,* the fifth-century emperors Richū and Ingyō went hunting on this island, and through mediums were given oracles by Izanagi, Awaji's guardian deity. Then, as the fishermen migrated to or traded with other areas, their myths and formal worship were diffused. The tenth-century *Engishiki* records several shrines dedicated to Izanagi and Izanami in the Kinki area (the area enclosed by Kyoto, Osaka, and Kobe). The oldest manuscript of the *Kojiki* describes the worship of Izanagi at the Taga shrine in Ōmi (now Shiga prefecture). In later ages the Taga shrine became the most famous and popular shrine for the worship of the divine couple.

BIBLIOGRAPHY

Aston, W. G., trans. *Nihongi: Chronicles of Japan from the Earliest Times to A.D. 697* (1896). Reprint, 2 vols. in 1, Tokyo, 1972.

Chamberlain, Basil Hall, trans. *Kojiki: Records of Ancient Matters* (1882). 2d ed. With annotations by W. G. Aston. Tokyo, 1932; reprint, Rutland, Vt., and Tokyo, 1982.

Matsumae Takeshi. *Nihon shinwa no shin kenkyū.* Tokyo, 1960.

Matsumoto Nobuhiro. *Nihon shinwa no kenkyū.* Tokyo, 1971.

Matsumura Takeo. *Nihon shinwa no kenkyū,* vol 2. Tokyo, 1955.

Philippi, Donald L., trans. *Kojiki.* Princeton, N.J.,1969.

MATSUMAE TAKESHI (1987)

J

JACOB, or, in Hebrew, Yaʿaqov, also called Israel; the son of Isaac and grandson of Abraham. The name *Yaʿaqov* is generally regarded as an abbreviation of *yaʿaqov el,* which probably means "God protects" and is attested among the Babylonians in the early part of the second pre-Christian millennium. The Bible relates it to forms of the Hebrew root *ʿqv,* meaning "heel" and "supplant," pertaining to Jacob's ongoing rivalry with his twin brother, Esau. That struggle originated in the womb, leading their mother Rebecca to seek a divine oracle from which she learned that the younger Jacob would rule over his brother. Esau was born first, with Jacob grasping at his heel (*ʿaqev*). The theme of fraternal rivalry continued when, as a young man, Jacob exploited Esau's hunger in order to buy his birthright (*bekhorah*) and then stole his brother's blessing (*berakhah*) by taking advantage of his father Isaac's blindness during Esau's absence.

A second period in Jacob's life was spent in Haran in northern Mesopotamia, where he fled to escape his brother's wrath. On the way, he had a vision of a stairway with angels climbing from earth to heaven and back again while God promised that his descendants would be numerous and possess the land all around. Jacob thus recognized the spot as God's house (Bethel), the gateway to heaven. In Haran, Jacob worked for his uncle Laban in order to obtain Rachel as a wife. After the stipulated seven years, Laban deceived Jacob by substituting Rachel's older sister Leah under cover of darkness, just as Jacob had exploited his father's inability to see in order to obtain the blessings intended for his older brother Esau.

During his return to Canaan, Jacob engaged in physical conflict with an apparently supernatural being (see *Hos.* 12:4), after which his name was changed to Israel (Heb., Yisraʾel). Although the historical etymology of this name is uncertain, the Bible explains it as meaning "he who has struggled with divine beings."

The final period of Jacob's life consists of various journeys and focuses primarily on the story of his son Joseph. Jacob eventually died at the age of 147 in Egypt, where he

---

Clockwise from top left corner. Tenth-century Gomateśvara in Sravanabelgola, India. *[©Gian Berto Vanni/Corbis]*; The Egyptian god Anubis weighs the heart of a deceased person against the feather of Maat, or truth, in the judgment hall of Osiris in a painting from the *Book of the Dead.* British Museum. *[The Art Archive/British Museum/Jacqueline Hyde]*; Menorah illumination by Joseph Assarfati, from the *Cervera Bible,* 1299. Biblioteca Nacional, Lisbon. *[©Giraudon/Art Resource, N.Y.]*; Stone relief of a jaguar from an Aztec sun calendar. *[©Michel Zabe/Art Resource, N.Y.]*; Medieval illustration of Joan of Arc arriving at Chinon Castle in 1428. *[©Bettmann/Corbis]*.

was embalmed before being brought back to Canaan to be buried in the family tomb at Machpelah.

Jacob's role as the third of Israel's patriarchs is central to the biblical account. The proper historical setting for all of the patriarchs is, however, currently a matter of scholarly disagreement. Although a wide range of possible dates have been proposed, most who accept the fundamental historicity of these figures date them to the middle or late Bronze Age on the basis of cultural similarities between the biblical descriptions and what is known of those periods from archaeological and epigraphic discoveries. One striking characteristic of these narratives is the way God is identified with individual patriarchs, as in the title *avir ya'aqov* (the "strong one" or perhaps "bull" of Jacob).

Many modern scholars consider the various patriarchal traditions to have come from different tribal groups. Some even regard Jacob and Israel as two originally separate figures, in which case Jacob probably comes from Transjordan (Gilead) and Israel from central Canaan (the region near Bethel and Shechem). These traditions were merged with those relating to Abraham and Isaac as the various tribes of biblical Israel coalesced. As his changed name attests, Jacob symbolizes the northern kingdom as well as the entire people of Israel, a perspective reflected also in the fact that his sons are named for the twelve tribes. Indeed, many actions, such as his entrance into the land and journey to Shechem and Bethel, foreshadow events involving the people as a whole.

Many interpreters have been troubled by the devious ways in which Jacob obtained his position of preeminence. Rabbinic tradition, in which he represented all of Israel even as his rival Esau came to stand for Rome, sought to minimize these negative traits, which seem so evident in the Bible. It must be recognized that from the biblical point of view these actions, whatever their moral character, serve primarily to ensure the fulfillment of God's design indicated even prior to Jacob's birth. Moreover, the Bible clearly describes how Jacob paid for his behavior: he was forced to leave his home, he was deceived by his uncle, he found his daughter raped, his favorite wife died in childbirth, and her son was kidnapped.

SEE ALSO Rachel and Leah.

BIBLIOGRAPHY

An excellent survey of modern scholarship on the patriarchs is Nahum M. Sarna's *Understanding Genesis* (New York, 1966); more recent historical information relating to the date and historicity of these figures is provided by Roland de Vaux's *The Early History of Israel,* translated by David Smith (Philadelphia, 1978). Rabbinic traditions on Jacob are collected in Louis Ginzberg's *The Legends of the Jews,* 2d ed., 2 vols., translated by Henrietta Szold and Paul Radin (Philadelphia, 2003). An insightful description of the Jacob story's literary characteristics is contained in Michael A. Fishbane's *Text and Texture: Close Readings of Selected Biblical Texts* (New York, 1979).

The literary and historical background of Jacob's rivalry with Esau and similar biblical stories is discussed in Frederick E. Greenspahn, *When Brothers Dwell Together, The Preeminence of Younger Siblings in the Hebrew Bible* (New York, 1994).

FREDERICK E. GREENSPAHN (1987 AND 2005)

JACOB BEN ASHER SEE YA'AQOV BEN ASHER

JACOB TAM SEE TAM, YA'AQOV BEN ME'IR

JADE. The term *jade* readily evokes the concept of a hard and precious, semitranslucent green stone. However, not only does jade appear in a wide variety of colors, such as white, brown, black, green, and even purple, but the term also describes two quite distinct stones, nephrite and jadeite. Nephrite, the stone of ancient China, is a silicate of calcium and magnesium and exhibits a felted, fibrous structure resembling wood grain as well as a soft, waxy luster. Jadeite, on the other hand, a pyroxene silicate of aluminum and sodium, has a cryptocrystalline structure, giving it an often grainy appearance. It is not only harder than nephrite, polishing to a glasslike finish, but it also appears in a wider variety of colors, including emerald green as well as rich blues and purples. Jade is universally admired for its beauty and durability as a precious stone, for its inexhaustible riches of color, and for its variety of grain and texture. In earlier times, however, in cultures as diverse as those of ancient China, Mesoamerica, and Polynesia, jade also had a religious value.

By the fifth millennium BCE various Chinese Neolithic peoples were working nephrite jade into beads, pendants, and other simple ornaments in both northern and southern China. To the north the Hongshan people (c. 4700–2920 BCE) created jade sculptures of cloudlike forms as well as early examples of the venerated dragon identified with rainmaking and rulership in traditional Chinese thought. Often termed *pig dragons* because of their blunt snouts, these Hongshan creatures typically appear as pendants, with the tightly coiled tail almost touching the mouth. Other jade carvings feature cicadas, creatures widely identified with resurrection in Chinese religion. The cicada is among the most frequently depicted creatures in traditional Chinese jade carving, as such objects were commonly placed in the mouths of the dead. Aside from Hongshan, there is the slightly later Liangzhu culture situated in the lower Yangtze River Basin to the south (c. 3200–2000 BCE). Excavations have revealed lavish Liangzhu graves containing massive amounts of jade. One of the most noteworthy forms is a hollow jade tube, squared on the outside. Series of finely incised, superimposed heads often appear on the corners of these remarkable objects, and it is quite possible that they refer to the four directions, thereby relating these jades to the concept of the four cosmic quarters and world center. Another jade type found in these graves is a flat disk with a large central perforation.

Both of these jade forms were commonly used in rituals during the later Zhou dynasty (1122–256 BCE). The *Zhou li* (Rites of Zhou) mentions six jade tablets that the *ta-tsung po* (master of religious ceremonies) used in paying homage to heaven, earth, and the four cardinal points. Aside from the jades of the four directions, heaven was worshiped by a blue flat jade disk called *bi,* while earth was represented by a yellow jade *cong,* a tube with four squared exterior sides. Whereas the *cong* was no longer used after the Han dynasty (206 BCE–220 CE), the jade *bi* has remained one of the most important symbols in the Chinese religious tradition. Jade was also used as a sacrificial substance. Round blue pieces of jade were offered to the Lord on High, and square yellow pieces were offered to Sovereign Earth. Several stories recount the offering of a jade ring to the god of the river to assure a safe crossing.

During the Zhou dynasty a large variety of jade objects played important symbolic roles in a religious and political system focused on sacred kingship. As symbols of political sovereignty, the jade insignia worn by the emperor and his officials were equally symbols of religious sanction. Ruling as the Son of Heaven, the emperor stood at the head of an elaborate ritual system, a sacral economy that found symbolic embodiment in a whole series of jade emblems. The emperor himself had the privilege of wearing ornaments of white jade, in particular the "large tablet" and the "tablet of power" that he wore as he offered the annual spring sacrifice to the Lord on High (Shangdi). His officials were given jade emblems that varied in size, shape, and color according to their rank.

Jade played a particularly important role in funeral practices. This was undoubtedly due to the belief that jade, as the embodiment of the power of heaven, would prevent the decay of the body after death. Accordingly one finds all manner of jade objects in the coffins of the deceased, often blocking the nine natural openings of the body. Especially common were jade tablets placed upon the tongue and carved in the likeness of cicadas, perhaps as symbols of renewed life. During the Han dynasty one also finds body-sized funeral suits made of jade.

Among the Daoists the religious symbolism of jade was given a more precise focus. The Daoists believed that jade embodied the principle of cosmic life and could thus ensure immortality if used in connection with certain alchemical practices. These practices included the actual ingestion of jade, because it was believed that jade could not only prevent the decay of the body after death but could actually regenerate it while alive. The importance of jade in Daoist thought is reflected in the name of the Daoist supreme being, the Jade Emperor.

In the New World, jade working is best known in connection with ancient Mesoamerica. Although nephrite does occur in this region, the material used was almost exclusively jadeite, a material that derived from the Motagua River region of eastern Guatemala. As early as 1500 BCE, beautifully polished jade celts were offered to a sacred spring at El Manati, Veracruz. The ritual context of these celts indicate that at this early date jade was already identified with water and agricultural symbolism. The later Olmec of the same region were the first Mesoamerican people to extensively work jade, and Olmec jade carvings constitute some of the finest jades known from Mesoamerica. The apogee of Olmec jade working occurred during the Middle Formative period (c. 900–500 BCE), during which fine translucent blue and green jades were fashioned into statues, pendants, and even life-size masks. In addition, jade celts continued to be worked, and at times these objects bear incised images of the Olmec maize god framed by four elements marking the world quarters. These images are schematic portrayals of the cosmos, with the maize god as the pivotal *axis mundi* at the world center. A number of Middle Formative Olmec caches feature jade celts oriented to the four directions, a pattern strikingly similar to the Chinese use of jades to mark the cardinal points. Among the later Classic Maya, jade was also identified with the maize god as the central world axis. A number of caches from Copán, Honduras, contain jade images of the maize god framed by other jades placed at the four directions.

Aside from being identified with verdant, life-giving maize, jade was also a basic symbol of life and the breath soul in ancient Mesoamerica. Among both the Formative Olmec and the later Classic Maya (c. 250–900 CE), breath is commonly portrayed as a bead floating before the face. The sixteenth-century chronicler Fray Bartolome de las Casas mentions that at the death of Pokom Maya kings, the expiring breath soul was captured in a precious bead. The common Mesoamerican funerary tradition of placing jade beads in the mouth probably concerned this breath soul, and this is probably also the case of the mosaic jade masks placed over the faces of Classic Maya kings. One example from Calakmul, Campeche, portrays breath volutes emerging from the nostrils and the corners of the mouth, much as if the jade mask constituted the breathing, living visage of the king. In Classic Maya art, jade beads and ear flares of floral form are often portrayed as exhaling breath. At times this breath or wind is embodied by a serpent that emerges from the cavelike opening of the ear flare, a convention also used by the later Aztec (c. 1250–1521 CE). In fact, the sixteenth-century *Florentine Codex* mentions that, according to Aztec belief, jade sources are surrounded by verdant growth due to the moist breath of the stone: "And thus do they know that this precious stone is there: [the herbs] always grow fresh; they grow green. They say that this is the breath of the green stone, and its breath is very fresh" (Sahagun, 1950–1982, 11:222).

Aside from identifying jade with breath and rain-bringing wind, the Aztec also compared jade to life-giving water. The Aztec referred to their goddess of terrestrial water as Chalchiuhtlicue, meaning She of the Jade Skirt. In Aztec art, water is commonly portrayed with jade discs interspersed with shells.

The Aztec appear to have shared with the Chinese a belief in the medicinal properties of jade. In particular jade seems to have been prescribed for relief from gastric pain—the term *jade,* in fact, derives from the early Spanish term for this purportedly medicinal stone, *piedra de ijada,* or "stone of the loins."

Aside from China and Mesoamerica, jade was also an esteemed ritual item in areas of Oceania. In New Caledonia, ceremonial nephrite axes of circular form denoted the rain-making powers of high chiefs. Nephrite jade, or *pounamu,* also attained a certain religious significance among the Maori of New Zealand, whose neck pendants, called *hei-tiki,* are made of jade. These are passed down from generation to generation, in the process becoming symbols of the ancestors. Many of these pendants appear to have been recarved from ceremonial adzes, which are in themselves symbols of chiefly status and power. Especially esteemed were jade hand clubs, or *patu pounamu.* Many of these were granted personal names and, with the *hei-tiki,* continue to be valued heirlooms in the early twenty-first century.

SEE ALSO Breath and Breathing; Dragons; Funeral Rites, overview article and article on Mesoamerican Funeral Rites; Symbol and Symbolism.

BIBLIOGRAPHY

The classic study of jade in ancient China remains that of Berthold Laufer, *Jade: A Study in Chinese Archaeology and Religion* (Chicago, 1912). To this may be added the more wide-ranging and less technical works of Louis Zara, *Jade* (New York, 1969), and Adrian Digby, *Maya Jades* (London, 1964). Roger Keverne, ed., *Jade* (London, 1991), contains many useful articles and excellent photographs. Frederick W. Lange, ed., *Precolumbian Jade* (Salt Lake City, Utah, 1993), discusses the geology and archaeology of ancient jadeite from Mexico and Central America. See also, Bernardino de Sahagun, *Florentine Codex: General History of the Things of New Spain,* translated by Arthur J. O. Anderson and Charles E. Dibble (Santa Fe, N.Mex., 1950–1982).

DAVID CARPENTER (1987)
KARL TAUBE (2005)

JAʿFAR AL-ṢĀDIQ

JAʿFAR AL-ṢĀDIQ (AHd. 148/765 CE) is one of the leading figures in early Islam expounding the teachings from the family of the Prophet. Active in Medina's scholarly circles, where he was born in 699 or 703, Jaʿfar al-Ṣādiq was the most frequently cited authority on points of law and tradition. His father, Muḥammad al-Bāqir, was an established scholar in Medina's learned circles. Jaʿfar al-Ṣādiq transmitted his family's wisdom to Muslims of diverse backgrounds and exponents of other religions, theosophers as well as Gnostics, who frequented his house in quest of knowledge.

In Shīʿī tradition, Jaʿfar al-Ṣādiq is a central figure and the last common *imām* recognized by both the Ithnāʿasharīs and the Ismāʿīlīs. After his death, the Shīʿī *imāmī* community became dispersed into several groups, two of which, the Ithnāʿasharīs following Mūsā al-Kāẓim and the Ismāʿīlīs accepting Ismāʿīl, have survived into the twenty-first century. Jaʿfar al-Ṣādiq's contribution and influence, however, are far wider. He is cited in a wide range of historical sources, Shīʿī as well as Ṣūfī and Sunnī, all of which acknowledge his insightful learning, clearly testifying to his influence.

Jaʿfar al-Ṣādiq inherited the position of Shīʿī leadership from his father, al-Bāqir, and was acknowledged as a Shīʿī *imām.* His family saw him as a last attempt to reconcile all the diverse groups of Muslims. The first two decades of Jaʿfar's imamate witnessed very turbulent times in early Islam, with active revolts from some extremist Shīʿah, the uprising of the Zaydīyah, and the ʿAbbāsid movement of Hāshimīyah unfolding from the Kaysāniyah. During this time, Jaʿfar al-Ṣādiq remained distant and somewhat overshadowed politically by the numerous claimants who became embroiled in the power struggle. Some of Jaʿfar al-Ṣādiq's difficulties were also doctrinal and came from certain individuals classed later as the *ghulāt.* His father had already repudiated some of them earlier. The fact that Jaʿfar managed to keep out of politics allowed him time to participate not only in scholarly activities, but also to hold private sessions at his home in Medina, thus maintaining his family's practice.

THOUGHT AND LAW. The Shīʿī community formed around Jaʿfar, who followed the foundations laid by al-Bāqir. Elaborating and consolidating some of the doctrines put forward by his father, Jaʿfar al-Ṣādiq developed an extensive system of law and theology so that under him the Shīʿah became very significant, with their own distinct rituals and religious doctrine. Al-Bāqir had already laid the foundations of the *madhhab ahl al-bayt* with specific views on rites, rituals, and practices of Islam, a contribution acknowledged in Jaʿfar's own words. Al-Bāqir's juridical views spring from his epistemology, which meant that the *imām* is endowed with the hereditary knowledge that rendered him an ultimate source of knowledge. It was on this basis that the legal pattern of the Shī ʿah was to change and develop within the circle of his adherents under the leadership of his son and successor, Jaʿfar al-Ṣādiq.

Jaʿfar al-Ṣādiq's own contribution is readily apparent in the numerous traditions recorded from him in the various Shīʿī, Ṣūfī, and Sunnī works. In Shīʿī literature (especially Ithnāʿasharī and Ismāʿīlī literature), the prominence of Jaʿfar's traditions represent a wide range of subjects comprising both the *ʿibādāt* and the *muʿāmalāt,* incorporating topics such as faith, devotion, alms, fasting, pilgrimage, and *jihād,* as well as food, drink, social and business transactions, marriage and divorce, inheritance, criminal punishments, and a host of other issues dealing with every conceivable aspect of life. As is well known, law in Islam is an all-embracing body of religious commands and prohibitions, consisting not only a proper legal system, but also of ordinances governing worship and ritual.

Jaʿfar al-Ṣādiq's teaching became so effective and influential that the Ithnāʿasharī legal school is called the *Jaʿfarī madhhab* after him. In addition, Fāṭimid Ismāʿīlī *fiqh* or jurisprudence, codified by al-Qāḍī al-Nuʿmān, is based mainly on the traditions of al-Ṣādiq and al-Bāqir. It is practically impossible to envisage the development of the Shīʿī tradition without Jaʿfar al-Ṣādiq; he is the most frequently quoted authority. Besides providing specific guidance to his own group, he was widely regarded as a central reference point for many others who sought his advice amidst the legal problems discussed and argued over in early Islam. Thus, within the context of his contemporaries in the Ḥijāz and Iraq, Jaʿfar was seen as a distinguished traditionist and jurist transmitting his family's views on a wide range of issues in his time.

Jaʿfar also represented his own distinct position among the theological issues of his day, such as those of the Murjiʾa, the Qādar ī yah, the Jahmiyah, and the Muʿtazilah, undoubtedly based on his own understanding of religious leadership. He taught a middle position on the question of determinism, following his father's views, which portrayed human responsibility but preserved God's absolute authority. Knowledge was a central theme in his teaching and a duty for all Muslims to acquire through *ʿaql* (intellect). For him, the intellect is that supreme faculty by which God is worshiped and through which the knowledge of good and evil is acquired; this knowledge, in turn, teaches people, among other things, how to struggle against tendencies of their own lower nature in order to purify the self. His views on the imamate and those on *ʿaql, ʿilm* (knowledge), *ʿamāl* (action), and *īmān* were therefore geared towards self-actualization. His concern for personal ethics and morality, as well as individual communion with God, is thus aimed at obtaining that receptivity in the heart and mind that he sometimes refers to as *maʿrifah* (not to be confused with its later usage).

***Imām* and Teacher.** For the Shīʿah, therefore, besides building an impressive edifice of Shīʿī law and theology, Jaʿfar al-Ṣādiq also played the role of a spiritual guide, *imām*, and teacher, initiating followers into the inner paths of knowledge and wisdom. An important aspect of Jaʿfar's thought was a search for *ḥaqīqah* (truth) in the revelation, and his teachings certainly reveal Shiism as the esoteric aspect of Islam. Undoubtedly, the crux of his teaching is the concept of the imamate, which perceives the perpetual need among humankind for an authoritative teacher who is both divinely guided and infallible.

The *amānah* or trust that the *imām* undertakes from God renders him a guarantor (*ḥujjah*) and a link (*sabab*) with the celestial world for individuals who accept his authority. This authority of the *imām* is part of the universal history, which begins with the pre-creation covenant, *yawm al-mithāq*, manifested through the chain of prophets and their legatees, the *imāms*. The *imām*'s task is therefore the purification of humanity in order to prepare appropriate receptacles for the *ḥaqīqah*, which is the *raison d'être* of history, restoring human beings to their original home. Jaʿfar's spirituality was not simply escapism, but expressed a genuine desire to articulate this experience for others to recognize and emulate. This was his role as an *imām*—to help others achieve this *maʿrifah qalbīyah* (cognition of the heart). This *maʿrifah* is channeled and communicated to the believers by the *imām*, who helps the faithful achieve *ḥaqīqah*. Although Jaʿfar's traditions communicate spirituality, he did not entertain extreme Gnosticism with the insular, individualistic, and anti-intellectual implications found in some later Ṣūfī movements. The vision of human hearts perceiving the realities of faith in human thought does not involve an esotericism refuting the authority of the intellect or that of the community. Self-sufficiency, a cardinal sin in the Qurʾān, can easily transpose into intellectual pride, and consequently according to Jaʿfar, human *ʿilm* is subordinated to God's gift of *maʿrifah,* and it is the prophets and the *imāms* who form the point of this contact between humans and God.

Jaʿfar al-Ṣādiq's ideas were especially pervasive in the development of the Ṣūfī movement, where the same issues were raised, though in a more individualistic manner. Jaʿfar's terminology made significant contributions to Ṣūfī thought, especially in employing experience as a hermeneutical principle. Paul Nywia (1970) emphasizes this contribution of Jaʿfar al-Ṣādiq, referring to his esoteric interpretation of the Qurʾān, collected by al-Sulamī (d. 1021). Muslim conscience is not in the world of imagination but in the living experience itself, and the external symbols have to be transformed by experience to become the truth. It is therefore important to internalize the letters or symbols in the Qurʾān through experience. Jaʿfar thus discerned in the Qurʾān a merger between the inner and the outer meanings, and he put forward a new exegesis that is no longer a reading of the Qurʾān, but a reading of the experience in a new interpretation of the Qurʾān *(taʾwīl).*

Jaʿfar al-Ṣādiq is also linked to several other major disciplines of divination, including alchemy; the science of *jafr*, which includes letter-number correspondences; and the occult arts, including pulmonancy (divination from body pulses) and hemerology (divination using calendars of auspicious and inauspicious days). Many of these were popular among the Turks and Persians, and they have been reported in works known as *fāl-nāmas*. On the Indian subcontinent the *fāl-nāmas* played an important role in the popular life of Muslims, as well as Hindus, evidence of which is found in Sindhi *pothīs* (private religious manuscripts). In South Asia, Jaʿfar al-Ṣādiq is credited with writing *khab-nāmas* (interpretations of dreams), sometimes referred to in Sindhi literature as *risāla* or *bayān.*

Jaʿfar's multiple roles are clearly evident in the development of intellectual and spiritual currents of his time. His seminal role in articulating Shīʿī thought provided a momentum for the development of law and theology, apparent in the monumental literature preserved in his name.

BIBLIOGRAPHY

Amir Moezzi, Mohammad Ali. *The Divine Guide in Early Shiʿism: The Sources of Esotericism in Islam.* Translated by David Streight. Albany, N.Y., 1994.

ʿAṭṭār, Farīd al-Dīn. *Tadhkirāt al-awliya'*, pt. 1. Edited by Reynold A. Nicholson. London, 1905.

Dhahabī, al-. *Tadhkirāt al-ḥufāz*, vol. 1. Hyderabad, India, 1955.

Ebeid, R. Y., and M. J. L. Young. "A Treatise on Hemerology Ascribed to Ǧāʿfar al-Ṣādiq." *Arabica* 23, no. 3 (1976): 296–307.

Fahd, T. "Ǧāʿfar al-Ṣadiq et la tradition scientifique arabe." In *Le Shiʿisme Imāmite Colloque de Strasbourg 6–9 mai 1968*, edited by T. Fahd, pp. 132–142. Paris, 1970.

Jafri, S. Husain M. *Origins and Early Development of Shiʿa Islam.* Beirut, 1979.

Kulaynī, Muḥammad ibn Yaʿqūb al-. *Al-Uṣūl min al-Kāfī.* Teheran, Iran, 1968.

Lalani, Arzina R. *Early Shiʿi Thought: The Teachings of Imam Muhammad al-Baqir.* London, 2000.

Nywia, Paul. *Exégèse coranique et le language mystique.* Beirut, 1970.

Qāḍī al-Nuʿmān, Abū Ḥanīfa al-. *Daʿāʾim al-Islām.* Edited by Asaf A. A. Fyzee. 2 vols. Cairo, 1950 and 1960. First volume translated and annotated as *The Pillars of Islam* by Ismail K. Poonawala. Oxford, 2002.

Sells, Michael A. "Early Sufi Qurʾān Interpretation." In *Early Islamic Mysticism: Sufi, Qurʾan, Miraj, Poetic, and Theological Writings*, translated and edited by Michael A. Sells, pp. 75–89. New York, 1996.

Ṭabarī, Abū Jaʿfar Muḥammad ibn Jarīr al-. *Taʾrīkh al-rusūl wa-al-mulūk. Annales.* Edited by M. J. de Goeje. Leiden, 1879–1901.

Taylor, John B. "Jaʿfar al-Ṣādiq: Spiritual Forebear of the Sufis." *Islamic Culture* 40 (April 1966): 97–113.

Taylor, John B. "Man's Knowledge of God in the Thought of Jaʿfar al-Ṣādiq." *Islamic Culture* 40 (October 1966): 195–206.

Yaʿqūbī, Aḥmad b. Ibn Wāḍiḥ al-. *Taʾrīkh*, vol. 2. Beirut, n.d.

ARZINA R. LALANI (2005)

JAGUARS.

JAGUARS. The jaguar (*Panthera onca*) is the largest native American cat, and for over three thousand years it has been one of Central and South America's most important symbolic animals. Sometimes associated with the puma (*Felis concolor*) and ocelot (*Felis pardalis*), the jaguar was a recurring motif in the religious iconography of many major pre-Columbian civilizations, including the Olmec, Maya, and Aztec in Mesoamerica and the Chavín and Moche in South America. In the twenty-first century, throughout tropical rain-forest areas, the jaguar still plays an important role in the spiritual beliefs of indigenous Amerindian societies.

As with all animal symbols, jaguar imagery is more than artistic depiction. It represents the symbolic joining of animal and human features and qualities and epitomizes the ways physical attributes and supernatural qualities could be fused to represent deities, spirits, shamans, and divine rulers. Beautiful and deadly, the jaguar's strength and agility made it a paragon of predatory male human virtues associated with hunters, warriors, sacrifice, and war. Its stealth, night vision, and nocturnal hunting habits identified it with sorcery and the spirit realm. Its widespread status as "Master of Animals" probably derives from its ability to hunt on land, up trees, and in water, and from the fact that while all animals are its prey, it is prey to none. Only humans kill jaguars, a fact that may account for the perception that both share a spiritual equivalence as equals.

In Mesoamerica the jaguar icon first appeared in the art of the Olmec civilization (1250–400 BCE) as monumental stone sculptures and intricate jade carvings, such as those found at sites such as La Venta and San Lorenzo in eastern Mexico. A common image is a half-human, half-feline creature with characteristic downturned snarling mouth, which has been interpreted as a were-jaguar—the supernatural offspring of Olmec rulers and mythical jaguar beings. Some sculptures depict what are regarded as shamans transforming into spirit felines. Broadly contemporary was the cult center of Chavín de Huántar in Peru (850–200 BCE), where startling images of jaguars and animals and humans with jaguar features were carved in stone, cast in gold, and worked in textiles and pottery. A decorative frieze at Chavín shows a procession of carved-stone jaguars and humans with feline fangs and claws, some of which appear associated with the hallucinogenic San Pedro cactus and which in turn indicates a shamanic religion.

Once established, the symbolic and spiritual relationship between the jaguar and human elites appears to have become a widespread phenomenon. As an icon linking spiritual dominance, rulership, sacrifice, and war, jaguar imagery became a recurring feature in art. Among Mesoamerica's Classic Maya (250–850 CE), jaguar pelts were worn by dynastic warrior kings and were used to cover royal thrones, themselves sometimes carved in feline form, as at Palenque and Chichén Itzá. Elsewhere, jaguar and ocelot apparel featured as war regalia, and jaguar imagery was associated with hieroglyphic texts referring to war and human sacrifice.

Royal titles incorporated the jaguar icon, and deceased kings were sometimes buried with the animal's skin, claws, and fangs. The sacrifice of fifteen jaguars by Yax Pac, king of Copán, to his ancestors suggests a spiritual identity between royalty and the jaguar, exemplified perhaps by the Classic Maya jaguar god of the underworld. At the later Toltec-Maya city of Chichén Itzá, jaguars appear eating what may be human hearts—perhaps symbolic representations of human sacrifice by a jaguar warrior elite. On Peru's north coast, jaguar imagery was similarly associated with warfare and human sacrifice in the Moche culture (100–650 CE). Master potters depicted sacrificial victims, perhaps prisoners of war, alongside jaguar figures, mountains, and possibly the

San Pedro cactus. Anthropomorphic figures appear with snarling jaguar fangs, giving the impression of a shamanic religion based on the transformation of powerful individuals into a supernatural jaguar being.

The jaguar played an equally important, though better documented, role in Mesoamerican Aztec religion and iconography. Known as *ocelotl,* it was regarded as the bravest of beasts, proud "ruler of the animal world." Its association with warfare was acknowledged in eponymous metaphors describing valiant soldiers, such as the elite Jaguar Warrior Society (*ocelomeh*). Religion, mythology, and astrology combined in the belief that those born under the calendrical sign *ocelotl* shared the jaguar's aggressive nature and were well suited to a warrior's life. Aztec sorcerers wielded the jaguar's pelt and claws as magical weapons during nocturnal rituals.

Aztec rulers also appropriated jaguar imagery. The emperor wore jaguar apparel in war and held court seated on thrones draped with the animal's pelt. Tezcatlipoca, the supreme Aztec deity, was patron of royalty and inventor of sacrifice whose alter ego was a huge jaguar known as Tepeyolotl. At the center of the Aztec universe—the Great Temple of Tenochtitlan (Mexico City)—complete feline bodies were interred with balls of jade gripped in their fangs. The temple was regarded mythologically as the "cosmic water mountain," jade symbolized water, and the jaguar was associated with fertility.

The metaphysical associations of the pre-Columbian jaguar survived into the colonial period, merging with the imagery of Old World lions and tigers and influenced by Christian beliefs. The animal's spiritual ambivalence, variously signifying good and evil, fertility and death, also persisted. In sixteenth-century Mexico sorcerers known as *nahuallis* were accused by the Spanish of devil worship, murder, insurrection, and changing into jaguars. Elsewhere in Mesoamerica the jaguar became Christ's defender, its pelt symbolizing its protective role in the passion. At the Maya village of Chamula, in the highlands of the Mexican state of Chiapas, there is a New Year ritual called the "Jaguar Skin Dance" understood as part of Christ's passion. During this dance, civil and religious leaders take turns to dance wearing a jaguar skin that symbolizes God's jaguar, which defended Christ against demons. The one who wears the skin impersonates the defender of Christ. Images of the jaguar also replaced the lion at the feet of St. Jerome, and for the Maya of Chamula only civic leaders and shamans could have the jaguar as their animal soul companion. In Colombia, by contrast, aggressive aspects of jaguar imagery were mobilized against the Spanish in the ferocious "tiger men" who fought the white invaders.

In modern Central and South America, jaguar masks and costumes are popular folk art items. In rural areas they are worn by dancers in religiously syncretic springtime festivals that mix Catholic beliefs with pre-Columbian ideas concerning the protection of crops and livestock. In remoter areas of Mexico echoes of ancient blood rituals survive in fiestas, where young men dressed as jaguars fight to spill blood for the jaguar deity, who then sends rain to fertilize the maize. Jaguar masks can be mainly decorative and made of wood or fabric and worn as part of dance costumes, as at the village of Totoltepec in the Mexican state of Guerrero. They can also be more like helmets, made from toughened wild pig skin, and worn as protection during violent ritualised fights between young men dressed as jaguars, as at the villages of Acatlán and Zitlala, also in the Mexican state of Guerrero.

In the tropical rain-forests of lowland South America, the jaguar remains a more visceral spiritual force as well as a feared and admired predator. In Amazonian mythology the jaguar was the original possessor of fire, though now only a reflected glow can be seen in its mirrored eyes. Jaguar metaphors signify bravery in battle and success in hunting, both in the physical world and the supernatural realm, where it is the spirit helper of shamans and chiefs. For Amazonian Indians, meeting a jaguar on a jungle path can be an unnerving experience, as one can never be sure whether it is the natural animal, the shade of an ancestor, or a malevolent shaman-turned-jaguar on a mission of vengeance against some enemy.

As the natural jaguar is the rain-forest's most powerful and resourceful hunter, so the supernatural jaguar is the most potent and dangerous spiritual force. Dominant shamans identify themselves with the jaguar, their reputation as successful curers based on their superior ability to defeat illness-bearing spirits. These jaguar-shamans may wear necklaces of jaguar fangs and claws, growl during trance, and eat the animal's magical strength-giving flesh. The spiritual equivalence between jaguars and shamans is sometimes made explicit in the widespread belief that, under the influence of hallucinogens, some shamans transform into jaguars in body as well as spirit.

See Also Mesoamerican Religions; South American Indian Religions.

Bibliography

Benson, Elizabeth P. "The Classic Maya Use of Jaguar Accessories." In *Fourth Palenque Round Table, 1980,* edited by Elizabeth P. Benson, pp. 155–156. San Francisco, 1985.

Benson, Elizabeth P. "The Lord, the Ruler: Jaguar Symbolism in the Americas." In *Icons of Power: Feline Symbolism in the Americas,* edited by Nicholas J. Saunders, pp. 53–76. London, 1998.

Furst, Peter T. "The Olmec Were-Jaguar Motif in the Light of Ethnographic Reality." In *Dumbarton Oaks Conference on the Olmec,* edited by Elizabeth P. Benson, pp. 143–175. Washington, D.C., 1968.

Kubler, George. "Jaguars in the Valley of Mexico." In *The Cult of the Feline,* edited by Elizabeth P. Benson, pp. 19–49. Washington, D.C., 1972.

Reichel-Dolmatoff, Gerardo. *The Shaman and the Jaguar: A Study of Narcotic Drugs among the Indians of Colombia.* Philadelphia, 1975.

Roe, Peter G. "Paragon or Peril? The Jaguar in Amazonian Indian Society." In *Icons of Power: Feline Symbolism in the Americas*, edited by Nicholas J. Saunders, pp. 171–202. London, 1998.

Saunders, Nicholas J. "The Day of the Jaguar: Rainmaking in a Mexican Village." *Geographical Magazine* 55 (1983): 398–405.

Saunders, Nicholas J. "Tezcatlipoca: Jaguar Metaphors and the Aztec Mirror of Nature." In *Signifying Animals: Human Meaning in the Natural World*, edited by Roy G. Willis, pp. 159–177. London, 1990.

Saunders, Nicholas J. "Architecture of Symbolism: The Feline Image." In *Icons of Power: Feline Symbolism in the Americas*, edited by Nicholas J. Saunders, pp. 12–52. London, 1998.

NICHOLAS J. SAUNDERS (2005)

JAINISM. Jainism is a South Asian religious tradition which takes its name from those (Sanskrit, *Jaina;* English, "Jain") who follow the teachings and example of authoritative teachers called Jina (conqueror). These teachers are also called "makers of the ford" (Sanskrit, *tīrthaṃkara*), signifying their construction of a community of monks, nuns, laymen, and laywomen that provides the means to cross the ocean of rebirth. Jain tradition holds that twenty-four Jinas appear in succession throughout regular temporal movements in the course of eternity and communicate the unchanging doctrine of correct knowledge (*samyagjñāna*), correct faith (*samyagdarśana*), and correct behavior (*samyagcāritra*).

As a soteriology, Jainism teaches that enlightenment in the form of omniscience and subsequent freedom from rebirth can be attained by progressive renunciatory withdrawal—manifesting itself most markedly as nonviolence (*ahiṃsā*)—from physical and sensory interaction with the surrounding world, which is constituted at all levels by embodied life monads.

According to the census of 1991, there are about 3.35 million Jains living in India, while an estimated 100,000 are domiciled abroad, largely in Africa, Britain, and North America.

BEGINNINGS. The historical origins of Jainism can be located in the teachings of Pārśva and Mahāvīra, who are traditionally regarded as the twenty-third and twenty-fourth Jinas of the present time-cycle. Both flourished in the Ganges Basin region of eastern India. The evidence of early Buddhist writings confirms that Mahāvīra was a contemporary of the Buddha, predeceasing him by some years. Since Western scholarship has reached near unanimity that the Buddha lived from approximately 480 to 400 BCE, Mahāvīra's dates must of necessity be changed from the traditional 599 to 527 BCE to about 490 to 410 BCE.

The Jain scriptures maintain that Pārśva lived around two centuries before Mahāvīra. He must therefore be dated to around the seventh century BCE. However, the evidence for the historicity of Pārśva is neither overwhelming nor contemporaneous. Buddhist references to Jain ascetics following four restraints (involving nonviolence, nonlying, not taking what has not been given, and nonpossession) of the sort traditionally attributed to Pārśva, as opposed to the five vows (the four restraints already mentioned, plus celibacy) taught by Mahāvīra, suggest that some sort of ascetic community descended from Pārśva was still in existence in the fifth century BCE, although it is not clearly identifiable subsequently. To argue that Mahāvīra reformed a preexisting style of ascetic practice promulgated by Pārśva and fitted it into a wider doctrinal setting is merely to frame a hypothesis, but it is one which makes sense of later Jain insistence that there was a link between the two teachers.

The broad trajectory of Mahāvīra's career as conveyed by tradition is stereotypical in that it was enacted by virtually all the other Jinas. The main events of his life involved the abandonment on reaching full maturity of a domestic life of royal ease, a subsequent austere search for knowledge, the gaining of full awakening, the subsequent conversion of followers and founding of a community, and death at an advanced age followed by a cremation appropriate for a king.

Mahāvīra's basic teachings, as opposed to the developed doctrine of classical Jainism that took final shape around the beginning of the first millennium CE (see below), can be reconstructed from what are accepted as being the oldest Jain texts. These teachings are anti-Brahmanic in their rejection of the validity of the Vedic sacrificial ritual, and they frequently intersect with elements of other contemporaneous renunciatory doctrines that circulated in the Ganges basin area. It was surely Mahāvīra's thoroughgoing analysis (quickly to be attributed to the quality of omniscience) of the multilayered living world which encompasses human beings, and his call for a heroic change of stance toward that world which provided a combination of the radically subversive and the inspirational, that was to render his teachings influential and long lasting.

According to Mahāvīra, the world is full of eternal life monads called *jīva* (from Sanskrit, *jīv* [live]; the oldest Jain texts also use the term *āyā,* equivalent to Sanskrit *ātman* [self], found in Brahmanic texts such as the Upaniṣads), which in their purest form possess the qualities of complete knowledge, energy, and bliss. However, those life monads, trapped in the world of rebirth (*saṃsāra*) as a result of their violent activities, are of necessity embodied in not just human and animal shape, but also in plant and insect form, extending down to those that exist in earth, water, air, and fire. Interaction with this world of visible and invisible life-forms, even through such basic activities as motion and breathing, inexorably effects destruction (*hiṃsā*) that leads through rebirth to further embodiment and gradual debasement of status. The only way to escape this perilous situation is to withdraw from performing, promoting, and approving physical, mental, and vocal "action" (*karman*). The sole appropriate mode of life that can facilitate the full practice of nonviolence (*ahiṃsā*) is ascetic renunciation.

HISTORY. A group of disciples (*gaṇadhara*), originally Brāhmaṇs, is credited with channeling Mahāvīra's teachings by putting them into textual form and taking over the direction of the community. Most significant among these *gaṇadhara* were Gautama Indrabhūti, portrayed in the scriptures as an interlocutor of Mahāvīra; Sudharman, credited by the Śvetāmbara sect (see below) with initiating its ascetic lineage; and Jambū, the last individual of this world age to gain enlightenment.

The early history of Jainism can be broadly reconstructed. Although the community never completely abandoned the area of its origins in the Ganges Basin, it quickly moved along the main trade routes of ancient South Asia, and by around the third to second centuries BCE it could be found in the northwestern city of Mathurā and in the Tamil country in the far south of the peninsula. Archaeological and inscriptional evidence from Mathurā bears witness to the existence there of ascetic lineages, a largely bourgeois lay community, and a cult centering on commemorative devotional worship of the Jinas in iconic form.

Mathurā and its environs seem to have been the center of a monastic community that styled itself *ardhaphālaka* (partially clothed), owing to its members being completely naked apart from a distinctive strip of cloth carried over the forearm. By the beginning of the common era, there existed a variety of styles of Jain monastic praxis, in which the wearing or abandonment of clothes were emblematic. This originally fluid situation became polarized by around the fourth to fifth centuries CE with the formation of two sects, the Śvetāmbara (white-clad), whose monks and nuns wear white robes, and the Digambara (sky-clad), whose monks go naked.

Further differences between these two groups were to emerge, although there was no disagreement about the central teachings of Jainism. The Digambaras were to reject the authenticity of the scriptural canon that emerged among the Śvetāmbaras (see below) and also claimed, unlike the Śvetāmbaras, that the fully enlightened individual (*kevalin*) transcended normal human behavior in not needing to eat, drink, or sleep. The Śvetāmbaras have always accepted that women are capable of gaining the goal of the religions in the same manner as men, whereas the Digambaras deny this on the grounds that women cannot, for social reasons, go naked like the true ascetic, and because they are incapable of any form of intense moral action. There are today only a small number of Digambara nuns who accept that because of the necessity to wear clothing they will only be able to make serious spiritual progress when reborn as males.

While other Jain sects existed, such as the Yāpanīyas who eventually disappeared around the beginning of the second millennium CE, the Śvetāmbara and Digambara sects have remained the two main pillars of the Jain community, with each claiming its interpretation of the practice of Jainism to be the more valid. The prestige of these two sects in the first millennium was enhanced by the achievement of a number of celebrated teachers, such as Siddhasena Divākara (Śvetāmbara; sixth century) and Akalaṅka (Digambara; ninth century). The Śvetāmbara Haribhadra (of uncertain date, possibly sixth or ninth centuries) left a particularly impressive body of writings in a wide variety of genres and became a major authority for later tradition.

Initially Jainism gained less consistent royal support than Buddhism, although at least one monarch, Khāravela (second century BCE) of the kingdom of Kaliṅga (modern Orissa in eastern India), was a devotee. However, Jainism subsequently deployed some of the imperial symbolism current in north India and presented itself in a manner congenial to aristocratic patrons as well as those of a trading background. This was particularly the case in medieval south India, where Digambara Jainism, with its ideology of spiritual transformation couched in the imagery of heroic conquest, was patronized by rulers and feudatories of prominent dynasties such as the Cālukyas and the Rāṣṭrakūṭas. The greatest Jain monument to the interaction between royal power and ascetic renunciation is the fifty-two-foot-high image, erected by the general Cāmuṇḍarāya in 951 at Śravaṇa Beḷgoḷa (south Karnataka), of Bāhubali, a prince who withdrew from martial violence to become an ascetic and was, according to Digambara tradition, the first individual of this world age to achieve liberation. The ritual anointment of this image, which occurs every twelve years, attracts huge numbers of onlookers and is one of India's most spectacular religious ceremonies. Although Jainism was an integral part of south Indian culture and Digambara monks played an important role in the early promulgation of literature in languages like Tamil and Kannada, the religion gradually lost its access to political power, and from the ninth to the thirteenth centuries vigorous anti-Jain Śaiva movements supplanted it in royal favor and effected large-scale conversions to Hinduism.

From the medieval period, the religious affairs of the image-worshiping Digambara community have been conducted by orange-robed celibate clerics called *bhaṭṭāraka* (a title signifying "learned"), specialists in ritual and the scriptures who occupy pontifical seats endowed with some of the trappings of secular kingship. The most well-known *bhaṭṭāraka* seats are at Śravaṇa Beḷgoḷa, Mūdbiḍrī, and Hombuja in Karnataka and Kolhāpur and Karāñjā in Maharashtra. Those Digambaras, largely to be found in Madhya Pradesh, who do not approve of image-worship and the presiding role of *bhaṭṭārakas* assign a prominent ritual position to sacred texts. The Digambara ascetic lineage was revived in the nineteenth century after becoming virtually defunct in the late medieval period. Today the Digambara Jains, around one million in number, remain a numerically small, although resilient community in Maharashtra, Karnataka, Rajasthan, and Tamil Nadu.

Since the fifth century CE, the main center of Śvetāmbara Jainism has been in Gujarat in western India. The Digambaras had lost serious influence in that region by the eleventh century, according to Śvetāmbara tradition, because of their failure in public debate. The greatest figure in medieval Gujarati Jainism was Hemacandra (1089–1172), a polymath monk who became court scholar of the Caulukya dynasty during the reigns of Siddharāja and his nephew Kumārapāla (1144–1173). Hemacandra is credited with having persuaded Kumārapāla to rule his kingdom in partial accordance with Jain ethical principles. The *Yogaśāstra,* written by Hemacandra as a compendium of lay behavior and still an authoritative text, may have been intended to guide Kumārapāla. Western India is the location of the most conspicuous exemplifications of Śvetāmbara religiosity, the great temple complexes built on Mount Śatruñjaya near Pālitāna, Mount Girnar near Junagaḍh, and Mount Ābū, the major initial impetus for which came in the eleventh century. Of particular note is the Dharnā Vihāra temple at Rāṇakpur in south Rajasthan, which was consecrated in 1441.

Beginning in the eleventh century a variety of Śvetāmbara sublineages (*gaccha*) appeared in western India, deriving from teachers who claimed to be reforming ascetic practice or who advocated ritual and calendrical innovations. While all represented themselves as promulgating the true form of Jainism reaching back to Mahāvīra's disciple Sudharman and converted numerous lay followers, only three of these have remained significant until the present day: the Kharatara Gaccha (founded in the eleventh century), the Añcala Gaccha (founded in the twelfth century), and the Tapā Gaccha (founded in the thirteenth century). Of these, the Tapā Gaccha is today by far the most prominent Śvetāmbara subsect in terms of numbers and intellectual and social prestige.

During the premodern period, Śvetāmbara Jainism in western India often found itself in an embattled situation because of the dominance of Islam. On occasion, however, Jain monks had access to political authority and were able to intercede to gain privileges for their community. Most notably, Hīravijaya Sūri (1527–1596), the head of the Tapā Gaccha, had a preceptorial relationship with the Moghul emperor Akbar (r. 1555–1605), at times prevailing upon him to abandon hunting and the slaughter of animals for food.

Controversies were to emerge within the Śvetāmbara Jain community in the early modern period. In the fifteenth century a layman called Loṅkā provided the impetus for the eventual appearance of new Śvetāmbara lineages that adopted a more radical approach to ascetic practice and abandoned temple-oriented Jainism and its attendant image cult. The Sthānakvāsī (Living in Lodging Houses) sect emerged in the seventeenth century, gaining its name from the fact that its ascetics took their temporary residence not in halls specially built beside temples but in dilapidated or unused buildings. Sthānakvāsī monks and nuns adopted the permanent wearing of the "mouth-shield" (*muhpattī*), hitherto only used on ritual occasions, in token of their continual adherence to nonviolence through minimizing injury to organisms in the air. The Sthānakvāsins have remained an important component of Jainism, particularly in Gujarat and Panjab.

In the eighteenth century a monk called Bhikṣu left the Sthānakvāsī community in the Marwar region of Rajasthan in rejection of its perceived laxity and founded a sect that came to be called Terāpanthī (Following the Thirteen Principles). This sect, recognizable by its ascetics' adoption of a mouth-shield more extended in shape than that of the Sthānakvāsins, was particularly radical in its espousal of a scripturally derived mode of life, and it accordingly claimed that the duty of the ascetic lay in the attainment of his or her own liberation, not in facilitating the gaining of merit. From Bhikṣu's time, sole authority in the Terāpanthī sect has been concentrated in the hands of each succeeding teacher, unlike the more fragmented situation prevailing in other Jain sects. In postindependence India, the Terāpanthī sect was associated with a campaign to uplift public morals and ban nuclear weapons.

SCRIPTURE. For Jain tradition, the scriptural corpus (*āgama*) formulated in identical manner by each Jina is eternal and totally authoritative in that it conveys the teaching of omniscient beings. Both the Śvetāmbara and Digambara sects maintain that there were originally fourteen texts called Pūrva (Prior) that eventually became lost, with some surviving texts representing a residue of what had once been a huge quantity of textual material.

Viewed historically, the Jain scriptural corpus as transmitted by the Śvetāmbaras developed over a considerable period of time, with the version current today apparently having been established at the council of Valabhī in the fifth century CE, in the last of a series of redactions. Only a relative chronology can be established. While some portions of the scriptures, such as the first chapter of the *Ācārāṅga Sūtra,* can realistically be dated back almost to the time of Mahāvīra, when composition and transmission were oral, others are (from the stylistic point of view) productions of the early common era, by which time writing had become the preferred method of transmission.

The language in which the canon was composed is called Ardhamāgadhī (Half Māgadhī), signifying a connection with the Magadha region of the Ganges Basin. Although having a vernacular base, this most likely functioned as a scriptural language only and was never spoken as a mother tongue. Some demonstrably later portions of the canon are composed in Mahārāṣṭrī Prākrit, a literary vernacular of the early common era.

The scriptural canon as accepted today by image-worshiping Śvetāmbaras consists of a large number of texts, divided into various subgroups. (There is no generally accepted number of texts, as the Sthānakvāsins and Terāpanthins omit thirteen from the total listed below and other enumerations have also been in circulation.) The first subgroup, the Twelve "Limbs" (*Aṅga*), consists of:

1. The *Ācārāṅga Sūtra,* which describes ascetic behavior and contains a biography of Mahāvīra.
2. The *Sūtrakṛtāṅga Sūtra,* which contains a wide range of material including accounts of non-Jain teachings.

3. The *Sthānāṅga Sūtra.*
4. The *Samavāyāṅga Sūtra,* encyclopedic texts listing significant categories for all aspects of Jainism.
5. The *Vyākhyāprajñapti Sūtra,* which records dialogues between Mahāvīra and his disciple Indrabhūti concerning a wide range of cosmological, ontological, and disciplinary issues.
6. The *Jñātādharmakathāḥ Sūtra,* exemplary and legendary narratives.
7. The *Upāsakadaśāḥ,* narratives of pious laymen.
8. The *Antakṛddaśāḥ,* narratives of those who ended rebirth.
9. The *Anuttaraupapātikadaśāḥ,* narratives describing those reborn as gods.
10. The *Praśnavyākaraṇāni,* questions and answers about doctrinal issues.
11. The *Vipākaśruta,* descriptions of the operation of *karma.*
12. The *Dṛṣṭivāda,* which were accepted as lost by the early common era.

The second subgroup, made up of the Twelve "Subordinate Limbs" (*Upāṅga*), includes:

1. The *Aupapātika Sūtra,* a description of a sermon by Mahāvīra and an account of non-Jain teachings and ascetics.
2. The *Rājapraśnīya Sūtra,* a discussion between King Prasenajit and a monk concerning ontological matters.
3. The *Jīvājīvābhigama Sūtra,* which describes the various categories of existence.
4. The *Prajñāpanā Sūtra,* which describes a wide range of epistemological and ontological topics.
5. The *Sūryaprajñapti Sūtra.*
6. The *Jambūdvīpaprajñapti Sūtra.*
7. The *Candraprajñapti Sūtra,* cosmological and astronomical texts.

8–12. A series of short narrative texts.

The third subgroup is formed by the *Cheda Sūtras*, which consist of seven texts dealing with disciplinary matters. The eighth chapter of the first, the *Ācāradaśāḥ,* is the *Kalpa Sūtra.* This text, which contains a biography of Mahāvīra, disciplinary recommendations, and the early lineage of the Jain ascetic community, is the focus of the most important period of the Śvetāmbara ritual year, Paryuṣan, when it is publicly recited and illustrations of it are displayed. The *Mahāniśītha Sūtra* is, on the grounds of language and content, later than the other texts, and its status was a source of controversy during the Medieval period.

The fourth subgroup consists of the "Fundamental" (*mūla*) Sūtras—namely, the *Uttarādhyayana Sūtra,* the *Daśavaikālika Sūtra,* the *Āvaśyaka Sūtra,* and (treated together) the *Piṇḍaniryukti* and *Oghaniryukti*—which set out the parameters of ascetic behavior and are to be studied at the beginning of the renunciant career.

The fifth subgroup consists of the "Mixed" Texts, which are, according to the most common enumeration, eleven short (and generally late) works describing subjects such as astrology and ascetic ritual.

Finally, the sixth subgroup consists of two hermeneutical texts, the *Nandī Sūtra* and the *Anuyogadvāra Sūtra.*

There is at present no definitive critical edition of the Śvetāmbara Jain scriptures. An extensive exegetical literature was produced from the early common era, with the oldest examples being the Prakrit mnemonic verses, called *niryukti,* attributed to the early–common era teacher Bhadrabāhu. The leading commentator in Sanskrit was Abhayadeva Sūri (eleventh century).

The Digambaras reject the authority of the Śvetāmbara scriptural canon in favor of texts that emerged at the beginning of the common era and are regarded as representing the residue of the ancient tradition. The Prakrit in which they are written, whose origins lie in the Mathurā region, is generally called Jaina Śaurasenī. The *Ṣaṭkhaṇḍāgama* (Scripture of Six Parts) attributed to the monk Dharasena (c. second century CE) and the approximately contemporary *Kaṣāyaprābhṛta* (Treatise on the Passions) are massive compilations dealing with the soul and its varying connections with karma. Also authoritative for the Digambaras are two early–common era works on ascetic behavior, the *Mūlācāra* (Basic behavior) of Vaṭṭakera and the *Bhagavatī Ārādhanā* (Revered accomplishing) of Śivārya. Of slightly more uncertain date are the influential verse treatises of Kundakunda, which adumbrate a radically interiorized, soul-oriented version of Jainism and have remained highly influential to the present day.

Unless they are scholars, Jains of both sects have generally had the scriptural tradition mediated to them in the form of practical canons consisting of short, often epitomizing texts that have sometimes been produced in relatively recent times. For the last two millennia, Jain writers have been major contributors to Indian literature in a wide variety of languages and in all the important literary genres. The literary language known as Apabhraṃśa was employed predominantly by Jain poets whose willingness to use popular song meters ensured their compositions wide circulation in western India between 1000 and 1300. A vast number of Jain hymns were composed in early forms of vernacular languages like Hindi and Gujarati.

TEACHINGS. Although tradition regards the teachings of Jainism as having been enunciated in full by Mahāvīra, it is possible to trace an evolution through the scriptural texts that reveals the intermittent influence of non-Jain philosophical positions and attempts to tighten up doctrinal structures. The introduction of the ontological categories of motion (*dharma*) and rest (*adharma*) and an atomic theory to explain the functioning of the material world are cases in point.

The textual catalyst for the formulation of a definitive version of the teachings is the *Tattvārtha Sūtra* (Sūtra on the meaning of the reals) by Umāsvāti, a monk belonging to a northern lineage who flourished around the fourth century CE. This sūtra is claimed, with some variants, by both the Śvetāmbaras and Digambaras. Using the medium of the short rule formulated in Sanskrit (*sūtra*), Umāsvāti identified and explained the main components of Jain teaching as they had developed throughout the canonical period in a manner that has remained authoritative until the present day.

Jainism is both dualist—in that it posits that the soul is different from nature—and pluralist—in its acceptance of the existence of a multitude of separate entities in the universe. Contrary to Brahmanic ideology, it teaches that there is no creator god and that the universe has existed and will continue to do so throughout eternity. Reality, identified as both permanent and subject to change, is composed of five (or six) categories: the *jīva,* or "life monad," and the four (or five) categories of non-*jīva,* namely motion, rest, atoms, and space (the Digambaras add time). The *jīva*—while eternal and in its purest form possessed of consciousness (including the faculty of understanding), energy, and bliss—embodies itself in six forms: earth-bodied, fire-bodied, air-bodied, water-bodied, stationary (in the form of plants and trees), and moving (including insects, animals, men, gods, and hell-beings). These embodiments are further differentiated by the number of senses they possess.

The cause of the external differentiation and psychic degradation of the *jīva* is *karma,* envisaged in Jainism as a fine material substance not dissimilar to dust. Each modulation of the *jīva,* whether physical, mental, or vocal, intentional or unintentional, attracts *karma* to itself. The more intense the modulation, the more karmic substance is attracted to the *jīva* to occlude the efficacy of its innate characteristics. Some awkwardnesses in this explanation had to be resolved by later Jain systematizers. For example, an allowance for the possibility of intention as motivating the quality of action was introduced to modify what might otherwise have been an excessively severe moral vision. Jain theorists were to develop, over almost a millennium and a half, a highly elaborate taxonomy of *karma,* charting in detail the subdivisions of the "harming" (*ghātiyā*) type, responsible for the diminution of faith, knowledge, and energy and the creation of false and deluded attitudes to the world, and the "nonharming" (*aghātiyā*), responsible for setting the parameters of existence in terms of birth, gender, length of life, and quality of experience.

Jainism is envisaged in ideal terms as a path of self-discipline that can progressively effect the "warding off" (*saṃvara*) of the influx of new *karma* and the "wearing away" (*nirjarā*) of that *karma* which has already been bound. When a human being (the only creature in the universe capable of this) destroys the harming *karmas* through the fire of asceticism (*tapas*), he gains pure omniscience and becomes an omniscient *kevalin* (Jinahood is reached by a particularly rare type of *karma*). When the karmically dictated period of life reaches its end, the *jīva* leaves its human shell to gain liberation (*mokṣa*) and moves in one instant to the roof of the universe, where it dwells in a state of pure energy, bliss, and knowledge along with but separate from all the other liberated (*siddha*) *jīvas*. Although the path is presented in universalist terms, Jainism posits the existence of a category of *jīva* called *abhavya* that is innately and eternally incapable of gaining liberation, thus ensuring that the world of rebirth will never be emptied.

Since any epistemological judgment short of that based on omniscience is necessarily incomplete, direct cognition and inference (along with two other advanced forms of knowledge accepted by Jainism, namely the ability to read other people's minds and clairvoyance) can only provide a partially correct understanding of a multiform world that is simultaneously permanent and changing. In acknowledgement of the complex nature of reality, Jain teachers formulated the "Many-pointed Doctrine" (*anekāntavāda*), which stipulates that any given object must be approached from seven standpoints (*naya*) in order to construct a valid judgment about it. The various judgments that can be formed are nonetheless provisional and should ideally be prefaced with the word *syāt* (maybe, perhaps).

In medieval times this pluralist style of analysis served the polemical purpose of destabilizing Brāhmaṇ claims concerning permanent essences and Buddhist teachings about impermanent constructed entities, both regarded by the Jains as partial and inadequate explanations of reality. In more modern times, the Many-pointed Doctrine has enabled liberal-minded Jains to present their religion as unique in terms of its tolerance and promotion of peace.

Renunciant Practice. Historically, the monk (most commonly, *muni, sādhu;* in the earliest period, *nirgrantha* [bondless]) has been the main representative of Jain values. This central role is commemorated within the most ubiquitous portion of Jain liturgy, the "Five Homages" (*Pañcanamaskāra*) *mantra,* in which homage is expressed in Prākrit to the omniscient teachers, the liberated souls, the teachers and preceptors, and all monks in the world.

According to the *Kalpa Sūtra,* an order of nuns was in existence at Mahāvīra's death that was three times as numerous as that of the monks, and female renunciation has been an important dimension of Jainism until the present day, with senior nuns having authority over the female order. However, the Jain nun has always been in a subordinate position to the monk and, invariably, female ascetic experience and its obligations were vectored through the prescriptions of male practitioners. No writings by nuns appear to have been produced before the modern period.

The nascent Jain order seems to have taken the broad structure of its practice from Brahmanic models. The Vedic term *vrata* (calling, vow) is used by the Jains to refer to the "Great Vows" (*mahāvrata*), the five main renunciatory vows defining the practice of an ascetic. Ascetic initiation, which is perceived as a form of radical transformation, is called *dīkṣā*, a term originally signifying the symbolic rebirth of the sponsor of the Vedic sacrifice.

In order to enter the Jain ascetic community, the novice (male or female) undergoes a preliminary initiatory period during which key texts are memorized and the implications of ascetic life conveyed. In the formal ceremony of initiation the presiding senior ascetic gives the novice, as tokens of entry into a transformed mode of life, a new name and various implements (among the Śvetāmbaras, a pair of robes, an alms bowl, a whisk emblematic of nonviolence, a staff, and, for Sthānakvāsī and Terāpanthī initiates, a mouth-shield; among the Digambaras the fully initiated monk who must henceforth go naked is given only a whisk and a water pot for cleaning himself after evacuating bodily wastes). In ancient times the novice pulled out his or her hair in token of sexual and social renunciation, although the general custom today is for the head to be shaved. Thereafter, the ascetic will be a member of a lineage which traces its teacher-pupil relationship back to Mahāvīra (in the case of the Digambaras) or his disciple Sudharman (in the case of the Śvetāmbaras) and will be under the control of senior ascetics who convey the wording and meaning of the scriptures and prescribe and keep watch over all aspects of behavior.

The life of the Jain ascetic is intended to provide the appropriate environment for the enactment of the requirements of nonviolence and the other vows, and thus effect a diminution of the passions. It is envisaged as involving a heroic struggle to overcome the various physical and mental discomforts (*parīṣaha*) that assail the renunciant. A continually watchful and controlled life is schematized in the form of three "Protections" (*gupti*) that involve the guarding of mind, body, and speech, and five "Careful Actions" (*samiti*) that enjoin continual care in movement, speech, seeking for food, receiving or putting down any object, and voiding the bowels.

Wandering mendicancy punctuated by short periods of fixed residence is obligatory, other than for those ascetics who are too infirm or engaged in scholarly activity and during the period of the rains, when the peripatetic life is suspended and monks and nuns live (separately) in lodging halls provided by the laity. Study, religious exercises, and preaching to the laity are the main occupations of ascetics during those periods when they spend time in villages and towns.

As Jain ascetics are not permitted to possess money, cook food, or grow crops, they must seek suitable vegetarian sustenance from (preferably) lay supporters or anybody appropriate who is disposed to give it. Acts of donation to ascetics are deemed to bring about merit for the donor. Śvetāmbara ascetics seek food (an activity called *gocari* [grazing], in token of its supposedly random nature) in the morning and before evening, consuming it out of sight of the laity, whereas their Digambara counterparts seek food only once in the morning, eating from their cupped hands in front of the donor. No Jain ascetic is allowed to eat after dark because of the possibility of unwitting destruction of life forms. Fasting, often over lengthy periods of time, is a regular feature of ascetic practice. Water can only be drunk after it has been boiled and filtered by laypeople.

An important structuring feature of Jain ascetic life is regular ritual activity, the standard model for which was in place by the early common era. The six "Obligatory Actions" (*Āvaśyaka*) to be performed daily are equanimity (*sāmāyika*), praise to the twenty-four Jinas (*caturviṃśatistava*), homage to the teacher (*guruvandaṇa*), repentance (*pratikramana*), laying down the body (*kāyotsarga*), and abandonment (*pratyākhyāna*). Equanimity is a form of temporary withdrawal of the senses, traditionally to be maintained for a period of forty-eight minutes; praise to the Jinas involves a strong devotional and commemorative element; homage to the teacher betokens Jainism's keen awareness of the transmission of the teachings (this ritual can be performed in front of a symbolic representation of a dead teacher); repentance, to be performed twice daily by the ascetic, as well as at various significant times of the year, expresses a desire to atone for acts of violence, witting or unwitting, inflicted on any living creature; laying down of the body is a temporarily assumed motionless pose; and abandonment relates to pledges to abstain from types of action or from consumption of food and drink in the future.

Equanimity is perhaps the nearest approximation in Jainism to what in other religious paths is called "meditation." However, little significant value is attributed to structured meditation by Jain tradition, no doubt because of the prestige of asceticism as the predominant means of eliminating karma. In the early common era, contemplative activity (*anuprekṣā*) directed toward subjects such as impermanence and human solitude was considered to be a component of asceticism. However, Digambara Jain teachers in the medieval period, such as Yogīndu (sixth century), did develop forms of soul-directed contemplative discipline, and in modern times the Śvetāmbara Terāpanthī sect has promoted a form of meditative practice drawing on eclectic sources.

The ideal ending to life for the Jain ascetic is the freely undertaken fast unto death called *sallekhanā*, literally "scouring out negative factors." This climactic and ritualized act of austerity, which should only be performed by developed practitioners (although in the medieval period laypeople often ended their lives in this manner), involves progressive withdrawal from food and drink and should conclude, in death, in a state of pious awareness. Such a heroic end will invariably ensure a positive rebirth. In modern times, *sallekhanā* has generally been practiced by aged or infirm ascetics near the conclusion of their lives and, most recently, by nuns of the Terāpanthī order.

Although the Jain renunciant life does involve unremitting austerity, the tradition has always stressed that benevolence, compassion, and friendship toward all living creatures are its predominant characteristics.

LAY PRACTICE. An emphasis on the renunciatory dimension of Jainism obscures the extent to which the religion has also been followed throughout history by laymen and laywomen (Sanskrit, *śrāvaka* [hearer]; fem., *śrāvikā*) for whom abnegation and social withdrawal do not inform the totality of their lives. Although most early texts of the Jain scriptural tradition are almost exclusively preoccupied with ascetics, later portions contain exemplary stories, probably dating from the early common era, of rich and pious laymen, often enduring attack by jealous demonic beings. These laymen, at this early period called "servants" (*upāsaka;* fem. *upāsikā*) in token of their support of the ascetic community, are depicted in idealized fashion as advanced followers of the Jain path whose lives gain fulfillment in ultimate abandonment of wealth and renunciation.

Such stories, and the extensive literature produced by monks during the medieval period that legislates (male) lay behavior, have encouraged a picture of the Jain laity as following a way of life that, if less intense in its ascetic enactment, is nonetheless like that of the initiated renunciant in being totally directed toward the gaining of deliverance (*mokṣa*). In actuality, the Jain tradition perceived as a whole is not oriented exclusively toward the realm of spiritual liberation and the values of *mokṣa*—it also markedly privileges social qualities such as prosperous well-being and auspiciousness that, while informed by renunciatory ideology, very much relate to positive attitudes toward worldly values. While Jain laypeople regularly involve themselves in pious and merit-generating activities such as fasting, it would be wrong to think of their lives as incomplete versions of those of monks and nuns.

The parameters of Jain lay life have been from early times textually defined as centering around five "Small Vows" (*anuvrata*) that parallel the five "Great Vows" (*mahāvrata*) of the ascetic. These are ethical injunctions that the typical layman must integrate into his public and domestic life, although they are almost invariably never formally assumed. Such an individual should take care to avoid any livelihood that might entail violence. He should not lie, particularly in business transactions. He should not steal, an interdict that can extend to any dishonest or improper dealings. He should avoid excessive sexual activity, and in his later years adopt total celibacy. He should not have excessive or conspicuous possessions and should unburden himself as much as possible of his wealth for charitable purposes. Further restrictions, embodied in the three "Subsidiary Vows" (*guṇavrata*), are placed upon the layman's behavior with regard to unnecessary movement, excessive enjoyment, and self-indulgent brooding. The four "Vows of Instruction" (*śikṣāvrata*) enjoin him to engage regularly in various forms of contemplative and pious activity, such as fasting.

In keeping with this idealized style of ethics that encourages self-development and an avoidance of activities that might lead to destruction of life forms, the standard occupations of lay Jains in modern times have been in business or professions such as law. More rarely, Jains are found as agriculturalists, particularly in the area of the Maharashtra-Karnataka border.

Jain laypeople, like ascetics, practice a stringent vegetarianism that represents a vital component of their self-perception. Particular care is taken with food, which, as with all Indian religions, is regarded as a potentially dangerous substance. In addition to rejecting meat, fish, and eggs, Jains will avoid root and bulb vegetables, such as potatoes and onions. At religiously significant times of the year, many Jains will also avoid green-leafed vegetables and, like ascetics, avoid eating after dark.

The source of a layman's social and business prestige is perceived as deriving from his liberality (*dāna*). The ancient ritual of meritorious giving of food and shelter to ascetics was transformed in the medieval period to include public enterprises such as temple building, the sponsorship of the copying of manuscripts, and the financing of public works. The thirteenth-century royal ministers Vastupāla and his brother Tejapāla are proverbial exemplars of such activities. Today, prominent members of the Jain community are celebrated for philanthropic work and their support for medical and educational establishments, social relief, and animal hospitals.

PRACTICAL RELIGIOSITY. Jainism may reject the possibility of a creator god who has the power to intervene in human affairs, but the religion is nonetheless strongly theistic and devotional in idiom. God (*Bhagavān*) is envisaged both as the totality of all the Jinas throughout eternity and as the spiritual principle within every living being, called by the Digambaras the "supreme self" (*paramātman*), which has the potential to actualize itself in enlightenment.

Devotion to the Jinas in iconic form, perhaps deriving from an original ritual involving homage to the teacher and the desire to commemorate the illustrious dead, stretches back at least to the beginning of the common era and is common to the majority of Jains. However, Śvetāmbara sects, such as the Sthānakvāsins and the Terāpanthins, as well as some Digambara groups, reject image worship on the grounds that it is not a significant feature in the scriptural tradition and involves a breach of the principle of nonviolence through digging in the earth to construct the temples in which images are housed.

Jain temples are envisaged as simulacra of the site of each Jina's first sermon. Allowing for regional and historical variation, they are structurally similar to Hindu shrines, most commonly having a series of halls (*maṇḍapa*) leading to an inner shrine where the image of the Jina, depicted in either seated or standing ascetic posture, is housed. Alternatively, a temple can take the form of an axial hall with a quadruple Jina image approached through doors located at each of the cardinal directions. It is not uncommon for laypeople to worship at small domestic shrines.

Images represent a devotional focus and means of recalling the message of Jainism, for the significance of the Jinas lies in the fact that having taught the doctrine they gained freedom from rebirth and are thus not directly accessible to human beings. While particular images are often regarded as having special powers, a temple with a central Jina icon will typically have ancillary shrines at its entrance dedicated to a tutelary deity credited by devotees with the ability to intercede in worldly affairs. Goddesses such as Ambikā and Padmāvatī, who emerged into prominence in the medieval period, are vital components of Jain religiosity.

The most basic type of worship of Jina images, practiced by ascetic and layperson alike, is "seeing" (*darśana*), in which the worshiper brings his eyes into focus with those of the icon. Worship of images (*pūjā*) with material substances, such as rice, flowers, camphor, and fruit, and often involving anointment with water or milk, can only be performed by laypeople (or, in their absence, temple servants). The idiom of this form of worship, which is not structured in any binding form, is one of abandonment, in that the offerings are given up (the Jina being worshiped cannot in any way consume them). The mind of the devotee is turned toward the qualities of the Jinas, with the resolve to emulate them. Ascetics are forbidden to have physical contact with images and can only engage in inner, mental worship.

A wide repertoire of hymns can be used by Jains when they worship. The *Bhaktāmara* (Immortal Devotees), composed by Mānatuṅga in the sixth century CE in honor of Ṛṣabha, the first Jina of this world age, is of particular popularity among all sects and the focus of much devotional and esoteric commentary. Today, the composition and performance of hymns, often set to current film tunes, is an important area of female religiosity.

The Jains are no different from the adherents of other religions in experiencing many of the modalities of their faith in the context of the rhythm of the sacred year. For the Śvetāmbaras, the central point of the year is Paryuṣan (Abiding), which takes place over a period of eight days in August and September when there are recitations of the *Kalpa Sūtra* by monks and displays of illustrations from copies of it. The last day is called Samvatsarī (Annual), during which laypeople express repentance and a request for forgiveness for any injuries committed during the previous year. The Digambaras, who reject the authority of the *Kalpa Sūtra,* listen to recitations of the ten chapters of Umāsvāti's *Tattvārtha Sūtra* over a ten-day period called Daśalakṣaṇaparvan (also referred to as Paryuṣan). Both sects celebrate the birth of the last Jina as Mahāvīra Jayanti during March and April, and they also have in common Akṣayā Tṛtīyā (Undying Third), which occurs in April and May and commemorates the first act of alms-donation of this world age: King Śreyaṃsa's giving of cane juice to the Jina Ṛṣabha.

MODERN DEVELOPMENTS. The nineteenth and twentieth centuries saw Jainism's engagement with modernity lead to a reassertion of certain traditional features of the religion and a reconfiguration of others to take account of altered circumstances.

Among both the image-worshiping Śvetāmbaras and Digambaras there has been a resuscitation of ascetic lineages that had come near to becoming defunct, and many senior monks regained the prestige and celebrity of earlier times. Noteworthy in this respect are Vijayavallabha Sūri (Śvetāmbara, 1870–1954) and Ācārya Śāntisāgara (Digambara, 1873–1955). At the same time, the lay community, while not seriously attempting to supplant ascetic authority, organized itself in associations such as the Dakṣiṇ Bhārat Jain Sabhā (South Indian Jain Society) in order to disseminate the values of Jainism, engage in educational projects, and mobilize membership in respect to issues of social reform, particularly relating to the reduction of caste influence.

There have also appeared neo-Digambara groups such as the Śrīmad Rājacandra movement and the Kānjī Svāmī Panth, whose leaders were laymen influenced by the mystical dimensions of Jainism as taught by the early–common era teacher Kundakunda and his successors, and in which initiated ascetics play less-pronounced roles than elsewhere in Jainism. Rāycandbhāī Mahetā (1867–1901), known as Śrīmad Rājacandra, was a Gujarati jeweler and mystic who was a confidant of the young Mohandas (Mahatma) Gandhi, while Kānjī Svāmī abandoned the Sthānakvāsī ascetic order to promulgate an intensely soul-oriented path that he claimed had been transmitted to him directly by Kundakunda. The Akram Vijñān movement, founded in western India in the 1960s by A. M. Patel, who was born a Vaiṣṇava Hindu, privileges spiritual gnosis as the road to salvation and rejects scriptural and institutional authority.

The most significant development during the second half of the twentieth century was the arrival of many Jains in the United Kingdom (generally via East Africa) and North America. It has not been easy for the full requirements of traditional Jainism to be followed in this new cultural context, in particular because image-worshiping Śvetāmbara and Digambara ascetics are not allowed to travel and teach outside India (although some Sthānakvāsī and lower-order Terāpanthī ascetics are now permitted to do so). Instead, elements of Jainism have been emphasized that are congenial to modern Western liberal opinion: nonviolence, vegetarianism, contemplative practice, and a style of environmentalism in which the Jain path is presented as a philosophy with an ecological message at its center.

SEE ALSO Ahiṃsā; Cosmology, article on Jain Cosmology; Jñāna; Karman, article on Hindu and Jain Concepts; Mahāvīra.

BIBLIOGRAPHY

Alphen, Jan van, ed. *Steps to Liberation: 2,500 Years of Jain Art and Religion.* Antwerp, 2000. An outstanding collection of illustrations of Jain religious art.

Balbir, Nalini. "Women and Jainism in India." In *Women in Indian Religions,* edited by Arvind Sharma, pp. 70–107. New Delhi, 2002.

Cort, John E. *Jains in the World: Religious Values and Ideology in India.* New York, 2001. A pioneering fieldwork-based study that foregrounds the worldview of the Śvetāmbara Jain laity in contemporary Gujarat.

Dundas, Paul. *The Jains.* 2d rev. ed. London and New York, 2002. A study of Jainism throughout history, with extensive bibliography.

Fischer, Eberhard, and Jyotindra Jain. *Jaina Iconography.* 2 vols. Leiden, 1978. Contains a large number of illustrations pertaining to Jain ritual, practice, architecture, and iconography.

Folkert, Kendall. *Scripture and Community: Collected Essays on the Jains.* Edited by John E. Cort. Atlanta, 1993. Contains a series of studies of the interaction between sacred texts and the Śvetāmbara Jain community.

Hemacandra. *The Yogaśāstra of Hemacandra: A Twelfth-Century Handbook on Śvetāmbara Jainism.* Edited and translated by Olle Qvarnström. Cambridge, Mass., 2002. A highly authoritative account prescribing Śvetāmbara lay behavior written for Hemacandra's patron, Kumarapāla Caulukya.

Jacobi, Hermann. *Jaina Sutras.* 2 vols. Oxford, 1884–1895. Pioneering translations of the *Ācārāṅga Sūtra,* the *Kalpa Sūtra,* the *Sūtrakṛtāṅga Sūtra,* and the *Uttarādhyayana Sūtra,* which, though outdated in many ways, have never been adequately replaced.

Jaini, Padmanabh S. *Gender and Salvation: Jaina Debates on the Spiritual Liberation of Women.* Berkeley, Calif., 1991. Richly annotated translation of key sources relating to the debate between the Śvetāmbaras and Digambaras concerning the religious status of women.

Jaini, Padmanabh S. *The Jaina Path of Purification.* Rev. ed. New Delhi, 1998. A clear account of doctrine and practice, invaluable for its Digambara perspective.

Jaini, Padmanabh S. *Collected Papers on Jaina Studies.* Delhi, 2000. An essential collection of often seminal studies.

Kelting, Mary Whitney. *Singing to the Jinas: Jain Laywomen, Mandal Singing, and the Negotiations of Jain Devotion.* New York, 2001. A study of female religiosity among a Śvetāmbara Jain community in Puṇe in the context of the production and performance of devotional hymns.

Pal, Pratapaditya, ed. *The Peaceful Liberators: Jain Art from India.* Los Angeles, 1994. Contains illustrations of many important images and manuscripts.

Schubring, Walther. *Die Lehre der Jainas, nach den alten Quellen dargestellt.* Berlin and Leipzig, Germany, 1935. Translated as *The Doctrine of the Jainas, Described after the Old Sources.* 2d rev. ed. Delhi, 2000. An authoritative account of canonical Jainism by the leading Western scholar of the last century. The German edition contains a still valuable bibliography of primary sources.

Shāntā, N. *The Unknown Pilgrims: The Voices of the Sādhvis: The History, Spirituality, and Life of the Jaina Women Ascetics.* Translated by Mary Rogers. Delhi, 1997. This diffuse study, originally written in French, presents Jainism from the historical and contemporary perspective of nuns of all sects.

Umāsvāti. *That Which Is: Tattvārtha Sūtra.* Translated by Nathmal Tatia. San Francisco, London, and Pymble, Australia, 1994. The classic summation of Jain doctrine.

Vallely, Anne. *Guardians of the Transcendent: An Ethnography of a Jain Ascetic Community.* Toronto, Buffalo, N.Y., and London, 2002. A study which focuses upon the religiosity of nuns of the Terāpanthī sect.

PAUL DUNDAS (2005)

JALĀL AL-DĪN RŪMĪ SEE RŪMĪ, JALĀL AL-DĪN

JAMĀʿAT-I ISLĀMĪ (The Islamic Society), a Muslim religio-political organization in the Indian subcontinent, was founded in August 1941 on the initiative of Abū al-Aʿlā Mawdūdī, who had issued a public invitation to all who were interested to meet in Lahore. In his earlier life Mawdūdī had worked as a journalist, but in 1932 he became editor of the religious monthly *Tarjumān al-Qurʾān,* which later served as the principal organ of the Jamāʿat. During the 1930s Mawdūdī participated in the debates about India's political future and opposed both the united Indian nationalism of the Indian National Congress and the Muslim nationalism of the Muslim League. All nationalism he thought contrary to Islam and insisted that the identity of Muslims derives from Islam alone.

In 1940 the Muslim League passed its famous Lahore Resolution calling for the creation of Pakistan as a homeland for Indian Muslims. Mawdūdī later said that the Lahore Resolution triggered his long-cherished plan to establish a society for the promotion of Islam. Earlier he had concentrated on criticism and reform of individual Muslim life; now, however, there was need for organized activity. At the initial meeting a constitution was adopted, and Mawdūdī was elected the first *amīr,* or leader. The Jamāʿat-i Islāmī has ever since been inseparably wedded to its founder. Not only was he its leader from the beginning until he retired in 1972, but his writings have provided the Jamāʿat's interpretation of Islam and its political beliefs.

The period between 1941 and 1947 was one of intense activity devoted to promoting the Jamāʿat. The organization's activities remained at the level of individual persuasion, however, and it had almost no influence on India. Although Mawdūdī opposed the nationalist view of Pakistan held by the Muslim League, and bitterly criticized their leadership, when India was partitioned in August 1947, he opted for Pakistan. He moved from East Punjab to Lahore with a portion of his followers, leaving another part of the Jamāʿat to remain in India. Since that time the Indian and Pakistani branches have been entirely separate, and the Indian one has been relatively less important.

HISTORY. In Pakistan the Jamāʿat first worked to assist the refugees pouring into the country from India. In early 1948, however, it leapt into political prominence by espousing the cause of the Islamic state and becoming the focal point of nationwide agitation. Pakistan, Mawdūdī reasoned, had been won in the name of Islam; it was, therefore, imperative that a truly Islamic system be established in the country. Since this position evoked a wide public response, it was troublesome for the liberal leadership of the Muslim League government, who could afford neither to reject the Islamic state nor to embrace it in the form demanded by the Jamāʿat-i Islāmī.

The Jamāʿat quickly came into confrontation with the government. Four things drew government wrath: (1) strident criticism of the leadership, (2) statements by Mawdūdī that the war against India over Kashmir was not a proper *jihād* ("war in the way of God"), (3) Mawdūdī's stand against oaths of unconditional loyalty to the government, and (4) a prepartition stand of the Jamāʿat against recruitment in the army. Mawdūdī and other leaders were arrested and held in jail for more than a year, but the campaign for the Islamic state continued.

When the Objectives Resolution of the Pakistan Constituent Assembly was passed in 1949, it was acclaimed by the Jamāʿat as Pakistan's declaration of intent to be an Islamic state; the issue then became election of a leadership to implement the Islamic ideal. Thus the way was opened for the Jamāʿat's active participation in elections. This decision to seek political office would subsequently, in 1957–1958, become the cause of a major rift in the Jamāʿat that would lead to the resignations of several important members.

In 1951 Mawdūdī reached the peak of his prominence in Pakistan and enjoyed respect even among the *ʿulamāʾ* ("religious scholars"), with whom he often differed. He was the principal figure at the conference of *ʿulamāʾ* convoked in Karachi in January 1951, in response to the controversial report of the Basic Principles Committee of the Constituent Assembly. The twenty-two points describing an Islamic state upon which the *ʿulamāʾ* agreed were largely due to his influence.

In 1952 and 1953 there was widespread agitation in Pakistan against the Aḥmadīyah sect, resulting in riots, loss of life, and destruction of property. Although the Jamāʿat did not officially sanction the "direct action" against the Aḥmadīyah, much of what happened had its tacit approval. Mawdūdī published a pamphlet entitled *Qādiyānī Masʾalah* condemning the group as non-Muslim. When martial law was declared in March 1953, he was again arrested, along with numerous Jamāʿat leaders, and was condemned to death. The sentence, however, was commuted, and he was released from prison in April 1955. During Mawdūdī's several imprisonments, others, such as Amīn Aḥsan Iṣlāḥī and Sulṭān Aḥmad, served as temporary amirs of the Jamāʿat.

When the 1956 Pakistani constitution was promulgated, the Jamāʿat-i Islami welcomed it as meeting most of the requirements of an Islamic state. It did so even though the constitution did not declare Islam the official religion of Pakistan, did not make the *sharīʿah* the law of the land, and did not make the specifically Islamic provisions enforceable in the courts. Acceptance of the constitution robbed the Islamic state issue of its viability, and the Jamāʿat turned to a campaign for "true democracy" in Pakistan centered upon a demand for separate electorates for Muslims and antisecularist propaganda.

In 1958 a military coup brought Field Marshal Muḥammad Ayyūb Khān to power in Pakistan. The Jamāʿat-i Islāmī fell under the ensuing martial law banning political parties and was thus not allowed to function until the promulgation of a new constitution in March 1962. The Jamāʿat bitterly opposed Ayyūb, whom it saw as a dictator who had frustrated democracy to keep the Islamic forces in check. It rejected the political system established by the new constitution but nonetheless worked within it. The Jamāʿat's ire was especially stimulated by the Muslim Family Law Ordinance, which introduced changes into Muslim personal law. Its activities led Ayyūb to ban the Jamāʿat and to arrest Mawdūdī once again in early 1964. The courts, however, declared the ban and the arrest illegal. During Ayyūb's time the Jamāʿat first adopted the policy of allying itself with other parties in combined opposition to the government. In the 1965 elections it supported Fāṭimah Jinnāḥ for president, despite its teaching that Islam disapproved a woman as head of state, and following the brief India-Pakistan war of 1965, it added its voice to the protests against the Tashkent Declaration. In the 1970 elections the Jamāʿat joined other right-wing groups in opposing both the socialism of Ẕulfiqār ʿAlī Bhutto and the demands of Mujīb al-Raḥmān's Awami League; these elections, however, were a crushing defeat for the Jamāʿat throughout the country. When Yaḥyā Khān launched military action against East Pakistan in March 1971, the Jamāʿat supported the actions of the government and the army and thereby lost the little support it had in Bengal. After Bhutto's rise to power it posed a demand for the Niẓām-i Muṣṭafā ("prophetic system") against the socialist tendencies of the People's Party. When Bhutto was overthrown by General Ẓiyā al-Ḥaqq (Ziya al-Haq), the Jamāʿat was at first favored by the new government by several appointments to cabinet posts, but it was soon reduced to impotence by the government's interdiction of all political activity.

ORGANIZATION. The Jamāʿat's constitution has been amended several times to compensate for changing circumstances. It provides for a highly centralized organization. Most power rests with the *amīr*, who is elected for a five-year term but who may hold office for life. Seven different central offices function under his direct supervision. He is assisted by a *majlis-i shūrā*, or consultative body, whose opinions, however, are not binding on him, and by a *majlis-i ʿumalāʾ*, or executive committee. There is also an executive assistant, the *qayyim*, who acts as secretary general. Duplicated at the district, circle, and provincial levels, this central organization is of great significance, for it is precisely that detailed for the ideal Islamic state. It was plainly the Jamāʿat's intention that it should become the government in the event of its political success. Membership in the organization, sharply restricted to persons meeting high standards of Islamic knowledge and personal conduct, has never been large. The majority of the Jamāʿat's associates are *muttafiqīn*, or sympathizers, who provide its principal political support and much of its finances. It is not uncommon for members to be expelled for misconduct or disinterest, and a number of the full members work full time for the Jamāʿat. Great attention is paid to training, and regular training sessions are held. Other activities include publication of journals and newspapers, the maintenance of reading rooms, mobile clinics, disaster relief, and work with labor unions. There are also associated organizations, the principal one of which is the Islāmī Jamāʿat-i Ṭulabāʾ, a militant student group with powerful influence in Pakistani universities.

THEOLOGY. The Jamāʿat-i Islāmī holds Islam to be an ideology comprising a complete set of principles for human life. Just as nature acknowledges the sovereignty of its creator by obedience to natural laws, so also should humans submit to the divine law for their existence. That law is known primarily through the Qurʾān and the *sunnah* of the Prophet. The Jamāʿat lays great emphasis on the all-inclusiveness of its ideology; Islam is not merely a matter of the relationship between the individual and God but must also govern social, economic, and political life. True Islamic faith demands that Muslims hold political power and that the state be ruled according to Islamic principles. There an be no political parties and no opposition in such a state since there is only one correct Islamic viewpoint. Neither can the state make law. Sovereignty belongs to God alone and all legitimate law must derive from his expressed will. Thus, the Jamāʿat insisted that policy-forming offices must be held by pious Muslims whose duties include suppression of rival ideologies. Non-Muslims have a protected status in the Islamic state but are treated as second-class citizens who must live under certain restrictions. The Jamāʿat envisages a totalitarian state united in obedience to a single ruler whose word prevails so long as it accords with the divine law. Such a state was considered democratic, however, since the ruler was elected and could be removed; it was also a welfare state obligated to meet the basic needs of its citizens. Despite the implicit authoritarianism of the ideology, the Jamāʿat has consistently held revolutionary violence to be illegitimate and the way to the Islamic state to lie in peaceful democratic methods.

BIBLIOGRAPHY

The role of the Jamāʿat-i Islāmī in the early phases of Pakistani history is treated fully by Leonard Binder in *Religion and Politics in Pakistan* (Berkeley, 1963) and by Keith Callard in *Pakistan: A Political Study* (London, 1957). The only full-length treatment of the organization in English is Kalim Bahadur's *The Jamāʿat-i-Islâmi of Pakistan* (New Delhi, 1977). I have discussed the society's ideology and teachings in "The Ideology of Mawlana Mawdudi," in *South Asian Politics and Religion*, edited by Donald Smith (Princeton, 1966), and "Mawdudi's Conception of the Islamic State," in *Voices of Resurgent Islam*, edited by John Esposito (Oxford, 1983).

There are also two accounts of the Jamāʿat's history by its founder: *Jamāʿat-i Islāmī, uskā maqsad, taʾrīkh, awr lāʾih-i ʿamal* (Lahore, 1952) and *Jamāʿat-i Islāmī kē 29 sāl* (Lahore, 1970).

New Sources

Esposito, John L., ed. *Political Islam: Revolution, Radicalism, or Reform?* Boulder, Colo., 1997.

Grare, Frédéric. *Political Islam in the Indian Subcontinent: The Jamaat-i-Islami.* New Delhi, 2001.

Nasr, Seyyed Vali Reza. *The Vanguard of the Islamic Revolution: The Jama'ati Islami of Pakistan.* Comparative Studies on Muslim Societies, vol. 19. Berkeley, 1994.

Nasr, Seyyed Vali Reza. "Democracy and Islamic Revivalism." *Political Science Quarterly*, 110 (Summer 1995): 261–286.

Sikand, Yogrinder. "The Emergence of the Jama'at-i-Islami of Jammu and Kashmir." *Modern Asian Studies*, 36 (July 2002): 705–752.

CHARLES J. ADAMS (1987)
Revised Bibliography

JAMĀL AL-DĪN AL-AFGHĀNĪ SEE AFGHĀNĪ, JAMĀL AL-DĪN AL-

JAMES, E. O. (1888–1972), was an English academic anthropologist, folklorist, and historian of religions. Edwin Oliver James was born in London on March 30, 1888. He was educated at Exeter College, Oxford, where he took a diploma in anthropology under R. R. Marett, and at University College, London. From 1911 to 1933 he served as a priest of the Church of England, chiefly in parishes in London and Oxford, while maintaining a scholarly interest in anthropology, comparative religion, and folklore. During the 1920s and 1930s he was associated with the diffusionist school of Elliot Smith and William James Perry, and with the "myth and ritual school" that emerged out of it. Thus he became one of the earliest British "myth and ritual" writers, contributing to the school's first two symposia. For *Myth and Ritual*, edited by S. H. Hooke (London, 1933), he wrote "Initiatory Rituals," and for its sequel, *The Labyrinth*, also edited by Hooke (London, 1935), "The Sources of Christian Ritual." Although he had published several books on anthropology, his first major work was *Christian Myth and Ritual* (1933), in which he applied the methods of the myth and ritual school to questions of Christian origins and to later Christian ceremonies.

In 1933 James became professor of the history and philosophy of religion at the University of Leeds, and in 1945 he moved to a similar post at the University of London (King's College), where he remained until his retirement in 1955. From 1960 until his death on July 6, 1972, he was chaplain of All Souls' College, Oxford. Throughout his active life he was a member of numerous learned societies, including the Folklore Society, of which he was president from

1930 to 1932, and in 1954 he was instrumental in founding the British section of the International Association for the History of Religions.

James published a large number of books and articles on a wide variety of subjects connected with anthropology and comparative religion. The best known were perhaps *Origins of Sacrifice* (1934), *Introduction to the Comparative Study of Religion* (1938), and *Prehistoric Religion* (1957). He was not, however, an original writer or theorist, being content for the most part to have assimilated, and to reproduce, the findings of others. In matters of controversy he habitually took a mediating position, which left him without a strong profile of his own. In theology he was an Anglo-Catholic; in anthropology he was initially an evolutionist but at a later stage was prepared to modify his views in response to changes of emphasis. He was not, for instance, despite his theological position, disposed to accept all the findings of the school of Wilhelm Schmidt concerning "high gods." Thus, although he wrote that "High Gods do in fact stand alone, head and shoulders above all secondary divinities," he insisted that "the belief in High Gods among low races cannot be described as a true monotheism" (*Prehistoric Religion*, pp. 206–208).

James's significance lay in his capacity to assimilate and interpret a vast body of material about comparative religion and to present it for a wider public. At a time when the study of religion in Britain was at a fairly low ebb, he served as an admirable interpreter, and as a mediator between positions that were often polarized internationally. His best work was done in the 1930s, for some of his later works were little more than compilations of material readily available elsewhere.

BIBLIOGRAPHY

A full bibliography of James's writings up to 1963 can be found in *The Saviour God: Comparative Studies in the Concept of Salvation, Presented to Professor E. O. James to Commemorate His Seventy-fifth Birthday*, edited by S. G. F. Brandon (Manchester, 1963). See also D. W. Gundry's "Professor E. O. James, 1888–1972," *Numen* 19 (August–December 1972): 81–83.

ERIC J. SHARPE (1987)

JAMES, WILLIAM (1842–1910), American psychologist and philosopher, was the eldest son of Henry James Sr. (1811–1882), a writer on social and religious subjects esteemed in his day but never famous. William was born in New York City on January 11, 1842. His early education at his father's hands was supplemented by much travel abroad and some schooling in Boulogne, France, and at the University of Geneva, where his scientific bent developed. Later he attended lectures at the University of Berlin and elsewhere in Germany. James was a voracious reader of philosophy and was particularly concerned with the question of science and materialism. Plagued by illness and "neurasthenic" by temperament, he was long uncertain about a career. He tried his hand at painting with fair success, but after joining the zoologist Louis Agassiz on a fifteen-month expedition to Brazil, James studied chemistry and medicine at Harvard, receiving his medical degree in 1869.

James soon decided against medical practice and began to teach anatomy and physiology at the university. The work of the new German school of physical psychology attracted him, and he prepared to teach the subject, establishing the first psychology laboratory in the United States (and perhaps in the world). After a few years, during which he produced some noted papers, he seized the opportunity in 1878 to add to his teaching a course in philosophy—later famous as Phil. 3. He spent the rest of his life teaching psychology and philosophy at Harvard and lecturing widely at home and abroad. He died in Chocorua, New Hampshire, on August 26, 1910.

JAMES'S WORKS. James's *Principles of Psychology*, which appeared in two volumes in 1890, was hailed as the summa of current knowledge, much of it based on his own previously published research. When it was reissued in the 1950s, reviewers in journals of psychology called it still able to inspire and instruct. James next published *The Will to Believe* (1897). Its title essay, first published in 1879, was his first mature statement on the nature of faith, including religious faith. His later volumes, *Pragmatism* (1907), *A Pluralistic Universe* and *The Meaning of Truth* (both 1909), and the posthumous *Some Problems of Philosophy* (1911) and *Essays in Radical Empiricism* (1912), rounded out his philosophic vision. Between the *Psychology* and these works James delivered the Gifford Lectures in Edinburgh, published as *The Varieties of Religious Experience* (1902). Both hailed and criticized, its influence was immediate and lasting. Widely read then and one hundred years later, it stands as a classic in the study of religion.

James framed *The Varieties* in terms of two questions, the first having to do with the nature and origin of religion and the second with its meaning and significance. The first was, for James, a historical question having to do with function and causation; the second was a question of value. In contrast to many scientists of his era, James maintained that the value of a thing should be assessed not on the basis of its origins but on the basis of its distinctive function.

For the purpose of his lectures, James defined religion in terms of religious experience, that is, "the feelings, acts, and experiences of individual men in their solitude, so far as they apprehend themselves to stand in relation to whatever they may consider divine" (James, 1985, p. 34). Although evangelical Protestants traditionally used the term *religious experience* to refer to the Protestant conversion experience, James imbued the term with a broader, more generic meaning, including under that rubric lectures on religious personality types (the healthy-minded and the sick soul), the divided self, conversion, saintliness, and mysticism. In keeping with the revival of interest in mysticism at the beginning of the twentieth century, James claimed "personal religious experience has its root and centre in mystical states of consciousness" (James, 1985, p. 301).

James utilized firsthand autobiographical accounts—mostly but not exclusively Christian—as his primary data. He was particularly interested in what he referred to as "'geniuses' in the religious line," persons who were frequently subject to extremes of experience, such as voices, visions, and falling into trance. (James, 1985, p.15). In contrast to many later psychologists of religion, James was convinced that the more extreme cases would shed the greatest light on religious experience as a whole. He utilized comparison both to explain the origins of such experiences and to identify their unique function. In many instances he adopted a method of "serial study," in which he arranged phenomena along continua of various sorts to better understand them. The distinction between origins and function allowed James to compare the more extreme forms of religious experience with experiences considered pathological without fear of discrediting religious experience in the process.

The central function of religion, in James's view, consists in the healing of the self through a connection with "the higher powers." All religions consist of two parts: an uneasiness and its solution. At the moment of salvation, the individual "becomes conscious that this higher part [of oneself] is conterminous with and continuous with a MORE of the same quality, which is operative in the universe outside of him" (James, 1985, p. 400). James considered the objective truth of "the more" by asking whether it originated in or beyond the self. He offered Frederick Myers's notion of the subconscious as a means of mediating between the claims of science and religion, while leaving the ultimate explanation of "the more" as a matter of "over-beliefs" informed by metaphysical convictions.

James's own metaphysical commitments were such that he did believe, as he indicated in his conclusion and postscript, that there were higher powers that might act through the subconscious self. James, however, did not link origins with value. Parallels between the experiences of geniuses, the religiously devout, and the mentally unstable led James to suggest their common subconscious origins and to insist that such experiences must be evaluated not in terms of their origins but in terms of their value for life. In the end, he stressed, the final test of a belief is "not its origin, but the way it works on the whole" (James, 1985, p. 24).

Interpretations of James. There has been considerable discussion among James scholars regarding the place of *The Varieties of Religious Experience* (VRE) in James's thought more generally. Scholars have traditionally located the VRE in the midst of James's transition from psychologist to philosopher during the late 1890s. Late twentieth-century scholarship has located that transition earlier (Taylor, 1996, 2002; Lamberth, 1999) and in some cases argued against the idea of a transition altogether (Reed, 1997; Gale, 1999; Cooper, 2002). Eugene Taylor argues that James's interest in psychology is evident throughout his intellectual career, but that his understanding of psychology shifts from the positivistic, cognitive psychology that predominates in *The Principles* to the humanistic understanding, grounded in developments in abnormal psychology and psychical research, that informs his metaphysics of radical empiricism during the late 1880s and early 1890s (Taylor, 1996, p. 39). This argument allows Taylor to read the VRE as a psychological text (Taylor, 1996, pp. 84–96). David C. Lamberth (1999), who is primarily interested in James's philosophy of religion, also argues for a shift from positivistic psychology to a metaphysics of radical empiricism, locating this shift in the early 1890s, again well prior to the publication of the VRE. Locating James's formulation of his metaphysics prior to the publication of the VRE allows Lamberth to read the VRE with an eye toward James's metaphysics of pure experience (Lamberth, 1999, pp. 97–145).

Edward S. Reed contends that Taylor and countless others "have (mis)interpreted *The Principles* as propounding a variant of the new positivist psychology when it was in fact an all-out assault on the turn psychology had taken in the 1870s" (Reed, 1997, p. 215). Reed points out that key essays published in *The Will to Believe* in 1897 were actually written in the late 1870s and early 1880s, arguing that "because James left these arguments out of *The Principles* . . . their connection with his psychological work has not been appreciated" (Reed, 1997, p. 215). In contrast to those that argue for a shift in focus, Reed argues that James's entire career was underpinned by his youthful interest in applying Darwinian ideas to the study of the mind. Reed's view supports Henry S. Levinson's (1981) Darwinian reading of the VRE, in which he argues that for James the ideas that emerge from the subconscious of religious geniuses are, in effect, spontaneous mental variations that survive when they prove themselves "fit" in a competitive environment.

Other scholars who, like Reed, see continuity over time, nonetheless question whether James's thought can be understood as unified at any given point in time. In *The Divided Self of William James* (1999), Richard Gale stresses the difficulties involved in reconciling the epistemological claims of his tough-minded pragmatism and his tender-minded mysticism. Wesley Cooper takes up Gale's challenge in *The Unity of William James's Thought* (2002), arguing for a "Two-Levels View" that distinguishes between empirical and metaphysical levels of truth. The unifying thread for Cooper, running from the *Principles* through his posthumous *Essays in Radical Empiricism*, is the "concept of sensation," which James later renamed as "pure experience." This metaphysically postulated concept, which is neither mental nor physical yet potentially either, is, according to Cooper, "the centerpeice of James's metaphysics" (Cooper, 2002, p. 140). The Gale-Cooper debate suggests that both psychological and metaphysical readings of the VRE are legitimate, while it leaves open the question of how they are related. Gale would argue that the scientist of religion and the metaphysician are two different and unintegrated Jamesian "selves." Cooper would read the VRE on two levels—empirical and metaphysical—and would argue, like Lamberth, that James's metaphysics of pure experience provides the theoretical link between them.

James and his family have had many notable biographers (e.g., Perry, 1935; Allen, 1967; Simon, 1998), most of whom have attended to James's difficulties deciding on a career and a wife, made note of his complicated relationship with his father, and speculated on James's personal stake in the writing of the VRE. Most agree that the VRE allowed James to work through his relationship with his father's religious views (see Taylor, 2002). In the process, most also make note of two first-person accounts in the VRE, one attributed to Henry James Sr., and one (the vision of the epileptic patient) William later ascribed to himself. Virtually all of James's biographers have associated the latter account with a period of near suicidal depression in the late 1860s that James ostensibly resolved while reading an essay by Charles Renouvier. The classic account of James's "crisis and recovery" has been undercut by Linda Simon (1998) and sharply challenged by Louis Menand (1998). Menand argues that there is no way to date the autobiographical fragment, and thus no way to link it to the Renouvier episode. Building on Simon's contention that James suffered from depressive episodes his entire life, Menand dismisses the crisis and recovery narrative as inadequate. In a move paralleling that of Gale and Cooper, Menand suggests that the story of the epileptic patient and the Renouvier entry in James's diary represent two enduring poles in James's emotional life: the optimism of the healthy-minded pragmatist and the pessimism of the sick soul.

Much attention has also been paid to James's life and thought in the context of late-nineteenth-century intellectual and cultural history. Bennett Ramsey (1993), Paul Jerome Croce (1995), Menand (2001), Kim Townsend (1996), and Charlene Haddock Seigfried (1996) all locate James's thought in relation to the erosion of intellectual certainty characteristic of the modern era. Ramsey emphasizes the perceived contingency of the self in the decades following the Civil War and James's response to it. Croce emphasizes the erosion of certainty with respect to both religious and scientific knowledge in the postwar period, describing James's thought as an effort to enjoy "the benefits of certainty witout an epistemology of certainty" (Croce, 1995, p. 229). Menand locates the rise of pragmatism with its emphasis on the mutability of ideas as a modernist response to the competing certainties of the Civil War. Townsend places James within the context of shifting cultural discourses of "manliness" among late-nineteenth-century Harvard intellectuals. Seigfried provides a feminist critique of James's relations with women. In the VRE the erosion of certainty is reflected in James's pragmatic criteria for ascertaining the value of religious experiences and the minimalism of his own "over-beliefs."

Within religious studies, much of the late-twentieth-century discussion of the VRE took place among philosophers of religion and scholars of mysticism. James's chapter on mysticism has often been cited in attempts to call upon religious (and specifically mystical) experience in defense of theism. Lamberth rejects this line of thinking, arguing instead for the relevance of James's metaphysics of pure experience understood socially (rather than individually) for contemporary philosophy of religion and theology. Matthew C. Bagger (1999) mounts a more extended critique of attempts to call upon religious experience to defend theism. G. William Barnard (1997) provides the most nuanced explication and defense of James's understanding of mysticism. Essays by David Hollinger, Wayne Proudfoot, and Richard Rorty in *William James and a Science of Religions* (Proudfoot, 2004) explore the relationship between religion, pragmatism, and science in the VRE. In many respects Henry S. Levinson (1981) still provides the most comprehensive treatment of James as a scientist of religion. David M. Wulff (1997) provides an excellent chapter on James as a psychologist of religion with an extensive discussion of the critical responses to the VRE. Carol Zaleski (in Capps and Jacobs, 1995) defends the VRE against its critics in an attempt to establish the contemporary relevance of the VRE for the study of religion. Ann Taves (2003) discusses the experimental research, both clinical and psychical, that underlies James's theory of the subconscious and calls for renewed attention to both his theory of the subconscious and his comparative method in the study of religion. Jeremy Carrette (2002) calls for the revitalization of the psychology of religion through an engagement of the writings of founders such as James with new research in the neurosciences.

SEE ALSO Psychology, article on Psychology of Religion; Religious Experience.

BIBLIOGRAPHY

Primary Sources

James, William. *The Varieties of Religious Experience.* (1902) Cambridge, Mass., 1985.

James, William. *The Works of William James.* Cambridge, Mass., 1975–1988.

James, William. *The Correspondence of William James.* Edited by Ignas K. Skrupskelis and Elizabeth M. Berkeley. Charlottesville, Va., 1992–.

Secondary Sources

Allen, Gay Wilson. *William James: A Biography.* New York, 1967.

Bagger, Matthew C. *Religious Experience, Justification, and History.* Cambridge, U.K., 1999.

Barnard, G. William. *Exploring Unseen Worlds: William James and the Philosophy of Mysticism.* Albany, N.Y., 1997.

Capps, Donald, and Janet L. Jacobs, eds. *The Struggle for Life: A Companion to William James's "The Varieties of Religious Experience."* West Lafayette, Ind., 1995.

Carrette, Jeremy. "The Return to James: Psychology, Religion, and the Amnesia of Neuroscience." In *The Varieties of Religious Experience*, centenary ed., pp. xxxix–lxiii. London, 2002.

Cooper, Wesley. *The Unity of William James's Thought.* Nashville, 2002.

Croce, Paul Jerome. *Science and Religion in the Era of William James.* Chapel Hill, N.C., 1995.

Gale, Richard M. *The Divided Self of William James.* Cambridge, U.K., 1999.

Lamberth, David C. *William James and the Metaphysics of Experience.* Cambridge, U.K., 1999.

Levinson, Henry Samuel. *The Religious Investigations of William James.* Chapel Hill, N.C., 1981. This is a comprehensive account of James's understanding of religion.

Menand, Louis. "William James and the Case of the Epileptic Patient." *New York Review of Books,* December 17, 1998.

Menand, Louis. *The Metaphysical Club.* New York, 2001.

Myers, Gerald E. *William James, His Life and Thought.* New Haven, Conn., 1986. Myers provides a thorough overview of James's thought.

Perry, Ralph Barton. *The Thought and Character of William James.* 2 vols. Boston, 1935. The classic starting point in James research.

Proudfoot, Wayne, ed. *William James and a Science of Religions.* New York, 2004.

Putnam, Ruth Anna, ed. *The Cambridge Companion to William James.* Cambridge, U.K., 1997.

Ramsey, Bennett. *Submitting to Freedom: The Religious Vision of William James.* New York, 1993.

Reed, Edward S. *From Soul to Mind.* New Haven, Conn., 1997.

Seigfried, Charlene Haddock. "The Feminine-Mystical Threat to Scientific-Masculine Other." In *Pragmatism and Feminism,* pp. 111–141. Chicago, 1996.

Simon, Linda. *Genuine Reality: A Life of William James.* New York, 1998.

Taves, Ann. *Fits, Trances, and Visions: Experiencing Religion and Explaining Experience from Wesley to James.* Princeton, N.J., 1999.

Taves, Ann. "Religious Experience and the Divisible Self: William James (and Frederick Myers) as Theorist(s) of Religion." *Journal of the American Academy of Religion* 71, no. 2 (2003): 303–326.

Taylor, Eugene. *William James on Consciousness beyond the Margin.* Princeton, N.J., 1996.

Taylor, Eugene. "The Spiritual Roots of James's *Varieties of Religious Experience.*" In *The Varieties of Religious Experience,* centenary ed., pp. xxxix–lxiii. London, 2002.

Townsend, Kim. *Manhood at Harvard: William James and Others.* New York, 1996.

Wulff, David M. *The Psychology of Religion: Classic and Contemporary Views.* 2d ed. New York, 1997.

JACQUES BARZUN (1987)
ANN TAVES (2005)

JANUS. According to most linguists, the word *ianus* seems to be based upon the root *iā,* which constitutes an extension of the Indo-European root *ei-* ("to go"). This abstract term, signifying "passage," alternates between the stem form *-u-* and the stem form *-o-*. From the first are formed the derivatives *Ianuarius* ("January"), *ianu-al* (a biscuit reserved for Janus), and *ianu-a* ("door"). From the second comes *iani-tor* ("porter"), *Iani-culum* (Janiculum Hill), and *Iani-gena* (daughter of Janus). In the Roman pantheon Janus is an original figure who has no Greek homologue (Ovid, *Fasti* 1.90). The Etruscan name *Ani,* which appears on the sculpture of an augur's liver found at Piacenza, is a borrowing from either Latin or an Italian dialect. Because, as Cicero emphasizes (*De natura deorum* 2.67), the god embodies the motive of "passage," it is characteristic of him to be at the beginning, in line with the scholar Varro's definition cited by Augustine (*City of God* 7.9): "To Janus comes everything that begins, to Jupiter everything that culminates" ("Penes Ianum sunt prima, penes Ioven summa").

This primacy is verified in the liturgy: Janus is invoked first in ceremonies. On the same basis he is patron, along with Juno (whence his epithet *Iunonius*), of all the calends. The first member of the priestly corps, the *rex sacrorum* ("king of the sacrifices"), offers him a sacrifice at the beginning of each month (Macrobius, *Saturnalia* 1.15.10). In the same way, the first official sacrifice of each year, the Agonium of January 9, is directed to Janus. Sculpted images of him with two faces—corresponding, according to the interpretations, to opening and closing or to past and future—gained for him the names of Janus Bifrons ("with double forehead"), Janus Biceps ("two-headed"), and Janus Geminus ("twin").

Other qualificatives have functional value. Thus tradition points to Janus Curiatius, who must have presided over a rite of passage of young men into the tribal subgroups called *curiae,* and to Janus Quirinus, mentioned in the "royal laws" as associated with the time when the third share of the *spolia opima* was allotted to the god Quirinus (Festus, ed. Lindsay, 1913, p. 204 L.). This last is the most ancient title given to Janus, who sits in the old Forum in the "ancient sanctuary provided with an altar" (Ovid, *Fasti* 1.275). According to whether its doors were shut or open, he "indicated the state of peace or war" (Livy, 1.19.2). Augustus, who restored this cult to a place of honor, boasted of having closed the temple on three occasions (*Res gestae* 13). This explains the appellation of Janus Quirinus: He is the god who presides over the passage from war to peace. This is the poet Horace's interpretation when he illustrates the "Quirinal" orientation of Janus by the expression "Ianus Quirini" (*Odes* 4.15.9), which he takes up elsewhere in a more prosaic and explicit phrase, "Janus, the guardian of peace" (*Epistles* 2.1.255).

BIBLIOGRAPHY

Dumézil, Georges. *Archaic Roman Religion.* 2 vols. Translated by Philip Krapp. Chicago, 1970.

Gagé, Jean. *Augustus, Emperor of Rome, 63 B.C.–14 A.D.: Res Gestae divi Augusti.* Paris, 1977.

Schilling, Robert. *Rites, cultes, dieux de Rome.* Paris, 1979. See pages 220–262 on Janus.

Wissowa, Georg. *Religion und Kultus der Römer.* 2d ed. Munich, 1912. See pages 103–113.

New Sources

Briquel, Dominique. "Le Fanum Voltumnae: remarques sur le culte fédéral des cités étrusques." In *Dieux, fêtes, sacré dans la Grèce et la Rome antiques,* edited by André Motte and Charles M. Ternes, pp. 133–159. Turnhout, 2003.

Capdeville, Gérard. "Les épithètes cultuelles de Janus." *Mélanges École Française Rome* 85 (1973): 395–436.

Gagé, Jean. "Sur les origines du culte de Janus." *Revue d'Histoire des Religions* 195 (1979): 3–33 and 129–151.

Pfligersdorffer Georg. "Ovidius Empedocleus. Zu Ovids Ianus-Deutung." *Grazer Beiträge* 1 (1973): 177–209.

Richard, Jean-Claude. "Ion-Janus ou de l'anonymat. À propos d'IGR, 2, 1–4." In *Hommages à Henri Le Bonniec. Res sacrae,* edited by Danielle Porte and Jean Pierre Néraudau, pp. 387–394. Brussels, 1988.

Simon, Erika. "Ianus Curiatius und Ianus Geminus im frühen Rom." In *Beitrage zur altitalischen Geistesgeschichte. Festschrift Gerhard Radke,* pp. 269–297. Münster, 1986.

Simon, Erika. "Culsu, Culsans e Ianus." In *Atti del Secondo congresso internazionale etrusco* (Firenze 26 maggio–2 giugno 1985), pp. 1271–1281. Rome, 1989.

Syme, Ronald. "Problems about Janus." *American Journal of Philology* 100 (1979): 188–212.

Thomas, Joël. "Janus, le dieu de la genèse et du passage." *Euphrosyne* 15 (1987): 281–296.

Turcan, Robert. "Janus à l'époque impériale." In *Aufstieg und Niedergand der Römischen Welt* 2.17.1, pp. 374–402. Berlin and New York, 1981.

ROBERT SCHILLING (1987)
Translated from French by Paul C. Duggan
Revised Bibliography

JAPANESE RELIGIONS

This entry consists of the following articles:

AN OVERVIEW
POPULAR RELIGION
THE STUDY OF MYTHS
RELIGIOUS DOCUMENTS

JAPANESE RELIGIONS: AN OVERVIEW

Like many other ethnic groups throughout the world, the earliest inhabitants of the Japanese archipelago constructed and lived in a religious world of meaning. To them the whole world was permeated by sacred power, authenticated by myths. In the early historical period, local traditions were consolidated around the emergent imperial cult in a form that later came to be designated as Shintō, or "the way of *kami.*" Many aspects of the archaic traditions have been preserved as basic features of an unorganized folk religion. Meanwhile, through contacts with Korea and China, Japan came under the impact of religious and cultural influences from the continent of Asia. Invariably, the religion of the people was changed as they adopted and adapted the concepts, symbols, rituals, and art forms of Confucianism, Daoism, the yin-yang school, and Buddhism. Although all of these religious and semi-religious systems kept a measure of their own prior identity, they were by no means considered by the people to be mutually exclusive.

It is worth noting in this connection that the term *shukyō* (religion) is a neologism not used prior to the nineteenth century. In Japanese traditions, religious schools are usually referred to as *dō, tō,* or *michi* (way), as in *butsudō* (the way of the Buddha) or *shintō* (the way of kami), implying that these are complementary ways or paths within the overarching Japanese religion. Various branches of art were also called *dō* or *michi,* as in *chadō* (also *sadō,* "the way of tea") in the medieval period. This usage reflects the close affinity in Japan between religious and aesthetic traditions.

PREHISTORIC BACKGROUND. The Japanese archipelago lies off the Asian continent, stretching north and south in the western Pacific. In ancient times, however, there were land connections between the continent and the Japanese islands. Animal and human populations thus were able to reach present Japan from different parts of the continent. Although we cannot be certain when and how the first inhabitants migrated to the Japanese islands, the scholarly consensus traces Japan's Paleolithic age back to between ten and thirty thousand years ago, when the inhabitants of the islands were primitive hunters and food gatherers who shared religious and cultural traits similar to their counterparts in other regions of the world.

Japan's prehistoric period is divided into two phases: (1) the Jomon period (*jomon* literally means "cord pattern," referring to pottery decoration), extending roughly from 8000 BCE to about 250 BCE, and (2) the Yayoi period (so named because pottery of this period was unearthed in the Yayoi district of present-day Tokyo), covering roughly the era from 250 BCE to 250 CE. Further subdivisions of both the Jomon and Yayoi periods, as proposed by various archaeologists, are not relevant for our purpose. Archaeological evidence reveals a gradual development in the use of fishing and hunting tools, but in the artistic qualities of pottery making and designs and in the living patterns of the Jomon people, we still have few clues regarding their religious outlooks or practices. Thus, we can only infer that the practice of extracting certain teeth, for example, probably indicates a puberty rite, while female figurines may have been used in fertility cults.

There is no clear-cut date for dividing the Jomon and the Yayoi periods, because the Yayoi culture emerged in western parts of Japan while the Jomon culture was still developing in the eastern parts. Nevertheless, the transition between these cultural forms was sufficiently marked so that some scholars even postulate the migration during the early third century BCE of a new ethnic group from outside. Yayoi pottery is more sophisticated in design and manufacturing techniques and more utilitarian than Jomon ware. Yayoi jugs, jars, and pots were used both for cooking and for preserving food. Moreover, Yayoi culture was based on rice cultivation, employing hydraulic technology. Evidently, communities were established in places of low altitude, and many farmhouses had raised floors, the space beneath them serving as storehouses for grain. As the Yayoi period coincided with the Qin (221–206 BCE) and the Han (206 BCE–220 CE) dynasties in China, and as Chinese political and cultural influence was penetrating the Korean peninsula, some features of continental civilization must have infiltrated into western Japan. This infiltration may account for the development in the Yayoi period of spinning and weaving and the use of iron, bronze, and copper. We cannot say with precision, however, what religious significance or uses bronze mirrors, bronze bells, dolmens (stone monuments), and funeral urns had.

The Ainu controversy and a culture-complex hypothesis. Although it is safe to assume that migrations of people to the Japanese islands were a part of larger movements of archaic peoples from Eurasia to North America, it is difficult to determine the ethnic identity of the first settlers in Japan. In this connection a heated controversy has been carried on in recent decades as to whether or not the Ainu—who have lived on the Hokkaidō, Sakhalin, and Kuril Islands, but who throughout history have never been fully assimilated into the cultural life of the Japanese—were indeed the original inhabitants of the Japanese islands. Scholarly opinion at the turn of the twenty-first century holds that the Ainu lived in northern Japan as early as the Jomon period, but that there was never, at least until the twentieth century, any significant amount of intermarriage between them and other inhabitants of the Japanese islands.

Although the exact identity of the Jomon people still remains unsettled, it is widely assumed that a number of ethnic groups came to the Japanese islands from various parts of the Asian continent during the prehistoric period, bringing with them various religious and cultural elements. A comprehensive culture-complex hypothesis proposed by Oka Masao in 1933 suggests that there were five major typological components in late prehistoric and early historic Japanese culture, mythology, religion, and social structure. According to Oka, various ethnic groups from South China and Southeast Asia with Melanesian, Austroasian, and Austronesian (Micronesian) cultural and religious traits—the secret society system; horizontal cosmology; female shamans; mythical motifs of brother-sister deities; initiation rites; cultivation of taro, yam, and rice; and other characteristics—provided the foundation for the agricultural society and culture of the Yayoi period.

A Tunguz group originally from Siberia or Manchuria, on the other hand, contributed a vertical cosmology, an exogamous patrilineal clan system, and a belief in deities (*kami*) who descend from heaven to mountaintops, trees, or pillars. Finally, an Altaic pastoral tribe that had subjugated other tribes in Manchuria and Korea migrated to Japan toward the end of the Yayoi period or the early part of the historic period, establishing itself as the ruling class over the earlier settlers. This group, which had an efficient military organization, shared with the Tunguz group religious and cultural traits such as a vertical cosmology, Siberian-type shamanism, and a patriarchal clan (*uji*) system. Its most powerful family emerged as the imperial house in the historic period.

Oka carefully avoids the question of the origin and development of the Japanese people and culture in a chronological sense. Although his hypothesis has been severely criticized by other scholars, it represents one of the most all-embracing efforts to explain the pluralistic nature of Japanese social structure, culture, and religion. Despite the lack of agreement concerning the details of the culture complex thus developed, it is widely agreed that, by the end of the Yayoi period, the inhabitants of the Japanese islands had attained a degree of self-consciousness as one people sharing a common culture.

The Yamatai controversy. One of the age-old controversies regarding Japan in the Yayoi period centers around the geographical location of the state of Yamatai (Yamadai), an important state in the Japanese islands and one that is mentioned in such Chinese dynastic histories as the record of the Eastern (Later) Han dynasty (25–220 CE) and that of the kingdom of Wei (220–265 CE). We learn from these documents that there were more than one hundred "states" in Japan, and that they acknowledged a hereditary ruler who resided in the state of Yamatai. These documents also record that the first Japanese emissary was dispatched to the Chinese court in 57 CE. A series of similar diplomatic missions followed in the second and third centuries. These same accounts reveal that during the second half of the second century, political turmoil developed in Japan owing to the absence of a ruler. An unmarried female shamanic diviner, Pimiko or Himiko, who occupied herself with magic and sorcery, bewitching people, then became the ruler, and order was restored. The Chinese court offered her the title Queen of Wo (Wa) Friendly to Wei. Evidently she lived in seclusion in a palace, protected by armed guards. She was attended by a thousand female servants, while only a single male relative transmitted her instructions and pronouncements, presumably utterances she made in a state of trance. When she died a great mound was raised, and one hundred attendants followed her to the grave. After her death a king was placed on the throne, but since the people did not obey him, a young girl of thirteen, Iyo, was made queen, and order was once again restored. From these Chinese records we learn, among other things, that political stability in prehistoric Japan depended heavily on magico-religious authority. The intriguing question still remains, however, whether or not the state of Yamatai was located in the western island of Kyushu, as some scholars now believe, or in the central part of the main island where the so-called Yamato kingdom was established in the early historical period.

EARLY HISTORICAL PERIOD. The early historical period of Japan corresponds to what archaeologists call the Kofun (tumulus) period (c. 250–600 CE), so named because of the gigantic mausoleums constructed during this time for the deceased of the ruling class in the present Nara and Osaka prefectures. These great tombs are the visible remains of the early Yamato kingdom. It is significant that Japan was not mentioned in Chinese records between the mid-third and the early fifth century. Many scholars conjecture that during this shadowy period, the Yamato kingdom was established in the present Nara prefecture and gained a foothold on the southern tip of the Korean peninsula. During the fourth century, according to Korean sources, Yamato became an ally of Paekche, one of the Korean states, and Korean artisans and scholars migrated to Japan, introducing new arts and techniques in weaving, ironwork, and irrigation, as well as the Chinese script and Confucian learning. In 391 Japanese expeditionary forces crossed the sea and fought against the northern Korean state, Koguryŏ, but were badly defeated. Following the military defeat in Korea, Yamato turned to the Chinese court to secure Chinese recognition and support for its claim of suzerainty over Korea. In fact, the *Sung shu* (a history of the Liu Song dynasty, covering the years 420–479) mentions the names of five Yamato rulers who sent emissaries to the Chinese court. During the sixth century, Yamato sought to restore its influence on the Korean peninsula. In this connection Buddhism was introduced officially from Paekche to the Yamato court in 538 or 552.

Prior to the introduction of Sino-Korean civilization and Buddhism, religion in the Japanese islands was not a well-structured institutional system. The early inhabitants took it for granted that the world was the land where they lived. They also accepted the notion that the natural world was a given. Yet their religious outlook had a strong cosmological orientation, so that their early religion might be characterized as a cosmic religion. Although they did not speculate on the metaphysical meaning of the cosmos, they felt that they were an integral part of the cosmos, which to them was a community of living beings, all sharing *kami* (sacred) nature. The term *kami*, a combination of the prefix *ka* and the root *mi*, signifies either a material thing or an embodied spirit possessing divine potency and magical power. The term *kami*, thus, refers to all beings that are worthy of reverence, including both good and evil beings. The people accepted the plurality of *kami* residing in different beings and objects, but their basic affirmation was the sacrality of the total cosmos.

Equally central to the early religious outlook was the notion of *uji* (lineage group, clan), which provided the basic framework for social solidarity. Although the *uji* was not based on the strict principle of consanguinity, some blood relationship, real or fictitious, was considered essential for communal cohesion. Each *uji* had clansmen (*ujibito*), groups of professional persons (*be*) who were not blood relations of the clansmen, and slaves (*nuhi*), all of whom were ruled by the *uji* chieftain (*uji no kami*). Each *uji* was not only a social, economic, and political unit but also a unit of religious solidarity centered on the *kami* of the *uji* (*ujigami*) who was attended by the *uji* chieftain. Indeed, sharing the same *kami* was ultimately considered more important to communal cohesion than blood relationship.

As far as we can ascertain, the early *kami* cults did not have fixed liturgies. Most religious functions took place either at home or around a sacred tree or sacred rock, in the paddy field, or on the seashore. Because the *uji* group tended to reside in the same locality, the *kami* of the *uji* often had the quality of local or regional *kami*. Also, there were numerous other spirits who controlled the health, fortune, and longevity of people. They were variously called *mono* (spiritual entities) or *tama* (animating spirits) and were believed to be attached to human and other beings or natural things. Equally prevalent was the notion of "sacred visitors" (*marebito*) or ancestral spirits who came from distant places to visit human communities. Celestial bodies (the sun, moon, and stars), meteorological phenomena (wind and storms), and awe-inspiring natural objects (mountaintops, tall trees, forests, the ocean, and rivers) were also considered sacred and, thus, were venerated. Not surprisingly, then, a variety of persons—fortune-tellers, healers, magicians, sorcerers, and diviners—served as intermediaries to these divine forces.

Religion and government. The early Yamato kingdom was a confederation of semiautonomous *uji*, each of which owned and ruled its respective members. The Yamato rulers paid tribute to China and in return received a monarchical title from the Chinese imperial court. Gradually, the Yamato rulers solidified their influence over other *uji* chieftains with their military power and with their claims to genealogical descent from the sun deity. They thus exercised the prerogatives of conferring such court titles as O-muraji ("great magnate," presented to the hereditary vassal families of the imperial *uji*) and O-omi ("chief of chieftains," conferred upon heads of former rival *uji* that had acknowledged the imperial authority); granting sacred seed at spring festivals to all *uji* groups; and establishing sacred sites for heavenly and earthly *kami*, as well as regulating *matsuri* (rituals) for them.

The term *matsuri* has the connotation "to be with," "to attend to the need of," "to entertain," or "to serve" the *kami*, the soul of the deceased, or a person of high status. Prior to a *matsuri*, the participants were expected to purify themselves and to abstain from certain foods and from sexual intercourse. It was understood that the most important duty of the Yamato emperor (*enno*) was to maintain close contact with the sun deity—the imperial family's tutelary and ancestral *kami*—and other heavenly and earthly *kami* by attending to their needs and following their will, which was communicated through oracles, dreams, and divinations and which concerned government administration (*matsurigoto*). Thus, in principle, at this level there was no line of demarcation between the sacred and the profane dimensions of life or between religious rituals (*matsuri*) and government administration (*matsurigoto*). Both were the prerogatives of the sovereign, who was by virtue of his solar ancestry the chief priest as well as the supreme political head of the kingdom. The sovereign, in turn, was assisted by hereditary religious functionaries and hereditary ministers of the court. This principle of the unity of religion and government (*saisei-itchi*) remained the foundation of Japanese religion when it later became institutionalized and acquired the designation of Shintō in contradistinction to *butsudō* (Buddhism).

Impact of Chinese civilization and Buddhism on Japanese religion. With the gradual penetration of Chinese civilization—or, more strictly, Sino-Korean civilization—and Buddhism during the fifth and sixth centuries, Japanese religion was destined to feel the impact of alien ways of viewing the world and interpreting the meaning of human existence. In order to create a designation for the hitherto relatively unsystematized religious, cultural, and political tradition, the Japanese borrowed two Chinese characters—*shen* (Japanese, *shin*) for *kami*, and *dao* (Japanese, *to* or *do*)—for "the way." The adoption of the name *Shintō* only magnified the profound tension between the indigenous Japanese understanding of the meaning of life and the world—authenticated solely by their particular historic experience on the Japanese islands—and the claims of Confucianism and Buddhism that their ways were grounded in universal laws and principles, the Confucian Dao (the Way) and Buddhist Dharma (the Law).

There is little doubt that the introduction of Chinese script and Buddhist images greatly aided the rapid penetration of Chinese civilization and Buddhism. As the inhabitants of the Japanese islands had not developed their own script, the task of adopting the Chinese script, with its highly developed ideographs and phonetic compounds, to indigenous words was a complex one. There were many educated Korean and Chinese immigrants who served as instructors, interpreters, artists, technicians, and scribes for the imperial court and influential *uji* leaders of the state. Over the course of time, the intelligentsia learned the use of literary Chinese and for many centuries used it for writing historical and official records. Poets, too, learned to express themselves in Chinese verse or, as in the *Man'yōshū*, the eighth-century poetry anthology, utilized Chinese characters as a form of syllabary to render their oral verses. The people accepted Chinese as a written, but not a spoken, language. Even so, through this one-sided medium the inhabitants of the Japanese islands gained access to the rich civilization of China, and Chinese culture became the major resource and model for the emerging state of Japan.

Through written media, the Japanese came to know the mystical tradition of philosophical Daoism, which enriched their aesthetic tradition. The Japanese also learned of the yin-yang school's concepts of the two principles (yin and yang), the five elements (metal, wood, water, fire, and earth), and the orderly rotation of these elements in the formation of nature, seasons, and the human being. The yin-yang school thus provided cosmological theories to the hitherto nonspeculative Japanese religion. It was also through written Chinese works that the society, which had been based on archaic communal rules and the *uji* system, appropriated certain features of Confucian ethical principles, social and political theories, and legal and educational systems.

The introduction of Buddhist art equally revolutionized Japanese religion, which despite its aesthetic sensitivities had never developed artistic images of *kami* in sculpture or painting. Understandably, when Buddhism was officially introduced to the Japanese court in the sixth century, it was the Buddha image that became the central point of contention between the pro- and anti-Buddhist factions there. Anti-Buddhist leaders argued that veneration of a "foreign *kami*" would offend the "native *kami*." After this initial controversy regarding statues of the Buddha, however, the chieftain of the powerful Soga *uji*s secured imperial permission to build a new clan temple in order to enshrine Buddha images. Soon, thanks to the energetic advocacy of the Soga, Buddhism was accepted by other aristocratic families, but not because the profound meaning of Buddhist law (the Dharma) was fully appreciated. Rather, Buddhist statues were believed to have magical potencies that would bring about mundane benefits. Thus the statues of Shaka (Śākyamuni), Miroku (Maitreya), Yakushi (Bhaisajyaguru), Kannon (Avalokiteśvara), and Amida (Amitābha) were venerated almost indiscriminately in the *uji*-based Buddhism of sixth- and early-seventh-century Japan.

PRINCE SHŌTOKU. The regency of Prince Shōtoku (574?–622?), who served under his aunt, Empress Suiko (r. 592–628), marks a new chapter in the history of Japanese religion. By that time Japan had lost its foothold on the southern tip of the Korean peninsula, while the powerful Sui dynasty had unified China after centuries of disunity. To protect Japan's survival in the precarious international scene, Shōtoku and his advisers attempted to strengthen the fabric of national community by working out a multireligious policy reconciling the particularistic Japanese religious tradition with the universal principles of Confucianism and Buddhism. Shōtoku's mentor here was clearly Emperor Wen (r. 581–605) of the Sui dynasty, who unified the races, cultures, and vast and diverse areas of China by utilizing Confucianism, Buddhism, and to a lesser degree Daoism as the arms of the throne. Moreover, his claim to semidivine status was sanctioned and authenticated by various religious symbols.

Shōtoku himself was a pious Buddhist and is reputed to have delivered learned lectures on selected Buddhist scriptures. Yet his policies, as exemplified in the establishment of the Chinese-style "cap ranks" of twelve grades for court ministers or in the promulgation of the Seventeen-Article Constitution, represented an indigenous attempt to reconcile Buddhist and Confucian traditions with the native Japanese religious tradition. Shōtoku envisaged a centralized national community under the throne, and he advocated the veneration of Buddhism as the final refuge of all creatures. Moreover, he held the Confucian notion of *li* (propriety) to be the key to right relations among ruler, ministers, and people.

Shōtoku was convinced that his policy was in keeping with the will of the *kami*. In his edict of 607, he states that his imperial ancestors had venerated the heavenly and earthly *kami* and, thus, the winter (yin, negative cosmic force) and summer (yang, positive cosmic force) elements remained in harmony, with their creative powers blended. He urged his ministers to do the same.

Prince Shōtoku took the initiative in reestablishing diplomatic contact with China by sending an envoy to the Sui court. He also sent a number of talented young scholars and monks to China to study. Although Shōtoku's reform measures remained unfulfilled at his untimely death, the individuals he sent to China later played important roles in the development of Japanese religions and national affairs upon their return.

THE RITSURYŌ SYNTHESIS. Prince Shōtoku's death was followed by a series of bloody power struggles, including a coup d'état in 645, which paradoxically strengthened the position of the throne. The Taika reforms of 645 and 646 attempted to consolidate the power of the centralized government by such Chinese-style measures as land redistribution, collection of revenues, and a census. During the second half of the seventh century the government, utilizing the talents of those who had studied in China, sponsored the compilation of a written law code. Significantly, those penal codes (*ritsu*; Chinese, *lü*) and civil statutes (*ryo*; Chinese, *ling*), which were modeled after Chinese legal systems, were issued in the name of the emperor as the will of the *kami*. The government structure thus developed during the late seventh century is referred to as the Ritsuryō (imperial rescript) state. Although the basic principle of the Ritsuryō state was in a sense a logical implementation of Prince Shōtoku's vision, which itself was a synthesis of Buddhist, Confucian, and Japanese traditions, it turned out to be in effect a form of immanental theocracy, in which the universal principles of Dao and Dharma were domesticated to serve the will of the sovereign, who now was elevated to the status of a living or manifest *kami*.

The government's effort to consolidate the Ritsuryō structure was initially resisted by the former *uji* chieftains and provincial magnates who had residual power in the court. Ironically, after usurping the throne from his uncle, Emperor Tenmu (r. 673–686) managed to bring new elements into the rank of court nobility and to reorganize the governmental structure. Tenmu ordered the compilation of two historical writings, the *Kojiki* (Record of ancient matters, completed in 712) and the *Nihongi* (or *Nihonshoki*, the Chronicle of Japan, completed in 720). Tenmu is also credited with canonizing Amaterasu, the sun deity, as the ancestral *kami* and with making her Grand Shrine of Ise the tutelary shrine of the imperial house.

One characteristic policy of the Ritsuryō state was to support and control all of the religious ways. Thus, the government enforced the Soniryo, or Law Governing Monks and Nuns, which was modeled after a Chinese code, the Law Governing Daoist and Buddhist Priests, of the Yonghui period (640–655). The government also elevated the Office of Kami Affairs (*Kanzukasa*) to a full-fledged Department of Kami Affairs (*Jingikan*), charged with supervising all officially sponsored Shintō shrines and overseeing the registers of the entire Shintō priesthood and other religious corporations. The Jingikan was given equal rank with the Great Council of State (*Dajokan*).

NARA PERIOD (710–784). During the eighth century Japanese religion reached an important stage of maturity under Chinese and Buddhist influence. It was a golden age for the Ritsuryō state and the imperial court. Thanks to the newly acquired Chinese script, the two mythohistorical writings—the *Kojiki* and the *Nihonshoki*—as well as the *Fudoki* (Records of local surveys), the *Man'yōshū* (Anthology of myriad leaves), and the *Kaifuso* (Fond recollection of poetry) were compiled. Also in this century, the Yoro Ritsuryō (Yoro penal and civil codes), the legal foundation of the Ritsuryō state, was fixed in writing.

The immanental theocratic principle of the Ritsuryō state was based on the myth of the solar ancestry of the imperial house. Similarly, the compilation of the *Kojiki* and the *Nihonshoki* was ordered by Emperor Tenmu in 673 to justify his accession to the throne. Thus, although the format of these chronicles was modeled after Chinese dynastic histories, their task was to sort out myths, legends, and historical events in such a way as to establish direct genealogical connections between the contemporary imperial house and the sun deity. With this objective in mind, the chroniclers worked out a transition from the domain of myths (narratives with divine actors), classified as the "age of *kami*," to the "historical" accounts of legendary emperors, who were presumed to be direct ancestors of the imperial house. Although the chronologies in the *Kojiki* and *Nihonshoki* were obviously fabricated, these mythohistorical writings provide a rich source of myths in which the ethos and meaning structure of early Japanese religion unfold. Later, under the guide of nativist scholars (*kokugakusha*), these two chronicles came to be regarded as semi-canonical scriptures of Shintō.

The *Man'yōshū* is as important as the chronicles for our understanding of early Japanese religion. In its literary form, the *Man'yōshū* utilized Chinese characters only for their sound value, disregarding their lexical meaning. Many of the poems in this anthology portray an interpenetration of what we now call religious, aesthetic, and political values. The *Man'yōshū* also reveals the crucial religio-political role oral poets played in public and ritual declamations of the sacred order of the heavens and the human realm.

In contrast to earlier periods, when Korean forms of Buddhism influenced Japan, early eighth-century Japan felt the strong impact of Chinese Buddhism. In 710 the first capital, modeled after the Chinese capital of Chang'an, was established in Nara, which was designed to serve as the religious as well as the political center of the nation. During the Nara period, the imperial court was eager to promote Buddhism as the religion best suited for the protection of the state. Accordingly, in every province the government established state-sponsored temples (*kokubunji*) and nunneries (*kokubunniji*). In the capital city the national cathedral, Tōdaiji was built as the home of the gigantic bronze statue of the buddha Vairocana. The government sponsored and supported six schools of Chinese Buddhism. Of the six, the Ritsu (Vinaya) school was concerned primarily with monastic disciplines. The other five were more like monastic schools based on different philosophical traditions than sectarian groups. For example, the two Hīnayāna schools—the Kusha (deriving its name from the *Abhidharmakóśa*) and the Jojitsu (deriving its name from the *Satyasiddhi*)—were devoted to cosmological and psychological analysis of elements of the universe, whereas the Sanron (Mādhyamika) school specialized in dialectic analysis of concepts in order to suppress all duality for the sake of gaining perfect wisdom. The Kegon school (deriving its name from the *Avataṃsaka Sūtra*) was a form of cosmotheism, viewing the cosmos itself as divine, and the Hossō (Yogācāra), probably the most influential system during the Nara period, stressed analysis of the nature of things and a theory of causality. Only those who had taken vows at one of the three official ordination platforms were qualified to be ordained monks. With government subsidies, the monks were able to devote their lives to the study of the doctrinal intricacies of their respective schools.

Despite such encouragement and support from the government, monastic Buddhism did not have much impact on the populace. More important were three new religious forms that developed out of the fusion between the Japanese religious heritage and Buddhism. The first new form was the Nature Wisdom school (Jinenchishu), which sought enlightenment by meditation or austere physical discipline in the mountains and forests. Those who followed this path, including some official monks, affirmed the superiority of enlightenment through nature to the traditional Buddhist disciplines and doctrines. The indigenous acceptance of the sacrality of the phenomenal world was thus reaffirmed.

Second, a variety of folk religious leaders, variously called private monks (*shidoso*) and unordained monks (*ubasoku*; from Sanskrit *upasaka*), emerged. Many of them were magicians, healers, and shamanic diviners of the mountain districts or the countryside who came under nominal Buddhist influence, although they had little or no formal Buddhist training. Their religious outlook was strongly influenced by the popular religious traditions and Daoism, but they also appropriated many features of Buddhism and taught simple and syncretistic folk Buddhism among the lower strata of society.

A third new form grew out of the interpenetration and amalgamation of the *kami* cults and Buddhism, whereby Shintō shrines found their way into the compounds of Buddhist temples and Buddhist chapels were built within the precincts of Shintō shrines. This development can be seen in the history of the construction of Tōdaiji, which was promoted by reported oracles from the Great Sun Deity of the Inner Shrine of Ise and from the *kami* Hachiman of the Usa Shrine in Kyushu. Indeed, Hachiman was explicitly equated with a Buddhist *bodhisattva*. This Shintō-Buddhist amalgamation, which began in the eighth century and later came to be called Ryobu (two aspects) Shintō, remained the institutional norm until the forced separation of Buddhism from Shintō shrines in the late nineteenth century.

Erosion of the Ritsuryō Ideal. In 794 the capital was moved from Nara to a remote site and then again ten years later to the present Kyoto. The new capital in Kyoto, called Heiankyo (capital of peace and tranquility), was modeled after the Chinese capital. Although Kyoto remained the seat of the imperial court until the nineteenth century, the Heian period covers only the period from the late eighth to the late twelfth century, when political power was concentrated in the capital. Eager to restore the integrity of the Ritsuryō system, the leaders of the Kyoto regime forbade the Nara Buddhist schools to move into the new capital. Instead, the imperial court favored, side by side with Shintō, two new Buddhist schools, Tendai (Chinese, Tiantai) and Shingon (Chinese, Zhenyan), introduced by Saichō (767–822) and Kūkai (774–835), respectively. Both Saichō and Kūkai had been disillusioned in their youth by the formalism and moral decadence of the Buddhist schools in Nara, both had studied in China, and both were to exert great influence on the further development of Japanese religion.

Saichō, also known by his posthumous name, Dengyō daishi, established the monastic center of the Tendai school at Mount Hiei, not far from Kyoto, and incorporated the doctrines of the *Saddharmapuṇḍarīka* (Lotus of the good law) *Sūtra*, esoteric (i.e., Tantric) forms of meditation and ritual practice, Zen (Chinese, Chan) meditation, and monastic discipline (Vinaya) into his teachings. He was conciliatory to the *kami* cults and his form of Shintō-Buddhist (Tendai) amalgam came to be known as Sannō Ichijitsu (one reality) Shintō. Shortly after Saichō's death, the Tendai school increasingly stressed its esoteric elements to the extent that it came to be styled Taimitsu (Tendai Esoterism). The Tendai monastic complex at Mount Hiei remained for centuries a most powerful institution and produced many prominent religious figures during the medieval period.

Kūkai, known posthumously as Kobo Daishi, established the Shingon monastic center at Mount Koya, not far from present-day Osaka. He also served as the head of the prestigious Toji (Eastern Temple) in Kyoto. As a result, Kūkai's teachings are often referred to as Tōmitsu (Eastern esoterism). Kūkai was noted for his exceptional erudition. His scheme of the ten stages of spiritual development included teachings from all the major Buddhist schools and also from Hinduism, Confucianism, and Daoism. Moreover, he taught that the essential truth of esoteric teaching could be revealed in art, thus affirming the mutual penetration of aesthetic and religious experiences. The Shingon school provided the theoretical basis for Ryobu Shintō, as mentioned earlier. According to both the Tendai and Shingon traditions of the Shintō-Buddhist amalgam, Shintō *kami* were believed to be manifestations (*suijaku*) of the buddhas who were the original realities (*onji*).

Meanwhile, in an important step toward restoring the Ritsuryō system, the government sponsored the *Shinsen shojiroku* (New compilation of the register of families), completed in 815. It divided the aristocracy into three categories: (1) descendants of heavenly and earthly *kami* (*shinbetsu*); (2) descendants of imperial and other royal families (*kobetsu*); and (3) descendants of naturalized Chinese and Koreans (*banbetsu*). The preface to this register acknowledged that provincial records had all been burned. Thus, in the absence of reliable documents, many commoners pretended to be scions of noblemen, while the children of naturalized Chinese and Koreans claimed to be the descendants of specific Japanese *kami*. Despite the admission of the impossibility of the task involved, the register presented the purported genealogies of 1,182 families as an essential instrument in the hands of the nation.

Nearly a century after the compilation of the *Shinsen shojiroku*, the government undertook the ambitious enterprise of collecting all supplementary rules to previously promulgated edicts and ceremonial rules known during the Engi era (901–922). Of the fifty books that comprise these documents, the *Engishiki*, the first ten are devoted to minute rules and procedures of dealing with various aspects of Shintō, such as festivals, the Grand Shrine of Ise, enthronement ceremonies, ritual prayers (*norito*), and a register of *kami*. Of special importance to the understanding of Japanese religion are the ritual prayers, some of which might be traced back to the mid-sixth century when ritualized recitation of prayers, inspired by the Buddhist example of reciting scriptures (sūtras) developed. The remaining forty books of the *Engishiki* are detailed descriptions of rules and regulations of all the bureaus under the Grand Council of State (Dajokan), including numerous references to affairs related to Shintō. The section on the Bureau of Yin-Yang (Onmyoryo), Book 16, mentions the duties of masters and doctors of divination and astrology in reciting the ritual prayers (*saimon*) addressed to heavenly and earthly *kami*.

The underlying principle of the *Engishiki*, which epitomized the Ritsuryō ideal, was that the imperial court was the earthly counterpart of the heavenly court. Just as the court of the Sun Deity included various functionaries, the imperial court included religious and administrative functionaries, and the stylized daily rituals of the court, properly performed, had great bearing on the harmonious blending of the yin and yang elements in the cosmos, as well as on the welfare of the people. Though the *Engishiki* was completed in 927, it was not put into effect until 967, by which time the very ideal of the Ritsuryō system was again eroding.

The foundation of the Ritsuryō system was the sacred monarchy, authenticated by the mythohistorical claim that Amaterasu, the Sun Deity, had given the mandate to her grandson, Ninigi, and his descendants to "reign" and "rule" the world, meaning Japan, in perpetuity. Ironically, during the Heian period the two institutions that were most closely related to the throne, namely, the Fujiwara regency and rule by retired monarchs (*insei*), undercut the structure of the Ritsuryō system. The regency had been exercised before the ninth century only by members of the royal family and only in times when the reigning monarch needed such assistance. But from the late ninth century to the mid-eleventh century, the nation was actually ruled by the regency of the powerful Fujiwara family. The institutionalization of the regency implied a significant redefinition of the Ritsuryō system by the aristocracy. The aristocratic families acknowledged the sacrality of the throne, but they expected the emperor to reign or act ritually only as the manifest *kami* and not to interfere with the actual operation of the government. The latter was believed to be the prerogative of the aristocratic officials. Moreover, the Fujiwaras, who had managed to marry off their daughters to reigning monarchs, claimed added privileges as the titular sovereigns' maternal in-laws.

The custom of rule by retired monarchs began in the eleventh century, when ambitious monarchs abdicated for the purpose of exercising power from behind the throne with the claim that they were still legitimate heads of the patriarchal imperial family. This institution of *insei* was weakened by the end of the twelfth century and effectively ended owing to the growth of political power held by provincial warrior families.

The Heian period witnessed the phenomenal growth of wealth and political influence of ecclesiastical institutions, both Shintō and Buddhist, equipped with lucrative manors and armed guards. However, among the members of the lower strata of society, who were largely neglected by established religious groups, magico-religious beliefs and practices of both indigenous and Chinese origins prevailed. In addition to healers, diviners, sorcerers, and the practitioners of *onmyōdō* (yin-yang and Daoist magic), mountain ascetics (*shugenja*)—heirs of the shamanistic folk religious leaders of the Nara period—attracted followers in places high and low. In the course of time, mountain ascetics allied themselves with the Tendai and Shingon schools and came to be known as the Tendai-Shugendo and the Shingon-Shugendo, respectively.

Female religious figures of various sorts also helped to spread Buddhism among the masses, while lay religious itinerants also helped to spread the fame of certain temple-shrine complexes. Such literary works as the *Genji monogatari* (Tale of Genji) by Lady Murasaki and the *Makura no soshi* (Pillow book) by Lady Sei-shonagon also reveal that during this period many calamities, ranging from earthquakes, fires, floods, and epidemics to civil wars, were widely believed to have been caused by the vengeance of angry spirits (*goryo*). Some of these spirits came to be venerated as *kami* and shrines were built to honor—but also to confine—them. Festivals for such angry spirits (*goryo-e*), with music, dance, wrestling, archery, and horse racing, as well as Shintō, Buddhist, and yin-yang liturgies, were held in order to pacify the anger of *goryo* and, thus, to protect the populace.

Frequent occurrences of natural calamities also precipitated the widespread belief that the apocalyptic age of the Latter Days of the Law *(mappō)* predicted in Buddhist scripture was at hand. This may also account for the growing popularity of the Buddha Amida (Sanskrit, Amitābha, the Buddha of Infinite Light, or Amitayus, the Buddha of Infinite Life), who had vowed to save all sentient beings and had promised rebirth in his Pure Land to the faithful. Amida Buddhism was to become a powerful spiritual movement in the following centuries. The Heian period, and the elegant culture it produced, vanished in the late twelfth century in a series of bloody battles involving both courtiers and warriors. It was followed by a new age dominated by warrior rulers.

Religious Ethos during the Kamakura Period. The country was ruled by warrior-rulers from the late twelfth to the nineteenth century, even though the emperor continued to reign throughout these centuries. This is a matter of considerable significance for the development of Japanese religions. There were three such feudal warrior regimes (*bakufu* or shogunates): (1) the Kamakura regime (1185–1333); (2) the Ashikaga regime (1338–1573); and (3) the Tokugawa regime (1600–1868). Unlike the Ritsuryō state, with its elaborate penal and civil codes, the warrior rule—at least under the first two regimes—was based on a much simpler legal system. For example, the legislation of the Kamakura regime consisted of only fifty-one pragmatic principles. This allowed established Shintō and Buddhist institutions more freedom than they had had under the cumbersome structure of the Ritsuryō state. It also set the stage for the development of new religious movements, many with roots in the folk tradition. Moreover, over time the power of major Buddhist institutions and schools, including the Tendai, Shingon, and the Pure Land, was severely curtailed by brutal wars waged by Oda Nobunaga (1534–1582) and other warriors against the *sōhei* (monk-soldiers) and adherents of these religious groups.

Unlike the Fujiwara noblemen and retired monarchs, who had wielded power from within the framework of the imperial court, the Kamakura regime established its own administrative structure consisting of three bureaus: military, administrative, and judiciary. The warriors, for the most part, were not very sophisticated in cultural and religious matters. Many of them, however, combined simple Buddhist piety with devotion to the tutelary *kami* of their families rather than those of the imperial Shintō tradition. In part, the cohesion of the warrior society, not unlike the early Yamato confederation of semiautonomous clans, was based on the *uji* and the larger unit of *uji* federation. Accordingly, the tutelary *kami* of warrior families (for example, Hachiman, the *kami* of war of the Minamoto *uji*, the founders of the Kamakura regime) increased in prominence. At the same time, the peasantry, artisans, and small merchants, whose living standard improved a little under the Kamakura regime, were attracted to new religious movements that promised an easier path to salvation in the dreaded age of degeneration *(mappō)*. On the other hand, the Zen traditions, which had been a part of older Buddhist schools, gained independence under the influence of the Chinese Chan movement and quickly found patronage among the Kamakura rulers.

Significantly, all the leaders of new religious movements during this period began their careers at the Tendai headquarters at Mount Hiei, but all had become disillusioned with the established schools for one reason or another. Three of these leaders altered their religious resolutions when they found certitude of salvation in reliance on the compassionate Amida by *nembutsu* (recitation of the Buddha's name). They then became instrumental in the establishment of the three Pure Land (Amida's Western Paradise) traditions. They were respectively, Hōnen (Genku, 1133–1212) of the Jōdo (Pure Land) sect, who is often compared with Martin Luther; Shinran (1173–1263) of the Jōdo Shin (True Pure Land) sect, a disciple of Hōnen, who among other things initiated the tradition of a married priesthood; and Ippen (Chishin, 1239–1289) of the Ji (Time) sect, so named because of the practice of reciting hymns to Amida six times a day. On the other hand, Nichiren (1222–1282), founder of the school bearing his name and a charismatic prophet, developed his own interpretation of the *Hokekyo (Lotus Sūtra)*, the *Saddharmapuṇḍarīka Sūtra*, as the only path toward salvation for the Japanese nation.

In contrast to the paths of salvation advocated by the Pure Land and Nichiren schools, the experience of enlightenment (*satori*) was stressed by Eisai (Yosai, 1141–1215), who introduced the Rinzai (Chinese, Linji) Zen tradition, and Dōgen (1200–1253), who established the Sōtō (Chinese, Caodong) Zen tradition. Zen was welcomed by Kamakura leaders, partly because it could counterbalance the powerful and wealthy established Buddhist institutions and partly because Zen priests could introduce other features of Song Chinese culture, including neo-Confucian learning. The Zen movement was greatly aided by a number of émigré Chan monks who settled in Japan.

Despite the growth of new religious movements, old religious establishments, both Shintō and Buddhist, remained powerful during this period. For example, both gave military support to the royalist cause against the Kamakura regime during the abortive Jokyu rebellion in 1221. On the other hand, confronted by a national crisis during the Mongol invasions of 1274 and 1281, both Shintō shrines and Buddhist monasteries solidly supported the Kamakura regime by offering prayers and incantations for the protection of Japan.

A short-lived "imperial rule" from 1333 to 1336 followed the decline of the Kamakura regime. This rule aided the Ise Shintō movement, which tried, not very successfully, to emancipate Shintō from Buddhist and Chinese influence. Ise Shintō influenced the royalist general Kitabatake Chikafusa (1293–1354), author of the *Jinnō shōtōki* (Records of the legitimate succession of the divine sovereigns). The imperial regime was also instrumental in shifting the centers of Zen and Song learning, established by the Kamakura regime in the Chinese-style Gozan ("five mountains") temples, to Kyoto.

ZEN, NEO-CONFUCIANISM, AND KIRISHITAN DURING THE ASHIKAGA PERIOD. Unlike the first feudal regime at Kamakura, the Ashikaga regime established its *bakufu* in Kyoto, the seat of the imperial court. Accordingly, religious and cultural development during the Ashikaga period (1336–1573, also referred to as the Muromachi period) blended various features of warrior and courtier traditions, Zen, and Chinese cultural influences. This blending in turn fostered a deeper interpenetration of religious and aesthetic values. All these religious and cultural developments took place at a time when social and political order was threatened not only by a series of bloody power struggles within the *bakufu*, but also by famines and epidemics that led to peasant uprisings. The devastating Ōnin War (1467–1477) accelerated the erosion of Ashikaga hegemony and the rise of competing daimyō, the so-called *sengoku daimyō* (feudal lords of warring states), in the provinces. In this situation of shifting fortunes and power vacuums, villages and towns sometimes developed something analogous to self-rule. Merchants and artisans formed guilds (*za*) that were usually affiliated with established Buddhist temples and Shintō shrines, whereas adherents of Pure Land and Nichiren sects showed themselves willing to defend themselves as armed religious societies. Into this complex religious, cultural, social, and political topography, European missionaries of Roman Catholicism, then known as Kirishitan, brought a new gospel of salvation to Japan.

Throughout the Ashikaga period, established institutions of older Buddhist schools and Shintō (for example, the Tendai monastery at Mount Hiei, the Shingon monastery at Mount Koya, and the Kasuga Shrine in Nara) remained both politically and economically powerful. However, the new religious groups that had begun to attract the lower strata of society during the Kamakura period continued to expand their influence, often competing among themselves. Some of these new religious groups staged a series of armed rebellions—such as Hokke ikki (uprisings of Nichiren followers) and ikkō ikki (uprisings of the True Pure Land followers)—to defend themselves against each other or against oppressive officialdoms. The Order of Mountain Ascetics (Shugendo) also became institutionalized as the eclectic Shugenshu (Shugen sect) and promoted devotional confraternities (*kosha*) among villagers and townspeople, competing with the other new religious groups.

Zen and neo-Confucianism. By far the most influential religious sect during the Ashikaga period was Zen, especially the Rinzai Zen tradition, which became de facto the official religion. The first Ashikaga shogun, following the advice of his confidant, Musō Sōseki established a "temple for the peace of the nation" (*ankokuji*) in each province. As economic necessity compelled the regime to turn to foreign trade, Sōseki's temple, Tenryūji, sent ships to China for this purpose. Many Zen priests served as advisers to administrative offices of the regime. With the rise of the Ming dynasty (1368–1644), which replaced Mongol rule, the third Ashikaga shogun resumed official diplomatic relations with China, again depending heavily on the assistance of Zen priests. After the third shogun regularized two Gozan (the five officially recognized Zen temples) systems, one in Kyoto and the second in Kamakura, Gozan temples served as important financial resources for the regime. Many Zen priests earned reputations as monk-poets or monk-painters, and Gozan temples became centers of cultural and artistic activities.

Zen priests, including émigré Chinese Chan monks, also made contributions as transmitters of neo-Confucianism, a complex philosophical system incorporating not only classical Confucian thought but also features of Buddhist and Daoist traditions that had developed in China during the Northern Song (960–1127) and Southern Song (1127–1279) periods. It should be noted that neo-Confucianism was initially conceived in Japan as a cultural appendage to Zen. Soon, however, many Zen monks upheld the unity of Zen and neo-Confucian traditions to the extent that the entire teaching staff and all the students of the Ashikaga Academy, presumably a nonreligious institution devoted to neo-Confucian learning, were Zen monks.

The combined inspiration of Japanese and Song Chinese aesthetics, Zen, and Pure Land traditions, coupled with the enthusiastic patronage of shoguns and daimyō, made possible the growth of a variety of elegant and sophisticated art: painting, calligraphy, *renga* (linked verse), stylized Nō drama, comical *kyogen* plays, flower arrangement, and the cult of tea. Some of these art forms are considered as much a religious "way" or discipline (*dō* or *michi*) as the "ways" of *kami* or the Buddha, implying that they are also soteriological paths.

THE COMING OF KIRISHITAN. When the Ōnin War ended in 1477, the Ashikaga regime could no longer control the ambitious provincial daimyō who were consolidating their own territories. By the sixteenth century Portugal was expanding its overseas empire in Asia. The chance arrival of shipwrecked Portuguese merchants at Tanegashima Island, south of Kyushu, in 1543 was followed by the arrival in Kyushu in 1549 of the famous Jesuit Francis Xavier. Although Xavier stayed only two years in Japan, he initiated vigorous proselytizing activities during that time.

The cause of Kirishitan (as Roman Catholicism was then called in Japanese) was greatly aided by the strongman Oda Nobunaga, who succeeded in taking control of the capital in 1568. Angry that established Buddhist institutions were resisting his scheme of national unification, Nobunaga took harsh measures. He burned the Tendai monastery at Mount Hiei, killed thousands of Ikko (True Pure Land) followers, and attacked rebellious priests at Mount Koya to destroy their power. At the same time, ostensibly to counteract the residual influence of Buddhism, he encouraged Kirishitan activities, a policy reversed after his death. Nevertheless, by the time Nobunaga was himself assassinated, there were reportedly 150,000 Japanese Catholics, including several daimyō.

The initial success of Catholicism in Japan was due to the Jesuits' policy of accommodation. Xavier himself adopted the name *Dainichi* (the Great Sun Buddha, the supreme deity of the Shingon school) as the designation of God. Later, however, the name was changed to *Deus.* Jesuits also used the Buddhist terms *jōdo* (pure land) for heaven and *so* (monk) for the title *padre.* Moreover, Kirishitan groups followed the general pattern of forming tightly knit religious societies as practiced by the Nichiren and Pure Land groups. Missionaries also followed the common Japanese approach in securing the favor of the ruling class to expedite their evangelistic and philanthropic activities. Conversely, trade-hungry daimyō eagerly befriended missionaries, knowing that the latter had influence over Portuguese traders. In fact, one Christian daimyō donated the port of Nagasaki to the Society of Jesus in 1580, hoping to attract Portuguese ships there, which would in turn benefit him, not least by supplying modern firearms. Inevitably, however, Jesuit-inspired missionary work aroused strong opposition not only from anti-Kirishitan daimyō and Buddhist clerics but from jealous Franciscans and other Catholic orders as well. Furthermore, the Portuguese traders who supported the Jesuits were now threatened by the arrival of the Spanish in 1592, via Mexico and the Philippines, and of the Dutch in 1600.

Meanwhile, following the death of Oda Nobunaga, one of his generals, Toyotomi Hideyoshi (1536–1598), endeavored to complete the task of national unification. Determined to eliminate the power of Buddhist institutions, he not only attacked rebellious monastic communities, such as those in Negoro and Saiga, but also conducted a thorough sword hunt in various monastic communities. Hideyoshi was interested in foreign trade, but he took a dim view of Catholicism because of its threat to the cause of national unification. He was incensed by what he saw in Nagasaki, a port that was then ruled by the Jesuits and the Portuguese. In 1587 he issued an edict banishing missionaries but did not enforce it until 1596, when he heard a rumor that the Spanish monarch was plotting to subjugate Japan with the help of Japanese Christians. In 1597 he had some twenty-six Franciscans and Japanese converts crucified. The following year, Hideyoshi himself died in the midst of his abortive invasion of Korea.

The Tokugawa Synthesis. The power struggle that followed the death of Toyotomi Hideyoshi was settled in 1600 in favor of Tokugawa Ieyasu (1542–1616), who established the *bakufu* in 1603 at Edo (present Tokyo). The Tokugawa regime, which was to hold political power until the Meiji restoration in 1868, was more than another feudal regime; it was a comprehensive sixfold order—political, social, legal, philosophical, religious, and moral—with the shogun in its pivotal position.

1. *Political order.* The Tokugawa form of government, usually known as the *baku-han,* was a national administration (*bakufu*) under the shogun combined with local administration by daimyō in their fiefs (*han*).
2. *Social order.* Under the Tokugawa regime, Japanese society was rigidly divided into warrior, farmer, artisan, and merchant classes, plus special categories such as imperial and courtier families and ecclesiastics. Accordingly, one's birth dictated one's status as well as one's duties to nation and family and one's role in social relations.
3. *Legal order.* The Tokugawas formulated a series of administrative and legislative principles, as well as rules and regulations (*hatto*) that dictated the boundaries and norms of behavior of various imperial, social, and religious groups.
4. *Philosophical order.* The Tokugawa synthesis was based on the neo-Confucian principle that the order of Heaven is not transcendental but rather is inherent in the sacrality of nation, family, and social hierarchy.
5. *Religious order.* In sharp contrast to the principle of sacred kingship that authenticated the immanental theocratic state as the nation of the *kami,* the Tokugawas looked to the throne to add a magico-religious aura to their own version of immanental theocracy. They grounded this notion in what they felt were the "natural" laws and "natural" norms implicit in human, social, and political order. The first shogun, Ieyasu, was deified as the Sun God of the East (Tosho) and was enshrined as the guardian deity of the Tokugawas at Nikkō. According to the Tokugawas, all religions were to become integral and supportive elements of the Tokugawa synthesis. However, they tolerated no prophetic judgment or critique of the whole system.
6. *Moral order.* Running through the Tokugawa synthesis was a sense of moral order that held the balance of the total system. Its basic formula was simple: the Way of Heaven was the natural norm, and the way of government, following the principle of benevolent rule (*jinsei*), was to actualize this moral order. This demanded something of each person in order to fulfill the true meaning of the relations (*taigi-meibun*) among the different status groups. Warriors, for example, were expected to follow Bushidō ("the way of the warrior").

Kirishitan under Tokugawa rule. The religious policy of the Tokugawa regime was firmly established by the first shogun, who held that all religious, philosophical, and ethical systems were to uphold and cooperate with the government's objective, namely, the establishment of a harmonious society. The first shogun stated in an edict of 1614: "Japan is called the land of the Buddha and not without reason. . . . *Kami* and the Buddha differ in name, but their meaning is one" (quoted in Sir Charles Eliot, *Japanese Buddhism,* p. 309). Accordingly, he surrounded himself with a variety of advisers, including Buddhist clerics and Confucian scholars, and shared their view that the Kirishitan religion could not be incorporated into the framework of Japanese religion and would be detrimental to the cause of social and political harmony. Nevertheless, the Tokugawa regime's initial attitude toward Catholicism was restrained. Perhaps this was because the regime did not wish to lose foreign trade by overt anti-Kirishitan measures. But in 1614 the edict banning Kirishitan was issued, followed two years later by a stricter edict. A series of persecutions of missionaries and Japanese converts then took place. Following the familiar pattern of religious uprising (such as Hokke ikki and ikko ikki), armed farmers, fishermen, warriors, and their women and children, many of whom were Kirishitan followers, rose in revolt in 1637 in Shimabara, Kyushu. When the uprising was quelled, Kirishitan followers were ordered to renounce their faith. If they did not do so, they were tortured to death.

The regime also took the far more drastic measure of enforcing national seclusion (*sakoku*) when it cut off all trade and other relations with foreign powers (with the exception of the Netherlands). Furthermore, in order to exterminate the forbidden religion of Kirishitan, every family was required to be registered in a Buddhist temple. However, hidden Kirishitan groups survived these severe persecutions and have preserved a distinct system of belief and practice into the twenty-first century.

Buddhism and the Tokugawa regime. The Tokugawa regime's anti-Kirishitan measures required every Japanese citizen to become, at least nominally, Buddhist. Accordingly, the number of Buddhist temples suddenly increased from 13,037 (the number of temples during the Kamakura period) to 469,934 during the Tokugawa period, although the latter number is disputed. Under Tokugawa rule a comprehensive parochial system was created, with Buddhist clerics serving as arms of the ruling regime in charge of thought control. In turn, Buddhist temples were tightly controlled by the regime, which tolerated internal doctrinal disputes but not deviation from official governmental policy. Since Buddhist temples were in charge of cemeteries, Buddhism was highly visible to the general populace through burial and memorial services. The only new sect that emerged during the Tokugawa period was the Ōbaku sect of Zen, which was introduced from China in the mid-seventeenth century.

Confucianism and Shintō. Neo-Confucianism was promoted by Zen Buddhists prior to the Tokugawa period. Thus, it was taken for granted that neo-Confucian scholars were also Zen clerics. Fujiwara Seika (1561–1619) first advocated the independence of neo-Confucianism from Zen. By his recommendation, Hayashi Razan (1583–1657), one of Seika's disciples, became the Confucian adviser to the first shogun, thus commencing the tradition that members of the Hayashi family served as heads of the official Confucian college, the Shoheiko, under the Tokugawa regime. Razan and many neo-Confucians expressed anti-Buddhist sentiments, and some Confucian scholars became interested in Shintō. Razan, himself an ardent follower of the Shushi (Chinese, Zhuxi) tradition, tried to relate the *ri* (Chinese, *li*, "reason, principle") of neo-Confucianism to Shintō. Another Shushi scholar, Yamazaki Ansai (1618–1682), went so far as to develop a form of Confucian Shintō called Suika Shintō. The Shushi school was acknowledged as the official guiding ideology of the regime and was promoted by powerful members of the Tokugawa family, including the fifth shogun. Especially noteworthy was Tokugawa Mitsukuni (1628–1701), grandson of the first shogun and the daimyō of Mito, who gathered together able scholars, including Zhu Shunshui (1600–1682), an exiled Ming royalist. He thereby initiated the Mito tradition of Confucianism. The *Dainihonshi* (History of great Japan), produced by Mito scholars, subsequently provided the theoretical basis for the royalist movement in the nineteenth century.

The second tradition of neo-Confucianism, Oyomeigaku or Yomeigaku (the school of Wang Yangming) held that the individual mind was the manifestation of the universal Mind. This school also attracted such able men as Nakae Toju (1608–1648) and Kumazawa Banzan (1619–1691). Oyomeigaku provided ethical incentives for social reform and came to have some characteristics of a religious system. Quite different from the traditions of Shushi and Oyomei was the Kogaku (ancient learning) tradition, which aspired to return to the classical sources of Confucianism. One of its early advocates, Yamaga Soko (1622–1685), left a lasting mark on Bushidō, while another scholar of this school, Ito Jinsai (1627–1705), probed the truth of classical Confucianism, rejecting the metaphysical dualism of Zhu Xi.

Throughout the Tokugawa period, Confucian scholars, particularly those of the Shushigaku, Oyomeigaku, and Kogaku schools, exerted lasting influence on the warriors-turned-administrators, who took up Confucian ideas on the art of governing and on the modes of conduct that were appropriate for warriors, farmers, and townspeople, respectively. Certainly, such movements as Shingaku (mind learning), initiated by Ishida Baigan (1685–1744), and Hotoku (repaying indebtedness), championed by Ninomiya Sontoku (1787–1856), were greatly indebted to Confucian ethical insights.

SHINTŌ REVIVAL AND THE DECLINE OF THE TOKUGAWA REGIME. With the encouragement of anti-Buddhist Confucianists, especially those of Suika Shintō, some Shintō leaders who were overshadowed by their Buddhist counterparts during the early Tokugawa period began to assert themselves. Shintō soon found a new ally in the scholars of Kokugaku (National Learning) notably Motoori Norinaga (1730–1801), whose monumental study, *Kojiki*, provided a theoretical basis for the Fukko (return to ancient) Shintō movement. Motoori's junior contemporary, Hirata Atsutane (1776–1843), pushed the cause of Fukko Shintō even further. The nationalistic sentiment generated by the leaders of the Shintō revival, National Learning, and pro-Shintō Confucians began to turn against the already weakening Tokugawa regime in favor of the emerging royalist cause. The authority of the regime was threatened further by the demands of Western powers to reopen Japan for trade. In time, the loosening of the shogunate's control resulted in political and social disintegration, which in turn precipitated the emergence of messianic cults from the soil of folk religious traditions. Several important messianic cults developed, including Kurozumikyo, founded by Kurozumi Munetada (1780–1850); Konkokyo, founded by Kawate Bunjiro (1814–1883); and Tenrikyō, founded by Nakayama Miki (1798–1887). These so-called new religions have survived down to the present and remain significant religious communities.

MODERN PERIOD. The checkered development of Japanese religion in the modern period reflects a series of political, social, and cultural changes that have taken place. These changes include rapid urbanization and demographic shifts; industrialization, modernization, and (in some ways) Westernization; the toppling of the Tokugawa regime (1868), followed by the restoration of imperial rule under the Meiji emperor (r. 1868–1912); the increasing influence of Western thought and civilization, as well as Christianity; the Sino-Japanese War (1894–1895); the Russo-Japanese War (1904–1905); the annexation of Korea (1910); World War I, followed by the short-lived Taisho Democracy; the economic crisis followed by the rise of militarism in the 1930s; the Japanese invasion of Manchuria and China followed by World War II; Japan's surrender to the Allied forces (1945); the Allied occupation of Japan; and postwar rebuilding and renewed economic prosperity. The particular path of development of Japanese religion was, of course, most directly affected by the government's religious policies.

Meiji era. Although the architects of modern Japan welcomed many features of Western civilization, the Meiji regime was determined to restore the ancient principle of the "unity of religion and government" and the immanental theocratic state. Their model was the Ritsuryō system of the seventh and eighth centuries. Accordingly, sacred kingship served as the pivot of national policy (*kokutai*). Thus, while the constitution nominally guaranteed religious freedom and the ban against Christianity was lifted, the government created an overarching new religious and ideological system called State Shintō, which was designed to supersede all other religious groups. In order to create such a new official religion out of the ancient Japanese religious heritage, an edict separating Shintō and Buddhism (*Shin-Butsu hanzen rei*) was issued. The feeling of leading bureaucrats and politicians was that the Shintō-Buddhist amalgam of the preceding ten centuries was contrary to indigenous religious tradition. After the abortive Taikyo Sempu (dissemination of the great doctrine) movement and the compulsory registration of Shintō parishioners, the government decided to utilize various other means, especially military training and public education, to promote the sacred "legacy of the *kami* way" (*kannagara*). This led to the promulgation of the Imperial Rescript to Soldiers and Sailors (1882) and the Imperial Rescript on Education (1890). Significantly, from 1882 until the end of World War II, Shintō priests were prohibited by law from preaching during Shintō ceremonies, although they were responsible—as arms of the government bureaucracy—for the preservation of State Shintō.

In order to keep State Shintō from becoming involved in overtly sectarian activities, the government created between 1882 and 1908 a new category of Kyoha (sect) Shintō and recognized thirteen such groups, including the "new religions" Kurozumikyo, Konkokyo, and Tenrikyō, which had emerged in the late Tokugawa period. Like Buddhist sects and Christian denominations, these groups depended on nongovernmental, private initiative for their propagation, organization, and financial support. Kyoha Shintō groups, however, have very little in common. Some consider themselves genuinely Shintō in beliefs and practices, whereas others are marked by strong Confucian features. Still others betray characteristic features of folk religious traditions, such as the veneration of sacred mountains, cults of mental and physical purification, utopian beliefs, and faith healing.

In the late nineteenth and twentieth centuries other "new religions" emerged. One of the most important historically is Omotokyō, founded by Deguchi Nao and greatly expanded under the leadership of her son-in-law, Deguchi Onisaburo. Numerous Omotokyō followers split off over the decades, founding their own religious movements and communities. In addition, it is important to note that women found leadership roles and positions of power in these religious movements by practicing and adapting older forms of shamanic mediumship and forms of faith healing. Figures such as Nakayama Miki, earlier in the nineteenth century, and Deguchi Nao represent the manner in which women used their experiences of divine possession as authorization to speak out against patriarchal oppression and governmental attempts to control religious beliefs and practices. An illiterate former ragpicker, Deguchi Nao came to be seen as a real threat to the national government and, consequently, was imprisoned; in addition, her group was repeatedly harassed by government authorities into the twentieth century. This fact testifies to the manner in which religious visionary experience became, in the hands of lay men and women in Japan, a powerful weapon of the weak.

Buddhism. The Buddhist establishment was destined to undergo many traumatic experiences in the modern period. The Meiji regime's edict separating Shintō and Buddhism precipitated a popular anti-Buddhist movement that reached its climax around 1871. In various districts temples were destroyed, monks and nuns were forcibly laicized, and the parochial system, the legacy of the Tokugawa period, eroded. Moreover, the short-lived Taikyo Sempu movement mobilized Buddhist monks to propagate *taikyo*, or government-concocted Shintō doctrines. Naturally, faithful Buddhists resented the Shintō-dominated Taikyo movement and advocated the principle of religious freedom. Thus, four branches of the True Pure Land sect managed to secure permission to leave the Taikyo movement, and shortly afterward the ill-fated movement itself was abolished. In the meantime, enlightened Buddhist leaders, determined to meet the challenge of Western thought and scholarship, sent able young monks to study in Western universities. Exposure to European buddhological scholarship and contacts with other Buddhist traditions in Asia greatly broadened the vista of previously insulated Japanese Buddhists.

The government's grudging decision to succumb to the pressure of Western powers and to lift the ban against Christianity was an emotional blow to many Buddhists who had been charged with the task of carrying out the anti-Kirishitan policy of the Tokugawa regime. Thus, a large number of Buddhists, including those who had advocated religious freedom, allied themselves with Shintō, Confucian, and nationalist leaders in an emotional anti-Christian campaign called *haja kensei* (refutation of evil religion and the exaltation of righteous religion). After the promulgation of the Imperial Rescript on Education in 1890, many Buddhists equated patriotism with nationalism, thus becoming willing defenders and spokesmen of the emperor cult that symbolized the unique national polity (*kokutai*). Although most Buddhists had no intention of restoring the historical form of the Shintō-Buddhist amalgam, until the end of World War II they largely accepted Buddhism's subordinate role in the nebulous but overarching superreligion of State Shintō.

Confucianism. Confucians, too, were disappointed by the turn of events during the early days of the Meiji era. It is well to recall that Confucians were the influential guardians of the Tokugawa regime's official ideology. In the late Tokugawa period, though, many of them cooperated with Shintō and nationalist leaders and prepared the ground for the new Japan. Indeed, Confucianism was an intellectual bridge between the premodern and modern periods. Although the new regime depended heavily on Confucian ethical principles in its formulation of imperial ideology and the principles of sacred national polity, sensitive Confucians felt that those Confucian features had been dissolved into a new overarching framework with heavy imprints of Shintō and National Learning (Kokugaku). Confucians also resented the new regime's policy of organizing the educational system on Western models and welcoming Western learning (*yogaku*) at the expense of, they felt, traditionally important Confucian learning (*jugaku*). After a decade of infatuation with things Western, however, a conservative mood returned, much to the comfort of Confucians. With the promulgation of the Imperial Rescript on Education and the adoption of compulsory "moral teaching" (*shushin*) in school systems, Confucian values were domesticated and represented as indigenous moral values. The historic Chinese Confucian notion of *wang-dao* (the way of true kingship) was recast into the framework of *kodo* (the imperial way), and its ethical universalism was transformed into *nihon-shugi* (Japanese-ism). As such, "nonreligious" Confucian ethics supported State Shintō until the end of World War II.

Christianity. The appearance—or reappearance, as far as Roman Catholicism was concerned—of Christianity in Japan was due to the convergence of several factors. These included pressures both external and internal, both from Western powers and from enlightened Buddhist leaders, who demanded religious freedom. Initially, the Meiji regime, in its eagerness to restore the ancient indigenous polity, arrested over three thousand "hidden Kirishitan" in Kyushu and sent them into exile in various parts of the country. However, foreign ministers strongly protested to the Meiji regime, which was then eager to improve its treaties with Western nations, and urged the government to change its anti-Christian policy. Responding to these pressures, the government lifted its ban against the "forbidden religion." This opened the door to missionary activity by Protestant, as well as Roman Catholic and Russian Orthodox, churches. From that time until 1945, Christian movements in Japan walked a tightrope between their own religious affirmations and the demands of the nation's inherent immanental theocratic principles.

The legal meaning of religious freedom was stated by Ito Hirobumi (1841–1909), the chief architect of the Meiji Constitution:

> No believer in this or that religion has the right to place himself outside the pale of the law of the Empire, on the ground that he is serving his god. . . . Thus, although freedom of religious belief is complete and exempt from all restrictions, so long as manifestations of it are confined to the mind; yet with regard to external matters such as forms of worship and the mode of propagation, certain necessary restrictions of law or regulations must be provided for, and besides, the general duties of subjects must be observed.

This understanding of religious freedom was interpreted even more narrowly after the promulgation of the Imperial Rescript on Education. Spokesmen for anti-Christian groups stressed that the Christian doctrine of universal love was incompatible with the national virtues of loyalty and filial piety taught explicitly in the Rescript. Some Christian leaders responded by stressing the compatibility of their faith and patriotism. Although a small group of Christian socialists and pacifists protested during the Sino-Japanese and Russo-Japanese wars, most Christians passively supported the war effort.

During the time of infatuation with things Western, curious or iconoclastic youths in urban areas were attracted by Christianity in part because of its foreignness. As a result, Westernized intellectuals, lesser bureaucrats, and technicians became the core of the Christian community. Through them, and through church-related schools, universities, and philanthropic activities, the Christian influence made a far greater impact on Japan than many people realize.

Christian churches in Japan, many of which had close relationships with their respective counterparts in the West, experienced difficult times in the 1930s. Under combined heavy pressure from militarists and Shintō leaders, both the Congregatio de Propaganda Fide in Rome and the National Christian Council of the Protestant Churches in Japan accepted the government's interpretation of State Shintō as nonreligious. In their view, obeisance at the State Shintō shrines as a nonreligious, patriotic act could be performed by all Japanese subjects. In 1939 all aspects of religion were placed under strict government control. In 1940 thirty-four Protestant churches were compelled to unite as the Church of Christ in Japan. This church and the Roman Catholic Church remained the only recognized Christian groups during World War II. During the war all religious groups were exploited by the government as ideological weapons. Individual religious leaders who did not cooperate with the government were jailed, intimidated, or tortured. The only religious freedom at the time was, as stated by Ito Hirobumi, "confined to the mind."

Japanese religion in the twentieth century. In the modern world, the destiny of any nation is as greatly influenced by external events as by domestic ones. As far as modern Japan was concerned, such external events as the Chinese Revolution in 1912, World War I, the Russian Revolution, and the worldwide depression intermingled with events at home and propelled Japan onto the world stage. Ironically, although World War I benefited the wealthy elite, the resultant economic imbalance it produced drove desperate masses to rice riots and workers to labor strikes. Marxist student organizations were formed, and some serious college students joined the Communist Party. Many people in lower social strata, benefiting little from modern civilization or industrial economy and neglected by institutionalized religions, turned to messianic and healing cults of the folk religious tradition. Thus, in spite of the government's determined effort to control religious groups and to prevent the emergence of new religions, the number of "quasi religions" (*ruiji shukyo*) increased from 98 in 1924 to 414 in 1930 and then to over one thousand in 1935. Many of them experienced harassment, police intervention, and persecution by the government, and some of them chose for the sake of survival to affiliate with Buddhist or Kyoha Shintō sects. Important among these groups were Omotokyō, founded by Deguchi Nao (1836–1918); Hito no Michi, founded by Miki Tokuharu (1871–1938); and Reiyukai, founded jointly by Kubo Kakutaro (1890–1944) and Kotani Kimi (1901–1971). After the end of World War II, these religious groups and their spiritual cousins became the so-called new religions (*shin shukyo*).

The end of World War II and the Allied occupation of Japan brought full-scale religious freedom, with far-reaching consequences, to Japan. In December 1945 the Occupation force issued the Shintō Directive dismantling the official structure of State Shintō; on New Year's Day 1946 the emperor publicly denied his divinity. Understandably, the loss of the sacral kingship and State Shintō undercut the mythohistorical foundation of Japanese religion. The new civil code of 1947 effectively abolished the traditional system of interlocking households (*ie seido*) as a legal institution, so that individuals were no longer bound by the religious affiliation of their households. The erosion of family cohesion greatly weakened the Buddhist parish system (*danka*), as well as the Shintō parish systems (*ujiko*).

The abrogation of the ill-famed Religious Organizations Law (enacted in 1939 and enforced in 1940) also radically altered the religious scene. Assured of religious freedom and separation of religion and state by the Religious Corporations Ordinance, all religious groups (Buddhist, Christian, Shintō—now called Shrine Shintō—and others) began energetic activities. This turn of events made it possible for new religions and Buddhist or Sect Shintō splinter groups to become independent. Sect Shintō, which comprised 13 groups before the war, developed into 75 groups by 1949. With the emergence of many more new religions, the total number of religious groups reached 742 by 1950. However, with the enactment of the Religious Juridical Persons Law (*Shukyo hojin ho*) in 1951, the number of government recognized religions was reduced to 379—142 in the Shintō tradition, 169 Buddhist groups, 38 Christian denominations, and 30 miscellaneous groups. This was done by subsuming some groups under others.

In the immediate postwar period, as many people suffered from uncertainty, poverty, and loss of confidence, a large number of men and women were attracted by what the new religions claimed to offer: mundane happiness, tightly knit religious organizations, healing, and readily accessible earthly deities or divine agents. The real prosperity of the new religions in Japan, though, came after the Korean War, with the intensification of urbanization. Not only did the urban population increase significantly, but much of the nation assumed the character of an industrialized society. In this situation some of the new religions, especially two Buddhist groups, Sōka Gakkai and Risshō Kōseikai, gained a large number of followers among the new middle class. Some of these new religions took an active part in political affairs. For example, as early as 1962, Sōka Gakkai scored an impressive success in the elections of the House of Councillors, running candidates under its own political party, Kōmeitō. In this way, Sōka Gakkai enjoyed a bargaining power that no other religiously based group had achieved in modern Japanese politics. Other groups have also attempted to gain political influence by campaigning for their favorite candidates for political offices. Under pressure, however, the formal ties between Sōka Gakkai and Kōmeitō were severed in the 1980s.

It has not been easy for older Buddhist groups to adjust to the changing social situation, especially since many of them lost their traditional financial support in the immediate postwar period. Also, religious freedom fostered schisms among some of them. Nevertheless, the strength of the older Buddhist groups lies in their following among the intelligentsia and the rural population. Japanese buddhological scholarship deservedly enjoys an international reputation. Japanese Buddhist leaders are taking increasingly active roles in pan-Asian and global Buddhist affairs, while at the same time attending to such issues as peace and disarmament at home.

For their part, some Shintoists now promote Shintō as a "green religion," an ecologically oriented nature religion.

In the highly technological industrial society of postwar Japan, nationalists, intellectuals, and the mass media have collectively created and promulgated the image of a timeless Japanese religiosity and spirituality. While historically untenable, this invented tradition has demonstrated a remarkable appeal both to the Japanese people and to foreigners. The construct of "Japanese religion"—singular—has come to mean for many people a nostalgic and comforting nature religion. Moreover, in the work of Japanese folklorists and foreign Japanophiles, Japanese religion is touted as proof that the social intimacy of the traditional village or small town is still accessible in spite of the alienating and isolating aspects of the high-tech and industrial world of global capitalism. The Japanese, we are told, still feel close to nature, still love poetry and the arts, and still observe numerous traditional rituals and *matsuri.*

A significant part of Japanese religious life continues to focus on family values and on observances performed in the home. In addition, many men and women of all social statuses still subscribe to fortune-telling, geomancy, and healing cults. While the Japanese are avid global travelers, for many, their world of meaning in some significant ways remains strongly tied to their land, language, customs, and traditions, no matter how recent in origin these might actually be. Shintō successfully transformed itself from State Shintō to Shrine Shintō in short order during the Allied occupation. Today, millions of pilgrims and worshipers continue to visit large and small Shintō shrines, Buddhist temples, and sacred mountains.

As noted, many persons have sought refuge in socially conservative new religions, while still others have turned to New Age religions. The latter groups are extremely diverse and eclectic in their beliefs and practices. Most such groups are media savvy and have exploited new communication technologies to gather followers. These groups are generally tolerated by the government and the public, but only if they do not threaten the status quo in any major way. The media frenzy and widespread fear of cults generated by the reporting on criminal acts of members of the religious group Aum Shinrikyō in the late twentieth century indicates the tenuous nature of religious freedom in contemporary Japan. Aum Shinrikyō gained international notoriety after it was implicated in the release of poisonous nerve gas in the Tokyo subway and the murder of some of its critics. The sarin gas attack was part of a misguided attempt to bring about the millennium that the members of the group expected. In the wake of the Aum affair, the government took what some have called draconian steps to police nontraditional religious groups now labeled "cults." In the late twentieth and the beginning of the twenty-first century, numerous examples of what the sociologist of religion Shimazono Susumu has labeled "postmodern religion" have emerged in Japan. Religion in its diverse manifestations remains an important component of the lives of many Japanese.

SEE ALSO Ainu Religion; Amaterasu Ōmikami; Amitābha; Buddhism, article on Buddhism in Japan; Bushidō; Christianity, article on Christianity in Asia; Confucianism in Japan; Dōgen; Domestic Observances, article on Japanese Practices; Drama, article on East Asian Dance and Theater; Gozan Zen; Hijiri; Hirata Atsutane; Hōnen; Honjisuijaku; Ippen; Jōdo Shinshū; Jōdoshū; Kami; Kingship, article on Kingship in East Asia; Kokugaku; Konkōkyō; Kurozumikyō; Li; Mappō; Motoori Norinaga; Musō Sōseki; Nakayama Miki; New Religious Movements, article on New Religious Movements in Japan; Nichiren; Nichirenshū; Norito; Ōmotokyō; Onmyōdō; Poetry, article on Japanese Religious Poetry; Reiyūkai Kyōdan; Risshō Kōseikai; Saichō; Shingonshū; Shinran; Shintō; Shōtoku Taishi; Shugendō; Sōka Gakkai; Tendaishū; Tenrikyō; Yinyang Wuxing; Zen.

BIBLIOGRAPHY

Reference Works on Japanese Cultural History and Religions

Collcutt, Martin et al. *A Cultural Atlas of Japan.* New York, 1988.

Hall, John W. et al., eds. *The Cambridge History of Japan.* 6 vols. Cambridge, UK, 1988–1999.

Itasaka Gen and Maurits Dekker, eds. *Kodansha Encyclopedia of Japan.* 6 vols. Tokyo, 1977.

Kamei Katsuichiro et al. *The Heibonsha Survey of Japanese Art.* 31 vols. New York, 1972–1979.

Surveys of Japanese Religious History

Anesaki Masaharu. *History of Japanese Religion.* London, 1930; reprint, Rutland, Vt., 1963.

Earhart, H. Byron. *Japanese Religion: Unity and Diversity.* 4th ed. Belmont, Calif., 2004.

Kasahara Kazuo, ed. *A History of Japanese Religion.* Tokyo, 2001.

Kitagawa, Joseph M. *Religion in Japanese History.* New York, 1966.

Ancient Japanese Religions

Aston, W. G., trans. *Nihongi: Chronicles of Japan from the Earliest Times to A.D. 697.* Tokyo, 1978.

Bock, Felicia G., trans. *Engi-Shiki: Procedures of the Engi Era, Books VI–X.* Tokyo, 1970.

Bock, Felicia G., trans. *Classical Learning and Taoist Practices in Early Japan: With a Translation of Books XVI and XX of the Engi-Shiki.* Tucson, Ariz., 1985.

Ebersole, Gary L. *Ritual Poetry and the Politics of Death in Early Japan.* Princeton, N.J., 1989.

Philippi, Donald L., trans. *Norito: A New Translation of the Ancient Japanese Ritual Prayers.* Tokyo, 1959.

Philippi, Donald L., trans. *Kojiki.* Tokyo, 1970.

Piggott, Joan. *The Emergence of Japanese Kingship.* Stanford, Calif., 1997.

Religions in the Medieval Period

Abe, Ryuichi. *The Weaving of Mantra: Kūkai and the Construction of Esoteric Buddhist Discourse.* New York, 1999.

Adolphson, Mickael S. *The Gates of Power: Monks, Courtiers, and Warriors in Pre-modern Japan.* Honolulu, 2000.

Breen, John, and Mark Teeuwen, eds. *Shinto in History: Ways of the Kami.* Richmond, U.K., 2000.

Faure, Bernard. *Visions of Power: Imagining Medieval Japanese Buddhism.* Princeton, N.J., 1996.

Faure, Bernard. *The Power of Denial: Buddhism, Purity, and Gender.* Princeton, N.J., 2003.

Grapard, Allan. *The Protocol of the Gods: A Study of the Kasuga Cult in Japanese History.* Berkeley, Calif., 1992.

Groner, Paul. *Saichō: The Establishment of the Japanese Tendai School.* Honolulu, 2000.

Klein, Susan Blakeley. *Allegories of Desire: Esoteric Literary Commentaries of Medieval Japan.* Cambridge, Mass., 2002.

Morrell, Robert. *Early Kamakura Buddhism: A Minority Report.* Fremont, Calif., 2002.

Payne, Richard K., ed. *Re-Visioning "Kamakura" Buddhism.* Honolulu, 1998.

Ruppert, Brian D. *Jewel in the Ashes: Buddha Relics and Power in Early Medieval Japan.* Cambridge, Mass., 2000.

Sharf, Robert H., and Elizabeth Horton Sharf, eds. *Living Images: Japanese Buddhist Icons in Context.* Stanford, Calif., 2002.

Stone, Jacqueline. *Original Enlightenment and the Transformation of Medieval Japanese Buddhism.* Princeton, N.J., 1999.

ten Grotenhuis, Elisabeth. *Japanese Mandalas: Representations of Sacred Geography.* Honolulu, 1999.

Tyler, Royall. *The Miracles of the Kasuga Deity.* New York, 1991.

Tyler, Susan C. *The Cult of Kasuga Seen through Its Art.* Ann Arbor, Mich., 1992.

Religions in Early Modern and Modern Japan

Davis, Winston. *Dojo: Magic and Exorcism in Modern Japan.* Stanford, Calif., 1980.

Davis, Winston. *Japanese Religion and Society: Paradigms of Structure and Change.* Albany, N.Y., 1992.

Hardacre, Helen. *Kurozumikyō and the New Religions of Japan.* Princeton, N.J., 1986.

Hardacre, Helen. *Shintō and the State, 1868–1988.* Princeton, N.J., 1989.

Hardacre, Helen. *Marketing the Menacing Fetus in Japan.* Berkeley, Calif., 1997.

Harootunian, H. D. *Things Seen and Unseen: Discourse and Ideology in Tokugawa Nativism.* Chicago, 1988.

Heisig, James W., and John C. Maraldo, eds. *Rude Awakenings: Zen, the Kyoto School, and the Question of Nationalism.* Honolulu, 1994.

Jaffe, Richard. *Neither Monk nor Layman: Clerical Marriage in Modern Japanese Buddhism.* Princeton, N.J., 2002.

Ketelaar, James E. *Of Heretics and Martyrs in Meiji Japan.* Princeton, N.J., 1990.

Nelson, John K. *Enduring Identities: The Guise of Shinto in Contemporary Japan.* Honolulu, 2000.

Nosco, Peter, ed. *Confucianism and Tokugawa Culture.* Princeton, N.J., 1984.

Ooms, Emily. *Women and Millenarian Protest in Meiji Japan: Deguchi Nao and Omotokyō.* Ithaca, N.Y., 1993.

Reader, Ian. *Religion in Contemporary Japan.* Honolulu, 1991.

Reader, Ian, and George J. Tanabe, Jr., eds. *Practically Religious: Worldly Benefits and the Common Religion of Japan.* Honolulu, 1998.

Smyers, Karen A. *The Fox and the Jewel: Shared and Private Meaning in Contemporary Japanese Inari Worship.* Honolulu, 1999.

Tanabe, George J., Jr., ed. *Religions of Japan in Practice.* Princeton, N.J., 1999.

JOSEPH M. KITAGAWA (1987)
GARY L. EBERSOLE (2005)

JAPANESE RELIGIONS: POPULAR RELIGION

In this article "popular religion" will be taken to include both "folk religion"—by which is meant the diverse and at most only locally organized attitudes, beliefs, and practices that together constitute a people's customary observance—and popular or lay aspects of ecclesiastical bodies whose organization and solidarity transcend local boundaries. What is not included, then, is the religion promoted by elites such as priests, monks, and nuns, as well as by governments upon occasion, including the rites, beliefs, and theoretical systematizations that such elites officially promulgate or defend. It should be understood that in practice often no sharp line can be drawn between any of these categories. Even religious elites often exhibit "folk" behavior and attitudes not justified by official doctrines; similarly, mutual diffusion can occur between official doctrines and folk attitudes and practices. These distinctions, however, are presented for the convenience of the student of religion and culture; they are usually not a part of the thought patterns of religious practitioners themselves.

For the purposes of this article, Japanese history will be divided into the following periods:

Prehistoric and protohistoric	–645 CE
Classical (Asuka, Nara, Heian)	645–1185
Medieval (Kamakura, Ashikaga)	1185–1600
Premodern (Tokugawa or Edo)	1600–1868
Modern (Meiji, Taishō, Shōwa)	1868–present

Popular religion in Japan is composed primarily of elements that can be assigned Shintō or Buddhist origins, although elements deriving from Chinese folk religion—usually labeled Daoist—are also important, along with those of an elite Chinese tradition, Confucianism, and, more recently, aspects of Christianity. In addition, the term *Shintō* must be understood in its most inclusive sense, namely, as denoting all of the indigenous religious attitudes and practices of the Japanese people prior to the influence of Chinese civilization (roughly beginning in the sixth century CE), as well as those that evolved from these native traditions in later centuries. Shintō itself reached the more complex status of an elite tradition only at the beginning of the classical period, with the establishment of an official cult with imperial patronage and the eventual promulgation of an official mythology, codification of rituals, and establishment of a priestly hierarchy. Even during this time, however, popular Shintō continued largely unaffected by these elite events; further, official Shintō itself clearly was derived from the vast reservoir of folk practices that had regulated the religious lives of the Japanese people from time immemorial.

INDIGENOUS FOLK RELIGION. The fundamental religious concept of Shintō past and present is *kami,* a widely inclusive term embracing the notion of sacred power from a *mana*-like impersonal force inherent in all things and concentrated in the unusual, to personal and therefore godlike beings such as culture heroes, the geniuses of particular places or things, species deities, and ancestors. Originally there were two major ways of interaction with *kami:* through *matsuri* ("rituals") that sought either to receive the blessings of the sacred powers or to turn aside their wrath, or through shamanic séances using the method of *kami* possession (*kamigakari*), by which the will of the *kami* could be made known through the oracular utterances of the shaman. Intermediate forms such as divination, omen reading, and oath swearing were also common. Although imperial recourse to *miko* (female shamans) is well documented in the legendary period, this element was largely lost to elite Shintō in the course of its development. *Miko* flourished among the common people, however, and have declined only in the modern period. On the other hand, public rituals, which take place at the thousands of Shintō shrines and mostly at regularly scheduled times throughout the year, have continued at all levels of Shintō.

An important class of *kami* were the *ujigami,* or ancestral deities of the large clans that came to dominate Japanese social, political, and religious organization in the protohistoric period; in modern times the *ujigami* survive at the village level, although without their former importance, as *dozokushin.* Indeed, the *ujigami* was probably the most important *kami* to the early Japanese; as high priest, the clan head needed the shamanic services of his wife to ensure that the will of this *kami* was carried out for the weal of all.

Probably the most important *kami* of popular religion has been Inari, the rice deity, whose shrines are found everywhere, even in modern urban settings. Although not a part of the official mythology, Inari became associated in later classical times with such mythic *kami* as Ugatama, the female *kami* of food and clothing; Sarutahiko, the monkey *kami,* whose special province was fecundity; and Ame no Uzume, the goddess who, through exposing her genitals in an ecstatic dance, wielded the feminine *kami* power to bring back the life-giving sun to a darkened and dying world. Such associations illuminate both the character of the folk deity Inari and the process by which popular religious elements were engrafted to the elite strata in Japan. Inari shrines still are places where farmers go to pray for abundant crops, but they are also places where both rural and urban dwellers pray for aid in conception, childbirth, and child rearing, as well as more generally for success in any endeavor.

The most famous Inari shrine is at Fushimi in the city of Kyoto, where the elaborate main shrine dedicated to the official cult is almost shouldered aside by the many popular shrines flanking the paths that meander about the mountain. Typical of the etiological tales associated with many shrines and temples is the legend that tells of the founding of Fushimi Inari shrine. In 711, many years before the founding of the capital at Kyoto, a nobleman was practicing archery by shooting at a ball of cooked rice tossed into the air. All at once the rice was transformed into a white bird that flew away and alighted at the peak of Mount Fushimi. There the nobleman built the shrine to the rice god.

Virtually all Inari shrines have statues of a pair of foxes flanking the main place of worship, a fact that illustrates syncretistic tendencies of popular religion. These foxes, now popularly understood to be the messengers of the rice god, or sometimes even identified with the god himself, were probably derived from popular Chinese lore concerning fox spirits. Certainly there exists in Chinese a large body of folk tales depicting the dangers of fox spirits, who usually take the form of a beautiful woman in order to seduce and ruin unsuspecting or weak-willed men. That these tales also have become naturalized in Japan discloses a much more general pattern of popular acceptance of Chinese cultural and religious elements; it also suggests the association of the fox as a symbol of sexual desire and Inari as a deity of fecundity and plenty.

IMPACT OF CHINESE CULTURE AND RELIGION. At the beginning of the classical period Japan experienced a cultural revolution brought about by the assimilation of Chinese technical, philosophical, aesthetic, and religious elements. Buddhism took its place as a more or less equal partner with Shintō in the official structure of government and in the religious practice of the aristocracy. Confucianism was adopted as a theory of government and a guide to personal conduct. Daoism was used to provide a ritual structure and to assist both Shintō and Buddhist efforts to ensure the well-being of the nation. To be sure, this revolution began among the Japanese elite and for many years was largely confined to it. By the Nara period, however, despite the government's attempts to control its spread, Buddhism had begun to reach the common people. The famous Buddhist tale collection, *Nihon ryōiki,* which used the folktale genre as a means of converting the masses and of inculcating Buddhist virtues, was produced by a monk for use by popular Buddhist preachers. The Nara period also saw the paradoxical rise of the *hijiri,* or holy men, who were popular preachers and miracle workers whose activities were proscribed by the government on the grounds that they "misled" the people. While not all *hijiri* were Buddhist, most combined a Buddhist understanding of a *bodhisattva*'s compassion with a sometimes indiscriminate mixture of magico-religious practices in attempting to ameliorate the physical as well as the spiritual condition of the masses. The most famous of the *hijiri* was Gyōgi, whose elevation to the head of the official Buddhist hierarchy by Emperor Shomu in 745 expressed not only the pious emperor's desire to unify the nation under the banner of Buddhism, but also the growing recognition on the part of the elite of the popular forms of that religion.

Another result of Buddhist penetration at the popular level was reinforcement of native belief in malevolent spirits, known in the classical period as *goryōshin.* Buddhism gave such beliefs a strongly moralistic tone; previously, it was believed that *kami* power was concentrated in many kinds of beings, some of which were by their nature destructive. Now, however, destructive supernatural power could be understood as justified by human events. Just as motivation was discovered in the Buddhist psychology and its expression ensured by the law of *karman,* so did Buddhism present a new problem to the people. *Goryōshin,* as particularly the ghosts of humans who had been wronged in life, had to be propitiated or exorcised by Shintō rites and saved from their suffering by Buddhist prayers and priestly magic.

MEDIEVAL POPULARIZATION OF BUDDHISM. The collapse of the classical social and political order, completed by the year 1185, not only brought on the medieval period of Japanese history but also resulted in the virtual destruction of official Shintō. To be sure, the imperial court continued to perform some of the old Shintō rituals in the name of the emperor and for the benefit of all the nation, but in fact these rites increasingly became the private cult of the imperial family and the ever more impoverished old aristocracy. But the relative decentralization of the times allowed a number of popular forms of Buddhism to become institutionalized independently of the old Buddhist schools. Among these, the Pure Land schools are especially noteworthy. These schools combined elite elements derived from monastic cults of the savior Buddha Amida (Skt., Amitābha) and popular practices of using Buddhist chanting to overcome evil influences. The so-called *nembutsu hijiri* had been at work among the common people throughout much of the classical period in healing and exorcising demons by chanting the Sino-Japanese phrase "Namu Amida Butsu" ("Hail to the Buddha Amitābha"). The Pure Land movement of the medieval period tended to convert this immediate concern for this-worldly problems to a concern for the ultimate salvation of the individual who, by complete faith in the power of Amida and by chanting of the Nembutsu, could be reborn at the end of this earthly life into the Buddhist paradise (the Pure Land).

It seems clear that neither major figure in the Pure Land movement, Hōnen (1133–1212) or his disciple Shinran (1173–1263), sought to found an independent Buddhist school. Instead, they were largely apolitical figures who intended to extend to the common people a share of Buddhist salvation hitherto reserved for monks. The result was a radical democratization and simplification of Buddhism—in short a truly popular form of that religion. In these schools, monasticism was abolished, priests were expected to marry, and the old elite Buddhism—what they called the Holy Path (*shōdomōn*)—was rejected as selfish and arrogant. This popular Buddhism had become a religion of lay participation, congregational worship, and acceptance of the social and political status quo. The elite quest of sanctification, of personal transformation, and of enlightenment was out of reach of the ordinary person; instead of working toward the transformation of self as in the Holy Path, the Pure Land schools (called, by way of contrast, *jōdomon,* or Path of Pure Land) brought about the transformation of Buddhism into an instrument of salvation open to all.

Another way in which Buddhism accommodated itself to the popular mind can be seen in the rise of the *yamabushi,* or mountain ascetics, whose tradition goes back to the classical period. Both of the dominant schools of Buddhism in the Heian period, Tendai, headquartered on Mount Hiei, and Shingon, headquartered on Mount Koya, established adjunct orders of *yamabushi.* Of these, one that was allied to Shingon, Shugendō, has survived into the modern age. The members of the *yamabushi* orders were differentiated by their varying degrees of initiation into the group's mysteries. In addition, the *yamabushi* did not follow the Buddhist monastic rules: they were laymen who lived ordinary lives except for certain times of the year when they would gather to go on pilgrimages and conduct their own secret rites deep in their sacred mountains. A famous *nō* play by Zeami (*Taniko*) depicts one of the Shugendo pilgrimages.

Belief in sacred mountains appears to be a native Shintō phenomenon in Japan, although both Daoism and Buddhism brought from China their own traditions of encountering the sacred among mountains, traditions that served to strengthen and sometimes modify indigenous attitudes. Mountains were the special abodes of the Daoist *xian* (Jpn., *sennin*), or immortals, as well as the saints and recluses that the personalistic side of that tradition promoted. These traditions, especially in the form of popular tales, were brought to Japan, where they found ready acceptance, mixing with the native *hijiri* tradition. In the Heian period, the Buddhists, themselves influenced by the Daoist tradition, especially sought out remote mountains as sites for monasteries as well as for retreats and hermitages for meditation. In addition, several mountains, such as Ontake and Fuji, were thought by the laity to be the special abodes of *bodhisattvas* or the entryways to the afterlife. All these cases show traces of the old Shintō notion that austerities practiced in mountains were especially efficacious for gaining spiritual power. The *yamabushi* demonstrate this connection by their habit of making long and arduous hikes through the mountains and by ritual bathing in icy mountain streams. Many sacred mountains in Japan were gathering places for *miko,* who served the common people by contacting the spirits of the dead or of Shintō, Daoist, or Buddhist saints and deities who were believed to inhabit such places.

The association and even amalgamation of Shintō and Buddhism among the people was aided by the *honjisuijaku* ("essence-manifestation") theory first promulgated in the classical period by Buddhist monks using Chinese models. Almost from the beginning of the Buddhist presence in Japan the people had assumed that Buddhist figures—saints, *bodhisattvas*, celestial Buddhas—were related in some way to native Shintō deities. The *honjisuijaku* theory simply gave official sanction to this popular view by stating that specific native figures were but the manifestation of certain Buddhist figures who were their true essence. This tendency to amalgamation can also be recognized in the practice, documented from the Nara period, of building small Buddhist temples within the confines of Shintō shrines, and vice versa. Thus the Shintō *kami* (deities) could be served by Buddhist rites, while Buddhist figures could be worshiped through Shintō rites. Sometimes the Buddhist rites were understood as attempts to bring the *kami* to Buddhist enlightenment; alternatively, they were thought of as a Buddhist accommodation to the parochial Japanese mentality, which often preferred native forms. By the medieval period, many local shrines and temples were served by priests who were both Shintō and Buddhist, performing the rites according to the figure addressed. Often, *yamabushi* would marry *miko* and carry on local priestly functions as a team within this popular amalgamation of religions.

DOMESTIC PIETY AND ANCESTOR REVERENCE. Even in the early twenty-first century most Japanese families have within the home both a Shintō *kamidana* ("god-shelf") and a Buddhist *butsudan* ("Buddhist altar"). At both, offerings of flowers and food are made from time to time and prayers are recited. Ancestral tablets will be found within the home, placed either in a special shrine or within the *kamidana* or *butsudan* according to the emphasis of the particular family. Theoretically, the Buddhist prayers are offered for the benefit of the departed, to aid them in their continuing postmortem quest for salvation in various hells or heavens or in rebirths in this world, while the Shintō prayers are acts of filial piety that address the spirits of the dead as present in the tablets, as still present family members who require service in death as in life. In practice, however, the popular mind often does not make such sharp distinctions.

An important example of attitudes toward the dead can be seen in the Obon festival, traditionally from the thirteenth to the sixteenth day of the seventh lunar month. Although its origins can be traced back even to pre-Buddhist Hindu ancestral cults, it clearly shows its folk Buddhist as well as Shintō colorations in Japan. Preparations for the festival include cleaning and decorating the *butsudan* and preparing special offerings there. Usually this is an occasion for the full cooperation of the *dozōku* in honoring its common ancestors. Fires are lit the first night before the door of each house as well as along the roads to the village to light the way of the dead, who are thought to return to the land of the living for these few days. The spirits are entertained in the home with food, gifts, and prayers, while in the village the entertainment takes the form of graceful dancing, the famous *bon odori,* of Shintō origin. During this time graves are visited and finally the spirits are sent off again with beacon fires.

Attitudes toward death among the Japanese people have been characterized by considerable ambivalance. On the one hand, the Shintō association of death with pollution or contamination has been strong from the first: touching, being in the presence of, or being kin to one who has just died make a person ritually unclean, requiring seclusion and ritual purification. A part of a larger and very ancient belief in the contagious nature of misfortune, this fear of the dead has resulted in a near monopoly of Buddhism in the conducting of funerals. On the other hand, much evidence, from prehistoric burial mounds as well as old Japanese poetry, attests to the continuing ties of affection and duty that the people maintained with the departed even in ancient times, while the continuing popularity of the Obon festival and of ancestral reverence in the home show that even today the continued presence of the dead, if properly handled through ritual, is still valued.

It should also be noted that Confucianism, another import from China, has played an important though amorphous role in promoting both ancestral reverence and family cohesion. From the beginning of the classical period the values of Confucian "familyism" were promoted by the government as the proper basis for a harmonious and prosperous nation. By the Tokugawa period Confucianism once again became an important philosophy of both government and personal life. Loyalty to the nation was one part of a value system that took the family as the model for all values. The native Japanese reverence for ancestors as well as for all *loci* of authority was thereby greatly reinforced.

Folk deities, often of mixed Shintō, Buddhist, and Daoist heritage, continue to be accorded some degree of reverence among the people. *Kami* of hearth, privy, and yard are still known, and, curiously in the modern world, deities or nameless powers of good or ill fortune remain popular. Some examples of these are Ebisu, the *kami* of good luck, having its origin among fishermen, Dōsojin, the *kami* of roads and gates and protector of children and of marital harmony, and Kōshin, a rather malevolent deity of Daoist origin whose calendar days, occurring once every sixty days throughout the year, are considered unlucky. Belief in lucky and unlucky days was greatly stimulated in classical times by *onmyōji* ("*yin-yang* masters"), who popularized Daoist ideas and promoted themselves as expert diviners and ritualists and who could discover in their books of astrology times and directions to avoid or to welcome in order to ritually protect one from the consequences of ill-considered actions. Modern fortune tellers continue this tradition and Shintō shrines usually have booths where fortunes are told and charms can be bought. These charms, or *omamori,* are usually blessed by the priests of a particular shrine.

FOLK TALES AS EXPRESSIONS OF POPULAR RELIGION. One important and often neglected expression of popular religion everywhere is the folk tale. Although in Japan as elsewhere this literary genre resists reduction to narrowly religious categories, in Japan especially many scholars have noted the close association of folk tale and popular religious sentiments. Many folk tales express deeply felt religious attitudes and values at variance with official codes set by ecclesiastical and governmental elites, yet many also reflect these more official views. Indeed, examples abound in which priests have made use of existing tales, either to create an official orthodoxy as in the construction of a mythology, or to teach certain religious values and behavior. In this latter category, the Buddhist use of folk tales in the *Nihon ryōiki* is an early example; later Shintō priests helped to invent the *okagura* dramas, which in part taught the old mythology to the masses at shrine festivals; similarly, the medieval Shintō-Buddhist world of ghosts and karmic retribution was combined with Zen-inspired aesthetics to create the famous *nō* dramas from folk tales and historical legends. In the Tokugawa period, popular pilgrimages, especially those to the great shrine dedicated to the sun goddess Amaterasu at Ise, spawned new tales of wonder, miracles, and divine retribution.

The well-known tale *Hagoromo* (The feather cloak), known in the West as *The Swan Maiden,* contributed significantly to the official mythology of Amaterasu, as well as to the Daijosai ritual, in which a new emperor is enthroned. Again, tales of Buddhist piety as found in the *Konjaku monogatari* collection of late classical times indicate both the power of Buddhist faith and charms sanctioned by elite religion—one notes especially the long section depicting rewards both in this life and in lives to come for those with faith in the *Hokekyō (Lotus Sūtra)*—and also an antinomian tendency that criticizes the faults and foibles of worldly clergy. A more purely folk phenomenon contained in these tales is the rejection of official unworldly values for such mundane goals as sexual fulfilment and the pursuit of wealth.

The greater portion of those folk tales that treat of supernatural phenomena have little to do with any official mythology, theology, or value system. To be sure, many promote such pan-Japanese values as loyalty, gratitude, and curbing of the appetites. However, the greatest number of tales as collected by professional folklorists in the twentieth century may be described as vaguely animistic in tone. The list of extrahuman powers and intelligences told of in such tales is very long and ranges from the ghosts of human beings to traditional *kami,* including many more fanciful entities such as the long-nosed *tengu,* hag-witches called *yamauba,* and mischievous fox-spirits. Not unusual are tales in which plants, especially trees, are endowed with powers that can cause much suffering among humans if insensitively treated. Perhaps the greatest error told of in these animistic tales is simply that of impiety: this world is a crowded place inhabited by myriads of powers, each of which the "good" man or woman treats with awe and respect, while the "bad" person ignores them to his or her peril.

Pilgrimage and Popular Drama. The rise of the pilgrimage as a popular form of religious expression can be traced to the sixteenth century, although the earliest Japanese literature shows that the aristocracy were wont to make journeys into sacred mountain fastnesses at least as early as the seventh century. It was not until the medieval period, however, that journeys to sacred sites, especially to Shintō shrines, became mass movements. The Ise Shrine, main cult center of Amaterasu, was the primary goal for the millions, mostly peasants, who undertook the often dangerous journey at the peak of the popularity of this phenomenon in the late eighteenth and early nineteenth centuries. A kind of frenzy, characterized by some as mass hysteria, caused many to drop their tools, abandon their domestic and economic responsibilities, and seek the abode of the *kami.* To be sure, motives were mixed, and nonreligious reasons such as a desire to break out of monotonous existence of toil must be considered. Still, popular tales of amulets mysterously falling from the sky, of healings, of misfortune to those who resisted or preached against the urge to participate in the pilgrimage, all powerfully reinforced the prevailing notion that it was the will of the *kami* that the people should pay their respects in this way.

It should also be pointed out that in the case of the Ise Shrine, these mass pilgrimages mark the last stage in a long history of slow democratization of the worship of Amaterasu. Originally, she was the *ujigami* of the imperial family and thus admitted only their exclusive worship. Apparently, her status as a national deity, always implied by her position as progenitor of the imperial lineage, had made of her a direct object of veneration for all in the course of a thousand years or more. It must also be noted that the outer shrine of Ise is dedicated to Toyouke, goddess of food and fertility, basic existential concerns of those close to the subsistence level of economy. From this point of view, the ritual pilgrimage, with its set forms of dress and gesture, its taboos and sometimes ecstatic dances, can be seen as a new means of carrying out village rites of cosmic renewal. The dangerous and rigorous journey was a long ascetic rite of abstinence and purification. The dancing (*okage odori*) is homologizable to the dances that accompany village festivals such as *bon odori,* in which the deities and spirits of the dead are entertained, or again to the ecstatic trance-inducing dances of the *miko* who communicate with the deities in shamanic rites. Prayers at the shrine of destination, and the distribution of amulets by the attending priests, are also a part of village shrine festivals.

The rise of popular drama can be seen to some extent as a part of the same movement toward popularization of what had been the exclusive property of official Shintō, namely the mythology as set down in the early eighth century in the *Kojiki* and *Nihonshoki. Okagura* dramas enacted with music and dance the creation of the world by the primordial parents Izanagi and Izanami, the struggle between Amaterasu and her impetuous brother Susano-o, the descent to earth of the imperial grandchild Ninigi, and many other official mythic themes. As such, they represent a successful attempt on the part of the local Shintō priesthood to keep alive the old traditions by bringing them to the common people. The *okagura* became a part of many village festivals in the medieval period and gave rise to other dramatic forms, most notably the *nō* drama, which in particular achieved a high level of artistic sophistication. But *okagura* have remained popular phenomena, and still may be viewed today. Indeed, they offer a valuable opportunity to observe the blending of folk values and forms with classical elite forms and themes. There is a good deal of humor and even ribaldry in *okagura,* as well as a clear infusion of universal folk concerns that blend with the more solemn and particular mythic motifs.

INSTITUTIONALIZATION OF POPULAR RELIGION. It can be said with some confidence that by the middle of the Tokugawa period the pattern of folk religion that can still be observed in village Japan had been established. The pattern bears two features that may at first sight seem contradictory: first is the high degree to which religious elements of disparate origin have become intermixed; second is the conspicuous division of labor among various religious institutions. This latter is expressed in the common formula that the Japanese are born and married by Shintō rites, buried by Buddhist rites, and live their everyday lives by Confucian principles. Yet both these features seem to stem from a single source, namely, a very pragmatic tendency among the Japanese people: they take those elements that seem immediately useful, employing them in a contextual framework all their own.

Another pattern that has emerged with special clarity—probably the result of Japan's relative isolation—is the process of interaction between elite and popular levels of religion. Within the long history of religion in Japan modern scholarship has been able to document much of the process through which elite elements are imposed upon or otherwise assimilated by the folk. Less well known is the reverse, in which folk elements are taken up into existing elite cultural strata or are institutionalized into what are often intermediate forms. Such popular movements often become churchlike institutions with more or less clear hierarchical organization and geographical boundaries that go beyond the local arena. Beginning perhaps with the *yamabushi* movements of the Heian period, continuing in the medieval popular Buddhist movements of the Nichiren and Pure Land schools, and still continuing into the modern period with the celebrated burgeoning of the so-called new religions (*shinkō shūkyō*), the religious institutions that have resulted have tended to combine simplified versions of old elite traditions—especially of monastic Buddhism and court Shintō—with popular values that center upon social interaction in this world and the maintenance of domestic health and prosperity.

The Shintō new religion Tenrikyō was founded in the nineteenth century by Nakayama Miki after she was possessed by several *kami,* who, in the old way of Japanese shamanism, spoke through her while she was in a trance. In the course of these possessions a new mythology was revealed that, while similar in many respects to the old classical Shintō cosmogonic myth, shows striking differences from it. Present are the familiar primordial parents, and many lesser episodes concerning the creation of life are common to both; conspicuous by their absence, however, are references to Amaterasu and her brother, the central characters of the old mythology. Also absent is the entire mythic apparatus that supported the imperial institution. The classical mythology was a seventh-century creation that took many fragmented clan traditions and worked them into a drama of the establishment and legitimization of the classical religious and political order. Nakayama is more concerned, however, with domestic values. The *kami* of Tenrikyō are called divine parents; humans are their children. The good and correct life is led in humble recognition of this most fundamental relationship; hence the cardinal virtues are loyalty, obligation, and gratitude. Diseases and all other misfortunes are caused by insensitivity to this basic parent/child (*oya-ko*) relationship. Specific cultic duties consist largely of participation in ritual dancing and in group activities such as shrine building and works of charity.

Another example, this time from the Buddhist tradition, can be seen in Sōka Gakkai (Value Creating Society), founded in 1937 by Makiguchi Tsunesaburō (1871–1944) and Toda Jōsei (1900–1958). Makiguchi was a schoolteacher who, during the difficult decades of economic hardship and increasing totalitarian repression in the 1920s and 1930s, developed a philosophy of life he called *sōka,* meaning "value creation." Initially his views seem to have been largely secular, although they borrowed heavily from Buddhist metaphysics in their fundamental insight into the relativity of all values (at least in the mundane sphere) and the necessity of overcoming dependence upon false absolutes. Only gradually did this view take on a more traditional Buddhist coloration. Eventually, however, through the efforts especially of Toda, Sōka Gakkai became affiliated with Nichiren Shōshū, one of the smaller branches of Nichiren Buddhism. Toda admired much of the Nichiren tradition, especially its unusual intolerance of other religions, its simple and straightforward rituals, its demand of absolute faith in ritual objects, in its founder, and in its sacred text (the *Lotus Sūtra*), and, perhaps more than anything else, the quasi-military hierarchical organization of the sect.

Now disaffiliated from Nichiren Shōshū, Sōka Gakkai calls itself a lay Buddhist organization; technically, it has no priests, its leaders remaining laymen. The society has been a tremendous success, with membership numbering in the millions. Typical of the new religions, and consistent with its origins, it stresses immediate attainment of all worldly goals and interprets the ancient Buddhist goal of enlightenment as something closely akin to "happiness." The mental culture of such a worldview is maintained through intense small group meetings that are partly testimonials, partly study sessions. Its very simplicity, as well as its emphasis on mundane problems and upon group solidarity, all have contributed to the success of this popular religion in meeting the needs of many Japanese in the modern industrial world, which constantly threatens to overwhelm them with anomie and rootlessness. Salvation is here and now, and the conviction of it is strongly reinforced by group rituals.

Another and very different new religion, Aum Shinrikyō, sought to mix the characteristic this-worldly emphasis of other popular religious movements and an elitist monastic organization with its goal of individual salvation.

As extensive interviews of past and continuing members conducted by Murakami Haruki show, this group also appealed to those out of step with the increasingly socially atomized modern Japanese society, but added an unusual rejection of that society's also rampant materialism. Granted official status by the Japanese government in 1989, Aum later became notorious for its engineering of the sarin gas attack in the Tokyo subway in 1995. Seeking to fill a spiritual void in their lives, its members unfortunately gave themselves over to the guidance of a charismatic but psychologically unstable and increasingly paranoid master who called himself Asahara Shōkō. Before the destructive aspect of this group was generally known, their proselytizing efforts by means of the distribution of pamphlets and the sale of books, as well as small group meetings, met with some success, especially among younger people. Its core was made up of as many as three thousand "renouncers," or *samana*, while considerably more of the less committed contributed money and studied the founder's books and sermons while passing through a series of initiations derived loosely from Vajrayāna Buddhism. Initially Asahara conceived the group's mission to be prevention of nuclear holocaust through the power of yogic meditation undertaken by increasing numbers of practitioners, which practice could also lead to the individual achievement of *nirvāṇa*. Eventually a broader apocalyptic vision emerged, which some scholars believe was influenced by science fiction as much as by any traditional religious ideas, whether eastern or western. The gas attack was apparently an attempt to bring about an end to the present hateful age, seen to be a jumble of meaningless ideas and threatening powers. The Aum group would become a surviving remnant, ready to rebuild the world as a utopian community. Thus did mass murder become a means of saving humankind.

SEE ALSO Amaterasu Ōmikami; Amitābha; Ancestors; Buddhism, article on Buddhism in Japan; Buddhist Religious Year; Confucianism in Japan; Domestic Observances, article on Japanese Practices; Drama, article on East Asian Dance and Theater; Foxes; Gyōgi; Hijiri; Hōnen; Honjisuijaku; Kami; New Religious Movements, article on New Religious Movements in Japan; Nianfo; Onmyōdō; Pilgrimage, article on Buddhist Pilgrimage in East Asia; Shinran; Shintō; Shugendō; Sōka Gakkai; Tenrikyō; Xian.

BIBLIOGRAPHY

Benedict, Ruth. *The Chrysanthemum and the Sword: Patterns of Japanese Culture.* Boston, 1946.

Blacker, Carmen. *The Catalpa Bow: A Study of Shamanistic Practices in Japan.* London, 1975.

Casal, U. A. *The Five Sacred Festivals of Ancient Japan.* Tokyo, 1967.

Earhart, H. Byron. *A Religious Study of the Mount Haguro Sect of Shugendo: An Example of Japanese Mountain Religion.* Tokyo, 1970.

Hearn, Lafcadio. *Glimpses of Unfamiliar Japan.* New York, 1894.

Herbert, Jean. *Shintō: At the Fountainhead of Japan.* London, 1967.

Hori Ichirō. *Wagakuni minkan shinkōshi no kenkyū.* 2 vols. Tokyo, 1953–1955.

Hori Ichirō. *Folk Religion in Japan.* Edited and translated by Joseph M. Kitagawa and Alan L. Miller. Chicago, 1968.

Kitagawa, Joseph M. *Religion in Japanese History.* New York, 1966.

McFarland, H. Neill. *The Rush Hour of the Gods: A Study of the New Religious Movements in Japan.* New York, 1967.

Philippi, Donald L., trans. *Norito: A New Translation of the Ancient Japanese Ritual Prayers.* Tokyo, 1959.

Seki Keigo. *Nihon mukashi-banashi shūsei.* 6 vols. Tokyo, 1950–1958.

Seki Keigo, ed. *Folktales of Japan.* Translated by Robert J. Adams. Chicago, 1963.

Yanagita Kunio, ed. *Japanese Folk Tales.* Translated by Fanny Hagin Mayer. Tokyo, 1954.

Yanagita Kunio, ed. *Japanese Folklore Dictionary.* Translated by Masanori Takatsuka and edited by George K. Brady. Lexington, Ky., 1958.

ALAN L. MILLER (1987 AND 2005)

JAPANESE RELIGIONS: THE STUDY OF MYTHS

Japanese mythology is typically identified with the *Kojiki* (Record of ancient matters) and *Nihonshoki* (Chronicle of Japan). Together referred to as the *Kiki* texts, they record the history of the Yamato court's rule, which extended throughout the Kinki region of Japan. Both the *Kojiki* (712 CE) and the *Nihonshoki* (720 CE) were compiled when the Ritsuryō state, which adopted Chinese legal codes and institutions, neared completion. Both texts begin with tales of deities, narratives that are today understood as myths.

The study of Japanese mythology has, until recently, been guided by the question of how to read the *Kojiki* and *Nihonshoki* in relation to themselves. That is to say, the texts alone provided the assumed framework for all readings, and the question of what position they occupied within the discursive space of the day—the space occupied by the *Kiki*—has rarely been asked. Moreover, from the modern period onwards, the *Kiki* texts have been understood in relation to the concept of myth. Given the Western origin of this concept, however, one must question how it has come to be applied to the *Kiki* texts, neither of which contains the term, and also how a modern understanding of these texts is altered as a result.

Issues of memory and amnesia within historical discourse have been discussed, to a large extent, within the field of modern history, but the problem posed by the limitations of historical material confronts all fields of historical research, regardless of theme or time period. Individual historical texts do not encompass or represent the discursive space of the time in question. The *Kiki* texts do not present themselves as collections of myths. Rather, they present themselves as histories and as narratives recorded and remembered as histories. Multiple written and orally transmitted narratives that have not been preserved must have existed alongside the *Kiki* texts.

Current research methods that discuss ancient Japanese mythology by focusing on the *Kiki* alone betray a textual approach typical of the era of the modern nation-state. An early manifestation of this textual approach can be seen in the works of Yoshimi Yoshikazu, a late Edo period scholar belonging to Yamazaki Ansai's Suika Shintō school. Yoshimi distinguished historical sources, whose dates of composition and authors were clear, from texts, including oral traditions, whose provenances were unclear. For example, Yoshimi rejected the Ise Shintō claim that the enshrined deity of the Outer Shrine, a shrine with close ties to the imperial house, was Kuni no Tokotachi no Mikoto by appealing to classical sources whose dates of composition were certain:

> It is clear that the Outer Shrine does not enshrine Kuni no Tokotachi no Mikoto. Those who make such claims believe only unofficial histories and mixed theories; they do not consult the national histories and official pronouncements. . . . Not a single word that pronounces Kuni no Tokotachi no Mikoto the enshrined deity of the Outer Shrine can be found in the true records jitsuroku.

As a result, the Five Books of (Ise) Shintō (*Shintō gobusho*) and the Shintō texts of the Yoshida house were determined not to be of ancient origin, as they claimed. In their stead, the *Nihonshoki* was granted the status of an authentic ancient source.

Later, scholars of Native Learning exalted the *Kojiki* above all other texts. As the modern emperor-system state (*tennōsei kokka*) took shape in the nineteenth century, accounts derived from the *Kiki* appeared in state-sponsored textbooks as official history. Thus, the *Kiki* functioned as the wellspring of the nation's (*kokumin*) historical identity and as the memory of a pure and continuous ethnic community (*minzoku*). Already in the late eighteenth century, Motoori Norinaga reread the Musubi deity of the *Kiki* as the origin of all things, including human beings: "All living things in this world. . .instinctively know well and perform those acts which they must each perform, and this all comes about through the august spirit of the Musubi no kami. Human beings are born into this world as especially gifted beings" (Motoori, 1997, p. 232). Familial *(ie)* documents that had been submitted to the court and clan *(uji)* records that were determined to be inauthentic by Yoshimi had originally functioned to connect specific groups to the *Kiki* texts. During the early modern period, however, the *Kiki* were separated from *uji* and family transmissions. In the process these texts became the repositories of a national memory no longer connected to specific groups or families.

The question of how the *Kiki* texts functioned in the ancient and medieval periods will next be considered. What follows is an examination of how the *Kiki* were related to *uji* traditions *(ujibumi)* and familial records *(kachō)*, *Kiki* commentaries, and Shintō texts (*shintōsho*). the transformation of that discursive space over time will also be traced.

Studies of the *Kiki* texts by Kōnoshi Takamitsu and Isomae Jun'ichi have examined the history of their interpretation in order to trace the change in worldviews that were read into the texts. Such approaches, however, have tended to compare chronologically arranged individual texts. Historians of religions have introduced the three textual categories of canon, scripture, and commentary, which have brought to light the discursive space created their interaction. As a result, texts such as the Bible or Confucian classics, which had previously been considered orthodox in an unchallenged manner, have been reexamined (Henderson, 1991; Levering, 1989). Scholars today speak of the canonization process rather than of a set canon. Applying this methodological approach to the *Kiki* may also yield critical insights. The modern textual category of the "(scholarly) essay" will also be added to the three textual categories in order to clarify the historical nature of present-day understandings of the *Kiki*—that is, the horizon of contemporary research.

THE ANCIENT DISCURSIVE SPACE. As already noted, the *Kiki* were compiled in close relation to the establishment of the Ritsuryō state's ruling structure. Although scholars have pointed out structural differences in the stories of the *Kojiki* and *Nihonshoki*, both texts sought to legitimate the hegemonic rule of the emperor-system state. It is helpful, however, to first examine the basic myth/history.

In the beginning, the orderless world divided into heaven and earth, and from between them a solitary deity emerged. After several generations, the male deity Izanagi and the female deity Izanami emerged. These two deities gave birth to all things, including the land of the Japanese archipelago, mountains, rivers, grass, and trees. In addition, three other major gods—Amaterasu Ōmikami, Tsukiyomi no Mikoto, and Susano-o no Mikoto—were born. Amaterasu ruled the heavens as the sun goddess and provided order to the mythical world of the *Kiki* as the ancestral deity to the imperial house. The story goes on to provide etiological accounts of the origin of human death in the conflict between Izanagi and Izanami and of the diurnal cycle of day and night in a fight between the god of the moon, Tsukiyomi no Mikoto, and the sun goddess, Amaterasu.

Eventually, the grandson of Amaterasu Ōmikami, Ho no Ninigi no Mikoto (a name referring to the ripening of rice) descended from the heavenly realm to the earthly realm, where he pacified the deities of earth, represented by Ōkuninushi no Mikoto. The stories of the *kami* end by demonstrating that the descendants of Ho no Ninigi no Mikoto (i.e., the emperors) possess the authority to rule the Japanese archipelago. The story then transitions from the age of deities to the age of humans, recounting how successive emperors, beginning with Emperor Jimmu, and princes, such as Yamato Takeru, brought the Japanese islands (and perhaps even the Korean peninsula) under their military, religious, and political control.

It is important to note from the outset that the audience for these texts was not the subservient population, but rather the aristocracy and officials of the Yamato court itself. As Tsuda Sōkichi has pointed out, the concept of divinity (*kami*) within the *Kiki* evidences a strong influence of Chinese Confucianism, with a clear conceptual bent that must have differed significantly from popular notions of the divine at the time. Furthermore, the characters within the *Kiki* texts belong largely to the imperial house and to the ruling elite. Other groups appear only as objects of conquest.

From the Nara period (710–784) through the early Heian period (794–943), commentaries on the Japanese chronicles (*Nihongi kōsho*) were produced periodically for the central aristocracy for the purpose of forming a unified textual understanding of the Ritsuryō state (Ōta, 1992; Seki, 1997). No evidence can be found of the *Kiki* having been read and explained to commoners in regional villages, or to the *bemin* slaves belonging to particular *uji.*

In other words, the *Kiki* texts did not propagate the cultural unity of the subservient masses from the perspective of the ruling elite, as is the case in the modern nation-state. The texts were compiled to form the communal memory of the ruling class. This can also be seen in the fact that the earlier imperial chronicles (*teiki*) and ancient tales (*kuji*), which formed the basis of the *Kiki* texts, were selected from familial documents belonging to the various clans.

At the time of the Yamato court, the texts were referred to as "national histories" *(kokushi)*, signifying their status as official state histories. The term *Kiki* was never employed. To be precise, the difference in social status between the *Nihonshoki* and the *Kojiki* was overwhelmingly clear. The *Nihonshoki* was included as the first of the Six National Histories (*rikkokushi*), while the *Kojiki*—whatever the initial intent behind its compilation might have been—was understood merely as a variant of the *Nihonshoki.* By late antiquity, the *Kojiki* was hardly read at all.

At the same time, the historical discourse recognized by the Ritsuryō state was not restricted to the national histories. As stated in the *Shoku Nihonshoki*: "these things are recorded in detail in the national histories and familial records." Each *uji* possessed its own transmitted tradition, and by incorporating passages from the *Nihonshoki* into it they claimed an intimate relationship to the imperial house and, by extension, the state. This structure can be seen within the *Kogoshūi* (Old things collected from the ground) of the Inbe clan, in the *Takahashi ujibumi* of the Takahashi clan, and in the familial histories included in the *Shinsen seishiroku* and the Six National Histories (Isomae, 1999a). The examination of both a passage from the *Nihonshoki* and the corresponding passage from the *Kogoshūi* can help to illustrate these textual relations

> Takamimusubi no Mikoto spoke and said, "I will raise up Amatuhimoroki and Amatsuwasaka, and truly have them bless my descendants. You, Ame no Koyane no Mikoto and Futodama no Mikoto, descend to the Middle Land of the Reed Plains with Amatsuhimoroki and also bless my descendants". . . .These two deities served within the palace and guarded it well. He also spoke and said, "Take the ear of rice from the sanctified garden [*yuniwa*] of our Plain of High Heaven and give it to our children". . . .For this reason, Ame no Koyane no Mikoto and Futodama no Mikoto, and the gods of the leading families with them, gave the rice to all. (*Nihonshoki*)

> Amatsumioya Amaterasu Ōhokami, Tamamimusuhi no Mikoto thus spoke and said, "We have raised Amatsuhimoroki and Amatsuiwasaka to bless our descendants. You two deities, Ame no Koyane no Mikoto and Futodama no Mikoto, descend to the Middle Land of the Reed Plains and bless our descendants. You two deities, both serve within the palace and guard it well. Take the ear of rice from the sanctified garden of our Plain of High Heaven and give it to our children. Futodama no Mikoto, lead the gods of the leading families and serve your lord, and do according to the command of heaven." Thus the various gods also came to serve. (*Kogoshūi*)

In a passage that closely mirrors the language of the *Nihonshoki,* the *Kogoshūi* inserts a section (italicized) wherein the ancestor of the Inbe *uji,* Futodama no Mikoto, is honored. Previous research has tended to view sections that do not overlap with the *Kiki* as the actual transmissions of the clans, while the overlapping sections were understood to be falsifications produced subsequent to the *Kiki* texts. Such an understanding, however, reflects the negative effects of the modern focus on the *Kiki* alone and treats the *uji* transmissions as mere variants of the *Kiki,* thus overlooking the differences in the social functions of the two. The function of the *uji* transmissions and the familial records was to chronicle the history of each group's service to the court, thus fulfilling the political function of advocating the legitimacy of their respective social positions within the court. Although the example above comes from the Heian period, there are many cases recorded in the Six National Histories, including a dispute between the Takahashi house and the Azumi house concerning the office of the imperial messenger who delivered offerings (*hōheishi*) to Ise Shrine, and the changing of familial names (*kaisei*), where *uji* and familial records were appealed to as legitimating documents. The state's basis for arbitrating such disputes was whether or not the clan traditions accorded with the Six National Histories, including the *Nihonshoki,* and the Ritsuryō code.

Against the backdrop of this political function, the Six National Histories, as the "historical canon" of the state, came to control the historical consciousness, and even the words, of the *uji* and familial records belonging to members of the court. By *canon,* we mean something that has been established as the "normative" text, which functions as a "law and rule, fundamental axiom, principle or standard" (Folkert, 1989, p. 173). It also includes the sense of being a "fixed" text (Levinson, 1997, p. 36). Conversely, however, the familial records developed their own unique narratives, not included in the national histories, by connecting them to passages in the Six National Histories. The familial records and *uji* transmissions, unlike the *Kiki*, were not closed records. As long as the group that they represented existed, they remained open texts that accumulated new narratives at each opportunity (e.g., by submitting records to the state). The structure of the *Takahashi ujibumi*, a document explaining the origins of court offices held by the Takahashi *uji*, and the production process of the *Nakaomi honkeichō* (the genealogy of the Nakaomi *uji*) both reflect such a structure of ongoing supplementation.

The expansion of the Ritsuryō state was accompanied by an increase in the number of officials serving the state. As the state's rule reached into the lower strata of society, the number of familial historical traditions must have increased as well. One indication of such a growth in historical records can be found in the large number of familial traditions included in the *Shinsen shōjiroku*, compiled in 815 CE.

In summary, with the compilation of national histories such as the *Nihonshoki*, state-related memory was fixed within the ruling class, and individual *uji* histories developed apart from, but in close relation to, these national histories. The *uji* records and familial documents submitted to the court functioned as a bridge between state memory and clan memories. Because of the existence of multiple group memories, the national histories became authoritative texts, the central memory of the ancient court, capable of bestowing social legitimacy on the individual *uji*. The dual structure of the rigid memory of the state and the multiple and developing memories of the various families constituted the shape of history in antiquity.

The modern understanding of the *Kiki* thus merely captures the unified memory that came only after the decline of the ancient court's political authority. As the court lost political power, the *Kiki* texts were no longer needed to determine the social status of court officials in relation to *uji* transmissions and familial records. Instead, the *Kiki* came to represent a national memory. In antiquity, those whose origins did not directly intersect with the *Kiki* must have possessed very different histories of private traditions.

One final point must be made regarding the position of the *Kiki* in antiquity. In the past, some scholars within the field of religious studies sought the origins of myth within ritual on the understanding that myths and rituals are closely related. In Japan, the *Kiki* narratives are understood to be myths, but the *Engishiki* (a text from the mid-Heian period) is understood to be a ritual text. The divine names and tales recorded in the *Engishiki* include some that are not included in the *Kiki*, but they all belong to common basic *Weltanschauung*. What is important to note is not a theory of origins concerned with which of the texts are more archaic, but rather the difference in their functions within the ancient Yamato dynasty. One the one hand, as already noted, the *Kiki* narratives were recognized as historical texts that regulated the *uji* traditions within ancient society. The *Engishiki*, on the other hand, contained prayers for the emperor, as the descendant of the heavenly deities, to recite before the multitude of deities inhabiting Japan, asking for peace in the land, a bountiful harvest, or for the emperor's own spiritual well-being (Nakamura, 1999; Saitō, 1996). In other words, the *Kiki* were, strictly speaking, declarative texts that recorded historical origins, and as such were expected to perform the function of regulating all other *uji* histories. The *Engishiki* was, in turn, a religious text recording human performances directed towards the deities, performances conducted by the emperor, the ritual celebrant who approached the deities or the spirits of deceased emperors in person. In recognizing this distinction, the difficulty of including within the category of myth all ancient Japanese texts dealing with deities should be apparent.

THE MEDIEVAL DISCURSIVE SPACE. What, then, was the discursive space of the medieval period, and what changes did it undergo as it bridged the ancient and modern discursive spaces? The pioneering works of Itō Masayoshi and Abe Yasurō concerning the medieval appropriations of the *Nihonshoki* provide important clues. The clearest indication of a shift from an ancient to a medieval discursive space is found in the terminological shift from national histories (*kokushi*) to Japanese chronicles (*nihongi*). Describing the corpus referred to as the Japanese chronicles, Abe makes the following observation: "What is most often found are explanations of meaning or origins that are told individual tales utterly unrelated to the main text of the *Nihonshoki*. At first glance, these tales simulate the form of a citation from a text called the *Chronicle of Japan*, and appear to belong to the scholarly genre of commentaries on ancient sources" (Abe, 1993, p. 199).

A fixed national history, as in the ancient official histories, can no longer be found within these texts. Instead, the content of the *Nihonshoki* is reread and rendered fluid by a multiplicity of voices. For example, in the section on Emperor Keikō in *Yamatohime no Mikoto seiki*, the spiritual power of the Kusanagi sword (one component of the imperial regalia) and how it came to be enshrined in Atsuta Shrine of Aichi prefecture is explained though Yamato Takeru's eastern conquest:

> (1) Winter, on the second day of the tenth month, Yamato Takeru departed on his journey. On the seventh day, he altered his route and worshiped at the shrine [*kamu miya*] of Ise. Taking his leave of Yamatohime, he said, "Under the order of the Emperor, I now go east to punish those who resist our rule. I take your leave." Then Yamatohime took the Kusanagi sword and gave it to Yamato Takeru, saying "Be reverent and do not be neglectful." Yamato Takeru reached Suruga for the first time that year, entered the wilderness, and woefully encountered a wildfire.
>
> (2) The prince's sword drew itself of its own accord and cut the grass around the prince. Because of this, the prince was saved. He named his sword Kusanagi [grass cutter].

(3) Yamato Takeru, having pacified the enemies of the east, reached the land of Owari on his journey home. There he stayed for a while with his wife, Miyazuhime. He untied his sword and left it at his house as he walked alone to climb Mount Ibuki. He died there, overcome by poisonous air. The Kusanagi sword is now at the shrine of Atsuta in the country of Owari.

Section (1) quotes the main text of the *Nihonshoki*; the section describing the wildfire in Suruga (2) comes from a variant of the *shoki*; and the passage describing the death of Yamato Takeru (3) is taken from the *Kogoshūi*.

Unlike the *Kojiki*, the *Nihonshoki* contains within it variants of the main text. Through the Heian period, these variants were cited only as references for the main text. The two were clearly differentiated by differences in the sizing of the characters. In *Yamatohime no Mikoto seiki*, however, the variant account of the Kusanagi sword moving of its own will to save Yamato Takeru is woven into the main text in order to create a tale demonstrating the spiritual power of the sword. The more powerful the sword was believed to be, the more authority the Ise Shrine, home to Yamatohime and the source of the sword, was thought to possess. This would have been an interpretation amenable to those affiliated with the shrine, who were responsible for the creation of this text. Furthermore, Yamatohime's words are prefaced with a "said" (*iwaku*) in the *Nihonshoki*, while they are prefaced with a "declared" (*notamau*) in *Yamatohime no Mikoto seiki*. This indicates a desire to elevate Yamatohime's status (Isomae, 1999b).

The medieval period saw the liberal alteration of the *Nihonshoki* text in the interest of producing tales that served the interests and positions of those who produced them. In regards to the legend of the Kusanagi sword's spiritual power, multiple texts emerged, including *Owari no kuni Atsuta taijingū engi* (an account of the origin of the Atsuta Shrine, thought to have been compiled by people affiliated with the shrine); *Jinnō seitōki* (a chronicle of deities and emperors by Kitabatake Chikafua, a central figure in the Southern Court); *Kanetomo senkenbon Nihon shoki jindaikanshō* (a Yoshida Shintō digest of the divine age section of the *Nihonshoki*); and the *Tsurugi no maki* (Tale of the sword) in military chronicles such as *Heike monogatari* and *Taiheiki*. In the Kakuichi variant of the *Heike monogatari*, for example, the tale begins with Susano-o gaining the Kusanagi sword by defeating the *Orochi* dragon. The sword is then enshrined in the Atsuta Shrine following Yamato Takeru's eastern conquest. Later, following the monk Dōgyō's failed attempt to steal the sword at the time of the Tenchi court and Emperor Yōzei's drawing of the sword out of madness, the Kusanagi sword is lost in the sea with the drowning of young Emperor Antoku. The tale concludes as follows:

A scholar among them offered this explanation: "The great snake killed at Hi River in Izumo by Susano-o longed for the spiritual sword deep in his head. As foretold by his eight heads and eight tails, he regained the sword after eighty generations of human rulers in the form of an eight-year-old emperor sinking with the sword to the depths of the sea." Having thus become the treasure of a divine dragon in the unfathomable depths of the sea, it will never return to human hands again.

An examination of *Heike monogatari* variants depicting the loss of the treasured sword reveals three distinct groups: (1) texts that claim a replica was forged during Emperor Sūjin's reign, which was then lost in the sea (*Engyō-bon*, *Yashiro-bon* [extracts], *Genpei jōsuiki*, *Shibukassenjo-bon*); (2) texts that claim a replica was forged, but that the real sword was lost (the Kakuichi variant quoted above); and (3) texts that mention no replica, but that depict the real sword being lost in the sea (*Yashiro-bon* [main text], *Hyakunijjuku-bon*). Takagi Makoto has explained the proliferation of these texts, observing that "each variant text refracts the other variants and denies a movement towards the creation of a single 'meaning.'" He sees "the totality of the relations [between the texts] as a corpus" (Takagi, 2001, pp. 227–228).

Within that corpus, little attention is paid to which text is historically accurate. Rather, an array of perspectives corresponding to varied positions exist side-by-side, containing mutual contradictions within their narratives. Additional new texts were produced by overlapping those multiple narratives. This is true not only of the *Heike monogatari* but also of the medieval Japanese chronicles as a whole. During this period, debates over whether or not texts were authentic rarely arose with any degree of seriousness.

The medieval period saw the warriors (*bushi*) assume real political power, while the court lost political influence. Paralleling that development, the *Nihonshoki*, compiled in order to legitimate the court's authority, could no longer maintain its position as a fixed referent. As a result, the various texts once subordinated to the *Nihonshoki*, such as the familial documents submitted to the court (*kachō*) and *uji* records (*ujibumi*), were replaced by genres with freer narrative content, such as Shintō texts (*shintōsho*), temple and shrine origins (*engi*), and military tales (*gunki*). As already noted, the familial documents and *uji* records were premised upon the political power of the court. They were political texts designed to be submitted to the court. At that time, the national histories, notably the *Nihonshoki*, functioned as the standard against which the content of the records and transmissions were judged. With the weakening of the court during the medieval period, however, the national histories lost this political function, and the ancient dual structure of "fixed authority/fluid familial records" crumbled.

At the center of the corpus referred to as the medieval Japanese chronicles lay the commentaries on the *Nihonshoki*. These were produced by priests of the Yoshida house and esoteric Buddhist monks in environs of the court. Commentarial activity on the *Nihonshoki* took place periodically from at least the Heian period in the form of the ritual "reading of the Japanese chronicles" (*Nihongi kōsho*). Private records of the official lectures have survived. These lectures, however, were conducted under the jurisdiction of the court. Most took the form of phonetic instruction (*kunchū*) with additional etymological discussion.

In the medieval period, the text was no longer literally interpreted as a record of actual events, as had been the case in the ancient court. Rather, focusing on the *Shindai no maki* (Scroll of the divine age), allegorical interpretations based on Buddhist metaphysics were used to reread the texts. The locus of commentary moved from the singular control of the court and spread throughout various aristocratic houses and schools. The difference between the ancient and medieval commentaries can be seen by comparing the following two passages:

> Kuni no Tokotachi no Mikoto. Query: Who first called this deity by this name? The teacher answers: the *Kana Nihongi*, *Kamimiyagi*, and the various ancient texts all contain this name. However, I have never seen the first instance of its use. There is no way to determine its origins in early antiquity (*jōko*). (*Nihonshoki shiki* [*teihon*; a private record of the official commentary])

> Kuni no Tokotachi no Mikoto—this deity is the one spirit of all the peoples' hearts. The heart of this deity is very clear, like a polished mirror reflecting light on its base. Because it contains no artifice and shines upon all things, it begat Amanokagami no Mikoto. To contain no artifice in the heart and to remain in nothingness [*kyomu*] is the essence of Shintō. (*Kanetomo Nihonshoki shindaikanmyō* [a Yoshida Shintō commentary])

The first commentary on the *Nihonshoki* entertains the question of who first named the deity Kuni no Tokotachi no Mikoto. Because the matter is not recorded in the sources, however, the question is abandoned. In contrast to this, Yoshida Kanetomo begins his commentary with the deity's name, but then develops a metaphysical argument regarding the essence of the human heart.

Shintō texts (*shintōsho*) were written as a result of this new form of commentary. In them, Buddhist metaphysics provided a means to construct a discourse that combined an interior "Way" with the historical ontology of Japan. At this time, the *Nihonshoki*—in some cases even the *Kojiki* and the *Sendai kujihongi*—was no longer treated as a "national history," but rather as scripture, a "divine text" that "tells the tales of the *kami*" (Yoshida Kanetomo). In Ryōbu Shintō's *Reikiki*, for example, Amaterasu Ōmikami's grandson Ho no Ninigi states his name as "imperial descendant Kotokukimi" and claims to have descended from heaven, not as the manifestation of the spirit of rice as depicted in the *Kiki*, but as the manifestation of the (Buddhist) diamond sword (*Kongōshō*) in order to spread throughout the land the true word (*shingon*) of Amaterasu Ōmikami's prime noumenon, Bontennō (Brahmā). The *Shindai no maki* was thus read as a text declaring the salvation of all people (*shujō*) by the Buddha. Its narrative form no longer strictly follows a historical chronology, but instead takes the form of topical sequences, such as a discussion of the three sacred treasures, or the imperial regalia. With commentary layered upon commentary, and, one provenance placed atop another, the discourse surrounding the Japanese chronicles swelled, all the while building centrifugal force.

These divine texts and commentaries on the *Nihonshoki* were transmitted and controlled as esoteric traditions by the houses and schools surrounding the surviving court, but no longer by the court itself. At the same time the military tales (*gunki*) and temple and shrine histories (*jisha engi*) that subsumed the medieval Japanese chronicles appear to have spread through society via regional lords and prominent temples and shrines. Both channels of textual transmission were located within the sphere of influence of political authority based in western Japan, with the surviving court at its apex. In eastern Japan, in contrast, the discourse of medieval Japanese chronicles was known to some extent, but it was either rejected or fundamentally reread. For example, one work describes Amaterasu-Ōmikami as "a deity who tells lies" (Nitta, 1989).

Moreover, while the divine texts and commentaries gained intellectual authority by virtue of being esoterically controlled, the origin tales and military chronicles circulated widely. For this reason, the reception of the *Kiki* during the medieval period appears to have followed two different trajectories. In one trajectory, the *Kiki* texts were hidden esoterically within the weakened court circles, with an ever-shrinking audience. In the other trajectory, the texts were pulled centrifugally beyond that boundary into broader segments of society.

In summary, in the course of the medieval period, the Six National Histories, especially the *Nihonshoki*, lost their centripetal force as classical sources (*koten*); Shintō texts, military chronicles, and temple and shrine histories emerged in place of the familial documents and *uji* records that had once been subordinated to the national histories. Among these, a distinct corpus called the "medieval Japanese chronicles" (*chūsei Nihongi*) took shape. These borrowed the title of the *Nihonshoki* but sought to present a reading beyond the meaning written into the text. In a sense, they sought to deconstruct the ancient worldview. The *honji suijaku* doctrine functioned within this corpus to ground the universal thought of Buddhism in the particular locus called Japan (Kuroda, 1975; Imahori, 1990).

At the same time, however, to the extent that these texts continued to claim some formal connection to the divine age of the *Kiki*, groups represented by the medieval texts still sought to ground their legitimacy in the historical tradition embodied in the emperor. In this, we can see the nature of the medieval state in western Japan mirrored in the corpus itself. The ranking aristocratic families and powerful Buddhist temples (*kenmon*), along with regional lords, increased their level of autonomy, while at the same time they sought the possibility of uniting all political forces beneath the emperor. While still lacking a true center, the discursive space of Buddhist metaphysics emerged wherein various texts took shape under the umbrella label of "Japanese chronicles."

With the demise of the Ritsuryō state, the divine rituals (*jingi saishi*), which possessed a different function from the national histories and familial records in antiquity, ceased to be performed. With the exception of private versions of these rituals, such as the Nakatomi purification ritual (*harai*), most court rituals were discontinued in the late medieval period. Under these circumstances, the difference between the concept of *kami* in the *Kiki* and that in the rituals and ritual texts grew ambiguous. The inconsistencies between the two were eventually unified, with the *Kiki* providing the basis for doing so. By this time, though, the *Kiki* texts had been fundamentally reread in relation to the discourses of Buddhist metaphysics and the medieval social structure, both very different from that of antiquity.

THE *KIKI* AS NATIONAL MEMORY. With the work of Yoshimi Yoshikazu in the late early modern period, texts with uncertain dates of composition were declared to be inauthentic, unlike such ancient texts as the national histories and official records. Furthermore, Motoori Norinaga's Native Learning (*kokugaku*) for the first time identified the *Kiki* as texts containing the memory of the ethnic-nation (*minzoku*) as a whole. Texts depicting the emperor existed in the early modern period, including Chikamatsu Monzaemon's Kabuki play, *Yōmei tennō shokunin kagami.* Yet such works dealt with the emperor strictly in terms of fiction and must be distinguished from any treatment of the *Kiki* as historical accounts. In the hands of scholars such as Yoshimi and Motoori, the status of the *Kiki*, which had become ambiguous during the medieval period, regained clarity. In the modern period, the *Kojiki* and *Nihonshoki* achieved canonical status as the repository of national memory. At the same time, the texts referred to as the medieval Japanese chronicles (*chūsei Nihongi*), such as the Shintō texts and temple/shrine origins, which had once subsumed the *Kiki*, were rejected as fabulous.

During the ancient period, the *Kiki* played a central role in explaining the origins of the social positions occupied by various *uji*. The status of the *Kiki* grew ambiguous during the medieval period, while the freedom enjoyed by Shintō texts and temple/shrine origins vis-à-vis the *Kiki* dramatically expanded. Still, for those represented by these new texts, the *Kiki* provided the basis for claims of historical origin, however perfunctory those claims may have been. The discursive space within which the *Kiki* possessed meaning from the ancient through the medieval period, however, did not comprehensively include all of the inhabitants of the Japanese islands, in terms of class and region. From the late early modern period onwards, however, this began to change. No longer tied to specific groups, the *Kiki* texts came to be held as the repositories of a shared, communal memory in correspondence with the emerging nation-state (Isomae, 2000). Needless to say, the homogeneity implied in such a discursive space functioned to elide social differences that nevertheless continued to exist.

Ancient *uji* records that survived into the early modern period ceased to connect the *Kiki* to specific groups. Instead, they came to be treated as mere variants capable of supplementing lacunae in the communal memory that the *Kiki* came to represent. By the early modern period, *shintōsho* could no longer exist independently, encompassing and altering the *Kiki.* They instead were relegated to the status of secondary texts that interpreted the canonical statements of the *Kiki.* The term *Shintō* itself came to be shunned in Native Learning. Although Shintō is once again placed at the center of the *kokutai* (national body) ideology in the modern period, new texts bearing the title *shintōsho* were never again produced.

During the modern period, the Ministry of Education's history curriculum and the Shintō shrines that, under the directives of State Shintō, came to enshrine deities from the *Kiki* served as the two primary conduits through which the *Kiki* texts were propagated to the nation (Kaigo, 1969; Murakami, 1970). Thus, public schools and shrines formed part of the foundation of the modern state's newly created administration. Both were expected to play a critical role in national indoctrination. History education was designed to "shape national thought," while "the rites of the state" were to be handled by the shrines. The identification and preservation of imperial tombs and palace sites mentioned in the *Kiki* expanded during this period as well.

In addition to such government vehicles, other books dealing with the *Kiki* sought to reread the state's official history in terms of liberalism or national essentialism (*kokusuishugi*). Such works spread through the nation via print media and the intellectual class. As early as the Edo period, however, woodblock print versions of the *Kiki* and other classics saw wide circulation. Many shrines also altered the names of their enshrined deities during this period in response to the growing influence of Yoshida Shintō.

Relatively large shrines possessed their own histories or oral traditions dating back to the medieval period. Confronted first with the Yoshida house's governmental mandate to license priests and with the modern state's shrine policies, however, such histories and traditions were too weak to resist alteration or outright erasure. In the case of small shrines lacking clear histories or defined deities, they were completely subsumed by the doctrinal system of Yoshida Shintō or the modern emperor system. The histories of newly formed branch families rarely reach farther back than a couple of generations. The state's history, with the *Kiki* at its core, supplemented this lacuna.

At the same time that the *Kiki* texts were fixed in their modern position, a liberal reading emerged, one premised on the *Kiki* texts but also subsuming them. The "academic essay" came to replace the "commentary." In the commentaries of the early modern period, the *Kiki* texts were treated as fact by the authors who strove to understand this content. Against this, the academic essay strives, not to enter into the *Kiki* themselves, but rather to grasp the "history" that came to exist separate from, yet surrounding, the texts. While commentaries were written under the restrictions of the text itself, the scholarly essay incorporates the *Kiki* texts into its own narrative, where the author employs it to develop his or her own thought.

Although a few commentaries were written in the modern era, they merely provided etymological interpretations and were no longer related to the understanding of history itself. Kazamaki Keijirō locates the supplanting of commentaries by academic essays in the Taisho era (1912–1926). He notes this shift in reference to studies of the *Kojiki*: "Looking at commentaries alone, there were twenty-six during the Meiji period. . .[but only] four commentaries on the *Kojiki* during the Taisho era. By contrast, there were twenty titles in the category of [scholarly] research. Just as the backgrounds of the scholars changed between the Meiji and Taisho periods, the nature of their research also changed" (Kazamaki, 1956, pp. 177–181).

Eventually, the commentaries themselves were incorporated into the essay form. The main body of the essay is treated as a text in its own right, while earlier commentaries are turned into authoritative works that support the author's own thought. This is clearly different from the fundamental distinction that had existed between the medieval commentaries and the metaphysical narrative of the Shintō texts.

At the same time, the *Kiki* texts continue to occupy a canonical position (even though the familial records and *uji* transmissions are absent in the modern period). The ancient and modern periods are fundamentally different, however, when it comes to the question of whether the *Kiki* are to be understood as history or as material for historical understanding. For example, in the ancient readings of the Japanese chronicles (*Nihongi kōsho*), when an undecipherable section of the text was reached, all attempts at judgment were suspended: "The way of the deities is unfathomable; the truth of this remains unknown. What is heard differs and explanations disagree." Because the text was held to be history itself, without a hint of modern rationality, commentators could not exceed the narrative of the text. If the *Kiki* maintained a sacred character before the modern era, it was the result of its identification with history itself. Even Norinaga understood the *Kiki* as the direct record of chronological events: "The ancient records merely recorded what has been transmitted from the age of the deities."

In contrast, because modern scholars separated history from the text of the *Kiki*, they could freely cut and weave texts. In some cases, they integrated *uji* transmissions and ancient texts in order to reach beyond the texts into the dimension of history.

The term *Kiki* first saw broad use in the Meiji period, but the term did not reflect simply combining the *Nihonshoki* and *Kojiki*. Rather, the term referred to the discursive space of history that appears in the background when the two texts are brought together. Naka Michiyo's argument concerning dating within the *Nihonshoki*, put forward in the 1880s, provides a clear example of this separation of the concept of history from the *Kiki*. By taking the Christian era into consideration, the measurement of time within the *Nihonshoki* and the *Kojiki*, the imperial reigns and the sexagenary cycle (*eto*), was rendered relative, and a different temporal axis was constructed outside of the *Kiki* texts (Tanaka, 1998). Dealing with the age of the deities, which lacked a calendar, created a problem though.

Motoori Norinaga's interpretation of the divine age during the transitional period to modernity was based on his declaration that all the content concerning the divine age was historical. Like Christian fundamentalists in the West, Norinaga forbade all allegorical interpretation of the ancient text. By the 1890s, however, Takagi Toshio and Anesaki Masaharu had absorbed the Western concept of "mythology." As a result, the descriptions of the divine age came to be understood in terms of psychological reality (Ōbayashi, 1973). The term *Kiki myths* broadly employed today originated at this time. In this manner, the sections of the *Kiki* concerning the divine age *(kamitsuyo no maki)* achieved a stable position as a form of "national history," although related in terms of the worldview of the past.

This perspective of treating such texts as historical products was applied not only to the divine age but also to the human age within the *Kiki* texts by the Taisho period, especially in the work of Tsuda Sōkichi. Consequently, the *Kiki* texts in their entirety came to be understood as reflecting the historical perspective of a specific class of people belonging to a specific time period (Ienaga, 1972). Not only was the concept of "hard history" detached from the *Kiki*, but simultaneously Japanese literary studies sought to reposition the *Kiki* within the axis of historical time.

Within the discursive space called "history," various debates regarding the *Kiki* intersect. These debates include competition between diverse approaches to the *Kiki*, such as: (1) treating the words as independent texts with distinct logical structures (*sakuhinron*); (2) searching for original texts that served as sources for the derivative *Kiki* (*seiritsuron*); (3) conflicts over the Western and imperial calendars in determining dates (*kinenron*); and (4) whether one should accept the depiction of the divine age as historical fact or as a product of psychological reality. The expansive discursive space today called "history" allows the discussant to read into history a variety of positions and perspectives.

By emphasizing the unique canonical status of the *Kiki* texts, the modern approach has treated them as the shared memory of the nation. The understanding of "Japanese mythology" is a discourse produced within these developments.

This discussion has traced the transformations that the discursive space surrounding the *Kiki* underwent through the ancient, medieval, and modern period. The ancient period, in the sense employed here, begins with the reign of Tenmu (673–686 CE) and ends in the early Heian period (tenth century CE). The medieval period stretches from the Kamakura period (1180–1333 CE) through the Muromachi period (1336–1573 CE). The modern period begins in the late Edo period (late eighteenth century onwards). The late Heian period, which produced the Japanese chronicle texts during the cloister governments of retired emperors (*inseiki*), corresponds to the transition from the ancient to the medieval period. Likewise, the early Edo period, with the strong influence of Confucian Shintō, corresponds to the transitional phase from the medieval to the modern period. Of course, this periodization is based on the types of textual analysis of the *Kiki* that were practiced. This chronology does not strictly correspond to the periodization employed by historians in general.

Whether or not current historical research can maintain its critical power depends upon whether we can move beyond acknowledging various historical products outside ourselves, and instead render our own horizon of understanding an object of analysis. To do so does not mean, as in the past, constructing another representation called the "true myths of the Japanese ethnic nation" in order to resist the authority of the emperor system and the *Kiki.* We can no longer immerse ourselves into the interior of existing texts. Nor does it mean, as in some scholarship on the medieval Japanese chronicles and ancient kingship, projecting modern and Western religious concepts, such as the sacred and profane developed by Euro-American religious studies, directly onto the past. The past must be faced in order to clarify how the structure of discursive space organizes subjectivity, and to understand what forces of integration and opposition are at work within that space. As part of that process, the significations contained within the concept of Japanese mythology must be historically examined in terms of their emergence as a discourse produced by native elites buffeted by waves of modern Westernization.

The discursive space that can be made an object of historical research, though, is only a small part of the memory that once existed within society as a whole, and a privileged part at that. At the same time, one must ask why the specific limited memory of the *Kiki* became the fountainhead of history, all the while altering the structure of the surrounding discursive space, and why it entranced those enmeshed in that space for so long. The field of research identified with Japanese mythology must now take up the task of confronting the historical inclinations that have been internalized.

SEE ALSO Amaterasu Ōmikami; Ame no Koyane; Izanagi and Izanami; Jimmu; Jingo; Ōkuninushi no Mikoto; Shintō; Susano-o no Mikoto; Yamato Takeru.

BIBLIOGRAPHY

Primary Sources

Motoori Norinaga. *Naobi no mitama. Motoori Norinaga zenshu,* vol. 9. Tokyo, 1968.

Motoori Norinaga. *Kojiki-Den: Book 1.* Translated by Ann Wehmeyer. Ithaca, N.Y., 1997.

Nishinomiya Kazutami, ed. *Kogoshūi.* Tokyo, 1985.

Nihon shoki shiki. Shintei zōho, Kokushi taikei. Tokyo, 1932.

Sakamoto Tarō, ed. *Nihon shoki. Nihon koten bungaku taikei,* vols. 67 and 68. Tokyo, 1965.

Yamatohime no Mikoto seiki. In *Shintei zōho, Kokushi taikei,* pp. 53–54. Tokyo, 1966.

Yoshida Kanetomo and Kiyohara Nobukata. *Kanetomo Nobutaka senken-bon nihon shoki kamiyo no maki myo.* Tokyo, 1984.

Yoshimi Yoshikazu. *Shobjo shashoku tomon.* In *Daijingū soshō: Watarai Shintō taisei; Kōhen.* Tokyo, 1955.

Secondary Sources

Abe Akio. *Yoshimi Yoshikazu.* Tokyo, 1944.

Abe Yasurō. *Nihongi to setsuwa. Setsuwa no Kōza,* vol. 3. Tokyo, 1993.

Folkert, Kendall W. "The 'Canons' of 'Scripture.'" In *Rethinking Scripture: Essays from a Comparative Perspective,* edited by Miriam Levering, pp. 170–179. Albany, N.Y., 1989.

Henderson, John B. *Scripture, Canon, and Commentary: A Comparison and Western Exegesis.* Princeton, 1991.

Ienaga Saburō. *Tsuda Sōkichi no shisōshiteki kenkyū.* Tokyo, 1972.

Imahori Taitsu. *Jingi shinkō no tenkai to bukkyō.* Tokyo, 1990.

Isomae Jun'ichi. "'Kokushi' to iu gensetsu kukan." In *Gendai Shisō* 27, no. 12 (1999a): 24–40.

Isomae Jun'ichi. "Myth in Metamorphosis: Ancient and Medieval Versions of the Yamatotakeru Legend." *Monumenta Nipponica* 54, no. 3 (1999b): 361–385.

Isomae Jun'ichi. "Reappropriating the Japanese Myths: Motoori Norinaga and the Creation Myths of the *Kojiki* and *Nihon shoki.*" *Japanese Journal of Religious Studies* 27, nos. 1–2 (2000): 15–39.

Isomae Jun'ichi and Fukazawa Hidetaka, eds. *Kindai nihon ni okeru chishikijin to shukyo: Anesaki Masaharu no kiseki.* Tokyo, 2002.

Ishimoda Tadashi. *Kodai kizoku no eiyu jidai: 'Kojiki' no ichi kosatsu* (1948). *Ishimoda chosakushū,* vol. 10. Tokyo, 1989.

Itō Masayoshi. "Chusei Nihongi no rinkaku: Taiheiki ni okeru Urabe Kanekazu-setsu wo megutte." *Bungaku* 40, no. 10 (1972): 28–48.

Kaigo Muneomi. *Rekishi kyōiku no rekishi.* Tokyo, 1969.

Kazamaki Keijiro. "Kojiki kenkyu no saishuppatsu." In *Kojiki taisei: Kenkyushi hen,* pp. 177–181. Tokyo, 1956.

Kōnoshi Takamitsu. *Kojiki no seikaikan.* Tokyo, 1987.

Kōnoshi Takamitsu, ed. "Kojiki Nihon shoki hikkei." *Besatsu Kokubungaku* 49 (1995): 6–10.

Kōnoshi Takamitsu. *Kojiki to "Nihon shoki": "Tenno shinwa" no rekishi.* Tokyo, 1999.

Kuroda Toshio. *Nihon chūsei no kokka to shūkyō.* Tokyo, 1975.

Levering, Miriam, ed. *Rethinking Scripture: Essays from a Comparative Perspective.* Albany, N.Y., 1989.

Levinson, Bernard M. "The Human Voice in Divine Revelation: The Problem in Religious Tradition in Biblical Law" In *Innovation in Religious Traditions: Essays in the Interpretation of Religious Change,* edited by Michael A Williams, Collette Cox, and Martin S. Jaffee, pp. 35–71. Berlin and New York, 1992.

Mizubayashi Takeshi. *Kiki shinwa to ōken no matsuri.* Tokyo, 1991.

Murakami Shigeyoshi. *Kokka shintō.* Tokyo, 1970.

Nakamura Hideo. *Kodai saishiroon.* Tokyo, 1999.

Nitta Ichirō. "Kyogen wo ōseraruru kami." *Rettō no Bunkashi* 6 (1989): 211–229.

Ōbayashi Taryō. *Nihon shinwa no kigen.* Tokyo, 1973.

Ogawa Toyoo. "Chusei no mechie: hensei suru Nihongi to 'Reikiki' Tensatsu no maki." In *Chūsei no chi to gaku: "chūshaku" wo yomu.* Tokyo, 1997.

Ōta Shōjirō. *Jodai ni okeru 'Nihon shoki' kōkyū* (1939). *Ōta Shōjirō Chosakushū,* vol. 3. Tokyo, 1992.

Saitō Hideki. *Amaterasu no Fukami e.* Tokyo, 1996.

Seki Akira. *Jodai ni okeru 'Nihon shoki' kodoku no kenkyu* (1942). *Seki Akira Chosakushū,* vol. 5. Tokyo, 1997.

Takagi Makoto. "Seitosei no shinwa ga hokai suru shunkan: Heike monogatari 'tsurugi no maki' no 'katari.'" In *Heike monogatari: sōzōsuru katari,* pp. 227–228. Tokyo, 2001.

Tanaka Satoshi. *'Joko' no kakutei: kinen ronso wo megutte. Edo no shisō* 8. Tokyo, 1998.

Tsuda Sōkichi. *Nihon koten no kenkyū: jo* (1948). *Tsuda Sōkichi zenshū,* vol. 1. Tokyo, 1963.

ISOMAE JUN'ICHI (2005)

JAPANESE RELIGIONS: RELIGIOUS DOCUMENTS

A vast number of religious documents were written, transmitted, and circulated in Japan in the course of history. Special note must be made at the outset of the particular importance in Japan of Buddhist texts, commentaries, and related works, including those imported from China or Korea, as well as original works by Japanese authors. Since this voluminous category of writings is covered elsewhere, however, it is only treated in outline in this entry.

Instead, this entry concentrates on certain literary, religious, and historical texts that were used in Japan to establish the legitimacy of the state, not only in the eighth century, when the texts were originally compiled for that purpose, but also in the medieval period and again in modern times. Politicians establishing the modern Japanese nation-state buttressed their ideology by drawing on eighteenth-century nativist philological writings about the early texts, thereby legitimizing the imperial system (*tennōsei*) and creating a cultural unity of the Japanese people (*kokuminsei*).These texts are treated in chronological sections: (1) the ancient period when the documents were first compiled; (2) the medieval period when they became part of syncretic discourse embracing teachings of Shintō, Buddhism, and Confucianism; (3) the early modern period when nativist scholars found in them a basis for a new mythology focusing on the common language and ethnic identity of the Japanese people; and (4) the modern period when, until the end of World War II, state mythology affirmed Japan as a nation-state under an emperor who had been authenticated by divine decree.

ANCIENT PERIOD. Important sources of written knowledge about Japan that predate the eighth century are passages treating "barbarians" in Chinese dynastic histories. The fullest account of Japan—known as the Land of Wa—is in *Wei zhi* (History of the Wei Kingdom, 220–264, of North China), which describes a territory of Wa called Yamatai that was ruled by a queen named Himiko, who was a shaman. Rulers of Wa maintained tributary relationships to China and were thus incorporated into the Chinese worldview. *Wei zhi* provides details about the customs of Yamatai. For example, people clapped their hands in worship, showed respect toward others by squatting or kneeling with both hands on the ground, and purified themselves in water after a funeral.

Between the third and the sixth centuries a state gradually evolved that came to be known first as Yamato and later as Nihon (land of the "sun's source"). Written sources all date from later, but archaeological evidence of this period indicates a variety of rituals and beliefs.

THE RITSURYŌ STATE. By the seventh century, rulers of Yamato or Nihon (Japan) declined to maintain the tributary relationship with China and set about establishing their own version of the Chinese imperial system and constructing the capital city of Nara in 710. Two texts in particular, *Kojiki* (Record of ancient matters; 712) and *Nihonshoki* (or *Nihongi*; Chronicle of Japan; 720), were compiled to legitimize the state, authenticate the political hegemony of the imperial Yamato clan, and establish comprehensive legal codes *(ritsuryō)* according to which political power emanated from an emperor or empress *(tennō)* who was above the law. Other key texts from this period include *Izumo fūdoki* (completed 733), a gazetteer of Izumo province in western Honshū; *Kogoshūi* (Gleanings of old narratives, 807); and *Man'yōshū* (Collection of a thousand leaves, late eight century), a collection of more than 4,500 poems.

Texts of the ancient period circulated in manuscript form. The oldest surviving manuscript by a Japanese author is a commentary on the *Lotus Sūtra* in the collections of the Japanese Imperial Household Ministry. The commentary was written by Shōtoku Taishi (574?–622?), regent to Empress Suiko and the leading cultural figure of his day. It is said to be in his own calligraphy.

Japanese monks traveled to China on missions to collect Buddhist texts several times in this early period. Of special note are collections of texts brought back by Saichō (767–822) and Kūkai (774–835) for which catalogs were made in the early ninth century. These catalogues are important milestones in the development of textual canons for Tendai and Shingon Buddhism in Japan. Imported Buddhist sūtras were copied in manuscript form to supply the many temples that proliferated in this period. Villages specializing in producing paper grew up in proximity to monasteries in order to meet the demand.

The earliest known printed documents in Japan also come from this period. They are ritual texts that were reproduced in a million copies, placed in small pagodas, and distributed to temples throughout the country in 764 on an order from Empress Shōtoku, following a protracted civil war. Known as the *Hyakumantō darani* (Dhāraṇī of one million pagodas), those texts were not in Japanese, but consisted of Sanskrit words (from a sūtra known in Japanese as *Muku jōkō dai daranikyō)* phonetically transcribed into Chinese characters. While the immediate motivation for printing them was evidently atonement for loss of life in the war, it has been suggested that the project also reflects Shōtoku's political sympathies for the Buddhist establishment rather than the court bureaucracy. Clearly not meant for reading, these ritual texts had both religious and political significance.

***KOJIKI* AND *NIHONSHOKI*.** Under Chinese influence, the Japanese began writing histories by at least the seventh century, but none have been preserved from that time. The project of historical compilation that resulted in the issuance of *Kojiki* in 712 and *Nihonshoki* in 720 was begun by Emperor Tenmu (r. 673–686), who had usurped the throne and wanted to legitimize his rule. According to the preface of *Kojiki*, Tenmu lamented that the records of the "various houses" (presumably the imperial and courtier houses) had been altered and falsified, and ordered a ritual reciter named Hieda no Are to memorize an imperial genealogy (*Teiki*) and a collection of narratives (*Kyūji*). These seem to have served as the basis for *Kojiki* and *Nihonshoki* in the next century.

Despite being based on the same sources and compiled for similar purposes, *Kojiki* and the *Nihonshoki* differ fundamentally, especially in the story of the origin of the imperial rule. *Kojiki* gives Amaterasu, the sun goddess, the key role as ancestress of the imperial house, while in *Nihonshoki* Amaterasu is a subordinate deity and plays no such role. It is likely that these two texts represent surviving exemplars of heterogeneous mythologies that eventually merged to form a single mythology of the origin of imperial rule. Furthermore, the text of *Kojiki* is in Japanese transcribed into Chinese characters, a cumbersome writing method that was later abandoned. So difficult is *Kojiki* to read that little attention was paid to it for more than a thousand years, until the scholar Motoori Norinaga (1730–1801) spent some thirty-five years translating it into vernacular Japanese. In contrast, *Nihonshoki* is in the Chinese language that was used at court, and it has always been relatively easy for educated Japanese to read.

According to both *Kojiki* and *Nihonshoki*, Ninigi, grandson of Amaterasu, descends to earth (Japan). In the *Kojiki* version Amaterasu gives Ninigi the Yasaka curved beads, mirror, and Kusanagi sword that became the regalia of emperorship, and decrees that Ninigi's family should rule Japan eternally. In the *Nihonshoki* there is no such role for Amaterasu and it is only after Ninigi's descendent, Emperor Jinmu, gains control over earth in 660 BCE that the legitimacy of imperial rule is established.

Kojiki is a book in three parts. Part one deals with the age of the gods from the time when the first deities appeared, as heaven and earth took shape, up to the birth of the emperor Jinmu. Part two covers the period from Jinmu through Ōjin, the fifteenth sovereign in the traditional chronology. Part three traces the imperial succession from Nintoku, Ōjin's son, through Empress Suiko (554–628), a historical figure who reigned from 592 to 628. The narrative comes to an end about a century before Suiko, and the last century of its coverage gives only a listing of sovereigns with genealogical data. Although the final part of *Kojiki* may be regarded as protohistory, the work as a whole is mythology.

In *Kojiki*, Amaterasu's role as the most important deity is evident in the story of the Heavenly Rock Cave. When Amaterasu hides in the cave, heaven and earth are plunged into darkness; only on her reemergence is order restored. Further, she bestows the rule of the land to the progeny of Ninigi, confirming that arrangement through ceremonial worship of the mirror, which represents her continuing support of the imperial line.

Nihonshoki is more than twice as long as the *Kojiki*, the later portions of its thirty chapters dealing in considerable detail with the events of the sixth and seventh centuries and ending with the abdication of Empress Jitō (645–720) in 697. While *Kojiki* gives only one version of each mythological story, the first two volumes of *Nihonshoki*, known as *The Age of the Gods*, often provide three or more. *Nihonshoki* begins with the story of the emergence of heaven and earth from a primal chaos, presenting a world view influenced by yin-yang philosophy. The intercourse of the deities Izanaki and Izanami gives birth to the world and all its deities (*kami*), with Amaterasu being a subordinate deity in this world order.

Although archaeological and other evidence indicates that, in fact, the historical ruling dynasty of Japan probably dates from only the early sixth century CE, the record of an unbroken imperial line beginning with Jinmu as found in *Kojiki* and *Nihonshoki* became the basis for the great myth of *bansei ikkei*, or "one dynasty to rule for a myriad generations"—that is, forever. Whereas in China there were frequent dynastic changes, justified by the mandate of heaven, in Japan it was established from early times that rulership had been given unequivocally and forever by Amaterasu to a single line of her descendants. According to *bansei ikkei*, Emperor Akihito, who was invested in 1989, is the 125th sovereign in direct descent from Jinmu.

While the genealogy of the imperial family is central to the mythology as presented in *Kojiki* and *Nihonshoki*, the pasts of leading courtier families are also woven conspicuously into it. A good example is the Nakatomi (later, Fujiwara) family, whose founder, according to the mythology, was Ame no Koyane, one of five deities (*kami*) who accompanied Ninigi on his descent from heaven. During the Heian period (794–1185), when the Fujiwara rose to dominance at court as imperial regents, they cited *Kojiki* and *Nihonshoki* in claiming that their right to "accompany" and "assist" in rule was as ancient and unassailable as the imperial family's right to rule.

IZUMO FUDŌKI. In 713 the newly established Nara court issued a decree to the provinces, calling upon each to report on its geography, natural resources, local traditions, and the like. The idea of requesting such reports was based on Chinese gazetteers and was intended as a means for the Nara government to extend its control more fully. Although bureaucratic in origin, these documents include details of local names, products, and legends, providing early (albeit limited) documentation of local religious practices. Of these reports, called *fudōki* (records of wind and earth), only one has survived intact: *Izumo fudōki.* Four others are preserved in fragments. Submitted to the Nara court in 733, *Izumo fudōki* comprises nine sections, each treating a district. Interspersed throughout are tales and legends that collectively constitute the mythology of Izumo.

Situated on the Japan Sea and relatively isolated by mountains, Izumo maintained its independence for a considerable period. The final conquest of Izumo was apparently an important step taken by the Yamato state in its march to hegemony, so the story was written prominently into the *Kojiki* and *Nihonshoki.* According to the mythology, Izumo, governed by the earthly deity Ōkuninushi (or Ōnamuchi), opposed repeated attempts by heaven to force it to submit to heavenly rule. Finally, however, Ōkuninushi and Izumo were persuaded to give in, thereby setting the stage for the dispatch of Ninigi to earth to found a ruling dynasty according to the mythology.

KOGOSHŪI. During the formative period of the Ritsuryō state, various strands of mythological systems were put forward that could not be completely reconciled with one another. New texts were then compiled that brought together ritual and mythology into a more coherent whole. The *Kogoshūi* (Gleanings from old narratives) is a prominent example.

In 807 the Inbe family of court ritualists compiled *Kogoshūi,* which includes stories not found in *Kojiki* and *Nihonshoki.* Many of these stories deal with the history of the Inbe clan itself. Their main purpose in compiling the text was to combat the ascendancy of the rival Nakatomi family at court. In *Kogoshūi* the family's role as key figures in imperial enthronement ceremonies and other court rituals was legitimized by a retelling of the story of Ninigi's descent that gave Futodama, an ancestral deity of the Inbe clan, a crucial role. This retelling presents a new version of the heavenly descent that incorporates elements from both *Kojiki* and *Nihonshoki,* along with new information not in either text. Further, *Kogoshūi* includes stories about the mirror and sword of the imperial regalia, their enshrinement at Ise, and rituals related to them, thereby creating a new mythology of the regalia.

Official lectures on *Nihonshoki* were presented six times from 812 through the end of the tenth century. Mythologies from *Kojiki, Nihonshoki, Kogoshūi,* and other sources were gradually synthesized into a single mythology and system of ritual practices at court. It was during this period, too, that Shintō and Buddhism coalesced (*shinbutsu shūgō*) and veneration of deities (*kami*) became part of Buddhist ritual practice in Japan, something that continued until the modern period when the Meiji government attempted to separate them.

MAN'YŌSHŪ. *Kojiki* contains more than one hundred songs and is thus the oldest body of written poetry in Japan. But Japanese poetic tradition truly began with the compilation of the *Man'yōshū* in the late eighth century. This anthology of more than 4,500 poems includes a majority (4,200) in the *tanka* or *waka* (short poem) form. Though its earliest poems are attributed to an empress of the fourth century, most verse in this collection dates from the mid-seventh to the mid-eighth centuries.

Like *Kojiki, Man'yōshū* is written in Japanese transcribed into Chinese characters. In the case of *Man'yōshū,* the writing system is called *man'yōgana,* or *Man'yō* syllabary, which became a forerunner of katakana and hiragana, the two syllabaries that were developed by the tenth century and that enabled the Japanese for the first time to write their own language with some ease. Since the creation of katakana and hiragana, Japanese has been written in a mixture of Chinese characters (for their meanings) and these two syllabaries (for their sounds).

The greatest poet of *Man'yōshū* was Kakinomoto no Hitomaro, who flourished in the late seventh century. A low-ranking courtier, Hitomaro served as a "court poet," engaged to compose poems on important public occasions, such as imperial hunts and other excursions, and the deaths of sovereigns.

Part of the fundamental "spirit" of the ancient Japanese that later scholars found in the poetry of *Man'yōshū* is the *kotodama* (spirit of words), manifested in *makura-kotoba* (pillow words), epithets that were evidently first employed for liturgical purposes. An example of a pillow word is *hisakata no* (far-reaching), as used in such phrases as "far-reaching heaven," "the far-reaching clouds," or even "the far-reaching capital." Here we see the great importance attached by the early Japanese to the native (Yamato) language, whose cadences were thought to possess both religious and magical qualities. Sacred verse and prose pieces known as *norito,* some of which purportedly date from the seventh century, illustrate the use of *kotodama.* Most surviving *norito* are found in *Engishiki* (Supplementary regulations of the Engi era), compiled in 927. In any case, all *norito* are based on seventh-century diction, and thus were later thought to retain the primitive spirit of the Yamato language.

MEDIEVAL PERIOD. Buddhist documents and ideas dominated Japanese religious and intellectual life in the medieval period. From the eleventh until the sixteenth century, printing of books in Japan was carried out exclusively at Buddhist monasteries. Sūtras and other works written in Chinese by both Chinese and Japanese authors were printed with woodblocks at major temples in and around Nara prior to the end of the twelfth century and in Kyoto thereafter. Especially influential were editions issued by the great Zen monasteries in Kyoto, Kamakura, and elsewhere that are known as *gozan-ban.* The earliest extant printed works in the Japanese language date from the fourteenth century and are associated with the Pure Land sect of Buddhism, which made special efforts to reach audiences unable to read Chinese. During this period Buddhist monasteries were seats of political and economic power, as well as religious authority, and the printing of Chinese religious and philosophical texts at such institutions had relevance in those realms, as well as within a religious context.

Throughout this long period, despite the availability of printing technology, most religious and other works written in the Japanese language circulated only in manuscript form. Of special interest are elaborate manuscripts combining texts and illustrations, known as *emakimono,* which included legends of the origins of temples and shrines, lives of famous monks, descriptions of festivals and rituals, and popular tales. Colophons on some manuscripts indicate that these scrolls were used in conjunction with performances and sermons that were religious in nature.

Japanese medieval manuscripts have survived in significant numbers. Especially noteworthy are large collections at medieval imperial Buddhist convents (*monzeki*) that were opened for the first time in the 1990s. These rich archives include manuscripts, paintings, diaries and other previously unknown primary sources that are especially relevant to studies of the role of women in Buddhism in medieval Japan.

With the establishment of the Kamakura *bakufu* (shogunate) at the end of the twelfth century, the government moved away from the imperial court in Kyoto. Changes in the role of the imperial court inevitably called for revisions in the imperial mythology reflecting the new world order. Commentaries on *Nihonshoki* along with new collections of legends from this period, called the "medieval *Nihongi*," present a syncretic view of the universe, in which Buddhist, neo-Confucian, and Shintō ideas are interwoven. In contrast to earlier texts on *Nihonshoki* that focused on legitimizing the Ritsuryō state, medieval commentaries present a pan-Asiatic worldview reflecting the widespread proliferation of Buddhist ideas.

Medieval scholars were particularly interested in *Nihonshoki*'s first section, the *Age of the Gods.* For example, Kitabatake Chikafusa (1293–1354) in his *Jinnō shōtōki* (Chronicle of gods and sovereigns, 1339), begins with a famous opening line: "Great Japan is the land of the gods." Writing to legitimize the Southern over the Northern imperial line during the war between the courts (1336–1392), Chikafusa emphasized the purity of imperial lineage, symbolized by transmission of the imperial regalia, which set Japan apart from other countries, making it superior in his view. However, his call for the restoration of imperial rule was not successful, and his thinking had more significance later than in his own time.

EARLY MODERN PERIOD. At the end of the sixteenth century, movable-type printing was brought to Japan from Korea as loot taken during the invasion of Toyotomi Hideoyoshi. Thereafter, printing of Japanese texts, including religious works, began and quickly spread. Sections of *Nihonshoki* were printed for the first time in 1599. Movable-type printing flourished under imperial and shogunal patronage until the mid-seventeenth century. Additionally, for a brief period starting in 1590, Jesuit missionaries in Japan published as many as one hundred titles that are known as *Kirishitan-ban.* Fewer than forty of those works have survived, due to severe censorship in the seventeenth century.

As commercial publishing took over, woodblock printing, providing greater economies of scale, was used until the nineteenth century. Between the mid-seventeenth and the mid-nineteenth centuries many ancient texts were printed in this manner, stimulating a great deal of scholarship about them, which also circulated in printed form.

Especially relevant to the topic at hand are works of eighteenth-century scholars of so-called *kokugaku* (national learning), a movement that embraced philological, literary, and political, as well as religious, concerns and was essentially motivated by the desire to "return to the past." A leading *kokugaku* scholar, Kamo no Mabuchi (1697–1769) saw *Man'yōshū* as a repository of the "forthright emotions" (*naoki kokoro*) and "sincerity" (*makoto*) of the Japanese people when they were still relatively "unpolluted" by Chinese culture. In fact, many of the most prominent poets of the *Man'yōshū* were well steeped in the culture of China, including Confucianism, Daoism, and Buddhism. Nevertheless, compared to the overly refined court poetry from the ninth century on, *Man'yōshū* poems seemed to *kokugaku* scholars to have a more youthful vigor, spontaneity, and breadth of emotion.

Mabuchi's most famous student was Motoori Norinaga. *Kojiki,* as noted previously, was scarcely comprehensible until he translated it. His study, *Kojikiden,* on which he worked from 1764 until his death in 1801, established *Kojiki,* rather than *Nihonshoki,* as the foundation text of Japanese history and as the repository of ancient Japanese language. Norinaga considered it a source in which to find the "ancient words" (*furukoto*) spoken by Japanese people in ancient times and expressing *mono no aware* (pathos of things). Norinaga's reading of *Kojiki* produced a new mythology different from that of the ancient texts that he studied. In particular, he did not focus on the legitimacy of the imperial system, but rather on the common language and ancestry of the Japanese people as the basis for allegiance to the emperor and opposition to outside lands, especially China. In Norinaga's interpretation the ancient myths have relevance for all Japanese people, not just the imperial and aristocratic families.

It should not be forgotten that Buddhist works continued to circulate widely in this period as well, especially in the seventeenth century, when they dominated commercial publishing. Huge compilations, such as the first Japanese editions of the Buddhist canon that were issued at this time, were private ventures of temples rather than commercial publishers, since such works would not be viable in the marketplace.

Perhaps the most extensively reprinted text of this period was the Confucian *Classic of Filial Piety* (*Xiao jing*), known in Japan as *Kōkyō*, which was first printed in Japan in 1599. Copies were continuously available, with surviving dated editions extant from almost every year between the 1650s and the 1860s. The popularity of this and other Confucian texts reflects the widespread influence of neo-Confucianism beginning in the medieval period and accelerating in the early modern period

While most documents that have survived prior to the modern period obviously are limited to works produced by educated elites, there are some extant sources from this period that reflect religious practices and beliefs of ordinary people. For the most part, such documentation is in the form of manuscripts written in cursive style (*komonjo)* that are held by local archives in Japan.

MODERN PERIOD. In the nineteenth century, as the Japanese nation-state was being formed, statesmen who visited Europe became aware of national literatures and poetic traditions through which people of each nation expressed their identity. With the introduction of Western-style movable-type printing in the 1870s, works of ***kokugaku*** scholars, as well as the ancient texts that they discussed, became readily available. In 1879 the government began sponsoring a project, not completed until 1914, to collect and classify the entire canon of Japanese classics into encyclopedic categories in a work entitled, *Koji ruien* (Classified collection of old documents). At the root of the project was a desire to establish a scientific and historical approach to the national literary and cultural heritage. Other projects initiated at the time, such as *Dai Nihon shiryō* (Japanese documents, 1901–) and *Dai Nihon komonjo* (Japanese manuscripts, 1901–), focusing on both collecting and publishing authoritative versions of historical texts in annalistic compilations, have been underway for more than a century.

Beginning in the 1880s, *Man'yōshū* was rediscovered in the course of the search for a national poetry anthology. From the time of its compilation almost a thousand years earlier, with the exception of ***kokugaku*** and other scholars, Japanese people in general had largely been unfamiliar with this work.

Building on the work of the ***kokugaku*** scholars, late nineteenth-century Japanese intellectuals focused on the role of language as a defining feature of a nation-state. Within that context, establishing a national literature, and particularly a poetry, that expressed the spirit of the people was seen as a way to prove the existence of a people united through a common language. Some scholars searched for the origins of Japanese culture in ethnographic studies of folk myths and songs, while others undertook philological studies of the ancient classics. Through this process, *Man'yōshū, Kojiki*, and *Nihonshoki* were established as repositories of such folk traditions. Motoori Norinaga's views of the superiority of *Kojiki* prevailed, and it assumed a privileged position as a national classic. Likewise *Man'yōshū* was established as the national poetry anthology, expressing both the national character (***kokuminsei***) and the ethnic or folk character of the people (minzokusei, minshūsei).

In the context of the Meiji (1868–1912) government's forcible separation of Shintō and Buddhism (***shinbutsu bunri***) and its suppression of Buddhism, the status of Shintō as an independent religion was constructed. Prior to this period, Shintō always existed within the context of Buddhism. Shintō as a separate religion dates from this period. Likewise the status of texts associated with Shintō, including *Kojiki, Nihonshoki*, and *Man'yōshū*, as national classics was constructed in this context.

In 1890 the *Imperial Rescript on Education* (*Kyōiku chokugo*) was promulgated in reaction to importation of Western culture, but quickly came to be seen as a statement of the spiritual unification of the Japanese people. Inoue Tetsujirō's (1855–1944) commentary on the text published in 1891 used figures from Western history, including George Washington and Joan of Arc, to show that loyalty and filial piety were universal ethical values. These values then became the foundation of the nation-state. Seeking to restore Shintō's role within the state, Shintō priests developed rituals, ceremonial readings, and other rites, and they began promoting adherence to the values not as an ideal, but as an obligation to the state. The *Rescript* became the basis of school curricula, supplemented by biographies of historical paragons of loyalty and filial piety worthy of emulation. Adherence to this was challenged by the Christian schoolteacher Uchimura Kanzō (1861–1930), who refused to pay obeisance to the *Rescript* when it was promulgated in 1891. He was removed from his position, at the time finding little support from Buddhist, Shintō, or even Christian communities in his protest of this limitation on religious freedom.

In 1937 the Ideological Control Bureau of the Ministry of Education issued *Kokutai no hongi* (Principles of the national essence of Japan), a patriotic educational work affirming Japan as a nation-state based on a system of continuous ancestry of the imperial family (*tennōsei*) and presenting the authority of the emperor as divinely decreed. In a section entitled, "Dai Nihon kokutai" (National essence of Japan), the mythological basis of ***kokutai*** (national essence) was detailed with quotations from *Kojiki* and *Nihonshoki* in perhaps the most extreme formulation of Japan as the emperor's country. By 1940 State Shintō was established as the national religion and ancient mythologies were being fully exploited for militaristic purposes.

Following the end of World War II the supreme commander for the Allied Powers issued the Shintō Directive, ordering the separation of church and state and guaranteeing freedom of religion in Japan. In January 1946 Emperor Hirohito issued the Declaration of Humanity, renouncing his divinity as well as that of his ancestors. The emperor continues to serve as "the symbol of the state and the unity of the people, deriving his position from the will of the people with whom resides sovereign power" under the 1946 constitution. This view of the emperor is based on the ideas of Watsuji Tetsurō (1889–1960), who reinterpreted *Kojiki* and *Nihonshoki* texts as expressing the moral authority of the emperor for the Japanese people.

SEE ALSO Kingship, article on Kingship in East Asia; Poetry, article on Japanese Religious Poetry; Shintō.

BIBLIOGRAPHY

Aoki, Michiko Y., trans. *Records of Wind and Earth: A Translation of Fudoki, with Introduction and Commentaries.* Ann Arbor, Mich., 1997.

Aston, W. G., trans. *Nihongi: Chronicles of Japan from the Earliest Times to A.D. 697* (1896). Tokyo, 1972.

Bock, Felicia, trans. *Engi-shiki: Procedures of the Engi Era.* Tokyo, 1972.

Chamberlain, Basil Hall. *The Invention of a New Religion.* London, 1912.

Chamberlain, Basil Hall, trans. *Kojiki: Records of Ancient Matters* (1882). 2d ed. Tokyo, 1932; reprint, Rutland, Vt., and Tokyo, 1982.

Ebersole, Gary L. *Ritual Poetry and the Politics of Death in Early Japan.* Princeton, 1989.

Gauntlett, John O., trans. *Kokutai no hongi: Cardinal Principles of the National Entity of Japan.* Cambridge, Mass., 1949; reprint, Newton, Mass., 1974.

Hardacre, Helen. *Shinto and the State, 1868–1988.* Princeton, 1989.

Hijiya-Kirschnereit, Irmela, ed. *Canon and Identity: Japanese Modernization Reconsidered: Trans-Cultural Perspectives.* Berlin, 2000.

Inoue Nobutaka, Itō Satoshi, Endō Jun, and Mori Mizue, eds. *Shinto: A Short History.* Translated by Mark Teeuwen and John Breen. London, 2003.

Isomae Jun'ichi. "Reappropriating the Japanese Myths: Motoori Norinaga and the Creation Myths of the *Kojiki* and *Nihon shoki.*" *Japanese Journal of Religious Studies* 27, nos. 1 and 2 (2000): 15–39.

Kato Genchi and Hoshino Hikoshiro, trans. *The Kogoshui: Gleanings from Ancient Stories.* 3d ed. Tokyo, 1926.

Kitabatake Chikafusa. *Jinnō Shōtōki: A Chronicle of Gods and Sovereigns.* Translated by H. Paul Varley. New York, 1980.

Kornicki, Peter. *The Book in Japan: A Cultural History from the Beginnings to the Nineteenth Century.* Leiden, 1998.

Kuroda Toshio. "Shinto in the History of Japanese Religion." Translated by James C. Dobbins and Suzanne Gray. *Journal of Japanese Studies* 7, no. 1 (1981): 1–21.

LaFleur, William. *Karma of Words: Buddhism and the Literary Arts in Medieval Japan.* Berkeley, 1983.

Levy, Ian Hideo. *Hitomaro and the Birth of Japanese Lyricism.* Princeton, 1984

Motoori Norinaga. *Kojiki-Den: Book 1.* Translated by Ann Wehmeyer. Ithaca, N.Y., 1997.

Nosco, Peter. *Remembering Paradise: Nativism and Nostalgia in Eighteenth-Century Japan.* Cambridge, Mass., 1990.

Philippi, Donald L., trans. *Kojiki.* Princeton, 1969.

Philippi, Donald L., trans. *Norito: A Translation of the Ancient Japanese Ritual Prayers* (1959). Princeton, 1990.

Sakamoto Tarō and John S. Brownlee, trans. *The Six National Histories of Japan.* Vancouver, 1991.

Shirane Haruo and Tomi Suzuki, eds. *Inventing the Classics: Modernity, National Identity, and Japanese Literature.* Stanford, Calif., 2000.

Suzuki Sadami. "The Reformulation of the Idea of History and the Publication of Historical Texts in Late Nineteenth-Century Japan." Translated by Jeffrey Angles. Edited by Joshua A. Fogel and James Baxter. In *Historiography and Japanese Consciousness of Values and Norms.* Kyoto, Japan, 2003.

Tsunoda, Ryusaku, et al., comps. *Sources of Japanese Tradition.* 2d ed. New York, 2001.

H. PAUL VARLEY (1987)
MAUREEN H. DONOVAN (2005)

JASPERS, KARL

JASPERS, KARL (1883–1969), was one of the most influential German thinkers of the twentieth century and a founder of modern existential philosophy. Born in Oldenburg, Jaspers studied law and medicine. After writing several works on psychopathology, he turned to philosophy, and in 1920 he became a professor at Heidelberg. He was dismissed from that position by Nazi authorities in 1937; after 1948 he taught at Basel, where he died.

For Jaspers, philosophizing is an effort to understand and to express the authentic experience of realities that can never be conceptually explained and are not objectifiable; therefore it cannot pretend to be knowledge in the same sense as scientific knowledge. Jaspers accepts the Augustinian maxim "Deum et animam scire cupio" (I want to know God and the soul), but neither God nor the soul are possible positive objects of metaphysical speculation. Their place is taken respectively by "the all-encompassing" (*das Allumgreifende*), or transcendence, and existence. The latter, even though it reveals itself in one's empirical being (*Dasein*), is not a psychological subject, not an empirically accessible reality, and the former is not God in the sense of any mythological tradition. Still, both realities are known not only negatively, not only as a realm of the unknown beyond knowledge, but they are inseparably linked with each other: The transcendence is there only for existence; it opens itself to one insofar as one is able radically to experience one's freedom. The presence of the transcendence cannot be described in metaphysical or scientific language; in other words, one does not hear God's voice in the empirical word. It speaks to humans through ciphers they can meet in all forms of being: in nature, in history, in art, in mythology. Yet ciphers are untranslatable. Therefore, in vain does one try to grasp God in metaphysical doctrines or in the dogmas of an institutionalized religion. The language of mythology, too, is a way that humankind has tried to commune with the transcendence, but this language is sui generis, it cannot be converted into a philosophical system. Therefore, Jaspers totally opposed Bultmann's project of "demythologization," which, he argued, implied that myths are theories in disguise, that they could be translated into a profane tongue so that a theologian could salvage elements that are acceptable to scientifically trained "modern man" and discard the "superstitious" rest.

Myths, according to Jaspers, are the means by which people gain access to ultimate reality, and although they have no empirical reference, they are an indispensable part of culture. All attempts of positive theology to reach God in metaphysical categories are useless; so are efforts to express the transcendence in the dogmatic formulas of one or another confession. But a personal existence, in an effort of self-illumination, is able to meet the transcendence as a pendant of its own reality. Existence is not a substance within the empirical word and it cannot survive death; it nevertheless reaches eternity as moments of timelessness within empirical time. Therefore, existence cannot avoid the ultimate defeat; one's death cannot be given a meaning. Still, the radical awareness of one's own finitude is not necessarily a reason for discouragement: In the very acceptance of inevitable defeat one finds the way to being. While existence and the transcendence become real only in an encounter which is expressible in ciphers, and not in any scientific or theological knowledge, this encounter does not make one's communication with other people or one's living participation in historical processes unimportant. One can never isolate one's self entirely from empirical realities, from history, and from one's fellow human beings; quite the contrary, it is only from within, not by a kind of mystical detachment, that people can understand their relationships with infinity; and yet, this understanding can never take the form of "objective" knowledge.

Jaspers tried, in his historical studies, positively to assimilate the entire history of European philosophy which, from various angles, supported his intuition. Both those who stressed the radical irreducibility of personal existence to "objective" reality (Augustine, Kierkegaard, Nietzsche) and those who attempted, however awkwardly, to grasp unconditional being conceptually (Plotinus, Nicholas of Cusa, Bruno, Spinoza, Schelling, Hegel) represented in his view the human effort to cope with the eternal tension between one's life among things and one's desire to reach the ultimate.

In interpreting religious phenomena Jaspers rejected all positivist or scientific attempts to reduce them to needs that might have an anthropological, social, or psychological explanation. On the other hand, he refused to believe that a rational theological or metaphysical enquiry might elucidate them. Both institutionalized Christianity and the tradition of the Enlightenment were unable, in his view, to express properly the relationship between existence and transcendence.

BIBLIOGRAPHY

Works by Jaspers

Allgemeine Psychopathologie. Berlin, 1913. Translated by J. Hoenig and Marian W. Hamilton as *General Psychopathology* (Chicago, 1963).

Die geistige Situation der Zeit. Berlin, 1931. Translated by Eden Paul and Cedar Paul as *Man in the Modern Age* (London, 1933).

Philosophie. 3 vols. Berlin, 1932. Translated by E. B. Ashton as *Philosophy* (Chicago, 1969).

Vernunft und Existenz. Groningen, 1935. Translated by William Earle as *Reason and Existenz* (New York, 1955).

Der philosophische Glaube. Zurich, 1948. Translated by Ralph Manheim as *The Perennial Scope of Philosophy* (New York, 1949).

Vom Ursprung und Ziel der Geschichte. Zurich, 1949. Translated by Michael Bullock as *The Origin and Goal of History* (New Haven, 1953).

Die Frage der Entmythologisierung. Written with Rudolf Bultmann. Munich, 1954. Translated as *Myth and Christianity* (New York, 1958).

Works about Jaspers

Bollnow, O. F. *Existenzphilosophie und Pädagogik.* Stuttgart, 1959.

Piper, Klaus, ed. *Offener Horizont: Festschrift für Karl Jaspers.* Munich, 1953.

Saner, Hans. *Karl Jaspers in Selbstzeugnissen und Bilddokumenten.* Reinbek bei Hamburg, 1970.

Saner, Hans, ed. *Karl Jaspers in der Diskussion.* Munich, 1973.

Schilpp, Paul A., ed. *The Philosophy of Karl Jaspers.* New York, 1957.

LESZEK KOLAKOWSKI (1987)

JĀTI SEE VARṆA AND JĀTI

JAVANESE RELIGION.

The Javanese occupy the central and eastern parts of Java, a moderately sized island over twelve hundred kilometers long and five hundred kilometers wide. The island constitutes only about 7 percent of the total land area of the Indonesian archipelago, which now constitutes the Republic of Indonesia. Javanese peasants have migrated to other islands in Indonesia and, because Dutch colonialists had for two centuries prior to Indonesia's independence moved Javanese unskilled laborers overseas, there are also Javanese communities in Cape Town, South Africa; in Surinam, Latin America; and in New Caledonia, Melanesia. They have in general retained the original Javanese culture and language.

Nearly all Javanese (i.e., about 97.3 percent) are Muslim, with the remainder either Roman Catholics, Protestants, Buddhists, or, in South Central Java, recent converts to Hinduism. The Javanese themselves recognize two variants of Javanese Islam: The one with the greatest number of adherents is syncretistic, incorporating Muslim, Hindu, Buddhist, and local religious elements; the other is more dogmatic and puritan. The first is called Agami Jawi ("Javanese religion") and the other, Agami Islam Santri ("Santri Islam religion"). Adherents of both variants are to be found in all Javanese communities, although in certain regions, one of the forms will predominate. In his study of Javanese religion, Clifford Geertz calls the first variant Abangan, and the second, Islam Santri.

JAVANESE RELIGIOUS HISTORY. Early Javanese religion must have been based on local forms of ancestor worship, and the belief in spirits, magical power in natural phenomena, and sacred objects in the human environment. Hinduism probably came to Java during the fourth century of the common era through the trade routes from South India, although the earliest traces of a Hindu-Javanese civilization can only be dated to the eighth century. During that period Javanese Buddhism also developed, and the remnants of ancient religious structures such as the Hindu Prambanan and the Buddhist Borobudur seem to indicate that Javanese Hinduism and Javanese Buddhism coexisted peacefully.

Although, initially, Hinduism and Buddhism had been spread along the trade routes, they were further disseminated by Indian *brahmans* and *bhikṣus,* who had quite likely been invited by Javanese rulers to act as consultants. Indian civilization was promoted and developed in the court centers of the ancient empires, first in Central Java during the eighth to tenth centuries, and later, during the eleventh to fifteenth centuries, in East Java, where it took on a specific Javanese character. Many elements of this Hindu-Javanese court civilization subsequently influenced Javanese folk culture.

Islam also came to Java through the trade routes, via North Sumatra and the Malay Peninsula between the fourteenth and seventeenth centuries. Islam in Java exhibits an emphasis on mystical ideas. Indeed, Islamic mysticism seems to have found fertile ground in Java because of the existing mystical elements in Javanese Hinduism: Muslim literary works written during the early period of Javanese Islamization show the importance of mystical Islam, or Sufism (Arab., *tasawwuf).* Dogmatic, puritan Islam, reformed Islam, and so forth arrived later, when Javanese devotees returned from making the pilgrimage *(ḥājj)* to Mecca.

As a new religion, Islam initially influenced the port towns and harbor states of Java's north coast, which subsequently became prosperous and powerful and undermined the declining power of the Majapahit empire of East Java. In the following period zealous Muslim missionaries who became holy men, called *wali* (Arab., *walī;* "saint, guardian") in Javanese folklore, spread Islam through the interior regions of East and Central Java. The Muslim religion, preached by the imam, included many mystical elements, a fact that probably facilitated the contact between the missionaries and the population, to whom mystical concepts and ideas had long been familiar. During the sixteenth and seventeenth centuries, students and disciples recorded notes of these teachings, which, presented as magical songs, have been compiled in books called *suluk.*

The court center of the Central Javanese empire, Mataram, traditionally resisted the penetration of Islam from the interior of Java. During the second half of the eighteenth century, however, Islam reached the heartland of the ancient Central Javanese civilization, although not always through peaceful means. The centers of the Hindu-Buddhistic civilization in Central Java merely had to accept the presence of Islam, and thus developed the syncretistic Agami Jawi variant of Javanese Islam.

AGAMI JAWI. The Agami Jawi belief system includes an extensive range of concepts, views, and values, many of which are Muslim in origin: the belief in God Almighty (*Gusti Allah*), the belief in the prophet Muḥammad *(kanjeng nabi Muḥammad),* and the belief in other prophets (*para ambiya*). The Javanese consider God Almighty to be the creator and ultimate cause of life and the entire universe. They believe that there is but one God ("gusti Allah ingkang maha esa"). All human actions as well as important decisions are done "in the name of God" (*bismillah*), a formula pronounced many times per day to inaugurate any small or large endeavor.

Divine beings. The Javanese literary tradition has elaborated extensively on the nature of God and humanity. The most important source for this subject is the seventeenth-century work, the *Dewaruci,* written in Javanese prose. In the mystical, pantheistic view of the *Dewaruci,* God is conceptualized as the totality of nature: He is a tiny divine being, so small that he can enter any human heart, yet in reality as wide as the oceans, as endless as space, and manifested in the colors that make and symbolize everything that exists on earth. Between the sixteenth and eighteenth centuries this religious concept of God was interwoven with Islamic concepts by the spiritual leaders and intellectuals who wrote the Agami Jawi literature, which includes voluminous books such as the *Serat centhini* and the magico-mystical *suluk* mentioned earlier.

In addition to the belief in God and the prophets, the Agami Jawi Javanese also believe in saints. Included among these holy persons are the nine semihistorical "apostles" (*wali sanga*), or first missionaries of Islam, religious teachers, and certain semihistorical figures who were known to the people through the Babad literature. The belief in these saints is usually kept alive by the veneration of their sacred graves (*pepundhen*). Local saints are also venerated, and many regions have their locally acknowledged sacred places. In certain village communities, one social class often associates itself with a particular legendary figure in order to obtain an exclusive status. Famous village leaders, *wayang* puppeteers (*dhalang*), healers (*dhukun*), or religious leaders (*kiyai*) may become holy men even while they are still alive, and their graves may turn into *pepundhen* and objects of veneration.

Many other elements, such as the belief in a great number of deities (*dewata*), are of Hindu-Buddhist origin, as one can see from their Sanskritic names. However, the roles and functions of several of the deities are different from those of the original ones. Dewi Sri, for instance, who originated from Sri, the wife of the Hindu god Viṣṇu, is in Javanese culture the goddess of fertility and rice. Bathara Kala was derived from the Hindu concept of time (*kāla*), and this destructive aspect of Śiva the creator is in Javanese culture the god of death and calamity.

An indigenous pre-Hindu element is the divine trickster Semar. The Javanese believe that Semar has the power to act as an intermediary between the world of mortals and the divine. In the dramatic *wayang,* the Javanese shadow-puppet play, he is a clown figure who acts as both the servant and guardian of the heroes of the *Bratayuda,* the Javanese version of the Hindu *Mahābhārata* epic.

Indigenous Javanese beliefs are primarily concerned with spirits, in particular, ancestral spirits (*ruh leluhur*), guardian spirits who care for the individual's well-being and are usually conceived of as the soul's twin (*sing ngemong*), and guardian spirits who oversee places such as public buildings, old wells, spots in a forest, turns in a river, old banyan trees, caves, and so forth. They also believe in a number of ghosts *(lelembut),* spooks *(setan),* and giants *(denawa),* who are frightening and malevolent creatures *(memedi),* and in fairies *(widadari)* and dwarfs *(thuyul),* who are considered benevolent.

The Agami Jawi has a cosmogony *(kang dumadi),* a cosmology (*bawanagung*), an eschatology *(akhiring jaman),* and messianic beliefs *(ratu adil).* While these are principally of Hindu origin, the Agami Jawi concepts of death and afterlife *(akherat)* have been influenced by Islam. Originating in pre-Hindu religious systems is their concept of magic, which imparts magical powers to certain people, parts of the human body, objects, certain plants, and rare animals.

Cultic life. The Agami Jawi ceremonial and ritual system differs essentially from the dogmatic teachings of Islam. The second pillar (*rukn*) of Islam, the *ṣalāt,* or ritual prayer performed five times daily, is considered unimportant and is often ignored. Instead, various kinds of sacred communal meals (*slametan*) are central to its ceremonial system. The family hosting the ceremony usually invites friends, neighbors, and important members of the community. A sacred meal consisting of particular, customary dishes is served after being blessed by a religious official from the mosque who recites of verses (*āyāt*) from the Qurʾān. A *slametan* ceremony often includes the *dhikr,* a monotonous chant of the phrase "La ilāha illā Allāh" ("There is no god but God"). This is repeated in chorus by all of the participants and may last for more than an hour without interruption.

The size, elaborateness, and cost of a *slametan* ceremony depend on the importance of the occasion and the financial resources of the host. The occasion may vary from celebrations of events associated with the individual's life cycle, of which circumcision and weddings may be considered the most important, to mortuary rites held on the day of the funeral and on the seventh, the fortieth, one-hundredth, and one-thousandth day after death. The *slametan* meals held as part of the funerary rites include elaborate *dhikr* chants.

Among the rural peasants, periodic *slametan* are held in connection with the stages of the agricultural cycle, whereas both rural and urban Javanese hold *slametan* meals on religious holidays of the Javanese Muslim calendar. Seasonal, community-sponsored *slametan* ceremonies, the *bersih dhusun,* are meant to purify the community. Intermittant *slametan* ceremonies are held in connection with disturbing events in the individual's life, such as a serious illness, accident, or bad dreams. More secular *slametan* are held to celebrate the move to a new house, the changing of one's name, the start of a long journey, an occupational promotion, or academic graduation, and the anniversaries of clubs and fraternal organizations, professional, functional, and recreational associations.

An equally important practice of the Agami Jawi is the veneration of the dead and ancestors, through visits to the graves of deceased relatives and ancestors (*nyekar*). Also indispensable to Agami Jawi observance are the numerous offerings (*sajen*) that appear in nearly all the ceremonies and may be performed independently as well. The latter type of offering, held at specific times, such as Thursday evenings, consists of bits of food (including tiny rice cones and an assortment of cookies), spices, and a variety of small items that are decoratively arranged on small trays of plaited bamboo. A careful analysis of the items reveals some consistency in their symbolic meanings, which relate to their names, appearance, colors, or use.

Fasting is not only practiced during the Muslim month of the fast, Ramaḍān, but on many other occasions as well. Other religious practices include deliberately seeking hardship (*tirakat*), asceticism (*tapabrata*), and meditation (*samadi*). The attainment of a state of trance is an integral aspect of a number of religious and semireligious folk dances, songs, and plays. Performances of certain *wayang* puppet dramas and religious concerts on sacred gamelan sets also accompany religious concepts and activities.

Agami Islam Santri. The Agami Islam Santri belief system of both rural and urban Javanese is composed of puritanical Islamic concepts about God, the prophet Muḥammad, creation, personal ethics, death and afterlife, eschatology, the day of resurrection, and so forth. These concepts are all clearly determined by dogmatic creed. Peasant Santri Javanese generally take these for granted and are indifferent about their interpretation. The urban Santri, however, are usually quite concerned about the moral and ethical backgrounds of the doctrine. In addition to having memorized certain parts of the Qurʾān, many have also been exposed to the exegetical literature (*tafsir*), and prophetic tradition (*ḥadīth*) during their education in more advanced religious schools (*pesan-*

tren). The Muslim belief system is organized and systematized in the *sharī'ah* (Islamic law); the dominant legal school (*madhhab*) in Java, and throughout Indonesia, is that of al-Shāfi'ī (d. 820).

The Santri Javanese practice a ceremonial and ritual system that follows the dogmatic rules of the Five Pillars (*arkān*, pl. of *rukn*) of Islam. The second pillar, the daily and Friday *ṣalāt* (Jav., *sembahyang*), is the central ceremony. *Ṣalāt*, often incorrectly translated as "prayer," is a series of religious acts of worship and prostration, accompanied by incantations that are fixed in form and content. The obligatory performance of the *sembahyang* is done individually five times per day and communally once per week, at noon on Friday. The Javanese also have voluntary personal prayers to God called *ndonga*, which may be performed at any time, using the Javanese vernacular rather than the prescribed Arabic. The third pillar is the gift to the poor, called *jakat* (Arab., *zakat*); the fourth is the fast (Jav., *siyam;* Arab., *ṣawm*); and the fifth, of great import to Javanese Santri Muslims, is the *ḥājj*, or pilgrimage.

Most of the Islamic calendrical ceremonial celebrations are observed by the Santri Javanese. Unlike the adherents of the Agami Jawi religion, the Santri do not prepare *slametan* meals on those holidays. They do, however, perform special *ṣalāt* rituals, recite verses from the Qur'ān throughout most of the night, listen to stories about the life of the Prophet, and attend *slawatan* performances consisting of religious songs accompanied by drums and tambourines.

Santri Javanese also perform rites to celebrate certain events in the life cycle of the individual. However, unlike the Agami Jawi Javanese, who hold numerous *slametan* ceremonies, they prefer to give *sedhekah* sacrifices in accordance with the *sharī'ah*. Their funerary ceremonies do not differ significantly from those of the Agami Jawi. The *ṣalātu 'jjināzah*, absent in the Agami Jawi, is a mortuary *ṣalāt* that is preceded by the act of cleansing oneself, and is performed in front of the body of the deceased person by those who come to show sympathy.

JAVANESE SPIRITUAL AND RELIGIOUS MOVEMENTS. There have always been adherents of Agami Jawi for whom recurrent *slametan* rituals, *sajen* offerings at fixed periods, and routine visits to graves represent a superficial, meaningless, and unsatisfactory religious life. Therefore, they search for a deeper understanding of the essence of life and spiritual existence. One response to the demand for a more spiritually meaningful life are the numerous *kebatinan kejawen* spiritual movements, which have emerged and disappeared, but have retained a constant following in the course of Javanese history. The term *kebatinan* refers to the search for truth, *batin* (Arab., *bāṭin*). Since the late 1960s, the number of these movements has increased significantly.

Most of the Javanese *kebatinan* movements have a local base with only a limited number of followers (usually not more than two hundred), and are officially called "small movements" (Indonesian, *aliran kecil).* Others, however, have thousands of followers, and are called "large movements" (Indonesian, *aliran besar*). The four largest are Susila Sudi Darma (SUBUD), Paguyuban Ngesti Tunggal (PANGESTU), Paguyuban Sumarah, and Sapta Darma. Although *kebatinan* movements are to be found throughout the Javanese area, the most important ones are located in Surakarta. In 1983 there were nineteen such organizations in that city, with a total of approximately 7,500 members. At the end of 1982, the entire province of Central Java listed ninety-three movements, with a total of more than 123,570 members. While most of the movements are based on mystical ideas, at least five other types can be distinguished: movements that focus on mysticism; moralistic and ethical movements that focus on the purification of the soul; messianic Ratu Adil ("just king") movements; nativistic movements, focusing on the return to original Javanese culture; and movements focusing on magical practices and occultism.

There are also movements with Santri orientation. These are usually based on a particular Islamic religious school (*pesantren*). Unification with God is the central objective of most of those Santri movements. In Indonesia, and particularly in Java, as in the rest of the Islamic world, Ṣūfīs are organized into movements called *tarekat* (Arab., *ṭarīqāt*). The *tarekat* are led by a charismatic teacher called *kiyai* in Javanese. Many Santri Javanese belong not only to these local *tarekat* movements, but also to various international Ṣūfī orders, such as the Qādirīyah, Wāḥidīyah, Naqshbandīyah, Shaṭṭārīyah, and Ṣiddiqīyah. In addition to spiritual movements with a mystical orientation, Javanese Santri have also initiated puritan religious reform movements. In the early twentieth century K. H. Achmad Dahlan (b. 1868) from Jogjakarta, brought Muslim reformist ideas to Java. Influenced by the Islamic modernist Muḥammad 'Abduh of al-Azhar University in Cairo, Dahlan founded the Muḥammadiyah in 1912 in his home city. Preaching the return of Islam to its two basic sources, the Qur'ān and the *ḥadīth*, Dahlan not only attacked the syncretistic Agami Jawi Islam, but also Islam Santri scholasticism and mysticism. The Muḥammadiyah developed into a nationwide movement, which applied itself not only to religious reform and modernization but also to education and social welfare.

SEE ALSO Drama, article on Javanese Wayang; Islam, article on Islam in Southeast Asia; Rites of Passage, article on Muslim Rites; Southeast Asian Religions, articles on Insular Cultures, Modern Movements in Insular Cultures.

BIBLIOGRAPHY

Alfian. *Islamic Modernization in Indonesian Politics: The Muhammadijah Movement during the Dutch Colonial Period, 1912–1942.* Madison, Wis., 1969. An excellent description of the history of the Javanese Muḥammadiyah modern reform movement, initiated by K. H. Achmad Dahlan in 1912.

Dhofier, Zamaksyari. *The Pesantren Tradition: A Study of the Role of the Kyai in the Maintenance of the Traditional Ideology of*

Islam in Java. Canberra, 1980. A good description of a Javanese Muslim religious school community.

Geertz, Clifford. *The Religion of Java.* Glencoe, Ill., 1960. A description of the two variants of Javanese Islam. The author has ignored the written indigenous religious literature; nevertheless, this book has dominated the literature on Javanese culture and society.

Hien, Hendrik A. van. *De Javaansche Geestenwereld en de Betrekking, die Tusschen de Geesten en de Zinnelijke Wereld Bestaat: Verduidelijkt door Petangan's of Tellingen bij de Javenen in Gebruik.* 4 vols. Semarang, 1896. An extensive description of the Javanese supernatural world, including lists of over one hundred names with brief annotations of Javanese deities, spirits, and ghosts.

Poensen, Carl. "Bijdragen tot de Kennis van den Godsdien-stigen en Zedelijken Toestand des Javaans." *Mededeelingen Vanwege het Nederlandsche Zendeling Genootschap* 7 (1863): 333–359 and 10 (1866): 23–80. An early description of two variants of Javanese Islam.

Soebardi. "Santri Religious Elements as Reflected in the Book of Tjĕntini." *Bijdragen tot de Taal-, Land- en Volkenkunde* 127 (1971): 331–349. A historical description of the absorption process of Muslim religious elements in the Hindu-Buddhist-Javanese syncretistic religion of the sixteenth and seventeenth centuries.

Zoetmulder, P. J. *Pantheïsme en monisme in de Javaansche soeloek-litteratuur.* Nijmegen, Netherlands, 1935. An analysis of the ancient Javanese mystical religious literature of the seventeenth and eighteenth centuries.

New Sources

Beatty, Andrew. *Varieties of Javanese Religion: An Anthropological Account.* New York, 1999.

Beatty, Andrew. "Islamic and non-Islamic Prayer in Java." In *Islamic Prayer Across the Indian Ocean,* edited by David Parkin and Stephen C. Headley, pp. 39–61. Richmond, U.K., 2000.

Doorn Harder, Pieternella van, and C. A. M. de Jong. "The Pilgrimage to Tembayat: Tradition and Revival in Indonesian Islam." *Muslim World* 91, nos. 3–4 (2001): 325–353.

Geels, A. *Subud and the Javanese Mystical Tradition.* Richmond, U.K., 1997.

Iyer, Alessandra. "Archaeology, Dance and Religion in Java: The Prambanan Complex." In *Case Studies in Archaeology and World Religion,* edited by Timothy Insoll, pp. 48–58. Oxford, 1999.

Yumarma, A. *Unity in Diversity: A Philosophical and Ethical Study of the Javanese Concept of 'Keselarasan'.* Rome, 1996.

Zoetmulder, P. J. *Pantheism and Monism in Javanese Suluk Literature: Islamic and Indian Mysticism in an Indonesian Setting.* Edited and translated by M. C. Ricklefs. Leiden, 1995.

R. M. KOENTJARANINGRAT (1987)
Revised Bibliography

JAYADEVA (late twelfth century?) was an Indian poet-saint who composed the dramatic lyrical poem *Gītagovinda.* Dedicated to the god Kṛṣṇa, the poem concentrates on Kṛṣṇa's love with the cowherdess Rādhā during a rite of spring. To express the complexities of divine and human love, Jayadeva uses the metaphor of intense earthly passion. The religious eroticism of the *Gītagovinda* earned sainthood for the poet and a wide audience for his poem.

There are conflicting traditions about Jayadeva's place of birth and region of poetic activity. Modern scholars of Bengal, Orissa, and Bihar have claimed him for their regions, but the most convincing evidence associates him with the Jagannātha cult of Puri in the latter half of the twelfth century. Although the poem originated in eastern India and remains most popular there, it spread throughout the Indian subcontinent in the centuries following its composition. As early as the thirteenth century it was quoted in a temple inscription in Gujarat (western India). Established commentatorial traditions and manuscripts exist in every part of India. The songs of the *Gītagovinda* are an important part of Vaiṣṇava devotional music and are still sung in temples from Orissa to Kerala. Its text represents one of the major subjects of Rajput painting.

Jayadeva is a name that the poet shares with Kṛṣṇa, the divine hero of his poem, whom he invokes in a song with the refrain "Jaya jayadeva hare" ("Triumph, God of Triumph, Hare!"). All versions of the legend of Jayadeva's life agree that he was born in a *brahman* family and became an accomplished student of Sanskrit and a skilled poet. However, he abandoned scholarship at a young age and adopted an ascetic life, devoting himself to God. As a wandering mendicant, he would not rest under any one tree for more than a night for fear that attachment to the place would violate his vow. His ascetic life ended when a *brahman* of Puri insisted that Jagannātha, Lord of the World, himself had ordained the marriage of Jayadeva with the *brahman*'s daughter Padmāvatī, who was dedicated as a dancing girl in the temple. Padmāvatī served her husband, who in turn shared her devotion to Jagannātha. As Jayadeva composed, Padmāvatī danced—and so the *Gītagovinda* was composed. In the process of composing the poem, Jayadeva conceived the climax of Kṛṣṇa's supplication to Rādhā as a command for her to place her foot on Kṛṣṇa's head in a symbolic gesture of victory. But in deference to Kṛṣṇa the poet hesitated to complete the couplet. He went to bathe, and in his absence Kṛṣṇa himself appeared, disguised as Jayadeva, and wrote down the couplet; the god then ate the food Padmāvatī had prepared for Jayadeva and left. When the poet returned, he realized that he had received divine grace by exalting Kṛṣṇa's love for Rādhā.

The poem's emotional drama unfolds in twelve movements of Sanskrit songs (*padāvalīs*) composed in recitative verses. The songs are meant to be sung with specific melodic patterns (*rāgas*) and rhythmic cycles (*tālas*). They are sung by Kṛṣṇa, Rādhā, and Rādhā's friend, who acts as an intermediary between the lovers.

Critical acclaim of the poem within the Indian literary and religious culture has been high, but its frank eroticism has led many Indian commentators to interpret the love between Rādhā and Kṛṣṇa as an allegory of the human soul's love for God. Through the centuries learned and popular audiences alike have appreciated the emotional lyricism expressed by the *Gītagovinda* in its variations on the theme of the passion felt by separated lovers.

BIBLIOGRAPHY

Miller, Barbara Stoler, ed. and trans. *Love Song of the Dark Lord: Jayadeva's Gītagovinda.* New York, 1977.

Sandahl-Forgue, Stella. *Le Gītagovinda: Tradition et innovation dans le kavya.* Stockholm, 1977.

Siegel, Lee. *Sacred and Profane Dimensions of Love in Indian Traditions, as Exemplified in the Gītagovinda of Jayadeva.* London, 1978.

New Sources

Jayadeva and Gitagovinda in the Traditions of Orissa. Edited by Dinanath Pathy, Bhagaban Panda, and Bijaya Kumar Rath. New Delhi, 1995.

BARBARA STOLER MILLER (1987)
Revised Bibliography

JEHOVAH'S WITNESSES are one of the few religious movements that originated in the United States. Like other sectarian Protestant groups founded in the later nineteenth century, they claim to restore Christianity to its original doctrines and practices. The organization adopted the name Jehovah's Witnesses in 1931 to emphasize the belief that the most accurate translation of the personal name of God in the Hebrew Scriptures is "Jehovah" (*Ps.* 83:18), and that as believers they are his "witnesses" (*Is.* 43:10; *Acts* 1:8). They fulfill the responsibility to witness by distributing literature, leading Bible studies, attending congregational meetings, and maintaining separation from secular culture. In matters of faith and practice, Jehovah's Witnesses submit to the theocratic authority of the Watchtower Society.

Central to Watchtower teaching is the belief that Jesus Christ will soon rule as king over the earth from heaven in fulfillment of prophecies. In the apocalyptic battle of Armageddon, Christ will destroy all human governments and establish the millennial kingdom of God. The vision of a perfect world order, in which people of all ethnic origins live in peace and justice in an earth restored to pristine condition, attracts followers across the globe. In 2002, Jehovah's Witnesses reported an active membership of over six million people in 234 countries. Over 80 percent of the members live outside the United States, with concentrations in Canada, Latin America, sub-Saharan Africa, Australia, and Scandinavia.

HISTORY. Jehovah's Witnesses trace the origin of their movement to Charles Taze Russell (1852–1916), who was raised in the Presbyterian tradition but became dissatisfied with Calvinist doctrines of original sin, everlasting punishment of unbelievers, and predestination. He was attracted to the Adventist teaching that Christ had returned in 1874 as an invisible presence, inaugurating a forty-year period of gathering true Christians. Russell began publishing his views in 1879 in Allegheny, Pennsylvania, in a monthly journal called *Zion's Watch Tower and Herald of Christ's Presence.* In 1884 he organized his readers, who met in small congregations of Bible students, into the Zion Watch Tower and Tract Society, and he began holding annual conventions in 1891. Russell traveled extensively, giving lectures on Bible prophecy and holding audiences spellbound with his dramatic oratory and charismatic presence. His followers, known popularly as "Russellites," gave him the honorary title of "Pastor."

Russell wrote prolifically, including a six-volume series of books called *Millennial Dawn* (1886–1904). In a pattern that continued into the twenty-first century, his students, called "publishers," distributed literature door-to-door, sometimes using phonographs and dioramas. Russell taught that the "presence" of Christ would begin to dawn with the end of Gentile domination over Israel (prophesied in *Lk.* 21:24), an event he later believed occurred with the onset of World War I. In 1909 Russell established operations in Brooklyn, New York, in a complex of buildings called Bethel, where Jehovah's Witnesses still serve as volunteers.

Russell's personal life was marked by controversies. He based some of his biblical interpretations on analyses of the Great Pyramid, he was committed to Zionism as a necessary condition for the fulfillment of prophecy, and he was accused of fraud in a commercial venture. His contentious divorce from Maria Ackley Russell arose from conflicts over her authority in the organization, resulting in her removal as associate editor of the *Watch Tower* (the original two-word spelling of the organization's journal). While Watchtower historians claim she was motivated by "her own desire for personal prominence" (*Jehovah's Witnesses: Proclaimers of God's Kingdom,* 1993, p. 143) critics charge that she was asserting her right to independent judgment.

The specific problem, according to the Watchtower Society, was that Maria "sought to secure for herself a stronger voice in directing what would appear in the *Watch Tower*" and resisted the editorial policy that required Charles's approval of the entire contents of every issue (*Jehovah's Witnesses: Proclaimers of God's Kingdom,* 1993, p. 645). Maria and Charles separated in 1897. In 1903 Maria published a tract with allegations of immoral conduct by Charles and initiated divorce proceedings, which were completed in 1908. Witnesses teach that a wife should respect and obey her husband as head of the family, whether he is a Christian or not (*Eph.* 5:22–24), and that she does not have authority to refuse sexual relations with her husband (*1 Cor.* 7:3–4). In that light, Maria serves for Jehovah's Witnesses as a cautionary example of a rebellious wife and a woman exceeding her authority as prescribed in the Bible. According to Watchtower Society interpretations of the New Testament texts, women are excluded from serving as overseers (elders) and ministerial servants (deacons) in Kingdom Halls, and from holding offices in the Watchtower Society.

Russell's death created a crisis of leadership that was resolved by the election of Joseph Franklin Rutherford (1869–1942) as president of the Watch Tower Society. Because Rutherford had trained as a legal apprentice and served occasionally on the circuit court, he was known as "Judge." While Rutherford was a charismatic speaker, his disposition was more confrontational than Russell's and his style of management more authoritarian. His forceful advocacy of refusal of military service led to his imprisonment in 1919, along with seven other directors of the Watch Tower Society, under the Sedition Act. They won release on appeal, but many members suffered harassment for their antigovernment teachings. Accusations of lack of patriotism, as well as disappointment in the failure of the kingdom to arrive after the end of the war, discouraged many. Rutherford responded by strengthening the efficiency and discipline of the organization. He introduced a monthly "service sheet" to record in detail the activities of members, increased the construction of Kingdom Halls, and began publishing a new monthly magazine called *The Golden Age* (later, *Awake!*). To reinforce apocalyptic hope he introduced the slogan, "Millions Now Living Will Never Die!"

Rutherford wrote extensively, revising many of Russell's views. He identified "Babylon the Great" of *Revelation* 17 with the League of Nations in alliance with the Roman Catholic Church and predicted the return of biblical patriarchs, for whom he built a mansion in San Diego. In 1935 Rutherford declared that membership of the "anointed class" of 144,000 Witnesses called to reign with Christ in heaven (*Rv.* 14:1) was "sealed" and that new members of the growing movement belonged to that "great crowd, which no man was able to number, out of all nations and tribes and peoples" (*Rv.* 7:9), who would not ascend to heaven but live in the earthly paradise.

Between the world wars Rutherford led Jehovah's Witnesses through a series of court battles over freedom of speech and press, right of assembly, and distribution of literature. His death from colon cancer in 1942 began the transition from charismatic to institutional authority.

Nathan Homer Knorr (1905–1977) became the third president of the Watch Tower Society in 1942. His presidency was marked by increased growth, greater uniformity in the programs of local congregations, and more effective methods of promotion, including training in public speaking through Theocratic Ministry Schools. Knorr traveled extensively and established international organizations in Asia, Latin America, the Middle East, and the Pacific Islands. He also began the Watchtower Bible School of Gilead for training missionaries. Known as "Brother," Knorr was more modest than his predecessors, and in 1943 he established a policy of anonymous publications on the principle that authority resides in official interpretations of the Bible, not in the views of any individual. In 1960 the Watchtower Society published its own *New World Translation of the Holy Scriptures.* During the cultural upheaval of the time, the society expelled many young people for sexual misconduct. This severe punishment, called "disfellowshipping," forbids social interaction with any Jehovah's Witnesses, including members of one's own family, and is based on *1 Corinthians* 5:9–11. Witnesses have also been disfellowshipped as apostates for renouncing official teaching.

Under Knorr's leadership the board of directors of the Watchtower Society reorganized into a Governing Body that issued binding directives, held all legal authority over the vast holdings of the Watchtower Society, approved all publications, and was the final arbiter of doctrinal and behavioral questions. Knorr also restored to local congregations the authority to elect their own ruling body of male elders. In his last years the organization faced a crisis of confidence. Based on *Watchtower* articles, many Jehovah's Witnesses began to expect that the kingdom would come in 1975. Despite official warnings that such hope was speculative, many left the organization when the kingdom failed to appear.

Frederick W. Franz (1893–1992), fourth president of the Watchtower Society, responded to the decline in membership after 1975 with a series of publications in defense of official teaching, including a revised reference edition of the *New World Translation* (NWT; 1984). Franz also expanded local programs of education and developed the Ministerial Training School in 1987. Under his leadership the number of pioneers (full-time evangelists) nearly tripled, and the list of congregations grew to seventy thousand. His emphasis on greater dedication led him to develop formal courses of instruction for newly baptized members of Kingdom Halls and to enforce stricter standards for disfellowshipping—resulting in the expulsion of his own nephew and member of the Governing Body, Raymond Franz.

Milton G. Henschel (1920–2003) rose to the presidency of the Watchtower Society in 1992 after decades of service at Bethel. During his administration the organization completed the transition from strong individual authority to corporate bureaucracy. Key to this move was severing the connection between the coming of the kingdom and the life span of the generation of 1914. Since the days of Rutherford, the official teaching was that the cohort of the anointed class would not all die until the kingdom arrives on earth, but by the mid-1990s they had dwindled to less than nine thousand. In 1995 the Watchtower Society revised its interpretation of Jesus' promise that "this generation will not pass away until all these things have taken place" (*Mt.* 24:34) to mean that there will always be those who oppose the truth until the kingdom arrives. Consequently, Jehovah's Witnesses began to teach that the time of the kingdom cannot be predicted by any human measure.

ORGANIZATION. In October 2000 the Watch Tower Bible and Tract Society of Pennsylvania, the parent corporation of Jehovah's Witnesses, separated its president and board of directors from the Governing Body of the Watchtower Society. Don Adams replaced Henschel as president, and the assets and properties of the Watchtower Society were assigned to separate corporations with their own presidents. The new officers were all younger men and were responsible for the management of ongoing operations. While the Governing Body has no legal authority, its members all belong to the anointed class and continue to provide guidance as the "faithful and discreet slave" (*Mt.* 24:45, NWT), to whom Christ gave spiritual authority on earth until his return. Critics charge that the change was instituted to protect the Governing Body from litigation over controversial practices, such as refusal of blood transfusions even for minor children (see article by Randall Watters in *Christianity Today* 45, no.4 [2001]: 25).

For administrative purposes, the global community of Jehovah's Witnesses is divided into thirty zones. Each zone is composed of branches; branches are made up of districts; and districts are divided into circuits. Each circuit includes twenty congregations. A circuit overseer visits each congregation twice a year. When membership in a Kingdom Hall (congregation) reaches two hundred, another congregation is formed. The 2002 *Yearbook* reported 94,600 congregations. Besides the national headquarters in Brooklyn, New York, there are Bethel complexes in Paterson, New Jersey, and Wallkill, New York, as well as several farms that produce food for the volunteers in these locations.

TEACHINGS. Jehovah's Witnesses claim that all of their beliefs are derived from the Bible, which they believe is inspired by God and is accurate in every statement. They interpret the Bible literally, except where they detect figurative language, and they offer "proof texts" for all of their teachings. They reject conventional Christian doctrines and practices that are not explicitly found in the Bible, such as the Trinity, deity of Christ, immortality of the soul, everlasting punishment of unbelievers, salvation by grace, and ordination of clergy. For Jehovah's Witnesses there is only one supreme God, known as Jehovah. He created the world in six "days" (each a period of time lasting several thousand years) without evolution but through the agency of Jesus in his preexistent form as the Word of God, also known as Michael the archangel. Jesus is not eternal, but he was the "firstborn of all creation" (*Col.* 1:15) and is properly called "a god" (*Jn.* 1:1, NWT). Jehovah's Witnesses pray to God in the name of Jesus. They understand "holy spirit" to refer to Jehovah's "active force."

Jehovah's Witnesses believe in a personal Devil, the rebellious angel who became Satan, the "adversary" of God. Satan tempted the first human couple to commit their free act of disobedience. As a result all humans became subject to sin, sickness, and the oblivion of death. As Adam became a living soul when God created him (*Gn.* 2:7), so the soul dies with the body: "The dead are conscious of nothing at all" (*Eccl.* 9:5). Their future existence depends upon resurrection in the kingdom. In the meanwhile, Satan opposes God's rule by leading humanity to worship the false gods of material success, sexual indulgence, and national pride. Because they believe the "world system" is under satanic control, Jehovah's Witnesses reject political, economic, and interfaith alliances. They insist that theirs is the only true religion.

To save humans from sin and death, Jesus was born through the virgin Mary and anointed at his baptism by God's holy spirit as Messiah. Jesus' sinless life qualified him to be the perfect sacrifice, a ransom that was the equivalent of the perfect life Adam forfeited in Eden. Christ's utter obedience to the divine will vindicated Jehovah's authority and restored the possibility of living eternally in earthly paradise for all who exercise faith in Jesus by following his example of obedience. In Watchtower interpretation, Jesus was executed on a "torture stake" rather than a cross, a symbol Jehovah's Witnesses associate with ancient false religions. Jehovah raised Jesus from the dead as an "immortal spirit person" (*1 Pt.* 3:18) with authority to rule over the messianic kingdom.

The anointed class, also called "little flock" (*Lk.* 12:32), will rule with Christ "as kings over the earth" (*Rv.* 5:10). They will not be resurrected but are raised upon death to heaven as "spirit beings." They are the subjects of the new covenant Jesus announced at his last meal, and therefore only they are qualified to partake in the annual Memorial. (A few younger members have declared a "heavenly calling" on the basis of inner conviction, and they are regarded as replacements for unidentified apostates.) They will administer divine government over the paradise on earth, populated by the "great crowd" of resurrected believers, also known as "other sheep" (*Jn.* 10:16). The present role of the "great crowd" is to assist the anointed class in bearing witness to Jehovah's kingdom.

Jehovah's Witnesses believe that 1914 is a key date in understanding Bible prophecy. Using numerical references in the books of *Daniel* and *Revelation,* they calculate that 1914 was when Christ returned to cast Satan out of heaven and be enthroned as king of the universe (*Rv.* 12:7–9). The natural disasters and human catastrophes that have occurred since then fulfill prophecies about worsening conditions in the last days. Jehovah's Witnesses regard such events as signs that the kingdom is imminent. Articles in the *Watchtower* often quote Jesus' promise that "the conclusion of the system of things" is near at hand (*Mt.* 24:3, NWT). As ruler of the kingdom Jesus will separate all people on earth into loyal "sheep" and rebellious "goats" (*Mt.* 25:31–34). The faithful will enter paradise, a thousand years of peace and harmony in a restored earth. All of those who opposed Jehovah's kingdom will not be resurrected and so will cease to exist. The dead who did not hear the gospel during their lives will be resurrected to join the "great crowd." At the end of the millennium, Satan will be released briefly to test all those on earth. Those who succumb to Satan's temptation will suffer "the second death" (*Rv.* 20:14–15) or annihilation. Only those who persevere in faith will be rewarded with eternal life.

WORSHIP. Jehovah's Witnesses meet several times a week in buildings with spare furnishings called Kingdom Halls. Services consist of serious study of the Bible using Watchtower literature and of training in techniques of promoting their teachings in local neighborhoods. Worship also involves singing hymns, written in a distinctive doctrinal vocabulary and sung to recorded music supplied by the Watchtower Society. All members are expected to "publish" their beliefs by door-to-door visitation. Those who spend fifteen hours a week in fieldwork are called "regular pioneers," whereas those who devote more time are designated "special pioneers." In 2002 Jehovah's Witnesses collectively recorded over one billion hours of service. To supply them with material, the Watchtower Society invests heavily in communications technology. The publishing center in Brooklyn annually produces millions of copies of the *Watchtower* (which is translated into 146 languages) and *Awake!* (printed in 87 versions). Jehovah's Witnesses do not broadcast on television, but the Watchtower Society maintains an official site on the World Wide Web.

Jehovah's Witnesses observe two rituals: water baptism and the Lord's Supper. They baptize only adults who have qualified by extended study. Baptisms are performed by public immersion, often at annual district conventions, as a sign of dedication to kingdom work. The Lord's Evening Meal, also called the Memorial, is observed once a year on Passover eve. The 2002 *Yearbook* reported that 8,760 of the anointed class partook of the "emblems" of bread and wine, and nearly 16 million attended the Memorial.

PRACTICES. Jehovah's Witnesses do not celebrate Christmas, Easter, or birthdays because they are associated with pagan celebrations. They abstain from tobacco and drugs and use alcohol in strict moderation, as required by the Bible. They denounce gambling because it is motivated by the sin of greed. Their sexual ethic forbids homosexuality, adultery, and premarital sex; abortion and some forms of birth control are also proscribed. Following the biblical injunction to "separate yourselves . . . quit touching the unclean thing" (*2 Cor.* 6:17, NWT), Jehovah's Witnesses shun occult practices, such as magic, divination, and necromancy.

While Jehovah's Witnesses respect secular authorities (*Rom.* 13:1), they imitate Jesus in maintaining strict neutrality toward human governments, refusing to serve in the military, pledge allegiance to national flags, or serve in public office. For their dissent they have been imprisoned in many countries, and in Nazi Germany they were consigned to concentration camps. However, they do not call themselves pacifists, mainly because they believe in the righteous war Christ will wage against worldly governments at Armageddon. Their right to refuse to engage in patriotic demonstrations was upheld by the Supreme Court in the case of *Barnette vs. West Virginia* (1943), which excused Jehovah's Witnesses schoolchildren from saluting the flag. That victory is one among many through which Jehovah's Witnesses have secured more civil rights by legal challenge than any other American religious group.

Jehovah's Witnesses place a high value on strong families. While women are not prevented from working outside the home, they are expected to fulfill traditional roles as wives and mothers. Watchtower Society publications also instruct husbands to respect and honor their wives. At the same time, women are excluded from leadership on the basis of biblical prohibitions against women speaking in church (*1 Cor.* 14:34–35) and the denial of permission for a woman "to teach or to have authority over a man" (*1 Tm.* 2:11–12).

Perhaps the most controversial Watchtower Society policy is the prohibition of intravenous blood transfusion, first made binding in 1945. Jehovah's Witnesses interpret the apostolic command to "abstain . . . from blood" (*Acts* 15:20) as unconditional because any means of taking blood into the body violates the principle that the "life (soul) is in the blood" (*Gn.* 9:4, *Lv.* 17:11). Transfusions of one's own blood are not allowed because storage would violate the Bible's command that the blood of a sacrifice must be poured on the earth "as water" (*Dt.* 12:16). Kidney dialysis is permitted as long as the blood circulates continuously through the filtering apparatus and returns to the patient's body. Since 1978, hemophiliacs have been allowed to choose treatment with blood components. Questions of parents' right to refuse transfusions for their children and of a pregnant woman to refuse transfusion that might save her life and that of her fetus, however, continued to challenge hospital ethics committees and courts in the early twenty-first century.

Jehovah's Witnesses maintain apocalyptic expectation of the imminent end of the world, a strict separation from popular culture, and adherence to a rigorous moral code, while abandoning attempts to set specific dates for the coming kingdom. The reorganization of the Watchtower Society separated religious from temporal authority, but critics continue to object to the conformity of thinking and behavior required by Watchtower Society teachings. Former Witnesses who have lost contact with family members through disfellowshipping bear bitter testimony to their experiences. While such exclusionary discipline strengthens group loyalty, it provides little opportunity for the free exchange of ideas that enables many religious movements to adapt creatively to changing historical conditions.

SEE ALSO Law and Religion, overview article; Millenarianism, overview article.

BIBLIOGRAPHY

The most important primary sources are official publications by the Watchtower Bible and Tract Society of New York. Besides the annual *Yearbook of Jehovah's Witnesses,* important works are *You Can Live Forever in Paradise on Earth* (Brooklyn, N.Y., 1982); *Revelation—Its Grand Climax at Hand!* (Brooklyn, N.Y., 1988); *Insight on the Scriptures* (Brooklyn, N.Y., 1988); *Jehovah's Witnesses: Proclaimers of God's Kingdom* (Brooklyn, N.Y., 1993), a compendium of the history, teaching, and organization of Jehovah's Witnesses that is free of the polemical tone of earlier writings; *Knowledge That Leads to Everlasting Life* (Brooklyn, N.Y., 1995); and *Worship the Only True God* (Brooklyn, N.Y., 2002). The Watchtower Society maintains a World Wide Website at http://www.watchtower.org, which includes current *Watchtower* articles. The complete works of Charles Taze Russell are available online from http://www.heraldmag.org. Jerry Bergman compiled a list of resources in *Jehovah's Witnesses: A Comprehensive and Selectively Annotated Bibliography* (Westport, Conn., 1999), and David A. Reed made a nonsympathetic survey in *Jehovah's Witness Literature: A Critical Guide to Watchtower Publications* (Grand Rapids, Mich., 1993). Herbert Hewitt Stroup wrote an early account that is analytical and scholarly in tone, *The Jehovah's Witnesses* (New York, 1945; reprint, 1967). Melvin D. Curry assessed academic scholarship in *Jehovah's Witnesses: The Millenarian World of the Watch Tower* (New York, 1992). James A. Beckford's *The Trumpet of Prophecy: A Sociological Study of Jehovah's Witnesses* (New York, 1975) analyzes the organization and ideology of the Watch Tower Society in Britain. Andrew Holden provides an ethnographic study in *Jehovah's Witnesses: Portrait of a Contemporary Religious Movement* (New York, 2002). Paul K. Conkin places Jehovah's Witnesses in the context of other forms of apocalyptic Christianity in *American Originals: Homemade Varieties of Christianity* (Chapel Hill, N.C., 1997), chap. 3. David L. Weddle, "A New 'Generation' of Jehovah's Witnesses: Revised Interpretation, Ritual, and Identity," *Nova Religio* 3, no. 2 (April 2000): 350–367, investigates the 1995 change in the status of the anointed class. William Kaplan traces the history of court cases in *State and Salvation: The Jehovah's Witnesses and Their Fight for Civil Rights* (Toronto, 1989).

Jehovah's Witnesses have drawn pejorative comment in many published studies, particularly by former members. See, for example, William J. Schnell, *Thirty Years a Watch Tower Slave: The Confessions of a Converted Jehovah's Witness* (Grand Rapids, Mich., 1956), and Heather Botting and Gary Botting, *The Orwellian World of Jehovah's Witnesses* (Toronto, 1984). David A. Reed has attacked both the teachings and the practices of the Watchtower Society in several books, including *Blood on the Altar: Confessions of a Jehovah's Witness Minister* (Amherst, N.Y., 1996). Two accounts by former members that provide more balanced reflections on the nature of their original commitments and eventual disappointments are Barbara Grizzuti Harrison, *Visions of Glory: A History and a Memory of Jehovah's Witnesses* (New York, 1978), and M. James Penton, *Apocalypse Delayed: The Story of Jehovah's Witnesses* (Toronto, 1985). For a revealing look inside the Watchtower Society, see Raymond Franz's account of his disfellowshipping as a member of the Governing Body in *Crisis of Conscience: The Struggle between Loyalty to God and Loyalty to One's Religion* (Atlanta, 1983). Greg Stafford mounts a detailed and reasoned response to critics in *Jehovah's Witnesses Defended: An Answer to Scholars and Critics*, 2d ed. (Huntington Beach, Calif., 2000).

David L. Weddle (2005)

JEN AND I See REN AND YI

JENSEN, ADOLF E.

JENSEN, ADOLF E. Adolf Ellegard Jensen (1899–1965) was a German ethnologist and historian of religions. He was born January 1, 1899, in Kiel. After World War I, Jensen studied mathematics, natural science, and philosophy at the universities of Bonn and Kiel. He received a doctorate in 1922 with a dissertation on the writings on natural philosophy of Ernst Mach (1838–1916) and Max Plank (1858–1947).

In the following year, Jensen took a position as research assistant at Leo Frobenius's newly founded Institute for Cultural Morphology in Munich. This position proved to be a turning point in Jensen's scientific ambitions, which from then on were directed toward the ethnological perspectives of Frobenius. When the institute was moved to Frankfurt in 1925, Jensen became a recognized lecturer at the university there. His thesis, "Beschneidung und Reifezeremonien bei Naturvölkern" (Circumcision and puberty rites among primitive peoples), was completed in 1933.

After the death of Leo Frobenius in 1938, Jensen was named director of the Institute for Cultural Morphology, which was eventually renamed for its founder. Also in 1938, Jensen succeeded Frobenius as director of the Municipal Ethnological Museum in Frankfurt, where he had served as curator since 1936. In 1946 Jensen received a chair in the University of Frankfurt's newly established department of cultural and ethnological studies. He directed research expeditions to South Africa (1928–1930), Libya (1932), Ethiopia (1934–1935, 1950–1951, and 1954–1955), and the Moluccan island of Ceram (1937). The works that grew out of these research trips proved decisive in influencing the structure of cultural history and morphology studies in the tradition founded by Frobenius.

In his work *Das religiöse Weltbild einer frahen Kultur* (1948) Jensen presented an array of complex cultural factors that, although widely dispersed, create the impression of sharing elements common to one central myth. The content of this myth reveals information about human existence as well as about the formation of essential cultural elements. According to this myth complex, which relates the activities of a tribe of *dema* (ancestral) deities, the body of a murdered deity was, in primeval times, transformed into the first useful plants. The present order of existence, in which man became a reproductive and mortal being, was then established. In this myth and its cultic form of expression, Jensen saw the nucleus of a worldview that was the ancient predecessor of that of the more advanced cultures, in which tubers were planted as a food crop. He maintained that contemporary "primitive" cultures could be viewed as living an earlier phase of human development, a fact that facilitates a reconstruction of the rise of culture.

Often honored for his work, Jensen was a member of various scholarly societies and was an honorary fellow of the Royal Anthropological Institute of Great Britain and Ireland. He died at his retirement home in Mammolsheim on May 20, 1965.

DISCUSSION OF THE *DEMA*. The ethnological research of Jensen attracted the attention of the Hungarian classicist, Károly Kerényi, who discovered remarkable similarities between the Indonesian myth of the girl Rabie-Hainuwele and that of the Greek Kore (a name that actually means young girl). In his opinion these similarities lay in the link between death and fertility that existed in both mythological systems. Just as Persephone is taken from her mother Demeter and carried off to Hades, from where she rises again in the form of vegetation on a cyclical basis, Hainuwele, whose name means Coconut Branch, is consigned to the ground during a ritual dance and the parts of her body thus buried are changed into tubers, which became the main food of the Ceramese.

According to Kerényi (1940–1941), who used the 1939 work of Jensen and H. Niggermeyer, this is an extremely widespread mythological theme, according to which the introduction of death into the world of man, coinciding with the movement from the mythological state to the present, leads to reproductive capability. Just as edible plants spring from the initial murder, so a new life comes about from every death, in the same way as in the lunar cycle the moon always disappears only in order to reappear again.

The myth complex, centered upon the character of the *dema* (the ancestors of the Marind-Anim of southern New Guinea), would have developed within a cultural context that Jensen calls "lunar," in which there was a more primitive form of the agriculture than the cereal cultivation that took place subsequently. In those societies that engaged in such economic activity, on the other hand, there would be a different idea of life (another *paideuma* as Frobenius would describe it), based on the Promethean myth of a demiurge who steals the seeds of grain from heaven for mankind.

The work that best illustrates Jensen's philosophy is *Mythos und Kult bei Naturvölkern* (1951) (*Myth and Cult among Primitive Peoples*, 1963), a collection of his most important contributions. A review of this work by a number of scholars was published in *Current Anthropology* in 1963 and provides a useful evaluation of the contribution of Jensen from both a methodological and ethnological perspective. For his own part, he states that the main assumption of his work is to regard the human being as invariably possessing the same spiritual and emotional capacities within different historical contexts, technical progress having no bearing on religious experience.

Furthermore, Jensen considers that myth and cult are derived from a creative act, and the agent does not address the question of its purpose nor reason logically in terms of cause and effect. In his opinion, man is interested in understanding the world, the place of the human being within it, and at the same time seeks to fit in with the order of reality, as he perceives and describes it. Mythological ideas are not an alternative to scientific explanations, but on the contrary seem to answer questions to which there could be no other response: Why are living beings mortal? Why do they reproduce?

These methodological assumptions, which characterize the opinions of his master Frobenius, are not shared by other writers. For example, Angelo Brelich (1963) criticizes the idea that the original religious behavior could represent the expression of an instinctive idea of the world, to which mankind would be attracted without subsequently remembering its meaning. This was why, according to Jensen, it had no purpose originally and would, over time, be changed into a repetitive way of behaving. In contrast, Brelich insists that religious institutions do have a purpose, even if believers are unaware of it, and that one can identify this by reestablishing the link between the social context and the religious life. In his opinion, Jensen's mistake lies in claiming to appreciate the present meaning of religious life on the basis of a past for which there is no evidence.

Carl A. Schmitz (1963) notes that Jensen is a Platonist and his work cannot be assessed with positivist argument because he suggests understanding some original religious ideas as implicitly contained in myth. Schmitz does not, however, share Jensen's view that the relation of tubers, the killing of the *dema* and the cereals, and the theft undertaken by a hero to the harming of a divine goddess would belong to different historical phases and occurred one after another. Furthermore, in his view, reasoning of this kind implies a materialist idea of religion, contrary to the thinking of Jensen himself.

Other criticisms were put forward by Ugo Bianchi (1971, p. 87), who emphasized that Jensen mistakenly made the *dema* the exclusive motif of a particular culture, linking it also with headhunting and ritual cannibalism, which were related to other cultural phenomena as well. Besides, according to Bianchi, his emphasis on the specific nature of the essential character of a culture—the contents of which were only accessible from within—led him to a kind of irrationalism. Vittorio Lanternari (1963) also identifies irrationalist themes in Jensen.

In a work published in 1968, however, Ileana Chirassi agreed with Jensen and contrasted the great agricultural myths of Bronze Age society, based around polytheistic gods such as Tammuz, Osiris, and Baal, with the myths of the *dema* known from the tuber planters, dating back to the late Paleolithic period (southern Asia), myths which can also be traced back in figures of Greek religion.

The work of Jonathan Z. Smith (1976) is central to discussion on the *dema*. He compares the Hainuwele myth to the Babylonian festival of Akitu, celebrated in order to reestablish proper political and cosmological order. In his opinion, the two religious complexes are similar in structure, because they are used in order to change a difficult and paradoxical situation. The Ceramese, colonized by the Dutch, got to know all about the possessions and strange goods of the Europeans, and they understood that relations were not based upon reciprocity. They lived in a *cargo situation*, developed in many parts of Oceania in the aftermath of colonization. In order to reverse this situation and restore reciprocity, they reverted to an ancient mythological theme, in which mythical beings were killed and hitherto unknown foods were produced by them, eaten, and thus assimilated within their culture. The same happens with Hainuwele, who excretes precious objects such as plates and Chinese gongs. In this myth the girl is killed and her body, from which come many precious objects like the European goods, is eaten as tubers, in the hope of transforming the goods into food that can be assimilated into the culture using the symbolism of ingestion. According to Smith (1976, p. 19) we should see in these religious motifs an attempt—albeit inadequate—to reach an understanding of (and change) a context or model that contradicts the previous historical situation.

Dario Sabbatucci (1986) once again goes through the theoretical explanation of Jensen in order to demonstrate the arbitrary nature of his conclusions. In particular, he claims that the discoverer of the *dema* interpreted foreign cultural phenomena on the basis of assumptions similar to institutions of the modern Western world. After all, the *dema* would thus have no existence per se, it would simply represent a restatement of the *dying god* of Frazer, and there would be no proof that it predated the latter nor that cereal cultivation derived from tuber cultivation (1986, pp. 322–323).

Ileana Chirassi (2001) has compared the mythical events of various Mediterranean deities as interpreted in the light of the Frazerian pattern of the dying and rising god, comparable to *dema*. From this comparison, based upon an accurate analysis of the various contexts, the conclusion is reached—as Chirassi writes, recalling Sabbatucci—that these events are diverse: the god may die or depart, but is not always linked to vegetation or dismembered, nor does he always rise again. Such details open debate concerning the category of the *dying god,* even to the extent of speculating on deconstructing it completely.

SEE ALSO Agriculture; Ecology and Religion, overview article; Food; Frobenius, Leo; Myth, overview article; Vegetation.

BIBLIOGRAPHY

"Book Review: *Myth and Cult Among Primitive Peoples*" in *Current Anthropology* 6 no. 2 (1963): 199–215, includes reviews of Jensen's work by Angelo Brelich, Ugo Bianchi, Carl A. Schmitz, Ake Hultkrantz, Vittorio Lanternari, Paul Leser, Egon Schaden, and others.

Bianchi, Ugo. "La storia delle religioni. Introduzione metodologica e storica." In *Storia delle religioni,* edited by Giuseppe Castellani, vol. 1, pp. 3–171. Turin, Italy. 1971.

Chirassi, Ileana. *Elementi di culture precereali nei miti e riti greci.* Rome, 1968.

Chirassi, Ileana. "Postfazione." In *Quando un dio muore: Morti e assenze divine nelle antiche tradizioni mediterranee,* edited by P. Xella, pp. 199–207. Verona, Italy, 2001.

Jung, Carl Gustav and Kerényi, Karoly. *Einführung in das Wesen der Mythologie.* Amsterdam and Leipzig, 1940.

Jensen, Adolf E. *Im Lande des Gada.* Stuttgart, Germany, 1936.

Jensen, Adolf E. *Die drei Ströme; Zage aus dem geistigen und religiösen Leben der Wemale.* Leipzig, 1948.

Jensen, Adolf E. *Das religiöse Weltbild einer frühen Kultur.* Stuttgart, Germany, 1948.

Jensen, Adolf E. *Mythos und Kult bei Naturvölkern.* Wiesbaden, Germany, 1951. Translated as *Myth and Cult among Primitive Peoples* (1969; 2nd ed., Chicago).

Jensen, Adolf E. *Altvölker Süd-Äthiopiens.* Stuttgart, Germany, 1959.

Sabbatucci, Dario. *Il dema. Mistica agraria e demistificazione.* Rome, 1986.

Schmitz, Carl A. "Die Problematik der mythologema 'Hainuwele' und 'Prometheus.'" *Anthropos* 55 (1960): 215–238.

Schmitz, Carl A. "Adolf Ellegard Jensen." *Paideuma* 11(1965): 1–7.

Smith, Jonathan Z. "A Pearl of Great Price and a Cargo of Yams: a Study in Situational Incongruity." *History of Religions* 16, no. 1 (1976): 1–19. Reprinted in *Imagining Religion.* Chicago, 1982. See pages 90–101.

OTTO ZERRIES (1987)
ALESSANDRA CIATTINI (2005)
Translated from Italian by Paul Ellis

JEREMIAH

JEREMIAH (c. 640–580 BCE), or, in Hebrew, Yirmeyah(u); biblical prophet. Jeremiah, son of Hilkiah, was born in Anathoth, some 3 miles (4.8 km) northeast of Jerusalem. The English name *Jeremiah* is based on the Greek *Hieremias* from the Septuagint and not on the received Hebrew Masoretic text. The Septuagint reflects a correct original Hebrew *Yarim-Yahu* ("Yahveh grants"), a name type whose antecedents can be traced to the third millennium BCE.

THE BOOK OF JEREMIAH AND THE BIOGRAPHY OF JEREMIAH. Most of our knowledge about Jeremiah's life comes from the biblical *Book of Jeremiah.* The book is not arranged chronologically, with the result that contemporary scholarly reconstructions of the prophet's life are highly subjective. Important background information is found in the Hebrew scriptures, in *1 Kings, 2 Kings, 2 Chronicles, Zephaniah, Nahum, Habakkuk,* and *Obadiah.* Other important sources are the Hebrew letters from Lachish, primary documents from Egypt and Mesopotamia, and the histories of Herodotos and Josephus Flavius. However, *2 Kings,* which describes in great detail events contemporary with Jeremiah, does not mention him.

Later generations regarded Jeremiah very highly. According to the Chronicler, the prophet was the author of a lament over Josiah, king of Judah (*2 Chr.* 35:25). His prophecies about the duration of the exile were cited in *2 Chronicles* 36:15–21 and by the author of the ninth chapter of *Daniel.* Later writers composed pious fictions about Jeremiah. The apocryphal *Letter of Jeremiah,* allegedly written by Jeremiah to the Jewish exiles in Babylonia, is styled in the manner of *Jeremiah* 29. According to the second chapter of *2 Maccabees,* Jeremiah secreted the ark and Tabernacle, a tradition based on *Jeremiah* 3:16. In the New Testament, Jeremiah is named in *Matthew* 2:17, and his vision of the "new covenant" (*Jer.*

31:31–34; cf. *Jer.* 32:38–40) is quoted in *Hebrews* 8:8–12 and 10:16–17. Jewish Talmudic tradition (B.T., *B.B.* 15a) ascribes to the prophet the authorship of *Jeremiah*, *Kings*, and *Lamentations* (the last probably on the basis of *2 Chronicles* 35:25).

Jeremiah was of priestly stock (*Jer.* 1:1) and probably of the Abiathar family, which had been banished to Anathoth by Solomon (c. 960) and had served at the Shiloh sanctuary before 1050. Yet there is no indication that Jeremiah ever functioned as a priest. Nonetheless, he generally had free access to the Temple and its chambers (*Jer.* 35:4). Apparently he was well off. He was able to spend seventeen shekels to buy a piece of property as a symbolic act (*Jer.* 32:9), and he was able to hire as a personal secretary one Baruch, son of Neriah, who thought the job would be lucrative and whose own brother was a high official (*Jer.* 45:2–5, 51:59). In addition, during the reigns of Jehoiakim (609–598) and Zedekiah (597-586), Jeremiah's counsel was regularly sought by the kings and their advisers. The powerful Shaphan family was particularly close to him (*Jer.* 26:24, 29:3, 36:10–12, 39:14, 40:5), and the Babylonian conquerors offered him special protection (*Jer.* 40:1–6). The high-ranking avengers of Gedaliah, son of Ahikam, sought him out as well, although they disregarded his counsel and forced him to accompany them to Egypt (*Jer.* 42). Perhaps a further indication of his affluence and influence is his relative lack of concern for the poor. Although he demanded justice for the oppressed (*Jer.* 7:6, 22:16), his denunciations of their suffering at the hands of the rich and powerful are not as frequent or as fervent as those of the prophets Amos and Isaiah. Josiah is praised as one who "ate and drank" at the same time as he dispensed justice and equity (*Jer.* 22:15). No particular class in society is singled out for condemnation (*Jer.* 5:1–5).

Among the details of his life, we hear that Jeremiah did not marry (*Jer.* 16:1–4), that he avoided social gatherings (*Jer.* 16:5–9), that he perceived himself as a man of strife and contention (*Jer.* 15:10), that he wished he had never been born (*Jer.* 20:15–17), and that his relatives had attempted to kill him (*Jer.* 10:21, 11:6), as had Jehoiakim (*Jer.* 36:26), the audience in the Temple court (*Jer.* 26:24), and some of Zedekiah's ministers (*Jer.* 38:4–6). Sometime after 586 Jeremiah and his amanuensis were forcibly taken to Egypt, which is probably where he died.

It is difficult to treat Jeremiah's thought systematically for a number of reasons. First, Israelite prophets did not write systematic treatises. Second, the textual history of the book is very complicated. The present book is found in two major recensions, the Masoretic text and the Septuagint, which is about one-eighth shorter. In addition to the divergence in size, the recensions differ in arrangement. The Masoretic text of *Jeremiah* consists of prophecies directed to Jeremiah's own people (*Jer.* 1–25), narratives about him (*Jer.* 26–45), prophecies directed to the Gentiles (*Jer.* 46–51), and a historical appendix (*Jer.* 52). The Septuagint, in contrast, places the oracles to the Gentiles in the middle of the book, following chapter 25, verse 13. The Hebrew fragments of *Jeremiah* from Qumran demonstrate that in the late pre-Christian era, the Hebrew text was circulating in shorter and longer forms. It is not always certain whether the longer is an expansion or the shorter an abridgment. In both recensions, there is material that can hardly be from the hand of the prophet. For example, the prophecy against Damascus (*Jer.* 49:23–27) dates from the eighth century BCE. Other sections, such as *Jeremiah* 33:14–16 (not found in the Septuagint), are later additions. In this same category are *Jeremiah* 15:4b, which attempts to harmonize Jeremiah's theology with that of *2 Kings* by blaming the fall on Manasseh, and the injunction to keep the Sabbath (*Jer.* 18:21–27), which recalls *Nehemiah* 10:15–21. Other suspicious prophecies are the Edomite oracle (*Jer.* 49:7–16; cf. *Ob.*) and the Moabite oracle (*Jer.* 48:45–46; cf. *Nm.* 21:28–29).

Some clues to the book's composition are provided in the text itself. In each case, a religious motivation is given. According to *Jeremiah* 30:2–3, which begins the section generally known as "The Little Book of Consolation," Jeremiah was told by Yahveh: "Commit to writing all the words I have spoken to you, for days are coming when I will restore the fortunes of my people . . . and bring them back to the land." The prophecies were to be written so that later generations would know that all had been foretold. Unfortunately, no date is given for this action. The prophecies themselves contain genuine Jeremianic utterances as well as later interpolations. More specific information is provided in *Jeremiah* 36, which is dated to the fourth year of the reign of Jehoiakim, synchronized in *Jeremiah* 25:1 with 605 BCE, the first regnal year of Nebuchadrezzar II, king of Babylon (605–562). In that year Yahveh commanded Jeremiah, "Get a scroll and write in it all the words concerning Israel, Judah and all the nations that I have spoken to you, from the days of Josiah until now. Perhaps when the house of Judah hear all the terrible designs I have on them they will turn away from their wicked ways so that I might pardon their wicked sins" (*Jer.* 36:2–3). The specific reason for writing the prophecies of twenty-three years was to demonstrate to the people that they had been warned early and frequently and that there was still time to avert disaster. Though Jeremiah knew how to write (*Jer.* 32:10), he found a secretary, Baruch. By the ninth month of Jehoiakim's fifth year, at the latest (*Jer.* 36:9), the scroll was complete. It was read three times on a public fast day. First Baruch read it to a crowd at the Temple (*Jer.* 36:10) and then to a group of royal officials (*Jer.* 36:15). Finally, it was read to King Jehoiakim, who destroyed it section by section (*Jer.* 36:22–23). The scroll probably contained no more than ten thousand words.

After the destruction of the original scroll, Jeremiah purchased a second, on which Baruch rewrote the destroyed prophecies. To this scroll were added prophecies similar in content to the original ones (*Jer.* 36:32). The text gives no information about the time period in which this second edition was produced. Our present book of Jeremiah most likely had its origin in this edition.

Historical Background and the Prophet's Position. It is impossible to understand the man Jeremiah or his prophecies apart from the turbulent historical period in which he lived. When Jeremiah was born, the Assyrian empire was the single most important political power in the Middle East and, consequently, in the life of the southern kingdom of Judah. By the time Jeremiah was in his early thirties, Assyria had disappeared as a political entity, and Judah's fate had become contingent on Egypt and on the Neo-Babylonian empire and its allies. Before Jeremiah turned sixty, Judah had lost its political independence entirely, and the prophet himself had become part of the Jewish Diaspora in Egypt.

Assyrian foreign policy had been important to Judah as early as the ninth century BCE, but the fall of the closely related northern kingdom of Israel and the establishment of the Assyrian province of Samaria on Judah's northern border was momentous. Judah maintained nominal political autonomy by becoming an Assyrian vassal, an arrangement that required the regular payment of tribute and the provision of troops for Assyrian campaigns. Between 720 and 627, Judah's political policy was very much in the Assyrian shadow. King Hezekiah of Judah (715–686) had attempted a revolt in collaboration with the Babylonian king Merodach-baladan II (Marduk-apal-iddina, 721–710) and with Egypt and various Philistine and Phoenician cities. The forces of the Assyrian king Sennacherib (704–681) quashed the rebellion, although they failed to take Jerusalem and left Hezekiah on his throne with a smaller domain and a larger tribute obligation.

If Jerusalem's deliverance appeared miraculous to some (*Is.* 37:33–38), it had a different moral for Manasseh, son and successor of Hezekiah. For most, and perhaps all, of his long reign (c. 692–639), Manasseh was a loyal Assyrian vassal. According to *2 Kings* 21:11, he was equally loyal in the service of foreign gods, outdoing everyone, the aboriginal Amorites included, in idolatry and wickedness. Some scholars have argued that Manasseh's religious and political policies were closely related, and have understood the worship of foreign gods as Assyrian vassal obligations. More recently, however, it has been noted that Assyria generally did not impose its forms of worship on its vassals. Even if we understand Manasseh's paganism as a somewhat voluntary attempt to curry favor with Assyria, we must keep in mind that the majority of the cults introduced or encouraged during his reign were not Assyrian (*2 Kgs.* 21:2–7). The bloodiness of his reign (*2 Kgs.* 21:16) surely reflects internal struggles, but we cannot tell what these concerned. Manasseh's death brought to the throne his son Amon, who was assassinated in a palace revolt of unknown motivation (*2 Kgs.* 21:23).

Amon's assassins were slain by *'am ha-arets* ("people of the land"), an influential body of Judahites who put on the throne his young son Josiah. The biblical books *2 Kings* (22-23) and *2 Chronicles* (34–35) have only praise for Josiah and devote much attention to his religious reforms, though each gives a different account. According to *2 Kings*, Josiah's reforms were initiated by Hilkiah's discovery of "the book of the *torah*" in the Jerusalem Temple (*2 Kgs.* 22:8). When the book, which is generally considered to be some form of *Deuteronomy*, was given by the scribe Shaphan to Josiah, the king rent his garments in contrition. In keeping with the book's message, the king centralized all sacrificial worship in the country, restricting it to Jerusalem. That same year (622 BCE), Josiah removed all traces of the foreign worship that Manasseh had encouraged. In addition, he abolished ancient rituals and institutions, which he considered antithetical to the cult of Yahveh.

In contrast, the Chronicler depicts a gradual reform in which important steps were taken in the king's eighth and twelfth years. Though chronologically more attractive, in this scheme the book is discovered in 622, by which time the major elements of the reform had been accomplished, with the exception of binding all the people of Judah by covenant to obey the book's provisions.

The wisest course is to combine elements from both our sources. The reforms must have been implemented gradually. At the same time, "the book of the *torah* [of the covenant]" must have been available at an early stage of the reform, when its reading would have had the greatest effect (cf. *Jeremiah* 36:24 with *2 Kings* 23:11). This is likely because, in the opinion of most current scholarship, the kernel of *Deuteronomy* was a northern Israelite work that had been brought to Judah after 720 BCE.

The political motivations for the Josianic reform have occasioned much debate. Some scholars have viewed the reform as a religious expression of anti-Assyrian nationalism; they have noted especially that Josiah destroyed the altar at Bethel, which was in Assyrian territory. Other scholars have remarked that neither *2 Kings* nor *2 Chronicles* imputes anti-Assyrian rebellion to Josiah, though both books describe revolts by "good" and "bad" kings of Israel and Judah (*2 Kgs.* 18:7, 24:1, 24:20; *2 Chr.* 32:10–11, 36:13). It is likely that Josiah's destruction of the Bethel altar had the motive of consolidating Davidic rule, for its original construction had been with the opposite intent (*1 Kgs.* 12:26–29, 13:2), but this could have been done with Assyrian acquiescence.

The role of Jeremiah in the Josianic reform has aroused much controversy. Some scholars depict the prophet as an early, ardent proponent of the reform who became disillusioned. At the other extreme, some scholars have revised the chronology of the prophet's life so that he begins to prophesy only after the death of Josiah in 609. If the Chronicler's chronology of the reform is accepted, then Jeremiah would have been an unlikely choice to consult about the book because of his tender age, and the prophetess Huldah a better candidate (*2 Kgs.* 22:14). It appears that sometime in the mid-twenties of the seventh century, during the reign of Josiah, whom he considered a just and righteous king (*Jer.* 22:12–15), Jeremiah preached "return" (repentance) to the northerners (*Jer.* 3:6, 3:11–18; cf. 31:2–23). If so, then he must have been enthusiastic at the outset, only to be disappointed later.

It is probably correct to say that for Jeremiah, the people's return could never be sufficient. He was too much of an idealist. He considers Judah's return to Yahveh "deceitful" (*Jer.* 3:10), whereas the people complain, "I have been cleansed. Surely his anger is turned away from me. . . . Will he be angry forever? Will he rage for all time?" (*Jer.* 2:35, 3:5). The author of *2 Kings* 23 is in fundamental agreement with the people rather than with Jeremiah. According to *2 Kings*, Josiah "returned to Yahveh with all his heart and soul and might, in complete accord with the teaching of Moses" (23:25). There is no indication that Josiah's contemporaries had not done enough or had been deceitful. Instead, the verse following says that although Josiah had repented (*shav*), Yahveh had not repented of his anger, because of the sins of Manasseh. For the writer of *2 Kings*, Manasseh's generation was so irredeemably wicked that the following generations were doomed no matter how they acted (*2 Kgs.* 21:1–16).

Some of Jeremiah's contemporaries expressed this same pessimistic attitude in the proverb "The ancestors ate sour grapes but the children's teeth are clean" (*Jer.* 31:29; cf. *Ez.* 18:1). That is, they believed that because the ancestors ate forbidden food, their children go hungry. But Jeremiah disagrees. He believes that his contemporaries are worse because they have returned (*shavu*) to the ancestral sins after supposedly repudiating them, and thus have broken the ancient covenant that demanded Yahveh's exclusive worship (*Jer.* 11:9–10, 16:10–12). The notion that returning to sin after allegedly repenting is worse than sinning without repentance is characteristic of Jeremiah. In *Jeremiah* 34, for example, the prophet rebukes the people who had first reinstated the provision for the release of Hebrew slaves under the leadership of Zedekiah, but then turned around (*va-yashuvu*) and enslaved them a second time.

The sin of insincere repentance underlies Jeremiah's attitude toward the cult of his time. Josiah's reforms had made the Jerusalem Temple the only legitimate Yahvistic shrine in the country, so that it could truly be called "Yahveh's palace" (*Jer.* 7:4) by the people, echoing the prophecies of the eighth-century prophet Isaiah (*Is.* 2:1–4, 31:4-5, 37:32–35). In contrast, Jeremiah taught, as had others (*Jer.* 26:18–20), that the Temple was not inviolable, nor was it any more permanent than the anciently destroyed Shiloh sanctuary (*Jer.* 7:14). Probably at the same time, he made the statement, "Add your whole burnt offerings to your other sacrifices and eat the meat. For when I brought your ancestors out of Egypt I did not speak with them to command them about burnt offerings and sacrifices. This rather is what I commanded them: Hearken to my voice so that I can be your God and you can be my people" (*Jer.* 7:21–22).

It would be inaccurate to say that Jeremiah advocated a cultless religion. He did not disagree that the Temple is God's place. Indeed, if the people mend their ways, then Yahveh will dwell with them in the Jerusalem Temple (*Jer.* 7:3, 7:7). But, for a number of reasons, the people's offerings are not "pleasing" (*Jer.* 6:20); the word used, *leratson*, is a technical term for an acceptable sacrifice (see also *Leviticus* 1:3, 19:5, 22:29; *Isaiah* 56:7). Most important, the popular view had it that other gods might be worshiped by Israelites as long as their worship of Yahveh was in purity. As Jeremiah says in his indictment, "Will you steal and murder and commit adultery and swear falsely and sacrifice to Baal and follow other gods with whom you have no [rightful] relation and then come and stand before me in this house which is called by my name and say 'we are saved' and then continue to commit all these abominations?" (*Jer.* 7:9–10).

It is clear that the people believed the cult could purify them of all their sins. If such violations as theft, murder, adultery, and false oaths could succumb to purificatory rituals, why could not the worship of foreign gods? In fact, such temporary rejection of foreign gods is ascribed to Jacob (*Gn.* 35:4) and to Joshua (*Jos.* 24). According to *Leviticus* 16:30, the priesthood claimed that its atonement rituals could remove all impurity caused by sin. (A priesthood could hardly claim otherwise.) Jeremiah did not accept this view because he saw it as insincere. In his eyes, Israel had been faithful to Yahveh only in the wilderness (*Jer.* 2:1). The people strayed as soon as they entered the promised land and so profaned it (*Jer.* 2:8, 3:2). Borrowing an image from Hosea, Jeremiah depicts the people of Judah as a faithless wife who had pretended to mend her ways (*Jer.* 3:1ff.). She knows that Yahveh has divorced the northern kingdom of Israel for infidelity (*Jer.* 3:8), but her heart is still uncircumcised (*Jer.* 4:4, 9:25). The entire people is guilty, for none has practiced true repentance—neither priests, teachers, kings, nor prophets (*Jer.* 2:8, 21:11–23:5, 23:9–40, 27–29). Jeremiah's mission is to bring the people to true repentance (*Jer.* 3:14, 3:22, 4:1). If he fails, then destruction of the land is inevitable, and even the gentiles will know the cause (*Jer.* 22:8–9; cf. *Dt.* 29:21–29, *1 Kgs.* 9:8–9).

Compared with sincere repentance, the obligations of the cult are secondary. Inasmuch as Jeremiah agrees with Amos that there was no organized sacrificial cult in Israel's forty-year wandering in the desert (*Am.* 5:25), the covenant between Yahveh and his people could not have been made through the cult. Conversely, the cult must be insufficient to sustain the bond.

In the tradition of those prophets who influenced him, notably Hosea, the political events of his time were to Jeremiah an indication of Yahveh's disfavor. In his early prophecies, Yahveh's judgment was described as being through the agency of an unnamed northern foe. The kings of the north would come "and set their thrones at Jerusalem's gates," where Yahveh would pronounce sentence against Judah for serving other gods (*Jer.* 1:14–16). It does not seem that Jeremiah actually identified the northern foe as Babylon until the Babylonian victory over the Egyptians at Carchemish in Syria in 605 (cf. *Jer.* 36:29). It is also likely that the description of the Babylonian officers sitting in the gate in Jerusalem (*Jer.* 39:3) is a "fulfillment" of the early prophecy.

At first Jeremiah teaches that Yahveh's punishment of the people at the hands of their foes can be averted by true repentance. The death of Josiah and the accession of Jehoiakim to the throne mark a turning point. Jeremiah does not accuse Jehoiakim of the worship of foreign gods but of social abuses. The king was unjustly impressing laborers into service so that he could build himself a lavish palace. He was shedding innocent blood and perpetrating fraud and violence (*Jer.* 22:13–17). In consequence, predicted Jeremiah, perhaps inaccurately (*2 Kgs.* 24:6), Jehoiakim would have a donkey's funeral rather than a king's.

During Jehoiakim's reign, Jeremiah first began to commit his prophecies to writing in order to bring the people to repentance. Baruch was sent to read the scroll publicly in the Temple on a fast day (*Jer.* 36:9). The reading did not have the desired effect: Jehoiakim destroyed the scroll and attempted to kill Jeremiah and Baruch (*Jer.* 36:26) just as he had slain Uriah, who preached a similar message (*Jer.* 26:23). The writer of *Jeremiah* 36 remarks pointedly that Jehoiakim and his courtiers "showed no fear and did not tear their garments," in order to contrast Jehoiakim with his pious father, Josiah, who had torn his garments upon hearing Yahveh's word from a book (*2 Kgs.* 22:11, 22:19). Jehoiakim's unjust behavior, coupled with the rise of Babylon, was proof enough to Jeremiah that the required change of heart had not taken place, that Jehoiakim was not the man to bring it about, and that Yahveh would use Babylon to punish Judah, just as he had used Assyria to punish northern Israel.

In consequence, Jeremiah began to preach submission to Babylonia as Yahveh's will. This was particularly offensive to Jehoiakim, who had rebelled against Nebuchadrezzar II after three years of vassalage (*2 Kgs.* 23:26). The counsel of submission of Babylonia intensified after the death of Jehoiakim, in 597. Jehoiakin, Jehoiakim's son and successor, was deposed after three months, following a siege of Jerusalem. He and many other Judahites were deported. Jeremiah thought little of Jehoiakin and predicted that he would die in exile (*Jer.* 22:24–30).

In the reign of Zedekiah, the last king to occupy the throne of Judah, Jeremiah articulated Yahveh's plan. Yahveh had given all the lands over to Nebuchadrezzar and would punish those people who would not submit to Babylonian rule. Nebuchadrezzar was Yahveh's servant (*Jer.* 27:6) whose rule had been ordained for three generations (*Jer.* 27:7), or seventy years (*Jer.* 25:11). Those people who submitted to Nebuchadrezzar and, consequently, to Yahveh's word would be permitted by Yahveh to remain on their own land, while those who resisted would be exiled (*Jer.* 27:10–11). For Jeremiah, people like the Yahveh prophet Hananiah, son of Azzur, who preached the speedy return of Jeconiah, son of Jehoiakim, and the Temple vessels (*Jer.* 28:3–4) and who counseled rebellion were no better than the pagan diviners who offered the same message (*Jer.* 27:9, 27:15). Just as false were those prophets from Judah in Babylonia who taught that the exile would be short (*Jer.* 29:8–9). Yahveh had not sent them. The exiled Judahites should consider themselves "good figs" and should do Yahveh's will by building homes and families in Babylonia (*Jer.* 24:5, 29:4–7). Those people of Judah who had not been captured and exiled in 597 and who continued to resist Nebuchadrezzar were "bad figs." Flight to Egypt in order to escape Babylonian rule was just as bad, as far as Jeremiah was concerned (*Jer.* 24:8, 42:10–16). Yahveh himself had turned against Judah (*Jer.* 21:4–8). This meant that the "way of life" was surrender and the "way of death" was resistance (*Jer.* 21:8–10). Jeremiah's insistence on surrender landed him in the stocks (*Jer.* 20:1–6), caused him to be accused of treason and subversion, and nearly cost him his life (*Jer.* 38:3–6).

PESSIMISM AND HOPE IN JEREMIAH. The *Book of Jeremiah* provides more information about its subject's inner life than does any other biblical book. Even if some elements, such as the disinclination to prophecy, are felt elsewhere, they are more articulate in *Jeremiah*. Jeremiah does not want to prophesy (*Jer.* 1:6), but he cannot contain himself with Yahveh's anger (*Jer.* 6:11, 20:9). Though a prophet is normally supposed to intercede (*Gn.* 20:7, 20:17), Jeremiah is told not to (*Jer.* 7:16, 15:1). At least once, Yahveh was about to remove him from his prophetic office (*Jer.* 15:19). In Jeremiah's eyes, Yahveh seduced and even raped him (*Jer.* 20:7). Jeremiah prayed for the death of his relatives (*Jer.* 12:3) and cursed the day of his own birth (*Jer.* 20:15–18). He depicted himself as a man of strife and contention (*Jer.* 15:10) who lacked the comfort of family and social gatherings (*Jer.* 16:1–13). Yahveh's word has been, he says ironically, his joyful wedding tune (*Jer.* 15:16).

Yet the moroseness of the man and the generally pessimistic tone of his prophecy give us only one side of his personality. For at least twenty-three years, he believed that Yahveh might avert disaster if the people would repent. Even afterward, he prophesied hope. Perhaps the most optimistic of his prophecies is that of the *berit ḥadashah* (new covenant or testament), which must be understood in terms of the sixth century BCE.

According to the authors of the Pentateuch, especially *Deuteronomy*, Yahveh and Israel were joined by covenant, or treaty. Yahveh had taken Israel as his people, and they had accepted him as their god and had assumed the obligation to worship him alone. Violation of the covenant would bring all manner of curses on the people (*Dt.* 28; cf. *Jer.* 11). Modern research has shown that the covenant form employed by *Jeremiah* and *Deuteronomy* is based on ancient Near Eastern political documents whereby a minor king becomes a vassal of a greater one. In such treaties, the suzerain promises land and protection to the vassal in return for the vassal's exclusive and undivided loyalty. The biblical religious covenants conceive of Israel as the vassal of Yahveh, who is, therefore, entitled to exclusive worship. Israel was entitled to remain on the land given it by Yahveh only as long as it served Yahveh alone (*Jer.* 11:5). Jeremiah was certain that his people had broken their covenant with Yahveh by following other gods (*Jer.*

11:10) and were therefore doomed to suffer the expected consequences. In *Jeremiah* 31, however, inspired by Hosea's teaching, the prophet arrives at a new idea.

Hosea speaks of Israel as a faithless wife who was to be cast out and divorced. But Yahveh realized that her inability to be faithful was inherent in her constitutional lack of the qualities of justice, equity, loyalty, compassion, and steadfastness. Yahveh would remarry Israel and would give her these qualities as betrothal gifts so that she would be able to be truly intimate with Yahveh (*Hos.* 2:18–21). He would even make it inherently impossible for her to pronounce the name *Baal.*

Jeremiah follows the same line of thinking, but he employs a political rather than a marital metaphor:

> In days to come I will make a new covenant with the house of Israel and the house of Judah. It will not be like the covenant which I made with their ancestors . . . a covenant which they broke, so I rejected them. . . . I will put my teaching inside of them and inscribe it upon their hearts. Then I will be their god and they will be my people. No longer will they need to teach one another "heed Yahveh," for all of them . . . shall heed me. (*Jer.* 31:31–34)

A similar notion is found in *Jeremiah* 32:38–41: "They shall be my people and I will be their god. I will give them an undivided heart and nature to revere me for all time. I will make an everlasting covenant with them and put reverence fore me in their hearts so that they cannot turn away from me. . . .Then I will plant them permanently in this land."

The new covenant is necessary because Israel and Judah lacked the innate abililty to keep the old one. Yahveh's recognition of the deficiency of his people inspires him to remedy it by a change of their nature. Once Yahveh has effected the change, his people will be able to keep his covenant and remain permanently on his land.

The new covenant itself was designed for the salvation of Israel and Judah. Yet its implications that a radical change of human nature is possible became universal. In a great irony of religious history, the words of the prophet who spent much of his career prophesying doom became to his direct and indirect descendants a legacy of hope.

BIBLIOGRAPHY

Bright, John, trans. and ed. *Jeremiah.* Anchor Bible, vol. 21. Garden City, N.Y., 1965. A readable translation with commentary, notes, historical introduction, and bibliography. A scholarly work but accessible to the nonspecialist.

Childs, Brevard S. *Introduction to the Old Testament as Scripture.* Philadelphia, 1979. Excellent bibliography and a succinct treatment of Jeremiah from the viewpoint of canon criticism.

Cogan, Morton. *Imperialism and Religion: Assyria, Judah and Israel in the Eighth and Seventh Centuries* B.C.E. Missoula, Mont., 1974. An examination of primary Assyrian sources to determine religious policy in Assyrian provinces and vassal states.

Ehrlich, Arnold B. *Miqra' ki-feshuṭo.* 3 vols. Berlin, 1899–1901. An excellent and erratic philological commentary.

Fohrer, Georg. *History of Israelite Religion.* Translated by David E. Green. Nashville, 1972.

Ginsberg, H. L. "Hosea, Book of." In *Encyclopaedia Judaica.* Jerusalem, 1971. An extremely important account of the background of northern Israelite prophetic thought and of Hosea's influence on *Deuteronomy.*

Kaufmann, Yeḥezkel. *The Religion of Israel, from Its Beginnings to the Babylonian Exile.* Translated and abridged by Moshe Greenberg. Chicago, 1960. An attempt to demonstrate that there was no great gap between prophetic and popular religion. Kaufmann argues that prophetic polemics against idolatry are mostly rhetorical exaggerations by idealists.

Nelson, Richard. "Realpolitik in Judah, 687–609 B.C.E." In *Scripture in Context,* edited by William W. Hallo, James C. Moyer, and Leo G. Perdue, vol. 2, pp. 177–189. Winona Lake, Ind., 1982. A critique of the theory that Josiah's religious policies were part of his anti-Assyrian nationalism.

Rowley, H. H. "The Prophet Jeremiah and the Book of Deuteronomy." In his *From Moses to Qumran,* chap. 6. London, 1963. A good summary of the problems involved in the relation between the prophet and the book. Good bibliography to 1950.

Soden, Wolfram von. *Akkadisches Handwörterbuch,* vol. 2. Wiesbaden, 1972. See the index, s.v. *rimu(m).*

New Sources

Berrigan, Daniel J. *Jeremiah: The World, the Wound of God.* Minneapolis, 1999.

Brueggman, Walter. *A Commentary on Jeremiah: Exile and Homecoming.* Grand Rapids, Mich., 1998.

Hunter, Michael J. *A Guide to Jeremiah.* London, 1993.

Jones, Douglas Rawlinson. *Jeremiah: Based on the Revised Standard Version.* Grand Rapids, Mich., 1992.

King, Philip J. *Jeremiah: An Archaeological Companion.* Louisville, Ky., 1993.

Lundbom, Jack R. *The Early Career of the Prophet Jeremiah.* Lewiston, N.Y., 1993.

Sharp, Carolyn J. *Prophecy and Ideology in Jeremiah: Struggles for Authority in the Deutero-Jeremianic Prose.* New York, 2003.

White, R.E.O. *The Indomitable Prophet: A Biographical Commentary: The Man, the Time, the Book, the Tasks.* Grand Rapids, Mich., 1992.

S. DAVID SPERLING (1987)
Revised Bibliography

JEREMIAS II (1530 or 1535–1595) was a Greek prelate, scholar, and patriarch of Constantinople. Jeremias II was born in the ancient city of Anchialus, Thrace (present-day Pomorie, Bulgaria), on the Black Sea; he was a descendant of the important Tranos family. Because there were no organized Greek schools in the Turk-dominated area, Jeremias was privately educated. In 1565 he was elected metropolitan of Larissa, and in 1572 he became patriarch of Constantinople at an uncommonly early age. As a result of the policy of the Ottoman rulers of changing patriarchs, Jeremias was deposed twice, in 1579 and again in 1584, but he was restored to his post by popular demand. He was patriarch from 1572 to 1579, 1580 to 1584, and from 1586 until his death in 1595.

While Jeremias was patriarch, he raised the standards of ecclesiastical and cultural life, both of which were at extremely low levels. He condemned simony among the clergy, and he undertook to restore the former austerity of the monastic life by abolishing the idiorrhythmic monasteries and strengthening the more centralized cenobitic life. He also forbade the establishment of monastic houses in secular environments without prior ecclesiastical consent. The authority of the patriarchate itself was strengthened as a result of his frequent visits to other Orthodox churches. At the insistence of Tsar Feodor I Ivanovich (r. 1584–1598), Jeremias raised the Russian church to the status of patriarchate, placing it in fifth place in the pentarchy after Jerusalem.

Jeremias would not accept the calendar sought by Pope Gregory XIII and suggested that the Orthodox church in the West should also follow the old calendar. For the Orthodox living in Italy, he transferred the see of Philadelphia to Venice, and Gabriel Severus, the scholar, was appointed the first metropolitan. Jeremias's reaction to the establishment of Western schools for proselytism during the period of Turkish occupation was to advise his bishops to establish Greek schools in their territories. He thereby made a contribution to the development of education.

Jeremias is, for the most part, remembered for his contacts and theological dialogues with the Protestant theologians of Tübingen. The Lutherans and the Greek Orthodox sought support in their disagreements with the church of Rome and therefore turned to one another for assistance. In 1573, two professors from Tübingen, Martin Crusius and Jakob Andreä, sent a copy of the Augsburg Confession (1531) to Jeremias. In his correspondence with the Lutheran theologians, Jeremias pointed out the serious differences in dogma that precluded any union of the Protestant and Orthodox churches. This correspondence went on for some time, and it was published as *The Three Dogmatic Answers to the Theologians of Tübingen.* In his various other works, Jeremias presented Orthodoxy as a continuation of the ancient catholic church, stressing, in particular, faithfulness and adherence to the original traditions of the church and avoidance of new doctrines and practices. Although his dialogues with the Lutheran theologians eventually deteriorated, Jeremias began the dialogues in a climate of love and friendship, and thus they became the forerunner of today's ecumenical dialogues.

BIBLIOGRAPHY

No English work on Jeremias II is readily available. Readers of Greek may consult Iōannēs N. Karmirēs' *Ta dogmatika kai sumbolika mnēmeia tēs Orthodoxou Katholikēs Ekklēsias,* vol. 1 (Athens, 1960), pp. 437–503. German readers are directed to *Wort und Mysterium: Der Briefwechsel über Glauben und Kirche, 1573 bis 1581 zwischen den Tübinger Theologen und dem Patriarchen von Konstantinopel* (Witten, 1958).

THEODORE ZISSIS (1987)
Translated from Greek by Philip M. McGhee

JEROME (c. 347–420), properly Eusebius Hieronymus; church father and biblical scholar. Born at Stridon in Dalmatia of a prosperous Christian family, Jerome was educated at Rome under Aelius Donatus, the most eminent grammarian of the fourth century. With Donatus he studied the principal Latin authors, of whom Cicero and Vergil exerted a lasting influence on him. His rhetorical training included the rudiments of philosophy, which held little interest for him, except for dialectics. Rhetoric and dialectics became the tools of his polemics. While in Rome he enjoyed those youthful indiscretions that he would later bitterly lament as immorality. Jerome was nevertheless baptized, perhaps in the year 366.

In his twentieth year Jerome continued his studies at Trier, where the ideal of monasticism took hold of him forever. In 374 he made a pilgrimage to Antioch in Syria, where he mastered Greek and began in earnest his lifelong study of the Bible. Recovery from a serious illness strengthened his resolve to become an anchorite in the nearby desert of Chalcis. While practicing asceticism, he learned Hebrew so that he could read the Old Testament without recourse to the Septuagint. Suspected of religious heterodoxy, he returned to Antioch in 378.

Ordained a priest at Antioch, Jerome was introduced to biblical exegesis by Apollinaris of Laodicea. Around the year 381 Jerome traveled to Constantinople, where he met the theologians Gregory of Nazianzus and Gregory of Nyssa and began his translations of Origen's works on the Bible. Origen was both Jerome's blessing and his bane. From Origen, Jerome derived substantially his own approach to biblical exegesis, but later he was often suspected of sharing Origen's heretical views.

In 382 Jerome returned to Rome and soon became secretary to Pope Damasus, who set him to revising the Old Latin versions of the New Testament. Jerome left Rome for the East in 389, soon to be joined by Paula and Eustochium, two religious Roman women. Together they established two monasteries at Bethlehem. Thereafter, Jerome lived the ascetic life of a monk and continued his study of the Bible. During these years there poured from his pen a river of Latin translations of the Bible from the Greek and Hebrew, translations of Origen's works on the Bible and commentaries of his own, polemical works, and letters to people throughout the Roman world. Although Jerome befriended Augustine of Hippo and the historian Paulus Orosius, he scorned Ambrose of Milan and hounded John Chrysostom. He died in 420. An obstinate monk, Jerome was combative, vindictive, and cantankerous. Nonetheless, as a biblical scholar he was the most learned of church fathers.

Jerome's voluminous writings fall into four broad groups: translations and studies of the Bible, polemics, historical works, and letters. By far the most important category deals with scripture, his towering achievement being his Latin translation of the Bible. Known as the Vulgate, it became the authorized version of the Bible in the Latin church. For the New Testament, Jerome corrected the Old Latin versions of the Gospels in the light of earlier Greek manuscripts. His work on the Old Testament took a more complicated course. He began by relying on the Septuagint, but the more familiar he became with Hebrew the more determined he was to base his translations on the Hebrew text. The result was a far more accurate version of the Old Testament than anything theretofore available in Latin.

Translation was only part of Jerome's biblical interests. In his quest to determine and understand the text, he wrote sixty-three volumes of commentaries and some one hundred homilies primarily concerned with explaining the Bible to the religious community at Bethlehem. Some of Jerome's commentaries are little more than Latin translations of Origen's Greek originals. In the areas of exegesis and homiletics, Jerome was influenced primarily by Apollinaris, Origen, and rabbinical thought, including the work of Akiva ben Joseph, one of the founders of rabbinical Judaism. From Apollinaris, Jerome learned the value of historical commentary and concrete interpretation of the Bible. Jewish exegesis also emphasized the literal sense of the Old Testament. In addition, his Hebrew teachers acquainted Jerome with Jewish oral traditions, a source unknown to most of his Christian contemporaries. Increasingly, Jerome respected the Hebrew text of the Old Testament, in his words, the *veritas Hebraica,* which ultimately led him to doubt the accuracy of the Septuagint. Origen influenced Jerome to go beyond literal and historical interpretation of scripture to discover its allegorical and symbolic meaning. Although Jerome often criticized Origen's approach, he too felt that under the literal text lay a level of deeper spiritual meaning.

Intellectually eclectic, Jerome used all three approaches to biblical exegesis. His usual method of exposition consisted of a literal explanation of every verse, including citations of variant readings and interpretations, frequently followed by an allegorical interpretation. For the Old Testament, he translated passages from Hebrew and from the Septuagint before commenting on them in turn. His treatment of the Hebrew text was generally historical and included discussion of Hebrew words, names, and grammar. Despite his high regard for rabbinical exegesis, Jerome never preferred it to orthodox Christian interpretation. The Septuagint was also often subjected to spiritual exegesis. Here especially Jerome relied heavily on Origen, whom he defended as a learned and gifted biblical scholar. Nonetheless, he often attacked Origen and steadfastly rejected his theology and dogmas. Origen's influence can be seen further in Jerome's tendency to give his own, original spiritual interpretation of the Septuagint.

The second major category of Jerome's writings is polemics. His early studies in Rome made their contribution in this area as well. The training in rhetoric and dialectics equipped him for controversy, and his mastery of Latin prose style gave him a clear, sometimes elegant, means of expression. Moreover, the young student had frequented the law courts and had enjoyed listening to the violent verbal exchanges of eminent lawyers. In addition to his well-turned Latin phrases, Jerome employed caustic and even disreputable abuse, his opponents generally being branded fools, charlatans, heretics, or all three. He was particularly adept at disparaging his opponents' literary style, which was all the more effective because he of all the church fathers wrote a Latin that was almost classically pure. These tools were valuable because Jerome was unimpressive as a theologian and a philosopher. His contribution was as a scholar, not as an original thinker.

Jerome employed his polemical works either to combat current heresies or to defend himself from the charge of heresy. His rebuttals often provide the best information about the nature of his opponents' views. Jerome unswervingly upheld the cause of orthodoxy. He entered the field of controversy in 378–379 with his *Altercatio Luciferiani et Orthodoxi* (Debate of a Luciferian and an orthodox), in which he attacked the views of the Sardinian bishop Lucifer. Using the orthodox believer as a sounding-board for his own views, Jerome argued in favor of Arian bishops' retaining their clerical positions upon recantation and defended the validity of Arian baptism. Chief among Jerome's religious views are his abiding faith in the Christian church and its apostolic authority, and his opposition to heresy as destructive to Christian unity. He never wavered from these beliefs.

In 383 Jerome combated the views of the Roman layman Helvidius, who denied the virginity of Mary after the birth of Jesus and who argued that the married and celibate states were equal in dignity. In *Adversus Helvidium,* a spirited pamphlet, Jerome used exegetical and scholarly arguments, along with his usual verbal abuse, to defend the perpetual virginity of Mary and to exalt the value of celibacy in Christian life. Jerome's triumph over Helvidius helped to establish the orthodox views of the Latin church on Mariology and celibacy. Next, in *Adversus Iovinianum* (Against Jovinian), written in 393, Jerome marshaled all his skills in exegesis, dialectics, rhetoric, satire, and obloquy to defend again the doctrines of Mary's virginity, the virgin birth of Jesus, the superiority of celibacy over marriage, and the advocacy of asceticism. In 404 Jerome wrote *Contra Vigilantium* (Against Vigilantius), a response to the polemics of Vigilantius, a priest from Aquitaine. In this controversy, Jerome defended devotion to the relics of martyrs and saints and the offering of prayers to them, and he endorsed all-night vigils at their shrines as acts of piety. He also again championed the ascetic way of life, including celibacy, monasticism, and fasting, and he approved sending alms to monasteries in Jerusalem as Paul had urged.

In two polemical works Jerome defended himself against the charge of sharing Origen's heresy, first in 397 with his *Contra Ioannem Hierosolymitanum* (Against John of Jerusalem) and again in 401, when his old friend Rufinus of Aquileia openly accused him of being a follower of Origen. In effect, Rufinus attacked Jerome's whole approach to the Bible. Jerome's response, *Apologia adversus Rufinum* (Apology against Rufinus), was a terrible counterattack, violent, satirical, scurrilous, and learned. Jerome successfully defended his life's work, including his use and translations of Origen's commentaries, his reliance on the Hebrew original of the Old Testament, and his respect for the Septuagint. Not denying his debt to Origen's learning, Jerome steadfastly denied sharing Origen's theology.

Jerome's last polemical work, *Dialogus adversus Pelagianos* (Dialogue against a Pelagian), written in 415, attacked the tenets of the Pelagian heresy, which was primarily concerned with the concepts of sin and grace. Against the Pelagian position that people can live free of sin, Jerome countered that humans constantly need divine help. He further insisted that humanity is given to sin, despite its possession of free will. Jerome also defended Augustine's concept of original sin and accepted the need for infant baptism. *Dialogus* exhibits the hallmarks common to the rest of Jerome's polemical works: personal abuse, biblical scholarship, and orthodoxy.

The last two categories of Jerome's work are more historical than religious in importance. Jerome either translated or wrote several historical treatises valuable for his study of the Bible. The first, published in 382, was his translation of Eusebius of Caesarea's *Chronikoi kanones* (Chronological canons), an annalistically arranged work that combined biblical and Near Eastern chronology with Greco-Roman chronology. Jerome added to its contents and continued its coverage to his own times, ending with the Battle of Adrianople in 378. *Chronicle* became the historical framework of his exegetical studies. In wider terms, Jerome's *Chronicle* became the standard authority in western Europe for the chronology of the ancient world.

In 392–393 Jerome published *De viris illustribus* (On famous men), a historical catalog of Christian literature in which he surveyed the lives and writings of 135 authors, overwhelmingly Christian with a sprinkling of Jewish authors, beginning with the apostle Peter and ending with himself. Although he relied heavily on Eusebius for the early part, and although he inserted authors whom he had never read, in the later part he contributed much information derived from his own reading. The work was continued by others into the fifteenth century.

For religious purposes, a trilogy of biblical studies is Jerome's most significant historical work. Between 389 and 391 Jerome produced his *Onomastikon* (Hebrew names), derived from Origen. *Onomastikon* is an etymological dictionary of proper names in the Bible, alphabetically arranged. Next came his *Liber locorum* (Book of places), a translation of Eusebius's *Onomastikon,* with meager additions drawn from his own knowledge of Palestine. The *Liber locorum* is an alphabetical listing of the place names and descriptions of the geographical features of the sites mentioned in the Bible. Last came his *Liber hebraicarum quaestionum* (Hebrew questions), a discussion of various problems in the text of the *Book of Genesis,* heavily dependent on rabbinical exegesis. The treatment is essentially linguistic, historical, and geographical. Rounding out Jerome's historical work are hagiographies of Paul, Malchus, and Hilarion.

Jerome's 154 letters also illuminate the religious climate of the time. In his correspondence, Jerome discussed prominent church leaders, satirized the Christian clergy, discussed the burning religious issues of the day, and provided much information about himself and his intellectual development. All his written work influenced the subsequent course of the Latin church. His greatest contribution can be put simply: when later generations read the Vulgate, they read the translation of Jerome and reaped the finest fruits of his superb scholarship.

BIBLIOGRAPHY

J. N. D. Kelly's *Jerome: His Life, Writings, and Controversies* (London, 1975) is easily the best treatment of Jerome's career. It is firmly based in the sources, and its approach is consistently sane. Philip Rousseau's *Ascetics, Authority, and the Church in the Age of Jerome and Cassian* (Oxford, 1978) is a much broader study of the religious and intellectual climate of the time. An excellent study of Jerome's polemics can be found in Ilona Opelt's *Hieronymus' Streitschriften* (Heidelberg, 1973), an exhaustive analysis of this genre. David S. Wiesen's *Saint Jerome as a Satirist* (Ithaca, N.Y., 1964) concentrates on one of the most salient aspects of Jerome's polemics and correspondence. Similarly, Harald Hagendahl's *Latin Fathers and the Classics* (Göteborg, 1958) devotes part 2, the heart of his book, to Jerome's use of classical writers. Francis X. Murphy, in *A Monument to Saint Jerome: Essays on Some Aspects of His Life, Works, and Influence* (New York, 1952), has assembled ten essays that discuss Jerome both as a religious figure and as an intellectual figure. The quality of the essays, however, is quite uneven.

JOHN BUCKLER (1987)

JERUSALEM

This entry consists of the following articles:

AN OVERVIEW
JERUSALEM IN JUDAISM, CHRISTIANITY, AND ISLAM

JERUSALEM: AN OVERVIEW

Jerusalem, an old Canaanite settlement in the uplands of Judaea, enters history rather offhandedly in the biblical narrative: David, king of Israel, then resident at nearby Hebron, decides to make this Jebusite city his capital. No reason is given—even today the site has obvious security advantages—and indeed Jerusalem shows no particular religious associations until David buys a Jebusite threshing floor atop Mount Moriah just north of his new "City of David" and builds an altar there, where the Lord had stayed the hand of his avenging angel. This spot may have been an earlier Canaanite high place, but it now became the site of a grandiose temple possibly planned by David and certainly built by his son Solomon.

The Temple of Solomon was an enormous structure with interior courtyards of progressively limited access, in the midst of which stood an ornately adorned sanctuary. Outside it stood the great altar of sacrifice, and within, in a curtained inner chamber, the Holy of Holies, was installed the ark of the covenant containing the Tablets of the Law and other tokens of the Israelites' deliverance from Egypt and sojourn in the wilderness of Sinai. And there too were reinstituted all the cultic acts commanded to Moses on Sinai, the daily sacrifices, the feasts of the New Moon and the New Year, the Day of Atonement, and the three great pilgrimage feasts of Passover, Shavuʿot (Weeks), and Sukkot (Tabernacles), all performed and managed by a body of Aaronite priests and ministering Levites.

There is no sign of this building today, because it was destroyed by the Babylonians in 587/6 BCE. Solomon's son Rehoboam could not maintain his father's empire intact, and the schism between the northern kingdom of Israel, with its own priests and shrines and its own rival temple atop Mount Gerizim in Samaria, and the southern kingdom of Judah, ruled from Jerusalem, persisted down to the fall of Samaria to the Assyrians in 721 BCE. Although the days of Judah were likewise numbered, the southern kingdom sustained itself under royal saints (e.g., Hezekiah) and royal sinners (e.g., Manasseh) long enough for the reformer king Josiah to centralize all Israelite cult practices in Jerusalem. This was in 621 BCE, and thereafter Jerusalem had few political rivals and no religious peers; for Jews, whether in Palestine or abroad, in what was known as the Diaspora, the Temple in Jerusalem was the unique site of Jewish sacrificial worship of God, and the divine presence dwelt there in a special way.

The Babylonians, then, took Jerusalem in 587/6 BCE, razed the Temple, and carried off many of the Jews into exile. And it is likely that at that time the ark of the covenant disappeared as part of the spoils; the Holy of Holies of later versions of the Jerusalem Temple was, at any rate, empty. Sometime after 538 BCE the Persian shah Cyrus II and his Achaemenid successors allowed the exiled Jews to return to Jerusalem. The city was rebuilt by Nehemiah, the Mosaic Law was repromulgated through the efforts of the priestly scribe Ezra, and under the auspices of Zerubbabel a reduced version of Solomon's Temple was constructed on the same site. The priesthoods were purified and God's cult restored. Jerusalem itself was rewalled and resettled and began to resume the growth that was already notable in the eighth century BCE. In the wake of Alexander the Great, Greeks succeeded to Persians in the late fourth century in Palestine, and after 200 BCE the Greco-Macedonian dynasty of the Seleucids ruled over what was a politically modest temple-state at Jerusalem.

The political straitening of Jerusalem was accompanied by an equally notable broadening of the religious character of the city. The chastening of the Israelites before, during, and immediately after their Babylonian exile produced a new type of religious leader in their midst, the prophet, and in their inspired visions Jerusalem became the symbol of and indeed identical with the Children of Israel and the Land of Israel, now cast down for its idolatry and fornication, now exalted, renewed, and glorified in the new age that would follow the present travails. Thus the historical Jerusalem, which often lay in ruin and misery, was transformed by Isaiah and Ezekiel, among others, into a heavenly and eschatological Jerusalem, a city whose holiness transcended the mere presence of the Temple but was rather coterminous with the glory of the Chosen People and served as a pledge of the presence of God.

The historical Jerusalem revived under Greek sovereignty, and a newly affluent upper class, including many priestly families, eased the way for the introduction there of the ideals and institutions of Hellenism. Under Antiochus IV Epiphanes (r. 175–164 BCE), the Hellenized Jews in Jerusalem requested and were granted permission by their sovereign to convert the city into a polis, a genuine Greek-style city. Subsequently, Antiochus and a significant number of Jews grew disenchanted with this Jerusalem experiment in cultural and political Hellenism, Antiochus because he scented treachery in the city, and Jewish pietists because they correctly perceived that Hellenism brought more than paved streets and gymnasiums; they saw that it was heavily freighted with spiritual values that constituted an attractive alternative and so a grave threat to Mosaic Judaism. The king instituted a full-scale attack on Judaism in Judaea and installed a Macedonian garrison and foreign cults in the Temple precinct. The outraged Jews mounted a bold resistance, and under the priestly family called the Maccabees they eventually drove most of the Greeks from Judaea and Jerusalem and in 164 BCE rededicated the Temple there to the cult of the Lord.

The Hasmonean dynasty survived until 37 BCE, when its own weaknesses permitted, and Roman choice dictated, the passage of power to the Idumaean Herod I (r. 37–34 BCE). Jerusalem was still growing—it now covered the western hill as well as the eastern hill where Solomon's Temple and the City of David had been located—and Hasmonean kingship had done nothing to inhibit its assimilation to a Hellenic-style settlement with notable public buildings and a regular street plan. The prodigious building activity of Herod increased the tempo of Greco-Roman urbanization. He extended the street plan, built an immense citadel at the western gate of the city, erected his own palace nearby, and sought to crown his labors by undertaking in 20 BCE a reconstruction of the Temple. This mammoth Herodian temple complex, with its newly extended platform, not only doubled the size of Solomon's installation, it dwarfed every known temple assemblage in the Greco-Roman Near East. Today only the platform and some of its gates are extant, having survived the Roman destruction of 70 CE. For Jews, the western wall, a retaining wall of the platform, has been a potent symbol of Jewish historical continuity since Talmudic times. The platform itself has been venerated by Muslims as the Ḥaram al-Sharīf, the Holy Sanctuary, since the late seventh century.

Jewish sovereignty over Jerusalem did not last very long; the Romans by contrast held the city, although they never ruled from it, for six and a half centuries, and different Muslim dynasties, who likewise preferred to put their palaces elsewhere, held sway over Jerusalem from the mid-seventh to the early twentieth century. But however brief the span, Jewish kings ruled over a Jewish state *in* Jerusalem; Roman governors, some pagan, some Christian, ruled *over* Jerusalem; and for a very long time the city was a part, often not a very important part, of some form or other of a Muslim political organization, although never its capital. Nor was it under any circumstances the capital of "the Christian people" or "the Muslim people" simply because there never were such.

Jesus was born under Herodian and died under Roman sovereignty. Although at home in Galilee, he taught, performed miracles, died, and was buried in Herodian Jerusalem. He worshiped in Herod's Temple, with which he identified himself and whose destruction he openly predicted. As he had foreseen, it happened in 70 CE, at the end of a Jewish insurrection against the Romans, but only after Jesus himself had been tried in Jerusalem, crucified outside the western wall of the city, and buried nearby, having said that he would rise again in three days. A century thereafter Jerusalem, too, had its resurrection. In 132 CE the Roman emperor Hadrian published his plans for a new, very Roman Jerusalem. This may have been the provocation for a new revolt; what was left of the city was razed in 135 CE, and it was only then that Hadrian was free to construct his new Aelia Capitolina, named after his house and his god. The Jews for their part were banned from the city and its near vicinity.

Researchers have a good idea of what Aelia Capitolina looked like from the Madeba map, a sixth-century mosaic map that lays out Jerusalem's plan and chief buildings in that era. But there are major new installations visible on that map. They were the work of Constantine and his Christian imperial successors. In 330 CE Constantine, with the urging or the assistance of his mother Helena, set about identifying the chief sites of Jesus' redemptive activity in Palestine. He enshrined them with major basilicas, notably the cave of the nativity in Bethlehem and the places, by then inside Jerusalem's walls, of Jesus' execution, burial, and resurrection. Jesus' tomb was housed under a splendid rotunda, and the site of the execution was enshrined at the corner of an open courtyard; abutting both was an extremely large basilica. The work was capped with both celebrity and authority when in the course of the construction Helena discovered the remains, verified by miracle, of Jesus' own cross.

It was Constantine's initiative that began the conversion of Jerusalem into a Christian holy city, or perhaps better, of Palestine into a Christian holy land, because the Christians held no brief for the city as such. For the early Christians the historical Jerusalem had been destroyed because of the perfidy of the Jews, and if Christians too, following Paul and the *Book of Revelation,* could savor the notion of a heavenly Jerusalem as the symbol of the New Covenant, it had no visible or even sentimental connection with the earthly Jerusalem. Nevertheless, in the wake of Constantine's building program, Christian pilgrims, particularly those from overseas, began to arrive in increasing numbers. What those visitors came to see, and to experience, was not Jerusalem, but the entire network of Palestinian sites connected with Jesus, his apostles, and the early Christian saints, who were being identified with enthusiastic liturgical and architectural celebration from the fourth century onward.

One Jerusalem holy place was not celebrated in either fashion: The site of Herod's Temple, twice reduced to ruins by the Romans, was left in that sad state in graphic and continuous fulfillment of Jesus' prophecy. Christian visitors went up onto the platform and looked about and reflected, but the only liturgy marked there was the piteous Jewish return once a year on Tishʿah be-Av, the anniversary of its destruction, to mourn the fallen sanctuary. In the rest of the city, meanwhile, the effect of imperial investment began to manifest itself in the network of churches, shrines, hospices, and even hospitals as marked on the Madeba map. Now, with no claim to either political or commerical eminence—even in the ecclesiastical hierarchy the city lost ground to nearby Caesarea and distant Antioch—Jerusalem was assuming a role it would have until 1967: that of a holy city supported and adorned for its holiness, and for the political benefits accruing from the official recognition of that holiness.

But throughout most of its history Jerusalem was also a contested city. The Jews were in no position to contest it with the Christians at this stage—they continued to be prohibited residence there by the Christian as well as by the pagan Roman emperors—but in 638 the Muslims came up from the south and took the city from them and their Christian Roman empire in almost perfunctory fashion. Among the Muslims' first acts was to build a mosque on the deserted Temple mount and, within a century, to erect in the middle of that same platform an extraordinary Muslim shrine called the Dome of the Rock.

Although subsequently rebuilt, the mosque on the Temple mount is still called al-Masjid al-Aqṣā ("the distant sanctuary," i.e., mosque), as it was from the beginning, and the reason reaches back to the Qurʾān itself, where God describes how he "carried his servant by night from the Sacred Sanctuary to the Distant Sanctuary" (*sūrah* 17:1). The servant was of course Muḥammad, and the "Sacred Sanctuary" was easily identified as al-Masjid al-Ḥaram and the Kaʿbah at Mecca. But the "Distant Sanctuary" provoked more discussion from the early commentators until here too a consensus developed that the reference was to Jerusalem and its Temple area. Quickly another tradition was worked into the first, that of Muḥammad's ascension into heaven where the mysteries of the prophets and of revelation were disclosed to him.

The Aqṣā, then, was the congregational mosque of Jerusalem, a prayer place that also commemorated that "Distant Sanctuary" mentioned in God's book and visited by the Prophet in the course of his "night journey." And what of the Dome of the Rock? It is in fact an ornate octagonal shrine over a rock, a bedrock outcropping of Mount Moriah, which, according to the Muslim tradition, marked part of the foundation of the Temple. The Muslim connection with Jerusalem, for them simply "the Holy" (al-Quds) or "the Holy House," runs back, then, both through the Bible to the Temple and through the Qurʾān to Muḥammad, and it centers precisely and exclusively on the Temple mount. Some Muslims, not a great many surely, settled in what was now their holy city in the years after 638 CE, and some Jews as well, because the Muslims permitted the latter to resettle in the city that had been forbidden to them for five centuries. The Jews did so with alacrity; they moved their chief rabbinical *yeshivah* from Tiberias to Jerusalem and may even have prayed somewhere on the Temple platform itself.

The relationship of Jews, Christians, and Muslims in Jerusalem, where a majority of the population was Christian and the political sovereignty Muslim, was more or less harmonious. But this holy city was and is a narrow place where emulation breeds envy, and envy, arrogance. In 1009 the assuredly arrogant and possibly envious Fatimid caliph al-Ḥākim burned down the Christians' Church of the Holy Sepulcher. It was eventually rebuilt, although on the reduced scale that separates the present church from its Constantinian predecessor, but some deep harm had been done. That harm was chiefly experienced in Christian Europe, which eventually launched a Crusade that took the city back from the Muslims in 1099.

The Western Crusade, with its religious propaganda and bloody violence, and the Muslims' response, which festooned the city with legends and blessings not unlike the Christians' own indulgences, poisoned relations between the two groups, and nowhere more disastrously than in Jerusalem itself. After the Muslim reoccupation of the city in 1187, Christians continued to come on pilgrimage, still following Jesus' "Way of the Cross" across the city, but now under the grimmest of circumstances; and the Muslim rulers, charged with the administration of an increasingly impoverished city, resorted to extortion against Jerusalem's only source of income, those same pilgrims. Between them were the Jews, too powerless as yet to be a political threat—the Christian pilgrims came from newly aggressive Christian nation-states, while the Jews found no European protectors until the nineteenth century—and almost too poor to be squeezed.

But power and poverty are not all. The Jews have always regarded themselves as a people, a single historical people, and so they alone, not the Christians or the Muslims, were capable of possessing, and did actually possess, a national capital, which was Jerusalem. No Christian pope or Muslim caliph—both quite different from a national king to begin with—ever had Jerusalem as his seat. Christian and Muslim governors Jerusalem has had and, during the Crusades, even a number of Christian kings, but that was either sectarian sovereignty or rule by delegated authority.

This line of thought is merely moving along the surface, however. Jerusalem is more than a city or even a national capital; it is an idea. And it is safe to say that it is a biblical idea. As the Bible unfolds, one can easily follow the progressive identification being drawn between the people of Israel, or the Land of Israel, and Jerusalem and its Temple. People, city, and Temple become one, linked in destiny and God's plan, and then transformed, apotheosized, into the Heavenly Jerusalem. By the time the Jews returned from their Babylonian exile and were granted limited sovereignty in Judaea and permission to rebuild the Temple in Jerusalem, the idea was firmly in place, so firmly indeed that even though the city was again lost to the Jews and then both the city and the Temple destroyed, the idea survived. It survived not as a vaguely conceived and fitfully remembered nostalgia but as a symbol solid as Jerusalem stonework built into the thought and liturgy of Judaism. Rabbis sitting in Galilean and Iraqi *yeshivot* two centuries and more after the actual Temple had disappeared could still cite the physical measurements of the entire complex and were still debating questions of priestly ritual performed there with as much vigor and conviction as if the Temple still stood in its glory. As indeed it did, in a tradition more perennial than stones or mortar or golden fretting.

The theme that Jerusalem is perennial was taken up and repeated in the synagogue liturgy that all Jews recite as part of their ordinary worship and that recurs throughout the art and literature, pious or prosaic, of the Middle Ages. "If I forget thee, O Jerusalem . . ." rolls like an anthem across Jewish history, and in the sense of those words of the psalmist all Jews have always been Zionists, whether they believed that the restoration of Jerusalem could be achieved by political means—as very few did from the final debacle of 135 CE down to the late nineteenth century—or that it would occur in some long-distant eschatological context. And their spiritual descendants inherited the notion from them, although without the same nationalist and tribal overtones: Christians and Muslims are both eschatological Zionists. Jesus saw as in a vision the eschatological destruction of Jerusalem and John's *Book of Revelation* saw its restoration as a heavenly city; in Islam the Kaʿbah itself will travel from Mecca to Jerusalem for the Day of Judgment.

SEE ALSO Biblical Temple; Crusades; Pilgrimage, articles on Contemporary Jewish Pilgrimage, Eastern Christian Pilgrimage.

BIBLIOGRAPHY

On the integration of the Jewish city into both ideology and the popular consciousness, see W. D. Davies's *The Territorial*

Dimension of Judaism (Berkeley, Calif., 1982); *The Temple of Solomon: Archaeological Fact and Medieval Tradition in Christian, Islamic and Jewish Art,* edited by Joseph Gutmann (Missoula, Mont., 1976); *Zion in Jewish Literature,* edited by Abraham S. Halkin (New York, 1961); and Zev Vilnay's *Legends of Jerusalem,* vol. 1, *The Sacred Land* (Philadelphia, 1973). Vilnay's work includes many of the Muslim legends. On the conversion of Jerusalem to a Christian holy city, see W. D. Davies's *The Gospel and the Land: Early Christianity and Jewish Territorial Doctrine* (Berkeley, 1974); E. D. Hunt's *Holy Land Pilgrimage in the Later Roman Empire, A.D. 312–460* (Oxford, 1982); *Peregrinatio Aetheriae: Egeria's Travels to the Holy Land,* rev. ed., translated by John Wilkinson (London, 1981); and John Wilkinson's *Jerusalem Pilgrims before the Crusades* (Warminster, U.K., 1977).

On Muslim Jerusalem, the best introduction is the double article in *The Encyclopaedia of Islam,* new ed., vol. 5, fasc. 83–84 (Leiden, 1980), under "al- Ḳuds"—"Part A: History," by S. D. Goitein, and "Part B: Monuments," by Oleg Grabar. Many of the Muslim historians' and travelers' accounts of the city are collected in *Palestine under the Moslems,* translated by Guy Le Strange (New York, 1890). Sections of this book dealing specifically with Jerusalem have recently been reprinted under the title *Jerusalem under the Moslems* (Jerusalem, n.d.).

For the most revealing travel accounts of the post-Crusader era, consult *Jewish Travellers: A Treasury of Travelogues from Nine Centuries,* 2d ed., edited by Elkan N. Adler (New York, 1966); *The Wanderings of Felix Fabri,* 2 vols., translated by Aubrey Stewart (1892–1893; New York, 1971); and *The Travels of* Ibn Battuta, A.D. 1325–1354, 2 vols., translated and edited by H. A. R. Gibb (Cambridge, U.K., 1958–1962).

On the ninteenth- and twentieth-century city, see Meron Benvenisti's *Jerusalem: The Torn City* (Jerusalem, 1976); N. A. Silberman's *Digging for God and Country: Exploration, Archeology and the Secret Struggle for the Holy Land, 1799–1917* (New York, 1982); and Walter Zander's *Israel and the Holy Places of Christendom* (New York, 1971). Finally, for visitors to the Holy City of all the faiths and in all eras, see my *Jerusalem: The Holy City in the Eyes of Chroniclers, Visitors, Pilgrims and Prophets from the Days of Abraham to the Beginnings of Modern Times* (Princeton, N.J., 1985).

New Sources

Armstrong, Karen. *Jerusalem: One City, Three Faiths.* New York, 1996.

Benvenisti, Meron. *City of Stone: The Hidden History of Jerusalem.* Translated by Maxine Kaufman Nunn. Berkeley, 1996.

Gonen, Rivka. *Contested Holiness: Jewish, Muslim, and Christian Perspective on the Temple Mount in Jerusalem.* Jersey City, 2003.

Janin, Hunt. *Four Paths to Jerusalem: Jewish, Christian, Muslim, and Secular Pilgrimages, 1000 BCE to 2001 CE.* Jefferson, N.C., 2002.

Shanks, Hershel. *Jerusalem: An Archaeological Biography.* New York, 1995.

Vaughn, Andrew G., and Ann E. Killebrew, eds. *Jerusalem in Bible and Archaeology: The First Temple Period.* Leiden and Boston, 2003.

Wasserstein, Bernard. *Divided Jerusalem: The Struggle for the Holy City.* New Haven, Conn., 2001.

F. E. PETERS (1987)
Revised Bibliography

JERUSALEM: JERUSALEM IN JUDAISM, CHRISTIANITY, AND ISLAM

Jerusalem both personifies and symbolizes the "sanctity of place" for all religions deriving from or responding to biblical scripture. The thousands of religious expressions, movements, sects, cults, and new religions that have emerged within the "clusters" or categories referred to as Judaism, Christianity, and Islam were born of spiritual environments that were formed, in part, through the paradigms established by the Hebrew Bible/Old Testament. The multifarious expressions of these religious institutions can even be described as part of a general "biblicist" civilization. Some might call this a "scriptural" religious civilization, but other religions include literatures that have sometimes been described as scripture. The generally accepted or paradigmatic concept of scripture itself is strongly influenced by Western biblical paradigms. In any case, this heterogeneous, biblicist religious civilization contrasts with other religious civilizations, for example, those deriving from Hindu-Buddhist or Confucian roots.

Whereas the religious impulse and regard for the sacred may be universal among humans and the social groups they form, each particular expression is shaped in limited paradigmatic ways that are themselves informed or shaped by cultural, intellectual, and symbolic context. The complex symbolic contexts through which the broad array of religious expressions noted above communicate their theologies and traditions include the authoritative symbolism of the Bible.

Jerusalem, therefore, because of its biblical centrality, serves as a definitive image and symbol of sacred place. But what is the origin of its sanctity? According to Mircea Eliade, sanctity of place reflects a hierophany or eruption of the sacred. This is something associated with a place that demonstrates it is not like just any other place. Whatever becomes associated with the sacred place causes that place to transcend the mundane nature of other places and puts it in the realm of the sacred (Eliade, 1954). Thus Jacob, after his dream of angels, realized that the place where he was laying was no ordinary place. He acknowledged this realization by changing its name from the mundane appellation of Luz to a name acknowledging the sacred, *Beth El,* meaning "abode of God" (*Gn.* 28:10–19).

The sacred nature of a place may also originate in something extraordinary in its physical nature. Extraordinarily large or beautiful trees, mountains, geological formations, or geothermal phenomena have all demonstrated or symbolized the transcendent, thus sacred, nature of places.

The sanctity of Jerusalem probably originates from the abundant flow from its natural source of water, a bountiful spring situated among barren desert hills. The spring is called *gihon* in the Bible (*1 Kgs.* 1:33, 38, 45; *2 Chr.* 32:30, 33:14), the root meaning of which conveys the meaning of bursting forth. The salvific waters of the desert spring thus burst forth in an unlikely place, attracting attention as a place of life-giving, transcendent power and meaning. The special nature of the spring is clarified by the use of the same name, *gihon,* for one of the rivers leading out of the Garden of Eden (*Gn.* 2:13); the nature or symbolism of the spring was powerful enough that it became the place wherein Solomon was anointed king of Israel (*1Kgs.* 1:33ff.).

Israelizing Jerusalem. Jerusalem was an important and, most likely, sacred place long before the Bible takes note of it. Eighteenth- and nineteenth-century BCE Execration texts mention Jerusalem, as do the late Bronze Age El-Amarna letters. But Jerusalem was not an Israelite city in those days; rather it was an Amorite and then Jebusite city. *Genesis* chapter 14 probably refers to Jerusalem (*yerushalayim* or *yerushalem*) when it places Abraham in or within the vicinity of a place named Shalem. Abraham encounters there a priest-king named Malki-Tzedek (meaning "king of righteousness") who is both the king of Shalem (*melekh shalem*) and priest of Great El (*kohen le'el 'elyon*).

Some eight centuries later, at the end of the eleventh century according to the biblical account, David conquered the Jebusite city known as *yevus* (*1 Chr.* 11:4–8; cf. *2 Sm.* 4–9), and Jerusalem became the political and religious capital of the people of Israel.

It is unlikely that the choice of Jerusalem was merely an arbitrary political decision (Smith, 1987, p. 86), given other hilltops in the Judean Hills that might have made a more effective fortress and Temple site. While the choice of place attributed to David certainly had a political component, in order to be effective it required a trans-political unifying element to be recognized as a capital of a dozen, often unruly, disparate tribes. The unifying element appears to have been an inherent aura of sanctity associated with Jerusalem. It became the site of the Temple and the center of the religious cult, and this centrality is attested by the abundant biblical poetry associated with Jerusalem in psalms of thanksgiving, victory, and mourning. Jerusalem served as the symbol of universal hope among the prophets, and its broken ramparts personify the bereavement of Israel and, by extension, humanity as a whole. As the location of the Temple, Jerusalem symbolizes the location of God's indwelling, the earthly center of the divine presence.

Perhaps the most striking aspect of Jerusalem's sanctity, however, is that all of the most authoritative biblical depictions of hierophanies occurred elsewhere. God's most powerful revelations occurred at the Red Sea and Mount Sinai, both outside of Jerusalem and even outside of the biblically defined Land of Israel. The theophanies described in relation to Abraham, Isaac, and Jacob occurred in Elon Moreh (*Gn.* 12:6), Eloney Mamre (*Gn.* 13:18, 14:13), 18:1ff.) Gerar (*Gn.* 20), Be'er Sheva (*Gn.* 21:32ff., 26:23f), Moria (*Gn.* 22:2), Luz/Beth-El (*Gn.* 28:10–29), and elsewhere. In fact, aside from the uncertain and enigmatic reference in Genesis chapter 14, Jerusalem is never even mentioned in the Torah (Pentateuch), the symbolic, literary, and religious core of the entire Hebrew Bible. The many deuteronomic references to "the site which [God] will choose" (*Dt.* 12: 5, 11, 21, 26; 14:25, and 15:6) do not refer specifically to Jerusalem, and the binding of Isaac in the "Land of Moria" is only associated with Jerusalem in the Second Temple period (*2 Chr.* 3:1). The prophets also received their messages outside the walls of Jerusalem.

This problem is resolved according to traditional Jewish and Christian commentators and theologians in a variety of ways that claim the primordial, divinely established prehistoric sanctity of Jerusalem for Israel. From the historical perspective, however, it must be noted that Jerusalem did not come under the full and consistent control of Israel until David, who lived in an era that is much later than that depicted in the Pentateuchal narratives. Jerusalem was chosen by David to be the political capital of an often-fractious group of tribes. It was not only the politically neutral nature of Jerusalem, located outside the established tribal areas, or the supposed geographic centrality of the city that caused it to become the capital of Israel. It was also the previously recognized pre-Israelite sanctity of the place that served to make Jerusalem an acceptable unifying symbol for the people of Israel. This is a noteworthy detail. To be precise, despite the Bible's consistent condemnation of Canaanite religion and the repeated command to destroy its ritual "high places," it was exactly such a place that became the most sacred space for Biblical religion. Jerusalem thus represents an early example of a sacred place that transcends cultural and religious boundaries. Ironically, perhaps, it was the pagan, non-Israelite sanctity of Jerusalem that made it not only an attractive place, but also a unifying center for the people of Israel and its emerging expressions of monotheism.

The challenge for the national record that would become the Bible was how to make the political capital of the Davidic chief-kings into the spiritual capital of a national religion whose memories of divine intervention all occurred elsewhere. Some of this process can be gleaned from the complex and layered writings of the Bible itself. One of its most powerful witnesses is the repeated reference in *Deuteronomy* (12:5, 11, 21, 26; 14:25, and 15:6) to an as-yet-unknown place where God will choose to cause the divine presence to dwell, the subtext of which is obviously Jerusalem. The authority of the divine word to Moses as depicted in *Deuteronomy* establishes Jerusalem even without specifically naming it, and David's and Solomon's divinely based authority as depicted in *2 Samuel* and *1 Kings* served to authenticate the priority of Jerusalem over Samaria and any other contending centers. The program was successful and Jerusalem would become the undisputed center, both physical and spiritual, for virtually all Jewish- and Christian-based religious movements, and one of the earliest and most important centers for religious expressions merging into and deriving from Islam.

The Extension of Sanctity. Just as the sanctity of Jerusalem moved across the religious boundary from Canaanite to Israelite religion, so would it become an important and perhaps necessary part of the sanctity that would define subsequent biblicist religious institutions. The defining act of the Crucifixion that would both symbolize and epitomize Christianity had to occur there, and even the divine authority of Jesus was established by his association with the holy city (*Lk.* 13:33–35). But the essential nature and meaning of Christian Jerusalem was not the same as Israelite Jerusalem. It had to be transformed in order for it to be a central and empowering institution for Christianity (*Mt.* 21:10–14). Jerusalem became spiritualized and delocalized in the early Christian context and therefore among its many derivative expressions. It is a "new Jerusalem" (*Rv.* 3:12), a "heavenly Jerusalem" (*Gal.* 4:26, *Heb.* 12:22), detached from the essentially defiling nature of physicality.

Similar to Christianity, the expressions of Judaism that emerged following the destruction of the Temple and the end of Jewish political power would also redefine the nature of the city, and their redefinition would find deep parallels with their sister Christian expressions. Although Jews, unlike Christians, would mourn the physical destruction of the city and its Temple (Babylonian Talmud [B.T.]: *Moʿed Katan* 16a), and pray daily for its rebuilding in future days, Jewish Jerusalem also became largely spiritualized (B.T.: *Baba Batra* 75B, *Midrash Tanhuma, Pequdey*) and it became, among other things, the gateway to heaven (*shaʿar hashamayim*) (*Pirqey deRabbi Eliʾezer* chapter 35).

Islam, too, would become deeply associated with this holy city, despite its preferential feeling for the sacred places of its origin in the Hijaz of west-central Arabia. As in the case of David and Solomon, the kings of Israel and Jesus, Muḥammad's divine authority was established through his personal association with Jerusalem (Qurʾān 17:1). But unlike the cases of these former personages, Muḥammad's entire mission took place in Arabia and not in Palestine.

From the perspective of the historian and student of religion, Muḥammad's association with Jerusalem is precarious, but from the perspective of the believer, it is deeply established and foundational. Anchored onto the first verse of the seventeenth chapter of the Qurʾān, known as the "Night Journey," the biographies of Muḥammad found in the *ḥadīth* and interpretive literatures prove his association with Jesus and the prophets of Israel in the holy city. Muḥammad's night journey to Jerusalem (*al-israʾ*) was not an end in itself, however, for the narratives always include his ascension (*miʿraj*) through Jerusalem, the gateway, to heaven. Although finding many parallels with Christian and rabbinic traditions, the Islamic association with Jerusalem remains unique. After arriving in the holy city (Arabic, *Al-Quds*), Muḥammad leads the other prophets in prayer; and through Jerusalem, the gateway to heaven, the Prophet enters and ascends the seven levels until he reaches the lotus tree beyond which no one can enter. At this highest level, Muḥammad receives a number of divine gifts, including divine guidance and knowledge of the divine will. These gifts guide him and authorize his *sunnah* or personal behavior to become the highest norm for Muslims throughout the world and throughout history. The record of Muḥammad's divinely guided *sunnah* was recorded over the centuries in an authoritative literature known as the *ḥadīth*, the most authoritative religious literature of Islam and second only to the Qurʾān. All of this is authorized and authenticated through the acknowledged sanctity of Jerusalem, the holy city.

Emerging Monotheisms and the Symbolic Polemics. Rodney Stark, in partnership with William Sims Bainbridge and Laurence Iannacone, has demonstrated how successful emerging religions invariably adopt symbols of previously established religions and use them to establish their own credibility (Stark and Bainbridge, 1966). In other words, newly emerging religions that fail invariably fail to integrate the symbolism of established religions and put them to their own use. The exact nature of Jerusalem's sanctity prior to the Davidic conquest of the city is unknown, but it is clear that the Bible took great pains to ensure that Jerusalem was recognized as sacred, particularly for the emerging religious institutions of Israel. At first Jerusalem provided a special credibility to the centralization of Israelite worship in the Temple. Later the Temple established the sacred nature of Jerusalem. Attempts by factions such as the Samaritans to compete with Jerusalem through the sanctification of other sacred sites failed, and Jerusalem became symbolic of authentic monotheism. Jerusalem was the Temple and the priesthood. As the location of the indwelling presence of God, Jerusalem became the center of the universe. By the pre-Christian Roman period of control, the sacred nature of the city was known throughout the Mediterranean world.

In order for Jesus' death and resurrection to have an impact as a significant and authentic event on the populations of the Eastern Mediterranean in the first centuries CE, they had to have occurred in Jerusalem, as *Luke* 13:33–35 makes clear. The numerous other prophets and messianic figures known to have missions in other places from that period all failed. But Christianity, as opposed to biblical religion, quickly moved away from the old Near Eastern model of religion centered around a physical sacred place. It required "ownership" of Jerusalem for its success, but physical ownership was impossible for the most formative period of its existence. It therefore spiritualized the symbolism of the holy city for Christianity and thus controlled it. No new physical Temple would be rebuilt for the True Israel (*verus israel*), that is, Christianity. The Temple of Israel became the Universal Church.

Early rabbinic Judaism, the most successful form of Judaism emerging from the ashes of the Second Temple destroyed by Rome, was ambivalent about the sanctity of Jerusalem's physicality. It found substitutes for animal sacrifice in family home ritual and for the priests and prophets in the rabbis or in all the Jewish people, but it also longed for the Temple and prayed that it be rebuilt. When Christianity won the spiritual battle for the Roman Empire in the fourth century, it became necessary for Christianity to demonstrate its absolute hegemony through the symbolism of Jerusalem. This was accomplished by shifting the spiritual focus of the city from the Temple Mount symbolizing the old Israelite/Jewish religion, to the Holy Sepulchre symbolizing the essential act of Christianity: the passion and resurrection of Christ.

To emphasize these intentions, the Byzantine rulers of Jerusalem made the Temple area into the city dump. The polemics of this statement could not be clearer. God had demonstrated through history the divine rejection of Judaism and the Jews on the one hand, and the divine love for Christ and his followers on the other. Jewish Jerusalem was impure and filled with refuse, whereas Christian Jerusalem was sublime. But whereas the physical sanctity shifted westward toward the Holy Sepulchre, it took on less of the sanctity of place that was so clearly exemplified by the Temple.

When the armies of the Arab Conquest reached Jerusalem in 638 CE, according to legend they were appalled at the condition of the Temple Mount. The caliph ʿUmar himself rolled up the sleeves of his robe and led his people in a clean up of the sacred Temple precinct. It became known later in Arabic as the Sacred Precinct *(al-haram al-sharif)*, and some of the old sanctity of place was renewed. To the conquering Arabs, Jerusalem was the city of the prophets, the most powerful and universal symbol of monotheism. Islam would then claim its hegemony over both Judaism and Christianity with the erection of a magnificent monument, symbolic of the purity and superiority of what it claimed as the most perfect expression of monotheism and the divine will. That construction was not a mosque, but rather a monument celebrating the presence and success of a new faith. Grabar described the Dome of the Rock, completed in 691 CE, as "the first consciously created masterpiece of Islamic art" (1986). Only later, next to this testimonial structure, was begun the monumental construction of the al-Aqsa mosque.

SACRED OFFSPRING. Although the sacred spring may have first brought attention to the place known as Jerusalem or *al-Quds* ("the holy"), there is no absolute certainty about the origin of Jerusalem's sanctity or an "original" Jerusalem, only that its sacred nature predates the Israelite occupation. Like other sacred places, Jerusalem emerged from the shadows of ancient days and acquired meaning that evolves and changes through the ages. The personality and significance of the place in the days of the Amorites and Jebusites has been lost, and, although the Hebrew Bible provided meaning and significance at a later time, the "Biblical Period" of Jerusalem itself spanned centuries and represents many distinctive political, cultural, social, and religious communities, none of which exist today. The spiritual offspring of those communities live today as Christians, Jews, and Muslims, and all have claimed to epitomize if not personify the true Israel or the pure and primordial monotheism of the biblical Abraham. Each has maintained that it is the true embodiment of God's religion. As such, each claims an exclusive right to Jerusalem, the symbolic center of monotheistic sanctity.

The sacred nature of Jerusalem continues to exert its pull in modern and postmodern history. It has become the symbol of Jewish nationalism known as Zionism, the "Zion" of which is a biblical appellation for Jerusalem (*1 Kgs.* 8:1; *Is.* 2:3, 4:9, 10:32, 52:1; *Ps.* 102:17). Jerusalem has become the symbol of Palestinian nationalism as well, a nationalism that has become increasingly Islamic and religious in nature. In this regard Christianity differs existentially from both Judaism and Islam in that it no longer considers itself a religious peoplehood, though the Crusades are witness to this sentiment in some premodern Christian expressions.

At least since the 1930s, but increasingly so after 1967, new prophets have found their way to Jerusalem. A phenomenon called the "Jerusalem Syndrome" takes hold of anywhere from a dozen to a hundred or more individuals per year, mostly tourists but occasionally locals as well, who believe that they are prophets or messianic figures. The behavior of those caught up in the fervor varies, but often includes bathing or engaging in some kind of ritual purification, dressing in white, and engaging in bizarre but usually harmless behavior. They are treated in a psychiatric duty hospital and are generally released after four or five days.

BIBLIOGRAPHY

Boyarin, Daniel. *Dying for God.* Stanford, Conn., 1999.

Bukhari, Muhammad b. Ismaʾil. *Sahih.* 9 vols. (English-Arabic). Lahore, Pakistan, 1983.

Demsky, Aaron. "Holy City and Holy Land as Viewed by Jews and Christians in the Byzantine Period: A Conceptual Approach to Sacred Space." In *Sanctity of Time and Space in Tradition and Modernity,* edited by A. Houtman, M. J. H. M. Poorthuis, and J. Schwartz, pp. 285–296. Leiden, 1998.

Eliade, Mircea. *The Myth of the Eternal Return.* New York, 1954.

Firestone, Reuven. *Journeys in Holy Lands.* Albany, N.Y., 1990.

Grabar, Oleg. *Encyclopedia of Islam,* 2d ed. Leiden, 1986.

Graham, William. *Beyond the Written Word.* Cambridge, Mass., 1987.

Guillaume, Alfred. *The Life of Muhammad: A Translation of Ibn Ishaq's Sirat Rasul Allah.* Oxford, 1955.

Guillaume, Alfred. "Where Was al-Masjid al-Aqsa?" *Andalus* 18 (1953): 323–336.

Ibn Hisham. *Al-Sira al-Nabawiyya,* 2 vols. Beirut, n.d.

Josephus, Flavius. *The Jewish War.* London, 1959.

Levine, Lee. *Jerusalem: Its Sanctity and Centrality to Judaism, Christianity, and Islam.* New York, 1999.

Smith, Jonathan Z. *Map Is Not Territory.* Leiden, 1978.

Smith, Jonathan Z. *To Take Place: Toward Theory in Ritual.* Chicago, 1987.

Stark, Rodney, and William Sims Bainbridge. *A Theory of Religion.* New Brunswick, N.J., 1996.

REUVEN FIRESTONE (2005)

JESUITS is the popular name for members of the Society of Jesus (S.J.), a religious order of clerics regular, founded by Ignatius Loyola (1491–1556) and canonically established by Pope Paul III in 1540.

PURPOSE AND ORGANIZATION. The order's purpose is twofold: to promote the salvation and perfection both of individual Jesuits and of all humankind. Jesuit organization, manner of life, and apostolic ministries are all designed to further this very broad goal. For the same reason, all Jesuits are expected to be ready to go to any part of the world and to engage in any work assigned to them, laboring always for the greater glory of God—hence the order's motto, "Ad Majorem Dei Gloriam" (A.M.D.G.). Much in the original structure was borrowed from existing orders, but several features were novel. These included the very extensive authority and lifelong tenure of the superior general; the lengthy training period and gradation of members; a distinct spirituality based on the *Spiritual Exercises* of Ignatius Loyola; and stress on the vow of religious obedience. Official directives can be found in a large body of writings, known collectively as the Institute, which includes pertinent papal documents; the *Spiritual Exercises* and the Jesuit Constitutions (also composed by Ignatius Loyola); decrees of the society's thirty-three general congregations; and instructions of superiors general.

Supreme authority, subject always to the pope, rests in an elective body, the general congregation, which selects the superior general (the sole elected superior) and which alone has full legislative power. Day-to-day government is highly centralized under the superior general, resident in Rome, who has complete authority over the entire order. In practice, however, much of this authority is delegated to superiors throughout the world and to others whom the superior general appoints. Members are priests, candidates for the priesthood (scholastics), or temporal coadjutors (brothers). After priestly ordination and a final period of spiritual training (tertianship), priests receive their final grade as spiritual coadjutors or they are professed of four solemn vows (poverty, chastity, obedience, and special obedience to the pope). No special privileges attach to this last group, although certain posts are open only to them.

EARLY HISTORY AND SUPPRESSION. The combating of Protestantism was a major preoccupation of Jesuits up to the mid-seventeenth century, although the order was not founded with this goal in mind. Education, both of young laymen and clerics (whose seminary training was largely in Jesuit hands), was the principal area of activity in Europe and in mission lands. The society accomplished its most effective work in the Counter-Reformation by means of its schools, all of which were tuition-free and which concentrated on the humanities. Uniform pedagogical norms were supplied by the *Ratio studiorum*, first published in 1599. By 1749 the order, with 22,589 members, was operating 669 secondary schools (*collegia*) and 176 seminaries; 24 universities were wholly or partly under its control. The academic renown of these institutions won Jesuits the reputation of being the "schoolmasters of Europe." Scholarship was also diligently pursued, especially in the ecclesiastical sciences. In theology those who gained lasting fame include Peter Canisius and Roberto Bellarmino (both doctors of the church), Francisco Suárez, Luis de Molina, Denis Petau (Petavius), Gregory of Valencia, Gabriel Vázquez, Leonard Lessius, and Juan de Ripal-da. The Bollandists, a group of Belgian Jesuits, are renowned for their contributions to Christian hagiography. Pastoral ministries were very diverse. The Jesuits placed special emphasis on preaching, popular missions, administration of the sacraments, retreat direction according to the method of the *Spiritual Exercises*, guidance of Marian Congregations (sodalities), and promotion of devotions, especially to the Sacred Heart. They had almost a monopoly on the post of royal confessor throughout Catholic Europe.

Next to education, missionary work was the chief preoccupation of the Jesuits. By the mid-eighteenth century the society was evangelizing more territory and sending out more missionaries than any other order. The overwhelming majority labored in the vast Spanish or Portuguese lands in the New World and Asia, with some also in Africa. Others toiled in the French possessions in North America. Jesuits first arrived in the present-day limits of the United States in 1566, along the southeastern coast. Up to the American Revolution almost all the Catholic clergy in the English colonies were Jesuits. In the Americas their missionary establishments, called Reductions, became famous. In Asia, however, the Jesuits' missiological method of accommodation to native cultures, beneficial as it proved in many ways, involved the order in long, bitter disputes over Chinese and Malabar rites of worship, the greatest of all mission controversies.

The Society of Jesus has never lacked opponents. During the third quarter of the eighteenth century disparate groups of enemies combined forces to engage the order in a losing battle for life. French Gallicans and supporters of monarchical absolutism resented Jesuit championship of the papacy. Jansenists were bent on the ruin of the group that had long supplied their chief theological critics. Most hostile of all were radical devotees of the rationalistic Enlightenment, whose ranks numbered highly placed government officials as well as such gifted authors as Voltaire. Between 1759 and 1768, governments expelled the society from Portugal and Spain and their overseas possessions, from the kingdom of the Two Sicilies, and from the Duchy of Parma. France outlawed the order. In 1773, Pope Clement XIV bowed to the demands and threats of the Bourbon courts, and by virtue of his supreme apostolic authority, dissolved the entire order. Complete suppression never actually occurred, for Russia refused the necessary official publication of the papal brief *Dominus ac Redemptor.* This permitted the society in Belorussia to continue its canonical existence. Pope Pius VII restored the order in the kingdom of the Two Sicilies in 1804 and allowed Jesuits everywhere to affiliate with their brethren in Russia. In 1814, Pius VII revoked the brief of suppression and completely restored the Society of Jesus.

ACTIVITIES SINCE 1814. After its restoration, the Society of Jesus spread throughout the world and came to exceed by far the numbers it had counted before 1773. Its membership totaled 36,038 in 1965, with 8,393 members in the United States. Educational and missionary endeavors continued to be its main areas of ministry. Scholarly traditions were revived, with more attention devoted to the social and physical sciences. The turbulence that has characterized life in the Catholic Church since Vatican II has not escaped the order, as is evident by its decline in total membership (to 25,952 in 1983; and to 20,170 in 2004) and among young scholastics (from 9,865 in 1965 to 3,347 in 1983). Efforts to meet the challenges of the age were the major preoccupations of the thirty-first general congregation (1965–1966) and the thirty-second (1974–1975), which decreed changes in the order's government, in the training and life of members, and in the choice of ministries. These general congregations also called for more emphasis on the struggle against atheism, on ecumenism, on closer relations with the laity, on the social apostolate, on use of the mass media, on service of faith, and on promotion of justice.

SEE ALSO Bellarmino, Roberto; Canisius, Peter; Christianity, articles on Christianity in Asia, Christianity in Latin America, Christianity in North America; Gallicanism; Ignatius Loyola; Missions, article on Christian Missions; Ricci, Matteo; Suárez, Francisco; Xavier, Francis.

BIBLIOGRAPHY

The literature concerning the Jesuits is enormous and often controversial. For extensive bibliography, see *Bibliography of the History of the Society of Jesus* by László Polgár, S.J. (Saint Louis, Mo., 1967), with 963 entries, and the same author's *Bibliographie sur l'histoire de la Compagnie de Jésus, 1901–1980,* 3 of 7 projected vols. to date (Rome, 1981–). Complete and well-ordered annual bibliographies appear in *Archivum historicum Societatis Iesu,* published since 1932. Important secondary works include *A History of the Society of Jesus* by William V. Bangert, S.J. (Saint Louis, Mo., 1972); *The Jesuits in History* by Martin P. Harney, S.J. (New York, 1941; reprint, Chicago, 1962); *Jesuiten-Lexikon: Die Gesellschaft Jesu einst und jetzt* by Ludwig Koch, S.J. (Paderborn, 1934; reprint, with a few additions by M. Dykmans, S.J., Louvain, 1962); and *The Jesuits: Their Spiritual Doctrine and Practice; A Historical Study* by Joseph de Guibert, S.J. (Chicago, 1964), an authoritative study. The reader should also consult Ludwig von Pastor's *The History of the Popes from the Close of the Middle Ages,* 40 vols. Volumes 12 through 39 devote in all several hundred pages to the Jesuits, giving a very detailed and lengthy treatment of the suppression.

New Sources

See also *Documents of the Thirty-Fourth General Congregation of the Society of Jesus,* ed. John L. McCarthy, S.J. (St. Louis, 1995); *The Jesuits: Cultures, Sciences, and the Arts,* ed. John W. O'Malley, et al. (Toronto, 1999); *Jesuits: Missions, Myths, and Histories,* by Jonathan Wright (London, 2004).

JOHN F. BRODERICK (1987)
Revised Bibliography

JESUS

JESUS. Jesus Christ (7–5 BCE – 30–33 CE) is the founder of the Christian religion.

TRADITIONAL IMAGES OF JESUS. From early times, Christians worshiped Jesus. John's gospel already speaks of him as divine (1:1–4), and the dominant Christian tradition makes Jesus' deity an article of faith. So just as human beings always make gods in their own image, so too have Christians done with Jesus. In popular piety, sophisticated theology, and modern historiography, he has been viewed through a half-silvered mirror: depending upon the light, one sees either one's reflection or what is on the other side. Often, the links between the historical Jesus of Nazareth and representations of him have been tenuous. At the same time, to the extent that the New Testament preserves memories of this individual, the potential influence of a real historical figure live on.

Savior. Although Christians have always considered Jesus their savior, no creed or church council has ever defined the nature of his redemptive work. The tradition in *1 Corinthians* 15:3–7 says that Jesus "died for our sins" but does not explain how this worked. Similarly, the accounts of the last supper, which have Jesus instituting the central rite of most churches, have him saying that his body is "for you" (*1 Cor.* 11:24) or that his blood is "poured out for many" (*Mk.* 14:24), but there is no accompanying explanation. In *Romans* 3:25, Paul speaks of Jesus' death as a "propitiation" or "expiation"—that is, in sacrificial terms. Yet again there is no theory of the atonement.

Later theologians made up the lack. Origen (c. 185–c. 254 CE) argued that Jesus became a ransom to the devil, who had, with the fall of Adam and Eve, acquired ownership over them and their descendants. A popular myth, growing out of *Colossians* 2:14 ("erasing the record that stood against us with its legal demands"), had the devil tricking the first human beings into an agreement that was written on a stone thrown into the Jordan River and destroyed by Jesus at his baptism.

In the East, Jesus' descent to hell, allegedly exegetically rooted in *Matthew* 27:51–53 and *1 Peter* 3:18–20, became the great act of redemption. After expiring, Jesus descended to the realm of the dead, to which the devil, who did not realize what he was doing, gave him entrance. Once there, Jesus revealed his true nature and destroyed the chains that held all in Hades. Having ruined Satan's realm, Jesus then ascended, taking with him Adam and Eve and the saints of old (and in a few versions of this story, everybody). Orthodox celebrations of the resurrection replay this act every Easter service when the priest knocks on the doors of the church, which then open and allow him and the congregation to enter and celebrate the feast.

Western thought has focused on the language of atonement. For Anselm (1033–1109), offence against the infinite dignity of God, who is owed perfect obedience, creates an infinite debt. Since human beings are finite, they cannot pay the debt. So God in the person of the Son deigned to make satisfaction; that is, the Son paid a ransom to the Father. Being divine, he had the ability to do this; being human, he had the right to pay for humanity. This basic scheme was retained by the Reformers and remains alive in much popular Protestant thought, where the spotlight has been on God's justice and the punishment it demands. Yet such thinking has always had its detractors. Abelard (1079–1142) urged an exemplarist theory of the atonement, according to which Jesus' death is primarily a display of his love; its value lies in our imitation of such love.

Moral model. Jesus, who in the Gospels says "Follow me," has often served as a moral model. *Romans* 15:1–7 supplies an early instance, and *Matthew* presents Jesus as a moral example by offering numerous correlations between Jesus' imperatives and his deeds (e.g., *Mt.* 5:17–20 and 8:4; 5:39 and 26:67; 27:30; 6:6 and 14:23). Ignatius wrote, "Be imitators of Jesus Christ, as he was of his Father" (*Phil.* 7:2). Origen was more expansive: "Christ is set forth as an example to all believers, because as he ever chose the good. . .and loved righteousness and hated iniquity. . .so, too, should each one of us. . . .By this means we may as far as is possible become, through our imitation of him, partakers of the divine nature; as it is written, 'The one who believes in Christ ought to walk even as he walked'" (*De prin.* 4.4.4). Christian monasticism shared the same outlook, taking Jesus' poverty, celibacy, and obedience to be imperatives.

The most influential presentation of Jesus as an ethical model is the fifteenth-century *Imitation of Christ,* written by Thomas à Kempis and translated into English many times. With the exception of the Bible, it is perhaps Christianity's most widely read work. The first chapter sets forth its theme: "'The one who follows me, walks not in darkness,' says the Lord. These are the words of Christ, by which we are admonished how we should imitate his life and manners, if we will be truly enlightened, and be delivered from all blindness of heart. So let our chief endeavor be to meditate upon the life of Jesus Christ."

Many Protestants have found this sort of devotion theologically problematic. Since Martin Luther (1483–1546), there has been a reaction against an unimaginative and literalistic *imitatio Christi* (such as that exhibited by Francis of Assisi). Some have condemned the notion of imitating the canonical Jesus as a purely human effort that, in the event, cannot be achieved. Others have argued that the idea fails to preserve Jesus' unique status as a savior whose accomplishments cannot be emulated: the Christian gospel is not imitation of a human hero.

Despite such criticism, Jesus has remained a moral model for many, including many Protestants. More than one hundred years ago, C. M. Sheldon's *In His Steps* (1896), in which Jesus appears more like a modern American than an ancient Jew, was a best-seller. The title indicates the main theme. Today, socially concerned Christians continue to appeal to Jesus' ministry to unfortunates as precedent for their charitable causes. Liberation theologians argue that Jesus fought social and political injustice and that his followers should do likewise. Others have supported women's causes by calling upon Jesus' supposed liberation of them. So the imitation of Christ continues to take various forms. Popular Christian jewelry worn in the West is inscribed with the question, "What would Jesus do?"

The face of God. Jesus' status as divine makes his attributes those of God. This has meant, among other things, that Christians have conceived of God as compassionate. In the Gospels, Jesus is the "friend of tax collectors and sinners"; he heals the sick and infirm; he refuses to cast the first stone. In line with all this, the traditional images of the Pantokrator (ruler of the universe) have the exalted Jesus, as lord of the universe, lifting his right hand in the posture of blessing and holding a book with the words, "Come to me all who labor and are heavy laden, and I will give you rest." Both Orthodox iconographers and Renaissance artists have favored the image of Mary embracing her infant son. Similarly, much popular Protestant art has depicted Jesus as welcoming children. This is the same compassionate Jesus to whom the so-called Jesus Prayer of Orthodox spirituality—"Lord Jesus Christ, Son of God, have mercy upon me a sinner"—is directed.

If Jesus has often been the face of divine compassion, no less often has he been the face of divine judgment. Already the Gospels depict him as warning repeatedly of hell, and *Matthew* 25:31–46 depicts him as the judge of the last day, sending some into eternal fire prepared for the devil and his angels. How such visions of judgment harmonize with the compassionate Christ is problematic. One thinks of Peter Paul Rubens's (1577–1640) astounding painting of Saint Francis crouched around and protecting the world from a Jesus Christ who wants to attack it with thunderbolts. Here Francis must become the compassionate savior because Jesus is the threatening judge.

The tension between the compassionate Jesus and the damning Jesus is such that many have thought the gospel portrait, which features both, cannot in this regard be historical. Can it be that a mind that was profoundly enamored of the love of God and that counseled charity toward enemies concurrently accepted and even promoted the dismal idea of a divinely-imposed, unending agony? Anticipating some modern scholarship, the poet Percy Bysshe Shelley (1792–1822) argued in his "Essay on Christianity" that the evangelists "impute sentiments to Jesus Christ which flatly contradict each other." According to Shelley, Jesus actually "summoned his whole resources of persuasion to oppose" the idea of justice inherent in hell; Jesus believed in "a gentle and beneficent and compassionate" God, not in "a Being who shall deliberately scheme to inflict on a large portion of the human race tortures indescribably intense and indefinitely protracted." Shelley argued that "the absurd and execrable doctrine of vengeance, in all its shapes, seems to have been contemplated by this great moralist with the profoundest disapprobation." The gospel texts suggesting otherwise are for Shelley unhistorical.

Perhaps the most distinctive image of Jesus and of Christian art, and certainly the most popular in the West, is that of Jesus being crucified. One of the earliest artistic evidences for Christianity is a crude graffito with inscription ("Alexamenos worships his god") on the wall of a house in Rome on the Palatine Hill. Reflecting the ancient world's abhorrence of crucifixion, it mocks the crucified Christ by giving him the head of a donkey. But, in accordance with Paul's paradoxical theology and his boasting in the crucified Christ, Christians transformed the ancient instrument of torture into the salvific instrument par excellence. The traditional icons of the crucifixion, which typically depict a serene and majestic Christ, even seeming to sleep, are on some level a response to the problem of evil. While this has no satisfactory intellectual solution, Christians have found solace in the notion that God the Son has also suffered. Blaise Pascal (1623–1662) famously wrote that Christ is on the cross until the end of time. In our own day, the Holocaust haunts all reflection about Jesus' suffering. The Protestant theologian, Jürgen Moltmann (1926–), has argued that Jesus' cry of dereliction on the cross should be taken at face value: on the cross, God abandoned Jesus. So the crucified Son reveals the reality of divine suffering. The Son is abandoned, the Father grieves, and God paradoxically forsakes God. In this way the reality of human suffering is taken up into the Godhead, and Christians do not feel alone in their suffering.

Images outside the church. Jesus belongs not just to Christians but also, in one way or another, to other religions and even to those with no religion. Most traditional Jewish thought, reacting against Christian polemic and persecution, turned Jesus into a deceiver, a false prophet who practiced illicit magic (see below). Not all Jewish opinion, however, has been negative. Anticipating many modern Jewish thinkers, the Kairites, a non-Talmudic sect of the Middle Ages, claimed that Jesus was an authentic Jewish martyr whose identity Christianity distorted. More recently, some, downplaying Jesus' originality, have tried to reclaim him for Judaism by turning him into a Pharisee or Essene. Martin Buber (1878–1965) spoke of Jesus as his "great brother," who has "a great place. . .in Israel's history of faith." Probably the most positive Jewish evaluation of Jesus has come from the Orthodox German scholar Pinchas Lapide (1922–). Denying that Jesus was the Messiah, Lapide nonetheless expressed belief in Jesus' resurrection and acknowledged him as God's prophet to the Gentiles.

In Islam, Jesus, whom the Qurʾān mentions over a dozen times, is in the honored line of prophets that culminates in Muḥammad. Jesus was born of a virgin and lived without sin. He was a wise teacher and worked miracles. He was sentenced to be crucified but never was, instead ascending to heaven, from whence many Muslims expect him to return. Some believe that he will help Muḥammad at the last judgment. Jesus is not, however, divine, and Islamic teaching has it that the Gospels are corrupt: they contain imperfect, distorted memories of Jesus.

Popular Hinduism, although it has no place for Jesus' atoning death, has sometimes regarded him as an avatar, or incarnation, of Viṣṇu. Mahatma Gandhi (1869–1948) further found Jesus' teaching in the sermon on the mount, or rather that teaching as Lev Tolstoi (1828–1910) interpreted it, to be profoundly true; it is reported that Gandhi was fond of several Christian hymns about Jesus. (Martin Luther King Jr.'s application of the sermon on the mount, with its emphasis upon nonviolence, was, to the extent it derived from Gandhi, also derived from Tolstoi.) Another twentieth-century Hindu, Sarvepalli Radhakrishnan (1888–1975), philosopher and president of India in the 1960s, offered a sophisticated, philosophical interpretation of Jesus. Radhakrishnan maintained the superiority of his native Hinduism over Christianity by accepting the authenticity of Jesus' religious experience but distinguishing that experience from its interpretations, which were suggested to Jesus and his followers by their human traditions. One should differentiate Jesus' discovery of the universal self from his culturally determined conception of that discovery as a revelation from without.

Of the negative evaluations of Jesus, three are especially characteristic of modern times. The Grand Inquisitor in Fedor Dostoevskii's novel *The Brothers Karamazov* (1879–1880) speaks for many when he asserts that Jesus "judged humanity too highly," for "it was created weaker and lower than Christ thought." In other words, Jesus was unrealistic. One cannot love one's enemies, or do away with anger, or turn the other cheek. His utopian ethic is just that—utopian: it does not work in the real world.

Friedrich Nietzsche (1844–1900) offered a different criticism. For him, certain teachings in the Gospels reflect a slave mentality that should be rejected. If the unfortunate and oppressed turn the other cheek, this is only because, being without power, they can do nothing else; they are resigned in the face of their own oppression. So Jesus' nonviolence simply baptizes the status quo.

The classical Marxist critique is related: Jesus' eschatological vision acquiesces to the evils of the present instead of demanding historical change. The promises of future reward and warnings of future punishment devalue this world and discourage critical engagement with it. It is exceptional when, in his attempt to counter an oppressive bureaucracy, Milan Machoveč in *A Marxist Looks at Jesus* (1976) finds value in Jesus' demand for personal transformation in the light of the future's penetration of the present.

THE MODERN QUEST FOR THE HISTORICAL JESUS. For seventeen hundred years the canonical Gospels were approached in two different ways. The dominant approach was that of the Christian church, which accepted the texts at face value. The Gospels were thought historically accurate because divinely inspired and written by eyewitnesses or their friends. Occasionally there was recognition of inconcinnities. Augustine of Hippo (354–430) admitted that sometimes the evangelists pass on the same saying with different wording and that the frailty of memory could put the same events in different orders. John Calvin (1509–1564) went so far as to assert that the sermon on the mount is not the record of what Jesus said on one occasion but an artificial collection of things he said on various occasions. For the most part, however, the Gospels were identified with history.

The second approach before the modern period was that of Jewish polemic. This saw Jesus and his followers as deliberate deceivers (note *Mt.* 28:11–15). The medieval *Toledoth Jesus* attributes Jesus' miracles, which it does not deny, to magic. This is typical. The *Toledoth* tends not to assert that this or that event never happened, but rather to dispute its Christian interpretation.

The eighteenth century. Matters began to change in the middle of the eighteenth century. Modern historical methods emerged out of the rebirth of learning in the Renaissance; the Protestant Reformation introduced critical analysis of traditional religious stories (e.g., Roman Catholic legends); and the growing secularism that followed the wars of religion and the Enlightenment fostered disbelief in miracles. All of this encouraged the critical examination of the Gospels.

The most important of the early critics was Hermann Samuel Reimarus (1694–1768), a one-time German pastor much influenced by the English deists. Unable to believe in miracles, he compiled objections to the Bible, including the Gospels. Reimarus may have been the first in the modern period—the third-century Greek philosopher Porphyry anticipated him in this—to distinguish between what Jesus himself said and what his disciples said he said. To the latter alone he attributed belief in the second coming and Jesus' atoning death. Reimarus also argued that Jesus' kingdom was basically political and that his tomb was empty because the disciples stole the body. Reimarus's goal was to take Christianity, subtract the bad and unbelievable things from it, and hand the world a new and improved religion.

Shying from controversy, Reimarus did not publish his own work, which did not appear until after his death, when the playwright and critic Gotthold Ephraim Lessing (1729–1781) edited and published it. As Reimarus was rhetorically powerful, and as his rationalistic arguments had substance, his work generated support, as well as the predictable opposition.

The nineteenth century. The next phase in research saw the proliferation of the so-called liberal lives of Jesus in Germany. Agreeing with Reimarus that miracles do not happen, but dissenting from much of his skepticism regarding the historicity of the Gospels, these liberal lives, like the old Jewish polemic, tended not to dispute the events in the Gospels but rather their supernatural explanations. Instead, however, of invoking deliberate deception, as did the polemic, these critics thought in terms of misperception. Jesus did not walk on the water; he only appeared to do so when disciples on a boat saw him afar off on the shore. Jesus did not raise anyone from the dead; rather, some he prayed over recovered from comas, leading to that belief. Jesus' own resurrection was also simple misinterpretation. He did not die on the cross; he revived in the cool of the tomb. But his disciples, who were simple and superstitious, thought he had in fact died and come back to life.

This school of thought began to lose its popularity in middle of nineteenth century for several reasons. Most important was the critical work of the German historian and theologian, David Friedrich Strauss (1808–1874), who disparaged the liberal lives, as well as the conservative harmonists. Like the liberals, Strauss disbelieved in miracles. Unlike the liberals, he believed the gospel narratives to be thoroughly unreliable (and he dismissed *John* entirely). He considered them, although not Jesus himself, to be mythological, mostly the product of reflection upon the Old Testament narratives. Illustrative for Strauss is the transfiguration, which is based upon the similar transfiguration of Moses in *Exodus* 24 and 34, as appears from the several motifs both share. In addition, the feeding of the five thousand is modeled upon *2 Kings* 4:42–44, as the striking similarities show. Strauss was able to pile up parallel after parallel and establish on a critical footing the intertextual nature of the Gospels. In doing this he was, from one point of view, just following Tertullian and Eusebius, church fathers who had also observed the parallels between the Testaments. These earlier theologians were pursuing apologetical ends: the coincidences showed the same God at work. Strauss used the very same parallels to show the mythological character of most of the tradition.

Some who came after Strauss argued that he had not gone far enough, that Jesus was not a historical figure who attracted myths but was rather a myth himself, no more real than Zeus. The future was not, however, with such radicalism, which could never really explain Paul or Josephus's two references to Jesus. Far more lasting in their influence were Johannes Weiss (1863–1914) and Albert Schweitzer (1875–1965), two German scholars who, more trusting of the synoptics than Strauss, argued that the historical Jesus was all about eschatology. When Jesus said that the kingdom was at hand, he was announcing the imminence of the new world or utopian order (compare *Mk.* 9:1; 13:30). His expectations were not fulfilled in Easter or Pentecost or the destruction of the temple in 70 CE. Jesus was rather a mistaken apocalyptic visionary, which is why his ethics are so unrealistic. They are not for everyday life, but are instead an ethic of perfection designed for a world about to go out of existence.

The twentieth century. Most scholars since Schweitzer would concede that he and Weiss largely set the agenda. Most have thought that they were right to the extent that the traditions about Jesus are indeed full of eschatological themes. The debate has been to what extent those traditions go back to Jesus and whether Schweitzer's more or less literal interpretation of them is correct. Schweitzer himself tried to force a choice between eschatology and historicity. That is, he urged that, if the synoptics are reliable, then we must accept that Jesus was an eschatological prophet. If, to the contrary, Jesus was not an eschatological prophet, then the synoptics are unreliable guides and we should resign ourselves to skepticism.

Joachim Jeremias (1900–1979) of Göttingen was probably the most important player after Schweitzer to implicitly accept Schweitzer's basic analysis. Jeremias thought that, with the exception of the miracle stories, the synoptics are relatively reliable, and he agreed with Schweitzer that Jesus believed in a near consummation, expected his death to inaugurate the great tribulation, and hoped for his own resurrection as part of the general resurrection of the dead.

Not all accepted Schweitzer's dichotomy. While Rudolf Bultmann (1884–1976), for instance, believed that Jesus was indeed an eschatological prophet, he was far more skeptical about the historicity of the synoptics than Schweitzer. Bultmann's views lie somewhere between Strauss's skepticism and Schweitzer's confidence. A form critic, Bultmann sought to isolate, classify, and evaluate the components of the Jesus tradition. Given that the order of events varies from gospel to gospel and that there is usually no logical connection between adjacent episodes, we cannot, Bultmann concluded, know the true order of events. When one adds that the church, in Bultmann's view, contributed as much to the sayings attributed to Jesus as did Jesus himself, it was no longer possible to write a biography of Jesus, only to sketch an outline of his teachings within a rather bare narrative.

Bultmann envisaged an oral stage during which various types of materials circulated. He attempted to reconstruct the setting in life for these types, to determine whether they were used in polemic, apologetics, moral teaching, or proclamation. Bultmann's tendency was to suppose that if a unit was used in Christian polemic, then Christian polemic created it. Yet despite his skepticism, he remained convinced that Schweitzer was basically correct about Jesus' eschatology, which Bultmann interpreted in existential terms. Assuming moderns could no longer share ancient eschatological expectations, Bultmann asked how the language functioned and, in response, stressed that it brought people to decision in the face of the future.

Another scholar who rejected Schweitzer's dichotomy was C. H. Dodd (1884–1973). Although he accepted the basic synoptic portrait (with the exception of *Mark* 13 and its parallels), he disagreed with Schweitzer regarding eschatology. Dodd famously urged that Jesus had a "realized eschatology." That is, the kingdom of God, Jesus' name for the transcendent order in which there is no before or after, had manifested itself in the crisis of his ministry. Further, Jesus expected vindication after death, which he variously spoke of as resurrection, the coming of the Son of man, and the rebuilding of the temple. But the church came to long for the future coming of the Son of man, now conceived of as Jesus' return. In this way eschatology ceased to be realized. The change of outlook was such that the church eventually, and according to Dodd regrettably, made *Revelation* its canonical finale.

Recent work. Probably the most prominent of recent scholars to reject Schweitzer's dichotomy is John Dominic Crossan (1934–). In his several books on Jesus he has argued that while most of the material Schweitzer used in his reconstruction of Jesus came from the church, we can still know a great deal about Jesus, who is very different from Schweitzer's vision of an eschatological visionary. For Crossan, Jesus was indeed utopian, but what he envisaged was not a traditional eschatological scenario. Jesus was a Jewish peasant whose revolutionary social program is best preserved in aphorisms and parables. These depict a Cynic-like sage who welcomes outcasts as equals. Traditional eschatology—resurrection, last judgment, heaven, hell—and their attendant violence do not make an appearance.

Crossan was one of the founding members of the Jesus Seminar, the other cofounder being Robert Funk (1926–). The Seminar is a loosely affiliated group of fewer than one hundred scholars who began, in the 1980s, meeting twice a year to discuss and vote upon questions concerning the historical Jesus. The upshot of their work is the conclusion that approximately 18 percent of the sayings attributed to Jesus in the synoptics go back to him or represent something that he said. Among their other conclusions, which have generated much controversy, are these: only one saying in *John* reflects something Jesus said (4:44); Jesus did not consider himself to be the messiah or Son of man; he said little or nothing about resurrection and judgment; he was a laconic sage known for pithy one-liners and parables; he did not keep kosher; and he did not often cite or refer to scripture. A major achievement of the Jesus Seminar, whose conclusions represent only one group of scholars, has been to bring contemporary critical work to public notice.

Many are now wont to divide the question for the historical Jesus into three stages. The first stage, it is claimed, was the nineteenth-century German endeavor so memorably reported by Schweitzer. The second was the "new quest" carried on in the 1950s and 1960s by some of Bultmann's students and a few others. The "third quest" is the name now often attached to the labors of the present moment. This typology, which obscures much more than it illumines, will, one hopes, eventually fall into oblivion. One fundamental failing is that it dismisses with silence the period between the first quest and the new quest. Some have even called this the period of "no quest," which scarcely fits the facts. The typology is also problematic because most work of importance that went on during and after the 1950s cannot be subsumed under the new quest, and because the third quest has no truly distinguishing features. Instead of dividing post-Schweitzerian activities into chronological segments or different quests, it is more useful to lay aside the diachronic in favor of the synchronic, to abandon periodization for a typology that allows the classification of a book, whether from the 1920s or the 1990s, with those akin to it. One should lump together books that present Jesus as a liberal social reformer, those that present him as forerunner of Christian orthodoxy, those that reconstruct him as an eschatological Jewish prophet, those that liken him to a wisdom sage, those that regard him as having been a political revolutionary, and so on. This is the best way to judge the progress of the discipline.

The most striking fact about recent research is that it resents easy generalization precisely because of its pluralism. Contemporary work has no characteristic method, it has no body of shared conclusions, and it has no common set of historiographical or theological presuppositions. Those who continue to speak of the third quest and delineate its distinctive features are engaging in an antiquated activity that needs to be deconstructed. The lists are all tendentious because the age of the easy generalization and the authentic consensus is over.

A Reconstruction. The most important sources for Jesus are found in the New Testament—Paul and the synoptics and their sources, including *Q*, the hypothetical sayings source used by *Matthew* and *Luke*. The *Gospel of John* is of less help, as are the various apocryphal gospels, although the *Gospel of Thomas* seems to contain some early and independent sayings of Jesus. Non-Christian sources—the Jewish historian Josephus, the Babylonian *Talmud*, the Roman historians Tacitus and Suetonius, and others—do little more than confirm Jesus' existence and his crucifixion under Pontius Pilate.

Scholars disagree on the reliability of the extant sources and so they do not concur on how much we can know about the historical Jesus. Discussions of method have led to no consensus. Many attempt to reconstruct Jesus by passing individual units through various criteria of authenticity. Such criteria are not particularly reliable. It seems safer to base one's major conclusions upon the larger patterns and themes that run throughout the various sources. It is probably in such patterns and themes, if anywhere, that the Jesus of history has been remembered.

Before the public ministry. Aside from *Matthew* 1–2 and *Luke* 1–2, first-century Christian writings have next to nothing to say about Jesus before his public ministry, and those two chapters are poor sources for history. Some agreements between *Matthew* 1–2 and *Luke* 1–2, however, preserve memory. Jesus' parents were named Mary and Joseph, and whether or not he was born in Bethlehem, he did later live in Nazareth (*Mt.* 2:23; *Lk.* 2:39). One can also plausibly defend Jesus' Davidic descent, his birth before the death of Herod the Great in 4 BCE, and perhaps the possibility that Mary became pregnant before Joseph and Mary began to live together.

John the Baptist and Jesus. John, who baptized Jesus, was an ascetic. The synoptics have him dwelling in the desert (*Mk.* 1:4; *Jn.* 1:23, 28), wearing camel's hair (*Mk.* 1:6), and eating locusts and wild honey (*Mk.* 1:6). *Matthew* 11:18 = *Luke* 7:33 (*Q*) characterizes him as neither eating nor drinking, and *Mark* 2:18 refers to the fasting of his followers.

John's asceticism was part of a moral earnestness linked to belief in an imminent consummation: he called for repentance in view of the coming judgment (*Mt.* 3:7–10 = *Lk.* 3:7–9 [*Q*]; *Mk.* 1:4). John the Baptist opposed the notion that all Israel has a place in the world to come. More than a few Jews probably hoped that their descent from Abraham would, as long as they did not abandon the Torah, gain them entry into the world to come. John thought otherwise (*Mt.* 3:9 = *Lk.* 3:8 [*Q*]).

That Jesus submitted to John's baptism shows his essential agreement with him on many, if not most, matters. This is confirmed by his praise of the Baptist (*Mt.* 11:7–19 = *Lk.* 7:24–35 [*Q*]). It is natural that Jesus was remembered as being, like John, a preacher of repentance, as being preoccupied with eschatology, and as being convinced that membership in the covenant guarantees nothing. There is not even fundamental discontinuity in the matter of asceticism, for the missionary discourses depict a very harsh lifestyle (*Mt.* 10:1–16 = *Lk.* 10:1–16 [*Q*]; *Mk.* 6:8–11), and some disciples abandoned families and business (*Mt.* 8:18–22 = *Lk.* 9:57–60 [*Q*]; *Mt.* 10:37 = *Lk.* 14:26 [*Q*]). Jesus himself was unmarried (presumably *Matthew* 19:12 was originally a riposte to the slander that he was a eunuch). He demanded the guarding of sexual desire (*Mt.* 5:27–28), issued strident warnings about money and property (*Mt.* 8:19–20 = *Lk.* 9:57–58 [*Q*]; *Mt.* 10:9–10, 13 = *Lk.* 10:4, 7–8 [*Q*]), and in general lived and demanded self-discipline and rigorous self-denial (*Mt.* 10:38 = *Lk.* 14:27 [*Q*]; *Mk.* 8:34).

Baptism and temptation. Although the baptismal narratives convey the theology of the church, one need not doubt that Jesus did, in fact, submit to John's baptism. This is not the sort of event the early church would have invented. It is, moreover, plausible that Jesus experienced his baptism as a prophetic call. This would explain why his public ministry was remembered as beginning shortly thereafter and why his followers narrated the event even though it involved Jesus submitting to John.

The accounts of Jesus' temptation also express the theology of the community. Even so, stories that do not reproduce history may convey it, and the temptation narratives highlight several themes that appear elsewhere in the sources. That Jesus overcomes Satan coheres with his being a successful exorcist. That Jesus is, as the devil's challenges assume, a miracle worker, harmonizes with the rest of the tradition. That Jesus does not perform miracles on demand matches *Mark* 8:11–13, where he refuses to grant a sign (see also *Mt.* 12:38–42 = *Lk.* 11:29–30 [*Q*]). And that Jesus is a person of great faith who, in need, waits upon God, also matches the rest of the tradition (see *Mt.* 6:11 = *Lk.* 11:3 [*Q*]; *Mt.* 6:25–34 = *Lk.* 12:22–32 [*Q*]).

Disciples. Because he was a teacher, Jesus had disciples. Not all scholars agree, however, that he gathered a select group of twelve. Doubt comes from the fact that they appear only once in *Q* (*Mt.* 19.28 = *Lk.* 22:28–30). Yet "the twelve" is already a fixed expression in *1 Corinthians* 15:5, which guarantees its antiquity. Furthermore, Judas, who was, according to the Gospels, chosen by Jesus himself, was known as "one of the twelve" (*Mk.* 14:10, 43). This is unlikely to be free invention.

In selecting a group of twelve, Jesus' intent was probably the creation of a prophetic and eschatological symbol: the twelve disciples represented the twelve tribes of Israel. Jesus presumably shared the expectation of the eschatological restoration of the twelve lost, or rather hidden, tribes. In line with this, *Matthew* 19:28 = *Luke* 22:28–30 (*Q*) promises Jesus' followers that they will "rule over" or "judge" the twelve tribes of Israel, which assumes that those tribes will soon return to the land.

If the twelve functioned as an eschatological symbol of Israel's renewal, they also served, along with others, to spread Jesus' message. This is likely why we have reliable information about Jesus in the first place. Pre-Easter itinerants, according to *Matthew* 10:7 = *Luke* 10:9 (*Q*), were instructed to proclaim the kingdom of God and its imminence. Although we do not learn what specifically they were to say, their message cannot have differed much from that of Jesus. Certainly their other activities were imitative, for their purpose was to enlarge Jesus' influence. So their proclamation must have been his proclamation. In other words, recitation of the teaching of Jesus predates the church.

The traditional image of Jesus wandering around Galilee with twelve male disciples is mistaken. Not only were the twelve presumably part of a larger group, but *Mark* 15:40–41 tells us that, when Jesus was crucified, some women looked on from a distance, among them Mary Magdalene, Mary the mother of James the younger and of Joses, and Salome. *Luke* 8:1–3, which in several particulars derived from non-Markan tradition, adds that Jesus was accompanied by "Mary, called Magdalene, from whom seven demons had gone out, and Joanna, the wife of Herod's steward Chuza, and Susanna, and many others, who provided for them out of their resources." This text and *Mark* 15:40–41 stand out from the rest of the synoptic tradition, which otherwise does not inform us that women were among the itinerants who followed Jesus. Notwithstanding its meager attestation in the extant sources, the existence of such a group is not a fiction.

Mark 15:41 says that the women "ministered" to Jesus. This may mean that they offered him financial support (so *Luke* 8:3) or served him at table. But *Mark* also says that the women "followed" Jesus, and this implies that they were, like the twelve, "disciples." Perhaps we should think of Mary Magdalene and the others as students of Jesus and genuine coworkers.

Eschatology. Jesus lived within an eschatological scenario, which he thought of as already unfolding. He anticipated the resurrection of the dead and the final judgment (*Mt.* 8:11–12 = *Lk.* 13:28–29 [*Q*]; *Mt.* 12:38–42 = *Lk.* 11:29–32 [*Q*]; *Mk.* 12:18–27). He spoke in terms of rewards for the righteous and recompense for the wicked (*Mt.* 10:32–33 = *Lk.* 12:8–9 [*Q*]; *Mk.* 8:35; 9:41–48; *Mt.* 25:14–30, 31–46). He prophesied trouble for the saints (*Mt.* 10:14–15 = *Lk.* 10:11–12 [*Q*]; *Mt.* 10:16 = *Lk.* 10:3 [*Q*]; *Mk.* 10:35–40; *Mt.* 10:23, 25). He envisaged a revised, second edition of earth with the earlier deficiencies corrected—paradise regained, heaven on earth. And he hoped all of this would transpire soon. There is no evidence that Jesus shared the expectation of some that the Gentiles would suffer destruction at the end, and the existence of an early Christian mission to Gentiles confirms that he did not anticipate their annihilation.

Jesus announced the beginning of God's reign in the present (*Mt.* 12:28 = *Lk.* 11:20 [*Q*]; *Lk.* 17:20) and otherwise indicated its arrival by speaking of the defeat of Satan (*Mt.* 12:28 = *Lk.* 11:20 [*Q*]; *Mk.* 13:27; *Lk.* 10:18). So eschatological expectations were being fulfilled: "Blessed are the eyes that see what you see! For I tell you that many prophets and kings desired to see what you see, but did not see it, and to hear what you hear, but did not hear it" (*Mt.* 13:16–17 = *Lk.* 10:23–24 [*Q*]). Matters are similar in *Matthew* 10:35–36 = *Luke* 12:53 (*Q*), which paraphrases the eschatological prophecy of family strife in *Micah* 7:6 and makes it a present reality. So once again Jesus' ministry fulfills an eschatological oracle. In this case, however, it is not the saving miracles of the end time that have entered the present, but the tribulation of the latter days.

Torah and ethics. In *Mark* 7:8–13 Jesus rebuts opponents by accusing them of not honoring their father and mother. In *Mark* 10:19 he enumerates and endorses the last half of the Decalogue. And in the Sabbath controversies he rejects the charge of being reckless. Jesus nowhere declares that the Sabbath has been abolished, as did some later Christians. Nor does he say that the true God did not institute the Sabbath. Instead of attacking the Sabbath, Jesus teaches that one imperative can trump another, that human need can, in some cases, overrule Sabbath keeping, which, it is assumed, remains intact. There is nothing revolutionary in this: Jewish law certainly knew that Sabbath observance might be the lesser of two goods (the law-observant Maccabees decided to take up arms on the Sabbath).

If tradition remembers Jesus upholding the Torah, it also shows another side. The question in *Mark* 3:33, "Who are my mother and my brothers?" does not honor Jesus' mother. Closely related is *Matthew* 10:37 = *Luke* 14:26 (*Q*): "Whoever comes to me and does not hate his own father and mother. . .cannot be my disciple." This is a deliberate contrast to *Exodus* 20:12 = *Deuteronomy* 5:16, "Honor your father and your mother." Even more far-reaching are *Matthew* 5:31–32 = *Luke* 16:18 (*Q*) and *Mark* 10:2–12 (cf. *1 Cor.* 7:10–11), where Jesus prohibits divorce, which Moses permits (*Dt.* 24:1–4).

The radical rhetoric is tied to eschatology. The kingdom relativizes Moses' imperatives by trumping them when the two conflict. If, moreover, the kingdom is at hand, then the renewal of the world is nigh; and if the renewal of the world is nigh, then paradise is about to be restored; and if paradise is about to be restored, then concessions to sin are no longer needed. This is the implicit logic of *Mark* 10:1–12. Because the last things will be as the first, and because, for Jesus, the last things have begun to come, so have the first. Jesus can therefore promulgate a prelapsarian ethic. Insofar as the law contains concessions to the fall, it requires repair.

That the coming of the kingdom impinges upon the law is explicit in *Matthew* 11:12–13 = *Luke* 16:16 (*Q*). Here Jesus distinguishes between the time of the law and the prophets on the one hand and the time of the kingdom on the other. This means that the time of the law has, in some sense, been superseded by the time of the eschatological kingdom.

The marginal. Jesus ministered to individuals with little social status. In *Mark,* he heals demoniacs, paralytics, a leper, and blind men. It is the same in *Q* (*Mt.* 11:2–6 = *Lk.* 7:18–23), in which Jesus blesses the poor, those in mourning, the thirsty, and the persecuted (*Mt.* 5:3–4, 6, 11–12 = *Lk.* 6:20–23) and announces that the humble will be exalted (*Mt.* 23:12 = *Lk.* 14:11). In *Luke,* Jesus takes the side of poor Lazarus, not the rich man (16:19–31), and he depicts Samaritans, traditionally enemies of Jews, in a good light (10:29–37; 17:11–19).

Even when one takes into account that healers necessarily minister to the sick, that the well have no need of a physician, one comes away with the impression that Jesus had a special interest in those on the margins of society. Perhaps this was part and parcel of the great eschatological reversal, which would see the humble exalted. Yet *Q* also has him healing the son or servant of a centurion, a person of great authority, without demanding any change of life (*Mt.* 8:5–13 = *Lk.* 7:1–10 [*Q*]); *Matthew* has Jesus giving advice to those who can afford to give alms (6:1–4); and *Luke* has him eating with a well-to-do toll collector, Zacchaeus (19:1–10), and being supported by "Joanna, the wife of Herod's steward Chuza," who must have been prosperous (8:3). So the tradition does not depict Jesus as engaging only those in the same socioeconomic circumstances but rather being expansive in his ministry and affections.

Miracles. Whether one explains the fact by appealing to divine intervention, parapsychology, or the psychosomatic phenomena of mass psychology, Jesus was known as a miracle worker during his own life. Surely the hope of being healed or beholding miracles brought much of his audience to him. His opponents themselves conceded his abilities when they attributed his success to an allegiance with Beelzebul (*Mt.* 12:27 = *Lk.* 11:19 [*Q*]; *Mk.* 3:22–27; cf. *Jn.* 7:20; 8:48; 10:20).

Although Jesus was a miracle worker, this does not guarantee the authenticity of any particular miracle story, and as they stand many of the stories are highly symbolic and vehicles of Christian theology. The transfiguration narrative in *Mark* 9:2–8 makes Jesus like the glowing Moses of *Exodus* 34 and so confirms him as the prophet foretold in *Deuteronomy* 18:15–18. The feeding of five thousand in *Mark* 6:32–44 and *John* 6:1–15 not only foreshadows the last supper but strongly recalls the miracle of *2 Kings* 4:42–44 and so makes Jesus like Elisha. The story of the widow of Nain in *Luke* 7:11–17 makes Jesus rather like Elijah because it is clearly modeled upon *1 Kings* 17:8–24. All this is typical.

The tradition interprets the miracles of Jesus as signs of eschatological fulfillment, and this was the interpretation of Jesus himself. According to *Matthew* 12:27 = *Luke* 11:20 (*Q*), if Jesus casts out demons by the finger of God, then the kingdom of God has come. The defeat of Satan's realm is what happens in the latter days, so if Satan's realm is now being conquered, the latter days have arrived.

Self-conception. That Jesus was arrested, not the disciples, shows that he was from the beginning the center of the new movement. This is confirmed by the title on the cross: Pilate charges Jesus alone with being "the king of the Jews" (*Mk.* 15:25; *Jn.* 19:19).

Some regarded Jesus as a prophet (*Mk.* 6:14–16; 8:28; *Lk.* 7:16), and the title appears on his own lips in *Mark* 6:4 and *Luke* 13:33. As *Matthew* 5:3–6, 11–12 = *Luke* 6:20–23 (*Q*, the beatitudes) and *Matthew* 11:2–6 = *Luke* 7:18–23 (*Q*, Jesus' answer to the Baptist) use the language of *Isaiah* 61:1–2, Jesus probably understood himself to be specifically the anointed prophet of Isaiah's oracle.

In addition to taking on the role of the prophet of *Isaiah* 61, there is a good chance that Jesus, like the early church (cf. *Acts* 3:22), reckoned himself the prophet like Moses of *Deuteronomy* 18:15 and 18:18 in the time of a new exodus. In *Matthew* 12:28 = *Luke* 11:20 (*Q*), Jesus alludes to *Exodus* 8:19 in claiming that he casts out demons by the finger of God, so in this respect at least he is like the miracle-working Moses. In reversing the commandment to love parents (*Mt.* 10:37 = *Lk.* 14:26 [*Q*]), Jesus sets his own words over against those of the first lawgiver. *Matthew* 5:21–22 and 27–28 do the same thing. He also characterizes his own generation with language originally descriptive of Moses' generation (cf. *Mt.* 12:38–42 = *Lk.* *Q* 11:29–30 [*Q*] with *Dt.* 1:35).

Traditionally, Christians have taken Jesus' favorite epithet in the synoptics, "the Son of man," to indicate his true humanity. Modern scholars, however, adopt other interpretations. Some suppose that "the Son of man" was a known messianic title that Jesus used of himself or another yet to come. For others, "the Son of man" goes back to an Aramaic idiom that meant something like "one"; it was an indirect way of talking about oneself, of speaking of the particular by way of the general (cf. "One must do one's duty").

The linguistic issues surrounding "the Son of man" in first-century Aramaic remain disputed. Further, even if the phrase was common and functioned like a pronoun, one can always take an everyday expression and do something interesting with it (cf. the use of "I am" in *John*). This is not an idle point given that Jesus was innovative in the linguistic sphere (e.g., in his use of "amen" at the beginning of sentences).

Some sayings link "the Son of man" with *Daniel* 7. Especially important is *Matthew* 10:32–33 = *Luke* 12:8–9, which probably goes back to Jesus. This *Q* saying echoes *Daniel* 7 in that it concerns the last judgment, has as its central figure the Son of man, depicts that figure as being "before" the divine court, sets the stage with angels, and speaks to a situation of persecution. This then is evidence that Jesus associated himself and his ministry with *Daniel's* vision of the judgment and "one like a son of man."

Regarding the promises to David and the title "messiah" (anointed one) or its Greek equivalent, "Christ," *Mark* 12:35–37 (on David's son and Lord) does not help, for even if it preserves an argument from Jesus, the point has been lost. Also less than helpful are *Mark* 8:27–30 (the confession at Caesarea Philippi) and 14:53–65 (the Jewish trial in which Jesus acknowledges his messiahship). For aside from how much history lies behind these passages, in neither does Jesus comment directly on the title "messiah." The very fact that "messiah" is so rare in the Gospels but so common in the epistles has suggested to many that the title betrays a post-Easter interpretation of Jesus.

Nonetheless, the Romans did execute him as a politically dangerous "king" (*Mk.* 15:26), and since they surely did not invent this charge out of nothing, somebody must have perceived Jesus as such. If Jesus identified himself with the eschatological prophet of *Isaiah* 61:1–2, he would have thought of himself as an anointed one, for that figure declares, "The Lord has anointed me." Again, if either *Matthew* 19:28 = *Luke* 22:28–30 (*Q*: Jesus is the leader of those who sit on thrones) or *Mark* 10:35–40 (disciples sit at Jesus' right and left in the kingdom) contains authentic material, Jesus must have thought himself king. The same result follows if he spoke of rebuilding the temple, for *2 Samuel* 7:4–17 foresees a descendant of David who will build God's house, and this was an eschatological prophecy in first-century Judaism.

Anticipation of death. Jesus presumably anticipated suffering and an untimely death. Not only do the prophetic and apocalyptic traditions, which so influenced Jesus, recognize that the saints must pass through tribulation before salvation arrives, but the Baptist's martyrdom must have served as a warning. A number of sayings furthermore depict Jesus enjoining his followers to reckon seriously with the prospect of both suffering and death; if any of them is authentic, then it is likely that Jesus himself expected to suffer and die before his time, for surely he would have anticipated for himself a fate similar to those around him.

Jesus likely imagined his future as belonging to the tribulation that would herald the end. *Matthew* 10:34–35 = *Luke* 12:51–53 *(Q)* applies *Micah* 7:6 to the present, and *Micah* 7:6 was widely understood as a prophecy of what the rabbis called "the woe of the messiah." In line with this, *Luke* 16:16 speaks of the kingdom of heaven suffering violence and seems to construe the death of the Baptist as belonging to the eschatological trial. According to *Mark* 9:49, everyone will go through the coming eschatological fire, and there is no reason to exclude Jesus from the generalization, as *Luke* 12:49–50, if authentic, confirms.

Jerusalem. Jesus went to Jerusalem in either 30 or 33 CE (*John* has him going up more than once, perhaps correctly). Whether Jesus wanted to provoke a confrontation, or even to die, *Mark* 11:1–10 and *John* 12:12–19 have him deliberately approaching Jerusalem not on foot but on a donkey, thereby making a public display of kingship (cf. *Zec.* 9:9). The scenario may be historical given Jesus' exalted self-conception, as well as the probability that he engaged in another prophetic action at the same time, turning over tables in the temple (*Mk.* 11:11, 15–17). Commentators tend to suppose that, by this disturbance, he was either symbolizing the future destruction of the temple or protesting certain corrupt practices, but the two interpretations need not be opposed. Protestation of abuses and an enacted parable of destruction probably went together.

Arrest and interrogation. Whether or not it was the incident in the temple that eventually led to Jesus' arrest, he was probably brought before some members of the Jerusalem Sanhedrin, although we should probably not speak of a formal trial (*Mk.* 14:53–65; *Jn.* 18:13–24). We can further accept the report that he was then accused of acting and speaking against the temple, and that the authorities, probably because they did not have the authority to execute him (*Jn.* 18:31), handed him over to Pilate (*Mk.* 15:1; *Jn.* 18:28), who ordered him to be crucified as a "king" or political pretender.

Resurrection. The traditions about Jesus' resurrection do not belong to the story of the historical Jesus but to church history. The explanations for them are manifold. (1) According to the traditional theological story, God raised Jesus from the dead. The tomb was empty, and people saw the glorified Jesus. (2) The tomb was empty, not because Jesus rose from the dead, but because followers visited the wrong tomb, because someone later moved the body to a permanent burial site (cf. *Jn.* 20:2, 14–15), or because the authorities, not wanting a venerated tomb, moved the body. Early Christians then interpreted the empty tomb in terms of their religious hopes and dreams, and some of them then had subjective visions. (3) To turn things around, the empty tomb was a late legend and Easter faith began with the subjective christophanies of Peter and the other disciples. (4) The visions were real because the disembodied Jesus survived death and communicated to his disciples, but the story of the empty tomb is late and legendary, the creation of people who believed, on the basis of their faith alone, that, if Jesus were alive, he had been resurrected, and so the body must have disappeared. (5) There was deliberate fraud. The disciples stole the body and concocted belief in the resurrection because they wanted to be leaders of a religious movement. (6) The disciples saw Jesus in terms of a traditional cluster of motifs surrounding the persecuted righteous individual whom God rescues from death (*2 Mc.* 7; *Wis.* 3–4), and after his death simply posited his vindication as an act of faith.

The appearance stories and empty tomb, however explained, emerged later and presuppose the resurrection.

SEE ALSO Atonement, article on Christian Concepts; Biblical Literature, article on New Testament; God, article on God in the New Testament; Justification; Redemption; Theology, article on Christian Theology; Trinity.

BIBLIOGRAPHY

Crossan, John Dominic. *The Historical Jesus: The Life of a Mediterranean Jewish Peasant.* San Francisco, 1991. The most discussed of recent books on Jesus.

Dawes, Gregory W. *The Historical Jesus Question: The Challenge of History to Religious Authority.* Louisville, Ky., 2001. An instructive review of the theological and philosophical issues raised by the modern quest for Jesus.

Funk, Robert W., Roy Hoover, and the Jesus Seminar. *The Five Gospels: The Search for the Authentic Words of Jesus.* New York, 1993. The results of the Jesus Seminar's voting on the words of Jesus.

Jeremias, Joachim. *New Testament Theology.* Translated by John Bowden. Vol. 1: *The Proclamation of Jesus.* London, 1971. A systematic presentation of Jesus' teaching by a famous German scholar.

Machoveč, Milan. *A Marxist Looks at Jesus.* Philadelphia, 1976. A sympathetic examination of Jesus from a Marxist perspective.

Meier, John P. *A Marginal Jew: Rethinking the Historical Jesus.* 3 vols. New York, 1991–2001. A detailed and comprehensive discussion of all the major issues and topics by a Roman Catholic.

Pelikan, Jaroslav Jan. *Jesus through the Centuries: His Place in the History of Culture.* New Haven, Conn., 1985. A learned overview of how Jesus has been interpreted from the first century to the twentieth century.

Sanders, E. P. *Jesus and Judaism.* London, 1985. An attempt to understand Jesus within his Jewish context that focuses first on what he did rather than what he said.

Schweitzer, Albert. *The Quest of the Historical Jesus.* The first complete edition. Translated by W. Montgomery, J. R. Coates, Susan Cupitt, and John Bowden. Minneapolis, 2001. The classic review of the eighteenth and nineteenth centuries that ends with Schweitzer's own interpretation.

Theissen, Gred, and Annette Merz. *The Historical Jesus: A Comprehensive Guide.* Translated by John Bowden. Minneapolis, 1998. The best contemporary introduction to all facets of the discussion.

Vermes, Geza. *Jesus the Jew: A Historian's Reading of the Gospels.* Philadelphia, 1973. A Jewish scholar's attempt to depict Jesus as a Galilean holy man.

Weaver, Walter P. *The Historical Jesus in the Twentieth Century, 1900–1950.* Harrisburg, Pa., 1999. A capable overview of Jesus research in the first half of the twentieth century.

DALE C. ALLISON, JR. (2005)

JESUS MOVEMENT refers to a communally oriented fundamentalist Christian movement that developed in the 1960s and 1970s among relatively affluent young people in the United States. Early Jesus Movement groups attracted considerable media attention and became the focus of some Christian religious leaders who were concerned about whether or not such groups were "truly Christian." Well-publicized lifestyle practices that included long hair and casual dress contributed to the controversy, as did overt efforts to proselytize other young people.

The movement gained much attention for about three decades and spread to other countries, becoming worldwide in scope. One controversial Jesus Movement group, the Children of God, at one time had outposts in nearly two hundred countries. The movement lost momentum in the 1990s, and by the early 2000s only a few Jesus Movement groups, such as Jesus People USA, centered in Chicago, and the Family (formerly known as the Children of God) were still in existence. Remnants of some Jesus Movement groups joined Pentecostal churches, such as Calvary Chapel, a new denomination that has many features akin to the Jesus Movement.

Most participants in early Jesus Movement groups were heavily involved with drugs, alcohol, tobacco, and premarital sex prior to joining. Participation in the Jesus Movement usually led to dramatic behavioral changes, with the notion of "getting high on Jesus" seeming to serve as a replacement for previous activities. The Jesus Movement seems to have served as a "halfway house" for many participants who had become disaffected from normal society and were involved with dissipated lifestyles.

Some Jesus Movement groups grew rapidly, attracting much media attention. Recruitment was aided by the establishment of communal centers where converts could find food, shelter, and friendship (along with the "message of Jesus"). This communal context also allowed more rigorous resocialization to take place in the relative isolation of such settings, with some Jesus Movement groups—such as Shiloh, which began in southern California in the late 1960s but shifted its headquarters to a rural setting in Oregon in the 1970s—developing sophisticated approaches to member training. Later, as the "target population" of young people decreased in number, recruitment became more difficult, forcing experimentation with new methods: "Jesus rock" concerts were held, Christian coffee houses were opened, and attention was paid to recruitment on college campuses, among other tactics.

Initial Jesus Movement recruits were mostly single young males, which contributed to the considerable geographic mobility that characterized the movement's early years. Members were not burdened with families and could be sent to faraway places for missionary activities. Members of several groups, such as the Children of God, could decide to "live on the road." Other groups were also quite mobile as they "spread the Word" in the United States and elsewhere.

Major media portrayed the large and energetic Jesus Movement as a sharp contrast to the considerable turmoil over the Vietnam War, race, and other issues in American society. Some societal leaders initially celebrated the apparent "return to religion" by many young people. Later, the media, as well as the general public and policymakers, soured on the recruitment efforts of most Jesus Movement groups. Unsavory actions, such as the Children of God's "flirty fishing," which for a time used sex as a recruiting tool, were revealed. In addition, most Jesus Movement groups were "high demand" religions that expected participants to "forsake all" to follow Jesus and obey group leaders.

When accusations of brainwashing and mind control were made against some Jesus Movement groups, authorities sought to exert control over the groups and to limit recruitment. Such accusations were refuted by scholars studying these groups, but such claims persisted and led to problems for some Jesus Movement groups. Indeed, the first recorded "deprogramming" of a member of a new religious movement (the first of many thousands in the United States and other countries) involved a member of the Children of God.

More females, including some with children, were attracted to the Jesus Movement groups, which were usually communal, facilitating the establishment of families. With the arrival of children (sometimes in large numbers, since most Jesus Movement groups did not practice birth control), life in the Jesus Movement underwent dramatic change. Groups with families as a large proportion of membership had to support the family units. Membership figures for the Family demonstrate the magnitude of this change. As of 2003, the Family had approximately ten thousand members worldwide, with well over half of them being children. The presence of families had a domesticating effect on Jesus Movement groups. Mobility had to be curtailed, making groups much more sedentary. This led to a lessening of missionary activities in other countries. Divisions of labor were established within the groups, so that fewer members traveled and proselytized, while most took care of children and sought ways to support growing families.

The presence of children sometimes led to conflicts with public officials over child care and schooling. Some Jesus Movement groups home-schooled their children in an effort to inculcate them with the group's values, thus drawing attention from local officials. Child-custody battles sometimes developed, brought on by a parent wanting to divorce his or her spouse and leave the group. The Children of God was even accused of child sex abuse as a result of the libertine lifestyle some adult members led for a time. In the 1980s and 1990s these accusations led to many children being temporary removed from Family homes in different countries, including France, Spain, Argentina, and Australia. The children were eventually returned to their families, and in Australia the government even had to pay damages for the actions taken toward the children.

Methods of group support varied considerably as members experimented with ways of raising money or engaging in activities that would support the group. Street solicitation for money was one successful method, but was not the most prevalent. The Children of God used this method, distributing their infamous "Mo Letters," which were tracts written by the Moses Davide Berg who established the group. Group members asked for money in exchange for the tracts, a fund raising method they called *litnessing*. The Children of God also scavenged for discarded fruits and vegetables from local markets, among other ways of finding sustenance. Other Jesus Movement groups, such as Shiloh, relied on work teams in agricultural and construction industries for support, as well as donations from members and their parents, and some even accepted contributions from governmental agencies. Some Jesus Movement groups also sold music tapes and put on concerts as they experimented with ways to support themselves.

The Jesus Movement still exits, even if some groups have changed markedly as a result of the material concerns discussed above. The apex of the Jesus Movement occurred in the 1970s and early 1980s, when there were Jesus Movement groups operating in many different areas of the United States, as well as in many other countries. The movement lost momentum as a result of fewer recruits, shifting societal circumstances, and problems deriving from the maturing of the membership and the establishment of families.

See Also Brainwashing (Debate); Family, The.

Bibliography

Di Sabatino, David. *The Jesus People Movement: An Annotated Bibliography and General Resource.* Westport, Conn., 1999. A good reference by an insider in the movement.

Ellwood, Robert S. *One Way: The Jesus Movement and Its Meaning.* Englewood Cliffs, N.J., 1973. An excellent early study by a major scholar.

Enroth, Ronald, Edward Ericson, and C. Breckinridge Peters. *The Jesus People: Old Time Religion in an Age of Aquarius.* Grand Rapids, Mich., 1972. One of the first major studies, filled with good descriptive material.

Lewis, James, and J. Gordon Melton. *Sex, Slander, and Salvation: Investigating the Family/Children of God.* Stanford, Calif., 1994. Edited volume with chapters from a number of major scholars, focusing on changes occurring in this controversial Jesus Movement group.

Richardson, James T., and Rex Davis. "Experiential Fundamentalism." *Journal of the American Academy of Religion* 51 (1983): 397–425. Article focusing on the melding of Christian fundamentalism with an experiential lifestyle, leading to some unexpected beliefs and behaviors.

Richardson, James T., Mary White Stewart, and Robert Simmonds. *Organized Miracles: A Study of a Contemporary Youth, Communal, Fundamentalist Organization.* New Brunswick, N.J., 1979. This book describes the second largest Jesus Movement group, Shiloh, from inception through the late 1970s.

Stewart, David T., and James T. Richardson. "Mundane Materialism: How Tax Policies and Other Governmental Regulation Affected Beliefs and Practices of Jesus Movement Organizations." *Journal of the American Academy of Religion* 67 (1999): 825–847. This article reports research on how material concerns of Jesus Movment groups affected every aspect of group culture, including beliefs.

Van Zandt, David. *Living in the Children of God.* Princeton, N.J., 1991. A detailed report on life in this controversial Jesus Movement group.

JAMES T. RICHARDSON (2005)

JEVONS, F. B.

JEVONS, F. B. (1858–1936), was an English classical scholar. Frank Byron Jevons played a significant role in popularizing the comparative study of religion in the English-speaking world during the two decades before World War I. Jevons, who was classical tutor at the University of Durham from 1882 to 1910, joined R. R. Marett, Andrew Lang, Gilbert Murray, and other Edwardians in applying the theoretical formulas of British evolutionist anthropology to the interpretation of Greco-Roman texts.

Magic was his special area of interest; he questioned the conclusion of James G. Frazer and others that magic necessarily preceded religion along a unilineal, evolutionary pathway. As he put it in his *Idea of God in Early Religions* (1910), magic and religion were "two moods" that were different from the beginning. Likewise, prayers and the worship of gods were phenomena that were originally separate from (and apparently as ancient as) spells and fetishism.

Jevons's most widely read work in England was *An Introduction to the History of Religion* (1896; 2d ed., 1902), complemented in the United States by his Hartford-Lamson Lectures on comparative religion for the American Board of Foreign Missions in 1908 (revised and published in 1910 under the title *Comparative Religion*). A liberal Anglican, Jevons thought that the religious quest of humanity reflected the divine will, and he maintained that all religions had their fulfillment in Christianity. He argued that Buddhism was not a religion but an etiolation of tendencies already present in ancient Brahmanism. Religious evolution, he believed, was above all the process by which the truth of monotheism came to be discerned. Following his appointment as professor of philosophy at the University of Durham in 1910, his books on *Evolution* (1910), *Personality* (1913), and *Philosophy* (1914) all find him espousing a species of nonmaterialist, creative, and dispersive (i.e., social) evolutionism influenced by Henri Bergson.

Jevons was principal of Hatfield Hall, Durham, from 1896 to 1923, and from there he corresponded with many scholars. His obvious theological orientation and evolutionism have led to a decline of interest in his work since World War I.

BIBLIOGRAPHY

Two important works by Jevons not discussed above are *Religion in Evolution* (London, 1906) and *An Introduction to the Study of Comparative Religion* (Cambridge, Mass., 1909). For works about Jevons, I refer the reader to Eric J. Sharpe's *Comparative Religion: A History* (London, 1975) and Jacques Waardenburg's *Classical Approaches to the Study of Religion,* 2 vols. (The Hague, 1973–1974).

New Sources

Davies, Douglas. *Frank Byron Jevons, 1858–1936: An Evolutionary Realist.* Lewiston, N.Y., 1991.

Davies, Douglas. "William Robertson Smith and Frank Byron Jevons: Faith and Evolution." In *William Robertson Smith,* pp. 311–319. Sheffield, U.K., 1995.

GARRY W. TROMPF (1987)
Revised Bibliography

JEWISH ETHICAL LITERATURE

JEWISH ETHICAL LITERATURE SEE JEWISH THOUGHT AND PHILOSOPHY, *ARTICLE ON* JEWISH ETHICAL LITERATURE

JEWISH LAW

JEWISH LAW SEE HALAKHAH

JEWISH PEOPLE

JEWISH PEOPLE. This entry discusses the sociological dimension of Judaism, in particular "Israel" in the historical sense of *ʿam Yisraʾel* (the "people of Israel," the Israelites). The article seeks to describe the factors shaping the transformation of Jewish peoplehood from the biblical period to modern times.

The Jews constitute a fellowship mandated and sustained by the Jewish religious tradition, a fellowship viewed in modern times as a social entity in its own right. In what sense Jewry is to be considered a nation or ethnic group depends on how these terms are defined. The Hebrew terms for nation, *goi, leʾum,* and above all *ʿam,* were applied to the collectivity in the Bible, where Israel is said to be "like all the nations" (*1 Sam.* 8:5) yet "a people dwelling alone and not reckoning itself among the nations" (*Num.* 23:9). This conceptual duality reappears in later eras.

Historical circumstances periodically intruded on the parameters of membership in the Jewish people. From time to time, uncertainty and even conflict have occurred as to who is a Jew (and who is not) according to Jewish law and more informal mores, the criteria for inclusion, the theological significance of Jewish survival, and exactly which religious actions or principles of faith were required of a Jew. Affected by changes in the historical context and worldly status of Jewry in its homeland and in the Diaspora, religious thinkers have interpreted the nature and destiny of Israel in various ways. This article seeks to explore the evolving conception of that fellowship, real and ideal, with special attention to the relationship of Jewish peoplehood to other faith communities that have emerged from the Israelite religious matrix and to modern concepts of ethnicity.

The Jewish religious fellowship can be illuminated by comparative considerations. Cultural variation between the various branches of Jewry for many centuries was virtually as great as that of the various branches of Christendom and Islam. A similar congruence of peoplehood and religion is found in some national forms of Christianity (e.g., the Armenian, Coptic, and Ethiopic Churches). The boundary between Judaism and Christianity has remained firm, however, unlike the aforementioned instances of subgroups within the Christian church. The centrality of salvation through Christ, along with related creedal and doctrinal formulations, facilitated a theology of the universal church that was different from the bonds sustaining the Jewish people. Most important, Judaism resisted definition by creedal formulation. In its emphasis on the centrality of religious law rather than salvation through faith in a messiah and sacramental grace, Judaism has a closer structural affinity to Islam. The "nation of Islam" is both a subject of religious law (four distinct systems of them) and conveys a sense of being a multinational corporate body, even though in Islam's early history it was in fact a religion of the Arabs and only afterwards became the religion of Persians, Turks, and subsequently many other peoples. Judaism never became the ruling religion of an empire or a congeries of states as did Islam, but Judaism is a "world religion" in its geographical and cultural diversity—and its impact in world history.

One major reason for the unique character of the Jewish communal bond was the quite different historical and political situation of Judaism and the Jews from that of Christendom and Islam. The origins of the Jewish people in ancient times predated the development of many of the central ideas and eventual customary practices of its religion. A considerable portion of the Hebrew Bible is the story of how the core of Israelite religion came into being. The mature religious tradition maintained the people's identity even when the Jews, in antiquity and later, were a small percentage of the population of the lands of their residence. At least since the last century before the common era, the Jews had become to a great extent a Diaspora population. Other peoples and religions have had diasporas, but the Jewish Diaspora is remarkable for its geographical dispersion and its ability to survive under many circumstances. (Indeed the term *diaspora* was first used in Jewish history.) After the fall of the Hasmonean kingdom of Judea in the first centuries BCE, except for the short-lived conversion of two medieval ruling elites to Judaism, there was no sovereign Jewish state until 1948, a duration of almost nineteen centuries. The political factor in these centuries of Jewish history involved semiautonomous communal institutions of various types, buttressed by the Gentile state and under the leadership of Jewish figures accorded authority in matters of legal exegesis and the right to issue authoritative interpretations. Therefore, during the long course of Jewish history in the Diaspora, common destiny and cohesiveness were maintained by a usual set of forces internal and external to the Jewish community working in tandem to facilitate the continuity of the Jewish tradition.

The principle of living in a condition of exile (*galut*) and awaiting ultimate redemption was a key subjective element in the self-identity inculcated by the tradition and constantly reinforced by the Jewish liturgy. At the same time, however, there has been the conspicuous presence of the Jewish people in the primary narratives of Christianity and Islam. In the New Testament the Jewish people are depicted as having spurned Jesus as the Messiah, even though he and his disciples were Jews. In the Qur'ān the Jews are depicted as having rejected Muḥammad as the "seal of the prophets," even though he acknowledged the divine source of their sacred book and certain features of Jewish belief and worship.

Acknowledgment by Christianity and Islam that the Jewish people have played an extraordinary role in the history of salvation, even when accompanied by doctrines that God had subsequently bestowed grace on another elect people, expressed the ambivalent attitudes toward Jewry of Christian and Muslim religious authorities: confirmation of Jewish specialness together with the scandal, if not outright anger, that the "stiff-necked" Jews denied self-evident (Christian or Muslim) truths. Conviction of possessing that truth and resulting disdain or even anger facilitated the imposition of social and legal restrictions on Jewish status and helped to rationalize periodic anti-Jewish persecutions. However, the peculiar conspicuousness of the Jewish people in the formative Christian and Muslim stories indirectly served to confirm the continued singularity of the Jewish people. In some sense (although not the Jewish sense), Israel was central to God's plan for history in both Christianity and Islam. The specialness of this role is a cardinal element of the Jewish tradition itself, and therefore a crucial reason for Jewish survival.

Another issue sometimes raised in connection with Jewish peoplehood is whether Judaism should be characterized as universalistic or particularistic. Judaism—more properly, Torah in its broad sense as divine "instruction"—holy teaching and action, is both. Gaining ultimate authority from the conviction that it is derived from revelation, Torah includes sacred literature and venerable religious practices (the key rabbinic terms are *mitsvot*, or commandments; *halakhah*, the correct way or religious law; and *minhag*, or custom). The values inculcated by rabbinic legal rulings and preaching as these unfold in time, as well as the understanding of the human condition expressed in Jewish religious teachings, are also Torah. Torah articulates concepts about God in relation to nature and history: that deity is one, eternal, creative, transcendent as well as immanent, revelatory, and personal—although Jewish religious thought has brought forth a variety of sometimes quite complex theological explications of these and other fundamental beliefs.

At the same time the rabbinic idea of Torah as instruction requires that there be a certain people among the nations of the world that exists to study and practice Torah as the raison d'être of its existence (and even of the existence of the universe, in rabbinic thought). The notion of a people elected by God to receive the complete set of his commandments hallows the people and locates their special role in the context of world history. Judaism conceives of this election not as a preordained, passive reception of revelation but as an active electing by the people to accept the "yoke" of Torah and the commandments. Thus, Jewish religious thought interprets the mundane factuality of the people's existence as expressing a joyful, voluntarily assumed obligation and responsibility. These introductory remarks indicate some of the complexities of Jewish peoplehood as fact and ideal, which will be dealt with separately in the following.

NAMES FOR THE JEWS AND JUDAISM. In the Jewish tradition, the Jewish people as a socioreligious entity is designated *ʿam Yisraʾel* (the people of Israel), *benei Yisraʾel* (children of Israel, Israelites), *beit Yisraʾel* (house of Israel), *keneset Yisraʾel* (assembly of Israel, in rabbinic literature), or simply as *Yisraʾel* (Israel). In the Hebrew Bible the patriarch Jacob, renamed Israel after wrestling with a divine being in *Genesis* 32:28, is the eponymous ancestor of the people of Israel through his progeny, the founders of the Israelite tribes. In contrast, a native of the modern state of Israel (*medinat Yisraʾel*), which possesses Christian and Muslim as well as Jewish citizens, is usually rendered by the modern Hebrew adjective *Israeli* (*Yisraʾeli*). The term *Jew* (Hebrew, *Yehudi*) is etymologically derived from *Judah* (*Yehudah*), the eponym of the tribe of Judah.

According to the biblical account, around 922 BCE the ten northern tribes rejected Solomon's son as ruler and formed the "kingdom of Israel" (*mamlekhet Yisraʾel*). Only the tribal territories of Judah and Benjamin and the Davidic capital of Jerusalem remained loyal to the dynasty founded by Solomon's father, David, early in the tenth century, thus becoming the separate, southern kingdom of Judah (*mamlekhet Yehudah*). When the northern kingdom was conquered by Assyria in 722 BCE, its population was deported and apparently assimilated, except for those who took refuge in Judah. The southern kingdom was destroyed by Babylonia in 586 BCE, but the Aramaic cognate *Yahud* remained the name for the region around Jerusalem in the Persian Empire. In *Esther* 2:5 the term *Jew* refers to a member of the whole people, even someone of the tribe of Benjamin; in *Esther* 8:17 and 9:27 the term refers to the act of Gentiles joining the Jews in some unspecified way. The Greek form *Ioudaia* was used in the Ptolemaic and Seleucid kingdoms and for the independent Jewish commonwealth established by the Hasmoneans in the second century BCE. The Latinized form was *Judaea*.

By Hellenistic times the term *Jew* (Greek, *Ioudaios*; Hebrew, *Yehudi*) had become a name not only for subjects of the Hasmonean state but throughout the Diaspora for those who were adherents of its religious tradition. The term *Judaism* for the distinctive religion of the Judeans used in Hellenistic times is first found in *2 Maccabees* 2:21 and 14:38. While accepting the term *Yehudi*, Jewish religious literature continued to prefer *Yisraʾel*, *benei Yisraʾel*, and so forth. (In the context of the traditional synagogue service, an "Israelite" is a Jew called to the reading of Scripture who is not a descendant of the priests or the Levites.)

Yet another relevant term is *ʿIvri* (Hebrew), which probably referred at first in the Hebrew Bible to a social status rather than to ethnic or Gentilic identification (this primary usage of *Hebrew*—as, for example, in *Ex.* 21:2—may have had a philological relationship to the second-millennium social category called in Akkadian the *habiru*). Several biblical instances when Hebrew can be construed as referring to an Israelite or to the ancestor of an Israelite (*Jon.* 1:8; *Gen.* 4:13) and as recalling Eber, a descendant of Noah's son Shem (*Gen.* 10:21, 11:14) may have led to its eventually becoming a synonym for the Israelites, and therefore their language. In the nineteenth century in some European countries, *Hebrew* became a polite equivalent for *Jew*, which had acquired negative connotations; in the twentieth century the positive force of *Jew* was regained in English, German, and other languages (but not in Russian).

COLLECTIVE EXISTENCE IN ANCIENT ISRAELITE RELIGION. A main theme of the Pentateuch is how, against the background of world history in the first part of *Genesis*, *ʿam Yisraʾel* came into being: a chain of narratives sets the stage for the enumeration of Israel's corporate duties to its God, YHVH (probably vocalized as *Yahveh*), after the Exodus during its wanderings in the wilderness. Accordingly, the ancestors of the children of Israel had lived in the land of Canaan as clans for several generations until they settled in Egypt, were enslaved, and after Moses' confrontation with the pharaoh, were redeemed by YHVH, who brought them to the wilderness of Sinai. There they entered a binding agreement with their God—a covenant that included a strict prohibition against worshiping other gods (*Ex.* 20:2–6). The theme of liberation from exile and return to Zion becomes a principal biblical model for future hopes of redemption. (Other biblical themes that served as paradigms for the Jewish people's traditional understanding of its history later included repeated cycles of sin followed by repentance and experiences of persecution followed by salvation.)

The Hebrew Scriptures represent a selection of the literature produced by and for the people of Israel mainly in the Land of Israel and over as many as eight to ten centuries. Modern historiography on the origins of the people in the context of the nations and social movements of the second millennium BCE involves considerable uncertainty as to the exact relationship of the direct ancestors of the Israelites to such ancient groups as the Amorites and the Hyksos, whether the proto-Israelites worshiped YHVH before the Exodus (compare *Ex.* 6:3 with *Gen.* 4:26), and the extent to which large numbers of Canaanites joined an Israelite tribal association in the thirteenth or twelfth centuries BCE, accepted its deity, and were absorbed in the Israelite people.

The exclusive divine authority of YHVH in relation to the collective existence of Israel is reflected in various and fundamental aspects of ancient Israelite religion. For example, Israelite tradition went to considerable lengths to disassociate ownership of the land of Canaan from the right of conquest. Israelite settlement was said to have been made possible by YHVH as Israel's supreme ruler; the Land of Israel was a territory on which the people could become a nation akin to other nations but devoted to carrying out its covenantal duties. The corporate aspect of landownership can be seen in the provision that land sold by individuals was to be returned periodically to the family to whom it was "originally" allocated (*Lev.* 25:2, 25:23).

Not only the framework, but a substantial portion of the covenantal duties preserved in the Pentateuch refer to Israel as a collective entity. Moral and legal obligations included many stipulations that regulated relations between sectors of Israelite society in addition to individual behavior. Besides offerings expressing personal thanksgiving or contrition, sacrifices are presented to God by the priests on behalf of the people to express collective gratitude or to expiate collective sin (e.g., *Num.* 28:2; *Lev.* 16:30). Ethical duties on the Israelites individually and as members of families are complemented by responsibilities to the "widow, orphan, and stranger," for which Israel as a whole is responsible (*Exod.* 22:21–22). The demand to create an equitable and just society figures prominently in the classical prophets.

Throughout the history of the Israelite kingdoms, prophetic messengers warned the people that if these collective obligations were not fulfilled, YHVH could take away the land he had given them and force them into exile (e.g., *Amos* 3:2, 7:11). This belief is reinforced by natural and military disasters affecting the people as a whole. The destruction of the northern kingdom of Israel in 722 BCE was interpreted in this manner by the so-called Deuteronomic movement, which probably acquired the opportunity to carry out an extensive program of religious reforms in the kingdom of Judah in the 620s (*2 Kings* 22–23; *2 Chron.* 34). The heart of the *Book of Deuteronomy* very likely reflects the position of this group, which emphasized that the corporate responsibility of Israel accepted at Sinai was binding on all their descendants, which was said to include (almost) all of the population of the late-seventh-century kingdom of Judah: to love YHVH, obey his commandments, avoid any taint of idolatry, worship him in the place—that is, Jerusalem—where he would "cause his name to dwell," where his only house and sacrificial altar were to be constructed (e.g., *Deut.* 6:4–5, 12:1–14).

When Judah was destroyed by the Babylonians in 586 BCE, the explanation offered was that the idolatry of the past, especially the later kings subservient to Assyria, such as Manasseh, had condemned the people to exile but that God continued to love them and held out a sure promise of redemption (*2 Kings* 24:3–4; *Jer.* 29). The experience of exile in Babylon brought to the fore the prophetic theme of the eternal nature of the covenant between YHVH and Israel. The religiosity of the exilic community was marked by an acceptance of the divine causation for the people's exile, a pervasive regret for the sins of the ancestors, and a heightening of the idealized role of the people in world history. While sustaining the concepts of a specific holy mountain (e.g., *Joel* 4:1), holy city (*Isa.* 2:3), and land of YHVH (*Isa.* 10:24)—all of which can be referred to poetically as Zion—exilic prophecy justified autonomous Israelite survival outside the precincts of these sacred spaces. (Contrast David's much earlier complaint that Saul banished him so that he could no longer serve YHVH, *1 Sam.* 26:19.) The exilic prophecies in the latter part of the *Book of Isaiah* portray the people as God's servant, a "light to the nations" that God's salvation be known to the ends of the earth (*Isa.* 49:6), anticipating that all Gentiles will eventually worship YHVH, who "makes weal and creates woe" (*Isa.* 45:7), bringing about universal peace and justice. (See relevant prophecies concerning a universal "End of Days" in *Isa.* 2:1–4; *Mic.* 4:1–4; *Isa.* 45:14, 45:22–24, 56:3–8; *Zech.* 8:20–23.)

The decisive difference between the historical development of Israelite religion and those of other ancient Near Eastern peoples was Israel's monotheistic elevation of its God to the status of the only deity, the sole creator of heaven and earth, supreme ruler of the world, and judge of all history—presumably a development that grew out of the unique combination of elements and features that comprised the early history of the Israelite people. Pre-Mosaic sources of the Israelite cult of YHVH are uncertain. Unlike other Near Eastern deities (Sin, Adad, Ishtar, Dagan, and so forth), YHVH did not have temples and shrines dedicated to him in various widely scattered localities around the Near East. YHVH was not incorporated into any other pantheon, confirming the attitude of the biblical authors that YHVH's name and reputation in the world depended solely on Israel. The dating of a full-fledged biblical monotheism has been a matter of longstanding scholarly controversy. For our purposes, determining when in Israelite history "other gods" came to be viewed as nondivine (in the biblical terminology, "idols," "the work of men's hands") is less important than the fact of the eventual emergence, in the course of the intellectual development of ancient Israel, of an explicit, sweeping, and radical demotion of other deities and elevation of one God, an action unprecedented in the history of ancient religion (*Isa.* 45:5–7). This transformation was accompanied by the reinterpretation of traditions concerning the human and Israelite past, rather than a dismissal of those traditions, from a monotheistic perspective.

The last redaction of the traditional material concerning human origins and the formative eras of Israelite history from the standpoint of radical monotheism may not have occurred until the postexilic period. The return to Zion of a portion (but not all) of the Babylonian exiles in the late sixth century and again in the midfifth century BCE laid the groundwork for the revival of Jerusalem, its Temple, and the land of Judaea in late Persian and Hellenistic times. By then Judaism had become a religion centered on a Scripture that defined the Jews as God's treasured possession, "a kingdom of priests and a holy people" (*Ex.* 19:4–6), necessary for his universal plan and goals.

From Biblical Israel to the Christian and Rabbinic Israels. The corporate and the individual dimensions of Israelite faith were further developed in succeeding centuries. Closely associated with the corporate aspect of salvation is the messianic idea (buttressed by various scriptural verses and prophecies concerning the end of days, the permanence of the Davidic dynasty, and the kingship of God) that there would arise a completely just, God-inspired king to rule Israel and establish everlasting peace and harmony in the world.

The individualistic dimension of postscriptural Judaism took the form of each person's accountability to carry out the *mitsvot*, including some that had primarily been the duty of the priesthood earlier. Individual immortality became a widely accepted doctrine of Judaism perhaps in the second century BCE (a late biblical allusion to the resurrection of the dead is *Dan.* 12:2, most likely dating from the Maccabean revolt; compare *2 Macc.* 7:9, 7:14, 9:29). Personal immortality was soon absorbed into most branches of Judaism (except the Sadducees) and was made binding in the second of the Eighteen Benedictions (*Shemoneh 'Esreh*, the *'Amidah*) that Jewish males were to recite three times daily. Jewish eschatological teachings of the last centuries BCE and the first century CE, for all their flux and uncertainty, emphasized the crucial significance of Israel ("And the kingdom and the dominion and the greatness of the kingdoms under the whole heaven shall be given to the people of the saints of the Most High," *Dan.* 7:27) and the transcendent value of membership in it. (The classical formulation came to be that, with some notable exceptions, "All Israel has a share in the world to come," *San.* 10.1) In what became the traditional formula, "this world" (*ha-'olam ha-zeh*) of history will be climaxed by the coming of the King-Messiah and a utopian messianic age. And this world is transcended by another realm, "the world to come" (*ha-'olam ha-ba'*), where the guilty will be consigned to a merited punishment for their sins and the righteous of all generations will be eternally rewarded with the radiance of the divine presence. In addition, control of the religious calendar designating when crucial holy days occur seems to have been an issue (as it was at times in the later history of Judaism as well) seriously threatening the unity of Israel.

Membership in the people of Israel was drastically transformed during the last centuries BCE and the first century CE with the emergence of formal procedures for conversion. By the time of the Jewish revolt of 66–70 CE against the Romans in Judaea, a majority of Jews were probably residing in the Diaspora, either in Persia under the Parthians (the Jewish community of Babylonia, dating from the exile of the sixth century BCE) or in the Hellenistic kingdoms and, later, the Roman Empire (Antioch, the cities of Asia Minor and European Greece, Alexandria and elsewhere in Egypt, as well as Rome and other locations around the Mediterranean). These new communities had been founded by Jewish settlers who had left Judaea for a variety of political and economic reasons but were significantly augmented by conversions to Judaism in the Diaspora, which occurred in Judea as well (including episodes of forced conversions by two Hasmonean kings).

Formal conversion to Judaism was a new phenomenon in Jewish life. Previously, non-Israelites had been accepted into Israel on an individual basis (the *Book of Ruth*, which may date from postexilic times, contains one such account). A contrary instance is depicted in accounts in the books of *Ezra* and *Nehemiah* demanding that the Judahites of their time separate themselves from their non-Israelite wives (*Neh.* 9:2, 13:3). At that time there was also a rejection of the inhabitants of Samaria (the heartland of the former northern kingdom of Israel) who worshiped YHVH but were considered not of the seed of preexilic Israel but rather foreign settlers brought in by Assyria almost three centuries earlier (*2 Kings* 17:29–34). (The Samaritans became the first religious tradition that stemmed from the biblical matrix but was separate from the Jewish people.) At the beginning of the common era, however, proselytism seems to have become a common occurrence (see, for example, *Matt.* 23:15; *Acts* 2:5; and B.T., *Shab.* 31a). In addition to formal conversion, which probably entailed circumcision for males, immersion, and the offering of a special Temple sacrifice, there is mention of pagans, referred to in ancient inscriptions as "God-fearers," who followed one or another element of the Jewish tradition, such as the Sabbath (Josephus, *Against Apion* 2.39; Tacitus, *Histories* 5.5).

The last two centuries BCE and the first century CE were a period of intense religious ferment, when new Jewish schools of thought and new elites competed with each other: Pharisees, Sadducees, Essenes, Zealots, early Judeo-Christians, apocalyptic visionaries in Judaea, and Hellenized philosophies (such as that of Philo of Alexandria) in the Diaspora. (There is no convincing evidence that Jewish religious authorities in the late Second Temple period condemned dissident groups for "blasphemy" or persecuted them for anything like heresy.) By the end of the first century CE, or at least by the late second century, after the last of the Jewish revolts against the Romans, rabbinic Judaism crystallized out of the Pharisaic movement, while Christianity became fully separated from the Jewish people.

After the Samaritans, Christianity was the second religious tradition that remained loyal to the witness of the Hebrew Scriptures but came to constitute a distinct community of faith. Christian writings held that the Jews ignored the Messiah and were collectively responsible for his death (*Matt.* 13:57, 27:25). Crucial elements in the parting of the ways between Judaism and Christianity were the former's rejection of Jesus of Nazareth as Messiah and Christianity's rejection (after a few years of uncertainty) of Jewish law. In what became the dominant Christian formulation, apparently articulated first by Paul of Tarsus, Torah law was held to have been divinely inspired but superseded by the atoning death of Jesus, the Christ (Greek for anointed, the root meaning of the Hebrew *mashi'ah*), who made available a full salvation that had been prophesied in the Hebrew Scriptures and that was not possible under "the law" (*Gal.* 3–4). By the end of the first century CE, to the basic Jewish prayers was added a benediction against sectarians (*birkat ha-minim*), which some historians believe was devised to exclude Christians from the synagogue.

By then most Christians were not of Jewish descent but were pagans converted directly to Christianity. This principled negation of Jewish law, especially ritual law, ceremonial practice, and *kashrut*, meant that experiencing the presence of Jesus as the Christ, accompanied by baptism, was the portal into the Christian people, now defined as the "new Israel" of the spirit (e.g., *Acts* 10; *Rom.* 9–11). In particular, the Jewish requirement of circumcision was rejected and baptismal immersion redefined as one's spiritual rebirth as a Christian. (According to rabbinic law, conversion is also a rebirth; the convert to Judaism terminates former family ties and is considered in the category of a newborn child. See *Gerim* 2.6.) In the New Testament, Christianity viewed the Hebrew Scripture through the concept of its fulfillment in Christ. For rabbinic Judaism, the Torah as divine law was a permanent feature of creation, a dynamic and ongoing process of articulating the tasks of God's people in history. Judaism viewed the written law of the Hebrew Scriptures as part of a comprehensive Torah that included the oral tradition as well—an oral law that was partly redacted in the Mishnah, God's "mystery" given only to Israel around 200 CE (*Pesiqta' Rabbati* 14b).

Eventually, the church did not reject the idea of religious law as such (it developed its own to regulate creeds, holy days, family status, religious hierarchies, and so forth), but the Christian theological rejection of the eternally binding character of Torah law meant the sharp separation of *'am Yisra'el* by the Jewish self-definition and the "new Israel" according to the Christian viewpoint. The two conceptions of holy peoplehood thus reflect the two contrasting modes of relating to the Hebrew Scripture as holy; Christianity in late antiquity pushed much further than Judaism the figural, allegoric, and symbolic interpretation of Old Testament figures, institutions, and prophecies.

Peoplehood in Rabbinic Judaism and Medieval Jewish Thought. According to rabbinic Judaism, Israel comprised the direct, physical descendants of the remnant of the preexilic people, augmented by those non-Jews who had accepted the yoke of the commandments and were adopted into the Jewish people through the conversion rituals required by Torah as interpreted by the rabbis. The biblical term *ger* (stranger, resident alien, sojourner) was understood to refer to a proselyte—a *ger tsedeq* in contrast to a *ger toshav*—who had rejected idolatry but not accepted the full burden of the *mitsvot.*

Even though most Jews were (and still are) Jews by birth, conversion is unquestionably a legitimate mode, in Jewish religious law, of acquiring the status of being a full member of the people of Israel. There are traditions that some of the most eminent rabbis were proselytes or their descendants and that God had special love for *gerim.* To be sure, a few sages are quoted as expressing suspicion of the motives and behavior of proselytes as conditions in the Roman Empire deteriorated. The prevailing position was that prospective converts should be warned that "this people was debased, oppressed, and degraded more than all other peoples." If they persisted, they were to be accepted with joy: "To whom are you cleaving? Happy are you! To him who spoke and the world came into being" (*Gerim* 1.1–5).

From the early fourth century CE on, however, Jewish proselytizing was anathema to the Christianized or Islamicized state; the Roman emperor Constantine made conversion to Judaism punishable by death, and a similar prohibition was part of the so-called Pact of Omar defining the status of Christians and Jews under Islam.

Certainly external obstacles were usually determinative in discouraging more than a trickle of conversions to Judaism from the early Middle Ages until the twentieth century. There were also, however, internal factors. Christianity viewed proselytism as its mission with a far greater intensity than did Judaism, and the church fathers insisted with far more rigor that there was no salvation outside the church. Rabbinic doctrine held that only the Jewish people had knowledge of and were bound by the full complement of divine commandments, but that there were seven Noahic laws binding on all humanity (usually enumerated as the prohibitions of idolatry, blasphemy, bloodshed, sexual sins, theft, and eating a limb of a living animal, together with a positive commandment to establish a legal system; B.T., *San.* 56a). On the salvation of non-Jews, the normative Jewish doctrine became the opinion of Yehoshu'a that the "righteous of all nations have a share in the world to come" (Tosefta, *San.* 13.2).

Who was Jewish according to rabbinic law? Since the second century CE the child of a Jewish mother and a Gentile father is a Jew, but the child of a Gentile mother and a Jewish father is a Gentile. This matrilineal principle is alluded to in the Mishnah (*Qid.* 3.12), which deals with marriages valid and invalid according to *halakhah* and the status of the offspring thereof. The relevant Talmudic ruling (addressed to the male) was Yonatan's that "your son by an Israelite woman is called your son, but your son by a heathen woman is not called your son but her son" (B.T., *Qid.* 68b); the later commentators emphasize the positive conclusion that the offspring of a Jewish woman is a Jew (see Moses Maimonides's *Code of Law*, Forbidden Intercourse 12.7). Various explanations, sociological and historical, have been offered for the adoption of the principle of matrilineal descent, including the influence of Roman law and the impossibility of confirming paternity. However, in premodern times the regulation was not of widespread practical consequence, since it was unlikely that many Jewish men would marry non-Jewish women who did not formally convert but would rear their children as members of the people of Israel.

In *halakhah*, Jews who converted to another religion were still considered Jews, although there are differences of opinion among the authorities over their specific *halakhic* rights. The relevant Talmudic principle was that such a person was a sinful Jew: "An Israelite, even though he sinned, remains an Israelite" (B.T., *San.* 44a). Thus the Jewish community accepted the return of Jews who had been forcibly baptized during the First Crusade in Europe, but acts of penitence and rituals of purification were required.

Impossible as it was in theory to leave the Jewish people, it was not so in fact. Although there might be psychological costs in apostasy, there could be tangible advantages to leaving a group that was of subordinate legal status and subject to periodic persecution. Individual Jewish converts were welcomed by Christian and Muslim authorities. Only in certain situations when large numbers of Jews were pressed into converting, such as in the Iberian Peninsula in the 1390s and again in the 1490s, did problems arise on the Christian side. In Spain there occurred a brutal "Old Christian" backlash against "New Christian" or *converso* (sometimes labeled *marrano* [Spanish for pig]) families, whose Christian faith was for many centuries considered suspect merely because of their Jewish bloodline. Procedures for readmitting to the status of Jews descendants of *conversos* several generations later was a *halakhic* problem that concerned rabbis in Jewish communities in North Africa, Ottoman Turkey, Amsterdam, and elsewhere.

Supplementing the halakhic problem of who was and who was not a Jew was the aggadic problem of why there was a people of Israel. Idealization of the chosenness of the Jewish people is evident in Jewish religious literature as epitomized in the benediction recited in the synagogue before the reading of the Torah: "Blessed art thou, Lord our God, ruler of the universe, who chose us from all the nations and gave us the Torah." The givenness or factuality of being a Jew—that Jews found themselves thrown into a Jewish destiny—was acknowledged in some coolly realistic Talmudic statements. Expounding the biblical verse "And they stood at the nether part of the mount" (i.e., Israel at Mount Sinai; *Ex.* 19:17), Avdimi bar Ḥama᾽ bar Ḥasa᾽ explained that the Holy One, blessed be he, tilted the mountain over the Israelites like a cask and said, "If you accept the Torah, well and good; and if not, there shall be your burial" (B.T., *Shab.* 88a). Most sages rejected this notion on the grounds that receiving the Torah under coercion could nullify the obligation to observe it. The rabbinic *aggadah* continues in the line of a theological idealization of the people by emphasizing the collective responsibility of all members of the people to each other and to God and the absolute centrality of Israel's collective presence in universal history. In a discussion concerning divine punishment, the principle is enunciated that "all Israel is surety one for the other" (B.T., *Shav.* 39a). Israel conciliates God only when it is one unity (B.T., *Men.* 27a).

According to rabbinic teaching, the Jewish people fulfill God's plan that his presence indwells in the world. A homily in *Ruth Rabbah* (1.1) ascribes to God the statement that if Israel had not accepted the Torah, the world would have reverted to void and destruction. A homily in *Exodus Rabbah* (47.3) attributes to God the statement that if this people had not accepted his Torah, he would not look upon them more than other idol worshipers. (The Talmudic dictum that "anyone who repudiates idolatry is called a Jew" [B.T., *Meg.* 13a], based on the biblical identification of Mordecai of the tribe of Benjamin as a *Yehudi* [Judean] in *Esther* 2:5, uses the term *Jew* in a theologically idealized, nonethnic, purely homiletic sense.) It was a merit for the Jews to have accepted the Torah, but ever since Sinai it was Israel's raison d'être to obey the 613 commandments contained in it. In contrast to the common Christian distinction of late antiquity and the Middle Ages between the "religious" and the laity, the goal of rabbinic Judaism was to raise all Israel to the level of masters of Torah, transforming the community into an academy, as it were, for the study and practice of Torah.

Despite a Diaspora stretching from the Atlantic to central Asia and eastward and from the Baltic to the Sahara and beyond to Ethiopia, medieval Judaism did not become multinational in quite the sense that Christianity or Islam did. Christianity became the official religion of the Roman Empire in the fourth century CE, followed by the conversion of the Frank, Germanic, Nordic, and Slavic peoples in the Middle Ages; Islam expanded beyond the Arab purview with the conversion of Persians, Berbers, and Turks (and later of peoples in sub-Saharan Africa and Southeast Asia), often spearheaded by their rulers. There were only two medieval instances where Judaism was adopted as the religion of a state: sixth-century Yemen briefly and the Khazar kingdom on the Volga between the eighth and tenth centuries. A wide diversity of Jewish subcultures did emerge: Jewries in the Middle East that were largely the continuation of the ancient homeland and Diaspora communities; Iranian and Kurdish Jews; Jewish tribal groups in the Caucasus Mountains; the various Jewish communities of India and China; Berber Jews in the Maghreb; Provençal and Italian Jews; Sephardic Jews in the Iberian Peninsula; Ashkenazic Jews in northern France, the Rhineland, and later eastern Germany, Poland, and Lithuania; and other communities with their own distinctive customs, dialectics, liturgies, and practices. As a result, in daily life medieval Jews spoke a wide variety of languages—Greek and Aramaic; Persian and Arabic; Spanish, French, and German—and they developed distinctive Jewish dialects of these languages, such as Ladino (a Jewish form of old Spanish) and Yiddish (a Jewish form of Middle High German), Hebrew being maintained for literary and liturgical purposes.

Some branches of medieval and early modern Jewry produced sophisticated courtier and banking classes and intellectual elites trained in the natural sciences and Aristotelian and Neoplatonic philosophies, whereas other Jewries were predominately folk cultures overwhelmingly engaged in menial occupations. Although in certain regions the Jewish population was large, compact, and had an agricultural or village component (e.g., the Galilee and Babylonia in late antiquity), political conditions under Christian and Muslim rulers necessitated that Judaism sustain itself increasingly as the religion of an urbanized minority mostly limited to crafts and trade (the specific list of the economic roles open to Jews differed widely from land to land and from era to era). In northwestern and eastern Europe, Jewish communities were founded and enlarged by Jews invited to settle in frontier areas, where the rulers considered them economically useful. However, given the interweaving of religion and the state in the countries in which medieval and early modern Jews resided, a Jewry could maintain itself only if permitted considerable legal autonomy—although the extent to which the Jewish leadership was dependent on the Gentile rulers or derived its authority solely from the consent of local Jewish communities varied considerably.

Through all of their history, the Jewish people, therefore, were hardly characterized by cultural or economic homogeneity. A sense of Jewish unity, inculcated by the prayers and religious law and by the Hebrew Bible and other literary works, was reinforced by the common condition of being a minority: a minority with a profound, if disputed, connection to the formative narratives of the ruling (Christian or Islamic) religion; a minority enjoying a precarious social status inasmuch as it was always susceptible to persecution but for considerable stretches of time better off than the local peasants and serfs; a minority with considerable training (especially through the Babylonian Talmud) in adjusting to living under Gentile governments while preserving the continuity of Jewish law; a minority possessing a far-flung Diaspora network linked together by scholars, traders, and other Jewish travelers and a steady stream of Jewish migration, sometimes westward, sometimes eastward; and above all a minority that defined itself as central to the history of creation.

The religious self-definition of the Jewish tradition, transmitted through Scriptures, rabbinic law and lore, and the *siddur*, reiterated the sanctity of being *Yisra'el*, *ʿamkha* (your people, as addressed to God who "has chosen his people Israel in love"). This God, who "because of our sins exiled us from our land," nevertheless "remembers the pious deeds of the patriarchs and in love will bring a redeemer to their children's children for his name's sake." He will "gather the dispersed of your people Israel . . . break the enemies and humble the arrogant . . . rebuild Jerusalem as an everlasting building and speedily set up therein the throne of David" (from the *Shemonehʿ Esreh*, basic to the Jewish liturgy) and "will remove the abominations from the earth, and the idols will be utterly cut off when the world will be perfected under the kingdom of the Almighty and all the children of flesh will call upon your name, when you will turn unto yourself all the wicked of the earth . . . for the kingdom is yours and to all eternity you will reign in glory" (from the *ʿAleinu* prayer at the conclusion of each service).

Indicative of the bonds maintaining a sense of Jewish peoplehood until modern times is the major schism of medieval Judaism: the Karaite movement of the eighth and ninth centuries CE in the Middle East. Calling for a return to the literal meaning of the Scriptures (Hebrew, *mik'rah*, from which the Karaites got their name) and denying the authority of the rabbis and the Talmud, the Karaites separated themselves from mainstream Judaism, developing their own religious law based on biblical precedents. Religious authority and the sources of divine law were the cruxes of the Karaite-Rabbinite conflict, although there may have been socioeconomic forces operating as well. Nevertheless, there were attempts, by Moses Maimonides (Mosheh ben Maimon, 1135/8–1204) and others, to encourage close contacts between the two religious communities. In modern times some Karaite groups have closely identified with the Jews (the Karaites in Egypt), whereas others disassociated themselves (the Karaites in the Ukraine).

Theorizing about the nature of the Jewish people was not an especially important theme in medieval Jewish philosophy but was implied in various formulations of the purpose of Jewish existence. In some streams of speculative Jewish thought, Jewish peoplehood was embedded in a theology that conceived of Judaism as an eminently rational faith, its doctrines of the oneness of God, the createdness of the universe, the rational component of prophecy, and the reasonableness of the commandments being logically justified by categories and arguments derived from ancient Greek philosophy as glossed by Jewish, Muslim, and Christian writers. For Saʿadyah Gaon, "our nation of the children of Israel is a nation only by virtue of its laws" that, because they are divine, can never be abrogated: "The Creator has stated that the Jewish nation was destined to exist as long as heaven and earth would exist, its law would, of necessity, have to endure as long as would heaven and earth" (Gaon, 1948, p. 158). Torah, as consonant with right reason and authentic revelation, provided the most reliable, expeditious, and truthful means to serve God, the raison d'être of Israel.

Maimonides presented Judaism as derived from Abraham's great insight into the divine nature:

> His father and mother and the entire population worshiped idols . . . but his mind was busily working and reflecting until he had attained the way of truth, apprehending the correct line of thought, and knew that there is One God, that He guides the celestial Sphere and created everything. . . . When the people flocked to him [in the land of Canaan] and questioned him regarding his assertions, he would instruct each one according to his capacity till he had brought him to the way of truth. . . . And so it went on with ever increasing vigor among Jacob's children and their adherents till they became a people that knew God. (*Mishneh Torah*, Idolatry 1.2)

Addressing a proselyte who asked if he could pray to the God of Abraham, Isaac, and Jacob as the "God of his fathers" (the first of the Eighteen Benedictions), Maimonides wrote that "Abraham our Father, peace be with him, is the father of his pious posterity who keep his ways, and the father of his disciples and of all proselytes who adopt Judaism" (*Letter to Obadiah the Proselyte*). He or she who believes in the basic principles of the Jewish faith, as Maimonides defined them, "is then part of that 'Israel' whom we are to love, pity, and treat, as God commanded, with love and fellowship"—otherwise he or she is an atheist, heretic, and unbeliever (Introduction to Pereq Heleq [*Sanhedrin* 10.1]). For Maimonides, those who affirm the unity of God as the cause of causes come as close as humanly possible to grasping divinity as such.

A second tendency in medieval Jewish thought was to emphasize the supermundane nature of Israel. In the philosophical tradition the exemplary exponent of this position was Yehudah ha-Levi, who suggested that "Israel among the nations is like the heart amid the organs of the body," at once the sickest and the healthiest of entities, exposed to all sorts of diseases and yet possessing through its relationship to the "divine influence" a unique proclivity that manifested itself as the gift of prophecy (Yehudah ha-Levi, 1946, p. 109). In another of ha-Levi's images, Israel is the seed "which transforms earth and water into its own substance," carrying this substance from stage to stage until it brings forth fruit capable of bearing the divine influence, so that the nations who at least follow part of God's law pave the way for the Messiah and will become God's fruit (Yehudah ha-Levi, 1946, p. 227).

The supernatural conception of Israel reached its apogee in Qabbalah, the medieval mystical tradition that originated in southern France and northern Spain. Thus, in a discussion of the *mitsvot* in the basic qabbalistic text, the *Zohar*, circumcision is a perquisite for carrying out the surface meaning of the divine regulations (although to be circumcised only and not carry out the precepts of the Torah is to be like a heathen); the deeper mystery is to understand that Torah, God, and Israel are indissolubly linked (*Zohar, Leviticus*, 73b). Drawing on ancient Midrashic teachings about Israel's central role in the cosmos and on medieval Neoplatonic metaphysics, the qabbalists taught an esoteric doctrine that Israel's carrying out of the commandments has direct, puissant effects on the highest spheres of Being. Fulfillment of the commandments by Israel with the proper intention (*kavvanah*) overcame forces making for cosmic disharmony, effecting unifications (*yihudim*) in the realm of divinity. After the expulsions from the Iberian Peninsula in the 1490s, the impact of the Qabbalah spread, protecting Judaism against loss of morale and providing a solace in times of degradation. In the sixteenth-century Lurianic version of Qabbalah, the exile of Israel was paralleled by the exile of God, while the ingathering of the sparks of divinity achieved by fulfilling the *mitsvot* can be seen as the metaphysical analogue of the eventual ingathering of Israel at the climax of history. The implications of these qabbalistic doctrines were felt in the seventeenth-century messianic movement surrounding Shabbetai Tsevi and, in a different way, in eighteenth-century Hasidism.

The Modernization of Jewish Peoplehood. The crisis of traditional Jewish peoplehood coincided with the overwhelming transformation of modernizing societies and the drastic shift in meaning of the term *nation* in Western and westernized societies. Previously, in many Western languages, *nation* had loosely designated a community connected by ties of birth and common geographical origin. Toward the end of the eighteenth century and especially during the era of the French Revolution, *nation* acquired a more specific connotation in relation to political geography and the nexus of sovereignty: the nation came to apply to the citizenry as a whole, in contrast to the "political nation" of the ancien régime, which was limited to the wellborn and the elite.

Inasmuch as revolutionary France and, later, other modernizing countries forged the unity of the nation-state by dissolving the remnants of traditional estates and semiautonomous corporate entities, the extension of legal equality to all citizens had profound implications for Jewish identity. As modern nationalist movements and ideologies called for the self-determination of one nation after the other on geographical, cultural, linguistic, and historical grounds, the status of the Jews, now on the road to legal and political emancipation—and apparently to economic and social integration—appeared exceptional and problematic. The almost seamless web of sociology, *halakhah*, and *aggadah* that had supported traditional Jewish peoplehood for centuries began to unravel.

In September 1791 the French revolutionary assembly acknowledged the citizenship rights of all French Jewry—Sephardic and Ashkenazic. In 1807 Napoleon invited a body of lay leaders and rabbis to clarify the status of the Jews of his realm with respect to the accusation that they were a "nation within the nation." In defense of their rights, an Assembly of Jewish Notables (and the following year a group given the grandiloquent title of Sanhedrin) distinguished between the religious requirements of Judaism, held to be timeless and absolute, and the political dispositions of biblical society, no longer applicable "since Israel no longer forms a nation." In effect, large areas of Torah law that dealt with civil and criminal matters were inoperative, and the fiscal and semipolitical autonomies that the Jewish communities had been awarded were acknowledged as no longer feasible—all this occurring at a time when the theological assumptions in which all traditional religious faiths were grounded were slowly being undermined by forms of thought influenced directly or indirectly by modern science and technology.

The course of Jewish emancipation in one Western country after another had to overcome considerable opposition by those who held to the Christian basis of the state or who continued to insist on the cultural alienness of the Jews. During the first three-quarters of the nineteenth century, Jews in central Europe tended to define Jewry as a purely religious body whose positive mission in the Diaspora was to preserve the doctrines of pure ethical monotheism. The national or ethnic component seemed to some, especially in Germany, to be obsolete. In their rejection of the traditional messianic notion of a particularistic Jewish redemption (the ingathering of the exiles to Zion, the rebuilding of the Temple in Jerusalem, the reinstitution of the Davidic monarchy), German Jewish Reformers preferred to eliminate these symbols from the liturgy, just as they preferred the language of the land in worship at the expense of Hebrew and otherwise sought to assure Jews and their neighbors that they were "Germans of the Jewish faith" or even "Germans of the Mosaic persuasion." To support this redefinition it was sometimes argued that nationhood had been a necessary aspect of the emergence of ethical monotheism in biblical times and had been the preservative of the truths of Judaism in the Middle Ages, but in an enlightened age, when Judaism would come into its own as a progressive, universalistic faith, it did not need an ethnic integument. Jewish unity was not of a political but of a spiritual character that in no way contravened the loyalty of Jews to their secular fatherlands.

Such ideas were echoed in almost all the trends of nineteenth-century Jewish thought in Europe and America that welcomed emancipation as a just and humane move to rectify the humiliation and segregation inflicted on Jewry for centuries and to recognize the historical role and intrinsic worth of Judaism. These conceptions of Jewish peoplehood were influenced not only by the novel political and social situation of modern Jews but also by the growth of Jewish historical scholarship that accompanied the emergence of *Wissenschaft des Judentums* (the modern scientific, or scholarly, study of Judaica). Having gained an appreciation of how Jewish religious institutions and ideas had undergone development in the course of time, some historians, and especially Jewish intellectuals in eastern Europe toward the end of the nineteenth century, turned to the Jewish collectivity as a social fact in its own right. Moreover, modern transportation and community facilitated the transformation of the Jewish people on a mundane level. As Lloyd P. Gartner noted, "In the middle of the nineteenth century emancipated European Jews took the first steps toward converting the intangible religious conception of 'community of Israel' (*knesset Yisra'el*) into the tangible reality of international Jewish organization, bound together by newspapers, philanthropy, and new range of organizations for the defense of the Jews in dangerous parts of the Diaspora" (Gartner, 2001, p. 147).

Just as the earlier phase of modern Jewish thinking had been influenced by the struggle for emancipation, so this phase was increasingly influenced by the rise of modern anti-Semitism, the growth of nationalist movements among the peoples of eastern Europe, and the emergence of modern Zionism. The term *anti-Semitism* was coined in the 1870s to indicate that dislike of the Jews was supposedly not for religious reasons but was a defense against "Semitic" aliens acting as a corrupting, dominating force in the national organisms of Europe. Drawing on the medieval negative image of the Jews as Christ-killers and allies of Satan, the new anti-Semitic ideologies assumed a variety of forms, economic, political, and cultural. Racist anti-Semitism insisted that the sinister characteristics of the Jews could never be corrected through cultural or theological reform because these traits were psychobiological in origin. Some anti-Semites held that even Christianity was infected with a Jewish virus.

The period between 1881 and 1914 also saw the reappearance of physical attacks on the Jews (the pogroms in Russia), restrictive quotas in education, blood libels of a medieval type in which Jews were again accused of killing Christian children for ritual purposes, and anti-Semitic congresses and political parties. These and other elements were to be synthesized by Adolf Hitler's National Socialist German Workers' Party (Nazis), founded in Germany after World War I, which came to power in 1933 with fatal results for the six million European Jews caught in Nazi-dominated Europe during World War II.

Zionism gained urgency from the spread of modern anti-Semitism but had roots in the Jewish tradition as well. Zionism sought to reconstitute the Jewish peoplehood in a tangible sociopolitical community rather than in the idealized versions of much previous nineteenth-century Jewish thought. From the mid-nineteenth century on, and especially after 1881, Zionist ideologues argued that one's Jewishness should not be based on a mission of Israel to convey pure ethical monotheism to the world, as some of the German Jewish reformers had proposed, but on natural pride in one's heritage and a healthy desire to identify with one's people rather than assimilating to one or another of the nationalisms of Europe.

This assertion of Jewish ethnicity in a secular rather than religious sense produced a broad continuum of movements in eastern Europe by the beginning of the twentieth century. Jewish socialism championed economic justice as well as emancipation for the Jewish working class, advocating sweeping Jewish ethnic and cultural rights. The Jewish Workers Bund of Russia, Poland, and Lithuania was sympathetic to an ideology of Diaspora Jewish nationalism that called for legally recognized rights of the Jews as a European cultural minority. Alongside Zionism, a Jewish "territorialist" organization looked for a land other than Palestine as the setting for a Jewish state. There was a growing interest in Jewish social and economic history and in the folklore of eastern European Jews and of the Sephardic communities. A literary renaissance in Hebrew and Yiddish produced a rich body of novels, drama, poetry, and prose in those languages.

Many of these secular concerns were also manifested in the world Zionist movement established in 1897 to create a modern Jewish home in the ancient homeland of the Jewish people. Zionism embraced the ideas that a Jewish homeland would serve as a creative center for the revitalization of Jewish cultural values in modern form, that anti-Semitism was a symptom of the abnormality of Jewish life in the Diaspora that could only be cured with Jewish "self-emancipation" made possible by a Jewish commonwealth, and that cooperative farming communities and a vigorous labor movement in the Land of Israel was the expression of a social revolution among the Jewish masses. Religious forms of Zionism developed as well. In post–World War I Europe, and especially after the Nazis came to power in Germany, the goal of a Jewish refuge—a home that the Jews could go to by right when threatened with political persecution, economic discrimination, or physical extermination—became an increasingly urgent concern.

The thrust of modern thinking around the theme of Jewish peoplehood in the twentieth century emphasized, therefore, the notion of *kelal Yisra'el* (the wholeness of the people of Israel). An influential American Jewish ideology that emphasizes cultural pluralism, Judaism as a civilization, and the centrality of Zion together with the international character of *kelal Yisra'el* is that of Mordecai Kaplan, who insisted on the continued relevance of Jewish religious values but denied on principle that the Jews were the "chosen people." Other American Jewish theologians rejected Kaplan's effort to normalize the Jewish tradition by stripping Jewish peoplehood of a transcendent uniqueness. After World War II, and especially by the late 1960s, "ethnicity" (a slippery concept, difficult to define) was more easily acknowledged as a positive force in Jewry in and of itself (as it has been among other groups), while belonging to the Jewish people has been assumed a far more voluntaristic character, expressed in a wide range of ways and unusual forms. After the Holocaust came noticeable improvement in Jewish-Christian understanding. And with the greater acceptance of Judaism and the social integration of Jews came a considerable increase in the United States in the numbers of converts to Judaism.

The establishment of the state of Israel in 1948 brought a new series of issues to the fore concerning Jewish membership and meaning. Will Israel, as a secular Jewish state, be fully legitimized in the international family of nations? And in what does the Jewishness of the state of Israel consist? What is to be its relation to the religious dimension of the Jewish heritage? The question of personal Jewish status has been raised several times in Israel's courts of law in connection with the law of return, which grants all Diaspora Jews immediate Israeli citizenship upon their immigration there. In the case of Oswald Rufeisen, a born Jew who became a Catholic priest, the supreme court of Israel ruled that although Rufeisen was a Jew by *halakhah*, his acceptance of Catholicism excluded him from the Jewish people, and therefore he was not to be granted automatic Israeli citizenship. In the 1968 Shalit case, involving children of a non-Jewish mother who were raised as nonreligious Jews, the children were not allowed, on purely secular grounds, to be registered as Jews on their identity cards.

The twenty-first-century definition of "who is a Jew" reflects a mix of *halakhic* principles and informal Jewish attitudes. Yet another issue involves whether the State of Israel will continue to recognize as authentically Jewish those Jews converted in the Diaspora not according to Orthodox authorities or strict *halakhic* procedures—that is, by Reform, Conservative, and Reconstructionist rabbis. This in turn directs attention to the legitimacy of religious pluralism within the Jewish people—a conspicuous fact in parts of the Diaspora but not in the State of Israel. In the United States the question of who is a Jew has been raised in connection with children of intermarriages where the non-Jewish mother does not convert to Judaism; the Reform and Reconstructionist movements, but not the Conservative and Orthodox, have argued for a recognition of patrilineal descent under certain circumstances. Underlying the question of who is a Jew is the issue of the contemporary authority of *halakhah*: how, to what extent, and by whom will Jewish religious law be adapted to modern times. Behind all these specifics, however, is the question of the transcendent meaning of Jewish peoplehood, which will surely remain a delicate and profound subject for Jewish theologians.

SEE ALSO Anti-Semitism; Christianity; Conservative Judaism; Essenes; Hasidism; Holocaust, The, article on History; Israelite Religion; Judaism; Kaplan, Mordecai; Karaites; Marranos; Orthodox Judaism; Paul the Apostle; Qabbalah; Reform Judaism; Sadducees; Samaritans; Torah; Zealots; Zionism.

BIBLIOGRAPHY

Three classic histories of the Jewish people are Heinrich Graetz's *Geschichte der Juden von den ältesten Zeiten bis auf die Gegenwart*, 11 vols. (Leipzig, Germany, 1853–1876), translated by Bella Löwy and Philipp Bloch as *History of the Jews*, 6 vols. (Philadelphia, 1891–1898); Simon Dubnow's *Vsemirnaia istoriia evreiskogo naroda*, 10 vols. (Berlin, 1924–1939), translated by Moshe Spiegal as *History of the Jews*, 5 vols. (South Brunswick, N.J., 1967–1973); and Salo W. Baron's *A Social and Religious History of the Jews*, 2d ed., 18 vols. (New York, 1952–1983, plus the index for vols. 9–18, 1993). The history of Judaism in relation to the Jewish people is covered in David Biale, ed., *Cultures of the Jews: A New History* (New York, 2002); Jacob Neusner and Alan J. Avery-Peck, eds., *The Blackwell Companion to Judaism* (Oxford, 2000, 2003); and Martin Goodman, ed., *The Oxford Handbook of Jewish Studies* (Oxford, 2002). Pertinent to the Jewish people in relation to the changing context of Judaism is S. N. Eisenstadt, *Jewish Civilization: The Jewish Historical Experience in a Comparative Perspective* (Albany, N.Y., 1992). A stimulating perspective on these transformations is Efraim Shmueli, *Seven Jewish Cultures: A Reinterpretation of Jewish History and Thought* (Cambridge, U.K., 1990).

An overview of the historiography of the origins of the people up to and including the settlement in Canaan is George W. Ramsey's *The Quest for the Historical Israel* (Atlanta, 1981). The uniqueness of Israelite monotheism is defended by Yehezkel Kaufmann in *The Religion of Israel: From Its Beginnings to the Babylonian Exile*, translated and abridged by Moshe Greenberg (Chicago, 1960). An earlier work by Kaufmann explains the primary role of religion in Jewish survival until modern times, *Golah ve-nekhar*, 2d ed., 2 vols. (Tel Aviv, 1954). On Jewish and Christian self-definition in antiquity, see Lawrence H. Schiffman's *Who Was a Jew? Rabbinic and Halakhic Perspectives on the Jewish-Christian Schism* (Hoboken, N.J., 1985). On biblical, Jewish, and Christian uses of the name *Israel*, see Samuel Sandmel's *The Several Is-*

raels (New York, 1971). Early *halakhic* aspects are treated by Shaye J. D. Cohen in "The Origins of the Matrilineal Principle in Rabbinic Law," *Association for Jewish Studies Review* 10 (Spring 1985): 19–53. The theological views of classic rabbinic Judaism are treated in Ephraim E. Urbach's *The Sages: Their Concepts and Beliefs*, 2d enl. ed., 2 vols., translated by Israel Abrahams (Jerusalem, 1979), see especially chapter 16.

Medieval Jewish views of Jewish identity in a Christian environment are discussed in Jacob Katz's *Exclusiveness and Tolerance: Studies in Jewish-Gentile Relations in Medieval and Modern Times* (London, 1961). A history of Jewish proselytism is in Joseph R. Rosenbloom's *Conversion to Judaism: From the Biblical Period to the Present* (Cincinnati, Ohio, 1978). The branches of the Jewish people around the world are surveyed in Raphael Patai's *Tents of Jacob: The Diaspora; Yesterday and Today* (Englewood Cliffs, N.J., 1971). Among the books on Jewish modernization are Jacob Katz's *Out of the Ghetto: The Social Background of Jewish Emancipation, 1770–1870* (Cambridge, Mass., 1973); Calvin Goldscheider and Alan S. Zuckerman's *The Transformation of the Jews* (Chicago, 1984); and Simon N. Herman's *Jewish Identity: A Social Psychological Perspective* (Beverly Hills, Calif., 1977).

Secular approaches to Jewish nationhood are defended in Simon Dubnow's *Nationalism and History: Essays on Old and New Judaism*, edited by Koppel S. Pinson (Philadelphia, 1958); and Ben Halpern's *The American Jew: A Zionist Analysis* (New York, 1956). A gamut of Zionist views, secular and religious, are in Arthur Hertzberg, ed., *The Zionist Idea: A Historical Analysis and Reader* (Garden City, N.Y., 1959). Most books that treat the main aspects of Jewish faith discuss the religious significance of Jewish peoplehood, but among the few important Jewish works that have taken it as their central theme are Mordecai M. Kaplan's *Judaism as a Civilization: Toward a Reconstruction of Jewish-American Life* (New York, 1934); and Michael Wyschogrod's *The Body of Faith: Judaism as Corporeal Election* (New York, 1983). A scholarly account of peoplehood in twentieth-century American Jewish religious thought is Arnold M. Eisen's *The Chosen People in America: A Study in Jewish Religious Ideology* (Bloomington, Ind., 1983). For a collection of statements on "who is a Jew" as this question has come to the fore since the establishment of the state of Israel, see Baruch Litvin, comp., *Jewish Identity: Modern Responsa and Opinions on the Registration of Children of Mixed Marriages*, edited by Sidney B. Hoenig (New York, 1956). A succinct treatment of Judaism in the context of the dilemmas of modernizing religions is R. J. Zwi Werblowsky's "Sacral Particularity: The Jewish Case," in his *Beyond Tradition and Modernity: Changing Religions in a Changing World* (London, 1976). A philosophically sensitive picture of the nature of Judaism is Leon Roth's *Judaism: A Portrait* (New York, 1961).

See also Saʿadyah Gaon, *The Book of Beliefs and Opinions*, translated by Samuel Rosenblatt (New Haven, Conn., 1948); Yehudah ha-Levi, *Book of Kuzari*, translated by Hartwig Hirschfeld (New York, 1946); and Lloyd P. Gartner, *History of the Jews in Modern Times* (Oxford, 2001).

ROBERT M. SELTZER (1987 AND 2005)

JEWISH PHILOSOPHY SEE JEWISH THOUGHT AND PHILOSOPHY, *ARTICLE ON* PREMODERN PHILOSOPHY

JEWISH RELIGIOUS YEAR. The Hebrew word *ḥodesh,* used in the Bible for "month," means "that which is renewed" and refers to the renewal of the moon. Hence the Jewish calendar is lunar, the first day of each month being Roʾsh Ḥodesh ("head of the month"). Some months have twenty-nine days, others thirty. When the previous month has twenty-nine days, Roʾsh Ḥodesh is celebrated as a minor festival for two days; when the previous month has thirty days, it is celebrated for one day. In the Pentateuch (*Ex.* 12:2), the month on which the Israelites went out of Egypt is counted as the first month of the year, so when the Bible speaks of the third month, the seventh month, and so on, these are counted from the month of the Exodus. But the festival of Passover, celebrating the Exodus, is said in *Deuteronomy* 16:1 to fall in the month Aviv ("ripening"). This is understood to mean that Passover must always fall in spring, and thus the Jewish lunar calendar presupposes a natural solar calendar like that used in most ancient societies. A process of intercalation was consequently introduced to enable the lunar year to keep pace with the solar. The method is to add an extra month to seven out of nineteen lunar years. During the Babylonian captivity, after the destruction of the First Temple, the Babylonian names of the months were adopted and are still used. These are Nisan, Iyyar, Sivan, Tammuz (its origin in the name of a Babylonian deity was either unknown or ignored), Av, Elul, Tishri, Marḥeshvan, Kislev, Tevet, Shevaṭ, Adar. When, in a leap year, an extra month is introduced at the end of the year, there is an Adar Sheni, or "second Adar."

THE DEVELOPMENT OF THE CALENDAR. There was no uniform method of dating years until the Middle Ages, when the current practice was adopted of reckoning from the (biblical) creation of the world. The French commentaries to the Talmud (*tosafot* to B. T., *Giṭṭin* 80b) observe that in twelfth-century France it was already an established practice to date documents from the creation. In the Talmudic literature it is debated whether the creation took place in Nisan (the first month) or in Tishri (the seventh month), but for dating purposes the latter view is followed, so that the new year begins on the first day of Tishri. This day is the date of the festival Roʾsh ha-Shanah (New Year). Thus the year 1240 CE is the year 5000 from the creation. Thus 1986 CE from January 1 to October 3 is the year 5746 from the creation; from October 4 (the date of Roʾsh ha-Shanah) it is 5747. This method of dating is used in legal documents, letters, and newspapers but has no doctrinal significance, so that it does not normally disturb traditionalists who prefer to interpret the biblical record nonliterally to allow for a belief in the vast age of the earth implied by science.

It is generally accepted in the critical study of the Bible that the recurring refrain in the first chapter of *Genesis*—

"and it was evening and it was morning"—means that when daylight had passed into evening and then night had passed into morning, a complete day had elapsed. But the Talmudic tradition understands the verses to mean that night precedes the day. For this reason the day, for religious purposes, begins at nightfall and lasts until the next nightfall. The Sabbath begins at sunset on Friday and goes out at nightfall on Saturday. The same applies to the festivals. The twilight period is a legally doubtful one, and there is also an obligation to extend the Sabbaths and festivals at beginning and end. Jewish calendars, consequently, give the time of the Sabbath as beginning just before sunset and as ending when it is fully dark. Pious Jews, in the absence of a calendar, will keep the Sabbath until it is sufficiently dark to see three average-sized stars in close proximity in the night sky.

Before the present fixed calendar was instituted (in the middle of the fourth century CE), the date of the new moon was arrived at by observation. If witnesses saw the new moon on the twenty-ninth day of the month, they would present their testimony to the high court and that day would be declared Ro'sh Ḥodesh, the beginning of the next month. If the new moon had not been observed on the twenty-ninth day, the thirtieth day automatically became Ro'sh Ḥodesh. Since the festivals falling in the month are counted from Ro'sh Ḥodesh, there was always some doubt as to which of two days would be the date of the festival. Except on Ro'sh ha-Shanah, which falls on the actual day of the new moon, special messengers could always inform the Jews of Palestine of the correct date of the festival. But for the Jews of the Diaspora, who resided in lands too distant for them to be informed in time, it became the practice to keep both days as the festival and thus avoid any possibility of error. Even after the calendar was fixed, the Talmudic sources state, the Jews of the Diaspora were advised by the Palestinian authorities to continue to hold fast to the custom of their ancestors and keep the "two days of the Diaspora." A post-Talmudic rationale for the two days of the Diaspora is that outside the Holy Land the extra festival day compensates for the absence of sanctity in the land. The practice in the state of Israel is thus to keep only one day (with the exception of Ro'sh ha-Shanah), whereas Jews living elsewhere keep two days. There is much discussion in the legal sources on the practice to be adopted by a Jew living outside Israel who visits Israel for the festival or vice versa. Reform Jews prefer to follow the biblical injunctions only, and they do not keep the two days of the Diaspora. Some Conservative Jews, too, have argued for the abolition of the second day because of the anomaly of treating as a holy day a day that is not observed as sacred in Israel.

THE HOLY DAYS. Similar festivals in the ancient Near East suggest that the biblical festivals were originally agricultural feasts transformed into celebrations of historical events. The most striking aspect of the Jewish religious calendar is this transfer from the round of the seasons to the affirmation of God's work in human history—the transfer, as it were, from space to time.

The holy days of the Jewish year can be divided into two categories: the biblical and the postbiblical, or the major and the minor. (Purim, though based on *Esther,* a book from the biblical period, is held to be a post-biblical festival from this point of view and hence a minor festival.) The first and last days of Passover and Sukkot, Shavu'ot, Ro'sh ha-Shanah, and Yom Kippur are major festivals in that all labor (except that required for the preparation of food and even this on Yom Kippur) is forbidden. On the days between the first and last days of Passover and Sukkot, necessary labor is permitted. All labor is permitted on minor festivals such as Purim and Ḥanukkah.

Each of the festivals has its own rituals and its own special liturgy. On all of them the Hallel ("praise"), consisting of *Psalms* 113–118, is recited in the synagogue, except on Ro'sh ha-Shanah, Yom Kippur, and Purim. Only part of Hallel is said on Ro'sh Ḥodesh, when labor is permitted, and the last six days of Passover, it being held unseemly to rejoice by singing the full praises of God since the Egyptians, who were also God's creatures, were destroyed. Festive meals are the order of the day on the festivals (except, of course, on Yom Kippur), and the day is marked by the donning of one's best clothes. It is considered meritorious to study on each festival the relevant passages in the classical sources of Judaism. On the fast days neither food nor drink is taken from sunrise to nightfall (on Yom Kippur and Tish'ah be-Av, from sunset on the previous night).

Following are major dates of the religious year, month by month.

- 15–22 Nisan (15–23 in the Diaspora): Passover, celebrating the Exodus from Egypt.
- 6 Sivan (6–7 in the Diaspora): Shavu'ot, anniversary of the theophany at Sinai.
- 17 Tammuz: Fast of Tammuz, commemorating the breaching of the walls of Jerusalem at the time of the destruction of the First Temple (587/6 BCE) and the Second Temple (70 CE).
- 9 Av: Tish'ah be-Av (Ninth of Av), fast day commemorating the destruction of the First and Second Temples and other national calamities.
- 1–2 Tishri: Ro'sh ha-Shanah, the New Year festival.
- 3 Tishri: Tsom Gedalyah (Fast of Gedaliah), commemorating the slaying of Gedaliah as told in *Jeremiah* 41:1–2 and *2 Kings* 25:25, an event that marked the end of the First Commonwealth.
- 10 Tishri: Yom Kippur (Day of Atonement), the great fast day.
- 15–23 Tishri (15–24 in the Diaspora): Sukkot (Feast of Tabernacles), celebrating the dwelling in booths by the Israelites in their journey through the wilderness after the Exodus.
- 25 Kislev: first day of Ḥanukkah (Feast of Rededica-

tion), celebrating the victory of the Maccabees and the rededication of the Temple. Ḥanukkah lasts for eight days.

- 10 Tevet: ʿAsarah be-Ṭevet (Fast of the Tenth of Ṭevet), commemorating the siege of Jerusalem by Nebuchadrezzar before the destruction of the First Temple in 587/6 BCE.
- 15 Shevaṭ: Roʾsh ha-Shanah le-Ilanot (New Year for Trees), a minor festival reminiscent of the laws of tithing in ancient times. Nowadays, this is a celebration of God's bounty, of thanksgiving for the fruit of the ground.
- 13 Adar: Taʿanit Ester (Fast of Esther), based on the account in *Esther* (4:16).
- 14 Adar: Purim (Lots), the festival celebrating the victory over Haman, who cast lots to destroy the Jews, as told in *Esther.*
- 15 Adar: Shushan Purim (Purim of Shushan), based on the account in *Esther* (9:18) that the Jews in the capital city of Shushan celebrated their deliverance on this day.

Major Festivals and Fast Days. The three festivals of Passover, Shavuʿot, and Sukkot form a unit in that, in Temple times, they were pilgrim festivals, when the people came to worship and offer sacrifices in the Temple. The connection between these three festivals is preserved in the liturgy in which there are references to the place of each festival in the yearly cycle. Thus, on Passover the reference is to "the season of our freedom," on Shavuʿot to "the season of the giving of our Torah," and on Sukkot to "the season of our rejoicing," since Sukkot, as the culmination of the cycle, is the special season of joy. The three major festivals of the month of Tishri have been seen as a unit of a different kind. Roʾsh ha-Shanah, the first of the three, is seen as the festival of the mind, when people reflect on their destiny and resolve to lead a better life in the coming year. Yom Kippur, the day when the emotions are stirred, is seen as the festival of the heart, because it is the day of pardon and reconciliation with God. Sukkot, the third in this triad, involves active participation in the building of the booth and eating meals there, and is seen therefore as the festival of the hand. Thus, head, heart, and hand are demanded in the service of God.

The days between Roʾsh ha-Shanah and Yom Kippur, inclusive, are known as the Ten Days of Penitence. This is a solemn season of reflection on life's meaning and sincere repentance. Similarly, the whole month of Elul, the last month of the old year, is a penitential season in preparation for the solemn period at the beginning of the new year. Roʾsh ha-Shanah and Yom Kippur are consequently known as Yamim Noraʾim, the Days of Awe.

Minor Festivals and Fast Days. In the annual cycle there are two periods of mourning during which marriages are not celebrated and tokens of mourning are observed. The first of these is the three-week period from the seventeenth of Tammuz to Tishʿah be-Av, the period of mourning for the destruction of the Temple and the sufferings of the people in subsequent ages. In many places the period becomes more intense from the first of Av in that the consumption of meat and wine is proscribed. The other, lesser, period of mourning is known as the ʿOmer period, forty-nine days from the second day of Passover to the festival of Shavuʿot (though, of course, there is no mourning during Passover itself). The *ʿomer* was a measure of meal brought as an offering in Temple times, and there is a biblical injunction to count these forty-nine days (*Lv.* 23:9–16; known as "counting the ʿOmer"). It has been suggested that the custom of mourning during the ʿOmer has its origin in the ancient belief, held by many peoples, that it is bad luck to marry during the month of May. The traditional sources state that the mourning is over the death by plague of many of the disciples of ʿAqivaʾ ben Yosef in the second century CE. The mystics introduce a different note. There are seven lower potencies or powers in the godhead, the *sefirot,* that become flawed as a result of human sin. Each one of these contains the others as well, so that each of the forty-nine days of the ʿOmer calls for repentance for the purpose of putting right these flaws. The mystics of Safad in the sixteenth century held that the eighteenth of Iyyar, the thirty-third day of the ʿOmer—Lag ba-ʿOmer—is the anniversary of the death of the great mystic Shimʿon bar Yoḥʾai, a disciple of ʿAqivʾa and the alleged author of the *Zohar.* The belief that at the saint's death his soul became united with its source on high is referred to as "the marriage of Shimʿon bar Yoḥʾai." This day, then, became a minor festival, and marriages are celebrated on the day.

The day of the new moon, Roʾsh Ḥodesh, is also a minor festival. From the juxtaposition of Roʾsh Ḥodesh with the Sabbath in a number of biblical passages, many biblical scholars conclude that in ancient times Roʾsh Ḥodesh was a major festival on a par with the Sabbath. Nowadays, however, the day is marked only by festivities in a minor key and by liturgical additions. An old custom frees women from the obligation to work on Roʾsh Ḥodesh, and this might be a vestige of the ancient sanctity the day enjoyed. The official reason given is that women refused to participate in the making of the golden calf and were, therefore, given an extra holiday. In the mystical tradition the moon symbolizes the Shekhinah, the female element in the godhead, the counterpart on high of the community of Israel, awaiting the redemption of the Jewish people and of all humankind with harmony restored throughout all creation. The waxing and the waning of the moon is thus a powerful mythological symbol. The Safad mystics consequently introduced a new ritual for the eve of Roʾsh Ḥodesh. This day is known as Yom Kippur Qatan (Minor Yom Kippur). As the name implies, it is a time of repentance and, for some, fasting.

There are a number of other lesser feasts and fast days. The Fast of the Firstborn has its origins in the early Middle Ages. In *Exodus* (13:1–16) it is related that the firstborn of the Israelites have a special sanctity because God spared them when he killed the firstborn of the Egyptians. Thus the custom of fasting on the eve of Passover, 14 Nisan, developed. Generally, nowadays, the firstborn, instead of fasting, attend a study session during which a tractate of the Talmud is completed. To partake of a festive meal on this occasion is held to be a religious obligation that overrides the obligation to fast.

Some pious Jews fast on the Monday, Thursday, and following Monday after the festivals of Passover and Sukkot—Beit He' Beit ("Two, Five, Two," referring to the days of the week). The reason given is that it is to atone for any untoward frivolity during the lengthy festival period.

In many Jewish communities the burial of the dead is attended to by a voluntary organization, whose membership is granted only to the most distinguished applicants. This organization is known as the *ḥevrah' qaddisha'* ("holy brotherhood"). The members of the *ḥevrah' qaddisha'* observe a fast on the seventh of Adar, the anniversary of the death of Moses, to atone for any disrespect they may have shown to the dead. But on the night following the fast they celebrate their privileged position by holding a special banquet.

There are also minor festivals observed by particular groups. For instance, on the analogy of Purim, many communities delivered miraculously from destruction celebrate ever after their day of deliverance as a "Purim." For example, the Hasidic master Shne'ur Zalman of Lyady (1745–1813), founder of the Habad school of Hasidism, was released from prison in Russia on the nineteenth of Kislev, after his arrest on a charge of treason, and his followers observe this day as a festival.

Two modern institutions are Yom ha-Sho'ah (Holocaust Day) on 27 Nisan, marking the destruction of six million Jews during the Nazi period, and Yom ha-Atsma'ut (Independence Day) on 5 Iyyar, the celebration, especially in the state of Israel, of the Israeli declaration of independence on that date. In many religious circles this day is treated as a full *yom tov,* and the *Hallel* is recited.

See Also Ḥanukkah; Judaism, articles on Judaism in Asia, Judaism in Northeast Africa; Passover; Purim; Ro'sh ha-Shanah and Yom Kippur; Shabbat; Shavu'ot; Sukkot.

Bibliography

The articles "Calendar, History of" and "Calendar" in the *Jewish Encyclopedia* (New York, 1906) are still the best general accounts. The article "Calendar" in *Encyclopaedia Judaica* (Jerusalem, 1971) contains more detail but is so technical as to be incomprehensible to all but the experts, who will have no need for it. Hayyim Schauss's *Guide to the Jewish Holy Days,* translated by Samuel Jaffe (New York, 1962), is a survey, from the rationalistic standpoint, with critical and historical notes. More traditional are Abraham P. Bloch's *The Biblical and Historical Background of the Jewish Holy Days* (New York, 1978) and Abraham Chill's *The Minhagim: The Customs and Ceremonies of Judaism, Their Origins and Rationale* (New York, 1979). A useful introduction to the traditionalist mood of thought on the significance of the festivals is *Seasons of the Soul: Religious, Historical and Philosophical Perspectives on the Jewish Year and Its Milestones* (New York, 1981), edited by Nisson Walpin. Similar meditations on the Jewish calendar year by a famous nineteenth-century Orthodox theologian are to be found in *Judaism Eternal: Selected Essays from the Writings of Rabbi Samson Raphael Hirsch,* vol. 1, translated from the German original by Isidor Grunfeld (London, 1956), pp. 3–152. *Ha-mo'adim ba-halakhah* (Jerusalem, 1980) by Shlomo Y. Zevin is a particularly fine and popular treatment of the legal principles behind the observances of the festivals and fast days. Part of this work has been published in English translation: *The Festivals in Halachah,* translated by Meir Fox-Ashrei and edited by Uri Kaploon (New York, 1981). Solomon Ganzfield's *Code of Jewish Law (Qitsur Shulhan 'arukh): A Compilation of Jewish Laws and Customs,* vol. 3, annot. & rev. ed., translated by Hyman E. Goldin (New York, 1961), is a comprehensive and clearly written but very pedestrian account.

Louis Jacobs (1987)

JEWISH RENEWAL MOVEMENT.

The Jewish Renewal movement is one of the most recent and creative expressions of Judaism's continued attempt to mold itself to the contours of modernity. It is, in many respects, an indigenous American religious movement but is expanding into a global Jewish phenomenon. This multifaceted development in contemporary Judaism is hard to categorize. It has the audacity of a reformation, the passion of a revival, and the optimism of a renaissance. Its critique and reconstruction of Judaism not only occupies the realm of ideas but reaches down to the organizational structure of Judaism in the Diaspora.

For most of the twentieth century Judaism in America developed along denominational lines. Each denomination has its own autonomy, its own rabbinical academies, its own fund-raising structure. The separation of church and state in America has enabled American Judaism to develop its own institutional and spiritual apparatus without any serious threat of one community dominating another. Renewal emerged from this denominational bedrock but has challenged the denominational structure. It is, perhaps, the prelude to, or first-fruits of, a postdenominational Judaism in America, growing out of the dissatisfaction many Jews have with the present ideological and practical structure of Judaism in the Diaspora, in North America in particular.

Origins. There are many factors that contribute to the breakdown or transformation of denominational Judaism in America and the emergence of a new approach to religion and culture. Three of the most prominent direct factors are the maturation of American Jews who did not experience firsthand the devastation of European Jewry in the Holocaust; the rise of a generation of Jews (many second generation Americans) who were dissatisfied with the materialism and spiritual vacuity of mid- to late-twentieth-century American Jewish life; and the shock-waves of the American counterculture, including the importation of Eastern religions to the American continent. More specifically, it is possible to pinpoint the beginning of Jewish Renewal in one seemingly benign event.

In 1948 the sixth Lubavitcher Rebbe, Rabbi Joseph Schneersohn (d. 1950), decided to inaugurate the missionary wing of his movement by sending emissaries to college campuses. He asked two young disciples, Zalman Schachter (later Schachter-Shalomi, b. 1924) and Shlomo Carlebach (1924–1994), to attend a Ḥanukkah party at Brandeis University (which opened its door that year) in a suburb of Boston, Massachusetts. Zalman and Shlomo (who prefer to be called by their first names) took various Hasidic books, tapes, and religious paraphernalia and attended the party intending to spread the message of traditional Judaism. Both were raised in Europe, studied there, and were refugees from the war, Schlomo escaping before the war and Zalman afterward. What they experienced that winter night at Brandeis University was the extent to which young American Jews lived in an intellectual universe that left no room for tradition the way they envisioned it. They both understood the extent to which unadulterated Hasidism simply could not be sold to an American audience raised on liberal democratic ideals. Zalman and Shlomo did different things with that realization, both of which contributed to Jewish Renewal, but the spark of what would become a new Jewish movement was ignited that evening. Zalman's meditation on those and other events was published as *Fragments of a Future Scroll* in 1975.

The next significant manifestations of nascent Jewish Renewal occurred on the two coasts of the American continent, in San Francisco and Boston, the former during the turbulent years of the late 1960s, the latter during its aftermath in the early 1970s. Shlomo opened what was known as the House of Love and Prayer in San Francisco in the late 1960s, what was, in effect, an early Chabad House—a small house, usually rented, run by members of the Chabad Hasidic sect that functioned as a synagogue, outreach and drop-in center, and a gathering place for Jews to express their Jewishness in whatever way felt comfortable. During the 1960s its purpose was often to provide a spiritual and countercultural Jewish alternative to compete with the myriad spiritualities that were emerging in the Bay Area after the Summer of Love in 1967.

In the early 1970s, Arthur Green, Zalman, and others founded Havurat Shalom in Somerville, Massachusetts, an egalitarian, experimental Jewish community devoted to study, prayer, and the exploration of Jewish spirituality. Zalman taught and served as Jewish chaplain for numerous years at the University of Winnipeg, and eventually settled in Philadelphia, founding a community called Bnei ʿOr (Sons of Light). Under the influence of feminism and his commitment to the egalitarian spirit it espoused, he changed its named to Pnei ʿOr (Faces of Light). This community and its numerous branches around the United States are often viewed as the first organized communities of the Jewish Renewal movement. Its experimental Judaism extended far beyond its Hasidic origins and beyond even the more restrained, albeit provocative, communities of Havurat Shalom (which is still operating) and the House of Love and Prayer (which disbanded in 1977; some of its members moved to a small community in Israel known as Moshav Me'or Modiim).

The Jewish Renewal movement has an umbrella organization called ALEPH, Alliance for Jewish Renewal, which has centers worldwide, training rabbis and spiritual leaders to serve in its own synagogues and the synagogues of other Jewish denominations. Jewish Renewal activities include an annual Kallah, a kind of Renewal pilgrimage where workshops, seminars, and communal celebrations are held in a rural setting. The Renewal centers are typical of a progressive experimental movement. They are strongest in places like Berkeley and San Francisco; Boulder, Colorado; New Mexico; Boston; New York; Philadelphia; and Los Angeles. Other centers exist in Miami, Florida; Hartford, Connecticut; and Washington, D.C. Much of the training of rabbis and leaders is accomplished through mentoring and correspondence.

INFLUENCES. In many ways Jewish Renewal is a good example of late twentieth-century religious syncretism in America. It does not intend to start a new American religion or subreligion, yet, in contrast to other Jewish denominations, it freely adopts ideas and practices from other religions, incorporating them into its developing Jewish model of worship. Renewal is antiorthodox in that it rejects the very notion that one way can embody the fullness of tradition. It seeks to create a spiritual context that can be utilized by Jews and non-Jews alike. In this sense, it is very much a product of American life, in that it exercises an kind of eclectic creativity, reaching beyond the confines of its own tradition, fully taking advantage of a society where freedom of religious expression is a matter of law. Influences include an amalgam of classical Jewish pietism, medieval Qabbalah, Hasidism, the Western version of Buddhism, Islamic Sufism, Christian monasticism, American pragmatism, Jewish Reconstructionism, religious existentialism, and progressive American political activism and environmentalism.

The most interesting thing about Jewish Renewal is that it is a decidedly non-Orthodox Judaism built on the pietism and ritualism of classical Jewish mysticism and Hasidism. It translates these insular forms of Judaism through the lens of an American counterculture devoted to progressive politics, global concerns, ecumenicism, equality of the sexes, and humanitarian universalism. Zalman Schachter-Shalomi employs his vast knowledge of Jewish sources to construct a Judaism that is an outgrowth of the American counterculture, presenting Judaism as a religion that can contribute to and be a source of inspiration for American Jews reared in the liberal democratic tradition who have been influenced by the spiritual renaissance of the 1960s. In many ways, Jewish Renewal is a pietistic antifundamentalism that is not apologetic for the tradition but views honest critique as a method of rebuilding a Jewish spirit lost in the dark ages of Jewish history. In this sense it sees itself as apostolic, reminiscent of Luther's Protestantism. It is solidly devoted to the concerns of living on the planet in a responsible and constructive manner and views its religiosity in global and activist terms.

The most direct and prominent influence on Jewish Renewal is Hasidism, a Jewish pietism from late-eighteenth-century eastern Europe that transformed world Jewry in the last two centuries. Both Zalman and Shlomo were trained in the Hasidic tradition and used Hasidic literature as the basis of their Renewal approach. Zalman, who is the architect of this movement, views the message of Hasidism as one that can be revamped, revalued, de- and recontextualized to complement an era of Jewish inclusiveness and tolerance. In many ways Martin Buber's modernization of Hasidism as Jewish existentialism plays an important role, as does Abraham Joshua Heschel's use of Hasidism as a source for his theology of pathos.

In his writings Zalman acknowledges his debt to Buber and Heschel yet seeks to take their initiative in a different direction. He does not relate to Hasidism as a movement but rather as an approach to Judaism, something that can be revalued and express contemporary sensibilities. While Hasidism is a usable model for this movement, some Renewal thinkers also view Hasidism as limited due to its unwillingness to extend its provocative teachings to their logical conclusion. This conclusion, which Zalman calls a paradigm shift, is the ideological foundation of Jewish Renewal and will be discussed below.

While American forms of Judaism have become fully comfortable with American life, in many respects the particularistic nature of Judaism and its relationship to the individual have prevented it from engaging in global issues as part of its devotional life. While Reform and Reconstructionist Judaism do address global concerns, their social activism is not as integrated into their devotional practices as in Renewal. A good example is the environmental movement in America. One of Renewal's original leaders, Arthur Waskow, has played a prominent role in contemporary environmentalism. His most popular works, *Seasons of Our Joy* and *Torah of the Earth: Exploring 4,000 Years of Ecology in Jewish Thought,* explore the connection between Judaism and environmentalism.

One very prominent feature of Jewish Renewal and an example of its commitment to integrating global issues into its devotional life is the concept of "eco-Kosher." This idea suggests that the traditional dietary laws (*kashrut*) should be augmented to include prohibitions against consuming any foods that exploit irreplaceable natural resources; are produced by companies that pollute the environment, are manufactured by using abusive labor practices, or support institutions that knowingly disregard environmental concerns. In Jewish Renewal there are differences of opinion as to whether these principles should replace existing restrictions or be added to them. This kind of debate is common in nascent religious reform and is reminiscent of the debate between the Jewish Christians and Paul regarding the continued efficacy of the law after Christ. Some Renewal Jews want to retain a more traditional relationship to Jewish law (*halakhah*) while others prefer to remain devoted to ritual yet not bound by existing legal decisions regarding those rituals and practices.

Ecumenicism and the use of other religious traditions and teachings to enhance and revise existing Jewish practice is another major aspect of Jewish Renewal. While modern American Judaisms often engage in ecumenical dialogue (before September 11, 2001, almost exclusively with Christians) they usually do not integrate the practices of other religions into their religious life. This speaks to the cautious way in which modern Judaisms view the "other" even in a free democratic society. Zalman is an ordained Ṣūfī teacher and many of Jewish Renewal's constituency practice and teach various forms of meditation, either adapted to Jewish sensibilities or not.

This raises yet another internal debate in this community common in fledgling religious movements. Should external influences be Judaized or made kosher or should other rituals and traditions be practiced without any Judaizing process? Elat Hayyim, the Jewish Renewal retreat center in upstate New York, holds regular mediation retreats as well as more traditional Jewish festival retreats and workshops. Serious engagement with other religious traditions, including inviting masters of other religious disciplines to speak at seminars and retreats and adapting some of their practices, illustrates Renewal's attempt to break out of the insular framework of traditional and even progressive Judaism.

Underlying this ecumenical approach is a fundamental belief that all religions hold some basic truths and that dialogue between religions, including openly borrowing various practices, can aid the healing of the planet and enhance religion's contribution to civilization more generally. This kind of applied universalist particularism is a new phenomenon in modern Judaism (most other progressive forms of Judaism, religious and secular, focus on Zionism and Israel as their global outlet). The implication here is that all religions have ossified and have lost some of their truth as a result of historical circumstances and that religious confluence can contribute to reconstructing some of these inherent truths. Jewish Renewal is sometimes accused of religious syncretism. This characterization is misleading, although not entirely false as the Jewish Renewal movement is making no attempt to develop a new religion. The starting and end point is always Judaism, but it is in fact Judaism transformed out of its insular and exclusivist mold.

Another important influence on Jewish Renewal is American pragmatism, viewed through the lens of Mordecai Kaplan's Reconstructionist Judaism. Reconstructionism argues that Judaism is, first and foremost, a civilization. Jewish law is viewed as a system of folkways that Jews developed in order to give themselves a unique identity as a people. These folkways must be maintained and protected as the people's identity is dependent upon them. However, Jewish ritual and practice must conform to the sensibilities of the people and not be foisted upon them as commandments.

This notion of Jewish practice came to be known as post-halakhic Judaism, a Judaism devoted to practice but one not based on unalterable and commanded law. Kaplan's battle was with the liberal Reform Judaism that abandoned law and practice completely and Conservative and Orthodox Judaism that were, in his view, living a law that was outdated, both in form and substance. Kaplan's influences included John Dewey and Émile Durkheim. His approach was rational and pragmatic and not generally metaphysical.

In many ways, Jewish Renewal took Kaplan's basic critique of contemporary Judaism and refracted it through Hasidism and mystical lenses. Renewal is one type of post-halakhic Judaism, one that fuses law and custom (not unlike many premodern Qabbalists) and views the Jewish attachment to its practices as essential for living an authentic and meaningful Jewish life. While it does view Jewish practice as commanded, it views commandedness largely as an outgrowth of the desire of the devotee to express love for the Creator and the creation and expression of Judaism's role (special but not necessarily unique) in promoting a healthy and organic global community. In other words, Renewal posits a theory of autonomous commandedness.

It is not coincidental that Renewal's headquarters in the 1970s and 1980s and the Reconstructionist Rabbinical College (RRC) were both located in Philadelphia (a city that was once a center of Conservative Judaism). Nor is it insignificant that Arthur Green, cofounder of Havurat Shalom in Somerville, Massachusetts, was president of RRC for ten years. During that time, there was a steady interaction between these two communities that resulted in, among other things, shared principles and ideals. If one had to cite the strongest influences on Jewish Renewal, Hasidism and Reconstructionism would top the list. This odd symbiosis is addressed by Zalman Schachter-Shalomi in a chapter entitled "Neo-Hasidism and Reconstructionism: A Not-Only-Imaginary Dialogue," in *Paradigm Shift,* edited by Ellen Singer.

Two other important influences are liberal/progressive politics and Zionism. While not a political movement, and, in many ways, strikingly apolitical, Jewish Renewal is loosely part of the new Jewish Left in North America. It champions progressive political positions on the environment, war, poverty relief, world hunger, AIDS, women's issues, globalization, and unilateral aggression. The two most prominent activists in this area of Renewal are Arthur Waskow and Michael Lerner. Both 1960s radicals who adopted Judaism as a center of their spiritual and political lives, Waskow and Lerner have been outspoken about many issues, both national and international, concerning Jews and society more generally. Lerner's bimonthly magazine *Tikkun* can be viewed as a political arm of Jewish Renewal, and many Renewal members write regularly for this publication. Two of Lerner's books, *The Politics of Meaning* and *Jewish Renewal,* offer a vision of Jewish Renewal dedicated to a Jewish approach to contemporary political issues and crisis (see, for example, *Jewish Renewal,* pp. 265–280).

Both Lerner and Waskow envision Renewal as contributing Jewish alternatives to the political arena. What is new and important here is that these Jewish resources are not employed to address issues of Jewish concern but rather to contribute to global concerns from a Jewish spiritual perspective. This illustrates the extent to which Jewish Renewal is a universalized Judaism with humanitarian concerns that extend far beyond the narrow boundaries of the Jewish people. This mixture of universal ideals coupled with a dedication to Jewish practice makes Jewish Renewal a unique phenomenon in contemporary Judaism.

The progress that Renewal made in diffusing the particularistic nature of traditional Judaism, however, is put to the test on the question of Zionism. While there is no official Jewish Renewal policy on Zionism, anecdotal evidence suggests that most members are Zionist if by that one simply means supporters of the State of Israel's right to exist. Given the prominence of Israel and Zionism in contemporary Judaism it is curious that the most sustained statement of Jewish Renewal, Zalman Schachter-Shalomi's article in *Paradigm Shift,* does not contain any serious discussion of Zionism or the State of Israel.

This omission is not insignificant and speaks to way in which Jewish Renewal is really a diasporic religious phenomenon (there is a growing Jewish Renewal movement in Israel which will no doubt confront these issues differently). While the minimalist definition of Zionism would include most of those involved with Jewish Renewal, many of its members advocate a progressive position on the Middle East crisis, are supporters of a Palestinian state along the 1967 borders, and view the occupation as both immoral and spiritually damaging to Israel as a nation and Judaism as a religion. While some in the larger Renewal community might not share this position, this appears to be the one that is dominant. This is surely the case with Waskow and Lerner, and the platform of *Tikkun* magazine.

Another important factor in Renewal is its engagement with Islam. Renewal members, and Zalman in particular, were early and continuous supporters of a dialogue with Palestinian Muslims, particularly Ṣūfīs. They were quite successful in opening lines of communication between Jews and Muslims on matters of spirituality and politics, particularly in the 1960s when there was almost no serious Jewish–Muslim dialogue. As progressive leftists, most sympathize with the plight of the Palestinian civilian population and view Israel as an occupying power in the territories.

Organizations like the New Jewish Agenda, the Abraham Fund, and Seeds of Peace, while not formally a part of

Jewish Renewal, are influenced by it. Renewal's stance on the crisis in the Middle East illustrates its decision to opt out of a fervent messianism (severing it from its roots in Lubavitch Hasidism, roots which now, with the Jewish settler movement, represent the most virulent examples of Jewish messianism) and reject the militant nationalism so common in Diaspora Judaism. Instead Renewal lobbies for a softer utopian vision where barriers between peoples are to be made more transparent rather than more opaque.

IDEOLOGY. Jewish Renewal is founded on a reformist ideology couched in a revivalist pietism. Like many such movements in the history of religion, its agenda is both apostolic and subversive. Its claim to have retrieved an internal meaning of Judaism is used to counter the status quo of what Judaism has become. In this sense it is also, to use more contemporary language, countercultural. The reformist predilection of Jewish Renewal is captured in what Zalman Schachter-Shalomi has termed a Paradigm Shift. The idea is not new, but is creatively adapted to the contours of the contemporary world.

The basic argument in the Paradigm Shift is that history can be divided into distinct historical epochs, each of which contains particular spiritual paths even within one particular religious tradition. As the epoch changes, so must the spiritual direction of that religion in order to insure an organicity between the external historic and cosmic environment (which are inextricable according to the Jewish mystical tradition) and individual and collective consciousness. This notion was suggested by the Christian monk Joachim of Fiore and is the basis of the anonymous fourteenth-century Jewish qabbalistic works *Sefer ha-temunah* and *Sefer ha-peliah.* In both premodern sources, each of which has underlying messianic pretensions, new paths of devotion are revealed as a new epoch emerges and those new paths must be followed in order to fully disclose the potential in the new era.

Jewish Renewal's rendition of this doctrine seems to have jettisoned the apocalyptic messianic flavor of these texts in favor of a belief in the slow and steady completion of the utopian redemption envisioned by some of the classical Hebrew prophets, a world without war, strife, and conflict. An analysis of the messianism of Jewish Renewal, born from a tempered reading of contemporary Lubavitch (Hasidic) messianism, is a desideratum in scholarship. What is also important here is that this doctrine is also foundational for the heretical Jewish movement of Shabbetai Tsevi in the seventeenth century.

The Shabbatean heretics argued that a new historical epoch was inaugurated by the Messiah Shabbetai Tsevi and this new era must be accompanied by a new Torah, a Torah that transcends the strict legalism of the old (rabbinic) law and expands God's presence into the mundane and even forbidden. While the language of Renewal is far more temperate and communal (it does not focus much attention on the centrality of the charismatic leader, or Zaddik, who serves as a foundation for Hasidic spirituality), it does argue that the theism (or deism) of past eras has now evolved into a pantheism of the present, thus requiring Jews to reaccess their relationship to Jewish theology and ritual practice. In Zalman's words:

> So where are we now? I'd like to say we are in the shift to the place where everything is God, pantheism. . . . We want Wholeness, a holistic understanding, now. . . . I believe that people are moving from theism to pantheism. There are some who don't like the word pantheism, the idea that God is everything. They prefer the word panentheism, which means that God is in everything. I, however, don't think the distinction is real. (Schachter-Shalomi, 2003, p. 20)

Using an astrological system (also used by the Shabbateans) filtered through the theosophical qabbalistic system of four worlds and the ten *sefirot* (cosmic potencies), Renewal claims that a new era, an Age of Aquarius, has emerged that requires Jews to respond by reconstructing the Torah of the past in preparation for a new era (on this see *Paradigm Shift,* pp. 277–298). While much of this is viewed by Renewal as rooted in Hasidic teachings, it is also quite reminiscent of the Shabbatean movement that also may have influenced early Hasidic doctrine. Because most Shabbatean texts remained (and largely remain) in manuscript (what Hebrew publisher would publish what had become viewed as blatant heresy?) most contemporary Jews are not familiar with them. It remains to be seen how the disclosure of these texts will affect both Hasidism and Renewal.

IMPACT. The impact of Jewish Renewal is already profound, yet, given that we are still in the midst of its full disclosure, still somewhat unknown. It is important to note that while Renewal was fed by the Baʾal Teshuva movement (new returnees to Judaism) in the late 1960s to mid-1970s, Renewal is not a part of that movement—in fact, in many ways it is its opposite. The Baʾal Teshuva movement was a movement of disenchanted Diaspora and Israeli youth who turned back to traditional Judaism as an alternative to the vacuous materialistic lives of their upbringing. The end-game of this movement was a return to Orthodoxy and a basic rejection of Western values. Renewal is not a return to the past but the construction of a future built on tradition but not bound to it. While many young Jewish seekers passed through Renewal on their way to Orthodoxy, those that stayed created a Judaism that was decidedly neither Orthodox nor accepting of the hegemonic claims of Orthodoxy's leadership.

Jewish Renewal has influenced all Jewish denominations in North America, from Orthodoxy to Reform. Orthodoxy absorbed Renewal's focus on joyful worship and the music of Shlomo Carlebach (who was not formally part of Renewal but floated freely between Jewish communities), some of the Hasidic teachings of Zalman Schachter-Shalomi, and the use of mediation and contemplative prayer developed by some Renewal members. Conservative and Reform Jewish communities in North America have seen the emergence of smaller prayer quorums (called Ḥavurah-style communities) in their larger synagogues among members who desire a more intimate and less formal prayer service.

Classes in Hasidism and mediation are held in many suburban American synagogues, largely due to the influence of members who attended Renewal retreats and brought the message of Renewal to their own communities. Secular Jews who had only negative views of Judaism as antiquated and irrelevant have found Renewal sympathetic to their needs and supportive of their own secular Jewish choices. Some of these Jews have found a political home in Renewal because it represents their politics and is decidedly and openly Jewish but not patriarchal, overly nationalistic, or xenophobic. In short, Jewish Renewal is leading a grassroots renaissance in Judaism, undermining tradition while espousing it, offering a progressive message that better suits the assimilationist ideology of classical Reform Judaism in the present multicultural climate and offers a non-Orthodox piety and metalegal alternative to Conservative Judaism.

The JewBu (Jewish-Buddhist) phenomenon is, in many ways, an extension of Jewish Renewal. This largely amorphous community consists of Jews who have taken on Buddhism as a religious and spiritual path, some attaining high ranks in Buddhist circles, and have taken their vocation and turned back to Judaism in an attempt to integrate Buddhist practice with Jewish worship. These practitioners and teachers have had an impact on Jewish communities by giving workshops throughout America and in Israel.

There has been a tendency to conflate Jewish Renewal and neo-Hasidism. They are, in fact, quite different. Neo-Hasidism was originally a literary movement among enlightened and ex-traditional Jews in the early part of the twentieth century who used Hasidism as a template for a kind of modern Jewish romanticism. Figures such as the Hebrew and Yiddish writer Yehuda Leib Peretz, the novelist and poet Shalom Ash, and the philosopher Martin Buber are counted among this circle. Contemporary neo-Hasidism is, perhaps, a second wave of that phenomenon, one that adopts the general tenor of Hasidic spirituality as a resource for contemporary Judaism. One example of neo-Hasidism would be the appearance of secular and contemporary adaptations of Hasidic music among some Israeli musicians in the 1970s.

Unlike Jewish Renewal, present-day neo-Hasidism has no discernible ideology, nor is it a constructive critique of Jewish life. It is primarily an artistic utilization and romanticization of a deeply theological movement. Religiously, it adopts certain Hasidic modes of worship in order to enhance Jewish ritual and practice. Neo-Hasidism is popular in all Jewish denominations as it does not demand any reordering of fundamental principles. It largely exists in the popularity of Hasidic texts and more prominently in music accompanying the liturgy. In this respect, the father of second wave neo-Hasidism is Shlomo Carlebach, whose music and Hasidic teachings have inspired Jews throughout the world. In contrast to Zalman and Jewish Renewal, Shlomo and neo-Hasidism have no real ideological or organizational agenda. While Jewish Renewal surely is a part of the more amorphous neo-Hasidism, it is not identical to it.

Jewish Renewal in Israel is just taking root and it is still too early to tell how it will affect Israeli society. Orthodoxy's hegemony in Israel and the deeply rooted secularism of Israeli Zionism will no doubt force Renewal to alter its message to accommodate the unique conditions in Israel. Renewal communities are beginning to emerge, reflecting secular Israel's fascination with Eastern spirituality and neo-Hasidic Jewish ritual and worship. Festivals held in rural areas on Jewish festivals like Roʾsh ha-Shanah (Jewish New Year) complete with drum circles, meditation, dancing, and the sounding of the *shofar* (ram's horn) are becoming commonplace. A new Israeli Renewal is surely emerging but, to date, it is still in its embryonic stages.

PERSONALITIES. Jewish Renewal is led by many talented individuals who contribute to the progress and expansion of the movement. Zalman Schachter-Shalomi remains the major force in this movement. Shlomo Carlebach's influence is deep and wide even as he offers a more inspirational than intellectual contribution. His dozens of recordings, many including stories and Hasidic teachings, began in 1959 and changed the face of contemporary Jewish music. Marcia Falk's *Book of Blessings* has had significant impact on Renewal liturgy.

Arthur Green is a major figure whose influence is both theological and organizational. His book *Seek My Face, Speak My Name* is perhaps the first systematic Renewal theology. Green was the president of RRC for more than a decade and fostered the important relationship between Reconstructionist Judaism and Jewish Renewal. Dovid Din, a lesser-known figure who died in the late 1980s, had a profound impact on many who are now in Renewal. He was a student of Zalman Schachter-Shalomi in Winnipeg in the 1960s and had a small community in Boro Park in Brooklyn.

Gershon Winkler is an important teacher in Renewal, as are Miles Krassen and Elliot Ginsburg. Other important figures include Sylvia Boorstein and Avram David, who teach Buddhist meditation, Jonathan Omerman and Rami Shapiro, who have both led Renewal communities, and Andrea Cohen-Keiner, who translated a work by a Hasidic master popular with Renewal entitled *Conscious Community,* and who has been very successful teaching Renewal to adolescents and young adults. Shefa Gold is a prominent Renewal musical personality who has composed and performed moving Jewish meditation chants based on Native American and Hindu traditions.

Arthur Waskow and Michael Lerner have both developed the political arm of Jewish Renewal and their work has influenced not only Jewish circles but also the U.S. and Israeli political arenas. Another thinker deserves recognition even as he might not feel comfortable identifying with Jewish Renewal. Aryeh Kaplan was an Orthodox Jew who inspired many with his works and translations. His forays into Jewish spirituality, especially with his *Meditation and the Bible* and *Meditation and the Kabbala,* have contributed greatly to the Jewish Renewal movement. While Kaplan's commitment to Orthodoxy remained strong, his works inspired many who would become important figures in Jewish Renewal. Finally, numerous professors of Judaism teaching in universities in the Diaspora are marginally or more formally connected to Jewish Renewal and have brought this orientation to their profession in many interesting ways.

CHALLENGES. Numerous challenges confront the relatively young Jewish Renewal movement. One major hurdle is the ability of Renewal to establish Jewish literacy among its members and create an educated lay community. Another challenge is how it will confront the radicalism of its own doctrine and develop a vision outside the shadow of more traditional Judaism. As is the case in many fledgling movements, Renewal tends to seek acceptance from the traditional branches of its religion. As it matures, it will have to decide how to negotiate this relationship on a more equal footing. The heterodox world of North America is fertile soil for such an endeavor.

In some respects, Jewish Renewal is following the path of early Hasidism. However, as scholars have argued, Hasidism's success in becoming normative was due, among other things, to its abandonment of some of its more radical doctrines. The contemporary situation is quite different from early-nineteenth-century eastern Europe, where the choices were more limited: either traditionalism or Enlightenment (or some combination of the two). In the present cultural climate, especially in North America, where the hegemony of Orthodoxy no longer exists, new religious movements can maintain less traditional positions and still survive and flourish among those seeking a spiritual alternative. Jewish Renewal may occupy a space between early Hasidism's more radical and audacious posture (which widened the margins of Jewish thought) and Shabbateanism (which abandoned Judaism altogether). Jewish Renewal seeks to offer a fresh critique of tradition, reconstructing a pietistic and contemplative alternative embedded in the spirit of universalism, activism, and tolerance.

SEE ALSO Hasidism; Reconstructionist Judaism.

BIBLIOGRAPHY

Aviad, Janet. *Return to Judaism.* Chicago, 1983.

Boorstein, Sylvia. *That's Funny, You Don't Look Buddhist.* San Francisco, 1997.

Carlebach, Shlomo. *Holy Brother.* Edited by Yitta Halberstam Mandelbaum. London, 1997.

Davis, Avram, ed. *Meditation from the Heart of Judaism.* Woodstock, Vt., 1997.

Falk, Marcia. *The Book of Blessings.* San Francisco, 1996.

Green, Arthur. *Seek My Face, Speak My Name.* Northvale, N.J., 1992.

Green, Arthur. *Ehyeh: A Kabbala for Tomorrow.* Woodstock, Vt., 2003.

Kaplan, Aryeh. *Meditation and the Bible.* York Beach, Maine, 1978.

Kaplan, Aryeh. *Meditation and Kabbala.* York Beach, Maine, 1982.

Kaplan, Aryeh. *Jewish Meditation: A Practical Guide.* New York, 1985.

Kaplan, Edward, and Shaul Magid. "An Interview with Rabbi Zalman Schachter-Shalomi." In *Merton and Judaism: Holiness in Words,* edited by Beatrice Bruteau. Louisville, Ky., 2003.

Lerner, Michael. *Jewish Renewal: A Path to Healing and Transformation.* New York, 1994.

Lerner, Michael. *The Politics of Meaning: Restoring Hope and Possibility in an Age of Cynicism.* Reading, Mass., 1996.

Schachter-Shalomi, Zalman. *Fragments of a Future Scroll: Hasidism for the Aquarian Age.* Germantown, Pa., 1975.

Schachter-Shalomi, Zalman. *Wrapped in a Holy Flame: Teachings and Tales of the Hasidic Masters.* San Francisco, 2003.

Serkez, Kalman, ed. *The Holy Beggars' Banquet.* London, 1998.

Shapiro, Rami. *Minyan: Ten Principles for Living a Life of Integrity.* New York, 1997.

Siegel, Richard. *The First Jewish Catalogue.* Philadelphia, 1973.

Singer, Ellen, ed. *Paradigm Shift.* London, 1993.

Strassfeld, Sharon. *The Second Jewish Catalogue.* Philadelphia, 1975.

Strassfeld, Sharon. *The Third Jewish Catalogue.* Philadelphia, 1980.

Waskow, Arthur. *God Wrestling.* New York, 1978.

Waskow, Arthur. *Seasons of Our Joy: A Handbook of Jewish Festivals.* New York, 1986.

Waskow, Arthur. *Torah of the Earth: Exploring 4,000 Years of Ecology in Jewish Thought.* Woodstock, Vt., 2000.

Winkler, Gershon. *The Place Where You Stand Is Holy: A Jewish Theology on Human Relationships.* London, 1994.

SHAUL MAGID (2005)

JEWISH STUDIES

This entry consists of the following articles:

JEWISH STUDIES FROM 1818 TO 1919
JEWISH STUDIES SINCE 1919

JEWISH STUDIES: JEWISH STUDIES FROM 1818 TO 1919

Although Judaism has long valued the study of sacred texts as an instrument of piety, the field of Jewish studies as an academic discipline is a product of the emancipation process and the westernization of Judaism in the nineteenth century. Born of a sense of the profound changes in the context of Jewish life and imbued with the academic ethos of the newly founded University of Berlin (1810) and with the philosophic rhetoric of German Idealism, *Wissenschaft des Judentums* heralded a series of disorienting intellectual shifts: from

Christian to Jewish scholarship on Judaism; from dogmatic to undogmatic, but not value-free, scholarship on Judaism; from a partial to a comprehensive conception of Jewish creativity; and from an exegetical to a conceptual mode of thought. What stands out in the subsequent development of the discipline over the next century, beyond its ceaseless growth and bifurcation, is the continued centrality of the German provenance down to the 1930s.

Early Academic Context. As launched by Leopold Zunz (1794–1886) and his friends in the Verein für Kultur and Wissenschaft der Juden (1819–1824), the application of the historical method to the study of Judaism by university-educated Jews challenged the undisputed Christian monopoly on the subject. Because economic utility had largely dictated the peripheral legal status of pre-emancipation Jews, their spokesmen had scarcely felt the need to transcend the insularity of the ghetto with an "insider's" depiction of Judaism for Christian consumption. In consequence, according to Zunz, "Rarely has the world been presented with more damaging, erroneous, and distorted views than on the subject of the Jewish religion; here, to render odious has been turned into a fine art" *(Etwas über die rabbinische Litteratur,* 1818). Against this backdrop, *Wissenschaft des Judentums* embodied a novel and sustained effort by Jews themselves to recount their history and expound their religion for non-Jews, to dissipate the miasma of misconceptions and prejudice with facts and empathy. From the outset, Zunz intuited the political payoff of the enterprise: Public respect for Judaism would be the only secure ground for lasting social intergration.

Symptomatic of the prevailing denigration was the exclusion of ancient Jewry from the vaunted field of *Altertumswissenschaft.* Admission was restricted to the Greeks and Romans, for they alone of the nations of antiquity had achieved the level of a learned culture. In his lectures on the discipline, Friedrich August Wolf, famed Homer scholar and one of Zunz's teachers, dismissed Israel's historical claim to equal treatment:

> The Hebraic nation did not raise itself to the level of culture, so that one might regard it as a learned, cultured people. It does not even have prose, but only half poetry. Its writers of history are but miserable chroniclers. They could never write in full sentences; this was an invention of the Greeks. (*Vorlesungen über die Altertumswissenschaft,* vol. 1, 1831, p. 14)

Thus, academically as well as philosophically, Judaism was relegated to a preliminary and long-surpassed stage of Oriental history, and hence was consigned to the periphery of Western consciousness.

The absence of any countervailing Jewish scholarship at the time is graphically illustrated by the plight of the young Heinrich Heine, then a member of the Verein, when he tried to convey an image of the attractiveness and pathos of medieval Judaism through the medium of a historical novel. The reasons for his failure to complete *Die Rabbi von Bacharach* (1840) are no doubt many, but among them surely is the total absence of empathetical historical works by Jews in German. With the primary Hebrew sources closed to him, Heine, under Zunz's tutelage, was forced to feed on the standard Christian fare, with the result that his imagination soon foundered. By way of contrast, Michael Sachs's evocative *Die religiöse Poesie der Juden in Spanien,* which appeared in 1845, did trigger Heine's poetic fantasy and led directly to his richly inventive and deeply felt collection, *Hebräische Melodien* (1851), an eloquent testimony to what he, and German academics, had lacked in 1824.

Wissenschaft des Judentums. In terms of method, *Wissenschaft des Judentums* raised an equally formidable challenge to the principles and parameters of traditional Jewish learning. Unfettered by dogmatic considerations, the alienated intellectuals of the Verein, at bitter odds with rabbinism but not prepared to convert, had formed "an association of consciousness" to begin conceptualizing Judaism afresh. Toward that end it embraced the research program enunciated in 1818 by Zunz in his profound, prescient, and determinative work *Etwas über die rabbinische Litteratur.* Convinced that emancipation spelled the end of the Hebraic-rabbinic period of Jewish history, Zunz called for its dispassionate historical assessment. In the process, he demonstrated with stunning detail its dimly realized cultural expanse and diversity. Postbiblical Hebrew literature was authored by Jews of all kinds, not only rabbis, and embraced all the interests of the human mind, not only matters of Jewish law. Given that scope, only the historian was equipped to speak of its genesis and character with any authority. The anticlerical thrust was unmistakable: The canons of modern scholarship were to be enlisted "in order to know and sort out the old which is useful, the antiquated which is detrimental, and the new which is desirable." History presumed to usurp the role of *halakhah* and philosophy as both the arbiter and expositor of Judaism. At issue was a grievously flawed method of learning overgrown with historical myth and error, indifferent to time and contextual analysis, hostile to all non-Hebraic and non-Jewish sources, and crippled by a truncated view of Jewish literature and a static concept of sacred texts.

The comprehensiveness of this vision of the Jewish experience extended into the present. As conceived by Zunz and amplified by Immanuel Wolf in his opening essay for the Verein's ephemeral *Zeitschrift für die Wissenschaft des Judentums* (1823), from whence the name, the field comprised not only the study of a remote past but of a living present. Both as an inner idea and a religious culture, Judaism was still of vital concern to a living community, which itself deserved scholarly attention. In the words of Wolf, "The history of the past is directly followed by the second main division of the subject, i.e., Judaism in the living form in which it lies before us—the general statistical position of the Jews in every country, with special reference to their religious and political circumstances" (*Leo Baeck Institute Year Book,* vol. 2, 1957, p. 202). It is precisely this sense of continuity and connectedness that distinguished the practitioners of *Wissenschaft des Judentums* from those of *Altertumswissenschaft.* For all its appeal and meaning to German neohumanists, *Altertumswissenschaft* was not the uninterrupted cultural legacy of a contemporary community. A century after the Verein, Ismar Elbogen (1874–1943), Weimar's premier Jewish historian, again emphasized this existential dimension of the field by defining it as "the academic study of a vital Judaism, standing in the stream of development, as a sociological and historical unity" (*Festschrift. . . der Hochschule für die Wissenschaft des Judentums,* 1922, p. 141). Its proper academic analogue, claimed Elbogen, was not the study of Greece and Rome but the world of Islam. Given this degree of contemporaneity, *Wissenschaft des Judentums* became the major medium for thinking through the dilemmas generated by Judaism's confrontation with modernity.

Zunz's contribution. What facilitated that use was the shift to a conceptual mode of thought. For all their anticipation of modern scholarship, the pathbreaking Hebrew commentaries accompanying Moses Mendelssohn's translation of the Torah and Wolf Heidenheim's edition of the German cycle of festival prayerbooks both adhered to the traditional exegetical mode, which bespoke the centrality of sacred texts. In consonance with the secular temper of the age, modern scholarship would render the text subordinate to larger issues that required thematic and synthetic treatment. No one searched for new sources more zealously or read old ones more trenchantly than Zunz, but all in the service of questions and constructs that defied the limitations of disjointed analysis. The modern scholarship of eastern European autodidacts, steeped in the thought patterns of rabbinic culture, often failed to reach the level of conceptualization, coherence, and systematization achieved by university-trained practitioners of *Wissenschaft* in the West.

Of the original members of the Verein, Zunz alone remained true to the promise of *Wissenschaft.* Years later Heine would celebrate him as one "who stood firm, constantly and unshakably, in a period of transition, hesitation, and vacillation. . . . A man of words and a man of action, he worked unceasingly, he did what needed doing, at a time when others lost themselves in dreams and sank to the ground, bereft of courage" (quoted in S. S. Prawer's *Heine's Jewish Comedy,* 1983, p. 470). For much of his productive life, Zunz focused his scholarly energy on a history of the synagogue, the institution that he regarded as "the expression of Jewish nationality and the guarantee of its religious existence." In 1832, his *Die gottesdienstlichen Vorträge der Juden* was published, which first exhibited the full sweep of Midrashic creativity in the synagogue from the third century BCE down to his own day, and from 1855 to 1865 he complemented that work with three volumes: *Die synagogale Poesie das Mittelalters* (1855), *Die Ritus des synagogalen Gottesdienstes* (1859), and *Literaturge-schichte der synagogalen Poesie* (1865), which unveiled the synagogue's undreamed of liturgical richness. The final volume alone included the treatment of some six thousand liturgical poems along with the identification of nearly one thousand poets.

That devotion to the history of the synagogue derived from Zunz's conviction that a culture deserved to be studied at its core, in its more quintessential expressions and not on the fringes of its creativity. Not only did he fearlessly refuse to dilute the "parochial" character of Jewish culture, but by portraying it with insight and warmth he meant to raise the self-respect and level of commitment of contemporary Jews. "Genuine scholarship," ran his motto, "gives rise to action." Historical consciousness could serve to augment the depleted forces for Jewish survival.

Concept of development. The upshot of Zunz's massive research on the synagogue was to introduce the concept of development, the trademark of modern historical thought, into the study of rabbinic literature. The urgency of the hour dictated the early agenda of *Wissenschaft* scholars: Emancipation seemed to challenge the very nature of a Judaism more rabbinic than biblical. Could subjects entangled in a seamless web of ritual obligations meet the demands of citizenship? Scholars soon moved beyond the inviting freedom of aggadic exegesis to the more problematic realm of rabbinic law to explore its genesis, evolution, and authority. Within two decades, works such as Levi Herzfeld's *Geschichte des Volkes Israel* (3 vols., 1847–1857), Naḥman Krochmal's *Moreh nevukhei ha-zeman,* edited by Zunz (1851), Heinrich Graetz's *Geschichte der Juden von den ältesten Zeiten bis auf die Gegenwart,* volume 4 (1853), Abraham Geiger's *Urschrift und Uebersetzungen der Bibel* (1857), Zacharias Frankel's *Darkhei ha-Mishnah* (1859), and Joseph Derenbourg's *Essai sur l'histoire et la géographie de la Palestine* (1867) had pierced the darkness of the Persian and Greco-Roman periods of Jewish history to illumine the dynamic origins of the halakhic system. For all the disagreement in detail and interpretation, the cumulative effect of their prodigious research was to dissolve a corpus of literature that had long been venerated as a single harmonious entity into its many historical components: namely, early sources, literary forms, exegetical modes, stages of complexity and composition, conflicting protagonists, and formative external influences. While it discomforted Orthodox spokesmen such as Samson R. Hirsch, and although it rested heavily on later rabbinic sources, the research served to show Christian scholars the unabated vitality of Judaism after the Babylonian exile and the responsive nature of rabbinic leadership.

Jewish sectarianism. At the same time, *Wissenschaft* chipped away at the static rabbinic monolith from yet another direction. As early as 1816, Krochmal, living in the midst of a still-unpunctured traditional society in eastern Galicia, had publicly defended the legitimacy of investigating the literature of the Karaites, who despite their halakhic deviance, had never distanced themselves from Jewish suffering. A few years later, Peter Beer of Prague published his *Geschichte, Lehren und Meinungen aller bestandenen und noch bestehenden religiösen Sekten der Juden und der Geheimlehre, oder Cabbalah* (2 vols., 1822–1823), an unabashedly antirabbinic history of Jewish sects (including medieval mystics), which provided a glimpse of the recurring resistance to Talmudic hegemony. At first, much of the interest in Jewish sectarianism focused on the era of the Second Commonwealth, but the steady publication of Karaite manuscripts in the ensuing decades, especially the rich cache by Simcha Pinsker in 1860, prompted works such as Isaak M. Jost's *Geschichte des Judenthums und seiner Sekten* (3 vols., 1857–1859), Heinrich Graetz's *Geschichte der Juden von den ältesten Zeiten bis auf die Gegenwart,* volume 5 (1860), and Julius Fürst's *Geschichte des Karärthums* (3 vols., 1862–1869), which reflect a renewal of the effort at a synthesis of Karaite history, though with insufficient attention to the Islamic ambiance. In Geiger's *Urschrift und Uebersetzungen der Bibel* (1857) and *Das Judentum und seine Geschichte* (3 vols., 1864–1871) the inherent link between sectarianism and halakhic development and the possible continuity of sectarian praxis were ingeniously integrated into a single overarching theory. Still more important, Geiger rehabilitated the Pharisees as the progressive party in ancient Judaism and claimed their patrimony for his own movement. The effect was to undercut the penchant among Reform leaders to connect their cause with the Sadducean-Karaite line, an affinity without much benefit.

Rabbinic and biblical literature. The absorption with rabbinic literature was a function of conception as well as need. When Zunz unfurled the agenda of *Wissenschaft des Judentums* in 1818, it was restricted to *"neuhebräische oder jüdische Literature."* By design he seemed to exclude, for the moment, the study of biblical literature, a subject firmly ensconced in the German university. If scholarship was to facilitate legislation, it had to concentrate on what was least known and most problematic: the nature and history of rabbinic Judaism. And, in fact, the modest amount of biblical scholarship produced by Jews in the nineteenth century bespeaks an avoidance intensified by dogmatic inhibitions but also born of political considerations.

Against this background, what was achieved, while not generally original, was not undistinguished. In *Die gottesdienstlichen Vorträge der Juden* (1832), Zunz already argued for a single author of *Ezra, Nehemiah,* and *Chronicles* and a post-exilic date for *Ezekiel.* In later essays, he analyzed the Pentateuch in terms of numerous constituent sources with none earlier than 900 BCE and *Leviticus* following *Ezekiel.* Though Geiger preferred to date *Leviticus* before *Deuteronomy,* he matched Zunz's documentary analysis of the Pentateuch and insisted on the fluidity of the biblical text long after composition. More conservative scholars like Krochmal and Graetz confined their research to the Prophets and the Writings, often taking leave of traditional views.

The most substantial and lasting Jewish contribution of the century to biblical research, however, came not from Berlin or Breslau but from Padua, where Shemu'el David Luzzatto, with an unsurpassed knowledge of the Hebrew language, renewed the long-disrupted genre of medieval Jewish exegesis of the Bible. Independent of Protestant scholarship and rooted in the distinctive style of Italian Judaism, Luzzatto's Hebrew commentaries were anything but doctrinaire. Unfortunately, by the last quarter of the century the rising tide of German anti-Semitism also seeped into the halls of the university and retarded the acceptance of the documentary hypothesis by Jewish scholars for decades. In 1910, the rabbinical seminary in Breslau still excluded modern biblical criticism from its curriculum.

Spanish Judaism. Zunz's modest proposal of 1818 ended with the charge to undertake the publishing of largely unknown but classical specimens of "rabbinic literature" in order to begin to banish the contempt in which it was held. By way of example, he declared his intention to bring out a scholarly edition with Latin translation of a Hebrew philosophical treatise by Shem Ṭov ibn Falaquera, a thirteenth-century Spanish Jew. The identification of the best of Hebrew literature with medieval Spain epitomized the Sephardic bias so vital to emancipated Ashkenazim in search of legitimacy. With roots going back to the seventeenth century, the attraction of Spanish Jewry and its descendants became a pervasive cultural force in nineteenth-century German Jewry, finding diverse expression in liturgy, synagogue architecture, literature, and, of course, scholarship.

Young scholars, whose own intellectual emancipation often started with Moses Maimonides' *Guide of the Perplexed* and the Hebrew literature of the Haskalah, gravitated naturally to the poetic and philosophical legacy of Spain. Ironically, the term *golden age,* which is used to highlight Jewish cultural creativity in Muslim Spain, is not of Jewish provenance. It was first bestowed by Franz Delitzsch, the greatest Christian scholar of Judaism in the nineteenth century, in his *Zur Geschichte der jüdischen Poësie* (1836), in which he depicted the two centuries from 940 to 1140 as the golden and silver ages respectively of Jewish poetic achievement. But the term accorded fully with the needs and perceptions of German Jewry, and despite the heroic effort by a penitent Zunz not to ignore the dissimilar but equally impressive cultural achievements of medieval Ashkenazic Jewry, the *Wissenschaft* of a long line of scholars served to deepen and solidify the bias. At the same time, their failure to generate much sympathy for the mystical side of Spanish Judaism was a consequence of their own rational bent, compounded by outrage at the unfounded historical claims of the mystics themselves.

The attraction to cultural history was reinforced by a decided aversion to political history. To work out a conceptualization that would have done justice to the unconventional political history of Diaspora Jewry would have produced more flak than self-esteem. The embattled position of German Jewry militated against the subject. When Michael Sachs decided to produce *Die religiose Poësie der Juden in Spanien* (1845), a volume of medieval religious poetry in translation, he settled on Spain because of the widely held view, going back to Shlomoh Yehudah Rappoport, that Sephardic poets addressed God as lonely believers, whereas Ashkenazic poets only lamented the fate of the nation. Sachs specifically asked of Luzzatto, who had agreed to supply him material, not to send any "national poems." Somewhat later, in volume five of his *Geschichte der Juden,* Graetz did declaim with courage that the medieval Jewish experience betrays a political dimension, but he failed completely to demonstrate it. Neither he nor his colleagues moved beyond the older Spanish conception of Jewish political history as one of recurring persecution, though they amplified it factually and emotionally. On occasion, isolated works of political history such as Selig Cassel's "Geschichte der Juden" in the *Allgemeine Encyklopädie der Wissenschaften und Künste* (1850), Otto Stobbe's *Die Juden in Deutschland während des Mittelalters in politischer, socialer und rechtlicher Beziehung* (1866), and a volume of *Regesten zur Geschichte der Juden in Deutschland während des Mittelalters* (1862) by Meir Wiener did reveal just how much the systematic use of non-Jewish archival sources could enlarge and enrich the conception of the subject, but Graetz, with whom Stobbe worked closely, remained skeptical about their large-scale utility.

Institutional standing. By the mid-1870s when the founders of *jüdische Wissenschaft* had completed most if not all of their work (only Zunz, Steinschneider, and Graetz were still living, though Zunz was no longer productive), the study of Judaism had all the signs of an academic discipline except one: inclusion in the structure of the German university, the premier research institution of the century. Though a direct product of its research imperative, *Wissenschaft des Judentums* matured entirely outside the framework of the university. Jewish scholars as its primary practitioners were never accorded the university's recognition and support. The occasional appointment of a *Privatdozent* or *Honorarprofessor* in a cognate field was but the trappings of academic respectability. Of course, that was exactly the kind of institutional affiliation, given their commitment to undogmatic scholarship and their resentment of rabbinic leadership, for which the founders yearned. Typical of faculty and bureaucratic resistance to the idea was the rebuff administered to Zunz in 1848 by the philosophy faculty of the University of Berlin to his request to create a chair in Jewish history and literature. Such a chair, it was felt, smacked of confessional interests and would merely strengthen Jewish parochialism. Misreading Zunz's intent, the faculty declared that it was not the function of the university to train rabbis. In the German context, such exclusion, which was, to be sure, experienced for a time by other nascent fields (such as history), meant the denial of the discipline's universal significance and doomed hardy aficionados to eke out a living in circumstances that were often trying. Increasingly, young scholars had little choice but to enter the ranks of a rabbinate in transition and to "make" the time for sustained research.

The creation of the Jewish Theological Seminary in Breslau in 1854 from the largesse of a single Jewish benefactor finally provided an institutional base for the floundering field and cemented its connection with the modern rabbinate. With a curriculum informed by *Wissenschaft des Judentums,* a small faculty immersed in it, and a scholarly journal promoting it, Breslau became the model for all modern rabbinical seminaries established during the next half-century in central and western Europe and the United States. Despite denominational differences, these institutions determined the scholarly character of the modern rabbinate, until it was modified again at the turn of the century by the changing social and political needs of the Jewish community. Its graduates brought to the pulpit a lively commitment to deepen as well as to disseminate the new mode of Jewish learning.

But Zunz and Moritz Steinschneider viewed these developments with dismay, regarding much of the scholarship coming out of Breslau as dogmatic and pretentious. Twice in the 1870s, Steinschneider, a man of awesome learning, prodigious output, and extensive personal contacts with non-Jewish scholars, preferred to turn down invitations from new seminaries in Berlin and Budapest and to stay at his modest post as director of the girls' school of the Berlin Jewish community. In 1876, he reaffirmed the original integrationist vision with typical acerbity:

> Institutions to preserve the rabbinate in the form acquired during the last centuries promote systematic hypocrisy and scholarly immaturity. What is scholarly about Jewish history and literature has no need to avoid the atmosphere of the university and must be made accessible to Christians. The task of our time seems to me, above all, to call for the temporary funding [obviously with Jewish money—I. S.] of unpaid instructorships for Jewish history and literature at philosophical faculties, so that governments will be prompted to create professorships and institutions in which matriculated Gymnasium students might prepare themselves for the study of Hebrew literature. (*Jewish Studies in Memory of George A. Kohut,* ed. Salo W. Baron and Alexander Marx, 1935, p. 521)

When Steinschneider shared his reasons for refusal with his old mentor and lifelong friend, Heinrich L. Fleischer, Germany's leading Orientalist, the latter, sensing the futility of such expectations, chided him for his errant purism: "If men like you deny your cooperation, have you then still a right to complain about the new institution's lack of success? Why not get involved from the outset in the hope that in this way the better will triumph?" (letter of July 1, 1875, Fleischer correspondence from the "Steinschneider Papers," archives of the Jewish Theological Seminary).

No scholar among the *Wissenschaft* pioneers contributed more to validating the right to university admission for Jewish studies than Steinschneider himself. With his matchless command of unpublished sources, he painstakingly reconstructed the unsuspected and seminal role that medieval Jews in the Islamic world had played in the transmission of Greco-Roman culture to the Christian West. His oeuvre, especially his massive *Die hebraeischen Übersetzungen des Mittelalters und die Juden als Dolmetscher* (2 vols., 1893), demonstrated for the first time the existence of a cultural unity in the medieval world that transcended religious differences, a theme that would continue to exercise Jewish scholars in the twentieth century. For instance, at Harvard, Harry A. Wolfson would try to integrate the parallel traditions of medieval religious philosophy into a single universe of discourse that operated from Philo to Spinoza. And at Princeton, on the basis of the inexhaustible documentary wealth of the Cairo Geniza, Shlomo D. Goitein would portray the social, economic, and material contours of a medieval Mediterranean society through the prism of Jewish life.

TURN OF THE CENTURY. The engagement of Jewish scholarship with the vital concerns of a dynamic community was, if anything, intensified by the unsettling events of Jewish history in the twentieth century. In particular, the resurgence and diffusion of anti-Semitism at the turn of the century added to the inherent momentum toward specialization and institutionalization which the discipline had already generated in the course of the century. Even without this intrusion, the remarkable sweep of early *Wissenschaft* works would hardly have survived the growing technical complexity of the field. In 1897 alone, Solomon Schechter brought back to Cambridge from the Cairo Geniza, which he had emptied, some 100,000 literary fragments pertaining to nearly fifteen hundred years of Jewish history in the Greco-Roman and Islamic worlds. Thus, new sources, interests, and anxieties expanded Jewish scholarship into a movement of international proportions.

HISTORICAL SOCIETIES. The last decades of the nineteenth century give evidence of a chain reaction across the Jewish world in the formation of national Jewish historical societies. With the overt intention of stimulating research on the antiquity, fate, and contribution of Jews in their respective lands of settlement, these societies betray all the anxiousness of insecurity. But they also testify to the emergence of a cadre of indigenous scholars. The first to be founded in Paris in 1880 was the Société des Études Juives, which published the triannual *Revue des études juives* (1880–), designed to accomplish two ends: By casting its net over the entire field of Jewish studies, the *Revue* served to challenge the German hegemony embodied in Breslau's *Monatsschrift für die Geschichte und Wissenschaft des Judentums* (1851–1939), a policy that accorded with the rancor sown by the Franco-Prussian War; at the same time, the *Revue* placed at the heart of its agenda the twofold intent of encouraging the study of Jews in the history of France and of French Jews in the history of medieval Judaism. By 1897 the new subfield could boast of a volume of universal Jewish import. In *Gallia Judaica* (1897) Henri Gross, Hungarian-born as were so many of the *Wissenschaft* circle, produced a geographical dictionary that listed, along with ample historical information, all French localities in which Jews are known to have lived according to medieval Hebrew sources. In the twentieth century, this accomplishment became the model for the *Germania Judaica* (1917–) of the Gesellschaft zur Förderung der Wissenschaft des Judentums and the *Sefer ha-yishuv* (1939–) of the Palestine Historical and Ethnographical Society.

AMERICAN SCHOLARSHIP. In America too, Jewish scholarship was enlisted to stem the growth in anti-Semitism set off by the massive influx of eastern European Jews. Jewish notables exploited the occasion of the four-hundredth anniversary of Columbus's discovery of America in 1892 to create an American Jewish Historical Society, which would restrict its mission to assembling data on the role of Jews in "the discovery, settlement, and development of our land." Its president Oscar S. Straus, who had served as the American ambassador to Constantinople a few years before, invited and funded a noted European scholar of Spanish Jewish history, Meyer Kayserling of Budapest, to write *Christopher Columbus and the Participation of the Jews in the Spanish and Portuguese Discoveries* (1894) to "bring to light the extent to which our race had direct part and share with Columbus in the discovery of our continent." Straus hoped that the historical confirmation of "this fact would be an answer for all time to come to anti-Semitic tendencies in this country."

Far more important than Kayserling's careful study of 1894 was the publication in 1901–1906 of the twelve-volume *Jewish Encyclopedia,* edited by Isidore Singer and Cyrus Adler, by the non-Jewish firm of Funk and Wagnalls. Produced in a land on the fringes of the *Wissenschaft* movement with no scholarly tradition of its own, this first Jewish encyclopedia represented a collective venture of huge proportions and astonishingly high quality, a magnificent summation of nearly a century of Jewish scholarship, and, above all, the transplantation of *Wissenschaft des Judentums* to America. But the level of scholarly attainment should not obscure the pragmatic concerns of its genesis. The preface alluded to the anxieties of the moment: ". . . the world's interest in Jews is perhaps keener than ever before. Recent events, to which more direct reference need not be made, have aroused the world's curiosity as to the history and condition of a people which has been able to accomplish so much under such adverse conditions." Accordingly, the editors were eager to present a balanced picture of Jews as both integrated and parochial, as both cosmopolitans and cultivators of their own traditions.

ANGLO-JEWISH SCHOLARSHIP. The founding of the *Jewish Quarterly Review* in 1888 and the Jewish Historical Society of England in 1893 certainly suggests a similar set of circumstances for Anglo-Jewry. The fact that Lucien Wolf launched the research program of the society in 1901 with his splendid edition of *Menasseh ben Israel's Mission to Oliver Cromwell* reflects the same need as felt in America for a "foundation myth" that intersects at a decisive juncture with the history of the nation. In one sense both Wolf's texts and the very idea of the society owed their patrimony to Henrich Graetz, who in his address to the immensely successful Anglo-Jewish Historical Exhibition of 1887 had called for an organized scholarly effort to study local history. The *Jewish Quarterly Review,* on the other hand, became the academic organ for a talented cluster of English scholars who had gathered around the charismatic figure of Solomon Schechter. For two decades it not only encompassed the full panoply of Jewish studies, but also often protested the jaundiced scholarship on ancient Judaism coming out of Germany.

RUSSIAN SCHOLARSHIP. Under the guidance of Simon Dubnow, the small and ever more beleaguered liberal sector of Russian Jewry also began to display an interest in the study of local history to firm up its sense of belonging and distinctiveness. Fully aware of the social role of Jewish scholarship in the West, the young Dubnow transformed his own religious alienation into a lifelong program for the cultivation of historical consciousness. In 1891 to 1892, he issued appeals in Russian and Hebrew to set up a Jewish historical society that would coordinate a nationwide effort to collect the diverse sources, fast disappearing, related to the nine-hundred-year history of Jews in Poland and Russia. He pointed with envy to what had been accomplished in the West and berated Russian Jews for failing to realize the cohesive power of historical consciousness. However, his own conception of Jewish history had already begun to diverge from that of his *Wissenschaft* mentors. While he too stressed the greater importance of the internal Jewish sources, he articulated for the first time a vision of Jewish political history in the Diaspora that went far beyond the passive endurance of persecution. In the institution of the *gahal,* Diaspora Jews, wherever they settled, had created a unique instrument of national self-government that preserved a large measure of political initiative. The still-unemancipated status and traditional character of Russian Jewry had sensitized Dubnow to the medieval political expression of Jewish nationhood, and he pleaded for the sources to study its history. In his *History of the Jews in Russia and Poland* (3 vols., Eng. ed., 1916–1920) and *Weltgeschichte des jüdischen Volkes* (10 vols., 1925–1929), Dubnow not only combined his many preliminary studies into a coherent narrative of a millennium of Jewish history in Poland and Russia, but also fully formulated and espoused his theory of Diaspora nationalism.

Dubnow's original proposal finally bore fruit in 1908 in Saint Petersburg with the founding of the Russian Jewish Historical Ethnographic Society by Maxim Vinaver and David Günzberg. Also at Saint Petersburg that same year, the scholarly, artistocratic Günzberg opened at his own expense an academy of Jewish studies in which Dubnow delivered public lectures on Jewish history and conducted seminars for advanced students, whose rank included some of the leading Zionist historians of the next generation. Most important of all, Dubnow's call to collect and record had become part of the credo of the nationalist Jewish renaissance emanating from Saint Petersburg. In the last three years before the war, the writer Solomon Anski led an ambitious ethnographic expedition sponsored by the society into the Jewish hinterland of the Ukraine to plumb its rich deposits of folklore and iconography, bringing back thousands of photographs, tales, folkways, manuscripts, and artifacts. In 1915, Issachar Ryback, a young art student, financed his own study of the wooden synagogues of White Russia, and in 1916 the society sent him and fellow artist El Lissitzky back to the Ukraine to do the same for its synagogues. In a far more somber vein, Anski in *Khurbm Galitsye* (1921) documented the agony of Galician Jewry inflicted by war in a monumental memoir of his heroic relief mission, and Elias Tcherikower, entirely in the spirit of Dubnow, organized and administered at great personal risk during the years 1918 to 1920 an archive to record the unparalleled slaughter of as many as seventy-five thousand Ukrainian Jews amidst the chaos of civil war.

FOLKLORE. The wholesale consumption of Jewish folklore in Russian exuded all the enthusiasm of the populist fervor unleashed by the socialist and Zionist rebellions at the turn of the century. But as an academic field, its origins lie in Germany, and as such it marked a sharp departure from the preoccupation with high culture that absorbed the founders of *jüdische Wissenschaft.* With fewer acknowledged luminaries than in the Sephardic world to distract them, the early students of Ashkenazic Judaism were forced to look at popular expressions of religious culture. The skein of development runs from the midcentury writers of ghetto novellas about central European Jewish life at the threshold of emancipation through the often overlooked collection of Judeo-German proverbs and expressions, *Sprichwörter und Redensarten deutsch-jüdischer Vorzeit* (1860) by Abraham Tendlau, the pioneering social histories of medieval Ashkenazic Jewry in Abraham Berliner's *Aus dem inneren Leben der deutschen Juden im Mittelalter* (1871), and Moritz Güdemann's *Geschichte des Erziehungswesens und der Cultur der abendländischen Juden während des Mittelalters und der neueren Zeit* (3 vols., 1880–1888), to Max Grunwald's work at the end of the century. A graduate of Breslau and at the same time rabbi in Hamburg, Grunwald delivered a manifesto in 1896 urging creation of a society, museum, and journal of Jewish folklore, and two years later he began publishing the first number of the *Mitteilungen der jüdischen Volkskunde* (1898–1929), which he was to edit singlehandedly in different formats for thirty volumes. That the first chair in Jewish folklore established at the Hebrew University in 1973 bears the name of this polymath is resounding testimony to his decisive role in launching the field.

The fascination with folklore signaled a broadly felt need to reconnect with the irrational, to reinvigorate an excessively cerebral tradition with the life-giving forces of imagination. Rabbinic Judaism as codified in the East or spiritualized in the West did not exhaust the record of Jewish lore and legend begun in the first decade of the twentieth century by scholars as diverse as Martin Buber, Ḥayyim Bialik and Yehoshuʿa Ravnitzki, Louis Ginzberg, and Micha Josef Berdyczewski. Ginzberg's monumental *The Legends of the Jews* (7 vols., 1909–1938), elegantly designed for scholar and layman alike, not only revealed the popular wellsprings of rabbinic religion, but also demonstrated the extent to which Jewish legends preserved and mediated the folklore of antiquity.

ART. Jewish art, as cultural expression and scholarly discipline, was similarly invigorated by the discoveries of folklore. In no area of contemporary Jewish life did creativity require quite as urgently the validation and inspiration of a historical tradition. Jewish artists and historians faced the same deep-seated stereotype, shared by friend and foe alike, that Jews by virtue of religion and race were singularly bereft of any aesthetic sensibility. But dramatic historical evidence to the contrary began to mount: the exhibition of the Isaac Strauss collection in Paris in 1878, the publication of the Sarajevo Haggadah in 1898 along with the recovery of a Jewish tradition of manuscript illumination, the formation of Jewish art societies and collections, the publication in 1916 of *Antike Synagogen in Galilaea* by Heinrich Kohl and Carl Watzinger of the first study of Galilean synagogues, and, above all, the plethora of folk art unearthed in the wooden synagogues of Russia. For artists projecting a secular Jewish culture, historians were supplying the resources of an indigenous past. In the beautiful pages of *Rimon,* a lavish magazine of Jewish arts and letters published in Berlin after the war in both a Hebrew and Yiddish edition, the artistic and historical dimensions converged symbiotically.

Sociology. From Jewish folklore to sociology was but a small step, for the interest remained primarily nonelitist. The impetus for this expansion of Jewish scholarship came directly from the nascent Zionist movement. Although Zunz had clearly foreshadowed the sociological study of the Jews in a programmatic essay in 1823, *Grundlinien zu einen künftigen Statistik der Juden,* it took the Zionist indictment of assimilation with all its putatively alarming consequences for Jewish survival to effect a scholarly shift to the present. At the fifth Zionist Congress in 1901, Max Nordau, who annually treated the delegates to a foreboding assessment of the Jewish situation, called for the systematic assemblage of data to confirm the Zionist consensus. The proposal took institutional form three years later in Berlin in the Bureau für Jüdische Statistik, manned by a small staff of unpaid Zionists, which for the next eighteen years would publish an invaluable journal for Jewish demography and statistics. Its first editor, till he went to Israel in 1908 to head the Palestine Office of the Zionist Organization, was Arthur Ruppin, who in 1904 had produced in his *Die Juden der Gegenwart* the first work of Jewish sociology. Not surprisingly, the first generation of scholars was drawn largely from the ranks of Zionists. By 1930 Ruppin's own research had grown into a sweeping two-volume *Soziologie der Juden* (1930–1931), and in 1938 he was the natural candidate for the Hebrew University's first professor of Jewish sociology.

Early Twentieth-Century Scholarship. The first century of Jewish studies ends where it began, in Berlin, with the formation of another association of young scholars still in rebellion against rabbinic ascendancy. In 1919 Eugen Täubler, this time with substantial Jewish backing, founded the Akademie für die Wissenschaft des Judentums. The idea was the outgrowth of a *cri du coeur* in 1917 by Franz Rosenzweig to German Jewry to revitalize its scholarly forces against the onslaught on ancient Judaism by the ever more confident scholarship of liberal Protestantism. Judaism's exclusion from the university remained unaltered, its incorporation into German society riddled with problems, and its laity unequipped for adversity. In final form, the academy, stripped of any polemical or educational intent, came to represent German Jewry's last attempt to bring *Wissenschaft des Judentums* out of its academic isolation and thereby to set its course for the twentieth century. In Täubler the academy had a classicist trained by Theodor Mommsen yet fully conversant with Jewish sources, a historical thinker of great conceptual power, and a proven administrator, who some years before had organized a national Jewish archive as the central repository for Jewish communal records.

As enunciated by Täubler, the mission of the academy was to end *jüdische Wissenschaft's* obsession with anti-Semitism and reliance on practicing rabbis and to reunite it with the highest standards of modern scholarship. This meant specialization, systematic use of non-Jewish archival sources, philological analysis broadly conceived, and contextual and comparative research. Talmudic research in particular still suffered from the absence of a firm philological basis. Täubler dreamed of creating eventually a library of critical editions of all Jewish texts prior to the eighteenth century. In the meantime, he divided the field of Jewish studies into nine distinct specialities, delineated the nature of ancillary instruments of resources, and funded the research of young scholars like Chanoch Albeck, Yitzhak Baer, David H. Baneth, Arthur Spanier, and Selma Stern.

Three years after Täubler died in 1950 in Cincinnati, he was eulogized in Jerusalem by Baer, Moshe Schwabe, and Ben Zion Dinur, three men whose lives he touched deeply. But the tribute signified more than personal indebtedness. The very conceptualization, ethos, and instruments of Jewish studies as they came to be embodied in the Hebrew University after 1924 were conceived by Täubler in Berlin. The professionalization of Jewish scholarship was under way, though communal concerns would continue to influence research agendas.

Bibliography

New Sources

Brenner, Michael, Vicki Caron, and Uri R. Kaufmann, eds. *Jewish Emancipation Reconsidered: The French and German Models.* Tübingen, 2003.

Gordon, Peter Eli. *Rosenzweig and Heidegger: Between Judaism and German Philosophy.* Weimar and Now, no. 33. Berkeley, 2003.

Hart, Mitchell Bryan. *Social Science and the Politics of Modern Jewish Identity.* Stanford Studies in Jewish History and Culture. Stanford, Calif., 2000.

Heschel, Susannah. "Revolt of the Colonized: Abraham Geiger's 'Wissenschaft des Judentums' as a Challenge to Christian Hegemony in the Academy." *New German Critique* 77 (1999): 61–85.

Iancu, Carol. "From the 'Science of Judaism' to the 'New Israeli Historians': Landmarks for a History of Jewish Historiography." *Studia Hebraica* 1 (2001): 114–126.

Lapin, Hayim, and Dale B. Martin, eds. *Jews, Antiquity, and the Nineteenth-Century Imagination.* Potomac, Md., 2003.

Reinharz, Jehuda. "Jewish Studies: A Historical Perspective." *Jewish Studies* 35 (1995): 5–9.

Schulte, Christoph. "Religion in der *Wissenschaft des Judentums:* ein historischer Abriss in methodologischer Absicht." *Revue des Etudes Juives* 161 (2002): 411–429.

Simon-Nahum, Perrine. "Exégèse traditionnelle et philologie: la 'Wissenschaft des Judentums.'" *Pardès* 19–20 (1994): 144–162.

Wiese, Christian. "Counterhistory, the 'Religion of the Future' and the Emancipation of Jewish Studies: The Conflict between the 'Wissenschaft des Judentums' and Liberal Protestantism 1900 to 1933." *Jewish Studies Quarterly* 7 (2000): 367–398.

ISMAR SCHORSCH (1987)
Revised Bibliography

JEWISH STUDIES: JEWISH STUDIES SINCE 1919

Between World War I and World War II in Europe, Jewish studies witnessed a parallel process of both professionalization and popularization. New professional institutions and associations were established to counterbalance the fact that the major Western universities, with only few exceptions, were still opposed to the inclusion of Jewish studies in their curricula. At the same time, grand projects, including encyclopedias, handbooks, and translations were underway to summarize the academic results of the first century of Wissenschaft des Judentums, as the academic study of Judaism and the Jews was called, for a broader audience.

Already in prewar years, the major rabbinical seminaries of central Europe (Breslau, Berlin, Vienna, Budapest), were no longer the only academic institutions occupied with the research and teaching of Jewish studies. In Germany, the Gesellschaft zur Förderung der Wissenschaft des Judentums (established 1902) became a central vehicle for the publication of major enterprises in Jewish studies. From the end of the nineteenth century Jewish historiography was increasingly influenced by new subdisciplines of Wissenschaft des Judentums, such as ethnography, sociology, and demography. The Gesellschaft fuer Juedische Volkskunde, a society of Jewish folklorists founded in 1898 and led by the Hamburg rabbi Max Grunwald, played a pioneering role in scholarly research into Jewish folk traditions around the globe. Its journal, the *Mitteilungen fuer Juedische Volkskunde,* published the most important findings in the field for almost three decades, from 1898 to 1929. In Russia, an expedition to the traditional communities of the Ukraine led by the playwright and folklorist An-Ski from 1912 to 1915 was the culmination of a long search for the remnants of rural Jewish life.

Jewish demographers created their own institutional framework when they established an office for statistics among the Jews in Berlin, which from 1904 published its own journal and was closely related to the burgeoning interest in Jewish sociology best expressed in the pioneering works of Arthur Ruppin. Most of these endeavors were clearly related to the Jewish renaissance propounded by the emerging Zionist movement. Zionist scholars reacted against what they alleged to be the orientation of nineteenth-century Jewish scholars exclusively to the Jewish past and broadened their interest to include contemporary issues within their research.

EUROPE AND PALESTINE BETWEEN THE WORLD WARS. The establishment of the Akademie für die Wissenschaft des Judentums in Berlin in 1919 was a major breakthrough for academic research in the field. For the first time, a secular organization was established to undertake broad research. However, due to the economic crisis of the early 1920s, the Akademie could not live up to its ambitious plans, originally conceived by the philosopher Franz Rosenzweig and later substantially transformed by the historian Eugen Täubler.

More decisive for the development of Wissenschaft des Judentums was the year 1925. In Jerusalem, the Hebrew University was officially opened, with Jewish studies as one of the three original disciplines (together with chemistry and microbiology). Scholars with a Zionist outlook formed a vaguely connected group of Jewish historians, sometimes referred to as the Jerusalem School, emphasizing the centrality of Palestine in the course of Jewish history. Their most outspoken representative, Benzion Dinur (Dünaburg), later became the Israeli minister of education. In 1935 he and medievalist Yitshak (Fritz) Baer, the first professor of Jewish history at the Hebrew University in Jerusalem, established the most important Hebrew-language historical journal, *Zion* (a first series of the journal had been aborted).

In the same year the Hebrew University was established, Simon Dubnov's ten-volume *World History of the Jewish People,* written in Russian, was first published in German translation (1925–1929). His work constituted a clear break from the earlier Germanocentric view of Jewish history and from the strong emphasis upon a history of suffering and scholarship, which had been typical for nineteenth-century German-Jewish historians. Motivated partly by his own political agenda—he was the founder of the autonomist Jewish movement which represented Jewish Diaspora nationalism in eastern Europe—his version of Jewish history centered on institutions of Jewish life in the Diaspora, most notably the *kehilla,* the semiautonomous Jewish community.

Dubnow was also among the founders of the YIVO Institute for Jewish Research, an institution established in Berlin 1925 (and subsequently transferred to then-Polish Vilnius) to systematically research the Jewish past and present in eastern Europe and other Ashkenazic communities. In contrast to the traditional German dominance of nineteenth-century Wissenschaft des Judentums and to Hebrew-language Zionist scholarship, the YIVO deliberately presented its research in Yiddish, the language spoken by the Jewish masses of eastern Europe. Although its emphasis was on the Yiddish-speaking world of eastern Europe, its offices in Berlin, Paris, and New York, and later also Buenos Aires, undertook some groundbreaking studies of Jews in the west, as well. YIVO published its own journal, *YIVO Bleter,* from 1931. From 1940, the *YIVO Bleter* were published in New

York, which subsequently became the center of its activities. In 1928, the Instytut Nauk Judaistycnych was established in Warsaw as the major center for Jewish studies in Poland, with a clear emphasis on historical studies. The center was supported by such eminent scholars as Majer Balaban, Mojzesz Schorr, and Ignacy Schiper.

Although European universities refused to establish professorships in Jewish studies, they opened slowly to the study of Jewish subjects. In Frankfurt am Main, Martin Buber became lecturer for religion and Jewish ethics in 1924. Christian studies of Judaism were no longer necessarily motivated by missionary motives. Thus, the Berlin Institutum Judaicum under its new director Hugo Gressmann became part of the theological faculty of the University of Berlin directed purely to the study of postbiblical Judaism. In Giessen, and from 1923 in Bonn, the theologian Paul Kahle became one of the most important researchers into the Masoretic text. One of his students was the noted Talmudic scholar Yechiel Jacob Weinberg, who later became the director of the Orthodox Berlin Rabbinical Seminary.

In Great Britain, Oxford and Cambridge expanded their role in Jewish studies. Cecil Roth became the first Jew to teach Jewish studies when he was appointed reader in postbiblical Jewish studies in 1939. In Lithuania, Simon Dubnow was close to obtaining a chair in Jewish history at the University of Kaunas in the early 1920s, but was finally refused the position, perhaps due to his lack of formal education.

Several major encyclopedias were edited in interwar Europe. Most notable were the German five-volume *Jüdisches Lexikon* (1927–1930) and the eleven volumes of the uncompleted *Encyclopaedia Judaica* (1928–1934), which was brought to an end at the letter *L* by the Nazi rise to power. The interwar period saw also the publication of comprehensive works and handbooks of lasting importance. In England, for example, Soncino Press of London undertook the first English-language editions of the Babylonian Talmud (1935–1948), Midrash Rabbah (1939), and the Zohar (1931–1934). In Germany, the bibliophilic Soncino Gesellschaft für das schöne jüdische Buch published several beautiful editions of Jewish classics and helped to establish a modern Hebrew typography. The comprehensive design and production of Hebrew typefaces in German-speaking regions between the two world wars, particularly the modern Frank-Rühl, which is still the most used Hebrew typeface for various purposes, was assisted by a group of scholars of Hebrew bibliography and booklore, including Isaiah Sonne and the brothers Alexander and Moses Marx.

The field of Jewish art was beginning to establish itself, with major publications and some impressive journals, such as the short-lived Hebrew *Rimon* (and its Yiddish edition, *Milgroyim*) published in Berlin from 1922 to 1924 and edited by Mark and Rachel Wischnitzer. Abraham Zvi Idelsohn was instrumental in establishing the academic study of Jewish music. His monumental ten-volume *Thesaurus of Hebrew Oriental Melodies* (1914–1932) remains an unsurpassed ethnographic work on Jewish music.

The United States until 1945. In the United States, there was a long tradition of including Semitic studies in the university canon. The 1920s, however, saw the first establishment of more broadly designed Jewish studies chairs at American universities: in 1925, Harry A. Wolfson became Littauer Professor of Jewish Literature and Philosophy at Harvard, and five years later Salo W. Baron was appointed Miller Chair for Jewish History, Literature, and Institutions at Columbia, where he taught for four decades. Despite rapidly growing Jewish student numbers, these two institutions remained until long after World War II the only examples of integrating Jewish studies into the broader university curriculum. Parallel to the establishment of the first modern Jewish studies chairs, the years following World War I saw also increasing academic anti-Semitism and restrictions on Jewish student enrollment. Thus, rabbinical seminaries, such as Hebrew Union College, the Jewish Theological Seminary, and Yeshiva University, as well as the secular Dropsie College, continued to be the academic home for most students in Jewish studies.

At almost at the same time as the Akademie was formed in Berlin, the American Academy for Jewish Research was established in 1920, and incorporated in 1929. New U.S. publications in Jewish studies included *Hebrew Union College Annual* (1924), *Jewish Social Studies* (1933), and *Historia Judaica* (1938–1961). The *Universal Jewish Encyclopedia* (1939–1943) had a special focus on American Jewish life.

Europe since 1945. Ironically, it was in Nazi Germany that Jewish studies first became part of the official structure of academic life, albeit in a distorted fashion described as research into the "Jewish Question." The Nazis set up research institutes in Munich, Frankfurt, and Berlin that tried to show the magnitude of Jewish influence in German and European societies. Some of the scholarly works on Jewish topics published in the 1950s and 1960s by historians and theologians who had by then become part of the academic establishment in postwar Germany originated in those institutes.

There were, however, other, more serious attempts to establish Jewish studies as an academic discipline. In Vienna, Berlin, and Cologne, Jewish studies (Judaistik) institutes were founded in the mid-1960s, followed by smaller institutes in Frankfurt am Main and a few other universities. The main focus of those institutes was ancient and medieval Judaism. At the same time, a young generation of German historians turned to topics of modern German-Jewish history. Those two approaches remained rather separate until the late twentieth century, when a number of new institutions were created to cover broad areas in Jewish studies, a development which began with the establishment of the Hochschule für Jüdische Studien in Heidelberg in 1979 and continued with the Salomon Ludwig Steinheim Institute in Duisburg, the Moses Mendelssohn Institute in Potsdam, the Simon Dubnow Institute in Leipzig, and new university chairs in Yiddish in Trier and Düsseldorf, in Jewish history in Munich, in Jewish philosophy in Halle, and in Jewish religion in Erfurt. In Switzerland, the universities of Luzern and Basel have Jewish studies positions.

In Great Britain, the Oxford Centre for Hebrew and Jewish Studies (formerly the Oxford Centre for Postgraduate Hebrew Studies) and the Department of Hebrew and Jewish Studies at the University College London developed into major centers of Jewish studies, but more recent institutes have been established in Southampton, Brighton, Birmingham, Manchester, and other cities. France, too, has seen an upsurge in Jewish studies in the late twentieth century. The field there was long dominated by Georges Vajda (1908–1981) and André Neher, with positions created in Paris, Lille, Strasbourg, Lyons, and Nancy. In contrast to other European countries, Sephardic studies as well as the history of Jewish art have been among the fields taught and researched in France. The Medem Library in Paris is one of the world's best resources in Yiddish literature. The CNRS (Centre national de la recherche scientifique) has a particularly strong tradition in Jewish studies. However, France lacks institutions with a full-fledged Jewish studies faculty analogous to Oxford or London.

The Scandinavian countries and Holland, Spain, and Italy traditionally had chairs in Hebrew and Bible studies, and in most of those countries new positions were added, especially to research the Jewish histories in those respective countries. More remarkable was the creation of new positions in Jewish studies in formerly Communist eastern Europe. The only institution of higher Jewish learning during the postwar period in all of those countries was the Rabbinical Seminary in Budapest. After the fall of Communism, the English-language Central European University in Budapest developed a program of courses in modern Jewish studies. Polish universities added Jewish studies, especially in the field of Polish-Jewish history, but the most visible changes happened in the former Soviet Union. Moscow and Saint Petersburg have a few centers of Jewish higher education, including research centers and rabbinical training. Kiev established a Jewish university, as did some other Russian and Ukrainian cities.

The increasing activities in Jewish studies found their expression in the establishment of the European Association for Jewish Studies in 1981, which holds a congress every four years. Its membership had grown enormously by the early twenty-first century. In 1998 it published the *Directory of Jewish Studies in Europe.* In 2003, the *Oxford Handbook of Jewish Studies,* edited by Martin Goodman, summarized global achievements in the field during the last few decades in over a thousand pages.

North America after 1945. Despite the increase in activities in Europe, the United States and Israel became the undisputed centers of higher Jewish learning after World War II. In the immediate postwar era, there was, however, little visible change in the United States. As a reaction to the restriction of Jewish student admissions at major American universities, Brandeis University was established in 1948 and soon developed its own Jewish studies center, drawing such eminent émigré scholars as Alexander Altmann and Nahum N. Glatzer. Emigré scholars also strengthened the faculties of the rabbinical seminaries and were instrumental in establishing the Leo Baeck Institute for the study of German-speaking Jewry in New York, London, and Jerusalem in 1955. The last historian who attempted a single-handed multivolume universal Jewish history was Salo W. Baron. His eighteen-volume *A Social and Religious History of the Jews* (1952–1976) reaches only the year 1650 and is characterized by an affirmative view of the Diaspora.

The period of most significant change began in the second half of the 1960s, with the proliferation of ethnic studies programs from which Jewish studies profited as well. In 1969 the Association of Jewish Studies was established and developed within the next three decades from a small circle of scholars into a major association with several hundred active members. This development reflects the spread of Jewish studies from a handful of rabbinical colleges and universities to almost any university campus in the United States and Canada. At most universities, Jewish studies are integrated into a variety of departments and loosely united in a Jewish studies center. At some universities, such as Brandeis or New York University, there exist separate Jewish studies departments. In contrast to earlier periods, when one professor covered vast areas of Jewish studies, most major research universities in the United States and Canada have numerous appointments in Jewish studies. Jewish studies has become part of the mainstream of American scholarship, as can be seen by the inclusion of Jewish studies publications in all major American publishing houses, whereas before the 1970s specific publishers, such as the Jewish Publication Society of America, were responsible for most publications in the field. Modern periodicals cover vast areas of Jewish studies, including *Modern Judaism, Prooftexts,* and *Jewish Thought,* as well as the revived *Jewish Social Studies* and publications such as *American Jewish History* and the *Journal of the American Jewish Archives.* The Association for Jewish Studies has published its *AJS Review* since 1976.

With the increase of teaching positions and publications, Jewish studies has become an accepted part of religious studies, and moreover, it has helped to transform a traditionally Christian-centered view within the field into a more pluralistic one. At the same time, modern trends within religious studies also shaped Jewish studies as a discipline. While it was common for research within the field to focus on its internal developments and concentrate on Jewish issues per se in the early twentieth century, a more comparative view, which takes the developments of the non-Jewish society more effectively into account, has become almost a given in modern research. As a consequence of relativizing and postmodern tendencies, first in literary theory and later in other fields as well, there seems to be no longer a search for what was or is Jewish culture, but rather for what constitutes the diverse *Cultures of the Jews,* the title of a collaborative work of twenty-three mainly American scholars published in 2002 and edited by David Biale. In contrast to the earlier postwar collaborative efforts of American Jewry, such as *The Jews,* edited by Louis Finkelstein (1949) or Israeli scholarship, as in *A History of the Jewish People,* edited by H. H. Ben-Sasson (1969), this volume neither summarizes the "contributions" of Jews to world civilization nor does it reduce the essence of the Jews to their peoplehood and connection to their own territory. Rather it defines Jewishness as an ever-changing category: "The present work is also the product of a particular time. Ours is a self-conscious age, when we raise questions about old ideologies and 'master' narratives and no longer assume as unchanging or monolithic categories like 'nation' and 'religion'" (p. xxx).

This volume may indeed be summarizing a larger tendency in Jewish studies, which began in North America and continued in Israel and Europe at the close of the twentieth century: the refusal to define clear categories for Jewishnes and Judaism, instead adopting theories of invention and the construction of tradition; the opposition to the still prevalent attitude outside academia of viewing Jewish history as a history of suffering, instead promoting the idea of integration into the non-Jewish world; and finally, the turn to previously lesser known and underrated areas of research, both thematic and geographical. This includes Jews in the Arab world and the history and culture of Jewish women, and also areas which had previously been taboo, such as Jewish magic and related phenomena and negative portrayals of Christianity in Jewish literature.

While those trends can be seen in numerous scholarly publications and campus teaching, another development often runs counter to its achievements. The relationship between Jewish studies and Jewish identity has become a major issue as a consequence of the rapid increase in Jewish studies positions. It differs from campus to campus. In some regions, especially those with a low Jewish enrollment, identity building through academic life plays a minor role. There are, however, many cases where Jewish identity is actively promoted through Jewish studies. The large percentage of privately endowed chairs in the field as well as the need for fund-raising in the broader Jewish community underline the growing connection between Jewish academic and communal interests. In this respect, North America differs profoundly from Israel and the United States.

The increasing centrality of the Holocaust as a field of teaching and research (with a significant research unit at the U.S. Holocaust memorial museum) and the large number of Jewish museums (both Holocaust and non-Holocaust related) have shaped the interest in Jewish studies in the last decades of the twentieth century.

ISRAEL. Jewish studies in a Jewish state naturally receive a different degree of attention than in Europe or North America. Indeed, Jewish studies is a central subject taught at all Israeli universities, often in its own faculties. The Hebrew University in Bar Ilan and Tel Aviv and Ben Gurion University of the Negev in Beer Sheva and Haifa have their own degrees in a variety of subjects within Jewish studies, and even the technical university in Haifa, the Technion, offers a nondegree program in the field. The first World Congress of Jewish Studies was held in Jerusalem in 1947, and has taken place there every four years since 1957. It has become the major meeting point for scholars in the field, and its sessions are published in several volumes.

There are also signs of crisis in Jewish studies at Israeli universities, mainly due to the growing divide between the secular and the religious. Many secular students come with little background or interest in pursuing Jewish studies on a university level. The growing radicalization of the Orthodox, on the other hand, leads to their rejection of university education in general, and academic Jewish studies in particular. Thus, while the Orthodox Talmud schools (*yeshivah*) claim increasing enrollment, the same cannot be said for the Jewish studies departments. In contrast to European and American traditions, Israeli universities or academic seminars (with the exception of the few non-Orthodox rabbis) have not taken on the education of rabbis in Israel, who are trained in traditional *yeshivah.*

The debate over post-Zionism has influenced large circles in Israeli studies, which became an increasingly important discipline, related to but not part of Jewish studies. From the late 1980s, the so-called New Historians and their colleagues in sociology began to question formerly fixed truths about the behavior of the Jewish leadership towards European Jews threatened by the Holocaust and about the origins of the Palestinian refugee problem. If the state was founded on the "original sin" of having expelled the Palestinians, this would have not only scholarly but also political consequences. In a time of continuing political crisis and existential threat, critical voices against the New Historians (not all of them post-Zionists) could be heard, arguing that a similar degree of archival access or free discourse does not exist in the Arab world.

CONCLUSION. The field of Jewish studies not only increased significantly in the late twentieth century, it also changed its nature. The emphasis on traditional Jewish sources has often been replaced by an interest in modern Jewish studies. The knowledge of Jewish languages can no longer be taken for granted among graduates and even professors of Jewish studies at many universities outside Israel. In postwar Europe and the United States for the first time, a significant number of students in Jewish studies are non-Jews. Two areas of enormous student interest have been Jewish mysticism and Holocaust studies.

In the last decades of the twentieth century, Jewish studies moved from its early Germanocentric and later Eurocentric emphases to a stronger integration of widely neglected communities. The experiences of Jews in the Muslim world have slowly been integrated into the general picture.

This is partly the result of the emergence of historians of Oriental background, mainly in Israel, but also of the establishment of a few academic positions concentrating on Sephardic Jewry at American universities. At the same time, research and teaching in Jewish studies spread outside its traditional centers. After its establishment in 1982, the Latin American Association for Jewish Studies has held regular conferences. It reflects not only the growing interest in Latin American Jewish history within the United States but also the new academic centers constructed in Latin America itself. There exists a China Judaic Studies Association, and Yiddish is being taught in Japan.

In the United States the history of Jewish women emerged as a subfield of gender studies, with significant publications in the 1990s about Jewish women in imperial Germany and in the United States, along with a historical encyclopedia of Jewish women. Postmodernism also has left its mark on the field. Some scholars have questioned whether Jewish studies constituted mainly an addition to the traditional university curriculum or a challenge to its strong emphasis on Christian and Greco-Roman roots. This opens the wider question of whether Jewish studies forms part of the classical canon of university subjects or if it should be grouped with the essentially modern disciplines like ethnic and gender studies in a multicultural university framework.

Overall, there are few disciplines that have made such significant inroads into mainstream scholarship in the twentieth century as did Jewish studies. From being banned from the academic curricula in the nineteenth century and restricted to a marginal existence in the first half of the twentieth century, Jewish studies was represented at most American and European universities by the end of the century. Moreover, other disciplines—ranging from theology to history and literature, from philosophy to art and political science—have integrated essential issues of Jewish studies. The burden of this success should not be overlooked: topics that prevail in the public discourse, such as the Holocaust and the Middle East conflict, have very often pushed the study of Jewish languages and crucial sources of Jewish tradition to the background. Overall, however, the fruitful integration of Jewish culture into the curriculum of modern academia has helped create a more open and diverse system of learning. Once the almost exclusive focus on Christian, Greco-Roman, and European traditions was successfully questioned by the inclusion of Jewish studies, the door was opened to other previously underprivileged subdisciplines as well.

Bibliography

Biale, David. *Gershom Scholem: Kabbalah and Counter-History.* Cambridge, Mass., 1979.

Brenner, Michael, and David N. Myers, eds. *Jüdische Geschichtsschreibung heute.* Munich, 2002.

Brenner, Michael, and Stefan Rohrbacher, eds. *Wissenschaft vom Judentum: Annäherungen nach dem Holocaust.* Göttingen, Germany, 2000.

Carlebach, Julius, ed. *Wissenschaft des Judentums: Anfänge der Judaistik in Europa.* Darmstadt, Germany, 1992.

Chulkova, L. A., ed. *University Teaching of Jewish Civilization in the Former Soviet Union.* Moscow, 1996.

Cohen, Shaye J. D., and E. L Greenberg, eds. *The State of Jewish Studies.* Detroit, 1990.

Davis, Moshe. *Teaching Jewish Civilization: A Global Approach to Higher Education.* New York, 1995.

Dobroszycki, Lucjan. "YIVO in Interwar Poland: Work in the Historical Sciences." In *The Jews of Poland between Two World Wars,* edited by Yisrael Gutman et al., pp. 494–518. Hanover, N.H., 1989.

Goodman, Martin, ed. *The Oxford Handbook of Jewish Studies.* Oxford, 2002.

Ilan, Tal. "Women's Studies and Jewish Studies: When and Where Do They Meet?" *Jewish Studies Quarterly* 3 (1996): 162–73.

Jospe, Alfred. "The Study of Judaism in German Universities before 1933." *Year Book of the Leo Baeck Institute* 27 (1982): pp. 295–319.

Jütte, Robert. *Die Emigration der deutschsprachigen "Wissenschaft des Judentums": Die Auswanderung jüdischer Historiker nach Palästina 1933–1945.* Stuttgart, 1991.

Liberles, Robert. *Salo Wittmayer Baron: Architect of Jewish History.* New York, 1995.

Marcus, Ivan G. "Judaic Studies in U.S. University and Jewish Institutional Settings." *Jewish Studies Quarterly* 3 (1996): 136–145.

Mendes-Flohr, Paul, ed. *Hokhmat Yisrael: Heiybetim historiyim u-filosofi'im.* Jerusalem, 1979.

Myers, David N. *Re-Inventing the Jewish Past: European Jewish Intellectuals and the Zionist Return to History.* Oxford, 1995.

Neusner, Jacob. *Judaism in the American Humanities: Essays and Reflections.* Chico, Calif., 1981.

Ritterband, Paul, and Harold S. Wechsler. *Jewish Learning in American Universities: The First Century.* Bloomington, Ind., 1994.

Schäfer, Peter. "Jewish Studies in Germay Today." *Jewish Studies Quarterly* 3 (1996): 146–161.

Schorsch, Ismar. *From Text to Context: The Turn to History in Modern Judaism.* Hanover, N.H., 1994.

Weitz, Yechiam. *Beyn chason le-revisia. Meah schenot historiografia zionit.* Jerusalem, 1997.

Winkelmann, Annette, ed. *Directory of Jewish Studies in Europe.* Oxford, 1998.

Michael Brenner (2005)

JEWISH THOUGHT AND PHILOSOPHY

This entry consists of the following articles:

PREMODERN PHILOSOPHY
MODERN THOUGHT
JEWISH ETHICAL LITERATURE

JEWISH THOUGHT AND PHILOSOPHY: PREMODERN PHILOSOPHY

Usually the term *medieval* designates a historical period falling "between" ancient and modern times. In the history of philosophy, then, the medieval period would occur between the last of the ancient Greek and Roman philosophers and Descartes. However, following H. A. Wolfson (1947), one may construe "medieval" philosophy as a style of thinking that, although prevalent during the Middle Ages, need not be temporally restricted. It is a style of philosophy that attempts to make use of two radically different sources of information for the establishment of a general worldview and way of life. These sources are human reason, particularly philosophy, and divine revelation, especially some sacred text. A medieval philosopher is someone whose intellectual outlook and language are shaped by both philosophy and prophecy.

Beginnings of Medieval Philosophy. Speaking from a strict historical perspective, one would have to say with Wolfson that the first medieval philosopher was Philo Judaeus (d. 45–50 CE). Most of Philo's many books are commentaries on various biblical narratives or legal codes, commentaries in which philosophical, especially Platonic, concepts are used to formulate and explain the text. In reading the Bible in this way, Philo introduced not only a new period in philosophy but also a novel style of philosophy, which we shall henceforth call "medieval." In general, Philo saw no fundamental cleavage between reason and revelation and optimistically sought to make "the sons of Japheth dwell in the tents of Shem." The subsequent story of medieval philosophy is in a sense a long and still ongoing drama on this Philonic theme. Nevertheless, a history of medieval Jewish philosophy cannot begin with Philo, who had little or no influence upon Jewish thought. Instead, it begins nine centuries later with Saʿadyah.

Saʿadyah Gaon. Originally an Egyptian, Saʿadyah ben Yosef (882–942), known as Saʿadyah Gaon, became the dean of the rabbinic academy in Baghdad, the most important in the Jewish world. Unlike Philo, Saʿadyah did influence subsequent Jewish thinkers who read his main philosophical work, *The Book of Beliefs and Opinions.* By Saʿadyah's time, the intellectual world had changed: whereas Philo had to contend with a dying paganism and several warring philosophical schools, Saʿadyah confronted the rival monotheistic religions of Christianity and Islam, Jewish sectarian movements, and the rejuvenated Greek philosophical traditions, now formulated in Arabic with a Muslim accent. Although *The Book of Beliefs and Opinions* is clearly a theological polemical treatise designed to vindicate rabbinic Judaism against its opponents, its method and language are philosophical. Saʿadyah makes use of the philosophical sources available to him through the Muslim theological tradition of *kalām,* the earliest philosophical school in Islam. The *mutakallimūn,* or Muslim theologians, attempted to defend Islam against its religious and philosophical rivals by using arguments and theories gleaned from Greek philosophy. Although *kalām* was initially polemical, rather than purely philosophical, in intention and method, it eventually evolved into a distinct philosophical style or school. Saʿadyah was in this sense a representative of Jewish *kalām.*

Since the only common ground among the various rivals in this religious-philosophical debate was reason, Saʿadyah begins *The Book of Beliefs and Opinions* with a defense of reason against the skeptics and fundamentalists who would disparage it on either philosophical or religious grounds. For Saʿadyah there are three main sources of truth, of which two belong to man's native powers: intellect and sense perception. In addition to these human capacities there is a prophetic tradition, which includes the original revelation to the prophets and the reliable, continuous transmission of their communications throughout a religious community, in particular the Jewish people. Saʿadyah clearly indicates that although prophetic tradition corroborates the two cognitive sources, it is ultimately based upon the senses and grounded in reason. It is based upon the senses since in a prophetic vision one *hears* God speaking or *sees* certain things. It is grounded in reason since the content of the revelation will be for the most part rational, or at least it will not be irrational. This epistemic foundation for revelation has an important practical consequence: a scriptural passage is to be understood according to its literal meaning *unless* it violates sense perception, reason, reliable tradition, or another passage whose meaning is clear. Thus the cognitive faculties serve as criteria for religious doctrine. A corollary of this "rationalistic bias" is that miraculous deeds performed by someone do not by themselves constitute proof of his prophetic authenticity if what he says violates reason.

Firmly convinced of the potency of reason, Saʿadyah offers his readers a rationalistic reconstruction of the Jewish faith, the goals of which are (1) to clarify the main dogmas of Judaism and to prove them where possible, and (2) to refute the opponents, internal and external, of Judaism. Saʿadyah's philosophical theology has, then, as its main purpose the transformation of our unreflective inherited opinions into rationally grounded beliefs. The "true believer" is thus someone who not only has true beliefs but in addition knows that they are true and why. Those who undertake this kind of inquiry will achieve something important and valuable—religious knowledge. Those who do not, but rather follow reliable tradition, will still merit divine favor so long as they willingly obey God's commandments. Saʿadyah's rationalism is thus not a religion of the intellectual alone.

Having laid these epistemological foundations, Saʿadyah next undertakes to prove basic principles of the Jewish faith, such as creation of the universe, the existence and nature of God, and man's free will. In general his argumentation follows the lines drawn up by the *kalām* on these topics, although it deviates considerably from the *kalām* on the subject of freedom. Like his *kalām* predecessors, Saʿadyah believed that the fundamental dogma of divine religion is creation *ex nihilo.* Once this principle has been demonstrated, he thought, it is easy to prove God's existence and to discover some information about his nature. Of the four proofs Saʿadyah gives for the creation of the universe, the first and fourth were to have considerable impact upon subsequent Jewish thought. The first argument asserts that if the universe is, as Aristotle admitted, finite in size, then it must have only finite energy. But a body of finite energy must ultimately decay and eventually disintegrate. However, if it disintegrates, then it must have had a beginning; for, as Aristotle argued, everything that is generated is corruptible, and the converse (Aristotle, *On the Heavens* 1.12). In this argument Saʿadyah cleverly uses Aristotle's physics to show that the Aristotelian claim that the universe is eternal is inconsistent with this physics. The fourth argument claims to show that on the hypothesis of infinite past time there would be an infinite series of moments and events prior to any chosen moment. But such an infinite series, *ex hypothesi,* can never be traversed such that the chosen moment is ever reached. But if this moment is never reached, then it never comes into being, which is *contra hypothesim.* Hence, past time is not infinite. A version of this argument appears in Kant's *Critique of Pure Reason* ("First Antinomy of Reason," B 454).

Convinced that these arguments are valid, Saʿadyah then proceeds to show that creation is out of nothing, which doctrine had become orthodox in Judaism, Christianity, and Islam by the tenth century. Of the various arguments in behalf of this dogma, one is especially significant: if there were some eternal matter out of which God fashioned the universe, as Plato had suggested in the *Timaeus,* this matter would be *co*-eternal with God and hence independent of him. But an independent entity may very well not want to be fashioned into anything! So God would in this view be beholden to matter if he were to create or not create at all.

Saʿadyah's defense of creation *ex nihilo* leads him to develop a theology that stresses God's creativity. First, the proof that the world has been created *ex nihilo* is proof also of God's existence, for a created world needs a creator. Second, Saʿadyah claims that it is the very nature of God to be creative: "In the beginning God created . . ." All the major divine attributes—power, wisdom, life, love—are different facets of God's essential creativity. Every other attribute is a corollary of this divine primal productivity. Hence corporeal characteristics cannot be applied to God, for such qualities can be true only of creatures, entities made by God out of nothing. To ascribe such features to God is to transform the creator into a creature. Saʿadyah is so convinced of the complete incorporeality of God that in his Arabic translation of the Bible he "cleanses" scripture of many anthropomorphic expressions. For example, "the hand of God" becomes "God's power." This conception of God also leads him to criticize the Christian doctrines of the Trinity and incarnation as contaminations of pure monotheism.

No matter how "pure" this monotheistic God may be, he is still a power that reveals himself to man. All the scriptural religions agree that God speaks to prophets and sends them to communicate God's will to man, usually in the form of divine law. Nevertheless, the question whether the Jewish law is a good and rational law or whether it has been superseded by another divine law revealed to a prophet other than Moses was controversial in Saʿadyah's day, as it is now. Saʿadyah's aim is to show (1) that a good God provides the means for his creatures to find their happiness and to receive divine reward; (2) that Mosaic law is based upon reason; and (3) that this law is still valid and cannot be abrogated.

For Saʿadyah it is rationally obligatory for a person to worship God, the creator, just as it is required that we respect and honor our parents. But it is also reasonable that God give us the means whereby we worship him and thereby obtain human perfection and reward. Unlike Paul and the religious antinomians, Saʿadyah sees divine grace as merited by good works; otherwise, the giving and receiving of grace would be arbitrary and undeserved. The Torah and its many commandments are therefore neither incitements to sin, as Paul claimed, nor a punishment of Israel, as Muḥammad believed. Just the contrary, they are expressions of God's love. But if this is so, the laws themselves cannot be capricious or irrational; otherwise, God would be a despotic tyrant, not a loving father and king. Accordingly, following the lead of both the earlier rabbis and the *kalām,* Saʿadyah initially distinguishes between those divine commands that obviously have some reason or purpose and those that do not readily exhibit such a rationale. The former he calls rational commands, the latter revelational commands. As examples of the former he gives the injunctions to abandon the worship of idols and to love our neighbor as ourselves; as examples of the latter he gives the festival laws and the laws concerning incest. Whereas the rational precepts are or can be derived from certain fundamental truths of reason, the revelational commands are neither dictated nor prohibited by reason.

However, as he proceeds to develop his account of law, it is clear that Saʿadyah virtually abandons this distinction and claims that on closer examination even the revelational commands are found to have some reasonable explanation and justification. For example, the selection of the Sabbath and other holy days may seem at first to be arbitrary. After all, neither the Greeks and Romans nor the Muslims have a complete day of rest on one specified day of the week. Yet, Saʿadyah argues, if we remember that "reason requires" (one of his favorite phrases) that we worship God, we have to worship him at some time, in some place, and in a certain way; otherwise, the initial rational precept to worship our creator is empty. Accordingly, our reasonable creator specifies for us through his prophet Moses the time, place, and manner of worship. If there were no uniform code of regulations, people would worship God at diverse times and in different ways. No community could survive such religious anarchy. Moreover, on practical grounds a Sabbath is quite beneficial: it affords not only physical rest but also mental relaxation and the opportunity to study Torah, to reflect, and to converse on spiritual matters. Although Saʿadyah does not, as did Philo, undertake to "rationalize" the whole body of Jewish law, he does suggest in outline how such an enterprise could and should be done. In this sketch he establishes the precedent for future medieval philosophers of Jewish law, such as Maimonides and Levi ben Gershom (Gersonides).

Of greater polemical urgency, however, is Saʿadyah's defense against the twin charges of falsification and abrogation in the Jewish law. The whole Jewish-Muslim-Christian debate in the medieval period turned on these issues. In reply to the Muslim accusation that the Bible in general, and Jewish law in particular, do not represent the pristine and true revelation, Saʿadyah appeals to the notion of reliable tradition, one of the original sources of truth referred to earlier. What is it that makes a religious text and tradition worthy of credence, Saʿadyah asks. Consider a tradition not based upon reliable evidence: it would be full of contradictions and discord. The Jewish tradition, at least as it existed prior to the nineteenth century, is unique in that it contains not only a text that one of its main rivals (i.e., Christianity) accepts as true and correct, but also a body of law that was almost universally accepted by its adherents. Were this tradition unreliable, such unanimity would be inconceivable.

But suppose one were to contend that the Torah is a true revelation but claim that it has been superseded by a more perfect divine law, such as the New Testament or Qurʾān. Saʿadyah counters this argument with several replies, some based upon reason, others on scripture, which, after all, the Christians accept as true. On purely rational grounds, the notion of a divine law being superseded by a totally different and in some cases contrary divine law is inconceivable, for two reasons. First, why would a perfect and immutable God give an imperfect law in the first place and then, only a few centuries later, replace it with a better but very different code? Wouldn't it have been more sensible to have revealed the better code at the outset? Moreover, does God really change his mind, as we do? Second, suppose the New Testament is more perfect than the Torah. But the Muslims claim that the Qurʾān is more perfect than both and hence supersedes them. Yet why stop at this point? Perhaps tomorrow God will reveal another law that abrogates the Qurʾān, and so on *ad infinitum.* To stop the regress at one point is just bias. So why concede a regress at all? Finally—and this argument is primarily directed against the Christians—the Torah, which the Christians accept in principle, testifies to its own eternal validity (*Jer.* 31, *Dt.* 33). The Christians, Saʿadyah implies, cannot have it both ways: either they should accept the whole Torah, especially if they see it as the basis for the messianic claim and role of Jesus; or they should drop it altogether and admit that their religion has no relationship at all to Judaism.

A rational and perfect law revealed by a reasonable and perfect lawgiver must, Saʿadyah continues, be such that its recipients are able to obey it, and in obeying it receive an appropriate reward. Man has to be a free agent in order to be a subject in the divine commonwealth and must have the conviction that his obedience to the law will have beneficial consequences for him. Otherwise, the lawgiver would be arbitrary and the law unrealizable. At this point in his inquiry, Saʿadyah grapples with one of the more thorny problems in classical theology, the alleged dilemma between divine omnipotence and omniscience and human free will, a problem that was especially vexing to the *kalām.* Saʿadyah unambiguously defends humanity against any divine encroachments: we are completely free agents, capable of assuming full responsibility for our actions despite God's omnipotence and omniscience. Unlike some Muslim theologians, Saʿadyah does not believe that God's infinite power would be curtailed if man had some power of his own; nor is it the case that whenever we do some deed God is the co-agent, as some other Muslim theologians claim. God is not so niggardly or envious that he would deprive human beings of any power to act from their own will, and the notion of one action with two co-agents is both implausible and unnecessary. To be an agent is *ex hypothesi* to be able to perform a deed. If I cannot do it myself, then I am not an agent! Nor is God's omniscience an impediment to my free action, as Cicero thought. Although God knows what I shall do tomorrow, he does not cause that action, just as my knowing what day it will be tomorrow does not bring about that day.

Saʿadyah maintains that each human soul is originally a pure and superior substance that is created by God to direct the body in their joint earthly undertaking. The soul needs the body to perform its mission as much as the body requires the soul for its guidance. No Platonic dualism, with its subsequent Christian overlay of original sin, infects Saʿadyah's optimistic religious psychology. The soul and body together act and bear jointly the responsibility for these actions. Upon death, the human soul will be separated from its body because it is a finer substance than the body, and it will reside in some supernal realm until the day of its eventual return to its original body, which will ultimately be resurrected with the soul. Saʿadyah recognizes two stages of resurrection: the first involves the righteous of Israel alone and is associated with the coming of the Messiah in this present world of human history; the second involves the resurrection of all humankind for ultimate judgment and initiates the world to come with its everlasting reward or punishment. These eschatological predictions are admittedly not the teachings of the philosophers but the promises of scripture, which, however, do not violate reason. Indeed, if God is able to create the world *ex nihilo,* why can he not resurrect the dead, not just once, but twice? With his establishment of these eschatological doctrines on both scriptural and rational grounds, Saʿadyah has completed his philosophical reconstruction and defense of Judaism.

SPANISH-JEWISH PHILOSOPHERS. Whereas the beginnings of both Islamic and Jewish philosophy were in the East, the second major phase in Jewish philosophy occurred in Muslim Spain, which became the philosophical-scientific center for the Jews for nearly the remainder of the Middle Ages. In Spain, the philosophical tradition that molded the Jewish mind was the "Neoplatonic" philosophy developed by the

Muslim *falāsifah* al-Fārābī and Ibn Sīnā as a synthesis of Aristotelian and Plotinian themes. For about two centuries both Muslim and Jewish philosophy developed within the metaphysical framework provided by Aristotle and Plotinus, as interpreted by Porphyry and Proclus. During this period Jewish cultural life in Spain flourished in virtually every domain, but especially in philosophy and poetry. Indeed, two of three leading thinkers in this epoch were poets as well as philosophers: Shelomoh ibn Gabirol and Yehudah ha-Levi.

Shelomoh ibn Gabirol. The philosophical fate of Shelomoh ibn Gabirol (c. 1021–c. 1058) is especially interesting. His major philosophical work, *The Fountain of Life*, was written in Arabic, as were most Jewish philosophical books until the fourteenth century; but the original Arabic text was lost and survives only in a Latin translation as *Fons vitae.* Its impact upon Jewish thought was minimal, and this is evidenced by the fact that no medieval Hebrew translation of the work was ever made; only a thirteenth-century Hebrew summary survives. The reason for this neglect in Judaism is that *Fons vitae* contains not one biblical or rabbinic reference. It is a pure philosophical treatise, having no obvious connection with the traditional theological problems that had preoccupied Saʿadyah and other Jewish thinkers. So it was soon forgotten by the Jews, although preserved by the Christians, who believed its author to be a certain Avicebrol, a Muslim, or perhaps a Christian Arab. It was not until 1846 that Solomon Munk proved that the author of *Fons vitae*, Avicebrol, was the famous Jewish poet Shelomoh ibn Gabirol.

Since Ibn Gabirol's *Fountain of Life* had no significant influence upon Jewish philosophy, we shall not discuss it here. Instead, we shall examine his poetry, and for two reasons. First, several of his poems are philosophical. Second, his poetry, including some of the philosophical poems, was popular among Spanish Jewry. One work in particular is deserving of study in this context: the forty-stanza philosophical poem *The Crown of Royalty* (*Keter malkhut*). This poem is part of the liturgy of Spanish Jewry and is recited on the holiest of the holy days, Yom Kippur.

Consistent with the hierarchical mode of thinking characteristic of the Middle Ages, and especially of Neoplatonic philosophy, the philosophical schema of *The Crown of Royalty* begins "on top," with an account of the divine attributes, expressing the apparently contradictory themes of Plotinian divine transcendence and ineffability and the biblical awareness of God in created nature. Then Ibn Gabirol proceeds down the "scale of being" to the mundane world of the four terrestrial elements, the home of man. Finally, he ascends the scale step by step through all the celestial spheres until the divine domain is reached. The *terminus a quo* turns out to be identical with the *terminus ad quem.* By beginning with God, Ibn Gabirol is telling us that the whole universe derives from and depends upon God, who is its creator and sustainer. Among all the standard attributes usually applied to God, it is the divine will that is, for Ibn Gabirol, most important, for God's will is responsible for creating the universe *ex nihilo.* God's will is of course "guided" by wisdom, which is for Ibn Gabirol "the source of life." Creation, then, is the very essence and purpose of reality.

As Ibn Gabirol ascends the ladder of being and reaches the sphere of the angels, or the supernal intellects, he indicates that man's true domicile is not the terrestrial domain of the four basic elements but the world of the intellect. It is here that the human soul has its origin, and it is here that the truly religious person will turn his attention. Committed to a current philosophical theory of immortality according to which man's ultimate reward (to use Alexander Altmann's phrase) consists in intellectual contact with some supernal intellect, Ibn Gabirol interprets the traditional Jewish idea of the world to come in these philosophical terms. The righteous will go beyond their original home of the sphere of the angels, or cosmic intellects, and reach the "seat of glory," a traditional Jewish metaphor referring to the divine domain itself. There the souls of the righteous are "bound up in the bundle of life," for they have reached the "source of life." But, Ibn Gabirol insists, this ascent is accomplished through a life of intellectual and moral discipline, in which philosophy plays a central role. For the soul is in its very nature and origin an intellect, and it is by virtue of intellectual perfection through philosophy that the soul attains immortality.

Baḥye ibn Paquda. The second representative of the Spanish school of Jewish philosophy was not a poet but a professional judge—Baḥye ibn Paquda (1080–1120). Baḥye's *Duties of the Heart* is perhaps the most widely read book of medieval Jewish philosophical literature. Not only was it studied and commented upon by scholars, but it has been read by ordinary Jews, who have regarded the book as a guide to religious and moral improvement. Its success lies in the emphasis it gives to the notion of personal piety, focusing upon both the individual's intellectual and emotional development and his progress toward the goal of complete love of God. Showing the external influences of both *kalām* and Neoplatonism on the philosophical side, and the Islamic mystical school of Sufism on the religious side, Baḥye wove these elements into the inherited fabric of the Bible and Talmud to produce a remarkably unified book of Jewish philosophical pietism, or "rationalistic mysticism." Contrary to the "duties of the limbs," which are concerned only with our external actions, such as what we eat, where we pray, and so on, the "duties of the heart" demand a specific mode of mental and emotional discipline whose ultimate purpose is to free us from the world of materiality and allow us to devote our whole being to God. This *methodos,* like Ibn Gabirol's ascent, stresses the primary and prior intellectual duty to reflect upon God and his created world in order to arrive at the most adequate understanding of God available to man. This duty leads Baḥye to embark upon a rigorous demonstration of God's existence and unity and his creation of the universe. Baḥye's arguments are an amalgam of *kalām* and Aristotelian and Plotinian elements, with the last's emphasis upon unity.

For Baḥye, God is virtually identical with the One of Plotinus, so much so that all the traditional biblical and rabbinic divine attributes are regarded as only concessions to the exigencies of human language. The only true attribute of God is unity, which expresses God's essence.

Once it is understood that God is the ultimate One from which everything else is derived, it is clear that we have another "duty of the heart": to devote our whole lives to the worship of this absolute unity upon whose existence everything depends. Most of Baḥye's treatise lays out a graded manual of emotional discipline whereby the reader is progressively prepared to serve and love his creator. Throughout these "purificatory" chapters concerning such topics as trust in God, humility, and self-examination, Baḥye proposes a form of asceticism that seems to be borrowed from the Muslim mystics but that is tempered by the Jewish insistence upon the duty to be a co-creator with God. Yet, it is evident that for Baḥye this world is not only a "vestibule" for the next, as the rabbis had suggested, but a school in which we are continually challenged, tested, and examined so as to prepare us for "real life," which in this case is the life with God. Our mind and emotions have to be cleansed from their corporeal contamination. For this purpose God has graciously given us both the duties of the limbs, which for Jews means the divine commandments of the Torah, and the duties of the heart, revealed to us through reason. Both help and lead us to the attainment of our goal, the love of God.

Yehudah ha-Levi. The third of our trio of Spanish-Jewish philosophers in this period of Neoplatonic philosophy was perhaps the greatest Hebrew poet since the biblical poets. Unlike Ibn Gabirol, Yehudah ha-Levi (1085–1141) was a philosopher turned against himself, for despite a youthful flirtation with the "wisdom of the Greeks" and his respectful appreciation of its "beautiful flowers," ha-Levi came to reject its "bitter fruits." These fruits contained, he believed, poison, but it was a poison that he himself had tasted. In this respect ha-Levi is like the modern religious thinker Søren Kierkegaard. Ha-Levi presents his critique of philosophy in the form of a "Platonic dialogue," whose main character is not a philosopher but the pagan king of the Khazars, a medieval Asiatic people living near the Black Sea who converted to Judaism in the middle of the eighth century. According to legend, the king decided to abandon paganism and summoned representatives of Judaism, Christianity (Greek and Roman), and Islam to prove in a debate which is the true religion. At the end of the debate the king was convinced by Judaism and hence converted. Ha-Levi uses this legend but modifies it in several ways. First, and most significant, he introduces a philosopher into the debate; indeed, it will turn out that philosophy is for ha-Levi the main intellectual rival of Judaism. Second, initially the king, despising the Jews as an inferior and persecuted people, resists inviting a Jew to the debate. It is only after both the Christian and the Muslim confess that their own religions presuppose the truth of Judaism for their own validity that the king invites a Jew to the discussion. Ha-Levi's book, usually referred to as the *Kuzari*, has as its complete title *The Kuzari, a Book of Proof and Argument: An Apology for a Despised Religion.* Like the books previously discussed, it was written in Arabic but soon translated into Hebrew, by Yehudah ibn Tibbon (1120–1190), the same translator who had rendered Saʿadyah's and Baḥye's works.

The opening paragraph of the book establishes the ground plan of the whole debate. The king receives a divine communication via an angel in a dream in which he is told that although his religious intentions are good, his pagan behavior is unacceptable to God. He then summons a philosopher to find out what behavior is acceptable to God. It is made quite clear why the philosopher is called first: ha-Levi's philosopher stresses that in his view God is not interested in actions, since God is not cognizant of, nor does he supervise, individual behavior. In expressing this belief the philosopher gives voice to the al-Fārābī-Ibn Sīnā denial of divine cognition of and providence for individuals. This philosopher is primarily concerned with the attainment of immortality through "conjunction" of the intellect with one of the angels, or supernal intellects, or perhaps with God himself. Whether one fasts or observes dietary laws is of no concern to this philosopher. He is dismissed immediately because the king has received a message from God. All the logical arguments adduced by the philosopher are not going to convince the king otherwise; since the philosophers are not noted for receiving prophetic revelations, they are not in the position of disparaging such experiences. The king expresses here his bias: experience is decisive over logic. Once dismissed, the philosopher does not physically return, although his ideas are frequently discussed in his absence.

The king now turns to a Christian theologian and then to a Muslim scholar, both of whom begin their speeches with a recital of theological dogma, supporting these beliefs by appealing to the Israelites and their Torah. Without Judaism there is no Christianity and no Islam. At this point the king realizes that he needs to summon a Jewish scholar, whose opening speech, unlike those of the Christian and the Muslim, is not a theological credo but a recitation of historical facts. Against the king's criticism that such facts have no significance to a non-Jew and hence Judaism is a "particularistic" religion, the Jew replies that the very historical facts are precisely the advantage of Judaism, especially over the philosopher. The last point intrigues the king, for he has already dismissed the philosopher precisely because of the latter's cavalier attitude to the facts. So now the king warms up to the Jewish scholar, who follows with a diatribe against philosophy, not so much for any specific philosophical theory as for its method. Since by definition philosophy is the *human* search for wisdom through *reason*, it is necessarily limited and subject to error. The clearest proof of this is the notorious inability of philosophers to agree on anything. This point is especially interesting to the king, who now listens avidly to the Jewish scholar. Later this epistemological skepticism is buttressed by another argument of a quasi-skeptical nature drawn from ethics: a purely philosophical morality, which the philosopher claimed was sufficient for man, is at best no better than a system of prudential maxims that may be broken at any time to suit one's convenience. Such a "morality" is insufficient to bind a society together or even to guide the individual in the complexities of moral action. Divine revelation alone can supply this required information.

And thus we are back to prophecy. Judaism, the scholar insists, rests upon the historical fact that God does speak to man. This belief is accepted by the Christian and the Muslim as well. Against the testimonies of sense experience, even if it is prophetic experience, logic is impotent, especially if the experience in question is attested to by over six hundred thousand people and unanimously reported. Here ha-Levi enunciates a philosophy of religious empiricism that emphasizes the role of experience over reason, prophecy over logic. When the king objects that experience is always subjective and particularistic, no matter how many people may be involved, the rabbi concedes the point but tries to turn it to his own advantage. Yes, prophecy is a special sense faculty that is found only in some people. After all, if everyone were a prophet, who would listen to any prophet? And again, even if prophecy is restricted to Israel, as ha-Levi somewhat excessively and heterodoxly insists, this is not so embarrassing, for again the Christian admits that the Israelites are God's chosen people, and the Muslim concedes that only Moses spoke to God directly. If the philosopher has trouble with this fact, so much the worse for him! After all, ha-Levi reminds us, the philosopher is really tone-deaf to prophecy. So why listen to him?

Convinced of both the irrelevancy of philosophy to his religious search and the derivative status of Christianity and Islam, the king converts to Judaism. The rabbi then instructs him in the basic teachings and practices of Judaism, of which one is especially pertinent to philosophy. Instead of giving the standard rabbinic distinction that *Yahveh*, God's proper name, expresses the divine attribute of love or mercy, whereas the name *Elohim* expresses the attribute of justice, ha-Levi distinguishes between two radically different ways of knowing, thinking, and talking about God. A philosopher—Aristotle, for example—arrives at his conception of the divine through a process of observation and logical inference. The outcome of this ratiocination is a first cause that serves as an explanatory hypothesis or entity. If Aristotle's theory is true, then its theological statements give an accurate description of reality, just as, if his astronomy is true, the astronomical statements correctly describe the heavens. But one does not pray to such a god! Ha-Levi's philosopher in book 1 of the *Kuzari* is right: the philosopher's god isn't interested in our world. But if this is so, how can we be interested in this god? "The God of Abraham, Isaac, and Jacob is not the god of the philosophers!" the rabbi insists. Through philosophy we may reach God; but this power is not the person who spoke to Abraham and Moses. This person is referred to in Hebrew by the tetragrammaton (*YHVH*), a name so holy that only the high priest pronounced it. This person is not known indirectly through inference but directly through prophecy. Here ha-Levi anticipates both Pascal's rejection of philosophical theology and Russell's distinction between knowledge by description and knowledge by acquaintance. The prophet "sees" and "tastes" the Lord (*Ps.* 34:9) with whom Moses at least spoke as friend to friend; the philosopher knows God as a hypothesis that, as the French mathematician Pierre La Place once said, may very well be superfluous. The former we may have to die for; the latter we can ignore with impunity.

MAIMONIDES. The next major figure in medieval Jewish philosophy, Moses Maimonides (Mosheh ben Maimon, 1135/8–1204), was also a native of Spain; but unlike his Spanish predecessors he was heir to a different philosophical tradition, in which Aristotle was "the Philosopher." Maimonides' mastery of this new intellectual outlook altered the whole philosophical scene in the medieval Jewish world. This renascent Aristotle is a "purer," more authentic Aristotle than the one who was encountered in the Neoplatonic-Aristotelian synthesis of Ibn Sīnā or Ibn Gabirol. Henceforth, until Spinoza, Jewish philosophers will have to cope with this Aristotle. Moreover, the power and style of Maimonides' own philosophical personality was such that his successors had to deal with him as well. This overwhelming influence is to be attributed to the character of Maimonides' chief philosophical work, *The Guide of the Perplexed*, translated from Arabic into Hebrew by Shemu'el ibn Tibbon (1150–1230).

Maimonides states at the outset that the *Guide* is no ordinary philosophical book. Although he indicates the goals of the book and his motives for writing it, he warns his readers that besides some stringent intellectual qualifications that they must possess before reading the *Guide*, they should not expect that the way out of their perplexities will be easily understood, clearly visible, or unambiguously stated. Indeed, it is one of the great ironies of this book that although one of its purposes is to discuss and clarify the various ambiguities in the Bible, and religious language in general, it is itself highly ambiguous, giving rise to all kinds of difficulties to its interpreters, both medieval and modern. Maimonides tells us that philosophical truth, especially in metaphysics, the divine science, cannot by its very nature be divulged and expressed in a public and discursive manner. In the first place, very few are fit to study and appreciate its problems. Second, by its very nature, metaphysical truth is not apprehended in a systematic, discursive, continuous manner; on the contrary, like lightning it comes suddenly, quickly, and discontinuously to those who do attain it. Rarely does a person reach a level of metaphysical knowledge that would enable him to set out its truths in a popularly accessible way. Do not expect, then, Maimonides tells us, that the *Guide* will be an easy book, since the book that it attempts to decipher—the Bible—contains the highest truths in science and philosophy formulated in language that is perplexing. In short, Moses was the greatest metaphysician, who via prophecy was charged with the assignment of disseminating these truths in a book containing many levels of meaning. Maimonides, on the other hand, set himself the task of uncovering some of these layers to the select few, whose philosophical-religious perplexities had reached such a pitch that a guide was needed.

Two basic methodological principles are laid down at the outset. First, the Bible cannot be read literally; otherwise it would be full of worthless doctrines and downright errors. Second, human reason has limits, especially in metaphysics, where the philosopher, in spite of his keen and deep desire for truth, must recognize the limited scope of his intellectual reach. The first of these rules is familiar, going back to both rabbinic and earlier philosophical sources, such as Philo and Saʿadyah. That the Torah "speaks the language of men" is a well-known Jewish hermeneutical principle. Thus, we must learn how to read the Bible, which for Maimonides is a philosophical book that has to be read philosophically. One consequence of this exegetical method is that we shall have to begin our new study of the Bible by applying a philosophical filter to purify the text of its anthropomorphic dross. Virtually all of part 1 of the *Guide* is devoted to this task. Maimonides philosophically translates many of the "offending" words and phrases; for example, the expression "face" in "my face shall not be seen" (*Ex.* 33:23) connotes God's essence, not any physical organ. The core of Maimonides' conception of God is a radical defense of the *via negativa:* the most accurate and appropriate way to speak of God is to say what he is not. Human language is essentially incapable of describing the nature of God.

In spite of this apparent theological agnosticism, Maimonides still holds that several of the basic beliefs of Judaism can be soundly proved by means of true philosophical principles, which have been established by Aristotle. To this extent a philosophical theology is possible, for we can demonstrate God's existence, unity, incorporeality, and simplicity philosophically. These "theological theorems" are as solid as the theorems of geometry or physics. Thus our "belief in God" is for Maimonides knowledge, not just "blind faith." But we have to remember that there are limits to reason. Some theological questions will remain recalcitrant to human reason: we shall not be able to resolve them decisively. This is essentially so in the issue of creation of the universe, a problem that becomes increasingly vexing with the spread of Aristotle's physics, one of whose "theorems" was the eternity of the universe. This question was regarded as crucial, since if the world is eternal, it would seem that divine providence would be idle or nonexistent, and hence miracles would be impossible. Saadyah believed that he could prove creation *ex nihilo*; the Muslim *falāsifah* claimed that they could prove the eternity of the universe. Here we have one of the earliest appearances of a metaphysical antinomy, two contrary theses with seemingly persuasive arguments. Like Kant seven centuries later, Maimonides attempts to show that none of the arguments pro or con are valid, that the question is not "decidable" for human reason.

Of course, Maimonides has a theological ax to grind: he wants to defend Moses against Aristotle; but he proceeds in manner quite different from the *kalām.* He first shows that with one exception all the *kalām* arguments are either invalid or rest upon false premises. The only argument that he finds acceptable is, however, inductive and thus does not constitute a decisive proof against Aristotle, since inductive arguments are falsifiable. Having removed the *kalām* from consideration, Maimonides then examines the Aristotelian arguments for the eternity hypothesis. These proofs divide into two classes: scientific and metaphysical. The first group rests, he claims, upon the assumption that the laws of physics are unrestrictedly applicable to every moment in the past including the first instant of time, which in the theory of creation begins the history of the world. Given this assumption, Aristotle argues that the hypothesis of a first instant is incompatible with the laws of physics; hence, such a hypothesis must be false (Aristotle, *Physics* 8.1). Maimonides claims, however, that this assumption is arbitrary, indeed a *petitio principii.* Must we say that at the very moment when the universe was created the laws of mechanics were true? Since for the creationist there is no history of the universe prior to or at the first instant of time, there is nothing that such laws would be true of. Maimonides believes that these laws are true after there is a universe, but not before or when it comes into being. Nor are the metaphysical arguments for eternity any less arbitrary; for they, too, assume that certain metaphysical principles are true of God such that creation would be precluded. But why say God is subject to such principles? After all, part 1 of the *Guide* has shown us how *different* God is from us!

From the inadequacy of the arguments both for creation and for eternity Maimonides infers that the question can be decided only by choosing one or the other hypothesis; neither has been proved true. Believers in the Bible will of course opt for creation, since it is this belief that makes their religion possible. For without creation there would be no miracles, and revelation is a miracle. But Maimonides does not leave the matter just to choice and religious pressure; he believes there is an inductive argument, drawn from the *kalām*, that renders the creation hypothesis more plausible than the eternity theory. The latter, Maimonides maintains, fails to explain certain specific natural phenomena; for example, why does the planet Venus emit a bluish color whereas Mars looks red, especially since both planets have, Aristotle claims, the same chemical structure? In eluding the reach of Aristotle's physics, these "accidental facts" are evidence for, but do not decisively prove, the creation theory. For in the latter theory these facts are explained by appealing to God's creative will. Finally, although Maimonides offers no philosophical argument for creation *ex nihilo*, as Saʿadyah did, he dismisses its rival Platonic model of creation from eternal matter as unproved. Accordingly, the way is open to accept the traditional belief in creation *ex nihilo.*

Since the ultimate purpose of Maimonides' defense of creation is to vindicate the possibility of miracles, Maimonides now proceeds to discuss a phenomenon that the religious believe to be the greatest miracle besides creation itself—prophecy. Given, on the one hand, the competing Islamic claim that Muḥammad was the last and most authoritative prophet and, on the other hand, the theory of the *falāsifah* that prophecy is a purely naturalistic phenomenon that requires no supernatural intervention for its occurrence, Maimonides was constrained to defend both the superiority of Moses against Muḥammad and the role of God in the granting of prophecy. Yet he was too committed to a scientific outlook indebted to Aristotle and al-Fārābī to dismiss altogether their explanation of prophecy as a necessary emanation from God through the Agent Intellect, or angel responsible for human intellection, to a properly prepared and qualified individual, in whom both the intellect and imagination have been perfected. His problem was to find an opening for divine intervention within this deterministic-naturalistic theory of prophecy. He discovered this opening by making two modifications in this theory. First, even though a person has satisfied the requisite conditions for prophecy, God can withhold the emanation. In this sense prophecy is "up to God." Second, in Moses' case the divine emanation reached his intellect free from any admixture of the imagination and without the mediation of the Agent Intellect. Thus, the Bible says of Moses, "he spoke to God face to face" (*Nm.* 12:8). This too, like creation, occurs outside the normal, natural course of events.

The third part of the *Guide* is devoted to the solution of several theological problems that were becoming increasingly vexing in the Aristotelian atmosphere surrounding Maimonides. Does God know particular events, especially the deeds of men? Is God's providence concerned with particular humans or just with the human race in general? Finally, are the commandments rational or just the whims of an arbitrary divine despot? The first two questions are treated together since they are different facets of the general question of how God relates himself to man. Contrary to both the philosophers' belief that God is so beyond man that he cannot know individual human deeds, especially their future actions, since such knowledge would mean that God would enter time and the events themselves would be necessitated, Maimonides claimed that the philosophers' fear again rests upon an illicit analogy drawn between divine and human cognition. Just as God's nature eludes our grasp, so too his way of knowing escapes our finite understanding. God does know particular human actions, and he knows them without their being necessitated. "Everything is foreseen; yet freedom is given" (*Avot* 3.15). The way out from this apparent dilemma lies in the realization that God's knowledge is not subject to the logic that our own knowledge obeys. Once it is admitted that God does know particular events, the question about divine providence is easily answered. If God can know particular men, he exercises his care over them as particulars; for man, unlike any other species, is directly linked to God by possessing reason. This link makes possible divine providence over individual human beings. Since these individuals will differ in their level of intellectual perfection, individual providence will vary; but this is only what one would expect.

The concluding chapters of the *Guide* focus on the question of the rationality of the divine commandments, which for the Jew are the supreme expression of God's care for man and for Israel in particular. Like Saʿadyah, Maimonides is committed to the general principle that the Mosaic legislation is a body of law based upon reason. God desires that human beings attain moral and intellectual perfection. Obviously, then, the laws must lead to these goals and hence cannot be without sense, as some of the *kalām* theologians had argued with respect to Muslim law. Unlike Saʿadyah, however, Maimonides proceeds to give a systematic and detailed analysis of Jewish law, showing that there is hardly anything in this whole legal corpus that cannot be understood. Take dietary laws, for example. Some of them are just good hygiene. (Remember that Maimonides was a practicing physician.) Others were designed to prevent assimilation with pagan nations. In general, Jewish law, for Maimonides, is a divinely revealed system of rational laws.

JEWISH AVERROISM AND GERSONIDES. By the beginning of the thirteenth century, Aristotle had overwhelmed the medieval intellectual world. Besides Maimonides, he had another ally, one who was even more influential: he was the Muslim philosopher Ibn Rushd (1126–1198), known in the West as Averroës. Like Maimonides, Ibn Rushd was born in Cordova, but unlike his Jewish colleague he remained there most of his life. The two never met, and Maimonides knew of Ibn Rushd's writings only after he had written the *Guide.* Had he known the Muslim's philosophy before the writing of the *Guide,* a much different book would have been written, for Ibn Rushd represents a less adulterated Aristotle, one virtually stripped of its Plotinian-Avicennian accretions. Nevertheless, this confrontation between Ibn Rushd and Maimonides does take place, but after their death and throughout almost all post-Maimonidean Jewish medieval philosophy. Indeed, the story of Jewish philosophy after Maimonides and prior to Spinoza is a drama whose main protagonists are Aristotle as interpreted by Ibn Rushd and Maimonides, although these roles are played by characters bearing different names.

Through his commentaries on Aristotle as well as by virtue of his own independent treatises, Ibn Rushd exerted an enormous influence upon Jewish thinkers, ultimately resulting in a "school" of philosophers who could be dubbed "Jewish Averroists." This circle included such figures as Yitsḥaq Albalag of northern Spain or southern France (fl. 1250–1280), Yosef Kaspi of Provence (1279–1340), and Mosheh Narboni of Provence (died c. 1360). One immediate consequence of this confluence of Ibn Rushd and Maimonides was that these Jewish Averroists read Maimonides from the perspective of Ibn Rushd's thought and arrived at an interpretation of their Jewish teacher that distinguished the exoteric teaching of the *Guide* from its esoteric meaning.

One Averroist thesis that is advocated by these three Jewish thinkers as part of Maimonides' esoteric message is the doctrine of eternal creation. This seeming cosmological oxymoron was advocated by Ibn Sīnā and explicitly rejected by Maimonides; but Ibn Rushd had reformulated it in terms of his new reading of Aristotle. In its new garb the theory asserts that the physical universe is a continuous emanation from God, who eternally sustains, and hence "creates," the world, his eternal product. In Narboni the relationship between God and the universe becomes so intimate that it almost results in pantheism. Another important Averroist thesis concerns human "eternity," or immortality, a topic on which the *Guide* is virtually silent. Ibn Rushd advanced the view that human immortality consists in a special "conjunction," or union, between man's intellect and the Agent Intellect, the cosmic power responsible for human intellection, prophecy, and terrestrial generation. Four features of this theory are especially important. First, immortality is literally intellectual, since it is of the intellect and attained through philosophical perfection. Second, in Ibn Rushd's psychology there is really only one human intellect, which is somehow "shared" by or exemplified in many individuals; this one intellect is, however, identical with the Agent Intellect, although only potentially so. Third, at death, or "decorporealization," a person's mind becomes actualized by being departicularized, that is, by "returning" to the Agent Intellect. Finally, in the Agent Intellect all previously particularized minds are now one and hence no longer individuated. Immortality is then for the Averroist literally *impersonal.* In this doctrine we have a kind of religiosity that several modern scholars have called "rationalistic mysticism."

Jewish Averroism did not go unchallenged, and its first important critic was thoroughly immersed in the literature of Ibn Rushd. Levi ben Gershom (Gersonides, 1288–1344) of Provence was an original, versatile, and prolific author whose writings encompass mathematics, astronomy, and biblical exegesis as well as philosophy. Although enamored of both Maimonides and Ibn Rushd, he took a critical stance toward both when he felt they were wrong; and they were wrong, he believed, on several important issues. To the elucidation and solution of these problems, Gersonides wrote in Hebrew *The Wars of the Lord,* which covers virtually all the main topics in medieval metaphysics, natural philosophy, and psychology, especially as they impinge upon religion. The common theme throughout the book is Gersonides' commitment to the power of human reason. Gersonides rejects ha-Levi's epistemological skepticism and Maimonides' moderate rationalism, and he expresses instead a robust confidence in man's intellectual powers. To use Kant's phrase, we can say that Gersonides attempted to bring "religion within the limits of reason alone."

The first major question discussed in *The Wars of the Lord* is human immortality, especially the doctrine of conjunction with the Agent Intellect. Although he retains the vocabulary and some of the principles of the psychology employed by the Muslim *falāsifah,* including Ibn Rushd, Gersonides rejects the possibility of construing human perfection in terms of such a conjunction. First, he criticizes the Averroist thesis that all human intellects are temporary manifestations of the one intellect, which in reality is the Agent Intellect. All of us, Gersonides maintains, have our own intellect, which persists after death and is different from all other human intellects. Its persistence and differentiation result from the cognitive capital that the individual intellect has accumulated throughout life. This knowledge is permanent but varies from person to person. Human immortality is then defined in terms of the knowledge possessed by each individual. The Agent Intellect helps us acquire knowledge but is identical neither with this knowledge nor with our intellects. Like God, the Agent Intellect is a transcendent power that continually influences us but eludes our grasp. No union with it is possible for man.

The next main issue Gersonides grapples with involves him in a struggle with both Maimonides and Ibn Rushd. On the question of whether God can know particulars, both of the earlier thinkers had appealed to the *via negativa* to solve all the apparent difficulties such a knowledge seemed to entail. Gersonides, however, rejects the *via negativa,* in general and especially in the case of God's cognition. He maintains that if God's knowledge or any other attribute is radically different from our knowledge, then we can know nothing about God, not even that he exists. After all, how could we justify an inference from our experience to God, if God is so different from any human attribute? Now turning to cognition in particular, Gersonides argues that God's knowledge is admittedly not like ours in every respect, but it is sufficiently like human cognition to apply to it certain basic epistemological and logical conditions. First, since it is required for our cognition of a spatio-temporal fact that we possess sense perception, God cannot know such facts, for since he has no sense organs, he has no sense perception. Second, God's knowing a future event is incompatible with its being contingent and free. Now we are back to the dilemma that Saʿadyah thought he had dissolved. Unlike most Jewish medieval philosophers, Gersonides is prepared to sacrifice God's knowledge of particulars, especially human actions, and to retain human freedom. Accordingly, he redefines divine omniscience as God's knowledge of all that is knowable. Future contingent events, however, are not knowable, as Aristotle pointed out, for if they were, they would not be contingent. Hence it is not an imperfection in God not to know them.

Another equally striking set of conclusions reached by Gersonides concerns his cosmology. Again he differs from both Maimonides and Ibn Rushd, not accepting the former's acceptance of creation *ex nihilo* and disbelief in a decisive proof on this topic and rejecting the latter's belief in the eternity of the universe. Gersonides shows Maimonides that it is possible to demonstrate the createdness of the world by giving several such proofs. One of these proofs goes like this: anything that exhibits teleological features must be made (for example, light); hence, the universe is made. Another proof, of which there are several varieties, shows that the Aristotelian hypothesis of a universe enduring for infinite time in the past is incompatible with Aristotle's physics and hence is false. For example, Aristotelian physics excludes an actual infinite, a magnitude all of whose infinite parts or members coexist. But if past time is infinite, Gersonides argues, we would have an actual infinite, since the past is in some sense actual insofar as all past events were real and have consequences. Infinite past time would be like a book so chock-full of facts that prior to any given page there are an infinite number of pages. Who could read such a book? Thus the universe is created at a definite moment, the first instant of time.

But how was it created? Saʿadyah, Ibn Gabirol, ha-Levi, and Maimonides all maintain *ex nihilo* creation, although only Saʿadyah undertook to prove it. Gersonides rejects this by-now orthodox doctrine and defends the Platonic view that the world was fashioned by God out of some formless preexistent matter. Here as before, his arguments are entirely philosophical. For example, if the world were created from nothing, then the matter that now constitutes the world would be preexisted by a vacuum, which it now partly fills. But a vacuum is impossible, as Aristotle had proved. Finally, unlike Saʿadyah but like Maimonides, Gersonides holds that the universe is everlasting. However, whereas Maimonides maintained this position on the basis of his interpretation of several biblical and rabbinic passages, Gersonides attempts to prove philosophically that the universe cannot be destroyed, not even by God. After all, what reason could he have for doing so? Spite, anger, regret, admission of a bad original job? Surely none of these human motives can be attributed to a perfect and immutable craftsman.

CRESCAS. Gersonides' thoroughgoing rationalism was to be most controversial; hardly any of his successors accepted its radical conclusions in cosmology or about divine cognition. His critics either reverted to some version of Maimonides' moderate rationalism or rejected completely the whole Aristotelian edifice upon which both Maimonides and Gersonides erected their philosophical reconstructions of Judaism. The best representative of the latter approach is Ḥasdai Crescas (1340–1410) of Spain, whose *Or Adonai* (Light of the Lord) consists both of a radical critique of Aristotle's natural philosophy and a redefinition of Jewish dogmatics on a different basis. Writing at the beginning of what would be the end of Spanish Judaism, Crescas claims that Maimonides committed a serious and fundamental mistake in attempting to establish Judaism upon Aristotelian foundations. One consequence of this error was Gersonides and the Jewish Averroists. So Crescas starts all over by first showing that Aristotle's natural philosophy is either false or weak, and that the natural theology based upon this "weak reed" is even more shaky. Crescas then proceeds to offer a new system of Jewish belief. The main thrust of his critique is his willingness to admit the twin Aristotelian horrors of the actual infinite and the void. After demonstrating the invalidity of the arguments against both these notions, Crescas seriously entertains the hypothesis that there may be an infinite vacuum surrounding our world, thus allowing for the possibility of a plurality of universes. Crescas was one of the earliest representatives of the modern theory of the "open universe."

The admittance of both an actual infinite and the void undermines, however, the arguments for several important theorems in medieval natural theology, such as the existence and unity of God and, in Gersonides' view, the impossibility of creation *ex nihilo.* Crescas is not unhappy with this conclusion and proceeds to draw out the theological implications of his new infinitist outlook. He does this by restructuring the Jewish creed, scrapping Maimonides' by-then famous Thirteen Articles and replacing them with his own "axiomatic reconstruction" of Jewish dogma. Arguing that Maimonides' list fails to exhibit the logical relationships among the various dogmas and omits any justification of why some of these articles are essential to Judaism, Crescas rearranges the creed into four categories: (1) the roots of religion, (2) the foundations of the Torah, (3) obligatory beliefs of Judaism, and (4) optional beliefs. Group 1 consists of the basic postulates of any monotheistic religion, such as the existence, unity, and incorporeality of God. Group 2 consists of the logical presuppositions of a revealed law, such as the Torah; among such postulates are divine cognition, prophecy, and omnipotence and human choice. Group 3 contains those beliefs taught in Judaism but not logically entailed by the fact of revelation; these ideas are contingent upon revelation but not essential to it. They include such beliefs as creation of the world, immortality of the soul, and resurrection of the dead. Finally, group 4, optional beliefs, includes opinions about a variety of topics, such as the plurality of universes or the truth of astrology, about which authoritative Judaism takes no definitive stand. On these matters Jews may believe as they wish.

Consider the existence of God—a root belief of any monotheistic religion. Since all the "classical" proofs have been undermined by his critique of their Aristotelian foundations, how does Crescas philosophically justify such a root belief? In the first place, for Crescas religious beliefs in general do not require a philosophical justification; the acceptance of religious authority, rather than the demonstration of logical proof, is decisive. Second, if philosophical argument is introduced into religion, say for explanatory or polemical purposes, it must be sound philosophy. And so Crescas provides a "new" argument for the existence of God, one which does not presuppose Aristotle's rejection of an actually infinite series of essential causes and effects. Crescas's proof purports to show that whether the causal series is infinite or finite, it is a series of contingent causes and effects and hence requires some necessary and eternal substance to bring it forth, for what is contingent is by its very nature a mere possible existent. As to God's unity and incorporeality, however, Crescas is doubtful whether philosophy is competent to prove such root beliefs; hence revelation must be the guide. On this latter point Crescas is close to the Christian Scholastic William of Ockham.

Crescas is most original and even radical in his treatment of the two closely related foundational beliefs of Judaism—divine cognition and human choice. Here he provides a deterministic solution to the classic dilemma between divine omniscience and human freedom. Rejecting Gersonides' equally radical indeterminist denial of divine cognition of future contingencies, Crescas claims that God's knowledge of some future event—say, Abraham's binding of Isaac—does fix the truth status of that event before its actual occurrence. True, Abraham's binding of Isaac takes place in time, but in God's "eternal vision" this event is eternally true and thus necessary. Abraham's freedom is, Crescas believes, ensured by virtue of the fact that from an abstract logical perspective, his binding of Isaac is a logically contingent state of affairs: in some other world it is possible that he would not bind Isaac. Here Crescas advances a view that, although novel in Judaism, is virtually identical with the doctrine of Boethius and Thomas Aquinas, but perhaps more pronounced in its deterministic flavor. Crescas's deterministic position is also reflected in his account of human choice. On purely psychological grounds he claims that human decisions, actions, and belief commitments are caused by a variety of factors. But if our choices, acts, and beliefs are all determined, are they free? Yes, so long as we have the correct understanding of what a free act, choice, or belief is. If we have not been compelled by an external cause to choose or act in a certain way and we feel no such compulsion, then we are free. As Hobbes and Hume were to say a few centuries later, as long as I can get up, move my legs, and walk, I am "at liberty" to walk, even though I have been conditioned to walk out of my office every time I hear the lunch bell. All of this, Crescas claims, is consistent with divine or human praise or blame, reward or punishment; for just as smoke naturally follows the kindling of a fire, so, too, does punishment follow the performance of an evil act. There is a divinely ordered moral plan in the universe whereby sins or crimes cause punishments and virtue brings about reward.

Crescas's account of creation is also original. Whereas almost all his predecessors and successors claimed that creation is either a "root" or a "foundation," Crescas contends that, although it is a belief taught by Judaism, it need not have been taught. If the Bible had begun with "From all eternity there was God and the universe," there could still have been a Jewish religion. After disposing of both Maimonides' and Gersonides' criticisms of the eternity cosmology, Crescas offers a "soft" defense of the eternal creation hypothesis, a doctrine that had been rejected by both Maimonides and Gersonides as internally incoherent. Crescas's presentation of this model is "soft" in the sense that he does not definitely commit himself to it. He allows for the view, occasionally expressed in rabbinic literature, that God has successively created a series of finitely enduring worlds, a series that may continue *ad infinitum.* On either of these models, Crescas claims, the universe is created, eternally or temporally, *ex nihilo,* since the universe is only a contingent being, whereas God is a necessary being, and as contingent, it depends upon God. This causal-ontological dependency means that it is created *ex nihilo.*

The Italian Renaissance. Crescas's radical critique of Aristotelianism and his own interpretation of some Jewish beliefs did not satisfy most of his successors in Spanish-Jewish philosophy. His pupil Yosef Albo, for example, rejected his determinism. For the most part, fifteenth- and sixteenth-century Spanish-Jewish philosophy reverts to some form of Maimonidean moderate rationalism. The new developments in Jewish philosophy take place on a different soil: Italy. With the emergence of Renaissance Platonism and the new physics of Galileo, different philosophic themes are sounded by several Italian-Jewish philosophical voices. The first of these "newer sounds" is of Spanish origin, Judah Abravanel (Leo Ebreo, c. 1460–1521), the son of the famous Spanish financier, biblical exegete, and philosopher Isaac Abravanel, who found asylum in Italy after the expulsion of the Jews from Spain in 1492. In Italy, especially in Florence, a "newer" Plato was discovered, who in many respects is closer to the historical Plato. Reading Plato directly either in the original Greek or from Latin translations of the Greek, Italian philosophers like Marsilio Ficino attempted to strip away the Aristotelian accretions to Plato that had accumulated during the Middle Ages, just as Ibn Rushd had tried to get at the real Aristotle. Judah Abravanel shows signs of this Platonic revival, even in the literary form of his philosophical work *Dialoghi d'amore,* which is a philosophical dialogue between two characters on the matter of love, both divine and human. This very topic betrays the new Renaissance spirit; for no previous medieval philosophical text, whether Jewish, Muslim, or Christian, made the Greek notion of *erōs* its central problem. But for a Platonic academy in Florence this was the problem *par excellence:* Plato's *Symposium* and *Phaedrus* had replaced the *Timaeus* and *Republic.*

Abravanel's *Dialoghi,* written most likely in Italian or perhaps in Spanish, represents an attempt to fit Plato's philosophy of *erōs* into a Jewish framework, even though there are in it citations drawn from classical mythology and even the New Testament. However, the Judaic orientation is clear. Not only are the Bible and rabbinic literature cited, but Maimonides and Ibn Gabirol are also referred to. Here Platonic *erōs* is legitimized by redefining it in terms of the Maimonidean motif that man loves God through his devotion to the life of the intellect. But man's intellectual love of God is reciprocated and complemented by God's love for man, indeed for the whole universe, which God creates freely out of love from preexistent matter. (Only Plato is cited on this point, not Gersonides.) Accordingly, the unifying and pervading power in the universe is *erōs,* redefined as man's intellectual love of God and God's creative love for man.

A very different tone is heard in the philosophical writings of another Italian-Jewish philosopher, Yosef Shelomoh

Delmedigo (1591–1659), who, although born in the Venetian colony of Crete, studied in Padua under Galileo and absorbed some of the latter's new ideas in astronomy and physics. He was the first Jewish philosopher or astronomer to adopt the Copernican-Galilean system, rejecting the Aristotelian theory of the celestial spheres with their "separate movers," which were identified with the biblical doctrine of angels. The angels, for Delmedigo, are natural forces or powers, primarily human faculties, an idea that was also suggested by Maimonides. Delmedigo also advocated Crescas's eternal-creation cosmology: after all, a God who is eternally active cannot not create; hence, the universe must be eternal. The denial of the world's eternity would be tantamount to the thesis that God's creative power is finite. This explicit espousal of eternal creation leads him in the direction of pantheism, which, however, he expresses tentatively.

The End of Medieval Jewish Philosophy. Despite Delmedigo's enthusiasm for the new science of Galileo, he still retained some medieval Aristotelian ideas and had an ambivalent attitude toward Jewish mysticism, which he criticized yet occasionally adopted. It is not without significance that he spent a few years in Amsterdam, the locale of the last act in our philosophical drama. Befriended by Menasseh ben Israel, one of the local rabbis, a philosopher and a publisher of Hebrew books, Delmedigo was able to get his major philosophical-scientific work published there shortly before he left for Frankfurt in 1630. Two years later the man who was to reject medieval philosophy completely was born in Amsterdam, and studied in the very same school in which Delmedigo had taught a few years earlier—Spinoza (1632–1676). Several scholars have claimed that the Delmedigo-Spinoza connection is not fortuitous, that features of the latter's formalistic philosophy either exhibit elements of or express explicitly doctrines of the former's more diffuse and ambiguous writings. Whether or not this is so, Spinoza clearly and definitively cuts the tie that linked philosophy with religion and advocates the new science with no reservations or fond reminiscences of Aristotle or Maimonides. Spinoza is the first modern philosopher, the first thinker who no longer sees philosophy either as theology's handmaiden or as fertilized by prophetic seeds. Philosophy is for Spinoza not only autonomous, as Descartes maintained, but self-sufficient as well, a thesis that Descartes was unwilling to admit, at least in public.

Spinoza's emancipation of philosophy from theology, based upon both philosophical and biblical-critical grounds, permits him to erect a naturalistic philosophical system in which metaphysics, logic, psychology, political theory, and moral philosophy are all comprehended. The pantheistic suggestions of Delmedigo are explicitly expressed in Spinoza's equation *Deus, sive Natura* ("God, or Nature"). No longer is there a hiatus between a transcendent, incorporeal, infinite God and a corporeal, finite universe. As both thought and extension, Spinoza's God is not divorced from man and the universe; as infinite and eternal, the physical world is inseparable from its cause. Crescas's eternal creation model is stripped of its medieval garb and shown for what it really is: a picture of an eternal, dynamic universe displaying infinite divine attributes. Moreover, nature is for Spinoza a thoroughly deterministic system in which scientific law reigns supreme. The laws of nature are for Spinoza God's decrees. Again, Spinoza pushes Crescas a step further: the latter's deterministic psychology becomes the universal rule of all nature. Such a system, however, allows for no miracles, especially divine prophecies. The wardens of the Amsterdam Jewish community in 1656 had considerable justification in viewing Spinoza as no longer of the Jewish faith. Indeed, he was no longer a medieval man. Medieval philosophy, and medieval Jewish philosophy in particular, had with Spinoza been terminated, and a new philosophical epoch had begun.

Bibliography

General

The best general philosophical study of Jewish philosophy is given by Julius Guttmann in his *Philosophies of Judaism*, translated by David W. Silverman (New York, 1964). Although a comprehensive historical survey beginning with the Bible and ending with Franz Rosenzweig, it contains five perceptive chapters on medieval thinkers. It has an excellent bibliography. Isaac Husik's *A History of Medieval Jewish Philosophy* (1916; reprint, New York, 1969) focuses upon individual thinkers. It is more detailed, but less analytical, than Guttmann's treatment. Harry A. Wolfson's *Philo: Foundations of Religious Philosophy in Judaism, Christianity and Islam*, 2 vols. (Cambridge, Mass., 1947), is the most comprehensive English study on Philo and establishes the conceptual framework adopted in this essay.

Saʿadyah and the Kalām

The most recent and comprehensive study of *kalām* is Wolfson's *The Philosophy of the Kalam* (Cambridge, Mass., 1976). The influence of *kalām* upon Jewish philosophy is discussed by Wolfson in his posthumously published *The Repercussions of the Kalam in Jewish Philosophy* (Cambridge, Mass., 1979). Saʿadyah's *The Book of Beliefs and Opinions* was translated by Samuel Rosenblatt as the first volume in the now extensive "Yale Judaica Series" (New Haven, 1948). The best biography and general survey of Saʿadyah's literary career is still Henry Malter's *Saadia Gaon: His Life and Works* (1921; reprint, Philadelphia, 1978).

Jewish Philosophy in Spain: The Neoplatonic Tradition

No complete English translation of Shelomoh ibn Gabirol's *Fons vitae* has appeared. A few excerpts were translated from the Latin into English by Arthur Hyman in the anthology *Philosophy in the Middle Ages*, edited by Arthur Hyman and James J. Walsh (New York, 1967), pp. 347–357. The most accessible introduction to the *Fons vitae* is still Solomon Munk's French translation of Shem Ṭov ibn Falaquera's medieval epitome, which is included in Munk's *Mélanges de philosophie juive et arabe* (1859; reprint, Paris, 1927). Ibn Gabirol's *Crown of Royalty* was translated by Israel Zangwill and annotated by Israel Davidson, and is included in Davidson's anthology *Selected Religious Poems of Solomon ibn Gabirol* (New York, 1973). Baḥye ibn Paquda's treatise has recently been translated from the Arabic by Menahem Mansoor as *The Book of Direction to the Duties of the Heart* (London, 1973). It has a full introduction.

Yehudah ha-Levi has fared better with respect to secondary literature but worse in translation. The only full English translation of the *Kuzari*, by Hartwig Hirschfeld (1905; reprint, New York, 1964), is inaccurate. Fortunately, the scholarly literature in English is excellent. Wolfson's essays should be consulted, especially the following: "Halevi and Maimonides on Design, Chance and Necessity" and "Halevi and Maimonides on Prophecy," both reprinted in his *Studies in the History of Philosophy and Religion*, edited by Isadore Twersky and George H. Williams, vol. 2 (Cambridge, Mass., 1977).

Maimonides

The most accurate English translation of *The Guide of the Perplexed* is that of Shlomo Pines (Chicago, 1963). Besides Pines's own fine introduction it contains a stimulating, although debatable, introductory essay by Leo Strauss. Surprisingly, there is no comprehensive English monograph on Maimonides' philosophy, although studies on separate facets of his thought abound. Leo Strauss's "The Literary Character of the *Guide for the Perplexed*," reprinted in his *Persecution and the Art of Writing* (1952; reprint, Westport, Conn., 1973), will introduce the reader into the "esoteric" interpretation of Maimonides. A more traditional but perceptive introduction is Simon Rawidowicz's "Knowledge of God: A Study of Maimonides' Philosophy of Religion," in *Studies in Jewish Thought*, edited by Nahum N. Glatzer (Philadelphia, 1974). Wolfson's more specialized studies have been reprinted in both volumes of his *Studies in the History of Philosophy and Religion* (cited above).

Gersonides and Crescas

A complete English translation of Gersonides' *Wars of the Lord* was published in three volumes by Seymour Feldman (Philadelphia, 1984–1999). A superb comprehensive study of Gersonides is Charles Touati's *La pensée philosophique et théologique de Gersonide* (Paris, 1973). For Jewish Averroism consult Alfred L. Ivry's "Moses of Narbonne's Treatise on the Perfection of the Soul," *Jewish Quarterly Review*, n.s. 57 (April 1967): 271–297.

No complete translation of Crescas's *Or Adonai* has been made. Wolfson translated most of book 1 in his masterful *Crescas' Critique of Aristotle: Problems of Aristotle's Physics in Jewish and Arabic Philosophy* (Cambridge, Mass., 1929). On Crescas's cosmology see Seymour Feldman's "The Theory of Eternal Creation in Ḥasdai Crescas and Some of His Predecessors," *Viator* 11 (1980): 289–320.

Jewish Philosophy in the Renaissance: Spinoza

A good descriptive survey of Italian-Jewish intellectual life, including philosophy, is given by Israel Zinberg in volume 4 of his *A History of Jewish Literature*, translated by Bernard Martin (New York, 1974). He discusses Judah Abravanel in chapter 1 and Yosef Shelomoh del Medigo in chapter 6. Isaac E. Barzilay has provided a good comprehensive study of Delmedigo in his *Yoseph Shlomo Delmedigo: His Life, Works and Times* (Leiden, 1974). Judah Abravanel's *Dialoghi d'amore* was translated into English by F. Friedberg-Seeley and Jean H. Barnes as *The Philosophy of Love* (London, 1937).

The literature on Spinoza is of course voluminous. A new translation of his *Ethics* was done by Samuel Shirley and edited by Seymour Feldman, *Ethics and Selected Letters* (Indianapolis, 1982). His *Theological-Political Treatise* was translated by R. H. M. Elwes (New York, 1951). Wolfson's *The Philosophy of Spinoza*, 2 vols. (Cambridge, Mass., 1934), and Leo Strauss's *Spinoza's Critique of Religion*, translated by E. M. Sinclair (1965; New York, 1982), are most helpful in relating Spinoza to the Jewish context.

New Sources

Borgen, Peter. *Philo of Alexandria: An Exegete for His Time.* New York, 1997.

Eisen, Robert. *Gersonides of Providence, Covenant, and the Chosen People: A Study in Medieval Jewish Philosophy and Biblical Commentary.* Albany, 1995.

Fox, Marvin. *Interpreting Maimonides: Studies in Methodology, Metaphysics, and Moral Philosophy.* Chicago, 1990.

Frank, Daniel H., and Oliver Leaman, eds. *The Cambridge Companion to Medieval Jewish Philosophy.* New York, 2003.

Goodman, Lenn E. *Jewish and Islamic Philosophy: Crosspollinations in the Classic Age.* New Brunswick, N.J., 1999.

Hyman, Arthur. *Eschatological Themes in Medieval Jewish Philosophy.* Milwaukee, Wis., 2002.

Kassim, Husain. *Aristotle and Aristotelianism in Medieval Muslim, Jewish, and Christian Philosophy.* Lanham, Md., 2000.

Leaman, Oliver. *Moses Maimonides.* New York, 1990.

Runia, David T. *Exegesis and Philosophy: Studies on Philo of Alexandria.* Brookfield, Vt., 1990.

Tirosh-Samuelson, Hava. *Happiness in Premodern Judaism: Virtue, Knowledge, and Well-Being.* Cincinnati, 2003.

SEYMOUR FELDMAN (1987)
Revised Bibliography

JEWISH THOUGHT AND PHILOSOPHY: MODERN THOUGHT

Modern Jewish religious thought is not simply a chronological category designating Jewish reflections that occur in the modern world. Rather, it is a category that denotes meditations by Jews about Judaism and Jewish destiny that take place within—or at least seek to take into account—the cognitive process distinctive of the modern world. Heir to the biblical image of knowledge, which is grounded in the concepts of divine creation, revelation, and redemption, modern Jewish thought seeks to come to terms with modern sensibilities and conceptions of truth. In this respect, of course, it is basically similar to modern religious thought in general. There are, however, specifics of the Jewish experience in the modern world that determine the agenda and peculiar inflections of modern Jewish thought.

INTRODUCTION TO THE MODERN WORLD. It should therefore be recalled that Jews first truly encountered the modern world during the protracted struggle for emancipation in the eighteenth and nineteenth centuries. This struggle was not merely a legal process but engaged Europe in an intense and wide-ranging debate reviewing Jewry's eligibility to participate in the modern world. In the course of this century-long debate, Jews became exceedingly sensitive to the prevailing image of Judaism in European culture. Not surprisingly, modern Jewish thought was thus often guided by an apologetic motive. This defensive posture was also prompted by the rise of modern political and racial anti-Semitism, which was not confined to the mob but gained vocal support from more than a few intellectuals. The integration of the Jews into the modern state and culture, which was achieved despite persistent opposition, led to a profound restructuring of Jewish life, both organizationally and culturally. The Jews were no longer under the obligatory rule of the rabbis and the Torah. In acquiring the political identity and culture of the non-Jewish society in which they lived, the Jews tended to lose much of their venerable culture, including, perhaps most significantly, knowledge of both Hebrew and the sacred texts of the tradition. Moreover, for many, Israel's covenantal relationship to God as a chosen people presently in exile but piously awaiting God's Messiah and restoration to the Promised Land was no longer self-evident and unambiguous.

Modern Jewish thought was thus charged not only with the task of explaining Judaism to both non-Jews and Jews estranged from the sources of their tradition, but also with that of rethinking some of the fundamental concepts of the tradition that bear on the nature of the Jews as a people (covenant, election, exile, the Messiah, and the promise of national redemption) and, in general, the meaning of Jewish community, history, and destiny. These questions gained a unique urgency in the mid-twentieth century because of the Holocaust and the establishment of the State of Israel. Thus, whereas medieval Jewish philosophy was primarily concerned with the relatively circumscribed issue of reconciling faith and reason, modern Jewish thought is broader and by necessity more protean, addressing the multiple dilemmas of the Jew in the modern world.

The beginnings of modern Jewish thought may be traced, paradoxically, to the heterodox sixteenth-century Dutch philosopher, Barukh Spinoza (1632–1677). This renegade Jew was to leave the Jewish community without taking the perfidious step of converting to another religion, a revolutionary precedent that opened the possibility of a secular, cosmopolitan Jew who, in discarding all primordial particularities, found a home in the religiously and ethnically neutral world of reason and common humanity. Universally adored by all votaries of the modern spirit, this iconoclastic but estimable figure has been an abiding challenge to the Jews of modernity to shed their ancestral faith for more supposedly noble, secular affiliations. Furthermore, Spinoza's harsh critique of Judaism as a religion has weighed heavily on modern Jews, not in the least because it has decisively influenced the negative image of Judaism in modern thought. Hence, despite his excommunication by the Jewish community of his native Amsterdam, Spinoza has remained preeminent in modern Jewish consciousness.

The First Modern Jew. In contrast to Spinoza, the eighteenth-century Berlin savant Moses Mendelssohn (1729–1786) represents the possibility that the Jew's creative participation in modern, secular culture need not negate a commitment to Judaism. Hailed by the Enlightenment as the German Socrates, he remained a proud and pious Jew. As a philosopher, he gained prominence for his disquisitions on aesthetics, epistemology, metaphysics, and psychology. Significantly, he based his arguments on reason alone, and although he made use of the metaphysical presuppositions of natural religion, his interest was strictly secular. He scrupulously refrained from introducing scriptural proof texts and certainly never referred to his Judaism. As such, he was not a "Jewish" philosopher. In fact, implicit in his writings is the assumption that his Judaism is irrelevant to his philosophical endeavor and is strictly an incidental and private affair.

Nonetheless, and to his great chagrin, he was repeatedly challenged to defend his continued devotion to his ancestral faith, a fidelity that many of his contemporaries found flagrantly inconsistent with his adherence to enlightened, philosophical culture. Mendelssohn sought to avoid confrontation on these matters, and at first he preferred to make a vigorous appeal to the principle of tolerance and not to engage in debates regarding his abiding commitment to Judaism. However, this proved insufficient to quiet his traducers, and finally in 1783 he penned his famous defense of his dual allegiance to the Enlightenment and Judaism: *Jerusalem oder über religiöse Macht und Judentum* (Jerusalem, or on religion and power in Judaism). Framing his argument in a careful explication of the principle of religious liberty, Mendelssohn holds that philosophical rationalism, which is grounded in the deistic assumption that the "eternal verities" and "human felicity" may be acquired without divine revelation, poses no special problem for Judaism. For the faith of Israel, as he declares, is "not a revealed religion but a revealed legislation." In contrast to Christianity, Judaism is founded not on doctrinal opinions and saving truths but rather on "laws, commandments, ordinances, rules of life, instructions in the will of God" (Mendelssohn, 1784/1983, pp. 89–90). Mendelssohn suggests that these commandments, particularly the most enduring ceremonial laws, serve as symbolic acts that alert one to the eternal truths of reason, thus preventing the Jews from succumbing to the idolatry of false ideas. Herein lies the extensive meaning of Israel's election. The Jews "were chosen by Providence to be a priestly nation . . . a nation which . . . was continually to call attention to sound and unadulterated ideas of God and his attributes. It was incessantly to teach, to proclaim and to endeavor to preserve these ideas among the nations, by means of its mere existence, as it were" (p. 118).

Mendelssohn thus reduced Judaism to a body of ceremonial laws while expanding it into a universal religion of reason. His effort in this respect characterizes much of modern Jewish thought: Unlike medieval Jewish philosophers, their modern descendents would no longer seek to reconcile revelation with reason as two distinct but homologous bodies of truth but would endeavor to demonstrate the significance of Judaism within the general framework of human reason and culture. Mendelssohn also anticipated another characteristic thrust of modern Jewish thought with his conception of Israel's mission to the nations, a notion that provided a universalistic justification of Judaism's continued particularity.

MENDELSSOHN'S LEGACY. Mendelssohn's definition of Judaism, however, was not unproblematic. His delineation of the distinctive essence of Judaism as "revealed legislation" exposed the religion to the charge—first developed by Mendelssohn's contemporary Immanuel Kant (1724–1804)—that Judaism is heteronomous religion of law that finds expression chiefly in religious ritual and ceremonies. In his *Religion within the Limits of Reason Alone* (1793), Kant regarded genuine religion to be the cultivation of moral autonomy; he correspondingly deemed ritual and ceremony to be pseudoservice to God and depicted Judaism as a religious illusion. Kant's indictment of Judaism, based largely on his reading of Mendelssohn and Spinoza, was repeated by many modern thinkers and has accordingly troubled many modern Jews, especially those who shared Kant's philosophical presuppositions. Moreover, Mendelssohn's definition of Judaism satisfied few Jews. The traditional Jew felt he ignored the unique creedal core of Judaism; the liberal Jew was unhappy (and not only because of Kant's critique) with his emphasis on the ceremonial laws. Nonetheless, Mendelssohn's *Jerusalem* still stands as a monument to a Jew who sought to secure the integrity of Judaism while actively pursuing modern culture.

Eager to accommodate Judaism to the modern spirit, Jews of varying theological tendencies claimed Mendelssohn as their spiritual progenitor. For Jewish opponents of the modern world, Mendelssohn became associated with the new order as a symbol, however, of betrayal. The *spiritus rector* of Jewish Orthodoxy as a self-conscious movement to guard the integrity of classical Judaism while fending off the putatively corrosive effects of the modern world, Mosheh Sofer (1762–1839; popularly known as Hatam Sofer), regarded Mendelssohn as the source of the contemporary Jew's beguiling infatuation with "alien culture." In his spiritual last will and testament, he cautioned all God-fearing Jews "not to turn to evil and never engage in corruptible partnership with those fond of innovations, who, as a penalty for our sins, have strayed from the Almighty and His law! Do not touch the books of Rabbi Moses [Mendelssohn] of Dessau, and your foot will never slip!" (cited in Mendes-Flohr and Reinharz, 1995, p. 172). The document, written some fifty years after Mendelssohn's death, is still immensely popular among some Orthodox Jews (sometimes called Ultra-Orthodox, as opposed to modern or Neo-Orthodox Jews who seek accommodation with the modern world).

The militant antimodernism of these Ultra-Orthodox Jews, who embraced much of the traditional Jewish community in the nineteenth century, especially in eastern Europe, is distinguished by a deliberate self-enclosure. Although not totally ignorant of the modern world, they failed to acknowledge its most significant epistemological presuppositions and social and political values. It would be erroneous, however, to assume that Ultra-Orthodoxy was moribund or spiritually stagnant; on the contrary, in its own terms the movement was (and is) dynamic and creative. The nineteenth century witnessed a renaissance of rabbinic learning; new *yeshivot* (talmudic academies) were established, and new methods and approaches to learning and piety were advocated. *Yeshivot* were established by Hatam Sofer in Pressburg, Hungary, (modern-day Bratislava, Slovakia) and by Hayyim ben Yitshaq (1749–1821) in Volozhin, Lithuania. Also notable are the pietistic movement, known as Musar, which was founded by another Lithuanian rabbi, Yisra'el (Lipkin) Salanter (1810–1883); and Hasidism, the movement of popular mystical piety, which flourished in the nineteenth century.

The opposition of the Ultra-Orthodox to modernism is not as much epistemological as it is axiological (value-related). They view the modern world, given its sociological and cultural implications, with profound suspicion, for in their judgment it leads to religious laxity and even defection. Even Hatam Sofer did not oppose secular studies per se, as long as they did not undermine the preeminence of Torah and Jewish tradition. With few exceptions, Orthodoxy has been indifferent to the epistemological (and ontological) issues raised by modern science and technology; its sole criterion for adjudging the developments in science has been to protect Torah observance.

Neither is science a salient issue for Jewish modernists. They have been principally exercised by the need to find a place for the Jews and Judaism in the modern world. Philosophically and theologically, this objective necessitated a delineation of Judaism's relevance to the historical unfolding of a universal, human culture. Within the orbit of nineteenth-century discourse, the principal vectors of this effort were provided by Kant, Friedrich Schelling (1775–1854), and G. W. F. Hegel (1770–1831).

JUDAISM AND MODERN HISTORICAL CONSCIOUSNESS. Proponents of religious reform of Judaism were particularly drawn to the historiosophical teachings of Schelling and Hegel. Solomon Formstecher (1808–1889) and Samuel Hirsch (1815–1889), prominent rabbinical leaders of the nascent Reform movement in Germany (which was later divided between a radical fringe and the liberal majority, which favored moderate reform), each in his own distinctive fashion recast the doctrines in support of religious reform and Jewish integration into modern society and culture. Because the philosophical idealism of Schelling and Hegel viewed spiritual truths as developing and maturing dynamically in history, it provided these advocates of religious reform with the conceptual perspectives justifying ritual and doctrinal change in Judaism: To be true to the spiritual truths with which it is entrusted, Judaism must be dynamic and evolutionary. The proposition of philosophical idealism that the historical unfolding of these truths leads to the progressive unification of human culture and sensibility also lent support to the Reformers' call for Jewish participation in general culture. However, their affirmation of a universal culture, in turn, posed a severe challenge to account for the enduring identity—and thus particularity—of Judaism, which they, like all Reform leaders, clearly upheld.

Formstecher and Hirsch reflected their generation's characteristic interest in history as a dynamic process fraught with cultural and spiritual significance. The historical imagination, especially with its critical, scientific bent, first had its impact in Jewish circles with the founding in Berlin in 1819 of a society promoting the scientific study of Judaism known as *Wissenschaft des Judentums.* The primary motive of this society—many of whose members were to be associated with religious reform—was to correct the calumnious opinions about Judaism and illuminate the varied, ongoing contribution of Judaism to the shaping of European civilization. It was hoped that the objective, scholarly study of Judaism would irrefutably demonstrate that the Jews sought to participate in modern European culture not as Asiatic interlopers but that they were, by right of this contribution, culturally and spiritually as much European as any other people.

This proposition was compatible with the presuppositions of Reform Judaism, which also shared the assumption that Judaism had made a decisive contribution to the historically unfolding spirit of Europe. The proponents of religious reform naturally supported *Wissenschaft des Judentums.* One of the founding proponents of Reform Judaism in Germany, Abraham Geiger (1810–1874), was also one of the most outstanding pioneers of *Wissenschaft des Judentums.* Critical historical scholarship, he maintained, would help identify the immanent forces in Jewish tradition sanctifying the change and renewal of Judaism that were deemed necessary by the advocates of reform. Implicitly adopting the Hegelian principle that history is the progressive revelation of the divine truth, Geiger presented the study of history as an alternative to *talmud Torah* (study of Torah) as the Jew's mode of reflecting on God's will.

Orthodox leaders, even those who supported to some degree the Jews' entry into the modern world, objected strenuously to what they perceived to be the historicist bias of *Wissenschaft des Judentums.* The founder of Neo-Orthodoxy in Germany, Samson Raphael Hirsch (1808–1888) bitterly remarked that the tendency of *Wissenschaft des Judentums* to compare Judaism to other historical phenomena—"Moses and Hesiod, David and Sappho"—in effect reduced Judaism to a "human and transitory [fact] of a by-gone age" (cited in Mendes-Flohr and Reinharz, 1995, p. 234). Similarly, the Italian Jewish religious philosopher Samuel David Luzzatto (1800–1865) plaintively observed with reference to the the votaries of *Wissenschaft des Judentums,* "They study ancient Israel the way the other scholars study ancient Egypt, Assyria, Babylon and Persia" (cited in Mendes-Flohr and Reinharz, 1995, p. 236). Luzzatto, although Orthodox, was a prolific author of scholarly studies of Judaism; nonetheless, he held that *Wissenschaft des Judentums* "must be grounded in faith"—as such it will "seek to understand the Torah and the prophets as the Word of God, [and] comprehend how, throughout our history, the spirit of God, which is our nation's inheritance, warred with the human spirit" (cited in Mendes-Flohr and Reinharz, 1995, p. 236).

Luzzatto's indictment of *Wissenschaft des Judentums* for its historicist bias may have been somewhat overstated, for the early scholars of *Wissenschaft des Judentums* were, in truth, not utterly devoid of the existential religious commitment that he called for. Nonetheless, the thrust of *Wissenschaft des Judentums* was largely philological and antiquarian, and its methodological assumptions unequivocally conformed to a historicist mold (which in the twentieth century, Jewish studies would seek to break). Naḥman Krochmal (1785–1840), for one, regarded the intellectual and spiritual dilemmas engendered by the historicism implicit in *Wissenschaft des Judentums* as the most exigent issue facing his generation. Krochmal, who lived in the politically and socially conservative Austrian provience of Galicia where emancipation and religious reform were remote prospects, published a monumental treatise in Hebrew on the challenge posed to Judaism by critical historical research. This work, published posthumously in 1851, was indicatively titled *Moreh nevukhei ha-zeman* (Guide of the perplexed of our time). The title alludes to Moses Maimonides's (1135/8–1204) famous *Guide of the Perplexed* (1190), and like the great Spanish rabbi in his day, Krochmal sought to offer guidance to the perplexed of his generation. The reference in the title to the perplexed *of our* (lit., *the*) *time* may be understood as both *of our time* and *by time* (i.e., by the category of time, by historical time).

Krochmal begins his treatise with the observation that Jewish youths are genuinely perplexed by the results of critical scholarship that cast doubt on the traditional view of events and, particularly, on the traditional view of the sacred texts, their composition, and, therefore, their authority. An observant Jew, Krochmal noted that the faith of these youths will surely not be fortified by an obscurantist response; the enjoining of dogma in the face of the fruits of scholarship would only exacerbate the estrangement of these youths. Faith, as Maimonides in his day indicated, must be allied with reason; now, Krochmal argued, faith must also be grounded in a proper philosophical understanding of history. This is what Krochmal's *Guide* sought to provide, hence its subtitle, *She'arei emunah tsurafah* (Gates to a purified faith).

JUDAISM AND MORAL THEOLOGY. With a few notable exceptions (e.g., Samuel David Luzzatto), virtually all Jewish religious thinkers in the nineteenth century who sought to accommodate Judaism to the modern sensibility were beholden to Kant's conception of ethical piety as the ultimate form of service to God. Even among those thinkers whose primary concern was to develop via Hegel and Schelling a philosophy of Jewish history, one discerns an attempt to come to terms with Kant's critique of Judaism as a heteronomous pseudoreligion. Nineteenth-century thinkers associated with every tendency in modern Judaism from Reform to Neo-Orthodoxy shared a conviction that the faith of Israel properly understood actually promotes ethical piety. Even Luzzatto, a staunch traditionalist who expressly rejected the very premises of Kant's ethical rationalism, argued that Judaism is fundamentally a religion of moral sentiment. Samson Raphael Hirsch developed an elaborate exegesis of the traditional precepts of Judaism, the *mitsvot* (commandments), demonstrating how each in its distinctive manner fosters the development of moral consciousness.

Moritz Lazarus (1824–1903), a professor at the University of Berlin from 1873 and prominent lay leader of Liberal Judaism in Germany, devoted numerous essays and a two-volume study, *Die Ethik des Judentums* (The ethics of Judaism; 1898–1911), to a systematic demonstration of Judaism's inherent compatibility with Kant's conception of morality. In developing his thesis, Lazarus drew on the principles he had formulated in founding the discipline of *Völkerpsychologie,* the comparative psychology of peoples. With respect to the psychological study of Judaism, he proposed an examination of the literary sources of classical Judaism as they most faithfully record the will, intent, and way of life of the Jews. By insisting that only on the basis of such a study could Judaism be properly characterized, Lazarus abjured the speculative approach of Formstecher and Samuel Hirsch. He introduced Kantian categories not as speculative presuppositions of his study but merely as heuristic principles that to his mind best organize and elucidate the empirical structure of Judaism and help illuminate the objective unity of its ethical structure.

Lazarus maintained that such a study demonstrates that Judaism in effect is a system of autonomous ethics; specifically, the rites and values of Judaism foster the development of what Kant celebrated as moral consciousness. The ethical piety engendered by Judaism may be best characterized as "holiness"—a quality of life that bespeaks neither a numinous nor a transcendent reality but, rather, the indomitable conviction that a moral life is the ultimate meaning and purpose of existence.

To Lazarus's profound disappointment, his *Ethics of Judaism* was severely criticized by the generation's foremost Kantian philosopher, Hermann Cohen (1842–1918), the founder of the Marburg school of neo-Kantianism. Cohen faulted Lazarus for locating the source of Judaism's ethical teachings in the Jewish "folk-soul." To Cohen, such a concept, grounded as it is in psychology and history, undermines the reliability and certitude required by a genuine ethical system. Ethics must derive its validity from rational, universal concepts. What renders Jewish ethics interesting, Cohen contends, is its distinctive dependence on the concept of a universal, unique God—and not just as a phantasm of the Jewish folk-soul but as a rationally defensible concept.

Like Lazarus, Cohen was prominently associated with Liberal Judaism, especially in his latter years, and he also sought to demonstrate the fundamental compatibility of Judaism with Kant's ethical idealism. Interpreting the master's teachings in a somewhat novel fashion, Cohen understood ethics not as primarily addressing the individual but in its fullest sense as summoning society to the task of molding the future according to the principle of a rationally determined, a priori *ought.* According to Cohen's most mature conception of faith and ritual, however, religion—in contradistinction to ethics—does not address the individual merely as representative of rational humanity; rather, it appertains to the individual as such, especially through the notion of sin, which Cohen understood as the individual's anguished realization of his or her own moral failings. This consciousness of sin, Cohen observed, bears the danger that the individual will despair of his or her own moral worth and abandon all subsequent moral effort. The self-estrangement attendant to sin requires the concept of a forbearing God who by the act of forgiveness serves to reintegrate the individual into an ethically committed humanity. The atonement of sin is not effected by God's grace but by the individual, who in acknowledging God's forgiveness becomes rededicated to the moral task.

Religion is thus preeminently a series of acts of atonement—rites and prayers expressing remorse and repentance and focused on the belief in a merciful, forgiving God. To Cohen, the reconciliation between God and humans thus achieved requires, in turn, that God be conceived not as an idea but as a being who relates to the finite, ever-changing world of becoming, of which humans are a part. Despite the fundamental ontological distinction separating them, being and becoming are interrelated through what Cohen called *correlation.* God and humans are correlated when the individual cognizant of God's mercy—God's love and concern—personally rededicates to emulating in his or her actions these divine qualities. Cohen spoke of correlation as a shared holiness in which God and humans are coworkers in the work of creation.

Cohen set forth these views in his posthumously published volume, *Religion der Vernunft aus den Quellen des Judentums* (1919, 1929; translated in 1995 as *Religion of Reason out of the Sources of Judaism*). In it he expounds his new conception of religion through a selective exegesis of the sources of classical Judaism in the Bible, the midrash, liturgy, and medieval Jewish philosophy. These traditional expressions of Jewish piety, Cohen avers, exemplify the most refined conception of religion.

The emerging portrait of Judaism as a faith of deep, personal significance has suggested to many commentators that Cohen anticipated the existentialist theology characteristic of much of twentieth-century Jewish thought, with its emphasis on the dialogic relation of the individual with a living, personal God. Cohen, however, continued to speak of the religion of reason, and his God remained the rational God of ethics. And although in a striking revision of his Kantian premises he accorded religion (defined by prayer) and ritual intrinsic significance, he still did not quite regard it as an utterly independent reality enjoying a unique ontological and epistemological status. Although not entirely absorbed into ethics, the religion of reason was for Cohen ultimately ancillary to ethics. Religion—and Judaism in particular—is conceived as an instrument for enhancing moral consciousness (i.e., moral reason) and commitment: It facilitates the acceptance of the kingdom of God.

JUDAISM AND RELIGIOUS EXISTENTIALISM. Despite the fact that Cohen's concept of correlation does indeed outline some important features of twentieth-century religious existentialism, his overarching moral theology renders him more a son of the previous century. Moral reason for Cohen was the heart of religion, and thus not surprisingly he identified it with revelation: "Revelation is the creation of Reason" (*Religion of Reason,* 1995, p. 72). This identification of reason and revelation was typical of nineteenth-century philosophical idealism.

Solomon Ludwig Steinheim. For religious existentialists the point of departure was revelation understood as a metarational category pointing to God's spontaneous and gracious address to the finite human. In this respect, the transitional figure from nineteenth- to twentieth-century Jewish thought is not Cohen but the little-known lay scholar Solomon Ludwig Steinheim (1789–1866). A physician by profession, Steinheim was not affiliated with any ideological camp within the Jewish community in his native Germany; indeed, he spent the last twenty years of his life mostly in Rome, isolated from organized Jewish life. As Hans Joachim Schoeps noted in *Vom Bleibenden und Vergänglichen im Judentum,* Steinheim was "the first [truly] Jewish theologian of the modern age. . . . He was twenty years too late, and one hundred years too early" (Schoeps, 1935, p. 81). If one views Jewish thought from Mendelssohn to Cohen as a sustained effort to interpret Judaism as a religion of reason par excellence, then Steinheim stands alone in the nineteenth century.

In his monumental study *Offenbarung nach dem Lehrbegriff der Synagoge* (Revelation according to the doctrine of the synagogue), Steinheim sought to remove religion from the tutelage of reason, maintaining that religious truths are the gift of supernatural revelation. In a manner recalling Søren Kierkegaard's (1813–1855) critique of Hegel, he held that the truths disclosed by revelation are incompatible with and irreducible to reason. Furthermore, the concept of supernatural revelation posits God as the creator who, unbounded by necessity, creates the world freely and out of nothing. As such, revelation confirms the irrefragable human experience of freedom that reason—burdened as it is by the principle of universal necessity perforce—denies. Accordingly, reason must acknowledge the primacy of revelation.

In that God is the logical presupposition of revelation, Steinheim observed, the affirmation of the possibility of revelation implicitly reestablishes the dignity and authority of God: "Our task is to present revelation [such that] we are constrained . . . to accept God. Therefore, it is for us to make a declaration the exact opposite of Mendelssohn's and to prove the Old Testament was given not to reveal law but the living God" (Steinheim, 1835, vol. 2, p. 38). Revelation, therefore, has a unique epistemic status, and its conceptual content corresponds to the postulates of Kant's moral reason: God, freedom, and immortality. It also follows that for Steinheim not only are these postulates granted in revelation, but that also the categorical imperatives of morality derive their authority from God and revealed will. Judaism represents the ideal ethical religion, for its moral code is commanded by the living God. Steinheim's conclusions regarding Judaism are hence not unlike those of other nineteenth-century Jewish thinkers; the crucial difference is that, for him, Judaism is a fact of supernatural revelation.

Franz Rosenzweig. Significantly, the philosophy of Franz Rosenzweig (1886–1929), whose path to Judaism from the midst of assimilation has become emblematic of much of twentieth-century Jewish religious thought, is grounded in his adoption of what he calls *Offenbarungsglaube,* a belief in revelation as a historical and existential reality. Such a belief must be the fulcrum of any genuine theology; otherwise, as Rosenzweig observes in his first essay on religious matters, "Atheistic Theology" (1914, but first published after his death), one arrives at the strange anthropocentric brew concocted by the nineteenth century, which by placing religion within the realm of human sensibility alone—be it called spiritual experience, moral consciousness, or national soul—is in effect godless. Theology, he contended, must proceed from the theocentric fact of divine revelation, the fact of God's address to humans. Rosenzweig developed his understanding of this address on the basis of a radical critique of philosophical idealism, with its quest for universal, timeless, abstract truths. In contrast to the logical reasoning of the philosophers, revelation is in time; it is an occurrence whereby God establishes a relation with specific time-bound individuals. Phenomenologically, this relation is what is celebrated in biblical tradition as love: the divine sounding of "Thou" to the temporally contingent "I" of the individual. God addresses the individual in his or her finite existence, calling each individual, as it were, by his or her "first and last name," which distinguishes each person existentially from all others. In revelation, the contingent existence of the individual is thus confirmed in love and blessed with the kiss of eternity.

Occurring in time, revelation is hence inaccessible to a reason that considers only timeless essences. Yet this conception does not contradict reason but merely delimits its sphere of validity. Properly understood, philosophical reason and faith are complementary. This affirmation of revelation allowed Rosenzweig to discern in Judaism what many of his generation of assimilated German Jews had denied—that Judaism was a theocentric faith of enduring existential significance. He elaborated his conception of faith and Judaism in his 1921 work *Stern der Erlösung* (Star of redemption).

Later, Rosenzweig sought to incorporate into his life and thought more and more extraliturgical aspects of traditional Judaism, from the commandment of keeping a kosher kitchen to that of Torah study. His approach to the *mitsvot*, however, was distinctive. Unlike Orthodox Jews, he could not accept the *mitsvot* on the basis of rabbinic authority, for, as he once remarked, "religion based on authority is equal to unbelief" (cited in Rosenstock-Huessy, 1971, p. 166). His approach to the Law, as he explained in a now-famous open letter to Martin Buber (1878–1965), was to encourage each individual Jew to explore the sacramental and existential possibilities of the *mitsvot* so as to determine which of these precepts he or she personally feels called on to fulfill. In an article entitled "The Builders: Concerning the Law," Rosenzweig further elaborated his position to Buber with reference to a rabbinic commentary to *Isaiah* 54:13, arguing that humans are not only God's obedient children (*banayikh*) but also "Your builders" *(bonayikh)*. As such, every generation has the opportunity—indeed, the task—to re-create for itself the Law (Glatzer, 1965, p. 72).

Rosenzweig's nondogmatic brand of traditionalism was, and continues to serve as, a guide to many who seek to reappropriate traditional forms of Jewish piety and to affirm Judaism as a relation to a living God. Furthermore, Rosenzweig inspired the serious, nonapologetic theological reflection characteristic of much Jewish religious thought in the twentieth century. Among those he most decisively inspired was his friend Buber, who emerged as a genuine religious thinker only with the publication of *I and Thou* (1923). Buber's previous writings on spiritual matters, Jewish and otherwise, belonged to a genre of Romantic mysticism that Rosenzweig had in mind when he wrote "Atheistic Theology"; these writings were virtually devoid of any reference to the God of revelation. With his treatise on I–Thou, or dialogic, relations Buber affirmed faith as grounded in the revealed word of God, and in so doing he developed a novel conception of revelation.

Martin Buber. For Buber, revelation is homologous with what he called dialogue. God, the Eternal Thou, addresses one through the varied life experiences—from the seemingly ephemeral and trivial to the grand and momentous—that demand a dialogic response, or a confirmation of the Thou, the unique presence, of the other who stands before one. In uttering "Thou" (the actual act of speech is superfluous), the self, or I, in turn finds its own presence confirmed. As a response to the continuously renewing presence and address of another, dialogue must be born ever anew. The I–Thou response thus requires spontaneity and cannot be determined by fixed expressions, gestures, and formulations. It also follows that God's address, as being refracted (revealed) through the addressing presence of the Thou who stands before one likewise, requires such spontaneity. Buber further contends that authentic service to God is found only in such a spontaneous response to the Eternal Thou, who turns to humans through the flux of life's ever-changing circumstances. Although not utterly dismissing prayer and ritual as bearing the possibility of spontaneous and hence authentic relation to God, Buber does not regard them as paradigmatic forms of religious service.

Clearly such a conception of divine revelation conflicts radically with the classical Jewish conception of a historical revelation (viz., the Torah) enjoying preeminence and enduring authority. Furthermore, Buber's antagonism toward liturgical prayer and the *mitsvot* as the proper form of divine service conflicts not only with tradition but also with all expressions of institutional Jewish religious life.

Acknowledging his anomalous position within Jewish religious thought, Buber insisted that he was not in a formal sense a theologian. He claimed he sought neither to justify revealed propositions about God nor to defend revealed scriptures and doctrine. He simply pointed to dialogue as a meta-ethical principle determining the life responses of an individual, ensuring that these responses will be informed by love and justice and crowned with existential meaning (i.e., the confirmation of the Thou). He taught that this principle is at the heart of all great spiritual traditions, but particularly that of Judaism. The concept of dialogue can thus be employed as a hermeneutical principle by which to read the Hebrew Bible and other formative religious texts in the Jewish tradition, such as those of Hasidism.

As a particular community of faith, Judaism is, in Buber's view, distinguished by its millennial and clarion witness to the dialogic principle both in its collective memory (enshrined in its central myths and sacred texts) and, ideally, in its current institutions. In fact, as a Zionist, Buber held that Jewish religious life in the Diaspora had been falsely restricted to the synagogue and the home, thus losing hold of the founding dialogic principle of Judaism and its comprehensive purview of divine service. By restoring to the Jews the sociological conditions of a full communal life, Zionism allows for the possibility that the Jews' public life, guided by the principle of dialogue, will once again become the essential realm of their relation to God. The reappropriation of the public sphere as the dialogic responsibility of the community of faith is consonant with the supreme injunction of the prophets of Israel and thus constitutes the renewal of what Buber called Hebrew, or biblical, humanism.

Buber's religious anarchism and often radical politics alienated him from many Jews committed to traditional forms of worship and conventional positions. Yet his philosophy of dialogue has manifestly inspired others, especially those eager for extrasynagogal expressions of Jewish spirituality. Furthermore, his—and Rosenzweig's—conception of dialogue as a way of reading sacred texts (viz., recognizing the divine voice in a text without necessarily accepting the written word uncritically) has had a seminal effect on contemporary Jewish studies and hermeneutical attitudes. Critical historical scholarship therefore need not be bound to antiquarian presuppositions or lead inevitably to a barren relativism. Guided by a dialogical hermeneutic, historiography and philology may be employed to bare anew the inner, eternal truth of Judaism. The dean of Jewish studies in the twentieth century, Gershom Scholem (1897–1982), for example, regarded *Wissenschaft des Judentums* as a means of uncovering dimensions and expressions of Jewish spirituality that may have been suppressed by Orthodoxy and, later in the nineteenth century, by apologetics in defense of specific conceptions of normative Judaism. Precisely because of its objective, nonprescriptive mode of inquiry, *Wissenschaft des Judentums* is capable of covering the full canvas of Jewish spiritual options to inspire religious renewal. To this end, Scholem devoted his prodigious scholarship to researching the surprisingly ramified and hitherto little-known or misperceived Jewish mystical tradition, Qabbalah.

Zionism and Religious Renewal. Like Buber, Scholem was a Zionist or, more precisely, a follower of Aḥad ha-ʿAm (1856–1927; literally, "one of the people"—the pen-name of Asher Ginzberg) and his vision of Zionism as effecting the reconstruction of Judaism as a secular, spiritually revitalized national culture. Having abandoned the religious Orthodoxy of his Hasidic upbringing in Russia, Aḥad ha-ʿAm was acutely aware of the spiritual crisis afflicting his generation of Jews, whose fidelity Judaism as a religious faith had ceased to engage. In ever-increasing numbers, young Jews were being drawn to the secular-humanist culture of the West—a culture, in Aḥad ha-ʿAm's judgment, whose intellectual, ethical, and aesthetic power one could not deny. In that the secular humanism of the contemporary world was sponsored by non-Jewish languages and national communities, the adoption of this new culture, by its nature, entailed a weakening of one's ties to the Jewish people and culture. To stem the consequent tide of assimilation, Aḥad ha-ʿAm taught that Judaism must be reformulated as a secular culture grounded in the autochthonous humanist values of Judaism (e.g., the ethical teachings of the Bible and the prophets) and in Hebrew as the national language of the Jewish people. In Zion, a culturally autonomous, Hebrew-speaking community would arise and, by force of the example of its spiritually vital and creative culture, inspire the Jews of the Diaspora to adjust Judaism to the new secular reality and at the same time maintain a firm Jewish national consciousness. For Aḥad ha-ʿAm the prevailing secularism implied an irrevocable eclipse of religious faith and culture; for Buber, Scholem, and other cultural Zionists, secularism was but a necessary historical stage that did not preclude the possible renewal of Judaism as a meaningful religious faith.

The idea of Zionism as a framework for the development of a Jewish religious humanism also inspired the teachings of Aharon David Gordon (1856–1922). One of the most remarkable figures in modern Jewish religious thought, Gordon discerned unique religious possibilities in Zionism, particularly in the ethos of the idealistic pioneers (*halutsim*), the select band of youths who, beginning in the 1890s, had gone to Palestine to prepare the Land of Israel for the ingathering of the exiles. At nearly the age of fifty, Gordon reliquished the comforts of affluence and bourgeois eminence in his native Russia and joined the youthful *halutsim* in the labor of draining the swamps and tilling the soil. Working tirelessly by day, this Jewish Tolstoy would write at night, exploring the religious significance of the pioneering endeavor. With a weave of Qabbalistic and Hasidic doctrine and Russian populist ideas about the pristine dignity of the peasantry and a life rooted in nature, Gordon developed a mystical pantheism in which he celebrated agricultural labor as a supreme act of personal, national, and cosmic redemption. Toil on the land, he taught, integrates one into the organic rhythms of nature and the universe. The resulting experience of the unity and purpose of the cosmos is the core religious experience—an experience that, he believed, had been largely denied to the Jews of the Diaspora. This cosmic experience ultimately leads one to God, regardless of one's intellectual attitude. For Gordon, an authentic relation to God has nothing to do with formal religious beliefs and ritual practices. In noting that God or the hidden mystery of the cosmos is approached through physical, especially agraian labor, he was quick to point out that biblical Hebrew employs the same word (viz., *ʿavodah*) to designate both work and divine worship.

Orthodox Jews have also seen Zionism as bearing extensive religious significance. The first chief rabbi of Palestine, Avraham Yitsḥaq Kook (1865–1935), was also profoundly inspired by the *halutsim,* whom, despite their often demonstrative irreligiosity, he regarded as instruments of God's *Heilsplan* (plan of salvation). Judging history from the perspective of the Qabbalistic teaching that external events are but symbols of a deeper, hidden reality, he interpreted the secular actions of the *halutsim* on behalf of the Jewish people's restoration to Zion as symbolically reflecting a divinely appointed cosmic process of restoring a fragmented world to its primal harmony. Kook, in general, saw the heightened secular movement of the modern world toward social and scientific progress as part of a providential design to quicken the eschatological conclusion of history with the return of the Jews to their ancient domicile as but the most glorious symbol of the eschaton.

Not all Orthodox Jews' support for Zionism was motivated by eschatological considerations. The principal theological motive prompting the founding of Mizrahi, the movement of religious Zionists created in 1902 by Yitsḥaq Yaʿaqov Reines (1839–1915) was a decidedly mundane endorsement of Theodor Herzl's (1860–1904) program of Jewish political sovereignty as a solution to anti-Semitism. Furthermore, Mizrahi welcomed the normalization of Jewish political and social life envisioned by Zionism as encouraging *halakhah* (Jewish religious law) to expand beyond the lamentably circumscribed scope allowed it by the conditions prevailing in the Diaspora. The prophetic vigor of the Torah would thus be restored as the comprehensive matrix of a holy and just life for the Jewish people.

The establishment of the State of Israel in 1948 generated special theological problems for Orthodox Jewish supporters of Zionism, foremost with respect to the messianic significance of the restoration of Jewish patrimony to the

Land of Israel. Many regard this as a miraculous event that pointed to the imminent advent of the Messiah and divine redemption. In the flush of messianic euphoria, the chief rabbis of the nascent state took the rare step of introducing a new prayer into the traditional liturgy, blessing God for causing "the beginning of redemption to flower." To be sure, a significant minority of Orthodox opinion continues to oppose Zionism, precisely because of what it deems to be the movement's messianic pretensions and its seemingly arrogant attempt to preempt God's judgment and redemptive deeds. On the other hand, Orthodox Jews who support Zionism and yet are unwilling to view its political achievements in eschatological terms are obliged to reckon with the absence of traditional theological categories to comprehend the anomalous situation posed by the reestablishment of Jewish political sovereignty in Zion as a process that is not the work of the divinely appointed Messiah.

Since the early 1940s these issues have acquired a sharp focus and popular attention through the sustained and invariably controversial efforts of Yeshayahu Leibowitz (1903–1993), a professor in biological chemistry at the Hebrew University of Jerusalem. A religiously observant and learned Jew, Leibowitz had—since his emigration to Palestine in 1935 from his native Latvia via Switzerland and Germany, where he earned degrees in medicine and chemistry—been a proponent of an approach to Zionist and religious questions that is rigorously rational and free from what he regarded as platitudes and sentimental pieties. For Leibowitz, Zionism and the State of Israel have no messianic import; he regarded messianism as fundamentally a folkloristic accretion to Judaism that is best ignored by serious, God-fearing Jews. He was particularly fond of citing Maimonides' admonition in his *Mishneh Torah* that one ought not preoccupy oneself with messianic speculations, for "they lead neither to fear [of God] nor to love [of Him]" (*Kings and Laws* 12.2).

Furthermore, Leibowitz argued, those who ascribe religious or any other intrinsic value to the state are committing the cardinal sin of idolatry (*'avodah zarah;* the worship of false gods). Leibowitz thus refused to regard Zionism as a religious phenomenon but viewed it simply as a movement for the political liberation of the Jewish people. He called on religious Jews to rejoice in this fact and greet the Zionist state as providing the framework for a fuller expression of *halakhah* and the Jewish people's religious vocation. He conceived of this vocation in strictly theocentric terms. By accepting the Torah and its commandments, Jews are foremost God's servants and not vice versa. Service to God must be for its own sake, without regard for spiritual, moral, or material enhancement. Judaism is not meant to render the Jews happier, more noble, or more prosperous. Even the perfection of society and history are extraneous to Judaism. (Although Leibowitz did not object to humanistic and progressive political endeavors, he insisted these are in the realm of humans and their fallible judgment and thus are not to be theologically sanctified.) Although he recurrently appealed to the authority of Maimonides, Leibowitz's theological position also betrays the decisive influence of Kant, Kierkegaard, and Karl Barth (1886–1968). His severe, almost priestly view of Judaism has evoked considerable, seminal discussion within both religious and secular circles of contemporary Israel.

JUDAISM AND THE AMERICAN EXPERIENCE. The reentry of the Jews into history as a sovereign nation has profoundly affected Jewish self-perception everywhere. In North America, Jewish thought is most strikingly distinguished by the effort to accommodate the new understanding of Jewish peoplehood, correlating it with the unique experience of life in an unambiguously free and pluralistic society. Mordecai M. Kaplan (1881–1983) developed a conception of Judaism that boldly articulates these apparently contrasting poles of the contemporary American Jewish reality. Regarding himself as a follower of Aḥad ha-'Am's cultural Zionism, Kaplan affirmed the centrality of the Land of Israel in Jewish life while upholding the creative and social viability of the Diaspora. In light of the secular definition of Jewish peoplehood legitimated by Zionism, Kaplan redefined Judaism as a civilization, a designation that allowed him to conceive of Judaism in the broadest social and cultural terms. As a civilization, Judaism is thus not in the first instance a system of religious beliefs and practices but the life of the Jewish people. The civilization of Judaism is religious in that it is set in a distinctive religious universe of discourse with a body of shared symbolic gestures and rituals.

Kaplan's understanding of religion and God, however, is neither traditional nor theistic. Indebted to the philosophical pragmatism of the American educator John Dewey (1859–1952), Kaplan viewed God as a functional concept pointing to a nonpersonal and nonmetaphysical power or process in the universe that bespeaks order, justice, and goodness and on which humans must rely to fulfill their destiny as human beings. This "Godhood of the cosmos" is a transnaturalistic principle: It is not a supernatural entity, nor is it to be understood simply as a metaphorical reification of human possibilities; it is, rather, an ontological concept that is continually being refined as human civilization advances on all fronts of knowledge—in the physical and normative sciences and in the imaginative arts. Religion and God thus have, for Kaplan, an ever-evolving pragmatic function of enhancing human well-being and dignity by "orienting us to life and eliciting from us the best of which we are capable" (*Judaism as Civilization,* p. 317).

Religion also has the more specifically sociological function of articulating and reenacting through certain ritualized practices (not necessarily liturgical or devotional) the collective self-consciousness and memory of its constituent community. As such, religion serves to foster the community's sense of historical continuity and shared values. Judaism so understood is unabashedly anthropocentric and humanistic. Moreover, as a religion that exists for the Jewish people and not vice versa (cf. Leibowitz), Judaism is not to be construed as a heteronomous discipline of ritual and codes, nor are its beliefs to be amplified catechistically.

Lest Judaism fail the contemporary Jew, Kaplan averred, it must respect each Jew's democratic and this-worldly temperament. Judaism therefore must be projected as an ongoing discourse that eschews all anachronistic, supernatural constructs of traditional religion and allows for diversity of opinion, especially with respect to questions of ultimate existential significance, such as the meaning of suffering, death, and evil. The specific theological function of Judaism, however, is to give focus to the needs and mutual responsibilities of the Jews as a people. Although the movement associated with Kaplan's conception of Judaism, known as Reconstructionism, has remained relatively small, Kaplan has given expression to the emerging folk religion of American Jewry, irrespective of formal denominational affiliation.

Whereas the ideology of Kaplan's Reconstructionism may have given expression to the regnant naturalism and ethnic orientation of American Jewry, the same community has paradoxically demanded of its religious elite (i.e., its rabbinical leadership) a theology that articulates, with due modifications, the theocentric, supernatural convictions that have classically defined Judaism. The image of Judaism even for the most theologically naturalist would seem to require a supernatural definition. Herein lies the explanation of why Reconstructionism, despite its fidelity to the folk religion of American Jewry, has remained numerically insignificant, and hence this also explains the receptivity of American Jews to the theocentric teachings of Buber and Rosenzweig.

European-educated religious thinkers, anchored in traditional Judaism and theological conviction, have also found in America a supportive environment. Emigrating to the United States in 1940, Abraham Joshua Heschel (1907–1972), a Polish-born descendent of Hasidic masters, developed for an appreciative American audience a lyrical theology that is more a persuasive personal witness than a conceptual argument. He presents a phenomenological explication of his own experience and prophetic consciousness. Blending Hasidic spirituality, which he held as resonating the innermost truths of traditional Jewish faith, with nuanced Western learning, Heschel sought to elaborate a conception of piety relevant to the contemporary Jew. Noting that the aptitude for faith of Western society has been dulled by technological, bourgeois civilization, in his writings Heschel endeavored to reawaken the *sensus numinus*—the a priori sense of wonder and awe evoked by the mystery of life, which he, with Rudolf Otto (1869–1937), regarded as the font of faith—by introducing his readers to the Hasidic-Qabbalistic teaching that all reality refracts the divine presence.

The life of traditional Jewish piety governed by *halakhah,* according to Heschel, creates an inner, holy reality that heightens one's sense of the divine presence. As a system of deeds, *halakhah* has also ritualized the prophetic teaching that faith is ultimately a leap of action: The individual responds to God's presence by making God's work his or her own. Indeed, the covenantal relation between God and Israel implies an intimate partnership between humans and God. The prophets, Heschel emphasized, were particularly conscious of the intimate, passionate relation between humans and God: An individual's sins anger and sadden God, and because the individual both fears and loves God, he or she resolves to bring God joy by sharing in God's work to crown creation with justice and compassion.

Despite his conviction that the prophetic consciousness captured the heart of traditional Judaism, Heschel's thought found its primary resonance not among the adherents of *halakhah* but among those Jews in need of an interpretation of Judaism that would authenticate their participation as Jews in the humane causes of their generation. Heschel's message of prophetic concern and responsibility spoke to a generation of American Jews in the 1960s and 1970s who felt themselves called on as Jews to join the struggle on behalf of civil rights for African Americans and to oppose the Vietnam War, which they regarded as unjust.

American-educated Orthodox Jews who are sensitive to the philosophical and religious questions raised by the contemporary West found their voice in Joseph Baer Soloveitchik (1903–1993), a descendant of renowned Lithuanian rabbis. Emigrating to the United States in 1932, he became one of the twentieth century's most esteemed Talmudists; he spoke with rare authority within the Orthodox community, pondering from the perspective of one firmly and unapologetically grounded in *halakhah* those questions generated by what he regarded as the ambiguous position of people of faith in a technological, pragmatic civilization shaped by pronouncedly secular bias. Assuming the self-evident validity of Judaism and religious faith, Soloveitchik did not challenge the premises of technological civilization but, rather, chose to defend within the context of that civilization the integrity of what he termed "the halakhic man." He achieved this by a phenomenological description of the religious consciousness of the halakhic man, elaborating his exposition with insights garnered from a subtle reading of modern philosophy, especially neo-Kantianism and existentialism. He concluded that those who follow the halakhic way are not antagonistic to the moral and cognitive concerns of the technological society; however, whereas the latter requires a social and gregarious personality, the halakhic follower accepts the individual's existential loneliness, overcoming the attendant isolation and anxiety through a redemptive love of God and Torah. The congregation of Jews forged by the Torah is a covenantal community that respects the solitary, existential reality of each of its members, who are joined to God and each other in a common covenantal relation sacrally objectified by the *halakhah.*

The European Jewish intellectual heritage has also inspired a generation of American-born Jewish religious thinkers, including Eugene B. Borowitz (b. 1924), Arthur A. Cohen (1928–1986), Will Herberg (1902–1977), David Hartman (b. 1931), Jakob J. Petuchowski (b. 1925), Richard L. Rubenstein (b. 1924), and Milton Steinberg (1903–1950). Characteristically, the writings of these individuals have been largely interpretative commentaries on the thought of their European predecessors. This dependence may be indicative not only of a pervasive sense of being the indebted heirs of the European intellectual tradition, but also of a portentous feeling of being their survivors. The tragic, catastrophic end of European Jewry created, in the words of Arthur Cohen, a profound caesura (a sudden silencing of sound) in Jewish collective and personal existence, engendering a sense of inconsolable mourning and obligation.

In reflecting on the tragedy of the Nazi era and its theological implications for the surviving remnant of Jewry, American Jews have been at their most original and probing. The resulting theology of the Holocaust may in many respects be viewed as a theology of survival—a theology that seeks to affirm the obligations of the remnant of Jewry to survive somehow as Jews. Auschwitz, according to Emil L. Fackenheim (1916–2003) issues a commandment to Jews to endure and to ensure the survival of Judaism. This commandment has also inspired the slow but impressive reconstruction of European Jewry, which has likewise witnessed the renewal of Jewish religious thought, most notably represented by Louis Jacobs (b. 1920) in England and Emmanuel Lévinas (1906–1995) in France.

Lévinas, one of the most esteemed philosophers of post–World War II France, represents a continuation of the existentialist thought pioneered by Rosenzweig and Buber. Employing the metaphysical phenomenology he developed as a critique of Edmund Husserl's (1859–1938) and Martin Heidegger's (1889–1976) concept of "the other," Lévinas sought to illuminate the religious meaning of Judaism. The moral experience of the other, borne by a compelling sense of responsibility toward that other, is the only genuine knowledge that can be attained of the other. Lévinas contrasts the antihumanistic tendency of Western culture, which masquerades as liberty but which is in fact bereft of responsibility for the other, with the biblical concept, especially as elaborated by the rabbis, of "a difficult liberty" (the title of his most important collection of essays on Judaism, *Difficile Liberté*). The Jew obtains transcendence, and thus liberty, by paradoxically living under God's law, which requires of the Jew ethical and social responsibility for the other. The biblical person, Lévinas observes with oblique reference to Heidegger, discovers a fellow person before anything else. As the custodian of biblical humanism, Lévinas avers, Judaism defiantly proclaims to the contemporary world that liberty entails responsibility and obligation.

For all Jewish thinkers who regard themselves as living in the shadow of Auschwitz, the State of Israel, born on the morrow of the Nazi nightmare, is the overarching symbol of Jewish survival and resolve to endure. Survival is affirmed, however, not simply in defiance of Satan and Satan's zealous agents but, rather, as an existential commitment to the God of Israel. Despite their horror and anguish, it is held, Jews must affirm God as the author of a purposeful and good universe. Fackenheim cites the Psalmist: "I shall not die but live, and declare the works of God" (*Ps.* 18:17).

This affirmation of Judaism as a living faith has led an increasing number of younger Jews—particularly, but not only, in America—to reappropriate the study of sacred Jewish texts as the axis of Jewish spirituality. Inspired by postmodernism and its critique of the Enlightenment's quest for one objective truth, these thinkers wish to revalorize Judaism as a community of study in which its foundational texts are continuously reinterpreted with no claim to the absolute validity of one's reading. The study of these texts and their inexhausitble interpretation is said to renew the traditional understanding of Torah study—broadly called midrash—as the principal medium of Israel's covenantal relation with God and God's revealed Word. As David Stern observes, Midrash was for the rabbis—and for their postmodern heirs—"a kind of conversation" enabling God "to speak to them from between the lines of Scripture, in the textual fissures and discontinuities that exegesis discovers" (Stern, 1996, p. 31).

See Also Holocaust, article on Jewish Theological Responses; Jewish Studies; Zionism.

Bibliography

An admirably lucid introduction to the major figures and themes of modern Jewish thought is provided in Robert M. Seltzer, *Jewish People, Jewish Thought: The Jewish Experience in History* (New York, 1980), chaps. 12, 13, 15, and 16. A nuanced weave of intellectual and social history, this volume illuminatingly places the development of Jewish thought within its cultural and historical context. A more strictly philosophical survey of the major protagonists of modern Jewish thought is Steven T. Katz, ed., *Jewish Philosophers* (New York, 1975). This volume is a useful compilation of articles on Jewish philosophers from the ancient period to the present that originally appeared in the *Encyclopaedia Judaica* (1971). The editor concludes the volume with a concise review of Jewish thought since 1945, dealing extensively with Heschel, Soloveitchik, post-Holocaust theologians, and other contemporary voices.

For authoritative scholarly analyses, which the general reader might find occasionally arcane, see Julius Guttmann, *Philosophies of Judaism: The History of Jewish Philosophy from Biblical Times to Franz Rosenzweig*, translated by David W. Silverman, with an introduction by R. J. Zwi Werblowsky (New York, 1964) and Nathan Rotenstreich, *Jewish Philosophy in Modern Times: From Mendelssohn to Rosenzweig* (New York, 1968). With somewhat less attention to philosophical detail, Heinz M. Graupe's *The Rise of Modern Judaism: An Intellectual History of German Jewry*, translated by John Robinson (Huntington, N.Y., 1978) provides an excellent and thorough discussion of the cultural history of Jewish thought in Germany from Mendelssohn to Rosenzweig. Graupe has also provided an excellent bibliography of the relevant German-language literature.

The best biography of Mendelssohn is Alexander Altmann's magisterial *Moses Mendelssohn: A Biographical Study* (University, Ala., 1973). Altmann has also written a most instructive introduction and commentary to Mendelssohn's *Jerusalem, or on Religion and Power in Judaism* (1783), translated by Allan Arkush (Hanover, N.H., 1983).

The impact of Kant, Schelling, and Hegel is subtly traced in Nathan Rotenstreich's *Jews and German Philosophy: the Polemics of Emancipation* (New York, 1984). Immanuel Kant's *Religion within the Limits of Reason Alone* (1793), translated with an introduction and notes by Theodore M. Greene and Hoyt H. Hudson (New York, 1960) provides a primary source for readers.

Fundamental documents with commentary of the *Wissenschaft des Judentums* may be found in Paul R. Mendes-Flohr and Jehuda Reinharz, *The Jew in the Modern World: A Documentary History,* 2d ed., rev. (Oxford, 1995), chap. 5. Ideological issues surrounding the founding of modern Jewish scholarship are discussed at length in Michael A. Meyer, *The Origin of the Modern Jew: Jewish Identity and Europoean Culture in Germany, 1749–1824* (Detroit, 1967), chap. 6. The problems posed to Jewish thought by *Wissenschaft des Judentums* and historicism are considered both historically and analytically in Nathan Rotenstreich, *Tradition and Reality: The Impact of History on Modern Jewish Thought* (New York, 1972), chaps. 2–4. Historical memory and the modern Jewish imagination are sensitively discussed in Yosef Hayim Yerushalmi, *Zakhor: Jewish History and Jewish Memory,* 2d ed. (New York, 1989), chap. 4. The relation between Jewish historiography and philosophies of Jewish history is the subject of Lionel Kochan, *The Jew and His History* (New York, 1977).

Hermann Cohen's basic Jewish writings are available in *Religion of Reason out of the Sources of Judaism* (1919), translated and with an introduction by Simon Kaplan, 2d ed. (Atlanta, 1995) and *Reason and Hope: Selections from the Jewish Writings of Hermann Cohen,* translated and edited by Eva Jospe (New York, 1971). For a sample of Gordon's writings, see Arthur Hertzberg, ed., *The Zionist Idea,* pp. 368–386 (New York, 1969). For an examination of Mordecai Kaplan's Reconstructionism, see Charles S. Liebman, "Reconstructionism in American Jewish Life," *American Jewish Year Book* 71 (1970): 3–99. Kaplan's most comprehensive presentation of his program is *Judaism as a Civilization: Toward a Reconstruction of American Jewish Life* (New York, 1936, reprint 1981).

Although the writings of Ludwig Steinheim are unfortunately not available in English, each of the above-mentioned general surveys of modern Jewish thought provides an overview of his thought. For a German reading, see Solomon Ludwig Steinheim, *Offenbarung nach dem Lehrbegriff der Synagoge* [Revelation according to the Doctrine of the Synagogue], 4 vols. (Frankfurt, Germany, 1835). For a detailed and critical examination of Steinheim's unique theological position, see Heinz M. Graupe's *The Rise of Modern Judaism* (Huntington, N.Y., 1978), pp. 231ff., and Joshua O. Haberman's "Solomon Ludwig Steinheim's Doctrine of Revelation," *Judaism* 17 (Winter 1968): 22–41. One should also consult the remarkable collection of essays in Hans Joachim Schoeps, Heinz Mosche Graupe, and Gerd-Hesse Goeman, eds., *Salomon Ludwig Steinheim zum Gedenken* (Leiden, 1966). Also see Hans Joachim Schoeps, *Vom Bleibenden und Vergänglichen im Judentum* (Berlin, 1935).

The best introduction to Rosenzweig remains Nahum N. Glatzer, *Franz Rosenzweig: His Life and Thought,* 3d ed. (Indianapolis, 1998). The most sustained and careful analysis of Rosenzweig's thought is Stéphane Mosès, *System and Revelation. The Philosophy of Franz Rosenzweig* (Detroit, 1992), which also includes a comprehensive bibliography of Rosenzweig's works in translation as well as the scholarly secondary literature. For primary readings, see Franz Rosenzweig, *Kleinere Schriften* (Berlin, 1937); *Stern der Erlösung* (Frankfurt, Germany, 1921), which was later published in English as *The Star Of Redemption,* translated by Barbara E. Galli (Madison, Wis., 2004); "The Builders: Concerning the Law," in *On Jewish Learning,* edited by Nahum N. Glatzer, pp. 72–92 (New York, 1965); and E. Rosenstock-Huessy, ed., *Judaism despite Christianity* (New York, 1971).

Buber's writings are widely available in English, and commentaries on his thought constitute a veritable library. Two excellent bibliographical guides to this literature are of immeasurable value: Margot Cohn and Rafael Buber, *Martin Buber: A Bibliography of His Writings, 1897–1978* (Jerusalem, 1980) and Willard Moonon, *Martin Buber and His Critics: An Annotated Bibliography of Writings in English through 1978* (New York, 1981). For a synoptic view of Buber's thought, see Maurice Friedman, *Martin Buber's Life and Thought,* 3 vols. (New York, 1981–1984). For a direct reading, see Martin Burber, *I and Thou,* translated with prologue and notes by Walter Kaufmann (New York, 1970).

For a representative selection of Leibowitz's writings, see Yeshayahu Leibowitz, *Judaism, Human Values, and the Jewish State,* edited by E. Goldman (Cambridge, Mass., 1992).

Lévinas has gathered his essays on Jewish themes in his *Difficult Freedom: Essays on Judaism,* translated by Sean Hand (Baltimore, 1990). For his reflections on Judaism, presented through weekly lessons on select passages of the Talmud and other rabbinic writings, see his *Nine Talmudic Readitings,* translated with introduction by Richard Al Cohen (Pittsburgh, 1999). For comprehensive discussions of Lévinas's conception of Judaism, see two works by Richard A. Cohen: "Emmanuel Lévinas," in Steven T. Katz, ed., *Intrerpretations of Judaism in the Twentieth Century,* pp. 205–228 (Washington, D.C., 1993) and *Elevations: The Heights of the Good in Levinas and Rosenzweig* (Chicago, 1994), as well as Robert Gibbs, *Correlations in Rosenzweig and Levinas* (Princeton, N.J., 1992). For a concise but judicious introduction to the issues of twentieth-century Jewish thought, with specific focus on Hermann Cohen, Franz Rosenzweig, Martin Buber, A. D. Gordon, and Rav Kook, see Samuel H. Bergman's *Faith and Reason: An Introduction to Modern Jewish Thought,* translated and edited by Alfred Jospe (Washington, D.C., 1961). A comprehensive and nuanced analysis of the abiding issues and unresolved tensions of modern Jewish religious thought is given in Gershom Scholem's "Reflections on Jewish Thought," in *On Jews and Judaism in Crisis,* edited by Werner J. Dannhauser, pp. 261–297 (New York, 1976).

The hermeneutic turn in Jewish thought inspired by postmodernism is documented in two collection of essays: Steven Kepnes, ed., *Interpreting Judaism in a Postmodern Age* (New York, 1996) and Peter Ochs and Nancy Levene, eds., *Textural Reasoning. Jewish Philosophy and Text Study at the End of the Twentieth Century* (Grand Rapids, Mich., 2002). The appeal of postmodern philosophers and literary critics to midrash is critically appraised by David Stern, *Midrash and Theory. Ancient Jewish Exegesis and Contemporary Literary Studies* (Evanston, Ill., 1996), especially chapter 1, "Midrash and Hermeneutics: Polysemy and Indeterminacy."

PAUL R. MENDES-FLOHR (1987 AND 2005)

JEWISH THOUGHT AND PHILOSOPHY: JEWISH ETHICAL LITERATURE

The Hebrew term *sifrut ha-musar* ("ethical literature") can be defined either very explicitly or in a general way. In a more proscribed sense it is a well-defined literary genre; the works belonging to it are easily recognizable because each chapter in these books deals with a specific religious and theological subject—belief in the unity of God, trust in God, repentance, fear and love of God, and so forth. The classical examples of books in this genre begin with Bahye ibn Paquda's *Ḥovot ha-levavot* (The duties of the heart) in the eleventh century and include Mosheh Ḥayyim Luzzatto's *Mesillat yesharim* (The path of the righteous) in the eighteenth century. In addition to the few dozen books written in this manner are some other minor genres, namely, *sifrut ha-tsavva'ot* ("ethical wills") and various monographs on subjects such as repentance.

In its broader meaning, the term *sifrut ha-musar* includes other religious literary genres, especially the vast literature of Hebrew homiletics, of which thousands of volumes were written between the twelfth and nineteenth centuries, as well as other popular works intended for the religious instruction of the masses. Hence, in general terms, "ethical literature" includes many literary genres; indeed, it refers to almost everything written for religious instruction except works of Jewish law (*halakhah*) or theology (philosophy or mysticism, i.e., Qabbalah).

Jewish ethical literature, in both its narrower and broader meanings, is not primarily intended to instruct the Jewish reader how to behave in certain circumstances. Practical instruction is reserved mainly for the literature of the *halakhah,* because Jewish law does not distinguish between religious and ethical commandments. Everything demanded by the Torah and the Talmud is included in the law, even subjects like the giving of *tsedaqah,* donations to the poor, or the proper behavior at a funeral. The main purpose of ethical literature is to explain to the Jew why it is necessary to follow the strict demands of Jewish law and ethical commandments. Thus, *sifrut ha-musar* is the literary genre that teaches the observant and devout Jew how to feel and how to organize his desires and intentions in order to be able to concentrate all his spiritual powers on the performance of the commandments that were enumerated by God in the ancient sources. The following brief description focuses on the development of Jewish ethical literature in its stricter sense, though reference will be made where possible to the broader field as well.

BEGINNINGS IN THE MIDDLE AGES. The first stage of the development of Jewish ethical literature in the Middle Ages signified a complete deviation from Jewish ethical works in the ancient period. While biblical and postbiblical Jewish literature included books dedicated specifically to the teaching of ethical values (*Proverbs, Ben Sira,* etc.), during the Talmudic period in late antiquity ethics was incorporated within the vast treasury of Midrashic homiletics and lost its standing as a separate literary genre. Rabbinic sayings dealing with ethical problems appear in Talmudic and Midrashic literature side by side, without any literary differentiation, with sayings dealing with astronomy, history, or medicine. The new insights and concepts in the field of ethics, which abound in this literature, were not expressed in a systematic way.

When Greek philosophy began to influence Jewish thinkers in the late Geonic period (tenth and eleventh centuries), ethical problems began to be treated in a special literary form and in a systematic way. The first Jewish philosophers who developed such systems in the tenth to the twelfth century saw themselves, with some justification, as innovators, formulating their concepts as if there were no previous Jewish ethical system. They were right in the sense that in previous Jewish literature it is impossible to find a systematic explanation of why a Jew should follow the divine commandments and how to educate oneself to accept and perform them.

One of the clearest examples of this approach is Saʿadyah Gaon's treatment of ethics in the first half of the tenth century. The tenth and last chapter of his great philosophical work, *Sefer emunot ve-deʿot* (The book of beliefs and opinions), is devoted to this subject. This chapter, which was probably written as a separate treatise, deals systematically with the main values of Jewish ethical behavior. According to Saʿadyah (882–942), God created the human psyche with thirteen different impulses or drives, each of which tends to impel him to fulfill it alone and thereby clashes with the others. Saʿadyah included in this list drives such as sex, laziness, revenge, and craving for food together with the urge to study the Torah and worship God. None of these, according to Saʿadyah, is either "right" or "wrong," "good" or "evil." Each of these drives is right and good if used in moderation, according to one's needs, and wrong and evil if it becomes one's sole or main preoccupation. Most of the chapter is dedicated to demonstrating the negative results of concentrating one's energies on the fulfillment of one drive alone, be it revenge or worship, eating or studying. Saʿadyah's arguments against such extreme behavior are mainly hedonistic: Complete submission to one drive turns even pleasure into pain and brings on suffering and ill health, while moderation and harmonic use of all of them together brings happiness, health, and long life. Saʿadyah uses some biblical and rabbinic references to strengthen his arguments, but his main thesis does not rely on Jewish sources; he is expressing, in fact, a secular conception of ethics.

A completely different approach was adopted by Baḥye ibn Paquda in Spain in the eleventh century. Like Saʿadyah, he wrote his ethical-philosophical treatise in Arabic, but his major work, *Ḥovot ha-levavot,* is the first book-length medieval Jewish work dedicated to the subject of ethics. In the introduction Baḥye complained that previous Jewish writers devoted all their works to the physical and material demands of Jewish religious life, neglecting completely the spiritual ones. His book was written in order to present the other, spiritual and ethical, side of the Jewish religion, which is, according to Baḥye, the most important and essential.

Baḥye's distinction between the physical and spiritual religious precepts was a major innovation in Jewish ethical thought. According to his system, prayer and religious studies cannot be included among the spiritual values because the human body and senses participate in their performance. Spiritual precepts, Baḥye explained, are those that are carried out completely "within the heart," that is, without any reliance or mediation of the limbs or the senses, and only the completely spiritual precepts have religious meaning and can be regarded as worship. The physical deeds, which include all the legal Jewish *mitsvot,* do not have any impact on one's religious life. A physical deed can have a religious meaning only if it is accompanied by spiritual concentration and intention—*kavvanah*—and even then its value is dependent on the spiritual intention and not on the deed itself. Thus Baḥye presented a completely spiritualized and internalized conception of Jewish religious life, which is a radical departure from the teachings of previous thinkers, who always insisted—as does Jewish law—that the physical performance of the *mitsvot,* both ritualistic and ethical ones, is the basis of Jewish worship.

Another new variation in the field of ethics in that period was introduced by Shelomoh ibn Gabirol (c. 1021–c. 1058), the great poet and philosopher, author of *Meqor ḥayyim,* which was known in Latin under the title *Fons vitae.* Ibn Gabirol wrote a short ethical treatise in Arabic, known in Hebrew as *Tiqqun middot ha-nefesh* (The correction of ethical attitudes). Ibn Gabirol's approach to ethics in this work is a physical-anthropological one. Characteristic human attitudes, he asserted, are dependent on the individual's complexion and physical harmony. Ibn Gabirol maintained that each of the twenty basic ethical attitudes is closely related to a certain combination of the four elements and the four liquids that constitute the human body according to medieval physiology. Using homiletical methods, Ibn Gabirol analyzed the ethical attitudes and arranged them in ten binary opposites (pride and humility, etc.), as an expression of the human physical constitution. Two such pairs are connected to each of the five senses. Ibn Gabirol's treatise is an attempt to give a scientific, secular, and physical basis to ethical human behavior and to correct every flaw in the same way that physical ailments are corrected.

The greatest Jewish philosopher of the Middle Ages, Moses Maimonides (Mosheh ben Maimon, 1135/8–1204), dedicated important discussions to ethical problems in several of his major works but did not write a special work on ethics. His philosophical works, commentaries, and legal works contain chapters and portions dealing with ethics. When writing in Arabic, he, like Saʿadyah Gaon and Ibn Gabirol, established Jewish ethics on scientific concepts, derived from psychological and anthropological analysis. The works of Aristotle and the Arab philosophers who followed him served as sources for Maimonides' own formulations. When writing in Hebrew, however, especially in *Sefer ha-maddaʿ* (The book of knowledge), the first book in his fourteen-book magnum opus of Jewish law, the *Mishneh Torah,* he very often based his ethical demands on old rabbinic ethical sayings.

Maimonides confronted the basic problems resulting from the meeting between rabbinic ethics and medieval philosophy and science in a profound way, taking pains to preserve the practical demands of ancient traditions while reconciling them with contemporary conceptions of spiritualized religious behavior. He contributed to the popularization in Hebrew literature of Aristotelian concepts like "the golden rule" of the "good" middle between two "evil" extremes, although their impact outside the immediate school of his followers was minimal. Even Maimonides, when dealing with the subject of ethics, saw himself not as a thinker who continued the deliberations of a long line of Jewish traditional teachers of ethics but as a philosopher who created a new system, relying mainly on non-Jewish scientific and philosophical sources and only assisted by biblical and Talmudic traditions.

EARLY HEBREW WORKS AND QABBALAH. While Saʿadyah, Baḥye, Ibn Gabirol, and Maimonides wrote mainly in Arabic and addressed themselves to Jewish intellectuals in the communities under Arab rule who were familiar with Arabic philosophy based on the Greek, almost no works were written in Hebrew and intended for a larger Jewish public. Only in the twelfth century does one find the beginnings of Hebrew medieval ethical literature written by Jewish thinkers in a contemporary manner. The first among these was Avraham bar Hiyyaʾ, who contributed to ethics his collection of four homilies, called *Hegyon ha-nefesh ha-ʿatsuvah* (The sad soul's deliberations), which was based on Neoplatonic philosophy. That same philosophy also influenced Avraham ibn ʿEzraʾ, the great commentator on the Bible, who dedicated to ethics a brief treatise called *Yesod moraʾ* (The foundation of the fear of God). It is typical that these two works were written in the first half and middle of the twelfth century by philosophers from Spain who traveled and visited Jewish communities in Christian Europe, where Arabic was not understood, and were aware of the need for such material.

The first school of writers of Hebrew ethical works in medieval Europe did not emerge in the areas influenced by Arabic culture but in the small town of Gerona in northern Spain ruled by the Christians in the first half of the thirteenth century. The four important writers of this school were Moses Nahmanides (Mosheh ben Naḥman), Yaʿaqov ben Sheshet Gerondi, Yonah ben Avraham Gerondi, and Asher ben David. All four belonged to the school of qabbalists that flourished in Gerona early in the thirteenth century. The mystical element in their ethical works is not dominant, and in the case of the best-known ethical writer among them, Yonah Gerondi, it is completely absent. If it were not for a letter written by Yitsḥaq the Blind, the great mystic of Provence, to the qabbalists in Gerona, naming Yonah Gerondi among them, it would never have been known for certain that he was indeed a qabbalist.

The most important innovation of the ethical works of this school of qabbalists is the revival of rabbinic ethics, almost completely neglected by their predecessors. Many parts of their works can be read as anthologies of Talmudic and Midrashic sayings concerning various ethical problems. It is clear that these writers intended to show, in contrast to the Jewish philosophers, that Judaism has an authentic ethical tradition which can answer every contemporary problem without relying on medieval philosophy and science. They tried to revive and reestablish the dominance of the traditional Jewish sources of antiquity as the normative guide to religious behavior. In this, their qabbalistic beliefs could have contributed to the spiritual depth and the pathos of their adherence to the traditional sources, but their works are not dependent on mystical symbolism.

The Gerona qabbalists viewed their concerted effort in the field of ethical works as a response to the threat that Jewish philosophy presented to Judaism. Extreme spiritualization on the one hand and profane, scientific systems of ethics on the other endangered the traditional conceptions of the primacy of ethical deeds and the observance of the practical precepts. Yonah Gerondi was one of the first Jewish thinkers to criticize Maimonides publicly and participated actively in the great controversy concerning Maimonides' works in 1232–1235. His ethical works, and especially his monograph on repentance, *Sha'arei teshuvah,* are intended to offer a traditional alternative to philosophical ethics. Nahmanides' ethical homilies include direct criticism of Aristotelian philosophy and indirect polemics against Maimonides.

Other writers of this period adopted the same attitude and created traditionalistic systems of ethics based on ancient sources as an alternative to the works of the philosophers. Prominent among them was Yeḥi'el ben Yequti'el of Rome, in the middle of the thirteenth century, whose ethical work *Ma'alot ha-middot* (The ascending ladder of ethical values) is an anthology of rabbinic paragraphs with some antiphilosophical undertones. Yeḥi'el was not a qabbalist, and his work proves that the return to the ancient sources in the realm of ethics was not motivated by mystical reasons alone.

Later in the thirteenth century another qabbalist, Baḥya ben Asher ibn Halawa, wrote one of the most influential works of Jewish ethics in a homiletical form, *Kad ha-qemaḥ* (A bowl of flour). In this work the author discusses ethical values, arranged in alphabetical order, dedicating a sermon to each. He seldom used qabbalistic symbolism, and the work is one of the most important books in medieval rabbinic ethics.

At the same time, Jewish philosophers continued to publish Hebrew books on philosophical ethics. The most prominent among them were Ya'aqov Anatoli in his collection of sermons, *Malmad ha-talmidim,* and Shem Ṭov ben Yosef Falaquera, who wrote several ethical treatises. Like other philosophers of the thirteenth century, these two relied heavily on the teachings of Maimonides, though very often their attitudes were more radical than those of their teachers.

In the thirteenth century in Spain, southern France, and Italy the two major schools of Hebrew ethical literature thus took shape, the philosophers, mostly Maimonidean, on the one hand, and the traditionalists, creators of rabbinic ethics, many of them qabbalists, on the other hand. New literary forms emerged in the two antagonistic schools, such as the ethical monographs, ethical homiletical literature, and ethical "wills," which summarize in a brief treatise a complete ethical system. From the thirteenth to the fifteenth century, Hebrew ethical literature is clearly divided along these basic ideological lines.

ETHICS OF THE ASHKENAZIC *ḤASIDIM*. While controversy raged in Spain, Italy, and southern France, an independent school of ethical thought was established in western Germany by the German-Jewish pietists, adherents of the esoteric, and often mystical, theology of Ashkenazic Hasidism. The main work of this school, which had a profound impact on Jewish ethical thought for many centuries, is the *Sefer Ḥasidim* (Book of the Pietists), written by Yehudah ben Shemu'el "the Pious" of Regensburg (d. 1217).

Sefer Ḥasidim is different from previous Hebrew ethical works in its concern with everyday behavior in minute details, relating to the performance of the religious precepts. Besides homilies that expound the theoretical basis of ethical ideas, the book, which is divided into brief, independent paragraphs, deals with specific ethical issues: how to choose a dwelling place; relationships with parents, teachers, neighbors, and the non-Jewish society; how to conduct business relations; attitude toward rabbis; and so forth.

The instructions of this book are based on a strict, radical ethical theory. The Ashkenazic Ḥasidim believed that God's presence in the world is evident only in the unusual and the miraculous. Natural and social laws are not a reflection of divine benevolence but are rather trials put before pietists by God in order to distinguish between the righteous and the wicked by testing their ability to obey God's commandments. Human life, according to the pietists, is a continuous struggle to prove one's devotion to God by overcoming all the obstacles that God himself put on the path of his believers. Ethical behavior, in this system, is choosing the most difficult and painful alternative. The pietist must always concentrate on the performance of that deed that most people around him neglect; by so doing he proves that this is the most difficult path, and following it gives him the maximum religious reward. This worldview is the complete reversal of the hedonistic tendencies found in the ethical works of Jewish philosophers of the Middle Ages such as Sa'adyah and Yeḥi'el ben Yequti'el.

Ashkenazic Hasidism both reflected and served as an ideological response to the massacres and persecutions that German Jewry suffered during the period of the Crusades. *Qiddush ha-shem* ("sanctifying the Holy Name") was regarded by the Ḥasidim as the supreme religious and ethical achievement, because it was the most total and difficult expression of devotion to God in spite of terrible hardships. If the sacrifice of one's life is the final goal, everyday life should reflect the same attitude and be conducted as if every religious and ethical deed had an element of sacrifice in it—the larger the sacrifice, the more meaningful the deed. Anything that negates the demands of the body has religious value, while every deed that satisfies physical needs signifies ethical surrender.

Ashkenazic Hasidic ethics are closely related to the esoteric theology of the teachers of Ashkenazic Hasidism. Whereas the theology did not continue to develop but was absorbed by qabbalistic mysticism, which spread in central Europe during the late thirteenth and the fourteenth century, the ethical teachings of the Ḥasidim survived for many centuries. Numerous ethical treatises written in Germany in the thirteenth to the fifteenth century are based on *Sefer Ḥasidim,* many of them dealing with the concept of repentance in Ashkenazic Hasidic ethics. Their teachings served as a basis for later Jewish ethical literature, even when Qabbalah began to develop its own specific mystical ethical literature.

Sixteenth- and Seventeenth-Century Qabbalistic Ethics. In the sixteenth century the study of Qabbalah became more and more popular among Jewish intellectuals, after being confined, during the thirteenth to fifteenth centuries, mainly to small circles of esoteric mystics. Since the sixteenth century, and especially in the seventeenth and eighteenth centuries, Qabbalah spread very rapidly and eventually became the dominant ideology in Judaism. This change was, to some extent, the result of the destruction of the great Jewish center in Spain in the expulsion of 1492 and of the rapid decline of Jewish philosophy at that time. The dissemination of Qabbalah among the Jewish masses was assisted mainly by the fact that in the sixteenth century qabbalists began to write and publish popular ethical works based on qabbalistic symbolism, which made Qabbalah easily accessible—and religiously relevant—to the Jewish masses.

Qabbalistic ethical literature appeared in sixteenth-century Safad, a small town in the Upper Galilee that served, after the expulsion from Spain, as a center for many Jewish halakhists, preachers, thinkers, and mystics. In this town Qabbalah became a way of life, so that ethical treatises explaining the close interdependence of human social and religious behavior and mystical occurrences in the divine world were relevant and meaningful. Mosheh Cordovero (1522–1570), the great qabbalist who wrote systematic works of Qabbalah that were very influential in the sixteenth century, wrote a brief ethical treatise, *Tomer Devorah* (The palm tree of Deborah), wherein he pointed out the ways by which the earthly ethical behavior of the righteous influenced the mystical processes in the divine world, the realm of the mystical *sefirot,* the divine hypostases central in qabbalistic symbolism. A disciple of Cordovero's, Eliyyahu de Vidas, followed suit by writing a major book on ethics, *Re'shit ḥokhmah* (The beginning of wisdom), in which he interpreted many sections of ancient qabbalistic works, mainly the Zohar, as explaining the central values of Jewish ethics. Ḥayyim Vital (Klippers), the great disciple of Isaac Luria, wrote a short ethical work, *Sha'arei qedushah* (The gates of holiness), describing the human spiritual ascension from involvement in secular life and sin up to the immersion of the human soul in the divine world. One of the great followers of Luria's mysticism, Yesha'yah Horowitz, wrote the largest ethical work of that time, *Shenei luḥot ha-berit* (The two tablets of the covenant), which remains to this day one of the most influential works of Jewish ethics ever written.

The new impact of Qabbalah on Jewish ethics was based to a large extent on the revolutionary mystical views introduced by Isaac Luria (1534–1572). Whereas previous qabbalistic systems were characterized by withdrawal from the contemporary world, Luria's Qabbalah was intensely messianic. According to his mythical symbolism, the world was created in order to serve as a battleground between the divine powers of good and evil, where good will ultimately be victorious. The historical orientation of this philosophy demands action from its followers. By righteousness and religious and ethical activity, humankind assists God in the struggle against the powers of evil that resided within God and that now, following an upheaval in the divine world, rule all on earth but the souls of the righteous.

Luria's theology brought a new intensity and a renewed, profound meaning to all religious and ethical demands. In his system, every word of every prayer, every humble ritualistic act, and all ethical human deeds become either messianic acts that facilitate the redemption or evil deeds that support the satanic powers in their struggle against God. There are no neutral acts; everything done or left undone carries enormous spiritual significance and may help decide the fate of all creation.

Following Luria, countless works of ethics and ethical homiletics were written by Jews in the East and the West during the seventeenth and eighteenth centuries. This period is undoubtedly the peak of the influence that Hebrew ethical literature had on Jewish life, social behavior, and historical activity. The spread of Lurianic theology served as a basis for the messianic theology of the Shabbatean movement beginning in 1665, and quite a few authors of ethical works were Shabbatean believers, like Eliyyahu ha-Kohen of Smyrna and Yonatan Eibeschutz of Prague. Some authors were influenced by Shabbateanism even though they themselves did not belong to the movement, among them Mosheh Ḥayyim Luzzatto, the Italian author of the popular *Mesillat ye-sharim.* The fusion between mysticism and ethics was complete in the eighteenth century.

Hasidism and Modern Trends. Hasidic ethics are, on the one hand, a continuation of the process of applying Lurianic mysticism to the field of ethics and, on the other hand, a response to the ideological crisis brought about by the Shabbatean messianic movement. The Hasidic *rebeyim*—who perpetuated the preachings of the movement's founder, the BeSHT (Yisra'el ben Eli'ezer, 1700–1760), and his disciples,

Yaʿaqov Yosef of Polonnoye and Dov Ber of Mezhirich (now Międzyrzecz, Poland)—based their ethical homiletics on qabbalistic terminology and the Lurianic myth. They had, however, to contend with a reality that the messianic theology of Natan of Gaza, the "prophet" of the messiah Shabbetai Tsevi, had greatly influenced, and with the deep disappointment that ensued when the movement engendered the antinomian heresy of the Frankist movement in the eighteenth century. Among the disciples of Dov Ber, especially in the works of Elimelekh of Lizhensk (now Lezajsk, Poland), a new theology emerged, attributing to the figure of the *tsaddiq,* the leader of a Hasidic community, powers to assist a sinner in obtaining forgiveness from God and influence in the divine realm over the affairs of every Hasidic adherent. The concept of the *tsaddiq* as an intermediary between the righteous and God (originally derived from Shabbatean theology) became one of the most important elements in the Hasidic movement, together with a new emphasis on mystical communion with God (*devequt*) and devotion to ethical behavior at the expense of intensive study of the Torah.

The *mitnaggdim,* the main "opponents" of Hasidism, developed ethical thinking, especially in the Musar ("ethics") movement, founded by Yisraʾel Salanter in the middle of the nineteenth century. This movement carried great weight in rabbinic academies (*yeshivot*) throughout eastern Europe in the second half of that century and the beginning of the twentieth. Yisraʾel Salanter did not use qabbalistic terminology, preferring instead a modern way of preaching, though at times it seems that the content of his ideas was still under the influence of Lurianism. The same can be said about the ethical works of the modern rabbi Avraham Yitsḥaq Kook (1865–1935), one of the most profound modern Jewish thinkers, whose thought is still influencing Jewish Orthodox movements in Israel today. He placed repentance in the center of his mystical theology as a way toward redemption, and his modern language sometimes hides Lurianic symbolism.

SEE ALSO Ashkenazic Hasidism; Halakhah; Hasidism, overview article; Midrash and Aggadah; Qabbalah.

BIBLIOGRAPHY

Works in Hebrew

Dan, Joseph. *Sifrut ha-musar ve-ha-derush* (Ethical and homiletical literature). Jerusalem, 1975. Includes a detailed bibliography.

Heinemann, Isaak. *Taʿamei ha-mitsvot be-sifrut Yisraʾel.* Jerusalem, 1956–1959.

Tishby, Isaiah. *Mishnat ha-Zohar* (The wisdom of the *Zohar*), vol. 2. Jerusalem, 1961.

Tishby, Isaiah, and Joseph Dan. *Mivkhar sifrut ha-Musar* (Hebrew ethical literature: Selected texts). Jerusalem, 1970.

Works in English

Barzilay, Isaac E. *Between Reason and Faith: Anti-Rationalism in Italian Jewish Thought, 1250–1650.* Paris, 1967.

Bettan, Israel. *Studies in Jewish Preaching: Middle Ages.* Cincinnati, 1939.

Bokser, Ben Zion. *From the World of the Cabbalah: The Philosophy of Rabbi Judah Loew of Prague.* New York, 1954.

Bokser, Ben Zion, trans. *Abraham Isaac Kook.* New York, 1978.

Cronbach, Abraham. "Social Thinking in the *Sefer Hasidim.*" *Hebrew Union College Annual* 22 (1949): 1–147.

Ginzberg, Louis. *Students, Scholars and Saints.* New York, 1928.

Ginzburg, Simon. *The Life and Works of Moses Hayyim Luzzatto.* Philadelphia, 1931.

Glenn, Mendel G. *Israel Salanter.* New York, 1953.

Husik, Isaac. *A History of Mediaeval Jewish Philosophy* (1916). New York, 1969.

Lazaroff, Allan. "Bahyā's Asceticism against Its Rabbinic and Islamic Background." *Journal of Jewish Studies* 21 (1970): 11–38.

Marcus, Ivan G. *Piety and Society: The Jewish Pietists of Medieval Germany.* Leiden, 1981.

Rosin, David. "The Ethics of Solomon Ibn Gabirol." *Jewish Quarterly Review* 3 (January 1891): 159–181.

Scholem, Gershom. *Major Trends in Jewish Mysticism* (1941). New York, 1961.

Werblowsky, R. J. Zwi. *Joseph Karo: Lawyer and Mystic.* London, 1962.

Werblowsky, R. J. Zwi. "Faith, Hope and Trust: A Study in the Concept of Bittahon." *Papers of the Institute of Jewish Studies* 1 (1964): 95–139.

New Sources

Borowitz, Eugene B., and Frances Weinman Schwartz. *The Jewish Moral Virtues.* Philadelphia, 1999.

Cohen, Hermann. *Ethics of Maimonides.* Translation and commentary by Almut Sh. Bruckstein. Modern Jewish Philosophy and Religion. Madison, Wisc., 2002.

Dan, Joseph. *Jewish Mysticism and Jewish Ethics.* 2d enl. ed. Northvale, N.J., 1996.

Gibbs, Robert. *Why Ethics? Signs of Responsibilities.* Princeton, N.J., 2000.

Novak, David. *Natural Law in Judaism.* Cambridge, U.K.; New York, 1998.

Pachter, Mordechai. "The Concept of 'Devekut' in the Homiletical Ethical Writings of 16th Century Safed." *Studies in Medieval Jewish History and Literature* 2 (1984): 171–230.

Shear, Eli M., and Chaim Miller. *The Rich Go to Heaven: Giving Charity in Jewish Thought.* Northvale, N.J., 1998.

Sigal, Phillip. "Reflections on Ethical Elements of Judaic Halakhah." *Duquesne Law Review* 23 (1985): 863–903.

JOSEPH DAN (1987)
Revised Bibliography

JIAO. The Chinese term *jiao* (sacrifice) in ancient times referred to a pledge in wine at the wedding ceremony or at the coming of age of a son. But the common meaning that we shall consider here is the sacrificial part of major Daoist services. In this connection *jiao* has historically been associated with *zhai,* the rites of abstinence and penitence. Under Buddhist influence, *zhai* took the form of rituals for the salvation of the individual and ancestors, whereas *jiao* sacrifices were performed by ordained Daoist priests to renew the community's covenant with the highest powers for blessings and protection. As practiced in Taiwan today, both these functions are generally covered by the single term *jiao.*

Although a dozen varieties of *jiao* are differentiated according to their purpose, in effect only four are performed nowadays with any frequency in Taiwan: (1) for peace and safety *(ping'an jiao),* (2) for the prevention of epidemics *(wen jiao),* (3) for blessings in general *(qingcheng jiao),* and (4) for protection from fire *(huo jiao).* Services may be held either at fixed intervals or irregularly, but the latter is much more common. However, in this as in the matter of their duration (from one to as many as seven days and nights) there is considerable variation according to custom and circumstance.

The essential difference between the Jiao and other large-scale religious services is that the powers addressed in the Jiao are the Three Pure Ones (San Qing), hypostases of the Dao, rather than the gods of popular religion. These Daoist powers receive only "pure" offerings—wine, tea, cakes, fruit—in contrast to the "blood sacrifices" of the popular cults. The public is allowed to attend and participate in the rituals of popular religion, but it is strictly barred from the sacred arena where the Daoists perform the Jiao. However, the people of the community prepare themselves for the visit of the Three Pure Ones by observing a fast for several days before the Jiao.

The sacred arena *(daochang)* of the Jiao is usually the community temple. But as the purpose of the Jiao is communion with the Three Pure Ones rather than with the deities of popular religion, the sacred arena is rearranged so that the main altar is reserved for the San Qing (represented by painted scrolls bearing the images of the deities) while the other deities are relegated to subsidiary or "guest" status at the altar of the three realms (that is, Heaven, earth, and the waters). The services, complex and protracted, consist of the following essential parts: announcement to the divine powers of the celebration of this Jiao, and an invitation for them to attend; feasting them when they have arrived; presenting official petitions seeking forgiveness of sins and expressing penitence; a formal negotiation for the renewal of the covenant between the highest powers and the community; sending off the eminent guests when this pact has been concluded. As part of the Jiao, rites for the salvation of all souls *(pudu)* are invariably included. The officiants include a high priest *(gaogong),* several assistants, and a small group of musicians, to whose accompaniment most of the actions are performed. Besides the official celebrants, prominent men of the community who have contributed heavily to the expenses of the Jiao are present within the sacred arena. At specified moments in the liturgy they follow the lead of the Daoist priests in making obeisances to the deities. This special privilege adds to the stature of the donors in the community and at the same time makes or generates religious merit for them.

The people of the community also earn merit by observing the preliminary fast, by contributing money, and through many kinds of assistance in preparation for the Jiao. Although they do not participate in the rituals that take place within the *daochang,* they do offer their own sacrifices in prepared areas outside the temple, to ancestors, gods, and bereaved spirits. At certain moments in the Jiao the celebrants appear before the public and perform rituals, usually at the several "outer altars" *(waitan)* that have been erected in vacant lots near the sacred arena. These altars, masterpieces of folk art, are dedicated to various important deities of popular religion.

The festivities which accompany the Jiao are many. One high point, so far as the people are concerned, is a colorful procession to the banks of a river (or ocean), where paper and bamboo rafts are launched. Bearing candles, the rafts float away to invite the souls of the drowned to come for their share of the feast provided by the community (this feast is the public part of the *pudu*). While the priests perform their esoteric liturgy within the temple, a great festival is taking place in the community. Mounds of sacrificial offerings, performances of drama, convivial entertainment of friends, relatives, and even strangers, and a general atmosphere of carnival draw huge crowds from near and far. All of this makes the Jiao not just a liturgical service, but a total community event.

For the Daoists, the Jiao is of more profound significance. According to the most ancient and basic theories of Daoism, to call down the highest powers of the macrocosm is in actuality to practice the exercises of "inner alchemy" *(neidan)* within the microcosm of the priest's body. While the high priest outwardly performs the liturgy, addressing the highest powers, he inwardly undergoes a regimen designed to produce the "immortal fetus." In the Jiao, then, the ultimate goal of the Daoist religion is still what it has always been: the attainment of immortality.

SEE ALSO Alchemy, article on Chinese Alchemy; Priesthood, article on Daoist Priesthood; Worship and Devotional Life, article on Daoist Devotional Life.

BIBLIOGRAPHY

The most detailed analytical description of the *Jiao* is Michael Saso's *Taoism and the Rite of Cosmic Renewal* (Seattle, 1972). A careful study of one of the constituent rites is in Kristofer Schipper's *Le Fen Teng: Ritual taoïste* (Paris, 1975). Édouard Chavannes gives a translation, with a wealth of annotation, of texts used in the *zhai,* in his *Le Jet des Dragons* (Paris, 1916). A rare account of the *Jiao* as practiced in imperial times is in J. J. M. de Groot's *Les fêtes annuellemment célébrées à Émoui (Amoy),* 2 vols. (1886; reprint., Taipei, 1977). For a good description written in popular style with color photographs, see Linda Wu's "The Biggest Festival of Them All," *Echo* 4 (January 1974): 28–44. General information on Daoism and specific information about Daoist communal rituals in pre-Tang times is given in the fundamental work of Henri Maspero, first published posthumously in *Les religions chin-*

oises (Paris, 1950), later published in expanded form in *Le taoïsme et les religions chinoises* (Paris, 1971). The latter has been translated into English by Frank A. Kierman, Jr., as *Daoism and Chinese Religion* (Amherst, 1981). The most complete and best informed overall treatment of Daoism since Maspero is the book by Kristofer Schipper, *Le corps taoïste* (Paris, 1982); see especially chapter 5, "Le rituel."

New Sources

Wickeri, P. L., et al. *Christianity & Modernization: A Chinese Debate.* Hongkong, 1995.

Wu, Y.-y., L. G. Thompson, and G. Seaman. *The Taoist Tradition in Chinese Thought.* Los Angeles, 1991.

Wu, Y.-y., L. G. Thompson, and G. Seaman. *Chinese Religious Traditions Collated.* Los Angeles, 1997.

LAURENCE G. THOMPSON (1987)
Revised Bibliography

JIEN (1155–1225), a Japanese Buddhist leader and renowned poet, was a highly influential figure at a critical time in the political, social, and religious life of Japan. Appointed abbot of the Tendai sect four times, he enjoyed close family ties with emperors and regents, composed poems that made him a leading poet of the day, and wrote Japan's first known interpretive history, the *Gukanshō.*

At the age of eleven, Jien was entrusted to the Enryakuji, a Buddhist temple, for training under a monk who was the seventh son of Retired Emperor Toba. Early poems by Jien, as well as entries in the diary of his distinguished brother Kanezane (1149–1207), indicate that he was a lonely child who was soon attracted to Buddhist teachings on transience and impermanence. A biography (the *Jichin kashōden*) states that when he was about twenty-five and was fasting at a temple on the Katsura River, he had a miraculous vision of the Buddhist deity Fudō Myō-ō.

Jien was ordained as a Buddhist monk, appointed to the headship of several important temples, and selected as personal priest to the emperor Go-Toba (r. 1183–1198) before reaching the age of thirty. When he was thirty-one, his elder brother Kanezane was designated regent, an appointment that further enhanced Jien's influence within Buddhist centers and at the imperial court. At the age of thirty-seven he received his first appointment as Abbot of Tendai. During the four years that he held the post, he devoted considerable time to the conduct of Buddhist rites in high places. He built new temples and promoted the practice and study of Buddhism in diverse ways.

In 1196 Jien and other members of his house (the Kujō) were ousted from office. Until his death nearly thirty years later, neither he nor his house ever again reached the dizzy heights attained during the Kanezane regency. For a time, Jien continued to be a favorite at court, largely because of his fame as a poet and his personal relationship with Go-Toba, but gradually the latter (who was now attempting to control state affairs as a retired emperor) moved to establish independence from *bakufu* control, rather than adopt the compromises favored by Jien and the Kujō house.

In the years immediately preceding the outbreak of civil war in 1221—a time of intense political rivalry within the court and between the court and the Kamakura *bakufu*—Jien turned frequently to written prayers, rituals, dreams, letters, and finally history in trying to convince Go-Toba and his advisers that drastic steps against the *bakufu* should be avoided. What Jien wrote in those troubled years suggests that he was especially interested in signs and revelations of what the native *kami* (gods) desired or had ordered.

Jien's history (the *Gukanshō*), written a year or so before the outbreak of war in 1221, was meant to show how national events had taken, and would continue to take, an up-and-down course in the direction of a political arrangement that would end the current crisis, an arrangement in which the Kujō house would figure prominently. He tried to show how a complex interplay of divine principles *(dōri)* was propelling events along that course: Some Buddhist principles were forcing it downward to destruction, and some *kami*-created (Shintō) principles were pulling it upward toward a state of temporary improvement.

Because Jien was primarily interested in *kami*-created *dōri* that would bring improvement, scholars have concluded that native Shintō belief was stronger than imported Buddhist ideas in his interpretive scheme, although the Buddhist flavor was strong. As the outbreak of civil war in 1221 attests, Go-Toba did not ultimately adopt the compromises that Jien favored and that the *Gukanshō* predicted as inevitable. But Jien remained convinced, to the end, that he had charted the "single course" of Japanese history correctly.

SEE ALSO Tendaishū.

BIBLIOGRAPHY

For a Jien biography, see Taga Munehaya's *Jien* (Tokyo, 1959), vol. 15 of "Jinbutsu Sōsho." His study of Japanese history has been translated by Delmer M. Brown and Ishida Ichirō in *The Future and the Past: A Translation and Study of the Gukanshō, an Interpretative History of Japan Written in 1219* (Berkeley, Calif., 1979).

DELMER M. BROWN (1987)

JIHĀD is the verbal noun of the Arabic verb *jahada,* meaning "to endeavor, to strive, to struggle." It is generally used to denote an effort toward a commendable aim. In religious contexts it can mean the struggle against one's evil inclinations or efforts toward the moral uplift of society or toward the spread of Islam. This last undertaking can be peaceful ("*jihād* of the tongue" or "*jihād* of the pen"), in accordance with *sūrah* 16:125 of the Qurʾān ("Call thou to the way of the Lord with wisdom and admonition, and dispute with them in the better way"), or involve the use of force ("*jihād* of the sword") as mentioned in *sūrah* 2:193 ("Fight them until there is no persecution and the religion is God's; then if they give over, there shall be no enmity save for evildoers"). In pious and mystical circles spiritual and moral *jihād* is emphasized. This they call "greater jihād" on the strength of the following tradition *(ḥadīth)* of the prophet Muḥammad: "Once, having returned from one of his campaigns, the Prophet said: 'We have now returned from the lesser *jihād* [i.e., fighting] to the greater *jihād*.'"

In view of the wide semantic spectrum of the word *jihād,* it is not correct to equate it with the notion of "holy war." And in those instances where the word *jihād* does refer to armed struggle, it must be borne in mind that Islam does not distinguish between holy and secular wars. All wars between Muslims and unbelievers and even wars between different Muslim groups would be labeled *jihād,* even if fought—as was mostly the case—for perfectly secular reasons. The religious aspect, then, is reduced to the certainty of the individual warriors that if they are killed they will enter paradise.

JIHĀD IN THE QUR'ĀN AND THE ḤADĪTH. In about two-thirds of the instances where the verb *jāhada* or its derivatives occur in the Qur'ān, it denotes warfare. Its distribution—and that of the verb *qātala* ("combat," "fight") for that matter—reflects the history of the nascent Islamic community. Both words are hardly used in the Meccan parts of the Qur'ān, revealed during the period when the Muslims were enjoined to bear patiently the aggressive behavior of the unbelievers, but abound in the Medinese chapters, sent down after the fighting between the Muslims and their Meccan adversaries had broken out. They are often linked with the phrase "in the way of God" (*fī sabīl Allāh*) to underscore the religious character of the struggle. And in order to indicate that warfare against the Meccans ought to be the concern of the whole community and not only of the direct participants in warfare, the words "with their goods and lives" (*bi-amwālihim wa-anfusihim*) are frequently added to these verbs.

Traditionally *sūrah* 22:39 ("Leave is given to those who fight because they were wronged—surely God is able to help them—who were expelled from their habitations without right, except that they say 'Our lord is God'"), revealed shortly after Muḥammad's Emigration (Hijrah) from Mecca to Medina in 622 CE, is regarded as marking the turning point in the relations between the Muslims and the unbelievers. Many later verses on *jihād* order the believers to take part in warfare, promise heavenly reward to those who do, and threaten those who do not with severe punishment in the hereafter. Some verses deal with practical matters such as exemption from military service (9:91, 48:17), fighting during the holy months (2:217) and in the holy territory of Mecca (2:191), the fate of prisoners of war (47:4), safe conduct (9:6), and truce (8:61).

Careful reading of the Qur'anic passages on *jihād* suggests that Muḥammad regarded the command to fight the unbelievers not as absolute, but as conditional upon provocation from them, for in many places this command is justified by aggression or perfidy on the part of the non-Muslims: "And fight in the way of God with those who fight with you, but aggress not: God loves not the aggressors" (2:190) and "But if they break their oaths after their covenant and thrust at your religion, then fight the leaders of unbelief" (9:13). Authoritative Muslim opinion, however, went in a different direction. Noticing that the Qur'anic verses on the relationship between Muslims and non-Muslims give evidence of a clear evolution from peacefulness to enmity and warfare, Muslim scholars have argued that this evolution culminated in an unconditional command to fight the unbelievers, as embodied in verses such as 5:9 ("Then, when the sacred months are drawn away, slay the idolaters wherever you find them, and take them, and confine them, and lie in wait for them at every place of ambush"). These "sword verses" are considered to have repealed all other verses concerning the intercourse with non-Muslims.

There is an abundant body of *ḥadīth* on *jihād.* Owing to their practical importance many of them were already recorded in special collections during the second century AH, before the compilation of the authoritative collections. The *ḥadīths* deal with the same topics as the Qur'ān but place more emphasis on the excellence of *jihād* as a pious act, on the rewards of martyrdom, and on practical and ethical matters of warfare. A typical *ḥadīth* from the last category is: "Whensoever the Prophet sent out a raiding party, he used to say, 'Raid in the name of God and in the way of God. Fight those who do not believe in God. Raid, do not embezzle spoils, do not act treacherously, do not mutilate, and do not kill children.'"

JIHĀD IN ISLAMIC LAW. The prescriptions found in the Qur'ān and *ḥadīth,* together with the practice of the early caliphs and army commanders, were, from the latter half of the second century AH on, cast in the mold of a legal doctrine to which a separate chapter in the handbooks on Islamic law was devoted. The central part of this doctrine is that the Muslim community as a whole has the duty to expand the territory and rule of Islam. Consequently, *jihād* is a collective duty of all Muslims, which means that if a sufficient number take part in it, the whole community has fulfilled its obligation. If, on the other hand, the number of participants is inadequate, the sin rests on all Muslims. After the period of conquests the jurists stipulated that the Muslim ruler, in order to keep the idea of *jihād* alive, ought to organize an expedition into enemy territory once per year. If the enemy attacks Muslim territory, *jihād* becomes an individual duty for all able-bodied inhabitants of the region under attack. Those killed in *jihād* are called martyrs (*shuhadā';* sg., *shahīd*). Their sins are forgiven and they go straight to paradise.

Shī'ī legal theory on *jihād* is very similar to Sunnī doctrine, with one important exception, however: the existence of the *jihād* duty depends on the manifest presence of a Shī'ī imam. Because the last of these went into concealment (*ghaybah*) in AH 260 (874 CE), the *jihād* doctrine should have lost its practical importance for the Shīʿah. However, in an attempt to strengthen their position vis-à-vis the state, Shīʿī scholars have claimed to represent collectively the Hidden Imam and, therefore, to be entitled to proclaim *jihād.* This explains why, during the last centuries, many wars between Iran and its neighbors have been waged under the banner of *jihād.*

The ultimate aim of *jihād* is "the subjection of the unbelievers" and "the extirpation of unbelief." This is understood, however, in a purely political way as the extension of Islamic rule over the remaining parts of the earth. The peoples thus conquered are not forced to embrace Islam: With payment of a special poll tax (*jizyah*) they can acquire the status of protected minorities and become non-Muslim subjects of the Islamic state (*dhimmīs*). In theory certain categories of non-Muslims are barred from this privilege: Some scholars exclude Arab idolaters—a class of mere academic interest after the Islamization of the Arabian Peninsula; others hold that only Christians, Jews, and fire worshipers (*majūs*) qualify. In practice, however, the definition of fire worshiper could be stretched to include all kinds of pagan tribes.

Before the final aim—Muslim domination of the whole world—has been achieved, the situation of war prevails between the Islamic state and the surrounding regions. This situation can be temporarily suspended by a truce, to be concluded by the head of state whenever he deems it in the interest of the Muslims. Most scholars stipulate that a truce may not last longer than ten years, the duration of the Treaty of al-Ḥudaybīyah, concluded in AH 6 (628 CE) between Muḥammad and his Meccan adversaries.

The *jihād* chapters in the legal handbooks contain many practical rules. Warfare must start with the summons in which the enemies are asked to embrace Islam or accept the status of non-Muslim subjects. Only if they refuse may they be attacked. Other prescriptions concern, for example, the protection of the lives of noncombatants, the treatment of prisoners of war, and the division of the spoils.

JIHĀD IN HISTORY. Throughout Islamic history the doctrine of *jihād* has been invoked to justify wars between Muslim and non-Muslim states and even to legitimate wars between Muslims themselves. In the latter case the adversaries would be branded as heretics or rebels to warrant the application of the *jihād* doctrine. In the eighteenth and nineteenth centuries there arose movements all over the Muslim world for whom *jihād* was so central to their teachings and actions that they are often referred to as *jihād* movements. Despite their wide geographical range—from West Africa to Southeast Asia—and the different social, economic, and political causes from which they sprang, they employed the same notions from the Islamic repertoire. *Jihād* for them meant the struggle within an only nominally Islamic society for the purification of religion and the establishment of a genuine Islamic community.

In combination with the *jihād* doctrine the obligation of *hijrah,* the duty of Muslims to emigrate from areas controlled by non-Muslims, was frequently appealed to. Often the notion of a Mahdi played a role, either because the leader proclaimed himself as such, or because he was regarded as a minister appointed to prepare the Mahdi's advent. The organizational framework of these movements was usually that of a Ṣūfī order. Although their main struggle was within their own society, many of these movements developed into formidable adversaries of the colonial powers once they collided with their expansionist policies.

Examples of *jihād* movements are the Wahhābīyah in Arabia, founded by Muḥammad ibn ʿAbd al-Wahhāb (1703–1792), the Fulbe *jihād* in northern Nigeria led by Usuman dan Fodio (1754–1817), the Padri movement in Sumatra (1803–1832), the West African *jihād* movement of ʿUmar Tāl (1794–1864), the *ṭarīqah-i muḥammadī* ("Muḥammadan way") in northern India founded by Aḥmad Barēlī (1786–1831), the Algerian resistance against French colonization, headed by ʿAbd al-Qādir (1808–1883), the Sanūsīyah in Libya and the Sahara, founded by Muḥammad ibn ʿAlī al-Sanūsi, and the Mahdist movement of Muḥammad Aḥmad in the Sudan (1881–1898). In the twentieth century the *jihād* doctrine lost much of its importance as a mobilizing ideology in the struggle against colonialism; its place was taken by secular nationalism.

THE CONTEMPORARY SIGNIFICANCE OF THE JIHĀD DOCTRINE. Since the nineteenth century attempts have been made to reinterpret the prevailing doctrine of *jihād.* One of the first thinkers to do so was the Indian reformer Sayyid Ahmad Khan (1817–1898). Believing that the interests of the Indian Muslims would be served best by close cooperation with the British colonizers, he sought to improve relations between both groups. Especially after the 1857 revolt (the so-called Mutiny), the British, who had laid the blame solely on the Muslims despite massive Hindu participation, had favored the latter on the grounds that collaboration with Muslims would pose a security risk because of their allegiance to the doctrine of *jihād.* By offering a new interpretation of the *jihād* duty, Sayyid Ahmad Khan wanted to refute these views and prove that Muslims could be loyal subjects of the British Crown. He rejected the theory that the "sword verses" had repealed all other verses concerning the relations with non-Muslims. On the basis of a new reading of the Qurʾān he asserted that *jihād* was obligatory only in the case of "positive oppression or obstruction in the exercise of their faith, impairing the foundation of some of the pillars of Islam." Because the British, in his view, did not interfere with the Islamic cult, *jihād* against them was not allowed.

In India this extremely limited interpretation of the *jihād* doctrine found some support. In the Middle East, however, reformers such as Muḥammad ʿAbduh (1849–1905) and Muḥammad Rashīd Riḍā (1865–1935) did not go so far. Yet their opinions differed considerably from the classical doctrine. They contended that peaceful coexistence is the normal relationship beween Islamic and non-Islamic territory and that *jihād* must be understood as defensive warfare, regardless, however, of whether the aggression on the part of the non-Muslims is directed against religion or not. In their view, then, *jihād* could indeed be proclaimed against Western colonial rule in the Islamic world. A recent development in modernist *jihād* literature is the presentation of an adapted and reinterpreted version of the *jihād* doctrine as Islamic international law, equating the notion of *jihād* with *bellum justum.*

Although modernist opinion is nowadays widespread, one ought not forget that there are also other schools of thought with regard to *jihād.* Apart from the conservative trend that contents itself with repeating the classical legal texts, there is the fundamentalist or revivalist tendency, whose adherents want to change the world according to Islamic principles. They view their struggle for the Islamization of state and society as *jihād,* explained by them as "the permanent revolution of Islam." They follow the classical doctrine and reject the modernist interpretation of *jihād* as defensive warfare. The most radical groups among them advocate the use of violence against their fellow Muslims, who, in their opinion, are so corrupt that they must be regarded as heathens. To this trend belonged the Tanẓīm al-Jihād ("*jihād* organization"), which was responsible for the assassination of the Egyptian president Sadat in 1981.

See Also ʿAbduh, Muḥammad; Ahmad Khan, Sayyid; Dan Fodio, Usuman; Ibn ʿAbd al-Wahhāb, Muḥammad; Muḥammad Aḥmad; ʿUmar Tāl; Wahhābīyah.

Bibliography

The most extensive and reliable survey of the classical doctrine of *jihād* is Majid Khadduri's *War and Peace in the Law of Islam* (Baltimore, 1955). The same author has translated the oldest legal handbook on *jihād,* written by Muḥammad al-Shaybānī (749–805) and published under the title *The Islamic Law of Nations: Shaybani's Siyar* (Baltimore, 1966). Muḥammad Hamidullah's *Muslim Conduct of State,* 6th rev. ed. (Lahore, 1973), is based on an extensive reading of the classical sources but is somewhat marred by the author's apologetic approach. In my *Jihad in Mediaeval and Modern Islam* (Leiden, 1977), I have translated and annotated a classical legal text and a modernist text on *jihād;* also included is a comprehensive bibliography of translations into Western languages of primary sources on *jihād.* Albrecht Noth's *Heiliger Krieg und heiliger Kampf in Islam und Christentum* (Bonn, 1966) and Emmanuel Sivan's *L'Islam et la Croisade: Idéologie et propagande dans les réactions musulmanes aux Croisades* (Paris, 1968) both deal with the *jihād* doctrine in the historical setting of the Crusades. In addition, Noth compares *jihād* with similar notions in Christianity. Hilmar Krüger's study *Fetwa und Siyar: Zur international rechtlichen Gutachtenpraxis der osmanischen Seyh ül-Islâm vom 17. bis 19. Jahrhundert unter besonderer Berücksichtigung des "Behcet ül-Fetâvâ "*(Wiesbaden, 1978) examines the role of the *jihād* doctrine in Ottoman international relations from the seventeenth to the nineteenth century. Mohammad Talaat Al Ghunaimi's *The Muslim Conception of International Law and the Western Approach* (The Hague, 1968) attempts to apply the notions of modern international law to the *jihād* doctrine and asserts that Islamic law, thus recast, could nowadays be applied in international relations. The political role and the interpretation of the *jihād* doctrine in the nineteenth and twentieth centuries are the main themes of my *Islam and Colonialism: The Doctrine of Jihād in Modern History* (The Hague, 1979). On the Egyptian *jihād* organization see Johannes J. G. Jansen's *The Neglected Duty* (New York, 1986).

Rudolph Peters (1987)

JIMMU, the first emperor of Japan, direct descendant of Amaterasu, the supreme deity, and generally regarded as the ancestor of the present Japanese emperor. Amaterasu's offspring, Ame no Oshiho-mimi, begot Ho no Ninigi, who descended from Heaven to earth. His offspring, Hikohohodemi, begot Ugaya-fukiaezu, whose offspring was Jimmu.

Jimmu is a Chinese-style name given to this emperor much later; his original name was Kamu-yamato-iwarehiko. *Kamu* means "divine," and *Yamato* is the name of the location of the ancient capital. The semantically significant portion of this name is *iwarehiko. Iwa* means "rock," and *are* means "to emerge." Since *hiko* means "a respectable person," Jimmu's original name, *Iwarehiko,* suggests "a respectable person who emerged (or was born) from a rock."

According to the early chronicles, Jimmu was born in the province of Himuka on the island of Kyushu in western Japan. He led a successful expedition to conquer the east and ascended the throne in Yamato in 660 BCE. Historians, however, reject this date because at that time the Japanese still lived in scattered tribal communities. It was only in the second century CE that a unified political organization emerged in western Japan. Although the date of 660 BCE is not acceptable, the description of the Jimmu expedition to Yamato is vivid and realistic. It is unlikely that the story itself was fabricated in later days to glorify the imperial ancestor. It is assumed that the army led by Jimmu entered Yamato in the early second century CE and that Jimmu played a major role in establishing the Yamato state.

See Also Amaterasu Ōmikami; Japanese Religions, article on The Study of Myths.

Bibliography

Aston, W. G., trans. *Nihongi: Chronicles of Japan from the Earliest Times to A.D. 697* (1896). Reprint, 2 vols. in 1, Tokyo, 1972.

Chamberlain, Basil Hall, trans. *Kojiki: Records of Ancient Matters* (1882). 2d ed. With annotations by W. G. Aston. Tokyo, 1932; reprint, Rutland, Vt., and Tokyo, 1982.

Kakubayashi, Fumio. *Nihonshoki Kamiyo-no-maki zenchushaku.* Tokyo, 1999.

Philippi, Donald L., trans. *Kojiki.* Princeton, 1969.

Kakubayashi Fumio (1987 and 2005)

JINGŌ (169–269?), a legendary Japanese empress, was the mother of Ōjin, Japan's first emperor, and symbol of Japanese female shamanism. Jingō is one of fifteen imperial figures fabricated by the authors of the oldest Japanese chronicles (the *Kojiki* and *Nihonshoki,* both seventh century) in order to fill the gap between the real beginning of Japanese history in the fourth century and its fictitious start in 660 BCE. Jingō, therefore, is not historical, but rather symbolic. She stands for the establishment of Japanese relations with the Asian mainland (Korea and China) and is representative of the important role of female shamans in early Japanese history and mythology.

The details of Jingō's legendary history are to be found only in the *Nihonshoki,* which records that she was born in the year 169, the daughter of Prince Okinaga no Sukune and Princess Takanuka of Katsuraki. Immediately after her death she was renamed Okinaga Tarashi hime no Mikoto ("The very witty and well-footed princess"). Almost three centuries later she was given a much shorter, Chinese-style honorary title, Jingō, still in use today. This title, literally "merit of the gods" or "divine merit," implies that she was either divine herself or served to convey divine commands. In this latter capacity she carried out Amaterasu's instructions to have temples erected to her throughout Japan.

In 194 Jingō married the emperor Chūai. In 201 she joined a campaign to subjugate the barbarous tribes of the Kumasō ("land spiders") in Kyushu. During this unsuccessful expedition, she lost her husband, who was probably hit by a Kumasō arrow. After his death, Jingō continued his reign for nearly seventy years.

Upon withdrawing from the campaign in Kyushu, Jingō was advised by the gods to conquer the three Korean states of Bakan, Benkan, and Shinkan, then known as Paekche, Silla, and Koguryō, respectively. Clad in male attire like an emperor, Jingō crossed the straits between Japan and Korea with an enormous army. Upon her arrival in Korea, she established on its south coast the protectorate of Mimana, the Japanese bridgehead from which for centuries to come Korean and Chinese religions and civilizations would spread to Japan. Within two months she had subdued the kingdom of Silla. After this, the kings of Paekche and Koguryō voluntarily agreed to continue yearly tribute to Japan.

Immediately after her return from Korea, Jingō gave birth to a boy, the future emperor Ōjin, whom she named Homuda or Honda. The chronicles of the thirty-ninth year of her reign quote the Chinese chronicles of Wei (composed in 445), in which the Japanese queen Himiko of Wa (in Kyushu) is reported to have paid tribute to the Chinese emperor. It is rather doubtful, however, whether Himiko (the real name of Jingō?) was the same person as Jingō, for the two resided in different regions of Japan. The *Nihonshoki* reports that Jingō died in the palace called Wakazakura (Fresh Cherries) at the age of one hundred.

SEE ALSO Japanese Religions, article on The Study of Myths.

BIBLIOGRAPHY

Aston, W. G., trans. *Nihongi: Chronicles of Japan from the Earliest Times to A.D. 697* (1896). 2 vols. in 1. Reprint, Tokyo, 1972.

Florenz, Karl. *Die historischen Quellen der Shinto-Religion aus dem Altjapanischen und Chinesischen übersetzt und erklärt.* Leipzig, 1919.

Kamstra, J. H. *Encounter or Syncretism: The Initial Growth of Japanese Buddhism.* Leiden, 1967.

J. H. KAMSTRA (1987)

JINGTU. The Chinese term *jingtu* ("pure land"), pronounced *jōdo* in Japanese, refers to the Chinese Buddhist tradition of devotion to Amitābha Buddha in order to be reborn into his Pure Land as a means of attaining enlightenment. Because many Amitābha devotees believed that sincerely chanting Amitābha's name guaranteed salvation in the next life, this practice became an auxiliary spiritual discipline for most Buddhists in East Asia and an important refuge for the laity, but often became a primary and sometimes exclusive orientation in times of crisis. At the heart of this exclusivistic tendency was despair about achieving enlightenment through traditional practices based on one's own effort, and enthusiasm over the compassionate vow of Amitābha to welcome devotees at death to the blessings of his Pure Land. Beginning in the seventh century CE, this tendency became recognized as a separate religious orientation called the Pure Land teaching (*jingtu-zong*).

Unlike counterparts in Japan, Pure Land devotees in China never developed into a centrally organized property-holding denomination with formalized methods of succession (except for the White Lotus movement during the twelfth to fourteenth centuries). Instead, the Pure Land devotional movement was a loosely knit association of individuals based on the promises of Indian scriptures interpreted by Chinese thinkers and supported by such practical devices as rosaries, paintings, liturgies, and stories about supernatural visions and deathbed miracles indicating successful rebirth into the Pure Land.

FORMATION OF CHINESE PURE LAND. The term *jingtu* was invented in China to refer to Sukhāvatī, the land of bliss created in the western regions by Amitābha, the Buddha of Infinite Life and Infinite Light, for the purification and enlightenment of beings. Mahāyāna Buddhists believe that all Buddhas have spheres of activity (Skt., *kṣetra,* "lands"), but Amitābha's land became most popular based on his vows that ordinary people can be reborn into his land through simple devotion and thereby attain a speedy, painless, and guaranteed enlightenment.

Beginning in 179 CE, when the *Banzhou sanmei jing* (Skt., *Pratyutpannasamādhi Sūtra*) was translated into Chinese, the visualization of Amitābha was recommended as a meditation practice for bringing a Buddha into one's presence. In the third century more Amitābha scriptures were translated, so that by the fourth century there are reports of the first Chinese Pure land devotees (Que Gongce and his disciple Wei Shidu), the first Pure Land lectures (by Zhu Faguang) and the first construction of images and pictures of Amitābha and his Pure Land.

In 402 CE, meditation master Lushan Huiyuan (334–416) formed a devotional group in South China. It consisted of Huiyuan and 123 laypeople and clergy who sought to support one another in visualizing and making offerings to Amitābha to facilitate rebirth in the Pure Land. Centuries later, this group came to be regarded as the original White Lotus Society. After the death of Huiyuan and his immediate disciples, little is heard of Pure Land practices in the south for the next few centuries.

The Shansi Pure Land movement. In response to the ravages of war, famine, and the uncertainties of the religious life during the sixth century, the monks Tanluan (c. 488–c. 554) and Daochuo (562–645) pioneered an independent Pure Land movement at the Xuanzhong Monastery in the remote hills of the Bingzhou area of Shansi Province in North China. By this time, the most important Indian Pure Land scriptures had been translated into Chinese. These included the *Amitābha Sūtra* (Chin., *Amitofo jing*), the "larger" *Sukhāvatīvyūha Sūtra* (Chin., *Wuliangshou jing*), the *Guan wuliangshou jing*, and the *Wangsheng lun*, attributed to Vasubandhu. These texts mention that enlightenment is difficult in our age because of the five afflictions (*wuzhuo*): war and natural disasters, deluded ideas, greed and hatred, infirmity of body and mind, and shortness of life. According to Tanluan, the compassionate aid of Amitābha is thus a necessity for salvation.

In his major work, the *Wangsheng lunchu* (a commentary to Vasubandhu's treatise), Tanluan divides Buddhism into two paths, the "difficult" and the "easy." The Difficult Path includes all traditional Buddhist practices based on self-effort. Later, Daochuo referred to this as the Path of the Sages (*shengdao*) and proclaimed that such practices were doomed to failure, not only because of the five afflictions but also because our age was the period predicted by the scriptures when true Buddhism would disappear (*mofa*; Jpn., *mappō*). Thus it became a key Pure Land idea that salvation through self-effort was impossible. Instead of the Difficult Path, Tanluan advocated the Easy Path made available through the forty-eight vows of Amitābha recorded in the *Wuliangshou jing*. Tanluan was the first in North China to emphasize how these vows promised rebirth in the Pure Land through the "other power" (*tali*) of Amitābha followed by the assurance of nonretrogression into lower rebirths and the speedy attainment of enlightenment.

Basing his teachings on the *Wangsheng lun*, Tanluan adopted as a curriculum of practice the five types of devotion to Amitābha (*nianfo*; Jpn., *nembutsu*) in order to ensure access to Amitābha's power: (1) to make prostrations to Amitābha and wish to be reborn in his land; (2) to sing praises to Amitābha and recite his name; (3) to make vows to be reborn into his Pure Land; (4) to visualize the appearance of Amitābha and the Pure land; and (5) to transfer these merits to all beings for their salvation. Tanluan and others emphasized the necessity of seeking the Pure Land not for its own pleasures but to attain enlightenment so as to return to this world to save others. This desire for enlightenment (*bodhicitta*) was held to be a primary condition for rebirth, thus demonstrating a continuity between the values of Pure Land and those of other forms of Buddhism.

Vocal recitation. The practice of vocal recitation and singing praises to Amitābha soon became the most striking form of Pure Land devotion in China. For Tanluan, this involved a mystical union with the name of Amitābha, which he believed had unlimited power, and required an exclusive and total concentration that precluded attention to other Buddhas and subordinated all other practices. Incessant vocal recitation then became a trademark of Daochuo, who made the first rosaries for counting recitations of Amitābha's name. By teaching this practice to laity, a popular religious movement developed with the slogan "Chant the Buddha's name and be reborn in the Pure Land" (*nianfo wangsheng*). His disciple Shandao (613–681) established scriptural arguments for vocal recitation of Amitābha's name as a minimal but sufficient practice to ensure the rebirth of ordinary people into the Pure Land. Although Shandao personally was preoccupied with visualization practices, he is most famous for his list of "five correct practices," in which he substituted chanting the scriptures and reciting Amitābha's name for making a vow and transferring merits. For Shandao, the recitation of Amitābha's name was the only "correct and determining action" necessary for salvation. In the next century, Fazhao furthured this trend by developing a five-rhythm melodic recitation of Amitābha's name, a practice still popular today. In the Song dynasty (960–1279), block printing enabled the distribution of devotional pamphlets and recitation cards in which one could record the number of one's recitations as a visible reminder to maintain one's practice.

Consolidation of the Pure Land school. Although Shandao studied under Daochuo, he spent his mature years in the national capital, Chang'an, where the stature of his achievements in meditation and the comprehensiveness of his writings firmly established the theory and practice of Pure Land devotionalism among Chinese Buddhist leaders. Besides his theoretical and liturgical writings, the *Guan wuliangshou chingshu*, *Guannian men*, *Banzhou zan*, *Wangshen lizanji*, and *Fashi zan*, Shandao brought added prestige to the movement by painting more than three hundred images of the Pure Land and, at the request of Empress Wu, supervising the construction of the great Vairocana Buddha image at Lung-men between the years 672 and 675. The ascendency of Pure Land devotion as a major force can be seen by the increasing number of sculptures of Amitābha, which in the

Lung-men caves came to outnumber those of Śākyamuni by a factor of twelve and those of Maitreya by a factor of ten in the period from 650 to 690.

In the generation after Shandao, Pure Land writings such as the *Shi jingtu chuni lun*, by Shandao's disciple Huaigan, and the *Jingtu shii lun*, based on the *Anloji* of Daochuo, summarized and applied the Pure Land doctrine in the question-and-answer format of a catechism. Studies of Indian Pure Land scriptures and essays on Pure Land subjects faded away in favor of ritual texts and manuals of practice. The *banzhou sanmei* ritual (based on the practice found in the *Banzhou sanmei jing*) was propogated by Huiri (680–748), Chengyuan, and Fazhao, whereas the more exclusive practice of verbal recitation was taught by Daxing and Daojing. Thus, by the beginning of the eighth century a cohesive core of Pure Land beliefs, values, and practices has emerged based upon a sense of the inadequacy or inappropriateness of all other Buddhist teachings and the attractiveness of Amitābha and his Pure Land. The Chinese Pure Land movement had reached its full definition and most exclusive form. One could safely live and die within a world of writings and practices devoted only to rebirth in the Pure Land and in which exclusive devotion to Amitābha was trumpeted as the only guaranteed method of salvation for all. For laity and those distressed by their inadequacies, Pure Land offered a simple but potent formula: (1) the miraculous power of *one* practice (*nianfo* as recitation), (2) directed toward *one* Buddha (Amitābha), (3) to achieve rebirth in *one* place (the Western Pure Land), (4) so that in *one* more rebirth Buddhahood could be achieved. Although other forms of Chinese Buddhist practice had not been abolished, for adherents of Pure Land they had been displaced as a major focus and obligation for the present life and largely postponed until rebirth in Sukhāvatī.

The spread of Pure Land. As early as Tanxian (d. 440), a member of Huiyuan's community on Lushan, advocates of Pure Land devotionalism had collected stories about those who had attained rebirth in the Pure Land. These stories recorded religious practices of devotees and unusual deathbed occurrences that were signs of rebirth in the Pure Land: music emanating from the sky, a sweet fragrance, five-colored clouds, visions of attendants welcoming one to the Pure Land, or pathways of light. The earliest surviving collection of Pure Land biographies is the *Jingtu lun*, compiled by Jiacai in the mid-seventh century. Of the twenty biographies he recorded, six are of monks, four of nuns, five of laymen, and five of laywomen. The enduring prominence of laity and of women in the movement makes it unique among the Buddhist traditions of China.

The Bingzhou area of North China remained the heart of Pure Land practice according to biographical records of eminent monks of the Tang dynasty (618–906). Among Pure Land collections, the *Wangsheng xifang jingtu ruiying zhuan*, compiled by 805 CE, lists 26 people from North China (Shansi and Shensi provinces) and only 7 from South China (Chekiang and Kiangsu provinces). By contrast, in the treatment of the Pure Land movement in the thirteenth century *Fozu tongji*, there are biographies of only 20 people from Shansi, 20 from Shensi, but 129 from Chekiang and 24 from Kiangsu. This marks a definite shift of the focus of Pure Land devotionalism from North to South China. In addition, the sequence of patriarchs offered by the *Fozu tongji* begins with a Southerner, Lushan Huiyuan, skips Tanluan and Daochuo, and goes on to Shandao, Chengyuan (713–803), Fazhao, Shaokang (d. 805), and Yenshou (904–975). This pattern also appears in the *Lobang wenlei*, compiled by Zongxiao (1151–1214), and it is a standard format in the Ming dynasty (1368–1644) lineages.

Opposition. Pure Land devotionalism did not spread without opposition. In the seventh century, yogācāra advocates argued against Shandao by claiming that the Pure Land was an expedient device for special circumstances that did not ensure final salvation, and that in any event ordinary people were not qualified to be reborn there. More vigorous attacks came in the early eighth century from the Southern Chan (Zen) school, which criticized Pure Land as dualistic, encouraging attachment, and promising future enlightenment as a delusive crutch for people of inferior spiritual capacities. Cimin Huiri (680–748) criticized Chan followers for their arrogant rejection of the many devotional practices recommended throughout Buddhist scriptures and in turn accused them of being ignorant of the higher forms of Indian *chan* (Skt., *dhyāna*, "meditation").

Integration and levels of nianfo. More constructively, the eighth-century *Wu fangpian nianfo men* interpreted both Chan and Pure Land as having five progressive levels of practice, each of which is regarded as an expedient device (*fangpian*; Skt., *upāya*). Insofar as practitioners have different spiritual needs and capacities, each level is valid but not exhaustive. The five expedient methods of *nianfo* are: (1) the Buddha's name is recited to attain rebirth in the Pure Land; (2) the form of the Buddha is visualized to eradicate sins; (3) all items of perception are seen as mere products of mind; (4) the mind and its objects of perception are both transcended; and (5) the perfect understanding of how true nature arises is gained. This scheme influenced the fourfold *nianfo* of Zongmi (780–841): (1) vocally calling the Buddha's name; (2) visualizing the Buddha's form as an image or painting to receive the five spiritual powers and see all Buddhas in the ten directions; (3) visualizing the major and minor marks of the Buddha to eradicate all sins; and (4) contemplating the absolute true nature wherein the Buddha has no marks and no name and one uses no-thought *(wui)* as the method to contemplate the Buddha (*nianfo*). Thus, at the highest level, Pure Land forms unite with Chan formlessness. This idea of the progressive levels of *nianfo* culminated in such thinkers as Zhixu (1599–1655), who proclaimed Pure Land devotion as supreme because it could include all Chan and Tiantai practices within different levels of *nianfo*.

Dual cultivation. The Chan patriarch Yungming Yenshou (904–975) is famous for advocating the "dual cultivation of Chan and Pure Land" (*chanjing shuangxiu*) as being doubly effective, like a "tiger wearing horns." His proposal was partially based on Feixi's idea that Chan and Pure Land were like the dialectic of emptiness and form, or underlying principle *(li)* and phenomenal events *(shi)*, and each would be incomplete without the other. In his *Wanshan tonggui* Yenshou considered Pure Land and Chan to be focused on phenomena and thus to represent only one aspect of the One Mind, namely its external functioning (*yong*). Basing his teaching on the *Dacheng qixin lun* (Awakening of faith in the Mahāyāna), Yenshou taught that phenomena must be balanced by the other aspect of the One Mind, namely its underlying nature *(ti)*. The Pure Land, like all phenomena, is perception-only (*weixin*), and the division between Pure Land and Chan is transcended when one is enlightened to the true nature of the One Mind.

Pure Land practices were an important part of the devotional life of many Chinese Buddhists usually identified with other traditions. Monks such as Zhiyi, Daoxuan, and Jizang, who are normally listed as the patriarchs of the Tiantai, Vinaya, and Sanlun schools, respectively, all employed Pure Land regimens in their practice. Tiantai Zhiyi (538–597) had a doctrine of four levels of Buddha lands and advocated a ninety-day practice of chanting Amitābha's name while constantly walking, a practice still undertaken in Japan. Tiantai became further identified with Pure Land when an eighth-century commentary on the *Guan jing* was attributed to Zhiyi. Later, Siming Zhili (960–1028) composed a subcommentary titled *Miaozong chao*, in which he presented his doctrine of "visualizing the Buddha in terms of the [mundane and absolute aspects of] mind" (*yuexin guanfo*). Basing his doctrine on the *Dacheng qixin lun*, he argued that all religious practices are the mind's external functioning *(yong)* and are for the sole purpose of revealing the mind's underlying nature *(ti)*. When our conditioned minds seek enlightenment by visualizing Amitābha, the underlying nature responds with an image in our minds so that there is temporarily a distinction between Buddhas and humans. However, in the act of seeking insight, practitioners are also united with the underlying enlightened nature. These two levels of activity reflect the two aspects of the One Mind; they are Zhili's interpretation of the *Guan jing* phrase: "This mind is the Buddha, this mind creates the Buddha." This doctrine had enormous influence, since Zhili's works became authoritative for Tiantai from the Song dynasty (960–1279) onward, and most Tiantai masters came to seek rebirth in the Pure Land.

The revival of Buddhism under the patronage of the Song dynasty was not marked by the intense textual and doctrinal studies of the Tang period; rather, the focus was on personal cultivation. In spite of Chan's initial antagonism to Pure Land, the Chan monastic code *Chanlin chinggui* (1311) recommended chanting Amitābha's name at funerals. Gradually, Yenshou's teaching of dual cultivation permeated all aspects of the Chan tradition and remains a model up to today. Various masters in the Wenyan Chan lineage taught that the Pure Land is a mental representation only. Cique Zongze formed a *nianfo* recitation society in 1089, asserting that "one's self-nature is Amitābha." Later teachers who used the practice of meditating on a question (*huatou*) such as Hanshan Deqing (1546–1623) urged that disciples ask "Who is it that recites the Buddha's name?" after each recitation of the name of Amitābha in order to achieve Chan enlightenment. Pure Land devotionalism as a supreme path was periodically championed by such figures as Zhuhong (1535–1615), Zhixu (1599–1655), the layman Peng Shaosheng (1739–1796), and his nephew Peng Xisu (who compiled the biographies of approximately five hundred Pure Land devotees).

White Lotus Society. Lay recitation societies flourished in the Song dynasty, the most famous being the White Lotus Society, formed by Mao Ziyuan (1086–1166) in Kiangsu in 1133. While appealing to Lushan Huiyuan's society as a model, Ziyuan added a number of later innovations: vocal recitations; married clergy; strict vegetarianism; the construction of hostels; the active leadership of women; the Tiantai theories of the four Buddha lands and the inseparability of mind-Buddha-living beings; and Zhili's teaching of visualizing the Buddha in terms of the mundane and absolute aspects of mind. He considered all religious practices to be valid insofar as they all have the same goal, all places are identical to the Pure Land, all phenomena are mind-only, and our own natures are identical to that of Amitābha. For ordinary people, however, Ziyuan urged the expedient means (*upāya*) of believing that the Pure Land is to the west and adhering to a gradual religious path based on correct faith, practice, and vows. Correct faith and vows were those that conformed to the teachings of Tanluan, Daochuo, and Shandao. Correct practice could be anything based on a person's abilities, but, like Shandao and Yenshou before him, Ziyuan stressed having correct mindfulness at the moment of death to seal rebirth in the Pure Land.

The White Lotus Society had a checkered history of political sponsorship and repression that culminated in its suppression in 1322. By that time it had developed from a centrally organized lay devotional society to a large property-holding movement with White Lotus Halls for charitable activities such as donating cloth to the populace, copying scriptures, and developing bathhouses, waterworks, mills, shops, boats, and land throughout Fukian Province. The reason for its suppression is uncertain, but as a lay society involving women, people from lower levels of society, and working people who met together at night, it probably provoked rumors of rebellion and immorality. The decree of abolishment became a template for branding and suppressing many later groups who developed followings independent of the state, but often with very different beliefs, until all so-called White Lotus groups were finally suppressed in 1813.

Modern status. A fundamentalist view of the Pure Land as an actual place and the need for moral purity was advocated by Yinguang (1861–1940), but in 1951 he was strongly opposed by Yinshun (1906–) in his *New Treatise on the Pure Land* (*Jingtu xinlun*). Arguing that the images of Amitābha and the Pure Land are culturally constructed and recitation is the lowest form of practice, Yinshun challenged the focus on funeral practices and rebirth in the Pure Land. Instead, practitioners should create an earthly Pure Land through inner cultivation and social service. Yinshun's this-worldly emphasis is now central to the two largest worldwide Chinese Buddhist movements, Fo Guang Shan and the Compassion Relief Tzu Chi Association, and the more exclusivistic tendencies of Daochuo, Shandao, and Yinguang are marginalized.

For the last thousand years Pure Land devotion was transmitted in conjunction with Tiantai and Chan, and most contemporary large monasteries include both a Chan meditation hall and a Pure Land recitation hall. Rosaries for reciting Amitābha's name (*nianzhu*) and the respectful greeting of "O-mi-to-fo" are found throughout Taiwan today, but rarely in mainland China. Nevertheless, wherever practice exists in a Chinese Buddhist temple, and no matter how it is understood, the melodic chanting of Amitābha's name echoes in its halls as an enduring part of Chinese culture.

See Also Amitābha; Daochuo; Huiyuan; Millenarianism, article on Chinese Millenarian Movements; Nianfo; Pure and Impure Lands; Shandao; Tanluan.

Bibliography

The most comprehensive scholarly study of *jingtu* is Mochizuki Shinkō's *Chūgoku jōdo kyōri shi* (Kyoto, 1942), which has an unpublished English translation by Leo Pruden (1982). The earliest Pure Land scripture translated into Chinese was studied by Paul Harrison, *The Samadhi of Direct Encounter with the Buddhas of the Present* (Tokyo, 1990). For issues in Pure Land thought, see Ken Tanaka, *The Dawn of Chinese Pure Land Buddhist Doctrine: Ching-ying Hui-yuan's Commentary on the* Visualization Sutra (Albany, N.Y., 1990). The primary Pure Land leader, Shandao, has two studies, Fujiwara Ryō-setsu, *The Way of Nirvana: The Concept of Nembutsu in Shan-tao's Pure Land Buddhism* (Tokyo, 1974) and Julian Pas, *Visions of Sukhāvatī: Shan-tao's Commentary on the Kuan Wu-liang-Shou-Fo Ching* (Albany, N.Y., 1995). Later historical developments are found in Peter Gregory and Daniel Getz, ed., *Buddhism in the Sung* (Honolulu, 2002), Daniel Overmyer, *Folk Buddhist Religion: Dissenting Sects in Late Traditional China* (Cambridge, Mass., 1976), Barend J. ter Haar, *The White Lotus Teachings in Chinese Religious History* (Leiden, 1992), Chun-fang Yu, *The Renewal of Buddhism in China: Chu-hung and the Late Ming Synthesis* (New York, 1981), and Charles Jones, *Buddhism in Taiwan* (Honolulu, 1999).

David W. Chappell (1987 and 2005)

JĪVA See INDIAN PHILOSOPHIES; JĪVANMUKTI

JĪVANMUKTI. The Sanskrit term *jīvanmukti* means "liberation as a living being." A person who has attained liberation in his lifetime is called *jīvanmukta.* Although these precise terms seem to have been popularized only by followers of Śaṅkara, late in the first millennium CE, the concept of a liberated person had become a commonplace of Indian religious thought many centuries earlier. This article will concentrate on the concept.

The final goal of every Hindu is to attain release (*mukti*) from *saṃsāra,* the endless cycle of death and rebirth that all living beings—gods, human beings, animals, and lower spirits—undergo. The cause of rebirth is *karman,* or intentional action. All intentional action originates from "passion" (*rāga*), or emotional involvement with the world. As *mukti* is release from *saṃsāra,* it is thus release from *karman* and its results; and this abandonment of *karman* is to be attained by cultivating "dispassion" (*vairāgya*), emotional disengagement from the world.

In those forms of Hinduism that see devotion to God as the means to salvation, such detachment from the world, and hence *mukti,* is to be attained only at death. However, in the religions that dominated Indian culture from about 500 BCE to late in the first millennium CE, salvation is due to a liberating insight, or *gnōsis.* It is a corollary of all Gnostic religion that liberation can be attained in this life. (In India this possibility is explicitly restricted to human beings.) Thus, there can be human beings who are already saved, who are devoid of passion and of the kind of intentionality that will cause them to be reborn: in such cases, at the death of the body, the sequence of cause and effect set in motion by the individual's *karman* will cease.

Although the content of this gnosis varies in detail from school to school, for all Hindus it involves the realization that one's essential nature is pure spirit, immortal and immutable. Whatever is not pure spirit is impermanent and liable to change; it is utterly other than one's essential nature. The Western distinction between mind and matter is a misleading analogy, for most of what Western thought assigns to mind Indian thought categorizes as nonspiritual. The only apparently "mental" characteristic allowed by all Hindus to the spirit is pure consciousness. All schools agree that the Gnostic who has successfully discriminated between his purely conscious spirit and the transient phenomena that comprise the rest of his apparent empirical personality is thereby freed from suffering (*duḥkha*); most go further and characterize this state as bliss (*ānanda*).

The earliest texts containing this kind of Gnostic religion are the early Upaniṣads (c. seventh century BCE). Buddhism and Jainism are religions of this Gnostic type; but the metaphysics of both are, in separate ways, different from those of Hinduism; and as the term *jīvanmukti* is never applied, even retrospectively, to Buddhist or Jain saints, this article deals only with Hindu formulations of the concept.

The Hindu Gnostic sees through the unreality of changing phenomena, in particularly their duality; he rises above pleasure and pain, good and evil. The enlightened person is thus beyond moral categories; but as he or she is free from all emotional attachments, the enlightened person will never do evil. The person seeking this gnosis will tend to renounce worldly life because it involves types of activity—sexual, economic—that cannot be carried on without attachment. Although the early Upaniṣads stress the intellectual pursuit of gnosis, in most schools it was pursued through the practice of yoga. On whether the liberated person continues to perform ritual, opinions differ sharply.

All later Hindu sects were influenced by the metaphysics of Sāṃkhya, an atheistic path to salvation. The spirit (*puruṣa/ātman*) is considered here as utterly other than nature/matter (*prakṛti*), which is one, though diversified. Spirits are many and are inactive and transcendent, mere conscious witnesses of the activity of *prakṛti,* the material cause of the phenomenal world, including all mental functions and intelligence. Involvement with the world and suffering arise from a failure of discrimination (*viveka*). Once one has dissociated one's spirit from mind and ego, one stands sheer and alone (*kevalin*), untouched by emotion. This isolation (*kaivalya*) of the spirit ensures that at death one is never reborn. The *kevalin* lives on after attaining gnosis because the *kevalin's karman,* which had begun to bear fruit, must exhaust its momentum, like the potter's wheel after the potter has stopped spinning it. The *Bhagavadgītā* describes such a person as *sthitaprajña,* "of serene wisdom."

The Advaita Vedānta school established by Śaṅkara virtually accepted the Sāṃkhya view of the *kevalin,* despite a different metaphysical basis. In the tradition of the early Upaniṣads, the Vedāntins regarded the plurality of individual souls (*ātman*) as an illusion: there is only one reality, *brahman,* with which all souls must realize their unity. *Prakṛti* is not only other than spirit; it is in fact nonexistent. One's entire view of a plural world is just a mistake. The person who has undone this mistake is *jīvanmukta.*

Hindu Tantric sects hold a different view of *mukti.* For these monotheistic Gnostics, salvation is achieved through God's grace, which is then instantiated in the successful efforts of the practitioner, who aims to change his or her impure body into the pure substance of *śákti,* God's energy, the source of all things. If successful, the practioner becomes a *siddha* ("successful one"). The idea occurs in the Śaiva Tantras, in the Vajrayāna Tantras, and in *haṭhayoga.* The pure body of a *siddha* was conceived by some to be immortal, so that *jīvanmukti* amounted to apotheosis. Specialists in alchemy (*rasaśāstra*) hoped to achieve immortality by ingesting mercury, the essence of Śiva, and some Tantrics continue to believe that breathing exercises can render them immortal, or at least ensure them very long life.

SEE ALSO Indian Philosophies; Tantrism, article on Hindu Tantrism.

BIBLIOGRAPHY

Brunner, Hélène. "Un chapître du *Sarvadarsanasamgraha:* Le Saivadarsana." In *Tantric and Taoist Studies in Honour of R. A. Stein,* edited by Michel Strickmann, vol. 20 of *Mélanges chinois et bouddhiques,* pp. 96–140. Brussels, 1983.

Dasgupta, Surendranath. *A History of Indian Philosophy,* vols. 1 & 2. Cambridge, U.K., 1922–1932. A traditional treatment of the views of Śaṅkara and his followers, including a lucid discussion of the Gnostic view of salvation. See especially pages 207, 268, and 291–292 in volume 1 and pages 245–252 in volume 2.

Eliade, Mircea. *Yoga: Immortality and Freedom.* 2d ed. Princeton, 1969. Still the best work on the yogic path of release.

Hiriyanna, Mysore. *The Essentials of Indian Philosophy.* London, 1949. A concise historical introduction. See especially pages 31–56 and 129–174.

Kaw, R. K. *Pratyabhijñā Kārikā of Utpaladeva: Basic Text on Pratyabhijñā Philosophy* (*The Doctrine of Recognition*). Sharada Peetha Indological Research Series, vol. 12. Srinagar, 1975. Includes a clear description of the Śaiva Tantra path of salvation.

New Sources

Fort, Andrew O. *Jivanmukti in Transformation: Embodied Liberation in Advaita and Neo-Vedanta.* Albany, N.Y., 1998.

Living Liberation in Hindu Thought. Edited by Andrew O. Fort and Patricia Y. Mumme. Albany, N.Y., 1996.

Srivastava, Lalit Kishore Lal. *Advaitic Concept of Jivanmukti.* Delhi, 1990.

SANJUKTA GUPTA (1987)
Revised Bibliography

JIZANG (549–623), Chinese Buddhist monk of the Sanlun (Three-Treatise) tradition. Although half Parthian by birth, Jizang's upbringing and education were entirely Chinese. At the age of ten he became a novice under the Sanlun master Falang (508–581) and resided at the Xinghuang temple in the Southern Dynasties (c. 420–589) capital of Jinling (modern Nanjing), the center of Buddhist culture in southern China. Until the age of thirty-two, he was under the tutelage of Falang, studying primary Sanlun sources as well as the important texts of his age, the Prajñāpāramitā (Perfection of Wisdom) canon, the *Saddharmapuṇḍarīka Sūtra (Lotus Sūtra),* and the Mahāyāna *Mahāparinirvāṇa Sūtra* (Sūtra of the great decease). Following Falang's death in 581, Jizang spent some eight years at the Jiaxiang temple, east of the capital on Mount Qinwang (his posthumous title, Master of Jiaxiang Temple, is derived from his residence at this temple). In 597 he was invited by the emperor Sui Yangdi (581–618) to reside at the Huiri Daochang, one of four monasteries built by that ruler in support of the religion. Jizang spent less than two years at this monastery and, again at the request of Yangdi, moved in 599 to the new imperial capital of Chang'an. There he resided at the Riyan temple, remaining there until his death at the age of seventy-four.

With the reunification of China in 589, Jizang witnessed the controlled revival of Buddhism at a time when the religion was sponsored not only for its own sake but also as a means by which the nation could be consolidated, expanded, and protected. Throughout his life Jizang participated fully in the optimism and luxury of imperial patronage. Under this patronage he produced twenty-six works, collected in some 112 fascicles, a number that makes him one of the most prolific Buddhist writers of his age. Jizang considered himself a specialist on the Perfection of Wisdom literature as well as on the major Mahāyāna sūtras then available to him in Chinese translation. Of his extant works, approximately fifteen are concerned exclusively with the exegesis of sūtras. They cover an extensive range of the topics found in the fertile symbols and ideas of the vast Mahāyāna textual corpus. As an exegete his writings account for some of the major doctrinal trends of Mahāyāna Buddhism and represent one of the earliest Chinese attempts to systematize its canon. Under the influence of the Mahāyāna *Nirvāṇa Sūtra,* the text that dominated Chinese intellectual thought during the fifth and sixth centuries, Jizang wrote extensively on its theme of "Buddha nature" (universal enlightenment). He was the first East Asian Buddhist to argue that even the nonsentient world of wood and stone had the potentiality for enlightenment. As a scholar of the Perfection of Wisdom tradition, he was best known for his essays on the Buddhist concept of the Two Truths, a theory of nonduality achieved through serial negation. These essays established one of the enduring ways by which later East Asian Buddhists came to approach and understand the Buddhist concept of emptiness (*śūnyatā*).

SEE ALSO Śūnyam and Śūnyatā.

BIBLIOGRAPHY

The most comprehensive work on Jizang and the Sanlun tradition is by Hirai Shun'ei, *Chūgoku hannya shisōshi kenkyū* (Tokyo, 1976). A review of this work and the questions it raises regarding the history of Sanlun Buddhism may be found in my study "'Later Mādhyamika' in China: Some Current Perspectives on the History of Chinese *Prajnāpāramitā* Thought," *Journal of the International Association for Buddhist Studies* 5, (1982): 53–62. Critical analyses of the Chinese contributions toward the Two Truths theory may be found in an article by Whalen Lai, "Further Developments of the Two Truths Theory in China: The *Ch'eng-shih-lun* Tradition and Chou Yung's *San-tsung-lun,*" *Philosophy East and West* 30 (April 1980): 139–161, and in an article I have written, "The Concept of Practice in San Lun Thought: Chi-tsang and the 'Concurrent Insight' of the Two Truths," *Philosophy East and West* 31 (October 1981): 449–466. Translations of selected portions of Jizang's writings can be found in Wing-tsit Chan's *A Source Book in Chinese Philosophy* (Princeton, 1963), pp. 360–369, and in *The Buddhist Tradition in India, China, and Japan,* edited by Wm. Theodore de Bary, Yoshito S. Hakeda, and Philip B. Yampolsky (New York, 1969).

New Sources

Fox, Alan. "Jizang (Chi-Tsang) [A.D. 549–623]." In *Great Thinkers of the Eastern World: The Major Thinkers and the Philosophical and Religious Classics of China, India, Japan, Korea, and the World of Islam,* edited by Ian P. McGreal, pp. 84–88. New York, 1995.

AARON K. KOSEKI (1987)
Revised Bibliography

JIZŌ SEE KṢITIGARBHA

JÑĀNA.

The Sanskrit root *jñā* is cognate with the Old English *knawan.* Hence on etymological consideration one normally translates *jñāna* as "knowledge." Although this translation seems harmless in many contexts, in a philosophical text that deals with epistemology, or *pramāṇa-śāstra,* it will often be wrong and misleading. In fact, in nontechnical Sanskrit *jñāna* often means knowledge. But when it is contrasted with *pramā* ("knowledge, knowledge-episode"), it means simply a cognition or awareness, and it is meant in an episodic sense. A cognition is an episode that happens in a subject, and when such a cognitive episode becomes true it becomes knowledge, as in *pramā.* Thus, one must say, only some cognitions are knowledge; others may be cases of doubt, misperception, error, false judgment, opinion, and so forth.

In epistemology, the problem is formulated as follows: What is it that makes a *jñāna* or a cognitive event a piece of knowledge, *pramā?* The general answer is that if the causal factors are faultless and no opposing or counteracting factor (*pratibandhaka*) intervenes, the result would be a true cognitive event, a piece of knowledge. The Nyāya school uses *jñāna* in the more comprehensive sense. For according to Nyāya, to be conscious means to be conscious of something, there being no such thing as "pure consciousness," and this again means to cognize or to be aware of something, that is, to have a *jñāna* of something. The conscious subject, or self, is analyzed as the subjunct that *has* cognition or *jñāna,* the obvious conclusion being that a *jñāna* or a particular cognitive event is a quality (*guṇa*) or a qualifier (*dharma*) of the self. The Buddhists, however, analyze the person or the self into five aggregates, of which the awareness series, or the awareness aggregate, is the main constituent. The self is therefore only an awareness series in this view where in each moment an awareness arises, conditioned by the preceding one, along with a number of attending factors. Feelings such as pleasure, pain, and anger are part of the awareness event, according to the Buddhists. But Nyāya wishes to introduce a distinction between the pleasure-event or pain-event and one's cognitive awareness (*jñāna*) of such events.

The Sāṃkhya view of *jñāna* is different. In this view the intellect (*buddhi*) and ego-sense or I-consciousness (*ahaṃkāra*) are all evolutes (*vikāras*) of matter. The spiritual substance is called *puruṣa* ("man"). Consciousness is the essential attribute of *puruṣa,* the spiritual reality. But because the intellect (a material evolute) is extremely transparent and mirrorlike by nature (Vācaspati's view), it reflects the consciousness of the *puruṣa,* that is, it becomes tinged with awareness, and thus an awareness-event arises. It is called a *vṛtti* ("modification") or transformation (*pariṇāma*) of the intellect. It is therefore the spiritual illumination of the mental form, that is, *buddhi* transformed into the form of an object, which makes *jñāna* possible. In Advaita Vedānta, a special manifestation of consciousness (the self-consciousness) is *jñāna* in the primary sense. But the *vṛtti* that the *buddhi* ("intellect") obtains is also called *jñāna* in a secondary sense. Of the two components, the *vṛtti* grasps the form of the object and destroys the veil of ignorance or the state of "unknowing" (*avidyā*), but the particular manifestation of consciousness is what actually *reveals* the object.

Jñāna has soteriological significance. It is almost unanimously claimed (except by the Cārvāka) that some sort of *jñāna,* or *tattva-jñāna* ("knowledge of the reality as it is") is instrumental in bringing about the final release from bondage. Here, of course, *jñāna* stands for "knowledge." Knowledge is what liberates one from human bondage. Even the *Nyāya Sūtra* states that the ultimate good (*niḥśreyasa*) springs from human knowledge (*tattva-jñāna*) of different realities. It is commonplace to say in Advaita Vedānta that *brahmajñāna* ("knowledge of the *brahman*") is the ultimate means for liberation: It is that which establishes the essential identity of the individual self with the ultimate Self or universal Self, *brahman.* One's congenital misconception (*avidyā*) creates a false disunity between the individual and the *brahman,* but *jñāna* establishes their ultimate union. In some Buddhist texts (cf. Vasubandhu, *Triṃśikā*) a distinction is made between *jñāna* and *vijñāna* where the latter is subdivided into *ālaya-vijñāna* and *pravṛtti-vijñāna.* The *pravṛtti-vijñāna* stands for all the ordinary cognitive events of life, cognition of blue for example; while the *ālaya* is said to be the seed (*bīja*) or the subterranean current that causes the "waves" of other cognitive experiences and in turn is fed back by such experiences to continue the process of *saṃsāra* ("the round of births and deaths"). But when the saint acquires *jñāna,* there is a complete reversal (*parāvṛtti*) of the base (*ālaya-āśraya*) in the saint. There is pure *jñāna,* which is also called *bodha* and which eliminates the *vijñāna* series. For there cannot be any *grāhaka* or *vijñāna* or apprehension when there is no *grāhya,* no apprehensible object. This is called the *dharmakāya* of the Buddha.

In certain religious or philosophical texts that promote syncretism, such as the *Bhagavadgītā,* three principal ways of attaining the final goal of salvation are mentioned. They are *karmayoga* (the path of action), *jñānayoga* (the path of knowledge), and *bhaktiyoga* (the path of devotion). The path of knowledge means that ultimate knowledge, or comprehension of the ultimate truth, is sufficient to bring about liberation. But sometimes this path is combined with the path of action, which means that religious and moral duties are performed with a completely unattached disposition (*niṣkāma karma*). One's actions with motivation to obtain results create bondage, but if one is unattached to the result one's actions cannot bind one. Hence knowledge of the Ultimate, when it is combined with such "unattached" action, opens the door to liberation. *Bhakti,* devotional attachment and complete surrender to the deity, is another way. Sometimes a situation is recognized as *jñāna-karma-samuccaya-vāda,* that is, it is claimed that *jñāna* and *karma* are like the two wings of a bird: It cannot fly with just one of them.

See Also Ālaya-vijñāna; Mīmāṃsā; Nyāya; Sāṃkhya; Vaiśeṣika; Vedānta; Yoga.

Bibliography

For *jñāna* in Nyāya-Vaiśeṣika, see chapter 2 of my *The Navya-nyāya Doctrine of Negation* (Cambridge, Mass., 1968). For the views of other schools, see Kalidas Bhattacharya's "The Indian Concept of Knowledge and Self," *Our Heritage* (Calcutta) 2–4 (1954–1956). For *jñāna-yoga,* one may consult Surendranath Dasgupta's *A History of Indian Philosophy,* vol. 2 (London, 1932), chap. 14. Editions and translations of the *Bhagavadgītā* are too numerous to be mentioned here.

Bimal Krishna Matilal (1987)

JOACHIM OF FIORE

JOACHIM OF FIORE (c. 1135–1202) was an Italian monk and biblical exegete. Joachim was born in Calabria, and after a pilgrimage to Palestine he returned to southern Italy, where he became successively abbot of the Benedictine, later Cistercian, monastery at Curazzo and founder of his own Florensian congregation at San Giovanni in Fiore. The Mediterranean was then a crossroads of history, with pilgrims and Crusaders coming and going and rumors of "the infidel" rife. Joachim was acutely aware of living in the end time and sought an interpretation of history through biblical exegesis illumined by spiritual understanding, a view elaborated upon in works such as *Liber Concordie Novi ac Veteris Testamenti* (1519), *Expositio in Apocalypsim* (1527), and *Psalterium decem chordarum* (1527).

Joachim recorded two experiences of mystical illumination (and hints of a third) in which the trinitarian understanding of history was revealed to him. He developed his theology of history through investigations into biblical concords, or sequences. The first sequence arises from the relation of the old and new dispensations. The second sequence, the procession of the Holy Spirit from both Father and Son, exemplifies his famous "pattern of threes": the first stage (*statusi*) that of the law, belongs to the Father and lasts until the incarnation of Jesus Christ; the second, that of grace, belongs to the Son and lasts until a near future point; the third, that of the Spirit, proceeding from the first two and characterized by love and liberty, runs until the second advent of Christ. Joachim found the clues for his scheme of history in particular biblical sequences, for instance, in the references to the twelve patriarchs, the twelve apostles, and the twelve expected future leaders, and in references to Noah's sending forth of a raven and a dove paralleling the mission of Paul and Barnabas, which he took as evidence for the future founding of two orders of spiritual people.

Joachim's originality lay in the concept of a third stage still to come, whereas in the standard threefold pattern (before the law, under the law, and under grace) the church had already entered the third stage. Joachim believed that the transition to the third *status* must be made only through the tribulation of the greatest Antichrist (the seventh dragon's head), who was imminent. This age to come, the age of the Spirit (equated with the seventh, or sabbath, age), was part of history and should be distinguished from the eighth day of eternity.

Joachim was recognized as a prophet in his lifetime. Richard I of England, leading the Third Crusade, interviewed him at Messina. In the thirteenth century his concept of the coming of two orders of spiritual people achieved a "prophetic scoop" when the Dominicans ("ravens") and Franciscans ("doves") were founded. In both orders, especially the Franciscan, some friars claimed the role outlined by Joachim, which successively fired the imagination not only of heretical groups—the Apostolic Brethren, Fraticelli, Provençal Beguines, and others—but also of some Augustinian hermits and Jesuits. Pseudo-Joachimist works spread the prophecies, and Joachimist influence is traceable as late as the seventeenth century in the myths of the Angelic Pope and the Last World Emperor. In 1254 occurred the "scandal of the eternal evangel," when a Franciscan proclaimed Joachim's works to be the new gospel, replacing the Old and New Testaments. This was widely documented and later referred to by Lessing, the eighteenth-century German philosopher whose *Education of the Human Race* was widely influential in promoting an optimistic view of the future age. Consequently, the nineteenth century saw a revival of interest in Joachim's third *status* among visionaries such as Jules Michelet, Edgar Quinet, Pierre Leroux, and George Sand who were antiecclesiastical but looked for a new gospel. Some scholars claim Joachim as the source of all later threefold patterns of history, but this is questionable.

BIBLIOGRAPHY

Bloomfield, Morton. "Joachim of Flora: A Critical Survey of His Canon, Teachings, Sources, Biography, and Influence." *Traditio* 13 (1957): 249–311. The best bibliographical survey, now updated in "Recent Scholarship on Joachim of Fiore and His Influence," in *Prophecy and Millenarianism,* edited by Ann Williams (London, 1980), pp. 23–52.

McGinn, Bernard. *The Calabrian Abbot.* New York, 1985. An account of Joachim's place in the history of Western thought.

Reeves, Marjorie E. *The Influence of Prophecy in the Later Middle Ages.* Oxford, 1969. Deals with Joachim's life and thought and traces his influence down to the seventeenth century.

Reeves, Marjorie E. *Joachim of Fiore and the Prophetic Future.* London, 1976. A brief account summarizing material in the preceding and the following book and incorporating some new material.

Reeves, Marjorie E., and Beatrice Hirsch-Reich. *The Figurae of Joachim of Fiore.* Oxford, 1972. A study of Joachim's use of symbolism, especially in his *Liber figurarum.*

West, Delno C., ed. *Joachim of Fiore in Christian Thought: Essays on the Influence of the Calabrian Prophet.* 2 vols. New York, 1975. Reprints essays from various journals, dating from 1930 to 1971.

MARJORIE E. REEVES (1987)

JOAN OF ARC (c. 1412–1431) was a French visionary; also known as the Maid of Orléans. Joan, who called herself Jeanne La Pucelle, used her claims to mystical experience to influence the course of French history in the fifteenth century. Led by her visions, she inspired the French army to turn the tide of the Hundred Years' War. Born around 1412 in Domrémy-la-Pucelle, a village on the border between Lorraine and France, Joan was a peasant who, in her own words, did not "know A from B." As she grew up she heard the magical lore and local saints' legends of Lorraine and reports of continuing French defeats at the hands of the English.

At age thirteen Joan began to hear a voice from God instructing her to go to the dauphin Charles, the uncrowned Valois king. Believing that she was called to drive the English out of France, Joan privately took a vow of virginity and prepared herself for the role of prophetic adviser to the king, a type of female mystic familiar in the late medieval period. At some point in these troubled years the voice became three voices, whom she later identified as the saints Catherine of Alexandria and Margaret of Antioch, both known for their heroic virginity, and the archangel Michael, protector of the French royal family.

Joan established her authority through her urgent sincerity, by identifying herself with prophecies about a virgin who would save France, and by accurately announcing a French defeat on the day it took place 150 miles away. No longer able to ignore her, the garrison captain at the nearby town of Vaucouleurs refused to endorse her mission to save France until she was exorcised, raising the issue that would haunt her mission henceforth: Did her powers come from God or from the devil? Not fully assured, the captain nonetheless gave her arms and an escort. Cutting her hair short and donning male clothing, Joan and her companions made their way through enemy territory, reaching the dauphin's court at Chinon in late February 1429.

Joan's indomitable belief that only she could save France impressed Charles, his astronomer, and some of the nobles. But they too moved carefully, requiring an examination for heresy by theologians at Poitiers, who declared her a good Christian, and a physical examination by three matrons, who certified that she was indeed a virgin. For a woman about to attempt the "miracle" of defeating the English, virginity added an aura of almost magical power.

Given the desperate nature of Charles's position, he had little to lose in allowing Joan to join the army marching to the relief of Orléans, which had been besieged by the English. Her presence attracted volunteers and raised morale.

Charging into the midst of battle, Joan was wounded and became the hero of the day. With Orléans secured, Joan impatiently counseled the army to move on. Town after town along the Loire fell, others offered their loyalty without battle. By late July, the dauphin could be crowned King Charles VII at Reims with Joan by his side.

But Joan's days of glory were brief. Driven by her voices, she disobeyed the king and continued to fight. Her attack on Paris failed, and several other ventures ended inconclusively. In May 1430, Joan was captured in a skirmish outside Compiègne. Neither Charles nor any of his court made an attempt to rescue or ransom her.

Determined to discredit Joan as a heretic and a witch, the English turned her over to an inquisitional court. Manned by more than one hundred French clerics in the pay of the English, Joan's trial in Rouen lasted from February 21 to May 28, 1431. Under inquisitional procedure she could not have counsel or call witnesses. As a layperson she had no religious order to speak for her, nor had she ever enlisted the support of a priest. Yet although she had spent months in military prisons, in chains and guarded constantly by men, Joan began with a strong defense. Reminding her interrogators that she was sent by God, she warned that they would condemn her at great risk. The charges came down to the question of ultimate authority: The judges insisted that she submit to the church's interpretation that her visions were evil, but Joan held to her claim that they came from God. Perhaps without intending it, Joan thus advocated the right of individual experience over the church's authority.

After weeks of unrelenting questioning, Joan began to break. Threatened with death by fire, she finally denied her voices and agreed to wear women's dress. It is not known precisely what happened next, but three days later she was found wearing male clothing again. She claimed that she had repented of betraying her voices; there are indications that her guards may have tried to rape her. Whatever her motivation, her actions sealed her fate. Declared a relapsed heretic on May 31, 1431, Joan was burned at the stake.

In 1450, because he was uneasy that he owed his crown to a convicted heretic, Charles instigated an inquiry into the trial, which led to a thorough papal investigation. Although the verdict of 1431 was revoked in 1456, the main charges against Joan were not cleared. Despite this ambiguity, Joan's memory received continuous attention from the French people through the centuries. It is ironic that in 1920 she was declared a saint, because none of the church's proceedings has acknowledged her right to interpret her divine messages, leaving the main issue for which she was condemned unaddressed.

BIBLIOGRAPHY

The basic materials relative to the trial are found in Jules Quicherat's five-volume *Procès de condamnation et de réhabilitation de Jeanne d'Arc* (Paris, 1841–1849; New York, 1960). For an updated edition of the trial in French and Latin, see *Procès de condamnation de Jeanne d'Arc,* 3 vols., edited by Pierre Tisset and Yvonne Lanhers (Paris, 1960–1971), and of the retrial, see *Procès en nullité de la condamnation de Jeanne d'Arc,* 3 vols., edited by Pierre Duparc (Paris, 1979–1983). An abridged English translation of the trial can be found in Wilfred P. Barrett's *The Trial of Jeanne d'Arc* (London, 1932), and of the retrial, in Régine Pernoud's *The Retrial of Joan of Arc,* translated by J. M. Cohen (London, 1955).

Of the vast secondary literature, the following biographies are good places to begin: Frances Gies's *Joan of Arc: The Legend and the Reality* (New York, 1981), Lucien Fabre's *Joan of Arc* (New York, 1954), and Victoria Sackville-West's *St. Joan of Arc* (London, 1936; New York, 1984). See also my study *Joan of Arc: Heretic, Mystic, Shaman* (Lewiston, N.Y., 1985) and Régine Pernoud's *Joan of Arc by Herself and Her Witnesses,* translated by Edward Hyams (London, 1964).

Anne Llewellyn Barstow (1987)

JOB. The biblical *Book of Job* is included among the Writings (*Ketubim*) in the Hebrew Bible and among the Poetic books in the Old Testament. Along with *Proverbs, Ecclesiastes,* and *Sirach,* it is part of the wisdom literature of ancient Israel. The character Job, however, is not an Israelite but a figure belonging to a broader ancient Near Eastern tradition. His name (Hebrew *'iyyōb*) is not a typical Hebrew name but is related to Amorite names attested throughout the second millennium BCE. Similarly, *Ezekiel* 14:14 mentions Job, along with Noah (the Israelite version of the Mesopotamian flood hero Utanapishtim) and the Canaanite king Dan'el, as figures legendary for their righteousness. The setting of the book of *Job* in the land of Uz and the homelands of Job's three friends (especially that of Eliphaz the Temanite) suggest that the Israelites may have acquired the story from Edomite sources. Although evidently familiar with a variety of ancient Near Eastern literary and folk traditions, the author of the biblical book has adapted these materials to his own specific religious and cultural beliefs. Few clues exist as to the date of composition. Though Job's world is described in terms that evoke a patriarchal setting, evidence from historical linguistics suggests that the book was composed in the early postexilic period.

Contents and Structure. The structure of the book has long puzzled scholars. It begins (1:1–2:13) and concludes (42:7–17) with a simple prose story that recounts how Job, a man of exemplary piety and extraordinary wealth, is tested through the loss of his family, property, and health. Refusing to curse God even in the depth of his suffering, Job's possessions are returned twofold, a new family is given to him, and he lives another one hundred and forty years. Between the prose beginning and ending, however, there are some thirty-nine chapters of erudite and highly sophisticated poetry. Chapters 3–27 contain a dialogue between Job and his three friends, Eliphaz, Bildad, and Zophar, concerning the significance of his suffering, the nature of God, and God's governance of the world. Though technically not cursing God, Job accuses God of heinous injustice, sadistic violence, and gross mismanagement of the world. A poem on the inaccessibility of wisdom follows the dialogue in chapter 28. Job resumes speaking in chapters 29–31, giving a defense of his life, swearing an oath of innocence, and challenging God to reply to him. Instead, the next several chapters (chapters 32–37) introduce a new character, Elihu, who attempts a further rebuttal of Job. At the conclusion of Elihu's speech, God appears "out of the tempest" to address Job (38:1–42:6). God does not speak directly to Job's complaints, however, but challenges his knowledge of creation and his inability to provide for the wild creatures of the earth as God does. Although Job retracts his accusations against God (40:1–5), God resumes with a second speech, describing the terrible magnificence of the legendary creatures Behemoth and Leviathan. In his final reply (42:1–6), Job acknowledges that he has spoken "without understanding," and having seen God "with my eyes," he recants. The prose conclusion then follows.

Although many ancient Near Eastern literary compositions incorporate a poetic text within a prose framework, the tensions between the prose and poetic parts of Job are striking. Where the prose story describes a character whose patient endurance is unwavering, the Job of the poetic section is an angry rebel whose accusations against God are only quelled by an encounter with the sublimity of the divine. Even those differences might be accommodated as features of a psychological portrait of acute suffering, but the transition from the poetry to the prose conclusion is jarring. Whereas in the poetic speech to Job God accuses him of "obscuring counsel" and speaking "without knowledge" (38:2), in the prose conclusion God rebukes the three friends because "you have not spoken the truth about me, as has my servant Job" (42:7).

With the rise of historical criticism in biblical studies, scholars argued that the prose narrative must be an ancient folk tale that the poet who wrote *Job* used to frame his new poetic composition, by removing the "original" dialogue between Job and his friends but otherwise not significantly changing the story. The Elihu speeches, which differ stylistically from the rest of the poetry and interrupt the dramatic structure, were regarded as a later addition. Some scholars argued that the wisdom poem, Job's final speech, and one or both of the divine speeches came from different hands. In reaction to historical-critical excesses, however, many recent commentators have attempted to understand the book as a more unified composition, though most still regard the figure and words of Elihu as a secondary addition. However the book was composed, the tensions between the prose tale and the poetic material remain fundamental for understanding the meaning of the book. The major components of the book are composed as different literary genres and address different aspects of the religious dilemma posed by the traditional figure of Job.

The Prose Tale. Although often referred to as a folk tale, the prose narrative is more accurately described as a didactic wisdom tale. In such stories, which include the stories about Joseph, Tobit, and Daniel, the protagonist embodies moral qualities valued by the culture. Within the story the moral coherency of the world is threatened when an antagonist menaces the hero. The suffering hero perseveres in his virtue, however, and is rewarded at the end, thus restoring the consistency of the moral order and recommending the virtue that the hero exemplifies. In *Job* the featured virtue is a disinterested piety that does not depend on reward. What is often overlooked is that this lack of concern for reward is not the typical way in which piety is described in the Bible. In *Deuteronomy,* in *Proverbs,* in *Psalms,* and elsewhere, devotion to God and blessings from God are seen as concomitant. God blesses the upright, whose gratitude expresses itself in further devotion to God. The Joban prose tale, far from being a simple folk story, is a narrative exploration and resolution of a potential problem within this religious framework. Does God's blessing corrupt piety? Or can one hold onto both concepts if one can imagine a form of piety that is truly disinterested? By depicting Job's piety as unchanged in good fortune and in bad, the writer can avoid potential contradiction. The restoration of Job at the end of the book serves to reunite the two values.

The character in the story who articulates the problem is the Adversary (*ha-śāṭān*), who argues that Job is pious only because he has been blessed and will curse God if all he has is taken away. This figure is not yet Satan, the dualistic opponent of God that he becomes in later Jewish and Christian thought. Rather, he is a member of the heavenly court charged with inspecting the earth and reporting instances of disloyalty or corruption. The same figure occurs in *Zechariah 3,* where he accuses the high priest of corruption. In these texts the term *satan* is a common noun, not a proper name. Nevertheless, in both cases the Adversary's accusations are rejected by God, and in *Job* he acts as something of an agent provocateur. Thus one can see how the character later develops into a figure of evil and an adversary of God himself.

The Wisdom Dialogue. The prose tale makes use of a suffering hero to examine the concept of piety. In wisdom circles in the ancient Near East, however, the enigma of suffering itself had long been a topic of reflection, and it is this aspect of Job's situation that the poetic parts of the book explore. Several poetic texts from Mesopotamia and Ugarit have been compared with Job, notably the Sumerian composition *A Man and His God* and the Babylonian text *I Will Praise the God of Wisdom.* These poems, however, are appeals and thanksgivings for relief from suffering, and as such are more comparable to biblical psalms of lament and thanksgiving than to the story of Job. The one text that bears a striking resemblance to the dialogue between Job and his friends is the so-called *Babylonian Theodicy,* composed around 1000 BCE. Here, as in the *Book of Job,* a sufferer repeatedly complains to his friend concerning the inexplicable evil that has befallen him, questioning the justice of the gods and the coherency of the moral world. His friend replies each time by offering the orthodox theodicies. Although direct literary dependency is unlikely, it is evident that the Job poet composed the dialogue portion of the book according to a well-known genre.

In the dialogue, although Job gives eloquent voice to his personal sufferings, the primary issue that concerns him is the nature of God. Since he cannot perceive his sufferings as in any way justifiable, he is forced to conclude that God is not only unjust but also sadistic and obsessed with seeking out and punishing vulnerable humans (e.g., 9:16–31; 14:18–22; 16:9–16). Job extends his critique to indict God's misgovernance of the world (e.g., 12:14–25 and 24:1–12). The most remarkable innovation in Job's religious thinking is his use of a forensic, or courtroom, model to explore his relationship with God. Although Israelite tradition sometimes described God's punishment of individuals or persons in terms of a legal judgment (e.g., *Ps.* 143:2; *Isa.* 3:13–14; *Mic.* 6:1–2), Job creatively reverses the force of the metaphor and attempts to imagine how a trial with God would allow him not only to hear God's charges against him but also to bring charges of his own (e.g., 13:18–27; 16:18–21; 23:2–7).

The role of the friends in the wisdom dialogue is to defend traditional understandings of divine justice against the skeptical onslaught of the sufferer. Though the friends are often read as simply "blaming the victim," their arguments are much more nuanced. Like many people in the ancient world, they believe that one could offend the deity unintentionally or unknowingly. Thus the only rational response to inexplicable suffering—especially for a righteous person—is to acknowledge any possible wrongdoing and to appeal humbly to God for deliverance (e.g., 5:1–16; 8:5–7; 11:13–20). Theirs is a thoroughly practical approach to the enigma of suffering. Only when Job persists in his blasphemous speech do they conclude that he must indeed be wicked (22:2–11), though their advice to him remains the same (22:21–30).

Thus what separates Job and the friends is not so much a question of Job's guilt or innocence as a conflict between two models of the divine-human relationship. The friends accept that a great gulf of being separates God and humans. In the face of that mystery, supplication of God's good favor is the only possible stance. Job, however, assumes that God and humans share a common set of values concerning justice and equity that can be rationally applied to both human and divine acts. Both perspectives are grounded in Israelite religious thought, making the dialogue a profound engagement of alternative worldviews.

JOB'S FINAL DEFENSE AND THE DIVINE SPEECHES. In his final speech (chapters 29–31) Job mounts a defense of his life and lays out the grounds on which he assumes he and God could address their differences. Job develops his view of the divine-human relationship as an extension of his self-understanding as a leader in his own community. The divine speeches, for which there is no parallel in the extant literature of the ancient Near East, are a fierce repudiation of an anthropocentric modeling of God and an implicit rejection of retributive justice as a part of the structure of the world. Although cast as a rhetorical repudiation of Job's pretensions ("Where were you. . . . Can you. . . . Do you know?"), their force is to challenge Job's construction of God as essentially a projection of an ancient Near Eastern patriarch on a cosmic scale. The divine speeches are difficult to interpret. Some commentators interpret them as a reaffirmation of the cosmos-creating deity who organizes the universe and restrains its chaotic elements. The difficulty with this understanding, however, is that the deity's final speech (chapters 40–41) appears rather to celebrate the place of the chaotic (exemplified in the legendary creatures Behemoth and Leviathan) alongside the accomplishments of the deity in establishing a stable order of creation (chapter 38). Indeed, the wild animals whom God nurtures (chapter 39) are precisely those that ancient Near Eastern thought considered to be emblems of the chaotic "other." Read in this way, the divine speeches are a radical challenge to traditional ancient Near Eastern theological assumptions.

JEWISH AND CHRISTIAN RECEPTION OF *JOB*. The *Book of Job* resists being read as a unified whole. Whether one deals with the tensions as evidence of successive editorial layers or as the construction of a subtle thinker who wished to juxtapose several different ways of engaging issues arising from human suffering, it remains a difficult book, the ambiguities of which have funded many different interpretations.

Early Jewish interpretation recast *Job* as an ethical testament in which a dying elder teaches his children the lessons of his life. The *Testament of Job*, probably composed in Alexandria in the first century BCE, depicts Job as opposing Satan's idolatry, for which he is told in advance that he will be persecuted. Thus he becomes a figure of endurance (cf. *James* 5:11), and his daughters are represented as mystics to whom he gives the gift of understanding the language of the angels. Other early Jewish interpretations of Job are more critical of him, casting him as one of Pharaoh's counselors at the time of the oppression of the Israelites. This identification of Job with the Egyptians in *Exodus* becomes the rationale for his suffering. The rabbis cited in the Babylonian Talmud (*b. Baba Batra* 15–16) debate whether Moses wrote the *Book of Job* (a manuscript from Qumran copies *Job* in paleo-Hebrew script, otherwise used only for the books of the Pentateuch and the name of God) and whether or not Job blasphemes. *B. Baba Batra* 16b subtly interprets *Job* 2:10, "And for all this, Job did not sin with his lips," to suggest that Job sinned in his heart—an interpretation that prepares the reader for the sudden transition from the pious Job of the prose tale to the rebellious Job of the poetic dialogue.

The early Christian church viewed Job as an "athlete of God" who perseveres through his suffering, and as an antitype of Christ, an interpretation most influentially presented in Pope Gregory's *Moralia in Job*. Ironically, since early postexilic Judaism did not have a conception of resurrection, certain passages in *Job* (especially 19:25–27) came to be cited during the patristic period as evidence for resurrection of the body. In the Middle Ages, Job became the patron saint of those who suffered from worms, leprosy, skin diseases, venereal disease, and melancholy. Calvin composed one hundred and fifty-nine sermons on *Job*, emphasizing the theme of divine providence.

The poetry of *Job* attracted considerable attention during the Romantic period, as *Job* became a prime example of the expression of the sublime in the writings of Robert Lowth (1710–1787; Bishop of London1777–1787), Johann Gottfried von Herder (1744–1803), and Edmund Burke (1729–1797). The most important Romantic interpretation of *Job,* however, is William Blake's series of illustrations, made around 1823, in which Job becomes an example of the cleansing of "the doors of perception," as he moves from misperception to true vision of God. In the early twentieth century, Rudolf Otto (*The Idea of the Holy*) claimed Job's encounter with God as a primary example of the experience of the holy. In the later twentieth century the figure of Job was invoked to exemplify psychological development (Carl Jung, *Answer to Job*); psychological illness (Jack Kahn, *Job's Illness*); absurdist existentialism (Robert Frost, "A Masque of Reason"; implicitly, Franz Kafka, *The Trial*); post-religious humanism (Archibald MacLeish, "J.B."); and the radical evil of the Shoah (Elie Wiesel, *The Trial of God*). In theological criticism *Job* has been critiqued as exemplifying the "evils of theodicy" (Terrence Tilley, *The Evils of Theodicy*), and from a liberationist perspective as an example of "how to speak about God" (Gustavo Gutiérrez, *On Job: God-Talk and the Suffering of the Innocent*). René Girard (*Job, the Victim of His People*) interprets Job as a type of scapegoat. Feminist critique has rehabilitated the maligned figure of Job's wife (Ilana Pardes, *Countertraditions in the Bible: A Feminist Approach*), and postmodernists have been drawn to the "self-consuming" structure of the internal contradictions of the *Book of Job* (Edward Good; David Clines; and Dermot Cox), or they have interpreted the book as modeling a dialogic play of voices in which no single character or perspective controls the meaning of the book. The richness and ambiguity of the book ensure that it will continue to be a provocative work that defies definitive interpretation.

See Also Resurrection; Satan; Suffering; Theodicy.

Bibliography

Baskin, Judith R. *Pharaoh's Counsellors: Job, Jethro, and Balaam in Rabbinic and Patristic Tradition.* Chico, Calif., 1983. An important comparative study of Jewish and Christian interpretation. Besserman, Lawrence L. *The Legend of Job in the Middle Ages.* Cambridge, Mass., 1979. Clines, David J. A. *Job 1–20.* Waco, Tex., 1989. The best and most comprehensive commentary. Contains an extensive bibliography. *Job 21–42* is to be published in 2005. Clines, David J. A. *What Does Eve Do to Help? And Other Readerly Questions to the Old Testament.* Sheffield, England, 1990. Cox, Dermot. *The Triumph of Impotence: Job and the Tradition of the Absurd.* Rome, 1978. Fohrer, Georg. *Das Buch Hiob.* Gütersloh, Germany, 1963. Insightful exegetical commentary. Good, Edward M. *In Turns of Tempest: A Reading of Job with a Translation.* Stanford, Calif., 1990. A provocative postmodern reading of Job. Habel, Norman C. *The Book of Job.* Philadelphia, 1985. An insightful commentary that emphasizes the literary features of Job, especially the legal metaphor. Keel, Othmar. *Jahwes Entgegnung an Ijob.* Göttingen, Germany, 1978. An innovative use of ancient Near Eastern iconography to illuminate the imagery of the divine speeches. Newsom, Carol A. *The Book of Job: A Contest of Imaginations.* New York, 2003. A reading of Job in light of Bakhtinian dialogism. Newsom, Carol A., and Susan E. Schreiner. "Job, Book of." In *Dictionary of Biblical Interpretation,* edited by John H. Hayes, pp. 587–599. Nashville, Tenn., 1999. History of interpretation, focusing on Christian sources. Extensive bibliography. Oberhänsli-Widmer, Gabrielle, *Hiob in jüdischer Antike und Moderne: Die Wirkungsgeschichte Hiobs in der jüdischen Literatur.* Neukirchen-Vluyn, Germany, 2003. The most comprehensive study of Job in Jewish tradition. Terrien, Samuel. *The Iconography of Job Through the Centuries: Artists as Biblical Interpreters.* University Park, Pa., 1996. An exceptionally valuable collection of materials. Wright, Andrew S. *Blake's Job: A Commentary.* Oxford, 1972. Important analysis of the illustrations by William Blake. Zuckerman, Bruce. *Job the Silent: A Study in Historical Counterpoint.* New York, 1991. Interpretation of the growth of the book of Job as a series of "misreadings," analogous to the documented misinterpretation of a Yiddish story.

Carol A. Newsom (2005)

JŌDO SHINSHŪ. The Jōdo Shinshū, or True Pure Land sect, is a school of Japanese Buddhism that takes as its central religious message the assurance of salvation granted to all beings by the Buddha Amida (Skt., Amitābha). Its founder, Shinran (1173–1263), a disciple of the eminent Japanese monk Hōnen (1133–1212), founder of the Jōdoshū (Pure Land sect), stands in a line of Buddhist thinkers who emphasize faith in the salvific power of Amitābha and the hope of rebirth in his Pure Land, a paradisical realm created out of the boundless religious merit generated by Amitābha's fulfillment of a series of vows taken eons ago while still the *bodhisattva* Dharmākara. Jōdo Shinshū, or Shinshū as it is often called, is but one of a number of "Pure Land" traditions in East Asia, and is today the largest of the denominations of Japanese Buddhism.

Pure Land devotionalism is a perennial element in both Chinese and Japanese Buddhism. Beginning nominally with the visualization cult of Amitābha inaugurated in the year 403 by the Chinese monk Huiyuan, Pure Land practices have served as adjuncts to the teachings of a variety of East Asian Buddhist traditions and, from the sixth century, as the foundation of several religious movements devoted more or less exclusively to the worship of Amitābha. These movements combine faith in the power of Amitābha with the practice of the Nembutsu, which various schools interpret in differing ways but that in general consists now of the formulaic recitation of the name of Amitābha. Although standing firmly within the Pure Land tradition of its Chinese and Japanese antecedents, Jōdo Shinshū is conspicuous in the interpretation it gives to Nembutsu practice and to the assurances of salvation found in the vows of Amitābha.

TEXTS. Like all Pure Land traditions, the core texts of the Shinshū are a cycle of scriptures originating in northwest India and, perhaps, Buddhist Central Asia, that detail the spiritual career of Amitābha, the glories of Sukhāvatī ("land of ease," i.e., the Pure Land) created by him, the vows he has undertaken for the salvation of all beings, or certain meditative techniques that the devotee can undertake in order to visualize Amitābha and his Pure Land. Although the texts of the so-called triple Pure Land scripture began as individual works (the visualization scripture appears of widely different provenance than the other two), the three Pure Land sūtras are considered by the Japanese to preach a wholly consistent religious message. These texts are the *Larger Sukhāvatīvyūha Sūtra* (Jpn., *Muryōjukyō;* T.D. no. 363), the *Smaller Sukhāvatīvyūha Sūtra* (Jpn., *Amidakyō;* T.D. no. 366), and a text no longer extant in Sanskrit, known in Japanese as the *Kanmuryōjukyō* (T.D. no. 365). The first and second contain elements of the mythic cycle of Amitābha; the third is a meditation scripture. Also important to Shinshū thought is the work of one of the patriarchal figures of Chinese Pure Land Buddhism, the *Wangsheng lunzhu* (Jpn., *Ōjōronchū;* T.D. no. 1819) of Tanluan (c. 488–c. 554). This text was held in great esteem by Shinran, who relied upon it in the composition of the founding document of the Jōdo Shinshū, the *Kyōgyōshinshō* (Teaching, practice, faith, and enlightenment).

SHINRAN. At the age of nine Shinran began his formal Buddhist training at the Tendai center on Mount Hiei. He remained there as a monk in the Jōgyōzammaidō for almost twenty years. At the age of twenty-nine, unable to attain peace of mind, Shinran decided to leave Hiei for Kyoto, where he became a disciple of Hōnen (1201). Despite, or perhaps owing to, the popularity of Nembutsu practices among the common people, monks from the established, traditional Buddhist sects began to denounce and censure Hōnen's Jōdoshū doctrines. This, coupled with certain improprieties of several of Hōnen's disciples, led to the official prohibition of Nembutsu Buddhism and the banishment of Hōnen and his main disciples from Kyoto. Shinran was defrocked and exiled to Echigo (in present-day Niigata prefecture) in 1207. During his years in exile Shinran lived as a layman—he took the humble name Gutoku ("old fool"), married, and raised a family. It was this experience that led Shinran to realize that enlightenment and rebirth in the Pure Land were not contingent on adherence to the monastic precepts, the study of scriptures and doctrine, or the severance of worldly ties. Shinran used his own experience as a model for the religious life, holding that salvation could be attained in this world and this life in the midst of one's common, daily activities. In this way, Shinran extended Hōnen's notions of universal salvation and completed Pure Land's transformation of Buddhism from a "religion of renunciation" to a "household religion."

The year 1211 saw Shinran officially pardoned. Thereafter, he lived with his family in the Kanto region, where he began proselytizing his new understanding of Pure Land doctrines. He attracted large numbers of followers—some estimate ten thousand—some of whom were instrumental in establishing and maintaining Shinshū centers after Shinran's death. During the period between 1235, when he returned to Kyoto, and his death Shinran was most prolific. It was during this period that he completed and revised the *Kyōgyōshinshō,* his most important work on Jōdo Shinshū doctrine. In this work Shinran traced the tradition of Pure Land teachings by collecting passages from scriptures and earlier commentaries, to which he added his own interpretations. The *Kyōgyōshinshō* represents an attempt by Shinran to lend legitimacy and orthodoxy to Shinshū teachings by establishing its affiliation with traditionally accepted authorities, an attempt necessitated by the virulent criticisms of the Jōdoshū by the monks of other Buddhist sects. Other of his works written during this period were intended to systematize his teachings for the guidance of his disciples and to settle the numerous small feuds among his followers in the Kanto region.

TRUE PURE LAND DOCTRINE. In his religious thought Shinran was influenced by Hōnen's division of Buddhist practices into two paths leading to enlightenment: the *shōdōmon* ("path of sages"), that is, the difficult path wherein enlightenment is dependent on the individual's "own power" (*jiriki*) and capability to adhere to the monastic precepts and to engage in arduous meditative practices and study; and the *jōdomon* ("path of Pure Land"), or the easy path in which one depends on "other power" (*tariki*), namely, the salvific power of Amida. Like Hōnen, Shinran held that during *mappō* (the "latter days of the Law"; i.e., an age of widespread degeneration and decadence) traditional Buddhist practices were all but useless for the attainment of enlightenment. In such an age, he claimed, faith in Amida and in the truth of his "original vow" (*hongan*) to save all sentient beings was the only path to salvation and rebirth in the Pure Land. As opposed to earlier forms of Buddhist practice, which uphold the path of wisdom (*prajñā*), meditation (*dhyāna*), and disciplined austerities (*śīla*), and are based on unlimited self-reliance, Pure Land practices provide a way to salvation in the face of the ineffectiveness of self-effort.

Struck by the very limitations of human capabilities and the inherent sinfulness of human nature, Shinran took Hōnen's advocacy of faith in Amida to an even greater degree. While Hōnen held that the individual must "choose" to have faith in Amida and that this choice must be continually reaffirmed through repeated invocations of the Nembutsu, Shinran argued that it was Amida who chose to save all humans. According to Shinran, what effectuates Amida's salvific power is the power of his Original Vow to save all beings as embodied in the Nembutsu. By participating in and allowing oneself to be permeated by this power, one transcends the world of causal necessity (*karman*). Implicit in the Pure Land teachings concerning the power of the

Original Vow is the belief that, even if the escape from this world of *saṃśara* (the round of birth and death of unenlightened existence) is possible through inspired insight alone, the ground of the possibility of that insight depends in turn on something higher or deeper than mere human insight: the divine power (Skt., *adhiṣṭhana*) of the Buddha. This divine power of the Buddha does not lie merely within his human career and character; it transcends his individual personhood, breaking through the limited framework of time and space to embrace all living beings eternally and without limitation.

This interpretation of faith led Shinran to reevaluate Hōnen's use of Nembutsu invocation. Like Hōnen, Shinran believed that the only means to apprehend Amida and to participate in his Original Vow was to invoke his name. By intoning the Nembutsu ("Namu Amida Butsu," or "Adoration be to Amida Buddha"), one accumulates boundless stores of merit and virtue. The necessary requisite is, of course, faith. Hōnen held that repeated invocations of the Nembutsu were necessary to build faith and to ensure rebirth in the Pure Land. Shinran, however, argued that one's practice must *begin* with faith. In any single invocation the devotee must direct his thoughts to the origins of that practice, that is, to faith in Amida's Original Vow. As such, the invocation of the Nembutsu is an expression of gratitude to Amida for being allowed to participate in the salvation promised by his vows. Yet Shinran did not deny the value of repeated invocations, for, although not leading directly to faith, the repeated invocation has the valuable function of awakening one's heart to Amida's existence. In this way, Nembutsu practice and faith come to be two sides of the same coin, with Shinshū emphasizing the moment of salvation and Jōdoshū stressing the process of arriving there.

INSTITUTIONALIZATION AND SUBSEQUENT HISTORY. After Shinran's death his tomb became the center of his movement's religious activities. Ten years later his youngest daughter, Kakushinni, built a mausoleum in the Higashiyama Ōtani area east of Kyoto in which she enshrined an image of Shinran and his ashes. In presenting the mausoleum and its grounds to her father's disciples, Kakushinni stipulated that the maintenance of the temple and the direction of the religious services held there were to be provided by Kakushinni and her descendants in perpetuity. While this marked the origin of the unique Jōdo Shinshū practice of hereditary succession, at the time it was not interpreted by Shinran's disciples as a move toward increasing authoritarian control over the movement. During this period the movement had still not been formally organized into a sect with a central temple under a single leader. Shinran himself had preferred to establish small, informal meeting places (*dōjō*) in the homes of his disciples, around which communities of followers (*monto*) could gather. Indeed, Shinran had no intention of becoming the founder of a new sect or religion. He considered himself the true successor to Hōnen's teaching and continued to think of his movement as part of the Jōdoshū. For this reason, there was a time when the disciples of Hōnen and those of Shinran, both claiming to represent the "true" Pure Land teachings, quarreled over the right to use the name Jōdo Shinshū. It was only in relatively recent times—in 1872—that this conflict was at last resolved and the name Jōdo Shinshū reserved for the groups stemming from Shinran. (Naturally, Shinshū adherents regard Hōnen as a patriarchal figure in his own right in the lineage of Pure Land teachers.) Prior to that date, Jōdo Shinshū was more commonly known as the Ikkōshū or the Montoshū. In the Kanto region, the *monto* evolved into large local organizations headed by the most powerful of Shinran's disciples. These groups took their names from the territories in which they were located and, for the most part, remained organizationally unrelated to other such groups.

After Kakushinni's death her son Kakunyo succeeded to the directorship of Shinran's mausoleum. His greatest wish was to consolidate and organize the various regional groups into a unified sect centered around the mausoleum. Toward this end, he transformed the mausoleum into a temple, naming it the Honganji (Original Vow Temple) and attempted to draw the local *monto* into the organization as branch temples. Kakunyo's efforts mark the establishment of the Jōdo Shinshū as a single, centralized organization. In 1332 the Honganji received official recognition as the central temple of the Shinshū movement. The government, however, still considered it an affiliate of the Tendai school. Kakunyo's plans met with resistance from the various local groups and movements, particularly in the Kanto. Many leaders began to erect temples and establish their own regionally based sects. As a result, numerous subsects of Jōdo Shinshū were founded throughout the country.

Although the Honganji continued to thrive, it was not without its problems. In 1456 the Honganji complex was burned to the ground by Tendai monks from Mount Hiei. This was not too serious a setback, for the Honganji had numerous affiliated congregations and temples throughout the country. However, the eighth successor to the head of the temple, Rennyo (1415–1499), was forced to move and ultimately established Shinshū headquarters in the Yamashina district of Kyoto. In the interim, Rennyo's determination to sever all ties with Tendai—he destroyed Tendai scriptures, scrolls, and images in his temples—and his plans to expand and strengthen the Shinshū organization aroused the anger of various Buddhist sects and local feudal lords (*daimyō*). The numerous attacks suffered by Rennyo and his followers at the hands of these detractors, led them to form an alliance with local peasants and samurai. During the Ōnin War such groups led armed uprisings known as *ikkō ikki* in an effort to protect their land holdings from the powerful daimyo. It was during this period that Jōdo Shinshū gained widespread acceptance and popularity among the masses. The success of his armed uprisings acquired for Rennyo the title "saint of the restoration of the Honganji."

The attacks against Shinshū followers continued throughout the Muromachi period. When the Honganji was again burned, this time by Nichiren monks, the tenth successor, Shōnyō, rebuilt the temple in the Ishiyama district of Osaka. It was under Shōnyō's leadership that membership in Shinshū began to spread beyond the peasant masses. The daimyo, recognizing both the potential of the armed peasant uprisings and the power of their affiliation with Shinshū, began to join the sect. When the eleventh successor to the Honganji, Kennyo, became the abbot of the temple, the sect was politically and militarily as powerful as any of the major aristocratic and military families in Japan. Shinshū's strength posed a serious threat to several of the contending military rulers, and in 1570 the powerful daimyo Oda Nobunaga attacked the Honganji. The temple, supported by peasant groups, samurai, and local daimyo, was able to ward off Nobunaga's troops for ten years. In 1580 the Honganji was forced to surrender, and Kennyo fled to Kii province. This siege marks both the height of Shinshū's power and the beginning of its decline. It also marks the end of the sect's involvement in armed peasant uprisings.

After Kennyo's death a dispute over succession divided and further weakened the Honganji. Two branches were formed: the Western Honganji (Honpa Honganji), led by Kennyo's second son, Junnyo, and the Eastern Honganji (Ōtani Honganji), led by his eldest son, Kyonyo. Both established their temple headquarters in Kyoto. It should be noted that the establishment of sects within the Jōdo Shinshū, from the earliest divisions during Kakunyo's leadership until the schism between Kennyo's sons, were all the result of factional, political, and succession disputes, and personality differences. Thus, there are few discernible differences in doctrine and practice among the various sects.

The major sects of today's Jōdo Shinshū religion were established between the latter part of the Kamakura period and the beginning of the Tokugawa. Today there are ten sects, of which the Eastern and Western Honganji sects are the most influential, each outnumbering the combined membership of all the smaller sects. These smaller sects include the Takada, Bukkōji, Sanmonto, Kibe, Yamamoto, Koshōji, Joshoji, and Izumoji groups. The practice of handing down the leadership of temples through family lines is upheld by all sects. The leaders of the Honganji sects claim descent from Shinran, and the leaders of the other sects trace descent to Shinran's direct disciples. In the post–World War II era the Honganji sects have undertaken foreign missionary activity, opening temples in Hawaii, North and South America, and elsewhere in countries with large Japanese populations.

SEE ALSO Amitābha; Hōnen; Huiyuan; Jingtu; Jōdoshū; Mappō; Nianfo; Pure and Impure Lands; Rennyo; Shinran; Tanluan; Worship and Devotional Life, article on Buddhist Devotional Life in East Asia.

BIBLIOGRAPHY

The most accessible works in English describing the history and thought of the Shinshū are D. T. Suzuki's *Collected Writings on Shin Buddhism* (Kyoto, 1973) and his *Shin Buddhism* (New York, 1970). Shinshū ideas presented in these works are skewed somewhat by Suzuki's own idiosyncratic interpretation of Pure Land doctrine. His earlier work in Japanese, *Jōdokei shisōron* (Kyoto, 1948), presents an easily understandable account of Jōdo Shinshū thought within the larger Pure Land tradition. English translations of Shinshū scriptures and texts are available in *The Shinshū Seiten,* 2d rev. ed., edited by Kōshō Yamamoto (San Francisco, 1978); in *The Kyō Gyō Shin Shō,* translated by Hisao Inagaki, Kōshō Yukawa, and Thomas R. Okano (Kyoto, 1966); and in the *Shin Buddhism Translation Series* (Kyoto, 1978–).

Many more sources on the Shinshū are published in Japanese. For example, good accounts of Shinshū history can be found in Inoue Toshio's *Honganji* (Tokyo, 1962); in *Shinshūshi gaisetsu,* edited by Akamatsu Toshihide and Kasahara Kazuo (Kyoto, 1963); and in *Honganjishi,* 3 vols., edited by the Honganji Shiryō Kenkyūjo (Kyoto, 1961–1969). A good treatment of the historical evolution of Jōdo Shinshū can be found in Akamatsu Toshihide's *Kamakura bukkyō no kenkyū* (Kyoto, 1957). *Shinshū nempyō,* edited by Ōtani Daigaku (Kyoto, 1973), provides a convenient one-volume chronology of Shinshū history. Hayashima Kyosei's *Ningen no negai: Muryōjukyō* (Tokyo, 1955) presents a straightforward commentary on the central scripture of Pure Land Buddhism, the *Daimuryōjukyō.*

The most widely cited collection of Shinshū scriptures and texts is *Shinshū shōgyō zensho,* 5 vols., 2d rev. ed., edited by the Shinshū Shōgyō Zensho Hensanjo (Kyoto, 1981–1984). Particularly useful commentaries on Shinran's central work, the *Kyōgyōshinshō,* include Yamabe Shūkaku and Akanuma Chizen's *Kyōgyōshinshō kōgi* (Kyoto, 1928); Takeuchi Yoshinori's *Kyōgyōshinshō no tetsugaku* (Tokyo, 1931); and Kaneko Taiei's *Kyōgyōshinshō sōsetsu* (Kyoto, 1959). Soga Ryojin's *Tannishō chōki* (Kyoto, 1961) is an outstanding exposition on the *Tannishō.* General outlines of Shinshū doctrine are available in Fugen Daien's *Shinshū gairon* (Kyoto, 1950) and in *Shinshū gaiyo,* edited by the Kyōka Kenkyūjō (Kyoto, 1953). More extensive discussions of Shinshū thought and development are found in Ishida Mitsuyuki's *Shinran kyōgaku no kisoteki kenkyū,* 2 vols. (Kyoto, 1970–1977). Concerning the religious organization of Jōdo Shinshū, see Uehara Senroku and Matsugi Nobuhiko's *Honganji kyōdan* (Tokyo, 1971). The most detailed reference work on Jōdo Shinshū is *Shinshū daijiten,* 3 vols., edited by Okamura Shūsatsu (Kyoto, 1935–1937).

New Sources

AmStutz, Galen Dean. *Interpreting Amida: History and Orientalism in the Study of Pure Land Buddhism.* Honolulu, 2002.

Bloom, Alfred. "Shin Buddhism in America: A Social Perspective." In *The Faces of Buddhism in America,* edited by Charles S. Prebish and Kenneth K. Tanaka. Berkeley, 1998.

Dobbins, James C. *Buddhism in Medieval Japan.* Honolulu, 2002.

Machida, Soho. *Renegade Monk: Honen and Japanese Pure Land Buddhism.* Berkeley, 1999.

HASE SHŌTŌ (1987)
Translated from Japanese by Carl Becker
Revised Bibliography

JŌDOSHŪ. The Jōdoshū, or Pure Land Sect, is a school of Japanese Buddhism founded in the twelfth century by the monk Hōnen (1133–1212), who took as the centerpiece of his religious teaching sole reliance on the power of the Buddha Amida (Skt., Amitābha) to save all beings. The Jōdoshū was the first of a series of independent Pure Land traditions to flourish in Japan, and continues to this day as a major force in the religion and culture of the nation.

In both China and Japan, Pure Land (Chin., *Jingtu*; Jpn., *jōdo*) practices and doctrines existed both as adjuncts to the teachings of most Buddhist sects and as independent traditions in their own right. Pure Land devotion emphasized faith in the salvific power of Amida, the desirability of attaining rebirth in his Pure Land, Sukhāvatī ("land of bliss"), and the efficacy of *nembutsu* practices (i.e., the recitation of the name of, or meditation on, Amida Buddha) for attaining salvation. For the precursors of the Jōdoshū, including Eikū, Ryōnin, and Genshin (942–1017), *nembutsu* meditation (Jpn., *nembutsu zammai*) involved the invocation of Amida's name while visualizing his body and circumambulating his image. Some, like Genshin, also advocated the practice of invoking Amida's name while engaging in the accompanying meditative exercise. While *nembutsu* meditation and invocation (although the latter was considered an inferior practice) were practiced by many monks of the Tendai sect, they were regarded at best as complements to other established practices. It was not until the Kamakura period (1185–1333), when Hōnen founded the Jōdoshū, that the invocation of the Nembutsu (here conceived as the formulaic recitation of the name of Amida) became the sole practice advocated by a sect as the superior method of attaining salvation.

BASIC TEXTS. Pure Land practices are founded upon a cycle of texts that emphasize either a technique of visualizing Amitābha and his Pure Land or that outline Amitābha's spiritual career, his vows to create a haven for suffering sentient beings, and the methods for winning rebirth there. A scripture of the first type, the *Pratyutpannasamādhi Sūtra,* was translated into Chinese as early as 179 CE and became the basis for the early Chinese worship of Amitābha on Mount Lu under the direction of the famous literatus-monk Huiyuan (334–416). By the fifth century another "meditation" scripture, the *Kuan wu-liang-shou-fo ching* (Skt., *Amitāyurdhyāna Sūtra**; T.D. no. 365) was also available in Chinese. Unlike the aforementioned *Pratyutpanna Sūtra,* which has as its aim the bringing into one's presence in meditation the "Buddhas of the ten directions," this text was devoted exclusively to meditation on Amitābha and his Pure Land. Techniques advocated in both of these texts were introduced to Japan principally through the Tiantai (Jpn., Tendai) system of meditation formulated by the Chinese monk Zhiyi (538–597). The scriptures of the latter type, those having to do with Amitābha's spiritual career and the glories of Pure Land, are two in number: the "larger" *Sukhāvatīvyuha Sūtra,* translated as many as five times into Chinese but known best to the Pure Land schools through Buddhabhadra's fifth century translation (traditionally attributed to Saṃghavarman), the *Wuliangshou jing* (T.D. no. 363), and the "shorter" *Sukhāvatīvyuha Sūtra,* first translated into Chinese as the *O-mi-t'o-fo ching* (T.D. no. 366) by Kumārajīva (343–409). The *Kuan-ching,* known in Japanese as the *Kanmuryōjukyō,* and the *Larger* and *Smaller Sukhāvatīvyuha Sūtras,* known as the *Muryō-jukyō* and the *Amidakyō,* respectively, together constitute the "triple Pure Land scripture," the core sūtra literature of the Chinese and Japanese Pure Land traditions.

The teachings of the Jōdo sect (and of its sister school, the Jōdo Shinshū) also draw their inspiration from the *Sukhāvatīvyuhopadeśa** (Chin., *Wuliangshou jing yu-p'o-t'i-che yüan-sheng chi*; T.D. no. 1524), a collection of hymns (*gāthā*), with autocommentary, on Pure Land topics by the eminent Indian *ācārya* Vasubandhu. The *Ōjōron,* as this text was known in Japan, was usually read in conjunction with the *Wang-sheng lun-chu* (Jpn., *Ōjōronchū*; T. D. no. 1819), a commentary on Vasubandhu's work by the Chinese Pure Land thinker Tanluan (476–542). Tanluan's commentary opens with reference to an "easy path to salvation" (Jpn., *igyōdō*) suitable to an era of the "five corruptions." This doctrine of an "easy path," worship of the Buddha rather than the more traditional practices of mental cultivation, Tanluan attributes to Nāgārjuna, the Mādhyamika thinker and alleged author of a treatise on Pure Land.

THE LIFE AND THOUGHT OF HŌNEN. Hōnen began his formal Buddhist training at the Tendai center on Mount Hiei, where he was ordained at the age of fourteen. Three years later, discouraged by the decadent and somewhat militaristic behavior of his fellow monks, Hōnen went to Kurodani to study under Eikū, a charismatic proponent of Pure Land devotion. For the next twenty-five years Hōnen studied Pure Land texts and practiced *nembutsu zammai* as advocated by Eikū, in accordance with Genshin's *Ōjōyōshū* (Essentials of Pure Land rebirth). During this period Hōnen also studied the doctrines, scriptures, and practices of the six Buddhist sects of the Nara period, Shingon (Vajrayāna), and Zen. Hōnen became convinced that Japan had entered the age, foretold in scripture, of *mappō* (the "latter days of the Law"), a period when Buddhist teachings had so degenerated that the attainment of salvation by one's own efforts was deemed all but impossible. In 1175, while reading the great Chinese Pure Land master Shandao's commentary on the *Kanmuryōjukyō,* Hōnen had a realization that the only path to salvation was to declare one's absolute faith in Amida's vow to save all sentient beings and to engage in "single-practice *nembutsu*" (*senju nembutsu*), which for Hōnen meant placing sole reliance on the invocation of Amida Buddha's name as a means to salvation. That year Hōnen left Kurodani for Kyoto, where he began to disseminate his teachings. This move marks the founding of Jōdoshū.

In 1197 at the request of the prime minister, Kujo Kanezane (1149–1207), Hōnen wrote his influential *Senchaku hongan nembutsushū* (Collection of passages on the original vow of Amida in which Nembutsu is chosen above all). This work establishes Hōnen's essential teachings as the foundation of the Jōdo sect. Following Daochuo (562–645), another Chinese Pure Land master, Hōnen divided Buddhist teachings into two paths, the *shōdōmon* ("gate of the sages") and the *jōdomon* ("gate of Pure Land"). Because it advocates reliance on one's own power and capabilities (*jiriki*) to attain salvation, Hōnen characterized the *shōdōmon* as the more difficult path. He argued that during *mappō* few people were able to attain rebirth in the Pure Land through the arduous practices of traditional Buddhism (e.g., adherence to the Vinaya, meditation, and study). Instead, he considered the *Jōdomon* as the easy path to salvation. Owing to its complete reliance on "other power" (*tariki*; i.e., dependence on Amida's saving grace), the *Jōdomon* is open to all people, masses and aristocracy alike. Hōnen argued that to be saved one need only make the "choice" (*senchaku*) to place absolute faith and trust in Amida's vow. In discussing Other Power and Self Power Hōnen agreed with Tanluan, who asserted that during this degenerate era reliance on Other Power is the easy but nevertheless superior path to salvation. However, he disagreed with Tanluan's characterization of diverse Buddhist practices as reliance on Other Power. For Hōnen, the only practice representing faith in Amida's grace was the invocation of Amida's name.

In addition to outlining these larger doctrinal issues, Hōnen discussed the need to repeat the invocation over a prolonged period of time. Constant repetition of the Nembutsu, he held, ensures the continual purification of one's mind and body and the dissolution of doubt. Moreover, it leads to a moment of awakening (*satori*) in this lifetime and, eventually, to rebirth in the Pure Land. To those detractors who argued that repeated recitations signified reliance on Self Power Hōnen answered that the necessary requisite of each invocation was the proper concentration and sincerity of the mind that comes only from absolute faith in Amida's salvific power. However, he never fully explicated the relation between faith, the Nembutsu, and Other Power.

Because of its appeal to members of all social classes, Hōnen's school soon gained widespread popularity. The monks of the established Buddhist sects, threatened by this popularity, sent a petition to the government charging the monks of the Jōdo sect with breaking the Vinaya precepts. In 1204 Hōnen, along with his main disciples, was compelled to compose and sign a seven-article pledge that would act as a guideline for his conduct. This quieted his enemies until 1205, when another petition was presented to the retired emperor, Go Toba, calling for the prohibition of *senju nembutsu.* In 1206 the situation was further aggravated when two of Hōnen's disciples were accused of attracting the attention of two court ladies while the emperor was absent from Kyoto. The emperor thereupon banned the teachings of the Jōdo sect and exiled Hōnen and most of his main disciples. Five years later Hōnen was pardoned and returned to Kyoto, where he died in 1212.

EARLY SCHISMS. After Hōnen's death his disciples were unanimous in calling for faith in Amida's vow and in promoting the invocation of the Nembutsu as a valuable practice for attaining rebirth in the Pure Land. However, they were left to grapple with many of the doctrinal and methodological issues that remained ambiguous in Hōnen's writings and in his way of life. As the debate over the correct interpretation of Self Power heightened, Hōnen's disciples became divided into two groups: those who moved toward the purest form of *senju nembutsu,* some of whom held that *ichinen* ("a single invocation") was sufficient for salvation, and those who compromised with other Buddhist sects, advocating the use of a variety of practices in conjunction with the Nembutsu. Benchō (1162–1238), considered the most orthodox of Hōnen's disciples, and Shōkū (1177–1247), who had helped compile the *Senchaku hongan nembutsushū,* both stressed the importance of repeated invocations of the Nembutsu, but disagreed on the value they accorded of other practices. The subsect founded by Benchō, the Chinzei-ha, advocated *senju nembutsu* and became the main school of Pure Land. Today, the Chinzei-ha is synonymous with Jōdoshū. Shōkū, on the other hand, in incorporating elements of Tendai and Esoteric Buddhism into his practice, argued that he was merely following the example of Hōnen, who engaged in meditative and ceremonial practices throughout his life. Because Shōkū was not an advocate of *senju nembutsu,* his sect, the Seizan-ha, was instrumental in gaining acceptance of Pure Land doctrines among other Buddhist schools.

The debate among the second group of disciples centered on the question of the relative value of one invocation of the Nembutsu, performed with absolute faith and sincerity, over and against repeated and continual recitation. Ryūkan (1148–1227), founder of the Chōrakuji subsect, argued that prolonged recitation was required as a prelude to salvation, which was attained only at the time of death. During the fifteenth century his sect was absorbed into the Jishū. Kōsai (1163–1247), founder of the Ichinengi sect, was perhaps the most controversial of Hōnen's disciples. Kōsai held that the continual invocation of the Nembutsu was futile since salvation was attained in one moment only, that is, that rebirth in the Pure Land was assured at any moment that the Nembutsu was chanted. Because many of Kōsai's followers were accused of excessively amoral conduct the sect did not enjoy the favor of other Buddhist sects. After Kōsai's death the school declined and many of his followers became members of Shinran's Jōdo Shinshū (True Pure Land sect).

Another form of Pure Land devotion to develop during the Kamakura period is best exemplified by Ippen (1239–1289), founder of the Jishū (Time Sect). Ippen began his Pure Land training at the age of fourteen when he went to Daizaifu to study under the Seizan-ha teacher Shōtatsu. According to legend, while visiting the Kumano shrine in 1276 Ippen had a divine revelation in which a *kami* told him that it is Amida's enlightenment that determines humankind's salvation and that an individual's faith was, therefore, inconsequential. Thereafter, Ippen traveled through the country, handing out *nembutsu* tablets and performing *nembutsu* dances, obtaining for himself the name Yugyō Shōnin ("wandering sage"). Believing that Amida existed everywhere, Ippen's disciples did not associate themselves with a particular temple but rather followed Ippen's example by wandering through the countryside. For Ippen, the name Jishū implied that the practice (i.e., the Nembutsu) accorded with the age (the "time"), that is, that the Nembutsu was the only appropriate practice in an age of *mappō*; for his followers, however, it came to mean that Nembutsu was to be chanted at all time and in all places. From its inception, the Jishū was an independent tradition, doctrinally related to, but unaffiliated with, the Seizan-ha.

Brief mention should be made of Shinran (1173–1263), founder of the Jōdo Shinshū, who considered himself the true successor to Hōnen's teachings. Shinran, however, rejected the Vinaya precepts (the code of monastic discipline), which the Jōdo sect had retained. Declaring himself "neither monk nor layman" he set an example for his disciples by marrying, eating meat, and otherwise living as a layman. While Shinran held that faith in Amida was an essential requisite for salvation, he also argued that such faith could not be ascribed to the individual's will but was entirely a result of Amida's grace as demonstrated by his vow to save all sentient beings. Unlike Hōnen, who claimed that one must make the "choice" to believe in Amida, Shinran was emphatic in stating that it is Amida who "chooses" all beings to be saved. Today, the Jōdo Shinshū is the largest Buddhist sect in Japan.

The Tokugawa, Meiji, and Modern Eras. During the Tokugawa period (1600–1868) Buddhism was particularly favored by the shoguns, who wished to minimize the influence of Christian missionaries. The Tokugawa rulers made Buddhism an integral part of the government organization, lavishly supporting the monks and temples of the established Buddhist sects. But the government also controlled ordinations, temple administration, and other activities, and prohibited sectarianism and factionalism. Thus, despite government patronage, Buddhism became spiritually stagnant. Within this context, the Jōdoshū was the personal favorite of the shoguns; the first shogun, Tokugawa Ieyasu, was a devotee of Jōdoshū, and his successors followed his example. The monks of the sect, however, indulged in this patronage and gradually became more corrupt and devoid of spiritual depth. Among the few who attempted to infuse new life into the Jōdoshū was Suzuki Shōsan (1579–1655), a practitioner of both Nembutsu and Zen. He combined Pure Land devotion and Zen notions of the value of work, teaching farmers that by reciting the Nembutsu while working in their fields they could sever their ties to earthly passions and ensure their attainment of the final awakening. Suzuki firmly believed that only by practicing in one's workplace could one attain salvation.

The Meiji era (1868–1912) saw a reversal in the government's attitude toward Buddhism. Shintō was adopted as the state religion, and neo-Confucianism continued to hold strong influence over the state ideology. Without the revitalization and modernization of its doctrines and practices, the very survival of Buddhism was threatened. Two trends that developed in the Jōdo sect during the Meiji period still continue to exert an influence on Pure Land practice today. The first stressed the attainment of salvation through the personal religious experience of Nembutsu practice. A representative of this position was Yamazaki Bennei (1859–1920), founder of the Kōmyōkai, who advocated intensive recitation of Nembutsu to attain an awakening in this very life. The members of his sect gather to invoke the Nembutsu continually for a few days at a time. Owing to its promise of salvation in this world and during this lifetime, Kōmyōkai practices became popular among adherents of Jōdoshū. However, because it demanded that members devote extended periods of time to their practice, the movement proved ultimately not suited to the lives of most lay people. The second trend emphasized that salvation is attained through social action. Shiio Benkyō (1876–1971), founder of Kyōseikai and a leading scholar of Buddhism, advocated purification and salvation of the entire world rather than the individual's rebirth in the Pure Land. The members of this movement place little emphasis on personal religious experience and instead participate in social work and welfare activities.

In the 1980s the total number of Jōdoshū temples and nuneries was approximately seven thousand. The Jōdoshū supports two Buddhist universities, many women's colleges and high schools, and has established numerous houses for the aged and orphaned.

See Also Amitābha; Benchō; Buddhist Meditation; Genshin; Hōnen; Huiyuan; Ippen; Jingtu; Jōdo Shinshū; Mappō; Nāgārjuna; Nianfo; Pure and Impure Lands; Shandao; Shinran; Suzuki Shōsan; Tanluan; Worship and Devotional Life, article on Buddhist Devotional Life in East Asia; Zhiyi.

Bibliography

Works in Japanese

Chionin Jōdo Shūgaku Kenkyūjo, eds. *Jōdoshū no oshie: reki-shi, shisō, kadai.* Tokyo, 1974.

Chionin Jōdo Shūgaku Kenkyūjo, eds. *Hōnen bukkyō no kenkyū.* Tokyo, 1975.

Fujiyoshi Jikai. *Jōdokyō shisō no kenkyū.* Kyoto, 1983.

Fujiyoshi Jikai, ed. *Jōdokyō ni okeru shūkyō taiken.* Kyoto, 1979.

Hattori Eijun. *Jōdokyō shisōron.* Tokyo, 1974.

Katsuki Jōkō. *Hōnen jōdokyō no shisō to rekishi.* Tokyo, 1974.

Katsuki Jōkō, ed. *Jōdoshū kaisoku no kenkyū.* Kyoto, 1970.

Takahashi Kōji. *Hōnen jōdokyō no shomondai.* Tokyo, 1978.

Tamura Enchō. *Hōnen Shōnin den no kenkyū.* Kyoto, 1972.

Todo Kyōshun. *Hōnen Shōnin kenkyū.* Tokyo, 1983.

Tsuboi Shunei. *Hōnen jōdokyō no kenkyū.* Tokyo, 1982.

Works in English

Coates, Harper H., and Ishizuka Ryūgaku. *Hōnen, the Buddhist Saint.* 5 vols. Kyoto, 1949. An introduction to Hōnen's life and thought.

Cowell, E. B., et al., eds. *Buddhist Mahâyâna Texts* (1894). Sacred Books of the East, vol. 49. Reprint, New York, 1969. Includes English translations of the Pure Land scriptures.

New Sources

Amstutz, Galen. *Interpreting Amida: History and Orientalism in the Study of Pure Land Buddhism.* Albany, 1997.

Blum, Mark Laurence. *The Origins and Development of Pure Land Buddhism: A Study and Translation of Gyōnen's 'Jōdo Hōmon Genrushō.'* New York, 2002.

Hasegawa Masatoshi. *Kinsei no nenbutsu hijiri Munō to minshū.* Tokyo, 2003.

Itō Yuishin. *Jōdoshū-shi no kenkyū.* Kyoto, 1996.

Kleine, Christoph. *Hōnens Buddhismus des Reinen Landes: Refirnm Reformation oder Häresie?* Frankfurt am Main, 1996.

Machida, Sōhō. *Renegade Monk: Hōnen and Japanese Pure Land Buddhism.* Berkeley, 1999.

Noda Hideo. *Meiji jōdoshūshi no kenkyū.* Kyoto, 2003.

Payne, Richard K., and Kenneth K. Tanaka. *Approaching the Land of Bliss: Religious Praxis in the Cult of Amitabha.* Honolulu, 2004.

Sakazume, Itsuko. *Asobi to kyōgai: Hōnen to Shinran.* Tokyo, 1990.

Terauchi Daikichi. *Hōnen sanka: ikiru tame no nenbutsu.* Tokyo, 2000.

Unno, Taitetsu. *River of Fire, River of Water: An Introduction to the Pure Land Tradition of Shin Buddhism.* New York, 1998.

FUJIYOSHI JIKAI (1987)
Revised Bibliography

JOHANAN BAR NAPPAHA SEE YOḤANAN BAR NAPPAḤA'

JOHANAN BAR ZAKKAI SEE YOḤANAN BEN ZAKK'AI

JOHN OF DAMASCUS,

JOHN OF DAMASCUS, also known as John Damascene, was an eighth-century Christian saint, church father, monastic, theologian, author, and poet. Little is known with certitude about John's life. The dates of both his birth and his death are disputed, as are the number of years that he lived. A conservative assessment of the evidence indicates that he was probably born about 679 and died at the age of seventy in 749. It is generally accepted that he was born into a Greek-speaking Syrian family of Damascus, known as Mansour ("victorious," or, "redeemed"). His father, Sergius, held the high position of *logothetes* in the Muslim caliphate at the end of the seventh century. John enjoyed a full course of instruction as a youth, including mathematics, geometry, music, astronomy, rhetoric, logic, philosophy (Plato and Aristotle), and theology.

Following the death of his father, John assumed an economic administrative position (*protosumboulos*) in the government of Caliph Walid (r. 705–715). He left public service just before, or shortly after, the outbreak of the Iconoclastic Controversy to become a monk in the famous Monastery of Saint Sava outside Jerusalem. He was ordained a priest by John V, patriarch of Jerusalem (r. 706–735). John Damascene left a rich legacy of writings reflecting the theology and religious tradition of Eastern Christianity and the spiritual tradition of the Greek fathers.

John was a prolific writer, who, though completely faithful to the Eastern church and its theological tradition, also evinced significant theological creativity. Several of his earlier writings were revised and enlarged after their original publication. John's works reflect his broad educational background and cover numerous areas of concern.

He wrote a number of exegetical works on the Old and New Testaments. Among the better known of these are a shortened version of Chrysostom's commentaries on the letters of Paul, to which he added some of his own observations. In the same manner he published an epitome of the sermons on the *Hexaemeron* attributed to Chrysostom but written by Severian of Gabala (c. 400).

John's major theological production was in the area of doctrinal writings: his most important work is *Pege gnoseos (Fount of Knowledge)*. This work has been translated into many languages and is the foundation of his reputation as a theologian and dogmatician. The work, divided into three parts, appears to have been revised several times, which explains why at least two dates for its composition are recorded, 728 and 743. Each of the parts is found in three versions, of differing length, indicating that they were written independently and at different times, revised, and subsequently gathered together into the unified work.

The first part of *Fount of Knowledge* consists of a treatment of general knowledge (the philosophical and physical sciences of his day) as an introduction to theology. Based primarily on Aristotle, this portion of the work is theologically important because of its holistic perspective. The method used is definitional, by which major terms are defined in brief sections or chapters, in two areas: theoretical (theology, physics, and mathematics), and practical (ethics, economics, and politics).

The second part of *Fount of Knowledge* deals with heresies, or various false teachings, from the perspective of orthodox Christianity. In large part it is a compilation and elucidation of other antiheretical writings, but the three chapters on Islam, Iconoclasm, and the *aposchistai* (wandering monks who rejected all sacraments), were written as new material by John. Additional chapters were added subsequently by others.

The most important part of this work is the third, an outline of orthodox theology (*Ekthesis orthodoxou pisteos*) consisting of 100 short chapters. In chapters 1–14 the doctrine of God is discussed; cosmology follows in chapters 15–44 dealing with angelology, demonology, good and evil, the created world, and anthropology; Christology and soteriology are discussed in chapters 45–73; and the last chapters deal with a variety of topics including Mariology, icons, self-determination (*autexousion*), faith, and the saints. The theological tenor of this work is basically Cappadocian, with perspectives from other theological streams of thought such as those derived from Dionysius the Areopagite, Chrysostom, Athanasius, and Maximos the Confessor.

A number of John's polemical works are doctrinal in character. Among these are *Concerning Faith against the Nestorians*, several works against monophysitism, *Against the Jacobites*, and a work concerning the Trisagion Hymn, in which he opposes a purely Christological reference to this popular and liturgical hymn. In his works *Concerning the Two Wills and Energies in Christ*, and *Against Monophysites and Monothelites*, John deals with the Monothelite Controversy. Between 726 and 731 he wrote three different studies titled *Concerning the Icons*, reflecting various early stages of the Iconoclastic Controversy. He also concerned himself with treating other religious traditions from an Eastern Orthodox perspective, including Judaism, Manichaeism, and Islam. John also dealt with ethical topics in a three-part work titled *Sacra Parallela: Concerning the Holy Fasts, The Eight Spirits of Evil*, and *Concerning Virtues and Vices.*

It has been difficult to determine which of the many sermons attributed to John of Damascus are genuine. Among those whose authenticity is in doubt are three sermons on the Dormition of the *theotokos*, one of two on the annunciation, sermons on the transfiguration of Christ, the fig tree, the birth of Christ, and Christ's presentation in the Temple. In addition there are a number of sermons on saints attributed to him.

Although disputed, it is now generally accepted that John also wrote a Christian version of an ancient Buddhist tale under the title *Barlaam and Joasaph*. It is essentially a story of the conversion to monastic Christianity of a young profligate through the hearing of a striking parable.

John of Damascus is highly regarded as a hymnodist. He is well known for the fourteen published collections of hymns known as canons. In addition, approximately ninety canons are attributed to him in the manuscript tradition. John is primarily responsible for the hymnology of the basic weekly cycle of Eastern Orthodox services found in the liturgical book the *Oktoēchos* (Eight tones). The hymns are characterized by theological exactness coupled with poetic warmth and power.

Tradition attributes to John of Damascus the epithet Chrusorroas ("golden-flowing"). His memory is commemorated by the Eastern Orthodox church on December 4, the date of his death, and by the Roman Catholic church on March 27. He is considered an authoritative voice for contemporary Orthodox theology. His writings were also an important source for Peter Lombard and Thomas Aquinas. Pope Leo XIII declared him a doctor of the Roman Catholic church in 1890.

Bibliography

Texts and Translations

Barlaam and Iosaph. Edited by Harold Mattingly; translated by G. R. Woodward. Loeb Classical Library, vol. 34. Cambridge, Mass., 1937.

Homélies sur la Nativité et la Dormition. Introduction, French translation, and notes by Pierre Voulet. Paris, 1961.

On the Divine Images: Three Apologies against Those Who Attack the Holy Images. Translated by David Anderson. Crestwood, N.Y., 1980. A readable translation.

Opera omnia quae exstant. Edited by Michel Lequien. Paris, 1712. Reproduced in *Patrologia Graeca*, edited by J.-P. Migne, vol. 94. Paris, 1860. The standard received text.

Die Schriften des Johannes von Damaskos. 4 vols. Edited by P. Bonifatius Kotter. Berlin, 1969–1981. These definitive critical texts have extensive documentation and textual critical material.

Hē Theotokos: Tesseres Theomētorikes Homilies. Edited by Athanasius Gievtits. Athens, 1970. Contains the text, with an introduction and commentary by the editor. Each of the four homilies has been rendered into modern Greek by a different translator.

Writings. Translated by Frederic H. Chase, Jr. Fathers of the Church, vol. 37. Washington, D.C., 1958. Includes only *Fount of Knowledge.* The best existing English translation. Contains an introduction by the translator that deals with many of the unresolved historical questions.

Studies

Barnard, Leslie W. "Use of the Bible in the Byzantine Iconoclastic Controversy, 726 to 843 A.D." *Theologische Zeitschrift* 31 (March–April 1975): 78–83. John's use of scripture is discussed as it relates to the Iconoclastic Controversy.

Chevalier, Celestin M. B. *La Mariologie de saint Jean Damascène.* Rome, 1936. A literary and theological examination of John of Damascus's teaching concerning the *theotokos.*

Sahas, Daniel J. *John of Damascus on Islam: The "Heresy of the Ishmaelites."* Leiden, 1972. A revision of a doctoral dissertation. The best detailed biographical treatment in English. It includes a careful treatment of the major problems regarding John of Damascus's teaching concerning Islam.

STANLEY SAMUEL HARAKAS (1987)

JOHN OF KRONSTADT SEE IOANN OF KRONSTADT

JOHN OF THE CROSS

JOHN OF THE CROSS (1542–1591), mystic, poet, saint, and doctor of the church. John was born Juan de Yepes y Álvarez in Fontiveros, Spain, the youngest of three sons. His father's untimely death left the family in poverty. Nevertheless, young John received an excellent education in the humanities at the Jesuit college in Medina del Campo, and in 1563 he entered the Carmelite order at the Monastery of Santa Ana. That same year he received the habit of the order and the religious name Juan de Santo Matía. He completed further studies at Salamanca and in 1567 was ordained to the priesthood.

Shortly after ordination the young friar returned to Medina del Campo, where he met the great Carmelite reformer Teresa of Ávila. Teresa, fifty-two years old at the time, recognized in the twenty-five-year old John the intelligence and holiness that would make him her spiritual and mystical compatriot and her collaborator in the reform movement, he doing in the masculine branch of the order what she was already accomplishing in the feminine branch. On November 28, 1568, after Teresa, as his spiritual mentor, had judged him ready, he professed the Primitive Rule and took the name Juan de la Cruz.

Captured by enemies of the reform movement and imprisoned in the calced (mitigated, or unreformed) monastery at Toledo, John spent nine months in a tiny cell. He was deprived of adequate food and was regularly scourged; yet his established holiness manifested itself in patient acceptance of these hardships and while in prison he began to write the exquisite religious poetry that was to place him among the greatest of the Spanish poets and form the kernel of his mystical legacy.

In 1578 he escaped from prison and began a twelve-year period of administration within the reformed branch of the order. He was a remarkably able superior and as spiritual director was much sought after by religious and laity alike. In 1590 John again became the object of persecution, this time by jealous confreres within the reform movement. An effort to have him expelled from the movement was frustrated by his death. John died at Ubeda on December 13, 1591, at the age of forty-nine.

John of the Cross was beatified in 1675 and canonized in 1726. In 1926 Pius XI declared him a doctor of the church under the title "Mystical Doctor." Besides a few letter, various maxims and counsels, and a number of extraordinarily beautiful poems, John left only four major works, and these have become the instruments of his remarkable influence on the history of Christian spirituality. All four were written from the vantage point of the full maturity of John's own mystical experience, and they reflect the wisdom of deep holiness well served by biblical and theological scholarship. Each consists of a poem followed by a long spiritual commentary.

The Ascent of Mount Carmel (1581–1585) and *The Dark Night* (poem, 1578 or 1579; commentary, 1584–1585) together form a treatise on the double purification (of the sensory and of the spiritual dimensions of the person) that leads to full mystical union. *The Spiritual Canticle* (poem, 1578, 1580–1584; commentary, 1584–1586) is the longest of John's poems, a rapturous overflowing of what he called "mystical wisdom" as he himself had experienced it. It describes four stages of the mystical journey, but the commentary sets forth the whole of that journey from its ascetical beginnings to total transformation in the mystical marriage, the last stage of the spiritual life. *The Living Flame of Love* (poem, 1582–1585; commentary in two redactions, 1585–1591) treats the most perfect experience of love within the highest mystical state of transforming union. The commentary frequently digresses from the poem's subject matter to treat various important aspects of the spiritual life as a whole.

Through the example of his sublime personal holiness and his wonderfully fruitful and very human friendship with Teresa of Ávila, his collaboration in the establishment of the Discalced Carmelite Friars, and especially, his unsurpassed poetic and doctrinal writings on mystical theology, John of the Cross continues to exercise an influence in Western Christian spirituality probably unequaled by anyone except Thomas, Augustine, Dionysius, and Teresa herself.

BIBLIOGRAPHY

The Collected Works of Saint John of the Cross. Translated by Kieran Kavanaugh and Otilio Rodriguez. Rev. ed. Revisions and introductions by Kieran Kavanaugh. Washington, D.C., 1991.

The Complete Works of Saint John of the Cross, Doctor of the Church. 3 vols. Translated by E. Allison Peers. London, 1953. Contains an extensive international bibliography useful for any study of John of the Cross.

God Speaks in the Night: The Life, Times, and Teaching of St. John of the Cross. Translated by Kieran Kavanaugh. Washington, D.C., 1991.

Matthew, Iain. *The Impact of God: Soundings from St. John of the Cross.* London, 1995.

Thompson, Colin. *St. John of the Cross: Songs in the Night.* Washington, D.C., 2003.

SANDRA M. SCHNEIDERS (1987 AND 2005)

JOHN THE BAPTIST.

Born of a poor priestly family in the hill country of Judea, John renounced the priesthood and entered upon an ascetic existence in the wilderness surrounding the Jordan River. There he inaugurated a baptism rite so unprecedented that he was named for it. His contemporary, Jesus, unhesitatingly ascribed the impetus for John's baptism to divine revelation (*Mk.* 11:30), and even though priestly lustrations in the Temple, the daily baths at Qumran, or even proselyte baptism (first attested in the second century CE) may provide certain parallels, they are wholly inadequate to account for John's demand that Jews submit to a once-only immersion in anticipation of an imminent divine judgment by fire. Rejecting all claims to salvation by virtue of Jewish blood or the "merits of Abraham," John demanded of each person works that would reflect a personal act of repentance. The examples preserved in *Luke* 3:10–14 indicate that John stood squarely in the line of the prophets, siding with the poor ("He who has two coats, let him share with him who has none; and he who has food, let him do likewise"). He demanded that toll collectors and soldiers desist from extorting unjust exactions from travelers and pilgrims. His dress was the homespun of the nomad, his diet the subsistence rations of the poorest of the poor (locusts and wild honey, *Mk.* 1:6). He even described the eschatological judge, whose near advent he proclaimed, in terms of a peasant or a man of the soil (chopping down trees, separating wheat from chaff).

Through baptism, John provided a means by which common people and other "sinners" (tax collectors and harlots, *Mt.* 21:32) could be regenerated apart from meticulous observance of the Jewish law. His influence on Jesus in this and other respects was profound. Jesus and his disciples were baptized by John. But whereas John demanded that people come out to him in the wilderness, Jesus went to the people in their towns and villages, rejecting an ascetic life (*Mt.* 11:18–19), and began to regard the future kingdom as an already dawning reality (*Mt.* 11:2–6). Despite these differences, Jesus continued to speak of John in terms of highest respect (*Mt.* 11:7–9, 11a).

John's execution by Herod Antipas was provoked by John's criticism of Herod for divorcing the daughter of the Nabatean king Aretas IV and entering upon an incestuous remarriage with Herodias, his half-brother's wife. John's attacks on Herod took place in Perea, a region controlled by Herod but bordered by Nabatean territory, an area inhabited by Arabs and infiltrated in winter by nomads. Herod's divorce provoked guerrilla warfare, and ultimately Aretas avenged his daughter's shame by a shattering defeat of Herod's army—a defeat that Josephus directly ascribes to divine punishment for Herod's execution of John (*Jewish Antiquities* 18.116–119). John's preaching must also have contributed substantially to popular disaffection from Herod.

Following the publication of the Dead Sea Scrolls, some scholars suggested that John might at one time have been an Essene. It is true that he preached but eight miles from Qumran, that he shared with the Essenes an imminent eschatological hope, and that he lived out (perhaps deliberately) the prophecy of *Isaiah* 40:3 and sought to prepare the way in the wilderness. Both John and the Essenes warned of a coming purgative fire associated with the Holy Spirit and with washing; both issued a radical call to repentance; both employed immersion in water as a religious rite; both believed that only an elect would be saved, and called the rest vipers; both condemned the priesthood and other authorities; both renounced society and abstained from strong drink.

These similarities, however, can in large part be accounted for: Both John and the Essenes belonged to the larger phenomenon of Jewish wilderness sectarianism. Their differences, in any case, are more decisive than all their similarities. John was a solitary. He established no settled community, moved around in the Jordan wastes, was inclusive rather that separatist, public rather than reclusive, addressing the whole nation rather than withdrawing into an isolated life. His baptism was granted once and for all, not daily, and for a forgiveness of sins on which eternal salvation hung, not for physical purity. His dress was camel's hair, not white linen. He did not require a long novitiate for his converts, nor did he organize them under rigid requirements. Almost all the other similarities with Qumran can be traced to common dependence on the prophet Isaiah. Indeed, if John had ever been connected with Qumran, his break was so radical that it scarcely seems necessary to posit any original connection at all. When he steps upon the stage of history, his message and mission are altogether his own.

All four evangelists treat John as "the beginning of the gospel." This reflects both the historical fact and the theological conviction that through John, Jesus perceived the nearness of the kingdom of God and his own relation to its coming. The church continued to treat John as the perpetual preparer for the coming of Christ, calling out for people to repent and let the shift of the aeons take place in their own lives, to "make ready the way of the Lord" (*Mk.* 1:2).

BIBLIOGRAPHY

Kraeling, Carl H. *John the Baptist.* New York, 1951. Despite more recent publications, this work remains definitive. Historical sleuthing at its best.

Scobie, Charles H. H. *John the Baptist.* London, 1964. Adds some interesting conjectures on the Samaritans.

Wink, Walter. *John the Baptist in the Gospel Tradition.* Cambridge, U.K., 1968. A critical study of the use made of the Baptist traditions by the evangelists.

WALTER WINK (1987)

JOHN THE EVANGELIST, according to ancient Christian tradition one of the Twelve chosen by Jesus; the son of Zebedee, brother of James, and author of the Fourth Gospel, the Johannine letters, and the *Book of Revelation.* Called by Jesus from his vocation as a fisherman, John is mentioned frequently in the synoptic Gospels, where with James and Peter he forms the inner circle of disciples. He appears in all four lists of the Twelve in the New Testament (*Mt.* 10:2, *Mk.* 3:17, *Lk.* 6:14, *Acts* 1:13). Usually he is mentioned after his brother James, which suggests that he is the younger, but in the *Acts of the Apostles* his name stands second, after Peter's. Moreover, he appears along with Peter in several of the Jerusalem scenes in the early chapters of *Acts* (e.g., 3:1, 3:4, 3:11, 8:14). Interestingly enough, the episodes in which John figures in the synoptic Gospels (e.g., the raising of Jairus's daughter, the Transfiguration) are missing from John's gospel, and the sons of Zebedee are mentioned only once, in the final chapter (*Jn.* 21:2).

Although, like the other Gospels, *John* is anonymous, it is ascribed to an unnamed beloved disciple (*Jn.* 21:24), who figures prominently in the passion and resurrection narrative of this gospel only. He always appears with Peter, except at the cross. Christian tradition has identified this disciple with John, although the gospel itself does not. In the late second century both Irenaeus and Polycrates ascribe the Fourth Gospel to John, and from that time on it becomes a commonplace that John wrote his gospel in Ephesus after the others had been composed.

Irenaeus traces the Johannine tradition to Papias and Polycarp, bishops during the first half of the second century (Eusebius, *Church History* 3.39.1–7, 4.14.3–8). This testimony is not without problems, however, as Eusebius recognized in reporting Irenaeus's statements about Papias. John's gospel was known in some circles throughout most of the second century; it was popular among Christians who were later condemned as heretics (the Gnostics) and was rejected by others, such as Gaius of Rome and the Alogoi, who objected to its departures from the synoptic Gospels. Such a reception raises questions about the status or recognition of the Fourth Gospel as an apostolic work during this period.

Nevertheless, when after several centuries the gospel, the letters, and *Revelation* had gained universal acceptance as Christian scripture, they were all regarded as the work of John the son of Zebedee. As early as the third century, however, Bishop Dionysius of Alexandria pointed out the stylistic and theological difficulty of regarding *Revelation* as the work of the author of the Fourth Gospel and the letters. Only *Revelation* is expressly the work of someone named John (*Rv.* 1:2), and this John makes no claim to being an apostle (cf. *Rv.* 18:20, 21:14). Both *2 John* and *3 John* are from "the elder," while *1 John* is anonymous. Modern scholars are inclined to see three or more authors represented in the Johannine corpus.

Evidence against the traditional view that John lived to an old age in Ephesus is provided by the silence of Ignatius, who wrote to the Ephesian church (c. 115) mentioning Paul's role at Ephesus prominently but John not at all. There is a strain of evidence, perhaps supported by Jesus' prediction in *Mark* 10:39, that John was martyred with James in Jerusalem during the 40s (*Acts* 12:2). However that may be, manifold difficulties stand in the way of tracing church tradition about John the Evangelist back through the second century.

Despite these difficulties, the *Gospel of John* and *1 John* clearly claim to be based on eyewitness testimony. The validity of that claim does not necessarily stand or fall with the traditional attribution of authorship, which reconciles John's gospel with synoptic and other data about Jesus' disciples. In Christian symbolism dating back to the second century, the fourth evangelist is appropriately represented by the eagle, for the Fourth Gospel goes its own way, apparently independent of the other Gospels and their traditions. John's feast is celebrated on December 27.

BIBLIOGRAPHY

Aside from the New Testament the most important primary source is Eusebius's *Church History*, which brings together earlier testimony of Christian writers on the origin and authorship of the Gospels. The most convenient edition is the two-volume "Loeb Classical Library" text and translation of Kirsopp Lake, J. E. L. Oulton, and Hugh J. Lawlor (Cambridge, Mass., 1926). The relevant early Christian texts have been conveniently collected by C. K. Barnett, *The Gospel According to St. John*, 2d ed. (Philadelphia, 1978), pp. 100–144.

Werner G. Kümmel's *Introduction to the New Testament*, rev. ed. (Nashville, 1975), pp. 234–246, succinctly states the modern, critical case against the tradition of Johannine authorship. In his more recent *Introduction to the New Testament* (New York, 1997), Raymond E. Brown defends the probability of a significant historical connection between the unnamed beloved disciple (*John* 21:24) and the composition of the *Gospel of John*. The most comprehensive treatment of the identity of John and the traditions about him is R. Alan Culpepper, *John the Son of Zebedee: The Life of a Legend* (Columbia, S.C., 1994), especially pp. 56–88.

D. MOODY SMITH (1987 AND 2005)

JOHN XXIII

JOHN XXIII (Angelo Giuseppe Roncalli, 1881–1963) was a pope of the Roman Catholic church (1958–1963). Born in Sotto il Monte, near Bergamo in northern Italy, on November 25, 1881, to a family of sharecroppers, Roncalli attended the local grammar school, was taught Latin by the parish priest, and entered the minor seminary at age eleven. Given a scholarship to the Roman seminary (the Apollinare), he was ordained a priest on August 10, 1904, after completing a year of military service. The following year he obtained a doctorate in theology (with Don Eugenio Pacelli, the future pope Pius XII, on his examining board) and became secretary to the bishop of Bergamo, Giacomo Radini-Tedeschi, an ecclesiastical activist in the social, economic, and political movements of the area. Roncalli accompanied the bishop on his visitations in the diocese and on frequent visits to France, Milan, and Rome, and so became acquainted with influential ecclesiastics, including Archbishop Giacomo della Chiesa (the future Benedict XV) and Monsignor Achille Ratti (the future Pius XI). Despite these contacts, both the bishop and his secretary came under suspicion during the heresy hunt that was occasioned by Pope Pius X's condemnation of modernism in 1907. Gravely affected by the accusation, as pope Roncalli corrected the record of the incident in the Vatican archives. His own attitudes were revealed in his granting of total freedom of theological expression to the Second Vatican Council.

At the outbreak of World War I, Roncalli was inducted into the Italian army as a sergeant in the medical corps and served on the front at Piave and as a chaplain in the nearby military hospitals. On his return to Bergamo he was engaged in diocesan education until 1921, when he was called to Rome by Pope Benedict XV and instructed to coordinate the activities of the Society for the Propagation of the Faith, a funding organ for foreign missions. After visiting the dioceses of Italy, he was persuaded to transfer the organization's headquarters from Lyons, France, to Rome.

Consecrated a titular archbishop of Aeropolis, Palestine, in March 1925, Roncalli was sent to Bulgaria as apostolic visitor to confront the problems of the Latin and other Eastern Christian Catholics in conflict with the Orthodox church and the local government. Settling in Sofia, he visited Catholic centers, brought relief to political and religious refugees from Thrace and Macedonia, organized a congress of Bulgarian Catholics in Yambol in 1928, and in 1930 arranged the canonical dispensation for the marriage of King Boris of Bulgaria, an Eastern Orthodox, to Princess Giovanna of Savoy, a Roman Catholic. Despite guarantees to the contrary, the marriage was repeated in the Orthodox cathedral in Sofia and so put the papal envoy "in a most difficult position." Nevertheless, in 1931 he regularized his position as apostolic delegate, encouraged the use of Bulgarian in the Catholic schools and liturgy, and became a welcome guest at cultural, social, and political events in the nation's capital.

In 1934, as titular archbishop of Mesembria (Thrace), Roncalli was appointed apostolic delegate to Turkey and Greece with residence in Istanbul, a difficult assignment. He had to contend with the secularization policies of the Turkish president Kemal Atatürk (r. 1923–1938), adopting civilian garb in public, and with the anti-Catholicism of the Orthodox clergy in Greece. While serving as parish priest for the small Catholic community in the Turkish metropolis, he visited the minute clusters of Catholics scattered throughout the country, called on the Orthodox patriarch Benjamin in the Phanar, the patriarchal residence in Istanbul, and introduced the use of Turkish in church publications and liturgy.

With the outbreak of World War II, Turkey became a center of political intrigue, and Roncalli, an intimate of the German ambassador Franz von Papen as well as of other diplomats, found himself a frequently consulted confidant, dispatching intelligence information to the Vatican. Aiding countless Jews and others fleeing persecution in central and eastern Europe, he established a unit of the Holy See's bureau for tracing missing persons, refugees, and prisoners of war. In 1942 he flew to Rome to urge Pius XII to persuade the British government to modify the blockade of Greece by allowing the import of food and medical supplies.

In December 1944 Roncalli was dispatched to France to replace Archbishop Valerio Valeri, the papal nuncio. On New Year's Day, as dean (ex officio) of the corps of ambassadors, he presented the ambassadorial body to the new French government of Charles de Gaulle. Together with reconciling the Catholic factions split by the resistance movement, he helped prevent the deposition of six or seven bishops accused of collaborating with the Pétain regime and initiated a renewal of the French episcopate, supporting Cardinal Suhard of Paris in his attempt to re-Christianize the country with his Mission de France. He inaugurated a seminary for training German prisoners of war for the priesthood and did his best to mitigate the Vatican's condemnation of the worker-priest movement. Through Monsignor Giovanni Battista Montini in the Vatican, Roncalli persuaded the Holy See to establish a permanent observer to the United Nations Educational, Scientific, and Cultural Organization (UNESCO). He smoothed over the displacements caused by the publication of Pius XII's encyclical *Humani generis* (Of the human race; 1950), which was used to censure such theologians as Yves Congar, Jean Daniélou, M.-J. Chenu, and Henri de Lubac, all of whom, as pope, John was to welcome as experts to the Second Vatican Council.

Roncalli was created a cardinal in January 1953 and, following an ancient custom, received the red hat from the ruler of France, the Socialist president Vincent Auriol, before taking possession of the See of Venice as its patriarch. On his arrival in the City of the Doges, he assured the faithful that he had always wanted to function as a parish priest and would end his days among them. Visiting the parishes of the archdiocese, he frequently wrote exhortatory letters in support of the vigorous religious, social, and labor movements then in vogue. He downgraded the left-wing faction of the Christian Democratic party and its weekly publication, *Il popolo Veneto,* and in an episcopal letter of 1955 he opposed the party's policy of "opening to the left." Changing precedents set by his predecessor, however, he accepted the Biennial Arts Festival of 1956 and welcomed the Italian Socialist party's congress in 1957. That same year he had organized a diocesan synod and was correcting the proofs of its ordinances when he was called to Rome on October 9, 1958, upon the death of Pius XII.

On October 28, the third day of the conclave, he was elected pope and supreme pastor of the Roman Catholic church. On accepting the election, he said that he would be called John XXIII and intended to imitate John the Baptist in making straight the path of the Lord. Within a month he created twenty-three cardinals, including Archbishop Montini of Milan and Monsignor Domenico Tardini; the latter he appointed his secretary of state. In January, to the consternation of the cardinals of the papal Curia, he announced plans for convening an ecumenical council aimed at updating the church's image and achieving Christian unity. By way of preparation he held a synod in Rome in 1960 and appointed a commission for the revision of canon law and a committee to deal with the moral aspects of birth control.

In outlining plans for the ecumenical council, John declared that it would be the work of the bishops and would not be under the control of the Curia. Nevertheless he appointed Cardinal Tardini as coordinator of the preparatory commissions and allowed Cardinal Alfredo Ottaviani of the Holy Office to dominate their activities. Under their aegis, prelates and professors from the Roman ecclesiastical institutions prepared seventy-two schemata, or topics for discussion, bulging with textbook theology as an agenda for an assembly of more than two thousand prelates that was to meet for one or two months. While saddened by the opposition of his curial advisers, John pushed ahead and in so doing gained the support of cardinals and prelates from the outside world, who at the council's start had reduced the number of schemata to seventeen.

In his opening address to the Second Vatican Council, on October 11, 1962, the pope said that the council had not been called to discuss the basic doctrines of the church; those were well known and defined. Instead, the assembly was aimed at restoring unity, first among Christians and then in the world. To do this the church would have to take a leap ahead *(balzo in avanti)* in penetrating the consciousness of contemporary men and women. While in the past, he asserted, the church had used severity in confronting error, now it was called upon to apply the medicine of mercy. Dismissing his opposition as "prophets of doom," John said that they knew no history. He insisted that "the truths of the deposit of faith are one thing; how they are expressed is another," and he said that the church had to restate its teaching in a medium that would employ the tools of modern scholarship and technology. Many of the prelatial listeners felt that the pope was close to heresy.

The council quickly took on a Johannine contour as it concentrated on updating the liturgy by introducing the vernacular languages for the celebration of the Mass and the sacraments; discussed the relationship between the Bible and tradition in formulating the church's teachings; and discussed the structure of the church itself and the way priests, the laity, nuns, and prelates were to conduct themselves in the contemporary world. Listening to the discussions on closed-circuit television, John seldom intervened, and then did so only to resolve a knotty impasse.

In preparing for the council, John invited Orthodox and Protestant churches to send observers. He presented these observers with the documents relating to the council, gave them permission to attend the debates, and provided informal settings where prelates, theologians, and observers got to know one another intimately. While concerned with the organized opposition to his liberalizing aims by a group of 250 prelates, John felt, as the first session drew to a close on December 8, that the intended updating (*aggiornamento*) had been initiated. Expressing his satisfaction that the "opening of the church's window" had been accomplished, he announced that the council's second session would begin in September 1963.

By early November suspicions were aroused regarding the pope's fatal cancer. John nevertheless continued his busy schedule, visiting parishes, receiving diplomats, and giving general audiences to pilgrims and visitors. During the Cuban missile crisis, he made a radio broadcast in which he admonished President Kennedy and Chairman Khrushchev to achieve a peaceful solution, thus enabling the two leaders to back off gracefully. On receiving telegrams of recognition for his efforts, he decided to leave the world a legacy in his noted encyclical *Pacem in terris* (Peace on earth), which was honored by a symposium at the United Nations in New York. His previous encyclical, *Mater et magistra* (Mother and Teacher), dealing with the world's social and economic needs, had caused some problems for conservative Catholics. And when the pope received the son-in-law of Khrushchev, Aleksei Adzhubei, in a private audience, there was talk of papal indiscretion. These incidents were compounded by John's reception of the Balzan Peace Prize, awarded by an international committee that included four Soviet members, in the spring of 1963, which was his last public appearance.

Throughout his career John proved a facile writer. As a young priest he produced a noted essay on the seventeenth-century church historian Cardinal Baronius. He also wrote a history of the practice of public charity in the diocese of Bergamo as well as a biography of Bishop Radini-Tedeschi. During the course of his diplomatic career he edited a five-volume, documented history of the effects of the Council of Trent on the diocese of Bergamo as it was administered by Cardinal Carlo Borromeo, one of John's favorite saints. From the journal of his seminary days he produced *Journal of a Soul* (New York, 1965), a spiritual diary that is the key to understanding his intimate relation with God and the placidity with which he accepted the ups and downs of everyday life, in keeping with his heraldic motto, "Peace and Obedience."

In the course of his pontificate, John named fifty-five cardinals; he did not hesitate to break with the tradition of holding the college of cardinals to seventy members. He canonized ten saints and beatified five holy men and women, including Elizabeth Seton of Baltimore. Labeled a transitional pope on his election at age seventy-six, John accepted the designation as a challenge and, as the most innovative pontiff in over five centuries, proceeded to revolutionize the church. When John died on June 3, 1963, he was mourned by the whole world; one newspaper carried the headline "A Death in the Family of Mankind."

SEE ALSO Vatican Councils.

BIBLIOGRAPHY

Aradi, Zsolt, et al. *Pope John XXIII: An Authoritative Biography.* New York, 1959.

Fesquet, Henri, ed. *Wit and Wisdom of Good Pope John.* Translated by Salvator Attanasio. New York, 1964.

Hales, E. E. Y. *Pope John and His Revolution.* Garden City, N.Y., 1956.

Hebblethwaite, Peter. *John XXIII, Pope of the Council.* New York, 1985.

John XXIII. *Scritti e discorsi, 1953–1958.* 4 vols. Rome, 1959–1964.

John XXIII. *Discorsi, messagi, colloqui del Santo Padre Giovanni XXIII.* 5 vols. Vatican City, 1961–1964.

John XXIII. *Souvenirs d'un nonce: Cahiers de France, 1944–1953.* Rome, 1963.

John XXIII. *Journal of a Soul.* Translated by Dorothy White. New York, 1965.

Murphy, Francis X. *Pope John XXIII Comes to the Vatican.* New York, 1959.

Murphy, Francis X. *The Papacy Today.* New York, 1981.

Trisco, Robert. "John XXIII, Pope." In *New Catholic Encyclopedia,* vol. 7. New York, 1967.

Zizola, Giancarlo. *The Utopia of Pope John XXIII.* Translated by Helen Barolini. Maryknoll, N.Y., 1978.

FRANCIS X. MURPHY (1987)

JONAH, or, in Hebrew, Yonah, was an Israelite prophet in the Bible who, as told in the book preserved in his name, was divinely commissioned to announce a prophecy of imminent doom to the Assyrian people of Nineveh (*Jon.* 1:1–2). Fleeing his task, Jonah hopped aboard a commercial vessel bound for Tarshish, in the west (*Jon.* 1:3). Subsequently, a violent storm broke out that was recognized through divination by lots to be due to a sin of Jonah's. The storm was quelled when Jonah was cast into the sea (*Jon.* 1:4–10). However, the Lord arranged for a great fish to swallow the prophet, who presumably repented his folly in attempting to flee divine destiny (*Jon.* 2:8). In any event, he was regurgitated upon the dry land and traveled to Nineveh, where he first announced doom to the city and its inhabitants and then witnessed the pagans' repentances and God's forgiveness (*Jon.* 3). Grieved at this expression of divine mercy, Jonah wished to die, but, in the parable of chapter 4, was given instruction and reproof by God in the form of a recinus plant that sprouted to shade him in the heat of the day but then as quickly withered. Jonah regretted its loss, although he had done nothing to care for it. How much more (he is asked rhetorically) should God have compassion for people like the Ninevites and their cattle—his creatures?

Both language and theology, as well as the inaccurate depiction of Nineveh, suggest that the *Book of Jonah* is a relatively late postexilic composition, from about the fourth century BCE (it is first cited in *Tobit*). The book is artistically organized and integrated: Chapters 1 and 3 deal with penitent pagans and their salvation from the wrath of Israel's God; chapters 2 and 4 deal with the Israelite prophet and his theological lessons in and by miraculous circumstances. But the concern of the text has, since antiquity, perplexed its readers.

In ancient Jewish Midrashic and aggadic literature, commentators have drawn out various lessons from the story of Jonah. In the failure of Jonah's flight they saw proof that a prophet could not escape his destiny. In his refusal to prophesy they detected a noble desire not to insult Israel, who—unlike the pagans—did not repent. In God's final response to the Ninevites, the rabbis underscored the power of repentance to affect the divine will. (Since antiquity the *Book of Jonah* has been the prophetic lection for the afternoon service of Yom Kippur, the Day of Atonement; see B.T., *Meg.* 31a.) Finally, in Jonah's refusal to utter a prophetic oracle of doom in the name of a merciful God, many interpreters have seen his fear of being killed as a false prophet. The church fathers, in contrast to the rabbis, argued that Jonah wanted by his prophecy to the Ninevites to teach a lesson to the stubborn Jews, and thus found in *Jonah* precedent and support for missions to the Gentiles.

Divine mercy, false prophecy, and repentance combined are the core of the prophetic meditation reflected in this book: Initially concerned that divine mercy would limit the dignity of prophecy and so make the divine oracular word conditional upon human behavior, Jonah rejected his office only to realize finally that repentance has no independent, magical effect, because divine mercy is an attribute of an utterly transcendent and free God. The asymmetry between the parable at the story's end, the prophet's situation, and the lesson derived from it, has often been regarded as support for this theological point. God will have mercy in the end upon whomsoever he chooses.

At another level, the ingestion and regurgitation of Jonah by a fish is a motif that dramatizes the inner transformation and spiritual rebirth of the prophet. Typologically, moreover, the three days spent by Jonah in the belly of the fish were seen in early Christian tradition as prefiguring the three days spent by Jesus "in the heart of the earth" (*Mt.* 12:40). The fish and salvation motifs are found frequently in the Roman catacombs and on the sarcophagi and were used extensively in Byzantine manuscripts and in medieval miracle plays. In Jewish Neoplatonic texts, the themes of the story of Jonah were understood allegorically in terms of the fate of the human soul in the world.

BIBLIOGRAPHY

Bickerman, Elias J. *Four Strange Books of the Bible: Jonah, Daniel, Koheleth, Esther.* New York, 1967.

Cohn, Gabriël H. *Das Buch Jona.* Assen, 1969.

Ginzberg, Louis. *The Legends of the Jews* (1909–1938). 7 vols. Translated by Henrietta Szold et al. Reprint, Philadelphia, 1937–1966. See the index, s.v. *Jonah.*

Goitein, S. D. "Some Observations on Jonah." *Journal of the Palestine Oriental Society* 17 (1937): 63–77.

Scholem, Gershom, ed. *Zohar, the Book of Splendor* (1949), vol. 6. Reprint, New York, 1963.

Urbach, E. E. "The Repentance of the People of Nineveh and the Discussions between Jews and Christians" (in Hebrew). *Tarbiz* 20 (1949): 118–122.

New Sources

Gaines, Janet Howe. *Forgiveness in a Wounded World: Jonah's Dilemma.* Studies in Biblical Literature, no. 5. Atlanta, 2003.

Person, Raymond F. *In Conversation with Jonah: Conversation Analysis, Literary Criticism, and the Book of Jonah.* Journal for the Study of the Old Testament Supplement Series, no. 220. Sheffield, 1996.

Sherwood, Yvonne. *Biblical Text and Its Afterlives: The Survival of Jonah in Western Culture.* Cambridge, U.K., and New York, 2000.

MICHAEL FISHBANE (1987)
Revised Bibliography

JONAS, HANS. Hans Jonas (1903–1993) was a theologian and philosopher whose intellectual development moved from research into the Gnosticism of late antiquity through a naturalistic philosophy of life and culminated in establishing an ethic of global ecological responsibility. Born in Mönchengladbach, Germany, into the liberal German-Jewish bourgeoisie, Jonas adhered to Zionist convictions early in life. His philosophical studies led him to Edmund

Husserl (1859–1938) in Freiburg, then—for a short time—to the *Hochschule für die Wissenschaft des Judentums* in Berlin, and finally into the circle of Martin Heidegger (1899–1976) in Marburg. There Jonas encountered his other influential teacher, Rudolf Bultmann (1884–1976), who was developing his method of existential interpretation and "demythologizing" of the New Testament. Bultmann aroused and intensified Jonas's interest in Gnosticism and in Gnostic ontology. On the road to his revolutionary attempt at a comprehensive philosophical interpretation of Gnosticism, the Heideggerian analysis of existence was especially helpful to Jonas, since it led him to a new, modern understanding of this religious-historical phenomenon of antiquity. In 1930, as an outcome of his dialogue with Bultmann and Heidegger, Jonas published the study *Augustin und das paulinische Freiheitsproblem,* in which he laid the foundation for his later reflections concerning freedom as the basic defining feature of human existence.

EARLY CAREER. When the first volume of *Gnosis und Späntantiker Geist* appeared, in 1934, Jonas had already left Nazi Germany and emigrated to Jerusalem, where he stepped into the German-Jewish intellectual circle of Gershom Scholem (1887–1982) and taught at the Hebrew University. In 1939, he volunteered to serve in the British army and in 1945 he returned to Germany as a member of the Jewish Brigade Group. There he learned that his mother had been deported to Lodz and had subsequently been murdered in Auschwitz. The passion with which Jonas, in his philosophy, attempted to justify the value of life resulted from his confrontation with the Nazis' utter abandonment of all that is human. In 1949, after being drawn into the army again during the Israeli War of Independence, Jonas left Jerusalem in order to accept an academic position in Canada, and in 1955 he accepted a post at the New School for Social Research in New York City.

GNOSTICISM. Jonas published the second volume of *Gnosis und Späntantiker Geist* in 1954; however, he devoted himself increasingly to other topics and continued to pursue his gnosis research as a peripheral activity. That most publications since the 1980s in the field of religious studies make only limited reference to Hans Jonas is due to the fact that current research—which is more strongly historical and sociological in its orientation—is capable, on the basis of the Nag Hammadi editions of the original sources, of elucidating the different currents of Gnosticism in a more thoroughgoing and detailed fashion than was possible for Jonas. Jonas did have access to an abundance of religious-historical sources, but these were primarily from the Patristic literature, the middle-Asian Manichean literature, the fore-Asian Mandean literature, and Neo-Platonism. However, his aim was first and foremost to effectuate a religious-philosophical interpretation of these sources. In later editions of his 1958 book *The Gnostic Religion,* he undertook to integrate new material into his understanding of Gnosticism, without changing his basic conception in any significant respects. In pursuing his work, he deliberately omitted offering any particular analysis of the religious-historical origins of Gnosticism, its development within the specific social and religious-cultural settings that engendered it, and its relationship to Judaism, Christianity, Zoroastrianism, or the Hellenistic philosophy. His goal was rather to achieve a philosophically based phenomenological survey of the mythological motifs, symbols, religious-existential attitudes and ethical concepts that characterized the appearance of Gnosticism in its diverse manifestations.

The permanent value of Jonas's interpretation lies in his hermeneutical approach, through which he led research on Gnosticism out of the narrow limits of theology and church history and at the same time went beyond a mere discussion of the religious-historical origins of the multifaceted, syncretistic Gnostic movement. Aided by the Heideggerian existential analytic—and proceeding also on the basis of Oswald Spengler's (1880–1936) cultural-morphological theses, which asserted that abstruse aspects were to be found hidden behind the historical expressions of religious phenomena—Jonas attempted to overcome the impression of chaos and pandemonium and identify the basic types of a Gnostic worldview. Particularly noteworthy in this connection were the belief in the essentially evil or alienating character of material existence and a tendency to devalue the demiurgic world (a world that could be overcome only by being renounced) on the basis of a fundamental anti-cosmic dualism. This interpretation formed the starting point of a whole generation of researchers in the field of Gnosticism; however, it has more recently been called in question, for example by Michael A. Williams, who has astutely disputed the idea of one Gnostic religion that can be understood in uniform categories and who has characterized this idea as a misleading typological construct.

ALIENATION AND ORGANIC BEING. Irrespective of whether Jonas's account of Gnosticism can stand in the face of more recent research in the field, it was a crucial determinant of his philosophical development after the war. In his 1952 essay "Gnosticism and Modern Nihilism," he endeavored to make use of his research on Gnosticism to effectuate a fundamental critique of Existentialism, which had been of great service to him as a hermeneutical key but which now had become the major challenge to his thinking. Above all, the politically ominous potential of Heidegger's attitude toward the world, which had made him susceptible to the inhumanity of the Nazi ideology, induced Jonas to set forth a counter-philosophy in opposition to modern nihilism. The "existentialist reading" of Gnosticism, with the help of Heideggerian categories (for example, the losing-of-self, abandonment into the nullity of the world, the foundationality of fear) helped Jonas decode the Gnostic myths and work out their nihilistic implications for self and the world—implications that are marked by the human feeling of alienation and suffering under the enslaving powers of the world and of the cosmos. He postulated a "Gnostic foundationality," comparable to Heidegger's "abandonment," which was diametrically opposed to the ontology of Greek antiquity, with its conception of the cosmos as a living, harmonious, and rational system affording security. The foundation myth that Jonas abstracted as Gnosticism's common feature tells of a radically disturbed metaphysical situation of the world, which—as a demiurgic creation—condemns the human being to existential abandonment, darkness and "not-at-home-ness." Liberation—which, in Gnostic thinking, was conceived of as a return of the imprisoned soul into an otherworldly, divine realm of light, wherein the human soul participates by virtue of the spirit even during its exile in the material world—is only possible by treading the path of revealed, occult knowledge (gnosis) and demands as an ethical consequence a conscious "renunciation of worldliness."

Jonas believed himself to have discerned a secularizing return to the Gnostic mode of thinking in spiritual streams that extended from Blaise Pascal (1623–1662) through Friedrich Nietzsche (1844–1900) and up to Heidegger; Jonas called these spiritual currents "cosmic nihilism" both because they viewed the human being as a lonely element within an altogether indifferent universe, an element separated from nature by an unbridgeable chasm, and because they advocated contempt for the world and escape from it. Jonas hoped to overcome this tendency through an antidualistic "philosophy of the organic," which he set forth in *The Phenomenon of Life* (1963). In this work, he expounded his understanding of organic being, which recognizes in the process of evolution a progressive development of freedom and danger, culminating in human beings, who do not have to experience the world as an inhospitable, hostile place where they are not at home if they will begin to see themselves as part of a nature that is meaningful in itself.

ETHIC OF RESPONSIBILITY. In his 1984 *The Imperative of Responsibility*, Jonas explored the ethical consequences of his speculative ontology. In view of the vulnerability of a world society that is able, through its actions, to damage life on earth irrevocably, and in opposition to the utopian thinking of Ernst Bloch (1885–1977), he demanded a "heuristic of fear" that would enable one to envision "evil suffered by coming generations" and set strategies of humility to counter the ominous euphoria of the Faustian dream, for example, strategies of self-limitation and reverence for the "holiness of life." In view of dwindling public trust in religion, he quite deliberately gave up theological arguments in order to be able to establish a universally plausible ethic for the global society. By contrast, when he addressed Jewish audiences, he gave a central role to human respect for the integrity of creation and to the notion that human beings are created in God's own image. Jonas viewed the power of science and technology to reshape the world, giving humanity the feeling of treading in the very footsteps of God, as the era's most important challenge. In the field of bio-ethics, he warned against unbridled genetic engineering, which, as he emphasized in his 1970 essay "Contemporary Problems in Ethics from a Jewish Perspective," seemed to him to endanger in a most dramatic fashion the very "image of the creation itself, including the human being."

In his 1987 essay *The Concept of God after Auschwitz*, Jonas radically transformed the question of theodicy into a question about the justification of the human being, who is created for freedom; he thus bid farewell to the idea that God is in absolute control of the course of history. Stimulated by ideas from the Lurianic Qabbalah, Jonas employed a speculative myth to unfold a process of theogony and cosmogony in which God, in the course of evolution, withdraws completely back into himself, relinquishes his omnipotence, and makes the world subject to human action, thereby giving over to human control the fate of his own divinity, which is deeply affected by the joy and suffering of life. These speculations lent the utmost urgency to his appeal to human responsibility for life. It is decisive for the whole of Hans Jonas's philosophy that his ethical-philosophical interpretation of the contemporary world's challenges cannot be understood in isolation from his existential confrontation with the abysmal depths of inhumanity revealed in Auschwitz, or from his belief in the transcendent responsibility of the human being. The underlying motif of the philosopher's cosmogonical suppositions is this: given the human formation of the world, in a time when genocide is practiced and technological self-destruction is possible, the very image of God is in peril.

SEE ALSO Ascension; Exile; Gnosticism; Hermeneutics; History of Religions.

BIBLIOGRAPHY

A comprehensive bibliography of the works of Hans Jonas, and of writings about him, is to be found in the appendix to Jonas's *Erinnerungen* (Memoirs), after conversations with Rachel Salamander, edited by Christian Wiese (Frankfurt am Main, Germany, 2003). Jonas's *Wissenschaft als persönliches Erlebnis* (Science as personal experience; Göttingen, Germany, 1987) contains further autobiographical reflections. Biographical perspectives provide good introductions to Jonas, especially Christian Wiese, *Hans Jonas: Zusammen Philosoph und Jude* (Hans Jonas: Philosopher and Jew; Frankfurt am Main, 2003); Olivier Depré, *Hans Jonas: 1903–1993* (Paris, 2003); and Alberto Prieri, *Hans Jonas* (Florence, Italy, 1998). A good overview of the different perspectives on Jonas's work can be found in Dietrich Böhler, ed., *Ethik für die Zukunft* (Ethic for the future; Münich, Germany, 1994). Introductions to Jonas's philosophy are provided by Franz Josef Wetz, *Hans Jonas zur Einführung* (Hamburg, 1994) and David J. Levy, *Hans Jonas: The Integrity of Thinking* (Columbia, Mo., 2003). Detailed interpretations of Jonas's life and research are found in two collections of essays, Wolfgang Erich Müller, ed., *Von der Gnosisforschung zur Verantwortungsethik* (Hans Jonas: From gnosis research to an ethic of responsibility; Stuttgart, Germany, 2003) and Christian Wiese and Eric Jacobson, eds., *Weiterwohnlichkeit der Welt* (Berlin, 2003).

Augustin und das paulinische Freiheitsproblem (Augustine and the Pauline problem of freedom; Göttingen, Germany, 1965) should be counted among Jonas's important religious-historical works. Other important books by Jonas include: *Ein philosophischer Beitrag zur Genesis der christlich-abendländischen Freiheitsidee* (A philosophical contribution toward the genesis of the Christian-Western idea of freedom; Göttingen, Germany, 1930); *Gnosis und spätantiker Geist. Die mythologische Gnosis zur Geschichte und Methodologie der Forschung* (Göttingen, Germany, 1934; expanded edition, 1964); *Gnosis und spätantiker Geist. Von der Mythologie zur mystischen Philosophie* (Göttingen, Germany, 1954); *The Gnostic Religion: The Message of the Alien God and the Beginnings of Christianity* (Boston 1958; expanded and revised edition, Boston, 1963).

Barbara Aland, with Ugo Bianchi et al., edited an important volume, *Festschrift für Hans Jonas* (Gnosis: commemorative volume for Hans Jonas; Göttingen, Germany, 1978), in which world-renowned specialists focus on Jonas's approach to Gnosticism and related subjects. Ioan P. Culianu, *Gnosticismo e pensiero moderno: Hans Jonas* (Rome, 1985) is also important in this respect. Eric Jakob, *Martin Heidegger und Hans Jonas* (Martin Heidegger and Hans Jonas; Tübingen, Germany, 1996) is devoted to elucidating Jonas's relationship to Heidegger. See also Wolfgang Baum, *Gnostische Elemente im Denken Martin Heideggers?: Eine Studie auf der Grundlage der Religionsphilosophie von Hans Jonas Gnostic* (Gnostic Elements in the thinking of Martin Heidegger?: A study of the foundations of Hans Jonas' philosophy of religion; Münich, Germany, 1997); and Richard Wolin, *Heidegger's Children: Hannah Arendt, Karl Loewith, Hans Jonas, and Herbert Marcuse* (Princeton, N.J. 2001). For criticism of the notion of Gnosticism as formulated by Jonas, see Michael A. Williams, *Rethinking "Gnosticism": An Argument for Dismantling a Dubious Category* (Princeton, N.J., 1996) and Michael Waldstein, "Hans Jonas' Construct 'Gnosticism': Analysis and Critique," *Journal of Early Christian Studies* 8, no. 3 (2000): 341–372.

Jonas develops his philosophy of the organic and brings out its ethical implications in *The Phenomenon of Life: Toward a Philosophical Biology* (New York, 1966); in *Philosophical Essays: From Ancient Creed to Technological Man* (Englewood Cliffs, N.J., 1974); and in *On Faith, Reason and Responsibility: Six Essays* (San Francisco, 1978). For Jonas's thoughts on the philosophy of responsibility and its ethical implications, see *Macht oder Ohnmacht der Subjektivität?: Das Leib-Seele-Problem im Vorfeld des Prinzips Verantwortung* (The power or powerlessness of subjectivity?: The mind-body problem underlying the imperative of responsibility; Frankfurt am Main, Germany, 1981); *The Imperative of Responsibility: In Search of an Ethics for the Technological Age* (Chicago, 1984); *Technik, Medizin und Ethik: Zur Praxis des Prinzips Verantwortung* (Technology, medicine and ethics: Toward practice of the imperative of responsibility; Frankfurt am Main, Germany, 1985); and *Philosophie: Rückschau und Vorschau am Ende des Jahrhunderts* (Philosophy: Review and preview at the end of the century; Frankfurt am Main, Germany, 1993). Important works for interrelated themes in the fields of ontology and ethics in Jonas are Wolfgang Müller's *Der Begriff der Verant wortung bei Hans Jonas* (Frankfurt am Main, Germany, 1988); Gilbert Hottois, *Hans Jonas: nature et responsabilité* (Hans Jonas: Nature and responsibility; Paris, 1993); Bernd Wille, *Ontologie und Ethik bei Hans Jonas* (Ontology and ethics in Hans Jonas; Dettelbach, Germany 1996); Nathalie Frogneux, *Hans Jonas ou la vie dans le monde* (Hans Jonas, or Life within the world; Brussels, Belgium, 2000); Marie-Geneviève Pinsart, *Hans Jonas et la liberté: Dimensions theologiques, ontologiques et politiques* (Hans Jonas and freedom: Theological, ontological, and political dimensions; Paris, 2002); Frank Niggemeier, *Pflicht zur Behutsamkeit?: Hans Jonas' naturphilosophische Ethik fuer die technologische Zivilisation* (Duty to be cautious?: Hans Jonas' natural-philosophical ethic for technological civilization; Würzburg, Germany, 2002).

Jonas' late metaphysical reflections are to be found in *Der Gottesbegriff nach Auschwitz: Eine jüdische Stimme (The concept of God after Auschwitz: A Jewish voice;* Frankfurt am Main, Germany, 1987); *Philosophische Untersuchungen und metaphysische Vermutungen* (Philosophical investigations and metaphysical suppositions; Frankfurt am Main, Germany, 1992); and *Mortality and Morality: A Search for Good after Auschwitz,* edited by Lawrence Vogel (Evanston, Ill., 2001). Thomas Schieder offers a critical polemic in *Weltabenteuer Gottes: Die Gottesfrage bei Hans Jonas* (God's cosmic adventure: The God question in Hans Jonas; Paderborn, Germany, 1998).

CHRISTIAN WIESE (2005)
Translated from German by Marvin C. Sterling

JONES, ABSALOM. Absalom Jones (November 6, 1746–February 13, 1818), the first African American priest ordained in the Episcopal Church, is commonly associated with the event that led to the formation of the African Methodist Episcopal denomination. Jones and Richard Allen (1760–1831) led a group of black worshippers out of Saint George's Methodist Church on a Sunday in November 1787 in protest of the church's decision to segregate black worshippers in the upstairs gallery.

Jones was born a slave in Sussex, Delaware. He taught himself to read during his early teens and learned to write after being taken to Philadelphia to work in his master's store as a clerk and handyman. In 1766 he began attending Anthony Benezet's school in the evenings. In 1770 Jones married another slave, whose freedom he purchased with the assistance of Quaker friends and his father-in-law. Jones later purchased his own freedom in 1784, after which he continued to work for his former master.

Jones was active at Saint George's Episcopal Church in Philadelphia and served as a lay preacher. His outreach efforts to Philadelphia's African American population gained greater success after Allen, who arrived in Philadelphia in 1786, joined the church. They formed the Free African Society on April 12, 1787, to provide aid and support to the sick, widows, and orphans. Philadelphia had the largest free African American population in the country, and the Free African Society was one of their major public gathering places. The number of black worshippers at Saint George's increased with the success of Jones and Allen's ministry and preaching. The white church leaders consequently restricted black worshippers to the balcony. On a Sunday in November 1787 Jones seated himself in a front pew in the balcony, but an usher insisted that he had to move to the rear of the balcony.

When Jones refused, the ushers attempted to physically move Jones from his seat, whereupon Jones, accompanied by Allen and the other black worshipers, left the church.

After they left Saint George's, Jones and Allen formed the African Church and held regular worship services. By 1792 the group had begun to raise funds for a church building, but the members disagreed over the appropriate denominational affiliation. Most of the members voted for affiliation with the Episcopal Church. Jones went with the majority, and Allen went with the minority that favored Methodism.

On July 17, 1794, the former group completed the construction of its new church building, which was consecrated Saint Thomas's African Episcopal Church, with Jones as its first minister in the official ecclesiastical capacity of licensed lay reader. The church was formally received into the Diocese of Pennsylvania on October 17, 1794. Jones was ordained as a deacon on August 6, 1795, and as a priest in 1804.

Jones was renowned as an orator and for the pastoral care he provided his members through house-to-house visitation. The church grew to a membership of 427 people, and under Jones the leadership organized schools, the Female Benevolent Society, and the African Friendly Society.

Although Jones and Allen followed separate denominational paths, together they founded Philadelphia's African Masonic Lodge in 1798, petitioned Congress and the state legislature for an end to slavery in 1800, and founded the Society for the Suppression of Vice and Immorality in 1808. In 1812 the Vigilance Committee approached Jones, Allen, and James Forten regarding efforts to defend the city, for which these men recruited 2,500 black men. In January 1817, Jones and Allen organized a convention to coordinate opposition to the American Colonization Society, which encouraged blacks to emigrate to Liberia.

BIBLIOGRAPHY

Appiah, Kwame Anthony, and Henry Louis Gates, Jr., eds. *Africana: The Encyclopedia of the African and African American Experience.* New York, 1999.

Douglass, William. *Annals of the First African Church in the United States of America.* Philadelphia, 1862.

Jones, Absalom. *A Thanksgiving Sermon, Preached January 1, 1808, in St. Thomas's (or the African Episcopal) Church, Philadelphia.* Philadelphia, 1808; reprint, Philadelphia, 1969.

Lammers, Ann C. "The Reverend Absalom Jones and the Episcopal Church: Christian Theology and Black Consciousness in a New Alliance." *Historical Magazine of the Protestant Episcopal Church* 51 (June 1982): 159–184.

JAMES ANTHONY NOEL (2005)

JONES, JIM. James Warren Jones (1931–1978), the charismatic leader of Peoples Temple who persuaded his followers to commit murder and suicide in Guyana in 1978, was born to James Thurman Jones and Lynetta Putnam Jones in Crete, Indiana, on May 13, 1931. Lynetta supported the family doing factory work in Lynn because the elder Jones suffered ill health resulting from injuries sustained in World War I. Although the family was irreligious, the younger Jones attended several local churches and by the age of ten was being groomed as a child evangelist by a female Pentecostal preacher.

As a high school student, Jones met Marceline Baldwin, a nursing student, at a hospital in Richmond where they both worked. They wed in 1949. After intermittently attending Indiana University and working at a series of jobs, Jones found himself drawn to the ministry, despite earlier expressions of atheism. He began an internship in 1952 at a Methodist church in Indianapolis but was expelled after he brought African Americans to services. He established his own congregation, Community Unity Church, which in 1955 became Peoples Temple. His ministry in Indianapolis, marked by Pentecostal and Holiness theology and black church tradition and style, attracted both black and white members drawn to his message of racial equality and social justice. He and Marceline adopted five children, including one white, one black, and three Koreans, and along with their biological son created what they called a "rainbow family." Jones's work as a white minister in an interracial congregation led to his appointment as director of the Indianapolis Human Rights Commission in 1961, where he served briefly before traveling to Hawaii and South America. When he returned two years later, he told the greatly reduced Indianapolis congregation that the church must move to northern California to be safe in the event of nuclear war.

A group of eighty parishioners relocated with the Jones family to Redwood Valley, a small town in the California wine country north of San Francisco. There members began to live and work communally, donating wages and income from outside jobs. The group sponsored several residential homes and outpatient services for the mentally ill and mentally retarded, which Marceline administered. Jim Jones continued to preach a social gospel message of service to the poor and encouraged expansion of the church to San Francisco, where membership grew with the inclusion of thousands of African Americans. The dynamic minister became a political force in San Francisco in the 1970s, a result of his delivering Peoples Temple members to demonstrations in support of freedom of the press, Native American rights, and antidevelopment efforts. Local, state, and national politicians frequented the Temple, where they were warmly greeted. The Temple also opened a church in Los Angeles, and during the mid-1970s Jones preached at all three California congregations, traveling the length of the state in a Temple-owned bus. He also led several cross-country caravans, preaching in Philadelphia, New York, and midwestern cities, attracting members at every stop.

In 1974 Jones signed a lease to cultivate 3,852 acres in the Northwest District of Guyana, the only English-speaking country in South America. Temple volunteers had been developing the site for three years when critical reports about the powerful minister emerged in San Francisco. Former members claimed that Jones forced sex upon them, encouraged corporal punishment of errant members by other members, and had faked faith healings and miracles. Some claimed that Jones had ordered ex-members to be killed. Negative publicity, coupled with a federal tax investigation, prompted Jones and a thousand members to immigrate to Guyana in mid-1977. Jones's mental and physical health deteriorated in the tropical climate, and his leadership became more erratic and abusive, as an addiction to tranquilizers worsened. A small leadership group, comprised mainly of women, carried out most day-to-day details, while Jones focused on what he believed were conspiracies against the community, now called Jonestown.

When U.S. Congressman Leo A. Ryan announced plans to visit Jonestown in November 1978 to investigate charges of kidnapping and abuse, Jones and the group protested, but then acquiesced once the congressman arrived in Guyana. On November 18 Ryan left Jonestown with about sixteen defectors. Gunmen, presumably from Jonestown, shot and killed Ryan and four members of his party and wounded a dozen others at the Port Kaituma airstrip, six miles from Jonestown. Meanwhile, in the community's central pavilion, Jones gathered residents who did not yet know of the death of Ryan and the others. As a tape recording made at the time indicates, Jones exhorted his followers to drink from a vat of poisoned punch. He asked mothers to quiet their children and allowed a dissenter to speak, although she was shouted down by other community members. His words indicate that he wanted the world to recognize their self-sacrifice as an act of "revolutionary suicide" to protest the conditions of an inhumane world. Jones was found shot to death, surrounded by his followers. An autopsy reported that his wounds were consistent with suicide, although the gun that killed him was found several feet away.

Jim Jones criticized traditional Christianity for being complacent and hypocritical in the face of massive suffering and injustice, and he disparaged otherworldly religion, which neglected the here-and-now. He advocated a type of "apostolic socialism," which followed the example of the early church (*Acts* 2:44–45, 4:32) in which everyone contributed to and shared in the common good. He wrote *The Letter Killeth,* a pamphlet that identified contradictions and injustices in the Bible, and during some services he would throw the Bible onto the floor in disdain. Modeling himself after Father Divine, the black leader of the Peace Mission, Jones encouraged followers to call him "Dad" or "Father." As opposed to Divine and other charismatic preachers, however, Jones eschewed the trappings that usually accompany celebrity. He wore used clothing and secondhand shoes, traveled and ate with his members, and shared the same type of housing. His modest lifestyle allowed him to attack "jackleg preachers" who drove Cadillacs and flaunted their worldly success.

As early as his years in Indianapolis Jones began to make claims about his own divinity, which eventually led him to declare himself "God, almighty God," in San Francisco. Once in Guyana, however, he dropped the religious language that had attracted thousands: Christian communalism gave way to political communism, as the group contemplated migration to North Korea, Cuba, or the Soviet Union. Jones's beliefs mixed religion, politics, and pragmatism into his own unique blend. In place of the sky god of Christianity, he encouraged people to believe in him and his divinity and to put their trust in his goodness. Ultimately that trust was betrayed.

See Also Father Divine; Jonestown and Peoples Temple.

Bibliography

Chidester, David. *Salvation and Suicide: An Interpretation of Peoples Temple and Jonestown.* Bloomington, Ind., 1988. A review of the theology of Jim Jones.

Hall, John R. *Gone from the Promised Land: Jonestown in American Cultural History.* New Brunswick, N.J., 1987. Detailed, scholarly history of Peoples Temple and Jonestown.

Maaga, Mary McCormick. *Hearing the Voices of Jonestown.* Syracuse, N.Y., 1998. History of Peoples Temple that focuses on the role of women in the movement.

Moore, Rebecca. *A Sympathetic History of Jonestown: The Moore Family Involvement in Peoples Temple.* Lewiston, N.Y., 1985. Personal account of a family whose relatives died in Jonestown.

Moore, Rebecca, and Fielding M. McGehee III. "Alternative Considerations of Jonestown and Peoples Temple." Available from http://jonestown.sdsu.edu. Website presenting primary and secondary source material on Jonestown and Peoples Temple.

Reiterman, Tim, with John Jacobs. *Raven: The Untold Story of the Rev. Jim Jones and His People.* New York, 1982. In-depth examination of Jim Jones and Peoples Temple.

Rebecca Moore (2005)

JONESTOWN AND PEOPLES TEMPLE

JONESTOWN AND PEOPLES TEMPLE was a communal religious settlement in the jungles of Guyana founded and led by the Reverend James Warren "Jim" Jones (1931–1978). Nearly 1,000 people had come to the South American country in the mid-1970s intending to build an integrated agricultural utopia. Things began to unravel, however, when California Congressman Leo Ryan (1925–1978), accompanied by journalists and former members, arrived to investigate persistent reports of brainwashing and abuse. After Ryan and four others were murdered by temple members, Jones commanded his followers to kill themselves and their children: Over 913 people died on November 18, 1978. In the aftermath, popular media and anticult activists depicted Jonestown as the epitome of dangerous "cults."

Rise and Demise. Jonestown began as a ministry of the Reverend Jim Jones, who blended Pentecostal religion, socialism, and racial harmony into a distinctive political theology. In 1955 he established the Peoples Temple Full Gospel Church in Indianapolis, Indiana, where he conducted faith-healing services, established social services, and campaigned for racial integration. In 1960 the Peoples Temple became formally affiliated with the Disciples of Christ; Jones was ordained as a minister in 1964. Although the Peoples Temple remained affiliated with the denomination until the end, the group's religious beliefs and practices of bore little relation to their parent organization.

When Jones had a vision of imminent nuclear destruction in 1967, he moved the Peoples Temple, choosing northern California because an article in *Esquire* magazine had identified it as one of "Nine Places in the World to Hide" in the event of such a catastrophe. With a nucleus of about 150 followers transplanted from Indiana, the Peoples Temple grew rapidly, expanding from its base to sponsor branches in San Francisco and Los Angeles. As his congregations multiplied during the early 1970s, Jones began to formulate an innovative theology.

In his sermons, Jones consistently discounted any God "out there," a notion that he ridiculed as the sky God, the mythological God, the spook God, or the buzzard God. But he celebrated a real God, a genuine God, which he defined as love, as sharing, as "God, Almighty Socialism." When he personally claimed to be God, the messiah, Jones could be understood to be asserting that he was an embodiment of this divine socialism. He promised his congregation that they also could be deified by dying to capitalism and being reborn in socialism.

In America, he argued, blacks, women, and the poor had been consistently treated as less than fully human. The Bible and Christian churches only sustained this dehumanizing subclassification. To be a human person, Jones argued, required liberation from the dehumanizing pull of America—and that could only be achieved through the superhuman power of divine socialism.

During the early 1970s, Peoples Temple members were told that as long as they lived in the United States they would be in captivity, exile, and eternal conflict. America, Jones argued, was the biblical ancient Egypt, where the children of Israel found only enslavement. America was the biblical Babylon, a place of exile, where refugees longed to return to Jerusalem. America was an imperial power, like first-century Rome, which Jones identified as the antichrist of the last days as described in the New Testament. Since America led the global, imperial crusade against God, Almighty Socialism, Jones claimed that people could only feel enslaved and exiled, defiled and dehumanized, by living within the United States.

A religious sense of origin and destiny was also cultivated within the Peoples Temple. Developing an innovative creation story, which depicted Eden not as a garden to be restored but as a prison from which to escape, Jones's sermons focused on an imminent rendezvous with nuclear destiny. Fashioned in the midst of Cold War politics, superpower conflicts, and the nuclear arms race, this religious worldview was forged in fear of a nuclear apocalypse and its prospect of a total planetary annihilation. Time, in this context, was running out.

Many shared this apocalyptic view. In 1950, during the early days of the nuclear age, American novelist William Faulkner accepted the Nobel Prize for literature, observing: "There is only one question: When will I be blown up?" In sermons twenty years later Jones declared that he would be glad to be blown up in a nuclear apocalypse if it meant the destruction of the world's capitalists. Self-sacrifice, even in a nuclear holocaust of extraordinary devastation, could be imagined as redemptive within the philosophy espoused by the Peoples Temple.

As Jones was developing his religious worldview during the early 1970s, temple membership grew to as many as 5,000. A former member estimated that up to 100,000 people may have heard a sermon by Jim Jones during this period. Most temple members were African Americans, many of them recent migrants from the rural South or Northeastern inner cities who had been drawn by extensive recruiting drives. The temple also attracted a number of white social activists who were drawn to Jones's integrated congregations as an alternative to the prevailing order of American society.

Jones portrayed communist countries such as the Soviet Union, China, and Cuba, as utopias in which divine socialism had already been established. In 1973 the Peoples Temple established a mission in the South American country of Guyana, which was then governed by the black socialist party of Forbes Burnham. By 1975 about fifty members were stationed there, clearing jungle land for the Peoples Temple Agricultural Project that came to be known as Jonestown.

In 1977 journalists Marshall Kilduff and Phil Tracy were preparing to publish an exposé of Jim Jones and the Peoples Temple in *New West* magazine. Their article was based in part on allegations by former members that Jim Jones was involved in questionable financial dealings, sexual impropriety, and the physical and mental abuse of followers.

Anticipating this negative publicity, Jones and many of his congregation moved to Guyana in a migration that came to be known as "Operation Exodus." By September of 1977 nearly 1,000 members were living in the compound. Jonestown residents were 75 percent black; 20 percent white; and 5 percent Hispanic, Asian, or Native American. Approximately two-thirds were women. Almost 300 were under the age of eighteen and over 150 were seniors past the age of sixty-five.

While trying to establish a viable agricultural commune in Guyana, Jones increasingly perceived the community to be under threat from external forces, especially the U.S. government, American media, and a group of former members who called themselves the Concerned Relatives. On November 17, 1978, an official fact-finding delegation led by Congressman Leo Ryan flew to Jonestown to investigate these charges. The visit became the flashpoint for the violence that exploded in murder and suicide. The delegation left the next day, taking fourteen dissatisfied Jonestown residents with them. As they gathered on the Port Kaituma airstrip, heavily armed Jonestown security guards drove up and opened fire, killing five, including Congressman Ryan, and wounding nine others.

Back at the temple and fearing retribution, Jim Jones commanded his followers to kill themselves. Vats of a cyanide-laced fruit drink were prepared and residents lined up to drink the poison. Although this event has usually been characterized as a mass suicide, it is clear that not everyone who died at Jonestown participated freely. Over 260 children, for example, had the poison given to them, while about forty adults escaped. For those who died willingly, however, collective suicide held a religious significance in the context of the worldview that had been cultivated in the Peoples Temple and Jonestown.

First, collective suicide was a ritual, signifying a purity of commitment to the community, which had been rehearsed a number of times over the past eighteen months. Referred to as "white nights," these ritual rehearsals of death affirmed, in the words of Jim Jones on the final night of Jonestown, that the members of the community were united as "black, proud socialists."

Second, collective suicide promised release from a world dominated by what Jones perceived as American racism, capitalism, and fascism. To avoid being captured and taken back to America, he urged his followers to step out of this world by taking "the potion like they used to take in ancient Greece."

Third, collective suicide was an act of revenge in which the guilt for these deaths would be transferred to the enemies of Jonestown. "They brought this upon us," Jones insisted. "And they'll pay for that. I leave that destiny to them."

Finally, collective suicide was regarded as redemptive. Many, perhaps most, of the adult participants believed this. What Jones called "revolutionary suicide" was meaningful for those who embraced it because it represented a superhuman act that would rescue them from dehumanization under the capitalist, racist, and fascist oppression they associated with America. "We didn't commit suicide," Jones declared. "We committed an act of revolutionary suicide protesting the conditions of an inhuman world."

Most Americans found the deaths at Jonestown unthinkable, something so obviously outside the mainstream of American cultural life that it stood as a boundary against which such values could be defined. In popular media they were depicted as not American, not religious, not sane, and ultimately not human. Resistance was mounted against allowing their bodies to be buried on American soil. Over 550 unclaimed bodies were stored for six months at the U.S. Air Force base at Dover, Delaware. The mayor of Dover expressed the feelings of many Americans by insisting the Jonestown dead should be cremated and their ashes scattered "beyond the continental limits of the United States." Twenty-five years later, survivors and family members were still struggling to create a suitable memorial for the Jonestown dead in America.

Interpretive Contexts. Academic analysis of the Jonestown murders and suicides has focused on three contexts: (1) the sociology of new religious movements; (2) the history and heritage of black religion in America; and (3) the phenomenology of redemptive sacrifice in the history of religions and religion in America.

In popular media and the anticult movement, Jonestown became the archetypal "cult," a deviant social organization masquerading as religion that was, in fact, its opposite—evil, dangerous, mind-controlling, financially exploitative, and politically subversive. *Time* and *Newsweek* proclaimed Jonestown the "Cult of Death." Jonestown was also viewed in light of the 1970s "cult controversy," in which some argued that every alternative, unconventional religious movement inevitably led to violence. This view was countered by the growing interest in the academic study of new, alternative, or unconventional religious movements.

Any understanding of Jim Jones, the Peoples Temple, and Jonestown, however, requires sustained attention to the broad and deep tradition of black religion in America. Although Jim Jones was white, he claimed to have a black soul, a black heart, and a black consciousness. He consistently identified himself as a black messiah advancing black liberation. His movement, which emerged from the racism and segregation of the 1950s, was fueled by contact with Father Divine's Peace Mission, the interests of a predominantly black membership, the attractions of a black socialist government in Guyana, and the sense of alienation experienced by many blacks in America.

Although in the aftermath of Jonestown mainline black religious leaders generally rejected the movement, most dramatically at the "Consultation on the Implications of Jonestown for the Black Church" in February of 1979, it is important to remember that many of Jones's followers had been drawn to his claims of embodying black consciousness, as well as his sermons, styles of worship, religious practices, and community formation, which were intentionally drawn from black religious traditions. Even white loyalist and former temple member Michael Prokes wrote a post-Jonestown suicide letter rejecting Jim Jones but retaining his identification with the Peoples Temple because it had given him a sense of community in which he learned what it meant "to be black and old and poor in this society."

In the history of religions, Jonestown-like collective suicides were seen in first-century Judea at Masada and among communities of seventeenth-century Old Believers in Russia. In these instances, as at Jonestown, groups of people chose death rather than what they perceived as defilement or dishonor by enemy forces. But the religious significance of redemptive sacrifice runs much deeper in the history of religions than such dramatic examples of collective suicide might suggest. As some analysts have argued, redemptive sacrifice goes to the heart of the meaning and power of religion, and has certainly been central to the religious and political history of the United States. For some analysts, Jonestown recalls the pervasive American religious commitment to redemptive sacrifice, which requires giving the greatest gift, paying the highest price, for a collective redemption.

Although the end of Jonestown entailed not only mass suicide but also the killing of infants and children, Jones insisted that truly loving people would kill their children before allowing them to be taken back to America to be tortured, brainwashed, or even killed by a society he regarded as fascist. That sentiment was echoed by a member of the community as he was surrounded by the bodies of the children who were in fact sacrificed: "I'd rather see them lay like that than to see them have to die like the Jews did." Members believed that death in Jonestown saved those children from a dehumanized life and death in America. If the children were captured by the Americans, this particular speaker concluded, "they're gonna just let them grow up and be dummies, just like they want them to be, and not grow up to be a *person* like the one and only Jim Jones." Sacrificial death, therefore, promised the redemption of an authentic human identity.

Saving children by killing them seems beyond the bounds of American religion. In the aftermath of Jonestown, however, from 1980 to 1988 the symbolic center of the American public order was occupied by President Ronald Reagan, a political figure who, on numerous occasions, idealized redemptive sacrifice, with specific attention to children. In a speech to the National Association of Evangelicals in Orlando, Florida, on March 8, 1983, Ronald Reagan related that a prominent young man in Hollywood told a public gathering during the early 1950s that there was nothing in the world that he loved more than his daughters but he was prepared to sacrifice them in the interest of a higher good. According to Reagan, this young father declared, "I would rather see my little girls die now, still believing in God, than have them grow up under communism and one day die no longer believing in God." In praising this young man, Reagan concluded that this willingness to sacrifice his children revealed "the profound truth" about "the physical and the soul and what was truly important." Revealing the "truth" of the American soul, this willingness to sacrifice promised to redeem that soul from a communist fate worse than death. According to Ronald Reagan, therefore, redemptive sacrifice was the "profound truth" at the heart of America.

The religious worldview of Jim Jones, the Peoples Temple, and Jonestown was forged in the Cold War between capitalism and communism. Jones's deification of God Almighty, Socialism, evolved during the second half of the twentieth century in which free-market capitalism was also being invested with religious significance. Although marginal to American society, the Peoples Temple and Jonestown nevertheless raised significant questions about religious authenticity, religion and violence, religions of the oppressed, and the religious and political role of redemptive sacrifice.

SEE ALSO Anticult Movements; Aum Shinrikyō; Brainwashing (Debate); Branch Davidians; Father Divine; Heaven's Gate; Jones, Jim; New Religious Movements, articles on New Religious Movements and Children, New Religious Movements and Millennialism, New Religious Movements and Violence; Temple Solaire.

BIBLIOGRAPHY

Following the demise of Jonestown, many journalistic accounts were published, the best of which is Tim Reiterman with John Jacobs, *Raven: The Untold Story of the Rev. Jim Jones and His People* (New York, 1982). For a social history and sociological analysis, see John R. Hall, *Gone from the Promised Land: Jonestown in American Cultural History* (New Brunswick, 1987; second edition published by Transaction Books, 2004). For a reconstruction of the religious worldview, see David Chidester, *Salvation and Suicide: Jim Jones, the Peoples Temple, and Jonestown,* second ed. (Bloomington, 2003), in which can be found all direct quotations in this entry from Jim Jones and his followers. See also Mary McCormick Maaga, *Hearing the Voices of Jonestown* (Syracuse, N.Y., 1998).

Jonestown has also been considered in analyses of new religious movements and violence. See John R. Hall, with Philip D. Schuyler and Sylvaine Trinh, *Apocalypse Observed: Religious Movements and Violence in North America, Europe, and Japan* (New York, 2000); Thomas Robbins and Susan J. Palmer, eds., *Millennium, Messiahs, and Mayhem: Contemporary Apocalyptic Movements* (New York, 1997); and Catherine Wessinger, *How the Millennium Comes Violently: From Jonestown to Heaven's Gate* (New York, 2000).

For discussions of the Peoples Temple and Jonestown in the context of African American religion, see Rebecca Moore, Anthony B. Pinn, and Mary R. Sawyer, eds., *Peoples Temple and Black Religion in America* (Bloomington, 2004). An early attempt to interpret Jonestown in the context of the history of religions was undertaken by Jonathan Z. Smith in "The Devil in Mr. Jones," *Imagining Religion: From Babylon to Jonestown* (Chicago, 1982): 102–120. Discussion of the role of redemptive sacrifice in the religious worldviews of Jim Jones, Ronald Reagan (including direct quotations from Reagan in this entry), and American popular culture can be found in David Chidester, "Saving the Children by Killing Them: Redemptive Sacrifice in the Ideologies of Jim Jones and Ronald Reagan," in *Religion in American Culture: A Journal of Interpretation* 1 (1991): 177–201; and David Chidester, *Authentic Fakes: Religion and American Popular Culture* (Berkeley, 2005).

Decades after the event, Jonestown has remained the focus of sensationalistic revelations by opponents, such as Deborah Layton, *Seductive Poison: A Jonestown Survivor's Story of Life and Death in the People's Temple* (New York, 1998), as well as counterarguments, including conspiracy theories, by defenders, such as Laurie Efrein Kahalas, *Snake Dance: Unravelling the Mysteries of Jonestown* (New York, 1998). In tracking the ongoing cultural, social, and religious history of Jonestown, dedicated scholarly research can be found on the website "Alternative Considerations of Jonestown and Peoples Temple," supported by the Department of Religious Studies, San Diego State University (http://www-rohan.sdsu.edu/~remoore/jonestown; May 20, 2004).

DAVID CHIDESTER (2005)

JOSEPH, or, in Hebrew, Yosef, was the firstborn son of Jacob's favorite wife, Rachel. The account of Joseph's life, which the Qurʾān (12:3) calls "the most beautiful of stories," is described in a uniquely detailed and sustained biblical narrative.

As Rachel's son, Joseph was treasured by his father. Resentful of Joseph's resulting conceit, his brothers sold him to a group of passing traders, who took him to Egypt, where he was purchased by one of pharaoh's officers. When Joseph, who is described as "attractive and good-looking" (*Gn.* 39:65), rejected the advances of the officer's wife, she accused him of attempted rape and had him imprisoned. In jail he demonstrated his ability to interpret dreams. He was therefore brought to pharaoh, whose dreams could not be otherwise understood. Joseph recognized them as warning that a period of abundance would be followed by famine. Elevated to high office to prepare Egypt for the coming threat, Joseph was given both an Egyptian name (Zaphenath-paneah) and wife (Aseneth).

As a result of Joseph's efforts, Egypt was ready for the difficult times that followed and even served as a resource for surrounding peoples. Joseph's brothers came from Canaan to purchase grain; he recognized and tested them before revealing himself and bringing the entire family to settle in the eastern Nile Delta. Joseph died at the age of 110; the Israelites took his bones to Canaan when they left Egypt during the Exodus.

Joseph's special status is attested by the ascription to him of two biblical tribes, named after his sons Ephraim and Manasseh. Ephraim came to dominate the northern kingdom of Israel, which is therefore also called the House of Joseph. Joseph's childhood dreams were thus fulfilled during the lifetimes of his descendants as much as during his own lifetime.

The story of Joseph is remarkable for its numerous human touches, which lead to the apparent absence of divine intervention so common elsewhere in *Genesis*. In fact, however, God is present, if not always visible, acting through human behavior (*Gn.* 45:5, 50:20). The narrative incorporates many elements found in other biblical tales, most strikingly in the stories of Daniel and Esther, which also describe an Israelite's rise in a foreign court. In postbiblical traditions, Joseph's fate is often connected to his personality: some present his experiences as a punishment for earlier wrongdoing; elsewhere they are seen as a trial intended to test his righteousness. Particular attention is devoted to his relationship with the wife of pharaoh's officer, elaborating on her efforts to attract Joseph or raising questions about his own role in the incident.

The historicity of the Joseph story has been defended on the basis of its incorporation of Egyptian vocabulary, customs, and narrative motifs. Historians since the first-century Josephus Flavius (*Against Apion* 1.103) have linked Joseph with the Hyksos, a West Semitic people who dominated Egypt toward the end of the middle Bronze Age. Their expulsion in the sixteenth century might then account for the Bible's statement that "there arose a new king over Egypt who did not know Joseph" (*Ex.* 1:8). However, none of these factors is sufficient historical proof. The author's knowledge of Egyptian culture hardly proves the story's historicity. The land of Canaan was long under Egyptian control, and there are several cases of apparently Semitic figures holding high positions in the Egyptian bureaucracy. As a result, such knowledge could have been acquired in any of several different periods.

SEE ALSO Jacob; Rachel and Leah.

BIBLIOGRAPHY

An overview of modern scholarship relating to the entire patriarchal period is in Nahum M. Sarna's *Understanding Genesis* (New York, 1970). This must, however, be read in conjunction with the historical information in Roland de Vaux's *The Early History of Israel,* translated by David Smith (Philadelphia, 1978). A detailed examination of the Joseph story, including both its literary characteristics and its Egyptian coloration, is in Donald B. Redford's *A Study of the Biblical Story of Joseph (Genesis 37–50)* (Leiden, Netherlands, 1970). The ways in which the story has been elaborated and their relationships to other traditions are explored in Shalom Goldman, *The Wiles of Women/The Wiles of Men* (Albany, N.Y., 1995); James L. Kugel, *In Potiphar's House* (San Francisco, 1990); and Maren Niehoff, *The Figure of Joseph in Post-Biblical Jewish Literature* (Leiden, Netherlands, 1992). Louis Ginzberg's *The Legends of the Jews,* 7 vols., translated by Henrietta Szold (Philadelphia, 1909–1938), contains an exhaustive collection of rabbinic lore relating to biblical stories.

FREDERICK E. GREENSPAHN (1987 AND 2005)

JOSEPH OF VOLOKOLAMSK (1439–1515), born Ivan Sanin, was a Russian Orthodox monastic saint. Joseph succeeded his spiritual father, Pafnutii, as abbot of the Borovsk monastery in 1477. But the reforms toward a stricter form of communal life that he sought there did not find favor with his community, and Joseph undertook an extensive tour of Russian monasteries in search of alternative models. Ultimately Joseph established an entirely new monastery at Volok or Volokolamsk (1479), where he remained for the rest of his life.

Since his early years at Volok, Joseph had been involved in politics, campaigning against the widespread reformationist heresy of the so-called Judaizers, the Novgorodian-Muscovite opponents of church order and Trinitarian teaching. Joseph was to urge consistently (and in 1504 finally attain) the physical elimination of the leading heretics at the hands of the state. In his view, even professions of repentance should not allow heretics to be spared. Joseph's zeal in this regard was expressed in his *Prosvetitel'* (The enlightener, c. 1502–1503; expanded version, c. 1511), a compilation of antiheretical writings. In 1507 Joseph transferred the allegiance of his now influential monastery to the Muscovite grand prince, a serious breach of ecclesiastical discipline, resulting in alienation from the Novgorodian archbishop.

More positive and more lasting than his work against heretics was Joseph's contribution to the shaping of Russian monastic discipline and piety. He composed two rules, the second (and longer) of which dates from his final years. The aim of each was to ensure sobriety and discipline in liturgy and daily life. Poverty was enjoined on the individual monk. Yet the community as a whole was expected to flourish for the service of society at large, especially at times of dearth or distress. As many as seven thousand people would be fed daily during a famine; an orphanage for fifty children was regularly maintained. The orderly and dutiful expression of Christian philanthropy was Joseph's dominant concern and principal contribution to Russian Orthodox tradition.

Joseph was the foremost proponent of the Possessors' school of thought; he insisted that monastics should own land and he effectively countered the contrary claim of certain Orthodox ascetics and of Ivan III (1440–1505). The Moscow church council of 1503 heeded Joseph and decided the question in favor of the Possessors. Had it been otherwise, Joseph might have felt impelled to act in accordance with the daring principle that obedience to a ruler was conditional on the ruler's righteousness, which he had enunciated earlier. An unjust ruler is "no tsar, but a tyrant." In the words of Georges Florovsky (1893–1979), Joseph bordered here on "justification of regicide." In fact, Joseph was to become ever more dependable a collaborator of the state.

It was Joseph's hope that his monastery would attract well-born postulants and that these would provide the bishops of the future. His expectations were fulfilled in the course of the sixteenth century. By the end of it his posthumous reputation was firmly established, and his local canonization (1578) was followed by the proclamation of his sanctity by the Russian Orthodox church as a whole in 1591.

BIBLIOGRAPHY

Joseph's *Prosvetitel'* was edited (anonymously) by Ivan I. Porfir'ev as *Prosvetitel' ili oblichenie eresi zhidovstvuiushchikh: Tvorenie prepodobnago ottsa nashego Iosifa, igumena Volotskago* (Kazan, 1857); while his prolific correspondence appeared more recently as *Poslaniia Iosifa Volotskogo*, edited by Aleksandr A. Zimin and Iakov S. Lur'e (Leningrad, 1959). Only one of Joseph's major writings has been translated into English: *The Monastic Rule of Joseph of Volokolamsk*, translated and edited by David Goldfrank (Kalamazoo, Mich., 1983). His spiritual counsels and regulations are surveyed in an orderly manner in Thomas Spidlík's *Joseph de Volokolamsk: Un chapitre de la spiritualité russe*, "Orientalia Christiana Analecta," no. 146 (Rome, 1956).

SERGEI HACKEL (1987)

JOSEPHUS FLAVIUS

JOSEPHUS FLAVIUS (37/8–c. 100 CE), born Yosef ben Mattityahu, was a Jewish general, historian, and apologist. Josephus was perhaps the most prolific, significant, and controversial of Jewish writers in Judaea during the Hellenistic-Roman era. Born in Jerusalem, he traced his paternal lineage from the priesthood and his maternal descent to the Hasmonean dynasty, and he claimed to have been educated not only within the priestly circles but also among the various Judaic sectarian movements of his day. In 64 he went to Rome and obtained the release of imprisoned Jewish priests, returning to Judaea on the eve of the Great Revolt, a Jewish uprising against Rome. Although he was a moderate, he was appointed to command the Galilean forces, and upon their defeat by Vespasian in 67 he surrendered after his comrades committed suicide. Josephus claims that while in captivity he predicted the accession of Vespasian to emperor, and two years later he was freed by the newly acclaimed ruler of Rome. Josephus accompanied Vespasian's son Titus during the siege and destruction of Jerusalem and the Temple. After the war, Josephus lived under imperial patronage in Rome, where he wrote four major works that survive thanks to their preservation by the Christian church.

Less than a decade after Jerusalem fell in 70, Josephus completed *The Jewish War*, a seven-book narrative of Judean history from the accession of the Seleucid king Antiochus IV (175 BCE) to the fall of Masada in 74 CE. This work was written first in Aramaic and later translated into Greek in order that readers in both the Parthian kingdom and the Roman empire would learn why the revolt occurred and how it failed. With Flavian approval, Josephus portrayed a Jewish nation tragically swept by a small band of fanatics into a war that could only demonstrate Rome's invincibility.

Jewish Antiquities, published in 93/4, recounts in twenty books the Jewish experience from earliest times until 66 CE. Josephus drew heavily from biblical and later Jewish and non-Jewish sources, which he carefully reworked and edited into a treatise modeled on the *Roman Antiquities* of Dionysios of Halikarnassos. The result is a highly creative *apologia* that within its Greek historiographic form emphasizes the antiquity and philanthropy of the Jews and Judaism even as it underscores biblical concepts of divine justice and providence. Josephus subsequently made these apologetic arguments more explicit in the two books collectively titled *Against Apion*, which quote and refute many anti-Semitic works from the Hellenistic age.

Finally, Josephus appended to *Jewish Antiquities* an autobiographical book that is almost entirely devoted to defending his conduct of the Galilean campaign. While in *The Jewish War* he portrayed himself as a committed, efficient general, in his autobiographical work, *The Life*, he emphasizes that he went to Galilee as a moderate who unsuccessfully attempted to restrain his countrymen.

Josephus and his works are no less controversial in modern scholarship than they were in their day. The literature is without equal in breadth and detail; therefore, paradoxically, questions about its reliability often cannot be resolved. Principal foci of contemporary analysis of Josephus include: (1) modes of Hellenization within Palestinian Judaism; (2) the nature of the Pharisaic, Sadducean, and Essene movements, among others; (3) Jewish and Roman political dynamics prior to and in the aftermath of the revolt; (4) Josephus's own motives and conduct, particularly during the revolt and then in light of his Flavian patronage; and (5) the brief, but extraordinary, passage in *Jewish Antiquities* that refers to Jesus but generally has been judged to be at least in part a forgery.

In sum, Josephus emerges as a crucial source for the reconstruction of Judaism and Jewish history in late antiquity. Many contemporary scholars eschew Jerome's claim that Josephus was the "Greek Livy," yet few would deny his contribution to current understanding of his era or his skill and passion in explaining and defending his people to their neighbors.

BIBLIOGRAPHY

The standard text and translation of Josephus's complete works is that of the "Loeb Classical Library," edited by Henry St. John Thackeray, Ralph Marcus, Allen Wikgren, and Louis H. Feldman in ten volumes (Cambridge, Mass., 1926–1965). A classic introduction is *Josephus: The Man and the Historian* by Henry St. John Thackeray (New York, 1929), republished with a new introduction (New York, 1967); and a fine, more recent overview is Tessa Rajak's *Josephus: The Historian and His Society* (London, 1983). The most complete annotated bibliography is Louis H. Feldman's *Josephus and Modern Scholarship, 1937–1980* (Hawthorne, N.Y., 1984).

DAVID ALTSHULER (1987)

JOSHUA, or, in Hebrew, Yehoshuaʿ, was an Israelite leader who flourished, according to tradition, in the thirteenth century BCE. The *Book of Joshua* tells how its namesake led the twelve tribes of Israel in a concerted military invasion and conquest of the land of Canaan, whose territory was divided among the tribes. Joshua attributes the success of the campaign to the direct involvement of YHVH, Israel's God (see *Jos.* 10:14, 23:3, 23:10)—a claim underscored by the miraculous nature of the defeats of the cities of Jericho (whose wall is toppled by the shouts of the Israelites) and Gibeon (where the sun stands still until the Israelites are victorious). After the conquest is completed, Joshua assembles the Israelites at Shechem to renew the covenant with YHVH made in the preceding generation through the mediation of Moses. He exhorts the people to remain devoted to YHVH and to keep his law.

Joshua's role as leader of the conquest is anticipated in the biblical narrative by his introduction as the field commander in the battle against Amalek (*Ex.* 17:8–13) and as a spy sent by Moses to reconnoiter Canaan (*Nm.* 13). Moses elevates Joshua's status by changing his name from Hosheaʿ to Yehoshuaʿ (YHVH is salvation) and by appointing Joshua as his successor. Indeed, the *Book of Joshua* frequently refers to Moses' tutelage of Joshua and shapes many aspects of Joshua's career to parallel similar aspects of the career of Moses. For example, Joshua's splitting of the Jordan River recalls Moses' splitting of the Sea of Reeds; Joshua's theophany (*Jos.* 5:13–15) specifically evokes that of Moses at the burning bush (*Ex.* 3–4); the image of Joshua holding out his spear until the city of Ai is taken (*Jos.* 8:26) recalls the image of Moses extending his arms until the Amalekites are routed (*Ex.* 17:12); and Joshua, like Moses, dispatches spies ahead of his army (*Jos.* 2). As though to highlight the parallel even further, in *Joshua* 12 a summary of Joshua's triumphs over Canaanite kings (*Jos.* 12:7–24) is juxtaposed with a summary of Moses' earlier triumphs over kings in the Transjordan (*Jos.* 12:1–6).

Because most of Joshua's military activities took place in what became the tribal territory of Benjamin and Ephraim, and because he is said to have been buried in an Ephraimite estate in Timnath-serah (*Jos.* 19:50), modern scholars surmise that Joshua was a legendary leader of the north-central Israelites. However, the *Book of Joshua*'s description of a massive takeover of Canaan by an army of invading Israelites is contradicted by a number of biblical passages (such as *Jos.* 13:1–5 and *Jgs.* 1). It is further contradicted by an increasingly clearer archaeological record, in view of which only some of the sites said to have been destroyed by Joshua were in fact destroyed in the late Bronze Age (thirteenth through twelfth centuries BCE), and those were destroyed over an extended period. The stories of Joshua's conquests, which were apparently written during the Judean monarchy (ninth through seventh centuries BCE), as well as the division of the land among the premonarchic tribes, tend to be regarded by historians as ideologically motivated. The clearance of Canaanite people and culture from the land of Canaan, as related in the *Book of Joshua,* is understood as a mythical expression of Israel's own self-definition (we are entirely distinct from them), and Joshua's military leadership is often interpreted as a projection or reflex of Judean imperial aspirations, such as those of Hezekiah (late eighth century) or Josiah (late seventh century).

When the compilers of the *Book of Joshua* combined traditions of the Exodus with traditions of the conquest, they cast Joshua as the lieutenant and successor of Moses. Thus they forged these once-disparate traditions into a unified narrative.

SEE ALSO Canaanite Religion; Moses.

BIBLIOGRAPHY

For a summary and discussion of the scholarly issues concerning the nature of the Israelite occupation of Canaan and of Joshua's role in it, see Manfred Weippert, *The Settlement of the Israelite Tribes in Palestine,* translated by James D. Martin (Naperville, Ill., 1971). For a summary of the pertinent archaeological evidence, see William G. Dever, *Who Were the Early Israelites, and Where Did They Come From?* (Grand Rapids, Mich., 2003). For a notable effort to trace the origins of the conquest tradition, see Nadav Na'aman, "The 'Conquest of Canaan' in the Book of Joshua and in History," in *From Nomadism to Monarchy: Archaeological and Historical Aspects of Early Israel,* edited by Israel Finkelstein and Nadav Na'aman, pp. 218–281 (Jerusalem and Washington, D.C., 1994). For a model analysis of Joshua as a type of a Judean king, see Richard D. Nelson, "Josiah in the Book of Joshua," *Journal of Biblical Literature* 100 (1981): 531–540. A close literary reading of the *Book of Joshua* is Robert Polzin's *Moses and the Deuteronomist,* pp. 73–145 (New York, 1980); and an ideologically oriented commentary is L. Daniel Hawk's *Joshua, Berit Olam* series (Collegeville, Minn., 2000).

EDWARD L. GREENSTEIN (1987 AND 2005)

JOSHUA BEN HANANIAH SEE YEHOSHU'A BEN ḤANANYAH

JOSHUA BEN LEVI SEE YEHOSHU'A BEN LEVI

JOSIAH, or, in Hebrew, Yo'shiyyahu, was a king of Judah (c. 640–609 BCE). Josiah came to the throne at eight years of age upon the assassination of his father, Amon. The account of his reign in *2 Kings* 22–23 is almost entirely taken up with a presentation of his cultic reform program in the eighteenth year. The parallel account in the much later history of *2 Chronicles* 34–35, which divides this reform activity between the twelfth and eighteenth years, probably has no independent validity and so should not be used in the reconstruction of the events of his reign.

The version in *Kings* states that during the course of the renovations of the Temple a "book of the law" (*sefer ha-torah*) was found. Its contents raised great consternation in the royal court and led to a large-scale reform program to purify the cult in Jerusalem. This last act meant the obliteration of other cult places throughout Judah and as far north as the region of Bethel, with the unemployed Levitical priests of "the high places" becoming wards of the state.

Because of the close match between the nature of the cultic reform program, especially the centralization of worship, and these same concerns in *Deuteronomy,* scholars have long identified "the book of the law" with this part of the Pentateuch. The time of Josiah is thus understood as a period of nationalistic and religious fervor resulting from the decline of Assyrian domination and influence in the west. It was within the context of these events that the framers of *Deuteronomy* were able to promulgate their reform program.

It must be kept in mind that the presentation of events in *2 Kings* 22–23 is shaped by a historian whose outlook is strongly influenced by *Deuteronomy.* It is possible, however, that both purification and centralization of the cult did not become firmly established until the Second Temple period, and even then there were exceptions. Some scholars have sought to offer archaeological evidence for the destruction of Judean sanctuaries at Arad and Beersheba in the late seventh century BCE, but the evidence is ambiguous and must be treated with caution.

Josiah is also credited with a brief revival of the Judean state and some expansion into the former Israelite kingdom to the north. About this, however, the Bible says little except for its reference to Josiah's destruction of the altar at Bethel. The archaeological evidence for Josiah's territorial control consists mostly of royal seal impressions on jar handles, which would limit his sphere of activity within the borders of Judah.

Apart from its description of the cultic reform, *Kings* contains only a few enigmatic remarks about Josiah's death at the hands of Pharaoh Necho at Megiddo while Necho was on his way to aid the Assyrians at Carche mish (*2 Kgs.* 23:29–30). The subsequent Babylonian hegemony led to the end of *de facto* Judean independence for the next four centuries.

The author of *Kings* rates Josiah highest of all the kings of Judah after David because of his religious reforms, and there is some further reflection of this esteem in *Jeremiah* 22:15–16.

BIBLIOGRAPHY

Treatments of the history can be found in John Bright's *A History of Israel,* 3d ed. (Philadelphia, 1981), and in the contributions by Hanoch Reviv, Yohanan Aharoni, and Yigael Yadin to *The World History of the Jewish People,* vol. 4, *The Age of the Monarchies,* edited by Abraham Malamat (Jerusalem, 1979), pt. 1, chaps. 9, 14; pt. 2, chap. 8. On the relationship of *Deuteronomy* to the reforms of Josiah, see E. W. Nicholson's *Deuteronomy and Tradition* (Philadelphia, 1967), Moshe Weinfeld's *Deuteronomy and the Deuteronomic School* (Oxford, 1972), and Hans-Detlef Hoffmann's *Reform und Reformen* (Zurich, 1980).

New Sources

Barrick, W. Boyd. *The King and the Cemeteries: Toward a New Understanding of Josiah's Reform.* Leiden and Boston, 2002.

JOHN VAN SETERS (1987)
Revised Bibliography

JÖTNAR (giants) constitute a supernatural tribe in Scandinavian mythology. Since the tribe includes fire giants and ice giants, the concept may have originated in the observation of natural phenomena. Giants are natural spirits and among the original inhabitants of the world. In Germanic cosmogony, life originated from the body of the primeval giant Ymir, who was eventually dismembered to create the world. A fire giant, Surtr, helps bring about the end of the current world age at Ragnarǫk, the giants' final conflict with the gods, in which both the Æsir and the giants perish. Although the mutual hostility of the gods and giants is implacable, they are biologically related and occasionally intermarry. The Æsir (the dominant group of gods) trace their descent from the giantess Bestla, and Óðinn's mistress Jörð, the mother of Þórr, is a giantess. Njǫrðr and Freyr, hostages from the second group of gods, the Vanir, marry giantesses, although the unions do not last. Óðinn also seduces a giantess as part of his efforts to steal the mead of poetic inspiration.

The Æsir fear that, left unchecked, giants will take over their citadel, Ásgarðr, and destroy all life on earth. Characteristically, Óðinn uses wisdom as his weapon, turning the giants' magic chants against them and stealing the mead of poetry, whereas Þórr uses brute strength to kill giants and giantesses. Heimdallr is another guardian of the gods against the giants. Yet giants are also depicted as brave and strong, old and wise, wealthy and (some at least) of high social status. For example, the Æsir enjoy drinking bouts at the home of the sea giant Ægir. It is a giant who builds Ásgarðr, the Æsir's stronghold. Giants are aligned with the natural when it is contrasted with the cultural, but this shows the natural to be unnatural and monstrous; superior to it is the cultural, which is of course associated with the Æsir.

Jötnar have been viewed as objects of cultic worship; as ancestors and primeval spirits; as the gods of a pre-Germanic population; as the powers of wintertime; and as forces of untamed nature, of death and infertility, and of chaos and destruction. It has also been argued that the giants continually try to steal the goddesses and symbols of order such as the sun and moon not because they are essentially disorderly, but because they have no opportunity for reciprocal exchange with the gods. Conversely, the Æsir practice violence, theft, deception, and oath breaking to gain what they want from giants, but their actions are depicted as justified. As time passed, the negative side of the giants became predominant in the mythology. A differentiation of the various types of giants was apparent in heathen times (*jötunn* is the generic term, whereas as *þurs* and *troll* designate malevolent giants), but the sources, which date from the late heathen or early Christian era, probably also reflect the Christian demonization of pagan mythological figures. Overall, Scandinavian mythology shows that the giants are not an external threat but are ineradicably part of divine society, both as mothers and monsters.

SEE ALSO Germanic Religion; Njǫrðr; Óðinn.

BIBLIOGRAPHY

Hilda R. Ellis emphasizes the benevolent aspects of giants in "Fostering by Giants in Old Norse Sagas," in *Medium Aevum* 10 (1941): 70–85, and Lotte Motz reassesses older views in "Giants in Folklore and Mythology: A New Approach," in *Folklore* 93 (1982): 70–84. Margaret Clunies Ross takes a sociological approach in *Prolonged Echoes: Old Norse Myths in Medieval Northern Society*, vol. 1 (Odense, Denmark, 1994). John Lindow surveys the scholarship in *Scandinavian Mythology: An Annotated Bibliography* (New York, 1988).

ELIZABETH ASHMAN ROWE (2005)

JOURNALISM AND RELIGION.

[*This entry discusses reporting on religious topics in the daily print and broadcast media in the United States.*]

Alexis de Tocqueville devoted a chapter of his *Democracy in America* (1835), "Of the Relation between Public Associations and the Newspapers," to the interdependence of communications media and other institutions in a democratic society. Tocqueville highlights this interdependence in the following observation:

> There is a necessary connection between public associations and newspapers; newspapers make associations, and associations make newspapers. . . . A newspaper can survive only on the condition of publishing sentiments or principles common to a large number of men. A newspaper, therefore, always represents an association that is composed of its habitual readers. This association may be more or less defined, more or less restricted, more or less numerous; but the fact that a newspaper keeps alive is proof that at least the germ of such an association exists in the minds of its readers. (Tocqueville, ed. Bradley, 1960, vol. 2, pp. 120, 122)

THE CREATION OF THE NEWS. Tocqueville's view ties newspapers and other media closely to their own associations of readers and viewers, and, at the same time, gives newspapers and other media a representative function. The representative function is actually twofold. First, the media represent the associations that make up their readerships and regular listeners, those in whose minds the germs of such associations exist. Second, the media, while being associations themselves, also represent other associations. They are both lamp and mirror in a society in which many groups seek to keep their own torches bright, thereby creating a need among the citizens for mirrors in which to perceive what is going on among the diversity of associations, each with its own self-interested agenda. In their preoccupation with matters of personal and neighborhood interest, the citizens "require a journal to bring to them every day, in the midst of their own minor concerns, some intelligence of the state of their public weal" (Tocqueville, p. 120).

In their interdependence the media and the associations they serve are among the central institutions in American society. Media shape and are shaped by the dynamic consensus of advocacy and counteradvocacy among the associations. To read a newspaper, listen to radio, or view television is to participate, whatever the attenuations, in a communion with the central institutions and ethos of the society, an act more powerful for being in large part symbolic and hence less obvious. The media, then, are a part of the consensus-making and consensus-reflecting exchanges that create a public out of a diverse and scattered population, encompassing even peoples of the globe, many of whom depend on American media for their news of the world.

Without an understanding of media as symbolic matrix, there can be no helpful understanding of "the news," much less the news of religion. The publication of the news is little noticed in its symbolic aspect, and the news becomes more powerful than it should be in a democratic society because the media through which news is mediated are disregarded. Why, then, are citizens not more critical of the media—not as institutions with their own affiliations, self-interests, and eccentricities, but rather in their symbolic function? Citizens are in fact critical of the media because of "bias" (writing and broadcast that takes words and images "out of context," or that touts a standard party line). Rarely, however, does criticism of the media touch on the means by which they make news out of persons, issues, movements, and events in the world. Why is this so? It is not possible to proceed to an examination of the way religion is reported in the media in the absence of some field against which to assess the ways in which aspects of various religions and religious practices become, and do not become, news. The "news" must be understood first.

News is not fact, but the mediation of facts through symbolic media, through conventions of writing and editing, and through inclusions and exclusions created in the practice of such conventions. This is not generally understood because the creators of the news and its readers and viewers are in common agreement on a key theory about what constitutes knowledge, particularly that form of knowledge called "news." News is not self-evident, because it is the creation of the media, but it is assumed to be self-evident because it is understood to be identical with "facts." Both reporter/editor and reader/viewer typically share a theory of knowledge that tacitly teaches them that news gets its status solely by reference to facts. What is published are matters of fact, a set of signs whose primary reason for being is to refer, copy, or imitate brute facts (the person who spoke, the event that occurred) or actions that happened beyond the pages and film, in the real world. On this view, news is reference; it is what is reported or photographed. The news-as-reference theory leaves unnoticed the nature of the media as symbolic matrices through which "facts" become "news."

CONVENTIONS OF STORYTELLING. The Princeton historian Robert Darnton, for an article in which he reflects upon his days as a reporter for papers in New Jersey and New York City, took as his epigraph a graffito he found in 1964 on the wall of the press room of the Manhattan police headquarters: "All the news that fits we print." Darnton called his article, which appeared in *Daedalus* in 1975, "Writing News and Telling Stories"; in it he tells how the reporting of facts becomes news through the repertory of conventions for writing stories. While the facts that can be reported are without limit, the conventions into which facts are translated are limited, though they may vary from medium to medium, from one journalistic tradition to another.

Conventions of writing include the type of story an event or set of facts is judged to be, the stereotypes and rhetorical modes common to reporters, and editors' norms of judgment. Darnton makes clear that reporters are not rote writers; they are enterprising in seeking new twists on old ways of telling stories, but they typically do so within an approved genre of storytelling. Facts may be observed, recorded, and quoted, but before the reader or viewer sees the results, the reporter, under supervision of editors, writes the news. This sequence is as true of television reporting as it is of radio and print media (one may note, for example, the beginning and ending sentences of every television report from "the scene").

These conventions of story writing compose the symbolic matrix through which the media translate facts into news. Thus the graffito "All the news that fits we print" captures in an aphoristic formulation the "neatness of fit that produces the sense of satisfaction like the comfort that follows the struggle to force one's foot into a tight boot. The trick will not work if the writer deviates too far from the conceptual repertory that he or she shares with the public and from the techniques of tapping it that he has learned from his predecessors" (Darnton, 1975, p. 190).

"Conceptual repertory" comes in the form of rhetorical conventions, descriptive types, and formulaic devices, and not in the form of explicitly held taxonomies of types of stories. The tacit sharing of these conventions of writing and reading (or viewing) stories is the underlayment that supports the public status of the media, that is, the means for publicity based on publicly shared symbolic forms. Even though they may be biased on specific issues, the media in this understanding are representative and consensual.

As a good historian of his own abandoned career as a reporter, Darnton recounts that the first move a reporter makes upon being given an assignment is to go to "the morgue" in search of relevant sheets, a cluster of examples that inscribe an exemplary way of telling the story. "The dead hand of the past therefore shapes his perception of the present" (ibid., p. 189). This is how journalistic traditions of writing are maintained. This practice demonstrates in important if little-noticed ways that news is old. "There is an epistemology of the *fait divers*" (ibid.). And this epistemology of tradition is displayed not as a theory of knowledge but as a set of slowly changing styles of writing, and through the rhetorical conventions of the trade.

Darnton reinterprets Tocqueville, or rather extends Tocqueville's observations by particularizing them. One important meaning of *association* is the communion between habitual readers and the newspapers, the sharing of "sentiments and principles" of which Tocqueville wrote; Darnton particularizes the devices of this sharing in arguing that an essential dimension of the media is their symbolic matrix. Many historians and critics of American journalism have neglected or overlooked what Darnton calls "the long term cultural determinants of the news," in part because they have neglected to consider the enduring styles of storytelling through which news is mediated to various publics. Darnton writes:

> Of course, we did not suspect that cultural determinants were shaping the way we wrote about crimes in Newark, but we did not sit down at our typewriters with our minds a *tabula rasa.* Because of our tendency to see immediate events rather than long term processes, we were blind to the archaic element in journalism. But our very conception of "news" resulted from ancient ways of telling stories. (ibid., p. 191)

The reason that newspapers and other media are consensus-making and consensus-made institutions is that stories fit a range of cultural preconceptions of news. These cultural preconceptions are expressed, not as such, but rather in the "fit" of the facts, the fit of a new story into available conventions for writing that story. To study the way the media report religion is to study some of the constitutive rules that govern the display of stories in the media, rules that are never stated as such but that are presented through the conventions of news writing.

Treatments of the news and how it becomes so are also examinations into the epistemology of power through the analysis of rhetorical forms and conventions that translate facts. The philosopher John Searle, drawing on earlier work by J. L. Austin and G. E. M. Anscombe, summarizes the hierarchical relations that obtain among facts, institutions, or associations, and those constitutive rules that order both: "The description of the brute facts can only be explained in terms of institutional facts. But the institutional facts can only be explained in terms of the constitutive rules which underlie them" (Searle, 1969, p. 52).

To understand how rules operate as norms and mediating symbols and to comprehend how they are refigured, historically, as they confront novel situations, requires an inquiry that can be usefully assisted by the work of historians of religion such as Jonathan Z. Smith. Especially helpful are two of Smith's essays, "Sacred Persistence: Toward a Redescription of Canon," and "The Bare Facts of Ritual," from his collection *Imagining Religion* (1982). Studies of revision in the canonical status of taxonomies that function as constitutive rules for the governance of facts through sanctioning of particular forms of storytelling would find many useful analogies from similar studies of canonical and ritual change occasioned by time and circumstance.

Media is an overlapping of associations: the association as institution, association as representing other associations, association between the media and habitual readers and viewers, and association as symbolic matrix. Through these complicated connections the news is made.

MEDIA AND RELIGION. With the larger context of the multiple meanings of media established, it is possible to move to the question of the media and religion. How do the media represent religion? It is necessary that the preceding discussion be joined to this key question at many points, because the long-term cultural determinants that decisively affect the play of the news in general affect the ways the media represent religion in particular. The discussion is focused on daily national media in the United States, not on local, state, or ethnic media, nor on the vast array of media owned by various religious organizations, nor on the weekly and monthly periodical press and television programs. The defining pressures of daily and hourly deadlines impose their "fits" on the representation of religion in the national media. This is the most illuminating case for understanding how the central associations in the society transmit and receive news about religion.

In the preceding paragraph this article has borrowed Darnton's term *cultural determinant* to refer to a catalog of conventions relied upon by reporters to write their stories. Yet one of the problems attending the effort to write with critical consciousness about religion is precisely that the available typologies and formulaic devices used to report on politics, war, sports, and other areas are used to write on religion.

Another sort of cultural determinant involves prevalent ideas among people working in the media about what religion is. Thus notions about religion in the American context determine not only how the news of religion is reported in this society, but also how religious leaders, movements, and traditions abroad are interpreted. Consensus about religion in this country, therefore, involves the ways that religions beyond this country are reported.

The ways the media represent religion through the mediations of their various conventions are different from the ways members of religious groups view their own and other religions, and different also from the ways scholars study religion. These differences account for many misunderstandings and criticisms. The representations of religion in the media are the combined results of both kinds of cultural determinations: the predetermination of story schema and the ideas held by writers and editors about religion, and the repertory of conventions and the conceptual repertories of ideas and images about religion. It is the interplay of these two sets of cultural determinations that make the constitutive rules that govern representations of religion in the media.

The first set requires that a story have a "hook" or "lead" that organizes its telling. The favorite convention or model for organization is some form of drama. Usually a type of conflict, this drama is something that can be grasped in a sharply delineated "take" that arrests the attention and woos the eye to read further. The dramatic, or conflict, scheme may come in cameo or in large-scale settings.

Those aspects of religious life that lend themselves to this prefiguration—namely, highly condensed, dramatic actions—are more likely to appear as stories: controversy, charge and countercharge, conversions, schisms, deviations of many sorts, novel conjunctions of tradition and modern style. Of special importance is the time sense required by this particular model or convention. This time sense is congruent with that that characterizes the entire world according to the media: a time sense made up of a series of discrete units, each more or less self-contained. Any religious practices that lend themselves to dramatic portrayal, that are of limited duration, and that are novel in appearance best meet these requirements. Of course, as has been noted, there is nothing in these requirements that is unique to religion. The way religion is reported must be regarded as essentially similar to the ways news of politics, economics, athletics, law, or military affairs is reported; there is no special category for "religious news" in contrast to "the news."

Formulaic pieces that report the visits of presidents and royalty, for example, work well for popes: the airport arrival, the crowds along the route of the motorcade, appearances in public places, presentations, brief speeches and testimonies, then departures—a series of sharp segments highly adaptable to the rhetorical inscription, transmission, and display requirements of the media. If drama, in one of its many variants, is the favored model, second in usefulness is the "personality" who dramatizes great conflicts in his or her gestures. Here two major genres for best coverage are those that focus on the spectacle or the personality. These genres, of course, are just as effective for athletic heroes, criminals, and political figures as they are useful in the portrayal of religious persons. Just as the presidential candidate's rally may have the form of a religious revival meeting, so papal visits have the form, according to the taxonomy relied upon by the media, of visits by heads of state. The substitutions of different events or personalities within the same format for writing or image making is a reminder of the power of the image types and story conventions that are used to schematize quite different situations in similar ways. "Facts" are not canonical for the media, but the forms within which they are organized have a canonical status worthy of the attention of scriptural scholars.

One idea that fits neatly with the conventions used to report religion is that religion is most authentically itself when it dramatizes itself, particularly in the lives of interesting human beings. Religion as ordinary living or as tradition, as a symbolic complex regularly reenacted, or as a complicated set of ideas with long histories (even with revolutionary consequences) does not attract the attention of the daily media. It is striking that the same features in religion—its symbolism, use of conventions, dependence on repetitions in institutional life and personal behavior—turn up in the media's analyses and that members of the media pay about as much attention to these aspects of religion as they pay to similar aspects in their own modes of operation. Personal lives and institutional histories do not lend themselves to translation into the major news-reporting conventions. In fact, the category of pastness and the category of the ordinary, so characteristic of much religious life and practice, are alien categories in the prevailing modes and ideas. The ways symbols work in the living of lives and in the continuities of institutional life, of habits of mind and textures of sensibility, of forms of conviviality, and of matters of taste legitimated by religious belief are outside the typical scope of the media—unless they are caught in the portmanteau category of "features," a prime location for worthy efforts that deviate from the prevailing norms and conventions.

The cultural historian will be intrigued by the hypothesis that the disposition to favor the drama of religion over the prose of religion is not original with the media, even though it happens that forms of storytelling most favored by the media conform to this dramatic idea of religion. This author's hypothesis is that one particular strand, a long and dominant strand, in Protestantism's religious practice has become thoroughly part of the media's ideas about religion: The media's dramatic model for religion is in fact derived from the conversion rituals so typical of evangelical Protestantism in particular and of a variety of conversion-oriented religions in general. Conversion and its opposite, deconversion, are metaphors that support the dramatic model for writing news about religion. Manifestly all dramatic stories about religion are not conversion stories, but the metaphor of conversion may serve as the tacit root for a variety of conflict models for use in the coverage of religion.

To write about the slow pace of institutional life and the erosions of change over time; to write about the variety of ways religious identity and sensibility affect other associations and expressions in society, the arts, manners, styles of living, family life; to describe ways of thinking about and imagining sexuality, work, leisure, competition, cooperation, war; and to analyze inside/outside group relations appear staggering tasks within the idioms and notions about religion that prevail in the media.

When necessary the media can do a competent job in reporting formal properties present in the collective life of religious groups, particularly when some of the properties—sexual ethics, for example—generate conflict within individual persons and families. But the distance is vast between the common forms and ideas about religion in the media and the remote but powerful ways religious symbols and behavior affect political and economic actions, for example.

When an understanding of religion moves beyond the personal and specifically institutional and goes in the direction of the less formal and more implicit ways religious belief and sensibility work themselves out in a variety of associations, such indeterminate but no less important aspects of religion place impossible strains on the media's conceptual framework, not to speak of the framework of its writing conventions. These elusive but important aspects of religion are rarely noticed in these idioms, and for good reasons, because they cannot be categorized within the prevailing forms of classification presupposed by reporters' assignments; by story types; by the specialized competences of reporters in politics, law, science, economics, sports; and, not least, by the departmentalization of media into corresponding sections on politics, law, science, economics, sports, and style. There is another set of reasons for large areas of religion's impact on society being dropped from notice by the media; it has to do with a set of intellectual traditions about religion that powerfully affect the outlooks of reporters, producers, editors, and columnists alike.

Some Specific Cases. Mary Catherine Bateson, an anthropologist, used the occasion of the Islamic Revolution to call to the attention of the editors and readers of the *New York Times* the consequences of the intellectual attitude toward religion that is held today by many experts upon whom the media wait for authoritative deliverances about such events as the mass suicide at Jonestown, Guyana, in 1978, and the Islamic Revolution of the late 1970s and early 1980s. She points to the failure of the media and of policymakers in the United States government, as others had pointed to the failure of the U.S. Central Intelligence Agency (CIA), to grasp the revolutionary forces at work in Iran. Such failures were extended in the systematic misrepresentations of the Ayatollah Khomeini by the American media, misrepresentations of a kind that will continue unless "there is a fundamental reappraisal of the role of religion in the world today" (letter to the *New York Times,* February 20, 1979).

What needs reappraising are notions about religion resident in large portions of the professions and among policymakers, as well as in the media. These ideas comprise an unsteady mixture of the Enlightenment idea that religion is at root superstition and liberalism's teaching that religious beliefs are primarily of interest in the private lives of persons. Neither attitude helps those who hold it to gain advanced notice of a crisis, much less write about many aspects of religion, until there is a dramatic crisis such as a revolution, something that is of course political and economic, not merely "religious"; this is particularly so because such a revolution would be unimaginable in America. Consensus reporting does not prepare the media to view religion as having the power to redirect the history of a nation, let alone affect the life of many other nations. Bateson notes that a new understanding of religion is necessary that will "transcend the fashionable tendency to see religion either as fanaticism or as a cloak for other interests; it must be premised on a recognition that for vast numbers of the world's people the symbols of religion sum up their highest aspirations."

When the media seek expert consultants on religious matters, they frequently call in members of the psychological profession, who are often disposed to see religion as a form of pathology, or other social scientists who see religion as a "cloak," or an ideology covering a variety of other interests, whether ethnic, economic, or political. Neither media notions of religion, derived from Enlightenment critique, nor courtship of the social sciences for authoritative enlightenment about unusual religious phenomena such as Jonestown, prepares the media to understand the power of symbols to inspire group visions other than those of progress and economic growth. The frequency of use of the term *medieval* in describing the forces led in Iran by Khomeini discloses much of the media's own misunderstanding of religion. The irony is that it was precisely this misunderstanding that led so many intellectuals in America to be surprised by the Islamic Revolution.

The media, then, work with conventions and ideas that reinforce each other in determining the ways religion is represented. In addition, the American press, used to the consensual reporting of religion in this country, is ill prepared to report on religion in other cultures where the manners of pluralism do not obtain and where religious power is often disintegrative of the existing social order instead of communing with it.

Just as there are working models in the media for what is authentically religious, so there is at work a pattern for the typical relationship between religion and the central social order. Nowhere is this model so clearly disclosed as when the media attempt to report minority or fundamentally different forms of religious practice, different ways of being religious than those practiced in the mainline associations and in the major religious traditions. Again, the ways the media report minority religious practices in American society indicate how foreign religions will be reported, or not reported.

On Sunday, June 8, 1980, the *New York Times* ran a story headlined "Police Seize Animals Prepared for Sacrifice by Cult in the Bronx," accompanied by a two-column picture of an officer of the American Society for the Prevention of Cruelty to Animals holding a lamb with the caption "Lamb Saved from Slaughter." The lead on this story was as follows: "Police officers and agents of an animal protection society raided a garage in the Southview section of the Bronx early yesterday and confiscated 62 animals that they said were apparently being held for sacrifice by a religious cult." The raid, following one that had occurred three weeks previously, was termed in the second lead paragraph "the first major successful raid on secret cults practicing animal sacrifice." The final sentence of the ten-paragraph story read "The animals used in the cultic rituals are usually killed by having their throats slit, according to Mr. Langdon," the officer pictured holding the saved lamb. The drama of the raid, as reported, was followed by lists and numbers of animals confiscated. Officer Langdon was the major source for the story, and apparently the quoted authority on the meaning and history of the cult. "People will give one of the sect's priests $100 to perform a sacrifice so that good things will happen, so they will get money, or become healthy," he said. Not until the seventh paragraph were any words attributed to a member of the group raided, and no leaders were quoted. There was no reference to scholarship on this form of religious practice. Not until the penultimate paragraph was any background information supplied about this group and its affiliations. Again, Officer Langdon was the informant quoted: "Mr. Langdon said that the people in the house belonged to a sect closely related to Santería, which, he said, was derived from a Nigerian religion called Yoruba that was brought to Cuba by slaves in the 18th century and which once practiced infanticide as well as animal sacrifice."

A generous critic of this story may doubt if many adherents of Santeria were assumed to be included in the *Times*'s readers that Sunday morning. All the key terms of the story—"raid," "sacrifice," "religious cult," "slaughter," "cruelty to animals," "sect," "a Nigerian religion called Yoruba," "slaves," "infanticide as well as animal sacrifice"—along with the quoted final sentence, combine to project a consistent image of the exotic. No reporter would describe a mainline religious group as "an American religion called X that was brought to this country in the seventeenth century by visionaries, refugees, indentured servants, and fortune seekers."

True to form, the story angles on a dramatic event, a police raid, followed by confiscation of the animals. But not so true to form is the hybrid mixture of conific offerings and demonstrating the qualities of taker. The alleged violations of city laws on the treatment of animals and on harboring farm animals in the city are in tension with the story of the religious rite interrupted by the raid, and nowhere is the issue of freedom to practice religion hinted at as an issue. The mixture of types struggling with each other here—the police raid; the exotic practices of a minority religion; the motivation for such practices as involving exchange of money with priests of the cult (a constant, formulaic consideration in reporting of religion); the sentimental story involving officers rescuing animals from danger (no pictures provided of goats or guinea hens, which were also saved)—disclose a clash of genre and, perhaps unwittingly, reveal the problematics of conventional treatments of the exotic for an intended majority readership. All information supplied about the minority religious group only highlights the alien, if not pathological and illegal, status of such groups and their practices.

The loosely braided character of the several story conventions at work demonstrates what happens when news that does not neatly fit gets published. Perhaps here was a telltale occasion when "All the news that's fit to print" prevailed over "All the news that fits we print." The misfits here illuminate the standard fits that prevail in most reporting of religion. The heterogeneity of the "brute facts" on which this story was based may have placed too much pressure on the ruling conventions for them to operate effectively.

The repitition of key words in the story shows how the alien and the minority is encoded for the familiar and majority. Terms such as "cult," "secret sacrifice," "infanticide," "slaughter," and the like had echoed through the media during the previous eighteen months, following the reporting of events at Jonestown, Guyana, in November 1978; at that time, other terms—"fanatical," "paranoid," and "bizarre"—were added to the code to alert readers and viewers to the alien and "other" status of such religious practices and leaders. These signals of differentness serve to reaffirm readers' and viewers' tacit association and to reassert the normative and "normal" status of the familiar and dominant. "Charismatic preacher" may work as a term of approval, but "cult leaders" become "self-proclaimed messiahs," while their believers become "victims."

The mix of conventions used to report the practice of Santeria in the Bronx bear close relations to similar encodings in the reporting of Jonestown and its leader Jim Jones and of the revolution in Iran and Khomeini, who was constantly referred to as a "madman," and whose country was classified as backward, if not primitive, by being called "medieval." The visual image of the shouting mob became the set for television reporting from Iran, recalling a scene type that goes back to the crowd imagery used by those writers hostile to the French Revolution.

Generalizations about the media as a consensual association enforcing what Tocqueville called "principles and sentiments" are routinely inscribed in the particulars of ordinary stories like the *Times* story discussed above. The ways that particular "facts" are represented contribute to the consensus while embodying many of the consensus's assumptions. Such representations not only define themselves and their constituents affirmatively toward their conception of the normal but also negatively toward the alien, the exotic, the criminal, the pathological, the animal, the medieval, the primitive, and so on. These terms of exclusion and their encoded idioms within the rhetorical commonplaces of news writing carry power to refamiliarize the normal by distancing the alien. Thus the rhetoric of the media bears close analogies to rituals of inclusion and of exorcism. In these ways the media make their contribution to the manners of discourse and good taste in a society that has shown a decided disposition to view religion as private, lest the plurality of prescriptive and assertive religions within its borders cease observing good form. This equivocal achievement is sustained by a studied absence of attention to the power of symbols, those of religion and those of the media, to affect the lives of the unreported many, who take the former with much more seriousness than the latter.

SEE ALSO Law and Religion, article on Law, Religion, and Human Rights; Religious Broadcasting.

BIBLIOGRAPHY

Anscombe, G. E. M. "On Brute Facts." *Analysis* 18 (1958): 69–72. A brief and influential article setting forth elementary distinctions among different kinds of facts and their relations. See Searle (1969), cited below.

Bensman, Joseph, and Robert Lilienfeld. *Craft and Consciousness: Occupational Technique and the Development of World Images.* New York, 1973. Journalists and intellectuals are among the occupational groups treated in this work in the sociology of knowledge. Alert to the power of images arising out of occupations, it is, in effect, a theoretical expansion of Kenneth Burke's dictum, "occupations engender preoccupations."

Cuddihy, John Murry. *No Offense: Civil Religion and Protestant Taste.* New York, 1978. While not directly about media in

American society, this work offers a provocative and controversial thesis about the function of discourses of civility and taste in a pluralistic society. Cuddihy's multiplication of examples from a variety of sources is a persuasive exercise in the hermeneutics of unmasking.

Darnton, Robert. "Writing News and Telling Stories." *Daedalus* 104 (Spring 1975): 175–194. Darnton shows himself to be a master of two conventions here, making the personal memoir serve the larger purposes of a historical and rhetorical analysis of the ways the news is prefigured. An exemplary approach suggesting literary and cultural analyses can be usefully combined with historical study of the media. Included is a selective and critical annotated bibliography.

Gans, Herbert J. *Deciding What's News: A Study of CBS Evening News, NBC Nightly News, Newsweek, and Time.* New York, 1979. Gans's analysis focuses on decision making. This is a standard approach in work on the media. The identification of sets of image traditions, however, such as the pastoral, makes his an important contribution to the symbolic analysis of the media.

Goethals, Gregor T. *The TV Ritual: Worship at the Video Altar.* Boston, 1981. While not strong on the history of the images employed on television, this art historian offers a novel thesis about the religious functions of television images in their various formats. An effort to suggest a ritual analysis of television image sequences.

Hughes, Helen MacGill. *News and the Human Interest Story.* Chicago, 1940. This is one of the earliest of the few works that stress the long-term cultural determinants at work in the conventions of news reporting. Like Darnton's memoir, it sets a good precedent for further work on the sociocultural determinants of news writing.

Innis, Harold A. *Empire and Communications* (1950). Reprint, Toronto, 1972.

Innis, Harold A. *The Bias of Communication.* Toronto, 1951. These two undervalued works have inspired more famous treatments of media, none of which have equaled Innis's cross-cultural scope and empirical incisiveness. Historians and anthropologists of religion can benefit from Innis's treatment of the role of intellectuals in various media in a variety of cultures, ancient and modern. Innis is particularly helpful in outlining, through comparative study, different time senses in various societies and within various strata of society.

Lippmann, Walter. *Public Opinion.* New York, 1922. Few subsequent works have approached the comprehensiveness of sweep and the use of telling detail of Lippmann's pioneering study. It is an extensive elaboration of many of Tocqueville's intuitions and notes. Most of interest to the student of religion is Lippmann's fine treatment of censorship and privacy, stereotypes (all of the third section of the book), the role of interests, and the recurrent attention to the function of rhetorical forms in media in a democratic society. A classic work meriting a new edition.

Rockefeller Foundation. *The Religion Beat: The Reporting of Religion in the Media.* New York, 1981. Papers by journalists and academic specialists in religious studies, followed by excerpts from a day's consultation, sponsored by the Rockefeller Foundation, Humanities Division, in the aftermath of Jonestown and the Islamic Revolution. A good collection of occasional pieces, many with bibliographical reference, for beginning an inquiry into the representation of religion in the news. Of particular note is the stress in several parts of the consultation on the interplay between the coverage of religion in America and the coverage of religion in other countries.

Schudson, Michael. *Discovering the News: A Social History of American Newspapers.* New York, 1978. A quality work clearly represented by its title. In the tradition of the Hughes book noted above.

Schudson, Michael. "Why News Is the Way It Is." *Raritan* 2 (Winter 1983): 109–125. Other than the Darnton article cited above, the single most useful article on the subject. Schudson is not held captive by any one theory but is deft in relating the reigning theories about the news to each other and in using them to criticize each other. The result, particularly because one of the theories he treats is the semiotic, is a minor classic of synthesis.

Searle, John. *Speech Acts: An Essay in the Philosophy of Language.* London, 1969. Drawing on the work of J. L. Austin and G. E. M. Anscombe, Searle is important for his placement of a philosophy of language in conjunction with questions of factuality, on the one hand, and institutional contexts, on the other, and he dialectically weaves the relations among them. An analysis that is useful to applied work in religion or in the media, or both.

Shils, Edward. "Center and Periphery." In *Center and Periphery: Essays in Macrosociology,* vol. 2, *Selected Papers,* pp. 3–16. Chicago, 1975. Shils offers a dialectic in the understanding of the central institutional system in a society, with dissensual forces imaged as "periphery." The bias toward the center is clear, though the delicacy of the analysis, if used to think about the functional and symbolic roles of media, is helpful. Should be supplemented by Shils's chapter on consensus in the same volume.

Smith, Jonathan Z. *Imagining Religion: From Babylon to Jonestown.* Chicago, 1982. Smith provides the only available treatment of Jonestown by a historian of religion. In addition, his essays "Sacred Persistence: Toward a Redescription of Canon" and "The Bare Facts of Ritual," included in this volume, not only illuminate problems in the history and anthropology of religion but are also helpful in understanding media as a canonical symbolic matrix and in exploring the problems attending changes in that canon.

Strauss, Leo. *Persecution and the Art of Writing* (1952). Westport, Conn., 1973. Strauss offers a hermeneutic for understanding writing performed under particular repressions, especially the threat of official censorship. The work's relevance ranges far beyond issues of writing and censorship if censorship is broadened to include a variety of forms of cultural suppression or exclusion.

Tocqueville, Alexis de. *Democracy in America.* Edited by Phillips Bradley. 2 vols. New York, 1960. This work is included because, in addition to the observations on newspapers in a democratic society, Tocqueville's chapters on language and speech in America are early instances that can now be seen to be a part of social semiotics.

New Sources

Buddenbaum, Judith, and Debra Mason, eds. *Readings on Religion as News.* Ames, Iowa, 2000.

Hangen, Tona. *Redeeming the Dial: Radio, Religion, and Popular Culture in America.* Chapel Hill, N.C., 2002.

Hoover, Stewart. *Religion and the News: Faith and Journalism in American Public Discourse.* Thousand Oaks, Calif., 1998.

Hoover, Stewart, and Lynn Schofield Clark, eds. *Practicing Religion in the Age of the Media.* New York, 2002.

Lundby, Knut, and Stewart Hoover, eds. *Rethinking Media, Religion, and Culture.* Thousand Oaks, Calif., 1997.

McDannell, Colleen. *Material Christianity, Religion and Popular Culture in America.* New Haven, 1998.

Schmalzbauer, John. *People of Faith: Religious Conviction in American Journalism and Higher Education.* Ithaca, N.Y., 2003.

Smith, Christian, ed. *The Secular Revolution: Power, Interests, and Conflict in the Secularization of American Public Life.* Berkeley, 2003.

RUEL W. TYSON, JR. (1987)
Revised Bibliography

JOURNEY SEE ASCENSION; DESCENT INTO THE UNDERWORLD; FLIGHT; PILGRIMAGE; QUESTS

JUANA INÉS DE LA CRUZ DE ASBAJE Y RAMIREZ. Sor Juana Inés de la Cruz (1648/1651–1695) was a compelling seventeenth-century Mexican scholar and writer whose work deserves a significant place in the history of Christian thought. Scholars who study her religious writings consider her to be the first female theologian of the Americas. Her poetry and dramas offer a theological voice through the medium of literature.

Juana Ramirez de Asbaje y Santillana, the daughter of unwed parents, was born in the town of Nepantla, Mexico, between 1648 and 1651. Her mother was a *criolla* (American of Spanish descent), and her father was a Spanish military officer. Around the age of thirteen, Juana went to live in the court of the viceroy of New Spain (colonial Mexico) as a lady-in-waiting. She stayed there for three years. In 1667 she entered into the ascetic, cloistered Roman Catholic order of Discalced Carmelites, which she left after a short time. Two years later she joined the order of the Hieronymites.

At a young age, Juana developed a passion for the intellectual life. She was an avid reader, primarily self-taught, and by her midteens she was recognized as the most erudite woman in Mexico. Her reputation as a scholar was a crucial factor in her gaining a position in the viceregal court. Her desire for a life of scholarship and study was perhaps a significant factor in her decision to enter cloistered life. During her time in the court, the Jesuit Antonio Núñez de Miranda encouraged Juana to enter the convent. Aware of her academic gifts, as well as her distaste for marriage, he felt the convent was the best venue from which to monitor Juana's growing public notoriety and intellectual aspirations. Juana hesitated to take the veil, fearing that convent life would impede her studies, and the reasons for her entry into a convent continue to be a matter of debate amongst *sorjuanistas* (Sor Juana scholars). Núñez de Miranda became Sor Juana's confessor for a significant portion of her cloistered life.

Sor Juana's time in the convent was focused primarily on fierce study and scholarship. She read in the fields of literature, philosophy, theology, and science. Estimates of the number of books in her library range from hundreds to thousands. She also collected scientific and musical instruments. Her poetry and plays were in high demand for both Church festivities and court occasions, and it is in these milieus that her writings were read, sung, and performed. Much of her corpus was written by request and for commission.

After enjoying a public life as a writer and intellectual, Sor Juana's situation took a dramatic turn when, in 1690, *La Carta Atenagórica*, her critique of a male theologian's analysis of Christ's greatest demonstration of love, was circulated without her authorization. The critique was circulated with a letter, written under the pseudonym Sor Filotea, criticizing Sor Juana's intellectual pursuits. Sor Juana scholars generally acknowledge that the author of the letter was the Bishop of Puebla, Manuel Fernández de Santa Cruz, and that Sor Juana was aware of his role in these events. Fernández names the object of Sor Juana's critique as a fifty-year-old sermon written by the prominent Jesuit theologian Antonio Vieira. Though the actual object of Sor Juana's critique is a matter of debate among *sorjuanistas*, the perceived target in the eyes of her contemporaries was Vieira. Sor Juana's response to these events, *La Respuesta*, an autobiographical defense of women's right to intellectual pursuits, was completed the following year. Within four years of the production of *La Respuesta*, Sor Juana renounced her public life. Two years later she died from an illness that she contracted while caring for the sick in her convent.

Three volumes of Sor Juana's works were published in Madrid between 1689 and 1700. Her corpus includes sixty-five sonnets, sixty-two romances, a large number of poems in other forms, two comedies, three *autos sacramentales* (allegorical dramas), sixteen sets of *villancicos* (poems sung on religious holidays), one *sarao* (a celebratory song accompanied by a dance), and two farces. Her writings incorporate an eclectic mixture of colonial Mexican philosophy and theology, including Thomism, Neoplatonism, and Hermeticism. A child of the Americas, Sor Juana incorporates indigenous and African sources and voices throughout her work. One of her most significant contributions to Christian theology is her defense of indigenous peoples and her understanding of indigenous religions as prefigurations of Christianity.

As a baroque figure, Sor Juana's writings are clearly marked by the excesses and ornamentation that characterize this era. She and other baroque writers of New Spain emulated the Spanish greats of the period, including Luis de Góngora (1561–1627) and Pedro Calderón de la Barca (1600–1681). The literature of this world was predominantly male, written to and read by men. Sor Juana, of course, is a notable exception, although not because she was a woman. There were other women writers in colonial Latin America, especially within the context of convent life. What distinguishes Sor Juana is her forays into what were understood as the masculine discourses of philosophy and theology, which contrast drastically with the mystical writings of other nuns. Today, Sor Juana is recognized as Mexico's most important colonial writer.

Sor Juana's corpus touches on a wide variety of theological themes through the lens of literature. In her poetry one finds a heavy Marian emphasis. The theme of beauty is pervasive in her work. Her Christological writings emphasize Jesus as a manifestation of God's glory and the beauty of humanity created in the image of God. Her allegorical drama *El divino Narciso* reinterprets the Ovidian myth of Narcissus into an account of Jesus' passion, death, and resurrection, highlighting the dramatic character of humanity's relationship with the divine. Her theological anthropology presents a relational humanity, constituted by the interconnectedness of the human community and its relationship with God. Sor Juana also defended women's right to an education, and she critiqued the social construction of gender. Poet, dramatist, theologian, and philosopher, Sor Juana is a Latin American Church mother and a key figure in the history of theology.

SEE ALSO Christianity, article on Christianity in Latin America.

BIBLIOGRAPHY

Bénassy-Berling, Marie-Cécile. *Humanisme et religion chez Sor Juana Inés de la Cruz: La femme et la culture au XVIIe siècle.* Paris, 1982.

Gonzalez, Michelle A. *Sor Juana: Beauty and Justice in the Americas.* Maryknoll, N.Y., 2003.

Juana Inés de la Cruz, Sor. *Obras completas.* 3d ed. Edited by Alfonso Méndez-Plancarte and Alberto G. Salceda. Vol. 1: *Lírica personal*; Vol. 2: *Villancicos y letras sacras*; Vol. 3: *Autos y loas*; Vol. 4: *Comedias, sainetes, y prosa.* Mexico City, 1995.

Kirk, Pamela. *Sor Juana Inés de la Cruz: Religion, Art, and Feminism.* New York, 1998.

Merrim, Stephanie, ed. *Feminist Perspectives on Sor Juana Inés de la Cruz.* Detroit, 1991.

Paz, Octavio. *Sor Juana Inés de la Cruz, or, The Traps of Faith.* Translated by Margaret Sayers Peden. Cambridge, Mass., 1988.

Tavard, George. *Juana Inés de la Cruz and the Theology of Beauty: The First Mexican Theology.* Notre Dame, Ind., 1991.

MICHELLE A. GONZALEZ (2005)

JUDAH

SEE YEHUDAH HA-LEVI

JUDAISM

This entry consists of the following articles:

JUDAISM: AN OVERVIEW

Judaism is the religion of the Jews, an ethnic, cultural, and religious group that has its origins in the ancient Near East, has lived in communities as members of collective polities and as individuals throughout the world, and now numbers about thirteen million people, chiefly concentrated in the State of Israel, North America, and Europe. However, not all Jews practice Judaism as a religion; nor does every form of Judaism constitute a religious expression. Judaism as a religion has since its emergence held to a belief in one God; believed that the Jewish people are bound to God by a sacred covenant; and read, interpreted, and followed what it sees as the terms of that covenant in God's revelation in the form of the Torah. But Jews' conceptions of God have ranged from extreme anthropomorphism to forms of pantheism; the idea that the covenant obliges Jews especially and personally has been challenged by certain Jewish religious movements in modern times; and ways and implications of interpreting the Torah have varied greatly, even in the most common forms of Judaism.

It is impossible to separate the history and description of Judaism from that of the Jewish people. Defining and describing Judaism for a reference work on religion therefore presents several questions, many of which do not arise when describing most other religions. How does one identify the Jewish people—a political, social, and religious entity that has ranged from antiquity to the present, that is not limited to one geographic region, and the members of which do not always agree on what constitutes membership in their community? Does this definition preclude any doctrinal or behavioral definition of Judaism? When members of that community depart from a set of beliefs or practices but still consider themselves Jews, are they still adherents to Judaism? Does one accept internal definitions of Judaism and Jews, or does one draw conclusions from the historical range of Jewish history?

Questions are not limited to those that concern identifying the Jews as an entity and simply describing their culture, the way one might define a geographic region such as southern India or ancient Mesoamerica and describe its indigenous religions. For Judaism as a religion has carried within it a concept of Jewish peoplehood. This concept is knit into the fabric of its myths, rituals, and theology. The Jewish people, usually designated as Israel in Jewish theological and mythic discourse, stands at the center of almost all major religious expressions of Judaism through the notion of a covenant between Israel and God. Religious conversion to Judaism entails not only joining a creed, set of rituals, and community, but an extended family as well: it is customary in Jewish legal and ceremonial practice for a convert to designate his or her parents as Abraham and Sarah, the progenitors of the Jewish people. Moreover, modern secular nationalist definitions of Judaism, such as Zionism, have drawn heavily from those religious conceptions of Jewish peoplehood and could not have developed without them. A few modern expressions of Judaism have sought to minimize or reconfigure the place of Jewish peoplehood in Judaism. Most notably some sectors of the Reform movement in the nineteenth and early twentieth centuries sought to redefine Judaism as a form of ethical monotheism open to all. However, a closer look at these expressions shows that they usually saw the dissolving of boundaries between Jews and non-Jews as the outcome of an enlightened, utopian future and furthermore saw Israel as a distinct entity charged with the mission of spreading Mosaic religion to the larger world.

In the light of the centrality of peoplehood in Judaism's conception of itself, the major historical entries on Judaism that follow will focus not only on myths, rituals, theologies, ethics, and factions that make up stages of Judaism but political and demographic data as well. After a brief discussion of criteria by which historians of religion can survey this subject, this article will proceed to a description of some of the major historical stages, themes, and practices that constitute Judaism.

DEFINITIONS. The term *Judaism* first appears in Hellenistic Jewish literature, most prominently *2 Maccabees* (a narration of the Judean revolt against the Seleucid Greeks in the second century BCE), where the word *Ioudaïsmos* seems to identify the ways and practices of the Jews in contradistinction with those of the "barbarians" (which in *2 Mc.* 2:21 actually means Greeks). There *Ioudaïsmos* is contrasted with *Hellenismos,* the ways and practices of the Greeks that the Maccabees' Jewish opponents wished to follow. Thus the term *Judaism* began as a way of distinguishing itself from the other. Likewise the Hebrew term *Yahadut* appears occasionally in the Middle Ages with a similar valence. In all of these premodern examples, *Judaism* refers to the whole of a religious behavioral system and is not given a substantive, doctrinal definition. From the Hellenistic period until the dawn of modernity, Jews would be most likely to describe their practices, beliefs, and theological thinking as *Torah.* This word originally meant "teaching" and in its simplest common meaning applies to the first five books of the Hebrew Bible (the Pentateuch). However, as shall be seen, the term came to encompass nearly the entirety of Judaic religious discourse.

It is in modern times that the word Judaism came most commonly to denote a full-fledged religious system that could be compared with Christianity, Islam, and other religions. From the nineteenth century to the mid-twentieth century it became common for Jewish thinkers to identify an "essence of Judaism," which consisted mainly of a set of doctrines authentic to the eternal character of Judaism as a religion. Books such as Leo Baeck's *The Essence of Judaism* (1961/1948) and Abba Hillel Silver's *Where Judaism Differed* (1987/1956) sought not only to present Judaism as a set of creeds and norms but to distinguish it from Christianity and other religions. Likewise much Jewish historiography in the nineteenth century was concerned with what was essential and nonessential to Judaism in Jewish history. As a result historians such as Heinrich Graetz dismissed large movements in Jewish history and thought as *unjüdisch* (see Biale, 1982).

This tendency was balanced by the efforts of historians of Jewish literature such as Leopold Zunz and Moritz Steinschneider, whose principal motivation was to uncover and catalog as many textual and cultural sources as possible. In the latter half of the twentieth century historians such as Gershom Scholem (who once described himself as a "religious anarchist"), Salo Baron, and others sought to describe Jewish cultures in their widest variety, privileging virtually no central idea or spiritual phenomenon over others. So too Jacob Neusner, describing the Jewish religious landscape in late antiquity, sees the major documents and genres of Jewish literature as constituting discrete "Judaisms" and not as one entity. Scholem's historiography, rejecting normative criteria for admitting phenomena into Jewish history, encompassed not only the Qabbalah but expressions of Judaism widely considered heretical, such as the messianic movements surrounding Shabbetai Tsevi and Jacob Frank, the extreme anthropomorphism of the Shiʿur Qomah literature of late antiquity, and "Jewish Gnosticism."

The earlier generation's effort at distinguishing the unique aspects of Judaism, however, was also paradoxically an attempt to place Judaism on a parity with other "world religions," especially Christianity. By describing it primarily as a set of doctrines, this discourse made Judaism a philosophical or spiritual system that could be compared with other systems of its class. This, no less than the status of Judaism as the spiritual ancestor of Christianity and Islam, granted Judaism pride of place in encyclopedias, textbooks, and other large-scale comparisons of Western religions.

Other historians and theorists of religions also had their uses for Judaism. For some historians of early Christianity and the matrix of first-century Judaism that produced it, Judaism was portrayed as a civilization whose nomocentrism, casuistry, and parochialism could be contrasted with early Christianity's spirituality, sincerity, and universality. For anthropologists from James Frazer (*Folklore in the Old Testament,* 1988) and W. Robertson Smith (*Religion of the Semites,* 2002/1956), Judaism could be held up to examination as an example of the persistence of ritual patterns, such as food taboos and sacrificial values, that also characterized "primitive" religions. From the nineteenth century, which saw the birth of the *Wissenschaft des Judentums,* the scholarly study of Judaism, historians of Judaism responded with a counterdiscourse that sought to prove that within Judaism's legal structure lay profound ethical and spiritual truths. Whereas, as mentioned above, this movement sometimes resulted in the tendency to gloss over aspects of Jewish history that did not conform to Western rationalist ideals of religion, this effort also succeeded in uncovering a sophisticated philosophical and literary civilization within the vast Jewish manuscript collections of Europe and the Middle East. With the increased integration of the study of Judaism into the Western academy, historians and critics have come to challenge conceptions of Judaism forged in these early conflicts. In addition, some students of the major non-Western religions, especially Hinduism and Buddhism, have come to see Judaism as a comperand for such themes as exile, scholasticism, purity, and discourse of sacrifice.

This has resulted in a productive tension between the effort to identify elements of Judaism that are enduring and indispensable on the one hand and on the other the tendency to see no form of Judaism as alien to the historian. It has led to synthetic studies tracing key motifs and ideas through long stretches of time; has brought to light genres, theological and experiential trends, and ritual patterns that otherwise might have been neglected; and keeps students of religion conscious of the complexity of their subject. It is likewise productive for an overview such as this, for it makes both writer and reader aware of the value of generalizations as well as their limits.

After a brief discussion of what constitutes Jewish identity in Judaism, this article will be organized historically, with an eye to understanding what each historical episode in the history of Judaism has contributed to the religion and culture as it stands in the early twenty-first century. This history will be described in five major stages.

1. The biblical period, second millennium to 536 BCE. In this period the Israelites coalesced into a divided kingdom under a Davidic royalty and a priestly caste. During this time the worship of YHWH rose to become the defining characteristic of Israel's religion and the Temple in Jerusalem the most important place of sacrifice and sacred space. In this period as well the scribes, priests, prophets, and poets dedicated to that God composed the writings that would become the Hebrew Scriptures.
2. The Second Temple period. After a fifty-year period of exile, the leadership of the nation of Judah returned from exile under Persian rule (538 to 333 BCE). With the advent of Greek, then Roman control of Judea and the introduction of Hellenism (333 BCE to 70 CE), political, economic, and cultural upheavals led to the formation of a Diaspora in the Greco-Roman world and the rise of competing sects and communities within Judea. During this period the writings of the biblical period were increasingly treated as a canon and were subject to diverse methods of interpretation. The civil strife that beset the commonwealth in the first century culminated in the destruction of Jerusalem and its Temple in 70 CE.
3. The rabbinic period, 70 CE to the sixth century. With the destruction of the Temple, a class of nonpriestly leaders called rabbis sought to construct a system whereby the worship of God centered around the study of the Torah as interpreted by its authoritative transmitters, the rabbis, and according to which the performance of individual commandments *(mitsvot)* could lead the person to a beatific life after resurrection. During this period synagogues became the primary locus of worship, and early forms of Jewish magic and mysticism took shape.
4. The medieval period, sixth to sixteenth centuries. During this period Jews increasingly lived in Europe, North Africa, and the Middle East among Christians and Muslims. This encounter with the two major religious civilizations that saw themselves as daughter and successor religions to Judaism produced tensions and new forms of discourse. Under Islam, Jews developed an extensive literature of systematic philosophy and secular poetry; under Christianity, Jewish intellectuals produced innovative systems of textual and legal interpretation.
5. The early modern and modern period, seventeenth to twenty-first centuries. During this period Jews in the Middle East and North Africa were affected by the fortunes of the Ottoman Empire and the colonization of those parts of the world by European countries. In eastern Europe new religious trends such as the Hasidic movement and the Talmudism of the Vilna Gaon changed the face of Jewish life. From the early nineteenth century onward Jews in the West increasingly became citizens of modern states, not members of autonomous Jewish communities. In some states in western Europe and in America it became possible for Jews to leave Jewish communities and disavow any Jewish identity without converting to another religion. By the twentieth century it also became possible to abandon Judaism as a religion while retaining a Jewish identity. During the modern period the religious denominations Reform, Orthodoxy, Conservative Judaism, and Reconstructionism formed over differences in the status and interpretation of Jewish law, the nature of revelation, and the role of the Jewish people in the modern world. In this period, in response to the growth of modern European nationalism as well as the rise of political anti-Semitism, the Zionist movement formed around the idea that the Jews could only find safety and fulfillment as a nation by returning to the Land of Israel.

Each historical stage will not be described comprehensively. Rather, those major elements of each period that contributed most to later stages will be emphasized. For more complete accounts, the reader is referred to the other major articles in this section. The article will conclude with a description of some of the most important forms, themes, and practices in contemporary Judaism, noting differences among the denominations where relevant. These include basic theological tenets, practices and rituals, and principles of ethics and polity.

WHO IS A JEW? The Hebrew Bible most often uses the word *Israel, Yisrael,* in such formulas as *Bene Yisrael,* "the children of Israel," or *'Am Yisrael,* the people of Israel. This term for the Jewish people has persisted in legal and religious discourse. Individually a Jew is known in Hebrew as *Yehudi,* Jew, or *Yisrael,* "member of Israel," the latter used principally to designate an individual in legal language from the Mishnah onward. However, the term Israel also refers to the kingdom that, according to the Hebrew Bible's historiography, formed when the descendants of Jacob (Israel) settled the land of Canaan, appointed kings, and in 722 BCE formed a separate kingdom from the southern Kingdom of Judah. Since this kingdom was conquered in 586 BCE and its leaders exiled, what remained was Judah. By the third century BCE its inhabitants became known as Judeans or *Ioudaïoi.* As a result of this history it is customary in English to use the term *Israelite* when referring to the people of biblical times before the Babylonian exile (that is, the second millennium to 585 BCE) and to use the term *Jew* to refer to the people after that period.

The criteria for membership in the Jewish people have not always been clear. In ancient Israel citizenship in the geographic and political entities that formed Israel and Judah were synonymous with being a member of the people. From the time of Ezra in the fifth century BCE onward (see *Ez.* 9), Jewish law has prohibited intermarriage between Jews and non-Jews. From at least the first century CE to the early twenty-first century it has been agreed that any child born of a Jewish mother is Jewish. However, some scholars have suggested that Jewish communities as late as the Hellenistic period considered the child of a Jewish father and a non-Jewish mother to be a Jew. At any rate the matrilineal definition held sway in Jewish law from the early rabbinic period until modern times. In the twentieth century the Reform and Reconstructionist movements declared that being the child of a Jewish father is sufficient to make one a Jew on condition that the parents raise the child as a Jew. However, this definition is controversial and is not accepted by the Orthodox and Conservative movements. The other way one becomes a Jew is by conversion. Since late antiquity, conversion in Rabbinic Judaism has been a legal procedure that involves accepting Judaism, circumcision for all males, and ritual immersion for all converts. That procedure thus changes the status of the individual and he or she is considered Jewish in every way. Whereas the Law of Return of the State of Israel grants citizenship to all Jews, the definition of the Jew for those purposes is still a matter of controversy, involving religious, political, and sociological considerations.

THE BIBLICAL HERITAGE. While the religion of ancient Israel differed in many dramatic ways from the Judaism that emerged from the Hellenistic era onward, several of the central ideas that were to define Judaism as a religion in this earliest stage of Judaism originated in this period. Two of the most fundamental are the sacred history of the Jewish people and the idea of their covenant with the one God. The narrative of the Torah, together with the "historical" books of the Bible, such as *Joshua, Judges, Samuel,* and the books of *Kings,* tell a story of the foundation, growth, and tribulations of a nation guided by its relationship to God. (God is known by several names, both generic and specific, in the Hebrew Bible; chief among them is a four-letter proper name whose original pronunciation is lost but whose letters correspond in English to YHWH. Based on some early sources, scholars often use the pronunciation Yahweh for this name.) This nation, according to *Genesis,* began with God's call to Abraham to go forth from his Mesopotamian homeland to form a holy nation (*Gn.* 12). In *Genesis* 17, God appears to Abraham as El Shaddai. He then makes the following charge to Abraham: "Walk in My ways and be blameless. I will establish My covenant between Me and you, and I will make you exceedingly numerous." He further stipulates that He will assign the land of Canaan to his children, and as a sign of that covenant Abraham is to circumcise himself and his male children. This practice is called *brit milah,* the covenant of circumcision.

The idea that a covenantal relationship exists between God and the children of Abraham is a driving force behind biblical and postbiblical Jewish theology and has informed every stage of Judaism. This covenant, like many political and religious treaties in the ancient Near East, is one of suzerainty, a solemn contractual relationship between unequal parties. At the same time it implies mutual obligations. In return for Israel's obedience, God will preserve the people and allow them to prosper. As a result, in biblical narration and prophetic rhetoric, Israel's misfortune was understood as a result of the nation's failure to live up to its terms in the covenant.

The covenant is tested and renewed several times in biblical narrative. It is tested when, in *Genesis* 22, God commands Abraham to sacrifice his son, thus putting the prospect of his having an heir into jeopardy (this, and not the ordinary love of father for son, was probably the source of the tension in the story for ancient readers, who were acquainted with the practice of sacrificing the first born). In *Exodus* 19–20, at Mount Sinai, God lays out, in the fashion of ancient Near Eastern suzerainty treaties, the terms of the covenant as they apply to the Children of Israel most permanently and dramatically through Moses, the paradigmatic prophet. The people, descendants of Jacob and his brothers who had settled in Egypt, had been liberated from slavery by God's intervention. God sets out the terms of their future relationship:

> You have seen what I did to the Egyptians, how I bore you on eagles' wings and brought you to me. Now then, if you will obey Me faithfully and keep My covenant, you shall be My treasured possession among all the peoples. Indeed, all the earth is Mine, but you shall be to Me a kingdom of priests and a holy nation.

After the people declare their acceptance of the covenant, the details of Israel's obedience are set forth in the Ten Commandments and the law code that follows. Those laws entail monolotry, that is, the requirement that Israel worship no god other than YHWH, social norms, and observance of the Sabbath. A result of the foundational status accorded to the Sinai experience, legal relationships tend to have deep emotional consequences in Judaism. One important biblical term for God's love of Israel is *Ḥesed*, which refers to the love that arises from God's fulfillment of his part in the covenantal relationship (see *Ps.* 136). Another poetic motif is that of marriage, a contractual relationship that carries strong emotional implications; for example, in the *Book of Hosea* the Sinai experience is seen as the honeymoon between Israel and YHWH. Israel's worship of other deities is depicted as adultery, and God's willingness to forgive the people is likened to the love of a forgiving husband.

The master narrative of the Hebrew Bible continues with its depiction of the people settling in Canaan under Joshua's leadership and forming a confederation of tribes led by a series of charismatic "judges," which then grows into a kingdom ruled by royalty descended from David. This kingdom divides into two, Israel in the north and Judah in the south. In 722 BCE Israel was conquered by the Assyrians, leaving Judah alone in the south. In 587 BCE Judah too was conquered by the Babylonians and its leaders exiled. They returned in 538 BCE under the Persian emperor Cyrus, who allowed them to rebuild the Temple and install a local government.

The early episodes of this grand narrative that weaves through the Torah and the historical and prophetic books of the Hebrew Bible do not always correspond with what historians can reconstruct of the early history of the Israelites. But after this narrative was codified in the Hebrew Bible and interpreted by generations of Jews from the postexilic period onward, it played a central role in determining not only Israel's self-conception but its ritual system, legal structure, and eschatology. The books that became the Hebrew Bible took shape over several centuries from the dawn of the first millennium BCE to the second century CE. The bulk of the Torah and the historical and prophetic books were probably composed from many sources during the period of the Judan monarchy, between the tenth and sixth centuries BCE.

Historians thus now present a complex picture of a society that emerged from diverse origins in the Fertile Crescent and came, in the first few centuries of the first millennium BCE, to understand itself as a nation unified by common ancestry and divine election. The Bible as it now exists is the product of a group of scribes, priests, and poets loyal to the cult of YHWH and so excludes much of the religious tendencies of ancient Israelites, including women. Archaeological finds of extrabiblical documents and close readings of the Hebrew Bible itself suggest that religion for some of ancient Israel's inhabitants included worship of deities such as Asherah, YHWH's consort; human sacrifice; and other phenomena condemned or ignored by biblical writers. Likewise students of the religion of ancient Israel believe that the Israelite idea of God evolved from a henotheistic religion to a monotheistic one. That is, ancient Israelite religion developed from a system whereby one local deity, YHWH, was believed to be a supreme God and further demanded excusive loyalty to one whereby only one God existed and all others were illusions. It became the common way of understanding God in the Hellenistic period. Even then, however, most Jews until modern times have believed in the existence of superhuman beings, such as angels and demons.

Integral to Israelite religion, like all Mediterranean religions in antiquity, was the system of sacrificial worship and seasonal pilgrimages. After several centuries this system came to be concentrated in the Temple in Jerusalem. In the climate of the Judean hills, a central concern was rain and the harvest. The festival system revolved around the agricultural cycle of that region. There were three major pilgrimage festivals. Pesaḥ, Passover, was a spring lamb sacrifice which was combined with the Feast of Unleavened Bread, Ḥag ha-Matsot. Shavuʿot, the Feast of Weeks, seven weeks after Passover, celebrated barley and wheat harvests and the offering of the first fruits. In time two of the festivals came to be associated with historical events. Sukkot commemorated Israel's sojourn in the Sinai Desert. The commandment to live in temporary harvest huts *(sukkot)* was associated with the tabernacles in which the Israelites lived in the wilderness. The spring festival of unleavened bread, Passover, commemorated the exodus from Egypt, when the Israelites had no time to let the bread rise in their haste to escape. By the rabbinic period the Shavuʿot became associated with the revelation at Sinai.The fall season began with a convocation of the nation at the beginning of the calendar year in Tishri (known by the rabbinic period as Roʾsh ha-Shanah) and, most important, a solemn sacrifice to cleanse the Temple of impurity and a day of fasting and atonement for sins (Yom Kippur).

Daily and seasonal offerings of slaughtered animals, grain, and fruits took up most of the activity in the Temple. Biblical stories make it clear that the sacrifice of animals on the altar was particularly pleasing to God if the individual who was sacrificing met with favor. In *Genesis* 8:20–22 Noah, having been spared the Flood, offers a sacrifice of thanksgiving. YHWH inhales the pleasing aroma of the burning meat and decides never again to doom the earth because of humanity's sins. On the other hand the prophets, often critics of the political authorities, warned that God would not accept the people's offerings if the sacrificers had not made provisions for a just society.

The sacrifice for Yom Kippur is another good illustration of the phenomenology and ritual system of biblical Israel. In *Leviticus* 16:2 God instructs Moses, "Tell your brother Aaron that he is not to come at will into the Shrine behind the curtain, in front of the cover that is upon the ark, lest he die, for I appear in the cloud over the cover." In this passage God is conceived as localized but volatile. His abode is in heaven, and he is able to come to earth under specific ritual circumstances. Those circumstances involve the presence of a sacred space—in this case the inner sanctum of the Tabernacle or Temple—that the deity is able to inhabit. Nor is

God invisible. In this case he comes enclosed in a cloud. Indeed there are several instances in which God is seen directly; the prophets Isaiah and Ezekiel have divine visions, and at Sinai, Moses, Aaron and his sons, and the elders of Israel "saw God, and ate and drank." At the same time direct encounter with the divine presence is a dangerous thing, and some biblical traditions think of the sight of God as fatal. In *Exodus* 33 God, replying to Moses' request to see him, says, "No one can see My face and live." Those who do see them, such as Isaiah, are frightened that they will die as a result (*Is.* 6:5).

What makes the encounter possible is observance of a system whereby ritual impurity, caused by such sources as corpses, dead reptiles, seminal flux, and menstruation, is purged from the Temple precincts, especially by means of water, sacrificial blood (which purges the sacrificial altar), and the purifying ashes of a red heifer. The creation of a pure space on earth allows God's presence to descend from the pure environment of the divine abode and bestow on the people the blessings of a complex agricultural society: safety from enemies, rain and prosperity, and children to carry on the family economy. But the terms of the covenant make that presence conditional on Israel's loyalty to YHWH as well as its observance of the ethical norms expected of God's people. In the period of the monarchy, a class of prophets warned the nation that divergence from those norms would result in God's withdrawal of that presence and military and political disaster.

The sociopolitical system of Israel too was sacralized. According to the *Books of Samuel,* the unsuccessful reign of the first king, Saul, gave way to the dynasty of David, who is anointed *(mashiaḥ)* by the prophet Samuel. David's descendants are seen by biblical narrative and by subsequent Jewish tradition as the only rightful heirs to the kingship. The prophets were critical of the kings for their failure to produce a just society as well as their tendency to allow worship of other gods, and some anticipated a time when a righteous Davidic king would usher in an era of peace and reverence.

In 722 BCE the Assyrian Empire conquered the northern Kingdom of Israel, exiled much of its population, and dissolved it as a political entity. In 587 BCE the Babylonians conquered the Kingdom of Judah and exiled its leaders. Fifty years later, under the Persians, they returned to reformulate a Jewish commonwealth under priestly leadership. Historians believe that this period, from the time of exile to the end of Persian rule in 333 BCE, was when key Judaic ideas were formed. Increasingly YHWH was seen not only as Israel's special deity but the only true God. It was probably during this period that diverse written and oral traditions of the ancient Israelites were gathered together to form the Torah and several of the central scriptural writings that became Judaism's sacred canon.

THE SECOND TEMPLE PERIOD. The conquest of the Persian Empire, including the Land of Israel, by Alexander in 333 BCE changed Judaism deeply and irrevocably. The Persians had been content to rely on local leaders and their cultures to preserve stability in the provinces they ruled. The Greeks on the other hand brought with them deep transformations in the nature of ancient societies. The effect of the exportation of Greek economic, social, and cultural patterns, called Hellenism, transformed the Mediterranean basin into an integrated economy. The instrument of that transformation was the polis, the Hellenistic city-state, which was used as a model for local governments. The polis carried with it a political structure based on the rulership of a local elite or boule; an economic program based on increasing urbanization and export of goods to other regions of the empire; and a cultural program based on Greek language, rhetoric, and religion—the latter spread through the teaching and interpretation of Homer and identification of local gods with the Greek pantheon.

Judea was not a major center of Hellenistic political or economic activity, and so the process of Hellenization came slowly there. In the late fourth century and early third century BCE gradual changes in architecture, demographic patterns, and cultural styles could be discerned. With the conflicts between the Ptolemaic and Seleucid successor empires to Alexander in the second century CE, Judea became a contested area because of its location between Egypt and Syria. Eventually Judea was ruled by Rome, who installed Herod, a descendant of Iduminean converts, as a client king. Roman economic and military pressure on the province of Judea as well as internal conflicts came to a head in 66 CE with a revolt against Rome. The revolt was suppressed by Romans with the destruction of Jerusalem and its Temple in 70 CE. By the first century as well there were substantial communities of Jews living in the Diaspora, that is, outside of the Land of Israel. There were Jews in many of the Greek-speaking communities of the Mediterranean, especially Alexandria, Rome, and Asia Minor. There was also a flourishing Jewish community in the Persian Empire, in Mesopotamia.

In Judea the changes in economic, social, and cultural organization brought on by Hellenism thus accelerated in the second and first centuries BCE. With them came increasing divisions within the society and differences of opinion about how God's word should be interpreted and followed. One effect of Hellenization was increased urbanization. This meant that Jerusalem, a modest community surrounded by the Judean hills, became a major regional center of economic and cultural as well as political activity. Another effect was cosmopolitanism. Each local government in the Hellenistic economic communities was called on to contribute to the trade in goods, pay taxes, and carry out political affairs in Greek. This entailed getting a Greek education and being conversant with Greek cultural norms and religious values, including exposure to Greek mythology and philosophy. The political leadership of Judea would therefore be increasingly associated with Hellenistic style and cultural symbols. Another result of Hellenization therefore was greater disparity in the social and cultural status of various sectors of society: rich versus poor, priests versus nonpriests, and urban versus rural. Some also saw these social differences in terms of a struggle between Hellenists, those inclined toward integrating Greek culture with their own, and anti-Hellenists, those who saw Greek ways of life as threats to the monotheism, legal norms, and ritual traditions of the Jews. These struggles came to a head in 167 BCE, when, after a period of unrest in the wake of political scandals in the Temple administration, the Ptolemaic emperor Antiochus IV imposed Seleucid rule on the Temple and turned it into a polytheistic shrine. This precipitated a revolt led by Judah Maccabee and his family. Their victory is commemorated in the holiday of Ḥanukkah, which celebrates the dedication of the Temple after the Maccabees retook it in 164 BCE. The Hasmonaean dynasty that then ruled Judea, first as a short-lived independent commonwealth and then as local rulers under the Seleucids, also provoked dissatisfaction. One therefore sees in this period a wide variety of religious communities ("sects") with political, ritual, and theological agendas.

The evidence for these social, cultural, and religious trends comes from a number of sources in addition to archaeological findings. One of the most important is the historian Josephus, a former priest of the first century CE who had joined the Roman army during the revolt against Rome and wrote several valuable historical and polemical works in Greek. There are also extant literary works written in Hebrew, Aramaic, and Greek. Some of these were translated into Greek and other languages and attained a canonical or deuterocanonical status in some Christian communities. Others, like the apocryphal *Book of Ben Sira (Ecclesiasticus),* survived in Hebrew as well as in Greek. One of the most valuable resources for an understanding of this period is the corpus of writings found in the Judean desert, especially the Dead Sea Scrolls, the library of a sectarian community formed in the second century BCE. However, these sources present difficulties for the historian. Josephus wrote his history with political and ideological goals in mind, and the apocryphal and sectarian writings, often written in a highly symbolic language or attributed pseudepigraphically to biblical personae, are cryptic about the historical circumstances of their composition.

The *Book of Ben Sira,* written at least thirteen years before the Maccabean revolt, provides a window into the type of piety that characterized the religious elite of the early Hellenistic period. This book is valuable because it was written by an individual, Yehoshuʿa Ben Sira, who signed his name to the book. The author was a priest who also apparently taught in the scribal schools of Jerusalem, perhaps in the Temple precincts. He wrote the book in the tradition of scribal wisdom, an ancient Mediterranean literary tradition represented in the Hebrew Bible by such works as *Proverbs* and *Job*. The *Book of Ben Sira* presents a type of piety in which the cultivation of wisdom, identified as practical social skills and, most important, the study of Torah, combines with reverence for the Temple and its personnel. The latter is represented by the figure of Simon, son of Yoḥanan, high priest from 219 to 196 BCE, who is depicted in rhapsodic poetry performing the daily sacrifice. Important to Ben Sira as well was reverence for the heroes of Israel's history, who are praised in an extensive encomium for their willingness to follow God's word and build Israel's institutions.

But this harmonious picture of a pious nation was not shared by all religious communities that formed in the wake of Hasmonaean rule. From Josephus as well as the Dead Sea Scrolls and later sources one can outline the main features of several of the sects and movements that flourished from the second century BCE to the fall of the Temple in 70 CE. One of the most important was the Pharisees, who are depicted in strikingly different ways in Josephus, the New Testament, and rabbinic literature. They are depicted by Josephus as a group that had much support among the general population and whose relationships with the ruling classes were unstable. The New Testament depicts them polemically as hypocritical intellectuals interested in the intricacies of ritual, especially ritual purity. The rabbis considered them their spiritual ancestors, sages who preserved traditions of Torah handed down from Moses, and defended them from heterodox sects such as the Sadducees. From these disparate portraits, a few commonalities emerge. The Pharisees held legal and ritual traditions that were not written down explicitly in Scripture, they counted priests and nonpriests in their ranks, and they were interested in extending purity rituals beyond the boundaries of the Temple and the officiating priests.

In rabbinic literature and in Josephus the opponents of the Pharisees are known as Sadducees. This term, which comes from the name of the priest Zadok (see *1 Kgs.* 1 and *Ez.* 40–48), designates a group that represented the families from which the high priests and principal officiants in the Temple were drawn. One can suppose that they represented the interests of the aristocratic priesthood and differed with the Pharisees on points of law. Josephus says that they did not believe in the resurrection of the dead.

The Sadducees left no texts, but the writings survive of another group that took Zadokite lineage seriously, the Qumran community, whose library was deposited in caves near the Dead Sea. This library, known as the Dead Sea Scrolls, tells about several things at once. The writings of the tightly organized community that preserved them yield a portrait of a sectarian eschatological community and its concerns. At the same time writings from what is now the biblical canon, apocryphal and pseudepigraphic literature, and liturgical poetry help round out the picture of the range of religious expressions in Greco-Roman Judea.

The Qumran community also demonstrates the growing prominence of two facets of Judaism: scripture as an object of interpretation and increasing concern with the eschatological future and the end results of historical process. This community, which may have been formed by Zadokite priests and their sympathizers who had been deprived of political power in the Temple establishment, formed soon after the Hasmonaean dynasty took hold. A legal epistle thought to be from the early history of the sect (the so-called halakhic letter or 4QMMT) suggests that the founders of the group split with the priestly establishment in Jerusalem over interpretations of Temple procedures and other legal and ritual issues. The group grew into a highly structured separatist sect that sought to live in accordance with its leaders' interpretations of Scripture. The most important function of this group, which saw itself as the true Israel, was to prepare its members for a future in which the forces of light, the sect and the angelic warriors, would fight on their behalf with the forces of darkness, the wicked nations of the world, Temple officials and priests whom they opposed, and the angels of darkness. For this purpose they were organized into a kind of Temple in exile, observed high standards of ritual purity, and held a liturgy in which they depicted the angels holding sacrifices in the heavenly camps in conjunction with their counterparts on earth.

Scripture, its interpretation, and the creation and preservation of new literary works were important facets of Qumran sectarian life. The sect developed the genre of *pesher,* in which a detail from a biblical book was taken to prophesy about current events. The sect also made innovations in interpretation of the laws of the Torah. For example, they extended the idea of ritual impurity to hold that an individual could be contaminated by committing such social transgressions as theft and false witness. These innovations were formed by a council of inspired interpreters *(moshav ha-Rabim),* whose founder was known as the "righteous teacher" *(moreh tzedek).*

In fact in this period one can locate what James Kugel has called "the rise of Scripture" (*Early Biblical Interpretation,* 1986). Although the Torah became the core of the Jewish canon by the Persian period, it was in the second and first centuries BCE that the canon began to coalesce and the interpretation of Scripture became a major issue. Writers composed works of "rewritten Bible," such as *Jubilees,* in which troublesome questions about biblical characters and concepts could be addressed through narrative. Rabbinic literature remembers the disputes between the Pharisees and the Sadducees as focused largely on differing interpretations of biblical law. The manuscripts found at Qumran include all books of the Jewish canon except for *Esther.*

From Qumran there are also examples in Hebrew and Aramaic of Jewish apocalyptic literature, a genre that otherwise would have survived largely in Greek translations and secondary translations into other languages of early Christendom. In this genre the secrets of the cosmos as well as the secrets of history are revealed to a human hero, usually a biblical figure such as Enoch or Ezra. The protagonist is often taken up to heaven and given a "guided tour" of its wonders. At this point the secrets of history are revealed to him by means of symbols that are interpreted by his heavenly guide. Usually these secrets not only demonstrate that the prior history of Israel has depended on a group of select pious people but that in the future there will be a day of reckoning when the forces of good, led by God and his armies, will defeat the forces of evil, on earth and in the supernatural realm. The genre may have its roots in Near Eastern wisdom tradition, in which cataloging the things that make up the cosmos played an important part. These works may also reflect dissatisfaction with the political and religious situation of the time, which, the writer implies, will be rectified in the time to come. The biblical book of *Daniel,* written during the crisis in the second century BCE that led to the Hasmonaean revolt, is an example of this genre.

Apocalyptic literature established certain ideas that were to influence esoteric and political trends in late antique and medieval Judaism: the idea that the boundaries between heaven and earth are permeable and the idea that history will end with a catastrophic battle between good and evil. The former idea survived in the literature of merkavah mysticism, which depicted rabbis ascending to heaven and gazing at the divine throne. Jewish apocalyptic literature influenced early Christian literature and was written occasionally in Hebrew well into the Middle Ages. Apocalyptic eschatology influences Jewish messianism even in the twenty-first century. Josephus, Philo (see below), and rabbinic literature also tell that there was an increasing diversity of opinion about the afterlife, a subject of no great importance to biblical writers. Whereas the Sadducees apparently did not believe in an afterlife, the Pharisees believed that at the end of time the dead would be resurrected. This became a central tenet of rabbinic Judaism.

The Greek-speaking Diaspora communities also left a literary legacy, which was forgotten by the rabbinic leaders in the Land of Israel but was preserved by the Christian community. Greco-Jewish works from the Hellenistic period include novelistic expansions of biblical works, such as *Joseph and Aseneth,* and apologetic works in the form of epistles, such as the *Letter of Aristeas,* and in the form of pseudepigrapha, such as the Sibylline Oracles. The Greek-speaking Jewish community in Egypt also produced the first major Jewish philosopher, Philo of Alexandria, who used middle Platonic metaphysics and Stoic allegorical hermeneutics to argue that the Torah was a supremely philosophical work.

When the Romans installed their own local officials in Judea in 6 CE, the political climate became more turbulent. While Herod, Rome's client king, had embarked on an elaborate building program that made Jerusalem and its magnificent Temple into one of the empire's great cities, oppressive taxation and dictatorial rule turned many against Rome. At the fringes of society, groups of zealots and dissenters advocated militant revolt against Rome and its Jewish representatives in Jerusalem; others took their promises of an imminent "kingdom of heaven" to small communities of followers. Most of these groups claimed that their leaders were the *mashiaḥ,* the righteous king foretold in the books of the prophets. Political enemies of the Roman order were often crucified, which most of the Jewish populace took as an indication that those individuals could not have been the victorious king to which those prophecies referred. However, two of those movements did carry dramatic consequences for the Jewish people and its religion. In 33 CE and the following decades one such movement, centered around Jesus of Nazareth, survived its leader's execution and went on to include non-Jews among its members, eventually forming the Christian community. In 66 CE another, more militant movement of zealots allied with other Jewish forces initiated a war against Rome that resulted in the destruction of Jerusalem and its Temple in 70 CE. In 132, another revolt against Rome led by Simon bar Kokhba broke out. It was repressed in 135 by the emperor Hadrian, who turned Jerusalem into a pagan city and renamed Judea Palestine.

THE DESTRUCTION OF THE TEMPLE AND THE RISE OF RABBINIC JUDAISM. Judaism as it is known in the early twenty-first century is largely a product of the first centuries after the destruction of the Temple in the Jewish revolt against Rome. It was following this event that many of the primary institutions, individual practices, values, and teleological underpinnings of classical Judaism were formed or refined. To be sure the defeat of the Jewish commonwealth by the Romans was a human catastrophe, but beyond the physical suffering it caused, it had profound religious and political significance. According to Jewish cultic theology, by which the Temple was the locus for God's presence on earth, the loss of that Temple meant the absence of that presence from the world. The Babylonian Talmud (b. *Bava Batra* 60b) paints a portrait of groups of first-century ascetics who abstained from meat and wine in mourning for the Temple. The apocryphal *Book of Baruch* reflects the response of apocalyptic communities that saw the cataclysm as a challenge to their eschatological expectations.

The centuries following the destruction of the Temple also saw the rise of the rabbinic movement. The Hebrew term *rabbi* means "my teacher" or "my master." In the New Testament, Jesus is occasionally addressed as rabbi, and the title appears as an honorific term in ancient inscriptions. In this discussion, however, the term *rabbi* refers to a class of leaders who came to define the character of Judaism for centuries to come. These scholars, who traced their heritage to the Pharisees, were not necessarily priests but laymen who held that by a life of study of the Torah, observance of the commandments, and ethical action the individual Jew could gain salvation in the form of resurrection in the messianic era. This system of everyday observance of a comprehensive system of sacred law, which came to be known as *halakhah,* depended on its constant teaching and refinement by masters—the rabbis—who considered their extrabiblical traditions to have been handed down as Torah from Sinai. These traditions came to be known as the Oral Torah.

The rabbis of late antiquity produced a series of texts and traditions that became a kind of second canon for Judaism. The Mishnah, compiled in 200 CE, sets forth rabbinic law and related matters in statements and formulae attributed to the sages of the Second Temple era and of the first two centuries CE. Whereas the rabbis considered rabbinic law to be based on Scripture, the Mishnah does not generally frame its laws as biblical commentary but rather states them in independent, apodictic form. Rabbinic study of the Mishnah resulted in the redaction of the great compendia of Mishnaic commentary, tradition, and lore known as the Talmuds. The Palestinian Talmud was redacted in the early fifth century and the Babylonian Talmud in the early sixth century.

The Babylonian Talmud became the source of legal decision, intense study, and reverence for most of the world Jewry in the Middle Ages and remains so for traditional Jews. As a result when people speak of "the Talmud," they are often referring to the Babylonian Talmud. The Talmud's commentary to the Mishnah is called the *Gemara'*. Besides commenting on the meaning and implications of the Mishnah's laws, the *Gemara'* discusses the relationship of the Mishnah to Scripture and extra-Mishnaic sources and includes tales of the sages, biblical exegesis, and folklore. While it is a commentary to the Mishnah, the *Gemara'* often takes the form of an ongoing conversation among sages, many of whom lived centuries apart from each other. This conversation is moderated, as it were, by an anonymous Aramaic text (called the *stam*) that can take the role of a skeptical observer, asking questions regarding opinions presented, pointing out contradictions and logical inconsistencies, and arranging source materials for comparison. This method of presentation can be considered a kind of dialectical argumentation about traditional sources for exegetical purposes.

Rabbinic scriptural exegesis, called midrash, found its way into compilations that were completed from the fourth century to the early Middle Ages. These compilations contain specific elucidations of the biblical text but also include postbibical legends, homilies, and discourses on biblical themes. Some of these were close readings of legal texts from the Torah *(midrash halakhah),* and others were more homiletical and narrative *(midrash aggadah).* In midrash one can occasionally find elements of the sort of theological speculation that might appear in systematic philosophical treatises in other cultures.

If one takes the Mishnah as the first systematic statement of rabbinic Judaism, one finds several striking ways in which it seems a departure from forms of Judaism that flourished in the Second Temple period. The first unit, or Mishnah, of the text, tractate *Berakhot* (Blessings) 1:1, indicates to the reader that new actions, notions of authority, and interests are in play:

> From what time is the Shema' recited in the evening? From the time when the priests enter to eat of their *terumah* [a portion of the harvest donated to the priests] until the end of the first watch. These are the words of Rabbi Eliezer. But the Sages say, Until midnight. Rabban Gamliel says: Until the rise of dawn.

The form of the passage and its social implications deserve mention. It begins with a question, which is answered immediately after. But this answer itself contains a detail—the end of the period when the Shema may be recited—that does not go unchallenged. What follows is a three-way controversy in which Rabbi Eliezer and Rabban Gamliel seem to stand against the entire community of sages. The Mishnah then conveys a sense of multivocality as well as the impression that revelation is a matter of dialectic. When one turns to the subject matter, one notices that the passage refers to rituals that would be understood by the rabbinic Jew if not the outsider. The Shemaʿ is the recitation of the declaration of God's unity in *Deuteronomy* 6:4 and accompanying scriptural passages. It is an essential part of the statutory liturgy for the individual (at least for men) in the evening and morning. Whereas the text to be recited is from the written Scriptures, the commandment to recite it in prayer is not. Indeed the whole tractate *Berakhot,* which specifies the order of prayers to be said on a daily basis, presupposes whole spheres of ritual law not anticipated in the Bible. The same can be said for such rituals as the lighting of candles and blessing of wine on the Sabbath. The Mishnah then relies on whole areas of law, such as rituals and regulations for the Sabbath, expansions of the dietary laws of *Leviticus* 11 and *Deuteronomy* 14, and procedures for marriage and divorce, that are not set out explicitly in Scripture.

It is therefore obvious that rabbinic Judaism relies on sources other than the written Bible for its authority and way of life. But at the same time it considers itself to be acting out God's will as expressed in the Torah. The argument for this authority is made most eloquently in the opening passage of the tractate *Avot,* "Fathers," a kind of manifesto of early rabbinic Judaism: "Moses received Torah from Sinai, and handed it down to Joshua, and Joshua to the Elders, and the Elders to the Prophets, and the Prophets handed it down to the Men of the Great Assembly" (M. *Avot* 1:1).

The text goes on to introduce the sayings by sages of the Great Assembly and continues with statements of a succession of sages until the later generations. This myth is a dramatic illustration of the idea of tradition. Revelation is not given anew to each sage or generation. Rather, it has come to Israel from Moses and has been transmitted through the succession of masters and disciples. Yet the Torah is not simply a document passed from one pair of hands to another. It is associated with a process by which the Torah's wisdom is elaborated by each successive generation. Human agency and wisdom thus play an essential role in the rabbinic theory of revelation. But more than that, since the agency is that of a succession of sages, this wisdom is cumulative. This distinguishes the rabbinic mode from the apocalyptic, in which the revelation is given by an angel to an individual, who is then charged to write it in a book that is made available to the community. By its inclusion of the sages from Moses to the later rabbis in its account of the transmission of Torah, *Avot* reinforces the authority of the rabbinic class. But this tractate does more than legitimize the rabbis. It sets the tone for a type of Judaism in which the act of study, epitomized by memorizing the words of the sages, becoming their disciple and watching their actions, and acting out those teachings in everyday activities, becomes a primary form of worship.

Returning to the first Mishnah in *Berakhot,* one also notices a curious historical dimension. The Mishnah was redacted in around 200 CE, 130 years after the Temple was destroyed and about 65 years after a revolt against Rome in 132–135 CE resulted in severe repression of Jewish teaching and rituals. Yet the Temple, where the priests enter to eat of their contributed produce, is alluded to in the present tense. In fact fully one-third of the Mishnah (the divisions of purities, holy things [covering sacrificial law], and some portions of tractates dealing with Passover and other rituals) concern the Temple and its rituals and laws. There are a few possible explanations for this anomaly. One is that the Mishnah is a utopian document, drawing an ideal picture of a redeemed society in which the Temple is restored and the sages have ultimate jurisdiction over their performance of the rituals. Another, proposed by Jacob Neusner, is that the framers of the Mishnah wished to assure the community that had endured historical catastrophe that life could go on as if that catastrophe had changed nothing. One must also remember that in the beginning of the third century sacrifice and sacrificial institutions were the norm and not the exception in the Mediterranean. It may simply have been inconceivable to describe a ritual and legal system without including the description of a Temple.

Yet for the rabbis the proper substitute for sacrifice was not to be found in the concept of sacred space but in sacred actions. Yoḥanan ben Zakkʾai, one of the founders of the rabbinic movement, is said to have declared, "We have another means of atonement, effective as Temple Sacrifice. It is deeds of loving kindness." Other statements assert that the study of sacrificial law, enshrined in the Mishnah and related sources, was equivalent to the performance of those sacrifices. Prayer in the synagogue was also considered to be a form of sacrifice. A famous rabbinic statement (y. *Ber.* 4:1 [7a]) declares prayer to be "the sacrifice in the heart" *(Avodah ba-Lev).* According to the Palestinian Talmud, when a prayer leader was called upon to begin the prayer service, the congregation would call, "Perform our sacrifice" (y. *Ber.* 4:4 [8b]).

The shift from a culture of sacrificial worship to one of prayer was part of a larger phenomenon: the shift from an emphasis on collective religious action to greater attention to individual religious action. To be sure the rabbis maintained a strong sense that the community of Israel was obliged to carry out its terms of the covenant and that it would be rewarded in the messianic future with the nation's return to the Land of Israel under divine sovereignty and the rebuilding of the Temple. At the same time rabbinic Judaism was structured around the idea that each individual was obliged to perform certain individual religious commandments, called *mitsvot,* by which he or she would gain merit. (While women had a place in this system, they were not held to the same specific *mitsvot* and were largely excluded from participation in the public dimensions of rabbinic life.) That merit would earn that individual resurrection in the messianic era or "world to come." Thus such actions as saying blessings before wine and bread, wearing phylacteries *(tefillin),* and giving to the poor functioned in several ways. They constituted *mitsvot* that contributed to salvation; they served as acts of witnessing God's sovereignty on earth; and they could be considered as bringing something of the divine presence to earth, an idea that Max Kadushin called "normal mysticism." Indeed there are statements in the Talmud that "wherever two speak words of Torah together, the Shekhinah [the indwelling presence of God] hovers over them." Such statements are an indication that some rabbis' conceptions of the divine presence had shifted from one that was localized and required special conditions to one that could be manifest in subtle ways at any place.

In pursuit of the proper way to carry out the *mitsvot,* the rabbis developed or codified significant innovations in ritual and civil law. For example, the dietary laws *(kashrut)* of *Leviticus* 11 and *Deuteronomy* 14 specify the animals that may and may not be eaten. In addition biblical law (*Ex.* 23:19, 34:26; *Dt.* 14:21) prohibits boiling a kid in its mother's milk. The rabbis interpreted this verse to mean that mixing any meat and milk products, including fowl, was prohibited (see M. *Hul.* 8:1). Other innovations addressed prohibition of carrying beyond the household on the Sabbath by allowing a community to construct a temporary boundary *(eruv)* that effectively turned an entire city into one household. *(M. Eruv.)*

In the sphere of civil legislation, rabbinic law codified the use of a marriage contract *(ketubah)* that specified the property rights of each party in the case of divorce. Rabbinic society did not deviate radically from the patriarchal norms of the Greco-Roman world. However, in the rabbinic legal system women were given a circumscribed set of rights and protections. One the one hand women are legally dependent on men when their status is that of daughters and wives. However, they gain their independence in the event of the death of the husband or divorce and therefore are granted full economic status in those circumstances.

The rabbis sought to expand their influence on the Jewish populations of Palestine and Babylonia through a system of courts governed by rabbinic law. It is not known to what extent the influence of this system took hold, but it was helped by the close alliance of the local Jewish authority, called the patriarch *(nasi),* with the rabbis. This was accompanied by a growing network of disciple circles and academies *(yeshivot),* which produced a form of dialectical reasoning preserved in the Talmuds.

Other spheres of cultural production intersected with the rabbinic class and were influenced by it. The synagogue emerged as an important institution during this period, particularly in Palestine. The synagogue (both the Greek word and the Hebrew term *bet kenesset* mean "place of assembly") began in the Second Temple period primarily as a place for study (although in the Diaspora synagogues were often called *proseuchē,* places for prayer). However, with the Temple in ruins, the synagogue became the primary locus for worship. There were many conceptual and practical differences between the Temple and the synagogue. Unlike the Temple, a synagogue could be built practically anywhere and could be of any size. Its space was not delineated as sacred in the same way as the Temple's. Whereas only priests were allowed to enter certain precincts of the Temple, nonpriests were allowed anywhere in the synagogue. (It is not clear to what extent women were allowed to participate; there is evidence for women being leaders of some Diaspora synagogues, although rabbinic literature specifies no liturgical or social role for women in the synagogue. Although the rabbis saw prayer as the "sacrifice of the heart," no animal sacrifice took place in the synagogue. Prayer could be led by any male Jew of the age of majority as long as he was fluent in the liturgy. By the sixth century CE synagogues, especially in the Galilee, had become prominent buildings decorated with fine sculptural stonework and colorful mosaics depicting central themes in Judaism's sacred lore.

The liturgy of the early synagogue has survived in the form of the liturgies of Jewish communities and in the form of manuscripts of prayer literature from the Middle Ages. In the ancient synagogue prayers were composed by prayer leaders who were considered to be representatives of the community and who improvised the texts of the prayers around rubrics predetermined by *halakhah.* In these prayers they expressed themes that were emphasized less in Talmudic literature, including the longing for the messianic era, the need for rain and prosperity, and the idea that Israel's patriarchs have accumulated merit *(zekhut avot)* on which the community can draw to plead for God's favor. In addition a substantial literature of liturgical poetry, known as *piyyut* (from the Greek *poetes*) flourished from the fourth to the seventh century. This ornate, allusive genre of synagogue poetry, composed by authors such as Yose ben Yose and Yanna'i, whose artistry earned them fame in Palestinian synagogues, served to embellish the standard liturgy with its recondite language, alliteration and acrostics, and references to themes popular among preachers and storytellers of the time. It is not known how closely the synagogue and the rabbinic school *(bet midrash)* were related. Synagogue literature and iconography draw on rabbinic midrash and law, but there are some interesting departures in emphasis and details. Most likely there were synagogues in which the community did not necessarily identify closely with the rabbinic movement, such as the synagogue in Sepphoris, which seems to reflect priestly interests, and others that did, such as the synagogue in Rechov in the northern Galilee, where passages from the Palestinian Talmud were used for the mosaic floor.

Other forms of Jewish religious behavior and literature from this period have come down from archaeological and manuscript sources. A corpus of Hebrew and Aramaic texts tells stories of how great rabbis, such as Rabbi Akiba and Rabbi Ishmael, ascended to heaven. In these texts the rabbinic heroes travel arduously through seven "palaces" or *hekhalot,* warding off the fierce angelic guardians, and finally reach the divine throne, which is conceived, in the manner of the visions of *Isaiah* 6 and *Ezekiel* 1, as a great chariot (merkavah) on which God is seated, surrounded by an angelic choir. The texts then state that anyone who fulfills the moral and ritual requirements for ascent may do the same. Other texts in this corpus give recipes for conjuring an angel known as the Prince of the Torah *(Sar ha-Torah),* who will impart to any man a prodigious memory and make him a great rabbi. Gershom Scholem, the founder of the modern study of Jewish mysticism, saw its authors as mystics who cultivated visions of the heavens and recorded their experiences as narrative and hymnology.

These texts were not written by the rabbis to whom they were attributed, but who their authors were is still a matter of debate. Most likely they were Jews who stood outside the rabbinic elite but shared some of its values. This literature is closely related to another corpus that is well attested in writings from this period: the literature of early Jewish magic. From ancient Palestine and its environs about three dozen amulets written on silver, lead, and copper foil survive. These amulets are formulaic incantations in Hebrew, Aramaic, and Jewish Greek adjuring angels and demons for such purposes as healing, love, and protection. A far larger corpus—indeed the single largest corpus of Jewish inscriptions from late antiquity—consists of hundreds of clay bowls found in the Mesopotamian region (Jewish Babylonia) on which Aramaic incantations are written. In these artifacts Jews address their daily needs by invoking divine power to command the intermediaries, using the powerful name of God as their authorization and weapon. The rabbis too believed in angels and demons and in the efficacy of magic, but these practitioners seem to have operated outside of their jurisdiction.

MEDIEVAL JUDAISM. If late antiquity represents a formative period for classical Judaism, the Middle Ages represents the period of its consolidation and expansion. It was in this period, beginning with the rise of Islam in the seventh and eighth centuries CE, that rabbinic Judaism spread through the influence of Talmudic academies and legal authorities to the Jewish population of the Diaspora. It was also in this period that new forms of discourse, especially philosophy and mysticism, took hold as significant ways of expressing Jewish religiosity.

By the ninth century a majority of Jews lived in the Diaspora. Jewish communities were scattered throughout the Mediterranean and the Middle East, especially Iran, Iraq, and North Africa, and had begun to form in western and central Europe. Both regions were dominated by the religions, Islam and Christianity, that saw Judaism as their precursors. This was an ambiguous legacy. On the one hand the Judaic heritage of both religions offered possibilities for dialogue and influence. Christianity was monotheistic; revered Hebrew Scriptures, which it accepted into its canon as the Old Testament; and held that Jesus was the Jewish Messiah. Islam made monotheism a central tenet of faith; understood Jewish biblical heroes, such as Abraham and Moses, to be prophetic forerunners to Muḥammad; and saw Ishmael as its progenitor. At the same time both religions considered themselves to have superceded Judaism with superior revelation and means to salvation. In particular Christianity saw Jews as having rejected the kingship of Jesus and therefore subject to rebuke or worse. Islam, which considers Jews and Christians to be "People of the Book," granted Jews and Christians the status of protected minorities *(dhimmī),* which assured them physical security while preventing them from attaining full status in Muslim society. Christianity since Augustine had developed a theology of tolerance of Jews. However, in practice Jewish communities could be welcomed into Christian lands or persecuted by Christian rulers, depending on the political and religious circumstances. So too in Islamic countries both the principles of subordinate status and tolerance were honored in the breach as well as in the observance.

The transformation of the southern Mediterranean into an Islamic region had deep consequences for Judaism. With the Muslim Empire centered in Baghdad in the eighth century, the political center of Jewry also shifted to Iraq—Jewish Babylonia—where a thriving Talmudic culture had produced a class of rabbinic scholars and legislators located in *yeshivot* in Baghdad. These eventually set the religious and halakhic agenda for Jewish communities, making rabbinic law the prevailing legal system throughout the Islamic world. This hegemony did not go unchallenged. Beginning in the eighth century a movement called Karaism opposed the authority of the Talmud and the rabbinic class, insisting on independent inquiry and a reading of the biblical text unmediated by Rabbinic interpretation. This movement gained a substantial following in Egypt, Palestine, and other Jewish communities before the eleventh century, and although the Karaite community is a small minority within Jewry, it still exists. The consolidation of rabbinic authority resulted in an increasing tendency toward disseminating legal rulings and toward legal codification. This took the form of halakhic epistles (responsa), Talmud commentaries, and eventually independent legal codes such as the *Mishneh Torah* of Moses Maimonides.

The first Muslim centuries were also a period of great cultural ferment. Islam's emphasis on the Qur'ān and its language brought with it intensive Arabic and scriptural study. Translations of Greek philosophical works brought philosophical concepts and methods into dialogue with Islamic monotheism. Mystical and pietistic movements sought direct experience of the divine. Judaism in the Islamic sphere was profoundly affected by these developments as well. Although philosophy had been introduced to the Hellenistic Jewish community of Alexandria through Philo, he left no mark on rabbinic Judaism in Palestine and Babylonia. However, in the intellectual environment of Islam in the ninth and tenth centuries, Jewish philosophy took hold for the first time. Jewish philosophy had begun largely as a way of defending rabbinic Judaism from freethinkers and Karaites who challenged rabbinic ways of thinking. However, by the eleventh century in Babylonia and Spain philosophical training and inquiry had become much more sophisticated. Moreover internal considerations impelled philosophical thinking among a Jewish elite in the Muslim world, especially in Spain from the tenth to the twelfth centuries. The prosperity of Spanish urban society during this period fostered the rise of intellectual classes dedicated to the ideal of *adab,* an Arabic term for proper social behavior and education. The *adib,* the cultured Mediterranean gentleman, had a profession such as law, trade, or medicine; acquired a traditional education, in the case of the Jewish *adib* in Bible, Talmud, and Hebrew grammar; learned to write sacred and secular poetry in Arabic or Hebrew; and also received a scientific education, which included philosophy. Philosophy in this period took on a particularly cosmopolitan tone. The Jewish philosopher Shelomoh ibn Gabirol (1020–1057) wrote *The Fountain of Life,* which was eventually translated into Latin though the original Arabic was lost. For centuries scholars debated whether it had been written by a Muslim, a Christian, or a Jew. Philosophy was designed not only to stimulate the religious thinking of these intellectuals but to protect them from religious doubt. Philosophy thus brought with it an ambivalence to Jewish tradition. On the one hand it strengthened concepts such as monotheism, the soul, and religious discipline. On the other hand it left open questions of whether biblical stories and traditional lore stood up to the rigorous demands of philosophical reasoning.

The philosophical patterns that prevailed during this period were influenced by several trends from the previous few centuries. From the *kalām* came the idea that God's unity was absolute; from Neoplatonism came the notion that creation was a process of emanation from a pure, spiritual, infinite God to physical matter; and from Aristotelianism came the idea of God as the unknowable unmoved mover. The greatest and most eloquent exponent of Jewish philosophy was Moses Maimonides (1135/8–1204), a physician and legal authority who was born in Spain but spent his adulthood in Egypt. Maimonides not only wrote philosophical works of great depth but attempted to codify philosophical principles in his monumental manual of *halakhah,* the *Mishneh Torah.* The tractate that begins that work, the *Book of Knowledge,* holds that it is a primary *mitzvah* to believe that God is one, unchangeable, and that he possesses no bodily form. Furthermore because God is unchangeable and not dependent on any other being, he cannot be affected by human action or prayer. These principles, formulated in elegantly rabbinic Hebrew, were notable as well for their departure from prephilosophical Jewish conceptions of God and his relationship with the world. The anthropomorphism familiar to readers of biblical and rabbinic literature gives way to a concept of a God who is utterly abstract and formless. For Maimonides as well prayer and the *mitsvot* are forms of religious discipline essential to the education of the moral person rather than direct interactions with a God who responds to the individual by guaranteeing salvation personally. The purpose of Judaism is to produce the ideal individual, the prophet, who achieves consummate knowledge of God through philosophical contemplation.

The medieval Jewish philosophical tradition ebbed by the fifteenth century, especially with the expulsion of Jews from Spain. Although some works continued to be read, medieval Jewish philosophy was largely rediscovered by nineteenth-century German Jewish scholars who saw in it antecedents for their own rationalism. It has therefore continued to be of interest not only to intellectual historians but to modern Jewish thinkers such as Hermann Cohen, Abraham Joshua Heschel, and Joseph B. Soloveitchik. But the most lasting effect of medieval Jewish philosophy has been the idea of Jewish philosophy. The idea that Judaism can be examined and explained through the same methods used to address other philosophical issues lies behind much influential Jewish thought of contemporary time.

Jewish philosophy, however, did not affect the majority of medieval Jews, who continued to live by the way of life, rituals, sacred stories, and forms of piety of prephilosophical Judaism. Fortunately a good deal of information about medieval Jewish culture in the Mediterranean is accessible thanks to the discovery a century ago of the Cairo Genizah, a storehouse of discarded Jewish manuscripts that contains everything from autographed letters from Maimonides to children's writing exercises. From the Genizah one can reconstruct a portrait of Jews as individuals and as communities steeped in biblical language and lore, looking up to Talmudic scholars for guidance and legal redress, concerned enough about divine disposition to their fate to take part in the Jewish magical tradition, and devoted to the life of the synagogue.

By the twelfth century another form of Jewish thought was taking shape in southern France and northern Spain among small groups of intellectuals and pietists that stressed the mystical contemplation of the divine nature. This form of mysticism picked up threads of esoteric lore and philosophy that had been circulating in the Mediterranean in the early Middle Ages and fused it with the Neoplatonic cosmology of medieval philosophy. Its adherents held that this form of mysticism had been passed down through esoteric tradition along with the exoteric Torah. They thus gave this form of religiosity the name *Qabbalah,* "tradition."

In the late thirteenth century qabbalistic literary creativity flourished in Spain, where speculative and richly symbolic writings were being produced. Moses de Leon, aided perhaps by some of his close associates, wrote a massive mystical commentary to the Torah called the *Zohar,* or Book of Enlightenment, which eventually became the most revered Jewish text after the Bible and the Talmud. The qabbalists were concerned about some of the effects of the new Maimonidean philosophy. If God did not need human prayer and virtue, they reasoned, what motivation would they have to do the *mitsvot*? If human beings can attribute no positive characteristics to God, as the Aristotelian Jewish philosophers had argued, how can God be worshiped meaningfully? For Maimonides, the love of God consisted of the wonder and awe that struck the enlightened devotee upon contemplation of the facts of God's creation and sustaining vitality. However, the qabbalists insisted that God did in fact have positive attributes that could be known by the person who understood how they were encoded in Scripture.

The qabbalah therefore developed a complex symbolic system in which God's attributes were unveiled in a process of ten emanations *(sefirot)* of the divine vitality from his infinite unknowable essence *(En Sof)* to his final manifestation *(Shekhinah)*. The idea of the *sefirot* emerged as a highly effective way of expressing divine attributes. They could be understood as parts of a divine body, as colors, as metaphysical principles, as cognitive and emotional facets of God's personality, and as letters of the divine name. For the *Zohar,* the Torah is not simply a book of stories and laws but an intricately coded treasury of mystical secrets, a kind of autobiography of God's manifestation of himself. The sefirotic system also addressed an important philosophical problem in an ingenious way. According to the philosophers, one could no longer conceive of God anthropomorphically. Maimonides considered the anthropomorphic language of the Bible to be an accommodation to the limitations of the human imagination; thus the expression "the hand of God" was a figurative way of speaking of divine power, which makes for all reality. The qabbalists likewise did not think of God as having a physical, anthropomorphic form. Rather, the "body of God" was the arrangement of the *sefirot.* Thus the right arm of God stood for the *sefirah* of supernatural mercy *(Ḥesed)* and so on. That hand was not merely a metaphor using the human hand as a symbol for a divine attribute—it was the real, supernal arm, the original to which the human arm, modeled in God's image, referred. In addition the Qabbalah introduced a new dimension of gender to the idea of God. The divine body was described as possessing male and female sides and male and female anatomy. Relationships between those male and female aspects were likened to the longing of men and women for each other. In the premessianic era God's male and female aspects were in exile from each other, only to be reunited in the age to come.

By contemplating the lower world, by searching the Scriptures, and by ecstatic contemplation, the qabbalist sought to gain a direct experience of the inner life of the godhead. At the same time qabbalists believed that knowledge of the inner workings of the *sefirot* enabled the mystics to draw down divine power for their own spiritual and material benefit. There was also an explicitly ecstatic dimension to the Qabbalah, epitomized especially by Abraham Abulafia, who instead of the theory of the *sefirot* developed such techniques as contemplation of Hebrew names and letter combinations with the goal of reaching the state of prophecy.

The resilience of this system is attested by the growth of Qabbalah from a small circle of mystics in the twelfth and thirteenth centuries to its prominence as a form of Jewish theology in the later medieval period and early modern period. With the expulsion of the Jews from Christian Spain in 1492, the Qabbalah spread to exiled communities in North Africa, Turkey, and Palestine. In the town of Safed in Palestine in the sixteenth century charismatic teachers such as Isaac Luria redrew the Qabbalah's cosmology and eschatology to construct a system whereby the individual, through the performance of a *mitzvah* fortified by meditation on divine names, could bring redemption and repair the broken pieces of the divine body. This system, which offered the worshiper a powerful motivation to perform the commandments, was popularized in subsequent centuries and is still deeply influential, especially in Middle Eastern Jewish communities. Through the Hasidic movement, the principal Jewish mystical movement of modern times, through modern scholarship, and through contemporary interest in mysticism, the Qabbalah continues to affect Jewish thought and practice.

Smaller Jewish communities existed in northern and central Europe from the ninth century, when they had been invited by Charlemagne to participate in the economy of the new empire. Longstanding communities were established in France and Germany, called Ashkenaz in Hebrew (a name that came to designate all of northern, central, and eastern European Jewry). However, with the crusades in the eleventh and twelfth centuries, relations between Jews and Christians took a turn for the worse. The massacres of Jews by crusading armies and Christian mobs and expulsions by local rulers left a deep imprint on these communities. Bitter poetic laments were written, describing how Jewish victims of these riots chose to martyr themselves and their families "for the sake of sanctifying the divine Name" (*ʿal qiddush ha-Shem*). However, there were also long periods of quiet if tense coexistence. Scholars are increasingly finding evidence of dialogue and mutual influence, both positive and negative, between European Christians and Jews.

The Ashkenazic communities distinguished themselves particularly in two areas of culture. The first was textual study. The region produced important schools of biblical exegesis. The most famous exegete of this community was a French scholar from Troyes named Shelomoh ben Yitsḥaq (1040–1105), known by the acronym Rashi. Rashi pioneered a type of terse, incisive biblical interpretation that focused on the *peshat,* or contextual ("plain") meaning of the text. His use of rabbinic midrash was highly selective, intended to draw out contradictions and nuances in the biblical text itself. Rashi's commentary is still an indispensable component of traditional study of the Torah. Rashi applied similar methods to his monumental Talmud commentary, which is still printed alongside of the Talmud text in nearly every edition. Rashi's method in his Talmud commentary was to draw out the essence of each position in the debates that constituted the main subject of the Talmud texts, without taking a clear position on the issue being discussed.

Rashi's grandson Yaʿaqov ben Meʾir Tam and his contemporaries pioneered a more wide-ranging and daring method of exegesis, which sought to probe each piece of the Talmud text for every possible internal contradiction and connection with other areas of the text. Over the next two centuries their successors compiled the work of several generations of this school of exegesis into "supplemental" commentaries *(Tosafot),* one of which is now printed opposite Rashi's in traditional editions of the Talmud. This method of exegesis was accompanied by a great deal of *halakhic* innovation, a trend encouraged by the structure of the Ashkenazic communities, which were more decentralized than the contemporary Spanish and Middle Eastern communities. Research suggests that this time and place saw an increasing textualization of Judaism, that is, it was the written text and its implications more than the way of life practiced by sages that came to determine how the law was shaped and followed.

A second important religious development of the early Ashkenazic community was one that affected a small group of elite Jewish scholars in twelfth- to thirteenth-century Germany. This group, called the German pietists or *Ḥaside Ashkenaz,* drew on a spiritual heritage that included the creation of liturgical poetry and collection of esoteric and magical lore. This group cultivated a type of austere pietism characterized on the one hand by the willingness to speculate on the mystical implications of the magical and visionary traditions of the Talmudic period and on the other hand an insistence on supererogatory discipline and punishment as a form of spiritual purification.

EARLY MODERN AND MODERN JUDAISM. It can be said that the changes to Judaism wrought by modernity were no less drastic than those wrought by the destruction of the Temple in the first century. By the twentieth century several conditions of Jewry were no longer valid. Jews were no longer living in autonomous communities governed by local Jewish leaders under the control of non-Jewish governments. In many countries Jews had full rights as citizens along with their non-Jewish neighbors. *Halakhah,* including civil law, was no longer binding on Jews. Jews were not exclusively religious; in several countries it was possible to abandon belief in God and still consider oneself a Jew. Many who were religious no longer saw themselves as carrying out an unchanging, sacred way of life that went back to God's revelation to Moses at Mount Sinai but as a religion in which they themselves could be agents of change. Finally, it was possible to leave the Jewish community entirely without converting to another religion—what sociologists and community leaders alike have come to call "assimilation." By the second half of the twentieth century two other radical changes had taken place. European Jewry was no longer a large part of the world's Jewish population, having been all but exterminated by Nazi Germany. There was also a Jewish state, Israel, with a democratically elected government, an army, and a national language, modern Hebrew.

These changes, however, did not come to all Jewish communities at the same time. For a small group of elite Jews in Germany, modernization came with the Enlightenment in the late eighteenth century, when liberal intellectuals contemplated giving Jews equal rights. For eastern European Jews, glimmers of modernity could be sensed in the eighteenth century, but several of its defining ingredients—science, secularism, liberalism and socialism, and nationalism—came only with the end of the nineteenth century. For Jews in the Muslim world, modernity was a product of colonialism, as it was to their Muslim neighbors. The nineteenth and twentieth centuries were also periods of great Jewish migration, from Europe to America (and prewar Palestine) and from the Middle East and North Africa to Israel.

It is difficult to say in what ways the tremors of the Enlightenment shaking western Europe were felt by the Jews living in Russia, Poland, and the Ukraine in the eighteenth century. But an important movement did change the nature of Judaism in those regions. Jewish communities at this time were still self-governed. The elite's authority rested on a network of *yeshivot* that stressed a rigorously intellectual approach to Talmud study. While this leadership accepted the principles of Qabbalah and revered the *Zohar,* mystical experience was not a priority. In this atmosphere Jewish healers and preachers flourished. Some of them were known as *baʿale shem,* masters of the (divine) name, that is, experts in the names of God that the magical tradition uses to achieve its ends. One of these figures, Rabbi Yisraʾel ben Eliʿezer (1700–1760), was known as the Good Master of the Name or Master of the Good Name, the Baʿal Shem Tov. He inspired a movement of spiritual revivalism whose adherents were known as Hasidim, "the pious" (this movement is not to be confused with Ashkenazic Ḥasidism, the pietistic movement of early medieval Germany described above). The movement spread, initially under the leadership of Dov Ber the Maggid of Mezhirich and then under charismatic leaders known as *tsaddiqim,* throughout eastern Europe.

Hasidism has been characterized, especially in the popular imagination, as an outpouring of simple religious enthusiasm, celebrated by singing, dancing, and heartfelt prayer. This image belies the complex theology and symbolism that Hasidic leaders developed in speculative writings as well as in stories and sermons. Hasidism took the qabbalistic ideas in new directions. Hasidic thinkers adopted a panentheistic approach to God's relationship with the world; that is, the universe existed within the infinitude of God's vitality and only existed in and of itself because of God's decision to create a boundary between himself and his creation. The earlier Lurianic Qabbalah had also argued that God needed to contract himself in order to create the world. But that movement presupposed a transcendent God who is apart from creation. Hasidism's notion of God was far more imminent. For Hasidism the human soul also carries within itself a model of the divine personality, and if one brings those inner *sefirot* to consciousness, it is possible to cleave to God. This process of attachment to the divine essence, known as *devequt,* is the constant goal of the Hasid. For the Hasidic movement, all actions—study, eating, prayer, and song—have the potential to raise the individual to a state of *devequt.* While the Hasidic leaders were usually well educated, studied Talmud, and were dedicated to *halakhah,* they also sought to address elements of the populace who did not have access to the elite centers of learning. They did so through the charismatic appeal of the *tsaddiqim,* through an emphasis on achieving *devequt* through everyday actions, and through skillfully wrought stories celebrating the Hasidic leadership and its way of life.

Another important dimension of the Hasidic movement was how it dealt with the longing for the messianic age that has characterized Judaism since the rabbinic period and that becomes especially potent in times of crisis. A century earlier the Jewish world had been convulsed by the failure of a popular messianic movement surrounding Shabbetai Tsevi. In the person of the *tsaddiq,* the Hasidim found a figure that took up something of Shabbetai's role of intervening between the ordinary man and God's will to redemption. Yet for most of the Hasidic movement, the *tsaddiq* was not the messiah himself but an extraordinarily endowed man who might one day "force the hand" of God to bring redemption. The Hasidic movement thrives in modern times, although most of its original population was decimated in the Holocaust. Several branches of Hasidism are known for their traditionalism, seeking to preserve the Hasidic way of life by maintaining their communal institutions and schools, ways of dress, and tightly knit social structures. However, the movement has also been influential. Hasidic thought has formed an important foundation for the theologies of modern Jewish thinkers such as Martin Buber, Abraham Joshua Heschel, and Arthur Green. In addition the Lubavitch movement, under the direction of Menachem Schneerson (1902–1994), initiated a major outreach effort after World War II to bring unaffiliated and non-Orthodox Jews into the Hasidic way of life.

In western Europe and the Western Hemisphere modernity affected Judaism more directly and with permanent consequences. Enlightenment thinkers in emerging modern states, especially Germany and France, argued that Jews should be granted full rights of citizenship. Eventually those states did relax restrictions on the personal, political, and professional rights of Jews. However, this came at the price of Jewish autonomy. It was a price that many Jews were willing to pay, and in Jewish intellectual circles in Germany, declarations of loyalty to the state could be heard. Modernization also meant that modern ways of thinking, such as individualism, liberalism, and science, could influence Jewish thought. Many Jews in Europe sought to change Judaism itself in a conscious way. Thus began the Reform movement in Germany in the second decade of the nineteenth century. The movement was begun by small circles of rabbis and laypeople and became a significant feature of Jewish life in Germany (and to a lesser extent in Britain, where it was called Liberal Judaism). Eventually it spread to the United States, where it grew exponentially in the atmosphere of almost unlimited religious freedom that Jews experienced there.

The goal of the Reform movement was to refashion Judaism into a religion that could take its place alongside the (post-Reformation) Christianity of its day, a religion that would also make sense to the growing numbers of Jews entering modern European society, speaking German, and acquiring a scientific and humanistic education. The Reformers declared that the Talmud and *halakhah* were no longer binding, that Jewish rituals, practices, and liturgy had to be remodeled to suit modern sensibilities, and that the Jews did not constitute a national group. To these ends they promoted changes in basic practices, doing away with aspects of traditional Jewish law, introducing prayers in the vernacular of the secular society, and applying historical methods of studying Judaism and Hebrew literature. At the same time Reform Judaism saw itself as carrying out a divine mission to spread ethical monotheism to the world and to use the freedom granted the Jewish people to carry out principles of social justice in the public sphere. The movement rejected the idea of a personal messiah, hoping instead for an ideal future when, as an American Reform prayer-book put it, "unbelief shall disappear and error be no more."

This movement did not go unopposed. A group of modernized Jews committed to *halakhah* argued that it was still possible to participate in modern society and observe Jewish law at the same time. The Orthodox movement, founded in the early nineteenth century in response to the Reform movement, took as its motto *Torah im derekh erets,* that is, full observance and study of the traditional Torah combined with a worldly occupation and demeanor. Thus, they argued, it was possible to wear modern clothes as long as one's head was covered according to tradition, to hold a job as a doctor or a lawyer, to observe Sabbath the way *halakhah* demanded, and to marry or divorce according to the dictates of Jewish civil law.

A third alternative was proposed by Zacharias Frankel (1801–1875), who founded Historical Judaism. For Frankel and subsequently for the Conservative movement in the United States, Judaism was best understood as a historical and national group. The preservation of Jewish culture and heritage was an essential goal of modern Judaism. Historical and Conservative Judaism held to the structure and centrality of the *halakhah.* However, halakhic change was permissible under controlled circumstances. Halakhic decision-making in the Conservative movement took into account modern scholarly textual criticism and the historical context of a legal issue, as well as changing circumstances. The movement grew in the United States with the mass immigration of Jews in the early twentieth century from eastern Europe. This community, unlike the German Jews who had formed Reform congregations in the mid-nineteenth century, were comfortable with the traditional liturgy and practices, but wanted the freedom of mixed seating and a more open approach to halakhah. One leader of the Conservative movement, Mordecai Kaplan, inspired by American pragmatism and twentieth-century social theory, broke with the theism and traditionalism of the movement and placed Jewish peoplehood at the absolute center of Judaism as a religion. For Kaplan, the collective spirit of Judaism, which he defined as an "evolving religious civilization," was the guiding force; personalistic and particularistic definitions of God were eschewed in favor of one that saw God more abstractly as "the power that makes for salvation." The movement Kaplan founded eventually became a separate American denomination of Judaism.

Yet all western European Jewish and American Jewish movements share many characteristics out of necessity. While the Orthodox might insist on practicing Jewish civil law, in the modern Western state such practice is ultimately a voluntary affair. The focus of Jewish life in North America and Europe is ritual, both at home and in the synagogue, which modern societies have designated as definitively private spheres.

The upheaval in Judaism that modernity caused has also given rise to an almost unprecedented degree of creativity in the religious sphere. Jewish philosophy was revived in post-Enlightenment Europe. Rationalists such as Moses Mendelsohn and Hermann Cohen took up the medieval intellectual tradition; existentialists such as Martin Buber and Franz Rosenzweig addressed Jewish theology from the standpoint of the condition of modern humanity. This tradition continues in Israel and North America, where such trends as poststructuralism and feminism inform Jewish religious thought. Ritual and liturgical creativity was a hallmark of the Reform movement, although not its exclusive provenance.

In the twentieth century two cataclysmic events shaped the nature of Judaism, not to mention the Jews as a nation: the attempt in 1941–1945 by Nazi Germany to exterminate world Jewry, what has come to be called the Holocaust; and the rise of Zionism, the settlement of Palestine by Jews, and the founding in 1948 of the State of Israel. The effects of both events are now essential elements not only of Jewish national life but of Judaism as a religion.

In western Europe, modern anti-Semitism, as opposed to most forms of premodern hatred of Jews, was directed not only at isolated and traditionalist groups of Jews but at those Jews who had integrated into Western society. In eastern Europe anti-Jewish riots (pogroms) accompanied the first stirrings of modernity in the early twentieth century. This and the influence of modern nationalism spawned the Zionist movement at the end of the nineteenth century. The movement was based on many principles central to Judaism as a religion, such as Jewish peoplehood, the hope for the nation's return to the Land of Israel in the messianic era, and the Hebrew language, which from the first century to modern times was used almost exclusively as a literary and liturgical tongue. There was also a religious Zionist movement, based on the principle that Jewish life, including the *halakhah,* could only be lived most fully in the Land of Israel and that the active return to the Land of Israel would be the first step in the messianic redemption. But there was also a revolutionary secular element to the movement. Inherent in Zionism was the idea that Jews would bring their own salvation rather than waiting for the Messiah. The movement also had a social and cultural dimension. Zionists sought to create a nation of "new Jews" who were not dependent on Gentiles for safety and livelihood but able to defend themselves militarily, work the land, and return to the vitality of biblical Israel. Since most of the early Zionist activists had received traditional educations and knew biblical and Talmudic literature thoroughly, they drew on those sources in their efforts to create a Jewish culture that was authentically Jewish yet radically different from that of the Diaspora. At the same time Zionists were for the most part starkly divided between secular and orthodox; a nonorthodox Zionist movement never took hold (the Reform and Conservative movements have small growing branches in Israel, but they are comparatively new developments). In Israel and North America most Jewish religious movements see the founding of the State of Israel and its survival under threats to its security as religiously meaningful events. A modern prayer for the welfare for Israel calls it "the beginning of our promised redemption." For some this takes on a specifically messianic connotation, and for others it is a more general wish for Israel to be the religious and cultural center of world Jewry.

European anti-Semitism culminated in the Holocaust (a term that came to be applied to that catastrophe in the 1950s and 1960s). Nazi Germany's attempted genocide of the Jewish people succeeded in wiping out the cultural and religious centers of European Jewry, including many of the major Hasidic communities, the most important *yeshivot,* the German academic seminaries of Jewish studies, and thriving communities of poets, writers, and theaters in Poland, Hungary, Lithuania, and elsewhere. On the surviving Jewish communities in North America, Israel, and Europe, this had several major effects. One was to galvanize support among Jewish movements for the State of Israel. Whereas some Reform Jews had opposed Zionism on the grounds that Judaism was most properly a religious not a national group, the Reform movement increasingly embraced Zionism and indeed ideas of Jewish nationhood. The strands of the Reform movement in North America that had since early in the twentieth century asserted Judaism's ethnic dimension were thus strengthened. In modern Orthodoxy too the element of religious Zionism has become more prominent from World War II to the twenty-first century.

Another effect has been a process of theological searching. The Holocaust seemed to break the paradigms of theodicy set by earlier generations of Jewish theologians. It could not be reasonably said that the millions of pious Jews who died in the death camps were being punished for their sins; nor was it any consolation to know that they would be rewarded for their martyrdom in the world to come. Much thoughtful meditation has been applied to these problems, but two approaches in particular have struck a chord with American Jews. Elie Wiesel's narrative works and essays stress the postwar Jewish community's responsibility simply to bear witness to the world, remember the victims and how they were victimized, and eschew easy lessons. Emil Fackenheim's response is to declare that there is a new commandment: "It is forbidden to grant Hitler any posthumous victories."

CONTEMPORARY JUDAISM. In the early twenty-first century religious Judaism in North America has inherited the denominationalism of the past two centuries, but other social and religious trends have rendered the structure of the community more complex. In the late 1960s and early 1970s, groups of young Jews, many of whom had been raised in the Conservative and Reform youth movements, began expressing their dissatisfaction with the large institutions and ethos of the major denominations by forming small, informal communities called ḥavurot. In these communities, no hired Rabbi or cantor presided over worship services or supervised education and programming. These communities were also deeply influenced by the egalitarianism and feminism of the postwar left as well as what they saw as the spontaneity and spirituality of the Hasidic movement. Some of the ḥavurot are independent; others are associated with the Jewish Renewal movement. Thus those Jewish denominations begun in the nineteenth century look quite different in the early twenty-first century. In the wake of the Holocaust and the founding of the State of Israel, practically no sector of religious Judaism accepts the notion that the Jews constitute a purely religious group—that is, a community defined only by common beliefs and not by common ancestry and tradition—and not a national or ethnic group. After World War II a major concern of all Jewish movements has been the worry that Judaism will disappear. Anti-Semitism is seen to present a physical threat to the Jews as a people, and conversely, it is feared that in an open society Jews will assimilate into the larger culture, intermarrying with non-Jews and leaving their religion and culture behind. This anxiety lies behind the arguments made by the major movements. Orthodoxy sees its dedication to *halakhah,* dietary laws, intensive traditional education, and commitment to religious Zionism as an effective way to fight assimilation. Nonorthodox movements argue that without adapting to the changing needs of society, Jews will be alienated from Judaism.

Israel is a different case. It is paradoxically a country with a secular Jewish majority in which orthodox institutions and authorities form part of the political and legal structure. One consequence of this structure is that religious and political movements are often closely related. Another result is that nonorthodox denominations are far smaller in Israel. Nonetheless, small groups of secular Israeli intellectuals that have formed to discuss what constitutes the "Jewish bookshelf"—a kind of Jewish canon for secular Israelis—include Jewish religious literature in that discussion. In addition, Israelis who have been influenced by travel to India or by New-Age spirituality form informal groups seeking religious experiences both inside and outside the framework of Judaism. More significant is the influence of large-scale immigration of Jews from Muslim countries in the 1950s. Those communities had not been divided deeply between orthodox and secular factions. As a result, Israelis of Middle Eastern background are often more sympathetic to religious traditions yet not always identifiable as Orthodox by conventional western criteria. The full consequences of this influence have yet to be determined.

Other trends are affecting Judaism at the beginning of the twenty-first century. One is feminism, which has affected the social, ritual, and theological life of contemporary Judaism. Especially since the 1960s Jewish feminists have argued for full equality both in Jewish communal life and in religious status. For nonorthodox movements, this has meant that after years of struggle women have won full participation in rituals, ordination as rabbis, and parity in Jewish law. For some orthodox communities, it has meant testing the boundaries of the *halakhah.* Jewish feminism has also resulted in a reexamination of Jewish theology and religious symbolism. This has taken several forms. One result is the interest in reexamining Jewish history from a feminist perspective, both to find historical precedents and alternative myths and symbols and to present a thorough critique of patriarchy within a Jewish cultural context. Another result is a reconsideration of gender in Jewish concepts of God. Jewish feminists have explored alternatives to masculine images and language for God. For example, some draw on elements of the Qabbalah that refer to the female within divinity (especially the idea of the *Shekhinah);* others believe that these categories will have to be redrawn considerably before they meet criteria for inclusive language. Jewish feminism has also resulted in the creation of new rituals or the reinvention of old ones. Thus the naming of a female baby becomes a (non-surgical) equivalent of *brit milah;* likewise, the New Moon celebration has become an occasion for Jewish women to gather for new ceremonies.

Another important trend that is affecting religious affairs all over the world is the rise of traditionalist, "fundamentalist," and militant religious movements. In Jewish communities this can be seen in the renewed vitality of traditionalist communities, such as Ḥasidim, that in the mid-twentieth century seemed on the verge of extinction. These trends are also in evidence with the growth of a movement of *ba'ale teshuvah,* Jews who "return" to Orthodoxy from nonaffiliated or nonorthodox backgrounds. In Israel, where politics and religion are inseparable, traditionalist religious parties and messianic movements have taken up a higher profile in public life. At the same time small numbers of Jews in North America who have not had a strong loyalty to the major denominations have become interested in spiritual trends, such as the Jewish Renewal movement, that adopt qabbalistic ideas and symbols but stress inner, personal goals.

However, certain constants prevail in contemporary Judaism, each of which can be seen as an inheritance from the long history described above. One common theme in religious Judaism, in all of its denominational manifestations, is the structure of a covenant between Israel and God. For traditional Jews, the terms of the covenant are to be found in the halakhic process, and understanding its details is vital to living a life devoted to God. For some nonorthodox movements, the covenant is the beginning point that initiates a process of dialogue with the tradition and the world.

Another constant is the Torah. The rabbis (M. *Avot* 5:22) said, "turn it over, turn it over, for everything is in it." Legends tell of how the Torah is literally as large as the world itself. Over the centuries the meaning of the term Torah has come to expand from individual biblical teachings, to the core of the canon, to traditions memorized and taught by rabbis and their disciples, to the entire Judaic tradition. Judaism sees Torah not simply as a body of textual material, but a form of activity. The Torah is read ritually in Hebrew in the synagogue from a scroll; the Oral Torah, written down in the Talmud and Midrash, is the focus of dialectical study and interpretation; and whether praying or making ethical decisions, religious Jews see themselves as translating the Torah into action.

It can be said that action, more than belief or inner experience, is seen as primary to Judaism. Ritual observance, whether in the synagogue or at home, remains a defining characteristic of Jews as individuals and as a community. Jewish religious communities are more likely to come together and divide over matters of ritual and practice than on theology or doctrine. Action can take the form of *halakhah,* observance of rituals, and engagement in social and ethical issues. In the late twentieth century and early twenty-first century, the experiential dimension has been emphasized increasingly by many communities; however, this dimension is usually associated with ritual and contemplative practices.

The persistent relevance of these themes are embodied in ritual, which often resonates particularly deeply with religious Jews. The Passover Seder can be taken as emblematic of the interplay of these themes in the way it illustrates the layers of history, interaction of myth and ritual, and affective nature of Jewish practice. The Seder is a meal held on the holiday of Passover, which celebrates Israel's liberation from slavery in Egypt. In the Torah (*Ex.* 12:1–28), an annual commemoration of the Exodus is prescribed as a reenactment of the original event. It consists of a lamb sacrifice eaten hastily by a family in the household; in time the sacrifice was linked to pilgrimage to the Temple in Jerusalem. With the destruction of the Temple, the sacrifice was no longer offered. However, by the time of the Mishnah the Passover celebration had become a meal in which symbolic foods were eaten and discussed and the biblical story of the Exodus was told and interpreted. For example, the participants not only eat the unleavened bread (*matsah*) and the bitter herbs (*maror*) as prescribed in *Ex.* 12:8, but explain their meaning as the bread eaten in haste by the Israelites and a symbol of the bitterness of slavery. Thus the participants internalize the historical experience both through the senses and discursively. As the Haggadah, the traditional narration for the Seder, puts it, "In every generation one should see oneself as having come out of Egypt." The Seder has become one of the most popular Jewish rituals in modern times, celebrated in homes not only by all religious denominations, but by secular Jews as well. For traditional Jews, the Seder has symbolized redemption and divine sovereignty; for many modern Jews, it represents national solidarity and political freedom. The ritual thus manages, in a series of gestures, to combine thought and action, history and the present, and the extraordinary and the everyday.

SEE ALSO Amoraim; Ashkenazic Hasidism; Conservative Judaism; Covenant; Dead Sea Scrolls; Halakhah, article on History of Halakhah; Hasidism; Israelite Religion; Jewish People; Jewish Religious Year; Jewish Renewal Movement; Jewish Thought and Philosophy; Midrash and Aggadah; Mishnah and Tosefta; Oral Torah; Orthodox Judaism; Patriarchate; Pesher; Qabbalah; Rabbinic Judaism in Late Antiquity; Reconstructionist Judaism; Reform Judaism; Sadducees; Synagogue; Talmud; Tannaim; Torah; Tosafot; Worship and Devotional Life, article on Jewish Worship; Zionism.

BIBLIOGRAPHY

General works

The best reference work for the study of Judaism is the *Encyclopedia Judaica,* 16 vols. (Jerusalem, 1971), although the earlier *Jewish Encyclopedia,* 12 vols. (1901–1906) is still of value. An excellent survey of the history of Judaism, balancing historical detail with religious ideas, is Robert Seltzer, *Jewish People, Jewish Thought.* A briefer, up-to-date historical survey is Raymond P. Scheindlin, *A Short History of the Jewish People: From Legendary Times to Modern Statehood* (New York, 1998). Judith Baskin (ed.), *Jewish Women in Historical Perspective* (Detroit, 1991), is especially useful for understanding the history of women in Judaism. An excellent introduction to the most important Jewish religious texts is Barry Holtz, *Back to the Sources* (New York, 1984). Harvey Goldberg, *Jewish Passages* (Berkeley, 2003) is a substantial description of the rituals of Jewish life that takes anthropological and historical methods into consideration. Two fine works on Jewish liturgy are Ruth Langer, *To Worship God Properly* (Cincinnati and Detroit, 1998) and Lawrence A. Hoffman, *Beyond the Text* (Bloomington, 1987).

On Jewish philosophy from antiquity to the twenty-first century see Daniel H. Frank and Oliver Leaman (eds.), *History of Jewish Philosophy* (London, 1997). The seminal work on Jewish mysticism, and one of the most important modern works of Jewish scholarship, is Gershom Scholem, *Major Trends in Jewish Mysticism* (New York, 1941). Other important studies of the Qabbalah and other types of Jewish mysticism are Moseh Idel, *Kabbalah: New Perspectives* (New Haven, 1988) and Elliot Wolfson, *Through a Speculum that Shines* (Princeton, 1994).

The biblical period

The best introduction to biblical religion, especially as a background for understanding Judaism, is Jon D. Levenson's

Sinai and Zion (New York, 1985). Mark S. Smith, *The Early History of God* (San Francisco, 1990; Dearborn, 2002) is also valuable. An important essay on the conception of God that underlies biblical ritual is Baruch A. Levine, "The Presence of God in Biblical Religion," in Jacob Neusner (ed.), *Religions in Antiquity* (Leiden, 1968), pp. 71–87. Susan Niditch, *Ancient Israelite Religion* (New York, 1997) is also notable for its consideration of archaeological data and the history of women in biblical Israel.

The Second-Temple and Rabbinic periods

Two valuable introductions to Judaism from the Persian period to the end of the talmudic period are Lawrence H. Schiffman, *From Text to Tradition* (Hoboken, 1991) and Martin S. Jaffee, *Early Judaism* (Upper Saddle River, N.J., 1997). Lawerence H. Schiffman's *Reclaiming the Dead Sea Scrolls* (Philadelphia, 1994) is a comprehensive introduction to the literature of the Qumran community; John J. Collins, *The Apocalyptic Imagination* (New York, 1984; Grand Rapids, Mich., 1998) is an excellent description of apocalyptic literature. An important statement on the Mishnah and how it reflects the earliest stage of Rabbinic Judaism is Jacob Neusner, *Judaism, the Evidence of the Mishnah* (Chicago, 1981). Solomon S. Schechter, *Aspects of Rabbinic Theology* (New York, 1909; reprint, 1969) is a collection of essays on Rabbinic thought that can still be read with profit. In *Imperialism and Jewish Society, 200 BCE to 640 CE* (Princeton, 2001) Seth Schwartz presents a provocative challenge to conventional understandings of Judaism in the Rabbinic period.

On women and gender in Rabbinic Judaism see Judith Romney Wegner, *Chattel or Person?* (New York, 1988); Judith Hauptman, *Rereading the Rabbis: A Woman's Voice* (Boulder, 1998); and Daniel Boyarin, *Carnal Israel* (Berkeley 1993). For the history of the ancient synagogue, Lee I. Levine, *The Ancient Synagogue: The First Thousand Years* (New Haven, 2000) and Steven Fine, *This Holy Place* (Notre Dame, 1997) integrate archaeological finds and textual research. Baruch Boxer, *The Origins of the Seder* (Berkeley, 1984) demonstrates the significance of the Passover Seder for the history of rabbinic Judaism. On Merkavah Mysticism, see Peter Schäfer, *The Hidden and Manifest God* (Albany, 1992).

The Middle Ages

For a social history of Jews in the Middle ages see Mark R. Cohen, *Under Crescent and Cross* (Princeton, 1994). S. D. Goiten synthesized the enormous range of sources found in the Cairo Genizah into a fascinating and comprehensive portrait of a medieval Jewish community in *A Mediterranean Society* (6 vols., Berkeley, 1971). On medieval Jewish philosophy see Colette Sirat, *A History of Jewish Philosophy in the Middle Ages* (Cambridge and Paris, 1985) and Julius Guttmann, *Philosophies of Judaism,* translated by David W. Silverman (New York, 1964). For the Qabbalah see the works of Scholem, Idel, and Wolfson cited above. On the spiritual world of medieval Ashkenazic intellectuals see Ephraim Kanarfogel, *Peering through the Lattices* (Detroit, 2000).

The modern period

An excellent portrait of the pioneers of Jewish modernity in Germany is Michael A. Meyer, *The Origins of the Modern Jew* (Detroit, 1967). Paul R. Mendes-Flohr and Jehuda Reinharz's *The Jew in the Modern World* (Oxford, 1980) is a valuable anthology of documents. For Judaism in the Middle East, see Norman A. Stillman, *The Jews of Arab Lands in Modern Times* (Philadelphia, 1991). For Judaism in the United States, see Jonathan D. Sarna, *American Judaism: a History* (New Haven, 2004). Charles S. Liebman's *The Ambivalent American Jew* (Philadelphia, 1973) also contains many good insights. For an overview of Zionism see Walter Laqueur, *A History of Zionism* (New York, 1989).

Among the many modern theologies of Judaism, several stand out as having made an impact on contemporary Judaism and are attentive to many aspects of Judaic experience. Though difficult, Franz Rosenzweig's *The Star of Redemption* (1930; trans. by William W. Hallo, New York, 1971) presented a system describing Judaism as a process of creation, revelation, and redemption that has been very influential. Abraham Joshua Heschel's *God in Search of Man* (New York, 1955) emphasized the experience of "radical amazement" and his poetic work *The Sabbath* proposed the values and worldview embodied in the Sabbath as an antidote to the sterility and cruelty of modern society. Joseph B. Soloveitchik's *Halakhic Man* and "The Lonely Man of Faith" (*Modern Judaism* 2:3 [1982]: 227–272) are important existential reflections from the modern Orthodox perspective. While not a work of theology per se, Elie Wiesel's works, especially *Night* (New York, 1972), have set the agenda in the starkest terms for Jewish considerations of the Holocaust. For two influential statements see Richard L. Rubenstein's *After Auschwitz* (Indianapolis, 1966) and Emil L. Fackenheim, *To Mend the World* (New York, 1982). Judith Plaskow, *Standing Again at Sinai* (New York, 1990), is a pioneering work of Jewish feminist theology.

Translations of major Jewish texts

Translations of most of the major Rabbinic texts are available; classic translations of the Mishnah, Babylonian Talmud and Midrash Rabbah (the principal Rabbinic commentary on the Torah and five other books) are *The Mishnah,* translated by Herbert Danby (Oxford, 1933); *The Babylonian Talmud,* 35 vols. (1935–1948; reprint in 18 vols., London, 1961); and *Midrash Rabbah,* 10 vols., translated by Harry Freedman et al. (London, 1939). A preliminary English translation of the Palestinian Talmud is *The Talmud of the Land of Israel,* translated by Jacob Neusner (35 vols.; Chicago, 1982). The *Mishneh Torah,* the great legal code of Maimonides, has been translated as *The Code of Maimonides,* 16 vols. to date (New Haven, 1949–). The best translation of Maimonides' philosophical *magnum opus* is *The Guide of the Perplexed,* translated by Shlomo Pines (Chicago, 1964). A translation of the Zohar into English that combines poetic language with critical acumen has been undertaken by Daniel C. Matt, *The Zohar* (two volumes published so far; Stanford, 2004–). The Jewish prayerbook (*siddur*) is an important source of information on Jewish values, implicit theologies, and sacred literature. The best translation of the traditional prayerbook is *Daily Prayer Book, ha-Siddur ha-Shalem,* translated by Philip Birnbaum (New York, 1949). The *Passover Haggadah,* edited by Nahum N. Glatzer (New York, 1969), is a good translation of the traditional text for the Passover Seder.

Other works cited in this entry

Baeck, Leo. *The Essence of Judaism.* Translated by Irving Howe and Victor Grubwieser. London, 1936; revised edition, New York, 1948.

Biale, David. *Gershom Scholem: Kabbalah and Counter-History,* 2d ed. Cambridge, Mass., 1982.

Frazer, James. *Folklore in the Old Testament.* New York, 1988.

Kadushin, Max, *Worship and Ethics.* New York, 1963.

Kugel, James L., and Greer, Rowan A. *Early Biblical Interpretation.* Philadelphia, 1986.

Silver, Abba Hillel. *Where Judaism Differed.* New York, 1956; reprint, Northvale, N.J., 1987.

Smith, W. Robertson. *Religion of the Semites.* New York, 1894; reprint, New Brunswick, N.J., 2002.

MICHAEL SWARTZ (2005)

JUDAISM: JUDAISM IN THE MIDDLE EAST AND NORTH AFRICA TO 1492

Judaism is indigenous to the Middle East. There in antiquity the Israelite people formed its unique identity. There the Bible came into being, and there by late antiquity Israelite religion was transformed into normative rabbinic Judaism. The basic texts of rabbinic Judaism—the halakhic *midrashim,* the Mishnah (compiled c. 200 CE), the two Talmuds, that of Palestine and that of Babylonia (compiled in the fifth and sixth centuries), and the first compilations of rabbinic lore (*aggadah*)—were all written in the Middle East. In the formative period of rabbinic Judaism, sectarian groups such as the religious communities of Qumran (the Dead Sea sects) manifested other varieties of Judaism. An esoteric mystical trend within rabbinic Judaism itself also grew in the Middle East of late antiquity. In Egypt in the first century CE, the Greek writings of Philo Judaeus of Alexandria gave voice to a Hellenized philosophical trend within Judaism.

Jews carried their religion to North Africa in late antiquity, where some form of Judaism penetrated the native Berber population, and to Arabia, where, in the seventh century, Judaism had some influence on the formation of the new religion of Islam. After the Middle East and North Africa were brought under the dominion of Islam, following the Arab conquests, and the centuries-old separation of Jewry into two branches, one living under Ssasanid-Zoroastrian rule, and the other living under a Roman-Christian regime, was brought to an end, Judaism underwent further change. Under Islam, rabbinic Judaism, faced with the unification of North African and Middle Eastern Jewry under one empire, became consolidated. In addition, as Jews adopted Arabic in place of Aramaic as both their written and spoken language, the intellectual culture of their host society became accessible to all layers of Jewish society for the first time in history. Responding to the challenge of dynamic Islamic civilization, perceived with unmediated intensity by Arabic-speaking Jewry, Judaism also experienced new developments in sectarianism, philosophy, and mysticism. These characteristic developments in Judaism between the Muslim conquests and the end of the fifteenth century will form the focus of this article.

THE BABYLONIAN CENTER. In the middle of the eighth century the capital of the Muslim caliphate was moved from Syria (where it had been located since 661 CE) to Baghdad. Under the Abbasid dynasty, Iraq became the center from which power and scholarly creativity radiated to the rest of the Islamic world. In this setting, the institutions of Babylonian Judaism were able to consolidate their own authority and religious leadership over the Jews living within the orbit of Islam. Successive waves of Jewish (as well as Muslim) migration from the eastern Islamic lands, long subject to the religious guidance of the Babylonian Talmud, to the Mediterranean and other western provinces of the caliphate, contributed substantially to this process.

The main instrument of this consolidation was the *yeshivah.* Though usually translated "academy," the *yeshivah* then was actually more than a center of learning. It was, as well, a seat of supreme judicial authority and a source of religious legislation. In pre-Islamic times there were already three *yeshivot,* one in Palestine, headed by the patriarch (the *nasi'*), and two in Babylonia, named Sura and Pumbedita. The Palestinian (or Jerusalem) and Babylonian Talmuds were redacted, respectively, in the Palestinian and Babylonian *yeshivot.*

After the middle of the eighth century the Babylonian *yeshivot* began to outshine their counterparts in Palestine. The heads of the *yeshivot* (first of Sura, later of Pumbedita, too) acquired a lofty title, "gaon" (short for *ro'sh yeshivat ge'on Ya'aqov,* "head of the *yeshivah* of the pride of Jacob," see *Psalms* 47:5). In an effort to assert the authority of Babylonian Judaism throughout the caliphate, the Geonim developed many types of halakhic (legal) literature. They were undoubtedly influenced by the intense efforts to consolidate Muslim legal traditions that were going on at the same time in Iraq. However, owing to the centrality of *halakhah* in Jewish life the consolidation of legal authority in the hands of the Babylonian Geonim also served the political purpose of endowing the Babylonian Gaonate with administrative hegemony over Islamic Jewry.

One of the most important literary vehicles used to this end was the system of questions and answers (*responsa*). Like its analogue in Roman and in Islamic law, a *responsum* (Heb., *teshuvah*) is an answer to a legal question. It can be issued only by a scholar of recognized authority. Something like the *responsa* seems to have existed in pre-Islamic Palestine, but the Babylonian geonim developed the legal custom into a major enterprise for the extension of their spiritual and political domination over the communities of the Islamic empire. Queries dispatched to Babylonia were accompanied by donations, which constituted one of the chief means of support for the *yeshivot* there.

A large number of *responsa* are extant from the mid-eighth century onward. They were sent to places as far away as North Africa and Spain and were transmitted mainly by Jewish merchants. In communities along the trade routes through which they passed, copies of the Geonic rulings were often made. In Old Cairo, for instance, a major commercial crossroads of the Islamic Middle Ages, many such *responsa* were discovered in the famous Cairo Genizah, where they had lain undisturbed for centuries owing to the Jewish custom of burying, rather than physically destroying, pages of sacred writings. Once a *responsum* reached the community that had sent the question, it was read aloud in the synagogue, a procedure that strengthened local reverence for the spiritual as well as the political authority of the Geonim.

The two Geonim from whom we have the largest number of *responsa* are Sherira᾽ and his son H᾽ai, whose consecutive reigns as gaon of the *yeshivah* of Pumbedita spanned the years 968–1038. The fact that very few *responsa* emanating from their rivals, the Palestinian Geonim, are known is a further measure of the success of the Babylonian *responsa* enterprise in creating a strong Babylonian orientation among the Jews of the Islamic world.

Another device employed by the Babylonian Geonim to universalize Babylonian Judaism was the *taqqanah* (legislative ordinance). These *taqqanot* were new laws, or modifications of existing laws, designed to adapt Talmudic law to realities not foreseen by the rabbis of the Mishnah and the *gemara᾽*. For instance, with the large-scale abandonment of agriculture by Jews and their increasing involvement in commerce, the issue of collection of debts by proxy became problematic. The Talmud permitted this only in conjunction with transfer of land. The Babylonian Geonim, conscious of the deagrarianization of Jewish life, promulgated a *taqqanah* stipulating that debt transfer could be effected even by the nonlanded by employing the legal fiction that every Jew owns four cubits of real property in the Land of Israel.

To further their ecumenical authority the Geonim also wrote commentaries on the Mishnah and Talmud. These originated as answers to questions about unclear passages in the Talmud that were posed by Jews living far from the center of living Talmud study in Babylonia. In their commentaries, the Geonim gave pride of place to halakhic sections, owing to the juridical priorities of the *yeshivot* and to the practical needs of the Jews. The Geonim also sought to make the Babylonian Talmud more accessible to those lacking training at the *yeshivah* itself. To this end they wrote introductions to that literature, explaining the methods, rules, and terminology of rabbinic jurisprudence. One type of introduction consisted of a chronological survey of Mishnaic and Talmudic teachers. This established their historical relationship and linked the rabbinic authority of the Geonim with the divine source of Jewish law at Mount Sinai. The most famous work of this type, which in form was actually a *responsum* sent to a North African questioner, is the "Epistle" (*Iggeret*) of Sherira᾽ Gaon, which forms our best single source for the history of Geonic rule.

The Geonim also compiled the first post-Mishnaic codes of Jewish law. The *Halakhot pesuqot* of Yehud'ai Gaon (in office 757–761 CE) is an abridged paraphrase of the Babylonian Talmud in Aramaic. A practical book, it omits nearly all of the *aggadah* (nonlegal literature) and the agricultural and sacrificial laws and concentrates on such practical subjects as precepts regarding festivals, commercial law, family law, and synagogue and other ritual observances. A more comprehensive work of this type was the *Halakhot gedolot* of Shim῾on of Basra (c. 825), a student at the *yeshivah* of Sura.

Like the Muslim legists, the Geonim composed specialized codes, extracting for handy reference Talmudic laws of inheritance, of deposit, of buying and selling, and of juridical procedure.

The first written prayer books in Jewish history were actually Geonic codes of liturgical procedure. The one by the ninth-century gaon Amram was sent in response to a request from a community in Spain for guidance in these matters. Sa῾adyah Gaon (882–942) also wrote a prayer book, one which, for the first time, used Arabic for the explanatory sections.

It was, however, not only by way of these various literary endeavors that the Babylonian Geonim imposed their authority on most of the Arabic-speaking Jewish world and universalized their form of Judaism; they further consolidated their spiritual and political sovereignty by training and licensing judges and by teaching Talmud to Jews who came from afar to hear lectures at the *yeshivah*'s semiannual conclaves (*kallot*). By the beginning of the eleventh century the process had been successfully completed. The Palestinian gaon Shelomoh ben Yehudah (in office 1026–1051) had to send his own son to the Baghdad *yeshivah* to complete his Talmudic education. Shelomoh's successor as gaon in Jerusalem, Daniyye᾽l ben ῾Azaryah, was a Babylonian scholar and a member of the family of the Babylonian exilarch, the descendants of the Davidic royal house who were living in Babylonian exile and were recognized by the caliph, as they had been by the pre-Islamic rulers of Persia, as "heads of the Diaspora." Ben ῾Azaryah, who died in 1062, brought Babylonian learning for a brief time to the *yeshivah* of Jerusalem.

New Centers in North Africa and Egypt. In the course of time, the very universalization of Babylonian Judaism and the dispersal of Babylonian-trained judges and scholars throughout the Diaspora in Islamic lands created a foundation upon which new independent centers of religious learning and authority could be built. This happened in North Africa in the tenth and eleventh centuries and in Egypt somewhat later.

Kairouan. In the ninth and tenth centuries, the Jews of Kairouan, the capital of Muslim Ifriqiya (modern Tunisia), were firmly within the camp of the Babylonian Geonim. Indeed, most of the Jewish settlers in Kairouan had originated in Iraq and Iran, the heartland of Geonic authority. But in these two centuries, Muslim Kairouan achieved considerable prosperity and became a major center of Islamic legal studies. Against this background, the local Jewish community began to create its own center of Talmudic scholarship. The first mention of a formal house of study in Kairouan—the term used was *midrash* rather than *yeshivah*—occurs at the end of the century. Led by Ya῾aqov bar Nissim ibn

Shahin, who belonged to a family whose origins lay in the East (probably Iran) and who was a loyal adherent of Babylonian Judaism, this *midrash* was not yet a rival institution to the Babylonian *yeshivot.* Detachment from Babylonian religious sovereignty became pronounced a generation later, following the arrival in Kairouan of a scholar, believed to have hailed from Italy, named Ḥushiʾel. Italian Jewry had been influenced more by Palestinian than by Babylonian traditions, so when Ḥushiʾel opened a second *midrash* in Kairouan, some Palestinian traditions were taught alongside Babylonian Talmudic scholarship.

In the first half of the eleventh century two of Ḥushiʾel's students placed native North African religious scholarship on a firm literary footing: his son, Ḥananʾel ben Ḥushiʾel, and Nissim, the son of Yaʿaqov bar Nissim (who had died in 1006/7). Ḥananʾel wrote *responsa,* commentaries on the Torah, on *Ezekiel,* on the dietary laws, and, most importantly, a comprehensive commentary on the Babylonian Talmud. In innovative fashion, this last-mentioned work employed material from the Palestinian Talmud to explain passages in the text, though, like the commentaries of the Babylonian Geonim, its primary focus was juridical.

Nissim (d. 1062) maintained his father's loyalty to the Babylonian Geonim. However, like his contemporary Ḥananʾel, he too wrote a fresh commentary on the Talmud utilizing material from the Palestinian text. Duplicating Babylonian Geonic efforts to disseminate knowledge of the Talmud, Nissim composed in Arabic his own "Introduction" entitled *The Book of the Key to the Locks of the Talmud.* Other religious writing of his include a chain of transmission of rabbinic tradition reminiscent of Sheriraʾ Gaon's "Epistle," *responsa* (of which many are extant), and a "Secret Scroll" (*Megillat setarim*), written in Arabic, that consisted of a potpourri of miscellaneous ritual laws. None of Nissim's rabbinic works has been preserved in its entirety and its original form; they are known of only from fragments or through quotations in the works of others.

Ḥushiʾel's disciples completed the process of fashioning an independent center of religious creativity in North Africa. Their period of activity coincided with the decline of the Babylonian Gaonate following the death of H'ai Gaon in 1038. However, the budding new center of rabbinic Judaism in North Africa was cut off abruptly in 1057 when Kairouan was destroyed by bedouin tribes sent by the Fāṭimid ruler of Egypt to punish his disloyal vassals, the Zirids, in that city.

Fez. Another creative center of Judaism in North Africa developed in Fez (present-day Morocco). *Responsa* addressed to Fez by the Geonim of Sura and Pumbedita testify to the presence of learned scholars in that distant North African city. The most famous rabbinic master from Fez, Yitsḥaq ben Yaʿaqov Alfasi (c. 1013–1103), wrote an abridged version of the Talmud that later became part of the apparatus of the standard printed Talmud text. He also wrote many *responsa.*

Egypt. In Egypt a local school of advanced religious study (a *midrash*) was established at the end of the tenth century by Shemaryah ben Elḥanan, a scholar educated at one of the Babylonian *yeshivot.* Egyptian Jewry at that time was subject to the political authority of the gaon of the Palestinian *yeshivah,* who was recognized by the Fāṭimid caliph in Cairo as head of the Jews in his empire (Egypt and Palestine). When Shemaryah's son and successor Elḥanan began to expand the activities of the Egyptian *midrash* by soliciting donations even from Palestine and by assuming some of the religious and political prerogatives of the Palestinian gaon, he was excommunicated by the Jerusalem *yeshivah.* This put a temporary halt to the growth of native Egyptian religious scholarship until, in the latter part of the eleventh century, several distinguished scholars settled in Egypt.

As in the case of Nissim ben Yaʿaqov of Kairouan, the writings of these scholars are known from fragments, from quotations in later works, and medieval book lists. One notable author was Yehudah ha-Kohen ben Yosef, who wrote commentaries on the Bible and on portions of the Talmud, a code of regulations concerning ritual slaughtering, liturgical poems, and a commentary on the mystical *Sefer yetsirah* (Book of creation). Another was a scholar from Spain named Yitsḥaq ben Shemuʾel, who wrote an Arabic commentary on some if not all of the Former Prophets, a commentary on at least one Talmudic tractate, *responsa,* and liturgical poems. Though neither of these scholars opened an academy of learning, they gave Egyptian Jewry a renewed sense of independence from the traditional sources of religious leadership in Babylonia and from the political dominion of the *yeshivah* in Palestine.

Related to the activity of these respected rabbinic scholars in Egypt toward the end of the eleventh century was the emergence there of a new Jewish institution of central leadership. This was the office of "head of the Jews" (Arab., *raʾīs al-yahūd*), more commonly known in Hebrew as the office of the *nagid.* The scholarly family of court physicians headed by the brothers Yehudah and Mevorakh ben Saʿadyah was the first to hold this position of dignity. The office of head of the Jews, inheriting the sovereignty formerly reserved for the Palestinian gaon, was invested with supreme religious as well as political authority over the Jews in the Fāṭimid empire.

In the third decade of the twelfth century the Palestinian *yeshivah,* which had been located outside the borders of Palestine since the Seljuk conquest of Jerusalem around 1071, transferred its own headquarters to the capital of Egypt. With this move the office of head of the Jews temporarily passed into the hands of the newly arrived Palestinian gaon, Matsliaḥ ha-Kohen ben Shelomoh. How much teaching went on in the relocated Palestinian *yeshivah* we do not know. However, the arrival of Moses Maimonides (Mosheh ben Maimon) in Egypt around 1165 established Egypt as a respectable center of Jewish religious scholarship. Maimonides attracted a circle of students and substituted the study of his own code of Jewish law, the *Mishneh Torah,* for the study of the Babylonian Talmud in the curriculum of Jewish higher education. The Babylonian Gaonate voiced opposition to Maimonides, who was seen as a threat to its efforts to reassert its former supremacy over world Jewry. Nevertheless, the Maimonidean tradition of learning in Egypt, modified by a distinctive mystical bent, was continued by his son Avraham and by a succession of Maimonidean descendants until the beginning of the fifteenth century.

Yemen. A center of Jewish learning much influenced by Moses Maimonides was to be found in Yemen. Already in late antiquity there was a small Jewish presence in South Arabia, as we know from the evidence of Hebrew inscriptions and from stories about the conversion to Judaism of rulers of the South Arabian kingdom of Ḥimyar (the last of these Jewish kings of Ḥimyar, who was also the last Ḥimyarī ruler, died in 525 CE). In the Islamic period the Jewish settlement was considerably strengthened by the migration of Jews from Babylonia and Persia. Naturally, from the outset the Yemenite community maintained loyalty to the Babylonian geonim and the Babylonian exilarch, supported the Babylonian *yeshivah* financially, and adhered to the Babylonian interpretation of rabbinic Judaism.

In the eleventh and twelfth centuries, however, Yemen and Yemenite Jews became closely connected with Egypt as a result of general political and economic developments. Thus, they identified in the twelfth century with the *yeshivah* of Matsliaḥ ha-Kohen in Cairo and especially with Maimonides after his arrival in Egypt. In the later Middle Ages a considerable indigenous religious literature developed among the Yemenite Jews, much of it consisting in commentaries on various works of Maimonides. In Yemen, moreover, Maimonides' *Mishneh Torah* became the principal code of Jewish practice. Among Yemenite works from the later Middle Ages that cite passages from Maimonides' œuvre is the voluminous anthology of homiletic and legal *midrashim* on the five books of the Torah compiled in the thirteenth century by David ben ʿAmram of the Yemenite port city of Aden, entitled *Midrash ha-gadol.*

KARAISM. Not long after the Muslim conquest, the most important religious schism in medieval Judaism, known as Karaism, occurred in the Middle East. The Karaites rejected the jurisdiction of the Talmud and of rabbinic Judaism in general, claiming exclusive reliance on the Bible. Some scholars believe that Karaism actualized a latent anti-Talmudism that had existed beneath the surface since the time of the Sadducees, who centuries earlier had denied the validity of the oral Law. Others identify in Karaism affinities with the religion of the Dead Sea sects, notably the asceticism shared by these two religious movements.

It is difficult to prove the influence of one sect on another separated from it in time by so many centuries. What is certain, however, in terms of immediate causes is that Karaism arose in opposition to the extension of the authority of rabbinic Judaism by the Babylonian Geonim in the early Islamic period and out of resentment towards the power wielded by the Jewish aristocracy of Iraq through the Davidic exilarchate.

The Iranian Plateau, fertile ground for sectarian rebellion in early Islam, spawned several antirabbinic Jewish revolts prior to the crystallization of a cohesive Karaite movement. One example was the sect of Abū ʿĪsā al-Isfahānī, whose period of activity is variously given as 685–705, during the reign of the Umayyad caliph ʿAbd al-Malik ibn Manṣūr, or at the time of the transition from Umayyad to Abbasid rule, between 744 and 775. His ascetic, anti-Talmudic program included the prohibition of divorce and a change in the daily liturgical cycle from three to seven prayers. Abū ʿĪsā was also driven by his belief in the imminent coming of the Messiah to take up arms against the Muslim government.

Abū ʿĪsā's sect was but one of many groups whose antirabbinic halakhic practices were collected together in the eighth century by ʿAnan ben David, an important link in the chain leading to the consolidation of Karaism in the ninth and tenth centuries. ʿAnan may have hailed from the Iranian Plateau, but he operated in the center of Geonic-exilarchal territory in Babylonia. He was, in fact, said to have been a member of the exilarchal family. A biased Rabbinite account of his sectarian rebellion ascribes his motives to personal disappointment after being passed over for appointment to the office of exilarch.

ʿAnan's principal achievement was to assemble scattered bits of sectarian *halakhah* into a code called *Sefer ha-mitsvot* (Book of commandments). In this book, he employed Talmudic methodology for his own end: his biblical exegesis served to lend credibility and respectability to the deviant practices that he codified. This use of rabbinic methods and language to establish the legitimacy of nonrabbinic Judaism constituted a serious challenge to the authority of the Geonim.

ʿAnan seems to have envisaged the creation of separatist communities of nonrabbinic Jews living in various locales within the Diaspora. One scholar has even proposed that he wished to gain government recognition for a second legitimate school of law within Judaism, coexisting with the school of the Babylonian Geonim much like the different *madhhabs* (schools of jurisprudence) in Islam.

Later Karaites attributed to ʿAnan the formulation of a principle, expressed as an apothegm: "Search thoroughly in the Torah and do not rely upon my opinion." This legitimated, in theory at least, the exclusive reliance on the Bible that distinguished Karaism from rabbinism and sounded the call for individualistic exegesis in place of slavish adherence to rabbinic tradition. It also justified a proliferation of non-ʿAnanite sects in the ninth and tenth centuries, such as the sect of Ismāʿīl al-ʿUkbarī (from ʿUkbara, near Baghdad), the sect of Mishawayh al-ʿUkbarī, the sect of Abū ʿImrān al-Tiflisī (from present-day Tbilisi, Republic of Georgia), and the sect of Malik al-Ramlī (from Ramleh, Palestine).

Much of our information about these groups comes from the law code, *Kitāb al-anwār wa-al-marāqib* (Book of lights and watchtowers), by the tenth-century Karaite thinker Yaʿqūb al-Qirqisānī, which contains an introduction on the history of sects in Judaism. Not surprisingly, for Qirqisānī it is the Rabbinites, beginning with the Pharisees, rather than the Karaites, who were the real religious deviants. ʿAnan ben David's role as reformer was to rediscover the long-suppressed true path.

The first to employ the term *Karaites* (*Benei Miqra'*, "children of scripture") was the ninth-century Binyamin al-Nahāwandī (of Nihāvand, Iran). He was known for his tolerance of observance of rabbinic laws, especially where biblical legislation failed to answer practical questions of everyday life. This liberalism with respect to Talmudic law was matched by an insistence on the right of every individual to interpret scripture as he saw fit. Troubled by the rationalist critique of biblical anthropomorphisms, Binyamin taught that the world was called into being by an angel created by God, and that all anthropomorphic expressions in the Bible were to be ascribed to that angel. A judge by profession, Binyamin wrote a *Sefer mitsvot* (Book of commandments) and a *Sefer Dīnim* (Book of laws). He also wrote biblical commentaries.

Daniyye'l al-Qūmisī, another Karaite thinker of the end of the ninth century, was a messianist who settled in Jerusalem in order to mourn for Zion (the group he headed was called Avelei-Tsiyyon, "Mourners for Zion") and to pray for redemption. In his approach to the Bible he rejected the liberal individualism of Binyamin al-Nahāwandī and the latter's theology of the creator angel. However, in his own exegesis, he was, according to some sources, a rationalist.

By the tenth century Karaism was sufficiently consolidated to pose an active threat to the Babylonian geonim. Saʿadyah Gaon took up the cudgels of defense on their behalf, writing a refutation of ʿAnan (*Kitāb al-radd ʿalā ʿAnan*) and opposing Karaite views in others of his writings. Saʿadyah's hostility inspired a Karaite counterattack. Indeed, he was the polemical object of much of the rich Karaite literature of the "golden age" of the tenth and eleventh centuries.

Several important figures of this Karaite golden age bear mention here. Yaʿqūb al-Qiriqisānī (tenth century) composed, in addition to the code of law, the *Book of Lights and Watchtowers*, commentaries on several books of the Bible, a refutation of Muḥammad's claim to prophecy, and a treatise on God's unity. Salmon ben Yeroḥam (tenth century) wrote a poetical tract against the Rabbinites, *The Book of the Wars of the Lord*, that bristles with polemic against Saʿadyah, and among other works, biblical commentaries on *Psalms* and the *Song of Songs*. Yefet ben ʿEli wrote commentaries in Arabic on the entire Hebrew Bible, accompanied by translations of Hebrew text into Arabic. Sahl ben Maṣliaḥ composed a *Book of Commandments*, only partly extant, and a letter to a Rabbinite disputant in Egypt extolling Karaism at the expense of rabbinism. Yūsuf al-Baṣīr (Yosef ha-Ro'eh, from Basra) wrote a *Book of Commandments* and important *responsa*, and initiated a liberalization of Karaite marriage laws which, on the basis of literal interpretation of the Bible, had multiplied the number of incestuous (and therefore forbidden) marriage combinations, thus threatening the biological continuity of the sect. Like al-Baṣīr, Yeshuʿah ben Yehudah composed a treatise refuting the Karaite laws of incestuous marriage. He also penned commentaries on books of the Bible.

Revival of Jewish Religious Philosophy. Several factors converged to bring about a revival of Jewish religious philosophy, dormant since Philo, among the Jews of the Muslim world, Rabbinites and Karaites alike. Most important were the new availability of Hellenistic philosophy in Arabic translation; Jewish awareness of the application of rationalist inquiry to theological questions in Islam; the critique of biblical anthropomorphism; the attack on the Bible by Jewish skeptics like Ḥiwi al-Balkhī; and the desire to prove that Judaism embraced the same universalistic truths as Islam. The lion's share of Jewish religious philosophy was written in Spain. However, the founder of Judeo-Arabic philosophy, Saʿadyah Gaon, and the most important philosopher of them all, Maimonides, wrote in the Middle East.

The earliest venture by Arabic-speaking Jews into rationalism followed the lead of the Muslim science of *kalām*. *Kalām* means "speech" and refers specifically to discussion of theological problems. The most rationalistic trend in the *kalām* was that of the Muʿtazilah, which originated in Iraq in the cities of Basra and Baghdad, and it was from this doctrine that Saʿadyah, who lived in Baghdad, drew the inspiration for his pioneering work of Jewish religious philosophy, *Kitāb al-amanat wa-al-Iʿtiqādāt* (The book of beliefs and convictions). Like the Muʿtazilah, he began his treatise with an epistemological discourse establishing the indispensability of reason as a source of religious knowledge. To this he added the category of reliable transmitted knowledge—doubtless in response to skeptics and Karaites who discredited the reliability of biblical stories and laws. The idea that reason and revelation lead to the same religious truths remained a cornerstone of all medieval Jewish religious philosophy after Saʿadyah. Like the Muʿtazilah, Saʿadyah placed the discussion of the creation of the world out of nothing (*creatio ex nihilo*) at the head of his treatise, since from the premise of creation flowed the belief in the existence of God and hence all other religious convictions.

The Muʿtazilah struggled with two major challenges to rationalism: scriptural anthropomorphisms that seemingly denied God's unity, and the question of the existence of evil in this world that appeared to contradict God's justice. Like the Muslim Muʿtazilah, Saʿadyah devoted separate chapters to these two subjects in his philosophical treatise. Divine unity was defended by invoking the principle that the Torah uses metaphor to describe God in terms understandable to human minds. The problem of divine justice was resolved with the Mu'tazilī solution of claiming freedom of the human will. Saʿadyah took other leads from the Muʿtazilah, for instance, in drawing a distinction between laws knowable through reason and laws knowable only through revelation, as well as in his treatment of retribution. In addition, he addressed Jewish eschatology in his chapters on resurrection and redemption.

The Muslim *kalām* influenced other Jewish writers in the Middle East. Before the time of Saʿadyah, David ben Marwān al-Muqammiṣ (ninth century) combined Muʿtazilī views with Greek philosophical notions. So did the Babylonian gaon Shemuʾel ben Ḥofni (d. 1013) in his commentary on the Bible. Nissim ben Yaʿaqov of Kairouan showed familiarity with Muʿtazilī teaching in his commentary on the Talmud. Finally, the Karaites, liberated from the commitment to tradition as a valid source of religious knowledge, adopted Muʿtazilī rationalism with even less reserve than its Rabbinite exponents. Prominent among the Karaite rationalists were the above-mentioned Yaʿqūb al-Qirqisānī, Yūsuf al-Baṣīr (eleventh century), and Yeshuʿah ben Yehudah (mid-eleventh century).

These Karaites went beyond the principle of the equivalence of reason and revelation and gave primacy to the former. It was, in fact, among the Karaites of Byzantium alone that Muʿtazilī *kalām* continued to have influence on Judaism after the eleventh century. In contrast, among the Rabbinites, Neoplatonism and especially Aristotelianism took over the role that Muʿtazilī thought had played during the pioneering phase of Jewish religious philosophy in the Islamic world.

Neoplatonism and Aristotelianism flourished mainly among the Jews of Spain. However, the first Jewish Neoplatonist, Yitsḥaq Yisraʾeli (c. 850–950), was born in Egypt and composed philosophical works in Arabic while serving as court physician to the Muslim governor in Kairouan. Of his works the *Book of Definition* and the *Book on the Elements* (extant only in Hebrew and Latin translations) and a commentary on *Sefer yetsirah* (Book of creation), revised by his students, show how he tried to incorporate the Neoplatonic doctrine of emanation into Judaism. Though he did not abandon the biblical premise of divinely willed creation out of nothing for a pure Neoplatonic cosmogony, he adopted the Neoplatonic conception of progressive emanation of spiritual substances in the supraterrestrial world. As with the Islamic Neoplatonists, some aspects of Yisraʾeli's philosophy of religion show the influence of Aristotelian ideas. For instance, his concept of reward for ethical conduct is based on the ascent of the human soul toward its final reunification with the upper soul. The phenomenon of prophecy, a problem for Muslim religious philosophers, similarly occupied Yitsḥaq Yisraʾeli; his theory employs the naturalistic explanation offered by the Islamic Aristotelians but leaves a place for divine will in connection with the form of the vision accorded prophets.

The most important full-fledged Jewish Aristotelian was Maimonides. Born in Spain, where in the twelfth century Aristotelianism replaced Neoplatonism as the preferred philosophy, Maimonides did most of his writing, including his philosophic magnum opus, the *Guide of the Perplexed*, in Egypt, where he lived out most of his life as a refugee from Almohade persecution in Spain and North Africa. Maimonides sought to achieve a workable synthesis between Judaism and Aristotelianism without glossing over the uncontestably incompatible elements in each of those systems. Writing for the initiated few in the *Guide*, he took up troublesome theological questions. He argued for the existence of God, which he demonstrated, not in the by-then-unsatisfactory manner of the old *kalām*, but by exploiting scientifically and logically more credible Aristotelian philosophical concepts. He upheld the unity of God, not by accepting the identity of God's attributes with his essence, as *kalām* would have it, but by combining the metaphoric interpretation of scriptural anthropomorphisms with the doctrine of negative attributes, which leaves the fact of God's existence as the sole bit of positive knowledge of divinity available to believers. He even addressed the problem of the creation of the world, which forced him to suspend Aristotle's doctrine of the eternity of the world in favor of the biblical account of the miraculous creation by the will of God.

Maimonides also attempted to bring an Aristotelian conception of Judaism within the reach of the philosophically uninitiated. This he did with a philosophical introduction to, and other occasional rationalistic comments in, his *Mishneh Torah* (Code of Jewish law); with an Aristotelian ethical introduction to the Mishnah tractate *Avot*; and by formulating a philosophic creed for Jews in his commentary on the Mishnah.

PIETISM AND JEWISH SUFISM. A new religious development in Judaism began in the Middle East in the twelfth and thirteenth centuries. Individual Jews began to be attracted to the pious asceticism of the Muslim Ṣūfīs. In his introduction to the Mishnah tractate *Avot*, called "The Eight Chapters," Maimonides chastises such people for engaging in extreme self-abnegation, thereby straying from the more moderate path advocated by Judaism.

In the thirteenth century in Egypt, some representatives of the Jewish upper classes (physicians, government secretaries, judges, and scholars) joined together in pietistic brotherhoods akin to the Ṣūfī orders that were then flourishing in Egypt under the patronage of the Ayyubid dynasty of Muslim rulers founded by Salaḥ al-Dīn (Saladin). These Jews called themselves *ḥasidim*, using the regular Talmudic word for the pious. They fasted frequently, practiced nightly prayer vigils, and recited additional prayers accompanied by bowings and prostrations more typical of Islam than of Judaism. Rather than exhibiting their pietism in public they maintained a private place of worship where they followed their special path. Rather than wearing wool outer clothing like the Muslim Ṣūfīs, they designated as the symbol of their asceticism the turban that they all wore (Arab., *baqyār* or *buqyār*).

The most illustrious member of this circle of *ḥasidim* was the *nagid* (head of the Jewish community) Avraham, the son of Moses Maimonides. He wrote a long code of Jewish law entitled *Kifāyat al-ʿābidīn* (The complete guide for the servants of God), which, in its fourth and final book, contains a program of mystical piety for the Jewish elite based on the ethical tenets of Sufism.

The *ḥasidim* in Avraham Maimonides' brotherhood made attempts to influence the general Jewish public to adopt some aspects of their pietism. Earlier, Moses Maimonides himself had introduced reforms in the Egyptian synagogue service aimed at imitating the more decorous environment of the mosque. Driven by pietistic zeal, his son went further. He tried to introduce the kneeling posture of Islamic prayer into the synagogue; he insisted that worshipers face the direction of prayer even while seated; and he required people to stand in straight rows during the Eighteen Benedictions, in imitation of the orderly, symmetrical pattern of the mosque. These and other pietistic reforms aroused much opposition, and some Jews actually denounced Avraham to the Muslim authorities for attempting to introduce unlawful innovations into Judaism. In response, Avraham wrote a vigorous defense of pietism, which has been found in the Cairo Genizah.

Avraham Maimonides' son ʿOvadyah wrote his own Ṣūfī-like book. Called *Al-maqālah al-ḥawḍīyah* (The treatise of the pool), it attempted to impart intellectual respectability to Jewish Sufism. In the later Middle Ages, some Jews in Egypt imitated the style of life of the Ṣūfī convents in the hills surrounding Cairo. In Egypt, too, Jewish thinkers, outstanding among them the descendants of Maimonides, continued to compose treatises in the Ṣūfī vein. This turn towards mystical piety in the Jewish world, at just about the time when Jewish religious philosophy reached its climactic stage in the Middle East in the writings of Maimonides, recalls the replacement of philosophy by Sufism as the dominant religious mode in Islam in the later medieval period. Possibly Jewish interest in Sufism similarly reflects a dissatisfaction with the answers given in the past by Jewish rationalism to religious questions. Only when the study of Jewish Sufism, still in its infancy, has progressed further will it be possible to gain a clear sense of its place in the history of Judaism in the Islamic world and of the influence it might have had on the Lurianic Qabbalah that sprouted in Muslim Palestine after the expulsion of Jews from Spain in 1492.

See Also Islam, overview article and article on Islam in North Africa; Jewish Thought and Philosophy, article on Premodern Philosophy; Karaites; Muʿtazilah; Polemics, article on Muslim-Jewish Polemics; Rabbinic Judaism in Late Antiquity; Sufism; Yeshivah.

Bibliography

The most thorough general work on Jewish history and religion is Salo W. Baron's *A Social and Religious History of the* Jews, 2d ed., rev. & enl., 18 vols. (New York, 1952–1980). A good introduction to Jewish life under Islam is to be found in *The Jews of Arab Lands: A History and Source Book*, compiled and introduced by Norman A. Stillman. An older but still valuable book on Jewish history and literature under early Islam is Simḥa Assaf's *Tequfat ha-geʾonim ve-sifrutah* (Jerusalem, 1955).

Regional studies include Jacob Mann's *The Jews in Egypt and in Palestine under the Fāṭimid Caliphs*, 2 vols. in 1 (1920–1922; reprint, New York, 1970); my *Jewish Self-Government in Medieval Egypt: The Origins of the Office of the Head of the Jews, ca. 1065–1126* (Princeton, 1980); Eliyahu Ashtor's *Toledot ha-Yehudim be-Mitsrayim ve-Suryah taḥat shilṭon ha-Mamlukim*, 3 vols. (Jerusalem, 1944–1970), which concerns the Jews of Egypt and Syria; his *The Jews of Moslem Spain*, translated by Aaron Klein and Jenny Machlowitz Klein, 3 vols. (Philadelphia, 1973–1984); and H. Z. Hirschberg's *A History of the Jews in North Africa*, 2d rev. ed., 2 vols. (Leiden, 1974–1981). On the Yemenite Jews see S. D. Goitein's *Ha-Teimanim* (Jerusalem, 1983) and David R. Blumenthal's edition and annotated translation of *The Commentary of R. Ḥōṭer ben Shelōmō to the Thirteen Principles of Maimonides* (Leiden, 1974). Goitein's magisterial work, *A Mediterranean Society*, 5 vols. (Berkeley, 1967–1983), presents a detailed portrait of Jewish life, in both its worldly and religious aspects, in the Mediterranean Arab world of the High Middle Ages. On Karaism, see *Karaite Anthology*, edited and translated by Leon Nemoy (New Haven, 1952), and the introduction to Zvi Ankori's *Karaites in Byzantium* (New York, 1959). Julius Guttmann's *Philosophies of Judaism*, translated by David W. Silverman (New York, 1964), and Georges Vajda's *Introduction à la pensée juive au Moyen Age* (Paris, 1947) offer excellent introductions to the subject of the revival of religious philosophy in medieval Judaism in the Islamic world. The major Jewish philosophical works mentioned in this article exist in partial or complete English translation, such as the selection of Yitsḥaq Yisraʾeli's philosophical writings translated into English in *Isaac Israeli: A Neoplatonic Philosopher of the Early Tenth Century* by Alexander Altmann and Samuel M. Stern (Oxford, 1958); *Saadia Gaon: The Book of Beliefs and Opinions*, translated by Samuel Rosenblatt (New Haven, 1948); and Maimonides' *Guide of the Perplexed*, translated by Shlomo Pines and introduced by Leo Strauss (Chicago, 1963). On pietism and Jewish Sufism, see the introduction to Paul Fenton's translation of Obadiah Maimonides' *Treatise of the Pool* (London, 1981) and Gerson D. Cohen's "The Soteriology of R. Abraham Maimuni," *ProceeDīngs of the American Academy for Jewish Research*, 35 (1967): 75–98 and 36 (1968): 33–56.

For additional bibliography on the general subject of Jewish life and culture in the medieval Islamic world, consult the *Bibliographical Essays in Medieval Jewish Studies*, edited by Yosef H. Yerushalmi (New York, 1976), especially my chapter, "The Jews under Medieval Islam: From Rise of Islam to Sabbatai Zevi," reprinted with a supplement for the years 1973–1980 as "Princeton Near East Paper," no. 32 (Princeton, 1981); and that by Lawrence Berman, "Medieval Jewish Religious Philosophy."

New Sources

Barclay, John M. G. *Jews in the Mediterranean Diaspora: From Alexander to Trajan (323 BCE–117 CE)*. Edinburgh, 1996.

Gil, Moshe. Tans. David Strassler. *Jews in Islamic Countries in the Middle Ages.* Boston, 2004.

Goldberg, Harvey E., ed. *Sephardi and Middle Eastern Jewries: History and Culture.* Bloomington, Ind., 1996.

Stillman, Yedida K., and Norman A. Stillman, eds. *From Iberia to Diaspora: Studies in Sephardic History and Culture.* Boston, 1998.

Wexler, Paul. *The Non-Jewish Origins of the Sephardic Jews.* Albany, 1996.

MARK R. COHEN (1987)
Revised Bibliography

JUDAISM: JUDAISM IN THE MIDDLE EAST AND NORTH AFRICA SINCE 1492

The year 1492 marks a turning point in the history of the Jewish people. The expulsion of the Jews from Spain closes a brilliant and complex chapter in Jewish history, releasing a massive group of talented and despondent refugees upon the shores of the Mediterranean. They were soon followed by other waves of Jewish émigrés from Portugal, France, Provence, and the various Italian states as a result of the forced conversions or expulsions in those countries in the late-fifteenth through mid-sixteenth centuries. Even within the tragic annals of the Jews, rarely had the contemporary scene appeared so bleak. With most of the gates of Europe closed, the refugees of western Europe fled to the world of Islam, injecting new life and much controversy into the Jewish communities there that had been living in a state of decline for at least two centuries. The emergent period was marked by fervent yearnings for redemption, painful attempts at evaluating why the Spanish Jewish experience had ended in such ignominy, a brief but brilliant renaissance of Jewish life in Turkey, the outburst of antinomianism in seventeenth-century Ottoman Jewry, and a final period of increasing intellectual stagnation of Jews in Muslim lands. Beginning in the nineteenth century, winds of change swept the Near East, propelled by the influence of the European powers. Jews were especially receptive to the attempts of western Jews to reform the eastern Jews and their situation, unleashing a chain of events and attempts at modernization whose effects are still being felt.

JEWISH LEGAL STATUS IN MUSLIM LANDS. From its inception, Islam exhibited an ambivalent attitude toward non-Muslims. The prophet Muḥammad had clearly enunciated his indebtedness to the faith of his monotheistic predecessors in the Qurʾān, tolerating their continued existence with certain provisos. Jews and Christians were to be recognized as possessors of scripture, *ahl al-kitāb* (people of the Book), were not to be forcibly converted, and were to be afforded a modicum of protection. Implied in the status of protection, *dhimma,* or of protected peoples—*dhimmis*—was the right of the Jews to exercise their Judaism provided they accepted a position of subordination.

Over the centuries Muslim jurists worked out elaborate codes of what constituted subordination and "signs of humiliation." Typically, Jewish and Christian houses of worship were to be inconspicuous, Jews and Christians were to wear distinguishing garments, such as special headgear or footwear and clothing of designated colors. They were prohibited from riding horses or engaging in occupations that would place them in a position of authority over Muslims. In addition, they were required to pay special discriminatory taxes on produce of the land and a special head tax *(jizyah).*

Implementation of the discriminatory decrees was never uniform; the earlier Middle Ages exhibited a far greater degree of tolerance than the later Middle Ages. On the peripheries of the Muslim empire, moreover, in Morocco, Persia, and Yemen, the Muslim regimes tended to enforce discriminatory codes much more rigorously than in the heartland. By the nineteenth century, the entire system of carefully balanced toleration tempered by discrimination had broken down and Jews increasingly turned to the European powers for protection. In general, however, Middle East society was marked by public displays of religiosity, which found particular expression in the family or clan unit. Judaism, too, was a family and communal tradition strengthened by generations of relative economic, social, and political isolation in Muslim lands. Known in Turkish as a *millet* (nation) in the Ottoman realm (from the mid-fifteenth century), Jews and Judaism enjoyed a relatively self-contained and protected position in the lands of Islam.

JEWISH DEMOGRAPHY IN MUSLIM LANDS: PRE- AND POST-1492. Population estimates of Jews in Muslim lands are extremely risky, since even at the height of the Muslim state its records of tax collection are partial and incomplete at best. It is generally accepted by historians that between eighty-five and ninety percent of world Jewry lived in the Muslim world in the period from the eighth through the tenth century. As that world became increasingly anarchic in the twelfth century, and as a result of the pogroms unleashed by the Almohads after 1147, Jewish population migrations to Christian lands increased. By the mid-seventeenth century, there were approximately three-quarters of a million Jews in the world, half of whom lived in the Muslim realm and half in Christian Europe (primarily Poland and Lithuania). During the sixteenth century acme of population growth in the Ottoman empire, the Jewish population in Istanbul alone reached forty thousand. At least as many Jews resided in contemporary Salonika. Perhaps as many as ten thousand Jews resided in Fez in Morocco, fifteen thousand in Iraq, and as many as fifteen thousand in the city of Safed (in Palestine) in the sixteenth century.

The Jewish population in the Ottoman empire began to decline dramatically in the seventeenth century as a result of fires, earthquakes, infant mortality, and increasing political insecurity. By the eve of World War II, Jews from Muslim lands numbered approximately one million out of the global Jewish population of approximately eighteen million. Since the Holocaust, Sephardic Jews (of Spanish origin) and Jews of Middle Eastern and North African origin have increased in demographic importance, both absolutely and relatively, since they significant percent of the Jewish population of Israel and a majority of the population of France, the second and third largest Jewish communities in the free world. (The term *Sephardic Jews* hereafter may include Middle Eastern and North African Jews, when their distinction is not necessary.)

The Exiles from Spain to the Maghreb. Jewish flight from Spain began as a mass movement, not in 1492, but in 1391. In that year, waves of violence inundated the Jews of Spain and the Balearic Islands, and while many Jews were martyred, others converted, and still others fled. One of the most important places of refuge of Spanish and Majorcan Jewry in 1391 was Algeria. Sephardic Jews met a mixed reception from the beleaguered indigenous Jews who feared that a large influx of Jews could ignite local anti-Semitism in the Muslim population. But they quickly assumed leadership positions in the community, providing a new élan to North African Jewish life. The scholar-refugee leaders Yitshaq ben Sheshet Perfet (1326–1408) and Shimʿon ben Tsemah Duran (1361–1444) have left a voluminous collection of rabbinic decisions and correspondence (*responsa*) revealing that Sephardic Jewry was troubled, not simply by the arduous task of communal reconstruction following flight, but also by very difficult questions of ritual and law as a result of the large-scale apostasy that had accompanied the waves of persecution. Questions of marital, ritual, and dietary law could not easily be resolved as demands for compassion clashed with real issues of communal continuity and Jewish identity.

The wave of refugees rose, and the question of secret Jews and forced converts (Marranos and *conversos*) grew more complex after 1492, as over 150,000 left Spain in haste. One of the favored refuges was Morocco, where Jews found asylum in the kingdom of Fez after a journey made perilous by unscrupulous captains and pirates. Chroniclers such as Avraham ben Shelomoh of Ardutiel, Avraham Zacuto, and Shelomoh ibn Verga dramatized the hazards of the flight from Spain. In Fez, Meknes, Marrakech, Safi, Arzila, and smaller towns the Sephardic refugees injected new leadership and frequent controversy into the midst of small indigenous communities. In the coastal regions they exploited their connections with the Iberian Peninsula, serving as commercial agents for the Spanish and Portuguese.

Wherever the Spanish refugees came, they brought with them great pride, loyalty, and nostalgia for their cities of origin. Many of their customs were unfamiliar to the local Jews, particularly the halakhic leniencies that they had devised in response to the religious persecution they had endured. But they considered their customs to be sacrosanct, and controversy raged among the Spanish Jews and between the Spaniards (known as *megorashim,* "expelled ones") and the indigenous Jews (known as *toshavim*). In Morocco, these communal divisions were reflected in a duplication of many communal institutions and a protracted communal debate in Fez that required Muslim intercession. Ultimately, Sephardic numerical preponderance and halakhic leadership prevailed and Moroccan Jewry emerged as a place of scholarship after centuries of quiescence.

In Tunisia, divisions between the refugees and the indigenous population were also institutionalized. They were aggravated by the influx of Jews from Livorno, Italy, who reinforced the separatism of the Spaniards. Two communities were established and the divisions between the newcomers (known as the *grana*) and the natives (*touansa*) persisted until the twentieth century. (This internecine struggle enabled local Turkish governors to exploit the Jews more easily.)

Jewish life in the Maghreb bore a number of distinctive features in the period following the advent of the Jews from Spain. On the one hand, most communities were torn by division as Sephardim attempted to impose their customs upon the local Jews. Given their large numbers, superior educational level, and self-confidence, Spanish Jewry assumed the helms of power in most of the Maghreb. New Jewish intellectual centers emerged in Fez (Morocco) and Tlemcen (Algeria), and the ordinances (*taqqanot*) of the Jews of Castile soon became the guide for natives as well as newcomers. In matters of personal status as well as questions of communal leadership, inheritance, and ritual slaughtering, the Sephardic way became the standard mode of behavior for most Maghrebi Jews.

North Africa was not, however, a mere replica of pre-1492 Spain. Local customs, such as worship at the tombs of saints, the special celebration at the end of the festival of Passover known as the Mimouna, and belief in the efficacy of amulets and talismans became part and parcel of Maghrebi Jewry as a whole. The special role of the emissary from Palestine, the *hakham kolel,* in the intellectual life of the Maghreb was already discernible by the fifteenth century. Through the *hakham kolel* the mystical movements of sixteenth-century Palestine spread rapidly in North Africa. North African Judaism was characterized by a melding of the study of Talmud with that of the Zohar and the pervasive spread in North Africa of Qabbalah or mysticism. This blending lent a special flavor to the scholarship of a long line of teachers, jurists, judges, and mystics.

The Aftermath of 1492: The Ottoman East. Even before the expulsion of 1492, Jews in the West began to hear that the Ottoman empire was welcoming Jewish immigration. Yitshaq Tsarfati reportedly addressed the Jews of northern Europe under the reign of Murad II (1421–1451):

> Brothers and teachers, friends and acquaintances! I, Isaac Sarfati, though I spring from French stock, yet I was born in Germany, and sat there at the feet of my esteemed teachers. I proclaim to you that Turkey is a land where nothing is lacking and where, if you will, all shall yet be well with you. The way to the Holy Land lies open to you through Turkey.

Indeed, Ottoman might appeared to be invincible for over one hundred years. By the reign of Süleyman I ("the Magnificent," 1520–1566) the Ottoman borders extended from Morocco in the west to Iran in the east, from Hungary in the north to Yemen in the south.

Throughout the sixteenth century, while the empire was reaching its acme, successive boats brought Jewish refugees ashore in the eastern Mediterranean, particularly to its fairest port on the Aegean, Salonika. Some of the refugees came directly from the Iberian Peninsula while others arrived after an initial stop in Italy or North Africa where many succeeded in recouping their assets. They were eagerly welcomed by the sultan Bayezid II (1481–1512), especially since many were reputed to be skilled munitions-makers who would undoubtedly be helpful allies in the repeated wars against the Habsburgs.

The newcomers to the Ottoman empire displayed a degree of separatism and individualism that surpassed that of their Sephardic coreligionists in the Maghreb. They tended to divide along geographic lines so that before long there were more than forty congregations in Istanbul and Salonika each. The very names of the congregations—Catalan, Castile, Aragon, Barcelona, Portugal, Calabria—evoked identification with their origins. Distinctive identities were reinforced by the separate formations of self-help societies of all sorts. The very mixture of Jews, not only various groups of Sephardim, but also Ashkenazim from Germany and Hungary, Greek-speaking Jews from the Balkans (known as Romaniots), and Italian Jews created strains and tensions. It was not long before the preponderance of Sephardim overwhelmed the smaller native communities and the Castilian language, with an admixture of Hebrew, Turkish, and Slavic words known as *Ladino,* became the primary language of Ottoman Jewry and it remained such until the twentieth century. Popular Jewish culture was sprinkled with Ladino proverbs and ballads and a veritable treasure trove of Iberian literature entered into the folk culture of Ottoman, especially Balkan Jewry.

The city of Salonika emerged as the preeminent Jewish community of the sixteenth century. The fame of its Talmud Torah (a rabbinic academy) spread far and wide, as did the rabbinic decisions of its rabbis Shemu'el de Medina (1505–1589) and his contemporary Yosef Taitasaq. The sixteenth-century Jewish historian Samuel Usque called Salonika in 1545 "a true mother in Judaism." Salonika's preeminence as a city of Sephardic culture remained down to its last days when, in 1943, the community was destroyed by the Nazis, its vast library sacked, and its four-hundred-year-old cemetery desecrated and dismantled.

One of the salient characteristics of the generation of exile was its melancholy brooding on the meaning of the tragic history of Israel, and especially of its Sephardic standard-bearers. A series of historians emerged among the Jewish people to record and comment upon the recent events. In his *Consolations for the Tribulations of Israel,* Samuel Usque, writing in Portuguese, adumbrated a lachrymose view of Jewish existence. His contemporary, Yosef ha-Kohen (d. 1578) in his *'Emeq ha-bakhah* compared Jewish history to a journey through a "valley of tears." A third sixteenth-century Sephardic commentator, Shelomoh ibn Verga, also sought to decipher the reasons for Jewish suffering in his *Shevet Yehudah* (Scepter of Judah). It has been suggested that this unparalleled outpouring of Jewish historical writing during the sixteenth century not only represented an intense intellectual attempt to understand what had happened but was also perceived by the very writers themselves as a *novum* in Jewish history. Jews were now seeking for the first time to understand the ways of oppressive nations, not only the ways of God. The chronicle *Seder Eliyyahu zuta'* by Eliyyahu Capsali of Crete is devoted in large part to discussions of Ottoman history. The events of the time also called forth two more enduring reactions in the mystical and messianic meanings ascribed to the Spanish Jewish tragedy.

Spanish Jews brought not only their contentiousness and tragic vision but also their critical intellectual and technological skills to the Ottoman realm. Among the most important of the technological skills was the fine art of printing. Soon after the expulsion, a Hebrew press appeared in Fez, and it was followed soon thereafter by Hebrew printing presses in Salonika (1500), Constantinople (1503), Safad (1563), and Smyrna (1764). Hebrew printing spread from there to Baghdad, Calcutta, and Poona and eventually to Jerba, Sousse, Algiers, and Oran. (Not until more than two hundred years after the establishment of the first Hebrew printing press in Turkey was the first Ottoman Turkish press established.) A large number of the works printed by the Jewish presses were tracts dealing with practical Qabbalah or mysticism. Indeed, the rapid spread of mysticism from sixteenth-century Safed throughout the Mediterranean world, as well as the *Zohar's* dissemination as a popular Sephardic text, can be attributed to the introduction of Hebrew printing in the Ottoman empire.

United under the umbrella of one dynamic and expansive empire, the Jews of Muslim lands enjoyed a cultural renaissance and an era of prosperity in the sixteenth century. Jewish physicians emerged in the royal courts of Constantinople to reassert their special role as courtiers and diplomats. Moshe Hamon (1490–1554), the personal physician to Süleyman I, managed to outlast the intrigues of the harem to excel as a physician, medical scholar, bibliophile, and protector of Jews against the blood libel (false accusation that Jews have committed a ritual murder). Rabbis Moshe Capsali (1453–1497), Eliyyahu Mizrahi (1498–1526), and Yosef ben Moshe di Trani (1604–1639) held considerable sway over the Ottoman Jews through their reputation as scholars rather than through any official position. By the eighteenth century, Izmir, as well, boasted a rabbinic leadership whose influence could be felt in the Near East.

Two personalities of sixteenth-century Ottoman Jewish history embody many of the qualities of the Sefardim in this generation. Gracia Nasi (d. 1568?), a Portuguese Marrano (whose *converso* name was Beatrice Mendès), Jewish banker, entrepreneur, and patron of scholars and schools, arrived in Constantinople amid great splendor. Her many activities in the Ottoman empire included the rescue of Marranos from the Inquisition, the restoration of Jewish learning through enormous charitable donations, and the judicious use of diplomatic levers to assist foreign Jews in distress. Gracia was assisted in her spectacular business undertakings by her nephew Yosef Nasi (1514–1579; that is, Joseph Mendès). Yosef was also adviser to Selim II, the sultan who awarded him a dukedom over the island of Naxos and a permit to recolonize the city of Tiberias. The awards were apparently made in recognition of the astuteness of Yosef's advice, particularly concerning the conquest of Cyprus in 1571.

Jewish life in the Arab provinces of the Ottoman empire also began to quicken as a result of the Ottoman conquests in the first quarter of the sixteenth century. Egypt produced David ibn Abi Zimra (1479–1573), one of the most prolific *responsa* writers of his day. Despite the Ottoman conquest of 1526, Iraq did not succumb to Ottoman control until the seventeenth century. Its small Jewish community, however, emerged from isolation and resumed contact with the outside Jewish world, turning, for example to the rabbis of Aleppo, Syria, for religious guidance. The Ottoman conquest of Arab provinces did not necessarily improve the lot of the Jews. For the Jews of Yemen, Ottoman incursions and conquest in 1546 destabilized an already precarious situation. Caught between warring Muslim forces, the Jews of Sanaa were subjected to severe discriminatory legislation, culminating in the destruction of synagogues and expulsions in the seventeenth century. Literarily, the community underwent a period of cultural flowering, despite these hardships, during the career of the Yemenite poet Shalom Shabbazi (1617–1680?).

Safed as a Center of Sephardic Search and Jewish Mysticism. The Sephardic refugees of the sixteenth century were a melancholy and restless generation, torn by guilty memories of community apostasy, perplexed by their continuing suffering and exile, and fevered by expectations of imminent salvation. Messianism ran deep in the community, easily aroused by flamboyant pretenders such as David Reubeni who went to Clement VII (1478–1534) and other Christian leaders with the offer of raising Jewish armies to help them recapture Palestine from the Ottomans. One of his most illustrious followers, a Portuguese secret Jew, Shelomoh Molkho (1501–1532), heeded Reubeni's call, circumcised himself, and set out for Italy preaching the advent of the Messiah. Ultimately he fell into the hands of the Inquisition and was burned at the stake in Mantua in 1532. His influence, however, spread as far as the settlement of Safed in Palestine.

After the Ottoman conquest of Palestine in 1516, Jewish migration to the Holy Land increased. Soon a remarkable galaxy of scholars and mystics emerged in Safed. Three generations of extraordinary mystics engaged collectively and individually in ascertaining practical means of hastening the redemption of the Jewish people while providing mythic formulations for comprehending the Sephardic catastrophe. These mystics were not recluses but were, rather, legal scholars actively engaged in history. One of their giants, Ya'aqov Berab (d. 1546), arrived in Safed after wanderings in North Africa and Egypt. Believing the time ripe for the messianic redemption of the Jewish people, Berab set out to restore the ancient rite of rabbinical ordination (*semikhah*) in 1538 as a prerequisite for the reestablishment of the Sanhedrin which was, in turn, prerequisite to the proper repentance of the Jewish people that would bring redemption. While his disciples eagerly accepted the new charge placed upon them, Berab's movement was ultimately thwarted by the forceful opposition of Levi ibn Habib of Jerusalem.

Another towering intellectual figure of that generation who eventually found his way to Safed after many years of wandering was Yosef Karo (1488–1575). Karo's halakhic authority was established by his major work *Beit Yosef.* He is remembered by posterity, however, through the utility of his comprehensive legal handbook *Shulhan Arukh.* In the *Shulhan Arukh* Karo presented numerous Sephardic as well as Ashkenazic practices in a readily accessible fashion, rendering his work one of the most useful codes for subsequent generations of Jews. Karo also possessed a mystical bent that emerges in his work *Maggid mesharim,* a mystical diary of angelic revelations, and he served as mentor to the remarkable cluster of mystics and pietists in sixteenth-century Safed.

With the arrival of Isaac Luria in Safed in the 1560s, Jewish mysticism reached its greatest heights. A charismatic personality with a stirring effect on his followers, Luria decisively influenced the development of Jewish mysticism in the following generations. Lurianic Qabbalah, with its doctrines of a cataclysmic scattering of divine sparks at creation and the unique role of Israel in liberating and reunifying these sparks, together with a belief in metempsychosis and new mystical modes of prayer, deepened the expectation of messianic redemption and altered the way many Jews thought about themselves for at least a century and a half.

The mystics of Safed delved into the vast corpus of Jewish literature, frequently using the Zohar as their point of departure. Many unusual personalities in this group were characterized by their frequent walks in the Galilee and fervent embellishment of the Sabbath and daily ritual actions. One of the participants was the poet Shelomoh Alkabets. He is best remembered for the poem *Lekhah dodi,* a Sabbath invocation welcoming the Sabbath as bride and queen that has been included in the Friday evening Sabbath services in all Jewish communities.

After Luria's death in 1572, his disciple Hayyim Vital (1543–1620) began to disseminate a version of the teachings of the Lurianic school of Safed. The prominence of the city itself did not last much longer. In 1576 the Ottoman sultan ordered the deportation of one thousand Jews from Safed to repopulate the newly conquered island of Cyprus. The order was rescinded soon thereafter, but many Jews had already left the city. The vitality of Safed's Jewish community was further sapped by the corruption of Ottoman provincial governors, the impact of devastating earthquakes, and the periodic depredations of local Arabs. Additionally, the mystical movement in Safed was severely compromised by the disastrous effects of the disillusionment in the wake of Shabbetai Tsevi's messianic movement. In the seventeenth century Safed reverted to its former role as an inconspicuous settlement in a backwater province while the qabbalistic ideas that had emerged there spread rapidly throughout the Diaspora.

INFLUENCE OF SHABBETAI TSEVI. The decline of the Jewish communities in Muslim lands was a slow process caused by a number of external factors. An especially prominent symptom of this decline is the bizarre and tragic career of Shabbetai Tsevi. Shabbetai Tsevi was born in the city of Smyrna in 1626, began to engage in mystical studies in 1648, and fell under the spell of Natan of Gaza in 1665, pronouncing himself the Messiah in that year. An anarchic outburst of antinomian activity and frenzy ensued as news of Shabbetai's bizarre behavior spread. Even his conversion to Islam in 1666 did not discredit the movement, but rather accelerated the tendency of that generation to perceive the Spanish experience as one with messianic overtones. The fact that Tsevi converted shook Marrano circles everywhere. Scholars in Italy and Amsterdam were agitated; poets in Kurdistan wrote poems on Shabbetean themes; Jewish followers of Tsevi, known as *Donmeh,* converted to Islam and continued to believe in Tsevi as the Messiah for generations after his death. The energy, confusion, guilt, and false hopes with which the Shabbatean movement had tried to break out of the mold of Jewish suffering left a hyperagitated Jewry deeply depressed.

Ultimately the messianic storm subsided, rabbis—especially in the Ottoman empire—began to destroy books with references to Shabbetai Tsevi, and concerted efforts were made once again to integrate mystical studies into rabbinics. Ultimately, Near Eastern Jewry repressed Shabbeteanism while retaining traces of it in its particular fondness for an integration of Judaism with such practices as saint worship and visiting holy sites (*ziyarah*), and a strengthened belief in the efficacy of practical Qabbalah such as the casting of lots or the interpretation of dreams.

Ottoman Jewish decline accelerated after the debacle of Tsevi. It was temporarily halted in 1730 when the first volume of the multivolume encyclopedia *Me'am lo'ez* appeared. This popular compendium of Oriental Sephardic lore by Ya'aqov ben Mahir Culi instructed while entertaining the masses with a vast array of legends, anecdotes, customs, and laws. Compositions in Ladino as well as Hebrew continued to be recited in the salons of Salonika, but the once vibrant Jewry of Ottoman lands found itself enfeebled by a series of natural catastrophies and by the mounting anti-Jewish hostility of Ottoman Christians as well as Muslims. While some of this hostility was the product of economic rivalry, some of it can also be traced to the influx of anti-Semitic notions from the West alongside the growing influence of Western, particularly French, power among the Christians.

NEAR EASTERN JEWRY ON THE EVE OF THE MODERN ERA. Jewish life in the easternmost part of the Ottoman empire did not share in the renaissance of sixteenth-century Ottoman Jewry. Persian Jews were particularly endangered by the campaign of forced conversion that the Shīʿī Safavid dynasty (1501–1732) undertook in the seventeenth century. Isolated from Ottoman Jewry, the forty thousand Jews of Persia were subjected to an especially harsh code of discriminatory legislation, known as the Jami Abbasi, which was operative until 1925. Even the increasing influence of the European powers could not spare the Jews of Mashhad from a forced conversion to Islam during the nineteenth century. The newly converted Jews of Mashhad continued to observe Judaism in secret, a fact that did not escape the notice of the surrounding Muslim population. When permitted in the twentieth century to revert to Judaism, new practices had crept into their observance. Foreign travelers to Persia (Iran) were struck by the abject conditions under which Jewish life endured.

Ottoman rule in Yemen (1546–1629) was succeeded by a harsh succession of independent *imāms* of the Zaydī sect. Despite the frequent expulsions from villages and towns and the implementation of the policy of kidnapping Jewish orphans to raise them within Islam, Yemenite Jews continued to produce a significant poetic and qabbalistic tradition during this period. Males were largely literate, the printed prayer books of the period attesting to the spread of Lurianic Qabbalah into the remote corners of the Ḥijāz. By the nineteenth century, even some of the tenets of Haskalah—European Jewish Enlightenment—had reached such communities as Sanaa. Change brought with it conflict and the Jews of Yemen were internally split. It was the worsening status of the Jews in Yemen, however, and not the ideological conflicts, that precipitated their mass migration from Yemen to Palestine in the 1880s. By the early twentieth century, Yemenite Jews formed a significant community in the city of Jerusalem.

Jews in the East had never ceased their close contact with other Jews even in the age of Ottoman military and political decline. Jews in the Ottoman realm (especially Sephardic Jews) continued to serve as merchants, diplomats, commercial agents, and interpreters throughout the period of Ottoman ascendancy and decline, reinforcing their ties with coreligionists. But by the nineteenth century, the Jewish position in Arab and Turkish lands was one of abject poverty, extreme vulnerability, humiliation, and insecurity. Pressures on the Ottomans to reform were brought to bear by the European powers, not so much to assist the Jews as primarily to assist the Ottoman Christians. Under these pressures the Ottoman reform movement, *Tanzimat,* ended special discriminatory taxation, agreed to protect the legal rights of non-Muslims, and granted civil equality to them. Reforming legislation, however, could not restore the Ottoman empire to good health. Jewish well-being came increasingly to depend upon the intervention of Western powers and Western Jews.

No incident highlighted this vulnerability and dependency more clearly than the Damascus blood libel in 1840. When the Jews of Damascus were falsely accused of murdering a Christian for ritual purposes, the community of Damascus, as well as other Syrian communities, faced grave danger. Through the intervention of Moses Montefiore of London (1784–1885) and Adolphe Crémieux (1796–1880) of Paris, the Jews of Damascus were rescued and the Sublime Porte was forced to publicly repudiate the blood libel accusation. During the course of their visit to the East, these European champions of Near Eastern Jewry became advocates of the introduction of modern schooling in the area and the importance of learning the languages of Europe and the local population. Soon after their successful intercession, tentative steps to introduce Western schooling began in Istanbul as well as Egypt. Despite this intervention, Near Eastern Jewry was subjected to a host of unfortunate blood libel accusations at the hands of the Greeks, Arabs, and Armenians in the nineteenth century. More than once the indefatigable Montefiore went to the Near East and the Maghreb to intercede personally on behalf of Jews.

Jewry in France. In 1860 the Alliance Israélite Universelle was founded in France. Among its guiding principles was the goal of protecting the Jewish communities of Muslim lands and modernizing and uplifting them from their abject state of poverty and ignorance. The altruistic goals of French Jewry dovetailed well with the political and imperial goals of the French government. The Jews of France set out with almost missionary zeal to transform the face of Near Eastern Jewry and to forge a community that would embody some of the cherished ideals of the French Revolution. Beginning with the establishment of their first school in Morocco in 1860, the Alliance Israélite Universelle proceeded to introduce modern, secular notions and technical skills to a new generation of Jews throughout the Near East. By World War I, over one hundred Alliance schools teaching the French language and secular subjects had been set up in Morocco, Algeria, Tunisia, Libya, Egypt, Iran, Turkey, and the Balkans. The Alliance schools succeeded in undercutting poverty and Jewish female illiteracy and, introducing secular studies to all Jews, prepared a new generation of Jews for entry into modernity. Its thoroughgoing insistence on modernization also dealt a near fatal blow to the preponderance of Ladino and its folk culture as Alliance schools insisted that their pupils discard the language in favor of French.

The introduction of Western-style education among Near Eastern Jews did not result in a parallel movement of religious reformulation and the building of a new, modern Jewish identity there. This was partially because Near Eastern Jews, unlike the Jews of Europe, were not presented with the option of entering their majority society provided they refashioned themselves since religion remained a fundamental basis of social and political organization in the Middle East. Many Jewish autonomous institutions ceased to exist as a direct result of European colonial legislation. For example, early in their administration, the French authorities in Algeria abolished the independent Jewish system of courts. While Jews were granted French citizenship in Algeria in 1870, elsewhere they adopted European culture without attaining the benefits of European citizenship. Their cultural identity with the European powers, especially in North Africa, ushered in a period of confusion of identities as local Arab nationalism began to flower. In some parts of the Arab world, such as Iraq, the Jewish minority became one of the segments of the population most active in creating modern Arabic literature. Yet, at the same time that they pioneered in the language, press, and modernization of the economy of the Arab states, Jews were increasingly isolated from the pan-Arab and pan-Islamic culture then capturing the hearts of the masses. For Middle Eastern Jews, however, the modern period of Western encroachment did not result in indigenous Jewish attempts to form new self-identifying modes of expression. Even the Zionist movement of national self-determination, a late nineteenth-century European Jewish response to emancipation and modernity, echoed only faintly in Muslim lands.

A vigorous movement of religious reform and its attendant strident denominationalism never took place in the Near East as occurred in Western Europe and America. Nevertheless, it would be incorrect to conclude that Judaism in the Near East was untouched by the currents of modernity. The traditional school declined as modern schools of the Alliance Israélite Universelle were founded from Morocco to Iran. From the beginning, the modernizing schools tried to stress the reforming, rather than revolutionary, nature of their innovations. Hebrew studies were relegated to a minor part of the curriculum and girls as well as boys were provided with vocational and linguistic skills. To smooth the path of its innovative schools, the Alliance received the endorsement of local traditional authorities by including them on their faculties as instructors of Judaica. Local rabbis were not simply co-opted, but sometimes eagerly endorsed the schools for their own children as it became increasingly evident that modern education would be the route out of poverty for their communities. Additionally, these schools provided the only alternative to the increasingly attractive option of the mission schools which the European powers were introducing in the area. Thus Rabbi Israel Moses Hazzan, chief rabbi of Alexandria from 1857 to 1863, endorsed the new curriculum and the learning of foreign languages. Rabbis Eliyyahu Bekhor Hazzan (1847–1908) and Raphael Ben Simeon (1847–1928) exhibited a gradualist approach to modernization in Egypt and Morocco respectively. For Rabbi Ben-Zion Meir Hai Uzziel (1880–1953), chief Sephardic rabbi in Israel, Jewish law had the inherent capacity to respond to the challenge of modernity

At the same time that many prominent nineteenth and twentieth century Sephardic rabbis adopted a moderate path with regard to modernization, the Near Eastern states continued to regard the rabbinical authorities as the final arbiters in family and personal law. Paradoxically, the actual power of the rabbinical courts increased. This scenario represented a sharp contrast to the increasing secularization of society characteristic of modern Europe and the sharp polarizations within Ashkenazic society. Respect for Near Eastern Jewish traditional leadership was undiminished even as Jewish traditional mores declined. Judaism as an expression of family solidarity remained as the bedrock of Sephardic and Near Eastern Jewry. Jewish life became increasingly secularized on a day to day basis.

CONCLUSION. Arab nationalism reached a crescendo in the post–World War II period. In the wake of the creation of the State of Israel and the emergence of Arab independent states in the post–World War II period, Jewish life became precarious in the extreme. Riots, forced incarcerations of Jews, panic and flight spread throughout the Near East and North Africa. The millennial communities of Jews in Muslim lands came to an abrupt and almost total end. By the year 2000 less than 10,000 of the former 250,000 Moroccan Jews remain in Morocco. All other Jewish communities have virtually disappeared except a small remnant in Turkey and Iran. The Judaism of the more than one million Jews who fled their ancestral homes for Israel or the West is a Judaism still in flux. Middle Eastern Jewish religiosity was always anchored in familial and communal action, especially in the post-1492 period. In the Muslim world, people had stayed in their communities for generations, passing on hereditary communal offices from father to son. Although these lines of tradition have been irrevocably cut with the great migration to Western, technological, modern societies, the Judaism of the Middle Eastern Jew has retained some remnants of former times. Among those remnants must be included the fervent love of the Land of Israel with its messianic and mystical overtones, the expression of religiosity within a familial context, and the special pride and quality imparted by a specific link with the Sephardic tradition.

Just as 1789 set in motion a crucial reorientation of Jewish identities and Judaism in western Europe, and just as 1881 set in motion a process of change that eventually led to a permanent transformation in the structure of Jewish politics among Ashkenazim, especially in eastern Europe, so too, one suspects, 1948 will be found to have marked a transforming date in the lives of Middle Eastern Jews. With the end of living on the fringes of Muslim society, the Jewish communities from the world of Islam have embarked upon a new path in Jewish history.

SEE ALSO Anti-Semitism; Folk Religion, article on Folk Judaism; Karo, Yosef; Luria, Isaac; Marranos; Messianism, article on Jewish Messianism; Pilgrimage, article on Contemporary Jewish Pilgrimage; Polemics, article on Muslim-Jewish Polemics; Qabbalah; Shabbetai Tsevi; Zionism.

BIBLIOGRAPHY

The best introductory volume on the subject is Solomon Dob Fritz Goitein's survey *Jews and Arabs: Their Contacts through the Ages,* 3d rev. ed. (New York, 1974). Norman A. Stillman's *The Jews of Arab Lands: A History and Source Book* (Philadelphia, 1979) provides a fine introductory essay and a large collection of documents translated from Arabic and Hebrew and a variety of Western languages. More recently, Bernard Lewis's *The Jews of Islam* (Princeton, 1984) has offered a fresh interpretation of the broad sweep of Middle Eastern Jewish history. André N. Chouraqui's *Between East and West: A History of the Jews of North Africa,* translated by Michael M. Bernet (Philadelphia, 1968), gives a balanced survey of the Jews of the Maghreb and is particularly informative for the modern period. For a more detailed examination of the Maghreb, see H. Z. Hirschberg's *Toledot ha-Yehudim be-Afriqah ha-Tsefonit,* 2 vols. (Jerusalem, 1965), translated by M. Eichelberg as *A History of the Jews in North Africa,* vol. 1, *From Antiquity to the Sixteenth Century* (Leiden, 1974) and vol. 2, *From the Ottoman Conquests to the Present Time* (Leiden, 1981). Hirschberg analyzes the political history of the Jews in Arab lands and the Maghreb extensively in his article "The Oriental Jewish Communities," in *Religion in the Middle East: Three Religions in Concord and Conflict,* edited by A. J. Arberry (Cambridge, 1969), pp. 119–225. Older multivolume studies of Ottoman Jewry such as Solomon A. Rosanes' *Divrei yemei Yisra'el be-Togarma,* 6 vols. (Jerusalem, 1930–1945) and Moïse Franco's *Essai sur l'histoire des Israelites de l'Empire Ottoman depuis les origines jusqu'à nos jours* (Paris, 1897) still contain valuable material culled from rabbinic sources. Volume 18 of Salo W. Baron's exceptionally important *A Social and Religious History of the Jews,* 2d ed., rev. & enl. (New York, 1983), updates these earlier studies, extending the geographic scope to include the Jews of Persia, China, India and Ethiopia as well as the Ottoman empire. Especially useful is Baron's discussion of demography. The problem of the general question of the legal status of the Jews under Islam has been treated by A. S. Tritton in *The Caliphs and Their Non-Muslim Subjects* (London, 1930). While Tritton is still the standard reference work on Muslim theories regarding the *dhimmis,* a methodical discussion can be found in Antoine Fattal's *Le statut légal des non-Musulmans en pays d'Islam* (Beirut, 1958). Four monographs of varying value treat the specific problems of individual Jewries based on rabbinic *responsa.* These studies are still useful as the sole English source on significant rabbinic figures and their age. Isidore Epstein's *The Responsa of Rabbi Simon B. Zemah Duran as a Source of the History of the Jews in North Africa* (1930; reprint New York, 1968), Israel Goldman's *The Life and Times of Rabbi David Ibn Abi Zimra* (New York, 1970), Morris S. Goodblatt's *Jewish Life in Turkey in the Sixteenth Century as Reflected in the Legal Writings of Samuel de Medina* (New York, 1952), and Abraham M. Hershman's *Rabbi Isaac ben Sheshet Perfet and His Times* (New York, 1943) explore the major problems of an age of transition and the response of a leading rabbinic luminary. A delightful account of the city of Safed and its Qabbalistic circles is Solomon Schechter's essay "Safad in the Sixteenth Century," which can be found in his *Studies in Judaism* (1908; reprint, Cleveland, 1958) and in *The Jewish Expression,* edited by Judah Goldin (New York, 1970). The Qabbalistic movement of Safed also can be seen in the excellent biography *Joseph Karo: Lawyer and Mystic* by R. J. Zwi Werblowsky (London, 1962). For an exhaustive and monumental treatment of the life and times of Shabbetai Tsevi, see Gershom Scholem's *Sabbatai Sevi: The Mystical Messiah, 1626–1676* (Princeton, 1973). More recent studies of the Shabbatean movement have enlarged the discussion to take into account parallel messianic and mystical movements in Christian and Muslim circles. See Matt Goldish's discussion of spirit possession and the intense religious contacts among Jews and Christians in the fifteenth and sixteenth centuries in *The Sabbatean Prophets* (Cambridge, 2004) and Lawrence Fine's *Safed Spirituality* (New York, 1982). Moshe Idel's ongoing scholarship has injected new scholarship and lively controversy in the growing literature on Qabbalah and the qabbalistic tradition. A one-volume introductory overview of Near Eastern Jewry with essays by leading scholars in the field can be found in *The Jews of the Middle East and North Africa in Modern Times*, edited by Reeva S. Simon, Michael M. Laskier, and Sara Reguer (New York, 2003). Norman Stillman's *Sephardic Religious Responses to Modernity* (Luxembourg, 1995) and Zvi Zohar's *Tradition and Change: Halakhic Responses of Middle Eastern Rabbis to Legal and Technological Change Syria and Egypt 1880–1920* (Jerusalem, 1993) [in Hebrew] offer extended discussions on how Near Eastern rabbinic authorities handled the challenges of modernity. The single best treatment of the Alliance Israelite Universelle can be found in Aron Rodrigue, *French Jews, Turkish Jews* (Bloomington, Ind., 1990). Esther Benbassa and Aron Rodrigue offer a comprehensive overview of Turkish and Balkan Jewry in *The Jews of the Balkans: The Judeo-Spanish Community, 15th to 20th Centuries* (Oxford, 1995), providing an essential one-volume text on the history of the Jews of the area from 1500–2000. For an exhaustive study of the Damascus Blood Libel see Jonathan Frankel, *The Damascus Affair* (Oxford, 1995). The latest studies on Jews in the Middle East can be found in such Israeli publications as *Sefunot* (Jerusalem, 1956–1966), *Pe'amin* (Jerusalem, 1979–), and *Mizrah u-ma'arav* (Jerusalem, 1919–1932). Interdisciplinary approaches can be fruitfully employed in this field, and the works of contemporary anthropologists such as Moshe Shokeid, Harvey Goldberg, Shlomo Deshen, and the late Walter Zenner have been especially illuminating in analyzing Middle Eastern Jewish communities in Israel. These studies frequently begin with considerations of individual Near Eastern Jewish communities in their traditional milieu and historical structure.

JANE S. GERBER (1987 AND 2005)

JUDAISM: JUDAISM IN NORTHEAST AFRICA

The Bēta Esraʾēl (Falāshā), or Beta Israel, formed an ethnic group that numbered around thirty thousand and resided in Northwest Ethiopia. Whereas some scholars and the Bēta Esraʾēl themselves contend that their religion was essentially an archaic form of Judaism, others view it as primarily Ethiopian in its origins, form, and content. Although the first of these hypotheses cannot be totally excluded, it is possible to demonstrate that numerous elements of the Bēta Esraʾēl religion, including its literature, liturgy, and clerical hierarchy, developed in Ethiopia after the fourteenth century. During the twentieth century Ethiopian Judaism ceased to exist in its customary form. Contacts with representatives of world Jewry led to changes in Ethiopia in the indigenous tradition, and the emigration to Israel of virtually all practicing Bēta Esraʾēl put an end to Jewish communal life in Ethiopia.

RELIGIOUS LIFE IN ETHIOPIA. The belief system of the Bēta Esraʾēl had at its core the belief in one God, the Lord of Israel. Both angels and demons, as well as hostile spirits known as *zar*, also figured prominently in their cosmology. The Bēta Esraʾēl did not believe divine intervention to be a regular occurrence; however, the judgment of souls after death forms one of the major themes in their literature. They also believed in a final judgment at the end of days.

The clerical structure of the Bēta Esraʾēl, which in the past included monks, priests, deacons, and clerics known as *dabtarotch*, showed a marked resemblance to that of their Christian neighbors. From the middle of the fifteenth century until the end of the nineteenth century, monks were the principal religious leaders of the Bēta Esraʾēl. The decline and virtual disappearance of monasticism during the twentieth century appears to be related to a disastrous famine (1888–1892) and criticisms from both Christian missionaries and representatives of world Jewry.

The Bēta Esraʾēl priesthood was not hereditary, nor was it limited to a particular family or clan. Priests recited prayers during the week and on the Sabbath and holidays. They also performed sacrifices and officiated at rites of passage, such as circumcisions, naming ceremonies, funerals, and memorials for the dead. Every Bēta Esraʾēl had a priest who was his or her confessor. During his training, a candidate for the priesthood served as a deacon. In this position he assisted in prayers, carried firewood and water, and cared for animals destined for sacrifice. He also learned to read and write, studied the Bible and other texts, and familiarized himself with the liturgy and ritual practice. A *dabtarā* (plural *dabtarotch*) was an unordained or defrocked cleric who assisted the in the liturgy. *Dabtarotch* were often skilled in the performance of sacred music and not only copied religious texts but also wrote charms. During the twentieth century the *dabtarotch* practically disappeared.

Bēta Esraʾēl religious life was centered around the prayer house (*ṣalota bēt*), also called a *masgid* (from the root *sagada*, "to bow"). Prayers were recited on all holidays and at major stages in the life cycle of the individual. The Bēta Esraʾēl also brought offerings of bread and beer to the prayer house on Sabbaths and other festivals. Another major feature of religious practice was the performance of sacrifices (*qwerbān*). During the twentieth century, however, there was a sharp decline in the frequency of sacrifice due to both economic distress and criticism voiced by foreign representatives of Judaism and Christianity.

For the computation of feasts *(baʿāl)* and fasts *(ṣom)*, the Bēta Esraʾēl used a lunar calendar composed alternately of thirty or twenty-nine days. Although this calendar drew from written sources, including the Pentateuch, *Enoch*, and *Jubilees*, there was no written calendar. The following are the most important Bēta Esraʾēl holidays and fasts.

Sanbat (Sabbath) observance is one of the major themes of Bēta Esraʾēl literature, and it holds a central place in their religious life. Sabbath observance was particularly strict: no work was done, no fires were lit (including Sabbath candles), no food was cooked, and no journey could be undertaken. Sexual relations were also forbidden. The Bēta Esraʾēl treated every seventh Sabbath with particular respect and viewed it as a day particularly suited for confession and the absolution of sins.

Most of the annual holidays observed by the Bēta Esraʾēl are based on biblical precedents and have parallels in the celebrations of other Jewish communities. These include Fāsikā in commemoration of the exodus from Egypt; Berhān Sharaqa, which marked the New Year; Astasreyo, which was similar to Yom Kippur; and Baʿāla Maṣallat, coinciding with Sukkot (Feast of Tabernacles). The holiday of Māʿrar (harvest), which corresponds to Pentecost, was celebrated on the twelfth day of the third month, seven weeks after the last day of Fāsikā. Another Māʿrar was celebrated in the ninth month, to better coincide with the actual harvest in the Ethiopian agricultural cycle. Although the Bēta Esraʾēl did not celebrate Purim, they did observe the fast of Esther (Ṣoma Astēr) in commemoration of *Esther* 4:16. Prior to the twentieth century Jewish festivals such as Simḥat Torah, Ḥanukkah, Lag ba-ʿOmer, the fast of Gedaliah, and Tu bʾshvat were not observed.

Sigd is a unique pilgrimage festival celebrated by the Bēta Esraʾēl on the twenty-ninth day of the eighth month. Some associate the holiday with the renewal of the covenant during the period of Ezra and Nehemiah (*Ezr.* 8–10), and passages from these texts were part of the holiday liturgy. However, scriptural texts concerning the revelation at Sinai and the Decalogue were also read.

Traditionally the Bēta Esraʾēl observed a number of monthly celebrations. The first day of each month was celebrated in keeping with biblical custom. The tenth, twelfth, fifteenth, and twenty-ninth of each month served as monthly reminders of Astasreyo, Mārʿar, Fāsikā, and Sigd. During the last decades of the twentieth century the observance of these holidays lapsed in Ethiopia.

Ritual purity played a central role in Bēta Esraʾēl observances both in the regulation of internal communal relations and the definition of the community's differences from its Christian neighbors. The Bēta Esraʾēl were particularly devoted to the laws that governed female purity during menstruation and after giving birth. According to Bēta Esraʾēl practice, a menstruating woman left her house and entered a menstrual hut, where she remained for seven days. This hut was located at the edge of her village, and only her children and other women, who brought her food, were allowed to enter it. Even when the observance of other purity laws began to decline, these rituals were maintained with a special tenacity.

Circumcision for Bēta Esraʾēl boys took place on the eighth day after birth. After the circumcision, the mother and the infant entered the birth hut, where they remained for thirty-nine days. Female circumcision was practiced by the Bēta Esraʾēl in Ethiopia, although the custom appears to have been in decline throughout the twentieth century. Unlike male circumcision, this ritual had no fixed day and minimal religious content. Female circumcision was only performed by women. Two weeks after the birth of a girl, the mother and child entered the birth hut, where they remained for sixty-six days. Forty days after the birth of a boy and eighty days after the birth of a girl, the mother and child ended their isolation. A priest gave the baby its name and immersed it in water. The Ethiopic text known as the *Book of the Disciples (Ardeʿet)* was read as part of this ceremony.

The Bēta Esraʾēl believed it to be of the utmost importance that the dead receive a proper burial and be properly commemorated. When a person felt death approaching, he or she offered a final confession to his or her spiritual guardian. Priests recited psalms and prayers of absolution at the funeral. For seven days after the funeral, close kin of the deceased abstained from work. On the seventh day, a sheep or goat was sacrificed, and a feast was prepared. A commemoration ceremony was also observed on the anniversary of the death.

LITERATURE. Any consideration of Bēta Esraʾēl literature must begin with biblical literature. Their version of the Old Testament, known as the *Orit*, is identical to that of the Ethiopian Orthodox Church. It also included such apocryphal and pseudepigraphical works as *Tobit*, *Judith*, *Ben Sira*, and most importantly *Enoch* and *Jubilees*. The Bēta Esraʾēl were not familiar with the Talmud or later rabbinic literature; however, they possessed a number of noncanonical works. One large group that includes *The Death of Moses*, *The Death of Aron*, and the testaments of Abraham, Isaac, and Jacob relates the deaths of biblical figures. *The Disciples* contains Moses' secret teachings to his disciples (the leaders of the twelve tribes). The *Conversation of Moses* contains a dialogue between Moses and God in which the divine essence and the punishment of the dead are explicated. The importance of the Sabbath forms the focus of *The Commandments of the Sabbath*, *The Teachings of the Sabbath*, and much of the homiletic work *Abba Elijah*. The fate of the soul after death is yet another central theme of Bēta Esraʾēl literature and is discussed in *The Book of Angels*, *Apocalypse of Baruch*, and *Gorgoryos*.

Almost without exception the literature of the Bēta Esraʾēl did not originate within their community, nor did it reach them directly through Jewish channels. Rather, the majority of Ethiopian "Jewish" texts reached the Bēta Esraʾēl through the mediation of Ethiopian Christian sources after the fourteenth century.

CHANGES IN THE TWENTIETH CENTURY. Although Bēta Esraʾēl religious practice developed and evolved throughout its history, changes became particularly obvious during the twentieth century as a result of contact with representatives of world Jewry. The arrival in Ethiopia in 1904 of Jacques (Yaʾacov) Faitlovitch marked a turning point in the relationship between the Bēta Esraʾēl and the outside Jewish world. Faitlovitch's introduction of external Jewish elements began a process that has continued into the twenty-first century. Following the establishment of the state of Israel, many Bēta Esraʾēl villages were exposed to aspects of external Jewry, including Hebrew prayers, Ḥanukkah, Purim, and the lighting of candles on the eve of the Sabbath. Elements of "normative" Jewish practice, such as the use of Torah scrolls, began to be introduced in the celebration of Sigd.

Although contact with representatives of world Jewry brought about certain changes in Bēta Esraʾēl belief and ritual in Ethiopia, these pale in comparison to the changes that occurred following the arrival of Bēta Esraʾēl in Israel beginning in 1977. Bēta Esraʾēl clergy in Israel were not allowed to retain their clerical status and lost the right to perform rituals such as weddings, circumcisions, or funerals. Moreover the resettlement of immigrants with no regard for previous village residence inevitably resulted in a disruption of previous ties between priests and their followers. Most priests, however, continue to perform some religious duties and to participate in ritual gatherings. A small number of younger priests have undertaken studies that enable them, at least in theory, to exercise some formal religious functions, and some priests are among the Ethiopians who have been trained as rabbis. Ethiopian synagogues have been established in a small number of communities, but these are the exception rather than the rule.

Ethiopian traditions of ritual purity have also weakened seriously since their arrival in Israel. Israeli authorities made a conscious decision not to facilitate the observance of menstrual separation. The comparatively late age of marriage of Ethiopian women in Israel, as well as their unprecedented presence in the educational system and workforce, are further factors that serve to discourage traditional menstrual observances. Although it is still possible for women to observe the days of separation after the birth of a child, this custom has changed dramatically. Most Ethiopians visit a woman after she gives birth, and some will kiss and touch a postpartum woman and her baby. Purification and naming ceremonies, forty or eighty days after birth, remain popular.

Most Bēta Esraʾēl holidays that parallel pan-Jewish observances have been assimilated to their non-Ethiopian equivalents in Israel. Sigd continues to be celebrated in Israel with a central national ceremony being conducted in Jerusalem. In the spring of every year, on the day that celebrates the Israeli reunification of Jerusalem in 1967, the Ethiopian community holds a ceremony in memory of those who perished in an attempt reach Israel.

The pressures on Ethiopian immigrants to adopt lifestyles similar to those of either their religious or secular Israeli neighbors have led to a large-scale abandonment of Ethiopian customs and practices. It appears unlikely that much more than remnants and scattered elements of Ethiopian Judaism will survive beyond the first decades of the twenty-first century.

BIBLIOGRAPHY

Aescoly, Aaron Z., ed. *Recueil de textes Falachas: Introduction, textes éthiopiens.* Paris, 1951. Geez religious texts with a French translation.

Halévy, Joseph, ed. and trans. *Teʾezaza Sanbat: Commandements du Sabbat.* Paris, 1902. The first major edition of Bēta Esraʾēl texts translated from Geez into French.

Kaplan, Steven. *Les Falāshās.* Turnhout, Belgium, 1990. A general survey discussing history, religion, and society, with selected texts in French translation.

Kaplan, Steven, and Hagar Salamon. "Ethiopian Immigrants in Israel: Experience and Prospects." *Jewish Policy Research Report* 1 (1998).

Leslau, Wolf. *Coutumes et croyances des Falachas.* Paris, 1957. An important survey of Bēta Esraʾēl religious life.

Leslau, Wolf, ed. and trans. *Falasha Anthology.* New Haven, Conn., 1951. A translation of Geez literature into English with an ethnographic introduction.

Quirin, James A. *The Evolution of the Ethiopian Jews: A History of the Beta Israel (Falasha) to 1920.* Philadelphia, 1992. A comprehensive history.

Salamon, Hagar. *The Hyena People: Ethiopian Jews in Christian Ethiopia.* Los Angeles, 1999. A reconstruction of Jewish life in Ethiopia based on interviews conducted in Israel.

Shelemay, Kay Kaufman. *Music, Ritual, and Falasha History.* East Lansing, Mich., 1986. A major study tracing the links between Christian monasticism and Bēta Esraʾēl liturgy.

Ullendorff, Edward. *Ethiopia and the Bible.* London, 1968. A classic work on the impact of the Bible on Ethiopian culture.

STEVEN KAPLAN (2005)

JUDAISM: JUDAISM IN ASIA

For as long as two millennia, perhaps even longer, there have been Jewish communities scattered throughout South, East, central, and Southeast Asia. Most have lived in port cities, such as Surat, Kochi (formerly Cochin), Mumbai (formerly Bombay), Kolakata (formerly Calcutta), Yangon (formerly Rangoon), Singapore, Bangkok, Kobe, Hong Kong, and Shanghai. Other Jewish communities were found at major trading centers along the Spice Route, which meandered westward from South India through Kabul, Herat, and thence Iran and Turkey. Jewish communities also thrived along the Silk Route at Bukhara, Tashkent, and Samarkand in central Asia and at Dunhuang, a cosmopolitan Gobi Desert oasis, but the best known was at the route's eastern terminus, Kaifeng.

Some of these Jewish communities are old, dating from at least the early medieval period if not ancient times, whereas some of them emerged when merchant houses in India established branches eastward during the nineteenth century. Some communities are newer: Bangkok's Jewish community dates from the first half of the twentieth century, and Shanghai's modern Jewish community has existed only since the establishment of diplomatic relations between China and Israel in 1992. Many of these Asian Diaspora communities have been in decline since the middle of the twentieth century due to emigration to Israel and elsewhere.

It is in the oldest of these Jewish communities that one finds the most profound interactions with the host culture. The best examples are Kochi in India and Kaifeng in China.

KOCHI, INDIA. According to local traditions, Jews first settled on India's southwest coast when the Second Temple was destroyed and the Romans exiled all Jews from Jerusalem in 70 CE. They fled along maritime trade routes, which had been in use since King Solomon's time; travel along these routes had recently become faster with the discovery of the monsoon winds by Greek navigators early in the first century. The Jewish refugees settled at Cranganore, among other towns, where they were granted political autonomy by local monarchs and flourished as agriculturists, international spice merchants, petty traders, and shipbuilders and in government service and the military. During the fourteenth century Jews migrated to Kochi. Their numbers in the Malabar rose as high as three thousand at the time of independence, but fewer than fifty remain at the beginning of the twenty-first century. Where there were once nine flourishing synagogues as well as Jewish schools, scribes, scholars, mystics, and poets, in the early twenty-first century the Cochin Synagogue, built in 1568, fails to obtain a prayer quorum of ten adult males unless there are Jewish visitors from elsewhere in India or abroad.

The Kochi Jews, always part of the Jewish mainstream both commercially and culturally, were knowledgeable about their religion and savvy about affairs of state and currency fluctuations even in far-off Europe, not to mention among the plethora of princely states of South India. Knowing the languages of the subcontinent, the Middle East, and Europe, they played invaluable roles in both commerce and diplomacy.

The Kochi Jews' religious life evidences a high degree of acculturation into their Indian context but not assimilation. For example, during their autumn holy days and at weddings, many customs of the Nayar (the local dominant caste) and symbols of royalty were adopted. At weddings, for another example, Kochi Jews borrowed an elephant from a neighboring Hindu temple to convey the bridegroom to the synagogue for nuptials. During the festival of Rejoicing in the Torah (Simḥat Torah), Kochi Jews added three elements to their celebrations that are found nowhere else in the Jewish world: they displayed their Torah scrolls on a temporary ark on the days just prior to the festival, during the afternoon prayers they performed outdoor circumambulations of the synagogue with their Torah scrolls, and at the conclusion of the festival they ritually demolished their temporary ark to the accompaniment of unique Hebrew songs. All of these behaviors reflect Hindu temple festivals, when the deity (*mūrti*) of the temple is first displayed, then taken on procession, and then (often) disposed of. None of these practices violates Judaic law (*halakhah*), so these borrowings from the local Hindu culture were judicious and reflected the Kochi Jewish community's firm Jewish identity, based on Judaic learning.

Another example of the acculturation of Kochi Jews is the position of women in the community. Kochi Jewish women were remarkably well educated, with fluency in Hebrew and knowledge of Judaic law. They were active in composing Malayalam folk songs, sung at weddings, during matzo baking, and on other occasions. These songs interweave Jewish and Malayali motifs and symbols, and they played an important role in establishing and celebrating the Indian Jewish identity of these Jewish communities. The high position of Jewish women in Kochi is also reflected symbolically. For example, liturgical events deemed important, such as Torah readings, were performed from a second bimah located in front of the *ezrat nashim* (women's section), which is up a flight of stairs. Women's ritual garments (*mundus*) were used to decorate the synagogue as well as for a *parochet* (curtain) in front of the holy ark. These unique expressions of the Judaism of the women reflect the religious and secular power of women of the local dominant caste, the Nayars, with whom the Jews had particularly close relationships.

KAIFENG, CHINA. The Kochi Jews were acculturated, which is to say they were culturally at home in their Hindu environment, without becoming assimilated, which involves a surrender of identity. Not so with the Jews of Kaifeng, China, at least not in the long run.

Jews came to China following two routes. Persian Jews came via the Silk Route. Judging from a Hebrew manuscript on Chinese paper discovered in a Buddhist library in Dunhuang as well as Muslim travelers' reports, Jews were established in China no later than the eighth century. Indian Jews came via maritime routes to the South China Sea and settled in port cities. The Kaifeng community is the only one that survived the Middle Ages, having been "discovered" as an isolated, moribund community by Jesuit missionaries during the early seventeenth century.

Jews lived in Kaifeng for nearly a thousand years, where they were traders, agriculturists, artisans, physicians, and government officials. More than a few passed the rigorous civil service examinations and became mandarins. They constructed a synagogue in Kaifeng in 1126 that included an ancestor hall, typical of Chinese temples. Through the years Kaifeng's Jews increasingly identified with Chinese high culture. A 1488 inscription in their synagogue proclaimed:

> Although our religion agrees in many respects with the religion of the literati, from which it differs in a slight degree, yet the main design of it is nothing more than reverence for Heaven, and veneration for ancestors, fi-

delity to the prince, and obedience to parents, just what is included in the five human relations, the five constant virtues, with the three principal connections of life.

To Western Jews it is striking to hear Judaism described in such Confucian terms. Similarly it is remarkable to see in the Cochin Synagogue reflections of Hindu temple behavior. But on the other hand, one can imagine that to an Indian or Chinese Jew it would be unnerving to know that their American coreligionists understand Judaism fundamentally as ethical monotheism; such a characterization might sound Protestant. The point is that Judaism, like any ancient religion, has many threads within itself, and one or another of these threads becomes highlighted in response to the ethos of the host culture in which a particular Jewish community finds itself. Such a process could be indicated by using a concept borrowed from Gestalt psychology, that of background and foreground. In relation to a background (the host culture), certain elements in a perceptual field rise to the foreground (the particular Judaisms of India, China, or the United States). As Judaism, or any religion, moves from culture to culture or as it moves through time, differing threads are foregrounded and others backgrounded, depending on the host culture and its vicissitudes.

CONTEMPORARY INDIAN JEWRY. India had and still has the largest number of Jews of any country east of Iran. Indian Jewish population peaked in 1950 at around thirty to thirty-five thousand, after which emigration to Israel and other places reduced their number to around four to six thousand by the beginning of the twenty-first century, more if the so-called Bʾnai Menashe and Bʾnai Ephraim are counted.

There have been three major distinct Jewish communities in India. The oldest group, which in the early twenty-first century numbers less than fifty, is found in and around Kochi in the southwestern state of Kerala. Perhaps five thousand Cochinim, as they are called in Hebrew, live in Israel. The largest group is known as Bene Israel and is found chiefly in and around Mumbai, with active communities in Pune also in Maharashtra state, in Ahmedabad in Gujerat state, and in New Delhi. All told, there are four to five thousand Bene Israel in India and forty to fifty thousand in Israel, where they make up a significant ethnic group (*edah* in Hebrew) known as *Hodʾim*, "Indians."

The most recently arrived group, which is known in India as Baghdadis, or Middle Eastern Jews, is made up mostly of Arabic speakers who migrated to India during the late eighteenth century, about the time the British arrived. These immigrants settled in India's port cities, especially Mumbai and Kolakata. Numbering about five thousand at their peak, they have declined to around one hundred, most all of whom are elderly. The Baghdadis played a significant role in the development of British India's ports. Beginning as jewelers and opium traders, Baghdadi entrepreneurs soon moved into textiles and shipping in Mumbai and real estate, jute, manufacturing, and tobacco in Kolakata. Replicating the Jewish experience in the United States, humble *boxwallahs* (door-to-door salespeople) settled down and became department store magnates. Of the three groups, only Bene Israel remains viable as a community.

Whereas most Bene Israel live in Mumbai, the nearby Konkan coast is their spiritual home. Bene Israel Jews trace their community back to seven couples from Israel who survived a shipwreck off Navgaon in the unknown distant past. Somehow the descendants of these Jews clung to vestigial Judaic observances despite centuries of isolation. Their tenacity in maintaining the Sabbath, ritual circumcision, Jewish dietary codes, and the Hebrew Shema (the affirmation "Hear O Israel! The Lord is our God, the Lord is One") set the stage for their unlikely transformation from an anonymous oil-pressing caste in the remote Konkan into modern, urban members of the world Jewish community. This evolution occurred over two hundred years, beginning in the middle of the eighteenth century.

A Kochi merchant heard rumors of a Konkani caste that rested on Saturday and circumcised their sons on the eighth day, so David Rahabi, the eldest son in Kochi's leading mercantile house, visited them. After spending time with the community, examining their dietary habits as well as their eccentric (by Hindu standards) religious observances, he concluded that they were lost Jews. Rahabi took three of them back to Kochi, where he educated them in Hebrew and the rudiments of Judaism and sent them back with the title of *kazi*, religious leader. This began a long-standing relationship between Bene Israel and Kochi Jews; as the Bene Israel prospered, they hired Kochi Jews to be their cantors, teachers, ritual slaughterers, and scribes. Bene Israel Jews recall these events as their "first awakening."

Subsequent encounters with British and American missionaries and with the nascent Baghdadi community of Mumbai built upon the sense of Jewishness among Bene Israel. This period is known as their "second awakening." They learned Bible stories from the missionaries, and they shared their synagogues (they built their first one in Mumbai in 1796) and cemeteries with the Baghdadis. Both the British and the Baghdadis offered opportunities in Mumbai, whether in the military, railway, or civil service or in the mills and docks of the illustrious Sassoons, and Bene Israel migrated to the new, glamorous city in search of their fortunes. It did not take long until there were more Bene Israel in Mumbai than in the Konkan.

Gradually the Baghdadis, in an effort to become accepted by the British as "European" rather than "Indian" (a label with tangible economic benefits as well as social snobbery), came to adopt British condescension toward all things Indian, including the Bene Israel Jews, who were unmistakably Indian in both appearance and culture. This condescension became all the more ugly when the Baghdadis began to cast aspersions upon the very Jewishness of the Bene Israel. The heart and soul of the newly found and hard-earned identity of the Bene Israel was under attack.

In Mumbai the Bene Israel learned about both the Zionist and Swaraj movements for independence from Britain in Palestine and India respectively, and they were rent by competing nationalisms. On the one hand, as Jews they had internalized the longing to return to Jerusalem and rebuild Zion. On the other hand, their unhappy experiences with the Baghdadis led them to mistrust foreign Jews, and as Indians they yearned for independence from the British. Moreover they were fond of the British, who were their employers and often patrons, and wanted to support them as well. Mahatma Gandhi appreciated their ambivalence. Leaders of the Ahmedabad Jewish community (where Gandhi had headquarters at his Sabarmati Ashram) asked the Mahatma what should be the stance of India's Jews vis-à-vis the independence movement. He is said to have replied that the Jews should "stand aside" because, as a small community, they would be crushed between the competing and overwhelming forces of the British Empire, Indian nationalism, and Muslim separatism. As a community they did stand apart, although many Bene Israel became involved as individuals. The bottom line, however, is that the great majority of Bene Israel emigrated to Israel.

By the beginning of the twenty-first century the Bene Israel community had stabilized. Those who intended to emigrate had done so, and most of those who remained intended to stay. Most are in Mumbai, where they work in the professions, education, industry, the military, and commerce. Most are educated and in the middle class. During the 1980s the Organization for Rehabilitation and Training (ORT) established two schools in Mumbai, one for boys and one for girls, to provide vocational training. The ORT schools became popular among Jews and non-Jews alike. Soon services expanded to include classes in religion, Hebrew, and Israel studies. The Joint Distribution Committee (JDC) also became active in Mumbai, sending rabbis from the United States to help meet the community's religious and educational needs. The Israeli consulate also serves as a community focus. Several of the synagogues in Mumbai have a full range of programs, from prayer services to singles groups to computer classes. Summer camps at a rural retreat center have provided an intense infusion of Jewish spirit to many of Mumbai's younger Jews. Kosher meat and wine, ritual objects, books, Indian Jewish calendars, and the accouterments of Judaic religious life are available, and India's generally tolerant attitude toward religions and religious pluralism bode well for the future of the Jewish community in Mumbai.

Smaller organized communities in Ahmedabad and Pune face more difficult challenges, but their synagogues are lively, and social and educational programs are well subscribed. In New Delhi there are only a handful of Bene Israel families, but they are augmented by Israeli and American diplomats and businesspeople. Regular prayers are held at the synagogue, and the Israeli embassy helps out with the community's Passover seder.

In Israel, despite initial difficulties in adapting to a new culture, climate, and economy, the sizeable Bene Israel community has maintained its own identity, largely through a singular ritual activity. Long devoted to the Prophet Elijah as a sort of patron saint, his veneration has become central to their new Israeli identity as *Hod'im.* The propitiatory rite known as *malida,* after a parched rice mixture served with fresh fruits and flowers, is often the culmination of a pilgrimage to an Elijah cave near Haifa.

In the mid-twentieth century several shamans and leaders of tribal people in extreme eastern India (the states of Mizoram, Manipur, and Tripura) and western Myanmar (formerly Burma) began having dreams and visions that told them of their lost, true identity—that they were Jews of the tribe of Menashe who had wandered from ancient Israel along the Silk Route to Kaifeng, China, then through Southeast Asia, finally settling in their current, remote mountainous homes. Their religious enthusiasm spread, such that in the early twenty-first century there are thousands of Kuki tribals on both sides of the border who are living as Jews. Some traveled to Israel, where they learned Hebrew, studied, and converted to Judaism; some later returned home as religious leaders. A number of synagogues sprouted up, and there are regular visits from Israeli and American coreligionists. Several hundred Kuki tribals now live in Israel, especially in the Yesha (settlements), but most wait for redemption at home. In the 1990s a similar group, who called themselves B'nai Ephraim, emerged in Andhra Pradesh, a state on the Bay of Bengal on India's southeast coast.

Most demographics of Indian Jewry do not include these tribals, and there are no reliable estimates of their number, but it is incontestable that some of them have undergone conversion and are therefore Jewish. It is also the case that most are sincere in their beliefs and aspirations, but their passionate yearning for Israel has provoked controversy. Israeli immigration officials generally take an unsympathetic, skeptical view, believing these groups to be opportunists who seek only a higher standard of living. Some accuse immigration authorities of racism, pointing out that many Russians who are white but are not Jewish have been welcomed in Israel, whereas these tribals, who are not white but who have at least some claim to Jewishness, receive only scorn. From the other side of the controversy, the Israeli and American supporters of these immigrants are criticized for settling them in disputed territories as a way of bolstering Israeli claims to Judea and Samaria (the West Bank).

CONTEMPORARY CHINESE JEWS. The ancient Jewish community at Kaifeng was on its last legs when Jesuits first visited in the seventeenth century. Even then local Jews bemoaned the withering away of traditions and observances, the dismal state of Hebrew learning, and the lack of a rabbi. Their synagogue was destroyed by a series of floods in 1841, 1849, and 1860, as it had been several times before, but by this time the community was too impoverished and isolated to rebuild it. Intermarriage was the rule, and assimilation had worn down their sense of Jewish identity.

However, due to the interest of Jewish tourists and then to the establishment of diplomatic relations with Israel, the community experienced something of a rebirth. Although virtually no Jews or Jewish descendants were found in Kaifeng during the 1980s, in the early twenty-first century hundreds of people in Kaifeng claim to be Jews. Some petition the Chinese government to be allowed to list their ethnicity as Jewish on their identity cards. Others hope to learn something about the religion of their ancestors. One Kaifeng Jew even attended rabbinical school in New York. There is also talk of building a Jewish museum in Kaifeng, but it seems that the Chinese bureaucracy is reticent.

In Shanghai and Hong Kong, on the other hand, Jewish life seems to be on the rise. Shanghai is more significant from a historical point of view, whereas Hong Kong has the more active Jewish life in the twenty-first century.

Modern Jewish communities in China date to 1844, when Elias Sassoon, one of the sons of the Mumbai industrialist David Sassoon, arrived in Shanghai. Elias Sassoon established his family's business interests, mostly in opium, and soon had offices in Guangzhou (formerly Canton) and Hong Kong. As soon as Japan was "opened" to Western trade in 1858, a branch office was opened in Tokyo. Jews from Kolakata, Iraq, and elsewhere soon followed. Shanghai's synagogues were built during the late nineteenth century, and soon the city's Jewish community had its own newspaper and glossy magazine, a religious school, a secular school, a hospital, and chapters of B'nai B'rith and various Zionist organizations.

At the same time that Shanghai's Sefardic community was coming of age, Ashkenazic Jews from Russia migrated east, following the overland trade route to Manchuria, especially to the city of Harbin, in northeastern China. These adventurers and furriers were joined by a wave of migration spurred by the 1917 Russian Revolution. Within a few years Harbin had thirteen thousand Jews, and there were more in Tianjin and other cities in the region. When the Japanese conquered Manchuria in 1931, most of these Ashkenazim moved to Shanghai, where they built their own synagogues and institutions. They were soon joined by German and Polish refugees from Adolf Hitler. At their peak there were more than thirty-thousand Jews in Shanghai, which was the only city in the world to remain open to Jewish immigration throughout World War II. The end of the war was followed by the Communist victory in China, at which time all but a handful of China's Jews left.

With China's opening to the West and especially the establishment of diplomatic relations with Israel, commercial opportunities in Shanghai enticed a number of Jews to take up residence there, with the result that a Jewish community may be in the process of rebirth. The Chinese government refurbished one of the old synagogues in Shanghai, but only as a museum. Prayers are forbidden.

Hong Kong is home to a thriving, prosperous Jewish community of about five hundred families. The community itself dates to the Sassoon and Kadoorie families, who arrived during the middle of the nineteenth century. Jews played a significant role in the development of Hong Kong, having electrified the city and established the famous Star Ferry. Even the city's main thoroughfare, Nathan Road, is named for a Jewish governor from the early twentieth century. The beautiful Ohel Leah Synagogue dates from the turn of the century, and the city has kosher facilities, a Jewish school, and a Jewish historical society and library, and prayers are held at several locations. The question facing Hong Kong's Jews is the same as that facing the entrepreneurial class as a whole, whose well-being is dependent upon a continued laissez-faire approach from Beijing. There is also a small Jewish community in Taipei composed of both Sefardic and Ashkenazic members as well as a handful of Jewish Chinese nationals.

JAPAN. Jews have lived in Japan since the Sassoons established themselves there in the mid-nineteenth century. Indian, Iraqi, and European Jews settled in Yokohama, Tokyo, Nagasaki, and Kobe.

Japanese attitudes toward Jews seem highly contradictory. Anti-Semitic literature enjoys great popularity among Japanese readers, who otherwise display no negative behavior toward Jews. Although Japan was allied with Nazi Germany during World War II, the country, nevertheless, afforded refuge to thousands of Eastern European Jews, including the entire Mir Yeshiva from Poland. Among the Jews of Japan are Russian-speaking former residents of Manchuria and Shanghai, Indian and Middle Eastern Sefardim, and a variety of foreign Jewish temporary residents. There are synagogues in Tokyo and Kobe.

Since World War II, Japan has been especially fertile ground for the emergence of new religions, and Japan's longstanding, ambivalent fascination with the Jewish people led to intriguing syncretic religious expressions. For example, there is a small but serious group of Japanese converts to Judaism led by Setsu Zau Abraham Kotsuji. Another group, the 50,000-strong Jewish-Christian Makuya, led by Abraham Teshima, believes itself to be the lost tribe of Zebulun. Although they accept the Christian Messiah, they study Hebrew and visit Israel frequently.

CENTRAL ASIA. Jews may have settled in central Asia, long associated with the legend of the ten lost tribes, earlier than in either India or China. Pottery shards bearing Hebrew names, which date from the first to third centuries CE, have been found in Turkmenistan, and it is believed that some of the many Jews of the Persian Empire were involved in the Silk Route trade when Persia ruled the region before the fourth century BCE.

Whether under the Persians, or the Hellenistic dominions of the Baktrian kingdom (fourth century BCE to third century CE), or the Buddhist Kushans (third to sixth centuries CE), Jewish traders and settlers were found in towns throughout central Asia. The mercantile Jewish Radanites and the semiheretical Karaites were bolstered when a neighboring Turkic tribe, the Khazars, converted to Judaism around 750 CE and dominated much of the Silk Route, the lifeblood of the community. It was toward the end of this period that Persian-speaking Jews made their way to China's Middle Kingdom and settled in Kaifeng.

After two hundred years of Arab rule and Islamicization, central Asia came to be dominated by "pagan" Mongols, led by Chinggis Khan, in the early thirteenth century. From the perspective of the Jews in the region, Chinggis and his Mongol successors often favored minority groups (Buddhists, Nestorian Christians, Jews, and animists) as a bulwark against the Muslims to their south. It has also been suggested that the Mongols were already familiar with Jews by the time they arrived at Samarkand, where they made their capital, from Kaifeng and elsewhere along their routes of conquest.

By the fourteenth century central Asian Jews were enjoying a cultural and religious revival, following two hundred years of hostile Islamicization. Timur Shah, known in Europe as Tamerlane, expanded the Mongol Empire, which under his reign extended as far north as the Volga River, as far west as Damascus, as far south as Delhi, and as far east as China. Although Timur adopted Islam, his rule was based more on the laws and traditions of Mongolia, which had been brought to the region by Chinggis Khan and were known as *Yasa*, than upon Islamic law, *sharī ʿah*. Jews were allowed to practice their religion freely and to pursue their livelihoods as physicians, translators, diplomats, merchants, agriculturalists, traders, and artisans.

For reasons unknown, Timur Shah became a devotee of the biblical prophet Daniel, and he is said to have reinterred Daniel at Samarkand, where a saint's cult emerged. The prophet became the "patron saint" of Bukharan Jews, and a number of epic and liturgical poems in Judeo-Persian (written in the Hebrew script) were composed about him. In this respect also the Bukharan Jews resembled their Indian counterparts. In Kochi the seventeenth-century qabbalist Nehemia Mota emerged as patron not only of local Jews but of the whole area; the Bene Israel have long had a similar special relationship with the Prophet Elijah, and the scribe Ezra sustained far-flung Baghdadis.

The fourteenth century was a time when Judeo-Persian literature flourished, and the religious saga, the *Musa-Nama*, has ever since embodied the mores and values of central Asian Jews, even those who migrated to Jerusalem centuries later. City-dwelling Bukharan Jews spoke Judeo-Persian for the most part, whereas their rural coreligionists spoke mostly Uzbek and Turkic. Most knew both.

It is also believed that Timur's closest adviser and prime minister was a Jew, David ha-Tsaddiq. Patterns resembling the Jewish experience in Kochi and Kaifeng were replicated in Samarkand under the Timurids. Like David ha-Tsaddiq in Samarkand, Yehezkel Rahabi was prime minister to an eighteenth-century Hindu maharaja in Kochi, and Kaifeng had its share of Jewish mandarins.

By the sixteenth century Islamicization led most of Samarkand's Jews to migrate to Bukhara. When the Timurids were defeated by the Persian Safavids a hundred years later, government policy supported forced conversion to Shīʿah Islam, and the ensuing persecution took its toll on the beleaguered community.

A late-eighteenth-century revival was sparked by the arrival of a shaliach (emissary) from the mystical city of Tsfat in the Holy Land. Yosef ha-Maʾaravi imported books and led a religious revival and by the same token instituted a Sefardic rather than a Mizraḥi ethos. A school for poets developed, and the literary outpouring was so great that a Russian bibliographer counted some 250 Judeo-Persian books and 20 manuscripts in the Jewish Museum of Samarkand in 1994.

When Shīʿah zealots forced conversion on the Jews of Meshed, the holy city in eastern Iran, many fled to Bukhara. A contemporary missionary reported some three hundred families of *anusim* (those forced to convert) among Bukhara's Jews. Fearful of Persian religious intolerance, many central Asian Jews flocked to territory newly conquered by Russia in the late nineteenth century. Sizable communities were to be found not only in Bukhara city but in Samarkand and Tashkent, all now in Uzbekistan, and in Turkmenistan as well.

Bukharan Jews began to migrate to the Holy Land as early as 1827, and by 1892 they had established the Bukharan Quarter in Jerusalem. There ensued ongoing travel between Bukhara and Jerusalem, sparking yet another period of intense literary activity. Some 170 books in Judeo-Persian were published in Jerusalem. The Bukharan Jews built synagogues in Jerusalem that one observer described as resembling a *masjid* (Muslim house of worship). Custom and architecture reflected central Asia: the prayer halls were carpeted, and men prayed shoeless, sitting on the floor. Religious leaders were called by the Persian title, mullah, and Torah cantillation resembled Qurʾān recitation.

Prior to World War II large numbers of Russian Ashkenazic Jews settled in the cities of Uzbekistan and Turkmenistan. Largely irreligious, they adapted to local traditions, which by the twentieth century had become indistinguishable from those in Iran or Afghanistan. At this time the region was home to sixty thousand Jews.

Judaism, like other religions, was suppressed under Soviet rule, and the Bukharan Jews devised ingenious techniques for practicing an attenuated form of the religion as well as for maintaining a Jewish identity under the suspicious eyes of Kremlin authorities. The annual memorial service became an emblematic ritual, performed in homes or community halls without prayer books. If an unfriendly eye should happen upon the event, it could appear as an innocuous meeting or meal devoid of religious content.

However, everything changed with the breakup of the Soviet Union. Almost immediately, in 1992, Israel became the third country to recognize an independent Uzbekistan, after only the United States and Turkey. In the early twenty-first century about twenty-eight thousand Jews remain in Uzbekistan, where there are sixteen synagogues. In Tashkent one finds the seat of the chief rabbinate of central Asia as well as the region's sole rabbinical seminary. Relations with Israel are cordial, and the community regularly receives Jewish visitors, pilgrims, and rabbis from Israel, the United States, and Europe. Bonds between resettled Bukharan Jews in Israel and the United States and their kin in Uzbekistan are strong, as they have been ever since the first Bukharans settled in Jerusalem in the nineteenth century.

SOUTHEAST ASIA. In the early nineteenth century Baghdadis from Kolakata pursued their fortunes to Yangon in Myanmar, gradually joined by Bene Israel and a few Kochi Jews. Later that century they built their synagogue, which still welcomes visitors to its well-maintained sanctuary. Satellite communities emerged in many of Burma's (Myanmar's) trade and shipping centers, including Mandalay, Myanmo, Moulmein, Bassein, Akyab, and Toungyi.

The community was virtually destroyed in the 1940s, when the Japanese, suspicious of Jews as potential British sympathizers, conquered Burma and drove most of its thirteen hundred Jewish inhabitants to Kolakata. About five hundred returned after the war. Burmese Judaism enjoyed a brief flowering after independence and the establishment of cordial Israeli-Burmese relations, based on the warm friendship between Prime Ministers U Nu and David Ben Gurion. After a military coup in 1962, the position of minorities in Burma degenerated, and most Jews left. A handful of Jewish descendants remain. Other Kolakata Jews migrated farther east to Singapore, Malaya, Bangkok, Indonesia, and the Philippines.

As soon as Stamford Raffles established a British settlement at Singapore in 1818, Indian Jews followed, mostly to pursue the opium trade. They settled in the Chinatown section that by the middle of the century had a synagogue and a cemetery. Twenty-five years later the community had migrated to what was then a suburban quarter, where they built the Maghain Aboth Synagogue, followed after another quarter century by Chesed El Synagogue and a religious school.

Out of a community that at one time numbered two thousand, David Marshall was undoubtedly the first citizen. The island nation's "father of independence," he was prime minister in 1955 and United Nations ambassador thereafter. In the early twenty-first century about three hundred Jewish families, mostly Sefardim, can be found in the prosperous, tiny state, enjoying a full religious life under the leadership of an emissary of the Chabad-Lubavitch movement.

A handful of Jews reside in Bangkok as citizens of Thailand, where the law requires that all nonethnic Thai citizens adopt a Thai name. This requirement has caused considerable distress among Muslims, the largest minority in Thailand. Jews have been the only group exempted from the law. The local Thai Jewish community, comprised of several hundred Sefardim and Ashkenazim, is augmented by a significant number of Jewish businesspeople and young Israeli backpackers. Two synagogues are maintained, one in a residential area and the other in the business district, both led by a Chabad-Lubavitch emissary.

As the Inquisition reigned in Spain, Spanish Jews and Marranos had an added impetus to join in Spanish and Portuguese voyages of exploration. They sailed to Mexico, the American colonies, Goa, the Philippines, and elsewhere. Sadly the Inquisition followed them, and by 1580 an auto-da-fé was held in Manila.

By the last quarter of the nineteenth century Jews from Alsace, Turkey, Syria, Lebanon, and Egypt began to settle openly. They were soon joined by Russian and central European Jews, who found their way to the Philippines via Harbin and Shanghai. After the Spanish-American War, American Jews added to Manila's community. In 1922 a formal congregation was established. In the early twenty-first century about 250 Jews live in the Philippines on a permanent basis.

CONCLUSION. The study of Asian Jewish communities uproots several common stereotypes. For example, the adage that "East is East and West is West" becomes transparent as a colonizing myth once a Jewish perspective is adopted. The study of these communities also reconfigures the common understanding of Judaism and the Jewish people. It is commonly held that Judaism is one of the sources of Western civilization and that Judaism is a Western religion. Such a view blinds one to Jewish experience in Asia; it silences the millennia-old, rich cultural interactions between Judaic, Indic, Sinitic, and Islamo-Mongol cultures. On the other hand, Jews have traditionally spoken of themselves as an *am-olam*, a "universal people," a cultural and mercantile bridge in a world bifurcated into an East and a West. The study of the Asian Jewish experience debunks the Jews-as-Westerners view and confirms the traditional self-understanding of Jews as a truly universal people.

BIBLIOGRAPHY

Ben-Zvi, Itzhak. *The Exiled and the Redeemed.* 3d ed. Translated by Isaac A. Abbady. Jerusalem, 1976.

Cooper, Alanna E. "Negotiating Identity in the Context of Diaspora: The Bukharan Jews and Jewish Peoplehood." Ph.D. diss., Boston University, 2000.

Elazar, Daniel J. *The Other Jews: The Sephardim Today.* New York, 1989.

Katz, Nathan. *Who Are the Jews of India?* Berkeley, Calif., 2000.

Katz, Nathan, and Ellen S. Goldberg. *The Last Jews of Cochin: Jewish Identity in Hindu India.* Columbia, S.C., 1993.

Lesley, Donald. *The Survival of the Chinese Jews: The Jewish Community of Kaifeng.* Leiden, Netherlands, 1972.

Pollak, Michael. *Mandarins, Jews, and Missionaries: The Jewish Experience in the Chinese Empire.* Philadelphia, 1980.

Roland, Joan G. *Jews in British India: Identity in a Colonial Age.* Hanover, N.H., 1989.

Shterenshis, Michael. *Tamerlane and the Jews.* London and New York, 2002.

NATHAN KATZ (2005)

JUDAISM: JUDAISM IN NORTHERN AND EASTERN EUROPE TO 1500

Although Jews lived in the northern European provinces of the ancient Roman Empire, long-lasting communal settlements began only in the tenth century, when Christian monarchs promoted the economic vitality of their domains by inviting Jewish merchants into the newly developing towns.

SETTLEMENT AND EARLY INSTITUTIONS. A pattern of early royal support followed by royal opposition and instability characterized Jewish political life first in western Europe and then later in the East. The earliest royal policy toward the Jews in northern Europe dates from Charlemagne and, especially, from his son, Louis the Pious, who issued three private charters (*privilegia*) to individual Jewish merchants in about 825. These texts indicate that Jews were among the international merchants doing business in the Carolingian empire and were granted protection of their lives, exemption from tolls, and guarantees of religious freedom. This Carolingian policy toward Jewish merchants was also pursued by subsequent rulers of the German empire, and it encouraged the Jewish immigration that became a factor in the demographic and urban expansion of early medieval Europe.

The first communities developed gradually in the Rhineland towns, where various family groups settled and intermarried. Of special significance were the Qalonimos family from Lucca, Italy; the descendants of Abun, a rabbi from Le Mans in northern France; and other families from France, which became the nucleus of the Mainz Jewish elite. Cut off from the Jewish political and religious authorities in Palestine and Babylonia, as well as Spain, the leaders of the Mainz community had considerable room to improvise and experiment with new patterns of autonomous local governance.

From the beginning, communal leadership assumed two overlapping but distinct forms. On the one hand, legal decisions were rendered by religious judges or rabbis who acquired expertise in the Talmud. On the other hand, communal control over nonlegal public affairs devolved upon the "elders," whose authority derived from their age, wealth, family lineage, and other personal qualities. They maintained public order, collected taxes for the Christian authorities and for support of Jewish social services, and were the liaison between the community and the gentile rulers.

In the period of first settlement the rabbis were merchants, like the rest of the community, and were among the elders who decided public policy. As communities grew in size and complexity, communal roles became more differentiated. A paid rabbinate gradually developed only in the thirteenth century.

The location of the early northern Jewish communities on a frontier prompted religious leaders and elders alike to be innovative. We see this in the legal decisions of Gershom ben Yehudah (d. 1028), the first major rabbinical figure in Mainz. Gershom functioned as an appeals judge on matters of Jewish law, and his legal opinions rarely mention the decisions and precedents of the Babylonian geonim. Rather, he answered questions by interpreting Talmudic or even biblical passages, thereby imitating rather than following the geonim. His ordinances against polygyny and a woman's involuntary divorce became binding precedents.

We also find signs of improvisation in the actions of the early community board *(qahal)* and communal leaders (*parnasim*) contemporary with Gershom, who undertook to maintain law and order, supervise the weights and measures in the market, and provide for the indigent. The institution of *maʿarufyah*, an individual Jewish merchant's trade monopoly with a specific Christian client, was widespread in the Rhineland, and boards adopted measures to protect it. As the Jewish population grew in the eleventh century, local community boards placed a ban on new settlement (*ḥerem ha-yishuv*) to prevent excessive economic competition.

By the middle of the eleventh century, questions about the limits of local autonomy had arisen in newer areas of settlement, like the duchy of Champagne. Yehudah ha-Kohen, Gershom's successor, decided that in the area of general public welfare and security each local Jewish community was completely autonomous, but if a community violated religious law, another community or outside religious authority could hold it accountable.

An additional sign of new communal development occurred in 1084, when some of the Mainz Jews moved to Speyer, where they were welcomed by Bishop Rüdiger, who issued them a formal charter. Modeled on the early Carolingian *privilegia*, this charter extended to the new community guarantees of life, religious protection, and exemption from tolls. Confirmed by the German emperor Henry IV in 1090, this continued the Carolingian policy of royal or imperial legal protection of European Jews until the late thirteenth century. The patterns of royal protection and local Jewish self-rule that had first developed in the German towns became the model for local Jewish communities in the regions of royal France, England, and central Europe.

DEVELOPMENTS IN THE HIGH MIDDLE AGES. The late eleventh and twelfth centuries were a time of social and cultural consolidation in northern Europe. New religious orders were founded; the popes renewed the claims of canon law to establish the primacy of the church over the empire in spiritual and even temporal affairs; and in Paris the university attracted students who eagerly came from all over Europe to sit at the feet of popular scholars like Peter Abelard. It is possible that the Christian Schoolmen were in part motivated to restate Christian doctrine in a clear and logically consistent way because Jews were raising doubts about Christianity in the minds of Christian townsmen. In return, an awareness of Christian religious innovation and ferment stimulated reappraisals of Judaism.

The First Crusade precipitated the first major crisis of Jewish cultural identity in northern Europe. Urban II's call for an armed pilgrimage to Jerusalem in the spring of 1095 led local German peasants and petty knights on their way to the Holy Land to riot in the towns of Mainz, Worms, Cologne, and Speyer. According to the Latin and Hebrew chronicles that recount what happened on this Peasants' Crusade, just before and during the Jewish holiday of Shavu'ot in the spring of 1096, the righteous Jews of Mainz and Worms ritually slaughtered their families and themselves in order to prevent the Christian rioters from forcibly baptizing or killing them. The victims included leaders of the rabbinical elites of Mainz and Worms as well as hundreds of innocent men, women, and children.

Many Jews escaped or were subjected to baptism by force, but the survivors' guilt only heightened the loss of the saintly martyrs, whose memory now cast a shadow over the following generations of German Jews. Among the liturgical memorials they instituted in Europe was the earlier geonic prohibition of celebrating Jewish weddings between Passover and Shavu'ot, still observed as an annual period of collective mourning. New prayers were written to recall the righteousness of the slain and to invoke God's vengeance on the guilty Christians. Each spring the martyrs' names were recited in the Rhenish synagogues in order to keep alive the memory of the sacrificed dead and to invoke their merit as a form of vicarious atonement for the living.

Two other important northern Jewish ideals emerged in the twelfth century; the first of these was the *ḥasid*, or pietist. By the second half of the twelfth century, an ascetic, pietistic movement emerged in Speyer, the one Jewish community that did not suffer major losses in 1096. It was led by descendants of the branch of the Qalonimos family that survived the riots of 1096. The pietists placed special emphasis not only on punctilious observance of Jewish law but also on certain spiritual exercises including concentrated prayer, physical self-denial, and the mystical and magical manipulations of Hebrew letter combinations that represent the secret names of God. One of the mottos of Shemu'el ben Qalonimos the Elder (fl. mid-twelfth century) is "be resourceful in the fear of God," a Talmudic dictum (B.T., *Ber.* 17a) that he reinterpreted to mean that the pietist, or truly God-fearing Jew, must search scripture resourcefully in order to infer additional prohibitions and higher degrees of self-discipline.

In *Sefer ḥasidim* (Book of the Pietists), written by Shemu'el's son Yehudah the Pietist (d. 1217), we find a sectarian fellowship of pietists, led by their own sages, who are constantly challenged and tested by their inner passions and by the harmful presence of nonpietistic Jews, whom the author calls "the wicked." Among Yehudah's innovations is the requirement that pietists who sin should confess their sins to a sage and receive penances proportional to the sinful act and to the pleasure experienced while sinning.

This new Jewish pietistic ideal, incorporating ancient Jewish mystical and ascetic practices, began as a regimen for religious virtuosos but became a common-place of European Jewish spirituality after the late twelfth century and continued to define the dominant style of Jewish piety in eastern Europe even after it was challenged by the eighteenth-century revival movement of Hasidism.

The second new mode of Jewish spirituality that developed in the twelfth century in northern France was the Talmud scholar who excelled in intellectual prowess by discovering new interpretations of difficult passages. At the very time that Christian Schoolmen were reconciling the logical inconsistencies in authoritative theological texts and scholars of canon and Roman law were resolving contradictions by making new distinctions, rabbinical scholars began to study systematically the entire Talmudic corpus and apply canons of logical consistency to it. This activity developed in northern France and not in the Rhineland for two reasons. On the negative side, the older academies of Mainz and Worms suffered a loss of leadership in the riots of 1096. On the positive side, the newer schools in Champagne were able to build on the foundations in Hebrew Bible and Talmud interpretation established by the late-eleventh-century rabbinic master Rashi (Shelomoh ben Yitshaq, 1040–1105).

In the duchy of Champagne, another Jewish frontier, the master of Troyes taught generations of students who were geographically and culturally removed from the living oral culture of rabbinic studies in Mainz and Worms. For them Rashi produced the first comprehensive running commentary on almost the entire Hebrew Bible and the Babylonian Talmud, the canon of the Ashkenazic curriculum. Because of his extraordinary sensitivity to the biblical usage of language and his knowledge of the Talmudic corpus, he succeeded in providing the one gloss to both the Hebrew Bible and the Babylonian Talmud that has remained standard for all students of those texts to this day.

The next generation's scholars, who glossed Rashi's commentary (*ba'alei ha-tosafot*), introduced a synoptic method of dialectical study designed to discover and resolve potential contradictions among different parts of the Talmud and between the Talmud and Jewish life in Christian Europe. The shift from the piecemeal to the synoptic study of the Talmud resulted in an expansion of the scope and detail of Jewish law. The new distinctions that resolved contradictions between divergent traditions added conceptual subtlety to categories of law that had been created for a Mediterranean society. Adjustments were also made to accommodate the Talmudic traditions, a product of ancient pagan and medieval Muslim societies, to the actual practices of the Jews living in Latin Christendom.

The Judaism that resulted from these encounters with Christian Europe in the twelfth century was more complex than the relatively homogeneous religious culture of the eleventh. The righteous self-image, the reverence of the dead martyrs, German Hasidism, and the scholasticism of the tosafists were part of a twelfth-century transformation of classical Judaism into a "traditional" Ashkenazic Judaism. Paralleling these developments were the creative philosophical synthesis of Moses Maimonides (d. 1204) in Egypt and the writing down for the first time of qabbalistic mystical traditions in southern France.

Expulsion and Resettlement in the Later Middle Ages. The pattern of royal support in return for Jewish economic usefulness appears in England in the twelfth century. Henry I (r. 1100–1135) issued a charter, no longer extant, similar to the continental ones, offering the Jews protection of life and toll exemptions backed by royal justice. Henry II (r. 1154–1189) extended Jewish privileges to include self-government under Jewish law. By this time, sizable Jewish communities existed not only in London but also in Norwich, Lincoln, and Oxford.

In addition to obtaining funds on demand from the community, the English kings turned to especially wealthy Jews, such as Aharon of Lincoln, for major loans. When Aharon died, in 1185, he had outstanding loans of fifteen thousand pounds, three-quarters of the annual receipts of the royal exchequer. To protect the safety of these financial records, Jewish and Christian officials were appointed to see to it that duplicate copies of loans were drawn up and deposited in chests (*archae*). By 1200 the office of exchequer of the Jews was filled entirely by Christians, called the justices of the Jews. Another centralized official of the end of the twelfth century was the *presbyter Judaeorum*, not a chief rabbi but a wealthy Jew appointed by the king to serve as the liaison between the court and the Jewish community.

Jewish money lending at immoderate interest, or usury, became a major factor in the decline of the Jewish communities in England and France in the thirteenth century. Although papal policy condoned Jewish lending at moderate rates of interest, canon lawyers opposed it absolutely, and in the late thirteenth century the English and French kings implemented policies based on the stricter position. These measures against usury were neither economically nor politically motivated; rather, they were successful royal efforts at spiritual reform undertaken at a time of waning papal authority.

In royal France, money lending with interest was made illegal in 1230. To support his crusade, Louis IX (r. 1226–1270) confiscated Jewish loans, as provided by the Council of Lyon (1245), expelled only Jewish usurers from France in 1248/9, and confiscated their property. In England, Edward I (r. 1272–1307) issued his Statute on the Jews (1275), which outlawed Jewish lending completely, and in 1290 the Jews were expelled from his kingdom. Philip the Fair (r. 1285–1314) expelled the Jews of royal France in 1306.

Whereas royal policy toward the Jews shifted from support in the period of settlement to antagonism in the late thirteenth century, papal policy remained relatively constant and supportive. But when heretical movements posed a threat to the church itself, measures adopted to fight heresy sometimes were directed against the Jewish infidel as well. Thus papal approval of the new urban reforming orders of the Franciscans and, especially, the Dominicans as disciplinary arms of the church in the early thirteenth century created a source of new pressure against Jewish distinctiveness. Individual friars, sometimes zealous apostates from Judaism, actively sought to persuade Jews to convert.

At the same time that the Jewish communities were eliminated in England and royal France in the late thirteenth and fourteenth centuries, organized Jewish life in the north shifted increasingly eastward to the politically fragmented German empire, the central European territories of Bohemia, Moravia, and Hungary, and Poland and Lithuania. The thirteenth and early fourteenth centuries were a time of continuous demographic expansion in Europe, and the Jewish communities in central and eastern Europe were augmented by natural increase and new immigration from the West.

The major turning point for central European Jewry was the Black Death of 1349, a trauma that reduced the population of some areas of Europe by as much as 50 percent. Unable to explain a catastrophe of such magnitude, the popular mind personalized the agents of destruction by blaming the Jews for poisoning the wells of Europe. Aside from being subject now to unpredictable waves of violence, whole Jewish communities were routinely expelled. The theme of death began to play an increased liturgical role in the religious sensibilities of Ashkenazic Judaism. In particular, the annual anniversary of a parent's death (Yi., *yahrzeit*) is first attested at the end of the fourteenth century. The regular recitation by mourners of the Qaddish prayer also seems to have begun around the fourteenth century, in this period of increased Jewish martyrdom and random violence.

As a gradual demographic and economic recovery slowly began, Jews were readmitted for specified periods into towns of early settlement, like Speyer, and into newer Jewish communities in Austria and Bohemia. The decline of imperial authority over and protection of the Jews is reflected in the growing influence of the Christian burghers, who reserved the right to expel "their" Jews at will. The elimination of effective royal protection added to the Jewish communities' increased political vulnerability in the later Middle Ages in the West.

In the late fourteenth and fifteenth centuries, Jewish legal authorities generally lost prestige and control in their communities. No intercommunal councils were established in the German empire after 1350, and local rabbis complained that the wealthy members of the community ignored them. To be sure, masters like Mosheh Mintz and Yisra'el Isserlein of Austria continued in the fifteenth century to exert their authority as great sages of the age, as had Gershom in the late tenth, but the influence of local rabbis declined after 1350.

Politically the proliferation of independent principalities and cities in the German empire constituted a safety valve for the Jews there. Whenever residents of one particular community were expelled, they could find refuge in another until the edict was rescinded. But as economic instability reduced the demand for Jewish money lending in the towns, some Jews began to settle in villages and on rural estates. Gradually they entered new occupations as agricultural merchants and middlemen. The decline in economic opportunities in the empire also led many Jews to join the eastward emigration of German Christian burghers attracted by new opportunities in Poland and Lithuania, still another frontier.

Although Jews had been settling gradually in the duchies of Poland and Lithuania for some time, official recognition of their communities appeared only in the thirteenth century. In 1264, Prince Boleslaw granted the Jews of Great Poland a charter modeled on those issued by Frederick II, duke of Austria, in 1244; Béla IV, king of Hungary, in 1251; and Otakar II, king of Bohemia and Moravia, in 1254. Unlike the Carolingian-type charters issued to Jewish merchants from the ninth through twelfth centuries, these were designed for Jews whose primary occupation was money lending. But like the earlier ones, the Polish charters provided for Jewish self-government and royal protection. In 1364, Casimir III (r. 1133–1170) issued a confirmation of these regional charters that was valid in the unified kingdom of Poland. Some Jews served the kings or dukes as money lenders and bankers; others managed estates forfeited to them for bad debts, lived in towns that the nobles founded, or farmed tolls. Jews were also prominent in the export trade of agricultural products to the German empire and the Crimea.

The Jews who migrated to Poland from Germany, Austria, and Bohemia brought along their familiar forms of communal government. The frontier model applies to Poland as it had before to the first settlements in western Europe, but with one important difference. The eastern immigrants could rely on support and spiritual guidance from their former homeland in the German empire.

The arrival of Ya'aqov Polak in Cracow, where he opened his innovative Talmudic academy, marks the beginning of advanced Jewish religious study in Poland and with it the first condition for cultural independence from the West. In 1503, Alexander I (r. 1501–1506) appointed him rabbi of Jewry there. Symbolically, a new era of centralized Jewish self-government and cultural ferment was about to begin.

SEE ALSO Ashkenazic Hasidism; Halakhah; Jewish Thought and Philosophy, article on Premodern Philosophy; Polemics, article on Jewish-Christian Polemics; Qabbalah; Rabbinate; Tosafot.

BIBLIOGRAPHY

Detailed critical discussions of the rich bibliography on this period can be found in my "The Jews in Western Europe: Fourth to Sixteenth Century" and Kenneth R. Stow's "The Church and the Jews: From St. Paul to Paul IV," both in *Bibliographical Essays in Medieval Jewish Studies* (New York, 1976). Despite its tendency to emphasize Jewish persecution in the Diaspora, parts of chapters 25–41 in *A History of the Jewish People*, edited by H. H. Ben-Sasson (Cambridge, Mass., 1969), contain important discussions of medieval Jewish communal life and also refer to many of the primary sources. On the Jewish communities of England, one still must turn to Cecil Roth's *A History of the Jews in England*, 3d ed. (Oxford, 1964), chaps. 1–5, and the more solid study by H. G. Richardson, *The English Jewry under Angevin Kings* (London, 1960). On northern France, Louis Rabinowitz's *The Social Life of the Jews of Northern France in the Twelfth to Fourteenth Centuries*, 2d ed. (New York, 1972), and Robert Chazan's *Medieval Jewry in Northern France* (Baltimore, 1973) should be supplemented by the pertinent studies of Gavin Langmuir, such as "'Judei Nostri' and the Beginnings of Capetian Legislation," *Traditio* 19 (1963): 183–244, and William Chester Jordan, such as "Jews on Top," *Journal of Jewish Studies* 29 (Spring 1978): 39–56. A synthetic scholarly treatment of German Jewry still does not exist but readers may consult with profit Guido Kisch's *The Jews in Medieval Germany*, 2d ed. (New York, 1970). Important trends in the early years of the European Jewish community are discussed by Avraham Grossman in "On 'The Early Sages of Ashkenaz,'" *Immanuel* 15 (Winter 1982–1983): 73–81, a summary of his book *Ḥakhmei Ashkenaz ha-ri'shonim* (Jerusalem, 1981).

The history and institutions of the medieval Jewish community are treated in depth in Salo W. Baron's *The Jewish Community*, 3 vols. (1942; reprint, Westport, Conn., 1972), which is out of date in some areas. On the major intellectual and religious trends discussed above, see Haym Soloveitchik's "Three Themes in the *Sefer Hasidim*," *AJS Review* 1 (1976): 311–357, especially on the influence of the Tosafists, and my book *Piety and Society: The Jewish Pietists of Medieval Germany* (Leiden, 1981) on German (Ashkenazic) Ḥasidism.

Two important studies on the deterioration of Jewish life in the thirteenth century are Kenneth R. Stow's "Papal and Royal Attitudes toward Jewish Lending in the Thirteenth Century," *AJS Review* 6 (1981): 161–184, and Jeremy Cohen's *The Friars and the Jews* (Ithaca, N.Y., 1982).

For Jewish life in central Europe during the late Middle Ages, see Shlomo Eidelberg's *Jewish Life in Austria in the Fifteenth Century* (Philadelphia, 1962) and Eric Zimmer's *Harmony and Discord* (New York, 1970). A basic work on eastern European Jewry that deals with the early period is Bernard D. Weinryb's *The Jews of Poland* (Philadelphia, 1972).

New Sources

Signer, Michael A., and John Van Engen, eds. *Jews and Christians in Twelfth-Century Europe*. Notre Dame, Ind., 2001.

IVAN G. MARCUS (1987)
Revised Bibliography

JUDAISM: JUDAISM IN NORTHERN AND EASTERN EUROPE SINCE 1500

As a result of a series of Jewish expulsions and of Poland's increasing economic attractiveness, in the sixteenth-century Ashkenazic world Poland was widely recognized as the most promising of the European communities.

POLAND AND LITHUANIA. The expulsion of Jews from numerous German cities and secular principalities and from much of Bohemia and Moravia, coupled with the final division of Hungary (previously relatively hospitable to Jews) into Habsburg, Ottoman, and Transylvanian sections, encouraged Jews to look eastward. Poland's rapid commercial expansion, the relative weakness until the late sixteenth century of its craft and trade guilds, and the religious toleration that characterized crown policy reinforced these migratory trends. Jewish adjustment to the new surroundings was eased because of German influences in the cities, which (despite the rapid polonization of the German immigrants) may have encouraged the retention by Jews of Yiddish. Greater occupational diversity was possible here than in Germany. Most Polish Jews worked in domestic trade, moneylending, and artisanry but some Jews also captured important roles in the trade between Constantinople and western and central Europe and in the export of Polish textiles, grains, and cattle. Others acquired the leases over minting and other crucial fiscal and administrative functions.

The increasing impact and militancy of the Roman Catholic Church in the wake of the Counter-Reformation and the rising antagonism of burghers toward Jews led to the partial expulsion of Jews from about fifty Polish cities by the end of the sixteenth century. Rarely were they completely barred; most often they were forced to move to suburban enclaves or to the *jurydyki* within the municipal boundaries but under the jurisdiction of the nobility. Jews continued to live in the same neighborhoods with Catholics in the cities where they were freely permitted to reside. However, the introduction of clauses permitting *non tolerandis Judaeis* and the effective unification of Poland and Lithuania with the Union of Lublin in 1569 encouraged Jewish migration to the southeastern Ukrainian expanses of Lithuania.

The *pacta conventa* of 1573, which confirmed the gentry's accumulation of considerable power at the expense of the crown, cemented close relations between the upper *szlachta* ("the magnates") and the Jews. The magnates frequently favored Jews as their commercial agents and lessees. Commerce, artisanry, and, in the southeastern regions, leaseholding (often tied to trade in agricultural goods) became the most common Jewish occupations. By the middle of the seventeenth century—when the Jewish community of Poland and Lithuania numbered, according to varying estimates, somewhere between 250,000 and 450,000—nearly 40 percent of the Jews lived, according to Samuel Ettinger, in the Ukrainian area.

Jewish participation in the Polish nobility's colonization of the Ukraine involved Jews in a system of pledges where Jewish lenders received a part of the income from estates pending the repayment of loans. What evolved was a more direct system of leaseholding, called the *arenda*, in which Jews leased agricultural properties from the nobility, generally for a period of three years, at a designated price. Profits would be extracted from taxes and fees on the local peasantry. The acquisition of a lease frequently constituted the beginning of a new Jewish community, since lessees would encourage other Jews to settle with them to run inns, flour mills, and so forth. Poland's rapidly growing population required ever-increasing supplies of agricultural and meat products, and the colonization of the Ukraine—in which Jews played an important and visible role—ensured a steady supply to domestic (and foreign) markets.

Jewish communal autonomy in Poland. A highly ramified system of Polish-Jewish autonomy with a centralized consultative council was created as Jews settled in Poland in large numbers. It was the product of several factors, including the Jewish community's wide geographic dispersion, the example of Jewish communal institutions in Bohemia and Moravia, pressures from the crown for a centralized Jewish leadership, and the diminishing power of the king, which motivated many sectors of Polish society to claim a measure of self-government. On the bottom tier of Jewry's system were the *qehalim*, or Jewish communal councils, which functioned alongside and were structured similar to the municipal councils of Polish cities. Above them were the district councils composed of representatives from the *qehalim*. At the uppermost tier were the supercouncils, which met, beginning in 1569 and perhaps even earlier, at the fairs of Lublin and less frequently at Jaroslaw. Representatives from all parts of Poland and Lithuania participated in these meetings of the Council of the Lands of Poland (until a separate Lithuanian council was established, for fiscal reasons, in 1623), where *taqqanot* ("regulations") were issued, individual and communal grievances were aired, and protests against *qehalim* were reviewed. The council deliberated on halakhic matters and, perhaps most important, intervened on behalf of the community before the authorities. From the vantage point of the state, the Polish Council was a tax-farming body but even the state recognized, at least tacitly, the council's more extensive functions.

Talmudic study in Poland and Lithuania. At the same time, the challenge posed by the distinguished Talmudist Mosheh Isserles of Cracow (1520–1572) in numerous works, particularly his *Darkhei Mosheh* to the Sephardic codification of Jewish law, the *Beit Yosef* of Yosef Karo, consolidated Poland's standing as the preeminent center of Ashkenazic learning. Isserles promoted the legitimacy of Polish-Jewish customs along with a rationalist-mystical understanding of *mitsvot*. The rich rabbinical literature of the period—which, in addition to Isserles, was represented by Shelomoh Luria, Yom Ṭov Lippman Heller, and many other Talmudic masters—was efficiently disseminated by the rapid expansion of printing in the sixteenth century.

Pilpul, a casuistic method based, in Poland, on the application of principles of logical differentiation to reconcile apparent Talmudic contradictions, was the focus of much of the *yeshivah* curriculum. This method was increasingly criticized beginning in the fifteenth century for its alleged obfuscation of the plain meaning of the texts. But it only declined in importance and was supplanted by an alternative pedagogical system in the early nineteenth century. Polish Jewry's wealth helped promote the spread of *yeshivah* study, but Polish-Jewish moralists, preeminently the late-sixteenth-century preacher Efrayim Luntshitz, argued that wealth was a certain sign of corruption and hypocrisy. By the seventeenth century the study of Torah was widely disseminated in Poland and Lithuania—though the Ukraine still provided fewer opportunities for serious study than more settled regions of eastern Europe.

The Khmel'nitskii uprising. Religious, economic, and ethnic tensions in the Ukraine erupted in 1648, and for the next twelve years the Polish state was faced with a series of Cossack uprisings (initially with Tartar support) and with invasions from Sweden and Muscovy. The Cossacks, led by Bogdan Khmel'nitskii, massacred rural and urban Jewish communities on both sides of the Dnieper river. Hatred of Jews—which had little influence in sparking the Deluge (as both Polish and Jewish accounts refer to it)—resulted nonetheless in the killing of large numbers of Ukrainian Jews and in the evacuation of nearly all the remainder. The Jews of Ukraine quickly rebuilt their communities after the uprising was put down, but it left its mark on the increasingly deleterious fiscal standing of the *qehalim* and the councils.

MOVEMENT WESTWARD. A westward trend in Jewish migratory patterns was now apparent. In particular, Jews from areas of Poland devastated by the Swedish invasion moved in large numbers to Silesia, Moravia, and elsewhere in central Europe. (To be sure, Germany had retained Jewish communities in the intervening period, despite the widespread expulsions, particularly in areas under imperial and ecclesiastical protection and in the central and southern parts of the Holy Roman Empire.) Small numbers of Polish Jews also found their way in this period to Amsterdam and London. Some joined the growing ranks of the central European *Betteljuden* or *Schnorrjuden* (Jewish beggars), but most were absorbed, if only marginally, into the economic life of the Empire, which offered greater opportunities for Jews after the Thirty Years' War.

The skill of Jewish agents and contractors during the war and the rise of absolutist and mercantilist tendencies in government policy helped improve the economic and even the social standing of German Jewry. Jews moved into new localities (especially noteworthy were the Sephardic settlement in Hamburg and the Ashkenazic enclave in suburban Altona) and, with the support of rulers, were permitted to participate in an increasingly wide range of occupations, particularly commerce. German princes, concerned about competition from Atlantic ports better able to trade with the New World, saw wealthy Jews as useful commercial allies. Central European armies had benefited from Jewish contacts with Poland during the Thirty Years' War, and the experience (and wealth) gained by some Jews in this period helped contribute to the eventual emergence of court Jews who served local princes.

Humanist appreciation for Hebrew and the gradual laicization of European culture that accompanied the appearance of humanism in the fifteenth and sixteenth centuries set the stage for some cultural collaboration between Jews and Christians. In the Ashkenazic world, the influence of humanist trends was most clearly reflected in a moderation of anti-Jewish sentiment in certain small but influential intellectual circles. In Johannes Reuchlin's (1455–1522) defense of the Jews against the anti-Talmudic charges of Johannes Pfefferkorn, for instance, he referred to Jews and Christians as "fellow citizens of the same Roman Empire [who] live on the basis of the same law of citizenship and internal peace." The religious wars, which culminated in treaties which acknowledged that religious toleration—at least toward other Christians—was essential if only to save Europe from ceaseless strife, led to arguments for tolerance. More important in this regard, however, were the Protestant sects, most of them marginal, which began to question the connection between religious truth and political rule and showed an often intense interest in the biblical constitution and an attachment to the people and language of the Bible. Such trends were most apparent in Cromwellian England, where the impact of the Judaizers, the growing appreciation for Hebrew, the spread of millenarianist sentiment, and the renewed search for the Ten Lost Tribes with the discovery of the New World created a suitable cultural climate for a receptiveness to Menasseh ben Israel's mission to promote Jewish readmission to England.

Around the time of the Whitehall conference of 1655, which considered the readmission of Jews to England but left the matter undecided, small numbers of New Christians as well as Ashkenazic Jews settled in England, mostly in London. This small community came from Amsterdam, where an increasingly sizable and economically prominent Jewish community had lived since the unification of the northern provinces of the Netherlands and their declaration that the new state would be free from religious persecution.

Within the Ashkenazic sphere, Jewish thought remained largely indifferent to indications (however uneven and contradictory) of changes in Christian attitudes toward Jews. Indeed, a renewed sense of cultural segregation, as Jacob Katz (1961) has characterized it, was apparent in the sixteenth and seventeenth centuries, as reflected in a complete lack of Jewish interest in anti-Christian polemics and in the formation of a set of Jewish attitudes toward non-Jews that saw differences between the two as inherent rather than doctrinal. This case was argued most coherently by Yehudah Löw ben Betsal'el (c. 1525–1609). Yet the same period saw the promulgation of important halakhic decisions that permitted Jews to trade in Gentile wine and even in rosaries (in contrast to earlier rabbinic prohibitions against such trade) on the grounds that the Talmudic prohibitions against trade with idol worshipers were not relevant to Christians, who, at least for practical purposes, did not fall under this category.

A stratum of well-placed Jews had, since the religious wars, played a significant role in the centralizing administrations of the absolutist German states. Jewish moneylenders, minters, and agents were selected to perform important administrative, fiscal, and even diplomatic functions because their loyalty to the princes was unaffected by guild attachments or local enmities. Close links were forged between Polish-Jewish agricultural exporters and wealthy Jewish importers in Leipzig, Frankfurt, and Hamburg. Court Jews, as some of these magnates were called, emerged as a group relatively free from Jewish communal and rabbinical control and with independent access to the Gentile authorities.

The wealth of the court Jews, their relatively easy access to the Christian elite, and the example of the acculturated Sephardim of Hamburg and elsewhere in central and western Europe encouraged some Ashkenazim to imitate Sephardic and even non-Jewish social patterns. In certain well-to-do German-Jewish circles in the early eighteenth century, dance lessons, the study of French, and even the cutting of beards was common. In the same circles, Polish Jews were frequently characterized as superstitious and culturally inferior.

However, until the late eighteenth century and the spread of the Enlightenment and emancipatory movements, distinctions between German and Polish Jews remained fluid. This essential fluidity was reflected, for instance, in the careers of Ya'aqov Emden and Yonatan Eibeschutz, the eminent rabbinic figures at the center of the most vociferous Jewish polemical battle of the eighteenth century, which spanned the major Jewish communities of eastern and central Europe. Cultural unity was also apparent in the response of Ashkenazic Jewry in the 1660s to the news of Shabbetai Tsevi, whose claim to be the Messiah was received with the greatest enthusiasm by Sephardim but who was supported, according to Gershom Scholem, by most of European Jewry.

Shabbetai Tsevi's conversion to Islam in 1666 led to the disintegration of the movement and to its rebirth, on a much smaller scale, as a secret network of sects. In Podolia, where the Frankist movement arose out of this Shabbatean network in the second half of the eighteenth century, it attracted the support of only small numbers of Jews, and its leader, Jacob Frank (1726–1791), along with about six hundred followers, eventually converted under some duress to Catholicism. The teachings of Frank, which combined an eclectic reliance on Qabbalah and an intense fascination with worldly power, had a limited impact outside Poland when Frank moved to Brno, Offenbach, and elsewhere in central Europe in the last years of his life. The sect served as a syncretistic pathway for some poor as well as rich Jews to a less insular, larger world.

HASIDISM. In contrast to Frankism, the Hasidic movement, which also arose in Podolia, gradually spread beyond the Ukraine after the death of its founder Yisra'el ben Eli'ezer (1700–1760), known as the Besht, and won widespread support in Poland, Belorussia, and, to a more limited extent, Lithuania. Completely devoid of the Christological tendencies that would attract some acculturated Jews to Frankism, Hasidism embraced qabbalistic concepts and built on Jewish spiritual yearnings stirred by the heretical mystical movements. At the same time, it effectively neutralized the potentially subversive elements of Lurianic Qabbalah.

The concept of *devequt* (cleaving to God), for instance, was shorn by Hasidism of its cosmic and elitist features and placed within a mundane framework. Hasidism promoted a strategy whereby Jews might focus on the prosaic and even the patently profane in order to transform and elevate them. Cosmic elements in Lurianic Qabbalah were transformed into individualized landmarks in the psychology of faith and repentance.

Hasidism's moderation helped it eventually gain the acceptance of rabbis sympathetic to mysticism. Its halakhic innovations were minor: the introduction of a sharper knife for ritual slaughter (perhaps to capture Hasidic control over a crucial communal sphere) and some liturgical changes, such as use of the Lurianic liturgy and a less punctilious attitude toward the traditionally designated times for prayer. Moreover, though Hasidism has come to represent for some modern interpreters a democratized form of Judaism, it promoted no concrete social program and, indeed, did not attract the support of the urban artisans who constituted at the time the severest critics of Jewish communal authority. Among its most ardent and earliest supporters were rural Jews, particularly arendators, who were unhappy with the inability of the *qehalim* to defend their traditional right of *ḥazaqah* (protection from competition) and whose interests were frequently protected by the Ḥasidim. In this respect communal decline helped to fuel the movement, and it is unlikely that it would have spread as quickly or widely—by 1800 close to one-half of the Jews of east Europe flocked to its banner—had the Polish and Lithuanian councils not been abolished by the state in 1764. When challenged, for instance, by a charismatic spokesman of the communal elite, as in Lithuania by Eliyyahu ben Shelomoh Zalman, known as the Gaon of Vilna (1720–1797), Hasidism's momentum was temporarily checked.

Rather than introducing a new egalitarian note into Jewish religious life, Hasidism's most influential innovation was the promotion of a new elite that differed from both the traditional rabbinic scholars and the qabbalistic ascetics. The Hasidic *tsaddiq* forged a link between the qabbalistic master and the Jewish masses by emphasizing his communal responsibilities (in contradistinction to the asceticism of the qabbalist). The eighteenth century witnessed a marked decline in rabbinical stature. Jewish popular sentiment, rather than feeling alienated from the rabbis because of their self-imposed scholastic isolation, criticized them for their inability to live up to their own austere and still widely accepted standards.

HASKALAH. The German-speaking lands produced at the same time a westernized, acculturated elite. It was shaped by the emphasis of enlightened absolutists on the state as a secular rather than a Christian polity; the compulsory education system introduced (briefly) into Austria; the Enlightenment's vision of a neutral society where religious distinctions were rendered irrelevant or, at least, subordinate to other considerations; and the French Revolution, which emancipated the Jews of France in 1791. Most central European Jews, particularly after the Polish partitions (1772–1795) when Galicia was absorbed by Austria and east Poznan was added to Prussia, were Yiddish-speaking and religiously traditional and remained so until the mid-nineteenth century. But the self-consciously "enlightened" elite that emerged emphasized the sensualist rather than the divine source of knowledge, the ultimate importance of earthly existence, and a revised understanding of the relationship between religion and state. As the leading German-Jewish Enlightenment figure, Moses Mendelssohn (1729–1786) argued that Judaism was able (better than Christianity) to fit into a new order constructed on the basis of natural truth, rationalism, and a clear distinction between the functions and tools of church and state.

Russian Jewry. The Prussian state did not repudiate Jewish autonomy as anticipated by Mendelssohn, but in Austria, France, and even, if somewhat ambiguously, in Russia, the unity of Jewish society had to be maintained despite the lack of support and even the hostility of the government. Russia had prohibited Jewish settlement before the Polish partitions but it absorbed in the late eighteenth century approximately eight hundred thousand Jews. The regime was unwilling, and perhaps unable, to integrate Jews into the existing estates, disinclined to believe that Jewish assimilation was possible, and suspicious of the potentially deleterious impact that the Jews might have on the Russian peasantry. The result was the creation of a large area in which Jews were permitted to live, called the Pale of Settlement, in the fifteen provinces of Lithuania, Belorussia, the Ukraine, and so-called New Russia (on the northern littoral of the Black and Azov seas). Jews were also allowed to live in the ten provinces of central Poland, although these were formally excluded from the Pale. Jews constitued an average of 12 percent of the total population in this area of west and southwestern Russia (and often the majority of the urban population) by the late nineteenth century. The classification of Jews as *inorodtsy* (in 1835), the legal category created for the semi-autonomous primitive and nomadic tribes at the periphery of the empire, highlighted their essentially anomalous status in Russian law, since the regime abolished the *qehalim* soon afterward, in 1844. Indeed, despite intermittent governmental attempts to assimilate Russia's Jews, the regime continued to share an abiding preoccupation (sometimes more and sometimes less acute) with their irredeemable separateness.

There was little intervention by the Russian state into the communal life of the Jews until the 1840s. Even after the *qahal* was abolished, a separate Jewish judiciary continued to function and many of the duties of the *qahal* were subsumed by other representative Jewish bodies (though Jewish autonomy was now checked by municipal supervision). The Russian Jewish community grew rapidly over the course of the century and by 1880 numbered four million; it increased in size to more than five million in 1897 despite the mass migration to the west in the same period. Rapid demographic increase, the legal discrimination suffered by Russian Jewry, and the sluggishness of those sectors of the Russian economy in which most Jews were employed contributed to the eventual politicization of the community and to its migratory trends in the late nineteenth and early twentieth centuries. At the turn of the twentieth century, more than 40 percent of the world's fourteen million Jews lived in the Russian empire; 7.5 million Jews lived in eastern Europe as a whole, including Galicia and east Prussia.

Rapid urbanization and economic change in the nineteenth century challenged the foundations of Russian Jewish social and economic life. Repeated expulsions from villages, moves against rural Jewish innkeepers, and the concentration of the liquor trade (which employed about 30 percent of prepartition Polish Jewry) in the hands of a small number of wealthy contractors contributed to the community's urbanization. Petty trade, on the other hand, was undermined by the decline of fairs, the rise of permanent markets, and the government's war on smuggling. Eventually the construction of railway lines destabilized previously crucial commercial and banking centers which were bypassed by the railroad. The decline of the commercial sector led to an overcrowding in others, such as artisanry, where Jews tended to concentrate in the garment trade and in shoemaking.

At the same time, improved transportation, renewed efforts at the exploitation of the agriculturally rich Ukrainian steppe, and the construction of major grain exporting ports (the most important being Odessa) where Jews played prominent economic roles all produced a stratum of successful Jewish entrepreneurs and merchants. Jews made substantial contributions to industrial manufacturing (particularly in Bialystok and Lódź), to the sugar trade (where Jews revolutionized marketing techniques), and the construction of railways. By 1851, 20 percent of the members of Russia's wealthiest merchant guild were Jews, though they constituted only about 2 or 3 percent of the total Russian population.

Jewish communal authority. In the absence of a state-recognized body that represented Russian Jewry (except for the infrequent, government-convened delegations of Jewish deputies and later the tepid rabbinical commissions), considerable pressure and responsibility was placed in the hands of *qehalim* and private associations. The authority of the *qehalim* was undermined by the 1827 statute which instituted the conscription of Jews and which placed responsibility for the draft in the hands of local *qahal* officials. This led to widespread abuse: the exemption of the rich, the forced conscription of the poor, the drafting of boys of twelve and younger who were subjected, once they were drafted and handed over to the military, to intense pressure to convert to Russian Orthodoxy. Protests by Jews against the *qahal* oligarchy erupted in Podolia, Minsk, Mogilev, and elsewhere, and the rabbinical elite—whose *yeshivah* students were protected by communal officials from the draft—mostly remained silent in the face of these abuses, which further eroded their popular stature.

Russian Haskalah. Nineteenth-century Russian Jewry nonetheless retained a traditional profile. There was little scope in Russia for acculturation; the multiethnic character of the empire mitigated assimilation and anti-Jewish sentiment remained pervasive among liberals and conservatives alike. Yet the introduction by the state in the 1840s and 1850s of a network of schools where secular as well as Jewish subjects were taught, the liberalization of government policy (and the emancipation of the serfs) under Alexander II (1855–1881) which excited Jewish hopes, and the example of an acculturating western and central European Jewry helped create a Russian Haskalah, or Jewish enlightenment movement. Haskalah stressed those aspects of Jewish life that non-Jews presumably considered positive: the purity of biblical Hebrew, the stability of Jewish family life, the Jews' financial aptitude, their agricultural past, and Judaism's philosophical legacy. On the other hand, the movement denounced aspects of contemporary Jewish life at variance with the beliefs of the larger society (and presumably with the true character of Judaism), such as mystical speculation, disdain for secular study, and ignorance of the vernacular.

In contrast to the exponents of the German-Jewish enlightenment in the decades after Moses Mendelssohn's death, Russian *maskilim* (Jews who subscribed to the goals of the Haskalah) hoped to see Jewry rendered acceptable to its neighbors without relinquishing its distinctive social or religious character. In their view, Judaism was to be purified but not entirely stripped of its idiosyncratic tendencies. The Haskalah movement gave rise to efforts to promote a secular Hebrew literature and periodical press and new types of philanthropic and self-help institutions, and it later had a decisive impact on Jewish nationalist and socialist movements. Its promotion of secular study also helped contribute (especially after the 1870s) to the precipitous rise in the number of Jews enrolled in Russian and secular Jewish schools.

Musar. The Musar movement was one response to modernizing trends within the traditional camp. It stressed self-discipline (an echo of the highly influential system of Eliyyahu ben Shelomoh Zalman, which saw the prodigious study of Torah as taking precedence even over the performance of *mitsvot*) but Musar's founder, Yisra'el Salanter (1810–1883), promoted a pedagogical system in which communal meditation and introspection were integrated into the traditional Talmudic curriculum. At the same time, a series of relatively well-funded and prestigious *yeshivot* were established in Lithuania to counter the inroads made by the Haskalah and secular education. Charismatic rabbinic figures, perhaps most prominently Yisra'el Me'ir Kagan (known as the Ḥafets Ḥayyim, 1838–1933), continued to represent the community's highest ideals in their personal piety, humility, and devotion to learning.

INTEGRATION AND EMANCIPATION. Nineteenth-century German and Austrian Jewry—with the major exception of the Jews of Galicia—eventually entered the middle class, discarded Yiddish for German, and produced ideologies of Reform and Neoorthodoxy which minimized or rejected aspects of Judaism considered as sacrosanct in the east. Joseph II's *Toleranzpatent* (1782) attempted to legislate against Jewish separatism while opening up new economic and educational options for some Jews. The long and contentious debate in Germany over the feasibility of Jewish emancipation made its small Jewish community (which constituted about 1.75 percent of the total population in 1871 when emancipation was finally granted) highly visible and particularly sensitive to the vagaries of public opinion. In Prussia, 58,000 of its 124,000 Jews were in fact emancipated by 1815; elsewhere in Germany restrictions on employment in the public and private sectors and limitations on Jewish residence were abolished, or at least substantially modified, by the 1850s. To be sure, the 1848 uprisings were followed by new restrictions in Austria and Bavaria, and they were also accompanied by a new anti-Semitic argument which identified Jews with the most disruptive and oppressive features of modern society.

In Galicia, where over 800,000 of Austria's 1.2 million Jews lived in 1900, 85 percent of the Jewish population, according to one report, subsisted at substandard conditions and worked as petty moneylenders, agents, and innkeepers. Yet the majority of Germany's Jews, who were concentrated until the mid-nineteenth century in petty trade, small retailing establishments, and artisanry had by 1871 entered the middle and upper-middle classes. The most telling indication of their social mobility was the disappearance of the *Betteljuden* (many of whom immigrated to the United States), who had, together with day laborers and domestic servants, made up 15 to 20 percent of the German-Jewish population in the late 1830s. German Jews continued to be concentrated in a cluster of occupations, but now these were wholesale trade, commerce, the money market, the professions, and journalism.

Emergence of reform. Attempts at integration by German Jews produced ideologies of religious reform that accepted the diminution of the national traits of Judaism as espoused by the larger society and emphasized those aspects of Judaism most conducive to cultural symbiosis. Abraham Geiger (1810–1874), Germany's major Reform exponent, saw Judaism as having evolved historically and asserted that every generation had to determine for itself what religious practices and concepts retained a contemporary relevance. Geiger identified monotheism and the teachings of the prophets as the quintessential message that had characterized Judaism throughout the ages and that constituted the basis for its ethical system. In a radical departure from the traditional understanding of *galut*, Geiger saw the Jewish dispersion as a positive condition, since it helped Jews promote the universalistic teachings of their faith. This emphasis on mission served to justify continued Jewish peculiarity and helped to reinforce, albeit within a substantially modified context, traditional assumptions of Jewish specialness and chosenness. The fundamental principles of Reform were elaborated in a series of rabbinical conferences held in the 1840s, and these assemblies constituted the culmination of a long period in which Reform promoted a substantially modified Jewish educational curriculum and alterations in synagogue service and decorum.

Emergence of Orthodoxy. The response of Pressburg's (modern Bratislava) influential Mosheh Sofer (Ḥatam Sofer, 1762–1839) to the emergence of Reform was summarized in his pithy "Ḥadash asur min ha-torah" ("everything new is forbidden by the Torah"), which denounced all change as undermining Judaism. The call for traditional Jews to segregate themselves from the increasingly Reform-dominated communities of Germany was promoted by many Orthodox rabbis, most prominently by Samson Raphael Hirsch (1808–1888), who argued for the universalizing of Judaism and, at the same time, for an uncompromising affirmation of its traditional commitment to *mitsvot.* Traditional Judaism in Germany, and elsewhere in Europe, began to employ the tools—and in Hirsch's case also the terminology—of the larger, secularizing world in order to combat Reform, and this led to the creation of Orthodox newspapers and political parties. The first such party was established in Hungary in 1867.

ACCULTURATION AND RESPONSES TO ANTI-SEMITISM. European Jewry's acculturation led, to be sure, to a diminution of the importance that Jewish concerns played in the lives of many Jews, but it also provided an increasingly westernized Jewry with new and sophisticated tools with which to promote Jewish interests. Jewish liberals and a small number of political radicals played a prominent role in the 1848 revolutions, in contrast to the political passivity of the Jews of France in 1789; another indication of the tendency of westernized Jews to employ new and innovative means to promote Jewish causes was the creation of a highly diversified Jewish press mostly published in European languages.

Jewish assimilation, whose goal was the fusion of Jewry into the majority culture, was most feasible in settings were Jews formed a small percentage of the population in large urban areas; where acculturation was widespread but anti-Semitism prevalent, the promotion of social integration was thwarted. A precipitous rise in anti-Semitism in societies where Jews had experienced substantial acculturation often contributed to an increase in the incidence of conversion. On average, 145 Jews converted annually in Prussia between 1880 and 1884 while, in the wake of the anti-Semitic agitation of the last decade of the century, the number doubled to 349 between 1895 and 1899.

Of the smaller Jewish communities of western and northern Europe, about 35,000 Jews lived in England in the 1850s, 80,000 in France, about 52,000 in Holland (in the 1840s), 64,000 in Belgium, and fewer than 1,000 in Sweden. In France and England, Jews were concentrated in the largest cities (a process that had begun earlier in England than in France). In both societies, despite the emancipation of French Jewry more than half a century before the Jews of England were admitted into the House of Commons in 1858, acculturation preceded the complete abrogation of Jewish restrictions. An absence of denominationalism was another feature common to both English and French Jewish life, and in the two communities Reform tendencies were absorbed or neutralized by the dominant religious institutions and they did not precipitate the sectarianism characteristic of German Judaism. The absorption into the middle class of most English and French Jews by the late nineteenth century helped encourage a privatization of Jewish identity, which was eventually challenged by the east European migration. Between 1881 and 1914 the English Jewish population increased, mostly as a result of the immigration of Russian Jews, from sixty-five thousand to three hundred thousand. Thirty thousand immigrants settled in Paris in the same period (arriving in particularly large numbers after 1905), and they introduced into the western urban Jewish milieu an ethnic dimension previously unknown. Indeed, between 1881 and 1924, about 2.5 million east European Jews (mostly from Russia) migrated to the West; two-thirds of them left their homes between 1903 and 1914 and the vast majority of immigrants moved to the United States. About 10–15 percent settled in western and central Europe. Russian Jews in particular emigrated in large numbers because of the oppressive tsarist legislation of the 1880s and 1890s, shrinking economic prospects, and often exaggerated rumors of economic prospects in the West.

East European Jewish immigrants became a special focus of attack by the anti-Semitic movement that erupted in western and central Europe in the late nineteenth century. This movement was the product of a general antiliberal reaction which promoted romantic conservatism over constitutionalism, a free market economy, and freedom of speech and assembly. Anti-Semitism (the term was coined in the 1870s) provided a seemingly plausible target for a wide range of social and economic frustrations. Its literature drew on secular (and often scientific) rather than religious terminology and sometimes, as in Edouard Adolphe Drumont's *La France juive* (1886), it drew on left-wing ideology in its case for the illegitimacy of Jewish wealth and position. Influential anti-Semitic parties appeared in Germany and Austria. Anti-Semitism became a cultural code, in Shulamit Volkov's characterization, for a wide range of groups that stressed militant nationalism, imperial expansion, racism, anticolonialism, antisocialism, and respect for authoritarian government.

The rise and resilience of the anti-Semitic movement compelled some European Jewish leaders to reassess their communal and political strategies. In Germany this gave birth in 1893 to the *Centralverein deutscher Staatsbürger jüdischen Glauben,* which departed from the classical Mendelssohnian stance both in its promotion of a conspicuously Jewish (as opposed to philo-Semitic, liberal, and Gentile-led) response to anti-Semitism and in its insistence that the Jewish case be aired and vindicated in courts of law. In Russia, as in the West, before the 1880s Jewish politics was seen as predicated entirely on the goodwill of Gentiles and its goal was the encouragement of Jewish emancipation. A new understanding took hold after the 1881–1882 pogroms, best encapsulated in the title of Odessa physician Leon Pinsker's *Auto-Emancipation* (1882), which called upon the Jews to cease their efforts to adapt themselves to the larger environment and to create instead a new one outside of Russia. A new type of Russian Jewish leader emerged in the same period: young, russianized (or partially so), who came to compete with the communal magnates of St. Petersburg and the rabbinical elite.

Zionism. Two major ideological currents emerged: Zionism and Jewish socialism. Zionism drew its constituency and vitality from eastern Europe but the Austrian journalist, Theodor Herzl (1860–1904), gave the small and Russian-based movement a measure of stature and international recognition in the 1890s and early twentieth century. Herzl's most important Zionist adversary was the Odessa intellectual Asher Ginzberg (better known as Aḥad ha-ʿAm, 1856–1927), who provided Zionism with influential ideological underpinnings very different from those of Herzl. From Herzl's perspective, the promotion by Zionism of a Jewish homeland would undercut the growth of anti-Semitism, restore Jewish economic productivity, and provide Jews throughout the world (as well as the threatened liberal order) with renewed stability. Ginzberg, on the other hand, saw Zionism as a framework that could allow Jewry to absorb Western values without having them submerge Jewish identity. He stressed the cultural benefits of the rebuilding of a Palestinian Jewish homeland and minimized its immediate economic impact.

Jewish socialism. A second Jewish political movement emphasized the need to transform Russia itself—a goal Russian Zionists also eventually adopted in their Helsinki platform of 1906—and the Jewish Socialist Labor Bund, established in 1897, charted a course between the two poles of nationalism and Marxism. Jewish socialism's following, not surprisingly, expanded in moments of revolutionary turmoil and contracted with rapidity in times of relative quiescence. But the heroism of the Jewish revolutionaries, their organization of self-defense groups during the pogroms, their participation in widespread philanthropic endeavors, and even their conspiratorial form of internal organization came to infuse them with an almost legendary respect in the Pale of Settlement.

WORLD WAR I AND ITS AFTERMATH. The war seemed at first to present a singularly unfavorable scenario for Jewish political activity but was, ironically, followed by a series of outstanding victories for Jewish leaders in the diplomatic sphere and by a new and apparently more encouraging political order. The Russian Revolution of 1917 brought down the imperial regime and emancipated Russia's Jews; the Balfour Declaration, issued by the British the same year, was Zionism's first concrete diplomatic achievement and it would serve, until the State of Israel was established in 1948, as a central focus of the movement's strategy. Moreover, the adoption of international guarantees for the observance of national minority rights in the new states of east central Europe (along with prewar Romania) was largely the product of the maneuvering of British and American Jewish leaders. The mass evacuation of hundreds of thousands of Galician and Russian Jews in 1914–1915 (the Russian ones evacuated under particularly degrading conditions) lent Jews a special visibility, which was reinforced by the fact that much of the war was conducted in regions heavily populated by Jews. Misperceptions of the strength and dimensions of Jewish influence (suppositions which gained worldwide notoriety after World War I with the dissemination of the anti-Semitic tract *Protocols of the Elders of Zion*) helped Jews wrest major political concessions for themselves. The Balfour Declaration, in which the British declared sympathy for Zionist aspirations in Palestine, resulted partly from the Allies' belief that Russian (and American) Jewish support was crucial in bolstering the war effort. The Russian liberalization of Jewish residence restrictions in 1915 was the product of a misperception that Jewish-controlled Western loans would be denied to Russia if it continued to be seen as brutally anti-Semitic. Western support for national minority rights in east central Europe was given special impetus in the wake of the Ukrainian pogroms of 1918–1919 in which more than five hundred Jewish communities were attacked and about seventy thousand Jews were killed. The effort of the Bolsheviks—who in November 1917 had overthrown the liberal anti-tsarist government that had been in power in Russia since the fall of the Romanovs earlier that year—to put down the anti-Jewish disturbances and to pacify the Ukrainian separatist movement won widespread (if somewhat equivocal) support for them among Russia's Jews.

The new Soviet government associated anti-Semitism with tsarist reaction and fought it vigorously, but Bolshevism also denied Jewish demands for national recognition on the basis of its authoritative statement on minority nationalism, *Marxism and the National Question* (1913). Nonetheless, Jewry's distinctive cultural and, implicitly, also its national needs were acknowledged by the regime, which was interested in consolidating Jewish support. Secular cultural activity in Yiddish was encouraged; Hebrew was barred as bourgeois and religious institutions and functionaries were harassed. By the early 1930s even Yiddish-language publishing, research, and pedagogical activity were restricted. At the same time, the Soviet Jewish population as a whole—which numbered about three million in 1926—benefited from the expanding economy, became urbanized (it was eventually concentrated in Moscow, Leningrad, and a few other large cities), and was absorbed, despite the existence of a residual popular as well as institutional anti-Semitism, into the industrial working class, the bureaucracy, the professions, and the sciences.

The Jews of interwar Poland (who numbered just under 2.9 million in 1921, 10.5 percent of the total population) underwent a process of acculturation different from that of Soviet Jewry. Ravaged as Poland was by the war and separated from its natural markets and sources of energy by the boundaries of the new Polish state, its postwar economic development was sluggish before 1929 and singularly depressed in the 1930s. Poland's depressed economic state reinforced a widespread integral nationalism that persuaded many Poles that the Jews, as members of a faith inimical to Christianity, had no place in Poland. Particularly after 1936, nationalist xenophobia, church-sponsored anti-Semitism, and economic decline combined to persuade Poles of varied political persuasions that anti-Jewish policies were a necessary cruelty. About one-third of Poland's Jews retained a largely traditional religious profile and promoted Orthodox interests with tenacity and some sophistication. Jewish acculturation was also vividly reflected in the growth of secular Jewish culture and widely diversified socialist and Zionist political activities, which took on different forms in various regions of Poland, Galicia, central Poland, and Lithuania-Belorussia.

THE HOLOCAUST. The vast majority of Germany's approximately 600,000 Jews (constituting about one percent of the population in the early 1920s) were solidly based in the middle class, though one-fifth of the Jewish population were foreign-born and maintained a less prosperous occupational profile. Anti-Semitic sentiment—which reached ferocious levels in the immediate post–World War I period when wide segments of the population associated the sudden loss of the war with the treachery of the Jews—was marginalized during the economic prosperity of 1923–1929. Anti-Semitism regained a mass following with the onset of the worldwide depression. Once Hitler was appointed chancellor in 1933, German Jewry was gradually segregated from the larger population, denied employment, and those who did not emigrate by 1939 were eventually deported and either worked to death or gassed in labor and death camps. Germany's invasion of Poland led to the effective segregation of its large Jewish community, and Jews elsewhere in Nazi-occupied or Nazi-dominated western and east central Europe were placed in ghettos where they too were starved, brutalized, and, in the end, sent to death camps. More than one million Soviet Jews were killed by Nazi mobile killing units during the German invasion of 1941; the introduction in 1942 of highly efficient means for mass extermination led to the construction of a series of death camps designed expressly for the extermination of European Jewry. Over the course of World War II during the Nazi Holocaust about 6 million Jews were killed: 4.5 million in Poland and the Soviet Union; 125,000 German Jews, 277,000 Czechs, 402,000 Hungarians, 24,000 Belgians, 102,000 Dutch, 40,000 Romanians, 60,000 Yugoslavs, 85,000 French, and tens of thousands in Greece and Italy.

POST-HOLOCAUST JEWISH COMMUNITY. The resilience of postwar anti-Semitism in Poland encouraged most Holocaust survivors to emigrate, and the Polish Jewish community, numbering about 30,000 in the late 1950s, was further decimated following the migration of large numbers of Jews in the wake of the 1968 anti-Semitic governmental campaign. Germany's 25,000 Jews in the late 1960s experienced a high rate of intermarriage (72.5 percent among males in the years 1951–1958) and a death rate that far exceeded its birthrate. The most culturally vibrant Jewish community of east central Europe was Hungary, where between 80,000 and 90,000 Jews in the 1960s maintained, eventually with government support, a wide range of religious and philanthropic institutions, including a rabbinical seminary. The post-1967 resurgence of Jewish nationalist sentiment among Soviet Jews led to a revival of (largely clandestine) cultural activity and helped precipitate a large migration of Jews to Israel and the United States. The centers of European Jewish cultural life in the postwar period were England and France. The French Jewish community, in particular, has demonstrated a marked vitality, encouraged by the migration of North African Jews, primarily from Algeria, in the 1960s.

SEE ALSO Agudat Yisra'el; Hasidism, overview article; Holocaust, The, article on History; Messianism, article on Jewish Messianism; Musar Movement; Orthodox Judaism; Reform Judaism; Shabbetai Tsevi; Yeshivah; Zionism.

BIBLIOGRAPHY

Early Modern Period

The most authoritative work in English on the Jews of Poland and Lithuania in the sixteenth and seventeenth centuries is volume 16 of Salo W. Baron's *A Social and Religious History of the Jews*, 2d ed., rev. and enl. (Philadelphia, 1976). For a sociological analysis of Jewish communal autonomy in eastern and central Europe, see Jacob Katz's *Tradition and Crisis* (New York, 1961). On Jews in the late medieval Germanic empire, see Selma Stern's *Josel of Rosheim* (Philadelphia, 1965). Useful methodological questions are raised in an article by Gershon David Hundert, "On the Jewish Community in Poland during the Seventeenth Century: Some Comparative Perspectives," *Revue des études juives* 142 (July–December 1983): 349–372. On the seventeenth century, there is interesting material in Jonathan I. Israel's "Central European Jewry during the Thirty Years' War," *Central European History* (March 1983): 3–30. The best treatment of Polish-Jewish cultural life in the same period is H. H. Ben-Sasson's *Hagut ve-hanhagah* (Jerusalem, 1959). Jewish migratory trends in the seventeenth and eighteenth centuries are studied in Moses A. Shulvass's *From East to West* (Detroit, 1971). On the readmission of English Jewry, see David S. Katz's *Philo-Semitism and the Readmission of the Jews to England, 1603–1655* (Oxford, 1982).

Modern Period

An incisive analysis of the social features of Hasidism may be found in Samuel Ettinger's "The Hassidic Movement: Reality and Ideals," in *Jewish Society through the Ages*, edited by H. H. Ben-Sasson and Samuel Ettinger (London, 1971), pp. 251–266. For a discussion of French Jewish identity, see Phyllis Cohen Albert's "Nonorthodox Attitudes in Nineteenth-Century French Judaism," in *Essays in Modern Jewish History: A Tribute to Ben Halpern*, edited by Frances Malino and Phyllis Cohen Albert (Rutherford, N.J., 1982), pp. 121–141. Michael Stanislawski's *Tsar Nicholas I and the Jews* (Philadelphia, 1983), and Hans Rogger's "Russian Ministers and the Jewish Question, 1881–1917," *California Slav-*

ic Studies 8 (1975): 15–76, study imperial Jewish policy. The essays in *Revolution and Evolution: 1848 in German-Jewish History,* edited by Werner E. Mosse, Arnold Paucker, and Reinhard Rürup (Tübingen, 1981), examine nineteenth century German Jewry, with particular emphasis on the community's socioeconomic transformation. Todd M. Endelman's *The Jews of Georgian England, 1714–1830* (Philadelphia, 1979) is a skillful social history. The political responses of east European Jews are studied in Jonathan Frankel's *Prophecy and Politics: Socialism, Nationalism and the Russian Jews, 1862–1917* (Cambridge, U.K., 1981). Ezra Mendelsohn reviews the interwar period in *The Jews of East Central Europe between the World Wars* (Bloomington, Ind., 1983). The best study of Soviet Jewry is Zvi Y. Gitelman's *Jewish Nationality and Soviet Politics* (Princeton, 1972). A particularly insightful essay in Yehuda Bauer's *The Holocaust in Historical Perspective* (Seattle, 1978) is his "Against Mystification: The Holocaust as a Historical Phenomenon."

New Sources

Gitelman, Zvi, ed. *The Emergence of Modern Jewish Politics: Bundism and Zionism in Eastern Europe.* Pitt Series in Russian and East European Studies. Pittsburgh, 2003.

Gruber, Ruth Ellen. *Virtually Jewish: Reinventing Jewish Culture in Europe.* Berkeley, 2002.

Israel, Jonathan Irvine. *European Jewry in the Age of Mercantilism, 1550–1750.* Oxford, 1998.

Sutcliffe, Adam. *Judaism and Enlightenment.* New York, 2003.

Wasserstein, Bernard. *Vanishing Diaspora: The Jews in Europe since 1945.* Cambridge, Mass., 1996.

STEVEN J. ZIPPERSTEIN (1987)
Revised Bibliography

JUDGE, WILLIAM Q. William Q. Judge (1851–1896) was a cofounder of the Theosophical Society in 1875, along with Madame Helena Petrovna Blavatsky (1831–1891) and Colonel Henry Steel Olcott (1832–1907). The society was dedicated to promoting universal brotherhood and the study of the hidden laws of nature and ancient scriptures. Judge was a close associate of Blavatsky during the years when she wrote *Isis Unveiled* (1877) until her death in 1891. She referred to him in a letter as "My dearest Brother and Co-Founder of the Theosophical Society" (H. P. Blavatsky to the American Conventions, Second Annual Meeting, April, 1888, p. 31). Blavatsky signed a letter to him, "yours until death and after" (*Lucifer,* June 1891). (Judge revealed the content of some of Blavatsky's letters in articles published after her death in the journal *Lucifer.*)

After Blavatsky's death, Judge continued to be a clear and notable expositor of her writings and of Theosophical concepts in general. Judge's *The Ocean of Theosophy* (1893) is a readable synopsis of Blavatsky's great work *The Secret Doctrine* (1888). Although he considered himself to be a disciple of Blavatsky and a line of mahatmas (masters) behind the Theosophical movement, Judge was an author, counselor, and teacher in his own right. In 1886, Judge began the *Path,* an independent journal published in New York. This publication continued for ten years and ran to ten volumes, mostly of Judge's own writings under pseudonyms such as Bryan Kinnavan, Eusebio Urban, and many others. The *Path* was renamed *Theosophy* in 1896.

Judge was born in Ireland, one of the seven children of Frederick Judge, a Freemason, and Mary Alice Quan. At the age of seven, the boy had a serious illness and indeed seemed to his family to have died, but he suddenly and miraculously recovered. After this near-death experience he showed remarkable abilities. He devoured books on Mesmerism, phrenology, religion, magic, and Rosicrucianism, which was surprising because no one had taught him to read. His family was simply puzzled by the change in his behavior. However, many theosophists believe he was an actually a Hindu initiate who had entered the body of the dying Irish boy to fulfill the vow of helping to bring the wisdom of the East to the West. In an April 1891 letter, he wrote to Annie Besant (1847–1933): "I am not in my own body and am perfectly aware of it. It is borrowed" (Ransom, 1938, p. 305). For this reason, some called him "the Rajah."

When Judge was thirteen, his family immigrated to New York. As a youth, he became a clerk and studied law in the offices of George P. Andrews. At twenty-one, he became a naturalized U.S. citizen and was admitted to the bar. He specialized in commercial law and developed a reputation for honesty and meticulous handling of cases. In 1874 he married Ella Smith, a strict Methodist who did not share his interest in occult and paranormal matters. The couple had a daughter who died as a small child. During this difficult time Judge read Olcott's *People from the Other World* (1875) and wrote to the author about their mutual interest in spiritualist phenomena. Olcott invited him to call on Madame Blavatsky in New York City. Judge wrote of his first meeting with Blavatsky: "It was her eye that attracted me, the eye of one whom I must have known in many lives past away" (*Lucifer* 8, no. 6 [June 15, 1891]). Blavatsky wrote in an 1889 letter that "H.P.B. would give. . . the whole esoteric brood in the U.S. for one W.Q.J., who is part of herself since several aeons" (*Theosophical Forum,* June 1933, pp. 192–193).

The period from 1878 to 1883 was particularly trying for the young disciple, for he was virtually penniless and could do little work for the society. In addition, Blavatsky and Olcott had sailed for India to carry on the work of the Theosophical Society while he remained in New York. In 1881 he traveled on business to Central and South America and Mexico where he contracted blackwater fever. He recorded his experiences in "A Weird Tale," one of the many spiritual allegories and stories he would write. Around this time Judge corresponded with Damodar K. Mavalankar, a disciple of Blavatsky in India, about being discouraged and depressed. He was himself called to India on June 11, 1883, by a summons on the back of a letter from Damodar printed in red pencil, "Better come, M. . ." Since Judge thought such messages were always from a master called Morya, he left as soon as possible. (Letter from the Adyar Archives, *Echoes of the Orient*, Vol.1, p. XXV, Sven Eek and Boris de Zirkoff.) After visiting Blavatsky in Paris for several months in 1884, he sailed to Bombay (Mumbai). Meeting there with Damodar and others about the future of the movement, Judge then traveled to several cities and gave lectures on Theosophy and the destiny of India.

Upon returning to New York in 1885, he was determined to preserve the Theosophical Society. Even when most of the membership had vanished, Judge held meetings, where he spoke and recorded the minutes himself. This work by Judge was instrumental in forming the American Section of the Theosophical Society, and he was elected its general secretary in 1886. In 1890 he was appointed vice president of the international Theosophical Society. Also in 1886, Mrs. Julia Campbell Ver Planck (later Mrs. Archibald Keightley) joined the Theosophical Society. Her correspondence with Judge (for which she used the name Jasper Niemand) became *Letters That Have Helped Me*, a valuable book concerning the trials of discipleship on the Theosophical path.

In 1890 Judge sued the *New York Sun* on behalf of Blavatsky, who had been libeled in the paper by Professor Elliot Coues. Coues had charged that Blavatsky had perpetrated a hoax by persuading Mabel Collins to claim that an adept had dictated her book *Light on the Path* (1885). He had also accused Blavatsky of sexual immorality, fraud, plagiarism, and deception. When the *Sun*'s attorneys found out that Coues's allegations were "without solid foundation," they were retracted in 1892.

After Blavatsky's death in London in 1891, Judge sailed to England as the representative of the U.S. section of the Theosophical Society. Judge published articles in the *Sun* and in the *Path* in tribute to Blavatsky's life and work. He also published a rendition of *The Yoga Aphorisms of Patanjali* (1889), introduced with a succinct discussion of Oriental psychology. In 1890 he published his version of the *Bhagavad Gita*, in which he sought to capture the original's meaning rather than to be strict to the letter of Sanskrit grammar. These works made a deep impact on Theosophy and the further introduction of Oriental psychology to the West.

In 1893 Judge made a lasting impression when he spoke to a large audience at the World Parliament of Religions in Chicago. However, his final years were clouded by the charges preferred against him by Besant and Olcott for misusing the mahatmas' names and handwriting. They claimed that no contact with the mahatmas could be proved to their satisfaction. Olcott ordered Judge to resign from the vice president's position. Judge refused, however, and defended himself by stating that he had in no way abrogated his duties as vice president, and that a trial could not be held without creating a dogma as to the existence of the masters, which was his personal belief.

Because both of these objections were held to be reasonable, in July 1894 he was reconfirmed as vice president of the Theosophical Society, based in Adyar, Madras (Chennai), India. However, personal feelings against Judge ran high, and there were renewed calls for his resignation. Because Annie Besant continued to press charges, the U.S. section declared complete autonomy from the Theosophical Society at its 1895 annual convention and formed an independent body, with Judge selected as president for life (1895). However, during the early part of 1896 the acrimony of these events had a detrimental effect on his health, which was still frail because of the blackwater fever contracted years earlier, and he died that same year on March 21 in New York. His last words were "There must be calmness. Hold fast. Go slow" (*Letters That Have Helped Me*, p. 29). Judge's teaching and life can be best summarized by his own words: "There is no room for sorrow in the heart of him who knows and realizes the Unity of all spiritual beings. While people, monuments and governments disappear, the self remains and returns again. The wise are not disturbed; they remain silent; they depend on the self and seek their refuge in It" (*Echoes of the Orient*, vol. 1, p. lxv). Katherine Tingley (1847–1929) became head of the Theosophical Society in the United States after Judge died, and she moved its headquarters to Point Loma, California. Judge's devoted student Robert Crosbie (1849–1919) seceded from this group and formed the United Lodge of Theosophists in 1909.

See Also Besant, Annie; Blavatsky, H. P.; Olcott, Henry Steel; Point Loma Theosophical Community; Theosophical Society; Tingley, Katherine.

Bibliography

Works by Judge

The Yoga Aphorisms of Patanjali. New York, 1889; reprint, Los Angeles, 1967. A rendition assisted by James Connelly, this is a valuable introduction to Oriental psychology.

Echoes of the Orient. New York. 1890; reprint, Los Angeles, 1950, and San Diego, 1987. A small pamphlet broadly outlining Theosophical doctrines.

The Bhagavad Gita: The Book of Devotion. New York, 1890; reprint, Los Angeles, 1947. Also done in collaboration with James Connelly. The *Notes*, covering the first seven chapters are by Judge, the rest by his student Robert Crosbie.

Letters That Have Helped Me. Compiled by Jasper Niemand. New York, 1891; reprint, Pasadena, Calif., 1953 and 1981. Contains correspondence between Judge and Jasper Niemand (Mrs. Archibald Keightley), Judge's notes for *"An Occult Novel,"* and information about his life.

The Ocean of Theosophy. 1893; reprint, Los Angeles, 1915.Originally published as a series of articles for the *Fort Wayne Sentinel.* The simplest and clearest exegesis of basic theosophical ideas and of Blavatsky's *The Secret Doctrine.*

Reply by Mr. Judge on Charges of Misuse of Mahatmas' Names and Handwritings. London, 1895. Reprinted as *Two Replies* (Los Angeles, 1992).

Practical Occultism. Edited by Arthur Conger. Covina, Calif., 1951. Contains private letters of William Q. Judge not previously printed.

Echoes of the Orient. 3 vols. San Diego, 1987. The most thorough publication of Judge's collected works.

See also *The Path,* vols. 1–10, New York, April 1886–March 1896. Judge owned this independent journal. It was renamed *Theosophy* in in 1896, and again renamed *Universal Brotherhood* in 1897. It became *Universal Broherhood Path* in 1900. After a series of changes, a similar journal began publication as *Sunrise,* issued by the Theosophical University Press in Pasadena. A journal with the same purpose has continued since 1912 in Los Angeles as *Theosophy.*

Works on Judge

Blavatsky, H.P. *H. P. Blavatsky, to the American Conventions, 1888–1891.* Pasadena, 1979. Blavatsky's messages to American Theosophists.

Deveney, John Patrick. "An 1876 Lecture by W.Q. Judge on his Magical Progress in the Theosophical Society." *Theosophical History* 9 (July 2003): 12. Discusses the young Judge's experiments with clairvoyance and astral travel as an effort of will not mediumship.

Forray, Brett. "William Q. Judge's and Annie Besant's Views of Brahmin Theosophists." *Theosophical History* 10, no. 1 (January 2004): 5–34. Discusses their divergent views on the Esoteric Section and on the importance of Hinduism for theosophy.

Gomes, Michael. "The Letters of H.P. Blavatsky to William Q. Judge." *Theosophical History* 6, p.129, Letter dated Nov. 19, 1890. Blavatsky praises Judge's loyalty and warns him about Olcott and the latter's possible resignation as president.

Greenwalt, Emmet A. *The Point Loma Community in California, 1897–1942: A Theosophical Experiment.* Berkeley, Calif., 1955. Discusses the association of Judge and Tingley, and of Tingley's "successorship."

Johnson, K. Paul. *Initiates of the Theosophical Masters.* Albany, N.Y., 1995. A discussion of a number of international figures of varying backgrounds who were "initiated" into theosophy.

Nethercot, Arthur H. *The First Five Lives of Annie Besant.* Kingswood, U. K., 1961. Examines the Judge–Besant association.

Nethercot, Arthur H. *The Last Four Lives of Annie Besant.* Chicago, 1963. Examines the Judge–Besant association.

Ransom, Josephine. *A Short History of the Theosophical Society.* Adyar, India, 1938.

Ryan, Charles J. *H. P. Blavatsky and the Theosophical Movement.* Pasadena, 1975.

United Lodge of Theosophists. *The Theosophical Movement, 1875–1950.* Los Angeles, 1951. Contains thorough discussions of Judge's relationship to Blavatsky and of Besant's allegations against Judge and his replies.

See also *Sunrise* (Vol. 45, April/May 1996); this entire issue of *Sunrise* magazine (published by Theosophical University Press) was devoted to articles about Judge in honor of the centennial of his death. *The Theosophical Forum,* Vols. VI-XXIX (Point Loma and Covina, 1929–1951), a monthly journal started by Gottfried de Purucker, is also of interest.

Websites

The website of the Theosophical Society (http://www.theosociety.org) includes biographies, letters, articles, and other useful information. The Theosophical University Press website (http://www.theosociety.org/pasadena/ts/tup.htm) also provides a plethora of information about Judge and Theosophy. The Theosophy Library Online (http://theosophy.org/JudgeWorks.htm) contains *The Ocean of Theosophy, The Yoga Aphorisms of Patanjali, Occult Tales,* and other books and articles by Judge.

Judy D. Saltzman (2005)

JUDGMENT OF THE DEAD.

JUDGMENT OF THE DEAD. In religions where a differentiation is made between the righteous and sinners in the hereafter, the decision to which category to assign each individual can be thought to take place in different ways. Sometimes it is an automatic process, as in the Indian doctrine of *karman*; each individual's deeds in this life determine his status in his next existence. In other cases, it is believed that the deceased has to pass over a narrow bridge; if he is good there is no difficulty, but if he is evil he is thrown down. This idea is found in ancient Iranian religion, and similar beliefs exist among the Algonquin Indians, the Mari (Cheremis) in Russia, and the Bojnang of the island of Sulawesi. Here no god or personal being seems to be involved in the decision. In other cases, however, a court scene is presupposed, with divine or semidivine judges passing on each individual.

Ancient Near East. The evidence from ancient Mesopotamia is scanty. One Assyrian text tells the story of a crown prince descending into the netherworld and appearing before its king, Nergal, who decides that he is to return to life. It seems likely that this text presents the mythical background of an incantation rite, and thus refers only to a decision in the netherworld whether a sick person should die or recover. It does not refer to a regular judgment of the dead. Texts from the sixth century BCE, found at Susa in southwestern Iran, mention some sort of judgment that gives the good some advantage over the wicked, but they hardly represent genuine Babylonian belief; possibly they were influenced by Iranian ideas.

Ancient Egyptian religion is especially known for its concern about life in the hereafter. However, in the Pyramid Texts, the oldest funerary texts at scholars' disposal, there is no reference to a judgment of the dead. Though there is found the idea that the king still carries out his earthly function as a judge, he is not said to judge the dead in general. Several tomb inscriptions from the Old Kingdom warn that anyone who violates the tomb will be "judged by the Great God at the place of judgment." But that again is no judgment of the dead. On the other hand, autobiographical texts from the same period express the wish that the author's name "may be good before the Great God." This seems to imply some kind of judgment in the hereafter. The same is true of inscriptions in which the dead person promises to defend anyone who respects his tomb "in the judgment hall of the Great God." But in the *Instruction for Merikare* (early Middle Kingdom) there is a clear passage referring to "the judges who judge the sinner" in the hereafter as not being lenient. Therefore individuals should remember that they must die, and that after their deaths their sins will be laid beside them in a heap. Anyone who lives unmindful of the judgment in the hereafter is foolish, but anyone who has not sinned will be like a god in eternal freedom.

A different outlook is reflected in the Coffin Texts. Here magical spells are used to secure various privileges for the deceased in the hereafter. There is also reference to a court of judgment presided over by the earth god Geb, who issues decrees to the benefit of the deceased in the same way as an earthly court might. Gradually it becomes customary to add to the name of the deceased person the epithet *maa kheru*, which denotes him as cleared by the court of an accusation. This title was also given to Osiris, when he had been declared righteous in the court of Geb and had been reinstated in his royal rights (though he was now in the netherworld). As it became customary to identify every dead person with Osiris, he was also certain of being *maa kheru*.

The final result of this development appears in the well-known judgment scene in the *Book of Going Forth by Day*. Chapter 125 describes how the deceased appears before Osiris, the divine judge of the netherworld, who is assisted by forty-two assessors, one for each of the provinces of Egypt. It seems that the reader is here confronted with two different sets of ideas. According to the text, the deceased addresses the assessors, asserting that he has not committed forty-two specific sins; this is often referred to as the "negative confession." The scene depicted, on the other hand, shows the deceased being led before the judges by Horus; in front of Osiris there is a balance, attended by the god Anubis. On one scale is put the heart of the dead man, on the other a feather, the symbol of the goddess Maat ("truth"). The wise god Thoth takes down the result of the weighing on his scribe's palette. The illustrations always present the scales in perfect equilibrium, indicating that the dead man's life has been in accordance with *maat*, the principle of order and truth. If such is the case, the deceased is declared to be *maa kheru*, "true of voice," that is, acquitted in the court of Osiris. If not, he will be eaten by the "devourer of the dead."

All this seems to imply high moral standards. But in fact this chapter of the *Book of Going Forth by Day* is hardly more than another magic spell, intended to protect the deceased from the perils of the other world. The negative confession is rather an expression of acceptance of the validity of certain moral principles (in the last count, of *maat*) than a real declaration that one is not guilty. In addition, there are also spells to prevent the heart from "standing up against" the deceased (*Book of Going Forth by Day*, chap. 30). Thus there is a tension between moral obligations on the one hand and recourse to magical spells on the other.

INDIA AND CHINA. Ancient Indian religion seems to know King Yama as the judge of the other world. A late Vedic text (*Taittirīya Āraṇyaka* 6.5.13) states that before Yama those who have been faithful to truth and those who have spoken lies will part company. There is no explicit reference to a judgment, but it may be implied. The weighing of good and wicked deeds is referred to in the Brahmanic texts.

This same Yama appears again in the pantheon of Mahāyāna Buddhism. In China he is called Yenlo or Yenlo Wang. Together with nine others of Chinese origin ("the Ten Kings") he is believed to be the administrator of the punishments of Hell. It is believed that all individuals are to meet him after death and be judged with the strictest impartiality. It is supposed that he fixes the hour of dissolution, and that once the decision is made, nothing can alter or postpone it. In Japanese Buddhism he is called Enma-ō.

ANCIENT GREECE AND ROME. In ancient Greece, one finds, in Homer and Hesiod, for example, the idea of a shadowy and dreary realm of the dead, called Hades, to which the "souls" of all dead come; but there are also at times the ideas of a miry place where the wicked are punished and of the Elysian Fields, where a few righteous are allowed to enter. But there is no information on how it is decided who is going where. Homer says that Minos gives laws to the dead but does not act as judge (*Odyssey* 11.567ff.).

Gradually, however, under the influence of the mystery cults and of the Orphic and Pythagorean movements, the ideas of judgment and retribution were developed. Pythagoras taught a judgment of souls (according to the biography of Iamblichus), and the Orphic judgment is depicted on a vase that shows Aiakos, Triptolemos, and Rhadamanthos as judges.

The ideas of the Orphics and Pythagoreans are reproduced by Pindar and by Plato in some of his dialogues (*Gorgias*, *Apology*, the *Republic*). Usually, the judges are three, Minos, Rhadamanthos, and Aiakos; in the *Apology* Plato adds Triptolemos. They give judgment in a meadow, at the parting of the ways, one of which leads to the Abode of the Blessed, the other to Tartaros.

In *Gorgias* Plato says that in the beginning the dead were sent to the Island of the Blessed or to the punishment in Tartaros; the judgment was pronounced on the day of death, but apparently it was sometimes influenced by the outer appearance of the person in question. Therefore Zeus decreed that souls should be judged naked, without their earthly frame. Punishment could serve for purification and improvement; but there are some evildoers who cannot be saved. Here, in part, Plato is using traditional ideas, possibly Orphic and other; but he may have created the eschatological myth he presents here to illustrate his philosophical ideas.

Such beliefs were probably widespread among the Greeks, as is shown by numerous references to judgment and the fate of souls in Lucian's satires, and by the caricatures of Aristophanes. The classical dramatists rarely mention a judgment of the dead, but there are a few references in Aeschylus, and it figures sporadically in other authors and in grave inscriptions. In Vergil's picture of the underworld, Minos judges certain crimes, and Rhadamanthos is judge in Tartaros (*Aeneid* 6.426ff., 540ff.).

JUDAISM. The writings of intertestamental Judaism contain occasional references to a judgment of the dead. The scene in the seventh chapter of the *Book of Daniel*, where the Ancient of Days opens the books and passes judgment, is not concerned with individuals, but with the kingdoms of the earth, and it is Israel that stands acquitted. But in chapter 50 of the Ethiopic *Apocalypse of Enoch* there is an explicit mention of judgment, in which the Lord of the Spirits will show himself righteous, sinners will be punished, and the righteous will be saved. Chapter 51 then speaks of the resurrection of the dead, and says that the Chosen One will sit on God's throne, probably as judge. The same idea is found in *2 Esdras* (chapter 7): The earth will give up those who are asleep in it, and the Most High will appear on the seat of judgment. The emphasis here, however, is not on the scene of judgment but on the resurrection, and on the destiny of the righteous and the wicked.

There are occasional references in these scriptures to books in which the deeds of indiviudals are recorded, and according to which they will be judged (Ethiopic *Apocalypse of Enoch* 47:3, 90:20), but the context does not mention a final judgment in connection with the resurrection. Thus, the weighing of people's works on a balance is referred to (ibid. 41:1, 61:8) without mentioning the judgment.

CHRISTIANITY. Jesus tells the parable of the last judgment in chapter 25 of the *Gospel of Matthew*. The Son of Man is to come and sit on his glorious throne, and all nations will gather before him; he will "separate them as a shepherd separates the sheep from the goats." Those who have acted in love for their neighbors will receive eternal life; those who have not will be sent away into eternal punishment.

Though this description of a final judgment is found only in the *Gospel of Matthew*, it is obvious from other occasional references in the New Testament that the idea was essential in early Christian preaching. Thus, in *Acts* 17:31, "God has fixed a day on which he will judge the world in righteousness by a man whom he has appointed [i. e., Jesus Christ]." In *Acts* 10:42, Christ "is the one ordained by God to be judge of the living and the dead"; in *2 Corinthians* 5:10, "we must all appear before the judgment seat of Christ [or, in *Romans* 14:10, of God], so that each one may receive good or evil, according to what he has done in the body." The last judgment is thus connected with the Parousia, or second coming of Christ.

In the *Gospel of John*, the idea of the judgment has been transformed in a peculiar way. Though it is stated that God the Father "has given all judgment to the Son" (5:22), the reader learns that one who believes "has eternal life" (here and now) "and does not come into judgment, but has passed from death to life" (5:24). In other words, the outcome of Christ's judgment is decided here and now, according to the belief or unbelief of each one; this should leave no room for a final judgment at the end of time.

The Christian church has placed considerable emphasis on the idea of the final judgment (that is, rather than on the judgment here and now). Both the Apostles' Creed and the Nicene Creed state that Christ "will come again (in glory) to judge the living and the dead."

ISLAM. In the preaching of Muḥammad the imminent day of judgment (*yawm al-dīn*) has a prominent place. Because many of the accompanying motifs correspond to Jewish and Christian ideas (not the least to the preaching of the Syriac church), it seems obvious that he has taken over the idea of judgment from these sources. The day is also referred to as the day of resurrection, the day of decision (Qurʾān, *sūrah* 77:13), the day of gathering (64:9), the day of eternity (50:34), and so forth. It is a day of great catastrophes that cause fear and terror on the earth. The judgment is individual. On that day "no soul will be able to help another, for the decision belongs to God" (82:19). Each soul must defend itself (16:112) and cannot bear the load of another (17:15, cf. 16:25); no soul will be able to give satisfaction or to make intercession for another (2:48); no ransom will be accepted (5:36). The works of each person will be documented in an irrefutable way. Books will be produced, in which "everything that they have done, great and small, is recorded" (54:52ff.). "The book will be put (before them), and you will see the sinners fearful at what is in it. . . . It leaves nothing behind, small or great, but it has numbered it. And they shall find all they did present, and your Lord shall not wrong anyone" (18:49). Every individual shall find a book wide open: "Read your book! Today you are yourself a reckoner against yourself" (17:13ff.). The idea of books that are opened is found in the Hebrew Bible (*Dn.* 7:10) and in other Jewish literature in connection with a judgment scene. In addition, it may be that Muḥammad, as a merchant, was familiar with the keeping of accounts.

There is also in the Qurʾān the idea of weighing human deeds. "We shall set up the just balances . . . so that not one soul shall be wronged anything; even if it be the weight of one grain of mustard-seed we shall produce it; and we know how to reckon" (21:49). "The weighing that day is true; he whose scales are heavy—they are the prosperous, and he whose scales are light—they have lost their souls" (7:8ff.; cf. 23:102 and 101:5ff.). There is here hardly any connection with the Egyptian ideas discussed above; the ideas of Muḥammad seem rather closer to those of the Jewish texts.

In the case of Islam, those who stand the trial will enter Paradise, and those who fail will be thrown into Hell. However, no one belief concerning the fate following judgment of the dead is common to all religious traditions. That fate is determined according to each tradition's conception of what happens after death. Just as the judgment of the dead is conceived in different ways within the different traditions, so too is the ultimate fate of the person who is judged.

See Also Afterlife.

Bibliography

A cross-cultural collection of sources on this topic is *Le jugement des morts: Égypte ancienne, Assour, Babylone, Israël, Iran, Islam, Inde, Chine, Japon,* "Sources orientales," no. 4 (Paris, 1961). For a treatment of the beliefs about the judgment of the dead in Egyptian religion, see *Die Idee vom Totengericht in der ägyptischen Religion* (Hamburg, 1935) by Joachim Spiegel. See also *The Dawn of Conscience* (New York, 1933), pp. 250ff., by James Henry Breasted. See my *Religions of the Ancient Near East,* translated by John Sturdy (Philadelphia, 1973), pp. 122ff., for a brief treatment of Mesopotamian ideas on the judgment of the dead. Volume 1 of H. C. C. Cavallin's *Life after Death: Paul's Argument for the Resurrection of the Dead* (Lund, 1974) treats the topic as it relates to Judaism. Two discussions of Christian beliefs about the judgment of the dead are John A. T. Robinson's *Jesus and His Coming* (New York, 1957) and his article "The Parable of the Sheep and Goats," *New Testament Studies* 2 (May 1956): 225–237. The only monograph on Greek ideas about judgment is in Latin: *De mortuorum iudicio* (Giessen, 1903) by Ludwig Ruhl. See also Fritz Graf's *Eleusis und die orphische Dichtung Athens in vorhellenistischer Zeit* (Berlin, 1974), pp. 79–150, and Franz Cumont's *After Life in Roman Paganism* (1922; reprint, New York, 1959). On Plato's treatment of the topic, see *Les mythes de Platon* (Paris, 1930) by Perceval Frutiger. Two studies of the Iranian view are *The Zoroastrian Doctrine of a Future Life* (New York, 1926) by J. D. C. Pavry, and R. C. Zaehner's *The Teachings of the Magi* (New York, 1956), pp. 131ff. Arthur Berriedale Keith's *Indian Mythology* (Boston, 1917), pp. 159ff., and Bimala Churn Law's *Heaven and Hell in Buddhist Perspective* (1925; reprint, Varanasi, 1973), pp. 96ff., present Indian and Buddhist ideas of judgment.

New Sources

Griffiths, John Gwyn. *The Divine Verdict. A Study of Divine Judgement in the Ancient Religions.* Leiden, 1991. The definitive cross-cultural survey by a scholar who is both a philologist expert in various domains and an insightful historian of religions. It includes a thorough well-organized bibliography.

Marguerat, Daniel. *Le jugement dans l'évangile selon saint Matthieu.* Geneva, 1995. A theological and historical study by a prominent New Testament scholar.

Helmer Ringgren (1987)
Revised Bibliography

JULIAN OF HALICARNASSUS

JULIAN OF HALICARNASSUS (d. after 518), Christian bishop and theologian. The place and date of birth of this prominent fifth- and early sixth-century churchman are unknown. Of his early life we know that as bishop of Halicarnassus in Asia Minor he had sojourned in Constantinople around 510, perhaps between 508 and 511. There he participated in the discussions as to whether the decisions of the Council of Chalcedon (451) ought to be abrogated in order to achieve church unity.

As bishop of Halicarnassus, Julian had been a protagonist of the monophysites, who maintained that Christ had only a divine nature, denying the reality of his humanity. At first Julian followed the moderate views of his friend Severus of Antioch, one of the leading critics of the Chalcedonian formula, according to which Christ is "one hypostasis [essence, entity] in two natures."

Julian's significance lies in the fact that he parted with the moderate monophysites. Deposed from his see in 518, he fled to Egypt, where he promulgated his theory known as aphthartodocetism (incorruptibility). Julian taught that, from the moment of its conception, the human nature of Christ was incorruptible, impassible, immortal, and free from all physical burdens such as hunger, thirst, and pain. Thus Christ's human sufferings were apparent rather than real, a theory similar to docetism. His followers in Alexandria established their own community and became known as Aphthartodocitae and Phantasiastai.

Not only the Orthodox Chalcedonians but also Julian's former friend Severus of Antioch attacked his teachings. Julian wrote a treatise entitled *Peri aphtharsias* (About incorruptibility), directed against Severus, and an *Apologia* defending his own teachings. Of his writings only two letters and fragments of his theological works, in the original Greek and in Syriac translation, have survived.

Bibliography

The sources for Julian's writings are *Spicilegium Romanum,* vol. 10, *Synodus cpolitana,* edited by Angelo Mai (Rome, 1844), pp. 206–211, and *Anecdota Syriaca,* vol. 3, edited by J. P. N. Land (Leiden, 1870), pp. 263–271. Studies of Julian include René Draguet's *Julien d'Halicarnasse et sa controverse avec Sévère d'Antioche sur l'incorruptibilité du corps du Christ* (Louvain, 1924) and "Pièces de polémique antijulianiste," *Le Muséon* 44 (1931): 255–317; Martin Jugie's "Julien d'Halicarnasse et Sévère d'Antioche," *Échos d'Orient* 24 (1925): 129–162, 257–285; and Robert P. Casey's "Julian of Alicarnassus," *Harvard Theological Review* 19 (1926): 206–213.

Demetrios J. Constantelos (1987)

JULIAN OF NORWICH

JULIAN OF NORWICH (1342–1416?), known as Lady Julian, Dame Julian, and Mother Julian, was an English mystic and Christian theologian. Julian lived in the century in which Europe was ravaged by the Black Death, and England and France were torn by the Hundred Years War. Against a background of war, plague, social turmoil, and religious unrest she shared in a flowering of English mysticism along with Walter Hilton, Richard Rolle, Margery Kempe, and the anonymous author of *The Cloud of Unknowing.*

Highly literate—despite a polite disclaimer in her book *Revelations* [or *Showings*] *of Divine Love*—and demonstrating a knowledge of the Vulgate rare for a layperson of her day, she was the first woman to compose a literary work in English. Although scholars have traced many general theological influences in Julian's book, specific influences are hard to identify, so thoroughly assimilated are they into a theology that is at once deeply traditional and highly original. She was probably familiar with the writings of William of Saint-Thierry (d. 1148) and Meister Eckhart (d. around 1327), but the only two writers whom she mentions by name are Dionysius the Areopagite (c. 500) and Gregory I (d. 604), from whose *Life of Saint Benedict* she quotes.

Little is known about Julian's life. In May 1373, when Julian was thirty years old, she became severely ill. At what seemed the point of death, she revived and received what she described as fifteen "showings of God's love"; on the following day she had a sixteenth such experience. Her mother, her parish priest, and possibly others were with her at these times. Some time later Julian wrote a description of these showings that is now referred to as the "short text" or "short version." Twenty years later, after profound meditation, she felt she had come to a fuller understanding of the showings, and she wrote a much longer version, concluding: "So I was taught that love is our Lord's meaning. And I saw very certainly in this and in everything that before God made us he loved us, which love was never abated and never will be" (Colledge and Walsh, *Showings,* p. 342).

At some time in her life Julian became an anchoress, living in a cell attached to the church of Saint Julian in King Street. It was probably from this saint that she took the name by which she is known.

The all-encompassing theme of Julian's *Revelations* is the compassionate love of God as universally manifested throughout the process of creation and as focused in the passion of Jesus, whose delight was to suffer for his beloved humankind. One aspect of Christ stressed by Julian is his "motherhood." Many earlier writers, including Anselm, had written of Christ's motherhood, but Julian wrote more extensively on this theme.

Julian's theology is eschatologically orientated. The resolution of the problem of evil (a problem over which she agonizes at length) will come through a "great deed ordained by our Lord God from without beginning, treasured and hidden in his blessed breast, known only to himself, through which deed he will make all things well" (Colledge and Walsh, *Showings,* pp. 232–233). This aspect of Julian's theology proved particularly interesting to T. S. Eliot, who quotes from her book and alludes to her thought in his mystical poem *Four Quartets.*

The enduring contemporary interest in Julian was expressed in an ecumenical celebration in Norwich in May 1973, the six-hundredth anniversary of her *Revelations.* Her influence continues at the Julian shrine in Norwich, where prayer and spiritual counsel continue in a chapel built where her cell once stood.

Bibliography

Basic information on Julian herself and on the six-hundredth-anniversary ecumenical celebration of *Revelations* is conveniently given in *Julian and Her Norwich: Commemorative Essays and Handbook to the Exhibition "Revelations of Divine Love,"* edited by Frank D. Sayer (Norwich, U.K., 1973). This book includes a useful bibliography of Julian publications prior to 1973: five manuscripts, twenty-six printed editions (in German, French, and Italian as well as English), and fifty-six books and articles about Julian and her thought. For works published since 1973, the *Fourteenth-Century English Mystics Newsletter* (Iowa City), published quarterly since 1974, is indispensable. Renamed *Mystics Quarterly* in 1984, this journal contains articles, book reviews, descriptions of scholarly studies in progress, and bibliographies of the many books and articles on Julian, including a Swedish translation and two French translations of *Revelations.* Among the post-1973 works, one of the most significant is the definitive edition of the original text prepared by Edmund Colledge and James Walsh, *Juliana, anchoret, 1343–1443: A Book of Showings to the Anchoress Julian of Norwich,* 2 vols. (Toronto, 1978). From this critical text Colledge and Walsh have made a modern translation, *Julian of Norwich: Showings,* "The Classics of Western Spirituality," vol. 1 (New York, 1978). Another significant English translation published since 1973 is *Revelations of Divine Love by Juliana of Norwich,* translated with a particularly good introduction by M. L. Del Mastro (Garden City, N.Y., 1977). The chaplain of the Julian shrine in Norwich, England, Robert Llewelyn, has written *With Pity, Not with Blame: Reflections on the Writings of Julian of Norwich and on The Cloud of Unknowing* (London, 1982). Many Julian publications are available at the shrine. In addition, the Norwich Public Library has a sizable collection of printed material on Julian.

BARBARA BISHOP (1987)

JUNAYD, AL- (d. AH 298/910 CE), whose full name is Abūʾl-Qāsim ibn Muḥammad al-Junayd, was a major representative of the Baghdad school of Sufism who is associated with its "sober" and socially responsible trend. He came from a family of Iranian merchants. Al-Junayd's father traded in glassware, and he himself earned his livelihood as a dealer in silk. Under the influence of his paternal uncle Sarī al-Saqaṭī, who is often viewed as one of the doyens of Baghdad Sufism, al-Junayd embraced its mystical ideals and ascetic ethos and eventually succeeded him as leader of the Baghdad school of mysticism. He received a solid juridical and theological training under the guidance of such famous Shāfiʿī scholars as Abū Thawr (d. 855 CE) and Ibn Kullāb (d. c. 855) and was qualified to issue legal opinions on various juridical issues. However, most of his teachers were associated with Ṣūfī circles. He cultivated the friendship of a famous Baghdad scholar and ascetic al-Ḥārith al-Muḥāsibī (d. 857) with whom he had long discussions of questions related to mystical experience and pious life. The influence of al-Muḥāsibī's mystical psychology and introspection on his young associate is abundantly attested in al-Junayd's epistles and logia.

The later Ṣūfī tradition portrays al-Junayd as the principal exponent of the "sober" type of mysticism, which was routinely juxtaposed with the "excesses" of its "intoxicated" counterpart represented by Abū Yazīd al-Bisṭāmī (d. 848 or

875), al-Shiblī (d. 945), al-Nūrī (d. 907), and al-Ḥallāj (d. 922). Al-Junayd's public sermons were not confined to his fellow mystics; they attracted many high-ranking state officials and respectable theologians as well, who showed a great respect for the Sūfī master. Modern western scholars share in this esteem. Thus, Arthur Arberry in *Sufism* (1969) described al-Junayd as "the most original and penetrating intellect among the Sufis of his time," who "took within his ranging vision the whole landscape of mystical speculation stretching below him, and with an artist's eye brought it to comprehension and unity upon a single canvas."

The Ṣūfī tradition also depicts al-Junayd as an eloquent exponent of "the science of God's uniqueness" *(ʿilm al-tawḥīd),* who was also proficient in the knowledge of the mystical states *(aḥwāl)* experienced by the mystical seeker. This statement is not entirely accurate: similar classifications of the *aḥwāl* were developed by some of his younger and older contemporaries. Al-Junayd's written legacy includes a number of "epistles" *(rasāʾil)* to his contemporaries and short treatises on mystical themes. The latter are simply commentaries on select Qurʾanic passages. The profoundly subtle and abstruse language of al-Junayd's mystical discourses may have been a deliberate strategy aimed at rendering his ideas impenetrable to exoterically minded scholars and thus eluding their criticisms. Al-Junayd's deliberately obscure style was imitated and elaborated by al-Ḥallāj, who, however, was much more outspoken in describing his mystical experiences than his older, and more cautious, contemporary.

Al-Junayd's discourses reiterate the theme, first clearly reasoned by him, that because all things have their origin in God, they must finally return, after their dispersion (*tafriqa*), to reside in him again (*jamʿ*). This dynamic of ecstatic rapture and subsequent return is captured in the mystical experience of passing away (*fanāʾ*) followed by the state of subsistence in God (*baqāʾ*). In the process of *fanāʾ* the human self is completely shattered by an encounter with the Divine Reality, which leads it to a mystic union with the divine. In describing this experience, al-Junayd writes:

> For at that time thou wilt be addressed, thyself addressing; questioned concerning thy tidings, thyself questioning; with abundant flow of precious wisdom, and interchange of visions; with constant increase of faith, and uninterrupted favors.

In accounting for his mystical experience he says:

> This that I say comes from the continuance of calamity and the consequence of misery, from a heart that is stirred from its foundations, and is tormented with its ceaseless conflagrations, by itself within itself: admitting no perception, no speech, no sense, no feeling, no repose, no effort, no familiar image; but constant in the calamity of its ceaseless torment, unimaginable, indescribable, unlimited, unbearable in its fierce onslaughts. (Translated by Arberry, 1969)

In meditating on the Qurʾanic image of the preeternal covenant between God and disembodied humanity (Qurʾān 7: 172), al-Junayd describes the entire course of history as people's quest to realize that covenant and return to the primeval state in which they were before they were. By endowing people with a separate, individual existence, God deliberately plunged them into the corporeal world of trial and affliction, where their bodily passions and appetites cause them to forget about their preeternal acknowledgment of God's absolute sovereignty. Through arduous, ascetic self-discipline and intense meditation, mystics strive to obliterate the last trace of the selfish impulses emanating from their imperfect bodies. If successful, they are reintegrated into the realm of the Divine Presence. They then return to this world by experiencing "survival" or "subsistence" in God (*baqāʾ*), which gives them a new, pure life in, and through, God. Yet, even in the blissful state of *baqāʾ*, the mystic remains separated and veiled from God. To accentuate the painful nature of this separation, al-Junayd employed the imagery of the lover yearning for the Divine Beloved and taking an intense joy in observing his reflections in the beauty in his handiwork. This agonizing vacillation between union and separation became the keynote of al-Junayd's entire legacy. Eschewing the extravagances of language that on the lips of the "intoxicated" mystics Abū Yazīd al-Bisṭāmī and al-Ḥallāj alarmed and alienated the orthodox, al-Junayd by his clear perception and absolute self-control laid the foundations on which most of the later Ṣūfī systems were built.

On the political and social plane, al-Junayd demonstrated a political conformism and docility that saved him from the persecutions against "heretics" that were common in this tumultuous age. Time and again, al-Junayd explicitly advised his disciples against challenging the temporary and religious authorities of the age. He viewed political and social activism as a sign of spiritual and intellectual immaturity and an attempt to rebel against the divine will. His cautious attitude came to the fore in his disavowal of the overpowering drunkenness of ecstasy that permeated the sayings of his contemporary Abū Yazīd al-Bisṭāmī. Al-Junayd's glosses on Abū Yazīd's ecstatic utterances (*shaṭaḥāt*) clearly show his preference for the state of sobriety over mystical intoxication. His discourses were firmly rooted in the Qurʾanic notions of God's uniqueness and absolute transcendence, and he was careful not to present the relationships between man and God as a union of two essences *(ittiḥād).* Rather, he never tired of stressing the purely experiential nature of this phenomenon.

Al-Junayd's age was rich in charismatic and mystical talent. Among his associates and disciples we find such consequential figures in Ṣūfī tradition as Abū Saʿīd al-Kharrāz (d. 899), Abū Ḥamza al-Khurāsānī (d. between 903 and 911), ʿAmr bin ʿUthmān al-Makkī (d. 903 or 909), Abūʾl-Ḥusayn al-Nūrī (d. 295/907), Ruwaym bin Aḥmad (d. 915) Abū Bakr al-Shiblī (d. 334/946), Abū Muḥammad al-Jurayri (d. 924), Abū ʿAlī al-Rudhbārī (d. 322/934), and Jaʿfar al-Khuldī (d. 348/959), to name but a few. Upon al-Junayd's death his disciple al-Jurayri replaced him as head of the Baghdad Ṣūfī school. Al-Junayd's life and work exemplify what Western scholars often call "the golden (or classical) age of Sufism."

BIBLIOGRAPHY

Ansari, Muhammad. "The Doctrine of One Actor: Junayd's View of Tawhid." *Islamic Quarterly* 27, no. 2 (1983): 83–102.

Arberry, Arthur. *Sufism: An Account of the Mystics of Islam.* London, 1968.

Ess, Josef van. *Theologie und Gesellschaft im 2. und 3. Jahrhundert Hidschra.* Berlin and New York, 1997, vol. 4, pp. 278–288 and index under "Ǧunaid."

el-Kader, Ali Abdel. *The Life Personality and Writings of al-Junaid.* London, 1962.

Knysh, Alexander. *Islamic Mysticism: A Short History.* Leiden, 2000. See pp. 52–56.

Singh, Darshan. "Attitudes of al-Junayd and al-Hallaj Towards the Sunna and *Ahwal* and *Maqamat.*" *Islamic Culture* 58, no. 3 (1984): 217–226.

Ẓāẓā, Zuhayr. *Al-Imām al-Junayd,* Damascus, 1994.

ALEXANDER KNYSH (2005)

JUNG, C. G. (1875–1961), was the originator of a distinctive variety of depth psychology. Until recently, accounts of the life and work of Carl Gustav Jung had emphasized the strong influence of Sigmund Freud (1856–1939) and had portrayed Jung as first an obedient follower of Freud and then a rebellious dissident. Although Jung's ideas were to a great extent influenced by his contact with Freud, Jung's originality preceded as well as followed his contact with Freud (see Bair, 2004, and Shamdasani, 2004). Jung's independence stems partly from his Christian background and is expressed in his mature conviction that depth psychology, his form of which he named analytical psychology, is inseparable from a religious appreciation of the world. Jung has had a greater influence on humanistic religious scholarship than has Freud, whose psychology has been more influential in the social sciences.

LIFE. Jung was born in the village of Kesswil, Switzerland, the son of a Lutheran minister. When he was four years old the family moved to Basel on Lake Constance, where Jung spent his childhood and youth. He took a medical degree from the University of Basel in 1902. Believing that psychiatry would allow him to combine his scientific with his humanistic interests, Jung joined the staff of the Burghölzli, the psychiatric clinic of the University of Zurich. There he worked under Eugen Bleuler, its highly regarded director. In 1903 he married Emma Rauschenbach and moved to Küsnacht, a small village near Zurich, on the shore of Lake Zurich, where he spent the rest of his life.

In 1900 Freud published what came to be his most famous book, *The Interpretation of Dreams,* and began to attract a talented following. Among the most gifted was Jung. The two corresponded and, in 1906, met. For the next seven years Jung's life was shaped almost entirely by his relationship with Freud. The two became intimate friends and corresponded extensively. Jung initially concluded that Freud's theories of the unconscious, dreams, childhood conflicts, and psychological illnesses (neuroses) were essentially correct, and he adopted them in his own psychiatric work. Freud considered Jung his most promising colleague.

The close collaboration did not last. Each man began to misunderstand the other, and heated resentments developed. Freud insisted on the sexual roots of neurosis, whereas Jung advanced a nonsexual approach. Jung maintained that he could discern a religious dimension in psychoanalysis, whereas Freud insisted that the basis of psychoanalysis was entirely scientific. The two broke off their correspondence and in 1913 abandoned all professional collaboration. From that time forward their personal lives, careers, psychological theories, and theories of religion diverged, and their bitterness toward each other never abated.

Freud survived his disappointment with Jung by turning his energies to his other followers and to the worldwide recognition that his ideas were receiving, but Jung had far less on which to fall back. Shaken by the break, he found it necessary to isolate himself. In 1913 he resigned from his teaching post at the University of Zurich and withdrew from the International Psychoanalytic Association. He had left the Burghölzli in 1909. Having made these breaks, Jung entered a period of intense inner stress during which he was beset by disturbing fantasies, visions, and dreams. For the next several years he occupied himself with analyzing the products of his own mind. Later he would look back on that turbulent time as the most creative period in his life. At its close he wrote what have become his two most important works, *Two Essays on Analytical Psychology* (1943 and 1928/1935 in German, 1953 in English) and *Psychological Types* (1921 in German, 1923 in English). These books established Jung's reputation as the founder of his own school of depth psychology.

For the remainder of his life, Jung practiced his approach to psychotherapy, wrote prolifically, and lectured and traveled widely. In addition to psychotherapy, two subjects of special interest to him were Western religion and the moral failures of modern society. His best-known books on these subjects are *Answer to Job* (1952 in German, 1954 in English) and *The Undiscovered Self* (1957 in German, 1958 in English). Near the end of his life Jung dictated an autobiographical memoir, *Memories, Dreams, Reflections* (1962 in German, 1963 in English).

ANALYTICAL PSYCHOLOGY AND RELIGION. The relationship between analytical psychology and religion is part of a broader topic: the relationship between modernity and religion. There are at least four views on this issue. The fundamentalist view pits religion against modernity and opts for religion. It denies modernity, or at least its inescapability. For fundamentalists, religion can continue to exist as it purportedly has done since the days of the apostles. Because fundamentalism ignores rather than confronts modernity, it cannot be taken seriously as a response to modernity.

The rationalist view is similar to the fundamentalist one in that it pits religion against modernity. For both fundamentalists and rationalists, there can be no modern religion, and the term *modern religion* is self-contradictory. However, rationalism, antithetically to fundamentalism, opts for modernity over religion. To rationalists, modernity itself is inescapable. One is born into the modern world. The question, then, is not, as for fundamentalists, whether modernity is acceptable to religion but whether religion is acceptable to modernity. The rationalist answer is no.

For rationalists, modernity is coextensive with science, and science, both natural and social, dooms religion. The scientific attribution of events in the physical world to impersonal processes is incompatible with the religious attribution of those events to the decisions of gods. Similarly, the social scientific attribution of human behavior to processes such as socialization and internalization is incompatible with the religious attribution of that behavior to phenomena such as sin and possession. Because rationalists are by definition scientific and cannot have both religion and science, they must reject religion for science.

Rationalists do not limit the function of religion to explanation. They recognize that religion serves many other functions as well, such as prescribing values. However, they insist that the nonexplanatory functions rest on the explanatory one. For example, acceptance of Jesus as a preacher of ethics depends on acceptance of Jesus as a resurrected being—a scientific impossibility. Religion can work only when its explanation is accepted, and science precludes the acceptance of that explanation.

For rationalists, the impact of science on religion is even more insidious. Science not only competes with religion but also accounts for it. Science explains not only the world but, through social science, religion itself. Religion does not merely cease to explain but becomes the explained. The explanation of religion typically provided transforms the chief function of religion from explanation into something sociological, economic, or psychological. To science is thus ceded not only the explanation provided by religion but also religion as an explanation. Religion remains irreconcilable with modernity because the nonexplanatory functions still depend on the explanatory one: if religion can no longer serve to explain the world to its adherents, it cannot exist, in which case it can scarcely serve to do anything else.

The romantic view breaks with both fundamentalism and rationalism in its refusal to oppose religion to modernity. Rather than forcing a choice between the two, it strives to reconcile them. Like fundamentalists, romantics prize religion as an eternal and invaluable possession. Nothing can supersede it. But unlike fundamentalists, romantics do not prize religion as an explanation. Religion for them serves to do almost anything but explain. It serves to express, to advocate, to comfort, to harmonize, or to give meaning. For rationalists, religion may serve a host of nonexplanatory functions alongside its explanatory one; those functions may be more important than the explanatory one; and those functions may overlap with the ones touted by romantics. But religion cannot exist once it stops being an explanation. By contrast, for romantics, religion can still exist and even thrive. In fact, the conflict with science gives religion the opportunity to rid itself of its explanatory baggage and to make explicit for the first time its nonexplanatory core. Far from undermining religion, science abets religion by compelling it to show that it has always been something other than an explanation. Romantics turn a necessity into a virtue.

The fourth view of the relationship between religion and modernity is the postmodern one. Like fundamentalists, postmodernists refuse to defer to modernity, but not in the name of religion, which they spurn as fully as rationalists do. In opposing modernity, they appeal not to prescientific religion but to postscientific culture. They reject science as the epitome of modernity, by which they mean above all the belief in objectivity, neutrality, and universal truth. They espouse subjectivity over objectivity, commitment over neutrality, and local truth over universal truth. Like fundamentalists and unlike both rationalists and romantics, postmodernists deny the inescapability of modernity. Indeed, for them the heretofore moderns have already escaped it, for they are now living in postmodern times.

CATEGORIZING JUNG. Jung was not a fundamentalist. He deferred to science and interpreted all aspects of religion nonliterally. He was not a budding postmodernist either. He proudly considered his discoveries, beginning with his association tests, scrupulously scientific. If nothing else, he antedated postmodernism. (For an attempt to see Jung as precociously postmodern, see Hauke, 2000.)

Jung was a grand rationalist insofar as he explained religion scientifically, that is, psychologically. No one psychologized religion more relentlessly than he. Certainly Freud lacked both the patience and the erudition to do so. In such essays as "A Psychological Approach to the Dogma of the Trinity" (Jung, 1953–1966, vol. 11, paragraphs 169–295) and "Transformation Symbolism in the Mass" (Jung, 1953–1966, vol. 11, paragraphs 296–448) Jung translated every aspect of the religious phenomenon into psychological terms. He psychologized not only the content but also the origin and function of religious belief and practice.

Yet Jung was a grand romantic insofar as he was indifferent to the explanatory function of religion. For him, religion was a psychological activity clothed in an explanatory or a metaphysical guise. Hence he continually characterized himself as a psychologist rather than a metaphysician and regularly distinguished his psychological use of the term *God* from any metaphysical one: "When I say 'God' this is a psychic thing. . . . This has nothing whatever to do with God *per se*" (Jung, 1973–1974, vol. I, p. 487). Jung bristled at his characterization, especially by theologians, as a metaphysician.

Conversely, Jung's rigid, Kantian-based distinction between the metaphysical and the nonmetaphysical realms allowed him to psychologize metaphysics without becoming metaphysical. Thus he objected as vigorously to theologians who denied him his psychological due as to those who mistook his psychology for metaphysics: "Psychology has no room for judgments like 'only religious' or 'only philosophical' despite the fact that we too often hear the charge of something's being 'only psychological'—especially from theologians" (Jung, 1963, p. 350). Even when Jung waxed metaphysical, as in *Memories, Dreams, Reflections,* he did so as a metaphysician, not as a psychologist, thereby preserving the distinction between the domains.

Jung found most theologians exasperating not only because they confused psychology with metaphysics but also because, as theologians, they focused on religious belief. For Jung, the heart of religion is experience, not belief. Experience shapes belief or creed rather than vice versa: "I want to make clear that by the term 'religion' I do not mean a creed. . . . Creeds are codified and dogmatized forms of original religious experience" ("Psychology and Religion," Jung, 1953–1966, vol. XI, paragraphs 9–10).

Jung's disdain for the creedal, explanatory, metaphysical side of religion does not by itself make him a romantic. Even a rationalist such as Freud would deem the main function of religion psychological rather than explanatory. The question is whether for Jung religion can exist after the rise of science. The question is whether for him religion can exclude belief yet remain religion. Where belief, like the rest of religion, can be psychologized, the acceptance of religious belief requires the acceptance of it as true about the external world, not merely as true about oneself. Therefore to say that for Jung belief was expendable because he psychologized belief is to miss the point.

JUNG'S STAGES OF PSYCHOLOGICAL DEVELOPMENT. To see the place of religious belief for Jung, it is helpful to plot the various stages of psychological growth into which he divides humanity (see Segal, 1992). The terms used here for some of the stages are this author's, not Jung's. The key divide for Jung is between primitives and ancients on the one hand and rationalists and romantics on the other. Both primitives and ancients are religious, and overtly so. By *ancients*—an admittedly imprecise term of this author's—is meant religious people up through the present, including not only ancient Sumerian, Egyptian, and Greek religions but also Judaism, Christianity, Islam, and Hinduism.

Primitives project themselves onto the physical world in the form of gods and, furthermore, identify themselves with those gods. Ancients also project themselves onto the physical world in the form of gods but do not identify themselves with their gods, who are taken as entities distinct from their worshippers. Today's fundamentalists are the heirs of the ancients. Primitives and ancients alike use religion to explain the world, but religion functions simultaneously and unconsciously to connect both groups to their unconscious. Religion operates circuitously by means of projection onto the physical world, so that one encounters oneself through encountering god. Still, religion consciously serves as an explanation, and the psychological function depends on the projection involved in the explanation.

By contrast, neither rationalists nor romantics are religious. Both groups have substantially withdrawn their projections from the physical world. For them, the world is natural rather than supernatural, impersonal rather than personified. It is explained by science, not religion: "Only in the following centuries, with the growth of natural science, was the projection withdrawn from matter and entirely abolished together with the psyche. . . . Nobody, it is true, any longer endows matter with mythological properties" ("The Philosophical Tree," Jung, 1953–1966, vol. 13, paragraph 395). Although some projections onto the external world remain, such as the anthropomorphizing of animals, most projections are now onto fellow human beings: "Projection is now confined to personal and social relationships. . . ." ("The Philosophical Tree," Jung, 1953–1966, vol. 13, paragraph 395).

Rationalists pride themselves on their rejection of religion, which they set against not only science but also their image of themselves as progressive, omniscient, and omnipotent—in short, modern. They, not any divine puppeteers, are the masters of their destiny. They reject not only religion as explanation but also the explanation religion offers, for that explanation subjugates humans to gods. In rejecting religion, rationalists unwittingly reject one of the best vehicles for encountering the unconscious. Of course, some rationalists reject the idea of an unconscious as contrary to their self-image. Others, notably, Freud, stress the hold of the unconscious on humans and consequently harbor a far more deterministic view of human nature. Still, for Freud, the unconscious lies within humans rather than outside them. It replaces god as the determinant of human destiny. For some rationalists, religion is nothing but an explanation, and for them science does all that religion has done. For other rationalists, including Freud, religion is much more than an explanation, but it is still partly an explanation, and the triumph of science over religion as explanation undoes religion altogether.

Although romantics no less than rationalists reject religion as an explanation, they do not applaud the demise of religion. On the contrary, they bemoan the loss of religion for its nonexplanatory functions, especially that of giving meaning. Romantics seek to preserve or revive religion by reconceiving it as other than explanatory and therefore as compatible with science.

JUNG'S RECONCILIATION OF RELIGION WITH SCIENCE. Jung did not fault religion for losing rationalists or even romantics to science. As an explanation of the world, religion must yield to science. Jung spurned sophisticated attempts to reconcile religious explanation with scientific explanation, for example, by placing God behind the scenes.

Similarly, Jung did not fault science for making atheists of rationalists and romantics. He celebrated, not condemned, science for its advances, and saw the development of psychology as part of the scientific enterprise, which for him encompassed social as well as natural science. He vaunted himself as a scientist of the mind and declared psychology to be the key science. Whether Jung is characterized as a rationalist or a romantic, he refused to deny the triumph of science over religion as an explanation of both the physical and the human worlds. Contrary to fundamentalists, he believed that science had supplanted religion as explanation. The only options left were to replace religion—the rationalist response—or to reconceive it—the romantic response. Jung opted, or seemingly opted, for the romantic route.

Jung's strategy was to separate mythology from the rest of religion and to offer mythology as a psychological, not an explanatory, phenomenon. Severed from the rest of religion, that is, from religion as explanation, mythology could continue to exist in the face of science. By mythology, Jung meant the stories of the lives of gods and heroes.

For Jung, mythology and religion traditionally had worked in tandem. Together with ritual, the other part of religion for Jung, mythology had provided the best entrée to God. In contrast to belief, which provides only information, myth offers experience: "The protean mythologem and the shimmering symbol express the processes of the psyche far more trenchantly and, in the end, far more clearly than the clearest concept; for the symbol not only conveys a visualization of the process but—and this is perhaps just as important—it also brings a re-experiencing of it" ("Paracelsus as a Spiritual Phenomenon," Jung, 1953–1956, vol. 13, paragraph 199).

Unlike early Christianity, present-day Christianity had failed to update its myths. That failure was part of its overall inability to reinvigorate itself. Sometimes Jung argued that Christianity had gone astray in trying to meet the challenge of science by severing belief from experience and relying only on belief. Jung's objection was that belief without experience is empty and that belief is in any case often incompatible with modern historical as well as scientific knowledge. At other times Jung contended that Christianity had gone astray by turning belief into dogmatic faith severed from knowledge. Jung's objection here was that even faith requires experience to sustain itself.

Although these criticisms did not involve myth, at other times Jung asserted that present-day Christianity had erred in its attempt to update itself by eliminating myth, for example, in the theological liberals' transformation of Jesus into a teacher of timeless ethics and in the theologian Rudolf Bultmann's project of "demythologizing," which Jung misinterpreted as eliminating rather than preserving myth. Jung objected that the supposed incompatibility of myth with modern knowledge stemmed from a false, literal interpretation of myth. Jung also believed that myth is indispensable to experience and therefore to religion. Christianity had sought to overcome the opposition between religion and modern knowledge by discarding belief that is at odds with knowledge—a rationalist kind of response in its preoccupation with belief. However, in eliminating myth, Christianity had eliminated experience as well.

By Christian mythology, Jung meant most of all the life of Christ. Read literally, the Gospels are incompatible with history and science alike. Taken psychologically, the Gospels sidestep these impediments. The life of Christ becomes a symbol of the archetypal journey of the hero from primordial unconsciousness (birth), to ego consciousness (adulthood), to the return to the unconscious (crucifixion), and to the reemergence from it to form the self (resurrection). Without denying the historicity of Christ, Jung maintained that Christ can be inspirational even as a mythical, that is, a psychological, hero. In arguing that the prime appeal of Christ has always been psychological rather than historical, Jung espoused a romantic position. The obstacles that modern historical and scientific knowledge pose to a literal rendition of Christ's life offer an opportunity to make clear for the first time the psychological meaning intended from the outset. Ironically, Jung's position was in fact close to Bultmann's. Both sought to show that Christian mythology had never been intended to be taken literally, so that the impossibility of continuing to accept it literally was a blessing in disguise.

Jung never faulted Christian mythology for its outdatedness, only its interpreters: "Our myth has become mute, and gives no answers. The fault lies not in it as it is set down in the Scriptures, but solely in us, who have not developed it further, who, rather, have suppressed any such attempts" (Jung, 1963, p. 332). By developing Christian mythology, Jung did not propose altering the psychological meaning of the life of Christ. He intended only to be explicating that meaning by filtering out the literal rendition.

At the same time Jung recognized that religion had ceased to be an option for many persons, even though he, unlike Bultmann, acknowledged that many others remain or seek to remain the equivalent of the ancients. For those for whom religion is no longer a possibility, such as rationalists, the alternative to psychologizing religious myths is to replace them with secular ones.

SECULAR MYTHS. For Jung, secular myths minimally take the form of a recasting of traditional, religious myths in secular garb:

> Mythological motifs frequently appear, but clothed in modern dress; for instance, instead of the eagle of Zeus, or the great roc, there is an airplane; the fight with the dragon is a railway smash; the dragon-slaying hero is an operatic tenor; the Earth Mother is a stout lady selling vegetables; the Pluto who abducts Persephone is a reckless chauffeur, and so on. ("Psychology and Literature," Jung, 1953–1966, vol. 15, paragraph 152)

Far more significant has been the creation of distinctively secular myths, of which Jung's best example is the belief in flying saucers. That belief is widespread and arouses the archetypal emotions of awe and fear. Flying saucers are invoked to explain events in the physical world, such as fast-flying objects and strange lights. Above all, these technologically advanced phenomena fit the present-day scientific self-image: "It is characteristic of our time that the archetype . . . should now take the form of an object, a technological construction, in order to avoid the odiousness of mythological personification. Anything that looks technological goes down without difficulty with modern man" ("Flying Saucers: A Modern Myth," Jung, 1953–1966, vol. 10, paragraph 624).

For primitives and ancients, myth functions outwardly as well as inwardly not merely in explaining the world but also in giving it meaningfulness. A personified world operates responsively, in accordance with the purposes of gods and the pleas of humans. To cite Jung's favorite example,

> The Pueblo Indians believe that they are the sons of Father Sun, and this belief endows their life with a perspective (and a goal) that goes far beyond their limited existence. . . . Their plight is infinitely more satisfactory than that of a man in our own civilization who knows that he is (and will remain) nothing more than an underdog with no inner meaning to his life. (Jung, 1968, p. 76)

Jung granted that most secular myths do not, like the myth of flying saucers, connect adherents to the physical world. Most myths presuppose the withdrawal of projections from the world, which now is experienced as impersonal and therefore meaningless. Most secular myths refer only to the human world and not to the physical one. For example, the myth of the Cold War as an apocalyptic struggle between the forces of good and the forces of evil demonizes Communists but not the earth. Still, Jung sought the existential, not merely the psychological, import of myths: connecting humans to the external world.

That continuing import is evinced above all in Jung's concept of synchronicity. Synchronicity restores to the physical world its meaningfulness even without its personality, which science precludes. Meaningfulness is now inherent in the outer world rather than imposed on it through projection: "Synchronistic experiences serve our turn here. They point to a latent meaning which is independent of [our] consciousness" (Jung, 1973–1974, vol. II, p. 495). Meaningfulness stems not from the existence of god, or personality, in the world but from the symmetry between human beings and the world. Still, the effect is the same as that once provided by gods: rather than being alien and indifferent to humans, the world proves to be akin to humans, not because gods respond to human wishes or because human wishes directly affect the world but because human thoughts correspond to the nature of the world. Jung continued to demand the withdrawal of projections from the world, but synchronicity restores to the world the meaningfulness that projections once provided.

Synchronicity is not itself myth. It is the experience of the world as meaningful. Myth would be an account of that experience. The payoff, however, would be less an explanation of the world than connectedness to the world. Secular myths that, like the myth of flying saucers, connect one to the physical world and not just to other human beings have the potential to duplicate the past existential as well as psychological functions of religious myths.

JUNG AS ROMANTIC. In conclusion, Jung was a rationalist insofar as he sought secular myths, that is, he sought alternatives to religious myths. As a rationalist, he could grant that the function of religious myths was no more explanatory than that of secular ones, but he would still argue that religious myths worked only for those who explained the world religiously. Secular myths were needed for those who now explained the world scientifically.

However, Jung was a romantic insofar as he considered secular myths to be secular versions of religious ones rather than secular alternatives to religious ones. He was thus retaining religion even in the face of science. First, he used the term *myths* in referring to secular myths, thereby linking them to religion. Second, the fullest secular myths, such as the myth of flying saucers, concern the physical world and thereby restore the symmetry between humans and the world formerly provided by religious myths. Third, the myth of flying saucers nearly brings back gods to the world in the form of the omniscient and omnipotent occupants of the saucers.

At the same time the link of secular myths to the physical world evinces a rationalist residue in Jung. Even if the myth of flying saucers primarily shapes the way the world is experienced and not the way it is explained, that myth does explain outer events. Moreover, the line between experience and explanation is blurry, and explanation affects experience. Rather than ceding the physical world to science, secular myths try to reclaim it.

Conversely, one might maintain, Jung so relentlessly psychologized (and existentialized) religion that religion replaced by psychology was religion as it had always been, whether or not this interpretation had ever been recognized by its practitioners. That is how Jung could trace a straight line from Gnostic religion to alchemy to analytical psychology:

> [W]hen I began to understand alchemy I realized that it represented the historical link with Gnosticism, and that a continuity therefore existed between past and present. Grounded in the natural philosophy of the Middle Ages, alchemy formed the bridge on the one hand into the past, to Gnosticism, and on the other into the future, to the modern psychology of the unconscious. (Jung, 1963, p. 201)

Analytical psychology represented an advance over Gnosticism and alchemy only in separating out what in them had been a mix of metaphysics and psychology. Taken this way, Jung was a consummate romantic.

BIBLIOGRAPHY

Bair, Deidre. *Jung: A Biography.* Boston, 2004. The fullest, most factual biography of Jung to date.

Campbell, Joseph. *The Hero with a Thousand Faces.* 1st ed. New York, 1949. 2d ed. Princeton, N.J., 1968. Reprint: Princeton, NJ, 2004. The classical application of Jungian psychology to hero myths. It provides a common plot for hero myths that symbolize the journey of the second half of Jung, from ego consciousness to the collective unconscious and back. This work is the Jungian counterpart to Otto Rank's Freudian *Myth of the Birth of the Hero*

Charet, F. X. *Spiritualism and the Foundations of C. G. Jung's Psychology.* Albany, N.Y., 1993. Argues that Jung, rather than conceding the explanation of the world to science, used spiritualism as a way to meld religion with science.

Clarke, J. J. *Jung and Eastern Thought: A Dialogue with the Orient.* London and New York, 1994. An examination of Jung and Eastern religions.

Hannah, Barbara. *Jung: His Life and Work.* New York, 1976. The standard hagiographical biographical account of Jung, whose psychology is attributed entirely to his genius and his inner life.

Hauke, Christopher. *Jung and the Postmodern: The Interpretation of Realities.* New York and London, 2000. A comparison of Jung's ideas with postmodern tenets.

Homans, Peter. *Jung in Context: Modernity and the Making of a Psychology.* Chicago, 1979.

Jung, C. G. *Collected Works of C. G. Jung.* Edited by Sir Herbert Read, Michael Fordham, and Gerhard Adler. Translated by R. F. C. Hull. New York, 1953–1966; Princeton, N.J., 1967–1979; London, 1953–1979.

Jung, C. G. *Memories, Dreams, Reflections* (1962). Edited by Aniela Jaffé. Translated by Richard and Clara Winston. New York, 1963.

Jung, C. G. "Approaching the Unconscious." In Jung et al., *Man and His Symbols,* pp. 1–94. New York, 1968 (originally published in 1964).

Jung, C. G. *Letters.* Edited by Gerhard Adler and Aniela Jaffé. 2 vols. Princeton, N.J., and London, 1973–1974.

Main, Roderick, ed. *Jung on Synchronicity and the Paranormal.* Princeton, N.J., and London, 1997. The best sourcebook on Jung and synchronicity.

Miller, David L., ed. *Jung and the Interpretation of the Bible.* New York, 1995.

Noll, Richard. *The Jung Cult.* Princeton, N.J., 1994. Argues that Jung, far from being committed to science, cloaked fundamentally antimodernist, atavistic, religious inclinations in a modern, secular guise.

Rowland, Susan. *Jung: A Feminist Revision.* Cambridge, U.K., 2002. The finest feminist assessment of Jungian psychology.

Ryce-Menuhin, Joel, ed. *Jung and the Monotheisms: Judaism, Christianity and Islam.* London and New York, 1994. A discussion of Jung and Western religions.

Segal, Robert A., ed. *The Gnostic Jung.* Princeton, N.J., and London, 1992.

Segal, Robert A., ed. *Jung on Mythology.* Princeton, N.J., and London, 1998. A sourcebook on both Jung and Jungians (Neumann, Von Franz, and Hillman).

Shamdasani, Sonu. *Jung and the Making of Modern Psychology: The Dream of a Science.* Cambridge, U.K., 2004. Argues that Jung was part of a group of leading psychologists who aimed to make psychology the queen of the sciences by incorporating the irreducibly subjective element in theorizing in any science.

Stein, Murray. *Jung's Treatment of Christianity: The Psychotherapy of a Religious Tradition.* Wilmette, Ill., 1985.

Stevens, Anthony. *Archetype: The Natural History of the Self.* London, 1982 (reprinted with the title *Archetypes* [New York, 1983]). An attempt to make analytical psychology scientific by explaining archetypes through ethology and neuropsychology.

Walker, Steven F. *Jung and the Jungians on Myth: An Introduction.* New York and London, 2002 (originally published in 1995).

PETER HOMANS (1987)
ROBERT A. SEGAL (2005)

JUNO. The name *Iuno* is a derivative of *iun-* and the ending *-on-*. It is very likely a shortened form of *iuven-*, as found in *iunix* ("heifer") and the comparative *iunior* ("younger"). The derivative *Iunius* (*mensis*), or "month of June," was linked by the ancients sometimes to *iunior* (Varro, *De lingua Latina* 6.33) and sometimes to *Iūno* (Servius, *Ad Georgica* 1.43). *Uni,* the name of an Etruscan goddess, is borrowed from the Latin *Iuno,* just as *Ani,* the name of an Etruscan god, comes from *Ianus.*

The goddess personifies creative youth. She oversees birth, both on a human and on a heavenly level. Upon beginning labor, women call upon Juno Lucina ("she who brings into light"), who is honored at the Matronalia of 1 March (cf. Plautus, *Aulularia* 692; Terence, *Adelphoe* 487). Juno Covella is the patroness, along with Janus, of each month's calends in order to further the labor of the young moon from the calends until the nones.

Several other ancient cults of Juno fall on the first of the month: February 1 (Juno Sospita); June 1 (Juno Moneta); September 1 (Juno Regina of the Aventine); October 1 (Juno Sororia). Exceptions to this rule are the cults of Juno that lost their autonomy. Thus Juno Caprotina is honored on July 7, the nones, in a ceremony "intended to strengthen the light of night" (Dumézil, 1975) and connected with the cult rendered to Jupiter in the Poplifugia of July 5. Similarly, Juno Regina of the Capitol is venerated, along with Jupiter, on September 13, the ides, in the left chapel of the Capitoline temple, the anniversary of which falls on that date (Livy, 7.3.5).

In Roman history Juno intervened in several instances. In 396 BCE the dictator M. Furius Camillus obtained the consent of Uni, the Etruscan homologue of Juno and the protectress of the hostile town of Veii, to be transferred from her besieged town to the Aventine in Rome. Thus a second Juno Regina, this one of foreign origin, was established in the capital (Livy, 5.21.3, 22.4–6). In 390 BCE the Capitol was saved from the Gauls by the honking of geese, birds sacred to Juno (Livy, 5.47.3–4). Was this an intervention of Juno Moneta ("the warner"; see Cicero, *De divinatione* 1.101)? In 344 BCE a temple was dedicated to her by the dictator L. Furius Camillus, the son of the aforementioned Marcus (Livy, 7.28.4). The establishment of a mint near this sanctuary to Moneta (*Ad Monetae;* Livy, 6.20.13) gave to the word *moneta* the meaning of "money."

Syncretism had little effect upon Juno. In the *lectisternium* of 217 BCE she was simply paired with Jupiter after the example of the Greek couple Zeus and Hera.

BIBLIOGRAPHY

Dumézil, Georges. *La religion romaine archaïque.* 2d ed. Paris, 1974. See page 299 on the etymology and pages 303–310 on the Italic Junoes. This work has been translated from the first edition by Philip Krapp as *Archaic Roman Religion,* 2 vols. (Chicago, 1970).

Dumézil, Georges. *Fêtes romaines d'été et d'automne.* Paris, 1975. See pages 271–283 on Juno Caprotina, written in partnership with Paul Drossart.

Schilling, Robert. *Rites, cultes, dieux de Rome.* Paris, 1979. See pages 233–239 on Juno Covella and pages 239–244 on Juno Sororia.

Wissowa, Georg. *Religion und Kultus der Römer.* 2d ed. Munich, 1912. See pages 181–191 for a general treatment.

New Sources

Champeaux, Jacqueline. "Religion romaine et religion latin: les cultes de Jupiter et Junon à Préneste." *Revue des études Latines* 60 (1982): 71–104.

Dury-Moyaers, Geneviève. "Aperçu critique relatif au culte de Junon." In *Aufstieg und Niedergang der Römischen Welt* 2.17.1, pp. 142–202. Berlin and New York, 1981.

Dury-Moyaers, Geneviève. "Réflexions à propos de l'iconographie de Iuno Sospita." In *Beiträge zur altitalischen Geistesgeschichte. Festschrift Gerhard Radke,* pp. 83–101. Münster, 1986.

Fabian, Klaus Dietrich. *Aspekte einer Entwicklungsgeschichte der römisch-lateinischen Göttin Juno.* Berlin, 1978.

Fabian, Klaus Dietrich. "Ex numine dea? Überlegungen zum numinosen Ursprung der römischen Göttin Iuno." In *Beiträge zur altitalischen Geistesgeschichte. Festschrift Gerhard Radke,* pp. 102–115. Münster, 1986.

Häussler, Reinhard. *Hera und Juno.* Wiesbaden, 1995.

Pailler, Jean-Marie, "Quaestiunculae Dumezilianae. 1. Origines de Rome, trivalence féminine, hagiographie." *Pallas* 48 (1998): 203–224.

ROBERT SCHILLING (1987)
Translated from French by Paul C. Duggan
Revised Bibliography

JUPITER.

The name *Iuppiter* is made up of two elements: the first, *Iou-,* stems from the Indo-European **dyeu,* the root of *dies,* or "day"; while in the second element we find the Latin word *pater,* meaning "father." *Iuppiter* therefore identifies the "god of heavenly light." Many of the ancients were aware of this meaning; Paulus-Festus for example, describes the epithet *Lucetius,* referring to the god, this way: "Lucetium Iovem appellabant quod eum lucis esse causam credebant" (Jupiter was called Lucetius since he was believed to be the author of light). The name *Iuppiter* belongs to the Indo-European domain, and is semantically related to the Greek *Zeus,* which stems from **dyeus.*

All Italians recognized Jupiter as their god, particularly the Latins, who honored him under the title of Jupiter Latiaris during the Feriae Latinae. This feast was celebrated each year under the auspices of Alba Longa on the summit of the Alban Hills. It continued in this location as a movable feast (*feriae conceptivae*) after Rome replaced Alba as the supervisor of this federal ceremony. Moreover, Jupiter is present in the Umbrian ritual of the Bronze Tables of Iguvium. This feast celebrates Jupiter, Mars, and Vofionus; Table VI lists the three identical prayers accompanying the sacrifices of three oxen, one to each of the deities. Tinia, the great god of the Etruscan pantheon, was equivalent to Zeus-Jupiter; he controlled three kinds of lightning. This supreme deity was often represented on mirrors, accompanied by *Uni* (Juno) and *Menrva* (Minerva), with background images from Greek mythology.

Ancient Rome honored Jupiter as the supreme god. His preeminence was never called into question, not even when syncretism brought in the *ritus Graecus* (Greek rite): in the *lectisternium* of 217 BCE, Jupiter, along with Juno, held the highest rank. Jupiter served as the keystone in the ancient triad of gods, along with Mars and Quirinus; later, in the Capitoline triad, his companions became Juno and Minerva. According to Latin and Greek historiography, and also according to archaeological evidence, the Capitoline temple of Jupiter, Juno, and Minerva with its three *cellae* was built at the end of the sixth century by Etruscan kings, the *Tarquinii.* Some scholars have also speculated on an Etruscan origin for the Latin triads, or another triad associating Ceres, Liber, and Libera (whose temple was dedicated on the Aventine at the beginning of the Republic).

The Jupiter of the archaic epoch, specified as Jupiter *Feretrius*—an epithet that the ancients traced to either *ferre* (to bear, carry) or *ferire* (to slay, strike)—was venerated in a chapel located on the summit of the Capitoline thought to have been built by Romulus. There, the first king of Rome consecrated the first *spolia opima* (spoils seized from a slain enemy commander) to Jupiter. According to Paulus-Festus, the sanctuary of Jupiter Feretrius contained "sceptrum per quod iurarent et lapidem silicem quo foedus ferirent" ("a sword for swearing oaths and a flintstone for concluding treaties"). Livy records that the Roman Fetialis, the college of priestly officials responsible for ritual declarations of war or peace, concluded a treaty in the name of the Roman people with the Alban people they prayed precisely to Jupiter

Feretrius to smite (*ferire*) the Roman people if they should deviate from the treaty, similar to the way the priest would strike the sacrificial pig with the flintstone. Plutrach records that near the sanctuary of Jupiter Feretrius, the Ludi Capitolini (Capitoline games) were celebrated each year on the ides of October; they consisted of hand-to-hand combat and foot races.

Jupiter is linked with Roman triumph. Romans believed their victories arose from two factors: the excellence of the general and from the favor of the supreme god who, as *optimus* and *maximus,* ensured the prosperity of the Roman Empire. Victory processions were directed towards Capitolium, where the victor would present a solemn offering to *Iuppiter Optimus Maximus;* the triumphator (victor) appeared to have achieved the rank of a god. The triumphator was clothed in the *vestis triumphalis:* the *tunica palmata,* thus called because of the palm-branches embroidered on it; and the *toga picta,* a name also owed to its rich embroidery; on his head, he wore the *corona laurea,* or crown of laurels, the symbol of the triumph. Scholars differ in their interpretations of the figure of the triumphator and the meaning of his insignia: some scholars saw the personification and embodiment of the god Jupiter, but others traced back the *insignia triumphalia* to the regal robes; consequently, they recognized the former *rex* in the triumphator. By wearing the *ornatus Iovis* and the *corona Etrusca,* by having his face painted with the red lead, and by exclaiming *triumpe,* the triumphator is viewed as the god manifesting himself. This idea may have originated in Etruscan kingship and thus can be explained against the background of Etruscan religion. These robes, which had originally become the state robes of the king when they had turned into *ornatus Iovis,* were, on the very day of the triumph, taken back from the god by the king, who then was characterized as both Jupiter and king.

Being god of heaven, Jupiter protected all the ides, or "days of full light," so called because those days were prolonged by a full moon. The ides were the thirteenth day of most months, but the fifteenth day in March, May, July, and October. On these days, the Romans offered Jupiter a sacrificial lamb (*ovis Idulis*). His cult was maintained by the *flamen Dialis,* who was "in the god's permanent service," and was "celebrated every day." His principal feast was celebrated on the Vinalia, which were divided into the Vinalia Rustica (August 19), marked by the consecration of grapes, and the Vinalia Priora (April 23), marked by the offering of wine. The feast of the Meditrinalia (October 11), celebrating the magical and medical power of the *vinum novum* also honored Jupiter. Together with Venus, he was venerated as the sovereign god, protector of the Romans. From a naturalistic point of view, scholars point to the gift of the wine to Jupiter as a proof of an "agrarian" god; in fact, Latin peasants honored Jupiter because his powers could endanger their crops and the vineyards. The link between Jupiter and wine and Jupiter and Venus (who is associated with Jupiter in the Vinalia) indicates his sovereignty and preeminence.

Many other epithets illustrate different aspects of Jupiter. Some correspond to his atmospheric manifestations, such as Jupiter Tonans (the thunderer) or Jupiter Fulgur (he who throws lightning). Others refer to his magical or juridical interventions, such as Jupiter Stator (he who immobilizes or Jupiter Fidius (loyalty warranter). During the historical epoch, however, his principal title was officially Jupiter Optimus Maximus. The anniversary of the founding of his temple on the Capitoline fell on the ides of September, and it was followed by the Ludi Romani (Roman games). On the calends of January, the new consuls would go there, accompanied by senators, magistrates, priests, and common people. The consul named to lead a military expedition would pronounce the *vota,* which were prayers and promises for gaining a victory. Upon his triumphant return, he would go to the temple to give thanks to the sovereign god.

SEE ALSO Fides; Flamen; Indo-European Religions, overview article; Juno; Minerva; Quirinus; Roman Religion, article on the Early Period.

BIBLIOGRAPHY

Banti, Laura. "Il culto del cosidetto tempio di Apollo a Veii e il problema delle triadi etrusco-italiche." *Studi Etruschi* 17 (1943): 187–224.

Brelich, Angelo. "Juppiter e le idus." In *Ex orbe religionum. Studia Geo Windengren oblata,* pp. 299–306. Leiden, 1972.

Cazeneuve, O. "Jupiter, Liber et le vin latin." *Revue d'Histoire des Religions* 205 (1988): 245–265.

Dumézil, Georges. *Jupiter, Mars, Quirinus, Essai sur la conception indo-européenne de la société et sur les origines de Rome.* Paris, 1941.

Dumézil, Georges. "Quaestiones indo-italicae, 14 (Jupiter et les Vinalia), 15 (Le mythe des Vinalia priora), 16 (Inter exta caesa et porrecta)." *Revue des Études Latines* 39 (1961): 261–274.

Dumézil, Georges. *La religion romaine archaïque.* 2d ed. Paris, 1974. Translated from the first edition by Philip Krapp as *Archaic Roman Religion,* 2 vols. (Chicago, 1970).

Fowler, W. Warde. "Juppiter and the Triumphator." *Classical Review* 30 (1916): 153.

Gantz, Timothy. "Divine Triads on an Archaic Etruscan Frieze Plaque from Poggio Civitate (Murlo)." *Studi Etruschi* 39 (1971): 1–22.

Koch, Carl. *Der römischen Juppiter* (Frankfurter Studien zur Religion und Kultur der Antike). Frankfurt-am-Main, Germany, 1937.

Montanari, Enrico. *Identità culturale e conflitti religiosi nella Roma reppublicana.* Rome, 1988.

Rufus, Fear Julius. "The Cult of Jupiter and Roman Imperial Ideology." *Aufstieg und Nidergang der römischen Welt,* II, 17, no. 1, 1981: 3–143.

Schilling, Robert. *Rites, cultes, dieux de Rome.* Paris, 1979.

Schilling, Robert. *La religion romaine de Vénus.* 2d ed. Paris, 1982.

Versnel, Henobrik Simon. *Triumphus. An Inquiry into the Origin, Development, and Meaning of the Roman Triumph.* Leiden, 1970.

Wissowa, Georg. *Religion und Kultus der Römer.* 2d ed. Munich, 1912.

ROBERT SCHILLING (1987)
CHARLES GUITTARD (2005)
Translated from French by Paul C. Duggan

JUSTICE SEE COSMOLOGY; DHARMA; ESCHATOLOGY; FATE; JUDGMENT OF THE DEAD; LAW AND RELIGION; THEODICY

JUSTIFICATION.

Christianity teaches that the ministry of Jesus Christ has established the conditions necessary for human beings to live in communion with God, both in the present and in eternity. The doctrine of atonement refers to the objective basis for this communion (i.e., how God's action in Christ makes such communion possible for humankind in general). By contrast, the doctrine of justification refers to its subjective basis (i.e., how this possibility is actualized in and for individual human beings). The justified person is one who has realized the possibility of communion with God established by Christ. The one who has not been justified has somehow failed to do so, and thus persists in the state of alienation or estrangement from God that Jesus was sent to overcome.

OVERALL PLACE OF THE CONCEPT IN CHRISTIANITY. The topic of justification has assumed particular importance in the history of Christian thought owing to internal disagreements over the way in which individuals appropriate the benefits of Christ's work for themselves. Although all sides have confessed the priority of God's grace in sending Jesus in the first place, consensus on the degree to which this gracious initiative needs to be complemented by some separate human action has been harder to achieve. The question at issue in these debates may be stated fairly easily. Granted that the aim of Christ's ministry was a transformation of the relationship between God and humankind, and granted that the concept of relationship implies the active participation of both parties, what are the respective roles of God and human beings in effecting justification?

Two concerns have tended to shape the ways in which Christians have attempted to answer this question. On the one hand, there has been a desire to minimize any talk of human activity with respect to justification in order to stress God's graciousness as the founder and guarantor of this relationship. On the other hand, there has been just as strong a desire to emphasize human activity as a means of avoiding any suggestion that God's graciousness undermines the freedom and responsibility of human beings as active participants in this relationship. Different groups' positions on justification can be interpreted for the most part as the result of an inclination to regard one or the other of these concerns as the more theologically pressing.

BIBLICAL ROOTS OF THE CONCEPT. *Justification* is one of many terms used in the New Testament to refer to the transformation of humanity's relationship to God as effected by Christ. Other terms draw on the imagery of healing (*salvation*), economics (*redemption*), and warfare (*ransom*), all of which suggest rescue or release from captivity to some alien power. By contrast, *justification* is a legal metaphor that connotes the vindication of an accused party before a judge and, more specifically, acquittal from self-incurred guilt. In biblical perspective, to be justified is to be reestablished in right relationship with God in spite of having violated that relationship: "Blessed are those whose iniquities are forgiven, and whose sins are covered; blessed is the one against whom the Lord will not reckon sin" (*Rom.* 4: 7–8, quoting *Ps.* 32: 1–2).

The language of justification reflects Christianity's roots in Judaism and, more specifically, the Jewish belief in God's covenant with the people of Israel. In ancient Judaism covenant was understood as a formal relationship, solemnly agreed between two parties, in which each has certain responsibilities to the other. For Israel, fidelity to its covenant with God was a matter of obedience to the law: the commandments, ordinances, and statutes given by God to Israel on Mount Sinai. These commandments structured common life by laying out the people's obligations to God and each other. God had promised to reward the keeping of the law with prosperity, but threatened those who broke it with judgment and punishment (see, e.g., *Deut.* 28).

The apostle Paul is the New Testament writer who deals most explicitly with the theme of justification. The language of justification is most prominent in his correspondence with the churches at Galatia (c. 54 CE) and Rome (c. 58 CE), though it is present in other letters as well. The key Greek terms relating to this concept in the Pauline corpus are the verb *dikaioun* (normally translated as "to justify") and its nominal and adjectival cognates *dikaiosune* and *dikaios* (normally translated as "righteousness" and "righteous," respectively).

In *Galatians,* Paul is arguing with a competing group of Christian missionaries who teach that Gentile Christians need to observe the Jewish law in order to be justified. Against this position, Paul maintains that the law does not justify. He breaks the conceptual link between justification and keeping the law by arguing that the covenant with Israel was established with God's promise to bless the descendants of Abraham, more than four hundred years before the giving of the law. The example of Abraham shows that the basis of justification is not keeping the law, but simply God's promise—and thus a matter of grace rather than works (*Gal.* 3: 17–18).

The letter to the Romans lacks the polemical context of *Galatians* and provides a more detailed development of Paul's views. He argues that all people, Jews and Gentiles, have violated the law and therefore stand under God's judgment (*Rom.* 3: 9, 23). It follows that justification cannot come by fulfilling the demands of the law; rather, people "are justified by [God's] grace as a gift, through the redemption which is in Christ Jesus" (3: 24). Once again, justification is the result of divine gift, rather than of human achievement (4: 6; 11: 5–6). Just as Abraham was justified by his faith in God's promises long before the law was given (4: 3–5), so now the basis for life in covenant with God is faith in Christ, through whom the justification obtained by Abraham has been made available to all peoples (4: 11–12).

JUSTIFICATION IN EARLY CHRISTIAN THEOLOGY. Though Paul's letters quickly acquired canonical status within the early church, his views on justification do not appear to have been accepted with great enthusiasm. The theme of justification is largely absent from the later, pseudo-Pauline letters that would eventually be included in the New Testament (though, see *Tit.* 3: 7), and still other biblical writers directly challenge the idea of justification by faith apart from works (*Jas.* 2: 14, 22–24). In short, it appears that while the memory of Paul was revered, his writings were seen as potentially dangerous (*2 Pet.* 3: 15–16), presumably because his emphasis on grace over works was seen as undermining ethical rigor in the church (a charge that Paul himself explicitly rejects in *Rom.* 3: 8 and 6: 1–2).

The general eclipse of Paul's teaching on justification within the church only increased in the first centuries after his death. The concern over a legalistic understandings of justification that had prompted Paul's letter to the Galatians evaporated with the rapid disappearance of a distinct Jewish presence within the church. Furthermore, in response to Gnostic Christians (who were understood to teach a kind of determinism with respect to human destiny), the leading theologians of the church's first centuries were anxious to stress the role of the human will in justification rather than echo Paul's emphasis on grace apart from works. This perspective, which stresses the way in which the incarnation renews the capacities of fallen human nature, remains dominant in the Eastern Orthodox churches to the present day.

It was not until the Pelagian controversy in the fifth century that justification again emerged as a central theme in Christian theology. Pelagius (died c. 420) was a British ascetic who wanted to instill greater ethical rigor into what he saw as a church that imperial patronage had rendered morally flaccid. To this end, he emphasized human beings' responsibility for their status before God: though he taught that divine grace was the ultimate source of human freedom, he insisted that justification depended upon the individual's use of that freedom and thus was finally a matter of human achievement.

Pelagius and his followers were opposed by Augustine of Hippo (354–430), who maintained that their position undermined the unmerited and gracious character of justification. In defending what he saw as clear Pauline teaching, Augustine challenged Pelagius's account of human freedom by defining a distinctly Western doctrine of original sin. Augustine argued that Adam's fall had corrupted not only his own will, but also that of his descendants in such a way that rendered human beings incapable of turning to God by their own power. The freedom of the will that Pelagius championed was therefore illusory. According to Augustine, human beings were justified exclusively by God's free gift of grace and not by their own efforts, to the extent that human salvation and damnation alike were determined exclusively by God's decree (the doctrine of double predestination).

DEVELOPMENTS IN THE MEDIEVAL PERIOD. Though Pelagianism was officially condemned at the Councils of Carthage in 418 and Ephesus in 431, Augustine's views did not win unconditional support. The Greek-speaking churches of the East did not accept his denial of free will. In the Latin-speaking West, the fifth and sixth centuries saw the rise of a so-called "semi-Pelagian" position that sought to strike more of a balance between human responsibility and divine grace than Augustine seemed to allow, arguing that freedom of the will had not been so damaged by the fall as to preclude all human initiative in the process of justification. Though semi-Pelagianism, too, was eventually condemned at the Second Council of Orange in 529, Western theology continued to be marked by debates over the relationship between human freedom and divine grace in justification throughout the medieval period.

The fifth-century condemnations of Pelagianism excluded any overt teaching of justification by works from subsequent Catholic theology. At the same time, the desire not to undermine the integrity of human beings as responsible agents before God tended to push many theologians away from Augustine's strict predestinarianism. Furthermore, the emergence in Western Europe of the careful distinctions of Scholastic theology in tandem with an increasingly intricate penitential practice led to an increasing understanding of God's righteousness as an impartial justice that could be satisfied only through individual human beings' acquisition of merit. Consequently, the degree to which human beings could be said to acquire merit before God without succumbing to Pelagianism became a central issue in medieval accounts of justification.

Gabriel Biel (c. 1425–1495) sought to avoid a crudely Pelagian account of justification by works while also leaving room for human initiative. He argued that while a person's deeds apart from grace are always objectively worthless (i.e., without merit) before God, God had determined for Christ's sake to reward with grace those who do their best (*facere quod in se est*) as though their deeds were meritorious. This theory seemed both to exclude justification by works (since it was acknowledged that human works had no objective merit), and to allow that human beings could dispose themselves for the receipt of justifying grace by their own natural powers.

Biel by no means represented the consensus position among his contemporaries. Many important theologians (especially members of the Dominican and Augustinian orders) rejected outright the idea that a person could ever be said to merit grace, even in the highly attenuated sense specified by Biel. Still, the "modern school" (*via moderna*) of which Biel was a representative was influential in many quarters, including the faculty of the University of Erfurt, where the German reformer Martin Luther (1483–1546) received his theological training.

The Role of the Concept in the Reformation and Protestantism. Luther soon began to have doubts about Biel's account of justification. His worries were at once theological and existential: Biel had taught that justification was conditional on doing one's best, but how was the individual to know if she or he had truly fulfilled this condition? Though Biel had conceived "doing one's best" as a minimal requirement, Luther, acutely conscious of his own sin, found he could never be sure that he had done even that much. After a thorough study of Paul, he eventually concluded that Biel's account was wrong: justification did not depend on humans meeting any prior condition.

Though Luther would go on to substantiate his claims by reference to Augustine's anti-Pelagian writings, his views on justification were in many ways quite distinct from those of Augustine and medieval Augustinians. Augustine had seen justification as the product of the divine gift of grace. Against the Pelagian claim that human beings could fulfill the commandments by an exercise of the will, Augustine had insisted that the will of fallen human beings was corrupted and could be healed only by a gift of grace that turned it to God. In short, for Augustine, God's grace justified human beings by giving them the capacity to be in right relationship with God.

By contrast, Luther denied that right relationship with God had anything to do with human capacities, whether in their natural state (as Pelagius had held) or as transformed by grace (as Augustine had argued). To suggest they did, he insisted, would cause human beings to look to themselves for evidence of their justification in a way that would lead either to arrogant presumption or crushing doubt regarding their status before God. Instead, Luther read Paul as teaching that the righteousness by which human beings were justified was Christ's rather than their own. It was therefore an "alien righteousness" (*iustitia aliena*) that remained always external to the justified (*extra nos*).

In arguing that justification consisted in God's ascribing Christ's righteousness to the individual (i.e., a matter of relation) rather than some objective change within the human being (i.e., matter of ontology), Luther concluded that even after being justified, the human being remained always also a sinner (*simul iustus et peccator*). As developed especially by Luther's colleague Philip Melanchthon (1497–1560), this emphasis on the externality of grace led to the specifically Protestant concept of "forensic justification." According to this interpretation of the doctrine, justification was best conceived along the lines of acquittal in a court of law (*forum* in Latin): to be justified was not a matter of being made (let alone of making oneself) righteous, but rather of being declared righteous by God.

Perhaps the most obvious mark distinguishing Protestant treatment of justification from that of classical Augustinianism is the role of faith. Where Augustine had defended justification by grace, Luther spoke of justification by grace through faith (*Eph.* 2: 8), or, still more succinctly, of justification by faith alone (*sola fide*). Because justification was rooted in God's promise to be gracious to humanity for Christ's sake, to be justified was nothing else than to have faith or believe in that promise as addressed to oneself. Importantly, the point of *sola fide* was not to make faith a condition of justification (as though faith were itself a meritorious work that earned God's favor), but rather to re-enforce the principle that trust was to be placed in Christ rather than oneself. For this reason, justification by faith alone has been characterized by Lutherans in particular as the article by which the church stands or falls (*articulus stantis vel cadentis ecclesiae*).

Role in Subsequent Theological Discussion. Though widely accepted by other Protestant reformers, including especially John Calvin (1509–1564), Luther's doctrine of justification was rejected by the Catholic magisterium at the Council of Trent (1545–1563). In its "Decree on Justification," the Council affirmed the priority of grace against both Pelagianism and the theology of Biel, but also taught that human beings actively cooperated in their own justification. Faith given by God was affirmed as the beginning of justification, but the idea of justification by faith alone and the associated teaching that grace was imputed rather than imparted were explicitly condemned. If Luther was worried that Catholic emphasis on human cooperation undermined trust in God as the sole source of salvation, Catholics charged that the Lutheran *sola fide* failed to honor God's creation of human beings as free and responsible agents.

Without seeking to minimize the differences between Protestant and Catholic positions on justification, it may be noted that representatives of the two traditions in the Reformation era frame the doctrine in very different ways. The Tridentine emphasis on faith as the beginning of justification is rooted in a vision of justification as a temporally extended process that includes the human growth in relationship with God. By contrast, Protestant emphasis on justification as a unilateral declaration of forgiveness led to a sharp distinction between divine action and human response. The latter (termed *sanctification*) was important, but was to be clearly distinguished from the question of human status before God (justification proper).

In the wake of the Second Vatican Council (1963–1965), dialogue between Protestant (especially Lutheran) and Catholic theologians has seen increasing convergence on the doctrine of justification. In 1997 representatives of the Catholic Church and the Lutheran World Federation issued the *Joint Declaration on the Doctrine of Justification* that reported a consensus on the basic truths in the doctrine and declared the mutual condemnations of the sixteenth century no longer applicable. Although this document has not met with universal approval within either communion, it does indicate a decisive move away from the intellectual hostility that marked Catholic and Protestant discussion of this topic from the Reformation period through the early twentieth century.

SEE ALSO Atonement, article on Christian Concepts; Free Will and Predestination, article on Christian Concepts; Grace; Incarnation; Merit, article on Christian Concepts; Redemption; Soteriology.

BIBLIOGRAPHY

The Lutheran-Catholic *Joint Declaration on the Doctrine of Justification* (Grand Rapids, Mich., 2000) is an accessible and even-handed introduction to the basic issues in the history of Western debate on this topic. For a critical response to this document from the Protestant perspective (and also a paradigmatic exposition of the traditional Lutheran view), see Eberhard Jüngel, *Justification: The Heart of the Christian Faith,* 3d. ed. (Edinburgh, 2001). Prominent Catholic studies of the question from an ecumenical perspective include Hans Küng, *Justification* (New York, 1964), and Otto H. Pesch, *Theologie der Rechtfertigung bei Martin Luther und Thomas von Aquin* (Mainz, Germany, 1967). An excellent introduction to Luther's thought is Paul Althaus's *The Theology of Martin Luther* (Philadelphia, 1966), especially pp. 224–250. Detailed studies of justification from a Catholic perspective include Bernard J. F. Lonergan, S.J., *Grace and Freedom* (New York, 1971), and Bernard Welte, *Heilsverständnis* (Freiburg, Germany, 1966). The most comprehensive historical survey of the topic in English is Alister E. McGrath's *Iustitia Dei: A History of the Christian Doctrine of Justification,* 2 vols. (Cambridge, U.K., 1986). For a survey of developments in the modern period, see Boniface Willems, "Soteriologie von der Reformation bis zur Gegenwart," in *Handbuch der Dogmengeschichte,* edited by Michael Schmaus, Alois Grillmeier, and Leo Scheffczyk, vol. 3, fasc. 2c (Freiburg, Germany, 1972).

IAN A. MCFARLAND (2005)

JUSTINIAN I (482–565), Roman emperor, was born in or near Skopje in Macedonia, a city where the local aristocracy spoke Latin. The trusted minister of his uncle, Justin I, from 518, Justinian was made his coemperor and succeeded him in 527. Justinian worked for the liberation of the Latin West from armies of occupation: Ostrogoths in Italy and Illyricum, Vandals in Africa and Sicily, Visigoths in Spain. To this end it was necessary to repair the breach between the court and church of Constantinople, and the church and city of Rome, which had been caused by concessions made in the East to those who held that the Council of Chalcedon (451) had pressed the distinction between the divine and human natures of Christ too far in a direction that could be called Nestorian.

Before the reign of Justinian, Chalcedonians in the East were a party opposed to anything that might obscure the distinction between the natures of Christ. During his reign, some Chalcedonians in the East came to stress what is common to the letters of Cyril of Alexandria, who wrote of a union of two natures in the incarnate Word, and of Leo of Rome, who wrote of one person in two natures. Both Cyril and Leo affirm that the manhood of Christ is the same as everyone's own and subject to suffering. John Mayentius and a group of Scythian monks from the Dobruja, who said that "one of the Trinity suffered in the flesh," had a cool reception in Rome in 519. But Justinian used their language in edicts in 529 and 533, which were included with a letter of approval from Pope John II (received in 534) in the definitive edition of his collection of Roman law, the *Corpus juris civilis* (535). So the suffering and death as well as the birth of the Son of God became part of the vocabulary of church and state in East and West.

The *Corpus juris* became the standard textbook of Roman law in the West, at Bologna and elsewhere, but Justinian did not succeed in restoring imperial government. In Africa the Vandals were eliminated, but the mountain tribes were not subdued. In Italy the Ostrogoths were defeated, but they fought on as guerrillas, preferred by the peasants to rent collectors and tax gatherers. Pope Agapetus I came from Rome to Constantinople in 536 in search of a diplomatic solution. He insisted on a purge of those whom he considered disloyal to the Council of Chalcedon and pressed the emperor to introduce a Chalcedonian patriarch into Alexandria. But when he died suddenly his successor at Rome was elected while the Ostrogoths were still in possession. Pope Silverius, deposed and exiled as soon as the imperial armies arrived, obtained a review of his case from Justinian, but he was deposed again and died in prison.

Vigilius, who replaced Silverius, was regarded as an intruder, an agent of Theodora, Justinian's empress, who patronized the Monophysite opponents of the Council of Chalcedon. In 543–544 Justinian issued the "Three Chapters" edict against the person and writings of Theodore of Mopsuestia, who, though the master of Nestorius, died in 428 before the Nestorian controversy broke out; and against criticisms of Cyril of Alexandria by Theodoret of Cyrrhus and Ibas of Edessa, who at Chalcedon were received as orthodox. In a revised form (551), which has been preserved, this edict contained a series of directions for the use of terms in appropriate contexts, for instance for the proper use of *in* and *of two natures.* Vigilius did not criticize these, but he kept up criticism of the "Three Chapters" before and after he was brought to Constantinople in 548 and during the Second Council of Constantinople (553), where a final version of the edict was approved.

The war in Italy continued until 553. After it was over, Vigilius consented to confirm the council, but he died on the way home. His successor at Rome, Pope Pelagius I, succeeded in limiting schism to a few places in northern Italy around Aquileia, but by this time the Monophysites in Syria had acquired their own hierarchy. There and in Egypt, where they kept control, their leaders were not extreme, but they feared to lose their followers if they accepted the orthodoxy of the Council of Chalcedon, as Vigilius feared to lose support in the West if he admitted their orthodoxy. Justinian continued to strive for a balance that can be seen in the architecture of the great churches built in his reign in Constantinople and Ravenna. He kept the West open to Eastern influence but failed to restore the unity of the East.

BIBLIOGRAPHY

A review of the political background can be found in George Ostrogorsky's *History of the Byzantine State,* rev. ed. (New Brunswick, N.J., 1969), pp. 68–79. For the history of theology, see Jaroslav Pelikan's *Christian Tradition,* vol. 1, *The Emergence of the Catholic Tradition, 100–600* (Chicago, 1971), pp. 267–279, and John Meyendorff's *Christ in Eastern Christian Thought* (Crestwood, N.Y., 1975), pp. 29–89.

GEORGE EVERY (1987)

JUSTIN MARTYR (c. 100–163/5) is generally regarded as the most significant Christian apologist of the second century. With him Christianity moved from competition with the popular Hellenistic mystery cults, which attracted chiefly persons of limited education and culture, to competition with philosophies that appealed to persons of higher education and culture. In his apologies he presented Christianity as "the true philosophy" uniting the wisdom of both Jews and Gentiles.

LIFE. Although born at Flavia Neapolis (modern Nablus) in Palestine, the site of ancient Shechem in Samaria, Justin claimed neither Jewish nor Samaritan ancestry. His grandfather was named Bacchius (a Greek name), his father Priscus (a Latin name), and, according to his own statements, he was uncircumcised, reared according to Gentile customs, and educated in the Greek fashion. His writings, however, reveal considerable familiarity with Jewish customs and thought, particularly in handling the Scriptures.

From his youth, Justin possessed a serious religious and philosophical interest. In quest of truth (God) he studied successively with Stoic, Peripatetic (Aristotelian), Pythagorean, and Platonist teachers. The Stoic, Justin reports, disappointed him; the teacher failed to help him further his knowledge of God. The Peripatetic evinced greater interest in collecting fees than in education. The Pythagorean, a philosopher of some note, rejected Justin when he found the latter had no acquaintance with music, astronomy, and geometry. Downcast but not despairing, Justin turned to Platonists, whose emphasis on the spiritual and on contemplation caused his spirit to soar.

Like many others after him, Justin crossed the Platonist bridge to Christianity. Witnessing the fearlessness of Christians in the face of death, he was convinced that they could not be living in wickedness and pleasure as their detractors charged. Further, he was influenced by an unidentified elderly Christian "philosopher," perhaps in his native Palestine or in Ephesus, where he went as a young man. Although some scholars have characterized Justin's account of his conversion to Christianity as an idealization, most have defended it as authentic, if somewhat stylized. The conversion itself entailed less a substantive shift than a change of commitment from Greek (Socrates and Plato) to Hebrew (the prophets and Jesus) truth. Justin opted for Christianity, he explained, "not because the teachings of Plato are different from those of Christ, but because they are not in all respects similar, as neither are those of the others, Stoics, and poets, and historians."

This philosopher-evangelist taught in Rome during the reign of Antoninus Pius (r. 138–161). His students included Tatian (fl. 160–175), the brilliant Assyrian founder of the Encratites, and Irenaeus (c. 130–c. 200), bishop of Lyons and noted antiheretical writer. Justin suffered martyrdom early in the reign of Marcus Aurelius (r. 161–180); he was betrayed by a Cynic philosopher named Crescens, whom he had bested in an argument. Summoned before the Roman prefect Rusticus, according to a reliable early martyrology, Justin and several companions who were apprehended at the same time refused to offer the sacrifices required by law, saying, "No right-thinking person falls away from piety to impiety." By command of the prefect they were scourged and beheaded. The date of his death is uncertain, but traditionally it has been commemorated in the Roman calendar on April 13 and 14.

WRITINGS. Although Justin was the first prolific Christian author, only three of his writings are extant in complete form. Works that have perished include the following treatises: *Against Marcion* (Marcion, d. 160?, was the founder of a heretical anti-Jewish sect); *Against All Heresies;* two titled *Against the Greeks; On the Sovereignty of God; Psaltes;* and *On the Soul.* The works that survive in their entirety are *1 Apology, 2 Apology,* and *Dialogue with Trypho, a Jew.* The second *Apology* is often characterized as an appendix to the first, but it seems to have been occasioned by different circumstances and probably was written several years later.

In *1 Apology,* addressed around 150 CE to the emperor Antoninus Pius, Justin weaves together a refutation of stock pagan charges against Christians and a positive case for Christianity as the true religion. He calls for a halt to punishment of Christians for the name alone and demands an impartial investigation of the common charges of atheism, immorality, treason, social aloofness, and theological absurdity. Justin holds that pagan sources reveal ample analogies to Christian teachings on the resurrection, the virgin birth, the life and death of Jesus, and Christ's Sonship. Thus while pagans have not been excluded from the truth, they have obtained this truth by imitation of the prophets or the Word, which became incarnate in Jesus, and they have mixed the truth with falsehood. Christianity alone expounds pure truth. Before Christ, the Word was in the world so that whoever lived reasonably, that is, according to the teaching of the Logos, the divine Word, or universal reason, such as Socrates or Heraclitus, was a Christian. Concluding *1 Apology* with an explanation of Christian baptism, the Eucharist, and the Sunday liturgy, Justin then appends the rescript of Hadrian.

In *2 Apology,* a very brief work addressed to the Roman Senate, Justin enters a plea for three Christians condemned to death by the prefect Urbicus at the urging of an irate husband whose wife divorced him for infidelity after she converted to Christianity. Confessing that he expects a similar fate because of the hatred of the Cynic Crescens for him, he offers to debate Crescens before the Senate itself. Why do not all Christians simply commit suicide if they love death so much? Because, replies Justin, the death of all Christians would mean the end of those instructed in divine doctrines and perhaps even the end of the human race, for God delays his final judgment for the sake of Christians. Christians do not differ from others in whom the Logos dwells, for all of these have suffered persecution inspired by demons. They differ only in the fact that they possess the whole truth because Christ "became the whole rational being, both body, and reason, and soul." Thus they do not fear death; rather, by dying, they prove the validity of their faith.

In *Dialogue with Trypho* Justin ostensibly reports a debate in Ephesus between himself and a Jew named Trypho, a recent refugee from Palestine during the Bar Kokhba Revolt (132–135). Some scholars have identified Trypho as Rabbi Ṭarfon, but this is improbable. Although the work could reflect an actual dialogue, in its present form it cannot be dated earlier than *1 Apology,* from which it quotes. Because Rabbi Ṭarfon remembered the Temple, destroyed in 70 CE, he most likely would not have been alive at the date required for the debate. Some scholars, moreover, have argued that the *Dialogue,* in which Justin makes skillful use of Jewish arguments based on scripture, was not an apology to Judaism per se but rather was addressed to Gentiles who cited Jewish objections to Christian claims (as did Celsus in his *True Discourse,* c. 175). It has also been argued that the *Dialogue* was designed as a treatise to prop up the faith of wavering Christians.

The longest of Justin's extant writings, the *Dialogue* consists of four major parts. After narrating at length the story of his conversion (chaps. 1–10), Justin proceeds to explain why Christians no longer keep the whole Mosaic law (11–31). Christianity, he claims, is the true Israel under a new covenant. The new covenant, requiring religion of the heart, has supplanted the old one, which required sacrifices, observance of the Sabbath, fasts, observance of dietary laws, and circumcision. Christians still keep the eternal (moral) law, but not the ritual law prescribed to Israel because of its hardness of heart and transgressions. In the longest section (32–114) Justin replies to Jewish objections to Christian claims concerning Jesus as fulfiller of Jewish messianic hopes and as Lord. He bases his argument wholly on the citing of Old Testament texts and types. In the final section (115–142) he makes a case for the conversion of the Gentiles by citing Old Testament texts. The rather one-sided "dialogue" ends with an appeal to Trypho but not with a conversion.

THOUGHT. Justin was not a theological giant. As his rejection by his Pythagorean teacher indicates, Justin lacked cultural depth. In his apologies, moreover, he wavered back and forth, relying now on citation of authorities and now on logical argument. As one of the first to grapple seriously with questions posed by more cultured Gentiles, he wobbled and tottered, very uncertain of his footing.

Nevertheless, because he tried, Justin established a permanent niche in Christian history. As a philosophical evangelist, he dared to undertake the difficult task of reinterpreting the biblical message in the idiom of what most scholars now recognize as Middle Platonism. Unlike other Christians of his day, even his own pupil Tatian, he acknowledged the truths found in Greek philosophical thought, especially Platonism. Although he sometimes ascribed such insights to borrowing from Moses and the prophets, he developed the more credible theory of illumination or inspiration by the preexistent Logos. Thus Socrates and Heraclitus, in advance of Jesus' advent, merited the title of "Christian." Whereas they, however, grasped truth partially, in Jesus the whole Logos dwelt bodily, thus vouchsafing to Christians the whole of truth.

The significant place that Christians ascribed to Jesus both in worship and in doctrine posed for Justin and other apologists an urgent theological problem: how to preserve belief in one God while recognizing Jesus as God. The eventual solution was the doctrine of the Trinity, but Justin's thinking did not reach that far. In his doctrine of God he wedded the Platonist idea of God as unknowable and transcendent, the unmoved first cause, nameless and unutterable, and the biblical conception of a living creator, the compassionate Father who has come near in Jesus Christ. Often the former idea dominated. For his understanding of the Logos he appropriated and developed elements of earlier Christian tradition in relation to either Stoic or Middle Platonist concepts. The Logos is God's personal reason—not only in name but numerically distinct from the Father—in which all partake but which in Jesus Christ became a man. Lest this dualism that he posits of God land him in ditheism, however, Justin emphasized the unity of the Father and the Logos prior to creation. The Logos is not eternal, as in later thought, but a product of the Father's will from the beginning, thus subordinate to the Father in person and function. His universal activity, Justin liked to say, is that of the *Logos spermatikos,* or Seminal Logos. Justin did not clearly differentiate the activity of the Holy Spirit from that of the Logos, though he evidently did believe in a personal Holy Spirit. The Spirit's chief office is prophetic inspiration.

Justin turned to Christian philosophy for the same reason that most people turned to one of the philosophies current in his time—as a means of salvation. Here he sounded two notes: truth and victory over demons. In line with his Platonist philosophical assumptions, he emphasized human freedom. In each person dwells a spirit or a part of the Seminal Logos. Thus each person has power of choice morally. None inherits sin or guilt; that comes from actual sin, which is the result of letting demons lead one into sin. Christianity offers two things to remedy this situation. One is the teaching and example of the Incarnate Logos, who was both divine and fully human. To live by his teaching is to avoid sin. The other is the power to overcome demons, the demons that Justin, like his contemporaries, believed to be everywhere in fearsome power. Through his death and resurrection Christ has triumphed. Demons, frequently exorcised in his name, are now subject to him.

Justin did not elaborate on his understanding of the church and the ministry, but he did supply some of the earliest extant evidence on Roman baptismal and liturgical practice in the second century, including the earliest liturgy. A period of instruction, the length of which is not indicated, preceded baptism. Prayer and fasting came immediately before. Baptism itself was in the name of the Trinity and accompanied by a confession, but Justin did not mention laying on the hands after baptism. The Eucharist was celebrated following baptism. The weekly liturgy combined a service of the word and a eucharistic service. Held on the "day of the sun," a designation Justin employed with some reservation, it consisted of reading "as long as time permits" the "memoirs" of the apostles or the writings of the prophets, exposition by the person presiding (presumably the elder or bishop), prayers said in a standing position, presentation of the bread and wine mixed with water, prayers and thanksgivings by the one presiding "to the best of his ability," distribution and reception of the bread and wine by those present, dispatch by the deacons of remaining portions to those absent, and a collection of alms for orphans, widows, the sick, visitors, and other needy persons.

Justin ascribed considerable significance to both baptism and the eucharistic meal. In baptism the Holy Spirit brings new birth (as promised in *John* 3:3–4). Baptism is "illumination" (*photismos*) by the Logos, which empowers one to live a truly moral life, thus achieving the goal of the philosopher. In the eucharistic meal the divine Logos unites with the bread and wine in such a way that they become the body and blood of the incarnate Jesus. This food, consecrated "by the word of prayer which comes from him," and thus no longer ordinary and common, fortifies the recipient with the mind and power of the Logos to live the Christian life. Although Justin uses the word *change* to describe the effect of consecration on the elements, his understanding should not be confused with the later doctrine of transubstantiation.

Suspended between two worlds, Greek and Hebrew, Justin sometimes did not know which way to lean. When in doubt, he opted for the biblical, as his eschatology (doctrine of "last things") indicates. In support of Christian messianic convictions he held tenaciously to his belief in the second coming of Christ, though he seems not to have worried about its delay. The first advent of Christ, he contended, was in lowliness; the second one will be in glory. The delay of the second coming, according to Justin, is a sign of God's patience with a recalcitrant humanity for the sake of Christians. Justin also sided with biblical authors on resurrection and the millennium. He was not wholly consistent here; in the *Dialogue* he envisioned the millennium inaugurated by a resurrection of the righteous and concluded by a general resurrection and judgment, as in the *Revelation to John*. He cited the judgment as a major part of his argument against persecution of Christians. Both human beings and angels would be judged according to their use or abuse of free will, and the wicked would be condemned to eternal fire. In his apologies Justin also spoke of a world conflagration, but his attention to this Stoic idea seems to have been more an accommodation to Gentile thinking than a contradiction of his belief in an eternal Jerusalem.

See Also Apologetics.

Bibliography

The standard critical edition of the text of Justin's writings is that by J. C. T. S. Otto, *Justini philosophi et martyris opera,* 3d ed. (Jena, 1875–1881). Reliable English translations of the three authentic works of Justin can be found in volume 1 of *The Ante-Nicene Fathers,* edited and translated by Alexander Roberts and James Donaldson (1867; reprint, Grand Rapids, Mich., 1975). A more up-to-date translation of the *Dialogue* is A. L. Williams's *Justin Martyr: The Dialogue with Trypho* (London, 1930). Excellent introductions to the life and thought of Justin are L. W. Barnard's *Justin Martyr: His Life and Thought* (Cambridge, U.K., 1967) and E. F. Osborn's *Justin Martyr* (Tübingen, 1973), which revise and correct Erwin R. Goodenough's one-sided judgments in *The Theology of Justin Martyr* (1923; reprint, Amsterdam, 1968). Willis A. Shotwell's *The Biblical Exegesis of Justin Martyr* (London, 1965) supplies useful information about Justin's knowledge of Judaism.

E. Glenn Hinson (1987)

JUVAROAN RELIGION See AMAZONIAN QUECHUA RELIGIONS

ISBN 0-02-865740-3
90000
9 780028 657400